ENCYCLOPEDIA OF
RELIGION
SECOND EDITION

ENCYCLOPEDIA OF RELIGION

SECOND EDITION

9

MARY
•
NDEMBU RELIGION

LINDSAY JONES
EDITOR IN CHIEF

MACMILLAN REFERENCE USA
An imprint of Thomson Gale, a part of The Thomson Corporation

THOMSON
GALE

Detroit • New York • San Francisco • San Diego • New Haven, Conn. • Waterville, Maine • London • Munich

THOMSON
GALE

Encyclopedia of Religion, Second Edition

Lindsay Jones, Editor in Chief

For more information, contact
Macmillan Reference USA
An imprint of Thomson Gale
27500 Drake Rd.
Farmington, Hills, MI 48331-3535
Or you can visit our Internet site at
http://www.gale.com

LIBRARY OF CONGRESS CATALOGING-IN-PUBLICATION DATA

Encyclopedia of religion / Lindsay Jones, editor in chief.— 2nd ed.
p. cm.
Includes bibliographical references and index.
ISBN 0-02-865733-0 (SET HARDCOVER : ALK. PAPER) — ISBN 0-02-865734-9 (V. 1) — ISBN 0-02-865735-7 (v. 2) — ISBN 0-02-865736-5 (v. 3) — ISBN 0-02-865737-3 (v. 4) — ISBN 0-02-865738-1 (v. 5) — ISBN 0-02-865739-X (v. 6) — ISBN 0-02-865740-3 (v. 7) — ISBN 0-02-865741-1 (v. 8) — ISBN 0-02-865742-X (v. 9) — ISBN 0-02-865743-8 (v. 10) — ISBN 0-02-865980-5 (v. 11) — ISBN 0-02-865981-3 (v. 12) — ISBN 0-02-865982-1 (v. 13) — ISBN 0-02-865983-X (v. 14) — ISBN 0-02-865984-8 (v. 15)
1. RELIGION—ENCYCLOPEDIAS. I. JONES, LINDSAY, 1954-

BL31.E46 2005
200'.3—dc22 2004017052

This title is also available as an e-book.
ISBN 0-02-865997-X
Contact your Thomson Gale representative for ordering information.

Printed in the United States of America
10 9 8 7 6 5 4 3 2

EDITORS AND CONSULTANTS

EDITOR IN CHIEF

LINDSAY JONES
Associate Professor, Department of Comparative Studies, Ohio State University

BOARD MEMBERS

DAVÍD CARRASCO
Neil Rudenstine Professor of Study of Latin America, Divinity School and Department of Anthropology, Harvard University

GIOVANNI CASADIO
Professor of History of Religions, Dipartimento di Scienze dell'Antichità, Università degli Studi di Salerno

WENDY DONIGER
Mircea Eliade Distinguished Service Professor of the History of Religions, University of Chicago

GARY L. EBERSOLE
Professor of History and Religious Studies, and Director, UMKC Center for Religious Studies, University of Missouri—Kansas City

JANET GYATSO
Hershey Professor of Buddhist Studies, The Divinity School, Harvard University

CHARLES HALLISEY
Associate Professor, Department of Languages and Cultures of Asia and Program in Religious Studies, University of Wisconsin—Madison

CHARLES H. LONG
Professor of History of Religions, Emeritus, and Former Director of Research Center for Black Studies, University of California, Santa Barbara

MARY N. MACDONALD
Professor, History of Religions, Le Moyne College (Syracuse, New York)

DALE B. MARTIN
Professor of Religious Studies, and Chair, Department of Religious Studies, Yale University

AZIM NANJI
Professor and Director, The Institute of Ismaili Studies, London

JACOB OLUPONA
Professor, African American and African Studies Program, University of California, Davis

MICHAEL SWARTZ
Professor of Hebrew and Religious Studies, Ohio State University

INÉS TALAMANTEZ
Associate Professor, Religious Studies Department, University of California, Santa Barbara

CONSULTANTS

GREGORY D. ALLES
Associate Professor of Religious Studies, McDaniel College
Study of Religion

SIGMA ANKRAVA
Professor, Department of Literary and Cultural Studies, Faculty of Modern Languages, University of Latvia
Baltic Religion and Slavic Religion

DIANE APOSTOLOS-CAPPADONA
Center for Muslim–Christian Understanding and Liberal Studies Program, Georgetown University
Art and Religion

DIANE BELL
Professor of Anthropology and Women's Studies, George Washington University
Australian Indigenous Religions

KEES W. BOLLE
Professor Emeritus of History, University of California, Los Angeles, and Fellow, Netherlands Institute for Advanced Studies in the Humanities and Social Sciences
History of Religions

MARK CSIKSZENTMIHALYI
Associate Professor in the Department of East Asian Languages and Literature and the Program in Religious Studies, University of Wisconsin—Madison
Chinese Religions

RICHARD A. GARDNER
Faculty of Comparative Culture, Sophia University
Humor and Religion

JOHN A. GRIM
Professor of Religion, Bucknell University and Co-Coordinator,

Harvard Forum on Religion and Ecology
Ecology and Religion

JOSEPH HARRIS
Francis Lee Higginson Professor of English Literature and Professor of Folklore, Harvard University
Germanic Religions

URSULA KING
Professor Emerita, Senior Research Fellow and Associate Member of the Institute for Advanced Studies, University of Bristol, England, and Professorial Research Associate, Centre for Gender and Religions Research, School of Oriental and African Studies, University of London
Gender and Religion

DAVID MORGAN
Duesenberg Professor of Christianity and the Arts, and Professor of Humanities and Art History, Valparaiso University
Color Inserts and Essays

JOSEPH F. NAGY
Professor, Department of English, University of California, Los Angeles
Celtic Religion

MATTHEW OJO
Obafemi Awolowo University
African Religions

JUHA PENTIKÄINEN
Professor of Comparative Religion, The University of Helsinki, Member of Academia Scientiarum Fennica, Finland
Arctic Religions and Uralic Religions

TED PETERS
Professor of Systematic Theology, Pacific Lutheran Theological Seminary and the Center for Theology and the Natural Sciences at the Graduate Theological Union, Berkeley, California
Science and Religion

FRANK E. REYNOLDS
Professor of the History of Religions and Buddhist Studies in the Divinity School and the Department of South Asian Languages and Civilizations, Emeritus, University of Chicago
History of Religions

GONZALO RUBIO
Assistant Professor, Department of Classics and Ancient Mediterranean Studies and Department of History and Religious Studies, Pennsylvania State University
Ancient Near Eastern Religions

SUSAN SERED
Director of Research, Religion, Health and Healing Initiative, Center for the Study of World Religions, Harvard University, and Senior Research Associate, Center for Women's Health and Human Rights, Suffolk University
Healing, Medicine, and Religion

LAWRENCE E. SULLIVAN
Professor, Department of Theology, University of Notre Dame
History of Religions

WINNIFRED FALLERS SULLIVAN
Dean of Students and Senior Lecturer in the Anthropology and Sociology of Religion, University of Chicago
Law and Religion

TOD SWANSON
Associate Professor of Religious Studies, and Director, Center for Latin American Studies, Arizona State University
South American Religions

MARY EVELYN TUCKER
Professor of Religion, Bucknell University, Founder and Coordinator, Harvard Forum on Religion and Ecology, Research Fellow, Harvard Yenching Institute, Research Associate, Harvard Reischauer Institute of Japanese Studies
Ecology and Religion

HUGH B. URBAN
Associate Professor, Department of Comparative Studies, Ohio State University
Politics and Religion

CATHERINE WESSINGER
Professor of the History of Religions and Women's Studies, Loyola University New Orleans
New Religious Movements

ROBERT A. YELLE
Mellon Postdoctoral Fellow, University of Toronto
Law and Religion

ERIC ZIOLKOWSKI
Charles A. Dana Professor of Religious Studies, Lafayette College
Literature and Religion

ABBREVIATIONS AND SYMBOLS USED IN THIS WORK

abbr. abbreviated; abbreviation
abr. abridged; abridgment
AD *anno Domini,* in the year of the (our) Lord
Afrik. Afrikaans
AH *anno Hegirae,* in the year of the Hijrah
Akk. Akkadian
Ala. Alabama
Alb. Albanian
Am. *Amos*
AM *ante meridiem,* before noon
amend. amended; amendment
annot. annotated; annotation
Ap. *Apocalypse*
Apn. *Apocryphon*
app. appendix
Arab. Arabic
ʿArakh. *ʿArakhin*
Aram. Aramaic
Ariz. Arizona
Ark. Arkansas
Arm. Armenian
art. article (pl., arts.)
AS Anglo-Saxon
Asm. Mos. *Assumption of Moses*
Assyr. Assyrian
A.S.S.R. Autonomous Soviet Socialist Republic
Av. Avestan
ʿA.Z. *ʿAvodah zarah*
b. born
Bab. Babylonian
Ban. Bantu
1 Bar. *1 Baruch*
2 Bar. *2 Baruch*
3 Bar. *3 Baruch*
4 Bar. *4 Baruch*
B.B. *Bavaʾ batraʾ*
BBC British Broadcasting Corporation
BC before Christ
BCE before the common era
B.D. Bachelor of Divinity
Beits. *Beitsah*
Bekh. *Bekhorot*
Beng. Bengali
Ber. *Berakhot*
Berb. Berber
Bik. *Bikkurim*
bk. book (pl., bks.)
B.M. *Bavaʾ metsiʿaʾ*
BP before the present
B.Q. *Bavaʾ qammaʾ*
Brāh. *Brāhmaṇa*
Bret. Breton
B.T. Babylonian Talmud
Bulg. Bulgarian
Burm. Burmese
c. *circa,* about, approximately
Calif. California
Can. Canaanite
Catal. Catalan
CE of the common era
Celt. Celtic
cf. *confer,* compare
Chald. Chaldean
chap. chapter (pl., chaps.)
Chin. Chinese
C.H.M. Community of the Holy Myrrhbearers
1 Chr. *1 Chronicles*
2 Chr. *2 Chronicles*
Ch. Slav. Church Slavic
cm centimeters
col. column (pl., cols.)
Col. *Colossians*
Colo. Colorado
comp. compiler (pl., comps.)
Conn. Connecticut
cont. continued
Copt. Coptic
1 Cor. *1 Corinthians*
2 Cor. *2 Corinthians*
corr. corrected
C.S.P. Congregatio Sancti Pauli, Congregation of Saint Paul (Paulists)
d. died
D Deuteronomic (source of the Pentateuch)
Dan. Danish
D.B. Divinitatis Baccalaureus, Bachelor of Divinity
D.C. District of Columbia
D.D. Divinitatis Doctor, Doctor of Divinity
Del. Delaware
Dem. *Demaʾi*
dim. diminutive
diss. dissertation
Dn. *Daniel*
D.Phil. Doctor of Philosophy
Dt. *Deuteronomy*
Du. Dutch
E Elohist (source of the Pentateuch)
Eccl. *Ecclesiastes*
ed. editor (pl., eds.); edition; edited by

'Eduy. *'Eduyyot*
e.g. *exempli gratia,* for example
Egyp. Egyptian
1 En. *1 Enoch*
2 En. *2 Enoch*
3 En. *3 Enoch*
Eng. English
enl. enlarged
Eph. *Ephesians*
'Eruv. *'Eruvin*
1 Esd. *1 Esdras*
2 Esd. *2 Esdras*
3 Esd. *3 Esdras*
4 Esd. *4 Esdras*
esp. especially
Est. Estonian
Est. *Esther*
et al. *et alii,* and others
etc. *et cetera,* and so forth
Eth. Ethiopic
EV English version
Ex. *Exodus*
exp. expanded
Ez. *Ezekiel*
Ezr. *Ezra*
2 Ezr. *2 Ezra*
4 Ezr. *4 Ezra*
f. feminine; and following (pl., ff.)
fasc. fascicle (pl., fascs.)
fig. figure (pl., figs.)
Finn. Finnish
fl. *floruit,* flourished
Fla. Florida
Fr. French
frag. fragment
ft. feet
Ga. Georgia
Gal. *Galatians*
Gaul. Gaulish
Ger. German
Giṭ. *Giṭṭin*
Gn. *Genesis*
Gr. Greek
Ḥag. *Ḥagigah*
Ḥal. *Ḥallah*
Hau. Hausa
Hb. *Habakkuk*
Heb. Hebrew
Heb. *Hebrews*
Hg. *Haggai*
Hitt. Hittite
Hor. *Horayot*
Hos. *Hosea*
Ḥul. *Ḥullin*
Hung. Hungarian
ibid. *ibidem,* in the same place (as the one immediately preceding)
Icel. Icelandic
i.e. *id est,* that is
IE Indo-European
Ill. Illinois
Ind. Indiana
intro. introduction
Ir. Gael. Irish Gaelic
Iran. Iranian
Is. *Isaiah*
Ital. Italian
J Yahvist (source of the Pentateuch)
Jas. *James*
Jav. Javanese
Jb. *Job*
Jdt. *Judith*
Jer. *Jeremiah*
Jgs. *Judges*
Jl. *Joel*
Jn. *John*
1 Jn. *1 John*
2 Jn. *2 John*
3 Jn. *3 John*
Jon. *Jonah*
Jos. *Joshua*
Jpn. Japanese
JPS Jewish Publication Society translation (1985) of the Hebrew Bible
J.T. Jerusalem Talmud
Jub. *Jubilees*
Kans. Kansas
Kel. *Kelim*
Ker. *Keritot*
Ket. *Ketubbot*
1 Kgs. *1 Kings*
2 Kgs. *2 Kings*
Khois. Khoisan
Kil. *Kil'ayim*
km kilometers
Kor. Korean
Ky. Kentucky
l. line (pl., ll.)
La. Louisiana
Lam. *Lamentations*
Lat. Latin
Latv. Latvian
L. en Th. Licencié en Théologie, Licentiate in Theology
L. ès L. Licencié ès Lettres, Licentiate in Literature
Let. Jer. *Letter of Jeremiah*
lit. literally
Lith. Lithuanian
Lk. *Luke*
LL Late Latin
LL.D. Legum Doctor, Doctor of Laws
Lv. *Leviticus*
m meters
m. masculine
M.A. Master of Arts
Ma 'as. *Ma'aserot*
Ma 'as. Sh. *Ma' aser sheni*
Mak. *Makkot*
Makh. *Makhshirin*
Mal. *Malachi*
Mar. Marathi
Mass. Massachusetts
1 Mc. *1 Maccabees*
2 Mc. *2 Maccabees*
3 Mc. *3 Maccabees*
4 Mc. *4 Maccabees*
Md. Maryland
M.D. Medicinae Doctor, Doctor of Medicine
ME Middle English
Meg. *Megillah*
Me 'il. *Me'ilah*
Men. *Menaḥot*
MHG Middle High German
mi. miles
Mi. *Micah*
Mich. Michigan
Mid. *Middot*
Minn. Minnesota
Miq. *Miqva'ot*
MIran. Middle Iranian
Miss. Mississippi
Mk. *Mark*
Mo. Missouri
Mo'ed Q. *Mo'ed qaṭan*
Mont. Montana
MPers. Middle Persian
MS. *manuscriptum,* manuscript (pl., MSS)
Mt. *Matthew*
MT Masoretic text
n. note
Na. *Nahum*
Nah. Nahuatl
Naz. *Nazir*
N.B. *nota bene,* take careful note
N.C. North Carolina
n.d. no date
N.Dak. North Dakota
NEB New English Bible
Nebr. Nebraska

Ned. *Nedarim*
Neg. *Negaʿim*
Neh. *Nehemiah*
Nev. Nevada
N.H. New Hampshire
Nid. *Niddah*
N.J. New Jersey
Nm. *Numbers*
N.Mex. New Mexico
no. number (pl., nos.)
Nor. Norwegian
n.p. no place
n.s. new series
N.Y. New York
Ob. *Obadiah*
O.Cist. Ordo Cisterciencium, Order of Cîteaux (Cistercians)
OCS Old Church Slavonic
OE Old English
O.F.M. Ordo Fratrum Minorum, Order of Friars Minor (Franciscans)
OFr. Old French
Ohal. *Ohalot*
OHG Old High German
OIr. Old Irish
OIran. Old Iranian
Okla. Oklahoma
ON Old Norse
O.P. Ordo Praedicatorum, Order of Preachers (Dominicans)
OPers. Old Persian
op. cit. *opere citato,* in the work cited
OPrus. Old Prussian
Oreg. Oregon
ʿOrl. *ʿOrlah*
O.S.B. Ordo Sancti Benedicti, Order of Saint Benedict (Benedictines)
p. page (pl., pp.)
P Priestly (source of the Pentateuch)
Pa. Pennsylvania
Pahl. Pahlavi
Par. *Parah*
para. paragraph (pl., paras.)
Pers. Persian
Pes. *Pesahim*
Ph.D. Philosophiae Doctor, Doctor of Philosophy
Phil. *Philippians*
Phlm. *Philemon*
Phoen. Phoenician
pl. plural; plate (pl., pls.)
PM *post meridiem,* after noon
Pol. Polish
pop. population
Port. Portuguese
Prv. *Proverbs*
Ps. *Psalms*
Ps. 151 *Psalm 151*
Ps. Sol. *Psalms of Solomon*
pt. part (pl., pts.)
1Pt. *1 Peter*
2 Pt. *2 Peter*
Pth. Parthian
Q hypothetical source of the synoptic Gospels
Qid. *Qiddushin*
Qin. *Qinnim*
r. reigned; ruled
Rab. *Rabbah*
rev. revised
R. ha-Sh. *Roʾsh ha-shanah*
R.I. Rhode Island
Rom. Romanian
Rom. *Romans*
R.S.C.J. Societas Sacratissimi Cordis Jesu, Religious of the Sacred Heart
RSV Revised Standard Version of the Bible
Ru. *Ruth*
Rus. Russian
Rv. *Revelation*
Rv. Ezr. *Revelation of Ezra*
San. *Sanhedrin*
S.C. South Carolina
Scot. Gael. Scottish Gaelic
S.Dak. South Dakota
sec. section (pl., secs.)
Sem. Semitic
ser. series
sg. singular
Sg. *Song of Songs*
Sg. of 3 *Prayer of Azariah and the Song of the Three Young Men*
Shab. *Shabbat*
Shav. *Shavuʿot*
Sheq. *Sheqalim*
Sib. Or. *Sibylline Oracles*
Sind. Sindhi
Sinh. Sinhala
Sir. *Ben Sira*
S.J. Societas Jesu, Society of Jesus (Jesuits)
Skt. Sanskrit
1 Sm. *1 Samuel*
2 Sm. *2 Samuel*
Sogd. Sogdian
Soṭ. *Soṭah*
sp. species (pl., spp.)
Span. Spanish
sq. square
S.S.R. Soviet Socialist Republic
st. stanza (pl., ss.)
S.T.M. Sacrae Theologiae Magister, Master of Sacred Theology
Suk. *Sukkah*
Sum. Sumerian
supp. supplement; supplementary
Sus. *Susanna*
s.v. *sub verbo,* under the word (pl., s.v.v.)
Swed. Swedish
Syr. Syriac
Syr. Men. *Syriac Menander*
Taʿ an. *Taʿanit*
Tam. Tamil
Tam. *Tamid*
Tb. *Tobit*
T.D. *Taishō shinshū daizōkyō,* edited by Takakusu Junjirō et al. (Tokyo,1922–1934)
Tem. *Temurah*
Tenn. Tennessee
Ter. Terumot
Ṭev. Y. *Ṭevul yom*
Tex. Texas
Th.D. Theologicae Doctor, Doctor of Theology
1 Thes. *1 Thessalonians*
2 Thes. *2 Thessalonians*
Thrac. Thracian
Ti. *Titus*
Tib. Tibetan
1 Tm. *1 Timothy*
2 Tm. *2 Timothy*
T. of 12 *Testaments of the Twelve Patriarchs*
Ṭoh. *ṭohorot*
Tong. Tongan
trans. translator, translators; translated by; translation
Turk. Turkish
Ukr. Ukrainian
Upan. *Upaniṣad*
U.S. United States
U.S.S.R. Union of Soviet Socialist Republics
Uqts. *Uqtsin*
v. verse (pl., vv.)
Va. Virginia
var. variant; variation
Viet. Vietnamese

viz. *videlicet,* namely
vol. volume (pl., vols.)
Vt. Vermont
Wash. Washington
Wel. Welsh
Wis. Wisconsin
Wis. *Wisdom of Solomon*
W.Va. West Virginia
Wyo. Wyoming
Yad. *Yadayim*
Yev. *Yevamot*
Yi. Yiddish
Yor. Yoruba
Zav. *Zavim*
Zec. *Zechariah*
Zep. *Zephaniah*
Zev. *Zevaḥim*

* hypothetical
? uncertain; possibly; perhaps
° degrees
+ plus
– minus
= equals; is equivalent to
× by; multiplied by
→ yields

M

CONTINUED

MARY

This entry consists of the following articles:

AN OVERVIEW
FEMINIST PERSPECTIVES

MARY: AN OVERVIEW

The New Testament description of Maria, or Mariam, includes Mary's virginal conception of Jesus. Preeminent among the saints, the Virgin Mary later became the object of piety and cult and, especially in the Roman Catholic church, of dogmas such as the immaculate conception and the assumption. Protestant treatment of her as a biblical saint varies. She is honored in the Qur'ān (*sūrah*s 3 and 19), Shīʿah speculation, and Ṣūfī mystical traditions (see Tavard 32–45, Pelikan 67–79). There is some Jewish interest in Mary as a Jewish mother and link to the people of Israel (Flusser).

Traditionally, Mary has been presented by combining all the references to her in the Gospels and *Acts of the Apostles* and viewing them in the light of the infancy narratives (*Mt.* 1–2, *Lk.* 1–2), which have been taken as her memoirs revealed years later to an evangelist. These accounts have then been psychologized and interpreted in light of later Marian thought. Further, *Revelation* 12, which speaks about "a woman clothed with the sun, with the moon under her feet, and on her head a crown of twelve stars," who gives birth to a male child who in turn is caught up to God after escaping a dragon on earth, has been regarded as a reference to Mary. Similarly, passages in the Hebrew scriptures have been said to refer to Mary; in *Genesis* 3:15 she (as the Vulgate reads) "shall bruise" the serpent's head; in *Isaiah* 7:14 (*Mt.* 1:23) a young girl (Septuagint, "virgin") shall give birth to a son; in *Proverbs* 8 and other passages about Wisdom (personified as a woman); and in the female figure of the daughter of Zion (e.g., *Zep.* 3:14–20). On Old Testament typologies in patristic sources, see Pelikan 23–36, 41–45.

CLOCKWISE FROM TOP LEFT CORNER. Mayan vase with relief depicting the head of the sun, c. seventh to tenth century. Naturhistorisches Museum, Vienna, Austria. *[©Giraudon/Art Resource, N.Y.]*; Greek vase depicting Circe mixing a magical potion to transform the companions of Odysseus into animals. *[Photograph ©2004 Museum of Fine Arts, Boston]*; Late-nineteenth-century Alaskan Eskimo mask representing the spirit of the moon as a face encompassed by the air (board), the cosmos (hoops), and the stars (feathers). Sheldon Jackson Museum, Sitka, Alaska. *[©Werner Forman/Art Resource, N.Y.]*; Ummayad Mosque in Damascus, Syria. *[©Christine Osborne/Corbis]*; The Abbey of Mont-Saint-Michel, France. *[©Archivo Iconografico, S.A./Corbis]* .

Modern scholarship finds differing pictures of Mary in each gospel. Earlier accounts can be ascertained from sources used by the gospel writers, and a "historical Mary" can be sought behind such sources. The concatenation of biblical images, together with evolving Marian piety and influences from other religions, led to post–New Testament developments that were initially connected with Christology, then with ecclesiology, but by the Middle Ages and certainly since the seventeenth century, Roman Catholic dogmatics were treated separately as Mariology. Pelikan treats her many titles like "the second Eve" and "black Madonna."

MARY IN THE NEW TESTAMENT. The *Gospel of Mark* (written about 70 CE) describes Jesus' mother and brothers on the edge of a crowd listening to him teach (*Mk.* 3:31–35). "His own" (3:20), likely "his family" (NRSV), have come to take him away because Jesus was, they thought, "out of his mind"; they are like the hostile scribes who claim that he is "possessed by Beelzebub" (3:22). In *Mark* 3:34–35, Jesus designates as "my mother and my brothers" those who do the will of God, thus contrasting his natural family, including Mary, with his "eschatological family" of disciples. The passage in *Mark* 6:1–6a, about the rejection of Jesus in his home synagogue, shows Mary and Jesus' brothers sharing the unbelief of those of the surrounding countryside; 6:3, "son of Mary," does not indicate either virgin birth or illegitimacy (contrast Schaberg). References to another Mary, in addition to Mary Magdalene, in 15:40, 15:47, and 16:1 do not denote Jesus' mother. Hence the overall picture of Mary in *Mark* is a negative one. (For details, see Brown et al., 1978, pp. 51–72, 286–287.)

In the *Gospel of Matthew* (perhaps before 90 CE), a more positive view of Mary results, especially from the first two chapters about the birth and infancy of Jesus, the fruit of meditation upon the Hebrew scriptures within the Matthean community. The genealogy (*Mt.* 1:1–17), from Abraham through David to "Jesus who is called the Messiah," mentions five women, including "Mary, of whom [fem.] Jesus was born" (1:16). This genealogy was probably designed to emphasize how God carried out his plan to save his people through Jesus the Messiah (1:21) in spite of "marital irregularities" in each of the cases of the five women. With Mary, the irregularity is that Joseph learns she is with child "from the Holy Spirit." But this is in accord with God's plan (*Mt.* 1:21–22). That the women were "threats" but "vulnerable" is stressed by Gaventa 32–46. The evangelist cites *Isaiah* 7:14 (Septuagint) to verify that a virgin has conceived and that the child will be "God with us" (*Mt.* 1:23).

Matthew's portrait of Mary during the ministry of Jesus is also ameliorated by other details. In the scene of Jesus' eschatological family (*Mt.* 12:46–50) no reference is made to Jesus' natural family coming to take custody of him. In the synagogue scene at Nazareth (*Mt.* 13:53–58), Matthew drops out the Marcan reference to "his own kin" in what Jesus says (13:57; cf. *Mk.* 6:4).

The most positive synoptic portrayal of Mary comes in the *Gospel of Luke* plus *Acts* (perhaps after 90 CE). In *Acts* 1:14, Mary is a member of the Jerusalem church. In *Luke* 1–2, Mary is described as Joseph's "betrothed" (*Luke* 2:1–20, where, however, a virgin birth is not mentioned). More striking are (1) the scene where the angel Gabriel tells Mary that she will bear "the Son of the Most High" and "The Holy Spirit will come upon you, and the power of the Most High will overshadow you" (God's creative activity, *Acts* 1:8; *Gen.* 1), and Mary responds, "Let it be with me according to your word" (*Lk.* 1:26–38, Mary's faith); (2) the story of Mary's visit to Elizabeth (*Lk.* 1:39–56) and Mary's song, the Magnificat (1:46–55, Mary as prophetess), in particular, the words about her blessedness (esp. 1:42 and 1:48); (3) the account of Mary in the Jerusalem Temple where she comes for purification after childbirth and where Jesus is presented to the Lord (*Lk.* 2:21–40); and (4) the story of Jesus in the Temple as a twelve-year-old (*Lk.* 2:41–52). These accounts show Mary's faith in God (*Lk.* 1:38, 1:45); tell of the virginal conception (*Lk.* 1:31–34, cf. 3:23) and of Mary's status as a "favored one" (*Lk.* 1:28; Vulgate, *gratia plena*), employing the term *hail (ave);* and relate Simeon's prophecy to Mary: "A sword will pierce your own soul too" (*Luke* 2:35; Mary, also, must transcend the natural bonds of family and come to faith in Jesus). This she does, for Jesus declares blessed not the womb that bore him but those who hear and keep God's word (*Lk.* 11:27–28). The rejection scene at Nazareth (*Lk.* 4:16–30) is presented very differently, and the saying about Jesus' eschatological family (*Lk.* 8:19–21) lacks any contrast with his natural family. In *Luke* 2:19 and 2:51, Mary ponders over Jesus' birth and thus grows in faith and discipleship.

The *Gospel of John* (c. 90) contains no reference to the virgin birth, in part because the preexistence and incarnation of the Word are emphasized (*Jn.* 1:1–18). The scenes involving "the mother of Jesus" (never "Mary") during Jesus' ministry are totally different from those in the Synoptic Gospels. In the story about a wedding feast at Cana (*Jn.* 2:1–11), his mother does not yet seem to have grasped that his "hour" does not parallel the wishes of his natural family. Although she accompanied Jesus to Capernaum (*Jn.* 2:12), perhaps this was because she was seeking to bring him home (cf. *Mk.* 3:20–35). The mother of Jesus appears in one other Johannine scene (*Jn.* 19:25–27), standing at the foot of the cross with the Beloved Disciple. This *stabat mater* reference occurs only in *John,* among all the Gospels.

Earlier New Testament writings, like Paul's letters (c. 50–60, *Gal.* 4:4, antidocetist), make no reference to Mary, nor does the Q source, a reconstructed collection of Jesus' sayings, presumed to have been used by Matthew and Luke. A pre-gospel tradition could be behind *John* 2:1–11, or a common source could be the basis of the Matthean-Lukan stories of Mary's conceiving and the genealogy. More likely these are deductions of post-Easter Christology, theologoumena, dramatizing the divine origins of Jesus.

Regardless of the backgrounds and symbolism of the scene in *Revelation* 12 that are suggested by scholarship in the history of religions, the passage is intended to assert God's triumph in Christ over Satan's attacks. The woman who gives birth to the Messiah is Israel and the church, Christ's suffering people. Marian applications to the passage developed only in the fourth century.

MARIAN PIETY AND MARIOLOGY. In the second century, references to Mary are rare, found chiefly in the letters of Ignatius of Antioch about the "mystery" of Jesus' birth (e.g., *Ephesians* 19.1) and in Justin Martyr (*Dialogue with Trypho* 100). Justin typologically compares Eve and Mary, a theme developed by Irenaeus (*Against Heresies* 3.21.10). The New Testament Apocrypha and gnostic documents from Nag Hammadi expand references to Mary (see Tavard 17–31). The *Protevangelium of James* (an infancy gospel and life of Mary, written mid-second century), with its hagiographic details, was to have great influence. It said that Mary remained a virgin while delivering her son *(in partu)* as well as after Jesus' birth (*virginitas post partum*). Growing Christian emphasis on asceticism, with Mary as virgin model, and contacts with "mother goddesses" in other religions, especially in Asia Minor, encouraged Marian themes. But even in the third century there is no trace of belief in Mary's assumption into heaven (Brown et al., 1978, pp. 241–282).

Popular piety concerning Mary usually developed first in the East, often involving icons (see Tavard 67–73) and in a liturgical context, sometimes involving groups deemed heretical. The West was often more sober in its piety (see Tavard 65–100). The prayer in the Byzantine liturgy *Sub tuum praesidium confugimus* ("Under your mercy we take refuge, O Theotokos . . .") has been traced back to the fourth century or earlier (for details, see O'Carroll, 1983). In the *Refutation of All Heresies* 78–79 (c. 375), Epiphanius, bishop of Cyprus, refers both to "opponents of Mary" who denied that she was perpetually a virgin (Gr., *aeiparthenos;* Lat., *semper virgo*), and to the Collyridians, women who offered cakes *(kollyrides)* to the Virgin as a goddess (cf. *Jer.* 7:18, 44:15–28). At the Second Council of Nicaea (787) clear distinctions were made: *latr(e)ia* ("worship") is for God alone; *d(o)ul(e)ia* ("reverence"), for the saints; and *huperdouleia* ("more than reverence"), for Mary.

In the Christological controversies of the fifth century, Mary took on more and more of the status of her Son. While Nestorius (d. 451) was willing to call Mary *christotokos* ("the one who bore Christ"), he boggled at the term *theotokos*, "God-bearer." This term became the rallying cry of Cyril of Alexandria (d. 444) and was proclaimed as a title for Mary at the councils of Ephesus (431) and Chalcedon (451). The intent was to assert that he whom Mary bore was, while "truly man," also "truly God." Use of the term *theotokos* also led to emphasis on Mary not simply as *Dei genitrix* ("she who gives birth to God") but also as *mater Dei*, the "mother of God" (see Tavard 49–64; Pelikan 55–65).

Marian festivals generally developed in the East and then spread elsewhere. They multiplied in number. Some had biblical roots, for example, the Annunciation on March 25 (*Lk.* 1:26–38) and the Purification on February 2 (*Lk.* 2:21–39, cf. *Lv.* 12). Others, like the Nativity of the Blessed Virgin Mary (September 8) and her Presentation in the Temple (November 21), have their roots in the *Protevangelium of James.* The fifteenth of August became the date for the Dormition, or "falling asleep" of the Virgin. Later there arose accounts of Mary's bodily assumption into heaven, paralleling Jesus' exaltation. Mary was regarded as now reigning with her Son, and thus she could be intercessor, or mediatrix, with Christ and God. A legend about Theophilus, who made a pact with the devil but obtained forgiveness through Mary, was an indication of her power to intervene. The Feast of the Immaculate Conception of Mary (December 8 or 9) arose around the theme of her sinlessness from the time of her birth (cf. *Protevangelium of James* 4). However, in the West there was a long debate over Mary's sinlessness in light of the Augustinian doctrine of original sin; the Franciscans promoted the feast, while the Dominicans (including Thomas Aquinas) opposed it.

Celebration of Mary had now moved from the realm of Christology to that of ecclesiology. Mary was Mater Ecclesiae ("mother of the church"), for she had brought forth Christ, the head of the church. One principle at work was *"potuit, decuit, fecit":* God *could* do a thing, it *was fitting* that God should, and therefore God *did* it—for example, God saw to it that Mary was born or exalted much like her Son. Other principles were exhibited by Bernard of Clairvaux's dictum "Everything through Mary" and the widespread medieval belief that one can never say too much about Mary. Reflections of this cascading piety can be seen in the Akathistos, a Greek hymn of the fifth or sixth century that has elaborate epithets for Mary, or in Western antiphons like *Alma redemptoris mater* (Sweet Mother of the Redeemer), or in the Ave Maria prayer ("Hail, Mary," *Luke* 1:28 and 1:48, with the later addition of "Pray for us sinners . . ."). Poetry, often outside the churches, e.g., by the English Romantics and pre-Raphaelites, and literature sometimes hailed Mary (see Tavard 153–167; Pelikan 165–175).

Some of the Protestant reformers (see Pelikan 153–163), including Ulrich Zwingli (see Tavard 104–109), grew up under the high Mariology of the late Middle Ages and its piety. Luther seems at times to have affirmed Mary's immaculate conception and even her bodily assumption and retained some Marian festivals, but with a Christological emphasis. More revealing is Luther's 1521 exposition of the Magnificat (*Works*, Saint Louis, 1956, vol. 21, pp. 297–358), where Mary is "the foremost example" of God's grace and of proper humility. The Lutheran confessions simply assume the virgin birth of Jesus Christ and even use stock phrases like *semper virgo.* But Calvin, who praised Mary as "holy virgin," expressed misgivings about calling her "mother of God." Protestant reaction to the post-Tridentine emphases in Roman Catholicism gave Mary less and less place (see Tavard 117–130; Dawe). Anglicanism often shares in (Roman) Catholic tradition about Mary, though not in the papal magisterium seen in the dogmas of 1854 and 1950 (see below; Tavard 134–152).

Eastern Orthodox regard for Mary has continued as living piety, but without the emphasis on dogmatic articulation found in Roman Catholicism (see Nikos Nissiotis, in *Concilium* 168, 1983, pp. 25–39, with bibliography). "Sophiology," Mary as created Wisdom (Sophia), developed especially in nineteenth-century Russian Orthodoxy (see Tavard 78–79; O'Carroll, *Theotokos* 332 and 90–92 on Sergius Bulgakov, 1817–1944). For Roman Catholic theology, the seventeenth and eighteenth centuries brought new developments in spirituality having to do with Mary (for example, the devotion to the Immaculate Heart of Mary promoted by Jean Eudes, 1601–1680). In Italy, Alfonso Liguori (1696–1787) gathered stories about the Virgin in his book *The Glories of Mary.* Emphasis on Mary was encouraged by reported visions and appearances (Pelikan 178–187), for example, at Lourdes in 1858, with the announcement, "I am the Immaculate Conception," at Fatima, Portugal in 1917, and Medjugore in Bosnia-Herzegovina, beginning in 1981 (appearances have been claimed more frequently in the twentieth century than any previous time, so Tavard 186); also by international Marian congresses; by Marian years proclaimed by the pope; and by pilgrimages (for example to Czestochowa in Poland, Guadalupe, Mexico).

Reflective of such popular piety was Pius IX's 1854 definition of the immaculate conception as dogma for Roman Catholics in *Ineffabilis Deus:* "The most blessed Virgin Mary . . . was preserved free from all stain of original sin." In 1950, Pius XII defined the assumption of the Blessed Virgin Mary as a dogma in the apostolic constitution *Munificentissimus Deus:* "The Immaculate Mother of God, the ever Virgin Mary . . . was assumed body and soul to heavenly glory." Protestant reaction was negative. The Orthodox reacted against the 1854 dogma because of their belief that everyone, Mary included, is afflicted with sin in the sense of human infirmity, but in 1950 they reacted only against papal claims of authority inherent in the proclamation (see Pelikan 189–213). Some Catholics have called for ecumenical rewriting of these dogmas (see Tavard 200).

Although some Catholic "maximalists" on Mary hoped that the Second Vatican Council would declare her coredemptrix with Christ, the council did not make such a statement. In fact, it voted in 1963 to include the material on Mary as chapter 8 of the Constitution on the Church, *Lumen gentium,* rather than to treat it as a separate schema. The dogmatic constitution treats her role in the economy of salvation, as Mother of God and of the Redeemer, as a model for the church, and as a sign of hope and solace for God's people in pilgrimage. There are also paragraphs on devotion to the Blessed Virgin, warning against exaggeration. However, the speech by Paul VI in 1964, promulgating *Lumen gentium,* proclaimed Mary as Mater Ecclesiae, and his apostolic exhortation in 1974, *Marialis cultus,* sought for renewal in devotion to Mary and called her "our sister." John Paul II has spoken frequently in traditional Marian terms, often devotionally (*Redemptoris mater,* 1987, announcing a Marian jubilee for 1987–1988, leading toward the bimillennium in 2000 of Jesus' birth). The net effect since Vatican II has generally been a greater restraint and balance in Roman Catholic Mariology and in Catholic devotional life. Some statements have suggested that Mary provides "the model of all real feminine freedom" (U.S. Catholic Bishops, *Behold Your Mother,* 1974). But for many feminists, Mariology, certainly in the church writers of the early centuries, has been all too androcentric (cf. Borrensen, Halkes, and Moltmann-Wendel, in *Concilium,* 168, 1983; contrast at points Tavard 49–57, 221–266). In ecumenical dialogues the fullest treatment has come in the United States "Lutherans and Catholics in Dialogue VIII," *The One Mediator, the Saints, and Mary,* ed. H. George Anderson, J. Francis Stafford, and Joseph A. Burgess (Minneapolis, 1992); "saints" and prayers for and to deceased saints proved more divisive than did Mary.

SEE ALSO Councils, article on Christian Councils; Cult of Saints; Goddess Worship; Jesus; Virgin Goddess.

BIBLIOGRAPHY

Walter Delius, *Geschichte der Marienverehrung* (Munich, 1963), and his *Texte zur Geschichte der Marienverehrung und Marienverkündigung in der alten Kirche,* rev. Hans-Udo Rosenbaum (New York/Berlin, 1973) are updated in *Die Religion in Geschichte und Gegenwart,* 4th ed., vol. 5 (Tübingen, 2002): 800–824, by Heinrich Petri, Reinhard Thöle, and Birgit Merz. More popular in tone are Hilda Graef's *Mary: A History of Doctrine and Devotion,* 2 vols. (New York, 1963–1965); Marina Warner's *Alone of All Her Sex: The Myth and Cult of the Virgin Mary* (New York, 1976); Christa Mulack's *Maria: Die geheime Göttin im Christentum* (Stuttgart, 1985); David Flusser, Jaroslav Pelikan, and Justin Lang, *Mary: Images of the Mother of Jesus in Jewish and Christian Perspective* (Philadelphia, 1986); George H. Tavard, *The Thousand Faces of the Virgin Mary* (Collegeville, Minn., 1996); and Jaroslav Pelikan, *Mary Through the Centuries: Her Place in the History of Culture* (New Haven, 1996). Sympathetic articles on persons, terms, and themes, with bibliography, will be found in Michael O'Carroll's *Theotokos: A Theological Encyclopedia of the Blessed Virgin Mary,* rev. ed. with supplement (Wilmington, Del., 1983). For biblical materials, treated with historical-critical methodology and ecumenically, see *Mary in the New Testament: A Collaborative Assessment by Protestant and Roman Catholic Scholars,* edited by Raymond E. Brown, Karl P. Donfried, Joseph A. Fitzmyer, and John Reumann (Philadelphia, 1978); Raymond E. Brown, *The Birth of the Messiah: A Commentary on the Infancy Narratives in Matthew and Luke* (Garden City, N.Y., 1977); Jane Schaberg, *The Illegitimacy of Jesus: A Feminist Theological Interpretation of the Infancy Narratives* (San Francisco, 1987); Mary Margaret Pazden, "Mary, Mother of Jesus," *The Anchor Bible Dictionary* (New York, 1992), vol. 4: 584–586; Ingrid Rosa Kitzberger, "Maria, Mutter Jesu," *Die Religion in Geschichte und Gegen-*

wart, 4th ed., vol. 5 (Tübingen, 2002): 798–799; Beverly Roberts Gaventa, *Mary, Glimpses of the Mother of Jesus* (Columbia, S.C., 1995), including literary approaches and "story." *Mary in the Churches,* edited by Hans Küng and Jürgen Moltmann, *Concilium* 168 (New York, 1983), surveys biblical origins and confessional attitudes today as well as trends in feminist and liberation theology and depth psychology and literature. *Mary's Place in Christian Dialogue,* edited by Alberic Stacpoole (Wilton, Conn., 1982), reflects work by the Ecumenical Society of the Blessed Virgin Mary, which also published Donald G. Dawe, *From Dysfunction to Disbelief: The Virigin Mary in Reformed Theology* (Washington, D.C., 1977). Stephen Benko's *Protestants, Catholics, and Mary* (Valley Forge, Pa., 1978) deals also with Josephology. Periodicals: *Marian Studies; Dialog* 31 (Fall 1992): 245–271.

JOHN REUMANN (1987 AND 2005)

MARY: FEMINIST PERSPECTIVES

The Virgin Mary has been a central figure in Catholic and Orthodox Christianity since the time of the early church. Although Marian devotion often has been aligned with papal power and Catholic imperialism, Mary also has been a focal point for popular devotional practices, legends, and folklore in Catholic culture, including those which express women's concerns with childbirth, motherhood, marriage, and religious life. Mary is a complex topic for feminist analysis, since the priorities and perspectives of a Western-educated feminist are likely to be different from those of a poor, illiterate Catholic woman, for whom the Virgin Mary nevertheless may be a potent source of inspiration and consolation.

FEMINIST PERSPECTIVES. The most common feminist critique of the Marian tradition focuses on the association between Mary and Eve, which is perceived as a destructive form of dualism that informs Christian concepts of womanhood. As the new Eve, Mary has been represented as the faithful, obedient virgin who brought life to the human race through her motherhood of Christ, whereas Eve has signified the disobedient virgin, the sexual temptress who brought death to the human race by eating the forbidden fruit and enticing Adam to eat it.

In parallel with the denigration of female sexuality in Eve's association with temptation, sin, and death, Mary's virginal motherhood is seen by feminist critics as representing an impossible ideal for women. The Christian understanding of female virtue has been constructed to a large extent around the contrast between Mary's virginal obedience, passivity, and modesty before God and Eve's disobedience, sexual incontinence, and susceptibility to temptation. This contrast has been exacerbated in the Roman Catholic tradition by the valuing of celibacy over marriage; as a result women have been identified with Eve as posing the ultimate threat to the spiritual and moral well-being of the celibate male.

CONTEMPORARY WRITINGS ON MARY. Although there is a long tradition of women's writings on Mary, contemporary feminist interpretations must be understood in the context of the Second Vatican Council (1962–1965). The question of Mary's place in the church generated some of the most heated debates in Vatican II (at which no women were present), and the council's teachings on Mary eventually were incorporated into Chapter 8 of the document on the church, *Lumen Gentium.* Although *Lumen Gentium* emphasizes the unique dignity and privilege of Mary in her role as Mother of God, it also portrays her as the model of Christian discipleship and prayer.

After Vatican II, Catholic interest in Mary declined dramatically, and thus it is not surprising that she attracted relatively little attention from early feminist theologians. Those who did write about Mary tended to follow the trend of Vatican II, emphasizing her biblical persona as the poor woman of Nazareth and an exemplary disciple rather than her transcendent mystical significance as the Mother of God or her cultic role in popular devotions and feasts (Ruether, 1993). Feminist liberationist theologians saw Mary as a source of inspiration for the struggles of the poor and the oppressed, identifying her with the words of the Magnificat attributed to her in Luke's gospel (1:46–55). The Brazilian theologians Ivone Gebara and María Clara Bingemer (1989) proposed a feminist liberationist understanding of Mary that seeks to reconcile her human significance as Mary of Nazareth and her transcendent universality as the Mother of God.

Alongside these liberal and liberationist perspectives, some feminist thinkers have attempted to reclaim Mary's significance as the unacknowledged goddess of the Christian tradition (Baring and Cashford, 1993). From this perspective, the early church only partially defeated the goddess religions of the ancient world. Those religions were subsumed and incorporated into Christianity in the status and devotion accorded to the Virgin Mary while being divested of their potent matriarchal significance in the context of a patriarchal religious culture.

This is one of the ideas explored by Marina Warner (2000) in her feminist analysis of the development of Marian devotion and doctrine. Warner presents the Marian tradition as historically significant but anachronistic in terms of the aspirations, values, and questions of contemporary secular society, although in more recent editions of her work she has modified this stance by acknowledging the enduring capacity of Mary to meet the religious need for a mother goddess figure. Others, such as Charlene Spretnak (2004), offer a more positive affirmation of the need to recognize Mary's potential in terms of a maternal feminine divine presence in the Catholic tradition. Spretnak criticizes the Second Vatican Council for divesting the Marian tradition of much of its power and argues for the rediscovery of Marian devotion as an important aspect of feminist spirituality.

Mary is also a significant figure in the writings of the psycholinguistic theorists Luce Irigaray and Julia Kristeva. For Irigaray she represents the missing feminine dimension of the Incarnation. Irigaray (1991) argues that the fertile, corporeal, and maternal aspects of the Christian story have been neglected in favor of a life-denying religion based on the patriarchal and sacrificial relationship between a Father God and his crucified Son. Kristeva (1987), drawing on the insights of psychoanalysis, sees the cult of the Virgin Mary as contributing to the sublimation rather than the repression of the maternal relationship in Catholic Christianity, including its associations with the body, desire, and death.

These theoretical insights have informed feminist Mariology, particularly in the work of Tina Beattie (2002). A different critical perspective is offered by Sarah Jane Boss (2000). Drawing on the critical theory of the Frankfurt school in her reading of the Marian tradition, Boss argues that the increasing trend toward the domination of nature and the female body is reflected in changing attitudes toward the Virgin Mary in Western culture.

As a visible and ubiquitous symbol of maternal femininity in the Christian tradition the Virgin Mary is a vast cultural presence and historical influence whose significance has not been recognized fully by many secular feminists. The traditions, theories, and practices that surround her are too diverse and enigmatic to lend themselves to a straightforward feminist analysis or theory. However, it is hard to see how any feminist approach to questions of religion, history, and ethics in Western culture can ignore the extent to which the Marian tradition has shaped attitudes toward women in ways that extend beyond the doctrinal beliefs and devotional practices of Catholic Christianity.

See Also Asceticism; Celibacy; Eve; Feminine Sacrality; Feminism, article on French Feminists on Religion; Feminist Theology, article on Christian Feminist Theology; Goddess Worship, overview article; Liberation Theology; Spirituality; Virgin Goddess; Virginity.

Bibliography

Baring, Anne, and Jules Cashford. *The Myth of the Goddess: Evolution of an Image.* London and New York, 1993. In this extensive study of goddess religions the authors argue that Eve and Mary are the repressed goddess figures of the Jewish and Christian traditions.

Beattie, Tina. *God's Mother, Eve's Advocate: A Marian Narrative of Women's Salvation.* London and New York, 2002. Beattie engages with French psycholinguistic theory in her reading of the Marian tradition. By comparing the symbolic significance of Eve and Mary in patristic theology with their representation in recent Catholic writings, she argues for the transformation of Marian symbolism through a feminist engagement with the beliefs of the early Church.

Boss, Sarah Jane. *Empress and Handmaid: Nature and Gender in the Cult of the Virgin Mary.* London and New York, 2000. This analysis of the development of the Marian tradition draws on both theology and sociology. In light of the critical theory of the Frankfurt school and its critique of domination, the author argues that changing attitudes toward nature and the female body in Western culture are reflected in Marian doctrine and devotion.

Gebara, Ivone, and María Clara Bingemer. *Mary: Mother of God, Mother of the Poor.* Tunbridge Wells, U.K., 1989. These Brazilian theologians draw on the insights of feminist and liberationist theologies to offer a Mariology that encompasses both the human dimension of Mary as a woman in history and the transcendent significance of Mary as a universal symbol of liberation and redemption.

Irigaray, Luce. *Marine Lover of Friedrich Nietzsche.* New York, 1991. The last chapter of this book, "Epistle to the Last Christians," offers the author's most sustained engagement with the Marian tradition, although references to the Virgin Mary are scattered widely throughout her work.

Johnston, Elizabeth A. *Truly Our Sister: A Theology of Mary in the Communion of Saints.* London and New York, 2003. The author rejects the iconic status of Mary in order to emphasize her humanity as a woman who struggles in solidarity with other women.

Kristeva, Julia. "Stabat Mater." In *Tales of Love.* New York, 1987 (first published in 1983). This lyrical essay, written as two sides of a dialogue, explores the relationship between the maternal body and Marian doctrine and devotion.

Ruether, Rosemary Radford. *Sexism and God-Talk.* London: 1992 (first published in 1983). Chapter 6, "Mariology as Symbolic Ecclesiology: Repression or Liberation?" proposes a feminist liberationist Mariology based on the identification of Mary with the church.

Spretnak, Charlene. *Missing Mary: The Queen of Heaven and Her Re-Emergence in the Modern Church.* Basingstoke, U.K., 2004. The author criticizes the Second Vatican Council for its minimalist approach to Mary and advocates a rediscovery of Marian devotion and mysticism as a potent expression of feminist spirituality.

Warner, Marina. *Alone of All Her Sex: The Myth and Cult of the Virgin Mary.* London, 2000 (first published in 1976). This scholarly and wide-ranging evaluation of the Marian tradition remains one of the most influential feminist critiques.

Tina Beattie (2005)

MARY MAGDALENE.

Mentioned by name in only fourteen verses in the New Testament, Mary Magdalene is nevertheless one of the most important and influential figures in the history of Christianity. Mary came from a prosperous town on the shores of the Sea of Galilee, which in the canonical gospels is called by its Aramaic name, Magdala. In Greek it is known as Tarichaeae. In antiquity the town had a reputation for exporting quality salt fish and fish oil. It is possible Mary herself was engaged in some business related to the fishing industry. This occupation is well attested for women in early Roman Palestine, and the Herodian court at nearby Tiberias regularly purchased goods from female suppliers. When Mary is introduced in *Luke* 8:2, she is in the company of Joanna, the wife of a Herodian official, suggesting Mary had contact with the court.

Luke presents Mary Magdalene as one who followed Jesus during his ministry in the Galilee. According to the third gospel, Jesus healed Mary of an unspecified disorder, which singles her out as the only close companion whom he cures. *Luke* also records that Mary "ministered" (the Greek verb means "to care for" or "to provide") to Jesus and his followers "out of [her] resources." The verse may recall Mary's patronage as a well-to-do businesswoman.

Whenever a group of women followers is listed in the canonical gospels, Mary is mentioned first, an indication of her preeminence. The gospels also relate that Mary is present at the crucifixion in Jerusalem. Finally, she is the only person to be named in all four gospels as a witness to the resurrection, subsequently qualifying her to receive the accolade of apostle.

MARY IN NON-CANONICAL LITERATURE. In the late nineteenth century fragments of an extra-canonical gospel written in the name of Mary Magdalene were found. The discovery of an incomplete Coptic manuscript was followed in the early twentieth century by the recovery of additional portions of the text in Greek. Scholars generally date its composition to the second century. The gospel portrays Mary as the recipient of a vision of Christ in which she is praised for her fidelity. Peter appears as an adversary, attacking Mary when she explains her vision. Peter asks incredulously whether Jesus really did "speak with a woman without our knowledge [and] not openly."

The *Gospel of Thomas,* also a second-century text, depicts Peter's attempt to discredit any authority Mary possesses among the disciples, attributing to him the declaration, "Let Mary leave us, because women are not worthy of life." The risen Jesus refutes Peter's dismissal, replying, "Look, I myself shall lead her so that I will make her male in order that she too may become a living spirit resembling you males. For every woman who makes herself male will enter the kingdom of heaven."

A large corpus of Gnostic literature found at Nag Hammadi, Egypt, in 1945 was published in the 1970s. The texts include a number of extra-canonical manuscripts concerning Mary Magdalene, notably the third-century *Pistis Sophia,* the *Gospel of Philip,* and the *Dialogue of the Savior.* The *Sophia of Jesus Christ* was dated to the early fourth century, although some scholars argue that it exhibits features suggesting an earlier date of composition. These writings aroused new interest in Mary's relationship with Jesus and in her authority among early Christians. They also indicate a wide diversity of teaching during the formative years of the new religious movement.

Mary is depicted in the Gnostic works as having a particularly intimate relationship with Jesus. She is praised as worthy of having received private teaching from him and she is presented as a leader within the Christian community. Of particular interest, the *Gospel of Philip* portrays Mary as the one whom Jesus loved more than the other disciples and as one whom he kissed frequently. The act of kissing as a greeting and sign of affection is well attested as a common practice among early Christians, as Paul's epistles witness. Jesus' kiss, therefore, does not necessarily imply a sexual relationship, though some twentieth-century commentators have interpreted it that way.

Peter appears in the Gnostic texts consistently opposing Mary's authority. As a result, some scholars suggest that the Gnostic writings reveal a struggle within the early church between a faction that recognizes in Mary a model for women's authority and leadership, and a Petrine group that opposes women's authority. Other scholars interpret Peter as representing the emerging orthodox position, while Mary stands for the Gnostic view.

"APOSTLE TO THE APOSTLES." Writing in *Galatians* 1:11–17, Paul intimates that an apostle is one who receives an appearance of the risen Lord and one who is commissioned to proclaim his message. In the canonical gospels Mary is recorded as fulfilling both of these conditions. Hippolytus, a third-century bishop, is generally thought to be the first person to name her as an "apostle to the apostles." Augustine of Hippo in the fourth century and John Chrysostom in the fifth also accord Mary this title. Some scholars argue that the appellation of apostle is honorific in Mary's case. However, as she meets the criteria, there seems no need to assume the title was anything less than recognition of her apostleship. The persistence and survival of the epithet confirm Mary's importance among early Christians.

In the sixth century Pope Gregory I (the Great) declared that Mary Magdalene was beloved of the savior and was the leader of a group of apostles. He also proclaimed that the Galilean Mary Magdalene, the Judean Mary of Bethany, and the other Mary were one and the same person, conflating three distinct women. In the West, pious myths arose based on the conflation. According to an eleventh-century tradition, Mary, now identified as the sister of Martha and Lazarus, introduced Christianity to France. In eastern Christianity the confusion did not arise, for the distinctions among the women were maintained.

MARY THE PENITENT. Mary's reputation as an apostle, preacher, and leader declined as male authority increased in orthodox Christianity. Gregory I not only conflated three Marys, he also made Mary Magdalene into a prostitute, declaring her a redeemed whore in a sermon in 591. Mary was stigmatized as a prostitute through an association with the unnamed sinner mentioned in *Luke* 7:36–50, an erroneous identification that endured for fourteen hundred years. In church teaching and Christian art, Mary was portrayed as a model of repentance and was used as a propaganda tool. Her misrepresentation served the purposes of a church promoting asceticism, by making her into a moral paradigm: the unfaithful harlot forgiven and restored.

Scholarly consensus since the 1980s has returned Mary Magdalene to her position of authority and leadership in early Christianity. The identification of her as a prostitute has been exposed as mistaken and rejected for lack of evidence. Study of the noncanonical literature has revealed that Mary's influence endured for at least six centuries prior to her conflation with Mary of Bethany and the so-called other

Mary. At the same time, the Gnostic literature has raised questions about early Christian teachings regarding the salvation of women. Mary's canonical role as a close associate of Jesus, a faithful disciple, and a witness to the resurrection, coupled with the noncanonical accounts of her as a preacher and missionary, have revised her memory as a role model for Christian women.

See Also Gender and Religion, article on Gender and Christianity; Gnosticism; Nag Hammadi.

Bibliography

Boer, Esther de. *Mary Magdalene: Beyond the Myth.* Translated by John Bowden. Harrisburg, Pa., 1997. De Boer revisits the tradition of Mary Magdalene as a redeemed prostitute. She examines both the canonical literature and the *Gospel of Mary,* placing the accounts in their historical, social, cultural, and theological contexts within formative Christianity. De Boer's work concludes that Mary was not a penitent whore, but a courageous and persistent disciple.

Brock, Ann Graham. *Mary Magdalene, the First Apostle: The Struggle for Authority.* Cambridge, Mass., 2003. This revised doctoral dissertation argues that the Magdalene fulfills the criteria of an apostle. Brock carefully and persuasively reexamines the canonical gospel portraits, particularly those of Luke and John, before turning to the Gnostic literature. Her treatment of a frequently hypothesized rivalry between proponents of the Magdalene and a Petrine group is especially instructive. Brock provides a comprehensive bibliography of the literature in French, German, Italian, and English.

Haskins, Susan. *Mary Magdalen: Myth and Metaphor.* London, 1993. Haskins explores how the story of the Magdalene has been transmitted through Christian history not only by means of biblical and early Christian texts, but also through visual representations from the mid-third century through the last decade of the twentieth century. Haskins's analysis of the texts seems rudimentary compared to subsequent studies, but as one of the first scholarly works on Mary Magdalene, her book remains an important contribution. It is particularly valuable for its medieval representations.

Jansen, Katherine Ludwig. "Maria Magdalena: *Apostolorum Apostola.*" In *Women Preachers and Prophets through Two Millennia of Christianity,* edited by Beverly Mayne Kienzle and Pamela J. Walker, pp. 57–96. Berkeley, Calif., 1998. Jansen notes that between the eleventh and sixteenth centuries medieval preaching circulated the story of the Magdalene as *apostola.* She looks at examples that draw upon pious traditions presenting Mary as a model missionary.

King, Karen. *The Gospel of Mary of Magdala: Jesus and the First Woman Apostle.* Santa Rosa, Calif., 2003. A scholar of Gnosticism, King argues the *Gospel of Mary* privileges inner spiritual knowledge over externally acquired knowledge. She examines the *Gospel's* teaching on various topics such as the body, women's authority, and visionary experiences, pointing out that the writing rejects Jesus' suffering and death as a path to eternal life.

Marjanen, Antti. *The Woman Jesus Loved: Mary Magdalene in the Nag Hammadi Library and Related Documents.* Leiden, 1996. This study, a revised dissertation, evaluates the descriptions of Mary Magdalene found in Gnostic literature. It concludes that she is presented as a prominent, even intimate, disciple of Jesus, who is a role model for women in early Christian communities. Marjanen observes a tension, however. Although Mary Magdalene is commended, the language subversively reflects a patriarchal culture that connects the male with the spiritual, perfect, and transcendent and the female with the sensual, incomplete, and mundane.

Robinson, James M., ed. *The Nag Hammadi Library in English.* Translated by members of the Coptic Gnostic Library Project of the Institute for Antiquity and Christianity. San Francisco, 1977.

Schaberg, Jane. *Resurrection of Mary Magdalene: The Legends, Apocrypha, and the Christian Testament.* New York, 2002. Drawing on canonical and extra-biblical literature, this feminist study approaches its subject through an analysis of legend, archaeology, and Gnostic traditions, employing Virginia Woolf's insights into structures of domination and communality.

Diane Treacy-Cole (2005)

MASCULINE SACRALITY is the designation of some domain of the supernatural universe as masculine. It is a feature of numerous religious systems in human societies around the world. A comparison of such systems reveals three levels of expression for the masculine valuation of the sacred.

At one level, certain natural symbols recur in religious systems in the form of hierophanies or sacred manifestations of masculine higher being. These natural symbols include sky, peaks and mountains, thunder, rain, and certain horned beasts, as well as such creatures of flight as eagles. At a second level of expression, religious systems often attribute certain cosmic functions to masculine metaphysical entities and/or specifically male supernatural beings. Thus gods as opposed to goddesses tend to be credited with such cosmic functions as creation of the mundane universe, establishment of the moral code, invention of the elements of mortal subsistence, and the like. Finally, in many religious systems there is a belief in the masculine orientation of certain sacred values. These commonly include order, stability, permanence, and essentiality. This level of religious expression may be basic to the social ethic and organization of a community, and may furnish it with a model and sanction for the pursuit of distinctive life patterns on the part of men and women.

A masculine being or entity of a particular system may have reality at more than one of these levels of expression and possibly at all three simultaneously. A brief illustration may be furnished by Indra, one of the highest gods in the Vedic religion of ancient India. An atmospheric divinity, he is credited with the unleashing of rain and storms, expressive of the masculine fecundating force. In general, Indra personifies cosmic vitality: he fertilizes the earth and makes rivers, sap, and blood alike to circulate; his retinue is the winds. He is also sagacious and deceptive, given to fooling his adversaries by changing his form. Finally, the power of Indra is sovereign: he is the chief of the heavenly council of gods, and in iconography he usually wears a crown.

As a figure of the Vedic religious universe, Indra exemplifies a particular set of conceptions about the masculine nature of the sacred. These are realized at the three levels of expression discussed above. At the level of natural symbols Indra is represented by lightning, his cosmic projectiles, and by the rainbow, whereby he dispatches those projectiles. At the level of cosmic functions, Indra is associated with fecundation and life-giving force. Finally, at the level of religious values, Indra has the meaning of sovereignty: he is the prototype of the ruler. He exemplifies the values pertaining to the proper relationship of ruler and ruled, for he is lauded and invoked more than any other deity in the oldest of Indian sacred texts, the *Ṛgveda.* As a secondary value, Indra represents a force of mystery and delusion, since he is a cosmic magician, able to generate new aspects and shapes at will.

From Indra's example it should be apparent that the levels at which masculine sacrality is expressed in religious systems frequently interrelate. It is difficult to discuss natural symbols, cosmic functions, and religious values of the masculine in isolation from one another. Nevertheless, these levels of expression should be borne in mind in the following discussion of the basic attributes of masculine sacred being.

PRIMORDIALITY. In religious systems, a form of higher being anterior to and/or prerequisite to other varieties of being tends to be masculine. Thus if differentiated forms of being are said to arise from some primordial undifferentiated entity, the latter is frequently masculine. The Arapaho of North America, for instance, believe in a supreme god out of whom the entire manifest world originated. Their name for him is Spider, presumably because the spider weaves his web out of himself.

Alternatively, the being that first dwells in or emerges from the undifferentiated cosmic mass tends to be masculine. In world mythologies, masculine first beings are abundant. The supreme god of the Flathead of North America is Amotken ("the old one"). Similarly, the supreme god of the Yahgan of Tierra del Fuego is Watauniewa ("the old, eternal, unchangeable one"). Among the Hawaiians, the supreme male divinity is the god who dwells primordially, at the dawn of sacred time, in Pō, the world of obscurity or darkness. Again, for the inhabitants of the Gilbert Islands, the earliest being in the primordial void is a male divinity, Na Areau the Elder. In Australian religions, during the primordial time called the Dreaming, over the earth roamed the first beings called Great Men, who are fathers to the creatures of the present world.

In mythology, feminine being tends to be secondary to masculine being. Thus, in the Navajo creation myth, First Man is paired with First Woman; both of them emerged from the union of primordial mists, but the emergence of First Woman follows that of First Man. In general, where there occur masculine and feminine forms of primordial being, the former tends to provide precedent for the latter: Eve emerges out of the body of Adam, not Adam out of Eve.

HEIGHT. Religious systems widely associate with masculine sacrality the attribute of height, as well as the corollaries of ascendancy and transcendence. Mircea Eliade points out in *Patterns in Comparative Religion* (1958) that belief in the celestiality of the divine being is nearly universal in religious systems. To this it may be no less validly appended that the highest entities and beings of religion and mythology overwhelmingly tend to be masculine. Moreover, the sky is the most fundamental of all natural symbols of masculine sacrality.

In cosmology, sky beings are preponderantly male as opposed to female. Io, meaning "raised up" or "on high," is the supreme god of the Maori, while the Yoruba of Africa call upon a god named Ọlọrun, "owner of the sky." In mythology, masculine first beings not infrequently represent sky divinities: Amotken, the previously mentioned first being of the Flathead, is also a celestial god, living in the crown of the cosmic tree.

In some mythologies, high gods originate elsewhere than in heaven, but journey there before the onset of profane time. This theme is particularly well attested in Australia. Bunjil, the god of the Wotjobaluk, for instance, lived on earth as a Great Man but later went to the sky. Among the Aranda, some earthborn first beings fell slumbering to the ground and reemerged into it, while others climbed sacred passages to the sky. The former are identified with totemic ancestors, the latter with high divinity—the sun, moon, and stars.

Because the nearly universal attribute of masculine sacrality is height—often expressed symbolically in terms of celestiality—the idea of access to godhood tends to be expressed through the imagery of ascent or, occasionally, of descent. In the Tantric tradition of southern Asia (India, Nepal, Tibet), the sublime is taken to be masculine; integration with it demands a technique of focusing and directing upward the feminine energies of the physiological microcosmos. In popular Hinduism, on the other hand, humans are said to approach the sublime at the god's instance, by his willful descent to the mundane world on a series of occasions called *avatāra.* Thus a popular myth cycle portrays the high god Viṣṇu mercifully descending upon earth to be born in a series of mortal forms: as a fish, as a boar, as King Rāma, as the rambunctious cowherd Kṛṣṇa, and so on. By contrast, while a mother goddess occurs in popular Hinduism and at times manifests herself on earth, she is not specifically credited with the capacity of *avatāra,* or divine descent.

As an attribute of masculine sacrality, height is fundamentally but not exclusively symbolized by sky and atmosphere. Height may also find expression in the symbolism of entities associated with loftiness. Sacred mountains are often the dwelling places of gods: the mythical Mount Meru of India and the Greek Olympus are well-known examples, as are certain peaks in Japan and other parts of the world. In some religious systems, height as an attribute of masculine sacrality finds expression in the natural symbolism of sky-dwelling creatures. Fabulous birds, especially eagles, tend to be associated with godhood. The Bella Coola of the northwestern coast of America, for instance, believe in an *axis mundi,* or sacred pole connecting heaven and earth, that was erected by the highest god; it is topped by a seated eagle. Elsewhere in the religions of North America, and in parts of Siberia as well, an important position is held by a mythical creature of eaglelike appearance, the Thunderbird. The Thunderbird's association with the awesome and fecundating masculine force of the sky is underscored by the fact that he is said to cause wind and thunder by flapping his wings, and lightning by opening and closing his eyes.

EFFULGENCE. Along with loftiness and sublimity, effulgence is a common attribute of masculine sacrality suggested by the natural symbolism of the sky. Various religious systems characterize the supreme god as white or shining. The Khanty and the Mansi of the Asian Arctic, for instance, describe their supreme god Num-Tūrem as luminous, golden, and white. One of the most powerful gods of Hinduism—dwelling, incidentally, on mountains—is Śiva, the "shining one." Devotional literature sometimes refers to him as "the lord white as jasmine." In Hawaiian mythology, at the dawn of sacred time the first light in the universe was that of the original being and high god. Navajo mythology has it that First Man and First Woman arose in unparalleled radiance from the primordial mists of the sky, the former in the place of sunrise and the latter in the place of sunset. While each burned a fire to light the firmament, the light of First Man's fire was stronger.

In cultic practices, sacred objects associated with masculine divinities tend to be chosen for whiteness or luminosity. This is true, for instance, of the crystal stones used in some Australian rituals. (The supreme god Baiame of certain southeastern Australian tribes sits on a crystal throne.) Similarly, the First Man of Navajo legend burned crystal for his fire and was accompanied at his birth by white corn.

Fire, of course, is a common accompaniment to religious ritual. In Vedic India, not only was fire itself a god, but it served as the purifier and sacred conveyance of sacrificial oblations to the high gods in heaven.

PERVASIVENESS. The attribute of being immanent in the universe is widely associated with masculine sacred being. It is not without significance that the name of the Hindu god associated with *avatāra* or divine descent, Viṣṇu, means "pervader." However, in relation to the concept of supreme godhood, the attribute of pervasiveness should be carefully qualified because sky gods, those quintessential exemplifications of masculine sacrality, are typically characterized as distant, remote, and inactive.

Accordingly, in many religious systems no special cult centers on the high being of the heavens. He may be left out of ritual and worship altogether, or be called upon only in times of extraordinary crisis. Many mythologies speak of the sky god as having once been actively engaged in cosmic business, but as having withdrawn from direct intervention in the universe for all time.

As *deus otiosus,* or retired divinity, the sky god nevertheless often remains in touch with mundane affairs and manifests his presence indirectly. A particularly widely held belief is that thunder is a manifestation of such a god. For instance, people of the Andaman Islands believe that thunder is the voice of their supreme god Puluga, and the Kansa Indians similarly maintain that thunder is the voice of their high god Wakantanka, whom they have never seen. Conceived of as a masculine epiphany, the growling sound of thunder may be imitated in ritual to invoke the presence of the sublime. In Australian ritual one of the most sacred objects is the bull-roarer, a piece of wood with a string tied through a hole in one end. When swung around, this object makes a growling sound suggestive of a bull's bellowing or of thunder; it is particularly used in boys' initiation rites. Similarly, in religious rituals, particularly male initiation ceremonies, of the North American Southwest, an instrument called a bull-roarer or whiner is used to invoke and evoke the presence of the high god.

As a variant on the treatment of thunder as a masculine epiphany, the growling force of volcanoes is occasionally regarded as a sign of the immanence of sacred masculine being. In South America, for instance, the Puruhá tribesmen of La Montaña occasionally sacrificed humans to a volcanic mountain inhabited by a god who made his presence felt from time to time.

Another way in which the high god, as *deus otiosus,* maintains an immanent presence in the affairs of the universe is by delegating authority to lesser supernaturals. The high god is often credited with initiating creation, but not always with completing it. In many mythologies the completion of the work is delegated to other figures of the high god's designation. For instance, the supreme god Gicelamu'kaong of the Delaware delegates creation to the sun, the moon, the thunder gods, the four winds, the earth mother, and the master of animals. It is common in mythology for the *deus otiosus* to withdraw, leaving his own son behind to carry on his cosmic activities. One of the many instances of this is found in the creation myth of the Gilbert Islands, where the divine protagonist Na Areau the Younger inherits the task of creation from his progenitor, Na Areau the Elder, the primordial being.

As son and successor to the high god, a secondary celestial may acquire considerable preeminence over the original high divinity. This preeminence is graphically symbolized in some belief systems by treating the high god's offspring and successor as a solar deity. Thus among the Tiv of Africa, the sun is the male child of the supreme being Awondo. Similarly, among the Wiradjuri and the Kamilaroi of southeastern Australia, the sun is the creator god's son.

In many mythologies, a type of supernatural who mediates between a withdrawn cosmic father figure and the mundane sphere is called the culture hero. A culture hero is usually portrayed as being with the high god in primordial times, and his sacred activities are sometimes performed at the high god's instance. As a stand-in for higher divinity, the culture hero may play a role in mythology that is more important than that of the high god. Culture heroes are sometimes represented anthropomorphically, but just as frequently the culture hero has a theriomorphic representation: as a coyote among some southwestern North American peoples, and as a great hare on the eastern North American coast; as a wolf or a raven in eastern Siberia; as a bat among the Paresí of Bolivia; and as a tapir in the Amazon Basin. Whatever his representation, the culture hero invariably serves to keep terrestrial society in touch with godhood, and almost without exception is portrayed as a male.

The activities of the culture hero are varied. In some mythologies he assists in the work of creation. This holds of the earth diver, a culture hero widely revered in North America who, at the instance of the high god, brings up the first land from the primal waters. Another typical task of the culture hero is to provide the elements of culture and/or the basic tools of subsistence to the ancestors of modern men. Among the Northwest Coast people and in eastern Siberia, for instance, the culture hero Raven brings light and various elements of culture to the mundane world in primordial time.

Acting as he does as a kind of rival to the ethically sublime high god, the culture hero is often portrayed as a schemer or trickster. He may assist men at the expense of higher being, as, for example, by stealing water, sun, or subsistence materials from the other world or by releasing game enclosed in a cave or other place inaccessible to humans. This aspect of the culture hero's character is exemplified by the fire-giver Prometheus of Greek mythology.

Culture heroes are also frequently portrayed as sacred ancestors of human descent groups. In the case of theriomorphic culture heroes, such beliefs may find expression through totemistic cults like those common in Australia and North America. More generally, religious systems commonly embody a belief that sacred substance, as an immanent component and inheritance of human individuals, is masculine—that is, it is derived from a high god, is transmitted by supernatural males acting in sacred time as ancestors of men, and is passed along in profane time through the male descent line. Thus, according to Hindu social theory and law, men alone pass the sacred substance of their lineage to their descendants, whereas the sacred substance inherited by a woman is not immutable, being transformed to correspond to that of her husband at the time of marriage. According to Hindu doctrine, then, women transmit to their offspring no sacred substance of their own but only that of their husbands.

Finally, regarding pervasiveness, it should be mentioned that the natural symbolism of the sky overlaying and embracing the supine earth powerfully suggests the immanence of the masculine sacred principle. A sexual dichotomy is commonly featured in religious systems, the sky being associated with the masculine and the earth with the feminine. Earth goddesses are not infrequently paired with sky gods. Moreover, earth and sky together constitute the prototype of the cosmic pair. A common theme in world mythologies is that of the primordial separation of the mutually embracing sky and earth. The creatures responsible for forcing sky and earth apart are variously represented as culture heroes, ancestors of the present earth dwellers, and/or the divine offspring of sky and earth themselves.

Contact between the separated celestial and terrestrial realms is frequently achieved in sacred time (and, by that precedent, is renewable in present, profane time) by means of certain sacred paraphernalia or entities of a fairly obvious sexual symbolism. Apertures in rocks or clouds are commonly portrayed as sacred means of passage, as are fabulous pillars, trees, ladders, mountains, and the like. In other words, Sky the father and Earth the mother are mediated by sacred holes and poles. These devices, moreover, contrast somewhat in their orientation: the sacred holes tend to be earth-directed, and the sacred poles sky-directed. Thus in the creation myth of the Gilbert Islanders the culture hero Na Areau the Younger walks in sacred time upon the rocklike upper surface of the sky, then pokes a hole down through it to apprehend the earth. From the bowels of the earth Na Areau then enlists an eel that braces himself against the earth with his tail in order to lift the sky upward by his snout. Thus the once direct contact between earth and sky comes to be mediated by the phallic force of that cosmic uplifter, the divine eel.

The performance of rituals for reestablishing primordial contact between the mundane world and the sublime is fairly common in religious systems. Such rituals tend to embody the symbolism of ascent, and the implements used in them are often of a phallic appearance. Thus to symbolize the *axis mundi*—the sacred connector of heaven and earth—a pole, ladder, or tree is often used; it may be ascended by a ritual specialist, who thereby symbolically journeys to heaven on behalf of his community. Such ascent rituals are typically performed in Siberia and other areas of the world by shamans, ritual specialists in techniques of healing and ecstasy.

FECUNDITY. Masculine sacred being is widely associated with generative and fecundating powers. This association seems to be based on the natural functioning of the sky, which fecundates the receptive earth by precipitation. One ritual of ancient India gives explicit expression to the association: the *Bṛhadāraṇyaka Upaniṣad* enjoins the husband to unite with the wife after uttering the formula, "I am the heavens, thou, the earth."

High gods and important male supernaturals tend to be credited with extraordinary potency and sexual capacity. These capabilities may be seen as independent of and additional to any role played by a given divinity in the creation of the cosmos. In popular Hinduism, for instance, the high god Śiva shakes the cosmos by the force of his copulation. A symbol of Śiva is the lingam, a stylized phallus usually given concrete realization in black stone.

In natural symbology, the masculine attribute of fecundity is often expressed by animals of high fertility. Bulls are a particularly common symbol. Śiva's cosmic vehicle is a fabulous bull, and the bull is also the form assumed by Zeus in the early Greek myth of Europa's ravishment.

As a symbol of the masculine, the bull tends to be cross-linked with the symbolism of thunderbolts. The latter are sometimes represented in the shape of stylized horns. Also, the bull's bellowing, like thunder, is an epiphany of godhood. Thus in the ancient Near East, the god Min had the epithet Great Bull, lightning was one of his attributes, and he was responsible for rain and for giving life. In Papua New Guinea, the culture hero Sosom is aurally evoked by the bull-roarer, which is his voice; his body is of stone, and he has an exaggerated penis, suggesting his sexual and fertile powers. Indeed, Sosom is credited with fertilizing man as well as soil.

Acculturation. Man's conception of order as a sacred force plausibly derives from observation of the events and entities of the heavens. Within the sky, which is itself unchanging and stable, celestial bodies move about according to a placid and unvarying rhythm. Because the sky is associated with the masculine, masculine sacrality comes to be seen more or less universally as the principle of permanence and order.

Thus, in mythology, the establishment of things that give permanence and stability to existence—rule, law, and the structured bases of things and institutions—tends to be treated as a masculine function. High gods and culture heroes delineate the features of the primordial landscape. They separate land from water and establish landmarks in the cosmos: sacred mountains, boulders, trees, rivers, and the like. Moreover, male supernaturals furnish society with the permanent institutions of culture, including law, moral code, and the forms of religious practice itself. At the same time, high culture tends to be perceived in religious communities as a domain proper to men. This is particularly true in regard to religion. Virtually without exception, human societies exclude women from the most sacred religious rites, as well as from manipulation of the most sacred objects of cult.

Where sacred values are associated with a dichotomy of gender, the usual tendency is for the masculine to be associated with stability and essentiality, and the feminine with change and materiality. The masculine may be identified with being's inner form—thought or structure—while the feminine is identified with being's outer forms—word or substance. The masculine may be associated with the potential, inactive form of being; the feminine, with kinetic, active being. The masculine is one and/or integrated; the feminine is plural and/or diffuse.

Thus in the Yoga and Sāṃkhya religious philosophies of India, the universe is said to be based on a polarity of two metaphysical principles. The masculine principle, *puruṣa* (which itself means "male" or "man"), is that of immanent and essential being, whose nature is immutable. By contrast, the feminine principle is associated with *śakti,* the energy that activates the ever-changing material universe. In the philosophical writings of the tradition, the masculine deprived of its *śakti* is compared to a lifeless god, while the feminine principle out of balance with the masculine is said to be rampant, capricious, and dangerous.

Navajo religion likewise associates dichotomies of cosmic function and religious value with the sacred masculine and feminine. In mythology the primordial being, First Man, creates a son and a daughter who are respectively Thought and Speech. The latter is called the outer form of Thought, and the former, the inner form of Speech; both are necessary for the creation of the inner forms of the present universe. As first boy and first girl, these entities are also said to have produced a daughter, a feminine deity identified with the earth. Her name, not insignificantly, is Changing Woman.

Gender dichotomies expressed in Navajo mythology are reflected with great consistency in the cultural and social patterns of the community. In *Language and Art in the Navajo Universe* (Ann Arbor, 1977), Gary Witherspoon points out that the Navajo associate the ritual and ceremonial domain with thought and the masculine. Thus most ceremonial practitioners are men. The ceremonies they conduct, moreover, are rigidly structured and must be performed without mistakes or modifications. Usually, Navajo ceremonies are concerned with restoring prior states of being. The fact that such ceremonies are the domain of men bespeaks a religious view that masculinity has to do with the origins of things and their culmination.

On the other hand, Navajo women are active in productive and domestic matters. They head most domestic groups and control land and sheep on behalf of those groups. This life pattern is consistent with the religious view of the feminine as the domain of growth, process, and change. For the Navajo, social and economic life concerns the generation of new conditions and new beings; it is characterized by movement, change, activity, and productivity. Here, then, it is appropriate that women dominate.

Summary. Belief in a masculine domain of the sacred universe is common in religious systems and tends to be associated with recurrent natural symbols, cosmic functions, and religious values. Based on the patterns discussed above, the following can be enumerated as more or less universal tendencies. (1) Primordial first beings of cult and/or mythology are most often male or masculine. (2) Cosmic functions pertaining to creation and fecundation are usually associated with masculine—as opposed to feminine—entities, principles, and beings. (3) Elements of culture tend to be associated with or attributed to masculine—as opposed to feminine—principles and/or supernaturals. (4) In community life, important differences in life patterns between the sexes have sanction and justification in beliefs about gender sacrality. In particular, manipulation of sacred objects and ceremonies tends to be seen as the appropriate domain of men. (5) The most exalted beings and entities of the masculine sacred universe are almost always associated with the natural symbolism of the sky and derive their attributes accordingly.

SEE ALSO Ascension; Axis Mundi; Bull-Roarers; Culture Heroes; Feminine Sacrality; Fire; Hieros Gamos; Kingship; Light and Darkness; Phallus and Vagina; Shamanism; Sky; Supreme Beings; Tjurungas; Transcendence and Immanence; War and Warriors.

BIBLIOGRAPHY

There is no single reference work devoted to the topic of masculine sacrality, though many pertinent sources are available. Concerning male supernaturals, a worthwhile and concise, if dated, treatment is Wilhelm Schmidt's "The Nature, Attributes and Worship of the Primitive High God." It appears in a volume edited by William Lessa and Evon Vogt, *Reader in Comparative Religion*, 4th ed. (New York, 1979). The standard reference work on comparative religions by Mircea Eliade, *Patterns in Comparative Religion* (London, 1958), contains much useful material on masculine sacrality.

Also worth citing are a number of studies on religious systems in particular world areas. For material on Australian systems, see Eliade's *Australian Religions* (Ithaca, N.Y., 1973). Some pertinent material on Papua New Guinea is found in Roy Wagner's *Habu* (Chicago, 1972). For a wealth of material on religious systems of the Western Hemisphere (and some references to northeastern Asia), see the valuable survey by Åke Hultkrantz, *The Religions of the American Indians* (Los Angeles, 1979). For Hawaiian and related Polynesian religions a standard source is Martha Warren Beckwith's *Hawaiian Mythology* (1940; Honolulu, 1970). A legend of the Gilbert Islanders that speaks for itself in the richness of its gender symbolism is reproduced by Arthur Grimble in "A Gilbertese Creation Myth," included in the Lessa and Vogt collection mentioned above.

On religious traditions of India and southern Asia there is a profusion of material related to masculine sacrality, among which several studies may be particularly recommended. Heinrich Zimmer provides a very accessible treatment on Indian sacrality in general, including much information on masculine sacrality, in *Myths and Symbols in Indian Art and Civilization*, edited by Joseph Campbell (1946; Princeton, 1972). Zimmer's *Philosophies of India*, also edited by Campbell (1951; Princeton, 1969), offers in its chapter "Sāṅkhya and Yoga" a penetrating discussion of the relationship of gender sacrality to the philosophical traditions of India. As a detailed account of sexual technique and symbolism in relation to metaphysics and philosophy within a single religious tradition, no study supersedes Mircea Eliade's classic *Yoga: Immortality and Freedom*, 2d ed. (Princeton, 1969). A stimulating treatment of masculinity and the sacred in Nepalese and Tibetan religious traditions is furnished by Robert A. Paul in *The Tibetan Symbolic World: Psychoanalytic Explorations* (Chicago, 1982). The joint monograph *Women in India: Two Perspectives* by Susan S. Wadley and Doranne Jacobson (Columbia, Mo., 1977) contains in Wadley's essay one of the best concise treatments available of *śakti* and its relationship to the Indian conception of the masculine and feminine sacred worlds.

Lastly, for a general anthropological perspective on the relationship of gender sacrality to social ethic and male/female life patterns, consult Sherry Ortner's "Is Female to Male as Nature Is to Culture?" in the collection *Woman, Culture, and Society*, edited by Michelle Rosaldo and Louise Lamphere (Stanford, Calif., 1974).

New Sources

Bodies, Lives, Voices: Gender in Theology. Kathleen O'Grady, Ann L. Gilroy and Janette Gray, editors. Sheffield, 1998.

Buddhism, Sexuality, and Gender. Jose Ignacio Cabezón, editor. Ithaca, N.Y., 1992.

Gender and Religion: On the Complexity of Symbols. Caroline Walker Bynum, Stevan Harrel and Paula Richman. Boston, 1986.

Invented Identities: The Interplay of Gender, Religion, and Politics in India. Julia Leslie and Mary McGee, editors. New Delhi and New York, 2000.

Shillony, Ben-Ami. *Divinity and Gender: The Riddle of the Japanese Emperors.* Oxford, 1999.

Spellberg, D. A. *Politics, Gender and the Islamic Past: The Legacy of Aisha bint Abi Bakr.* New York, 1996.

Suchocki, Marjorie. "The Unmale God: Reconsidering the Trinity." *Quarterly Review* 3 (1983): 34–49.

Wickremeratne, Ananda. "Shifting Metaphors of Sacrality: The Mythic Dimensions of Anurādhapura." *Journal of Developing Societies* 2/2 (1986): 193–207.

M. H. KLAIMAN (1987)
Revised Bibliography

MASHTOTSʿ, MESROP

MASHTOTSʿ, MESROP (c. 345–440), inventor of the Armenian alphabet and saint of the Armenian church. The major source for his biography is the *Life of Mashtotsʿ* written by his pupil and associate, Koriwn. The name *Mesrop*, the etymology of which is still unknown, does not appear in the works of Armenian writers until after the fifth century.

Mashtotsʿ was born to a peasant named Vardan in the village of Hatsʿekatsʿ, in the district of Tarōn (present-day Muş, Turkey). He was educated in Greek letters as a youth. As a young man he entered military service, becoming a clerk in the royal army stationed at Vagarshapat (present-day Echmiadzin). Led to solitary life by his interest in the scriptures, Mashtotsʿ became an anchorite. He evidently headed a *kellion* (a small group of anchorites) in the 390s. While proselytizing the people of the district of Goghtʿn (Nakhichevan, Azerbaijan), he conceived the idea of inventing an alphabet for the Armenian language and making the scriptures available to the common people. After deliberating with Bishop Sahak of Armenia and King Vṛam-shapuh of Persarmenia, he learned that a certain Syriac bishop by the name of Daniel had in his possession an alphabet for Armenian, which was immediately solicited. Finding Daniel's alphabet unsuited to the phonetic structure of Armenian, Mashtotsʿ and his pupils set out for Edessa to do research, and there in 404 Mashtotsʿ himself invented an alphabet consisting of thirty-six letters.

Returning to Armenia, Mashtotsʿ founded schools and continued the task of translating the scriptures that he had begun in Edessa. He devoted the rest of his life to literary, educational, and missionary works. At first his activities were concentrated in the southeastern and eastern parts of historical Armenia (i.e., Armenia Magna). He preached in Goghtʿn and then in Siwnikʿ, where he founded schools and established an episcopal see. Subsequently, he went to Georgia, where he invented a script for Georgian and preached the teachings of the Christian church. His concern for the Armenians on the Byzantine side of the border led him in the 420s to Constantinople, where he met the emperor Theodosius and the patriarch Atticus. Having received from them the necessary permission for carrying out cultural work, he returned to Byzantine Armenia, where he established schools and introduced the new script. During his stay there he persecuted an obscure sect known as the Barbarianos and invented a script for Albanian.

After his return to Persarmenia, Mashtotsʿ went to preach in Caucasian Albania (corresponding to parts of present-day Azerbaijan and Dagestan). He then visited those districts of historical Armenia that had been annexed to Georgia and Albania in 363. An important contribution of Mashtotsʿ was to unify the Armenians of these districts through linguistic bonds.

Mashtotsʿ spent the final two decades of his life in Armenia devoting himself to writing homilies and letters, none of which has survived. Some scholars identify Mashtotsʿ with the chorepiscopus Mastoubios of Armenia. Mashtotsʿ died on February 17, 440 and was buried in the village of Oshakan. A martyrium was built over his grave and he was venerated as a saint. The Armenian people consider him the father of the Armenian literary tradition and the creator of the Armenian national identity. His grave is still a major site of pilgrimage.

BIBLIOGRAPHY

Akinian, Nerses. *Der hl. Maschtotz Wardapet: Sein Leben und sein Wirken, nebst einer Biographie des hl. Sahak, mit einer deutschen Zusammenfassung.* Vienna, 1949.

Koriwn. *Varkʿ Mashtotsʿi.* Yerevan, 1941. Translated into English by Bedros Norehad as *Koriun: The Life of Mashtots* (New York, 1964).

Marquart, Josef. *Über den Ursprung des armenischen Alphabets, in Verbindung mit der Biographie des heil. Maštʿocʿ.* Vienna, 1917.

Peeters, Paulus. "Pour l'histoire des origines de l'alphabet arménien." In *Recherches d'histoire et de philologie orientales,* vol. 1, pp. 171–207. Brussels, 1951.

KRIKOR H. MAKSOUDIAN (1987)

MASKS

MASKS. This article will not attempt to establish a comprehensive inventory of masks and their various ritual uses because even larger works have only been able to do this imperfectly. Rather, as a general introduction to this field, it will concentrate on some of the general concepts and theories that have arisen from the study of masks. Its geographical focus will be Africa, Melanesia, and the Americas because these regions provided the data on which the theories discussed were based.

HISTORICAL OVERVIEW. Although the importance of descriptions by travelers, missionaries, and topographers from at least as early as the sixteenth century should not be overlooked, it can be argued that effective study of ritual masks began only in the nineteenth century. At this time the first interpretations and general theories about European folk traditions emerged, following (among others) the work of the Grimm brothers, Jacob Grimm (1785–1863) and Wilhelm Grimm (1786–1859), for whom folktales revealed traces of beliefs and myths connected with ancient pagan gods. Later, Wilhelm Mannhardt (1831–1880) took an interest in the folk religion of his time, in particular that of the rural communities. Collecting vast amounts of data, Mannhardt underscored the predominance of beliefs in fertility spirits and in the existence of a connection between vegetal and human life. Under his influence, a number of mask rituals came to be understood as incorporating ancient beliefs dealing with fertility, and masks were interpreted as representing demons of the vegetal world.

At the same time, E. B. Tylor (1832–1917) began to establish anthropology as a science of human beings and their culture. He described the evolution of civilization from the first humans, who in his eyes were in large part represented by contemporary "primitive" peoples, up to the civilized human of his day. To this end he used a comparative method to organize an impressive number of facts and documents in support of his evolutionary perspective. He also analyzed the process whereby elements belonging to an older stage of evolution survive into later stages in which they do not function adequately.

Therefore, the various elements that formed the core of the study of masks by folklorists as well as anthropologists up to World War II were present as early as the last quarter of the nineteenth century. These elements are: (1) the evolutionist perspective, following which the history of Western society can be reconstructed by classifying all known societies according to the degree of civilization they have reached; from this point of view, the peoples studied by ethnology enabled modern humans to relive, as it were, stages experienced by the Western world thousands of years ago; (2) the notion of "survival," used to describe those remnants of ancient customs that resisted evolution and survived beyond the period in which they were truly meaningful; and (3) intensive use of the comparative method—on the basis of what ethnology reported on traditional communities of Africa, Oceania, or the Americas, it was thought possible to reconstruct the earlier stages in the evolution of a society and to recover the original meaning of a particular custom.

By the end of the nineteenth century, scholars were in possession of an ever-increasing amount of comparative data on masks. In 1883 Adolf Bastian wrote a general study on the role of masks. In 1886 Richard Andree published an overview and summary of far-ranging documents from various periods. He thus made a large database on masks available to other scholars while organizing it into categories that have been constantly taken up ever since. Finally, in 1898 Leo Frobenius linked masks, seen as representing spirits of the dead, to secret societies. From his perspective this relationship originated as a male reaction to matriarchy and provided an explanation for the exclusion of women from practically all mask rituals. These early theories of ritual masks marked the anthropological and folkloric study of masks for several decades.

In a well-known article published in 1933, Karl Meuli formulated a general theory of "primitive" masks that he then applied to European traditions. According to him, there is a close connection between masks and so-called matriarchal societies. Furthermore, the majority of primitive masks represent spirits, primarily spirits of the dead. Indeed, the strange appearance of masked figures indicates that they do not belong to the human realm. Their behavior reinforces this interpretation: the masks beg while threatening, they reprimand, and they punish, after which they distribute gifts and grant wishes of prosperity and then disappear. Meuli explains this behavior as the result of a primitive belief that no death is natural, every death being the result of the malevolence of a living person. At particular times during the transition from an end to a beginning (the passage from one year to the next, for example), the underworld opens up, allowing the dead to return among the living. The masked figures represent these dead, who first seek revenge. By letting them pilfer and chastise as they please, one gives them the opportunity to calm down, after which they again bestow benevolence.

This interpretation, applicable equally to the masks described by ethnology and to European folk masks, is a synthesis of the theories founded on evolutionism, the notion of survival, and the comparative method, to which it adds psychoanalysis. Influential both within and outside scholarly circles, Meuli's theory played an important role in the history of the study of masks. It appeared, however, at a time when anthropology itself was gradually turning away from the ambitious theories developed at the beginning of the century to focus instead on elaborate and detailed localized research, employing a more demanding method. A similar trend emerged somewhat later, after World War II, in the study of folk traditions.

Up until then, because of the survival theory, a given culture was not studied as a coherent contemporary phenomenon but rather as a patchwork of various elements that could be analyzed somewhat independently of each other. Critics noted, however, that a custom should not be considered as a mere relic: it survived because it still had a role to play in the society in which it was observed. From then on studies increasingly tended to consider each custom as part of a contemporary system, analysis of which would illuminate the function of each of its components. Similarly, comparison was no longer applied to isolated elements; rather, scholars compared systems of relationships. Finally, the problem of the continuity of culture and cultural traits was tackled on a new basis: the historic dimension was reintroduced into the analysis and replaced the notion of survival, which focused interest on the question of origins and, in effect, canceled out history.

For instance, earlier authors had interpreted Carnival as either an old agrarian rite of purification and fertility aiming at driving out the bad spirits of winter or as a survival of the Roman Saturnalia. However, as Suzanne Chappaz-Wirthner (1995) points out, integrating history into the study of Carnival reveals that the imagery linked to secular and religious power, as manifest in court festivals and liturgical celebrations, played a decisive role in the development of a repertoire of carnivalesque images unique to the Christian West; individuals as well as social groups resort to it to play out their conflicts and express their aspirations. Carnival therefore can be considered a language with cosmic resonance enabling a dramatization of social dynamics.

The traditional populations studied by ethnology were again placed in the historical framework that general theories considering them as "primitive" had somewhat obscured. Thus, anthropologists and art historians as well as folklorists came to carry on their research within concrete historical frameworks. They now deal with notions of identity, creativity, change, exchange, power, and politics among other elements that shape a particular mask ritual at a particular time.

PROBLEMS OF DEFINITION. Although everybody seems certain of what a mask is, the definition of the term poses important problems. In the narrow and usual sense of the word, a *mask* is a false face behind which one hides one's own face for purposes of disguise. In ethnology, mask also refers to headpieces that do not cover the face, as well as elements of costumes that are worn over the face (such as veils, fringes) and other full or partial adornments of the body or face. The term *mask* is also used to refer to any representation of a face, whether or not it is worn on the face of a dancer. Consequently this includes mannequins; effigies; faces painted, molded, or carved on buildings and boats; and pendant masks as well as finger or pocket masks. Finally, the definition is sometimes widened to include face or body paintings and tattoos. Since scholars do not agree on the denotation of the term, confusion permeates the literature on the subject. As M. C. Jedrej (1980) puts it, the word "mask" identifies no coherent class of institutions of any use to social anthropologists.

It is important to keep in mind this problem of definition when trying to understand some of the ideas frequently advanced on the subject of masks; for example, the claim for universality of the mask: it is only when makeup, paintings, and tattoos are included in the definition of mask that one can say that masks can be found in virtually all cultures. But is such a broad definition justified? No one can say, for this question has not yet been systematically investigated.

It is important to note that the focus on the face that museums, art galleries, and books on masks often maintain gives a distorted view of the ritual mask. This interest in the face has encouraged a tendency to relegate to the background the many masks that, lacking a face, are simple hoods or fringes of fibers or beads falling in front of the face of the wearer. Fascination with the face has also tended to minimize interest in the costume of the mask, which has often been hastily dismissed either as fundamentally designed to conceal the wearer or as merely accompanying the mask. The mask must, however, be considered from a larger perspective so as to include the costume, the headdress, and the possible accessories, as well as immaterial factors such as the behavior, the dance steps, and the songs or texts pertaining to the mask. As Eberhard Fischer (1980) points out, among the Dan of Liberia and the Ivory Coast it is the headdress, and not the face, that immediately signals a mask's type. Consequently, the first step in the transformation of a mask from one category to another is the alteration of the headdress. The Dan also have "night masks," which comprise no tangible face but may include feathered headdresses. In ancient Egypt the priests' masks were adorned only with animal heads. The priests playing the roles of anthropomorphic deities did not require masks: the headdresses and the specific emblems of the gods were enough to identify them.

The face, therefore, is not necessarily the place where the meaning of the mask is concentrated. It follows that, when faced with an ensemble that includes all the elements of a mask (costume, headdress, dance), it is rather difficult to decide that there is no mask simply because the face of the dancer is painted rather than covered with a hood or false face. In any case, some scholars see a continuity between face paintings and masks because of the similarities between the two phenomena: both are temporary adornments, both appear on special occasions (initiation, marriage, death, or the lifting of a prohibition), and both seem to have comparable functions. On the other hand, the inclusion of tattoos in the definition of masks creates more problems than it resolves, for it is difficult to see how masks and paintings, which are temporary, could simply be classified with tattoos, which are permanent.

THE GEOGRAPHY OF RITUAL MASKS. A narrower definition of masks—one that takes as a fundamental criterion the existence of one element of costume (false face, hood) worn in front of the face—forces the realization that even in regions that are traditionally considered the privileged domains of masks there exist extensive zones in which masks are not used. In Africa, for instance, masks are found mostly along a strip that cuts across the center of the continent from west to east and curves toward the south. In the Americas, intensive use of masks is most frequent in the western heights of both North and South America. Finally, in Oceania the mask is practically absent from Polynesia. It is extremely widespread in Melanesia, although it is not used among most of the highland peoples of New Guinea, in the main part of Irian Jaya and in eastern Papua New Guinea, in parts of the Bismark Archipelago, in the central and Southeast Solomons and the Santa Cruz group, and in the Fiji group.

Several hypotheses have been put forward to explain the gaps in the distribution of masks. According to one, peoples without masks simply lack the wish to express themselves plastically and use other means to formulate and express their beliefs. Besides being an example of circular reasoning, this explanation runs against a number of exceptions that it cannot explain, particularly among peoples that have a statuary but no masks. The absence of masks in certain regions of Africa has also been attributed to the influence of Islam. However, anthropologists have demonstrated that the Islamicization of a given region did not necessarily lead to the elimination of the art of masks. On the contrary, as René Bravmann (1977) showed, some African societies created new masks after the advent of Islam in order to represent the *jinn.* Masks have also been said to be more characteristic of agricultural peoples. This hypothesis, however, accounts only imperfectly for the presence of masks among hunters in Asia and the Americas. The most successful general theory has been that of the historical cultural school, which explained the distribution of masks by arguing for their relationship with so-called matriarchal societies. An examination of the available data has, however, discredited this hypothesis as well. To date no global model is available to explain the geographic distribution of masks.

As a matter of fact, since being forced to abandon the broad theories of the nineteenth century and beginning of the twentieth century, scholars have no longer shown much interest for the study of questions of this amplitude. Most have focused instead on the in-depth analysis of a particular society, avoiding any far-reaching comparative evaluation they consider responsible in part for those past mistakes.

Nevertheless, some interesting localized studies have attempted to specify the status of masks within certain populations. Some try to elucidate the relationship that may exist in particular societies between the mask and other religious and sociopolitical structures. Others look for the provenance of the masks of particular groups or even attempt to reconstruct its history. For instance, Jean Guiart (1966) showed that, in certain parts of New Caledonia, the development of the art of masks seems to have been linked to the development of chieftainships in the same region. And according to William Siegmann (1980), the use or nonuse of masks to manifest spiritual forces in West Africa seems directly related to the dominant features of social organization in particular areas, and especially to the role of lineages and political structures. But still lacking is a general model that explains the distribution of ritual masks, an extremely important element of this institution.

The Dating of Masks. How far back can one trace the appearance of the ritual mask? Many scholars do not hesitate to go as far back as the Early Stone Age, but this raises a number of problems. The documents on which they base their conclusions are far from clear and admit of various interpretations. A workable example is that of the well-known "Sorcerer" of Les Trois Frères cave (Ariège, France, middle Magdalenian Age; c. 12,000 BCE). It is often presented as the oldest representation of a masked human, whereas paleontologists now prefer to see in it the portrayal of a mythical mixed being (half man and half beast). Such a figure may or may not be linked to the existence of masks; it may or may not constitute the inception or consequence of mask use. In any case, one cannot be categorical about it. This is true as well for an important number of the documents that have been interpreted as representing masked beings because they showed anthropomorphic figures with stylized or animal heads.

Ofer Bar-Yosef (1985) reports that, in a cave at Nahal Hemar in the Judean Desert, archaeologists have discovered fragments of several stone masks dating back to the prepottery Neolithic B period (seventh millennium BCE). It seems unlikely that these stone masks were affixed to the face of a wearer during ceremonies. They might be funerary masks or the facial part of effigies, or even masks that were hung from poles. Nothing allows a decision in favor of one or the other of these hypotheses. Nevertheless, these stone artifacts are the oldest reliable dated documents testifying to the existence of masks in the seventh millennium BCE. One cannot conclude from this find that there existed at the same time masks worn by living human beings during ceremonies. The oldest document from this point of view seems to belong to Egypt, where the representation of a masked figure appears on a fragment of a wall of the funerary temple of King Sahoure (fifth dynasty, c. 2500 BCE). From a general point of view, however, it may be assumed that the plausibility of the existence of ritual masks increases with the advent of the Late Stone Age, particularly in parts of the Middle East, Africa, and Europe.

What Does the Ritual Mask Represent? Throughout the principal regions in which ritual masks are found—Africa, Melanesia, and the Americas—the majority of the figures depicted in masks are primordial beings, mythical ancestors, culture heroes, and gods. In fact, in most cases the mask is not limited to representing a particular figure: it evokes the events in which said figure played a role. These events are not necessarily enacted as on a theatrical stage; they can be recalled by a dance, by a song or chant, by a piece of costume, or by the recital of a text that accompanies the performance of the mask. They can even be implicit: the mask intervenes in certain circumstances, because the figure it represents was implicated in similar circumstances at the time of origins—a fact known to the initiates at least.

Among the Senufo of Ivory Coast, for instance, the *kponiougo* (head or face) of the Poro, the men's secret society, recalls the original state of the world as it is described in mythological narratives. Among the Dan the mask of the toucan recalls the events that led God to create the earth. Although knowledge of Melanesian myths is only fragmentary, many masks of that part of the world seem to strive to recall paradigmatic events. For instance, the performance of the Mai masks of the middle Sepik of New Guinea is accompanied by the recital of totemic names and mythical texts through a bamboo megaphone. Another mask represents a feminine spirit, who, along with a masculine being often represented in the form of a crocodile, is the protagonist of events that accompanied the creation of the present world.

On the northwest coast of North America, Bill Holm (1972) has noted that the great majority of Kwakiutl masks are worn in representations, in stylized dance form, of incidents from hereditary family myths. In some cases the dance dramatizes the mythical adventure of the ancestor, whereas in others it re-creates a dance given to the ancestor by a mythical being with whom he came in contact. And according to Frank G. Speck (1949), among the Iroquois, at the beginning of each reunion of the False Faces, the chief recalls the confrontation between the original False Face and the Great Spirit, in memory of which the False Faces wear masks with crooked noses. Before entering the home of sick people to minister to them, the False Faces produce weird noises. These nasal sounds are said to be in imitation of the utterances the original False Face made during one episode of his challenge of the Great Spirit.

In the southwest United States the masked dances of the Zuni represent various episodes of their mythology. In the Shalako ceremony, for instance, some dances consist of a mimetic representation of the actions of the kachinas when they want to send rain to the Zuni.

In South America the mask rituals and their symbolisms often have an elementary character. However, careful analysis of the ceremonies reveals that many commemorate the principal episodes of the tribal mythology. The Carajá, who live along the middle course of the Araguaia River, have masks that portray a pair of supernatural parrots whose descent to humankind is related in myth. The Aruana, a dance performed in the same region, bears the name of a fish whose form the Carajá bore before they became human beings.

The use of masks may reflect the will to enact certain events as much as the desire to portray certain figures. At times, masks represent no particular character at all but only events. For instance, Carl Laufer (1970) reports that, among the Mali-Baining of the Gazelle Peninsula of New Britain, the main purpose of the Mandas festival is to represent the events that took place in the primordial mythic time. While a choir of women chants the story of creation, eighty masks enact its various phases: the birth of the sea, the appearance of the earth, the primordial forest, the flora, the winds, the animals and birds, and, when the stage has thus been set, the appearance of the first human couple and their sons. In this festival the *ngoaremchi* masks portray whirlpools and explain thereby the birth of the sea, which swirled forth in all directions, and the *ngavoucha* masks show how the earth was separated from the waters.

The Dogon of Mali have a mask called *sirige,* a term that can be translated literally as "two-storied house." This mask consists of a rectangular face surmounted by a high sculpted mast sometimes over five meters high. Marcel Griaule (1938) was told that the *sirige* was recent and profane, a mere sculpture inspired by the view of a two-storied house, and that the wide movements traced by its mast served only to allow the wearer to show off the power of his jaw and neck. Later, French anthropologists were given a more complex idea of Dogon cosmology, and it appeared that both the mask and the house recalled the same series of mythical events.

When the masks are shown in the main square of a Dogon village, the rich ensemble of things, animals, and human figures is a reproduction of the world, a catalog of both the live and extinct fauna of the cliffs and the plains. This display recalls all of the public functions, the trades, the ages; it presents a host of strangers, friends, or enemies; it mimics a wide variety of essential activities, all in a specified order, at least theoretically. It is truly a cosmos. When the mask society gets under way in the public square, it dances the march of the world; it dances the system of the world.

In some cases the system within which a population lives may be represented not by the ensemble of masks but by one particular mask that summarizes the entire system. Among the northern Igbo of eastern Nigeria, the mask *ijele* is a lofty tableau of figures with trappings hanging from its bottom edge to conceal the performer, who carries the whole structure on his head. According to John S. Boston (1960), the theme of the tableau that occupies the upper section of the *ijele* is the life of a typical Igbo community. Marie-Claude Dupré (1968) also tells that, among the Bantsaya group of the western Téké, the mask of the Kidumu dancer is a true summary of the culture of the group.

Masks are thus closely linked to the founding events of a society and its institutions, as well as to its values. It is therefore easy to understand why among many peoples the mask is linked to conservative forces and plays an important role in social control, assuming even a quasi-police function. The few examples given above also show that the primary function of masks is to represent rather than to conceal.

Sometimes the masks lose their ritual value at the end of the ceremonies of which they have been a part. This widespread phenomenon has often surprised observers. For instance, Francis E. Williams (1940) wondered why the *hevehe* masks of the Elema of New Guinea had to be killed and destroyed at the end of the ritual cycle, only to be re-created in the next cycle, when they might pass from one cycle into the other as if living throughout. He was puzzled to see the products of years of industry and art so readily consigned to the flames. This surprise in the face of the abandonment or destruction of the masks once they have been used reveals the bias of Western interpreters. First, Western interest in the mask as an artifact highlights the finished product and underestimates the ritual value involved in its making. Further, the Western tendency is to consider the masked ceremonies as theatrical performances and to think that all the preparations that precede them find their meaning only in the performance itself. This is a distorted view of those ritual cycles; often the making of the mask is in itself a ritual that reproduces the various phases of the creation of the archetypal mask. Therefore it is vitally important that the following cycle start anew at the beginning; that is, with the making of the mask. This is probably the reason why masks can be destroyed or left to rot without regret at the end of a cycle.

The Mask and Its Wearer. The notion of a "primitive mentality" was prevalent among writers at the beginning of the twentieth century. One of the principal characteristics of this mentality was the supposed inability to truly differentiate between the being and its appearance, the thing and its image, the signifier and the signified. Influenced by this view, most of the books on ritual masks spread a theory according to which the wearer of the mask not only represented a certain figure (ancestor, culture hero, god) but actually became this figure. For these authors, therefore, to put a mask on was akin to undergoing a real transformation. Some scholars took this theory even further and claimed that it provided an explanation for the phenomenon of masking itself. According to them, masks stemmed from the possibility they gave people to liberate themselves, to repudiate their current personalities, to undergo metamorphosis.

The conditions of ethnographic fieldwork do not always lend themselves to an evaluation of the precise level of reality on which the presence of a mythical being is located in a given ritual. But in light of available knowledge, the range in which the various hypotheses mentioned above may apply is becoming narrower and narrower. The best studies show that cultures that utilize masks are perfectly capable of distinguishing between the thing and its image.

For instance, in 1938 Griaule wrote that the Dogon did not fit the prevalent assumption about the attitude of Africans toward the images they create. Far from being fooled by the appearances or the material effects of the ritual, they were definitely aware of the difference between the thing represented and its image. They even had a word, *bibile,* to express the concept of reproduction, image, resemblance, or double. A photograph was the *bibile* of the person it represented. The shadow of a living being was considered a *bibile* because it reproduced the silhouette, the posture, and the movements of that person. A masked dancer was called *imina bibile,* meaning appearance or reproduction of the mask. Similar findings have been made among numerous other societies of Africa, Oceania, and the Americas.

Other factors also seem to reduce the applicability of the metamorphosis thesis. For example, masks are rarely associated with possession of the wearer, although that would be in the logic of the hypothesis. Also, the initiates in those communities in which masks are found constantly stress the fact that only the uninitiated believe they are actually in the presence of a spirit or a god. These statements are difficult to reconcile with the metamorphosis thesis. They have from the very first forced the proponents of that thesis to embark on often complicated explanations in order to bring their theory into harmony with the ethnographic data.

Similarly attempts to explain the ritual mask phenomenon by a desire, a need, even an instinct of the wearer were probably influenced by theories geared to explain the persistence of Carnival masks in the Western world. In one example of what Edward Evan Evans-Pritchard (1965) called the "if I were a horse" type of guesswork, the feeling of liberation experienced by Western mask wearers was projected onto African, American, or Melanesian mask wearers. Even if such a feeling may exist among some of these people, it cannot be used as a general explanation of the masked-ritual phenomenon.

Moreover, wearing a mask often carries social responsibilities that make it a service rather than a liberation. This service is often compulsory: reprobation, a fine, or worse await those who try to sidestep it. Either one particular person or a category of people is compelled to perform this service: one or several members of the family of the deceased, all members of a brotherhood, all circumcised males, and so forth. Although wearing a mask can bring honor and prestige, it also burdens the wearer with various duties, such as the payment of a tax to purchase the right to wear a particular mask or several months of preparation during which the mask wearers learn the dance steps, intensively rehearse combined movements, and may have to memorize complicated texts, sometimes in a secret language.

Among the Asmat of Irian Jaya, for example, it takes four to five months to prepare the masks for the ritual called Jipae. H. C. van Renselaar reports that, during all of that time, the mask wearers have to support the mask makers (van Renselaar and Mellema, 1956). The relatives of the deceased for whom the Jipae is celebrated must in turn give daily supplies of food to the mask wearers. Furthermore, the mask wearers must act as the surrogate for the dead and adopt and provide for the children of the deceased.

The Mask and the Dead. One mask has been constantly associated with the representation of the dead: the skull mask. Some experts, such as Hans Nevermann, have considered it the most primitive form of masking (Nevermann, Worms, and Petri, 1968). Those partial or complete skulls, worn on the top of the head or in front of the face, decorated, remodeled, or covered with tight skin, have provoked a number of speculations. Frobenius considered them part of a logical continuum of mask making that began with the use of a complete skull and moved to the use of a skull mask, concluding with the mask carved out of wood. Skull masks are found in the three main mask regions. In Africa such masks are sometimes tightly covered with skin in a manner peculiar to the Cross River region, where Keith Nicklin (1974) reports this same technique is used also to cover the wooden supports of masks. In Mesoamerica the Aztec often combined the techniques of remodeling and decorating the skulls (e.g., with turquoise).

However, as noted by Hans Damm (1969), the Melanesian masks have given rise to the most speculation. In Melanesia the skull is partially or entirely remodeled or molded over with a kind of wax; it is then painted and often adorned with human hair. These techniques are not, however, limited to the making of masks. They are also used in the making of funerary effigies (for example the *rambaramp* of Malekula) and in the remodeling of heads that are preserved in cult houses and in dwellings. The same techniques are also used to mold human heads on wooden supports.

Because of the radical changes these traditions have undergone, many of the assumptions made and questions raised about them may never be checked or resolved. However, an examination of some other Melanesian masks portraying deceased historical persons (as opposed to those that portray the dead as a class) help define a general context in which the skull mask can most probably be placed.

In the Jipae ceremony of the Asmat, for example, masked men represent the dangerous dead, especially children, great warriors, and the victims of headhunters. Beginning at dusk the masqueraders dance, imitating the waddle of the cassowary bird. At sunrise the dancers move toward the men's house followed by the women. Suddenly the men of the village attack the masks with sticks, forcing them to enter the men's house and thus ending the ritual. In the Jipae the mask represents a specific dead person, but several solar characteristics are also ascribed to it. This ritual begins at nightfall, when, according to the Asmat, the sun puts on its mask to descend into the land of the dead. The dancers imitate the cassowary, which the Asmat associate with the sun. Finally, the ritual ends at sunrise; that is, when the sun leaves the land of the dead and removes its mask.

To understand the meaning of a ceremony of this type one must keep in mind that for a large number of societies, in Melanesia as well as in other parts of the world, it is not death itself but ritual that opens the way toward the next life. This ritual fulfills several functions linked together: it prevents the spirit of the dead from wandering among the living; it allows deceased persons to enjoy the status due to their rank in the hereafter; it removes the risk that—in despair about their unresolved fate—the deceased might act against the living to force them to celebrate the appropriate ritual. This ritual may also mark the end of mourning, it may be the occasion of the redistribution of the land, or it may serve as a framework or a background for initiations. It is mostly during this kind of ritual that masks representing deceased individuals intervene.

Early-twentieth-century scholars were so preoccupied with the idea that the mask wearer was adopting a new personality that they overlooked one of the mask's main purposes—which may have been to identify the dead with his or her paradigm (the first dead human, a culture hero) and not just to associate the mask wearer with the spirit of the dead. This is nevertheless one of the important elements of such rituals as the Malanggan of New Ireland, the Ne-leng of Malekula, the Horiomu of the Kiwai, the Jipae of the Asmat, and the Mbii-kawane of Mimika (New Guinea).

This identification can take various forms that fall between two extreme poles. In some cases nothing is done to bring the appearance of the masked figure, as it is defined by tradition, closer to that of the deceased. In those cases it is mainly the attitude of kin that expresses this identification; they act toward the masked figure as they would toward the departed they are mourning. The ceremony called Mbii-kawane described by Jan Pouwer (1956) is close to this type. In other cases a considerable effort is made to ensure that the masked person will resemble the deceased as closely as possible. In this case the identification with the paradigmatic figure is made through the text, which is sung or recited, and through the dance steps. This seems to be the case with the Horiomu of the Kiwai as reported by Gunnar Landtman (1927).

The above remarks also pertain to a number of funerary masks. This term has been used to categorize various types of masks found on mortal remains, on mummies, on funerary urns, or among the funerary furnishings found in certain tombs. Some of these masks are realistic and seem like portraits, and they have on occasion been molded directly onto the dead person's face. Others, sometimes called "idealistic," reveal traits that obviously did not belong to the deceased. In between those two categories, variations such as idealized or stylized portraits are found. Others, finally, do not have a real face. In some cases the mask could have been worn by somebody during a burial ritual, whereas in other cases there is no evidence to support that interpretation.

Given the extensive variations that may be found from one tradition to the next, funerary masks seem to have two basic purposes: (1) to prevent the spirits of the dead from wandering among the living (by offering them a new support, by luring or forcing them away from the living); and (2) to insure that the deceased will safely reach his or her resting place in the hereafter. The identification with a paradigm should not be overlooked as a means to achieve this goal.

MASKS, WOMEN, AND SECRET SOCIETIES. According to the Viennese school of the "culture circles," in a former era women played a leading role in society, and in order to resist their economic, social, and religious supremacy, men created secret societies. The theory postulated a quasi-organic link between secret societies and masks, the latter being the means used by men to seize power from women and secure their own domination. This link was even noted by authors who did not necessarily accept the hypothesis of matriarchy. Here, summarized in four points, is how Felix Speiser (1923) expressed it: (1) the goal of secret societies is to terrorize the uninitiated, in particular women; (2) this is achieved through the use of masks representing spirits; (3) for masks to represent spirits the wearer must not be recognizable; and (4) it follows that originally masks must have disguised the wearer's entire body.

This theory was immensely popular, for it offered a logical and unique framework for an array of puzzling facts. However, along the road taken by anthropology since the 1930s, every one of its elements was disputed and abandoned. Regarding secret societies, the apparent simplicity of the theory stemmed from the fact that its authors had amalgamated extremely diverse institutions under the term *secret society* (e.g., brotherhoods of men, age-group organizations, initiation societies, societies based on social rank, and more or less restricted cultic societies). Furthermore, later studies showed that masks could very well exist independently of secret societies and that many secret societies had no masks, while others had only recently adopted them. Therefore the concept of a primary and original link between masks and secret societies could no longer be taken uncritically.

As for secrecy, it is true that, in many societies with masks, the uninitiated must not speak of matters concerning masks, or they must only speak of them in a certain manner, or they are supposed to remain ignorant of certain things. However, the best-documented reports from Africa, Melanesia, and the Americas acknowledge that women in particular know the true nature of masks and that a large gap often separates that which they are supposed to know from that which they actually know. Secrecy, or the pretense of it, is but one element that helps delineate and maintain the identity of the various groups in a given society, but it cannot be taken literally.

The theory contended that masks were meant to terrorize women. However, because in many cases women were aware of the true nature of the masks, they could not be fooled by a ritual, the purpose of which would be to deceive them. Yet they display emotions, sometimes violent ones, during the performance of certain masks. If they are not fooled by appearances, then how can those feelings be explained?

When women express fear when confronted with the masks or when they recognize in them the deceased of their own families and implore them with cries and tears, one is forced to wonder if such a display of emotions is not an essential part of the ritual itself. There is no doubt that women are frightened in many societies. But they are afraid of the consequences that would follow if they did not behave as tradition requires or if they breached the prohibitions surrounding the masks. Depending on the situation and the society, a fine would be levied; a sacrifice would have to be made; the woman would become sick, sterile, or even die; the men might kill her; the mask wearer would die; or the entire community would disappear. But this does not mean that women act merely out of fright and that their emotions (for instance, their grief) are not genuine. Indeed this does not rule out sincerity in any way, but a sincerity that is addressed to what is represented in the ritual and a sincerity that cannot be understood unless one first accepts that all the participants may experience the ritual at the level of what is being represented while remaining perfectly aware of the means used to create the performance. The deeper meaning of masked rituals can only be perceived if one acknowledges that the behavior of everyone concerned is meaningful, the women's as well as the men's, both contributions being at once necessary to the ritual and constitutive of it.

The elegant "culture circles" hypothesis presented the relationship between masks and women as one of incompatibility, ignorance, and credulity. A detailed examination shows that the situation is more complex and differentiated. Indeed the prohibitions to which women are subject sometimes only cover a particular part of the mask or a special circumstance. It is also impossible to ignore the particular position that certain women occupy within the masking society (among the Dogon, the Kono, or the Mende, for instance). In certain cases women contribute to the preparation of masks or dancers or are entrusted with the care and preservation of the masks and other ritual objects otherwise prohibited to women. In addition, the wives of chiefs and the wives of the heads of initiation societies are sometimes initiated into the secrets of masks, and, from a more general point of view, numerous elderly women are exceptions to the "rule" that all women be excluded from masking rites. Last but not least, there are of course cases—attested in Africa, Melanesia, and the Americas—when masks are worn by women, often during women's initiations. Due to the anthropocentrism of early scholarship, little information was available on these ceremonies when the theory was proposed. Fortunately, since the 1970s this situation has been changing rapidly (for instance, see Sidney L. Kasfir and Pamela R. Franco [1998]).

However, even taking into consideration the numerous cases mentioned above, a simple statistical study will show that in most instances masks are worn by men, even though women are said to have discovered and owned them to begin with. Thus, if the masked ritual must be viewed in the context of a symbolism shared by men and women, the dialectic between the two sexes that the ritual reveals must not be neglected. It comes back to the sacredness peculiar to each sex and to the ambivalent attitude of men toward the extraordinary power of women: particularly with regard to women's ability to conceive and to self-regulate their uncleanness through their menstrual cycles.

SEE ALSO Ancestors, article on Mythic Ancestors; Bodily Marks; Carnival; Culture Heroes; Dogon Religion; Griaule, Marcel; Kulturkreiselehre; Paleolithic Religion.

BIBLIOGRAPHY

Andree, Richard. "Die Masken in der Völkerkunde." *Archiv für Anthropologie* 16 (1886): 477–506.

Bar-Yosef, Ofer. *A Cave in the Desert: Nahal Hemar.* Jerusalem, 1985.

Bastian, Adolf. "Masken und Maskereien." *Zeitschrift für Völkerpsychologie* 14 (1883): 335–358.

Bastin, Marie-Louise. *Introduction aux arts d'Afrique noire.* Arnouville-lès-Gonesse, France, 1984.

Bédouin, Jean Louis. *Les masques.* Paris, 1967.

Biebuyck, Daniel P. *Lega: Ethics and Beauty in the Heart of Africa.* Brussels, 2002.

Boston, John S. "Some Northern Ibo Masquerades." *Journal of the Royal Anthropological Institute of Great Britain and Ireland* 90 (1960): 54–65.

Bravmann, René A. "Gyinna-Gyinna: Making the Djinn Manifest." *African Arts* 10, no. 3 (April 1977): 46–52, 87.

Chappaz-Wirthner, Suzanne. *Le turc, le fol, et le dragon: Figures du carnaval haut-valaisan.* Neuchâtel, Switzerland, 1995.

Cole, Herbert M., ed. *I Am Not Myself: The Art of African Masquerade.* Los Angeles, 1985.

Craig, Barry, Bernie Kernot, and Christopher Anderson, eds. *Art and Performance in Oceania.* Honolulu, 1999.

Crumrine, N. Ross, and Marjorie Halpin, eds. *The Power of Symbols: Masks and Masquerade in the Americas.* Vancouver, 1983.

Damm, Hans. "Bemerkungen zu den Schädelmasken aus Neubritannien (Südsee)." *Jahrbuch des Museums für Völkerkunde zu Leipzig* 26 (1969): 85–116.

Dupré, Marie-Claude. "A propos d'un masque des Téké de l'ouest (Congo-Brazzaville)." *Objets et Mondes* 8, no. 4 (1968): 295–310.

Eban, Dan, Erik Cohen, and Brenda Danet, eds. *Art as a Means of Communication in Pre-Literate Societies.* Jerusalem, 1990.

Ebeling, Ingelore. *Masken und Maskierung: Kult, Kunst, and Kosmeti: Von den Naturvölkern bis zur Gegenwart.* Cologne, Germany, 1984.

Emigh, John. *Masked Performance: The Play of Self and Other in Ritual and Theatre.* Philadelphia, 1996.

Evans-Pritchard, Edward Evan. *Theories of Primitive Religion.* Oxford, 1965.

Fischer, Eberhard. "Masks in a Non-Poro Area: The Dan." *Ethnologische Zeitschrift Zürich* 1 (1980): 81–88.

Frobenius, Leo. *Die Masken und Geheimbünde Afrikas.* Halle, Germany, 1898.

Griaule, Marcel. *Masques Dogons.* Paris, 1938.

Guiart, Jean. *The Arts of the South Pacific.* New York, 1963.

Guiart, Jean. *Mythologie du masque en Nouvelle-Calédonie.* Paris, 1966.

Hartmann, Günther. *Masken südamerikanischer Naturvölker.* Berlin, 1967.

Holm, Bill. *Crooked Beak of Heaven: Masks and Other Ceremonial Art of the Northwest Coast.* Seattle, 1972.

Inhaber, Herbert. *Masks from Antiquity to the Modern Era: An Annotated Bibliography.* Lanham, Md., 1997. Inhaber reviews about twelve hundred books, articles, dissertations, videos, and other media that primarily discuss masks.The entries are filed geographically and according to criteria such as historical aspects, dramatic aspects, and philosophical and psychological aspects. An index completes this extremely useful bibliography.

Jedrej, M. C. "A Comparison of Some Masks from North America, Africa, and Melanesia." *Journal of Anthropological Research* 36 (1980): 220–230.

Kaeppler, Adrienne L., Christian Kaufmann, and Douglas Newton. *Oceanic Art.* Translated by Nora Scott and Sabine Bouladon. New York, 1997.

Kasfir, Sidney Littlefield, and Pamela R. Franco, guest eds. "Women's Masquerades in Africa and the Diaspora." *African Arts* 31, no. 2 (1998): Special issue.

Landtman, Gunnar. *The Kiwai Papuans of British New Guinea: A Nature-Born Instance of Rousseau's Ideal Community.* London, 1927.

Laufer, Carl. "Die Mandas-Maskenfeier der Mali-Baining." *Jahrbuch des Museums für Völkerkunde zu Leipzig* 27 (1970): 160–184.

Lawal, Babatunde. *The Gèlèdé Spectacle: Art, Gender, and Social Harmony in an African Culture.* Seattle, 1996.

Lévi-Strauss, Claude. *The Way of the Masks.* Translated by Sylvia Modelski. Seattle, 1982.

Lommel, Andreas. *Masks: Their Meaning and Function.* Translated by Nadia Fowler. New York, 1981.

Lupu, François, ed. *Océanie: Le masque au long cours.* Rennes, France, 1983.

Mack, John, ed. *Masks and the Art of Expression.* New York, 1994.

Malin, Edward. *A World of Faces: Masks of the Northwest Coast Indians.* Portland, Ore., 1978.

Mauldin, Barbara. *Masks of Mexico: Tigers, Devils, and the Dance of Life.* Santa Fe, N.Mex., 1999.

Mead, Sidney M., ed. *Exploring the Visual Art of Oceania: Australia, Melanesia, Micronesia, and Polynesia.* Honolulu, 1979.

Meuli, Karl. "Maske, Maskereien." *Handwörterbuch des Deutschen Aberglaubens.* Vol. 5, pp. 1744–1852. Berlin, 1933. Reprinted in Karl Meuli. *Gesammelte Schriften.* Pp. 69–162. Basel, Switzerland, 1975.

Nevermann, Hans, Ernest A. Worms, and Helmut Petri. *Die Religionen der Südsee und Australiens.* Stuttgart, 1968.

Nicklin, Keith. "Nigerian Skin-Covered Masks." *African Arts* 7, no. 3 (1974): 8–15, 67–68, 92.

Norris, Karen, and Ralph Norris. *Northwest Carving Traditions.* Atglen, Pa., 1999.

Nunley, John W., and Cara McCarty. *Masks: Faces of Culture.* New York, 1999.

Pernet, Henry. *Ritual Masks: Deceptions and Revelations.* Translated by Laura Grillo. Columbia, S.C., 1992. This "problem-oriented" and thematic book deals in greater depth with the questions raised in this article. It also provides abundant references, a twenty-seven-page bibliography, and an index.

Phillips, Ruth B. *Representing Woman: Sande Masquerades of the Mende of Sierra Leone.* Los Angeles, 1995.

Pouwer, Jan. "A Masquerade in Mimika." *Antiquity and Survival* 5 (1956): 373–386.

Ray, Dorothy Jean. *Eskimo Masks: Art and Ceremony.* Seattle, 1967.

Reed, Daniel B. *Dan Ge Performance: Masks and Music in Contemporary Côte d'Ivoire.* Bloomington, Ind., 2003.

Siegmann, William C. "Spirit Manifestation and the Poro Society." *Ethnologische Zeitschrift Zürich* 1 (1980): 89–95.

Smidt, Dirk A. M., ed. *Asmat Art: Woodcarvings of Southwest New Guinea.* New York, 1993.

Speck, Frank G. *Midwinter Rites of the Cayuga Long House.* Philadelphia, 1949.

Speiser, Felix. *Ethnographische Materialien aus den Neuen Hebriden und den Banks-Inseln.* Berlin, 1923.

Strother, Zoë S. *Inventing Masks: Agency and History in the Art of the Central Pende.* Chicago, 1998.

Sturtevant, William C., gen. ed. *Handbook of North American Indians.* 17 vols. Washington, D.C., 1978–2001 (13 of 17 vols. published as of 2001).

Van Renselaar, H. C., and R. L. Mellema. *Asmat Art from Southwest New Guinea.* Amsterdam, 1956.

Washburn, Dorothy K., ed. *Hopi Kachina: Spirit of Life.* Seattle, 1980.

Wherry, Joseph H. *Indian Masks and Myths of the West.* New York, 1974.

Williams, Francis Edgar. *Drama of Orokolo: The Social and Ceremonial Life of the Elema.* Oxford, 1940.

Wyatt, Gary. *Spirit Faces: Contemporary Native American Masks from the Northwest.* San Francisco, 1995.

HENRY PERNET (2005)

MAṢLAḤAH is the Arabic term for the Islamic concept of public interest or general welfare of the community of Muslims. Consideration for the public interest (*istiṣlāḥ*) is held by Muslim legal scholars to be ancillary to the four canonical sources of Islamic law, namely the Qurʾān; the *sunnah*, or normative behavior of the Prophet; *ijmāʿ*, or the historical consensus of the community; and *qiyās*, analogical extension of accepted law or judgment. Although these sources are meant to provide guidelines for all eventualities, there have always been instances that seem to require abandoning either the specific ordinances of the Qurʾān and *sunnah* or the results of analogical reasoning, because of the overriding nature of the public interest.

In positive or applied law, considerations of *maṣlaḥah* in social and economic matters have usually led to the inclusion of pre-Islamic or non-Islamic local laws and customs in regional local practice. Historically, the concept of *maṣlaḥah* has been associated more often with Mālikī school than with the other Sunnī schools of law. This is largely due to the attention the Mālikī scholars of Morocco have given it in their recognition of the validity of local practice (*ʿamal*), even though they thereby allow institutions that strict Mālikī theory would reject. But the association of *maṣlaḥah* with the Mālikīyah should not be overemphasized; all Sunnī schools of law have contributed to its development and utilization.

The early and medieval Muslim scholars who wrote on *maṣlaḥah* defined it in various ways. Some approached it purely from a practical point of view; others considered it a problem of the philosophy of law and discussed its moral and ethical aspects. They all indicated, however, that the investigation of *maṣlaḥah* involved concern for the spirit rather than the letter of the law. Focusing on this feature of *maṣlaḥah*, a few twentieth-century Muslim reformers have put forward the idea of redefining *maṣlaḥah* in terms of the needs of contemporary society and then using *istiṣlāh* as a vehicle for modernizing and revitalizing Islamic law. Thus far, at least, their efforts have not been successful.

BIBLIOGRAPHY

Aghnides, Nicolas P. *Muhammadan Theories of Finance.* New York, 1916. Very useful and detailed introduction to the sources of Islamic law.

Kerr, Malcolm H. *Islamic Reform: The Political and Legal Theories of Muhammed Abduh and Rashid Rida.* Berkeley, 1966. Discusses the history of *maṣlaḥah* and some modern attempts to utilize it for Islamic reform.

Schacht, Joseph. *An Introduction to Islamic Law.* Oxford, 1964. The authoritative general introduction, with a very valuable bibliography.

SUSAN A. SPECTORSKY (1987)

MASORAH SEE BIBLICAL LITERATURE, *ARTICLE ON* HEBREW SCRIPTURES

MASPERO, HENRI

MASPERO, HENRI (1883–1945), French Sinologist and pioneer of Daoist studies. Son of the Egyptologist Gaston Maspero, Henri Maspero did his first research in 1904 in Cairo on the financial system of ancient Egypt. In 1907 he obtained his *licence en droit* and his diploma in Chinese. From 1908 to 1920, he was a member of the École Française d'Extrême-Orient (EFEO) and was stationed in Hanoi, whence he traveled extensively throughout Southeast Asia and China. He was in Beijing during the winter of 1908–1909, at the time of the death of Emperor Tezong and the Dowager Empress Cixi, and he witnessed some of the ensuing revolutionary agitation. His research and publications covered an amazing range of subjects: the administrative geography of ancient Indochina, the beginnings of Buddhism in China, Chinese epigraphy, history of law, architecture, art, and astronomy, as well as linguistics. His articles on the Thai languages and on the phonetics of Annamese were the first serious studies of Southeast Asian languages. The Chinese elements in Annamese led him, before Bernhard Karlgren, to the study of ancient Chinese phonology.

In 1914, on a study mission to China, Maspero began an investigation of contemporary Chinese religious life, which he continued among Chinese expatriates in France during World War I. This fieldwork enabled him later to describe the modern Chinese folk religion in a remarkably lively fashion.

Maspero initiated and supervised, until 1920, the vast EFEO collection of Indochinese documents, a unique repository of the history of this region. Some of this material served him for comparative studies on modern Thai and ancient Chinese religion, studies that confirmed the results of Marcel Granet's epoch-making work (1919) on the *Book of Odes.*

In 1920 Maspero was recalled to Paris and appointed the successor of Édouard Chavannes at the Collège de France. The only book he published in his lifetime, *La Chine antique* (1927), is a history of China from the beginnings to the third century BCE. The remaining years of his life were devoted to a thorough preparation of a second volume dealing with Chinese history up to the Tang dynasty.

The summaries of Maspero's courses at the Collège de France (1921–1944) show that, among many other aspects of Sinology that he treated in numerous articles, he was most interested during this period in the emergence of the Daoist religion. This was virgin territory, uncharted not only by Western scholars but also by Chinese scholars, who traditionally had despised everything Daoist except the philosophers Lao-tzu and Chuang-tzu. In 1926 the sole remaining complete set of the Daoist canon was published in 1,120 Chinese-style volumes. Maspero was the first to start extracting from this huge store of documents (dating from the fourth century BCE, in the case of the early Daoist mystical writings, to the sixteenth century CE) a chronology of texts and a coherent history of the origins and the first five centuries of the Daoist religion. He discovered that this religion, far from being the popular hodgepodge of superstitions described by missionaries, or the illiterate and seditious demon-worship denounced by the Chinese scholarly elite, was in fact the native high religion of all classes of Chinese society, with a literate tradition going back to the second century CE. Realizing the importance in Daoism of physiological longevity techniques and of mystical techniques for gaining union with the Dao (and participating in its immortality), Maspero devoted a detailed study to them.

On July 27, 1944, Maspero was expected in vain at a session of the Académie des Inscriptions et Belle-Lettres, of which he was president at the time. He had been arrested by the German occupation forces because of his son's activities in the French Resistance. On August 15, 1944, he was aboard the last prisoner transport to Germany before the liberation of Paris. He succumbed to disease amid the horrors of Buchenwald on March 17, 1945, less than one month before the liberation of this concentration camp by American troops.

SEE ALSO Granet, Marcel.

BIBLIOGRAPHY

Maspero's *La Chine antique* (Paris, 1924) has been translated as *China in Antiquity* (Amherst, Mass., 1979), and the majority of Maspero's studies on Daoism have been collected in *Le daoïsme et les religions chinoises* (Paris, 1971), translated as *Daoism and Chinese Religion* (Amherst, Mass., 1981). Among Maspero's writing on Buddhism are "Le songe et l'ambassade de l'empereur Ming" and "Communautés et moines bouddhistes chinois au deuxième et troisième siècles," both of which appear in the *Bulletin de l'École Française d'Extrême-*

Orient (Hanoi) 10 (1910): 95–130 and 222–232, respectively, and "Les origines de la comunauté bouddhiste de Loyang," *Journal Asiatique* 225 (1934): 88–107. On mythology and popular religion, see "Légendes mythologiques dans le Chou king," *Journal asiatique* 204 (1924): 1–100; "The Mythology of Modern China," in *Asiatic Mythology*, edited by Joseph Hackin and others (New York, 1932); and "Les ivoires chinois et l'iconographie populaire," in *Les ivoires religieux et médicaux chinois d'après la collection Lucien Lion*, edited by Maspero, René Grousset, and Lucien Lion (Paris, 1939).

An obituary by Paul Demiéville, including a useful bibliography, appears in *Journal Asiatique* 234 (1943–1945): 245–280, and Demiéville's summary of Maspero's contribution to Chinese studies, "Henri Maspero et l'avenir des études chinoises," can be found in *T'oung pao* 38 (1947): 16–42.

ANNA SEIDEL (1987)

MASS SEE EUCHARIST

MASSIGNON, LOUIS

MASSIGNON, LOUIS (1883–1962), French Islamicist. Louis-Fernand-Jules Massignon grew up in Paris, where he enrolled at the university and pursued various disciplines, including Arabic. He spent most of the period 1906–1910 studying in Cairo and carrying out research in Iraq and Istanbul, and in 1912–1913 he was visiting professor at the Egyptian (later Cairo) University. In 1922 he submitted his two requisite doctoral theses on al-Ḥallāj and early Islamic mysticism to the University of Paris; published in two volumes as *La passion d'al-Hosayn-ibn-Mansour al'Hallâj, martyr mystique de l'Islam exécuté à Bagdad le 26 mars 922* (1922), his *thèse principale* has since become a classic. A second, greatly enlarged edition appeared posthumously (1975). In 1926 Massignon was elected professor of sociology and sociography of Islam at the Collège de France in Paris, and in 1933 he was appointed director of studies for Islam at the École Pratique des Hautes Études, also in Paris, in the section of *sciences religeuses*. In the same year he was elected a member of the new Academy of the Arabic Language in Cairo, where he spent several weeks working each winter.

Born and raised a Roman Catholic, Massignon underwent a particular inner experience in 1908, which he spoke of as his "conversion." As a result he became once more a loyal member of the Roman Catholic church, increasingly with a spiritual vocation with regard to Islam. In 1931 he became a third-order Franciscan, and in 1934 he founded the Badaliya sodality, the members of which were inspired by compassion and devoted themselves to "substitution" for their Muslim brethren. (The idea of substitution involves one person's taking another's suffering upon himself.) After joining the Greek Catholic (Uniate) church in 1949, Massignon was ordained a priest on January 28, 1950, in Cairo. Even though ordination in this church is possible for a married man, as Massignon was, the Vatican imposed the condition that Massignon's priesthood, which turned out to be an essential element in his spiritual life and vocation, should remain secret. Even after his retirement in 1954 Massignon continued to take an active part in defending victims of violence (e.g., Palestinians and Algerians) until his death on October 31, 1962, in Paris.

Massignon's work is the accomplishment and creation of a mind of remarkable stature, illuminated by flashes of genius but capable of being carried away, to the verge of aberration, by ideas. A reader is confronted with the difficult task of recognizing the particular perspectives in which Massignon interpreted his subject matter and correcting them according to the scholarly criteria of factual interpretation and validity. If Massignon's unique spiritual commitments made his oeuvre one of the richest in the whole field of Islamic studies, one must recognize that it drew its strength from an existential position unrelated to scholarship. While its originality deserves respect and admiration, the lack of scholarly standards must also be recognized.

Massignon's monumental study of al-Ḥallāj will probably remain his lasting contribution to the study of Islam and religion generally. It is more than a careful historical reconstruction of facts and bygone spiritual worlds. It is the record of a spiritual encounter in which a scholar fascinated by a religious truth meets a mystic of the past in whom this truth is recognized. Were it not for Massignon, such spiritual dimensions might not have been revealed in al-Ḥallāj, but to what extent the spiritual al-Ḥallāj discovered by Massignon is the result of valid hermeneutics of the texts and not a spiritual creation born of the religious needs and passions of Massignon as a person is a question that haunts the reader. Massignon's inner experiences of May and June 1908, as a result of which he received a "new life" of adoration and witnessing, welded together for him the figures of al-Ḥallāj and Christ, the existence of God and the experience of divine grace. Thereafter, al-Ḥallāj, Christ, and their witness Louis Massignon could no longer be separated either by Massignon himself or by those studying his reconstruction of the Hallajian drama.

Massignon's second contribution is his precise technical investigation of the religious, particularly the mystical, vocabulary in Islam. Apart from his claim that the spiritual realities to which these words allude can be rediscovered through the study of the words themselves—and that the researcher at a certain moment finds himself confronted precisely with that reality to which the mystic testifies—his technical achievements were enormous and have inspired such scholars as Paul Nwyia to proceed with their researches on religious vocabulary along the same line.

Massignon's third major contribution is to have succeeded, in a period of ever-growing specialization, in retaining a global view of what may be called the world of Islam in its various material and spiritual dimensions. He could see it all as forming a meaningful whole under the sign of Islam, just as he could see Islam as meaningful in the perspective of al-Ḥallāj. Thus his "minor works," collected in *Opera minora* (1963), include articles on widely varying subjects. Throughout these articles we find a complex hermeneutics of texts, personalities, and ideas directed to revealing not only their literary, historical, and semantic meanings but also their spiritual intentions. In his hermeneutical research, Massignon showed both an immense erudition and an extraordinary sensitivity, particularly to religious and devotional realities. His sensitivity extended to those realities that exist partly in the realm of dreams and partly in that of fact, realities to which the religious mind and what was once commonly called the "Oriental mind" are so attuned.

BIBLIOGRAPHY

Massignon's principal work is his monumental study of al-Ḥallāj, the second, greatly expanded version of which appeared posthumously in four volumes (Paris, 1975), and has been translated by Herbert Mason as *The Passion of al-Ḥallāj: Mystic and Martyr of Islam,* 4 vols. (Princeton, 1982). Another classic study is his *Essai sur les origines du lexique technique de la mystique musulmane,* 3d ed. (Paris, 1968), which deals with the development of mystical vocabulary during the first centuries of Islam. A number of mystical texts were edited by Massignon in his *Recueil de textes inédits concernant l'histoire de la mystique en pays d'Islam* (Paris, 1929). A translation of al-Ḥallāj's poems, the *Dîwân* (1955; reprint, Paris, 1981), was also published by Massignon. Of Massignon's other books, mention should be made of *Mission en Mésopotamie, 1907–1908,* 2 vols. (Cairo, 1910–1912), and of the various editions of the important *Annuaire du monde musulman* that were compiled by Massignon (1st ed., Paris, 1922–1923; 2d ed., Paris, 1926; 3d ed., Paris, 1929; 4th ed., Paris, 1954). (The last of these volumes was accomplished with the collaboration of Vincent Monteil.) A collection, edited by Youakim Moubarac, of 205 of Massignon's articles has been published under the title *Opera minora,* 3 vols. (1963; reprint, Paris, 1969); two more volumes have been announced.

Bibliographies of works by and about Massignon appear in Youakim Moubarac's *L'œuvre de Louis Massignon* (Beirut, 1972), pp. 7–107; the book is, however, difficult both to find and to use, and is incomplete. A definitive bibliography with complete references has yet to be compiled. Most accessible at present is the succinct bibliography given in my *L'Islam dans le miroir de l'Occident,* 3d ed. (The Hague, 1970), pp. 351–358. These bibliographies may be supplemented by that contained in Guy Harpigny's penetrating study of Massignon's work and spirituality, *Islam et christianisme selon Louis Massignon* (Louvain-la-Neuve, 1981), pp. 295–301. To celebrate the one hundredth anniversary of Massignon's birth, UNESCO issued a useful brochure titled *Centenaire de la naissance de Louis Massignon, 1883–1962* (Paris, 1983).

New Sources

Baldick, Julian. "Massignon: Man of Opposites." *Religious Studies* 23, no. 1 (1987): 29–39.

Burrell, David E. "Mind and Heart at the Service of Muslim-Christian Understanding: Louis Massignon as Trail Blazer." *Muslim World* 88 (1998): 268–278.

Gude, Mary Louise. *Louis Massignon: The Crucible of Compassion.* Notre Dame, 1996.

Harpigny, Guy. "Louis Massignon: L'Hospitalité et la visitation de l'étranger." *Recherches de Science Religieuse* 75, no. 1 (1987): 39–64.

Mason, Herbert. *Memoir of a Friend: Louis Massignon.* London, 1988.

JACQUES WAARDENBURG (1987)
Revised Bibliography

MATERIALISM. As a philosophical doctrine, materialism can be given a deceptively simple definition: the view that matter is all there is. The simplicity is deceptive because, of course, the term *matter* can itself be understood in so many different ways. It is more illuminating, perhaps, to define materialism in terms of what it denies. It excludes the existence of entities that are radically different in kind from, and in some sense superior to, the matter of our ordinary experience. It rejects, therefore, a God or gods on whom the universe would depend for its existence or mode of operation; it denies the existence of angels or spirits that can affect the material order while ultimately escaping its limitations; it questions the notion of a soul, if taken to be an immaterial entity separable in principle from the human body it informs. Its two main targets are, therefore, theism and dualistic views of human nature.

Materialism has, in the past, usually derived from one or the other of two sources. The first is the conviction that the world can be understood in terms of a single set of categories derived from our everyday physical experience, without having to introduce a second set of "immaterial" entities of an altogether different kind. The second is the criticism of organized religion on the grounds of its superstitious or politically oppressive character and a linking of religion with belief in gods, angels, souls, miracles. The former allies materialism with naturalism. The stress in both is on "natural" modes of explanation; "supernatural" forms of action are rejected as unnecessary or even incoherent. Materialism also resembles reductionism, since both seek to reduce the diversity of the explanations offered for events in the world to a single category, or at least to a minimal number of categories. There are, for the same reasons, overtones in it of positivism, at least to the extent that both lay stress on science as the only legitimate source of knowledge about the causalities of the world. Where classic materialism would differ from these other philosophic emphases would be mainly in the specificity of its objections to the category of "spirit" on which religious belief is taken to rely.

BEGINNINGS. It is to Aristotle (384–322 BCE) that we owe the first explicit articulation of a concept of "matter," that is, an underlying substratum to which reference must be made in explaining physical change. Aristotle criticizes the Ionian physicists, his predecessors of two centuries earlier, because of their supposedly exclusive reliance on a common underlying "stuff" (water, air, fire) in explaining change in nature. Such a stuff would retain its own identity throughout all change; substantial change would, therefore, be excluded and the apparently fundamental differences between different kinds (different species of animal, for instance) would be reduced to mere differences in arrangement of the fundamental "stuff." Aristotle rejected this "materialist" doctrine. But he did not believe the Ionians to be materialists. He notes that Thales thought all things to be "full of gods" and to be in some sense "ensouled"; similar views are attributed to the other major figures in the early Ionian tradition. Though these men made the first known attempt to explain physical changes in a systematic way, they did not question the traditional explanatory roles of the gods and of soul.

A century later, the founders of atomism, Leucippus and Democritus, came much closer to a clear-cut materialist doctrine. Their view that all things consist of "atoms," imperceptibly small, indivisible, eternal, and unchanging entities, derived from the metaphysical arguments of Parmenides regarding the One, not from an empirical starting-point in observation. Change is nothing more than the movement and redistribution of atoms in the void. The planets, the stars, and even the earth itself have come to be by the aggregating of vortices of atoms. Since space is infinite, there will be infinitely many worlds produced in this way. Sensation is to be understood in purely physical terms; the soul itself consists of atoms, admittedly smaller and finer than even the particles of fire, but still of the same general kind as other atoms. All interaction is thus mechanical and explanation in terms of final causes is prohibited. Yet the atomists do not appear to have excluded the gods. Though Democritus is critical of those who would base ethical behavior on religious sanctions, he does seem to allow that the gods may visit men. This may, of course, have been no more than a concession to the orthodoxy of the day. Yet it would seem more likely that he had not yet reduced the gods, as he had done soul, to matter.

Epicurus (341–270 BCE) took this further step. The gods are situated in the intervals between the innumerable universes; they too must be composed of atoms, and they live in a state of bliss undisturbed by the affairs of mortals. Lucretius (99–55 BCE) popularized the teachings of Epicurus in the Roman world through his great poem, *De rerum natura*, which was the most complete expression of materialist doctrine in ancient times. The gods here seem to be dismissed entirely; insofar as there is a deity it is nature itself. Lucretius views the state religion of Rome as a primarily political institution and sees no reason for any exception to the atomist claim that all there is, is atoms and void.

The Renaissance. With the growth of Christianity, the attraction of Epicurean materialism diminished. During the Middle Ages, atomism was sometimes discussed by philosophers, but the Aristotelian arguments against it seemed overwhelming. There could be no serious defense of materialism in an age when the influence of spirit, in all its forms, seemed so palpable and when no plausible argument had been found for the claim that all change can be explained in atomic or material terms only. It was only when the "new science" of mechanics made its appearance in the seventeenth century that the outlines of an argument became faintly visible. Galileo and Descartes took for granted that matter is composed of a multitude of tiny corpuscles whose properties ("primary qualities") are precisely those required to make them subject to, and entirely predictable by, mechanical law. There was no real evidence for this, but it seemed plausible to extend the realm of the new mathematicized mechanics to the very small and thus make all types of physical change explicable, perhaps, in mechanical terms.

Pierre Gassendi (1592–1655) could now revive the ancient Epicurean atomism and present it as the best available (though admittedly hypothetical) scientific explanation of the sensory qualities of things. However, he did not carry his Epicureanism all the way to materialism; though an opponent of the claims to demonstrative knowledge made by scholastics and Cartesians alike, he was not disaffected with religion and saw no reason to extend atomism to the soul or to use it to deny the need for a creator God. His friend Thomas Hobbes (1588–1679) had no such scruples. A severe critic of institutional religion, he argued that mechanical modes of explanation must be extended not only to sensation but to thought, which is no more than the motion of material particles in the brain. Nothing other than body can exist, so that God, if he exists (and Hobbes's real views on this issue are very difficult to discover), must be corporeal.

Reductive Materialism. If all material things are to be understood by a single set of laws, the general laws of mechanics, it would follow that human action, too, can be reduced to mechanical law. This is the conclusion Hobbes reached; Descartes avoided it only by placing within man an immaterial mind. Reductive materialism or sharp dualism—these seemed to be the only options, if one decided to bring the entire domain of physical interaction under one science. Most philosophers of the seventeenth and eighteenth centuries found the alternatives unappealing, but it was not at all evident where a stable solution might be found. In France, where reaction against royal as well as ecclesiastical authority continued to mount, reductive materialism found favor with a number of writers, of whom the most original was Denis Diderot (1713–1784), editor of the great *Encyclopedia*. Influenced by George-Louis Buffon's *Natural History* (1749), he speculated about the sort of developmental laws that might have brought about the organic world we know from an initial chaos of material particles. A number of medical writers, of whom the most notable was Julien de La Mettrie (1709–1751), were at the same time developing a materialist physiology in which human action is reduced to simple mechanical causes. Paul d'Holbach (1723–1789), on the other hand, was much more metaphysical in his approach. His *Système de la nature* (1770) was the most thoroughgoing materialist statement of the century; in it, the two sources of classic materialism are especially evident: a conviction that because matter is one, only one sort of explanation is permissible, and a strong hostility to religion.

But the weaknesses of this kind of material monism were still evident. The claims to explain in mechanical terms the operations of the human body, to reduce sensation and thought to mechanical action between molecules, and to derive the profusion of organic species from an original undifferentiated matter were still almost entirely promissory. Materialism was still, at best, a program, not an achieved philosophy. To become something more, a genuine materialist science would have to be available to serve as support. And one of the fundamental premises of classic materialism, its reductionist principle, might have to be abandoned.

Major philosophers of the day were struck by the crudity, as they saw it, of the materialist doctrine. Hegel, in particular, attacked the mechanistic presuppositions of Newtonian science, its assumption that all motion can be explained by the single science of mechanics. In its stead, he attempted to construct a philosophy of nature and a theory of history in which spirit is the moving force. Motion involves contradiction, since for it to occur, a body has to be "both here and not here at the same time." Thus, contradiction pervades both nature and society; it is out of the consequent struggle and opposition that advance comes.

DIALECTICAL MATERIALISM. The most influential form of nonreductive materialism is undoubtedly that of Marx and Engels. Marx took over much of the structure of Hegel's account of society and of social change, retaining the discontinuities of the Hegelian "dialectical" method, but inverting the order of matter and mind. Mind originates from matter (as the reductive materialists had held), but in a discontinuous way that makes it irreducible to the categories of matter (which they had denied). Beliefs in God or in an immortal soul are no more than the projections of those who would rationalize an unjust social order instead of trying to change it. All knowledge of the world and of society must be based on sense experience and ultimately on science.

Marx's "historical materialism" is restricted to human history; by taking economic and industrial factors as the fundamental agencies of change, Marx believed that he could give a thoroughly "materialist" (i.e., empirical, naturalistic, scientific) account of history. Engels went on to a broader focus on nature. His "dialectical materialism" (as Plekhanov later called it) is first and foremost a philosophy of nature in the Hegelian tradition. He rejects Ludwig Büchner's claim that the sciences alone suffice; in Engels's view (and this has become a central tenet of Marxist-Leninist thought), positivism is inadequate because the sciences have to be supplemented by a unified and guiding philosophy. This philosophy is "dialectical" because it recognizes the presence of contradictions and of discontinuous change in nature and is unified insofar as it proposes a scheme that can grasp things in their totality. Engels characterizes as "idealist" any philosophical view that would deny that mind and spirit must originate from matter. Thus, anyone who believes in a transcendent God or in the dualism of soul (mind) and body would automatically qualify as "idealist" in this new sense.

The attempt on the part of Marx and Engels to "materialize Hegel" led to notable internal strain (many have argued, incoherence) within the materialism they proposed. On the one hand, there is the stress on the primacy of sense-experience (which is said to "reflect" the world) and consequently of science. On the other, the dialectical element (which is crucial to Marx's political theory) is difficult to sustain by science alone, unless it be almost emptied of content. This tension is even more evident in Lenin's version of dialectical materialism, which tries to mediate between positivism and Hegelian idealism, utilizing a rather naive realist epistemology.

CHRISTIANITY AND MATERIALISM. The progress of science since the mid-nineteenth century has undercut the older reductive materialism by showing that the categories of mechanics at any one time are never definitive and that there are, besides, different levels of explanation that are probably not reducible to one another, not in the sense in which reduction was supposed to be possible, at least. On the other hand, the progress of science has also demonstrated the strength of the naturalistic program of explanation. More and more, it seems possible to explain the entire order of nature in a single interlinked set of categories that leave no gaps "of principle" into which a different order of causality has to be interposed in order to render a coherent account of world process. It is hard *not* to be a "naturalist" in that sense.

Nonetheless, there are unsolved philosophical problems about the relation of mind and body, about the reality of human freedom in a world scientifically fully explicable, that have led to the formulation of alternatives besides that of a sophisticated nonreductive materialism, alternatives that would still maintain a broadly naturalist orientation. These would differ from materialism in the degree of stress they would lay on causal categories that derive from the domain of mind and freedom rather than from that of mechanical action even if the term *mechanical* be construed as broadly as it could plausibly be.

When naturalism/materialism is carried to the point of denying the possibility of a creator God or an afterlife for man, a conflict with religious, and specifically with Christian, belief is unavoidable. Christian theologians, however, have gone to some lengths to try to show that the notions of the natural order as sufficient in its own right, or of resurrection as independent of a strong dualism of soul and body, are perfectly compatible with—indeed entirely faithful to—the Christian tradition. The grounds for the materialist exclusion in principle of God or of a personal afterlife are thus brought into question.

Some have gone further to argue the propriety of a "Christian materialism" that would draw on the positive insights of the materialist tradition, particularly in its Marxist form. Such a view would suggest that all that happens in nature and in history is in principle explicable at its own level without directly invoking the intervening agency of God. "Christian materialism" would note and deplore the manner in which Christianity, like other religions, has often allowed itself to become the ideological legitimation of structures of social domination. It would oppose the "idealism" that would make Christianity a set of doctrines to be believed rather than a doctrine of redemption that finds its reality first in action and transformation.

The limits of such a view are set by the Christian doctrines of the dependence of nature and history on divine grace and of the entrance of the Word of God, as man, into the human story. There would be the reality to acknowledge of a God whose action entirely transcends the categories of nature. And that is something that materialism cannot do without ceasing (it would seem) to be materialism.

SEE ALSO Aristotle; Descartes, René; Earth; Empiricism; Hegel, G. W. F.; Idealism; Marx, Karl; Naturalism; Newton, Isaac; Positivism; Skeptics and Skepticism.

BIBLIOGRAPHY

The most detailed general history of materialism is still Friedrich Lange's *Geschichte des Materialismus* (Marburg, 1865), translated by E. C. Thomas as *The History of Materialism* (London, 1925). Many helpful essays will be found in *The Encyclopedia of Philosophy*, edited by Paul Edwards (New York, 1967); see, in particular, Keith Campbell's "Materialism"; H. B. Acton's "Dialectical Materialism" and "Historical Materialism"; G. E. R. Lloyd's "Leucippus and Democritus"; R. S. Peters's "Hobbes, Thomas"; and Norman L. Torrey's "Diderot, Denis." For a survey of the varied roles played by the concept of matter in the history of philosophy and of science, see *The Concept of Matter*, edited by me (Notre Dame, Ind., 1963), especially the essay by Nicholas Lobkowicz, "Materialism and Matter in Marxism-Leninism," pp. 430–464. For further reading on Marxist versions of materialism, see Gustav A. Wetter's *Der dialecktische Materialismus* (Vienna, 1952), translated by Peter Heath as *Dialectical Materialism* (London, 1958). For a useful historical study of the strains within the Soviet development of materialism, see David Joravsky's *Soviet Marxism and Natural Science, 1917–1932* (London, 1961). In his *A Matter of Hope: A Theologian's Reflections on the Thought of Karl Marx* (Notre Dame, Ind., 1982), Nicholas Lash defends the view that "it is the 'materialist' rather than the 'idealist' forms of Christianity which conform most closely to the demands of obedience to the gospel" (p. 148).

New Sources

Carrier, James. *Gifts and Commodities: Exchange and Western Capitalism since 1700.* New York, 1995.

Gillet, Carl, and Barry Loewer, eds. *Physicalism and Its Discontents.* New York, 2001.

Lund, David. *Perception, Mind, and Personal Identity: A Critique of Materialism.* Lanham. Md., 1994.

Melnyk, Andrew. *A Physicalist Manifesto: Thoroughly Modern Materialism.* New York, 2003.

Miller, Daniel, ed. *Unwrapping Christmas.* New York, 1993.

Vitzthum, Robert. *Materialism: An Affirmative History and Definition.* Amherst, N.Y., 1995.

Wallace, Alan. *The Taboo of Subjectivity: Toward a New Science of Consciousness.* New York, 2000.

ERNAN MCMULLIN (1987)
Revised Bibliography

MATERIALISTS, HINDU
SEE CĀRVĀKA

MATHER FAMILY.

Members of three successive generations of the Mather family were Puritan ministers in the Massachusetts Bay Colony in New England: Richard (1596–1669), Increase (1629–1723), and Cotton (1663–1728). Each achieved fame as a preacher and writer, and collectively they exerted a formative influence on the religious life of colonial America.

Richard Mather, who was born in Lowton, near Liverpool, matriculated at Brasenose College, Oxford, in 1618 but studied there for only a few months. He was preaching at Toxteth Park when, late in 1633, he was removed from the pulpit. His offenses are not known, although they were doubtless ecclesiastical; he did not conform to the practices of the Church of England in all ways. He and his family then immigrated to Massachusetts Bay, arriving in mid-August 1635. The people of Dorchester, Massachusetts, after failing to organize a church in April 1636, succeeded in August of that year, and Mather was immediately called to the church as its teacher.

In the pulpit in Dorchester, Mather served quietly and faithfully. Although in most ways he probably resembled most Puritan ministers of his time in Massachusetts Bay Colony, in several notable accomplishments he differed. He published defenses of the "New England Way," as the church polity of the Bay Colony was called; he helped to write the Cambridge Platform (1648) defining ecclesiastical polity; he contributed to the definition of Puritan baptismal practice in the so-called Halfway Covenant (1662); and he served as an overseer of Harvard College.

Increase Mather, sixth son of Richard, was the outstanding minister of his generation. Born in Dorchester, he entered Harvard College when he was twelve years of age; after graduation he went to Ireland, where he took an M.A. at Trinity College, Dublin. Preaching followed at Torrington in Devonshire, to the garrison on Guernsey, and in Gloucester. However, his heterodox opinions made life in England dangerous for him after the Restoration, so in 1661 he returned to New England. There he was soon asked by the Second Church in Boston (Boston North Church) to fill its pulpit.

Increase Mather spent his life expounding the "New England Way." He was not an innovator in religion; like his father he defended nonseparating Congregationalism. But Increase Mather was a much more imaginative man than his father and a more passionate one. The Puritan vision of New

England as a redemptive society was one of the passions of his life. He saw his American homeland as the one place on earth where true church polity might be established and the Protestant Reformation completed. The defense of New England carried him to England a second time shortly after the Glorious Revolution. He returned with a charter that protected much of the colony's—and its Congregational churches'—autonomy. Increase Mather's other achievements were varied: he acted as president of Harvard College; he wrote about science, especially astronomy; he advised governors; he helped to halt the persecution of those accused in the Salem witchcraft episode; and he preached and published on New England Christianity.

Cotton Mather was the first of Increase Mather's nine children. Although he never left New England, his visible achievements outnumbered those of his father. After a brilliant performance at Harvard College (A.B., 1678), Cotton Mather was ordained a minister in his father's church in 1685; the two served there together until Increase Mather's death almost forty years later. In 1689, while his father was in England securing a new charter for the colony, Cotton Mather played an important role in the expulsion of Sir Edmund Andros, governor of Massachusetts and head of the Dominion of New England. He also supported the witchcraft trials in Salem in 1692, although he was uneasy and had reservations about the proceedings.

Most of Cotton Mather's life was not spent in public affairs. He was a scholar of great learning and power and an immensely successful preacher. His learning extended to almost all fields of knowledge, although theology was the subject he knew most profoundly. Cotton Mather wrote histories, the greatest being his *Magnalia Christi Americana* (London, 1702), biographies (many first appearing in sermon form), scientific treatises, practical guides to medicine, prophetical works, and guides to conduct for the young, for sailors, and for almost every other order of society; most of his works, however, were sermons. He preached a "practical divinity," filled with exhortation and advice on the Christian life. Many of his sermons were intended to convert his listeners; others provided solace and nourishment to believers. Much of his work remains in manuscript, including "The Biblia Americana," his massive commentary on the scriptures.

Like his father, Cotton Mather was obsessed with the history and the future of New England. His great hope was that the second coming of Christ would take place in his lifetime and that New England would in reality prove to be the site of the New Jerusalem. He never surrendered his faith in the Congregationalism of his country, but he did come to preach an ecumenism embodied in his conception of a Christian Union, a worldwide league of believers. Cotton Mather earned a reputation in his day as a splendid preacher and scholar, but he was also widely disliked for the excesses of his style and expression. Despite his pride in his family and his attainments, he died feeling unappreciated and, to some extent, unfulfilled.

Bibliography

The standard bibliographies of the works of the Mathers are those edited by Thomas J. Holmes: *The Minor Mathers: A List of Their Works* (Cambridge, Mass., 1940), for Richard Mather; *Increase Mather: A Bibliography of His Works*, 2 vols. (Cleveland, 1931); and *Cotton Mather: A Bibliography of His Works*, 3 vols. (Cambridge, Mass., 1940). Useful studies of the Mathers include Kenneth Murlock's *Increase Mather: The Foremost American Puritan* (Cambridge, Mass., 1926), my own *The Mathers: Three Generations of Puritan Intellectuals, 1596–1728* (New York, 1971), and Kenneth Silverman's *The Life and Times of Cotton Mather* (New York, 1984).

Robert Middlekauff (1987)

MATRES. The *matres* or *matrae* ("mothers"), Celtic feminine divinities, are attested throughout the ancient continental and insular Celtic domain (with the exception of nonromanized Ireland) by abundant Romano-British and Gallo-Roman epigraphic and iconographic testimony. The word is Latin, but it can only be the translation or adaptation of a Celtic word, as the Gaulish inscription at Nimes consecrated to the *matrevo namausikavo* ("Nimesian mothers") witnesses. On the evidence, the *matres* as a group are very diverse, and it would be difficult to propose a single explanation for them. A *matre* may be conceived in terms of a particular locale, a certain function, or a principle and sphere of sovereignty. Specific instances are frequently multiple: the Suleviae, solar goddesses who have been unduly transformed into psychopomps; the Iunones, who are multiple forms of the Latin goddess Juno; the simple Triviae or Quadruviae, who watch over crossroads (but may not be truly Celtic).

Thus the term *matres* has come to designate several types of feminine divinities who are in some instances anything but mother goddesses or protectors of fecundity. At first, prior to the identifications and multiplications, there was certainly a single feminine divinity. Described briefly by Caesar under the name of Minerva in his account of Gaulish religion, she is at once mother, spouse, sister, and daughter of the gods.

This unique goddess in multiple form may be identified, in the context of Irish myth, with a range of feminine deities. There is Brighid, daughter of Daghdha, but also mother of the gods and protector of leeches, poets, and smiths. There is Boann, who is wife to Elcmhaire but bears a son to Daghdha. Also, and preeminently, there is Édaín, sovereign and ancestor of a long line of Irish kings. Further, there is Morríghan ("the great queen"), goddess of war and wife of Daghdha, she who washes the bloody remains of heroes who have died in combat. There is Macha ("plain" or "level land"), eponym of Emhain Mhacha, capital of Ulster. There is the gentle Fann ("swallow"), wife of the god Manannán, who loves and tempts Cú Chulainn, and there is Tailtiu ("earth"), foster mother of Lugh. Finally, there are the allegorical personifications of Ireland and queens of the Tuatha Dé Danann: Ériu, Banbha, and Fódla.

BIBLIOGRAPHY

Guyonvarc'h, Christian-J., and Françoise Le Roux. *Textes mythologiques irlandais,* vol. 1. Rennes, 1980.

Mac Cana, Proinsias. *Celtic Mythology.* Rev. ed. Feltham, U.K., 1983.

FRANÇOISE LE ROUX (1987)
CHRISTIAN-J. GUYONVARC'H (1987)
Translated from French by Erica Meltzer

MATTHEW THE EVANGELIST, traditionally the author of the first canonical gospel, which bears his name. His exact dates are unknown, but the gospel was probably written in the last quarter of the first century, possibly in Syrian Antioch.

The name *Matthew* appears in every list of the twelve disciples of Jesus (*Mt.* 10:3, *Mk.* 3:18, *Lk.* 6:15, *Acts* 1:13). In the *Gospel of Matthew* Jesus calls him from his toll booth and his role as a despised tax collector to be a disciple (9:9–10), and in that gospel's list of the Twelve he is called Matthew the tax collector. Otherwise, Matthew does not appear in the gospel narratives or in the rest of the New Testament.

Mark 2:13–14 and *Luke* 5:27–28 relate the calling of a tax collector whose name is Levi, rather than Matthew (in *Mark* 2:14 he is called the son of Alphaeus; cf. "James the son of Alphaeus" in all the lists of the Twelve). Otherwise, the stories are quite similar, and in each case the call is followed by Jesus' eating at table with tax collectors and sinners and saying that he has come to call not righteous people, but sinners. (Tax collectors were regarded as egregious sinners, because the government sold the right to collect taxes to private entrepreneurs, who then realized as large a profit as possible at the expense of the public.)

The tradition of Matthean authorship of the first gospel has been questioned by critical scholarship for significant reasons. Matthew the tax collector turned disciple would have been an eyewitness of the events he narrates. Yet the close relationship between the narrative attributed to Matthew and that of Mark, which is generally accounted to be earlier, suggests that *Mark* was the principal narrative source. The fact that *Mark* was written in Greek (not Jesus and Matthew's native Aramaic) by someone who was not one of the Twelve makes it unlikely that the apostle Matthew would have relied upon it. Moreover, the gospel attributed to Matthew seems to have been written after the destruction of Jerusalem in the Roman War (70 CE; cf. *Mt.* 22:7), rather late for an apostolic writing. Quite possibly the name Matthew has been substituted for Levi in the call story of the first gospel, in which he is also singled out as the tax collector in the apostolic list.

Ancient church tradition, nevertheless, unanimously ascribes the gospel to the apostle Matthew. The fourth-century church historian Eusebius cites Papias (bishop of Hierapolis in Asia Minor during the first half of the second century) who wrote that "Matthew collected the sayings of the Lord in the Hebrew language, and each one interpreted them as he was able" (*Church History* 3.39.16). Later church authorities attribute a gospel to Matthew, agreeing that it was written in Hebrew. Matthew is frequently said to have preached among Hebrews. Interestingly, modern gospel criticism continues to see a pervasive Jewish or Jewish-Christian dimension in Matthew's gospel, whether in its tradition or intended audience. The statement of Papias concerning Matthew's collection of Jesus' sayings has sometimes been taken to refer to an earlier source (which can be discerned in *Matthew* and *Luke* and is usually called Q by biblical scholars) rather than to the present gospel. This interpretation avoids the difficulties of attributing the gospel to the apostle directly and helps to explain why the name of a relatively obscure disciple became attached to the most prominent gospel, but it remains at best a plausible conjecture.

Legends about Matthew grew in time. He is said to have worked among Gentiles in remote lands toward the end of his career. He came to be revered as a martyr (although tradition is not unanimous on this point), and he is commemorated in the Western church on September 21. However, we know nothing for certain of his career or fate. Since the second century Matthew has been represented in Christian symbolism as a winged man, said by Irenaeus to represent the humanity of Christ.

BIBLIOGRAPHY

Aside from the New Testament the most important primary source is Eusebius's *Church History,* which brings together earlier testimony of Christian writers on the origin and authorship of the Gospels. The most convenient edition is the two-volume "Loeb Classical Library" text and translation of Kirsopp Lake, J. E. L. Oulton, and Hugh J. Lawlor (Cambridge, Mass., 1926).

The most important testimonies of patristic authors are collected in *The Gospel According to St. Matthew,* edited by A. H. McNeile (London, 1915), pp. xxx–xxxii. For a concise statement of the modern, critical view of Matthean authorship, see Werner G. Kümmel's *Introduction to the New Testament,* rev. ed. (Nashville, 1975), pp. 119–121. Raymond E. Brown, *Introduction to the New Testament* (New York, 1997), pp. 208–212, also rejects ascription of the Gospel of Matthew to the disciple of Jesus, although he does not dismiss Papias's attribution of a sayings collection to Matthew. The same is true of W. D. Davies and Dale C. Allison, Jr., *The Gospel According to Saint Matthew,* vol. 1 (Edinburgh, 1985)., p. 17, who think there may be a connection between the collection and Matthew's Gospel.

D. MOODY SMITH (1987 AND 2005)

MĀTURĪDĪ, AL- (d. AH 333/944 CE), more fully Abū Manṣūr Muḥammad ibn Muḥammad ibn Maḥmūd al-Samarqandī al-Māturīdī, was a Muslim theologian, jurist, and Qur'ān commentator. The name Māturīdīyah is also the eponym of a school of theology that represented an intermediate position between the Ḥanbalī traditionalists and the Muʿtazilah, advocates of religious rationalism in Islamic theology. Māturīdī was born in Māturīd, near the Central Asian city of Samarkand. Under the Persian Samanid rulers (874–999), al-Māturīdī lived in a setting of intense cultural and intellectual activity. He was trained by scholars of the Ḥanafī school of Islamic law. Not much is known of his life except that he wrote several books on theology, jurisprudence, and heresiology, as well as a commentary on the Qurʾān entitled *Kitāb taʾwilāt al-Qurʾān.* He is said to have led a simple and ascetic life. Some sources attribute to him miracles *(karāmāt)*—an obvious reference to his devout religious life. He died in Samarkand. Subsequent generations remember him by the honorific title Imām al-Hudá (leader of the right guidance).

Despite his fame in the Sunnī world today, no source earlier than the fourteenth century mentions a school of theology carrying Māturīdī's name. The manuals speak of the Māturīdīyah together with the Ashʿarīyah, or followers of al-Ashʿarī (d. 935), as the theological spokesmen of the *ahl al-sunnah wa-al-jamāʿah* (people of the prophetic norms and the community), the majority group in the Muslim world, commonly known as Sunnīs. Al-Ashʿarī lived in Baghdad and was a contemporary of al-Māturīdī, but there is no indication that they were aware of each other's work. Many similarities in their theological formulations have been noted. Al-Ashʿarī is much better known than his Ḥanafī counterpart, but recent studies have shown that the latter came nearer to providing a bridge between traditionalism and philosophical theology than did the Baghdad scholar. Substantial differences between the two are few, but they are sufficient to have created some rivalry between their respective schools.

The Māturīdīyah school spread in the tenth and eleventh centuries mostly due to the earnest efforts of Turks, mainly the Saljūqids, whose historic conversion to Islam had occurred in the preceding century. This was combined with the ardent support of the newly converted Turks for Ḥanafism. The famous cursing of al-Ashʿarī and his ideas in the Turkish-controlled Khorasan region on the order of the Saljūqid ruler Tughrul Beg points to a period of confrontation between the Māturīdī and Ashʿarite schools of *kalām* in the eleventh century. As the Māturīdī school was identified with Ḥanafism and Ashʿarism with the Shāfiʿī school of law, this led to some factional tensions and clashes between the Ḥanafis and the Shāfiʿīs in some Saljūqid-controlled areas. The Māturīdī school gained prominence between the eleventh and fourteenth centuries. A number of attempts were made to ease the tensions between the two schools during the Mamlūk period. The Ashʿarī Shāfiʿī jurist-theologian Tāj al-Dīn al-Subkī composed a poem in which he tried to explain away the theological differences between the two as mostly terminological and rhetorical. This trend continued in later *kalām* history and reached a point where Māturīdism was redefined as a branch of Ashʿarism.

Al-Māturīdī, like al-Ashʿarī, was firmly grounded in the Qurʾanic revelation, but he also developed a rational epistemology, giving a high place to human reasoning—a sign of his strong Ḥanafism. He was much concerned with proofs for the existence of God and with the doctrine of creation, questions that probably reflect the intellectual climate of Samarkand and the terms of his encounter with other currents of religious thought. Al-Māturīdī accepted the reality of human freedom, as against the determinism of al-Ashʿarī, but he also opposed the Muʿtazilī view of human beings as creators of their own deeds. He maintained that every act of humankind is at the same time the result of human capacity and a divine creation. Using somewhat the same language as al-Ashʿarī and as his opponents, the Muʿtazilah, he nevertheless described a balance between divine omnipotence and human freedom that was distinctive.

Even though Māturīdī was opposed to the general thrust of Muʿtazilism, he agreed with some views of the Muʿtazilites. Like the Muʿtazilites, he believed in the human ability and, in fact, obligation to know God and worship him through unaided reason even in the absence of a specific prophetic revelation. While rejecting some interpretations of the Muʿtazilites, Māturīdī accepted the necessity of interpreting anthropomorphic expressions in the Qurʾān through metaphors and symbols rather than understanding them literally. On the question of the attributes of God, he took a position opposite to the Muʿtazilites and considered divine names and qualities described in the Qurʾān to be eternally subsisting in God's essence. Like al-Ashʿarī, he affirmed the negative formula that God's names and qualities are neither identical with the divine essence nor distinct from it. He accepted the possibility of beatific vision *(ruʾyat Allāh),* that is, the idea that human beings will be able to see God in the hereafter, but he rejected the specification "by the eyes," endorsing in some ways the famous Ḥanbalī position of "without [asking/knowing] how" *(bilā kayf).* Against al-Ashʿarī he held that faith, as the act that makes a person a member of the Muslim community, is immutable, incapable of either decrease or increase. This tenet was a part of the Ḥanafī doctrinal heritage. Furthermore, he defined faith *(al-imān)* as "consent by the heart" *(taṣdīq bi al-qalb)* and "confession by the tongue" *(iqrār bi al-lisān).* Like the Ḥanafīs and the Murjiʿas before him, Māturīdī held that works *(aʿmāl)* are not part of the doctrinal confession of faith.

BIBLIOGRAPHY

The most comprehensive work on Māturīdī and his school is Shams al-Dīn Salafī Afghānī's *al-Māturīdīyyah,* 3 vols. (Taʾif, Saudi Arabia, 1998), in which the author analyzes Māturīdī's thought and its subsequent development. Mustafa Ceric provides a systematic analysis of Māturīdī's thought in *Roots of Synthetic Theology in Islam: A Study of the Theology of Abū Manṣūr al-Māturīdī* (Kuala Lumpur, 1995). Fatḥallah Khulayf prepared a critical edition of *Kitāb al-tawḥīd* (Beirut, 1969), thus making available for the first time the printed Arabic text of al-Māturīdī's most important existing theological work. The editor has provided a 43-page introduction in English, describing in an incomplete and somewhat unsystematic way the contents of *Kitāb al-tawḥīd* W. Montgomery Watt furnishes a brief introduction to the Ḥanafī theologian in *The Formative Period of Islamic Thought* (Edinburgh, 1973), pp. 312–314; reprint, Oxford, 1998. Michel Allard provides a more detailed summary and discussion of the contents of *Kitāb al-tawḥīd* in *Le problème des attributes divins dans la doctrine d'al-As'ari et de ses premiers grands disciples* (Beirut, 1965), pp. 419–427. A section of Daniel Gimaret's *Théories de l'acte humain en théologie musulmaneé* (Paris, 1980), pp. 175–190, deals in a perceptive and detailed way with the discussion in *Kitāb al-tawḥīd* concerning the relationship between human acts and divine sovereignty. Hans Daiber provides a discussion of *Kitāb al-tawḥīd* in "Zur Erstausgabe von al-Māturīdī, Kitāb al-Tawḥīd," *Der Islam* 52 (1975): 299–313.

Muḥammad Ibrāhim Fayyūmī's *Ta'rīkh al-firaq al-islāmīyah al-siyāsī wa-al-dīnī* (Cairo, 2003) contains an extensive chapter on Māturīdī and his school. Another monograph on Māturīdī's life and thought is Balqāsim Ghālī's *Abū Manṣūr al-Māturīdī: ḥayātuhu wa ārā'uhu al-'aqdiyah* (Tunis, Tunisia, 1989). Saim Yeprem's *İrade Hürriyeti ve Imām Māturīdī* in Turkish (Istanbul, 1984) is a detailed survey of Māturīdī's concept of free will and determinism. Kemal Işık's *Māturīdī'nin Kelam Sisteminde İman, Allah ve Peygamberlik Anlayışı* (Ankara, Turkey, 1980), another monograph in Turkish, deals with the concepts of faith, God, and prophethood in Māturīdī's system.

Even though somewhat outdated, A. K. M. Ayyub Ali's chapter on the life, thought, and influence of al-Māturīdī in *A History of Muslim Philosophy,* vol. 1, edited by M. M. Sharif, pp. 259–274 (Weisbaden, Germany, 1963), is based on an examination of *Kitāb al-tawḥīd,* existing only in manuscript at the time, and *Ta'wīlāt al-qur'ān,* al- Māturīdī's multivolume commentary on the Qur'ān. The latter, existing in several manuscript copies, was described for the first time by Manfred Götz in an article, "Māturīdī und sein Kitab Ta'wīlāt al-Qur'ān," *Der Islam* 41 (1965): 22–70. The most extensive study of the spread of Maturidism is Wilferd Madelung's "The Spread of Maturidism and the Turks," in *Actas do IV Congresso de Estudos Arabes e Islamicos Coimbra-Lisboa 1968* (Leiden, 1971), pp. 109–168. See also his two entries "al-Māturīdī" and "Māturīdīyyah," in the *Encyclopedia of Islam,* 2d ed., vol. 4, edited by C. E. Bosworth et al., pp. 846a–847a (CD-ROM edition, Leiden, 2003). Ulrich Rudolph's *Al-Māturīdī und die sunnitische Theologie in Samarkand* (New York, 1996) places Māturīdī and his thought in a historical context. There is also a short commentary on Abū Ḥanīfa's *Fiqh al-akbār* attributed to Māturīdī.

R. MARSTON SPEIGHT (1987)
IBRAHIM KALIN (2005)

MĀUI is the most versatile, popular, and widely known supernatural hero in South Pacific mythology. Islanders as far west as the Micronesian island of Yap narrate how Māui, with his enchanted fishhook, pulled up a big "fish": an island complete with people, villages, and gardens of new food plants. Māui is, however, primarily a Polynesian hero; inhabitants of every island from Hawai'i to New Zealand and from Mangareva to Tonga and Samoa narrate versions of his exploits in separate myths or unified myth cycles. In the traditional culture, islanders recited his spells for success in their mundane lives; priests converted secular, humorous myths about Māui to their own serious purposes.

Māui is not only the earth-fisher but also the Polynesian sun-snarer, sky-raiser, fire-stealer, monster-slayer, seeker of immortality, and, in fact, the hero of so many mischievous exploits that Tuamotuans nicknamed him Maui-of-a-Thousand-Tricks and Tupuatupua ("super-superman"). To Hawai'ians he was *aīwaīwa* ("wonderful") because he was marvelously skilled, yet weird, bad, and notorious. His best-known cognomen, Maui-tikitiki-a-Taranga (or cognates), originated, the New Zealand Maori claimed, when his mother, Taranga, wrapped him—her last born and a miscarriage—in a topknot *(tikitiki)* of hair and cast him with a prayer into the ocean. Ocean and sky gods rescued and reared him until, as a boy, he rejoined his family. His tricks finally ended when he entered the womb of the sleeping goddess Hine-nui-te-po ("great Hine of the underworld") in order to gain immortality. He intended to depart through her mouth, but when his bird companion laughed at the sight, the goddess awoke and crushed Māui to death.

Māui was a shape-shifting trickster and, usually unintentionally, a culture hero. He was also the quintessential demigod, neither wholly god nor wholly man, a misfit, who continually tested his magic and *mana* against the cosmogonic gods and against his father and elder brothers in his attempts to usurp their privileges, to humiliate them, and to demonstrate his superiority. He was also a bridge in time between the ending of the era of creation and the beginning of the era of human migrations.

Polynesians believed that by using his incantations and referring to his deeds they would sanctify their work and, at its conclusion, lift taboos on the workers. New Zealand provides the clearest examples of this. A priest of bird-catching rituals regarded the sun as a great bird and would chant Māui's sun-snaring spell to ensure a good catch. To kindle sacred new fire he would recite the incantation by which Māui had overpowered the fire deity and learned to make fire. A priestly expert on the ceremonies accompanying the planting and harvesting of *kumara* (sweet potato) would chant Māui's "song of plenty" over a feather-ornamented, crescent-topped digging stick. The song recalled how Māui, in the guise of a pigeon, had perched on his father's stick after having sneaked after him to his underworld sweet potato garden. Using Māui's charm, fishermen would weaken a large fish's reluctance to leave the ocean, and hostile invaders would recite it to unnerve people and force them to leave their homes. High priests who had been influenced by Western religion rejected the common version of the earth-fishing story and divulged its esoteric, "real" meaning. The high god Io, they explained, gave Māui, his brothers, and their descendants—the Maori—possession of the earth (i.e., New Zealand).

Wherever Māui was known he was claimed as an ancestor. In the Hawai'ian Islands the claim received royal recognition in the genealogical prayer chant, the *Kumulipo* ("source in deepest darkness"), which belonged to the family of King Kalakaua (1836–1891) and his sister Queen Lili'uokalani (1838–1917), and which described the family's descent from the time of primary gods to that of deified chiefs. Eighteen lines of the fifteenth of the sixteen chants comprising the *Kumulipo* cryptically list the principal events in Māui's life. The sixteenth chant opens with the names of Māui and his wife and ends with that of Lono-i-ka-makahiki. High chiefs once intoned this two-thousand-line prayer to consecrate an infant sacred chief; they gave him the revered name of Lono-i-ka-makahiki and activated his *mana* by naming his ancestors (who included spiritualized natural phenomena, cosmogonic gods, demigods like Māui, and deified chiefs). In 1778, high chiefs chanted the *Kumulipo* over Captain James Cook, welcoming him as a returned god whose name, like the sacred child's, was Lono-i-ka-makahiki.

Priests exploited Māui for several reasons. To Society Islands priests, Māui was a submissive helper who raised the low-lying sky and regulated the time of the sun's journey to enable his eldest brother, a priest, to build temples. In Rarotonga in the Cook Islands, high priests interpreted Māui as a giant who, the first time he stood up, pushed up the sky with his head; later Māui became the weary avenger of insults made by other gods against Tangaroa, his foster father.

References to worship of Māui are obscure, rare, and based on unsupported hearsay. Tongans, it is said, formerly had a shrine and priest of Māui. One Hawai'ian priest declared that Hawai'i had long ago had a Māui cult and priests; another informant stated that Kamehameha I had built a temple to honor Māui. Most Polynesians usually respected Māui as an ancestor, despite his tricks, and they appreciated the benefits derived from his craftiness. But rather than to worship him, it seems that they preferred simply to enjoy the stories of how he humiliated many senior gods and earthly elders.

BIBLIOGRAPHY

Lessa, William A. *Tales from Ulithi Atoll: A Comparative Study in Oceanic Folklore.* Berkeley, 1961. Included are previously unrecorded versions of the earth-fishing myth, a description of its distribution in the Pacific, and a detailed comparative analysis of the versions.

Luomala, Katharine. *Oceanic, American Indian, and African Myths of Snaring the Sun.* Honolulu, 1940. A detailed study of the distribution and versions of sun-snaring myths in three parts of the world.

Luomala, Katharine. *Māui-of-a-Thousand-Tricks: His Oceanic and European Biographers.* Honolulu, 1949. The most comprehensive general survey to date on Māui in Oceanic culture, the major myth cycles that interpret his character and exploits, and the many theories of European scholars about him.

Luomala, Katharine. *Voices on the Wind: Polynesian Myths and Chants.* Honolulu, 1955. Includes a chapter on Māui and, with chapters on other heroes and on Polynesian narrative art, puts him in a broad setting.

KATHARINE LUOMALA (1987)

MAURICE, FREDERICK DENISON (1805–1872), Anglican theologian, founder of Christian Socialism.

John Frederick Denison Maurice was born near Lowestoft, Suffolk, England, the only son of a Unitarian minister, Michael Maurice, and Priscilla Hurry Maurice. Childhood memories of bitter family religious dissension (his mother and three older sisters abandoned Unitarianism for a form of Calvinism) left the young Frederick with a thirst for unity that was to motivate him all his life.

At Cambridge from 1823 to 1826, Maurice was influenced by Coleridge. During his intense conversion experience beginning in 1828, Maurice was deeply affected by the Scottish theologians Edward Irving (1792–1834) and Thomas Erskine (1788–1870). He decided to read for holy orders as an undergraduate, this time at Oxford, and was rebaptized and ordained in the Church of England in 1834.

At the core of this experience was Maurice's desire to know God directly as an actual, living person, in contrast to the abstract God of the Unitarians. This was not merely a romantic reaction to Western rationalism, but the discovery of a biblical, Christocentric, Pauline worldview, the great paradox of Christian faith, in which the holy and invisible God was at the same time in the person of a man. For Maurice, the fundamental, unchanging relationship at the heart of reality was that between God as revealer and man, the creature formed to know God. Man as the receiving image possesses no nature or life of his own. Man's sin is his assertion of independence, his striving hard not to be a receiver. Christ, the perfect image of the Father, is the image after which man was created. Christ is in every man, but the condemnation of every man is that he will not believe or act as if this were true. Maurice found the objective structure of this subjective faith in the articles, creeds, and liturgy of the English church. These formed a permanent witness to the fact that God had established a spiritual and universal kingdom on earth.

Maurice applied this worldview consistently to what he perceived as the basic need of his time: the rediscovery of revelation as the ground of faith. A divine-human struggle has marked all human history through man's distortion or denial of God's revelation. Instead of receiving and living within the given, divine order or constitution of the universe, man has been busily creating theories, systems, and opinions of his own as substitutes. These have resulted in the fragmentations of religious and political sects, parties, and factions and in philosophical attempts to bring heaven and earth within the terms of the intellect, Hegel being the latest offender. Maurice's method was the reverse: to be a digger, uncovering the original purpose and intent of all institutions, in order to show they were meant to be signs to the world of something invisible and permanent, the lineaments of an actual, existing kingdom of Christ.

In his writings, Maurice deliberately took the offensive, impelled by an urgent sense that a serious crisis of faith was growing among the young and that what passed for religion was a perversion of the Judeo-Christian faith that could not win their allegiance. His experience with young men was considerable: with medical students as chaplain of Guy's Hospital, London (1836–1845); as professor of English literature and history and then of theology (1840–1853) at King's College, London; with law students as chaplain of Lincoln's Inn, London (1846–1860). His luminous personal qualities and passionate devotion to truth attracted a growing circle of young men who were deeply influenced by him. These close contacts increased his concern about their questionings and doubts. They were being dosed with religion about God rather than with the living God himself: "Religion against God: this is the heresy of our age."

The revolutions of 1848 and the potentially explosive social situation in England found Maurice as spiritual leader of the short-lived but significant Christian Socialist movement (1848–1854), together with John Malcolm Ludlow (1821–1911) and Charles Kingsley (1819–1875). Convinced that cooperation, not competition, was the true foundation of a Christian society, their practical focus became that of cooperative associations for tailors and other trades. For Maurice the kingdom of Christ was the actual constitution of the universe, the "great practical existing reality which is to renew the earth." Society was not to be made anew but regenerated through uncovering its true functions and purpose, a view opposed to Ludlow's aim for reorganizing society on a socialist base. Maurice's interest in the education of the young was extended through his experience with workers, resulting in the founding in London of the Working Men's College (1854) to express his conviction that the true ground of human culture was not utilitarian but theological, the original purpose for which the ancient universities had been founded. His concern to set high standards for the education of governesses led to the founding of Queen's College, London, early in 1848.

Negative reactions to Maurice's theological and social views and to his growing influence reached a climax with the publication of his *Theological Essays* in 1853. These essays were written with the doubts and questions of the young in mind, as an alternative to the prevailing evangelical orthodoxy, which presented only theories and systems about God, Judgment Day, the verbal inspiration of the Bible, and everlasting punishment. This last Maurice viewed as a cosmic struggle between two eternal opposites: eternal life, which God presents to man, and eternal death, which man chooses for himself. But Christ's gospel reveals an abyss of love below that of death. This view was interpreted by the religious press as a denial of everlasting punishment and led finally to Maurice's expulsion from King's College in 1853 for unsettling the minds of the young.

Despite such controversies, increasing recognition and acceptance came to Maurice in his lifetime and he is viewed today as one of the most original thinkers of the Church of England. His permanent influence remains that of a prophet whose writings formed a sustained, passionate critique of the religious world of his time, comparable in depth to that of Søren Kierkegaard in the nineteenth century and of Karl Barth in the twentieth.

BIBLIOGRAPHY

Works by Frederick Denison Maurice

The Life of Frederick Denison Maurice Chiefly Told in His Own Letters, edited by his son, Frederick Maurice (London, 1884), is a major source for understanding Maurice's thought. For a selection of the letters, see *Toward the Recovery of Unity,* edited by John F. Porter and William J. Wolf (New York, 1964). Characteristic themes appear in his early work *The Kingdom of Christ, or, Hints on the Principles, Ordinances, and Constitution of the Catholic Church in Letters to a Member of the Society of Friends* (1838; revised, London, 1842). A new edition by Alec Vidler, based on the 1842 edition, has been published in two volumes (London, 1958). The post-Reformation religious bodies—Protestant, Roman Catholic, and Anglican—have turned their true principles into separate systems and theories, thereby losing sight of that church universal that existed before these systems and whose signs are indicated in the book's title. A variation of this theme is applied to the history of philosophy in *Moral and Metaphysical Philosophy: Philosophy of the First Six Centuries,* 2 vols., 2d ed., rev. (1854; reprint, London, 1872), begun in 1835, which contrasts man's independent search for wisdom with that Wisdom that first sought him. A lengthy controversy over Henry L. Mansel's Bampton Lectures of 1858 resulted in an important statement of the actual revelation of God to man presented in two works: *What Is Revelation? A Series of Sermons on the Epiphany* (Cambridge, 1859) and *A Sequel to the Inquiry, What Is Revelation?* (Cambridge, 1860). Some of the flavor of Maurice's views on Christian Socialism may be gleaned from *Politics for the People,* weekly papers from May through August 1848 (London), and *Tracts on Christian Socialism* (London, 1850).

Works on Frederick Denison Maurice

Among the works by the many distinguished twentieth-century Anglicans interested in Maurice, Alec Vidler's pioneering study *Witness to the Light: F. D. Maurice's Message for Today* (New York, 1948), his later *F. D. Maurice and Company* (London, 1966), and Arthur M. Ramsey's *F. D. Maurice and the Conflicts of Modern Theology* (Cambridge, 1951) are outstanding. Frank M. McClain's *Maurice: Man and Moralist* (London, 1972) is a perceptive account of how Maurice's personal relationships shaped his outlook on those givens of the Kingdom: the self, the family, the nation, and the church as universal society. My own *Frederick Denison Maurice: Rebellious Conformist* (Athens, Ohio, 1971) is a historical study emphasizing the centrality of Maurice's conversion from Unitarianism to Anglicanism and assessing his stature as a major Victorian figure. The Danish scholar Torben Christensen's *The Divine Order: A Study of F. D. Maurice's Theology* (Leiden, 1973) is a detailed analysis of Maurice's thought as a fusion of the message of the Bible and the Platonic idea of reality, in which Christianity is adjusted to Platonism. See also his excellent critical work *Origin and History of Christian Socialism, 1848–1854* (Aarhus, 1962).

OLIVE J. BROSE (1987)

MAUSS, MARCEL (1872–1950), the father of French ethnography, has had a profound influence on human and social sciences and has left behind an incredibly rich intellectual legacy. He is automatically linked with his uncle and teacher, Émile Durkheim (1858–1917). Some would say that he was "in the shadow of Durkheim" when describing his scholarly output, produced in direct cooperation with him.

Born to a family of merchants and rabbis at Épinal in 1872, Mauss studied philosophy at Bordeaux under Durkheim. After gaining his *agrégation* (teaching exam) in philosophy in 1895, he gave up the standard career path of secondary teaching, turning his attention instead to sociology of religion. During his studies at the École Pratique des Hautes Études and a trip to Holland and England, he also gained a solid grounding in philology, the history of religions, and ethnology. From his university days Mauss was also politically active, supporting Dreyfus and the socialists. He worked with the *Mouvement socialiste* and he took part in founding the new *Société de librairie et d'édition* with Lucien Herr and Charles Andler. Once he became a professor, Mauss was involved in the cooperative movement and the Socialist Party and published numerous articles in *L'Humanité,* of which he had been one of the founders.

Marcel Mauss produced his first major work together with his friend and colleague Henri Hubert (1872–1927), titled "Essai sur la nature et la fonction du sacrifice" (1899) [Essay on the nature and function of sacrifice]. The essay appeared in *L'Année sociologique,* which Durkheim had just founded in 1898. In charge of the section on religious sociology, Mauss was one of its leading contributors. At the École Pratique des Hautes Études, where he succeeded Léon Marillier in 1901, Mauss was responsible for teaching the history of the religion of primitive peoples. Frequently comparative and backed up with detailed evidence, the research undertaken by Mauss was set out as part of a program that had as its subject the ritual expressions of religious life and as its purpose the development of a theory of the sacred. His work quickly went beyond the boundaries of the sociology of religion to deal with the theory of knowledge, as can be seen from the essay written with Durkheim, titled "Quelques formes primitives de classification" (1903) [Some primitive forms of classification]. Concerning sociology, the supporters of Durkheim were quick to point out that it was a collective psychology with the purpose of studying collective representation.

The main debate in Durkheim's first books at the end of the nineteenth century revolved around the conflict between the individual and society, one of the problems faced by sociology since its inception being its specific nature and its relation to other disciplines, particularly psychology. This debate not only pitted Durkheim against his opponents, such as Gabriel Tarde, it also divided his colleagues, as can be seen from the initial volumes of *L'Année sociologique.* Célestin Bouglé, who, like his friend Paul Lapie, was undecided regarding the theoretical framework proposed by Durkheim, recognized the role of the individual and sought to go beyond the conflict between the individual and society, talking of interaction, association between individuals, communication of conscious awareness.

In the work of Mauss was the intention to soften the dogmatic tone of Durkheim. In an essay titled "Sociologie" [Sociology] which he co-authored with Paul Fauconnet in 1901 for *La Grande Encyclopédie,* he stressed the psychological aspect of social life, beliefs and communal feelings. "The very core of social life is a collection of representations," he wrote. "In this sense then, it could be said that sociology is a kind of psychology . . ." (Mauss, 1901). He clearly means a psychology different from that of the individual. Together with Henri Hubert, in 1904 Mauss published in *L'Année sociologique* the important "Esquisse d'une théorie générale de la magie" [Outline of a general theory of magic], demonstrating that here the laws of collective psychology transgress the laws of individual psychology. "It is belief that creates the magician," they wrote, "and the effects he unleashes" (Mauss, 1904). The use of the concept of *mana,* as the source idea of magic, stirred up a long-lasting controversy.

After the First World War, a tragedy which resulted in the death of Durkheim, his son André and several contributors to *L'Année sociologique,* and during which Mauss had volunteered and served as an interpreter, the latter undertook the difficult task of replacing his uncle and he attempted to relaunch *L'Année sociologique,* but only two volumes appeared, in 1925 and 1927. He also kept up intense political activity, undertaking the editing of an important work on the State and, after publishing his "Observations sur la violence" [Observations on violence] in *Vie socialiste,* he planned a book on Bolshevism. Then, encouraged by the current exoticism, which was attracting a new public to ethnology, Mauss worked together with Lucien Lévi-Bruhl and Paul Rivet, and in 1925 he set up the Institut d'ethnologie de l'université de Paris. The Institute attracted many students and researchers—Jeanne Cuisinier, Alfred Métraux, Marcel Griaule (1898–1956), Georges Dumézil (1898–1986), Denise Paulme, Michel Leiris, Germaine Dieterlen, Louis Dumont, André-Georges Haudricourt, Jacques Soustelle, Germaine Tillion, and others—who led many field studies, particularly in Africa, and organized the first important ethnological expeditions.

A man of tremendous intellectual curiosity and exceptional erudition, Mauss undertook research in a large number of areas: from magic, to body technique via the idea of the individual, he rectified the anti-psychological attitude of his uncle. Mauss set new "Rapports réels et pratiques de psychologie et de la sociologie" [Real and practical relationships of psychology and sociology], in an article which he published in 1924 in *Journal de psychologie.* The following year, he published in the new series of *L'Année sociologique,* his "Essai sur le don. Forme et raison de l'échange dans les sociétés archaïques" [Essay on the gift. The form and reason of exchange in archaic societies].

Durkheim's nephew had never before been so interested in concerning himself with work undertaken by psychologists, and he took part in the projects of the Société de psychologie, becoming its president in 1923. His friends included Charles Blondel, Georges Dumas and above all Ignace Meyerson, the managing editor of the *Journal de psychologie normale et pathologique.* "Sociology, psychology, physiology, everything should be combined," wrote Mauss. The intention is thus to take as a subject "the entire, actual human being" and to analyze "the phenomena as a whole." In 1936 then, again in the *Journal de psychologie,* he published a study on the "Effet physique chez l'individu de l'idée de mort suggérée par la collectivité" ["Physical effect upon the individual of the collectively suggested idea of death"]. Mental confusion, inhibitions, delusions, and hallucinations were all phenomena in which Mauss had a keen interest, but which, contrary to the opinions of psychologists, he did not perceive as pathological symptoms.

Marcel Mauss was elected to the Collège de France in 1930 and he became head of sociology. The texts he published at this period include "Les techniques du corps" [Body techniques] which appeared in 1935 in the *Journal de psychologie,* and "Une catégorie de l'esprit humain: la notion de personne, celle de « moi », un plan de travail" [A category of the human spirit: the idea of the person, the idea of 'self' a plan], in the *Journal of the Royal Anthropological Institute.* His last academic presentation was in 1941 and consisted of the paper, "Les techniques et la technologie" [Techniques and technology], delivered to the Journée de psychologie et d'histoire du travail et des techniques organized in Toulouse in 1941 by Ignace Meyerson. Marcel Mauss died on February 11, 1950, aged sixty-seven.

Mauss's writings were first collected by Claude Lévi-Strauss in 1950 in *Sociologie et anthropologie,* then in 1969, by Victor Karady in three volumes, *Œuvres.* As for his extensive *Écrits politiques*—Mauss was a very active militant socialist—they were only collected by Marcel Fournier in 1997. The political work of Mauss consists of a large number of reflections and invaluable "reflections" where he combines and expresses, as he recognizes himself, the fervor of the scholar and the politician. He had no doubt at the end of his "Essai sur le don" [Essay on the gift] concerning the worth of ancient moral values, such as charity, and he put forward a morality based upon solidarity and reciprocity.

BIBLIOGRAPHY

Primary Writings

Mauss, Marcel. "Essai sur la nature et la fonction du sacrifice" ("Essay on the nature and function of sacrifice"). *L'Année sociologique* (1899).

Mauss, Marcel, and Paul Fauconnet. "Sociologie"("Sociology"). In *La Grande Encyclopédie.* 1901.

Mauss, Marcel. "Esquisse d'une théorie générale de la magie" ("Outline of a general theory of magic"). *L'Année sociologique* (1904).

Mauss, Marcel. "Observations sur la violence" ("Observations on violence"). *Vie socialiste.*

Mauss, Marcel. "Rapports réels et pratiques de psychologie et de la sociologie" ("Real and practical relationships of psychology and sociology"). *Journal de psychologie* (1924).

Mauss, Marcel. "Essai sur le don. Forme et raison de l'échange dans les sociétés archaïques" ("Essay on the gift. The form and reason of exchange in archaic societies"). *L'Année sociologique* (1925).

Mauss, Marcel. "Les techniques du corps" ("Body techniques"). *Journal de psychologie* (1935).

Mauss, Marcel. "Une catégorie de l'esprit humain: la notion de personne, celle de « moi », un plan de travail" ("A category of the human spirit: the idea of the person, the idea of 'self' a plan"). *Journal of the Royal Anthropological Institute* (1935).

Mauss, Marcel. "Effet physique chez l'individu de l'idée de mort suggérée par la collectivité" ("Physical effect upon the individual of the collectively suggested idea of death"). *Journal de psychologie* (1936).

Mauss, Marcel. "Les techniques et la technologie" ("Techniques and technology"), paper delivered to the Journée de psychologie et d'histoire du travail et des techniques, 1941.

Mauss, Marcel. *Sociologie et anthropologie.* Edited by Claude Lévi-Strauss.Paris, 1950.

Mauss, Marcel. *Œuvres.* Three volumes. Edited by Victor Karady. Paris, 1969.

Mauss, Marcel. *Écrits politiques.* Edited by Marcel Fournier. Paris, 1997.

Secondary Writings

Allen, N. J. *Categories and Classifications: Maussian Reflections on the Social.* New York, 2000.

Cazeneuve, Jean. *Sociologie de Marcel Mauss.* Paris, 1968.

Fimiani, Mariapaola. *Marcel Mauss e il pensiero dell'origine.* Naples, 1984.

Karsenti, Bruno. *L'Homme total: sociologie, anthropologie et philosophie chez Marcel Mauss.* Paris, 1997.

Kirchmayr, Raoul. *Il circolo interrotto: figure del dono in Mauss, Sartre e Lacan.* Trieste, Italy, 2002.

Lévi-Strauss, Claude. *Introduction to the Work of Marcel Mauss.* Translated by Felicity Baker. London, 1987.

MARCEL FOURNIER (2005)

MĀWARDĪ, AL- (AH 364–450/974–1058 CE), more fully Abū al-Ḥasan ʿAlī ibn Muḥammad ibn Ḥabīb; Muslim jurist and political theorist. Al-Māwardī was born in Basra but spent most of his life in Baghdad. He studied Islamic law in both cities with eminent legists of the Shāfiʿī school of jurisprudence. Because of his reputation as a scholar, he was appointed judge in several towns, including Ustuwā in Iran and Baghdad in Iraq. In Baghdad the caliph al-Qādir (991–1031) chose him to write a resumé of Shāfiʿī jurisprudence; al-Qādir's successor, al-Qāʾim (1031–1074), used al-Māwardī for diplomatic missions to the Buyid and Seljuk rulers of Iran.

Although al-Māwardī is remembered primarily as the author of *Kitāb al-aḥkām al-sulṭānīyah* (Book of governmental ordinances), he wrote other books on jurisprudence and government, as well as treatises on such varied topics as Qurʾanic exegesis, the prophethood of Muhammad, the conduct of judges, proverbs and traditions, and Islamic ethics. The report that he did not permit circulation of his books until after his death is regarded as apocryphal. While his book on ethics, entitled *Kitāb adab al-dunyā wa-al-dīn* (Book of manners in worldly and religious affairs), is still read by Muslims, it is seldom taken into account in discussions of al-Māwardī's importance in the development of Islamic thought; surprisingly enough, the same holds true even for his works closely related in subject matter to *Al-aḥkām.* Accordingly, in the absence of any comprehensive study of al-Māwardī's complete works, estimates of his significance must be regarded as tentative despite the fact that the place assigned him in political thought by Western scholars is firmly fixed and widely accepted.

The date of composition of *Al-aḥkām* is not known, nor is the nature of the relationship of this book to a similar, in many respects identical, book of the same title written by al-Māwardī's contemporary, the Ḥanbalī jurist Abū Yaʿlā ibn al-Farrāʾ. However, scholars assume, without documentation, that since al-Māwardī's *Al-aḥkām* seems to be a mature work, it must have been written toward the end of his life; since, moreover, al-Māwardī was sixteen years older than Ibn al-Farrāʾ, it is believed that the latter must have borrowed, without acknowledgment, from the former. Clearly these are problems that need to be solved before al-Māwardī's originality and development as a thinker can be understood. In the meantime, an indication of the content of *Al-aḥkām* and its possible connection with the author's milieu must suffice.

According to al-Māwardī he wrote *Al-aḥkām* at the behest of a ruler, perhaps a caliph, as a convenient compendium of ordinances relating to government, culled from manuals of jurisprudence. This work, and Abū Yaʿlā's, are rightly regarded as the first books of jurisprudence to be devoted exclusively to the principles and practice of Islamic government. The parts of *Al-aḥkām* that have attracted most attention discuss the three highest offices of the medieval Islamic state: the caliphate, the vizierate, and the emirate by usurpation, even though at least two-thirds of the work is devoted to lesser administrative and judicial offices, taxation, and land policy. Scholars are divided as to whether the book, either as a whole or in parts, reflects actual political conditions prevailing in al-Māwardī's time or constitutes a program for establishing an ideal state or for reasserting the power of the caliphate in the face of threats posed by secular, military rulers. The prevailing view is that al-Māwardī was a supporter of al-Qāʾim and al-Qādir in their struggle against the Buyids and the Seljuks. His support, never explicitly expressed as such, came in the form of arguments derived from the Qurʾān, tradition (*ḥadīth*), and jurisprudence (*fiqh*) for the necessity of maintaining the caliph as executor of Islamic law and for the duty of the Muslim community to obey him. Admittedly, this dual principle seems remote from the realities of al-Māwardī's day, when generals exercised political power in Islamic states. But al-Māwardī tried to come to terms with this reality and to accommodate it within the scope of Islamic law in his chapter on the emirate by usurpation. There he argued that rule by emirs based on force was to be sanctioned as long as they acknowledged the authority of the caliphs and implemented Islamic law. In effect, such an admission constituted a first step toward concession to political expediency, which was characteristic of the subsequent development of medieval Islamic political thought. Be that as it may, al-Māwardī's formulation of the character of the Islamic state has been regarded as authoritative by many Muslim thinkers and Western scholars alike.

BIBLIOGRAPHY

The fullest published study of al-Māwardī is the long article by Henri Laoust, "La penseé et l'action politiques d'al-Māwardī," *Revue des études islamiques* 36 (1968): 11–92. I discuss problems that Laoust does not treat in my article "A New Look at *al-aḥkām al-Sulṭāniyya*," *Muslim World* 64 (January 1974): 1–15. *Al-aḥkām al-sulṭānīyah* has been translated into French by Edmond Fagnan as *Les statuts gouvernementaux* (Algiers, 1915).

DONALD P. LITTLE (1987)

MAWDŪDĪ, SAYYID ABŪ AL-AʿLĀ (1903–1979), popularly known as Mawlānā Mawdūdī; Indian (later Pakistani), writer, religious thinker, political figure, and founder and leader of an Islamic revivalist movement. Mawdūdī was born into a religious family in Aurangabad, British India. With the exception of a short period in a Hyderabad *madrasah,* his education was gained at home or through his own efforts. His earliest occupation was journalism, and in 1920 he became editor of the highly influential newspaper of the Jamʿiyat-i ʿUlamāʾ (the organization of Indian *ʿulamaʾ*), where he remained for seven years. As one of the Indian Muslim leaders outraged by Gandhi's abandonment of the Swarāj movement for independence, he began to argue that Muslim interests could not be reconciled with those of Hindus. Although Mawdūdī had participated in the religio-political Khilāfat movement, he and his brother criticized the Khilāfat leaders for the fiasco of the *hijrah* ("emigration") movement from India to Afghanistan.

In the mid-1920s, in response to Hindu attacks on Islam resulting from the murder of a Hindu leader by a Muslim fanatic, Mawdūdī wrote a series of articles in defense of Islamic beliefs, subsequently published as *Al-jihād fī al-Islām* (Religious War in Islam). He later said that this volume, his first serious work on Islam, represented his true intellectual and spiritual conversion to the religion.

Mawdūdī left journalism in 1927 for literary and historical pursuits. In the following years he wrote a history of the Seljuks and an unfinished history of the Asafi dynasty of Hyderabad. From 1932 he was associated with a Hyderabad religious journal, *Tarjumān al-Qurʾān*, which he edited from 1933 until his death; this publication has been the principal instrument for the propagation of his views. Criticizing the westernized class of Indian Muslims, Mawdūdī began to call for the mobilization of Muslims in the cause of Islam. In the political debates of the late 1930s he rejected both the Indian nationalism of the Congress and the Muslim nationalism of the Muslim League, calling instead for an Islamic order in India. His views from the period are collected in three volumes called *Musalmān awr mawjūdah siyāsī kashmakash* (The Muslim and the Present Political Struggle).

In 1941 Mawdūdī founded the Jamāʿat-i Islāmī, an organization for the promotion of Islamic principles, and was elected its chief, or *amīr*, which he remained until 1972. From 1941 until the partition of Indian he devoted his time to building the organization and to writing. In 1947, despite his unhappiness with the Muslim League, Mawdūdī moved to Pakistan, where he and his group became the leading spokesmen for an Islamic state. The Jamāʿat-i Islāmī sought political power, and its activities attracted the disapproval of government. Mawdūdī and his principal followers were imprisoned on several occasions; he himself was condemned to death by a military court after the anti-Aḥmadīyah disturbances of 1953, but the sentence was never carried out. His ideas and activities brought criticism from both modernist and conservative Muslims as well as from secularists.

Mawdūdī's teachings are set out in a large number of writings that include a six-volume commentary on the Qurʾān, *Tafhīm al-Qurʾān*. These writings have been translated into numerous languages, and he is at present one of the most widely read authors in the Islamic world. He believed Islam to be an ideology that offers complete guidance for human life, laid down by God in his holy book, the Qurʾān, and through his prophet, Muḥammad. The task of Muslims is to follow the eternal divine law by building an Islamic state, by creating an Islamic society as well as an individual Islamic life. The paramount feature of his teaching is the demand for an Islamic state, which he intended to be realized in the form of the Jamāʿat-i Islāmī. His vision of society was rigorous, puritanical, authoritarian, antisecular, and antidemocratic but was based upon a deeply held conviction that people must live according to the law of God.

BIBLIOGRAPHY

A sympathetic discussion of the import of Mawdūdī's perspective for many aspects of life is *Islamic Perspectives: Studies in Honor of Mawlana Sayyid Abul Aʿlā Mawdudi*, edited by Khurshid Ahmad and Zafar Ishaq Ansari (Leicester, 1979). Kalim Bahadur's *The Jamāʿat-i Islāmī of Pakistan* (New Delhi, 1980) is informative as to the history of that organization. Leonard Binder's *Religion and Politics in Pakistan* (Berkeley, 1963) gives the Pakistani background. Charles J. Adams's "The Ideology of Mawlana Mawdudi," in *South Asian Politics and Religion*, edited by Donald Smith (Princeton, 1966), pp. 371–397, is a balanced account; see also his "Mawdudi and the Islamic State," in *Voices of Resurgent Islam*, edited by John Esposito (New York, 1983), pp. 99–133.

SHEILA MCDONOUGH (1987)

MAWLID is an Arabic word that literally means the time and place of a birth, but the word is used in particular for the birth of the prophet Muḥammad (*mawlid al-nabī*). In some Islamic countries it also refers to the festival days of local saints (*walīs*). The actual birth date of the prophet Muḥammad is unknown, but the anniversary of his birth is celebrated on 12 Rabīʿah al-Awwal of the Islamic lunar calendar, a day prior to the anniversary of his death (in 632 CE).

Muḥammad is portrayed in the Qurʾān as a messenger of God who was an ordinary mortal in other respects. Only in later centuries did many Muslims begin to assert a higher sanctity for his person. The first recorded celebrations of his birth occurred during the latter part of Fatimid rule in Egypt (909–1171). As Shīʿī Muslims who held descendants of the Prophet in particularly high esteem, the Fatimid elite similarly observed the *mawlids* of Muḥammad's son-in-law ʿAlī, his daughter Fāṭimah, and the reigning caliph. Palace dignitaries and religious notables held daylight processions and delivered sermons, a practice briefly prohibited but later revived. The Sunnī majority in Egypt took no part in these ceremonies.

The first popular *mawlid* occurred in 1207. Muẓaffar al-Dīn Kökbürü, brother-in-law of the famed Ṣalāḥ al-Dīn (Saladin), arranged for a festival in Arbalāʾ, a town near Mosul in present-day northern Iraq. As described by the historian Ibn Khallikān (d. 1282), a native of the town, the *mawlid* became an elaborate annual event, attracting scholars, notables, preachers, and poets from throughout the region. The deeds and person of Muḥammad were celebrated in religious poetry and songs and culminated on the eve of the *mawlid* in a torchlight procession led by the prince. Followers of Ṣūfī orders were also prominent in the celebrations, and gifts were lavishly distributed to participants.

Some aspects of early *mawlids* appear to have been influenced by Middle Eastern Christian traditions of the period, such as lavish entertainments and nighttime processions in honor of saints. Even as *mawlids* also developed for saints and other holy persons, especially in Egypt, the Prophet's *mawlid* continued to be the most elaborate. *Mawlids* quickly became highly popular occasions associated with mysticism, during which Ṣūfī orders congregated in public, reciting rhythmical chants in praise of God and in some cases entering into trance. From Egypt, *mawlids* spread to many other parts of the Islamic world.

The popularity of *mawlids* met initial resistance from some theologians. Ibn Taymīyah (d. 1328) and others condemned the Prophet's *mawlid* as a harmful innovation (*bidʿah*). After considerable discussion, most theologians, except those precursors of the later Wahhābī movement, who espoused Islam in its most idealized and fundamental form, tolerated the *mawlid* as a praiseworthy innovation (*bidʿah ḥasanah*), since it inspired reverence for the Prophet. The central activity of *mawlids* is the recital of long panegyrical poems and legends commemorating Muḥammad and his deeds, recitations so popular that they are repeated on festive occasions throughout the year.

The acceptance of popular practice by theologians shows the Islamic principle of consensus (*ijmāʿ*) at work. A key doctrinal tenet in Islam is that the community of believers cannot agree upon error. The legal opinions of religious jurists appear to have had minimal influence in reducing the popularity of *mawlids*, so that most jurists were encouraged to accommodate theological doctrine to social realities.

As with other Islamic celebrations and rites of passage, *mawlids* show considerable differences throughout the Islamic world. In some contexts, the *mawlid* is minimally distinguished from other festive occasions; elsewhere, it is one of the most important annual religious events. In nineteenth-century Cairo, *mawlid* celebrations started on the first day of Rabīʿah al-Awwal. Large tents were pitched in one of Cairo's quarters and decorated with lamps and Qurʾanic inscriptions. Each night Ṣūfī orders carried their banners in procession to their tents, where they chanted the name of God, recited poems in praise of Muḥammad, and provided refreshments to guests. In the daytime, dancers, clowns, and storytellers entertained the audience in a carnival atmosphere. Festivities climaxed on the eleventh and twelfth evenings of the month, with elaborate poems and songs in praise of Muḥammad that continued until morning. In recent times government restrictions against large public gatherings sought to curtail these events. Nonetheless, the Prophet's *mawlid* and to a lesser extent those for local saints continue to be large communal festivals attracting hundreds of thousands of people in Egypt's larger towns.

Elsewhere in the Islamic world, religious orders play a less central role in *mawlid* festivities. In Morocco, the month in which the Prophet's birthday occurs is popularly known as *mulūd*, the local pronunciation of *mawlid*. Children born during this month are considered especially fortunate and are often named after it, and it is a good time to circumcise boys. Celebrations last a week, culminating with recitations of panegyrics of Muḥammad in decorated and illuminated community mosques. On the final night, recitations continue until daybreak. Some families offer a feast and distribute food to the poor; women decorate their hands and feet with henna and visit cemeteries. In Java, a feast is offered for the *mawlid*, which is one of the two most important calendrical ceremonies in a region given over to elaborate festival cycles. A popular Javanese belief is that the giving of feasts for the Prophet's birthday and the end of Ramaḍān distinguishes Muslims from non-Muslims and humans from animals; this view of the importance of the occasion is not necessarily shared by those Javanese who have a more elaborate understanding of Islamic doctrine and ritual.

The symbolism of the *mawlid* is especially highly developed among Swahili-speaking East African Muslims. In the town and island of Lamu, located off the northern coast of Kenya, most Muslims hold that the prophet Muḥammad, created of dust, like all other persons, carried "light" to the earth in this month. The discipline of fasting during the month of Ramadan emphasizes the separation of nature and culture and the distance between actual human society and the Islamic ideal. Likewise, the month of Muḥammad's birth is regarded as a joyous occasion that emphasizes life as lived here and now, combined with belief in the Prophet's willingness to intervene on behalf of his people and to accept them in full recognition of their individual shortcomings. It is said that during this month the Prophet lives on the earth like a human being and loves and hates just as they do. The first twelve days of the month are marked by processions, singing, and the music of tambourines and flutes. Intense competitions are held on successive evenings in the mosques and religious associations of the various quarters in Lamu. Each quarter vies in enthusiasm to praise Muḥammad's life and deeds in song and prose and to show its love for the Prophet. *Sharīfs*, descendants of Muḥammad, are especially honored in Lamu during this period.

Sharīfs are invited to recite poems in praise of Muḥammad in most of the nineteen mosques of Lamu town. In beautiful performances on successive evenings, assemblies of young boys from mosque schools and musicians perform songs and poems that have been rehearsed for months. Brightly colored tunics, donated by wealthy Muslims, are worn for the ceremonies. The freeborn and the ex-slaves, members of two important local social categories, compete with one another during these celebrations to express a willingness to use earthly wealth—the offer of food and refreshments to guests—and talent to show their love for the Prophet. If not enough effort is put into the preparations for quarter festivities, the *sharīfs* are said to participate with less enthusiasm and to attract fewer blessings for the quarter. Love of the Prophet is said to join together the world of nature and the world of culture. Ceremonies include the sacrifice of cows, highly valued on the island, visits to cemeteries, and the distribution of rose water by *sharīfs* to symbolize Muḥammad's ability to cleanse his followers of their sins. Until the 1970s distinctions between freeborn and ex-slave and *sharīf* and commoner remained significant for many East African Muslims, although in recent years such distinctions have been eroded under pressure from reformist Muslims.

Bibliography

In his *Muhammadan Festivals* (New York, 1951) G. E. Von Grunebaum discusses the early history of the *mawlid* and includes translations from original source materials. For the *mawlid* in more recent times, see Edward W. Lane's *An Account of the Manners and Customs of the Modern Egyptians*, 3d ed. (1846; reprint, New York, 1973), which includes a description of the celebrations as he saw them in Cairo in 1834. Michael Gilsenan's *Saint and Sufi in Modern Egypt* (Oxford, 1973) provides a brief commentary on contemporary Egyptian practices. For Morocco, Edward A. Westermarck's *Ritual and Belief in Morocco*, vol. 2 (1926; reprint, New Hyde Park, N. Y., 1968), remains the best-documented ethnographic account, while Pessah Shinar's "Traditional and Reformist Mawlid Celebrations in the Maghrib," in *Studies in Memory of Gaston Wiet*, edited by Myriam Rosen-Ayalon (Jerusalem, 1977), pp. 371–413, provides a richly analytic account of how *mawlid* practices have changed over time throughout North Africa. In *The Religion of Java* (Glencoe, Ill., 1960) Clifford Geertz mentions the *mawlid* only briefly but fully situates it in a highly elaborate ritual context. By far the most extensive discussion of the symbolism of occasion as elaborated in one local context is Abdul Hamid M. el-Zein's *The Sacred Meadows: A Structural Analysis of Religious Symbolism in an East African Town* (Evanston, Ill., 1974).

Dale F. Eickelman (1987)

MAWU-LISA is a complex deity worshiped in coastal West Africa by the Fon and most of the Ewe. Occasionally Mawu and Lisa are considered as separate deities; sometimes they are seen together as a complementary sexual pair. The issue is complicated because the Ewe peoples use the term *mawu* both to refer to God in a general way or to a specific deity.

As a specific deity, Mawu is seen as a creator, but she rarely has shrines, priests, or rituals dedicated to her. Among peoples such as the Fon, Mawu is conceived of as a female deity associated with the moon, and it is in this manifestation that she is most often paired with Lisa. Among the Fon, the cult of Mawu-Lisa was centered in Abomey, the capital of the old kingdom of Dahomey. Mawu is depicted as an elder female figure in conjunction with Lisa, a younger male consort. Other complementary qualities are seen in them. For example, whereas Mawu is associated with the moon (night) and is cool (gentle and forgiving), Lisa is associated with the sun (day) and is hot (fierce and punitive). Sometimes even their actions are complementary. In one mythic tradition, Mawu created the earth and then retired to the heavens. When she saw that things were not going well with men, she sent Lisa to make tools and clear the forests so that men could farm and live a civilized life.

The name *Lisa* among the Fon appears to be derived from the nearby Yoruba people, who use the word *oriṣa* (or *orisha*) to refer to lesser deities. Lisa is an analogue for the Yoruba *oriṣa* Ọbatala and is variously described as the twin brother, husband, or son of Mawu. This paired complementarity is not all that unusual in West Africa. Other pairs of spiritual beings include Nana-Buku of central Benin and Togo, Dada-Sogbo of the Ewe, and Eṣu-Legba of the Yoruba. Their pairing need not refer to sexuality but merely to the unity of duality, however that may be defined.

Mawu also creates human souls and rules their destinies. The soul is called *mawuse* (the Mawu within a person). At first, Mawu made people out of clay, but after running short, she began to make them out of reused bodies (hence we can see resemblances in people). Mawu upholds moral law and also metes out rewards and punishments after death.

The priests of Mawu wear white, and at Abomey there is a rare statue of Mawu. The figure, painted red, has large breasts and holds a crescent moon. The cult of Mawu is not limited to West Africa. There are scattered instances of Mawu's cult in the New World. For example, in Yoruba houses in São Luiz, Brazil, there is said to be an *encantado* (spirit) of Mawu. There, as in West Africa, Mawu connotes a generalized notion of divinity.

Bibliography

Herskovits, Melville J. *Dahomey: An Ancient West African Kingdom.* 2 vols. New York, 1938. An excellent description by one of the great ethnographers of Africa.

Pelton, Robert D. *The Trickster in West Africa.* Berkeley, 1980. Includes a good discussion of Mawu-Lisa and the role played by Legba, the Fon trickster figure.

James S. Thayer (1987)

MAXIMÓN is a trickster deity from Santiago Atitlán, Guatemala. His origin as a Mesoamerican merchant and lineage deity originates in the pre-classic Maya world (c. 500 BCE). His cult has spread throughout the highlands of Guatemala alongside the proselytizing evangelical movement among the Maya of the highlands. His image, in various forms, can now be found throughout the republic, but this essay concentrates on the deity found in Santiago Atitlán while recognizing the many similarities between the various Maximón cults found in different highland towns. Maximón is particularly important to all those people who want more out of life than simple sustenance; he specializes in giving everything that is "extra" in this world. His cult has thus grown to satisfy the focus of material wealth that is now so important to the people who inhabit the towns and villages of the Guatemalan highlands.

Maximón is a name derived from two different origins: first, from the Catholic Simón Pedro (Ximón Pedro) the first apostle of Christ who was given the keys to heaven and the power of "binding and loosing"; second, from the Tz'utujil term meaning "Mr. Knotted," derived from *ma* (mister) and *ximon* (to have knotted). Maximón is the trickster who waits at the portal of fate, where he either captures and binds his prey or loosens the knotted one from the trap of a predator. Like Simon Peter, he is seen as the gatekeeper of all those souls who are out on the road, at the crossroads of life, or in the marketplace where happenstance can change one's luck. Maximón is the one who opens or closes the road to opportunity, creates an accidental meeting at the crossroads, or finds the needed connection in the marketplace.

Maximón is Lord of Merchants, similar to God L and God M of the ancient Maya. He is a tireless walker of roads without end; his wanderings lead him to wherever he is called, as well as to all those places where he creates problems that he alone can solve. He is the shape-shifter who alters his shape to the changing shape of the world in which he exists as trickster, and because of this his disguises are infinite.

He is *versipellis*, a being who changes its skin to imitate another being or an environment, a completely flexible being whose way is "no way." Maximón is ever-present in his many forms, but mostly he is known to take the form of one of the following: a young girl, the old man, the latina temptress, the poor beggar, the wealthy plantation owner, the hummingbird, the blue jay, the skunk, the donkey, the wild mountain dahlia, the "divining tree," a whirlwind, a night breeze, a earth tremor, a fly, a mosquito, a wafting scent of a cigar, or even a ripple across still water.

Like all tricksters he makes himself known to his followers through signs given on the road, where a heightened sense of insecurity is always felt. All of his disguises or changes give messages to those who follow his guidance to safe passage and profitable markets. He is lord of all those portals of opportunity where tax collectors let one pass unmolested, where obstacles are lifted, where government officials look the other way, where traps are avoided, and where doors of opportunity are flung wide open. He is lord of the crossroads where destinies accidentally come together for better or worse. He is lord of the marketplace where abundance is turned into wealth and where finding a new product or person brings about a life reversal. Maximón is guide to souls in need, both in this lifetime and at death; it is he who is the *k'amal b'iey* (pathfinder) who ushers us towards the direction we must be taking. Sacred history tells that Maximón was made of the "Tz'ajtel tree" (*erythrina corallodendron*), a type of "divining wood" used by shamans, diviners, matchmakers, midwives, and oracles to see into the future or back into the past.

Maximón is also known as Mam or Rilaj Mam, Ancestor or Great Ancestor. *Mam* means both "grandfather" and "grandchild," making him a deity that replaces the ancestors with future ancestors in such a way that the lineage never dies. Mam is also known as "Year Bearer" in a Mayan world where the sun is carried on the back of humanity through ritual sacrifice. The Year Bearer carries the year, and the ritual practitioners carry the Year Bearer through rituals of sacrifice. The Year Bearer is a sacred being who occupies the four corners of the world in a quadripartite fashion. In Maya timekeeping, each year had one of four styles, each of which had a Mam from one of the four world corners. As one year ended, the Year Bearer of that year was dismembered, purified, and then put back together as another Mam, another Year Bearer. In this way years are seen as human ancestors that continuously replace one another throughout time.

Mam also signifies the five dangerous days of the Uayeb', a short, five-day month between two 360-day years, each of which is made up of eighteen months of twenty days. During this short five-day month of the Uayeb', the Mam was celebrated as one year ended and another began. Mam is thus the Lord of Middle, where years end and begin, as well as lord of endless generations of ancestors, or Mam, and their replacements, also known as Mam.

Mam has many similarities with God N, or Pawahtuun, of the classic Maya. Pawahtuun was depicted as an aged sky-bearing deity who went about dressed in a conch shell or turtle carapace, linking him to waterways, lakes, and seas of merchant people. He was an old man who loved a party, where he would indulge himself in drunkenness as well as the affections of wild young women. As a quadripartite deity he was closely associated with the Chaks, or rain deities, and may have been the rain deities' earthly counterpart. Mam, like Chak, is a deity of the four corners; as a mountain god, he personifies the stones or mountains that support the sky at each of the four corners. Mam in his most beloved form is an elderly lord of the earth, thunder, and the ancestors.

Tz'utujil tradition of Santiago Atitlán states that Mam was created by immortals known as Nawales, who were merchants and in much need of a guardian who would watch over their women while they were on the road and in the marketplaces of distant towns. As soon as Mam was brought to life by the Nawales as a replication of their perfection, he began doing what he had been ordered to. Pretty soon he was making love to all the wives of those who had created him. Eventually, Mam was dismembered and put back together in such away that he could never misuse his human body again: his head was twisted around backwards, and his arms and legs were left short. This is the image that is found today in the Cofradia of Santa Cruz in Santiago Atitlán. Like all tricksters, Mam's appetites cause his fall from prescriptive culture, and so teaches people how not to act in the world.

The present-day image of Maximón stands about four-feet tall in a brand new pair of boots. He is adorned in many silk scarves, which once may have been feathers. On his gourd skull is a wooden mask of an old man. On the backside of his head is another mask, giving Mam a 360-degree view. Upon this head of twin masks are two modern Stetson cowboy hats, signifying the duplicity inherent in this capricious being. (The Stetson hats are given as gifts to Maximón by wealthy Indian merchants, who wear them themselves to manifest their high status in the Indian world.) His body is made of pieces of divining wood that are tied together with sashes of traditional cloth and string. This ritually bundled core is adorned in traditional clothing from Santiago Atitlán and other towns from the lake region, creating a deity that looks much like it must have when the Nawales first formed it.

Mam, or Maximón, is a boundary crosser and a liminal character that lives at the threshold of this world of humans and the other world of the gods. He is the go-between and messenger that relays communication between humanity and their deities. In this middle ground between humans and gods he takes his payment in the form of offerings, including only flowers, incense, candles, liquor, tobacco, sweet-smelling waters, song, and prayers. He takes part of all that once was given only to the gods, and in this way he makes a good living by existing between and betwixt two worlds.

See Also Mesoamerican Religions.

Bibliography

Carlsen, Robert S. *The War for the Heart and Soul of a Highland Maya Town.* Austin, Tex., 1997. Analysis of cultural continuity and change in Santiago Atitlán, including considerable discussion of the Maximón cult.

Hyde, Lewis. *Trickster Makes This World.* New York, 1998. A profound and creative analysis of the religious archetype of the trickster and his power to create and recreate this world.

Stanzione, Vincent J. *Rituals of Sacrifice: Walking the Face of the Earth on the Sacred Path of the Sun.* Albuquerque, N.Mex., 2003. An in-depth study of religion and ceremony in Santiago Atitlán, this creative and exciting study by a historian of religion focuses on the cult of Maximón and his trickster relationship with Jesus during the rituals of sacrifice at the time of Lent and Easter Week in Santiago Atitlán.

Tarn, Nathaniel. *Scandals in the House of Birds: Shamans and Priests on Lake Atitlán.* New York, 1998. A complicated yet comprehensive anthropological study of religious symbolism in Santiago Atitlán.

Vincent Stanzione (2005)

MAXIMOS THE CONFESSOR

MAXIMOS THE CONFESSOR (c. 580–662), Byzantine theologian, Eastern Orthodox saint, ascetic writer, and opponent of monothelitism. What is known about Maximos's life largely derives from an anonymous biography.

Born in Constantinople, Maximos received a good education, which was rare for his time. Indicative of his abilities was his appointment as first secretary to the emperor Heraclius (r. 610–641), but Maximos soon recognized his ecclesiastical calling. He entered the Monastery of Philipikos, in Chrysopolis (present-day Üsküdar, Turkey), probably in 614, where he eventually became abbot. Because of attacks by the Persians, Maximos and the other monks were forced to flee to the Monastery of Saint George, at Cyzicus (present-day Kapidagi, Turkey). Two years later Maximos was again obliged to flee because of Persian expansionism. His path likely took him through Crete, and probably Cyprus, to North Africa (626). It is well known that he was in Carthage on Pentecost of 632. At the Eucratas Monastery he became acquainted with Sophronios, another refugee, who later became patriarch of Jerusalem (634–638). Maximos was greatly influenced by Sophronios and later called him his forerunner, father, and teacher.

The two monks journeyed to Alexandria in an effort to overturn an agreement of union with the monophysites but were unable to persuade the former patriarch, Cyrus of Alexandria (d. 641), to their cause. Because such concessions to monophysitism were likely to terminate in the heresy of monoenergism, Sophronios had turned against the agreement; Maximos continued in the struggle against the union but acted in a reserved way. After Heraclius published his *Ecthesis* (638), and a monothelite direction was given to the heresy, Maximos cut off relations with the patriarch Pyrrhus and began his own antimonothelite activities.

Important stages of Maximos's struggle against monothelitism are his dialogue with the deposed Pyrrhus in Carthage; the convocation in North Africa of three antimonothelite synods, where he explained his position; and the continuation of his endeavors in Rome (646), which had become the new center of antimonothelitism. Maximos's efforts were now carried out with unmitigated zeal. He composed treatises and letters to the emperor, the pope, and the patriarch of Constantinople. His antiheretical struggle prompted the convocation of a synod in Rome (649) where he condemned monothelitism.

Maximos's initiatives were regarded by the imperial authorities as hostile to its policy of union and reconciliation. Therefore, Maximos and his companions, one of whom was the papal legate, were taken to Constantinople for questioning. (This was in 655, not, as is commonly reported, during the reign of Pope Martin I.) Although the charge that he had betrayed the interests of the empire was not proved, Maximos was exiled (along with his two disciples) to Byzia in Thrace for refusing to sign the new conciliatory declaration, the *Typus* of Constans II, under Patriarch Peter (655–666). Maximos was called back to Constantinople in 656 for another investigation, but after refusing once again to sign, he was exiled and imprisoned at Perbera. Although his opponents were determined, Maximos's intransigence in matters of faith prevented him from giving in to them. Six years later, Maximos, Pope Martin, and Sophronios were anathemized. There followed exchanges of messages, rumors of torture (some say Maximos was beaten, his tongue cut out, and his right hand lopped off), and further exiling. Maximos was finally imprisoned in the fortress of Schimaris, where after two months he died, on August 13, 662.

Maximos composed numerous works on the interpretation of scripture and on the teachings of the fathers. His doctrinal writings consist largely of short treatises against monophysitism, a more important series against monothelitism, and numerous other ascetical writings. He wrote commentaries on mystical theology and on the work of Dionysius the Areopagite (Pseudo-Dionysius). Also extant are many letters by Maximos, including the letters and disputation that he wrote to Pyrrhus. Some other writings exist only in manuscript.

The teachings of Maximos developed in two directions: on the one hand, in a theoretical direction, with strong metaphysical emphasis; and on the other, in an existential direction, which elaborated a spiritual way of life. In his theology of the unity and trinity of God, Maximos follows the ontological method and the teachings of the Greek fathers. The interpretation by some Western theologians that Maximos agrees with the view that the Holy Spirit proceeds from the Father and the Son cannot be demonstrated definitively. For example, Maximos sees in the Trinity the relation of three persons who participate jointly in one essence and jointly express a common divine energy: the Father, "by grace"; the Son, "by self-operation"; the Holy Spirit, "by synergy."

Maximos believed that the world was created by God so that beings could participate in his goodness. Accordingly, man holds the dominant place in creation and is the natural link between God and creation; further, all will is united to God through man. The first man, Maximos thought, was created with an orientation toward God and was meant to bridge the distance between "image" and "likeness." For Maximos, disobedience to the divine will constitutes deliberate sin, in which man's will is distorted and his nature corrupted; thus, man loses the grace of *apatheia*. Also, corruptibility in human nature is inherited; therefore, there is no human possibility of self-regeneration or of exemption from death. However, what man has done out of negligence, the man Christ has corrected.

Maximos's Christology is devoted to his struggle against monophysitism and monothelitism. For Maximos, in Christ, human nature, which had no previous existence as such, became substantial and received existence in the preexisting substance of God the Word (the Logos). As one being, Christ has the same humanity as man but he also has divinity. However, as in the Trinity, in Christ's being one essence is confessed without confusing the two natures.

The resolution of the question of whether there are one or two energies (or one or two wills) in Christ lies in the determination of their origin, that is, whether in the nature or in the person of Christ. For the monoenergists, Christ has only one energy because he has only one active element. For the monothelites, he has only one will because nature, according to doctrines of natural philosophy, is governed by the rule of necessity.

In order to oppose monophysitism, Maximos attempts to define the operational autonomy of the person on the basis of the dynamism of nature. He argues that nature, which is both noetic and created, "has no necessity" (*Patrologia Graeca* 91.293). Will, as a reasonable desire, presupposes the habit of nature, which is movement and energy, not stasis. The will governs this nature within the functions of the person. For example, sight and speech are capacities inherent in nature, but "how" one sees is dependent upon the person. In this way, Maximos distinguishes between the natural origin of the will and its personal (that is, "gnomic") orientation. As such, will does not violate the order of nature but diverts its movement and, in this case, expresses the ethical responsibility of the person.

According to Maximos, Christ is recognized as God and man from his divine and human qualities. Christ willed, or acted, as God and man. Maximos sees a "divine-human will" and a "divine-human energy" in Christ's very nature. In distinction from his opponents, Maximos argues that if will is identical with persons (and not nature), then the Trinity, which is a trinity of persons, and not of natures, would have to comprise three wills. Further, if the energy were to flow from persons, there would be three energies in the Trinity, and Christ would be cut off from the energy of the Father and that of the Holy Spirit.

The human will of Christ is, by the logic of nature, the same as ours, but its manifestation in Christ is directed by the person of God the Word. Hence, Christ's will experienced everything human except sin. The famous phrase "My Father, if it is possible, let this cup pass from me; nevertheless, not as I will, but as thou wilt" (*Mt.* 26:39) expresses the will of the human nature in Christ, that is, his resistance to death as well as his acceptance of it. This is an indication that salvation is completed by the human will. Thus Maximos's intention is to defend the human will of Christ, which also constitutes a defense of the freedom of man in relation to God. Under such presuppositions, Christ healed and divinized corruptible human nature. Christ also formulated a new way of existence for man, free from sin and death. Furthermore, it is through the work of the church, Maximos believed, that familiarization with these gifts of Christ can occur. Likewise, in his dogmatic teaching, Maximos describes the spiritual life as a pedagogical way to salvation and divinization.

The three factors, according to Maximos, that mold man are God, human nature, and the world. It is man's will that moves him in relation to these factors. *Being* refers to the essence of man, *well-being* to the call of God to pass from the "image" to the "likeness" of God; *eternal being* is granted to those worthy of the grace of God. The development of the inner life cultivates the gift of baptism, through which human nature is renewed by Christ's existence. The discovery of freedom and the acquisition of virtues, especially of love, promote the social life of the person and union with God. Spiritual formation, which is carried out through natural and theological vision, follows. In the principles of creation and in the principles of human nature, God is discovered. In the divine Word we possess the unity of the Creator and creation, as the revelation of his person and work to the world.

Spiritual formation is fulfilled in the work of the Holy Spirit, which enlightens man, enabling him to understand beings, the meaning of the scriptures, and the mysteries of worship. At the very center of their existence Christians participate in the divine energy and receive awareness of the spiritual presence of God. Such a process—internal, moral, and spiritual—makes the person capable of *theōsis* (deification), that is, exemption from the corruption of creation and acquisition of union with God. Finally, full communion and union in the second coming of Christ is awaited as a consummation of our own personal lives, just as resurrection was the consummation of Christ's life.

Maximos's contribution to the intellectual support of orthodox views, his ecclesiastical conduct, and his witness as a confessor were recognized by the Third Council of Constantinople (680–681). The basic themes of his teaching, such as the distinction between nature and divine energy, the principles of nature and human will, the communion and synergy of God and man as persons, the participation of man in God, and *theōsis*—all of these influenced the spirituality and later direction of orthodox theology. For example, Maximos's authority was invoked during the hesychast dispute of the fourteenth century. The successful application of Aristotelian dialectic in theology was inaugurated by Maximos, and his teaching has provoked interest in modern theological circles.

BIBLIOGRAPHY

Works by Maximos

Maximos's collected works are available in *Patrologia Graeca*, edited by J.-P. Migne, vol. 4 (Paris, 1857) and vols. 90–91 (Paris, 1860). *Questions to Thalassius* is available in *Corpus Christianorum, Series Graeca*, vol. 7 (Turnhout, 1980). *The Ascetic Life* has been translated by Polycarp Sherwood in "Ancient Christian Writers," edited by Johannes Quasten et al., vol. 21 (Westminster, Md., 1955).

Works on Maximos

Balthasar, Hans Urs von. *Kosmische Liturgie: Das Weltbild Maximus', des Bekenners*. 2d ed. Einsiedeln, 1961.

Garrigues, Juan Miguel. *Maxime le confesseur: La charité, avenir de l'homme*. Paris, 1976. Includes a complete bibliography.

Karazafiris, Nicholas. *Hē peri prosōpou didascalia Maximou tou Homologētou*. Thessaloniki, 1985.

Léthel, François-Marie. *Théologie de l'agonie du Christ*. Paris, 1979.

Matsouka, Nikos. *Kosmos, anthrōpos, koinōnia kata ton Maximon ton homologētēn*. Athens, 1980.

Piret, Pierre. *Le Christ et la Trinité selon Maxime le confesseur*. Paris, 1983.

Radosavljevic, A. *To musterion tes soterias kata ton hagion Maximon ton homologeten*. Athens, 1975.

Riou, Alain. *Le monde et l'église selon Maxime le confesseur*. Paris, 1973.

Sherwood, Polycarp. *An Annotated Date-List of the Works of Maximus the Confessor*. Rome, 1952.

Thunberg, Lars. *Microcosm and Mediator: The Theological Anthropology of Maximus the Confessor*. Lund, 1965.

Volker, Walther. *Maximus Confessor als Meister des geistlichen Lebens*. Wiesbaden, 1965.

NICHOLAS KARAZAFIRIS (1987)

MĀYĀ.

MĀYĀ. is one of the key terms in Indian religious tradition. Its original meaning may be "creation" or "construction" (from the Sanskrit *mā*, "measure" or "mete out"), but the term can be used in several connotations, implying a power, a process, and the result of that process.

Development of the concept. In the history of Indian thought the term *māyā* is used with remarkable consistency, to express, define, and explain the enigma of life and the material world. The viewpoint expressed by Śaṅkara, admittedly pivotal, is often stressed too much, at the cost of other opinions conceived by intelligent minds from the time of the Vedas to the modern period. For the Vedic authors, *māyā* denoted the faculty that transforms an original concept of creative mind into concrete form, a faculty of immense proficiency and shrewdness such as is suggested by the English word *craft*.

In the Vedas, performances of *māyā* are mainly ascribed to divine beings, *devas* ("gods") or *asuras* ("countergods"). Each god works *māyā* in his own way and for his own ends. Thus, through *māyā* Varuṇa metes out the earth and creates order in nature (*Ṛgveda* 5.85.5 et al.), and Indra employs it to defeat the demon Vrtra or to transform himself into another shape (*Ṛgveda* 6.47.18: "By his powers of *māyā*, Indra goes around in many forms," an oft-quoted phrase). The reality of all these mayic creations, however incomprehensible to common man, is never questioned. The Upaniṣads develop a metaphysical notion of *māyā* as the emanation of the phenomenal world by *brahman*, the cosmic Self. In post-Vedic Hinduism, the term can be used to convey a metaphysical, epistemological, mythological, or magical sense, depending on the immediate context.

METAPHYSICAL ASPECT. In Indian thought, *māyā* is the metaphysical principle that must be assumed in order to account for the transformation of the eternal and indivisible into the temporal and differentiated. Beginning with the Upaniṣads (*Chāndogya Upaniṣad* 6.1.4–6), empirical reality is most often conceived as a polymorphous modification or transformation of the Absolute, and thus maintains a "derived reality." Mahāyāna Buddhism, however, developed a concept of the world as a "substitution" or "delusion" conjured up by *māyā* as by an act of illusionism. The world process and our experience of it are devices to hide the inexpressible total void (Nāgārjuna, second century CE?), or cosmic consciousness. Even the Buddha's teaching is said to belong to this sphere of secondary reality. An attitude of nihilism is avoided by the concept of two levels of reality developed by Nāgārjuna: *pāramārthika* ("ultimate") and *vyāvahārika* ("practical"). It is therefore not correct to state that for these thinkers the world of *māyā* is a mere illusion.

In Hindu philosophy (especially the Vedānta school), the concept of *māyā* follows the Vedic tradition of a mysterious power of self-transformation. The Buddhist doctrine of an ultimate void is emphatically denied: the nonexistent cannot be the source of creation, just as a barren woman can never have a son, says Gauḍapāda (sixth century CE?). After him, Śaṅkara (c. eighth century CE) and later scions of the Advaita ("Nondualist") school also deny ultimate reality to the phenomenal world. But creation is not totally unreal either, since it cannot be separated from the truth that is *brahman* (what else could be its cause?), and also because it retains a pragmatic validity for the individual as long as the liberating experience of all-oneness has not been reached. "Illusion" thus implies the mysteriously different, not the *nihil.*

Other Vedānta theorists tend to emphasize the reality of the mayic transformation. According to Rāmānuja (eleventh century CE), the world is a mode of existence of *brahman,* related to it as the body is to the soul. The Śaiva and Śākta schools of thought also held a realistic view of *māyā.* In the recent period, Vivekananda, Aurobindo, and others have endeavored to restate the doctrine of *māyā* in reaction to objections by other philosophical systems without deviating in essentials from the tradition.

EPISTEMOLOGICAL ASPECT. *Māyā* deludes cosmic consciousness into associating itself with individuality, sense perception, and the sensory objects of phenomenal reality. Gauḍapāda interprets this process as a misconception *(vikalpa)* of the pure and undivided self-consciousness of the *ātman,* just as in darkness a rope is mistakenly perceived as a snake. To dispel false perception is to attain true insight into the undivided Absolute. Śaṅkara prefers the term *avidyā* ("nescience") or *ajñāna* ("ignorance"). This is not just the absence of insight but a positive entity, the cause of superimposition of external experience on the undefiled self-consciousness. Besides, there is a metaphysical *avidyā* assumed by Śaṅkara as a necessary cause for cosmic evolution in order to vindicate the doctrine of the static unity of *brahman.* Śaṅkara rejects the equation of ordinary waking experience with dream experience held by the Mahāyāna theorists and Gauḍapāda. In modern Hindu philosophy, the epistemological aspect of *māyā* is emphasized: *māyā* does not imply the denial of the reality of the world, but refers only to the relative validity of our experience.

OTHER ASPECTS. The speculative concept described above has often been clothed in religious myth and popular legend. In the popular mind, the power of *māyā* often amounted to feats of magic or illusionism *(indrajāla).* In the epic *Mahābhārata* (and elsewhere), this power is said to be wielded by God to beguile and delude mankind. "The Lord plays with his subjects as a child with its toys" (*Mahābhārata* 3.31.19f.). In other contexts, the phenomenal world is likened to a bubble on the water, a drop trickling from a lotus leaf, evanescent autumnal clouds, a colorful patch, or a circle of fire created by a torch. Several legends express the same view in allegorical form. Such religious imagery remains very important in later Hinduism. In religious poetry, *māyā* is sometimes embodied as a tempting or fear-inspiring woman; she can be the consort of the male supreme being (Śrī for Viṣṇu, Rādhā for Kṛṣṇa, Devī for Śiva) or, in Śāktism, a manifestation of the Cosmic Mother in her own right as Māyādevī or Bhuvaneśvarī (Goddess of the World).

SEE ALSO Avidyā; Vedānta.

BIBLIOGRAPHY

Discussions of *māyā* and its place in Indian religious and philosophical thought are dealt with in several books of more general scope. A very scholarly, thoughtful, and dependable survey by a classical Indologist can be found in Jan Gonda's *Change and Continuity in Indian Religion* (The Hague, 1965), pp. 164–197. Gonda's discussion of *māyā* in this work is a summary and restatement of two of his earlier studies. Also very readable as an introduction is Paul D. Devanandan's *The Concept of Māyā: An Essay in Historical Survey of the Hindu Theory of the World, with Special Reference to the Vedānta* (London, 1950; Calcutta, 1954). The author's Christian viewpoint is not stressed. Anil K. Ray Chaudhuri's *The Doctrine of Māyā,* 2d rev. & enl. ed. (Calcutta, 1950), is a philosophical study with special emphasis on the epistemological doctrine of nescience in the Vedānta. A concise book that focuses mainly on *māyā* in twentieth-century Hindu philosophy is Ruth Reyna's *The Concept of Māyā from the Vedas to the Twentieth Century* (London and Bombay, 1962). My own book, *Māyā Divine and Human* (Delhi, 1978), is a study of Indian and Balinese sources in Sanskrit concentrating on the magical side of the *māyā* concept. Predating all of these works is Heinrich Zimmer's *Maya, der indische Mythos* (Stuttgart, 1936), which contains a wealth of legends and personal interpretations.

TEUN GOUDRIAAN (1987)

MAYA RELIGION, like many aspects of Maya civilization, is part of a widespread and long-lasting tradition of belief and culture shared by numerous ethnic groups in Mesoamerica. Neighboring cultures with whom the Maya interacted throughout their history, including the Mixe, Zapotec, and Mexica-Aztec, shared numerous aspects of this tradition, and indeed Maya religion, particularly in its present-day forms among traditional communities in southern Mexico and Guatemala, is difficult to distinguish as a separate tradition within the greater framework of Mesoamerican theology. These cultures shared a distinctive pantheistic model of belief and a specific calendar system defined by important numerological and ritual cycles. Maya religion is distinct, however, in that archaeological and textual data extend the direct evidence of its history and practice back some two thousand years, thus providing a time-depth unlike that available for any other Native American religious tradition. The vast majority of such ancient sources date from the so-called Classic period (250–850 CE), when particularly expressive religious monuments and inscriptions were widespread. In the post-Conquest world, Maya religion has adapted and transformed, adopting elements of Christian ideology while at the same time adhering to many ancient concepts and ceremonies. Today, political empowerment and activism by Maya in Guatemala, in particular, has led to the revitalization of native cultural identity; religious expression, often based on appropriated ancient symbols and idea, occupies an important place in this modern movement.

COSMOLOGY AND DEEP TIME. Numerous spatial categories defined the basic elements of Maya cosmology: prominent among these are the earth's surface (*kab*), the sky (*chan*), the sun (*k'in*) and moon (*uh*) and their recurring paths, caves (*ch'een*), and mountains (*witz*). These and a few other terms were the vocabulary of space and the cyclical processes that inhabited them. In the Classic period, the word that most closely translates as "world" or "universe" was *chan ch'een,* "sky-and-cave," which comprised the two vertical extremes of existence, above and below the earthly realm of everyday human experience, where various gods dwelled.

Mountains, caves, and springs are of special importance in defining Maya sacred landscapes. Among many traditional communities, mountains are seen as animate beings, sometimes as manifestations of the earth lord. Other individual mountains are seen to be localized gods or "containers" for important ancestral figures. Communication with ancestors and earth lords took place through caves, which have from the earliest times been important settings for Maya ritual.

The earth and sky share a fundamental quadripartite organization corresponding more or less to the modern notion of the four cardinal directions. According to some conceptualizations, the four points of the sun's emergence and entrance on the horizon at summer and winter solstice marked the division of space into four quarters: east (*elk'in*), north (*xaman*), west (*ochk'in*), and south *(nohol).* Each direction was associated with its own color (red, white, black, and yellow, respectively), which corresponded to the basic color variations of maize grown in Mesoamerica. Several deities had directional aspects or manifestations and were colored accordingly, including the storm gods called *chaak.* Many temples and ceremonial plazas were built to evoke this four-part structure of the world, and such layouts of built spaces have persisted to this day. Sacred mountains were considered to be distributed in the natural landscape according to this four-part directional model.

Maya communities both ancient and modern are spatially arranged to evoke and reproduce certain aspects of cosmic organization. In pre-Columbian times the most prominent architectural form was the terraced pyramid, which clearly often served as an artificial ritual mountain. Buildings and architectural groups are often oriented toward important astronomical phenomena (such as the winter solstice sunrise, for example), and roadways entering towns were sometimes radiated out toward the four cardinal directions. Town centers were nodes of ritual activity due to their importance as cosmological centers.

Agriculture and the cyclical growth of human sustenance, based largely on maize, have left indelible marks on cosmological beliefs and Maya religion in general. The four colors associated with the cardinal directions in Maya cosmology (red, white, black, and yellow) find replication in the four principal varieties of maize. Maize, being the basic staple of the Maya diet throughout history, was also equated with the human body and its substance. Robert Carlsen and Martin Prechtel note in "Flowering of the Dead" (1991) that cycles of growth and harvest were and are seen as a general metaphor for human and universal patterns of change and regeneration, or what the modern Tzutujil Maya call *jaloj-k'exoj,* perhaps best translated as "change and renewal."

The ancient Maya made ample use of a complex calendar system that was shared to some degree among all Mesoamerican cultures. The solar year, computed as 365 whole days, was subdivided into a set of eighteen twenty-day "months," plus a remaining five-day liminal period (the *xmak'abak'inob* or "days without name" among the Yukatek Maya) associated with renewal. The months bore names suggesting that they were originally tied to important agricultural periods, but they also served as a basic framework for the scheduling of ritual festivals throughout the solar year. Running concurrently with this was a separate reckoning of days based on a 260-day cycle, wherein a given day was expressed as one of a set of twenty named days accompanied by a numeral coefficient of 1–13. Today this same calendar remains in use among conservative "day-keepers" in the highlands of Guatemala, where it is used in rites of divination.

A separate calendar system widely known as the *Long Count* operated concurrently with the 260-day and 365-day rounds described above. The Long Count was different in its structure, presenting a more linear reckoning of days by means of a place-notation arrangement that expressed an accumulation of elapsed days from a set starting point in the distant past. The temporal scope of the Long Count was therefore much greater than the 260-day and 365-day components of the Calendar Round. The three systems—the Long Count, the 260-day round, and the approximate solar-year cycle—together constituted a triumvirate of calendars used throughout Maya history.

The standard Long Count has five units, each standing for a set period of time. These are, in increasing order, the *K'in* (the single day), the *Winal* (each equaling twenty *K'ins*), the *Tun* (eighteen *Winals,* or 360 days), the *K'atun* (twenty *Tuns,* or 7,200 days), and the *Bak'tun* (twenty *K'atuns,* or 144,000 days). In writing Long Count dates in hieroglyphic form, the periods assume the opposite order, beginning with the *Bak'tun* and descending to the *K'in.* It can be seen that the system reflects the basic vigesimal (base-twenty) structure of Maya numeration, with larger periods composed of twenty units of the next lower period. The exception to this vigesimal pattern is the *Tun,* which is made up of eighteen *Winals* (360 days), seemingly so as to approximate the solar year of 365 days. In the notation system, a numerical coefficient was assigned to each of these units to convey a certain amount of elapsed time from a specific starting date. A comparison to an automobile's odometer is perhaps apt, for the Long Count represented a perpetual accumulation of days.

In most circumstances, the standard Long Count of five periods provided an adequate mechanism for the tracking of time, yet it was structurally limited for recording and computing very large numbers of days. In certain ritual or mythical texts, however, scribes felt the need to compute greater time amounts—sometimes much greater—and in these records and calculations they employed time periods above the *Bak'tun.* The standard five-part Long Count is, in fact, a truncated version of a larger system composed of at least twenty-five periods that can be called the Grand Long Count. The standard Long Count represents the last five positions in this much larger cyclical arrangement. Textual evidence now points to the existence of twenty-one periods in the complete Grand Long Count, the highest period being equivalent to 20^{22} *Tuns* (that is, 20^{22} times 360 days). The conception of linear and cyclical time encompassed within this system is truly vast, and of course dwarfs the age of the universe as presently understood by Western science.

Ritual texts describe gods performing rituals millions of years in the past, but they also consistently refer to a "change" in the cosmic order on the day 13.0.0.0.0 4 *Ajaw* 8 *Kumk'u,* corresponding to August 13, 3114 BCE. This day, cited in numerous texts all over the Maya area, can rightly be called the traditional creation date in the ancient sources.

CREATIONS AND THE *POPOL VUH*. According to two related ancient sources, the creation of the present era on 13.0.0.0.0 saw the "placing in order" of various gods in the dark underworld. Another text on Stele C from Quirigua relates that a group of gods placed a set of three stones in the sky, reproducing the form of a domestic hearth. In many texts this particular location is described as being at "the sky's edge, the new hearth place." The establishment of the new cosmic order thus replicated the placement and dedication of a house, an idea that is no doubt based on the widely shared belief among Mesoamerican peoples that the sky is the roof of a vast cosmic house, with support posts corresponding to the four cardinal points.

The most detailed ancient sources for creation mythology are the extensive inscriptions from Palenque, Mexico. Inscribed wall tablets in numerous temples record primordial myths from the time of the creation, the most important being the birth of three sibling gods known to Mayanists as the Palenque Triad, who later play important roles as supernatural patrons of the royal dynasty of Palenque. Chief among these gods was the first brother, known today as GI, who seems to have associations with the rising sun and perhaps also to Venus as the morning star. According to one important inscription, GI was a king in the pre-13.0.0.0.0 era who oversaw the ritual sacrifice of a cosmological crocodile, perhaps a symbol of the earth. This act of sacrifice set the stage for the creation of a new era that saw the rebirth and reestablishment of a new cosmic order, with the Triad occupying a central role, at least at Palenque. Significantly, no other Maya kingdoms cite the Palenque Triad as a significant assembly of gods, suggesting the many communities had differing narratives of creation and the supernatural beings that participated in it.

Of all the primary written sources now extant, the most important is the *Popol Vuh,* or "Community Book," written by a Kiche' scribe probably during the mid-sixteenth century from an earlier pre-Columbian pictorial document. The manuscript was discovered in the early eighteenth century by Friar Francisco Ximénez at his parish in San Tomas Chichicastenango, Guatemala. His meticulous copy of the lost original is preserved today and is the source for several published versions and translations. Other accounts of world creation exist from other regions in the Maya area, but these are relatively short fragments for the most part; the *Popol Vuh* is truly epic in its scope and narrative.

Portions of the *Popol Vuh* clearly tell old and elemental stories of Maya mythology. It opens with an account of the "sowing and the dawning" of the world and its inhabitants, partly by two creator beings named Tz'aqol and B'itol, best translated as "Builder" and "Shaper," respectively. They act in concert with one another and with another more prominent creator being named Uk'u'xkaj, "Heart of the Sky," and together they create earth and the animals that roam it. The gods demand veneration from "the deer and the birds," but the animals cannot speak their names and worship them properly. In a series of trials and failures, Builder, Shaper, and Heart of the Sky therefore attempt to create humans, first with mud, then with wood. Before "proper" worshipful people are made, however, the story of creation shifts focus to the so-called Hero Twins, Hunahpu and Xbalanque. These brothers defeat a series of malevolent figures, including the proud primordial sun, Seven Macaw, and ultimately through cunning, trickery, and athleticism they defeat the lords of Xibalba, the realm of death. The twins are then resurrected as the sun and moon. Once this celestial and moral order is established, Builder and Shaper once more attempt the creation of humanity.

The ancient sources repeat certain elements of this story involving the Hero Twins—they are depicted in many examples of Maya art from a very early date—but creation narratives from Classic times suggest that several different accounts coexisted among various kingdoms. Palenque's complex mythological narrative, for example, is not found elsewhere, and it may well be that different ancient communities had different stories of sacred origin and creation.

GODS, SOULS, AND CONCEPTS OF THE SACRED. There is good reason to believe that the Maya religion saw the "sacred" as a pervasive and unifying feature of their natural and domestic world; the universe possessed this concept of deity (*k'uh*), but it was manifested most clearly and powerfully in specific places, objects, and individuals. This notion reflects a wider pantheistic organization of religious ideas within Mesoamerican philosophy. It is difficult to distinguish this widespread notion of "divinity" from the related notion that the natural and cultural worlds possess a pervasive vital essence that lends Maya religion a certain "animistic" quality.

The souls of humans are also expressions of this vital force. Recent ethnographic work has shown that complex concepts surrounding the human soul operate to orient human experiences and life events in a cosmological framework. Terms for the soul vary considerably from community to community, but there is a basic consistency to many of the ideas, which are also reflected to some degree in ancient religious texts and artworks. The well-studied soul concepts among the Tzotzil Maya of Zinacantan, Chiapas, Mexico, offer a good illustration of these ideas and how they help to explain a Maya conception of the sacred. In Zinacantan, humans possess two basic types of souls called *ch'ulel* and *chanul.* The *ch'ulel* is the animating life spirit of the individual that inhabits the heart and blood of the person, and it consists of thirteen parts. A *ch'ulel* soul can also inhabit nonhuman things and materials, such as musical instruments, crosses, and even salt, perhaps because these create important sensations (sound, emotion, and taste). The *chanul* is a person's animal alter ego, sometimes perceived through dreams. In Zinacantan, the animal souls of the community are closely guarded by ancestors called "mothers-fathers," who corral them within one of the important sacred mountains near the town. Both *ch'ulel* and *chanul* souls are key to understanding complex social relationships within the community. Through the *chanul* the ancestors exert powerful social and moral controls. As Evon Vogt states, "the most important interaction in the universe is not between person, nor between persons and objects, as we would perceive them; it is, instead, between the *ch'ulel* souls possessed by these persons and objects" (1976, p. 141). In ancient times, Maya kings derived much of their authority through their possession of an especially powerful *ch'ulel* soul, through which they expressed their divine role in the community and the cosmos.

The word *ch'ulel* derives from the word for *god* (*k'uh,* or its variant form *ch'uh*), and the term was applied to many sacred entities or objects. Ancient sources contains images and references to a great variety of deities that ranged from animate natural forces to localized patron figures and deified ancestors. Indeed, in the Classic inscriptions the collective term for the multitude of supernatural figures was *hunpikk'uh,* literally, "the eight thousand gods."

For the Classic Maya, demons and fantastic beasts called *way* were considered personifications of disease and illness, images of which often decorated ritual ceramic vessels. These curious entities remain poorly understood, but they seem to have been important in complex ideas of witchcraft and its association with royal power. Individual dynasties and kingdoms appear to have had their own "patron beasts" that were important to the expression of supernatural prowess within and among communities.

Among the major gods are several animated natural forces, most prominent among them being K'inich Ajaw, the sun god, who occupied a celestial throne and may have had the feminine moon as his wife. Another was the maize god, who embodied the principal staple of the human diet in Mesoamerica and thus served as the focus of numerous cosmological and agricultural rituals. Chaak, the rain or storm god, had four aspects, each associated with one of the cardinal points. A more complex figure was K'awil, who is described as a god of agricultural fertility and sustenance at the time of European contact, but who in the more ancient sources from the Classic period seems to have also served as the embodiment of dynastic power and royal ancestry.

The god Itzamnah was the most prominent of deities at the time of the Conquest, and is described as the patron of learning, esoteric knowledge, and the arts. Classic period sources suggest that he was also a ruler of the celestial sphere, and he may well have been an aspect of the sun god who existed in the primordial time before creation. One of his principal aspects or manifestations was the Principal Bird Deity, a large bejeweled avian creature that perched atop the cosmic tree and served as an important symbol of rulership in the pre-Classic and early Classic periods. This bird is probably a distant ancestor of the solar deity named Seven Macaw, who plays an important role in the *Popol Vuh.*

Human ancestors often are active and important members of Maya communities, and in ancient times certain illustrious figures became the focal points of important ancestral "cults" heavily invested with political and cosmological symbolism. Perhaps the best known royal ancestor from the Classic period is the venerated king K'inich Yax K'uk' Mo' ("Great Sun Green Quetzal Macaw"), who was the dynastic founder at Copan, a major Maya kingdom in present-day Honduras. He reigned at Copan in the early fifth century, when he celebrated the turn of the *Bak'tun* cycle (9.0.0.0.0) in 435 CE. Over the next four centuries, later Copan kings declared themselves successors of the illustrious founder, and temples to him were continually refurbished and rebuilt over his resting place in the main acropolis. Excavations of this sacred *axis mundi* at Copan have revealed a series of superimposed buildings, ornately modeled and painted with iconography evoking the deified ancestor and his origin in distant time. All kings became divine ancestors upon death, and those who were more historically significant, such as "founders," came to be especially venerated.

In the ideology of Classic Maya kingship, the category of historical ancestors easily melded with gods and mythological characters of the very distant past. At Palenque, for example, late Classic rulers traced their political and religious authority not only to dynastic founders but also to semimythical beings that were said to live thousands if not millions of years in the past. For example, the king K'inich Janab Pakal (603–683 CE) linked his accession in 615 to a deity who had assumed the status of rulership more than twenty-five million years in the past. Such like-in-kind juxtapositions of primordial time and human history were consistently featured in Classic Maya political ideology.

Ritual and Religious Specialists. The traditional keepers of religious and divinatory knowledge were named *ajk'in,* "he/she of the day(s)" or "day-keeper." This was sometimes simply translated as "priest" in colonial era sources, but the term was probably more specifically reserved for ritual specialists who possessed esoteric knowledge of the days and their varied meanings and prognostications. Today among the Kiche' Maya of highland Guatemala, for example, *ajq'ij* refers to priest-shamans who oversee rites of curing, marriage, death, and burial, as well as more mundane divination ceremonies. Given the complex social hierarchies of Maya communities throughout history, there were no doubt different categories of priests and religious officials at various times and places.

In the Classic period the ruler, or *k'uhul ajaw* (literally, "holy lord"), occupied the most prominent and public position in the religious hierarchy. Ancient Maya kings oversaw the passage of important stations in the long count calendar, and were even symbolically equated with the time periods themselves (all period endings in the Long Count calendar fall on the day named *Ajaw,* which also means "lord" or "king"). On these and other occasions rulers were said to "conjure" (*tzak*) the spirits of ancestors and fertility, known generically as *k'awil.* This process, evidently achieved through bloodletting, was among the principal royal duties, and was made possible through the kings' special ability to wield a force known as "creation and darkness" (*ch'ab ak'ab*). This enigmatic term probably relates to the widespread notion that birth and creation derive from "darkness," which then came to be embodied through the procreative powers of rulers in a cosmological setting.

Other rituals recorded in ancient inscriptions seem to have been anchored to political events like accession to power and anniversaries. Important rites included ceremonial bloodletting, incense burning, and dance, and in many ways these activities overlapped and occurred in combination with one another. Formulaic prayers and orations are today key aspects of ritual performance, as they were no doubt in ancient times as well. The ancient texts are also replete with records of dedication rites for temples and other important religious monuments or spaces. The ritual activation of a temple or house was called *och k'ahk,'* or "fire-entering," and presumably involved the placement of censers and other ritual fires within shrines and on interior temple floors. Such rites seem to be an obvious antecedent to house dedication ceremonies found among many Maya communities in modern times.

Religious Art and Architecture. Arguably all public art produced by the ancient Maya can be considered religious or ritual art in some sense. The ubiquitous type of sculpture from Classic period was the stele, an upright stone slab or column that typically bore hieroglyphic inscriptions and a portrait of a ruler engaged in ritual activities. Stelae were usually erected in the open plazas before pyramids and platforms, and served to mark important stations in the Long Count calendar or significant events of political history.

Maya cities of the pre-Classic and Classic periods were dominated by large ritual structures, often in the form of imposing pyramids. The remains of the largest pyramids are also the earliest, found at ruins such as Nakbe and El Mirador in present-day northern Guatemala, and dating from about 200 BCE to 200 CE. These manmade mountains are in fact some of the largest structures ever built in pre-Columbian America. Their terraces were typically decorated with massive plaster sculptures of deities and cosmological symbolism, clearly marking them as microcosmic spaces. Later Maya pyramids at centers such as Uaxactun and Tikal were likewise conceived as replicas of cosmological structures, though at smaller but still impressive scales. Structures were often dedicated to particular deities or to venerated ancestors who were buried in their centers. The temples atop pyramids were often adorned with interior paintings, sculpted stone panels, or plaster decorations. Some contained inner shrines that held effigy figures of clay or stone, and the burning of copal incense was pervasive in such sacred spaces.

Revivalism and Modern Change. The process of conquest and conversion by Europeans began in the early sixteenth century, and today, after several centuries, most Maya would consider themselves devout Christians. Yet elements of pre-Columbian belief and religion have persisted, often interwoven and tightly integrated with old traditions of "folk Catholicism." Today a core of basic beliefs still exerts a strong presence in Maya spirituality, and these vary widely among the communities of Guatemala, Belize, and Mexico. In recent years, indigenous political movements, in Guatemala in particular, have led to more open expressions of non-Christian ideas long hidden from view, as well as the appropriation of ancient ideas and symbols. Maya religion is increasingly being portrayed as a unified and unifying cosmovision and ideology, different in some ways from its Classic period expression, but with roots nonetheless in the deep pre-Columbian past.

Bibliography

Carlsen, Robert, and Martin Prechtel. "Flowering of the Dead: An Interpretation of Highland Maya Culture." *Man* 26 (1991): 23–42.

Friedel, David, Linda Schele, and Joy Parker. *Maya Cosmos: Three Thousand Years on the Shaman's Path.* New York, 1993.

Girard, Rafael. *Los Maya Eternos.* Mexico City, 1962.

Gossen, Gary H. *Chamulas in the World of the Sun: Time and Space in a Maya Oral Tradition.* Cambridge, Mass., 1974.

Guiteras-Holmes, Calixta. *The Perils of the Soul: The Worldview of a Tzotzil Indian.* Glencoe, Ill., 1961.

Houston, Stephen, and David Stuart. "Of Gods, Glyphs, and Kings: Divinity and Rulership among the Classic Maya." *Antiquity* 70 (1996): 289–312.

Lounsbury, Floyd G. "Maya Numeration, Computation, and Calendrical Astronomy." In *Dictionary of Scientific Biography,* edited by Charles C. Gillespie, vol. 15, pp. 759–818. New York, 1978.

Stuart, David. "Kings of Stone: A Consideration of Stelae in Classic Maya Ritual and Representation." *Res: Anthropology and Aesthetics* 29/30 (1996): 148–171.

Taube, Karl A. *The Major Gods of Ancient Yucatan.* Washington, D.C., 1992.

Tedlock, Barbara. *Time and the Highland Maya.* Albuquerque, 1982.

Tedlock, Dennis, trans. and ed. *The* Popol Vuh: *The Definitive Edition of the Mayan Book of the Dawn of Life and the Glories of Gods and Kings.* New York, 1985.

Vogt, Evon Z. *Tortillas for the Gods: A Symbolic Analysis of Zinacanteco Ritual.* Cambridge, Mass., 1976; reprint, Norman, Okla., 1993.

Watanabe, John. *Maya Saints and Souls in a Changing World.* Austin, Tex., 1992.

DAVID STUART (2005)

MAZDAKISM is a socioreligious movement that flared up in the reign of the Sasanian king Kavād (488–531 CE) under the leadership of Mazdak, son of Bāmdād. Its genesis, however, seems to go back to an earlier period, possibly the fourth century, when Zarādusht, a Zoroastrian priest, attempted through new interpretations of the Zoroastrian scriptures, to purify the faith.

A populist and egalitarian movement, Mazdakism socially preached in its acute form what modern scholars have called a communistic agenda, advocating an equitable distribution of property and breaking of the barriers which placed the concentration of wealth and women into the hands of the privileged classes. In terms of religious doctrine it exhibited some Gnostic features and apparently entertained a qabbalistic notion of the significance of numbers and the letters of the alphabet. The followers of the sect called themselves Derest-dēnān (of the right faith). Kavād favored the movement for a while, but it was brutally suppressed by his son and successor, Khusrau I (531–579 CE). It went underground as a result and reappeared in various sectarian forms after the advent of Islam and the fall of the Sasanian Empire in the mid–seventh century.

THE SOURCES. No work of the Mazdakites has survived. Nearly all the information on Mazdakism derives from hostile sources. These can be divided in two categories: contemporary and post-Sasanian. The first consists of Syriac and Greek (Byzantine) works. Chief among them are Procopius' *Persian Wars* and Agathias's *Histories,* both in Greek; Pseudo-Joshua the Stylite's *Chronicle* and Malalas of Antioch's, *Chronographia* in Syriac. The second comprises Middle Persian, Arabic, and New Persian sources. The latter two are believed to have generally derived their information from *Khwaday-nāmag,* a compendium of Iranian history, myths, and legends, reflecting the views of the Sasanian nobles and clergy, transmitted orally until it was committed to writing in the sixth century. Its translation into Arabic by Ibn al-Muqaffa (died c. 757) now lost, served as the chief source for subsequent Islamic histories of Persia. These focus on the events of the reigns of Kavād and Khusrau I, including the Mazdakite revolt. They emphasize the communistic features of the doctrine, lingering in particular—as do the Middle Persian passages—on sharing of women as common property and its evil consequences.

Among the most important is the report by the heresiographer Shāhrastānī (died 1153) which provides us with a glimpse of Mazdakite religious beliefs and theology. His source, Abu Isâ Hārūn al-Warrāq (died 861), a Manichaean or Zoroastrian convert to Islam, seems to have had access to some genuine Mazdakite source.

MAZDAKITE DOCTRINE. According to Shāhrastānī's account, the Mazdakites believed in two primordial principles, Light and Darkness. Light is endowed with knowledge and feeling and acts by design and free will, whereas Darkness is ignorant and blind and acts randomly and without direction. The admixture of the two is the result of pure accident, as will be their separation. From their mingling, two beings arose, the Manager of Good and the Manager of Evil. The Supreme Being is seated on his throne in the world above, as the [Sasanian] king of kings is seated in the world below; four Powers stand before him: Discernment, Understanding, Preservation, and Joy. There are four high-ranking officials before the king of kings, including the Chief Priest and Judge *(Mōbadān Mōbad),* the Chief *Hērbad* (religious doctor), the Commander of the Army *(Spāhbad),* and the Entertainment Master *(Rāmishgar).* The four Powers direct the world with the help of seven viziers (cf. the seven planets) who act within a circle of twelve spiritual forces (cf. the zodiac). When the four Powers and the Seven and Twelve come together in a human being, he becomes godly *(rabbānī)* and no longer subject to religious observances (implying antinomianism). The Supreme Being reigns by the power of the letters, of which the total sum constitutes the Supreme Name *(al-Ism al-a'zam).* Men who come to understand something of these letters have found the key to the Great Secret *(al-sirr al-akbar).* Those who are deprived will remain in blindness, ignorance, neglect and dullness (opposites of the four Powers).

From this brief but precious account the character and basic tenet of Mazdakite theology may be adduced and summarized as belief in:

1. A fundamental dualism, not far from that of Zoroastrianism or Manichaeism;
2. Three elements, compared to Zoroastrian four and Manichaean five;
3. The remoteness of the supreme deity, as evinced by the postulation of the two demiurgical "managers";
4. A spiritual macrocosm, reflected in the mesocosm of our world and mirrored in the microcosm of humans;
5. The symbolic power of letters, words, and numbers as keys to the redemptive knowledge; and

6. Irrelevance of religious obligations and, therefore, the outward meaning of religious prescriptions, once a revelatory knowledge of the essence of the "secret" of religion is gained.

Such beliefs, which are typical of Gnostic religions, bring Mazdakism unmistakably within the orbit of the syncretistic faiths which developed in the early Christian centuries with an admixture of Iranian, Syro-Babylonian, and Hellenic thought. However, Shāhrastānī's report probably reflects a late phase of Mazdakism, particularly since the terms used for the twelve spiritual forces are mostly New Persian rather than Middle Persian of Sasanian period. (Shāhrastānī's account, however, leaves us in the dark on many essential matters such as Mazdakite eschatology, or the nature of revelation and prophethood, and the origin of the Evil principle.)

One of the fullest accounts of the social aspects of Mazdakite doctrine in Islamic sources appears in *Ghurar akhbâr mulûk al-Furs*:

> Mazdak declared that God placed the means of subsistence *(arzāq)* on earth so that people divide them among themselves equally, in a manner that no one of them could have more than his share; but people wronged one another and sought domination over one another; the strong defeated the weak and took exclusive possession of livelihood and property. It is absolutely necessary that one take from the rich for giving to the poor, so that all become equal in wealth. Whoever possesses an excess of property, women or goods, he has no more right to it than another. (p. 600)

The noted Muslim historian al-Tabari (d. 923) adds in *The History of al-Tabari* that Mazdak believed that such deeds were "an act of piety that pleased God and was rewarded by Him with the best of rewards" (vol. 1, p. 893).

In his verse rendering of *Khwadāy-nāmag,* Firdawsi (d. c. 1026) provides some further detail on the moral philosophy of the sect (vol. VIII, p. 46): men are turned from righteousness by five demons (envy, wrath, vengeance, need [*ā niyāz*], and greed) to prevail against these and to tread the path of the good religion, wealth and women must be made common. The sources do not specify any rules or regulations that Mazdak may have prescribed for a just distribution of women and wealth; they mostly concentrate on the alleged community of women, the resulting promiscuity, and its confusing effect on the line of descent.

Many modern scholars, including Mansour Shaki (1978) and Patricia Crone (1991), have taken the sharing of women at its face value, ignoring the impracticability of such a provision in a large, tradition-based society as was Sasanian Iran, and where virtue depended as much on race and lineage *(gowhar, nasab)* as on personal accomplishments *(honar, hasab).* It would have gone against the grain of all the Zoroastrian faithful and would have destroyed the social fabric of the country. What appears to be true is that Mazdak advocated a number of measures, such as prohibiting accumulation of women or having more than one wife; reducing the financial requirement of marriage, such as the dowry (and marriage portion for the wife [*kābin*]); and breaking of the harems and allowing intermarriage among social estates. Hostile sources have cast such prescriptions in the mold of a standard accusation against all heretics as a juicy and scandalizing weapon against the Mazdakites. There is no evidence of promiscuity among the offshoots of the Mazdakism that sprang up in Islamic times and from which one learns more about the Mazdakites.

BIBLIOGRAPHY

Selected Primary Sources

Agathias. *Histories.* Translated by Joseph D. Frendo. Berlin and New York. 1975.

Bīrūnī, Abu Raihān. *al-Athār al-bāqiya.* Translated by Eduard Sachau as *The Chronology of Ancient Nations.* London, 1879.

Firdausī, Abulqāsim. *Shāhnāma.* 9 vols. Moscow, 1963–1971.

Ibn al-Nadīm. *al-Fihrist.* Edited by Rizā Tajaddod. Tehran, 1971. Translated by Bayard Dodge. 2 vols. New York, 1970.

Malalas of Antioch. *Chronographia,* in Jacques Paul Migne, ed., *Patrologiae Cursus Completus,* Series Graeca XCVII. Paris, 1860.

Pseudo-Joshua the Stylite. *Chronicle.* Edited and translated by WilliamWright. Cambridge, 1882.

Shahrastānī, Muhammad. *al-Milal wa'l-nihal.* Edited by William Cureton. Leiden, 1846.

al-Tabari, Muhammad b. Jarīr. *Ta'rīkh al-rusul wa'l-mulūk.* Translated as *The History of al-Tabari* by a number of scholars; vol. 5. by C. E. Bosworth and Clifford Edmunds. New York, 1999.

Tha'ālibī, Abū Mansūr. *Ghurar akhbār mulūk al-Furs.* Edited and translated into French by Hermann Zotenberg. Paris, 1900.

(For fuller listing of the primary sources see Yarshater and Crone, below.)

Studies

The first scholar to bring Greek, Syriac, and Islamic sources systematically together was Th. Nöldeke, *Geschichte der Perser und Araber* (Leipzig, 1879), pp. 284–291. A. Christensen devoted a monograph, *Le règne du roi Kawādh I et le communisme mazdakite* (Copenhagen, 1925) to a full discussion of the Mazdakite revolt, believing mistakenly, however, that Mazdakism was an offshoot of Manichaeism. Gholam Hossein Sadighi's *Les mouvemets religieux iraniens au IIe et au IIIe siècle de l'hégire* (Paris, 1938) is particularly useful for its close examination of the Khorramis and some other Islamic sectarians with Mazdakite roots. Nina Viktorovna Pigulevskaya, in her *Les villes de l'état iranien aux époques parthe et sassanide* (Paris, 1963), pp. 195–230, reflects the Marxist point of view and considers the movement born of the peasant protests against Kavād's and Khusrau I's land survey and tax reforms. In 1957, Otakar Klima, the Czech scholar, published in Prague his monograph *Mazdak,* a comprehensive study of the movement (in the context of Sasanian history and Middle Eastern religions), conceiving Mazdakism as a social movement in religious garb brought about by social and economic conditions in Sasanian Iran. He followed later with another monograph on Mazdakism, *Beiträge zur Gesch-*

ichte des Mazdakismus (Prague, 1977), where he considered the absence of the Mazdak's name in contemporary sources as the result of a deliberate attempt on the part of Khusrau I to delete his name from all records and force oblivion of his memory. In 1978 Mansour Shaki published "The Social Doctrine of Mazdak," based on Middle Persian passages in the Zoroastrian encyclopedic work *Dēnkard*, written in the ninth or tenth century but based on Sasanian materials; he provided a new translation of these difficult and corrupted passages, attempted earlier by Marijan Molé in 1961, emphasizing the communistic aspects of Mazdakism and the sharing of women and property by all.

In 1982 Heinz Gaube, pointing to the absence of Mazdak's name in the contemporary sources and also a number of contradictions in the Islamic reports, doubted even the very existence of Mazdak and thought it likely that the revolt had to do with the tax reforms initiated by Kavād and followed up by Khusrau I, who later manipulated the reports and placed the blame for the upheavals on Mazdak, possibly an invention of him, in order to save the reputation of his father—a view which has not found favorable reception (see Crone, pp. 22–23).

Ehsan Yarshater's chapter on Mazdakism in the *Cambridge History of Iran* III/2 (Cambridge, 1983), pp. 991–1024, provides a comprehensive presentation of Mazdakite doctrine and analysis of the sources and discusses the Islamic sects, mostly of an esoteric nature, that derived from Mazdakism in the first centuries of Islam.

In a second article, "The Cosmogonical and Cosmological Teachings of Mazdak" (*Acta Iranica* XI, 1985, pp. 527–543), Shaki tried to make sense of a number of terms reported in the work of Shahrastānī.

In 1988, Werner Sundermann, who had written an article in 1977 about Mazdakite uprising, "Mazdak und die mazdakititischen Volksaufstände," *Das Altertum* 23, pp. 245–249, offered a German translation of the very obscure and laconic passage of Book VII of the *Dēnkard*, which differs somewhat from that of Shaki but still remains far from clear in all its details.

In 1991, Patricia Crone, in "Kavād's Heresy and Mazdak's Revolt" (*Iran* 29: pp. 21–42), presented a thorough analysis of the sources with a view of finding a solution to the existing contradictions in the reports about Mazdak and the historical events related to him. She, too, considered the revolt as a result of Khusrau I's cadastral reform and the hardship it caused the peasantry.

EHSAN YARSHATER (2005)

MAZE SEE LABYRINTH

MBONA (sometimes also spelled M'Bona or M'bona) is the name of the patronal deity of a famous shrine near the township of Nsanje in the Republic of Malawi (southeastern Africa). Although he is usually referred to as a rain god, Mbona is also invoked on the occasion of locust plagues, floods, epidemic diseases, and other acute threats to the productive and reproductive capacities of the land and its population.

Mbona's is a territorial cult, which may be defined as a cult whose constituency is a territorial group identified by common occupation of a land area, so that membership, in the final instance, is a consequence of residence and not kinship or ethnic designation. The cult is supervised by local chiefs and headmen under the chairmanship of a high priest and a chief administrator. In addition to these officials, there is also a spirit medium, a man or woman who on occasion claims to be possessed by Mbona and who comments on a variety of urgent political issues while possessed. Formerly, the cult also maintained a spirit wife, a woman consecrated for life to Mbona's service, who was supposed to receive revelations from the deity in her dreams and was regularly consulted by chiefs and other important people. There no longer is a permanent spirit wife, but on ceremonial occasions her place is taken temporarily by a local woman. Although the oldest known written documents on the cult date only from the middle of the nineteenth century, it is much older, predating even the Portuguese penetration of the southeast African interior in the first half of the sixteenth century.

According to oral tradition, Mbona was a celebrated rainmaker who, on account of his great popularity, came into conflict with the secular and religious authorities of the day, who in the end had him killed. Following his death, the local populace is said to have erected a shrine to his name and thus to have initiated the cult. The story of Mbona's life and death is known in many versions, but all follow a common structure and can be reduced to three streams or clusters depending on whether the events of the narrative take place in a stateless setting, an emergent state, or a highly centralized kingdom. The mightier the state, the more Mbona is portrayed as a marginal person. Mbona's diminishing status therefore seems to symbolize the increasing subjection of the commonalty to the aristocracy at successive stages of state formation.

As stated before, there are no known written documents on the cult prior to the middle of the nineteenth century; nevertheless, certain names and events referred to in the Mbona legends are also found in Portuguese documents pertaining to the sixteenth and seventeenth centuries. From a comparison between the legends and the historical texts it can be inferred, among other things, that the cult underwent major organizational and theological changes about 1600 and that, probably under Portuguese missionary influence, Mbona was attributed certain Christ-like traits. After this radical transformation, the cult gained its widest geographical acceptance and became one of the most influential religious organizations on the north bank of the Zambezi. In the twentieth century, however, its importance diminished to the extent that as of 1985 the cult had little more than local significance.

BIBLIOGRAPHY

Discussions of various aspects of the Mbona cult can be found in essays I have contributed to several special collections. Among them are "The History and Political Role of the

M'Bona Cult among the Mang'anja," in *The Historical Study of African Religion,* edited by T. O. Ranger and Isaria N. Kimambo (Berkeley, Calif., 1972); "The Interaction of the M'Bona Cult and Christianity, 1859–1963," in *Themes in the Christian History of Central Africa,* edited by T. O. Ranger and John Weller (Berkeley, Calif., 1975); "Cult Idioms and the Dialectics of a Region," in *Regional Cults,* edited by R. P. Werbner (New York, 1977); "The Chisumphi and Mbona Cults in Malawi: A Comparative History," in *Guardians of the Land,* edited by J. Matthew Schoffeleers (Gwelo, 1978); and "Oral History and the Retrieval of the Distant Past: On the Use of Legendary Chronicles as Sources of Historical Information," in *Theoretical Explorations in African Religion,* edited by Wim van Binsbergen and J. Matthew Schoffeleers (London, 1984).

New Sources

Schoffeleers, J. Matthew. *River of Blood: The Genesis of a Martyr Cult in Southern Malawi c. A.D. 1600.* Madison, Wis.,1992.

Schoffeleers, J. Matthew. *Religion and the Dramatisation of Life: Spirit Beliefs and Rituals in Southern and Central Malawi.* Blantyre, Malawi, 1997.

J. MATTHEW SCHOFFELEERS (1987)
Revised Bibliography

MCPHERSON, AIMEE SEMPLE (1890–1944),

American Pentecostal evangelist and divine healer. McPherson was born Aimee Elizabeth Kennedy on a farm near Ingersoll, Ontario, Canada. Raised in the Salvation Army, she was converted to Pentecostalism through the preaching of Robert James Semple, whom she married in 1908 and accompanied to China, where they served as missionaries until Semple's death in 1910. Two subsequent marriages ended in divorce.

In 1917, McPherson embarked upon an evangelistic and divine healing career in the United States that quickly brought her national and international fame. In 1923, she settled in Los Angeles and built the five-thousand-seat Angelus Temple, a center of welfare services, and in 1927, she incorporated her large network of churches as the International Church of the Foursquare Gospel. She also founded a ministerial institute, later named the Lighthouse of International Foursquare Evangelism (LIFE) Bible College.

McPherson's turbulent personal life, involving her alleged kidnapping, rumors of romantic liaisons, dozens of lawsuits, conflicts with her mother and daughter, and divorce from her third husband, brought her much notoriety. Nevertheless, she retained the unswerving loyalty of her followers. Her denomination grew to four hundred congregations in the United States, two hundred mission stations abroad, and a worldwide total of twenty-two thousand members at the time of her death.

McPherson's Foursquare Gospel was a restatement of standard Pentecostal doctrine focusing on Jesus Christ as savior, baptizer in the Holy Spirit, healer, and coming king. She wrote several autobiographical books, published numerous pamphlets and articles, edited two periodicals, and composed some eighty hymns and five sacred operas. In her preaching she avoided condemnation and appeals to fear, emphasizing instead the love and joy that religion provides.

McPherson was unique in her evangelistic style. Her mastery at promoting herself and her work through the media made "Sister Aimee," or simply "Aimee," a household name. She was a pioneer in religious broadcasting, establishing the first church-owned radio station (KFSG) in the United States in 1924. She adapted the techniques of vaudeville and the theater to evangelism, using costumes, lighting, scenery and props, orchestras and brass bands, huge choirs, and dramatizations to achieve an unforgettable emotional impact on her audiences. Endowed with enormous energy and optimism, a powerful, melodious voice, rare acting ability, and a physical attractiveness heightened by an aura of sexuality, she was acclaimed a spellbinding platform personality by the millions to whom she preached.

BIBLIOGRAPHY

Bahr, Robert. *Least of All Saints: The Story of Aimee Semple McPherson.* Englewood Cliffs, N. J., 1979. A popular, fictionalized account that captures much of the whirlwind spirit of McPherson's career and temperament.

McLoughlin, William G. "Aimee Semple McPherson: Your Sister in the King's Glad Service." *Journal of Popular Culture* 1 (Winter 1968): 193–217. An analysis and evaluation that places McPherson's life and career in their cultural context, by an eminent historian of American religion.

McPherson, Aimee Semple. *This Is That: Personal Experiences, Sermons, and Writings.* Los Angeles, 1923. A reconstruction of McPherson's early years as she wanted others to see them, and a collection of sermons and tracts that reveal her public message.

McWilliams, Carey. "Aimee Semple McPherson: 'Sunlight in My Soul.'" In *The Aspirin Age, 1919–1941,* edited by Isabel Leighton, pp. 50–80. Los Angeles, 1949. A sympathetic interpretation of McPherson's life that reveals the tragic element behind the radiant facade.

ROBERT MAPES ANDERSON (1987)

MEAD, MARGARET (1901–1978)

was America's best-known anthropologist of the twentieth century. She grew up in Pennsylvania, briefly attended DePauw University in Greencastle, Indiana, and moved to New York City where she received her B.A. in psychology from Barnard College. Mead completed her education with an M.A. in psychology and a Ph.D. in anthropology from Columbia University. In the mid-1920s she became a curator of anthropology at the American Museum of Natural History in New York, where she spent her entire professional life. In a career that lasted over fifty years, Mead was an energetic researcher, prolific author, sought-after public speaker, influential public thinker, and tireless champion for the young discipline of anthropology.

Mead's research on several cultures in the South Pacific during the 1920s and 1930s, including Samoans, Manus, Balinese, and the Arapesh, Mundugumor, Tchambuli, and Iatmul of New Guinea, led to a number of popular books and professional monographs. Her research focused primarily on childhood, youth, and adolescence, as well as kinship and social organization. She is also known as the founder of the culture-and-personality school of cultural anthropology. Although Mead is not well known for her contributions to the study of religion, she nevertheless wrote about religion for both professional and popular audiences.

Mead's research on religion in her professional work is reflected in her detailed monograph on Arapesh supernaturalism (1940). It is her most comprehensive description of an indigenous religious system, containing extensive data on this New Guinea tribal culture's cosmology, myths, ritual beliefs, and practices. In this work, she gave special attention to rites of passage. Mead also published articles on taboo, magic, and men's houses in New Guinea. Based on her extensive fieldwork on the island of Manus, off the coast of New Guinea, she wrote about the belief in animism among adults and children, as well as long-term religious change in *New Lives for Old* (1956). She also described a revitalization movement on Manus (1964).

In *Balinese Character* (1942), Mead and Gregory Bateson used photographic analysis to comprehend Balinese trance. Their documentary, *Trance and Dance in Bali* (1952), is considered a classic in ethnographic film. In most of Mead's work on indigenous cultures, though, religion was tangential to other topics. For example, in *Coming of Age in Samoa* (1928), she briefly discussed the role of Christianity in the lives of adolescent girls. Mead viewed Christianity as playing a relatively benign role in adolescent socialization and was subsequently criticized by anthropologist Derek Freeman for not fully addressing what he viewed as the harsh and puritanical Christian morality of the time (Freeman, 1983). Mead also wrote a chapter on the child and the supernatural in *Growing Up in New Guinea* (1930) and one on religious institutions in *The Changing Culture of an Indian Tribe* (1932).

Although she wrote about religion based on her fieldwork, Mead's detailed ethnographic work on religion did not provide major contributions to theories of religion. She favored a more scientific, psychological, and developmental approach to religion that was superseded by more humanistic, symbolic approaches in anthropology. Mead's pioneering descriptions published in the 1930s and 1940s yielded to the interpretive ideas of Clifford Geertz, Victor Turner, and Mary Douglas in the 1960s and thereafter. And, while Mead was a forerunner of feminist approaches to the study of culture in general, she did not offer a feminist approach to the study of religion.

Mead wrote a good deal about religion in her role as a public intellectual, especially in her later life. She was very interested in religion in her own life, in the United States, and in the world at large. Although her parents were atheists, at age eleven Mead asked to be baptized. Her first husband, Luther Cressman, was an Episcopalian minister, and early in their courtship Mead planned to be a minister's wife. As she became a professional anthropologist, her goals changed. Yet Mead continued to be a religious person, unlike most of her colleagues in anthropology. Unknown to many of her friends, she secretly maintained her Christian faith.

In the 1960s, she saw a new role for Christianity in the world community, involving issues like civil rights and ecumenism. She was asked to be a representative for the Episcopal Church to the World Council of Churches, which she attended for several years. Mead was deeply involved in this project and authored *Twentieth Century Faith: Hope and Survival* (1972) about religion in the age of technology. Mead also wrote a number of opinion pieces on religion for the lay public in religious magazines and for her long-running column in *Redbook* magazine. She discussed the spiritual dimensions of birth control, the right to die, women as priests, the contemporary fascination with the occult, and other issues of the day. Mead saw no conflict between religion and science, and she envisioned a world where the faiths of other cultures would not be considered inferior. In her role as a public intellectual, she wrote more extensively on religion for a popular audience than she had for her peers in anthropology.

BIBLIOGRAPHY

Freeman, Derek. *Margaret Mead and Samoa: The Making and Unmaking of an Anthropological Myth.* Cambridge, Mass., 1983.

Gordan, Joan. *Margaret Mead: The Complete Bibliography, 1925–1975.* The Hague, 1975.

Howard, Jane. "Bishops May Not, but Anthropologists Do." In *Margaret Mead: A Life,* pp. 339–354. New York, 1984.

Mead, Margaret. *Coming of Age in Samoa: A Psychological Study of Primitive Youth for Western Civilisation.* New York, 1928.

Mead, Margaret. *The Mountain Arapesh;* Vol. 2: *Supernaturalism.* The Anthropological Papers of the American Museum of Natural History, vol. 37, pt. 3, pp. 317–541. New York, 1940.

Mead, Margaret. *New Lives for Old: Cultural Transformation—Manus, 1928–1953.* New York, 1956.

Mead, Margaret. "The Paliau Movement in the Admiralties." In *Continuities in Cultural Evolution,* pp. 192–234. New Haven, Conn., 1964.

Mead, Margaret. *Blackberry Winter: My Earlier Years.* New York, 1972.

Mead, Margaret. *Twentieth Century Faith: Hope and Survival.* New York, 1972.

PAUL SHANKMAN (2005)

MECCA SEE PILGRIMAGE, *ARTICLE ON* MUSLIM PILGRIMAGE

MEDIA AND RELIGION. The media have come to play an ever more prominent role in social and cultural life since the emergence of the so-called "mass media" in the late nineteenth century. Before that time, even though the media through which social and cultural knowledge were shared (oral transmission, ritual performance, writing, visual representation, and printing) were vital, they were more tacit and transparent to the processes they enabled. Today, in a range of social and cultural contexts, the media are foregrounded, even determinative.

The mass media emerged as the result of interacting technological and social developments. Mechanized printing, which developed with the industrial revolution and found its way into mass-market communication in Britain in the 1870s, brought about major changes in production, in reception, and in the political economy of media. Mass production allowed media to be financially supported by advertising instead of direct sales of newspapers or magazines. The resultant economic logic saw readers as audiences and sought to maximize their numbers. This coincided with the increasing concentration of populations in urban settings, removed from the social and cultural supports of the village and town. These audiences began to be thought of as "mass" audiences, and the content of media began to reflect more generalized class tastes.

A debate has raged ever since over how the resulting relationship between the mass audience and the mass media is to be seen. To some observers, the media ideologically dominate the audience. To others, the media act as a kind of cultural canvas on which is inscribed the more or less common themes, ideas, and discourses of the culture. To still others, the media are important as palliatives, replacing the lost connectedness of pre-industrial village life. For most, the class and taste orientation of mass media necessarily has meant that they are at least not the preferred communicational context for the authentic business of the culture.

These structural realities and social assumptions have come to condition the way the media function in relation to culture, and therefore, religion. The media are connected with generalized "mass" tastes. They are industrial and technical and thus are seen as artificial and their abilities to authentically articulate cultural and social artifacts, symbols, and values are suspect. They are commercial, and thus necessarily traffic in commodified culture and cultural experience. At the same time, though, they are intrinsically articulated into the fabric of modernity in ever-deepening ways. Thus, while social and cultural structures and institutions might wish to exist outside the boundaries of media culture, it is increasingly difficult for them to do so. These realities define the role that media play in the evolution of modern and late-modern religious institutions and practices.

The role of the media is not only social-structural, it is also geographic and semiotic/aesthetic. And, as the scholarly study of the interaction between religion and media has developed in recent years, it has become obvious that these three aspects of mediatization interact in interesting ways in the formation of the religious-media landscape. A phenomenology of media and religion in the twenty-first century would see media and religion in a number of different relationships.

RELIGION USING MEDIA. There is of course a long and deep history of mediation of religion. Various religions have been typified by means of their relationship to various media. It is commonplace to think of the development of the religions of the modern West as having been affected in major ways by moveable-type printing. In the twentieth century, a number of religions developed specific and particular relationships to the mass media. In most cases, these relationships were defined by the assumption of a kind of dualism, separating the "sacred" sphere of authentic religious history, claims, faith, and practice, from a "profane" sphere represented by the media. Islam, for example, is widely thought to eschew mass mediation, and particularly mediated visual depiction. The asceticism of Buddhism is also thought to separate it from a media sphere dominated by materiality and material concerns. Jewish scholarship has stressed the importance of "the book," but has tended to think that other modes of communication and representation were less worthy.

At the same time that Christian thought has assumed the sacred-profane dualism, Christianity in the modern and late-modern West has come to exhibit a range of responses and relationships to mass media, and the Christian relationship has come to be in some ways definitive, due to the fact that the media of the Christian West have come to dominate the media worldwide (a situation that has begun to change in small ways). Christian groups were among the earliest publishers in both Europe and North America. The evangelical impulse in Christianity seems, over time, to have given it a particular cultural interest in publication. All Christian groups (and most non-Christian groups and other religious movements in Europe and North America) have historically produced printed materials such as tracts, pamphlets, newsletters, magazines, Sunday school materials, and books. Missions programs, including Bible societies, have also been prolific publishers.

The nonprint media have been a less comfortable context for most religions, however. In the twentieth century, as the establishment religions of Europe and North America confronted the emergence of the mass media, these groups began a struggle for definition and cultural ascendancy that continues unabated. The dualist assumption brings with it a suspicion of the media of the "profane" sphere. While the medium of print has long been understood by religions to be an appropriate context for the conveyance of religious ideas and values, the succeeding waves of non-print "new" media have been seen differently. Probably as a result of their association with secular entertainment and thus secular values, film, broadcasting, television, and digital media has, in its turn, met with suspicion on the part of religion and religious authorities.

The most significant exception to this has been the case of Evangelical Protestantism. Beginning with the earliest days of radio, Fundamentalist and later Evangelical individuals and groups have seen great promise in these new technologies. It can even be argued that through the careful use of film, radio, and television, that what now is known as "neo-Evangelicalism" found its place in the religious landscape. Billy Graham, for example, who became one of the most significant Evangelical leaders of the twentieth century, was an active producer of media of all kinds, and is widely regarded as having risen to prominence in part as a "media figure." This further suggests a central role for mass media in religious evolution, as the mediation of Graham and the Evangelical movement generally played a large part in establishing their legitimacy. The phenomenon of televangelism, which emerged in the 1970s in North America and then spread, as a form, to much of the world, further contributed to the definition of religious and political landscapes. Such use of media by religion is not without its dangers, however. As a number of scholars have noted, religion has had to make compromises in order to fit into the structural and other conditions and limitations of the media form.

Media Using Religion. Traditionally, the media have been most involved in the presentation of religion through journalism. The mass media era began with the development of a mass press, and in addition to the development of new audiences and new economies, it also developed new content. Before the mass press, most press in Europe and North America were partisan in one way or another, beholden to political, clerical, even corporate authority. The new economy of mass publication meant that the press could be freed from patronage, and that new readers and audiences would be coming to the press for a wider range of material than in the past. The result was the notion of newspapers and magazines as public records, presumably speaking from positions outside the narrow perspectives of special interests. This kind of journalism needed to find its voice, and new models of journalism and new roles for journalism in public and political life emerged.

In the case of North America, religion has not necessarily been part of that mix. For most of the twentieth century, religion was seen by journalism to be a story of religious institutions and their practices and prerogatives. At the same time, these institutions were treated with deference, when treated at all. There was much evidence that religious institutions, at least, were of fading importance as the century progressed, and journalism generally assumed that secularization was moving ahead apace. It was not until late in the century that religion came to be seen as "hard" news, largely as the result of news events such as the Islamic Revolution in Iran in 1979, the rise of traditionalist religious movements worldwide, and the emergence of Evangelicalism as a political force in North America. The terrorist attacks of September 11, 2001, on New York, Washington, D.C., and Pennsylvania, put religion much more squarely on the "news agenda," with increasing coverage of religion per se among European and North American journalism.

Religion and Media Converge. The entertainment media have had an independent relationship to religion and religious content. There has been a tendency for these media to see the relationship in dualistic terms, evidenced by such things as the separate best-seller lists maintained for religious and non-religious book titles. The religious "market" for commercialized religious films, magazines, and books is now a multi-million-dollar industry worldwide, but is still thought of as a separate field from the dominant, and larger, "secular" market.

In that secular market, there are important examples in most major media and across most of the century. Early in the century, the so-called "Biblical Epics" such as *The Ten Commandments* and *The Robe* became major breakthrough films, attracting large numbers of conservative Christians and Jews to theaters for the first time. Later in the century, an explosion of book and magazine publishing devoted to spirituality, therapy, and self-help became one of the major trends in that industry.

In entertainment television, a range of new programs and series began to appear in the 1990s, featuring both explicitly and implicitly religious themes. Globally syndicated U.S. programs such as *Touched by an Angel*, *The X-Files*, *Buffy: Vampire Slayer*, *The Simpsons*, and *Northern Exposure* integrated a wide range of religious sensibilities, from traditional, to spiritual, to New Age, to Pagan and Wiccan. The situation became even more diverse in the digital media of the internet.

These trends resulted from changes in both religion and the media. For the media, rapid change in the structure and regulation of the electronic and digital media led to an exponential increase in the ubiquity and number of such channels fed into homes worldwide. A simultaneous increase in the differentiation of printed media into smaller and smaller "niche" markets meant that the media were both motivated to seek out new content and audiences, and to become increasingly able to provide material suiting specialized tastes. At the same time, religion was also undergoing great change, described in the case of North America as a "restructuring" that de-emphasized the traditional religious institutions. At the same time, religion increasingly became focused in the religious practices and meaning quests of individuals.

This new, more autonomous religious individualism, called "seeking" or "questing" by sociologists, naturally articulates with a mediated culture that can and does increasingly provide resources related to that project. Thus, a market for commodified religious symbols, rituals, and other resources arises, made possible by emerging attitudes oriented to religious and spiritual issues, and by a media system that can provide for increasingly specialized and focused tastes. The result is the gradual erosion of whatever bright line might have once existed between the "sacred" world of legitimate religious media and a "profane" world of secular media. At the beginning of the twenty-first century, that division is less and less obvious. It has become, for all practical purposes, one media culture.

There are important antecedents to this convergence of religion and media. In the case of North America, which largely led these developments, Protestantism has long tolerated, even encouraged, the development of religious commodities, religious markets, and religious spectacles. American Christianity has thus long had a nascent culture of mediated religious commodities and has cultivated in succeeding generations tastes and interests in such approaches to faith and spirituality.

RELIGION AND MEDIA INTERACT. The evolving relationship between media and religion, then, is best seen as an interaction between them rather than an effect or influence one may have on the other. Increasingly, scholars of religion and media are describing this interaction in its reception and the experiences of individuals and groups as they encounter media culture and work to inhabit religious lives in relation to it. This can be seen on both radically local and radically global levels. On the local level, in a wide range of contexts, the interaction between media culture and religious culture comes alive in the ways individuals and groups use the various cultural resources available to them to make meaning in their lives. This is seen most readily in the field context, where observers encounter evidence of negotiated relations between the lived local and the mediated non-local. As anthropologist Lila Abu-Lughod reflects in her essay, "The Interpretation of Cultures after Television":

> In *Writing Women's Worlds*, I suggested that we could write critical ethnographies that went "against the grain" of global inequalities, even as we had to remain modest in our claims to radicalism and realistic about the impacts of these ethnographies. Television, I believe, is particularly useful for writing against the grain because it forces us to represent people in distant villages as part of the same cultural worlds we inhabit—worlds of mass media, consumption, and dispersed communities of the imagination. To write about television in Egypt, or Indonesia, or Brazil is to write about the articulation of the transnational, the national, the local, and the personal. Television is not the only way to do this, of course . . . [b]ut television makes it especially difficult to write as if culture and cultures . . . were the most powerful ways to make sense of the world. (Lila Abu-Lughod, 1999, pp. 110–135)

On the global level, media and religion interact in events such as the national and international experience of the September 11 attacks and their aftermath. The direct experience of the attacks was mediated, and the fact that the attacks in New York took place in the world's leading media center made the images available and accessible, live and in real time. Whatever national and international processes of existential reflection and ritual mourning ensued, those processes were largely mediated as well. Media were also implicated in the widespread impression of distance and misunderstanding that was invoked. The media should be the primary means by which the developed West knows the Islamic East and vice versa. That the Islamic East was self-defined in large measure by religious identity places the media at the center of whatever misunderstanding may have led to or exacerbated the attacks. Further, a measure of the Islamic critique of Western culture is rooted in a moral reaction to the profanity and licentiousness found in the largely American popular culture that floods the developing world. Thus the media are taken to represent religious culture whether they intend to or not. Finally, the media were and are the primary context for the national and global rituals of commemoration and mourning around the event, thus assuming a role not unlike a "civil religion" in this regard.

IDENTITY, REFLEXIVITY, AND GLOBALIZATION. Beyond the evolution in media and religion already discussed, the convergence and interaction between religion and media in late modernity are responsive to a number of social and cultural trends. Three stand out. First, the convergence and interaction are most clearly felt in the project of the self and religious identity. As theorists of late modern social life have suggested, the project of the self is perhaps the dominant concern of the age. As social life has become more and more complex and rationalized, the means of support available in the social sphere have withdrawn, leaving individuals increasingly to their own devices. This has driven individuals inward, to a quest for the self. This quest turns outward, however, to seek and appropriate resources relevant to its task, and the commodities of the media sphere are among the most obvious and available such resources. To the extent that the project of the self is a religious project, this becomes an important role for media in the formation and shaping of religious identity.

The second of these trends is reflexivity. Prominent theorists of late modernity recognize the role of mediation in the encouragement of a reflexive mode of consciousness. Reflexivity results from the access to sources and contexts of knowledge that offer individuals a self-consciousness of place that is historically unprecedented. With this reflexive knowledge comes a sense of autonomy in spheres of normative action, including self and identity. In late modernity, mediation plays a major role in our knowledge of place and location, and thus is implicated in important ways in the reflexivity that today defines much of the religious quest for self and identity.

Finally, globalization and what is coming to be called "glocalization," the blending of a global concept to a local application, are definitive trends. The media are major global and globalizing industries, of course, but their implications extend well beyond their structural and economic relations. To the extent that globalization is a fact, it results in large measure from the capabilities of the media to provide global interconnectivity, socially, culturally, and religiously. The media are, after all, "consciousness industries," and among their capabilities is the conveyance of cultural symbols, forms, and texts related to the deepest human desires for connection and belonging. They can transcend space and time, and frequently do provide, for a variety of "imagined communities," a connectivity across space and time that is unprecedented in its depth and speed.

Increasingly, the media can be seen to be active in the negotiative frameworks that underlie glocalization as well. The media are no longer thought of as determinative or dominant, as noted. Instead, they provide, to reflexive individuals and communities, senses of the structured relations of local, national, and global life, and symbolic and other resources relevant to making sense of that life. This involves the constructive negotiation of that consciousness, those contexts and those resources. What results is an imbrication of the global and the local, a reflexive consciousness of place within those frameworks, and senses of self and group identity relevant to this awareness. Religion is a fundamental quest, as well as an important dimension of these relations. Thus religion and mediation interact in fundamental ways in the ongoing development of global and glocal consciousness.

But the globalized world is not only a place of harmony, it is also a place of conflict and struggle. Among the social and cultural relations increasingly accessible today are those between conflicting worldviews. In the case of religion, the media can and do offer much information about the religious "other," but that does not necessarily lead to increased understanding. The Anglican Church, for example, learned during their struggles over gay ordination in the early part of the twenty-first century, that a global media context made those deliberations accessible worldwide, increasing the intra-communal tension as African Anglicans could have real-time access to the debates taking place among North-American Anglicans. As globalization and glocalization move ahead, international media will continue to place before religion challenges to self-understanding and inter-religious understanding.

MEDIA EFFECTS ON RELIGION. Given this discussion, there remain a number of ways that the media affect religious institutions and practices. First, the media increasingly set the context for religion and spirituality, and help define their terms in contemporary life. The 2004 film *The Passion of the Christ,* for example, both invoked a public debate about contemporary religious faith and presented a new set of images and symbols through which that aspect of the Christians' story will be understood for years to come. The performer Madonna, through songs and music videos, presented influential interpretations and juxtapositions of important Catholic symbols and artifacts. Because of their position in the culture, the media are now the context within which the most widely-held discourses in national and global culture take place, and religion and religious discourses must find their way within that larger context.

A second effect of media on religion is in the area of commodification. Contemporary social and cultural experience is becoming increasingly commodified, and the media sphere plays a major role in this trend. Religion is not immune to commodification, and indeed, there is a long and deep history of it in some traditions. In the mass media age, it makes sense to think of culture as a marketplace of symbols and ideas. Cultural commodities of all kinds, including religious ones, are valued and exchanged in that marketplace.

The third effect of media on religion is in the consumption and reception of religious symbols and discourses. The secular media define the terms of access for religious and spiritual material as it enters the public sphere. In the field of contemporary Christian music, for example, the ability of religiously motivated musicians to "cross over" into the mainstream, a desire by some, is constrained by a set of expectations established by the conditions under which the public, secular, mass media operate. The primary one is the expectation that to be public, such material must appeal to general as opposed to narrower, sectarian tastes. In both popular music and book publishing, separate "lists" continue to be maintained.

The fourth effect, then, is that in this and many other ways, religions can no longer control their own stories if they wish to be present in the public sphere and in public discourse. The terms of reference, the language, the visual and linguistic symbols, and the conditions under which religion becomes public are all matters determined by media practice. It is possible for religious groups and individuals to remain separate from this process, but they then surrender opportunities to be part of the public culture. Even groups that aspire to separation, such as the Amish, find it increasingly difficult to do so.

This relates to a fifth effect, that it is no longer possible for religions to retain zones of privacy around themselves. Increasingly, and as a result of the reflexivity of late-modern consciousness, individuals today expect a level of openness from public institutions. As religious groups and movements interact with the commercial and governmental spheres, they begin taking on the attributes of publicness and are thus seen to be subject to media scrutiny, journalistic and otherwise. Both the Roman Catholic Church, in its struggles over scandals and vocations crises, and the Anglican Communion (and other Protestant bodies) as they face the question of gay rights, have found that the conversation is not and cannot be a private one any more.

A sixth effect is that, as was noted earlier, the media bring individuals the religious and spiritual "other." In the context of globalization/glocalization, this is felt in the increasing cross-national and cross-cultural exchange of information, symbols, images, and ideas, circulated through journalism, through popular culture, and through the personal media of the digital age. In the context of the increasing international flow of persons, both through travel and through immigration, the media have become active in providing information about the "others" who are now arriving next door or in the next town. The media are now becoming the authoritative context for interreligious contact and dialog. At the same time, they can and do provide information about some traditions that other traditions find to be scandalous.

A seventh effect of media has been discussed in some detail already. That is that the media are today a major source of religious and spiritual resources to the "seeking" and "questing" sensibilities that increasingly define religion in the developed West. This is related to an eighth effect, that it has been suggested that the media have the potential to support the development of "new" or "alternative" religions. This has been thought by some to be a particular potential of the new digital media. The Internet provides opportunities for interactive relations among focused networks of like-minded people. Thus they might well be a context where those networks could develop into religious movements of their own. This of course remains to be seen.

Finally, an effect of media on religion is the central role that the media play in national and global rituals around major public events. Beginning with the Kennedy assassination and continuing through royal weddings and funerals, crises such as the *Challenger, Columbia,* and Columbine tragedies, the death of the Diana, Princess of Wales, and of course the September 11 attacks, the media have come to accept a central role in a new civil religion of commemoration and mourning.

The relationship between media and religion is a profound, complex, and subtle one. While the media have grown in cultural importance over the past century, and religious institutions and movements have contemplated how to respond and experimented with ways of accommodating to this new reality, a relationship has developed that now determines, in important ways, the prospects and prerogatives of religion into the twenty-first century.

SEE ALSO Religious Broadcasting.

BIBLIOGRAPHY

Abu-Lughod, Lila. "The Interpretation of Culture(s) after Television." In *The Fate of "Culture,"* edited by Sherry B. Ortner, pp. 110–135. Berkeley, Calif., 1999. A provocative scholarly reflection by an anthropologist on the extent to which television is now integrated into cultural and religious life, as a local and worldwide phenomenon.

Appadurai, Arjun. "Global Ethnoscapes: Notes and Queries for a Transnational Anthropology." In *Recapturing Anthropology: Working in the Present,* edited by Richard G. Fox, pp. 191–210. Santa Fe, 1991. An influential survey that reveals and assesses the phenomenon of emerging global cultures.

Brasher, Brenda. *Give Me That Online Religion.* San Francisco, 2001. A pioneering study of internet religion, which considers the possibility of the digital media coming to a central place in emerging religious practice.

Bunt, Gary R. *Islam in the Digital Age: E-Jihad, Online Fatwas, and Cyber Islamic Movements.* London, 2003. The first comprehensive account of Islam in the internet age. Provides evidence of a growing accommodation between Islam, in both traditional and non-traditional forms, and the digital media.

Clark, Lynn Schofield. *From Angels to Aliens: Teenagers, the Media, and the Supernatural.* New York, 2003. A fieldwork-based cultural analysis of emerging religious sensibilities in youth culture articulated by and through the media culture.

De Vries, Hent, and Samuel Weber, eds. *Religion and Media.* Stanford, Calif., 2001. An influential compendium of essays and field reports focusing on the intervention of media into religious memory, history, and practice.

Eisentstein, Elizabeth. *The Printing Press as an Agent of Change.* New York, 1974. The definitive study of printing and its relationship to clerical and state authority. Contains important insights into how printing became publishing and thus the foundation of the modern mass media.

Ginsburg, Faye, Brian Larkin, and Lila Abu-Lughod, eds. *Media Worlds: Anthropology on New Terrain.* Berkeley, Calif., 2002. A significant and influential collection that has helped define the development of a scholarly discourse on media within anthropology. Many of the contributions deal with religion in specific contexts.

Habermas, Jürgen. *The Structural Transformation of the Public Sphere: An Inquiry into a Category of Bourgeois Society.* Cambridge, Mass., 1991. An influential social history of the emergence of public discourse and its integration into social, political, and communicational contexts.

Hendershot, Heather. *Shaking the World for Jesus: Media and Conservative Evangelical Culture.* Chicago, 2004. A comprehensive study of Evangelical relations to the media and popular culture. Contains important insights into Evangelical self-understanding and understanding of the possibilities in media technologies.

Hoover, Stewart M. *Mass Media Religion: The Social Sources of the Electronic Church.* London, 1988. The first field study of religious television audiences, it established the extent to which these programs had important symbolic value in representing the ascendancy of Evangelicalism in the culture more generally.

Hoover, Stewart M., and Knut Lundby, eds. *Rethinking Media, Religion, and Culture.* Newbury Park, Calif., 1998. An edited collection focused on the emerging scholarly field of media and religion studies. Largely social-scientific in orientation, the contributions look at media and religion in a variety of contexts worldwide.

Hoover, Stewart M., and Lynn Schofield Clark, eds. *Practicing Religion in the Age of the Media: Studies in Media, Religion, and Culture.* New York, 2002. A collection concentrating on humanistic, historical, and critical analysis of the practice of religion in the media age.

Mahan, Jeffrey, and Bruce Forbes, eds. *Religion and Popular Culture in America.* Berkeley, Calif., 2000. An edited volume containing significant scholarship from the field of religious studies focused on media culture and popular culture.

McDannell, Colleen. *Material Christianity, Religion, and Popular Culture in America.* New Haven, Conn., 1998. A field-based study of major contexts of popular religious culture. Provides an excellent introduction to the commodities and artifacts that have historically defined American religion.

Morgan, David. *Visual Piety: A History and Theory of Popular Religious Images.* Berkeley, Calif., 1999. The definitive account of the role of material culture in American Protestant piety, with special attention to visual artifacts. It includes both historical and contemporary reception analysis.

Roof, Wade Clark. *Spiritual Marketplace: Baby Boomers and the Remaking of American Religion.* Princeton, N.J., 1999. The definitive account of the individualistic "seeker" phenomenon among baby-boom and post-boom generations in the West and in the United States more specifically. Gives particular attention to the role that cultural commodities, including media commodities, play in religion and spirituality among these generations.

Schultze, Quentin J. *Habits of the High-Tech Heart: Living Virtuously in the Information Age.* Grand Rapids, Mich., 1992. A thoughtful reflection on the implications of the digital age for religious community and religious practice. Contrasts the mediated digital context with religious community in traditional terms.

Underwood, Doug. *From Yahweh to Yahoo!: The Religious Roots of the Secular Press.* Urbana, Ill., 2002. An award-winning history of media and religion that looks at the institutional relations and integration of religious and non-religious media.

Winston, Diane. *Red-Hot and Righteous: The Urban Religion of the Salvation Army.* Cambridge, Mass., 2000. An in-depth historical look at the central case of religion encountering publication and commodification in the nineteenth and twentieth centuries. The Salvation Army proves to be an excellent case-study of the costs and benefits of the interaction between religion and media.

Wuthnow, Robert. *After Heaven: Spirituality in America since the 1950s.* Berkeley, Calif., 2000. An influential account of the relationship between individualistic religion and the contexts of faith.

STEWART M. HOOVER (2005)

MEDIATORS

SEE ANGELS; ATONEMENT, *ARTICLE ON* CHRISTIAN CONCEPTS; DEMONS; LOGOS; PRIESTHOOD; PROPHECY; SHAMANISM; SPIRITUAL GUIDE

MEDICAL ETHICS.

Religious beliefs are central to the process of deliberation in medical ethics. An awareness of the rich diversity of perspectives both within and among different religious traditions is critical to the development of respectful dialogue. This entry will focus on the religious traditions of Christianity, Judaism, and Islam. Readers interested in Hinduism are referred to S. Cromwell Crawford's *Hindu Bioethics for the Twenty-First Century* (2003) and those interested in Buddhism are referred to Damien Keown's *Buddhism and Bioethics* (1995).

OVERVIEW OF MEDICAL ETHICS. Medical ethics is the application of principles and rules of morality to healthcare (Clouser, 1974). It is a multidisciplinary field grappling with perplexing questions created by rapidly evolving scientific, technological, and social developments. There is not a single systematic theory of medical ethics. Rather, medical ethics has matured into a discipline that is enriched by a plurality of voices from clinical medicine, religious traditions, philosophy, literature, politics, and the social sciences.

One of the earliest articulations of ethical guidance for physicians is the oath of Hippocrates, which dates from as early as the fourth century BCE. Two statements in the Hippocratic oath—"into whatsoever house you shall enter, it shall be for the good of the sick to the utmost of your power" and "you will exercise my art solely for the cure of patients"—are the basis for the well-known principle of "above all do no harm" when caring for patients (Dorman, 1995; Carey, 1928).

In contrast to the personal expression of ideal conduct embodied in the Hippocratic oath, in 1803 Thomas Percival published *Medical Ethics or a Code of Institutes and Precepts* (Percival, 2000). This code became the basis of the American Medical Association's first *Code of Ethics* adopted in 1847 (Baker, 2000). The development of a code of ethics marked a radical transition from a personal ethic that focused primarily on elucidating the proper demeanor for physicians (Jonsen, 2000) to a collective professional ethic that renewed concern for the place of values in the practice of medicine.

By the middle of the twentieth century advances in medical science radically changed the ability of physicians to diagnose and treat illness. These developments created a moral crisis that cried out for a rethinking of the moral obligations of physicians. Notably, the condemnation of research without patient consent, codified as the Nuremberg Code in 1947, transformed the interaction of physician-investigators and patients in research. In 1950 an era of organ transplantation began, eventually forcing society to reassess the definition and criteria for death (*Defining Death*, 1981). In 1953 the structure of DNA was discovered and set the groundwork for the genetic revolution in the early twenty-first century. In 1961 hemodialysis became a reality, raising questions about the allocation of scarce resources and the appropriateness of using technology to prolong life. In 1973 the U.S. Supreme Court's *Roe v. Wade* decision affirmed the right of a woman to obtain an abortion during the first trimester of pregnancy. The 1970s also ushered in vigorous debates about who should live and who should be allowed to forgo lifesaving treatment. These questions were stimulated by the seminal cases of Karen Quinlan (*Quinlan* 70 NJ, 335A2d, 1976) and Donald "Dax" Cowart (Kliever, 1989) and continued into the 1990s with questions about the ethics of euthanasia and assisted suicide (*Deciding to Forgo Life-Sustaining Treatment,* 1982; *Washington et al. v. Glucksberg et al.*, 1997; and *Vacco, Attorney General of New York, et al. v. Quill et al.*, 1997). More recently, greater emphasis has been placed on the quality of end-of-life care and how to improve it. The advent of managed care has invigorated debates on resource allocation and the role of physicians as managers. The twenty-first century heralded in an era of genetics with the mapping of the human genome and questions about the acceptability of stem cell research and cloning (Shapiro, 1999; Nuffield Council on Bioethics, 2000). These questions are part of a gradual shift in the discipline from internal professional concerns to matters of public debate.

RELIGIOUS APPROACHES TO MEDICAL ETHICS. Theologians were among the first to contribute to the modern dialogue of medical ethics, and they were instrumental in shaping the emergence of the discipline (Callahan, 1990). Religious approaches to medical ethics share a common grounding of ethical positions in religiously based claims (Lammers, 1998; Williams, 1997). A brief discussion of the theological principles that guide each religion's vision of healthcare follows.

Catholic medical ethics. There is a long tradition of Catholic medical ethics dating from Augustine's writings on suicide and Thomas Aquinas's doctrine of natural law to modern-day directives on euthanasia and reproductive technologies (O'Rourke, 1999). The church's ethical and religious directives govern Catholic medical ethics (*Ethical and Religious Directives for Catholic Health Care Services*, 2001). The directives are grounded in the natural law approach of Catholic moral theology from which the church has derived its understanding of the nature of the human person, of human acts, and of the goals that shape human activity.

Fundamental to Catholic bioethics is a belief in the sanctity of life. Life is understood as a gift from God, and human beings are its steward (Wildes, 1997). The Catholic belief in the resurrection of Christ and an afterlife, however, influences the attitude toward life. Catholicism believes that human life and personhood begin at conception. Thus, a human fetus at any stage of development is a person who has a right to life. Central to Catholicism is a belief in a metaphysical conception of human beings as both body and soul. The presence of a living body, even if it has diminished or absent intellectual capabilities, is the defining characteristic of personhood. This belief has implications for ethical questions at the beginning and end of life.

As in most religions, there is a diversity of opinion within Catholicism. Richard McCormick has articulated a teleological ethic in which good is judged in relation to the common good. He argues for a proportionalist perspective in which an action viewed as evil might be justifiable if it brings about a good that is proportionate to or greater than the associated evil (McCormick, 1981b). This position is in opposition to Catholic beliefs in the absolute ontic nature of moral acts. McCormick has a dynamic understanding of Catholic theology that emphasizes an individualized and context-sensitive approach to moral problems (May, 1987 and 1994). According to McCormick actions should be judged based on what values they advance or denigrate within the context of an objective hierarchy of values (Rae, 1999). McCormick connects moral values to moral rights and duties. Thus the right to self-determination is linked to the moral value of human freedom.

Protestant medical ethics. Protestant medical ethics is rooted in the teachings of Martin Luther and such Reformation themes as "the freedom of a Christian," as well as biblical principles, such as love (Johnson, 1978). There are many strains of Protestant theology, and so there are diverse approaches to Protestant medical ethics. It is therefore difficult to define a uniquely Protestant approach to medical ethics, and most Protestants would view secular medical ethics as compatible with their personal religious beliefs (Pauls and Hutchinson, 2002). Paul Ramsey and James Gustafson are two prominent Protestant thinkers who have developed a Protestant approach to medical ethics. Ramsey develops an ethic that is rooted in the biblical concept of a covenantal relationship and the biblical conception of righteousness. His ethical positions are directed at meeting the needs of others (Ramsey, 1950). It is therefore not surprising that he focuses on the obligations of physicians to patients and those of researchers to human subjects. He leaves no room for consideration of the common good that might diminish the priority of care for individual patients. The individual's welfare is always first and foremost (Ramsey, 1970b). Ramsey also developed a phenomenological conception of Protestant natural law and argues that natural laws are discovered "in the course of active reflection upon man in the context of moral, social, and legal decisions" (Ramsey, 1962, p. 216). This is consistent with the historical Protestant emphasis on personal freedom and has contributed to the establishment of patient autonomy as a central concept within the moral framework of medical decision-making.

James Gustafson has emphasized the web of human relationships in which individuals are situated (Gustafson, 1965). The starting place for his ethical reflection is ordinary human existence rather than church doctrines or scriptural passages; nevertheless, Gustafson developed a theocentric ethic. Although he argued that Christian ethics should begin with human experience, human action should be judged primarily by the will of God and not by the welfare of human beings.

Jewish medical ethics. Jewish medical ethics is rooted in the application of the scriptural texts of the Five Books of Moses, the Talmud, codes of Jewish law, and the *responsa* literature to contemporary ethical questions in medicine. The Talmud is the primary sourcebook of Jewish law; it entails expositions and debates by rabbis about how to apply principles to different circumstances. The *responsa* literature is a compilation of written decisions and rulings by rabbis in response to questions posed about Jewish law. The questions are usually practical, and often concern new situations for which no provision had been made in prior codes of law. *Responsa* begin to appear in the sixth century CE, and all denominations within Judaism continue to formulate *responsa.* In recent years they have addressed many contemporary questions relating to medical ethics.

The presence of a well-defined corpus of religious legal texts does not mean, however, that there is one authoritative

Jewish position on questions of medical ethics. Within Orthodox Judaism (Freedman, 1999; Waldenberg, 1963) and among Orthodox, Conservative, Reform, and Reconstructionist Judaism there is a diversity of opinions on how to apply traditional sources to contemporary ethical problems. For some, Jewish medical ethics is constrained by the scriptural rules and precedents accumulated over thousands of years (Tendler, 1998; Jakobovits, 1975; Rosner, 1979). This approach is in tension with those who look more broadly at the values behind Jewish law and apply them to modern-day situations (Newman, 1995; Zohar, 1997; Gordis, 1989). What sources are selected and what methodological approach is used in the interpretation of traditional Jewish texts will influence the ethical decision that is reached. Jewish ethicists dispute fundamental questions about how concrete examples discussed in the Talmud can be extrapolated to modern-day questions in medical ethics.

In an effort to grapple with contemporary questions from a Jewish perspective, Elliott Dorff (1998) has articulated several fundamental beliefs underlying Jewish medical ethics. He argues that the following beliefs should inform the Jewish response to modern-day questions in medical ethics: a belief that human bodies belong to God, human worth flows from being created in the image of God, the human being is an integrated whole where body and soul are judged as one, the body is morally neutral and potentially good, there is an obligation to heal, and Jews have an obligation to engage in action that sanctifies God's name. Dorff thus puts forth a methodology of Jewish medical ethics that goes beyond strict legalism. He interprets Judaism's general rules not as inviolable principles, but as guiding policies that need to be applied with sensitivity to the contexts of specific medical cases.

Islamic medical ethics. Islamic medical ethics is based on *sharīʿah,* Islamic law, which is founded on the Qurʾān and the *sunnah.* The Qurʾān is the holy book of all Muslims, and the *sunnah* contains aspects of Islamic law based on the prophet Muḥammad's teachings. As in Judaism, Muslim scholars of religious law are called upon to determine religious practice and resolve questions in medical ethics. The application and interpretation of Islamic law is dynamic and flexible within the confines of a sacred set of values and texts (Van Bommel, 1999). In 1982 Abdul Rahman C. Amine, M.D., and Ahmed Elkadi, M.D., proposed an Islamic code of medical ethics that addresses many fundamental questions in contemporary medical ethics (Rahman, 1982). In Islam, life is sacred and every moment has value even where the quality of life is diminished. Full human life begins after the ensoulment of the fetus, and most Muslim scholars agree that this occurs at about 120 days after conception (Al Bar, 1986). A minority of scholars believes that ensoulment occurs at forty days after conception (Al Bar, 1995). Saving a life is considered a duty informed by the guiding principle mentioned in both the Qurʾān and in the Talmud, "If anyone has saved a life, it would be as if he has saved the life of the whole of mankind" (Qurʾān 5:35; and Mishnah *Sanhedrin* 4:5). Death is considered to occur when the soul leaves the body, but since this cannot be determined with certainty, physical signs are used to diagnose death. The concept of brain death was accepted by a majority of Islamic scholars in 1986 (Al Bar, 1995).

REPRODUCTION. Many religious traditions share the assumption that human life is sacred. This understanding of life has implications for the permissibility of abortion. Catholicism's official opposition to abortion has been based on two fundamental beliefs (Pope John Paul II, 1995). One is the belief that a human fetus is a person from the moment of conception, and thus aborting a fetus is tantamount to murder. The Second Vatican Council (1962–1965) condemned abortion unconditionally as an "unspeakable crime" (Pope Paul VI, 1965). The second belief that underlies the Catholic position on abortion, contraception, and assisted reproduction is that sex is permitted only when it is integrated into marriage and has procreative intent. In opposition to the antiabortion stance of the church, some Catholic theologians have tried to revive a more liberal position that claims that the male fetus acquires a soul forty days after conception, while the female fetus only acquires a soul eighty days after conception (Dombrowski, 2000). This position is based on the teachings of Augustine of Hippo (354–430), and it is strikingly similar to Jewish understandings of the fetus, but it was never held as a universal truth by everyone in the church.

Protestant views on abortion are diverse. Conservative groups believe that life begins at conception; however, some liberal denominations are pro-choice, believing that freedom of choice is an important principle. Exceptions to the duty to preserve life include medical indications, pregnancy resulting from rape, or social and emotional conditions that would not be beneficial to the mother or future child (Gustafson, 1970).

In Jewish law an embryo is considered to be mere water until the fortieth day (Epstein, 1935–1952). This leads some to argue that abortion is permissible during the first forty days of pregnancy (*Responsa Seridei Esh,* 1966). A fetus has the status of a potential human life, and thus Judaism permits abortion under certain circumstances. Where the mother's life is in jeopardy, abortion is mandatory. The Talmud speaks directly to this question where it says: "if the fetus threatens the life of the mother, you cut it up within her body and remove it limb by limb if necessary, because its life is not as valuable as hers. But once the greater part of the body has emerged, you cannot take its life to save the mother's, because you cannot choose between one human life and another" (Mishnah *Ohalot* 7:6). Thus a fetus becomes a person when the head emerges from the womb. As with most questions in Judaism, there is a diversity of opinion on when abortion is permitted (Feldman, 1980; Lubarsky, 1984; Bleich, 1968). Some authorities permit abortion in the case of rape, and some will permit abortion in the first trimester if the fetus would be born with an abnormality that would cause it to suffer. One Orthodox authority has argued that abortion is permissible until the end of the second trimester if the fetus has a genetic mutation that would be lethal and would cause great suffering (Waldenberg, 1980).

Islam discourages abortion, but permits it under certain circumstances. Abortion has been allowed after implantation and before ensoulment in cases where there are adequate reasons. However, many Shīʿah and some Sunnis have prohibited abortion after implantation unless the mother's life is in danger (Ebrahim, 1989).

END-OF-LIFE CARE. Advances in medical technology have made it possible to prolong life through the use of ventilators, artificial organs, intravenous feeding, and ventricular assist devices. The monotheistic religions of Judaism, Christianity, and Islam uphold a duty to protect life that is on temporary hold from God. These faiths have uniformly rejected suicide. Within the Catholic tradition the failure to use ordinary measures to preserve life is morally equivalent to suicide. This does not imply, however, that there is a duty to prolong life in all circumstances, regardless of the patient's condition. Catholic theologians have distinguished ordinary and extraordinary life support, arguing that a person is obligated to use ordinary measures but that there is room for choice with regard to the use of extraordinary measures (Cronin, 1958). The directives outline compassionate care for the dying, which includes pain management but also respects informed and competent refusal of life-sustaining treatment. McCormick argues that Catholic moral theory connects self-determination with the duty to preserve life, but it places limits on this duty. "Life is indeed a basic and precious good, but a good to be preserved precisely at the condition of other values" (McCormick, 1981a, p. 345). He affirms the right of competent patients to reject life-sustaining treatment, arguing that individual patients will be in the best position to determine which treatments have a reasonable benefit and which treatments are accompanied by an unreasonable burden. McCormick urges patients to make a proportionate, reasoned decision in considering the rejection of life-sustaining treatment. This would include a consideration of the value of preserving life, human freedom, and lack of pain (McCormick, 1981a, p. 399).

Gustafson argues that life is not an absolute value, and yet he is also quick to say that life is the "indispensable condition for human values and valuing" (1971, p. 140). Thus we should neither worship life nor should we be quick to end life. Gustafson puts forth four religious qualifications to consider about life and death: (1) Life is a gift since human beings are dependent creatures; (2) Only God is absolute, and human life is of relative worth; (3) Human beings are accountable to God and responsible for how they treat life; (4) Human beings are participants in life who must respond to the developments and purposes that are made possible by God (Gustafson, 1968).

Jewish perspectives on end-of-life care are also informed by a belief that human life is sacred, and thus the preservation of life surpasses almost all other commandments. Most would argue, however, that this belief does not translate into a mandate to preserve all human life under all circumstances and at all costs (Herring, 1984). Although hastening death is prohibited, if something is an impediment to the natural process of death, it is permitted to withdraw that impediment. For example, if a person is certain to die, and is only being kept alive by a ventilator, it is permissible to withdraw the ventilator, which is impeding the natural process of death. Judaism attempts to balance the thrust to prolong life and the recognition that life may become unbearably difficult and painful (Rosner, 1979).

Islam considers the intentional hastening of death to be the equivalent of murder and thus denounces suicide and assisted suicide (Ebrahim, 2000). Islam does not condone the secular concept of a right to die. Like Judaism, however, Islam acknowledges that when treatment becomes futile, it ceases to be mandatory. A patient may refuse treatment when it will not improve his condition or quality of life. Although continued medical care, including the use of a ventilator may not be required, hydration, nutrition, and pain control should not be withheld (Khomeini, 1998).

GENETICS. The completion of the finished sequence of the Human Genome Project in 2003 marks the beginning of a new era of genetic manipulation. The potential for disease prevention, early detection, and improved treatment of diseases for which there is an identified genetic basis, however, is accompanied by concern about the ethical, social, legal, and psychological implications of genetic information (Andrews et al., 1994). One of the most promising and controversial areas of genetics is stem cell research. Stem cells are unique in their ability to differentiate into any cell of the human body. They have been isolated from adults, aborted fetuses, and embryos shortly after conception, and many believe stem cells are the key to developing treatments and cures for some diseases. Others, however, argue that using these cells is the equivalent of taking a human life, and even if their use leads to saving lives, it is not morally permissible to destroy embryonic stem cells.

Embedded within religious perspectives on the use of stem cells and cloning are varying theological assumptions that each religion has about a human embryo, the religious duty to procreate, and the relationship between human beings and technology. These assumptions lead to varied conclusions about the permissibility of stem cell research and cloning.

The Catholic Church has been unequivocal in its denunciation of the use of embryonic stem cells. This position is based on the belief that human life begins at conception and thus embryos must be respected (*Donum Vitae*, 1987). Because Protestant theology is pluralistic, there is not a unified position on the use of embryonic stem cells. The general synods of the United Church of Christ have regarded human embryos as due great respect, but they have not regarded embryos as the equivalent of a person (Cole-Turner, 1997). Other Protestant views consider the dangers of not respecting the weakest human being, namely the embryo, to be greater than any medical benefit that might be achieved through stem cell research.

Since Judaism does not consider an embryo to have significant moral status prior to forty days of gestation, the majority of Jewish authorities believe that embryos may be used for research (National Bioethics Advisory Commission, 1999; Breitowitz, 1996).

The successful cloning in 1996 of Dolly the sheep through the somatic cell nuclear transfer technique has raised the possibility of cloning humans. Some Catholic and Protestant thinkers have reiterated past opposition to cloning (Cahill, 1997; Verhey, 1994; Ramsey, 1966 and 1970a). The foundations of these claims are an opposition to "playing God," the view that cloning represents a violation of the unitive aspect of marriage, and a belief that cloning is a violation of human dignity (Haas, 1997; Moraczewski, 1997).

However, some Protestant thinkers have expressed qualified support for cloning research and for creating children using somatic cell nuclear transfer techniques. This view is based on an understanding of the meaning of human partnership with ongoing divine creative activity. Ted Peters argues that human begins are called to "play human" and assume the role of co-creator through the acquisition of knowledge aimed at improving humanity (Peters, 1996). According to this view there are no theological principles that the cloning of humans necessarily violates.

Jewish perspectives on cloning are guided by the biblical injunction to procreate and "master the world" (*Gn.* 1:28). The fulfillment of this biblical mandate is understood as permitting people to modify nature to make the world a better place (Dorff, 1997). Cloning is one example of mastery over the world, and it is not theologically problematic in the Jewish tradition (Tendler, 1997; Luria, 1971).

The model of a partnership with God in the creative process also appears in Islamic thought (Sachedina, 1997). Understood in this light, cloning may in some circumstances be an example of using human creative potential for good. Islamic scholars have argued that scientific discovery is ultimately a revelation of the divinely ordained creation. Scientific knowledge is therefore understood as a symbol of God's creation and an opportunity given by God to human beings (Hathout, 1997).

See Also Bioethics; Buddhist Ethics; Christian Ethics; Genetics and Religion; Hippocrates.

Bibliography

Al Bar, M. A. *Human Development as Revealed in the Holy Qur'an and Hadith (The Creation of Man Between Medicine and the Qur'an).* Jeddah, Saudi Arabia, 1986.

Al Bar, M. A., ed. "Organ Transplantation: An Islamic Perspective." In *Contemporary Topics in Islamic Medicine.* Jeddah, Saudi Arabia, 1995.

Al Bar, M. A., ed. "When Is the Soul Inspired?" In *Contemporary Topics in Islamic Medicine*, pp. 131–136. Jeddah, Saudi Arabia, 1995.

Andrews L. B., Jane E. Fullarton, Neil A. Holtzman, and Arno G. Motulsky, eds. *Social, Legal, and Ethical Implications of Genetic Testing: Assessing Genetic Risks.* Washington, D.C., 1994. See pages 247–289.

Baker, Robert, et al., eds. *The American Medical Ethics Revolution: How the AMA's Code of Ethics Has Transformed Physicians' Relationships to Patients, Professionals, and Society.* Baltimore, 2000.

Behoref Hayamim: In the Winter of Life: A Values-Based Jewish Guide for Decision Making at the End of Life. Philadelphia, 2002. A Reconstructionist perspective on medical ethics.

Bleich, J. David. "Abortion in Halakhic Literature." *Tradition* 6 (1968): 73.

Breitowitz, Yitzchok. "Halakhic Approaches to the Resolution of Disputes Concerning the Disposition of PreEmbryos." *Tradition* 31, no. 1 (1996): 64–92.

Cahill, Lisa S. "Cloning: Religion-Based Perspectives." Testimony before the National Bioethics Advisory Commission, March 13, 1997.

Callahan, Daniel. "Religion and the Secularization of Bioethics." Special supplement to the *Hastings Center Report. Theology, Religious Traditions, and Bioethics* 20, no. 4 (1990).

Carey, E. J. "The Formal Use of the Hippocratic Oath for Medical Students at Commencement Exercises." *Bulletin of the Association of American Medical Colleges* 3 (1928): 159–166.

Clouser, K. D. "What Is Medical Ethics?" *Annals of Internal Medicine* 80, no. 4 (1974): 657–660.

Cole-Turner, Ronald, ed. "Statement on Cloning by the United Church of Christ Committee on Genetics." In *Human Cloning: Religious Responses*, pp 147–151. Louisville, Ky., 1997.

Committee on Doctrine of the National Conference of Catholic Bishops. *Ethical and Religious Directives for Catholic Health Care Services.* 4th ed. Washington, D.C., 2001.

Committee on Jewish Law and Standards of the Rabbinical Assembly. *Responsa 1991–2000.* New York, 2002.

Congregation for the Doctrine of the Faith. *The Gift of Life (Donum Vitae): Instruction on Respect for Human Life in its Origin and the Dignity of Procreation: Replies to Certain Questions of the Day.* Washington, D.C., 1987. Available at: www.nccbuscc.org/prolife/tdocs/donumvitae.htm.

Crawford, S. Cromwell. *Hindu Bioethics for the Twenty-First Century.* Albany, N.Y., 2003.

Cronin, D. A. *The Moral Law in Regard to the Ordinary and Extraordinary Means of Conserving Life.* Rome, 1958. See pages 47–87.

Dombrowski, Daniel A., and Robert Deltete. *A Brief, Liberal, Catholic Defense of Abortion.* Urbana, Ill., 2000.

Dorff, Elliot N. "Human Cloning: A Jewish Perspective." Testimony before the National Bioethics Commission, March 14, 1997.

Dorff, Elliot N. *Matters of Life and Death: A Jewish Approach to Modern Medical Ethics.* Philadelphia, 1998.

Dorman, J. "The Hippocratic Oath." *College Health: Journal of the American College Health Association* 44 (1995): 86.

Ebrahim, Abul F. M. *Abortion, Birth Control, and Surrogate Parenting: An Islamic Perspective.* Indianapolis, Ind., 1989.

Ebrahim, Abul F. M. "The Living Will (Wasiyat Al-Hayy): A Study of its Legality in the Light of Islamic Jurisprudence." *Medical Law* 19 (2000): 147–160.

Epstein, I., ed. *Yevamot* 69b. In *Babylonian Talmud.* Complete English translation. London, 1935–1952.

Feldman, David. *Birth Control in Jewish Law: Marital Relations, Contraception, and Abortion as Set Forth in the Classic Texts of Jewish Law.* New York, 1980.

Freedman, Benjamin. *Duty and Healing: Foundations of a Jewish Bioethic.* New York, 1999.

Ginzberg, Louis. *Responsa of Professor Louis Ginzberg.* Edited by David Golinkin. New York, 1996.

Golinkin, David. *Responsa in a Moment: Halakhic Responses to Contemporary Issues.* Jerusalem, 2000.

Gordis, Daniel H. "Wanted—The Ethical in Jewish Bio-Ethics." *Judaism* 38, no. 1 (1989): 28–40.

Gustafson, James M. "Context vs. Principles: A Misplaced Debate in Christian Ethics." *Harvard Theological Review* 58 (1965): 171–202.

Gustafson, James M. "The Transcendence of God and the Value of Human Life." *Catholic Theological Society of America Proceedings* 23 (1968).

Gustafson, James M. "A Protestant Ethical Approach." In *The Morality of Abortion,* edited by John T. Noon, pp. 403–412. Cambridge, Mass., 1970.

Gustafson, James M. "God's Transcendence and the Value of Human Life." In *Christian Ethics and the Community,* p. 140. Philadelphia, 1971.

Haas, J. M. Letter from the Pope John Center, submitted to the National Bioethics Advisory Commission. March 31, 1997.

Hathout, M. "Cloning: Who Will Set the Limits?" *The Minaret* 19, no. 8 (1997): 81–85.

Herring, Basil F. *Jewish Ethics and Halakah for Our Time: Sources and Commentary.* New York, 1984.

Jakobovits, Immanuel. *Jewish Medical Ethics.* New York, 1975.

Johnson, James T. "Protestantism: History of Protestant Medical Ethics." In *Encyclopedia of Bioethics,* edited by Warren T. Reich, vol. 3, pp. 1364–1372. New York, 1978.

Jonsen, Albert R. *A Short History of Bioethics.* Oxford, 2000.

Keown, Damien. *Buddhism and Bioethics.* New York, 1995; reprint, 2001.

Khomeini, R. "Rulings on the Final Moments of Life." In *Ahkam-e Pezeshki,* edited by M. Rohani and F. Noghani, p. 306. Rulings nos. 1–3. Tehran, 1998.

Klein, Isaac. *Responsa and Halakhic Studies.* New York, 1975.

Kliever, L. D. *Dax's Case: Essays in Medical Ethics and Human Meaning.* Dallas, Tex.,1989.

Lammers, Stephen E., and Allen Verhey, eds. *On Moral Medicine: Theological Perspectives in Medical Ethics.* 2d ed. Grand Rapids, Mich., 1998.

Lander, E. S., L. M. Linton, B. Birren, C. Nusbaum, M. C. Zody, J. Baldwin, et al. "Initial Sequencing and Analysis of the Human Genome." *Nature* 409, no. 6822 (2001): 860–921.

Lubarsky, Sandra. "Judaism and the Justification of Abortion for Nonmedical Reasons." *Journal of Reform Judaism* 31 (1984): 1–13.

Luria, Rabbi Judah of Prague. "Bu'ir Hagolah." In *Maharal Me-Prague,* pp. 38–39. Jerusalem, 1971.

May, William E. "Feeding and Hydrating the Permanently Unconscious and Other Vulnerable Persons." *Issues in Law and Medicine* 3 (1987): 208.

May, William E. *An Introduction to Moral Theology.* Huntington, Ind., 1994.

McCormick, Richard A. *How Brave a New World? Dilemmas in Bioethics.* Garden City, N.Y., 1981a. See "To Save or Let Die: The Dilemma of Modern Medicine" (p. 345) and "The Quality of Life, the Sanctity of Life" (p. 399).

McCormick, Richard. A. *Notes on Moral Theology: 1965–1980.* Washington D.C., 1981b. See pages 709–711.

Moraczewski, Albert S. "Cloning and the Church." Testimony of the Pope John Center before the National Bioethics Advisory Commission, March 13, 1997.

National Bioethics Advisory Commission. "Stem Cell Research and Therapy: A Judeo-Biblical Perspective." *Ethical Issues in Human Stem Cell Research,* Vol. 3: *Religious Perspectives.* Rockville, Md., 1999–2000.

Newman, Louis E. "Woodchoppers and Respirators: The Problem of Interpretation in Contemporary Jewish Ethics." In *Contemporary Jewish Ethics and Morality: A Reader,* edited by Elliot N. Dorff and Louis E. Newman, pp 140–160. Oxford, 1995.

Nuffield Council on Bioethics. "Stem Cell Therapy: The Ethical Issues." 2000. Available from the Nuffield Foundation: www.nuffieldfoundation.org/bioethics/publication/stemcell/p_0022221.html.

O'Rourke, Kevin D., and Philip Boyle. *Medical Ethics: Sources of Catholic Teachings.* 3d ed. Washington, D.C., 1999.

Pauls, Merril, and Roger C. Hutchinson. "Bioethics for Clinicians: Protestant Bioethics." *Canadian Medical Association Journal* 166 (2002): 339–343.

Percival, Thomas. "Medical Ethics or a Code of Institutes and Precepts, Adapted to the Professional Conduct of Physicians and Surgeons." In *Cross-Cultural Perspectives in Medical Ethics,* edited by R. M. Veatch, pp 29–38. 2d ed. Boston, Mass., 2000.

Peters, Ted. *Playing God? Genetic Determinism and Human Freedom.* New York, 1996.

Pope John Paul II. *Evangelium Vitae, On the Value and Inviolability of Human Life.* Vatican City, 1995.

Pope Paul VI. *Pastoral Constitution on the Church in the Modern World* (1965). Boston, 1966.

President's Commission on Ethical Problems in Medicine and Biomedical and Behavior Research. *Defining Death: A Report of the Medial, Legal, and Ethical Issues in the Definition of Death.* Washington, D.C., 1981.

President's Commission on Ethical Problems in Medicine and Biomedical and Behavior Research. *Deciding to Forgo Life-Sustaining Treatment: A Report on the Ethical and Legal Issues in Treatment Decisions.* Washington, D.C., 1982.

Proceedings of the Committee on Jewish Law and Standards of the Conservative Movement: 1927–1970. Edited by David Golinkin. New York, 1997.

Proceedings of the Committee on Jewish Law and Standards of the Conservative Movement: 1980–1985. New York, 1998.

Proceedings of the Committee on Jewish Law and Standards of the Conservative Movement: 1986–1990. New York, 2001.

Rae, Scott, and Paul Cox. *Bioethics: A Christian Approach in a Pluralistic Age.* Grand Rapids, Mich., 1999.

Rahman, Abdul, and Ahmed, Elkadi. "The Islamic Code of Medical Ethics." *World Medical Journal* 29 (1982): 78–80.

Ramsey, Paul. *Basic Christian Ethics.* New York, 1950.

Ramsey, Paul. *Nine Modern Moralists.* Englewood Cliffs., N.J., 1962.

Ramsey, Paul. "Moral and Religious Implications of Genetic Control." In *Genetics and the Future of Man,* edited by John D. Roslansky, pp. 107–169. New York, 1966.

Ramsey, Paul. *Fabricated Man: The Ethics of Genetic Control.* New Haven, Conn.,1970a.

Ramsey, Paul. *The Patient as Person: Explorations in Medical Ethics.* New Haven, Conn., 1970b.

Responsa for Today. Schecter Institute for Jewish Studies. Available at: www.responsafortoday.com/eng_index.html.

Responsa Project: The Global Jewish Database at Bar-Ilan University. Available at: www.biu.ac.il/JH/Responsa. A compendium of classical Jewish texts.

Responsa Seridei Esh, vol. 3, no. 127. Jerusalem, 1966.

Rosner, Fred, and J. David Bleich, eds. *Jewish Bioethics.* New York, 1979.

Rosner, Fred. "Jewish Attitude Toward Euthanasia." In *Jewish Bioethics,* edited by Fred Rosener and J. David Bleich, pp. 253–265. New York, 1979.

Sachedina, Aziz. "Islamic Perspectives on Cloning." Testimony before the National Bioethics Advisory Commission, March 14, 1997.

Shapiro, H. T. "Ethical Dilemmas and Stem Cell Research." *Science* 285 (1999): 2065.

Tendler, Moshe. "Testimony before the National Bioethics Advisory Commission." March 14, 1997.

Tendler, Moshe, ed. and trans. *Responsa of Rav Moshe Feinstein,* vol. 1: *Care of the Critically Ill.* Hoboken, N.J., 1998.

Van Bommel, A. "Medical Ethics from the Muslim Perspective." *Acta Neurochir* 74, supplement (1999): 17–27.

Verhey, A. "Cloning: Revisiting an Old Debate." *Kennedy Institute of Ethics Journal* 4, no. 3: (1994): 227–234.

Waldenberg, Eliezar. *Tzitz Eli'ezer* (Jerusalem) 7 (1963): 190.

Waldenberg, Eliezar. *Tzitz Eli'ezer* (Jerusalem) 8 (1965): 218–219.

Waldenberg, Eliezar. *Tzitz Eli'ezer* (Jerusalem) 9 (1967): 225–240.

Waldenberg, Eliezar. *Tzitz Eli'ezer* (Jerusalem) 15 (1980): 43.

Walter, Jacob. *The Fetus and Fertility: Essays and Responsa.* Pittsburgh, Penn., 1998.

Walter, Jacob, and Mose Zemer, eds. *Death and Euthanasia in Jewish Law: Essays and Responsa.* Pittsburgh, Pa., 1995.

Wildes, Kevin, and Alan C. Mitchell, eds. *Choosing Life: A Dialogue on Evangelium Vitae.* Washington, D.C., 1997.

Williams, John R. *Christian Perspectives on Bioethics: Religious Values and Public Policy in a Pluralistic Society.* Toronto, 1997.

Zohar, Noam J. *Alternatives in Jewish Bioethics.* Albany, N.Y., 1997.

LISA SOLEYMANI LEHMANN (2005)

MEDICINE MAN SEE SHAMANISM

MEDITATION.

MEDITATION. The terms *meditation* and *contemplation* are applied to a variety of manifestations throughout the historical and cultural geography of world religions. *Meditation* and *contemplation* are used in English to translate a number of specialized terms in several different languages. Attention will be paid here to the etymologies of these terms in English, so that the reader may determine the suitability of their application to foreign terms. Some general categories through which meditative and contemplative systems can be described will be introduced.

Confusion sometimes arises when the words *meditation* and *contemplation* are used interchangeably. However, a working distinction between the two terms can be suggested. Meditation is considered preparatory and contributory to the achievement of contemplation. Meditation involves concentration, the narrowing of the focus of consciousness to a single theme, symbol, catechism, or doctrine, yet it remains cognitive and intellectual. Meditation is usually rumination on a particular religious subject, while contemplation is a direct intuitive seeing, using spiritual faculties beyond discursive thought and ratiocination. In the felicitous phrase of Richard of Saint-Victor, a Christian theologian of the twelfth century, "Meditation investigates, contemplation wonders."

The English word *meditate* comes from the Latin *meditari. Meditari* connotes deep, continued reflection, a concentrated dwelling in thought. Contemplation is derived from the Latin *cum* ("with") and *templum* ("a consecrated place"). Frequently, contemplation is itself a spiritual state and serves as the end of an ascetic quest. Particularly in the monotheistic traditions of Judaism, Christianity, and Islam, this state is sometimes considered tantamount to the beatific vision bestowed upon the individual through the grace of God. This distinction between *meditation* and *contemplation* will serve for an examination of the following materials, but the reader should bear in mind the difficulty of translating these concepts from one language and culture to another.

As for the morphology of the theories and practices indicated by the terms *meditation* and *contemplation,* it may be useful to mention some categories of spiritual discipline. Meditation leading to contemplation can be apophatic. Involved here is an emptying procedure, in which the individual systematically removes from consciousness any content that is not the object of the quest. In Christian mysticism, this type of path is referred to as the *via negativa;* it is also an important technique in Buddhism.

Other forms of meditation and contemplation may be termed cataphatic. In this type of practice, a specific image, idea, role, or deity is held in the mind's eye. The object of the individual is to assimilate, or to participate in some way with, the chosen object. Apophatic forms of meditation tend to be more speculative, cognitive, and intellectual, at least in their early stages. They tend to be centered in the mind. Cataphatic forms of meditation and contemplation, on the other hand, tend to be more emotional and devotional. They tend to be centered in the heart. In what follows, meditation and contemplation represent a continuum, with different systems and traditions illustrating shifting perspectives within a descriptive framework that opposes the apophatic and speculative to the cataphatic and affective.

WESTERN TRADITIONS. The practice of prayer has always held a central place in the Western traditions of Judaism, Christianity, and Islam. Although prayer may devolve into meditation and even into contemplation, these are more directly the concerns of the mystical and, in many instances, the monastic dimensions of these traditions.

Judaism. Meditation and contemplation in the Jewish tradition acknowledge the centrality and authority of the Hebrew scriptures. Reading and interpreting the Torah require concentration and discursive meditation. This meditation led to the development of commentary, such as the Mishnah and the Talmud, and schools came into being that fostered an experiential approach. Heavily influenced by gnosticism and Hellenism, this movement is referred to as *heikhalot* mysticism. Ascetical practices culminated in a contemplative ascent of the soul through seven heavens to reach its final home in a state of beatitude. The final state is viewed as one in which the mystic stands before the throne of God and sees and hears directly. There is no experience of mystical union, and God remains "wholly other." This tradition remained essentially cataphatic and nonaffective, although the symbolism of the ascent and the attainment of ecstatic consciousness is characteristic of Jewish contemplation.

A more immanentist approach to the contemplation of God developed within the Hasidic tradition. One can trace here the influence of Philo Judaeus, a Jewish philosopher of the first century CE who later was to have an important influence on Christianity. In Hasidic contemplation, the transcendent majesty of God is preserved by making the object of contemplation the *shekhinah,* or the spirit of the living God. God can be contemplated directly only at the end of the world, or the Day of Yahveh. The Jewish contemplative almost always retains a sense of the distance between himself and God. The quest ends not with mystical union but with a sense of adhesion (or being joined) to God, which is short of an actual union.

The qabbalistic school from the thirteenth century onward produced some major developments in the Jewish meditative and contemplative tradition. A major exponent of this school was the Spaniard Avraham ben Shemuʾel Abulafia. He developed a meditative technique designed to release the individual from bondage to the sensible forms and images that one must deal with in everyday life and that delimit the soul. Meditation is an avenue through which the soul can come to apprehend more than the forms of nature. Abulafia looks for a means to deautomatize the human faculties from the normal preoccupation with daily events. He seizes upon a system of meditation based on the Hebrew alphabet. The letters of the alphabet are sufficiently abstract so as not to preoccupy the mind with any specific meaning, but concrete enough to supply an object of intense focus and concentration. The letters of the alphabet are regarded by the meditator as constituents of the holy name of God. The meditator is instructed to combine and recombine the letters of the alphabet without any attempt to form words, thereby constructing a kind of nonrepresentational mystical logic. Such exercise produces interior freedom and detachment from natural objects and prepares the adept for the final achievement: the pure contemplation of the divine name.

Christianity. Meditation and contemplation, particularly within monastic circles, reached a high degree of differentiation and sophistication in the Christian tradition. The practices of the early church took form in an atmosphere influenced by Hermetic literature and the philosophy of Neoplatonism. Syncretic in nature, the Hermetic books present the theme of a mystical ascent to the knowledge of God. This important image (found also in Jewish mysticism) becomes central to the mysticism of Christianity. The idea of an ascent from the many to the One is taken over from the thought of the Neoplatonist Plotinus. Plotinus describes four movements in the ascent to divine knowledge: (1) purgation in the practice of virtue; (2) the development of thought beyond sense perception; (3) the transcendence of thought in the achievement of union; and (4) the final absorption in the One. In the Christian circles of third-century Alexandria, these non-Christian ideas came to be absorbed into the tradition and to exert an important influence. Two important figures of this development were Clement and Origen.

For Clement, meditation led to the apprehension of the intelligible realities and then, through *gnosis* as a gift of Christ, to hidden spiritual realities. Reflective reading of, and meditation on, the scriptures in order to discern this hidden meaning was important. Within this metaphorical framework, Origen introduces the symbol of a contemplative marriage between the soul and the Logos (Christ).

Anchoritism, or withdrawal into the desert, was a form of spirituality in the early church that gave full rein to ascetic and meditative practices. Disengagement from the concerns of ordinary life provided a favorable atmosphere for the awakening of the spirit to the word of God. The austere life of the desert could produce a deep, inner quiet and was conducive to a life of continual meditation on the scriptures in an attempt to hear the word of God and to ascend the ladder of perfection through grace.

Within this context, as early as the third century, a life of constant prayer developed as an ideal for the anchorite.

The beginnings of the prayer of the heart, or the Jesus Prayer, are found here. The Jesus Prayer is an apothegm translated as "Lord Jesus Christ, Son of God, have mercy on me." The first reference to this prayer comes from the seventh century. The practice of the Jesus Prayer became important in Eastern Orthodox spirituality and in the development of the movement known as hesychasm. Meditation came to be seen, in a movement away from Neoplatonism, as more properly centered in the heart rather than in the mind. Control of breathing and the fixation of the gaze were important ancillaries to the constant repetition of the apothegm. This tradition has survived down to the present day in its major center on Mount Athos, in Greece.

The sixteenth and seventeenth centuries in the Roman Catholic church were a period of rationalization and the systematization of meditative and contemplative processes. This movement looked back to a medieval interest in the methodology of meditation developed among the Franciscans. A major figure in this movement was Bonaventure (1217–1274). In his *De triplici via,* he gives an exemplary statement for Western Christianity on the three processes of meditation: purgation, illumination, and union.

Ignatius Loyola (1495–1556), the founder of the Jesuits, wrote a treatise entitled *Spiritual Exercises,* in which he outlines a progression in meditative practice. His notions of meditation may not be so exalted as others, but his methods are of interest insofar as they involve cataphatic visualization techniques that bear some resemblance to Hindu and Buddhist practices. For example, Ignatius's fourth method requires that the practitioner choose a specific image, such as the passion or the resurrection of Jesus, and apply each of the five senses to that image. Thus, through seeing, hearing, smelling, tasting, and touching, the image is vivified in the consciousness of the meditator.

Teresa of Ávila (1515–1582) was a member of the Carmelite order. In her *Autobiography,* she narrates her meditative experiences and describes a period of spiritual desiccation followed by a series of ecstatic experiences. Teresa describes the latter in sexual images and draws upon the symbolism of the bride and the bridegroom, a symbolism that dates back at least to the time of Origen. In the *Autobiography* she catalogs degrees of meditation, using the symbolism of the husbandry of plants. She compares discursive meditation to watering the garden, bucket by bucket; recollection is analogous to the use of a water wheel, and quiet, to springs of water. Union is compared to a drenching rain.

Teresa's contemporary and fellow Carmelite, John of the Cross (1542–1591), modified the three ways of meditation developed by Bonaventure. Purgation is retained but illumination is replaced, using the bridal imagery, with betrothal, and union with spiritual marriage. Both Teresa of Ávila and John of the Cross describe a stage in contemplation referred to as the "dark night of the soul," an experience of alienation and isolation preparatory to illumination through the grace of God. This theme continues a long-standing tradition of a vision of God that includes the perception of darkness.

A major figure of the French church involved in codifying meditation was Francis of Sales (1567–1622). In his *Introduction to the Devout Life,* he teaches a five-step meditation. The preparatory stage of meditation involves three steps: (1) placing one's self in the presence of God, (2) praying for divine assistance, and (3) imagining a scene from the life of Jesus. The second step builds on the first through identification with those images that most affect the practitioner. In the third step feelings generated in the second are converted into acts of understanding and will. The fourth step involves thanksgiving and offering up the results of the meditation as a sacrifice, and petition for the putting into practice of the insights gained. The fifth step is the development of the "spiritual nosegay" or the preparation of some content of the meditation to sustain one in daily affairs.

Islam. The prophet Muḥammad (b. 570) considered his prophecy to be a continuation and reaffirmation of the Judeo-Christian tradition. The word *islām* means "submission" in Arabic; thus a Muslim is one who submits. Islamic theology emphasizes the transcendent majesty and unity of God. Humanity is considered to exist face to face with this transcendent majesty without intercessors. Humans are not expected to try to share the secrets of God.

In the more orthodox forms of Islam, daily prayer (*ṣalāt*) is one of the obligatory observances. Usually this prayer is conducted communally. Although it is also recommended that a Muslim perform *dhikr,* or remembrance of God, these practices are external formalities and not necessarily related to contemplation and meditation in the present sense.

By the eighth century, strict Muslim orthodoxy began to be challenged by Sufism, the generic term for Islamic mysticism. The Ṣūfī movement favored an interiorization and esotericization of the basic institutions of Islam. The orthodox religious attitudes of fear and obedience before the transcendence of God changed in Sufism to an attitude of ecstatic love of God and hope of union with him through a transcendence of the phenomenal self. Meditative and contemplative practices became an important part of this quest, and *dhikr* became a constant practice of the presence of God.

Ecstasy is the goal of the Ṣūfī path, and *dhikr,* in an expanded and intensified form, becomes a means to the goal. Techniques familiar in other traditions such as control of the breath, visualization of sacred words, and repetition of sacred phrases were adopted as important means to this end. The goal is termed *fanāʾ,* or annihilation of the lower self, which enables God through his grace to bestow on the mystic the rapture of union with him.

The Ṣūfīs developed sacred dance as a technique for the induction of ecstasy. The turning and whirling movements of the dance accompanied by hypnotic music and chanting of poetry bypassed the intellectual faculties and created a trancelike state of centeredness and concentration. The Mevlevi order of Ṣūfīs founded by Jalāl al-Dīn Rūmī institutionalized this practice as the foundation of its worship.

EASTERN TRADITIONS. Sophisticated psychologies and techniques of contemplation and meditation were developed within the spiritual traditions of India and China. These traditions, which antedate the beginning of the common era, developed independently until the introduction of Buddhism into China in the first century CE. Thereafter, India's techniques of meditation strongly influenced Chinese religious thought.

India. A concern for meditative asceticism, which runs through Indian religious history, can be traced as far back as the Indus Valley civilization of the third millennium BCE. Artifacts recovered from this civilization can be interpreted as representing individuals or deities in meditative attitudes.

Yoga. An early systematization of meditative technique is found in the *Yoga Sūtra* of Patañjali, dating from the third century BCE. Patañjali defines *yoga* as "the cessation of the modifications of the mind." This statement forms the basis of much of pan-Indian spirituality. The Yoga system is one of the classical *darśana*s, or "viewpoints," of Indian philosophy. The object of meditation and other ascetic practices is to still the mind and the emotions with which the individual usually identifies. When this is accomplished, consciousness can reflect the pure absolute spirit (or *puruṣa*), which is the principle of consciousness itself. Realization of the *puruṣa* as one's true and ultimate identity brings with it release (*mokṣa*) from the tendency to identify with temporal experience.

The mind (*citta*) in Yoga philosophy is considered to be the repository of *saṃskāra* (the root impressions of past deeds). These impressions are stored from present and past lives in unconscious layers of the psyche and, in turn, produce binding proclivities, good and bad habits, and all forms of limited vision and false identification, which modify and determine a person's life in the unenlightened state. The unenlightened mind is modified by its past ignorant experience and in turn perpetuates such modifications into the indefinite future. (This is the pan-Indian doctrine of *karman,* which becomes axiomatic for much of Indian spirituality.) Hence the importance of causing the modifications of the mind to cease so that the pure unconditioned spirit may become manifest in meditation.

A primary object of Yoga discipline is to bring the mind into a state of one-pointedness or intense concentration. Moral and ethical abstinences and observances form the first two limbs of an eightfold prescription for attaining this state. A comfortable posture (*āsana*) is recommended, especially one that enables the practitioner to keep the spine correctly aligned and one that can be comfortably held for protracted periods of time as the mind becomes abstracted from the body. Breath control (*prāṇāyāma*) is then recommended, since states of breathing and states of consciousness correspond closely to each other. A calming and quieting of the breath produces a corresponding calming and quieting of the mind.

As concentration deepens, the next limb of Yoga, *pratyāhāra* (withdrawal of the senses from their objects), contributes to a further interiority. The next step is *dharaṇa,* or the concentration of the mind on a single object. This is followed by *dhyāna,* or the achievement of an uninterrupted nonverbal current of consciousness focused on the meditative object. The eighth and last limb of this meditative program is *samādhi,* in which the goal of complete cessation of the modifications of the mind is achieved, and a transcendent awareness of one's ultimate identity as *puruṣa,* or unconditional spirit, is attained. In this state of ecstasy, the normal ego sense and the experience of a dichotomy between subject and object is overcome. Yoga discipline in a variety of forms becomes an important ingredient in several Indian spiritual traditions and religions, including Jainism, various forms of Hinduism, and Buddhism.

Hinduism. *Hinduism* is a generic term used to refer to a variety of religious manifestations within the Indian subcontinent and other areas subject to Indian influence. In the early history of Hinduism, a stage referred to as Brahmanism, there was a movement away from the practice of exoteric ritual and toward meditative interiority and realization. As the tradition developed, Hindus came to be divided into three main sects: the Vaiṣṇava, the Śaiva, and the Śākta.

Vaiṣṇavism. The Vaiṣṇavas, worshipers of the god Viṣṇu and his many incarnations, developed a form of active, affective, and cataphatic meditation in which chanting, singing, and dancing were used to induce transic absorption into the deity. Perhaps the most popular incarnation of Viṣṇu is the deity Kṛṣṇa, whose worship is *bhakti* ("devotion"). In addition to performances of chanting and dance, a devotee was expected to remain ever mindful of his object of devotion. In turn, the deity extends his grace and love to the devotee. In both Vaiṣṇava and Śaiva forms of theistic meditation, the emotions are given a much freer rein than in the more abstract classical Yoga system. Transmutation of the emotions through devotion to Viṣṇu, Śiva, and their *avatāra*s became popular and had a far-reaching effect on Indian art and literature.

Devotional theism borrowed some of its elements from Sanskrit poetics. The term *bhāva,* which refers to an intense personal emotion in poetic theory, was adapted by the Vaiṣṇavas to refer to the meditative attitude that a devotee assumes toward Kṛṣṇa. There are four types of contemplative mood, determined by the form of relationship with the deity. These range from a relationship to Kṛṣṇa as supreme deity, as friend, as brother, and, perhaps most importantly, as lover. A devotee's chosen *bhāva* was to be cultivated through meditation, chanting, and dance until he experienced himself as the friend or lover of Kṛṣṇa. Continual absorption into these various roles enabled the adherent to experience the love and the personality of the deity.

Śaivism and Śaktism. The devotees of Śiva developed their own forms of contemplative worship. One is the growth of a cult dedicated to Śakti, the female consort of

Śiva. Śakti is the active female energy of the universe in contradistinction to the passive contemplative energy of Śiva himself. Śaktism became an important part of the Tantric manifestations of Hinduism. Tantric Hinduism developed several techniques of meditation, including the use of the *yantra.* A *yantra* is a geometric diagram that represents an abstract form or manifestation of a deity. Deities are essentially formless in their own nature but are thought to manifest themselves in a movement from the subtle to the gross, in the forms of sound, the geometric forms of the *yantra,* and the *mūrti* (or sculpted) image. A *yantra* is a series of triangles, squares, and circles emanating from a central point, which serves to focus the mind of the meditating yogin.

Visualization of a sculpted or painted form of the deity became important in Tantric meditation. The object was to achieve a high degree of absorption in the outward form so that it could be reproduced in complex detail within the mind of the meditator. When this stage was reached the outward form could be dispensed with. The general goal of Tantric meditation is the complete unification of the body, speech, and mind of the Tantric yogin with the body, speech, and mind of his chosen divinity. *Mantras*, symbolic sounds or phrases for the sound form of the divinity, were used in this practice. *Mudrās* were used in meditation also as symbolic gestures of the hands and body representing various stages of the unification process.

In *kuṇḍalinīyoga,* the macrocosmic Sakti is further identified, within the microcosm of the human body, as *kuṇḍalinī. Kuṇḍalinī* literally means "coiled" and refers to the visualization of Sakti as an energy within the body in the form of a sleeping serpent. This energy is associated with a meditative physiology of the subtle body of the human. The meditator visualizes six vital centers called *cakras* placed along the spine from its base to the crown of the head. The *cakras* are connected to each other by a central vein with two lesser veins, or channels, on either side. The object of the meditation and physical exercises of this form of Tantric yoga is to wake the latent energy of Śakti coiled at the base of the spine and to cause it to enter the central vein. As *kuṇḍalinī* ascends and is drawn upward through meditation, it energizes the six *cakras* until it reaches the topmost *cakra,* where it is reunited with Śiva. At this point the body of the yogin and the body of the cosmos are resolved into the primal unity.

Buddhism. Buddhism is a tradition that seeks to penetrate the veil of appearances and social conditioning and, through meditative insight, to achieve a vision of the truth of reality. This vision leads to liberation from the round of karmic cycles and the achievement of ultimate freedom in *nirvāṇa. Nirvāṇa* is the goal of Buddhist ascesis subsumed under the term *bhāvana,* or meditation. *Bhāvana* has two secondary objectives: the first is the achievement of *śamatha,* or calm; the second is *vipaśyanā,* insight or higher vision.

As a foundation for other Buddhist meditation practices, a monk starts with the practice of mindfulness (Pali, *sati).* This practice is basic to both *śamatha* (Pali, *samatha*) and *vipaśyanā* (Pali, *vipassanā*) and can be used for both calming and higher vision. The practice of mindfulness, or total awareness, takes place in four main areas: the body itself, the sensations, thought, and mental objects. Mindfulness of the body begins with the observation of breathing. Strict attention is paid to inhalation and exhalation, note being taken of the duration of each as the practitioner becomes aware of this usually unconscious activity. Such concentration involves narrowing of the mind's focus. The effects of mindfulness of breathing include a refined awareness of the entire body and a sense of tranquillity.

Mindfulness of the body is next applied to a monk's postures and movements. Every bodily action is performed with complete awareness and consciousness. This discipline brings into awareness bodily activity, which normally goes on beyond the conscious level. As activities are performed, mindfulness tranquilizes, calms, and controls the body; mindfulness can then proceed with an examination of the constituent parts of the body, external and internal, and a breakdown of the body into its primary physical elements. These practices break up any tendency to identify with the body.

Mindfulness is then applied to the sensations that are discerned as pleasant, unpleasant, or neutral. In a continuing progression, from the gross to the more subtle, mindfulness is then applied to the mind, or thought itself, and its objects. Attention is paid to each thought as it occurs, whether it is with or without such factors as passion, hatred, delusion, or freedom. The objective is detachment and a loosening of the tendency to identify with any factors of experience. With the achievement of detachment, the monk has an increased ability to respond actively to the actual circumstances of life.

Through concentrative attention, a monk sees the momentary quality of life, and sees that a moment of experience arises based on temporary causes and conditions. The monk thus can see the real nature of experience, which had previously been obscured by incorrect mental fabrications and the false projection of permanent identity on a transient stream of moments.

The Buddhist *śamatha* practices are associated with *dhyāna,* or the achievement of meditative absorption. *Dhyāna* practice continues the work of mindfulness into an even greater experience of detachment, one in which contact with the normal content of worldly experience is gradually attenuated and almost altogether eliminated. The *dhyānas* (absorptions) are as follows: four absorptions with form, four absorptions without form, and finally the cessation of conception and feeling. These stages represent a gradual elimination of the verbal, discursive, and affective contents of the mind. They lead a monk gradually out of the world of sense-based experience to a new, detached interior dimension. These stages are increasingly independent of the external world and signify a developing autonomy on the part of the monk. The monk is no longer bound by the accidental and chaotic sensory stimuli of the world of ordinary experience or by intellectual concerns, and begins to acquire the power of turning away from the "given world" and toward the ability to "create" an interior world of attenuated, simplified, and peaceful content. This is the meaning of *śamatha,* the calming of the contents of consciousness, and the attainment of release from subjection to external circumstances.

Calming, transic absorption and insight are important features of Buddhist ascesis; they continue to be fundamental in both Hīnayāna and Mahāyāna schools. The Vajrayāna, or Tantric form of Buddhism, also developed elaborate visualization meditations in which carefully delineated images of deities, or *maṇḍalas*, were reproduced with great exactitude within the mind of the meditator. The Tantric form of Buddhist meditation became firmly established in Tibet.

China. Contemplation and meditation have held a position of high importance in Chinese religious traditions. This is particularly true of the indigenous Daoist tradition and the various schools of Buddhism imported from India.

Daoism. Daoism in its early literary form (here referred to as "classical Daoism") and its later offshoot, which is usually termed "Neo-Daoism," are usually thought of as the primary province of contemplation in the Chinese indigenous tradition.

Laozi (seventh century BCE?) and Zhuangzu (365–290 BCE?) are the two main figures of classical Daoism. Since their existence as historical figures is questioned, here they shall be referred to only by their works, now known as the *Laozu* (or *Dao de jing*) and the *Zhuangzi.* These two books contain the early formulation of the Daoist worldview and ethos. In Daoism there is a contrast between the superficialities of conventional reality and the insight achieved by the Daoist sage. The task of Daoist contemplation is to move from a partial and self-centered view of things to a holistic view of the cosmos and its spontaneously functioning dynamism.

The Dao is the primary object of contemplation and meditation in the Daoist tradition. It is the ultimate principle beyond phenomenal manifestations and yet within which all phenomenal manifestations are brought forth and undergo change. The first chapter of the *Dao de jing* emphasizes the ineffability of the true Dao:

> The Dao (Way) that can be told of is not the Eternal Dao;
> The name that can be named is not the eternal name.
> The Nameless is the origin of Heaven and Earth;
> The Named is the mother of all things. (Zhan, 1963, p. 139)

The Dao is the substratum that remains when all verbal and physical phenomena are discarded. Awareness of the Dao can be reached through apophatic contemplation and meditation, that is, only through direct meditative experience. In order to attain inner illumination, the Daoist sage has to follow a way of unknowing, of abandoning learning in favor of looking directly into himself. Real education for the Daoist, in the phrase of Zhuangzu, is "sitting and forgetting."

Buddhism. From the time when Buddhism entered China from India and Central Asia around the first century BCE, the Chinese were exposed to a bewildering variety of Buddhist teachings. The major Indian schools were represented, including the Madhyamika (Sanlun) and the Yogacara (Faxiang). Another school that developed in China, the Tiantai, promulgated an elaborate meditative regime based on a variety of scriptural sources. The Huayan school developed a teaching and meditative discipline that led to a vision of the harmony of totality and the mutual interpenetration of all things.

Two schools of Chinese Buddhism, the Chan and the Jingtu (Pure Land school), developed different understandings of meditation practice, a difference often referred to as that between "self-power" and "other-power." "Other-power" refers to a reliance on the grace of a deity for the achievement of salvation, an idea characteristic of the Pure Land school. The idea behind this emphasis is that human beings are not strong enough to bring themselves to *nirvāṇa* through their own meditative practices. Paradoxically, an adherent of this school is advised to call on the name of the saving deity (Amitabha; Chin., Omituo Fo; Jpn., Amida) with an undivided mind, thus constituting a mantralike form of apophthegmatic practice. Meditation in the "other-power" schools tends toward the affective and cataphatic.

"Self-power" schools, like Chan (Jpn., Zen) Buddhism, are more austere and apophatic. The word *chan* is a transliteration of the Sanskrit term *dhyāna,* which means "meditation" or "contemplation." The Chan school emphasized "self-power" and sitting in formless meditation. Because of its exclusive emphasis on meditation, Chan developed an iconoclastic attitude toward other forms of religious observance. In Chan, personal enlightenment through intense meditation was the goal, and nothing was allowed to stand in the way of this pursuit, not even the religious and doctrinal trappings of Buddhism itself.

In Chan monasteries, meditation occupied a major part of the daily routine. Formal meditation usually took place in a separate building erected for the purpose and was supervised by a senior monk. Attention was paid to details of technique, including posture in the lotus position, with an erect spine, and the achievement of comfort and relaxation therein. Chan meditation focuses on the process of breathing, leading to a gradual withdrawal from external stimuli. A monk is instructed simply to observe the thoughts, feelings, and visions that may come into consciousness, and let them pass away of their own accord. When a monk is successful in detaching from both external and internal stimuli, the result is an experience of stillness and emptiness. This breaks up the tendency to identify with the body and mind and provides a new perspective on ordinary experience, marked by detachment, equanimity, and freedom from a sense of the ego as a reference point for experience. This is a realization beyond doctrine and beyond words themselves. The semilegendary founder of Chan in China, Bodhidharma, is said to have described Chan as "a special transmission outside the scriptures; no dependence on words and letters; direct pointing at the mind of man; seeing into one's own nature and the attainment of Buddhahood."

SEE ALSO Alphabets; Attention; Breath and Breathing; Dhikr; Eremitism; Mantra; Mudrā; Mystical Union in Judaism, Christianity, and Islam; Mysticism; Nianfo; Postures and Gestures; Samadhi; Via Negativa; Yantra; Yoga.

BIBLIOGRAPHY

Chan, Wing-tsit, trans. and ed. *Instructions for Practical Living, and Other Neo-Confucian Writings by Wang Wangming.* New York, 1963.

Chan, Wing-tsit, trans. and comp. *A Source Book in Chinese Philosophy.* Princeton, 1963.

Chang Zhongyuan, trans. and ed. *Original Teachings of Chan Buddhism.* New York, 1969.

Conze, Edward. *Buddhist Meditation.* London, 1956.

de Bary, Wm. Theodore, Wing-tsit Chan, and Burton Watson, comps. *Sources of Chinese Tradition.* New York, 1960.

Ernest, John, J. E. L. Oulton, and Henry Chadwick, eds. *Alexandrian Christianity: Selected Translations of Clement and Origen.* London, 1954.

Francis of Sales. *Introduction to the Devout Life.* Rev. ed. Translated and edited by John K. Ryan. New York, 1972.

Kadloubovsky, Eugènie, and G. E. H. Palmer, trans. *Writings from the Philokalia on Prayer of the Heart.* London, 1951.

Naranjo, Claudio, and Robert E. Ornstein. *On the Psychology of Meditation.* New York, 1971.

Needleman, Jacob. *Los Christianity.* New York, 1980.

Radhakrishnan, Sarvepalli, and Charles A. Moore, eds. *A Source Book in Indian Philosophy.* Princeton, 1957.

Schimmel, Annemarie. *Mystical Dimensions of Islam.* Chapel Hill, N. C., 1975.

Scholem, Gershom. *Major Trends in Jewish Mysticism* (1941). New York, 1961.

Suzuki, D. T. *Zen and Japanese Culture.* 2d ed., rev. & enl. Princeton, 1959.

Tart, Charles T. *States of Consciousness.* New York, 1975.

Tsunoda, Ryusaku, Wm. Theodore de Bary, and Donald Keene, comps. *Sources of Japanese Tradition.* 2 vols. New York, 1958.

FREDERIC B. UNDERWOOD (1987)

MEGALITHIC RELIGION

This entry consists of the following articles:

PREHISTORIC EVIDENCE
HISTORICAL CULTURES

MEGALITHIC RELIGION: PREHISTORIC EVIDENCE

In Neolithic western Europe, large stones, or megaliths (from the Greek *megas*, "great," and *lithos*, "stone"), were used for construction of tombs, temples, rings, alignments, and stelae. The largest number of some fifty thousand megalithic monuments are in Spain and Portugal, France, Britain, southern Sweden, and northern Germany. The terms *megalithic culture* and *megalithic religion* have been applied to the massive stone monuments. However, neither a separate megalithic culture nor isolated megalithic religion existed. The culture that produced megalithic monuments was a part of the western European Neolithic and Aeneolithic (a transitional period between the Neolithic and Bronze ages). It consisted of a number of regional culture groups whose religion can be understood in the context of the gynecocentric Old European (i. e., pre-Indo-European) religion inherited from Upper Paleolithic times. Huge stones were used wherever they were readily available. Monumental architecture, motivated by religious ideas, emerged synchronically with the rise of a sedentary way of life.

Carbon-14 dating has established that western European megaliths were built over a span of at least three thousand years, from the fifth to the second millennium BCE. They were constructed earlier than the Egyptian pyramids and do not descend from forms in the Near East; the majority of archaeologists now believe that their development was indigenous. If there was any diffusion of ideas, it occurred along the seaboard and from the Atlantic coast toward the interior.

Megalithic structures fall into four main categories. The first is the temple, found in the Mediterranean islands of Malta and Gozo. Maltese temples have solid walls of very large stone slabs, and their floor plan has apses that recall the shape of a seated or standing goddess. The second and largest category of megalithic structures is the burial chamber, which is subdivided into dolmens (monuments of two or more upright stones supporting a horizontal slab), passage graves, court tombs, and gallery graves. Some passage graves are monumental buildings whose chambers have corbeled vaults; for example, Newgrange in the Boyne River valley, Ireland, which dates from 3200 to 3000 BCE, rises twenty feet above the ground. The third category is the single upright stone, or menhir (the word comes from the Welsh *maen*, "a stone," and *hir*, "long"). Some of the menhirs found in Brittany are as high as six meters. A special kind of menhir, called a statue menhir, is sculpted to represent a divinity. The fourth category consists of grouped standing stones, placed either in rows or in elliptical rings.

Archaeologists once assumed that these megalithic monuments had evolved from simple to more complex forms, but the new chronology shows that some very elaborate buildings predate the simple gallery graves.

Temples and tombs were built in the likeness of the Mother of the Dead or Mother Earth's pregnant belly or womb; this is the key to understanding megalithic structures and their floor plans. The idea that caves and caverns are natural manifestations of the primordial womb of the goddess is not Neolithic in origin; it goes back to the Paleolithic, when a cave's narrow passages, oval-shaped areas, clefts, and small cavities were marked or painted entirely in red, a color that must have symbolized the color of the mother's generative organs. The rock-cut tombs and hypogea of Malta, Sicily, and Sardinia are usually uterine, egg-shaped, or roughly anthropomorphic. Red soil is found under each temple of Malta.

In western Europe, the body of the goddess is magnificently realized as the megalithic tomb. The so-called cruciform and double-oval tombs, as well as Maltese temples, are unmistakably human in shape. Some monuments replicate the ample contours of figurines of the pregnant goddess.

The earliest form of the grandiose chamber tombs is the passage grave, which consists of a corridor and principal chamber. The natural cave, with its connotations of the goddess's womb (vagina and uterus), was probably the inspiration for the aboveground monumental structures that were erected later. The basic form of the passage grave—a shorter or longer passage and a round, corbel-roofed chamber—dates from the fifth millennium BCE in Portugal, Spain, and Brittany.

The interior structures of many Neolithic court tombs found in Ireland are outlined in a clearly anthropomorphic form. In addition to a large abdomen and head, some structures have legs and even eyes. The term *court cairns* or *court tombs* comes from the semicircular entrance, built with large stones, that characterize these structures. In many instances, the court and one or more chambers attached to the middle of the edifice are all that remain of the cairn (De Valera, 1960, pls. ii-xxx). However, better-preserved examples show that the court marks the inner contour of the anthropomorphic figure's open legs; the chambers or a corridorlike structure next to it, which leads into the very center of the mound, represents the vagina and uterus. The same symbolism is manifested in different areas and periods. The Sardinian *tombe di giganti* of the third and second millennia BCE, consisting of a long chamber entered through the center of a semicircular facade, do not differ in symbolism from the Irish court tombs.

The other type of grave is a long barrow whose shape resembles that of a bone, a symbol of death. Like the court tombs, this type of grave has an entrance at the front that leads into an anthropomorphic or uterus-shaped chamber.

Megalithic monuments were built to be seen. Careful excavations and reconstructions have shown that much attention was paid to their outer walls and facades. For example, a reconstruction of a monument at Barnenez, Brittany, dating from the fifth millennium BCE (Giot, 1980), revealed a concentric series of walls with the upper parts of the internal walls visible. Another great structure, dating from the first half of the third millennium BCE, was reconstructed at Silbury, Wiltshire, in southwestern England (Dames, 1976). Later excavations revealed that there were once wooden structures on top and beside the megalithic monuments that were just as important as the monuments. Postholes (indicating the presence of structures) have been observed in low barrows in Brittany, Britain, and Denmark. Traces of a timber facade, a porch at the front end of the barrow, and palisade enclosures have also been discovered (Madsen, 1979). The exquisite decoration in bas-relief on stones at entrances (as at Newgrange) implies that ceremonies took place in front of the cairns. Settlement debris in Irish court cairns has led some scholars to believe that chambered tombs and long barrows should be considered not burial places but shrines. However, excavations of megalithic chambers over the past two centuries have revealed skeletons, suggesting that the monuments served as repositories and were used collectively by the community. Some tombs have yielded as many as 350 disarticulated skeletons; others contain only 5 to 20 skeletons, discovered in compartments where they were placed after the flesh had decayed. In a few instances, skulls were found stacked carefully in corners.

Long cairns in Britain have yielded so-called mortuary houses, which were constructed of timber or stone and had plank floors. The rectangular mortuary houses found at Lochhill and Slewcairn contained three pits; the central one had two posts while the end pits held large split tree trunks (Masters, in Renfrew, 1981, p. 103). Mortuary houses are also known from Denmark (Becker, in Daniel and Kjaerum, 1973, pp. 75–80; Madsen, 1979). These mortuary buildings yielded deposits of charcoal, dark soil, cremated bone, an occasional child's skull, and flint tools, indicative of rituals including sacrifices. It seems that megalithic structures and long barrows, not unlike Christian cathedrals and churches, served as shrines and ossuaries. No doubt the large monuments, exquisitely built and engraved with symbols on curbstones and on inner walls, such as those at Knowth and Newgrange (O'Kelly, 1983), Ireland, and Gavrinis, Brittany, were sacred places where funeral, calendrical, and initiation rites took place. These monuments should be called not "tombs" but rather "tomb-shrines." The egg-shaped mound that covers the tomb-shrine of Newgrange is sprinkled with white quartz and looks like a huge egg-shaped dome. Probably it was meant to represent a gigantic cosmic egg, the womb of the world.

It is very likely that not all rituals were connected with death of humans and of all nature; some may have been initiation rites. Typically, the entrances to the tombs are narrow, resembling vulvas. One enters the mortuary house by either crawling or crouching along a narrow passage of stone. A wall of large curbstones, forming a forecourt, supports the mouth of the passage entrance on both sides. The structure may be a replica of the narrow and difficult entry into the mother goddess's womb.

In megalithic gallery graves of France, Switzerland, and the Funnel-necked Beaker culture in Germany, partition walls sometimes have round holes. Their meaning is apparent if the still-extant veneration of stones with holes is considered; belief in the miraculous power of holed stones is still found in Ireland, Scotland, England, France, and in many other European countries. Trees with holes play a related role. By crawling through the aperture of a stone or tree, a person is symbolically crawling into Mother Earth's womb and giving oneself to her. Strengthened by the goddess's powers, he or she is reborn. The crawling constitutes an initiation rite and is similar to sleeping in a cave, that is, "sleeping with the mother," which means to die and to be resurrected. Well-known sculptures of sleeping women from the Hal Saflieni hypogeum in Malta, dating from approximately 3000 BCE, most likely represent such an initiation rite.

The pregnant mother's (or earth mother's) generative potential is emphasized by the symbol of a mound and omphalos (navel), which is found engraved or in bas-relief on stone slabs. For example, relief engravings completely cover the surface of twenty-three erect slabs within the passage grave of Gavrinis, rendering an overall impression of symbolic unity. This sanctuary, one of the richest megalithic monuments in Brittany, is situated on a small island in the Gulf of Morbihan. The extensive use of wavy and concentric arc motifs is in harmony with the monument's aqueous environment. The dominant symbol found in this sanctuary is the concentric semicircle, interconnected with or surrounded by multiple wavy lines and serpentine forms. Several slabs are decorated with concentric arcs, piled one on top of the other in vertical columns. The arcs in the center are larger than the rest and have an omphalos-like protrusion. In my opinion, this image is a glyph of the goddess's rising generative force. Emphasis is on the anthropomorphic vulva or cervix sign in the center. (For other illustrations, see Twohig, 1981, pp. 172–175.)

Symbolically related to the passage grave of Gavrinis is the roughly triangular backstone of a passage grave from La Table des Marchands in Brittany. It has a vulva at its center, flanked by energy signs—four rows of hooks—meant to stimulate the life source. This symbolism is similar to that found on ancient Greek vases, in which the young goddess (Semele, Gaia) is depicted within an artificial mound surrounded by satyrs, goatmen, and Dionysos, who stimulate her generative powers. On other passage-grave slabs, the symbol of an artificial mound surmounted by a knob is surrounded by axes, another energy symbol, or in association with serpentine lines or snakes and footprints. Still other engravings of the same image (called a "buckler" in the archaeological literature, where it has been seriously misunderstood) show wavy lines emanating from the upper part, which may signify the resurgence of plant life. The beehive-shaped chamber, topped with a flat stone, found in passage graves appears to be a pregnant belly and an omphalos. The so-called buckler sign replicates the same idea in an engraving.

In his analysis of the Silbury Hill monument, Michael Dames shows that in Neolithic Britain the hill functioned as a metaphor for the goddess's pregnant belly (Dames, 1976). The entire structure forms an image of the goddess: the hill is her belly, the ditch forms the rest of her body in a seated or squatting position. The circular summit of Silbury Hill is the goddess's navel, or omphalos, in which her life-producing power is concentrated. Veneration of sacred hills was found in Europe until the twentieth century. Worship of the earth mother was celebrated on mountain summits crowned with large stones.

The second deity associated with the symbolism of the megalithic monuments is the goddess of death and regeneration in the guise of a bird of prey, usually an owl. Her image is engraved or modeled on statue menhirs, slabs of passage and gallery graves, and on walls of subterranean tombs. She herself, her eyes, or her signs appear also on schist plaques, phalanges (bones of toes or fingers), and stone cylinders laid in graves.

The characteristic features of the owl—round eyes and hooked beak—can be seen on the statue menhirs of southern France and Iberia, as well as in reliefs and charcoal drawings in the hypogea of the Paris Basin. The face is frequently schematized as a T shape or depicted with only eyes and brows or with a square head, surrounded by chevrons, in the center of the forehead. On the slabs of gallery graves of Brittany, only breasts and necklaces are shown in relief as *pars pro toto* of the owl goddess. The images of the owl goddess on schist plaques in the passage graves of Portugal have a prominent nose or beak, schematized arms, three horizontal lines or bands across the cheeks, occasional indications of a vulva, and a chevron design on the back. The goddess's owl face appears on a very fine sculpture discovered at Knowth West, Ireland. Her visage is immersed in a labyrinthine design probably symbolic of the life source or life-giving waters; a vulva is in the center. Images of the owl goddess on vases from Almería in Spain are at times associated with a honeycomb design—a maze of Vs, triangles, and lozenges.

The symbols associated with the owl goddess—wavy lines, hatched or zigzag band, net, labyrinth, meander, honeycomb, tri-line, hook, ax—all seem to be life-source, energy, or life-stimulating signs. Their association with the owl goddess emphasizes regeneration as an essential component of her personality. The agony of death is nowhere perceptible in this symbolism.

The round eyes of the owl goddess stare from bone phalanges and stone cylinders deposited in megalithic tombs in Spain and Portugal. The eyes and brows are incised in the upper part of the bone or stone cylinder and are surrounded by chevrons, triangles, zigzags, and nets. Again, the symbols of death (bones, light-colored stone) are combined with aquatic, life-source symbolism.

The goddess's impressive, divine eyes gave rise to one of her names, which came into use after the publication of *The Eye Goddess* by O. G. S. Crawford in 1957. The goddess of the title was said to have originated in the Near East, her cult then diffusing across the Mediterranean to western Europe. Indeed, the resemblance of figurines from the temple of Tell Brak, eastern Syria (c. 3500 BCE), with their staring eyes and brows joined over the beak, to the stone idols of Spain and Portugal with their oculi motif is astonishing. The similarity, however, most probably resulted from a universally held symbolic concept of divine eyes, from which western variants developed. The western European eye goddess dates from the fifth and fourth millennia BCE (in Crawford's day considered to be the third and second millennia BCE). She has close parallels in southeastern Europe and certainly cannot be an imported goddess.

Small stone hourglass figurines, sometimes with triangular heads, are frequently found in Iberian megalithic tombs of the Los Millares type, dating from the end of the fourth or early third millennium BCE. Hourglass figures also are painted on Neolithic cave walls in Spain and are engraved on stones of Irish passage graves. The shape may have originated as a doubling of the pubic triangle (vulva) sign, connected at the tip. In Sardinian hypogea, vulva and hourglass signs are interchanged. Engraved triangles and hourglass shapes also appear to be associated on Irish megaliths. Not infrequently, hourglass symbols are engraved in triunes or next to three encircled round holes, as on Curbstone 52 from Newgrange. The number three may reflect the triple nature of the goddess. In vase painting, the hourglass sign appears in association with nets, serpentiforms, and snake meanders, which link this symbol with the life source and water of life symbolism. Bird feet or claws that appear attached to some hourglass figures on vases of the Cucuteni culture (northeastern Romania and western Ukraine) and of the Sardinian Ozieri culture speak for the association with the bird-of-prey goddess. The hourglass shape itself may symbolize an incipient form of life in which the goddess of death and regeneration emerges from graves or caves. This sign is related to the butterfly, a horizontal hourglass and symbol of new life. The origins of the goddess's image as a bird of prey are rooted in the Paleolithic, as is documented by portrayals of owls in Upper Paleolithic caves and by the large birds and wing bones of large fowl found in Paleolithic graves.

Disarticulated skeletons and skulls in megalithic tombs are proof that excarnation was practiced. Corpses were offered to the goddess, who was embodied in birds of prey. This practice is illustrated in frescoes of vulture shrines of Çatal Hüyük, central Anatolia. Large birds were also buried in megalithic tombs, probably as sacrifices to the goddess. Excavations have uncovered a large deposit in a chambered tomb at Isbister in Orkney, Scotland. The greatest number of bones came from the white-tailed eagle. Others were from short-eared owls, great black-backed gulls, rooks or crows, and ravens (Hedges, 1983). All these birds feed on carrion.

Geometric engravings on Irish megaliths—crescents, circles, and concentric circles; serpentiforms or zigzags with thirteen to seventeen turnings (the number of the moon's waxing days); subdivisions into four, six, or eight and twelve—suggest a preoccupation with the cycles of time. The involvement of the goddess in configurations of cycles of nature and human life is certain. She must have been the overseer and controller of life and moon cycles.

Many western European tomb-shrines have been constructed so that the entrances align with the winter solstice. The alignment of tomb entrances according to the moon's position at the winter solstice suggests the importance of lunar influences on burial customs and suggests the association with the lunar goddess, who was a cosmic regenerator. These monuments were not built to serve as lunar or solar observatories, as claimed by A. Thom (1979) and other scientists writing on the importance of megalithic astronomy. Rather, their orientation according to lunar and solar phases served essentially for the regeneration of life. Rebirth was in the power of the goddess. In megalithic symbolic art we see the link between the time-measuring symbols and the symbols of her regenerative power, between sundials and divine eyes, and between the gnomon and the cupmark, symbols of the life source and rebirth. Other associated symbols are expressions of regenerative aquatic or plant forces.

Ceremonial ships are engraved on inner tomb walls in megalithic tombs in Brittany and Ireland. All depictions of ships are highly abstracted; some are just a row of vertical lines connected by a bar at the bottom. However, frequently there is a zoomorphic or spiral head, probably that of a serpent, on the keel. Sometimes an abstracted image of the goddess is shown being pulled by what may be a snake or ship. If the ship and serpent are interchangeable symbols (as they are on Egyptian artifacts and on Scandinavian rocks from the Bronze Age), then many winding serpents engraved on tomb walls are life-renewal symbols. Perhaps it is not accidental that some of the winding snakes a and zigzags in Knowth and Newgrange are joined to a triangle or lozenge (two triangles joined at their bases), the special signs of the goddess of death and regeneration, just as the feet of the birds of prey are attached to the prow of the ship on Cycladic platters dating from the middle of the third millennium BCE.

Folk stories associate megalithic tombs with fearsome goddesses, such as the goddess Gráinne, the Old Hag of Celtic myths (Burl, 1981, p. 66). The original meaning of *Gráinne* is "ugliness." Some cairns are said to be composed of stones dropped from the apron of the Old Hag. At least forty chambered tombs in Ireland are nicknamed "Diarmaid and Gráinne's Bed." The passage grave at Knockmany, County Tyrone, is called "Annia's Cave," a reference to the home of the hag Anu, guardian of the dead. Breast-shaped hills in County Kerry, Ireland, are still called the "Paps of Anu." Anu is related to the Breton goddess Ankou ("death") and to other death goddesses with similar names (such as the Slavic *Yaga*, from **Enga*; the Proto-Samoyed **Nga*; the Near Eastern *Anat*, etc.). Thus the lunar goddess represented in figurines as the White Lady, or Death, is still alive in folk memories.

In sum, the art of the megalithic monuments reveals the association with the two aspects of the prehistoric Great Goddess, the chthonic and the lunar. The underlying idea of the ground plan and shape of the monuments was the belief in the self-creating Mother Earth who was also the Mother of the Dead. The sculptures (figurines and stelae), bas-reliefs, and engravings represent the lunar goddess in an anthropomorphic shape as White Lady (Old Hag) and in the guise of a bird of prey, usually the owl. This second aspect is the other side (the side associated with necrosis, night, and winter) of the life giver in anthropomorphic or water-bird shape.

See Also Feminine Sacrality; Goddess Worship; Prehistoric Religions, article on Old Europe; Stones.

Bibliography

Almagro Basch, Martín, and Antonio Arribas. *El poblado y la necrópolis megalíticos de Los Millares.* Madrid, 1963.

d'Anna, A. *Les statues-menhirs et stèles anthropomorphes du midi méditerranéen.* Paris, 1977.

Arnal, Jean. *Les statues-menhirs: Hommes et dieux.* Paris, 1976.

Brennan, Martin. *The Stars and the Stones: Ancient Art and Astronomy in Ireland.* London, 1983.

Burl, Aubrey. *Rites of the Gods.* London, 1981.

Crawford, O. G. S. *The Eye Goddess.* London, 1957.

Dames, Michael. *The Silbury Treasure: The Great Goddess Rediscovered.* London, 1976.

Dames, Michael. *The Avebury Cycle.* London, 1977.

Daniel, Glyn E. *The Megalith Builders of Western Europe.* London, 1958.

Daniel, Glyn E. *The Prehistoric Chamber Tombs of France.* London, 1960.

Daniel, Glyn E., and Poul Kjaerum, eds. *Megalithic Graves and Ritual.* Copenhagen, 1973. A collection of essays, including "Problems of the Megalithic 'Mortuary Houses' in Denmark" by C. J. Becker and "The Relations between Kujavian Barrows in Poland and Megalithic Tombs in Northern Germany, Denmark and Western European Countries" by Konrad Jazdzewski.

De Valera, Ruaidhrí. "The Court Cairns of Ireland." *Proceedings of the Royal Irish Academy* 60, sec. C, 2 (1960): 9–140.

De Valera, Ruaidhrí, and Seán Ó Nualláin. *Survey of the Megalithic Tombs of Ireland,* vol. 3, *Counties.* Dublin, 1972.

Eogan, George. *Excavations at Knowth.* Dublin, 1984.

Giot, P. R. *Barnenez, Carn, Guennoc.* Rennes, 1980.

Giot, P. R., Jean L'Helgouac'h, and Jean-Laurent Monnier. *Préhistoire de la Bretagne.* Rennes, 1979.

Hedges, John W. *Isbister: A Chambered Tomb in Orkney.* Oxford, 1983.

Henshall, Audrey S. *The Chambered Tombs of Scotland.* 2 vols. Edinburgh, 1963–1972.

Herity, Michael. *Irish Passage Graves: Neolithic Tomb-Builders in Ireland and Britain, 2500 BC.* New York, 1974.

Leisner, Georg, and Vera Leisner. *Die Megalithgräber der iberischen Halbinsel: Der Süden.* Berlin, 1943.

L'Helgouac'h, Jean. *Les sépultures mégalithiques en Armorique: Dolmens à couloir et allées couvertes.* Alençon, 1965.

MacKie, Evan. *The Megalith Builders.* Oxford, 1977.

Madsen, Torsten. "Earthen Long Barrows and Timber Structures: Aspects of the Early Neolithic Mortuary Practice in Denmark." *Proceedings of the Prehistoric Society* 45 (December 1979): 301–320.

Masters, Lionel J. "The Lochhill Long Cairn." *Antiquity* 47 (1973): 96–100.

Müller-Karpe, Hermann. *Handbuch der Vorgeschichte,* vol. 3, *Kupferzeit.* Munich, 1974.

O'Kelly, Michael J. *Newgrange: Archaeology, Art and Legend.* London, 1983.

Renfrew, Colin, ed. *The Megalithic Monuments of Western Europe.* London, 1981. A collection of essays, including "The Megalithic Tombs of Iberia" by Robert W. Chapman, "The Megaliths of France" by P. R. Giot, "Megaliths of the Funnel Beaker Culture in Germany and Scandinavia" by Lili Kaelas, "Chambered Tombs and Non-Megalithic Barrows in Britain" by Lionel J. Masters, "The Megalithic Tombs of Ireland" by Michael J. O'Kelly, and "Megalithic Architecture in Malta" by David Trump.

Thom, A. *Megalithic Remains in Britain and Brittany.* Oxford, 1979.

Twohig, Elizabeth Shee. *The Megalithic Art of Western Europe.* Oxford, 1981.

Marija Gimbutas (1987)

MEGALITHIC RELIGION: HISTORICAL CULTURES

Megaliths are simply monuments built of large stones. In Southeast Asia and Oceania, a variety of megaliths are found, some thousands of years old, others brand new. Early studies of these structures viewed them primarily in the context of theories suggesting prehistoric migrations of megalith builders. In 1928 the eminent Austrian archaeologist Robert Heine-Geldern wrote the first of a series of influential articles, in which he argued that megaliths were created during two great waves of prehistoric migrations into Southeast Asia. The first group, the "Older Megalithic Culture," was thought to have ushered in the Neolithic age, while the second, the "Younger Megalithic Culture," was credited with the introduction of metal.

Heine-Geldern's view of megaliths as stepping-stones by which archaeologists could trace prehistoric migrations dominated Southeast Asian archaeology for many years, giving rise to extensive debates on the "problem of megaliths." In the past few decades, however, fresh waves of archaeologists, equipped with superior tool kits for prehistoric research, have passed over the territory first explored by Heine-Geldern. As the picture of prehistoric Southeast Asia became clearer, Heine-Geldern's theory of migratory megalith builders had to be abandoned. Several prominent archaeologists subsequently issued a joint statement, for the benefit of those who might not have kept up with the current state of archaeological research, that "the label 'megalithic culture' cannot reasonably be applied to any of the phases or levels of social integration recognizable in the recent or prehistoric past of South East Asia" (Smith and Watson, 1979, p. 253). In the wake of the reaction against comprehensive theories linking megaliths to prehistoric migrations, little effort has been made to sort out the historical relationships among the various builders of megaliths in Southeast Asia and the Pacific. But, as we shall see, megaliths play an important role among many societies in the region, particularly those which share a common Austronesian cultural heritage. As Peter Bellwood, a leading authority on Pacific prehistory, observed recently, "The wide occurrence of megalithic monuments and statues in Oceania suggests that their origins may go very deep into the Austronesian past, possibly at least into the first millennium B.C." (Bellwood, 1978, p. 226).

Many types of megaliths are found in the Indo-Pacific region, including menhirs (erect stones), dolmens (flat stones resting on two stone pillars), stone seats, stepped stone pyramids, and various types of stone tombs and sarcophagi. Active megalithic traditions exist today on several Indonesian islands, possibly related to megalithic customs still found among hill tribes of Northeast India such as the Nagas. In Southeast Asia, the most elaborate and well-documented megalithic traditions are found on the island of Nias, which lies about seventy miles off the northwest coast of Sumatra. In Nias, stones were put to many uses, foremost among them being the large menhirs and dolmens erected as monuments to chiefs.

In 1907 a Dutch colonial administrator, E. E. W. G. Schröder, photographed the erection of a dolmen as a monument for a chieftain who had died the previous year. A rectangular stone forty centimeters thick, three and one-half meters long, and two meters wide was dragged by means of logrollers from a quarry to the summit of a hilltop village, a distance of about two kilometers. There it was set on two stone pillars outside the former chief's house as a monument to his glory and as a home for his spirit, whenever the chief might choose to visit the village. The project was organized by his son and successor, who mobilized 525 kinsmen and allies to transport the stone. Schröder's dramatic photographs show the chief's son atop the stone as it is being dragged uphill; he is wearing a warrior's costume and waving his sword.

Such megaliths, called *darodaro*, were personal monuments erected about a year after the death of a chief by his kinsmen and allies. Often the chief's skull was placed in a niche in the *darodaro*, along with his sword and other regalia. The larger the *darodaro*, and the more people who participated in dragging the stone and celebrating the funeral feast, the greater the chief. The same logic also applied to a second type of megalith erected in honor of chiefs, the *batu nitaru'o*, which was an upright stone or menhir placed in front of a living chief's house. The erection of such monuments were important political events, with roots in the fundamental structure of Niasian chiefdoms. Niasian society was divided into patrilineal descent groups, and rank order within each lineage was determined by a cycle of feasts. Every adult male had to give the first six feasts in the cycle. But the "heads" (*ulu*) of lineage branches had to give up to six additional feasts, each more elaborate than the last. Each man would invite to his feasts his personal *öri* ("circle")—a circle of kinsmen, friends, and allies linked by marriage ties or reciprocal feasting. The supreme feast, given only by lineage heads, drew together an *öri* of several lineages and villages, and established the boundaries of a chiefdom: a chiefdom was nothing more than the *öri* of a chief. This supreme feast was called the *batu nitaru'o ba wa'ulu* ("chief's feast of the *nitaru'o* stone"). The larger the stone, the more people belonging to the chief's *öri* who participated, the greater the chief. Political authority was not vested automatically in a man born as a lineage head; it had to be demonstrated through the feast cycle. The *öri* of the chief whose funeral Schröder photographed included sixteen villages.

In addition to the chief's monuments, Niasians also erected smaller megaliths for a variety of purposes related to their belief that stones provided temporary shrines for various spirits. Each village had its *batu banuwa* (village stone) celebrating the origin of the village. Childless women, especially those of high rank, were considered likely to become dangerous ghosts. So they were often provided after their deaths with small *darodaro* in case they should visit the village. Schröder, who spent several years exploring the island in the first decade of this century, recorded a wide variety of megaliths in different villages. In one village, stones had been placed near a bathing place "for the spirits to dry their clothes." In another, he found stone seats with footprints below for childless women, because "she who dies without children leaves no footprints on the earth."

The advent of Christianity brought an end to most of the megalithic customs of Nias in the past few decades, but on the island of Sumba three thousand kilometers to the southeast, megaliths even larger than those of Nias continue to be erected in honor of important chiefs. On Sumba, there is no parallel to the Niasian *batu nitaru'o* (the stones erected by living chiefs), but the death of a chief calls for the erection of a stone sarcophagus reminiscent of the *darodaro.* Like the Niasians, the Sumbanese usually build their villages on hilltops, and the center of the village is dominated by an array of these megaliths, which may weigh as much as thirty tons. Stones (*ondi*) are cut from native limestone, and placed atop a wooden platform (*tena*) which the Sumbanese liken to a ship, complete with a figurehead in the shape of a horse's head. Dragging the stone to the village may take weeks and call for the efforts of several hundred men. As in Nias, a chief (*rato*) stands on the stone and gives directions. Stone dragging is dangerous, and responsibility for managing things so that the stone does not slip and kill or injure someone rests with the chief. Every day, numbers of water buffalo and pigs must be slaughtered to feed the whole party.

As in Nias, Sumbanese social organization is based on alliances between clans, and the strength of an alliance is demonstrated by the number of allies who arrive to participate in the megalithic funeral, bringing gifts of water buffalo and pigs. As many as a hundred buffalo and pigs may be slaughtered for a major funeral, their horns and jawbones later tied to the chief's house as mementos of the feast. The more such trophies, and the larger the stone slab, the greater the chief. At the conclusion of the funeral, the chief's body is placed in the tomb and his favorite horse is killed so that the horse's spirit may lead him to the spirit world.

A different sort of megalithic tradition is found on the island of Bali, a tradition nicely exemplified by a chance discovery made in 1935 by the first archaeologist to work in Bali, William F. Stutterheim. Near a spring sacred to the early Hindu kings of Bali, he found a stone with a weatherworn inscription.

> None of the Balinese could decipher the old engraved letters, nor were the contents of the inscription known to anyone. The stone stood there, as every villager of Manukaya knew it from childhood, wrapped in a white cloth and provided with regular offerings. I was told, however, that on the fourth moon of every year, at full moon, this stone (which is also said to have fallen from the sky) is carried to the holy waters of Tirta Mpul and bathed therein—much to the detriment of the stone, by the way, which is a big slab of soft grey tufa covered as usual with a thin layer of cement. Deciphering the inscription, I found that it was none other than the charter of Tirta Mpul's foundation, made in the fourth month, at full-moon day, in the year 962 A.D. Thus the people have kept alive the connection between the stone and the watering place for a thousand years, and have always celebrated its anniversary on the correct day, but of the true meaning of this connection every recollection was lost. (Stutterheim, 1935, p. 7)

Bali is now famous as the last surviving Hindu-Buddhist civilization of Indonesia. But the stone of Manukaya draws our attention to deeper, pre-Hindu roots of Balinese religion. Although the Balinese worship Hindu gods, they do so in temples that resemble ancient Polynesian *marae* much more than traditional Indian temples. Balinese temples, like Polynesian *marae*, are basically rectangular walled courtyards open to the sky, with a row of menhirlike shrines at one end. While the Balinese shrines may be much more elaborate than those typical of Polynesia, occasionally replacing stone with wood, the two types of shrines perform the same function of providing a temporary resting-place for visiting spirits of gods or ancestors. Both Balinese and Polynesians believe that the gods are not continuously present, but temporary, invisible visitors who like to alight in menhirs or similar objects for brief visits. Even the details of worship are often quite similar—both Balinese and ancient Polynesians wrapped cloths around the stones for important festivals. Unlike the Balinese, but very much in the spirit of the Niasians and Sumbanese, the ancient Polynesians buried important chiefs within their temples, and sometimes consecrated them with human sacrifices.

The largest Polynesian *marae* were stepped stone pyramids, of which the greatest was the *marae* of Mahaiatea in Tahiti (now destroyed). Mahaiatea was a rectangular pyramid of eleven steps, with a base measuring eighty-one meters by twenty-two meters. Similar structures were once common in Bali, such as the village temple (Pura Desa) of the village of Sembiran, although in Bali such pyramids may be interpreted in a Hindu idiom as *prasada* ("cosmic mountain").

We have noted several common uses for megaliths in the Indo-Pacific region—as tombs and monuments to the power of chiefs, and as temporary shrines or resting-places for ancestral spirits and gods. In Polynesia, we encounter also a different type of megalith, the importance of which is only beginning to be recognized—navigational "sighting stones." These stones, which are found on several islands, appear to have served three related purposes: as markers to align beacons (watch fires?) for ships sailing to neighboring islands; as the centers of navigational schools where students could learn the movements of useful stars by watching star after star appear at a particular point on the horizon marked by a stone, according to the seasons; and as timekeeping devices, predicting the position of sunrise and sunset at the solstices. For example, on the island of Arorae, in the Kiribati (Gilbert Islands), nine stones at the northernmost tip of the island point accurately toward three neighboring islands. Each stone points about five degrees out, perhaps to allow for the drift caused by the equatorial current in different seasons. Although no longer in active use, these megalithic "sighting stones" may have played an important role in prehistoric Pacific voyaging. Much remains to be learned about the functions of these stones and the other megaliths of the Indo-Pacific.

BIBLIOGRAPHY

There are two useful references for locating sources on particular megalithic customs. For Southeast Asia, see H. H. E. Loofs's *Elements of the Megalithic Complex in Southeast Asia: An Annotated Bibliography* (Canberra, 1967), which reflects, however, an outdated theoretical perspective. For Oceania, the literature on megaliths is surveyed in Peter Bellwood's comprehensive *Man's Conquest of the Pacific* (Oxford, 1978). More recent information on megaliths in Southeast Asia is contained in R. B. Smith and William Watson's Early *South East Asia* (Oxford, 1979), in which Glover, Bronson, and Bayard comment on Christie's presentation of the "Megalithic Problem." The megalithic traditions of Nias are described and illustrated in exemplary detail in E. E. W. G. Schröder's *Nias: Ethnographische, Geographische, en Historische Aantekeningen* (Leiden, 1917). A brief summary in English based on Schröder may be found in Edwin M. Loeb's *Sumatra: Its History and People* (1935; Oxford, 1972), which also contains an appendix by Robert Heine-Geldern on "The Archaeology and Art of Sumatra," summarizing his views on megaliths. On navigational stones in the Pacific, see Brett Hilder's article in *Polynesian Navigation*, edited by Jack Golson (Wellington, 1963), and Thomas Gladwin's *East Is a Big Bird: Navigation and Logic on Puluwat Atoll* (Cambridge, Mass., 1970). Sumbanese megalithic customs are outlined in

Christiaan Nooteboom's *Oost-Soemba, Een Volkenkundige Studie*, Proceedings of the Royal Anthropological and Linguistic Institute, no. 3 (The Hague, 1940), and in Janet Alison Hoskins's "So My Name Shall Live: Stone-Dragging and Grave-Building in Kodi, West Sumba," *Bijdragen tot de Taal-, Land- en Volkenkunde* 145 (1986): 1–16. William F. Stutterheim's *Indian Influences in Old-Balinese Art* (London, 1935) sketches the major monuments of ancient Bali.

New Sources

Rao, S. K. "Megalithic Religion among Savara of Srikakulam District, South India." *Eastern Anthropology* 42, no. 3 (1989): 289–293.

Van Tilburg, Jo Anne, and James L. Amos. "Moving the Moai: Transporting the Megaliths of Easter Island: How Did They Do It?" *Archaeology* 48, no. 1 (January–February 1995): 34–43.

J. STEPHEN LANSING (1987)
Revised Bibliography

MEHER BABA (1894–1969), born Merwan Sheriar Irani, was a spiritual master who declared himself the avatar (descent of God into human form) of this age. Beginning in 1925 he observed silence for the rest of his life, communicating at first by pointing at letters on an alphabet board and later through hand gestures. Meher Baba (Compassionate Father) stated that his silence and the breaking of his silence would bring about a universal transformation of consciousness through a release of divine love in the world.

Meher Baba was born on February 25, 1894, in Pune, India, into a Zoroastrian family of Persian descent. In 1913, while attending Deccan College, he met the first of five "perfect masters" (fully enlightened or God-realized individuals), who made him aware of his identity as avatar. Stating that he had come "not to teach but to awaken," Meher Baba demonstrated the essential oneness of all life through acts of love and service. Throughout his life he served the poor, the physically and mentally ill, the "God-intoxicated" aspirants whom he called *masts,* and others in need. He indicated that his outer activities were symbolic of the inner awakening that constituted his real work. Giving no importance to the divisions of caste or creed, he drew followers from many faiths and social classes.

In the early days of his mission, Meher Baba forewarned his disciples that his "universal work" would require of him great suffering, including the shedding of his blood on American and Indian soil. Outwardly, the suffering took the form of two automobile accidents, the first in the United States (1952) and the second in India (1956). In one the entire left side on his body was injured, and in the other the entire right side was severely damaged. In spite of his suffering, Meher Baba gave *darshan* (personal blessing) to thousands of people during the 1950s and early 1960s.

Since his death (the "dropping of his body") on January 31, 1969, Meher Baba's worldwide following has grown modestly in the West, especially in the United States, Europe, and Australia, judging by the number of people attending gatherings devoted to Meher Baba in those countries. More rapid growth has taken place in India. It is difficult to calculate the precise number of followers around the world because there is no formal membership or central authority. Many Meher Baba devotees remain active participants in the world's major religious traditions. Nevertheless, a variety of organizations have been founded in his name in the West and East to spread his message of divine love and the oneness of all life.

Meher Baba's followers (often called "Baba lovers") attempt to heed his wish to found no new religion or sect by resisting efforts to impose any one creed or interpretation of his writings. They feel themselves to be in an individual lover-beloved relationship with Meher Baba, believing that he inwardly guides them in their spiritual journey to eliminate the ego (false self) and to realize God as the "true Self." Many of his followers gather informally in groups to share experiences of his love and guidance and to discuss his life and work.

Among Meher Baba's close circle of companions, Mehera J. Irani was his chief woman disciple, a role Meher Baba compared to that of Sītā for Rāma and Rādhā for Kṛṣṇa. During Meher Baba's lifetime, Mehera was strictly cloistered from the outside world. After his death, Mehera played a more public role, greeting pilgrims and sharing stories of her life with Meher Baba. Mehera passed away on May 20, 1989, and is buried next to Meher Baba at Meherabad, near Ahmednagar, India.

Two sites associated with Meher Baba's life have become places of pilgrimage for his followers. The most important is his tomb shrine at Meherabad, where tens of thousands of devotees gather every January 31 to commemorate the day Meher Baba left his physical body. Meherabad is also the site of a free school, medical clinic, hospital, and other institutions established at Meher Baba's directive to serve those in need. The other place of pilgrimage is Meher Spiritual Center in Myrtle Beach, South Carolina, where Meher Baba stayed during his three visits to the United States in the 1950s. This center is now a place of spiritual renewal and retreat for thousands of people each year.

SEE ALSO Indian Philosophies; New Religious Movements, articles on New Religious Movements in Europe, New Religious Movements in the United States.

BIBLIOGRAPHY

Works by Meher Baba

The most comprehensive book containing Meher Baba's guidance concerning spiritual life is *Discourses* (Myrtle Beach, S.C., 1987). For a detailed explanation of his cosmology, see *God Speaks: The Theme of Creation and Its Purpose*, 2d ed. (New York, 1973). Both of these books were dictated by Meher Baba on an alphabet board. Many later discourses given through hand gestures are collected in *The Everything and the Nothing* (Myrtle Beach, S.C., 1989).

Works about Meher Baba

The most reliable biography is C. B. Purdom's *The God-Man* (Myrtle Beach, S.C., 1971), which also contains an interpretation of Meher Baba's life and message. For an extensive account of Meher Baba's work with the God-intoxicated, advanced aspirants, *sādhus*, and poor, consult William Donkin's *The Wayfarers* (San Francisco, 1969). An intimate look at life with Meher Baba is in Kitty L. Davy's *Love Alone Prevails: A Story of Life with Meher Baba* (Myrtle Beach, S.C., 1981).

CHARLES C. HAYNES (1987 AND 2005)

ME'IR (second century CE), Palestinian tanna. According to legend, Me'ir was descended from a family of proselytes that traced its line back to the Roman emperor Nero. He allegedly studied with both ʿAqiva' ben Yosef and Yishmaʿe'l. Me'ir was one of the five rabbis secretly ordained by Yehudah ben Bava' during the Hadrianic persecutions that followed the collapse of the Bar Kokhba Revolt (c. 132–135 CE), and he was one of the seven disciples of ʿAqiva' who issued a famous edict concerning the intercalation of the year that was crucial to the maintenance of the Jewish festivals.

Me'ir is associated with Elishaʿ ben Avuyah, a heretic also known as Aḥer, "the Other." Some rabbinic sources depict Me'ir as a sometime student of Elishaʿ (B.T., *Ḥag.* 15a).

The tomb of the legendary Me'ir Baʿal ha-Nes in Tiberias, a famous place of pilgrimage, is identified in some accounts as the burial place of Me'ir. Other Talmudic traditions suggest that Me'ir died in self-imposed exile in Asia Minor, where, at his request, he was buried beside the sea so that he could be near the waters that wash up on the shores of the Land of Israel (J.T., *Kil.* 9.4, 32c).

Me'ir is prominently linked to the major rabbinic legislative and political activities of his generation. He served as the *ḥakham* ("sage") of the revived Sanhedrin that met at Usha in the Galilee. His ability to defend both sides of opposing legal viewpoints was greatly extolled. Ultimately, his opposition to the authority of the *nasi'* Shimʿon ben Gamli'el was the basis for his exile from Israel.

Legal rulings ascribed to Me'ir make up an important part of the earliest rabbinic compilations, the Mishnah and the Tosefta. The Talmud states that all anonymous rulings in the Mishnah are to be attributed to Me'ir. Epstein (1957) believes that the corpus of his teachings was one of the primary documents used in the redaction of the Mishnah. Since the laws in the Mishnah form the basis for much of Talmudic and later rabbinic thought and practice, it is fair to say that Me'ir is one of the most influential classical rabbinic figures.

Me'ir's dicta deal with most of the central values of rabbinic Judaism; he placed extreme emphasis on the study of Torah and strongly castigated the unlettered. One tradition attributed to him indicates his understanding of rabbinic ritual as a coherent system of practice that demanded punctilious observance: "Rabbi Me'ir used to say, 'There is no man in Israel who does not perform one hundred commandments each day [and recite over them one hundred blessings]. . . . And there is no man in Israel who is not surrounded by [reminders of the] commandments: [Every person wears] phylacteries on his head, phylacteries on his arm, has a *mezuzah* on his doorpost and four fringes on his garment around him'" (Tosefta, *Ber.* 6.24–25). Many Midrashic teachings and several fables are also attributed to Me'ir.

SEE ALSO Tannaim.

BIBLIOGRAPHY

No systematic critical analysis has been made of the rich and extensive corpus of traditions associated with Me'ir. Two biographical treatments of Me'ir are Adolf Blumenthal's *Rabbi Meir: Leben und Wirken eines jüdischen Weisen* (Frankfurt, 1888), which is a classical treatment of rabbinic biography, and Naomi G. Cohen's "Rabbi Meir: A Descendant of Anatolian Proselytes," *Journal of Jewish Studies* 23 (Spring 1972): 51-59, which critically examines the sources pertaining to Me'ir's lineage. Jacob N. Epstein in his *Prolegomena ad Litteras Tannaiticus* (Jerusalem, 1957) discusses, in Hebrew, the role of Me'ir's materials in the formation of the Mishnah. Robert Goldenberg's analysis in *The Sabbath-Law of Rabbi Meir* (Missoula, Mont., 1978) is confined to the examination of Me'ir's contribution to the laws of a single tractate. *Rabbi Meir: Collected Sayings* (Jerusalem, 1967) is a compendium, in Hebrew, of all the references to Me'ir in rabbinic literature, edited by Israel Konovitz. Avigdor Shinan in his "The Brother of Rabbi Meir," *Jerusalem Studies in Hebrew Literature* 2 (1983): 7–20, analyzes a Midrashic story about Me'ir.

New Sources

Kushelevsky, Rella. "The Image of Woman in Transition from East to West: The Tale of R. Meir and His Friend's Wife in the 'Book of Comfort' and in Manuscript Parma 2295 de Rossi 563." *Aschkenas* 11 (2001): 9–38.

TZVEE ZAHAVY (1987)
Revised Bibliography

ME'IR BEN BARUKH OF ROTHENBURG (c. 1220–1293), known by the acronym MaHaRaM (Morenu ha-Rav Me'ir ["our teacher, Rabbi Me'ir"]); German Talmudist, authority on rabbinic law, and communal leader. Me'ir's early years were spent studying under Yitsḥaq ben Mosheh of Vienna and Yeḥi'el of Paris; he witnessed the famous Paris disputation of 1240 and saw the Talmud burned publicly in 1242. Eventually he settled in Rothenburg and with the passing years was universally recognized by contemporaries as the greatest of Ashkenazic rabbis. With the increasingly precarious situation of German Jewry in the latter decades of the thirteenth century, culminating in Rudolph I's imposition of the status of *servi camerae* ("servants of the chamber") on all Jews and, in 1286, his confiscation of the properties of Jews who left his domain, many fled. Me'ir himself was apprehended in Lombardy in an attempt to flee Germany and was imprisoned—possibly because of his role as a leader of the mass exodus. He remained in prison for the rest of his life, mostly in Ensisheim Castle in Alsace. Communal efforts to ransom the master never succeeded and, indeed, it was not until 1307 that his body was released for burial in exchange for a huge sum. In the sixteenth century Shelomoh Luria cited a tradition that Meʾir himself forbade payment of the exorbitant price, and Irving Agus has further claimed that the crux of the matter was its nature—was it to be ransom or tax? In these interpretations, Meʾir becomes a martyr for Jewish law and the integrity of the community. Sources contemporary with events more soberly indicate that Meʾir died in the course of protracted negotiations for his release.

Meʾir's preeminence is indicated by the express statements of his contemporaries, the scope and quantity of his *responsa,* and his impact on subsequent halakhic history. Though it is unlikely that Meʾir was ever officially appointed chief rabbi of Germany, he undoubtedly fulfilled that function. Close to one thousand of his *responsa* have been preserved, a number far exceeding the combined mass of all other tosafist *responsa.* On the whole, Meʾir avoids prolix discussions, combining care and decisiveness in his writing. Acknowledging fully the authority of the Talmud, he maintains an independent stance in relation to his contemporaries, even when their rabbinical posture is allied with communal and economic power. About one hundred of his *responsa* deal with community governance and organization. These texts are of great significance; they provide invaluable data on the social history of the period and offer substantial insight into Meʾir's political ideology. In general, Meʾir walks a thin line between the protection of individual rights and the need to give the community the legal weapons necessary for its survival and well-being.

In addition to his *responsa,* Meʾir wrote and edited *tosafot* ("additions") to many tractates of the Talmud; during his latter years in prison he was allowed access to some books and could be visited by students. His habits were noted and recorded by his students, who became the rabbinic leaders of the next generation. Meʾir's magisterial figure is prominent in subsequent Ashkenazic rabbinic development, and many of the decisions and customs recorded in Mosheh Isserles's glosses to the *Shulḥan ʿarukh,* authoritative for Ashkenazic Jews, derive from his work.

See Also Judaism, article on Judaism in Northern and Eastern Europe to 1500; Tosafot.

Bibliography

Irving A. Agus's stimulating *Rabbi Meir of Rothenburg,* 2 vols. (Philadelphia, 1947), is the most detailed analysis of Meʾir's life and achievement; Agus also provides translations of a large number of Meʾir's *responsa.* A more sober treatment is E. E. Urbach's *Baʿalei ha-tosafot,* vol. 2, 4th ed. (Jerusalem, 1980), pp. 521–570. Salo W. Baron's *A Social and Religious History of the Jews,* vol. 9, 2d ed. (New York, 1965), pp. 135–193, gives historical background.

Gerald J. Blidstein (1987)

MEISTER ECKHART See ECKHART, JOHANNES

MELANCHTHON, PHILIPP

MELANCHTHON, PHILIPP (1497–1560), born Philipp Schwartzerd; German theologian and major sixteenth-century reformer, writer of Protestantism's first systematic theology, organizer of the Protestant public school system, and author of two statements of Lutheran belief: the Augsburg Confession and its apology. Although he was a close friend of Martin Luther for twenty-eight years, his humanism and stance on nonessentials brought charges of corrupting Lutheranism.

Born in Bretten, Germany, and orphaned at ten, Melanchthon received tutoring from his grandfather John Reuter and the linguist John Unger. He attended the Pforzheim Latin School where his granduncle John Reuchlin, the Hebraic scholar and humanist, supervised him for two years. For achievement in Latin and Greek, Reuchlin named his nephew Melanchthon—Greek for Schwartzerd, meaning "black earth." He entered Heidelberg University in 1509, at the age of twelve, and was awarded the B.A. in 1511 but was rejected as too young to pursue the M.A. At Tübingen University he received the M.A. in 1514, edited for Thomas Anshelm's press, and published translations of Plutarch, Pythagoras, and Lycidas, comedies of Terence in verse, and his popular *Rudiments of the Greek Language* (1518). Called in 1518 to teach Greek at Wittenberg University, Melanchthon became Luther's lifelong colleague. While teaching, he studied theology and earned a bachelor's degree in 1519, his only theological degree. Thenceforth, Melanchthon taught classics and theology. In 1530 he married Katherine Krapp, who bore him four children.

In 1521 Melanchthon's *Loci communes rerum theologicarum* appeared, Protestantism's first systematic theology, which was highly lauded by Luther. It dealt with basic Reformation tenets on sin, law, and grace, and went through many enlarged editions. Besides maintaining an extensive correspondence, Melanchthon produced classical treatises, translations, commentaries, theological works, and numerous textbooks. He was called Germany's preceptor for reorganizing numerous schools and universities. The Augsburg Confession (1530), Lutheranism's basic statement of faith, was conciliatory toward Roman Catholicism without sacrificing evangelical views; the *Apology for the Augsburg Confession* (1531) was boldly assertive. Melanchthon encountered criticism when in the *Variata* of 1540 he changed the Augsburg Confession to allow a Calvinistic interpretation of the Eucharist. His ecumenical efforts brought temporary unity between Martin Bucer and Luther in 1536 on the real eucharistic presence of Christ. However, his irenic agreement with Cardinal Contarini on justification was rejected by Luther and the papacy. Fearful of antinomianism, Melanchthon, with Luther's support, insisted that good works follow faith, but this view seemed too Roman Catholic for some critics. Melanchthon's contention that the Word, the Holy Spirit, and the consenting human will have a part in conversion evoked charges of synergism—cooperation between God and man. Melanchthon was accused by many of being too humanistic, though not by Luther.

Following Luther's death in 1546 and the Lutheran military defeat at Mühlenberg in 1547, Melanchthon accepted some Catholic views as nonessentials, or *adiaphora,* in the Augsburg-Leipzig Interim of 1548–1549, in order to avoid civil war and the destruction of Wittenberg. Although Melanchthon boldly rejected the Augsburg Interim as too contrary to Protestant views, he later reluctantly accepted the Leipzig Interim after securing justification by faith, clerical marriage, and confession without enumeration of all sins, though scriptural authority was left vague. Other provisions—episcopal rule, baptism as in ancient times, confirmation, extreme unction, repentance, pictures, clerical dress, and numerous Catholic ceremonies—he agreed to as nonessentials. Strict Lutherans strongly objected. The Formula of Concord later asserted that nothing during persecution should be deemed nonessential. Melanchthon died in Wittenberg on April 19, 1560.

BIBLIOGRAPHY

Manschreck, Clyde L. *Melanchthon: The Quiet Reformer.* New York, 1958. Good, full, biographical study of Melanchthon.

Manschreck, Clyde L., trans. and ed. *Melanchthon on Christian Doctrine* (1965). Grand Rapids, Mich., 1982. Translation of Melanchthon's late *Loci communes* (1555).

Maxcey, Carl E. *Bona Opera: A Study in the Development of the Doctrine in Philip Melanchthon.* Neieuwkoop, Netherlands, 1980. Good study of Melanchthon's controversial views on good works.

Pauck, Wilhelm, ed. *Melanchthon and Bucer.* Philadelphia, 1969. Library of Christian Classics, vol. 19. Translation of *Loci communes* (1521).

Rogness, Michael. *Philip Melanchthon: Reformer without Honor.* Minneapolis, 1969. Short, good appraisal of Melanchthon's views.

CLYDE L. MANSCHRECK (1987)

MELANESIAN RELIGIONS

This entry consists of the following articles:

MELANESIAN RELIGIONS: AN OVERVIEW

Anthropologists have disagreed about the exact geographical boundaries of Melanesia, some using the term to designate only the islands east of New Guinea, though without arguing that New Guinea is culturally distinct. Others have suggested that Fiji, because of its links with Tonga, should be considered part of Polynesia. Here, following the most common usage, Melanesia will be understood to extend from New Guinea in the west to Fiji in the east, encompassing the islands of the Torres Straits, the Bismarck archipelago, the Solomons, Vanuatu (formerly the New Hebrides), New Caledonia, and many smaller islands.

Within the northeastern part of this region, a few islands are inhabited by people whose languages and cultures are classified as Polynesian, such as the inhabitants of Tikopia and Bellona. Although these peoples' homes now belong to the same political units as the Melanesian islands, scholars consider them part of Polynesia. Nevertheless, it is difficult to draw a line between the cultures of Melanesia and of Polynesia to the east, Indonesia to the west, and Micronesia to the north, and many continuities exist with these neighboring regions. Furthermore, given its small total land area, Melanesia contains a much larger number of distinct languages and cultures than any other part of the world. This diversity greatly hampers generalization about Melanesia; it is only possible to mention features that recur with some regularity, while acknowledging that a single culture might fail to exhibit any of them.

As has happened elsewhere, an additional complication was introduced by foreign missionaries bringing their own religions and seeking to replace the indigenous ones. The westernmost portion of the island of New Guinea was somewhat influenced by Islam, coming via Indonesia, but in the rest of Melanesia various Christian denominations have greatly altered most traditional religious practices and beliefs. These were further affected by encounters with other foreigners, whose very existence and whose technology changed traditional worldviews; colonial governments also forbade a range of practices, such as ways of dealing with corpses, that often were closely tied to religion. Both missionaries and government officers arrived in some parts of coastal Melanesia in the nineteenth century, but did not enter the Highlands (mountainous interior) of New Guinea until the 1930s. Fifty years later there are still a few parts of this island not yet exposed to missionary influence. Inevitably, our ideas about Melanesian religion derive mainly from a small sample of societies that were either contacted late or that, unlike most, resisted conversion to Christianity. Most of these are found in the interior of New Guinea and of some large islands in the Solomons and Vanuatu, but the group includes a few small islands, such as Manus (Great Admiralty Island) and Wogeo, both north of New Guinea, whose societies were described by anthropologists before the missionaries arrived.

As regards the rest of Melanesia, because conversion has often been recent and not so thorough as to eradicate all traditional beliefs, it is still possible in most cases to learn much about certain aspects of indigenous religion. Theories about the magical causes of disease, sexual attraction, and bad weather often persist long after orthodox Christian ideas about the destiny of the soul have been accepted. Rarely, however, is any religious belief or practice of Melanesians living in the twenty-first century precisely like that of their ancestors. The accelerated spread of ideas from other societies as the result of pacification and wage labor, the introduction of modern technology, new conditions such as foreign diseases, and an altered worldview produce changes even in such practices as garden magic and birth ritual. In the vast majority of cases, contemporary Melanesian religions are highly syncretic, and only in a handful of scattered societies is it possible to appreciate the full complexity and emotional impact of the original systems. Given the persistence of many ideas, however, it is still possible to use the present tense to describe selected aspects of the religions, as will be done here.

The Spirit World. One of the few valid generalizations about Melanesian religions is that they all include a belief in a variety of spirits, some of human origin and some not, who interact with living human beings.

Souls. All people are assumed to have a spiritual component or soul (and sometimes more than one). Depending on the culture, it may derive from the descent group of one parent, in which case the child is usually born with it, or it may be inserted into the child by another supernatural being, often well after birth. Belief in reincarnation is found only sporadically. In line with a widespread Melanesian tendency not to speculate about origins, many societies have no theory about the source of the human soul. It is usually thought to be only lightly attached to the body, and to wander in dreams; often it is considered dangerous to awaken a sleeper suddenly, lest he suffer soul loss that can lead to madness or death. The souls of babies are particularly vulnerable to attack or capture by other spirits, whereas the souls of adults are more likely to be captured by human sorcerers performing magic over personal leavings, such as food crumbs, that are thought to contain part of the victim's soul-stuff. Specialist curers may undertake soul rescue in dreams, or sometimes a suspected sorcerer can be persuaded to perform countermagic that releases the soul-stuff.

Ghosts. At death the human soul is transformed into a ghost that usually retains its identity but not necessarily its antemortem personality. In some societies ghosts are expected to be malevolent, resentful of the living, and likely to attack or kill them; in others, they are thought generally to be benevolent, especially toward their close kin; and in others it is assumed that their new condition makes them capricious or unpredictable. Sometimes the ghosts of those who die in particular ways, as in battle or childbirth, are feared even when other ghosts are considered benevolent; so may be the ghosts of former sorcerers.

There is usually a traditional abode of the dead, or a series of abodes, often a different one for each clan. Occasionally these are underground or in the sky, but usually they are on the earth and physically close to human habitations. Although it may be difficult for the ghost to reach the land of the dead, especially if the correct funeral rites have not been performed, very rarely is there any idea of punishment after death for those who have misbehaved in life. The land of the dead is usually much like that of the living, though perhaps somewhat more pleasant; in most societies all of the dead share the same sort of afterlife, gardening, marrying, and behaving much like the living. Ghosts of the newly deceased are thought most likely to stay around their old villages for some time before really severing ties with their kin, but often people have contradictory ideas about the behavior of ghosts, simultaneously believing that they proceed immediately to the land of the dead and that they continue to haunt the village and its environs. In Manus the skull of a particular dead kinsman, in which his ghost resided, would be kept to serve as guardian for each adult man but was banished into a sort of limbo when it failed to confer benefits or when its "ward" died. In many other societies men summon the ghosts of dead kin to help with specific enterprises such as hunting or weather control; they may be aided in this endeavor by keeping some relic of the corpse such as fingernails, but the Manus practice of harboring ghosts within the dwelling house seems to be shared only with the people of Sarera Bay in Irian Jaya. Much more often ghosts are thought to reside either in bones or in special paraphernalia kept in men's houses or cult houses, far from the women and children. In a few societies, however, ghosts are summoned to join the living on special occasions, as at the famous harvest festival of the Trobriand Islands.

Spirits of the dead always have abilities both to aid and to harm that transcend those of living human beings; but they may be thought to take little interest in those left behind, who in turn are primarily concerned to avoid meeting ghosts. As those who remember them die, the names of specific ghosts are forgotten, and conceptually they may be assimilated to spirits of the bush or sea that were never human. In some societies, however, the long deceased are more important and influential than the recently dead, especially if they were the founding ancestors of large descent groups such as clans. Judging from myths, such founding ancestors may have had supernatural attributes even when alive, but in other cases they have been raised near to the status of deities by the period of time that separates them from the living or by the ceremonies carried out on their behalf. Where ancestors are accorded great powers and are regularly appealed to, it is possible to talk of ancestor cults or ancestor worship. The beliefs that ancestors are greatly concerned with the health, fertility, and morality of their descendants and that they can be induced by ritual means such as sacrifice (usually of domestic or wild animals) to grant benefits to the living are found much less often in Melanesia than in surrounding areas, but these beliefs form a prominent part of the religion in many parts of eastern Melanesia and also in the Highlands of New Guinea.

Masalai. Spirits that have never been human play some part in all Melanesian religions, but their nature and importance vary greatly from one society to another. In western Melanesia, including New Guinea and the nearby islands, one of the most important is a type known in Pidgin English as *masalai. Masalai* live in wild places and, although they may assume human form, are typically animals of abnormal appearance—gigantic, brightly colored, sometimes wearing human ornaments such as earrings. Often they are associated with descent groups whose members they aid in distress—if, for instance, they are lost in the bush or drowning—but they do so only if the person has observed relevant rules concerning marriage and food taboos. Offenders may be punished by the *masalai,* who also attack outsiders who stray into their territory. Monstrous births may be attributed to the child's having been conceived in a *masalai* place (and possibly actually being its child); getting lost in the bush can result from being led astray by them; and sudden illness after eating wild animals or plants may be ascribed to either having ingested the *masalai* itself, in one of its transformations, or having "stolen" a food that actually belonged to the *masalai.* (The spirit may later visit the victim in a dream to explain its action.) Melanesia has few dangerous wild animals, but the uninhabited bush and the deep sea teem with dangerous spirits, and many people are uneasy about moving far outside the area of human settlement and cultivation. In some societies, men—as hunters, fishermen, traders, and warriors—think of the bush as peculiarly their own, free of the threat of sexual contamination by women, while in others women are banished from the village when they are in a dangerous condition (e.g., menstruation and childbirth). Usually the village is regarded as uniquely safe from supernatural threat, at least during the day; after dark, spirits more easily invade the human domain. Belief in menacing beings that assume a harmless form at daybreak is widespread in Melanesia.

Deities and culture heroes. Many spirit beings appear only in mythology and play no part in contemporary society apart from being remembered when origins and migrations are discussed. Some societies even lack such mythological figures. In a relatively small number of Melanesian cultures, however, people believe in uniquely powerful spirits who maintain an interest in the whole society rather than in specific descent groups. They are sometimes referred to in the scholarly literature as "deities," especially if they seem well disposed toward humankind; otherwise they may be called "demons" by outside observers. The large majority of Melanesian religions cannot be described as ethical; spiritual beings and forces rarely support the rules of society except in very limited spheres. Exceptions exist, especially in the east (where influence from Polynesia may be involved in some cases) but also in the New Guinea Highlands. In these societies, deities may punish misbehavior with crop failure, human infertility, sickness in the pig herds, or volcanic eruption. If procedures exist for ascertaining the will of the deity, it may be possible to placate him or her, usually with offerings. Otherwise people simply try to avoid or prevent behavior likely to evoke the wrath of the gods, and sometimes explain that they must do everything just as they were told to in the remote past lest disaster befall them.

Interestingly, several Melanesian societies in which the status of women is low have male cults devoted to the worship of female goddesses who promote male interests alone. Much more common are deities who are concerned with only one activity or one aspect of life, such as fishing for bonito, or warfare. Less powerful spirits may be invoked to aid with other activities such as gardening.

Whether or not deities remain near, or accessible to, human settlements after performing initial acts of creation, they may be mentioned in magical spells as a sign that the magic too derives from them. In a number of societies along the north coast of New Guinea, it is reported that meticulous maintenance and performance of ritual secrets imparted by these deities and culture heroes ensures success in a wide range of activities. Other societies are not so conservative, and their members try out any new rituals that seem promising. To the extent that deviations from morality are punished in these, the actual penalties are usually carried out by men wearing masks and manipulating ritual noisemakers such as flutes and bull-roarers to represent the voice of the spirits. The men may not believe that the spirits are present, but women and children are said to be deluded.

In a few areas there exist religious cults that are dedicated to a particular deity or other powerful being, or to the semideified collection of ancestors. In historical times such cults, typically involving secret rituals held in special structures, have spread widely in the New Guinea Highlands, honoring beings who promote health, strength, and fertility. Elsewhere, cults center on dispelling disease and other ills, so that cult performances tend to be triggered by disasters. Whatever their nature, cults, like most major religious activities in Melanesia, tend to involve only mature males.

RELIGIOUS SPECIALISTS. Officiants who intervene between deities and ancestors and the ordinary people have often been called priests, even though they are never full-time specialists. Throughout Melanesia the most esteemed religious expert is a man of mature age who possesses detailed knowledge of ritual, either through training by another expert or by attaining the higher grades of a secret society. Where he is expected to communicate with the ancestors, he is ideally their senior male descendant, but ability to learn and perform rituals may outweigh pure seniority. By contrast with some other parts of the world, ritual specialists are rarely set apart psychologically or sexually, although they may report many direct encounters with spirits in dreams or, while purportedly fully conscious, in waking life. They are taught what they know rather than being inspired. In a number of Melanesian societies mediums are possessed by spirits, like the Manus women who communicate with ghosts through their own deceased young sons, and the curing shamans of the Baktaman of New Guinea, who must be possessed by a particular spirit before assuming their roles. Such people are rarely the most esteemed experts; the mediums of the Kaluli of New Guinea described by Edward L. Schieffelin (1976) are exceptional in this respect.

That for most of Melanesia religious experts have been described as magicians rather than as priests or shamans reflects the most widely reported attitude toward the supernatural. Power lies in the hands of human adepts rather than with gods or other spirits. Given sufficient knowledge, men can control rain, sun, and wind; they can bring success to themselves and their kin and misfortune to others—making gardens flourish or blighting them, luring a pig into a trap or a rival's garden, sending a snake or crocodile to kill an enemy or causing him to fall from a tree, or enticing a woman from her husband. In some societies they accomplish their ends by manipulation of spirit beings, while in others the results follow automatically if ritual is performed correctly. Particularly as regards eastern Melanesia, much has been written about the concept of an invisible supernatural power, called *mana* (or some cognate term), which can be manipulated by the magician. As originally described by R. H. Codrington in *The Melanesians* (1891), *mana* was thought to be a power derived from "spiritual beings," but the term came to be understood by some other anthropologists as designating power that is impersonal and independent of spirits. Certainly the term exists in both eastern Melanesia and Polynesia, but there have been many debates about its exact significance, as Roger M. Keesing points out in *Kwaio Religion* (1982).

It is generally agreed that even when terms like *mana* are used, the speakers tend to have no clearly defined and expressed concept of just what this supernatural power is and how it operates. What interests them are results that can be duplicated. If an act seems to be effective, it does not matter just how the effect is produced. Typically, Melanesian magic involves the recitation of spells that must be carefully memorized; the use of substances thought to be potent in themselves, such as ginger; ritual acts that may involve imitation of the results desired; and maintenance of a state of potency by the observation of taboos, as on washing and sexual intercourse. Failure to achieve the desired results is usually attributed to countermagic performed by someone else, but it may also be blamed on failure to learn or perform correctly. All magic is not this complicated; sometimes only the spell or the act is needed. With the simpler forms, it may be difficult to distinguish magic from technology, and often distinctions are made by an outsider that would seem artificial to the local people. Trying to make a woman conceive by simply putting spider eggs into her food is an example of such a borderline case.

In Melanesia, intent is always involved in magic; there is no equivalent of the African witch or European possessor of the evil eye who harms others involuntarily. In most cases, too, evaluation of the act depends on the relation between the performer and those affected. In a few societies, such as that of the Tangu on the northern coast of New Guinea, there exists a belief in wholly malicious sorcerers all of whose attacks are condemned, but in many other societies a sorcerer is admired so long as he does not attack members of his own group. Usually all men know a little magic—for gardening, hunting, fishing, and sexual attraction—but only a few specialists know the major types such as those dealing with weather control, warfare, sorcery, and the curing of serious diseases. In most Melanesian societies all deaths except those of the very young and the very old tend to be attributed to supernatural causes—sorcery, spirits, or the breach of a taboo—and so do all major accidents and serious illnesses. Diviners and curers seek to ascertain the cause of sickness or death, to help cure the sickness (possibly by identifying the person responsible), and to direct vengeance in the case of death. Magicians are often paid fees when they perform outside their kinship group, unless their work benefits themselves along with others, as is the case with garden magicians. Usually each community contains a number of different specialist magicians, but political leaders are likely to control more than one major form of ritual, either through their own knowledge or by being wealthy enough to hire others. Political leadership is reinforced by religious knowledge, but only in a few coastal societies are there official magicians at the service of the leaders.

Taboos and Totems. The English word *taboo* is derived from a Polynesian word (Tongan, *tabu*), and its cognates appear in many of those Melanesian languages that are related to Polynesian languages. Similar concepts, called by different terms, are found among speakers of unrelated languages. There is debate about the range of meaning of these terms, but they normally include the concept of "forbidden," and often "sacred" as well. The words meaning "taboo" may be nouns, adjectives, or active verbs. The source of taboos varies from one society to another, and so does the kind of thing encompassed by them. Sometimes they can be traced to edicts by deities in mythological times, as is usually the case with incest taboos. So too can special attitudes toward totemic animals or plants. These are species associated with particular descent groups, perhaps because people are thought to be descended from similar but supernatural beings; perhaps because they emerged from the underworld together with these species, as is believed in the Trobriand Islands; or perhaps because of aid given by a member of the species to a human ancestor. Whatever the reason for the connection, members of the descent group are usually forbidden to kill or eat members of their totemic species; if they break the taboo, they may sicken or die. Those who punish such breaches of taboo may be the creatures themselves, their ghosts (which may be possessed by animals and plants as well as people), the ghostly founders of the descent groups, or some impersonal force that acts automatically. All associations between people and natural species are not totemic; sometimes members of a particular descent group simply claim to have first discovered a food plant, or to have particular success in hunting certain animals. Where totems do occur, however, they are a significant part of the religion, but in a different category from spirits.

Many other taboos are tied in with aspects of the local worldview. For example, if the soul is called by the same term as the reflection and shadow, as is often the case, it may be taboo to stare at one's own reflection or to step on someone's shadow, for fear of soul loss. Traditional systems of belief typically involve the observation of many taboos, some of which result from revelation by spirits and some from simple deduction. An unexpected event such as an earthquake may be ascribed to the breach of a previously unknown taboo, the nature of which may be revealed by a supernatural being in a dream. Equally often, however, it is simply decided that any action out of the ordinary that immediately preceded the event actually caused it, especially if the action took place in the wild. To avoid further trouble, it may be decided and announced, for instance, that never again should anyone put a stick down a rat hole. Since taboos acquired in this way rarely form a coherent system, they can seem arbitrary and almost meaningless once their origin has been forgotten, but it may be strongly believed that the maintenance of society and of human life depends on meticulous observation of them.

WOMEN AND RELIGION. Melanesia is famous in the anthropological literature for what has been called sexual antagonism, most often expressed in male fears of contact, which can be dangerous and weakening, with women. At their mildest, such fears and avoidance are no greater than those found in many societies outside Melanesia. Men's reluctance to sleep with menstruating women, and their belief that sexual intercourse saps the strength of a warrior and is antithetical to the practice of religion, can be found almost everywhere. More characteristically Melanesian is the frequently encountered belief that fertile women in themselves are polluting to men, particularly, but not exclusively, when menstruating and during and immediately after childbirth. While menstruating, they may be forbidden to cook for men or to enter gardens, and in many societies have to retire to menstrual huts in the bush. If menstrual blood is feared, so too is the blood shed in childbirth. Not only does a man avoid the scene of childbirth, which also may be relegated to the bush, but he may consider both mother and baby to be polluted for months after the birth. It may be considered dangerous for a man to touch a young baby, surrounded as it is by the dangerous aura acquired from its mother. Later little boys may need to be ritually cleansed of female influences before they will be able to become mature men or to participate in male ceremonies. Where fears of female pollution are high, men usually spend much of their time in men's houses separate from the family dwellings. Such structures may be taboo to women and even to little boys, who will have to undergo special rituals before they can begin to sleep there. In a number of Melanesian societies, fertile women are thought to pollute anything that they step over, such as food, firewood, or human beings. Men must take care never to be physically below women, nor to drink downstream from where women bathe. In extreme cases, as among the Kwaio of Malaita in the Solomons, the whole village is built on ridges so that everything pertaining to men, including ancestral shrines, is uphill from the area assigned to women.

The situation is not always so simple as it seems at first glance. In some societies, such as Wogeo, women too are thought to be endangered by the sexual secretions of men, and menstrual blood may also be considered polluting to a woman (who then has to take great care while eating or chewing betel nut during menstruation) as well as to a man. Furthermore, it has been argued that women actually enjoy and profit from the periods of seclusion associated with menstruation and childbirth, rather than feeling that they are suffering because they are unclean. Certainly women's labors may be lightened if it is thought that crops planted by them will not grow well and that men will sicken if they eat food cooked by women. Furthermore, the possibility that an angry wife might put menstrual blood into the food of a husband who beats her, and so "poison" him, gives her some control over his behavior. If, however, women are thought to be innately malevolent, or to become malevolent because they are subject to discrimination in such matters as diet, their ability to harm men may count against them in that they are likely to be accused of causing deaths, and to be killed in revenge.

In most of Melanesia, however, the low status accorded women also keeps them from being considered powerful magicians. An exception is the so-called Massim region off the eastern tip of New Guinea (including the Trobriand Islands), where female status is relatively high, and where cannibalistic female witches who fly abroad seeking victims are blamed for many deaths. In most other parts of Melanesia, those deaths not attributed to spirits are more likely to be blamed on male sorcerers. If women know magic at all, it typically deals with female fertility and childbirth, and with the growth and health of small children. Nevertheless, women may play a role in religious life insofar as their dreams may be taken as seriously as those of men, so that they too may have meaningful encounters with spirits and can act as soul rescuers, as well as sources of information about the world of spirits. The most respected female adepts are likely to be women past menopause, who are exempt from many of the restrictions of their juniors, and who may even be identified with men.

Where women are considered unfit for the most esteemed activities, the reason may simply be that they are thought to be physically and mentally weaker than men. Often, however, it is held that femininity in itself, or because of its association with female blood and milk, is repulsive to spirits and to wild animals, who flee hunting and fishing equipment if women touch it. Sometimes it is the odor of sexual intercourse rather than of women specifically that is thought to repel other beings; nevertheless, even in those societies that do not practice the sorts of discrimination just described, women are usually forbidden to touch certain male tools and weapons, and warriors must avoid too much contact with women or risk death in battle. Usually these effects are automatic. If women are really feared and avoided in other contexts, boys are likely to need formal rites of separation from their mothers before they can join the men in their exclusive domain.

RITES OF PASSAGE. Whether changes of status during life are marked ritually depends on the society and on the individual's position within it. If there is a class system, as in many coastal areas, members of the upper class receive much more ceremonial attention than do ordinary people. Elsewhere ritual may be focused on the firstborn child, regardless of sex, in the belief that some benefits will extend to younger siblings. Often ceremonies mark the first time that the child engages in any new activity, such as going to the gardens or having his first haircut. Although rites of passage always mark a change of status, they need not contain a religious element. Ceremonies revolving around children or grandchildren are often sponsored by older men to enhance their own prestige, and the complexity and amount of display has little to do with the significance of the event except as a marker of wealth and social status. Of all the rites of passage commonly held in Melanesia, weddings are least likely to be religious ceremonies, whereas funerals almost invariably are.

Birth. A first pregnancy, and the birth of a first child, may be celebrated for the mother as marking her final shift of responsibility from her parents to her new status as a parent herself. Unless she experiences difficulties in childbirth, religious rituals are not usually involved except for the observation of many taboos on acts that might affect her or her child. The husband may need to observe these as well. After birth, however, the baby is vulnerable to many inimical forces, and is normally kept in seclusion until his survival seems likely, when his skin has darkened and the umbilical cord has dropped off. He may then be given a name and formally introduced to the community. Both parents continue to observe taboos on behavior that might affect him, staying away from spirit places and wild foods that might be associated with spirits. Spells are recited to promote his health and growth, and rituals may be performed in connection with such events as the appearance of teeth. Among the Siuai of Bougainville, the young child is the object of an elaborate ritual that summons spirits to help him, after which he is a full member of society; usually, though, the most complex rites are reserved for puberty.

Puberty and initiation. In many parts of Melanesia it is taken for granted that once the perils of early childhood are past, a child will mature naturally; supernatural aid is invoked only for illness. In others, boys especially are thought to need the aid of both society and the supernatural if they are to reach healthy adulthood. Puberty rites for boys are likely to be communal events occupying long periods of time. A girl very often undergoes a ceremony at menarche that may involve a period of seclusion, both because of attitudes about menstrual blood and because her emergence afterward is likely to mark her transition to the new status of marriageability. Sometimes elaborate rituals surround the whole period of isolation.

In a very few societies, such as the Orokaiva of New Guinea, boys and girls go through puberty ceremonies together. But much more often boys are separated from all females. In many parts of New Guinea they are subjected to rituals involving vomiting and bloodletting designed to rid their bodies of the pernicious effects of their former contact with women. In some societies, such as the Wogeo, male bloodletting is equated with female menstruation: designed to rid the body of "bad" blood, it is practiced throughout life. By contrast, in a group of societies in south central New Guinea, it is held that boys will mature only if they are "fed" with semen, and highly secret ceremonies involving ritual homosexuality form the center of the puberty rites. Where much secret knowledge is imparted at this time, puberty rites are indistinguishable from initiation into men's societies or cults; but usually the religious content of the rites is limited to the use of spells and practices to promote health, growth, and beauty. Various taboos are connected not only with separation from women but with the healing of any operations on the penis, nose, ears, or skin that also signal the change of status. At the end of the rituals, the boys emerge fully decorated in a new social persona, but may still avoid marriage for some years.

Men's societies forbidden to women extend from New Guinea to Vanuatu; only in this last island group are women reported to have similar societies of their own. Often the male societies are basically political rather than religious, a way for older men to dominate women and boys; but in some areas much secret knowledge of rituals essential to the maintenance of society is in the hands of the few individuals who have passed through various grades of initiation, typically with severe associated ordeals. Passing through all the grades may take a lifetime, and, in parts of Vanuatu, a fortune. Sometimes the actual secrets are minor, apart from the frequent revelation that purported spirits are simply human impersonations; the initiates may only learn how masks are made or how the "voices" of the spirits are produced. In these cases it could be argued that belief in the existence and nonhuman nature of these beings is part of the religion of the uninitiated but not of the initiates. A measure of deception need not, however, indicate the absence of other levels of belief among the initiates. Several recent studies of rites still being carried on in the interior of New Guinea reveal that often the older adepts really believe that they alone are able to keep society functioning; their activities are serious behind the facade of deception and frequent revelations of trivia. Overall, however, there is no necessary connection between the elaborateness of the ceremonies, the degree of hazing involved, and the care with which the secrets are guarded from noninitiates, and the actual religious content. Perhaps because of the way they spread from one society to another, rites that look very similar on the surface may differ greatly in function.

Mortuary rites. Death triggers the ceremonies most characteristic of Melanesia, particularly of the coastal and lowland regions. Beginning with the funeral, these may culminate years later in great festivals involving dances and masked performances and the dispersing of vast amounts of pork and other food to the participants. In most societies formal funerals are held for everyone, though they may be abbreviated when the corpse is that of a baby or an old woman who lacks close kin. At the wake that enables mourners to view the body, diviners often attempt to ascertain the cause of death from the ghost, which then may be ritually dispatched to the land of the dead. Although cremation is practiced in a few places, in many others initial disposal of the body is temporary. It may be exposed on a platform or buried for a few months until decay is complete, but thereafter some or all of the bones may be subject to special treatment. This varies according to local ideas about the relations between body and soul, and about the symbolic significance of bones and of specific parts of the body such as the head.

The period following initial disposal of the body is typically one of intense mourning for the surviving kin, who abstain from work, keep a restricted diet, make themselves as physically unattractive as possible, sometimes lop off a finger joint, and often go into complete seclusion. The heaviest restrictions fall on the widow, whose willingness to submit to them may be taken as evidence that she did not help to kill her husband by magical means. Only in Dobu, a matrilineal society in the D'Entrecasteaux Islands, east of New Guinea, is mourning for the widower more arduous than for the widow. In a number of lowland societies extending as far as Fiji, the wife or wives of prominent men or chiefs were formerly killed to join them in the afterlife, and in southwest New Britain all widows were killed and buried with their husbands, whose ghosts would linger around the settlements until their wives joined them. A widow cannot resume normal life in other parts of Melanesia until she has been formally released from mourning, in ceremonies that mark her reintegration into the community.

Personal possessions of the dead may be broken, trees cut down, and pigs killed either as signs of grief or so that their spiritual essence can be released to accompany the deceased into the afterlife. It may also be considered supernaturally dangerous for survivors to remain in close contact with the personal possessions, which are imbued with soul-stuff. Much of the remaining property, especially pigs and garden crops, is likely to be used in feasts celebrating the lifting of taboos from the mourners. When this is done, relics of the dead, such as the house in which the person died, may be destroyed. But if further ceremonies are planned, some relic will be preserved for use in these.

Major mortuary ceremonies are not held for everyone. Men of high status are usually honored in this way by their kin; but equally often, a leader or a man who aspires to that status sponsors such a ceremony primarily for the personal glory that he will gain. The dead person may be any type of kin, such as a young child or a mother-in-law; their importance as individuals in life or after death may be wholly subordinate to that of the sponsor. Throughout Melanesia leaders attain or ratify their positions by sponsoring ceremonies in which they try to outdo each other in display and generosity. Some of the food dispensed at mortuary ceremonies may derive from that left by the deceased, and so be taboo to some of those who attend. Furthermore, the specific parts played by those attending may reflect their relation to the dead as well as to the sponsor, and if relics are displayed, those holding them are likely to be close kin, who weep as they remember the dead. Unless the ghost is thought to attend, however, the religious content of such ceremonies may be confined to magic designed to produce a successful occasion, as by preventing rain and ensuring that the food supply is adequate. The deceased may be present only in memory. It is, however, common for a few final mortuary taboos to be lifted on these occasions, such as those prohibiting use of the fruit trees and the house site of the deceased.

In some societies apparently similar ceremonies have the deepest religious significance. Ghosts of the dead, sometimes including those of distant ancestors, may be summoned to attend, and rites are directed at them in an attempt to win their favor and avert their wrath. When pigs are killed, their blood soaking into the ground or burnt portions of their bodies are specifically intended as offerings to the ghosts. The fate of the bones of the dead varies with the sorts of continuing relations desired between their former owners and the living, but often they are deposited in sanctuaries such as caves, or in structures that serve as temples in which the bones will be a focus for future rituals. If bones are reburied or deposited in village or garden sites, their presence may create continuing prosperity, fertility, and safety for the descendants who use the land.

Art and Religion. The spectacular art of most of lowland Melanesia is usually, but not invariably, connected with religion. In some societies, such as those of the area around Lake Sentani in Irian Jaya and of the Massim Islands east of New Guinea, almost all utilitarian objects are decorated, and in most cases the decorations have no religious significance. The most dramatic Melanesian sculptures, paintings, and constructions are, however, produced either specifically for religious ceremonies or to honor and commemorate particular spirits. Some of the most colorful constructions, made of painted barkcloth or woven fiber decorated with colored leaves and feathers, may be quite ephemeral; perhaps inhabited by spirits during a ceremony, they are destroyed or dismantled with the departure of the spirits for their own realm. The sculptures and painting that represent spirits may also be kept permanently hidden inside men's houses or ceremonial structures forbidden to noninitiates; viewing of these pieces, and explanation of their meaning, often forms a major part of initiation ceremonies. Women may never see them. The manufacture of ceremonial art, including even the gathering of leaves to conceal the bodies of maskers, is usually carried out in great secrecy, with women and children threatened with death if they approach the area or voice any suspicion that the supposed spirits are actually human creations. Spirits may indeed be summoned into the art objects after they are complete, and sometimes the actual process of manufacture introduces the spirit, as when eyes are painted on the masks of the Tolai of New Britain. In many societies, however, simple impersonation is involved, but magic is usually employed to ensure that the impersonations are successful, and sorcery is used to punish those who speak disrespectfully of the ceremonies.

When carvings are made for rituals—such as those connected with puberty and death—that honor specific individuals, they often include motifs associated with that person's descent group, such as totems and *masalai.* True portrait sculpture is rare but is found in a few areas, as in memorial carvings in parts of the Solomons and most notably in the modeling of features over the dead person's skull in parts of Vanuatu, New Britain, and the Sepik River region of New Guinea. Often memorials are destroyed when the mortuary ceremonies end, and anthropomorphic sculptures that remain permanently in place usually represent more distant ancestors or deities. Such sculptures are prominently displayed in many regions, forming the doorjambs and finials of houses in New Caledonia, and standing outside men's houses and clubhouses in parts of the Solomons, Vanuatu, and Sepik River region.

The ritual art of other areas focuses not on ancestors but on supernatural beings who are only partly human in form, like the shark god of parts of the Solomons or the culture hero with the body of a snake of western New Britain. Still other beings, such as those painted on the facades of Sepik ceremonial houses or constructed elsewhere for ceremonies to bring fertility or drive away sickness, have little or no trace of humanity in their appearance. Particularly in the New Guinea Highlands, divine power may reside in objects such as stones or boards that are painted with abstract designs of uncertain meaning.

Art objects collected for museums have often been arbitrarily identified as representing gods, ancestors, or totems, without any real evidence that they were so regarded by their creators. Detailed studies of Melanesian art in its context are few, and have demonstrated in some cases that people may be uncertain about the precise significance of designs that may still be thought to form an essential part of a ritual. Some anthropologists argue that art and ritual express and communicate messages that cannot be conveyed verbally, so that it is useless to expect native exegesis. The field is then open for the outsider to proffer his own explanations, and many have taken advantage of the opportunity. Some experts, especially those trained in a German tradition of reconstructing culture history in terms of postulated waves of migration, tend to see evidence in art of the previous existence of earlier religious attitudes such as sun worship. Anthropologists have more often relied upon psychoanalytic theory or a structuralism modeled on that of Claude Lévi-Strauss to explain what is being represented at a subconscious level. The same types of interpretation have been applied to myth and ritual.

In some societies, however, the local experts are willing and able to discuss art objects and their relation to religious concepts. As with other aspects of religion, many details remain inexplicable, simply a traditional way of doing things that is not questioned. It may also, of course, be improper to discuss esoteric matters with noninitiates; but outsiders have often been admitted to discussions that are closed to female or junior members of the society itself.

SACRED AND PROFANE. In describing Melanesian societies, many observers have hesitated both to use the word *sacred* and to contrast it with the *profane.* The reasons are several. First, the discovery that often masked men impersonate supernatural beings without feeling any religious awe emphasizes the secular character of many ceremonies. Second, the widespread tendency to rely on magic in which impersonal forces are manipulated by individuals, and the rarity of communal rites dealing with supernatural beings, makes it difficult to apply labels derived from other religious systems. Third, the frequent observation that Melanesian religions tend to be highly pragmatic, concerned with securing benefits in this life rather than rewards in another world, and not concerned with problems of good and evil, has led some to deny that they are really religions at all. The fact that supernatural beings are rarely all-powerful, awesome in appearance, wholly incorporeal in nature, or far removed from human habitations, and in fact that ordinary people so often encounter them in the bush or in their dreams, makes them seem part of everyday life rather than being set apart, natural rather than supernatural.

The rituals of some societies do, however, strike some observers as embodying concepts that can be labeled sacred. Communion with ancestral spirits by priests and other specialists in Fiji, Vanuatu, the Solomons, and Highlands New Guinea; first-fruits rites in New Caledonia; the invocation of powerful nonhuman spirits along the Sepik: all these seem on emotional and cognitive grounds to indicate that the term is applicable. *Sacred* has also been applied to the state of religious practitioners while carrying out ritual, and of those who are temporarily removed from normal society during rites of passage. In these instances it is suggested that women, children, and noninitiates belong to the realm of the profane, and doubly so as regards women if they are regarded as intrinsically polluting to men and antithetical to religious enterprises. Several investigators have, however, argued that such labels and dichotomies are misleading. If men are taboo when sacrificing to the ancestors and women are taboo when menstruating, they are seen as similar rather than separate (see Keesing, 1982, p. 66). Furthermore, the fact that women usually do interact with the spirit world and control some magical techniques of their own invalidates the assumption that they are excluded from the realm of the sacred.

When *sacred* is used today, it tends to be in two contexts. Places consecrated to spirits, such as burial caves, ancestral shrines and groves, and cult houses, may be permanently sacred, as are places inhabited by important supernatural beings such as *masalai.* By contrast, people may be only temporarily sacred during a religious performance; eventually they return to their normal state and to the everyday world. In this, the usual processes of life continue to involve them in contact with supernatural beings and forces, so frequently that it seems meaningless to characterize what is not sacred as profane.

SEE ALSO Christianity, article on Christianity in the Pacific Islands; Homosexuality; Solomon Islands Religions; Taboo; Totemism.

BIBLIOGRAPHY

Most of the earlier descriptions of Melanesian societies written by anthropologists and missionaries contain lengthy and relatively straightforward accounts of religious beliefs and activities. On the theoretical side they may devote much time to out-of-date controversies about such matters as the nature of totemism or the possible connections between Melanesian religions and those of other parts of the world. Only a few of the better-known examples are mentioned here, but many others exist. Later investigators more often begin with varying theories about the nature of religion and ways to study it, producing works that differ greatly from each other, in which the author's role as interpreter is usually made explicit, and in which the study tends to focus on a particular problem rather than attempt to cover the entire field. Many recent books are consequently both narrower and deeper than earlier ones. The earlier works are particularly useful for an overview and for descriptions of long-vanished ceremonies, while the later works may be considerably more difficult to read but may expose the student to a wide range of theoretical problems and current controversies in the field of religion both in Melanesia and in other parts of the world where small-scale societies still exist.

Allen, Michael. *Male Cults and Secret Initiations in Melanesia.* Melbourne, 1967. An out-of-date but useful survey of the nature and distribution of these institutions, which also examines various theories attempting to account for them and settles for one in which social structure is the important variable.

Barth, Fredrik. *Ritual and Knowledge among the Baktaman of New Guinea.* New Haven, 1975. An interesting attempt to use the author's investigation of an elaborate initiation system as a basis for generalizing about the nature of ritual and the communication of knowledge in other societies.

Bateson, Gregory. *Naven* (1938). 2d ed. Stanford, Calif., 1958. A classic attempt to analyze certain rituals of a Sepik River society with approaches this writer later made famous in such fields as communications theory.

Codrington, R. H. *The Melanesians: Studies in Their Anthropology and Folklore* (1891). Reprint, New Haven, 1957. Based mostly on interviews with Melanesian mission students, supplemented by some visits to the islands of eastern Melanesia, this work is often incorrect in ethnographic detail but contains the classic discussions of *mana* and taboo, and useful descriptions of now-vanished rituals.

Deacon, A. Bernard. *Malekula.* Edited by Camilla H. Wedgwood. London, 1934. Incomplete, having been edited from field notes after the author's death, but the most accessible account of the elaborate New Hebrides (now Vanuatu) graded societies, with much information on religions.

Fortune, Reo F. *Sorcerers of Dobu* (1932). Rev. ed. New York, 1963. Includes a general account of ritual in small islands east of New Guinea, with particular attention to the importance of sorcery beliefs and practices.

Fortune, Reo F. *Manus Religion: An Ethnological Study of the Manus Natives of the Admiralty Islands* (1935). Reprint, Lincoln, Neb., 1965. A famous account of a religious system uncommon in Melanesia for its ethical content and for the role of ancestral ghosts.

Gell, Alfred. *Metamorphosis of the Cassowaries: Umeda Society, Language, and Ritual.* London, 1975. An innovative attempt to interpret a fertility ritual in a New Guinea society by analyzing the associated language and symbols. The arguments are complex.

Herdt, Gilbert H., ed. *Rituals of Manhood: Male Initiation in Papua New Guinea.* Berkeley, 1982. A collection noteworthy for the attention paid to psychological as well as social and religious aspects of initiation. Contains several detailed descriptions of ceremonies in their wider context.

Hogbin, Ian. *The Island of Menstruating Men: Religion in Wogeo, New Guinea.* Scranton, Pa., 1970. Based on fieldwork carried out in 1934, this general account, written for the nonspecialist, pays particular attention to concepts of pollution and taboo, and contains some discussion of theories about magical ritual.

Keesing, Roger M. *Kwaio Religion: The Living and the Dead in a Solomon Island Society.* New York, 1982. Includes not only description of belief and rites among pagans on Malaita, but discussion of many theoretical issues concerning concepts of pollution, *mana* and taboo, symbolism and meaning, and the social consequences of religious beliefs and practices. Addressed to a general audience.

Lawrence, Peter, and M. J. Meggitt, eds. *Gods Ghosts and Men in Melanesia.* Melbourne, 1965. A series of descriptive essays, all but one dealing with the religions of Australian New Guinea (now Papua New Guinea), with an introduction in which the authors attempt to generalize about Melanesian religions as a whole. A very useful survey, though authors of the essays have not all dealt with the same topics. But it has been rendered somewhat out of date by more recent studies.

Lewis, Gilbert. *Day of Shining Red.* Cambridge, 1980. An interesting and readable critical examination of the usefulness of various theories of ritual in helping to understand the nature and meaning of puberty rites in a New Guinea village.

Malinowski, Bronislaw. *Magic, Science and Religion.* New York, 1948. Contains three famous essays setting forth Malinowski's theories about the differences between magic and religion and the functions of these practices and of mythology, as well as a description of Trobriand beliefs and rituals concerning the dead. Malinowski's theories continue to influence a number of scholars, and are clearly explained here.

Rappaport, Roy A. *Pigs for the Ancestors: Ritual in the Ecology of a New Guinea People* (1968). Rev. ed. New Haven, 1984. A well-known and widely quoted attempt to explain ritual in adaptive terms. In the revised edition, the author answers his critics and presents the results of further thinking on such topics as the importance of sanctity ("sanctified understandings") in human societies.

Schieffelin, Edward L. *The Sorrow of the Lonely and the Burning of the Dancers.* New York, 1976. A short and readable account and analysis of a set of ceremonies in a New Guinea society, with particular attention to their emotional content.

Tuzin, Donald. *The Voice of the Tambaran: Truth and Illusion in Ilahita Arapesh Religion.* Berkeley, 1980. A complex and detailed examination of the meaning of the numerous rituals associated with male initiation, which are characterized by spectacular religious art in a New Guinea society. Questions of belief and psychological reactions to the rituals are discussed as well.

Williams, Francis E. *Drama of Orokolo: The Social and Ceremonial Life of the Elema.* Oxford, 1940. A detailed description of one of the most elaborate and spectacular ceremonial cycles ever recorded for Melanesia, and the implications of its decline and neglect in the colonial period.

New Sources

Finnegan, Ruth, and Margaret Orbell, eds. *South Pacific Oral Traditions.* Bloomington, Ind., 1995.

Knauflt, Bruce M. *From Primitive to Postcolonial in Melanesia and Anthropology.* Ann Arbor, 1999.

Krieger, Michael H. *Conversations with the Cannibals: The End of the Old South Pacific.* Hopewell, N.J., 1994.

Lambek, Michael, and Andrew Strathern, eds. *Bodies and Persons: Comparative Perspectives from Africa and Melanesia.* New York, 1998.

May, John D'Arcy. *Transcendence and Violence: The Encounter of Buddhist, Christian and Primal Traditions.* New York, 2003.

Sillitoe, Paul. *An Introduction to the Anthropology of Melanesian Culture and Tradition.* New York, 1998.

Strathern, Andrew. *Body Thoughts.* Ann Arbor, 1996.

Trompf, G. W. *Melanesian Religion.* New York, 1991.

Trompf, G. W. *Payback: The Logic of Retribution in Melanesian Religions.* New York, 1994.

Whitehouse, Harvey. *Arguments and Icons: Divergent Modes of Religiosity.* New York, 2000.

ANN CHOWNING (1987)
Revised Bibliography

MELANESIAN RELIGIONS: MYTHIC THEMES

The myths of all known Melanesian peoples are subtly, intricately, and often tacitly bound to fundamental matters of worldview, ethos, and personhood in religious systems of meaning. Yet the study of myth in Melanesia has a long, largely unvaried tradition of being descriptively rich but analytically impoverished. Indeed, this fascinating field of study remains a vast *terra incognita* in important respects and lags significantly behind the study of Melanesian ritual, in which significant theoretical and comparative advances have been made. Relatively few ethnographies of Melanesian cultures and societies have focused exclusively or even primarily on making theoretical or comparative sense of the marked diversity and remarkable intricacy of the mythology of this area. Most ethnographic studies contain some references to myth, but in general, myth tends to be merely a secondary feature of the central analytic endeavor and is explored—if at all—largely to enhance the primary interests of analysis. Only recently has Melanesian mythology begun to attract focal analytic attention on its own.

STUDIES OF MELANESIAN MYTH. The legacy of earlier studies of Melanesian myth still burdens present endeavors to summarize and to synthesize what is archivally available. In the late nineteenth and early twentieth centuries, scholars working among the myriad indigenous peoples of the Dutch, French, English, and German Melanesian colonies compiled extensive collections of mythic narratives in many forms. These often simplistic assemblages of myths, however, were ethnographically sterile and left ample room for varied academic fancies and fantasies to supplant Melanesian mythic realities. The collections were sometimes linguistically suspect and often unidentified by genre of oral literature and by sociocultural group. Thus, various kinds of myths, legends, folk tales, and other conventional classes of oral literature, sometimes from different regions, would often be merged in one collection regardless of local or analytic senses of genre. Compilations tended to include an emphasis on origin myths, mythic charters of institutional forms, and myths and legends of culture heroes and migrations. These early collections revealed little about other important aspects of Melanesian myth—of its role in or as a sacred performance and as an assertion of ideology or belief, a map of supernatural landscapes, a model of personhood, a mode of ethnohistorical discourse, a social or ritual charter, and a shared but also contestable collective representation (in the Durkheimian sense). They usually ignored the significance of myth as a vital, flexible, and changing but also enduring aspect of a lived, remembered, and imagined sociocultural reality among those islands of the southwest Pacific that constitute Melanesia.

The boundaries of mythology in Melanesia are sometimes obscure, for the analysis of myth as sacred narrative has been simplistic, uncritical, imprecise, and inconsistent and has not encompassed the many diverse kinds of regional oral traditions. Moreover, scant attention has been given to local genres of narrative, such as the Daribi *namu po* or *po page,* Kalauna *neineya,* Kamano *kinihera,* Keraki *ninyi-ji,* Kewa *lidi* or *ramani,* and Trobriand *kukwanebu, libogwo,* or *liliu.* Indeed, there are few ethnographic portraits of the classificatory complexity exhibited in the seventeen genres of Bimin-Kuskusmin oral tradition, or analytic frameworks that could accommodate such complexity. Nonetheless, the sacred qualities of myth often do seem to be marked in a more or less distinctive manner throughout Melanesia. Thus, myths may be distinguished by certain modes of discourse or language (as among Bimin-Kuskusmin, Daribi, or Kwaio); embedded formulas or linked songs or chants (as among Gende, Kamano, or Trobriand Islanders); tacit contextual associations and symbolic allusions (as among Baktaman, Bimin-Kuskusmin, Fore, Gende, Gimi, Gnau, Hua, Huli, Iatmül, Jate, Kai, Kamano, Keraki, Siane, Telefolmin, Umeda, or Usurufa); entitlements to know, to explicate, and to narrate bound to a complex sociology of sacred knowledge and related rules of secrecy, taboo, and revelation (as among Baktaman, Bimin-Kuskusmin, Elema, Kera-ki, or Marind-Anim); and intricate linkages with forms of art, magic, music, and ritual (as among Abelam, ʾAréʿaré, Elema, Ilahita Arapesh, Kwaio, or Sambia). Most myths are cast in the form of narratives and are sometimes interconnected in complex cycles; examples of these mythic cycles are the delicate mosaics of origin myths among the Nalum of the Star Mountains of Irian Jaya, the narratives of the founding ancestress Afek in the Mountain-Ok region of Papua New Guinea, the key Massim myths of canoe voyages and *kula* exchange transactions, and the mythic culture-hero cycles that pervade the whole of Melanesia. Other myths, however, may also be both danced and sung (Waropen), embedded in linked cycles of songs (Kiwai), or enacted in magical or ritual dramas (Elema, Marind-Anim) to enhance their performative efficacy or elocutionary force in creating a sacred cognitive-affective experience.

Despite their occasional entertainment value, the casual way in which they are often told, and their abstract literary qualities, the myths of Melanesia are profoundly anchored to the local foundations of sociocultural existence. They are portraits of various phenomena of sacred significance, "charters" (in Bronislaw Malinowski's sense) that both elucidate and legitimate fundamental institutional forms and practices, and narrated performances that are believed to affect the course of events of concern to human communities. The performance aspects of myth in Melanesia are less well understood than similar features of ritual, although there have been numerous studies of the place of myth vis-à-vis male initiation ritual (as among Awa, Baktaman, Bimin-Kuskusmin, Chambri, Gnau, Ilahita Arapesh, Mianmin, Ndumba, Sambia, or Telefolmin) and noteworthy analyses of myth by Jan van Baal (1966) on Marind-Anim, Catherine H. Berndt (1955) on the Kai-nantu area (Fore, Jate, Kamano, Usurufa), Kenelm O. L. Burridge (1969) on Tangu, S. Hylkema (1974) on Nalum, John LeRoy (1985) on Kewa, Roy Wagner (1978) on Daribi, and Michael W. Young (1983) on Kalauna. A linguistically and symbolically sophisticated approach to the ethnography of mythological discourse in Melanesia, however, is evident only in incipient and rudimentary form. Attention has been directed primarily toward more descriptive, functional, or structural characteristics of portrayals of mythic personae, landscapes, origins, migrations, and other sacred phenomena. Analysis of these mythical portraits has focused on varied aspects of their subjects' cultural, existential, psychological, social, or even theological significance in times of both stability and change.

Personae of Melanesian Myth. Characters in Melanesian myth are variously and loosely identified as deities or primordial creator spirits, culture heroes, remote or recent ancestors, totemic figures, local spirits, demons or ogres, forest spirits, and tricksters. The notion of a supreme deity or creator is found rarely, or remains doubtful as an interpretation of local belief, in most areas of Melanesia, with the possible exceptions of the hierarchical societies of eastern Melanesia (notably Fiji) and the northwest and northeast coasts of Papua New Guinea. Certain renowned and omnipotent figures sometimes also appear in Melanesian myths, such as Enda Semangko (Kyaka Enga); Honabe (Huli); Marunogere (Kiwai); Oma Rumufa (Siane); Ora Rove Marai (Roro); Parambik (Ngaing); Sinatu, Mubu, and Obomwe (Garia); and Ye (Rossel). Although creative or regulative beings are known in most of the area's mythologies (except among the Tangu), such spirits rarely have the elaborate Polynesian features of the Kalou-Vu and other deities of the Fijian pantheon. Indeed, in eastern Melanesia at the Polynesian frontier cosmogonic myths and their portraits of the generative powers and acts of mythic creators are generally more intricate and are interwoven with representations of social hierarchy. In this subregion, myths tend to place greater emphasis on ideas of duality; totemic concepts; complex culture-hero or trickster cycles (at times almost as elaborate as those of the Polynesian Maui myths); images of regeneration, reproduction, or reincarnation (often in serpentine form and less bound to ideas of garden fertility than in western Melanesia); regional integration; and autochthonous origins—all in support of fundamental creation in and of the cosmos. In other parts of Melanesia, however, mythic creators are usually assigned less than cosmogonic tasks.

Myths of Cosmogony. Myths of origin, found in almost every cultural repertoire of Melanesian myth, generally assume the preexistence of the fundamental characteristics of the cosmos. When described at all, the primeval era is often portrayed either as a mosaic of basic elements, structures, and processes—earth, water, sky, astronomical bodies, the underworld, and the forces of wind, rain, tide, and temperature (Huli, Iatmül, Mae Enga, Marind-Anim, Mbowamb, Rossel)—or as a period of chaos, marked by cataclysms, storms, fires, floods, volcanic eruptions, eclipses, comets, and earthquakes, to be eventually put in order (Bimin-Kuskusmin, Orokaiva, Tangu, Trans-Fly, Waropen). Indeed, this primordial chaos is often paralleled by the mythical moral disorder attributed by many Melanesian peoples to the fringes of their known world (Bimin-Kuskusmin, Marind-Anim, Trans-Fly).

More often, however, such myths largely ignore cosmogony, focusing instead on subsequent modifications or transformations of terrain or seascape, flora, fauna, humankind, and culture or society brought about by important creators, culture heroes, totemic figures, or ancestors. Some of these mythic characters are both creative and regulative. Responsible for particular facets of cosmic order, they dwell in or near human settlements and supplicants, taking an interest in human affairs and often intervening in them. Other mythological beings are primarily or only regulative, possessing few if any creative powers but monitoring and intervening in human affairs after the establishment of the essential cosmic, moral, and social orders.

Culture heroes, on the other hand, are usually only creative. Soon after completing their acts of creation, they abandon human society, taking no further interest in its continuing affairs. But ancestral and totemic figures—through genealogical or ethnohistorical links with social groups founded on principles of descent or locality—tend to be significantly associated with the ongoing sociocultural life of particular communities. They model, validate, and also regulate aspects of the social, economic, moral, political, and ritual orders.

ORIGINS OF HUMANITY. In most Melanesian origin myths, primordial transformations reveal little sense of an original paradise and are attributed to various forms of hostility, to breaches of morality, and to conflict—often incest (Bimin-Kuskusmin, Huli, Marind-Anim, Waropen) but also adultery, desecration, homicide, rape, rebellion, sibling rivalry, suicide, treachery, and theft. The first humans are sometimes created through primeval acts of incest, although myths of ancestral parthenogenesis or virgin birth are also known (Bimin-Kuskusmin, Sambia, Trobriand Islanders). The original humans are depicted as emerging not only from the bodies of primordial humanoid forebears, but also from various sacred or mysterious cassowaries (Bimin-Kuskusmin), earthworms (Ndika), eggs (Rossel), stems (Kiwai), pigs (Tangu), palms (Keraki), and ground holes (Trobriand Islanders). Sometimes they emerge from other sources and sites—land, sea, sky, or perhaps some unknown, unmapped netherworld. Although they are occasionally completely formed, the first humans most often are molded or hardened by hand or by fire or sun into fully human form. They are then endowed with sensory, sexual, reproductive, and judgmental capacities, as well as other attributes of personhood (Bimin-Kuskusmin, Ilahita Arapesh, Marind-Anim, Trans-Fly). Once they are minimally human, these early beings are usually further endowed not only with the essential cultural artifacts—of gardening, fishing, hunting, and other productive activities—but also with such institutions as marriage, childrearing, ritual, magic, exchange, warfare, sorcery or witchcraft, and other foundations of Melanesian ideas of ethics, morality, and social order.

If the mythic bestowal of life, humanity, and sociality is complex and profound, the advent of death is usually associated with an apparently trivial incident that could well have had a different outcome—often involving some kind of acquisition or display of improper knowledge, emotion, or behavior and sometimes cast in the image of the shedding of skins and the apparent immortality of various lizards and snakes (Bimin-Kuskusmin, Kiwai, Trobriand Islanders). Yet Melanesian ideas of immortality tend to be ambiguous, and mythic beings are often given corporeal forms and mortal fragilities despite their recognized invisibility and supernatural powers. In turn, the complex symbolic relationships of birth, death, rebirth, and regeneration are commonly articulated in myths focused on and perhaps embedded in fertility, initiation, funerary, cannibalistic, and head-hunting rituals (Bimin-Kuskusmin, Gimi, Hua, Keraki, Marind-Anim, Trobriand Islanders).

CONTOURS OF THE COSMOLOGICAL LANDSCAPE. Myths of origin in Melanesia are often concerned with the primordial roles of sun, moon, stars, and other celestial phenomena and with the fundamental separations of water and land, earth and sky, valley and mountain, plain and river, night and day, and other key contours of a cosmological landscape (Bimin-Kuskusmin, Kyaka Enga, Tolai). The distinctions of forest, garden, and hamlet, or of sea, shore, and inland village, however, are often relegated to a later time when the sense of domesticated space and human community became apparent. Separations of the realms of natural and supernatural or living and dead are more problematic in both conception and representation, for many mythic spirits are imagined to live near human settlements and to be involved with their affairs. Indeed, these spiritual abodes are sometimes described as mirror images of, or as significantly overlapping with, the social world of the living.

The acquisition of fire commonly marks the inception of humanity and community. According to many Melanesian myths, the original fire, which is denied to beings other than the morally human, is usually brought by spirits, created by sacred lightning, or hidden in the body of an ancestral being—perhaps an old woman or a totemic animal (Bimin-Kuskusmin, Marind-Anim, Nalum, Trans-Fly). Sometimes the advent of fire is linked to the origin of a major food or of ritual plants and animals—especially taro, sweet potatoes, yams, sago, and valued wild flora, as well as cassowaries, dogs, pigs, marsupials, pythons, fruit bats, crocodiles, dugongs, and sharks. Such foods and the taboos applied to them are mythically portrayed as key sociocultural markers of self and person (Bimin-Kuskusmin, Hua, Manga, Ndumba). The common mythic theme of interwoven animal, plant, and human fertility is often bound to ideas of the generative powers of male and female substances, anthropophagic symbols, and images of human heads and acts of headhunting (Bimin-Kuskusmin, Marind-Anim, Rossel, Trans-Fly).

ORIGINS OF SOCIETY AND CULTURE. Throughout Melanesia, the beginnings of particular societies are attributed to both autochthonous origins and primordial migrations, which are often revealed in different contexts and serve distinct functions in the domains of ritual and ethnohistory (Bimin-Kuskusmin, Kwermin, Lagaip Enga, Umeda). It is in the context of these migrations that the culture heroes of Melanesia are often found. These culture heroes—including figures known over wide regions, such as Qat (Banks), Sido (Kiwai), Sosom (Marind-Anim), Souw (Daribi), Tagaro (Vanuatu), and Warohunuga (Solomons)—establish key aspects of sociocultural order, test the limits of morality, institute basic productive practices, introduce significant flora and fauna, and otherwise determine or shape the foundations of community. Often coming from a nearby land, the culture hero journeys across the known world, explores new frontiers, discovers new horizons, encounters strangers, enemies, or unknown women, travels to the realm of the dead, and shapes the world of the living. His exploits transform him profoundly and lend significance to the present condition of humankind. As he embarks on his odyssey of discovery, intrusion, indiscretion, insight, and creation, he is often cast as one member of an elder-younger sibling or cross-cousin set, and he marks the cultural boundaries of both cross-generational and male-female relationships. In exploring the moral boundaries of a community, the culture heroes exhibit some affinity with various local spirits, demons, ogres, fools, and tricksters, such as Gabruurian and Kamdaak Waneng (Bimin-Kuskusmin), Kakamora (San Cristoval), Masi (Ulawa), Muu-muu (Mala), Pakasa Uru and Tulagola (Lakalai), Tukis (Buka), and Yevale (Yéi-nan), but these figures never have the creative capacities of Melanesian culture heroes.

The myths of culture heroes introduce the sociological themes that are the foci of so many Melanesian narratives. Matters of egalitarian and hierarchical ethos and social order pervade the mythologies of western and eastern Melanesia, respectively. Ancestor spirits are genealogically and mythically marked in the descent ideologies of patrilineal, matrilineal, and cognatic Melanesian societies in different ways, but most of these societies—except in the patrilineal Highlands of New Guinea and hierarchical eastern Melanesia—emphasize the recently dead and largely ignore more remote ancestors. Although the myths of the classic New Guinea Highlands are substantially lacking in totemic figures or emblems, many fringe Highland and other Melanesian myths do associate totems with clans or moieties (Abelam, Bimin-Kuskusmin, Dobuans, Iatmül, Lakalai, Mountain Arapesh, Ngaing, Orokaiva, South Pentecost). Such mythic totemic figures may have few ritual implications (Keraki, Kiwai, Yéi-nan) or be associated with elaborate ancestor cults (Bimin-Kuskusmin, Marind-Anim).

Although Melanesian myths concerning ancestors and totems serve significantly as a community's corporate property, as charters of local or descent groups, and as the basis of claims on various social resources, many myths subtly depict a range of relations—between siblings, men and women, and generations—as a model extending from the family to the widest contours of social structure. Sibling relations are significant in almost all Melanesian myths. Emphasis is placed on either elder-younger (brother-brother, sister-sister) or male-female (brother-sister) configurations, with implications for matters of either generation or gender in transformations of the mythic sibling model (Bimin-Kuskusmin, Ilahita Arapesh, Mae Enga, Murik). Mythic portraits of generational relations tend to explore themes of authority and sexuality between parent and child and of amity in grandparent-grandchild relationships (Bimin-Kuskusmin, Mae Enga, Mountain Arapesh, Sambia). In turn, myths depicting gender relations tend to focus on substance, power, purity, and pollution; on the sexual division of labor; and on cultural images of virgins, wantons, witches, and female elders. These myths develop local ideas of primordial matriarchy and their ritual and political consequences (Asaro, Awa, Benabena, Bimin-Kuskusmin, Fore, Gadsup, Gahuku-Gama, Gimi, Hua, Jate, Kamano, Sambia, Siane, Tairora, Usurufa, Yagaria).

New Fields of Study. Although the themes noted above have significantly shaped the described or analyzed character of Melanesian myths as they have been portrayed in more than a half century of anthropological study, several other foci are also worthy of special note. First, there is now a quite considerable tradition of concern with syncretic myths, which are subtly linked to mission Christianity or to various millenarian or messianic cargo cults. These analyses, which introduce the critical element of sociocultural change into the study of Melanesian mythology, extend to all major areas of the cultural region. Second, studies conducted in the second half of the twentieth century on Daribi and Kewa myths stressed the flexibility, metaphoric character, and creative potential of Melanesian myths, which are seen as complex forms of communication that play on ambiguity, trope, and innovation. Third, analyses of Kalauna and Tangu mythology emphasize the ways in which mythic understandings become variously embedded in both personal and public senses of self, person, experience, and symbol. In these studies, the analysis of Melanesian mythology has finally come to the forefront of anthropological interest, field research, and theoretical concern and promises to enrich this field of inquiry beyond traditional measure.

Bibliography

The literature on Melanesian myths is immense and enormously varied, although it has remained primarily descriptive until quite recently. In the earlier periods of scholarly interest in Melanesia, the journals *Anthropos* (Salzburg, 1906–), *Baessler-Archiv* (Berlin, 1959–), *Folk-Lore* (London, 1890–), *Journal de la Société des Océanistes* (Paris, 1945–), *Journal of the Polynesian Society* (Wellington, New Zealand, 1892–), *Journal of the Royal Anthropological Institute of Great Britain and Ireland* (London, 1871–), *Man* (London, 1901–), *Oceania* (Sydney, 1930–), *Zeitschrift für Morphologie und Anthropologie* (Leipzig, 1899–), *Deutsche Gesellschaft für Anthropologie, Ethnologie und Urgeschichte* (Braunschweig, Germany, 1870–1920), and other publications printed myriad unannotated texts of Melanesian myths. Despite the sterility of this early practice, the tradition of presenting such textual materials on mythology is being continued not only in some of the periodical literature listed above, but also in the exemplary anthologies of the Summer Institute of Linguistics, the Société d'Études Linguistiques et Anthropologiques de France, and the Institute of Papua New Guinea Studies, as well as in the journals *Bikmaus* (Boroko, Papua New Guinea, 1980–) and *Oral History* (Boroko, Papua New Guinea, 1973–). The vital importance of providing appropriate ethnographic context, however, is now recognized in these endeavors to establish an archive of Melanesian oral traditions.

There are many early but altogether excellent ethnographic studies of Melanesian cultures and societies based on the tradition of field research that give detailed and significant—if not focal—attention to mythology. A fine, sensitive, but highly descriptive presentation of numerous mythic and other texts that provides a rich sense of their ethnographic contexts is to be found in Gunnar Landtmann's *The Folk-Tales of the Kiwai Papuans* (Helsinki, 1917). A somewhat similar study is well represented in G. Camden Wheeler's *Mono-Alu Folklore (Bougainville Strait, Western Solomon Islands)* (London, 1926), which provides extensive annotations of many texts and thoughtful comparisons with diverse Melanesian myths, but which portrays a somewhat superficial sense of relevant ethnographic context.

The problem-centered, theoretical analysis of Melanesian myth, however, becomes more prominent in the era of functionalist concerns, which emphasize the intricate embeddedness of mythology in the cultural fabric of social institutions. Thus, the place of myth in a system of morality enforced and sanctioned through oracles is splendidly illustrated in Reo F. Fortune's *Manus Religion* (Philadelphia, 1935). The intertwined cultural, social, and psychological characteristics of myth and its key functions as a charter of magical, ritual, and social institutions is remarkably portrayed for Trobriand gardening beliefs and practices in Bronislaw Malinowski's *Coral Gardens and Their Magic*, 2 vols. (London, 1935), and for the theoretical and comparative study of myth in Malinowski's *Magic, Science and Religion and Other Essays* (New York, 1948), which draws heavily on a range of Trobriand myths. A sensitivity to the psychocultural nuances of Melanesian mythology, however, is not generally a hallmark of the functionalist tradition and, beyond Malinowski's work, is perhaps best carried forward in John Layard's *Stone Men of Malekula* (London, 1942), which marvelously explores the cultural, psychological, and ritual character and context of myth on the islands of Malekula and Vao in the New Hebrides (now Vanuatu).

The analysis of Melanesian myth moves well beyond a simplistic concern with both function and charter in the seminal but little-recognized studies of the Keraki and other Trans-Fly groups and of the Elema, documented in Francis Edgar Williams's *Papuans of the Trans-Fly* (Oxford, 1936) and *Drama of Orokolo* (Oxford, 1940). A master of ethnography and no slavish adherent of functionalist dogma, Williams challenges the foundations of Malinowski's faith in mythic charters and opens new ground by raising significant questions about the cultural embeddedness, semiotic construction, and psychological importance of myths in Melanesia and elsewhere. In these several regards, Williams's central concern is to address the subtle relationships between mythic and ritual forms—an issue that is also richly explored in the magnificent studies of the Marind-Anim portrayed in Paul Wirz's *Die Marind-Anim von Holländisch-Süd-Neu-Guinea*, 2 vols. (Hamburg, 1922–1925), and in Jan van Baal's *Dema* (The Hague, 1966).

The classic study of the mythology of New Caledonia is beautifully represented in Maurice Leenhardt's *Do Kamo: Person and Myth in the Melanesian World* (1947; reprint, Chicago, 1979). In his exploration of matters of experience, epistemology, and personhood through myth and the nuances of the anthropological study of myth, Leenhardt provokes a depth of insight into Canaque myth that provides inspiration from Lucien Lévy-Bruhl to Claude Lévi-Strauss in the unraveling of Melanesian *mythologiques*. Yet the contemporary study of New Caledonian mythology, as admirably exemplified in Alban Bensa and Jean-Claude Rivièrre's *Les chemins de l'alliance* (Paris, 1982), is far less philosophical in its theoretical foundations and reflective in its methodological moorings and attempts to promote a more "scientific" emphasis on ethnosemantic classificatory schemas and sociopolitical patterns implicated in mythic narratives.

The state of the art in the anthropological study of Melanesian mythology is well examined and summarized for the period ending in the early 1960s in *Gods, Ghosts and Men in Melanesia*, edited by Peter Lawrence and M. J. Meggitt (Melbourne, 1965). This overview suggests how little progress had been made in the study of the myths and religions of Melanesia before the 1960s, which represented what might be called a renaissance of academic interest in Melanesian religions. Prior to this time, there is particularly little exploration of mythology in the New Guinea Highlands, with the notable exception of the monumental study of Fore, Jate, Kamano, and Usurufa origin, *kinihera*, and other genres of myth in Catherine H. Berndt's "Myth in Action" (Ph.D. diss., London School of Economics, 1955).

The modern era in the study of Melanesian mythology exhibits two particularly significant trends: (1) a comparative examination of mythological and other aspects of millenarian, nativistic, or cargo cult movements; and (2) a new emphasis on mythology as the focus of ethnographic interest and theoretical analysis. In the first instance, mythological portraits of the significance of sociocultural change, of altered conceptions of personhood, self, society, and cosmos, and of revitalized traditional or newly syncretic images are compared throughout much of Melanesia in Peter Worsley's *The Trumpet Shall Sound* (London, 1957) and in Kenelm Burridge's *New Heaven, New Earth* (New York, 1969).

In the second instance, however, the study of Melanesian myth comes fully into the mainstream of the best academic explorations of myth. These new and exciting analytic undertakings are perhaps best represented in a limited set of exemplary articles and in the monographic work of five scholars. The mythic exploration of moral ambiguities and dilemmas is insightfully examined in a Kamano text in Catherine H. Berndt's "The Ghost Husband: Society and the Individual in New Guinea Myth," *Journal of American Folklore* 79 (1966): 244–277. Subtleties of the conceptual images and internal paradoxes of Kaliai culture and society as represented in a single myth are unraveled in Dorothy Ayers Counts's "*Akro* and *Gagandewa:* A Melanesian Myth," *Journal of the Polynesian Society* 89 (1980): 33–64. These analyses show the power of exploring the nuances of a single mythic narrative in elaborate sociocultural context. In contrast, a comparative examination of the dialectical relationship between sociocultural experience, moral order, and mythic representation in the Eastern Highlands region of Papua New Guinea is admirably constructed in John Finch's "Structure and Meaning in Papua New Guinea Highland Mythology," *Oceania* 55 (1985): 197–213.

Whether focusing within or beyond a particular sociocultural community, the monographic endeavors variously attend to problems of the comparative analysis of myth. The complex and subtle relations between mythology and matters of personhood, self, morality, and experience in Tangu society are elegantly dissected in Kenelm Burridge's *Tangu Traditions* (Oxford, 1969), which delicately probes the intricate way in which myth is variously embedded in diverse ethnographic contexts and which forcefully demonstrates how myths become crystallizations of cultural themes and of both social and personal experiences. Exploring a tension between the disclosure of immoral realities and the revelation of existential truths, enigmatic and oracular Tangu myths unveil dilemmas of the local human condition. How such mythic crystallizations are constructed and manipulated creatively and through complex understandings of cultural tropes is analyzed admirably for Daribi mythology in Roy Wagner's *Habu* (Chicago, 1972) and *Lethal Speech* (Ithaca, N.Y., 1978), which also attend to broader comparative issues in assessing the commonalities and peculiarities of Daribi myth in New Guinea and in Melanesia. The significance of variations among versions of myths with respect to the cultural discrimination of social differences and to the transformational characteristics of a corpus of myths within a particular society is illustrated in exemplary fashion for Nalum mythology in S. Hylkema's *Mannen in het Draagnet* (The Hague, 1974). The subtle interplay between narrative compositions and pragmatic experiences, between intertextual resonances and textual references, between the surfaces and the depths of constructed layers of meaning, and between the fanciful and the factual of cultural contradictions and social conflicts, is marvelously explored in the "fabricated worlds" of Kewa *lidi* myths in John LeRoy's *Fabricated World* (Vancouver, 1985), which is usefully complemented by a fine collection of the analyzed myths in *Kewa Tales*, edited by LeRoy (Vancouver, 1985). Finally, the problem of how myths—usually conceived as particular forms of collective representations (in the Durkheimian sense)—become articulated with personal symbols and subjective experience and embedded in autobiographical narratives is superbly examined in Michael W. Young's *Magicians of Manumanua* (Berkeley, 1983). These new studies reach well beyond the descriptive and analytic limits of their predecessors and hold much promise for the future of academic understandings of the subtleties of mythological constructions in the Melanesian cultural region.

New Sources

Burridge, Kenelm. *Mambu: A Melanesian Millennium* (1960). Princeton, N.J., 1995.

Kahn, Miriam. "Stone-Faced Ancestors: The Spatial Anchoring of Myth in Wamira, Papua NewGuinea." *Ethnology* 29 (January 1990): 51–66.

MacDonald, Mary N. *Mararoko: A Study in Melanesian Religion.* New York, 1990.

Pech, Rufus. *Manub and Kilibob: Melanesian Models for Brotherhood Shaped by Myth, Dream and Drama.* Papua New Guinea, 1991.

Fitz John Porter Poole (1987)
Revised Bibliography

MELQART, whose name means "king of the city" (*milk qart*), was the patron god of the Phoenician city of Tyre and one of the major gods of the Phoenician and Punic pantheons. He was also known as Baal Sur (Lord of Tyre) and was identified with Herakles (Hercules) since at least the sixth century BCE. There is no longer any doubt about his link with Tyre (the "city" of his name) since the publication in the 1990s and early 2000s by Pierre Bordreuil of explicit epigraphical evidence, including a seal, tesserae, dedication, weight, and sling balls.

Phoenicia and Syria. The earliest epigraphical evidence on Melqart appears on a statue found near Aleppo (Bredj), Syria, dating from about 800 BCE. The royal Aramaic votive inscription bears the name of Barhadad, who probably was king of Arpad. This document is an important trace of commercial and cultural contacts between Northern Syria and Phoenicia, especially Tyre, which explains why an Aramaic king made such an offering to a Tyrian god. Melqart is represented on the stela, standing, striding from right to left, with a naked torso and bare feet, bearded, with a loincloth and a dome-shaped hat, a fenestrated ax on the shoulder (a royal symbol) and carrying what may be an ankh or a lotus flower in the right hand (a symbol of immortality). This is clearly a composite image, with Egyptian and Syro-Hittite affiliations. The same iconography, with a standing or seated god (on a throne), is also attested in different Mediterranean contexts (Cyprus, Carthage, Ibiza, Sardinia), but it is not certain that it always refers to Melqart.

Although the first reference to Melqart belongs to the beginning of the first millennium BCE, different literary sources link him with the founding of the city of Tyre, and Herodotus (II, 44) reports that, according to the priestly traditions, Melqart's Tyrian sanctuary was as old as the city itself. It is likely that Melqart's cult was based on a longtime religious tradition, the cult of royal ancestors, which is well attested in Mesopotamia and Syria until the third millennium BCE. However, Melqart became the poliadic god of Tyre, with this specific name, only at the beginning of the first millennium BCE, when Tyre became a great commercial center with a Mediterranean dimension. In fact, Josephus (*A.J.*, VIII, 145–146; *C.Ap.* I, 117–119) records that Hiram I, the king of Tyre during the tenth century BCE, built new temples for Melqart (Herakles) and Astarte in the city and celebrated for the first time the *egersis*, which was the resurrection ritual of Melqart, in the month of Peritios (February–March). During this annual ritual, the god "died" (perhaps in a fire) and was awakened or resuscitated, perhaps through a sacred marriage (*hierosgamos*) with the goddess Astarte. In this celebration, the Tyrian king probably played the role of the god, and a priestess played the role of the goddess.

Later in Cyprus and in the Punic world, a ritual title applied to important citizens is attested, surely in connection with Melqart's *egersis*: "The one who makes the god(s) awaken, bridegroom of Astarte(?)." In Greek inscriptions found in Amman, Ramleh, and Ashkelon, this function is translated as "*egerseites* of Herakles." On a vase, presumably from Sidon, there is a probable iconographical representation of the main moments of Melqart's *egersis.* In addition, in Gades (Spain), Hercules/Melqart's bones were kept (Pomponius Mela III 46). These elements seem to fit well with the known Frazerian pattern of the "dying and rising god," but this pattern has been critically challenged because it is an artificial construction that does not reflect the great diversity of the historical and "theological" backgrounds of the so-called dying and rising gods, a category that includes Osiris, Dumuzi, Attis, Adonis, and others. In Melqart's case, it appears clear that the annual ritual death and resurrection means that every year the natural, cosmic, sociopolitical, and religious order was renewed with and through the king. It is not simply a "naturalistic" ritual, but a way to assure fertility, order, peace, and wealth for all the people, because, as the Semitic royal inscriptions say, the king—mythical and historical—"makes his people live." It is also interesting to notice that Astarte seems to be the mother and *paredros* (companion) of the god. According to Cicero (*N.D.* III, 42) and Philo of Byblos (Eusebius, *P.E.*, I, 10, 27, 3), the Tyrian Herakles was the son of Zeus Demarous (from *Dmrn*, the "Warrior," possibly an epithet of Baal) and Asteria (Astarte); he was killed by Typho in Libya and was brought back to life by the goddess, who made him smell roasted quails (Eudoxus of Cnidos, fr. 284).

Direct evidence. After the Aleppo inscription, Melqart appears in two vassal Assyrian treaties. First, Melqart is mentioned in the treaty of 754 BCE between Matiel, king of Arpad (Northern Syria) and Ashurnirari V, king of Assyria. Here Melqart is included in the group of gods who warrant the treaty; together with Eshmun (the Baal of Sidon), Melqart is also named in the treaty of 675–670 BCE between the kings Esarhaddon of Assyria and Baal of Tyre. This treaty regulated the shipping and overland trade routes, and Melqart is included in the group of Tyrian gods, together with Astarte and Eshmun: "May Melqart and Eshmun deliver your land to destruction and your people to deportation; may they [uproot] you from your land and take away the food from your mouth, the clothes from your body, and the oil for your anointing" (Parpola and Watanabe, 1988, vol. II, p. 27).

Various scholars hold that the cult of Baal that King Ahab and his wife Jezebel, a Tyrian princess, introduced into Israel in the ninth century BCE (1 *Kgs.* 16), and against which the prophet Elijah fought on Mount Carmel (1 *Kgs.* 18:20–40), was in fact a cult of Melqart. The text that narrates the challenge between Elijah and Baal's prophets alludes to a god who sleeps and travels, like Melqart, the god of the *egersis* and the companion of the Tyrian expansion on the Mediterranean shores. But the god Baal Shamin (Lord of the Heaven) is another good possibility for the Carmel episode. In the sixth century BCE, Ezekiel's oracle against Tyre (*Ez.* 28:1–19) probably refers to the cultural background of the Tyrian kingship when he places in the king's mouth these words: "I am a god, I sit on a divine throne, in the heart of the seas." The Tyrian betyls (standing stones) that symbolize the city's power (*Ez.* 26:11) are probably the two stelae that Herodotus (II, 44) describes in Melqart's shrine and that are represented on the city's coinage. They were a symbol of his dominion, as were, later, the columns of Herakles at the end of the Western world (Libya, then Gibraltar). These elements prove that an aniconic tendency, maybe the older form of the cult, was still present in the worship of Melqart, especially in Tyre and Gades, though anthropomorphic figures are also known. On the Tyrian coinage, the Heraklean symbols occur frequently in the Hellenistic and Roman period. In the fifth century BCE a sea god riding a hippocampus is depicted, which could be Melqart represented as the protector of commercial expansion, but this is not certain.

When Alexander the Great reached Tyre in the fourth century BCE and began the siege, because of his Heraklean genealogy he tried to manifest his devotion to the Tyrian Herakles (Melqart), making several offerings in his temple (Arrian, *Anab.* II, 16–24). But by that time the Hellenization of the cult was already deep, and it is difficult to distinguish the local Semitic god and its Greek interpretation; one deals with a syncretistic figure (Melqart/Herakles) in a syncretistic context (the Hellenistic period). The Greek iconographical language completely covers the original Phoenician image, which is very poorly attested.

Just as the Tyrian influence expanded through the Mediterranean by way of trade and colonization, so did the cult of Melqart. The "Lord of Tyre" was also the "sailors' god" (Diodorus XX, 14), who traveled with the population. Melqart thus became one of the major figures of the ancestral religious traditions for the western Phoenicians (Punic people). For example, it is known that the Tyrian founders of Carthage and Gades brought on their ships, together with their families, relics of Melqart (Justin XVIII, 4, 15; XLIV, 5, 2). In these colonial contexts, the foundation of a sanctuary for Melqart, often *extra muros,* was probably one of the first concerns of the new inhabitants because the sanctuary was a neutral and sacral space that offered an adequate context for the first commercial and social contacts with the local populations. Melqart's temples probably had an important economic function, perhaps serving as "treasuries" of commercial exchanges through a system of tithe, but this aspect of his cult is still hypothetical because of the lack of documentation.

Elsewhere in Phoenicia and Syria, Melqart is mainly attested in Amrith (together with Eshmun), Sarepta (if he is the "holy god" of the inscriptions), Umm el-Awamid (under the name of Milkashtart), Jamnia, and Ascalon.

BEYOND PHOENICIA AND SYRIA. From Phoenicia, Melqart's devotion expanded in the eastern Mediterranean.

Cyprus. The first step was Cyprus. There Melqart is documented in several places: Kition, Amathus, Idalion, and Larnaka, which were the major centers of Phoenician colonization since the ninth century BCE. In Kition-Bamboula, Melqart's sanctuary was near Astarte's, while in Kition-Batsalos there is epigraphical evidence of a common cult to Melqart-Eshmun. In many Cypriot cult sites, a Heraklean iconography, similar to that present on the Syrian coast (Amirth) since the sixth to fifth centuries BCE, is present. It may allude to Melqart, but probably also alludes to other cults, including Reshef /Apollo and some anonym Cypriot god, as if the Heraklean shape were a standard male god iconography. Cyprus was thus a crucial place for the iconographical assimilation between Melqart, the royal god, perhaps associated with the lion (as in the Eastern iconography of the smiting king or god), and the Greek Herakles, who became the god with the *leonte*, the bow and the club. The Idalion cup (eighth century BCE) is the best illustration of this assimilation process.

Greece. Although there is little specific evidence of Melqart in Greece, it is probable that Samos was an important stage on the road that brought Melqart/Herakles from Phoenicia and Syria to Greece, through Cyprus and perhaps Rhodi, where an "awakener of the god" is attested, surely in connection with Melqart's cult. In Samos, where Hera looks much like Astarte, there is a famous pectoral (625–600 BCE) with the first Heraklean image of the hero with the *leonte*. Otherwise, Melqart's name never appears on Greek soil.

Herodotos reports (II, 44) that Melqart was venerated in Thasos as the *archegetes* of the city, just as the Thasian Herakles was venerated in Tyre, but excavations have not provided any evidence of this. In Crete, the Phoenician presence (at least in Kommos) is well documented, but Melqart does not appear, although the Cretan Herakles Daktylos may have some relationship to him and to the Egyptian Bes. Another important site in the religious map of the Greek world is Delos, where different oriental communities settled for commercial reasons. The Tyrian group considered Melqart as their patron god and therefore took the name of Heracleistes. Their decree (ID 1519) records that on the Aegean island they regularly practiced Melqart's cult as their *archegetes* during the second century BCE.

Africa. Though the monarchy disappeared in Carthage, Melqart, the royal god par excellence, remained popular as a symbol of the Phoenician roots of Carthaginian people, like the goddess Astarte. The divine couple, Melqart and Astarte, already attested in Phoenicia, survived in the Punic context and was often translated in Greek and Roman sources through the *interpretatio graeca* or *latina*: Herakles/Hercules for Melqart, and Aphrodite/Venus or Hera/Juno, especially but not exclusively, for Astarte. In Carthage, Melqart's cult provided one of the most important occasions to maintain the relationships between Tyre and its major Punic colony. Every year during Melqart's feast a tithe was sent from Carthage to Tyre to demonstrate the people's fidelity to the great ancestral god and to Tyrian traditions. When the Carthaginians interrupted this custom, they were badly punished by the god with war and epidemics, as reported by Diodorus of Sicily (XX, 14). In the famous treaty between Hannibal and the Macedonian king Philippus V in 215 BCE, Herakles (with the Carthaginian daimôn and Iolaus), who must surely be Melqart (Polybius VII, 9, 2–3), is mentioned among the Punic gods.

Elsewhere in Africa, Melqart is present in Leptis Magna (as Milkashtart, together with Shadrafa), Sabrata (as Hercules), El Hofra, and Lixus, where the classical authors placed the Hesperian garden.

Spain. In Spain, where Phoenician people founded emporia as early as the eighth century BCE, the main center of Melqart's cult was Gades. The evidence is entirely Greek and Latin, and relatively late, so it is difficult to determine what belongs to the Phoenician god and what to his later classical brothers. It is likely that Phoenician, Greek, and Roman cults were practiced together in a clearly syncretistic context, where each believer was able to recognize his own god.

Milkashtart, who could be a god similar to Melqart and who was also assimilated to Herakles/Hercules, appears in Gades in the second century BCE. His name alludes to a royal god (Milk) of Ashtarot, a Palestinian place name, and not to Ashtart/Astarte. The cult of Melqart/Herakles/Hercules propagated in several places in southern Spain, as demonstrated by local coinage with Heraklean symbols or images, including Herakles' head, bowl, and club, but the chronology of such a phenomenon is not clear. It is probable that the brief Punic dominion on Spain in the third century BCE under the leadership of the Barcides, a family who had a special devotion for Melqart, reinforced the god's presence in Spain. The Barcides imitated Alexander's coinage with the Heraklean head.

The cult of Melqart is also known through epigraphical and iconographical evidence to have been present in Ibiza. Scholars are not aware of any mythological cycle of Melqart's adventures similar to those surrounding Herakles, neither in Ibiza, the far West, or the East. The Western episodes of Herakles' myth are particularly important because they constitute the antecedent of his death and apotheosis. The West, the Sun's house, was considered to be the end of the world, a fabulous land where a person could communicate with the netherworld. But nothing similar is known about Melqart, and the old idea that the "city" contained in his name was the city of the dead is not convincing.

Italy, Malta, and Great Britain. Melqart is found in all Phoenician colonies, including Sardinia, Sicily, and Malta. In Sardinia, there is little evidence of Melqart's presence in Tharros, the most important Phoenician colony on the island, apart from a temple, known from an inscription. Astarte is much better documented, particularly on iconographical grounds, and these two gods probably formed a divine couple, as they frequently did elsewhere. Melqart is also documented in the Sid/Sardus Pater's sanctuary in Antas.

In Sicily, the name of Melqart occurs as a theophorous element in the onomastics, but there is no cultural evidence.

He was nevertheless probably venerated in different places, for example in Selinus, where the cult of Herakles is well documented, and in Mozia, where the famous statue of the Young of Mozia (fifth century BCE) has been interpreted as Heraklean iconography. Melqart also appears in the place-name Roshmelqart (Cape of Melqart), which is documented in inscriptions and on the coinage but has not yet been definitively identified. In Sicily, the Heraklean presence is strong and is reinforced through the interaction (often violent, in the form of a conquest and assimilation) with indigenous cults.

In Malta, Melqart certainly had a temple, which is mentioned by Ptolemy as Herakles' temple; the location was revisited in 2003 by Nicholas Vella. The twin stelae with double bilingual inscriptions in Phoenician and Greek were probably offered in this temple to Melqart, Baal of Tyre, and to Herakles, *archegetes* of the Tyrians, that is, the founder, the "leader of the foundation" (Donner and Ršllig, 2002). These texts enabled Jean-Jacques Barthèlemy to decipher the Phoenician scripture in 1758. Astarte's cult is also well attested in Tas Silg in Malta.

Pyrgi is the most important site in continental Italy, which has something to do with Melqart. The evidence is both epigraphical and iconographical. The bilingual Phoenician and Etruscan inscription on the laminae includes a dedication to Astarte/Uni from the local king on a special occasion: "the day of the burial of the god" (Donner and Ršllig, 2002). The name of this god is not explicitly mentioned, but the iconographical evidence may indicate that he was Melqart—in the decoration of Pyrgi's temples (A and B), Heraklean motifs are common, probably in connection with the cults practiced there. In the Forum Boarium on the Ara Maxima in Rome, the local Hercules had economic and commercial functions. Because of the relationships between archaic Rome and different oriental groups (Cypriots and Phoenicians, maybe through the Etruscans), the Forum Boarium's Hercules could have some oriental connotations, just like he also has deep Greek shapes, but he is surely not *sic et simpliciter* Melqart.

Phoenician traders probably settled in Corstopitum in Great Britain, the cult site of both their ancestral gods, during the Imperial period. Melqart, translated as Herakles, and Astarte (*Inscriptiones Graecae,* XIV, 2253–2254) remain together, even in such a remote place.

From the rich evidence discussed above, from all the Mediterranean shores, scholars conclude that Melqart was one of the most important gods of the Phoenician and Punic world. He was primarily a royal god who was linked with the Syro-Mesopotamian background of the cult of royal ancestors and who had some chthonic, salvific, and healing connotations. Because of the commercial vocation of Tyre and its expansion in the West, Melqart became a god of the sea, who took the Tyrian people to the colonial world. He was not simply a vegetation god, an example of the dying-god typology, but rather a king who protects the population and assures security, victory, wealth, fertility, and stability. Melqart was thus the king's prototype in historical times. His cyclical death, recorded in a special ritual that involved the king, means that without the king's mediation between the divine and the human sphere the world cannot function, fertility ceases, and fecundity disappears, as in the Ugaritic Kirta myth. The annual death and resurrection (*egersis*) of Melqart must demonstrate what a society without a king (a catastrophic event) means and how it is important to reestablish and confirm the primary importance of the king in the balance between life and death, power and destruction, fertility and desolation. This pattern surely includes the life of nature and vegetation, but it goes far beyond.

SEE ALSO Dying and Rising Gods; Eshmun; Heracles.

BIBLIOGRAPHY

Bonnet, Corinne. *Melqart: Cultes et mythes de l'Héraclès tyrien en Méditerranée.* Louvain, Belgium, 1988.

Bonnet, Corinne. "Melqart est-il vraiment le Baal de Tyr?" *Ugarit-Forschungen* 27 (1995): 695–701.

Donner, Herbert, and Wolfgang Ršllig, eds. *KanaanŠische und aramŠische Inschriften,* 5th ed. Wiesbaden, 2002.

Gibson, J. C. L. *Textbook of Syrian Semitic Inscriptions.* Oxford, 1973–1982.

Lipiński, Edward. *Dieux et déesses de l'univers phénicien.* Louvain, Belgium, 1995. See pages 226–243.

Mettinger, Tryggve N. D. *No Graven Image? Israelite Aniconism in its Ancient Near Eastern Context.* Stockholm, 1995.

Mettinger, Tryggve N. D. *The Riddle of Resurrection: "Dying and Rising Gods" in the Ancient Near East.* Stockholm, 2001. See pages 83–111 for a discussion on the dying-god typology.

Parpola, Simo, and Kazuko Watanabe, eds. *Neo-Assyrian Treaties and Loyalty Oaths.* Helsinki, 1988.

Ribichini, Sergio. "Melqart." In *Dictionary of Deities and Demons in the Bible,* 2d ed., edited by Karel van der Toorn, Bob Becking, and Pieter W. van der Horst, pp. 563–565. Leiden, Netherlands, 1999.

Xella, Paolo. "Da Baal di Ugarit agli déi fenici: Una questione di vita o di morte." In *Quando un dio muore: Morti e assenze divine nelle antiche tradizioni mediterranee,* edited by Paolo Xella, pp. 73–96. Verona, Italy, 2001.

Xella, Paolo. "Le soi-disant 'dieu qui meurt' en domaine phénico-punique." *Transeuphratène* 22 (2001): 63–77.

CORINNE BONNET (2005)

MEMORIZATION, as the act of storing information in the memory, is distinguished by the fact that it can be either mechanical or deliberate. It is through practice and imitation, through the mechanical repetition of the traditional gestures and speech of his social group, that the individual, without actually realizing it, memorizes most of the information necessary for proper social and religious behavior. Taken in this sense, memorization culminates in the acquisition of the innumerable actions, of behavior, thought, and sensibility, that define a social and cultural identity. From the classic texts of Maurice Halbwachs on social memory and Marcel Mauss on bodily techniques to the more recent studies of André Leroi-Gourhan on mechanical operatory chains and Erwin Goffman on interaction rites, this type of memory acquisition has been the object of numerous investigations that need not be considered here. It is sufficient to emphasize that, in contrast to this kind of memorization, there exists another, deliberate form, the techniques of which become especially prominent when certain individuals are momentarily separated from their usual social group in order to take part in an initiatory ritual or to become part of an educational institution. These extreme cases do not apply to all members of a community, however, and those to whom they do apply are never required to memorize everything, but only those gestures, techniques, and special narratives that are of particular importance, as for example certain ritual formulas, declarations of faith, religious chants, prayers, and rules of religious behavior. Deliberate memorization thus appears to be a specialization of the more natural process of acquiring knowledge and techniques, religious or otherwise, that unconsciously determine a person's membership in a particular tradition.

To this initial distinction, between mechanical and deliberate memorization, can be added another, which does not coincide with it, but applies to each term independently: the techniques and practices of memorization, be they mechanical or deliberate, vary according to whether they are associated with orality or writing. Studies by Laura Bohannan, E. A. Havelock, and Jack Goody have established that memory is organized differently when written records and models are available; without writing, memory does not function as exact reproduction, but rather as generative recollection that ties repetition to variation. It would be wrong to think that this second distinction is historical. Oral memory and memory determined by writing can easily coexist in the same culture, as the Greek, Jewish, Celtic, and Hindu examples to be mentioned below will show. This is also still the case in contemporary cultures. In the exposition that follows, which must be limited to only a few examples, will be traced a line that leads from the oral to the written. At each stage it is necessary to respect the double contribution of mechanical memorization and deliberate memorization.

In societies without writing, riddles, proverbs, myths, fables, and stories depend upon a memory that is more or less shared by the entire community. In this sense, one can speak of "social memory" or "shared knowledge." However, memorization is often an activity left to the free choice of individuals, to their tastes, affinities, and personal gifts. Henri Junod (1936) recalls a woman among the Tsonga who could tell riddle after riddle until late into the night. He met storytellers of every age and of both sexes: "Such a narrator might know only one story, and repeat it on every occasion, as did Jim Tandane, who told the story of an ogre, Nwatlakoulalambibi, with such enthusiasm that he was nicknamed after his hero! But others can tell six, ten, or twenty stories" (p. 159).

In certain societies, in particular among the Native Populations of North America, the knowledge and the possession of a myth or chant may be the privilege of an individual, who alone may pronounce it. It is for this reason that a Navajo of New Mexico may give as a sign of his poverty the fact that he does not own a single chant. A chant thus becomes a piece of "property" that concerns his own social and spiritual identity.

Most often, however, it is because certain stories are of an important collective interest that they are entrusted to the vigilant memory of one or more persons. The task of memorization is then taken up by a specific institution, often religious. These institutions are generally controlled by an elite close to power. In Rwanda, the oral tradition of the Ubwiiru, in which the rites to be performed by the king were described, was divided into eighteen rituals that were kept strictly secret. In an essay on this oral tradition Pierre Smith (1970) notes that "the individuals in charge of remembering and repeating it word for word—errors could be punished with death—were the most important dignitaries in the kingdom, and the most important three among them, the only ones who knew the text as a whole, partook of the sacred character of royalty" (p. 1385). Such "memory specialists" can be found wherever a community expresses in narrative its needs to preserve its identity. In Oceania, the experts in oral tradition, the "holders of memory," were assembled in colleges analogous to religious confraternities. The most famous among them, portrayed by Victor Ségalen in *Les immémoriaux,* were the *harepo* of Tahiti, who were the keepers of the genealogies, myths, and epics.

> These orators were given true responsibility only after a serious examination, composed of difficult tests. The least mistake in memory was enough to eliminate a candidate, whose preparation was the responsibility of the priests. It is said that the *harepo* practiced in complete isolation, during long nocturnal walks. The transmission of ancestral knowledge rested with them. These story tellers were surrounded by a whole set of religious rituals. (O'Reilly and Poirer, 1956, pp. 1469–1470)

On Easter Island, the *rongorongo,* from noble families often attached to the king, used to teach chants and oral traditions in special huts. Alfred Métraux (1941) describes how this oral tradition is learned: "The student's memory was perfectly trained. During their first years of schooling, they had to learn certain psalms by heart, which they recited while playing cat's cradle: each figure . . . would correspond to a chant to be recited" (p. 168).

Among the Inca, the education of the nobility was the responsibility of the *amautas*, who were of aristocratic descent. Their instruction lasted four years. The first year was devoted to the learning of the Quechua language; the second year to learning the religious traditions; and the third and fourth years to the handling of the famous knotted strings, the *quipu.*

Memorization, as it is practiced by such specialists, becomes a technique that can be taught, and that has its appropriate equipment. The Peruvian *quipu,* the *kou-hau* made by the *rongorongo* on Easter Island, the skeins of coconut fiber adorned with knots made in the Marquesas Islands, the wooden tablets of the Cuna Indians in Panama, and the pieces of bark of the Ojibwa Indians of North America do not, strictly speaking, constitute writing systems, but they do represent mnemotechnical means pertaining to oral memory. The same is true of certain systems of pictographic notation, such as the Aztec ideograms. Fernandon de Alva Ixtlilxóchitl recalls that the Aztec used to have writers for each type of history:

> Some would work with the *Annals* [Xiuhamatl], putting in order the things which took place each year, giving the day, the month, and the hour. Others were charged with the genealogies and ancestries of the kings and lords and persons of lineage. . . . Others took care of the paintings of the boundaries, the limits, and the landmarks of the cities, provinces, and towns, and [recorded] to whom they belonged. (quoted in Léon-Portilla, 1963, p. 157)

These "writers" used pictographs to construct a mnemonic system that later historians could refer to, provided that they also referred to the purely oral tradition of the chants (ibid., p. 156), since as a system of notation it was not sufficient in itself for the total preservation of information. It was necessary in addition to have recourse to the memory that was transmitted by word of mouth through the traditional chants. One finds a similar situation, *mutatis mutandis,* in the early days of Islam, when to read the Qurʾān it was necessary that one already know it, since writing was still too rudimentary to be the sole means of transmission.

In oral cultures, memorization remains closely tied to the conditions of performance, despite the use of mnemonic techniques. Between listening and repeating, the absence of a fixed model does not allow for exact word-for-word repetition. Variability is essential, even though the transformations from one speaker to another often go unnoticed. There is no original version that others could reproduce, or from which they could depart. Claude Lévi-Strauss suggests that there is nevertheless a logical model, which follows certain laws of transformation. Although reproduction is not determined by the ideal of fidelity to an original (a "text"), this does not mean that it thereby becomes prey to arbitrariness. Its flexibility, its adaptability, respects certain formal conditions. "Understood in this way," notes Dan Sperber,

> the facts presented by Lévi-Strauss, these peculiar correspondances and regularities, represent the intellectual capital available for primitive thought, and more particularly . . . for storing and retrieving information in the absence of the external memory which writing provides. Thus the study of myths can clarify the nature of human thought itself, in some of its least known aspects. (*Le savoir des anthropologues,* Paris, 1982, p. 115)

As logical as these rules of transformation can be, and as apt be enlightening on the workings of the human mind, they are not incompatible with trivial motives. Take, for instance, what Edmund Leach (1954) reports of the Kachin of Burma:

> Kachins recount their traditions on set occasions, to justify a quarrel, to validate a social custom, to accompany a religious performance. The story-telling therefore has a purpose; it serves to validate the status of the individual who tells the story, or rather of the individual who hires a bard to tell the story, for among Kachins the telling of traditional tales is a professional occupation carried out by priests and bards of various grades *(jaiwa, dumsa, laika).* But if the status of one individual is validated, that almost always means that the status of someone else is denigrated. One might then infer almost from first principles that every traditional tale will occur in several different versions, each tending to uphold the claims of a different vested interest. (Leach, 1954, pp. 265–266)

This amounts to saying that the priestly bard adjusts his stories to the requirements of the audience who hired him. The horizon of expectation, the "reception," appears to be a constitutive component of oral memory, a component that conditions the very notions of fidelity and truth.

Oral memory does not like writing; there are numerous examples of this. This is not simply because it knows that writing can place it in contradiction with itself. It is primarily because the standard of truth is different for each. To understand this phenomenon better, one may turn to cultures where the two types of memory coexist. First the Celts, where the specialists of the sacred, the druids, ran their own schools, in which the main subject was memorization. According to an Irish judicial treatise, the *ollam* (the highest ranking scholar) was considered the equal of a king; he could recite 350 stories, 250 long ones, and 100 short ones. "As for the tenth-ranked *oblaire,* who makes do with leftovers at a feast, and whose escort is small, only seven stories suffices." The druids, who were the only Celts who knew how to write, refused to use their skill for religious purposes. "They say," wrote Caesar,

> that they learn a great number of verses by heart: some spend twenty years at their school. They believe that religion forbids the use of writing for this purpose, unlike any other purpose such as recording public or private stories, for which they use the Greek alphabet. It seems to me that they established this usage for two reasons. On the one hand, they did not want their doctrine to spread among the people; on the other hand, they did not want those who study to rely on writing and neglect their memory, since it often happens that the use of texts has the effect of reducing efforts to memorize by heart and weakens the memory. (*Gallic Wars* 6.13)

Georges Dumézil (1940) comments on this testimony as follows: "knowledge is reincarnated in each generation, in each student; it is not received as a deposit; it assumes a form which, even while retaining its meaning and its essential traits, rejuvenates it and in a certain measure actualizes it." It is this dynamic, flexible, and adaptable character of oral memory that is threatened by writing. This is apparent from recent testimonies as well, such as that of a native of New Guinea (Humboldt Bay), who told an ethnologist, "in putting down our myths and legislative rules in writing you just kill them." According to Freerk C. Kamma (1975) "he meant to say: to fix or stabilize a progressing living reality means to cut it off from accompanying the living community."

In India, the *brahmans* who teach the Vedas are specialists in the techniques of memory, even though the Vedas have for a long time been fixed in writing. Louis Renou has noted that

> there is something fascinating in the process of memorizing the verses. The master stares at the student while feeding him the verses, so to speak, with an implacable regularity, while the student rocks back and forth in a squatting position. After looking on for a few moments in such a recitation class, one better understands the hymn of the *Rgveda* (7.103) in which this monotonous delivery has been likened to the croaking of frogs. (Renou, 1950, p. 36)

A precise description of the techniques of memorization in the Vedic schools can be found in the fifteenth chapter of the *Rk Pratisakhya,* an old phonetic and grammatical treatise.

E. A. Havelock and Marcel Detienne have insisted on the coexistence of two types of memory in ancient Greece up until the time of Plato: (1) written memory and (2) social memory that is still dependent on oral tradition. Thus it is noteworthy that, although archives were available from the end of the fifth century BCE, it never occured to Greek historians to refer to them as historical sources more reliable than the tradition transmitted by the works of their predecessors (appraised according to their degree of verisimilitude) or transmitted by the experience of sight *(autopsía)* or hearing (testimony). And yet, already from about 470 BCE, Pindar and Aeschylus employ the metaphor that represents memory as an inscription, on the tablets of the soul, of what is fit to be remembered. Shortly before, the poet Simonides is said to have invented the art of memory, a technique built upon the metaphor of writing, which will undergo an important development, passing by way of Roman rhetoric (Quintillian) to the Renaissance. At the beginning of the fourth century BCE, Plato is obviously preoccupied with the negative effects of the invention of writing on memory. And Antisthenes of Athens recommends according more trust to personal memory than to the external memory of written annotations.

Although Homer appears to have been a necessary reference point in ancient Greece, since his written text was learned by heart in the schools and was recited by specialists at religious festivals, there was no religious text that had authority over others. Nor was there a class of religious specialists, comparable to the *pontifices, flamines,* and other Roman colleges, or to the Celtic druids or Vedic brahmans. Essentially pluralist and political, Greek religion was a religion without dogmas. It obeyed customs, which varied from region to region, and from one sanctuary to the next. As a result, correct practice depended on diverse forms of information derived from a variety of sources: the family, the tribe, the town, and so on. Certain religious practices, such as those connected with the mysteries or with divination, were sometimes reserved for certain families or circles of initiates (for example, the Eumolpides and the Ceryces, the Iamides, the Trophoniades), but every Greek, regardless of social status, was capable of addressing a prayer to the gods or performing the actions indispensable to a sacrifice. Deliberate memorization, and for that matter writing as well, appeared as religious practices only in the context of such marginal devotions as Orphism and Pythagoreanism.

In the Judaic tradition, memorization plays a different role in the study of the written Torah than it does in the study of the oral Torah. The written Torah is taught through reading. The transmission of the text, teaching of the scriptures, and public readings, must all be done from a book. Even if these activities eventually result in the memorization of the text, and in fact many rabbis do know the text by heart, it is specified that the written Torah must never be copied from memory. On the other hand, the oral Torah is taught through repetition from memory, even though written notes may be used as a mnemotechnic device, and even though, at an early date, the Mishnah, and then the Talmud, was committed to writing. The masters of the oral Torah, the *tannaim* ("teachers"), were like living memories, capable of reproducing an impressive number of traditions. Their knowledge, often mechanical and lacking in reflection, was used as a reference source by the rabbis and colleges. A famous example is Natronai ben Ḥavivai (eighth century), who wrote down the entire Talmud from memory after immigrating to Spain.

In the Christian tradition, the role of memorization seems to be much less important, although from the fourth century there are references to religious schools where the Psalms, the words of the apostles, prayers, and passages from the Old Testament, were learned by heart. In the Divine Office, for instance, the use of a breviary, even though required to be recited aloud, served as a substitute for memorization. Thus blindness could relieve a monk of the obligation of reciting the hours, save for what he knew from memory.

In Islam, which is a religion of the word as much as a religion of the book, memorization was essential from the very beginning. The words of the Prophet, which repeated the Archangel Gabriel's reading of the archetypal book, were transmitted orally by a group of the companions of the Prophet and by specialists in memorization before the Qurʾān was finally written down. From the time of the third caliph, writing made possible the fixation of the tradition, but it never did away with recourse to memory. In effect, to read the Qur'ān in its primitive form, it was necessary to know its contents. Later, writing and memorization continued to be closely related practices. The Qur'anic schools (*madrasahs*) were tied to a mosque. Children came to learn the Qur'ān by heart, even before they could read. These schools also taught the *ḥadīths*, the tradition that was guaranteed by a chain of authorities, or *isnad.* Before being written down in such texts, such as that of al-Bukhari, this tradition was transmitted orally. The information it gives about the acts and words of the Prophet are used to regulate daily life down to the smallest details, in profane as well as in religious matters. The tradition represents the Prophet himself, sitting in the mosque and teaching the *ḥadīths*. His words are repeated three times by all present, until they are known by heart.

SEE ALSO Anamnesis; Dhikr; Oral Tradition; Tilāwah.

BIBLIOGRAPHY

General Works

For a general discussion of memorization and of method, see Maurice Halbwachs's *Les cadres sociaux de la mémoire* (Paris, 1925) and *La mémoire collective* (Paris, 1950); Marcel Mauss's "Les techniques du corps," *Journal de psychologie* 32 (March–April 1935): 271–293, reprinted in Mauss's *Sociologie et anthropologie* (Paris, pp. 365–383); André Leroi-Gourhan's *Le geste et la parole,* vol. 2, *La mémoire et les rythmes* (Paris, 1965); Laura Bohannan's "A Genealogical Charter," *Africa* 22 (October 1952): 301–315; Jack Goody's *The Domestication of the Savage Mind* (Cambridge, 1977); Jan Assmann, *Das Kulturelle Gedächtnis. Schrift, Erinnerung und politische Identität in frühen Hochkulturen* (München, 1992); Jan Vansina's *Oral Tradition: A Study in Historical Methodology,* translated by H. M. Wright (Chicago, 1965); Ruth Finnegan's *Oral Poetry: Its Nature, Significance and Social Context* (Cambridge, 1977); W. Kelber, "Modalities of Communication, Cognition, and Physiology of Perception: Orality, Rhetoric, Scribality," *Semeia* 65 (1995): 193–216.

Specific Cultures

The following works discuss the role and nature of memorization in specific regions and religious traditions.

Africa

Henri A. Junod, *Mœurs et coutumes des Bantous,* vol. 2, *Vie mentale* (Paris, 1936). Pierre Smith, "La lance d'une jeune fille: Mythe et poésie au Rwanda," in *Échanges et communications: Mélanges offerts à Claude Lévi-Strauss a l'occasion de son soixantième anniversaire,* edited by Pierre Maranda and Jean Pouillon, vol. 2 (The Hague, 1970), pp. 1381–1408.

North America

Marcelle Bouteiller, "Littérature indienne d'Amérique du Nord," in *Histoire des littératures,* edited by Raymond Queneau, vol. 1 (Paris, 1956), pp. 1513–1523. Robert H. Lowie, *Primitive Society* (New York, 1961), pp. 224–232.

Oceania

Patrick O'Reilly and Jean Poirer, "Littératures océaniennes," in *Histoire des littératures,* edited by Raymond Queneau, vol. 1 (Paris, 1956), pp. 1461–1492. Alfred Métraux, *L'Ile de Pâques* (Paris, 1941), pp. 165–179.

The Inca

M. L. Locke, *The Ancient Quipu or Peruvian Knot-Record* (New York, 1923). Rafael Karsten, *A Totalitarian State of the Past: The Civilization of Inca Empire in Ancient Peru* (1949; reprint, Port Washington, N. Y., 1969).

The Aztec

Miguel León-Portilla, *Aztec Thought and Culture: A Study of the Ancient Nahuatl Mind,* translated by Jack Emory (Norman, Okla., 1963).

Burma

Edmund Leach, *Political Systems of Highland Burma: A Study of Kachin Social Structure.* (Cambridge, Mass., 1954).

New Guinea

Freerk C. Kamma, trans. and comp. *Religious Texts of the Oral Tradition from Western New-Guinea (Irian Jaya),* pt. A (Leiden, 1975).

The Celts

Georges Dumézil, "La tradition druidique et l'écriture: Le Vivant et le Mort," *Revue de l'histoire des religions* 121 (March–June 1940): 125–133. Françoise Le Roux and Christian-J. Guyonvarc'h, *Les druides,* 3d ed. (Rennes, 1982).

India

Louis Renou, *Sanskrit et culture* (Paris, 1950). Louis Renou, *Les écoles védiques et la formation du Véda* (Paris, 1957).

Ancient Greece

E. A. Havelock, *Preface to Plato* (Cambridge, Mass., 1963). Marcel Detienne, *L'invention de la mythologie* (Paris, 1981). M. Simondon, *La mémoire et l'oubli dans la pensée grecque jusqu'à la fin du cinquième siècle avant J.-C.: Psychologie archaïque, mythes et doctrines* (Paris, 1982). Marcel Detienne (ed.), *Les savoirs de l'écriture en Grèce ancienne* (Lilles, 1988).

Judaism

Birger Gerhardsson, *Memory and Manuscript: Oral Tradition and Written Transmission in Rabbinic Judaism and Early Christianity,* translated by Eric J. Sharpe (Uppsala, 1961).

Christianity

Theodor Klauser, "Auswendiglernen," in *Reallexikon für Antike und Christentum,* vol. 1 (Stuttgart, 1950).

Islam

Dale F. Eickelman, "The Art of Memory: Islamic Education and Its Social Reproduction," *Comparative Studies in Society and History* 20 (October 1978): pp. 485–516. Pierre Crapon de Caprona, *Le Coran: Aux sources de la parole oraculaire* (Paris, 1981), pp. 147–162; Alfred-Louis de Prémare, *Les fondations de l'Islam. Entre écriture et histoire,* Paris, 2002.

PHILLIPE BORGEAUD (1987 AND 2005)
Translated from French by Marie-Claude Hays-Merlaud

MEMORY SEE ANAMNESIS; MEMORIZATION

MENCIUS SEE MENGZI

MENDELSSOHN, MOSES

MENDELSSOHN, MOSES (1729–1786), German-Jewish philosopher and public figure of the Enlightenment period. Born in Dessau, the son of a poor Torah scribe, Mendelssohn received a traditional education that, rather exceptionally, included the study of the philosophy of Moses Maimonides. In 1743 Mendelssohn followed his teacher to Berlin to continue his Jewish studies. There he was able to acquire considerable knowledge of contemporary mathematics, philosophy, poetry, and classical and modern languages. The German dramatist and critic G. E. Lessing encouraged Mendelssohn to publish his first German essays and used him as the model for the tolerant and modest Jew in his play *Nathan the Wise.* In 1763 Mendelssohn received first prize from the Prussian Royal Academy of Sciences for a treatise on evidence in metaphysics; in the same year he was granted the status of "protected Jew" with rights of residence in Berlin. Mendelssohn supported himself successively as family tutor, bookkeeper, manager, and partner of a Berlin Jewish silk manufacturer; his home became a gathering place for Berlin intellectuals. In the nineteenth century members of the Mendelssohn family (most of whom converted to Christianity after Moses' death) achieved considerable financial, academic, and artistic prominence.

General Metaphysical and Religious Writings. Mendelssohn's philosophical position was derived from the English philosophers John Locke (1632–1704) and Shaftesbury (1671–1713) and especially from the German rationalists Gottfried Wilhelm Leibnitz (1646–1716) and Christian Wolff (1679–1754). The publication of Mendelssohn's *Phädon* (1767), a work on the immortality of the soul and named after Plato's dialogue, established his reputation among the enlightened public. Drawing on Leibnitz's theory of monads, Mendelssohn argues that souls are primary, imperishable elements that impose unity on the changing features of the body. Continued personal consciousness of the soul after death is guaranteed by God, inasmuch as divine wisdom and goodness would not allow the soul to relapse into nothingness without fulfilling its natural impulse to self-perfection. *Morgenstunden, oder Über das Dasein Gottes* (Morning hours, or lectures on the existence of God, 1785), the most methodical of Mendelssohn's major works, moves from a discussion of epistemological issues to the importance of a belief in God, providence, and immortality for man's happiness, to a formal ontological proof of God's existence.

Jewish Writings and Activities. In the mid-1750s Mendelssohn collaborated in a short-lived Hebrew weekly and published a commentary to Maimonides' treatise on logic. He was forced to speak out as a Jew, however, after 1769, when he was publicly challenged to explain why he, an enlightened man, did not convert to Christianity. In a reply to the Swiss pastor, Johann Kasper Lavater, Mendelssohn rejected the implication that his loyalty to Judaism was inconsistent with his innermost enlightened religious convictions and devotion to rational inquiry. In the 1770s Mendelssohn used his influence with liberal Christians to deflect threatened anti-Jewish measures in Switzerland and Germany. In connection with efforts to protect the Jews of Alsace, Mendelssohn encouraged Christian Wilhelm von Dohm to write his classic defense of the civic betterment of the Jews but demurred from Dohm's support of limited judicial autonomy for Jews and the right of Jewry to excommunicate recalcitrant Jews.

Mendelssohn's translation of the Pentateuch into German was published in 1780. It was accompanied by a commentary (the *Bi'ur*) that draws on both traditional exegesis and modern literary aesthetics. Often reprinted, the translation drew the ire of some traditionalist rabbis but served as an important bridge to modern culture for many young Jews in the nineteenth century.

Jerusalem, or On Religious Power and Judaism. Mendelssohn's principal contribution to Jewish thought was the result of yet another challenge by a Christian, this time concerning an alleged inconsistency in his supporting the abolition of excommunication while remaining loyal to biblical law, which condones coercion. Mendelssohn's reply, *Jerusalem, oder Über religiöse Macht und Judenthum* (1783), was one of the first works in German to plead for freedom of conscience in religious matters, separation of church and state, and (indirectly) civil rights for the Jews. According to Mendelssohn both states and church have as their final goals the promotion of human happiness. The state is permitted to enforce specific actions, whereas the church's task is to convince its followers of their religious and ethical duties through persuasion alone. To the question of the continued authority of Jewish law, which was adumbrated by Spinoza in the *Tractatus Theologico-Politicus,* Mendelssohn replied that the ceremonial law stemming from the Hebrew Bible is binding solely on the Jewish people; Judaism is a religion of revealed legislation, not of revealed beliefs. The existence and unity of God, the reality of divine providence, and the immortality of the soul are to be affirmed on the grounds of natural reason, not miracles or supernatural revelation. Mendelssohn acknowledges the importance of Spinoza in the history of philosophy but vigorously rejects Spinoza's pantheism. Spinoza's primary concern was the noninterference by the state or religious authorities in the intellectual freedom of the philosopher and scientist. Mendelssohn, while still affirming the continued authority of Jewish law, was concerned with freedom inside one religion as well as freedom of religion for minority communities.

Mendelssohn argued that the identification of church and state in biblical Israel ceased with the destruction of the ancient commonwealth; laws remaining in force are personal religious duties that preserve the universal principles of Jewish faith against lapses into idolatry and polytheism. These laws will not lose their force until God arranges another indubitable supernatural revelation to the Jewish people to supersede that of Mount Sinai. Loyalty to the Jewish law, however, does not prevent Jews from assuming the legitimate duties of citizenship in an enlightened society.

The Place of Mendelssohn in the History of Jewish Thought. Although Mendelssohn's synthesis of philosophical theism and traditional religious observance was viewed as outdated by the next generation of Jewish thinkers influenced by Kant and Hegel, Mendelssohn could be seen as forebear of the conflicting trends of nineteenth-century German Jewry: Reform, for his openness to change; and Neo-Orthodoxy, for his insistence on the binding nature of Jewish ceremonial law. Mendelssohn's disciples among the writers who collaborated with him in the *Bi'ur* were prominent in the Jewish Enlightenment (the Haskalah) that emerged in Prussia in the 1770s and later spread to eastern Europe. Mendelssohn was revered by the Enlighteners (*maskilim*) for having moved from the ghetto to modern society without abandoning the Jewish tradition or the Jewish people. In the 1880s, however, at the end of the Haskalah period, Mendelssohn was assailed for having paved the way to the loss of Jewish distinctiveness and, therefore, to assimilation. In retrospect, his thought and life can be seen to have posed some of the fundamental issues of Jewish religious survival in secular, liberal society.

BIBLIOGRAPHY

The standard edition of Mendelssohn's writings is *Gesammelte Schriften Jubiläumsausgabe*, 7 vols., edited by Fritz Bamberger and others and incompletely published between 1929 and 1938; a completed edition in 20 volumes is being prepared under the editorship of Alexander Altmann (Stuttgart, 1971–). The most recent English translation of *Jerusalem* is by Allan Arkush, with an introduction and commentary by Alexander Altmann (Hanover, N.H., 1983). Useful is *Moses Mendelssohn: Selections from His Writings*, edited and translated by Eva Jospe (New York, 1975). The magisterial biography of Mendelssohn is Alexander Altmann's *Moses Mendelssohn: A Biographical Study* (University, Ala., 1973). On Mendelssohn's role in the intellectual history of Judaism, see Michael A. Meyer's *The Origins of the Modern Jew: Jewish Identity and European Culture in Germany, 1749–1824* (Detroit, 1967), chap. 1; Julius Guttmann's *Philosophies of Judaism*, translated by David W. Silverman (New York, 1964), pp. 291–303; and H. I. Bach's *The German Jew: A Synthesis of Judaism and Western Civilization, 1730–1930* (Oxford, 1984), pp. 44–72).

New Sources

Arkush, Allan. *Moses Mendelssohn and the Enlightenment.* Albany, 1994.

Berghahn, Cord-Friedrich. *Moses Mendelssohns "Jerusalem:" ein Beitrag zur Geschichte der Menschenrechte und der pluralistischen Gesellschaft in der deutschen Aufklärung.* Tübingen, 2001.

Sorkin, David Jan. *Moses Mendelssohn and the Religious Enlightenment.* Berkeley, Calif., 1996.

ROBERT M. SELTZER (1987)
Revised Bibliography

MENDICANCY. As a religious term, *mendicancy* (from the Latin *mendicare*, "to beg") denotes renunciation of all worldly possessions and the practice of begging alms from door to door. The custom is of ancient origin and, although its observance has varied in character from place to place, the general impetus for the phenomenon seems to have derived from an idea that the discipline of living solely on alms is conducive to the attainment of spiritual goals. Early in the Vedic period, *brahman* mendicants had precise rules for soliciting alms, and among the ancient Greeks, mendicant priests went from place to place in quest of alms on behalf of their favorite deities (e.g., Isis and Artemis Opis). Among the Romans, certain priests who were bound by vows of temperance received support from public almsgiving. (According to some critics, these mendicants had occasionally to be reminded to restrain their extravagant demands; see Cicero, *On the Laws* 50.) Although religious mendicancy is a phenomenon that still finds acceptance in varying degrees in a number of cultures, it is chiefly within the Hindu, Buddhist, Christian, and Islamic traditions that it has won sanction as a religious practice.

In the Hindu tradition, pious men with sons to carry on the family line have long had open to them a renunciant ideal by which they may give away their possessions to *brahmans* and go forth into homelessness, first as a hermit (*vanaprastha*) and later as a mendicant (*saṃnyāsin*) who begs from door to door. Individuals from different ranks of society have sometimes chosen to devote themselves to a life of poverty and meditation, dependent for support upon others. The Hindu mystic's quest for illumination, for union with ultimate reality, generally promotes such an attitude of indifference to worldly concerns, and, since liberation (*mokṣa*) from them is one of the recognized aims of a Hindu's life, the asceticism of the mendicant is perceived as a positive means for achieving that goal.

In Buddhism, the monastic enterprise instituted by Gautama Buddha was probably derived from even more ancient Vedic ascetic movements. For the Buddhist, renunciation of the world is considered meritorious in that it allows the devotee to dedicate his or her energies to the task of delivering people from suffering. Both laypersons and monastics subscribe to mendicancy as a practice leading to the lessening of attachment and, hence, ultimately to *nirvāṇa.* The daily life of the monastic mendicants usually includes regular rounds from house to house for the purpose of gathering alms; whatever food is placed in their bowls is to be accepted gratefully. Monks and nuns are exhorted to follow specific rules (e.g., not discriminating between houses when begging, eating solely from an alms bowl, eating only one meal per day, etc.). They are instructed that no real value obtains in external performances; only if alms-gathering is attended by the desire for *nirvāṇa* can this discipline be meritorious. Although the practice of begging food and alms still prevails in most countries where Buddhist monasticism exists, meals are also often brought to the monasteries so that the laypeople may acquire extra merit.

In early Christian history, pious mendicants (Lat., *solitarii, gyrovagi*) wandered through city and countryside, preaching and begging alms, but they usually did not meet with popular acceptance. Jerome, for example, complained that some of these *solitarii* were accustomed to wandering from house to house, often leading people astray and living a life of luxury at the expense of other Christians. Monastic or semimonastic communities were in existence by the beginning of the fourth century and, although their inhabitants may have had to resort to begging during hard times, they generally sustained themselves by their own labors. It was not until the time of Francis of Assisi and Dominic (twelfth and thirteenth centuries) that mendicant orders as such arose and eventually became sanctioned by the church hierarchy. The appearance of these mendicant orders ensued as a protest against the corruption within certain established monastic communities (a problem with which the mendicant orders themselves had to deal at a later time, when abuses crept into their own communities).

Four mendicant orders were approved by the Council of Lyons (1274): Franciscans, Dominicans, Carmelites, and Augustinians. Francis insisted that his followers own nothing whatever, for they were to be "pilgrims and strangers in this world," living with confidence in God's care and subsisting on alms received from those among whom they preached and worked. After the deaths of Francis and Dominic, however, church authorities mitigated the orders' rules to allow for possession of worldly goods. From time to time, members of the Roman Catholic and Greek Orthodox churches have, in an attempt to return to the simplicity of the message of the Gospel, initiated reform movements that included mendicancy. Their belief was that through ascetic practices such as begging, Christians might rid themselves of the imperfections and sins that kept them from union with God—especially by placing one's daily life in God's hands (*divina providentia*)—by complete reliance on God for subsistence one might more quickly achieve that union with the divine. Toward the end of the Middle Ages, mendicancy as a religious practice was prohibited by the Roman Catholic church because of various abuses that had crept into the system.

Within Islamic tradition, there has generally been disagreement as to the value of mendicancy. Some have argued that, since the Qur'ān contains injunctions against begging, it is debatable whether dependence upon others for one's sustenance is more virtuous than having independent means. Mendicancy on a broad scale came into vogue with the ninth-century Ṣūfīs; these were Muslim ascetics who interpreted *zuhd* ("renunciation") in a strictly spiritual sense, viewing it as the abandonment of all that diverts one from God.

Many of the early Ṣūfīs carried the Islamic theory of *tawakkul* ("trust [in God]") to an extreme, defining it as renunciation of all personal initiative and volition. Since everything is in God's hands, Ṣūfīs were neither to beg nor work for pay but to depend on what God has sent as a gift, either directly or through the generous alms of others. This system often proved ineffective, and some Ṣūfīs wandered from place to place, trusting in God to provide their livelihood. At times, the result was starvation and, gradually, Ṣūfīs concluded that trust in God and seeking a livelihood were not mutually exclusive. The words *faqīr* and *darwīsh* (Arabic and Persian for "poor") are terms for religious mendicants who ask for food or money in the name of God. They profess a life of poverty and withdrawal from worldly pursuits for the purpose of deepening their spiritual insights and communing more intimately with God. Some mendicants follow their careers independently, and others (like their Christian counterparts) live communally. The doctrines of these mendicants and their orders are derived from Ṣūfī principles and beliefs, particularly those that stress dependence upon God.

Within these four religious traditions, mendicancy has generally connoted withdrawal from worldly possessions and worldly pursuits for the purpose of demonstrating and experiencing a sense of dependency upon God and/or a supreme life principle. Wherever mendicancy has become accepted as a religious practice, almsgiving also has been elevated to an act of merit whose efficacy is rarely surpassed by other virtues. It, too, is considered in positive terms as a way of distancing oneself from society in order to transcend the material world.

SEE ALSO Almsgiving; Eremitism; Religious Communities, article on Christian Religious Orders; Saṃnyāsa.

BIBLIOGRAPHY

Although there are no specific monographs on mendicancy, the following encyclopedias, dictionaries, and texts provide relevant material on the topic.

Boyle, L. E. "Mendicant Orders." In *New Catholic Encyclopedia*, vol. 9. New York, 1967.

Brandon, S. G. F., ed. *A Dictionary of Comparative Religion.* London, 1970.

Hastings, James, ed. *Encyclopaedia of Religion and Ethics.* 13 vols. Edinburgh, 1908–1926. See the index, s. v. *Mendicant orders.*

Hughes, Thomas P. *A Dictionary of Islam.* London, 1885.

Macdonald, D. B. *Religious Attitude and Life in Islam.*

Parrinder, Geoffrey. *Dictionary of Non-Christian Religions.* Philadelphia, 1971.

Spiro, Melford E. *Buddhism and Society.* New York, 1970.

Stutley, Margaret, and James Stutley. *A Dictionary of Hinduism.* London, 1977.

New Sources

Bailey, Michael. "Religious Poverty, Mendicancy and Reform in the Late Middle Ages." *Church History* 72 (September 2003): 457–484.

Jotischley, Andrew. *The Carmelites and Antiquity: Mendicants and Their Pasts in the Middle Ages.* New York, 2002.

Lawrence, C. H. *The Friars: The Impact of the Early Mendicant Movement on Western Society.* New York, 1994.

Lu, Hanchao. "Becoming Urban: Mendicancy and Vagrants in Modern Shanghai." *Journal of Social History* 33 (Fall 1999): 7–37.

Munzer, Stephen. "Heroism, Spiritual Development and Triadic Bonds in Jain and Christian Almsgiving." *Numen: International Review for the History of Religions* 48 (2001): 47–80.

ROSEMARY RADER (1987)
Revised Bibliography

MENG-TZU SEE MENGZI

MENGZI.

The name *Mengzi,* meaning literally "Master Meng," is the honorific epithet of Meng Ke (391–308 BCE), known in the West as "Mencius." Mengzi defended and developed Kongzi's (Confucius's) teachings in response to various challenges in the highly diverse and contentious intellectual world of fourth-century BCE China. In the process, he expounded innovative views about heaven, human nature, the mind, and self-cultivation that proved to be of profound and enduring importance in the later Confucian tradition.

Mengzi was a native of Zou, a small state located at the base of the Shandong peninsula. Traditional accounts claim that he studied under Zisi, Confucius's grandson, but it is more likely that he was a student of one of Zisi's disciples. Mengzi's teachings bear some similarities to parts of the *Li ji* (Book of rites), which tradition ascribes to Zisi. One also finds common themes and ideas in recently excavated texts, which show that Mengzi was participating in an ongoing debate about the nature of the emerging Confucian tradition.

The earliest information we have about Mengzi's life comes from the text that bears his name. In its present form, the *Mengzi* consists of seven books, each of which is divided into two parts, which are further subdivided into sections of varying length. The shortest sections consist of brief dicta, while the longest extend to over two thousand words. These purportedly record the teachings of Mengzi and conversations he had with various disciples, friends, royal patrons, and rivals. Some accounts claim that Mengzi himself composed the text, others that it was compiled by his disciples with his approval and advice. In the second century CE, the *Mengzi* was edited and several "chapters" were discarded by Zhao Qi, who also wrote the first extant commentary.

The *Mengzi* had a place, but not a distinguished position, among Confucian writings until its remarkable ascent toward the end of the Tang dynasty (618–907). In the following Song (960–1279), Yuan (1206–1368), and Ming (1368–1644) dynasties it came to occupy a singularly important place in the Confucian scriptural pantheon. The great Zhu Xi (1130–1200) wrote a highly influential commentary on the *Mengzi* and included it, along with the *Analects, Great Learning,* and *Doctrine of the Mean,* as one of the "Four Books"—a collection intended to serve as the gateway to Confucian learning. In 1315 the Mongol court recognized the *Mengzi* as a classic and secured its preeminent position within the tradition. Since that time the text has enjoyed remarkable influence and prestige. It is one of the most highly studied Confucian classics among contemporary scholars.

CENTRAL TEACHINGS. Mengzi is renowned for advocating the theory that "human nature is good" (*xing shan;* 6A2, 6A6). A central claim of this theory is that heaven has endowed human beings with nascent moral "sprouts" (*duan*), which are the defining features of human nature (2A6). These innate moral tendencies are active and observable aspects of human nature, but they do not exhaustively describe the nature of human beings. They are the beginnings of morality, but like all sprouts they require a period of growth, care, and the right kind of environment in order to reach maturity (2A2, 6A7). The sprouts of morality are sensibilities of the heart-and-mind (*xin*), which is also the seat of human cognition, emotion, and volition. For Mengzi, the task of cultivating one's nature begins with an awareness of the moral aspects of the heart-and-mind, and consists in mobilizing the various faculties of the *xin* to protect, nurture, and develop these nascent moral assets. Successfully cultivating the moral sprouts, and thereby fulfilling one's nature, is the proper way to serve heaven, and in the course of this process one comes to understand heaven's decree (7A1).

Mengzi claims that four moral sprouts constitute the core of human nature; these serve as the bases of his four cardinal virtues: benevolence, righteousness, propriety, and wisdom (2A6). Throughout one's life, these moral sprouts regularly spring up—even though one often fails to notice or cultivate them. In certain contexts, in unguarded moments, they break through accumulated bad habits and indifference to manifest themselves in small, spontaneous moral acts. One of Mengzi's main tasks as a moral teacher is to help people notice, appreciate, and focus attention on such "giveaway" actions.

Giveaway actions are one of several types of evidence Mengzi adduces for the existence of the moral sprouts. He also supports his claim about innate moral tendencies by posing hypothetical scenarios or thought experiments designed to illustrate the universal presence of moral feelings in human beings. For example, he asks us to imagine what one would feel if one were suddenly to see a child about to fall into a well (2A6, 3A5). Mengzi claims that every person facing such a scene would feel alarm and concern for the child. This spontaneous feeling of compassion shows that by nature we are creatures who care for one another.

Mengzi argues further that there is a heavenly endowed structure and hierarchy to human nature (6A14–15). Each of our various parts has a natural station and function that determine its place within the hierarchy and its relative value. No one who is aware of the natural hierarchy and its different functions would act against them, nor would such a person sacrifice a part of greater importance for one of lesser importance. The natural function of the *xin* is to reflect on and determine the relative merit of different courses of action because it alone has the capacity to consider, weigh, and judge among the various alternatives we face.

Mengzi never claimed that our innate moral tendencies alone guarantee moral development. These are only the beginnings of virtue; they need attention, effort, and the right kind of environment to attain their full forms. Without sustained and concerted work, human beings will not become moral. His central metaphors for self-cultivation are agricultural (not merely vegetative) and farming requires attention, persistence, and a great deal of hard work. According to Mengzi, people are not born good; but rather are born for goodness (6A6). Our moral sprouts must ripen, as grain must ripen (6A19), before our true nature is revealed.

NEO-CONFUCIAN REVIVAL. Toward the end of the Tang dynasty, Mengzi and his teachings became a rallying point for a broad revival that modern scholars call neo-Confucianism. This important movement was propelled by a series of political, military, economic, and social crises that together motivated many Chinese intellectuals to regard their contemporary culture as corrupted, weak, and ineffective and to seek a renewal in an older, indigenous Chinese culture. A number of influential late Tang thinkers pointedly criticized Buddhism and Daoism for eroding and undermining Chinese culture. The former was especially castigated as a "foreign" and baleful influence on indigenous culture and was held responsible for a litany of social problems. Accompanying such criticisms were calls for a return to "traditional" Chinese culture, and the *Mengzi* proved to be one of the most important texts singled out for renewed interest.

Modern scholars tend to describe this rediscovery of the *Mengzi* in strategic terms. That is to say, the *Mengzi's* teachings on human nature and the cultivation of the mind offered a version of the tradition that could effectively engage the sophisticated philosophies found in Buddhist and Daoist rivals. While there is some truth in this, such an account obscures the degree to which these "rival" traditions transformed the way all Chinese intellectuals thought about themselves and their world. It is more accurate to say that the *Mengzi* and other early texts favored by neo-Confucians, such as the *Doctrine of the Mean* and the *Great Learning*, were chosen because they fit what had become a new, general paradigm of thought, one that owed a great deal to the influence of Buddhism and Daoism.

Among the features of this new paradigm was a belief in a hidden, pure, fundamental nature and a manifest, defiled, physical nature. The former defines what we and other creatures *really* are while the latter corrupts our "original" nature and gives rise to everything bad. Our fundamental nature is shared with all things in the universe and unites us not only with all other human beings but with all creatures and things as well. Those who fully appreciate the true character of their nature understand this, and such insight allows them to "form one body" with all things. However, the understanding of most people is beclouded by the errant aspects of their physical nature, which give rise to and are reinforced by "selfish desires." The task of cultivating one's original heavenly nature consists primarily of eliminating the obscuring influence of such errant aspects. As a practical matter, this entails the elimination of selfish desires, a process that enables one to find the "Mind of the Way" (*daoxin*) within the "Human Mind" (*renxin*).

Under the influence of this new paradigm, neo-Confucians reappropriated Mengzi's teachings about a heavenly-conferred, morally good nature, along with its focus on the cultivation of the heart-and-mind. However, seen through this new lens, Mengzi's original teachings took on a dramatically different form. For example, while Mengzi had advocated the sustained and gradual development of moral sprouts, neo-Confucians sought to discover and bring into play a fully-formed moral mind. This change generated a new and unprecedented belief in the inherent perfection of all human beings and a corresponding concern with "enlightenment" as a religious goal. Mengzi did not employ the stark contrast, common to most neo-Confucian thinkers, between a pure, fundamental nature in opposition to a corrupt yet reformable physical nature. Nor did he ever envisage anything resembling the way neo-Confucians deployed these basic metaphysical notions to construct a scheme in which human nature was fundamentally united with the rest of the universe. Nevertheless, the major neo-Confucian thinkers all saw themselves as inheritors and defenders of Mengzi's line of the Confucian tradition.

The neo-Confucian revival was a vast, complex, and exceedingly rich movement that continued for more than a thousand years. However, many of its main themes were defined by the Lu-Wang and Cheng-Zhu schools. Both of these "schools" are loosely defined in terms of their respective emphases regarding the nature of the *xin* and the proper methods of self-cultivation. The former takes the thought of Lu Xiangshan (1139–1193) and Wang Yangming (1472–1529) as its primary sources of inspiration, whereas the latter looks to Cheng Yi (1033–1107), Cheng Hao (1032–1085), and Zhu Xi. Roughly speaking, members of the former school express a greater faith in the inherent purity and power of the *xin*. As a result, they tend to emphasize an extreme form of particularism in which every ethical decision and action is strongly dependent upon context, and moral progress is primarily a matter of personal reflection and struggle. They distrust rules, precedents, and conventions and advocate a radical independence on the part of individuals. Followers of the Cheng-Zhu school have an equally strong faith in the existence of a fundamental nature. However, they believe that human beings are guided to this nature primarily through a course of careful and dedicated study, practice, and reflection. They view adherents of the Lu-Wang school as self-indulgent and undisciplined and see their teachings and practices as the road to spiraling selfishness and deepening delusion.

Later Confucian thinkers such as Yan Yuan (1635–1704) and Dai Zhen (1723–1777) sharply criticized the followers of both the Lu-Wang and Cheng-Zhu schools for abandoning Mengzi's original legacy. Both of these Qing dynasty (1644–1911) critics accused earlier neo-Confucians of incorporating too much Buddhism and Daoism into their philosophy. They rightly pointed out that much of the metaphysical speculation underlying both Lu-Wang and Cheng-Zhu thought was alien to Mengzi and his age. Moreover, these foreign elements worked to obscure some of the most profound insights of Mengzi's original vision. Prominent among these is his emphasis on certain shared human reactive attitudes as the basis of the moral life. Both Yan and Dai insisted that our physical, embodied life, with all its feelings and desires, is the site of both our best and worst aspects. We must not look to obscure metaphysical theories for moral guidance. Heaven has endowed each of us with the means, and the Confucian tradition provides all of us with the Way. The challenge is to understand and practice the Way in order to develop the best parts of our nature to their full potential.

IMPLICATIONS OF MENGZI'S THOUGHT FOR RELIGIOUS ETHICS. Traditionally, religious ethics has had a difficult time bringing together a more anthropological, descriptive account of what is good for human beings and the prescriptions of revealed religion. An echo of this tension is seen as the central problem of modern philosophical ethics as well: how to reconcile one's personal interests with the demands of morality. Mengzi's thought appears to avoid many of the problems associated with at least the religious version of this type of challenge. For according to Mengzi, heaven has created us in such a way that we live the best lives possible for creatures like us only when we fully realize our heavenly endowed moral nature. Moreover, part of what heaven instills in us is a natural tendency and taste for morality and a natural aversion for what is morally bad. On such a view, there is no conflict between human flourishing and what heaven commands. In fact, a life in service to heaven is the only way to the most satisfying and pleasant life that human beings can have.

Such a view might lead one to ask if *heaven* is just an honorific term used to express approval for what human beings naturally find most satisfying. Does heaven place restrictions on what constitutes the human good? One possible response, which incorporates early Confucian concerns about the importance of natural harmony, is that heaven does constrain conceptions of the human good by serving as the source of all things in the universe. Humans seek harmony within the natural order but cannot fundamentally alter or damage this order without violating heaven's plan. While heaven is not a personal deity for Mengzi, it is an agent with a plan for the world, and that on occasion acts in the world to realize its will.

Mengzi's description of the religious life in terms of the *dao* and the degree to which knowledge of the Way is accessible to human beings are also issues of interest for religious ethics. Mengzi's reverence for Confucian learning, with its legacy of sacred texts, rituals, and sagely teachers, seems to privilege those within this tradition. On the other hand, he insists that heaven has endowed all human beings with the nascent sprouts that are the basis of moral knowledge. This seems to open up the Way to all who are prepared to dedicate themselves to the task of self-cultivation. In thinkers like Wang Yangming, these aspects of Mengzi's teachings find expression as a profound faith that each and every person has a pure and perfect divine guide within.

These brief remarks only sketch Mengzi's thought and offer some suggestions about its value as a source for religious ethical reflection. What is beyond dispute is that his religious vision has inspired many of the best minds throughout East and Southeast Asia for more than two thousand years, and the *Mengzi* continues to challenge and inspire contemporary thinkers throughout the world.

SEE ALSO Cheng Yi; Dai Zhen; Li; Lu Xiangshan; Mozi; Ren and Yi; Wang Yangming; Zhu Xi.

BIBLIOGRAPHY

Translations

Lau, D. C., trans. *Mencius.* Harmondsworth, U.K., 1970. A readable and reliable translation with indispensable introduction and appendices.

Legge, James, trans. *The Chinese Classics;* Vol. 2: *The Works of Mencius* (1861). Reprint, Hong Kong, 1970. A classic translation with Chinese text, extensive notes, and supporting material. This edition includes Arthur Waley's notes on translation.

Nivison, David S. "On Translating Mencius." *Philosophy East and West* 30 (1980): 93–122. A remarkable and philosophically revealing review of translations of the text into English and other languages.

Secondary Works

Chan, Alan K. L., ed. *Mencius: Contexts and Interpretations.* Honolulu, 2002. A conference volume exploring Mengzi's thought from a variety of perspectives.

Ivanhoe, Philip J. *Confucian Moral Self Cultivation.* 2d ed. Indianapolis, 2000. An introduction to the Confucian tradition focused on the work of seven major figures, including Mengzi and several others discussed in this entry.

Ivanhoe, Philip J. *Ethics in the Confucian Tradition: The Thought of Mengzi and Wang Yangming.* 2d ed. Indianapolis, 2002. A study comparing Mengzi's philosophy with that of the neo-Confucian Wang Yangming.

Liu, Xiusheng, and Philip J. Ivanhoe, eds. *Essays on the Moral Philosophy of Mengzi.* Indianapolis, 2002. An anthology of classic and contemporary works on Mengzi's moral philosophy.

Nivison, David S. *The Ways of Confucianism: Investigations in Chinese Philosophy.* Edited by Bryan W. Van Norden. LaSalle, Ill., 1996. An anthology containing a number of seminal essays on Mengzi's thought and its later influence.

Shun, Kwong-loi. *Mencius and Early Chinese Thought.* Stanford, Calif., 1997. A thorough, meticulous, and carefully argued study of various aspects of Mengzi's moral philosophy with particular emphasis on how it has been read by traditional and contemporary interpreters.

Tu, Wei-ming. *Humanity and Self-Cultivation: Essays in Confucian Thought.* Berkeley, 1979; reprint, Boston, 1998. A collection of essays on historical figures and contemporary issues from the most influential spokesman for the contemporary Mengzian religious vision.

Yearley, Lee H. *Mencius and Aquinas: Theories of Virtue and Conceptions of Courage.* Albany, N.Y., 1990. An excellent and revealing comparison of Mengzi and Thomas Aquinas as virtue ethicists with a focus on courage as a virtue.

PHILIP J. IVANHOE (2005)

MENNONITES. The Mennonites, a Christian denomination, were first called Menists, or Mennonites, in 1541 by Countess Anna of Friesland after the group's primary leader, Menno Simons (1496–1561). She used this name in order to distinguish the Mennonites, as peaceful settlers whom she welcomed in her lands, from other, revolutionary, groups. Historically and theologically, Mennonites are the direct descendants of sixteenth-century Anabaptists, a radical reform group in Europe.

EARLY HISTORY AND DOCTRINE. One of the most significant influences upon Mennonite history and identity has been the experience of decades of persecution during the sixteenth and seventeenth centuries. Numerous martyrologies, including the classic *Martyrs' Mirror* (1660), testify to this experience. The Mennonites lived in an age that was not ready for religious or social pluralism. In their insistence upon a church constituted of believers only, and in their embodiment of the principles of voluntary church membership and the separation of church and state, they represented a counterculture that society could not tolerate. In their reading of the Bible, however, they found these principles to be self-evident, particularly in the teaching and example of Jesus Christ. In keeping with the vision of their Anabaptist forebears, the Mennonites also shared the vision of a New Testament church restored both in essence and in form.

A church-world dualism was implicit in the Mennonites' theology and social view. It had been given early expression in the "Brotherly Union" of 1527, sometimes called the Schleitheim Confession of Faith, article four of which states:

> Now there is nothing else in the world and all creation than good or evil, believing and unbelieving, darkness and light, the world and those who are [come] out of the world, God's temple and idols, Christ and Belial, and none will have part with the other.

Toleration came to the Mennonites first in the Netherlands in the 1570s and somewhat later in other parts of Europe, except in Switzerland, where severe restrictions against them remained until the eighteenth century. Increasing freedom in the north led to rapid growth in membership, until by 1700 the Dutch congregations included 160,000 members. The sectarian virtues of frugality and hard work led to considerable affluence and to urbanization. Soon Mennonites became prominent patrons of the arts in the Netherlands. Numerous artists, poets, and writers from among their ranks achieved lasting fame. But the Enlightenment spirit of rationalism and secularism was also a part of these developments, and by 1837 there were only 15,300 members left in the Netherlands. Late-nineteenth- and twentieth-century developments resulted in another increase in membership.

The early pattern of survival through withdrawal from society led to numerous migrations. Records indicate that emigration from the Netherlands eastward to Hamburg and along the coast to Danzig (present-day Gdańsk) began as early as 1534. Eventually large settlements developed in the Vistula delta. In 1788, migrations began from there to the Ukraine. By 1835 some 1,600 families had settled on Russian lands. By 1920 this population had grown to 120,000. But migration began again, this time from Russia beginning in the 1870s, primarily to North America.

A similar pattern prevailed among the Swiss and South German Mennonites. Many escaped Swiss persecution by migrating to the Palatinate or to central Germany. Others immigrated to the United States and Canada, beginning in 1663. The first permanent Mennonite settlement in the United States was established at Germantown, six miles north of Philadelphia, in 1683. Yet the total number of western European Mennonites coming to North America did not exceed 8,000, which, along with the approximately 55,000 immigrants from Prussian, Polish, and Russian lands, contributed to a core immigration to North America of no more than 70,000 up to the mid-1980s. There have also been migrations from North America, primarily from Canada to Mexico, Paraguay, Bolivia, and other Latin American locations. Thus pilgrimage has been central to Mennonite identity.

While Mennonites are non-creedal and affirm the Bible as their final authority for faith and life, they have written numerous confessions throughout their history. Chief among these are the *Brotherly Union* (1527) and the *Dordrecht Confession of Faith* (1632). In these the nature of the church as a believing, covenanting, caring, and obedient fellowship is central, as would be in keeping with the vision of restoring the New Testament church. The importance of the new birth and the authority of the Bible are stressed. Peace, including absolute pacifism, is considered an integral part of the gospel and, therefore, part of the discipleship of the believer. This discipleship is possible within the context of an Arminian theology, which acknowledges free will rather than Augustinian determinism. The second Adam, Christ, has undone the damage of the first Adam, making possible a gradual transformation of the disciple's life into the image of Christ himself. Ethics is a part of the Good News. Grace is necessary for discipleship rather than being antithetical to it. The believer who has experienced this grace is ready to receive baptism as a covenanting member of the "Believers' Church," a term commonly used since the 1950s to refer to those who are baptized as adults.

LATER DEVELOPMENTS. Partly through migration and natural increase, but particularly through twentieth-century missionary activities, Mennonites were scattered across the globe by the late twentieth century. In the early 1990s their total membership worldwide was approximately 800,000. The

Mennonite World Conference, begun in 1925, meets every five or six years for fellowship and the sharing of ideas, as well as for worship and celebration. It is not a delegate conference, and no decisions binding upon world membership are made.

The extent to which contemporary Mennonites hold to the doctrines of early Anabaptism varies from nation to nation, from group to group, and even from congregation to congregation. Mennonites do form regional and national conferences, but they are basically congregational in polity. The Amish, who split off from Swiss and Alsatian Mennonites in 1693–1697, as well as the Hutterites and some conservative Mennonites, do not form conferences. Historically, Pietism, more than other socioreligious movements, has influenced Mennonite theology; fundamentalism has also had an impact in North America. Both movements strengthen the inner, personal, and experiential aspect of faith but weaken social concern, pacifism, and the inherent church-world dualism of the sixteenth century. An enthusiastic recovery of the Anabaptist vision, led by Harold S. Bender (1897–1962), has modified these influences since the 1940s.

Anabaptists Four Centuries Later (Kauffman and Harder, 1975) provides a profile of late-twentieth-century North American Mennonite religious attitudes and practices. In relation to two doctrinal orthodoxy scales established in the study, 90 percent of the respondents chose the most orthodox response on a liberal-orthodox continuum. About 80 percent of the members could identify a specific conversion experience. The practice of daily personal prayer ranged from a low of 73 percent in one conference to a high of 82 percent in another. More than 80 percent reported regular Sunday school participation, with teenagers having the highest rating. Fewer than 2 percent of the membership had experienced divorce or separation. Some 85 percent considered sexual intercourse before marriage as always wrong. The early emphasis on church-world dualism, pacifism, not taking oaths, and church discipline was affirmed by a range of from 60 to 80 percent, depending upon the conference.

This religious stance is nurtured through worship, attendance at denominational schools, devotional practices, small-group Bible study, and involvement in mission and service projects. Church buildings are generally functional and relatively austere. Worship services are usually sermon-centered. Most congregations enjoy singing, often a cappella. The Lord's Supper is celebrated two to four times annually. Some congregations practice the rite of foot washing.

Numerous liberal arts colleges are maintained in North America; they were established originally to train workers for church vocations. Seminaries, Bible schools, secondary schools, and other church institutions are maintained by Mennonites around the world as political and economic conditions permit. Retirement centers, community mental health centers, and medical and disaster aid services are maintained particularly in North America and Europe. The concern for united help for needy people around the world led to organization of the Mennonite Central Committee (MCC) in North America in 1920. A Dutch Mennonite relief agency had been organized two hundred years earlier. In 2003, the MCC had a cash and material aid budget in excess of $62 million, spent on projects both abroad and in North America. In the same year, about 1400 long-term and over 800 short-term workers were involved in projects in over sixty countries.

These activities are a direct extension of the Mennonite conviction that word and deed must be one and that love must be visible. It may, however, also be that these and related activities serve the less altruistic function of legitimizing the social significance and usefulness of a traditionally pacifist and persecuted people. Nevertheless, most Mennonites are deeply concerned about the futility of war and nuclear weapons, as well as about global poverty and the need for peaceful steps toward economic and social justice. These concerns are part of the total global mission to which Mennonites continue to feel committed.

BIBLIOGRAPHY

The standard reference work in English is *The Mennonite Encyclopedia,* 4 vols. plus index, edited by Harold S. Bender and C. Henry Smith (Scottdale, Pa., 1955–1959). Nelson P. Springer and A. J. Klassen have compiled a helpful bibliography, the *Mennonite Bibliography, 1631–1961,* 2 vols. (Scottdale, Pa., 1977). A revised edition of *An Introduction to Mennonite History,* edited by Cornelius J. Dyck (Scottdale, Pa., 1981), provides a basic account of the entire Anabaptist and Mennonite movement worldwide from the sixteenth century to the present. J. Howard Kauffman and Leland Harder's *Anabaptists Four Centuries Later* (Scottdale, Pa., 1975) is a statistically rich and well-interpreted study of Mennonite religious attitudes and practices at the time of its publication. A particularly useful volume for a country-by-country study of world Mennonitism is the *Mennonite World Handbook,* edited by Paul N. Kraybill (Lombard, Ill., 1978).

New Sources

Driedger, Leo. *Mennonites in the Global Village.* Toronto, 2000.

Driedger, Leo, and Donald B. Kraybill. *Mennonite Peacemaking: From Quietism to Activism.* Scottdale, Pa., 1994.

Jost, Lynn, and Connie Faber. *Family Matters: Discovering the Mennonite Brethren.* Hillsboro, Kans., 2002.

CORNELIUS J. DYCK (1987)
Revised Bibliography

MEN'S STUDIES IN RELIGION is part of the unfolding concern within religion to address the effects of gender and sexuality upon religious faith and practice. As a new field of scholarly inquiry, it reflects upon and analyzes the complex connections between men and religion, building upon gender studies, feminist theory and criticism, the men's movement, and the increasing number of subdisciplines in the academic study of religion. Methodologically men's studies in religion is an open field; its object of inquiry is "men" as gendered beings in relation to religion. But the precise delineations of this inquiry are not yet determined. Distinctions between the academic study of men in religion, on the one hand, and affirmation of socially accepted forms of male religiosity, on the other, are not always drawn with sufficient clarity.

The compelling simplification that this new field is constituted by "men writing about religion" is misleading because it does not recognize that the sphere of the sacred has been traditionally male-centered and male-dominated. In many religions, religious norms and male experiences are indistinguishable, making men the beneficiaries of religiously sanctioned hierarchies. The task of men's studies in religion is to bring gender consciousness to the interpretation and analysis of men in relation to any aspect of religion. Simply put, the writing of a religious man is not the same as the scholarly study of a male author's gendered text and context.

Studies in this new field are, on the one hand, critical of normative models of masculinities and, on the other, also supportive of men struggling to find their place in religion and society. These studies may examine male religious authority, analyze societal attitudes toward men, or study religious practices that enforce gender norms. They may probe theologies that justify patriarchal hierarchies or investigate men's participation in religiously sanctified oppression. They may also suggest alternative devotional and spiritual practices for men and reenvision men's roles as caregivers in both the profane and sacred realms.

Historical Precedents. A trajectory can be identified from secular feminism to the current concerns of men's studies in religion. Feminists of the 1960s and 1970s drew attention to the devastating effects of patriarchy and heterosexism in Western culture. Their analyses deeply influenced women scholars of Christianity and Judaism so that by the 1980s feminist interpretations of Scripture and theology had become part of the theological norm. Also in the 1980s men outside religion began to respond to the feminist critique of patriarchy and to study the effects of hegemonic masculinity upon men themselves, drawing particularly on the fields of sociology, anthropology, and psychology.

Within the field of religion, in response to secular feminism, religious feminism, secular men's studies, and the rise of the gay liberation movement, gay men's issues in religion began to be addressed in the 1980s. One of the early controversial academic works was John Boswell's *Christianity, Social Tolerance, and Homosexuality* (1980). By 1988 gay men's issues in religion became a recognized group within the large, North American–based organization of the American Academy of Religion (AAR). Finally, in the 1990s men's studies in religion emerged as a field in its own right at the AAR. Stephen Boyd's "Domination as Punishment: Men's Studies and Religion," published in *Men's Studies Review* (1990), was probably the first public articulation of the need for such an inquiry, arguing that "in light of recent research in and theories of men's studies, the relationship between religion and male experiences" must be examined (Boyd, 1990, pp. 8–9).

Generally speaking, there is a difference between the men's movement (secular and religious) and the academic study of men in religion. Whereas the former tends to favor biological, essentialist, and archetypal models, the latter tends to see men as culturally constructed, gendered, and performing contradictory roles due to constantly changing ideologies of masculinity. Men's studies in religion then analyzes and understands "the role of religion in supporting or resisting unstable masculine identities" (Boyd et al., 1996, p. 286). The following trends within the field can be observed.

Men Reclaiming Religion and Faith. In the twentieth century the mythopoetic movement and various conservative men's movements have attempted to reclaim spirituality and faith-based attitudes toward male identity and toward larger social issues, such as family values. These movements can be viewed as essentialist responses to a perceived threat of feminism.

Mythopoetics is based on the archetypal theories of C. G. Jung, James Hillman, and Joseph Campbell. It was made popular outside Christian churches by Robert Moore and Douglas Gillette's *King, Warrior, Magician, Lover* (1990) and remained relatively marginalized in Christian communities until the writings by Robert Bly and John Gray. The mythopoetic movement generally assumes that biological and genetic differences between men and women preordain irreconcilable differences in gendered behavior and thought, often presuming an essential masculinity that can be threatened when men become too much like women. In response men need to be nurtured socially, religiously, and spiritually in ways that match their masculine nature, generally with a preference for male images of the divine.

Evangelical Christian men's movements arose in the nineteenth and twentieth centuries in the Western world out of the panic that women were moving into the sphere of the sacred and were taking over religious institutions. The first such development in the first half of the nineteenth century was known as Muscular Christianity. It was followed by the Freethought movement (1880–1920), which characterized Christian churches as feminized, numerically dominated by women, and therefore weak, sentimental, and irrational. The third development, the Men and Religion Forward movement (from about World War I through to the 1950s), coined the slogan "More Men for Religion, More Religion for Men." The fourth movement was spearheaded by the evangelist Billy Sunday, who uttered the famous statement at a sermon in Chicago in 1916: "Lord save us from off-handed, flabby-cheeked, brittle-boned, weak-kneed, thin-skinned, pliable, plastic, spineless, effeminate, ossified three-karat Christianity" ("Sunday, the Fighting Saint," *Trenton Evening Times*, January 6, 1916). Finally, in the 1990s two prominent movements emerged in the United States that strengthened the faith of their male constituencies: the

Promise Keepers, intended to draw men back to Christianity, and the Million Man March, organized in 1995 by the Nation of Islam leader Louis Farrakhan, that mobilized African American men to commit themselves to religiously based values. Both argued for man's rightful position as head of the family.

SPIRITUAL AND CONFESSIONAL WRITINGS. The religious traditions have accumulated a wealth of spiritual journals and autobiographies, mystical journeys, and confessional testimonies written by men. They constitute a vast source for examining individual as well as collective presentations of the male self. Bringing a gender-conscious perspective to these texts yields critical insights into the male psyche and forms of male embodiment, intimacy, and sexualities.

The literature reflecting on men's spiritual and autobiographical voices often blends scholarly analysis with a more personal and existential style. The borders between critical analysis and an envisioned spiritual renewal are intentionally porous. Areas of concern in the Jewish and Christian traditions are issues of embodiment, sexual theologies, and the deconstruction of traditional masculine roles. The male body is reclaimed as a positive part of a male religious identity, so that the threats of impotence, disease, aging, mortality, and homophobia are turned into valuable spiritual resources. Rather than denigrating men's sexual nature, the sexual body is demystified and understood as an important source of theologies of intimacy and friendship with humans and the divine. These writings usually shun the privileging of hegemonic masculinity in order to engage otherness in the form of race, class, and sexual orientation. Particularly they counter the crippling effects of homophobia and abusive behavior toward women as well as culturally or sexually marginalized men. Instead, new forms of masculine spirituality are located in relationality, shared power, the aesthetics of the male and female body, creativity, ritual, and the living out of social justice through quiet service.

Another aspect of men's studies in religion is to reflect critically on confessional modes of male discourses on religion. Still an underutilized approach, most of this work is located within the Christian tradition, largely due to the lasting influence of Augustine's (354–430 CE) *Confessions* and the thought of the French philosopher Michel Foucault (1926–1984). In his *History of Sexuality* (1978) and "The Battle for Chastity" (1982), Foucault mapped out an influential theory about the Christian monastic roots of the modern concern over sexual practices, desires, and politics. The monastic orders, especially as envisioned by John Cassian (360s–430s CE), created intimate male-male spaces for the confession of sins that developed into "very complex techniques of self-analysis" (Foucault, 1982, p. 195). A Foucaultian framework helps analyze religious men's desire for intimate self-revelations; at the same time it can be used to investigate both subjugated and liberating knowledge of male sexualities as revealed in confessional, spiritual, and autobiographical writings.

THEOLOGICAL AND BIBLICAL INVESTIGATIONS. Men's studies in religion investigates the scriptural traditions as well as the Christian and Jewish theological heritages. Boyd (1995) identifies six cultural barriers that prevent white Christian men from enjoying true intimacy with the multiplicity of God's creation: classism, anti-Semitism, racism, homophobia, sexism, and femiphobia. This list can be completed by adding men's obsession with work as a source of identity, disappointments with biological fathers (and by extension with monotheistic father gods), tolerance of violence, body unconsciousness, and emotional deadness. By accepting such restrictive constructions of masculinity, men inhibit themselves from living into their potential of a creatively embodied *imago Dei.*

A number of writers interact critically with Christian thinkers such as Augustine, Martin Luther, Dietrich Bonhoeffer, Matthew Fox, Alfred North Whitehead, Richard Niebuhr, Malcolm X, Desmond Tutu, and Howard Thurman. Other writers focus more on the psychology of male characters in the biblical Scriptures, highlighting the problems of contemporary men struggling with relationship and identity issues. Christian writers in this field generally focus on Jesus, Jewish writers on God and the rabbinic tradition when addressing such issues as boyhood and parenting, friendship and intimacy, community and accountability, and the experiential dimension of the male body, pain, and sacrifice.

Another trend in men's studies in religion is to examine how Christianity and Judaism have framed the discourse on masculine ideologies, especially in their formative periods of late antiquity. Following feminist scholars, who have reconstructed the complexity of religious women's lives, new studies show that notions of masculinity were far from stable in the culturally diverse Hellenistic world. During the waning of the Roman Empire and the rise of new religions (Catholicism in the West, Orthodoxy in the East, Rabbinic Judaism in the exilic communities, and eventually Islam), male identities had become fragile and contested, even among the educated upper-class men who were still the beneficiaries of male privileges. As inconsistencies grew between ancient ideals and new social realities, Jewish and Christian men began to redefine male sexuality and manly virtues. Christianity succeeded in replacing the Roman ideas of vigor and military strength with the virtues of a spiritual strength and sexual constraint.

While scholars of masculinity in early Christianity and late antiquity have stressed the rapid rise of a subordinate ideology of manliness to dominant status, Jewish scholarship has described rabbinic masculinity as subjected to and colonized by first the Roman then Christian supremacy. Talmudic discussions of what it means to be or to become a man differed greatly from the theologies of the Christian Church Fathers, not at least due to their profoundly different assessments of male celibacy. But both Jewish and Christian discourses converged on the issue of the male desire to be close to God. Positioning themselves as symbolic "woman" in relation to a (male) God, men excluded actual women from the sacred sphere. To hide the homosocial and homoerotic nature of this relation to the divine, they inscribed heterosexual norms by effeminizing subordinate and disloyal men. In Christianity the desire for male humility was a gesture of submissiveness toward God, not women. In Rabbinic Judaism, Jewish men saw themselves figuratively in the place of woman in the presence of God. Torah study itself became a highly eroticized passion from which (actual) women were excluded. Although the feminization of Jewish men is one of the enduring anti-Semitic stereotypes in Christianity, one scholar has suggested embracing "the feminized Jewish male" as an act of resistance to dominant Christian masculinities (Boyarin, 1997, p. xiv).

The debate about male-divine relations is echoed in a number of writings about the theological conundrum that both Christianity and Judaism posit a God who is ungendered and unsexed. How do men reconcile a craving for a male God when hegemonic masculinity demands that desire be felt and expressed (or denied) only between men and women? The monotheistic traditions offer no clear models for such homosocial desire. Judaism sees penile circumcision as a theological and covenantal act of mature obedience, while Christianity offers a more metaphorical interpretation: the circumcision of the heart. Neither religion answers the question about whether circumcision is a part of the *imago Dei* or an act of male violence toward males.

GAY AND QUEER STUDIES IN RELIGION. Gay men's religious studies have generally developed separately from men's studies in religion despite some significant overlap. Gay studies challenge hetero-normativity by focusing on diversity, pride, and liberation. Some writers understand gay spirituality as a theology from the margins, defining itself by difference, otherness, and intimacy. Sexuality is often conceived as an act of sacramental Eros and gay spirituality as an act of political protest. Gay men's studies walk a fine line between mainstream integration and resistance to Christian scriptural and theological heterosexism. They may focus on mapping out gay spirituality, developing theodicies on AIDS, or criticizing the attitudes of religious institutions toward homosexual clergy and faithful laity.

The work of the British clergyman and poet Edward Carpenter (1844–1926), a gay theologian of the early modern period, was not really built upon until after three disasters hit the international gay community: the trial of Oscar Wilde (1895), the Nazi extermination of gay men in the concentration camps (1940–1944), and the Stonewall riots in New York City (1969). In the early 1980s the theologian James Nelson may have been the first nongay in the men's movement to adamantly oppose double standards in sexual ethics that separate straight and gay. Others have divided gay men's spirituality into four types: the apologetic (the reasoned defense of homosexuality), the therapeutic ("coming-out" as a spiritual journey), the ecological (emphasizing liberation theology and right relation), and the autobiographical (Boisvert, 2000). This typology must be expanded to include the growing repertoire of transgressive and queer theologies and spiritualities. In general gay spirituality is earthed, embodied, daily mundane, and informed by feminist and Native American spiritualities.

Just as there are no fixed demarcations between men's and gay men's studies in religion, gay studies overlap in multiple ways with queer theory. Queer theory, which made its public debut in 1990, is less concerned about the same-sex orientation of men but instead focuses on sexualities in their multitudes. Queer theory questions any theoretical or practical system that claims sexuality as natural or biological categories, and it moves beyond the binary restrictions of men and women, of hetero- and homosexuality. Queer theory refuses hetero-normativity because it "recognizes that human desire . . . is queer, excessive, not teleological or natural" (Boyarin, 1997, p. 14). Scholarship on queer theory that engages issues of religion and masculinity includes biblical studies, Jewish studies on masculinity, and queer theology (the latter defined as a political theology that questions theological assumptions about sexuality).

OUTLOOK. Men's studies in religion as an emerging field of inquiry is still heavily located within the scholarly traditions of the West, specifically Christianity and Judaism. It has not yet sufficiently engaged other religious traditions and been tested seriously as a topic of interreligious dialogue within an increasingly globalized community. Men's studies in religion has the potential to offer a sustained, gender-conscious critique of foundational religious texts and practices in order to envision nonhegemonic models of masculinity and to allow all men and women to participate in religious life fully and equally.

SEE ALSO Feminism, article on Feminism, Gender Studies, and Religion; Gender and Religion, overview article, article on History of Study; Gender Roles; Homosexuality; Human Body, article on Human Bodies, Religion, and Gender; Patriachy and Matriarchy; Spirituality; Women's Studies in Religion.

BIBLIOGRAPHY

Boisvert, Donald L. *Out on Holy Ground: Meditations on Gay Men's Spirituality.* Cleveland, Ohio, 2000.

Boswell, John. *Christianity, Social Tolerance, and Homosexuality.* Chicago, 1980. A study by a Yale historian of the treatment of gays and lesbians throughout the history of the church. Consulting theological, literary, legal, and cultural sources, it offers a witty and unrelenting argument for tolerance and repentance.

Boyarin, Daniel. *Unheroic Conduct: The Rise of Heterosexuality and the Invention of the Jewish Man.* Berkeley, Calif., 1997. A Talmudic scholar interprets ancient and modern Jewish sources with the aim of articulating an alternative rabbinic model of masculinity. Rather than objecting to the image of the feminized Jewish male, the author employs queer theory in his intertextual readings to argue that such an image provides a new space for being male without submitting to the Christian (and later European) hegemonic notions of masculinity.

Boyd, Stephen. "Domination as Punishment: Men's Studies and Religion." *Men's Studies Review* (Spring 1990): pp. 1, 4–9.

Boyd, Stephen B. *The Men We Long to Be: Beyond Domination to a New Christian Understanding of Manhood.* San Francisco, 1995. A historian of Christianity consults a range of traditional and contemporary theologians about their assumptions about masculinity. Rather than arriving at conclusions that defend traditional gender roles, he uses his critique of Christian sources to envision a Christian masculinity which is authentic, nurturing, caring, and challenging of cultural socialization.

Boyd, Stephen B., W. Merle Longwood, and Mark W. Muesse, eds. *Redeeming Men: Religion and Masculinities.* Louisville, Ky., 1996. This collection of essays demonstrates some of the diversity of the scholarly research on and methodological approaches to issues of men and religion. The contributors investigate dominant religious and historical constructions of masculinity by taking seriously the challenges posed by the feminist critique.

Burrus, Virginia. *Begotten Not Made: Conceiving Manhood in Late Antiquity.* Stanford, Calif., 2000. This book is a study of manhood in late antiquity presented by a feminist cultural historian of the early church. It is a close reading of texts of the Christian Church Fathers Athanasius of Alexandria, Gregory of Nyssa, and Ambrose of Milan. All three were instrumental in further interpreting and disseminating the Nicene Trinitarian doctrine.

Claussen, Dane S. *The Promise Keepers: Essays on Masculinity and Christianity.* Jefferson, N.C., and London, 2000.

Comstock, Gary David, and Susan E. Henking, eds. *Que(e)rying Religion: A Critical Anthology.* New York, 1997.

Culbertson, Philip. *New Adam: The Future of Male Spirituality.* Minneapolis, 1992. The author employs his experience in pastoral theology and biblical studies to re-examine the psychology of five masculine role models in Scripture. Based on close textual readings, he explores a number of stumbling blocks to the development of a healthy male spirituality and ends with a critique of Robert Bly's mythopoetic approach.

Culbertson, Philip. *The Spirituality of Men: Sixteen Christians Write about Their Faith.* Minneapolis, 2002. Scholars in men's studies in religion explore in this collection of essays the gendered nature of their own journeys in Christian faith. Intended for both academics and Christian laity, the essays take a broad approach to the empirical nature of masculine thought and behavior among men committed to the church.

Eilberg-Schwartz, Howard. *God's Phallus and Other Problems for Men and Monotheism.* Boston, 1994. A Jewish studies scholar explores how the concept of masculinity has been affected negatively by the disappearance of God's sexual body in the narrative corpus of ancient Judaism. Close readings of passages in the Hebrew Scriptures, Talmud, and Midrash are frequently informed by psychoanalytically informed styles of interpretation.

Foucault, Michel. *The History of Sexuality.* New York, 1978.

Foucault, Michel. "The Battle for Chastity." In *Religion and Culture,* selected and edited by Jeremy R. Carrette, translated by Anthony Forster, pp. 188–197. New York, 1999. First published in France in 1982.

Goss, Robert E. *Queering Christ: Beyond Jesus Acted Up.* Cleveland, Ohio, 2002.

Hall, Donald, ed. *Muscular Christianity: Embodying the Victorian Age.* Cambridge, U.K., 1994. A professor of English traces the development and long-term effects of the mid-nineteenth-century religious and social movement known as Muscular Christianity. The study's emphasis is on hypermasculinity as a response to spiritual and class anxieties about faith, gender, and national identity.

Krondorfer, Björn. "Revealing the Non-Absent Male Body: Confessions of an African Bishop and a Jewish Ghetto Policeman." In *Revealing Male Bodies,* edited by Nancy Tuana, William Cowling, Maurice Hamington, Greg Johnson, and Terrance MacMullan, pp. 245–268. Bloomington, Ind., 2002.

Krondorfer, Björn, ed. *Men's Bodies, Men's Gods: Male Identities in a (Post-) Christian Culture.* New York, 1996. Contributors to this volume reflect on the complex and often ambiguous religious forces that shape male bodies and identities in the Christian traditions and post-Christian cultures. Questions of male spirituality are raised in view of men's diverse cultural and ethnic backgrounds and sexual orientations. Visual and textual representations of men in contemporary religion and culture are also addressed.

Kuefler, Mathew. *Manly Eunuch: Masculinity, Gender Ambiguity, and Christian Ideology in Late Antiquity.* Chicago, 2001. This historical study explores the manly ideal of emerging Christianity in late antiquity. It examines how Christianity was able to reformulate the virtues of manliness and convince Roman men to transfer their allegiance from the one to the other. The book also addresses Christian and pagan notions of eunuchs, castration, holy transvestites, and gender equality.

Lippy, Charles. "Miles to Go: Promise Keepers in Historical and Cultural Context." *Soundings* 80, nos. 2–3 (Summer/Fall 1997): 289–304.

Moore, Robert, and Douglas Gillette. *King, Warrior, Magician, Lover: Rediscovering the Archetypes of the Mature Masculine.* San Francisco, 1990.

Moore, Stephen D. *God's Beauty Parlor: And Other Queer Spaces in and around the Bible.* Stanford, Calif., 2001. Written from the perspective of a New Testament scholar, this book brings queer theory and masculinity studies into conversation with biblical studies. It is critical commentary and cultural interpretation of select biblical texts and theologies, addressing issues of sexuality, violence, homoeroticism, and ideologies of beauty and of masculinity.

Nelson, James B. *Between Two Gardens: Reflections on Sexuality and Religious Experience.* New York, 1983. One of the earliest books to examine the relationship between human sexuality and Christian experience, the author asks what sexuality says about faith. He argues for the liberation of men from the gender assumptions of traditional Christianity and exposes Christian hypocrisy in holding out conflicting standards for heterosexual and homosexual men.

Nelson, James B. *The Intimate Connection: Male Sexuality, Masculine Spirituality.* Philadelphia, 1988. Seeking to promote "whole men" as opposed to "real men," Nelson discusses the human need for intimacy and sensuousness. He asks why men have trouble establishing deep friendships and how God's transforming love can work among men who take risks. In particular this book is known for offering a healthy spirituality of male genital desire.

BJÖRN KRONDORFER (2005)
PHILIP CULBERTSON (2005)

MENSTRUATION. It is questionable whether late-modern scientific, detraditionalized Western societies can still be said to institute a menstrual taboo. Today in westernized cultures, menstrual blood is more likely to be considered a bodily waste product whose disposal is more a matter of hygiene and social etiquette than a threat to the cultic order. However, the contemporary world is only partially and unevenly secularized, and the role and status of women in the world's religions cannot be fully understood without reference to the negative powers generally ascribed to menstrual blood. And more than that, while menstrual taboos vary in practice and intensity in the world's religious cultures, menstruation remains central to the construction of female difference.

Where early anthropologists and historians of religion claimed that menstrual taboo was universal, more recently Thomas Buckley and Alma Gottlieb (1988) have argued that the Western repugnance for menstrual blood and Western cultural alienation from female biological processes have been projected onto the interpretation of indigenous menstrual practices. The power of menstrual blood may not, in fact, be universally regarded as negative, but sometimes as positive and, if handled with due care, life-giving. Indeed, menstruation, and especially menarche (the onset of menstruation) can for North American Indians, such as the Sioux, confer honor and power on a woman rather than stigmatize her.

Nonetheless, in both historical and contemporary practice, the major world religions share an overwhelmingly negative view of menstruation as a pollutant of sacred public and domestic space, which requires some form of separation of the menstruant from the family or community. Menstrual blood is a contact pollutant and excludes women from religious acts either during their menstruation or simply because they are persons who menstruate. These exclusions owe much to the symbolic and material ambivalence of menstrual blood. On the one hand, it is a defiling natural excretion whose cyclic flow is not susceptible to (masculine) cultural control. Menstrual blood actually and metaphorically represents the loss or abortion of a potential life, yet it causes a woman no painful threat to her life. On the other hand, menstrual blood belongs to the mysterious, quasi-divine processes of creation: the gestation and birth of a new life.

MENSTRUATION IN THE WORLD RELIGIONS. Given the complexity of religious traditions, the following remarks are necessarily very general and may not pertain to all forms of a specific religion. Nonetheless, it is broadly the case that in Brahmanical Hinduism, menstrual blood is considered polluting and requires a woman to separate from her family for the first three days of her period. During this time she cannot perform religious acts of devotion and, secluded from her family, cannot cook, look after children, brush her hair, or wear jewelry. She must perform a purificatory bathing rite before normal relationships and activities can resume.

Similarly, in Buddhism, menstrual pollution prevents a woman from undertaking pilgrimage or entering a temple. The prohibitions differ according to context: some temples in northern Thailand do not allow women to circumambulate the stupas, fearing the pollution of relics held at their center. However, contemporary Buddhist apologetics frequently disown the menstrual taboo as non-Buddhist and as originating in the older purity codes of host countries such as India and Japan.

In the Qurʾanic view (2:223), menstruation is polluting and requires the Muslim woman's seclusion from her husband. The *ḥadīth* literature prohibits a menstruant from reciting prayers, fasting, entering a mosque, and touching the Qurʾān until she has finished her menses and taken a full bath *(ghusl)*. This purification ritual allows her to resume sexual relations with her husband. There are, however, some notable variations in practice: the Khārajīs, for example, believe that a menstruant should continue to fast and pray.

In Judaism, the menstrual taboo derives from the priestly codes of the Hebrew Bible and from rabbinic law. After Judaism's post-biblical transformation from a religion of cultic sacrifice to one of law, the rabbis reinforced the injunctions of *Leviticus* 12:1–5 and 15:19–32 by ruling that a menstruant is impure for the five or so days of her menses and for at least seven days afterwards. After this time has elapsed, the menstruant (*niddah*) visits a ritual bath (*miqveh*) and, after immersion, physical relations with her husband can be resumed. However, the power of menstrual blood to defile Jewish sacred objects and spaces is limited: the touch of a menstruant cannot pollute the Torah scroll, and menstruating women are not excluded by law, though sometimes historically by custom, from the synagogue. Only the ultra-Orthodox are punctilious in observing the laws of menstruation (customarily termed "the laws of family purity"), but the contemporary apologetic emphasis is on the laws' alleviation of sexual boredom in marriage, rather than on a superstitious or cultic repugnance for menstrual blood as such. Conservative Judaism has modified the laws of menstrual purity, and Reform Judaism has abolished them as irrelevant, archaic, and offensive to women.

The Christian tradition is historically and denominationally diverse in its view of menstruation. In the New Testament, Jesus is presented as having abolished the Jewish menstrual taboo among other distinctions between the clean and the unclean. Most significantly, in a story found in all three synoptic Gospels, Jesus heals the menstrual disorder of a woman whose touch he experiences not as a defilement but as a mark of her faith. Nonetheless, Christian feminists have argued that, as the church developed, a legacy of Greek philosophical misogyny, ancient Mediterranean menstrual superstition, Gnostic asceticism, the institution of a celibate priesthood, and the authority of the Old Testament combined to reinstate the view of menstrual blood as unclean. To this day, the Christian menstrual taboo informs the disqualification of women from ordination because in most quarters of the church (notably the Orthodox and Catholic Churches) it is believed, if not always stated, that a woman's biological presence pollutes the sanctuary.

By contrast, the menstrual taboo would appear to have fallen into disuse in the contemporary Protestant denominations. In the Anglican Church, for example, the practice of churching (derived from *Leviticus* 12:2–8), where a woman undergoes a purification ritual forty days after she has given birth to mark her return to the community, is no longer observed. Whether Protestantism's apparent indifference to women's menstruality is a function of its egalitarian, word-centered, and anti-priestly ecclesiology, or whether it is ignored because it is considered socially unmentionable, remains a matter of debate.

Feminist Subversions of the Menstrual Taboo. From the mid-1970s to the 1990s, a number of influential feminist studies of menstruation were published in which Jewish, Christian, and Goddess feminists critiqued, subverted, and reclaimed the menstrual taboo, broadly construing its various forms as the fear, appropriation, and regulation of women's sacral power. Two central arguments were proposed. First, it was observed that the gendering of blood underpins gendered inequalities of religio-political power. That is, whereas the cultural, controlled flow of the blood of male animals spilled in the Israelite Temple cult in the covenantal circumcision of Jewish boys—and the sacrificial passion and crucifixion of Jesus—reunited the world and God, the natural cyclic flow of female blood has separated them, leaving female time, space, and bodies unfit for direct contact with the divine presence or its revelation. Second, it has been noted that if menstrual blood is, as it were, repulsive of divine presence, then that has left women historically vulnerable to unjust charges of unreason and maleficence.

While some religious feminists find menstrual taboos distasteful and irrelevant, others have interpreted the apparent reverence of some of the world's pagan traditions for menstrual blood as suggestive of a more ecological and feminist approach to religion and spirituality. The anthropology of indigenous ritual seclusion practices has been read selectively to suggest ways for menstruating women to gather together in rest and friendship to celebrate the female transformation mysteries. In these, as in some Jewish feminist circles, menstruation is experienced as a time of creative energy rather than lassitude and depression; daughters' menarches are celebrated as affirmatory rites of passage into womanhood, and menopause is marked by rituals that allow women to reflect with other women on their passage through time into greater wisdom and independence. Rejecting, then, the demystifying secular feminist view of menstruation as what Germaine Greer once called the "liquidification of abjection," these spiritual feminists have together produced a new menstrual praxis that celebrates the connections of menstrual flow to the phases of the moon and the tides. Spiritual feminists have reclaimed the magic-natural charge of menstruation and put it to regenerative ends, sometimes using menstrual blood in rituals, and they have ritualized political direct action to protest the masculine wasting or spilling of blood in war.

See Also Blood; Human Body; Purification; Rites of Passage.

Bibliography

Buckley, Thomas, and Alma Gottlieb, eds. *Blood Magic: The Anthropology of Menstruation.* London, 1988. A re-reading of native cultures' attitudes and practices regarding menstruation that refuses to project Western associations of menstruation and evil onto the objects of its ethnographical research.

Grahn, Judy. *Blood, Bread, and Roses: How Menstruation Created the World.* Boston, 1993. A spiritual feminist examination of the role of menstruation in the creation of human culture.

Joseph, Alison, ed. *Through the Devil's Gateway: Women, Religion, and Taboo.* London, 1990. A collection of essays in which women from a number of different faith traditions outline their perspectives on menstruation.

Knight, Chris. *Blood Relations: Menstruation and the Origins of Culture.* London, 1991. An anthropological study of menstruation, theorizing prehistoric African women's role in the emergence of civilization.

Laws, Sophie. *Issues of Blood: The Politics of Menstruation.* London, 1990. A secular study, rejecting supernaturalist views of menstruation. Laws construes menstrual taboos as political instruments for maintaining gender hierarchy.

O'Grady, Kathleen. "Menstruation." In *Encyclopedia of Women and World Religion,* edited by Serinity Young, vol. 2, pp. 649–652. New York, 1999.

Raphael, Melissa. *Thealogy and Embodiment: The Post-Patriarchal Reconstruction of Female Sacrality.* Sheffield, U.K., 1996. A study of post-Christian feminist conceptions of female sacrality, attending to the cosmological and political implications of spiritual feminism's subversion and reclamation of the menstrual taboo.

Shuttle, Penelope, and Peter Redgrove. *The Wise Wound: Menstruation and Everywoman.* London, 1978; rev. ed., 1986. A Jungian interpretation of menstruation, urging women not to suppress its healing, generative power.

Steinberg, Jonah. "From a 'Pot of Filth' to a 'Hedge of Roses' (and Back): Changing Theorizations of Menstruation in Judaism." *Journal of Feminist Studies in Religion* 13 (1997): 5–26. This article observes how Orthodox Judaism's discourse on menstruation has shifted from repugnance to an emphasis on the marital benefits of separation during women's "impure" days.

Wansbrough, Paula, and Kathleen O'Grady. "Menstruation: A List of Sources." Available from http://www.inform.

umd.edu/EdRes/Topic/WomensStudies/Bibliographies/menstruation. A useful annotated bibliography compiled and regularly updated by two experts in the field.

MELISSA RAPHAEL (2005)

MERCIER, DÉSIRÉ JOSEPH (1851–1926), a leading figure in Roman Catholic neoscholastic philosophy at the end of the nineteenth century and Cardinal Primate of Belgium (1906–1926). Born November 21, 1851, in Braine-l'Alleud, near Waterloo, Mercier studied philosophy and theology at Malines and earned a licentiate in theology at Louvain University (1877). Subsequently, he studied psychiatry in Paris.

Ordained a Roman Catholic priest in 1874, Mercier became a staunch supporter of Pope Leo XIII's call for a revival of Thomistic thought in the encyclical *Aeterni patris* (1879). Initially a professor of philosophy at the Malines seminary in 1877, Mercier then became the first holder of a new chair for Thomist philosophy at Louvain University in 1882. He soon sought papal approbation for a new institute at Louvain, and in 1889 Leo XIII approved the Institut Supérieur de Philosophie with Mercier at its head. Calling former students together from around the globe, he assembled an international group of disciples.

Working in opposition to Mill's positivism, and above all to neo-Kantian idealism, Mercier became a major figure in the development of Roman Catholic neoscholastic thought, which sought to mediate between modern natural science and traditional Thomistic metaphysics. While neoscholastic thought of the nineteenth century was concerned mainly with questions of epistemology and the soul-body relationship and locked its responses to these problems into a rigid anti-Kantian tradition, Mercier strove to make Thomistic philosophy dependent upon the thought of his time: to see the "new" in the "old." His main area of concentration was psychology, and in 1892 he founded the first experimental laboratory at his institute in that discipline; later laboratories, emphasizing his regard for experimental methods, followed in cosmology, chemistry, and physics.

In contrast to most Roman Catholic thinkers of his time, Mercier saw philosophy as distinct from theology, and above all as an enterprise that should be free of all apologetics. Without abandoning all tradition, he sought to imbue philosophy with the same ethic of investigation that marked other university disciplines; philosophy must address the people, their times, and their problems. Even when dealing with such questions as truth and certitude, Mercier appealed to human experience. This led to his system of "illationism," which admitted that truth and certitude came from intellectual reflection, but that the content of such abstract thought always had its origins in concrete experience. Though this direction produced much controversy in neoscholastic circles, it was unable to sustain itself as a "school" at Louvain University. Mercier gave expression to his thought in a series of textbooks (his *Course in Philosophy*) that dealt with logic, psychology, metaphysics, and the criteria for truth and certitude (1892–1899). In addition, he founded the influential *Revue néo-scolastique de philosophie* (1894), in which many of the movement's most important debates were carried out.

Appointed archbishop of Malines in 1906, Mercier was created a cardinal by Pius X in 1907. Though never a leading figure in the controversy of modernism that rocked the Roman Catholic church at the beginning of the twentieth century, he did issue a famous Lenten pastoral letter in 1908 against the work of George Tyrrell (1861–1909), a prominent Irish modernist thinker; his letter prompted a vitriolic but brilliant rejoinder by Tyrrell in his *Medievalism* (1908). As a pastorally concerned leader of his diocese, Mercier was deeply involved in the spiritual life and development of both his clergy and the laity; indeed, he sought greater cooperation between both groups as well as advances in social justice. Though Mercier never became a strong political figure in Belgium—his attachment to French culture hindered his understanding of the Flemish and their problems—he did become a figurehead for the Belgian people during the German occupation of World War I (1914–1918), strengthening their morale through sermons and pastoral letters. This proved so effective that the Germans placed him under house arrest, which earned him great prestige among the Belgian people and much praise from the Allies after the war.

Mercier's final years after World War I were dedicated to more universal problems, particularly those of church reunion. He founded the Institute of the Monks of Union at Chevetogne in Belgium in order to further reunion and reconciliation with the Eastern churches and made perhaps his most influential and lasting effort in hosting and participating in the famous "Malines Conversations" (1921–1925). Suggested by Lord Halifax (Charles Lindley Wood, 1839–1934), these meetings were concerned with aiding the mutual understanding and relations between the Roman Catholic and Anglican churches. Mercier's most famous moment came in the fourth session when he presented his paper on "The English Church United Not Absorbed," in which he proposed that the archbishopric of Canterbury be made a patriarchate, that the Roman code of canon law not be imposed in England, that England be allowed its own liturgy, and that all of the historical English sees be left in place while the newly erected Roman Catholic sees (1850) be suppressed. These suggestions generated much controversy and opposition in Rome, and Mercier's death on January 26, 1926, in Brussels effectively meant the end of the "Conversations."

BIBLIOGRAPHY

Works by Mercier

Mercier's main work, the *Cours de philosophie*, 4 vols. (Louvain, 1894–1899): vol. 1, *Logique* (1894); vol. 2, *Métaphysique générale, ou Ontologie* (1894); vol. 3, *La psychologie* (1899); and vol. 4, *Critériologie générale, ou Théorie générale de la certitude* (1899), represented his sequence of philosophy courses given at the Higher Institute for Philosophy at the University of Louvain. Many of Mercier's writings and public utterances were collected in the *Œuvres pastorales* (Brussels and Louvain, 1911–1929), in seven volumes. Finally, his famous exchange of letters with the commandant of the German occupation forces during World War I appeared as *La correspondance de S. E. cardinal Mercier avec le gouvernement général allemand pendant l'occupation, 1914–1918,* edited by Fernand Mayence (Brussels, 1919); in English translation as *Cardinal Mercier's Own Story* (New York, 1920). The most complete bibliography of Mercier's published writings should be consulted in the commemorative volume *Le cardinal Mercier, 1851–1926* (Brussels, 1927), pp. 341–372.

Works about Mercier

Of the several biographies of Mercier, one may profitably consult John A. Gade's *The Life of Cardinal Mercier* (New York, 1934). A full-scale and scholarly biography of Mercier, taking advantage of the many particular studies that have appeared since his death, and which would place him more accurately in the troubled and multifaceted context of his time, still must be written. Among the most important of these investigations are Alois Simon's major studies, particularly *Le cardinal Mercier* (Brussels, 1960), which provide an assessment of Mercier's contributions both to renewed scholasticism and the general philosophical conversation at the turn of the century in Europe. For new information concerning Mercier's ecumenical activities, one should consult Roger Aubert's "Les conversations de Malines: Le cardinal Mercier et le Saint-Siège," *Bulletin de l'Academie Royale de Belgique* 53 (1967): 87–159; and R. J. Lahey's "The Origins and Approval of the Malines Conversations," *Church History* 43 (September 1974): 366–384.

GARY LEASE (1987)

MEREZHKOVSKII, DMITRII (1865–1941),

chief proselytizer of the religious renaissance in Russia in the early twentieth century. Scion of an eminent Saint Petersburg aristocratic family, Merezhkovskii was educated at the Third Classical Gymnasium and at the Historical-Philological Faculty of the University of Saint Petersburg (1884–1888). Interested in metaphysical and existential issues, he dissented from the positivism and materialism of his contemporaries and searched, all his life, for a new and all-encompassing higher ideal.

In the 1890s, he championed mystical idealism as the bridge between the atheistic intelligentsia and the believing peasantry, campaigned against mandatory social didacticism in literature, introduced Russians to French symbolism and the philosophy of Nietzsche, and reintroduced them to classical antiquity and the Renaissance. Versatile and erudite, he expressed his ideas in poetry, literary criticism, essays, novels, and plays. Major works of this period are *Symbols* (1892), a book of poems; "On the Causes of the Decline of Russian Literature and on the New Trends in Poetry" (1893), an influential essay sometimes considered the manifesto of Russian symbolism; *New Verse* (1896); and *The Outcaste* (1895), later retitled *Death of the Gods,* a historical novel about Julian the Apostate. Attracted by pagan values of earthly happiness and Christian ideals of personal immortality and love, and unable to choose between them, by 1896 Merezhkovskii had concluded that Christianity and paganism were two halves of a yet unknown higher truth.

Around 1900, Merezhkovskii advanced a new interpretation of Christianity, designed to synthesize the "truth of heaven" and the "truth of the earth," and based on the second coming of Christ and on a forthcoming third testament. Proclaiming a new religious consciousness that stressed the human need for faith and religious quest, he dismissed historical Christianity as obsolete and rejected the asceticism, altruism, and humility preached by Russian Orthodox Christianity. Major works of this period include *Tolstoy as Man and Artist with an Essay on Dostoevskii* (1901–1902), which treats these writers as exemplars of the religious principles of the flesh and the spirit respectively; *Birth of the Gods: Leonardo da Vinci* (1901); and *Antichrist: Peter and Alexis* (1905). Together with *Julian the Apostate,* the last two comprise his historical trilogy, *Christ and Antichrist.*

To disseminate their views (sometimes called "God-seeking views"), Merezhkovskii, his wife Zinaida Gippius, and Dmitrii Filosofov founded the Religious Philosophical Society of Saint Petersburg (November 1901–April 1903). The society, which featured debates between intellectuals and clergymen on burning issues of the day, became a focal point of the religious renaissance. The minutes of the meetings were published in the Merezhkovskiis' review, *Novyi put'* (New Path, 1902–1904), founded as a showcase for the new trends in art and thought. Permitted to reopen in 1907, after the Revolution of 1905, branches of the society were later founded in Moscow and in Kiev. Through these public activities and through his writings, Merezhkovskii's ideas reached a wide audience, challenged traditional verities, inspired other reinterpretations of Christianity, and even stimulated the Bolshevik secular religion of "God-building," which featured worship of the collective spirit of humanity instead of God.

The Revolution of 1905 led Merezhkovskii to consider social and political questions. He interpreted it as the first stage of a great religious revolution that would usher in the kingdom of God on earth. He denounced autocracy as a tool of the Antichrist, and advocated religious community, viewed as a kind of Christian anarchism, as the solution to social conflict. Hostile to Marxist materialism and collectivism, he claimed that socialism stifles creativity and argued that Jesus Christ is the supreme affirmation of the individual. Major works of this period are *Dostoevskii: Prophet of the Russian Revolution* (1906), *The Coming Ham* (1906), and *Not Peace but a Sword* (1908). He opposed Russia's entry into World War I, welcomed the February Revolution, but regarded the Bolshevik regime as the reign of the Antichrist. He cooperated with attempts to overthrow it, both before and after his emigration in 1919, until his death in Paris, in 1941.

BIBLIOGRAPHY

Most of Merezhkovskii's important works can be found in *Polnoe sobranie sochinenii,* 24 vols. (Saint Petersburg, 1911–1914). Works in English translation include *Death of the Gods* (London, 1901), *The Romance of Leonardo da Vinci* (London, 1902), *Peter and Alexis* (London, 1905), *The Menace of the Mob* (New York, 1921), and an abridged version of *Tolstoi as Man and Artist* (Westminster, England, 1902). Useful secondary literature includes my own *D. S. Merezhkovsky and the Silver Age* (The Hague, 1975); Charles H. Bedford's *The Seeker: D. S. Merezhkovskiy* (Lawrence, Kans., 1975); *D. S. Merezhkovskii: Mysl' i slogo* (D. S. Merezhkovskii, Thought and word), edited by A V. Keldysh, I.V. Koretskaia, M. A. Nikitina, and N. V. Koroleva (Moscow, 1999); and *D. S. Mereshkovskii: pro et contra,* edited by D. K. Burlak et al. (St. Petersburg, 2001).

BERNICE GLATZER ROSENTHAL (1987 AND 2005)

MERIT

This entry consists of the following articles:

AN OVERVIEW
BUDDHIST CONCEPTS
CHRISTIAN CONCEPTS

MERIT: AN OVERVIEW

The terms *merit* and *merit making* are used in connection with religious practices that have the calculated aim of improving the future spiritual welfare of oneself or others. However, the number of contexts in which a specific terminology such as *merit* (Lat., *meritum*) or its older analogue, the Buddhist *puṇya* (Pali, *puñña*) has developed are surprisingly few. It is probably for this reason that most well-known systematic or phenomenological studies of religion have little or nothing to say on the subject. Elsewhere, the use of these terms in writing on religion is widespread but extremely sporadic, occurring mainly in discussions of generally related subjects such as judgment, reward and punishment, grace, and salvation.

In religion west of India, the earliest specific teaching on merit, or merits, is found in rabbinic Judaism, although merit was not the subject of formal definitions. From the third century CE, the concept played an increasingly significant role in Western Christianity; it reached a high point in the Middle Ages, only to be drawn into the vortex of Reformation debate on grace and the relation between works, faith, and man's justification in the sight of God.

Recent years have seen a smooth and indeed justifiable transfer of the English term *merit* (as well as of European equivalents such as the German *Verdienst*) to that area of Buddhist practice and interpretation covered by the Sanskrit term *puṇya* and its equivalents. The term *merit making* implies an observational, analytic stance not usually found in studies of merit in Christianity, which have been more doctrinal or theological in tone. Nevertheless, interesting parallels can be drawn between Buddhism and Christianity as regards merit. Elsewhere, the relationships are much less clear, and comparative questions have to be suggested much more loosely insofar as they are relevant at all. The following observations should be understood as indicating the general context in which specific teachings on merit have arisen in rabbinic Judaism, Buddhism, and Christianity.

INDIA AND CHINA. That religious action has practical effects in this existence and others has been widely assumed in the religious systems of Asia, though with many variations. In the Indian context, the common assumption of post-Vedic religion is that of a series of existences, each conditioned by the *karman,* or accrued causal momentum, of the previous existence. Since *karman* can be either bad or good, there is room for improvement through religious practice or moral effort. Thus, loose analogies exist with other religious teachings on reward and punishment, religious works, and spiritual development. The main characteristic of Indian assumptions on the subject, whether Hindu, Jain, or Buddhist, is that karmic cause and effect are in principle self-regulating, not subject to divine decision, arbitration, or satisfaction.

In Jainism, seven "fields of merit" (*puṇyakṣetra*) are recognized as conducive to a pleasantly advanced rebirth. These have been presented by Padmanabh S. Jaini in *The Jaina Path of Purification* (Berkeley, 1979) as seven categories of meritorious activity: donating an image, donating a building to house an image, having the scriptures copied, giving alms to monks, giving alms to nuns, assisting laymen in their religious or practical needs, assisting laywomen similarly. The concept of *karman* should not in itself, however, be regarded as amounting to a doctrine of merit. This would push the analogy beyond its limits.

In Chinese religion, two relevant strands are discernible. First, there is the tradition of self-discipline and cultivation, in Confucian form oriented socially and pragmatically, in Daoist form linked to the achievement of supernormal powers, longevity, and even immortality. The idea of achieving supernormal physical and psychical powers through strenuous self-discipline is also present in Indian religions, including Buddhism, and hence in all cultural areas influenced by China and India. At the same time, this motivation for religious practice and achievement is not directly related to any concept analogous to merit.

Second, Chinese religion also knows the theme of postmortal judgment, presided over by Yen-lo (counterpart of the Indian god Yama) as god of death and ruler of the hells. Aided by his assistants, Yen-lo brings out the inexorable law of *karman,* and many illustrated works depict this as a warning to the living. (See, for example, the illustrated volumes *Religiöse Malerei aus Taiwan: Katalog* and *Die Höllentexte,* publications 1 and 2 of the Religionskundliche Sammlung der Philipps-Universität Marburg, 1980, 1981.) Religious imagery of this kind, though clearly related, does not entail a distinct doctrine of merit except insofar as it is influenced by Buddhism.

Egypt and Ancient Near East. In ancient Egypt, the diffusion of the cult of Osiris as lord of the underworld who had died, been judged, and risen again, provided the first common focus for postmortal expectation and concern. Elaborate funerary rites were accompanied by preparations for judgment before Osiris assisted by assessors. The candidate for new life asserted his innocence of numerous moral transgressions and saw his own heart weighed on scales against a feather representing truth in the sense of divine order (*maat*). Gradually, efforts were made to organise the outcome of the judgment in advance by preparing in advance lists of good deeds and declarations of innocence. This process was ritualized and commercialized through the sale of appropriate rolls of text to be filled in with names before death, modern scholars have named these texts collectively *The Book of Going Forth by Day.* On the other hand, these phenomena may be regarded as the earliest indication of attempts to establish an individual's worth—in effect to "make merit" for him, in order to achieve a desired effect after death.

The idea of merit apparently did not develop in Mesopotamia, where notions of existence after death remained shadowy and pessimistic. Nor did Canaanite or early Hebrew views of death include a postmortal goal toward which the individual could work. The Hebrew concept of She'ol as a silent, forgotten abode beneath the earth was related at least in type to the Babylonian.

The clearly delineated cosmological dualism of Iranian religion gave prominence to the alternatives awaiting the individual after death. The spiritual position of the soul was determined in accordance with its behavior before departure from the body. In principle, the thinking is analogous to the Egyptian conceptions mentioned above, for there is evidence of attempts to influence the judgment. Eschatologically, Iranian ideas strongly influenced developing Judaism, so that She'ol became the place of postmortal punishment, while up to seven heavens were enumerated as abodes of pleasure and bliss.

Theistic Religions. A theistic worldview in the Abrahamic tradition does not necessarily entail a detailed doctrine of merit, as may be seen in the cases of the Qumran community, very early Christianity and, later, Islam. In both the teachings of Qumran and of the New Testament, the concept of calculable merit is entirely lacking. What is required is total, inward obedience to the law, or will, of God. The subsequent development of Christian teachings on merit has been variously described and interpreted. Historical priority must be ascribed to the rabbinic teachings on merit, or merits, which, in a transposed form, underlay Paul's interpretation of the death of Jesus. (This relationship has been skillfully delineated by W. D. Davies in *Paul and Rabbinic Judaism,* 2d ed., London, 1955, pp. 227–284.)

The rabbinic doctrine of merit, though articulated in detail in the first four centuries of the common era, is based on two fundamental ideas which reach much further back in Jewish tradition. These are, first, that keeping the Mosaic covenant with God (i.e., observing the Torah), will lead to blessing and welfare and, second, that the responsibility and benefit of this covenant are essentially corporate and pass from generation to generation. Stated negatively, disobedience leads to punishment in the form of social or political suffering, but this punishment can be moderated by credit accumulated by previous generations. Looking forward, the idea of caring for one's children spiritually as well as physically was a motivating force for assiduousness in religious duty and charitable works. The justifiableness of a man, his standing before God in these respects, is summed up in the term *zakkut.*

As Davies points out, this line of thought is not without variations: some rabbis taught that the dividing of the waters at the exodus took place on account of the merits of Abraham, or the combined merits of Abraham, Isaac, and Jacob, while others stressed the meritorious faith of the Israelites at the time. The underlying spirit of the teaching is neatly expressed in Arthur Marmorstein's summary of the ideas of Rabbi Yanna'i: "A man who kindles light in daytime for his friend when it is light, what benefit has he derived? When does he obtain any advantage from light? In case he kindles it in the night-time, in darkness. The affection Israel has shown in the wilderness was kept for them from that time, from the days of Moses" (Marmorstein, 1920, p. 17). From regarding the keeping of the Torah as meritorious, and beneficial for future generations, it was not far to the idea that God gave the Torah so that merit could be achieved or even the idea that the whole of creation was designed to this end.

As to life beyond death, reference to this was by no means lacking, and it was considered possible that some individuals, through lack of merit, might fail to be rewarded. Nevertheless, the calculation of one's credits and debits was always regarded as ultimately in the hands of God, so that while relatively good men might tremble, even the wicked might hope. In practical terms, merit was typically considered to accrue through "faith, charity, hospitality, the circumcision, Sabbath and festivals, the study of the Torah, repentance, the Holy Land, the Tabernacle, Jerusalem, the tithe, and the observances in general" (ibid., p. 65).

With Islam, it was, and is, expected that realizable duties will be fulfilled. However, God, and only God, knows what is actually possible for each individual; moreover, he is patient of human weakness. Thus, insofar as it is possible, the pilgrimage to Mecca is required of Muslims. This may be regarded as a negative doctrine of merit in that every Muslim has to assess whether or not he or she is able to make the pilgrimage. While Islam has always recognized that some acts are not strictly required but are nevertheless praiseworthy, any assessment of human behavior for the purpose of achieving salvation was quickly ruled out by the strong emphasis on the preeminent knowledge and grace of God, which amounted to predestination. A broadly similar doctrinal structure was to appear, in the Christian world, in Reformation theology, and in Jansenism.

Comparative Reflections. A simple typology of religions with respect to concepts of merit and broadly related aspects of religiosity may be delineated in four parts.

First, it should be noted that much religion simply has not included the concept of merit, especially when notions of the future are shadowy, when a future existence is prepared for by elaborate funerals for royalty only, or when life after death is understood in any case to be the same for everybody. Thus, primal religions—even, for example, the highly developed Japanese Shintō—presuppose neither a radical dividing of the ways based on merit nor any elaborate path of cumulative spiritual development for the individual. Such religions naturally bear powerful religious values, such as a sense of cosmological orientation and belonging. Transactional religiosity, however, is directed in this context towards proximate, this-worldly, goals such as social and economic well-being, the avoidance of disaster and sickness or, in a modern differentiated economy, personal welfare and success.

Second, when clear-cut conceptions of future existence have developed, we see an extension of transactional religiosity into the future, as in Egyptian and Iranian religions, or, in a very different way, in Indian religion. The same holds for Chinese religion, though not without influence from Indian Buddhism. Such transactionalism may or may not be morally differentiated. The key feature here is that an element of future-directed management and even calculation is introduced to cope with an assumed judgment to come or with implications of the present for future existences. In principle, responsibility lies with the individual, although he may seek the assistance of priests, or, in the interesting variation of rabbinic Judaism, draw on the worthy performance of previous generations. Islam also belongs to this type, although in this case there is little interest in calculation and a great reliance on God's compassionate appraisal of what could realistically be expected from each individual in the circumstances of life.

The third type is represented above all by Buddhism and Christianity, although these emerged from quite different assumptions. Here we see that specific doctrines of merit arose at the point of intersection between transactional religiosity and soteriological concern. The natural, or primal, community is left on one side, and the possibility of the transfer of merit from transcendental or intermediate beings is envisaged. Interestingly, this latter idea did not go unopposed in Theravāda Buddhism, where it was criticized on ethical grounds. At the same time, the recommendation of merit-creating activities by the priesthood becomes normal.

Fourth, Buddhism and Christianity are similar not only in having produced an individualized soteriology based, at times, on a doctrine of merit. They have also both seen movements within the tradition which radically internalized the reception of spiritual assistance or grace. For Christianity, this is connected with the Reformation; for Buddhism, such movements are associated with the teachings of the Japanese patriarchs Hōnen (1133–1212) and, above all, Shinran (1173–1263). The latter argued, for example, that there was no value in reciting the Nembutsu (calling on the name of Amida Buddha) on behalf of the deceased because as a human work it could not benefit them in any way. All that was possible was reliance on the grace of Amida Buddha to effect rebirth in the Pure Land in the western heavens. Thus, the soteriological focus was internalized and the idea of merit was transformed from within. These subjectivizing trends within the Buddhist and Christian traditions, though influential, have not become dominant, and, broadly speaking, the vocabulary of merit continues to play a distinctive role in both.

See Also Judgment of the Dead.

BIBLIOGRAPHY

Davies, W. D. *Paul and Rabbinic Judaism,* 2d ed. London, 1955.

Jaini, Padmanabh S. *The Jaina Path of Purification.* Berkeley, 1979.

Marmorstein, Arthur. *The Doctrine of Merits in Old Rabbinical Literature.* London, 1920.

Religiöse Malerei aus Taiwan: Katalog and *Die Höllentexte,* Publications 1 and 2 of the Religionskundliche Sammlung der Philipps-Universität Marburg, 1980, 1981.

New Sources

Brokaw, Cynthia J. *The Ledgers of Merit and Demerit: Social Change and Moral Order in Late Imperial China.* Princeton, 1991.

Kammerer, Cornelia Ann, and Nicola Tannenbaum, eds. *Merit and Blessing in Mainland Southeast Asia in Comparative Perspective.* New Haven, 1996.

Lehtonen, Tommi. *Punishment, Atonement and Merit in Modern Philosophy of Religion.* Helsinki, 1999.

Schopen, Gregory. "Two Problems in the History of Indian Buddhism: The Layman/Monk Distinction and the Doctrines of the Transfer of Merit." *Studien zur Indologie und Iranistik* 10 (1985): 9–47.

Wawrykow, Joseph P. *God's Grace and Human Action: 'Merit' in the Theology of Thomas Aquinas.* Notre Dame, 1995.

Michael Pye (1987)
Revised Bibliography

MERIT: BUDDHIST CONCEPTS

The notion of merit (Skt., *puṇya* or *kuśala;* Pali, *puñña* or *kusala*) is one of the central concepts of Buddhism, and the practice of merit-making is one of the fundamental activities of Buddhists everywhere.

The idea of merit is intimately bound up with the theory of *karman,* the Indian law of cause and effect. According to this theory, every situation in which an individual finds himself is the result of his own deeds in this or a previous lifetime, and every intentional act he now performs will eventually bear its own fruit—good or bad—in this or a future lifetime. Thus present felicity, wealth, physical beauty, or social prestige may be explained as the karmic reward of past deeds of merit, and present suffering, poverty, ugliness, or lack of prestige may be attributed to past acts of demerit. In the same manner, present meritorious deeds may be expected to bring about rebirth in a happier station as a human being or as a deity in one of the heavens, and present demeritorious deeds may result in more suffering and in rebirth as an animal, a hungry ghost (Skt., *preta*), or a being in one of the Buddhist hells. A mixture of meritorious and demeritorious acts will bear mixed karmic results.

This basic understanding of the workings of merit and demerit can be traced back to the time of the Buddha, or the sixth to fifth centuries BCE. It received its fullest elaboration later, however, in the vast collections of *jātakas* (stories of the Buddha's previous lives), *avadānas* (legends), and *ānisaṃsas* (tales of karmic reward), which were and continue to be very popular in both Hīnayāna and Mahāyāna Buddhism.

MERIT-MAKING ACTIVITIES. There are, according to the Buddhists themselves, many ways of making merit. One of the most comprehensive listings of these is the noncanonical catalog of "ten meritorious deeds" (Pali, *dasa-kusalakamma*), which has been widely influential in South Asia. It comprises the following practices:

1. Giving (*dāna*)
2. Observing the moral precepts (*sīla*)
3. Meditation (*bhāvanā*)
4. Showing respect to one's superiors (*apacāyana*)
5. Attending to their needs (*veyyāvacca*)
6. Transferring merit (*pattidāna*)
7. Rejoicing at the merit of others (*pattānumodana*)
8. Listening to the Dharma, that is, the Buddha's teachings (*dhammasavana*)
9. Preaching the Dharma (*dhammadesanā*)
10. Having right beliefs (*diṭṭhijjukamma*)

It is noteworthy that most of the deeds on this list (with the possible exception of the ninth, which is more traditionally a monastic function) can be and are practiced both by Buddhist laypersons and by monks. It is clear, then, that merit making in general is a preoccupation not only of the Buddhist laity (as is sometimes claimed) but also of members of the monastic community, the *saṃgha*. In this regard, it is interesting too that meditation—a practice that is sometimes said to be an enterprise not concerned with attaining a better rebirth but aimed solely at enlightenment—is also seen as a merit-making activity and is engaged in as such by both monks and laypersons.

Another noteworthy item on this list is *sīla*, the observance of the moral precepts. For the laity, this consists of following the injunctions against killing, stealing, lying, sexual misconduct, and intoxication. On certain occasions, however, *sīla* may also involve the voluntary acceptance of three additional precepts, sometimes counted as four, against eating after noon, attending worldly amusements, using ornaments or perfumes, and sleeping on a high bed. Monks, who by their very status are thought to be more filled with merit than the laity, are expected to observe all the above precepts at all times; in addition, there is a tenth injunction for monks against the handling of money.

The most meritorious practice on this list, however, is giving, or *dāna*. In many ways, this is the Buddhist act of merit *par excellence*. Monks engage in it by giving the Dharma to laypersons in the form of sermons or advice, or by the example of their own lives. Laypersons practice it by giving to the monks support of a more material kind, especially food, robes, and shelter. The ideology of merit thus cements a symbiotic relationship between the *saṃgha* and the laity that has long been one of the prominent features of Buddhism.

Not all lay acts of *dāna* make equal amounts of merit. The specific karmic efficacy of any gift may depend on what is given (quantity and quality can be significant), how it is given (i.e., whether the gift is offered with proper respect, faith, and intention), when it is given (food offerings, for example, should be made before noon), and, especially, to whom it is given. Although *dāna* may sometimes be thought to include gifts to the poor and the needy, offerings made to the *saṃgha* are seen as karmically much more effective. Thus, making regular food offerings to the monks, giving them new robes and supplies, funding special ceremonies and festivals, building a new monastery, or having a son join the *saṃgha* are all typical lay acts of *dāna*. These activities share a common focus on the monks and are consistently ranked as more highly meritorious than other types of social service; they are even more highly valued than observation of the moral precepts.

Metaphorically, acts of merit are seen as seeds that bear most fruit when they are planted in good fields of merit (Skt., *puṇyakṣetra*), and the most fertile field of merit today is the *saṃgha*. This obviously has had tremendous sociological and economic implications. In Buddhist societies, the *saṃgha* often became the recipient of the excess (and sometimes not so excessive) wealth of the laity, and thus from its roots it quickly grew into a rather richly endowed institution.

Traditionally, however, the best "field of merit" was the Buddha himself. The model acts of *dāna* that are recounted in Buddhist popular literature often depict gifts that are made to him. Today, in addition to donations to the monks, offerings are made to images and other symbolic representations of the Buddha and are still thought of as highly meritorious. The roots of *dāna*, therefore, lie not only in a desire to do one's duty to the *saṃgha* but also to express one's devotion to the faith in the Buddha. This experiential cultic side of merit-making has often been overlooked, yet it is frequently emphasized in popular Buddhist literature.

Aims of the Merit Maker. In addition to expressing individual faith and devotion, the merit maker may be said to be interested in three things. First, an individual wants to obtain karmic rewards for himself in this or the next lifetime. Thus, for example, he might wish, by virtue of his acts of merit, to enjoy long life, good health, and enormous wealth, and never to fall into one of the lower realms of rebirth where suffering runs rampant, but to be reborn as a well-to-do person or a great god in heaven. Many such statements, in fact, may be found in the inscriptions left by pious Buddhists throughout the centuries to record their meritorious deeds, and in anthropologists' descriptions of present-day merit-making practices.

Second, the merit maker may also be interested in enlightenment. It is sometimes claimed that this is not the case, that beyond receiving karmic rewards the merit maker has no real ambition for *nirvāṇa.* To be sure, in the oldest strata of the Buddhist canon *nirvāṇa* is not thought to be attainable by merit-making alone, but Buddhist popular literature soon tended to take a different view. In the Avadānas, for example, even the most trivial acts of merit are accompanied by a vow (Skt., *praṇidhāna*) made by the merit maker to obtain some form of enlightenment in the future. This enlightenment may be a long time in coming, but when it does it is portrayed as the fruit of the merit maker's vow and act of merit, and not as the result of any meditative endeavor.

In present-day Theravāda practice, these same vows take the form of ritual resolves to be reborn at the time of the future Buddha Maitreya and to attain enlightenment at that time. Far from rejecting the possibility of *nirvāṇa*, then, the merit maker, by means of a *praṇidhāna*, can link an act of merit to that very soteriological goal.

The Transfer of Merit. Third, the merit maker may also wish to share his or her merit with others, especially with members of the family. By clearly indicating whom the merit maker intends to benefit by a good deed, an individual can transfer the merit accrued to that other person. This does not mean that one thereby loses some of one's own merit; on the contrary, one makes even more, since the transfer of merit is in itself a meritorious act.

Such sharing of merit is sometimes thought to be in contradiction to one of the basic principles of *karman*, according to which merit-making is an entirely individual process whereby one reaps only what one has sown oneself. While this may be correct theoretically, and while it is true that the transfer of merit is not mentioned explicitly in the earliest canonical sources, the practice quickly became very common. It had always been the case, of course, that an individual could undertake an act of merit on behalf of a larger social group. Thus, the housewife who gives food to a monk on his begging round makes merit not only for herself but for her whole family. Buddhist inscriptions and popular literature, however, testify also to the wishes of donors to have their merit benefit somewhat more remote recipients, such as a deceased parent or teacher, the suffering spirits of the dead, or, more generally, all sentient beings.

Probably one of the motivations for such sharing of merit was the desire to continue, in a Buddhist context, the Brahmanical practice of ancestor worship. The transfer of merit by offerings to the *saṃgha* simply replaced the more direct sacrifice of food to the spirits of the dead.

The literalness with which this transfer was sometimes understood is well illustrated by the story of the ghosts of King Bimbisāra's dead relatives. They made horrible noises in his palace at night because they were hungry, for the king had neglected to dedicate to them the merit of a meal he had served to the *saṃgha.* Therefore he had to make a new offering of food to the monks and properly transfer the merit. Once fed, the ghosts no longer complained.

It is worth noting in this story the crucial role played by the field of merit—in this case the *saṃgha*—in successfully transmitting the benefits of meritorious deeds to beings in the other world: the monks act as effective intermediaries between two worlds. They continued to enjoy this role in China and Japan, where their efficacy in transferring merit to the ancestors was much emphasized.

Merit-Making and the Bodhisattva Ideal. Although the doctrine of the transfer of merit has its roots in the Hīnayāna, it was most fully developed in the Mahāyāna. There it became one of the basic practices of the *bodhisattva* (buddha-to-be), who was thought to be able freely to bestow upon others the merit accrued during a greatly extended spiritual career.

Actually, there are two stages to a *bodhisattva*'s meritorious career. In the first, while seeking enlightenment, he amasses merit by good deeds toward others. In this, his actions are not much different from those described in the Jātakas and attributed to the Buddha in his former lives. In the second stage, the *bodhisattva* (or, in Pure Land Buddhism, the Buddha Amitābha), infinitely meritorious, dispenses merit to all beings.

After initially awakening in himself the mind intent on enlightenment (Skt., *bodhicitta*), the *bodhisattva* begins his career with the path of accumulation of merit (*saṃbhāramārga*), during which he performs great acts of self-sacrifice over many lifetimes and begins the practice of the perfections of giving, morality, patience, energy, meditation, and wisdom. In all of this, his actions are governed by his vow for enlightenment (*praṇidhāna*). Unlike the vows of the Hinayanists, however, those of a *bodhisattva* can be quite elaborate (especially in Pure Land Buddhism), and generally involve his willingness to postpone individual attainment of final *nirvāṇa* in order to be able to lead all sentient beings to enlightenment.

As a result of such altruism, certain great *bodhisattvas*, such as Avalokiteśvara, Mañjuśrī, Kṣitigarbha, or Samantabhadra, came to be seen as having stored up virtually inexhaustible supplies of merit, which they can now dispense to sentient beings in order to allay their sufferings. The mechanism by which this is done is that of the transfer of merit, but this is now seen as a more total and compassionate act than in the Hīnayāna. Not only does the *bodhisattva* confer on others the benefit of specific deeds, but he also seeks to share with them his entire store of merit, or, to use a different simile, his own actual roots of merit (*kuśalamūla*). In this, all desire for a better rebirth for himself has disappeared; the only sentiment remaining is his great compassion (*mahākaruṇā*) for all sentient beings in their many states of suffering.

SEE ALSO Bodhisattva Path; Karman, article on Buddhist Concepts.

BIBLIOGRAPHY

Four kinds of sources are most useful in considering the practice of merit-making in Buddhism.

First, there are anthologies of popular Buddhist stories illustrating the workings of merit and demerit. These are too vast and numerous to be described here, but they include the Jātakas (tales of Buddha's former lives), the Avadānas (legends about the lives of individual Buddhists), and innumerable stories of karmic rewards either included in commentaries on canonical works or gathered in separate collections. For translations of examples of each of these three types, see *The Jātaka*, 6 vols. (1895–1905; London, 1973), edited by E. B. Cowell; *Avadāna-çatakạ: Cent légendes bouddhiques*, translated by Léon Feer (Paris, 1891); and *Elucidation of the Intrinsic Meaning: The Commentary on the Peta Stories*, translated by U Ba Kyaw, edited by Peter Masefield (London, 1980).

Second, there are the descriptions and discussions of merit-making practices in present-day Buddhist societies by anthropologists and other observers in the field. For a variety of these works, which also present significant interpretations of merit making, see, for Sri Lanka, Richard F. Gombrich's *Precept and Practice* (Oxford, 1971), chapters 4–7; for Thailand, Stanley J. Tambiah's "The Ideology of Merit and the Social Correlates of Buddhism in a Thai Village," in *Dialectic in Practical Religion* (Cambridge, 1968), edited by Edmund Leach; and, for Burma, Melford E. Spiro's *Buddhism and Society* (New York, 1970).

Third, there are the inscriptions left by merit makers in India and elsewhere to record their acts of merit. Various examples of these invaluable and fascinating documents may be found in Dines Chandra Sircar's *Select Inscriptions Bearing on Indian History and Civilization*, vol. 1, *From the Sixth Century B.C. to the Sixth Century A.D.*, 2d ed. (Calcutta, 1965).

Finally, there are the more specialized scholarly studies of specific aspects of merit-making. Only a few of these can be mentioned here. For a fine discussion of the various connotations of the word for "merit," see Jean Filliozat's "Sur le domaine sémantique de puṇya," in *Indianisme et bouddhisme: Mélanges offerts à Mgr. Étienne Lamotte* (Louvain, 1980). For two very helpful studies of the transfer of merit in Hīnayāna Buddhism, see G. P. Malalasekera's "'Transference of Merit' in Ceylonese Buddhism," *Philosophy East and West* 17 (1967): 85–90, and Jean-Michel Agasse's "Le transfert de mérite dans le bouddhisme pāli classique," *Journal asiatique* 226 (1978): 311–332. The latter is an especially suggestive article and has an English summary. For a social scientist's view of the way in which merit-making combines with other forces in defining social roles and hierarchies, see L. M. Hank's "Merit and Power in the Thai Social Order," *American Anthropologist* 64 (1962): 1247–1261. Finally, for a clear discussion of the place of merit in the development of the *bodhisattva* ideal, see A. L. Basham's "The Evolution of the Concept of the Bodhisattva," in *The Bodhisattva Doctrine in Buddhism* (Waterloo, Ontario, 1981), edited by Leslie S. Kawamura.

New Sources

Bechert, Heinz. "Buddha-field and Transfer of Merit in a Theravada Source." *Indo-Iranian Journal* 35 (1992): 95–108.

Boucher, Daniel. "Sutra on the Merit of Bathing the Buddha." In *Buddhism in Practice*, edited by Donald S. Lopez, Jr., pp. 59–68. Princeton, 1995.

Cousins, Lance. "Good or Skilful? *Kusala* in Canon and Commentary." *Journal of Buddhist Ethics* 3 (1996): 136–64. Available from http://jbe.la.psu.edu.

Herrmann-Pfandt, A. "Verdienstübertragung im Hīnayāna und Mahāyāna." In *Suhrllekhāḥ: Festgabe für Helmut Eimer*, edited by Michael Hahn, Jens-Uwe Hartmann and Roland Steiner, pp. 79–98. Swisttal-Odendorf, 1996.

Schopen, Gregory. "Two Problems in the History of Indian Buddhism: The Layman/Monk Distinction and the Doctrines of the Transfer of Merit." *Studien zur Indologie und Iranistik* 10 (1985): 9–47.

JOHN S. STRONG (1987)
Revised Bibliography

MERIT: CHRISTIAN CONCEPTS

The term *merit* derives directly from the Latin *meritum* as used by theologians in Western Christianity beginning with Tertullian (160?–225?). Earlier Christian apologists had stressed the importance of postbaptismal works as a preparation for eternal life, and indeed this line of thought can be traced back in a general way to various New Testament writings. The important question as to whether the third-century teaching on merit emerged naturally out of early Christianity or whether it was a distortion, or at best a countertheme, is variously assessed by Catholic and Protestant theologians. Thus, in an article on merit (1962), Günther Bornkamm emphasized the absence of any concept of merit in the New Testament, while his co-writer Erdmann Schott roundly declared that "only the Roman Catholic church developed a doctrine of merit." However, both of these writers recognize the presence of those elements in early Christian writings, including the New Testament, which writers with a Catholic viewpoint see as the basis for the development of the doctrine. These elements are none other than judgment, reward, and punishment. Thus according to Anselm Forster (1965) references to such themes are so numerous that the apostolic fathers and the apologists simply brought the idea of merit into their proclamation of salvation as circumstances required, without any need for systematic reflection at that time.

The New Testament writers certainly made much use of this complex of ideas, as seen for example in the vision of judgment in *Matthew* 25. However, such ideas do not in themselves amount to or necessarily require the development of a doctrine of merit, as may be observed in parallel situations in the history of religions. Historically, there certainly was no general belief in the New Testament writings that some sufficient degree of merit either should or even could be accumulated for any purpose. The main thrust of early Christian teaching was rather to overcome any calculating religiosity in favor of a trusting reliance on the promises of God and spontaneous, uncircumscribed works of love. This holds good both for the teaching of Jesus himself, as far as this can be precisely ascertained, and also for the teaching of the major theological exponents, John and Paul. A doctrine of merit as such did not clearly arise until the third century.

PATRISTIC VIEW OF MERIT. With Tertullian, well known for his legal metaphors, the doctrine of merit came into semiformal existence. He distinguished between good works as a source of merit and nonobligatory good works as a source of extra merit, thus introducing an element of calculation. He also taught that human sinners are required to render satisfaction to God, a satisfaction that could be fulfilled by the offering of merits. Other church fathers accepted Tertullian's teaching, above all with a view to the care of postbaptismal life within the church.

Thus Cyprian (c. 205–258), bishop of Carthage, taught that sins could be purged by charitable works and by faith. This did not refer to those sins contracted before baptism, for they were purged by the blood and sanctification of Christ. But, Cyprian says in *On Works and Charity*, "sic eleemosyne extinguet peccatum" ("as water extinguishes fire, so charitable work extinguishes sin") and "eleemosynis atque operationibus iustis" ("as the fire of Gehenna is extinguished by the water of salvation, so the flame of transgressions is assuaged by almsgiving and just works"). He goes on to say that God is satisfied by just works and that sins are purged by the merits of mercifulness (*misericordiae meritis*). Indeed, by charitable works our prayers are made effective, our lives saved from danger, and our souls liberated from death.

Of importance for later understanding of the doctrine was the debate between Pelagius, Augustine, and others in the first part of the fifth century. Pelagius, whose teaching was current in Rome and North Africa, stressed the power of man through free will to choose and practice the good, and he viewed grace conveyed by the example and stimulus of Christ as a welcome but theoretically not absolutely essential extra. Augustine considered Pelagius's teaching to present a faulty doctrine of man and to render Christian salvation all but superfluous. For the present subject the debate is of importance in that it had the effect of subordinating teaching on merit to the doctrine of grace. Since Pelagianism was condemned as heretical at the councils of Milevum and Carthage (in 416 and 418), Augustine's treatment of the subject set the framework for later Western definitions and ultimately for the divergence that broke out at the Reformation.

It may be noted in passing that the concept of merit was never worked out in detail and did not become a matter of controversy in the Eastern (Orthodox) churches because the operation of divine grace and human free will were and are seen in terms of synergy. By this is meant a cooperation of powers that are unequal but both essential. Although human response and action are necessary within the event of salvation, the preeminent role of grace means that calculations are of no relevance. The perfect example of synergy is provided by Mary, honored as the mother of God (*theotokos*).

MEDIEVAL AND REFORMATION VIEWS OF MERIT. In medieval Latin Christendom an increasingly carefully defined doctrine of merit was current. This doctrine was, with minor variations, consistent from Peter Abelard up until the Reformation. Both obligatory and nonobligatory (supererogatory) works were regarded as meritorious in the sense that they contributed, within the overall economy of divine grace, to the ensuring of salvation. Grace itself can be understood at various levels: all-important was *gratia praeveniens*, but Peter Lombard distinguished between the self-effective *gratia operans* and the *gratia cooperans* that assists in the creation of merit. Widespread in the Middle Ages was the distinction between acts that ensure divine recognition and acts that merely qualify for it at divine discretion. These two types of merit are referred to as condign merit (*meritum de condigno*) and congruent merit (*meritum de congruo*) respectively. However, the sovereignty of God was maintained by the teaching, for example of Thomas Aquinas, that while merit arises equally from free will and from grace, the effective status assigned to condign merit was itself still dependent ultimately on grace. The underlying idea here, not usually made explicit, is that the church in its teaching function can reliably assert the positive availability of grace in such circumstances. Some discussion centered on the possibility of regaining a state of grace through merit after committing deadly sin, which Bonaventure considered possible and Thomas impossible. Another aspect arose with John Duns Scotus, who emphasized the crucial role of the divine acceptance of merit over against the value inherent in the work itself. This permitted the assertion that God recognizes the merits of supernaturally assisted works within the economy of salvation rather than of those performed by man in his natural state simply because he so wishes. (For more details on these and other aspects of the medieval doctrine of merit, see Schott, 1962.)

The doctrinal subtlety of many medieval theologians was clearly directed toward safeguarding the principle of the prior, determinative grace of God over against any idea that salvation could be ensured by calculated acts on man's part. However, not all medieval Christians had the ability, or, in their often short and hard lives, the leisure, to appreciate these points. Since theology had a place for individual acts that might be meritorious, that is, of assistance in securing salvation rather than damnation, the common assumption was that some of these acts had better be performed. It was plainly believed that bad things had to be compensated for by good things if lengthy or eternal punishment was to be avoided, and this meant in daily religious life: penance, good works, and the sacraments. Thus salvation became for many a transaction, albeit a mysterious one. The sale of indulgences in respect of a plenary remission of sins may be regarded as an extreme example of this and was understandably criticized at the Reformation as an abuse. That the element of weighing, or paying, had become a standard feature of Western Catholic tradition, was evident also, however, in the large numbers of chantries endowed for masses to be said for the patron's benefit, via a transfer of merit, after his death.

The Reformation saw a massive reassertion of grace and a straightforward rejection of reliance on works of any kind. With Martin Luther the language of justification was central but was used paradoxically, as in Pauline literature, to refer to God's gracious justification of man through Christ, even though man himself is not able to stand before God in judgment. With this fundamental shift of emphasis, which became increasingly critical of current religious practice, the doctrine of merit related to works was swept away. Yet the vocabulary of merit did not immediately disappear. Indeed the traditional terminology of condign and congruent merit occurs in Luther's *Dictata super Psalterium* (Lectures on the Psalms) and serves as the basis for a gradual transposition of the concept of merited salvation into that of unmerited salvation (cf. Rupp, 1953, esp. pp. 138f.). Thus the idea of the insufficiency of merit or of works provided Luther at one and the same time with a polemical differentiation from the existing tradition of Western Christianity and an invitation to faith in the saving and transforming power of grace leading to good works as the fruit of Christian life. As far as these matters were concerned, the position of other reformers, including John Calvin with his formula *sola gratia* (by grace alone), was essentially similar. As a result, wholesale changes occurred in the practical forms of religion. At the same time the transactional aspect was concentrated in the doctrine of atonement through the merits of the death of Christ.

Merit in Catholicism. The positive significance of merit in the context of the religious life was reaffirmed for Western Catholicism at the Council of Trent (1545–1563), the relevant definitions and thirty-three anathemas being contained in the sixteenth chapter of the text for the sixth session: "De fructu justificationis, hoc est, de merito bonorum operum, deque ipsius meriti ratione" (Denzinger, 1965). The argument is tightly linked to the concept of justification, which is viewed as a process within the believer that leads to meritorious good works. Since the merit of good works was considered to bring about specific results contributing to the increase of grace in the present life, to eternal life itself, and to the increase of glory, room was left for the continued pastoral management of religious life in terms of relative achievement, within the overall context of divine grace. This has essentially been the basis of Catholic religiosity ever since.

Thus the marketing of indulgences was abandoned, but the attainment of an indulgence through devotional practice (e.g., on "the first nine Fridays") or through special sets of prayers (Our Fathers, Ave Marias, etc.), leading to a reduction of the number of days required to be spent in purgatory (by 500, 1,000, etc.), has continued down to the present. Moreover such remissions can, via the communion of saints and the work of Christ himself, be applied to the suffering of souls already in purgatory, through prayer, fasting, alms, and the saying of Mass. As one popular nineteenth-century work put it: "She [the church] appears before the tribunal of the judge, not only as a suppliant, but also as the stewardess of the treasure of the merits of Christ and his saints, and from it offers to him the ransom for the souls in purgatory, with full confidence that he will accept her offer and release her children from the tortures of the debtor's prison" (F. J. Shadler, *The Beauties of the Catholic Church*, New York, 1881, p. 404). One could hardly hope to find a clearer statement both of the idea of the transfer of merit and of the transactional manner in which merit is, or can be, understood. Other presentations content themselves with a loose statement of the need for both grace and works, thereby allowing elaboration at the pastoral level. Thus a modern catechism declares: "We can do no good work of ourselves toward our salvation; we need the help of God's grace," but also: "Faith alone will not save us without good works; we must also have hope and charity" (Catholic Truth Society, *A Catechism of Christian Doctrine*, London, 1971, pp. 22f.). The consciousness of ordinary Catholic believers may be summed up in the view that while one cannot ensure one's own salvation one is certainly expected to make a contribution.

In recent years theological controversy about merit in the context of Christianity has lost much of its sharpness for three reasons. First, the theme is subsumed, for Protestants, into the greater theme of faith and grace over against works. From this point of view relying on merits or merit is simply a variant form of relying on works and therefore hardly requires separate consideration. Second, although the concept of merit is retained by Catholics, it is usually made clear, at least in formal accounts, that the prior grace of God is an essential condition. Although, admittedly, this does not meet Protestant objections to all and every form of reliance on works, it does mean that from the Catholic side, too, attention is directed fundamentally toward man's position in the overall economy of divine grace. Third, and this applies to Protestant and Catholic theologians alike, interest is directed toward other issues such as the historical and social responsibilities of Christianity, questions arising through the encounter with non-Christian traditions, and philosophical reflections about the very nature of religious language. In such a perspective, while theological viewpoints regarding merit remain distinct, it is not currently considered to be a matter requiring intense or urgent debate.

See Also Atonement, article on Christian Concepts; Free Will and Predestination, article on Christian Concepts; Grace; Justification.

BIBLIOGRAPHY

Bornkamm, Günther, Erdmann Schott, et al. "Verdienst." In *Die Religion in Geschichte und Gegenwart*, 3d ed., vol. 6, pp. 1261–1271. Tübingen, 1962.

Cyprian. *Quellen zur Geschichte des Papsttums und des römischen Katholizismus.* Edited by Carl Mirbt. Tübingen, 1911. Includes the Latin text of Cyprian's *On Works and Charity.*

Denzinger, Heinrich, ed. *Enchiridion Symbolorum.* Freiburg, 1965. Includes definitions formulated by the Council of Trent. See especially pages 376ff.

Forster, Anselm. "Verdienst (Systematisch)." In *Lexikon für Theologie und Kirche*, vol. 10, cols. 677–680. Freiburg, 1965.

Jedin, Hubert. *A History of the Council of Trent*, vol. 2. Translated by Ernest Graf. London, 1960.

Raemers, W. *Indulgenced Prayers to Help the Holy Souls.* London, 1956.

Rupp, E. G. *The Righteousness of God: Luther Studies.* London, 1953.

Ware, Timothy. *The Orthodox Church.* Harmondsworth, 1963.

New Sources

Hallonsten, Gösta. *Meritum bei Tertullian: Überprüffung einer Forschungstadition II.* Malmö, 1985.

Moule, Charles Francis Digby. *Forgiveness and Reconciliation and Other New Testament Themes.* London, 1998.

Wawrykow, Joseph P. "God's Grace and Human Action: 'Merit.'" In *Theology of Thomas Aquinas.* Notre Dame, Ind., 1995.

MICHAEL PYE (1987)
Revised Bibliography

MERLIN.

MERLIN. The origins of Merlin, the magician, prophet, and guardian of the legendary British king Arthur and a central figure in medieval Arthurian romance in both French and English, are to be found in a number of early Welsh poems and related material in Latin. The name *Merlin* was created by the twelfth-century pseudohistorian Geoffrey of Monmouth, who described the conception of "a fatherless boy" by a nun who had been impregnated by an incubus in the South Wales town of Caerfyrddin (modern-day Carmarthen). The omniscient boy's advice to King Vortigern suggests that Geoffrey modeled his Merlin on an earlier Welsh story of the wonder-child Ambrosius. Although two later exploits, the removal of Stonehenge from Ireland to England and the disguising of Uter Pendragon as Gorlois so that he might sleep with the latter's wife (a ruse that results in the conception of Arthur), are not found in the earlier sources, Merlin's major role as a political prophet in Geoffrey's *Historia regum Britanniae* is traditional.

The prophet's birth at Caerfyrddin is a sure sign that he is in fact the Welsh Myrddin, whose name is variously spelled *Merddin, Merdin,* and *Myrtin,* which Geoffrey changed to *Merlin* to avoid unfortunate associations with the French *merde.* There are extant a large number of medieval Welsh poems claimed to have been composed by a fictional Myrddin. The majority of these are post hoc vaticinations and contemporary comments on political events attributed to the famed prophet, who had acquired this role by the tenth century, as the poem *Armes Prydein* (c. 935) shows, a role he was to retain throughout the Middle Ages. There may also be discerned, however, a substratum of story to which other pre-twelfth-century poems allude and which can be reconstituted from these and other sources. Myrddin, a member of the court of King Gwenddoleu, became insane at the Battle of Arfderydd (fought in 573 in modern-day Cumbria). He fled in terror from King Rhydderch of Strathclyde to the Caledonian Forest (in the Scottish Lowlands), and lived there the life of a wild man (his Welsh epithet is *Wyllt,* "wild"). He was befriended by his sister, or lover, Gwenddydd, to whom he prophesied events at court. These traditions were used by Geoffrey of Monmouth in his poem *Vita Merlini,* which is designed to correct the nontraditional elements and to supplement the picture he had earlier given in his *Historia.* His two Merlins appeared to contemporaries as distinct characters named Merlinus Ambrosius (in the *Historia*) and Merlinus Silvestris (in the *Vita*), but it is better to regard the distinction as being due to Geoffrey's imprecise knowledge of the genuine tradition at the time of his writing of the *Historia.*

The northern Myrddin is found under the name *Lailoken* in the twelfth-century *Vita Kentigerni* of Joceline of Furness, and he has an analogue in the ninth-century Irish character Suibhne Geilt. Lailoken's tale was relocated in South Wales, and, according to the claims of A. O. H. Jarman, the madman was given a new name derived from *Caerfyrddin.* Rachel Bromwich, stressing Myrddin's status as a poet in Welsh bardic tradition, suggests that he was a sixth-century historical poet, none of whose work is extant but who developed legendary features, as happened to Taliesin. There is little doubt that the sagas of two characters have influenced one another, and they are linked in a pre-twelfth-century dialogue poem which may have been known to Geoffrey of Monmouth, who used the device of dialogue in the *Vita.* Although Welsh literature does not show the influence of later Arthurian romance in the character of Myrddin, late medieval Welsh poetry does contain allusions to his imprisonment and death and to erotic elements in the legend.

BIBLIOGRAPHY

A good and concise account of the development of the theme of Myrddin/Merlin is presented in *The Legend of Merlin* (Cardiff, 1960) by A. O. H. Jarman. Consult, also, Jarman's article titled "A oedd Myrddin yn fardd hanesyddol," *Studia Celtica* 10/11 (1975–1976): 182–197. This article is written in response to Rachel Bromwich's piece, "Y Cynfeirdd a'r Traddodiad Cymraeg," *Bulletin of the Board of Celtic Studies* 22 (1966): 30–37. A thorough review of the important issues is found in *Trioedd Ynys Prydein: The Welsh Triads,* 2d ed. (Cardiff, 1978), which was edited and translated by Bromwich. For views on Merlin's historical origins see Nikolai Tolstoy, *The Quest for Merlin* (London, 1985).

BRYNLEY F. ROBERTS (1987 AND 2005)

MERTON, THOMAS (1915–1968), Roman Catholic monk, author, and poet. Merton pursued a career that may be divided into three distinct phases: secular, monastic, and public. The secular career encompasses the first twenty-six years of his life and culminates with his entrance into the abbey of Gethsemani, Kentucky, in 1941. The basic elements that influenced his later life were set in place during this period. Merton was born on 31 January 1915 in Prades, France, the first child of artist Ruth Jenkins Merton of Zanesville, Ohio, and artist Owen Merton of Christchurch, New Zealand. The family moved to New York City the next year to escape World War I. The loss of his mother while still a child, his father at age sixteen, and a younger brother in World War II, contributed to Merton's sense of the tragic contingency of human life and, possibly, to his decision to enter monastic life. The influence from two parents who were artists and instinctive pacifists bore fruit in their son's pursuits as writer, poet, and prophet of nonviolence.

Merton attended school in the United States, Bermuda, France, and England before commencing higher education. He entered Clare College of Cambridge University on scholarship and completed his undergraduate education at Columbia University in New York. His friendships with Professor Mark Van Doren, the Pulitzer Prize poet, and fellow student Robert Lax, the future poet, helped to develop his already existing interests in mysticism, poetry, and monasticism. He converted to Roman Catholicism in 1938, completed an M.A. in literature from Columbia in 1939, and entered the abbey of Gethsemani in 1941 while working on a never-completed Ph.D. thesis on Gerard Manley Hopkins and teaching English at Saint Bonaventure University in New York State.

The second phase of Merton's career is his life as a monk of the Cistercian Order of the Strict Observance. The rigor of this life is characterized by perpetual silence, a lifelong vegetarian diet, and many hours of daily prayer starting at 2:00 AM. The purpose of this regimen is the development of a contemplative life. Many of those who knew Merton well believe he became a mystic during these years. The last three years of his life were also lived as a hermit, removed from the communal life of the monastery.

The third phase of Merton's life, the public career, is somewhat coincident with the second and is marked by an intense involvement in writing, social protest, and Asian spirituality. The most famous of his sixty books is *Seven Storey Mountain*, an autobiography about a personal search that brings him from unfocused activism to contemplation and from a life of self-indulgence to self-discipline. The writings of Merton include eight volumes of poetry and some six hundred articles.

If a career in writing was unconventional, Merton's involvement in social protest was even less part of the monastic model. He objected vehemently to the United States' involvement in the Vietnam War, the nuclear arms race, violations of the rights of black Americans, and the dehumanizing effects of technology. This protest caused him difficulty at times with readers who favored a pietistic style of writing, with church superiors, and with members of his monastic community. He persevered in putting his views forward, however, believing that mystics owed their contemporaries the value of their own unique witness.

In the final years of his life, Merton was committed to Hindu and Buddhist spiritual wisdom without diminishing his attachment to Catholic Christianity. Zen Buddhism, most especially, appealed to Merton because of its emphasis on experience rather than doctrine. Merton searched for God through participation in the ancient spiritualities of Asia on a long journey to the East that was his personal pilgrimage and a metaphor of his life. He died of accidental electrocution in Bangkok, Thailand, on December 10, 1968.

BIBLIOGRAPHY

The authorized biography of Thomas Merton, Michael Mott's *The Seven Mountains of Thomas Merton* (Boston, 1984), is an exhaustively researched and yet readable study. It may suffer from lack of a central interpretive theme but sets a standard for subsequent work on Merton. *Merton: A Biography* by Monica Furlong (New York, 1980) is a reliable account, although little attention is given to Merton's monastic vocation or his involvement with Asian spirituality. *Thomas Merton: Monk and Poet*, by George Woodcock (New York, 1978), is a perceptive analysis of the creative dynamics in Merton's literary work. The author, himself a poet and novelist, is sensitive to the religious dimension of Merton's life. My own book, *The Human Journey: Thomas Merton, Symbol of a Century* (New York, 1982), draws out the correlations between Merton's personal life and the tensions and aspirations of the twentieth century. It traces the appeal of Merton to his capacity to assimilate the problems and promise of his own time.

ANTHONY PADOVANO (1987)

MESOAMERICAN RELIGIONS

This entry consists of the following articles:

MESOAMERICAN RELIGIONS: PRE-COLUMBIAN RELIGIONS

Through several millennia and up to the present, complex forms of indigenous belief and ritual have developed in Mesoamerica, the area between North America proper and the southern portion of isthmic Central America. The term *Mesoamerica*, whose connotation is at once geographical and cultural, is used to designate the area where these distinctive forms of high culture existed. There, through a long process of cultural transformation, periods of rise, fall, and recovery occurred. On the eve of the Spanish invasion (1519), Mesoamerica embraced what are now the central and southern parts of Mexico, as well as the nations of Guatemala, Belize, El Salvador, and some portions of Honduras, Nicaragua, and Costa Rica.

Distinctive forms of social organization began to develop in this area from, at the latest, the end of the second millennium BCE. Parallel to these social and economic structures, various forms of religion also flourished. Most contemporary researchers agree that Mesoamerican religion, and the Mesoamerican high cultures in general, developed without any significant influence from the civilizations of Asia, Europe, and Africa. But whereas it is generally accepted that the various forms of high culture that appeared in Mesoamerica shared the same indigenous origin, a divergence of opinions exists regarding the question of how the various religious manifestations are ultimately interrelated.

According to some scholars (e.g., Bernal, 1969; Caso, 1971; Joralemon, 1971, 1976; Léon-Portilla, 1968; Nicholson, 1972, 1976), there was only one religious substratum, which came to realize itself in what are the distinct varieties of beliefs and cults of peoples such as the Maya, the builders of Teotihuacan, the Zapotec, the Mixtec, the Toltec, the Aztec, and others. A different opinion (maintained by, among others, George Kubler [1967, 1970]) postulates the existence of various religious traditions in ancient Mesoamerica. Those adhering to this view nonetheless admit to reciprocal forms of influence and even to various kinds of indigenous religious syncretism.

This essay on pre-Columbian religions postulates the existence of what is essentially a single religious tradition in Mesoamerica, without, however, minimizing the regional differences or any changes that have altered the continuity of various elements of what can be labeled "Mesoamerican religion" (Carrasco, 1990).

The assertion about the existence of a single religious tradition rests on various kinds of evidence:

1. All over Mesoamerica there were identical calendrical systems which guided the functioning of religious rituals in function of which religious rituals were performed.
2. The Mesoamerican pantheon included a number of deities that were universally worshiped, including the supreme Dual God, Our Father our Mother; an Old God known also as God of Fire; a Rain god; a Young God of Maize; Quetzalcoatl, Kukulcan, god and priest; a Monster of the Earth; and others. The gods also had calendrical names.
3. Rituals performed included various kinds of offerings such as animals, flowers, food and human sacrifices.
4. Self-sacrifice also played an important role.
5. There was a complex priestly hierarchy.
6. The temples were built in a basically similar architectural pattern, truncated pyramids with sanctuaries on top.
7. Recorded texts show the existence of a similar worldview, which included the sequence of several cosmic ages and spatial symbols such as cosmic trees, birds, colors, and deities.

EARLIEST RELIGIOUS MANIFESTATIONS. Because of lack of evidence, scholarship does not extend back to the religious concerns of the earliest inhabitants of Mesoamerica (c. 25,000 BCE). Nevertheless, some archaeological findings show that the early hunter-gatherers had at least some metaphysical or religious preoccupations. Reference can be made to their rock art: paintings and petroglyphs, some of which date to about 10,000 BCE, several of which suggest religious or magical forms of propitiation through hunting, fishing, and gathering.

Objects that are more obviously religious in function date only from 2500 to 1500 BCE, when the earliest village-type settlements appeared in Mesoamerica. By that time, after a slow process of plant domestication that probably began around 6000 BCE, new forms of society began to develop. It had taken several millennia for the hunter-gatherers to become settled in the first small Mesoamerican villages. In the evolution of Mesoamerican culture, what has come to be known as the Early Formative period had commenced.

Those living during this period employed an ensemble of objects indicative of their beliefs about the afterlife, and of their need to make offerings to their deities. At different sites throughout Mesoamerica (especially in the Central Highlands, the Oaxaca area, and the Yucatán Peninsula), many female clay figurines have been found in what were the agricultural fields. Scholars hypothesize that these figurines were placed in the fields to propitiate the gods and ensure the fertility of crops. Burials in places close to the villages (as in Asia, Africa, and Europe) also appear, with a large proportion of the human remains belonging to children or young people. These burial places are accompanied by offerings such as vestiges of food and pieces of ceramics.

OLMEC HIGH CULTURE. Villages of agriculturists and potters, who evidently were already concerned with the afterlife and with "sacred" fertility, became gradually more numerous in Mesoamerica, with the villages established in hospitable environments experiencing significant population growth. Among these, the communities in the area near the Gulf of Mexico in the southern part of the Mexican state of Veracruz and neighboring Tabasco underwent extraordinary changes around 1200 BCE. Archaeological findings in the centers now called Tres Zapotes, La Venta, and San Lorenzo reveal that a high culture was already developing and, with it, a strong religious tradition.

Olman (land of rubber), the abode of the Olmec, with its large buildings mainly serving religious purposes, stands out as the first high culture in Mesoamerica. The center of La Venta, with its mud-plastered pyramids, its semicylindrical and circular mounds, carved stone altars, tombs, stelae, and many sculptures, anticipates the more complex ensembles of religious structures that proliferated centuries later in

Mesoamerica. The central part of La Venta, built on a small island in a swampy area sixteen kilometers from the point where the Tonala River empties into the Gulf of Mexico, was no doubt sacred space to the Olmec. The agriculturist villagers who had settled in the vicinity of La Venta were already developing new economic, social, political, and religious institutions. Although many villagers continued their subsistence activities—especially agriculture and fishing—others specialized in various crafts and arts, commercial endeavors, the defense of the group, and—of particular significance—the cult of the gods. Government at this point was most likely left to those who knew how to worship the gods.

Olmec religious iconography. Olmec religious representations have been described as "biologically impossible" (Joralemon, 1976, p. 33). Human and animal features are combined in these representations in a great variety of forms. Early researchers pointed out the omnipresence of a jaguarlike god, who seemingly had the highest rank in the Olmec pantheon. One early hypothesis stated that the main traits of what later became the prominent Mesoamerican rain god derived from these jaguarlike representations.

A more ample and precise approach to Olmec iconography has led Peter D. Joralemon (1971, 1976) and Michael D. Coe (1972, 1973) to express the opinion that the variety of presentations of the jaguarlike god portray distinct, though closely associated, divine beings. A number of divine identities integrate various animal and human attributes. The animal features most frequently used in combination with the basically human-shaped face are a jaguar's nose, spots, and mighty forearms, as well as a bird's wings, a serpent's body, and a caiman's teeth. Thus, one finds beings that might be described as a human-jaguar, a jaguar-bird, a bird-jaguar-caiman, a bird-jaguar-serpent, a jaguar-caiman-fish, a human-bird-serpent, a bird-caiman-serpent, and a bird-mammal-caiman (Joralemon, 1976, pp. 33–37).

Iconographic comparisons between representations of these kinds and other religious Mesoamerican effigies from the Classic (c. 250–900 CE) and the Postclassic periods (c. 900–1519 CE) reveal that the nucleus of the Mesoamerican pantheon was already developing in the Olmec epoch. One god is sometimes represented as a kind of dragon, frequently featuring a jaguar's face, a pug nose, a caiman's teeth, and a snarling, open, cavernous mouth with fangs projecting from the upper jaw, a flaming eyebrow, various serpentine attributes, and at times a hand/paw/wing linked to the occipital region. Other, more abstract, motifs include crossed-band designs in the eyes, crossed bands and a dotted bracket, four dots and a bar, and the symbols for raindrops and maize.

This god, probably the supreme Olmec deity, was worshiped in his many guises, as the power related to fertility, rain, lightning, earth, fire, and water. In him, various forms of duality—an essential feature in the Classic and Postclassic Mesoamerican universe in both its divine and human aspects—can be anticipated. Prototypes of other gods that were later worshiped among the Maya, as well as the peoples of the central highlands and those of Oaxaca, can also be identified in the Olmec pantheon. Among these are the Maize God, the One Who Rules in the Heavens, the Old Lord (protector of the sacred domestic hearth), and the Serpent, who has birdlike attributes and is a prototype of the Feathered Serpent.

Other researchers have recognized that, in additon to emphasizing the appearance of the omnipresent Olmec god as a kind of a dragon with a jaguar's face, it must also be identified by its equally visible serpentine traits. Román Piña Chan summarizes such an interpretation:

> We can say that during the period of maximum Olmec development they gave birth to new religious concepts: [. . .] rattle snake representations, or bird-serpents, that began to symbolize the god of rain or celestial water. (Piña Chan, 1982, p. 194)

Chan and others have recognized that the god with serpentine traits is the antecedent of Tlaloc, the rain god of the central plateau, known also as Chac among the Maya, and as Cocijo among the Zapotec of Oaxaca. It can be asserted that iconographic studies support this view.

The Olmec thought of their gods as endowed with interchangeable traits and attributes. Thus, a kind of continuum existed in the sphere of the divine, as if the ensemble of all the godlike forms was essentially a mere manifestation of the same supreme reality. This distinctive character of the divine—represented through ensembles of symbols, often shifting from one godlike countenance to another—perdured, as will be seen, in the religious tradition of Mesoamerica. That continuity, subject to variations of time and space, did, however, undergo innovations and other kinds of change. One important change derived from the relationship that was to develop between the perception of the universe of the divine and the art and science of measuring periods of time (i.e., the development of calendrical computations).

Origins of the calendar. The earliest evidence of calendrical computations—inscriptions discovered in places influenced by Olmec culture—also conveys other related information. Of prime importance is the indication that the political and social order was not only closely linked to the universe of the divine, but was also conceived in terms of the measurement of time—all of whose moments are bearers of destiny. In the Stelae of the Dancers (a stele [pl. stelae] is an engraved upright stone slab), at Monte Albán I (epoch I) in Oaxaca (c. 600 BCE), where Olmec influence is present, the human figures, described "as an expression of political and ritual power" (Marcus, 1976, p. 127), are accompanied by hieroglyphs denoting names of persons (probably both human and divine), place names, and dates.

The calendar was doubtless the result of assiduous astronomical observation. Its early diffusion throughout various parts of Mesoamerica implies an old origin (probably 1000–900 BCE) for this calendar that later came to determine all divine and human activities. Humans are represented in several Olmec monuments, such as the Basalt Altar 4 in La Venta, as emerging from the mouth or cave of the supreme "dragon" deity, signifying humankind's birth into a universe where time moves in sacred rhythms. The recurring Olmec symbols—quadruple and quintuple patternings (indicative of the four corners and the center of the earth), stylized maize plants, and other motifs—seem to reveal that a prototype of what became the classic Mesoamerican image of sacred space had been developed as far back as Olmec times.

Maya Religion. Olmec civilization acted as a ferment of many cultural transformations. Archaeological research has identified the traces of its ample diffusion. In addition to the numerous sites excavated in the Olmec heartland of Veracruz-Tabasco, many villages of the Early Formative type in the Central Plateau—in the western region along the Pacific coast in Oaxaca—and in the land of the Maya, show evidence of having undergone processes of rapid change. (The Maya territories include the Yucatán Peninsula and parts of the present-day Mexican states of Tabasco and Chiapas, as well as Guatemala, Belize, and parts of Honduras and El Salvador.)

Antecedents of cultural grandeur. Some notable findings have highlighted the processes that culminated in the grandeur of Maya high culture. These findings reveal that a preoccupation with the sacred cycles of time resulted in extraordinary achievements as early as several decades BCE. One of the findings is Stele 2 of Chiapa de Corzo, Mexico, where a date corresponding to December 9, 36 BCE is expressed in what modern researchers describe as the calendar's Long Count (see below). Two other inscriptions, registered in the same Long Count, have been found in places closer to the ancient Olmec heartland, one on Stele C at Tres Zapotes, Veracruz (31 BCE), and the other on the Tuxtla (Veracruz) Statuette (162 CE). The deeply rooted Mesoamerican tradition of measuring the flow of time, a tradition whose oldest vestiges appear in Monte Albán I, Oaxaca (c. 600 BCE), became more sophisticated around 200 to 100 BCE with the complexities and extreme precision of the Long Count. To understand its functioning and multiple religious connotations, one needs to be familiar with two basic systems—the 365-day solar calendar and the 260-day count—described later in this article.

Other vestiges that have been unearthed point to cultural changes that were taking place during this period, called the Late Formative. In the Pacific plains of the southernmost Mexican state of Chiapas and in adjacent parts of Guatemala, several centers boasted impressive religious buildings, temples, altars, stelae with bas-reliefs, and a few calendrical inscriptions. Archaeologists rightly consider these centers to be the immediate antecedents of Maya culture. The centers of Izapa, Abaj Takalik, and El Baúl contain monuments that are outstanding. Stele 2 at Abaj Takalik contains a carved image of a celestial god and an inscription of a date, which, though partly illegible, is expressed in the system of the Long Count. In El Baúl, other calendrical instriptions correspond to the year 36 CE. Maya culture—one of the variants of Mesoamerican civilization—was about to be born.

Stele 5 of Izapa in Chiapas is particularly remarkable; in it a vertical image of the world is represented. One sees in it the cosmic tree of the center, and at its sides, the figures of Our Father and Our Mother, as they appear on pages 75 to 76 of the Maya *Codex Tro-Cortesiano.* In the stele, two feathered serpents surround the scene, which at its bottom shows the terrestrial waters and at its top the celestial ones. This stele, as well as others from the same center and from nearby sites, provides a glimpse at the beginnings of what was to become the vision of the world and of the supreme deity in Maya culture.

Chronology and sources. A Classic period (c. 250–900 CE) and a Postclassic period (c. 900–1519 CE) have been distinguished in the cultural development of the Maya. The most magnificent of their religious and urban centers flourished during the Classic period: Tikal, Uaxactún, and Piedras Negras in Guatemala; Copán and Quiriquá in Honduras; Nakum in Belize; Yaxchilán, Palenque, and Bonampak' in what is now the Mexican state of Chiapas; and Dzibililchaltún, Cobá, Kabáh, Labná, Chichén Itzá, Uxmal, Río Bec, and others in the Yucatán Peninsula. At these sites, sophisticated forms of spiritual development emerged. Even Diego de Landa, the Spanish friar who in the sixteenth century set fire to many of the written records of the Maya, could not refrain from remarking on "the number, the grandeur, and the beauty of their buildings" (Landa, trans. Tozzer, 1941, p. 170), especially those devoted to the cult of their gods. Besides Maya architecture—which included among its techniques the corbel vault—also deserving of special mention is their sculpture, mural painting, and bas-relief carving on stone stelae, stairways, lintels, panels, and plaques of jade. On them, thousands of hieroglyphic inscriptions have been found, some related to the universe of the gods and others having more mundane historical content. These inscriptions at times accompany carved images of gods as well as of rulers and other dignitaries.

To compensate for the obscurities that still surround the spiritual achievements of the Classic period, one has to look for whatever is indicative of a cultural continuity in the Postclassic. From the latter period, three pre-Columbian books—or codices—survive; and, even more significantly, a considerable number of indigenous testimonies, in Yucatec-Maya, Quiché-Maya, and other linguistic variants, have come down to us in early transcriptions done by Maya priests or sages who survived the Spanish conquest and learned to use the Roman alphabet. Among these testimonies, the *Popol Vuh* (The Book of counsel) of the Quiché-Maya, the several *Chilam Balam* books of the Yucatec-Maya, and the *Book of Songs of Dzitbalche* (from the Yucatán) stand out as conveyers of the religious wisdom of this remarkable people.

The Maya image of the world. To approach the core of the religious worldview of the Classic Maya, one has to analyze an ensemble of elements—some with antecedents in the Olmec culture, yet enriched and often transformed. The most significant of these elements include the Mayan image of the earth and universe, their calendrical concerns and ideas about time, and the ultimate meaning of the divine and of humans within their spatial and temporal universe.

In several Classic monuments, as well as in Postclassic books and other representations, the surface of the earth is conceived as being the back of a huge caiman with saurian, ophidian, and feline attributes that sometimes resemble those of the so-called Olmec Dragon. The monstrous creature is surrounded by vast waters. In Palenque, in the Tablet of the Cross and the Tablet of the Foliated Cross, cosmic trees rise from the earth monster. In some representations, one sees a double-headed serpent in the sky. The creature also appears with other attributes of the Olmec Dragon, such as crossed bands and various celestial symbols. The double-headed serpent covers and embraces the earth. It was this celestial serpent that, dividing the terrestrial monster into two parts, activated this universe and introduced life on earth. Thus, a primeval duality presides over and gives rise to the universe.

The surface of the earth, as in the case of the Olmec prototype, is distributed into four quadrants that converge at a central point: the navel of the world. One finds in Classic inscriptions and Postclassic codices hieroglyphs for each of the world quadrants and their associated colors. Cosmic trees and deities reside in the "red east," "white north," "black west," "yellow south," and "green central point." Above and below the surface of the earth are thirteen heavens and nine underworld levels, where thirteen celestial gods and nine "lords of the night" have their respective abodes.

MAYA DEITIES. The comparative study of religious iconography, the contents of the three extant Pre-Columbian Maya codices, and the relatively numerous texts of diverse origin within this culture allow us to surmise that the idea of a divine duality was deeply rooted in Mesoamerican thought since at least the Classic period, if not since the Olmec. The Dual God resides in the uppermost of the celestial levels. In the *Popol Vuh* of the Quiché-Maya, he-she is addressed both as E Quahalom (Begetter of Children) and as E Alom (Conceiver of Children). In the first of the *Songs of Dzitbalche* appears the following reference to the father-mother god:

> The little yellowbird, and also the cuckoo, and there is the mockingbird, they all delight the heart, the creatures of the Father, god, so likewise the Mother, such as the little turtle dove. . . (Edmonson, 1982, p. 176)

Our Father Our Mother has other names as well. There is evidence to identify him-her with the Postclassic Itzamná (Lizard House), the name probably referring to the primeval celestial and terrestrial being of monstrous countenance, whose house is the universe. This supreme creator-god is invoked at times with the feminine prefix *Ix-*, as in Ix Hun Itzam Na. To him-her—that is, to the "begetter-conceiver of children"—the Maya ultimately attributed the creation of the earth, heavens, sun, moon, plants, animals, and, of course, humans. As in the case of the Olmec nuclear deity, traits of caiman, bird, serpent, and jaguar can be perceived at times in the god's iconography.

The quadruple patterning expressed in certain Olmec monuments proliferated in Maya religious representations. The divine duality, "begetting and conceiving" children, develops a quadruple being—the various ensembles of gods that have to do with the four quadrants of the universe. The Red Itzamná appears in the East, the White in the North, the Black in the West, and the Yellow in the South. Other quadruple sets are the four Bacabs, supporters of the sky at the four corners of the world; the four Chacs, gods of rain; the four Pahuatuns, deities of wind; the four Chicchans (Owners of Thunder), godlike giant snakes; and the four Balams (Tigers), protectors of the cultivated fields.

Divine reality also permeates the upperworld and underworld levels. Itzamná is at once a celestial, a terrestrial, and an underworld god. The Oxlahum-ti-ku (thirteen gods) rule in the thirteen heavens, and the Bolom-ti-ku (nine gods) preside over the nine inferior levels.

Prominent in the Maya pantheon is Kin, the sun god, who, wandering above, creates the day and the cycles of time. When he reaches his home in the West, he enters the fangs of the earth monster and journeys through the obscure regions of the underworld to reappear in the East, from the same monster's fangs. Although the sun god himself cannot be considered the supreme deity of the Maya, his frequent association with the worlds above and below, with the four quadrants of the world, and with all the calendar's periods makes him a multifaceted god with innumerable religious connotations. He is often related to Itzamná as a celestial deity, and also to Yum Kimil (Lord of Death) who abides in the netherworld, the region visited at night by the sun god disguised as a jaguar. The abode of Yum Kimil is also the place to which most of the dead go. Only a few dead—chosen by the Chacs, the gods of rain—attain a sort of paradise, a place of pleasure situated in one of the heavens. It is not clear whether those who go to the abode of the lord of death are to remain there forever, are eventually reduced to nothing, or if, after a period of purification, they are transferred to the celestial paradise.

Other gods worshiped by the Maya include the moon goddess Ixchel (another title of the mother goddess, often described as wife of the sun god). The "great star" (Venus), whose heliacal risings and conjunctions were of great interest to Maya skywatchers, received at times the calendrical name *1 Ahau* (1 Lord), but it was also associated with five other celestial gods, whose identification implies the assimilation of cultural elements in the Postclassic from the Central Plateau of Mexico. There also appear to have been patron gods of specific occupational groups, such as merchants, hunters, fishermen, cacao growers, medicine men, ball players, poets, and musicians.

With regard to the "feathered serpent god," a distinction has to be made. On the one hand, serpent representations—in association with bird's elements such as plumage, or with traits belonging to other animals such as the caiman or jaguar—had been extremely frequent since the early Classic period. As previously mentioned, these complex figures—sometimes described as celestial dragons, earth monsters, cosmic lizards, and so forth—are representations of gods like the Chicchan serpents, deities of rain, or of the multifaceted Itzamná. On the other hand, the idea of a particular god and culture hero, Kukulcan, corresponding to central Mexico's Quetzalcoatl (Quetzal-Feathered Serpent), was borrowed from that subarea in the Postclassic.

Priests and forms of worship. The existence of a priesthood, and of the many sacred sites and monuments reserved for the various kinds of cult, imposed a canon to be observed in the communication with the universe of the divine. The chiefs, *halach uinicoob* (true men), could perform some religious ceremonies; but for the most part, the cult of the gods was the duty of the priests. Above them was a class of high priests, who in Postclassic texts were named "rattlesnake-tobacco lords" and "rattlesnake-deer lords." These priests were in custody of the ancient religious wisdom, the books and the calendrical computations. They were considered prophets and acted in the most important ceremonies. Of a lower rank were the *ah kinoob,* the priests whose title can be translated as "those of the sun." Their duty was to interpret the calendrical signs, to direct the feast-day celebrations, and to "read" the destinies of humans. To some of the *ah kinoob* fell the performance of offerings and sacrifices, including human sacrifices.

Bearers of the rain god's name were the *chac* priests, assistants in the sacrifices and other ceremonies. The lowest rank was occupied by the *ah men* (performers, prayer makers), who were concerned mostly with the local forms of cult. Women who lived close to the sacred buildings assisted the priests in their duties.

Obviously, great differences existed between the ceremonies performed in the important religious centers and those that took place at a more modest level in a village or at home. Most ceremonies were preceded by different forms of fasting and continence. Thus, the gods would be appeased by their acceptance of what people were expected to offer as payment for what they had received from the gods. A recurrent belief—not only among the Maya but also in other Mesoamerican subareas—was that, in a primeval time, "when there was still night," the gods entered into an agreement with humans: humans could not subsist without the constant support of the gods; but the gods themselves needed to be worshiped and to receive offerings.

The Maya practiced autosacrifice in various forms, as can be observed in multiple representations of both Classic and Postclassic monuments. Most often, blood was offered by passing a cord or a blade of grass through the tongue, the penis, or some other part of the body. Offerings of animals (quail, parrots, iguanas, opossums, turtles) and of all sorts of plants or plant and animal products (copal, flowers, cacao, rubber, honey) were also frequent.

Human sacrifice was performed following various rituals. The most frequent form required opening the breast of the victim to offer his or her heart to the god. Other kinds of human sacrifice included shooting arrows at a victim tied to a frame of wood, beheading, and throwing the victim—usually a young girl or child—into a cenote (Maya, *dz'onot,* a natural deposit of water in places where the limestone surface has caved in) or into a lake, as in certain sites in Guatemala. Human sacrifices—never so numerous among the Maya as they became among the Aztec—were performed during the sacred feasts to repay the gods with the most precious offering: the life-giving blood.

A considerable number of prayers in the Maya languages have been preserved. Among them one can distinguish sacred hymns (hymns of intercession, praise, or thanks) from those accompanying a sacrifice and from those to be chanted in a domestic ceremony.

Religion and the calendar. The calendar provided the Maya with a frame of mathematical precision, a basis for understanding and predicting events in the universe. Thus, all the sacred duties of the priests—the ceremonies, sacrifices, and invocations—were not performed at random but followed established cycles. Observation of the celestial bodies and of whatever is born and grows on the earth demonstrated that beings undergo cyclical changes. The Maya believed that if humans succeeded in discovering and measuring the cyclical rhythms of the universe, they would adapt themselves to favorable situations and escape adverse ones. The belief that the gods and their sacred forces are essentially related to the cyclical appearances and intervals of the celestial bodies—which are their manifestations—led the sages to conclude that the realm of the divine was ruled by a complex variety of cycles.

The Maya saw the manifestations or arrivals of the gods in these cycles; all the deities were thought of as being endowed with calendrical presences, and so the gods were given their respective calendrical names. As for humans, the divine presences along the counts of time could not be meaningless: they brought fate, favorable or adverse, and all dates had therefore to be scrutinized to discover the destinies they carried. This probably explains why calendrical and religious concerns became so inseparable for the Maya.

The calendar systems they employed were not a Maya invention (although they added new forms of precision to these systems). Two forms of count were at the base of the complexities of all Mesoamerican calendars. One count is that of the solar year, computed for practical purposes as having 365 days and subject to various forms of adjustment or correction. The other count, specifically Mesoamerican, is the cycle of 260 days. In it a sequence of numbers from 1 to 13 is employed. A series of 20 day names, each expressed by its respective hieroglyph, is the other essential element of the calendar.

The solar-year count and the 260-day count meshed to make it possible to give a date not only within a year, but also within a 52-year cycle, as well as in the so-called Long Count. To represent the calendar's internal structures and forms of correlation is to represent the precise mechanism that provided the norm for the order of feasts, rites, and sacrifices; astrological wisdom; economic, agricultural, and commercial enterprises; and social and political obligations. This mechanism was also the key to understanding a universe in which divine forces—the gods themselves and the destinies they wrought—became manifest cycle after cycle.

The 260-day count places the numbers 1 to 13 on a series of 20 day names, whose meanings in the Maya languages are related to various deities and other sacred realities. The 20 days have the following names and associations: *Imix* (the earth monster); *Ik* ("Wind" or "Life," associated with the rain god); *Akbal* ("Darkness," associated with the jaguar-faced nocturnal sun god); *Kan* ("Ripeness," the sign of the god of young maize); *Chicchan* (the celestial serpent); *Cimi* ("Death," associated with the god of the underworld); *Manik* ("Hand," the day name of the god of hunting); *Lamat* (day name of the lord of the "great star," Venus); *Muluc* (symbolized by jade and water, evokes the Chacs, gods of rain); *Oc* (represented by a dog's head, which guides the sun through the underworld); *Chuen* (the monkey god, the patron of knowledge and the arts); *Eb* (represented by a face with a prominent jaw; related to the god who sends drizzles and mists); *Ben* ("Descending," the day name of the god who fosters the growth of the maize stalk); *Ix* (a variant of the jaguar-like sun god); *Men* (associated with the aged moon goddess); *Cib* (related to the four Bacabs, supporters of the sky); *Caban* ("Earthquake," associated with the god/goddess of the earth); *Etz'nab* ("Obsidian Blade," linked to human sacrifice); *Cauac* (day name of the celestial dragon deities); and *Ahau* ("Lord," the radiant presence of the sun god).

During the first 13-day "week" of the 260-day cycle, the numbers 1 through 13 are prefixed to the first 13 day names. At this point, the series of numbers begins again at 1, so that, for example, *Ik,* whose number is 2 during the first week, has the number 9 prefixed to it during the second week, 3 during the third week, and so on. The cycle begins to repeat itself after 260 (20 x 13) days. In this 260-day count, one also distinguishes 4 groups of 65 days, each of which is broken into 5 "weeks" of 13 days (each presided over by a particular god).

The solar count of the *haab,* or year, is divided into 18 groups—*uinals,* or "months"—of 20 days each (18 x 20 = 360), to which 5 *uayebs* (ominous days) are added at the end of the cycle. These 18 "months" of 20 days and the 5 final days are the span of time along which the 260-day count develops. The intermeshing of the two counts implies that in each solar year there will be a repetition in the 260-day combination of numbers and day names in 105 instances (365 - 260 = 105). As the number and the day name together form the basic element to express a date, the way to distinguish between such repetitions is by specifying the position of the days in the different 18 months of 20 days of the solar count.

Thus, if the day *13 Ahau* (13 Lord) is repeated within a 365-day solar count, one can distinguish two different dates by noting the day to which it corresponds in the series of the 18 months. For example, *13 Ahau, 18 Tzec* (the day *13 Ahau* is related to the 18th day of the month of *Tzec*) is different from *13 Ahau, 18 Cumhu* (the day *13 Ahau* is related to the 18th day of the month of *Cumhu*).

The number of possible different interlockings of the two counts comprises 18,980 expressions of the day name, number, and position within the month. Such a number of differently named days integrates a Calendar Round, a cycle of 52 years. Each of these 18,890 calendric combinations was designated as the bearer of a distinct divine presence and destiny, obviously not of that many different gods, but of a complex diversification of their influences—favorable or adverse—successively oriented towards one of the four quadrants of the world.

The Long Count System. But the Maya, like some of their predecessors who were exposed to Olmec influence, could also compute any date in terms of the Long Count, in which a fixed date, corresponding to a day in the year 3133 BCE (probably representing the beginning of the present cosmic age), was taken as the point of departure. The end of the Long Count's cycle will occur on a date equivalent to December 24, 2011. The Long Count was conceived to express dates in terms of elapsed time, or *kin* (a word that has cognates throughout the Maya family of languages and that means "sun, sun god, day, time, cosmic age"). Periods within the Long Count were reckoned in accordance with Mesoamerican counting systems, which employed base 20. These periods, each of which had its presiding deity, were registered in columns of hieroglyphs, beginning with the largest cycle, as follows:

> *Baktun* (7,200 days x 20 = 144,000 days) *Katun* (360 days x 20 = 7,200 days) *Tun* (20 days x 18 = 360 days) *Uinal* (20 days) *Kin* (1 day)

By means of their dot, bar, and shell— numerical signs for 1, 5, and 0, respectively—the Maya indicated how many *baktuns, katuns, tuns, uinals,* and *kins* had, at a given moment, elapsed since the beginning of the present cosmic age. The date was finally correlated with the meshed system of the 365-day solar calendar and the 260-day count, which thus became adjusted to the astronomical year.

Besides these precise forms of calendar, the Maya developed other systems devised to measure different celestial cycles, such as those of the "great star" and of the moon. The inscriptions on Maya stelae allow us to understand some of the main reasons for their astronomical and calendrical endeavors. To the Maya, dates conveyed not only the presence of one god on any given day, but also the sum total of the divine forces "becoming" and acting in the universe. The deities of the numbers, of the day names, of the periods within the 260-day count, of the *uinals* (or months of the year), and of the divisions within a 52-year cycle—as well as of the many other cycles within the Long Count system—converged at any given moment and exerted their influences, intrinsically coloring and affecting human and earthly realities.

Through color symbolism and indications like those of the "directional hieroglyphs of the years," one can identify the cosmic regions (quadrants of horizontal space and also celestial and inferior levels) to which specific cycles and gods address their influence. For the Maya, space separated from the cycles of time would have been meaningless. When the cycles are finally completed, the consequence will be the end of life on earth, the death of the sun, the absence of the gods, and an ominous return to primeval darkness.

The priests known as *ah kinoob* (those of the sun and of the destinies) whose duty was to recognize and anticipate the divine presences, as well as their beneficial or dangerous influences, were consulted by rich and poor alike. Thanks to special rites and sacrifices, favorable destinies could be discovered that would neutralize the influence of adverse fates. In this way one escaped fatalism, and a door was opened to reflection and righteous behavior. The wisdom of the calendar was indeed the key to penetrating the mysterious rhythms of what exists and becomes. This probably explains why the priests were also interested in the computation of dates in the distant past. On Stele F of Quirigua is inscribed a date, *1 Ahau, 18 Yaxkin,* that corresponds to a day 91,683,930 years in the past!

In the Postclassic period, the Long Count fell into oblivion and the simplified system of the Count of the *Katuns* (13 periods of 20 years) was introduced. The destinies of the *katuns* remained an object of concern and a source of prophetic announcements. In spite of the Spanish Conquest, the burning of the ancient books, and the efforts of Christian missionaries, elements of the ancient worldview and religion have survived among the contemporary Maya, as has been documented by the ethnographer Alfonso Villa Rojas (León-Portilla, 1973, pp. 113–159).

Epigraphy and religion. For a long time, the reading of the Maya inscriptions in monuments, codices, and other objects was limited (for the most part) to the calendar's registrations and the names of some gods and feasts. In the 1950s the Russian Yuri Knorosov made a basic contribution that opened the entrance into the realm of Maya inscriptions. In opposition to the opinion of well-known scholars such as Günter Zimermann and J. Eric S. Thompson, who insisted upon the ideographic nature of Maya writing, Knorosov asserted its basically phonetic character.

Knorosov's Rosetta Stone was found in Friar Diego de Landa's *Relación de Yucatán,* where a supposed Maya alphabet was included. Knorosov carefully analyzed de Landa's work and reached the conclusion that, far from dealing with an alphabet, he was confronted with a syllabary. Further research led him to identify a large number of syllables as well as glyphic markers of morphological relations (Coe, 1992).

Following Knorosov's steps, a growing number of Mayists, including American, Mexican, and European scholars, have advanced in deciphering a writing that for centuries remained a mystery. As a result, readings of many inscriptions have been achieved that provide a better understanding of the religion and history of the Maya. Whereas in the past it was thought that most of the inscriptions were of calendrical and astronomical nature, today it is recognized that they provide first-hand information on the dynasties of the rulers and their deeds, and on their relations with the gods and the realm of the beyond.

Linda Schele, Mary Ellen Miller, and David Freidel have made substantial contributions in this respect. Their books, *The Blood of Kings: Dynasty and Ritual in Maya Art* (1986), and *A Forest of Kings: The Untold Story of the Ancient Maya* (1990), offer readings that have unveiled the dynastic sequences of those who ruled in a good number of Maya centers. With respect to the religion, these authors have revealed the various ways in which the Maya conceived of the relationship of their *Ahauob* (lords or rulers), and the people in general, with the universe of the gods and ultimate realities.

The readings of hundreds of inscriptions and the iconographic approaches to the inscriptions' accompanying imagery carved into panels, lintels, stelae, and other monuments and objects—as well as the unveiling of the architectural planning of the temples, palaces, and ballcourts situated close to great plazas—has led to a better understand of how the Maya maintained the relationship between the rulers and the universe of the gods.

Cerros, an important Maya center near the mouth of a river that empties into the Bay of Chetumal in the southern part of the Yucatán Peninsula, appears as one of the earlier sites where, kinship having been formally established, new religious symbols and rites were introduced. Pyramids were erected on broad platforms; a stairway was built to reach the summit of the temple; and below, in the open space of the great plaza, the people would attend the rituals performed on top of the pyramid. There, the *ahau,* or high ruler, would proceed towards the front door of the temple—he was about to leave earthly space to penetrate the realm of the divine.

A ritual represented in several monuments, that of self-bloodletting was practiced by the *ahau.* The imagery and inscriptions carved in dintel 25 from a temple of Yaxchilan in Chiapas illustrate the performance and meaning of such ritual. One sees there a kneeling noblewoman, Lady Xoc. She holds in her hands obsidean lancets, a spine, and bloodied paper. She is looking upwards, contemplating the vision of a great serpent; she is having a revelation. Lady Xoc is recalled in the lintel in commemoration of the accession to the throne of Yaxchilan of the Lord Shield Jaguar.

Scenes like this one of self-bloodletting are not rare in several Maya centers. These scenes represent the ritual by which nobles would pay the gods for their creation and accession to a throne from which they were destined to rule in permanent communion with the gods.

Among other forms of representation of the relation of the *ahauob* with the gods, there is one in which a perdurable life for the rulers is asserted and parallels are established between the rulers and the deities. This is the case with a carved panel from temple 14 of Palenque. Its imagery includes the effigy of Chan Bahlum dancing after his victory over the Lords of Xibalbá (the underworld). His mother, Lady Ahpo-Hell, welcomes him, lifting an image of the god Ah Bolon Tzacab, a primordial deity that has been described as the Maya equivalent to the Nahua god Tezcatlipoca.

The inscription on the left side of the panel registers the date in which the tablet was erected: a day *9 Ik* and the month *10 Mol*, corresponding to November 6, 705 CE. Lord Chan Bahlum had died three years before. On the right side, the inscription correlates the event represented with happenings that took place in a previous cosmic age, more than nine hundred thousand years before. The mother of Chan Bahlum, also represented in the tablet, "is likened to Moon Goddess" (Schele and Miller, 1986, p. 272).

Those who rule—the *ahauob*—are likened to the gods, and it is on them that the people depend. The *ahauob* are in communion with the Otherworld, and this is why their memory shall be kept. Rulership and royal dynasties were thus forever linked to the ritual and beliefs of the Maya.

ZAPOTEC AND MIXTEC RELIGIOUS VARIANTS. Mountain ranges that encompass several valleys, as well as the slopes that lead to the Pacific plains in the Mexican state of Oaxaca, have been the ancestral abode of the Zapotec, Mixtec, and other indigenous peoples. The Zapotec reached their cultural zenith in the Classic period, whereas the Mixtec achieved hegemony during the Postclassic period. Although linguistically different, the Zapotec and the Mixtec were culturally akin. Olmec culture had influenced the Zapotec since the Middle Formative period.

Zapotec religion. From 200 to 800 CE, the Zapotec developed forms of urban life and built magnificent religious buildings in their towns (Monte Albán, Yagul, Zaachila). Their sacred spaces included large plazas around which the temple-pyramids, altars, ball courts, and other religious monuments were raised.

Mainly through what has been discovered in subterranean tombs near the temples, reliable information can be offered about Zapotec gods and other beliefs. In paintings preserved on the walls of the tombs, prominent members of the Zapotec pantheon appear, accompanied at times by inscriptions. Pottery—urns in particular—also tell about the attributes of the Zapotec gods and their ideas of the afterlife.

As in the case of the Maya, a supreme dual god, Pitao Cozaana-Pitao Cochaana, presided over all realities, divine and human. Addressed as a single god, he-she was Pije-Tao (Lord of Time), principle of all that exists. Godly beings often appear with the symbolic attributes of the serpent, bird, caiman, and jaguar—motifs also familiar to the Olmec and Maya. Cocijo, the rain god, also had a quadruple form of presence in the world. Pitao Cozobi was the god of maize.

Zapotec writing (since its early beginnings in Monte Albán 1, c. 600 BCE) appears to be the source of the forms of script later developed by the Mixtec and transmitted to the groups of central Mexico. The study of Zapotec writing reveals their calendrical concern.

Zapotec pottery urns, used mostly as containers of water, were placed near the dead in the tombs. Most of the urns include the molded representation of a god—often the rain god Cocijo. The headdress of the god conveys his emblem, in which the combined traits of serpent, jaguar, and bird are often visible.

It is known that the Zapotec of the Classic period believed in a supreme dual god. They also worshiped several deities revered in other Mesoamerican areas. The Zapotec were so much concerned with death that they placed their dignitaries' remains in sumptuous tombs close to their temples. The Zapotec also knew about time computations.

Mixtec religion. The Mixtec founded new towns, and they conquered and rebuilt places (c. 1000 CE) in which the Zapotec had ruled. The Mixtec were great artists, excelling in the production of metal objects, many of which bear religious connotations. Several Mixtec books of religious and historical content have survived. These books constitute one of the most precious sources of the cultural history of a Mesoamerican subarea.

In the Mixtec books known as *Codex Selden* and *Codex Gómez de Orozco*, an image of the Mixtec worldview is offered. It is a worldview that closely corresponds to that of the Maya: the earth is represented by the monstrous animal with traits of caiman, serpent, and jaguar; below it is the underworld; while above the earth nine levels of the upperworld (not thirteen as in the Maya worldview) are represented. The sun and the moon and the stars are there. The dual god, with the symbols of time and of his-her day names, resides on the uppermost level.

According to other traditions, this dual god caused the earth to rise out of the waters. Later he-she built a beautiful place on the top of a large rock. The children he-she engendered and conceived are the gods of the various quadrants of the world—the gods of rain and wind, gods of maize, and so on. According to Mixtec belief, the earth and the sun had been destroyed several times; the Mixtec believed the gods waged combat in a celestial ball court. (This is represented in a gold pectoral found with other religious objects in Tomb 7 within the sacred space of Monte Albán, the site that had been built by the Zapotec but that was later conquered by the Mixtec).

Another extraordinary Mixtec book, known as *Codex Vindobonensis*, conveys the beliefs of this people about their origins in the present cosmic age. They had come from a place called Yuta Tnoho (River of the Lineages). There they were born from a cosmic tree. The Mixtec calendar systems corresponded to the 260-day count and the 365-day solar year computed by the Zapotec and the Maya. (Caso, 1965, pp. 948–961).

TEOTIHUACAN. As in the Maya and Oaxaca areas, some Early Formative–type villages in the Central Plateau experienced important changes. Places like El Arbolillo, Zacatenco, Tlatilco, Cuicuilco, and others received the ferment of Olmec influence. Special areas began to be reserved for religious purposes; temple pyramids and round platforms were built. Clay images of the fire god Huehueteotl (Old God), who much later was also worshiped by the Aztec, have been dated to the Late Formative period (c. 500 BCE).

In Tlapacoya, not far from where Teotihuacan was to be established, another important Late Formative center flourished (c. 300–100 BCE). Here, temple pyramids, tombs, and mural paintings anticipate, in many respects, what was to be the grandeur of Teotihuacan.

Teotihuacan ("the place where one becomes deified") marks the Classic period's climax in the Central Plateau. Archaeological research has revealed that it was here that whatever is implied by the idea of a city became a reality. It took several centuries (100–500 CE) for generations of priests and sages to conceive, realize, modify, enlarge, and enrich the city, which probably was planned to last forever. Beside the two great pyramids of the Sun and the Moon, the Temple of the Feathered Serpent, and the Palace of the Quetzalpapalotl (quetzal butterflies), many other enclosures, palaces, schools, markets, and other buildings have been unearthed. Large suburbs, where members of the Teotihuacan community had their homes, surrounded the religious and administrative center. The pyramids and palaces were decorated with murals. Gods in the forms of human beings, fantastic serpents, birds, caimans, lizards, and jaguars, as well as flowers, plants, priests, and even complex scenes—such as a depiction of Tlalocan, the paradise of the rain god—were represented in the paintings.

Teotihuacan was the capital of a large state—perhaps an empire—the vestiges of whose cultural influence have been found in Oaxaca, Chiapas, and the Guatemalan highlands. According to annals preserved by the Aztec, "In Teotihuacan orders were given, and the chiefdom was established. Those who were the chiefs were the sages, the ones who knew secret things, who preserved old traditions" (from *Codex Matritense,* trans. Léon-Portilla, folio 192r).

The inhabitants of Teotihuacan worshiped several deities whose iconography is similar to that of gods later revered by other groups in central Mexico: the Toltec (900–1050 CE), the Acolhua, and the Aztec (1200–1519 CE). The Aztec called these gods by the following names: Tlaloc and Chalchiuhtlicue, god and goddess of the waters, who together constitute one aspect of divine duality; Quetzalcoatl (Quetzal-Feathered Serpent); Xiuhtecuhtli, the fire god; Xochipilli (The One of the Flowery Lineage); Xipe Totec (Our Lord the Flayed One); Itztlacoliuhqui (Stone Knife), whose traits resemble those of the Toltec and Aztec god Tezcatlipoca (Smoking Mirror); Tlahuizcalpantecuhtli, the god of the morning star, and Xolotl, the god of the evening star, who were also aspects of the divine duality; and Yacatecuhtli, the god of merchants (Caso, 1966; Séjourné, 1966).

In addition to these gods, a large number of other symbols and a few hieroglyphs identified in the mural paintings, sculptures, and ceramics persisted in the corresponding Toltec and Aztec ensemble of religious expressions.

Although some researchers have dismissed the validity of comparing iconographic symbols of one culture with those of another culture from a subsequent epoch, the evidence supporting a common Mesoamerican religious tradition, and the fact that one is not dealing with isolated cases of iconographic similarity but rather with ensembles of symbols, seem valid reasons for rejecting the skepticism of those who deny this cultural interrelation. Archaeological finds have shown that Teotihuacan actually influenced Toltec and Aztec cultures, which the religious iconographic similarities are obvious.

It is reasonable to assert that the arrangement of sacred space at Teotihuacan, and the gods worshiped there, was prototypical for the future religious development of central Mexico. In part because of the relative abundance of the Postclassic historical testimonies of Toltec and Aztec cultures, scholars now have a better understanding of Teotihuacan symbols.

Aztec consciousness of Teotihuacan as the ultimate source of their own culture led Aztec to see the sacred space of the Place Where One Becomes Deified as a kind of primordial site, where, *in illo tempore,* the Fifth Sun (the present cosmic age) had its beginning. An Aztec text that describes the four previous Suns, or cosmic ages, and their successive violent destructions says about the fifth and new age, "This Sun, its day name is 4-Movement. This is our Sun, the one in which we now live. And here is its sign, how the Sun fell into the fire, into the divine hearth, there at Teotihuacan" (from *Annals of Cuauhtitlan,* trans. Léon-Portilla, folio 77).

The Aztec myth about the beginning of the Fifth Sun at Teotihuacan tells how the gods met there to discuss the remaking of the sun and moon, and of human beings and their sustenance. "When there was still night," the text relates, the gods gathered for four days around the divine hearth at Teotihuacan to determine which god would cast himself into the fire and thus become transformed into the sun. There were two candidates, the arrogant Tecuciztecatl (Lord of the Conch Shells) and the modest Nanahuatzin (The Pimply One). Tecuciztecatl made four attempts to throw himself into the flames, but each time he backed away in fear. Then it was Nanahuatzin's turn to try. Closing his eyes, he courageously hurled himself into the fire, was consumed, and finally appeared transformed as the sun. Tecuciztecatl, fearful and too late, was only able to achieve transformation into the lesser celestial body, the moon.

To the surprise of the other gods, the sun and moon did not move. The way to solve this problem was through sacrifice. To give the sun energy, the gods sacrificed themselves, offering their blood, a primeval act that had to be reenacted by humans—for it is only through the bloody sacrifice that the sun and life exist; only through the sacrifice of human blood could existence be prolonged. With their own blood, human beings had to repay the divine sacrifice that had prevented the cataclysms that put an end to previous suns. Here was the seed that later flowered as the Aztec rituals of human sacrifice.

QUETZALCOATL AND TOLTEC RELIGION. It appears that Teotihuacan came to a sudden, and still unexplained, end around 650 CE. Its collapse, however, did not mean the death of high culture in Mesoamerica. From among those cultures that inherited numerous cultural elements from the Classic glory of Teotihuacan, the city of Tula stands out. Tula is about eighty kilometers north of Mexico City. Its name, Tula, means "large town, metropolis," which is what the Toltec, following the advice of their high priest Quetzalcoatl, actually built.

Quetzalcoatl, a legendary figure, was believed to have been a king who derived his name from that of the "feathered serpent god," in whose representations two of the pan-Mesoamerican iconographic elements—the serpent and the plumage of the quetzal—became integrated. It is said that Quetzalcoatl, while still young, retired to Huapalcalco, a village not far from Teotihuacan, to devote himself to meditation. He was taken there by the Toltec to serve as their ruler and high priest.

Native books attribute to him whatever is good and great. He induced his people to worship benevolent supreme dual god, Ometeotl. This same god was also invoked as the Precious Feathered Serpent or Precious Feathered Twins. Both meanings are actually implied by the term *Quetzalcoatl,* at once the name of the god and that of his priest. The original Toltec text says,

> And it is told, it is said,
> That Quetzalcoatl invoked, took as his God,
> The One in the uppermost heaven:
> She of the starry skirt,
> He whose radiance envelops things;
> Lady of Our Flesh,
> Lord of Our Flesh;
> She who is clothed in black,
> He who is clothed in red;
> She who endows the earth with solidity,
> He who covers it with cotton.
> And thus it was known
> That toward the heavens was his plea directed,
> Toward the place of duality,
> Above the nine levels of Heaven. (from *Annals of Cuauhtitlan,* trans. Léon-Portilla, folio 4, 1995)

The dual god Ometeotl—who in the night covers his-her feminine aspect with a skirt of stars, but who during the day reveals himself as the sun, the greatest of the light-giving stars—-appears also as the Lord and Lady of Our Flesh, as he-she who vests himself-herself in black and red (colors symbolizing wisdom), and, at the same time, as the one who gives stability to the earth. Thus the priest taught the Toltec how to draw near to Ometeotl-Quetzalcoatl, the god who dwells in the uppermost heaven:

> The Toltec were solicitous of the things of God; they had but one God; they held him to be their only God; they invoked him; they made supplications to him; his name was Quetzalcoatl. The guardian of their God, their priest, his name was also Quetzalcoatl. And they were so respectful of the things of God that everything that the priest Quetzalcoatl told them they did, and they did not depart from it. He persuaded them; he taught them: This one God, Quetzalcoatl is his name. He demands nothing except serpents, except butterflies, which you must offer to him, which you must sacrifice to him. (from *Codex Matritense,* trans. Léon-Portilla, folio 179r.)

The Toltec understood the doctrine of Quetzalcoatl. Under his guidance they were able to relate the idea of the dual god with the ancient image of the world and the destiny of man on earth. *Codex Matritense* is clear on this point:

> The Toltec knew that the heavens are many; they said that there are thirteen divisions, one upon the other. There abides, there lives the True God and his Consort. The Heavenly God is called the Lord of Duality, and his Consort is called Lady of Duality, Heavenly Lady. Which means: He is king, he is lord over the thirteen heavens. Thence we receive our life, we men. Thence falls our destiny when the child is conceived, when he is placed in the womb. His fate comes to him there. It is sent by the God of Duality. (From *Codex Matritense,* trans. Léon-Portilla, folio 175v)

The golden age of the Toltec produced all sorts of achievements: palaces and temples were built; many towns and peoples accepted the rule of Quetzalcoatl. Only some enemies—most likely religious adversaries—attempted to bring about the downfall of that age. Some texts speak of the appearance of one named Tezcatlipoca, the Smoking Mirror, a god who came to Tula to force Quetzalcoatl to abandon his city and his followers. According to these accounts, the departure of the wise priest precipitated the ruin of Tula. Other texts speak of two different critical moments. The first was that of the flight of Quetzalcoatl. Although tragic, it did not bring about the complete downfall of Tula. The second crisis took place several decades later. Huemac was the king ruling at that time. His forced departure and death, around 1150, marked the total collapse of Tula. The ruin of the Toltec also meant a diffusion of their culture and religious ideas among various peoples, some distant from Tula. The existence of the Toltec is recorded in annals such as those of the Mixtec of Oaxaca and the Maya of Yucatán and Guatemala.

Henry B. Nicholson has written an excellent volume on Quetzalcoatl. Originally written as a Ph.D. dissertation and presented at Harvard University in 1957, this work has retained its value as "the most thoroungh and insightful analysis of a large part of Mesoamerican ensemble of primary sources ever done in a single volume" (Carrasco and Matos Moctezuma, 2001, VI). It was revised by Nicholson and published in 2001 as *Topiltzin Quetzalcoatl. The Once and Future Lord of the Toltecs.*

Nicholson analyzes a large number of primary sources from Central Mexico (Nahuatl and non-Nahuatl); from Oaxaca (Mixtec and Zapotec); and from Chiapas and Guatemala, Tabasco-Campeche, as well as the Yucatán (Maya); and he elaborates on interpretations of the data presented. One can assert that his book, although by now several decades old, remains a fresh and relevant approach to the complexities surrounding the figure of Quetzalcoatl, a subject that in many forms permeates Mesoamerican religion and ethnohistory.

While Quetzalcoatl is an extremely important figure in the history of Mesoamerica, he has been the subject of several divergent interpretations (see Nicholson 2000 and Carrasco 2003).

On the one hand, attending to the meaning of his name, "Feathered Serpent," it can be inferred that he was worshipped in Teotihuacan since the Classic period. There, at the so-called Temple of Quetzalcoatl, one can see heads of serpents with quetzal feathers.

Quetzalcoatl was also the name of a prominent priest and sage, portentously conceived by his mother, who lived in Tula-Xicocotitlan in the ninth century. A legendary figure, he had taken his name from that of the "feathered-serpent god" and became the ruler and guide of the Toltec.

THE AZTEC RELIGIOUS VARIANT. By the end of the thirteenth century CE, new chiefdoms existed in central Mexico. Some were the result of a renaissance in towns of Toltec or Teotihuacan origin. Others were new entities made up of the cultures of semibarbarian groups from the north (the so-called Chichimecs) and the remnants of Toltec civilization.

At the same time, other peoples made themselves present in the Central Plateau. Their language was Nahuatl, the same that the Toltec had spoken. The various Nahuatlan groups—among them the Aztec, or Mexica—had been living in northern outposts, on the frontier of Mesoamerica. In the Nahuatlan texts they repeat, "Now we are coming back from the north. . ." The Aztec return (or, as it is often described, their "pilgrimage") was a difficult enterprise. They had to overcome many hardships until finally they were settled (c. 1325 CE) on the island of Tenochtitlan (in the lake that then covered a large part of the Valley of Mexico). It took the Aztec a century to initiate the period of their greatness in Mesoamerica.

Cultural and religious heritages. The Aztec's worldview, beliefs, and cultural forms, which by the time of Aztec hegemony were already fully integrated as elements of their own culture, had diverse origins. The Aztec preserved ancient traditions that were the common inheritance of many peoples of Mesoamerica, such as the worship of the "Old God," Huehueteotl, who had been revered since several hundred years before the beginning of the common era. Other beliefs and practices were probably derived from the cultures that had flourished along the coast of the Gulf of Mexico, such as the veneration of Xipe Totec ("Our lord the flayed one"), a god of fertility.

Some deities, such as Tlaloc, Chac, or Cocijo (different names of the rain god, whose presence in Mesoamerica since the Classic period is amply manifested in the archaeological evidence), also became members of the Aztec pantheon. So did the two Toltec gods Quetzalcoatl and Tezcatlipoca. Besides individual gods and ensembles of gods, Aztec culture incorporated the old Mesoamerican spatial image of the world, with its four quadrants, central point, and upperworld and underworld levels (as well as the symbolic meanings attached to these divisions), and it integrated the solar calendar, the 260-day count, and the Mesoamerican system of writing.

To this heritage, the Aztec's own beliefs must be added. Among these are the Aztec patron gods Huitzilopochtli (Hummingbird of the South, or Hummingbird of the Left) and Coatlicue (She of the Skirt of Serpents).

Consciousness of divine destiny. Aztec accounts speak of the place in the north from which they had come, Aztlán Chicomoztoc (The Place of the Herons, or The Place of the Seven Caves). There they had been oppressed by a dominant people. One day, the "portentous god," Tezcatlipoca, spoke to the Aztec high priest, Huitzilopochtli. Tezcatlipoca offered to liberate the Aztec from their rulers. He would lead them to a place where they could enjoy freedom and from which they would extend themselves as conquerors into the four quadrants of the world. This he would do if the Aztec promised to be his vassals and to have him as their tutelary god. The Aztec then began their march to their promised land. On the way, Huitzilopochtli died, but the spirit and power of Tezcatlipoca entered into Huitzilopochtli's bones, and from that moment on the god and the priest were one person. When the Aztec, in their search for their predestined land, arrived at Coatepec (Mountain of the Serpent), they learned that the mother goddess Coatlicue was present there and that their own god Huitzilopochtli was to be miraculously reborn as Coatlicue's son. Huitzilopochtli's birth occurred at the precise moment when another goddess, Coyolxauhqui (She of the Face Painted with Rattles), was about to kill Coatlicue because of the offense Coatlicue had caused her and her four hundred brothers, the Warriors of the South, when it became known that Coatlicue was inexplicably pregnant. As Coyolxauhqui and her four hundred brothers were climbing Coatepec, Huitzilopochtli was born to Coatlicue, and he immediately used his weapon, the Fire Snake, to hurt Coyolxauqui and to cut off her head. He then pursued the Warriors of the South, driving them off the top of the mountain and destroying them. Huitzilopochtli stripped the four hundred brothers of their belongings and made them part of his own destiny. Later, when the Aztec had established themselves on the island of México-

Tenochtitlan, they constructed their main temple (the so-called Templo Mayor) to Huitzilopochtli in the form of the mountain Coatepec, and there they ritually reenacted Huitzilopochtli's portentous birth. A representation of the goddess Coatlicue stood near Huitzilopochtli's shrine on top of this "pyramid mountain," as did representations of the beheaded goddess Coyolxauhqui, the Fire Snake, and the four hundred Warriors of the South. The gods' primeval confrontation was reenacted on the feast of Panquetzaliztli (When the Flags are Raised). Objects found during the excavations of the Templo Mayor (Great Temple), undertaken from 1979 through 1990, have corroborated the native texts: all of the symbols of the Mountain of the Serpent and the story of Huitzilopochtli's birth have been recovered from the temple site.

Tributary wars and the reenactment of the sacrifice at Teotihuacan. The Aztec knew the story of the sacrifice at Teotihuacan, where the gods gave their blood and lives to strengthen the "Giver of Life" (the sun) whose movement was enabled by the sacrifice. The Aztec, believing they had to imitate the gods, took on the mission of continuing to provide the sun with vital energy. They deemed themselves called to offer the sun that same precious liquid that the gods had shed, and they obtained it from human sacrifice.

As if hypnotized by the mystery of blood, the Aztec proclaimed themselves the chosen People of the Sun. Ceremonial warfare—the principal manner of obtaining victims for the sacrifice—became the dominant activity in the Aztec's social, religious, and national life. Thus, they developed what can be described as a mystical imperialism: they devoted themselves to conquest in their effort to maintain the life of the sun and to keep the age of 4 Movement alive. The theme of war in Aztec visual art and in Aztec literature is everywhere linked to that of national greatness. In the primeval myth of Teotihuacan, mention is also made of the eagle and the ocelot (or jaguar), who were present at the divine hearth into which the gods had hurled themselves. Eagles and ocelots therefore became the symbols of warriors.

Fire, which had blazed in the hearth at Teotihuacan, and water, without which nothing green grows on earth, were strangely linked in the minds of the priests. Jointly, fire and water conveyed the idea of the mystical warfare that makes the life of the universe possible. *Atl/tlachinolli* (water/fire), *quauhtli/ocelotl* (eagle/ocelot), *mitl/chimalli* (arrow/shield), *yaoxochitl/xochiaoctli* (flowery wars/flowery liquor), *quauhtli/nochtli* (eagle/prickly pear, or the sun/the red heart): these are some of the binary forms of symbolic expression that recur in Aztec hymns, chants, and discourses and echo the Aztec's official worldview:

> From where the eagles rest, From where the ocelots are exalted, The Sun is invoked. Like a shield that descends, So does the Sun set. In Mexico night is falling, War rages on all sides. O Giver of Life! War draws near, Proud of ifself Is the city of México-Tenochtitlan. Here no one fears to die in war. This is our glory. This your command, O Giver of Life! (Cantares Mexicanos, trans. by León-Portilla, fol. 19 v.)

Divine duality. Paintings and ideograms in some of the native books corroborate what is proclaimed in the songs of the Aztec warriors. Again, binary forms of expression—captains' headdresses in the forms of eagles and ocelots, the hieroglyphs for fire and water coupled, and so on—appear consistently related to the universe of the gods, who are essentially dual entities.

Below, in the abode of the dead, reign Mictlantecuhtli and Mictlancihuatl, the god and goddess of that region. On the surface of the earth is Our Father-Our Mother, who is at once the Old Lord, He-She of the Yellow Face, and Creator of Fire. And above, in the various celestial levels, other dual divine manifestations exist: Tlaloc and Chalchiuhtlicue (god and goddess of rain and of the terrestrial waters); the precious twins Quetzalcoatl and Cihuacoatl (the feathered serpent and the female serpent); Tezcatlipoca and Tezcatlanextia (the mirror that obscures things and the mirror that makes them brilliant); and, above all other deities, the dual god Ometeotl, a supreme being endowed with both male and female countenances.

In both Aztec and Maya religion, the Dual God, in an unfolding of his-her own being, gave birth to four sons, who are primordial divine forces. In Aztec thought these are known as the four Tezcatlipocas—White, Black, Red, and Blue—who presided over the successive cosmic ages. Their actions connoted confrontations between opposing forces as well as diverse kinds of alteration and becoming. Tezcatlipoca sometimes appears as the adversary of Tlaloc, at other times of Quetzalcoatl. Tezcatlipoca also often becomes identified with other deities—as in the story related above of Huitzilopochtli's transformation.

An iconographic analysis of the Aztec gods confirms that they shared the attribute of "divine becoming"—that is, of procession through a series of transformations. There are representations in which this "divine becoming" is evident, where, for example, Tlaloc, the rain god, is portrayed as if he were Tlahuizcalpantecuhtli, the god of the morning star; Mictlantecuhtli, the god of death; or Xochipilli, the god of dance and song. This "becoming" of the gods was linked to the Aztec canon of religious celebrations. Abundant information about the feasts along the 365-day calendar can be found in several of the indigenous texts: the *Borbonicus*, *Matritense*, *Florentine*, *Magliabecchianus*, *Tudela*, *Ixtlilxochitl*, *Telleriano-Remensis*, and *Vaticanus A* codices.

SACRIFICE AND OTHER RITES. Penance, abstinence, and the offering of a variety of animals and vegetables were frequent in Aztec celebrations. Intonation of sacred hymns was accompanied by music and dances. More than any other Mesoamerican people, the Aztec practiced human sacrifice during their celebrations. A sort of perpetual drama developed in which the primeval events were reenacted, with the victims playing the roles of the gods who *in illo tempore* offered their blood to make life on earth possible. The forms of human sacrifice were similar to those that had been practiced by the Maya. The largest number of sacrifices took place at the Templo Mayor at the center of México-Tenochtitlan.

Afterlife. Some manners of dying promised glorious destinies: death in battle, death while trying to take captives, the death of a sacrificial victim, and the death of a woman in childbirth (while bearing a future warrior). To die in any of these ways meant that one would travel, after death, to the House of the Sun, to be his-her companion in the heavens. Persons chosen by the rain god for a special kind of death (by drowning, being struck by lightning, or through a serious disease such as dropsy) were destined to enjoy Tlalocan, the rain god's paradise. Others of the dead were said to go to Mictlan (the place of the dead), which was also known as Ximoayan (the place of the fleshless) and Tocempopolihuiyan (our common destination, where we lose ourselves).

Doubt and skepticism. In contrast to the officially accepted beliefs, there are some indigenous texts from the Aztec epoch in which doubts are expressed. A conviction that the mystery that surrounds human existence will never be completely unveiled appears again and again in these compositions. These beautiful poems, written by the sages (*tlamatinime,* "those who know something"), at times convey pessimism and even a sort of natural skepticism. Their core question seems to be whether or not it is possible to say true words about the beyond, the universe of the gods, or one's survival of death. The following example is eloquent:

> Even if we offer the Giver of Life Jade and precious ointments, If with offering of necklaces You are invoked, With the strength of the eagle and the jaguar, With the force of the warriors, It may be that on earth No one speaks of truth. (from *Cantares Mexicanos,* trans. by Léon-Portilla, folio 13r)

The contrast between the official religious militarism of the Aztec and the questionings of these sages seems to reflect the vitality of the spiritual world of Mesoamerica.

The Templo Mayor. Testimonies that encompass the history of a single monument are seldom found in the available Mesoamerican sources. In the case of the Aztec Templo Mayor, a good number of testimonies permit the interpretation of the many symbols incorporated into it during its successive enlargements. The testimonies include pictorial manuscripts of indigenous provenance, some of them produced a few decades after the destruction of the temple as a consequence of the Spanish Conquest. There are, as well, texts in Nahuatl derived from the native orality and put in written form by means of the Latin alphabet by Nahua scribes. To this, one has to add descriptions in Spanish done by several friars and others interested in the subject.

Among the testimonies thus produced are descriptions of the Templo Mayor; of its various buildings; of the sacrifices and ceremonies held therein; of the sacred hymns that were entoned and the prayers that were recited; and, in sum, copious references about what the temple was and how it functioned as the most important precinct dedicated to the cult of the Aztec gods.

It can be asserted that the Templo Mayor was conceived as a plastic representation of the Coatepetl or "Mountain of the Serpent," situated near Tula—the ancient Toltec metropolis—where the Aztec patron god Huitzilopochtli was born. His shrine was built on top of the pyramid. Close to it, a sculpture of Huitzilopochtli's mother, the goddess Coatlicue, was placed. At the botton of the same pyramid the Aztec placed the effigy of Coyolxauhqui, the rebel sister of Huitzilopochtli. She appeared beheaded and dismembered by her brother who, once born, resisted her attack and killed her with his invincible weapon, the Xiuhcoatl (Fire Serpent). A stone sculpture of the Xiuhcoatl stood near the shrine of Huitzilopochtli. This complex of symbols, repeated in each enlargement of the temple, corresponds to what is proclaimed in a Nahuatl hymn that recalls the birth of Huitzilopochtli.

The Aztec reenacted Huitzilopochtli's portentous birth on the feast of Panquetzaliztli (Raising of Banners). A young warrior representing Huitzilopochtli carried his image, and he would have to fight in front of the temple against Coyolxauhqui and her allies. The young warrior's victory symbolized the triumph of the Sun against the forces of the night.

A shrine dedicated to Tlaloc, the rain god, was placed on top of the twin pyramid close to that of Huitzilopochtli (both pyramids were built on a common platform to symbolize divine dualism). Tlaloc, although called by various names, was a universally worshiped god in Mesoamerica. By placing his adoratory side by side with that of Huitzilopochtli, the Aztec were proclaiming at once their veneration to their own tutelary god and also to the one omnipresent in Mesoamerica, known as Tlaloc in central Mexico.

The sources that describe the rituals performed in the temple along the eighteen groups, or "months," of twenty days demonstrate that Aztec religious beliefs and practices somehow centered upon two temporal axes. One was that of *Tonalco,* "the time of the heat and the Sun"; the other was *Xopan,* "the time of verdor," when water abounds. In both periods, however, Huitzilopochtli and Tlaloc were present, intertwined with several gods and goddesses with which they were associated. During *Tonalco,* the dry and hot season, Tlaloc and Chalchuihtlicue (the goddess of the terrestrial waters), as well as their servants, the Tlaloques, and the gods related to maize, were asked to protect the people against eventual famines. Sacrifices, including those of adults and babies, were performed in the main temple.

When the feast of Tlaxochimaco ("flowers are given") took place in the ninth "month," people went to the fields looking for flowers to celebrate the god Huitzilopochtli. Banquets, music, and dances were held in his honor. Tlaxochimaco marked the beginning of the second half the year. In the following months—and already in the rainy season—once again Huitzilopochli, Tlaloc, and the gods of maize, salt, and fire, as well as Tonantzin (Our Mother), invoked under various names, entered the temporal and spatial scene of the Templo Mayor. Then and there the Aztec asked for abundant harvests and would practice the sacrifices that could propitiate them.

The great temple of Mexico, Tenochtitlan had become not only an extraordinary architectural monument and precinct, as its surviving vestiges indicate; it was also a living stage where a sort of perpetual drama was played out by the Aztec. These were a people who thought of themselves as "chosen" by the primordial sacrifice of the gods and who, therefore, had to repay them in a similar form to foster the existence of their present cosmic era.

In *The Aztec Templo Mayor, a Visualization* (2001), Antonio Serrato-Combe presents computer-generated, three-dimensional color imagery of Tenochititlan, conceived to explore the architectural configuration of the main temple and its whole precinct. The author describes his method in the book as a "digital modeling process," and the book adds interesting contributions to what is known about the largest and most important sacred monument in Aztec Mesoamerica.

MESOAMERICAN SACRED LITERATURE. Mention has been made of the available archaelogical and documentary sources for the study of Mesoamerican religion. One must also take into consideration the material that is properly labeled "Mesoamerican sacred literature." Notwithstanding the many destructions and consequences of the Conquest, indigenous texts do exist that can be considered part of a corpus of Mesoamerican sacred literature.

A clear distinction can be made pertaining to these texts that allow the corpus to be divided into two eras: (1) those works of a pre-Spanish provenance; and (2) those texts produced after the Conquest, either as transcriptions of older testimonies or as surviving documentary manifestations of native religiosity.

The works clearly of a pre-Spanish provenance include inscriptions in monuments excavated by archaeologists, mainly from the Maya area, and some of the fifteen extant codices or "books" (i.e., those of religious content, such as codices from Central Mexico known as *Borgia, Vaticanus B, Cospi, Fejérváry-Máyer,* and *Laud;* those from the Maya known as *Dresden, Tro-Cortesiano, Paris;* and those from the Mixtec of Oaxaca, such as *Vindobonensis.*

Transcriptions from older documents or from the oral tradition, produced after the conquest, include the Quiché *Popol Vuh,* or Book of Council; the Maya *Books of the Chilam Balamob;* the Nahua *Huehuehtlahtolli,* or Testimonies of the Ancient Word (the conveyors of the moral discourses, as well as the expression of the wisdom of the elders); and the collections of *Mexican Songs,* manuscripts preserved at the National Library of Mexico and the Nettie Lee Benson Latin American Collection of the University of Texas at Austin. The surviving documentary manifestations of native religiosity encompass texts like those collected in the seventeenth century by Hernando Ruiz de Alarcón in what is today the State of Guerrero.

In this corpus of Mesoamerican sacred literature one finds testimonies on the pre-Columbian religious beliefs and practices (feasts, sacrifices, and offerings); on the relationship of the gods and rituals with the calendrical computations; and on prophetic ennunciations, incantations, moral precepts, prayers, hymns, and a variety of songs and poetry.

AFTER THE CONQUEST. The Spanish Conquest, which, in the case of the Aztec, was completed in 1521, brought with it the burning of native libraries, the demolition of temples, and the annihilation of whatever appeared to the conquistadors to be "idolatrous." Nevertheless, neither the Conquest nor the zealous activity of some Christian missionaries who followed in its wake succeeded in completely erasing all of the ancient traditions. It is extraordinary to discover that contemporary Maya, Mixtec, Zapotec, Nahuatl, and other groups keep remembrances of the old mythic traditions as part of their lore.

Studies of contemporary Mesoamericans' worldviews and religious attitudes reveals that Christianity and indigenous Mesoamerican traditions have combined to form several kinds of syncretistic systems. Whereas in some cases a Christianized paganism has developed, in others one can see that new forms of Christianity, embedded in an indigenous Mesoamerican world of symbols, have been born.

Syncretism is present among contemporary Indians and other peoples in Mexico who reinterpret the Christian dogma of the Holy Trinity partially through indigenous conceptions. For instance, instead of speaking of the Trinity or the Father, the Son and the Holy Spirit, people refer to Our Father Jesus and Our Mother, the Virgin of Guadalupe, in an implicit reference to the dual supreme god, Our Father, Our Mother. Another example of syncretism in religious practices is provided by contemporary acts of self-sacrifice that follow the admonition "to pay" for what the gods have done for us in the creation of various forms of life. Today such practices of self-sacrifice or repayment to the gods are performed in pilgrimages to sanctuaries such as those of Chalma, Talpa, Tepeyac and others, as well as in determined Christian feasts.

SEE ALSO Aztec Religion; Calendars, article on Mesoamerican Calendars; Human Sacrifice, article on Aztec Rites; Maya Religion; Olmec Religion; Quetzalcoatl.

BIBLIOGRAPHY

Annals of Cuauhtitlan. In *Codice Chimalpopoca,* edited by Primo Feliciano Velázquez. Mexico City, 1995. Nahuatl text and Spanish translation. A basic source of Mesoamerican indigenous tradition; includes important references to religious beliefs and practices.

Bernal, Ignacio. *The Olmec World.* Berkeley, Calif., 1969. A readable account of the archaeological findings in the Olmec area.

Broda, Johanna, Davíd Carrasco, and Eduardo Matos Moctezuma. *The Great Temple of Tenochtitlan: Center and Periphery in the Aztec World.* Berkeley, Calif., 1987.

Cantares Mexicanos (Collection of Mexican Songs). A sixteenth-century manuscript that includes a large number of compositions, in Nahuatl, of pre-Columbian origin. It is preserved at the Biblioteca Nacional de México in Mexico City. Translations of some of these songs appear in *Pre-Columbian Literatures of Mexico,* edited by Miguel Léon-Portilla. Norman, Okla., 1969.

Carrasco Davíd, *Religions of Mesoamerica: Cosmovision and Ceremonial Centers,* San Francisco, Calif., 1990. A lucid discussion of the core aspects of religion in Mesoamerica.

Carrasco Davíd. *Quetzalcoatl and the Irony of Empire: Myths and Proprecies in the Aztec Tradicion.* Rev. ed. Norman, Okla., 2000.

Carrasco, Pedro. "Pagan Rituals and Beliefs among the Chontal Indians of Oaxaca, Mexico." *Anthropological Records* 20 (1960): 87–117. Discusses Christian and pagan elements in contemporary religious ceremonies of this indigenous group.

Caso, Alfonso. "Zapotec Writing and Calendar." In *Handbook of Middle American Indians,* edited by Robert Wauchope et al., vol. 3. Austin, Tex., 1965. A concise, well-documented presentation of religious inscriptions of the Zapotec.

Caso, Alfonso. "Mixtec Writing and Calendar." In *Handbook of Middle American Indians,* edited by Robert Wauchope et al., vol. 3. Austin, Tex., 1965. A valuable complement to the previously listed article.

Caso, Alfonso. "Dioses y signos Teotihuacanos." In *Teotihuacan onceava mesa redonda,* vol. 1. Mexico City, 1966. Well-researched study on the gods worshiped at Teotihuacan.

Caso, Alfonso. "Religión o religiones mesoamericanos?" In *Verhandlungen des XXXVIII Amerikanistenkongresses,* vol. 3. Excellent synthesis of the evidence that supports the existence of one religious tradition common to the various Mesoamerican groups.

Codex Maggliabecchianus, XIII: Manuscrit mexicain post-Colombien de la Bibilothèque Nationale de Florence (1904). Graz, Austria, 1970. Contains summaries in English and Spanish. *Codex Matritense.* 3 vols. Madrid, Spain, 1905–1907. Nahuatl texts of the Indian informants of Fray Bernardo de Sahagún (sixteenth century). A classic collection of texts of the indigenous tradition, extremely rich in religious materials, including sacred hymns, speeches, and descriptions of feasts and sacrifices.

Coe, Michael D. *America's First Civilization.* New York, 1968. Excellent introduction to the study of Olmec culture.

Coe, Michael D. "The Iconology of Olmec Art." In *The Iconography of Middle American Sculpture* (an anthology of conference papers, Metropolitan Museum of Art, New York). New York, 1973. Summary and lucid discussion of the meaning of Olmec religious art.

Coe, Michael D. *Breaking the Maya Code.* New York, 1992. The story of the deciphering of Maya writing.

Edmonson, Munro S., ed. and trans. *The Book of Counsel: The Popol Vuh of the Quiché Maya of Guatemala.* New Orleans, La., 1971. An excellent introduction and English version of this classic of sacred Mesoamerican literature.

Edmonson, Munro S. "The Songs of Dzitbalché: A Literary Commentary." In *Tlalocan: A Journal of Source Materials on the Native Cultures of Mexico* 9 (1982): 173–208. A new translation of, and commentary, on these sacred Maya compositions.

Glass, John B. "A Survey of Native American Pictorial Manuscripts." In *Handbook of Middle American Indians,* edited by Robert Wauchope et al., vol. 14. Austin, Tex., 1975. A comprehensive guide to these primary sources for the study of Mesoamerican cultures.

Joralemon, Peter D. *A Study of Olmec Iconography.* Washington, D.C., 1971. A pioneer interpretation of the religious iconography of the Olmec.

Joralemon, Peter D. "The Olmec Dragon: A Study in Pre-Columbian Iconography." In *Origins of Religious Art and Iconography in Preclassic Mesoamerica,* edited by Henry B. Nicholson. Los Angeles, 1976.

Kubler, George. *The Iconography of the Art of Teotihuacan.* Washington, D.C., 1967. Objects to the idea of a single Mesoamerican "cotradition."

Kubler, George. "Period, Style, and Meaning in Ancient American Art." *New Literary History* 1 (1970): 127–144. Adds arguments in support of the point of view expressed in the previously listed paper.

Landa, Diego de. *Landa's Relación de las Cosas de Yucatan.* Trans. and ed., with notes, by A. M. Tozzer. Cambridge, Mass., 1941. The best critical edition of this sixteenth-century classic study of Maya culture and religion.

Léon-Portilla, Miguel. *Aztec Thought and Culture: A Study of the Ancient Nahuatl Mind.* Norman, Okla., 1963. A study of the Aztec worldview about ultimate reality; includes numerous Nahuatl texts from the indigenous pre-Columbian tradition.

Léon-Portilla, Miguel. "The Ethnohistorical Records for the Huey Teocalli of Tenochtitlan." In *The Aztec Templo Mayor,* edited by Elizabeth Hill Boone, Washington, D.C., 1983. Registers the main sources for the study of the symbolism embedded in the Templo Mayor.

Léon-Portilla, Miguel. *Pre-Columbian Literatures of Mexico.* Norman, Okla., 1969. An introduction to the extant texts of the Aztec, Maya, Mixtec, Otomí, and other Mesoamerican groups.

Léon-Portilla, Miguel. *Time and Reality in the Thought of the Maya.* Boston, 1973. An ethnohistorical approach to Maya religion and worldview with an emphasis on the Mayan concern for time.

Léon-Portilla, Miguel, ed. *Native Mesoamerican Spirituality: Ancient Myths, Discourses, Stories, Doctrines, Hymns, Poems from the Aztec, Yucatec Quiche-Maya, and Other Sacred Traditions.* New York, 1980. An annotated anthology, with commentary of texts from the pre-Columbian traditions.

Nicholson, Henry B. "Religion in Pre-Hispanic Central Mexico." In *Handbook of Middle American Indians,* edited by Robert Wauchope et al., vol. 10. Austin, Tex., 1971. A classification of the principal cult themes and deity complexes.

Nicholson, Henry B. *Topiltzin Quetzalcoatl: The Once and Future Lord of the Toltecs.* Boulder, Colo., 2001. Comprehensive descriptions of the sources on Quetzalcoatl and an interpretation of them.

Norman, V. Garth *Izapa Sculpture,* part 2. Provo, Utah, 1976. Includes a careful description of Stele 5. Piña Chán, Román. *Los Olmecas antiguos.* Mexico, 1982. A comprehensive approach to Olmec culture by a distinguished archaeologist.

Sahagún, (Fray) Bernardino de. *Historia de los cosas de la Nueva España* (compiled 1569–1582; first published 1820). Translated by Arthur J. O. Anderson and Charles E. Dibble as *Florentine Codex: General History of the Things of New Spain,* 13 vols. Santa Fe, N. Mex., 1950–1982. Vivid descriptions of temples, rituals, paraphernalia, and mythology can be found in several of this work's volumes, especially volumes 2 and 3.

Schele, Linda, and Mary Ellen Miller. *Blood of Kings: Dynasty and Ritual in Maya Art.* New York, 1985. This and the following book offer readings of a large number of inscriptions.

Schele, Linda, and Davin Freidel. *A Forest of Kings: The Untold Story of the Ancient Maya.* New York, 1990.

Serrato-Combe, Antonio, *The Aztec Templo Mayor: A Vizualization.* Salt Lake, Utah, 2001.

Thompson, J. Eric S. *Maya Hieroglyphic Writing: An Introduction.* Norman, Okla., 1960. A basic work for the study of Maya symbols and inscriptions.

Thompson, J. Eric S. *Maya History and Religion.* Norman, Okla., 1970. An ethnohistorical approach in which a large number of sources are analyzed by a great scholar who devoted his life to research on the Maya.

Valliant, George C., ed. *A Sacred Almanac of the Aztecs.* New York, 1940. Translation of *Codex Borbonicus: Manuscrit mexicaine de la bibilothèque du Palais Bourbon,* edited by Jules Theodore Ernest Hamy (Paris, 1899).

MIGUEL LÉON-PORTILLA (1987 AND 2005)

MESOAMERICAN RELIGIONS: FORMATIVE CULTURES

Religious practices during Mesoamerica's Preclassic, or Formative, period (1500 BCE–250 CE) can only be inferred from the archaeological remains. One of the most thoroughly investigated regions is the lacustrine Basin of Mexico in the central highlands, where remains of pottery and figurines provide a yardstick for determining the cultural sequence within the Basin and adjacent regions. Throughout the Preclassic this region witnessed a steady population increase and a locally diverse progression from small farming communities with developing social stratification to large towns with complex political hierarchies. The period is divided in four major phases. Different time spans for the major phases, as well as local subphases, have been proposed by various researchers. These are consolidated in the following chronology: Early Preclassic, 1500–800 BCE; Middle Pre-classic, 800–500 BCE; Late Preclassic, 500–150 BCE; Terminal Preclassic, 150 BCE–250 CE. (Piña Chan, 1972; Sanders et al., 1979).

BASIN OF MEXICO. During the Early Preclassic, the Ixtapaluca subphase (1400–800 BCE) in the southern part of the Basin of Mexico contains pottery strongly related to the Olmec style of San Lorenzo on the Gulf Coast. The Olmec tradition is also evident in figurines of great refinement, found in large numbers in the Tlatilco cemeteries, which have since been engulfed by present-day Mexico City. Most of these figurines are female. Some indicate advanced pregnancy, suggestive of a concern with human as well as agricultural fertility. Other figurines show two heads on one body or heads with three eyes and two noses, believed to perhaps represent diviner-healers. In general the Tlatilco figurines, which include both Olmec and local styles, are thought to be merely grave offerings without explicit religious function. Olmec influence in the Basin was only marginal; its impact was stronger in the states of Morelos, Puebla, and Guerrero.

In the Middle Preclassic new hamlets appeared around the system of lakes in the Basin of Mexico (which have now virtually disappeared). At Zacatenco and Ticomán, figurines abound but are cruder. As they were no longer placed in graves but appeared in refuse middens, it is assumed that they served as fetishes in household cults. There are no representations of gods or goddesses that can be recognized as such with reference to the iconographic system prevalent in the Classic and Postclassic periods (250–1521 CE). Nor is there definite evidence of civic-ceremonial architecture. It has been argued that a society capable of supporting potters not engaged in full-time food production should also be able to maintain religious practitioners, such as shamans. Certain figurines depicting masked dancers in peculiar costumes have been identified as magicians (shamans) and ballplayers but they are part of the Olmec component, as are the pottery masks (Coe, 1965). Concrete evidence of shamanism, amply demonstrated for North and South America, is lacking for Preclassic Mesoamerica.

In the Late Preclassic, pyramidal mounds of modest proportions occur at some sites in the southern part of the Basin of Mexico and indicate the beginning of ceremonial activities outside the immediate household clusters. This period is notable for a veritable population explosion. Cuicuilco became the dominant political center, with five to ten thousand inhabitants, while Ticomán remained only a minor village. At Cuicuilco several small pyramids were located in the residential zone and may have served the local populace. By 400 BCE a large, oval, truncated pyramid of adobe bricks with rough stone facing was built in tiers or stages, each of which contains an altarlike structure. Access was by a ramp facing east, toward the sunrise. The town and the lower parts of the pyramid were covered by a lava flow that, according to latest estimates, occurred around 400 CE, when Cuicuilco had long ceased to be a dominant center (Heizer and Bennyhoff, 1972). However, earlier eruptions from the nearby Xitle volcano, with spectacular displays of fire, smoke, and molten lava, led to the creation of the first deity in Mesoamerica, the "old fire god." He is portrayed in clay and later exclusively in stone sculpture as an old, toothless male with a wrinkled face who bears on his head a large basin for the burning of incense. Known by his Nahuatl (Aztec) name Huehueteotl ("old god"), he became one of the major deities of the Teotihuacán pantheon and, after the Toltec interlude, reappeared in the Aztec pantheon in different guise as Xiuhtecuhtli ("turquoise lord" or "lord of the year"). The burning of incense as an offering for petitioning the gods became general practice throughout Mesoamerica, both in household and in elaborate temple rituals. This is indicated by the great variety and number of ceramic incense burners that have been excavated.

Between 150 and 1 BCE, Teotihuacán occupied an area of about six square kilometers and was a highly stratified agrarian community. It developed into an urban center of twenty-five to thirty thousand people in the Tzacualli phase (1–150 CE), when the grid system of the town was laid out with a main north-south axis, known as the Street of the Dead (so named by the Spanish, who thought the place a necropolis). On either side of the axis were erected numerous complexes, each with three temple-pyramid and a central courtyard. The monumental Pyramid of the Sun (sixty-three meters high) and the substructure of the Pyramid of the Moon were completed in this phase during a single fifty-year construction episode. (Again, these names were given by the Spanish.) The ceremonial precinct, over four kilometers in length, served civic and religious functions and became a pilgrimage center. Dependence on seasonal rainfall for agriculture gave rise to a cult of a god of rain and lightning, Tlaloc, who became the supreme deity and continued to be one of the major gods in later cultures up to the Spanish conquest (1521). The establishment of a hierarchical priesthood can be inferred from the art and architecture of this period. In the Classic period (250–750 CE) the pantheon expanded, and Teotihuacán became the largest city of the New World.

WESTERN MEXICO. In Guanajuato, to the northwest of the Basin of Mexico, elaborate pottery and finely modeled figurines of the Chupícuaro tradition (500–1 BCE) were lavishly used for tomb offerings, and ceramic flutes, whistles, and rattles were interred in children's graves. Ceremonies included the practice of decapitation, related to warfare. This custom, however, did not become widespread until the Middle and Late Classic.

The Preclassic cultures of western Mexico (in the present-day states of Michoacán, Colima, Jalisco, and Nayarit) remained outside the Mesoamerican cotradition until about 350 CE when the Teotihuacán and Gulf Coast cultures began to penetrate the area and introduced their culture and ideology.

Most noteworthy among these loosely united chiefdoms was their concern for the dead, as evidenced by the Shaft Tomb Complex (c. 200 BCE–400/500 CE). Unparalleled in other parts of Mesoamerica, it extends in a great arc from south-central Nayarit through central Jalisco to Colima. The tombs consist of vertical entrance shafts 1.5 to 8 meters deep, with narrow, short tunnels at the end leading to one or more vaults carved in the hard volcanic soil (*tepetate*). After interment the shafts were completely filled with rubble and hand-packed dirt; stone slabs prevented the fill from entering the burial chambers. Grave offerings comprise large, hollow ceramic figures in varied local styles, representing men (some of them tomb guards with armor and weapons) and women in different poses and attitudes. The human figures have stylized features and disproportionate bodies but they are very expressive, approaching portraitlike countenances. They reflect the customs, dress, and ornaments of the ancient inhabitants (von Winning, 1974).

Funeral processions and mourning scenes modeled in clay depict rites preceding interment. They show the mourners in orderly arrangement following a catafalque being carried to a house, or groups of mourners surrounding a corpse. Other kinds of grave offerings include complex scenes of villagers and their huts, family gatherings, ball-court scenes, bloodletting and cheek-perforation rituals, and dancers with musicians, all consisting of small, crudely modeled figurines attached to clay slabs. The variety of ceramic house models of one or two stories, some of them multichambered, is interesting inasmuch as no masonry architecture existed in this area. They replicate constructions of wattle daubed with mud, covered with a thatched roof. These were tomb offerings intended as shelters in the afterlife.

Among the smaller, solid figurines are those showing a female strapped to a slab. They appear to represent corpses on biers laid out for funeral rites, ready to be lowered through the shaft into the burial chamber. Similar ceramic "bed figures" occur in coeval contexts in Ecuador, and sporadically in the Old World (von Winning and Hammer, 1972).

A variety of large, hollow animal effigies occur also in the shaft tombs. In Colima dog effigies abound, their well-fed appearance indicates that they had been deliberately fattened to provide food for the departed. (In Aztec times fattened dogs were sold in the market for human consumption.) Skeletons of carefully buried dogs have been found in graves at Tlatilco and Chupícuaro, and it is generally believed that the dogs were supposed to help the souls of the deceased on their paths through the perils of the underworld.

The generally held view that the ceramic sculptures of the Shaft Tomb Complex portray secular subjects indicative of everyday village life has been rejected by Peter T. Furst (1975). Based on ethnographic comparisons—mainly with the beliefs and shamanistic practices among the modern Huichol Indians whose remote ancestors occupied part of the Shaft Tomb zone—he concludes that the art of western Mexico was no less religious than that of the rest of Mesoamerica. However, none of the figures display attributes that clearly identify them as deities or deity impersonators in the manner of other Mesoamerican religion and iconography. Tlaloc and Huehueteotl effigies occur only after the end of the Shaft Tomb period. Lacking temple pyramids and relevant documentary sources, the ceramic sculptures provide the only evidence for a ceremonialism that emphasized a cult of the dead.

GUERRERO AND THE PUEBLA-TLAXCALA AREA. Preclassic ceremonialism was introduced into this area by Olmec intruders. For the period after the decline of Olmec influence (after 800 BCE), information on social, political, and religious aspects is lacking. The Mezcala region of Guerrero produced a remarkable number of highly stylized anthropomorphic figures and masks, ranging from the Preclassic Olmecoid to Teotihuacanoid types, but the stylistic sequence is not datable. Among the small stone sculptures are flat models of temple facades with doorways in which a human figure occasionally stands on top of the stairway. However, masonry temples of this type have not been reported from the Mezcala region, and the date of these artifacts is unknown. These temple sculptures probably were made in the Classic period. In the Tehuacán Valley, developments from early village life to urban communities paralleled those in other parts of Mesoamerica. The archaeological remains give no indication of religious activities.

In sum, the Preclassic figurines that appear all over Mexico north of the eighteenth parallel are similar insofar as their features were incised and clay fillets added. Neither these nor the Shaft Tomb figures represent well-defined deities with determinative attributes such as occur in later periods. With the exception of the Olmec intrusive layer and the emergence of the old fire god at Cuicuilco, and the rain god Tlaloc in Teotihuacán, in all other regions the gods, as Ignacio Bernal once said, had not yet been born.

SEE ALSO Olmec Religion.

BIBLIOGRAPHY

Coe, Michael D. *The Jaguar's Children: Pre-Classic Central Mexico.* New York, 1965. An explicit exposition of the Olmec art style and its distribution. Numerous good illustrations of pottery vessels, figurines, masks, and other artifacts from the Mexican highlands.

Furst, Peter T. "House of Darkness and House of Light: Sacred Functions of West Mexican Funeral Art." In *Death and the Afterlife in Pre-Columbian America: A Conference at Dumbarton Oaks, October 27th, 1973,* edited by Elizabeth P. Benson, pp. 33–68. Washington, D.C., 1975. Elaborating his earlier published views that western Mexican funerary art objects have a religious rather than a secular or anecdotal significance, Furst considers the Nayarit house models as houses of the dead, the *locus mundi* of the soul.

Heizer, Robert F., and James A. Bennyhoff. "Archaeological Excavations at Cuicuilco, Mexico, 1957." In *Research Reports, 1955–1960 Projects, National Geographic Society,* edited by Paul H. Oelsen, pp. 93–104. Washington, D.C., 1972. A revision of the cultural sequence of the Late and Terminal Preclassic periods in the Valley of Mexico. A preliminary summary of the authors' work appears in their article "Archaeological Investigation of Cuicuilco, Valley of Mexico, 1957," *Science* 127 (January 1958): 232–233.

Piña Chan, Román. *Historia, arqueología y arte prehispánico.* Mexico City, 1972. Includes the only comprehensive chronological chart of all the pre-Columbian cultures of Mexico published so far by a Mexican archaeologist.

Sanders, William T., Jeffrey R. Parsons, and Robert S. Santley. *The Basin of Mexico: Ecological Processes in the Evolution of a Civilization.* New York, 1979. An up-to-date synthesis of the sociocultural evolution based primarily on settlement pattern surveys.

von Winning, Hasso. *The Shaft Tomb Figures of West Mexico.* Los Angeles, 1974. A classification according to thematic significance of the ceramic figures of Colima, Jalisco, and Nayarit.

von Winning, Hasso, and Olga Hammer. *Anecdotal Sculpture of Ancient West Mexico.* Los Angeles, 1972. A copiously illustrated and annotated exhibition catalog of ceramic house models and figurine groups from Colima, Jalisco, and Nayarit, with two essays on related topics.

HASSO VON WINNING (1987)

MESOAMERICAN RELIGIONS: CLASSIC CULTURES

The Classic period in the Valley of Mexico and its environs (150 BCE–750 CE) was one of florescence and of great achievement and intellectual advancement in the fields of art, government, and ideology. These centuries saw urbanism defined. Intense trade developed along established routes, diffusing ideas and material goods from one corner of Mesoamerica to another and consolidating religious thought and ceremonial.

Data for Classic period religion is based on archaeology; while no written documents from that period have come down to us, we can rightly regard mural painting, architecture, and other works of art as valid documents. Sixteenth-century chronicles describing Aztec religious belief and custom—about eight centuries after the decline of Teotihuacan—nevertheless can help us interpret earlier cultures, if used with caution. Ethnographic evidence can also shed light on ancient cultures, since in many cases there seems to be a continuity of tradition. It is significant, too, that Mesoamerica constituted a unified culture area, unlike the Mediterranean civilization that had interaction with totally different cultures from very early times on. In addition to the shared urbanism of its cultures, pre-Columbian Mesoamerica was in many ways unified by a common ideological system, with regional and temporal variation. This apparent underlying tradition of many basic beliefs allows us to compare one culture with another, but only to a certain extent and allowing for changes over time.

During the Classic period the characteristics of Mesoamerican religion were formalized. Patterns in belief, ritual, and iconography, some of them derived from earlier cultures, were set, and they formed the basis of later societies, especially those of the Toltec and the Aztec. The belief that natural forces were animate, the measurement of time as coordinated with sacred space, and the observation of heavenly bodies were some of the main characteristics. There was an intense ceremonialism supported by iconography and by oral mythic tradition. The gods were numerous, often human in form and often conceived as animals that were the gods' doubles. Religion was integrated with social organization, politics, economy, art, music, and poetry. There was a patron deity for virtually every activity, and all objects received homage and offerings, from certain flowers reserved for sovereigns to humble implements for planting and harvesting. The world was considered a sacred structure, an image of the cosmos.

Sites and structures (and probably human activities such as processions and ritual dancing) were oriented to the sun, moon, stars, and to sacred geographical places. Architectural splendor was manifested in pyramid platforms surmounted by temples; many were painted in symbolic colors, their exteriors and interiors covered with murals. The temple in each city was the *axis mundi*, the center of the universe. Sculpture depicted religious themes, and much pottery was decorated with images of the gods. The worldview of Classic Mesoamerica was peopled with deities who intervened in every phase of life. Men who governed were deeply enmeshed in ritual. Every ruler had his priestly duties, and the priests themselves controlled the ritual calendar and thus the agricultural cycle, which was a basic part of the economy.

TEOTIHUACAN. During the Classic period, Teotihuacan, which means "place where the gods are made," became the center of the Mesoamerican world. A vast settlement occupying more than eight square miles in the valley of the same name, a subvalley of the Basin of Mexico, the city of Teotihuacan was the leading Classic center and the most highly urbanized center in the New World. Although Teotihuacan at its height ruled the trade routes and set religious patterns for many other cultures, in its early period it barely set the stage for its later grandeur.

Founding and early history. Around the beginning of the common era, a small settlement was established in the northern part of what we now call the Teotihuacan Valley. After the eruption of the Xitle volcano in the southern part of the Basin of Mexico (c. 1000 BCE), some residents of Cuicuilco, which had been covered by lava in the eruption, probably moved to the east, into the Teotihuacan area. The refugees would have brought their own deities, especially the fire god. We see him in the Teotihuacan braziers of Huehueteotl ("old god"), who may have originated in Cuicuilco. At an early period Teotihuacan also was strongly influenced by the Puebla-Tlaxcala peoples. During the Patlachique (150–1 BCE) and the Tzacualli (1–150 CE) phases, Teotihuacan experienced explosive growth. People from the eastern and southern parts of the Basin of Mexico concentrated around this center, raising the population of Teotihuacan to eighty thousand or more (Sanders et al., 1979, pp. 184ff.; Millon, 1981, p. 221). This population concentration was reflected in the city's direct control of agricultural production and of the obsidian industry, as well as in its importance as a regional economic center, which at the same time stimulated religious manifestation.

Toward the end of the Tzacualli phase the great Pyramid of the Sun was erected, standing more than 63 meters high and measuring 225 meters on each of its four sides. Shortly after this the Pyramid of the Moon was built with the Avenue of the Dead leading up to it. (These structures were named by the Aztec; we do not know what the Teotihuacanos called them.) The orientation of the Avenue of the Dead is 15°25° east of north and the major structures were aligned with this axis, slightly "skewed" from the cardinal directions. From the Tzacualli phase on, an exuberance of construction filled Teotihuacan with splendid structures, all carefully planned on a grid pattern.

Caves and cults. The most sacred place in the Teotihuacan complex was the spot where the Sun pyramid stood, underneath which lies a sacred cave. Caves were considered sacred throughout Mesoamerica, and this one designated the site for the construction of the great pyramid. Teotihuacan was a powerful religious magnet and attracted pilgrims from all over. The influx of large groups of pilgrims undoubtedly created the need for more spectacular structures and probably provided the economic means and hands for the work. According to Mircea Eliade in *The Sacred and the Profane* (New York, 1959), sacred time is relived in a sacred space by means of a pilgrimage, and divine space is repeated by building one holy place over another. In Teotihuacan this repetition took place when the great pyramid was erected over a primitive shrine, itself built over a subterranean cave. A cult of long standing existed in this cavern and was one reason that Teotihuacan became a religious center. The presence of drainage channels through which water was brought into the cave (Millon, 1981, p. 234) indicates the performance there of rituals associated with water, and the remains of ritual fires suggest a symbolic juxtaposition of fire and water, which juxtaposition was basic in Mesoamerican religion. It is likely, René Millon suggests, that the guardians of beliefs and cults in the sacred cave had awesome prestige and that this prestige and the importance of religion and ritual in general played a major part in the shaping of Teotihuacan's hierarchical society and in the legitimation of the authority of the state.

Orientation, symbolic planning, and architecture. Urban planning, architecture, myth, and ritual were interrelated in ancient Mexico. The blending of religious-cosmological conceptions with an acute awareness of nature constituted much of the Classic worldview. The orientation of Teotihuacan's major axis, the Avenue of the Dead, was astronomically and calendrically determined. The star group Pleiades was also influential since some structures were oriented to its rising position. The main facades of most of the pyramids, except the Pyramid of the Moon, faced west (that is, in the direction of the setting sun), as did monuments in later Mesoamerican cultures. An astronomical symbol found in strategic positions all over the city was also one of the determinants of the orientation of streets and structures. This symbol is the "pecked cross," actually a quartered circle consisting of dots whose number probably referred to a calendrical-ritual count. It was carved on the floors of ceremonial buildings and also on rocks on the periphery of the city, which were aligned with the monuments (Aveni, 1980, p. 223).

There are more than seventy-five temples in the city. Some, found on the Avenue of the Dead, are grouped into complexes of three, perhaps a symbolic number. More than two thousand residential compounds are located in Teotihuacan, and every residential compound had one or more local temples within it. Even within smaller units a miniature temple is often found in the center of a courtyard. That the natural environment and nearby topographical features were part of the worldview of Teotihuacan and that they figured in the planning of the city is evident from the relation of Teotihuacan to the mountains, caves, and bodies of water in its environs. On the mountaintops, rites to the rain gods were held, for here the clouds gathered and formed the precious liquid. Chronicles referring to the Aztec, whose practices can perhaps give us an insight into the earlier period, tell us that mountains were seen as female; water was thought to be held inside them as if in the womb. The mountain north of the Avenue of the Dead, whose form was mirrored by the Pyramid of the Moon, was called Tenan, "the mother" (i.e., of people) by the Aztec. Hills and waterholes were considered sacred, as were trees, for they protected people and provided sustenance in the form of leaves, fruit, and roots.

Teotihuacan, like most of Mesoamerica, was basically an agricultural society. Observance of the seasons was controlled by a ritual calendar and the invocation of rain through propitiation of the gods was an important ceremony. Lake Tezcoco, the great body of water that covered a large part of the Basin of Mexico, came almost to the borders of Teotihuacan and provided aquatic foods and a waterway for transportation. So for the Teotihuacanos, the gods of water were associated with "Our Mother" (as the lake was called in Aztec times) as well as with rain and mountaintops. This setting of natural abundance was enhanced in Teotihuacan by local deposits of obsidian, which was considered divine.

The Avenue of the Dead extends almost two thousand meters from the Sun and Moon pyramids to the Ciudadela (Span., "citadel"), Teotihuacan's religious and political center during much of the metropolis's existence. The vast quadrangle (4.4 hectares) is surrounded on each of its four sides by wide platforms topped by four low pyramids on three sides, and by three at the east or rear (Millon, 1981, p. 203). Entrance to the complex is only from the Avenue of the Dead on the west and from the north, suggesting that entrance to and exit from the area were strictly controlled. Living quarters in the northeast and southeast of the Ciudadela could have housed about 250 persons, probably high cult officials. George L. Cowgill states that while the head of state must have resided in the Ciudadela, his presence here was largely ceremonial and the real governing activity was carried out elsewhere (Cowgill, 1983). A square platform with a staircase on each of its four sides in the middle of the quadrangle suggests large-scale rites; theatrical performances of a religious character evidently were held here.

At the eastern end of the Ciudadela stands the majestic pyramid known as the Temple of Quetzalcoatl, so called because of the feathered serpents that decorate its facade—although the temple was not necessarily dedicated to Quetzalcoatl, who in the Postclassic period was a god of civilization, creation, and the arts. Also on the facade are heads of fire serpents that have been identified erroneously as representations of the rain god Tlaloc. The spectacular Temple of Quetzalcoatl was erected in the second construction period of the Ciudadela (probably 150–200 CE), coeval in part with the Sun and Moon pyramids, and was used (and at times rebuilt) up until the end of Teotihuacan, around 750 CE. But at one period in the city's history (c. 300 CE), another smaller pyramid, the Adosada (Span., "affixed") was attached to its facade, partly blocking the earlier building. The Adosada seems to have enhanced rather than eclipsed the Temple of Quetzalcoatl's religious importance. Perhaps this was an architectural rather than an ideological renovation. According to Cowgill (1983), the religious and political significance combined in the Ciudadela and the Quetzalcoatl pyramid cult was intimately associated with Teotihuacan's rulership. He also suggests that increased activity associated with the Quetzalcoatl temple may have necessitated the building of this extra structure.

A pyramid platform in the southern part of the Ciudadela is decorated with red X designs and with green circles, symbols of water, "that which is precious." The X is clearly an *ollin,* symbol of motion (or of the movement of the sun, according to later Aztec tradition). The joining of water and fire (in this case, the sun) are thus represented during this early period. Although the combination symbolized war in the Postclassic period, here in Teotihuacan it may have had astronomical significance.

Another enormous area of dwellings, pyramids, platforms, temples, and courtyards occupying many hectares along the major avenue, and known as the Avenue of the Dead Complex, has been tentatively identified as the center of governmental functions. The *talud* ("sloping panel") combined with the *tablero* ("vertical panel") is the characteristic Teotihuacan facade for religious structures and has long been recognized as the sign that a building faced in such a way is a temple (Millon, 1981, p. 229). This convention was also applied to public buildings and residential compounds, thus consecrating the entire avenue, as well as giving a sacred character to buildings in other zones that incorporate the *talud-tablero* mode of facing. Juan Vidarte de Linares (cited in Cowgill, 1983) has interpreted the Avenue of the Dead, lined with temple platforms thus built, as a great open-air cathedral.

Art. The art of Teotihuacan is intensely religious. Mural painting (one of the major art forms) on buildings, temples, and shrines, leads Clara Millon (cited in Millon, 1981, p. 213) to consider it the "official graphic medium for transmitting ideas and beliefs . . . ideologically acceptable and desirable." Murals were an ideal medium for communication because they were out in the open for all to see. In the interior of palaces, where the paintings usually had a religious context, their messages, perhaps understood only by priests, must also have constituted a type of didactic "book" on the walls. Sculpture in Teotihuacan was usually architectural: roof merlons with year-sign motifs, serpentine balustrades on stairways (later seen at Tenayuca, Chichén Itzá, and other sites), zoomorphic stone heads on the facades of buildings (on, for example, the Temple of Quetzalcoatl and at one time on the Pyramid of the Sun), and stone figures perhaps representing gods, such as the old fire god. A relief panel recently discovered in the West Plaza of the Avenue of the Dead Complex represents a personage with rain god characteristics holding a rattle in either hand. According to Noel Morelos, the archaeologist who discovered it, the image is somewhat similar to Tlaloc figures in the Tetitla and Tepantitla murals at Teotihuacan. Another rich source of information is pottery, painted or decorated with other techniques, that depicts rituals and either deities or priests.

The large braziers found at Teotihuacan are sometimes called "theaters" because the masks surrounded by symbolic elements that are attached to them are reminiscent of the stage. *Candeleros* (Span., "candle-sticks") must have been used for copal incense; the Teotihuacanos had no candles. The use of clay figurines can only be guessed at. Some may have been used on household altars or kept by pilgrims as souvenirs from sacred places. "Portrait figurines," sometimes called "dancers," are small, nude, sexless people in animated positions. Other clay figures are "puppets," with movable arms and legs, nude bodies, and carefully made and adorned heads. Lack of body adornment on the portrait figurines and puppets suggests that they were dressed in bark paper, a ritual material, for ceremonial use. Clay dogs may, as among the Aztec, have represented the animal that accompanied the deceased to the afterworld.

A possible warrior cult, involving relations with other regions of Mesoamerica, is indicated by representations of military figures in the murals, on decorated pottery, and in figurines. Some of the figurines wear warrior vestments, including animal helmets. Painted representations of people holding excised hearts on knives, as in a mural in the Atetelco (another architectural complex, or palace), may indicate the existence of a warrior cult, although they might represent human sacrifice practiced for ritual reasons. Citing the work of Hasso von Winning and George Kubler, Esther Pasztory (1978, p. 133) notes that war-related iconographic themes in Teotihuacan include the sun god as a raptorial bird and as a feline, warriors in animal disguise, and an owl-and-weapon symbol.

Burials. Funerary customs also shed light on the religion of Teotihuacan. Cremation was practiced and was possibly related to the later Aztec belief that a person's possessions must be burned in order to travel to the afterworld, where they would be turned over to the lord of the dead. Interment was also practiced; burials were accompanied by grave goods—vessels whose contents may have been food or other necessities for the other world and miniature objects that were symbolic offerings. Mica decorated some of the large braziers and urns and has been found under floors. Its meaning is obscure, but it is mirrorlike and mirrors were used for divining.

Deities. Names of Teotihuacan gods are unknown to us; therefore we refer to them by their characteristics or symbols, sometimes comparing them to Aztec deities whose iconography and function are similar. Esther Pasztory (1973, p. 147) has noted that the structure of Teotihuacan iconography is in many ways similar to that of the Aztec, for which we have written data, and image clusters have been identified in Teotihuacan that have elements similar to representations of Aztec deities. The presence of water-agricultural deities is indicated by aquatic symbols such as streams, water dripping from shells, fish, frogs, and water lilies. The god associated with rain and the earth is distinguished by traits found on the Aztec deity Tlaloc—goggle eyes and fangs, for example—but also by a water lily in his mouth, a lightning staff, a vessel with water, a year-sign headdress, and crocodilian traits. Pasztory calls him "Tlaloc A." "Tlaloc B" appeared later on the scene when there was a trend toward militarism in Teotihuacan. Some of Tlaloc B's diagnostic traits are a bifurcated tongue, a *bigotera* (Span., "mustache"), and jaguar features. Both "Tlalocs" are associated with water, although the latter, because his image is found in foreign centers and is related to persons who may be representatives of the Teotihuacan state, seems to be connected with military and foreign relations as well. Pasztory (1978, p. 134) sees Tlaloc B, or the "Jaguar Tlaloc," as possibly being the patron deity of Teotihuacan, and claims that the "patron deity cult," later practiced among the Toltec and Aztec (which was different from a cult to deified ancestors) originated in Teotihuacan. She also notes that Teotihuacan was the first culture in Mesoamerica to develop a state cult from the earlier agricultural fertility cult. To this must be added the importance of aquatic sustenance from the nearby lake, to which many of the water symbols may refer.

Evidence of other deities is scanty, but among those believed to have existed in Teotihuacan are Huehueteotl, whose brazier, which was designed to be carried on the head, suggests he is a fire god, and an earth mother figure who may have been associated with water and vegetation. She is represented in the Tepantitla murals surrounded by fertility symbols such as plants, drops of water, seeds, and birds. Formerly she was thought to be a male water god, and in Aztec times she had a number of names, including Xochiquetzal ("precious flower"). A precursor of this goddess may be represented in some figurines whose headdresses bear flowers, usually the characteristic mark of Xochiquetzal. A majestic stone statue discovered near the Pyramid of the Moon may have water association, due to the "meanders" (water symbols) on her garments. The agricultural fertility cult was associated with gods of earth, water, rain, crops, sun, and moon. A large stone disk, with rays surrounding a skull head, seems to represent the sun. It was painted red, the color applied to bodies of the deceased; thus it may represent the setting sun that dies in the west. Deformed figures represented on the walls of the Atetelco suggest Nanahuatzin, the sick god of the Aztec tradition who became the sun, although these may not actually portray him. Another god portrayed is the feathered serpent, but there is no way of knowing if he is the same god the Aztec worshiped under the name Quetzalcoatl. There is also a "flayed god," represented in clay figurines and on pottery vessels. One statue depicts a flayed god (or his surrogate) wearing a human skin. This deity may be related to the later Xipe Totec, Aztec god of vegetation, although this large clay figure dates from the beginning of the Postclassic era.

There may also have been a "dual complex," a male-female creative force, such as existed later in Aztec cosmology. This could be inferred from the two major pyramids. Innumerable figurines with hollow interiors that in turn contain one or more miniature figures fully dressed may represent a creator deity. But the most convincing evidence indicates that the pantheon was built around forces of water and fertility.

Creation of the sun in Teotihuacan. Animals portrayed in a mural painting called the Mural of the Mythological Animals may be an early version of the myth of the four Suns, or eras, that form part of Aztec mythology (Millon, 1972, p. 7). Jaguars devouring fish, a type of *cipactli* (crocodilian) earth creature, and evidence of a cataclysm are seen in the Teotihuacan mural. The creation of the Fifth Sun in Teotihuacan (the Aztec mythical celestial plain), in which the poor deformed god Nanahuatzin threw himself into the fire to become the sun, constitutes one of the great Mesoamerican myths. This myth may have been invented *a posteriori* by the Aztec in order to explain the creation of their own era, the Fifth Sun, associated with the "place where the gods are made" (i.e., Teotihuacan) and with their sacred ancestors, the Teotihuacanos. The impact of Teotihuacan religion and myth on the Aztec is evident from the orientation of the sacred precinct in Tenochtitlan, the Aztec capital. This was based on the fact that, in the myth of the Fifth Sun, the gods in Teotihuacan, after the birth of the sun, faced the four directions to see where it would rise. Four gateways facing these directions were made in Tenochtitlan in memory of the myth. The desire of the Aztec to view Teotihuacan as the sacred ancestral place can be seen here and also in the fact that the Aztec sovereign worshiped there every twenty days.

Ritual. Ritual, as represented in many paintings, was clearly an important aspect of Teotihuacan religion. One example of such a representation is that of the priests, depicted in profile, who face the great central figure in the Tepantitla mural, and who evidently are carrying out a ceremony involving this earth-god figure. Men (as gods' surrogates) in ritual attitudes are also depicted on decorated pottery. The very layout of the major avenues and structures of the city brings to mind the probability of dramatic processions led by religious leaders, involving a large part of the population and possibly pilgrims. Processions would probably have stopped at the small altar-platforms in the center of the avenues, where rites would have been performed. Fray Diego Durán (1971, p. 296) writes about didactic yet amusing skits involving deities that were performed during the later Aztec religious festivals, which may provide us with parallels of earlier ritual celebrations. Colonial chronicles describe Aztec processions in which the costumes of the participants, the materials of which they were made, and their colors were all significant: yellow face paint symbolized maize; "popcorn" garlands represented the dry season. People walked, danced, and sang in the processions; the beat of the drum, the shrill sound of a native flute, and the rhythmic tone of chanted poetry set the pace for their steps. Large braziers may have been carried at the head of the procession, smoke from resin incense floating upward as a medium for communication with the gods. A ritual liquid such as *pulque* may have been poured on the ground. Hands pouring precious symbols in streams are depicted in Teotihuacan murals, representing this type of libation. Processions like these would have been public rituals to celebrate seasonal, calendrical, religious, political, and agricultural events. The changing of the seasons and their effect upon the crops, for example, called for constant celebration and/or propitiation of the gods.

Parallel with the public rituals would have been rites performed at small temples in residential compounds. Household worship probably occurred at times when major events took place but also in relation to the more private cycles of the household. People close to the soil practice innumerable ceremonies important to their well-being. In postclassic times rites were performed annually (as they still are today) to honor agricultural implements; permission is still ritually requested of the earth to break the surface in order to plant; clay figurines are buried in the fields as offerings; terracotta frogs or water-deity figures are thrown into waterholes; food and clay images are placed in caves for the "owners of maize" and plants. Evidence of some concern in Teotihuacan culture for human fertility is provided by figurines of pregnant women, which were most likely used in rites of fecundity.

The end of Teotihuacan and its heritage. The eclipse of Teotihuacan took place around 750 CE, when much of the city was burned, the destruction centering on religious and public buildings. Statues of the gods were broken and their faces mutilated (Jarquin and Martínez, 1982, p. 36). (In the pictorial manuscripts from Postclassic Mexico the conquest of a city is generally depicted by the burning of its temples.) Burning occurred mainly in the heart of Teotihuacan—four hundred instances of burning are evident in the Avenue of the Dead zone alone (Millon, 1981, pp. 236–237)—but to date there is no evidence of foreign invaders, such as non-Teotihuacan weapons or the like. The burning of temples and smashing of images implies ritual destruction, and René Millon points out that many religious structures in Mesoamerica were ritually burned and then reconstructed. The destruction of Teotihuacan's temples was so complete, however, that in spite of later building at the site, the city never again rose to even a portion of its former grandeur.

Meanwhile, other peoples had filtered into the valley, including the Toltec and the Chichimec. As Teotihuacan fell other centers rose. Sites in Tlaxcala expanded. Cacaxtla adopted many Teotihuacan motifs and possibly its cultural ideas as well. Xochicalco, a critical point on a trade route from the south, became powerful. El Tajín acquired more importance in the Gulf Coast region. Teotihuacan as a live metropolis disappeared, but its fame and influence lived on. South to the Maya region, east to the Gulf, west to the Pacific, and north to Alta-vista (near what would become the United States border), Teotihuacan religion, art, myth, and tradition spread and were adapted to other cultures. This great civilization and religious center took its place as the revered ancestor of many later cultures.

CHOLULA. About two hundred kilometers to the southeast, Cholula was a sister city to Teotihuacan during the Classic period; Quetzalcoatl was its principal god. According to archaeologist Eduardo Merlo, the earliest pyramid at Cholula (c. 150 BCE), was constructed over a sacred spring, paralleling the Teotihuacan tradition of building over a consecrated spot. The Mural of the Bebedores (Span., "drinkers"; c. 200 CE) in Cholula, at the west side of the great pyramid, portrays elaborate scenes of ritual drinking of *pulque.* This mural is dedicated to agricultural fertility and to *pulque* gods. The main Classic period deity here was the water goddess, and it is interesting that the patron saint of present-day Cholula, whose sanctuary is built on top of the great pyramid, is the Virgin of Los Remedios, whose special province is the control of the water supply (Olivera, 1970, pp. 212–213).

Cantona, in the Puebla-Tlaxcala Valley, was contemporary with early Cholula and Teotihuacan but was evidently eclipsed by the dramatic rise of the latter. Cantona must have been an important religious pilgrimage center and was possibly a Gulf Coast link with the central highlands. More than sixteen square kilometers in area, this site dates from the Late Preclassic into the Middle Classic and exhibits strong Veracruz influence, as seen in the ball-game cult, represented by sixteen courts. There are thousands of unexplored mounds, many dwellings, one excavated igloo-type sweat bath, and the unexplored remains of about twenty more of these structures. According to archaeologist Diana Lopez, these were used for ritual bathing.

MONTE ALBÁN AND OAXACA. The Valley of Oaxaca is an archaeologically rich area in the central part of the present state of Oaxaca in south-central Mexico. Ecological advantages, effectively exploited, contributed to the rise of urbanism here centuries earlier than in other nearby regions north and west of the valley (Paddock, 1966, p. 242). In this setting the splendid Zapotec civilization of Monte Albán arose. This city was built on five artificially leveled hills just east of today's city of Oaxaca and covered a total area of six and a half square kilometers. Monte Albán's main plaza, 150 by 300 meters, dominates the central hill, producing a whole that can be seen as the center and four corners of the universe. This central hill contains both religious and residential buildings: pyramid platforms, a main plaza and smaller ones, a ball court, the royal residence, and subterranean tombs whose entrances are protected by gods and whose interiors were filled with funerary urns in the form of gods. Richard Blanton (in Flannery and Marcus, 1983, p. 84) suggests that Monte Albán, constructed on a hilltop not easily accessible, yet near a rich alluvial plain, was the principal center of the region. Its hilltop location probably was in part a defensive measure against possible incursions, although many other important centers in Oaxaca also were built on mountaintops: for example, Monte Negro, Quiotepec, and Guiengola. There could also have been a religious motivation in this, in that the summits of mountains were often held to be sacred in ancient Mesoamerica and are dedicated to gods of rain.

Although Monte Albán has traditionally been seen as indebted to Teotihuacan for much of its religion, art, and ideas, Kent V. Flannery, Joyce Marcus, and John Paddock (Flannery and Marcus, 1983, p. 161) point out that the Zapotec autonomous tradition was thousands of years old when Monte Albán was built (c. 100 BCE) and that hieroglyphic writing was developed there before Teotihuacan was founded. Strong influence and exchange between the two centers did exist, however. There was an enclave of Oaxaca people in Teotihuacan, whose residents lived in their own zone, produced Oaxaca-style pottery, constructed a stone-lined Oaxaca tomb and stela, or tomb jamb, and who worshiped their own gods, if one may judge from two funerary urns representing a god with serpent buccal mask found in the tomb (Millon, 1973, I, pp. 141–142). Although no comparable Teotihuacano enclave has been found at Monte Albán, Teotihuacan personages are represented on some of the city's monuments. They carry copal incense bags (characteristic of priests) and wear identifying deity, animal, or "tassel" Teotihuacan headdresses. A Teotihuacan-style temple is also depicted. Marcus (Flannery and Marcus, 1983, p. 179) interprets these scenes as visual proof that Teotihuacan and Monte Albán had emissaries who consolidated agreements through rituals, thus placing these treaties in a sacred context.

Early history. Monte Albán has a long history, beginning about 500 BCE. Between 200 BCE and 100 CE (Monte Albán I–II) this center of ten thousand inhabitants constructed large defensive walls and masonry tombs. Three hundred carved stone monuments with calendrical and military themes have been found dating from this period, along with hieroglyphic writing and effigy vessels possibly representing gods (Marcus, in Flannery and Marcus, 1983, pp. 52–53, 95). The nude figures in distorted poses known as *danzantes* (Span., "dancers") were carved on stone slabs along with symbols of sacrifice. They represented captives and as such may refer to ritual death. They also may represent a symbolic display of power. Fear-inspiring propaganda of this type was repeated—in ritual, not sculpture—many centuries later by the Aztec, who invited their enemies to witness mass sacrifices of war captives. Toward the end of this early period there were highly developed traits such as a complex pantheon of deities, ceremonial architecture, a stratified society, increased population, and political, economic, and military influence outside the Valley of Oaxaca (Paddock, 1966, pp. 111–119). The plan of the Zapotec temple at this time, with an inner chamber reserved for members of the cult, points to the existence of full-time priests and an incipient state religion (Flannery, in Flannery and Marcus, 1983, p. 82).

Florescence of Monte Albán. Classic Monte Albán (Monte Albán III) covers the period from 100 to 600 CE. This was a period of florescence during which the population reached its maximum size and both the main plaza and neighboring hills became covered with monumental structures. Restricted entrance to the main plaza suggests that its use may have been mainly for religious and civil leaders, yet its size would indicate that on some occasions rites were celebrated involving the general populace, which Blanton (in Flannery and Marcus, 1983, pp. 131–133) estimates at approximately thirty thousand. The temples had full-time priests plus a high priest (Flannery, in Flannery and Marcus, 1983, pp. 132, 134). As in other Mesoamerican societies, the Zapotec ruler was given a year of religious training, and the priesthood was drawn from noble families. The ruler worshiped at a special shrine.

Tombs, funerary urns, and Zapotec gods. Typical of Monte Albán is the subterranean cruciform tomb, probably constructed during its future occupant's life and over which a temple or residential structure was built. Living quarters over these tombs indicate that the descendants of the deceased (probably usually rulers) practiced ancestor worship (Flannery and Marcus, 1983, pp. 135, 345). Personages represented in the murals of Tomb 104 and Tomb 105, described by Alfonso Caso as gods, evidently depict royal couples dressed in the garb of deities. As in Asia, the dead ruler or forefather had to be propitiated in order to protect the living. The people portrayed in these tombs, then, are the royal, deified ancestors of those buried here. The four rooms of the building over Tomb 105 are oriented to the four cardinal directions, indicating a cosmic plan in the building of Monte Albán. In a niche above the entrance to each tomb is a funerary urn. Within the tomb more urns appear. Urns have been found, too, as offerings in temples and caches. Most of the urns are anthropomorphic in form; many wear zoomorphic masks and headdresses and they are adorned with numerals and glyphs.

One type of urn, the *acompañante* (Span., "companion" or "attendant"), has been found either with the deceased or with the major urns themselves. There are two schools of thought regarding the funeral urns. Alfonso Caso and Ignacio Bernal (1952) define them as gods, while Joyce Marcus (in Flannery and Marcus, 1983, pp. 144–148) interprets them as deceased ancestors. Sixteenth-century chronicles associate calendric names with personages but not with gods. The Spanish at that time did not understand this reference to ancestors because they were unfamiliar with the system of naming forefathers with dates; therefore they often mistook figures of dead rulers for deities, and this confusion has persisted. Because they had no knowledge of Zapotec, Europeans often mistook titles of nobility or references to natural forces (such as *cocijo*, which means "lightning") for names of deities.

Caso and Bernal (1952), who believe them to be gods, identify the figures depicted on the funerary urns as follows: Cocijo, the rain god (who also has maize aspects, judging from the corn cobs in his headdress on some urns); Pitao Cozobi, god of maize and grains; other maize-sustenance deities such as 5 Flower Quiepelagayo and a god referred to as "with bow in the Headdress"; a Zapotec version of Quetzalcoatl; a flayed god (Xipe?), represented carrying a disembodied head; an old god associated with caves and the underworld; 13 Serpent, an earth mother; and animal deities such as the parrot (associated with the sun), the jaguar (associated with rain), and the bat and the *tlacuache* (opossum), both associated with maize.

Natural forces. Joyce Marcus (in Flannery and Marcus, 1983, pp. 345–351) stresses the importance in Zapotec religion of animism—the animate character of things such as trees, stars, hills, but especially powerful natural and supernatural forces. A vital force was *pèe* ("wind, breath, spirit") and this existed in man, animals, the 260-day ritual calendar, light, the sun, the moon, clouds, lightning, rain, fire, and earthquakes. *Pitào,* the augmentative form of *pèe,* means "great breath" or "great spirit," and refers to a sacred quality. Lightning, (*cocijo*) was a highly revered element among the Zapotec because it brought rain. According to Fray Juan de Córdova's *Arte del idioma zapoteca* (1578), the thirteen-day period in the pre-Hispanic calendar (13 numbers x 20 day names = 260 days constituting the ritual-divinatory calendar) was called *cocijo* or *pitào.* Thus the gods were identified with time periods and with phenomena associated with the calendar.

Clouds were held as sacred by the Zapotec. In fact, they considered themselves descended from clouds, just as the Mixtec regarded trees as their primordial ancestors. After death, the Zapotec believed, they once again became clouds. The Zapotec not only had an organized priesthood, temples, and elaborate ritual, but they also considered places such as caves, mountains, certain trees, springs, and other natural sites to be sacred shrines.

Other Oaxaca sites. Monte Albán was the major Zapotec civil and religious center, yet it was not the only sacred place in Oaxaca. Dainzú, a place distinguished by stone reliefs of masked ball players, was coeval with early Monte Albán. The ball players, some in jaguar disguise, are evidently engaged in a ritual game. A number of these carved slabs are set into the lowest level of a pyramid-temple structure. They are similar to Monte Albán's *danzantes*. Stones of the same type have turned up in many sites in the Oaxaca Valley, among them Macuilxochitl and Tlacochauaya. Other sites in the valley, of which there are many (Yagul, Caballito Blanco, Mitla, Loma Larga, Lambityeco) were contemporary in part with Monte Albán and shared the same religious beliefs and practices. Many of these were not occupied until after the Classic period and thus fall outside this discussion. But Oaxaca is rich in archeological zones, many dating from the Classic. In the Ñuiñe culture in the lower Mixtec region (northern Oaxaca and southern Puebla), the pantheon was similar to that of Monte Albán, containing gods of earth, rain, wind, death, fire, jaguar, and perhaps vegetation represented by flayed figures (Moser, in Flannery and Marcus, 1983, p. 212). San José Mogote was largely a Preclassic settlement, but in the Classic period (corresponding to Monte Alban II), there were numerous temples there and, as at Monte Albán, a court for the ritual ball game.

El Tajín and the Gulf Coast Region. About three hundred kilometers east of Teotihuacan lies the lush, humid Gulf of Mexico region, home of numerous archaeological sites. The most important of these is El Tajín, dating from around 100 BCE and continuing through the Classic period and into the early Postclassic. El Tajín continued to be occupied, by the Totonac, on a small scale for a few centuries after this. Although this rich region is called Totonacapan, the Totonac, for whom it was named, were a late group; the modern inhabitants are still Totonac. El Tajín was built by the Maya-related Huastec people. It may be that the baroque flavor in El Tajín art derives from a Maya heritage, but probably this reflects the natural environment with its lush vegetation. *Tajín* means "lightning," "hurricane," "thunder" and names these forces. Like the Zapotec, the Totonac believed that lightning brings rain, but near the Gulf of Mexico the rain often comes in the form of hurricanes, for this is a region of violent winds and precipitation. Thus, Tajín and the god Huracán are often seen as one, the god of tropical storms, who, like the Aztec god Tezcatlipoca, can be both beneficial and destructive.

Religion at El Tajín followed the typical Mesoamerican pattern of temple-pyramids, formal priesthood, a pantheon of gods, ritual calendar, pilgrimages to its center district, periodic festivities, sacrifice and bloodletting, and other traits already mentioned. But El Tajín and the Gulf Coast region exemplify certain distinct characteristics not found elsewhere. For example, the main pyramid at El Tajín is lavishly decorated with niches, which is typical of this site and of nearby Yohualichan ("house of night") in southern Puebla. The ball court, although common in Mesoamerica, occupies a primary importance in El Tajín, where there are ten (Wilkerson, 1980, p. 219). Their wall panels are decorated with spectacular scenes of ritual and sacrifice.

El Tajín became the major religious and administrative center of the region in the first few centuries of the current era. El Tajín's peak, in size, population, wealth, and religious importance, was between 600 and 900 CE, toward the end of the Classic period. This great city has been partially excavated by Mexico's Instituto Nacional de Antropologia e Historia. Its most spectacular building is the Pyramid of the Niches, dedicated to rain and wind gods, whose 365 niches are thought to be related to the solar calendar. Originally the pyramid's facade was painted in various colors, mainly red, the color of life and also of death. A *xicalcoliuhqui*, a fret in stone mosaic, decorates the balustrades on either side of the pyramid's stairway. The *xicalcoliuhqui*, popular in ancient Mexican sites, especially Mitla, but probably of Maya origin, may be symbolic of serpents of rain and wind. Originally, grotesque wind-rain serpents framed the panels of ritual scenes at the top of the temple.

The ball-game cult. Typical of the Gulf area is the *yugo-hacha-palma-candado* (Span., "yoke-ax-palm-padlock") complex, consisting of objects sculptured similar to these forms. The elements of this complex seem to form part of the ritual ball game. In the Maya zone, players are depicted wearing padded waist protectors formed like yokes, and figures are often seen wearing *palmas* in their belts. S. Jeffrey K. Wilkerson (1980, p. 219) states that at El Tajín the paraphernalia of the ball game became cult objects when carved in stone, and that stone copies of the wooden waist protectors, or yokes, were symbols of the jaws of the earth, into which the wearer descended after death. In El Tajín and probably all over Mesoamerica the ball game was a ritual act and concluded with one of the players, usually impersonating a god, being decapitated. Burials in the Veracruz region were frequently accompanied by elaborately carved stone yokes and other ball-game symbols. The ball-game cult started in the Preclassic, probably among the Olmec. The Gulf area was the home of rubber and the cult most likely originated here and then spread out to other regions, diffused by traders who took cacao and rubber (as well as their ideology) from the lowlands to the highlands. Both the cacao tree and ballplayers are represented in murals at Teotihuacan. In the Maya region, some Classic period ball-court markers were associated with symbols of the sun, water, and vegetation. The purpose of the sacrifice of a player at the end of the game, as seen on El Tajín reliefs, was the rejuvenation of agricultural and solar fertility, the cycle of death and rebirth in nature (Pasztory, 1978, p. 139). The stone reliefs at El Tajín portray ballplayers, rites to the rain god and to a deity of pulque, autosacrifice from genitals, decapitation of a ballplayer and his descent into the underworld, and sacrifice by extraction of the heart (Kampen, 1972).

Smiling figures and divine women. Among the ritual manifestations of the Classic period of the Gulf area are the "smiling figures" from Remojadas and El Zapotal, murals from Higueras, and lifesize terracotta sculptures of *cihuateteo* ("divine women"). El Zapotal, located in southern Veracruz near the Olmec site of Cerro de las Mesas, had its florescent period from 500 to 800 CE. Unlike the Zapotec and Mixtec, who had a cult to the dead, this Totonac culture apparently maintained a cult to death itself. In a major temple at El Zapotal there is an altar 1.6 meters high with a seated terracotta figure of the death god. His skeletal form is surrounded by skulls. Equally dramatic are the monumental clay figures called by the Postclassic term *cihuateteo.* Colonial chronicles identify the *cihuateteo* as women who died in childbirth and who then were deified, joining dead warriors in the task of helping the sun cross the sky. They were considered warriors because they lost their lives while taking a "prisoner," that is, the child. These striking figures wear skirts fastened by large serpent belts and carry trophy-head staffs in one hand. Each woman seems to be covered with a flayed skin, which might indicate a cult to a female vegetation deity (Gutiérrez Solana and Hamilton, 1977, p. 146). The presence of the serpent around the waist may refer, however, to a Serpent Woman who was, in Postclassic times, a goddess (the Aztec goddess Cihuacoatl) associated with war, sacrifice, and political power. Among the other deities represented in the monumental El Zapotal sculptures are male gods of rain, an old fire god—whose presence shows Teotihuacan influence—and a flayed god. Skeletal remains at this site, found in burials where offerings of terracotta sculptures were placed, reveal decapitation and dismemberment on a vast scale, probably as a result of sacrifice. Next to one rich offering of sculpture was an ossarium containing eighty-two skulls, many of them women's. The female skulls may indicate a death-fertility cult because, in a later period, sacrifice by decapitation represented the harvesting of first fruits, especially the cutting of an ear of corn. At El Zapotal, yokes, axes, and smiling figures have also been found, although the latter are more typical of Remojadas, a site north of El Zapotal noted for its splendid clay sculpture. The smiling figures are just that: their mouths are open in broad smiles, their legs are apart in an attitude of dancing, their arms flung wide. These have been interpreted as representations of a cognate of Xochipilli, the Aztec god of song and dance, but it is possible that they portray surrogates of the gods, drugged as they go to their sacrifice. The colonial chronicler Durán described the pre-Hispanic custom of giving these god-representatives drinks containing hallucinogens so they would laugh, dance, and fling out their arms on the way to the sacrificial knife. If they were not "happy" this was considered a bad omen.

Las Higueras is a late Classic Totonac site (600–800 CE), with outstanding mural paintings. Represented here are the ever-present Huracán, shown supine at the bottom of the sea, surrounded by sharks; water or "flood" gods, pouring liquid over the land; a female moon; the sun; and a crocodilian earth god. Priests with incense bags, a temple, and ball courts are also represented (Arellanos et al., 1975, pp. 309–312).

SEE ALSO Caves; Maya Religion.

BIBLIOGRAPHY

Alcina French, José. "Los dioses del pantéon zapoteca." *Anales de Antropología* (Mexico City) 9 (1972): 9–40.

Arellanos, Ramon, et al. "El proyecto de investigacion 'Higueras'." In *Sociedad Mexicana de Antropologia XIII mesa redonda.* Mexico City, 1975.

Aveni, Anthony F. *Skywatchers of Ancient Mexico.* Austin, Tex., 1980.

Caso, Alfonso, and Ignacio Bernal. *Urnas de Oaxaca.* Mexico City, 1952.

Cowgill, George L. "Rulership and the Ciudadela: Political Inferences from Teotihuacan Architecture." In *Civilization in the Ancient Americas: Essays in Honor of Gordon R. Willey,* edited by Richard M. Leventhal and Alan L. Kolata, pp. 313–344. Cambridge, Mass., 1983.

Durán, (Fray) Diego. *Los dioses y ritos* and *El calendario* (c. 1581). Translated as *Book of the Gods and Rites and The Ancient Calendar* by Fernando Horcasitas and Doris Heyden. Norman, Okla., 1971.

Flannery, Kent V., and Joyce Marcus, eds. *The Cloud People: Divergent Evolution of the Zapotec and Mixtec Civilizations.* New York, 1983.

Gutiérrez Solana, Nelly, and Susan K. Hamilton. *Las esculturas en terracotta de El Zapotel, Veracruz.* Mexico City, 1977.

Jarquín Pacheco, Ana María, and Enrique Martínez Vargas. "Exploración en el lado este de la Ciudadela." In *Memoria del proyecto arqueologico Teotihuacan 80–82,* edited by Rubén Cabrera Castro, Ignacio Rodríguez, and Noel Morelos, pp. 19–47. Mexico City, 1982.

Kampen, Michael Edwin. *The Sculptures of El Tajín, Veracruz, Mexico.* Gainesville, Fla., 1972.

Millon, Clara. "The History of Mural Art at Teotihuacan." In *Sociedad Mexicana de Antropologia XI mesa redonda: Teotihuacan,* pp. 1–16. Mexico City, 1972.

Millon, Clara. "Painting, Writing, and Polity in Teotihuacan, Mexico." *American Antiquity* 38 (1973): 294–314.

Millon, René, ed. *Urbanization at Teotihuacan, Mexico,* vol. 1, *The Teotihuacan Map.* Austin, Tex., 1973.

Millon, René. "Teotihuacan: City, State, and Civilization." In *Supplement to the Handbook of Middle American Indians,* vol. 1, *Archaeology,* edited by Jeremy A. Sabloff, pp. 198–243. Austin, Tex., 1981.

Olivera de Vazquez, Mercedes. "La importancia religiosa en Cholula." In *Proyecto Cholula,* edited by Ignacio Marquina, pp. 211–242. Mexico City, 1970.

Paddock, John. "Oaxaca in Ancient Mesoamerica." In *Ancient Oaxaca,* edited by John Paddock, pp. 83–242. Stanford, Calif., 1966.

Pasztory, Esther. "The Gods of Teotihuacan: A Synthetic Approach in Teotihuacan Iconography." In *Atti del XL Congresso Internazionale degli Americanisti,* vol. 1, pp. 108–142. Genoa, 1973.

Pasztory, Esther. "Artistic Traditions of the Middle Classic Period." In *Middle Classic Mesoamerica: A. D. 400–700,* edited by Esther Pasztory, pp. 108–142. New York, 1978.

Sanders, William T., Jeffrey R. Parsons, and Robert S. Santley. *The Basin of Mexico: The Ecological Processes in the Evolution of a Civilization.* New York, 1979.

Séjourné, Laurette. *Arquitectura y pintura en Teotihuacan.* Mexico City, 1966.

Wilkerson, S. Jeffrey K. "Man's Eighty Centuries in Veracruz." *National Geographic* 158 (1980): 203–231.

DORIS HEYDEN (1987)

MESOAMERICAN RELIGIONS: POSTCLASSIC CULTURES

This entry is devoted to a summary of the religious patterns of the leading peoples of that portion of the Mesoamerican area cotradition located west of the Isthmus of Tehuantepec in the Postclassic period (c. 900–1521 CE). Western Mesoamerica was a complex mosaic of linguistic-ethnic groups organized into various polities, but certain ones stand out most prominently: the Aztec, Tarascan, Otomí, Huastec, Totonac, Mixtec, and Zapotec. Although those who spoke the same language normally shared most cultural characteristics, including religious-ritual patterns, rarely were they unified politically. The more advanced groups were organized into what can be called city-states. Occasionally an especially powerful one of these, usually confederated with others, embarked on an imperialistic course, extending its military and political control over a wide area. The earliest well-documented empire of this type, one that may have dominated much of central Mexico, was that of the Toltec, so named from their capital, Tollan (or Tula), north of the Basin of Mexico. The flowering of the Toltec empire appears to have been essentially coterminous with the Early Postclassic period (c. 900–1200 CE). Coverage will begin with a concise review of what is known concerning Toltec religion.

TOLTEC RELIGION. At the time of the Conquest, many traditions were extant concerning the Toltec, the prestigious political and cultural predecessors of the Aztec. Whereas they emphasized dynastic themes primarily, they occasionally included some references to religious-ritual aspects. Together with the archaeological evidence, they provide a picture, however incomplete, of a rich religious tradition directly ancestral to that which prevailed in central Mexico at the time of the Conquest.

Many Aztec deities were anticipated in the Toltec pantheon. The most prominent was Quetzalcoatl, symbolized by a rattlesnake covered with feathers. In Aztec religious ideology this deity particularly expressed creativity and fertility, with emphasis on the vivifying and fructifying role of the wind (or breath), Ehécatl, which Quetzalcoatl bore as an additional appellation. The fusion of snake and bird in his icon can be interpreted as the creative coupling of earth and sky. The Toltec concept of Quetzalcoatl was probably similar, but the situation is complicated by the merging of the supernatural personage with a Toltec ruler, Topiltzin, apparently a particular devotee of the god, whose name he also carried as a title. A rich corpus of traditional narratives surrounded this remarkable figure, Topiltzin Quetzalcoatl, who was the archetype of the Toltec and Aztec priesthood and credited with introducing autosacrificial rituals into the cult. Topiltzin Quetzalcoatl was forced to abandon Tollan, persecuted by the omnipotent, capricious god of gods, Tezcatlipoca. Moving down to the Gulf Coast with a band of followers, Topiltzin Quetzalcoatl died and was cremated, and his soul ascended into heaven and became the Morning Star. He was considered to have been the founder of all "legitimate" political power in central Mexico, and the rulers of Mexico Tenochtitlán, the Aztec capital, claimed direct dynastic descent from him—with the expectation that he would some day return to reclaim his royal dignity.

Other Toltec deities mentioned in the traditions include the androgynous creative deity with various names, among them Ometecuhtli/Omecihuatl; Xipe Totec, who expressed the concept of fertility in a macabre fashion as his devotees ritually donned the skins of sacrificed human victims; Tlazolteotl-Ixcuina, a major earth and fertility goddess whose cult was reputedly introduced from the Huastec; and Tlaloc, the ancient, preeminent rain and fertility deity. Archaeological evidence confirms the importance of these supernaturals in the Toltec pantheon and indicates the presence of various others: the *pulque (octli)* gods, as well as Mayahuel, the female personification of the maguey plant, the source of the intoxicating beverage *pulque;* the Venus deity, Tlahuizcalpantecuhtli, closely related to Quetzalcoatl; the hunting and war deity, Mixcoatl; Itzpapalotl, another earth and fertility goddess allied to Mixcoatl; and, possibly, the old fire god, Xiuhtecuhtli-Huehueteotl. The Toltec pantheon probably included many other deities not mentioned in the traditions or evidenced by archaeological remains, and it is likely that at the time of the Conquest most were still propitiated in some form in central Mexico.

Toltec ceremonialism was probably similar to the overall system prevailing in the Late Postclassic, especially as regards the calendrically regulated ritual. It is virtually certain that the two basic Mesoamerican calendric cycles, the 260-day (13 x 20) divinatory cycle, called the *tonalpohualli* by the Aztec, and the 365-day (18 x 20 + 5) vague solar year *(xihuitl),* were well established by Toltec times and possibly much earlier. Most of the names employed for the twenty day-signs and apparently at least ten of the eighteen twenty-day periods, the "months," were the same as those used in the Aztec system. The major Toltec public ceremonies were undoubtedly geared to the eighteen months and followed the same basic ritual patterns as those current at the time of the invasion of Spanish forces under Hernán Cortés.

Archaeological evidence at Tula (ancient Tollan) and other Toltec-influenced sites, such as Chichén Itzá in Yucatán, demonstrates that Toltec religious architecture was essentially similar to that of the Late Postclassic. Basic continuities are manifest, especially in the forms of the temples and other sacred structures such as skull-racks (Nah., *tzompantli*) and small platform altars (Nah., *momoztli*). Certain specific Toltec traits, exemplified by *chacmools,* the reclining anthropomorphic images positioned in the vestibules of shrines, and reliefs of files of warriors decorating the faces of stone benches (banquettes) along the walls of rooms in structures adjoining the temples, were closely replicated in Aztec sacred architecture, most notably in the Templo Mayor precinct of the imperial capital, Mexico-Tenochtitlán.

After a series of disasters, the Toltec hegemony collapsed, probably in the late twelfth or during the thirteenth century, and barbarous newcomers, collectively known as the Chichimec, flowed in from the north. In the mid-fourteenth century a powerful new Basin of Mexico city-state, Azcapotzalco, arose. Under a remarkably vigorous ruler, Tezozomoc, the Tepanec, as the people of Azcapotzalco were called, established a central Mexican imperial system on the Toltec model. However, it did not long survive the death of Tezozomoc in 1426, and by 1434 the final pre-Hispanic political order emerged in central Mexico. This was headed by two former tributaries of Azcapotzalco, Mexico-Tenochtitlan and Tezcoco, joined, as a junior partner, by Tlacopan, an erstwhile ally of, and of the same Tepanec affiliation as, Azcapotzalco. This so-called Triple Alliance generated great military power and by the time of the Conquest dominated much of western Mesoamerica. Most of the leading ethnic-linguistic groups within this area had fallen completely or partially under its sway. The Tarascan of Michoacán, however, successfully maintained their independence and ruled a sizable empire of their own in western Mexico. Most of the Huastec-speaking communities, in the northeastern sector of Mesoamerica, also remained beyond Triple Alliance control.

AZTEC RELIGION. The following summary applies primarily to the Nahuatl-speaking communities of the Basin of Mexico and adjoining territory, whose culture is traditionally labeled "Aztec," although fundamentally similar religious systems prevailed over a much more extensive area. Following this overview of the Aztec religious-ritual system, what is known concerning the religions of the major non-Nahuatl-speaking groups will be summarized, emphasizing aspects that appear to have been especially distinctive to each particular group.

Cosmogony and cosmology. Four great cosmic eras, or "suns," were believed to have preceded the present age. The inhabitants of each era were destroyed at that era's end—with the exception of single pairs that survived to perpetuate the species—by different kinds of cataclysmic destructions: respectively, swarms of ferocious jaguars, hurricanes, rains of fire, and a devastating deluge. The first era was assigned to the earth, the second to the air or wind, the third to fire, and the fourth to water. Different deities presided over each, and each age was also ascribed to one of the four cardinal directions and to its symbolic color. The last era, the Fifth Sun, was to be terminated, with the annihilation of humanity, by shattering earthquakes.

At the commencement of this final period, two major creative deities, Tezcatlipoca and Quetzalcoatl, dispersed the waters of the great flood and raised the sky, thus creating a new earth. Fire was next produced, followed by a fresh human generation. Quetzalcoatl traveled to the underworld, Mictlan, to obtain from its ruler, Mictlantecuhtli, the bones and ashes of previous human beings. With them the assembled gods created the primeval human pair, for whom they also provided sustenance (above all, maize). A new sun and moon were next created by the cremation in a great hearth at Teotihuacán of two gods, one a diseased but courageous pauper and the other wealthy but cowardly, who were thereby transformed into, respectively, the orbs of day and night. The gods then sacrificed themselves to provide food and drink (hearts and blood) for the rising sun. But the sun's terrible sustenance had to be supplied constantly to satisfy his insatiable appetite and unquenchable thirst. War, for the purpose of obtaining victims for sacrifice, was therefore instituted—and this perpetual obligation was laid on humankind.

The earth was conceived by the Aztec in a schematized geographic fashion and mystically and metaphorically as well. In the first conception the earth was visualized as a quadrilateral landmass surrounded by ocean. From its center four quadrants extended out to the varicolored cardinal directions, which, with the center, played a very important cosmological role as a basic principle of organization of numerous supernaturalistic concepts. At each direction stood a sacred tree upon which perched a sacred bird. In the fashion of Atlanteans, four deities supported the lowest heaven at each cardinal point. In the second terrestrial image, the earth was conceived both as a huge crocodilian monster, the *cipactli,* and as a gigantic, crouching, toadlike creature with snapping "mouths" at its elbows and knees and a gaping, teeth-studded mouth, called Tlaltecuhtli, which devoured the hearts and blood of sacrificed victims and the souls of the dead in general. Both creatures were apparently conceived as floating on the all-encompassing universal sea.

There was also a comparable vertical organization of the universe. The heavens were conceived as a series of superposed varicolored tiers to which various deities and certain natural phenomena were assigned. The commonest scheme featured thirteen celestial layers and nine subterrestrial levels.

Gods. A crowded pantheon of individualized, essentially anthropomorphic deities was believed to control the various spheres of the universe. Almost every major natural and human activity was embodied in at least one supernatural personality. This plethora of deities was organized around a few fundamental cult themes. Within each theme can be discerned "deity complexes," clusters of deities expressing various aspects of what amount to subthemes. Three major themes stand out: (1) celestial creativity and divine paternalism; (2) rain-moisture-agricultural fertility; (3) war, sacrifice, and the sanguinary nourishment of the sun and earth. Included within the first theme were such important deities as Ometeotl (Ometecuhtli/Omecihuatl or Tonacatecuhtli/Tonacacihuatl), the androgynous creative deity; Tezcatlipoca, the omnipotent "supreme god"; and Xiuhtecuhtli Huehueteotl, the old god of fire. Prominent within the second theme were Tlaloc, the paramount fertility deity and producer of rain; Ehécatl Quetzalcoatl, the wind god; Centeotl Chicomecoatl, the maize deity (with both male and female aspects); the *octli (pulque)* deity, Ometochtli, who had many individualized avatars, each with its own name; Teteoinnan Tlazolteotl, the earth mother, with many aspects; and Xipe Totec, the gruesome "flayed god." The third theme featured Tonatiuh, the solar deity; Huitzilopochtli, the special patron of Mexico Tenochtitlán, who had strong martial associations; Mixcoatl Camaxtli, the Chichimec hunting and war god; Tlahuizcalpantecuhtli, the god of the planet Venus; and Mictlantecuhtli, the death god. Many minor deities presided over various crafts and occupations, the most important of which was Yacatecuhtli, the merchant deity. A major, protean god who defies neat categorization was Quetzalcoatl, whose creative function especially stands out and, as indicated, with whom a semilegendary Toltec ruler was inextricably entwined.

Ritual. The ritual system was intricate, variegated, and often highly theatrical. Some of the Spanish missionary ethnographers, influenced by Christian ceremonialism, divided the public, calendrically regulated rituals into those that were "fixed" (geared to the *xi-huitl,* the 365-day vague solar year) and those that were "movable" (geared to the *tonalpohualli,* the 260-day divinatory cycle). The eighteen "fixed" ceremonies, which were normally celebrated at the end of each "month," or twenty-day period, together constituted the most important series of rituals in the whole system, closely linked to the annual agricultural cycle. Many were primarily concerned with fertility promotion and involved the propitiation of deities that most explicitly expressed this theme. The "movable" *tonalpohualli*-geared ceremonies were generally more modest in scope, but some were quite impressive, especially that which occurred on the day 4 Ollin dedicated to the Sun, which featured a strict fast and ritual bloodletting by the whole community. The sacrifice of war captives and condemned slaves and ritual cannibalism often, but not invariably, accompanied these major ceremonies. There were numerous other significant ritual occasions: key events in the life cycle of the individual, dedications of new structures and monuments, before and after battles, triumphs, investitures (especially royal coronations), and the like. There was also considerable daily domestic ritualism, centered on the hearth fire and the household oratory. Many ceremonies were also conducted in the fields by the cultivators.

The profession of the full-time, specialized priest, *teopixqui* ("keeper of the god"), was highly important. Practitioners were numerous and well-organized, with formal, hierarchic ranking. Much sacerdotal duty also devolved on "rotational priests" who served successive shifts for particular periods of time. Priests usually lived together, practicing sexual abstinence, in a monastic establishment *(calmecac)* in the temple compound. They were obligated to perform a rigorous daily round of offertory, sacrificial, and penitential exercises. Religious activities were focused on the temple *(teocalli)* and the sacred precinct, usually walled, within which it was situated. These precincts also contained the priestly dormitories and schools, sacred pools for purificatory bathing, skull racks, platform altars, courts for the ritual ball game, giant braziers for perpetual fires, gardens and artificial forests, arsenals, and so on. The typical *teocalli* consisted of a solid, staged substructure with a balustraded stairway on one side. At the top was the shrine containing the image—of stone, wood, or clay—of the deity to whom the temple was dedicated. The space between the door of the shrine and the head of the stairs was the usual position for the sacrificial stone.

As indicated, the calendric cycles were intimately interconnected with the ritual system. The most basic cycle, the *tonalpohualli,* a permutation cycle of twenty days and thirteen numbers (totaling 260 days), was employed largely for divinatory purposes. Each day, which possessed an inherent favorable or unfavorable augury, was patronized by deities in two series, one of thirteen ("lords of the day") and one of nine ("lords of the night"), plus the thirteen "sacred birds." The days were also grouped into various divisions; the most common arrangement consisted of twenty periods of thirteen-day "weeks," each of which was patronized, as a unit, by a deity or deity pair. These complex batteries of influences, for good or evil, were carefully taken into account by the diviners *(tonalpouhque),* particularly when "casting the horoscope" of the newborn child on the basis of the day of his or her birth.

No sharp division existed between the religious-ritual system that served the community as a whole and that was administered by the formally organized, professional priesthood and the more private system dominated by procedures usually defined as magical and practiced by "magicians" and diviners or, as anthropologists usually prefer to call them, shamans. Aztec shamanism was richly developed. Often neglected in general treatments of Aztec religion, its importance deserves special emphasis.

The most generic term for shaman was *nahualli,* also applied to his "disguise," usually a kind of animal familiar into which he could transform himself. The power of the *nahualli* could be used for beneficial or harmful ends. The malevolent practitioner employed a variety of techniques to inflict harm on his victim, including the application of sympathetic magic to destroy the victim by burning his effigy. One of the most important activities of the benevolent shaman was divination. Aside from calendric divination, mentioned above, various techniques were employed: scattering maize kernels and beans, knotting and unknotting cords, scrying by peering into a liquid or an obsidian mirror, and so on. Divining by ingesting various hallucinogens was also practiced. Divination to ascertain the cause of disease was important in curing, which usually involved magical procedures, although many genuinely efficacious empirical therapeutic techniques were also employed. Both the intrusive-harmful-object and soul-loss concepts of illness were recognized.

Various illusionistic tricks were performed on occasion, such as animating wood images, burning structures without actually damaging them, and the shaman's dismembering himself, also without inflicting real harm. Interpreting omens, auguries, and dreams was another important function of the *nanahualtin,* who were frequently consulted at times of crisis. A famous example occurred after the arrival of Cortés, when a bewildered Motecuhzoma Xocoyotzin (Moctezuma II), the ruler of Mexico Tenochtitlan, turned to the diviners in desperation in an unsuccessful attempt to understand the implications of the sudden appearance of these strange newcomers on the shore of his empire.

The Spanish missionaries were generally successful in eliminating the established native priesthoods, but the individualistic practitioners of magic managed to carry on their activities with little interference. Their repertoire was actually enriched by their adoption of various congenial European magical practices. In the less-acculturated Mexican Indian communities of today, the basically indigenous shamanistic tradition still thrives.

TARASCAN RELIGION. The Tarascan-speakers, the Purepecha, centered in the modern state of Michoacán in the area around Lake Pátzcuaro, were a numerous and vigorous people who, contemporaneously with the rise of the Triple Alliance empire in central Mexico, built up a smaller but still sizable dominion in western Mexico that effectively blocked Aztec expansion in that direction. Pre-Hispanic western Mexico shared most fundamental Mesoamerican culture patterns but often expressed them in a distinctive fashion. The Tarascan religious-ritual system, which is only incompletely known, was typical in this respect. Compared to that of the Aztec, it appears to have been somewhat less elaborated, with a smaller pantheon and a simpler ceremonialism.

The most important deity seems to have been Curicaueri, the special patron of the Tarascan royal house. Curicaueri was connected with fire, the sun, and warfare, and he was symbolized by the eagle and a flint sacrificial knife. The Tarascan ruler was apparently considered to be his incarnation. Urendecuaucara, the god of the planet Venus, was also of some importance. Other significant members of the pantheon included a deity of *pulque,* a god related to the Aztec Xipe Totec, and a death god, in addition to numerous lesser deities, among them various local patrons. Two goddesses stand out: Xaratanga, an important fertility deity linked with Curicaueri, and Cuerauaperi, the old earth-mother goddess, seemingly cognate with the Aztec Teteoinnan Tlazolteotl (flaying and skin-wearing rituals were common to both cults).

The Tarascan priesthood was well organized, with a hierarchy of various specialists headed by an influential high priest. Like Aztec priests, the Tarascan priests wore badges of office and carried gourd vessels for tobacco pellets, but unlike Aztec priests they were not celibate. Shamanism was also well developed, and divination by scrying (peering into a liquid surface or a mirror) was of special importance. Tarascan temples *(yacatas),* consisting of straw-roofed shrines atop massive, partly circular, staged substructures, were sometimes large and elaborate (e.g., the five major temples at Tzintzuntzan, the imperial capital). Sacred images of both wood and stone (and often portable) represented the major deities.

The ceremonial system featured fire rituals. In each temple was a perpetual fire, and even the ruler was obligated to cut and collect wood for these sacred fires. The principal ceremonies, during which the most prominent deities were propitiated, were geared to the standard Mesoamerican annual calendar (18 x 20 + 5 = 365). The basic ritual patterns appear to have been quite similar to those of other Mesoamerican groups, featuring abundant offerings, human and animal sacrifices, and dancing.

OTOMÍ RELIGION. After the dominant Nahuatl-speakers, the Otomí constituted the most important group in central Mexico. Their center of gravity lay northwest of the Basin of Mexico, but they were also numerous, interdigitated with the Nahuatl-speakers, in the Basin itself. While Otomí were much deprecated, and considered backward rustics by Nahuatl-speakers, there actually seems to have been no sharp cultural division between the two groups. Their religious-ritual systems were quite similar, although that of the Otomí did exhibit some distinctive features. They clearly shared most of the leading deities of the pantheons of their Nahuatl-speaking neighbors.

A particularly important Otomí cult revolved around a fire-death god who bore various names—Otontecuhtli ("lord of the Otomí"), Xocotl, and Cuecuex—and who was merged with Xiuhtecuhtli Huehueteotl, the standard fire god of the Nahuatl-speakers. He was especially important in the cult of the Tepanec, who from their capital at Azcapotzalco had dominated a large area of central Mexico before the rise of the Triple Alliance. Indeed, Otontecuhtli was considered to have been the divine ancestor of the Tepanec, among whom the Otomian ethnic element was very strong. His particular annual ceremony featured various rituals surrounding the erection of a tall pine pole at the top of which was affixed a special, mortuary version of the god's image formed of amaranth seed dough. Boys scrambled up this pole on ropes, competing to be first in grabbing the image. Both the Otomí- and Nahuatl-speakers called this ceremony the Great Feast of the Dead. It was also designated Xocotlhuetzi ("Xocotl falls") by the Nahuatl-speakers, who had widely adopted it. An integral part of this ceremony was the sacrifice of a victim who was first roasted on glowing coals, then dispatched by the usual heart extraction method.

One source ascribes even greater importance among the Otomí to another deity named Yocippa. He can apparently be identified with Mixcoatl-Camaxtli of the Nahuatl-speakers, who was especially associated with the more nomadic, hunting lifestyle of the Chichimec, with whom some of the less sedentary Otomí were connected. His special annual feast probably can be equated with Quecholli, dedicated by the Aztec to Mixcoatl Camaxtli, which involved camping out in the fields and hunting and sacrificing deer and other game animals Chichimec-style. In the cult of the major Otomí center of Xaltocan in the northern Basin of Mexico, during the fourteenth century a significant imperial capital in its own right before its conquest by Azcapotzalco, a lunar goddess was preeminent. Lunar deities also appear to have been important in the northeast Otomí-speaking region.

The overall Otomí ritual system was essentially similar to that of the Nahuatl-speakers. It also featured human and animal sacrifice, autosacrifice, incensing with copal and rubber, vigils, fasts, dancing, processions, chanting, and so on. Their calendric systems, including both the 260- and 365-day cycles, were also basically the same.

HUASTEC RELIGION. The Huastec occupied the northeast corner of Mesoamerica, mainly in northern Veracruz, southern Tamaulipas, and eastern San Luis Potosí. They spoke a language of the Mayan family, although their territory was separated from that of the other Mayan-speakers by a considerable distance. The Huastec were regarded by the Aztec as possessing numerous exotic traits: head deformation, filed teeth, tattooing, exaggerated nasal septum perforation for insertion of ornaments, yellow and red hair dying, no loincloths worn by males, tendency to drunkenness and general lewdness, and a reputation as great sorcerers, especially illusionists. Nahuatl-speakers had encroached on their territory, and some of their southernmost communities had been subjected to Triple Alliance imperial control. Most, however, were still independent—and often in conflict with each other—at the time of the Conquest.

Huastec religion is not well documented, but it appears to have been as richly developed as most Mesoamerican systems. The pantheon must be largely reconstructed from Aztec sources that refer to various deities associated with the Huasteca and that were represented wearing Huastec costume and ornamentation. The clearest example is Tlazolteotl Ixcuina, a licentious earth-fertility goddess, who was regularly portrayed with costume elements and insignia of Huastec type. It has been suggested that her alternate name, *Ixcuina,* may actually be a Huastec word meaning "lady of the cotton," a substance with which Tlazolteotl was intimately associated and that flourished in the hot, humid lowlands of the Huasteca. Flaying rituals were important in her cult, and these also seem to have been an element in the Huastec ceremonial complex (possibly also reflecting the presence of a version of Xipe Totec).

Another important deity with strong Huasteca connections, both iconographically and in tradition, was the wind and fertility deity, Ehécatl Quetzalcoatl. The numerous *pulque* deities, with the common calendric name *Ome Tochtli (2 Rabbit),* were more connected in Aztec sources with the area south of the Basin of Mexico, centered on Morelos. But in the Codex Borgia group of ritual-divinatory pictorials, which probably originated in southern Puebla, western Oaxaca, or Veracruz, these deities typically display Huastec insignia. The alcoholic tendency attributed to the Huastec would support this connection. It is further evidenced by the survival in modern Huastec communities of the ancient deity of earth and thunder, Mam, also considered to be the god of drunkenness. Another Aztec deity, Mixcoatl, usually ascribed to the Chichimec, the barbaric hunting peoples of the north, was also frequently depicted with patently Huastec features. Some version of this god, therefore, probably also figured in the Huastec pantheon.

Archaeological remains from the Huasteca, including engraved shell ornaments, stone images and reliefs, and wall paintings, evidence the presence of other deities, including a death god, whose identifications often remain obscure. Archaeological evidence also indicates that Huastec temples were often circular in form, both the staged substructures and the shrines on top of them. These have sometimes been connected with round temples dedicated to Ehécatl Quetzalcoatl, whose Huastec iconographic affiliations I have mentioned above.

The Huastec ritual system is barely known, but human sacrifice and autosacrifice are well attested both ethnohistorically and archaeologically. The modern survival of the Volador, or Flying Pole ceremony, indicates its ancient importance. There is also archaeological evidence for the existence of the 260-day divinatory cycle, while one colonial source lists a few apparent Huastec names for the eighteen twenty-day periods of the 365-day annual cycle. It seems likely, therefore, that, as elsewhere in Mesoamerica, the major Huastec ceremonies were geared to these cycles, but no further data are available.

TOTONAC RELIGION. The speakers of Totonac, a language unrelated to Nahuatl but perhaps remotely related to the Mixe-Zoquean and Mayan linguistic families centered farther to the east, occupied the lowland tropical area of central Veracruz, extending into the high mountains edging the Mesa Central to the west. At the time of the Conquest their principal community was Zempoala (Cempoallan) near the coast, the first large Mesoamerican urban center visited by the Europeans, a few days after Cortés's landing farther south near the present city of Veracruz. Zempoala and most of the other Totonac-speaking towns had been conquered by the Triple Alliance some years earlier. Totonac culture patterns were basically Mesoamerican, reflecting strong influence from their Nahuatl-speaking neighbors and conquerors, but the Totonac also exhibited various distinctive features, some of which they shared with their northern Gulf Coast neighbors, the Huastec.

The rather thin amount of knowledge of pre-Hispanic Totonac religion derives from the incompletely known archaeology of the area and, especially, from a lost account, apparently written by the young page reportedly left at Zempoala by Cortés in August 1519 to learn Totonac. Preserved in part in three later missionary chronicles, this source describes a Totonac trinity of deities: the Sun, Chichini; his wife, the great mother-fertility goddess; and their son, who was expected to return at some future time as a kind of redeemer. The goddess might have been a version of Tlazolteotl-Ixcuina, known to have been important in the cults of the Gulf Coast groups, perhaps merged with the maize goddess. The son might be identified with the youthful male maize deity called Centeotl by the Nahuatl-speakers. Some Christian influence here seems obvious, but the basic nature of these deities might have been accurately reported with the possible exception of the redeemer aspect of the son. From archaeological evidence, principally at Zempoala, the cults of other deities are discernible, including those of Ehécatl Quetzalcoatl and Xochipilli Macuilxochitl. The latter, the Aztec young god of flowers, dancing, music, and sensuality in general, also had solar associations and overlapped with Centeotl. Undoubtedly the Totonac pantheon was much more extensive than this, but more specific information is lacking.

The early Spanish account mentioned provides some interesting information on the Totonac priesthood. A hierarchy of six major priests is described whose attire and functions were essentially similar to those of Aztec priests. Lesser religious functionaries assisted them, particularly in tending the sacred fires. The priests also instructed children between the ages of six and nine in the tenets of the religious-ritual system. The importance of two elderly penitent "monks," dedicated to the cult of the "great goddess," is stressed. Consulted regularly by the other priests as oracles, they lived in a retreat on a mountaintop, spending most of their time painting ritual books.

The same source describes various aspects of Totonac ritual, including incensing, fasting, circumcision, human sacrifice, autosacrifice involving the passing of straws through a perforation in the tongue, ritual cannibalism, confession of sins to a priest, and child sacrifice followed by the ingestion, "like the sacrament of communion," of a concoction of rubber and seeds mixed with the young victims' blood. The Totonac calendar appears to have been typically Mesoamerican. Although the key early account speaks of only three major ceremonies annually, all of which featured human sacrifice on a limited scale and ritual cannibalism, there is evidence that the usual round of eighteen principal ceremonies was celebrated at twenty-day intervals. The importance of the Volador ceremony is known from modern survivals. Archaeological evidence, especially at the site of Zempoala, demonstrates that Totonac temples were basically similar to those of the Aztec. The sacred images they contained seem to have usually been carved of wood. No specimens survive.

Mixtec Religion. The speakers of Mixtec, a language remotely related to Otomí and closely allied to Zapotec, occupied an extensive region centered in western Oaxaca. Generally characterized by a very broken topography, the Mixteca featured numerous small city-states, politically autonomous but closely linked by an intricate network of dynastic marital alliances, a basically common language, and a shared religious ideology. Although it has recently been claimed by some scholars that the Mixtec religious-ritual system might have been quite different from that which prevailed in central Mexico, it appears to have been similar in most fundamental features. The influence of the adjacent Nahuatl-speakers to the north was very strong in late pre-Hispanic times, and most of the Mixtec city-states were tributary to the Triple Alliance at the time of the Conquest.

No systematic account of pre-Hispanic Mixtec religion is available, but its basic outlines can be reconstructed from a variety of sources. Among these are an unusual wealth of pictorial histories that include much material relevant to the Mixtec pantheon, ritual system, cosmogony, and cosmology. What is known of Mixtec versions of their beginnings indicates that cosmogonical concepts were intertwined with dynastic origins and ritualized community foundations throughout the four quarters of the Mixteca. A "celestial prologue" to Mixtec royal history involved the creation by a primordial demiurge male-female pair (probably corresponding to the Aztec Ometecuhtli/Omecihuatl) of a culture hero, apparently also conceived in twin form, who iconographically and functionally closely resembles Ehécatl Quetzalcoatl of the Nahuatl-speakers. Descending from the celestial realm, he presided over dynastic and community initiations and consecrations and was apparently considered to have been the divine ancestor of Mixtec royalty. Other dynastic ancestors were believed to have emerged from a cosmic tree near the northern Mixtec community of Yutatnoho/Apohuallan (Apoala).

These semidivine ancestral heroes, as in the Nahuatl-speaking world, interacted closely with various deities, and no sharp line can be drawn between gods and men at this stage. Although it has been suggested that the central Mexican concept of deity, *teotl*, does not conform to its putative Mixtec equivalent, *ñuhu*, the two concepts were probably not dissimilar. In any case, the pictorial iconography of Mixtec supernaturalism was quite close to that of central Mexico. Costume elements and insignia of personages often bear striking resemblance to those of recognized Aztec deities. Each major Mixtec community appears to have had a special patron deity or deities, and the names (mostly calendric) of many of these are known. More than in any other Mesoamerican pantheonic system, the Mixtec supernaturals were designated, both in the texts and pictorially, by their calendric names. Only in part do they agree with their central Mexican counterparts. A number of their verbal names are also known, such as *Dzahui*, name of the basic rain and fertility deity, cognate with the Aztec Tlaloc.

Mixtec ceremonialism was richly developed, particularly that revolving around "sacred bundles." Human sacrifice and autosacrifice were a regular part of propitiatory ritual. Here too the Volador ceremony was important, as was the ceremonial ball game played in formal I-shaped courts. The widespread cult of Xipe Totec, featuring flaying rituals, was well established in the Mixteca, including its attendant ceremony, the "gladiatorial sacrifice," wherein the victim perished in ceremonial combat. As elsewhere, much of the ritual was calendrically regulated. Mixtec temples were often represented in the pictorials and were very similar to those of central Mexico. The holiest shrine of all, the Mixteca—seat of a far-famed oracle—was located on a mountain top near Ñuudeco/Achiotlan in the heart of the Mixteca Alta—with a subsidiary shrine in a cave in the valley of Yodzocahi/Yanhuitlan to the north.

The Mixtec priesthood was well organized and influential. Candidates were ordinarily recruited when quite young from the ranks of the nobility and underwent a rigorous training for at least a full year as novices. All future rulers received this same sacerdotal education, also being required to serve their yearlong novitiate. Following their training, most future priests apparently returned to secular life and married until called to their term of office, during which they usually served a particular deity and were required to be strictly celibate. Maintained by the rulers and constantly consulted by them, in control of all "higher education," they exerted great power in their communities. Shamanism was also well developed. Mixtec practitioners of magic and sorcery particularly specialized in calendric divination but also employed many other techniques, sometimes aided by ingestion of hallucinogens.

ZAPOTEC RELIGION. The Zapotec-speakers occupied an area of considerable ecological diversity in the eastern portion of Oaxaca. Like the Mixtec, who were close cultural and linguistic relatives, the Zapotec were not politically unified. In the Valley of Oaxaca, Zaachila/Teozapotlan dominated a wide area, and its political offshoot, Daniguibedji/Tehuantepec controlled much of the southern Isthmus of Tehuantepec. At the time of the Conquest most of the major Zapotec communities were tributary to the Triple Alliance.

The Zapotec heritage was an ancient one. Most students believe that the great Classic period (c. 100–700 CE) civilization of Monte Albán was mainly the creation of Zapotec-speakers. By the time of the Conquest, Zapotec supernaturalism was typically Mesoamerican in its richness and complexity. As in the case of the Mixtec, it has recently been suggested that the Zapotec lacked the concept of individualized anthropomorphic deities. It seems likely, however, that Zapotec religious concepts were not that different from those of other advanced Mesoamerican cultures. A large number of Zapotec names for what the Spaniards, at least, regarded as *dioses* (Span., "gods") were recorded in various colonial textual sources. Some appear to have been appellations and general designations of godhead rather than proper names in the usual sense.

A typically Mesoamerican abstract, creative godhead was of considerable importance, known by various appellations: Coquixee, or Coquixilla ("lord of the beginning"), Piyetao ("great spirit"), and others, described in 1578 by Fray Juan de Córdova as the "god without end and without beginning, so they called him without knowing whom," and "god of whom they said that he was the creator of all things and was himself uncreated." Overlapping this deity was Pitao Cozaana (procreator) with an apparent female counterpart, Pitao Huichana (procreatrix). This Zapotec creative power was obviously cognate with a similar concept among the Nahuatl-speakers, known, among other titles and appellations, as Tloque Nahuaque ("master of the near and the adjacent"), Ipalnemoani ("he through whom one lives"), and Ometeotl ("dual deity").

The fertility theme, as usual, received special emphasis and was expressed by various supernatural personalities. Standing out was Cocijo ("lightning"), the fundamental male fertility and rain deity, cognate with the Aztec Tlaloc and the Mixtec Dzahui, along with Pitao Cozobi, a deity of maize and foodstuffs in general, cognate with the Aztec Centeotl. Pitao Xicala (Pecala), "god of desire and dreams," would also seem to fit in this category; he has been equated with the Aztec Xochipilli-Macuilxochitl.

Apparently a widely venerated deity, sometimes even stated to have been the principal Zapotec god, was Pitao Pezelao, lord of death and the underworld. This deity was especially connected with the greatest of the Zapotec oracular shrines, Liobaa/Mictlan (Mitla), which provided a ritual focal point for the Zapotec communities in and adjacent to the Valley of Oaxaca. This god was also closely connected with the veneration of royal ancestors, whose tombs were prominently featured at Liobaa. The macabre Aztec "flayed god," Xipe Totec, whose cult was virtually pan-Mesoamerican but was especially connected with the Oaxaca-Guerrero area, clearly played a role of some importance in Zapotec religion, although the local sources provide scant information. Many more names of ostensible Zapotec deities are extant, but their importance and precise functions are obscure. As was common throughout Mesoamerica, each community featured a special supernatural patron or patrons, including, at times, deified ancestors. These were sometimes important, widely venerated deities; in other cases their cults were apparently only local. As in the Mixteca, they were often designated by calendric names.

Zapotec ceremonialism seems to have displayed virtually all known major Mesoamerican ritual patterns, including human sacrifice and its attendant ritual cannibalism. Oracular sanctuaries, often in caves, were important. In addition to that at Liobaa, one famous cave was situated on an island called in colonial times Laguna de San Dionisio, east of Daniguibedji/Tehuantepec, the capital of the Isthmus Zapotec. Here the deity venerated as "the soul and heart of the kingdom" appears to have been an earth god, perhaps known as Pitao Xoo, and related to Tepeyolotl of the Nahuatl-speakers. The professional priesthood played an influential role in Zapotec society; it was headed by a high priest, *uijatao* ("great seer"), assisted by lesser functionaries: *copa pitao* ("guardians of the deities"), *ueza eche* ("sacrificers"), and *pizana* (or *vigaña*, "young or student priests"). Shamanistic diviners called *colanij* were also important, particularly in calendric divination. As elsewhere, much of Zapotec ritual was calendrically regulated, particularly the vital pancommunity fertility-promoting ceremonies geared to the annual agricultural cycle.

CONCLUDING REMARKS. This capsule survey of the religious-ritual systems of the major western Mesoamerican groups in the Postclassic period reveals that they all displayed numerous fundamental ideological and ceremonial similarities in spite of expectable regional differences in gods' names and ritual emphasis. The importance throughout western Mesoamerica of the two basic calendric mechanisms, the 260- and 365-day cycles, in ceremonial regulation and in divination, deserves special emphasis as a common ideological structure linking the various subregions. The question arises, therefore, as to whether one is dealing here with a single fundamental religious-ritual system with numerous regional variants or with various essentially independent systems that happened to share, due largely to historical contacts, most basic features. One way of addressing this question is to ask whether Aztec, Tarascan, Otomí, Huastec, Totonac, Mixtec, and Zapotec priests, if brought together (assuming an effective method of linguistic communication) to compare notes could adequately understand each others' cultic systems. The evidence appears to indicate that the similarities would have far outweighed the differences and that they might well have had no difficulty in basic comprehension. If this view is valid, the religions of these groups could be likened to an essentially common language divided into a number of mutually intelligible dialects—all of which would underscore the fundamental cultural unity of the Mesoamerican area co-tradition.

SEE ALSO Aztec Religion; Human Sacrifice, article on Aztec Rites; Toltec Religion.

BIBLIOGRAPHY

Alcalá, Jerónimo de. *Relación de las ceremonias y rictos y boblación y gobernación de lost Indios de la provincia de Mechuacan,* coordinated by Moises Franco Mendoza. Morelia, Mexico, 2000. The best edition of the prime sixteenth-century source on Tarascan history and culture, with essays by leading ethnohistorians and color photoreproductions of all of the illustrations in the manuscript (Escorial, Madrid, c. IV.5). It contains virtually all that is known about pre-Hispanic Tarascan religion.

Alcina Franch, José. "Los dioses del panteón Zapoteco." *Anales de antropología* 9 (1972): 9–43. A useful summary and discussion of the principal deities of the Zapotec-speaking peoples of eastern Oaxaca derived from sixteenth- and seventeenth-century ethnohistorical sources.

Beyer, Hermann. "Shell Ornament Sets from the Huasteca, Mexico." In Tulane University, Middle American Research Institute, publication no. 5, pp. 155–216. New Orleans, 1934. A scholarly study of a series of shell ornaments from the Huasteca that feature what appear to be representations of deities, which are perceptively discussed in relation to their iconography in the ritual-divinatory pictorial manuscripts of central Mexico and in the Codex Borgia group.

Carrasco Pizana, Pedro. *Los Otomíes: Cultura e historia prehispánica de los pueblos mesoamericanos de habla otomiana* (1950). Reprint, Mexico City, 1979. A thorough, well-documented survey of the late pre-Hispanic and Conquest period culture of the Otomí speakers of central Mexico that includes an excellent section on the religious-ritual system.

Caso, Alfonso. *The Aztecs: People of the Sun.* Norman, Okla., 1958. A very useful, well-illustrated, popular summary of Aztec religion.

Caso, Alfonso. "Religión o religiones Mesoamericanas?" In *Verhandlungen des XXXVIII. Internationalen Amerikanistenkongresses, Stuttgart-München, 12. bis 18. August 1968,* vol. 3, pp. 189–200. Stuttgart, 1971. After a broad comparative survey of the religious-ritual systems of the major peoples of pre-Hispanic Mesoamerica, the author concludes that one fundamental religion (rather than various religions) prevailed in this area cotradition.

Dahlgren de Jordán, Barbro. *La Mixteca: Su cultura e historia prehispánicas.* Mexico City, 1954. The most comprehensive treatment of late pre-Hispanic and Conquest period Mixtec culture, based on ethnohistorical sources, both textual and pictorial. It includes an extensive section on religion.

Jansen, Maarten. *Huisi Tacu: Estudio interpretativo de un libro Mixteco antiguo, Codex Vindobonensis Mexicanus 1.* 2 vols. Amsterdam, 1982. A significant study of Mixtec cosmogony, cosmology, and ritual patterns, focusing on the obverse of one of the most important of the pre-Hispanic Mixtec pictorial screenfold histories. It includes pertinent observations on Mixtec religion in general.

Krickeberg, Walter. *Los Totonaca: Contribución a la etnografía histórica de la América Central.* Translated from German by Porfirio Aguirre. Mexico City, 1933. A comprehensive account of the culture of the late pre-Hispanic and Conquest period Totonac, derived largely from ethnohistorical sources. A major section of the book is devoted to the religious-ritual system.

Léon-Portilla, Miguel. *Aztec Thought and Culture: A Study of the Ancient Nahuatl Mind.* Norman, Okla., 1963. A broad survey of Aztec religious ideology, based on relevant primary textual and pictorial sources and stressing the more philosophical aspects.

Marcus, Joyce. "Zapotec Religion." In *The Cloud People: Divergent Evolution of the Zapotec and Mixtec Civilizations,* edited by Kent V. Flannery and Joyce Marcus, pp. 345–351. New York, 1983. A concise summary of Zapotec religion. Marcus suggests that individualized anthropomorphic deities were lacking in the Zapotec pantheon.

Mateos Higuera, Salvador. *Enciclopedia gráfica del México antiguo, I: Los dioses supremos; II–III; Los dioses creadores; IV: Los dioses menores.* Mexico City, 1992–1994. Encyclopedic overview of the religious pantheon of the peoples of Late Postclassic Central Mexico. Profusely illlustrated in color with depictions of deities and ceremonies in the native tradition pre-Hispanic and early colonial periods, plus drawings of stone carvings of prominent gods and goddesses.

Meade, Joaquín. *La Huasteca: Época antigua.* Mexico City, 1942. The most comprehensive available treatment of the archaeology and ethnohistory of the Huastec. It includes considerable material on the religious aspect.

Miller, Mary, and Karl Taube. *The Gods and Symbols of Ancient Mexico and the Maya: An Illustrated Dictionary of Mesoamerican Religion.* London, 1993. Scholarly, well-illustrated catalog of the major deities, rituals, and religious concepts of the Mesoamerican peoples.

Nicholson, H. B. "Religion in Pre-Hispanic Central Mexico." In *Handbook of Middle American Indians,* vol. 10, edited by Robert Wauchope, Gordon F. Ekholm, and Ignacio Bernal, pp. 395–441. Austin, 1971. A concise overview of the Conquest period Aztec and Otomí religious-ritual systems, based on primary textual and pictorial sources. It includes a proposed typology of the complex Aztec pantheon.

Nicholson, H. B. *Topiltzin Quetzalcoatl: The One and Future Lord of the Toltecs.* Boulder, Colo., 2001. Detailed summary and analysis of the numerious primary accounts of the rise and fall of the most prominent ruler of legend-thronged Tollan, who was merged with the major wind/creator deity, Ehecatl Quetzalcoatl, and was expected to return to reclaim his royal dignity.

Olivier, Guilhem. *Moqueries et metamorphoses d'un dieu aztéque: Tezcatlipoca, le "Siegner au miroir fumant."* Paris, 1997. Wide-ranging analysis and interpretation of the protean, paramount deity of the Nahuatl-speaking peoples of Cental Mexico at the time of the Conquest.

Pohl, John. "The Lintel Paintings of Mitla and the Function of the Mitla Palaces." In *Mesoamerican Architecture as a Cultural Symbol,* edited by Jeff Karl Kowalski, pp. 176–197. New York, 1999. Comprehensive interpretation—building on the pioneer effort of Eduard Seler—of the fragmentary wall paintings, in a variant of the Mixteca-Puebla style, decorating the stone buildings of this paramount Zapotec oracular shrine. Views them as a blend of the cosmographical biography of the dynastically interrelated polities of the "easter Nahua" (Puebla-Tlaxcala, La Mixteca, and Zapotecapan).

Sahagún, Bernardino de. *Historia general de las cosas de la Nueva España* (compiled 1558–1569; first published 1830). Paleography and English translation by Arthur J. O. Anderson and Charles E. Dibble as *Florentine Codex: General History of the Things of New Spain, Fray Bernardino de Sahagún,* "Monographs of the School of American Research," no. 14, parts 1–13, Santa Fe, N.Mex., 1950–1982, plus revised editions of parts 2 (1970), 3 (1981), 4 (1978), and 13 1975).

Seler, Eduard. "The Wall Paintings of Mitla." *Smithsonian Institution, Washington, D.C., Bureau of American Ethnology Bulletin* 28 (1904): 242–324. The first adequate reproduction and interpretation of the wall paintings of the great Zapotec sanctuary in the valley of Oaxaca. It includes the pioneer scholarly account of Zapotec deities and religious conceptions.

Seler, Eduard. *Eduard Seler, Collected Works in Mesoamerican Lingusitics and Archaeology. English Translations of German Papers from Gessamelte Abhandlunger zur Amerikanischen Sprach und Alterthumskunde,* translated by Theodore Gutman; edited by Frank Comparato. Culver City and Lancaster, Calif., 1900–1998. Vol. IV, pp. 3–66.

Spores, Ronald. "Mixtec Religion." In *The Cloud People: Divergent Evolution of the Zapotec and Mixtec Civilizations,* edited by Kent V. Flannery and Joyce Marcus, pp. 342–345. New York, 1983. A concise summary of Conquest period Mixtec religion by a leading Mesoamerican ethnohistorian-archaeologist specializing in this area.

Stresser-Péan, Guy. "Ancient Sources on the Huasteca." In *Handbook of Middle American Indians,* vol. 11, edited by Robert Wauchope, Gordon F. Ekholm, and Ignacio Bernal, pp. 582–602. Austin, 1971. A well-documented account of what is known concerning Conquest period Huastec culture, including a brief but informative treatment of the religious-ritual system.

H. B. Nicholson (1987 and 2005)

MESOAMERICAN RELIGIONS: COLONIAL CULTURES

The colonial period in Mesoamerica began with the founding of Spanish colonies in the 1520s to the 1540s and ended with the emergence of independent states during the 1820s. The Spanish Conquest and the imposition of colonial rule was often violent, disruptive, and accompanied by epidemic disease. In the long run, however, most Mesoamerican communities enjoyed local self-rule and flourished under the relative stability of the *pax colonial.* The native subjects of what the colonists called New Spain were exploited economically, but many aspects of native culture persisted under Spanish rule, influenced only gradually by contact with non-Mesoamerican cultures. However, the one dimension of Mesoamerican culture that Spaniards were implacably dedicated to destroying was its religion.

Arguably, therefore, the colonial institution that most profoundly affected indigenous life in Mesoamerica was the Catholic Church. Its impact was initiated by the earliest arrival of Spaniards in Mesoamerica; by the time Hernando Cortés and his men arrived in Tenochtitlan on November 8, 1519, for example, they had destroyed native temples, erected wooden crosses, and criticized indigenous religious practices, often against the advice of the Spanish priests in their company. Cortés's efforts were allegedly showcased during one of his first conversations with Moctezuma, the Mexica (or Aztec) emperor. According to Bernal Díaz, a Spaniard who accompanied Cortés, the Spanish conquistador sought out Moctezuma in his palace. There he promoted the worship of Christ, grieved about the Mexica worship of devils, and begged Moctezuma and his party to become Christian. Moctezuma's often-quoted reply was:

> I understand what you have said to my ambassadors about the three gods and the cross, and what you preached in the various towns through which you passed. We have given you no answer, since we have worshipped our own gods here from the beginning and know them to be good. No doubt yours are good also, but do not trouble to tell us any more about them at present. (Díaz, 1963, pp. 222–223)

Moctezuma's response speaks to the Mesoamerican tendency to incorporate new religions into their own belief system rather than replace them. This incident foreshadowed indigenous responses to subsequent, more systematic evangelization efforts in Mesoamerica. As influential as the church remained throughout the colonial period, indigenous individuals and communities played an equally significant role in the development of Mesoamerican Catholicism.

THE SPIRITUAL CONQUEST. Coming in the wake of (or preceding) military invasions, campaigns of evangelization have often been viewed as manifestations of the Conquest. The best-known example of such a view is Robert Ricard's use of a term coined by colonial-era Franciscans, "spiritual conquest," in his seminal work on Christian evangelization efforts in Mexico, *La conquête spirituelle du Mexique* (1933). Since then, spiritual conquest has come to denote the methodical proselytization of indigenous Mesoamericans led by the mendicant orders—primarily the Franciscans, Dominicans, and Augustinians, but also the secular clergy and later the Jesuits. Although Ricard argues for the success of Christianization efforts in Mexico, scholars have challenged traditional assumptions about the evangelization of Mesoamericans, specifically the notion that native peoples were "spiritually conquered," since the 1970s. This work began with the study of the Nahuas of central Mexico. In 1974, for example, Miguel León-Portilla published the first study examining Nahua reactions to evangelization. Building upon this research, in 1982 J. Jorge Klor de Alva outlined a typology of diverse and complex Nahua responses to Christianity, and in *The Slippery Earth: Nahua-Christian Moral Dialogue in Sixteenth-Century Mexico* (1989), the anthropologist Louise Burkhart analyzed native-language catechetical texts, arguing for a reciprocal model of evangelization, essentially a Nahuatilization of Christianity (see also Dibble, 1974). Other scholars, working with texts in Spanish and Nahuatl, have reinterpreted indigenous responses to Christianity through the lens of resistance, subversion, and dissent, particularly in examining sacramental confession (e.g., Gruzinski, 1989; Klor de Alva, 1999). Not surprisingly, the development and treatment of native agency during the "spiritual conquest" parallels the progress of scholarship regarding native agency in other areas of the Conquest and colonialism.

Although priests accompanied the conquistadors in their earliest expeditions to the mainland (most significantly the Mercedarian Fray Bartolomé de Olmedo in Cortés's party), the effective Christianization of Mesoamerica did not begin until the arrival of the Franciscans in Mexico City, which rose on the ruins of Tenochtitlan as the capital of the viceroyalty of New Spain. In 1523, Fray Pedro de Gante (Peter of Ghent), a Flemish lay Franciscan, and his two priest companions were the first to arrive in New Spain. It was the 1524 appearance of twelve Franciscans in Mexico City, however, that initiated the systematic evangelization of Mesoamerica. Led by Fray Martín de Valencia, "The Twelve" landed at Veracruz and walked the entire distance to Mexico City. One of them, Fray Toribio de Benavente, changed his surname to Motolinía when he noticed natives pointing to his tattered garments and realized it was their word for "poor person." Motolinía's response exemplifies the Franciscan preoccupation with native language and culture that characterized Franciscan activity in the early colonial period and continued to some extent to its end. For their part, the Nahuas of Tenochtitlan were impressed by the reverence with which Cortés and the other conquistadors received these men.

Mesoamericans witnessed the appearance of numerous mendicants in the early post-Conquest period. Another religious order, the Dominicans, sent a group of twelve friars to New Spain in 1526, led by Fray Tomás Ortiz. Because the Franciscans had already begun extensive evangelizing in the central plateau, the Dominican presence was confined to the valley of Mexico and the Zapotec and Mixtec lands, obliging them to base their evangelization efforts in Oaxaca. By the time a group of seven Augustinians, the third major mendicant order, reached New Spain in 1532, they found themselves relegated to the lands unoccupied by the other two orders. In these early years, the religious were among the only Spaniards living in the Mesoamerican countryside. When Spaniards eventually founded a permanent colony in Yucatan in the 1540s, it was likewise the Franciscans who led evangelization efforts and claimed the most lucrative parishes.

IBERIAN CHRISTIANITY. Understanding the Castilian Catholicism that the Spanish conquistadors and mendicants brought with them to Mesoamerica is essential to understanding the progression of the "spiritual conquest." This form of Roman Catholicism developed in the Iberian Peninsula in part due to the *Reconquista*, the eight-century-long struggle to expel the Moors, who had invaded the Visigoth kingdom in Iberia as new converts to Islam in 711. In 1492 the last Moors were driven from Granada, their remaining Iberian kingdom. Led by the expansionist central kingdom of Castile, the *Reconquista* represented a reinterpretation of the Iberian past and the promotion of the present as a Christian crusade, one that aggressively persecuted Jews and Muslims. Fresh from the unifying experience of fighting for Christian restoration in their homeland, sixteenth-century conquistadors and mendicants simply transferred their exclusionary mentality from Islamic ritual to Mesoamerican religious practices. Oftentimes they also possessed a militaristic approach to evangelization that was not adverse to the use of force for religious purposes. This attitude was reinforced by the doctrine that salvation resided in the Catholic Church alone as the true church founded by Christ. Not yet affected by the religious upheaval resulting from the secession of Martin Luther (in 1517), sixteenth-century Iberians nevertheless struggled with the presence of crypto-Jews who publicly professed Catholicism yet privately participated in Jewish rituals. It was from this crusading atmosphere that the conquistadors and mendicants arrived in Mesoamerica, intent on the complete conversion of the peoples they encountered.

Within the Franciscan order during the colonial period another form of spiritual urgency existed. Certain members of the order, often called Spiritual Franciscans (as opposed to Conventional Franciscans), embraced millenarianism, the belief in the imminent second coming of Christ, which they saw as dependant upon mass conversion of the newly discovered peoples in Mesoamerica. As John Leddy Phelan explains in *The Millennial Kingdom of the Franciscans in the New World* (1956), Fray Gerónimo de Mendieta was the most notable colonial Franciscan advocate of this mystical interpretation of the Conquest. He based his ideology on the parable of the banquet in *Luke* 14:16–24. In addition to the host (whom Mendieta identified as Christ), the parable names three groups of people: the guests initially invited to the banquet who refuse to come; those from the streets who are invited in their stead; and those compelled to attend to fill the hall. According to Mendieta, these groups represented the Jews, the Christians, and the Gentiles in Mesoamerica respectively, with the understanding that once the last group had entered the hall (i.e., become Christian), God's plan for the world would be fulfilled and it would come to an end. The influence of this belief among the Franciscans persisted until late in the colonial period, evidenced by Fray Junipero Serra's founding of his California missions in the northern frontier of New Spain in the eighteenth century. Not all Franciscans advocated millenarianism, but for those who did, evangelizing the natives in Mesoamerica was seen as an extraordinary opportunity to become active participants in the unfolding of God's eternal plan.

ESTABLISHING CHURCHES IN MESOAMERICA. Rather than implement a completely new system of church buildings and dioceses in Mesoamerica, the friars turned existing native communities into parishes and deliberately constructed churches upon the ruins of Nahua, Mixtec, and Maya temples. Mexico City's cathedral, for example, was erected adjacent to the foundation of Tenochtitlan's central temple. In many instances, the temple's ruins provided the construction materials as well as the site for the new Christian church. In important native towns such as Cholula (central Mexico) and Izamal (Yucatan), churches were built on top of the preserved pyramidal platforms of former temples using the same stones. Not only did the mendicants raze Mesoamerican temples and rebuild Christian churches, but they also destroyed images associated with native religious practice and dismantled the native priesthood—inadvertently driving its remnants underground. Afraid of what might be contained in "pagan" religious documents, the friars confiscated and burned numerous native codices. This method ensured a rapid transition to Christianity—at least outwardly—that allowed the more pressing matter of evangelization to begin; its unintentional side effect was to stimulate complex and largely clandestine native attempts to reconcile aspects of the new religion to old beliefs and practices. These efforts were viewed as heretically recidivist by the Spanish priests who discovered them; they also believed that hieroglyphic and painted books aided such spiritual resistance.

The friars' motivation for establishing churches in this manner was both pragmatic and symbolic; they desired to extirpate any native attachment to paganism and idolatry (which were more or less the same in Mesoamerica, due to the devil's influence, according to the Jesuit Fray José de Acosta), and to eliminate any reverence for previous Mesoamerican holy sites. On a spiritual and psychological level the friars hoped to channel Mesoamerican religious loyalty towards Christianity and its manifestation by erecting new structures on traditionally sacred land. For the mendicants then, new church buildings served as powerful symbols of the spiritual superiority of Christianity and the permanence of its establishment. Not surprisingly, Mesoamericans often used their own religious language to identify these new structures; the Nahuas referred to the church as *teocalli* (sacred house) and the Mayas used the word *kuna* (god-house). They also imbued new churches with local cultural and political meaning, painting and decorating them elaborately (in Mexico) or adding impressive towers (in Yucatan and in the Mixteca) with an enthusiasm that friars interpreted as spiritual zeal, rather than as a continuation of the competitive community pride that had given rise to pyramids and other monumental pre-Conquest structures.

During the colonial period, native parishes were called *doctrinas* (doctrines) rather than *parroquias* (parishes) to emphasize indigenous status as neophytes engaged in the process of conversion. This also differentiated native religious communities from local Spanish churches. Because of the limited numbers of Spanish clergy in Mesoamerica, only the larger urban native communities had resident priests; smaller towns would receive only occasional visits from a priest living nearby, at which time he would celebrate Mass, baptize those born since his last visit, hear confessions, and preside at weddings. Certain Mesoamerican communities criticized negligent or incompetent clergy whose visits were infrequent or whose lackadaisical attitude resulted in mediocre spiritual attention. Accusations of physical abuse or sexual molestation by priests, as well as complaints that clergy charged exorbitant fees to administer the sacraments, surfaced with some regularity. Those priests who were dedicated, particularly if they were fluent in the native languages of these communities, remained in high demand throughout the colonial period. In 1567, for example, Maya parishioners petitioned the king to send them Franciscans who "speak well to us, truly and clearly preaching to us, [and] wish to learn our language here," but not secular clergy, who spoke no Maya and "really ask and ask for a great deal of money" (quoted in Restall, 1998, pp. 160–165). Native community *cabildos* (town councils) made skillful and often successful use of their access to the colonial legal system to petition for the removal of abusive, negligent, or unpopular priests.

NATIVE LANGUAGES AND CHRISTIANITY. From its earliest interactions with native Mesoamericans, the church evangelized them in their own languages, a policy that was formally accepted at the First Mexican Provincial Council in 1555. Members of the religious orders developed extensive linguistic and cultural training programs both in the New World and in Spain. Beyond the immediate goals of communicating with the natives under their care, preaching to them in the open patios of their churches, and hearing their confessions, the friars ultimately sought to understand native culture and religious practice in order to identify and eradicate it. Knowledge of local custom and language also enabled them to compose new sacred texts such as catechisms and instruction manuals for confessors that replaced the burned native codices. The mendicants developed native-language dictionaries and grammars by establishing schools where they trained male nobles and their sons to write their languages in the Roman alphabet. In the sixteenth century alone, numerous native-language dictionaries, confession manuals, grammars, catechisms, and dramas were published.

The Franciscans dominated linguistic and ethnohistorical studies in the colonial period (native complaints that priests did not speak the local language tended to be leveled against secular clergy). Some of the most important native-language work was done by the Franciscan Bernardino de Sahagún, who arrived in Mexico in 1529 and remained until his death in 1590. Sahagún devoted his life to a methodical study of native history, customs, and language, using a cadre of native assistants to produce a monumental, twelve-volume work, the *Historia universal de las cosas de Nueva España.* Usually referred to as the *Florentine Codex,* these volumes remain an invaluable resource for numerous aspects of fifteenth- and sixteenth-century Nahua (especially Mexica) culture and history; their study has become a veritable subfield of scholarship, complete with a debate on whether Sahagún's project was essentially medieval (e.g., Browne, 2000) or modern (e.g., Klor de Alva et al., 1988).

The challenge of indigenous language acquisition remained more complex than simply translating Spanish texts into native languages. The translation of Christian doctrine and such concepts as the Trinity and the Eucharist required careful attention to the nuances of individual native languages. Spanish clergy often resorted to incorporating words such as *Dios* (God), *Espiritu Santo* (Holy Spirit) or *obispo* (bishop) into their sermons or sacred texts, hoping—often in vain—that by introducing a foreign word the concept would remain purely Christian. When the friars did use native words, however, the result was often ambiguous. For example, the Nahuatl word that was used to convey the Christian idea of "sin," *tlahtlacolli,* meant "destruction, error, or crime," while the word used for "devil," *tlacatecolotl,* meant "owl-person," a Mesoamerican malevolent night creature who could make people sick, sometimes fatally. Similarly, the terms Dominican friars used to convey Christian concepts in Ñudzahui, the Mixtec language, illustrate the linguistic and conceptual difficulties that priests experienced in replacing pre-Conquest religious ideas with Christian ones: "idolater" was *tay yoquidzahuico,* "person who makes feasts"; and "the devil" was *tiñomi ñaha,* "owl-person," or *ñuhu cuina,* "deity who robs or tricks." Understandably, Mixtecs accused of sins or crimes in the sixteenth century sometimes claimed that "the devils deceived me" (quoted by Terraciano, 2001, p. 304).

The Native Clergy Debate. In the early post-Conquest years, from about 1521 to 1542, the majority of churchmen, both religious and secular, looked favorably upon the prospect of ordaining native clergy. Spanish priests and lay brothers generally considered natives capable of Christianization and education, as well as full cultural Hispanization. In particular, the Franciscans believed that "Indians" were raw material waiting to be formed in the Christian faith, and that God had given the Franciscan Order a unique opportunity to bring souls to Christ to counterbalance the numbers who were leaving the church to follow Luther. Given this attitude, it is not surprising that the 1532 *Junta Apostólica,* a quasi-official gathering of clergy who met to draw up guidelines for New Spain's young church, made a statement in favor of the native capacity to accept Christianity. More importantly, this *Junta* took the preliminary steps toward approving natives for priestly ordination by declaring that educated natives and mestizos could be admitted into the minor orders, a preparatory step toward the priesthood. Despite these favorable beginnings, the *Junta Apostólica* of 1544 declared that native peoples could never be fully civilized and Christianized. Furthermore, the First Mexican Provincial Council of 1555 not only forbade the ordination of natives to the sacramental priesthood, but also prohibited them from touching the sacred vessels. The official church position regarding native clergy in New Spain reflected the attitudes present throughout Mesoamerica, so that with very few exceptions—in some Jesuit missions or frontier regions—native men were not allowed to become priests (see Poole, 1989).

Among the secondary schools founded in Mesoamerica, the Franciscan College of Santiago Tlatelolco played the most significant role in the native clergy debate. Established in a Mexico City neighborhood in January 1536, the school trained the sons of Nahua nobles in reading, writing, music, Latin, rhetoric, logic, philosophy, and indigenous medicine. Given the Franciscan position in the debate, the student body, the daily educational structure, and the subjects offered, this school appears to have been intended as a seminary. Although its numbers grew in the first year, by the 1570s the project was abandoned; not one of its students received holy orders. The persistent opposition of the Dominicans, the secular clergy, and the general Spanish population to the college's goals may have contributed to its demise. Within its brief existence, however, the Franciscans' most beloved student was a Nahua named Antonio Valeriano, a brilliant Latinist who became one of Sahagún's collaborators. In sharp contrast to Valeriano was a former Tlatelolco student named don Carlos of Texcoco, a native leader accused of heresy and executed in 1539 by Fray Juan de Zumárraga, an inquisitor and the first bishop of Mexico City.

The Role of the Inquisition in Maintaining Christianity in Mesoamerica. From the 1530s to the 1560s, Inquisition-like proceedings, usually led by Spanish bishops, often resulted in the torture and execution of Mesoamericans accused of heresy or idolatry. One of the most extensive—and, eventually, infamous—of these proceedings was the campaign to extirpate idolatry in Yucatan led by the Franciscan Fray Diego de Landa in 1562, during which some four thousand Mayas were interrogated under torture (hundreds died). The much-publicized execution of don Carlos, of which most crown and church officials disapproved, instigated a debate that was settled in the wake of Landa's auto-da-fé; Spanish policy finally recognized the inappropriateness of subjecting a people in the process of learning Christianity to inquisitorial persecution as heretics. Importantly, the church defined a heretic as a baptized person who obstinately denied some aspect of Catholic doctrine, a condition that did not apply to most indigenous neophytes. Removing natives from persecution also reflected a common paternalistic attitude towards Mesoamericans that persisted among clergy throughout the colonial period. Nevertheless, in remote regions native priests continued to practice traditional rituals quite openly, although many were prosecuted. For example, a Mixtec priest named Caxaa, arrested in 1544, testified that he and two colleagues had continued to perform rites such as human sacrifice since before the Conquest.

Consequently, when the Holy Office of the Inquisition was formally established in Mexico City in 1571 to uncover and penalize crimes against Catholicism, native people were exempt from prosecution. Although Mesoamericans did not fall under Holy Office jurisdiction, the bishop-controlled *Provisorato de Indios* (also known as the *ordinario*) monitored religious adherence in native communities. The church's policy toward indigenous Christians remained in effect until the Inquisition was dissolved in the nineteenth century.

OFFICIAL INDIGENOUS PARTICIPATION IN COLONIAL CHURCH LIFE. Although native men could not enter the priesthood, and the early decades of evangelization were often accompanied by violent campaigns of extirpation, Mesoamericans exercised considerable control over their religious lives during the colonial period. Not only were churches built on pre-Conquest holy sites, but friars preserved aspects of Mesoamerican religious social and political structure. Again, this decision was motivated by practical concerns, since there were so few priests available to administer to the thousands of native parishes scattered throughout Mesoamerica.

Within each parish the mendicants appointed a hierarchy of native officials to hold positions of importance. This hierarchy was usually drawn from the community's male elite; both before and after the Conquest, elite men represented local noble families, enjoyed privileged access to political office, and were responsible for organizing activities around the temple and palace complex (pre-Conquest) or parish church (post-Conquest). They became lay catechists who were trained by the friars in the basic tenets of Christianity, instructed in the Spanish language, and expected to assist in the recitation of the daily office. When Spanish priests were not present these native officials handled most of the day-to-day affairs in their church, organized the community religious festivals, and otherwise supervised matters of faith in the parishes. With this system the mendicants found yet another method of easing the transition between Mesoamerican religious ritual and the introduction of Christianity. By reinforcing the pre-Conquest Mesoamerican inter-association of religious and political offices, friars also reinforced the status of local elite families at a time when socioeconomic differences among natives were lessened by colonial exploitation.

Each parish hierarchy consisted of several specialized positions. The *fiscal* was the most important religious official; he acted as the priest's assistant or deputy. His duties included overseeing local matters such as teaching catechism to the parish children, monitoring the village Mass attendance, and updating the parish birth, marriage, and death records. The parish records that have survived are now some of the most valuable sources of information for historians studying family structures, naming patterns, and demography. Other religious officials included the *sacristanes* (sacristans), who supervised the upkeep of the church buildings and who, with the *maestros de capilla* (chapel choirmasters), translated prayers and hymns into native languages for use during Mass.

Music was an integral part of daily church life, particularly during Mass and other services, so that the native position of *maestro de capilla*, or alternately the *maestro de coro* (choirmaster), brought considerable status. For his services the choirmaster occasionally enjoyed such privileges as tribute exemption and might receive a small salary. Often, the other native members of the parish choir (i.e., the singers and musicians) shared these benefits. Despite this honor, native salaries did not compare to the wages received by choir members in the Spanish parishes. In addition to these important religious officials, several minor religious positions existed that often varied by parish. In Nahua (and even in some non-Nahua) parishes, the Nahuatl term *teopan tlaca* (church people) labeled those responsible for such tasks as preparing bodies for burial, digging graves, cleaning the church, and decorating the altar with fresh flowers and other seasonal adornments.

Over time, the elite members of these religious hierarchies—as native representatives of the church—became a link between the local communities and the regional Spanish representatives of the church. They also interacted on the community's behalf with crown representatives of the Inquisition and *Provisorato* responsible for monitoring the purity of the faith. Influential in their communities and benefiting from their position as representatives of the crown, native elites became instrumental in shaping church doctrine and developing devotional practices according to local custom.

COFRADÍAS. Because parish hierarchy was limited to the native male nobility, the most important institution in native religious life was the *cofradía* (confraternity, religious brotherhood, or sodality). Everyone was welcome to participate in *cofradías*, including women and children. Importantly for women, they could assume informal leadership roles in a manner unavailable to them within the parish hierarchical structure, thereby gaining community status while actively participating in local religious life. Already widespread in Europe, the *cofradía* gained popularity rapidly in Mesoamerica, even as it adapted to local custom. These voluntary organizations of local residents devoted themselves to some aspect of Catholic belief, devotion, or to a particular saint. A *cofradía* dedicated to the Virgin Mary, for example, could focus on the assumption, the rosary, the immaculate conception, or any of her numerous forms. If a *cofradía* chose Christ as its patron, it might be devoted to the child Jesus, the passion of Christ, or the Eucharist. Small villages usually had only one or two confraternities; larger towns could support a dozen confraternities; and cities might have several confraternities associated with each local church.

Since each confraternity was responsible for sponsoring a public religious celebration associated with its devotion, the name of the confraternity became important in dictating the schedule of community festivals. If a *cofradía* was dedicated to the assumption of the Virgin Mary, for instance, the Virgin's image would be carried in an elaborate procession through the streets on August 15. The members of the *cofradía* might even sponsor and reenact the event by configuring a platform with pulleys to raise an actress posing as the Virgin heavenward while onlookers sang a Marian hymn. The souls in purgatory, another popular devotion among confraternities, would celebrate its feast day on November 2, All Souls' Day. In addition to the standard procession, this celebration might include a visit to the local cemetery with offerings of food and flowers or a donation to the priest to offer Masses for the souls of departed relations.

These elaborate religious celebrations were financed by the confraternity's treasury, to which each member contributed yearly dues. These funds were often invested in *cofradía* properties or other enterprises, such as cattle ranches. The treasury was also used to cover the cost of members' funerals, to sponsor Masses for the souls of the dead, and to purchase flowers, candles, costumes, and other accessories necessary for religious celebrations. Additional duties included caring for images in local churches and manufacturing priestly vestments and processional platforms to be used when religious images were carried outside the church. Along with their spiritual duties, members attended to the physical needs of other members, particularly orphans and widows. *Cofradías* were by no means exclusively native organizations, however, since each group was formally instituted and overseen by the Catholic Church. Nevertheless, at a local level they allowed communities to unite and organize their own religious festivals, and they offered a counterbalance to the spiritual leadership of the local foreign priest. As economic and political organizations, as well as social and religious ones, Mesoamerican *cofradías* were connected to all aspects of native life.

THE QUESTION OF NATIVE CONVERSION. The existence and popularity of *cofradías* implied a homogeneity within native communities that did not always exist. Although most natives were baptized within decades of Spanish rule, throughout the colonial period priests complained that Mesoamericans resorted to their prior beliefs even after appearing to accept Christianity. In 1588, for example, a Jesuit criticized his native parishioners for worshiping Christ only at the urgings of priests or judges; he disapproved of their apparently superficial veneration and doubted they believed the faith wholeheartedly. Clerical responses to the problem of native conversion ranged from a paternalistic pardoning of their actions as childlike confusion and innocent misunderstanding to fiery allegations of inherent indigenous laziness, incompetence, malicious intent, or even possession by the devil. The aspirations of the mendicants who arrived in the sixteenth century intending to convert Mesoamericans within a generation or two were never realized. In fact, localized versions of Christianity influenced by native practices continue to evolve in Mexico and Guatemala today.

The numerous similarities and possibilities for identification between native religions and Christianity complicated attempts to determine the sincerity of native conversion. For example, in addition to the successful introduction of the *cofradía,* the Christian cult of saints gained popularity throughout Mesoamerica. The patron saint of the local church became the symbolic head of the community, replacing or even merging with the area's pre-Conquest deity. Mesoamericans at times organized religious feasts for these saints, who were listed on the new Catholic calendar, on days devoted to deities in their own religious calendars. Similarly, during the colonial period the identity of Christ was often associated with one of the manifestations of the ancient sun god. Despite the outward appearance of Christianity and the efforts of the Spanish priests, pre-Conquest beliefs remained in wide circulation.

Even if Mesoamericans wanted to accept the Christian belief system, misunderstanding or reinterpreting Catholic concepts in terms of their own cultural and ideological principles was inevitable. Significantly, many fundamental Christian principles had no Mesoamerican equivalent—concepts such as heaven, hell, and the devil. With respect to the latter, for example, Fernando Cervantes has shown that the pre-Conquest Mesoamerican belief that notions of the demonic and the divine were "inextricably intertwined" contributed to early colonial diabolism (Cervantes, 1994, p. 40). When priests confronted Mesoamericans caught in apparent anti-Christian activities, the native defense was often to claim deception by the devil; in the 1530s, for example, Andrés Mixcoatl made such a claim when arrested for casting spells and claiming to be a god, as did Tacaetl for making rain sacrifices to the devil, and Culoa Tlaspicue, who claimed to be a prophet responsible for "the care of the devils" (Cervantes, 1994, p. 46). These men were not simply resisting Christianity, but attempting to reconcile the new religion with old practices and beliefs—to preserve sacrifice, which was so important to Mesoamerican religions but which the friars insisted was the work of the devil.

Thus the cultural divide that existed between Spanish priests and their native parishioners prevented either side from engaging in dialogue on an equal plane. For the priests, conversion was an act of exclusionism, but for Mesoamericans, accepting Christianity did not signify a rejection of prior beliefs, since incorporating the gods of their conquerors into their own systems of belief was an orthodox religious practice. For this reason, even as Catholicism outwardly replaced indigenous religion, ancient practices often combined with Christian forms to develop into highly individualized local traditions. The paucity of priests in Mesoamerica throughout the colonial period contributed to the inconsistent native response to Christianity, so that the Christianization process in the sixteenth and seventeenth centuries was often a confused and reactive one; natives in rural communities responded in unorthodox ways to inadequately explained and alien concepts, then absentee priests responded in turn when these unorthodoxies created local tensions.

The religious syncretism that often emerged from native responses to evangelization had larger cultural implications. Priests sought to regulate not just belief and ritual, but also family life, gender relations, and sexual identity; in these areas too, native ideas and practices persisted while being gradually influenced and altered by Catholic culture. Scholars examining native conversion continue to uncover indications of personal decisions and forms of devotion by colonial Mesoamericans. These are illustrated by the explanation made to the Dominican fray Diego Durán by an "idolatrous" Nahua that natives were "still *nepantla* . . . which means, to be in the middle" (quoted in Burkhart, 1989, p. 188; Cervantes, 1994, p. 57). Scholars have interpreted *nepantlism* variously as a form of syncretism, as representing a middle ground between faiths, as reflecting the lack of a middle ground between mutually exclusive alternatives, or as a panacea for myriad personal accommodations. Personal responses are also revealed in baptism patterns (which cannot solely be explained by priestly activity, since natives often requested the sacrament for religious, social, or political reasons), in the religious formulas that open the testaments dictated and recorded in Mesoamerican languages (formulas based on Spanish models but exhibiting local and even individual variations that hint at personal piety), and in the keeping and bequeathing of saint images.

Indeed, the prevalence of personal syncretic devotions remains most evident within the private rather than the public sphere. At the household level, a family altar became the center of religious devotions. Called *santocalli* (saint's house) in Nahuatl, Christian images such as saints, rosaries, and crucifixes were displayed alongside figurines associated with indigenous deities without concern for religious inconsistency. Families gathered before these altars to recite Christian prayers in their native languages, to make offerings of flowers or food, and to clean and sweep around it. These altars even became the focus of native wills that specified the types of offerings and reverence the inheritor was to perform.

The Persistence of Folk Religious Cultures. Mesoamerican altars were only one aspect of native folk religion that developed in the colonial period and that continues to this day. Indigenous curers, midwives, and conjurers maintained their practices after the introduction of Christianity, often with the inclusion of Catholic prayers, rituals, or objects. Kevin Terraciano's observation that "conventional European distinctions between priests and sorcerers, religion and magic, did not apply in the Mixteca" was true to some extent throughout Mesoamerica (Terraciano, 2001, p. 271). The confusion created by Christianization further blurred the line between native medicinal practices and the persistence of Mesoamerican religion at the folk level—as well as that between medicinal practitioners or healers and the underground post-Conquest native priesthood. The abovementioned Andrés Mixcoatl, for example, confessed to the Inquisition that he had preached that "the [Franciscan] brothers' sermons were good for nothing, that I was a god, that the Indians should sacrifice to me." (quoted in Gruzinski, 1989, p. 36), but he also behaved much like the shamans who could be found in many regions of Mesoamerica throughout the colonial period and beyond—practicing divination with grains of corn (a Maya *h-men* might have used cacao beans), healing the sick, and using hallucinogens such as mushrooms.

Mixcoatl was but one of hundreds of non-Spaniards investigated by Inquisition or *Provisorato* priests for crossing over, in speech and deed, the religious lines drawn by the church in New Spain in its Sisyphean efforts to forge Catholic orthodoxy. The patterns contained in these cases are still being studied by scholars, but the following simplification may be made: in the sixteenth century, Spanish priests were more likely to associate native shamanism with idolatry; in the seventeenth century they were more likely to condemn shamanism as witchcraft or as superstition. This gradual shift reflected the ongoing syncretism of Mesoamerican religion and Christianity with unorthodox native practices less readily identified by Spaniards as idolatrous; it also reflected the impact of African folk religious and healing practices as the quarter of a million black slaves imported into New Spain before 1650 and their Afro-Mexican descendents began to mix culturally and biologically with Mesoamericans.

The Tzeltal Revolt. Although most Mesoamericans accepted Christianity at least outwardly, the colonial period witnessed numerous resistance movements among native peoples. Many forms of dissent remained personal, such as refusal to accept baptism, persistence in polygamous relationships even after promising Spanish clergy to become monogamous, or refusal to attend religious services. Yet even when resistance became communal, Mesoamericans usually sought to form their own Christian cults that incorporated native beliefs rather than completely reject Catholicism. Localized native resistance may be read as an assertion of the right to govern local religious development rather than rely on a foreign (i.e., nonlocal) clergy. Rebellions typically began as a reaction against negligent or abusive priests, and generally centered on an individual who appropriated the identity of the Virgin Mary, Christ, or another saint.

One of the most well-known religious rebellions took place in Chiapas in 1712 among the Tzeltal Maya. Often called the Tzeltal Revolt, this event remains unusual, for although small local riots and revolts were commonplace, large regional revolts such as this, amounting to a localized revolution in ideological terms, were not. The revolt began when the Virgin Mary appeared to a thirteen-year-old Tzeltal Maya girl named María López (later known as María de la Candelaría) as she walked along the outskirts of Cancuc. María's father, Augustín López, a sacristan in his community's parish, was instrumental in advertising the miracle and gaining local support to build a small chapel on the site at the Virgin's request. Fray Simón de Lara, the Dominican priest assigned to Cancuc, investigated the event, denounced it as instigated by the devil, and flogged María and Augustín. He did, however, allow the chapel to remain.

Events escalated quickly; later that month several citizens from Cancuc were imprisoned after they traveled to Chiapas to ask the bishop's permission to maintain the chapel. Religious authorities also imprisoned Cancuc's civic leaders, but their prompt escape only served to strengthen the cult. Its members removed the Christian images from their local church, placed them in their own chapel, and proceeded to participate in a ceremony imitating Mass during which native priests were ceremoniously ordained. A letter signed by "the Most Holy Virgin Mary of the Cross" circulated among the townspeople encouraging them to revolt against Spanish rule since there was neither God nor king.

The people of Cancuc were joined in the Tzeltal Revolt by twenty neighboring native villages. These rebels not only raided Spanish towns, killing clergy and militiamen and forcing women to marry Maya men, but they also attacked indigenous towns that remained loyal to the colonial regime. Their movement was eventually repressed by a Spanish and native army and its leaders flogged or executed; Cancuc was razed and its residents forcibly resettled. By February 1713, nine months after the apparition outside Cancuc, the last of the rebel leaders abandoned the cause, and the Spaniards initiated strict laws regarding apparition stories or claims of miraculous occurrences.

The Virgin of Guadalupe. Significantly, the two most successful religious devotions to emerge from the colonial period in Mesoamerica, the cults of the Virgin of Remedies (La Virgen de los Remedios) and the Virgin of Guadalupe, were not born in revolt. Both have been, at various times, highly controversial, but nonviolent debate seems to have encouraged rather than diminished the popularity of, and a widespread devotion to, these Virgins—especially Guadalupe—that has persisted to this day.

The Virgin of Remedies has enjoyed several phases of devotion in central Mexico. She first appeared during the Conquest, allegedly assisting the Spaniards against the Mexica during the war of 1519 to 1521. Twenty years later she appeared to a Nahua nobleman, Juan de Tovar, who maintained a shrine to her, at first in his home but later among the ruins of a pre-Conquest temple on Tetoltepec hill. Then, in the 1570s, the Mexico City council appropriated this cult, founded a new church and *cofradía* for her, and made her the patron saint of the city. Over the following half-century, despite competing stories relating to the appearance of the Virgin and numerous lawsuits over the shrine, the image of a benevolent Mary associated with local Nahua followers gradually replaced the earlier Conquest-related Virgin of Remedies. In other words, "the symbolism of Remedies was altered to correspond to changing colonial reality" (Curcio-Nagy, 1996, p. 374). By 1700, the statue of the Virgin had been carried into Mexico City nineteen times; she made the journey another thirty-two times between then and 1810, while a second image of her, known as the *Peregrina*, made regular visits to native communities in and around Mexico City, many of which also claimed her as their patroness. The Virgin of Remedies was eventually replaced, at both an official and popular level, by Guadalupe, but her festival—featuring native dance performances—still takes place on top of Tetoltepec hill.

From its earliest days in the sixteenth century, when a small shrine to the Virgin of Guadalupe was dedicated at Tepeyacac hill outside Mexico City, the devotion to Guadalupe divided the Spanish clergy, disrupted communities who embraced it, became the topic of passionate sermons and polemical colonial writings, as well as the subject of hundreds of colonial paintings. The reason for the Guadalupe debate was and continues to be the lack of contemporary historical evidence to support the tradition's origins. In fact, the first extant source that references the Guadalupe story is *Imagen de la Virgen Maria, Madre de Dios de Guadalupe* (Image of the Virgin Mary, Mother of God of Guadalupe), a Spanish account written in 1648 by a Spanish Mexican priest named Miguel Sánchez. The following year, a priest named Luis Laso de la Vega published a similar account in Nahuatl, known as *Huei tlamahuiçoltica* (and whose full title translates as "By a great miracle the heavenly queen, Saint Mary, our precious mother of Guadalupe, appeared here near the great Altepetl of Mexico in a place called Tepeyacac"), which was destined to replace Sánchez's version as the standard apparition account.

According to Catholic tradition, popular Mexican belief, and these accounts, the Virgin Mary appeared to a widowed 57-year-old Nahua peasant and recent convert named Juan Diego as he walked to Tlatelolco for Saturday morning Mass. After departing from his village of Cuauhtitlan on December 9, 1531, Juan Diego suddenly heard the singing of many birds as he passed Tepeyacac hill near Mexico City. The singing ceased as suddenly as it began, replaced by a vision of a beautiful brown-skinned lady standing amidst the rocks and shrubs. Summoning him tenderly, she identified herself as the Virgin Mary, Mother of God, and requested that he approach the bishop so that he might build a chapel at that site to signify her love for Mexico's indigenous people. After several meetings with Fray Juan de Zumárraga, the first bishop of Mexico City, and subsequent meetings with the Virgin, to whom Juan Diego reported his failure, the bishop asked him for a sign from the lady to prove that she was indeed the Mother of God.

On December 12 the Virgin asked Juan Diego to walk to the top of Tepeyacac hill and gather the roses he would find growing there, which she arranged in his cloak (*tilmatli*, now known as *tilma*) with her own hands. When Juan Diego unfolded his *tilma* before the bishop, the roses fell to the ground to reveal a miraculous imprint of the Virgin. Fray Zumárraga fell to his knees, realized his error in not believing the humble Nahua, and took the image to his private chapel until construction of the Virgin's chapel was completed on December 26, 1531.

The story of Guadalupe remains one of the most treasured accounts in Mexican popular culture from the colonial period, inspiring writers over the centuries to debate the case for it as truth or legend. Stafford Poole's *Our Lady of Guadalupe: The Origins and Sources of a Mexican National Symbol, 1531–1797* (1995) points out several internal inconsistencies within the Nahuatl document in de la Vega's *Huei tlamahuiçoltica*. For example, he notes that although the text refers to the Franciscan presence in Tlatelolco, sources indicate that these friars had not yet established missions there by 1531, but had, in fact, resided in Juan Diego's hometown of Cuauhtitlan as early as 1525. In addition, native commoners in 1531 did not usually take double Christian names. Most important is the name of the devotion itself, taken from the Spanish Virgin of Extremadura, but whose pronunciation would have been difficult for Nahuatl speakers, since there is no *d* or *g* in their language. Poole also challenges scholarship that accepts Tepeyacac hill as the site of pre-Conquest Nahua worship of the mother goddess, Tonantzin, pointing out that native sources never mention this. He notes that Fray Bernardino de Sahagún first made this identification and remains the principal source of this error perpetuated by subsequent chroniclers. All of these complications lead Poole to conclude that the chapel at Tepeyacac hill dedicated to the Virgin of Guadalupe predated the apparition account. Many historians agree with this conclusion, including Nahuatl scholars Lisa Sousa and James Lockhart, who together with Poole published a new English translation and transcription of the *Huei tlamahuiçoltica* in 1998. Nevertheless, considerable scholarship exists to support the historicity of Juan Diego and his sixteenth-century vision, especially in Mexico, beginning with priest and professor Luis Becerra Tanco's two books of 1666 and 1675 in defense of the tradition, and the polymath Carlos de Sigüenza y Góngora's devotion to Guadalupe later that century. By the late nineteenth century, when Joaquín García Icazbalceta concluded that the tradition was not historically credible, he was "savagely attacked" by a large body of apparitionists (Brading, 2001, p. 10). The Jesuit church historian Mariano Cuevas also defended the cult in the 1920s, as did priest and honorary basilica canon Lauro López Beltrán, with great passion, from the 1940s to 1980s. The position adopted by the influential Angel María Garibay (a Nahuatl scholar and basilica canon) in the 1950s was ambiguously neutral on the issue of historicity, prompting criticism from Edmundo O'Gorman, who argued in the 1980s that Antonio Valeriano was the original author of the Nahuatl account (the official position today of the Mexican Catholic Church). Even so, O'Gorman did not believe that this supported the historicity of the apparition story. Since Poole published his 1995 book, there has been no shortage of Mexican scholars, José Luis Guerrero prominent among them, to respond to him and his colleagues.

Despite the persistent controversy over the historicity of the apparition, the Catholic Church approved the Guadalupe tradition in official declarations beginning in the eighteenth century. In 1723, Our Lady of Guadalupe was proclaimed the "Patroness of Mexico City" and in 1737 she was named the "Patroness of New Spain" from California to El Salvador. Pope Benedict XIV approved these declarations for universal devotion by proclaiming Guadalupe the "Patroness of Mexico" in 1754. Official recognition gained further momentum in the late twentieth century. Pope John Paul II beatified Juan Diego on May 6, 1990, at the Basilica of Our Lady of Guadalupe, declaring December 9 as his feast day. On July 31, 2002, he canonized Juan Diego before a crowd of millions at the Basilica, making him the first indigenous American saint of the Catholic Church.

Because the worlds of academic discourse and personal faith do not often intersect, the debate over Guadalupe will remain controversial both within its colonial context and in its modern form. Considered alternately as being of indigenous origin, an invention of the sixteenth-century Spanish clergy to argue for their successful evangelization efforts, a seventeenth-century development to promote unity among clergy born in the New World, or as an authentic apparition story, the Virgin of Guadalupe has become the national symbol of Mexico and an important aspect of Latin American life today. Despite the roles of the colonial Spanish clergy and of modern Mexican politics in the development and perpetuation of the Guadalupe cult, the Virgin also represents the importance of the native influence on the evolution of Mesoamerican Catholicism. Christianity was not just imposed on Mesoamerica; it was in numerous ways appropriated by indigenous peoples and made Mesoamerican—that is, made meaningful in local, native terms.

SEE ALSO Afterlife, article on Mesoamerican Concepts; Colonialism and Postcolonialism; Temple, article on Mesoamerican Temples.

BIBLIOGRAPHY

Brading, David. *Mexican Phoenix, Our Lady of Guadalupe: Image and Tradition across Five Centuries.* Cambridge, UK, 2001.

Browne, Walden. *Sahagún and the Transition to Modernity.* Norman, Okla., 2000.

Burkhart, Louise M. *The Slippery Earth: Nahua-Christian Moral Dialogue in Sixteenth-Century Mexico.* Tucson, Ariz., 1989.

Burkhart, Louise M. *Holy Wednesday: A Nahua Drama from Early Colonial Mexico.* Philadelphia, 1996.

Carmack, Robert M., Janine Gasco, and Gary H. Gossen, eds. *The Legacy of Mesoamerica: History and Culture of a Native American Civilization.* Upper Saddle River, N.J., 1996.

Carrasco, Davíd. *Quetzalcoatl and the Irony of Empire: Myths and Prophecies in the Aztec Tradition.* Rev. ed. Boulder, Colo., 2000.

Cervantes, Fernando. *The Devil in the New World: The Impact of Diabolism in New Spain.* New Haven, 1994.

Chuchiak, John F., IV. "The Indian Inquisition and the Extirpation of Idolatry: The Process of Punishment in the Provisorato de Indios of the Diocese of Yucatan, 1563–1812." Ph.D. diss., Tulane University, 2000.

Cline, Sarah. "The Spiritual Conquest Reexamined: Baptism and Christian Marriage in Early Sixteenth-Century Mexico." *Hispanic American Historical Review* 73, no. 3 (1993): 453–480. Reprinted in John F. Schwaller, ed. *The Church in Colonial Latin America.* Wilmington, Del., 2000.

Curcio-Nagy, Linda A. "Native Icon to City Protectress to Royal Patroness: Ritual, Political Symbolism, and the Virgin of Remedies." *Americas* 52, no. 3 (1996): 367–391. Reprinted in John F. Schwaller, ed. *The Church in Colonial Latin America.* Wilmington, Del., 2000.

Díaz del Castillo, Bernal. *The Conquest of New Spain* (c. 1570). Translated by J. M. Cohen. London and New York, 1963.

Dibble, Charles E. "The Nahuatilization of Christianity." In *Sixteenth Century Mexico: The Work of Sahagún,* edited by Munro S. Edmonson. Albuquerque, New Mex., 1974.

Farriss, Nancy M. *Maya Society under Colonial Rule: The Collective Enterprise of Survival.* Princeton, 1984.

Gruzinski, Serge. *Man-Gods in the Mexican Highlands: Indian Power and Colonial Society, 1520–1800.* Stanford, Calif., 1989.

Gruzinski, Serge. "Individualization and Acculturation: Confession among the Nahuas of Mexico from the Sixteenth to the Eighteenth Century." In *Sexuality and Marriage in Colonial Latin America,* edited by Asunción Lavin. Lincoln, Neb., 1989. Reprinted in *The Church in Colonial Latin America,* edited by John F. Schwaller. Wilmington, Del., 2000.

Klor de Alva, J. Jorge. "Spiritual Conflict and Accommodation in New Spain: Toward a Typology of Aztec Responses to Christianity." In *The Inca and Aztec States, 1400–1800: Anthropology and History,* edited by George A. Collier, Renato I. Rosaldo, and John D. Wirth, pp. 345–366. Stanford, Calif., 1982.

Klor de Alva, J. Jorge. "'Telling Lives': Confessional Autobiography and the Reconstruction of the Nahua Self." In *Spiritual Encounters: Interactions between Christianity and Native Religions in Colonial America,* edited by Nicholas Griffiths and Fernando Cervantes, pp. 136–162. Lincoln, Neb., 1999.

Klor de Alva, J. Jorge, H. B. Nicholson, and Eloise Quiñones Keber, eds. *The Work of Bernardino de Sahagún: Pioneer Ethnographer of Sixteenth-Century Aztec Mexico.* Austin, Tex., 1988.

León-Portilla, Miguel. "Testimonios nahuas sobre la conquista espiritual." *Estudios de cultura Nahuatl* 11 (1974): 11–36. Reprinted in *Handbook of Latin American Studies,* vol. 38. Gainesville, Fla., 1976.

Lockhart, James. *The Nahuas after the Conquest: A Social and Cultural History of the Indians of Central Mexico, Sixteenth through Eighteenth Centuries.* Stanford, Calif., 1992.

Osowski, Edward. "Saints of the Republic: Nahua Religious Obligations in Central Mexico, 1692–1810." Ph.D. diss., Pennsylvania State University, 2002.

Phelan, John Leddy. *The Millennial Kingdom of the Franciscans in the New World: A Study of the Writings of Gerónimo de Mendieta (1525–1604).* Berkeley, Calif., 1956.

Poole, Stafford. "The Declining Image of the Indian among Churchmen in Sixteenth-Century New Spain." In *Indian-Religious Relations in Colonial Spanish America,* edited by Susan Ramirez, pp. 11–19. Syracuse, N.Y., 1989.

Poole, Stafford. *Our Lady of Guadalupe: The Origins and Sources of a Mexican National Symbol, 1531–1797.* Tucson, Ariz., 1995.

Restall, Matthew. *The Maya World: Yucatec Culture and Society, 1550–1850.* Stanford, Calif., 1997.

Restall, Matthew. *Maya Conquistador.* Boston, 1998.

Ricard, Robert. *The Spiritual Conquest of Mexico: An Essay on the Apostolate and the Evangelizing Methods of the Mendicant Orders in New Spain: 1523–1572.* Translated by Lesley Byrd Simpson from *La conquête spirituelle du Mexique* (1933). Berkeley, 1966.

Sigal, Pete. *From Moon Goddesses to Virgins: The Colonization of Yucatecan Maya Sexual Desire.* Austin, Tex., 2000.

Sousa, Lisa, Stafford Poole, and James Lockhart, eds. and trans. *The Story of Guadalupe: Luis Laso de la Vega's Huei tlamahuiçoltica of 1649.* Stanford, Calif., 1998.

Tavárez, David. "Idolatry as an Ontological Question: Native Consciousness and Juridical Proof in Colonial Mexico." *Journal of Early Modern History* 6, no. 2 (2002): 114–139.

Taylor, William B. *Magistrates of the Sacred: Priests and Parishioners in Eighteenth-Century Mexico.* Stanford, Calif., 1996.

Terraciano, Kevin. *The Mixtecs of Colonial Oaxaca: Ñudzahui History, Sixteenth through Eighteenth Centuries.* Stanford, Calif., 2001.

VERONICA GUTIÉRREZ (2005)
MATTHEW RESTALL (2005)

MESOAMERICAN RELIGIONS: CONTEMPORARY CULTURES

Since long before the arrival of the first Europeans to Mesoamerica, the area's indigenous inhabitants have understood their world and indeed the cosmos to be an inherently unstable place whose continuity has demanded periodic human intervention in the form of religious rituals. It is ironic that a tendency for the world to slip into chaos has provided a primary organizing force, one which links the Mesoamerican with his or her individual community, its leaders, and ultimately with the cosmos beyond. This ritually forged cultural nexus has been pivotal in the cultural survival that has characterized the post-Conquest history of many regional towns. A widespread belief that a given town's leaders are uniquely capable of performing the rituals needed to maintain cosmic order has functioned in a centripetal manner to strengthen the community at its political center. This in turn might buttress the capacity of a town to negotiate with outside religious, political, and economic interests.

These dynamics help explain a common characteristic of post-Conquest Mesoamerican religion: its distinctly local orientation. In various places, such as Zincantan, Mexico, and Momostenango, Guatemala, the town has been understood by its inhabitants to be the literal center of the cosmos. Whereas this sense of sacred center manifest on a local level has identifiably pre-Conquest origins, with the arrival of Europeans it came to include key elements of Catholicism, such as the saints, Jesus, and the Virgin Mary. In marked contrast to this syncretistic blending of indigenous and European religious expressions are other Mesoamerican locales that have been fully integrated into the European cultural sphere. The capacity of a given town or region to avoid this type of integration—and similarly to maintain its customary local orientation—has often been a function of geographic or economic isolation.

In the early twenty-first century the dynamics of globalization are fully engaged in undermining that isolation. Diverse global forces, such as the North American Free Trade Agreement (NAFTA), loss of land to agribusiness, massive internationally based missionization, and cable television mean that in the struggle between tradition and change, the defining currents are steeply slanted toward change. The capacity of local communities to maintain any sort of viable autonomy is being overwhelmed. As a result modern Mesoamerica has witnessed changes in the religious landscape not seen since the Conquest nearly five hundred years ago. As the traditional religious-based political hierarchies have lost their capacity to successfully negotiate with outside interests, the local citizenry has turned away from both those hierarchies and traditional religious beliefs as well. In some cases secular national political parties have replaced the customary indigenous hierarchies. In other cases new religious-based political movements have ascended to power. Notable in this regard has been the politics of Guatemalan Efraín Ríos Montt. Founding his politics on an overt platform of evangelical Protestantism, Ríos Montt reigned over an exceedingly violent military junta in the early 1980s. He remains perhaps the most influential politician in the country in the early twenty-first century.

Despite the success of recently introduced religions in contemporary Mesoamerica, especially Protestantism, aspects of the older religious forms are still evident. In fact the religious landscape of Mesoamerica is highly diverse. The range of religious identifications and behaviors exceeds just indigenous expressions with deep historical roots and recently introduced religions with unmistakable foreign characteristics but also includes such expressions as revitalization movements representing a backlash against outside intrusions.

CUSTOMARY RELIGIOUS EXPRESSIONS. Before the arrival of the first Europeans to Mesoamerica, the region's indigenous inhabitants conceived of the cosmos as square. At its center was an axis mundi, typically in the form of a mountain, a tree, or a maize plant. There was a general consensus that the cosmos was layered and populated by multiple deities. Whereas the specifics of the configuration varied regionally, the subterranean realm(s) included an association with death and similarly with ancestors and the past. Although this realm seems to have evoked frightful emotions—to the K'iche' it was even called Fright Road—it was also understood by many of the region's inhabitants to be a source for the regeneration of the living present. Whether pertaining to humans, plants, or the vital life-nurturing rain, life was thought to come from death. Another widespread characteristic was a belief that religious ritual, typically performed by specialists, was needed to insure the recycling of death into life and ultimately back into death. These beliefs contributed to a ritual focus that was circular and repetitive in nature and all the while aimed backward to the ancestral past. This death to life cycle was sometimes expressed using vegetation metaphors, underscoring the centrality of agriculture in daily life.

In 1519 Hernan Cortés and the first large contingent of Spaniards arrived in Mesoamerica. While primarily motivated by the desire for wealth, these conquistadores also sought to convert the region's indigenous population to Catholicism. Although within a few decades newly built churches—often constructed on the sites of pre-Conquest temples—were to be encountered in all but the most isolated areas of Mesoamerica, the Europeans soon discovered that the "spiritual conquest" of the region was far more difficult than its military subjugation. A general dearth of Spaniards and a preference for the company of their own countrymen, compounded by their attraction to areas rich in readily exploitable economic resources, insured a high degree of indigenous self-administration, particularly in peripheral rural areas. In his book *Catholic Colonialism,* Adriaan van Oss observes that "by approaching the conversion of Indian communities through their traditional leaders, missionaries insured that the persons who played an active role in the establishment of the new cult, for example as sacristans, acolytes, catechists, etc., would in many cases be exactly the same individuals who before the conversion had occupied comparable positions in the spiritual life of the community, with obvious implications for the kind of Christian observance which took root" (van Oss, 1986, p. 21). The effects of that situation are evident in the religious lives of many Mesoamericans even in the twenty-first century.

COSTUMBRE. Central to the "Christianity" that took root in post-Conquest Mesoamerica is a shadowy construct known simply as *costumbre. Costumbre,* which can be defined as "old inherited ways of knowing and doing," is often employed in verb form, as in to "do *costumbre.*" For most of the past five hundred years life in many Mesoamerica communities has been molded by it. To be a member of the community was to be a Costumbrista, a practitioner of *costumbre. Costumbre* can be performed in myriad forms, from praying to the gods to planting maize. This vastly important component of post-Conquest culture tends to be shrouded in secrecy. In *Corn Is Our Blood* the anthropologist Alan Sandstrom observes that the Nahua of Amatlán, Mexico, passively avoid revealing anything about *costumbre* to outsiders by simply never revealing where or when a ritual is held. He writes that "so effective is their method of concealment that I had spent almost five months in Amatlán before I was aware that there was any ritual activity in the village. I was beginning to wonder whether perhaps I had discovered the first human group without rituals or religion" (Sandstrom, 1991, p. 231). The stealth aspect of *costumbre* hints of a certain anti-Spanish underpinning to the construct.

THE FIESTA SYSTEM. A primary venue for the performance of *costumbre*, and certainly a key element in the understanding of the evolution of post-Conquest indigenous society, has been the fiesta system. Variously referred to in the literature as the "cargo system," "*cofradía* system," and "*mayordomía* system," the fiesta system is the institutionalized celebration of regularly occurring fiestas. Whereas there is strong evidence for pre-Hispanic antecedents, in its strict sense the fiesta system is Catholic. Most of the fiestas are celebrated in accordance with Catholic saints' days. In its modern form the fiesta system typically includes some form of "cargoes," non-paying periodically rotated positions. This usage of the term *cargo* comes from Spanish and means position, duty, and responsibility. Attached to the cargo positions is a characteristic hierarchical structure. At some point the religious hierarchies in many Mesoamerican communities assumed political leadership duties as well. The resulting "civil-religious hierarchies" eventually shaped the subsequent cultural development of the communities over which they presided. The cultural forms, which emerged often, resembled pre-Hispanic forms, hence undermining the desires of the church and state alike.

One defining aspect of the emergent culture that echoes the pre-Hispanic era is the fiesta system's ritual focus on the ancestral past. In many locales, such as Tlayacapan, a town in Morelos, Mexico, the connection with the past is vestigial and faint. The focus on the ancestral past is more evident in the Day of the Dead ceremonies celebrated in many Mesoamerican communities, though in some regions, such as in the Purepecha area of Michoacán, Mexico, it is performed in a heavily Catholic infused milieu. In other cases the pre-Hispanic connection is far stronger. For instance, in the Tz'utujil town of Santiago Atitlán, Guatemala, the fiesta system (*cofradía* system) is directly associated with the ancestral World Tree, the axis mundi thought to exist at the center of a four-cornered world. For Costumbristas in that town, the ancestors are said to lie at the root of the Tree, and the people of the town are its leaves and flowers. The leader of the system is believed to be the trunk (he is literally called Trunk), and his ritual input is thought to be vital for the world's orderly functioning.

Although this type of belief can be traced to the pre-Conquest past, it would be incorrect to conclude that it represents some pristine form of ancient culture. Instead, even when having significant links to the past, the indigenous cultural expressions of post-Conquest Mesoamerica have been "reconstituted" in entirely new ethnic and class contexts. Clearly when the Spanish arrived and began their attempts to subdue and to control the indigenous inhabitants—to conquer them—that population's embrace of the ancestral past took on significant new political implications. While in the words of one scholar the foreigners sought to "put an end to everything indigenous, especially in the realm of ideas, even so far as to leave no sign of them," many Mesoamericans simply refused to cooperate (K. Garibay in Anderson, 1960, p. 33). By aiding and abetting the refusal of their own spiritual conquest, the embrace of the ancestral past assumed subversive ethnic dimensions that had not previously existed.

***COFRADÍA* BARTER AND BARRIER.** The Catholic fiesta system was introduced into Mesoamerica within a decade of the Conquest with the importation of the first *cofradías. Cofradías* had long existed in Spain and Portugal as voluntary lay organizations whose primary purposes were the veneration of a particular saint and providing funerals and taking care of members' widows. The initial Mesoamerican *cofradía* prototype matched closely its European counterpart, including the provision of social services. However, the Spaniards' reasons for the institution's introduction had little to do with such altruism. Rather, it was intended that *cofradías* (1) provide for the collection of revenues and (2) further the indigenous population's integration into the church. Catholic priests, who were often poor, itinerant, and living in distant towns, came to be reliant on the funds paid by *cofradías* for the saying of mass on saints' days. Because they had neither direct control over the *cofradía* funds nor over the amount of the stipend, it is of little surprise that they were forced to concede to certain indigenous demands. Bluntly, in various parts of Mesoamerica the local population utilized *cofradía* revenues to buy off otherwise intrusive outsiders, particularly priests, and in that way to subsidize a degree of cultural autonomy. Although outsiders did manage to successfully exploit *cofradías* for personal economic gain, that success came at a significant cultural and theological price.

This "barter" aspect has allowed many communities to subvert the second Spanish motivation for the introduction of *cofradías*: the facilitation of the local population's integration into the church. Evading the scrutiny of their pious overlords living in distant towns, many communities have used the *cofradía* system to transfer aspects of pre-Conquest religious ritual, refabricating the institution in the process. Given that the *cofradía* system was ostensibly Catholic, as long as what the church looked upon as patently "idolatrous gear" was kept from sight, the system was on the whole at least minimally acceptable. (This is certainly not to say that "idolatry" disappeared. To the contrary: in some locales it has flourished, and in important ways the *cofradía* system has provided the platform for that survival.) Whereas enough of the accoutrements of Catholicism are generally present in the *cofradías* to deflect direct intervention, at the same time the system can constitute a "barrier," the occult side of which offers a venue for the celebrations of characteristically indigenous religious expressions.

THE SAINTS. A particularly salient component of post-Conquest Mesoamerican religious expression is the cult of the Catholic saints. Whereas the role of the saints in the religious life of the region's inhabitants has changed considerably over time, in many cases they continue to resonate with what Nancy Farriss in *Maya Society under Colonial Rule* identifies as the "chameleon nature" of the pre-Hispanic gods. Writing about the Yucatecan Maya, she observes that the saints lining the walls and altars of the *cofradías* and parishes in many cases merely came to represent aspects of far more inclusive local deities. According to Farriss, "the addition of one more guise to the multiple permutations each deity already possessed would hardly have fazed the Maya theologians" (Farriss, 1984, p. 313). In some cases in the early twenty-first century the relation of pre-Hispanic deities with Catholic saints is only vaguely discernible. For instance, in Tlayacapan, Mexico, there is a faint relation of the central Mexican rain deity Tlaloc with John the Baptist. In other cases the conflation of ancient gods with Catholic saints is evident. In Santiago Atitlán, Saint Peter (called don Pedro) has a strong association with the ancient Mayan god Mam. In the town the "saint" is typically called Mam. Moreover both Mam and Saint Peter have associations with the *uayeb*, the five "delicate" days of the Mayan solar calendar.

Evident in these examples is the difference of interpretation in the significance of the saints encountered from community to community. This variation is further underscored in local understandings of the saints' origins. In many communities the saints are believed to have come from foreign lands, though they may now be thought to inhabit nearby mountains. Other accounts of the origins of the saints may be more ambivalent, with some interpretations citing a local indigenous pedigree and others (at times coming from the same informant) describing a foreign origin. The regional variation in the significance of the saints is also evident in the specific roles and importance attached to them. For instance, in one town (Santiago Atitlán) Saint John might be associated with wild animals, whereas in another town (Amatlán) he might be linked to water.

Mesoamerican saints commonly behave in humanlike fashion, which is to say that they do not always display "saintly" behavior. Karl Wipf observes that the saints "may lie, lose their composure, take revenge, have love affairs, and so on" (Wipf, 1987, p. 430).

JUDAS. A tendency for Mesoamericans to interpret the "saints" in ways that differ from orthodox Catholicism is evident in understandings of Judas, again underscoring the church's limited success in regulating the ideological and social contexts of Mesoamerican religious expression. Although in many communities Judas is reviled—just as he is in most of Christianity—in other communities he is venerated as a saint. These wide differences in interpretation notwithstanding, in various instances interpretations of Judas find common ground in their reflections of indigenous Mesoamericans' conflicts with the competing dominant national ethnic sector. In a classic study of Mayan passion plays, June Nash writes that in the Chiapas town of Amatenango del Valle, Judas is associated with the devil and the leader of the Jews. She adds that this disdained entity also prevents corn—the indigenous staff of life—from growing. Particularly significant is that in Amatenango "the Indians, with all the subtlety and intensity of the dominated, have transmogrified the despised villain of the anti-Semitic Christian passion into an icon of their own oppressor, the Christian Ladino" (Nash, 1968, p. 323). The fact is that in Amatenango Judas is unequivocally equated with Ladinos (non-Indians).

Starkly contrasting with Amatenango, in Santiago Atitlán, Guatemala, the local Judas figure is revered. Exemplifying the diversity of Mesoamerican Judas figures, in Atitlán Judas does not represent Ladinos but instead is said to have been created by local rain gods (*nawals*) and is typically considered to be Mayan. Moreover the deity embodies various definitively ancient Mayan aspects, including calendric associations. Connections with the ancient Mayas notwithstanding, the deity clearly embodies an anti-Catholic dimension. By elevating the enemy of orthodox Catholicism to a deified status, the local Mayas reaffirm their separation from the dominant ethnic sector. These ethnic underpinnings of the Judas figure indicate that the local adoption and subsequent reworking of foreign cultural elements has been integral in mediating the external hegemonic threat, of which the adopted elements originally were a part.

MAXIMÓN. Judas veneration in Guatemala is generally linked to the worship of a rum-chugging, cigar-puffing deity commonly called Maximón. In fact Judas is but one facet of Maximón, a complex deity who is worshipped in various cult centers around the country. The most important centers are located in Zunil, San Andrés Itzapa, and Santiago Atitlán. The god is addressed by a multitude of names, including San Judas, San Simón, don Pedro, Lord Skunk, and Lord Tobacco. Unlike virtually all other aspects of traditional indigenous religion in Guatemala, the Maximón cult may actually be growing. There is no central organization to the cult, explaining in part why the appearance and significance of the deity varies from town to town.

In customary usage the name Maximón is specific to the cult as it exists in the Tz'utujil town Santiago Atitlán. Only in the late twentieth century was the name adopted elsewhere. (Previously the other shrines generally employed the name San Simón.) Indicative of the deity's complexity, the name Maximón has multiple meanings. It is a conflation of Mam, an ancient Mayan god and one of Maximón's primary names, with the biblical Simon. Additionally in Tz'utujil the name means Mr. Knotted, this in reference to the deity's manner of construction. While the exact nature of Maximón's construction is a secret, it is widely known that the figure is made of tied tz'ajtel wood sticks. Its mask is carved from the same wood, accounting for another of its names, Lord Tz'ajtel. The god, who stands about four feet tall, wears two Stetson hats, one atop the other, and is draped in scarves, hence the name Lord Scarves. Varying from the other centers, where the deity is depicted as a seated Ladino (non-Mayan) wearing European-style clothing and dark glasses, in Atitlán it stands, wears the local style of handwoven dress, is Mayan, and never wears dark glasses.

Devotees in Atitlán recognize Maximón as the Lord of Looking Good. This is related to the deity's fancy garb but also pertains to sexual aspects. According to some scholars, this dimension may have its roots in an antecedent deity: the cigar smoking, lecherous ancient Mayan god L. Sexuality certainly underscores Maximón's creation. According to myth, Maximón was created in the primordial past by rain deities—*nawals*—to watch over their unfaithful wives. Contrary to plan, Maximón displayed unbridled hypersexuality, forcing the *nawals* to break the deity's neck to curb its behavior and power. Maximón nonetheless retained a capacity to transform into unworldly beautiful women or men. However, should one succumb to Maximón's sexual temptations, the price is insanity and death.

The ambivalent gender of Maximón reflects one of the god's more esoteric dimensions. Mayan cosmology has long emphasized binary opposition, including the world's never-ending transformations of male into female aspects, of dry into wet, and of life into death. As Lord of the Center, Maximón occupies the space between opposites and is the power that attracts one to the other. This underscores Maximón's Judas aspect, which devotees understand to be requisite to Christ's resurrection, hence the world's transformation of death into life and similarly of the dry into the rainy season.

SUN, MOON, AND EARTH. Whereas Maximón is recognized and worshipped in numerous Guatemalan towns, other deities of unquestioned pre-Hispanic origin have even wider representation in Mesoamerica. Central among those deities are the sun, the moon, and the earth. Like the Maximón cult, specific interpretations of these deities tend to vary from region to region. In fact in the primary Maximón cult center, Santiago Atitlán, Maximón includes the sun among his attributes. In that town the annual solar cycle is equated with waxing and waning of sexual "heat" and the evolution of Maximón (Mam) from his young to old forms. Local residents often refer to the sun as father. The sun is also called father by the Nahuas of Amatlán, Mexico, where it is considered to be the most powerful of the spirits. In marked contrast to Santiago Atitlán, where the sun is associated with Maximón-Judas, in Amatlán it is associated with Jesus. A pairing of Jesus and the sun is also found in the Tzotzil town of Chamula and elsewhere.

In numerous Mesoamerican towns the moon is equated with Mary. This association is found in communities that are generally thought of as traditional, such as Chamula, and also in those that are highly acculturated, such as Tlayacapan. No doubt one reason for the salience of this association is that in Catholic iconography the Virgin of Guadalupe is generally depicted standing on a crescent moon. Not all towns that recognize a moon goddess pair her with Mary. In Santiago Atitlán, the moon, who is revered as "Grandmother," is not linked with Mary. In that town, the moon goddess' association with childbirth and weaving points to an origin in the ancient Mayan deity Ix Chel, who was also a moon goddess and associated with birth and weaving. For the Nahua of Amatlán, the moon is related to the revered goddess Tonantsij, Our Honored Mother, but is also associated with the feared Tlahuelilo, "Wrathful One." This ambivalent understanding reflects both the moon's relationship to birth and fertility but also to the feared underworld and hence death.

This ambivalence about fertility and life on the one hand and death on the other stems from a Mesoamerican understanding of the earth in general. Writing about Amatlán, Sandstrom notes that "people are considered to sprout from the earth like the corn plant, and they are placed back in the earth when they die. The earth is the womb and tomb, the provider of nourishment and all wealth, home to the ancestors, and the daily sustainer of human life" (Sandstrom, 1991, p. 241). The idea of the earth as "womb and tomb" is also widespread in highland Guatemala, as is the association of the human body with corn. So important is the earth in this regard that it is deified. In several Mayan languages the word for earth is *ruchiliew,* "face of the land," which to Costumbristas refers to an understanding that the surface of the earth is the literal face of the deity. The Mixe of Oaxaca believe that the earth deity is female and call her Na·swi·ñ, or "earth surface." In some parts of Mesoamerica the earth deity is called simply Dios Mundo, World God.

LOCAL GODS. The local orientation of traditional Mesoamerican culture and religion translates into a certain local orientation for all the gods, even those such as the sun and moon that have wide regional recognition. This orientation is even more pronounced in a diverse set of gods explicit to individual Mesoamerican towns and subregions. For instance, many Mesoamericans believe deities inhabit local mountains. In Zinacantan these important deities are called Father-Mothers and are linked with ancestors. For the Tz'utujil of Santiago Atitlán, the primary surrounding mountains are thought to be the abodes of rain deities identified by a variety of names, including *nawales* and *achijab* (warriors). In Atitlán these deities, who are often conflated with the New Testament apostles, are believed to have wives, variously called the Marias and *ixok ajauwa* (lady lords). Several of the Marias are believed to be deified parts of the backstrap loom. Mountain gods and goddesses in the Q'eqchi' region of Guatemala are generically called *tzuultaq'a,* from the word *tzuul* (mountain) and *taq'a* (valley). The *tzuultaq'a,* who may be equated with saints and are thought to have a human form, live deep inside the mountain in a "house" (a cave). At the same time, a given mountain is thought to be the physical body of the god. Citing a Q'eqchi' informant,

Richard Wilson writes that "a tzuultaq'a feels pain when we clear the brush with machetes and jab the planting sticks into the earth" (Wilson, 1995, p. 54). Wilson adds that a given mountain is believed to have a face, a head, a body, and a cave that is either its mouth or womb. In various Mesoamerican towns the local mountain gods are said to be the "owners" of a particular mountain or volcano.

"Shamanism." Numerous published studies of contemporary Mesoamerican towns cite the presence of "shamans," sometimes including the indigenous term for the specific type of practitioner and sometimes not. A careful reading of this literature shows that the activities of the different practitioners vary significantly. This wide range of practices is at the basis of fierce scholarly debate about the use of the term *shaman* for ritual practitioners in Mesoamerica and elsewhere. One camp in this debate argues vehemently that shamanism is a viable concept that refers to an identifiable human activity. Others counter that it is really just a "made-up, modern, Western category." Critics contend that the literature stereotypes a vast array of religious specialists and behaviors from widely differing cultural, historical, and class backgrounds when it presents those specialists under the tidy rubric "shaman."

Whereas it may be useful and accurate to have a single term shaman, there is no doubt that in reference to Mesoamerica the category combines a wide range of differing ritual specialists. Among the different types of Mesoamerican specialists often labeled as shamans are herbalists, indigenous calendar specialists, bonesetters, midwives, snake and spider bite healers, and spirit mediums. Further underscoring these differences is that shamans in communities such as Amatlán and Momostenango are generally respected, whereas in other communities, such as Santiago Atitlán and San Antonio Ilotenango, they are not. A primary reason for the negative association, where it exists, is suspicion of witchcraft.

Syncretism and Transculturation. Over most of the past five centuries a defining characteristic of Mesoamerica has been what one scholar describes as "radically asymmetrical relations of power" (Pratt, 1992, p. 7). Since the Conquest the region's indigenous inhabitants have been subordinate to Spaniards and later to Ladinos. In this environment temples were sacked and churches built in their places. The indigenous inhabitants had to watch as the Spaniards brought in the cult of the saints and *cofradías,* as they introduced new artistic styles, even new forms of clothing. Over time few aspects of indigenous cultural expression were left untouched by European contact. In the wake of this contact many indigenous societies were completely integrated into the European cultural sphere.

Yet a survey of Mesoamerican religious practices and behaviors demonstrates that the region's inhabitants have not been passive witnesses to their own history. Reflecting cultural resilience and transformative capacity, in many generally rural areas significant cultural aspects could be traced to the pre-European past. Evident in the Mesoamerican cult of the saints—or the fiesta system—is that defining aspects of the post-Conquest cultures commonly have a European outer form but retain an identifiably indigenous meaning. In fact the Mesoamerican cultural landscape presents a textbook example of syncretism, the blending of two formerly discrete cultural traditions leading to the formation of new one. A simple observation of syncretism, however, leaves an important question unanswered. To what extent did Mesoamericans purposefully hold on to their pre-European traditions and in that way attempt to subvert the agendas of their would-be overlords?

Syncretism can be the natural outcome of subconscious thought processes and need not indicate purposeful intent. All people tend to interpret novelty according to preexisting understandings. In that light it is not surprising that Mesoamericans understandings of the saints, for instance, came to closely resemble those of their traditional gods. Whereas this sort of subconscious dynamic helps to explain Mesoamerican religious beliefs, it cannot account fully for the situation in towns where purposeful attempts to retain pre-European beliefs have occurred. In places like Amatlan, Momostenango, and Santiago Atitlán, traditionalists are aware that their *costumbres* differ from church teachings. An element of antichurch sentiment may also be apparent, as is evident in the Maximón cult or in the phenomenon of *cofradía* barter. These types of situations are explained by transculturation, the process in which marginal groups select and invent from materials transmitted to them by a dominant or metropolitan culture. In *Imperial Eyes,* a book about transculturation, Mary Louise Pratt points out that "while subjugated peoples cannot readily control what emanates from the dominant culture, they do determine to varying extents what they absorb into their own and what they use it for" (Pratt, 1992, p. 6). Mesoamericans may have had to watch as the Spaniards brought in the saints. Yet far from converting the Mesoamericans to Catholicism, Mesoamericans converted the saints to their own identifiably Native American religion.

Emerging Religious Expressions. On March 15, 1873, Guatemalan president Justo Rufino Barrios signed the Freedom of Worship Act, eliminating Catholicism as the state religion and opening the country to Protestant missionization. A few years later the president went to New York, where he successfully petitioned the Board of Foreign Missions of the Presbyterian Church to commence a presence in Guatemala. Barrios's petition had little to do with his personal religious conviction. Instead, Barrios, a Catholic, sought to attract foreign entrepreneurs otherwise ill-disposed toward Catholic countries. Although the early decades of the twentieth century did see a significant increase in the number of foreign entrepreneurs, it is not possible to determine how much of that was due to Barrios's strategy on religion. What is clear is that the strategy had little impact on conversion to Protestantism. Fully a half century later, in 1940, less than 2 percent of Guatemalans identified themselves as Protestant. Guatemala remained solidly Catholic, though often with a substantial infusion of the *costumbres.* That situation has now changed.

PROTESTANTISM. Contemporary Mesoamerica is experiencing a surge in Protestant growth. In Mesoamerica, as elsewhere in Latin America, the category Protestant, *evangélico* in Spanish, lumps a diverse group of religious identities, including Mormon, Jehovah's Witness, Pentecostal, and mainline denominations (predominantly Baptist, Presbyterian, and Lutheran). Since the 1970s Guatemala has witnessed particularly impressive Protestant growth, mostly among Pentecostal denominations. As many as one in three Guatemalans now identify themselves as Protestant. In fact three of the past seven heads of state have been Protestant. While the number is far lower in neighboring Mexico—around 5 percent of the country's roughly 100 million people—that country is now also witnessing significant Protestant growth, especially among the indigenous population. This growth is in part explained by conversions from Catholicism. Yet a Catholic migration explanation may be oversimplified, particularly when Costumbristas are lumped with orthodox Catholics. A different picture emerges when these groups with scant mutual resemblance are treated separately. In Santiago Atitlán, the town for which the best data are available, growth in orthodox Catholicism has actually outpaced the otherwise impressive Protestant growth. In both cases the growth has come at the expense of the Costumbristas, whose numbers declined precipitously in the late twentieth century.

There are multiple reasons for the surge in new religious identities and similarly for the abandonment of the *costumbres.* Where Protestant converts typically point to the Holy Spirit as the cause, scholars tend to look to an interplay of local, national, and international socioeconomic variables. The complexity of the situation, even on just the local level, is evident in consideration of population dynamics. Studies in Guatemala indicate that explosive local population growth has contributed to land scarcity, with catastrophic implications for religious systems founded on agriculture. In contrast, an analysis of the abandonment of the *costumbres* in the area in and around Tenango de Doria in Hidalgo, Mexico, by anthropologist James Dow, shows that an actual decline in the number of males, and hence of potential candidates to assume positions in the cargo system, has been a factor. In her book *Protestantism in Guatemala,* Virginia Garrard-Burnett observes that new religious identities held little appeal as long the so-called "traditional community" remained in tact. "But when the center began to give, through the erosive processes of 'development,' migration, and war, many beliefs, practices, and institutions that shaped identity gave way with it. It is, at least in part, the attempt to re-create some sense of order, identity, and belonging that has caused so many to turn to Protestantism in recent years" (Garrard-Burnett, 1998, p. xiii). Other factors, which may add to the local appeal of Protestantism, can be its opposition to the sometimes excessive alcohol consumption associated with the *costumbres.* Additionally the relative quickness and efficiency of the Protestant seminary track has allowed a widespread network of local churches staffed by local ministers. This is in contrast to a severe shortage of Catholic priests.

ECONOMIC UNDERPINNINGS OF CONVERSION. Various Mesoamerican scholars have written about a correlation between social and economic marginalization and religious conversion. Sandstrom's observation in Amatlán is typical in this regard. Sandstrom notes that early converts were from the most impoverished households in the village and included three alcoholics, one suspected thief, and another who was a "deadbeat" that refused to pay his debts. All were villagers who had lost hope that they could succeed in the prevailing socioeconomic environment. Similar dynamics are also evident in the Kaqchikel town San Antonio Aguascalientes, Guatemala. Sheldon Annis writes in *God and Production in a Guatemalan Town* that "to those who are economically marginalized by an abject poverty or socially marginalized by increased entrepreneurial activity, Protestantism says: Come to me" (Annis, 1987, p. 141). The attraction of Protestantism to the poor may be enhanced by "prosperity gospel," a message conveyed by some missionaries that conversion will bring concrete material gain. Sandstrom writes about statements by missionaries in Amatlán that local residents are poor because the *costumbre* religion is of the devil and conversely that all people of the United States are Protestants and "it is because of their religion that God has rewarded them with such great wealth" (Sandstrom, 1991, p. 352).

Whereas it might seem logical to simply dismiss any economic validity to prosperity gospel, there is evidence of a relation between Protestant conversion and economic advantage. Arguments for such advantage—what mission theorists sometimes call "redemption and lift"—usually point out that the cargoes attached to the traditional fiesta system are expensive and entail a trade of significant personal wealth for political power and prestige. Although this sort of economic redistribution and leveling may be socially stabilizing in a functioning subsistence-based agricultural society, it is anathema to entrepreneurship and the market economy. In his study on San Antonio Aguascalientes, Annis argues that ecological crisis, made worse by inequitable distribution of land, has pushed local residents toward Protestantism and its largely pro-entrepreneurial ethic. He observes that Protestants dominate a successful capitalist stratum in the town.

CONVERSION AS SOCIAL BACKLASH. One key factor benefiting Protestant entrepreneurs in San Antonio Aguascalientes has been convenient access to markets in the bustling nearby city Antigua. Much of rural Mesoamerica does not have that sort of economic advantage. One town that does not is San Antonio Ilotenango, Guatemala, as described by Ricardo Falla in his book *Quiché Rebelde.* Although Falla, who is both a Jesuit priest and an anthropologist, notes that some early converts in the 1970s did experience upward economic mobility, he points out that not all did. Hence Falla's study underscores both the possibilities and the limitations of religious conversion in effecting economic change. His study is also notable because the converts he describes are primarily orthodox Catholics. Large-scale religious conversions often represent a backlash against existing power structures. In San Antonio Ilotenango, as in much of Mesoamerica, that power structure has not been orthodox Catholic so much as the *costumbre*-based indigenous religion and its civil-religious hierarchies. It should be recalled that in Mesoamerica the customary religion has often included a steadfast embrace of the ancestral past. That embrace elevated traditionality—and thus an emphasis on nonchange—to the level of religious dogma. Yet the undermining of traditional cultural forms, including subsistence based agricultural economies, now demands change. In what one scholar has called a "revolt against the dead," as the traditional forms have eroded, many Mesoamericans have converted to new religious beliefs and identities (Brintnall, 1979).

EMERGENT CATHOLIC IDENTITIES. As the word *catholic* implies, the Catholic Church has always included a wide range of religious behaviors and identities. In the aftermath of the reign of the *costumbres* in rural Mesoamerica, several primary identities have emerged as dominant. One particularly salient expression, charismatic renewal, is the subject of considerable ambiguity in Catholic ranks. Mesoamerican *carismáticos* de-emphasize the saints and sometimes the central role of the Virgin Mary as well. Similarly they de-emphasize priestly liturgical participation, at times even refusing to conduct their religious services in the church building. Like their charismatic counterparts in other regions and countries, Mesoamerican *carismáticos* emphasize the role of the Holy Spirit and the reception of divine gifts, charisma. Given the similarities to Protestantism, particularly Pentecostal, some critics suggest that charismatic renewal represents a "Trojan horse" to the church, that it is a grave danger to legitimate Catholic belief and ritual. Others contend that *carismáticos* are really just Protestants-in-becoming. Whereas it is certain that some *carismáticos* may gravitate to Protestant Churches, for those that do not it may provide a bulwark to Protestant expansion. Charismatic worship may also help to "recapture" former Catholics.

An emphasis on the reception of divine gifts helps to explain charismatic renewal's near total disregard of social and political issues. That disregard contrasts with another emergent Catholic group in Mesoamerica, Catholic Action. Although originally established by Pope Pius XI (r. 1922–1939) to be a nonpolitical lay organization, Catholic Action has generally worn the mantle of politics. This has been particularly evident in Guatemala, where, following on the heals of the organization's role of attempting to stem the tide of communism and secularism in Franco's Spain, it was employed in 1935. Largely confined to Guatemala City in its early years, the scope of the movement increased significantly in 1944, when a revolutionary regime with secular leftist tendencies assumed the Guatemalan presidency. Additionally that year the church took particular notice of its deteriorating state, as evidenced by the fact that a mere 120 priests attempted to serve the entire country. Under the direction of Bishop Rossel y Arellano, Catholic Action was introduced throughout the countryside. Newly formed lay groups were instructed in Catholic orthodoxy and in the sins of nonsanctioned religious ritual. In this way the Guatemalan architects of Catholic Action intended that it serve both as a defense against Protestantism and communism and that it target the *cofradías* and shamans.

Although by the time of the introduction of Catholic Action into the countryside the efficacy of the traditional civil-religious hierarchies was already eroded, that introduction did cause considerable social turmoil and backlash in communities such as San Andrés Semetebaj and San Antonio Ilotenango. Perhaps most notable in that regard was Santiago Atitlán, where in 1950 leading members of Catholic Action were involved in the stealing of the head of Maximón and the temporary outlawing of the god's cult. Ironically it was the intercession of town Protestants on the side of the Costumbristas and against the Catholics that restored the legal status of the cult. The occasional Costumbrista triumph such as this notwithstanding, Catholic Action has become a dominant social and religious force in rural Mesoamerica.

LIBERATION THEOLOGY. Augmenting the strategic introduction of Catholic Action in the fight against secularism, communism, and Protestantism, the Catholic Church began to aggressively place new priests in the indigenous countryside. Of particular note in Guatemala was the introduction in the late 1940s and 1950s of number of Maryknolls, based in the United States, and Belgian Sacred Heart brothers, who arrived a year after the church-supported overthrow of the leftist government in 1954. In Mexico the appointment in 1949 of Samuel Ruiz to be bishop of the heavily Mayan diocese of Chiapas proved significant. On his arrival to San Cristobal de las Casas, where the diocese is centered, Ruiz was shocked to find that the indigenous peoples were prohibited even from walking on the sidewalks. The Maryknolls and Sacred Heart brothers were equally shocked by the poverty and squalor in the indigenous communities to which they were sent and the inhumane treatment of the population by some in the dominant Ladino sector.

Because of the crisis state of the local economies in both Guatemala and Chiapas, including an increasingly critical shortage of available agricultural land, many residents were forced into seasonal plantation work. In that highly exploitative environment, people from all over intermingled and talked. Gradually they became aware of national social and political issues. Some even learned that the plantation land now owned by international agribusiness was former Indian land that had earlier been expropriated. Many of these migrant workers were catechists, members of Catholic Action. Garrard-Burnett notes that, in stark contrast to the local orientation of the Costumbrista civil-religious hierarchies, "catechists were outwardly focused leaders informed by contemporary ideas of development and, more recently, by concepts of social justice as defined by liberationist Catholicism as introduced by the foreign priests" (Garrard-Burnett, 1998, p. 129).

Beginning in the 1960s and gaining full momentum with the 1971 publication of *A Theology of Liberation* by the Peruvian Catholic priest Gustavo Gutierrez, many Latin American priests embraced liberation theology. In Mexico, Bishop Ruiz became probably the leading figure in the movement. At the forefront of that trend in Guatemala were the Maryknoll and Sacred Heart orders. Ironically, though it had originally been intended that those orders be a firewall against communism, liberation theology is founded on a Marxist substrate. In particular liberation theology fully embraced the notion of dependency theory and its argument that the economic development of the core developed countries entailed the subsequent underdevelopment of the Third World. The radical clergy aggressively sought to break the ties of that dependency. Finding a particularly receptive base within their newly activist parishioners, the liberationist priests embarked on program of *conscientización* (consciousness raising) and economic development. Central to the liberationist strategy was the establishment of base ecclesial communities (CEBs), which were groups of twenty to thirty lay members who regularly met with a nun or priest to discuss issues of philosophy and religion and to initiate strategies for liberation.

THE NEW JERUSALEM. On March 23, 1982, a military coup established General Efraín Ríos Montt as the head of state in a Guatemala embroiled in a lengthy civil war. That night on national television the born-again Protestant proclaimed, "I am trusting my Lord and King, that He shall guide me." A week later Ríos Montt appeared on *The 700 Club,* where the host Pat Robertson appealed to viewers to pray around the clock for the general and pledged $1 billion for Guatemala's reconstruction. With Guatemala now firmly established in the holy war against godless communism, Ríos Montt oversaw what one scholar has called "total war at the grassroots" (Jonas, 1991, p. 148). In sanctioning this campaign the "born-again" general time and again noted Guatemala's central role in divine providence. "We are the chosen people of the New Testament," Ríos Montt said. "We are the new Israelites of Central America" (Annis, 1987, p. 4). Deflecting charges that his policies, which ultimately led to the total destruction of more than four hundred Maya communities, amounted to a "scorched earth" campaign, the dictator replied that it was in fact a "scorched communist" campaign.

The great majority of those "scorched" were Maya living in the countryside. Particularly hard-hit was the Department of El Quiché, the primary area served by the Maryknoll and the Sacred Heart orders. Suspected as being communist, the nuns and priests and their parishioners in the base ecclesial communities were common targets for state-sponsored violence, though many Protestant Maya were also killed or displaced. Garrard-Burnett notes that for Ríos Montt, "communism represented the ultimate rejection of morality and God-given authority; it had to be countermanded by his divinely sanctioned 'final battle against subversion,' which he conceptualized in nearly apocalyptic terms" (Garrard-Burnett, 1998, p. 145). The dictator talked of the "rottenness of mankind," which he said had a name "communism, or the Antichrist, and all means must be used to exterminate it" (Garrard-Burnett, 1998, p. 148). Although Ríos Montt was only in power for seventeen months before being toppled in another military coup, the number of people killed during his regime far eclipsed any other head of state in Guatemala's thirty-year civil war.

THE ZAPATISTA UPRISING. On New Year's Day 1994 the world awoke to the surprising news of a massive revolt in Chiapas, Mexico. As stunning as the "Zapatista" uprising itself was its coincidence, to the day, with the implementation of the North American Free Trade Agreement (NAFTA). In hindsight the uprising perhaps should have come as no surprise. Amid incessant heralding of the widespread benefits that free trade must inevitably bring, even proponents of NAFTA confessed that its implementation would entail certain "adjustments" for some of those involved. Simply put, those that took to arms in the mountains and jungles of Chiapas believed that they themselves were in danger of being adjusted. Of particular concern was NAFTA's dismantling of Article 27 of the Mexican constitution. That article, which grew out of the *Tierra y Libertad* (Land and Liberty) rally cry of Emiliano Zapata's followers in the Mexican Civil War, is a constitutional guarantee of land for all Mexican citizens.

For some years prior to the uprising, displaced peasants from highland Chiapas and elsewhere in Mexico began forming communities in the sparsely populated jungle areas of eastern Chiapas. Included in the population were thousands of Protestant Tzotzil and Tzeltal Maya who had been expelled from their towns because of their religious beliefs. One town, Chamula, has expelled more than thirty-two thousand mostly Presbyterian evangelicals in the previous twenty years. The 1990 census showed that Protestants numbered between 20 and 51 percent of the population in the *municipios* (towns) of eastern Chiapas. Included in the population is a mix of Seventh-day Adventists, Presbyterians, Baptists, Pentecostals, Jehovah's Witnesses, and Mormons. In part to counter the growth of Protestantism, the Catholic Church ramped up its community building efforts in the region, concentrating much of their efforts in a group of settlements lying in the Lacandón rain forest near the border with Guatemala.

The anthropologist George Collier, perhaps the leading authority on the Zapatista rebellion, argues that the social mix of eastern Chiapas provided fertile ground for the rise of the EZLN, the Zapatista National Liberation Army. Because most of the residents were recent immigrants, there were few established power structures to limit the emergence of participatory democratic communities. Moreover the newly arrived religious groups established functioning networks for building those communities. Another key factor in the incipient peasant movement was the input of liberationist dialogue, mostly coming from Bishop Ruiz and his colleagues. Of particular significance was the church-sponsored 1974 Chiapas Indigenous Congress. Collier observes that the demands issued at the conference on issues of land, food, education, and health were almost identical (suspiciously so) to those the EZLN issued twenty years later.

The catechist delegates took the lessons of the Indigenous Congress with them when they returned to their communities in eastern Chiapas. Ultimately they were stymied in getting their message out by the region's religious pluralism. Collier observes that only truly secular movement appealing to pluralism and democracy could unite the peasant communities across the chasm of religious diversity. Ultimately the EZLN filled that role. Although the level of direct involvement of Bishop Ruiz and his catechist colleagues in the formation of the EZLN remains unclear, some level of involvement is certain. Critics have charged the bishop with being a primary architect of the movement. Others claim that his lessons were merely an inspiration. For its part the EZLN declares that "we have no links to Catholic religious authorities, nor with those of any other creed . . . . Among the ranks, the majority are Catholic, but there are also other creeds and religions" (Collier, 1999, p. 65).

Fully a decade after first seizing the world's attention, the EZLN steadfastly declares that "land is for the Indians and peasants who work it, not for the large landlords. We demand that the copious lands in the hands of ranchers, foreign and national landlords, and other non-peasants be turned over to our communities" (Collier, 1999, p. 64).

PAN-MAYANIST ACTIVISM. Activist demands for land and human rights in Mesoamerica are not limited to those emanating out of the Zapatista communities in eastern Chiapas. Of particular note in this regard is Pan-Mayanism, a coordinated activism bringing together Maya from far-flung locales. Whereas there are indications that this movement may be starting to take hold in Mexico, it is primarily associated with Guatemala. In fact in many ways it was the social turmoil created by the civil war and aggravated by such factors as globalization and ecological crisis that provided the impetus for Maya to unite in demands for the halt of racism, ethnocide, poverty, and violence. Joining in that demand has been a loosely knit group of foreign intellectuals and scholars who have provided organizational and technical support to the movement. A challenge for those involved has been to refocus Maya culture and ethnic identity from its customary local orientation to a national level of identity. Stated differently, the challenge has been to create a sense of Maya nationalism. It has been helpful that various key indigenous leaders of the movement have been educated in urban universities, where they could share perspectives and kindle their activism. The outgrowth of the Pan-Mayanism can be seen in dozens of indigenous organizations dedicated to the preservation of Maya languages, cultural research, publishing, and civil rights. The movement was also influential in the inclusion of a plank recognizing Maya culture and indigenous rights in the peace accord ending Guatemala's civil war.

This activist substrate to Pan-Mayanism is explained in part by its having built on the Catholic Action pattern of leadership. Given the original anti-*costumbre* agenda of Catholic Action, it might seem curious that many Pan-Mayanists embrace a "decolonized" form of the *costumbres.* In a classic display of revitalization, they have attempted to remove all traces of Christianity. Yet revitalization movements never fully succeed in purifying themselves, and they typically include new beliefs and behaviors. This is evident in the use of laptop computers to calculate Maya calendar dates by the movement's "Maya priests" or in their embrace of New Age concepts. Ironically, in the attempt to recreate the original form of Mesoamerican religion, Pan-Mayanism may actually have created its newest form. In any case apparent is the agency, creativity, tragedy, and sense of hope that has always characterized religion in Mesoamerica.

SEE ALSO Gender and Religion, article on Gender and Mesoamerican Religions; Roman Catholicism; Shamanism, article on South American Shamanism; Syncretism; Transculturation and Religion, overview article.

BIBLIOGRAPHY

Anderson, Arthur J. O. "Sahagun's Nahuatl Texts as Indigenist Documents." *Estudios de Cultura Nahuatl* 2 (1960): 33.

Annis, Sheldon. *God and Production in a Guatemalan Town.* Austin, Tex., 1987. Analysis of religious conversion and economic performance in San Antonio Aguascalientes, Guatemala.

Brintnall, Douglas E., *Revolt against the Dead: The Modernization of a Mayan Community in the Highlands of Guatemala.* New York, 1979. Study of the abandonment of the *costumbres* in Aguacatán, Guatemala.

Carlsen, Robert S. *The War for the Heart and Soul of a Highland Maya Town.* Austin, Tex., 1997. Survey of religious continuity and change in Santiago Atitlán, including considerable discussion of the Maximón cult and *cofradías.*

Collier, George A., and Elizabeth Lowery Quaratiello. *Basta!: Land and the Zapatista Rebellion in Chiapas.* 2d ed. Oakland, Calif., 1999. Comprehensive study of the Zapatista uprising, including consideration of the role of religion.

Dow, James W., and Alan R. Sandstrom, eds. *Holy Saints and Fiery Preachers: The Anthopology of Protestantism in Mexico and Central America.* Westport, Conn., 2001. Quantitatively based analysis of Protestant growth.

Falla, Ricardo. *Quiché Rebelde: Religious Conversion, Politics, and Ethnic Identity in Guatemala.* Austin, Tex., 2001. Analysis of the rise of Catholic Action in San Antonio Ilotenango, Guatemala.

Farriss, Nancy M. *Maya Society under Colonial Rule: The Collective Enterprise of Survival.* Princeton, N.J., 1984. History of the post-Conquest Maya in Yucatán.

Garrard-Burnett, Virginia. *Protestantism in Guatemala: Living in the New Jerusalem.* Austin, Tex., 1998. Comprehensive historical survey of Protestantism in Guatemala.

Garrard-Burnett, Virginia, and David Stoll, eds. *Rethinking Protestantism in Latin America.* Philadelphia, 1993. Theoretic and historic analysis, with considerable attention given to Mesoamerica.

Gossen, Gary H. *Chamulas in the World of the Sun: Time and Space in a Maya Oral Tradition.* Prospect Heights, Ill., 1974.

Anthropological analysis of traditional beliefs in Chamula, Mexico.

Ingham, John M. *Mary, Michael, and Lucifer: Folk Catholicism in Central Mexico.* Austin, Tex., 1986. Analysis of the history and beliefs of an acculturated Tlayacapan, Mexico.

Jonas, Suzanne. *The Battle for Guatemala: Rebels, Death Squads, and U.S. Power.* Boulder, Colo., 1991.

Klein, Cecilia, Eulogio Guzman, Elisa C. Mandell, and Maya Stanfield-Mazzi. "Shamanism in Mesoamerican Art: A Reassessment." *Current Anthropology* 43 (2002): 383–401. Contribution to the critical literature on the category "shamanism."

Lipp, Frank J. *The Mixe of Oaxaca: Religion, Ritual, and Healing.* Austin, Tex., 1991. Overview of traditional religion in Oaxaca, Mexico.

Nash, June. "The Passion Play in Maya Indian Communities." *Comparative Studies in Society and History* 10 (1968): 318–327. A classic study that focuses on Judas in Mesoamerican passion plays.

Pratt, Mary Louise. *Imperial Eyes: Travel Writing and Transculturation.* New York, 1992. A definitive study on transculturation.

Sandstrom, Alan R. *Corn Is Our Blood: Culture and Ethnic Identity in a Contemporary Aztec Indian Village.* Norman, Okla., 1991. Cultural analysis of Amatlán, Mexico, a traditional Nahua community.

Stanzione, Vincent. *Rituals of Sacrifice: Walking the Face of the Earth on the Sacred Path of the Sun.* Albuquerque, 2003. Comprehensive study of the Maximón cult in Santiago Atitlán, with a focus on the Holy Week pilgrimage.

Stoll, David. *Is Latin America Turning Protestant? The Politics of Evangelical Growth.* Berkeley, Calif., 1990. A definitive study on religious change in contemporary Latin American, with considerable attention given to Ríos Montt.

Tarn, Nathaniel. *Scandals in the House of Birds: Shamans and Priests on Lake Atitlán.* New York, 1998. A comprehensive source on Maximón.

Tedlock, Barbara. *Time and the Highland Maya.* Albuquerque, N.M., 1982. In-depth study of the continued use of the traditional Maya calendar in Momostenango, Guatemala.

Van Oss, Adriaan C. *Catholic Colonialism: A Parish History of Guatemala, 1524-1821.* Cambridge, Mass., 1986. Detailed historical survey of Catholicism in Guatemala.

Vogt, Evon. Z. *Zinacantan: A Maya Community in the Highlands of Chiapas.* Cambridge, Mass., 1969. Classic analysis of traditional culture and religion in Zinacantan, Mexico.

Warren, Kay B. *The Symbolism of Subordination: Indian Identity in a Guatemalan Town.* 2d ed., Austin, Tex., 1989. Theoretically rich study of ethnic and religious identity in San Andrés Semetebaj, Guatemala.

Warren, Kay B. *Indigenous Movements and Their Critics: Pan-Maya Activism in Guatemala.* Princeton, N.J., 1998. A comprehensive analysis of Pan-Mayanism.

Watanabe, John M. *Maya Saints and Souls in a Changing World.* Austin, Tex., 1992. Sensitive treatment of the cult of the saints in Santiago Chimaltenango, Guatemala.

Wilson, Richard. *Maya Resurgence in Guatemala: Q'eqchi' Experiences.* Norman, Okla., 1995. Political violence and religion among the Q'eqchi' of eastern Guatemala.

Wipf, Karl A. "Mesoamerican Religions: Contemporary Cultures." In *The Encyclopedia of Religion*, edited by Mircea Eliade. New York, 1987. The antecedent article to the present treatment of contemporary Mesoamerican religion.

ROBERT S. CARLSEN (2005)

MESOAMERICAN RELIGIONS: MYTHIC THEMES

Myths emphasize realities and events of the origins and foundations of the world, of humanity, of staple food, and of supernatural beings—of gods and cultural heroes.

In the case of Mesoamerican pre-Hispanic myths, the various primary written sources have often survived in fragmented form. As for present Mesoamerican peoples, most scholars count on ethnographic material collected by anthropologists in the twentieth century.

Mesoamerica shares a common cosmovision and therefore many similar myths with a diversity of cultures. The sources that describe the aboriginal cultures were written mostly in Spanish—and primarily about Central Mexico—in the sixteenth and seventeenth centuries; some were written in Nahuatl by the conquerors themselves, by friars who began to evangelize, or by converted indigenous peoples. Whereas a few complete texts remain—such as the creation of the sun and moon in Teotihuacan and the story of Quetzalcoatl—most of these texts contain only fragments of the myths. There is the long, well-structured Mayan cosmogonic myth of the *Popol Vuh*, written around 1551. This myth was written in Roman characters, in Quiché, with the intention to be read in their secret ceremonies (a tradition that is still alive among the present indigenous peoples).

The ethnographic data cover wider areas, but share some mythic themes with each other, as well as with pre-Hispanic myths. Much Christian syncretism also exists, because many saints and virgins become merged with old deities.

Many symbols of the pre-Hispanic myths that have not reached us are shown iconographically in the archaeological remains, like the cosmic tree, the earth monster, or the jaguar.

Mesoamerican thought is dominated by a concept of duality. The Nahua Supreme God is known as Ometeotl ("Lord Two") who represents a unity of contraries. He-she lives in Omeyocan ("Place Two"), which has been identified with Tamoanchan ("the house where they came down") and Xochitlicacan ("the place where the flowers raise") and is located above the thirteen heavens. When Ometeotl unfolds, he-she becomes Omecihuatl ("Lady Two") and Ometecuhtli ("Lord Two") who together create four gods—the creators of the rest of the gods and of the world: fire, the calendar, the lord of the land of the dead, a great sea, aquatic gods, the earth monster, and twelve more heavens. Omecihuatl and Ometecuhtli then made a man and a woman, the first sorcerers and the parents of humankind.

In the middle of Tamoanchan, the heavenly paradise, rises a marvelous flowering tree. According to one version of the myth, the beautiful goddess Xochiquetzal lived there in happiness and plenty, but she was seduced by Tezcatlipoca. In another version of the myth, the gods tear the branches off the tree, cutting off its flowers in the process. For this deed they are punished by the supreme gods Tonacatecuhtli and Tonacacihuatl and thrown out to earth and to the underworld.

Alfredo López Austin (1994), has written about Tamoanchan and the actions that took place there, working from the fragments of myth and from Nahuatl poems. López Austin concludes that through the actions of the gods for which they were punished, they originated sex, created other space, other beings and other time. The gods had been contaminated with death, but they could now reproduce.

Michel Graulich writes that the main theme in the origins of Mesoamerican myths is the passage from one era to another, by the way of a rupture between the sky and the earth as a consequence of a transgression (1997). When the gods are banished from Tamoancham, Tollan, Tlalocan, and Aztlan—places mentioned as paradises or ideal lands which represent the union of opposites—a state of unity and harmony is achieved where the primordial couple and their children lived in perfect tranquility. When the creators punish the gods, they are sent to darkness. However, they return to light following a sacrifice

COSMOGONIC MYTHS. The concept of cyclic time and the cosmogonic ages (or "suns") is based on the idea that the gods created the universe to be inhabited by humans so that they would serve, worship, and feed the gods. This concept emerged through a cyclic process of creation and destruction through which the beings (humans) that the gods wanted to serve them evolved progressively.

> In central highland Mexico there were held to have been four previous Suns or eras, each of which ended in a cataclysm, then a fifth which is the present world. The fist age was called 4 Ocelotl (4 Jaguar) and Tezcatlipoca became it's Sun. Giants lived during this time but were devoured by jaguars when the Sun ended. The second era was 4 Ehecatl (4 Wind), when Quetzalcoatl Ehecatl was the sun. This epoch was destroyed by great winds, the survivors turned into monkeys. The third creation was 4 Quiauitl (4 Rain), the Sun of the rain god Tlaloc. This world ended in a rain of fire and the few survivors became butterflies, birds and dogs. In the fourth age, 4 Atl (4 water), Chalchiuhtlicue, the water goddess, was the Sun. The world disappeared in a great deluge and any survivors became into fish. The force of the flood caused the sky to fall down, so Tezcatlipoca and Quetzalcoatl became into great trees and raised it back into place. The name of the Fifth Sun 4 Ollin (4 movement), refers to the movement of the solar phenomena; This era was presided by the earth god Tlaltecuhtli and was to be destroyed by an earthquake. (Heyden, 1987).

According to Mayan myth, in the first creation the gods made the animals but these animals did not praise the gods; they only cried, croaked, or screeched. The gods then made some men out of mud, but they were destroyed by water, so they in turn made man out of wood and woman out of reeds. These creations also could not serve the gods and were destroyed by the rebellion of their domestic animals, their household objects, and by a flood. The remaining humans became monkeys. At last the gods created four men who were so intelligent and with eyesight that was so perfect that they could see all that exists. The gods realized, however, that they had once again failed; if humans were perfect they would then equal the gods and would not propagate. So "Heart of Heaven" threw his breath on the eyes of these four men and blurred their sight, preventing them from seeing only that which was nearest to them. Thus, their wisdom was destroyed. This myth can still be found among the Lacandon.

In another Maya version, thirteen men and twelve women were created by Hurakan and the other gods by their mixing maize dough with the blood of a snake and a tapir.

Many modern Mayan groups still believe in the different cosmic ages, with the various beings inhabiting them. In the modern era, however, these beliefs have expanded to also include Adam, Eve, Jesus, and Mary. These groups have also lost the idea that humans were made to worship and sustain the gods.

THE DELUGE AND THE CREATION OF MEN. The last creation was destroyed by water. The version of the deluge and the creation of the new humanity is told in pre-Hispanic versions, but it is also widely known among many modern ethnic groups. In the pre-Hispanic version of the myth, Tezcatlipoca chose a couple, Tata and Nene, to be saved from the deluge. He asked them to make a canoe out of a hollow tree and save themselves. When the water receded they broiled a fish, but the smoke reached heaven and the gods became angry. So, Tezcatlipoca came down and converted Tata and Nene into dogs.

The more widely spread ethnographic version of this myth says that a man was saved from the deluge on the advice of a supernatural being. The man took with him on his boat maize and a bitch. When the waters receded, he went to the field to work. Every time he returned home he found that food had been prepared. One time the man hid and found that the bitch was in fact a woman who had taken off her bitch skin; it was she that was doing the cooking. The man burned the skin and took the woman as a wife, and from the descendants of that couple the earth was inhabited again.

In some pre-Hispanic myths humans are also created from the bones of people of other ages. This creation myth has been explained by López Austin (1994) as the generic creation of human beings against the differentiated birth of human groups from Chicomoztoc (Seven caves). When the world had been restored, the gods got together and asked themselves: who is going to inhabit the world? They decided to send Quetzalcoatl to the underworld to get the bones to create the new humankind. (Another version of this myth claims that it was Xolotl who was sent to the underworld.) Quetzalcoatl went to the underworld and asked for the bones of the Lord of the dead. Quetzalcoatl was given the bones, but at the last minute the Lord changed his mind. After persisting, Quetzalcoatl at last retrieved the bones and brought them to Tamoanchan, where the goddess Cihuacoatl Quilaztli ground them and mixed the powder with the blood from Quetzalcoatl's penis. With this material the new humanity was created.

OTHER CREATIONS OF MAN. The first four gods created by the primeval couple made a man and a woman, Oxomoco and Cipactonal, who were ordered to till the soil and to spin and weave. Then they were given maize kernels for divination. Oxomoco's and Cipactonal's children formed early mankind. The *Historia de los Mexicanos por sus pinturas* (1964) relates that when the sky fell and Quetzalcoatl and Tezcatlipoca raised it again, they had to create four men to help.

In yet another myth, when the first four gods made a sun to light the world and this was fed hearts and blood to help it move, war was invented; humans were created in order to wage that war. In the Tlaxcala tradition, Camaxtli, the hunting and war god, hit a great rock with his staff and four hundred Chichimecs came out to settle the land. The Chichimec, who later changed their name to Otomí, regarded both Camaxtli and the rock as their mythical ancestors. According to accounts from Tetzcoco, related in *Historia de México* (1964), an arrow shot from the sky landed near Tetzcoco and formed a great hole in which appeared a man and a woman. But they were in the form of busts, with half bodies. This man and woman copulated with their tongues and had children who settled Tetzcoco. Another account states that Citlalicue ("skirt of stars," i.e., the Milky Way) sent sixteen hundred sons and daughters to Teotihuacán, but all perished there. According to Mendieta (1945), Citlalicue gave birth to a flint knife. This frightened her other children, and they threw the knife out of the sky and it landed in Chicomoztoc ("seven caves") near Acolman in the vicinity of Teotihuacan.

However, the sixteen hundred sons and daughters sent by Citlalicue (or who miraculously came from the flint knife) were more divine than human; they demanded that their mother provide people to serve them (Heyden, 1987).

SUN, MOON, AND STARS. The myth of the Fifth Sun (the present era) is one of the best known in Mesoamerica: when all was in darkness, the gods gathered at Teotihuacan (identified in historical tradition with the historical city of Teotihuacan) to create a new sun. Two gods offered to sacrifice themselves: the rich Tecuciztecatl, who performed penance with costly objects; and Nananhuatzin, who was poor and diseased and whose offerings were only reeds, grass balls, maguey spines, and paper. After four nights of penance, both gods were led to a sacred fire. Tecuciztecatl was terrified by the strength of the fire and withdrew, whereupon Nanahuatzin threw himself into the flames, which purified him and turned him into the sun. Inspired by this metamorphosis Tecuciztecatl also leaped into the fire. But it had died down and no longer burned brightly, so he turned into a lesser light. He became the moon (Heyden, 1987). When the moon came out, one of the gods hit its face with a rabbit, the mark of which can still be seen. After this, the sun stopped in the sky and refused to move unless all of the gods were sacrificed. (A version of this myth was recorded in 1949 by R. Barlow in Tepoztlan, Morelos, and another version is still told among the Huichol people.)

The Maya version of the sun creation myth is included in the *Popol Vuh* and it relates the adventures of the twins called Hun Hunahpu ("1 hunter") and Vucub Hunahpu ("7 hunter"). One hunter had two sons who were both wise men, painters, and diviners. The twins were fond of playing ball and the noise they made bothered the Lords of Xibalba (the underworld). These lords incarnated different diseases. They called the twins to their realm and had them pass through a series of trials until they ended up sacrificed and buried. The head of Hun Hunahpu was placed in a gourd tree. Ixquic, the daughter of one of the Lords of Xibalba, approached the tree and the head of One hunter spat on her hand and made her pregnant. Ixquic was condemned to be sacrificed because of this, but escaped with the help of her would-be executioners, who were two owls. Ixquic went to the surface of the earth and gave birth to another pair of twins, Hunahpu ("Hunter") and Xbalanque ("Deer jaguar") who are taken care of by their grandmother. After some adventures—which include converting their half brothers into monkeys—they also start playing the ball game; again they are called to Xibalba, but this time they pass the trials, deceiving the lords of the underworld. At last, however, Hunter and Deer jaguar decide to burn themselves, thus becoming the sun and the moon.

The creation of Venus is also the result of the sacrifice of Quetzalcoatl, ruler of Tollan, who after having been deceived by his rival gods, Tezcatlipoca and Huitzilopochtli, leaves his city and goes to a land called Tlillan Tlapallan, the land of red and black. It is here that he burns himself and becomes the morning star.

SACRIFICE. Sacrifice as a means of creation, transformation, sustenance of the world is an important mythic theme, as has been seen in the cosmogonic myths in which not only the sun, moon, and Venus have to incinerate themselves to become stars, but so too do the rest of the gods have to sacrifice themselves so that the sun agrees to move on in the sky.

Sacrifice is also mentioned in the story of how the Sun made four hundred men, the Mimixcoa, wage war and give to him the blood and hearts of their captives to eat. The Mimixcoa, however, occupied their time hunting and having fun and failed to do their duty; therefore, the sun decided to create four other men and a woman, ordering them to kill the first four hundred and to feed the sun and the earth. The division of the primeval androgynous monster to create heaven and earth is a form of sacrifice, as the earth would not give her fruits if she was not given to eat men's hearts and was not irrigated by their blood.

Sacrifice is also demanded by the Tlaloque—the gods of water—as a requirement for the ability to grow edible plants. In the last days of the Toltecs, there was a period of storms and destruction of crops; to stop this, the tlaloque asked for the sacrifice of the Mexica Tozcacuex's daughter; he did did this, and received as his prize good crops of maize.

The Origin of Maize and Other Edible Plants. Because maize was the staple food of Mexico, much of the ritual life was guided towards its production. In pre-Hispanic as well as in modern times, plenty of myths relate to it; most of them are ethnographic.

According to the pre-Hispanic version, Quetzalcoatl saw a red ant carrying a maize kernel and asked the ant many times from where she had obtained it. Eventually the ant told him that she received it from the Tonacatepetl ("hill of our sustenance"). So, Quetzalcoatl transformed himself into a black ant and got the kernels, which he took to Tamoanchan; there the gods chewed them and put the kernels into the mouths of humans to make them strong. They then sent Nanahuatl to break Tonacatepetl, and the tlaloque collected the maize of four colors and other edible seeds to make them available to humans.

In another version, maize and all edible plants came from the body of the god Cinteotl ("god of maize") who "enters" the earth. In some ethnographic versions, one can still find the stories of the ants hiding the maize kernels.

Ethnographic versions of a maize child are very widely spread all over Mexico. His name may be Oxchuk, Dipak, Piltontli, or many others. This myth was discovered by George Foster (1945). In it, the child who has golden hair is found inside an egg by two old people. The child has marvelous powers, as well as good and bad relations with animals. Afer a while, the elderly couple tries to kill and eat him, but he discovers their intentions and kills them first. The child then has more adventures, in one of which he has an encounter with Hurakan, a god of the sea and/or of thunder, whom he defeats.

In the Totonac version (Ichon 1973), the father's child is killed because he likes to play the violin. Shortly after the child is born, he dies and is buried by the mother, and from his tomb a plant of maize grows. She cuts some kernels and throws some grains to the water; there, a turtle keeps one on her shell, and from that grain the maize child is born again. The child then has many adventures, including creating thunder and the clouds of rain.

Maguey was a very important plant in Central Mexico, from which, among other things, the intoxicating drink *octli* or *pulque* was (and is) made. The story says that Quetzalcoatl went to heaven to look for a maiden goddess called Mayahuel. He found her among other maidens who were being taken care of by their grandmother, a *tzitzimitl* (a monster). Quetzalcoatl woke Mayahuel up; he told her that he was taking her to earth, which he did, transforming them both into a tree with two branches. One branch was Quetzalcoatl, the other Mayahuel. When the *tzitzimitl* discovered that Mayahuel was missing she went after her, found the tree, and broke Mayahuel's branch and, along with other *tzitzimitl*, ate her up. Quetzalcoatl gathered Mayahuel's bones and planted them, and from these bones the first *maguey* was born.

Mythologized Cultural Heroes. The hero acts as a point of intersection between different times that may be both mythic and historic; he gets close to beings who travel through the three cosmic levels: heaven, earth, and underworld, and are capable of supernatural feats. Many heros must pass through initiation trials. They also have miraculous births. Heroes may act as tricksters, they are deified, and they are expected to return.

The first example of a hero is Quetzalcoatl, born miraculously—according to different versions—from Chimalma, who swallowed a green stone or was made pregnant by Mixcoatl. Quetzalcoatl's jealous uncles or brothers try to kill him, but they fail and instead kill his father. He takes revenge and kills the uncles or brothers, then begins searching for his father's bones. Quetzalcoatl becomes the wise ascetic king of the city of Tollan, which becomes very prosperous under him. He spends his time praying; he bans human sacrifice. However, Quetzalcoatl's eternal enemy, Tezcatlipoca—along with other gods—deceive him by making him drunk and then introducing into his chambers a woman: his sister or a prostitute.

When Quetzalcoatl recovers from his drunkenness he feels so ashamed that he decides to leave Tollan and goes to the west until he reaches the coast of the sea. In a land called Tlillan Tlapallan he burns himself, thus becoming the Morning Star. Before he becomes the star, however, he first promises that he will return. Quetzalcoatl is also said to have gone to the Maya area, where he is known and worshipped as Kukulkan.

Quetzalcoatl, along with Tezcatlipoca, is one of the gods in charge of creation. These two gods divided the primeval monster and created heaven and earth, keeping heaven and earth separate. Both gods had been suns in the past ages. Quetzalcoatl went to the Land of the Dead to get the bones to create man. He also brought maize from the Tonacatepetl and helped with the creation of maguey.

Much has been written about the mythic hero Quetzalcoatl, by Alfredo Lopez Austin, Blas Castellón, David Carrasco, and H. B. Nicholson. According to Nicholson, Topiltzin Quetzalcoatl "was conceivably a genuine historical figure prominently involved with an early stage of Toltec history. . . if so he later seems to have become blended and, occasionally, to some extent confused with certain supernatural personalities, particularly an ancient fertility/rain/wind creator deity, Ehecatl Quetzalcoatl." After several other appreciations he concludes that "the evidence for a widespread belief in his eventual return to reclaim his power, which might have influenced Motecuhzoma II of Mexico Tenochtitlan—who apparently was considered to be the direct dynastic successor of Topiltzin Quetzalcoatl—during his initial dealings with Cortés, is quite strong" (1992, p. 291).

Huitzilopochtli, the patron god of the Mexica's story, is connected with the Mexica pilgrimage and with their success as conquerors of almost all of Mesoamerica. He seems to have been a shaman priest who was in communication with the god Tetzauhteotl, who may have been a form of Tezcatlipoca. Huitzilopochtli was the one who took the Mexica out from Aztlan and guided them during their pilgrimage. He dies on the way and on his bones incarnates the god Tetzauhteotl and then continues guiding them. According to the best known story, Hutzilopochtli is born from Coatlicue ("Skirt of snakes") who was made pregnant by a ball of feathers that fell from the sky while she was sweeping the temple and which she put under her dress. Her other children, the four hundred Huitznahua, led by the sister Coyolxauhqui, felt ashamed of their mother and tried to kill her. But Huitzilopochtli, born in full warrior's regalia, fights and defeats them. He cuts off Coyolxauhqui's head and dismembers her, then annihilates the rest of the brothers. Huitzilopochtli then leads the Mexica to their final destination, giving them orders and advice and setting the rules for the privileges given to warriors who distinguish themselves in battle by offering more prisoners for sacrifice.

Hunahpu and Xbalanque are examples of mythic heroes, as well. Among the ethnographic mythic heroes, one can also include the maize child, in addition to Kondoy, Fane Kantsini, and Tepozteco from the Mixe, Chontales from Oaxaca, and the Nahua from Morelos.

Kondoy and Fane Kantsini were born from an egg and raised by adoptive parents. Both developed rapidly and became great hunters, fighting against the Zapotecs. Both Kondoy and Fane Kantsini disappeared but promised to return to help their people.

The other cultural hero is Tepozteco, whose mother became pregnant by a bird that flew around her for a time. Tepozteco was not liked by the grandparents. When he grew up, he did a marvelous deed, however, by placing the bells on the towers of Mexico City's cathedral in a very strong wind. Tepozteco then returns to his town and builds a house on the top of the hill of the Tepozteco, where he remains to this day. He is the one who causes the winds to blow; he is worshipped by the inhabitants of Tepoztlan.

TRICKSTERS. Tezcatlipoca has many traits which can identify him as a pre-Hispanic trickster. One of his names is *yaotl* ("the enemy"), he who introduces all disagreement in the world. Yaotl seduces Xochiquetzal in Tamoanchan, and therefore is one of the main transgressors. He cheats Quetzalcoatl and makes him leave his kingdom. He also does many evil things against the Toltecs, thus causing their destruction; at the same time, however, he is also a creator.

But the typical trickster is the Huichol cultural hero Kauymali, or Kauyumaric, who appears through all the mythical time of the Huichol. He is the son of the Sun. He is called "Big Brother"; he is the inventor of many useful things for his people; and he is a great teacher who provides the Huichol with most of their knowledge. Kauymali guides the way of the shaman to their pilgrimage to Wirikuta, the sacred place where the peyote is collected. He disguises himself as a deer and as several other animals, and he is inclined to sexual excesses. He also has a voluble character, is mischievous, and at times even evil. In one of his adventures he fights against the women of vagina dentata.

The Mayan Hunahpu and Xbalanque, as do many of the ethnographic heroes that have been mentioned have also many trickster traits.

TWINS. Twins appear in many of the myths, not only those of Mexico, but in all of the Americas. In pre-Hispanic Mexico, Quetzalcoatl and Xolotl are supposed to be twins. Xolotl sometimes transforms himself into a double maize kernel, or into a double *maguey* cactus. In the ethnographic material, many twins are cultural heroes and tricksters, born in a miraculous way, most found by an elderly couple who try to kill and eat them. The twins, however, after several successful attempts at subterfuge, eventually save themselves and end up killing the elderly couple.

A version of the killing of the elderly couple appears in many stories of cultural heroes—not necessarily twins—who are raised by the grandmother who has a husband-lover who is a deer. When the twins discover this, they kill the deer, stuff his skin with wasps and bees, and when the old woman goes to meet him, the insects come out of the skin and kill her.

Sometimes the twins have to kill a serpent and get hold of the eyes, one of which becomes the sun and the other the moon.

PILGRIMAGE. Another mythic theme is the pilgrimage, on which one seeks a final destiny from an original home of the different ethnic groups. Typically these groups come from caves located in a hill called Chicomoztoc (seven caves). From each cave a different group emerges that is guided by a powerful person who carries a "sacred bundle," within which are contained the relics of the person's patron god, with whom he or she is in communication. The guide later becomes deified. The promised land is marked by a sign.

Even though most Mesoamerican ethnic groups have a story of their pilgrimage, the best known story is the Mexica's, who are guided by Huitzilopochtli till they reach the promised land, which is marked by the sign of the eagle standing in the prickly pear cactus.

Graulich finds the same structure of the banishment of the gods from Tamoanchan in the expulsion of the land of origin, and, after wandering in darkness, they arrive in the light at the promised land.

The pilgrimage of the Huichol to Wirikuta, the sacred land of the peyote, was performed for the first time by the ancestors, who formed the first group of "peyoteros" who reached the desert of "Real de Catorce." Here, by trying the psychotropic cactus for the first time, they could become gods and could be transformed in all the elements of nature that their descendants, the human beings, needed in order to live. The route and the adventures that take place in this pilgrimage are sung to the Huichol children by the shamans in a special ceremony. This allows them to travel with their imaginations (Anguiano and Fürst, 1976).

ANIMALS. Animals play an important part in several myths. In many ethnographic groups it was believed that animals and human beings participated in original life together. The Huichol called their mythical predecessors *hewi*, who were animal and person at the same time. In many parts of Mexico, every person has an animal companion that may live in a mountain near the village; when the animal companion suffers an injury, or is killed, the person suffers the same fate. This is a very widespread belief, and since pre-Hispanic times powerful people have believed that they can transform themselves into animals called *nahual*.

In many myths, especially those of the Mayans, it is frequently seen that some animals had previously been human. or that they—the animals—inherited their characteristics from people who lived in other ages (like the *tepezcuintle*, armadillo, squirrels, coatis, racoons and monkeys).

There are also "lords of the animals" who take care that the animals and are not killed in exaggeration by hunters; sometimes the lords of the animals will punish the hunters.

The earth monster is apparently a crocodile in Central Mexico, as well as among the Maya. The very Supreme Creator of the Maya Itzamna is an iguana. Some of the creator gods of the Maya have animal names: *tlacuache*, coyote, great white coati, great boar, and *guacamaya*.

Although there are lots of iconographic representations of the snake, no myths exist about the serpent. The name of the Quetzalcoatl, "Feathered serpent," seems to be also the name of an old fertility god that blended with the mythical cultural hero. Also among the Maya, the cultural hero and demiurge is called Gukumatz ("feathered serpent"). Among the Huicholes and Coras, a serpent of the West is the personification of nocturnal sky without stars that is conceived as water, and which is pierced by an arrow every morning. Also among the Huichol, water in the form of a snake, associated with thunder, is conceived of as an aquatic goddess who lives in the center of rain clouds.

The dog carries the soul of the dead over the river of the underworld, and a bitch is the ancestor of the human race. The god Xolotl is depicted as a dog.

The opossum steals the fire from the gods, is killed, then made into pieces; it revives; however, and takes the fire to men. López Austin identifies her with Quetzalcoatl.

The people who lived in the second cosmic era were transformed into monkeys. And Hunahpu and Xbalanque transformed their half brothers into monkeys.

SEE ALSO Human Body, article on Myths and Symbolism; Myth, overview article; Sacrifice; Tricksters, overview article and article on Mesoamerican and South American Tricksters.

BIBLIOGRAPHY

This article is based on Doris Heyden's article on "Mythic Themes" in the 1987 edition of the *Encyclopedia of Religion.* Included in this entry for the second edition are new approaches by Alfredo López Austin and Michel Graulich about Tamoanchan and themes related to—as well as themes about—sacrifice, cultural heroes, pilgrimage, twins, tricksters, and animals.

The principal sixteenth- and seventeenth-century books from which most of the Pre-Hispanic myths are taken are:

Bierhorst, John, trans. *History and Mythology of the Aztecs: The Codex Chimalpopoca.* Tucson, Ariz., 1998.

Dennis, Tedlock, trans. *Popol Vuh: The Mayan Book of the Dawn of Life.* Rev. ed. New York, 1996.

Durán, Fray Diego. *The History of the Indies of New Spain.* Translated, annotated, and with an introduction by Doris Heyden. Norman, Okla., 1994.

Garibay, Angel María, ed. *Teogonía e historia de los Mexicanos; tres opúsculos del siglo xvi.* Mexico City, 1964. This book includes three important short manuscripts written in the sixteenth century: *Historia de los mexicanos por sus pinturas, Historia de México,* and *Breve Relación de los Dioses y Ritos de la Gentilidad.*

Mendieta, Fray Gerónimo de, ed. *Historia Eclesiástica Indiana.* Porrua, Mexico, 1971.

Muñoz Camargo, Diego. *Historia de Tlaxcala.* Tlaxcala, Mexico, 1998.

Sahagún, Fray Bernardino de, ed. *Historia General de las Cosas de la Nueva España.* Porrúa, Mexico, 1956.

Books by Modern Authors on Mesoamerican Myths

Blas Roman Castellón. *Analisis estructural del mito de Quetzalcoatl. Una aproximación a la lógica en el mito del México antiguo.* Mexico City, 1997.

González Torres, Yolotl. *Diccionario de mitología y religión mesoamericana.* Mexico City, 1999.

Graulich, Michel. *Myths of Ancient Mexico.* Translated by Bernard R. Ortiz de Montellano and Thelma Ortiz de Montellano. Norman, Okla., 1999.

López Austin, Alfredo. *Tamoanchan, Tlalocan: Places of Mist.* Translated by Bernard Ortiz de Montellano and Thelma Ortiz de Montellano. Boulder, Colo., 1997.

López Austin, Alfredo. *The Myths of the Oopossum: Pathways of Mesoamerican Mythology.* Translated by Bernard Ortiz de Montellano and Thelma Ortiz de Montellano. Albuquerque, 1993.

Monjaraz Ruiz, Jesus, comp. *Mitos cosmogónicos del México Indígena.* Mexico City, 1987. This useful book includes in five chapters a résumé of myths from different areas of Mexico written by different authors: Mayan myths, pre-Hispanic and modern, by Mercedes de la Garza; Oaxacan myths by Doris Heyden; Nahua pre-Hispanic myths and modern nahua myths by Blas Román Castellón; as well as Myths from West of Mesoamerica and Northwest Mexico by María Eugenia Olavarría.xico.

Nicholson, H.B. *Topiltzin Quetzalcoatl: The Once and Future Lord of the Toltecs.* Boulder, Colo., 1992.

Ethnographic Bibliography

There is an enormous amount of ethnographic material which cannot be mentioned in this bibliography. Mentioned here are only a few from where data has been taken for this article. Many of these books are not recent; however, the information contained within them is still valid and is always considered in the new ethnographies.

Baez, Jorge, Félix. *Dioses héroes y demonios.* Xalapa, Veracruz, Mexico, 1997. Two articles of this book are of interest here: "Homshuk y el simbolismo de la ovogenesis en Mesoamerica," and "Kauymali las vaginas dentadas."

Barabas, Alicia and Miguel Bartolomé. "Héroes culturales e identidades étnicas; la tradición mesiánica de mixes y chontales in El héroe entre el mito y la historia." In *UnAM* (2000): 219–234.

Foster, G. H. "Sierra Popoloca Folklore and Beliefs." In *American Archaeology and Ethnology* 42, no. 2 (1945): 117–250.

Fürst, Peter and Marina Anguiano. "'To Fly as Birds': Myth and Ritual as Agents of Enculturation among the Huichol Indians of Mexico." In *Enculturation in Latin America: An Anthology,* edited by Johannes Wilbert. pp. 95–181. Los Angeles, 1976.

Ichon, Alain. *La religión de los totonacas de la Sierra de Puebla.* Mexico City, 1973.

DORIS HEYDEN (1987)
YOLOTL GONZÁLEZ TORRES (2005)
DAVÍD CARRASCO (2005)

MESOAMERICAN RELIGIONS: HISTORY OF STUDY

A number of diverse primary sources exist for the study of the religious systems of ancient Mesoamerica, foremost among them being archaeological remains. The investigation of these remains provides the only means of obtaining information about Mesoamerican cultures from the Preclassic period (beginning c. 1500 BCE) to the period shortly before the early sixteenth century CE, when the Aztec empire was destroyed by the Spanish. Most of the archaeological remains are structures that were devoted to religious purposes.

EARLY TEXTS. Eighteen pre-Hispanic pictorial documents were saved from the religious zeal of the Spanish conquerors. A number of these are *tonalamatls,* or "books of destiny," which deal with the ritual divinatory calendar of 260 days. They are of special importance for the study of pre-Hispanic religion because they contain in their screenfold pages illustrations of the religious aspects of the calendar, as well as other esoteric paintings that deal with Mesoamerican astronomical conceptions. Some of these books have not been completely deciphered or interpreted.

The most important *tonalamatls* are six of the Borgia group (originally from the Mixteca-Puebla region), the Dresden Codex (from the Maya area), and the Codex Borbonicus from the Mexican Plateau. Besides these pre-Hispanic manuscripts are others that the Spanish priests and rulers commissioned for their own purposes; these were usually executed in a Spanish pictorial style. Among these commissioned works, the Codex Magliabecchiano and the Florentine Codex, both of which contain important religious data, deserve special mention.

During the century following the Conquest a number of manuscripts were written by priests whose special interest in the religious beliefs and practices of the Indians was dictated by their desire to suppress the indigenous religious systems. Toribio Motolinía was one of the first twelve Franciscan friars to travel, in 1524, to the recently conquered "New Spain" to evangelize the Indians. His work is one of the earliest testimonies on native Mesoamerican culture; unfortunately, only a portion of his writing survives. A reconstruction by Edmundo O'Gorman of the original work has been published under the title *Memoriales, o Libro de las cosas de la Nueva España y de los naturales de ella* (1971).

Without any doubt, the most important work about the customs of the ancient Mexicans is that compiled by Fray Bernardino de Sahagún. His informants were native elders who dictated in Nahuatl to young Indians who had been trained by Sahagún. They produced several manuscripts that have been named after the places where they are now kept: the Florentine Codex and the Matritense Codex. The former is the more celebrated; it is also known under the title given it by Sahagún, *Historia general de las cosas de la Nueva España.* Produced in twelve volumes between 1569 and 1582, it was first published in 1820. It has been translated into English by Arthur J. O. Anderson and Charles E. Dibble and published as *Florentine Codex* (13 vols., 1950–1982). The first five books of Sahagún's work, which deal with the gods, myths, calendar, temples, and priests of the Aztec capital, Tenochtitlan, constitute the most important source for the study of the religion of the ancient Mexicans.

Fray Diego Durán, a Dominican, arrived in New Spain as a child and learned Nahuatl and some of the old traditions from the native people of the Valley of Mexico. He also had access to old manuscripts. He devoted the second volume of his *Historia de las Indias de Nueva España e Islas de Tierra Firme* (concluded 1581) to descriptions of the gods, rites, and calendar of ancient Mexico. Fray Diego de Landa, who was responsible for the burning of massive numbers of precious ancient Maya manuscripts in the city of Mani in 1562, was also the author of the most important early book about Maya culture and religion, *Relación de las cosas de Yucatan* (first published in 1864). Fray Juan de Torquemada, a Franciscan, was the first person to write a "comparative" history of the peoples of New Spain. He was deeply interested in historiography, and many of the long digressions in his book *Monarquia indiana* (1615), which utilize biblical and classical references, were designed to show that the aboriginal Indian cultures followed universal laws of history. Four chapters of his book contrast native religion with the "true" religion, Christianity. Also of interest to the study of religion are the *Códice Chimalpopoca, Anales de Cuauhtitlan, and Leyenda de los soles,* three manuscripts written in the second half of the sixteen century, two anonymous in Nahuatl and one in Spanish by Pedro Ponce and the *Historia de Tlaxcala,* written in the sixteenth century in Spanish by the mestizo Diego Muñoz Camargo.

THE EIGHTEENTH CENTURY. The Jesuit priest Francisco Javier Clavigero was fluent in Nahuatl and had some knowledge of other Indian languages. He was the first to write a work devoted solely to the history of Mexico, his *Storia antica del Messico* (1780–1781), written and published in Italy during his exile there. The work contains an excellent chapter on religion. Although in his writings Clavigero tends, as might be expected given the time during which he wrote, to use Christian scripture and theology as norms of judgment, this tendency hardly colors his description of native religion. Indeed, it surfaces only in one passage within which he characterizes the ancestral religion of the Indians as a jumble of mistaken, cruel, and childish practices—the knowledge of which might help the ancient Indians' descendants to see the great advantages of Christianity. Clavigero shared the belief, widespread among his contemporaries, that the ancient Mexicans displayed knowledge of biblically recorded events, and he reiterates the belief, then common, that Quetzalcoatl was none other than Thomas, the disciple of Jesus, who had traveled to America to evangelize its inhabitants. Clavigero's book was widely read, and it helped to further a growing interest in the history and culture of ancient Mexico. It also fostered the spirit of nationalism among New Spain's mestizo population.

MEXICO AFTER INDEPENDENCE. Shortly after Mexican independence in 1821, the Museo Nacional was established to house pre-Conquest antiquities. In conjunction with the museum's founding, a number of studies of Mexico's ancient culture were carried out. Influenced by current liberal, positivistic ideas, a group of Mexican scholars began to study the ancient Mexican civilizations. Manuel Orozco y Berra, Francisco del Paso y Troncoso, Cecilio A. Robelo, and Alfredo Chavero were the first to investigate Mesoamerican religions in this new manner. The first volume of Orozco y Berra's *Historia antigua y de la conquista de México* (4 vols., 1880–1881), is devoted to a study of native myths and thought, which he compares to Pythagorean and Hindu philosophies, doubtless with the purpose of demonstrating the universal value of Nahuatl ideas. Among other works of scholarship produced were Paso y Troncoso's erudite and well-documented commentary, *Codex Borbonicus: Descripción historia y exposición del códice pictórico de los antiguos náuas* (1898). Robelo compiled a *Diccionario de mitología nahuatl* (2d ed., 1911), which contains source material and scholarly interpretation about ancient Mexican religion in general. Chavero wrote several works on ancient Mexican religion, including *Historia antigua y de la conquista* (1888), the first volume of an ambitious publication project directed by D. V. Riva Palacio and titled *México a través de los siglos* (Mexico through the Ages). In this volume, Chavero espouses the belief that religious ideas provide a means of measuring the degree of advancement of the Mexican people and of determining their social tendencies. He maintains the thesis that native Mexican religion was materialistic inasmuch as it did not include a belief in a spirit or a soul. Later scholars have dismissed Chavero's interpretations as sheer fantasy.

The commencement of the publication of the periodical *Anales del Museo Nacional de México* in 1877 marked the transformation of research from a private endeavor into an academic pursuit in Mexico. During the second half of the nineteenth century, the Mexican contribution to the reconstruction of the Indian past was greater than that of any other national group.

OTHER NATIONAL SCHOOLS OF THOUGHT. The German traveler, naturalist, and man of letters Alexander von Humboldt visited New Spain in 1803–1804 and brought back to Europe a vision of the New World that had up until then eluded the attention of European scholars. Humboldt was so impressed by the vestiges he saw of the ancient pre-Columbian cultures that he proclaimed these civilizations comparable to that of ancient Egypt. He published his most important books on the Americas in French. In one of them, *Vue des Cordillères, et monuments des peuples indigènes de l'Amérique* (1810), which contains paintings and images that captured interest, he deals extensively with the pre-Hispanic calendars, myths, and rituals. By the second half of the nineteenth century, waves of European travelers were visiting Mexico. They made drawings and took photographs of the pre-Hispanic ruins and carried off ancient manuscripts and objects, thus broadening interest in the ancient Mesoamerican cultures.

France. In 1858, a group in France founded the Société des Américainistes de France and started a specialized journal. As an outgrowth of this, the first Americanist congress was held in Nancy in 1874. Some of the first French scholars to write about Mesoamerican religion were Albert Réville (*Les religions du Mexique de l'Amérique Centrale et du Pérou,* 1855), Hyacinthe de Charency (*Le mythe du Votan,* 1871), and Léon de Rosny (*L'interprétation des anciens textes Mayas,* 1875, among dozens of other works). Much later, the ethnologist Jacques Soustelle, of the French sociological school, worked in the field of Mesoamerican religion. In his book *La pensée cosmologique des anciens Mexicaines* (1940), Soustelle claimed that the Mexican image of the universe reflected the people who created it, and he asserted that the gods Huitzilopochtli and Quetzalcoatl corresponded to the ideals of a distinct faction of the dominant class of Aztec society.

Germany. From von Humboldt's time up to the present, German scholars have been producing studies on the subject of Mesoamerican religion, either as parts of works about religion in general (e.g., Friedrich Majer's *Mythologische Taschebuch oder Darstellung und Schilderung der Mythen: Religiösen Ideen und Gebrauche aller Völker,* 2 vols., 1811–1813) or in the form of monographs specifically focusing on Mesoamerica (e.g., J. G. Müller's *Geschichte der amerikanischen Urreligionen,* 2d ed., 1867; and Konrad Haebler's *Die Religionen mittleren Amerika,* 1899). From the analysis of the Mayan Codex Paul Schellhas extracted the first classification of the Mayan gods (*Die Götter festallen der Maya Handschriften. Ein Mythologisches Kulturbild aus dem Alten Amerika* 1897).

Perhaps the most eminent scholar of Mesoamerican religion that Germany produced was Eduard Seler. He was influenced in his interpretations of the origin of myths by his contemporary F. Max Müller (1823–1900), and even more by Ernst Siecke's ideas concerning lunar mythology. Seler's most important work was his commentary on *Codex Borgia: Eine altamerikanische Bilderschrift der Bibliothek der Congregatio de Propaganda Fide* (3 vols., 1904–1909). The first part of volume 4 of Seler's collected works (*Gessamelte Abhandlung zur amerikanischen Sprach- und Altertumskunde,* 5 vols., 1902–1915) is devoted to the mythology and religion of the ancient Mexicans. Hermann Beyer, one of Seler's followers, published more than forty articles (1908–1924) relating to pre-Hispanic religion and symbolism which were published in 1965 in vol. X of *El Mexico antiguo.* Beyer tried to prove that the Aztec's vision of the cosmos was monistic and pantheistic.

Another of Seler's disciples, Konrad T. Preuss, was the first to use pre-Hispanic Mesoamerican religion as the basis for ethnographic studies. His most important work was *Die Nayarit-Expedition,* volume 1, *Die Religion der Cora-Indianer* (1912). Walter Krickeberg in 1928 published a compilation of American myths, *Märchen der Azteken und Inkaperuaner, Maya und Muisca;* in 1956 he brought out *Altmexikanische Kulturen,* in which he emphasized the strong connection between religion and art in Mexican thought.

England. The interest in American antiquities was stimulated in England by E. K. Kingsborough's project, *Antiquities of Mexico,* which eventually produced nine huge volumes (1830–1848). For the most part, British scholars specialized in Maya archaeology. Among them was J. Eric S. Thompson, who from 1927 to 1972 published a number of books and articles and contributed to the deciphering of Maya hieroglyphic writing. In *Maya History and Religion* (1970), Thompson summarized all his research. In his last years, he expressed doubts about the possibility that Maya religion will ever be thoroughly understood, especially given the kind of data that are available to scholars.

Lewis T. Spence, the British historian and mythologist, took quite a different approach; he was one of the few students of Mesoamerica who were primarily specialists in religion. Besides his books on the Americas (e.g., *The Mythologies of Ancient Mexico and Peru,* 1907; *The Civilization of Ancient Mexico,* 1912; *The Myths of Mexico and Peru,* 1913; *The Gods of Mexico,* 1923; and *The Magic and Mysteries of Mexico,* 1930), he wrote about the legendary continents of Atlantis and Lemuria and about the mysteries of ancient Britain and Spain and those of Egypt, Rome, Babylonia, and Assyria. Spence is noted for introducing some ideas that retain importance for contemporary scholars. For instance, he claims that Quetzalcoatl's cult was a "wisdom"-type religion that taught a highly developed form of mysticism and that was similar to the mystery religions that flourished in ancient times in Britain, Greece, and Egypt. The differences between Old and New World systems were superficial, he said, and they arose from a variance in magical practices. The Mesoamerican mystery religion was basically a complex rain cult upon which the solar cult and, later, the Quetzalcoatl rain cult had been superimposed.

United States. Another important researcher in the field of Mesoamerican mythology was Daniel Garrison Brinton. His most important works were *The Myths of the New World: A Treatise on the Symbolism and Mythology of the Red Race of America* (1868) and *Nagualism: A Study in Native American Folklore and History* (1894). Brinton claimed to be using modern methods of scholarship and, in contrast to prevailing scholarly consensus, maintained that the gods of the American tribes had their origins in the observation of natural phenomena rather than in historical chiefs or heroes. He tried to prove that the gods of Mesoamerica were human and benign, that they were loved rather than feared, and that their worship carried within it the seeds of benevolent emotion and sound ethical principles.

One of the great scholars of Maya ritual and religion was Alfred Tozzer who did important archaeological work in Tikal and Chichén Itzá and who developed a meticulous method for organizing his field work. Tozzer looked for contemporary survivals of the prehispanic Maya ritual. In his 1907 *Comparative studies of the Maya and the Lacandon* he dedicated more than half the book to the description of rites and ceremonies, which the author had the opportunity to witness.

The Norwegian scholar Carl Lumholz led a Mexican expedition that was sponsored by American Institutions during the last decade of the nineteenth century, which uncovered vivid examples of religiosity and daily life among tribes of the western Sierra Madre. He was allowed to photograph places and ritual practices as well as interview and collect oral traditions and myths. His *Symbolism of the Huichol Indians* (1900) and *El México desconocido* (1904) provide important data about the world view and ritual life of the Huichol and the Tarahumara peoples.

CONTEMPORARY PERSPECTIVES. During the 1930s and 1940s there was some pioneer ethnographic and historical research done, like Alfonso Villa Rojas's *Dioses y espíritus paganos de los mayas de Quintana Roo* (1941), George Foster's

Nagualism in Mexico and Guatemala (1944), and Robert M. Zingg's *The Huichol, Primitive Artists* (1938). In 1949 the Sociedad Mexicana de Antropología started organizing their Round Tables in which important Mesoamerican themes were discussed.

During the 1950s several important books on the subject of Prehispanic Mesoamerican religions appeared. One of these, *El pueblo del Sol* (1953), by the Mexican archaeologist Alfonso Caso, was the first book written on a popular level to give a general overview of Aztec religion. Caso distinguished three levels of religiosity in Aztec culture: the popular and polytheistic, the priestly, and the philosophical, which, according to Caso, almost attained monotheism. He stressed that the Aztec's actions and, indeed, their very sense of life were derived from the belief that they were a people with a mission. The Aztec conceived of themselves as a people favored by the Sun, allied to the forces of goodness and engaged in a moral struggle against the forces of evil.

One of the most articulate voices on Mesoamerican philosophy and religion is Miguel Léon-Portilla, whose many books and articles have set a standard for writing about worldview, metaphor and poetry. His first book, *La filosofía náhuatl* (1956; *Aztec Thought and Culture,* in English, 1956), attempted to demonstrate that among the ancient Mexicans there was a group of genuine philosophers distinct from the class of priests. He argued that there existed among the ancient Mesoamericans two opposite points of view regarding life and the universe. One was mystic-militaristic, oriented toward war and bloody sacrifice (the main purpose of which was to preserve the life of the sun, which was menaced by the threat of final cataclysm). The other worldview, represented by the Nahuatl symbol for knowledge, Quetzalcoatl, was philosophical and attempted to find the meaning of life through intellectual means. Léon-Portilla, in his *Tiempo y realidad en el pensamiento Maya* (1968; *Time and Reality in the Thought of the Maya,* in English, 1973), provides us with a useful overview of how time and the passage of time was understood to permeate every level of daily life and reality among the Maya. He later wrote other books, including *La religión de los nicaraos* (1972) and *Mexico Tenochtitlan, su espacio y tiempo sagrados* (1978). Appended to *Tiempo y realidad* was included Villa Roja's important essay "Los conceptos de espacio y tiempo entre los grupos mayences contemporaneos."

Corona Núñez wrote two books on the Tarascan: *La religión de los tarascos* (1957) and *Mitología tarasca* (1962). Pedro Carrasco (1950) wrote an ethnohistorical study on the Otomí, and Barbro Dahlgren (1954) on La Mixteca with very important sections on the religion of these ethnic groups.

French archaeologist Laurette Séjourné's *Burning Water: Thought and Religion in Ancient Mexico,* (1957) synthesizes her interpretations of Mexican religion. According to her, the myth of Quetzalcoatl constitutes the paradigmatic revelation at the heart of Aztec tradition, and can be compared to some of the world's great religions. For Sejourne, the chief difference from other great religions was to be found in the distinctive symbolic language of the Quetzalcoatl tradition, which reveals that the human soul passes thorough different stages and ordeals until it reaches a liberated consciousness.

From the 1950s and especially in the 1960s there was an increase in the ethnographic research with an emphasis in indigenous cosmologies and religious practices, including beliefs related to medicine, Indian and Spanish syncretic religion. Most of these studies were made under research projects of the University of Chicago and Harvard University. Many themes are still relevant, including: fertility associated with death; the importance of agricultural myths—especially the ones associated with the rain cycle; the concepts of cold and hot, of the soul, of *tona* and *nagual;* diseases related to the spiritual sphere; and the ritual specialists who had as their main task curing people. While much of this research was synthetized in articles published in the *Handbook of Middle American Indians,* one article in particular constitutes a watershed in the study of Mesoamerican religions, H. B. Nicholson's classic study "Religion in Prehispanic Central Mexico" which appeared in Vol. X (1971) provides us with a thorough account of prehispanic Central Mexican religion. This essay gives special atttention to cosmogony, cosmology, major cult themes, deities, and ritualism based on the archaeological, documentary and pictorial sources, and on the authors who had dealt with the themes up to his publication.

In volumes VII and VIII devoted to Ethnology, specialists wrote about the different ethnic groups, each with a section on religion. Volume VI on Social Anthropology (1967) included several articles related to religion: William Madsens' "Religious syncretism," Frank Canciani's "Religious and Political organization," and Michael E. Mendelson's "Ritual and Cosmology," based on his own investigations and the ethnographic studies published so far by several authors. He directs his attention to Indian and Spanish acculturation, giving priority to the Mayan people, to the distribution of ritual personnel, and to the general study of the forms of ritual and the contents of myth.

Other important books written during these years were Guiteras Holmes's *Perils of the soul* (1961); Holland's, *Medicina maya en los Altos de Chiapas* (1963); Aguirre Beltrán's *Medicina y magia, el proceso de aculturación en la estructura colonial* (1963); and Alain Ichon's *La religion des totonaques* (1969).

In 1972 the twelfth "round table" of the Sociedad Mexicana de Antropología was held in Cholula, Mexico. During the conference, which was titled "Religion in Mesoamerica," ninety-six scholars presented papers, most of which were later published in a volume (1972) and were the seeds of new full investigations. Discussion at the conference centered on a perennial question in Mesoamerican studies: is "Mesoamerican religion" one religious system or many? On one side of the argument were Alfonso Caso and Jiménez Moreno, who posited the unity of the Mesoamerican religions. On the other side was George Kubler, who argued for a Mesoamerican co-tradition following Bennet's 1948 proposal for Peruvian co-tradition. The problem of methodology was raised again during the conference by Kubler's critical voice against the validity of using modern ethnological analogies explaining prehispanic religion. In fact, Kubler was against using even sixteenth century colonial analogies to interpret prehispanic religion explaining older Mesoamerican cultures. He proposed instead Panowsky's principle of disjunction.

Modern Mesoamerican ethnographic studies have proven a unity of Mesoamerican culture, including cosmovision and religion. In 1973 the first Round table of Palenque organized by Merle Green took place and has continued to the present publishing the proceedings, which are the results of important studies.

From the late 1970s, new discoveries in the fields of Mesoamerican ethnography, archaeology and Maya epigraphy have led to an increasing amount of research dealing with the religious systems of Mesoamerica. It includes new types of theoretical trends, such as Marxist, structuralist, cognitive anthropology, symbolic anthropology, phenomenology, hermeneutics, and the scientific study of religion. The increase in publication is so vast that it is impossible to mention all the names involved, therefore only the most significant will be noted.

Eva Hunt, in her book *The Transformation of the Hummingbird: Cultural Roots of a Zinacantecan Mythical Poem* (1977), claims to employ the social-scientific theories of Auguste Comte, Karl Marx, Émile Durkheim (1858–1917), Sigmund Freud (1856–1939), Claude Lévi-Strauss, and Victor Turner—among others—as tools of interpretation. She interprets a modern Maya-Zinacantecan poem in light of its antecedents in Mesoamerican mythology. She concludes that Mesoamerican religion is of a type characteristic of agrarian states, and that it is based upon an agrarian paradigm of space and time.

Other authors who wrote important books on mayense groups include Gary Gossen, *Los chamulas en el mundo del sol* (1979), and Evon Z. Vogt, *Ofrenda para los dioses* (1983).

Alfredo López Austin has contributed many new ideas to the field of Mesoamerican religions. His book *Cuerpo humano e ideología* (1980) examines Nahuatl concepts concerning the human body (of which the soul was considered a part) from within a frame constructed through an understanding of the society from which these concepts arose. López Austin's interpretations of what he calls "soul entities" represent a new kind of reading of ancient Mesoamerican religious thought. He has also put forward the hypothesis of a "hard nucleus" of Mesoamerican culture, a complex of ideas quite resistant to change, but with a dynamic cultural unity which admitted cultural variations, and is followed by almost all Mexican Mesoamericanists.

In his publications *Los mitos del tlacuache* (1990) and *Tamoanchan* (1993), he studies cosmic typology and its significance, the foundation of Mesoamerican mythology from prehispanic times to the present, and proposes an archetype of vegetable type with concepts concerning vegetation and the life and death cycle, which emphasizes the preeminent role of maize.

López Austin also develops cosmological conceptions of the duality of the mythic Tamoanchan and Tlalocan. For him Tamoanchan is the great cosmic tree situated in the center of the universe, which sinks its roots into the underworld and extends its foliage into heaven. Through its two intertwisted trunks, in a helicoidal form, run the streams of opposite forces which, in their struggle, produce time.

A number of scholars, including Michael Graulich, Doris Heyden, Johanna Broda and Yolotl González, have explored the diversity and complexity of Mesoamerican mythologies. Graulich believes that a fundamental pattern in mythology follows the transgressions of the gods and their expulsion from paradise, resulting in human strategies of sacrifice in order to return, in some symbolic or actual way, to a glorious world. Doris Heyden's work has shown how plants, caves, and stones were understood to be imbued with mythic powers and thereby became substances that enabled commoners and elites alike to participate in the worlds of the gods. González Torres shows us how myths of sacrifice not only served as models for ritual sacrifice but also functioned to weave political authority and hegemony together with religious power and prestige. Broda has given special importance to rituals, above all to agricultural rituals and to hills as models of the universe and as *axis mundi*—the center of the world. She sees in all these a reflection of the observation of nature and the cosmos.

Among the many authors who have written about the religion of the Mayans is Mercedes de la Garza, whose methodological approach is the science of religion. She considers Maya religion as a cultural phenomenon by itself, leaving behind interpretations of archeology and other disciplines. Her books include: *El universo sagrado de la serpiente en el mundo maya* (1984) and *Sueño y alucinación en el mundo nahuatl y maya* (1999).

Other authors who have written about Maya religion, are Karl A. Taube, *The Major Gods of Yucatan* (1992), Linda Schele and Mary Ellen Miller, *The Blood of Kings* (1989), and David Freidel, Linda Schelle, and Joy Parker, *Maya Cosmos: Three Thousand Years on the Shaman's Path* (1993). The authors of these books analyze through iconography and epigraphy sacrificial practices and the development of Maya religion and cosmology. Since the 1990s, epigraphic discoveries of David Stuart and Stephen Houston on supernatural domains and spiritual essences have added to the religious knowledge of the Classic Maya.

TYPES OF STUDY. The study of Mesoamerican religions has been the domain of archaeologists, ethnologists, art historians, historians of religion, and sociologists. Most of the literature has been published in anthropological journals, such as *American Anthropologist* (Washington, D.C., 1899–), *Anthropos* (Salzburg, 1906–1979), *Zeitschrift für Ethnologie* (Berlin, 1869–), *Anales del Museo Nacional* (Mexico City, 1877–1945), *Estudios de cultura náhuatl* (1959–), *Estudios de cultura maya* (1962–), *Tlalocan* (1943–) and many other magazines. A newer one is *Arqueología* (1993–), which has articles on Mexican anthropology and history superbly illustrated, with religion occupying an important place. There have been other articles on "Mexican gods," "sacrifice," "rituals" and so on, written by specialists on the particular subjects.

Several museums in Mexico, the United States, Europe, and Asia have held exhibitions of prehispanic objects, most of which are religious, having been found in burial sites and ceremonial centers. These exhibitions have added to the knowledge and the diffusion of prehispanic culture and religion. The most relevant have been: "The Blood of Kings," Forth Worth, Tex. (1986); "Aztec, the World of Moctezuma," Denver, Colo. (1992); "Teotihuacan. Art from the City of Gods," San Francisco (1993); "Gods of Ancient Mexico," Mexico City (1995–1996); "The Mayans," Venice and Mexico City (1999); "A Trip Through the Land of the Gods," Amsterdam (2000); and "Aztecs," London (2002) Berlin (2003) and Washington (2004).

Some exhibitions' catalogues reprint material already discussed in other publications, while others offer new research and become texts in their own right.

There are articles written by different scholars about Mesoamerican religion in encyclopedias of world mythologies or religion (*Larousse World Mythology,* 1988, *Man and His Gods,* 1971) or general histories of religion, like Francisco Diez de Velasco's *Introducción a la Historia de las Religiones* (2002). Dictionaries of Mesoamerican religion have also been published, including: Yolotl González's 1991 *Diccionario de Mitología y Religión mesoamericana* and Mary Ellen Miller and Karl Taube's 1993 *The Gods and Symbols of Ancient Mexico.*

Many research and educational institutions, especially in Mexico, are doing research on Mesoamerican religion, including: the National Institute of Anthropology and History (INAH) with its different museums and regional centers; several research institutes of the National Autonomous University (UNAM); and many other universities and educational centers. The French Center for Latin American Studies (CEMCA), the Italian Mission Italiana and the Polish Center for Latin American Studies have produced books like J Gallinier's *La mitad del mundo en la cosmovisión otomí* (1990); Guillaume Olivier's 1997 *Moquerie et metamorphosis d'un dieu azteque. Tezcatlipoca* (*Mockeries and Metamorphoses of an Aztec God: Tezcatlipoca,* in English); Anne-Marie Vié-Wohrer's 1999 *Xipe Totec, Notre Seigneur l'Ecorché;* Italo Signorini and Alessandro Lupo's *Los ejes de la vida, alma, cuerpo y enfermedad entre los nahuas serranos* (1989); Lupo's *La Tierra nos escucha* (1995); and Andrez Wiercinski's *Tlillan Tlapallan. Estudio de la religión mesoamericana* (1998).

Alcina Frank has written "Dioses zapotecas," 1972, and *El temazcal* (Mesoamerican steam bath), 1999. Rivera Dorado wrote *Religión maya* (1986).

The study of Mesoamerican religions received a major stimulus from the stunning discoveries made in downtown Mexico City by Proyecto Templo Mayor between 1979 and 1985. Led by Eduardo Matos Moctezuma, this truly multidisciplinary excavation uncovered the primary religio-political shrine of the Aztec Empire. The dig uncovered seven complete rebuildings of the Great Temple. Most amazing were the excavations of over 115 ritual caches buried by the Aztecs at key religious cermonies between the fourteenth and sixteenth centuries. Among the many important works written about these discoveries is Leonardo López Luján's excellent synthesis "Offerings of the Templo Mayor of Tenochtittlan." This is one part of Templo Mayor studies developed in a twenty-year collaboration between Eduardo Matos and Davíd Carrasco, who set up the Mesoamerican Archive at the University of Colorado in 1984. Together they have organized important investigations of archeological, ethnohistorical and ideological analysis of sacred space, urban plans and ceremonial practices in ancient Mesoamerica. At Harvard University's Peabody Museum, the archive, in collaboration with the University Press of Colorado, launched a series "Mesoamerican Worlds" which has published results in books, including *To Change Place: Aztec Ceremonial Landscapes* (1991). Carrasco is the author of *Religions of Mesoamerica: Cosmovision and Ceremonial Centeres* and was the editor-in-chief of the three-volume *Oxford Encyclopedia of Mesoamerican Culture* (1999).

Mesoamerican religion is a topic—and sometimes main theme—of numerous meetings of institutions and associations, including: Americanists Congress, American Anthropological Association, Dumbarton Oaks Foundation, and recently, the International Congress of the History of Religion.

The Instituto de Investigaciones antropológicas de la UNAM and the Sociedad mexicana de Estudios de la Religión A.C. organized three coloquia under the name of Historia de la Religión en Mesoamérica y áreas afines. Its proceedings were published by Barbro Dahlgren in 1987, 1990, and 1993.

Recent years have seen an explosion of ethnohistorical and interpretive publications. Significant work has been performed by art historians who have developed a new grasp on the iconographic traditions relating religiosity to politics and art styles. Especially important are the works by Doris Heyden, George Kubler, H. B. Nicholson, Esther Pasztory, Richard Townsend, Elizabeth Boone and Carmen Aguilera. The growing community of Mesoamerican scholars who have developed intensive dialogues among themselves has resulted in a loss of interest in cross-cultural analysis between Mesoamerica and other parts of the world. This is due in part to the recent discrediting of the diffusionist approach of earlier scholars. It may be that in time, new comparative studies will result in useful tools for developing broader views for the rise and complexity of state societies. While historical interpretations of myths continue to dominate the scholarship, a small but potent series of publications drawing on the structuralist approach continue to contribute to our understanding of religion an ideology.

The problem of myth and history has continued to engage scholars such as López Austin, González Torres, Enrique Florescano, Davíd Carrasco and H. B. Nicholson, particularly in regard to the Toltec tradition. Carrasco (*Quetzalcoatl and the Irony of Empire*) and Florescano (*Quetzalcoatl y los mitos fundadores de Mesoamérica*) argue, in different ways, that Teotihuacan either stimulated the idea of Tollan in the minds of Mesoamerican people, or was the original Tollan. In a recent celebrated publication, H. B. Nicholson (*Topiltzin quetzalcoatl: The Once and Future Lord of the Toltecs*) outlines the possibility of some degree of historicity in the Topiltzin Quetzalcoatl of Tollan tale. Others, including López Austin and López Luján, emphasize that Quetzalcoatl and Tollan were understood primarily as mythic sites and figures.

Due in part to the leadership of Anthony Aveni, Franz Tichy, Johanna Broda, S. Milbrath and Y. González, Mesoamericanists have placed an increasing emphasis on astronomical alignments, appearances and patterns in their interpretations of Mesoamerican religions and societies. New fields of study, including archaeoastronomy and ethnoastronomy, have emerged as a result of their publications, and a series of productive conferences in Mexico, the United States and Europe have taken place.

Other studies explore the relationships between energy, man, and the cosmos in ancient and modern Mesoamerican thought. These concepts have been associated with the concept of *mana*. Several authors have linked these concepts with hot (positive) and cold (negative) energy which circulates between the underworld, earth and the supraworld through cosmic trees, and also with the acute consciousness of entropy—which, according to Christian Duverger in his *La fleur létale: Économie du sacrifice aztèque* (1979), characterized the thought of the Aztec.

Concepts about the relation of man to nature and the cosmos present in beliefs, symbols, and rituals permeate almost all Mesoamerican research. Important also has been the research about religious specialists: *rezanderos* (shamans and healers) and *graniceros* (diviners and witches).

For a long time, the main task for all scholars studying Mesoamerican traditions has been to gather all available ethnohistorical and ethnographic material and to attempt, on the basis of this evidence, to reconstruct the different aspects of Mesoamerican cultures, including their religious systems. This reconstruction continues, as new archaeological and ethnographic discoveries are constantly providing new data. New ethnological studies have shown that it is possible to use knowledge of modern Indian religions to help interpret data concerning pre-Conquest religion, and vice-versa. It shows the unity and continuity of Mesoamerican cosmovision, in spite of the superimposition of Catholicism, which has led to the syncretic religion that has been called "popular religion" and has become a wide field of study. One of the most prolific writers on this field is Félix Baez Jorge, the author of *Los oficios de las diosas* (1988), *Las voces del agua* (1992), *La parentela de María* (1994), and *Nahuales and Santos* (1998). Also important is James Dow, author of *Santos y Supervivenicas* (1974), *Giménez Gilberto* (1978), *Cultura Popular y religión en Anahuac, Gonzalo Aguirre Beltrán* (1986), and *Zongolica: encuentro de Dioses y Santos Patronos.*

Isabel Kelly (1961), Isabel Lagarriga (1975) and Silvia Ortiz Echaniz (1991) have studied the "espiritualismo trinitario mariano," a widespread popular religion which gives great importance to spiritual healing.

The role of religion and identity consciousness has also become an important aspect of study, linked to nativism and revival religions. One area in particular has received scholarly attention, resulting in three powerful publications: The contemporary religious practice in communities near Lake Atitlan in Guatemala have been effectively studied by Robert Carlsen (*War for the Heart and Soul of a Highland Maya Town*), Vincent Stanzione (*Rituals of Sacrifice: Walking the Face of the Earth on the Sacred Path of the Sun, a Journey Through the Tz'Utujil Maya World of Santiago Atitlan*) and Nathaniel Tarn and Martin Prechtel, (*Scandals in the House of Birds: Shamans and Priests on Lake Atitlan*).

Indian symbolic reelaboration of Christian stories and calendric festivals like the celebration of the Holy Cross in May and the day of the death in November, as well as the carnival and Holy Week, sanctuaries, pilgrimages, religious dances and the cult of the Virgin of Guadalupe, so strongly linked to Mexican identity, have produced a number of investigations (De la Maza 1981, Nebel 1992, Noguez 1993). Since the 1980s there has been a rapid spread of Protestantism in Mesoamerican communities, especially among the mayense groups of Mexico and Guatemala. This, and the influence of the Catholic Liberation movement, has greatly changed the cosmovision of the different ethnic groups and has led to much religious conflict.

Also appearing are revival and nativist movements, formed mostly by non-Indians, influenced by New Age ideas and pan Indian movements. They try to revive an idealized Aztec religion, denying the practice of human sacrifice. They have adopted as one of their main rituals the "concheros" or Aztec dance and claim that the main archaeological sites are their places of worship, charged with the sacredness of "their ancestors," especially in the equinoxes and the solstices. Some groups have adopted the North American Lakota dance of the sun as their most important ritual. These revivalist religious movements are spreading rapidly throughout Mexico, among the Mexican Americans, and even in Europe. There is also a group of priests, who after the Second Vatican Council (1962–1965), where it was decided that the people had cultural and religious rights, have followed what they call the Indian theology. They argue that the Indians have had their own theology since prehispanic times and that now there should be a dialogue between the Christian theology and the religiosity of the Indian populations.

See Also Calendars, article on Mesoamerican Calendars.

Bibliography

Beyer, Herman. *Mito y simbología en el México antiguo.* Mexico, 1965.

Carrasco, Davíd. *Quetzalcoatl and the Irony of Empire: Myths and Prophecies in the Aztec Tradition.* Chicago, 1982.

Carrasco, Davíd, ed. *To Change Place: Aztec Ceremonial Landscape.* Niwot, Colo., 1992.

Carrasco, Davíd, ed. *The Oxford Encyclopedia of Mesoamerican Cultures,* 3 vols. New York, 2001.

Dahlgren, Barbro, ed. *Historia de la Religión en Mesoamérica y areas afines: Coloquios.* Mexico, 1987, 1990, 1993.

Florescano, Enrique. *Quetzalcoatl y los mitos fundadores de Mesoamérica.* Mexico, 1994

González Torres, Yolotl. "La religión y la cosmovisión mesoamericanas." In *Historia General de la Antropología en México,* pp. 599–617. Mexico, 1988.

González Torres, Yolotl. "The Revival of Mexican Religions: The Impact of Nativism." In *Numen,* vol. 43, pp. 1–31. Leiden, 1993.

González Torres, Yolotl. "Nativisim in México." In *Religion and Society: Procedings of the Seventeenth Quinquennial Congress of the International Association of the History of Religions, México 1995,* edited by Michael Pye and Yolotl González Torres, pp. 29–47. Cambridge, U.K., 2003.

González Torres, Yolotl. "The history of religion and the history of religion in Mexico" In *Perspectives on Method and Theory of the Study of Religions. Adjunct Proceedings of the XVIIth Congress of the History of Religion,* edited by Geerz, A., and Russell McCutcheon, pp. 38–48. Boston, 2000.

Gossen, H. Gary, and Miguel Leon Portilla. *South and Mesoamerican Native Spirituality: From the Cult of the Feathered Serpent to the Theology of Liberation.* New York, 1993.

Hvidtfeldt, Arid. *Teotl and Ixiptlatli: Some Central Conceptions in Ancient Mexican Religion.* Copenhagen, Denmark, 1958.

Litvak, Jaime, Neomí King, and Tejero Castillo, eds. *Religión en Mesoamérica. XII Mesa Redonda.* México, 1972.

Maza, Francisco de la. *El guadalupanismo mexicano.* Mexico, 1981.

Medina, Andrés. "La cosmovisión mesoamericana. Una mirada desde la etnografía." In *Cosmovisión, ritual e identidad de los pueblos indígenas,* edited by Johanna Broda and Félix Baez-Jorge, pp. 67–158. Mexico, 2001.

Nebel, Richard Santa Maria Tonantzin. *Virgen de Guadalupe: Religiose kontinuität und transformation in Méxiko.* Immensee, 1992.

Nicholson, Henry B. *Topiltzin Quetalcoatl: The Once and Future Lord of the Toltecs.* Boulder, Colo., 2001.

Noguez, Xavier. *Documentos guadalupanos: Un estudio sobre las fuentes de informatión tempranas en tomo a las mariofanías en el Tepeyac.* Mexico, 1993.

Wauchofe, Robert, ed. *Handbook of Middle American Indians.* Vols. VI, VII, VIII and X. Austin, Tex., 1967, 1969, 1971.

Yolotl González Torres (1987 and 2005)

MESOPOTAMIAN RELIGIONS

This entry consists of the following articles:

AN OVERVIEW [FIRST EDITION]
AN OVERVIEW [FURTHER CONSIDERATIONS]
HISTORY OF STUDY

MESOPOTAMIAN RELIGIONS: AN OVERVIEW [FIRST EDITION]

Ancient Mesopotamia is the country now called Iraq. Its northern part, down to an imaginary line running east-west slightly north of modern Baghdad, constituted ancient Assyria, with the cities of Ashur (modern Qalʾat Shergat), which was the old capital; Calah (Nimrud); and Nineveh (Kouyundjik), which took its place later, at the time of the Assyrian empire in the first millennium BCE. The country consists of rolling plains resting on a bed of rocks. Rainfall over most of the area is sufficient to sustain a cereal crop. The main river is the Tigris, which traverses the country from northwest to southeast. The language spoken in historical times was Assyrian, a dialect of Akkadian, a Semitic language related to Hebrew and Arabic.

The southern part of Mesopotamia, south of the imaginary line mentioned, was ancient Babylonia, with Babylon (Babil) as its capital. The country here is flat, alluvial plain, and the average rainfall is too scant to allow a cereal crop. The country thus depends on artificial irrigation for its agriculture. It was in antiquity crisscrossed by a formidable net of rivers and canals. Such rains as fall are, though, sufficient to bring up pasture of grasses and herbs in the desert for a short grazing season in the spring. The language spoken was the Babylonian dialect of Akkadian.

The designations *Assyria* and *Babylonia* are appropriate only for the second and first millennia BCE, or, more exactly, from about 1700 BCE on, when Ashur and Babylon rose to political prominence. Before that time the later Assyria was known as Subartu, while what was to become Babylonia consisted of two main parts. Dwellers of the region north of an imaginary line running east-west slightly above Nippur (Nuffar) in historical times spoke Akkadian, while those of the region south of it spoke Sumerian, a language unrelated to any other known language or language family. The northern region was known as Akkad in Akkadian and as Uri in Sumerian, while the southern one was called Sumer or, more correctly, Shumer in Akkadian, Kiengir in Sumerian.

The capital of Akkad was in early times the city of Kish (Uheimir); later on, the city Akkad (not yet located) took its place. The country was traversed by two rivers, the Tigris flowing along the eastern border areas and the Euphrates farther to the west. The course of the Euphrates was, however, not the same then as it is today. Its main branch flowed by

Nippur and east to Shuruppak (Fara), then south to Uruk (Warka), and on to Ararma (in Akkadian, Larsa; now Senkereh) and Ur (Muqayyir). Above Nippur an arching branch, the Arah-tu, took off in a westerly direction, flowing by Babylon before rejoining the main course; another branch flowed south to Isin (Ishan Bahriyāt). In an easterly direction a major arching branch, the Iturungal, took off, flowing by Adab (Bismāya) to Zabalam (Bzeikh), Umma (Joha), and Patibira (Medina) before rejoining the main course at Ararma. At Zabalam the Iturungal sent a branch east, then south, to serve Girsu (Tello), Lagash (Tel al Hiba), and Nina (Zurghul). The main course of the Euphrates south of Uruk sent a branch south to Eridu (Abu Shahrein).

Economically, as mentioned, both Akkad and Sumer depended mainly on irrigation agriculture. There were, however, also other important economies. The region around Uruk and south along the Euphrates was, then as now, famous for its date groves; herding of sheep and oxen provided wool and dairy products as well as meat; fishing and hunting were important along the rivers and in the southern marshlands.

Capital cities in Sumer were Uruk and Ur; later on, Isin and Ararma. Of central religious and political importance was Nippur, seat of the god Enlil.

HISTORY. The earliest settlement of Mesopotamia of which we have evidence took place in the north, in the plains of the later Assyria. Here small agricultural villages, dependent essentially on rain agriculture and herding, occurred as early as the seventh millennium BCE. In the south, the later Babylonia, settlement began in the sixth millennium only, with what is known as the Ubaid period. The people who settled were most likely the forebears of the later Sumerian-speaking people of the region. Their settlement form seems originally to have been one of campsites and seminomadic small villages located along natural watercourses. They depended partly on irrigation hoe agriculture, partly on herding and fishing. Each tribe had a fixed center, a "treasury" in which it kept stores and religious objects that would have been inconvenient to take along on wanderings. Such tribal centers appear to have formed the nuclei of many of the later cities and central sanctuaries, to judge from their names.

The period of the earliest occupation, the Ubaid period, was a long one, and it saw, toward its end, the rise of the first cities. They lined the edge of the southern marshes and may well have owed their existence to a combination of the varied economies of the region: irrigation farming, herding, fishing and hunting; the key requirement for the rise of a city is the availability of economies able to sustain a massing of population on a small space.

Among these first cities were Eridu, Ur, and Uruk, and with the Uruk period, which followed in the late fifth millennium, the cities and the lifestyle they fostered had grown to a point where, as the period was coming to an end around 3500 BCE, we can speak for the first time of true civilization, characterized by magnificent sculpture, monumental architecture, and—most important of all—the invention and development of writing.

As to political forms then in vogue, the occurrence of the term for general assembly (*unkin*) in the early inscriptions is of interest. It belongs in a political pattern called "primitive democracy." Supreme power was vested in a general assembly, which served as a court, as a legislative assembly, and as the authority for electing officers, such as the religio-economic manager, the *en*, and in times of crisis, a war leader, the *lugal*, who served for the time of the emergency only. This pattern made its imprint on early myths and survived as a feature of local government down into the second millennium. In the following Jemdet Nasr and Early Dynastic periods there are suggestions that the pattern of primitive democracy was extended from a local to a national scale with the formation of a league of the city-states along the Euphrates, which met for assembly in Nippur. What specific circumstances could have induced these city-states to forget their local rivalries and join in a common effort is not known for certain, but a plausible guess would be that pressure from invading Akkadian-speaking nomads from the west, which should date to about this time, would have constituted a danger clear and present enough to impose unity, at least for a while.

Whatever unity may have been imposed by the common need to stem the Akkadian advance can have been of short duration only. The Early Dynastic period quickly became one of wars between city-states, which vied with one another for hegemony over the country. The first city to achieve such status was Kish in the north, and its rulers maintained that status long enough to make the title "king of Kish" a term for overlordship over all of Sumer and Akkad. After Kish, various other cities, prominent among them Uruk and Ur, held the hegemony for shorter periods, always precariously and open to successful challenge.

The warlike conditions of life made their mark on the kind of political leadership that had evolved, that of the en and the *lugal*. The *en* was basically a person who produced abundance. He or she participated as spouse of the city deity in the yearly fertility drama of the Sacred Marriage, and generally, through personal charisma, managed city affairs productively. One might speak of a "priest-king" or "priest-queen." The *lugal* was quite different. The term means "great householder," not "great man," as it is generally translated, and the *lugal* was originally the son of a major landowner, chosen in the assembly for his military prowess and for the house servants of his paternal house, who would form the core of the army and its high command. As times grew more warlike—and evidence for war appears already with the late Uruk period—the *en*, if he wished to retain his leadership, was forced to turn his abilities to military leadership also, while the *lugal*, who originally had been chosen for the term of an emergency, tended to become permanent as the threat of war became so. This imposed on him responsibility also for the religious, administrative, and economic tasks that belonged originally to the *en,* so that the functions of the two offices tended to merge. The old title of *en* was continued in Uruk. Almost everywhere else that of *lugal* was preferred. A new title of rather more restricted claim, which made its appearance in the Early Dynastic period, was that of *ensi,* "productive manager of the arable lands." It designated the official in charge of plowing, and thus of the city's draft animals, which in war would serve the chariotry of its army. The *ensi,* therefore, tended to become the political head of the community, its ruler.

At the very end of the Early Dynastic period a ruler of the city of Umma succeeded in extending his domain to include all of Sumer and Akkad. After an unsuccessful campaign in the north he was defeated and his realm taken over by Sargon of Akkad (c. 2334–2279). Sargon's successors kept a precarious hold on the south until, at the accession of Naram-Sin (c. 2254–2218), that region made itself independent. Akkad continued to flourish, however, deriving its wealth from its position on the major overland route from the Mediterranean to Iran and India, a route the Akkad rulers carefully policed. The city's wealth may have been the cause of an attack on it by a coalition of neighboring countries. Naram-Sin met their armies one by one and defeated them, thus regaining control of all of Mesopotamia. This feat so awed his fellow citizens that they deified him and chose him city god of Akkad. Under Naram-Sin's successors Akkad went into decline, and the Gutians, invaders from the eastern mountains, for a while took control. They were defeated, and the country liberated, by Utuhegal of Uruk, who in turn was succeeded by the famous third dynasty of Ur. Under that dynasty a well-integrated administrative system was developed. The formerly independent city rulers now became governors appointed by, and responsible to, the king and his corps of central officials.

The third dynasty of Ur ended in disaster. A breakthrough of Mardu tribes, nomads of the western desert, disrupted communications and isolated the former city-states from the capital, Ur, which lost control of all but the immediately adjacent territory. Eventually the city fell to an invading force from Elam and was mercilessly looted. Its fall spelled the end of Sumerian civilization even though the language, as the vehicle of culture and learning, continued to be taught in the schools.

The third dynasty of Ur was followed by two long-lived dynasties, one of Isin and one of Larsa, which divided the country between them. They in turn gave way to the short-lived rule of all of Babylonia by Hammurabi of Babylon (fl. 1792–1750), famous for his law code, and his son Samsuiluna. Late in the latter's reign the south and middle of Babylonia again made itself independent, now under the name of the Sea Land. It covered much the same territory as had Sumer, and its kings consciously stressed their role as heirs to Sumer's ancient language and culture. The dynasty of Babylon fell to a raid by the faraway Hittites around 1600 BCE. When the Hittites had withdrawn, invaders from the mountains, the Kassites, took control and ruled Babylonia for a substantial length of time. One of these Kassite kings, Ulamburiash, conquered the Sea Land and thus unified Babylonia once more. The major rivals of the Kassite kings were the rulers of Assyria, which since the time of Hammurabi had grown in power and influence.

The Kassite dynasty fell before an attack by Shutruk-Nahunte of Elam, who controlled the country for a while. Then a move to regain independence developed in Isin, and the energetic ruler Nebuchadrezzar I (1124–1103) completely liberated the country, defeated Elam, and brought back the statue of Marduk, the city god of Babylon, which the Elamites had earlier taken as booty. From this time on begins the rise of that god to a position of supreme power in, and creator of, the cosmos. Before then the traditional view with Enlil as supreme god had held sway as the officially accepted one.

The following centuries saw a steady rivalry between Babylonia and Assyria, with the latter eventually victorious. After a gradual extension of their authority over Syria by the Assyrians, Tiglath-pileser III (745–727) conquered Babylonia, and under his successors, Sargon II, Sennacherib, Esarhaddon, and Ashurbanipal, it remained an Assyrian dependency even though at times it had its own Assyrian-appointed king and a semblance of independence. Throughout this time, however, Babylonia remained a thorn in the side of its Assyrian overlords. It even drove Sennacherib to the extreme of obliterating the city, only to have it restored by his son Esarhaddon.

Assyria fell in 609 BCE, after the capital, Nineveh, had been captured in 612 in a combined attack by the Medes and the army of Babylonia. Here an Aramean, Nabopolassar, had achieved freedom from the Assyrian yoke and founded a dynasty. After participating with the Medes in the destruction of Nineveh and Assyria, he turned to the conquest of Syria, which was accomplished by the crown prince Nebuchadrezzar, who followed his father to the throne in 605.

In 539 BCE Babylon opened its gates to the Persian king Cyrus. The last indigenous ruler, Nabonidus, had incurred the hatred of the Marduk priesthood through his championship of the moon god Sin of Harran and his attempts at religious reform. For part of his reign he left rule in Babylon to his son Belshazzar and withdrew himself to the Tema Oasis in Arabia. With him ended Babylonian independence.

DIVINE FORMS: THE NUMINOUS. Basic to all religion, and so also to ancient Mesopotamian religion, is, I believe, a unique experience of confrontation with power not of this world. The German theologian and philosopher Rudolf Otto called it the numinous experience and characterized it as experience of a *mysterium tremendum et fascinans,* a confrontation with a "wholly other" outside of normal experience and indescribable in its terms. It is the human response to it in thought (myth and theology) and action (cult and worship) that constitutes religion.

Since what is met with in the numinous experience is not of this world, it cannot be described, for all descriptive terms necessarily reflect this-worldly experience and so fall short. At most, therefore, it will be possible to seek to recall and suggest the human response to the numinous experience as closely as possible by way of analogy and evocative metaphor. Every religion, accordingly, has evolved standardized versions of such metaphors. They form the link from firsthand to secondhand experience, become the vehicle of religious instruction, and form the body of collective belief. They will differ, naturally, with the different civilizations in which they are grounded and from which their imagery is taken. Study of any given religion must thus begin with the study of its favorite and central metaphors, taking due care not to forget that they are but metaphors and so are no end in themselves but are meant to point beyond.

Physiomorphism. Turning, then, to the world of ancient Mesopotamian religion, its most striking characteristic seems to be an innate bend toward immanence. The numinous was here experienced as the inwardness of some striking feature or phenomenon of the situation in which it was encountered, as a will and power for that phenomenon to be in its particular form and manner and to thrive. It was therefore natural that it should be considered to have the form and name of the phenomenon whose inwardness it constituted. It was also natural that the early settlers should have been drawn particularly to those numinous forces that informed phenomena vital to their survival, the early economies, and that they should have wished to hold onto them and maintain them through cult and worship.

The original identity of numinous powers with the phenomena they were thought to inform is indicated by divine names such as *An* ("heaven") for the god of heaven, *Hursag* ("foothills") for the goddess of the near ranges, *Nanna* ("moon") for the moon god, *Utu* ("sun") for the sun god, *Ezen* ("grain") for the grain goddess, and so forth. Occasionally an honorific epithet, such as *en* ("productive manager, lord") or *nin* ("mistress"), was added, as in *Enlil* ("lord wind") and *Nintur* ("mistress birth-hut"). In some cases the mythopoeic imagination elaborated on a phenomenon to bring out its character more vividly, as when the numinous thundercloud Imdugud ("rain cloud") takes form as an enormous bird floating on outstretched wings and emitting its thunderous roar through a lion's head, or when Gishzida ("wellgrown tree") is given form as the stock of a tree entangled in roots having the form of snakes, thus visualizing the belief of the ancients that tree roots could come alive as snakes.

The early selectivity of powers experienced in phenomena of vital economic importance to the settlers shows in the distribution of city gods, who must be considered coeval with their cities, over the various regional economies of the country. The extreme south is marshland with characteristic economies such as fishing, fowling, and hunting. Here was Eridu, the city of Enki, whose other names were *Daradim* ("wild goat fashioner") and *Enuru* ("lord reed-bundle"), signifying power in the marsh vegetation and in the reed bundles with which reed huts were constructed. Farther east, in Nina, resided Enki's daughter Nanshe, goddess of fish, the numinous force producing the teeming schools of fish that gave the fisherman his livelihood. South of Nina, in Kinirsha, was the home of Dumuzi-Abzu ("producer of healthy young ones of the marsh"), the mysterious numinous will and power for the young of marsh fauna to be born healthy and unimpaired. Through the marshlands along the Euphrates runs also the country of the ox herdsman and the orchardman. To the ox herdsman's pantheon belonged the bull god Ningublaga and his consort Nineiagara ("lady of the creamery"). In Ur resided Nanna, the moon god envisaged by the herdsman as a frisky young bull with gleaming horns—the new moon—grazing in the pasture of heaven. In Ararma, farther up river, resided the sun god Utu, whose round face was seen as the round face of a bison. At Uruk, finally, was the cow goddess Ninsuna ("mistress of the wild cows"), who was herself visualized as cow-shaped, and her bull-god husband, Lugalbanda. The ox herdsmen grazed their herds on the young shoots of reed and rushes in the marshes along the Euphrates. Closer to the river itself was the country of the orchardmen, who depended on the river for the irrigation of their plantations. To them belonged Ninazu of Enegir, seemingly a god of waters, and his son Ningishzida ("master of the good tree") of Gishbanda, a deity of tree roots and serpents. His wife was Ninazimua ("mistress of the well-grown branch"). Damu, city god of Girsu on the Euphrates, was a vegetation god, especially, it would seem, the power for the sap to rise in plants and trees in the spring. Farther up still, at Uruk—in antiquity as today a center of date culture—there was Amaushumgalana, the power for animal growth and new life of the date palm, and his consort Inanna, earlier Ninana ("mistress of the date clusters"), a personification of the date storehouse.

At Uruk the country of the orchardmen and the oxherds joins that of the shepherds; called the *edin*, it is a wide, grassy steppe in the heart of Sumer, ringed around by the Euphrates and the Iturungal. Here on the western edge is Uruk with Inanna of the shepherds, goddess of the rains that call up verdure and grazing in the desert, and her young husband, Dumuzi ("producer of healthy young ones"). This pair was also worshiped in Patibira on the southern edge, and in Umma and Zabalam on the eastern edge. On the southern edge lies also Ararma with the sun god Utu and his son Shakan, god of all four-legged beasts of the desert, and to the north is the domain of Ishkur, god of the thundershowers that turn the desert green like a garden in the spring.

North and east of the *edin*, finally, lay the plowlands with cities dedicated to cereal and chthonic deities, or deities of the chief agricultural implements, the hoe and plow. Shuruppak on the Euphrates was the home of Ansud, goddess of the ear of grain and daughter of Ninshebargunu ("mistress mottled barley"). Farther up the river was Nippur with

Ansud's divine husband, Enlil; and since Enlil's winds were the moist winds of spring that made the soil workable, he also was god of the oldest and most versatile agricultural implement, the hoe. Nippur—the city rather than its sacred quarter around Enlil's temple, Ekur—was also the home of Enlil's son Ninurta ("master plow"), god of the younger implement, the plow, and charged in Nippur with the office of plowman (*ensi*) on his father's estate. Identified by the ancients with Ninurta were the gods Pabilsag ("first new shoot"), who in Isin was husband of the city goddess Nininsina ("mistress of Isin"); and Ningirsu ("master of [the city] Girsu"), who in Girsu, southeast of the *edin*, was essentially a god of the thundershowers and the floods of spring. Farther north, in Cutha, resided the netherworld gods Meslamtaea ("the one issuing from the luxuriant mesu tree")—presumably originally a tree deity—and Nergal. In Kish resided Sabbaba ("ever spreading the wings"), a god of war and originally, perhaps, of the thundercloud. In Babylon Merodakh, or Marduk ("calf of the storm"), was the city god. He was a god of the thunderstorm envisaged as a roaring young bull.

Anthropomorphism. It seems reasonable to consider the physiomorphic forms the original and oldest forms under which the gods were envisaged, yet one should probably not altogether exclude the possibility that the human form may be almost equally early. The two forms were not mutually exclusive, and a deity might well choose to appear now under one, now under another. Seal impressions from the late Uruk period show the ritual scene of the sacred marriage with the goddess Inanna in her physiomorphic form of storehouse gateposts on some, in her human form on others. A later example is a statement about Gudea, ruler of Lagash (fl. c. 2144–c. 2124 BCE), who lived shortly before the third dynasty of Ur and whose goddess mother was the cow goddess Ninsuna. He is said to have been "born of a good cow in its woman aspect." As late as the early first millennium, a hymn to the moon god revels in attributing to the god physiomorphic and anthropomorphic forms alike: he is a prince, a young bull, a fruit selfgrown, a womb giving birth to all, and a merciful, forgiving father.

Although human and nonhuman forms thus could coexist peacefully, there are indications that they were not always equally favored. The human form was clearly seen as more dignified and appropriate than the nonhuman one and tended to eclipse it.

One outcome of this attitude was representations in which the two different kinds of form were blended but with the human features dominant. In Girsu, for instance, at the end of the Third Early Dynastic period a mace head dedicated to Ningirsu, god of thundershowers and floods, shows the donor in a pose of adoration before the god in his old form of a thunderbird. Somewhat later, when Gudea saw the god in his dream, Ningirsu was essentially human in form although he retained the thunderbird wings and merged the lower part of his body with a flood. From the time of Gudea stems also a vase dedicated to Ningishzida that shows the god in his cella with the door open and flanked by two gatekeepers in dragon form. The god appears in his original form of the stock of a tree entwined by serpent-shaped roots. To this same period belongs a relief that shows Ningishzida introducing Gudea to Ningirsu. Here he is in completely human form except for two heads of serpents peeping out from his body at the shoulders. In much similar fashion, vegetation deities on seals are shown with branches and greens protruding from their bodies as if—in the words of the archaeologist Henri Frankfort—their inner being was seeking to burst asunder the imposed human form.

Composite forms such as the above still recognize the relevance of the nonhuman forms and preserve their essential characteristics even if the human form clearly dominates; but more radical trends away from the physiomorphic representation deliberately separated the deity from the phenomenon which he or she informed. The deity became a power in human shape; the phenomenon subsided into a mere thing owned or managed by the deity, and the form derived from it into a mere emblem.

Thus, for instance, the goddess Hursag ("foothills") ceased being the deified foothills themselves and became instead Ninhursaga ("mistress of the foothills"). Similarly, the deified wild cow became Ninsuna ("mistress of wild cows"). Gishzida ("good tree") turned into Ningishzida ("master of the good tree"). Ningirsu's form of thunderbird was referred to by Gudea as his emblem, and it adorns—and perhaps protects—Ninurta's war chariot on the famous Stela of the Vultures. Inanna, as goddess of the morning and evening star, had the physiomorphic form of the small, round disk which that star looks like in the Near East. That too became an emblem carried as a standard by the contingent from her clan when Gudea called it up for work on the temple he was building.

As so often with religious beliefs, so also here: no change is ever a clean break. Although demoted to emblems, the old forms did not altogether lose their potency. It is in these forms, as standards, that the gods followed the army in war and gave victory, and it is in these forms that the gods sanctioned oaths. Oaths were taken by touching them.

At times the aversion felt for the older, nonhuman forms must have been intense enough to engender open enmity. This seems to have been the case with the thunderbird, which from being Ningirsu's early shape became first a mere emblem of his and then was listed by editors of the myth about him, called *Angim*, among the god's captured enemies pulling his triumphal chariot. In still later time the bird—often shown as a winged lion rather than as a lion-headed bird—even became the god's chief antagonist. Thus in the Akkadian myth of Anzu (the Akkadian name of the bird) the god victoriously routs and subdues his own former self. A pictorial representation of the battle graced his temple in Nimrud. In these later materials Ningirsu is called by the name of Ninurta, the god of Nippur with whom he was early identified.

Sociomorphism. Man is a social being: he exists in a context of family and society generally, so in attributing to the gods human form the ancients almost unavoidably attributed to them also social role and status. One such basic context implied in the human form was that of family and household. In the case of major deities the household could be sizable, resembling that of a manorial lord.

The factors that determined the grouping of deities into a given divine family are not always obvious and may have been of various kinds—similarity of nature, complementarity, spatial proximity, and so forth. Similar character probably dictated the grouping of seven minor cloud goddesses as daughters of the god of thundershowers, Ningirsu. The nature of their mother, Ningirsu's wife, Baba, is less clear; she may have been a goddess of pasture. Ningirsu's son Igalima ("door leaf of the honored one") appears to be a deification of the door to Ningirsu's court of justice. Since clouds were seen to rise as mist from the marshes, the positing of the raincloud god Asalluhe as son of the god of the marshes, Enki, seems understandable. So too does the marriage of Amaushumgalana, the power producing the date harvest, to Inanna, the goddess of the storehouse. A logical connection seems observable also between the aspect of Enlil in which he is god of the older agricultural implement, the hoe, and that of his son Ninurta, god of the younger implement, the plow; but only too often no explanation readily suggests itself.

Our most complete picture of a major divine household is given by Gudea in the hymn known as Cylinder B. It lists the minor gods who served as functionaries in Ningirsu's house, that is, his temple, lending divine guidance to the human staff. Thus Ningirsu's oldest son Shulshagana served as majordomo, the traditional role of the eldest son. His brother Igalima functioned as chief gendarme responsible for the maintenance of law and order on the estate. Ningirsu's septuplet daughters served as his handmaidens and also presented petitions to him. He had two harpists—one for hymns, one for elegies—and a chambermaid, who bathed him at night and saw to it that his bed was provided with fresh straw. For the task of administering his estate and sitting in judgment in disputes that might arise, the god had a divine counselor and a secretary *(sukal)*. There were two generals, and an assherd to look after the draft animals. Goats and deer on the estate were cared for by a divine herder of deer; a divine farmer looked after the extensive agricultural holdings; a tax gatherer supervised the fisheries; and a ranger protected the wildlife of the estate against poachers. A high constable and a night watchman kept the estate safe.

In addition to their local functions of looking after their estates, most of the major deities had also wider, national responsibilities as officers of the divine polity into which the sociomorphic view was gradually transforming the cosmos. Highest authority in this divine state was a general assembly of the gods, which met in Nippur in a corner of the forecourt of Enlil's temple, Ekur, called Ubshuukkinna. An and Enlil presided; the gods took an oath to abide by the decision of the assembly, and voted by saying "Heam" ("May it be!"). The assembly served as a court—it once even banned Enlil himself—and it elected cities and their rulers to hold sway over all of Sumer and Akkad. The election was for a term only, and when the assembly decided a term was ended, it voted to overthrow the reigning city and transfer its kingship to another city and ruler.

Besides the office of king, the divine state knew also more permanent offices. For the most part these offices, which were called *me* ("office, function"), were reinterpretations of functions already innate in the gods in question, the phenomena and processes of which they were the indwelling will and power; they were now envisaged as the official duties of members of a divine bureaucracy. A comprehensive statement of this view of the cosmos is found in the myth *Enki and the World Order*, which tells how Enki, acting on behalf of Enlil, institutes the proper course of natural phenomena and the manner of engaging in human industries, appointing in each case a divine official to be responsible for them. The regime of the Tigris and the Euphrates thus comes under the administration of the "inspector of canals," the god Enbilulu. Other officials are appointed for the marshes and the sea; the storm god Ishkur is made the official in charge of the yearly rains. For agriculture the farmer god Enkimdu and the grain goddess Ezinu are appointed; for the wildlife, the god of beasts, Shakan; for the flocks, Dumuzi, the shepherd; for just boundaries, the god of justice, Utu; for weaving, the spider goddess, Uttu; and so forth.

THE PANTHEON. A pantheon seeking to interrelate and to rank the innumerable deities the ancient Mesopotamians worshiped, or merely recognized, in cities and villages throughout the land evolved gradually through the diligent work of scribes, who produced lists of divine names as part of their general lexical endeavors. The resulting scheme as it is known to us from old Babylonian copies was based primarily on the prominence in the cosmos of the cosmic feature with which the deity in question was associated, secondarily on his or her family and household ties. It is thus anthropomorphic and sociomorphic in character. First came the deities of heaven, the winds, the eastern foothills, and the underground fresh waters, each with his or her family and household. Then followed deities of smaller entities such as the moon, the sun, and the morning and evening star. A following section dealing with deities of the Lagash region was probably not part of the original list, since that region was considered enemy territory down to the time of the third dynasty of Ur. Last came the deities of the netherworld. In its main lines, and necessarily highly selectively, the pantheon may be presented as follows (Akkadian names, when different from the Sumerian ones, are given in parentheses).

An. An (Anum) was god of the sky and father of the gods. The main center of An's cult seems to have been in

Uruk. An was given form mythopoeically as a mighty bull whose bellowing was heard in the thunder. The rain was seen as his semen impregnating the earth (*ki*) and producing vegetation. As the cloudy skies vanished with the spring, An as Gugalanna ("great bull of heaven") was thought to have been killed and gone to the netherworld. A different tradition saw An (Anum) as the sky in its male aspect married to An (Antum), the sky in its female aspect. She, like her husband, was given bovine form and seen as a cow, whose udders, the clouds, produced the rain. An important aspect of An was his relation to the calendar, the months having their characteristic constellations that announced them. To this aspect belonged monthly and yearly festival rites dedicated to An.

Enlil. God of wind and storms, Enlil was the most prominent member of the divine assembly and executor of its decrees. The city of Enlil was Nippur (Nuffar), with his temple, Ekur. He was married to the goddess Ninlil ("lady wind"), who was also known as Ansud ("long ear of grain"). Her mother was Ninshebargunu, the barley goddess, and her father, Haya, was keeper of the seal with which the doors of Enlil's granaries were secured. Originally in keeping with the agricultural ambience of his wife, Enlil would seem to have been the power in and for the moist winds of spring that soften the hard crust on the soil and make it tillable. Thus he was also god of the oldest tool of tillage, the hoe. With the hoe, after he had invented it, he broke—according to one myth—the hard crust on the earth at Uzumua ("flesh-grower"), in Nippur, so that mankind could shoot up like plants from the earth.

Two quite different myths deal with the wooing of Ninlil or Ansud by Enlil. In one he follows successfully established procedures for winning her. In the other, more primitive one, Ninlil, disregarding her mother's instructions, deliberately tempts Enlil to take her by force by bathing in the canal of the town. Enlil is then banished from the city by the assembly of gods for his misdeed and leaves for the netherworld. Ninlil, pregnant with the moon god Suen (Sin), follows him. On the road Enlil, posing successively as gatekeeper of Nippur, man of the river of the netherworld, and ferryman, persuades her to lie with him that she may conceive a further child, who may take Suen's place in the netherworld. Thus Suen's netherworld brothers, Meslamtaea, Ninazu, and Ennugi, are engendered. The myth ends—oddly to a modern reader—with a paean to Enlil as a source of fertility: "A lord of great consequence, a lord of the storehouse are you! A lord making the barley grow up, lord making the vines grow up are you! Lord of heaven, lord of abundance, lord of earth are you!"

The aspect of Enlil in which he was the benevolent provider of abundance is clearly an old one, and it was never lost sight of. With time, however, his character took on also more grim features. As leader of the divine assembly and executor of its decrees, he became the power for destruction of temples and cities, the all-obliterating storm with which the assembly overthrew dynasties and their capitals as it shaped history. This later aspect of Enlil is prominent in laments, where more and more the will of the assembly becomes subsumed in his will, and it is for him alone to relent and to restore what he had destroyed. In the first millennium, as Marduk of Babylon rose to preeminence, Enlil, as representative of the often-rebellious south, even came to be treated as enemy and evil in northern Babylonia, as is clear from his role in ritual texts; or he was totally ignored, as in the late creation epic *Enuma elish*, which celebrates Marduk as the creator and ruler of the cosmos.

Besides the tradition which had Ninlil or Ansud as consort of Enlil, there existed a variant one in which he was paired with the goddess Ninhursaga, the older Hursag ("foothills"). Here probably also belongs an aspect of Enlil in which he was seen as a mountain deity, his name in that capacity being Kurgal ("great mountain") and that of his main temple, Ekur ("mountain house"). The connection between this mountain aspect and his aspect as god of the wind appears to correlate with the fact that the ancients believed the home of the winds to be in the mountains. Enlil would thus originally have been specifically the east wind, *imkura* ("wind of the mountains").

On Ninhursaga, Enlil begat the seasons of the year, Winter and Summer, and he also fathered the god of the yearly flood of the Tigris, Ningirsu. In the form the myth of the latter takes in Gudea's references to it, Ningirsu is the semen of Enlil reddened in the deflowering. This may be taken to refer to the waters of the melting snow in the high mountains in Iran (Enlil as Kurgal) in the spring. The waters make their way through the foothills (*hursag*), where the clay they absorb gives them a reddish hue, to pour into the Tigris, swelling it to flood, Ningirsu.

Ninurta. In Nippur, the town itself—as distinct from the sacred area around Ekur—had as city god a son of Enlil called Ninurta, whose wife was the goddess Nin-Nibru ("queen of Nippur"). Ninurta's name may be interpreted as containing a cultural loanword, *urta* ("plow"), thus identifying him as god of that implement, much as his father, Enlil, in one aspect was god of the older agricultural tool, the hoe. Ninurta held in Nippur the office of plowman (*ensi*) for Ekur, and at his yearly festival the king opened the plowing season behind a ceremonial plow. Ninurta was early identified with Ningirsu of Girsu, and myths pertaining to the latter were freely attributed to him, so that it often is difficult to determine which traits are original to whom.

A clear case is that of the myth *Lugale*, which can be shown to belong originally to Ningirsu. It depicts the god as a young warrior king who learns that a rival has arisen in the mountains and plots to kill him. He sets out with his army for a preemptive strike, attacks impetuously, and faces disaster, but is saved by advice from his father to send out a heavy rain, which lays the dust that his adversary, one Azag, had raised against him, nearly suffocating him. He then succeeds in killing Azag and goes on to organize the regime of the Tigris, bringing its waters down for irrigation. Before that they had flowed into the mountains, where they froze. To hold the waters on their new course, Ningirsu constructs a barrier of stone, the foothills (*hursag*), and when his mother comes to visit he presents it to her as a gift, renaming her Ninhursaga ("mistress of the foothills"). Last he sits in judgment over Azag's warriors, various kinds of stones that he had captured, and imposes rewards or punishment according to their conduct in the war. His judgments determine the nature and the distinguishing traits of the stones in question for all time. He finally returns victoriously home.

To Ningirsu probably also belongs the myth *Angim* (mentioned above), which describes the god's victorious return from war and how he has to tone down his boisterous behavior lest he upset his father, Enlil. The basis for the tale would seem to be a spell for averting thunderstorms—Ningirsu was god of the thunderstorm—from Nippur. Conceivably a hymn praising Ninurta in his relation to various stones could be in origin Ningirsu material.

So perhaps also is a myth telling how the thunderbird stole the tablets of destiny from Enki in Eridu, how Ninurta set out to recover them, intending to keep them for himself, and how, when his weapon stunned the bird, it let go its hold of the tablets, and they of themselves returned to Enki. Frustrated in his ambition, Ninurta then raised a flood against Eridu, but Enki craftily had a turtle dig a pit, and he lured Ninurta into it. Underlying the myth is apparently a concept of the rain cloud rising as mist from the swamps, Enki's underground waters (*apsu*), and, moving in over the mountains, the flight of the thunderbird. The return of the waters in the flood is seen as the god's jealous attack on Enki, and his imprisonment in the turtle's pit must stand for the eventual dwindling of the flood to a trickle between towering banks, the pit.

Nusku. To Enlil's household belonged Nusku, in origin a god of lamps. He served as Enlil's trusted vizier and confidant.

Ninhursaga. Ninhursaga ("mistress of the foothills"), earlier simply Hursag ("foothills"), was the power in the fertile near slopes of the eastern mountains, the favorite grazing grounds in the spring. Her cities were Kesh, not yet identified, and Adab, the modern mound Bismaya. In addition to the name *Ninhursaga*, the goddess was also known as *Ninmah* ("august mistress"), Dingirmah ("august deity"), and *Nintur* ("mistress birth-hut"), her name as goddess of birth. Her Akkadian name was *Beletili* ("mistress of the gods"). She, An, and Enlil formed in the third millennium the ruling triad of cosmic powers.

Enki. Enki (Ea) was god of the underground fresh waters that come to the surface in rivers, pools, and marshes. The Sumerians imagined them as a vast subterranean freshwater sea, which they called Abzu or Engur. Enki's city was Eridu (Abu Shahrein), where he resided in the temple called Eengura ("house of the deep"). A myth tells how he built it and celebrated its completion with a feast for his father, Enlil, in Nippur. Enki's mother was the goddess Namma, whom the scribes listed as Enlil's housekeeper. Other evidence suggests that she was the deified riverbed that gave birth to the god of the river, Enki. Her name seems to mean "mistress vulva," and it may be that the mythopoeic imagination of the ancients saw the chasm of the empty riverbed as the vulva of the earth. Enki's spouse was called Damgalnunna ("great spouse of the prince"), a name that tells us little about her. Enki's vizier was a Janus-faced god, Sha (Usmu).

The name *Enki* means "productive manager [lord] of the soil," which must seem highly appropriate for the god of river waters in a society dependent on irrigation agriculture. In a hymn he describes himself in this aspect, saying: "When I draw near unto heaven, the rains of abundance rain down; when I draw near unto the earth, the early flood at its height comes into being; when I draw near unto the yellowing fields, grain piles are heaped at my command." Water not only slakes the thirst of men, animals, and plants, it also serves to cleanse. In that aspect, as power to cleanse, Enki appears in rituals of purification from all that defiles, including evil spirits attacking man, causing disease and uncleanness. One such elaborate ritual, meant to purify the king of possible evil caused by an eclipse, has the form of a trial before the sun god in which Enki sends a messenger, the exorcist, to speak for the claimant, the polluted king, and undertakes to enforce the verdict. This he does by washing all evil away with his water. The ritual is called Bitrimki ("bathhouse"). In other rituals Enki provided the effective incantation and prescribed the needed cleaning and healing acts, and it is not too much to say that he occupied a central position in all white magic for combating demons of illness.

Since Enki always knew what to do to drive away demons, he generally rated as the most resourceful and ingenious of the gods. He was skilled in every craft, and under different names he served as patron deity for most of them. His practical ingenuity also made him a born organizer. He was the one who organized the cosmos for Enlil in the myth *Enki and the World Order*, discussed above. Enki in the myths told about him never uses force; instead he gains his point by cunning deftly exercised. An example is the story of Adapa, the steward of Enki, or rather of Ea, for the text uses his Akkadian name. When Adapa once was summoned to appear before Anu in heaven for having broken the wing of the south wind, Ea told him how to gain the goodwill of the two gods who guarded the gate so that they would intercede for him. Ea also warned him not to eat and not to drink, for he would be offered the bread of death and the water of death. All went as planned, and Anu was appeased by the intercession of the doormen. When Adapa refused food and drink, however, Anu was surprised and asked why. Adapa told him, and Anu burst into laughter. The food and drink would actually have made Adapa immortal, which Ea knew and did not want to happen.

A rather more momentous occasion on which Enki showed his cunning was when he saved the human race from destruction at the hand of Enlil. We are told about it in the Sumerian story of the flood, which forms part of the myth called the *Eridu Genesis.* Mankind, having been created and provided with leadership—in the form of kings—by the gods, prospered and proliferated, to the extent that the noise they made became so irksome to Enlil that he persuaded the assembly of the gods to wipe out man with a universal flood. Enki, who was present, was able to warn the pious King Ziusudra to build an ark. Ziusudra followed the advice and was eventually accepted among the gods and granted eternal life as reward for saving all living things.

A far more detailed—and conceivably more original—version of this story is found in the Akkadian tale of Atrahasis ("the surpassingly wise"), who here takes the place of Ziusudra. The story falls into two halves, each clearly originally a separate tale. The first half tells how in the beginning the gods themselves had to work for their food, digging the needed irrigation canals. They eventually rebelled, and Ea thought of the solution, creating man to do the hard work. To that end a god was killed and his blood mixed into the clay from which man was to take form. The mother goddess gave birth to him, and there was general rejoicing. The second half tells how mankind proliferated on earth and with their noise kept Enlil from going to sleep. Enlil therefore tried to cut down on man's numbers by a succession of diseases and famines, but each time Ea found ways of stopping the evils before it was too late, and soon man again proliferated as before. Finally Enlil decided on a desperate means: wiping out mankind with a flood. Again Ea frustrated the plan, by having Atrahasis build an ark in which he survived with his family and the animals. As he emerged from the ark he offered a sacrifice, and the gods were delighted, for all through the flood, with no humans to offer sacrifice, they had suffered severely from hunger. Only Enlil was wroth, but him Ea appeased by instituting plans for population control: barrenness, child disease, and so forth. Thus harmony in the universe was reestablished. As given in the tale of Atrahasis, the story of the flood is the most detailed we have. A shorter version—shorn of any motivation for the flood—was added to the *Epic of Gilgamesh* by the later editor Sinliqiunnini. In the story of Adapa, Enki used his ingenuity against Anu; in the flood story, against Enlil.

A third myth, *Enki and Ninmah,* pits Enki against the third in the triad of highest deities, Ninhursaga, whom the myth calls Ninmah. Like the Atrahasis story, this composition consists of two separate myths only very loosely connected. The first of these is a Sumerian counterpart to the first part of the Atrahasis story, where the refusal of the gods to work had Enki propose the creation of man. Here he is fathered by "the engendering clay of Abzu," which once also fathered Enki, and he is given form and is borne by Enki's mother, Namma. The second myth begins with a party given by Enki to celebrate the birth of man. As he and Ninmah, who had assisted Namma as birth helper, drink deeply, Ninmah begins to boast that she controls men's fortunes, determining whether they will be good or bad. (That makes little sense if she was, as here, a mere midwife. Apparently, in the original myth underlying this part of the composition she was, as in the Atrahasis story, the one who gave shape to the embryo of man and bore it as an infant.) Enki accepts her challenge, waging that he can counter anything she can think up. She then creates a series of misshapen or otherwise defective human beings, but for each one Enki is able to think of a place in society where it can function and support itself. When Ninmah finally gives up, Enki proposes that he try his hand and that she find a place for his creature. He then fashions an embryo and has it given premature birth by a woman provided by Ninmah. There is nothing Ninmah can do for it, and she breaks out in lament. Enki, however, calms her with a conciliatory speech, pointing out that it is precisely her contribution, the maturing of the embryo in the womb, that it lacked. The man's contribution to the engendering of a child is not enough by itself; the woman's is needed too. And so he praises her powers.

The question thus raised, of the respective share of the male and the female partner in procreation, seems to have been variously answered at different times. The first part of *Enki and Ninmah* gives the woman all the credit. Man was engendered from clay, formed, and given birth—as it specifically states—without a male being involved. Somewhat similarly, the tale of Atrahasis has man created from clay and divine blood and formed and given birth by Nintur, that is, by Ninmah. Enki's contribution in both cases was chiefly the idea of making man. In the second part of *Enki and Ninmah,* however, this changes. Enki's power to create an embryo, although not to mature it and give it birth, is stressed; and finally, in the account of the creation of man in *Enuma elish* at the turn of the first millennium, the birth goddess has vanished, and Enki does the creation all by himself.

One final odd composition with Enki as its hero remains to be mentioned, *Enki and Ninhursaga.* It begins with praise of the island of Dilmun (modern Bah-rain) and its pristine purity at the beginning of time. It then tells how Enki provided it with fresh water and made it a port and an emporium. Next we hear how Enki attempts to seduce Ninhursaga but is rejected until he proposes marriage, making her his wife. She gives birth to a daughter, whom Enki seduces as soon as she becomes nubile, fathering a second daughter, whom in turn he seduces and makes pregnant. Her daughter, Enki's granddaughter, is Uttu, the spider goddess, and Ninhursaga warns her against Enki. Uttu therefore refuses to let him into the house unless he brings wedding gifts of fruits. He does so, and when Uttu lets him in, he takes her by force. Uttu's screams bring Ninhursaga, who removes Enki's semen and sows it. From it eight plants grow up. Later, passing by, Enki notes the plants, and as his vizier gives them names, Enki eats them. Ninhursaga, discovering what has happened, vows never to look upon him with her life-giving eye. The plants, Enki's semen, which he swallowed, then begin to develop as embryos in his body. Being male, he is unable to give birth to them, and so falls critically ill. The gods are greatly distressed, but the Fox offers to bring Ninhursaga. It does so; she is released from her vow, places Enki in her vulva, and successfully gives birth to eight deities, who are named and given status, their names serving as grotesque puns on the words for the part of Enki's body from which they come. The last is the goddess of Dilmun.

The stress on Dilmun, and on Enki's amorous success with his daughter, granddaughter, and, in one version, great-granddaughter, the "comely spider goddess Uttu," is hardly meant to be taken seriously. Presumably, the earthy humor of the composition was intended to amuse visiting sailors from Dilmun when they were entertained at the court of Ur.

Asalluhe. Asalluhe ("man-drenching Asar"), city god of Kuar, near Eridu, and god of rain clouds, was Enki's son. He appears predominantly in incantations against all kinds of evil doings. Floating as a cloud above the earth, he was in a position to observe what was going on below and duly reported it to his father, Enki, who was not in a similar, favorable position to observe. On hearing Asalluhe's account, however, out of his profound knowledge he was able in each case to tell how the evil was to be countered. Identified with Asalluhe in later times was Marduk.

Marduk. Marduk, or preferably Merodakh, city god of Babylon, was an old Sumerian deity who, like Ninazu in Eshnunna (discussed below) and Meslamtaea in Cutha, was taken over by the Akkadian invaders. His name, abbreviated from *(A)marudak* ("calf of the storm"), characterizes him as a god of thunderstorms visualized as a bellowing young bull. The thundershowers of spring mark the appearance of verdure in the desert and of plowing and sowing; thus Marduk's chief festival, the Akiti (Akitu), or "time of the earth reviving," was further described as "of the seed plowing." His city was Kadingira ("gate of the god"), translated into Akkadian as Babilim. The name indicates a settlement grown up at the entrance to a sanctuary, presumably Marduk's temple Esagila ("house with head held high"). Throughout the third and second millennia, it would seem, Marduk's status was little more than that of a local city god. With the advent of the first millennium, however, began his rise to supreme god of the universe and his rivalry for that honor with Ashur of Assyria.

Marduk's claim to supremacy was celebrated in the creation epic *Enuma elish,* in which he is presented as savior of the gods and creator and organizer of the cosmos. The myth begins by tracing world origins from a watery chaos of fresh waters, Apsu, and salt waters, Tiamat, the sea. From them stemmed various generations of gods: Lahmu and Lahamu; Anshar and Kishar, the horizon; Anu, heaven; and Nudimmud or Ea. The younger gods, getting together to dance, proved disturbing to the older generations, who prized peace and quiet. Tiamat, as a long-suffering mother, bore with it, but Apsu decided to get rid of the troublemakers. However, before he could carry out his evil design he was overcome and slain by Ea, who then built for himself a house on top of Apsu's body. There Ea engendered his son Marduk. Anu, inordinately fond of his grandchild, fashioned the four winds for little Marduk to play with. The winds disturbed the still surface of the sea, creating billows. This greatly vexed the older gods, and they were able to rouse Tiamat to action. An army was assembled to destroy the younger gods and was placed under the command of Tiamat's paramour Kingu. The threat to the gods was serious and caused consternation among them. Both Ea and Anu, who were sent to cope with the crisis one after the other, failed and turned back. Finally, since the gods were in deepest despair, Ea suggested to the leader of the gods, Anshar, that Marduk be summoned to champion the gods. Marduk came and was willing to undertake the task, but he demanded full authority. The gods agreed, gave him the power for his word to come true, and made sure by a test that his word now had that effect. Marduk then rode to battle on his storm chariot. The sight of him overwhelmed the enemy; only Tiamat dared face him, but after an angry exchange of words, as she opened her maw to swallow him, he drove in the winds and then killed her with an arrow. Her army he took captive, enclosing it in a net held by the four winds. Out of the carcass of Tiamat Marduk then created the extant universe. He split her in two, and made out of one part heaven; out of the other, earth. To prevent her waters from escaping he provided bolts and guards. In heaven, directly opposite Ea's Apsu, he built his own house, Esharra, which the text says was the sky. He then fashioned the constellations, organized the calendar, fixed the polestar, and gave the moon and sun orders about their motion.

When Marduk returned home, he was hailed by the gods, who reaffirmed their allegiance to him. His first demand of them, then, was that they build him a city, to be called Babylon. He then pardoned the captive gods, who gratefully hailed him as king and savior and promised to build his city for him. Their willingness moved Marduk to think of a means of lightening their labors, and he decided to create man. An assembly was called. Kingu was denounced as the instigator of the rebellion and was slain, and out of his body Ea fashioned man. Marduk then divided the gods into two groups, one celestial and one terrestrial. The gods for the last time took spade in hand and built the city Marduk wanted, Babylon. At a great housewarming party to celebrate the completion of Babylon, Marduk was appointed permanent king of the gods. The myth ends with the gods naming Marduk's fifty names, each of which expressed a power that he held. Marduk's consort was the goddess Sarpanitum; his son, the god of Borsippa near Babylon, was Nabu, god of the scribal art.

Nanna. Nanna (also Suen or Sin) was the god of the moon. His city was Ur (Muqayyir); his temple there, Egishnugal. His wife was Ningal. His own name, *Nanna,* would seem to designate him as the full moon, while *Suen* would be the name of the sickle moon. He was regularly envisioned in a bull shape, an image that the hornlike shape of the sickle moon may have encouraged. He was also visualized as a herder driving his herd—the stars—across the pastures of heaven, or as riding in the heavens in a boat, the sickle moon. A late myth—actually an incantation to ward off the evils of an eclipse of the moon—tells how he was attacked by storm demons after they had lured the storm god, Ishkur, and Inanna, who aspired to queenship of heaven, to their side. The attack was noted, however, by Enlil, who alerted Enki and had him send Marduk to the rescue.

Utu. The god of the sun and of justice and fair dealings was Utu (Shamash). His cities were Ararma (Larsa) in the south and Sippar in the north. His temple in both cities was called Ebabbar; his wife was Ninkurra (Aya). As judge, Utu presided each day in various temples at specific places called "the place of Utu." He was greeted in the morning as he rose on the horizon, heard cases all day, and was sped on his way in the evening, at sundown. During the night he sat in judgment in the netherworld. The cases he heard, whether by day or by night, were apparently normally such as were brought by the living against ghosts and demons that plagued them.

Ishkur. Ishkur (Adad) was the god of rains and thunderstorms. A text, basically a spell to avert a threatening thunderstorm from Nippur, tells him to go away so as not to disturb his father, Enlil, with his clamor. His original form seems to have been that of a bull. In many ways he resembles Ningirsu, but he seems to be more specifically a herder's god, the power in the spring rains that bring up pasture in the desert.

Inanna. Inanna (Ishtar) was earlier called *Ninana*, which can be understood as either "mistress of the date clusters" or "mistress of heaven." The center of her worship was, in the south, at Uruk, in the temple called Eana, and in the north at Hursagkalamma, near Kish. Characteristic of her is her great complexity and many-sidedness. It is apparent that a variety of originally different deities were syncretized in her and also that the ancients had been able to blend these differences into a fascinating, many-faceted, and convincing character. Normally she was envisioned as a rather willful, highhanded, young aristocratic girl of marriageable age or else as a young bride. Her lover or husband is a form of the god Dumuzi (Tammuz). In the complex image the goddess presents it seems possible to distinguish the following aspects, presumably once independent figures.

1. As goddess of the storehouse of dates, Inanna was at home in Uruk, situated in a famous date-growing region. Her name *Ninana* here stands for "mistress of the date clusters"; the name of her temple, *Eana*, for "house of the date clusters." Here, at the gate of the storeroom (*egida*), she received her bridegroom, Amaushumgalana ("the one great source of the date clusters"), that is, the one great bud that the date palm sprouts anually. He was the power that made the date palm produce; their wedding and his entering Inanna's house constitute a mythopoeic view of the bringing in of the date harvest. As the rite of this marriage was performed later, the ruling king not only took the role of, but actually became, Amaushumgalana, while the goddess would have been incarnate in the queen, Ninegala ("mistress of the palace"). In the literature relating to Inanna's wedding she is therefore often called by that epithet, and in love songs written for that occasion it is often difficult to tell whether they celebrate Inanna's love for Amaushumgalana or perhaps rather that of the human queen for her husband. The cult of Inanna in her aspect of goddess of the date storehouse was a happy one. There was no sense of loss, no "death" of the god. The dates, eminently storable, were always with the community, and so was the power they represented.
2. Rather different was another aspect, also at home in Uruk, but in the Uruk of sheepfolds rather than of date groves. In this aspect Inanna was the power of the thundershowers of spring, on which the shepherds depended for pasturage in the desert. In this aspect she was paired with Dumuzi, the shepherd. Her early form was apparently that of the lion-headed thunderbird, which remained with her as an attribute. Besides it, and more or less replacing it, was also the form of the lion alone.
3. Closely related to Inanna's aspect as goddess of the thunderstorm was her aspect as goddess of war. The thunderous rumble of the primitive war chariot made it easy to see and hear thunder as the chariot's counterpart in the sky. The ferocious nature of other forms such as lions and bulls fitted easily into the image. As goddess of war, Inanna led the Dance of Inanna, the moving of the battle lines toward each other as if they were lines of dancers. In the myths about her she subdues the insubmissive Ebeh mountain range in southern Assyria.
4. An astral aspect of both Inanna and the Akkadian Ishtar is that of goddess of the morning and evening star, with which she forms a triad with her father, the moon god, and her brother, the sun god. Her precise function in this role is not clear except insofar as her appearance marked the beginning and the end of the working day. As goddess of the morning and evening star her name was understood to mean "mistress of heaven," and her celestial affinities conceivably also encouraged an interpretation of the name of her temple, *Eana*, as "house of heaven" and a belief that it had originally descended from heaven. There is even evidence that in later times she managed to supplant the goddess of heaven, An (Antum), as spouse of the god of heaven, An (Anum), and became queen of heaven. In the *Eclipse Myth* she unsuccessfully conspires with the storm demons to obtain that position, but in a later myth, the *Elevation of Inanna*, the august assembly of the gods itself petitions An to marry her, and she is invested with supreme powers among the gods.
5. Finally, as protector of harlots, Inanna was herself envisaged as a harlot. Her original form in this aspect was that of the owl, which, like the harlot, comes out at

dusk. Correspondingly her name as harlot was *Ninnina* ("mistress owl"). In Akkadian her name was *Kilili.*

In the myths dealing with Inanna a frequently occurring motif is her insatiable desire for power. In the *Eclipse Myth,* as noted, it leads her to conspire with the evil storm demons; in *Enki and the World Order* she complains bitterly that all other goddesses have offices and only she has none, so Enki tries to assuage her. In the myth *Inanna and the Parse,* that is, Inanna and the divine offices called in Sumerian *me,* we are told how she visited Enki in Eridu, how he drank deeply at the party welcoming her, and how in an expansive mood he conferred upon her one office after another. Wisely, she decided to leave immediately for home with her newly won offices, so that when Enki woke up sober and wanted the offices back it was too late. The myth lists the offices one by one; they constitute a formidable list. Owing, probably, in large part to the syncretistic background of the image of Inanna, the offices attributed to her show little unity or coherent pattern; rather, they form a motley collection of variorums. That did not trouble the ancients though; instead, they gloried in Inanna's versatility, and a major hymn to her even makes a point of praising her as goddess of opposites, of insult and veneration, downheartedness and good cheer, and so on.

Inanna's lust for power is also an important motif in the best known of the myths about her, *Inanna's Descent to the Netherworld.* It prompts her to descend to the realm of death to wrest queenship over it from its rightful queen, Ereshkigal. The attempt fails, and Inanna is killed and turned into a cut of meat gone bad and hung on a peg. When she fails to return, her loyal handmaiden Ninshubura seeks help, first from Enlil in Nippur, then from Nanna in Ur, and finally from Enki in Eridu. Only Enki can think of a means to help. He creates two creatures from the dirt under his fingernails and sends them to the netherworld with instructions to condole with Ereshkigal, who, as is her custom, laments children who have died before their time. Then, when moved by the creatures' concern she grants them a wish, they are to ask for the tainted meat hanging on a peg and to throw on it the grass and water of life which Enki has given them. They follow the instructions, and Inanna rises alive. As she is about to leave the netherworld, however, its ruling gods stop her and decree that she must provide a substitute to take her place. So she is accompanied by a detachment of netherworld police to ensure that she will designate a substitute to go back with them.

On the journey back to Uruk she is met by one loyal servant after another, all clad in mourning for her, and she refuses to hand any of them over to the demons. When they reach Uruk, however, they come upon her young husband, Dumuzi, sitting in fine clothes and enjoying himself listening to the music of reed pipes. This flagrant lack of concern infuriates Inanna, and in a flash of jealous rage she hands him over to the demons, who carry him off. In his distress he calls upon his brother-in-law, Utu, god of justice and fairness, and asks Utu to change him into a gazelle—in another version into a snake—so that he can escape his captors. Utu does so, and Dumuzi escapes, only to be again caught; again he escapes, until finally he is caught for good in his sheepfold. The story ends with Dumuzi's sister Geshtinanna, the goddess of the grapevine, seeking him. Eventually, advised by the Fly, she finds him and joins him in the netherworld. In distress at the undeserved misfortune of both Dumuzi and his sister, Inanna decrees that they may share the obligation to serve in the netherworld as her substitute: Dumuzi will serve half a year below; then he will return to the world above while his sister takes over. She in turn will return after half a year as he goes below.

This ends the tale, and a closer look at it will suggest that *tale* rather than *myth* is the proper designation, for it is most easily understood as a composite of dead myths put together for dramatic effect by the storyteller and haphazardly embellished. The myth of Inanna's death and transformation into a cut of spoiled meat is best understood as an original myth in which she represents the underground storehouse for meat; she becomes like a grave when the meat rots in summer, but she is revived—as the storehouse is restocked with fresh meat from the flocks fed on the grass and water of life, the pastures of spring. The myth has nothing to do with Inanna's aspect as the morning star, in which the storyteller has her present herself when she seeks entry into the netherworld. The second part of the tale was originally a separate myth dealing with Dumuzi rather than with Inanna, and it has also come down, in slightly variant forms, as a separate, self-contained myth.

Dumuzi. Like Inanna, and perhaps even more so, does her lover and bridegroom, Dumuzi (Tammuz), present a highly complex, syncretized image, one in which it is not always easy to sort out cleanly the various strands woven into it. Some fairly distinct aspects do, however, stand out and may reasonably be assumed to represent originally separate, independent deities. They are the following.

1. *Dumuzi as Amaushumgalana,* the power for productivity in the date palm. His marriage to Inanna as numen of the storehouse celebrates the bringing in of the date harvest. His cult was based in Uruk.
2. *Dumuzi the shepherd,* the power causing ewes to produce normal, well-shaped lambs. His bride was Inanna as goddess of the spring rain showers that call up verdure for pasture in the desert. The vanishing of the power he represented when the lambing season came to an end was seen as the death of the god, to be observed with wailing and lament.
3. *Dumuzi of the beer.* No separate distinctive name sets apart this aspect of the god. The texts dealing with it sometimes use the name *Dumuzi,* sometimes *Damu.* They involve the search for him after his death by his sister and mother.
4. *Damu the child,* the power for the sap to rise in plants

and trees in the spring. Considered lost during the dry summer, he was sought by his mother and found coming down the river, presumably with the beginning of the early flood in spring. His cult was based in Uruk.

5. *Damu the conscript*, an aspect of the god under which he was seen as a young boy liable for military service. He has been taken forcibly from his mother by brutal recruiters, and she seeks him, gradually realizing that he is dead. What precise power he represented is not clear; most likely it was one connected with the welfare of cattle herds. His cult was based in Girsu (Tello) on the Euphrates.

The myths about these various aspects of Dumuzi naturally fall into two groups, those dealing with wooing and wedding and those dealing with his death and the search for him. To the first group belongs a dialogue between Inanna and Dumuzi in which he has found a house for them near her parents. She does not know that they have chosen him as her future husband, and he teases her, stating that his family is like her family, as it were. Eventually he enlightens her, and she is well pleased. The Inanna of this tale seems very young. Slightly older, she appears in a tale in which Dumuzi's sister Geshtinanna tells him that Inanna invited her in and told her how she, Inanna, suffered from love for her brother. Dumuzi is quick to ask leave to go, and is off to ease the damsel's suffering. At about the same age, Inanna appears in a different story, awaiting Dumuzi toward evening. They had met and fallen in love the day before, and when Dumuzi appears he impetuously propositions her. She promptly turns him down and apparently—the text is broken here—makes him propose properly. When the text resumes they are on their way to her mother's house to announce the engagement.

Another story tells how Inanna's brother Utu has arranged a marriage for her but is unsure about how she will receive the news. He therefore speaks obliquely, proposing to bring her fresh flax for a linen sheet. He does not say that it is to be her bridal sheet, but she immediately understands. Afraid to hear her brother's choice in case it turns out to be a wrong one, she postpones the crucial question, pretending that she has nobody to ret the flax, spin it, double the thread, weave it, dye it, and bleach it, but each time Utu offers to bring the flax already prepared. So at last she has to come to the point: who is to lie down with her on it? When Utu tells her it is Amaushumgalana, she is overjoyed. The wedding itself is recounted in a tale which begins with Inanna sending for her bridegroom and attendants, specifying what gifts they are to bring. They appear before the house, but Inanna is in no hurry. She bathes and dresses in all her finery and listens to instructions from her mother about the obedience due to her parents-in-law. Eventually she opens the door to Dumuzi—the formal act that concludes a Sumerian marriage—and presumably (the text is broken here) leads him to the bridal chamber for the consummation of the marriage. A wedding feast probably follows the next morning. When the text resumes, Dumuzi is leading his young bride to his house and wants first to take her to his personal god that he may bless the marriage. But Inanna is thoroughly frightened, so Dumuzi tries to hearten her by telling her what an honored position she will occupy in the household and how no domestic work whatever will be demanded of her.

The other group of myths, centering on the death of the young god, is perhaps best represented by the myth called the *Dream of Dumuzi*. In it, Dumuzi has an ominous dream that Geshtinanna interprets as boding death for them both. Dumuzi sends her up on a mound as lookout, and she reports the arrival of a boat with evil recruiters. Dumuzi decides to hide in the desert, but first he tells his sister and colleague where he will be. When the recruiters land and offer bribes for information, Geshtinanna is steadfast; however, the colleague betrays his friend. Dumuzi is captured but appeals to Utu to help him escape by turning him into a gazelle. Utu does so, and Dumuzi does escape, only to be again caught. This repeats itself until he flees to his fold. The pursuers break in, wrecking everything on their way, and Dumuzi is killed. A similar myth, the *Most Bitter Cry*, also describes the attack on the fold and the rude awakening of Dumuzi, naked and a prisoner. He manages to escape and flees toward Uruk. As he tries to cross the Euphrates, however, he is swept off by the flood and drowns before the eyes of his horrified mother, Duttur, and wife, Inanna.

Lugalbanda and Ninsuna. Lugalbanda ("fierce king") and Ninsuna ("mistress of the wild cows") were apparently city god and goddess of Kullab, a city that was early absorbed into Uruk. Both were deities of cattle, but with the absorption of his city Lugalbanda seems to have lost definition, and even his divine status. He appears in historical times predominantly as an ancient king of the first dynasty of Ur, and his achievement in the extant epic about him, that of a supernaturally gifted messenger, was probably tacked on precisely because nothing else was known about him. Ninsuna for her part managed to keep her divine status. She was the tutelary goddess of Gudea of Lagash and, curiously enough, in that role was the consort of Ningishzida, not of Lugalbanda.

Ningirsu. Ningirsu ("master of Girsu") was the city god of Girsu, with the temple Eninnu. His wife was the goddess Baba. Ningirsu was god of the thunderstorms in spring and of the spring flood of the Tigris. His early form was that of the thunderbird, an enormous eagle or vulture with a lion's head out of which thunder roared. Ningirsu was early identified with Ninurta of Nippur, and a great deal of his mythology was therefore transferred to the latter (it has been discussed above). *Ninurta* was also the name under which the god was borrowed by the Assyrians when he became prominent as god of war.

Gatumdug. Gatumdug was goddess of the city of Lagash (Al Hiba), south of Girsu. The meaning of her name is not clear, but other evidence suggests that she was also a goddess of birth giving.

Nanshe. The goddess of fowl and fish was Nanshe. She was city goddess of Nina (Zurghul), with the temple Siratr.

She was, according to Gudea, the interpreter of dreams for the gods.

Ninmar. City goddess of Guabba and seemingly a goddess of birds was Ninmar.

Dumuzi-Abzu. Dumuzi-Abzu was city goddess of Kinirsha, and the power for fertility and healthy new life in the marshes.

Nininsina. Nininsina ("mistress of Isin") was city goddess of Isin (Ishan Bahriyat), south of Nippur, which served as capital of Sumer for most of the time after the third dynasty of Ur until the advent of the Old Babylonian period. She seems to have been envisaged in the shape of a dog and was presumably the goddess of dogs. Her special powers were those of the physician. Her daughter Damu—different from the boy of Girsu on the Euphrates—followed in her mother's footsteps as goddess of healing.

Ereshkigal. The name of the goddess Ereshkigal (Allatum) meant "queen [of the] greater earth." The ancients believed that there was a "larger heaven" above the visible sky that connected with a "larger earth" below the observable earth. In the larger earth was the realm of the dead, of which Ereshkigal was queen, although a variant—and conflicting—belief located the realm of the dead in the eastern mountains. The ancients imagined it as a walled city. As with cities on earth, the wall served not only to keep out enemies but also to keep in people—as, for instance, the slaves—who were not free to leave the city. It had its own police and a court where the sun god presided during the night. Existence there was dreary. If one had no son to make funerary offerings, one lived like a begger, but with many sons one could enjoy a degree of comfort. Reasonably well off were also young men killed in battle—they had their parents take care of them—and small children, who played with golden toys. In the second and first millennia ideas about existence below seem to have become even darker: dust was said to cover all; the dead were clad in feathers like birds; and when an Assyrian prince visited the netherworld in a vision, he found it full of horrifying monsters. Ereshkigal herself was cast in the image of a mourning woman, pulling her hair and raking her body with her nails for grief as she lamented the children dead before their time. In the late myth of Nergal and Ereshkigal she plaintively tells of her joyless life: even when young she never played as other young girls did. Ereshkigal's husband seems to have been originally Gugalanna ("great bull of heaven"). A variant, perhaps later, tradition has Ninazu as her spouse, and finally Nergal became king of the netherworld with Ereshkigal as his queen.

Ninazu. The meaning of the name *Ninazu* is not clear, but it apparently has to do with water. Most likely, since he was a netherworld god, his name refers to the waters underground. His wife was Ningirda ("mistress [well-]rope"), a daughter of Enki. In the north, in Eshnunna (Tel Asmar) in the Diyala region, where his Akkadian name was *Tishpak* ("outpouring"), he was a god of rain storms. His city in the south was Enegir on the lower Euphrates.

Ningishzida. Ningishzida ("master of the well-grown tree") was the god of trees, especially the powers in the root that nourish and sustain the tree. As god of tree roots he was naturally seen as an underground, netherworld power. His office there was that of throne bearer, an old title for the head of the constabulary. Ningishzida's wife was Azimua ("well-grown branch"). His city was Gishbanda on the lower Euphrates. The ancients thought that there was a common identity between tree roots and snakes, the latter being roots moving freely. Accordingly, Ningishzida was also the god of serpents, and his older form, as noted above, was that of the stock of a tree around which serpent roots wind, the whole resembling the Greek caduceus.

Nergal. The other names of Nergal ("lord great city"), originally probably designating different gods, were *Meslamtaea* ("the one issuing from the luxuriant *mesu* tree") and *Irra. Meslam* or *Emeslam* ("house Meslam") was the name of Nergal's temple at Cutha, in Akkad.

A myth preserved in a copy found at Tell al-ʿAmarna in Egypt and dating from the thirteenth century BCE tells how Nergal came to be king of the netherworld. Once when the gods were feasting they sent a message down to Ereshkigal inviting her to send up her vizier, Namtar, to fetch her a portion of the delicacies. She did so, and when he arrived all the gods rose respectfully except one, Nergal, who rudely remained seated. When Namtar reported this, Ereshkigal furiously demanded that the offending god be delivered up to her so that she could kill him. But when Namtar came for Nergal, Ea had changed his appearance so that Namtar did not recognize him. Later, however, Ea told Nergal to take a throne down to Ereshkigal to placate her. Nergal was understandably reluctant, but Ea insisted and gave him demons to hold open the gates of the netherworld so that he could get out fast if needed. However, he met with no resistance, pulled Ereshkigal down from her throne by the hair, and threatened to kill her. When she pleaded for her life, offering marriage and rule over the netherworld, Nergal accepted, kissed her, and wiped away her tears, saying wonderingly, "It was but love you wanted of me from months long ago to now." A later version greatly enlarges on the tale. It has Nergal visit the netherworld twice, the first time to bed Ereshkigal against Ea's advice and to escape, the second time to stay after Ereshkigal has passionately pleaded with the gods for his return.

Another myth, the *Irra Epic*, celebrates Nergal under the name *Irra* (an Akkadian name meaning "scorched earth"), which most likely originally designated a separate god. The epic tells how Irra was roused to action by his weapon, Sibittu (the name means "heptad"), and how he persuaded Marduk to leave him in charge of the world while Marduk went to have his jewels cleaned. Irra's first act was to foment rebellion in Babylon and have it ruthlessly put down by the commandant of the Assyrian garrison in that city. Next Irra had riots, rebellions, and wars spread all over the country, and might have destroyed it completely had not his vizier,

Ishum, reasoned with him and persuaded him to leave a remnant. The epic ends with self-praise by Irra, who nowise regrets his deeds of violence—rather, he suggests that he may cut loose again at any time.

Ashur. Ashur was city god of Ashur (Qal'at Shergat) and chief god of Assyria. No recognizable features characterize him other than those that belong to his role as embodiment of the political aspirations of his city and nation. Even his wife and the name of his temple are not truly his own; they were borrowed from Enlil as part of Ashur's aspiration to the universal dominion for which Enlil stood. Basically, thus, he may in origin simply have been a *numen loci*—a spirit inhabiting a place and imbuing it with its character—named from the place where his presence was sensed.

THE TEMPLE. The earliest Mesopotamian temples may have been in origin storehouses in which nomadic or seminomadic tribes kept their sacred objects and provisions, which were too cumbersome to carry along on their wanderings. Very soon, though, these structures would have been considered, as always later, dwellings of the gods to whom they belonged. The earliest recognizable form was that of a dwelling house with a large, rectangular middle room from which two smaller rooms projected at the end, creating a T-shaped effect. With time the projecting rooms disappeared and left a rectangular room that was entered from a door in one of the side-walls near its end. At the short end-wall farthest from the door was a dais that kept the seat of the owner, in this case the god, out of the floor-level draft. In later times a niche in this end-wall steadied a baldachin, or tentlike aedicula, further protecting the god. Before the dais a curtain shielded him from profane eyes. On low benches along the side-walls stood statues of worshipers to remind the god of the people they represented and their needs. The god himself was, to judge by depictions dating from as early as the late Uruk period, represented by a statue in physiomorphic or anthropomorphic form. Facing it—conceivably inside the hanging—stood a large vase with greenery of various kinds, sometimes placed over a drain, into which petitioners received in audience by the god would pour libations before presenting their petitions.

Temples were by preference built on existing high ground; in addition, frequent rebuildings, during which stumps of the old walls were left while their upper parts were dumped in the space between them as fill to make a new building site, tended to create a small mound under the new rebuilding. In fact, this development, by which a temple came to stand on the walls of earlier ones, became in later time so much a part of the concept of a temple that builders created underground artificially filled-in walls for the actual walls to rest on. Such a filling was known as a temple terrace (*temen*). At the time of the third dynasty of Ur, possibly already in the time of the dynasty of Akkad, these mounds were built high, with stairs leading up to the temple on top, and were squared off to form a stage tower, the so-called ziggurat. With larger temples it became customary in early dynastic times to surround them with a protective oval wall, called an *ibgal.* The pattern for this may conceivably have been the long curved pile of camel-thorn gathered for fuel with which bedouins—then as now—ringed their camps in the desert. It served the double purpose of protection and a handy fuel supply. Inside the oval, along its sides, were the various storerooms, kitchens, and workshops for the temple personnel, while the house on top of the terraced tower constituted the god's living quarters: bedroom, bath, and so on. Often a few side rooms were added to the central structure.

In time—as can be seen by comparisons of temple plans from Khafaje with those for the later one at Ishchali—a tendency toward squaring off the oval and greatly enlarging the plan of the temple on the high terrace led to a new concept of the older design. The central room was enlarged so that its lower parts with the door became the size of a court. At its end the hanging or hangings were replaced with walls having doors in the middle, thus creating a rectangular cella with the niche and dais at the middle of the far side-wall, a so-called broad-room cella, which became standard for Sumero-Akkadian and Babylonian temples from the third dynasty of Ur on. The remainder of the original central room developed into a court with surrounding rooms. A gate and covered landing midway up the stairs leading to the temple above often served as court of justice in which the god sat in judgment. In Assyria the development from the bent-axis approach took a different course. There the door was relocated around the corner nearest to it to the middle of the end-wall facing the wall with the niche and dais, thus creating the long-room type of temple.

The temple, rising over the houses of the community, was visible and tangible proof of the god's presence and, more, that he was himself a member of the community and had a stake in it, with his house, his servants, his oxen and sheep, and his fields in grain. To have the temple was a privilege. To build it or rebuild it needed divine approval, which was not always granted. The story of the *Cursing of Akkad* told of the dire consequences of King Naram-sin's willful decision to rebuild Ekur in Nippur without Enlil's permission. Even rebuilding after enemy attack and demolition needed divine cooperation. The god had to be roused from his state of shock after the catastrophe to make him able to act, so laments to soothe him and to recall past happiness were part of the ritual. Originally these laments had clear reference to a specific historical situation; later they were generalized for wider use. In later times they became obligatory for any rebuilding, since that implied demolition of the existing structure, and some even became part of the daily program of temple music and were used to awaken the temple personnel in the morning. Older than the laments for the destruction of a temple are, it would seem, hymns to temples. They celebrate the specific powers inherent in the temple to uphold the welfare of the country. The Cursing of Akkad tells how the peace of the country, its harvest of grain, and so on vanish when corresponding parts of Ekur are demolished. In fact, the temples shared in inordinate measure in the particular kind of holiness that characterizes the gods inhabiting them, and it is often difficult to distinguish between god and temple. The temple shares name and function with its god as if it were his embodiment.

The Cult. The communal cult of the gods was of two kinds, celebrating the appropriate festivals of the various gods at appropriate times and providing daily services such as would be required by any high human dignitary. The earlier of these are undoubtedly the festivals, most of which are best understood as communal magic rites for prosperity developed into cult dramas performed by community representatives. There is evidence for various types of such dramas: the Sacred Marriage, the Death Drama, the Journey Drama, and the Plowing Drama. Others may have existed.

The Sacred Marriage is attested in Uruk as early as the late Uruk period. The ruler (*en*) "became" the god of the date palm, Amaushumgalana, and brought the harvest as wedding gift to the date storeroom of the temple. His wife—one presumes—similarly "became" the goddess of the storehouse, Inanna, and opened the door for him, thereby concluding the marriage and lasting union of the powers for producing and storing the dates. Their meeting at the gate is depicted on the famous Uruk Vase and on contemporary cylinder seals. In this early form the source of abundance clearly was the god. In later times—as shown by materials from Isin and Larsa—emphasis oddly changed, and the goddess came to be seen as the conveyor of bounty. The high point was now a blessing by the goddess of the marital couch after the king had proved his prowess as bridegroom. By Isin-Larsa times, too, focus was no longer narrowly on dates but on prosperity generally. A special form of the rite—perhaps at home among herders—saw it still quite directly as sympathetic magic for fertility. Here the rising of the king's member in the sexual congress of the rite immediately made plants and greenery shoot up.

The Death Drama had the function of performing for the dying god of fertility—characteristically Dumuzi—the rites of lament due to the dead. Such data as we have suggest that processions of mourners went into the desert in early summer lamenting the god of dirges sung by representatives of his mother, sister, and young widow. The rite was a magic strengthening of the emotional bonds with the god, a seeking to have him back.

In the Journey Drama, the god, perhaps represented by his image or an emblem, traveled to visit a god in some other city. There are references to a yearly visit to Eridu by Ningirsu traveling from the Lagash region, and similarly there are texts connected with such a journey by Ninurta of Nippur. Whether in so traveling these gods conferred a boon on Enki and Eridu, or conversely were themselves the beneficiaries, is not always clear. In a myth about Enmerkar, founder of Uruk, a ritual journey he made to Eridu is mentioned in terms suggesting that he was reconfirmed or enhanced in his office of lord (*en*), that is, of provider. Most likely also the myth of Inanna and the offices she obtained from a not-too-sober Enki preserves memories of a rite in which Inanna's various offices were authenticated from Eridu. A rather full statement of a ritual journey is given in a text describing how Nanna of Ur travels up by boat to visit his father, Enlil, in Nippur, bringing first fruits from the products of the south. He is warmly received and leaves to go back to Ur with matching gifts from the agricultural lands around Nippur. The Plowing Drama of Ninurta's festival that opened the plowing season in Nippur is thus far unique. The king himself guided the plow, and a report was made to Enlil.

Last there is the Battle Drama. It seems to be at home with gods of the thunderstorms of spring, Ninurta and Marduk, and it is conceivable that it was once performed to activate these powers, to rouse the thunderstorms that were seen—as in the relevant myths—as the divine warrior attacking the mountains. There is, however, no evidence so far to indicate performance in such terms. The name of Marduk's main festival, Akitu ("time of the earth reviving"), does, as mentioned earlier, refer to an early aspect of him as the power causing natural abundance, but there is no indication of any battle drama. Such ritual evidence as we have for this type of drama all shows a later, completely politicized form behind which little if any trace of earlier implications survives. The materials for the Battle Drama are contained largely in cultic commentaries from Ashur, which, however, are clearly Babylonian in origin and reflect the bitter political rivalry between Babylon and the Sea Land to the south. Braziers and torches are lighted to signify the burning of Kingu, Anu, and Enlil. A chariot arriving with great show of martial prowess is Nabu, who was sent against Enlil and now returns victorious. A loaf of bread is bounded by the king and a bishop, who represent Marduk and Nabu. The loaf is the heart of Anu, whom Marduk bound and whose heart he tore out.

The Babylonian epic of creation, *Enuma elish*, which tells how Marduk "vanquished Tiamat and assumed kingship," reflects the same political conflict, with Marduk representing Babylon and Tiamat representing the sea and the Sea Land. It is generally—and perhaps rightly—assumed to be a cult myth corresponding to a dramatic ritual reenactment of this primordial battle each new year. However, our knowledge about the actual ritual of the Akitu festival in later times is scant in the extreme. We know that *Enuma elish* was read on one occasion and that Sennacherib, when he tried to transfer the festival to Assyria with Ashur as its hero, decorated the gates to his Akitu house with a relief showing the battle with Tiamat, but that is all. Otherwise such information as we have indicates that on the tenth of the month of Nisan, Marduk traveled by boat to the Akitu house, where a feast was celebrated on the eleventh, and that he then returned to Babylon. That is all. Not usable, unfortunately, for reconstructing the festival is a lengthy commentary called—not too happily—*Death and Resurrection of Marduk.* It has been shown to be an Assyrian, anti-Babylonian propaganda pamphlet, and it does not mention any death of Marduk.

The trend toward sociomorphism imposed on the gods the patterns of the human family and household, and this in turn implied service such as was rendered to a human magnate in providing for his bodily comfort and assisting in the running of his estate. All of this became the daily temple cult, as described earlier. A further implication of anthropomorphism and sociomorphism was that since the god had become ruler of the community, it was essential to know what he wanted done. Thus a variety of methods of communication was developed. Some of these left the initiative to the god: he might show signs in the stars or on earth that the initiated could interpret. Others were available when man needed to know the divine will. The earliest of these methods of communication of which we have evidence are dreams sought by incubation in the temple, and inspection of the liver of a sacrificed kid for propitious or nonpropitious shape. This latter method was used by Gudea as a check on the message obtained when he was dreaming. An extensive and highly detailed literature serving as textbook for these and many other manners of prognostication developed during the second and first millennia. Originally meant as guides for rulers and war leaders, this literature soon broadened its scope to take in the fortunes of ordinary citizens.

For conveying human wishes and needs to the gods and asking for help, a ritual of seeking audience to present petition and prayers was developed. The petitioner was led in before the deity with his greeting gift, usually a lamb or a kid. Here he libated water or wine in a huge vase with greenery that stood before the deity, and he spoke a formal greeting prayer. He then presented his petition. As the ritual for seeking an audience with the god was an occasional one, dependent on special circumstances, so the cult comprised other rituals for use in exceptional situations. I have mentioned the elaborate one called Bitrimki ("bathhouse"), which aimed at lustration of the king when he was threatened by the defiling evil of an eclipse of the moon; others were available for the rebuilding of a temple or for making or replacing a cult statue. In this last ritual great pains were taken to nullify by powerful incantations the fact that the statue was a work of human hands, and to make of it instead a god born in heaven.

The cult so far described was the communal, public cult. There was, however, a private cult as well. City life and its ever-greater differentiation between the fortunes of families and individuals and those of other families and individuals encouraged feelings that special success was due to a god's personal interest in a man and his family, while, conversely, misfortune would seem to be due to the god's abandonment of his ward for some reason or other. Thus the term for having luck became "to acquire a god." Since no achievement could be had without divine help, that of engendering a child necessarily implied such intervention. A god and goddess entered the body of the human father and mother and made the mother conceive. Thus the god and goddess who were assumed to have helped became family deities and were visualized in the image of a father and mother. As such they also took on the protective roles of parents, chief among which was to defend their wards against demons of disease and inspire successful thought and action. They had their altars and received daily offerings in the house of their wards, and prayers and petitions were addressed to them there.

The close connection between the personal god and success could not but raise problems, for experience showed that virtue was not always rewarded; rather, a virtuous man might fall ill or suffer other miseries such as should have happened to evildoers only. The obvious solution, that the virtuous man unwittingly must have offended his god, was accepted in a measure, and prayers often asked for enlightenment as to how a sufferer had sinned, so that he could do penance and mend his ways; but as a general explanation it did not carry full conviction, and the vexing problem of the righteous sufferer arose. It is dealt with in two major compositions datable to Middle Babylonian times. One is called *Ludlul* ("let me praise"), after its beginning, "Let me praise the possessor of wisdom." It tells of a pious and just man who suffers one misfortune after the other but does not lose his trust in Marduk. Eventually Marduk takes pity on him and restores him to health and prosperity. No real answer to the problem of why he had to suffer is attempted; the text merely holds out the conviction that the gods can have a change of heart and take pity. The other composition is known as the *Theodicy.* It is in the form of a dialogue between two friends about the fact that evil men appear to prosper, whereas good men fall on evil days. Here, too, there is no real answer, only a conviction that eventually retribution will come to evildoers.

The question of the innate justice—or, rather, injustice—of existence is also dealt with in a famous work known as the *Epic of Gilgamesh.* It tells how Gilgamesh, an ancient ruler of the city of Uruk endowed with exceptional vigor, drives his people too hard. They complain to the gods, who create Enkidu, a wild man who becomes a friend and brother of Gilgamesh. Together they set out to kill a famous warrior, Huwawa, who lives far away in the cedar mountains. They succeed. After their return to Uruk, Gilgamesh scornfully turns down a marriage proposal from the city goddess Ishtar. In her anger at being rejected she borrows the bull of heaven in order to kill Gilgamesh, but he and Enkidu overcome it. Then, however, things catch up with the two friends: the gods decide that Enkidu must die for having killed Huwawa. Gilgamesh is inconsolable at the loss of his friend and at the thought that he, too, must die. He therefore sets out on an arduous journey to an ancestor of his, Utanapishtim, who had gained eternal life. Eventually Gilgamesh reaches him, but Utanapishtim has no solace to offer. He invites Gilgamesh to try fighting Sleep—Death's younger brother, so to speak—but Gilgamesh fails miserably to keep awake. So Utanapishtim gives him clean clothes and sets him on his way home. There is no escape from death, however unjust it seems that man may not live forever.

It seems likely that the original epic ended here. At a later date, probably in the Middle Babylonian period, a certain Sinliqiunnini reworked the epic from a radically different point of view. Where the outlook of the earlier epic was tragic—a tale of a quest for eternal life that failed—the reworking saw Gilgamesh as a heroic traveler to romantic foreign parts who recovered hidden knowledge of the ancient times. A long story about the flood was added, as well as a further tale about a plant with the power to rejuvenate, which Gilgamesh obtained only to lose it again by carelessness. An introduction and conclusion stressed Gilgamesh's achievements, including lasting fame as builder of the city walls of Uruk. Finally, part of a Sumerian tale in which Enkidu describes conditions in the netherworld was tacked on, perhaps by some copyist. Passionate protest against existential evil thus became pleasure in romantic quest for hidden knowledge in faraway lands.

SEE ALSO Adad; Akitu; An; Anthropomorphism; Ashur; Atrahasis; Divination; Drama, article on Ancient Near Eastern Ritual Drama; Dumuzi; Dying and Rising Gods; Enki; Enlil; Enuma Elish; Gilgamesh; Hierodouleia; Hieros Gamos; Iconography, article on Mesopotamian Iconography; Inanna; Kingship, article on Kingship in the Ancient Mediterranean World; Marduk; Nabu; Nanna; Nergal; Ninhursaga; Ninurta; Pyramids, overview article; Temple, article on Ancient Near Eastern and Mediterranean Temples; Utu.

BIBLIOGRAPHY

Bottéro, Jean. *La religion babylonienne.* Paris, 1952.

Dhorme, Édouard. *Les religions de Babylonie et d'Assyrie.* Paris, 1945.

Dijk, V. van. "Sumerische Religion." In *Handbuch der Religionsgeschichte,* vol. 1, edited by Jes Peter Asmussen, Jørgen Laessøe, and Carsten Colpe, pp. 431–496. Göttingen, 1971.

Frankfort, Henri, et al. *Before Philosophy.* Harmondsworth, 1949. First published as *The Intellectual Adventure of Ancient Man* (Chicago, 1946).

Hooke, S. H. *Babylonian and Assyrian Religion.* New York, 1953.

Jacobsen, Thorkild. *The Treasures of Darkness: A History of Mesopotamian Religion.* New Haven, 1975.

Laessøe, Jørgen. "Babylonische und assyrische Religion." In *Handbuch der Religionsgeschichte,* vol. 1, edited by Jes Peter Asmussen, Jørgen Laessøe, and Carsten Colpe, pp. 497–525. Göttingen, 1971.

Meissner, Bruno. *Babylonien und Assyrien,* vol. 2. Heidelberg, 1925.

Pritchard, J. B., ed. *Ancient Near Eastern Texts relating to the Old Testament.* 3d ed. Princeton, 1969.

Ringgren, Helmer. *Religions of the Ancient Near East.* Translated by John Sturdy. Philadelphia, 1973.

THORKILD JACOBSEN (1987)

MESOPOTAMIAN RELIGIONS: AN OVERVIEW [FURTHER CONSIDERATIONS]

The Sumerians, who built human civilization over their thousand-year history, from 3000 BCE to 2000 BCE approximately, were not the only players on the Mesopotamian social and political stage. As we turn the pages of their history, we find that there is another ethnic group, of Semitic origin, living in the same territory at almost the same time, a people conventionally known as the Akkadians, who came to power and took control of the entire region in 2350 BCE under their king Sargon the Great, founder of a dynasty of the same name.

At least until the 1950s and 1960s, there was a lively debate amongst Assyriologists—on the one hand, those who believed that there was an ethnic link between the Sumerians and the Akkadians, almost a direct symbiosis, and on the other, those who, while not overemphasizing that they were different racial groups, stressed that their ways of life were basically different, in their model of political thought, in their cultural traditions, even in the different languages that they spoke. The Sumerians spoke an agglutinative language ("Sumerian"), whereas the Akkadians spoke an inflected Semitic language ("Akkadian").

In 1970 F. A. Kraus, holding that the use of a different language did not necessarily relate to different ethnic origins, concluded that "the Sumerian and Akkadian texts are evidence of the same culture, namely Babylonian" (pp. 1ff.) In the following year Giovanni Pettinato published *Das altorientalische Menschenbild und die sumerischen und akkadischen Schöpfungsmythen,* in which he maintained exactly the opposite position—that, at the very least, language is an important piece of evidence in the investigation of the cultures of these two peoples. Simply on the basis of mythological texts concerning the creation and conception of the human race, Pettinato reached the conclusion that, contrary to what is published in books on Mesopotamian history and civilization, the Sumerians and the Akkadians, the two main peoples that inhabited Mesopotamia, had very different approaches to such matters, and this is central to our understanding of their thinking. The Sumerians and the Akkadians were exponents of two quite distinct cultures, with mutually incompatible principles and ideals. Thus the opinion put forward by Assyriologists concerning this symbiosis seemed to be completely incorrect and not borne out by the surviving documentary evidence, which has been even more firmly established and developed in recent years.

In 1992 W. G. Lambert proposed a comparison between Sumerian and Akkadian tales of the creation of the human race and stated that the two traditions had certain fundamental motifs in common, concluding: "for the moment it is most sensible to consider the two mythological corpora as expressions of a single culture" (Lambert, 1992, p. 130). He comes to the same conclusion when he compares the Sumerian narratives of the Descent of Inanna with the Akkadian versions concerning Ishtar. The studies of Steinkeller (1992) and Durand (1993), which demonstrated the existence of a Semitic mythology that was completely different and alien to the Sumerian, were of no avail, because all this left Heimpel completely unmoved; for him, Kraus's theory remained unchanged and unchangeable. In fact, Falkenstein was probably right when he stated that the Sumerians and the Semites (= Akkadians) maintained and propagated two very different traditions. Subsequent studies have confirmed the views of Pettinato (1971), and the discoveries at Ebla, in ancient Syria, have provided us with evidence of a level of civilized development and a cultural heritage to match the richest and most abundant in the Sumerian world. For these reasons, it is both useful and necessary to examine the two cultures, the Sumerian and the Akkadian, separately, because only in this way will we be able to join the dots together and thus understand the interchange between different cultures, something which is now a primary duty of our research.

Sumerian Beliefs. To understand the essentials of Babylonian religion we should refer to the beliefs of the first inhabitants of Mesopotamia, the Sumerians. Only a few key aspects of Sumerian religious literature were of interest to the Babylonians; for example, there was no information concerning the origin of the cosmos, which interested the Babylonians keenly. What was of far greater significance to the Sumerians was the organization of their own world, in which the divine intervened regularly. The Sumerians had two leading gods in their divine pantheon: Enlil, the poliad god of Nippur, and Enki, the poliad god of Eridu. The first is the undisputed head of the Sumerian pantheon, the second is the god of wisdom par excellence. Besides these two main divinities, another god, the father of both, plays a prominent role in the Sumerian religious outlook—An, the god of the sky. These three gods formed the supreme triad of the Sumerian pantheon around which all the other gods revolved. Their role in the world was well defined and constantly overseen by the assembly of the gods. It is no coincidence that Babylonian astronomy was based upon these three Sumerian divinities, nor indeed that the astrological series *Enuma Anu Enlil* begins with these words: "When the gods Anu, Enlil, and Ea prepared the outline of heaven and earth. . . ." (Ea is the Semitic name of the god Enki, and Anu is the Semitic form of the Sumerian An.)

There were naturally other important gods, such as the seven mother goddesses led by Ninhursag, the mother of all creatures, and the three astral gods of the sun, moon, and Venus, respectively called Utu, Nanna, and Inanna. The sun god, whose watchful eye never falters, guarantees justice; the moon god lights up the earth by night and lets travelers find their way in the dark; Inanna (Venus) is the goddess of love and war, a very important figure in the pantheon, who along with her two brothers Nanna and Utu controls the smooth progress of events, but in particular guarantees the kingship. It is no less important to note that Inanna was the poliad goddess of Uruk, as Utu was the god of Sippar and Nanna of Ur, cities of major historical importance from 3000 BCE onwards.

From the mythological literary compositions dealing with the creation of the human race, which the traditions of Nippur and Eridu attribute respectively to the gods Enlil and Enki, we learn that the main gods had various spheres of influence, as follows: An, the sky; Enlil, the earth; and Enki, the waters of the deep. Thus Enlil is the ruler of the earth and everything that happens there is in a certain sense controlled and determined by him.

Humanity's attachment to the divine world is expressed in terms of a deliberate, and perhaps even joyful, obedience. The human race, as the Sumerians considered it, had been created to carry on with the gods' work of putting the world in order. Well aware of the onerous nature of the work they had been created to carry out, the Sumerians accepted this burden willingly, confident of leaving a permanent impression, just as the gods had done when they had created the world. What the texts emphasize, from different angles, is the presence within human beings of a divine element, bestowed by either Enki or Enlil, according to the two different traditions, which allows them to survive the finality of death; there is firm belief in an afterlife. There were some attempts to overcome death, as in the effort of Gilgamesh, but the firm laws established by the gods from the time of creation were accepted without argument by the Sumerians.

Although the creation texts, because of their concise nature, do not indicate the evolution of the human race, both Sumerian documents referring to the Nippur tradition and the Chaldean Berosus, dealing with the Enki variant, stress in no uncertain terms that man became a city dweller by going through various stages of development. In the Nippur tradition, after human beings had been created they were living like wild animals and behaved as such. It was only after Enlil instilled in them the vital spiritual spark, that is, the divine element, that the human race was ready to undertake the task of organizing the world. The story told by Berosus of the early stages of human development is even more significant: in this tradition too, human beings were ignorant of the benefits of civilization, so Enki, the god of wisdom, had amphibian creatures that were half-fish, half-human emerge from the ocean depths and live with human beings, teaching them how to behave in a civilized way, and instructing them in all the arts. These are the renowned *apkallu,* known from cuneiform literature, who after this first stage of human development served the king of the earth as his advisers when the gods sent down the kingship from heaven. Gilgamesh, the mythical king of Uruk, was the first to have a purely human adviser, signifying in its way a break in the history of humanity as decisive as the first real break, which was caused by the direct intervention of the gods—the Universal Flood.

Early Babylonian Beliefs. The Sumerians transmitted their religious ideas in myths, hymns, and wisdom texts, which the Babylonians, once they arrived in Mesopotamia, began to copy and translate so that the knowledge of the Sumerian world would not be lost. In the schools of Babylon and in other centers of learning, knowledge of the previous peoples was preserved and began to be developed, and it was adapted to later people's own beliefs. It should not be forgotten either that the Assyrians, although mainly preoccupied with war, did not scorn the culture of the Sumerian and Babylonian schools, as shown in that miraculous monument to human history, the library at Nineveh, from which the vast majority of the literary texts written by the inhabitants of the "land between the two rivers" now come. Although it had the highest regard for the previous tradition, which she welcomed in toto, Babylon nonetheless was faced with a problem of enormous proportions—how to introduce the principal Babylonian god, Marduk, into the established Sumerian pantheon.

The Mesopotamian kingship was regarded by the inhabitants of the region as a gift from the gods; it had descended from heaven, in fact. For the Sumerians, the protector of the kingship was the god Enlil, who was both the city god of Nippur and the ruler of the earth. For the Babylonians, on the other hand, the guardian of the kingship was Marduk, a god who had no role in the religious tradition of Mesopotamia. Even in the Old Babylon period, around 1800 BCE, during the reign of Hammurabi, Marduk was not only seen as the poliad god of the city, but also the controller of the kingship of the Babylonian sovereigns. There was nothing new in terms of the religious and political situation in Mesopotamia; just as in the past, local rulers received their sovereign powers from their own city god. The problem occurred when one city tried to predominate over the others; only then was it necessary to resort to the god of the earth, Enlil, the god of Nippur, to be invested with sovereignty.

Later too, in the Middle Babylonian period, around 1100 BCE, it is still Marduk who conferred the kingship on the Babylonian sovereigns. In the New Babylonian period (c. sixth century BCE) the position changed: Babylon wanted to become the political center of the whole of Mesopotamia, and Marduk was sufficient in stature to secure such an expectation. Yet, the rulers of Babylon called Marduk "ruler of all the gods," "source of the kingship." What happened in the preceding centuries? Did a religious revolution occur, so that no one could accuse the kings of Babylon of blasphemy? In fact, Babylonian scholars devised a new myth, reintegrating the theology that underpinned Babylonian hegemony in the religious and political environment of ancient Mesopotamia.

The prologue to the Code of Hammurabi provides information on the Babylonian pantheon: the gods were subdivided into two categories, the Anunnaki and the Igigi, who were respectively the greater and lesser gods. Anu, Enlil, and Enki, the supreme triad, clearly belonged to the Anunnaki, together with the classical divinities of the Sumerian world, and Marduk was part of the second group, the Igigi; in the prologue he is called "firstborn of Enki" and "leader of the Igigi." Yet, this description shows that we are still a long way from the moment when Marduk, following his actions in the *Enuma elish,* became the new head of the Babylonian pantheon.

In the myth of Atrahasis, too, the pantheon is divided in two, the Anunna and the Igigi; the triad Anu, Enlil, and Ea belongs to a group of seven, the greater gods, whereas the Igigi, the lesser gods, are obliged to put up with the burden of hard work. The roles that they are given are the same as those assigned by the Sumerians, so the change has not yet taken place. (It is interesting that the god Marduk is not mentioned once in the myth of Atrahasis.) The Sumerian religion was still very much alive in the period that followed, and any radical change of a religious nature would have had enormous difficulty in being accepted.

ENUMA ELISH. The situation is completely different in *Enuma elish* (end of the second millennium BCE), the greatest religious poem of Babylonian literature. The scribes had grasped that there were two possible ways to elevate their poliad god to a central position in the pantheon: either to link Marduk to the god of Nippur or—certainly more subtle—to relate him to the god Enki. It may be surprising that they chose to establish a father-son relationship between Enki and Marduk, since the latter had never historically guaranteed the kingship, but the choice of the scribes shows a quite remarkable intelligence: they wanted to overturn historical reality and turn it to something of universal significance.

All of the Sumerian traditions assigned the position of principal god in their pantheon to Enlil, but at the same time they emphasized that the first seat of the kingship before the Flood was the city of Eridu, the home of the god Enki, who was therefore regarded as the first holder of royal power on earth. Hence the decision of the scribes to make Marduk the son of Enki. Their syllogistic reasoning is clear: if Enki the king is Marduk's father, then Marduk becomes the king. And that is not all:if Eridu is the home of Enki and at the same time the location of his kingship, then Babylon, the home of Marduk, is automatically the one true location of the kingship. So when we read the words of Berosus, that the first royal capital on earth was Babylon, we begin to understand how convincing the syllogism devised by the scribes of Babylon had become for later generations.

To make such a revolutionary idea acceptable, those responsible for creating the poem *Enuma elish* were obliged to confront subjects never dealt with by mythological texts of the preceding period. The seven tablets on which the poem is set down refer back to the primordial world, to the beginning of everything, which preceded the present cosmos. Thus they began the tale in the time before the birth of the sky god An, the future head of the Sumerian pantheon. The description of the situation that preceded the birth of the god of the sky was completely new, even if it may have been indirectly reconstructed from known sources. First of all, there existed only the primordial waters, the sweet and salt waters,

Apsu and Tiamat. These two beings joined in marriage and produced pairs of completely shadowy beings, until the couple Anshar and Kishar brought forth the god of the sky, An. The text then goes on to describe the generation of the god Enki and his son Marduk, thus ensuring that Marduk is given a definite place in the Mesopotamian pantheon.

Yet the priestly scribes went still further. They were anxious to install the Babylonian god in a leading position, and they accomplished their task in a most admirable way. Marduk could only become the ruler of the gods if he performed some quite exceptional act. The facts are quickly set out: the young gods were disturbing the rest of the primordial gods with their noise, so Apsu became angry and intended to punish them. Tiamat, their mother, did not want the young gods to die—they were still her children, after all—but Apsu was unyielding. The younger generation, led by An and Enki, refused to accept the decision of Apsu, and Enki killed his grandfather by trickery. At this, Tiamat declared all-out war on the entire set of young gods and there ensued a cosmic battle setting the old generation against the new. The forces of the primordial gods were led by Tiamat herself, and on Enki's advice, the task of commanding the young gods' army was given to Marduk. After various ups and downs, Marduk was victorious over Tiamat, thus doing away with the power of the primordial gods; only then did the gods unanimously agree to make Marduk their leader. The tale goes on to detail all of Marduk's actions, including the creation of the present cosmos with the constellations and planets (especially the sun and the moon), the setting up the calendar, and the foundation of Babylon, the new capital of the world.

The revolutionary idea underlying this poem should not be underestimated: all religious thinking had to be revised, and yet the Babylonian scribes did not actually omit anything from the religious situation. Among the Sumerian literary texts copied in the schools of Babylon, a prominent place was given to lists of Mesopotamian gods handed down from the Sumerians, but here an innovation occurred in the drafting of the texts: the divinities were subject to a great theological reworking that organized all the gods into a well-defined family structure—that is, into a pyramid with Marduk at its head, as a result of his victory over Tiamat. Not one of the great Sumerian gods was ousted—not An, nor Enlil, nor Enki—and they are the ones who elevate the young god and choose him as their undisputed new leader.

OTHER BABYLONIAN RELIGIOUS LITERATURE. We would be mistaken, however, if we thought that the Babylonians stopped at what we might term institutions. The ancient scribes believed, as we do, that ideas are truly revolutionary when they are popularly accepted. The mythological texts were accompanied by wisdom texts in which the scribes dealt with the problem of humanity, its suffering, its pain, and its eventual death. Although they recognized various solutions, the scribes directed their response towards the god Marduk. The poem *Ludlul bĒl nĒmeqi* is a document of unusual beauty which puts forward Marduk as the true savior of every human being. Similarly, individual prayers rediscovered in the libraries of Babylon, as well as all the theophoric onomasticons (names made up of divine constituent parts), provide irrefutable evidence that the cultural mission undertaken by the theological schools had been spread amongst the populace, and had become a fundamental idea within Babylonian culture.

If we turn our attention to the plan devised by the Babylonians to attain supremacy, which they would not be able to gain through political means, we see a genuine religious and intellectual revolution brought about by some exceptional minds. Precisely because Babylon was a city that had been recently founded, the learned priests of Marduk, the supreme god of Babylon, needed to find some means of incorporating their city and their god in his proper position in the primordial world from which their civilization had developed, and from which the kingship had originated. In the religious and historical texts of the Sumerians, the first inhabitants of Mesopotamia, we find a quite precise list of the order in which the first cities were founded and power was given to mankind by the gods. Even the divine world is duly ordered, with the principal gods, Anu, Enki, Enlil, and Inanna, allotted their specific roles and tasks, so that the world is organized and unchanging. At that time, Babylon did not yet exist, so later Babylonian priests needed to find a way for their city and their god to re-enter the Sumerian schema, or Babylon would share the same fate as many other cities, such as Ashur and Nineveh—powerful politically, but completely irrelevant in the intellectual and religious spheres. Of course, the priests of Marduk had one weapon on their side, and that was the actual ancestry of the god himself. Marduk was indeed the son of Enki, the Sumerian god of wisdom and one of the four main Sumerian gods, and thus it was in principle possible to link him with the existing Sumerian traditions, so that he could enter fully into a cultural framework from which newcomers had been excluded.

In *Marduk, the Heir of Enki,* there is clearly a subtle change in the Sumerian tradition which the Babylonian priests referenced: Enki is the creator of the human race and organizes the world, but he is also the father of Marduk. This is highly significant, because it is not only Marduk, but also Babylon that is elevated to the status of legitimate heir to Sumerian civilization, the first civilization in Mesopotamia. Marduk, as creator of the human race, is also the guardian of the kingship, of the exercise of power, which he grants to whomsoever he chooses, but in his chosen city, and thus Babylon becomes the legitimate home of the kingship. In the festival of the New Year the god Marduk solemnly renews his choice of the Babylonian sovereign and once again grants his trust to the shepherd of his people.

In the Babylonian schools a plan was set in motion to rework all previous knowledge, both religious and secular. Thus Babylon became the repository of Mesopotamian learning, once again invoking the divine world. Marduk has a son, the god Nabu, heir to the knowledge and wisdom of his grandfather Enki; Nabu oversees all intellectual endeavor and is the patron of the prestigious class of scribes.

AKKADIAN LITERATURE. The mythological texts of Assyro-Babylonian literature are in fact a product of the Semitic people who replaced the Sumerians around 2000 BCE, and correctly identified with the large-scale migration there of the Amorites, who were able to create new dynasties and a new series of capitals, such as Babylon in the south and Ashur in the north. As early as the start of the Old Babylonian period there was sudden, intense literary activitywhich was faithful to tradition, in particular regarding the role of the principal triad An, Enlil, and Enki/Ea, but which also included a number of properties and personalities with characteristics that appear to be the product of exclusively Semitic thinking. For the typical nature of Sumerian civilization, which adapted to the dictates of the divine world without a murmur, there was substituted a much more typically Semitic character that was rebellious and in a certain sense inimical to the preordained plan of the divine world. There is sympathy for the view that the Semitic scribes expressed a way of thinking that was different and perhaps also at variance with the norm, in certain verses giving their assessment of cosmic and human reality.

Some historians of Akkadian literature stress that the Assyro-Babylonians needed several hundred years to produce literary and mythological compositions, which reached the height of the works created by the Sumerians. This conclusion is probably incorrect, as shown by the myth of Atrahasis, already in existence in the Old Babylonian period, at the beginning of settlement in Mesopotamia by the Semitic Amorites. Of course, until 1966, the Old Babylonian version of this myth was not known, because it was buried in the vaults of the British Museum. However, there were already sufficient other literary texts providing evidence of the literary maturity of the Babylonian scribes to prevent this kind of mistake.

In addition to the myth of Atrahasis, which had a long tradition and reworking that lasted until the New Babylonian period, we should recall the following as definitely attributable to the same period of Hammurabi: the myth of Etana, the myth of Ninurta and Anzu, the myth of Adad and the dragon, *Belet-ili and Lillu,* and the first draft of the *Epic of Gilgamesh.* Naturally, successive periods saw the reworking of these myths, along with the editing and composition of new myths, such as, for example, the *Descent of Ishtar to the Underworld* and *Nergal and Ereshkigal,* and in the Neo-Assyrian period there were the wonderful compositions of *Enuma elish* and the myth of Erra, which reached new and unequalled literary heights. Other texts that are considered mythological include the series of incantations that have introductory passages which refer to cosmological or human events (as well as serving as introductions to the actual spells themselves). There are also various hymns to divinities that allude to events which are, in the true sense of the word, mythological.

In conclusion, then, it can be stated that Akkadian mythology was certainly not in any sense inferior to Sumerian, and indeed was at least its equal, if not somewhat superior on account of its underlying distinctive, dynamic, and vigorous nature.

SEE ALSO An; Atrahasis; Enlil; Enuma Elish; Marduk; Utu.

BIBLIOGRAPHY

Bottéro, Jean. *La religion babylonienne.* Paris, 1952.

Durand, Jean-Marie. "Le Mithologème du combat entre le dieu de l'orage et la mèr in Mésopotamie." *MARI* 7 (1993): 41–61.

Falkenstein, Adam. "La Cité-Temple sumérienne." CHM I 4 (1954): 784–812.

Heimpel, Wolfgang. "Mythologie (mythology). I. In Mesopotamien." *Reallexikon fur Assyriologie* 8 (1997): 537–564.

Jacobsen, Thorkild. *The Treasures of Darkness: A History of Mesopotamian Religion.* New Haven, Conn., 1975.

Kraus, Franz R. *Sumerer und Akkader.* Amsterdam, 1970.

Laessoe, Jorgen. "Babylonische und assyrische Religion." In *Handbuch der Religionsgeschichte,* vol. 1, edited by Jes Peter Asmussen, Jorgen Laessoe, and Carsten Colpe, pp. 497–525. Göttingen, Germany, 1971.

Lambert, Wilfred G. "Studies in Marduk." *Bulletin of the School of Oriental and African Studies* 47 (1984): 1–9.

Lambert, Wilfred G. "The Relationship of Sumerian and Babylonian Myth as Seen in Account of Creation," *CRRAI* 38 (1991): 129–135.

Pettinato, Giovanni. *Das altorientalische Menschenbild und die sumerischen und akkadischen Schöpfungsmythen.* Heidelberg, Germany, 1970.

Pettinato, Giovanni. *Mitologia Sumerica.* Turin, Italy, 2001.

Ringgren, Helmer. *Religions of the Ancient Near East.* Translated by J. Sturdy. Philadelphia, 1973.

Steinkeller, Piotr. "Early Semitic Literature and Third Millennium Seals with Mythological Motifs," *QdS* 18 (1993): 243–275.

van Dijk, Jan J. A. "Sumerische Religion" In *Handbuch der Religionsgeschichte,* vol. 1, edited by Jes Peter Asmussen, Jorgen Laessoe, and Carsten Colpe, pp. 431–496. Göttingen, Germany, 1971.

GIOVANNI PETTINATO (2005)
Translated from Italian by Paul Ellis

MESOPOTAMIAN RELIGIONS: HISTORY OF STUDY

The study of ancient Mesopotamian religions, like the study of ancient Mesopotamia in general, was severely hampered in its early phases by an imperfect understanding of Sumerian and Akkadian, the languages of its source materials, and by the relatively limited and fragmentary nature of the materials then available. To some extent, similar difficulties still exist, and new finds as well as new insights may challenge even seemingly assured results.

General Presentations. The earliest attempt at a comprehensive presentation of ancient Mesopotamian religions is François Lenormant's *La magie chez les Chaldéens et les origines accadiennes* (1874). Lenormant posited an early Sumerian (then called Akkadian) animistic stage of belief in spirits that were controlled by magicians. Contrasting with this was the religion of the Semitic inhabitants (now called Akkadians), a debased form of monotheism in which hypostases of the supreme god, called Ilu, had become separate powers in natural phenomena, especially astral phenomena. These two competing kinds of beliefs were eventually unified into a single system under Sargon of Akkad, whom Lenormant dated at about 2000 BCE. Part of this systematization included the ordering of local deities into the later pantheon.

The next major contribution to the study of Mesopotamian religions, and one of a wider scope, was A. H. Sayce's *Lectures on the Origin and Growth of Religions as Illustrated by the Religion of the Ancient Babylonians* (1887). Sayce's book deals with various Babylonian deities, such as Bel-Merodakh (Marduk), Tammuz, and Istar (Ishtar), among others. He also discusses what he called "the sacred books of Chaldea," as well as cosmogonies and astro-theology. Sayce saw evidence of totemism in the animal forms that many of the gods could assume. Because Prometheus brought fire to man, Sayce saw him as a parallel to the deity Lugalbanda ("fierce king"). In his overall view of religious development, Sayce essentially followed Lenormant.

The Sumerian beliefs in spirits that were controlled by a body of medicine men was termed by Sayce "organized animism." The Sumerian word for spirit was thought to be *zi,* and "the *zi* was simply that which manifested life, and the test of the manifestation of life was movement" (p. 327). The spirits in those major cosmic elements that were considered good gradually developed into gods. The level of power of motion possessed by an object, or in a force of nature, was the test of its supernaturalism (that is, of the existence of a spirit within it). Sayce writes:

> The spirit of the moon, for example, developed into a god, but the god was abstracted from the visible moon itself, and identified with the creative force of the lunar orb which manifested itself in motion. The new god might in turn be abstracted from the creative force, more especially if he was assimilated to the sacred steer; in this case the creative force would become his spirit, in no way differing, it will be seen, from the spirit that was believed to reside in man. (p. 334)

Sayce attributed to the Semitic-speaking Akkadians a change from the gods as creators to the gods as fathers, a change encouraged by anthropomorphism and the creation of a family-based pantheon.

In his later *Religions of Ancient Egypt and Babylonia* (1902), Sayce modified his position and rejected the idea that the gods might have developed out of older spirits. He assumed instead that the idea was brought in by immigrants from the south, who founded a tradition centered on the god Ea of the ancient city of Eridu.

Much more comprehensive than any previous treatment was Morris Jastrow's *The Religion of Babylonia and Assyria* (1898). Jastrow discusses the land and peoples of Babylon and Syria, the general traits of the Old Babylonian pantheon, the gods and their consorts prior to the days of Hammurabi, the pantheon of Hammurabi, Gudea's pantheon, and the minor gods in the period of Hammurabi. The book also deals with the gods appearing in temple lists and in legal and commercial documents of the area. Other topics that Jastrow investigates rather extensively are the animism that survived in Babylonian religions, the Assyrian pantheon, the triad and the combined invocation of the deities, the Neo-Babylonian period, and the Babylonian cosmology. Jastrow's work also examines the religious literature—magical texts, prayers and hymns, penitential psalms, oracles, omens, the *Epic of Gilgamesh,* and other myths and legends. There is also a discussion of the Babylonian view of life after death, and of the temple and cult in Babylonia and Syria.

Because Jastrow avoided theorizing as much as possible, his treatment is sober and descriptive. He also deliberately avoided distinguishing Sumerian from Akkadian contributions. Jastrow argued that animism was still basic to the religion of Babylonia and Assyria, and he observed that the gods had evolved from their role as spirits of the settlement plots. As these settlements grew into cities, the spirits grew correspondingly in stature and importance. The detailed bibliography of the field up to 1898 that Jastrow included in his book is particularly valuable. A later work by Jastrow, *Die Religion Babyloniens und Assyriens* (1905–1912), although never completed, is essentially a lengthy study of divination texts.

To the third edition of *Die Keilinschriften und das Alte Testament* (1903), which was edited by Eberhard Schrader, the German Assyriologist Heinrich Zimmern contributed his study *Religion und Sprache,* discussing the religious system of the Babylonians; the formation of the pantheon; local cults; the Semitic and Sumerian elements still evident in Babylonian religion; the Babylonians' reliance on the heavens in the formation of beliefs, practices, and myths; and the Babylonian view of life. Zimmern's presentation was strongly influenced by the school of *Astralmythologie* that flourished in Germany at the time, so an overabundance of gods were seen as solar in character. For example, Marduk was said to represent the sun of morning and spring; Ninurta (whose name was then read as Ninib) represented the eastern or western sun; the destructive glowing south, noon, and summer sun were represented by Nergal; and so on. The purview of the book called for comparisons with biblical materials (twenty-one pages were devoted to a comparison of Marduk and Christ), but the methods used have since been discounted.

In 1910 Édouard Dhorme's *La religion assyro-babylonienne* was published; the materials are organized with such clarity and relevance that the book remains one of the most notable early treatments of Mesopotamian religions.

Dhorme's work focused on the sources of the Assyrian and Babylonian religions and their conception of the divine, including the gods, gods of the cities and of kings, gods and men, moral laws, prayers, sacrifice, and the priesthood. A new, enlarged edition was published in 1945 under the title *Les religions de Babylonie et d'Assyrie.* Although it achieved a far greater coverage of detail, it lost the enlightening clarity that characterizes the earlier work.

A most useful, purely factual, and well-documented presentation was given by Bruno Meissner in the second volume of his *Babylonien und Assyrien* (1925). For ready access to the main data of pantheons, cults, divination, and magic, it remains unrivaled.

Jean Bottéro, in his *La religion babylonienne* (1952), sought to present the development of Babylonian religion among the Semitic-speaking inhabitants of Mesopotamia during the last two millennia before the Common Era. The work is marked by a great sensitivity and respect for the ancient achievement. A few of the subjects Bottéro discusses are deserving of special mention: religious sentiment, the theology of the divine, and cults of adoration and sacrament. His method of treatment is reminiscent of what is known as the phenomenology of religion.

A different approach, one that belongs to the Myth and Ritual school, is represented by S. H. Hooke's *Babylonian and Assyrian Religion* (1953), a well-written and very readable account of the essentials of its subject that is free of any extreme positions. Other general presentations include L. W. King's *Babylonian Religion and Mythology* (1899), Giuseppe Furlani's *La religione babilonese e assira* (1928–1929), Charles F. Jean's *La religion sumérienne* (1931), Hans Hirsch's *Untersuchungen zur altassyrischen Religion* (1961), and W. H. P. Römer's article "Religion of Ancient Mesopotamia" in *Historia Religionum,* volume 1, *Religions of the Past,* edited by C. Jouco Bleeker and Geo Widengren (1969). Also important are J. van Dijk's "Sumerische Religion" and Jørgen Laessøe's "Babylonische und assyrische Religion," in volume 1 of *Handbuch der Religionsgeschichte,* edited by Jes P. Asmussen, Jørgen Laessøe, and Carsten Colpe (1976). In this, as well as in other works, van Dijk refers to Eliade's phenomenological approach.

Thorkild Jacobsen's *The Treasures of Darkness: A History of Mesopotamian Religion* (1976) is a pivotal study of Mesopotamian religion. Jacobsen based this work on Rudolf Otto's theory on numinous experience, but when he set that theoretical approach in the history of Mesopotamia, he gave the book an evolutionist structure, a structure that is, however, absent in his entry "Mesopotamian Religion" in the first edition of this encyclopedia. Jacobsen provides an overall reconstruction of the poems describing the love and death of Dumuzi and Inanna, and he discusses a pre-urban historical phase, a period when the village communities were struggling to survive and the gods were conceived as providers (as stated in the title of Chapter 2 in *Treasures of Darkness.*). With the development of urban life, the gods became rulers in a society living in a state of endemic war. The book also includes important insight into personal religion, the epic of Gilgamesh, and the apotheosis of Marduk.

General presentations that appeared after Jacobsen's work include Helmut Freydank's "Religion Mesopotamiens" in *Kulturgeschichte des alten Vorderasien,* edited by Horst Klengel (1989); Joachín Sanmartin's "Mitología y Religíon" in *Mitología y Religíon del Oriente Antiguo,* edited by Gregorio del Olmo Lete (1993); and Jean Bottéro's *Plus vieille religion en Mésopotamie* (1998), translated into English by Teresa L. Fagan as *Religion in Ancient Mesopotamia* (2001).

SPECIAL STUDIES. As important as the general presentations on ancient Mesopotamian religions are, a wealth of special studies are in many cases even more essential for understanding these religions' major aspects. Unfortunately, considerations of space do not allow any comprehensive and systematic treatment; it is only possible to comment on a somewhat random and necessarily subjective selection.

The nature of the concept of divinity in Mesopotamia is treated in Johannes Hehn's *Die biblische und die babylonische Gottesidee* (1913) and in Elena Cassin's *La splendeur divine: Introduction à l'étude de la mentalité mesopotamienne* (1968). Rich in materials is Knut Tallquist's *Akkadische Götterepitheta* (1938). For discussion of the pantheon, Anton Deimel's *Pantheon Babylonicum* (1914) and part one of his *Sumerisches Lexikon,* volume 4, *Pantheon Babylonicum* (1950), are still standard references.

The origins and development of the pantheon were dealt with by Tharsicius Paffrath in his book *Zur Götterlehre in den altbabylonischen Königsinschriften* (1913) and by W. G. Lambert in his article "The Historical Development of the Mesopotamian Pantheon: A Study in Sophisticated Polytheism" in *Unity and Diversity,* edited by Hans Goedicke and J. J. M. Roberts (1975).

A representative collection of myths and epics in translation may be found in *Ancient Near Eastern Texts Relating to the Old Testament* (3d ed., 1969), edited by J. B. Pritchard. Thorkild Jacobsen's *The Harps That Once—Sumerian Poetry in Translation* (1987) translates a selection of significant religious poems from the Sumerian, and Stephanie Dalley's *Myths from Mesopotamia* (1989) does the same for Akkadian. Jean Bottéro and Samual Noah Kramer's *Lorsque les dieux faisaient l'homme* (1989) includes translations of almost all the Sumerian and Akkadian mythological poems.

Treatments of mythology include Samuel Noah Kramer's *Sumerian Mythology* (1944; rev. ed., 1972); D. O. Edzard's article "Mesopotamien," in the first volume of *Wörterbuch der Mythologie,* edited by H. W. Haussig (1965); Giorgio R. Castellino's *Mitologia Sumerico-Accadica* (1967); and Alexander Heidel's *The Babylonian Genesis* (1942; 2d ed., 1963) and *The Gilgamesh Epic and Old Testament Parallels* (1949; 2d ed., 1963).

Aspects of the daily cult are the focus of Agnès Spycket's book *Les statues de culte dans les textes mesopotamiens* (1968).

Other books of interest include Friedrich Blome's *Die Opfermaterie in Babylonien und Israel* (1934) and Yvonne Rosengarten's *Le concept sumérien de consommation* (1960). For the times of the annual festivals, there is Benno Landsberger's magisterial (and still standard) work, *Der kultische Kalender der Babylonier und Assyrer* (1915). The *raison d'être* of the festivals was first clarified by Svend Aage Pallis in his book *The Babylonian Akitu Festival* (1926). Of crucial importance because it dismissed once and for all some serious misunderstandings of the Akitu is Wolfram von Soden's article "Gibt es ein Zeugnis dafür das die Babylonier an die Wiederauferstehung Marduks geglaubt haben?" (Is there any proof that the Babylonians believed in the resurrection of Marduk?), which appeared in *Zeitschrift für Assyriologie* 51 (1955). Beate Pongratz-Leisten's *Ina Šulmi Īrub* (1994) examines textual material on the Akitu festival. *Ritual and Sacrifice in the Ancient Near East,* edited by J. Quaegebeur (1993), offers additional insights into this topic. Thorkild Jacobsen's "Religious Drama in Ancient Mesopotamia" in *Unity and Diversity,* edited by Hans Goedicke and J. J. M. Roberts (1975), gives a general treatment of festival rites.

Rites of divine journeys are treated in *Nanna-Suen's Journey to Nippur,* edited by A. J. Ferrara (1973), and in Daniel David Reisman's Ph. D. dissertation, "Two Neo-Sumerian Royal Hymns" (University of Pennsylvania, 1969). Royal inauguration rituals are discussed in Karl Friedrich Müller's *Texte zum assyrischen Königsritual* (1937), which is the first volume of his *Das assyrische Ritual.* Ritual meals are treated in Rintje Frankena's *Takultu: De sacrale maaltijd in het Assyrische ritueel* (1954).

The religious aspects of kingship are the subject of René Labat's *Le caractère religieux de la royauté assyro-babylonienne* (1939) and of Henri Frankfort's *Kingship and the Gods* (1948). An interesting strand in the fabric of kingship is treated in Ilse Siebert's *Hirt, Herde, König* (1969). To this research must be added the important articles by Å. Sjöberg, "Die göttliche Abstammung der sumerisch-babylonischen Herrscher," *Orientalia Suecana* 21 (1972); Piotr Michalowski, "History as Charter: Some Observations on the Sumerian King List," *Journal of the American Oriental Society* 103 (1983); and Claus Wilcke, "Genealogical and Geographical Thought in the Sumerian King List," in *Studies in Honor of Å. Sjöberg,* edited by Erle Leichty (1989).

Communal laments are covered in Raphael Kutscher's book *Oh Angry Sea (a-ab-ba-hu-luh-ha): The History of a Sumerian Congregational Lament* (1975). Penitential psalms are the focus of Julian Morgenstern's *The Doctrine of Sin in the Babylonian Religion* (1905), Walter Schrank's *Babylonische Sühnrites* (1908), Walter G. Kunstmann's *Die babylonische Gebetsbeschwörung* (1932), and Geo Widengren's *The Accadian and Hebrew Psalms of Lamentation as Religious Documents* (1936) and *Hymnes et prières aux dieux de Babylonie et d'Assyrie* (1976). Excellent translations may be found in Adam Falkenstein's *Die Haupptypen der Sumerischen Beschwörung literarisch untersucht* (1931). An updated study of the rich material on this topic has been accomplished by Werner Meier, *Untersuchunen zur Formensprache der babylonischen "Gebetsbeschwörungen"* (1976).

Divination is treated in Georges Conteneau's *La divination chez les Assyriens et les Babyloniens* (1940) and C. J. Gadd's *Ideas of Divine Rule in the Ancient Near East* (1948). Important studies include Ivan Starr's *The Rituals of the Diviner* (1983), Ulla Jeyes's *Old Babylonian Extispicy* (1989), and Barabara Böck's *Die babylonisch-assyrische Morphoskopie* (2000). An overview of celestial divination can be found in Ulla Koch-Westenholz's exhaustive *Mesopotamian Astrology: An Introduction to Babylonian and Assyrian Celestial Divination* (1995).

On magic, L. W. King's *Babylonian Magic and Sorcery* (1896) and B. A. van Proosdij's *L. W. King's Babylonian Magic and Sorcery* (1952) are joined by the pivotal study by Erica Reiner, *Astral Magic in Babylonia* (1995). Studies of exorcistic traditions include Markham J. Geller's "Freud and Mesopotamian Magic," in *Mesopotamian Magic,* edited by Tzvi Abusch and Karel van der Toorn (1999), and Tzvi Abusch's *Mesopotamian Witchcraft: Toward a History and Understanding of Babylonian Witchcraft Beliefs and Literature* (2002). The subject of wisdom has been comprehensively treated in W. G. Lambert's *Babylonian Wisdom Literature* (1960).

In Mesopotamian thought, the cosmos were conceived of as a unity in which the gods, the impersonal powers, and all the realities of the tangible world were a part. Aspects of this cosmology are investigated in the seminal study by Jean Bottéro, "Le noms de Marduk, l'écriture et la 'logique' en Mesopotamie ancienne," in *Ancient Near Eastern Studies in Memory of J. J. Finkelstein,* edited by Maria de Jong Ellis (1977), and developed in his *Mésopotamie: L'écriture, la raison, et les dieux* (1987), translated into English by Zainab Bahrani and Marc Van De Mieroop as *Mesopotamia: Writing, Reasoning, and the Gods* (1992).

Connections between writing and speculative thought have been investigated by Alasdair Livingstone, *Mystical and Mythological Explanatory Works of Assyrian and Babylonian Scholars* (1986); Antoine Cavigneaux, "Aux sources du Midrash: l'herméneutique babylonienne," in *Aula Orientalis* 5 (1987); Paul-Alain Beaulieu, "New Light on Secret Knowledge in Late Babylonian Culture," in *Zeitschrift für Assyriologie* 82 (1992), and "Theological and Philological Speculations on the Names of the Goddess Antu," in *Orientalia* 64 (1995); Morgen Trolle Larsen, "The Mesopotamian Lukewarm Mind: Reflections on Science, Divination, and Literacy," in *Language, Literature, and History: Philological and Historical Studies Presented to Erica Reiner,* edited by Francesca Rochberg-Halton (1987); Dietrich Otto Edzard, "La vision du passé et l'avenir en Mésopotamie," in *Histoire et consience historique dans les civilisations du Proche-Orient Ancien* (1989); Piotr Michalowski, "Mental Maps and Ideology: Reflections on Subartu," in *The Origin of Cities in Dry-Farming Syria and Mesopotamia in the Third Millennium B.C.,* edited by H. Weiss (1986); Bent Alster, "Dilmun, Bahrain, and the Alleged Paradise in Sumerian Myth and Literature," in *Dilmun: New Studies in the Archaeology and Early History of Bahrain,* edited by Daniel I. Potts (1983); Jean-Jaques Glassner, "La philosophie mésopotamienne," in *L'univers philosophique I,* edited by A. Jacob (1989), and his more detailed "V. Religion sumérienne," in *Supplément au dictionnaire de la Bible,* edited by H. Cazelles, J. Briend, and M. Quesnel (2002); P. Michalowski, "Presence at the Creation," in *Lingering over Words,* edited by T. Abusch et al. (1990); Pietro Mander, "General Considerations on Main Concerns in the Religion of Ancient Mesopotamia," *Studi in Memoria di P. L. G. Cagni,* vol. 2, edited by S. Graziani (2000).

The study by Simo Parpola, "The Assyrian Tree of Life: Tracing the Origin of Jewish Monotheism and Greek Philosophy," in *Journal of Near Eastern Studies* 52 (1993) deserves attention despite its problematic methodology. Thorkild Jacobsen's last work, "The Historian and the Sumerian Gods," in *Journal of the American Oriental Society* 114 (1994), is devoted to methodological approaches in which Jacobsen employs the concept of *epoché,* derived from Husserl's phenomenology.

For attempts to reconstruct the historical development of Mesopotamian religion, see Wilfred George Lambert, "Ninurta Mythology in the Babylonian Epic of Creation," in *Keilschriftliche Literaturen: Ausgewählte Vorträge der XXXII Rencontre Assyriologique Internationale,* edited by K. Hecker and W. Sommerfeld (1986); Claus Wilcke, "Politik im Spiegel der Literatur, Literatur als Mittel der Politik im älteren Babylonien," in *Anfänge politischen Denkens in der Antike,* edited by K. Raaflaub et al. (1993); and William W. Hallo, "Sumerian Religion," in *Kinattûtu sha darâti,* edited by A. F. Rainey et al. (1994).

Studies dedicated to the interpretation of anthropogonic mythology and concepts about the human condition and the universe include W. G. Lambert and A. R. Millard, *Atra-hasis: The Babylonian Story of the Flood* (1969); W. L. Moran, "Some Considerations of Form and Interpretation in *Atra-hasis,*" in *Language, Literature, and History: Philological and Historical Studies Presented to Erica Reiner,* edited by F. Rochberg-Halton (1987); Anne Draffkorn Kilmer, "Speculations on Umul, the First Baby," in *Sumerological Studies in Honour of Samuel Noah Kramer,* edited by B. L. Eichler (1976), and "The Symbolism of the Flies in the Mesopotamian Flood Myth," in *Language, Literature, and History: Philological and Historical Studies Presented to Erica Reiner,* edited by F. Rochberg-Halton (1987); W. G. Lambert, "The Theology of Death," in *Death in Mesopotamia: Papers Read at the XXVIe Rencontre assyriologique internationale,* edited by B. Alster (1980); Isaac M. Kikawada, "The Double Creation of Mankind in Enki and Ninmah, Atrahasis I 1–351, and Genesis 1–2," in *Iraq* 45 (1983); W. G. Lambert, "The Pair Lahmu-Lahamu in Cosmology," in *Orientalia* 54 (1985), and "The Cosmology of Sumer and Babylon," in *Ancient Cosmologies,* edited by C. Blacker and M. Loewe (1975); Marten Stol, *Birth in Babylonia and the Bible: Its Mediterranean Setting* (2000); and Karel van der Toorn, *Family Religion in Babylonia, Syria, and Israel: Continuity and Change in the Forms of Religious Life* (1996).

On the topic of the so-called personal god, see Jacob Klein, "'Personal God' and Individual Prayer in Sumerian Religion," in *Archiv für Orientforschungen-Beiheft* 19 (1982), and Brigitte Groneberg, "Eine Einführungsszenze in der altbabylonischen Literatur: Bemerkungen zum persönlichen Gott," in *Keilschriftlichen Literaturen,* edited by K. Hecker and W. Sommerfeld (1985).

For information on specific topics in Mesopotamian religion see the entries in *Reallexicon der Assyriologie* (1932–1957) and *Dictionary of Deities and Demons in the Bible,* 2nd ed. (1999), edited by K. van den Toorn, B. Becking, and P. W. van der Horst. The published volumes of the proceedings of the Melammu Symposia deserve a particular mention: *Mythology and Mithologies,* edited by R. M. Whiting (2001) and *Ideologies as Intercultural Phenomena,* edited by A. Panaino and G. Pettinato (2003). Jeremy Black, Anthony Green, and Tessa Rickards's *Gods, Demons, and Symbols of Ancient Mesopotamia: An Illustrated Dictionary* (1992) is both accessible and accurate.

UNCERTAINTIES. The script and languages of ancient Mesopotamia continue to present great difficulties to the modern student. These are so serious that almost no translations of Akkadian texts made prior to the twentieth century can safely be taken at face value; they need to be checked by a competent Assyriologist. As for Sumerian, at present no consensus about basic features of writing and grammar exists, and translations of one and the same text may differ radically. Extreme caution is thus indicated.

Since the late 1970s, however, in spite of the many difficulties, many important religious texts in Sumerian and in Akkadian have been published. While not aimed at the nonspecialist, this great mass of philological work does provide the essential basis for further knowledge.

Last but not least, important work has been published by scholars looking for patterns that show the influence on the Greek religious world. Outstanding studies include Geoffrey S. Kirk's *Myth: Its Meaning and Functions in Ancient and Other Cultures* (1970), and *The Nature of Greek Myths* (1974), Martin L. West's *Early Greek Philosophy and the Orient* (1971), and *The East Face of Helicon* (1997), and Walter Burkert's *Griechische Religion der archaischen und klassischen Epoche* (1977), and *The Orientalizing Revolution: Near Eastern Influence on Greek Culture in Early Archaic Age* (1992).

SEE ALSO An; Ashur; Dagan; Dumuzi; Enlil; Inanna; Marduk; Nabu; Nanna; Nergal; Utu.

THORKILD JACOBSEN (1987)
PIETRO MANDER (2005)

MESROB SEE MASHTOTSʿ, MESROP

MESSIANISM

This entry consists of the following articles:

AN OVERVIEW
JEWISH MESSIANISM
MESSIANISM IN THE MUSLIM TRADITION
SOUTH AMERICAN MESSIANISM

MESSIANISM: AN OVERVIEW

The term *messianism* is derived from *messiah,* a transliteration of the Hebrew *mashiaḥ* ("anointed"), which originally denoted a king whose reign was consecrated by a rite of anointment with oil. In the Hebrew scriptures (Old Testament), *mashiaḥ* is always used in reference to the actual king of Israel: Saul (*1 Sm.* 12:3–5, 24:7–11), David (*2 Sm.* 19:21–22), Solomon (*2 Chr.* 6:42), or the king in general (*Ps.* 2:2, 18:50, 20:6, 28:8, 84:9, 89:38, 89:51, 132:17). In the intertestamental period, however, the term was applied to the future king, who was expected to restore the kingdom of Israel and save the people from all evil.

At the same time, prophetic oracles referring to an ideal future king, though not using the word *messiah,* were interpreted as prophecies of this same eschatological figure. These passages include *Isaiah* 9:1–6 and 11:1–9, *Micah* 5:2–6, and *Zechariah* 9:9, and certain of the "royal" psalms, such as Psalms 2, 72, and 110. Precedence for this later conception lies in the royal ideologies of the ancient Near East, where the king played the role of the savior of his people: every new king was expected to bring fertility, wealth, freedom, peace, and happiness to his land. Examples are found both in Egypt and in Mesopotamia. The French scholar Édouard Dhorme, in his book *La religion assyro-babylonienne* (1910), quoted some texts indicating such expectations under the heading "The Messiah King."

JUDAISM. In the Judaism of the intertestamental period, messianic expectations developed in two directions. One was national and political and is most clearly set out in the pseudepigraphic *Psalms of Solomon* (17 and 18). Here the national Messiah is a descendant of David. He shall rule in wisdom and righteousness; he shall defeat the great powers of the world, liberate his people from foreign rule, and establish a universal kingdom in which the people will live in peace and happiness. The same kingly ideal is expressed in the description of the rule of Simon in *1 Maccabees* 14:4, which echoes the messianic prophecies of the Old Testament.

Some apocryphal documents, especially the *Testament of Levi,* speak also of a priestly messiah, one who is to bring peace and knowledge of God to his people and to the world. The Qumran community even expected two anointed ones, a priest and a king, but very little is known about their functions.

The other line of development is found above all in the Ethiopic *Apocalypse of Enoch (1 Enoch)* and in *2 Esdras* (also called *4 Ezra*). It centers around the term *son of man.* This term is used in the Old Testament to refer generally to a human being (*Psalms* 8:5, 80:18 [English version 80:17] and several times, addressing the prophet, in *Ezekiel*). In the vision recorded in *Daniel* 7, the term is used in verse 13 with reference to a "man-like being," which, in contrast to the usual four animals representing the four great powers of the ancient world, stands for Israel in its prominent role at the last judgment.

In the apocalyptic books mentioned, the son of man is a transcendental figure, more or less divine, preexistent, and at present hidden in heaven. At the end of time he will appear to judge the world in connection with the resurrection of the dead. The pious will be freed from the dominion of the wicked, and he will rule the world forever in peace and righteousness. He is often referred to as "the chosen One" but only occasionally as "the anointed One," that is, the Messiah. Obviously, this interpretation of *Daniel* 7:13 takes "son of man" to refer to a person and not to an object of comparison. The problem is the extent to which these passages are pre-Christian. *2 Esdras* was definitely written after the fall of Jerusalem in 70 CE, and those parts of *1 Enoch* in which references to the son of man occur do not appear among the Aramaic fragments of the same work found at Qumran. On the other hand, the New Testament seems to presuppose this same interpretation of *Daniel* 7:13.

CHRISTIANITY. Early Christianity took many of the Jewish ideas about the Messiah and applied them to Jesus. *Messiah* was translated into Greek as *Christos,* that is, Christ, thereby identifying Jesus with Jewish messianic expectations. Matthew interpreted *Isaiah* 9:1 (EV 9:2), "The people who walk in darkness shall see a great light," as fulfilled in Jesus (*Mt.* 4:14–18). *Micah* 5:1 (EV 5:2) is quoted to prove that the Messiah should be born in Bethlehem (*Mt.* 2:6). *Zechariah* 9:9 is read as a prediction of Jesus' entry into Jerusalem (*Mt.* 21:5), and if the story related by Matthew is authentic, it must mean that Jesus wanted to proclaim himself as the Messiah. *Psalms* 2:7 ("You are my son") is quoted or at least alluded to in connection with the baptism of Jesus (*Mt.* 3:17, *Mk.* 1:11, *Lk.* 3:22). (The Jewish Messiah, however, was not regarded as God's son.) *Psalms* 110:1 is used to prove that the Messiah cannot be the son of David (*Mt.* 22:44); other parts of Psalm 110 are behind the exposition in *Hebrews* 5, 6, and 7. However, the New Testament rejects the political messiahship described in the *Psalms of Solomon.* Jesus refused to be made king (*Jn.* 6:15); he proclaimed before Pilate: "My kingdom is not of this world" (*Jn.* 18:26). Despite this, he was accused of pretending to be "the king of the Jews" (*Jn.* 19:19).

The New Testament, however, although maintaining that the Messiah is the Son of God, also uses the epithet "Son of man." According to the Gospels, Jesus uses it of himself. In a few cases it could possibly mean simply "a human being" or "this man" (*Mk.* 2:10, *Mt.* 11:8, and parallels; *Mt.* 8:20 and parallels). A number of passages refer to the coming of the Son of man at the end of time (*Mt.* 24:27, 24:37; *Lk.* 18:18, 18:22, 18:69; *Mt.* 10:23; *Mk.* 13:26); these imply the same interpretation of *Daniel* 7:13 as that implied by *1 Enoch* and *2 Esdras* but add a new element in that it is Christ who is to come a second time, returning as the judge of the world. A third group of "Son of man" references allude to the suffering and death of Jesus, sometimes also mentioning his resurrection (*Mk.* 8:31, 9:9, 9:31, 10:33, 14:21, 14:41; *Lk.* 22:48 and others). These introduce the idea of a suffering messiah, which is not entirely unknown in Jewish messianism but is never linked with the Son of man. (If the latter is sometimes described in terms of the "servant of the Lord," the chapter on the suffering servant, *Isaiah* 53, is never applied to him.) In the *Gospel of John* the Son of man is almost always the glorified Lord as king and judge; he is also described as preexistent in heaven (*Jn.* 1:51, 3:13, 8:28). *Hebrews* 2:6–8 applies Psalm 8, in which "son of man" was originally meant as "human being," to Jesus, thus giving the expression an eschatological meaning.

A new feature was introduced in New Testament messianism by the identification of Jesus with the suffering servant of *Isaiah* 53. *Mark* 9:12 says that it "was written of the Son of man that he should suffer many things and be treated with contempt" (cf. *Is.* 53:3). *Acts of the Apostles* 8:32 explicitly quotes *Isaiah* 53:7–8 as fulfilled in Jesus, and *1 Peter* 2:22–24 quotes or alludes to parts of *Isaiah* 53 as referring to him. It would seem that this identification is an original creation of Jesus (or, possibly, of the early church).

Thus, New Testament Christology utilizes a great many traits drawn from Jewish messianism. At the same time, it adds a new dimension: the idea that Jesus, though he has already in person fulfilled the messianic expectations, is to return in order to bring them to their final fulfillment.

ISLAMIC MESSIANISM. Ideas comparable to that of the second coming of Christ are found in Islam, probably owing to Christian influence. While the Qurʾān envisages God as the judge on the Day of Judgment, later Muslim tradition introduces certain preparatory events before that day. Muḥammad is reported to have said that the last day of the world will be prolonged in order that a ruler of the Prophet's family may defeat all enemies of Islam. This ruler is called the Mahdi, "the rightly guided one." Other traditions say that he will fill the world with justice as it is now filled with wrong, an apparent echo of ancient kingship ideology. Some identify the Mahdi with Jesus (Arab., ʿIsā), who is supposed to appear before the end of the world to defeat al-Dajjāl ("the deceiver"), the false messiah, or antichrist. Such traditions were utilized by founders of new dynasties and other political or religious leaders, especially among the Shīʿah. The last such example was the rebel leader Muḥammad Aḥmad of Sudan, who from 1883 temporarily held back the British influence in this area.

"NATIVISTIC" MOVEMENTS. With some justification the concept of messianism is used to describe a number of "nativistic" cults in different parts of the world that have emerged as the result of a clash between colonialist Christianity and native religions. Following Vittorio Lanternari (1965), however, a distinction should be made between messianic and prophetic movements. "The 'messiah,'" he says, "is the awaited savior, the 'prophet' is he who announces the arrival of one who is to come. The prophet himself can be the 'messiah' after he has died and his return is expected as a redeemer, or when the prophet himself, leaning upon an earlier messianic myth, declares himself to be the prophet-messiah" (p. 242n.).

Examples of such movements are known from all parts of the aboriginal world. As early as the sixteenth century, successive waves of Tupi tribes in Brazil moved to the Bahia coast, impelled by a messianic quest for the "land without evil." Another such migration to find the "land of immortality and perpetual rest" is reported to have inspired the Spaniards' idea of El Dorado. Similar migrations took place in later centuries, led by a kind of prophet described as "Man-God" or "Demi-God," that is, local shamans who came to the natives as religious leaders and reincarnations of the great mythical heroes of native tradition and announcing an era of renewal.

The Ghost Dance movement in the western United States was initiated in 1869 by a certain Wodziwob, who had visions through which the Great Spirit announced that a major cataclysm would soon shake the entire world and wipe out the white man. The Indians would come back to life, and the Great Spirit would dwell among them in the heavenly era. Wodziwob's son, Wovoka (John Wilson), established contacts with the Mormons in 1892 and was considered by them to be the Messiah of the Indians and the Son of God.

In the Kongo region in Africa, Simon Kimbangu, who had been raised in the British Baptist Mission, appeared in 1921 as a prophet to his people. His preaching was a combination of Christian and indigenous elements. He prophesied the imminent ousting of the foreign rulers, a new way of life for the Africans, and the coming of a golden age. Both he and his successor, Andre Matswa, expected to return after death as the liberators of their people. Several movements of a similar kind are known from other parts of Africa.

In the early twentieth century, Melanesia and New Guinea saw the emergence of the so-called cargo cults. Common to them all is the belief that a Western ship (or even airplane), manned by whites, will come to bring riches to the natives, while at the same time the dead will return to life and an era of happiness will follow. Some prophets of these cults were regarded as incarnations of spirits.

It would seem that all these movements originated among people under oppression and gave expression to their longing for freedom and better conditions. Obviously, the conditions under which Christianity arose are somewhat comparable.

SEE ALSO Cargo Cults; Kingship, article on Kingship in the Ancient Mediterranean World; Millenarianism; Revival and Renewal.

BIBLIOGRAPHY

The standard work for early Jewish messianism is Sigmund Mowinckel's *He That Cometh* (Oxford, 1956). Briefer, but including the Egyptian and Mesopotamian texts referred to in the article, is my book *The Messiah in the Old Testament* (London, 1956). A good introduction to the Son of man question is Carsten Colpe's article "Huios Tou Anthrōpou," in the *Theological Dictionary of the New Testment*, edited by Gerhard Kittel (Grand Rapids, Mich., 1972). See also Rollin Kearns's *Vorfragen zur Christologie*, 3 vols. (Tübingen, 1978–1982), and Maurice Casey's *Son of Man: The Interpretation and Influence of Daniel 7* (London, 1979). Islamic messianism has been dealt with most recently by Hava Lazarus-Yafeh in her book *Some Religious Aspects of Islam* (Leiden, 1981), pp. 48–57, and by Jan-Olaf Blichfeldt in *Early Mahdism* (Leiden, 1985). On Islam see also my article "Some Religious Aspects of the Caliphate," in *The Sacral Kingship* (Leiden, 1959). Edgar Blochet provides some early observations in *Le messianisme dans l'hétérodoxie musulmane* (Paris, 1903). A comprehensive survey of the millenarian movements is found in Vittorio Lanternari's *The Religions of the Oppressed* (New York, 1965). Lanternari's book includes a good bibliography.

New Sources

Baigent, Michael, Richard Leigh, and Henry Lincoln. *The Messianic Legacy.* New York, 1986.

Beuken, Wim, Seán Freyne, and Antonius Gerardus Weiler. *Messianism through History.* London, 1993.

Charlesworth, James H. *The Messiah: Developments in Earliest Judaism and Christianity.* Minneapolis, 1992.

Katz, David S., and Richard Henry Popkin. *Messianic Revolution: Radical Religious Politics to the End of the Second Millennium.* New York, 1999.

Szeminski, Jan. "Last Time the Inca Came Back: Messianism and Nationalism in the Great Rebellion of 1780–1783." In *South and Meso-American Native Spirituality: From the Cult of the Feathered Serpent to the Theology of Liberation.* See pages 279–299. New York, 1993.

HELMER RINGGREN (1987)
Revised Bibliography

MESSIANISM: JEWISH MESSIANISM

The term *messianism* denotes a movement, or a system of beliefs and ideas, centered on the expectation of the advent of a messiah (derived from the Hebrew *mashiaḥ*, "the anointed one"). The Hebrew verb *mashaḥ* means to anoint objects or persons with oil for ordinary secular purposes as well as for sacral purposes. In due course the nominative form came to mean anyone with a specific mission from God (i.e., not only kings or high priests), even if the anointing was purely metaphorical (prophets, partiarchs), and ultimately it acquired the connotation of a savior or redeemer who would appear at the end of days and usher in the kingdom of God, the restoration of Israel, or whatever dispensation was considered to be the ideal state of the world.

This specific semantic development was due to the Jewish belief that the ultimate salvation of Israel, though wrought by God, would be presided over or realized by a descendant of the royal house of David. He, the "son of David," would be the Lord's anointed *par excellence.* From its original Jewish context the word *mashiaḥ* then passed into general use, denoting movements or expectations of a utopian character or otherwise concerned with the salvation of society and the world. The messianic complex appears at times as restorative in character (the *Paradise Lost-Paradise Regained* syndrome), in the sense that it envisages the restoration of the past and lost golden age. At other times it appears as more utopian, in the sense that it envisages a state of perfection the like of which has never existed before ("a new heaven and a new earth"); the Messiah will not merely renew the days of yore but will usher in a "new age."

The term *mashiaḥ* in this specific eschatological sense does not occur in the Hebrew scriptures. *Isaiah* 45:1 calls the Persian king Cyrus II the Lord's "anointed" because it was evidently as the chosen instrument of God that he permitted the Israelite exiles to return from Babylonia to Jerusalem. Using later terminology one may, perhaps, commit a technical anachronism and describe as "messianic" those scriptural passages that prophesy a future golden age, the ingathering of the exiles, the restoration of the Davidic dynasty, the rebuilding of Jerusalem and the Temple, the era of peace when the wolf will lie down with the lamb, and so on.

Such is the nature of messianism that it develops and flourishes in periods of suffering and frustration. When the present is satisfactory it need not be redeemed but should be perpetuated or renewed (e.g., by periodic or cyclical renewal rites). When the present is profoundly unsatisfactory, messianism emerges as one of the possible answers: the certainty of a satisfactory natural, social, and historical order (and this certainty was particularly strong in Israel, based as it was on God's promise enshrined in his eternal covenant) is projected on the horizon of an ideal future. As the biblical account amply shows, already in biblical times the present was generally perceived as far from satisfactory (wicked and sinful kings, enemy incursions, defeats), and hence ideas concerning an ideal order under an ideal Davidic king began to crystallize.

The tendency to look toward future fulfillment was reinforced by the destruction of the First Temple (587/6 BCE), the Babylonian exile, and the subsequent return to Zion under Cyrus, hailed by "Second Isaiah" as an event of a messianic order. But this "messianic" salvation proved a sad disappointment. The severe persecution under the Syrian Seleucid ruler Antiochus IV (r. 175–163 BCE) similarly led to messianic-eschatological hopes, as evidenced by the *Book of Daniel*, the composition of which is generally dated in that period. But the great salvation wrought by the victory of the Maccabees similarly proved, in the long run, a sad disappointment. The revolts against the oppressive "kingdom of wickedness," Rome in 65–70 CE (which ended with the destruction of Jerusalem and the Second Temple) and again in 132–135 CE (the Bar Kokhba Revolt, which ended in the practical destruction of Palestinian Jewry) no doubt had messianic elements. Thereafter messianism was a mixture of firm and unshakable hope in ultimate redemption, on the one hand, and, on the other hand, fear of the dangers and disastrous consequences of messianic explosions—"messianic activism," as the historian would call it, or "premature messianism," as the theologian would call it.

The messianic doctrines that developed during the second half of the Second Temple period from approximately 220 BCE to 70 CE (also called the "intertestamentary" period) were of diverse kinds, reflecting the mentality and spiritual preoccupations of different circles. They ranged from this-worldly, political expectations— the breaking of the yoke of foreign rule, the restoration of the Davidic dynasty (the messianic king), and, after 70 CE, also the ingathering of the exiles and the rebuilding of the Temple—to more apocalyptic conceptions, such as the spectacular and catastrophic end of "this age" (including a Day of Judgment), the ushering in of a new age, the advent of the kingdom of heaven, the resurrection of the dead, a new heaven and a new earth. The main protagonist might be a military leader, a kingly "son of David," a supernatural figure such as the somewhat mysterious "son of man" mentioned in some books of the Hebrew scriptures as well as in apocryphal apocalyptic texts. Many scholars think that Jesus deliberately avoided the use of the term messiah because of its political overtones (especially as he was announcing a kingdom that was not of this world) and preferred the unpolitical term "son of man." On the other hand, those responsible for the final redaction of the *Gospel of Matthew* thought it necessary to provide Jesus with a lineage proving his descent from David in order to legitimate his messianic status, since the *mashiaḥ* (Gr., *christos*) had to be identified as the "son of David."

These examples, incidentally, also show that the origins of Christianity have to be seen in the context of the messianic ferment of contemporaneous Jewish Palestine. Messianic ideas developed not only by way of interpretation of biblical texts (e.g., the *pesher* of the Qumran community and the later *midrash* of rabbinic Judaism) but also by "revelations" granted to apocalyptic visionaries. The latter tradition is well illustrated by the last book of the New Testament, the *Book of Revelation.*

But messianic ideas and expectations could also be based on "rational" (i.e., nonvisionary) insights, especially when the interpretation of scriptural prophecies took the form of calculations and computations of the dates allegedly hinted at in the obscure symbolism of the texts. Jewish messianic enthusiasts would often base their calculations on the *Book of Daniel* (much as Christian millenarians would compute the end time from the "number of the beast" mentioned in *Revelation* 13:18). Since the high-pitched hopes generated by these calculations would often lead to disaster (or at best to severe disappointment), the Talmudic rabbis had very harsh words about "those who compute the [messianic] end."

One tradition, probably influenced by *Zechariah* 3–4, appears to have held a doctrine of two messianic figures, the one a high-priestly "anointed one" of the house of Aaron, the other a royal messiah of the house of David. This belief, which was held by the Qumran community (also known as the Dead Sea Sect), obviously implies that these complementary messianic figures are not so much saviors and redeemers as symbolic types presiding over the redeemed and ideal social order. Echoes of this doctrine seem to be present in the (apparently polemical) insistence of the New Testament *Letter to the Hebrews* that Jesus was both king and high priest. The doctrine seems to have survived into the Middle Ages (by what channels is not quite clear), for it is found also among the Karaites.

Another version of the "double messiah" developed in the second century CE, possibly as a reaction to the catastrophic failure of the Bar Kokhba Revolt. The messiah of the house of Joseph (or Ephraim)—a possible echo of the motif of the ten lost tribes—falls in battle against the forces of Gog and Magog (the Jewish counterpart to the Battle of Armageddon). He is thus not a suffering messiah but a warrior messiah who dies a hero's death, to be followed by the victorious messiah of the house of David. This view of a double messiah also expresses an essential duality in Jewish (but not only in Jewish) messianism: messianic fulfillment is preceded by cosmic, natural, and social upheavals and catastrophes. (The Christian transformation of the Jewish motif is the idea of the Antichrist let loose to rule the world before being finally vanquished at the Second Coming.) Hence, whenever severe sufferings and tribulations were visited on the Jewish people, these could be, and often were, interpreted as the predicted premessianic catastrophe (the "birth pangs" of the messianic age, in the language of the Talmud) heralding an imminent messianic consummation.

Messianism in the wider sense of an ideal future need not imply the belief in a particular, individual savior or redeemer figure. While *Isaiah* 11 and 2:2–4 envisage a peaceful and utopian world under a Davidic king, the parallel text *Micah* 4:4 has even fewer miraculous elements and speaks of an earthly happiness, with every man dwelling under his vine and under his fig tree. For Jeremiah too, though his vision of the future also emphasizes the moral dimensions—compare *Jeremiah* 31:30ff. and 32:36–44 with Ezekiel's "new heart" and "heart of flesh" instead of the previous heart of stone (*Ez.* 2:4, 11:19, 18:31, 32:9, 36:26)—the promised boon is that "there shall enter into the gates of this city [Jerusalem] kings and princes sitting upon the throne of David, riding in chariots and on horses" (*Jer.* 17:25). Noteworthy in this text is not only its this-worldly ideal, with Jerusalem as a bustling royal city, but also the reference to kings, in the plural. The idea of the *one* messianic savior-king had not yet developed.

In later, especially modern and secularized, versions of messianism, the idea of a personal messiah increasingly gave way to the notion of a "messianic age" of peace, social justice, and universal love—conceptions that could easily function as progressive, liberal, socialist, utopian, and even revolutionary transformations of traditional messianism. Thus the Philadelphia program of American Reform Judaism (1869) substituted for the belief in a personal messiah the optimistic faith in the advent of a messianic era characterized by "the unity of all men as children of God in the confession of the One and Sole God," and the Pittsburgh Platform (1885) spoke of the establishment "of the kingdom of truth, justice and peace." Twentieth-century disillusionment with the idea of progress seems to have given a new lease on life to more radical and utopian forms of messianism.

In the intertestamentary period, messianic beliefs and doctrines developed, as we have seen, in a variety of forms. Messianism became increasingly eschatological, and eschatology was decisively influenced by apocalypticism. At the same time, messianic expectations became increasingly focused on the figure of an individual savior. In times of stress and crisis messianic pretenders (or forerunners and heralds announcing their advent) would appear, often as leaders of revolts. Josephus Flavius as well as the author of *Acts* 5 mentions several such figures. Moreover, the Messiah no longer symbolized the coming of the new age, but he was somehow supposed to bring it about. The "Lord's anointed" thus became the "savior and redeemer" and the focus of more intense expectations and doctrines, even of a "messianic theology." Compare, for example, the implications of Paul's reading of *Isaiah* 52:20, "and the Redeemer [i.e., God] cometh to Zion," as "the Redeemer [i.e., Christ] cometh *from* Zion" (*Rom.* 11:26).

Since many Jews of the Diaspora lived under Christian domination, which meant also Christian persecution and missionary pressure, theological polemics inevitably centered on christological—that is, messianic—themes. (Is Jesus the promised messiah? Why do the Jews refuse to acknowledge him? Because of carnal blindness or diabolic wickedness?) Since both religions recognized the Hebrew Bible as holy scripture, polemic often assumed an exegetical character (i.e., it claimed a correct interpretation of the "messianic" prophecies in the Bible). As a rule, Jewish messianism never relinquished its concrete, historical, national, and social expectations and was little impressed by the "spiritual" character of Christian doctrine.

Christian polemics, from the early church fathers to the Middle Ages and later, accused the Jews of an inferior and crude materialism that made them read the scriptures *kata sarka*, with eyes of flesh rather than with eyes of the spirit. Paradoxically, the Jews considered this reproach as a compliment, since for them the claim that the Messiah had come was, in an unredeemed world plagued by wars, injustice, oppression, sickness, sin, and violence, utterly meaningless. In the famous disputation of Barcelona (1263), forced upon the Jews by Dominican missionaries and held in the presence of King James I of Aragon, the Jewish spokesman, the great Talmudist and qabbalist Moses Nahmanides (Mosheh ben Naḥman, c. 1194–c. 1270), simply quoted *Isaiah* 2:4 and observed that His Most Christian Majesty, in spite of his belief that the Messiah had come, would probably find it difficult to disband his army and send home all his knights so that they might beat their swords into plowshares and their spears into pruning hooks.

Throughout Jewish history there has existed a tension between two types of messianism, already briefly mentioned before: the apocalyptic one, with its miraculous and supernatural elements, and a more "rationalist" one. Throughout the Middle Ages old, and usually pseudepigraphic, apocalypses and messianic *midrashim* were copied and new ones were produced by messianic enthusiasts and visionaries. The rabbinic attitude, at least the official one, was more sober and prudent: too many messianic outbursts had ended in disaster, namely, cruel suppression by the gentile rulers. A burned child dreads the fire, and the rabbinic hesitations (probably a result of the traumatic experience of the Bar Kokhba Revolt) found eloquent expression in the homiletic interpretation of *Song of Songs* 2:7: " 'I charge you, you daughters of Jerusalem, that you stir not up nor awake my love till he please'—this verse contains six charges to Israel: not to rebel against the kingdoms of this world, not to force the end of the days . . . and not to use force to return to the Land of Israel" (B. T., *Ket.* 111a). On a more theoretical level, already one Talmudic master had given the opinion that "there is no difference between this age and the messianic age but the oppression of Israel by the heathen kingdoms [which will cease after Israel regains its freedom under a messianic king]."

The great medieval authority, the philosopher-theologian Moses Maimonides (Mosheh ben Maimon, 1135/8–1204), although he enumerated belief in the advent of the Messiah among the basic articles of faith, was careful to rule in his legal code as follows:

> Let no one think that the messianic king would have to perform signs or miracles . . . and let no one think that in the messianic era the normal course of things would be changed or the order of nature altered. . . . What scripture says on the subject is very obscure, and our sages [too] have no clear and explicit traditions in these matters. Most [of the prophecies and traditions] are parables, the real meaning of which will become clear only after the event. These details are therefore not articles of religion, and one should not waste time on their interpretation or on the computation of the date of the messianic advent, since these things are conducive neither to the love of God nor to the fear of God. (*Mishneh Torah*, Kings 11, 12)

In Maimonides' own lifetime, messianic movements occurred in parts of the Diaspora, and as the acknowledged leader of his generation he had to do his best, without offending the messianic enthusiasm of the pious folk, to prevent disasters and backlashes by carefully preaching his more sober approach (e.g., in his *Epistle to Yemen* and *Epistle on the Resurrection of the Dead*). Nevertheless, messianic longing and apocalyptic imagination, fired by persecutions and suffering, continued to flourish and to ignite messianic outbursts. There was no dearth of messianic pretenders ("pseudomessiahs") or precursors announcing the advent of the Redeemer, provided the people would prepare themselves by appropriate means (e.g., penitential austerities).

But no matter whether messianic hopes and beliefs were apocalyptic or more sober, a matter of feverish agitation or of theological dogma, they had become an essential part of the Jewish faith and of the Jewish experience of life and of history. The apocalyptic texts might be rejected by some as too fantastic, but the heritage of messianic prophecy was accepted by all—not only in its biblical form but even more decisively in its subsequent rabbinic development. The most influential factor was, perhaps, the constant emphasis of messianic beliefs (the ingathering of the exiles, the restoration of the Davidic kingdom, the rebuilding of Jerusalem and the Temple) in the daily liturgy, in the grace recited after every meal, and especially in the prayers on Sabbath and holy days. This is not the only instance in the history of religions that illustrates how the prayer book and the liturgy can exert a more pervasive influence than theological tracts.

Messianic movements accompanied Jewish history throughout the Middle Ages, and there were probably many more than have come to our knowledge through chronicles, rabbinic *responsa*, and other incidental references. Most of them were local phenomena of short duration. The movement usually petered out after its suppression by the authorities or the disappearance (or execution) of the leader. In this respect the movement inspired by the seventeenth-century messianic pretender Shabbetai Tsevi is an exceptional case. Messianic movements are attested in Persia from the eighth century (Abū ʿIsā al-Isfahānī and his disciple Yudghan) to David Alroy (Menaḥem al-Dūjī) in the twelfth century. Abū ʿIsā, who proclaimed himself the messiah of the house of Joseph, duly fell in battle against the Abbasid forces against which he had marched with ten thousand followers, while David Alroy (known best from Disraeli's fanciful novel) staged a revolt against the sultan. Several messianic pretenders appeared in the eleventh and twelfth centuries in western Europe, particularly in Spain. Later, under the influence of Qabbalah, messianic activism became more mystical and even magical. Spiritual activism, when all realistic and practical outlets are closed, easily becomes magical activism, and Jewish legend tells of masters who undertook to force the messianic advent by means of extreme mortifications, special meditations, and qabbalistic incantations. These legends, the most popular of which was that concerning Yosef della Reyna, usually end with the qabbalist adept falling prey to the demonic powers that he had sought to vanquish.

To understand the various messianic movements properly, one would have to examine carefully, individually, and in detail the specific historical circumstances and external pressures as well as internal tensions that precipitated them. The common fate of Jews everywhere as a despised and persecuted minority, existing in a hostile environment yet sharing the same religious culture and messianic hope, provides a general framework; nevertheless it is clearly inadequate as an explanation of specific messianic movements. The permanent presence of messianic dynamisms is also attested by the phenomenon of smaller or larger groups of Jews leaving their countries of origin in the Diaspora in order to settle in the Holy Land. While less blatantly millenarian than the acute messianic outbursts, these movements often had messianic motivations. Although the Messiah had not yet appeared or called the faithful to the Promised Land, the motivation was often "preeschatological" in the sense that a life of prayer and ascetic sanctification in the Holy Land was thought to prepare or even hasten the advent of the Redeemer.

With the emergence of Qabbalah after the thirteenth century, and especially its development after the expulsion of Jews from Spain and Portugal, qabbalistic mysticism became a major element and driving social force in Jewish messianism. This process requires a brief elucidation. As a rule mystical systems have little or no relationship to time or to the process of time, history, and hence to messianism. After all, the mystic aspires to a supratemporal sphere, the anticipation of timeless eternity and the "everlasting now" rather than to the crowning consummation of history. It is therefore not surprising to find messianic tension decreasing in inverse proportion to the mystical tension. This principle seems to hold true also regarding classical Spanish Qabbalah. The new Qabbalah, Lurianic Qabbalah, that developed after the Spanish expulsion in the great centers of the Ottoman empire, but especially in Safad in the Holy Land, was remarkable for its high, one would almost say explosive, messianic charge, especially in the form that it received at the hand of the most original, charismatic, and outstanding qabbalist in that group, Isaac Luria (1534–1572).

Lurianic Qabbalah interpreted the history of the world in general, and Israel's exile, suffering, and redemption in particular, in an idiom of a type that might be called gnostic, that is, in terms of a cosmic, or rather divine, drama in which God himself was involved. One might also describe the system as a theosophical *Heilsgeschichte*. According to this strangely "gnostic" myth, a primordial catastrophe or "fall" occurred—long before Adam's original sin—at the moment when the divine light-essence externalized itself with a view to creating the world. The vessels that were to carry and transmit the divine light collapsed (the "breaking of the vessels") and the divine light-sparks fell into chaos and have since been imprisoned and "exiled" there, where—and this is part of their tragedy—they sustain the life of the demonic realm.

Israel's exile and suffering thus merely reflect on the historical, material, and external level the more fundamental mystery of the exile and suffering of the divine fallen sparks. Redemption thus means the liberation of the divine sparks from the defiling embrace of the demonic powers and their return to their divine source, no less than the liberation of Israel from subjugation to the Gentiles and its return to the

Holy Land. Indeed, the latter process would follow as natural consequence from the former, which it was Israel's true and mystical vocation to bring about by a life of piety and holiness. This is spiritual activism at its most extreme, for here God has become a *salvator salvandus*. To the harassed and hounded Jew, exile became meaningful because it was seen as a reflection of, and participation in, the profounder exile of God, and God himself required Israel's cooperation in the redemption of himself, his people, and his creation. It is not surprising that, at least at first, the personality of the Messiah played a relatively minor role in this system. He was not so much a redeemer as a sign and symbol that the mystical messianic process had been consummated. In fact, the messianic doctrine of Lurianism comes close, at least structurally, to an evolutionist scheme.

This qabbalistic system provided the background of one of the most remarkable messianic episodes in the course of Jewish history—the movement centered on the person of Shabbetai Tsevi. The ignominious debacle of Shabbateanism, with its aftermath of heresy, antinomianism, and apostasy, left a trail of spiritual confusion and disarray as a result of which both Qabbalah and messianism declined, at least in their public and social role. Apart from a few minor messianic convulsions, "automessianism" (as Martin Buber called it) declined steadily. The messianic idea remained alive in Judaism, influencing no doubt also non-Jewish ideologies of utopia and hope (see the influential work of the Marxist thinker Ernst Bloch, *Das Prinzip Hoffnung*), but no more messianic pretenders appeared. Orthodox Judaism continued to believe in the traditional doctrine of a personal messiah but *de facto* retreated into a shell of strict halakhic observance. The myth had lost its power to trigger messianic movements.

Hasidism, the great spiritual revival launched in eighteenth-century eastern Europe by the Besht (Yisraʾel ben Eliʿezer, 1700–1760), certainly did not relinquish traditional messianic beliefs, but its main emphasis was on closeness to God through spiritual inwardness or (at times) ecstasy. Gershom Scholem has described this process (though the subject is still a matter of scholarly debate) as a "neutralization of the messianic element." But while Hasidism attempted to provide an answer, in a traditional idiom, for the spiritual seekers as well as for the pauperized masses in the ghettos of eastern Europe, the Jewry of western and central Europe entered the modern age (civil emancipation, assimilation, Reform Judaism).

The implications of these developments for Jewish messianism are still a matter for research. Many of the modern ideologies undoubtedly preserved some of the traditional messianic overtones. At times they made deliberate use of messianic terminology. Of course the progressive liberals and later socialists, and needless to say the national revival known as Zionism, did not think in terms of Armageddon, or a heavenly Jerusalem descending from above, or the "son of David" riding on an ass, but rather of civil liberties, equality before the law, universal peace, all-around ethical and human progress, the national emancipation of the Jewish people within the family of nations, and so on. But all these aspirations were somehow surrounded with a messianic halo. Jews rarely asked the literalist questions so congenial to Christian fundamentalism. They do not, as a rule, inquire whether a particular historical event is the "fulfillment" of a particular biblical prophecy. But it is impossible, for most of them, to pass through apocalyptic events such as the Holocaust, or to experience the end of exile and the reestablishment of Israel as a sovereign commonwealth, without the stirring of messianic chords in their souls.

In fact, since the Yom Kippur War, a trend toward a "messianization" of politics has become noticeable in Israel, especially among groups advocating settlements on the West Bank or Jewish rights on the Temple Mount. Some of this messianized Zionism goes back to the teaching of Avraham Yitsḥaq Kook, chief rabbi of Palestine from 1921 to 1935. In the Prayer for the State of Israel the chief rabbinate refers to the state—in an incredibly primitive dispensationalist fashion—as "the beginning of the sprouting of our Redemption." Others, however, feel that messianism as an eschatological concept should be kept out of the pragmatics and ambiguities of current politics, since it tends to demoralize and mythologize them instead of moralizing them (in the prophetic sense). It is still too early for a definitive historical and sociological evaluation of these conflicting tendencies, and of the nature and role of messianism in contemporary Judaism.

SEE ALSO Apocalypse, articles on Jewish Apocalypticism to the Rabbinic Period, Medieval Jewish Apocalyptic Literature; Eschatology; Polemics, article on Jewish-Christian Polemics; Qabbalah; Shabbetai Tsevi; Zionism.

BIBLIOGRAPHY

Cohen, Gerson D. "Messianic Postures of Ashkenazim and Sephardim." In *Studies of the Leo Baeck Institute*, edited by Max Kreutzberger, pp. 115–156. New York, 1967.

Friedmann, H. G. "Pseudo-Messiahs." In *Jewish Encyclopaedia*. New York, 1925. A history of messianic pretenders throughout Jewish history.

Klausner, Joseph. *The Messianic Idea in Israel, from Its Beginning to the Completion of the Mishnah*. New York, 1955.

Mowinckel, Sigmund. *He That Cometh: The Messianic Concept in the Old Testament and Later Judaism*. Translated by G. W. Anderson. Oxford, 1956.

Scholem, Gershom. *The Messianic Idea in Judaism and Other Essays on Jewish Spirituality*. New York, 1971.

Silver, A. H. *A History of Messianic Speculation in Israel*. Rev. ed. Boston, 1959.

Werblowsky, R. J. Zwi. "Messianism in Jewish History." In *Jewish Society through the Ages*, edited by H. H. Ben-Sasson and Samuel Ettinger, pp. 30–45. New York, 1971. A short survey and analysis.

New Sources

Goldish, Matt, and Richard M. Popkin, eds. *Millenarianism and Messianism in Early Modern European Culture: Jewish Messianism in the Early Modern World.* Boston, 2001.

Idel, Moshe. *Messianic Mystics.* New Haven, Conn., 1998.

Kavka, Martin J. *Messianism and the History of Philosophy.* New York, 2004.

Liebes, Yehuda. *Studies in Jewish Myth and Jewish Messianism.* Translated by Batya Stein. Albany, 1992.

Magid, Shaul. *Hasidism on the Margin: Reconciliation, Antinomianism, and Messianism in Izbica and Radzin Hasidism.* Madison, Wis., 2003.

Pomykala, Kenneth. *The Davidic Dynasty Tradition in Early Judaism: Its History and Significance for Messianism.* Atlanta, 1995.

Ravitzky, Aviezer. *Messianism, Zionism, and Jewish Religious Radicalism.* Chicago, 1996.

Saperstein, Marc, ed. *Essential Papers on Messianic Movements and Personalities in Jewish History.* New York, 1992.

R. J. Zwi Werblowsky (1987)
Revised Bibliography

MESSIANISM: MESSIANISM IN THE MUSLIM TRADITION

Islamic messianism has taken two main forms: one is the *masīḥ*, or "messiah," which is the title given to the prophet ʿĪsā (Jesus) in the Qurʾān; the other is the *mahdī*, or the "divinely guided one." These two messianic figures are closely associated with *al-masīḥ al-dajjāl*, or the "false messiah." In its most basic definition, Islamic messianism consists of the belief that at the end of time, when the world has degenerated into moral corruption and depravity, a *mahdī* will be sent by God to revive Islam, restore faith in God, and bring justice and prosperity to the world. The arrival of the *mahdī* will trigger the emergence of the *dajjāl*, which will in turn be followed by the return of the prophet ʿĪsā. The *dajjāl* will then be defeated by the *mahdī*, by *ʿĪsā*, or by both. Finally, these events will bring about the end of the world and the advent of Judgment Day. For Muslims, this doctrine is one of hope in the face of a world that at times may seem to have strayed very far from the path to God. While Islamic messianism refers primarily to the return of the *mahdī*, it is important to begin with the Muslim understanding of the role of ʿĪsā al-Masīḥ (Jesus the Messiah) and his perceived relationship to the false messiah, or *al-masīḥ al-dajjāl.*

ʿĪsā al-Masīḥ (Jesus the Messiah). In the Qurʾān and *ḥadīth*, the title *masīḥ* (messiah) is given to ʿĪsā (Jesus the son of Mary). In addition to countless *ḥadīth*, there are nine Qurʾanic verses referring to Jesus as the messiah (3:45, 4:157, 4:171, 4:172, 5:17, 5:72, 5:75, 9:30, and 9:31). While these verses clearly refer to Jesus as the messiah, the Islamic scripture conceives of a messiah somewhat differently from the Jewish and Christian traditions. In Islam, Jesus is viewed as a Muslim prophet who was miraculously conceived and was sent to deliver the Islamic message and scripture. This view is part of the broader Muslim belief that Christianity is a divergence from the primordial Islam, which has existed since the creation of the universe.

Muslims believe that Jesus was a prophet in a chain of thousands of Muslim prophets, beginning with Adam and ending with Muḥammad, who were sent by God to preach Islam. According to this view, Jesus is considered to be entirely human and does not share in any way in God's divinity. In fact, many of the Qurʾanic references to Jesus as the messiah specifically reject the Christian conception of the Trinity. For example, Qurʾān 4:171 states:

> O people of the Book [i.e., Jews, Christian, Zoroastrians, and some other monotheists]! Commit no excesses in your religion: nor say of God aught but the truth. Christ [*masīḥ*] Jesus the son of Mary was (no more than) an apostle [i.e., a prophet who brought scripture] of God, and His Word, which he bestowed on Mary, and a Spirit proceeding from Him: so believe in God and His apostles. Say not "Trinity"; desist: It will be better for you: for God is One God: glory be to Him: (Far Exalted is He) above having a son. To Him belong all things in the heavens and on earth. And enough is God as a Disposer of affairs. (Abdullah Yusuf Ali translation)

While Muslims consider Jesus to be one of many prophets, he is still viewed as a somewhat unique prophet. Like Muḥammad, Abraham, Moses, and David, Jesus is one of the few prophets who brought actual scripture, rather than merely being divinely inspired to preach God's word. Unlike other prophets, Jesus is also believed to be returning at the end of time. However, since Muḥammad is universally accepted as the final prophet, Jesus' mission is not understood to be a prophetic mission in the strict sense of the term. Rather, Jesus is believed to be returning for a specific purpose, which is to bring justice to the world by reaffirming God's religion on earth and by destroying the false messiah, either by himself or in cooperation with the *mahdī*, thus paving the way for the end of the world and the coming of the Day of Judgment. In some traditions the concepts of *masīḥ* and *mahdī* have been conflated, but the majority of Muslims make a clear distinction between the two. Jesus is viewed as a prophet who is returning for a specific purpose. The *mahdī*, on the other hand, is not represented as a prophet at all. Rather, he is viewed as a divinely guided man with a religious mission, but not a prophet. For example, it is not believed that he will bring any new scripture.

This conception of the return of Jesus is based primarily upon *ḥadīth* and popular religious beliefs. For example, in one *ḥadīth* the prophet Muḥammad is reported to have said "[Jesus the] son of Mary will shortly descend among you people (Muslims) as a just ruler" (Bukhārī, 3.34.425). In another *ḥadīth* Muḥammad explains:

> The *dajjāl* will appear in my *ummah* [i.e., Muslims] and he will stay (in the world) for forty—I cannot say whether he meant forty days, forty months, or forty

> years. And Allāh will then send Jesus son of Mary who will resemble ʿUrwah ibn Masʿūd. He (Jesus) will seek him out and kill him. Then people will live for seven years in which there will be no conflict between any two people. (Muslim, 41.7023)

***Al-Masīḥ al-Dajjāl* (The False Messiah).** The false messiah, or *al-masīḥ al-dajjāl,* is portrayed by Muslims as an evil but powerful human being, with a blind right eye that protrudes like a grape. He symbolically represents everything that is evil in human nature, namely greed, atheism, arrogance, malice, tyranny, and deception. For Muslims, his appearance serves as a test of faith in this world, because his power and ability to seduce the hearts of humanity is supposed to separate pious believers from "those who are more concerned with this world than with the next." It is believed that he will come to oppress humanity and to spread disbelief by trying to convince people to worship him as a god. In one *ḥadīth* the prophet Muḥammad is quoted as saying:

> He (the *dajjāl)* will be a young man with twisted, curly hair, and a blind eye. . .he will appear somewhere between Syria and Iraq and will spread mischief right and left. . .We said: "Allāh's messenger, how long will he stay? He said. . .For forty days, one day like a year, and one day like a month and one day like a week and the rest of the days would be like your days." He went on to explain how the *dajjāl* will oppress humanity and try to lead people away from faith. Then he said ". . .and it will be at this very time that Allāh will send the messiah, Jesus son of Mary, and he will descend at the white minaret in the eastern side of Damascus wearing two garments lightly dyed with saffron, while placing his hands on the wings of two Angels. . .He will then search for him *(dajjāl)* until he will catch hold of him at the gate of Ludd and will kill him." (Muslim, 41.7015)

The *Mahdī*. Although Muslims consider Jesus to be the messiah, the focal point of messianism among Muslims is not Jesus. Rather, it is the *mahdī* (the guided one). The term *mahdī* in this context is also understood to mean that he will guide Muslims. Its grammatical function is therefore simultaneously active and passive. While *mahdī* has always been a common Muslim name, when used in the context of religious doctrine it has a very specific meaning. The doctrine of the *mahdī* is based on *ḥadīth* and popular consensus, rather than the Qurʾān. The following are two samples of such *ḥadīth*: "[Muḥammad] said 'There will be a caliph in the last (period) of my *ummah* who will freely give handfuls of wealth to the people without counting it'" (Muslim, 41.6961). This *ḥadīth* is understood by many to refer to the *mahdī*. Another *ḥadīth* states, "The Prophet (peace be upon him) said: 'The *mahdī* will be of my stock, and will have a broad forehead, and a prominent nose. He will fill the earth with equity and justice as it [previously] was filled with oppression and tyranny, and he will rule for seven years'" (Abū Dāʾūd, bk. 36, no. 4272).

Ibn Khaldūn (d. 1406) gives an account of the doctrine during his time:

> It has been well known (and generally accepted) by all Muslims in every epoch, that at the end of time a man from the family (of the Prophet) will without fail make his appearance, one who will strengthen Islam and make justice triumph. Muslims will follow him, and he will gain domination over the Muslim realm. He will be called the *mahdī*. Following him, the antichrist [*al-masīḥ al-dajjāl*] will appear, together with all the subsequent signs of the hour (the Day of Judgment), as established in (the sound tradition of) *ṣaḥīḥ* [*ḥadīth*; afterwards, the *mahdī*] ʿĪsā (Jesus) will descend and kill the antichrist. Or, Jesus will descend together with the *mahdī*, and help him kill (the antichrist), and have him as the leader in his prayers. Such statements have been found in the traditions [*ḥadīth*] that religious leaders have published. They have been (critically) discussed by those who disapprove of (the matter) and have often been refuted by means of certain (other) traditions. . .a number of leaders have published traditions [*ḥadīth*] concerning the *mahdī*, among them at-Tirmidhī, Abū Dāʾūd, al-Bazzār, Ibn Mājah, al-Ḥakīm, al-Tabarānī, and Abū Yaʿlā al-Mawsilī. (Ibn Khaldūn, *The Muqaddimah*, 1958, pp. 156–157)

The concept of the *mahdī* has evolved over the centuries, but there are several basic characteristics of the doctrine that are common to most definitions. Most Muslims believe that a descendant of the Prophet will return at the end of time, when the world has descended into moral depravity, to revive and restore both his community and the religion of God. It is also believed that he will spread prosperity and goodwill. He is usually described as being a handsome young man with long dark hair, a broad forehead, and a high and prominent nose. He is usually considered to be a descendant of the Prophet. It is often believed that in the process of uniting Muslims and the whole world, he will defeat the *Rūm* (Romans, Greeks, etc.) and will conquer Jerusalem and Constantinople. Some believe that he will make himself first appear in the Levant, while others claim that he will come from Mecca or even Khorasan in northeastern Iran.

The role of the *mahdī* is closely linked to two concepts in Islam: *iṣlāḥ* (to reform Islam through purification) and *tajdīd* (to renew or revive Islam). Both concepts encompass the basic Muslim conception of reform, correction, or purification of the faith. *Iṣlāḥ* is mentioned in the Qurʾān, whereas *tajdīd* is based on interpretations of *ḥadīth.* The core principles in these doctrines is that the Muslim community, which is always in danger of straying from the commandments of God and the examples set by the prophet Muḥammad, must continually be reformed and revived. The primary method for realizing such reforms is to expunge heretical elements from the faith. Reform, therefore, equals purification. For example, if cultural or regional customs enter into the faith (as they usually do), these are often criticized by Muslims as "heretical innovations" (*bidʿah*). Likewise, when people convert from another religion to Islam, they sometimes carry over their previous beliefs and practices. All these are labeled as *bidʿah,* and are condemned. It is not surprising that accusations of *bid'ah* have always been among the more common tactics used by Muslims in sectarian, ideological, and political polemics. Sectarian views that are regarded as heresies are often dealt with in the same way, by labeling their doctrines as *bid'ah,* and calling for the need to purge Islam of these heretical innovations.

In its most general sense, *tajdīd* and *iṣlāḥ* are considered to be the duty of every Muslim. However, in the more specific doctrinal sense, it is believed that this sort of reform should be carried out by a religious leader who is supposed to come at certain intervals (usually once per century) to revive and purify Islam. As one would expect, different groups of Muslims have normally disagreed on exactly who these leaders are, based on sectarian, ideological, and political divisions. For example, al-Ghazālī (d. 1111) and Ibn Taymīyah (d. 1328), whose views were often diametrically opposed to one another, have both been referred to as *mujaddids* (*tajdīd* reformers). The *mahdī* is often treated as a special type of *mujaddid* in that much greater success, power, and influence are attributed to him, and he is divinely guided in a supernatural way. In fact, in some traditions, the *mahdī* is considered to be the last in a chain of *mujaddids.* The fact that he is singled out for mention by the Prophet gives him an added symbolic significance. Most importantly, Muslims believe that he will help to bring about the changes that will set the stage for the end of the world and bring about the Day of Judgment. This gives him a much more specific and important eschatological function compared to other *mujaddids.*

The title *mahdī* has also been used by some Muslims to refer to such early Muslim leaders as Abū Bakr, ʿUmar ibn al-Khaṭṭāb, ʿUthmān ibn ʿAffān, and ʿAlī ibn Abī Ṭālib (these four caliphs, who ruled from 632 to 661, were sometimes collectively referred to as al-Khulafāʾal-Rāshidīn al-Mahdīyyīn). The title *mahdī* has also been used to refer to Ḥusayn ibn ʿAlī (d. 680), the Umayyad caliph ʿUmar II (d. 720), and ʿAlī's son by a Ḥanafī woman, Muḥammad ibn al-Ḥanafīyah (d. 700). Several Umayyad, Abbasid, and Fāṭimid caliphs were also referred to as *mahdī.* In fact, the term *mahdī* was used often during the Umayyad and Abbasid periods as a polemical device to legitimize a wide variety of religious leaders.

The most dynamic period of Muslim history with regard to the concept of the *mahdī* is without a doubt the seventh century (especially following the Battle of Karbala in 680) through the twelfth century. The main reason for this is the relative diversity of religious views during this period. The wide variety of heterodox views that proliferated during these centuries, along with the ideological civil wars that were underway, provided an ideal environment in which political and religious leaders were considered to be the *mahdī.* In many cases these early *mahdīs* were Shīʿī leaders of various sorts, like Muḥammad ibn al-Ḥanafīyah, his son Abū Hāshim (d. 717), Mūsá Kādhim (d. 799), and others. However, some of these early *mahdīs* were associated with the Sunnī community, such as Umayyad caliph ʿUmar the II; the founder of the ʿAbbāsid dynasty, al-Saffāḥ (d. 754); and other Abbasid caliphs. (For a detailed discussion of these early uses of the term *mahdī,* see Madelung, 1986.)

One of the most significant divisions among Muslims on the doctrine of the *mahdī* is between Shīʿah and Sunnīs. The primary difference between the Sunnī definition of the *mahdī* and the Shīʿī view is his identity, and by extension his sectarian affiliation. Generally, the Twelver Shīʿah consider the *mahdī* to be a vanished *imām* who will return at some future time. While Sunnīs and Shīʿah generally accept that the *mahdī* will reward the faithful and punish the wicked, for most Shīʿah the *mahdī* will also vindicate the Shīʿī cause by showing Sunnīs and other non-Shīʿah the errors of their ways, thus reaffirming Shiism and the doctrine of the *imāmat.*

A typical *ḥadīth,* attributed to the first *imām,* ʿAlī ibn Abī Ṭālib, sums up the Shīʿī doctrine:

> Soon God shall bring forth a group whom He Loves and they too are His lovers and the one who is like a stranger amongst them shall take over the Government. Verily, he shall be the 'MAHDĪ'; his face rosy and hair golden in color. He will fill the earth with justice without any difficulty. In his very childhood, he shall get separated from his mother and father and from the viewpoint of training he shall be rare and matchless. He shall rule over the Muslim countries with utmost calm and security and time shall be favorable and friendly toward him. His words will be accepted; the young and the old shall humbly obey him. He shall fill the earth with Justice just as it had previously been filled with oppression. Then, at that moment his *imāmat* shall reach its perfection and Viceregency will be established for him. Moreover, Allāh will make the dead to rise from their graves and return them back to this world. Then, like people who get up from their sleep, they shall see nothing but their own houses. The land will flourish and by blessing of his [i.e., *mahdī's*] existence, it shall become fresh and fruitful. Seditions and disturbances shall vanish and blessings and welfare will increase manifold. (Ṣadr Iṣfahānī, 1994, pp. 39–40)

While Shīʿah and Sunnīs have historically disagreed on the identity of the *mahdī,* they have agreed on many of the basic details surrounding his return. For example, they generally accept that the *mahdī* will be a descendant of the Prophet who returns at the end of time, when corruption and tyranny are widespread, in order to spread justice and renew Islam. Shīʿah have relied on both Shīʿī and Sunnī *ḥadīth* to articulate their definition of the *mahdī.* For example, the prominent Shīʿī scholar Ṣadrudīn Ṣadr Iṣfahānī, in his book *Al-Mahdī* (1994), quotes Sunnī *ḥadīth* from Abū Dāʾūd, Tirmidhī, Aḥmad ibn Ḥanbal, and Ibn Majah in which the Prophet is quoted as saying: "If there remains not more than a day from the life of the earth, indeed God shall make a person from my progeny to appear" (p. 33). He also quotes another *ḥadīth* of Aḥmad ibn Ḥanbal: "*Qiyāmat* shall not be established until the earth is filled with cruelty and oppression. Then a person from my progeny shall appear and fill it with equity and Justice" (p. 33).

However, since Shīʿī groups have different definitions of the imamate, they also differ on the identity of the *mahdī.* For example, the most widespread Shīʿī group, called the Ithnā ʿasharīs (Twelvers) or Imāmīs, believe that the *mahdī* will be the twelfth *imām* Muḥammad al-Mahdī, who was believed to have gone into occultation in 874. For other Shīʿah, the *mahdī* is (or was) believed to be a different *imām,* such as ʿAlī ibn Abī Ṭālib, Ḥusayn ibn ʿAlī, Ḥasan al-ʿAskarī, Jaʿfar al-Ṣādiq, Ismāʿīl ibn Jaʿfar, Mūsá al-Kāẓim, Muḥammad ibn al-Ḥanafīyah, the *imāms* of the Fāṭimid dynasty, or other *imāms.*

The earliest historical record we have of a clearly Shīʿī conception of the *mahdī* was shortly after the massacre at Karbala of the Prophet's grandson Ḥusayn along with his family in 680. This traumatic event inspired many Muslims to call for an uprising of someone from the Prophet's progeny to take vengeance on the Umayyad regime. It was within this context that in 685 to 687 Mukhtār led an uprising in the name of Ḥusayn's half brother, Muḥammad ibn al-Hanafīyah. He said: "Al-Mahdī Muḥammad ibn ʿAlī [i.e., ibn al-Ḥanafīyah], the son of the *Wāṣī,* sent me to you as his trusted man, minister, and chosen supporter, and as his commander. He ordered me to fight against he blasphemers and claim vengeance for the blood of the people of his House, the excellent ones" (Jafrī, 1979, p. 262). Eventually, Mukhtār and his follows were killed, but once Muḥammad ibn al-Ḥanafīyah died he was considered by many to have gone into occultation. Following this precedent, several Shīʿī claimants emerged, and others were given the title with or without their own acknowledgement.

Another variation on the *mahdī* doctrine is the Ṣūfī view, which stresses the mystical lineage of the *mahdī* and his role as Ṣūfī master. Overall, the Ṣūfī view does not fundamentally differ from the views articulated by other Muslims, except in one very important respect. Whereas the Sunnīs expect the return of a pious Muslim reformer, and Shīʿah expect the return of a vanished *imām,* the Ṣūfīs generally expect the *mahdī* to be the final link in a long change of masters and disciples in the Ṣūfī tradition. In that sense, this continuous chain or lineage begins with Muḥammad and ends with the *mahdī.* The *mahdī* is therefore viewed as the final and most perfect Ṣūfī master, who is able to guide Muslims to God. As the "divinely guided guide of humanity" he will occupy a place between the believers and God. This is not to say that the *mahdī* will be divine in any way. Rather, it is to say that he will serve as the axis of human faith in God, or stated differently, he will serve as a doorway of sorts on the path to God.

It is not surprising that throughout Muslim history there have been numerous political and religious leaders who either claimed to be the *mahdī,* or were considered by others to be the *mahdī.* These mahdist movements usually have involved a combination of charismatic leadership, religious reformism, and revivalism, and some sort of military struggle, either against non-Muslims or against Muslim leaders who were deemed to be morally corrupt. One interesting historical trend is that for Shīʿah the *mahdī* rebellions tended to be restricted to the early centuries of their movements, at a time when Shīʿī doctrines were more heterodox than orthodox. There are some later exceptions to this general rule, such as Ismāʿīl Safavī's (d. 1524) mahdist claims in the fifteenth century. Ismāʿīl was accepted as a messianic figure by his tribal followers, the Qizilbāsh, who have been accused by some of going so far as to deify him. While Ismāʿīl and his followers were technically Shīʿī, his movement was based more on a particular strain of rural Ṣūfī beliefs that tended toward Shiism. His military successes helped to bolster his religious legitimacy. However, after the Safavid Empire was established in 1501, the state shifted toward orthodox Shīʿī doctrine, according to which he could not be considered a messianic figure.

While for Sunnīs, mahdist movements have not been particularly widespread, they have occurred throughout Islamic history. In fact, mahdist movements continued to emerge as late as the early modern period, after which there was a noticeable reduction in the frequency of their occurrence. Often these movements had roots in Sufism. The most famous mahdist movement in recent history occurred in the Sudan in the 1880s. A local Ṣūfī leader named Muḥammad Aḥmad declared himself the *mahdī* in 1881. His movement was centered on a rejection of the religious legitimacy of the Egyptian Ottoman rulers, whom he accused of straying from Islam by tolerating (or even promoting) gambling, prostitution, music, dancing, and the drinking of alcohol. His followers were called the Anṣār, and they believed that his military successes were due to divine intervention. The state he established in Khartoum lasted until 1899. This movement was in many ways typical of Sunnī mahdist movements in that it was built around a charismatic leader who took up a local political cause by pursuing armed struggle against the state. It was also similar to many mahdist movements in that it was at the political periphery of the empire and was associated with rural Sufism and heterodox Islam.

In recent decades, the use of the *mahdī* doctrine in political discourse has been less common. One of the reasons for this has been the relative displacement of traditional popular religious ideals by modernist religious orthodox sentiments. Muslim political movements have tended toward orthodox legalism, which is usually hostile to Sufism, Shiism, and popular Islam. A similar trend in orthodox Shiism can be seen, because anyone who claims to be the *mahdī* would necessarily have to be the vanished *imām* as well.

See Also Eschatology, article on Islamic Eschatology; Modernism, article on Islamic Modernism; Nubūwah.

BIBLIOGRAPHY

Ali, Shaukat. *Millenarian and Messianic Tendencies in Islamic History.* Lahore, Pakistan, 1993.

Blichfeldt, Jan-Olaf. *Early Mahdism: Politics and Religion in the Formative Period of Islam.* Leiden, 1985.

Daftary, Farhad. *The Ismāʿīlis: Their History and Doctrines.* Cambridge, UK, 1990.

García-Arenal, Mercedes. *Mahdīsme et millénarisme en Islam.* Aix-en-Provence, France, 2001.

Hussain, Jassim M. *The Occultation of the Twelfth Imam: A Historical Background.* London, 1982.

Jafrī, S. H. *Origins and Early Development of Shiʿa Islam.* London, 1979.

Khaldūn, Ibn. *The Muqaddimah: An Introduction,* vol. 2. Translated by Franz Rosenthal. New York, 1958.

Madelung, Wilferd. "Mahdī." In *The Encyclopedia of Islam, New Edition,* edited by C. E. Bosworth, E. Van Donzel, B. Lewis, and Ch. Pellat, vol. 5, pp. 1230–1238. Leiden, 1986.

Momen, Moojan. *An Introduction to Shīʿī Islam: The History and Doctrines of Twelver Shi'ism.* New Haven, 1985.

Mūfīd Shaykh al-. *The Book of Guidance into the Lives of the Twelve Imams (Kitāb al-Irshād).* Translated by I. K. A. Howard. Elmhurst, N.Y., 1981.

Sachedina, Abdulaziz Abdulhussein. *Islamic Messianism: The Idea of the Mahdī in Twelver Shīʿīsm.* Albany, N.Y., 1981.

Ṣadr Iṣfahānī, Ṣadr al-Dīn. *Al-Mahdī (A.S.).* Translated by Jalil Dorrani. Tehran, 1994.

Salih, Mohamed Osman. "Mahdīsm in Islam up to 260 A.H./874 A.D. and Its Relation to Zoroastrian, Jewish, and Christian Messianism." Ph.D. diss., University of Edinburgh, 1976.

KAMRAN SCOT AGHAIE (2005)

MESSIANISM: SOUTH AMERICAN MESSIANISM

Messianism is not a universal religious phenomenon. It appears in some, but not all, societies of the world, and in some religious systems but not in others. South America is one of those regions prone to the development of messianism, regardless of the nature of a society. This entry shall explore how expressions of messianism may be found among the peasant inheritors of the high civilizations that developed in the Andes, as well as among hunters and gatherers of the Amazonian region. Although most evidence derives from the postconquest period, it is possible to identify certain structural concomitants and cultural motives associated with South American messianism that are different from Christian and European forms of this religious phenomenon. Hence the kind of messianism that this entry will discuss is a non-Western variety, although in some cases it may disguise itself in Christian trappings.

In contrast to Christian messianism, South America messianism is generally accompanied by a cyclical or static conception of time, which is believed to be encapsulated in fixed ages that are represented under a symbolic number, generally five or three. For Mesoamericans, these ages were also conceived as having ended as a result of a cosmic cataclysm that closed a period lasting either one thousand or five hundred years. In the Andes, the Quechua name for this catastrophic event was *pachacuti,* which literally means "transformation of the earth." The name for the thousand-year period was *capac huatan,* or "great year." Since the beginning of time, four *capac huatan* were thought to have taken place, along with nine *pachacuti,* given that during every *capac huatan,* an internal *pachacuti* divided it into two periods of five hundred years. Linked to this schema was the idea that the Incas, when they were conquered by the Spanish, were seen as emerging after an elapse of 4,500 years, after which they would eventually disappear at the close of the 5,000-year period.

In Mexico the means devised to avoid the interruption of the circulation of the sun, which produced the end of the ages, was the sacrifice of human beings. Among the Incas, however, the king was believed to have a divine nature, raising him to the level of the gods. Divine kingship was common to both cultural areas, but as Henri Frankfort noticed when comparing the Egyptian pharaohs with the kings of Mesopotamia and Israel, the position of the Inca king was next to the celestial gods, whereas the kings of Mesoamerica were considered to be closer to mortal beings. As such, the Inca king could command and punish the divinities, and he could even stop time. Consequently, some of the human sacrifices that took place in the Andes were intended to maintain the health of the Inca king, given that what really endangered the cosmic order was his death.

A paradigm of the capacity to maintain and restore order embodied in each Inca king can be found in one of the Incas who are generally listed as members of a dynastical order. His name is Pachacuti, and he occupies the ninth position within the dynastical list that is commonly found in old chronicles. Pachacuti holds the same name as the cataclysm described above because as the restorer of order and the initiator of a new age he is also part of the interregnum that marks the transition from chaos to order. Interestingly, Pachacuti's ninth position corresponds to the most ordered time cycle within the sequence of five ages—the last Inca dynasty that started in the 4,500th year.

It is under this conceptual framework that postcolonial Andean messianism tended to develop. It is manifested more clearly in a chronicle written during the sixteenth and early seventeenth centuries by a Peruvian Indian named Felipe Guamán Poma de Ayala (1526–1614). The title of this manuscript is *El primer nueva corónica y buen gobierno* (First new chronicle and good government), but given its messianic overtones, it could more properly be titled "Letter to the King." A careful reading reveals that for the author the Spanish conquest was not properly a historical event but a *pachacuti* that had been triggered by the intermingling of Spaniards and Indians, who represented two separate principles within a dualistic conception of order that conceived the principles as separate and in equilibrium. As a consequence of this cosmic event, the world was turned upside down. The social order had been altered by the introduction of circumstances that enabled the possibility of change, and the Indians lost their property and suffered innumerable injustices.

The best evidence that the conquest was seen as a *pachacuti*-type cataclysm is that throughout his chronicle Guamán Poma speaks about the existence of five ages, with the Incas being located in the fifth age. However, when he is forced to incorporate the conquest and its aftermath, he expands his schema of ages to include a tenth age, naming the sixth *Pachacuti*. But even more important is the fact that Guamán Poma estimates the duration of the world since its beginnings to be 6,613 years, a figure he obtains by adding the year in which he was writing his chronicle (1613) to a mythical 5,000-year period corresponding to the closing period of the five ages.

Having conceived in these terms the sorrowful sentiments awakened by colonial domination, the only solution sought by this Indian writer is that somebody proportional to the cosmic nature of the crisis might overcome it. For him this person was the king of Spain, but the king of Spain conceived as an Inca king—that is, as a kind of metaphysical being capable of confronting a problem whose solution was beyond the power of common mortals. Guamán Poma thus addresses his chronicle to the king of Spain, not as a humble Indian but as the descendant of the "Second Person" of the Inca (who, as king of Chinchaysuyo, was a leader next in hierarchy below the Inca king and the one who held the highest position among the kings of the four quarters) and as the unified voice of the Indians of the four quarters. This perhaps explains why he chose to call himself *Guaman* (a bird associated with the upper realm) and *Poma* (a feline linked to a lower moiety), since this image conveys a sense of unity through complementary opposites.

After Guamán Poma, the figure of the Inca king became central to the numerous messianic expressions that developed in the Andes, even up to the present day. However the first messianic movement recorded for this area does not clearly show that this heroic figure would have been present. Instead, those who figure prominently are a type of Andean divinity known as *guacas*.

The first messianic movement known to have emerged in the Andean region was the *Taqui Onqoy*, a Quechua term that literally means "dance illness." One of the characteristics of this movement was that followers entered a state of trance provoked by dancing and oscillating their heads under the rhythm of a repetitive chant and the consumption of large amounts of coca leaf and brewed maize. This movement dates from around 1564; a priest named Cristóbal de Albornoz had an important role in its discovery and in its extirpation. Through him and other priests we learn that the preachers of this movement explained to their followers that the Spaniards dominated the Indians because their God had defeated the *guacas*. However, a change was taking place, and the *guacas* were becoming stronger and were in the process of defeating the Christian God. Under the framework of a dual conception of the world, the followers of the movement grouped around two important religious centers—one associated with an upper moiety, and the other with a lower one. The first site had as its central divinity the god Pachácamac and was located towards the north in Chinchaysuyo; the second had the god Titicaca and was located in Collasuyo, towards the south. To attain final triumph, which would consist of a reversal of time analogous to a *pachacuti*, the preachers directed the Indians to avoid Christian practices and resume those from before the Hispanic period.

Perhaps because the Inca rulers were still actively resisting the Spanish in Vilcabamba, this messianic movement does not recall the presence of an Inca image (as in later movements), and instead addresses the *guacas*. However, the movement shares with Guamán Poma's messianism the expectation of a cosmic reversal of the world associated with a cyclical view of time and an image of a unified Indian world, an image represented by the two most important religious centers located in opposite but complementary moieties.

Evidence of the centrality of the Inca in Andean messianism can be found in the movements headed by Juan Santos Atahuallpa (forest of central Peru) and José Gabriel Condorcanqui (Cuzco) during the eighteenth century. Two representative movements of the nineteenth century are those of Atusparia (Ancash) and Rumi Maqui (Puno). The twentieth century witnessed the vast expansion of the Inkarri myth and the embodiment of this myth in such messianic leaders as Ezequiel Ataucusi Gamonal, the founder of the Israelites of the New Universal Covenant. The Inkarri myth has many versions, but those with more messianic connotations describe a hero named Inkarri (a combination of *inka* and *rey*, or king), who is the offspring of the Sun and a herder woman. After being beheaded by the Spaniards, Inkarri was said to be in the process of magically reconstituting himself. Once this process was complete, order would be reintroduced to the Andean world.

This myth was prominent primarily in the highlands, although stories of a hero known as "Inca" (or "Inka") spread among the inhabitants of the Amazonian lowlands. This figure also carried messianic overtones, but they were unlike those associated with the highland hero. Rather, this figure resembled other Amazonian heroes who suggest the Cargo cults of Melanesia. For the Ashaninka of the Peruvian central Amazon, Inka was the ruler of their territory and a great shaman "who voyaged downriver on a raft at a time when a great flood was produced by the Caucasians. This enabled the Caucasians, whose territory is downriver, to capture Inka and force him to manufacture the superior artifacts which they now possess. Inka remains a captive downriver to this day, wishing to return to his people but restrained by the Caucasians. If he ever did return, the existing relationship between the Campa and Caucasians would of course be reversed" (Weiss, 1969, p. 109).

In other Ashaninka versions of this myth, the owner of these attributes is Pachakamaite, the son of the Sun and his wife, Mamantziki. Pachakamaite has the power to manufacture guns, ammunition, pots, salt, and other objects important to the wider society. Stéfano Varese's informants told him that in the past their ancestors, who were poor, could obtain these objects by acceding to this divinity after a long journey during which they met a number of dangerous beings. But this is no longer possible because white people have appropriated these goods to sell them to the Ashaninka. They have thus interrupted the route to Pachakamaite's realm by raising fences to keep natives from obtaining what Pachakamaite has promised them (Varese, 1973, p. 360).

Mythical heroes with similar characteristics are also found among other Peruvian Amazonian groups, including the Amuesha and Machiguenga, and among natives of other South American countries. Among some Ge Indians of central Brazil, for example, heroes of this nature are reported with names associated with their particular dialects. Some of these heroes became the focus of messianic movements. This is the case with the Ramkókamekra-Canelas Indians of Maranhao, who in 1963 developed a messianic movement headed by a woman prophet called Kee-khwei. According to William Crocker, Kee-khwei predicted that civilized people would be thrown into the forest to live as hunters, and the Indians would go to the cities, where they would direct road construction and pilot planes. Kee-khwei obtained this prediction from a revelation granted to her by a mythical hero known as Aukhé, who spoke to her through a daughter she carried in her womb. The unborn daughter was thought to be the hero's sister, and it was explained that she was coming to this world because her brother was tired of the ill treatment that white people imposed on Indians. Certain rituals consisting mostly of dancing were conducted to ensure the materialization of this prediction, which was to occur at the moment the child was born. The more intense the dance and the greater the offerings, the more plentiful the wealth that would be received in the new life. Not performing the rituals or contributing money to the movement would result in severe punishments from a group of youngsters who served Kee-khwei. In addition, followers were free to seize the cattle of any person because the cattle was said to belong to Aukhé. Followers did not fear repression because it was stated that the mythical hero would divert bullets and that a great fire would annihilate aggressors (Crocker, 1976, p. 516).

Almost twelve years before this movement, around 1951, a similar messianic movement had developed among the Krahó, an eastern Timbira group. Here again the expectations focused on appropriating material objects belonging to white people through the mediation of a divine hero. Although the characterization of this divinity as a bearded man with curly hair and holding a gun do not correspond to the mythical pantheon of this group, the linkage of this hero with rain makes him similar to Aukhé (Sullivan, 1988, p. 584). According to Julio César Melatti, the movement unfolded around a prophet named Rópkur Txortxó Kraté, also known as José Nogueira, who incorporated the powers of the divinity to punish Christians and to transform the Indians into civilized people. Because the divinity was associated with rain, thunder was the main weapon with which he was to inflict his punishments, which were considered revenge for Indians who had been killed and a means for the Indians to avoid being dispossessed from their lands. Among the methods suggested for becoming civilized was the building of a big house to store the merchandise that would arrive in a riverboat and the performance of both traditional and Western dances on certain days of the week. In addition, the consumption of specified foods, particularly meat, during certain days was prohibited in order to accelerate the Indians' transformation into civilized people.

As reported by Roberto Da Matta (1967, 1970), Julio César Melatti (1972), and Lawrence Sullivan (1988), all of these movements were inspired by the image of Aukhé, a hero who became widely known among several Ge groups. This personage was always associated with water and with the wealth of the whites, which the Indians believed was rightfully destined to belong to them. The resemblance of this hero with the Amazonian Inka and Pachakamaite is well known. All these cases, however, can be contrasted with the messianism that developed in the Andes. Whereas that of the Amazon suggests an inclination to accede to Western civilization, the messianism of the Andes suggests a wish to express a rejection. In both cases, white people are evil, but in the Amazon it is because they have developed obstacles to the Indians' access to wealth, whereas in the Andes it is because white people have altered the Indians' normal conditions of existence.

Another South American messianic expression that has attracted the attention of scholars is the search for the land without evil by several native groups, in particular the Tupi-Guaraníes. Curt Nimuendajú (1978) and Alfred Métraux (1973) suggest that this search began before the arrival of Europeans. Once more this expression incorporates an idea of temporal cycles that end in cataclysms, the presence of a divine figure, various beliefs about the afterlife, and the presence of shamans as leaders. The most overt manifestation of this kind of messianism is the mobilization of vast contingents of Indians throughout Brazilian, Peruvian, and Paraguayan territory. These were led by shamans who preached the imminent destruction of the world, with the only possible salvation being to settle in a land without evil. In traditional mythology this place was the settlement of Nanderuvusú, the creator, and of his wife, Ñandesy. It was described as a realm where plants grew without being cultivated and fruits ripened at the spot. It was commonly said to be located at the center of the earth, which was identified as existing in the east. Only the souls of the children could arrive there after overcoming dangers. It was also said that if the creator had the power to create the world, he could destroy it. By ordering his son Ñanderikey to remove the east-west–oriented pole located at the center world, Nanderuvusú could cause the world to collapse. However, there was a magical solution for escaping this threat. The solution involved dancing and migrating in an easterly direction.

Among the Quechua Indians of southern Peru, an equivalent to this land without evil is Paititi. A settlement with this name, located towards the east in the southern forest, was known as early as the sixteenth century. Even the eighteenth-century rebel Tupac Amarú II mentioned Paititi as part of his dominion as an Inca. Today, Paititi is described as a kind of urban paradise, with golden buildings where Incas from the past continue living. According to some versions, only Indians who speak an uncontaminated Quechua language are permitted to enter Paititi. Ezequiel Ataucusi Gamonal, the prophet of the Israelites of the New Covenant, is sometimes included as one of its visitors.

Such is the permanence and expansion of this belief that not only did the Israelites of the New Covenant succumb to it, but other syncretic movements did as well, including that developed in the Peruvian Amazon by José Francisco de la Cruz, who began his movement in the 1960s in Brazil, Paraguay, Uruguay, Argentina, Peru, and Colombia. In Peru the name of the church he founded is Cruzada Católica Apostólica Evangélica del Perú (Catholic, Apostolic, Evangelical Crusade of Peru). In Peru this church has about four thousand followers. In Brazil, where there are approximately twenty thousand followers, the main center of the church is located in the village of Vila Santa next to the Putumayo river, an area regarded as a land without evil (Regan, 1993, p. 341). Like many syncretic messianic movements, this one departs from the idea of salvation in the face of an imminent end of the world. To overcome this threat, the symbol of the cross and the search for the land without evil is assigned an important role, which has had great appeal among natives of the Tupi Guarani family and acculturated Cocamas, Cocamillas, and Omahuas, who believe that those who search for the land without evil will have larger harvests (Regan, 1993, p. 360).

Another syncretic movement—this time of Andean origin—that has incorporated belief in a land without evil is the Israelites of the New Universal Covenant. Followers of this movement hold that salvation in the face of the imminent end of the world will be possible only by becoming a member of this religious organization, whose leader, Ezequiel Ataucusi Gamonal, is seen as the new Christ and the incarnation of the Holy Ghost, as well as a new Inca. They call themselves "Israelites" because they have incorporated into their movement the ancient ritual practices of the Israelites of the Old Testament including wearing the kinds of garments the Hebrews used in the past during their celebrations. To this form of nativism they also proclaim a restoration of Inca practices, and it is according to these practices that they model the colonies they have developed in the Amazonian region. Moreover, this Inca "utopia" became the headquarters of the political party the group established to support the candidacy of Ezequiel Ataucusi Gamonal to the presidency of the Republic of Peru.

The colonies, therefore, represent the materialization of the Inca utopia, and as such they become the land without evil, where all the Israelites should go to wait for the end of the world; it is from here that they will be transported to Canaan, once more located in the east, to attain complete salvation. The Israelites of the New Covenant represent a synthesis of almost all the varieties of messianism that developed in South America, although this group added a biblical dimension that is a variation of Adventism.

BIBLIOGRAPHY

Crocker, William. "O movimiento messianico dos canelas: Uma introducao." In *Leituras de etnologia Brasileira,* edited by Egon Schaden, pp. 515–527. São Paulo, Brazil, 1976.

Da Matta, Roberto. "Mito e autoridade doméstica: Uma tentative deanalise de um moto timbira en suas ralacoes com estrutura social." *Revista do Instituto de Ciencias Sociais,* U.F.R.J., IV, no. 1 (1967): 93–141.

Da Matta, Roberto. "Mito e anti-mito entre os timbira." In *Mito e linguagem social.* Rio de Janeiro, 1970.

Frankfort, Henri. *Kingship and the Gods: A Study of Ancient Near Eastern Religion as the Integration of Society and Nature.* Chicago, 1948.

Graciano, Frank. *The Millennial New World.* Oxford, 1999.

Melatti, Julio César. *O messianismo krahó.* São Paulo, Brazil, 1972.

Métraux, Alfred. *Religions et magies indiennes d'Am'éroqie do sud.* Paris, 1967. Tranlsated into Spanish as *Religión y magias indígenas de américa del sur* (Madrid, 1973).

Nimuendajú, Curt. *Los mitos de creación y de destrucción del mundo como fundamentos de la religión de los apapokuva-guaraní.* Lima, Peru, 1978.

Ossio, Juan M., comp. *Ideología mesiánica del mundo andino.* Lima, Peru, 1973.

Regan, Jaime. *Hacia la tierra sin mal.* Lima, Peru, 1993.

Sullivan, Lawrence E. *Icanchu's Drum: An Orientation to Meaning in South American Religions.* New York, 1988.

Varese, Stéfano. "Pachhacamaite." In *Ideología mesiánica del mundo andino,* compiled by Juan M. Ossio, pp. 359–374. Lima, Peru, 1973.

Weiss, Gerald. "The Cosmology of the Campa Indians of Eastern Peru." Ph.D. diss. University of Michigan, Ann Arbor, 1969.

Juan M. Ossio (2005)

METALS AND METALLURGY. Archaic, nonliterate peoples, as well as prehistoric populations, worked meteoric iron long before they learned to use the ferrous ores occurring on the earth's surface. They treated certain ores like stones, that is, they regarded them as raw material for the manufacture of lithic tools. A similar technique was applied until recently by certain peoples having no knowledge of metallurgy: they worked meteorites with silex (flint) hammers and fashioned objects whose shapes resembled their stone models in all respects. This was how the Greenland

Inuit (Eskimo) made their knives out of meteoric iron (Andrée, 1984, pp. 121ff.). When Cortés asked the Aztec chieftains where they had gotten their knives, they pointed to the sky. Like the Maya of Yucatan and the Inca of Peru, the Aztec used only meteoric iron, which they valued more highly than gold. In fact, excavations have revealed no trace of terrestrial iron in the prehistoric deposits of the New World (Forbes, 1950, pp. 401ff.).

Paleo-Oriental peoples presumably held similar ideas. The Sumerian word *an-bar*, the earliest vocable designating iron, is written with the signs for "sky" and "fire." Campbell Thompson renders it "celestial lightning (or meteorite)," but it is usually translated "celestial metal" or "star-metal" (Eliade, 1978, p. 22; Bjorkman, 1973, pp. 114ff.). For a long period the Egyptians too knew only meteoric iron, and the same is true of the Hittites: a text of the fourteenth century BCE states that the Hittite kings used "the black iron of the sky" (Rickard, 1932, vol. 1, p. 149). Iron, therefore, was scarce, and its use was principally ritual.

THE DISCOVERY OF SMELTING. It required the discovery of the smelting of ores to inaugurate a new stage in the history of mankind. Unlike the production of copper or bronze, the metallurgy of iron very soon became industrial. Once the secret of smelting magnetite and hematite was discovered, there was no longer any difficulty in obtaining large quantities of iron, for deposits were very rich and easy to exploit. But the handling of telluric ores differed from that of meteoric iron, as it did also from the smelting of copper and bronze. It was not until after the discovery of furnaces, and particularly after perfecting the technique for "hardening" metal brought to the point of white heat, that iron achieved its preeminent position. It was the metallurgy of terrestrial iron that made this metal fit for everyday use. The beginnings of iron metallurgy on an industrial scale can be fixed at a period between 1200 and 1000 BCE, in the mountains of Armenia. From there the secret of smelting spread across the Near East, the Mediterranean, and central Europe, although, as I have noted, iron, whether of meteoric origin or from superficial deposits, was known in the third millennium in Mesopotamia, in Asia Minor, and probably also in Egypt (Forbes, 1950, p. 417; Eliade, 1978, pp. 23ff., 201ff.).

MINES: THE WOMB OF MOTHER EARTH. The discovery of furnaces had important religious consequences. Besides the celestial sacredness of the sky, immanent in meteorites, there was now the telluric sacredness of the earth, in which mines and ore share. Metals "grow" in the bosom of the earth. Caves and mines are assimilated to the womb of Mother Earth. The ores extracted from mines are in some sense "embryos." They grow slowly, as if obeying a temporal rhythm different from that of vegetable and animal organisms; nevertheless, they do grow, they "ripen" in the telluric darkness. Hence, their extraction from Mother Earth is an operation performed prematurely. If they had been given the time to develop (that is, if they were to come to term in geological time), ores would become ripe, "perfect" metals. Belief in the natural growth, and thus in the metamorphosis, of metals is of very ancient origin in China and is also found in Vietnamese Annam, in India, and in the Malay archipelago. The peasants of Vietnamese Tonkin, for example, have a saying: "Black bronze is the mother of gold." They believe that gold is engendered naturally by bronze, but only if the bronze has lain a sufficiently long period in the bosom of the earth. "Thus the Annamites are convinced that the gold found in the mines is formed slowly *in situ* over the centuries and that if one had probed the earth originally, one would have discovered bronze in the places where gold is found today" (Przyluski, 1914, p. 3). Similar beliefs survived even into eighteenth-century Europe (Eliade, 1978, pp. 46ff.).

The Egyptians, who, according to Plutarch and Diodorus, hated iron—which they called "the bones of Seth"—considered that the flesh of gods was made of gold; in other words, that the gods were immortal. That is why, after the model of the gods, Pharaoh was also assigned flesh of gold. Indeed, as repeatedly proclaimed in the Hindu Brahmanas, "Gold is immortality." Consequently, in many cultures, to obtain the elixir that transmutes metals into alchemical gold is tantamount to obtaining immortality.

In Eastern as in Western alchemy, the transmutation of metals into gold is equated with a miraculously rapid maturation. The elixir (or the philosopher's stone) completes and consummates the work of nature. One of the characters in Ben Jonson's play *The Alchemist* (1610) asserts that "lead and other metals . . . would be gold if they had time," and another character adds, "And that our Art doth further." That is to say, the alchemist prolongs the dream and the ideology of miners and metalworkers: to perfect nature by accelerating the temporal rhythm, with the difference that the *aurum alchemicum*—the elixir—confers health, perennial youth, and even immortality. As is well known, by the end of the eighteenth century alchemy was supplanted by the new science of chemistry. But the alchemist's ideals survived, camouflaged and radically secularized, in nineteenth-century ideology.

In many parts of the world miners practice rites involving a state of purity, fasting, meditation, prayers, and cultic acts. The rites are governed by the nature of the intended operation, for the performance of them is meant to introduce the worker into a sacred zone, supposedly inviolable: he enters into contact with a sacrality that does not participate in the familiar religious universe, for it is a deeper and also a more dangerous sacrality. The miner feels that he risks entering a domain that does not rightfully belong to man: the underground world with its mysteries concerning the slow mineralogical gestation taking place in the womb of Mother Earth. All the mythologies of mines and mountains, their countless fairies, genii, elves, phantoms, and spirits, are the multiple epiphanies of the sacred presence that the individual confronts when he penetrates the geological levels of life (Eliade, 1978, pp. 53ff.).

Thus, the Melanesians opened a new mine only after long rituals and ceremonials. The Malay *pawang* (medicine man) derived a very fair revenue from propitiating and scaring those spirits who had to do with mines and mining (W. W. Skeat, quoted in Eliade, 1938, p. 92). Among many African peoples, the chief, surrounded by a shaman and the workers, recites a special prayer to his ancestral spirits, who preside over the mine, and only then does he determine where the digging shall be done (Cline, 1937, p. 119). In Europe, until the end of the Middle Ages, miners opened a mine only after the celebration of a religious ceremony (Sébillot, 1894, p. 421).

FURNACES AND THE "GROWTH" OF THE ORE. Laden with this dark sacrality, the ores are taken from the mine to the furnaces. Then begins the most difficult and riskiest operation. The artisan takes the place of Mother Earth in order to hasten and perfect the "growth" of the ores. The furnaces are in some sense a new, artificial womb in which the ore completes its gestation. Hence the countless precautions, taboos, and rituals that accompany smelting.

In Africa, camps are set up in the vicinity of the mines, and there the workers live, in a state of purity, throughout the mining season, which sometimes lasts for several months (Cline, 1937, p. 119). The Kitara believe that if the bellows-maker has had sexual relations during the course of his work, the bellows will constantly fill up with water and refuse to function (ibid., p. 121). The belief that the sexual act can in some way compromise the success of the work is general throughout sub-Saharan Africa. This prohibition is even stated in the ritual songs sung during the work. Indeed, smelting represents a sacred marriage—the mixture of "male" and "female" ores—and consequently all the sexual energies of the workmen must be kept in reserve, to ensure the magical success of the union that is taking place in the furnaces. The nuptial symbolism is present in many metallurgical ceremonies. The Kitara smith treats the anvil like a bride. When men bring it into the house they sing as though for a nuptial procession. In accepting it, the smith sprinkles it with water so that it "may bear many children" and tells his wife that he has brought a second wife home to help her (ibid., p. 118).

THE MAGICO-RELIGIOUS POWERS OF THE SMITH. The metallurgist, like the blacksmith and before him the potter, is a "master of fire." It is by means of fire that he brings about the passage of a material from one state to another. Smelting proves to be not only the means of "acting faster" but also of acting to make a different thing from what already existed in nature. This is why, in archaic societies, smelters and smiths are held to be masters of fire, along with shamans, medicine men, and magicians. But the ambivalent character of metal—laden with powers at once sacred and demonic—is transferred to metallurgists and smiths: they are highly esteemed but are also feared, segregated, or even scorned. Thus, in West Africa, smiths play important roles in secret societies, enjoy the prestige normally accorded magicians, and form separate clans. In the Kongo and surrounding regions, they have a close association with priests and chiefs (and sometimes are one and the same); elsewhere (e.g., among the Chagga, Hamitic Bantu-speaking agricultural workers) the smith is both feared and respected. By contrast, in pastoral Hamitic cultures and among steppe hunters, smiths are despised and form a caste set apart (Eliade, 1978, pp. 90ff.; see also Dieterlen, 1965, pp. 10ff.). In Indonesia and elsewhere in South Asia, the smith and the smelter are much respected for their secret powers (O'Connor, 1975, pp. 177ff.).

The tools of the African smith share this sacred quality. The hammer, the bellows, and the anvil are considered animate and miraculous; they are regarded as capable of operating by their own magico-religious force, unassisted by the smith. The art of creating tools is essentially superhuman—either divine or demonic (for the smith also forges murderous weapons). Remnants of ancient mythologies belonging to the Stone Age have probably been added to, or woven into, the mythology of metals. The stone tool and the hand ax were charged with a mysterious power; they struck, inflicted injury, caused explosions, and produced sparks, as did the thunderbolt. The ambivalent magic of stone weapons, both lethal and beneficial, like the thunderbolt itself, was transmitted and magnified in the new instruments forged of metal. The hammer, successor to the ax of the Stone Age, becomes the emblem of the powerful storm gods. Indeed, storm gods and the gods of agricultural fecundity are sometimes conceived as smith-gods (for examples, see Eliade, 1978, pp. 92ff.; Dieterlen, 1965, passim).

In many mythologies divine smiths forge the weapons of the gods, thus insuring them victory over dragons or other monstrous beings. In the Canaanite myth, Koshar-wa-Hasis (literally, "adroit-and-clever") forges for Baal two clubs with which he will kill Yamm, lord of the seas and underground waters. In the Egyptian version of the myth, Ptah (the potter god) forges the weapons that enable Horus to conquor Seth. Similarly, in the Vedas, the divine smith Tvaṣṭṛ makes Indra's weapons for his battle with Vṛtra; Hephaistos forges the thunderbolt that will enable Zeus to triumph over Typhon. But the cooperation between the divine smith and the gods is not confined to his help in the final combat for sovereignty of the world.

The smith is also the architect and artisan of the gods, supervises the construction of Baal's palace, and equips the sanctuaries of the other divinities. In addition, this god-smith has connections with music and song, just as in a number of societies the smiths and braziers are also musicians, poets, healers, and magicians. Thus, the mythic African smith is a culture hero. He has been enjoined by God to complete creation, to organize the world, to educate men, that is, to reveal to them the arts and the religious mysteries. For this reason, in many African cultures, smiths play the central role in puberty initiations and in male secret societies. Similarly, in early Greece, certain groups of mythical personages—Telchines, Cabiri, Curetes, Dactyls—were both secret guild associations performing initiations of young boys and corporations of metalworkers (Eliade, 1978, pp. 101ff.). Blacksmiths were equally important in the initiatory rituals of the ancient Germans and in the Japanese male societies. In old Scandinavia there was a close connection between the profession of the smith and the art of the poet and musician. The same associations are to be found among the Turco-Tatars and Mongols, where the smith is linked with horses, singers, and poets. Tzigane nomads are, even today, a combination of smith, tinker, musician, healer, and fortune-teller (ibid., pp. 98ff.). It seems, then, that on many different levels of culture (an indication of great antiquity) there is an intimate connection between the art of the smith, occult techniques (shamanism, magic, healing, etc.), and the arts of song, of the dance, and of poetry.

All these ideas and beliefs articulated around the trades of miners, metallurgists, and smiths have markedly enriched the mythology of *homo faber* inherited from the Stone Age. But the wish to collaborate in the perfecting of matter also had other important consequences. In assuming the responsibility for changing nature, man took the place of time; what would have required eons to ripen in the subterranean depths, as the artisan believed, he could obtain in a few weeks, for the furnace replaced the telluric womb. Millennia later, the alchemist did not think differently.

See Also Alchemy, overview article; Blades; Elixir; Gold and Silver.

Bibliography

Aitchison, Leslie. *A History of Metals.* 2 vols. London, 1960. A classic work.

Andrée, Richard. *Die Metalle bei den Naturvölkern mit Berücksichtigung prähistorischer Verhältnisse.* Leipzig, 1884. Outdated but still useful.

Bjorkman, Judith Kingston. *Meteors and Meteorites in the Ancient Near East.* Center for Meteorite Studies, Publication no. 12. Tempe, Ariz., 1973.

Cline, Walter. *Mining and Metallurgy in Negro Africa.* Menasha, Wis., 1937. Indispensable; should be completed and corrected by the most recent publications of French Africanists.

Dieterlen, Germaine. "Contribution à l'étude des forgerons en Afrique occidentale." In *Annuaire, 1965–1966, École Pratique des Hautes Études, cinquième section, Sciences religieuses,* vol. 73, pp. 3–28. Paris, 1966. An important study.

Eliade, Mircea. "Metallurgy, Magic and Alchemy." *Zalmoxis: Revue des études religieuses* 1 (1938): 197–203.

Eliade, Mircea. *The Forge and the Crucible.* 2d ed. Chicago, 1978. Originally published under the title *Forgerons et alchimistes* (Paris, 1956).

Forbes, R. J. *Metallurgy in Antiquity.* Leiden, 1950. A valuable synthesis with an excellent bibliography.

Lechtman, Heather. "Andean Value Systems and the Development of Prehistoric Metallurgy." *Technology and Culture* 25 (January 1984): 1–36. Important.

O'Connor, Stanley J. "Iron Working as Spiritual Inquiry in the Indonesian Archipelago." *History of Religions* 14 (1975): 173–190.

Przyluski, Jean. "L'or, son origine et ses pouvoirs magiques." *Bulletin de l'École Française d'Extreme Orient* 14 (1914): 1–16.

Rickard, T. A. *Man and Metals: A History of Mining in Relation to the Development of Civilizations.* 2 vols. New York, 1932.

Sébillot, Paul. *Les travaux publics et les mines dans les traditions et les superstitions de tous les pays.* Paris, 1894. Old but still useful.

Singer, Charles, Eric J. Holmyard, and A. R. Hall. *A History of Technology,* vol. 1, *From Early Times to the Fall of Ancient Empires.* Oxford, 1954. Indispensable.

Mircea Eliade (1987)

METAMORPHOSIS See SHAPE SHIFTING; TRANSMIGRATION

METAPHYSICS

METAPHYSICS is generally understood as a philosophical inquiry into the fundamental nature of reality. The word *metaphysics* derives from the Greek *meta ta phusica* ("after the things of nature"), a classificatory rubric used by commentators on and editors of Aristotle's corpus to refer to an untitled group of texts concerned with "first philosophy." Western medieval and modern philosophers often have construed metaphysics as the most basic and most comprehensive of philosophical inquiries, one that is primarily focused on the ontological status of objects, the existence of entities that transcend nature, and the generic features exhibited in experience. African and Eastern philosophers usually have conceived of metaphysics (in the sense implied by the word's etymology) as more closely interwoven with the axiological (or value-laden) character of the cosmos and the moral quality of human community.

A distinctive feature of Western metaphysics is the attempt to understand the universe by means of a logical investigation of concepts rather than an empirical inquiry based on sensory evidence. Such metaphysical sentiments rest upon a relative distrust of the variable, visible, and sensible world and involve a quest for the invariable, invisible, and intelligible world. They also assume a basic unity of thought and being, of logic and the world. Rationally coherent and logically consistent systems of thought are believed to reveal the way the world really is.

The origins of Western metaphysics go back to Parmenides of Elea (c. 515–475 BCE). In the poem usually titled *On Nature,* Parmenides provides the first exemplary philosophical argument of Western metaphysics. In the form of a journey to the heavens to receive wisdom from "the goddess," Parmenides attacks the reality of the physical world, condemns difference as illusory, and proposes that fundamental reality is invariable, invisible, and intelligible, as well as single, indivisible, and homogeneous. This metaphysical viewpoint rests upon the deployment of the basic binary opposition of reality and appearance, in which the realm of the former is qualitatively different from and superior to the realm of the latter.

Parmenides' metaphysical conception of being, grounded in his logical reasoning and monistic conclusions, has been a major influence in Western metaphysics. This Parmenidean legacy can be seen in Plotinus's One, Spinoza's God, and Hegel's Absolute. The most immediate influence of Parmenides is found in Plato's *Phaedo,* in which, despite subtle gradations, the reality/appearance distinction is appropriated to undergird the existence of a separate order of Forms accessible only to the mind and more real than the senses. In his heroic efforts to refute the skepticism of the Sophists, Plato (427–347 BCE) extends the ontological binary opposition of reality/appearance to epistemology, morality, and politics, thus including distinctions such as knowledge/opinion, nature/convention, and philosopher/sophist. In this way, Plato's metaphysics, like that of some African and Eastern thinkers, is inseparable from ethics and political philosophy.

The religious significance of Plato's metaphysics is his doctrine of recollection, which defends the immortality of the soul. In *Meno,* Plato portrays Socrates interrogating a slave boy, an interrogation that results in the boy arriving at a geometric truth. Socrates then argues that since this truth was not told to the boy but rather elicited from him, the truth must reside in the boy at birth and in a previous existence: his questions merely prompted the boy to remember what he had forgotten from an earlier life. Similar arguments, related to the existence of a separate order of Forms, are found in the *Phaedo,* while a more speculative account of the transmigration of souls, life after death, and the soul fleeing the bondage of the body is put forward in the tenth book of the Republic.

Aristotle (384–322 BCE) set forth the first Western metaphysical system, including a new vocabulary, an articulation of the central issues, and a thorough treatment of these issues. He conceives of metaphysics as a "first philosophy" that investigates the fundamental principles presupposed by the other sciences. Aristotle's metaphysics can be viewed as a profound and persistent polemic against the notions of indeterminacy and infinity. Its aim is to establish a fixed beginning point, the limits of inquiry, the determinateness of concrete individual objects, and the termination of epistemic chains of justification. Aristotelian notions of causality (material, formal, efficient, and final), substance, being, essence, form, and actuality set the terms for Western metaphysical discourse through the twentieth century. The legacy of Aristotle's metaphysics in religious thought is found most clearly in the Christian systematic theology of Thomas Aquinas and the neo-Thomist tradition of the Catholic church exemplified in thinkers such as Étienne Gilson (1884–1978) and Jacques Maritain (1882–1973).

The last great metaphysical system of classical antiquity was the Neoplatonism best represented by the Hellenized Egyptian philosopher Plotinus (205–270 CE), his pupil Porphyry (232–306?), the Syrian school of Iamblichus (250–330?), the Athenian school of Proclus (c. 410–485), and the Latin Christian school of Boethius (480–524). This system (and its various versions) is rooted in Plato's devaluation of the sensible world and elevation of the intelligible world. Yet, as in certain themes in Plato's second and seventh letters, Neoplatonism promotes a kind of mysticism and asceticism that deeply influenced the Christian theology of the African thinker Augustine (354–430). This mysticism is based on an intuition of the unity and wholeness of being, the One, which differentiates itself downward into lesser degrees in spirits, souls, and, lastly, physical objects. This process of emanation from undifferentiated unity to modes of differentiated disunity results in a return (or epistrophe) to unity and wholeness.

The Syrian philosopher Porphyry not only made Plotinus's lectures available but also wrote a short introduction to Aristotle's *Categories,* titled *Isagoge,* that directed attention to the relation between the essential and accidental attributes of things and the status of universals. This influential text, translated into Latin by Boethius, provided the framework and language for metaphysical reflection in the early Middle Ages by Christian theologians such as John Scottus Eriugena (fl. 847–877), Anselm (c. 1033–1109), and Bonaventure (c. 1221–1274).

The thirteenth-century translations of Aristotle and his Arabian commentators into Greek and Latin by Robert Grosseteste and William of Moerbeke facilitated the crowning achievement of Western metaphysics in the late Middle Ages: the magisterial system of Thomas Aquinas (c. 1224–1274) and the critical nominalism of William of Ockham (c. 1280/1285–1349?). Thomas creatively appropriated Aristotelian metaphysics into a Christian philosophy, whereas William paved the road for the new "modern way" (*via moderna*) by separating metaphysics from Christian faith and thereby emphasizing religious faith and church tradition. William influenced major figures of the Reformation.

The modern conception of metaphysics in the West begins with René Descartes (1596–1650), who tried to apply the rigor and standards of mathematics and geometry to metaphysical claims. Descartes's quest for indubitability within the immediate awareness of a thinking self and his call for clarity and distinctness in truth-claims reflect an ingenious and influential philosophical response to the rise of modern science, especially the wedding of quantitative models with physics and chemistry. Barukh Spinoza (1632–1677) and Gottfried Wilhelm Leibniz (1646–1716) followed the Cartesian project of scientific rigor and philosophical boldness by setting forth deductive metaphysical systems. Spinoza's mechanical and deterministic view of the universe, in which the only two known attributes of substance are thought and extension, yielded a pantheistic conception of God as identical with nature. This conception would inspire later forms of German idealism. Leibniz's rationalist commitments to a priori reasoning, the analysis of concepts according to logical necessity and rational intelligibility, produced refined versions of ontological arguments for the existence of God that sharpened modal logical tools for subsequent efforts by Christian theists.

The crisis of modern Western metaphysics begins with the major empiricists: John Locke (1632–1704), George Berkeley (1685–1753), and, especially, David Hume (1711–1776). All three assumed the Cartesian starting point for philosophical reflection as within the arena of immediate awareness of a thinking self. But in contrast to Descartes, Locke argues that sense impressions are the primary data for knowledge of the world, self, and God. This restriction requires that we cannot have "clear and distinct ideas" of substance and essence, only empirical access to their properties and powers. Therefore, the most privileged notions in traditional Western metaphysics, such as substance and essence, were rendered problematic. Berkeley further questioned the distinction between ideas of objects and properties of objects that cause ideas, thereby radically calling into question material substance. Hume changed the course of Western metaphysics by dissolving philosophical conceptions of the self, subject, and mind into mere bundles of sensations and perceptions. By replacing philosophical notions of necessity and causality with psychological accounts of imagination and sociological notions of habit and custom, Hume defended an inescapable skepticism regarding the possibility of metaphysics. This position presented religious thinkers with the options of a rational agnosticism or a nonrational religious faith.

The significance of Immanuel Kant (1724–1804) lies in his rescue of Western metaphysics by specifying the limits of human knowledge. This rescue took the form of rejecting the dogmatism of Cartesian metaphysical projects and circumscribing the skepticism of Hume's empiricism. The result was a critical idealist metaphysics that preserved the objectivity of knowledge-claims yet prevented human access to ultimate reality. The aim of Kant's metaphysics was to disclose the universal conceptual scheme that people employ in theoretically ordering the world and practically acting within it. For Kant, religious faith became a mere appendage to ethics, a practical postulate for moral behavior.

The last great metaphysical system in the modern West—a response, in part, to Kant—was that of Georg Wilhelm Friedrich Hegel (1770–1831). Like Plato, Aristotle, and the Neoplatonists, Hegel attempted to penetrate to the fundamental nature of reality by means of rational deliberation. Yet he conceived of this reality as a historical and dialectical process intelligible only to the discerning and retrospective philosopher. Hegel's metaphysics emphasized the radical dependence of God upon the world and promoted a divine immanent presence in human history.

Western metaphysics has been under severe attack since Hegel. Apart from the ambitious project of Alfred North Whitehead (1861–1947), the vitalistic program of Henri Bergson (1859–1941), the versions of logical atomism of Bertrand Russell (1872–1970) and the early Ludwig Wittgenstein (1889–1951), and Paul Ricoeur's (b. 1913) recent metaphysics of narrativity, post-Hegelian philosophy has been strongly antimetaphysical. The Christian existentialism of Søren Kierkegaard (1813–1855) and the transcendental phenomenology of Edmund Husserl (1859–1938) inspired the ontological hermeneutics of Martin Heidegger (1889–1976), which claims to have "destroyed" the Western metaphysical tradition. The logical positivism of the Vienna Circle (Otto Neurath, Moritz Schlick, Rudolf Carnap, and others) and ordinary-language philosophy served as steppingstones for the later Ludwig Wittgenstein's linguistic conventionalism, which claims to have "dodged" the bewitching traps of Western metaphysics. The perspectivism of Friedrich Nietzsche (1844–1900) and the structuralist vocabulary of Ferdinand de Saussure (1857–1913) provided resources for the present-day poststructuralist skepticism of Jacques Derrida (1930–2004), which claims to have "deconstructed" the Western metaphysical tradition. Lastly, the pragmatism of William James (1842–1910) and John Dewey (1859–1952) and the epistemological holism of W. V. Quine (1908–2000) and Nelson Goodman (1906–1998) are employed by Richard Rorty (b. 1931) in his contemporary attempt to "demythologize" the Western metaphysical tradition. Whether the influential attacks of Heidegger, Wittgenstein, Derrida, and Rorty on Western metaphysics are skeptical moments in the history of Western philosophy (like those of Pyrrho and Montaigne in times past) or proleptic precursors of a new stage remains an open question. The religious significance and implications of these attacks—within and outside the West—remain relatively unexplored.

BIBLIOGRAPHY

Ayer, A. J. *Philosophy in the Twentieth Century.* New York, 1982. A noteworthy and well-written sequel to Bertrand Russell's *A History of Western Philosophy* (1945) by a major figure active on the contemporary scene since the 1930s.

Hancock, Roger. "Metaphysics, History of." In *The Encyclopedia of Philosophy*, edited by Paul Edwards, vol. 5. New York, 1967. The best short and concise article-length treatment of major historical developments in Western metaphysics. An extensive bibliography on central figures and periods is included.

Passmore, John. *A Hundred Years of Philosophy.* 2d ed. Middlesex, U.K., 1970. The most comprehensive and detailed history of academic Western philosophy dealing with post-Hegelian developments. Reliable reportage and exposition, but lacks an overarching interpretive framework.

Rorty, Richard. *Philosophy and the Mirror of Nature.* Princeton, 1979. A highly provocative, imaginative, and learned interpretation of Western philosophy that puts forward devastating critiques of metaphysics.

Russell, Bertrand. *A History of Western Philosophy.* New York, 1945. The most informative, stimulating, and engaging history of Western philosophy available in one volume in English, by one of the most brilliant thinkers of the twentieth century.

New Sources

Levinas, Emmanuel. *Otherwise than Being: Or Beyond Essence.* Translated by Alphonso Lingis. Pittsburgh, Pa., 1998.

Lewis, David. *On the Plurality of Worlds.* Oxford, U.K., 2000.

McCumber, John. *Metaphysics and Oppression: Heidegger's Challenge to Western Philosophy.* Bloomington, Ind., 1999.

Miklowitz, Paul. *Metaphysics to Metafictions: Hegel, Nietzsche, and the End of Philosophy.* Albany, N.Y., 1998.

Silverman, Allan Jay. *The Dialectic of Essence: A Study of Plato's Metaphysics.* Princeton, 2002.

CORNEL WEST (1987)
Revised Bibliography

METEOROLOGICAL BEINGS. Religious people of very different times and cultures have tended to "humanize" meteorological phenomena by telling stories about the displays of celestial power and fruitfulness they witnessed, converting those events into elements of a sacred narrative intended to explain how the world and humankind have come to be the way they are. The experience of life in a properly religious world differs radically from our experience of life today. For one thing, it makes no distinction between the natural and human realms. Whereas for us a storm is invariably an "it," the storm has been much more a "thou" for the better part of human history. It is not the storm that religious people have worshiped but the sacred power, will, and qualities that are somehow revealed there, although it would be quite incorrect to speak of the "personification" of inanimate nature or, for that matter, to invoke some sort of animistic theory to explain why meteorological phenomena play the important roles in religious life that they do. For religious people, storms are everywhere manifestations of the sacred. As such they engage the whole human person—meaning his or her emotional, imaginative, and intellectual faculties taken together—in a vital relationship.

Moreover, the various qualities of storm and rain have suggested, both to our religious forebears and to our contemporaries living in the so-called traditional societies, countless analogies that have enabled them to express—perhaps even to discover—certain important truths about their experience of life and their religious aspirations. For example, by analogy with atmospheric lightning, Iglulik Inuit shamans refer to a mystical experience called *qaumaneq* ("lightning" or "illumination") that confers clairvoyance. Indeed, lightning, or dreams about it, typically figures in shamanic initiations or callings; and by the same token the rapidity or suddenness of spiritual "illumination" has been compared to lightning in many of the religions of history.

Storms have both a benign, life-sustaining aspect, because they bring rain, and a dark, chaotic one, owing to their potential for destruction. The high winds and distant roll of thunder that in one instance may announce an imminent end to prolonged drought may in another have inspired an apocalyptic vision, or a collective memory preserved in myth, of the world's complete destruction by flood. The storm gods, for their part, often garner trust as senders of the moisture upon which living things depend, but just as often they are feared as agents of divine punishment, retribution, or simply inexplicable malevolence. Symbols derived from the phenomena of storm thus express quite effectively humankind's deeply rooted ambivalence toward the sacred. Or, put another way, they express the profound anxiety that men and women have felt about the sacred powers that sustain the world, powers over which human beings have little if any control.

Finally, and what is most important, storm symbols function the way other religious symbols do in making it possible for the human situation to be translated into cosmological terms and vice versa. They reveal a fundamental oneness between human life and the structure of the world and so have led people out of their isolation in subjectivity, beyond the human condition as it were, toward a stance vis-à-vis their own experience of life that one could easily describe as a kind of transcendence. That much, at least, accounts for the essentially religious character of these symbols.

In this article I propose to continue the morphological description of sky symbols begun elsewhere, concentrating now on the divine figures connected with dramatic meteorological events, chiefly thunder, lightning, and rain. No single explanation can account for the uniformity and variety of the storm gods in history. Some are also supreme beings, some appear in animal guise. All of them display in varying proportions what I have chosen to call "two kinds of sovereignty," the one more "spiritual" and derived from the ideas and values associated with the sky and sky gods, the other more "physical" and connected with the earth and its fertility.

STORM DEITIES AND THEIR FORMS. If all the sky gods were arranged on a line according to their dominant powers and attributes, the result would be a broad array with, at one end, deities who display most fully the characteristics that make them creators, sovereigns, lords of the universe, law givers, and moral overseers. To the second half of the array would belong a collection of progressively more varied and colorful deities whose chief traits describe a generative, vitalizing mission in the world. These latter are typically male deities, often spouses of the Great Mother, and givers of rain, hence prone to develop into more specialized storm gods and fecundators. All are epiphanies of force and violence, those necessary sources of energy on which biological life and civil order in the world depend; and, over a broad geographical expanse throughout Africa, Europe, and Asia, many have a connection with the bull. (The bull and the thunderbolt appear historically very early in connection with the storm gods. The Kannada word *ko*, which means "ox, sky, or lightning, ray of light, water, horn, mountain," preserves intact the full semantic range of this complex of symbols.)

The so-called specialization of the sky gods either in the direction of *dei otiosi* or into the gods of storm and rain derives from the ambivalent structure of the sky symbols generally and has led scholars to speak of the "passive," transcendent nature of the sky gods and, conversely, of their tendency to give way to more active, vital divine forms. Of course nowhere in history does one find either specialized type, the far-off ruler whose celestial attributes predominate, or the storm god-fecundator, in isolation; invariably there are mixtures of the two. Sometimes both functions belong to a single deity's sphere of activity; elsewhere a rather clear division of labor prevails, with the storm god usually subordinate to a celestial ruler who is often the storm god's father. In certain cases the storm deity represents the exercise of legitimate force on behalf of some higher authority; in other cases his link with agriculture is more important.

Specialization usually brings with it a radical change of form: that is, the storm gods can be said to have abandoned absolute transcendence in favor of powers and attributes that did not belong to their original celestial make-up. For that reason they are apt to betray foreign influences too. For example, Parjanya, the Indian god of hurricanes and son of Dyaus, the ancient Indo-Aryan sky god, was said to rule the waters and all living things. He made the whole universe tremble with his storms. His specialization, though, rendered him no longer omniscient like his father (with whom the authors of the *Ṛgveda* sometimes confused him) nor a sovereign like Varuṇa. As a result, in Vedic times he yielded his place to Indra, a warrior king, also god of rain and easily the chief god of the *Ṛgveda.* Indra, for his part, is always compared to a bull or a ram, two animals associated with Rudra, a non-Aryan divinity, many of whose attributes Indra would absorb over the course of time. In fact Indra's connection with bulls, soma, and the Maruts (to the degree they personified the wandering souls of the dead) would suggest that he also acquired certain lunar prerogatives: that is, Indra *qua* symbol expanded in the direction of a larger integrated expression of life's power and sacrality, one that included even elements belonging to the symbolism of the moon.

The point is that storm gods, no matter how early in time they appear and no matter what type of culture they belong to, always show evidence of long and complicated histories. Thus, in using the term *specialization* here to account for the forms the storm gods take, I do not mean to imply that storm, rain, and fertility gods are necessarily late developments, for we have no reason to doubt the antiquity of dramatic, stormy elements in the sky god's make-up. There is a unity of structure to the sky symbolism that we can only assume has been present from the very beginning, and that unified structure includes both distant supreme soverignty and active, even violent, involvement with life processes in the human world.

METEOROLOGICAL PHENOMENA AS ATTRIBUTES OF A SUPREME BEING. Some religious people have seen none other than the supreme sky deity behind the stormy atmospheric displays that, for them, attest to his all-knowing presence, will, and power. The Andaman Islanders know such a deity in Puluga, whose breath is the wind and whose voice is thunder. Hurricanes signal his anger, and lightning bolts are the punishment he executes against those who violate his laws.

The tribes of Southeast Australia report that Baiame created all things out of nothing, but Baiame is creative in another sense, for in causing the rain to fall he makes the whole earth new and green. Natives can discern his voice in thunder. On the east coast of Australia other tribes worship Daramulun, who also speaks in thunder and sends them rain. Daramulun is said to have created the first ancestor during his stay on earth, giving him the laws and customs that have passed from one generation to the next ever since. Most importantly, Daramulun left behind the initation ceremony, which entails, among other things, a solemn display of the bull-roarer, said to make a noise like thunder and to represent the supreme being's continued presence among his people. Indeed, almost all the Australian sky gods communicate their presence in thunder, lightning, the wind and the rainbow, which is to say that meteorological traits belong inseparably to their supreme, celestial modes of being.

THE AMBIVALENCE OF THE STORM DEITIES: CREATIVITY AND CHAOS. Stormy attributes help to express the dual nature of supreme beings, who on account of their power over life and death are apt to inspire both trust and fear in equal measure. For example, the Maasai of Kenya pray to a supreme being named Ngai ("sky" or "rain") who lives high above our world where the winds circulate through his nostrils. Lightning is the dreadful glance of his eye, thunder a cry of joy at something he has seen, and raindrops are the joyful tears he sheds at the sight of fat beehives during the rainy season when cattle grow sleek. By analogy with the sky's polychrome appearance, the Maasai refer to a black, red, gray, and white Ngai, but they ultimately reduce those four to the black and red Ngai alone, two opposed and complementary forms of deity. The black Ngai is good because, like the black, cloudy sky, he brings rain; whereas the red Ngai, like the red, hot sky, withholds it. (In Babylonian mythology it is the gigantic bird Imdugud that rescued human beings from drought. It covered the sky with the black storm clouds of its wings and consumed the Bull of Heaven, whose hot breath had scorched the crops down below.)

The Inca of pre-Columbian times worshiped Illapa (whom the Aymara knew as Thunupa). Both dreaded as a storm god and adored as a bringer of rain, Illapa was pictured as a man with club and sling who draws water from a heavenly stream (the Milky Way) using pitchers that he leaves in the safekeeping of his sister until he breaks them with his thunder club.

By some early accounts the Aztec rain god Tlaloc has four pitchers, and according to the one he uses, the result will be a good maize crop or a harvest spoiled by vermin and frost. No Aztec deity enjoyed a more active or widespread cult than he. Tlaloc, the giver of rain, but also the wrathful deity of lightning, was conceived in multiple form as *tlaloques* (lesser, sometimes dwarflike, storm deities) assigned to the four directions, or as the leader of a group of *tlaloques*, who were said to dwell on mountaintops in caves, where storm clouds brew. Descriptions of Tlaloc's heavenly paradise supply further clues about his ambiguous nature. It is a place of infinite abundance and perpetual verdure where those who had died by drowning or had been struck by lightning or were suffering from such afflictions as leprosy, venereal disease, skin ailments, gout, and dropsy enjoyed eternal happiness. They were the only dead whom the Aztec did not bury; all others were cremated.

According to Juan Ignacio Molina and other writers of the second half of the eighteenth century, the Mapuche knew a supreme being with many forms of address. One of his epithets, "two faces" (black and white), apparently referred to the rain and sunshine prayed for in public rites but also to the deity's ambivalent attitude—both indulgent and severe—toward his worshipers. Older sources dating back to the seventeenth century call this deity Pillán; he was said to produce thunder and lightning and all manner of violent and destructive weather phenomena such as volcanic eruptions, river floods, tidal waves, and epidemics. On the other hand, Pillán was considered a protector of the crops and hence a beneficent weather god as well.

Two Kinds of Sovereignty. It is not uncommon for storm gods to display this dual character, especially in parts of the world where sudden, unpredictable shows of meteorological force dominate the landscape and must surely have compelled people to theological reflection. For example, by contrast with the reassuring periodicity of the Egyptian cosmos, the environment in which Mesopotamian civilization grew and flourished could only have led men and women to conclude that order was not a given but rather something to be achieved through the continual integration of many different competing wills, each one powerful and frightening. As a result, the Mesopotamians envisioned a huge cosmic state that included human beings, animals, inanimate objects, natural phenomena, and even such abstractions as justice, righteousness, and the form of a circle. An assembly of gods presided over this "state," led by Anu (An), the god of heaven, and next to him in rank, Enlil his son, the god of storm. So far as the Mesopotamians were concerned, Enlil had revealed himself both in nature and in history. The violence that fills a storm and is expressed there *was* Enlil.

But a meteorological analogy also made it possible to interpret such catastrophic events as the destruction of Ur by the Elamite hordes sweeping down from the eastern highlands as Enlil's handiwork too: that is, in some deeper, truer sense those barbarians were also a storm, Enlil's storm, in and through which the god himself had executed a verdict passed on Ur and its people by the divine assembly. In keeping with the Mesopotamian vision of a cosmic bureaucracy, Enlil's specialized juridical role was distinguished from that of another diety, Enki, known as "lord of the earth," who administered the waters, specifically, rivers, canals, irrigation, and the organization of all productive forces. Enki's ministerial role derived from the sovereignty exercised by Anu and Enlil. Anu and, later, Marduk represent the magical or "spiritual" component of that sovereignty, whereas Enlil's sovereignty is of a more physical kind; and the latter's stormy attributes, though in this case they have little to do directly with fertility, have everything to do with the problem of legitimate force, especially the legitimate force that must have been an important concern—and a deep source of anxiety—for the citizens of such a highly regulated cosmos.

While it is true that in many cases the sky god withdrew in favor of storm gods and other divinities with more specific and concrete functions, in other instances the sky god assumed a new role. That is certainly what happened in the Greek and Roman traditions, where Zeus and Jupiter stood for both kinds of sovereignty, being at once divine guarantors of cosmic order, supreme rulers, moral arbiters, even personifications of law, as well as gods of rain and fertility. Zeus preserves in his name the Sankrit root *div* ("shine" or "day"), leaving no doubt as to his celestial nature and shared heritage with the ancient Indo-European sky god Dyaus. However, scholars in the past were so quick to seize upon the etymology of Zeus's name as the key to his religious significance that they usually inquired no further into Zeus's unique and complicated mode of being, much of it vividly expressed in his meteorological attributes.

The many epithets for Zeus in Homer explain why he came to be equated with weather deities elsewhere in Asia Minor: he is called at various times Ombrios and Hyetios ("the rainy one"), Ourios ("he who sends favorable winds"), Astrapios ("sender of lightning"), and Bronton ("thunderer"). Other epithets tell of an affinity with crops and the dark earth: Georgos ("the farmer"), Chthonios ("earth-dweller"), and even Zeus Katachthonios ("the underground Zeus"). Zeus's theriomorphic aspect—he is sometimes a bull, as in the myth of Europa, or a wolf to whom sacrifice was performed in time of drought or storm—is further evidence of his link to agriculture and rain.

The transforming quality of lightning that accounts for its role in shamanic initiations may help to explain yet another of Zeus's prerogatives, for whatever was used to purify from sin and much of what pertained to rites of initiation fell directly or indirectly under his control. Lightning marked his direct epiphany, and wherever it struck, a sanctuary was raised to Zeus Descending.

The whole complex of ideas, powers, and attributes belonging to Zeus's stormy aspect reappears on a different level of symbolic expression in the divine twins. The Dioscuri, or "Zeus's sons," like many other pairs of mythic twins, issued from the union of a god and a human mother and thus represented in a peculiar way the sacrality of the sky god on earth. In the Indo-European tradition, the twins are usually sons of the sky god, warriors, magic healers, saviors, and fertility gods; as gods of light, they are often associated with the dawn, the morning and evening stars, and the pair, thunder and lightning. The Dioscuri, for example, became popular as rescuers from personal distress, especially from danger at sea. Saint Elmo's fire, the electric discharge from the ship's mast during a thunderstorm, was widely regarded as their corporeal epiphany. Also, like Herakles, they were said to have been initiated at Eleusis. The various pairs of divine twins in the Indo-European tradition—the Germanic Freyr and Ñord, the Vedic Asvins, and the Dioscuri, to name three—were invoked to witness the swearing of oaths. Likewise, at Olympia a statue of Zeus Horkios ("Zeus of the oath"), before which competitors took their oaths, had in either hand thunderbolts with which to punish false swearers; and according to the Homeric formulas of oaths, Zeus was always the first deity called upon to guarantee an oath and punish any violation that might occur.

In ancient Rome when a building was struck by lightning, fulgural ritual prescribed that an opening be made in the roof over the spot so that the god could always have free access to the place he had chosen for his sanctuary. The most solemn oath was that sworn in the name of Iuppiter Lapis ("Jupiter present in the thunderstone"). The sacred stone was used when the *fetiales* took an oath and made sacrifices upon allying themselves with a foreign power. We know from Vergil that such an alliance received its highest sanction from the storm god himself. The priest, pronouncing a curse on the contractor who should first violate the sacred compact, hurled the stone at the sacrificial swine saying, "Jupiter, strike down the Romans as I now strike this pig, and strike them more heavily, for your power is greater than mine." This action represented in ritual form the stroke of lighting, and it has survived in the practice of Masurian (East Prussian) peasants who hurl a stone ax in a ritually designated manner against the door to protect their homes from lightning. Comparable practices are documented for other traditions.

Yahveh developed along lines that in some ways parallel the development of Zeus and Jupiter. Throughout the history of Israel, he shows himself a god of sky and storm, omnipotent creator, absolute sovereign, author of the norms and laws that make human life possible and good. By contrast Indra's exaggeratedly "physical" sovereignty develops into a personification of cosmic and biological energy. Indra is not a creator; instead the creative function is specialized in Indra's case into a generative, vitalizing one. Of course the *Ṛgveda* does feature a sky father called Dyaus Pitṛ, a cognate form of *Zeus Pater* and *Jupiter*, but by Vedic times Indra had already assumed the role of celestial sovereign in India, and storms are the supreme manifestations of his creative force. He wields the thunderbolt, frees the waters, absorbs fabulous amounts of soma, fertilizes the fields and bestows fertility on human women, displays fantastic sexual powers himself, and leads an army of lesser storm gods, the Maruts, to victory for the Indo-Aryan invaders.

The Germanic deities Óðinn (Odin) and Þórr (Thor) offer a clear example of a storm god's specialized function and the two kinds of sovereignty implicit in this cosmic division of labor. Óðinn belongs primarily to a category of divine sovereigns that includes the Chinese Tian, the Indian Varuṇa, and Ahura Mazdā of Zoroastrian belief, although in the course of his development, he took on certain attributes of agricultural and fertility gods as well, becoming in the process a chthonian master of the souls of dead heroes. Óðinn typifies what the great Indo-Europeanist Georges Dumézil has called "the magical sovereign" because, like Varuṇa, he employs the power to bind and discerns the future. Þórr, on the other hand, god of tempests and combat, represents a second, more physical and less spiritual, kind of sovereignty, and his "physicality" takes in more than his martial qualities. Modern Scandinavian folklore studies, the remnants of old agrarian cults, and archaeological findings have all tended to prove that Þórr was originally much more than a warrior. Through rain, the happy side-effect of his atmospheric battles and the exploits of his hammer, he assisted the growth of crops; and Swedish peasant names for him recall the Saami (Lapp) cult dedicated to a fertility god who gives rain or sun according to the needs of the soil and sees to it that growing things mature and bear fruit.

STORM ANIMALS. The world's mythology and folklore describe a whole host of animals associated with thunder, lightning, and rain. The goat, the ram, or horses, for example, frequently accompany the storm god or pull his thundering vehicle across the sky. But the most common and widespread of the storm animals are probably the thunderbird or woodpecker, the dragon, and the bull.

North American Indians worship various supernatural beings in avian guise who produce thunder by the whir of their wings and lightning with flashes—a winking or twinkling—of their eyes (Cree, Hare, Tlingit, and other tribes). The distribution of this thunderbird belief is very wide, but the kind of bird in question ranges from a crane (Pawnee), jackpine partridge (Beaver), or humming bird (Lilloet) to a gigantic eagle (Sauk, Hare, and others). In eastern North America, the thunderbirds are typically four in number, one for each of the cardinal directions; and over the same region, they are considered to be locked in a cosmic struggle with evil water spirits, panthers, or horned serpents. This antagonism on the level of myth finds cultic expression in the division into sacred moieties characteristic of the eastern tribes who rely on agriculture for their subsistence. However, it may also reflect a dualism known elsewhere in world mythology that usually pits the thunder god against a reptilian water monster (the way Indra opposes Vṛtra or the way Marduk battles Tiamat). The same sort of struggle recurs, for example, in northern Siberia and among the Buriats around Lake Baikal, this time between the ruler of birds (a great eagle) and a many-headed water snake. The thunderbird motif also appears in the Gran Chaco, in Ecuador, and among the Carib-speaking peoples on the northern coast of South America. In fact the thunderbird's range would seem to indicate it was a much more vital presence in the minds and hearts of religious people in earlier times than now.

Across Europe, around the Mediterranean, and in parts of Inner Asia, at least, the woodpecker was believed to have supernatural powers because of its association with thunder, rain, and fertility. There is much evidence to suggest that the belief arose in Neolithic times with the spread of cultivation by means of the hoe and, later, the plow. In many places the woodpecker also has a connection with divine twins and, like the storm gods, with war and agriculture. For example, according to Roman legend Romulus and Remus were cared for not only by the she-wolf but also by the woodpecker; and Mars, god of war and at one time a god of agriculture, was said to have fathered the two by the vestal virgin Rhea Silvia. In other words the woodpecker has a dual nature corresponding to the storm's ambivalent values: destructive power and fertility.

Among the classes of dragons in China, there is first the dragon (*jiao*), originally an evil, snakelike creature that lived and always stayed in water. Then there is a river-god dragon, the *long-wang*, a form strongly influenced by the Indian *nāga*, originally a snake and, in fact, a version of the *jiao* that spread to India along with other elements of coastal culture. Under Indian influence the *jiao* dragon became a *long-wang*, or river god, with cults in many places along major waterways in China.

The *long* dragon associated with storms is neither the dragon *jiao* nor the *long-wang*. It too lives in water but has the unique ability to ascend to Heaven in the springtime and to summer there as the rain dragon. The *long* can frequently be seen in the sky during thunderstorms and is basically a benevolent animal that produces rain and ensures fertility. In the Chinese classics it sometimes corresponds to Heaven itself and therefore also to the emperor. (Later Chinese myths describe a thunder god whose characteristics derive from the wild boar, the promoter of wet-field agriculture.)

The mythologies of India, Africa, Europe, and Asia regularly associate a divine bull with the gods of the atmosphere and fertility, Indra and Rudra being two such examples. In pre-Aryan India the cults of Mohenjo-Daro and Baluchistan included important bull cults, and temples dedicated to Śiva are full of his bovine images. At Ur in the third millennium, the god of the atmosphere was a bull; in ancient Assyria men swore by a god in the form of a bull; and the supremacy achieved by such storm gods as Teshub, Hadad, and Baal in the religions of the Near East is notable for their connections with bulls. What is venerated in these and other bull gods of lightning who are married to the great earth goddess is both their transcendence, expressed in violent weather phenomena, and their physical potential as fecundators. In other words the interdependence of the "celestial" and "generative" functions in the figure of the bull seems abundantly clear. The same could be said of storm gods and of every storm hierophany.

See Also Hierophany; Rain; Sky.

Bibliography

I do not know of a monograph devoted to the storm gods or to the symbolism of meteorological phenomena. One general source, however, is Mircea Eliade's "The Sky and Sky Gods," chapter 2 of his *Patterns in Comparative Religion* (New York, 1958), pp. 38–123. A bibliography devoted specifically to storm gods in the Near East and their relation to the bull can be found on page 120. Other general sources are James G. Frazer's *The Worship of Nature*, vol. 1 (New York, 1926), Raffaele Pettazzoni's *The All Knowing God*, translated by H. J. Rose (London, 1956), and C. Blinkenberg's *The Thunderweapon in Religion and Folklore* (1911; New York, 1977).

Literature on the divine twins is quite extensive. Two old but still fascinating studies are Rendel Harris's *The Cult of the Heavenly Twins* (Cambridge, 1906) and *Boanerges* (Cambridge, U.K., 1913). For excellent bibliographies on the subject, see Donald J. Ward's *The Divine Twins: An Indo-European Myth in Germanic Tradition* (Berkeley, 1968) and Raymond Kuntzmann's *Le symbolisme des jumeaux au Proche-Orient ancien: Naissance, fonction, et évolution d'un symbole* (Paris, 1983).

On the range of the thunderbird belief, see Trumen Michelson's *Contributions to Fox Ethnology II*, United States Bureau of American Ethnology (Washington, D.C., 1930), pp. 51–56. For its religious meanings, a reliable source is Åke Hultkrantz's *Religions of the American Indians*, translated by Monica Setterwall (Berkeley, 1979).

On the woodpecker as a thunderbird, see "The Thunderbird," chapter 6 of Edward A. Armstrong's *The Folklore of Birds: An Enquiry into the Origin and Distribution of Some Magico-Religious Traditions*, 2d ed., rev. & enl. (New York, 1970), pp. 94–112. See also Rendel Harris's *Picus Who Is Also Zeus* (Cambridge, U.K., 1916).

The standard work on the dragon in China and Japan is still M. W. de Visser's *The Dragon in China and Japan* (Amsterdam, 1913). A more recent and probably more useful source is Wolfram Eberhard's *The Local Cultures of South and East China*, translated by Alide Eberhard (Leiden, 1968), pp. 238–250.

New Sources

Deighton, Hilary J. *The 'Weather-God' in Hittite Anatolia: An Examination of the Archaeological and Textual Sources.* Oxford, U.K., 1982.

Dijkstra, Meindert. "The Weather-God on Two Mountains." *Ugarit-Forschungen* 23 (1992): 127–140.

Reed, M. "Weather God of the Hittites." *Weatherwise* 44, no. 2 (April 1991): 38–40.

Sayers, William. "Weather Gods, Syncretism, and the Eastern Baltic." *Temenos* 26 (1990): 105–114.

Schwemer, Daniel. *Die Wettergottgestalten Mesopotamiens und Nordsyriens im Zeitalter der Keilschriftkulturen: Materialien und Studien nach den schriftlichen Quellen.* Wiesbaden, 2001.

Peter C. Chemery **(1987)**
Revised Bibliography

METHODIST CHURCHES. Methodism arose from the search of John Wesley and his brother Charles for a deepened religious life within the ordered ways of the Church of England, which John described as "the best constituted national church in the world." He sought no drastic reform in doctrines but rather a greater emphasis upon a personal experience of God's saving and perfecting grace and more opportunity for a spiritual quest within Christian groups, undeterred by denominational barriers. He downplayed the divisive element of his movement, publishing in 1742 an elaboration of Clement of Alexandria's description of a perfect Christian as *The Character of a Methodist* and offering this simple definition in his *Complete English Dictionary* (1753): "A Methodist, one that lives according to the method laid down in the Bible."

John Wesley, both as the living leader and later as the almost legendary "Mr. Wesley" of "the people called Methodists," so greatly influenced the developing thought of Methodism that he demands a far greater proportion of attention than if he had been the mere titular founder of a new denomination.

After his heart was "strangely warmed" on May 24, 1738, Wesley began to preach salvation by faith with the conviction of personal experience, and he gathered around him an organized society in London, the first of many that spread throughout the British Isles. These societies were intended to supplement, not supplant, the worship of the church. In his *Rules* (1743) he argued that a society was simply "a company of men 'having the form, and seeking the power of godliness,' united in order to pray together, to receive the word of exhortation, and to watch over one another in love, that they may help each other to work out their salvation." There was only one condition for membership, "a desire . . . to be saved from [their] sins." To test and reinforce his followers' sincerity, however, the *Rules* insisted that members should avoid evil, do good, and seek holiness, for which illustrative examples were given in all three categories.

In order to proclaim his message and administer his societies Wesley enrolled a steadily increasing number of lay preachers to join the handful of sympathetic clergy who engaged in an itinerant evangelical ministry under his supervision. In 1744 he called these together in London to confer about doctrine and organization. This was the first annual conference of Wesley's Methodism, although the Welsh Calvinistic wing of the movement, who looked to George Whitefield as their chief inspirer, had been holding their "Associations" for several years.

The primary purpose of the Conferences of 1744–1747 was to formulate the major doctrinal emphases of Methodist preaching: salvation by grace through faith, confirmed and exemplified by good works; the witness of the Holy Spirit to a person's salvation from the penalties of past sin and to his power over present temptations to sin; and the theoretical possibility of personal triumph over temptation, under the title of Christian perfection, which Wesley defined as perfect love to God and man, though consistent with human error and with no guarantee of permanence. These doctrines, as taught and illustrated in Wesley's first four volumes of *Sermons* (1744–1760) and his *Explanatory Notes upon the New Testament* (1755), formed the basis of all Methodist preaching.

The early Conferences also consolidated the organization of Methodism into a *connexion*, a network of societies served by lay preachers itinerating regularly on a circuit, or round, covering a district such as a county in tours lasting from four to six weeks, but also itinerating between circuits periodically—at first every three months, then every six, and eventually every year. Each year Wesley's own preaching and administrative journeys took him over most of England. In 1747 Ireland was added to his tour, and in 1751, Scotland. Wesley and his itinerant preachers developed a strong family identity among the societies.

This connectional unity became so strong that in 1749 Wesley published two sets of extracts from the minutes of his conferences, each with the same title—*Minutes of Some Late Conversations between the Revd. Mr. Wesleys and Others*—one summarizing Methodist teaching, the other Methodist organization. In effect they constituted a declaration that Methodism had become an established ecclesiastical body. Inevitably this process of consolidation aroused much criticism of Methodism: the preachers' teaching, so unfamiliar to non-Methodists, was incorrectly described as unorthodox; their vigor, warmth, and ebullience were pejoratively labeled "enthusiasm"; and Wesley's unconventional preaching in the open air and in other parishes, and, worse still, his authorizing laypeople to preach, were regarded by even sympathetic clergy as a grave breach of ecclesiastical order. Preachers and people were occasionally mobbed, but the somewhat quiescent church authorities took no concerted action.

The chief threat, indeed, came from within the movement. The people's desire to receive the sacraments from their preachers fed the preachers' natural ambitions to improve their status and to transform the society into a church. John Wesley was inclined to let things run their course, but the vehement opposition of his brother Charles led him to tighten the rein on his preachers, most of whom from 1752 onward signed agreements "never to leave the communion of the Church of England without the consent of all whose names are subjoined." Avowed separation from the church was narrowly averted at the Conference of 1755, when all agreed "that (whether it was *lawful* or not) it was no ways *expedient*." This deferred any open separation for almost thirty years.

Meanwhile, British and Irish immigrants brought Methodism to America, where it became so firmly rooted that Wesley responded to their plea for help by sending out matched pairs of itinerant preachers in 1769, 1771, 1773, and 1774, of whom by far the best known and most influential was Francis Asbury, who remained throughout the Revolutionary War (1775–1783). With some difficulty Asbury persuaded the American Methodists not to sever their ties with Wesley in their eagerness for religious independence, and thus Wesley himself was able to assist Americans in the birth of the first independent church within Methodism.

The year 1784 was "that grand climacteric year of Methodism." Aided by Dr. Thomas Coke, Wesley prepared a deed poll (in which one party binds himself or herself without reference to obligations undertaken by another) that legally defined the term *Conference,* and made that body heir to British Methodism after Wesley's death. Wesley also entrusted to Coke a major part in publishing a revision of *The Book of Common Prayer* for the use of American Methodists, and discussed with him a complementary plan for securing a threefold ministry in American Methodism. Already convinced that in any ecclesiastical emergency the power of ordination resided in presbyters, Wesley ordained two of his preachers, first as deacons and then as elders. With their assistance he then commissioned Coke as "superintendent" of the American flock, with instructions to share his new authority with Asbury upon his arrival in America.

At the Christmas Conference in Baltimore (1784–1785) with Wesley's blessing, a new denomination was launched, the Methodist Episcopal Church. In England Methodism still remained a society, governed by a presbyter of the Church of England and at least theoretically within the fold of that church. After Wesley's death in 1791, however, under the terms of his deed poll, the Conference of preachers became the ruling body, with a modified presbyterian system of government rather than the modified episcopalian polity that was being developed in America. Although some of Wesley's Anglican friends had occasionally referred to "the Methodist church" during his lifetime, not until 1893 did the class tickets indicating membership in the Wesleyan Methodist Society carry the word *church.*

When in 1739 Wesley had written, "I look upon all the world as my parish, " he was defending his disregard of ecclesiastical boundaries in Britain, but in fact he did also cherish a vision of a world renewed in the image of Christ, and was convinced that his liberal, pragmatic approach to theology and to churchmanship should make good missionaries of his people—as indeed it did. He heartily supported Coke's missionary plans, and a month before his death wrote to a native American preacher, "Lose no opportunity of declaring to all men that the Methodists are one people in all the world." Within a century after Wesley's death immigrants and missionaries from both sides of the Atlantic had planted Methodism on each continent and in almost every country.

Methodist missionary expansion during the nineteenth century varied little whether it came from the British or the American type of church polity, because polity was overshadowed by ethos, and the ethos sprang from Wesley, Methodists everywhere remained within a tightly knit *connexion* governed by a conference. They followed Wesley in assigning major responsibilities to laypeople, and were progressive in enrolling women as leaders, and even as preachers. They emphasized evangelical preaching and continued to experiment with an adventurous and flexible organization. While making good use of their rich heritage of Charles Wesley's hymns they observed those almost uniquely Methodist forms of worship, the watch-night, the covenant service, and the love-feast, as well as the close fellowship of the class-meeting and the bands, with their cherished tickets of membership. They constantly remembered their early rules, by "avoiding evil of every kind—especially that which is most generally practised," and by "doing good of every possible sort, and as far as is possible to all men."

It is true that the full appreciation of some of these features fell off even during the nineteenth century, and a few were almost forgotten in the twentieth, such as Wesley's constant charge, "Press on to perfection." Human frailty brought about fragmentation into many independent denominations, a process furthered during the twentieth century by the hiving off of national churches from the parent bodies.

The first major division in England, the Methodist New Connexion (1797), was a revolt against the autocracy of the leading Wesleyan preachers, but the Primitive Methodists (1811) and Bible Christians (1819), though also favoring more lay leadership, left because they wished to restore evangelism. The Wesleyan Methodist hierarchy came under increasing attack from 1849 onward in a disruptive pamphlet warfare that led to eventual democratic reforms at the cost of losing many thousands of members. Happily, some of these breaches were progressively healed through the formation of the United Methodist Free Churches in 1857, the United Methodist Church in 1907, and the Methodist Church in 1932.

In America, where membership had almost drawn level with that in the British Isles by Wesley's death, Methodism expanded and divided far more rapidly than in Britain during the nineteenth and twentieth centuries. The controversy over the institution of slavery and other disruptive forces similar to those in England were at work in America. Coke and Asbury had unsuccessfully sought to eradicate slavery from the Methodist Episcopal Church, but even in the abolitionist strongholds of New York and Philadelphia race remained an issue among Methodists. There, blacks forsook their second-class membership to form their own congregations, which eventually became the African Methodist Episcopal Church (1816) and the African Methodist Episcopal Zion Church (1820), with communities of 3.5 million and 1.2 million respectively, in the 1990s. In 1844 the whole Methodist Episcopal Church split north and south over the issue, though other factors were also at work, including varying views of the episcopacy. In 1870 the Methodist Episcopal Church South blessed the incorporation of their own black members into the Colored (now "Christian") Methodist Episcopal Church. Slavery was also a factor in the formation of the Wesleyan Methodist Connection (1843), which did not name itself a church until 1947, and which also sought a return to earlier Wesleyan evangelism and the abolition of the episcopacy. The Free Methodist Church (1860) arose after lengthy preliminaries from a widespread desire to recover Wesley's teaching upon Christian perfection. A similar emphasis within American Methodism upon the need to recover scriptural holiness led to the piecemeal formation of the Church of the Nazarene.

In American Methodism and its missions, as well as in the British Commonwealth, a measure of consolidation took place during the nineteenth and twentieth centuries, notably in the union of the northern and southern churches with the Protestant Methodists in 1939 to form the Methodist Church, which in 1968 united with the Evangelical United Brethren (itself a union of churches with a German-speaking background) to form the United Methodist Church, with a membership of eleven million out of a total world Methodist community of around fifty million. At the beginning of the twenty-first century the total world Methodist community numbered around thirty-five million.

These and other unions were consummated largely because of the coming together in Christian fellowship of representatives from dozens of autonomous Methodist churches and missions from all over the world, first decennially from 1881 in the Ecumenical Methodist Conference, then quinquennially from 1951 in the World Methodist Council. Welcome guests at these gatherings are representatives from churches where Methodism has subsumed its identity in an interdenominational union, such as the United Church of Canada (1925), the Churches of North and South India, the Uniting Church in Australia, or other such unions in Belgium, China, Ecuador, Japan, Pakistan, the Philippines, and Zambia. As an important element in the World Council of Churches, Methodism remains true to the spirit of its founder, who gloried in the catholicity of his early societies, open to persons of all creeds, and who firmly maintained, in spite of attacks by his critics, that "orthodoxy, or right opinions, is at best but a very slender part of religion."

SEE ALSO Asbury, Francis; Coke, Thomas; Wesley Brothers; Whitefield, George.

BIBLIOGRAPHY

A valuable summary of the history, doctrines, spread, activities, and leaders of Methodism in its many branches through more than two centuries can be found in *The Encyclopedia of World Methodism,* 2 vols., edited by Nolan B. Harmon (Nashville, 1974). The unplanned development of Methodism from a movement into a denomination is described by Frank Baker in *John Wesley and the Church of England* (Nashville, 1970). Fuller details of some British aspects of Methodism, especially in their later stages, are given in *A History of the Methodist Church in Great Britain,* 3 vols., edited by Rupert Davies and Gordon Rupp (London, 1965–1984), and the rise and development of the main stream in the United States is portrayed in *The History of American Methodism,* 3 vols., edited by Emory Stevens Bucke (Nashville, 1964). The latter work should be supplemented by Frank Baker's *From Wesley to Asbury: Studies in Early American Methodism* (Durham, N.C., 1976), which traces the transition of British Methodism to the American scene, and by Frederick A. Norwood's *The Story of American Methodism* (Nashville, 1974), which traces later developments in the history of the United Methodists.

New Sources

Craske, Jane, and Clive March, eds. *Methodism and the Future: Facing the Challenge.* New York, 2000.

Wigger, John H., and Nathan O. Hatch, eds. *Methodism and the Shaping of American Culture.* Nashville, 2001.

FRANK BAKER (1987)
Revised Bibliography

METHODIUS SEE CYRIL AND METHODIUS

MEYKAṆṬĀR

MEYKAṆṬĀR (thirteenth century CE), Tamil Śaiva Siddhānta author and theologian. Meykaṇṭār ("he who saw the truth") was the first of the four *santāna ācāryas* ("hereditary teachers," here referring to four successive theologians) of the Tamil Śaiva Siddhānta school of philosophy-theology. Originally called Svētaraṉam, Meykaṇṭār, who lived in Tiruveṇṇainallūr, received the name by which posterity recognizes him from his guru Parañcōti Muṉivar. Meykaṇṭār's prominence rests almost entirely on his composition of a single work, the *Civañāṉapōtam* (Skt., *Śivajñānabodha,* The understanding of the knowledge of Śiva). The *Civañāṉapōtam,* written in the early thirteen century, is held to be the *mutaṉūl* ("primary treatise") of the fourteen theological texts that have canonical status in Tamil Śaivism. These fourteen texts are collectively called the *Meykaṇṭaśāstra,* although Meykaṇṭār is the author of only one of the fourteen, but the fundamental one, the *Civañāṉapōtam.*

The *Civañāṉapōtam* consists of twelve Tamil sūtras along with two sets of glosses, the *cūttirakkaṇṇaḻivu* (the words of the sūtra divided into sentences) and the *cūrṇikai* (a brief gloss on the sentences setting forth their meaning in simple prose), as well as a commentary composed of articles (*atikaraṇam*), each consisting of a thesis *(mēṟkōḷ),* reason (*ētu*), and illustrative verses (*utāraṇam*). The twelve sūtras of the *Civañāṉapōtam* are also found in the *Rauravāgama,* one of the Sanskrit Āgamas also held sacred by Tamil Śaivas. Whether Meykaṇṭār translated the sūtras from Sanskrit into Tamil or the author of the *Rauravāgama* borrowed from the *Civañāṉapōtam* is difficult, if not impossible, to ascertain and is a subject about which there is no scholarly consensus. Suffice it to note here that possession of a Sanskrit Agamic prototype for the authoritative text is hardly surprising when one considers the concern of medieval Hindu sectarian schools to establish their legitimacy.

The *Civañāṉapōtam* is a highly systematic and logical presentation of basic Śaiva Siddhānta ideology. The first six sūtras establish the existence, attributes, and interrelations of the three fundamental components of Śaiva Siddhānta ontology: *pati* (the Lord, i.e., God, Śiva), *pacu* (the soul), and *pācam* (the bondage that enslaves souls and separates them from knowledge of God). Meykaṇṭār cites the fact that the world evidences intelligible processes of creation, maintenance, and dissolution to establish God's existence. God is claimed to be both immanent in souls and yet different from them. The soul's knowledge of reality, however, is clouded by its being conjoined with an innate impurity (*cakajamalam*, i.e., *āṇavamalam*, the basic component of *pācam*). But the soul can be illuminated by the Lord's grace and overcome its bondage. The soul is thus an entity that is defined by its relations—either to "bondage" (*pācam*), "impurity" (*malam*, i.e., the structure of finite, phenomenal existence), or to the Lord *(pati)*, who bestows divine knowledge and bliss. Specific aspects of the soul's realization of its *advaita* relation with *pati* are the subject of the final six sūtras of the *Civañāṉapōtam*. Here in germ are the basics of a Śaiva Siddhānta path of spiritual realization: the necessity of a guru who is free of bondage and hence manifests the Lord, the use of the five-syllabled mantra ("*nama śivāya*"), and above all the centrality of devotional love (*bhakti*; Tam., *aṉpu*) for God, and the value of associating with other *bhaktas* (devotees).

See Also Māṇikkavācakar; Umāpati Śivācārya.

Bibliography

The *Civañāṉapōtam* has been translated into English several times. Of these, the most complete, accurate, and accessible is *Śiva-ñāna-bōdham: A Manual of Śaiva Religious Doctrine*, translated and interpreted by Gordon Matthews (Oxford, 1948). Closely following the *Civañāṉapōtam* in its summary of the Śaiva Siddhānta is John H. Piet's *A Logical Presentation of the Śaiva Siddhānta Philosophy* (Madras, 1952). A valuable study of the entire canonical corpus of Śaiva Siddhānta theological texts, which also contains in appendices both the Tamil and Sanskrit sūtras of the *Civañāṉapōtam* and the *Rauravāgama* along with English translations, is Mariasusai Dhavamony's *Love of God according to Śaiva Siddhānta* (Oxford, 1971). A large volume on Śaiva Siddhānta thought, occasionally marred by a Protestant Christian bias but nonetheless still useful for its thoroughness and occasional insight, is H. W. Schomerus's *Der Çaiva-Siddhanta: Eine Mystik Indiens* (Leipzig, 1912).

New Sources

Muthupackiam, J. X. *Mysticism and Metaphysics in Saiva Siddhanta: A Study of the Concept of Self in the Sivajnanabodham of Meykantar Deva in Relation to the Mystical Experience of Appar.* New Delhi, 2001.

Glenn E. Yocum (1987)
Revised Bibliography

MIAO RELIGION See SOUTHEAST ASIAN RELIGIONS, *ARTICLE ON* MAINLAND CULTURES

MICAH (fl. eighth century BCE), or, in Hebrew, Mikhah; Hebrew prophet whose prophecy is recorded in the biblical *Book of Micah*. Although the *Book of Micah* employs a personal approach in which the prophet occasionally speaks directly in the first person to reveal his deep feelings (e.g., 1:8, 3:8 [citations herein follow the English version]), the prophet reveals neither his personal life nor his background, in contrast to many other prophets, including his contemporary, Isaiah. He does not even provide an account of his call. We know only his general period of time as stated in the superscription (1:1), which is derived from a later hand. There is also a reference to Micah's hometown, Moresheth (cf. Moresheth-gath, 1:14), which is located southwest of Jerusalem. Interestingly, this information is repeated later, in *Jeremiah* 26:18, demonstrating the strong impact of Micah's prophecy.

According to the superscription, the period of Micah's activity was during the time of Jotham, Ahaz, and Hezekiah, kings of Judah in the second half of the eighth century BCE. It was a politically stormy time dominated by the Syro-Ephraimite war and Assyrian military threats against Judah. Yet these major military events, which underlie Isaiah's prophecy, are not specifically addressed in Micah's speeches, for he was mainly concerned with the internal situation—the social and moral injustices of the rulers of Judah. Micah's attack on the false prophets (3:5–12) is noteworthy in that he was the first to devote an entire speech to the problem.

A large part of *Micah* concerns prophecies of salvation and the "new age." Many scholars consider the relationship between oracles of doom and prophecies of salvation to be mutually exclusive, and tend to distinguish between the oracles of doom, that is, the authentic Micah, and prophecies of salvation, which they consider later additions. As a rule, these scholars consider the major parts of chapters 1–3 (except, perhaps, 2:12–13) the core of Micah's own prophecy, with the remainder reflecting thinkers of later periods who were influenced by Micah (as in *Jer.* 26:18) and sought to update the outcome of the old prophecies.

This distinction between Micah and his later editors is based upon a particular modern scholarly understanding of the nature of the authentic prophecies. Stylistic and linguistic criteria, however, are not the decisive factors in determining the original text as opposed to additions. This distinction is based upon theme rather than stylistic literary analysis. We should, however, take into consideration the possibility that prophecies of judgment may mingle with oracles of salvation, that the prophet did not merely record his surroundings but also developed a specific perspective on the new age, which he sought to share with his audience. Micah's criticism of his present world leads to his prophecy of the new age, the period of peace and justice. A distinction between original prophecies of doom and supplementary prophecies of salvation would therefore be misleading.

Much has been written about the relationship between the two contemporaries, Micah and Isaiah, because of the similarity between the visions of the "new age" in *Micah* 4:1–5 and *Isaiah* 2:1–4 (or 5). Since Micah's vision is not in chapters 1–3 of *Micah,* which contain oracles of doom (considered to be the words of Micah himself), scholars tend to regard this vision as inauthentic. Isaiah's vision is likewise regarded as an addition, since it is a prophecy of salvation. It has been stated above, however, that the distinction between oracles of doom and prophecies of salvation may be an artificial one. Notice should be taken of Micah's conclusion: "For all the people walk each in the name of its god, but we will walk in the name of the Lord our God for ever and ever" (4:5, RSV). Insofar as this differs from Isaiah's emphasis on the universality and centrality of the mountain of God, the house of the God of Jacob, Micah's national approach here conveys a message that contrasts with Isaiah's universalism. Furthermore, Micah speaks specifically about the total destruction of Jerusalem (3:2; cf. *Jer.* 26:18), while Isaiah avoids such a description of the holy city. In this context we may also question Micah's criticism of the other prophets. For instance, when he condemns them for calling for peace (3:5), is he referring to Isaiah's call for peace during the Syro-Ephraimite war (*Is.* 7:4–9)?

There are no definite criteria for determining where Micah's various speeches begin and end in the text. He starts with the subject of Judah's military troubles, and then in chapter 2 presents a sharp social criticism of those who oppress the poor and take their houses and property. In chapter 3 this attack is addressed more directly to rulers who tyrannize their citizens. In 3:5–12, Micah admonishes the prophets for misleading the people concerning the political situation. The style of discourse of chapters 1–3 maintains the characteristic prophetic conception of cause and effect: that the political and military situation reflects social and moral misbehavior. Wars and political disasters do not occur in a vacuum: political events are initiated by God as a punishment; they are God's response to the moral misconduct of the rulers of Judah.

Micah 4:1–5 describes the new age, the period of peace, while 5:1–5 concentrates on the new ruler of Israel, a descendant of the house of David, who will come from the town of Bethlehem. At 5:9 a prophecy begins concerning the destruction of the state's symbols of power—the military horses, chariots, and fortresses—as well as the destruction of foreign religious idols. It prophesies a conflict between God and Israel in which God condemns Israel for its betrayal. The speech ends with a moral-religious revelation (6:6–8). The lament of 7:17 is followed by a prophetic liturgy (7:8–20), which concludes with God's praise and the assurance that God will continue to protect his people as he has done in the past.

Despite numerous textual difficulties, Micah's message is clear and precise, and he clarifies the role of the prophet:

> But as for me, I am filled with power, with the Spirit of the Lord, and with justice and might, to declare to Jacob his transgression and to Israel his sin. (3:8)

Above all, the book lucidly states the meaning of Yahvistic religion in terms of God's demands upon the worshipers. Micah stresses the elements of justice, love, and kindness as God's preference in worship (6:6–8).

Bibliography

Hillers, Delbert R. *Micah.* Philadelphia, 1984.

Mays, James Luther. *Micah: A Commentary.* Philadelphia, 1976.

Wolff, Hans Walter. *Mit Micha Reden.* Neukirchen, 1978.

Wolff, Hans Walter. *Micah the Prophet.* Philadelphia, 1981.

New Sources

Alfaro, Juan I. *Justice and Loyalty: A Commentary on the Book of Micah.* International Theological Commentary. Grand Rapids, Mich., and Edinburgh, 1989.

Jacobs, Mignon R. *The Conceptual Coherence of the Book of Micah.* Sheffield, U.K., 2001.

Luker, Lamontte M. "Beyond Form Criticism: The Relation of Doom and Hope Oracles in Micah 2-6." *Hebrew Annual Review* 11 (1987): 285–301.

McKane, William. *The Book of Micah: Introduction and Commentary.* Edinburgh, 1998.

Wessels, Wilhelm (Willie) J. "Conflicting Powers: Reflections from the Book of Micah." *Old Testament Essays* 10 (1997): 528–544.

Yehoshua Gitay (1987)
Revised Bibliography

MICHAEL CERULARIOUS See CERULARIOS, MICHAEL

MICHAEL PSELLUS See PSELLUS, MICHAEL

MICRONESIAN RELIGIONS

This entry consists of the following articles:

MICRONESIAN RELIGIONS: AN OVERVIEW

In 1838, the French explorer Dumont D'Urville divided up the Pacific into Polynesia, Melanesia, and Micronesia. Scholars since then have debated whether or not these three terms do justice to the diversity of cultures in these areas, especially in Micronesia, where the first settlers arrived at various times and brought with them different cultures and languages. The Micronesians' exposure to Western influences also varied. The people of the Marianas, for example, were Christianized by the Spanish by 1700 CE. The Caroline island of Ifalik, on the other hand, became Christian only after World War II.

When the missionary Luther Gulick arrived on the central Pacific island of Pohnpei in 1852 he found the native priests dying out, and their shrines, like the megalithic Nan

Madol, were almost abandoned. Populations were decimated by whaling ships that left behind diseases to which the local people had no immunity; the Caroline island of Kosrae, one of the hardest hit, was left without a population large enough to support elaborate priestly hierarchies and religious title holders. Western governments raced to the islands to claim their shares of the new colonies in the Pacific, and so Micronesia became a patchwork of Spanish, German, British, Japanese, and American trusteeships, protectorates, and colonies. In the twenty-first century all of the Micronesian islands except Guam, a U.S. territory, are independent.

Few of the "little islands" that give Micronesia its name were unified at the time of first contact. Kosrae was the only island with a centralized government under a single paramount leader, and the smaller islands sometimes had several chiefs. The geology of the islands varies greatly. Some, like Pohnpei, one of what are called the high islands, are volcanic with lush vegetation. Others are coral atolls of a few acres only a few feet above sea level. The Marshall Islands, for example, are made up of coral atolls and islands with a total dry land area of 74 square miles spread over 375,000 square miles of ocean. Kosrae, on the other hand, is a single high island of 42 square miles with its highest point, Mount Finkol, at 2,064 feet above sea level.

In spite of the diversity within Micronesia, its cultures and old religions demonstrate certain shared patterns. These patterns can be seen in three areas: the Micronesian conception of the cosmos, the spirit inhabitants of this cosmos, and the patterns of interaction between spirits and humans.

Why these common traits exist when the Micronesian islands were settled by different peoples who spoke different languages and were widely separated from each other isn't entirely clear. Certainly the fact that the Micronesians were and still are some of the Pacific's finest boatbuilders and navigators is part of the explanation; they had the technology to make the Pacific Ocean not an obstacle but a means of colonizing and trading over long distances. Evidence of traffic in precontact Micronesia includes a highly organized trading and exchange system called the *sawei* (basket) that joined the people of Yap and the central Caroline atolls, with the Ulithi islands as the intermediary. Pottery exchanges show that this system began in the seventh century CE.

THE MICRONESIAN COSMOS AND ITS SPIRITS. Their image of the cosmos allowed the Micronesians to explain how things work and why things happen (as is the case with the Polynesians and Melanesians). The cosmos defined the spheres of activity between spirits and humans. Within the cosmos are places for gods, ancestral spirits, and living humans. There are places where people go after death, places where the dead are put to various tests, and places where the living can interact with their deceased kin.

Most Micronesian views of the cosmos are of a sky world as an inverted bowl, with several layers populated by different categories of deities. The islands of Micronesia are seen as columns projecting up from the bottom of the sea, and the bottom of the sea has a trapdoor that opens not into an underworld but into an undersea world. This is where the people of some islands believe they do when they die.

Early ethnographers recorded descriptions and even collected drawings depicting the cosmos, including a surviving sketch made by a native of Puluwat in 1910. The inverted bowl is the most widespread image, but there are variations. In Pohnpei the vault of the sky was like the roof of a ceremonial meeting house. In the Marshalls there were four heavenly post-men who held up the heavens in each of the four cardinal directions. But as the post-men fell asleep the heavens at each corner collapsed, and then the vault of heaven became an inverted bowl. On the Kiribati atolls the cosmos are depicted as a gigantic clamshell that the god Naurea tried to pry open to let the light come in. He persuaded Riki to help him. Riki succeeded in opening the shell and was rewarded by losing his legs and becoming the eel or snake in the sky: the Milky Way.

Curiously the sun, moon, and stars—all important to navigators—are not of widespread importance in most Micronesian religions, with Kiribati the notable exception. Kiribati is influenced by Polynesian religions, where the sun and moon play prominent roles in myth and ritual. One also finds occasional myths about the sun and moon on Palau, and the constellations Antares and the Pleiades play a role in Marshallese mythology. In the Marshall Islands story, Liktanur, the mother of two brothers, asks the older brother Tumur (Antares) to take her along with him in a canoe race, but he does not want the extra weight. Jebro (Pleiades), the younger son, does take his mother, and as the race begins Liktanur opens a parcel and sets up the first sail and rigging. As Jebro begins to overtake his older brother, Tumur commandeers the sailing boat. But clever Liktanur keeps some of the rigging, and Tumur is unable to change course. Liktanur and Jebro finish the race first and hide in the bushes. Tumur lands and proclaims himself winner and chief. Then Liktanur and Jebro emerge from hiding, and Liktanur proclaims young Jebro the new chief.

This is what is known as a charter myth and is typical of Micronesian mythology. In this case it demonstrates the unwritten law that the rank of chief (*irooj, lerooj,* or *iroojlaplap*) is determined by the mother's lineage. This myth has been reinterpreted by contemporary Christians on the remote atoll of Ujelang, who see the rising of Jebro/Pleiades, which comes into view about the time of Christmas, as symbolic of Jesus' birth.

The people of Pohnpei have the same myth, which also has both political and religious meanings. A woman named Likitanir creates the starts. None of her children wants to listen to her, with the exception of the smallest one, Margiregir, who obeys her and takes her in his canoe. She teaches him sailing and proclaims him *nahnmwarki* (a paramount chief, the equivalent of *iroojlaplap* in the Marshalls). Margiregir becomes Margigi on Yap and is a mythic foundation for both the political and religious centers of Yap. This story, like many others, transcended the boundaries of ocean and language to become one of the common features of Micronesian mythology.

The spirit population. The spirit population of the cosmos exemplifies the Micronesian characteristic of great diversity with certain common features. Many of the islands use the same term to describe the myriad spirits in their cosmos: *énú,* or some cognate of this Chuukic term, which is applied to various kinds of spirits. Across Micronesia, these spirits fall into the following main categories:

- Sky gods, often called the great spirit. An example is the Chuukic Enúúnap. Frequently the sky god's son or brother, the spirit Luk or Nuuk (among other variations), works for the sky god.
- Patron deities. They may live in highest heaven but are still deeply involved in helping humans. They sometimes bring culture and technology, like Liktanur of the Marshalls, who taught humankind the all-important art of sailing.
- Ancestors of the family, the lineage, or the clan. These are the spirits who take possession of their living kin and offer advice, help, and predictions. The Micronesian attitude toward these spirits ranges from what we commonly refer to as ancestor worship to a veneration that is more akin to filial piety.
- Nature spirits (tolls, ogres, and wee people). These spirits are geographically bound to certain locations, like the reef spirits of the Chuuk Main Lagoon.
- Trickster spirits. The trickster is a common mythic symbol throughout Polynesia and Micronesia. He is Olifat (Wonofáát) in the Chuukic islands, Letau in the Marshalls, Nareau in Kiribati, and Maui in Polynesian Hawai'i. In some places he is pure trickster, the archetypal character who does everything wrong, breaks all the rules, and hops into bed with his brother's wife. In others he is cruel, and in many stories he kills one of his brothers. He can also be helpful: on some islands it is the trickster who brings fire to humankind. In general, he functions more as the central figure in a cycle of morality stories illustrating how not to behave than as a supernatural sanction against breaking cultural rules.

A further assortment of divinities does not fit into the above categories. Most cultures have a local deity whose activities overshadow all the others in importance. On the central Carolinian atoll of Ifalik this is Tilitur, who was sent by the high sky god Enúúnap to take care of the people of this atoll. Anthropologists just after World War II recorded the reverence the people of Ifalik showed for Tilitur and his interactions with them. He frequently possessed his chosen vehicles.

Two types of spirits are either rare or completely missing in Micronesia: an omnipotent and uncreated deity and a purely evil deity. The Micronesian pantheon generally lacks an uncreated creator of all things who existed before the universe and before other gods. Naurea of the Kiribati opens a cosmic clamshell to let light into the world, for example, but that world was already in existence. There is one known exception: ethnologist Wilhelm Müller recorded, and in 1917 published, a Yapese story about an uncreated deity who, merely by thinking, brought into existence the other deities, who in turn created islands, people, plants, and fish (p. 505). However, Dobbin, writing in 1996, found that no contemporary Yapese knew of this god, who was called Gavur li yel yel.

The Micronesian pantheon also lacks a genuinely omnipotent deity and an incarnation of evil like Satan or the devil in Western cosmology, despite the ideas of early Christian missionaries, who identified Enúúnap with the Judeo-Christian God and the trickster figures with Satan. Enúúnap, like Zeus or Jupiter in Greco-Roman mythology, is caught up in the foibles of his children and nagged by his wife. Whatever else he may be, he is not omnipotent. In the category of evil spirits, none is totally evil like the Christian Satan. The tricksters Letau, Nareau, Wonofáát, and Yalifath are a glorious mixture of evil, stupidity, and cleverness, acting at various times as gift givers, killers, and slapstick comics.

Another kind of spirit found only in rare instances occurs when a dead human being returns to possess the body of a living person. William Lessa (1961) traced one of the few examples to an infant boy from Ulithi named Marespa, born in the mid-nineteenth century. The infant's father was possessed by his deceased child, and the spirit of Marespa quickly inspired a cult for healing and curing that spread to other islands, including Yap, Ngulu, and the atolls south of Palau.

Roles in the spirit world. While it is possible to draw a genealogical chart of the spirits for most islands, who begat whom is notoriously inconsistent. The spirits' characteristics vary as well. Olifat (Wonofáát) is a trickster and sometimes a cruel spirit in eastern Micronesia, but on Yap he is Yelafath the Elder (a god who creates the other gods) and Yelafath the Younger (the trickster). This pattern also occurs in Kiribati, where one manifestation of Nareau is a creator and the other is the trickster. In Chuuk tradition, Luk and Lukenleng (or Nuuk and Nuukeyinen, literally "middle of heaven") are one and the same god, a god who is something of an heir apparent who does most of the work of Enúúnap. In Yap tradition, however, Lug (Luk) is the god of death who flies about snaring humans in his net, and Lukenlang is a different god.

Patron deities were active in the everyday work of craftspeople, healers, medicine makers, and navigators, and helped assure a bountiful harvest or successful fishing trip. The blending of religion and daily life involved more than just blessing a new canoe or house or praying for the safe return of the fleet. The famed navigators of old learned their craft through training filled with religious ritual. They were initiated into the profession with an elaborate ceremony and performed complex rituals before setting sail. In medicine the healing chants and formulas for making up medicines ultimately came from the spirits through dreams, possession and trace, or from an elder who passed on these spirit-given gifts.

The creator deities, the sky gods, had different ways of working with the cosmos and human beings. Some of the great sky gods were aloof from the lives of humankind, having finished their creating work and retired to the bliss of one of the high heavens. But in the Chuuk tradition the priest-chiefs (*itang*) invoked the sky gods Enúúnap and Luk as they led their men into battle. The Marshallese creation myth resembles the first chapters of *Genesis,* where God says, "Let there be . . ." and lo, there it is, only in this case the chief Marshallese sky gods send a divinity to earth to teach canoe building, sailing, and tattooing.

Pohnpei mythology offers an interesting contrast. The Pohnpei universe is created by divinities and humans working together. A supernatural octopus directs the first human settlers to the place where the rocks will be deposited to become Pohn-pei, literally "upon a stone altar"). The god Dau Katau confers the first title of Soumenlang on the priest at Salapwuk; this according to oral historian Bernart Luelen is the beginning of religion and the title system on Pohnpei. After the Sau Deleu dynasty was destroyed, the god Luk appeared in a canoe floating in the sky. The current priest-chief, Soukisenlang, and the ruler of Ant Island are brought to the canoe, and they talk with Luk. Together they determine the political structure of Pohnpei: autonomous states (*wehi*) each led by a paramount chief, the *nahnmwarki.*

The relative importance of each type of spirit varies from island to island, again following the Micronesian pattern of diversity and similarity. In the Chuuk Main Lagoon and nearby atolls the spirits of the ancestors were of primary importance. On nearby Pohnpei the high gods like Dau Katau or Luk were more important.

WHERE SPIRITS AND HUMANS MEET: PLACES. There is no doubt that Micronesians of old believed that the divine met the human at certain physical sites, and the belief in the sacred or taboo nature of some of these sites continues in the early twenty-first century.

Household shrines were common through much of Micronesia. In the eastern Chuuk-speaking islands hanging shrines or altars, often in the shape of miniature double-hulled canoes, provided a place for the spirits of the ancestors to be with their kin. Here offerings of flowers and food were made, and it was at the household shrine that the ancestor spirits could possess a living family member, enabling the possessed one, called the *wáátawa,* to answer questions in the voice of the spirit, predict events and even deaths, and give advice to the living.

Sacred places were often combined with living spaces. The Palauan *kerong* (a possessed and entranced diviner like the *wáátawa* of Chuuk) often conducted their rituals in part of their own house. The raised-rock platforms (*taliuw*) on Yap were both the sacred dwelling sites of the gods and the residence of priests. On Pohnpei a variety of natural rock formations were considered to be sacred sites where the gods gave the island its physical shape and its culture.

Sacred places were created in other ways. On Kiribati collections of ancestral skulls became a kind of portable shrine that the living talked to in their homes and took to dances in the giant meeting houses, the *maneba.* The cult of the skulls, as Sir Arthur Grimble called it, gave the character of a sacred spot to the place where the skulls were kept.

WHERE SPIRITS AND HUMANS MEET: RITUAL. Micronesians also sought interaction with the spirit inhabitants of the cosmos by means of ritual.

Household rituals. Probably the simplest and most widespread ritual around Micronesia was conducted in the family dwelling or boathouse and dedicated to the remembrance of deceased kin. Rituals were conducted at household shrines throughout Micronesia, even in places with gigantic cult centers like Kosrae's Lelu. On Nauru the household shrine was located at the center pole of the house, where gifts of food were placed for the ancestors (later replaced by Roman Catholic converts with a picture of Jesus). The hanging altar or shrine of the Chuukic-speaking islands, the *faar,* was basically a household shrine for the lineage. Flowers, wreaths, and food could be place in this hanging altar. In some areas the ritual was even simpler. On Palau the ancestor's betel nut bag (a purse holding the ingredients needed to chew betel nuts) might be hung on the wall of the house and offered a tidbit of food. The Kiribati kept their ancestors' skulls in the house and treated them quite informally, talking with them, offering them cigarettes, and blowing cigarette smoke into the skull.

Divination. Micronesians had a bevy of divination rituals to call on to help them make decisions and forecast the future. The simplest methods were perhaps not religious at all, but, like tarot cards, horoscopes, and palm reading, simply a way of probing into the unknown. Micronesian divination involved analyzing the number and sequence of knots made from fresh young palm fronds. Sometimes the palm knots were replaced by stones thrown on the ground. A Micronesian equivalent of tea-leaf reading analyzed the lines on the inside of a coconut shell. These were forms of do-it-yourself divination, although some people were known to be better at it than others.

Professional diviners worked in a variety of ways. The *kerong* of the Palauans might, for a price, offer to make predictions or answer questions in their own dwellings, from behind a screen, possessed by a spirit but apparently not in a trance. In some cases they had special huts next to their houses reserved for divining. Or they might rapidly chew and spit betel nut in order to stimulate a trance state, during which they spoke as a possessing spirit. Sometimes another person interpreted the words of the entranced diviner.

In some Palauan villages a god or goddess ruled the village, and the leading *kerong* passed along its decisions. At times these diviners or oracles became threats to the political chiefs. One of the few nativist movements in Micronesia involved a revival of the diviners' arts. In 1915 a *kerong* named Tamadad developed a syncretistic religion that combined elements of the old ecstatic rituals and healing and curing with Christian elements. The religion, known as Modekngei, still exists.

Ecstatic rituals. In Micronesia divination ritual leads logically to ecstatic ritual, which involves trances or altered states of consciousness that are often interpreted as possession. Trances or possession can be found in the past or present culture of almost every atoll or island of Micronesia. The priests at the great cult centers on Pohnpei and Kosrae used trances in divining rituals. The *ibonga* of Kiribati, whom Sabatier variously described as soothsayer, magician, divine, doctor, prophet, miracle worker, and charlatan, used trance. On the atoll of Ifalik, women who fell into trances were often the inspiration for new songs; the same was true of certain people on Yap.

The best-recorded tradition of trance and possession is on the Chuukic-speaking atolls and especially in the Chuuk Main Lagoon. Ancestor spirits were believed to descend onto the shoulders of a living relative and possess them. Those chosen as vessels by the ancestors were called the *wáátawa* or *wáánaanú*, literally "the canoe of the spirit." This possession did not happen automatically, however, and there was often speculation at the wake and burial about whether the deceased would be a helping spirit or a harmful one. The hope was that the spirit would descend from the hanging shrine (*faar*) and possess one of the living kin, who would become the *wáánaanú* for the family or lineage and offer valuable advice to the living. Some reports indicate that this tradition is still alive on certain atolls, but by the end of World War II the *wáánaanú* as an official status within the community was rare.

What did continue in Chuuk communities is a more voluntary form of spirit possession and trance, especially among young girls. The signs of an altered state are clearly present in the transformation of the individual's persona. Dobbin has argued that the possession trance is a culturally sanctioned way for young females to protest problems, especially family problems that their cultural status prohibits them from otherwise confronting. If a girl is possessed by her mother or grandmother, the matrilineal Chuuk social system allows the senior woman to berate male family members. Contemporary possession trance is reported in other Micronesian islands, but it is rare. The Chuuk case is a classic example of continuity and change in Micronesian ritual.

Funeral rituals. Funeral rituals vary throughout the islands of Micronesia. The wake and burial rituals on Palau focused on the transfer of the deceased's title (if he or she was a titleholder) and determination of why the person died. The leading women of the group, which might be a clan, extended family, or village, gathered together, and one woman held a bouquet of *sis* branches (*Cordyline fruticosa*). The women would shout out potential reasons for the death, and if the *sis* bouquet shook, this indicated that the correct cause had been found. Sometimes someone known to be good at this type of divining was invited to the ceremony. Early reports indicated that the woman holding the branches was believed to be possessed by the deceased's spirit, but the evidence is vague. Palauan funerals may still feature trances without possession, as they did in the past.

Burial rituals also vary greatly from island to island. On Yap the dead are considered a source of spiritual pollution, and the immediate kin leave the deceased's house as quickly as possible. They may remain in seclusion and eat a restricted diet for as long as a hundred days. In some areas upper-caste people are buried by landless lower-class people who are beholden to them (this tradition is still observed on Yap). In the past burial was often at sea among the Chuuk, while burial on the family homestead was common on Kosrae. In some places the interment of the body in the ground was temporary, and the bones and skulls were exhumed and given places of honor, often in the home. In some of the matrilineal societies where Christian cemeteries have replaced older burial sites, some of the old ways continue.

The rituals of medicine. Traditional or local medicine is still commonly used in Micronesia, as it is in many parts of the Pacific. How much of it is tied to spirit beliefs and ritual is impossible to gauge. On islands that are overwhelmingly Christian, nobody wants to be known as a pagan, so the use of traditional healing rituals is often disguised. The physical ingredients of a medicine may be used without the traditional chants or with the chants mumbled. Dobbin, however, describes how the mother in a devout Christian family was in the process of becoming a medicine expert and received curing chants in a dream.

The local medicine system may begin with an informal diagnosis of an illness, but there is also a more formal system in which a diagnostic specialist uses divination to determin which spirit power is responsible for an illness. In some cases another specialist will then be called in who has the means to cure the illness. Sometimes these are one and the same person. The curing ceremonies are generally public events that require the presence of family and friends. The location of medicinal plants and details of the recipes, however, may be kept secret.

Occasionally a medicine specialist in Chuuk will receive chants and recipes for medicines while in a trance state, but the more common source of local medicine, as it is called now, is through dreams sent by spirits. One can learn the specifics from an elder or even buy the formula, but ultimately medicine, especially on Chuuk and Pohnpei, comes from the spirits.

Fertility and increase rituals. This category includes rituals designed to help mothers with pregnancy and childbirth and to insure a good harvest and a bountiful catch from the land and sea. On Yap the *tamarong* (priest, magician, conjuror, or diviner) visited the pregnant woman at distinct periods during pregnancy and offered ritual words or chants (*pig*) to insure the healthy birth of a child. Chuuk had elaborate rituals to ensure the fertility of crops, probably some of the most elaborate among the smaller Micronesian communities.

Breadfruit was the staple starch of the Chuukic world, and the spirits of the breadfruit were believed to live in the mystic south of the cosmos. A breadfruit caller would beckon the spirits to come to the community's breadfruit trees so that the flower would blossom and produce large breadfruits. So important was the caller that his larynx or entire body might be mummified when he died, lest he take the breadfruit spirits with him when he went on to Ewúr, the mystic home of the breadfruit gods and goddesses.

As a breadfruit season approached, the caller began his rounds, blowing on a conch horn and calling the spirits or souls of the trees to come and blossom. Some of these prayers and petitions are still remembered on Puluwat, where the caller was a ritual specialist of high honor. He petitioned, and he begged, and he prayed. He assembled the leading men of the island in a procession. The caller led the way, chanting, and the followers responded as he waved a spear-like rod from side to side. They stopped at each complex of extended family residences, where the caller plunged the rod into the ground and put some of the earth into a basket. He deposited the earth in his own land, and repeated the ritual around the atoll.

The incarnate breadfruit god, a conger eel called the *Hewanu,* appeared on the shores of Puluwat every few years. When one arrived, the breadfruit caller took the eel, wrapped in mats, to a meeting house; only the caller (or priest, as the early reports call him) knew what the sacred eel was saying. The eel's presence sometimes meant that one of the select few who traditionally took care of the eel was going to die, and the ritual became a dirge for the coming death. In other cases the eel was checking up on the Puluwatese, and inquired of the breadfruit caller as to how hard they were working. The eel was put on a special platform bedecked by the women with sweet-smelling wreaths of flowers, and the men brought coconuts as offerings. At first all could come and pay their respects to the breadfruit god, later only men were allowed, and finally only the select few who served the eel god maintained the vigil. Eventually the eel was returned to the sea.

The eel was an important symbol throughout Micronesia. The Kosraean breadfruit goddess, Sinlanka, was symbolized by an eel, and the grand ritual at Pohnpei's Nan Madol included the sacrifice of a turtle to a ravenous moray eel. Myths abound on Pohnpei about the smaller freshwater eels as well.

The grand rituals at Nan Madol and Lelu. Nan Madol at Pohnpei and Lelu at Kosrae were elaborate stonework constructions that functioned as the residence of the leading political authorities and groups of hierarchically ranked priests, and also served as ceremonial centers.

Kosrae had a centralized chief or king, the *tokosra,* and several priesthoods, each dedicated to a leading deity such as Sinlanka. Some priests stayed in the ritual and political center of Lelu at Kosrae. Others lived at shrines scattered across the island, and on certain occasions these rural priests led processions into Lelu. One of the most important rituals they led celebrated the coronation of the king and his queen.

Nan Madol was the residence of the leading chief of the Sau Deleur dynasty with a section for the attending priesthoods. Next to the Sau Deleur residence and court was the tiny islet of Idet, where a turtle was sacrificed to a sacred moray eel. To what extent Nan Madol controlled all of Pohnpei is debatable, but other ritual centers with priest-chiefs continued to exist as independent entities.

The turtle–eel ceremony may have been the culmination of a longer, more ancient ritual. Its symbolism is debated. Rufino Mauricio, a Pohnpeian archaeologist and specialist in oral histories, has suggested that the Nan Madol ritual combines an older ritual focused on sacred sites with newer rituals worshipping living animals like the eel. Another interpretation focuses on the meaning of *wehi,* the turtle, which is also the name for the main sections of Pohnpei, and says that three *wehis* sacrificed their independence and autonomy to the ravenous appetite of the Sau Deleur dynasty.

Neither interpretation is compelling, especially since the ritual outlived the fall of the Sau Deleurs and then was stopped by one of the paramount chiefs (*nahnmwarki*) of the Nan Madol area after a priest killed the eels because he did not get his share of the turtle meat. After about 1860 the priesthoods disappeared along with the animal sacrifices. Nan Madol is now abandoned, a monument to the Pohnpeian fear of centralization.

The political structure after the fall of the Sau Deleurs mirrors a shift in the evolution of Pohnpeian religion. One or two priestly centers of worship predate Nan Madol and the Sau Deleur dynasty, with a high priest who also was the political chief of the area. At least one of these the high priests and chiefs, the *soukisenleng* (literally "the master of the part of heaven"), eventually joined the post-Sau Deleur structure of autonomous, paramount chiefs (*nahnmwarkis*) and took or was given the highest title of *nahnmwarki.* His priests took lesser noble titles. The ruler or *nahnmwarki* of the southern *wehi* of Wene is still called the *soukisenleng,* and the other nobles of Wene still have the old priestly titles. Mauricio judges this shift to be an early form of secularization. Of the priesthoods only the titles remain, although it is not known when they lost their religious functions.

Some elements of the old priestly rituals are maintained in the ceremonial houses (*nahs*) of the *nahnmwarkis.* Ritual offerings of *sakau* (kava, *Piper methysticum*) are made to the god as they were in days of old. *Sakau* offering is part of a formal reconciliation ritual led by the chiefs; it is now incorporated into the Roman Catholic sacrament of forgiveness. In modern times *sakau,* which is made into a slightly narcotic drink, has been secularized, and can be enjoyed in *sakau* bars.

The dance as sacred ritual. On some islands the dance tradition has all but disappeared. On Guam a so-called ritual fire dance is performed by Filipino entertainers for visiting tourists at the Guam Hilton hotel. Palau is struggling to revive its dance traditions. But in two areas the dance needs no revival: on Kiribati and on Yap. The extent to which Kiribati dance is considered holdy or sacred is uncertain, although the dancers of old were thought to be inspired by the spirits. But on Yap the sacred dance still exists. Sometimes the men or women of a village perform the dance for their village, with no outsiders allowed to attend. Yap is now largely Roman Catholic, and the sacred dance is regularly performed as part of the liturgy. At the adoration of the cross on Good Friday, the women perform the mourning dance and dirge; at the Easter vigil, the hymn of the resurrection, the *Exultat,* is danced. At the ordination of a priest or deacon, the dancing comes after the Roman Catholic ritual. As one Yapese remarked after the Catholic ceremony was finished, "now the real liturgy begins."

In the late nineteenth century on the Mortlock islands of Chuuk, a strong outbreak of dancing occurred. Protestant missionaries, fearing both its inspiration by the spirits and also what they saw as its obscene forms, thought this a return to the old pagan ways, although the German colonial authorities encouraged it. Different denominations reacted differently to the old ways. On Kosrae and in the Marshalls, where Boston-based Congregationalism became the dominant Christian denomination, the bare-breasted women were required to wear the all-encompassing muumuus. In Yap, the Catholic services are filled with bare-breasted women and men in scanty wraparounds that cover only the genitals.

WHAT HAPPENS AT DEATH. An almost universal Micronesian belief is that the soul and/or the spirit leave the body three or four days after death. On some islands, like the Marshalls, early writers could not find a clear notion of soul among the locals, probably because the Micronesians did not distinguish between soul and spirit, or perhaps because the spirit functioned like the soul of Western traditions. The people of Yap and Chuuk believe in two spirits within a single individual: a good-spirit soul, *ngúnúyéech,* and an evil-spirit soul, *énúngngaw.* The good spirit was a spiritual double of the living person and hence could appear to the living. The Chuukese also had a separate word for soul, *gnúnú.*

Another almost universal belief in Micronesia is that a departed spirit can be helpful to its living kinfolk. This is the basis for what early writers called ancestor worship, but the term is misleading. Although the deceased might be put in the same general category as the sky deities, for example, in other cases, such as on Chuuk, the good *ngúnúyéech* might become an *énú,* which is the global Micronesian term for gods and goddesses, patron deities, and harmful land or sea spirits. Various islands also had a combination term that identified the *énú* as a spirit that originated as a human being (*énúúyaramas* in Chuukese).

Widespread ambivalence among the living regarding recently deceased kin is common throughout Micronesia. On the one hand, people hope the deceased will be helpful to his or her relatives, and even take possession of one of the living who will function as the family or lineage medium. On the other hand, they may burn the possessions of the deceased, hoping that the spirit will climb on the column of smoke away from the living and up to the heavens.

Few Micronesian islands seem to have had a version of eschatological judgment, where one's accumulated merit is rewarded or punished at death, although this is debated. Various reports, like Father Cantova's interviews in the 1720s with Chuuk-speaking atoll dwellers who were stranded on Guam or records from the Russian expedition of 1927 speak of an afterlife involving reward and punishment. Spiro's investigations on Ifalik found a highly developed morality, but the sanctions for enforcing the morality came from the chiefs, not the gods or the religious specialists. He saw no evidence of an afterlife of reward and punishment.

The destination of the dead is often determined by a test rather than the record of a good life. Pohnpeians at death came to a swinging bridge over water. If the deceased could not sing well, the swinging bridge dumped the poor singer into the "place of no return." Yapese could not ascend to the sky layer unless their ears were pierced. On Ulithi a bad person might be destined for a sticky garbage pit. Many traditions include a long journey to the place where the deceased would ultimately live, sometimes on the mystic island of Matang. It was also commonly believed that one went to a part of the cosmos associated with one's occupation, like the deceased breadfruit callers who went to the south part of the heavens where the spirits of the breadfruit came from.

THE PRACTITIONERS OR LEADERS OF THE OLD RELIGIONS. Religious leaders in Micronesia generally performed a combination of roles, including soothsayer, magician, divine, doctor, prophet, and miracle worker. The biggest problem in describing them is to find an appropriate word for, say, the Palauan *kerong,* the Chuuk breadfruit caller (*sowuyótoomey*), or the Marshallese diviner and magician (*drijikan*). Three of the high islands, Kosrae, Pohnpei, and Yap, had distinct hierarchies of priests. The Kosraean and Pohnpeian priests disappeared in the nineteenth century, and the last practicing Yap priest (*peq'taliuw*) performed his final rituals, unattended by anybody, after World War II. Saipan or Guam had no religious hierarchies, and the Palauan *kerong* generally worked alone. The religious status these leaders hold is given or inherited, not chosen or earned. The spirits have selected these people to receive their spiritual gifts.

Many religious practitioners were part-time functionaries, as is still the case for the Chuuk healers, the *sowusáfey,* and for the Yap masters of the weather, the *tamarong.* Certain practitioners were also craftspeople, experts, and possessors of exotic lore. Classic examples include navigators and the priest-chiefs (*itang*). The navigators had to have technical skills as well as spirit-given knowledge and power to succeed. The priest-chiefs had the technical knowledge to plan wars and also the power of the spirits to lead battles with success. The *itang* were actual combatants poised ahead of their own battle lines. In a sea battle they stood in the lead canoe, blowing the conch horn, waving a spear, leading the men in battle chants and prayers to the war god. When the German colonial powers banned warfare, the *itang* became the respected repositories of traditions, old customs, and lineage histories. Functionally speaking, the *itang* are now the equivalent of the Pohnpeian oral historians, the *soupoadoapoad.* In the twenty-first century about five or six *itang* are reportedly still working in the Chuuk Lagoon. They seem to be confined to the eastern Chuukic islands. The names of some of the *itang* training schools are the same as the navigators' schools in the central Chuuk atolls, where perhaps the navigators were also *itang.* The priest-chiefs found it valuable to know both the skills of the *itang* and of the navigators.

THE UNSOLVED DISTINCTIONS AND TERMS. Many of the neat terminological distinctions made by scholars about the Pacific religions cannot be sustained in Micronesia, including the distinction between magic and religion. When the Ulithian masters of the weather gather near the ocean side of the lagoon and make their pleas and petitions to the gods, is this magic or religion? Some of the chants certainly are petitions and not an attempt to manipulate the powers of the cosmos. Some priests also worked as diviners, and some of the breadfruit callers functioned like priests when they recalled the legends of the breadfruit spirits and petitioned the breadfruit spirits to come and bless the trees with a good harvest.

Every Micronesian culture has words for taboo (forbidden) and sacred (holy). On the islets of the Kwajalein atoll, the places where the chiefs were buried and medicine was made were called sacred, but they could just as easily have been called taboo. And the *taliuw*—the platforms used by the Yap priests of old, which had a shrine for the site's god of goddess on top of the platform—were sacred because of the deity dwelling there, and access was prohibited to anyone but the priests, making them both holy and taboo. Many English translations or glosses for Micronesian words and religious terms are less that perfect fits. Their meanings were frequently distorted by observers who did not understand the theology or cosmology they were reporting.

WAS THERE A SINGLE MICRONESIAN RELIGION? The pre-Christian religions of Micronesia underwent a long period of evolution and change. Pohnpei is the best example of the shift in religion from the cult centers of the priest-chiefs to hierarchical priesthoods at various sites, followed by an attempt at centralization under the Sau Deleurs and new rituals involving the sacrifice of living beings, and ultimately the secularization of priestly titles in the polity of the autonomous states (*wehi*) under paramount chiefs, the *nahnmwarkis.*

Rituals and religious organizations varied from region to region. Patterns such as the prominent role of divination and the widespread use of trance and possession cut across the diversity in Micronesia, although they are carried out differently in different regions. Certain types of gods are universal: sky and creator divinities, patron gods and goddesses, evil spirits bound to certain locations on land and sea, and of course ancestors. The main categories are the same, but the emphasis given to various gods varies greatly. A test or trial to determine who goes where in the cosmos after death is widespread, and the general lack of eschatological judgment to allot rewards or punishment in the afterlife is a common feature across Micronesia.

Because of the regional differences fostered by geographic distances as well as varying degrees of influence from adjacent culture areas, an overall character cannot be assigned to Micronesian religion. It is a mélange of many elements: celestial and terrestrial deities, nature spirits, demons, and ancestral ghosts, with a strong infusion of magic, taboo, and divination. No one trait dominates the system, but many common patterns run through the overarching diversity.

BIBLIOGRAPHY

Aoyagi, M. "Gods of the Modekngei Religion in Belau." In *Cultural Uniformity and Diversity in Micronesia,* edited by Iwao Ushijima and Ken-ichi Sudo. Osaka, 1987. Burrows, Edwin G., and Melford E. Spiro. *An Atoll Culture: Ethnography of Ifaluk in the Central Carolines.* New Haven, Conn., 1953. A classic Freudian interpretation and good description of the workings of religion in the Chuuk-speaking atolls. Dobbin, J. D., and F. X. Hezel. "The Distribution of Spirit Possession and Trance in Micronesia." *Pacific Studies* 19 (1996): 105–148. Erdland, August. *The Marshall Islanders: Life and Customs, Thought and Religion of a South Seas People. Translation in part by Richard Neuse.* New Haven, Conn., 1961. In *Die Marshall-Insulaner: Leben und Sitte, Sinn und Religion eines Südsee-Volkes.* Münster, 1914. The best study of religion on the Marshall Islands. Goodenough, Ward H. *Under Heaven's Brow: Pre-Christian Religious Traditions in Chuuk.* Philadelphia, 2002. Limited to the religion of the Main Chuuk Lagoon. Grimble, Arthur. *Tungaru Traditions: Writings on the Atoll Culture of the Gilbert Islands.* Honolulu, 1989. Grimble, Arthur, and Grimble, Rosemary. *Migrations, Myth, and Magic from the Gilbert Islands: Early Writings of Sir Arthur Grimble.* London, 1972. Hanlon, David L. *Upon a Stone Altar: A History of the Island of Pohnpei to 1890.* Honolulu, 1988. Rich data about the evolution of religion on Pohnpei. Kubary, Jan S. "Die Religion de Palauer." In *Allerlei aus Volks- und Menschenkunde,* edited by Adolf Bastian. Berlin, 1888. A 1969 translation is located at the University of Hawaii's Pacific Collection. Kubary's article on the religion of the Palau is short by highly detailed. Lessa, William A. *Tales from Ulithi Atoll: A Comparative Study in Oceanic Folklore.* Berkley, 1961. Lessa, William A. *Ulithi: A Micronesian Design for Living.* New York, 1966. The best analysis of the folklore of the Chuuk-speaking islands and atolls. Mahony, F. *A Trukese Theory of Medicine.* Ph.D. diss., Stanford University, 1970. Lucid analysis of the role of medicine in the Chuuk-speaking isles. Mauricio, R.ufino. *Ideological Bases for*

Power and Leadership on Pohnpei, Micronesia: Perspectives from Archaeology and Oral History. Ph.D. diss., University of Oregon, 1993. Müller, Wilhelm. *Yap.* Hamburg, 1917–1918. Parmentier, Richard J. *The Sacred Remains: Myth, History, and Polity in Belau.* Chicago, 1987. Parmentier, Richard J. "Transactional Symbolism in Belauan Mortuary Rites: A Diachronic Study." *Journal of the Polynesian Society* 97, no. 3 (1988): 281–312. Sabatier, Ernest. *Sous L'Equateur du Pacifique: Les Isles Gilbert et la Mission Catholique.* Paris, 1939. Reprinted as *Astride the Equator: An Account of the Gilbert Islands,* translated by Ursula Nixon. Melbourne, 1977. Sarfert, Ernst G. "Kosrae: Results of the South Sea Expedition." In *Kusae,* edited by Ernst Sarfert. Hamburg, 1919–1920. A translation from the German by Elizabeth Murphy is located at the Pacific Collection of Hamilton Library, University of Hawaii at Manoa, 1919. The only extensive ethnography of the old religion. Tobin, Jack A. *Stories from the Marshall Islands.* Honolulu, 2002.

WILLIAM A. LESSA (1987)
JAY DOBBIN (2005)

MICRONESIAN RELIGIONS: MYTHIC THEMES

Micronesian myths (as distinguished from folktales) have been primarily the domain of clan elders and sometimes of trained specialists, who cite them in regard not only to community land claims, rights, values, authority, and prestige but also to functions of deities, sequences of rulers, and origins of place-names. On Chuuk, in the Caroline Islands, the specialists *(itang)* narrate myths according to the practice of the school that has trained them; they observe taboos, and they speak a secret jargon consisting of standard words with altered meanings, archaic expressions, and words spoken backward. On Pohnpei, also in the Carolines, the sacred narratives, called "establishing the foundation," tend to be organized into a cultural and historical developmental sequence about the origins of physical objects and of society and about migrations, wars, and religion; the narratives also include songs that are based on myths. In the Marshall Islands, *rebwebwenato* (storytellers) are the repositories of oral narratives that explain the origins of physical reality as well as the human and spiritual worlds. The Kiribati and Banaba Islanders systematize their sacred narratives so that they begin with creation, continue with traditions about the migrations of clan ancestors from Samoa and about their settlement and experiences in the Kiribati, and usually end with the narrating clan elder's genealogy.

CREATION AND COSMOGONIC DEITIES. Even within the same archipelago or on the same island, diversity and contradiction characterize the myths about the origins of the world, the pantheon, the islands, living beings, and customs. In the Carolines, for example, the functions of named gods often shift from island to island. However, a persistent Micronesian theme is that a preexistent god or goddess created and generated everything or delegated all or part of the work to newly created subordinates.

According to the Jesuit missionary Diego Luis de Sanvitores, who wrote between 1668 and 1672, the Chamorros of Guam believed that parentless Puntan and his unnamed sister lived before the earth and sky existed. Concerned for the welfare of humankind, which was as yet uncreated, Puntan at his death gave all his powers to his sister, enabling her to fashion the earth and sky from his breast and back, the sun and moon from his eyes, and the rainbow from his eyebrows.

On Chuuk, the Carolinian earth mother is replaced as the primal deity by Enuunap (or Anulap, great spirit). Enuunap either creates the world himself or has Nikowupwuupw (or Ligoupup, bearer or nurturer)—his wife, whom he made from his blood—do it. Their children commit incest and, along with a girl who is born from a boil that afflicts Enuunap, found the clans, for which Nikowupwuupw establishes social rules and to whom she gives healing medicines. Faraulep Islanders state that Solal, a god who was half man and half fish, planted his staff in the primeval sea; it grew mightily, after which his brother Aluelap, who was also half man and half fish, climbed it to sprinkle down earth and so make land. Aluelap now rules the sky while Solal rules the sea and the district under it.

In the Marshall Islands, parentless Lowa is said to have glanced down and murmured until a reef, islands, plants, and a white tern rose from the primeval sea. The tern then created the sky by flying back and forth as if weaving a spiderweb. Lowa's commands produced deities, each with specific duties. A couple born from a blood tumor on his leg had two children who tattooed nearly every living being. Because the sky rested on people's heads, two maternal nephews of Iroojrilik (god of the west and of reproduction), netted it and raised it by flying about in the same way as had the tern. His brother, Lomotal, created the seas, lagoons, fish, and seabirds in the same way with his voice.

The myths of the Kiribati show much Polynesian influence; they poetically and metaphorically elaborate the themes of creation from a person's body, of the planted staff, of divine incest, and of sky raising. They may indeed have a broader base in ancient Austronesian culture. Their primordial deity, Na Areau (Na Areao or Nareau), may be not only the creator but also a world transformer, shape-shifter, and trickster, or there may be two Na Areaus, an elder who creates the world and a younger who puts the world in order. Although Na Areau's name means "Sir Spider," the Kiribati rarely think of him as such. Na Areau brooded alone on the rock-hard carapace of the undifferentiated universe, called "the darkness and the cleaving together." With his potent staff he penetrated its hollow interior, where, some say, the last child of Rock and Nothingness (who were the offspring of Sand and Water) was Na Areau the Younger. The elder Na Areau then vanished to leave the work to the younger, who, after naming and activating the preexistent, recumbent Fools and Deaf Mutes, had them free and raise the carapace of the universe, which became the sky.

In one version, Na Areau the Younger took the eyes of the elder Na Areau to form the sun and the moon, his brains to make the stars, and his spine for the Ancestral Tree on Samoa, a land that Octopus and Wave had formed. Humanlike and nonhumanlike deities, male and female, grew happily on and under the tree, each in his or her place, until Red-tailed Tropic Bird, who lived at the crest of the tree, defecated on those below. Na Areau then burned the tree, forcing the ancestors to seek new homes in the Kiribati, which had been created by Na Areau's commands (or other means). Red-tailed Tropic Bird then settled in Makin, where it ate people until the ever-benevolent Titua-bine, whose pet it was, ordered it killed. Red-skinned men grew on what had been its pandanus perch, and women grew on the coconut tree that had been planted by the goddess on her pet's grave. These newcomers (both male and female) became chiefs in the local assembly house. Other Kiribati also have local ancestral trees that have sprung from an ancestor's grave.

Some Kiribati replace Na Areau in his role as the transformer with Auriaria, son of Tituabine and Tabakea (hawksbill turtle), who are sister and brother born as a result of Earth and Sky rubbing together. According to this alternative version, Na Areau sprang from Tabakea's head. When Auriaria, having directed the separation of Earth and Sky, struck Heaven with the staff given him by Tabakea, the islands on top of Heaven tumbled upside down into the sea with Tabakea under Ocean Island. Then Auriaria planted his staff on Samoa, which he had raised from the sea, so that the staff could grow into the Ancestral Tree. Later he married Na Areau's daughter, whose descendants now live in the Kiribati.

The high god who had been described in most detail, Enuunap of the Chuuk area, lives in a mansion, one part for himself, the other for his ten siblings. Flounder, who has both eyes on the same side, guards Enuunap; while Sandpiper, on the clashing rocks at Enuunap's door, shrieks as souls of the dead try to enter, allowing only the worthy to pass safely between the rocks. The now aged, white-haired, long-breasted, weak, and virtually inactive god has two men to raise his eyelids so that he can see; they also open his mouth and raise his upper lip so that he can eat. Like Puntan, Enuunap does not receive worship. Nonetheless, he is omniscient, the creator, the ruler of the pantheon, and with his brother Semenkooror (Father of Determining), he is the god of wisdom, the greatest *itang*. Among the high gods there are others of similar inactivity.

The Ifaluk high god Aluelap's only activity is to advise his son Lugeilang (middle of heaven), who raises Aluelap's eyelids to get his attention. Yet there are also high gods who actively help people. Yalafath of Yap, a most helpful deity, had Dessra, the thunder god, bring people fire; Yalafath also sent his wife as a frigate bird to scout a flooded island's needs, and once, after resuscitating a dead boy, he gave the boy and his mother sand to form islands and seedlings to plant.

HUMAN ANCESTORS. Except in those Micronesian mythic traditions in which the primal deity and his or her spouse have children, it is usually unclear how the first people originated. Rather, attention is paid to particular individual mythic figures, male or female, and the role of the opposite sex is often denied. Husbandless females, human or animal, bear human beings and animals and so establish clans. Children also emerge from parts of the body or from maggots on the body of a deity who is more often male than female. Even trees bear people, as in the Kiribati, and in some traditions a tree growing from a person's head splits open to release children. In one story the earthly parentage of a clan's female ancestor is denied when she, a fingertip-size baby, falls from heaven.

A female animal ancestor often becomes her clan's totem. In one of several variations on the "swan maiden" theme, a Yap man, by hiding the fins of a dolphin girl who came ashore to dance, captures and marries her. Years later, on finding her fins, she leaves her human family to return to the sea, and her daughters establish the Dolphin totemic clan. Occasionally a totem animal is helpful, as in the Pohnpei story in which stingrays blanket the sea, tossing a disrespectful minor chief from one to another until they finally kill him for sending their totem descendant, the king, a pregnant woman's corpse instead of the bananas he had requested.

Many traditions include the tale of an animal mother's beautiful daughter who marries a king who has never seen his mother-in-law. For example, in one version Good Lizard makes channels on Pohnpei Island as she crawls to visit her daughter, who was married to the king, holder of the dynastic title Sau Deleur (Lord of Deleur). When the husband brings his mother-in-law her food, she tells him not to look at her. He disobeys, panics, and sets fire to the enormous guesthouse he had prepared for his wife's mother. His wife runs into the flames; he, for love of her, follows, and the three perish.

There are numerous myths about marriages between sky gods and mortal women. Olofat, the Caroline Islands trickster, is the son of Lugeilang and an earthly woman, from whose head he emerges. Like many culture heroes, he grows precociously. Later he flies to his sky father on a column of smoke. A Kiribati semidivine clan ancestor, Bue (burn), snares his father the Sun to demand knowledge and magic; Bue is not, like the Polynesian Maui who performed a similar feat, trying to regulate the sun's speed.

On both Pohnpei and Kosrae it is said that Isokelekel (Ijokelekel, shining noble or wonderful king) is the son of the Pohnpei thunder god Nansapwe (Nan Djapue) and the latter's aged clan sister from Katau (which may be Kosrae or a spiritual place to the east). The tart lime given to her by Nansapwe makes her pregnant, and in her womb Isokelekel learns that he is to take revenge on the irreverent Sau Deleur, the ruler who had once imprisoned Nansapwe for seducing his wife. When he is a young adult, Isokelekel sails against this Sau Deleur with 333 warriors and their families. Isokelekel defeats his enemy, seizes power, and puts an end to a long line of increasingly oppressive rulers who had set their subjects impossible tasks. For instance, a certain Sau Deleur had demanded a rare shell; a boy, aided by fish, went under the sea to get the shell, but on his return he and his family committed suicide to escape having to perform any further such tasks.

TRICKSTERS AND DEATH. Cycles of myths tell of divine and semidivine tricksters who are magicians, shape-shifters, transformers, and gross adulterers. When the demigod Olofat (Chuuk Wonofaat Stamper), who is known throughout the Carolines, was insulted by boys in the sky world, he gave their pet sharks teeth and their stingrays barbs such as they have now. Pretending ignorance of his relationship to him, Olofat jealously kills his half brother. When Half-Beak kills Olofat for stealing his wife, Lugeilang resuscitates him. Na Areau also enrages gods and men. When carpenters jam a house post down on him, Na Areau, like Olofat in a similar story, has a side passage ready. With red earth and coconut he simulates blood and flesh and deceives his enemies into thinking he is dead; then he appears and mocks them.

In the myths of the Marshall Islands, Etao and Jemaluut are either the sons of Iroojrilik and Lijebake (Libage Lady Turtle) or spring from the thunder god Wullep's head. Etao constantly outwits his elder brother and others, and like Na Areau he plays the oven trick. Telling his host of an easy way to get food, he lies down in a hot earth oven, is covered over, and later strolls up from the beach to uncover an oven full of fish and taro. His foolish host, imitating him, perishes, and the trickster takes his wife. This is an Austronesian-wide mythic theme found, for example, among the people of New Hanover in Papua New Guinea.

In these Micronesian myths there is little interest in the origin of permanent death. Olofat decrees that all must die and stay dead, and his sister adds that Olofat too, but not the gods, must die when the world ends. Forgetfulness leads to permanent death when children forget to dig up their mother's corpse as directed or when those who, having learned a man's god-given secret of eternal life, forget a part of the secret and fail to revive him. Stories of temporary death and resuscitation are frequent. When the Belauan semidivine Milad dies in a flood, the gods whom she had once sheltered restore her to life and send Mud Hen, a personified mythic bird (progenitor of *Rallus pectoralis*), to fetch the "water of immortality" in a leaf. However, selfish Mud Hen has a hibiscus bush pierce the leaf. While the spilled "water" makes the hibiscus immune to harsh conditions, Milad loses the chance of immortality. The angry gods, striking Mud Hen's head, give it a red stripe to make it a symbol of wickedness and ugliness. All mud hens now have that stripe.

THE LAND AND ITS FRUITS. According to the myths of the area, numerous islands and islets developed not only from sand but also from taro, flowers, branches, and the like that were cast on the sea, often by disgruntled women leaving home. Dead bodies could also be the bases of islands. Belau developed from a giant's corpse and the people of Belau from its maggots; Lelu developed from a whale-mother's corpse. Except on Fais and Mile, island fishing is less important in the myths of Micronesia than in those of Polynesia. When Motikitik (a cognate of Mauitikitiki, or Maui) fishes up Fais, his dead mother's signal confirms that he, not his brothers, owns it and can divide it into its present three parts. Because it acquired the magical hook, a Yap district dominates Fais politically; were the hook lost, Fais would sink. Etao capsized Mile to test some diviners' skill in coconut-leaf divination; they located the island, fished it up, and made a drain hole that is now a taro pit. Stories of building an island, usually with rocks flying magically into place, are common. Aided by an octopus, explorers found an exposed reef on which to build Pohnpei and shelter it with mangroves and a barrier reef. Later Olsihpa and Olsohpa constructed eighty or ninety artificial islets, Nan Madol, as sites for a ceremonial center, now in ruins. Olsohpa was perhaps the first to bear the royal title Sau Deleur. According to some folk beliefs, bands of "little people," also known in other islands, did the actual work of construction. In most accounts the work is communal, and the heaviest labor is accomplished by magic and a couple of large, strong people.

The principal cultivated plants or certain varieties of these came directly or indirectly from celestial beings, usually women. Even modern Micronesian gardeners think any new variety of plant has fallen from heaven. When three swamp taros *(Cyrtosperma)* fell into the sea from the Kiribati sky, they became porpoises, swam to Arorae, turned back into taros, and were planted by a man whom Tituabine instructed. Two sky men gave taro to Majro Atoll after Namu had rejected it. Milad taught the people of Belau to cultivate *Colocasia* taro; each island learned differently.

More than one mythical woman who bore both human beings and food plants had a coconut son. Limkade, Iroojrilik's sister, planted her coconut son Tobolaar after he told her of benefits that would grow from him and therefore prove his value to his hostile, older, human brother. Like other Pacific Islanders, Micronesians tell of coconut trees growing from the head or the grave of an eel or a person. Nikowupwuupw saw her first child's eyes and mouth in the nuts from the coconut tree growing on his grave. When a female eel, which Yalafath sent to Yap to populate the island with people, was killed generations later, a coconut tree grew from her buried head, a banana plant from her middle, and a swamp taro from her tail.

On Pohnpei, kava grew from a bit of the god Luhk's flesh that he gave a kind woman to plant, and sugarcane grew on the grave of a man he had ordered buried. Observing that rats stupefied themselves on kava and then chewed sugarcane as a chaser, people imitated them, as did the sky dwellers.

According to the myths, easy ways to get food eventually fail through envy or carelessness. Jealous neighbors who chopped down Milad's god-given tree, which produced breadfruit and fish, thereby caused a life-destroying flood; carved wooden storyboards from Belau portray the scene. Travelers bring home new foods or carry them elsewhere. Yalafath, on sending his guest Galuai flying home on a chicken-festooned pole, said that if he took proper care of the chickens they would excrete yams. Soon Galuai became careless, and the hungry chickens, by eating the yams, lost their magic (as in another tale did another man's mistreated money-excreting bird). Travelers, including gods, who eat from an inexhaustible taro plant, coconut tree, or fishpond in an alien land or from a tree growing in midocean must watch out for supernatural hazards.

ORIGIN OF FIRE AND TECHNOLOGY. People ate only sun-baked food until male spirits, usually from the sky and consigned to earth against their will, rewarded helpful women or boys with the knowledge of fire and cooking. Etao taught a generous boy; a disoriented spirit (only a head) instructed a Mortlock boy who escorted him home (and also restored the life of the boy's brother). When a Yap woman extricated the thunder god from a prickly pandanus, he put two sticks under his arm to imbue them with fire and then demonstrated how to make fire with them and cook; he also taught her pottery making. Fire from a god's body is a recurrent motif in Austronesian mythology. On Chuuk, Rat, a personified mythic being, taught a sympathetic woman to make fire and cook after Nuukeyinen (Lugeilang) had set Rat's muzzle on fire and driven him from heaven for thievery. On Mortlock and Namoluk, Olofat, after escaping from being burned alive for his tricks, became the god of fire and the condemned and sent fire to earth in a starling's beak.

In the myths of the Kiribati, fire came from the ocean. Because the sunbeam that was caught by the boy Te-ika (the fish) set numerous fires in the ocean world, his father Bakoa (shark), Lord of the Ocean, exiled him. On earth, Tabakea, Lord of the Land, beat Te-ika and his sunbeam to death with sticks that absorbed the fire. Subsequently he revived Te-ika with the same sticks because of Bakoa's grief, but the fiery boy died at the water's edge. Like Maui in Polynesia, Na Areau in the Kiribati repeatedly demanded fire from its keeper (here, Lightning); but unlike Maui, Na Areau did not want to learn the secret of making fire. He wished only to provoke the thunder god Tabuariki to a wrestling match and to weaken him by breaking his arm.

Spirits keep secret their fishing techniques, gear, and magic except from generous and deserving individuals. A woman to whom a sea spirit has divulged family secrets in exchange for her new yellow skirt has to flee from the sea spirit's angry father to another island where, however, she sells her secrets. In exchange for secretly borrowing his canoe, spirits later show a Ulithi man how to make fish traps. According to a complex myth, the people of Chuuk did not know how to fish until the god Solal taught a neglected one-legged boy, whose success then led villagers to make him chief.

Because of the enormous hazards of seafaring, experts in the practice, lore, and magic of canoe building and navigation are highly prized by the islanders. Experts from the Marshall Islands fear that they may at sea forget their mnemonic, informational, magical, and courage-inspiring chants; others fear watchful Jemeluut (Rainbow), who might punish them for mistakes at sea. In Ulithi, when Palulop (great navigator), a sky man residing on earth, teaches his sons navigation, the as yet unborn Ialuluwe (Aluluei) listens. As elsewhere in the Caroline Islands, he subsequently became the supreme sea god. Like the Polynesian Tinirau, he has two faces, one looking ahead and the other looking back at dangers people cannot see. Of his sons, Rongerik studies diligently under his father, as a future navigator should, and later has to rescue his brother Rongolap, who had thought only of women and had neglected his studies.

Three women who transmitted navigational lore to people are the Yap goddess Legerem, who taught canoe building, navigation, and star lore; the Kiribati ancestress Branch of Buka, whose grandfather taught navigation and bonito fishing to her rather than to her selfish brothers; and in the Carolines, Aluluei's daughter, who, having given three navigation gods an inexhaustible drinking nut, received from them knowledge that was as yet unknown to her father.

Certain mythical canoes made of rock, sand, taro tubers, or pandanus drupes obey verbal commands even if the owner is not aboard. Others skim through the air, reflecting Micronesian interest in flying by magic over their vast island area; in one myth a man's hollow wooden bird carries him to his abducted wife. More pragmatically two Pikinni (Bikini) men are said to have invented the Tridacna adze and the paddling canoe. Subsequently the Marshall Islanders learned about Loktanur's invention of masts and sails, with which she had enabled Jebro, youngest of her five sons, to win a race to become chief. Like other Pacific Islanders, a canoe maker may find his or her felled tree restored by an offended spirit. When this happened to Rongerik, Aluluei told him to first greet a trilling bird named Seilangi, god of carpenters. This done, happy Seilangi made Rongerik's canoe in one night to start him on his great career as a navigator.

POLITICS AND POWER. Throughout Micronesia knowledge is power. Those who possess the narratives hide things, change things, and selectively reveal things that will give a certain shape to political and social reality. While myths seem to speak of the past, certain themes, such as the resistance to hegemony found in trickster stories, address the present and offers hope for the future. On Pohnpei, Isokelekel's victory over the increasingly despotic Sau Deleur becomes a motif for resistance to the regionalizing tendencies of the Federated States of Micronesia. In the Marshall Islands, Etao does prevail against the more powerful gods and thus becomes a symbol of hope in the struggle of the people of Pikinni, Anewetak, and Epja against the American military weapons program.

SEE ALSO Myth; Nature, article on Worship of Nature.

BIBLIOGRAPHY

The following publications are organized according to three eras of collection of mythological materials.

First Era

The Belief among the Micronesiana, the third volume of James G. Frazer's *The Belief in Immortality and the Worship of the Dead* (London, 1913–1924), gives English translations from the first era of Spanish and German collections of myths, tales, and legends that, despite Frazer's title, relate to more than simply death and immortality. These collections date up to and include 1914. The volume also contains many examples from Wilhelm Müller's *Yap* (Hamburg, 1917–1918), which is contained in *Ergebnisse der Südsee-expedition, 1908–1910* (ESSE), edited by Georg Thilenius, a work that is conventionally identified as ESSE II. B. II.1–2. Frazer's *Myths of the Origin of Fire* (London, 1930) includes Micronesian examples from English sources, such as Frederick William Christian, *The Caroline Islands* (London, 1899; reprint, London, 1967), and English translations of Spanish and German sources, including examples from several ESSE volumes.

As almost every ESSE volume includes myths (some are devoted entirely to narratives and chants), the series is an indispensable primary source. Also during the first era, the series Anthropos Bibliothek published August Erdland, *Die Marshall-Insulaner* (Münster, Germany, 1914), and Laurentius Bollig, *Die Bewohner der Truk-inseln* (Münster, Germany, 1927), both of which take into account the islanders' own classification of genres. Paul Hambruch, *Südseemärchen aus Australien, Neu-Guinea, Fidji, Karolinen, Samoa, Tonga, Hawaii, Neu-Seeland* (Jena, Germany, 1921), has valuable notes on the distribution of certain myths.

Second Era

As the first era was that of Spanish, and then German, political control of the Marianas, Carolines, and Marshalls (the Gilberts remained British), the second era of collection was that of the Japanese between the two world wars. Lack of translation from the Japanese has made largely inaccessible such publications as those by Masamichi Miyatake and Masaachi Noguchi for Palau (now Belau) and especially Hisataka Hijakata for Palau and Satawal. Until Hijakata taught Palauans to carve portable storyboards, they had carved mythic scenes only on men's clubhouses.

Third Era

The third collecting era in the three archipelagoes began after World War II with the Coordinated Investigation of Micronesian Anthropology (CIMA) and led many Americans to do fieldwork in the area. A work of special note is Edwin Grant Burrows's *Flower in My Ear: Arts and Ethos of Ifaluk Atoll* (Seattle, Wash., 1963), which discusses myths and chants in terms of style and social values. Roger E. Mitchell, *Micronesian Folktales* (Nagoya, Japan, 1973), includes notes on distribution. Seventeen pages of annotated listings of Micronesian, including Kiribati, mythology are in Margaret Orbell, *A Select Bibliography of the Oral Tradition of Oceania* (Paris, 1974).

Collections by Micronesians themselves are increasing. Particularly remarkable is John L. Fischer, Saul H. Riesenberg, and Marjorie G. Whiting, eds. and trans., *The Book of Luelen: Luelen Bernart* (Honolulu, 1977). Luelen (1866–1946?), a Ponapean man, wrote and dictated between 1934 and 1946 what he considered significant for his family to know about Pohnpei, including its myths, oral history, and song texts. John L. Fischer, Saul H. Riesenberg, and Marjorie G. Whiting, eds. and trans., *Annotations to the Book of Luelen* (Honolulu, 1977), adds explanations, variants, and comparative data.

Yale University's Human Relations Area Files (HRAF) has produced English translations of parts of the German ESSE and other works. An example is the complete translation into English of the German work by Augustin Krämer and Hans Nevermann, *Ralik-Ratak (Marshall-Inseln)* (ESSE II. B. XI; Hamburg, 1938), as HRAF no. 1003. Most Micronesian school readers retell the traditions, but Pensile Lawrence et al., eds., *Pohnpei ni Mwehin Kawa: Old Po-nape* (Saipan, 1973), uses Paul Hambruch's *Ponape* (ESSE II. B. VII.3; Hamburg, 1936), quoting his Ponapean texts and translating into English Hambruch's free German translations.

There have been significant attempts to collect, preserve, and use Micronesian myths. Students have become more aware of their heritage, as evidenced in Gene Ashby, comp. and ed., *Never and Always: Micronesian Stories of the Origins of Islands, Landmarks, and Customs,* 2d ed. (Eugene, Oreg., 1983). Museums and libraries have begun to collect local myths, for example, the Alele Museum on Majro, the Belau National Museum, the libraries at Belau Community College and the Community College of Micronesia, and the Oceania and Special Collections at Northern Marianas College. These and other sources contributed to Bo Flood, comp., *Marianas Island Legends: Myth and Magic* (Honolulu, 2001), and Bo Flood, Beret E. Strong, and William Flood, comps., *Micronesian Legends* (Honolulu, 2002).

Anthropologists continue to develop an understanding of Micronesian myths. Glenn Petersen explores the meanings and political uses of narratives in *Lost in the Weeds: Theme and Variation in Pohnpei Political Mythology,* Occasional Paper 35 (Honolulu, 1990). Ward H. Goodenough analyzes the relationship between myth and personhood in *Under Heaven's Brow: Pre-Christian Religious Tradition in Chuuk* (Philadelphia, 2002). A notable collection of myths is Jack A. Tobin's *Stories from the Marshall Islands: Bwebwenato jan Aelon Kein* (Honolulu, 2002). Tobin provides texts collected over the last forty years in both Marshallese original and English translations.

There have been some creative attempts to bring myths to bear on present realities. Robert Barclay probes the neocolonial arrangement on Kwajalein through parallel story lines juxtaposing life in the expatriate American community, life in the Marshallese labor community, and life in the spiritual world of Etao and Jemaluut in *Melal: A Novel of the Pacific* (Honolulu, 2002).

KATHARINE LUOMALA (1987)
MICHAEL A. RYNKIEWICH (2005)

MIDRASH AND AGGADAH [FIRST EDITION].

Regardless of what specifically the Hebrew word *midrash* stands for in its two occurrences in a postexilic book of the Hebrew scriptures (*2 Chr.* 13:22, 24:27), where the reference is clearly to something written or written in (Heb., *ketuvim*; Gr., *gegramménoi*), by the last century BCE it stands for oral interpretation, that is, interpretation of the Torah, the Law of Moses; and one who interprets the Law is referred to as *doresh ha-torah.* This we learn from the literature of the Dead Sea sectarians (*Damascus Covenant* 6.7, 7.18f., 8.29; *Manual of Discipline* 6.6, 8.15; see also *Ecclesiastes* 1:13). Indeed, it is possible that already at the beginning of the second century BCE there were in existence schools where Torah interpretation was going on. In the Hebrew of *Ben Sira* (c. 200–180 BCE), the author, Simeon ben Joshua ben Sira, or Sirach, by whose time "wisdom" is already equated with the Torah, speaks as follows: "Turn to me, you who are untaught, and lodge in my school [*beit midrash*; literally, 'house, or place, of *midrash*'; *en oikō paideias*]." *Midrash* is therefore a school activity. In the *beit ha-midrash*, the school, learning is to be found, wisdom is to be acquired, there is a master, and there are disciples; through interpretation, understanding of the Torah is attained: "The book of the covenant of the Most High God, the Law (Torah) which Moses commanded us . . . fills men with wisdom, like the Pishon, and like the Tigris at the time of the first fruits. It makes them full of understanding like the Euphrates, and like the Jordan at harvest time" (*Sir.* 24:23–26)—and there is more to this effect.

Origins of the Midrash. A question that may never be answered satisfactorily is that of when, precisely, the interpretation of the Torah began. For from the moment any text is adopted as a rule or guide of life, some interpretation—added explanation, commentary—inevitably becomes necessary. In scripture itself, though most commandments are lucidly drawn up, there are four occasions when even Moses was in need of further instruction regarding procedures for laws already established (*Lv.* 24:10–23; *Nm.* 9:4–14, 15:32–36, 27:1–11). The *Midrash* also calls attention to Moses facing difficulty in understanding specifically what God has ordered (*Mekhilta'*, ed. Jacob Lauterbach, 1.15; cf. *Sifrei Zuṭa'*, ed. Saul Lieberman, 6.16; but see also Harry Fox in *Tarbiz* 49, 1980, 278ff.). In scripture such cases are reported probably to underscore that no human legislator, not even Moses, is the originator of biblical laws, that Moses only transmits what the Lord ordains; the Law of Moses is God's law which he communicates through Moses. But these cases at the same time illustrate that no written code can be operative without supplementary instruction. And supplementary instruction is what *midrash* provides.

There is therefore a measure of justice to the traditional view that the written Torah had to be accompanied from the outset by expository teachings of some kind, transmitted and inherited orally (the oral Torah). But we are in no position to fix the time when precisely such very ancient supplementary teaching began. In legendary lore there are views that, for example, statutory prayer services were first established by the patriarchs (B.T., *Ber.* 26b); that benedictions of the grace after meals were added by Moses, Joshua, David, and Solomon (ibid., 48b); and that already at Sinai at the giving of the Ten Commandments interpretation was taking place (*Mekhilta'* 2.267). But such statements have no historical value and perhaps are not meant to be taken as history in the strict sense. They represent a tendency to project later institutions farther and farther back in time in order to suggest high antiquity and that these are not recent unauthorized inventions.

Whatever very ancient interpretation may have been like (reflected also in glosses, popular etymologies, and parables within the Hebrew scriptures themselves; cf. I. L. Seeligmann in *Supplement to Vetus Testamentum*, vol. 1, 1953, pp. 150–181), it is unquestionable that from roughly 250 BCE, when the Pentateuch was translated into Greek (as the Septuagint), and continuing for seven hundred years and beyond, when major collections of midrashic literature continued to be redacted, *midrash* flourished in the Jewish academies of Palestine. From the end of approximately the second century CE, *midrash* flourished to a lesser extent in the Babylonian Jewish academies as well, though it was principally a Palestinian creation.

Hellenistic-Roman influence on intellectual and cultural life in Jewish Palestine affected midrashic activity, as can be seen in the penetration of Greek (and other foreign) terms, the terminology for some rules of interpretation, the circulation of tales and epigrams, the parables drawn from royal and imperial establishments, a few cultic details, and the significance given to the numerical value of Hebrew words (*gimaṭriyyah*). In short, while it would be inexcusably uncritical to assume that wherever there is influence there is simultaneously direct dependence and borrowing, the rich and constant intellectual preoccupation with explanation of the language and content of scripture by teachers to students in the schools, and to the public at large by means of sermons in the synagogues, is an echo of the stimulation provided wherever—not only in Palestine—the spirit of Greek learning and letters came to the attention of the learned classes. Native traditions were not necessarily abandoned; indeed, they might now be held onto more tightly, but they would also be interpreted in ways comprehensible to those who lived in an age when Greek models of thinking and expression dominated the overall intellectual climate.

Aggadic Midrash. *Midrash* (i.e., interpretation, commentary, exegesis, amplification) was applied to all of scripture, and in tannaitic times (approximately the first two centuries CE), especially to four books of the Pentateuch, *Exodus* through *Deuteronomy*, because these contained the bulk of biblical *halakhah*, the regulations governing the conduct of society as well as individual practice. However, even in these books there is considerable nonhalakhic material, what is called *aggadah*, and the first book of the Pentateuch, *Genesis*, is almost entirely *aggadah*. Aggadic subject matter was therefore also commented on in the tannaitic *midrashim*, and some of the leading masters of *halakhah* were also leading masters of *aggadah*. Thus we have aggadic *midrashim* not only on *Genesis* but also in the midrashic compilations on the other Pentateuch books as well, and aggadic discussion is thus included not only in the tannaitic *midrashim* but in subsequent works devoted to all the books of the Hebrew Bible.

The word *aggadah* may be rendered as "narrative, recitation, account based on scripture," but the term, the concept, implies and refers to very much more in the midrashic and Talmudic corpora. By *aggadah* is meant that which strictly speaking is not classified as *halakhah*, as required, normative practice. *Aggadah* includes narratives, historical composition, poetry, speculation, genealogical records, fanciful interpretation, moral exhortation—in short, the exposition of the whole variety of scriptural contents beyond the codified, legislative, and juristic, prescribed courses of action which constitute *halakhah*.

There are instances where a sharp line between aggadic comment and halakhic cannot be drawn easily; see, for example, *Keritot* 6.3 (and cf. Eliʿezer in *Keritot* 6.1). On the whole, however, a halakhic discussion is easily distinguished from an aggadic one. In the former, legalistic concern is uppermost, norms of practice are sought, there is close attachment to what the sages regard as literal meaning, argument by authorities is erudite and acute, there is constant resort to tradition, rules of interpretation are followed with due regard for their function (those of Hillel in the first century, those of ʿAqivaʾ and Yishmaʿeʾl in the second century), and casuistry is employed as in all legal and scholastic disciplines. On the other hand, *aggadah* is unrestrained contemplation and interpretation associated with the vocabulary and themes of all parts of the Bible. There is free application of the subject of one verse in scripture to another verse far removed from it, so that, for example, in undertaking to comment on *Leviticus* 1:1, the teacher or preacher introduces *Psalms* 103:20 and by skillful adaptation can demonstrate that the *Psalms* verse explains the intention of the *Leviticus* verse. *Aggadah* is very often sermonic, interpretation for the benefit of the folk in the synagogue, and therefore, though there are, so to speak, rules of interpretation for *aggadah* as well, they do not really confine the *aggadot* within strictly drawn hermeneutical perimeters.

Considerable liberty of interpretation was permitted to and practiced by the authors of *midrash aggadah*, who employed all the rhetorical devices common among textual scholars of their time, used, for instance, in the interpretation of Homer. Thus much is made of punning, of homophones, of methods of dream interpretation, of figures of speech, and of acronyms. A frequent form of interpretation is the parable of kings and their subjects. Verses receive not just one but many interpretations, which indictes not the rejection of previous explanation but the simultaneous legitimacy of a number of meanings which the biblical, divinely revealed text contains and hence, also, beneath-the-surface lessons. *Midrash aggadah* is employed for polemic purposes, against internal challengers as well as antagonists from the outside. For example, when Pappos interprets *Job* 23:13 as a statement of God's omnipotent and arbitrary power, ʿAqivaʾ hushes him up by means of an alternative interpretation that every decision of God is just, (*Mekhiltaʾ* 1.248). Or when Israel is mocked because the Temple was destroyed (presumably, a sign of God's rejection of Israel), one sage declares that this was, on the contrary, a sign of God's love for Israel, in that he let out his wrath on the sticks and stones of the structure (his own habitation) rather than on the people themselves (*Lam. Rab. on Lam.* 4:11 ed. Buber, 74b). Comments like these were obviously made as a consolation after profound tragedy. And they reveal too the ready resort to paradox: even misfortune may be for the good (see also *Genesis* 45:5–8; for paradox in *halakhah*, see *Tanḥumaʾ* on *Numbers*, ed. Buber, 52a–b).

Along with polemics, *midrash aggadah* does not hesitate to indulge in varieties of apologetics. Thus examples of questionable behavior of the patriarchs and Israel's heroes (the twelve sons of Jacob, David, and Solomon) are frequently excused and presented in a positive light, while their enemies' characters are in almost all respects regarded as wicked—typical folkloristic treatment. Events in scripture are identified as foreshadowings of experiences later in the sages' own times and of the age to come. By means of *midrash* the protests and resentments of later generations find eloquent outlet, and this in turn leads to attempts at theodicy. In the retelling of biblical narratives legendary lore is drawn upon in order to emphasize particular values and ideals; so, too, to contrast the ways of the nations of the world with Israel's ways. And in virtually all interpretation, especially where more than immediate, literal meaning is sought, the aim of aggadic *midrash* is moral and didactic. This is particularly noteworthy in the stories told about famous sages: in these, fancy and fact are so closely intertwined it is rare that the one can be separated from the other.

Aggadic *midrash* also preserves evidence of Gnostic speculation by certain rabbis on the theme of creation, on the chariot spoken of by Ezekiel, on the overpowering reality of the godhead and his celestial retinue, on major historic experiences of Israel (at the sea after the redemption from Egyptian bondage and at the Sinai revelation), on the contrast between the fate of man after the Fall and before it and what might have been otherwise.

With such latitude available to aggadic *midrash*, all aspects of life come under review—the relations of man to God and of man to fellow man. Piety of conduct (in the light of the law and in action surpassing legal prescription) and piety of thought are exemplified. Public virtue and private virtue are discussed in the light of moral expectation, related to biblical verses, which are quoted and given novel interpretation, and interrelated with the particular theme in the mind of the teacher or preacher.

For example, scripture (*Ex.* 19:1–2) reports that "On the third new moon after the Israelites had gone forth from the land of Egypt, on that very day, they entered the wilderness of Sinai. Having journeyed from Rephidim, they entered the wilderness of Sinai and encamped [here the verb is plural: *va-yaḥanu*] in the wilderness. Israel encamped [here the verb is singular: *va-yiḥan*] there in front of the mountain."

To draw the moral of these verses the homilist first invokes a verse from *Proverbs* in which the subject is the excellence of wisdom, which for the homilist and his audience is already understood as the Torah. Then *Proverbs* 3:17—"Its [wisdom's] ways are ways of pleasantness, and all its paths are peace"—is made to shed light on the *Exodus* report. Thus the Holy One, blessed be he, actually wished to give the Torah to Israel at the time they left Egypt, but the Israelites kept quarreling with each other, saying all the time, "Let us head back to Egypt" (*Nm.* 14:4). Note what is written (*Ex.* 13:20): "They set out from Succoth and encamped at Ethan"—both verbs are in the plural, for as the Israelites moved on ("set out"), they quarreled, and as they halted ("encamped"), they quarreled; but when they reached Rephidim, they all made peace and became a united assembly (a single band). (And when is the Almighty exalted? When Israel forms a single band, as it is said [*Am.* 9:6], "His band he founded on the earth" [*Lv. Rab.* 30.12, 710]—possibly an appeal not to break up into conflicting sects.) How do we know that they all became a united assembly? For the verse (*Ex.* 19:2) says, "Israel encamped there in front of the mountain," and this time the verb is in the singular: *va-yiḥan*; it is not written, "they encamped," with the verb in the plural, *va-yaḥanu*. Said the Holy One, blessed be he, the Torah, all of it, is peace (-loving); to whom shall I give it? To the nation that loves peace. Hence (*Prv.* 3:17), "and all its paths are peace" (*Mekhilta'* 2.200; *Lv. Rab.* 9.9, 188; *Tanḥuma'* on *Ex.*, ed. Buber, 37b, 9).

A number of elements, typical of *midrash* as a whole, appear in this passage. To begin with, there is the association of a verse "far removed" (in *Proverbs*) with the particular verse (in *Exodus*) to be interpreted—which is meant to demonstrate that all parts of scripture endorse each other and that it can be shown, when necessary, that they are not in conflict. Second, there is meticulous attention to minutiae—the significance even of shifts from plural to singular (by dropping one consonant)—from which an important lesson can be derived. Third, verses are cited at every opportunity to serve as proof text; in many *midrashim* this feature is even more lavishly exhibited than in our passage, and there is no trace of their authors' possessing concordances to help them in their search for apt quotations. Finally, of course, there is the chief theme with which the *midrash* may be concerned, in our case, the theme of peace (which may be a warning against sectarianism or even an exhortation not to contemplate rebellion against the ruling powers). That study of the Torah thrives on peace and leads to peace is what the midrashic and Talmudic sages frequently tried to stress.

GOALS AND THEMES OF THE MIDRASH. There are very many *midrashim* even more complex in their structure and content, but basically it may be said that all midrashic teaching undertakes two things: (1) to explain opaque or ambiguous texts and their difficult vocabulary and syntax thus supplying us with what we would call literal or close-to-literal explanation or, for lack of that, purely homiletical guess; (2) to contemporize, that is, so to describe or treat biblical personalities and events as to make recognizable the immediate relevance of what might otherwise be regarded as only archaic. As we have seen, a scene from the account of the revelation of the Ten Commandments becomes a homily on Torah and peace. Patriarchs will be described as mourning for the destruction of the Temple. Esau comes to represent the Roman empire. The twelve sons of Jacob become extraordinary military heroes. And so it goes for the rest of scripture: the past addresses the present, directly or indirectly, and drops hints of the future. There are midrashic interpretations that grow out of both a lexical problem in the verse and the desire to apply the explanation to the thinking and need of the later age. For example, for *ve-anvehu* ("and I will glorify him" [*Ex.* 15:2]) Abba' Sha'ul says, "Take after him [*ani ve-hu'*; lit., 'I and he'], even as he is gracious and compassionate, so should you be gracious and compassionate"; thus a meaning of the problematic *anvehu* is provided and along with that the moral lesson of *imitatio dei* (*Mekhilta'* 2.25).

Although, as I have said earlier, the midrash takes into account whatever scripture refers to, there are at least three themes to which much reflection and commentary are devoted. The first is the absolute unity and incomparability of God. The cue for this is of course in scripture (*Dt.* 6:4 and elsewhere), but the kind of emphasis given is essentially post-biblical—that is, that no dualism or plurality of gods is to be tolerated; no worship of God is to be modeled after pagan worship; that regardless of what overtakes Israel, God's justice is not to be denied; that unlike frequent frivolous treatment of their gods by the pagan world, Israel must love God absolutely, with no reservations, come what may. In the *midrash* God may be spoken of anthropomorphically; this does not embarrass the sages; they know that such speech is metaphorical and inevitable (therefore its presence in scripture itself); what they fear is blasphemy and anything that can lead to the desecration of God's name.

A second recurring theme is Israel—that is, Israel of the biblical past, Israel of the present, and the ideal Israel of the age to come. To the patriarchs of Israel there had already been the promise that God would maintain a unique relationship with their descendants. And though God may grow angry at them and visit them with punishments and disasters, the bond between God and their people is a permanent one (see also *Ezekiel* 20:30–44). Israel is under obligation to carry out his commands, and in midrashic and Talmudic centuries this meant not merely the commands as formulated "briefly" in the scriptures but as interpreted at length by the sages: "'If you do not hearken unto me' (*Lv.* 26:14), that is, if you do not hearken to the interpretation, the instruction [*midrash*] of the sages" (*Sifra'* 111b; see also *Sifrei, Dt.* 49, ed. Finkelstein, 114f.). Along with this fundamental view come all sorts of promises of ultimate reward for adherence to the terms of the covenantal relationship and all sorts of regulations concerning how Israel is to remain distinct from the nations of the world in whose midst Israel of the present must live. The self-consciousness demanded by the original covenant and its subsequent reaffirmations is not merely taken for granted or left implicit; it is repeatedly articulated.

No less pervasive is the third theme, that of Torah, which has two meanings, often simultaneous but often also distinct, and it is not always easy to decide which is intended. The word *torah* can stand both for the study of the Torah and for putting into practice the teachings of the Torah. While obedience to the commands of the Torah is already a frequent biblical injunction, what especially characterizes the demands of the sages in the *midrash* is their tireless exhortation that all must study Torah, that neglect of study is not just a sign of a poor education but a deficiency in one's role in life. The sages do not deny that one may merit a share in the life of the world to come even if he is not a scholar or student. But this hardly satisfies them, and ever and again they return to the duty and privilege of Torah study. It is a person's required curriculum from the time he begins scripture study at the age of five—from the time he begins to speak, he should be taught selected verses on the theme of Torah—until the day of his death. Many hyperbolic sayings occur in this connection, and these are indicative of the lengths to which the sages were prepared to go in order to impress on all classes in society, rich and poor, the supreme obligation and value of Torah study. It is the emphasis on Torah study, indeed, that gradually transformed the originally prophetically oriented religion of Judaism into an intellectually directed religious experience in which scholars are the elite.

The Process of Composition. The bulk of aggadic *midrash* commentary which we possess very likely came into being as homilies in connection with the Torah reading as part of synagogue worship. Unfortunately, it is still impossible to fix the time when public Torah reading was first institutionalized. It was certainly in existence by the end of the last century BCE and the first century CE, for Philo Judaeus, Josephus Flavius, and the New Testament all refer to the study and exegesis of Torah (and prophetic selections) as a weekly Sabbath program. The weekly reading (in Palestine, according to a three-and-a-half-year cycle) served as the principle of organization, the scheme of arrangement for the midrashic homilies.

The different midrashic compilations display a certain variety of composition—there are *midrashim* that comment on the biblical text verse by verse (exegetical *midrashim*; e.g., *Genesis Rabbah*) and those that comment only on the opening verse or verses of the pericope and then move on to the next biblical unit (homiletical *midrashim*; e.g., *Leviticus Rabbah*) In these exegetical and homiletic *midrashim*, before the principal midrashic interpretation there may be an introductory homily or homilies, petiḥta', petiḥata', or proems, as a kind of overture to the principal interpretation; perhaps (as suggested by Joseph Heinemann in *Scripta Hierosolymitana*, 1971) these served as brief sermons before the Torah reading. Tanḥuma' Yelammdenu *midrashim* tend to introduce the aggadic discourse by citation of a halakhic question and answer, doubtless not only to convey a rule of practice but to underscore that *halakhah* and *aggadah* are one in aim. There are midrashic texts drawn up for the round of special days in the year, feasts and fast days and other appointed occasions (e.g., *Pesiqta' de-Rav Kahana'*). There are still other compilations, but what is significant is that in all these texts, regardless of stylization, there is created an intellectual, didactic, hortatory tone which all the *midrashim* share, and thus all the *midrashim* sound as though they all were in manner or approach alike. At a later time (from about the seventh century on), midrashic views are combined to create a literary composition—for example, on the sacrifice of Isaac or Abraham, on the rabbinic martyrs of the Hadrianic period, on Abraham's discovery of and commitment to the one God, on the death of Moses, and so forth.

There seem occasionally to have existed books of *aggadah* even in rabbinic times, but the rabbis disapproved of them. Like all other branches of study, except for scripture, aggadic *midrash* was delivered and attended to as part of the oral law, that branch of the total tradition that was not to be put in writing: midrash, Mishnah, targum, Talmud, the *halakhot* and the *aggadot*—in other words, what the rabbis taught.

The creators of the aggadic *midrashim* were the rabbis, but this does not mean that they drew only on scholarly sources or had only scholarly exposition in mind. The rabbis did draw on these, especially when biblical terms were difficult; but they also drew on folklore, on popular legends, on anecdotes, on deliberately imaginative identifications which would make the passage they were interpreting intelligible and also surprising to their audience. They might use current Greek words and epigrams to add special vividness to their interpretation. They might adopt allegorical methods of explanation. Everyone, including women and children, attended the synagogue to hear the preacher. Midrashic method became so popular that even nonscholarly men could express themselves in the form, or so the *midrash* relates. For example, a rabbi's ass driver undertakes to refute a Samaritan when the rabbi himself is at a loss for a proper retort (*Gn. Rab.* 32.10, 296f.); an unlearned man offers an interpretation of a verse the rabbi had not thought of, and the rabbi promises the man that he will use that interpretation in a sermon in the man's name (ibid., 78.12, 932f.). When a homily is admired, one might praise it as "a precious gem."

Exposure and attention to aggadic *midrash* were certainly widespread, especially when the hearts of the people craved comforting. But aggadic *midrash*, as I have mentioned, was also part of the oral law and was also a subject of the *beit ha-midrash*, the academy. There is no lack of comments emphasizing the value of this study, but the very repetitions in favor of *aggadah* create the impression that scholars had to be encouraged again and again not to neglect it. Early allegorists said, "If you wish to recognize him who spake and the world came to be [i.e., if you wish to have correct thoughts about the creator of the universe], study *aggadah*, for it is thus that you will recognize him who spake and the world came to be and cleave to his ways" (*Sifrei Dt.* 49, ed. Finkelstein, p. 115). The superlative estimate of *aggadah* is here evident: what leads one to a proper knowledge of God and to attachment to his ways is to be found not in pursuit of halakhic studies (alone?) but in reflection on the acts of God as described in many places of the *aggadah*. But the feeling is inescapable that such sentiments imply a criticism of those scholars who, because they are chiefly masters of the law, experts in the complex disciplines of dialectic and halakhic subtleties, tend to regard *aggadah* condescendingly. The very freedom of speculation it permits and its very lack of fixed rules of mandatory conduct probably make the sages uncomfortable. Moreover, the exacting analytic exercises demanded by *halakhah* may have made single-minded halakhists feel superior to that which appealed to popular taste. On the other hand, for the folk as a whole the *aggadah* was a perennial refreshment of spirit and of the courage to endure. This the scholars did not deny, and that experience of refreshment remained true for centuries to come.

PRINCIPAL COMPILATIONS. The following is a list of the principal midrashic compilations and treatises; critical editions are listed briefly within parentheses. Particular but noncritical editions are listed without parentheses.

First are the tannaitic *midrashim*; these are essentially halakhic, but they contain a good deal of aggadic material as well:

1. *Exodus: Mekhilta' de-Rabbi Yishma'e'l* (edited by Jacob Lauterbach; a second edition was edited by Hayyim Horovitz and Israel Rabin) and *Mekhilta' de Rabbi Shim'on bar Yoḥ'ai* (edited by Jacob Epstein and Ezra Melamed).
2. *Leviticus: Sifra'*, edited by I. H. Weiss. There is also an edition by Meir Ish Shalom [Friedmann] that is critical but only a beginning; Louis Finkelstein has published Vatican Manuscript Codex Assemani LXVI of the treatise with a long and instructive introduction. Finkelstein's critical edition of *Sifra'* has begun to appear.
3. *Numbers: Sifrei de-vei Rav*, and *Sifrei zuṭa'* (both edited by Horovitz).
4. *Deuteronomy: Sifrei* (edited by Finkelstein) and *Midrash Tanna'im*, edited by David Hoffmann.

The following are aggadic *midrashim* from the amoraic period (c. third through fifth or sixth century) to the thirteenth century:

1. The collection known as *Midrash* Rabbah on the Pentateuch and the Five Scrolls (*Song of Songs*, *Ruth*, *Lamentations*, *Ecclesiastes*, and *Esther*). The individual works were drawn up in different times: *Genesis Rabbah* (edited by Julius Theodor and Chanoch Albeck), from the late fourth to early fifth century, is the earliest, and just a little later is *Leviticus Rabbah* (edited by Mordecai Margulies). For *Deuteronomy Rabbah*, see also the edition by Saul Lieberman. On this collection as a whole, see Zunz (1892).
2. *Tanḥuma'* on the Pentateuch and *Tanḥuma'*, edited by Solomon Buber.
3. *Pesiqta' de-Rav Kahana'* (edited by Bernard Mandelbaum).
4. *Midrash Tehillim* (Midrash of the Psalms), edited by Buber.
5. The Yemenite *Midrash ha-gadol* on the Pentateuch, by David ben Amram Adani (thirteenth century), which draws on earlier midrashic compilations (some no longer extant) and even Maimonides to form a collection of its own: *Genesis* and *Exodus* (edited by Margulies); *Leviticus* (edited by Nahum Rabinowitz and Adin Steinsalz); *Numbers* (edited by Solomon Fisch; a second edition was edited by Tsevi Rabinowitz); *Deuteronomy* (edited by Fisch).
6. *Yalquṭ Shim'oni*, also of the thirteenth century, by a rabbi Shim'on, which gathers its material from many earlier *midrashim* and covers the whole of Hebrew scriptures.

SEE ALSO Biblical Exegesis, article on Jewish Views; Torah.

BIBLIOGRAPHY

On all this literature see the classic presentation by Leopold Zunz, *Die gottesdienstlichen Vorträge der Juden* (1832; 2d ed., Hildesheim, 1966) but even better the Hebrew translation thereof, *Ha-derashot be-Yisra'el* (Jerusalem, 1947), which is brought up to date and corrected by Chanoch Albeck in the light of later research. Other midrashic collections not listed here, albeit of considerable importance, are also described and discussed in this work.

The best presentation of the sages as aggadic teachers is Wilhelm Bacher's *Die Agada der Tannaiten*, 2 vols. (1884–1890; reprint, Berlin, 1965–1966); *Die Agada der palästinischen Amoräer*, 3 vols. (Strasbourg, 1892–1899); and *Die Agada der babylonischen Amoräer* (Strasbourg, 1878). Bacher introduces each of the principal teachers separately, organizes the teachings around major categories as embodied in many scattered sayings, and comments on them. This work is also available in Hebrew translation by A. Z. Rabinowitz). See also E. E. Epstein-Halevi's *Ha-aggadah ha-historit biyyogerafit le-or meqorot Yevaniyim ve-Laṭiniyim* (Jerusalem, 1973).

The nature of Judaism as a religion as it emerges from aggadic *midrash* especially (but not exclusively) is best represented by Solomon Schechter's *Some Aspects of Rabbinic Theology* (London, 1909), reprinted as *Aspects of Rabbinic Theology* (New York, 1961); George Foot Moore's *Judaism in the First Three Centuries of the Christian Era, the Age of Tannaim*, 3 vols. (1927–1940; reprint, Cambridge, Mass., 1970); Joseph Bon-sir-ven's *Palestinian Judaism in the Time of Jesus Christ*, translated by William Wolf (New York, 1964); and E. E. Urbach's *The Sages: Their Concepts and Beliefs*, 2 vols., translated from the second Hebrew edition by Israel Abrahams (Jerusalem, 1975). For additional reading one may consult the selected titles listed below.

Albeck, Chanoch. "Introduction." In *Genesis Rabbah*. Edited by Chanoch Albeck and Julius Theodor. Berlin, 1931. Reprinted under the title *Midrash: Rabbath Genesis*. Jerusalem, 1965.

Bickerman, Elias J. "La chaîne de la tradition pharisienne." *Revue biblique* 59 (1952): 44–54.

Fischel, Henry A. *Rabbinic Literature and Greco-Roman Philosophy: A Study of Epicurea and Rhetorica in Early Midrashic Writings*. Leiden, 1973.

Ginzberg, Louis. *Legends of the Jews*. 7 vols. Translated by Henrietta Szold et al. 1909–1938. Reprint, Philadelphia, 1946–1955.

Goldin, Judah. *The Song at the Sea*. New Haven, 1971.

Halperin, David J. *The Merkabah in Rabbinic Literature*, American Oriental Series, no. 62. New Haven, 1980.

Heinemann, Isaak. *Darkhei ha-agadah*. Jerusalem, 1970.

Heinemann, Joseph, ed. *Derashot ba-tsibbur bi-tequfat ha-Talmud*. Jerusalem, 1970.

Heinemann, Joseph. "The Proem in the Aggadic Midrashim: A Form-Critical Study." In *Studies in Aggadah and Folk Literature*. Edited by Joseph Heinemann and Dov Noy, pp. 100–122. Scripta Hierosolymitana, vol. 22. Jerusalem, 1971.

Kasher, M. M. *Torah sheleimah*. 37 vols. New York, 1927–1982.

Lieberman, Saul. *Hellenism in Jewish Palestine*. New York, 1962.

Marrou, Henri I. *A History of Education in Antiquity*. Translated by George Lamb. New York, 1956.

Scholem, Gershom G. *Jewish Gnosticism, Merkabah Mysticism, and Talmudic Tradition*. 2d ed. New York, 1965.

Spiegel, Shalom. "Introduction." In *Legends of the Bible* by Louis Ginzberg. New York, 1956.

Spiegel, Shalom. *The Last Trial*. Translated by Judah Goldin. New York, 1964.

Stern, David M. "Rhetoric and Midrash: The Case of the Mashal." *Prooftexts* 1 (1981): 261–291.

Strack, Hermann L. *Introduction to the Talmud and Midrash*. 5th ed., rev. Philadelphia, 1931.

JUDAH GOLDIN (1987)

MIDRASH AND AGGADAH [FURTHER CONSIDERATONS]. Scholarship on midrash and aggadah grew exponentially during the last two decades of the twentieth century. As a result, many of the areas covered by Judah Goldin in the first edition of this *Encyclopedia* have been subjected to further academic scrutiny and changed consensus. New avenues of inquiry have opened and are discussed here. This essay primarily covers the ideas and works of authors who have been active since the 1980s. The updated bibliography briefly annotates the works cited here.

ORIGINS OF MIDRASH. Goldin's assumptions regarding the biblical origins of midrash have been buttressed in a number of works. This insistence on biblical antecedents has been exhaustively demonstrated by Michael Fishbane (1985) and also linked to the scribal and wisdom circles of the late Second Temple era by James Kugel (1986, 2001). It should be noted that this tracing of the lineage of the midrash to its biblical roots is somewhat apologetic in nature in that it depicts rabbinic activity as preexistent within the canon and as the natural outgrowth from it. Nevertheless, the prerabbinic origins of midrash and aggadah are now considered well established.

COMPARISON WITH OTHER LITERATURES. The work of comparison of rabbinic literature and its exegetical activity with that of Hellenistic authors continues apace. Henry Fischel (1977) edited an anthology of essays on the issue, and he appended a thoroughly annotated bibliography. It is now a given in scholarly circles that midrashic literature sits quite comfortably within a Hellenistic milieu, as demonstrated in the Stroum Lectures by Lee Levine.

At the same time, scholarly attention has turned to comparison of the midrashic works of the rabbis with those of the Church Fathers. Here, the commonalities of their exegetical techniques are explored, and areas of rabbinic polemic against the church are also considered. The work of Burton L. Visotzky (1995) includes a consideration of methodology in these areas as well as a survey of recent scholarship on the topic. This comparison of rabbis and Church Fathers builds on the earlier comparative work done with Hellenistic literature and recognizes the common intellectual patrimony that both rabbis and Church Fathers owe to their Hellenistic forbears.

TEXTUAL CRITICISM AND TRANSLATION. The production of critical editions of rabbinic works of midrash and aggadah also continues. New editions, such as those of *Exodus Rabbah—Part I* (Shinan, 1984), *Midrash Mishle* (Visotzky, 1990), and *Pesiqta Rabbati* (Ulmer, 1997), now share a place on scholarly bookshelves. Other scholars, including Menahem Kahana (1999) and Menahem Kister (1998), published preliminary studies to critical editions. Although a debate continues between scholars such as Peter Schäfer (1986) and Chaim Milikowsky (1988, 1996) regarding the proper form such a critical edition should take, there is a growing interest in the use of electronic media in the production of online virtual editions and CD-ROM texts with search capabilities. This trend promises to enhance further scholarly activity in the study of midrash and aggadah and potentially obviate the debate regarding printed text editions.

A broad variety of translations into English were published in the last two decades of the twentieth century. Four principal publishing programs have enhanced this scholarly translation movement. Jacob Neusner and his students translated much of the library of rabbinic literature, including works on midrash and aggadah. The Yale Judaica Series and the Jewish Publication Society also have continued to produce high quality, annotated English translations of classic rabbinic works. Finally, the Soncino Press continues to reprint their earlier, yet still reliable translations. All in all, most major works of midrash and aggadah now are available in English translation.

From History to Literature. During the two-decade period that closed out the twentieth century, under the influence of the work of Morton Smith and his students (e.g., Jacob Neusner, Lee Levine, Shaye J. D. Cohen, and Seth Schwartz), there has been a decisive move away from treating works of midrash and aggadah as evidence for the history of the rabbinic period. This group of historians, writing primarily in North America, determined that rabbinic literature is largely undependable for historic documentation. The reasons for this vary, but include the lack of reliable attributions of traditions to given named rabbis, the insecure dating of traditions within rabbinic documents, and the didactic literary forms of the legends themselves.

In place of this negativist assessment and concomitant with the growth of postmodern literary studies in the greater academy, the study of midrash and aggadah has turned more and more to literary critical techniques for its methodology, as exemplified in the works of Jonah Fränkel (1981) and James Kugel (1990). Treating midrash and aggadah as literature values these texts in their own right and also yields differing results regarding the role of the literature. The recent attention to deconstruction and other postmodernist trends in the broader literary world has also affected the study of midrash and aggadah. The work of Susan Handelman (1982) sought to compare midrash and deconstruction (decisively criticized by David Stern, 1984). A broader anthology of essays linking the postmodernist literary critical movement with midrash was edited by Geoffrey Hartman and Sanford Budick (1986). The thoughtful work of David Stern (1996) is an excellent example of the move to literary theory on midrash and aggadah. In the late twentieth and early twenty-first century there has been a much broader interest in and study of midrash and aggadah as literature than at any time in modern history.

Richard Sarason (1981) led the way in treating midrash as literature rather than as historic documentation. His work caused scholars to cease looking for synagogue settings for what had been presumed to be the collected sermons and homilies of the rabbis. Instead, the works currently are treated as intertextual exegetical exercises by Daniel Boyarin (1990), as miscellanies of various literary and homiletic materials by Burton Visotzky (2003), and artfully edited anthologies by scholars as diverse as Jacob Neusner (1985) and Norman Cohen (1981).

A form of midrash called the *petihah*, or its Aramaic form, *petihta*, best exemplifies the debate regarding the question of synagogue setting versus literary compilation. Some scholars, including Joseph Heinemann, hold the opinion that this form, which is sometimes translated as a "proem," is a redacted sermon or an introduction to the weekly triennial Torah lection in the synagogues of the Land of Israel—although they are careful to refer to the form as a "literary homily." Other scholars, including Sarason (1982) and Visotzky (2003), imagine the *petihah* as a primarily literary or editorial construct, devised as a means of ordering and anthologizing earlier textual and oral traditions. The current trend toward treating midrash and aggadah first and foremost as literature is readily apparent, even when scholars continue to use the historical-critical tools of analysis associated with the old school of *Wissenschaft des Judentums*, such as philology and traditions-history. Günter Stemberger's (1992) update of Hermann Strack's classic *Introduction to the Talmud and Midrash* remains the best summary of the now-waning historical-critical avenue of research.

Orality and Folklore. Scholars are also currently considering a newly nuanced view of the oral nature of the midrash and aggadah. Obviously, all of the midrashic works extant are literary, in that they are preserved in a written text form. In the past, however, the debate regarding the origins of these traditions was framed as either there are oral or written materials, with no middle ground. Today, the scholarship of Martin Jaffee (1998, 2001) advocates a blurring of the relationship between the possible oral origins of midrash and aggadah and their written record. Jaffee suggests that each sermon may have been an oral performance of traditional materials and that texts as they now exist may thus be *librettos* or snapshots of given performances of these traditions. Jaffee's theory helps explain the existence of variant textual traditions, allows for the literary development and editorial redaction of these rabbinic works, and potentially maintains a grip on the theory of oral origins in the "performance" of the synagogue sermon. This area of scholarship offers great promise for future research on understanding the origins and transmission of midrash and aggadah.

Another direction of research related to oral performance is the treatment of some parts of the corpus of midrash and aggadah as folk literature. Particularly in Israel, folklorists such as Dov Noy and Galit Hasan-Rokem treat elements of aggadah as folklore, subjecting it to the types of analyses common in that cross-cultural field of study. Another field of study, still operating under the assumption of an original synagogue setting for midrash and aggadah, displays a growing interest in the nexus of midrash and aggadah with the Aramaic translations of the Torah called *Targum*, notably in the scholarly writings of Avigdor Shinan (1992). Yosef Yahalom explores the relationship of both of these genres of rabbinic literature with synagogue liturgical poetry, *Piyyut*.

Other Subcategories of Midrash. There is growing interest in the subcategories of midrashic literature, as evidenced by the studies in the *petihah* and the genres of *Targum* and *Piyyut*. The parable *(mashal)* in the midrash garnered the interest of David Stern (1981, 1991) and Daniel Boyarin (1985), who debated the role of the *mashal* in the pages of a journal of Jewish literary history. The *mashal* continues to be of interest to those who would compare it to the New Testament parable and forms of Hellensitic *allegoresis*.

The religious ideas expressed in midrash and aggadah also remain of great interest to students and scholars alike. The theological ideas of the literature and their relation to Christian or Hellenistic philosophical thought of the Late Antique period of Roman history are discussed by a broad range of both Jewish and Christian scholars. Rabbinic theology is decidedly unsystematic and is expressed, instead, through *mashal*, various exegeses, and narratives. Michael Fishbane (2003) has considered the varying modes of rabbinic mythopoesis, the ways in which the rabbis reshape and expand earlier biblical and ancient Near Eastern myth. The beginning of a broad intellectual history of rabbinic thought has also been ably explored by David Kraemer (1990).

Midrash and Aggadah. This discussion of the ideas of midrash and aggadah leads to a consideration of rabbinic literature as composed of two interrelated, yet distinct modes of narrative. In the first, midrash, the rabbis perform exegesis of Scripture, playfully yet seriously unpacking the Sacred Writ. However, rabbinic exegesis of Scripture, which might be construed as narrowly focused explication of biblical words and phrases, can and often does yield narrative, as demonstrated by Israeli scholars Ofra Meir (1987) and Fränkel.

In the second mode of narrative, aggadah, the rabbis employ a style less directly tethered to Scripture, often in the form of Sage Tales about one another. These Sage Tales, although emphatically not biography, are a form of religious didactic fiction, a Jewish version of the legends or *Lives of the Saints.* This latter aggadah is the subject of intensive study relying on literary techniques such as New Criticism in the works of Fränkel and his American student Jeffrey Rubenstein (1999). Further consideration of this type of rabbinic narrative has been done under the rubric of new historicism by Daniel Boyarin (1993). The results of these various studies yield a corpus of rabbinic short stories, as it were, which express the religious and social ideas of the rabbis through tales and legends about the characters who are the very authors of the literature itself.

Impact of Feminism. Feminist theory is one of the other manifestations of postmodern literary criticism that has had a profound impact on the study of midrash and aggadah. In this arena, there is still a great deal of criticism needed, and such studies as those of Judith Baskin (2002) help lay the groundwork by explicating texts about women in rabbinic literature. The work of Miriam Peskowitz (1997) offers a gendered reading on all aspects of rabbinic literature and bears a great deal of fruit as a sophisticated methodology with roots in feminist studies.

Feminism and this new approach to midrash also gave birth to an outpouring of creative writing about women in biblical narratives. In some instances, a Bible story is retold from the perspective of a woman character. In further instances, voice is given to female characters who otherwise are silent. Works such as Anita Diamant's *The Red Tent* (1997) achieved enormous commercial popularity. Many other studies offer feminist perspectives on biblical narratives, and these, too, contribute to what is being called modern midrash. Norma Rosen's *Biblical Women Unbound* (1996) is a representative work of this latter genre of current fiction.

Other Forms of Modern Midrash. In addition to feminist studies, other types of modern midrash are burgeoning in creative areas as diverse as fiction, poetry, television and film. In fiction, older works such as that of Thomas Mann's *Joseph and His Brothers* (1948) have been supplemented by writings such as Israeli author Shulamit Hareven's *The Miracle Hater* (1988). The nexus of midrash and aggadah with poetry is ancient, going back to classical *piyyut.* In the modern era, Israeli writers in particular offer poetry that contemplates biblical themes, such as the works of Dan Pagis and Yehuda Amichai. Again in Israel, a great deal of television programming has been devoted to midrashic explorations of the Bible. In the United States, in addition to the regular fare of costume-dramas, public television has taken up "Genesis: A Living Conversation," in a ten-hour series hosted by Bill Moyers. Finally, even Hollywood produced modern midrash, most notably the animated feature *Prince of Egypt.*

In summary, the study of midrash and aggadah continues to expand in both academic and popular settings. The annotated bibliography that follows offers sources for more in-depth study.

Bibliography

Baskin, Judith. *Midrashic Women.* Hanover, N.H., 2002. Scholarly studies of the women mentioned in rabbinic literature.

Boyarin, Daniel. "An Exchange on the Mashal, Rhetoric and Interpretation." *Prooftexts* 5 (1985): 269–280. Boyarin debates David Stern.

Boyarin, Daniel. *Intertextuality and the Reading of Midrash.* Bloomington, Ind., 1990. Applies postmodern critical theory to his study of early rabbinic exegetical traditions.

Boyarin, Daniel. *Carnal Israel.* Berkeley, Calif., 1993. An attempt at feminist criticism of rabbinic literature.

Cohen, Norman. "Leviticus Rabbah, Parashah 3." *Jewish Quarterly Review* 72 (1981): 18–31. Considers the thematic unity of composition of a chapter of this literary work.

Diamant, Anita. *The Red Tent.* New York, 1997.

Fischel, Henry. *Essays in Greco-Roman and Related Talmudic Literature.* New York, 1977. An anthology of scholarly writings on the relationship of Hellenism and rabbinic Judaism, with an annotated bibliography.

Fishbane, Michael. *Biblical Interpretation in Ancient Israel.* Oxford, 1985. An exhaustive cataloging of inner-biblical midrash.

Fishbane, Michael. *Biblical Myth and Rabbinic Mythmaking.* Oxford, 2003. Traces rabbinic mythopoesis from the Bible through the Zohar.

Fraade, Steven. *From Tradition to Commentary.* Albany, N.Y., 1991. A study book for the Sifre to *Deuteronomy,* tracing the early history of rabbinic exegesis.

Fränkel, Jonah. *'Iyyunim BeOlamo HaRuhani Shel Sippur HaAggadah.* Tel Aviv, 1981. Basic literary criticism on a number of well-known aggadot.

Goldin, Judah. *Studies in Midrash and Related Literature.* Philadelphia, 1988. A collection of historical and literary-critical essays by the master.

Handelman, Susan. *The Slayers of Moses: The Re-emergence of Rabbinic Interpretation in Modern Literary Theory.* Albany, N.Y., 1982. Seeks to find a historical antecedent for literary deconstruction in midrash.

Hareven, Shulamit. *The Miracle Hater.* San Francisco, 1988.

Hartman, Geoffrey, and Sanford Budick, eds. *Midrash and Literature.* New Haven, Conn., 1986.

Hasan-Rokem, Galit. *Web of Life: Folklore and Midrash in Rabbinic Literature.* Stanford, Calif., 2000. An exploration of various folktales found in rabbinic midrash and aggadah.

Heinemann, Joseph. "The Proem in the Aggadic Midrashim." *Scripta Hierosolymitana* 22 (1971): 100–122. A form-critical study that places the proem in a hypothetical synagogue setting.

Jaffee, Martin. "The Oral-Cultural Context of the Talmud Yerushalmi." In *The Talmud Yerushalmi and Graeco-Roman Culture I,* edited by Peter Schäfer, pp. 27–61. Tübingen, Germany, 1998. A first statement of Jaffee's oral *libretto* theory.

Jaffee, Martin. *Torah in the Mouth: Writing and Oral Tradition in Palestinian Judaism 200 BCE–400 CE.* Oxford, 2001. A full-length study of the rhetoric of oral Torah and its implications for modern study.

Kahana, Menahem. *HaMekhiltot LeFarashat Amalek.* Jerusalem, 1999. A prolegomenon to a new critical edition of the Mekhilta to *Exodus.*

Kister, Menahem. *ʿIyyunim BaAvot DeRabbi Nathan.* Jerusalem, 1998. A prolegomenon to a new critical edition of Avot de-Rabbi Nathan.

Kraemer, David. *The Mind of the Talmud.* Oxford, 1990. Aptly subtitled "An Intellectual History of the Bavli."

Kugel, James. *In Potiphar's House.* San Francisco, 1990. Traditions-history of the midrash and aggadah on the Joseph stories.

Kugel, James. "Ancient Biblical Interpretation and the Biblical Sage." In *Studies in Ancient Midrash,* edited by James Kugel. Cambridge, U.K., 2001. An attempt to trace midrash to the late Second Temple scribal schools.

Kugel, James, and Rowan Greer. *Early Biblical Interpretation.* Philadelphia, 1986. Back-to-back attempts to prove that rabbinic midrash and patristic exegesis each flow organically from the Hebrew Bible.

Levine, Lee. *Judaism and Hellenism in Antiquity.* Seattle, 1998. A consideration of the relation between Judaism and Hellenism.

Mann, Thomas. *Joseph and His Brothers.* New York, 1948.

Meir, Ofra. *HaSippur HaDarshani.* Tel Aviv, 1987. On the nexus of biblical exegesis and rabbinic narrative.

Milikowsky, Chaim. "The Status Quaestionis of Research into Rabbinic Literature." *Journal of Jewish Studies* 39 (1988): 201–211. More debate on critical editions.

Milikowsky, Chaim. "On Editing Rabbinic Texts." *Jewish Quarterly Review* 86 (1996): 409–417. Debates Peter Schäfer on what makes a proper critical edition.

Neusner, Jacob. *Development of a Legend.* Leiden, 1970. Neusner's watershed work in which he begins to back away from positivist historical rabbinic biography.

Neusner, Jacob. *The Integrity of Leviticus Rabbah.* Chico, Calif., 1985. A consideration of the literary-philosophical qualities of the rabbinic midrash on *Leviticus.*

Noy, Dov. *Motif Index of Talmudic-Midrashic Literature.* Bloomington, Ind., 1954. A landmark listing of rabbinic motifs as part of world folklore.

Peskowitz, Miriam. *Spinning Fantasies.* Berkeley, Calif., 1997. A profoundly fruitful study of rabbinic rhetoric from a gender perspective.

Rosen, Norma. *Biblical Women Unbound.* Philadelphia, 1996.

Rubenstein, Jeffrey. *Talmudic Stories.* Baltimore, 1999. "New criticism, plus" as a literary approach to Talmudic narratives.

Sarason, Richard. "Towards a New Agendum for the Study of Rabbinic Midrashic Literature." In *Studies in Aggadah, Targum and Jewish Liturgy in Memory of Joseph Heinemann,* edited by Ezra Fleischer and Jacob Petuchowski, pp. 55–73. Jerusalem, 1981. Sarason takes seriously the scholarly challenge of considering rabbinic texts as literature.

Sarason, Richard. "The Petihtot in Leviticus Rabba: 'Oral Homilies' or Redactional Constructions?" *Journal of Jewish Studies* 33 (1982): 557–567. The aptly titled article reconsiders Heinemann's location of the *petihta* in a synagogue setting.

Schäfer, Peter. "Research into Rabbinic Literature: An Attempt to Define the Status Quaestionis." *Journal of Jewish Studies* 37 (1986): 139–152. Focuses on critical editions of texts; debated by Milikowsky.

Schwartz, Seth. *Imperialism and Jewish Society, 200 BCE to 640 CE.*. Princeton, N.J., 2001. How, if at all, one may use rabbinic literature in reconstructing Jewish history of the period.

Shinan, Avigdor. *Midrash Shemot Rabbah.* Tel Aviv, 1984. A critical edition of the first half of the work.

Shinan, Avigdor. *Targum VaAggadah Bo.* Jerusalem, 1992. On the relationship of midrash and aggadah to *Targum.*

Stemberger, Gunther. *Introduction to the Talmud and Midrash.* Minneapolis, 1992. The standard handbook on the literature.

Stern, David. "Method, Rhetoric and Midrash: The Case of the 'Mashal.'" *Prooftexts* 1 (1981): 261–291. Debates Boyarin.

Stern, David. "Moses-cide, Midrash and Contemporary Literary Criticism." *Prooftexts* 4 (1984): 193–204. An incisive reply to Handelman.

Stern, David. *Parables in Midrash.* Cambridge, U.K., 1991. A thorough study of the role of the *mashal* in Midrash.

Stern, David. *Midrash and Theory.* Evanston, Ill., 1996. On the relation between midrash and postmodern theory and its implications.

Ulmer, Rivka. *Pesiqta Rabbati.* Atlanta, 1997. A synoptic edition of the text.

Visotzky, Burton. *Midrash Mishle.* New York, 1990. A critical edition of the work.

Visotzky, Burton. *Fathers of the World: Essays in Rabbinic and Patristic Literatures.* Tübingen, Germany, 1995. On the interrelations of rabbinic and patristic exegeses and polemics.

Visotzky, Burton. *Golden Bells and Pomegranates.* Tübingen, Germany, 2003. Studies of the form and contents of Leviticus Rabbah.

Yahalom, Yosef. *Piyyut UMetziyut BeShilhei HaZeman He'Atiq.* Tel Aviv, 1999. On the historic setting of ancient liturgical poetry.

BURTON L. VISOTZKY (2005)

MIGRATION AND RELIGION. Migration almost always affects religion. This is so because when people migrate to a new place they alter routines of daily life, and new experience inevitably acts upon even the most tenaciously held religious tradition. Conversely, religion often inspires migration.

RELIGIOUS MOTIVES. Organized religious groups may decide to move to a place where their pursuit of holiness will face fewer obstacles. Some successful colonies of this kind played important historic roles by defining patterns of conduct for larger, less religiously incandescent communities that succeeded them.

Among Christians and Muslims, though rarely for other religions, armed migration also played an important part in spreading and defending the faith. Crusade and *jihād*, between them, defined the frontier between *Dār al-Islām* and Christendom for more than a millennium, from the first Muslim conquests of the seventh century until the secularized statecraft of the eighteenth pushed religious antipathy to the margins of military enterprise. The Muslim conquest of India (eleventh to seventeenth century) was likewise sustained by a flow of fighting men who came to Hindustan in order to combat infidelity, and, perchance, to acquire fame and wealth in the process.

Personal and private pursuit of holiness has also inspired innumerable pilgrims to visit shrines that are usually located where their religion originated or had its earliest efflorescence. A contrary flow of holy men beyond the frontiers of the society of their birth has often led to the conversion of strangers, even across linguistic and cultural barriers. Overall and in general we may therefore say that religiously inspired migration, whether peaceable or warlike, had a great deal to do with the definition of civilizational and cultural frontiers in historic times.

Pilgrimage affirmed and helped to homogenize religious and secular culture within each civilization. It became especially important for Islam. Long after the caliphate collapsed, the thousands of pilgrims who traveled to Mecca each year from all over the Muslim world maintained a loose but effective unity among the community of the faithful. Holy war and peaceable conversion on the other hand, enhanced heterogeneity by bringing new populations within the circle of one or another religion from time to time. Diversity did not bother Hindus and Buddhists very much, but new frictions arose among Jews, Christians, and Muslims with every missionary success, since converts inevitably retained some remnants of older "pagan" outlooks and habits. For these faiths, therefore, local and sectarian diversity remained in perpetual conflict with the ideal of uniform and punctilious obedience to God's will as authoritatively defined by religious experts and administrators.

Second only to crusade and counter-crusade, religiously inspired collective migrations offer the most dramatic manifestations of how human motility and religiosity interact. The migrants' goal, of course, is to find a place where the will of God can be more perfectly obeyed. Undoubtedly, most sectarian enterprises of this sort do not last very long. The mass suicide of Jim Jones's followers in the jungles of Guyana in 1978 was a reminder of how such ventures may collapse in grisly failure. At the other extreme, the Puritans of Massachusetts and the Mormons of Utah dominated their chosen localities for generations and still influence the mainstream of American life. In Russia, communities of Old Believers played almost as prominent a part, for they, too, throve on the frontiers and influenced the wider community around them by pioneering privately managed trade and industry in the eighteenth and nineteenth centuries.

In the deeper past, monastic communities offered the most important examples of collective migration undertaken for religious reasons. Buddhist, Daoist, Shintō, and Christian monasteries were often set up in remote rural localities where the monks' devotion and learning propagated and sustained the faith among surrounding populations while also providing a focus for economic exchange and (at least sometimes) for political activity as well. Such monastic centers were especially important in times and places where towns were absent or poorly developed, and tended to become marginal in proportion to the rise of secular urban centers.

The initial establishment of such monasteries was achieved by deliberate, collective migration of bodies of monks or nuns. Subsequent recruitment came from far and wide, since the inhabitants did not reproduce themselves. Monastic establishments thus depended on and could only thrive by retaining connection with the currents of personal migration in search of holiness that flowed within (and sometimes between) each of the Eurasian civilizations.

Private, personal migration for religious reasons is difficult to document since itinerant holy men, living on alms, seldom recorded their experience in writing. The forest retreats of ancient India where the Upaniṣads were generated constitute the oldest attested examples of personal, private migration away from the toils of ordinary society in order to pursue religious enlightenment and truth. They were, perhaps, archetypical. At any rate, India's warm climate was propitious since it allowed seekers after holiness to survive on little food and with little clothing. The ascetic way of life, in turn, encouraged and sustained mystic visions of transcendental reality—visions that validated the holy way of life and confirmed the aspiration of escaping from the ills of this world by entering into contact with suprasensory reality.

Transient and personal master-disciple relationships among Indian holy men took a new and enduring form among the followers of Gautama, the Buddha. For, on the occasion of his death (484 BCE), the Buddha's followers defined a holy way of life that combined itinerant mendicancy with periods of rest and recuperation in specially constructed monasteries. Following this regimen, Buddhist monks soon penetrated far beyond the borders of India, traveling along the caravan routes of Asia to the Far East and boarding merchant vessels bound for Southeast Asia as well. In ensuing centuries, holy men of other faiths (Manichaeans and Nestorian Christians especially) adopted similar modes of life. Later still, Daoists and adherents of Shintō established monastic communities modeled more or less closely on the Buddhist prototype.

Wandering holy men, whether of the Buddhist or some other persuasion, had much in common with the merchant-peddlers who frequented the same trade routes. Indeed, these itinerant holy men *were* a kind of merchant whose stock-in-trade consisted of esoteric knowledge and personal experience of the transcendental world. They lived, in effect, by exchanging their special access to the supernatural for the alms that sustained their bodily wants.

Mainstream Christianity and Islam went in opposite directions in developing the Buddhist pattern of religiously motivated migration. Early in the history of Christian asceticism, monastic rules inhibited the private pursuit of holiness by itinerant almstakers. Yet this did not prevent the systematic establishment of new monasteries at distant frontier locations. Rather, monasteries played a leading role in spreading Christian civilization beyond the borders of the Roman Empire, both in the west among Germanic peoples and in the east among the Slavs. Then, after the voyages of discovery by Europeans during the sixteenth century, missionary orders met with enormous success in converting Amerindians to Roman Catholicism, but failed to win many Asians or Africans to their faith. Protestant missions flourished mainly in the nineteenth century, and probably converted more Asians and Africans to the secular aspects of Western civilization than to their various versions of Christianity.

Within the realm of Islam, on the other hand, the initial effort to make the entire community perfectly obedient to God left no room for monks or any other kind of specially holy personages. The Qur'ān accordingly forbade monastic vows. As a result, when the first burst of conquest came to a halt, pious Muslim merchants took over the missionary role that had been exercised for other faiths by monks and other religious specialists. Thus with the advent of Islam the convergence between missionary and merchant, already apparent in Buddhist practice, became complete.

To be sure, from the twelfth century onward, dervish communities, somewhat analogous to the monastic orders of other religions, arose within Islam. They flourished most in the frontier lands where the expanding Turkish power encountered the Christian populations of Asia Minor and the Balkans. Dervish forms of piety had an important role in converting Christians to Islam along that frontier, but the dervishes never escaped the taint of heterodoxy.

There is profound irony in the upshot of all these various religiously motivated patterns of migration. Puritans of New England as much as Old Believers in Russia, along with all the variegated company of monks and holy men who propagated Hinduism, Buddhism, Christianity, and other faiths along remote frontiers, all sought to escape from the corruptions of civilized society as exemplified in their initial homelands. Yet the net effect of their efforts at withdrawal and pursuit of a more perfect obedience to the precepts of their religion was to spread civilized skills and knowledge among previously simpler societies. Institutional success in the form of flourishing monastic or civil communities, dedicated to holiness though they might be, perversely propagated the very corruptions of civilization which the founders had so earnestly wished to escape from. Of course, discrepancy between intentions and accomplishments is normal in human affairs, but the gap is seldom so patent as in these instances.

SECULAR MOTIVES. Migration undertaken for other than religious reasons also had the overall effect of spreading civilized complexity. Its immediate impact on religion was usually to provoke some sort of blending of old and new traditions as immigrants encountered new peoples and new conditions of life along with alien faiths and religious practices. But religious interactions exhibited many variations, depending on conditions of the encounters and on choices individual leaders and teachers made in coping with unprecedented novelties.

If one seeks to make sense of such diversity it is useful to distinguish between migrations that carry a particular population up a cultural gradient and migrations that carry people in an opposite direction toward frontiers where civilized institutions weaken or disappear.

A people that moves up a cultural gradient may do so as conqueror or captive. Peaceable infiltration of individuals or small family groups is also theoretically possible but remained statistically unimportant until the nineteenth century, when the advent of superior public peace, efficient communications, and mechanically powered transport made that kind of migration feasible on a mass scale for the first time. It follows that the Israelites' conquest of Canaan on the one hand and the African slave trade on the other are the appropriate models for most historical migration, unlike the sort of individual and family migration that did so much to populate the United States between the 1840s and 1920s.

In matters of religion, conquerors and captives alike have three options when arriving in lands whose skills are superior to their own. The newcomers may accept the established religion of the land to which they have come, retaining only a few telltale traces of their own older practices. The Akkadian invaders of ancient Sumer seem to have accepted this option at the very beginning of civilized history; Turks coming into the realm of Islam either as slaves or as conquerors did the same. So did the African slaves imported to North America to work on plantations.

Slaves had little choice as a rule. Forcibly separated from the social context that had nurtured them, they could not, as more or less isolated individuals, carry very much of their native religion with them. Conquerors, however, were in a position to choose. Nevertheless, simple maintenance of accustomed rites and ideas was seldom possible. New experiences, ideas, and circumstances crowded in on successful conquerors. To resist their subjects' religions took a special effort, all the more difficult in view of the fact that the established rituals of the land were already adapted to the circumstances of civilized and agricultural life.

The Bible record shows how hard it was for the Israelites to maintain their desert faith in the land of Canaan after settling down to an agricultural existence. Energetic, violent means were needed to repress Baal worship. This was the work of kings and prophets, who in reaffirming the old religion in fact transformed it. That transformation is what made Judaism so enormously influential in the world at large, but its influence also attests the exceptional character of the prophetic response to the conditions of agricultural civilization.

Other invaders who rejected the religion of the land they had conquered were nonetheless affected by contact with people of a different faith. This happened even when the subjected population accepted the faith of their conquerors en masse. The contamination of Turkish Islam with Christian elements was a pronounced feature of Ottoman life, for example, while the Mughals in India alternated between a policy of permitting and resisting the parallel contamination of their faith with Hindu practices and ideas. A similar situation prevailed in the crusading states of the Levant, and when the Mongol Empire was at its height, Khubilai Khan's policy of patronizing all available religions, so as not to foreclose any avenue of access to the supernatural, shocked and puzzled Christians and Muslims alike.

A third policy that attracted many "barbarian" conquerors was to try for the best of both worlds by espousing a heretical form of civilized religion. This marked the conquerors off from their subjects and helped to maintain a collective *esprit de corps* among the invaders, while also allowing the new rulers to benefit from advantages of civilized religion—for example, literacy, an authoritative scripture, and a hierarchical priesthood. The German tribesmen who adhered to Arian Christianity when invading the Roman Empire in the fourth and fifth centuries followed such a policy. The Uighurs, who became Manichaeans, and the Khazars, who became Jews, illustrate a variation on the same theme, for the religions of their choice served to mark them off from neighbors and subjects while at the same time offering rulers the support of a fully civilized faith.

Nevertheless, such barbarian polities were transitory and so were the heresies they found attractive. The reactions that mattered were assimilation to civilized forms of religion on the one hand and inventive rejection on the other that has been so central in the history of Judaism, of Shintō, and, since the mid-nineteenth century, to the evolution of Hinduism and Islam as well.

Migrations undertaken for economic or political reasons that carry a people to lands less developed than those they leave behind ordinarily have less impact on traditional religious practices. The Chinese migration from north to south that created the imposing mass of contemporary China, for example, had no very obvious effect on Chinese religion. The same may be said of Japanese expansion northward through their islands and of the German *Drang nach Osten.*

Only in modern times did it become possible for family groups and isolated individuals to migrate safely toward an open frontier. In such circumstances, of course, pioneers left organized religion behind. This prepared the ground for itinerant revivalists. Emotionally vibrant forms of established religion fared best in such circumstances, with conspicuous individual conversion the goal.

Proletarian migrants into cities faced circumstances similar in some important respects to the deculturation and individual isolation of the rural frontier. It is not really surprising therefore that the Methodists who first addressed themselves to unchurched urban populations of Great Britain were also among the most successful on the American frontier.

Other varieties of religious revivalism are currently flourishing among urban immigrants, both in the United States and beyond its borders. Islamic revivalism is the most politically prominent of such movements, but sectarian forms of Christianity also have a vigorous life in American cities and in many developing nations, while offshoots of Buddhism can also be observed making headway in urban contexts, both Eastern and Western. Marxism, too, is no more than a secular heresy competing in this environment for human commitment to its materialist doctrines.

CONCLUDING REMARK. In the world at large, as populations increase and migratory flows swell to unexampled proportions, religious interminglings and interactions—both hostile and pacific—are sure to intensify. The future history of humankind will in all likelihood be written around the clash of religions and cultures that is taking place around us, for secular thought and abstract reasoning are weak reeds by comparison with the tidal flows of faith and feeling that govern human conduct today as much as at any time in the past.

SEE ALSO Crusades; Jihād; Mendicancy; Missions; Monasticism; Pilgrimage; Zionism.

BIBLIOGRAPHY

Curtin, Philip D. *Cross-Cultural Trade in World History.* Cambridge and New York, 1984. An in-depth discussion of trade between people of different cultures and of the complex cultural exchanges between diverse human societies that were brought about by trade.

Diesner, Hans-Joachim. *The Great Migration: The Movement of Peoples across Europe, AD 300–700.* London, 1978. A splendidly illustrated, thoroughly researched study on the main groups of migratory (barbarian) peoples that crisscrossed Europe during the Middle Ages and on the emergence of new societies and civilizations as a result of this diaspora.

Folz, Robert, et al. *De l'antiquité au monde médiéval.* Paris, 1972. A minute and erudite discussion of the period of the most spectacular migrations, invasions, and conquests in both western European and Islamic worlds.

French, Allen. *Charles I and the Puritan Upheaval.* London, 1955. A background of the Puritan exodus, the "Great Migration."

Goblet d'Alviella, Eugène. *The Migration of Symbols.* London, 1894. Groundbreaking work on the circulation of religious symbols as a result of movements of peoples.

Kirsten, Ernst, et al., eds. *Raum und Bevölkerung in der Weltgeschichte: Bevölkerungs-Ploetz.* 3d ed. 4 vols. Würzburg, 1965–1966. A collection of demographical data from the beginnings of recorded history until late 1950s, from every part of the inhabited world.

Knowles, David. *Christian Monasticism.* New York, 1969. A learned and concise history of monasticism. Monks' religious fervor, mobility, and political influence made them ideal for the spread of religion in the remotest corners of the world.

Mayer, Hans Eberhard. *The Crusades.* Oxford, 1972. Succinct work on the history of the Crusades and on all the territorial and population changes connected with these holy wars.

McNeill, William H., and Ruth S. Adams, eds. *Human Migration: Patterns and Policies.* Bloomington, Ind., 1978. A collection of essays by scholars in the field that stands as a standard reference source for the complex topic of population movements.

Noth, Albrecht. *Heiliger Krieg und Heiliger Kampf im Islam und Christentum.* Bonn, 1966. A comparative study on the ideology and practice of holy war in Islam and Christianity, reviewing aspects of population displacements and territorial changes in the western Mediteranean region.

Parry, J. H. *The Age of Reconnaissance.* London, 1963. Probably the best study on the history of European colonization between the fifteenth and seventeenth centuries.

Price, A. Grenfell. *The Western Invasions of the Pacific and Its Continents: A Study of Moving Frontiers and Changing Landscapes, 1513–1958.* Oxford, 1963. An investigation into the physical and cultural changes suffered by the Pacific territories as a result of the white peoples' invasions.

Rawley, James A. *The Transatlantic Slave Trade: A History.* New York, 1981. A comprehensive analysis of the African diaspora as a result of the slave trade during European and American colonial history.

Simon, Marcel, et al., eds. *Les pèlerinages de l'antiquité biblique et classique à l'occident médiéval.* Paris, 1973. This volume focuses on the pilgrimage traditions of the Jews, Christians, and Muslims of the Mediteranean basin and of ancient Greece. It also provides an important theoretical treatment of the notion of pilgrimage.

Strobel, August. *Der spätbronzezeitliche Seevölkerstum: Ein Forschungsüberblick mit Folgerungen zur biblischen Exodusthematic.* Berlin, 1976. A remarkable contribution to the controversial study of the "sea people" and the great migration that turned around the history of the ancient Near East.

Yeivin, Samuel. *The Israelite Conquest of Canaan.* Istanbul, 1971. An exemplary investigation, based on literary and archaeological evidence, of the Israelite invasion.

New Sources

Eickelman, Dale F., and James Piscatori. *Muslim Travelers: Pilgrimage, Migration, and the Religious Imagination.* London, 1990.

Fisk, William L. *The Scottish High Church Tradition in America: An Essay in Scotch Irish Ethnoreligious History.* Lanham, Md., 1995.

Geaves, Ron. "Religion and Ethnicity: Community Formation in the British Alevi Community." *Numen: International Review for the History of Religions* 50 (2003): 52–71.

Gregg, Robert. *Sparks from the Anvil of Oppression: Philadelphia's African Methodists and the Southern Migrants, 1880–1940.* Philadelphia, 1993.

Landman, Christina. "Telling Sacred Stories: Eersterust and the Forced Removals of the 1860s." *Religion and Theology,* 6 (1990): 415–428.

Péres y Mena, Andrés Isidora. *Speaking with the Dead: Development of Afro-Latin Religion among Puerto Ricans in the United States: A Study into the Interpenetration of Civilizations in the New World.* New York, 1991.

Sennet, Milton C. *Bound for the Promised Land: African American Religion and the Great Migration.* Durham, N.C., 1997.

WILLIAM H. MCNEILL (1987)
Revised Bibliography

MI LA RAS PA (MILAREPA) (1028/40–1111/23)

was a highly revered Tibetan yogin, famous both for his austere hermetic lifestyle and for the Tantric instructions he imparted through songs of realization. Mi la ras pa is considered an early founder of the Bka' brgyud (Kagyu) sect of Tibetan Buddhism, and therefore an heir to the Tantric tradition of the Indian *siddhas,* or spiritual adepts, Tilopa (fl. tenth century), Nāropa (c. 1016–1100), and Maitrīpa (1007–1085). He is also esteemed throughout the Himalayan Buddhist world as an exemplar of religious dedication, perseverance through hardship, and meditative accomplishment. Themes principally associated with his life story—purification of past misdeeds, faith and devotion to the *guru,* ardor in meditation and yogic practice, and the possibility of attaining liberation in a single lifetime—have shaped the development of Buddhist teaching and practice in Tibet. Mi la ras pa's biographical tradition also inspired works of significant literary achievement in which readers found not only the portrait of an exemplary life but an exhortation to lead such a life themselves.

As a child, the yogin was called Thos pa dga' (Delightful to Hear) and was later given the Tantric initiation name Bzhad pa'i rdo rje (Laughing Vajra). But the master is ubiquitously known as Mi la ras pa. *Mi la* was his clan name; *ras pa* is derived from the single cotton robe (*ras*) worn by Tibetan anchorites—an attire Mi la ras pa retained for most of his life. The name is therefore an appellation, perhaps translated as "The Cotton-Clad Mi la." He is universally addressed with the title *rje btsun*, a word difficult to translate (it is often rendered as "Venerable Lord") but which carries the meaning of both skillful guide and unsullied master.

Mi la ras pa's life story has been the subject of a vast hagiographic tradition in Tibet. Perhaps the earliest record of the yogin's life and teachings is found in an extensive work known as the *Bu chen bcu gnyis* (The twelve great disciples version), purportedly written toward the end of Mi la ras pa's life by a group of his close disciples. Accounts of the biography soon proliferated, and Tibetan authors writing several centuries later mention the existence of more than one hundred versions of the life story.

In the late fifteenth century, the iconoclastic author Gtsang smyon Heruka (1452–1507), the so-called Madman of Central Tibet, completed what would become Mi la ras pa's definitive portrait. Beginning in 1488 he published two major works concerning the yogin: a sacred biography, often known simply as the *Mi la ras pa'i rnam thar* (The life of Mi la ras pa), and a collection of versified teachings organized within short framing tales, the *Mi la ras pa'i mgur 'bum* (Hundred thousand songs of Mi la ras pa). Cast as a first person narrative, the *Life* draws upon traditional models of Buddhist hagiography (including the historical Buddha's pursuit of enlightenment), poignantly describing Mi la ras pa's childhood, his search for a Buddhist master, and his rigorous practice of solitary meditation. The latter collection presents Mi la ras pa's teaching career, his assembling of disciples, subjugation of harmful spirits, and forging of a sacred landscape across the Himalayan region. As its name suggests, the work also preserves Mi la ras pa's primary legacy: his songs of practical instruction and inner realization. The number "one hundred thousand" in the title is a conventional reckoning used to signify a great quantity. Compilations called one hundred thousand songs (*mgur 'bum*) became a popular genre of Tibetan writing, of which Mi la ras pa's was arguably the most famous example.

While clearly based on earlier accounts, these two works became classics in Tibet. As literary masterpieces of the highest order, they quickly eclipsed all previous accounts of Mi la ras pa's life. They were also promoted, and promptly accepted, as presenting the authorized version of the saint's life, which came to be known by generations of readers around the world. Innumerable Tibetan authors refer to Gtsang smyon Heruka's editions; modern scholars continue to hail Mi la ras pa as "Tibet's most celebrated saint," largely based on the popularity of these two works.

Although his dates are debated, biographies agree that Mi la ras pa was born to a prosperous family in the Gung thang region of southwest Tibet. At an early age, after the death of his father, he lived with his mother and sister under the care of a paternal uncle, with the family estate stipulated to return to the boy upon his reaching majority. The rapacious uncle instead appropriated the estate for himself, reducing Mi la ras pa and his family to lives of poverty and privation. At the behest of his mother, Mi la ras pa sought out instruction in black magic and hail making in order to exact revenge upon their manipulative relatives.

In central Tibet, Mi la ras pa found several skilled teachers, fervently applied himself to their instruction, and quickly showed signs of success. Traditional sources describe how, through the power of a particularly effective magical rite, he murdered thirty-five people gathered one evening for the wedding reception of his uncle's family, sparing his aunt and uncle only so that they could bear witness to his revenge. In retaliation, the surviving relatives conspired to kill Mi la ras pa's mother. To defend her, Mi la ras pa once again applied himself to the practice of magic, this time destroying the crops of his village under a great hailstorm. Eventually, through the ensuing tumult, Mi la ras pa came to realize the magnitude of his misdeeds. Feeling deep contrition for his past actions, he sought to redeem himself from their karmic effects through the practice of Buddhism. He secured the support of his former magic instructor, promised to devote himself to the *dharma*, and set out in search of a Buddhist master.

Mi la ras pa briefly studied Rdzogs chen (dzogchen, Great Completion) practice under one lama before meeting his principal *guru*, the great translator of Indian texts Mar pa Chos kyi blo gros (Marpa Chokyi Lodro, 1002/1012–1097). The relationship that developed between Mar pa and Mi la ras pa would become a celebrated example of the link forged between *guru* and disciple in Vajrayāna Buddhism, emphasizing the central role of faith and devotion in the reliance upon a spiritual guide. It is said that the mere mention of Mar pa's name caused Mi la ras pa's body to shake with devotion. Mar pa, however, was famous for his quick-tempered and demanding personality, and he did not immediately teach his new disciple. He instead subjected Mi la ras pa to repeated abuse, segregating him from other students and forcing him to undergo various ordeals, such as the famous trial of constructing immense stone towers. Pushed to the brink of despair, Mi la ras pa contemplated escape, and later suicide. Mar pa finally assuaged his disciple, revealing that the trials were actually a means of purifying previous negative *karma*. He explained that Mi la ras pa was, from the beginning, a disciple prophesied by Mar pa's own *guru*, the Indian *siddha* Nāropa. Mi la ras pa received numerous Tantric initiations and instructions—especially those of *mahāmudrā* and the practice of *gtum mo* (*tumo*), or yogic "inner heat"—together with the command that he should persevere against all hardship, meditating in solitary caves and mountain retreats.

Mi la ras pa spent the rest of his life practicing meditation in seclusion and teaching small groups of disciples, mainly through spontaneous poetry and songs of realization. He had little interest in philosophical discourse and no tolerance for intellectual pretension. His songs are composed in vernacular idioms, abandoning the highly ornamental formal structures of classical poetry in favor of a simple, direct, and often playful style. Employing metaphors from everyday Tibetan life, they illuminate the nature of mind, emphasize meditation over study, and reflect a love for solitude in nature.

Mi la ras pa traveled widely across the Himalayan region where he attracted a devout following among ascetics and householders alike. Dozens of locations associated with the yogin have become important pilgrimage sites and retreat centers. He spent much of his life in southern Tibet, at caves sites such as Brag dkar rta so (Drakar Taso, White Rock Horse Tooth), La phyi (Lapchi), and Chu dbar (Chubar),and he visited Nepal on several occasions. According to tradition, he secured Mount Kailâsa (Kailash) as a Buddhist pilgrimage site after defeating a priest of the Bon religion in a contest of magic. One account records his stay at the acclaimed Stag tshang (Taktsang) hermitage in Bhutan, first consecrated by the eighth-century Indian adept Padmasambhava. Mi la ras pa's disciples, including the illustrious Sgam po pa Bsod nams rin chen (Gampopa Sonam Rinchen, 1079–1153) and Ras chung pa Rdo rje grags (Rechungpa Dorje Drak, 1084–1161), established a lineage of Bka' brgyud masters that continues to play an important role in the dissemination of Tibetan Buddhism.

The figure of Mi la ras pa has likewise remained deeply embedded within the Tibetan religious world. Buddhist practitioners of all sectarian affiliations throughout the Himalayan region still memorize his songs; elaborate temple murals and scroll paintings record episodes from his life story in great detail; monastic dances reenact his meetings with important disciples; Tantric rituals and *guruyoga sādhanas* invoke his presence as an enlightened being; and new generations of Buddhist yogins embark on solitary meditation retreats, often in caves that he is said to have inhabited, with him as a chief inspiration. Mi la ras pa's biographical tradition also played a central role in the study of Tibet by early European and American scholars. Beginning in the late nineteenth century, the *Life* and *Hundred Thousand Songs* were among the first Tibetan texts to receive widespread attention. Compilers of the earliest Tibetan-English dictionaries made frequent use of passage from these works as models of Tibetan literary usage and style. The figure of Mi la ras pa, the tales of his life, and the penetrating wisdom of his songs persist as part of a living tradition within Tibetan Buddhist communities, and now serve as potent symbols of Tibet to the rest of the world.

SEE ALSO Buddhism, article on Buddhism in Tibet; Buddhism, Schools of, article on Tibetan and Mongolian Buddhism; Mahāsiddhas; Mar pa.

BIBLIOGRAPHY

The first complete English translation of Mi la ras pa's life story was edited by W. Y. Evans-Wentz (in collaboration with the Sikkimese translator Kazi Dawa Samdup), published as *Tibet's Great Yogī Milarepa* (Oxford, 1928). A modern translation by Lobsang P. Lhalungpa, *The Life of Milarepa* (New York, 1977), has now largely superseded this pioneering effort. The standard collection of Mi la ras pa's songs appears in Garma C. C. Chang, trans., *The Hundred Thousand Songs of Milarepa: The Life-Story and Teaching of the Greatest Poet-Saint Ever to Appear in the History of Buddhism* (New Hyde Park, N.Y., 1962). Two further volumes of Mi la ras pa's stories and songs have been translated by Lama Kunga and Brian Cutillo in *Drinking the Mountain Stream* (Novato, Calif., 1978) and *Miraculous Journey* (Novato, Calif., 1986). These works are of particular interest since they include material left out of Gtsang smyon Heruka's versions and may therefore offer, in the translators' words, "pieces from the cutting-room floor."

ANDREW QUINTMAN (2005)

MILLENARIANISM

This entry consists of the following articles:

MILLENARIANISM: AN OVERVIEW

Millenarianism, known also as millennialism, is the belief that the end of this world is at hand and that in its wake will appear a New World, inexhaustibly fertile, harmonious, sanctified, and just. The more exclusive the concern with the End itself, the more such belief shades off toward the catastrophic; the more exclusive the concern with the New World, the nearer it approaches the utopian.

MILLENARIAN THOUGHT. Complexity in millenarian thought derives from questions of sign, sequence, duration, and human agency. What are the marks of the End? At what stage are we now? Exactly how much time do we have? What should we do? Although warranted by cosmology, prophecy, or ancestral myth, the End usually stands in sudden proximity to the immediate era. The trail of events may at last have been tracked to the cliff's edge, or recent insight may have cleared the brier from some ancient oracle.

The root term, *millennium*, refers to a first-century eastern Mediterranean text, the *Apocalypse of John* or *Book of Revelation*, itself a rich source of disputes about the End. John of Patmos here describes in highly figured language a penultimate battle between forces of good and evil, succeeded by a thousand-year reign of saintly martyrs with Jesus, and then the defeat of Satan, the Last Judgment, a new heaven, and a new earth. This interim, earthly reign is literally the millennium (from Lat. *mille*, "thousand"; Gr., *chil*, whence "chiliasm," sometimes applied pejoratively to belief in an indulgent, carnal millennium, or "chiliad"). Not all millenarians expect an interim paradise before an ultimate heavenly assumption; not all anticipate precisely one thousand years of peace; not all stipulate a messianic presence or a saintly elite. Like John, however, they have constant recourse to images, for millenarians are essentially metaphorical thinkers.

In theory, as a speculative poetic enterprise, millenarianism is properly an adjunct of eschatology, the study of last things. In practice, millenarianism is distinguished by close scrutiny of the present, from which arise urgent issues of human agency. Once the fateful coincidence between history and prophecy has been confirmed, must good people sit tight, or must they gather together, withdraw to a refuge? Should they enter the wilderness to construct a holy city, or should they directly engage the chaos of the End, confront the regiments of evil? Millenarians answer with many voices, rephrasing their positions as they come to terms with an End less imminent or less cataclysmic. Where their image of the New World is that of a golden age, they begin with a restorative ethos, seeking a return to a lost purity. Where their image is that of the land of the happy dead or a distant galaxy of glory, their ethos is initially retributive, seeking to balance an unfortunate past against a fortunate future. Few millenarians remain entirely passive, quietly awaiting a supernatural transformation of the world; those who go about their lives without allusion to the looming End customarily escape notice. Most millenarians conflate the restorative and retributive. They act in some way to assure themselves that the New World will not be unfamiliar. Images of a fortunate future are primed with nostalgia.

A millenarian's sense of time, consequently, is neither strictly cyclical nor linear. However much the millennium is to be the capstone to time, as in Christian and Islamic traditions, it is also in character and affect the return of that carefree era posited for the start of things. However much the millennium is to be an impost between two of the infinite arches of time, as in Aztec and Mahāyāna Buddhist traditions, it is for all mortal purposes a release from pain and chaos for many generations.

To the uninitiated, the millenarian mathematics of time may seem mysteriously scaled: how can one account for that arbitrary algebra that assigns the value 3,500 years to the locution "a time, and times, and half a time" (*Rv.* 12:14)? Millenarian thought is figurative in both senses of that word—metaphorical and numerological. Intricate play with numbers of years is founded upon a faith in the impending aesthetic wholeness of the world-historical process. Millenarian searches for laws of historical correspondence between the individually human and the universally human bear a formal similarity to one another, whether the searchers are nineteenth-century social visionaries (the Saint-Simonian Gustave d'Eichthal, the young Hegelian August von Cieszkowski, the Confucian reformer Kang Yuwei), seventeenth-century theologians (the Puritan chronologist Joseph Mede, the natural philosopher Isaac Newton, the Shīʿī Neoplatonist Muḥammad Sadr al-Dīn), or twelfth-century monastics (the abbess Hildegard of Bingen, the abbot Joachim of Fiore, the White Lotus monk Mao Ziyuan). Each discerns a pattern of historical ages that promises both completion and recapitulation.

World religions have known two deep reservoirs of millenarian thought, one noumenal and Gnostic, the other phenomenal and nomothetic. When the reservoirs empty into each other—when mathematicians allude to secret knowledge or contemplatives allude to laws of physics (as in fifth-century southern China, seventeenth-century Western Europe, twentieth-century North America)—millenarianism waxes strong. Alchemy and astrology, nuclear physics and molecular genetics share with qabbalistic magic and Tantric yoga an appreciation for techniques of prediction and mutation. Popularly set in sharp contrast to millenarian "fanatics," scientists and mystics have in fact been crucial to the cultural continuity of millenarian thought; they have preserved an intense concern with processes of transformation and the pulsing of time.

Among the world religions we can locate two constellations of millenarian thought about an epochal pulsing of time, one Zoroastrian-Jewish-Greek-Christian, the other Hindu-Buddhist-Daoist-Confucian. In the Mediterranean littoral, an epochal aesthetic was elaborated by scribal elites who were resistant first to Greek rule (thus producing the Jewish *Book of Daniel* and the lost sources for the Mazdean *Apocalypse of Hystaspe*), then to Roman rule (producing the Egyptian *Potter's Prophecy* and Judeo-Christian apocalypses such as *Enoch* and the *Epistle of Barnabas*), and finally to Muslim rule (producing the Syrian-Christian *Revelations* of Pseudo-Methodius). Feasting upon a cosmopolitan diet of Zoroastrian cosmology, Jewish notions of Sabbath, and Greco-Roman ideas of historical recurrence, these literati stamped the disturbing flux of empires with the template of the divine creative week, which they saw being played out again at length in human history through a reassuringly predictable series of world kingdoms over a period of six or seven thousand years. At the end lay a millennial sabbath, transposed from a time of perpetual rest to a time of truce and earthly reward prior to the final onslaughts of the dragon, tyrant, or false messiah.

This demonic figure of imperium acquired a righteous cousin, the Last World Emperor, whose inexplicable abdication would open the way to his black kin. The dialectic between devious shape-changing evil and prematurely vanishing good, played out against a Christian backdrop that placed a redemptive event close to the center of Roman history, gradually reversed epochal theory, which had begun with a fourfold schema of decadence from golden antiquity. The upshot by the fourteenth century was a progressive tripartite schema bounded on one side by fall and flood, on the other by fire and judgment, and aesthetically framed: here a primordial earthly paradise spoiled by a fork-tongued beast; there a climactic earthly paradise spiked by a horned beast, the antichrist. Between these ran three broad historical ages, each with its bright dawn and horrid nightfall. These ages were identified with other trinities (Father-Law-Justice, Son-Faith-Grace, Spirit-Love-Freedom). Over the next centuries, the millennium itself was annexed to the third age and enshrined in historical rhetoric (classical, medieval, renaissance; feudal, capitalist, socialist). Nineteenth-century exponents of infinite progress had only to remove the limiting aesthetic frame.

Across East Asia, a millenarian aesthetic developed within contexts far less adversarial, and we find no figure antiphonal to the universal perfect ruler (the Hindu *cakravartin*, the Buddhist Rudra Cakin, the Javanese hybrid *Ratu Adil)* or to the future incarnate savior (the Hindu Kalkin, the Maitreya Buddha, a reborn Laozi). Furthermore, the epochal scheme was overwhelmingly degenerative: it fixed all recorded history within the last of the four increasingly chaotic eras (*yugas*) of the aeon (*kalpa*). The problem here was not to expand the prophetic horizon but to foreshorten the 4.3 million-year Indian *kalpa* cycle so that hundreds of thousands of distressing years of the fourth era, the *kaliyuga*, did not still lie ahead.

Each *kalpa* was to end in a cosmic disaster that would, after some blank time, initiate a new cycle whose first *yuga* was always a golden age. Strategic foreshortening brought present catastrophe stern to snout with a renewed world. The foreshortening began in northern India with early Mahāyāna Buddhist images of *bodhisattvas*, compassionate enlightened beings who chose to work in this world for the benefit of others rather than withdraw into final *nirvāṇa*. Almost simultaneously, Chinese commentators during the Later Han period (25–220 CE) alloyed the Confucian golden age of antiquity, the Datong, to the Daiping golden age, which according to Daoist sexagenary cycles could be both ancient and imminent, as the Yellow Turban rebels in 184 sincerely hoped. By the sixth century, the colossal four-cycle Indian cosmology had collapsed under the weight of Daoist alchemy, pietist Pure Land Buddhism, and popular Chinese worship of the Eternal Mother (Wusheng Laomu) and the *bodhisattva* Prince Moonlight (Yueguang Tongzi).

There were then three accessible ages, associated cosmologically with the Daoist Former, Middle, and Latter Heavens, typologically with the three Buddhas (Lamplighter, Śākyamuni, and Maitreya), and synecdochically with the Buddhas' lotus thrones of azure, red, and white. Each age begins with a new buddha and then declines, again in triplets: True Doctrine, or Dharma; Counterfeit Doctrine; and Last Days of Doctrine. Since the days of the historical Buddha, Śākyamuni (and, traditionally, of Confucius and Laozi), we have squatted uncomfortably in the dissolute Last Days, awaiting Maitreya or his predecessor, Prince Moonlight, who is due to sweep in at the height of catastrophes one thousand years after Śākyamuni's *parinirvāṇa*. Profitably vague as it was, such a schedule made it clear that Venerable Mother, responsible for sending each of the buddhas, intended our imminent return to the Pure Land, the Western Paradise.

The upshot of this foreshortening was an epochal aesthetic which, by the fourteenth century, called for rounded contours to a humanly proportioned history, and a millenarian White Lotus rebellion, which in 1351 drew the curtain on the Yuan dynasty and set the stage for the Ming (from Ming Wang, the Chinese name for the Manichaean "perfect ruler," the Prince of Radiance). This aesthetic survived to inform the White Lotus uprisings of the eighteenth century, the Taiping Rebellion of 1851 to 1864, the Dao Lanh sect founded in 1849 by the Vietnamese Buddha Master of Western Peace, Doan Minh Huyen, the Ōmotokyō, founded in 1892, by the Japanese farmer Deguchi Nao, and the Saya San rebellion in Burma from 1930 to 1932.

Stretched between the Mediterranean and East Asian constellations, Manichaeism and Islam transected both. Mani's lithe dualism darkened the antichrist and highlighted the Amitābha (Pure Land) Buddha and the Ming Prince of Radiance. Islam shared with the Mediterranean a demonic end-time imposter, al-Dajjāl, and with East Asia a degenerative epochal theory, but more important was its caravan of redeemers. By 1300, Shīʿī Muslims had at least four candidates for the job of world-renewer: the twelfth spiritual guide, or *imām,* who had disappeared in the ninth century and was in hiding or occultation; a twelfth caliph, under whose reign would appear the restorer of the faith, the Mahdi, to usher in a short golden age before the End; and ʿĪsā (Jesus) who would do military honors at the End. Ismāʿīlī and Ṣūfī emphasis on the hiddenness of the *imām* may have colored later Christian visions of a Last World Emperor dying (or vanishing) prematurely, and Shīʿī Mahdism certainly splashed across North India and Indonesia. Eventually, *imām,* caliph, and Mahdi merged; in Africa even ʿĪsā had joined ranks by the mid-1800s. Two epochal motifs also merged then, a punctual one, according to which a renewer of the faith would appear at the end of each Islamic century, and a symmetrical one, according to which the twelfth *imām* would reappear in the thirteenth century AH (1785/6 to 1881/2 CE), which was a century of worldwide Mahdist movements—northern Nigeria (1804), India (1810, 1828, and 1880), Java (1825), Iran (1844), Algeria (1849, 1860, and 1879), Senegal (1854), and the Sudan (1881).

Common to millenarian aesthetics in all the world religions is this epochal scenario: a calm inaugural and a riotous finale to each act; the circling of two protagonists near the End, one imperial, the other sacramental; and a time at the End that is at once encore, intermezzo, and the throwing open of the doors.

Millenarianism stands therefore in contrast to the modern pessimism that paints miniatures of global devastation yet mounts no panorama of a future marvelous world. Though flood, plague, famine, or war may summon visions of collective death, millenarians promise more than an accurate prediction of catastrophe. They promise an earth lifted beyond safety to grace. Even at their most catastrophic, millenarians insist that a classical tragedy must be fought through only to reach a genuinely good time. From this conviction of drama derive those socially uncompromising rituals of breaking—obscenity, nudity, fasting, celibacy, rebellion—so coincident with millenarian movements. At their most utopian, millenarians tone down the nightmare of the final act: the earth will be transformed by sheer unanimity. Through evangelism, prophecy, and technologies of translation (speaking in tongues, polyglot scriptures, computer mailing), people will, in the face of local despair, embrace the same faith. A single faith, warmly bespoken, must entail a universal community whose very existence will effect the harmony, sanctity, and security long sought. A time of crisis thus becomes a time of redemption.

Characteristically, millenarians are least specific concerning the millennium itself, a time of instant and perfect communication whose seamlessness makes anatomical detail unnecessary. Millenarians are, rather, diagnosticians of bodies in metastasis. It is hardly coincidental that millenarianism in such diverse contexts as central Africa, western Europe, and northeastern Brazil has been chartered by homeopathic healers, who best appreciate the dramatic working-through of crisis. Not all healers become prophets, but most millenarian prophets claim therapeutic powers that extend from the ailing human body to the ailing body politic. Themselves usually colporteurs of regional symbolic systems, the prophet-healers take millenarianism from diagnosis to prescription, from philosophy to jubilee.

Millenarian Movements. If millenarian thought is curled inside calendar scrolls, millenarian movements are engraved on maps. Their rhetoric has to do less with time than with place. Just as millenarian thought focuses upon golden ages, so millenarian movements have golden places: Heaven on Earth, the Pure Land, the Blessed Isle, the Land without Evil, California (this last from a sixteenth-century Spanish romance read by Hernán Cortés). And since in most iconographies what is closest to perfect is closest to the eye of the storm, millenarians are sure that any migration they make is no retreat but a step toward the New World. Millenarian crying of doom and recruitment of the elect must be understood as the epochal duty of taking into the calm center the kernel of humanity.

Prime metaphor of millenarian movements, migration can also become the prime experience, palpable or vicarious. Millenarians encourage those sensations of the migrant that observers may mistake for motives: exile and wandering, put in scriptural tandem with the peripatetic Buddha, the Wandering Jew, the itinerant Jesus, and Muḥammad's Hijrah; nostalgia for lost lands; contrary moods of excited expectation and deep remorse; inflation of the spiritual benefits of transit, sustained by epics of a terrifying, miraculous crossing; ambivalence toward the New World as both brave and strange.

Whether a millenarian group solicits new gods or extorts aid from the old, it will confuse old home with new. Imagery of migration brings into view earlier mythical dislocations (deluge, expulsion) even as it makes evident the need to accommodate to a new land. The more intransigent the notion of home, the more people must provide themselves with apologies for imagined or actual movements away from it, and the more they will tend toward migration as a commanding metaphor.

We know that the English Puritan settlement of "New" England, like the Spanish Franciscan conquest of "New" Spain, had such millenarian resonance that neither Puritans nor Franciscans were able to acknowledge the historical integrity of the so-called Indians. We know also that for many societies, visitors of a different complexion already had a millenarian role in myths of migration and ancestry (the pink-skinned Europeans for the Fuyughe of the New Guinea highlands, the white-skinned Europeans for the MuKongo of the region of the Kongo, the dark-skinned Mongols, or "Tartars," for western Europeans). For victor as for vanquished, millenarian vertigo has conditioned initial contacts, later misunderstandings, violence, and oppression.

If millenarianism is the religion of the oppressed, it is no less the religion of the oppressor. What prompts the oppressed to envision a new moral order is likely to be the same as what, some decades earlier, prompted the oppressor to move on or over or through. So millenarianism may be both cause and result of migration. This is seen most vividly in the conjunction of Sudanese Mahdism with long-term migration south from an expanding Saharan desert, accelerated pilgrimage across the Sudan to Mecca during the thirteenth century AH, and Egyptian disruption of slave trade from 1850 to 1880.

There is, to many millenarian movements, a primary ecology dependent upon this experience of migration, whether lived or fantasized. Millenarians commonly foresee an End in which the elements of the world are used up, consumed by fire, lava, or flood. As the faithful migrate, the world does too, its elements recombining. How else could that ultimate harmony between the human and the natural be established? Although the elemental reshuffling may be divinely operated, millenarians have typically excited notice by their own human, mimetic acts of violence, their putative disregard for the wealth of the world and the bonds of social life. Cattle killing or pig killing, bonfires of earthly possessions, neglect of crops—these are more than public commitments to prophets or prophecies; they are attempts to act in concert with what seems to be a driving rhythm of history—humanity and nature cracking apart in war and earthquake or crumbling more silently through immorality and faithlessness.

The New World implied by most millenarian movements presumes not only a new natural physiognomy but also a new human physiognomy, one that is messianic in import. We can make no easy distinctions between messianic and millenarian movements. Few messianic leaders appear without heralding an instantaneous New World. Obversely, where there are no focal messianic leaders, as in the Chinese Eight Trigrams Rebellion in 1813, millenarians usually take upon themselves a collective messianic mantle, with cloth enough to redress themselves and the world.

For those who follow prophets toward a New World already marked out—Jan Beuckelzoon's Münster (Germany, 1534), Jemima Wilkinson's Jerusalem (New York, 1788–1794), Antonio Conselheiro's Canudos (Brazil, 1893–1897), Julian Baltasar's Cabaruan (the Philippines, 1897–

1901), Rua Kenana's Maungapohatu (New Guinea, 1907–1916)—the millennium begins in miniature as a sacred prologue. For civic millenarians—the Japanese of Nichiren's Tokaido region in the 1250s, the Italians of Girolamo Savonarola's Florence in the 1490s, the Americans of the 1860s in Emanuel Leutze's mural *Westward the Course of Empire Takes Its Way* in the Capitol, Washington, D.C.,—the burden of pointing the way toward the millennium lies not upon any prophetic enclave or diasporal elite but upon the entire population. The city, the city-state, the state itself becomes the vehicle for world renovation.

So millenarianism may beat at the heart of aggressive nationalism, as in the French revolutionary anthem "La Marseillaise" (1792) or at independence day extravaganzas everywhere. It has underlain beliefs in a Russian mission to redeem civilization, as promoted by the novelist Johann Heinrich Jung-Stilling, the occultist Baroness Barbara Juliane von Krüdener, and Tsar Alexander I before his Holy Alliance of 1815; a Hungarian mission, as in *The Entry of the Magyars*, (1892–1894), a cyclorama celebrating Hungary's "millennial constitution"; a German mission—the Nazi Third Reich; and a Greek mission—the Zoeist Fraternity of the 1950s. Ancient westerly migrations from the Asian steppes by Huns, Magyars, Aryans, and Dorians have thus been rousted out of annals, written into history, and gilded to serve as a national mandate. Talk of a "Third World" as the last hope for a failing planet is a contemporary extension of the same civic millenarian ideal.

"First World" scholars tend to link civic millenarianism with modern Christian postmillennial theology, which holds that Jesus' second coming will postdate the start of the millennium, and that no great tumult will intervene between this world and the New World. Millenarians of this type may be told only by their rhythms from the gentler rocking of reformers. In contrast, premillennialists, paradoxically considered both more primitive and more revolutionary, actively prepare for the advent. The New World, inaugurated by Jesus, ruptures the historical chain and affirms the supernal nature of deity. ("Amillennialists," such as Augustine of Hippo, run the millennium concurrently with the life of the church, so that there can be no separate future earthly kingdom.)

Millenarian movements do not settle conveniently into a pre- or postmillennial stance; even within Latin Christianity, these categories had little bearing before the nineteenth century. From the time of Lucius Lactantius (c. 240–320) until the Reformation, the issue for millenarians was whether the millennium would occur before or after the advent of the antichrist. When early Protestants convinced themselves that the Roman papacy was the antichrist, their heirs had to rephrase the advent debate in terms of the reappearance of Jesus. In the seventeenth century, another generation built up historical arguments in favor of Protestantism by adducing a theory of dispensations through which God progressively revealed divine law. Their heirs mustered courage to reread the *Book of Daniel* and the *Book of Revelation* as if these books could at last be compassed. Such courage led John Nelson Darby (1800–1882) to lower from the flies a startlingly theatrical machine that inspired many subsequent premillennial scenarios: the "secret rapture," an unannounced ascension of the living elect while Jesus returns to do battle on the earth below (cf. *1 Thes.* 4:17). Certified by the widely distributed Cyrus Scofield Bible commentary (1909; amended 1919), this machine resembles Hellenistic blueprints of the Gnostic sage's ascent to the lower heavens during world conflagration. Both tend to cloud the supposedly radical thrust of premillennialism.

In larger perspective, it is less useful to distinguish between conservatives and radical millenarians than to note that millenarian movements go through phases: an expansive phase during which believers move out to a ripening world and an astringent phase during which they pull in toward a holy refuge. These phases are equally political. In the stubbornest withdrawal to the most undesirable, inaccessible places (like Jim Jones's village in the Guyanese jungle from 1972 to 1978), millenarians become *prima facie* political threats, whether or not they speak of loyalty to earthly regents. Total withdrawal so often suggests cabal that the more a millenarian group seeks full disengagement, the more the ruling elite may suspect conspiracy and subversion. Similarly, in their expansive phase, millenarians may be the missionary outriders of empire (Christopher Columbus, for example, his monogram qabbalistic, his "Christ-bearing" mission self-consciously prophetic) or the counterforce to empire (the Plains Indian Ghost Dance of the 1880s, the Contestado of Brazil in the 1910s, the New Mexican La Raza movement in the 1960s); they may be the impetus for nationalism (the Tana Bhagat of India, 1915) or the barrier against it (the Watchtower and Kitawala movements in south-central Africa since 1909, Alice Lenshina's Lumpa Church in Zambia in the 1960s); they may be universalists (the International Workers of the World and their general strikes of 1905 to 1920) or ethnic separatists (Juan Santos presenting himself in 1742 as Apu-Inca, descendant of the last Inca, Atahuallpa, or the Altai Turks in 1904 awaiting the Oirot Khan's return and freedom from the Russians). Expansive or astringent, millenarian movements are inherently political but not inherently reactionary or revolutionary.

Typologies of millenarian movements. Altogether, as a system of thought and social movement, millenarianism spins on two axes: golden age or new era; primitive paradise or promised land. This oscillation leads perplexed observers to depict millenarian movements as volatile, metamorphic, undirected, and ephemeral. Journalistic or academic, administrative or missiological, works on the subject abound with images that have shaped policy. Millenarianism is described in five iconic sets:

1. a contagion to be quarantined (as with Mormonism in Utah in the later 1800s);
2. a quicksand to be fenced off (as in the legal actions

against the American Shakers in the early 1800s and the present-day anticult campaigns against the Unification Church);

3. a simmering stew to be watched, on the premise that a watched pot never boils (as in police surveillance of the group surrounding Catherine Théot in Paris in 1793 and 1794);
4. a boil to be lanced (as in the English kidnapping of the prophet Birsa from Munda country in northeastern India in 1895 or the Belgian imprisonment of Simon Kimbangu and his first disciples from 1921 to 1957);
5. an explosion to be contained (the German war against the Maji Maji of German East Africa [modern-day Tanzania] in 1905 and 1906 or the Jamaican government's preemption of Rastafarian music and rhetoric).

Millenarianism appears here as an epiphenomenon, a symptom of or a pretext for something more sinister. These images (and policies) have an august history. Church councils in Latin, Byzantine, and Protestant Christianity, legal scholars of Sunnī Islam and rabbinic Judaism, the presiding monks of Buddhist *saṃghas*—all have long regarded millenarianism as a disguised attack on codes of behavior that are meant to govern faith and cult. Rulers and their bureaucracies—Confucian, Islamic, Hindu—have regarded millenarianism as a ritual mask worn by crafty rebels.

Present-day typologists are somewhat more sympathetic. For them, millenarianism is emblematic, a ceremonial flag waved furiously over swamps of injustice. Such an interpretation was codified by the French and German Enlightenments, then refurbished by liberals in the nineteenth century until positivist denials of a religious instinct made religion itself seem epiphenomenal. Latter-day social scientists have made millenarianism doubly emblematic, for they describe it as the sign of transition from a religious to a secular society.

Current typologies work along three scales: temporal focus, soteriology, and sociopolitical engagement. On the first scale, typologists range those movements oriented toward (1) the reconstitution of an earlier social structure (called nativist, traditionalist, conservationist, restorative), (2) the imaginative making of peace with change (called acculturative, adjustive, perpetuative, revitalist, reformative), and (3) the creation of an ideal future society (called messianic or utopian). The second scale runs from those movements concerned exclusively with individual salvation (called redemptive, revivalist, thaumaturgic) to those that demand an overhaul of economy and etiquette (called transformative or revolutionary). The third scale starts at total isolation and finishes with collective assault on the state. This scale especially has been plodded and plowed by rhetoric (re-actionary/progressive, passive/active, prepolitical/political, mythological/ideological). Like mule teams, these binary terms are hardworking but perpetually sterile, since millenarians delight in the yoking of opposites.

Dynamic typologies, plotted by such scholars as Mary Douglas (1970), James W. Fernandez, (1964), and Wim M. J. van Binsbergen (1981), are quadrivalent, balancing social pressures against social structures. Douglas uses two variables, social cohesion and shared symbolic systems. Fernandez takes acculturation as his ordinate, instrumentality as his abscissa. Van Binsbergen considers both the source of disequilibrium (infrastructural, superstructural) and the nature of the threat ("peasantization," "proletarianization"). Such typologies, more appreciative of the complexity of millenarian movements, still hesitate before the phase shifts through which most movements go.

Motives for the fabrication of typologies may themselves be classified as prophylactic or exploitative. Most typologies mean to be prophylactic. Political scientists, for example, may hope to forestall the rise of charismatic tyranny; anthropologists in colonial settings may want to persuade authorities to handle millenarian movements more reasonably and with less show of force; missionaries may wish to avoid spawning highly independent churches or syncretic cults. Other typologies are exploitative. Marxist and capitalist alike place millenarians on a sociohistorical ladder so as to direct their obvious energies upward, toward national liberation and socialism or toward modern industrialism and oligopoly. Occultists and irenic church people place millenarians on one rung of the ladder of spiritual evolution so as to draw them toward higher consciousness, the Aquarian age, or one broad faith.

Explanations for millenarian movements. Despite the many typologies, there are but two current scholarly explanations for the birth of millenarian movements. The first asserts that millenarianism arises from feelings of relative deprivation in matters of status, wealth, security, or self-esteem. Millenarian movements appear in periods of crisis, when such feelings become most painful. The crisis may be as blatant and acute as the sack of a city or as subtle and prolonged as the passage from isolated agrarian community to industrial megalopolis. Whichever it is, the crisis engenders personal fantasies of invulnerability and escape, which are transformed by charismatic individuals who are often members of displaced elites. These prophets shape public expressions of protest at a time when more straightforward political action seems useless. In the necessarily unsuccessful aftermath, millenarians master the cognitive dissonance between expectation and failure by perpetuating millenarian beliefs within a revised chronology and a new missionary plan. The underlying causes for feelings of deprivation will not have been resolved, so a millenarian tradition, halfway between social banditry and the politics of party, burns on.

The second, complementary explanation says that millenarian movements spring from contact between two cultures when one is technologically far superior to the other. Millenarianism spreads within the settled, inferior culture, whose polity is critically threatened. The newcomers, usually white and literate, disrupt traditional systems of kinship, healing, and land rights. Most wrenching are the factorial economics introduced by the newcomers, whose quantitative uses of time and money rasp across the qualitative webs of social reciprocity. The indigenes must redefine their notions of power, status, and law, or they must stave off the well-armed traders, their navies, and their missionaries. Acknowledging the superiority of the newcomers' technology but not that of their ethic of possessive individualism, the indigenes begin to speculate about the true origin of the goods and gods of the stingy, secretive newcomers. The result is the contact cult (also called a "crisis cult" or "cargo cult") devoted to frenzied preparation for the receipt of shiploads of goods (cargo) that will dock unaccompanied by whites or in the company of fair-skinned but unselfish ancestors. Already under intense pressure, the people ceremonially destroy sacred objects and standing crops. They believe that this world is ending and a new one must begin, best with the newcomers gone and themselves masters of the secret of wealth.

Contact is the sociology for which deprivation is the psychology. Contact leads to millenarianism when one group feels unalterably deprived vis-à-vis a new other. The two explanations, compatible with stock images of eruption and contagion, rely on the premise of a closed system. At the millenarian core lies frustration; out of frustration squirms fantasy, and fantasy breeds violence. Early Freudian analyses of hysteria, psychosis, and schizophrenia have been employed here to wire the circuit between individual fireworks and collective explosion.

Deprivation theories prevail despite decades of criticism for their being slackly predictive. Scholars have noted that relative deprivation does not account specifically for millenarianism; it may as easily induce fracas, sabotage, or personal depression. Conversely, millenarian movements have not "burst out" where relative deprivation has been most apparent: eighteenth-century Ireland, nineteenth-century Ethiopia, the southeastern coast of modern India. Indeed, as critics may add, where across this imperfect world has relative deprivation ever been absent or a crisis lacking?

At this point, theorists invoke a *homo ex machina*, the charismatic prophet who processes the raw stuff of frustration. As a person whose life portends or echoes social crises, the prophet articulates the myth-dream of the people and so becomes invested with the power to direct its expression. Wherever gambols a weak social theory about religious movements, sure to follow is the fleece of charisma. For face-to-face groups, as W. R. Bion showed in his *Experiences in Groups* (New York, 1961), prophetic leaders may embody group fantasies of rebirth. For larger groups—like most millenarian movements—charisma becomes narcotic, a controlled substance rather than a theory of social relations.

Theorists have given particularly short shrift to the remarkable prominence of women as millenarian prophets. In all but Islam and Judaism, women have stridden at the head of millenarian movements, with men as their scribes, publicists, and ideologues. The list is long; a few examples must do: Priscilla and Maximilla of the New Prophecy (the Montanists) in Asia Minor in the late second century; Guglielma of Milan and her women disciples in the late thirteenth century; Dona Béatrice's Antonine movement in the Lower Congo from 1703 to 1706; Joanna Southcott with perhaps twenty thousand followers in England before her death in 1814; Ellen Gould White, chief oracle of the Seventh-day Adventists in the United States, in the late nineteenth century; Jacobina Maurer of the Brazilian Muckers movement from 1872 to 1898; the visionary Gaidaliu in Assam from 1929 to 1930 and 1961 to 1965; Mai Chaza's Guta ra Jehova (City of Jehovah) in Rhodesia from 1954 to 1960; Kitamura Sayō's Dancing Religion (Tenshō Kōtai Jingukyō) founded in Japan in 1945.

Deprivation theories maintain that women, an injured group, use religion as a means to power otherwise denied them by patriarchies. This makes religion a negative (compensatory) vehicle for women and a positive (creative) vehicle for men, and it fails to explain the power that women gain over men through millenarian movements. There is as yet no sufficient discussion of female charisma. Indeed, where prophetic leadership is male, analysis customarily proceeds from the instrumental, socioeconomic background to doctrine and political tactics; where female, it proceeds from affective, sexual background to ritual and spirit possession. Active men, reactive women: a contact theory of the sexes.

Contact theories are tricky. Amazed by discoveries of previously unknown tribes in the Amazon region and in the Philippines, industrial societies exaggerate the isolation of nonindustrial people. Nonetheless, contact is always a matter of degree: from armies with bulldozers abruptly grading runways in Melanesia to pandemics of smallpox hundreds of miles from (European) vectors. Contact is never so much a shock that some prophecy or other has not already accumulated around a piece of strangeness that years before drifted in on a storm tide or fell from the clouds.

In addition, we have sparse evidence that a number of peoples—the Guaraní of South America, the Karen of Burma, the Lakalai of the island of New Britain, and perhaps the Pacific Northwest Indians—had myths, rituals, and cults whose motifs were millenarian and whose origins were prior to contact with an in-pressing "superior" (Eurasian) culture.

Furthermore, not every uneven contact lights a millenarian "fuse." While the same material imbalance between Europeans and natives faced both Polynesians and Melanesians, millenarian movements have been infrequent among the politically stratified societies of Polynesia. More loosely bunched and socially fluid, Melanesians had inadequate etiquette by which to carry out diplomacy between distinctly separate orders. The customary structure of discourse, not contact itself, seems to have been a key variable in the general absence of cargo cults in Polynesia and their flowering in Melanesia, where consistently powerful Europeans could not be dealt with as easily as could another and analogous order.

At best, deprivation predisposes, contact precipitates. There are six other factors whose presence predisposes to millenarian movements:

1. permeable monastic communities and lay sodalities that extend loyalties beyond the family;
2. itinerant homeopathic healers who carry ritual and rumor across regional borders;
3. a mythopoetic tradition in popular drama and folktale, which makes history prophetic and the people the bearers of prophecy;
4. numerology and astrology, which encourage people habitually to search out relationships between number, event, and time;
5. rituals of inversion, such as carnival or exhaustive mourning, in which endings and beginnings are willfully confused;
6. migration myths that call for the return to an ancestral land or for the return of the dead to a renewed land.

There are negatively prejudicial factors as well. Millenarian movements are least likely at the extremes of the economic spectrum—that is, among those who have complete freedom of mobility and among those absolutely constrained. No millenarian movements occur within groups whose positions are secure, comfortable, and protected by mechanisms of caste (classical North Indian, Japanese, and Roman aristocracies). Nor do millenarian movements occur within groups whose mobility has been severely restricted by political oppression (prisoners, inmates of concentration camps), economic oppression (slaves), physical illness (hospital patients, the starving), or mental illness (asylum inmates, the autistic).

This verges on tautology: millenarian movements happen where physical movement is possible. But the near tautology is suggestive. Where cultural ideals of physical movement differ, so, correspondingly, may the nature of social movements. For example, to be harshly schematic, Western Europeans have stressed vertical, direct, outbound motion in their sports, their dancing, their tools, and their manners; the head and shoulders lead, with the mass of the body in tow. Sub-Saharan Africans such as the Dogon have a kinesthetic of orchestral, highly oppositional, polyrhythmic motion in which the body twists at the hips. The northern Chinese have in their martial arts, their medicine and calligraphy a kinesthetic of sustained circular motion, an integrated body linked to the flow of universal energy. These differences may be expressed in the European proclivity for a tight echelon of prophets leading an undifferentiated millenarian body, the African tendency toward coextensive and fissiparous leadership, the Chinese history of generational continuity from one guiding millenarian family to the next. Kinesthetic differences may also determine the relative importance of the precipitants of millenarianism: where a society looks for whole-body motion, the triggering instances must affect the entire society; where a society looks for articulated or isolated motions, the triggering instances may be more local.

The following four factors recur cross-culturally as major precipitants of millenarian movements:

1. the evangelism of foreign missionaries whose success requires the reordering of native patterns of marriage, family, diet, and calendar;
2. displacement by refugees or invaders, or as a result of persecution, economic decline, or natural calamity;
3. confusion about landholdings due to shifting settlement, the superposition of a new legal grid, or the advent of new technologies, as foreshadowed most particularly by census taking, geological surveys, rail laying, and road building;
4. generational distortion, where the traditional transfer of loyalties and moral authority is profoundly disturbed by war deaths, schooling, long-distance migrations, or urbanization.

These are, of course, related. Threaded throughout are anxieties about inheritance, boundaries, and language (its intelligibility, its capacity for truth-telling). Set within a matrix of predisposing factors, granted some rumors and good weather, these anxieties should specifically engage the wheels of millenarianism, with its special freight of ages, places, and figures of speech. Expansive millenarianism occurs when believers are imperiled or impressed by forces within their society; astringent millenarianism occurs when the forces seem foreign.

Patterns of millenarian movements in world history. The world's great religions share a larger historical pattern of millenarian activity (although Vedānta Hinduism may be a partial exception). Founded on the fringes of empire or at the fracture line between competing kingdoms, these religions find themselves several centuries later at the center of an empire. Millenarian thought then appears in canonical form, drawing its impetus from those forces of imperial expansion that compel the recalculation of calendars, histories, distances, and sacred geography. The new arithmetic signals a shift in scales of measurement, mediated as much by mystics as by scientists. When an empire seems to have reached its limits, millenarian movements flourish, usually several generations before the dynastic collapse.

When the millennium does not arrive, or when millenarian movements are co-opted by a new dynasty, as in Ming China or Safavid Iran, millenarianism does not fade away. End-of-the-world images linger in the dreams and speech of the people, and end-time ideas are filtered through monasteries, lay brotherhoods, and scientific communities. As these are gradually attracted to the nodes of political power, millenarian movements reappear either as adjuncts of conquest or as resistance to it. Millenarian activity peaks again when the limits of territorial coherence are felt within the empire and along its colonial periphery.

This sequence may obtain for other than the great world religions (e.g., for the Aztec, Iroquois, and Ba-kongo), but materials are lacking that would sustain such an argument for the many preliterate cultures. It is tempting, in the same way that millenarianism itself is tempting, to offer a global explanation—such as climatic cycles—for its rhythms. The quest for global explanations, however, like the quest for a fountain of youth, tells more about the explorers than it does about the territory.

CONTEMPORARY FASCINATION WITH THE END. Why does millenarianism presently seem in such need of some kind of covering law? The answers to this question have to do with the characteristics of the North Atlantic ecumene, which is responsible for most of the law making.

A first answer is that millenarians tend not to fall within the bell of the ecumene's emotional curve. Although sternly depressed about current affairs, millenarians are at the same time exultant about the prospects for a New World. European and North American psychologists interpret ambivalence as a symptom of inner discord; the greater the ambivalence, the more serious the illness. But "sensible" middle-class citizens join UFO cults, buy fifteen million copies of Hal Lindsey's *The Late Great Planet Earth* (Grand Rapids, Mich., 1970), and order bulk goods from End Time Foods, Inc., in Virginia. Why?

A second answer is that millenarians threaten the stability of the ecumene, upsetting the development of outlying colonies. Millenarians seem haphazardly amused by industrial investment and international tariffs. Why do they keep popping up to make a hash of foreign policy, and why do they prefer the "magical" to the "practical"?

A third answer is that the wars of the twentieth century burned the mark of the beast on North Atlantic arts, philosophy, and history. The beast roared through the no-man's-lands of World War I and the gas chambers and radioactive cinders of World War II. Apocalypse has lost its reference to millennium; it has become simply a synonym for disaster.

We can also trace the growth of a catastrophic mood in North Atlantic science over a century of work in astronomy, cosmology, ecology, climatology, and, recently, morphogenetics and mathematics (the last two united by catastrophe theory, which accounts topologically for instant changes of state). The mood has prevailed in popular science from Henry Adams's 1909 essay on the second law of thermodynamics ("The Rule of Phase Applied to History") to the syzygy scare of the so-called Jupiter effect (1974–1982).

A fourth, more upbeat answer is that archaeology, theology, politics, and the Gregorian calendar have conspired to regenerate the utopian side of millenarianism. Although no millenarian movements and exceedingly few prophecies were geared to the year 1000 (few then used such a calendar), the historical myth persisted because it seemed to many that the year 2000 would be truly millennial. The discovery of the Dead Sea Scrolls since 1947 has underscored the contention, popularized by Albert Schweitzer in 1906, that eschatological hope was vital at the time of apostolic Christianity and should therefore be part of all true Christian belief. Israel's statehood in 1948 and its 1967 reunification of Jerusalem have convinced fundamentalist Christians of the nearness of the Second Coming, for which a principal sign is the Jews' return to Zion. So we see in the ecumene a telephone hot line for news of the latest scriptural prophecies fulfilled, an international conference on end-of-world prophecies (in Jerusalem in 1971), and a new perfume called Millennium: "In the life of every woman's skin there comes a turning point, a time when her face begins to look older. Now there is an alternative."

Outside the ecumene, detached from Christian dates, Hindu and Buddhist revivalists (Hare Krishna, Divine Light Mission, Sōka Gakkai) preach the last era, the *kaliyuga* or *mappō.* Shīʿīs awaiting the Mahdi at century's end (AH1399/1979–1980 CE) experienced instead the Iranian revolution. Mexican intellectuals of the Movement of the Reappearance of Anauak, following the Aztec calendar, find this a time of cataclysm. Marxists, flipping through an economic almanac, tear off the leaves of late capitalism.

The fifth answer, then, is that from within and without the ecumene, notions of change have taken on a prepotently millenarian cast.

THE SIGNIFICANCE OF MILLENARIANISM. Claims for the significance of millenarianism, either as a system of thought or as a tradition of social movements, range from the thoughtfully deprecatory (that it is one more index to the predicament of capitalism) to the modestly dismissive (that it is an expression of a universally human fantasy of returning to the womb and resuming unhindered power in a practically timeless world) to the complimentary (that it is a rich mode of dissent where other modes are either unavailable or unavailing) to the genuinely laudatory (that in the form of the myth of the eternal return and its rituals of cosmic renewal, it is the taproot of religion and revolution). The truth, as usual, lies athwart.

SEE ALSO Eschatology; Exile; Golden Age; Utopia.

BIBLIOGRAPHY

Millenarian scholarship, chiefly a phenomenon of the North Atlantic ecumene, has followed the same patterns of historical change.

During the sixteenth century, while European merchants redefined time as fortune, millenarians appeared in Roman Catholic histories of heresy and Protestant martyrologies. For Catholics and for the Magisterial Reformers, millenarianism was occasioned by lust (impatience, appetite without love); for radical Protestants, millenarianism came of a desperately loving desire to return to the apostolic model. Then, as today, the bell cows of any overview were the communalistic Taborites in fifteenth-century Bohemia, Thomas Müntzer's rebels in the German Peasants' Revolt of 1524–1525, and the antinomian Anabaptist kingdom at Münster in 1534. In these three episodes the consequences of the millenarian program were so played out that most subsequent commentaries used them to distinguish between legitimate and illegitimate visions of religious and social renewal.

Early seventeenth-century histories, written in a confusing era of religious warfare, tended to describe millenarianism as the confused or gangrenous extension of piety, for which in English was coined the word *enthusiasm,* an outlier of the syndrome of melancholia. Melancholics seemed to resemble the age itself, mixing categories and muddling the practical, the extravagant, and the fantastic.

After the near revolutions of midcentury—the French Fronde with its *illuminés,* the English Civil War with its Levellers and Fifth Monarchists—millenarianism was implicated in political plotting and secret communication. So the medical figure of contagion, used earlier against witchcraft, was resurrected in works about millenarians, who might be possessed or mad or deluded but were likely first to have been infected by conniving knaves. Every one of these explanations was offered for the mass appeal of the great Jewish false messiah, Shabbetai Tsevi, who in 1666, at the height of his career, converted to Islam under penalty of death.

Eighteenth-century accounts, although sometimes pietist and sympathetic to millenarians, moved toward a vaguely biological description: millenarianism was seen as corpuscular, nervous, iatromechanical. In an era of newly accurate clocks and mortality statistics, historical source-criticism and the propaganda of Newtonian science, millenarians seemed to have lost their sense of time and power of memory.

Most modern assumptions about millenarianism were in place soon after the French Revolution. Encyclopedias of religion and dictionaries of sects sank the stakes: millenarianism was a personal reaction to internal chemical imbalance or to feelings of envy or lust; it was a social ploy or a disguise for politicking, money making, or ambition. Later in the century, under the impact of revivalism and labor agitation, millenarianism became part of the sociology of crowds; as a personal disorder it was associated homologically with *dementia praecox* (soon to be called schizophrenia). Anthropologists worked with Europocentric genetic metaphors: if millenarian movements occurred within Western civilization, they were classified as throwbacks to the spiritual childhood of religion; if outside, they were seen as infantile tantrums of primitive societies.

At least three thousand studies of millenarianism have been printed in this century, more and more often with a sympathetic preamble. Even so, because millenarians seem destined to inevitable disappointment, people of all political persuasions have resented the millenarian label, none more so than revolutionaries who want to make it clear that their programs for a New World are neither illusory nor doomed. Since Ernst Bloch's *Thomas Müntzer als Theologe der Revolution* (Munich, 1921), millenarian scholarship has been especially sharpened by political as well as religious polemic.

At midcentury, out tumbled a spate of works insisting on the centrality and continuity of millenarianism: for European culture, Normal R. C. Cohn's *The Pursuit of the Millennium* (1957), 3 ed. (New York, 1970); for peasant culture, Eric J. Hobsbawm's *Primitive Rebels* (New York, 1959); for world culture, *La table ronde*'s full issue on "Apocalypse et idée de fin des temps" (no. 110, February 1957); and the human condition, Mircea Eliade's *Cosmos and History: The Myth of the Eternal Return* (New York, 1954). Simultaneously, in *When Prophecy Fails* (1956; reprint, New York, 1964), Leon Festinger, Henry W. Riecken, and Stanley Schachter developed a theory of cognitive dissonance to explain the endurance of millenarian beliefs from the point of view of social psychology. The capstone was a conference in 1960 sponsored by *Comparative Studies in Society and History* (The Hague, 1958–), the journal that is still the most active in millenarian studies. The event set the agenda for at least a decade of research, prompting scholars to fashion typologies and to formulate distinctions between varieties of millenarian activity. The conference results were published in book form in *Millennial Dreams in Action: Essays in Comparative Study,* edited by Sylvia L. Thrupp (The Hague, 1962).

Although the works discussed above remain the most consistently cited sources in millenarian studies, their popularity is largely a measure of the comfort they have afforded a North Atlantic ecumene that is increasingly upset by liberation movements and cold war apocalypse diplomacy. Millenarianism, they assure us, has a history, a tradition, a phenomenology, a philosophy, and a psychology.

Henri Desroche's *Dieux d'hommes: Dictionnaire des messianismes et millénarismes de l'ère chrétienne* (Paris, 1969), although incomplete and outdated, codified much earlier scholarship. That year also saw a general turn away from theories of social pathology and mental illness to explain millenarian movements. Sophisticated analysis has turned toward the creative and polysemous nature of millenarianism. The following are some of the most thoughtful and evocative works published in English since 1969.

The oxymorons of millenarian thought have been deftly handled by Marjorie E. Reeves in *The Influence of Prophecy in the Later Middle Ages: A Study of Joachimism* (Oxford, 1969) and *Joachim of Fiore and the Prophetic Future* (London, 1976), which should be supplemented by a series of articles by Robert E. Lerner, including "Medieval Prophecy and Religious Dissent," *Past and Present* 72 (1976): 3–24; J. G. A. Pocock's *Politics, Language and Time* (New York, 1971), especially his essay "Time, History and Eschatology in the Thought of Thomas Hobbes," pp. 148–201; and Sacvan Bercovitch's *The Puritan Origins of the American Self* (London, 1975), which is excellently extended in his article "The Typology of America's Mission," *American Quarterly* 30 (Summer 1978): 135–155. Theodore Olson's *Millennialism, Utopianism, and Progress* (Toronto, 1981) moves heroically from the Greeks to the present, slipping and sliding along the way but always serious and sometimes passionate. Joseph Needham's purview is even broader; Needham masterfully draws out the similarities as well as the differences between European and Chinese approaches to time, in "Time and Eastern Man" in his *The Grand Titration: Science and Society in East and West* (Buffalo, N.Y., 1969), pp. 218–298. Like Needham, Charles Webster underlines the philosophical but also the social relations between science and millenarianism in his *The Great Instauration: Science, Medicine and Reform, 1626–1660* (New York, 1976).

Social anthropologists have been at the forefront of theory about millenarian movements. Alluded to in the text were Mary Douglas's *Natural Symbols: Explorations in Cosmology* (New York, 1970); James W. Fernandez's "African Religious Movements," *Annual Review of Anthropology* 7 (1978): 195–234, and "African Religious Movements: Types and Dynamics," *Journal of Modern African Studies* 2 (1964): 531–549; and Wim M. J. van Binsbergen's *Religious Change in Zambia* (Boston, 1981). Highly influential for his sophistication and for his theory of differential access to redemptive media is Kenelm Burridge's *New Heaven, New Earth* (New York, 1969). An interesting and thoroughgoing Marxist approach is presented by Berta I. Sharevskaya in *The Religious Traditions of Tropical Africa in Contemporary Focus* (Budapest, 1973); more accessible may be her article "Toward a Typology of Anticolonial Religious-Political Movements in Tropical Africa," *Soviet Anthropology and Archaeology* 15 (1976): 84–102. Less anthropological but nicely eclectic is Stephen Sharot's *Messianism, Mysticism, and Magic: A Sociological Analysis of Jewish Religious Movements* (Chapel Hill, N.C., 1982).

For particularly well done case studies of millenarian movements, see Mangol Bayat's *Mysticism and Dissent: Socioreligious Thought in Qajar Iran* (Syracuse, N.Y. 1982); Pierre Clastres's *Society against the State,* translated by Robert Harley and Abe Stein (New York, 1977), concerning the Guaraní of South America; Hue-Tam Ho Tai's *Millenarianism and Peasant Politics in Vietnam* (Cambridge, Mass., and London, 1983); Susan Naquin's *Millenarian Rebellion in China: The Eight Trigrams Uprising of 1813* (New Haven and London, 1976) and *Shantung Rebellion: The Wang Lun Uprising of 1774* (New Haven, 1981); my own *The French Prophets: The History of a Millenarian Group in Eighteenth-Century England* (Berkeley, 1980); and Anthony F. C. Wallace's *The Death and Rebirth of the Seneca* (New York, 1972).

Further bibliographies may be found in my "The End of the Beginning: Millenarian Studies, 1969–1975," *Religious Studies Review* 2 (July 1976): 1–15; Harold W. Turner's *Bibliography of New Religious Movements in Primal Societies,* 4 vols. (Boston, 1977–); and Bryan R. Wilson's *Magic and the Millennium* (New York, 1973), pp. 505–531.

New Sources

Bowie, Fiona, and Christopher Deacy, eds. *Christian Millenarianism: From the Early Church to Waco.* London, 2001.

Emmerson, Richard, and Bernard McGinn, eds. *Apocalypse in the Middle Ages.* Ithaca, N.Y., 1992.

Greenspoon, Leonard J., and Ronald A. Simkins, eds. *Millenialism from the Hebrew Bible to the Present.* Lincoln, Neb., 2003.

Landes, Richard A., ed. *Encyclopedia of Millennialism and Millenial Movements.* New York, 2000.

McGinn, Bernard, John J. Collins, and Stephen J. Stein, eds. *Continuum History of Apocalypticism.* New York, 2003.

Robbins, Thomas, and Susan J. Palmer, eds. *Millenium, Messiahs, and Mayhem: Contemporary Apocalyptic Movements.* New York, 1997.

Rowland, Christopher, and John Barton, eds. *Apocalyptic in History and Tradition.* London and New York, 2002.

Trompf, G. W., ed. *Cargo Cults and Millenarian Movements: Transoceanic Comparisons of New Religious Movements.* Berlin and New York, 1990.

HILLEL SCHWARTZ (1987)
Revised Bibliography

MILLENARIANISM: CHINESE MILLENARIAN MOVEMENTS

The yearning for a utopia where one is free from want and where peace and prosperity reign supreme has been very much an integral part of Chinese religion since pre-Qin times (before 221 BCE). Confucius (551–479 BCE) maintained the notion of a golden age when Sage-Kings such as Yao and Shun reigned effortlessly in perfect harmony. Laozi also espoused the idea of small agricultural communities where life was simple and government was noninterfering. The Moist concept of undifferentiated and nondiscriminating love was expressed in the form of *datong* ("grand unity" or "great equality"), which had been incorporated into the Confucian text *Liji* (The classic of rites). However, all these utopian states were understood to have existed in the distant past. As time progressed, the conceptualization of utopia became more concrete and contemporary. During the Qin-Han period (221 BCE–220 CE), mysterious lands in the extreme east and west of China were regarded either as paradises inhabited by immortals, or as idealized countries where justice and honesty prevailed. The realm of Xiwangmu or Queen Mother of the West, on Mount Kunlun in the west and the three fairy islands of Penglai ("proliferating weeds"), Fangzhang ("square fathom"), and Yingzhou ("ocean continent") in the eastern seas belonged to the first category, while the land of "Great Qin" (Da Qin), an idealized version of the Roman Empire, belonged to the second.

In contrast to pre-Qin utopias, all these ideal realms were understood to be contemporaneous with those who visited or reported on them. However, they were accessible to only a few privileged members of society. The Queen Mother of the West, for example, entertained only emperors and regaled them by her turquoise pond with her peaches and wine of immortality. The three fairy islands were similarly inaccessible to ordinary mortals; they either sank into the ocean when approached, or caused big storms to drive people off course.

EARLY MOVEMENTS. Two major soteriological movements developed in China in the second century of the common era. Both had appeal to the masses. The first, centered in western China (present-day Sichuan and Shaanxi), was headed by Zhang Lu, who created a theocratic state between 186 and 216 CE. Tracing his teaching to his grandfather Zhang Daoling (34?–156? CE), Zhang Lu taught that illness was a sign of sin and could be healed by confession. Furthermore, he advocated the establishment of communal facilities to expedite the realization of his utopia on earth. These facilities provided free food for the needy and undertook all kinds of public works for the good of the commonweal. Zhang's movement, known as the Five Pecks of Rice (Wudoumi) or Way of Celestial Masters (Tianshi dao), survived the Han-Wei dynastic transition because of his accommodation with political authorities. It became the recognized orthodox Daoist tradition in China, and Zhang Daoling was revered as the first Daoist patriarch.

There was another religious movement in eastern China that, under the leadership of Zhang Jue (d. 184 CE), existed contemporaneously with Zhang Lu's and in many ways resembled the latter in both belief and organization. It was called the Way of Highest Peace (Taiping dao) because of its alleged subscription to the text *Taiping jing* (Classic of highest peace). However, it differed from Zhang Lu's movement in that it rebelled in 184 and was ruthlessly crushed by the Han imperial forces. This rebellion, known as the Yellow Turban Rebellion because of the color of the headgear worn by the rebels, represented the first large-scale religiously inspired rebellious movement in Chinese history.

Some scholars argue that the impetus for the militancy of the Yellow Turbans came from the *Taiping jing* which, despite its Confucian and perhaps even Buddhist borrowings, was obviously a Daoist text concerned with eschatology and changing the course of history. Compiled in the form of a continuing dialogue between the Celestial Master, an emissary of Dao, and his disciples, the *Taiping jing* offers description of an ideal society and provides expectation of a renewal of the world through heavenly agents. The significance of the text's eschatology lies in the fact that it relativizes the validity of the existing society. It sees drastic change in the course of history as imminent and desirable, for the demarcation between this world and the beyond will be broken down, and the dawning of a mystical new order will be at hand.

Thus, from the original view of an ideal world existing in the remote past, through the transitional view of the utopia existing in distant lands contemporaneously, Chinese religion finally came to the view of the perfect realm existing in the future, the arrival of which would signal the end of the present age.

THE MEDIEVAL PERIOD. The several centuries after the collapse of the Han dynasty were a time of burning religious zeal, caused in part by the people's desire to seek solace from a rapidly disintegrating society brought about by "barbarian" invasions and incessant warfare. With Confucianism in eclipse, both Daoism and the newly introduced Buddhism made great inroads into the hearts and minds of the Chinese. Especially attractive to the suffering masses was the promise of messianic deliverance offered by both Daoist and Buddhist sectarian groups. It was during this time, specifically from the fourth century on, that a Chinese-style millenarianism developed, complete with the identification of an eschatological crisis, the appearance of a messianic figure, the apocalyptic battle, the guaranteed survival of the elect, and the portrayal of the "New Jerusalem."

In sectarian Daoism, millenarianism was expressed in the cult of Laozi, which now assumed the name of Li Hong the Perfect Lord. Between the fourth and the fifth centuries numerous rebel leaders, claiming to be incarnations of Li Hong, staged uprisings. As described in the *Dongyuan shenzhou jing* (Classic of divine spells from the deep cavern), a Daoist text compiled in the early fifth century, the millenarianism of the Li Hong cult contains the following themes:

1. There is an impending crisis of cosmic proportions caused by the accumulation of evil. The time of reckoning will be the year *renchen* (which occurs once every sixty years in the Chinese calendar, but was generally understood to specify the year 392 CE), when floods surging upwards of several thousand feet and epidemics of every imaginable kind will afflict the world.
2. The savior Li Hong will appear to deliver his believers from this cataclysmic disaster and to eradicate all nonbelievers, who will be discarded as chaff. This apocalyptic battle will result in the total triumph of Li Hong and his chosen ones.
3. An era of unutterable joy and peace will ensue. The ravages of war will be eliminated. The cosmos will be reconstituted. The entire earth will be covered with seven treasures. One sowing will yield nine crops and human lifespan will be extended to three thousand years, after which it will be renewed again. All men and women will be sages and evil people will no longer exist.

This Daoist millenarianism was paralleled by a Buddhist version of the same period. Centered around the messianic figure of "Prince Moonlight" (Yueguang tongzi), a minor character in the legendary biography of the Buddha, this Buddhist millenarianism has essentially all the features of its Daoist counterpart, with the same expectation of apocalyptic happenings designated to take place in a specific year. In fact, the similarity between the two versions of millenarianism is so striking that one is compelled to assume that Daoism and Buddhism must have overlapped or merged together at the popular level during their parallel development at this time.

Prince Moonlight was later superseded by a much more powerful and famous Buddhist savior—the Buddha Maitreya. In Buddhist mythology, Maitreya was the Buddha who "has yet to come." He was believed to dwell in the Tusita heaven, waiting to descend to earth to save all believers. There is the further understanding that when he arrives the world will be experiencing the last days of the Buddhist *dharma* (an age known as the *mofa*), and that with one bold stroke he will rid the world of all evil elements and usher in a new golden age. The Maitreya Buddha was thus perceived as a savior, as his coming would signal the end of existing misery and injustice. Unlike Amitābha Buddha, who promised salvation in the form of rebirth in his Pure Land and made no attempt to improve this world, the Maitreya Buddha served as a world redeemer who would radically and dramatically change the status quo and transform the world into a realm of bliss and abundance. What made Maitreya worship even more subversive was the belief, pervasive since the fifth century, that his coming was imminent (rather than in the distant future as originally believed). This immediately turned him into a symbol for numerous antidynastic movements, all of which aimed at the speedy toppling of the existing order.

In addition to Daoist Li Hong and Buddhist Maitreya, there was yet another millenarian tradition in medieval

China—Manichaeism. Originally introduced from Persia during the early Tang dynasty (618–907), Manichaeism subscribed to a dualistic view of the world wherein the forces of Light, under the leadership of Mani, would engage in a fierce struggle with the forces of Darkness. Followers of this tradition held the belief that cosmic history progressed in three stages: the first stage characterized by a clear division between the realms of Light and Darkness, the second by a blurring of this division that resulted in the struggle between the two, and the third by the ultimate triumph of Light over Darkness and the creation of a realm of everlasting peace. Believing themselves to be living near the end of the second stage, followers of Mani led a pure and puritanical life in order to guarantee victory over the forces of Darkness and evil. They practiced strict vegetarianism, refused to worship spirits, ghosts, and even ancestors, and buried their dead naked. Indeed their vegetarian diet had become such a distinguishing feature that they were pejoratively referred to as "vegetable eaters and devil (Mani) worshipers" (*chicai shimo*). Their antinomian values, demonstrated by such practices as naked burial and nonobservance of ancestral rites, earned them further suspicion from the authorities.

THE LATE IMPERIAL PERIOD. All the above-mentioned millenarian traditions interacted with one another as they evolved. By the fourteenth century, such a substantial merger had taken place among them that they were collectively known as the White Lotus, a catchall label used by the government to encompass most of the proscribed millenarian groups, all of which had their own respective names. In fact, White Lotus had a very distinguished beginning. It was allegedly the name of a lay Buddhist group organized in 402 by the eminent monk Huiyuan to worship the Buddha Amitābha. Later, the Pure Land master Mao Ziyuan (1086–1166) also used this name to designate his pious vegetarian group. In any event, White Lotus had obviously metamorphosed into a millenarian sectarian movement under the leadership of Han Shantong (d. 1355) toward the end of the Yuan dynasty (1206–1368). Combining Maitreyan with Manichaean elements, Han boldly declared the "incarnation of Maitreya Buddha and the birth of the Manichaean Prince of Light." Although he was captured and executed, Han was the symbol of the religious movement that eventually brought an end to the Yuan regime.

During the ensuing Ming dynasty (1368–1644) (some scholars even argue that the very name *Ming,* which means "light," is indicative of the Manichaean influence on the founder of the dynasty), the folk sectarian tradition generally labeled by the government as White Lotus became even more systematized. Central to this mature sectarian belief was the notion of Wusheng laomu, or the Eternal Mother, who, as progenitor of the human race, had vowed to save all her repentant children from certain demise. She would deliver them to the *zhenkong jiaxiang* ("native land of true emptiness") where they would enjoy peace and affluence forever. This dual concept of the Eternal Mother and her Native Land of True Emptiness became the identifying creed of these late imperial Chinese sectarians. It served as a profession of faith and a powerful bond that drew all the sect members together into one big religious family. This concept also enabled them to relativize their attachment to their earthly parents and their native communities, and allowed them to see that this world was not the best of all possible worlds, that a "new beginning" would arrive in time to replace the existing order, and that this new beginning would sit in judgment over the entire past.

Like the Manichaeans before them, the Ming-Qing sectarian believers maintained that time progressed in three major epochs: the age of the Lamplighting Buddha of the past, the age of the Śākyamuni Buddha of the present, and the age of the Maitreya Buddha of the future. Crucial to this time scheme was the expectation that the third or future age was imminent, to be ushered in by an apocalyptic conflagration that would scourge the world to remove all evil elements. (Some sects used the epithets Blue Sun, Red Sun, and White Sun to represent the respective ages.) This cataclysmic turning point was known as the kalpic transition *(jie),* characterized by floods, epidemics, earthquakes, and all kinds of unspeakable disasters during which the whole cosmic order would be torn asunder and the elect and the doomed would be separated. When the Maitreya Buddha finally appeared as the messenger of the Eternal Mother to deliver the surviving faithful, the world would be reconstructed and the reunion between the Mother and her lost children would take place. The saved would enjoy the new order, which, according to the description of the *baojuan* ("precious scrolls")—a special genre of religious tracts compiled by the sectarians in profusion during the sixteenth and seventeenth centuries—would be peaceful, immortal, and egalitarian.

Because of this millenarian and antinomian orientation of the sectarians, they were feared and ruthlessly persecuted by successive dynasties. Their very expectation of the advent of the third age was a negation of the present age, thus undermining the authority as well as the legitimacy of the existing regime. As it turned out, this obsession with salvation in the future age did occasionally inspire ambitious individuals within the sects to proclaim the descent of the Maitreya Buddha and to raise the banner of rebellion in an attempt to usher in the third age. To be sure, the correlation between millenarianism and rebellion was never a direct one, yet the government was always suspicious of millenarians, who, it had reason to fear, were not averse to using violence in order to hasten the end of the present age. There was only a fine line separating the anticipation of the kalpa from the expedition of its arrival. Given the fact that the leaders of these sectarian groups were often uprooted, restless, and disgruntled elements in society, this official apprehension is understandable.

Suspicion was further reinforced by the vicarious sibling relationship of the sect members, which undermined the Confucian emphasis on blood ties, as well as the relative equality of the sexes within the sectarian group, flouting the orthodox insistence on strict sexual distinctions. Sectarian organization itself, though lacking centralization, was nevertheless capable of forming large-scale regional networks in a short time because of shared beliefs among the majority of the sects. Quite often, different groups in different geographic areas would subscribe to the same precious scrolls, thus espousing the same doctrines. Many of these tracts had been handed down through generations of sect leaders, allowing the creation of a hereditary folk religious elite. Notable groups such as the Dacheng sect of Wang Sen (d. 1619) maintained an uninterrupted hereditary transmission for at least two centuries. This resilience of the sects was a great source of worry for the government.

The Taiping Rebellion. The most famous and spectacular millenarian movement in traditional China was, of course, the Taiping Rebellion (1850–1864) led by Hong Xiuquan (1813–1864). Hong was a frustrated examination candidate who had received Christian literature from a Chinese convert. With that minimal exposure, he wove together a religion that was a mixture of traditional Chinese eschatology and Christian salvationism. He also organized the God-Worshipers Society, which, reacting to ethnic tensions and prompted by Hong's own sense of mission, rebelled in 1850.

Hong Xiuquan's religion is best understood through the designation he chose for his movement after 1850. He named it Taiping tianguo ("heavenly kingdom of highest peace"). Taiping, it should be recalled, was the ideal of the Yellow Turbans who rebelled in 184, and had inspired various millenarian groups throughout Chinese history. *Tianguo* was derived from the Judeo-Christian notion of God's kingdom. Together, the two compound terms indicate Hong's unshakable faith that God's kingdom, in the form of Highest Peace, could be realized on earth, and that he himself would be the instrument through which this momentous task would be accomplished. Declaring himself to be the second son of God and the younger brother of Jesus, Hong saw himself as the redeemer of China, if not of the world as well. At once anti-Confucian and anti-Manchu, his brand of messianic salvationism was by far the most radical China ever witnessed.

Hong's Heavenly Kingdom was characterized by the proclaimed equality of all men and the liberation of all women. To be sure, there was the inevitable discrepancy between theory and practice. Yet this Taiping ideal was unequivocally enunciated and applied to concrete situations in the form of policy promulgations such as the land tenure system. This system provided equitable land redistribution, going so far as to observe no distinction between the sexes in land allotment.

When the Taiping army captured the city of Nanjing in 1853, Hong made it his Heavenly Capital. Nanjing, scene of the signing of the treaty that concluded the Opium War between China and Great Britain only eleven years earlier, was seen by Hong as the "New Jerusalem" promised in the *Book of Revelation.* But internal strife, coupled with Manchu military reforms and growing Western hostility toward the Taipings, finally resulted in their crushing defeat in 1864.

Chinese millenarianism can thus be seen having a history that goes back to the early medieval period. It can still be detected among certain religious groups on the mainland, in Taiwan, and in Southeast Asia. It has exerted its greatest appeal among marginal or peripheral members of society who, though not necessarily economically deprived, were denied access to power and prestige in the orthodox world. Through mutual aid and group solidarity these people were able to gain self-respect and a sense of worth from their affiliation with sectarian organizations. The charismatic and talented among them might even achieve positions of power and influence within the sect. This was particularly true of women, who were otherwise totally barred from meaningful contacts outside of their families. Ethically relativistic because of their orientation toward the future millennium, members of these movements often invited the wrath and oppression of the authorities. They interpreted times of economic distress, social turmoil, and natural disasters as signals of the advent of the third age, an age when they would emerge triumphant in their combat against exploitation and injustice, as well as against death itself. They therefore became agitated and expectant, if not openly rebellious, and always potentially subversive. Their antinomian values and behavior posed a direct challenge to the orthodox tradition, while their millennial yearning to build a better world often implied their rejection of the present one. In a certain sense, twentieth-century Chinese revolutionaries, including the Communists, operated much in the same mode as the earlier millenarian sectarians in their attempt to change the world.

See Also Huiyuan; Maitreya; Manichaeism, overview article; Zhang Daoling; Zhang Jue; Zhang Lu.

Bibliography

Bauer, Wolfgang. *China und die Hoffnung auf Glück.* Munich, 1971. Translated by Michael Shaw as *China and the Search for Happiness: Recurring Themes in Four Thousand Years of Chinese Cultural History.* New York, 1976. A delightful work that details the history of utopian thought in China. Full of insights and lengthy quotes.

Groot, J. J. M. de. *Sectarianism and Religious Persecution in China* (1903–1904). Reprint in 2 volumes, Taipei, 1963. First published around the turn of the twentieth century, this work examines the beliefs and rituals of the Chinese sects through official records and decrees.

Liu, Kwang-ching, and Richard Shek, eds. *Heterodoxy in Late Imperial China.* Honolulu, 2004. A symposium volume that contains numerous chapters dealing with chiliastic and millenarian movements in medieval and late imperial China.

Naquin, Susan. *Millenarian Rebellion in China: The Eight Trigrams Uprising of 1813.* New Haven, 1976. An interesting work that traces the unfolding of a millenarian rebellion through the analysis of the confessions of the rebels.

Naquin, Susan. *Shantung Rebellion: The Wang Lun Uprising of 1774.* New Haven, 1981. Another work by Naquin using the same valuable rebel confessions for another rebellion.

Overmyer, Daniel L. *Folk Buddhist Religion: Dissenting Sects in Late Traditional China.* Cambridge, Mass., 1976. A trailblazing work on Chinese sectarianism, particularly the White Lotus movement. It contains insightful comparisons with European religious movements.

Overmyer, Daniel L. *Precious Volumes: An Introduction to Chinese Sectarian Scriptures from the Sixteenth and Seventeenth Centuries.* Cambridge, Mass., 1999. The most thorough study in English of the teachings of late imperial Chinese sectarian writings.

Seidel, Anna. "The Image of the Perfect Ruler in Early Daoist Messianism: Lao-tzu and Li Hung." *History of Religions* 9 (November 1969–February 1970): 216–247. A celebrated work on Daoist messianism in the early medieval period. The Li Hong cult is analyzed.

Spence, Jonathan D. *God's Chinese Son: The Taiping Heavenly Kingdom of Hong Xiuquan.* New York, 1996. The most recent study of Hong Xiuquan and the Taiping movement, with an emphasis on Hong's religious beliefs.

Ter Haar, B. J. *The White Lotus Teachings in Chinese Religious History.* Leiden, 1992. A revisionist study of the White Lotus tradition that corrects some of the misconceptions regarding the movement.

Zürcher, Erik. "'Prince Moonlight': Messianism and Eschatology in Early Medieval Chinese Buddhism." *Toung bao* 68 (1982): 1–75. A seminal work on Buddhist millenarianism in the fourth and fifth centuries. Contains full translation of the pertinent Buddhist text.

RICHARD SHEK (1987 AND 2005)

MĪMĀṂSĀ. The word *mīmāṃsā* means "investigation" in ordinary Sanskrit. Since the term is applied to an important South Asian philosophical school, it must originally have meant "the investigation of the proper interpretation of the Vedic texts." The Mīmāṃsā school is thus better known as the Purva-mīmāṃsā school, which is sometimes called the Dharma-mīmāṃsā (inquiry into the nature of *dharma* as laid down by the Vedas, the supreme authority). Uttara-mīmāṃsā is the descriptive name for the Vedānta school, which deals with the nature of *brahman* as laid down in the latter part (*uttara*) of the Vedas, and in the Upaniṣads, hence also called Brahma-mīmāṃsā (inquiry into the nature of *brahman*). The word *dharma* is of prime importance in this context. It stands here for one's "duty" (*codanā*) enjoined by the Vedas, which includes both the religious or sacred duties or actions and the moral duties as well. *Dharma* also denotes the "virtue" attainable by performing such duties or following such courses of actions. Thus *dharma* is the main topic for discussion in the Mīmāṃsā school.

The Vedic scriptures were seriously attacked by the Śramaṇas (mendicant Brahmanic philosophers) about 500 BCE, and as a result its authority was apparently being devastated by criticisms. Hence the Mīmāṃsā school originated among the Vedic priests who wanted to reestablish this authority by resolving the apparent contradictions and other textual problems found in the Vedic scriptures. The Mīmāṃsā school in this way developed the science of exegesis. A *Mīmāṃsā Sūtra* was compiled as early as the first century BCE, and it was ascribed to an ancient sage, Jaimini. It is regarded as the key text of the school.

Regarding *dharma,* Mīmāṃsā maintains a form of fundamentalism. It claims that the scriptures are the only means of knowing what is *dharma* and what is not. Only by following the injunctions of the scriptures can we attain *dharma,* or the "good," that cannot be attained by any other means. Other means of knowledge (perception, inference, reasoning, etc.) are of no help in the realm of *dharma,* for concerns of *dharma* are with transcendental matters, the imperceptibles and the unverifiables, such as the afterlife, heaven, and the moral order. Hence the Mīmāṃsā school defines the essence of the Vedas (*vedatā*) as that which informs us about such a transcendental realm. And the authority of the Vedas in such matters is self-evident. The truth of the scriptural statements is self-validating. The Vedas are to be regarded as eternal and uncreated. The scriptures are *revealed* texts, there being no author of them. In short, the truths of the Vedas are transempirical, hence no empirical evidence can conceivably bear on them.

The problem of interpretation has led the Mīmāṃsā school to the study and discussion of topics which are of great philosophical interest. The Mīmāṃsā developed itself into a kind of philosophical discipline, incorporating into it a theory of knowledge, epistemology, logic, a theory of meaning and language, and a realistic metaphysic. With its emphasis on the philosophy of language and linguistics, the Mīmāṃsā has sometimes been called the *vākya-śāstra* ("theory of speech"). It also formulated various rules of interpretation in order to resolve and eliminate the apparent inconsistencies of the scriptural texts.

Later on, the Mīmāṃsā school was divided into two subschools (c. 600–700 CE), following the two important exponents of the school, Kumārila Bhaṭṭa and Prābhākara. They are called the Bhāṭṭa school and the Prābhākara school. Of the many minor differences between the two subschools, only a few of the more notable ones have been noted here.

Kumārila speaks of six *pramāṇas* ("legitimate ways of knowing")—perception (*pratyakṣa*), inference (*anumāna*), verbal testimony (*śabda* or *aptāvacana*), comparison (*upamāna*), presumption (*arthāpatti*), and nonapprehension (*anupalabdhi*). Prabhākara accepts the first five only. Since he rejects "absence" (*abhāva*) as a separate reality, as a "knowable" entity (*prameya*), he does not need "nonapprehension" to establish such entities. For the Bhāṭṭas, a cognition is not a perceptible property, but it is inferred from the "cognizedness" (*jñātatā*) of the object cognized: since this pot is cognized by me, a cognition of it must have occurred in me. For the Prābhākaras, a cognition is self-cognized—it perceives itself. But both regard knowledge to be self-validating. Kumārila admits both Vedic and non-Vedic *śabda* (sentences, speech) to be *pramāṇa.* Prabhākara holds that real *śabda-pramāṇa* is the Vedic *śabda*. Both try to establish the Vedic authority not on God but on such transcendental reality as *dharma* and *mokṣa*. The Bhāṭṭas explicitly hold the *jñāna-karma-samuccaya-vāda*, that both knowledge and action lead to liberation. The Prābhākara view does not seem to be very different.

The two subschools differ in their views about the correct incentive for man's action (which includes both moral and religious acts). The Prābhākaras say that it is only the sense of duty while the Bhāṭṭas argue that both sense of duty and the desire for benefit constitute the correct incentive for action. On another rather technical matter, the two disagree. The Bhāṭṭas believe that the sentences get their meanings from their atomistic constituents, the individual word-meanings, while the Prābhākaras believe that the words directly constitute the sentence-meaning as a whole only insofar as they are syntactically connected (*anvita*) with other words in the sentence.

SEE ALSO Vedānta.

BIBLIOGRAPHY

Jha, Ganganath. *Prābhākara School of Pūrva-mīmāṃsā*. Allahabad, 1911.

Rāmānujācārya. *Tantra-rahasya* (1923). 2d ed. Edited by Rudrapatha Shamasastry and K. S. Ramaswami Sastri. Gaekwad's Oriental Series, no. 24. Baroda, 1956. Contains an introduction by the editors.

Shastri, Pashupatinath. *Introduction to Pūrva Mīmāṃsā* (1923). 2d ed. Edited and revised by Gaurinath Sastri. Varanasi, 1980.

New Sources

Bhatta, V. P. *Epistemology, Logic, and Grammer in the Analysis of Sentence-Meaning*. Delhi, 1992.

Sarma, Rajendra Nath. *Mimamsa Theory of Meaning: Based on the Vakyarthamatrika*. Delhi, 1988.

Studies in Mimamsa: Dr. Mandan Mishra Felicitation Volume. Edited by R.C. Dwivedi. Delhi, 1994.

BIMAL KRISHNA MATILAL (1987)
Revised Bibliography

MIND SEE ARTIFICIAL INTELLIGENCE; CONSCIOUSNESS, STATES OF; EPISTEMOLOGY; NEUROSCIENCE AND RELIGION, *ARTICLE ON* NEUROEPISTEMOLOGY

MINERVA, a Roman goddess, was the protector of intellectual and manual skills. The oldest form of her name, *Menerva*, may derive from the Indo-European root **men-*, which is expressive of mental processes. Various Etruscan transcriptions of the name, though earlier attested than any Italic form, probably should be regarded as borrowed from the Latin.

Minerva appears neither in the so-called Numan calendar, which registers the oldest public festivals in Rome, nor in connection with a priesthood. Her first occurrence is with Jupiter and Juno as a member of the divine triad that was worshiped on the Capitoline Hill in Etruscan-ruled Rome at the end of the sixth century BCE. Archaeological findings in Santa Marinella and Veii-Portonaccio bear witness to a contemporaneous cult of Minerva in southern Etruria.

Images of the goddess show many features of the Greek Athena: helmet, shield, spear, and aegis stamped with the likeness of a Gorgon. Recent discoveries in Pratica di Mare (the ancient Lavinium) show that the influence of Greek art did not exert itself exclusively through the Etruscan medium. The mythological episodes that were selected in Italy represent the goddess as a patroness of warlike heroes and gods (especially Herakles and Mars) and as a palladium (a token of invincibility).

Minerva was worshiped throughout Italy and on several Roman hills: with Jupiter and Juno on the Capitoline and the Quirinal and alone on the Aventine. There were also sanctuaries of the "captive Minerva" (brought from Falerii in 241 BCE) on the Caelius and of Minerva as patroness of physicians on the Esquiline. The emperor Domitian (81–96 CE), a prominent votary of the goddess, increased the number of her cult places.

Minerva was the special patroness of craftsmen, and at least from the time of Augustus (27 BCE–14 CE) craftsmen attended the festival of the Quinquatrus (March 19–23). The festival was publicly solemnized by gladiatorial exhibitions and included a *tubilustrium* (a ritual purification of war trumpets), further evidence of a link with Mars and war. Flute players celebrated a festival of their own ("little Quinquatrus") on June 13.

The cult of Minerva, supported by the municipal institution of capitols (imitations of the Roman temple of the Capitoline triad) and the devotion of craftsmen and soldiers, diffused widely throughout the Roman Empire until the beginning of the common era.

BIBLIOGRAPHY

Articles in three classical encyclopedias provide detailed and cautiously interpretative views of the subject: Franz Altheim's "Minerva," in *Real-Encyclopädie der klassischen Altertumswissenschaft* (Stuttgart, 1932); Filippo Coarelli's "Minerva," in *Enciclopedia dell'arte antica* (Rome, 1963); and Konrat Ziegler's "Minerva," in *Der kleine Pauly: Lexicon der Antike* (Stuttgart, 1969). The most recent discoveries are commented on by Ambros J. Pfiffig in *Ein Opfergelübde an die etruskische Minerva* (Vienna, 1968), for Santa Marinella, and by F. Castagnoli in *Il culto di Minerva a Lavinium*, "Problemi attuali di scienza e di cultura," no. 246 (Rome, 1979), for Pratica di Mare.

New Sources

Cunliffe, Barry. "The Sanctuary of Sulis Minerva at Bath: A Brief Review." In *Pagan Gods and Shrines of the Roman Empire*, edited by Martin Henig and Anthony King, pp. 1–14. Oxford, 1986.

Girard, Jean-Louis. "Domitien et Minerve: une prédilection impériale." In *Aufstieg und Niedergang der Römischen Welt.* Berlin and New York, 1981. See pages 233–245.

Girard, Jean-Louis. "La place de Minerve dans la religion romaine au temps du principat." In *Aufstieg und Niedergang der Römischen Welt.* Berlin and New York, 1981. See pages 203–232.

Graf, Fritz. "Athena and Minerva: Two Faces of One Goddess?" In *Athena in the Classical World.*, edited by Susan Deacy and Alexandra Willing, pp. 127–139. Leiden, 2001.

Köves-Zulauf, Thomas. "Minerva Capta." In *Religio Graeco-Romana: Festschrift für Walter Pötscher,* edited by Joachim Dalfen, Gerhard Petersmann, and Franz Ferdinand Schwarz., pp. 159–176. Horn, 1993.

Martin, Luther H. "Why Cecropian Minerva? Hellenistic Religious Syncretism as System." *Numen* 30 (1983): 131–145.

Massa-Pairault, Françoise-Hélène. "De Preneste à Volsinii: Minerve, le 'fatum' et la constitution de la société." *Parola del Passato* 42 (1987): 200–233.

Sauer, Eberhard. "An Inscription from Northern Italy, the Roman Temple Complex in Bath, and Minerva as a Healing Goddess in Gallo-Roman Religion." *Oxford Journal of Archaeology* 15, no.1 (1996): 63–93.

JEAN-LOUIS GIRARD (1987)
Revised Bibliography

MINISTRY. The term *ministry* traditionally refers to offices of leadership in the Christian church, but there has been a growing recognition that it also describes the way the mission of the whole church is conducted. Both in terms of specific offices (ministers) and in terms of the work of the church in general, ministry has biblical roots. In Hebrew, *sheret* ("to serve") applies to temple officers and was normally translated *leitourgein* in the Septuagint. This use was carried over into the New Testament, where the various linguistic forms of *leitourgein* are used not only for general acts of service to others (*Rom.* 15:27, *2 Cor.* 9:12, *Phil.* 2:30) but also for worship (*Acts* 13:3) and particularly for priestly and Levitical functions under the Old Covenant (*Lk.* 1:23; *Heb.* 8:2, 8:6, 9:21, 10:11). But the New Testament introduced the words *diakonia* ("service") and *diakonein* ("to serve"), referring to the menial work done by a *diakonos* ("servant") or *doulos* ("slave") to indicate the quality of ministry in the church. These words represent not status but the serving relationship of the minister to the one served: following the example of Christ (and, subsequently, the example of the apostle Paul) is at the heart of the Christian understanding of ministry (*Jn.* 13:1–20; *1 Cor.* 4:16, 11:1; *Phil.* 3:17).

Scholars dispute how far the New Testament reflects a uniform and obligatory pattern of ministerial orders. Roman Catholic scholars generally hold that it does, but most Protestant scholars believe that the New Testament offers several patterns of ministry (*Eph.* 4:11–12; *1 Cor.* 12:27–31; *1 Tm.* 3:1–13, 4:11–16, 5:3–10, 5:17–22). The former view maintains that the orders of ministry are fixed by tradition and that their authority is transmitted by historical succession from the apostles through bishops or the pope as the vicar of Christ (apostolic succession). The latter view regards ministerial orders as essentially functional and focused on faithful transmission of the apostolic testimony.

There is, however, agreement that all ministry traces its authority to Jesus Christ and to the apostles who testified to his saving work and resurrection (*Mt.* 16:13–24, 18:18, 28:18–20; *Jn.* 20:23). Although the apostle Paul could not claim personal connection with the Galilean ministry, he did claim commission from Jesus Christ as the heart of his own call to apostleship (*Gal.* 1:1, 1:11–24, 2:1–21). Churches also generally agree that officers in the church's ministry (i.e., the clergy) have particular responsibility for preaching, for administration of the sacraments (or ordinances), and for the oversight and nurture of their congregations.

By the beginning of the second century, three principal orders of ministry—bishop or pastor (*episcopos,* "overseer"), presbyter or priest (*presbuteros,* "elder"), and deacon (*diakonos,* "servant")—had become widely accepted, and although various confessional groups may not agree how far or when these orders became dependent on the Roman pontiff, the primacy of the pope seems to have been widely acknowledged by the time of Leo I (d. 461) and continued in the West until the Reformation. In the Eastern church the break with Rome, the Great Schism, is often given the date 1054, but scholars recognize that this was the end of a process of estrangement over centuries. However, the threefold ministry remained unchanged in both halves of Christendom through a millennium of Christian history.

Catholic branches of the church claim unbroken succession with this earlier history and believe that these offices are prescribed (i.e., *iure divino*) and guaranteed by apostolic succession. Ordination is a sacrament whereby the Holy Spirit is transmitted through the bishop's imposition of hands, which imparts special grace to administer the sacraments and to exercise authority in the church. In the Roman Catholic Church these powers derive ultimately from the pope, while among the Orthodox it is exercised by the bishop within the corporate authority of the Orthodox community. Old Catholics and Anglo-Catholics hold a position on apostolic succession close to that of Rome but do not acknowledge the infallible authority of the papacy.

The sixteenth-century Reformation challenged the absolute authority of ecclesiastical tradition and its priesthood. Protestants turned from papal authority to the authority of the Bible, which led to revisions in their understanding of the church and its ministry. In the main, they claimed to restore the New Testament pattern, and in reaction to ecclesiastical legalism they tended to appeal to the Bible as a divine law book. New Testament "restorationism" appears in the early Luther, based on a primary appeal to scripture and on scripture exegeted by "the priesthood of all believers." Luther may be described as advocating a form of "evangelical pragmatism," since he accepted any pattern consistent with scripture that served the effective preaching of the word and the proper administration of the sacraments. Lutheranism has therefore adopted episcopal, consistorial, and congregational forms of churchmanship.

Attempts to restore a more biblical pattern of church and ministry are to be found in almost every form of Reformation church, and not least the Reformed church. Differences between Ulrich Zwingli (1484–1531) and the Anabaptists (Swiss Brethren) were not over the primacy of scripture but over its interpretation. John Calvin (1509–1564) systematized the Reformed position, claiming that church and ministry are of divine institution (*Institutes* 4.1, 4.3). Like many in his day, he regarded apostles, prophets, and evangelists as peculiar to the apostolic age, although he recognized that they might be revived "as the need of the times demands." Pastors and teachers, he argued, were indispensable. Pastors exercised general oversight discipline and preached and administered the sacraments; teachers were responsible for doctrine. Calvin also recognized the New Testament office of deacon in care of the poor (within which he included the office of the "widow"). He insisted on both the inward call of a minister and the recognition by the church of that call. In matters of discipline the pastor was to share power with a consistory of elders so that power would not be exclusively in the hands of a single person.

Calvin's fourfold ordering of ministry was taken over by the Reformed church and the Puritans in the British Isles and colonial America in the Presbyterian and Congregational churches. Similar forms of ministry arose out of English Separatism (e.g., Baptist churches) and the Christian Church (Disciples of Christ) movement of the American frontier. Differences between the classic Reformation positions and later restoration movements turned not so much on the appeal to the Bible as on other matters affecting scriptural interpretation: the relationship of the church to civil authorities, insistence on the church's purity, ministerial training, and how far literal appeal to scripture may be modified by the Holy Spirit revealed in scripture. Extreme restorationists reject any deviation from the New Testament pattern; at the other extreme, the Society of Friends (Quakers) claims that the spirit of the scriptures requires no specially ordained ministers.

A different modification of the church's ministry is seen in the Anglican settlement. In the sixteenth century, Henry VIII sought to separate from Rome without changing the shape of the national church, and his daughter, Elizabeth I, followed his lead. She wooed English Catholics by maintaining traditional vestments, liturgy, and forms of church government (episcopal). From the first the Church of England tried to reconcile appeal to scripture and to church tradition. Originally the settlement was based on the authority of the crown (the divine right of kings), but at the turn of the seventeenth century appeals to the divine right of the episcopacy began to appear. Differences concerning the role of the episcopacy are reflected in the so-called high church (Anglo-Catholic), broad church (Latitudinarian), and low church (Evangelical) traditions within Anglicanism.

In the eighteenth century, John Wesley, founder of Methodism, refused to separate from the Church of England. He finally became convinced that priests and bishops were of the same order in the New Testament and that he had the right to ordain ministers for America, but he refused to designate bishops and instead appointed superintendents. The decision to employ the term *bishop* in American Methodism probably arose from the determination to assert independence from Anglicanism. But although Wesley believed that the threefold order of ministry is scriptural, he offered an essentially pragmatic interpretation of these offices. His position was fundamentally the evangelical pragmatism seen in Luther.

By the mid-1980s there was no acceptance of the ordination of women in the Roman Catholic and Orthodox branches of the church, but a growing acceptance of women into the ordained ministry of Protestant denominations and in some provinces of Anglicanism was evident. Protestant and Anglican practices stem from the theological belief that the call to ministry is open to all God's people. The ecumenical movement has also prompted many churches to reexamine earlier claims and to recognize that they have much to learn from each other. Statements on ministry prepared for the Consultation on Church Union (1984), which reflected the views of ten American Protestant denominations, and by the World Council of Churches (1982) indicate a significant and growing consensus. This consensus reveals an emphasis on the servanthood of ministry as evidenced in the ministry of Jesus; an awareness that the whole church is the proper context in which the ordained ministry should be considered; an awareness that the doctrines of church and ministry cannot be separated; and a recognition that the traditional threefold ordering of ministry should not be lightly discarded. This growing consensus shows that many Christian churches seek to manifest their essential unity and to arrive at a point where their ministries may be mutually recognized.

SEE ALSO Anglicanism; Apostles; Church; Discipleship; Ecumenical Movement; Leadership; Methodist Churches; Ordination; Papacy; Priesthood, article on Christian Priesthood; Reformation.

BIBLIOGRAPHY

The tendency today is to consider the doctrines of church and ministry holistically, and in any reading list on ministry, books about the doctrine of the church should find a place. Among the older books considering ministry, *The Apostolic Ministry,* edited by Kenneth E. Kirk (London, 1946), and T. W. Manson's *The Church's Ministry* (Philadelphia, 1948) must be mentioned because they illustrate a classic debate on apostolic succession in relation to episcopacy. For a general account of where the churches stand on the issues, *The Nature of the Unity We Seek,* edited by Paul Minear (Saint Louis, 1958), may be consulted, and also the relevant documents in *The Documents of Vatican II,* edited by Walter M. Abbott (New York, 1966), for the Roman Catholic position.

One of the most thorough historical studies to be conducted in the United States is *The Ministry in Historical Perspectives,* edited by H. Richard Niebuhr and Daniel D. Williams (New York, 1956), and H. Richard Niebuhr's theological interpretation of that evidence, *The Purpose of the Church and Its Ministry* (New York, 1956), underscores the recognition that church and ministry cannot be separated. *The Pioneer Ministry,* by Anthony Tyrrell Hanson (London, 1961), an important biblical study of ministerial leadership in the Pauline churches, responds to assumptions made earlier in Kirk's book, while my own book *Ministry* (Grand Rapids, Mich., 1965) places this Anglo-Saxon debate within its ecumenical context. Ronald E. Osborn's *In Christ's Place: Christian Ministry in Today's World* (Saint Louis, 1967) arrives at similar conclusions on the basis of New Testament evidence.

The most important recent documents on ministry are those coming out of bilateral conversations, such as *The Ministry in the Church* (Geneva, 1982), published by the Roman Catholic/Lutheran Joint Commission; the documents produced by the Consultation on Church Union, such as the *Digest of the Plenary Meetings* (Princeton, 1979–) and *The COCU Consensus: In Quest of a Church of Christ Uniting* (Princeton, 1985); and the documents published by the World Council of Churches, particularly the "Lima Document," in *Baptism, Eucharist and Ministry,* "Faith and Order Paper no. 111" (Geneva, 1982).

New Sources

Barrett, C. K. *Church, Ministry, and Sacraments in the New Testament.* Grand Rapids, Mich., 1985.

Best, Thomas F., and Dagmar C. Heller. *Eucharistic Worship in Ecumenical Contexts: The Lima Liturgy–and Beyond.* Geneva, 1998.

Fahey, Michael A., ed. *Catholic Perspectives on Baptism, Eucharist and Ministry.* Lanham, Md., 1986.

Limouris, Gennadios, and N. M. Vaporis, eds. *Orthodox Perspectives on Baptism, Eucharist, and Ministry.* Brookline, Mass., 1985.

Oden, Thomas C. *Ministry through Word and Sacrament.* New York, 1989.

Wood, Susan K. *Sacramental Orders.* Collegeville, Minn., 2000.

ROBERT S. PAUL (1987)
Revised Bibliography

MINOAN RELIGION SEE AEGEAN RELIGIONS

MIQVEH.

MIQVEH. In Jewish tradition, a *miqveh* (plural *miqva'ot*) is a pool of water, either natural or constructed, used for ritual purification of persons and objects.

BIBLICAL PERIOD. Biblical texts concerning contraction of ritual impurity, such as *Leviticus* 15 (impurity from bodily emissions), *Numbers* 19 (impurity from contact with a corpse), and *Numbers* 31:22–23 (impure objects), ordain that immersion in water is required to remove ritual uncleanness in some instances. However, biblical legislation does not specify the nature of the pool or the source or amount of the water in which ritual immersion is to take place, nor does the word *miqveh* appear in the Hebrew Bible in this context. It seems likely that immersion in the biblical period was generally restricted to priests who were required to be ritually pure before partaking of the freewill offerings (*terumah*) given by the people.

SECOND TEMPLE PERIOD. The earliest archaeological remains of ritual bath installations date from the Hasmonaean period (second century BCE), when concern for ritual immersion appears to have become a public matter, possibly under influence from Hellenism, with its strongly developed bathhouse culture. More than three hundred *miqva'ot* dating from Hasmonaean times through the Roman period have been discovered in Judea and Galilee, half in the Jerusalem area; many were built beside agricultural installations (wine and olive presses) in both cities and villages, and others were constructed in the private dwellings of wealthy, often priestly, families. Hasmonaean ritual baths have been discovered in Jericho, Qumran, and Gezer, and it seems likely that some of the Roman period ritual baths were also in earlier use.

The most common use of such *miqva'ot* in the Second Temple period was purification prior to entering the area of the Temple. Many *miqva'ot* were located on the Temple Mount (over forty have been excavated south of the Double and Triple Gates), and the Temple itself contained pools for priests. A large number of valid *miqva'ot* were also available to festival pilgrims in towns and villages around Jerusalem. Rabbinic sources indicate that the Jewish court (*bet din*) supervised the construction, the validity, the measurements, and the cleanliness of the *miqva'ot* that served these crowds of visitors to the Temple. Because stored rainwater was always a scarce commodity, water from caves, springs, and rivers was utilized whenever possible in building *miqva'ot.*

RABBINIC PERIOD. *Miqva'ot,* the sixth tractate in the order *Tohorot* (purities) of the Mishnah (edited in the Land of Israel in the third century CE), discusses the characteristics of a valid *miqveh,* various ways of constructing a *miqveh,* and the nature and sources of the water necessary for a valid *miqveh*; it also delineates what constitutes valid immersion. According to this tractate, a *miqveh* must be hewn out of rock or built into the ground; it must also be made watertight, usually with plaster, because any leakage invalidates it. A *miqveh* must contain a minimum of forty *se'ah* (approximately one hundred gallons) of free-flowing clean water, sufficient for full immersion either vertically or horizontally. Rain- or springwater is valid, as is water diverted from a river, lake, or ocean. Once a *miqveh* contains the minimum of at least forty *se'ah* of valid water, drawn water of any amount may be added. Similarly if an upper *miqveh* contains forty *se'ah* of valid water and drawn water is then added to it and at least forty *se'ah* flows into the lower pool, that lower pool is also a valid *miqveh.* Because water must not flow through metal vessels or other materials that are susceptible to ritual uncleanness, all pipes and other accessories are attached to the ground. The *miqveh* may not be emptied through a drain in the bottom; such a drain could allow leakage, and any drain plug would be regarded as an unacceptable vessel. A variety of construction methods based on these principles have developed over time.

MEDIEVAL PERIOD. *Miqva'ot* have been essential features of Jewish communities over the centuries. A recently discovered *miqveh* complex in the old Jewish quarter of Siracusa in Sicily probably dates from the sixth century CE and may be the oldest surviving ritual bathing area in Europe. Medieval *miqva'ot* have been discovered at a number of other European sites, including Cologne (c. 1170), Speyer (c. 1200), London (c. 1200), and Friedberg (c. 1260). The *miqveh* in Worms (c. 1190), a subterranean building with Romanesque architectural elements, is typical: from an aboveground structure, nineteen steps descend to an entrance hall, and then another eleven steps descend to the *miqveh.* A similar medieval underground *miqveh* also exists in Cairo. In many instances the *miqva'ot* of the Middle Ages also served as bathhouses because of orders from Christian rulers forbidding Jews to wash in rivers.

***MIQVEH* USE HISTORICALLY.** Most biblical laws of ritual impurity lapsed with the destruction of the Second Temple in 70 CE, and since the rabbinic era the *miqveh* has been used most frequently by women who immerse prior to marriage, at a specified time in each menstrual cycle, and following the birth of children. *Miqveh* immersion is also obligatory according to *halakhah* (rabbinic legislation) as part of the ceremony of conversion to Judaism. Some Jewish groups have encouraged *miqveh* immersion for men on the eve of the Sabbath and festivals. The *miqveh* has also been used, in accordance with *Numbers* 31:22–23, to immerse new metal and glass vessels and vessels purchased from non-Jews.

The requirements of *miqveh* immersion for women are detailed in rabbinic *halakhah,* particularly in the Talmudic tractate *Niddah,* which discusses the practical consequences of women's menstrual and nonmenstrual discharges. In this rabbinic legislation biblical ordinances are expanded into a complicated system of rules for avoiding not only sexual intercourse but any physical contact between husband and wife during the wife's menses and for an additional seven days following the cessation of flow. On the eighth "white day" the wife must immerse in the *miqveh* before marital relations may resume (interestingly, immersion following menstruation is not a biblical commandment). The rabbinic *halakhah* is concerned with preserving men from the ritual pollution that would follow from any contact with their ritually impure wives. However, procedures for calculating the interval of time when spousal contact is forbidden relies heavily on a woman's knowledge of the stages of her cycle. Fidelity to the rules of self-examination and expedient immersion as soon as legally possible comprise one of the three areas of ritual obligations specifically incumbent on women (together with separating a part of the dough used to make Sabbath loaves and kindling Sabbath lights). Jewish girls were traditionally taught to comply strictly and promptly with the regulations connected with the *niddah* (the menstruating woman). The process of immersion, which includes the recitation of a benediction, takes place only after the body has been thoroughly cleansed and must be complete; whereas one total immersion is sufficient according to the *halakhah,* three have become customary. Postmenstrual and postpartum women have usually visited the *miqveh* at night, often accompanied by other women.

CONTEMPORARY *MIQVEH* USE. In the first half of the twentieth century female *miqveh* observance appears to have declined significantly in North America, even among nominally traditional families, despite Orthodox exhortation in sermons and written tracts on the spiritual and medical benefits of *taharat hamishpahah* (family purity regulations), as these laws came to be called. Factors militating against *miqveh* use included disaffection of Americanized children of immigrants with their parents' Old World ways, the success of liberal forms of organized Judaism (the Reform, Conservative, and Reconstructionist movements) that did not advocate *miqveh* use, and the deterrent effect of ill-maintained and unhygienic *miqva'ot.* Many Jewish feminist writers of the late twentieth century also condemned *taharat hamishpahah* regulations as archaic expressions of male anxiety about the biological processes of the female body that reinforced the predominant construction in rabbinic Judaism of women as other and lesser than men.

However, the 1980s and 1990s saw a resurgence in the numbers of Orthodox Jews and a new sympathy for various previously discarded practices of traditional Judaism in Reform, Conservative, and Reconstructionist Judaism. In this period positive new interpretations of *miqveh* immersion developed, accompanied by construction of attractive modern *miqva'ot* in many Jewish communities. Contemporary Orthodox advocates of *taharat hamishpahah* regulations praised the ways in which they enhanced the sanctity of marriage and human sexuality, maintaining that traditional Judaism recognizes and values the fluctuating rhythms of human relationships by mandating a monthly separation between husband and wife when spousal communication and empathy must be enhanced in nonphysical ways. Supporters commended the elevating value of fulfilling a demanding divinely ordained mandate. They also praised the consciousness of the body and its functions that these rules impose on women and the feeling of personal renewal and rebirth following each immersion.

At the beginning of the twenty-first century *miqveh* immersion has became a symbolic expression of a new spiritual beginning for both women and men in all branches of Jewish practice beyond the domain of *taharat hamishpahah.* In addition to conversion to Judaism, rituals have developed that incorporate *miqveh* immersion as part of bar mitzvah and bat mitzvah (coming of age); before Jewish holidays; prior to marriage; in cases of miscarriage, infertility, and illness; and following divorce, sexual assault, or other life-altering events. An indication of the probable long-term impact of this trend is the increased construction of *miqva'ot* by non-Orthodox Jewish communities.

SEE ALSO Conversion; Purification, article on Purification in Judaism.

BIBLIOGRAPHY

Adler, Rachel. "'In Your Blood, Live': Re-Visions of a Theology of Purity." In *Lifecycles*, vol. 2: *Jewish Women on Biblical Themes in Contemporary Life*, edited by Debra Orenstein and Jane Rachel Litman, pp. 197–206. Woodstock, Vt., 1997. Revisionist feminist response to Orthodox apologetics.

Baskin, Judith R. "Women and Ritual Immersion in Medieval Ashkenaz: The Sexual Politics of Piety." In *Judaism in Practice: From the Middle Ages through the Early Modern Period*, edited by Lawrence Fine, pp. 131–142. Princeton, N.J., 2001. Medieval primary texts and feminist analysis.

Ginsberg, Johanna R. "Dipping into Tradition: The *Mikveh* Makes a Comeback." *Jewish Theological Seminary Magazine* 10, no. 3 (2001): 12–13, 19–21. Discussion of resurgence of *miqveh* use in contemporary American Conservative Judaism.

Levine, Lee. "The Age of Hellenism: Alexander the Great and the Rise and Fall of the Hasmonean Kingdom." In *Ancient Israel: From Abraham to the Roman Destruction of the Temple*, edited by Hershel Shanks, rev. ed., pp. 231–264. Upper Saddle River, N.J., 1999. Includes archaeological perspectives on *miqva'ot* in the Second Temple period.

Levitt, Laura, and Sue Ann Wasserman. "Mikvah Ceremony for Laura." In *Four Centuries of Jewish Women's Spirituality: A Sourcebook*, edited by Ellen M. Umansky and Dianne Ashton, pp. 321–325. Boston, 1992. A contemporary *miqveh* ritual in the aftermath of sexual assault.

Slonim, Rivkah, ed. *Total Immersion: A Mikvah Anthology*. Northvale, N.J., 1996. Contemporary reflections on *miqveh* use from Orthodox points of view.

Wasserfall, Rahel R., ed. *Women and Water: Menstruation in Jewish Life and Law*. Hanover, N.H., 1999. Scholarly essays on women and *miqveh* immersion with a strong ethnographical slant.

JUDITH R. BASKIN (2005)

MIRABAI (b. circa 1500 CE) is the most famous medieval woman saint of *bhakti*, or devotional Hinduism. Known for her unwavering devotion to God in the form of Kṛṣṇa (the amorous incarnation of Viṣṇu) and for her suffering and perseverance in the face of extreme opposition to that love, Mirabai's lifestory and songs are performed throughout India and beyond. Like other *bhakti* saints, her sainthood was not conferred by any institutional authority but rather by countless subsequent devotees who have found in her an exemplar of the ideal devotee and a spiritual guide.

According to hagiographic and legendary accounts, Mirabai was born to a minor royal family in Merta, Rajasthan, in western India, probably around the beginning of the sixteenth century. Devoted to Kṛṣṇa from childhood, she was married into the royal family of the neighboring kingdom of Mewar, but she refused to honor her new husband or his family, seeing Kṛṣṇa as her true husband and Lord. Her in-laws found her behavior as a woman intolerable, particularly her public dancing and singing in temples and her conversing openly with holy men. Attempts were made first to stop her and then to kill her, the method of choice being poison. Who tried to kill her varies by account. Some say she was a devoted wife and it was only after her husband's death that an evil brother-in-law began to persecute her, but many more name her husband as her would-be killer.

The Mughal emperor Akbar is said to have come in disguise to see this renowned devotee of God, her appeal extending across religious boundaries. But eventually she grew weary of persecution and left her marital home to become a wandering saint, going first to Kṛṣṇa's holy city of Vrindavan. There Jiv Goswami, disciple of Caitanya (1486–1533), initially refused to meet her, having vowed not to speak to women, but he then welcomed her after she reminded him that all souls are feminine in the presence of the decidedly male Lord Kṛṣṇa. She settled in Dvaraka until a delegation of Brahmin priests arrived from her marital family to escort her back, threatening to fast to death if she refused. Entering the temple to take leave of Kṛṣṇa, she disappeared, merging with his image.

Other stories also speak of Mirabai taking the untouchable leatherworker Raidas as her guru, an act which places her under male authority but also adds defiance of caste to her transgressions. The story of Mirabai's life has inspired not only devotees of God, but also oppressed low-caste people; women whose suffering, longing, and independence parallel hers; Indian nationalists seeking heroic Indian women to inspire their struggle against the British; and such figures as Mahatma Gandhi (1869–1948), for whom she was an ideal practitioner of non-violent resistance. Upper-caste male historians have also sought to write the definitive historical biography of Mirabai, but historical sources record little about her, and Parita Mukta has even argued that Mirabai's marital family sought to actively suppress her memory. The resulting biographies, like the stories told by others, are—and indeed must be—shaped significantly by the values and assumptions of the tellers. The dates they give for events in her life and the assignment of Bhoj Raj, son of Sanga, as her husband must be treated as speculative.

Like other *bhakti* saints, Mirabai expressed her devotion in songs which have been primarily preserved and disseminated through oral traditions. No early extensive written collections of her songs exist, though such collections are available for male saints like Kabīr (c. 1450–1525) and Surdas. Unlike them, Mirabai was never formally adopted by any institutionalized branch of devotional Hinduism—she remained well loved but outside such structures, in all likelihood because of her independent behavior as a woman.

Among the songs attributed to her, those actually composed by the sixteenth-century woman cannot be distinguished from those composed by others in her name and style.

These songs speak in the first person of deep love and longing for God and of Mirabai's persecution and rejection of the royal world of her husband. They traverse the range of emotions connected with love—longing, anticipation, the ecstatic joy of union, adoration, jealousy, and anger—but also speak of a merger with the One who transcends all distinctions and forms. Throughout her stories and songs, the overriding theme is absolute love of God, with complete disregard for the consequences.

The variations in the telling of Mirabai's story show a deep appreciation for her devotion coupled with a recognition of the depth of opposition she faced and consequent suffering she endured. However, they also reflect the ambivalence that continues to surround a woman's defiance of social norms even out of devotion to God. Mirabai remains immensely popular as a saint but also both powerful and controversial as an exemplary woman.

See Also Bhakti; Hindi Religious Traditions; Poetry, article on Indian Religious Poetry; Vaisnavism, article on Bhāgavatas.

Bibliography

For a comprehensive study of the saint, see Nancy M. Martin's *Mirabai* (New York, 2005). Shorter introductions to the saint with translations of selected songs can be found in John Stratton Hawley and Mark Juergensmeyer's *Songs of the Saints of India* (New York, 1988) and in Madhu Kishwar and Ruth Vanita's "Poison to Nectar: The Life and Work of Mirabai," *Manushi* 50–52 (January–June 1989): 74–93. More extensive English translations are available in A. J. Alston's *Devotional Poems of Mira Bai* (New Delhi, 1980). Detailed studies of low caste traditions surrounding Mirabai, the search for the historical Mirabai, and Mirabai's role as a model for Indian women can be found in Parita Mukti's *Upholding the Common Life: The Community of Mirabai* (New Delhi, 1994); Nancy M. Martin's "Mirabai in the Academy and the Politics of Identity," in *Faces of the Feminine from Ancient, Medieval and Modern India,* edited by Mandakranta Bose (New York, 2000); and Nancy M. Martin's "Mirabai: Inscribed in Text, Embodied in Life," in *Vaisnavi: Women and the Worship of Krishna,* edited by Steven Rosen (Delhi, 1996).

Nancy M. Martin (2005)

MIRACLES

This entry consists of the following articles:

MIRACLES: AN OVERVIEW

The history of religions has preserved the record of miracles, that is, events, actions, and states taken to be so unusual, extraordinary, and supernatural that the normal level of human consciousness finds them hard to accept rationally. These miracles are usually taken as manifestations of the supernatural power of the divine being fulfilling his purpose in history, but they are also caused to occur "naturally" by charismatic figures who have succeeded in controlling their consciousness through visions, dreams, or the practices of meditation. Although miracles have assumed diverse forms, healing miracles and exorcisms have often attracted most attention.

However diverse the forms may be, miracles are preeminently sociological phenomena. It is, of course, true that no miracles exist without miracle workers who often claim religious authority of one kind or another based on their performance of miracles; but as the etymological meaning of the word *miracle* (Lat., *miraculum*) may suggest, one of the conditions indispensable for the creation of miracles is the presence of those people, spectators, who take the performance of miracle workers to be wonderful, extraordinary, and worthy of admiration. These people are often the followers of miracle workers, witnesses of miracles, or professional priests or laymen of the cults at whose shrines, temples, or caves miracles have occurred, and it is they who are often responsible for the creation and propagation of miracle stories in which the saving power of the divine beings and the extraordinary personality of miracle workers are extolled.

Miracles in the "Primitive" Tradition. In primitive societies religious specialists, such as magicians, medicine men, sorcerers, and shamans, are known for their performance of miracles as well as for their exercise of magico-religious powers. They have acquired such miracle-working powers through the practices of meditation, vision quest, or a series of initiatory sicknesses and dreams.

In some parts of Asia, Australia, and North America, it is believed that illness is caused by the intrusion of a magical object into the patient's body, or through his possession by evil spirits. Healing is effected by magicians, sorcerers, or medicine men through the extraction of the harmful object or the expulsion of demons. Among the Aranda in central Australia, for example, a man is initiated into the profession of medicine man through a series of hardships and rituals: one of the older medicine men pierces the index finger of the novice with a pointed magical wand. By this operation the novice acquires the ability to drive out the objects causing illness in his future patients. The old medicine man also seizes the tongue of the novice and cuts a hole in it with a sharp stone knife. This is done to enable him to suck out the evil magical forces to be found in the bodies of his patients.

The vision quest among the Indians of North America is a means of acquiring supernatural power through personal contact with the divine. In California, the vision is sought by shamans wishing to effect a cure. The shaman occupies a unique place among religious specialists due to his ability, in a trance state, to make the ecstatic journey to the beyond. He is engaged in the spiritual journey most often when he has to cure the sick; when he finds that the illness of a sick person has been caused by the loss of his soul, the shaman searches for the lost soul in heaven, in distant space, and most frequently in the underworld.

The shaman acquires the power of healing as well as other magico-religious powers through his unique psychic experience. In Siberia, as a rule, the future shaman is sick for an indefinite period of time; he stays in his tent or wanders in the wilderness, behaving in such eccentric ways that he could be mistaken for a madman: he becomes suddenly frenzied, loses consciousness, feeds on tree bark, or flings himself into water and fire. These pathological symptoms can properly be interpreted in terms of initiatory trials, which the future shaman is destined to undergo in order to be miraculously transformed into a "new being."

Significantly, in the state of sickness, dreams, and visions, the future shaman has the experience of being dismembered, reduced to bones, and then given entirely new internal organs. For example, a Tunguz shaman (Ivan Cholko) states that before a man becomes shaman he is sick for a long time, his head being in a state of confusion. The spirits of the dead shaman-ancestors come, cut his flesh in pieces, and drink his blood. They also cut off his head and throw it into a caldron. According to a Buriat shaman (Mikhail Stepanov), before a man becomes shaman he is sick for a long time. Then the spirits of dead shamans come and teach him; he becomes absentminded, speaking with the dead shamans as if he were with living persons. He alone is able to "see" the spirits. They torture him, strike him, and cut his flesh in pieces with knives. During this surgical operation the future shaman becomes half dead; the beating of his heart is scarcely heard, his breathing is weak, and his face and hands are dark blue. A Yakut shaman (Petr Ivanov) gives further details concerning the initiatory ordeal of dismemberment, followed by the renewal of the body: his limbs are removed and disjointed with an iron hook by the spirits of ancestral shamans; the bones are cleaned, the flesh scraped, the body fluids thrown away, and the eyes torn out of their sockets. After this operation all the bones are gathered up, joined together with iron, and new eyes are put in place. He is thus transformed into a new being, a shaman.

The experiences described above by no means exhaust the shaman's transforming initiatory trials. The Inuit (Eskimo) shaman, for example, acquires the *qaumaneq* (mystical light). "The first time a young shaman experiences this light," Knud Rasmussen states, "it is as if the house in which he is suddenly rises; he sees far ahead of him, through mountains, exactly as if the earth were one great plain, and his eyes could reach to the end of the earth" (*Intellectual Culture of the Igtulik Eskimos*, Copenhagen, 1930, p. 113). According to Franz Boas: "When a person becomes shaman, a light covers his body. He can see supernatural things. The stronger the light is within him, the deeper and further away he can see, and the greater is his supernatural power. The light makes his whole body feel well. When the intensity of this light increases, he feels a strong pressure, and it seems to him as though a film were being removed from his eyes which prevented him from seeing clearly. The light is always present with him. It guides him, and enables him to see into the future and back into the past" (*The Eskimo of Baffin Land and Hudson Bay*, New York, 1901, p. 133).

Shamans must demonstrate to spectators the new, superhuman condition that they have acquired: they gash themselves with knives, touch red-hot iron, and swallow burning coals. Shamans are masters over fire. They also incarnate the spirit of fire to the point where, during séances, they emit flames from their mouths, noses, and whole bodies. The practice of fire walking is imposed on shamans and medicine men in, for instance, Australia, Indonesia, China, and among the Manchu. Sometimes a shaman must prove his miraculous powers by resisting the most severe cold or by drying a wet sheet on his naked body. Among the Manchu, for example, nine holes are made in the ice during winter; the candidate has to dive into the first hole, come out through the second, and so on to the ninth hole. A young Labrador Inuit obtained the title of *angakkoq* (shaman) after remaining five days and nights in the icy sea and proving that he was not even wet. A shaman sometimes shows his miraculous powers to the public by climbing a ladder of knives. Among the Lolo in southern China, a double ladder made of thirty-six knives is built, and the barefoot shaman climbs it to the top, then comes down on the other side. Similar feats are also attested in other parts of China and among the Chingpaw of Upper Burma.

MIRACLES IN THE MEDITERRANEAN WORLD. In archaic Greece, Abaris, Aristeas, and Epimenides were known for their wonders and miracles. Abaris was a shamanic figure; carrying the golden arrow in his hand, he passed through many lands, dispelling sickness and pestilence, and giving warning of earthquakes and other disasters. He was also known to fly through the air on his arrow, a symbol of magic flight. Aristeas of Proconnesus could appear at the same time in two places far apart, sometimes assuming the form of a crow. Epimenides was a master of the techniques of ecstasy, well known for his miraculous powers; he journeyed through many lands, bringing his health-giving arts with him, prophesying the future, interpreting the hidden meaning of past occurrences, and expelling the demonic evils that arose from misdeeds of the past.

Especially noteworthy is Pythagoras, whose image in the Hellenistic Mediterranean world was quite complex in nature. According to his biographies by Porphyry and Iamblichus dating from the third and fourth centuries CE, Pythagoras was a "divine man" (*theios anēr*), combining the figure of the popular miracle worker, the portrait of the philosopher, and the idealized image of the practical statesman. His image as miracle worker was enhanced by several recurring motifs: (1) Pythagoras was seen in two cities at the same time; (2) he could recall his previous existences; (3) he was endowed with the ability to stop an eagle in flight; and (4) he could predict events in the future. It is highly probable that, as Neo-Pythagoreanism gained popularity among ordinary people, the image of Pythagoras the thaumaturge was promoted by a circle of followers quite distinct from those who wished to cultivate his reputation as a philosopher and scientist.

Apollonius of Tyana, a wandering Pythagorean philosopher of the first century CE, also worked miracles. It is generally accepted that early traditions about his activity as a miracle worker were incorporated into subsequent accounts of his life, which were apologetically intended to present him as a philosopher. Apollonius described exorcisms and instances of healing the blind, the lame, and the paralytic in India (see Philostratus, *The Life of Apollonius of Tyana* 3.38–39); more important than that, he performed similar miracles himself. Apollonius reportedly performed even the miracle of raising the dead while he was in Rome (4.45): a girl had died just before her marriage, and the bridegroom was following her bier lamenting; the whole of Rome lamented with him, for she belonged to a consular family. Apollonius, meeting the funeral procession, said, "Put down the bier, for I will put a stop to your tears for the girl." Then he asked her name. The crowd thought he was going to deliver a funeral oration, but he merely touched her and said something in secret over her, and thus he awoke her from her seeming death. In the magical papyri, his name is attached to a spell, a fact indicating his considerable popularity as a magician. According to Dio Cassius, the Roman emperor Caracalla (r. 211–217) built a temple in honor of Apollonius, who was a "perfect example of the magician."

The figure of Moses was one of the most important propaganda instruments that Jews of the Hellenistic period used in their competition with non-Jewish schools and cults. In *Deuteronomy* 34:10–12, Moses is described as the greatest prophet in Israel, known for his signs and wonders as well as for his mighty powers and great and terrible deeds. This Moses was presented to the Hellenistic world as a miracle-working philosopher, as is exemplified in Philo Judaeus's *On the Life of Moses.*

There are many stories in late Judaism narrating how rabbis worked miracles of healing. The best known, perhaps, is the healing of the son of Yoḥanan ben Zakk'ai by Ḥanina' ben Dosa'. Both rabbis lived in Palestine around 70 CE. Ḥanina' ben Dosa' went to study the Torah with Yoḥanan ben Zakk'ai, whose son was seriously ill. Yoḥanan requested: "Ḥanina', my son, pray for mercy for him that he may live." Ḥanina' ben Dosa' laid his head between his knees and prayed, and then the boy was cured (B.T., *Ber.* 34).

Miracles of healing were performed also by kings, for example, the Roman emperor Vespasian (r. 70–79). While the emperor was in Alexandria, a blind man approached him, acting on the advice of the god Sarapis; he fell at Vespasian's feet, demanding with sobs a cure for his blindness and imploring the emperor to moisten his eyes with the spittle from his mouth. Another man with a maimed hand, also inspired by Sarapis, asked Vespasian to touch it with his heel. "To the great excitement of the bystanders," states Tacitus, Vespasian "did as the men desired him. Immediately the hand recovered its functions and daylight shone once more in the blind man's eyes" (*Histories* 4.81; see also Dio Cassius, *Roman History* 65.8, and Suetonius, *Vespasian* 7.2–3).

Throughout late antiquity, Epidaurus was a holy site especially celebrated for the epiphany of Asklepios, the divine healer. According to Strabo, Asklepios was believed to "cure diseases of every kind." His temple was always full of the sick as well as containing the votive tablets on which treatments were recorded (*Geography* 8.6.15). Asklepios would appear to the sick sleeping in his temple—more precisely, in the innermost chamber (*to abaton*) of the sanctuary; he would approach the sick in dreams and visions, or, as Aelius Aristides put it, in a "state of mind intermediate between sleep and waking." This practice of temple sleep, incubation (*incubatio*), was of vital importance to the sick; it was in the state of such dreams and visions that one was healed or given instructions by Asklepios. The healing god would touch his patient's body with his hands, apply drugs, or undertake surgical operations. Consequently, the eyesight of the blind would be restored, the lame would walk, the mute would speak, and the man whose fingers had been paralyzed would stretch each of them one by one. Some examples of Asklepios's miracles follow.

Ambrosia of Athens, blind in one eye, came to Epidaurus to seek help from Asklepios. But as she walked around the temple, she mocked at the many records of divine healings: "It is unbelievable and impossible that the lame and the blind can be cured by merely dreaming." In her sleep she had a dream: Asklepios approached and promised to heal her; only in return she must present a gift offering in the temple—a silver pig, in memory of her stupidity. After saying this, Asklepios cut open her defective eye and poured in a drug. Her sight was soon restored. The following miracle story about a man with an abscess inside his abdomen reminds us of the initiatory dreaming of Siberian shamans. While asleep in the temple, the man saw a dream: Asklepios ordered the servants who accompanied him to hold him tightly so that he could cut open his abdomen. The man tried to escape but could not. Then Asklepios cut his belly open, removed the abscess, and stitched him up. Sometimes, the healing power of Asklepios reached the patient far away from his temple. Arata, a woman of Lacedaemon, was dropsical. While she remained in Lacedaemon, her mother slept in the temple on her behalf and saw a dream: Asklepios cut off her daughter's head and hung up her body in such a way that her throat was turned downward. Out of it came a huge quantity of fluid matter. Then he took down the body and put the head back onto the neck. After the mother had seen this dream, she went home and found her daughter in good health; the daughter had seen the same dream.

The Mediterranean world knew Egypt as the home of thaumaturgy, theosophy, and esoteric wisdom. There, the goddess Isis was praised for her miraculous healings; she was credited with bringing the arts of healing to men and, once she had attained immortality, taking pleasure in miraculously healing those who incubated themselves in her temple (Diodorus Siculus, *The Library of History* 1.25.2–5). At her hands the maimed were healed and the blind received their eyesight. According to the inscriptions found on the island of Delos dating from about the first century BCE, Isis worship was attended by a functionary specifically called an *aretalogos*, an interpreter of dreams, who may have functioned as a proclaimer of miraculous events. The temple of the god Sarapis at Canopus, not far from Alexandria, was also famous for its divine healing; Sarapis would visit those who slept in his temple, giving them advice in dreams.

YOGINS, DAOIST CONTEMPLATIVES, AND YAMABUSHI. Indian ascetics practicing Yoga are well known for their miraculous powers. The yogin sits cross-legged and firm on a flat space with his eyes fixed on a certain object beyond him. He has to master, at the same time, the breathing techniques (*prāṇāyāma*); at first, the breath is kept for one minute and then exhaled. This practice goes on for days, weeks, and months until the period of retention of the inhaled breath is gradually increased.

According to the Indo-Tibetan Tantric tradition, the ascetic is able to produce "inner heat" on the basis of rhythmical breathing and various "visualizations." During a winter-night snowstorm, the degree of his progress is tested by his ability to dry a large number of soaked sheets draped directly over his naked body. "Sheets are dipped in the icy water," reports Alexandra David-Neel. "Each man wraps himself in one of them and must dry it on his body. As soon as the sheet has become dry, it is again dipped in the water and placed on the novice's body to be dried as before. The operation goes on until daybreak. Then he who has dried the largest number of sheets is acknowledged the winner of the competition" (*With Mystics and Magicians in Tibet*, London, 1931, pp. 227–228).

The yogin acquires the "miraculous powers" (*siddhis*) when he has reached a particular stage of his meditational discipline called *saṃyama*, referring, more specifically, to the last stages of yogic technique, that is, concentration (*dhāraṇa*), meditation (*dhyāna*), and *samādhi*. For example, by practicing *saṃyama* in regard to the subconscious residues (*saṃskāras*), the yogin knows his previous existences; through the practice of Yoga, he arrives successfully at the state of mind in which he is one with the things meditated, namely, his subconscious residues. This enables him to ideally relive his former existences. Through *saṃyama* exercised in respect to notions (*pratyaya*), the yogin also knows the mental states of other men; he sees, as on a screen, all the states of consciousness that notions are able to arouse in their minds. Some of the yogin's "miraculous powers" are even more extraordinary: he can make himself invisible by practicing *saṃyama* concerning the form of the body. "When the yogin practices *saṃyama* on the form of the body," Vācaspatimiśra comments, "he destroys the perceptibility of the color (*rūpa*) that is the cause of perception of the body" (Eliade, 1958, p. 87).

In India, the yogin has always been considered a *mahāsiddha*, a possessor of miraculous powers, a magician. However, a yogin is still far from attaining his final goal of absolute freedom so long as his miraculous powers serve him as his "possession." As soon as he consents to use the magical forces gained through his ascetic discipline, the possibility of his realizing absolute freedom diminishes; only a new renunciation, a determination not to use the miraculous powers, would lead the ascetic to a higher spiritual horizon.

Daoists in ancient China are convinced that man can become an "immortal" (*xianren, shenxian,* or *shengren*), that man is able to transcend his human condition by various means, including the practice of meditation. The *Zhuangzi* tells of one such extraordinary man living on a remote mountain: "He does not eat the five grains, but sucks the wind, drinks the dew, climbs up on the clouds and mist, rides a flying dragon, and watches beyond the four seas" (chap. 1). Moreover, "by concentrating his spirit, he can protect creatures from sickness and plague and make the harvest plentiful" (ibid.). Abstention from cereals belongs to a basic requirement in Daoism for nourishing life, as is illustrated by Ge Hong's *Baopuzi* dating from the early fourth century CE. "Sucking the wind" and "drinking the dew" are technical terms in Daoism for breathing exercises. It is certain that the story speaks about a Daoist contemplative on his ecstatic journey, transcending the universe. Especially interesting in the story is the fact that he is able to "concentrate his spirit," that is, to solidify his spiritual potency. The ability to solidify the spiritual potency or light belongs to the privilege of such religious specialists as shamans, yogins, and Daoist saints. According to Max Kaltenmark, the solidification of the spiritual potency points to an essential feature of the Daoist technique of meditation, which consists in freezing the faculties of the soul, concentrating them in a single point.

The practice of meditation essential for attaining immortality leads inevitably to the possession of miraculous powers. According to the *Baopuzi*, the Daoist immortal Ge Xuan, one of Ge Hong's paternal uncles, would stay at the bottom of a deep pond for almost a whole day in hot summer weather. This "miracle" was possible because of his mastery of "embryonic respiration": he was able to accumulate his breaths and to breathe like a fetus in its mother's womb. Ge Xuan was a disciple of the famous Daoist immortal Zuo Ci, of whom it is said that, despite abstinence from eating cereals for almost a whole month, his complexion remained unchanged and his vitality stayed normal (*Baopuzi*, chap. 2).

Mountain ascetics in Japan known as *yamabushi* acquired magico-religious powers through a series of disciplines. The *yamabushi* was the master of heat and fire; he walked barefoot on red hot charcoals without injury; he proved his extraordinary power when, with only a white robe on his naked body, he entered a bath of boiling water and came out entirely unscathed; and he surprised his spectators by climbing a ladder of swords, the sharp edge facing upward. Like a shaman, he was a spiritual being. In his inner consciousness he was a bird in control of cosmic space; at the culminating moment of a ceremony, the *yamabushi* in a trance would spread his arms and fly in the sky in imitation of a bird. In view of the extraordinary powers at his disposal, it is not surprising that he cured the sick, exorcised demons, and fought triumphant battles against evil spirits.

MIRACLES IN FOUNDED RELIGIONS. The founders of three major religions of the world—Buddhism, Christianity, and Islam—have each taken a different attitude toward miracle; Jesus Christ was utterly positive in working miracles, whereas Muḥammad, as represented in the Qurʾān, categorically rejected them. Significantly, the Buddha took the middle course, so to speak. Despite this remarkable divergence among these founders, the subsequent history of these religions demonstrates unmistakably that miracles and miracle stories have been an integral part of man's religious life.

Buddhism. The Buddha was well aware that the practice of meditation essential for attaining enlightenment leads eventually to the possession of "miraculous power" (Skt., *siddhi*; Pali, *iddhi*). But he did not encourage his disciples to seek *siddhi*s. "O *bhikkus*," the Buddha said, "you must not show the superhuman power of *iddhi* before the laity. Whoever does so shall be guilty of an evil deed" (*Vinaya Texts*, trans. T. W. Rhys Davids and Hermann Oldenberg, vol. 3, Delhi, [1885] 1965, p. 81). The true task was not to acquire miraculous powers but to transcend the world of pain and suffering and to attain the state of enlightenment (see *Dīgha Nikāya* 24.3). Moreover, the possession of one miraculous power or another in no way promoted, in the Buddha's mind, the propagation of the central message of Buddhism; yogins, ecstatics, and other ascetics could perform the same miracles.

"Miraculous powers" are one of the five classes of "superknowledge" (Skt., *abhijñā;* Pali, *abhiññā*), which are (1) *siddhi*, (2) divine eye, (3) divine hearing, (4) knowledge of another's thought, and (5) recollection of previous existences. By virtue of deepening meditation, the Buddhist saint is able to acquire the *siddhi* in its various forms: he becomes invisible at his own will; he goes, without feeling any obstacle, to the far side of a wall or rampart or hill, as if through air; he penetrates up and down through solid ground, as if through water; he walks on water without breaking through, as if on solid ground; and he travels cross-legged in the sky, like the birds on the wing (*Dīgha Nikāya* 2.87, 11.4).

According to biographical sources, the Buddha himself was sometimes led to work miracles; for example, when he returned to his native city, Kapilavastu, for the first time after attaining enlightenment, he rose in the air, emitted flames of fire and streams of water from his body, and walked in the sky (see *Mahāvastu* 3.115). According to Aśvaghoṣa's *Buddhacarita* (19.12–13), in order to convince his relatives of his spiritual capacities and prepare them for conversion, the Buddha rose in the air, cut his body to pieces, let his head and limbs fall to the ground, and then joined them together again before the amazed eyes of the spectators. Among the eminent disciples of the Buddha, Moggallāna (Skt., Maudgalyāyana) was well known as the "chief of those endowed with miraculous powers."

As Buddhism was transplanted to China, its missionaries often resorted to the display of miraculous powers. Especially in northern China, Buddhist saints performed magical feats for evangelical purposes; Fotudeng, who came to China at the beginning of the fourth century CE, worked the miracles of producing rain, creating a lotus out of a bowl of water, and drawing water from dried-up wells. The fame of the monk Dharmaksema was based not only on his scholarly contributions but also on his supernatural powers to produce rain and foretell the outcome of political events or military campaigns. One may not be prepared to accept all of these miracle stories told by pious biographers, but they were undoubtedly created with the good intention of glorifying the Buddha, who was able to endow his ardent followers with such miraculous powers.

Christianity. Jesus Christ performed the miracles of healing and exorcism. In the miracle stories that, together with his sayings and passion narratives, occupy an important place in the Synoptic Gospels, Jesus of Nazareth is presented as the supreme thaumaturge, the great miracle worker, the magician. In fact, there was a charge that Jesus was in league with Beelzebul (*Mk.* 3:22, *Mt.* 12:24, 12:27) and, according to a rabbinic tradition (see B.T., *San.* 43a), Jesus was executed for his practice of sorcery, misguiding the people of Israel.

Typically, the miracle stories of healing and exorcism in the Synoptic Gospels all emphasize three motifs: (1) the history of the illness, (2) the actual process or techniques of the healing, and (3) a demonstration of the cure to the satisfaction of spectators. There is no doubt that the miracle stories were utilized internally for the strengthening of Christian faith and externally for propaganda purposes in a world in which such stories were commonly told of heroes of faith.

Particularly interesting are the techniques that Jesus employed for healing and exorcism. There is no question that he considered prayer to be essential for working miracles (*Mk.* 9:29). But, as a thaumaturge, he had to work up his emotions; in healing a leper Jesus was moved with "anger" (*orgistheis*), stretched out his hand, and touched him (*Mk.* 1:40–45). Jesus displayed the emotional frenzy of the thaumaturge (see also *Lk.* 4:39). In the story of the deaf and mute man (*Mk.* 7:32–37), Jesus puts his fingers into his ears, spits and touches his tongue. Looking up to heaven, he sighs and says to him, "Ephphatha" ("Be opened"). In *Mk.* 8:22–26 Jesus heals a blind man by spitting on his eyes and laying his hands on them. Groaning sighs and spittle were often used by the thaumaturges. As to the use of Semitic words for healing purposes, the account in the *Gospel of Mark* (5:41) of Jesus restoring a girl to life by saying, "Talithȧ Koum" ("Little girl, stand up"), retains the original Aramaic words even in otherwise translated versions. According to the German theologian Martin Dibelius, the preservation of such foreign words and phrases may show that the stories were utilized as a kind of handbook to Christian miracles and magic. The image of Jesus as the thaumaturge can still be identified in the *Gospel of John* (see 9:6, 11:33, 11:35, 11:38, 11:43).

Especially interesting is a cycle of miracle stories in the *Gospel of Mark* (4:35–5:43) that includes the stories of the Gerasene demoniac, the woman with an issue of blood, and the daughter of Jairus. Each of these has all the characteristics of the popular miracle story, and each contributes to the impression that Jesus is a "divine man," tempting New Testament scholars to talk about the development of "divine man Christology" in the *Gospel of Mark*; the miraculous power of Jesus is such that the Gerasenes beg him to leave their district, the touch of his clothes effects a cure, and he raises the dead by strange-sounding words. Moreover, Jesus is presented as performing the miracles of stilling the storm (4:35–41), feeding the five thousand people (6:34–44; see also 8:1–9), and walking on water (6:45–52).

Jesus Christ was followed by his apostles in working miracles (*Acts* 2:43, 5:12), and it seems that they worked the miracles of healing and exorcism "in the name of Jesus Christ" (*Acts* 3:6, 16:18; see also 19:13–17). Stephen and Philip demonstrated great wonders and signs among the people (*Acts* 6:8, 8:5–7), while Peter healed the lame and the paralytic, restoring the dead to life (*Acts* 3:1ff., 9:32ff., 9:36ff.). Even his "shadow" was believed to have healing power (*Acts* 5:15). Paul is also presented in *Acts* as a great miracle worker: he healed a cripple at Lystra (14:8ff.), performed an exorcism in the name of Jesus Christ (16:18), and cured Publius's father, who was sick with fever and dysentery, by putting his hands on him (28:8). Even handkerchiefs and aprons that had touched Paul's body were believed to be effective for curing sickness and exorcism (19:11–12). In *Acts* 13:4–12, Paul evokes belief in the proconsul Sergius Paulus by showing his superior thaumaturgy over the Jewish magician Bar-Jesus and another magician, Elymas.

As we can see from the portrayal of these apostles in *Acts*, the Christian community in the Hellenistic Mediterranean world had a tendency to view its heroes as "divine men"; Paul's opponents in Corinth, especially those he argued against in 2 *Corinthians*, understood a Christian apostle as one who exhibited the aura and power of a "divine man," and they claimed it of themselves and wanted Paul to demonstrate it of himself. Accordingly, Paul had to write to the Corinthians that he had shown the signs of a true apostle among them, "with signs and wonders and mighty works" (2 *Cor.* 12:12; see also *Rom.* 15:18–19a; 1 *Cor.* 12:9–10; *Gal.* 3:5).

Jesus Christ and his apostles in the first century set the examples to be followed by the faithful. In the subsequent history of Christianity, charisma or divine gift of "power" was represented on earth by a limited number of exceptional charismatic figures, such as the martyrs of the second and third centuries, the bishops of the late third century, and, finally, the succession of great Christian saints of ascetic origin, from Anthony onward.

Islam. Muḥammad, the "seal of the prophets," rejected every request to pose as a miracle worker; in contrast to Moses and other Hebrew prophets, as well as Jesus, who all worked miracles (*muʿjizāt*), Muḥammad made no attempt to advance his religious authority by performing miracles, although people demanded them, saying, "Why does he not bring us a sign from his Lord?" (*sūrah* 20:133). To those people who wondered why signs, that is, miracles, had not been sent down on him from God, Muḥammad responded: "The signs are only with God, and I am only a plain warner" (29:49; see also 13:27–30, 17:92ff.).

According to Muḥammad, as presented in the Qurʾān, all the existing things in the universe are the signs (*āyāt*; sg., *āyah*) pointing to the reality of God in action. Natural phenomena, such as rain, wind, the structure of heaven and earth, the rhythmical alternation of day and night, and so forth, are not simply "natural" occurrences; they should be understood as "signs" or "symbols" manifesting God's mercy and compassion for man's well-being on earth. God declares, "We shall show them our signs in the horizons and in themselves" (41:53; see also 51:20–21). The universe is thus miraculously transformed into a forest of symbols; human beings dwell within the forest of divine symbols, and these symbols can be deciphered by anyone if he is spiritually prepared to interpret them as symbols. There should be no miracles except for these "signs."

However, the majority of the Islamic community has never ceased to expect miracles. Muḥammad is presented in the traditions (*ḥadīths*) as having worked miracles in public on many occasions. It was especially Ṣūfī saints who performed miracles (*karāmāt*). Often called the "friends of God" (*awliyāʾ*, sg. *walī*), they worked miracles by divine grace. On the one hand, it is often said by the Ṣūfīs that saints must not seek after the gift of miracle working, which might become a serious obstacle in the path to the union with God. On the other hand, the biographies of leading Ṣūfīs abound in miracle stories that certainly have been utilized for evangelical purposes: saints traveled a long distance in a short time; walked on water and in the air; talked with such inanimate objects as stones, as well as with animals; miraculously produced food, clothing, and other necessities of life; and made predictions of future events. Even after their death, saints are believed to work miracles at their own graves on behalf of the faithful, and their intercession is piously invoked.

See Also Asklepios; Dreams; Healing and Medicine; Magic; Shamanism; Spittle and Spitting; Supernatural, The; Yoga.

Bibliography

There is no comprehensive book dealing with the topic of miracles in the general history of religions. On the problem of interpretation concerning miracles and magico-religious powers in "primitive" societies, see Ernesto de Martino's *Il mondo magico* (Turin, 1948), translated by Paul S. White as *The World of Magic* (New York, 1972). On the miracles and miraculous powers of shamans, there is an admirable account in Mircea Eliade's *Shamanism: Archaic Techniques of Ecstasy,* rev. & enl. ed. (New York, 1964). This book contains an excellent bibliography.

Richard Reitzenstein's *Hellenistische Wundererzählungen* (1906; reprint, Darmstadt, 1963) still remains a classic for the study of the miracle stories in the Hellenistic Mediterranean world. Otto Weinreich has offered a detailed analysis of some of the major motifs appearing in the Greco-Roman stories of healing miracles. See his *Antike Heilungswunder: Untersuchungen zum Wunderglauben der Griechen und Römer* (Giessen, 1909). Valuable information on the miracle stories pertaining to the cult of Asklepios is presented in Emma J. Edelstein and Ludwig Edelstein's *Asclepius: A Collection and Interpretation of the Testimonies,* 2 vols. (Baltimore, 1945). See also Károly Kerényi's important study *Die göttliche Arzt: Studien über Asklepios und seine Kultstätten,* rev. ed. (Darmstadt, 1956), translated by Ralph Manheim as *Asklepios: Archetypal Image of the Physician's Existence* (New York, 1959). Miracle stories in rabbinic Judaism have been collected by Paul Fiebig in his *Jüdische Wundergeschichten des neutestamentlichen Zeitalters* (Tübingen, 1911).

On the miraculous powers of yogins, there is a brilliant account in Mircea Eliade's *Yoga: Immortality and Freedom,* 2d ed. (Princeton, 1969), still the standard work on the theory and practice of Yoga. On Daoist immortals and their miraculous powers, there is a brief but excellent account in Max Kaltenmark's *Lao Tseu et le daoïsme* (Paris, 1965), translated by Roger Greaves as *Lao Tzu and Taoism* (Stanford, Calif., 1969).

On miracles in the life of the Buddha, see a valuable account in Edward J. Thomas's *The Life of Buddha as Legend and History,* 3d rev. ed. (London, 1949).

The modern study of the miracle stories in the Synoptic Gospels was initiated shortly after the end of World War I by such brilliant form critics as Martin Dibelius and Rudolf Bultmann. See a fascinating study by Dibelius, *Die Formgeschichte des Evangeliums,* 2d rev. ed. (Tübingen, 1933), translated by Bertram Lee Woolf as *From Tradition to Gospel* (New York, 1935). See also Bultmann's admirable analysis of the miracle stories in his *Die Geschichte der synoptischen Tradition,* 3d ed. (Göttingen, 1958), translated by John Marsh as *The History of the Synoptic Tradition* (New York, 1963). More recently, Gerd Theissen has studied the miracle stories from the perspective of the sociology of literature. See his *Urchristliche Wundergeschichten: Ein Beitrag zur formgeschichtlichen Erforschung der synoptischen Evangelien* (Gutersloh, 1974), translated by Francis McDonagh and edited by John Riches as *The Miracle Stories of the Early Christian Tradition* (Philadelphia, 1983). David L. Tiede, in his very useful study *The Charismatic Figure as Miracle Worker* (Missoula, Mont., 1972), distinguishes between the aretalogy of the sage-philosopher and the aretalogy of the miracle worker. On Christian saints and their miracles, there is an excellent study by Peter Brown, *The Cult of the Saints: Its Rise and Function in Latin Christianity* (Chicago, 1981).

On Muḥammad's reinterpretation of the concept *āyah* ("sign"), there is an admirable account by Toshihiko Izutsu, *God and Man in the Koran: Semantics of the Koranic Weltanschauung* (Tokyo, 1964), pp. 133ff. Reynold A. Nicholson has written on Muslim saints and their miracles in his *The Mystics of Islam: An Introduction to Sufism* (1914; reprint, London, 1963), pp. 120–147. See also a fascinating account by Annemarie Schimmel, *Mystical Dimensions of Islam* (Chapel Hill, N.C., 1975), pp. 204ff.

New Sources

Cavadini, John, ed. *Miracles in Jewish and Christian Antiquity: Imagining Truth.* Notre Dame, Ind., 1999.

Davis, Richard, ed. *Images, Miracles and Authority in Asian Religious Traditions.* Boulder, Co., 1998.

Earman, John. *Hume's Abject Failure: The Argument against Miracles.* New York, 2000.

Harline, Craig. *Miracles at the Jesus Oak: Histories of the Supernatural in Reformation Europe.* New York, 2003.

Kahl, Werner. *New Testament Stories in Their Religious-Historical Setting: A Religionsgeschichtliche Comparison from a Structural Perspective.* Göttingen, 1994.

Korte, Anne-Marie. *Women in Miracle Stories: A Multidisciplinary Exploration.* Boston, 2001.

Mullin, Robert Bruce. *Miracles and the Modern Religious Imagination.* New Haven, 1996.

Woodward, Kenneth. *The Book of Miracles: The Meaning of the Miracle Stories in Christianity, Judaism, Buddhism, Hinduism, Islam.* New York, 2000.

MANABU WAIDA (1987)
Revised Bibliography

MIRACLES: MODERN PERSPECTIVES

The attitude toward miracles in the Western world is a strange combination of belief and disbelief. Most of the Mediterranean cultures that laid the groundwork for Western thinking believed that human beings have two modes of coping with animate and inanimate reality. One is the ordinary way, the other the religious or miraculous way. (Most nineteenth-century Western anthropologists called the second way magical.) Humans act in the ordinary way when they use habit, conventional thinking processes, or acquired skills. When these methods fail, when humans cannot adequately deal with the physical world, or when other human beings are hostile or unchanged by threats, war, contracts, or persuasion, another option is available: they can seek the help and intervention of a spiritual or nonphysical dimension of reality, which exists alongside and interpenetrates the ordinary physical dimension. This supplication can be quite conscious or it can be performed unconsciously through actions that imply control over these powers. Help can be invoked through concentration, meditation, ritual, spell, or ecstatic trance. Aid can be sought for knowledge, protection, or deliverance. The spiritual powers called upon can be either beneficent, malignant, or neutral. When a result appears in response to such an action, a miracle is said to occur. The miracle may occur within an individual or in the external world.

Four different attitudes toward miracles are to be found in Western cultures at the present time. (1) Christianity's view, which has remained quite consistent from the teachings and practice of Jesus to the present time, holds that miracles are natural manifestations of God. (2) Rational materialism maintains that material reality accounts for all data of experience and infers therefrom that spiritual reality is an illusion and that miracles do not exist. This view has encouraged liberal Christianity to doubt the reality of the miracles found in the New Testament and to rule out the possibility of their happening at present. This view has influenced conservative Christianity as well, for conservatives believe that miracles did occur within the dispensation of God at the time of Jesus but that they do not occur now. (3) A resurgence of interest in and study of phenomena not accounted for within the framework of materialism constitutes yet another approach to miracles, which has recently engaged the scientific community. (4) A fourth attitude toward miracles prevails in Hinduism, Buddhism, and Western Christian Science. In this view, material reality is seen as illusion. A miracle occurs once an individual realizes this truth. This approach is increasingly popular in the West, for it provides an alternative to rational materialism.

Christianity and Miracle. Christianity is both a historical religion and a living one. The historic Christian faith is one of the few in which miracles are seen as constituent of the orthodox faith. It continues the Old Testament tradition of God acting powerfully in the physical world. As C. S. Lewis (1947) points out, historical Christianity sees the incarnation of God in the world as the greatest miracle that culminates in the crucifixion and resurrection. Through this invasion of God the powers of evil are defeated and the kingdom of heaven begins to manifest itself on earth. Reginald H. Fuller (1963) sees the New Testament miracles as signs of the breakthrough of the kingdom into the ordinary world, though he questions the historicity of most miracles.

I have shown in detail in *The Christian and the Supernatural* (1976) that the miraculous in the ministry of Jesus and the apostles described in the New Testament falls into six categories:

1. The most common miracles are physical and mental healings, from curing ailments like a fever (*Mk.* 1:30) to raising the dead.
2. Another class of miracles involves exorcism, or healing through the expulsion of a spiritual force causing mental or physical illness. Most mental and physical sickness was perceived not as the action of God but as the infiltration of negative spiritual powers at war with God, an infiltration that morally caused sin, physically caused disease, and mentally caused madness or possession.
3. The third category comprises communication with the spiritual world and with God through dreams, visions, revelations, or prayer. Such communication is a basic principle of the teachings and practice of Jesus.
4. Nature miracles comprise a fourth category. Examples include Jesus walking on the water (*Mk.* 6:48), the stilling of the storm (*Mk.* 4:38), physical disappearance (*Lk.* 4:30), and the feeding of the multitudes (*Mk.* 6:35).
5. In another category of miracles Jesus shows telepathic, clairvoyant, and precognitive power (*Mk.* 2:6, *Jn.* 1:47, *Mk.* 11:1). Sometimes his statements are prophetic, as when he foretells his own death and resurrection, relates the destruction of Jerusalem, and speaks of the coming of the Kingdom.
6. In the final category of miracles are the resurrection appearances of Jesus, which combine both the physical and the spiritual in a religious experience that is dynamic and transforming.

Similar miracles are reported among the apostles after the ascension of Jesus in *Acts of the Apostles* and in other books of the New Testament. This tradition of miracles continued without interruption in both Roman Catholicism and Orthodox Christianity; services for healing and exorcism are found in the official service books of both. Writing during the fifth century, Sozomenos reports that miracles began to occur again at the end of the Arian controversy, when churches held by Arians were returned to Orthodox pastors (*Ecclesiastical History* 7.5). Throughout Christian history miracles have been reported to occur around saintly people. To this day several attested miracles are required by the Roman Catholic church before a saint is canonized.

During the Reformation, both Luther and Calvin wrote that the age of miracles was over and that their occurrence should not be expected. At the same time Protestantism was overwhelmed by the rationalism and materialism of the Enlightenment, and discussion of the miraculous nearly disappeared. The Roman Catholic church upheld its practice without trying to defend it intellectually, and shrines like Lourdes drew great crowds. The academic Protestant community came to believe that the practice of Christianity was largely a matter of morality and that neither God nor the spiritual world contacted or influenced practical human life to any great extent. Rudolf Bultmann presented this thesis consistently and thoroughly.

Philosophical Materialism. Materialism as an adequate explanation for all things originated in the thinking of several classical Greek thinkers, was developed by Aristotle, and came to fruition in the eighteenth and nineteenth centuries. My book *Encounter with God* (1972) traces this development from its first beginnings to its full-blown denial of any aspect of reality not perceived by the five senses and not objectively verifiable. This view, diametrically opposed to the view of Hinduism and Buddhism, dominated the intellectual and academic life of the West in the nineteenth and early twentieth centuries and influenced nearly all disciplines from psychology and anthropology to comparative religion and Christian theology. In several books B. F. Skinner dismisses human consciousness as the ghost in the box. Melvin Konner in *The Tangled Wing* (New York, 1982) writes that there is only the blind action of natural selection, sifting material genes. A person is only a gene's way of making another gene. This skeptical materialism has arisen many times in human history—in China, Greece, and Rome—but only recently has it effectively taken over nearly a whole culture.

This worldview considers all miracles and all contact with any dimension of reality other than the concrete physical one absurd, the result of ignorance, superstition, or the refusal to search long enough for the purely physical causes. Supposedly intelligent people will classify miracle with magic and ignore any experience purporting to be miraculous.

SCIENTIFIC STUDY OF PARANORMAL EXPERIENCE. Since the mid-twentieth century, when man succeeded in splitting the atom and the implications of Heisenberg's principle of indeterminacy and Einstein's theory of relativity were fully realized, theoretical physics has become much less certain that it can provide final answers. In *Physics and Philosophy* (New York, 1962) Werner Heisenberg suggests that we live in an open universe and that the conventional words describing God and spirit may have greater correspondence with reality than the highly developed words of physics. The mathematical thinking of Kurt Gödel, the analysis of scientific theory presented by Thomas S. Kuhn in *The Structure of Scientific Revolutions* (Chicago, 1962), the findings of psychosomatic medicine, the work of modern anthropologists, the data in Andrew Greeley's *The Sociology of the Paranormal: A Reconnaissance* (1975), the scientific study of parapsychological phenomena, and the theory underlying the depth psychology of C. G. Jung all cast doubt on Western materialist determinism.

In the heyday of materialism in London a group of serious scientists organized the Society for Psychical Research in 1882. An American society was organized three years later in which William James was active. Sigmund Freud was a member of the original society and contributed to its publications. Jung too studied and published on the subject of paranormal experience; he discussed synchronicity, mediumship, and telepathy and provided models for understanding these events. Joseph Banks Rhine at Duke University did many scientific studies of events that did not fit into the materialistic paradigm.

Finally, the professional organization calling itself the Parapsychological Association was accepted as an affiliate by the American Association for the Advancement of Science in 1969. One of the most comprehensive surveys of scientific parapsychology to date is that of Robert F. Jahn (1982). Jahn describes four categories of psychic phenomena; three of these are divided further. These categories are similar to the Christian ones. In the following outline, I have added explanations of the terms.

I. EXTRASENSORY PERCEPTION (ESP)

A. Telepathy: information passing from mind to mind without physical means

B. Clairvoyance: perception of events or happenings at a distance in space

C. Precognition/Retrocognition: perception of events in future time or past time

D. Animal ESP

II. PSYCHOKINESIS (PK): THE AFFECT OF MIND OR PSYCHE OR SPIRIT ON A MATERIAL ENVIRONMENT

A. Physical Systems

1. deliberate, actually effected by conscious intent

2. spontaneous, as in poltergeist phenomena

B. Biological Systems

1. psychic healing

2. plant PK

III. SURVIVAL: EXPERIENCES OF THE DECEASED

A. Reincarnation: evidence of a former life of the individual

B. Apparitions: experience of the person deceased or spiritual reality

C. Mediumship: using others to make contact with this nonphysical domain

IV. OUT-OF-BODY EXPERIENCES (OOBE): THE EXPERIENCE OF HAVING EXISTENCE AS A PSYCHE, BUT NO LONGER TIED TO THE PHYSICAL BODY. Once it is acknowledged that human beings can receive verifiable information through means other than the five senses and that this reception breaks the rules of space and time, the serious scientific study of miracle becomes possible. It becomes possible to examine critically data that are not easily verifiable, such as communication from the deceased and the transformative power of religious experience. A strict materialistic framework considers communication through nonphysical means as absurd as a miracle, because it assumes that some physical signal has to enter the closed system and move the cogs so that the message can get through. An alternate theory of perception is required to avoid such an impasse.

Since the first decade of the twentieth century the medical profession has come to realize that a materialist point of view cannot explain or heal all human disease. Both James and Jung point out that the experience of meaninglessness is a disease causing both emotional and physical sickness. In *The Broken Heart* (1977) James J. Lynch describes the medical consequences of loneliness and calls organized religion to task for not providing ways to meet this human need, which is largely ignored in a mechanistic, materialistic society. O. Carl and Stephanie Simonton have described a meditative treatment for cancer in *Getting Well Again* (1978). Herbert Benson describes what he calls the faith factor in *Beyond the Relaxation Response* (1983).

In *The Structure and Dynamics of the Psyche* (1960), Jung presents a theory of synchronicity developed in conjunction with the Nobel Prize-winning atomic physicist Wolfgang Pauli. He offers a hypothesis as to how events can be influenced both by physical causality operating within the material world and by other forces as well. Jung never denied physical causality, but he concluded that it could not explain all happenings, a conclusion also reached by other scientists. Those events not explainable in purely causal terms Jung called acausal or synchronous. In his theory each instant of time contains meaning; there is a coherence in each period of duration, and these coherences have their source in the nonphysical, psychoid, or, in Christian terminology, the spiritual aspect of reality. The Chinese call this the Dao, and the Chinese book of oracles, *I ching*, is based upon this principle. Miracles exemplify synchronous events. In oracular information, dream interpretation, religious experience, healing, and nature miracles the synchronous appears autonomously or through mediation.

The most recent studies seem to suggest that the issue of miracle or paranormal experience remains an open question in the Western world.

See Also Otherworld; Philosophy, articles on Philosophy and Religion, Philosophy of Religion.

BIBLIOGRAPHY

Benson, Herbert, and William Proctor. *Beyond the Relaxation Response.* New York, 1984.

Eliade, Mircea. *Shamanism: Archaic Techniques of Ecstasy.* Rev. & enl. ed. New York, 1964. The authoritative study of the shaman and the technique of esctasy by which the otherworld is mediated to the physical world.

Frank, Jerome D. *Persuasion and Healing.* Baltimore, 1961. A comparative study of the various schools of modern psychotherapy, healing in primitive society, religious revivalism, and Communist thought reform.

Fuller, Reginald H. *Interpreting the Miracles.* London, 1963. An attempt to study New Testament miracles using the framework of Rudolf Bultmann.

Greeley, Andrew M. *The Sociology of the Paranormal: A Reconnaissance.* Beverly Hills, Calif., 1975. Hard sociological data on the incidence of religious experience and its effect on human beings.

Jahn, Robert F. "The Persistent Paradox of Psychic Phenomena: An Engineering Perspective." *Proceedings of the Institute of Electrical and Electronics Engineers* 70 (February 1982): 136-170. The finest and most up-to-date summary of parapsychological research.

Jung, C. G. *The Structure and Dynamics of the Psyche.* Translated by R. F. C. Hull. New York, 1960. Gives Jung's theory of personality and synchronicity.

Kelsey, Morton. *Dreams: The Dark Speech of the Spirit.* Garden City, N.Y., 1968. An analytical and historical study of dreams as conveyors of information from the space-time world. Republished without appendix as God, Dreams and Revelation (Minneapolis, 1974).

Kelsey, Morton. *Encounter with God.* Minneapolis, 1972. Provides a study of the development of Western philosophical materialism and the evidence that points beyond its worldview.

Kelsey, Morton. *Healing and Christianity.* New York, 1973. A study of the miracles of healing and exorcism found in the ministry of Jesus and in the history of the Christian Church, together with a consideration of their psychological, medical, and philosophical base.

Kelsey, Morton. *The Christian and the Supernatural.* Minneapolis, 1976. An analysis of miraculous elements in the New Testament.

Kelsey, Morton. *Companions on the Inner Way: The Art of Spiritual Guidance.* New York, 1983. Contains both a philosophical base for religious experience and miracles and an analysis of the nature of religious experience.

Lewis, C. S. *Miracles* (1947). Rev. ed. New York, 1968. An excellent analysis of the subject from a Christian viewpoint.

Lynch, James J. *The Broken Heart: The Medical Consequences of Loneliness.* New York, 1977. A serious medical study of the effect of human and religious values on health.

Simonton, O. Carl, Stephanie Simonton, et al. *Getting Well Again.* Los Angeles, 1978. The theory and practice of using meditation for the treatment of cancer.

New Sources

Cavadini, John C., ed. *Miracles in Jewish and Christian Antiquity: Imagining Truth.* Notre Dame, 1999.

Geisler, Norman L. *Miracles and the Modern Mind: A Defense of Biblical Miracles.* Grand Rapids, Mich., 1992.

Grosso, Michael. "Miracles: Illusions, Natural events, or Divine Interventions?" *Journal of Religion & Psychical Research* 20, no. 4 (October 1997): 182–198.

Mullin, Robert Bruce. *Miracles and the Modern Religious Imagination.* New Haven, 1996.

Rao, Ursula. "How to Prove Divinities? Experiencing and Defending Divine Agency in a Modern Indian Space." *Religion* 32, no. 1 (January 2002): 3–12.

Saunders, Nicholas. *Divine Action and Modern Science.* Cambridge, U.K. and New York, 2002.

ter Haar, Gerrie. "A Wondrous God: Miracles In Contemporary Africa." *African Affairs* 102, no. 408 (July 2003): 409–429.

Morton Kelsey (1987)
Revised Bibliography

MIʿRĀJ. The belief that Muḥammad ascended to heaven in the course of his life and beheld the secrets of the otherworld as no other person had ever beheld them is shared by all factions of Islam. In Muslim religious literature, the idea of the Miʿrāj, Muḥammad's ascension to heaven, is closely associated with that of the Isrāʾ, his nocturnal journey. Neither term appears as such in the Qurʾān, yet both developed in close connection with crucial, though ambiguous, Qurʾanic passages.

Qurʾanic Associations. The term *isrāʾ* is taken from surah 17:1, "Glory be to him who carried his servant by night from the Holy Mosque to the Further Mosque, the precincts of which we have blessed, that we might show him some of our signs." It is reasonably certain that "his servant" refers to Muḥammad, "the Holy Mosque" to Mecca (*sūrahs* 2:144, 2:149, 2:150, 2:191, 2:196, 2:217, 5:2, 8:34, 9:7, 9:19,

9:28, 22:25, 48:25, 48:27), and "by night" to a journey begun by night (44:23), without reference to the journey's miraculous nature. Far less certain, however, is the intended meaning of "the Further Mosque" (*al-masjid al-aqṣā*). Since the earliest prophetic traditions (*ḥadīth*), this term has been explained either as a sanctuary on earth ("terrestrial" Jerusalem, the temple precinct) or in heaven ("celestial" Jerusalem, the environs of the divine throne). There is no apparent connection between the *isrāʾ* verse and a dream (*ruʾyā*) shown to Muḥammad by God and mentioned in the same *sūrah* (17:60), although the *ḥadīth* would interpret this dream as a vision of Jerusalem that Muḥammad communicated to the unbelieving Meccans.

The association of "the Further Mosque" with the terrestrial Jerusalem, which became the most widely accepted explanation, seems to be supported by the Qurʾanic phrase "the precincts of which we have blessed," referring to the Holy Land (21:71, 21:81, 7:137, 34:18), although Palestine in general is referred to as the "nearer part of the land" (30:3). This explanation was favored under the Umayyads, who were intent on glorifying Jerusalem as a holy territory rivaling Mecca, then ruled by their opponent ʿAbd Allāh ibn Zubayr. The interpretation of "the Further Mosque" as al-Jiʿrānah, a place on the fringes of the holy precinct of Mecca from which Muḥammad set out on his pilgrimage (*ʿumrah*) of Dhū al-Qaʿdah 630, has been rejected on decisive evidence (Maurice Plessner, "Muḥammad's Clandestine ʿUmra in the D̲ū'l-Qaʿda 8 H. and Sūra 17,1," *Revista degli studi orientali* 32 [1957]: 525–530; Rudi Paret, "Die 'ferne Gebetsstatte' in Sure 17,1," *Der Islam* 34 [1959]: 150–152).

The association with the celestial Jerusalem was favored in the classical sources of *ḥadīth* and Qurʾān commentary, which tended to use *isrāʾ* for the ascension to heaven and thus linked Muḥammad's night journey with his ascension. This explanation, which also included the purification of Muḥammad's heart as a preparatory stage, tended to interpret the story as Muḥammad's divine initiation to his prophetic career.

As a term for ascension, the word *miʿrāj*, literally "ladder," appears to conceal a vaguely understood reference to Jacob's ladder (*Gn.* 28:12). The term was probably borrowed from the Ethiopic *maʿāreg* (*Ethiopic Book of Jubilees* 21:37) as a translation of the Hebrew *sullām.* The background for the cryptic references in the Qurʾān may be provided by various motifs: the apocalyptic images of a heavenly ladder that recur in Jewish *heikhalot* literature; symbolic notions of a seven-runged ladder on which the soul ascends through the gates of heaven, found in the liturgy of Mithras; and gnostic ideas of the ladder as a means of ascending to heaven, as in the Mandaean *sumbilta* and the Manichaean pillar of glory.

In fragmentary Qurʾanic references, God is called "the Lord of the Stairways" (*dhū al-maʿārij*, 70:3; see also 43:33, 40:15), to whom the angels, the spirit, and the divine command "mount up" (*taʿruju, yaʿruju*) in a day (70:4, 32:5). God knows what comes down from heaven and what goes up to it (34:2, 57:4). The notion of heavenly ascent appears to be implied when Pharaoh gives orders to build a tower so that he may reach the cords of heaven and climb up to the god of Moses (40:36–37), or when Muḥammad is challenged by his opponents to go up into heaven (17:93). To this he replies, "Let them ascend the cords" (38:10) and "Stretch up a rope to heaven" (22:15), for even if God opened to them "a gate in heaven" (15:14), or if they had "a ladder" into heaven (*sullam*, 52:38, 6:35) and were climbing to it (6:125), they would not believe.

Three Qurʾanic passages not explicitly referring to heavenly ascent appear nevertheless to be linked with Muḥammad's visionary experiences of heaven. *Sūrahs* 81:19–25 and 53:1–12 give a parallel account of a vision in which Muḥammad saw a divine messenger on the horizon, and *sūrah* 53:13–18 gives an account of a vision in which he beheld the greatest signs of God near the lote tree on the edge of Paradise. In both cases the heavenly messenger approaches the Prophet from a distance but does not carry him off.

On the basis of the Qurʾanic evidence it appears certain that *miʿrāj* and *isrāʾ* refer to experiences Muḥammad had prior to his emigration from Mecca to Medina in 622, since the relevant Qurʾanic passages can be traced back to that period. It cannot be ascertained, however, whether or not these experiences occurred toward the beginning of Muḥammad's prophetic activity in Mecca, although they seem to have their natural setting in that time.

NARRATIVE LORE. The Qurʾanic references became associated with legends that proliferated rapidly during the first two centuries of Islam through the activity of the *quṣṣāṣ*, pious and popular storytellers. Their stories in turn were taken up and recast in the *ḥadīth* methodology of the Prophet's biography (*sīrah*) with the aim of establishing a scholarly consensus (*ijmāʿ*) concerning this legendary and mainly oral tradition. This consensus, reflected in the *Sīrat Muḥammad* by Ibn Isḥāq (d. 767), revised by Ibn Hishām (d. 834), admitted both interpretations of "the Further Mosque" and harmonized the two by assigning *isrāʾ* the particular meaning of the nocturnal journey to Jerusalem. This harmonization implied the elimination of an earlier tradition that made Mecca the starting point of the ascension and the substitution of Jerusalem, the starting point of Christ's ascension, where, perhaps since ʿAbd al-Malik's caliphate (685–705), the Prophet's footprint was shown to Muslim pilgrims.

Sīrat Muḥammad. Ibn Isḥāq's account of the miraculous events occurring during a single night combines all features in a continuous narrative, yet inverts the events. One night Muḥammad is asleep near the Kaʿbah at Mecca (or in the house of Umm Hāniʾ) when he is awakened by the angel Gabriel, who leads him to a winged animal called Burāq. Gabriel places the Prophet on the back of this steed, and they journey together to Jerusalem. In Jerusalem they meet several prophets, notably Abraham, Moses, and Jesus. By leading a public prayer service (*ṣalāt*), Muḥammad takes precedence over all the other prophets assembled there. When the Prophet finishes all that has to be done in Jerusalem, so the narrative continues, the beautiful ladder (*miʿrāj*) on which the dying fix their eyes, and which the human souls ascend to heaven, is brought. Gabriel makes Muḥammad ascend it and brings him to the gates of the seven heavens, one after the other. At each gate Gabriel is asked to identify Muḥammad and testify that revelation has already been made to him. Then follows a long description of Muḥammad's experiences in the heavens, in each of which he meets one of the prophets. Finally, Muḥammad beholds the garden of Paradise (as, from the first heaven, he has witnessed the tortures of Hell) and appears before God's throne to converse with him. God then reduces the number of obligatory daily prayers incumbent on the Muslim community from the original fifty to five. Muḥammad returns to Mecca and the next morning informs the Meccans that during the night he has gone to Syria and come back again. The public, including his close companion Abū Bakr, is naturally skeptical at first, and many of the Prophet's followers apostatize.

Ḥadīth. Influenced in part by the Jewish and Christian apocalyptic traditions, *ḥadīth* literature embellished the basic narrative of the Prophet's ascent to heaven with a great variety of detail that focused on the preparation for the ascent, the riding animal, and the experiences in heaven. It was also at this point that the story of the purification of Muḥammad's heart was prefixed to the ascension narrative. As Muḥammad is sleeping in the neighborhood of the Kaʿbah, angels appear, lay him on his back, open his body, and, with water from the well of Zamzam, wash his heart and bowels, cleansing them of doubt, idolatry, ignorance, and error. They then bring a golden vessel filled with wisdom and belief and fill his body with faith and wisdom. Purified in his heart and dedicated to be a prophet, Muḥammad is taken up to the lowest heaven.

The animal that carries Muḥammad to Jerusalem, Burāq (etymologically probably Arabic, "little lightning flash"), is depicted as a miraculous beast of exceptional fleetness. It is described as a brilliant steed of either gender, saddled and bridled, in size between a donkey and a mule, with a long back, shaking ears, and "a cheek like that of a man." Wings on its shanks propelled legs that moved in one stride as far as its eyes could reach. It was the riding beast of prophets in the past, Abraham in particular, and more recently Jesus. Upon the arrival in Jerusalem, according to some traditions, Gabriel tied it to a rock or ring, while, according to others, Burāq served as a flying steed for Muḥammad's ascension, taking over the function of the ladder. In its pictorial representations Burāq received a human face, a woman's head, and a peacock's tail. From the earliest extant image in a 1314 manuscript of Rashīd al-Dīn's Jamīʿ al-tawārīkh (Universal history) to the most splendid Persian and Turkish miniatures of later centuries, the steed, its rider, and its guide became a highly cherished motif of Islamic painting and poetry. Beautiful miniatures of Muḥammad's *miʿrāj* can be found, for example, in the fifteenth-century *Miʿrāj-nāmah* translated into Eastern Turkish by Mīr Ḥaydar and calligraphed in Uighur script by Mālik Bakhshī of Herat (see Marie-Rose Séguy, *The Miraculous Journey of Mahomet*, New York, 1977).

The meeting of the Prophet with Abraham, Moses, and Jesus at Jerusalem may be modeled on accounts of the transfiguration of Jesus on Mount Tabor (*Mt.* 17:1, *Mk.* 9:1, *Lk.* 9:28). Muḥammad encounters Adam as judge over the souls of the dead in the first heaven, Joseph in the third, and Enoch/Idrīs in the fourth. Jesus and John the Baptist appear together in the second heaven, whereas Aaron and Moses appear separately in the fifth and sixth. Moses weeps, realizing that Muḥammad is higher than himself in God's esteem and that his followers will be more numerous than his own. Muḥammad refuses his advice to ask God to reduce the obligatory daily prayers to fewer than five. Finally, in the seventh heaven, that of Abraham, Muḥammad finds himself in the presence of God's throne, reaches the lote-tree marking the limit of knowledge that creatures possess, and beholds the rivers of Paradise, where he is offered vessels of water, wine, milk, and honey but partakes of the milk alone.

ADAPTATIONS AND INTERPRETATIONS. The theme of the Prophet's ascension found its place in the literature of Islamic theology, philosophy, and Sufism. Muslim theologians were preoccupied with the question, already discussed since early times, of whether the night journey and ascension took place in a literal or a spiritual sense. Al-Ṭabarī (d. 923) strongly favored the belief, shared by the majority of Muslims, that the Prophet was transported literally, with his body and while awake. Others, in particular the Muʿtazilah, held that he was carried in spirit to Jerusalem and heaven while his body remained at Mecca; this view was supported by a statement attributed to Muḥammad's favorite wife, ʿĀʾishah. Al-Taftāzānī (d. 1389) states that the event happened in body and spirit but does not rule out its possible occurrence in sleep or in spirit alone. The question of whether or not Muḥammad saw God face to face on the occasion of the ascension constituted another debate within Islamic theology, in particular against the background of the controversy concerning the beatific vision of the believer.

The Neoplatonic philosophers of Islam gave an allegorical meaning to the Prophet's ascension. The *Epistles* of the Ikhwān al-Ṣafāʾ (Brethren of Purity), completed in 969, adopted the pattern of cosmological descent and eschatological ascent and interpreted the latter as the ascent *(miʿrāj)* of the human soul that abandons its bodily existence and returns to its angelic state of pure spirituality. Abū al-ʿAlāʾ al-Maʿarrī (d. 1057) wrote a parody, *Risālat al-ghufrān* (The epistle of forgiveness), on the traditional accounts of the *miʿrāj*. Two treatises of al-Ghazālī (d. 1111) are focused on the theme of ascension: his *Miʿrāj al-sālikīn* (The ladder of those who follow the path) elucidates the theme from seven different topical angles, while his *Mishkāt al-anwār* (The niche for lights) offers a Neoplatonic interpretation in purely psychological terms. Ibn al-Sīd al-Baṭalyawsī (d. 1127), in his *Kitāb al-ḥadāʾiq* (Book of gardens), describes the ascent of the purified spirits to the supernal world on "the ladder of ascensions" *(sullam al-maʿārij)* that follows a straight line connecting the terrestrial and celestial spheres.

For the Ṣūfīs, the night journey and ascension of the Prophet became the prototype of the soul's itinerary to God as it rises from the bonds of sensuality to the height of mystical knowledge. It is doubtful whether, as is frequently asserted, Abū Yazīd al-Bisṭāmī (d. 875) claimed to have experienced *miʿrāj* himself, leading to mystical union with God. Al-Ḥallāj (d. 922) meditated on the theme in his *Kitāb al-ṭawāsīn.* Al-Qushayrī (d. 1074) collected accounts current among moderate Ṣūfīs in his *Kitāb al-miʿrāj* and included in it a discussion of the ascension attributed to Enoch/Idrīs, Abraham, Elijah, Moses, and Jesus. He reserved ascension in body and spirit for the prophets and conceded to the Ṣūfīs only the dream experience of ascent to heaven. Al-Hujwīrī (d. 1077) makes a clear distinction in his *Kashf al-maḥjūb* (Elucidation of the secrets) between the ascension of prophets, which occurs outwardly and in the body, and that of the saints, which takes place inwardly and in the spirit only. Ibn al-ʿArabī (d. 1240) expounded the Prophet's night journey and ascension as a symbol of the soul's itinerary toward mystical union in his *Kitāb al-isrāʾ* and also devoted two lengthy sections of his *Futūḥāt* (Revelations) to the subject. In one section he has a mystic and a philosopher make the journey together; the philosopher has to stop short at the seventh heaven, while no secrets remain hidden from the mystic. In the other section applies the Prophet's ascension to the mystical experience of Ṣūfī ecstasy, recording his own mystical ascent and his conversations with the prophets about mystic themes.

The Miʿrāj provided an ideal type for the symbolic narratives created by Ṣūfī philosophers and poets intent on explaining the spiritual heights of mystical union. In the fine Persian *Miʿrāj-nāmah,* attributed to Ibn Sīnā (d. 1037) or Yaḥyā Suhrawardī (d. 1191), yet probably written by an anonymous eleventh-century author, the theme of the postmortem ascent of the soul to heaven under conduct of the angel is overshadowed by the ecstatic ascent of the mystic to the divine throne in imitation of the ascension of the Prophet, the archetypal mystic. This symbolic narrative may be understood, topically although not historically, as bridging the gulf between Ibn Sīnā's Arabic allegory, *Ḥayy ibn Yaqẓān,* and ʿAṭṭār's (d. 1220) grandiose mystical Persian epic, *Manṭiq al-ṭayr* (Conversation of the birds), both of which, in their respective ways and not unlike the Persian *Miʿrāj-nāmah,* move from the level of the symbolic interpretation of the narrative to the plane of the existential exegesis of mystic ascent experienced in the human soul.

The theme of *miʿrāj* appears in many aspects in Persian Ṣūfī poetry from Rūmī (d. 1273) to Iqbal (d. 1938). For Rūmī the Miʿrāj became the symbol of the radical difference between discursive reason and mystical union. Gabriel, the symbol of reason and the guide of the heavenly journey, remains outside the divine presence while the Prophet, the symbol of the true lover of God, enjoys "a time with God" in the chamber of union and mystery. The *Jāvīd-nāmah* of Iqbal describes a contemporary version of the spiritual journey made by the poet from earth through and beyond the spheres to the presence of God.

Later popular accounts of the Prophet's ascension collect and systematize the material scattered in the older sources, largely augmenting the matter without increasing its depth. Al-Suyūṭī (d. 1505) presents a fine disquisition on the traditions of *isrāʾ* and *miʿrāj,* discussing their nature, time, place, and details in *Al-āyah al-kubrā fī sharḥ qiṣṣat al-isrāʾ.* Al-Nuʿmānī, a disciple of Ibn Ḥajar al-ʿAsqalānī (d. 1449), collects a medley of traditions, theological views, and mystical statements concerning the Prophet's night journey and ascension in *Al-sirāj al-wahhāj* (The glowing lamp). The most popular *miʿrāj* book down to modern times is the *Kitāb al-isrāʾ wa-al-miʿrāj* of al-Ghaythī (d. 1573), on which Dardīr (d. 1786) wrote a gloss. Al-Barzanjī's (d. 1766) *Qiṣṣat al-miʿrāj* appears to be modeled on al-Ghaythī's work. The Uighur *Miʿrāj-nāmah,* composed in 1436/7, documents the spread of the legend in Central Asian languages.

The Christians of the Middle Ages possessed a certain knowledge about the Muslim legends surrounding Muḥammad's miraculous journey to heaven. This is evidenced by the famous Latin version of the legend, apparently prepared by Ibrāhīm al-Ḥakīm, a Jewish physician active at the court of Alfonso X of Castile (1264–1277). This Latin version (*Liber scalae*) and a French translation from Latin (*Eschiele Mahomet*) became the focal point of the discussion surrounding the question of Dante's Muslim sources in his *Commedia* (raised by the Spanish Jesuit Juan Andrès about 1780, again advanced by Ozanam in 1838 and Labitte in 1842, and clearly formulated by Blochet in *Les sources orientales de la divine comédie,* Paris, 1901).

See Also Muḥammad.

Bibliography

Historians of religions have long realized the significance of Muḥammad's ascension as a theme in comparative religion. D. W. Bousset's groundbreaking study "Die Himmelsreise der Seele," *Archiv für Religionswissenschaft* 4 (1901): 136–169, 229–273, set the stage for an inquiry into the soul's ascent to heaven in world religions. Following Bousset's line of research and Edgar Blochet's study of the theme in "L'ascension au ciel du prophète Mohammed," *Revue de l'histoire des religions* 40 (1899): 1–25, 203–236, Geo Widengren has traced the Iranian motifs of Muḥammad's Miʿrāj in two works, *The Ascension of the Apostle and the Heavenly Book* (Uppsala, 1950) and *Muḥammad, the Apostle of God, and His Ascension* (Uppsala, 1955), which attempt to establish an "ideal" ritual of the Prophet's ascension. Marie-Thérèse d'Alverny documents the theme of the soul's ascent in Latin sources of medieval philosophy in "Les pérégrinations de l'âme dans l'autre monde d'après un anonyme de la fin du douzième siècle," *Archives d'histoire doctrinale et littéraire du Moyen-Âge* 15–17 (1940–1942): 239–299, while Alexander Altmann demonstrates the impact of Muslim sources on the theme of the ascension in Jewish religious philosophy in "The Ladder of Ascension," *Studies in Mysticism and Religion Presented to Gershom G. Scholem*, edited by E. E. Urbach, R. J. Zwi Werblowsky, and Chaim Wirszubski (Jerusalem, 1967), pp. 1–32. The problems of typological similarity between Muḥammad's Miʿrāj and shamanic experiences of ascension are outlined by Mircea Eliade in *Shamanism* (New York, 1964) and taken up by J. R. Porter in "Muḥammad's Journey to Heaven," *Numen* 21 (1974): 64–80.

The question of Muslim sources in Dante's *Commedia* has been treated systematically by Miguel Asín Palacios in his important work *La escatologia musulmana en la Divina comedia* (Madrid, 1919), translated and abridged by Harold Sunderland as *Islam and the Divine Comedy* (New York, 1926). The controversy Asín Palacios's book stirred up is recorded in the second Spanish edition (Madrid and Granada, 1943). The basis of the discussion was significantly broadened with the independent publication of the French and Latin versions of the legend: *Il "Libro della scala" e la questione delle fonti arabo-spagnole della Divina commedia*, edited by Enrico Cerulli (Vatican City, 1949), and *La escala de Mahoma*, edited by José Muñoz Sendino (Madrid, 1949). The trends of more recent discussion on the point can be traced in Peter Wunderli's survey "Zur Auseinandersetzung über die muselmanischen Quellen der Divina Commedia," *Romanistisches Jahrbuch* 15 (1964): 19–50, and Enrico Cerulli's *Nuove ricerche sul Libro della scala e la conoscenza dell'Islam in Occidente* (Vatican City, 1972).

GERHARD BÖWERING (1987)

MIRIAM, or, in Hebrew, Miryam; Israelite prophetess who flourished, according to tradition, in the thirteenth century BCE. Biblical tradition recalls Miriam as the sister of Moses and Aaron who helped Moses lead the Hebrew slaves out of Egypt (*Mic.* 6:4). *Exodus* 15:20–21 describes how she led the women of Israel in a hymn of victory to YHVH, Lord of Israel, after he had split the Sea of Reeds, enabling the Hebrews to pass through and escape their Egyptian pursuers:

> Miriam the prophetess, sister of Aaron, took the drum in her hand. All the women went out after her with drums and dances. Miriam declared to them: "Sing to the Lord, for he has triumphed; horse and its rider he has hurled into the sea."

Modern scholars now tend to view the sibling relationships between Miriam, Aaron, and Moses as an embellishment on earlier traditions. Miriam was originally identified as an associate of Aaron, Israel's first priest, and later as his sister. When biblical tradition similarly developed a sibling relationship between Aaron and Moses, the great leader, prophet, and lawgiver of Israel, Miriam became known as the sister of Moses too (*Nm.* 26:39). In the story of Moses' birth (*Ex.* 2:2–7), the unnamed older sister who guards him is assumed by Jewish and Christian tradition to have been Miriam. If her name were of Egyptian origin, as some have explained, that would reinforce the conclusion that she was of the priestly tribe of Levi, as several prominent Levites bore Egyptian names.

Miriam figures primarily in one episode in the Pentateuch, *Numbers* 12:1–16, in which she and Aaron reproach Moses for having taken a Cushite wife—who may or may not be identified with his Midianite wife, Zipporah—and in which they challenge the superiority of Moses' prophetic stature to their own. YHVH responds to their challenge by asserting the unique and intimate nature of his revelations to Moses and responds to their reproach by afflicting Miriam with leprosy. Moses intercedes on Miriam's behalf at Aaron's request—thereby demonstrating his intimacy with God—and after a seven-day quarantine, Miriam's health is restored. The legendary quality of the episode is suggested by the fact that Miriam's leprosy became an admonition to any who would fail to heed the priests (*Dt.* 24:8–9). Miriam predeceased Aaron and Moses (*Nm.* 20:1) and, so far is known, never married.

The references to Miriam's leadership in *Micah* 6:4, to her prophetic status in *Exodus* 15:20, and to her importance to the Israelites in *Numbers* 12:15, create the impression that Miriam was an even more significant figure than the present form of the Pentateuch suggests. According to rabbinic legend, Miriam was on par with Moses and Aaron. The Israelites were sustained by water drawn from Miriam's well, which traveled with the Israelites on their journey in the wilderness.

BIBLIOGRAPHY

On the difficulty of establishing Miriam's historical position, see Martin Noth's *A History of Pentateuchal Traditions*, translated with an introduction by Bernhard W. Anderson (Chico, Calif., 1981), pp. 180–183. Miriam is most extensively discussed in connection with the challenges to Moses, for analysis of which see G. B. Gray's *A Critical and Exegetical Commentary on Numbers* (Edinburgh, 1903), pp. 120–128. The most exhaustive, but a very technical, analysis is Heinrich Valentin's *Aaron: Eine Studie zur vor-priesterschriftlichen Aaron-Überlieferung* (Göttingen, 1978), pp. 306–364; Valentin also discusses (pp. 377–384) *Exodus* 15:20. Martin Buber's *Moses: The Revelation and the Covenant* (New York, 1958), pp. 167–169, attempts to connect the two challenges to Moses. On Miriam's name, see Alan H. Gardiner's "The Egyptian Origin of Some English Personal Names," *Journal of the American Oriental Society* 56 (1936): 189–197, esp. pp. 194–197.

On the apparently suppressed significance of Miriam, see Phyllis Trible, "Bringing Miriam out of the Shadows," *Bible Review* 5/1 (February 1989): 14–25, 34. Rabbinic lore on Miriam's well is gathered in Louis Ginzberg's *The Legends of the Jews*, vol. 3, translated by Paul Radin (Philadelphia, 1911), pp. 50–54, 307–308.

EDWARD L. GREENSTEIN (1987 AND 2005)

MIRRORS. Object and symbol, instrument of knowledge and type of reflection or speculation (the Latin word for mirror is *speculum*), means of visual perception and hallucination: there is scarcely a single culture that has not been interested in the mirror, first in its primitive form—a bowl filled with water, a sparkling stone (jade, obsidian)—then in more elaborate guise—polished metal discs (bronze, silver, or steel), a mirror of balloon-shaped mediaeval glass—and, finally, in the form of the plane mirror, clear as rock crystal. Because it reflects an image of the self that the eye is unable to see directly, because it traps light, because the effect of the reflection is to reveal an unseen "other," and because it faithfully reproduces its subject while making it seem different—that is, reversed—religions have made the mirror central to the mystical life and knowledge of self.

What is the nature of that which can be learned from a mirror? It can be used in divination, metaphor, analogy, or mimicry. In the West, meditation on the mirror image originates with Plato. Before him, the reflected image was seen as a living animate form, the double that attracted Narcissus from beneath the surface of the water. One can see this myth in its original form as expressing ancient beliefs in the existence of a double or in the idea of the soul taking shape, concepts still found in primitive cultures up until the present day. It was not until the philosophy of Classical Greece had reached a certain stage of development that the reflection came to be seen as a flimsy illusion, a snare.

COSMIC PROCESS AND MYSTIC EXPERIENCE. Is the reflection in the mirror merely a deceitful trick? According to Plato, it has another function: by producing an immaterial form, it invites the mind to free itself from what is perceived by the senses and to ascend to the world of ideas. Although itself devoid of reality, a reflection provides access to the thing it signifies. It is not an optical illusion but a revelation of something hidden, an apparition rather than an appearance. Pausanias says that a mirror adorned the entrance of the temple of Lycosoura in Arcadia, and that anyone who looked in it before entering the sanctuary saw a reflection unlike any they had seen before. Thus they had to shed their appearance and assume a new identity.

According to the Neoplatonists, what is produced by the world of the senses comes about in the way that a mirror "creates" reflections. Plotinus (*Enneads* 4.3) regards the world of the senses as a mirror image emanating from the world of eternal forms, and the body as a reflection that the soul produces when it comes into contact with matter, in the same way as a human being produces a reflection when facing a polished surface: the spiritual exercise or mystical experience consists of once again ascending from the light of the body to the earlier light, without allowing oneself to be mesmerized by an illusion (like Narcissus).

Christian thinking, derived from Judaism and infused with Neoplatonist thought, has developed the concept of the symbolic double to explain the resemblance of the human being to God and the indirect knowledge of God that can thus be obtained through analogy. According to *Genesis*, God created man in his image and likeness. The soul is a reflection of the beauty of God, but because sin has made the mirror darken, one must look in the mirror of the Bible, a book and a mirror without blemish, to restore the likeness that has been lost. The mirror is also a model of knowledge. According to Saint Paul (*1Cor.* 13:12), the knowledge that mankind has of God here on Earth is like an image "seen through a glass darkly": the mirror gives no more than an indirect image of the Truth. At the end of time, however, humans will see the vision of God not through the intervening reflection, but clearly, face to face. In mystical experience, the mirror is the juncture point where the visible face sees its invisible face: "We shall be like God, because we shall see him as he is," says Saint John (*1 John* 3:2). Teresa of Ávila describes this union in the mirror: "My entire soul appeared before me like a clear mirror, back, top and bottom, everything was lit up. In the center appeared Jesus Christ" (*Autobiography,* ch. 49). Faithful and flexible, the mirror no longer indicates a different vision but the receptive nature of the person who gazes into it.

Islamic mysticism, inspired by Neoplatonism, has not ignored the reflection, that likeness by which individual essence sees itself as part of the divine being. If the body is the dark reflection in the mirror, writes the Persian poet Farīd al-Dīn ʿAṭṭār, the soul is the "clear one." According to a famous *ḥadīth,* the more the reflective surface of the soul is purified by asceticism, the more it will be fit to reproduce the truth faithfully, so that the believer actually becomes a mirror for another believer. As Louis Massignon and Louis Gardet point out in *Mardis de Dar-el-Salam* (1951), the back-to-front image of the face reflected in the mirror is a symbolic indication of one who has been straightened out, in accord with his essential reality. For Ṣūfīs, the entire universe is an array of mirrors in which the eternal essence may be gazed upon in many forms, all emanations of the One Being.

The Far East has developed a rich mythology concerning the reflective power of mirrors. According to a Chinese tradition going back to the third century BCE, the divine intelligence that is symbolically identified with the sun is reflected in a mirror that is circular in shape—but the mirror is also a lunar symbol, because the moon reflects the light of the sun. Huge vats filled with water were used to attract sunlight, a method subsequently replaced by the use of bronze mirrors. The idea of a link between the mirror and the sun became widespread in Japan around about the first century CE. A well-known Japanese myth describes how the goddess Amaterasu, the Divine Light, retreated into a cave following some wrongdoing by her brother, plunging the Earth into darkness. The gods arranged a ceremony, and when the goddess was attracted by this and appeared at the entrance of the cave, she saw her image reflected in a mirror that had been set up by another god. Surprised at the existence of another similar goddess, she leaned out of the place where she had retreated far enough to be seized. The cave was sealed shut behind her and she lit up the world.

Buddhism has made "mirror knowledge" one of the four stages of the path of Awakening, along with three other kind of knowledge: of equality, of clear-sightedness, and of the task to be completed. The mirror is used metaphorically in the Mahāyāna literature to suggest that Reality contains everything in the same way that a mirror contains images. The images in the mirror are clear and distinct; although not unreal, they are nonetheless not taken as real, because they cannot be grasped. Having obtained knowledge of mirrors, the consciousness of the *bodhisattva* no longer involves a division of subject and object, but becomes a clear omniscient consciousness, capable of reflecting images of everything in the universe, while also being one with what it reflects. With an understanding of universal equivalence based on the recognition of the emptiness of all things, and with the achievement of clear-sightedness concerning the nature most appropriate to each thing, the *bodhisattva,* having achieved awareness of the mirror, the peak of the mystic life, reaches Awakening. There is no more intention, no more projection; consciousness merges with the mirror. Consciousness, according to Asaṅga, is "a mirror, because in it there appear reflected images, delights, buddha-ness and knowledge" (*Mahāyānasūtrālaṃkāra* 9:69).

MAGIC MIRRORS AND DIVINATION MIRRORS. The shining brilliance of the reflective surface gives rise to all kinds of hallucinations and lends itself to divination: like dreams, mirrors can reveal what is not visible. Divination by mirror (or catoptromancy), which originated in Persia, is described in many texts. In the *Oneirocritica* (translated as *The Interpretation of Dreams*), for example, the Greek Artemidorus Daldianus (second century CE) devotes several paragraphs to the art of reading the future in mirror images. The magical use of mirrors to learn the future, namely, to know if one will have a long life, is frequently mentioned in European folklore. In central Asia, shamans practiced divination by mirror by pointing mirrors toward the sun or moon, which were themselves considered as mirrors in which was reflected everything that took place on Earth. In the Congo, soothsayers sprinkled reflective surfaces with kaolin (a fine, usually white, clay) in order to question the spirits.

The belief that reflections could reveal secrets rested in turn upon an ancient belief in the existence of a double. This mysterious spiritual double, as close as possible to the bodily self, was a representation of the idea of the soul and offered the possibility that one could deny death by splitting in two. Yet whereas the double guaranteed immortality and implied fertility, it also continually reminded a human being of the end; it was the specter of repressed death. In ancient Greece, for example, looking at one's reflection or seeing it in a dream could lead to death or be a premonition of death. An old European tradition requires that mirrors in the house of someone who has died be covered, to prevent them from absorbing the soul and forcing the deceased to remain on Earth. The fear of having one's portrait painted or photograph taken, widespread all over the world, stems from the same concern: the soul represented by its image may be imprisoned by a stranger and subjected to evil spells.

Containing both the potential for harm and beneficent power, the mirror is regarded ambivalently in every culture. Small children are stopped from looking into the glass in case the sight of their reflection brings them bad luck; pretty girls who look at themselves see the devil suddenly appear; anyone looking at themselves at night risks losing their reflection, and anyone losing their reflection loses their creative force. In the Christian West, the mirror of God could become the mirror of the devil—something produced by the fear of death. Like all magicians, those who practiced magic with mirrors were persecuted by the Inquisition: in 1326 Pope John XXII excommunicated "those who have made a pact with Hell, manufacturing a mirror to secure demons." Daoists believe a mirror reveals evil influences and that one may protect oneself by placing a mirror over the door of a house. In the Middle Ages, Christian pilgrims sewed small mirrors into their hats in order to absorb grace from relics that were exposed during processions. Because of what water and mirrors have in common, the Bambara people use mirror fragments or cups of water to make rain fall. In China, a mirror is a sign of harmony and fertility, but a broken mirror means that a separation will occur, particularly in marriage. The mirror has an important place in marriage ceremonies: in modern India, the couple, instead of looking at each other directly, exchange looks in a mirror hung at the far end of the room and see their faces looking up, as they will be in eternal life.

MIRROR AND SELF-KNOWLEDGE. From the start of the common era onward, mythological tradition concerning the mirror has given rise to philosophical commentaries, focused not so much on revealing a universal process as on describing a moral and spiritual condition: the disorder in the minds of those who allow themselves to be bewitched by their own reflections. The misfortune of Narcissus lies in his inability to love someone else. A later myth, in a version by Olympiodorus, recounts that the child Dionysus, fascinated by his reflection, let himself be cut into pieces by the Titans, who scattered the pieces all over the world. Commentators see in this the fate of a mind so seduced by its own reflection that it lets itself be torn to pieces by its passions. A number of such collective motifs still remain current today, along with their accompanying taboos, and modern psychology suggests new interpretations of them. The demon that appears in the mirror is the projection of repressed images. The death of Narcissus signifies the failure to transfer youthful libido to another person and fixation upon oneself in a process of autoerotic regression.

As for the double (shadow or reflection), nineteenth-century writers (Alfred de Musset, E. T. A. Hoffmann, Edgar Allan Poe, Guy de Maupassant, Rainer Maria Rilke) spent much effort exploring its deadly significance and the regions of the unconscious mind: the image in the mirror is no longer seen as a visual effect, but as a real alter ego. Psychiatry has described the defense mechanisms by which a pathologically self-centered subject seeks to create a double by expelling a part of himself that is associated with his shameful desires, so that the double, having become a rival, both assuages his anxiety and threatens him with a powerful feeling of guilt.

The importance of the reflection in the mirror in the inception of the ego has been stressed for more than a century in the work of a number of neuropsychiatrists and psychoanalysts, including Henri Wallon, Geza Roheim, and Paul Schilder. In 1938 Jacques Lacan made the "mirror stage" an essential part of his theories on the psychological development of the infant. The infant in front of the mirror moves from awareness of his body in pieces to perceiving his reflection as a single being, and thus acquires a new grasp of symbolic function at the same time that he or she comes to understand the difference between the body and its reflection. The process of visual perception is the reverse of what befell Dionysus, because by looking at themselves infants avoid dismemberment. Françoise Dolto considered this emphasis on visual perception misleading, and preferred the idea of the "unconscious image of the body" created by all the senses. Later, Lacan introduced into his outline the necessary presence of a symbolic third party, the mother whose approval and smile validate the task of recognition. The infant thus returns to the adult: he tests the formative image that the reflection in the mirror has shown him, but he also tests, in turning back to the other, everything which is absent there, the absence of desire. It is indeed this absence, this hidden part, this "other" that the human being continues to seek by questioning the mirror.

BIBLIOGRAPHY

Frazer, James G. *The Golden Bough*, vol. 3, *Taboo and the Perils of the Soul.* 3d ed., rev. and enl. London, 1911.

Grabbes, Herbert. *Speculum, Mirror, und Looking Glass: Kontinuität und Originalität der Spiegelmetapher in den Buchtiteln des Mittelalters und der englischen Literature des 13. bis 17. Jahrhunderts.* Tübingen, Germany, 1973. Translated by Gordon Collier as *The Mutable Glass: Mirror-Imagery in Titles and Texts of the Middle Ages and Renaissance* (Cambridge, U.K., 1982).

Hadot, Pierre. "Le mythe de Narcisse et son interprétation par Plotin." *Nouvelle Revue de Psychanalyse* 13 (1976): 81–108.

Hartlaub, G. F. *Zauber des Spiegels: Geschichte und Bedeutung des Spiegels in der Kunst.* Munich, 1951.

Litvinskii, B. A. *Orudiia truda i utvar' iz mogil'nikov Zapadnoi Fergany.* Moscow, 1978.

Martinet, Marie-Madeleine. *Le Miroir de l'esprit dans le théâtre élisabéthain.* Paris, 1981.

Melchior-Bonnet, Sabine. *The Mirror: A History.* New York, 2001.

Rank, Otto. *Der Doppelgänger: Eine psychoanalytische Studie.* Leipzig, Germany, 1925. Translated by Harry Tucker Jr. as *The Double: A Psychoanalytic Study* (Chapel Hill, N.C., 1971).

Schimmel, Annemarie. *The Triumphal Sun: A Study of the Works of Jalaloddin Rumi.* London, 1978.

Swallow, R. W. *Ancient Chinese Bronze Mirrors.* Beijing, 1937.

Wayman, Alex. "The Mirror as a Pan-Buddhist Metaphor-Simile." *History of Religions* 13 (1974): 251–269.

Wayman, Alex. "Notes on Mirror Words and Entities in the Area of India." *Ural-Altaische Jahrbücher* 47 (1975): 204–206.

Züchner, Wolfgang. *Griechische Klappspiegel.* Berlin, 1942.

SABINE MELCHIOR-BONNET (2005)
Translated from French by Paul Ellis

MISHNAH AND TOSEFTA. The Mishnah is a law code and school book, containing the legal and theological system of Judaism. It was brought to closure about 200 CE under the auspices of the head of the Jewish community of the Holy Land at that time, Yehudah ha-Nasi', and has remained the foundation stone of Judaism from that time to the present. The Tosefta is a collection of supplements to the Mishnah, with approximately three-fourths devoted merely to citation and amplification of the contents of the Mishnah. The other fourth of the whole is constituted by laws essentially autonomous of, but correlative to, the Mishnah's laws. The Tosefta has no independent standing, being organized around the Mishnah. Tosefta was formulated and gathered together some time in the centuries following the closure of the Mishnah, with the fifth century being a safe guess for the time of closure. These two documents together are extensively cited and analyzed in the two Talmuds, one produced in Babylonia about 500 CE, the other in the Land of Israel about 400 CE.

The Mishnah (with the Tosefta) is important in Judaism because it is represented, from the time of its closure onward, as part of "the one whole Torah of Moses, our rabbi," that is, as revealed to Moses at Sinai by God. The Mishnah and all of the documents flowing from it later on, beginning with the Tosefta and the two Talmuds, thus form an integral part of the canon of Torah, that is, of Judaism. The Torah myth distinguishes two Torahs of Sinai. One is in written form, the other, oral. This oral Torah, encompassing the Mishnah and its continuators and successors, was revealed alongside the written Torah. But it was transmitted in a different way. While, as its name indicates, the one was written down, the other was formulated for memorization, and it was then transmitted in this easily memorized form.

Viewed structurally, the two Torahs of Judaism may be compared to the conception of an old and a new testament in Christianity, thus:

Old Testament = Written Torah (Hebrew scriptures)
New Testament = Oral Torah (Mishnah and its continuators)

The top line on both sides speaks of the same holy book, but with the words particular to Christianity and Judaism, respectively. That is to say, the biblical books that Christians know as the "Old Testament," Judaism knows as the "written Torah." The Mishnah is the first and principal expression of this other Torah, the oral Torah revealed to Moses at Sinai. It thus is as important to Judaism as the New Testament is to Christianity.

CONTENTS. Six divisions, or orders, comprise the Mishnah's system: Zeraʿim (Seeds, or Agriculture), Moʿed (Appointed Times), Nashim (Women), Neziqin (Damages, i.e., civil law), Qodashim (Holy Things, i.e., cultic law), and Ṭohorot (Purities, i.e., cultic taboos). Each division is divided into tractates, and each tractate into chapters and paragraphs. There are, in all, 63 tractates, divided into some 531 chapters.

The critical issue in economic life (i.e., in farming) is treated in the Mishnah's first division, Agriculture, or Seeds. This is in two parts. First, Israel, as tenant on God's holy land, maintains the property in the ways God requires, keeping the rules that mark the land and its crops as holy. Next, the hour at which the sanctification of the land comes to form a critical mass, namely, in the ripened crops, is the moment ponderous with danger and heightened holiness. Israel's will so affects the crops as to mark a part of them as holy, the rest of them as available for common use. The human will is determinative in the process of sanctification.

In the second division, Appointed Times, what happens in the Land of Israel at certain special times, especially in the lunar year, marks off areas of the land as holy in yet another way. The center of the Land of Israel and the focus of its sanctification is the Temple. There the produce of the land is received and given back to God, the one who created and sanctified the Holy Land. At these unusual moments of sanctification, the inhabitants of the Holy Land in their social being in villages enter a state of spatial sanctification. That is to say, the village boundaries mark off holy space, within which one must remain during the holy time. This is expressed in two ways. First, the Temple itself observes and expresses the special, recurring holy time. Second, the villages of the Holy Land are brought into alignment with the Temple, forming a complement and completion to the Temple's sacred being. The advent of the appointed times precipitates a spatial reordering of the land, so that the boundaries of the sacred are matched and mirrored in village and in Temple. At the heightened holiness marked by these appointed times, therefore, the occasion for an affective sanctification is worked out. Like the harvest, the advent of an appointed time, a pilgrim festival, also a sacred season, is made to express that regular, orderly, and predictable sort of sanctification for Israel that the system as a whole seeks.

If for the moment we now leap over the next two divisions, the third and fourth, we come to the counterpart of the divisions of Agriculture and Appointed Times. These are the fifth and sixth divisions, Holy Things and Purities. They deal with the everyday and the ordinary, as against the special moments of harvest, on the one side, and special time or season, on the other.

The fifth division, Holy Things, is about the Temple on ordinary days (i.e., not during appointed times). The Temple, the locus of sanctification, is conducted in a wholly routine and trustworthy, punctilious manner. The one thing that may unsettle matters is the intention and will of the human actor. This actor, the priest, is subjected to carefully prescribed limitations and remedies.

The division of Holy Things generates its companion, the sixth division, Purities, the one on cultic cleanness. In the sixth division, once we speak of the one place of the Temple, we address, too, the cleanness that pertains to every place. A system of cleanness, taking into account what imparts uncleanness and how this is done, what is subject to uncleanness, and how that state is overcome—that system is fully expressed in response to the participation of the human will. Without the wish and act of a human being, the system does not function. It is inert. Sources of uncleanness, which come naturally and not by volition, and modes of purification, which work naturally, and not by human intervention, remain inert until human will has imparted susceptibility to uncleanness, until, that is, human will introduces into the system some object of uncleanness—food and drink, bed, pot, chair, or pan—that becomes subject to contamination. The movement from sanctification to uncleanness takes place when human will and work initiate it.

This now brings us back to the middle divisions, the third and fourth, Women and Damages, respectively. They take their place in the structure of the whole by showing the congruence, within the larger framework of regularity and order, of human concerns of family and farm, politics and workaday transactions among ordinary people. For without attending to these matters, the Mishnah's system does not encompass what, at its foundations, it is meant to comprehend and order: Israel's whole life. So what is at issue is fully cogent with the rest.

In Women, the third division, attention focuses upon the point of disorder marked by the transfer of that disordering anomaly, woman, from the regular status provided by one man to the equally trustworthy status provided by another. That is the point at which the Mishnah's interests are aroused: once more, predictably, the moment of disorder.

In Damages, the fourth division, are two important concerns. First, there is the paramount interest in preventing the disorderly rise of one person and fall of another, in sustaining the status quo of the economy, of the house and household, of Israel, the holy society in eternal stasis. Second, there is the necessary concomitant in the provision of a system of political institutions to carry out the laws that preserve the balance and steady state of persons.

The third and fourth divisions take up topics of concrete and material concern, the formation and dissolution of families and the transfer of property in that connection, the transactions, both through torts and through commerce, that lead to exchanges of property and the potential dislocation of the state of families in society. They deal with the concrete locations in which people make their lives, household and street and field, the sexual and commercial exchanges of a given village.

So the six components of the Mishnah's system insist upon two things: first, stability, second, order. They define as a problem something out of line, therefore dangerous. Laws for a woman must be made, in particular, when she changes hands, moving from father to husband, or, in divorce, from husband to father. Laws for the governance of civil transactions must make certain that all transactions produce equal and opposite results. No one emerges larger than when he entered; none is diminished. Equal value must be exchanged, or a transaction is null. The advent of sacred time, as we shall see, not only imposes the opposite of the Temple's rules upon the village. The holy day also has the effect of linking the Israelite to one place, a particular place, his or her village. So for a moment sacred time establishes a tableau and creates a diorama, a still place of perfection in a silent and perfected moment.

CONTEXT. The Mishnah came into being during the first and second centuries of the common era. The document contains ideas likely to have circulated even before the destruction of the Temple in 70 CE, among people whose traditions were carried forward and ultimately written down in the Mishnah itself. But the structure of the system presented by the Mishnah is well attested only after the Bar Kokhba War (c. 132–135). It is attributed principally to authorities who flourished in the middle of the second century. Accordingly, using antecedent ideas and laws, the document came into being at the end of two wars—the first war against Rome (66–73), culminating in the destruction of the Temple, and the second, Bar Kokhba's. Since the Mishnah emerges after a time of wars, the one thing we should expect to find is a message about the meaning of history, an account of events and their meaning. Central to the Mishnah's system might well be a picture of the course of Israel's destiny, in the tradition of the biblical histories—*Samuel*, *Kings*, or *Chronicles*, for instance—and in the tradition of the prophets of ancient Israel, the several Isaiahs, Jeremiah, and the rest.

The Mishnah's principal point of insistence is the opposite. It speaks of what is permanent and enduring: the flow of time through the solar seasons, marked by lunar festivals and Sabbaths; the procedures of the cult through the regular and enduring sacrifices; the conduct of the civil society through norms of fairness to prevent unjust change; the pursuit of agricultural work in accord with the rules of holiness; the enduring, unchanging, invisible phobias of cultic uncleanness and cleannesss. The Mishnah has no division devoted to the interpretation of history. There is no pretence even at telling what had just happened. There is scarcely a line to address the issue of the meaning of the disasters of the day.

The Mishnah does not address one-time events of history. Its laws express recurrent patterns, eternal patterns as enduring as the movement of the moon and sun around the earth (as people then understood it) and as regular as the lapping of the waves on the beach. These are laws on plowing, planting, harvesting; birth, marriage, procreation, death; home, family, household; work, rest; sunrise, sunset—private lives, not the stuff of history. The laws speak of the here and now, not of state or of tradition, past or future. Since, in the time in which the ideas of the Mishnah took shape, most other Jews expressed a keen interest in history, the contrast cannot be missed. The Mishnah imagines a world of regularity and order in the aftermath of the end of ancient certainties and patterns. It designs laws after the old rules all were broken. It speaks of an eternal present—generally using the continuous present tense and describing how things are—to people beyond all touch with their own past, its life and institutions.

Since, as we know, in the aftermath of the war against Rome in 132–135, the Temple was declared permanently prohibited to Jews, and Jerusalem was closed off to them as well, the Mishnah's laws in part speak of nowhere and not now. Why not? There was no cult, no Temple, no holy city, to which at this time the description of the Mishnaic laws applied. Much of the Mishnah deals with matters to which the sages had no material access. They had no practical knowledge at the time of their work on cultic law. They themselves were not members of the priestly caste. Yet we have seen that the Mishnah contains a division on the conduct of the cult, namely, the fifth, as well as one on the conduct of matters so as to preserve the cultic purity of the sacrificial system along the lines laid out in the *Book of Leviticus*, the sixth division.

There is a further point of unreality. Many of the tractates of the first division, on agriculture, deal with the rations provided for the priests by the Israelite farmers out of the produce of the holy land. The interests of the division overall flow from the Levitical taboos on land use and disposition of crops; the whole is an exercise of most acute interest to the priests.

Furthermore, a fair part of the second division, on appointed times, takes up the conduct of the cult on special days, the sacrifices offered on Yom Kippur, Passover, and the like. Indeed, what the Mishnah wants to know *about* appointed seasons concerns the cult far more than it does the synagogue, which plays a subordinate and trivial role.

The fourth division, on civil law, for its part, presents an elaborate account of a political structure and system of Israelite self-government based on Temple, priesthood, and monarchy, in tractates *Sanhedrin* and *Makkot*, not to mention *Shavu'ot* and *Horayot*. This system speaks of king, priest, Temple, and court. Not the Jews, kings, priests, and judges but the Romans conducted the government of Israel in the Land of Israel in the time in which the second-century authorities did their work.

Well over half of the document—the first division, the second, part of the fourth, all of the fifth, and most of the sixth—speaks of cult, Temple, government, priesthood. But these things did not yet exist. They derived, moreover, from other groups in Israelite society. The Mishnah takes up a profoundly priestly and Levitical conception of sanctification as the principal statement on Israel's condition. Sages had no control of these matters. Furthermore, in the very time the document was written, the Temple lay in ruins, the city of Jerusalem was prohibited to all Israelites, and the Jewish government and administration, which had centered on the Temple and based its authority on the holy life lived there, were in ruins. So the Mishnah's sages could not report any facts they had observed on their own. Much of the Mishnah speaks of matters not current at the time it was created because the Mishnah's sages wished to make a statement on what really matters: the holiness of Israel as they defined it.

LATER DEVELOPMENTS. From what has been said, we should never be able to account for the persistence of the Mishnah as half of the whole "Torah" of Judaism. The bulk of the document was irrelevant to its own time, all the more so to the ages that would follow. The two Talmuds, indeed, pick and choose what they want from the Mishnah, and, in so doing, revise the system of the whole. The Talmud of the Land of Israel, for example, provides elaboration and commentary for only thirty-nine of the Mishnah's sixty-two tractates, omitting reference to the fifth and nearly the whole of the sixth division. The Babylonian Talmud, for its part, treats the fifth division but ignores nearly all of the first. What both Talmuds do in common is ignore the system and structure of the whole and divide the Mishnah into tiny bits and pieces. These were then subjected to close and thorough analysis. The upshot is that the two Talmuds took up the whole. By continuing what Yehudah ha-Nasi' had treated as concluded, they carried forward the unending process of revelation and canon. That is to say, the heirs of the Mishnah revered the document but also took responsibility for interpreting it. In the very process of their quite accurate and careful reading, they in fact accomplished a considerable reformation of the Mishnah itself.

SEE ALSO Talmud; Tannaim.

BIBLIOGRAPHY

Tosefta

The best edition is Saul Lieberman's *Tosefta*, 3 vols. (New York, 1955–1967), including *Zera'im* (1955), Mo'ed (1962), and Nashim (1967), together with a monumental commentary by the same scholar. For the other three divisions, M. S. Zuckermandel's *Tosefta'* (1881) is available. I have made an English translation of the second through the sixth divisions in *The Tosefta, Translated from the Hebrew*, vols. 2–6 (New York, 1977–1981). A brief scholarly account is Moshe David Heer's "Tosefta," in *Encyclopaedia Judaica*, vol. 15 (Jerusalem, 1971).

Mishnah

The best available edition, including a commentary, is Chanoch Albeck's *Shishah Sidrei Mishnah* (Tel Aviv, 1952ff.). No critical edition exists. Herbert Danby has made a one-volume translation in *The Mishnah* (London, 1933), and I have made a complete translation and commentary on the second through the sixth divisions of the Mishnah and Tosefta in *A History of the Mishnaic Law* (Leiden, 1974–); included in the latter work are Appointed Times, 5 vols. (1981ff.), *Women*, 5 vols. (1980), *Damages*, 5 vols. (1983–1984), *Holy Things*, 6 vols. (1979–1980), and *Purities*, 22 vols. (1974–1977). An account of how the Mishnah has been studied in classical and modern times is given in my edition of *The Modern Study of the Mishnah* (Leiden, 1973), and the religious world view of the Mishnah is described and interpreted in my book *Judaism: The Evidence of the Mishnah* (Chicago, 1981). A brief introduction, presenting a quite different approach, is E. E. Urbach's "Mishnah," in *Encyclopaedia Judaica*, vol. 12 (Jerusalem, 1971).

New Sources

Cohen, Shaye J. D., ed. *The Synoptic Problem in Rabbinic Literature.* Providence, R.I., 2000.

Hauptman, Judith. "Does the Tosefta Precede the Mishnah: Halakhal, Aggada, and Narrative Coherence." *Judaism*, 50 (Spring 2001): 224–241.

Houtman, Alberdina. *Mishnah and Tosefta: A Synoptic Comparison of the Tractates Berakhot and Shebiit.* Tübingen, 1996.

Neusner, Jacob. *How the Talmud Shaped Rabbinic Discourse.* Atlanta, 1991.

Neusner, Jacob. *The Place of the Tosefta in the Halakhah of Formal Judaism: What Alberdina Houtman Didn't Notice.* Atlanta, 1998.

Perkins, Carl M. "The Evening Shema: A Study in Rabbinic Consolation." *Judaism* 43 (Winter 1994): 27–37.

JACOB NEUSNER (1987)
Revised Bibliography

MISSIONS

This entry consists of the following articles:

MISSIONARY ACTIVITY
BUDDHIST MISSIONS
CHRISTIAN MISSIONS

MISSIONS: MISSIONARY ACTIVITY

Many records and some suggestive studies of the foundations, motivations, dynamics, techniques, and sociocultural effects of missionary activity in specific locales exist. Most of them are written from the perspective of the missionaries or are based on the study of records, letters, or fund-raising reports they have left. Certain encounters between the major religious orientations in various parts of the world have also been documented, but few systematic, cross-cultural, and comparative studies of missions and missionary activities have been produced.

There is no lack of material dealing with the dissemination of and conversion to a specific religion from the standpoint of that religion's advocates, nor of the theological warrants or mandates given by a particular faith for its propagation. Cultural historians and social scientists have also studied the effects of religious change in specific periods, and psychologists have attempted to identify the psychodynamics of conversion. Still, systematic overviews of organized proselytism and the basic ideational, social, and institutional foundations on which it rests remain sparse.

In the nineteenth century, to be sure, certain evolutionary theories of the development of "high" cultures offered rather triumphalist accounts of the spread of "ethical religions" over territories where "animistic" or "polytheistic" faiths previously claimed the loyalties of the people. And in the early twentieth century certain theories of religio-cultural "diffusion" attempted to comprehend world historical development in ways that would also account for the spread of religions by analogy with the spread of artifacts such as the plow or the clock. Theories of political-economic and cultural imperialism have gained considerable prominence as a framework for interpreting missionary activity, a fact that will require comment here. None of these efforts, however, has resulted in a compelling account of the nature, character, and dynamics of missionary activities that bear cross-cultural scrutiny.

Near the end of the twentieth century, after the end of the cold war that occupied much of the world's attention, many became aware that governments, policies, and economic systems pass away, but that religions endure and seem to be able to renew themselves, even in areas where they were thought to be surpassed. The idea that modernization meant "progress" and inevitable secularization seems to have died a thousand deaths. In fact, the religions have undergone a substantial resurgence and have amazed and troubled no small number of social theorists, historians, and liberal religious scholars. The troubling part of this resurgence for many is that the world religions have reasserted themselves in conservative and fundamentalist forms. Some religions are local, tribal, or ethnic in character, and they often seek to recover eroding identity in the face of globalizing developments. More amazing is the fact that an enormous range of peoples have converted to Christianity and, to a somewhat lesser degree, to the other great world religions in the age that was assumed to be, according to enlightened orthodoxy, an age in which the religious illusions of the past were demystified by scientific fact. It turns out that the facts suggest that the religions in their conservative forms are engaging in vigorous missionary activity and converting the world. Why this is so is not altogether clear to observers and critics. Yet the evidence is rather clear. Evangelical, Pentecostal, fundamentalist, and heterodox (e.g., "Mormonism") forms of Christianity have been growing around the world at a record pace, as have the more militant forms of Islam, Hinduism, and Buddhism. Tribal religions, reemerging as ethnic identity religions, have erupted into fits of violence and "ethnic cleansing." The study of these dynamics continues, with many dynamics being obvious, though the are causes not.

FOUNDATIONS AND MOTIVATIONS. Nonetheless it is possible to venture some generalizations about missionary activity that seem relevant for all the great missionizing religions. The first point is that they all seem to be impelled by a unique revelation or a great discovery about the nature of being and existence, the discovery of which prompts a momentous personal transformation and a revitalization of social and cultural purpose given by an awareness of transcendence that brings spiritual and moral renewal. This generates a salvific metaphysical-moral vision that is not only of intense personal meaning but also thought to be of universal import for humanity. This vision induces a passion that intellectually, morally, and emotionally is felt by those grasped by it from magical practices of local deities and cults, from familial, clan, caste, or ethnic loyalties, from feeble or dysfunctional political-economic conditions, and from "meaningless" or ineffective rites and rituals. The missionary impulse that grows from this source becomes "homeless," for it finds its true home in a realm that relativizes all that is understood to be natural or conventional, which it then tries either to escape or to transform. It further evokes a desire to bring about the universal acceptance and application of the vision, which it holds to be universally true in principle, even if it is not universally accepted.

Every missionizing religion thus is by definition transcultural; where it is not entirely transmundane, it is cosmopolitan. It endows its advocates with a transcendental, ecumenical, cross-cultural, and global perspective, and it understands humanity to be trapped in chaotic states of mental, spiritual, social, or physical oppression from which humanity must be delivered by accepting a new foundation of meaning and a new discipline. It thereby promises to liberate humanity from evil and falsehood and bind humans to the good and true—although the precise definitions of the causes of the evil and the nature of the good, the marks of falsehood and the indicators of the true, and the means that are able to move humanity from one to the other are what divide these religions from each other.

A missionary is one who seizes or is seized by a universalistic vision and who feels a mandate, a commission, or a vocation to bring the vision and its benefits to "all." Thus missionary activity, both domestic and foreign, is the most intense in those moments when the metaphysical-moral vision of a religion is engendered or revitalized and held to be particularly pertinent in changing conditions. "Home" missions often take the form of new programs for youth, "purification" of religious and cultural practice, proselytism of marginal groups, protest against lax practices among the social elite (including the established clergy), and often moral or spiritual attempts to put domestic social, political, and economic policies on a new foundation. "Foreign" missions attempt to take the vision beyond the land of origin and thereby to lay the foundations for a new spiritual world order by transforming the souls and minds of individuals and the social habits of society. Missionary activity always alienates its converts from previous belief and practice to some degree, for it introduces a different way of organizing faith and life. Both domestic and foreign missionary activity is marked by intense intellectual activity, for the whole of reality has to be reconsidered from the new perspective. It also is the breeding ground of freedom, for in conversion a person finds that he or she can make an ultimate choice about, or be drawn by grace into, a new relationship to the truly divine. Such a person no longer has an identity determined by age, gender, class, custom, status, ethnicity, or the dictate of any lesser authority—parental or political, cultural or economic. Having been drawn into freedom, all other areas of life are subject to reevaluation and reconstruction.

One or another universalistic vision has provided the foundations and motivations for Buddhism, Christianity, Islam, and that fading secular "civil religion," Communism, to name but four of the most obvious missionizing faiths. Certain strands and periods of Judaism, Zoroastrianism, and "syncretistic" religions, such as Bahaʾi, Sikhism, and the Unification Church (Moonies) have a similar dynamic. A universalistic metaphysical-moral vision is less pronounced, however, in the beliefs of the primal religions, Daoism and Shintōism, and is less overt in Confucianism and most strands of Judaism and Zoroastrianism. However great their spiritual, moral, and intellectual achievements, these latter religions are constitutively tied to specific sociopolitical contexts and often to ethnic particularities. These religions may also claim to possess a universalistic message—they may welcome converts, and aspects of their metaphysical-moral visions may be honored or adopted by other religions, but they spread more by the migrations of peoples or by the gradual incorporation of immediate neighbors than by organized missionary activities. They are, as some say, the "staying" religions, in contrast to the "going" religions.

Hinduism represents a special and exceedingly complex case, for while it is similar to nonmissionizing traditions in many respects, and while it seems to have spread essentially by a process called sanskritization (the gradual adoption of Vedic practices and Brahmanic authority by non-Aryan peoples on the Indian subcontinent), it has had periods of vigorous missionary activity. Indeed, active missions have not only been carried out by "evangelical" forms of Hinduism, such as the Ramakrishna Mission, the International Society for Krishna Coinsciousness (ISKCON), and the organizations supporting the teachings and charitable works of Sai Baba, but are being actively pursued in another way by the *Hindutva* movement. Represented in its political mode by a Hindu nationalist party that presently heads the Indian government, a series of related "safron" groups (made up of priests and "holy men") and lay militant activists are seeking to "convert" Dalit and tribal groups into their "original" status as part of the religious and cultural fabric of the "Indic" peoples and to "deconvert" former Hindus who have become Muslim, Christian, or neo-Buddhist. Their methods often include persuasion, aid in building local temples, and promised access to educational and medical opportunity, but they also sometimes use violence against mosques, churches, and stūpas; against minorities who resist their efforts; or against missionaries from such religions. Many see this movement as a threat not only to other faiths but to the democracy, socialism, and human rights guaranteed by the Indian constitution, principles that, since Gandhi, have been held by many as almost sacred.

Most initial efforts to spread the faith focus rather strictly on the message of salvation, presented in its simplist forms. This is partly a matter of conviction. It is often also a matter of necessity—in authoritarian cultures, it is dangerous to begin pointing out all the social implications that a conversion might eventually entail. This is not to say that when missionizing religions expand they cease to have cultural, political, ethnic, or economic content and become purely transcendental, for that is seldom the case. Rather, missionaries often believe that they have a message based on a salvific metaphysical-moral vision, which is in fundamental respects separable from accidental sociohistorical trappings and thus able to be transplanted into new cultural settings. This is true even if the bearers of the message believe that at its core are implications for ethical changes in society that ought also to be spread for the well-being of humanity. Those living religions that claim the most universalistic visions and evidence the most extensive missionary zeal beyond the place of origin—Buddhism, Christianity, Islam, and indeed Communism—have never been able to extricate themselves fully from the social contexts in which they were developed nor from the unintended consequences that follow from the transplanting of the faith.

KEY DYNAMICS OF MISSIONARY ACTIVITY. As a population is missionized, new patterns of educational, familial, cultural, political, and economic life are introduced, and the indigenous "tradition" is reshaped on new foundations. The tendency to identify the universalistic message with the newly established patterns of life within the converted group is widespread. The vision "for all" once again becomes a vision "for us," until such time as a new burst of piety and learning renews the awareness of the universalistic vision and revitalizes missionary efforts, demanding a purging of false tendencies to syncretism and closed localistic identity. Missionary religions are continually or episodically engaged in religious renewal and reformation from within. The great missionizing religions are in part to be contrasted with the occasionally proselytizing, primal, and localistic religions precisely by the enduring and recurring vitality of their universalizing, in contrast to the particularizing and syncretizing tendencies of the localistic religions. It is not surprising that missionary religions are those with authoritative scriptures and "orthodox" doctrines that serve as the standards for periodic renewal.

The great universalistic teachings of the missionizing religions are, however, always treasures borne in "earthen vessels," to paraphrase Paul, the model of all Christian missionaries. And the line between the treasure and the vessel is frequently extremely fine. Early Buddhist missionaries, to cite another example, were sent out presumably armed with nothing but the pure and unadulterated message of Gautama's great discovery of the secret of true enlightenment. Wittingly or not, however, they carried with them both the philosophical presuppositions of Indian religious thought, which were the terms in which and through which the Buddha found his truth, and the political, social, and cultural patterns of Indian society. Theravāda Buddhism, as it missionized in Sri Lanka, Burma, and Thailand, brought with it metaphysical-moral assumptions and sociopolitical principles that derived from Hindu traditions and which, in part, the Buddha had sought to overcome and transcend. In Mahāyāna Buddhism as well, careful scholars can speak of the "Indianization of China."

Later, when this stream of Buddhism became wedded to motifs from Confucian and Daoist sources, its movement into Korea and Japan carried powerful elements from Chinese traditions, elements that also became wedded to Korean shamanism and Japanese Shintōism. And it is well known that both Christianity and Islam carried Greco-Roman patterns of thought, medicine, and political theory—as well as Hebraic understandings of ethical monotheism—with them as they expanded in the medieval periods. Islam has also always borne a certain Arabic cultural stamp wherever it goes, and Communism bears everywhere the marks of Germanic philosophy, French revolutionary zeal, and British economic dynamics from the days of the industrial revolution. Along with the gospel, modern Christian missions transmit Western definitions of human rights, democracy, and scientific methods in the fields of education, medicine, management, agriculture, and corporate organization. These cursory examples serve to illustrate the point that, while missionary activity must always be understood first of all in terms of the universal metaphysical-moral vision that calls it into being and gives it its transcultural raison d'être, it is always laden with particular philosophical, social, and cultural elements.

Missions and Cultural Imperialism. The inevitable presence of intellectual and social assumptions and implications, even in the "purest" of faiths, has made missionary activity subject to the charge of cultural imperialism. But two factors differentiate missionary expansion from it. First, the truly religious missionary recognizes a distinction between the message and the accoutrements, the universalistic kernel and the incidental husk. However difficult it is to distinguish the two, the primary concern is with the former. Transformation of the latter is allowed in terms of and for the sake of the former. The imperialist understands the message only in terms of its sociocultural trappings in highly particularist ways. Imperialism obtains when, for example, Buddhism in Myanmar becomes identical with and a tool of the Burman peoples as opposed to those of the Chin, Kachin, or other Burmese peoples; when Christianity becomes "Aryanized" in the Nazi period or sanctifies apartheid as in South Africa; when Islam in, for instance, Malaysia, Iran, or Saudi Arabia is understood to be coterminous with the fate of the countries themselves; or when Communism is thought to be identical with "socialism in one country" and celebrated with a personality cult. These forms of cultural imperialism have had their vicious corollaries in many lands wherever a particular social group, political hegemony, or economic advantage is confused with a universalistic religious message and spread by coercive means to colonize peoples in the name of religion.

Second, missionary activity is rooted in the fundamental assumptions that, once people are exposed to "the truth" that has been proclaimed, they will choose this truth and that they ought to be free to encounter and choose even "foreign" truth. Missions presuppose that a truly universalistic vision is convincing to the mind, compelling to the will, and attractive to the heart. Missions thus require, or provoke, a situation in which freedom of thought, choice, and affection can create new communities of conviction to celebrate and exercise what the will, mind, and heart have come to hold dear. However much missionary activity has been carried out hand in hand with cultural arrogance, military power, and economic opportunism, there has been and remains in principle a sharp tension between missionary efforts and imperialistic imposition of religion by force or "mind control," a fact increasingly documented by missiologists examining the relative validity of the charge that missions are but the ideological instrument of colonial practice. Those incapable of imagining a fundamental transformation of thought, disposition, and loyalty by conversion to a new religious insight, however, always attribute the change to nefarious interests.

It is certainly true that every missionizing religion has had periods during which something like the classic Islamic pattern could be documented. H. A. R. Gibb wrote of Islam that, "while the faith itself was not spread by the sword, it was under the wing of Muslim dominance that its missionaries found most favorable conditions for their activities of conversion. This view of Islam . . . was universally held by its adherents; the theologians found justification for it in the Koran, the jurists made it the basis of their expositions of Muslim law, and the mass of the people accepted it as a self-evident fact" (Gibb, 1932/1973, p. 56). Comparable patterns could be cited regarding periods of Buddhist expansion at the hands of pious war lords, Christian missions in Latin America, or Communist movements in eastern Europe. Nevertheless, the Qurʾān and the authoritative teachings of every other missionizing religion agree that forced conversion is false and that truly universal religion must depend on the freely convinced mind, will, and heart of the convert (although Communists held that changing the social conditions themselves would bring about the fading of religion and the turning to the true ideology of humanity). Thus, wherever missions go and do not immediately preclude other missionary efforts by force, they open up new vistas for mind, will, and heart, and thus for new social practices to which people are invited to turn.

Reactions of Missionized People. Every missionary religion must be received as well as propagated. Where it is not received, missionary activity dies, and doubt about the universality of the originating vision sets in. Where it is received under coercion, and not in the mind, will, heart or the transformed customs of the people, the indigenous religion goes underground, eventually resurfacing as a revitalized rallying point to overthrow "foreign gods" or as a heterodox or heretical religion in contention with the one brought by missions. Where the missionary religion is received in the heart, will, and mind, newly converted people soon send out their own missionaries. But it is almost never received as given. It is filtered through the philosophical, sociopolitical, and historical perspectives of the recipients. The old traditions are almost never entirely abandoned. They are inevitably active in interpreting and modifying the new message, helping to at least partially purge it of missionary-borne incidental elements that can be seen as merely cultural biases or sociopolitical interests.

One of the most fascinating studies of the reception of a religion is that by Kenneth Ch'en (1973) of the way in which Buddhism was modified, acculturated, and indigenized in China. A message, such as that exported by Indian Buddhism, that called for the breaking of family ties and demanded that kings give honor to monks simply did not make sense in a culture where filial piety and homage to the emperor were absolutely central to both belief and social order. Ch'en demonstrates that, if one speaks of the "Indianization of China" with the spread of Buddhism, one must also speak of the "sinicization of Buddhism." In China, key Buddhist texts were given fresh interpretation; apologetic literature, new poems, and new regulations for the community of monks were promulgated that modified or transformed aspects of the Buddhist message so that it could fit into, and in some ways revitalize, both the indigenous folk religions and of the Confucianism and Daoism of that land. Comparable stories can be told of every missionizing religion: the Christianity of the Copts in Northeast Africa is not the same as that of the Kimbanguists of West Africa; the Islam of Morocco differs from that of Mindanao in significant ways; Communism in North Korea is distinct from that of Cuba. This is so in spite of the fact that each of these great traditions tends to press the local society and culture in a distinctive direction.

In this connection it must be noted that some religions engage in missionary activity precisely as a result of being invited, sought, or adopted with great eagerness. In several places where traditional systems have been displaced by exploitative cultural contact, war, crop failure, or the failure of a social system to survive its own internal strains, missionary groups bearing universalistic messages are readily embraced, for they offer new symbolic and cognitive models by which life and its perplexities may be interpreted. Often the appropriation of a new religion is accompanied by a quest for new technological, educational, and sociopolitical frameworks for organizing the common life. Missionaries often agree that such a quest is implied by the core of their metaphysical-moral vision. Certainly a comparable phenomenon has occurred in quite different locales, as John Garrett (1982) has shown in regard to the Pacific Islands and Frederick S. Downs (1983) has demonstrated concerning the Christianization of tribal peoples of Assam in the twentieth century. More ancient examples are the historic reception in the sixth and seventh centuries of Chinese Buddhism (and Confucianism) into Japan at the hands of the imperial court; the reception in the ninth to eleventh centuries of Eastern Orthodox Christianity into Russia, bringing with it Byzantine art, literature, and political theory; and the reception in the twelfth to fifteenth centuries of Islam (as mediated through India) in the Malay archipelago that was accompanied by aspects of mysticism and caste-related social patterns.

In almost no instance, however, is a new religion received without some resistance. This resistance is sometimes easily overcome. When the indigenous faith is a highly literate and complex religion, however, the resistance is usually prolonged and powerful. One of the dramatic examples of this resistance is that, while Buddhism originated in India and at one time had nearly swept the subcontinent, in the twenty-first century can be found there only in forms of neo-Buddhism newly reintroduced by Bhimo Rao Ambedkar and the Dalai Lama. This is because Hinduism reasserted itself by a ten-century-long process involving the adoption of some aspects of Buddhism (especially the revitalization of devotional practice in *bhakti*), the bloody slaughter of Buddhist monks, extensive philosophical argumentation, and an effort that was more organized than that of Buddhism. But the neo-Buddhism being introduced is taken as protests against the Hindu caste system, recently celebrated by some Dalit (outcaste) Christians. Similarly, Confucianism reasserted itself in China during the "neo-Confucian" period of renewal in the ninth century by a similar process—one that relegated the Buddhists and Daoists to an inferior status while borrowing some motifs from them. Islam encountered intellectual and military resistance when it threatened expansion into Europe from the time of Charlemagne through the Crusades. The Christianity that expanded into central Asia has been essentially stamped out, and what remains in western Asia is now weak and scattered because of Islamic resistance. Most Western Jews and Christians resist the Hindu, Islamic, and Buddhist missions as well as the host of hybrid or syncretistic cults rooted in these, or in some heterodox Christian faith, found in most of the major cities of the West. Meanwhile, indigenized forms of Christianity from Africa, Latin America, and Asia are challenging the kinds of Christianity that have developed in the West.

One notable feature of the phenomenon of "mission" and "resistance" is that missions that do not succeed among the intellectual and political-economic elites of a new country but that do succeed among the people become fatefully drawn into perennial tensions between the rulers and the ruled. If conversion is successful among the masses but not among leadership, intense resistance results. If conversion occurs only among marginal groups, ethnic conflict is frequent, and minorities are suspected of being agents of foreign powers. If missions are successful among some sections of the leadership and among wide segments of the people, the stage is set for revolutionary change.

Types of Missionaries. In surveying mission and missionary activity, however, one must not only note the primacy of the metaphysical-moral vision—its relationship to social and cultural patterns, its patterns of reception, and resistances to it—one must also consider certain similarities of institutional form that are characteristic of missionary activity. What groups or classes of people undertake missionary activity, and how do they organize to do so?

On missionaries, merchants, and mercenaries. The earliest missionaries are, more often than not, traders or travelers with them. One does not have to accept the Marxist interpretation of the relationship between commercial exploitation and religion to observe that the spreading of a new religious insight repeatedly follows commercial traffic lanes—and that this insight is frequently borne by merchants. Further, it must be noted that both commercial and missionary activities can only be conducted in conditions of relative peace and stability. When that is disrupted, soldiers are frequently brought in to establish it, and they are accompanied by new waves of chaplains, who become missionaries. Since traders and soldiers vary widely in their behavior, from the relatively congenial to the simply marauding, missionary activity has often been conducted within networks of shifting alliances, both economic and military, on the far end of trade routes. It is not possible to make any single generalization about these relationships, however, for missionaries have resisted exploitative trade as often as they have benefited from it, and they have fought imperial "pacification" as often as they have been protected by it.

The cross-cultural frequency of missionary activity by merchants, however, invites speculation as to why this general class has played so significant a role in missionizing. Perhaps it is because merchants are people who seek increased opportunity by taking the risk of leaving the settled and accepted patterns of life at home. The very act of engaging in trade on a cross-cultural basis, however crass the individual motivation might be, requires a somewhat more cosmopolitan perspective on the world than is frequently present in those societies where religion and morality run in channels circumscribed by fixed economic roles and duties for people of each specific ethnic, gender, age, and class status. In addition those societies that send merchants farthest and equip caravans or ships the most extensively for trade are usually the more highly developed economically, politically, militarily, and socially. It would not be strange for them to hold the view that their "superiority" in this respect is due, in substantial part at least, to the "superior" religious, spiritual, and ethical foundations of their faith. In an influential study, Edward Said (1995) has argued that this accounts for the various condescending projections on Eastern cultures by Western merchants, soldiers, and missionaries.

Professional missionaries. New religions are seldom, if ever, however, fully developed in a new location by the sometimes quite unholy alliance of missionaries, merchants, and soldiers, or by general processes of cultural diffusion that accompany them. The introduction of a religion through commercial channels (the character and quality of which influence reception or resistance) has everywhere been succeeded by the arrival of professional missionaries. For most religions throughout most of history, the professional missionary has been monastic, that is, organized into ascetic, trained, and disciplined religious orders intentionally "homeless" for the sake of the metaphysical-moral vision held to be universally true.

Missionary monks and nuns attempt to spread their religious convictions by public proclamation and commentary on sacred texts at both popular and learned levels; by teaching hymns, chants, and prayers; by establishing new centers of worship where the truth they know can be celebrated; and by service—that is, by medical, educational, pastoral care, social relief, and advocacy. Needless to say all missionary religions have relied on "wondrous," magical, or technological demonstrations of "spiritual" power from time to time. The stories well known in the West about saintly missionary monks, such as Patrick (387–493), Columba (c. 521–597), Boniface (d. 755), Ramón Lull (1232–1316), and Francis Xavier (1506–1552), are paralleled in the lore of Buddhism, in the formation of the *maṭhas* as a Hindu reaction to the challenge posed by Buddhism, and in the roles played by the "schools" of jurists and even more by the Ṣūfī orders of Islam.

To carry out their tasks, missionaries have four requirements. First, they must have a dedication, a commitment—a piety, if you will—linked to learning. Missionaries must be able to articulate the faith and to interpret it in intellectual and cultural terms that are foreign to them. They must be able to understand and put into perspective whatever they encounter in the course of their work. It is no accident that several sciences, including modern comparative linguistics and anthropology, to a large extent have their roots in missionary activity. Everywhere professional missionaries are given to literary activity—they have published apologetics, tracts, propaganda, and commentaries, and they are responsible for the composition and dissemination of poetry, song, and history.

Second, missionary professionals require a reliable institutional foundation, a polity, to sustain them. Missionary orders and societies are surely among the world's first transnational, nonprofit corporations. These polities, however, are ever subject to incorporation into the existing polities of the host countries. Thus the Buddhist *saṃgha,* spread under the protectorate of kings, is ever tempted to become simply an instrument of state. Some converted Christian communities in India are always in peril of becoming more a subcaste than a church, and the *ṭarīqahs* of Islam tend to become simply trade guilds or sanctified tribal brotherhoods.

Third, missions require funding. Economic support may derive from state funds, charitable bequests, the establishment of plantations, handicraft manufacturing centers, agricultural communes, and religious taxes. The economic ties of a missionary enterprise with its country of origin or with the elites of the host country are the source of enormous distrust of missionary activity.

And fourth, missionaries must have a clear policy, one that coordinates strategies and tactics and prevents divergent teachings from confusing potential converts. These policies must cover such matters as how much of the indigenous culture to allow and what to disallow, how to deal with marriage practices, "pagan" festivals, various "fraternities" that are marginally stamped with traditional religious practices, and the like.

Indigenous missionaries. While most professional missionaries are sent to a foreign land, they can measure their success by whether or not they are replaced by indigenous lay or clerical missiological leaders. The mark of successful reception is that the newly converted themselves become motivated to spread the message to which they have been converted, both to others in their own land and to other lands, and to develop institutional and financial support systems for their own missionaries. It was largely Chinese Buddhists who missionized not only many parts of China but Korea and Japan after Indian and Tibetan Buddhists established monasteries in China and trained Chinese novices. It was Malay Muslims who missionized Indonesia and Mindanao after Arabic traders and missionaries brought the faith to the region. And it is Chinese, Indian, and Korean Christians who are spreading the faith in South and East Asia after most Western missionaries only come as short-term visitors or to provide support for specific projects. And in Africa and Latin America, local leadership has become the spearhead of massive growth. The direct knowledge of the language, culture, common worldviews, lifestyles, felt needs, and life's difficulties allows the message to become more directly pertinent and more thoroughly embedded in the life of the people. It also alters the contours of the faith and renders fresh theological perspectives, as seen in Christian history by the names of major branches of the Christian faith: Greek Orthodoxy, Roman Catholicism, German Lutheranism, Dutch Calvinism, the Anglican Church, and American Evangelicalism. Sometimes the organizations that once sent missionaries abroad find that the work is better done by believers who live there and that they must attend to the fact that the faith at home has become cool, routine, and so deeply enculturated that it needs renewal. They turn to the reevangelization of their home cultures or to fresh views of the global mission.

MODERN PRACTICES. Modern missionary efforts have been pursued not so much by monastic orders (although these orders continue to missionize around the world) as by nonmonastic missionary "societies." This situation is prompted primarily by the rather unique developments of "free-church" Protestant polities, economic support systems, and policies. While the established churches in Europe had been sending out monastic missionaries for centuries and the Moravians anticipated later developments, the formation of the London Missionary Society in 1795 inaugurated a new form of paraecclesial organization that continues in the twenty-first century and is emulated by non-Christian missionaries. Missionary societies, of which there are hundreds, raise funds by freewill contributions and form nonmonastic "voluntary associations" staffed by a combination of nonparochial clergy, lay professionals, and volunteers not only to save souls from "paganism" but to sweep away superstition and oppression; to offer agricultural, technical, medical, and educational assistance; and to engender a desire for democratic institutions, human dignity, self-sufficiency, and social liberation. Some modern theorists indeed suggest that these efforts at social service and social change are the very core of missionizing and theological renewal.

A notable example of the side effects of this pattern can be illustrated by reference to the Young Men's Christian Association (YMCA). The association was formed in England in 1844 as a part of a "home mission" voluntary association for youth flocking to the cities to get jobs in factories, and it attempted to provide a wholesome place where young men could find physical, mental, social, and spiritual benefit on a biblical foundation. The movement spread to North America and to most of the countries around the world where missions were active. It was often the agent of evangelization and the womb of efforts at social change by young men who came under its influence. Other religions responded by forming counterorganizations on a comparable basis. One can find not only the YMCA but the Young Women's Christian Association (YWCA), the Young Men's Buddhist Association, the Young Men's Hebrew Association, and the Young Men's Muslim Association, as well as youth hostels for Hindus scattered throughout much of Asia and in many parts of Africa and South America. Comparable developments could be documented regarding schools, colleges, presses, hospitals, orphanages, institutions for the handicapped, human rights advocacy groups, organizations for battered women, or substance abuse centers, all organized outside of traditional political, familial, and clerical control. Examples of such independent organizations exist in all the world religions. This not only introduces new principles of organization in more closed societies, it suggests the possibilities of converting traditions without converting whole populations. The proliferation of communities of a faith-based, voluntary-associational type is one of the most remarkable and explosive social effects of missionary activity in the twentieth century, one not fully documented on a comparative basis.

Increasingly, the great missionizing religions are confronting not only the primal or folk religions, where missionary activity has been most pronounced, and not only the social needs in various contexts, where missionary activity has been remarkable, but one another. Thus far missionary efforts with regard to the other great missionary religions have been only marginally successful. This is in part because of severe restrictions on missionary activities in especially Islamic and Marxist lands and in parts of India, where induced conversion has been criminalized, but also because the world religions that have shaped complex civilization rarely had to confront one another directly and tend to do so only in intercivilizational clashes. In a globalizing age, however, when economic, political, educational, scientific, medical, technological, and cultural traditions shaped by these religions are interacting with great intensity and frequency, encounter is unavoidable. Although some theorists have argued that these religions are moving toward a great synthesis of world faiths (an essentially Hindu argument), others have attempted to find analogous meanings in shared symbolic patterns present in all religions as manifestations of the development of the species (an evolutionary argument), and still others have sought the common ethical teachings that can prevent mutual assassination (a natural-law argument). Still the way these religions will continue to deal with one another is not at all certain. None of the great faiths can be satisfied with a complete relativism, but some can recognize diversity. It is contrary to a deep faith and to missionary activity to hold that what is ultimately true about the divine and the realities of this world is only true for some in specific cultures, times, or places, even if all agree that people perceive the true state of affairs in somewhat different ways due to the influece of context, time, and space. Few think the world will soon, or ever, be converted to one faith only.

In the face of this development, a new set of writings about "theologies of religions" has begun to emerge. It is, in brief, an attempt to identify what the religions hold in common, where they differ, and in some measure how they have, can, or could mutually enrich and correct one another without loosing integrity. It is the likely case that dedicated evangelists for one or another faith will confront the questions sooner or later, and it is surely the case that these questions are the most lively ones to be faced intellectually.

See Also Religious Communities.

Bibliography

An-Na'im, Abdullahi Ahmed. *Toward an Islamic Reformation.* Syracuse, N.Y., 1990. A study of the Islamic tradition in its legal and political dimensions and a call for its revision, in accord with neglected themes, toward human rights and democracy.

Athyal, J. M. *Relevant Patterns of Witness: People as Agents of Mission.* Teruvalla, India, 2000. A documentation of popular and grassroots Christian concerns and mission movements among minority, tribal, and Dalit (formerly "untouchable") peoples of India.

Barrett, David B., George T. Kurian, and Todd M. Johnson. *World Christian Encyclopedia.* 2d ed. Oxford, 2001. An exhaustive and authoritative statistical documentation of the modern spread of Christianity in comparison and contrast to other religions.

Berger, Peter L., ed. *The Desecularization of the World.* Grand Rapids, Mich., 1999. Key sociological essays that challenge the nineteenth-century assumption, repeated often, that secularization inevitably accompanies modernization.

Bosch, David J. *Transforming Mission: Paradigm Shifts in Theology of Mission.* Maryknoll, N.Y., 1991. The widely acclaimed "new classic" that traces the changing theories of missiology and proposes a postcolonial, post-Christendom understanding of the *missio dei.*

Bulliet, Richard W. *Conversion to Islam in the Medieval Period.* Cambridge, Mass., 1979. A major study of the expansion of Islam by conquest and by persuasion in the centuries of its most rapid growth, widest reach, and highest cultural development.

Ch'en, Kenneth K. S. *The Chinese Transformation of Buddhism.* Princeton, N.J., 1973. A landmark study of the reception of a foreign religion by China and the alterations the adoptive cultural and religious tradition brought about on the classical tradition.

Christensen, Torben, and William R. Hutchison, eds. *Missionary Ideologies in the Imperialist Era, 1880–1920.* Århus, Denmark, 1983. The interaction of missiological theories, cultural expansion, "civilizing" intentions, and imperial designs in the colonialization of the world by, especially, European powers.

Clarke, Sathianathan. *Dalits and Christianity.* Delhi, India, 1998. Ways the Dalit (outcaste) communities of South Asia that have converted to Christianity have used themes from this faith to find dignity and preserve their culture.

Downs, Frederick S. *Christianity in North East India.* Delhi, India, 1983. An authoritative documentation of the adoption of evangelical (mostly Baptist) Christianity by the tribal peoples of that "Assamese" corner of India.

Dunn, Edmond J. *Missionary Theology: Foundations in Development.* Lanham, Md., 1980. The development of reformist Roman Catholic missional theory at the hands of radical priests and nuns in the context of, especially, Latin American anticolonial movements.

Foreman, C. W. "A History of Foreign Mission Theory in America." In *American Missions in Bicentennial Perspective,* edited by R. Pierce Beaver, pp. 69–140. South Pasadena, Calif., 1977. An overview of American theologies and programs of missions by major church bodies and the most important "independent" missionary organizations.

Garrett, John. *To Live among the Stars.* Suva, Fiji, 1982. The stories of missions to the South Sea Islands and how different peoples responded to various efforts according to the "fit" of their tradition with the polity of the missionaries.

Gibb, H. A. R. *Whither Islam* (1932). New York, 1973. A prescient analysis of the tendencies and directions of Islamic development in the twentieth century by one of the major missionary scholars of the period.

Guder, Darrell L., ed. *Missional Church.* Grand Rapids, Mich., 1998. A fresh attempt to identify the missionary mandate of the churches in a postcolonial era in which Christians are often more respectful of other traditions than in times past.

Harvard Tercentenary Conference of Arts and Sciences. *Independence, Convergence, and Borrowing in Institutions, Thought, and Art.* Cambridge, Mass., 1937. An older, still-valuable study of how cultures and religions maintain their distinctive qualities while adopting from other traditions and finding ways to reduce conflict.

Hefner, Robert W., ed. *Conversion to Christianity: Historical and Anthropological Perspectives on a Great Transformation.* Berkeley, Calif., 1993. A substantive descriptive analysis of peoples who have been evangelized into the Christian faith and who often are grateful and want the missions to continue.

Heim, S. Mark. *Salvations.* Maryknoll, N.Y., 1995. A groundbreaking interpretation of the world religions that sees them as sharing much but having distinctive views of what humanity needs to be saved from and for.

Huntington, Samuel P. *The Clash of Civilizations and the Remaking of World Order.* New York, 1996. The much-debated thesis that civilizations are founded on religious "tectonic cultural plates" that may include a number of societies but tend to violence when they clash.

Jeganathan, W. S. M. *Mission Paradigms in the New Millennium.* Delhi, India, 2000. An attempt to critically analyze the major alternative approaches to missions for the twenty-first century, with particular attention to their social effectiveness.

Jenkins, Philip. *The Next Christendom: The Coming of Global Christianity.* New York, 2002. A treatment of new "conservative" movements, Protestant and Catholic, that are rapidly developing in Africa and South America and may displace Euro-American traditions.

Kim, Yon-t'aek. *Protestant Church Growth in Korea.* Toronto, Canada, 1998. An analysis of the growth of Korean Christianity, among the most rapidly growing missionary movements in the world, with many social effects in South Korea and abroad.

Kopf, David. *British Orientalism and the Bengal Renaissance.* Berkeley, Calif., 1969. A classic study of the relationship of the British raj and the missionary movement, with careful attention to the effects they had on changing the character of Hinduism.

Latourette, Kenneth Scott. *A History of the Expansion of Christianity.* 7 vols. New York, 1937–1945. An extensive historical treatment of the growth of Christianity and its encounter with other religions and cultures.

Macy, Joanna. *Dharma and Development.* West Hartford, Conn., 1983. A study of the social development and community organization efforts undertaken by Theravāda Buddhist monks and their devotees in Sri Lanka.

Martin, David. *Pentecostalism: The World Their Parish.* Oxford, U.K., 2002. A summary of Pentecostal expansion around the world, with attention to vibrant movements in Latin America, Africa, and Asia and the rebound effect in the West.

Marty, Martin E., and R. Scott Appleby, eds. *The Fundamentalism Project.* 7 vols. Chicago, 1991–1995. An extensive study of the resurgence of fundamentalist movements in most of the world religions, with attention to the motives and probable consequences.

Mattam, J., and P. Arockiadoss. *Hindutva: An Indian Christian Response.* Bangalore, India, 2002. A study of the militantly "evangelizing" form of Hindu nationalism that has grown since independence and taken control of the government in India.

Neville, Robert Cummings, ed. *The Human Condition.* New York, 2001.

Neville, Robert Cummings, ed. *Religious Truth.* New York, 2001.

Neville, Robert Cummings, ed. *Ultimate Realities.* New York, 2001. These three Neville works constitute a process philosophical analysis of the common features of the great religious traditions and spiritual perspectives that seeks to identify convergences and areas for dialogue.

Pachuau, Lalsangkima, ed. *Ecumenical Missiology.* Bangalore, India, 2002. A fresh summary of the developments in ecumenical thought as it bears on prospects for a revitalized program for missions, with special reference to ethnic conflicts.

Queen, Christopher S., and Sallie B. King. *Engaged Buddhism: Buddhist Liberation Movements in Asia.* Albany, N.Y., 1996. A study of "activist" Buddhism as it adopts missionizing and "social witness" techniques from other traditions and adapts them to Asian settings.

Rambo, L. R. "Current Research on Religious Conversion." *Religious Studies Review* 8, no. 2 (1982): 146–158. A key summary and evaluation of research conducted in the third quarter of the twentieth century.

Reed, James. *The Missionary Mind and American East Asia Policy, 1911–1915.* Cambridge, Mass., 1983. An argument that American policy toward East Asia has been shaped by the experience of missionaries (and their children) in the region, giving policy a moralistic flavor.

Said, Edward W. *Orientalism.* New York, 1994. A sharp critique of the views Westerners have projected on the East due to the interlock of colonial, imperial, and missiological interests that have justified oppressive policies.

Sanneh, Lamin O. *West African Christianity.* Maryknoll, N.Y., 1983. A study of the ways Christianity came to Africa, learned from its new environment, exploited the people, and simultaneously offered the resources for cultural renewal.

Song, C.-S. *The Compassionate God.* Maryknoll, N.Y., 1982. One of several key examples of how indigenization and cultural synthesis enters into the process of theological construction as religions move into new contexts.

Srinivas, M. N. *Caste in Modern India.* Bombay, India, 1962. A classic study of how a "nonmissiological" religion expands by the incorporation of primal communities and redefines their social rights, duties, and statuses.

Stackhouse, Max L. *Creeds, Societies, and Human Rights.* Grand Rapids, Mich., 1984. A comparative analysis of how differing worldviews and religious orientations support or inhibit the development of human rights, pluralistic society, and democratic polity.

Stackhouse, Max L., with Peter J. Paris, eds. *God and Globalization.* 4 vols. Harrisburg, Pa., 2000–2005. A compendium of essays by an international team of scholars on how religions and ethics have shaped the dynamics and structures of globalization and are being shaped by them.

Trimingham, J. Spencer. *The Sufi Orders in Islam.* London, 1973. An analysis of the ways this heterodox movement in Islam has been among the major forces spreading the Muslim faith, especially among "brotherhoods" of traders.

Walls, Andrew F. *The Missionary Movement in Christian History.* Edinburgh, U.K., 1996. A study of the process by which converts to a tradition seldom leave their older traditions behind entirely but bring them into the new faith and generate new syntheses.

MAX L. STACKHOUSE (1987 AND 2005)

MISSIONS: BUDDHIST MISSIONS

The term *Buddhist mission* was invented in the 1830s to explain the religion's diffusion throughout Asia, and "missionary spirit" has been treated as an essential dimension of Buddhist spirituality in virtually all English-language works about Buddhism composed since. By the 1870s "Buddhist mission" had been theorized further by early historians of religions as a key plank in the subsequently ubiquitous disciplinary distinction between "missionary" or "world" religions (Buddhism, Islam, and Christianity) and "national" or "indigenous" religions (all the rest) which did not expand far beyond traditional geographical borders. Two proof-texts were singled out for citation in Western writings on Buddhist mission, namely, the Buddha's so-called great commission, and stories about the transmission of his religion associated with the age of King Aśoka (third century BCE).

The "great commission" is an ancient passage found already reworked in three canonical Buddha biographies, the *Mahāvagga* of the *Vinaya*, the *Mārasaṃyutta* of the *Samyutta Nikāya* and the *Mahāpadānasutta* of the *Dīgha-nikāya.* According to these accounts, after attaining enlightenment and gathering together his first followers (later reckoned to be sixty in number), the Buddha, realizing that all of them were already saints (*arhats*) who required no further guidance, gave them leave to depart, saying:

> Wander about on wanderings, monks. For the good of many folk, for the happiness of many folk, out of compassion for the world, for the good and happiness of gods and men, don't two of you go by one [road]. Preach the *dharma,* monks, which is lovely at the beginning, lovely in the middle, lovely at the end, in meaning and sound. Demonstrate the purified celibate life which is fully complete. There are beings with little dust in their eyes; they are falling away from the *dharma* for not hearing it. There will be people who understand, monks.

According to later reckonings this occurred just after the concluding ceremony (Pali, *pavāraṇa*) of the first-ever Buddhist rains retreat (Pali, *vassa*), which for subsequent monastic and lay Buddhists became an annual time of renewal and recommitment.

The Buddha's actions in this moment were important to later Buddhists as a watershed in the history of the monastic community (*saṃgha*), especially in the emergence of monastic discipline (*Vinaya*). At that time none of the monastic rules had yet been promulgated—as perfected saints, the first sixty monks did not require rules. According to the *Mahāvagga* account, however, permitting them to preach to others while wandering about ultimately required the Buddha to promulgate the rules one after another because the people who heard them preach, and sometimes then joined the order, were not yet themselves enlightened. The passage in question was not portrayed as a commission to all Buddhists; the point was that only the first sixty (and presumably subsequent) saints were free to wander forth unguided by the monastic discipline. But removed from such literary contexts, constructed grammatically to make the wandering dependent upon the preaching rather than the other way around (which is possible, though against the grain of the commentarial tradition), and translated into biblical English, this passage was easily read as a much-remarked parallel to Jesus' great (or apostolic) commission (*Mt.* 28:18–20).

All versions of the legend of King Aśoka agree that some favored patriarch of his, directly connected through pupillary succession to the Buddha himself, convened a great council at the conclusion of which monks were sent to "establish the Buddha's dispensation" (Skt., *śāsana*; Pali, *sāsana*) in various regions. The patriarch himself (or some special disciple) is said to have taken it to a region that the Buddha or the patriarch had foreseen would be a future Buddhist center. These legends, which emerged in oral traditions shortly after Aśoka and were composed in their surviving written forms beginning around the first century CE, include colorful stories about these monks' encounters in various regions, emphasizing their supernormal attainments. Though the oft-repeated claim that Aśoka himself sponsored this event is unfounded—in the texts the patriarch, not the king, always provides the impetus to hold the council and send the dispensation to some far-off region(s)—the portrayal of these texts as "missionary" is understandable, for the basic themes also constituted important dimensions of nineteenth-century Christian missionary discourse.

But the wide divergence among various versions of this narrative—especially as regards the identity of the patriarch, his lineage, his sectarian affiliation, and the future Buddhist center—suggests that they are better viewed as specific, even polemical, claims about their own times than as windows into actual Aśokan history (there is no mention of Buddhist councils, nor of the dispensation-transmission, in the known Aśokan epigraphs; scholars now agree that the legendary "missions" cannot be read into the diplomatic embassies Aśoka does mention). As elaborated below, these stories enjoyed wide significance among later Buddhists, but in precolonial times these did not include the claim of nineteenth- and twentieth-century writers that Aśoka, the patriarch, or the "missionaries" (often said to be trying to fulfill the Buddha's great commission) were manifesting "missionary spirit," nor is there warrant for assuming that these legends were read as paradigms and guides for missionary service in the same way that the apostolic missions were significant to Christian missionaries.

Little else is cited in writings about "Buddhist mission," not only because these problematic examples were considered sufficient proof, but also because apart from them premodern Buddhists demonstrated no concern with "mission" in its nineteenth-century trappings. Aspects of what Christians consider "mission"—preaching, modeling, and advocating proper behavior; reproducing and disseminating texts; confronting religious others; traveling—certainly did concern Buddhists from ancient times, but the premodern tradition lacked specialized vocabulary for discussing them as "mission" (nor were there words for conversion, missionary spirit, or mission field), and the premodern tradition never produced missiological literature as such. "Mission" never figured in the systematic lists of practices, virtues, or spiritual attainments so carefully articulated by Buddhists around the world.

Indeed, until the late nineteenth century it was notoriously the case for Christian missionaries serving in Buddhist countries that then-contemporary Buddhists lacked any glimmer of "missionary spirit." During the early nineteenth century, Buddhist monks allowed Christian missionaries to use their temples for rallies and politely refused challenges and taunts that they debate comparative doctrine or salvation; missionaries regularly complained that Buddhists would listen to sermons and even enact approbation without undergoing the existential "conversion" that was a hallmark of Christian missionary discourse and expectations. Rather than catalyze revision of the (Western, Christian) presuppositions that made "mission" an essential dimension of Buddhist religiosity, however, this actual lack of it was treated as a failure of Buddhists to live up to their own essence.

Nineteenth- and twentieth-century writings on Buddhist (and Muslim) mission made available for study an "other" mission to juxtapose with Christian mission. This comparative framework originally contributed to Christian missionary self-confidence, portraying their approach as a middle-ground between overly forceful (Muslim) mission and overly tolerant (Buddhist) mission. Beginning in the 1870s, however, a growing number of Western Buddhist sympathizers turned this discourse upside-down, using the "tolerance" of Buddhist mission to chastise Christian evangelism, a comparison that, eventually internalized by missionaries themselves, played an important role in the general abandonment of evangelical missions by mainstream Protestant churches since World War II. At the same time, as mentioned above, Buddhist mission was central to the classification of religions into "world" and "national" types, a classification whose persistence (sometimes in modified language) belies its foundation in fact, despite the problematically "missionary" framework through which the global reach strongly characteristic only of Buddhism, Christianity, and Islam has been theorized.

But "Buddhist mission" was an inadequate tool for understanding pre-nineteenth-century Buddhist history, sometimes misconstruing the spread of the dispensation and the functioning of the pan-Buddhist world on the basis of Christian presuppositions about how religions expand. Increasingly employing the context-appropriate language of traditional Buddhist historians—who discussed the "spreading out" or "establishment" of (some particular sectarian version of) the dispensation—recent scholars have been able to better understand the various important phenomena hitherto lumped together as "Buddhist mission."

The Spread of the Dispensation. Scholars agree on the basic chronology of this spread of the dispensation because its formal establishment regularly resulted in Buddhist construction projects that survive as archaeological evidence, the creation of monastic lineages and schools, and textual accounts of the event(s), preserved and embellished in the different regions. Even during the Buddha's lifetime his community certainly had grown into a sizeable institution spread throughout the kingdoms of northeastern India; traditional accounts claim that thousands of people ordained or participated in the early community as laypeople. The Buddhist presence there and beyond was bolstered by Aśokan stupa building and other Buddhist projects that he and his successors undertook from the third century BCE to the third century CE. The earliest archaeological evidence of Buddhist practice in the northwest (Kashmir) and far south (Tamil Nadu and Sri Lanka) dates from about Aśoka's time, while Buddhist texts agree in narrating the establishment of the dispensation in these secondary centers (Kashmir and Sri Lanka) as part of the Aśoka legend itself. The texts chronicle the northern transmission from Kashmir to modern Iran and Central Asia from the first century CE onwards in various kingdoms (the last was Tibet, during the seventh to eighth centuries) and China (first century), and from the latter to Korea (fifth century) and thence to Japan (sixth century); and the southern transmission from northeast and central India to Sri Lanka, and from there (or India directly) to kingdoms in modern Burma (fifth century), the Maldives (seventh century), the Malay Peninsula and Indonesian archipelago (fifth century), Thailand (seventh century), Cambodia (fifth century), southern Vietnam (fifth century), and Laos (twelfth century). Later Buddhists as far afield as China and southeast Asia sometimes directly extended the Aśoka legend—or even the Buddha's own preaching career—to include their own kingdoms.

Like any schematization, however convenient, this one is deceptively neat. Archaeological and textual evidence suggests that Buddhists were present in various regions prior to the formal establishment of the dispensation there, and the sources leave no doubt that transregional transmissions continued to occur long after. Such efforts included numerous organized Chinese endeavors to bring additional texts and practices from India and Sri Lanka (especially from the fourth to seventh centuries) and corresponding Indian, Central Asian, and Sri Lankan embassies to China (during the first to ninth centuries); imperial exchanges of texts and *dharma*-masters through which Chinese Buddhist schools were transplanted in Korea, Japan, and northern Vietnam (especially during the seventh to the ninth and twelfth centuries); formal diplomatic embassies to reestablish monastic higher ordination (*upasampada*) and transmit texts that traded the dispensation back and forth among the Theravāda Buddhist traditions of Sri Lanka, Burma, Thailand, Cambodia, and Laos (from the tenth to twenty-first centuries); and discussion and comparison of pan-Buddhist philosophies and practices at multicultural Buddhist universities (such as

Nālandā in modern Bihar, which flourished in the last centuries of the first millennium CE) and pilgrimage sites (most importantly Bodh Gayā, also in modern Bihar, which continued to function as a transregional Buddhist center from the time of Aśoka until about the thirteenth century, and has regained that significance from the nineteenth century to the present). Chinese translation of Sanskrit and Pali texts obtained in India and Sri Lanka (which was often compared with the voluminous output of Christian mission presses) lasted at least until the eighth century, while Tibetan translations of Indian and Chinese texts only began in the eighth century and Mongolia only received the dispensation, from Tibet, in the sixteenth century. Many vernacular translation projects around the globe are still on-going. In addition to these formal transmissions, groups of Buddhists periodically, from the Buddha's time to the present, have moved into new regions, establishing at the grass roots their own versions of the dispensation, at least through their presence, and often with much more lasting effect.

Further complicating the picture, these transmissions did not occur according to modern geographical and sectarian boundaries. Thus there were Buddhists in the Burmese kingdoms of Thaton, Pyu, and Arakan by the fifth century, but the (Theravāda) dispensation was formally established in Bagan in the eleventh century, while the continuing presence of northern Buddhist cults and texts in this subsequently officially Theravāda Buddhist region make certain that transmissions there were more multiple still. Moreover, in all regions the fortunes of a variety of different Buddhist schools (with different transmission histories) waxed and waned vis-à-vis each other as well as non-Buddhist religious orders. And throughout the Buddhist world, especially after it was dislocated by the rise of Asian Islam and virulent "national" religions such as Hinduism in India and Confucianism in China (tenth to twelfth centuries) there occurred a process of popularizing Buddhist teachings and practices through vernacular literatures and preaching, which effectively involved transmissions to people who ostensibly had already been Buddhist for centuries. These medieval popularizers—ranging from the authors of Sinhala devotional writings to charismatic Japanese figures like Ippen, Shinran, and Nichiren—expressed motivations to increase universal access to the *dharma*, which represents the closest Buddhist approximation of missionary spirit (mostly confined to what Christians called *home mission*). Clearly, the dispensation did not become established fully formed in a single moment anywhere in the Buddhist world.

No single reason accounts for all these transmissions; scholars have suggested various factors that contributed to the spread of the dispensation. One was certainly a willingness to share the *dharma*, which has characterized the whole tradition. In the earliest Buddha biographies the Brahmanical God implores a Buddha who is not inclined to preach that he nevertheless do so "for the good of many folk," echoing the precise language the Buddha uses later in these same texts to dismiss the first sixty saints. The underlying virtue that motivates the Buddha to assent to preach is compassion (*karuṇā*), one of the four "godly states" (*brahmavihāra*) that constitutes buddhahood. Compassion is also singled out in the "great commission" passage as the reason monks should bother to preach while wandering about, and in the Aśoka legends compassion motivates the patriarch and his associates who established the dispensation abroad. Unlike missionary spirit or the desire to convert others, such compassion for others' suffering figures prominently in lists of virtues and accomplishments across the Buddhist tradition. In texts about the establishment of the dispensation, the corresponding emotion, on the part of the recipient, is pleasure (*pasāda*); in Buddhist hagiography such feelings of pleasure in Buddhist contexts prove ultimately salvific, whether in this or future lives. One of the few technical terms developed by early Buddhists that could correspond to *missionary* was *pasādaka*, or "pleaser," signaling the importance of generating this emotion on the part of those who would transmit the *dharma.*

The exercise of such compassion was facilitated by the fact that—unlike contemporary Jains and Ājīvikas—Buddhists suffered virtually no restrictions on travel; unlike contemporary Brahmans they did not have to adhere to inhibiting dietary or purificatory regimens. Coupled with the consistent attraction to Buddhist teachings and practices—perhaps in part for these reasons—evinced by an urban middle class that from the time of Aśoka onward was increasingly involved in transregional trade, these factors simply allowed Buddhists to be more mobile than their would-be competitors. Because there were also few restrictions on public preaching and no secret doctrines to be guarded, explications of the *dharma* must have occurred quite often and naturally wherever Buddhists went. The public, and no doubt publicized, support that Aśoka and subsequent Indian emperors gave the Buddhists would have increased their presence and prestige in various extra-Indic courts and cities.

In the process, what we might think of as Buddhist technologies quickly circulated across the northern (land-based) and southern (sea-based) Silk Routes. These technologies included magical and medical practices and texts (which overwhelmingly dominate the manuscript finds at archaeological sites along the northern Silk Route); meditative strategies; sociopolitical principles and organizational forms; banking and even the minting of coins; funerary rites; stone architecture and sculpture; literature and manuscript preparation; and a vernacular (*prakrit*) language that with minor modifications served as a *lingua franca* throughout South, Southeast, and Central Asia and through systematic translation intersected the east Asian *lingua franca* (Chinese). Such technologies could be adopted or participated in without any further claim upon the participant because there was no formal "conversion" requiring the renunciation of previous religious ideas and practices. The line between Buddhist and non-

Buddhist was left gray, it being unproblematic (as far as Buddhists were concerned) to continue practicing previous religions, save perhaps in terms of their unproductiveness in the Buddhist context. Those whose interest became more serious were always free to adopt the five, eight, or ten precepts of a layperson, or even to take robes. Another beneficial absence among Buddhists was exclusion based on wealth, class, caste, gender, age, or educational/professional background. These higher levels of participation involved increasingly strict disciplinary codes but still nothing approximating the nineteenth-century idea of "conversion."

As the Buddhist presence in various kingdoms grew, and sectarian identities crystallized, Buddhist historians—like their nineteenth- and twentieth-century Western counterparts—tidied up this messy history by composing the regional accounts of the establishment of the dispensation (usually attached to Aśoka legends) mentioned above. These narratives hierarchically ordered various regional Buddhists within a single sectarian framework by making the entire regional dispensation derivative of (or preparatory for) a single original transmission portrayed in the sectarian garb of the monks and nuns who composed any particular account. These accounts always involve the approbation of a paradigmatic regional king (and archaeological evidence leaves no doubt that the support of royal families and other wealthy elites did contribute to the religion's success wherever it went), thereby entailing sectarian appeals to royal power and patronage as well. On the other hand, these narratives located such regional Buddhist kingdoms and sectarian groups within the larger pan-Buddhist imperial situation and the larger universal *saṃgha* of a given period. These larger organizational structures involved their own hierarchical orderings based on highly contested interpretations of the Buddha's teachings and practices and early Buddhist history; the different accounts of the establishment of the dispensation were therefore consequential in terms of transregional political and religious diplomacy, alliance and enmity, and prestige. As late as the fifteenth century, Burmese ambassador-monks greeted Sri Lankan hosts by invoking their shared version of the Aśokan transmission legend, and even in the nineteenth-century Burmese chronicle *Sāsanavaṃsa*, new claims associating this transmission with the kingdoms of peninsular southeast Asia were advanced.

This simultaneously local and transregional significance helps explain the widespread literary and sometimes liturgical veneration of the different enlightened monks and nuns who established any particular instance of the dispensation, like Mahinda and Sanghamittā in Sri Lanka, Sona and Uttara in Burma, Madhyantika in Kashmir, Padmasambhava in Tibet, Bodhidharma in China, and Upagupta throughout the northern Buddhist world. It also helps explain why the details are so contested across the different versions. But because they were deeply connected with Buddhist identity and portrayals of exemplary saints, these stories certainly also had more specifically religious significance through the ages. Beyond the polemics and politics they also effected feelings of gratitude for the efforts made by the "pleasers" who brought the dispensation to their kingdoms, renewed commitment to practice and, at least in the case of Upagupta, hope for worldly and spiritual assistance, and would have helped cultivate that compassion for others that lies at the heart of the tradition.

MODERN BUDDHIST MISSIONS. If the term *Buddhist mission* shows up the danger in cross-cultural application of categories derived from particular religions, it also exemplifies the powerful impact that scholarly discourses can have upon the actual practice of the religions they analyze. Reared on accounts that read mission into their sacred texts and history, beleaguered by criticisms that nonmissionary Buddhism is moribund, provoked to respond to Christian missionaries, and befriended by Westerners (including Christian and Jewish converts to Buddhism, among the first Buddhist missionaries proper) who though sympathizers with the Buddhists remained deeply immersed in missionary thinking, Buddhists throughout the twentieth century (especially in Sri Lanka, Burma, Thailand, and Japan) created actual Buddhist missionary societies in the very image of what Western writers said they ought to possess.

Beginning with the founding of the Maha Bodhi Society in Sri Lanka in 1891, these organizations—now numbering in the thousands and spread throughout the world—incorporated "missionary spirit" as such into their explications of Buddhist religiosity (often based on the "great commission" passage) and declared (first at the World Parliament of Religions in Chicago in 1893) a world Buddhist mission that has witnessed considerable success in the last century, especially in the West. Simultaneously, they adopted and transformed into particularly Buddhist enterprises numerous Christian missionary strategies, such as scripture and tract publication and distribution; "Sunday school" and other youth movements like the Young Men's Buddhist Association (YMBA); revival rallies, temperance, and other social-reform movements; transregional ecumenical organization (most notably the World Fellowship of Buddhists, founded in 1956); study of foreign religions (and other schools of Buddhism) and interfaith dialogue; and the sponsorship of foreign Buddhist missions (ranging from Sri Lankan missionaries in India, Nepal, Cambodia, Vietnam, and Singapore to Japanese missionaries in Hawai'i and California).

Branch offices and full-fledged temple-monastery complexes representing a variety of Buddhist traditions have been established to serve immigrant Buddhist communities in major cities throughout the world, while simultaneously reaching out to non-Buddhists there. The twentieth century produced a vast discourse in English (and many other European and Asian languages) that is properly missiological: biographies of famous Buddhist missionaries and eulogistic histories of various Buddhist missions, treatises on Buddhist missionary strategies and calls for expansion of Buddhism based on global conversion statistics, discourse about competitor religions, missionary annuals and keepsake volumes, and missionary newspapers and websites. In addition, vernacular vocabularies have been developed; the term for *Buddhist missionary* used in southern Buddhist countries, *dharmadūta* (Skt., "emissary of the teachings," sometimes wrongly conflated with the *dhammamahāmātas* or "righteous ministers" of the Aśokan inscriptions) was first coined as a Sinhala translation of the English word in a Christian missionary dictionary, published the same year the world Buddhist mission was declared. And in the late twentieth century, Buddhist missionaries in the West even developed formal conversion ceremonies to match the expectations of converts there.

This transformation of the religion (especially in elite, Westernized Buddhist circles) as appropriate to the nineteenth- and twentieth-century missionary-dominated global context for understanding and participating in human multireligiosity reflects its unique adaptability to changing local circumstances (what has been called its "missionary tolerance"), perhaps the most important factor underlying all these instances of *dharma*-transmission. The creation of modern Buddhist missions was continuous with a long history of taking up and "Buddhicizing" non-Buddhist religious forms, ideas, and practices that truly does stretch back to the time of the Buddha himself; it has been nurtured in this case by an ability to find new meanings in the ancient Buddhist texts about preaching and hagiographies of the various "pleasers" of significance to different traditions, and by relaxing monastic discipline in contexts where specific minor rules prove unfeasible. Its results represent a modern transmission of the dispensation broader in scope even than the legendary accounts of the time of Aśoka.

See Also Aśoka; Saṃgha.

Bibliography

For all its ubiquity in Buddhological scholarship, "Buddhist mission" has actually received little direct scholarly attention. Though the details of the spread of the dispensation and later exchanges of it, in specific situations, have become increasingly well known, the idea itself has remained virtually unexamined since the 1830s. Probably the earliest use of the English term *Buddhist mission* was in George Turnour's "Examination of the Pali Buddhistical Annals," *Journal of Asiatic Society of Bengal* 7, no. 2 (1838): 687, 716–717, 1050. Prior to Jonathan S. Walters's "Rethinking Buddhist Missions," Ph.D. diss. (University of Chicago, 1992), only in one instance (C. A. F. Rhys Davids, *Outlines of Buddhism: A Historical Sketch* [London, 1938], pp. 90–96) was the construct "Buddhist mission" even questioned (Rhys Davids pointed out its inapplicability to the texts about Aśoka and its inconsistency with the utter lack of missiological literature in the premodern tradition, though she did not totally abandon the concept). But it was subsequently mentioned—and often made the underlying historical force—in virtually every English-language work on Buddhism, world religions, and especially Buddhist history published from Turnour's day up to and including the present; in this sense the bibliography on Buddhist mission nearly overlaps with the entire bibliography on Buddhism or, for that matter, "world religions."

For an important theoretical statement of the idea of Buddhist mission and the configuration of the history of religions according to the distinction of "missionary" and "nonmissionary" religions, see F. Max Müller, *On Missions: A Lecture Delivered in Westminster Abbey, on December 3, 1873* (New York, 1874). Walters's dissertation (cited above) explores the sociohistorical context in which "Buddhist mission" was invented, reviews the whole genre of nineteenth- and twentieth-century writings on the topic, and contains extended emic analyses of the "great commission" and legends of the Aśokan establishment of the dispensation. The role of Buddhist mission in the big picture of nineteenth- and twentieth-century Buddhology, and alternatives to it, are explored further in Walters's *Finding Buddhists in Global History* (Washington, D.C., 1998).

The most comprehensive and scholarly treatment of the global spread of the religion as a whole, which treats it in a specifically "missionary" framework, remains Erik Zürcher, *Buddhism: Its Origin and Spread in Words, Maps, and Pictures* (New York, 1962); on China in particular see Zürcher's *The Buddhist Conquest of China* (Leiden, 1959; reprint, 1972). There have been many similar accounts of the rise and spread of Buddhism in India and abroad, more or less consciously reproducing this framework; a classic, much-read, and still readable example of the larger genre is James Bissett Pratt, *The Pilgrimage of Buddhism and a Buddhist Pilgrimage* (New York, 1928). For a reliable scholarly review of the rise and spread of the early tradition within India, also explained as Buddhist mission, the standard source remains Étienne Lamotte, *History of Indian Buddhism, from the Origins to the Śaka Era*, translated by Sara Webb-Boin (Louvain-la-Neuve, Belgium, 1988). Egil Lothe, "Mission in Theravada Buddhism," Ph.D. diss. (University of Oslo, 1986), is an innovative attempt to read Pali scriptures about preaching for missiological insight. For more recent scholarship on the spread of the dispensation to the different Buddhist regions and their mutual exchanges (in much of which this "missionary" explanation has been abandoned or at least displaced), see the separate entries on those regional traditions and their bibliographies. Readers seeking a general introduction to the rise and extent of the pan-Buddhist world would also do well to consult Heinz Bechert and Richard Gombrich, eds., *The World of Buddhism: Buddhist Monks and Nuns in Society and Culture* (New York, 1984), a richly illustrated collection of essays on the different regions composed by eminent scholars.

For translations of early texts containing the great commission passage in its original literary frames, see C. A. F. Rhys Davids, trans., *The Book of Kindred Sayings* (*Saṃyutta-nikāya*), vol. 1, pp. 128–159 (London, 1917) (S i.103–27=*Mārasaṃyutta*); T. W. and C. A. F. Rhys Davids, trans., *Dialogues of the Buddha* (*Dīgha-nikāya*), vol. 2, pp. 1–41 (London, 1959) (*Mahāpadānasutta*=D. ii. 1–54); and I. B. Horner, trans., *The Book of the Discipline* (*Vinaya-piṭaka*), vol. 4: *Mahāvagga*, pp. 28–29 (Oxford, 1993). For texts of the legends of Aśoka and Chinese pilgrims' accounts see the separate entry on Aśoka and its bibliography. An engaging primary source for memories of Indian and central Asian *dharma*-transmitters in China is Kathryn Ann Tsai, trans., *Lives of the Nuns: Biographies of Chinese Buddhist Nuns from the Fourth to Sixth Centuries* (Honolulu, 1994). For the original text of a legend of a famous monk revered tradition-wide for success (and adventure) preaching to others, see Joel Tatelman, trans., *The Glorious Deeds of Pūrṇa: A Translation and Study of the Pūrṇāvadāna* (Surrey, U.K., 2000).

An enormous amount of primary ephemera related to modern Buddhist missions exists, but there is not yet a comprehensive scholarly account of them. The fieldwork presented in Lothe's dissertation (cited above) provides a useful entry point. A valuable collection of essays by Sri Lankan Anagārika Dharmapāla (1864–1933), the world's first Buddhist missionary proper, is Ananda Guruge, ed., *Return to Righteousness: A Collection of Speeches, Essays, and Letters of the Anagarika Dharmapala* (Colombo, Ceylon, 1965). The best documented modern Buddhist mission is to the United States; for important accounts of the establishment of the dispensation there (and in the West more generally), see Rick Fields, *How the Swans Came to the Lake: A Narrative History of Buddhism in America* (Boulder, Colo., 1981); Thomas A. Tweed, *The American Encounter with Buddhism, 1844–1912: Victorian Culture and the Limits of Dissent* (Bloomington, Ind., 1992); Stephen Batchelor, *The Awakening of the West: The Encounter of Buddhism and Western Culture* (Berkeley, 1994); Richard Hughes Seager, *Buddhism in America* (New York, 2000); and Charles S. Prebish and Martin Baumann, *Westward Dharma: Buddhism beyond Asia* (Berkeley, 2002). Paul David Numrich's *Old Wisdom in the New World: Americanization in Two Immigrant Theravada Buddhist Temples* (Knoxville, Tenn., 1996) analyzes fascinating field data on the sociology of Buddhist mission in Los Angeles and Chicago.

JONATHAN S. WALTERS (2005)

MISSIONS: CHRISTIAN MISSIONS

Mission, the extension of the church beyond its existing frontiers, has been characteristic of the Christian fellowship from its earliest beginnings. In its claim to universal relevance, the Christian church resembles the other great missionary religions, Buddhism and Islam, which are also alike in looking back to a single historic founder. "Go forth, therefore, and make all nations my disciples" (*Mt.* 28:19). It is perhaps doubtful whether Jesus of Nazareth expressed himself in precisely these terms; but there is no reason to suppose that his followers gravely misunderstood his intentions. His personal ministry was directed to Jews; but when he found among non-Jews what he recognized as adequate faith, he showed no inclination to exclude them from his fellowship.

THE EARLY FOLLOWERS OF JESUS. The earliest followers of Jesus seem to have understood the universal dimension of their faith as the fulfillment of Old Testament prophecy *(Isaiah, Zechariah),* according to which all nations would come up to Jerusalem to receive the law of the Lord in the form of the new covenant in Jesus. Two new factors reversed this original Christian understanding. The first was persecution, which led to many Christians being dispersed from Jerusalem. The second was the adventurous spirit of certain Greek-speaking Jews who crossed over a well-marked boundary and in Antioch began to proclaim the gospel to non-Jews, apparently with considerable success. This new Christian perspective was rationalized by Saul of Tarsus, also called Paul, who, believing that he had received a commission as apostle of the Gentiles, worked out a master plan for establishing Christian groups in all the main centers of the Greco-Roman world. He looked to Rome, and beyond that even to Spain, the western limit of the Mediterranean world.

So great a project was far beyond the strength of one man, but the impulse given by Paul never died. The Christian proclamation was carried out almost entirely anonymously; indeed, the names of the founders of the great churches of the Roman empire remain for the most part unrecorded. Yet this early work had surprisingly rapid success. Within a century of the death of the founder, churches came into existence in many parts of Asia Minor, in Greece, in Italy, in Egypt, almost certainly in France and Spain, and perhaps even as far away as India. To this day, the Thomas Christians in Kerala claim that their church was founded by the apostle Thomas in person.

Whence this rapid success? By around AD 100, many more Jews lived outside Palestine than within its borders. The strict monotheism of the Jewish faith, and the high moral standards inculcated by their law, had attracted many to at least a partial acceptance of the Jewish faith, and this served for some as a preparation for the Christian gospel. In that hard and often cruel world, a fellowship of people who really loved one another and cared for one another's needs clearly had attractive power. The fervent expectations of the Christians, both for the world and for the individual, must have come as a message of hope to those who had none. Jesus became known as the Savior of the world.

PERSECUTION AND STABILIZATION. The persecutions to which the early Christians were periodically exposed seem to have done little to hinder the advance of their faith. Not all Christians were being persecuted all the time, and the number of martyrs was greatly exaggerated in tradition. To be sure, there were signs of hysteria among the faithful, and some failed to stand fast. But persecution often undermined its own purpose because the courage, dignity, and charity shown by martyrs often won the allegiance and admiration of some who might otherwise have remained indifferent. This has been a recurring phenomenon through the centuries up to the great persecution in Buganda in the 1880s, and in more recent events in Germany and Russia.

The great change in the Christian situation came in 313 when Constantine made Christianity the religion of the empire at a time when its followers cannot have numbered more than about 10 percent of the population. From that time on, the resemblance between Christianity and the other missionary religions has been startlingly close. From the time of Asoka in India (third century BCE) to Sri Lanka and Thailand in 1983, Buddhism has always maintained close relations with the ruling powers. In all Muslim countries, and in all those which have come under Marxist domination, the identification of the state with religion or ideology has been undisguised and taken for granted. But since Christians claim to be followers of the Prince of Peace, close connections between interests of state and interests of religion have proved a burden and an embarrassment rather than a help. Justinian, who reigned from 527 to 565, seems to have been the first Roman emperor to accept coercion as a legitimate instrument of conversion to Christianity.

By the year 600, the Mediterranean world was almost entirely Christian, with outliers among the Goths, in the approaches to Inner Asia, in Ethiopia, and in what is now Sudan. At the end of the century, Gregory the Great (540–604) saw the importance of the world which lay north of the Alps and which was yet to be converted. Hence the pope's mission to the Angles in Kent. This was the first mission of the church to be officially organized; it paved the way for the central control over the missions which Rome exercised for many centuries.

A Long Period of Uncertainty. In the year 600, it might have seemed that the gospel was destined to carry all before it. Then suddenly everything went into reverse. In 610 an obscure prophet named Muhammad began to preach a new faith to the tribes of Arabia. By the time of his death he had given to these tribes unity, a simple demanding creed, and a sense of destiny. Only a century later, the Muslim armies were at Tours, in the very heart of France, and were repelled only by the vigor and military skill of Charles Martel (685–741). By that time the Christian churches had almost disappeared in Palestine, Syria, and Egypt, and were gravely threatened in Persia, North Africa, and large parts of Asia Minor. In 1453, the Turks succeeded in capturing Constantinople and destroying the Eastern Empire, which for a thousand years had been the bulwark of the Christian world. Many causes have been adduced for the disappearance of so many churches. Military weakness was no doubt one, but there were others as well: dissensions among Christians, the rise of national feeling in Egypt and elsewhere, and the superficiality of conversion in such areas as North Africa, where the church had failed to express Christian truth in the languages of the local people.

In this period, the wisdom of Gregory was vindicated. During the centuries between 632 and 1232, the Christian faith spread west, north, and east until the conversion of Europe was complete. There was a dark side to this advance. When at the end of the eighth century Charlemagne succeeded in conquering the long-refractory Saxons, he agreed to spare their lives on the condition that they accept baptism. It was only one of many regions in which cross and sword went together. In Scandinavia, conversion proceeded more easily. In many areas the ruler was the first to accept the faith, and this brought about a quiet revolution. Iceland seems to have been unique in accepting the faith (around 1000) by genuinely democratic methods. With the conversion of Jagiello (1383), king of the Lithuanians, conversion seems to have reached its natural term.

Monks and nuns played a creative part in the building of churches. In the remote places where they settled they introduced better methods of agriculture and new crops. They laid the foundations of literature in the languages of Europe. They gave to isolated peoples a sense of belonging to one great unity: the Catholic Church. Out of these beginnings grew the splendid cultures of medieval Europe.

Missionary activity sometimes took on the form of conflict between the old and the new. Such actions as Boniface's felling the oak of Thor at Geismar must not be misinterpreted as mere missionary vandalism. The people of that time believed that the powerful spirit who inhabited the oak would be able to take condign vengeance on any intruder, thus they expected Boniface to fall dead upon the spot. When he survived, they concluded that the god whom he preached was more powerful than their own.

The Eastern church, with its base in Constantinople, beginning with the conversion in 988 of Vladimir, grand duke of Kiev, created the great Slavonic cultures, the Christian origins of which are not disputed even by Marxist opponents of religion. These cultures survived the fall of Constantinople. During the fifteenth century, the faith was received by more remote peoples to the east and north, a process that continued until by the end of the nineteenth century it had reached the shores of the Pacific Ocean.

With the great Franciscan and Dominican movements of the thirteenth century, the missionary enterprise of the Western church looked beyond the limits of Europe; the "friars travelling abroad in the service of Christ" reached strange lands far afield. One of their most remarkable achievements was the creation of an archbishopric in Beijing; the first archbishop to fill the post, John of Monte Corvino, lived there from 1294 to 1328, greatly respected by all. But the church's hope of converting the Inner Asian peoples was frustrated by the Muslims' success in winning them to the Islamic faith. The lines of communication with Inner Asia were too tenuous, however, and in the fifteenth century the mission to China faded away. For the moment Christian expansion seemed to be at an end.

The Colonial Period. The last decade of the fifteenth century saw the discovery of America by Columbus in 1492 and the opening up of the sea route to India by Vasco da Gama in 1498. These two events changed the relationships between the nations of the world and in time gravely affected the presentation of the Christian gospel to the non-Christian world.

Roman Catholic monopoly. For two centuries the greater part of the missionary enterprise of the Western church was in the hands of the Portuguese, who, following the precedent of Muslim evangelism in Europe, expected their converts to accept Portuguese names, manners, and customs. There was, however, never total adoption of this principle. By the end of the sixteenth century, the Portuguese had on their hands three considerable blocks of Indian Christianity. In those possessions which they directly controlled, the process of Europeanization was almost complete. The Thomas Christians in Kerala and the Parava converts on the coast of Coromandel, on the other hand, declared and maintained their intention to be and to remain Indian Christians, a stance from which they have not departed in four centuries.

Moreover, in these years two notable attempts were made to adapt Christian thought to the ideas and ways of Asia. The Italian Matteo Ricci in 1601 succeeded in reaching Beijing. He and his Jesuit colleagues, by mastering the Chinese language, winning the favor of the emperor and other leaders by their skill in astronomy and other sciences, and by adapting Christian faith to Chinese ideas, were able to maintain their mission, albeit with varying fortunes, through nearly three centuries. In southern India another Italian, Roberto de Nobili, learned Tamil and Sanskrit, and in order to win over the brahmans turned himself into a brahman, and not without success. Unfortunately, in 1744 Rome condemned all such efforts at adaptation, thereby sterilizing the Roman mission for the next two hundred years.

Internationalization of missions. The Lutherans sent their first missionaries to India in 1706. In 1794 the English Baptists, represented by their great pioneer William Carey and his colleagues, set up their work in Bengal. Thus the enormous resources of the English-speaking world, followed by those of the Dutch, the Swiss, and Scandinavians, were let loose throughout the world.

From this time on, relations between the Western governments and Christian missionary forces became unimaginably complicated. On the whole, the British maintained an attitude of lofty neutrality toward missionary activity, modified by the personal interest of a number of Christian government officials. But as government financial aid became available for educational and medical programs and for other forms of service, the Christian missionaries in the forefront of such enterprises profited greatly, perhaps excessively, from the provision of such aid. On the other hand, in British India the Indian rulers prohibited all Christian propaganda in their areas; religious freedom in India was proclaimed not by the British but by the government of independent India after 1947. In northern Nigeria, the British clearly favored Islam at the expense of Christianity.

In German, Dutch, and Belgian colonies, the association of governments with missions was undesirably close. In China, because of Napoleon III's decision that all missionaries, of whatever nationality, must be in possession of French passports, Roman Catholic missions were inevitably stigmatized as dangerous and foreign. By contrast, Hudson Taylor, the director of the largest Protestant mission, instructed his missionaries that in case of trouble they were to turn not to consular authorities but to the local representatives of the Chinese governments.

A new factor emerged when the Japanese government showed itself as the great colonial power in the East. American missionaries in Korea sympathized deeply with Korean national aspirations and were opposed, though quietly and discreetly, to Japanese colonial enterprise.

Varieties of missionary enterprise. Over two centuries there has been significant diversification of missionary enterprise, including the activities of women missionaries, which indeed have been far more numerous and diverse than those of men. Almost every conceivable means of communication has been employed. Education, on the basis of the Christian conviction that all truth and all knowledge are from God, has been emphasized. Together with this priority has gone the widespread distribution of Christian literature in countless languages. Medical and social services were conceived and have been rendered by Christians, not as propaganda but as manifestations of the universal love of Christ, and they were perceived as such by many who were served. Public lectures to interested non-Christians have in many areas left deep impressions on the minds of the hearers, though debates between the adherents of different religious systems have tended more to exacerbation than to conviction. Preaching in the open air in villages and public places has made many hearers aware of the existence of alternative systems of belief. Quiet study groups, under the guidance of sympathetic Christians, have helped to clarify questions about Christian belief. Where no open propaganda has been permitted, the mere presence of loving Christians as neighbors has proved remarkably effective as witness to the faith.

The nature of conversion. No full and scientific study of the process of conversion in the non-Christian world has as yet been written. Undoubtedly in a number of cases the desire for social advancement and a better manner of life has played a powerful part. But is this a blameworthy motive in the case of those who have been subjected for centuries to ruthless oppression reinforced by religious sanction? For many, the gospel comes with promise of deliverance from the power of evil forces which are believed at all times to threaten and beleaguer the well-being of humans. For some, the gospel represents an immense simplification of religion. It has been stated that in India more people have been converted to Christianity by reading the first three chapters of *Genesis* than in any other way, for the majestic simplicity of these chapters appeals deeply to those perplexed by the complexity of Hindu mythology. Other converts, oppressed by the burden of sin, are drawn by the promise of forgiveness in Christ, so different from the inexorable law of *karman* in Hinduism. Others, conscious of moral infirmity, have come to believe that Christ can offer the inner rehabilitation which they feel they need. Yet others have been impressed by the intensity of mutual love manifest in the society of Christian believers. Varied as the process may be, in all there is a central unity. Christ himself stands at the center of everything. Only when the risen Christ is seen as friend, example, savior, and lord can genuine Christian conversion be expected to take place.

Conversion to Christ is not necessarily identical with acceptance of the church; but in the vast majority of cases this follows, though this second acceptance may prove to be more difficult than the first.

Missionary motives. For more than four centuries the Western powers have exercised a dominating influence on the destinies of the rest of the world. Since so many people, especially in Muslim countries, have identified the West with the Christian West, there has been a natural tendency to regard Christian missionary enterprise as no more than an expression of Western aggression and imperialism. How far is there any adequate basis for this equation?

Many careful studies of missionary motivation have been made. Clearly no human motives are entirely pure. But only in a minority of cases can it be shown that national and imperialistic motives have played a strong part in missionary devotion. More frequently the glory of Christ has been the central and dominant motive. Some missionaries have gone so far in identifying with those they have come to serve as to renounce their own nation and to accept naturalization in the countries they have made their own. All have accepted some measure of acculturation in new surroundings. All who have served long years in alien lands have accepted with equanimity the destiny of becoming strangers in their own homes. The number of missionary martyrs is legion, their sacrifice equaled only by the devotion of their friends in many nations around the world who have also given their lives in the service of Christ.

The Twentieth Century. When in 1910 the first World Missionary Conference was held at Edinburgh, twelve hundred delegates from all over the world (including, however, no Roman Catholic or Orthodox Christians) could look back on a century of almost unimpeded progress. Converts had been won from every form of religion. In almost every country—a notable exception being Tibet—churches had come into existence, and the process by which the foreign mission was being transformed into the independent self-governing church was well advanced.

The years which followed were marked by a number of major setbacks to Christian missionization, such as the Russian revolution and the fading of religion in many Western communities. Yet the *World Christian Encyclopedia*, edited by David B. Barrett (1982) makes it plain that the achievements of the prior seventy years had been greater than those of the preceding century. For the first time in history the possibility of a universal religion appeared a reality. Roughly one-third of the inhabitants of the world had come to call themselves Christians. The progress of Christian missions continues in almost every area of the world. In India, Christians, already the third largest religious community after Hindus and Muslims, are also the most rapidly increasing in number.

Hostile critics of the Christian enterprise have maintained that the gospel has failed to touch deeply the mind and conscience of peoples outside the West, that the Christian churches in these areas are fragile and exotic blooms that came with the colonial powers, have been dependent exclusively on foreign aid and support, and that with the disappearance of the colonial powers these churches will also disappear. The twentieth century has shown that there is no ground at all for these expectations. After the communist takeover in China (1949), it was held even by a number of Christians that "missionary Christianity" in China had no roots and that there was little if any chance of its survival. When relaxation of government control occurred in 1980, however, it was revealed that several million Chinese had remained faithful to the Christian church. Chinese Christians have made known their determination to be fully independent of every kind of foreign control and to work out for themselves a form of Christian faith which will be genuinely Chinese. Elsewhere, if all foreign support has been compulsorily withdrawn, as in Burma, the churches have simply declared their maturity and have planned for a future of self-support and radical independence. Where this has taken place, accessions to the Christian faith have been more numerous than they were in the flourishing colonial days.

Changing world order. As a world phenomenon, the Christian church has not remained unaffected by the violent changes that have taken place in the troubled modern world. During the nineteenth century the dominant nations and the churches which were dependent on them assumed that they could plant Christian missions wherever they pleased, sometimes imposing their will by force on unwilling peoples. In the twentieth century all this has changed. A number of nations (e.g., Burma, Guinea, Saudi Arabia) prohibit all religious activity by foreigners which is directed at native citizens. A number of others make it very difficult for missionaries to obtain visas or residence permits. Yet others (e.g., Nepal) admit missionaries with few restrictions, but only on condition that they engage in what the government regards as nation-building activities (such as educational or medical services). Where all access is made impossible, churches in neighboring areas fall back upon the help that can be rendered by prayer alone.

The churches have gladly accepted the claim of these nations to independence and national dignity. No case is on record of a missionary leaving his or her assignment through unwillingness to accept the changed conditions of service. Christian witnesses have desired to stay on and to become in fact what they always wanted to be—servants of those to whom they came to minister. Even in China missionaries stayed on until it became clear that there was no longer any useful service that they could render. From Burma and other areas, foreigners withdrew because they felt that their work was done, since the local churches could carry on without their aid, and that their continued presence might embarrass—and possibly endanger—their Christian friends. Some have been deported, at very short notice, for political reasons.

Anti-Western sentiments and resentments have been strong in many countries of the world since the end of the nineteenth century. Since 1947, decolonization has taken place with quite unexpected rapidity. Yet wounds remain. Some nations have desired to emancipate themselves from Western influences, but this has proved impossible. The more far-sighted leaders have seen it as their task to retain all that is valuable in the Western inheritance and at the same time to assert or to rediscover the integrity of their own national traditions.

From foreign mission to independent church. The major change in the twentieth century was the process of transfer of power from foreign mission to independent local church, a process almost complete by the end of the century in almost every country in the world. The churches in some emerging nations think that the process has not gone fast enough or far enough; that it is on the way cannot be doubted by any observer of the process of change. Where churches are still wrestling with the problems and the prejudices of the past, they may be unwilling to accept the help of foreigners. Where they have reached maturity, as in India and Korea, and are becoming aware of the immense tasks still before them, they are in many cases glad to accept the help of foreigners, provided that these are prepared to keep their proper place and to accept only such responsibilities for service or leadership as the local church may lay upon them. Nor need it be supposed that all missionaries will be from the Western world; missionary interchange among developing nations is one of the most interesting features of the contemporary situation.

The independence of churches outside Europe and North America is increasingly shown in a number of remarkable ways. One that has attracted considerable attention is the rise of African independent churches, all of which have grown out of the mission-controlled churches of the past. Some of these are unorthodox. But the great majority desire to remain part of the main lines of the Christian tradition and have yet to create for themselves a place in which to feel at home, to think out the gospel for themselves, and to decide for themselves which of the ancient traditions of Africa can be retained within the Christian structure. Many Christians, even in the mainstream churches outside the West, are rethinking their own past in the light of divine providence, expecting to find signs of the working of God no less in their own pre-Christian history than in the special history of which the Old and New Testaments are the record. Some in India, for example, have suggested that the Upanisads are the real "old testament" of the Indian Christian and should take rank at least on the same level as the Hebrew scriptures. The nature of this quest is neatly summed up in the title of a book by Raimundo Panikkar, *The Unknown Christ of Hinduism* (New York, 1981). Genuinely indigenous theology is still in its beginnings, and it has to be confessed that the reapings in this field are still rather scanty; but what there is gives promise of a richer harvest in days to come.

One reason for the Christian quest to discover Christ beyond the historical bounds of Christendom is to be found in the remarkable resuscitation in the twentieth century of the ancient non-Christian faiths. Rediscovering the treasures of their own past, non-Christians feel able to approach Christians with renewed confidence and a sense of security. The Buddhist knows himself to be in contact with the great mystery of nothingness, the Hindu to be in contact with the unchangeable mystery of infinite being, the Muslim with the mystery of the infinite exaltation of God. There need be no Christian doubt about the greatness of these religions. Christian and non-Christian alike have much to teach one another in a manner different from that of the past.

The basis of this approach is a conventional rationale of mutual respect. Through centuries millions of men and women have lived by the teachings that they have received in these various religions, and, therefore, these may not be treated as though they did not matter, even though some of their teachings may be displeasing to the adherents of other religions. So one who engages in dialogue with those of faiths other than his own must come to it in the spirit Chaucer described in the words "gladly would he learn and gladly teach." Confident in the value of what he has experienced through his own faith, the Christian is able to delight in everything that he learns from others of what is true and good and beautiful, and at the same time maintain his hope that those who have seen in their own faith what he must judge to be partial may come to find the full-orbed reality of the true, the good, and the beautiful as he himself has seen it in Jesus Christ. If mission is understood in this sense, some of the asperities of the missionary approach in the past may be mitigated.

A NEW UNDERSTANDING OF MISSION. Almost all Christians who are members of churches outside Europe and North America are conscious of belonging to a single great worldwide fellowship, regardless of the denominational label they may bear. Several, though not all, are ardent supporters of contemporary ecumenical movements for the unity and renewal of the church. But they too are almost at one in holding that reconsideration of the meaning of the term *mission* is long overdue. Those who have traveled in the lands of older Christian traditions and sensed the decay in Christian allegiance of many in these countries are inclined to think that mission should be labeled as a product intended for universal and international export. In the past, the gospel traveled across continents and oceans almost exclusively in one direction. Has not the time come to establish two-way traffic, to have the gospel travel across continents and oceans in many directions? If this is true, the word *mission* may be in need of new and contemporary definition.

SEE ALSO Christianity; Constantinianism; Ecumenical Movement; Persecution, article on Christian Experience.

BIBLIOGRAPHY

The *World Christian Encyclopedia: A Comparative Study of Churches and Religions in the Modern World, A. D. 1900–2000,* edited by David B. Barrett (Oxford, 1982), is an astonishing repertory of information about the Christian faith and all other faiths in all the countries of the world. The *Concise Dictionary of the Christian World Mission,* edited by Stephen C. Neill, Gerald H. Anderson, and John Goodwin (Nashville, 1971), gives in much more condensed form information on almost every aspect of the Christian mission. By far the most extensive survey of the whole field is K. S. Latourette's *A History of the Expansion of Christianity,* 7 vols. (New York, 1937–1945), to be supplemented by the same writer's *Christianity in a Revolutionary Age: A History of Christianity in the Nineteenth and Twentieth Centuries,* 5 vols. (New York, 1958–1963). My own *Christian Missions* (Baltimore, 1964) has gathered together information from many parts of the world.

No satisfactory history of Roman Catholic missions exists; the best so far is *Histoire universelle des missions catholiques,* 4 vols., edited by Simon Delacroix (Paris, 1956–1958). No English work on Eastern Orthodox missions can be recommended. Two works in German by Josef Glazik, *Die russisch-orthodoxe Heidenmission seit Peter dem Grossen* (Münster, 1954) and *Die Islammission der russisch-orthodoxe Kirche* (Münster, 1959), are classic.

Special studies of many areas are available. For China, K. S. Latourette's *A History of Christian Missions in China* (New York, 1929), is authoritative up to the date of publication. A reliable survey of what has been happening in China since 1948 remains to be written. My *History of Christianity in India,* 2 vols. (Cambridge, 1984–1985), provides substantial coverage. For Africa, C. P. Groves's *The Planting of Christianity in Africa,* 4 vols. (1948–1958; reprint London, 1964), is a work of patient research but is overweighted on the Protestant side.

Countless lives of Christians, Western, Eastern, and African, have been written, but almost all the older works need to be rewritten in the light of modern knowledge. As a notable example of a biography of a twentieth-century saint, mention may be made of Hugh Tinker's *The Ordeal of Love: C. F. Andrews and India* (New York, 1979). Georg Schurhammer's *Francis Xavier: His Life, His Times,* 4 vols. (Rome, 1973–1982) is a superb example of what can be achieved by intense industry continued over almost sixty years.

Peter Beyerhaus's *The Responsible Church and the Foreign Mission* (London, 1964) is a pioneer work on the transformation of a foreign mission into an independent local church. The works of Roland Allen, especially *Missionary Methods: St. Paul's or Ours?,* 6th ed. (London, 1968), let loose questionings and discussions which have continued to the present day.

On the Christian confrontation with the non-Christian religions, the World Council of Churches in Geneva has published a whole series of valuable books, under the editorship of Stanley J. Samartha. On contemporary trends in mission thinking and theology, the interconfessional and international series "Mission Trends," edited by Gerald Anderson and Thomas Stransky (Ramsey, N. J., 1974–), will be found full of up-to-date and relevant information on almost all matters related to the Christian mission.

STEPHEN C. NEILL (1987)

MITHRA. After Ahura Mazdā and together with Anāhitā, Mithra is one of the major deities of ancient Iran, one that later crossed the borders of the Iranian world to become the supreme god of a mystery religion popular throughout the Roman Empire. In the Avesta and the later Zoroastrian literature Mithra turns up frequently; indeed, an entire Avestan hymn is dedicated to him (*Yashts* 10). He was also the subject of the Mithrakāna, a great festival that took place annually in the seventh month of the Zoroastrian calendar, which was itself dedicated to him. He is known to us from many other sources: in the inscriptions of the Achaemenids, beginning with Artaxerxes II (404–359 BCE), he is mentioned and invoked together with Ahura Mazdā and Anāhitā; on the coins of the Kushan empire he is named as Mioro and is depicted as a solar deity; in Parthian and Sogdian Manichaeism he is the *tertius legatus*; in Persian Manichaeism, he appears as the *spiritus vivens*; and so forth.

Mithra is essentially a deity of light: he draws the sun with rapid horses; he is the first to reach the summit of Mount Harā, at the center of the earth, and from there watches over the entire abode of the Aryans; he shines with his own light and in the morning makes the many forms of the world visible. If his name is synonymous with the word *mithra,* meaning "contract, covenant," as Antoine Meillet (1907) suggests, his functions are not restricted to merely personifying that notion. In the Iranian world, besides being a deity of light with strong solar characteristics (which explains his identification with the Mesopotamian Shamash), Mithra has a clear significance as a warrior god. Thus, in relation to the gods of the Indo-Iranian pantheon, he is closer to Indra than to the Vedic Mitra. He also, however, has the traits of a divinity who ensures rain and prosperity and who protects cattle by providing it ample pasturage.

The cult of Mithra, together with that of Anāhitā, constitutes the principal innovation of Zoroastrianism as it evolved after Zarathushtra (Zoroaster) and represents its major compromise with ancient polytheism. It was probably Mithra's role as defender and guardian of *asha,* truth and order—the fundamental principle of earlier Indo-Iranian religion, as well as of Zoroastrianism—that redeemed him from Zarathushtra's original general condemnation of polytheism.

BIBLIOGRAPHY

Bivar, A. D. H. *The Personalities of Mithra in Archaeology and Literature.* New York, 1998.

Boyce, Mary. "On Mithra's Part in Zoroastrianism." *Bulletin of the School of Oriental and African Studies* 32 (1969): 10–34.

Boyce, Mary, and Frantz Grenet. *A History of Zoroastrianism,* vol. 3. Leiden, 1991.

de Jong, Albert. *Traditions of the Magi. Zoroastrianism in Greek and Latin Literature.* Leiden, 1997.

Dumézil, Georges. *Les dieux souverains des Indo-Européens.* Paris, 1977.

Gershevitch, Ilya, trans. and ed. *The Avestan Hymn to Mithra.* Cambridge, 1959.

Gershevitch, Ilya. "Die Sonne das Beste." In *Mithraic Studies*, edited by John R. Hinnells, vol. 1, pp. 68–89. Manchester, 1975.

Gnoli, Gherardo. "Sol Persice Mithra." In *Mysteria Mithrae*, edited by Ugo Bianchi, pp. 725–740. Leiden, 1979.

Lentz, Wolfgang. "The 'Social Functions' of the Old Iranian Mithra." In *W. B. Henning Memorial Volume*, edited by Mary Boyce and Ilya Gershevitch, pp. 245–255. London, 1970.

Meillet, Antoine. "Le dieu indo-iranien Mitra." *Journal asiatique* 10 (1907): 143–159.

Schmidt, Hanns-Peter. "Indo-Iranian Mitra Studies: The State of the Central Problem." In *Études mithriaques*, edited by Jacques Duchesne-Guillemin, pp. 345–393. Tehran and Liège, 1978.

Thieme, Paul. *Mitra and Aryaman.* New Haven, 1957.

Windischmann, Friedrich. *Mithra: Ein Beitrag zur Mythengeschichte des Orients.* Abhandlungen für die Kunde Morgenlandes, vol. 1.1. Leipzig, 1857.

GHERARDO GNOLI (1987)
Translated from Italian by Roger DeGaris

MITHRAISM. The name *Mithraism,* with its equivalents in other languages, is a modern term for a cult known, at least to Christian writers and in later antiquity, as "the mysteries of Mithras," but for which the most neutral term is "the Roman cult of Mithras." Its usual organization was based on small, exclusively male groups that gathered for sacrificial meals in honor of the originally Indo-Iranian god Mitra/Mithra/Mithras. Owing to the virtually total loss of ancient discursive accounts, almost all important aspects of the cult are more contentious. Much of what passes as received knowledge about Mithraism has little or no evidential basis.

HISTORY OF RESEARCH. The mythological compilations of the High Renaissance, particularly L. G. Giraldi's *De deis gentium* (1548), assembled virtually all the classical texts relating to the god Mithras, then identified with Helios-Apollo, but these provided no coherent account either of the god or of the Roman cult. However, a handful of inscribed reliefs from Rome and elsewhere showing Mithras stabbing a bull to death enabled antiquarians such as Martin de Smet/Smetius (c. 1525–1578) and Steven Pigge/Pighius (1520–1604) to correctly identify them. Throughout the early modern period to 1700, the key text was *Statius Thebais* 1.719f.: *Persaei sub rupibus antri—indignata sequi torquentem cornua Mithram,* "[Apollo addressed as the god] who, beneath the rocks of a Persian cave, twists the resistful horns—Mithras." The god's act in stabbing the bull to death was understood as an allegory of the Sun's role in furthering agricultural fertility; indeed the god himself was often interpreted as the Good Husbandman. This assumption that Mithras was simply another name for the Sun-god underpinned all important studies over the following two centuries; such progress as was made consisted in the description of new statues and reliefs, but much Mithraic imagery remained unintelligible, and thus prey to speculative evocation.

Given the essentially enigmatic character of the iconographical evidence, the device of allegorical interpretation could only be challenged by an appeal to history. Although Georg Zoega (1755–1809) had stressed the possible role of the Persian magi and the Cilician pirates mentioned by Plutarch, *Pompeius* 24, 631c, in transmitting the cult of Mithra from the East, a substantial effort at historicization was only possible once James Darmesteter (1849–1894) published his translation of the Iranian sacred books, the *Zend-Avesta* (1892–1893).

In 1889, inspired by the model of the Egyptian cult of Isis, the Belgian scholar Franz Cumont (1868–1947) advanced a view of the cult of Mithras as a syncretistic borrowing from Zoroastrian dualism, through the medium of Greek-speaking Iranian priests *(magousaioi)* who, he claimed, remained active in Anatolia after Alexander's conquest of the Persian Empire (336–330 BCE). Although no Iranian antecedent could be found for Mithras killing a bull (rather than Ahriman, the principle of evil; or the Saoshyant, at the end of the world), much of the iconography could, he thought, be referred to Zoroastrian precedent and thus explained. Cumont's main work (1896–1899), supported by a full archaeological inventory, provoked what would now be called a paradigm shift and continued to be the dominant account until the early 1970s. Its decline was provoked by two independent developments. First, the ever more hypothetical claims made by certain Iranists, for example Geo Widengren's (1907–1996) theories about ancient, non-Zoroastrian, Iranian religion, including the role of Aryan warrior-societies (*Männerbünde*) and supposed analogies with a Mazdakite revivalist sect, the al-Babakiyah, or Leroy A. Campbell's obsessively precise translation (1968) of every particular of Roman Mithraic imagery into Zoroastrian terms, tended to discredit the very idea of direct transmission. Second, it came to be realized that the Roman cult was much more independent of its presumed Iranian origins than Cumont allowed—by contrast with the cases of Cybele, Isis, and Iuppiter Dolichenus, for example, which were certainly maintained in the western Empire at least in part by actual Anatolian and Egyptian priests, there were traces in the West neither of the magi *(magousaioi)*, nor of a fire-cult, nor of Mithra as god of the contract. As a result, with one or two exceptions, Iranists have now abandoned Mithraism to classical archaeologists and historians of Greco-Roman religion.

Since the 1970s, research has moved in three directions, all of which emphasize in different ways the Greco-Roman character of the cult. The first, picking up a suggestion by the Swedish scholar Martin P. Nilsson that Mithraism was the invention of an unknown religious genius, starts from the assumption that it was founded in Rome or Italy in the first century CE and stresses its integration into the hierarchical social system of the Empire (Merkelbach, 1984; Clauss,

2000). Another approach has concentrated on the enigma of the bull-killing scene, and, in a reversion to Renaissance techniques of allegory, read it as a star-map, evoking either a particular season or an identification between Mithras and a constellation (Orion, Perseus, Auriga . . .) (e.g., Ulansey, 1991). A third approach has emphasized the cult's local diversity in the Roman world, employing the techniques of the "new" archaeology to establish new facts—for example, the contrast between the "Italian" sacrificial diet of at least some Mithraists in the northwest Empire (chickens, piglets) and the "Gallo-German" diet of local soldiers (mainly beef), or the probable date of particular celebrations (Martens and de Boe, 2004). Such facts have little to do with belief as traditionally understood, but emphasize instead the cult's lived ritual practice. At the same time, the archaeological evidence has greatly increased both in quantity and in quality: well over sixty Mithraic temples (modern term: *mithraeum*) were excavated between 1934 and 2004.

ORIGINS. Generally speaking, Iranists have wanted to find, like Cumont, a strong Iranian kernel, an actual pre-existing Iranian cult or myth. The main obstacle here has always been the energetic filtering of nonorthodox traditions from the Pahlavi sacred books of Zoroastrianism. Moreover it is difficult to isolate a meaningful group of distinctively Iranian features of the Roman cult. Indeed, one can list only the god's name itself, the god Areimanius, and two apparently Old Persian words, *nama* ("Hail!") and *nabarze(s)*, the latter of which is not recorded as such in Iranian sources but is found in the aristocratic personal name Nabarzanes. Moreover, if the cult had entered the Greco-Roman world from the eastern part of Anatolia (Cappadocia, Armenia Minor, Commagene), or from Parthia, one would have expected, as with Cybele, Isis, Iuppiter Dolichenus, and early Christianity, a clear pattern of evidence documenting its progress from east to west.

It is because it appears to provide such a bridge that Plutarch's statement that the Cilician "pirates" worshiped Mithra by means of special rites *(teletai)* on Mount Olympus in Lycia-Pamphylia during the late Republic (c. 67 BCE), and still did so in his own day, has to many seemed so decisively important. However to single out this cult (which is not Cilician but Lycian) is to overvalue one among several attested local cults of Mithra) in Hellenistic Anatolia simply because it happens to be found in a written text and to take for granted what needs to be demonstrated, namely that Plutarch mentions it because he already knew about "our" Mithraism. While that is not absolutely impossible in the period 110 to 120 CE, it is much more likely that Plutarch was interested in Mithra(s) for the same reason that he was interested in Isis and Osiris, namely because, as a Platonist, he welcomed the late Stoic view that foreign mythologies contained traces of the truth revealed in primitive religion. However that may be, archaeologically speaking the cult is documented only 170 to 190 years later, in the mid-Flavian/early Trajanic period, more or less simultaneously in a number of widely scattered sites, sometimes in military contexts, such as at Heddernheim/Frankfurt (Germania) and Carnuntum (Pannonia); sometimes in connection with the organized collection of tolls, such as at Novae (Moesia Inferior) and Pons Aeni (Raetia); and elsewhere again in relation to private harbour activities (Caesarea Maritima, Judaea). The earliest datable evidence from Rome, of the same period, is a statue, dedicated by a trusted, evidently rich slave of the Praetorian Prefect, of Mithras killing the bull. Such a pattern provides no clear support either to any strong Iranian thesis yet proposed nor to the more recent idea that the cult was founded in Italy; nor does the idea of a transition between a Lycian mountain-top cult and a private dining cult celebrated in pseudo-caves seem especially compelling.

Three weak Iranian scenarios have been offered, two of them emphasizing the cult's interest in astral-astrological phenomena. One of these is that a group of Stoicizing philosophers in Tarsus (Cilicia) seized upon the phenomenon of the "precession of the equinoxes" (the very gradual movement of the fixed stars around the pole of the ecliptic) supposedly discovered by Hipparchus in the late second century BCE. This group interpreted it as a "movement of the great cosmic axis," and made this into the central secret of a preexisting local cult of Mithras, now identified as the constellation Perseus (Ulansey, 1991). Each one of these claims has been hotly disputed; the thesis rests undeniably upon misunderstandings both of Hipparchus and of his ancient reception. The second scenario is that the cult emanated from the court of Commagene, which had both the requisite Irano-Hellenic culture and familiarity with astrological lore, and which was dispersed early in the Flavian period (72 CE) (Beck, 1998). By contrast, the third, quasi-Cumontian scenario focuses on the Mithraic magical gems and sees the origins of the Roman cult in the lore of Hellenized magi offering magical healing at centers of existing mystery-cults, such as Samothrake (Mastrocinque, 1998).

Whatever the merits of these suggestions, it seems intuitively more plausible to suppose that the Roman cult developed, or was created, in the late Hellenistic or early imperial period out of the debris of ancient Iranian cult in Anatolia rather than that it was a genuine esoteric development among certain pre-Sassanian Zoroastrians somehow mediated across the culture gap between the Parthian and Roman Empires. Theophoric names, such as Mithres, Mithradates, and Mithratochmes, are widespread in Anatolia; by contrast with the case of Anāhīta, no major temple of Mithra survived the conquest, and such worship of him as continued must have been mainly private and local. Yet hints of the sporadic existence of public cult have turned up in western Anatolia, including Mithras-Helios at Oenoanda (Lycia) and a tantalizing but hopelessly fragmentary link between Mithras and the magi in relation to a temple in northwest Phrygia. One possibility is that the Mithrakana, the Iranian Fall festival, which continued to be celebrated in some places, was apparently restricted to men, and involved bull-sacrifice, provided the stimulus for the invention of a private Hellenistic cult of moral self-affirmation, of the kind known from Philadelphia (Lydia), whose rules were allegedly revealed to a certain Dionysios by Zeus Eumenes around 100 BCE (Barton and Horsley, 1981).

However it is to be explained, the reappearance within the Roman cult of four themes already linked with Mithra in the Avestan Mithra-Yašt cannot be accidental: association with light, mighty strength, the bestowal of life and fortune, and knowledge of human actions. It is certainly important to remember that there is no archaeological trace of Christianity's westward progress in the first and second centuries CE, but, unlike Christianity, worshipers' relation to Mithras was to a significant degree based on vows and votive offerings, which required fixed places of worship where they could be set up. This point suggests a rapid, almost explosive, expansion in the Flavian period of one among several local Anatolian cults of Mithras, a cult which must already have been a bricolage of Iranian, Anatolian, and Hellenic themes. The scheme of the tauroctony itself is evidently borrowed from that of Nike (Victory) sacrificing, a type which experienced a marked revival in the Flavian, then in the Trajanic, period. Whether this successful cult was first practiced in Commagene, further north (Cappadocia, reduced to provincial status by Vespasian), or further west (Phrygia, Lycia) is unknown; the handful of Anatolian *mithraea* so far discovered are later and may be due to Roman influence.

THE ROMAN CULT. Two main difficulties, both exemplified in the work of Cumont (and many others), have stood in the way of an adequately historical account of Mithraism. One is the unitarian belief that evidence widely scattered in space and time could legitimately be fitted together to produce an account of a single, essentially unchanging, religion; the other is its classification as an oriental mystery-cult. The first legitimated the reading of monuments from different periods as evidence for the same unchanging reality; perhaps even more seriously, texts were treated as atemporal sources, blithely disregarding the argumentative contexts within which the supposed information occurred. The second meant that Mithraism was absorbed into a larger discourse about the originality and status of pagan religious thought, whose real subject was the priority or otherwise of the truth-claims of Christianity: the category *mystery-religion* was an invention of German Protestant historiography of the 1880s. Although the construction of typologies, for example, that of Ugo Bianchi (1979), may help to highlight major similarities and distinctions, they necessarily depend on received views and cannot respond to the implications of new discoveries, which may be considerable in the case of cults for which, as with Mithraism, the evidence is almost entirely archaeological. Moreover, it seems advisable on principle to disregard all evidence attested solely by Christian sources and wherever possible to rely on internal Mithraic evidence, such as the verse-lines from the Santa Prisca Mithraeum in Rome, circa 210 to 230 CE (Vermaseren and Van Essen, 1965).

A Weberian model would suggest a wide initial appeal crossing social boundaries, followed by consolidation within a relatively homogeneous social stratum. The evidence, such as it is, however, indicates instead a continuous expansion of social and geographical range well into the fourth century, and a gradual acceptance as a Roman cult. A list of ninety-eight members accruing to a *mithraeum* in Virunum (Noricum) over a period of some eighteen years (183–201 CE) confirms that the typical urban adherent either occupied some function within imperial or local administration, as at Poetovio (Pannonia Superior), or belonged, as at Ostia, to the more prosperous urban craft-population descended from freedmen: the great majority of *cognomina* are Latin, implying that their holders were at least second-generation citizens; there are twenty-three Greek *cognomina,* two Celtic names, and only one (private) slave. Moreover, not a single woman is listed: the repeated attempts to show that women might belong to the cult are wishful thinking (Piccottini, 1994). Recent discoveries in the northwest provinces suggest that the belief that the cult was mainly attractive to soldiers is an error based on the accident of excavation: in this area, practically every *vicus,* even some villas (large farms), now appear to have had a *mithraeum.* Nevertheless, the discovery of a late second- to early third-century *mithraeum* inside the house of the military tribunes of senatorial rank (*tribuni laticlavii*) in the permanent camp of Legio II Adiutrix at Aquincum (Pannonia Inferior) both attests to the continuation of the early association between Mithraism and the military and suggests one likely means whereby the cult eventually came to the notice of the social elite.

The early archaeological evidence in the West confirms that three fundamental features of the cult were already established on its appearance in the Roman world: Mithras's cult title as *(Deus) Sol Invictus Mithras,* "Mithras, the divine never-vanquished Sun"; the interpretation of Mithras's act of killing the bull in both a cosmological and an anthropological sense; and a highly original conception of the *mithraeum* as sacred space, ambiguous between natural cave and human construct, between temple-cella and sacrificial dining room, and between a meeting place and a coded representation of the cosmos as a whole. Although the earliest evidence for a narrative that framed and commented on the central bull-killing act is late-Antonine, parts of it must have existed long before: the earliest evidence (140–160 CE) for an initiation ritual is the representation on a krater from Mainz (Germania Superior) of a seated member of the highest grade, Pater (Father), aiming an armed bow at a cowering naked initiand, in a clear reference to Mithras's mythical act in shooting an arrow to produce a stream that gushes from a rock (Beck, 2000). This in turn suggests that one motive for representing scenes of the sacred narrative was to establish mythic charters or analogies for initiatory and other ritual events. On the other face of the Mainz vessel is the earliest surviving representation of at least three of the grades: Miles (Soldier), Pater, and Heliodromus (Messenger of the Sun), who form a procession moving to the left. The rear is taken up by a smaller, fourth figure with a raised staff, perhaps a Corax (Raven). This procession has been interpreted as a ritual reenactment within the *mithraeum* of the sun's course along the ecliptic (Beck, 2000).

All this suggests that what was initially attractive about the cult of Mithras was its integration of a distinctive (albeit generically familiar) cosmogony and cosmology with an image of a physically and morally steadfast hero, submissive to the will of the gods, a sort of Persian Herakles. One of the few genuinely internal statements we possess, from the Santa Prisca Mithraeum in Rome, runs: *Atque perlata humeris tuli[t] m[a]xima divum,* "And he has borne on his shoulders the gods' behests, to the very end" (Vermaseren and Van Essen, 1965: 204–205, line 9). Mithras offered a model, directed exclusively at men, of personal submission. This model was enforced, in evidently dramatic ways, by the humiliation, pain, and fear to which initiates were exposed, as on the Mainz vessel, and still more clearly in the podium paintings at S. Maria Capua Vetere (c. 220–240 CE) (Vermaseren, 1971).

At the same time, the death of the bull was interpreted as salvific: another (damaged) line at S. Prisca reads: *Et nos servasti . . . sanguine fuso,* "And you have saved us . . . by shedding (the) blood" (Vermaseren and Van Essen, 1965: 217–221, line 14). This salvation could be understood in different ways. In the early second century it was probably evoked primarily in the usual sense of divine protection and guidance. Salvation no doubt continued in some contexts and geographical areas always to be understood in those traditional terms. However, a generation later than the Mainz vessel, the Middle Platonist philosopher Celsus alludes (Origen, *Contra Celsum* 6.22) to an elaborate Mithraic scheme of a ladder representing the soul's ascent to the fixed stars (c. 175–180 CE). In the mid-third century the Neo-Platonist philosopher Porphyry cites a certain Euboulus for the claim that the Persian prophet Zoroaster was the first to dedicate a cave to Mithras, "creator and father of all," a cave which was artfully marked out with the symbols of the cosmos whose demiurge was Mithras (*De antro* 6); and the related claim that North and South (of the *mithraeum*) were associated with the entry and departure of souls into and out of the world (*De antro* 24). Turcan has argued that such claims represent a systematic distortion of Mithraic belief by Platonists for their own purposes (Turcan, 1975). Beck, on the other hand, has urged that Porphyry's data are to be taken at face value: the Mithraists designed and constructed their *mithraeum* as an image of the cosmos so as to be able to reenact a ritual of the descent and return of souls (Beck, 2000). The image of Mithras killing the bull is, inter alia, a representation of Mithras "seated at the equinoxes" (*De antro* 24). It is also a kind of explanatory commentary on the two central, albeit enigmatic, claims of Mithraism, that Mithras both is and is not identical with the Sun (*Deus Sol Invictus Mithras*), and that the universe is sustained by the "harmony of tension in opposition" (Beck and Gordon, 2005).

If Mithras's heroic feat of subduing and killing the bull began as a hunt, it ended as a sacrifice, the primal sacrifice, which established the terms of the asymmetrical relationship between gods and men. It also offered a distinctive myth of the origin of cosmic order and civilized life (fire, agriculture). Ethically, the cult seems to have imposed strict self-discipline (Porphyry, *De antro* 15); soteriologically, it offered the promise of a gradual, differentiated, self-identification with Mithras. For example, the bull-killing scene has rightly been seen as representing an epiphanic moment (Zwirn, 1989); the grade Leo (Lion) evidently had a mystic link with that animal, which exists simultaneously on earth and in heaven (the constellation) and appears in numerous, albeit to us unintelligible, contexts in the iconography; the Pater in the procession scene at S. Prisca is represented as the god receiving the initiates. The principal ritual means of this self-identification was the shared sacrificial meal, which alluded to that eaten by Mithras and Helios/Sol (the Sun-god) immediately after the butchery of the bull, on a couch (*kline*) covered by its skinned hide, during the course of which the gods ate the grilled *splangkna* (heart, liver) and drank pure, unmixed wine. The krater containing this wine appears together with a snake and a lion on many German reliefs, and usable reproductions of it have been found widely in *mithraea,* such as at Tienen (Belgica), where the vessel was constructed in such a manner that the heated wine and water could be poured (or sucked) through the snake's mouth. The vine itself could be given a Mithraic meaning: on a probably Syrian relief now in the Israel Museum, Mithras, who, being born from a rock, had no mother whose milk he could drink, is depicted as a baby drinking the juice extruded from bunches of grapes—the wine of the feast is the civilized version of that primitive, natural juice.

Mithraism thus constituted an elaborate, self-conscious, meritocratic form of the cult community widespread in the western Roman Empire, whose most striking feature was that, despite being supra-regional (indeed, in the northwest and northeast provinces, virtually universal), it tenaciously retained its private character, and (except in military contexts) resisted absorption by the religio-political rhetoric of public religious institutions. Its self-consciousness as a cult is epitomized by the fact that, despite the marked regional variation, individuals could and did pass from one end of the Empire to the other and find a cult of Mithras recognizably the same as that which they already knew: there are several examples of miniature reliefs suitable for packing in one's luggage and several examples of reliefs fabricated in the Danube area but found in Germany, Italy, and Israel.

Another source of self-consciousness was the sense of being a foreign cult: relatively unhampered by implication in local (politico-social) meanings, Mithraism was able constantly to reinvent itself, not least among those with intellectual pretensions. An important recourse here was astronomy-astrology; another was the Greco-Roman reception of Persia. Statius, writing in the decade 80 to 90 CE, knew already that the bull was sacrificed inside a Persian cave, and we have no reason to doubt Euboulus's statement (mid-third century) that the cult claimed to have been founded by the Persian sage Zoroaster. The systematic association that Celsus attests between planets and metals looks typical of the occultic preoccupation with (fanciful) list-making, whereas both Euboulus and a certain Pallas, cited by Porphyry, *De abstin.* 4.16, evidently tried to explain Mithraism by invoking metempsychosis and soul-journeys, beliefs which they knew to be "Persian" probably because they, or their sources, found them in pseudonymous texts purportedly by Zoroaster (the so-called Zoroastrian pseudepigrapha). At the same time there is evidence that some *mobeds* (Zoroastrian priests) in the Sassanian period did indeed believe in metempsychosis. The "Mithras Liturgy" in the Great Paris magical codex, which gives every appearance of including a mystic vision of the god, may also have been influenced by such ideas (Betz, 2003).

Mithraists themselves certainly drew upon analogous texts: the existence of a Mithraic god Areimanius, known from Rome and Aquincum, is best explained as a backformation within Roman Mithraism owed to familiarity with descriptions of Persian religion by historians such as Theopompus and philosophers such as Eudemus of Rhodes and Hermippus "the Callimachean." These accounts commonly represented Ahriman as Hades, god of the Underworld (de Jong, 1997). The Persian magi are cited in the *mithraeum* at Dura-Europos (Syria) as authority for the idea of "fiery breath," possibly in relation to the end of the world, but more probably in relation to punishment for sin. The most striking example of a reference to Iranian ideas, however, is a fresco (c. 370–380 CE) in the *mithraeum* of Hawarti/Huarte near Apamea (Syria), where a group of ghastly decapitated human and demonic heads is depicted strung along a city-wall, each pierced, like representations of the evil eye, by a spear. The simplest explanation is that they evoke the descriptions of Mithras's savage destruction of the enemies of religion, human and demonic, in the Mithra-Yašt, and that this is an example of late Mithraic borrowing—self reinvention—from authentic Sassanian Zoroastrianism. Such knowledge was probably passed through frontier cities such as Nisibis, which was ceded to the Sassanians in 363 CE, but continued even thereafter to be an important commercial and cultural bridgehead.

SEE ALSO Hellenistic Religions; Iranian Religions; Roman Religion.

BIBLIOGRAPHY

Barton, S. C., and G. H. R. Horsley. "A Hellenistic Cult-Group and the New Testament Churches." *Jahrbuch für Antike und Christentum* 24 (1981): 7–41.

Beck, Roger L. "Mithraism since Franz Cumont." In *Aufstieg und Niedergang der römischen Welt,* edited by Hildegard Temporini and Wolfgang Haase, II 17.4, 2002–2115. Berlin, 1984.

Beck, Roger L. *Planetary Gods and Planetary Orders in the Mysteries of Mithras.* Études préliminaires, 109. Leiden, 1988.

Beck, Roger L. "The Mysteries of Mithras: A New Account of Their Genesis." *Journal of Roman Studies* 88 (1998): 115–128.

Beck, Roger L. "Myth, Ritual, Doctrine, and Initiation in the Mysteries of Mithras: New Evidence from a Cult-Vessel." *Journal of Roman Studies* 90 (2000): 145–180.

Beck, Roger L., and Richard L. Gordon. *Mysteries of the Unconquered Sun: The Cult of Mithras in the Roman Empire.* Oxford, 2005.

Betz, Hans-Dieter. *The "Mithras-Liturgy": Text, Translation, and Commentary.* Tübingen, Germany, 2003.

Bianchi, Ugo. "Prolegomena: The Religio-Historical Question of the Mysteries of Mithra." In *Mysteria Mithrae,* edited by Ugo Bianchi pp. 3–47. Études préliminaires 80. Rome, 1979.

Clauss, Manfred. *Cultores Mithrae: Die Anhängerschaft des Mithras-Kultes.* Stuttgart, 1992.

Clauss, Manfred. *The Roman Cult of Mithras: The God and His Mysteries.* Edinburgh, 2000. English translation with revisions of *Mithras: Kult und Mysterien.* (1990). The most balanced introduction, with ample illustrations and an updated bibliography of English-language publications.

Cumont, Franz. *Textes et monuments relatifs aux Mystères de Mithra.* Brussels, 1896–1899. The "Conclusions" alone translated by T. J. McCormack as *The Mysteries of Mithra* (New York, 1913 and continually reprinted). Monumental, but now of only historical importance.

De Jong, Albert. *Traditions of the Magi: Zoroastrianism in Greek and Latin Literature.* Religions in the Graeco-Roman World 133. Leiden, 1997.

Martens, Marleen, and Guy de Boe, ed. *Roman Mithraism: The Evidence of the Small Finds.* Archeologie in Vlanderen, Monogr. 5. Brussels, 2004.

Mastrocinque, Attilio. *Studi sul Mitraismo (Il Mitraismo e la magia).* Rome, 1998.

Merkelbach, Reinhold. *Mithras.* Königstein, Germany, 1984. Well-illustrated, but very speculative.

Nock, Arthur Darby. "The Genius of Mithraism." *Journal of Roman Studies* 27 (1937): 108–113, reprinted in *Essays on Religion and the Ancient World,* edited by Z. Stewart, pp. 452–458. Oxford, 1972. Still well worth reading.

Piccottini, Gernot. *Mithrastempel in Virunum.* Aus Forschung und Kunst, 28. Klagenfurt, Austria, 1994.

Turcan, Robert. *Mithra et le mithriacisme.* Paris, 2000 [1981]. A concise, reliable survey, with good bibliography and excellent appendices, but under-illustrated.

Ulansey, David. *The Origins of the Mithraic Mysteries: Cosmology and Salvation in the Ancient World.* New York and Oxford, 1991 [1989]. A tendentious popular revelation of "the truth" about the cult of Mithras.

Vermaseren, Maarten J. *Corpus Inscriptionum et Monumentorum Religionis Mithriacae,* 2 vols. The Hague, 1956–1960. The fundamental catalogue of the archaeological remains, now however rather seriously out of date.

Vermaseren, Maarten J., and C.C. Van Essen. *The Excavations in the Mithraeum of the Church of S. Prisca in Rome.* Leiden, 1965.

Vermaseren, Maarten J. *Mithriaca I: The Mithraeum at S. Maria Capua Vetere.* Études préliminaires, 16.1. Leiden, Netherlands, 1971.

Widengren, Geo. "Reflections on the Origins of the Mithraic Mysteries." In *Perennitas: Studi in onore di A. Brelich*, pp. 645–668. Rome, 1980.

Zwirn, Stephen. "The Intention of Biographical Narration on Mithraic Cult-Images." *Word and Image* 5 (1989): 2–18.

RICHARD GORDON (2005)

MOABITE RELIGION. In ancient times the land of Moab comprised the narrow strip of cultivable land on the Transjordanian Plateau east of the Dead Sea, between the escarpment and the Arabian Desert. This was an area about twenty-five kilometers wide and, during its periods of greatest strength, about ninety kilometers long, stretching the length of the Dead Sea. The main Moabite plateau extended from the Wādī al-Ḥesā (the biblical river Zered) at the south end of the Dead Sea to the Wādī el-Mūjib (the biblical river Arnon) at the midpoint. The northern portion of Moab from the Wādī el-Mūjib up to around Tell Ḥesbān (biblical Heshbon), however, was historically not as secure and seems to have been open to incursion, a fact that is illustrated by the Moabite Inscription (MI), the largest preserved Moabite text. Not many details are known about Moabite history, but Moab as an independent kingdom probably arose in the last centuries of the second millennium BCE and disintegrated in the mid–first millennium BCE (that is, c. 1300–600 BCE), falling first to the Assyrians and then to subsequent conquerors.

The Moabite religion seems to have shared several features with that of other Iron Age kingdoms in the region, such as Israel, Edom, and Ammon, and all of them probably inherited much from their Bronze Age "Canaanite" predecessors. However, while it used to be commonplace to claim that all four kingdoms had their own national god (Kemosh for Moab, Yahweh for Israel, Qaws for Edom, and Milkom for Ammon), it is perhaps better to be more cautious in view of the meager evidence outside the Bible. At any rate, the MI shows that King Mesha of the Moabites worshipped a patron deity (Kemosh), in whose name Mesha conducted warfare, made sacrifices, and consecrated sanctuaries and even the peoples he had defeated (compare the biblical *ḥerem,* or "sacred ban"). The Moabite religion probably slowly disappeared as new religions such as that of the Nabateans entered the region at the end of the first millennium BCE.

SOURCES. The most important of the scarce textual sources concerning Moab and the Moabites are the Mesha Inscription (Donner and Röllig, 1966–1969) and the Hebrew Bible (Old Testament). Other relevant written evidence is preserved in a few other fragmentary Moabite inscriptions, several Moabite seals with inscribed personal names, and a handful of references to Moabite place or personal names in Assyrian and Egyptian texts. Archaeological remains have been uncovered as well; in addition to various regional surveys of the Transjordan, there are excavated sites such as Dhībān and Tell Ḥesbān to analyze.

DEITIES. Kemosh (or Chemosh) was presumably the chief deity of the Moabites, although they doubtless worshipped other gods as well. Kemosh is known from earlier times in Syria-Palestine, with the consonants *kmš* or *kmṯ* variously vocalized, having the phonological forms *kam(m)iṯ* or *kam(m)uṯ*. For instance, at Ebla in the third millennium the deity was known as Kamish (ᵈ*Ga-mi-iš* or ᵈ*Ga-me-iš*), and he played a significant role; he received sacrifices, possessed a sanctuary, and even had a month named after him. The deity may even have been the chief god of the city of Carchemish/Kār-Kamiš in northern Syria, since the very name signifies "quay or port of Kamiš." In Akkadian texts from the second millennium onward, the divine name appears as Kam(m)ush (ᵈ*Ka-am-muš* or ᵈ*Ka-mu-uš*). Alphabetic texts from fourteenth-century Ugarit preserve *kmṯ* in combination with another divine name *ẓẓ* (*ẓẓ.w kmṯ*), and the resulting compound (perhaps pronounced *Ẓiẓẓu-wa-Kamāṯu*), may or may not be related to the later Moabite deity. In Moabite texts (also written without vowels), the name is given as *kmš* and was possibly pronounced Kam(m)ash or Kam(m)ush (note the two Moabite royal names that appear in Akkadian as ᵐ*Ka-ma-aš-ḫal-ta-a* and ᵐ*Kam-mu-su-na-ad-bi*). Finally, in the Bible, the name is written once as *Kĕmîš* (*Jer.* 48:7) but otherwise as *Kĕmôš*, which has become the conventional way of pronouncing this deity's name ever since.

The meaning of the name Kemosh in its nonbiblical forms may be "conqueror, subduer," from variously an adjective (*qaṭṭil*-pattern), a causative verbal adjective *(qaṭṭul)*, or a nomen agentis *(qaṭṭāl)*, from the same root as Akkadian *kamāšu* or *kamāsu*, which means "to bow or kneel." The Masoretic pronunciation *Kemosh* (*Kĕmôš*) as it appears most often in the Bible is difficult to explain. The Greek Septuagint and Latin Vulgate versions of the Bible have instead *Khamós*/ *Chamos*, hinting that the correct vocalization of the Hebrew *Kemosh* should have been *kāmôš* from an original *kam(m)âš*. One suggestion for the Masoretic twist in pronunciation is that it was given the same vowels as *bĕʾôš*, "stench." A similar treatment was given to other divine names in the Bible; for example, Baʿal, which is sometimes rendered as *bōšet,* "shame," or the pronunciation *ʿAštōret* (ʿAshtoreth, for the goddess Astarte), whose two final vowels also reflect those of *bōšet.*

Personal names containing the element Kemosh attest to the god's popularity. The father of Mesha was possibly *kmšyt* (Kamash-yat, "Kemosh has given [a son]"). In seals, one finds among others the names *kmšyḥy* (may Kemosh live), *kmšmʾš* (Kemosh is [my] gift), *kmšʿm* (Kemosh is kin), *kmšʾl* (Kemosh is god), *kmšṣdq* (Kemosh is righteous or Kemosh has done justly), *kmšdn* (Kemosh has judged), and *kmšntn* (Kemosh has given). In Assyrian texts recording tributes from Moab, one also finds royal names with *kmš*: Kamush-nadbi (ᵐ*Kam-mu-su-na-ad-bi*, "Kemosh is my abundance"), Kamash-ḫalta (ᵐ*Ka-ma-as-ḫal-ta-a*, "Kemosh is strength").

Characteristics of Kemosh. In the MI, Kemosh is portrayed as a god of war who delivers his people, the Moabites, up to their enemies when he is angry and then "delivers" them and "returns" their land. Scholars as far back as Eusebius (c. 260–330 CE) have equated Kemosh with the Greek god of war, Ares, based especially on the fact that there was a town named Areopolis in the center of the Moabite region (although this may be a folk etymology). The so-called Shīḥān Warrior Stele, with its javelin-wielding figure, has also been interpreted as depicting a warrior deity, perhaps Kemosh.

Also in the MI, Kemosh accepts the consecration of the massacred populace under the name "ʿAshtar-Kemosh" (*ʿštr.kmš*, MI, line 17). The "ʿAshtar" element is most likely the name of a well-known West Semitic astral deity ʿAshtar/ʿAthtar, combined with Kemosh in a compound name, as is not uncommon with West Semitic divine names (see above *ẓẓ.w kmṯ* at Ugarit). Another less likely option is that the name is that of Kemosh's consort, a goddess—for example, the goddess Ishtar or Astarte. However, in West Semitic the goddess's name should have a final *-t*, and the compound should thus have more likely been spelled *ʿštrt.kmš*. At any rate, the basis for the association of Kemosh with ʿAshtar is unknown, as the compound only appears in this single inscription.

In the Bible, the name Kemosh appears eight times (*Nm.* 21:29; *Jgs.* 11:24; *1 Kgs.* 11:7, 33; *2 Kgs.* 23:13; and *Jer.* 48:7, 13, 46), and Kemosh is said to be the god of the Moabites or, as in *Judges* 11:24, the god of the Ammonites.

Since Kemosh was worshipped throughout Syria-Palestine, one may also look to non-Moabite sources for relevant information. For instance, Kemosh may well have had a chthonic nature. In a Middle Assyrian copy of a Mesopotamian god list (*Cuneiform texts from Babylonian tablets in the British Museum* 24, 36:66), the Akkadian name ᵈ*Ka-am-muš* is equated with Nergal (god of war, death, and the netherworld). In a Mesopotamian lexical list, Kamush (ᵈ*Ka-mu-uš* or ᵈ*Ka-muš*) appears as one of several possible readings of the Sumerogram GUD, which sometimes stands for Akkadian *eṭemmu*, "ghost, spirit" (Ea IV 142 = *Materials for the Sumerian Lexicon*, vol. 14, p. 361). In three Ugaritic invocations of gods (*KTU* 1.100:36; 1.107:41'; and 1.123:5 —the last two are incantations against serpent bites), there is a deity with a double divine name that may refer to Kemosh: *ẓẓ.w kmṯ* (*Ẓizzu-wa-Kamāṯu*). The *ẓẓ* element perhaps means "mud, clay" (compare Akkadian *ṭīṭu*, Hebrew *ṭîṭ*), a substance that in ancient Near Eastern texts is often said to be abundant in the netherworld. The location of the main cult place of *ẓẓ.w kmṯ* is said to be *ḫryt(h)* (see *KTU* 1.100:36), perhaps one of the two or three towns known by the name Hurriya in Syria and northern Mesopotamia.

Other Moabite Deities. On the basis of Moabite place and personal names, it is possible to perhaps identify other deities in addition to Kemosh that were known or worshipped by the Moabites. The several occurrences of Baʿal (*bʿl*) as a theophoric element in personal names (e.g., *bʿlntn*, "Baʿal has given") and in place names (Baʿal-peʿor, Bamoth-baʿal, Baʿal-meʿon) might mean one of two things: either they indicate that the deity Baʿal was worshipped by Moabites or else the word *baʿal* was used to mean merely "lord" and could have referred to Kemosh himself. There are also combinations with ʾEl in Moabite personal names, as in *mšpṭʾl* or Mishpaṭʾel, "El (or the god) is justice." However, in these cases as well one does not know if the Canaanite deity ʾEl is meant or simply the generic definition "god." The Moabite place name Nebo in the MI (*nbh*) and the Bible may indicate that the Mesopotamian god Nabu was worshipped. The name Shalamanu (*Sa-la-ma-nu*) for a Moabite king in a Tiglat-Pileser tribute list may attest to worship of the god Shalman, and other Moabite personal names in published seals may perhaps attest to the knowledge of further deities in Moab. The name of the god Ḥoron may appear in the place name Ḥawronen (*ḥwrnn*) in the Mesha Inscription (line 32, compare the biblical *Ḥōrōnayim, Jer.* 48:34). Ḥoron was known as a deity of magic and exorcism in especially Ugaritic and Egyptian texts. Finally, the Bālūʿa stele bears iconographic witness to what is probably a god and goddess in front of a worshipper. The stele, which has Egyptianizing artistic elements, may or may not reflect Kemosh and a female consort.

Sanctuaries or Temples. According to the MI, King Mesha built a "high place" (*bmt*, compare the Hebrew *bāmāh*) for Kemosh at Qarḥoh (perhaps a name for the acropolis or royal quarter of the city of Dibon, modern Dhībân). In another inscription also found at Dhībân, a sanctuary is mentioned that may have been devoted to Kemosh too (only the *k* of the god's name is preserved). Excavations at Dhībân in 1955 suggested that the Iron Age II structure in Section L was the palace complex of Mesha, on the east side of which there may have been a sanctuary. In this vicinity a terra-cotta incense stand was found along with two female figurines. The fact that there was a Nabataean-Roman temple built much later on that site may indicate a continuous sacred tradition. There may also have been a sanctuary of Kemosh in Kir-hareseth (modern Kerak), and the Bible retains a tradition that Solomon made a high place to Kemosh at Jerusalem (*1 Kgs.* 11:7–8; *2 Kgs.* 23:13).

Cultic Practices. Information about sacrifices and rituals is scarce. In the Bible, however, Moabites are said to make sacrifices (presumably to Baʿal) in *Numbers* 22:40–23:30 and to make sacrifices and burn incense in *Jeremiah* 48:35. *Numbers* 25:1–5 mentions sacrifices again as well as orgiastic practices carried out by Israelites with Moabite women in honor of Baʿal of Peʿor. Most shockingly of all, in *2 Kings* 3:4–27 the Moabite king Mesha is said to offer a human sacrifice. On this occasion, a campaign of King Jehoram of Israel (son of Ahaziah, son of Ahab) against Mesha ends with a siege at Kir-hareseth, the city in which Mesha had taken refuge. The Israelites are said to have withdrawn after Mesha sacrificed his oldest son on the city wall. Although one may doubt whether or not this story reflects merely a pejorative tradition about the practices of Israelite enemies, there are other clues that suggest at least the possibility that the Transjordanian peoples were acquainted with human or child sacrifice. One notes that the Deir ʿAllā inscriptions from the mid-eighth century BCE, which relate to a certain prophet Balaam (compare the biblical non-Israelite prophet of the same name in *Nm.* 22–24), have several key words that might indicate child sacrifice was practiced in the region (e.g., *nqr* "sprout" or "scion" for a human sacrificial victim, *mlk* as the word for a kind of offering). In fact, child sacrifice constitutes a highly debated topic in modern scholarship concerning the Phoenician and Punic world.

PRIESTS AND PROPHETS. *Jeremiah* 48:7 refers to priests of Kemosh, but evidence for other cultic practitioners is unknown. It has been suggested that line 32 in the MI, "Kemosh said to me, 'Go down, fight against Ḥawronen,'" indicates divination of some sort, requiring a prophet or the like to obtain an oracle or vision from the deity. The hiring of Balaam by King Balak of Moab to curse the Israelites in *Numbers* 22–24 perhaps also indicates that the Moabites used seers and diviners.

SACRED WARFARE AND DIVINE INTERVENTION. In the MI, King Mesha says he dedicated to Kemosh the Israelite inhabitants of the cities ʿAṭaroth and Nebo. The idea of sacred battles and a consecrated massacre of peoples (including men, women, and children) is shared with the Hebrew Bible's theological accounts of the Israelite conquest of Canaan, in which Yahweh is said to demand such a destruction (with use of the root *ḥrm* in, for example, *Dt.* 7:2, 20:16–17; *Jos.* 6:17–19, 21; *1 Sm.* 15:3; compare line 17 of the MI). In fact, the MI can actually be seen as a religious document that has the same theological tone and envisions the same divine involvement in human affairs as the Hebrew Bible.

AFTERLIFE. There is no textual evidence for Moabite beliefs in an afterlife. However, the Iron Age II rock-cut tombs at Dhībân from around the time of Mesha contain mortuary goods such as pottery, jewelry, and at least one anthropoid clay coffin, suggesting a Moabite concern for proper burial with an eye to needs in the afterlife. There has also been some speculation that since Kemosh was perhaps associated with the gods of the netherworld, Moabites might have believed in some form of continued existence after death.

BIBLIOGRAPHY

An important modern body of studies on the MI and Moab is Andrew Dearman, ed., *Studies in the Mesha Inscription and Moab* (Atlanta, 1989); see especially Gerald L. Mattingly's "Moabite Religion," pp. 211–238. Other studies include A. H. van Zyl, *The Moabites* (Leiden, Netherlands, 1960); Herbert Donner and Wolfgang Röllig, *Kanaanäische und aramäische Inschriften, I-III,* 2d ed., no. 181 (Wiesbaden, Germany, 1966–1969); H. P. Müller, "Chemosh," in *Dictionary of Deities and Demons in the Bible,* 2d ed., edited by Karel van der Toorn, Bob Becking, and Pieter W. van der Horst, pp. 186–189 (Leiden, Netherlands, 1999); H. P. Müller, "Die Inschrift des Königs Mesa von Moab,"in *Texte aus der Umwelt des Alten Testaments* I/6, edited by O. Kaiser, pp. 646–650 (Gütersloh, Germany, 1985); U. Worschech, "Der Gott Kemosch: Versuch einer Characterisierung," *Ugarit Forschung* 24 (1992): 393–401; U. Worschech, "Pferd, Göttin, und Stier: Funde zur moabistischen Religion aus el-Bālūʿ (Jordanien)," *Ugarit Forschung* 24 (1992): 385–391; Jo Ann Hackett, "Religious Traditions in Israelite Transjordan," in *Ancient Israelite Religion: Essays in Honor of Frank Moore Cross,* ed. Patrick D. Miller et al., pp. 125–136 (Philadelphia, 1987); W. Lambert, "Kammuš," *Reallexikon der Assyriologie,* vol. 5 (Berlin, 1976–1980), p. 335. For the Ugaritic texts *(KTU),* see now Manfried Dietrich, Oswald Loretz, and Joaquín Sanmartín, *The Cuneiform Alphabetic Texts from Ugarit, Ras Ibn Hani, and Other Places (KTU)* (Münster, Germany, 1995), 2d ed. of *Die keilalphabetischen Texte aus Ugarit* (Neunkirchen, Austria, 1976).

Archaeological studies include Nelson Glueck, *The Other Side of the Jordan,* rev. ed. (Winona Lake, Ind., 1970); Rudolph Henry Dornemann, *The Archaeology of the Transjordan in the Bronze and Iron Ages* (Milwaukee, Wis., 1983); A. D. Tushingham, *Excavations at Dhiban in Moab* (Cambridge, Mass., 1972); and Piotr Bienkowski, ed., *Early Edom and Moab: The Beginning of the Iron Age in Southern Jordan* (Sheffield, U.K., 1992). For additional translation sources, see the *Cuneiform Texts from Babylonian Tablets in the British Museum* 24 (1896–): 36–66, and Benno Landsberger's *Materials for the Sumerian Lexicon* 14 (1937–1985): 361.

TAWNY L. HOLM (2005)

MODERNISM

This entry consists of the following articles:

ISLAMIC MODERNISM
CHRISTIAN MODERNISM

MODERNISM: ISLAMIC MODERNISM

As is the case with a number of other Islamic discourses, it can be hard to locate the precise boundary of Islamic modernism. Few Muslims explicitly self-identify as "Muslim modernists," instead referring to themselves simply as Muslims, Muslims involved in the process of reform and renewal, Muslims committed to democracy, or even Muslims intent on reviving the original spirit of Islam. In this essay, Islamic modernism is defined as those discourses of Islamic thought and practice in the last two centuries in which modernity itself is seen as a viable category to be engaged and drawn upon, not merely dismissed or used as a foil to define oneself against. In other words, advocates of Islamic modernism are not simply modern Muslims but those Muslims who see something (if not all) of modernity as a constitutive element of their worldview and practice.

As is the case with other intellectual and religious traditions, Islamic engagements with modernity have been neither static nor uniform. Traditions ranging from the revivalism of the eighteenth and nineteenth centuries to the rationalizing and Salafī tendencies of the early twentieth century, as well as liberal movements of the twentieth century onto the progressive Muslim movement of the twenty-first century, can all be discussed under the broad parameter of Islamic modernism. At times, it has been difficult to locate the boundary between Islamic modernists and some nineteenth- and early twentieth-century Salafī thinkers. While both advocated fresh interpretations of the Qurʾān, the modernists tended to engage modernity explicitly, while many Salafīs couched their language in terms of the "righteous forefathers" (*al-salaf al-salih*), the generation of Muslims living with and immediately after the Prophet Muḥammad in the seventh century. As the Salafī movement has become more intertwined with Wahhabism in the later half of the twentieth century, the overlap between modernists and Salafīs has greatly been reduced.

The discourse of modernity itself has not stayed static, as it has come under severe critique and contestation from feminists, environmentalists, Marxists, subalterns, and others. As the discourse of modernity continues to change, so do the Muslims' engagement with modernity.

There has also been a long-running tendency among Western journalists and even some scholars to look at the more conservative articulations of Islam (such as those of some traditional religious scholars) and even Muslim extremists as somehow representing "real" Islam. Subsequently, these same sources have not adequately engaged Muslim modernists, who are unfairly dismissed as lacking a constituency or influence. Even more problematic is the view that any explicit reimagination of Islam is no longer proper Islam. Lord Cromer, the British high commissioner in colonized Egypt, once said: "Islam reformed is Islam no longer." That attitude misses out on the vigorous and dynamic debates that are going on within not only modernist circles but also much wider segments of Muslim societies.

WESTERNIZATION AND ISLAMIC PARADIGMS. Part of the difficulty in establishing the proper boundaries of Islamic modernism has to do with the way that the legacy of Islamic thought in the modern era is conceived. Many Western scholars (such as Bernard Lewis and others) have seen modernity as the exclusive offspring of the West. As a result, they approach any other civilization that engages modernity through the lens of "westernization." There is no doubt that the encounter with Western institutions and thought has had a profound impact on Islamic modernism both positively (emphasis on human rights, constitutional forms of government, adoption of science, etc.) and negatively (colonialism, support for autocratic regimes). At the same time, many of the issues that Islamic modernism engages today, such as human rights, democracy, gender equality, and the like, are truly seen as universal struggles. Furthermore, most Muslims who engage these issues frame their own discourse not as a borrowing or "influence" from Western discourses but rather as a part of indigenous Islamic interpretations. Positioning the Muslims' struggles in these universal arenas as perpetually derivative vis-à-vis Western paradigms robs them of their own legitimacy and dynamism.

The above debate is also related to when one begins the history of Islamic modernism. The older paradigm that viewed Islamic thought as being hopelessly stagnated before being jolted into a renaissance by its interaction with European colonialism is now critiqued by many scholars. Without diminishing the profound experience of responding to the shock, inspiration, and violation of the colonial experience, it is also important to realize that some of Islamic modernism also taps into important reform traditions such as Shāh Walī Allāh of Delhi (d. 1762) and many others that predate the full-blown experience of colonialism.

Many Muslim modernists have readily acknowledged their interactions with Western models, institutions, and figures. At the same time they have been careful to cast their movement in decidedly Islamic terms. Perhaps the most common strategy for presenting modernism as an indigenously and authentically Islamic movement is through the framework of *ijtihād. Ijtihād* initially had a narrower meaning, referring to the process whereby Muslim jurists would arrive at rulings for unprecedented cases. Modernists have gradually expanded the definition of *ijtihād* to mean critical, independent reasoning in all domains of thought. In other words, the proper domain of *ijtihād* was taken to be not just Islamic law but rather all aspects of thought. In an egalitarian move, modernists often hold that it is not just jurists but all Muslims who have the responsibility to carry on *ijtihād.* The majority of Islamic modernist writers emphasize the need for *ijtihād,* often juxtaposing it polemically against *taqlīd.* As with *ijtihād,* modernists often came to reinterpret *taqlīd. Taqlīd* had originally meant simply following a school of Islamic law, or a designated authority (*marjaʿ*) in the case of Shīʿī Muslims. For modernists, who wished to highlight independent critical reasoning, *taqlīd* came to mean blind imitationism, becoming a symbol of everything they held to be wrong with Islamic thought.

Like many other Muslims, modernists have also cast their own struggles as perpetuating the spirit of the Qurʾān and the teachings of the Prophet Muḥammad. Modernists often insist that the egalitarian spirit of the Qurʾān in areas ranging from women's rights to religious pluralism should take precedence over more conservative later rulings. The distinction between essence and manifestation (universals and particulars, or other similar dichotomies) is a common motif in the history of modern religious thought. Many modernists also argue for a situated and contextualized reading of the Qurʾanic revelations.

Modernists find Qurʾanic precedence for their own critique of tradition-embedded injustice by pointing to Qurʾanic voices (such as Abraham and Muḥammad) who challenged their own community, which had insisted on continuing "the ways of the forefathers." In appealing to prophetic legitimization, many modernists have recorded the conversation between Prophet Muḥammad and a companion named Muʿādh ibn Jabal (d. 627). Muʿādh stated that if he found no explicit guidance in the Qurʾān or the prophetic *sunnah*, he would rely upon his own independent reasoning. While the systematic nature of this anecdote may well belie a later juridical desire to legitimize their own methodology, it has served as a powerful tool for modernists to sanctify their own appeal to *ijtihād*.

Modernists also tapped into other traditions of Islamic legitimacy that predated the encounter with Europe. One of their most powerful means of legitimizing themselves was by adopting the title of "renewer" *(mujaddid)*, which recalled a statement attributed to the Prophet Muḥammad: "God sends to this nation at the beginning of every century someone who renews its religion." In doing so, modernists could lay claim to carrying the mantle of Islamic renewal, following established masters such as Abū Ḥāmid al-Ghazālī (1058–1111) whose *Iḥyā' ʿ ulūm al-dīn* (*Revivification of Religious Sciences*) had explicitly evoked the theme of rejuvenation and renewal after death and stagnation.

RELIGIOUS AUTHORITY. The crisis of contemporary Islam is inseparable from the struggle over defining Islam and the concomitant question of who gets to define Islam, using what sources and which methodologies. The question of authority in Islam is today—and has always been—a contested one. It has often been noted that there is no formal church structure in Islam, thus making the base of religious authority more fluid. However, the lack of a formal structure of authority does not mean that there is *no* religious authority in Islam. Competing groups of Muslims claim authority for themselves by appealing to religious language and symbols. Foremost among them have been the religious scholars (*ʿulamā'*) and the mystics (Ṣūfīs) of Islam. However, Sufism is a contested category today, and many in the Muslim community who gravitate towards Salafism view Ṣūfīs with skepticism. For example, the mainstream Muslim organizations in the United States, such as the Islamic Society of North America (ISNA) and the Islamic Circle of North America (ICNA), avoid almost all mention of Sufism (and also Shiism). Ismāʿīlīs, particularly those under the leadership of the Aga Khan, are arguably the most cosmopolitan and modernity accommodating of Muslims, yet they too are seen by some conservative Sunnī Muslims as suspect.

The majority of Muslims turn to the *ʿulamā'*, religious scholars, for religious guidance. However, many *ʿulamā'* today are ill equipped to handle the more sophisticated aspects of modernity. Traditional *madrasah* institutions in many Muslim-majority countries no longer offer the highest level of critical thought. Whereas these institutions historically attracted the brightest minds in the community, today they are often a haven for those who have been unable to gain admittance to more lucrative medicine, engineering, and computer science programs. By and large, there are very few *madrasahs* for the training of *ʿulamā'* in a curriculum that takes modernity in the sense of engagements with modern philosophy, sciences, politics, economics, and the like seriously. Ironically, while it is precisely modernist Muslims who are often best suited to handle those decidedly modern parameters, many community members view the same scholars with some skepticism because modernists are not usually products of the *madrasah* system. This skepticism of the community members reveals a great deal about the presuppositions of many contemporary Muslims regarding the "purity" of Islamic knowledge and how it may be "contaminated" by Western training. Ironically, this compartmentalized view of knowledge contradicts both medieval philosophical notions and certain contemporary rigorous interpretations of Islam. As early as the ninth century, the philosopher al-Kindī had stated: "We should not be ashamed to acknowledge truth and to assimilate it from whatever source it comes to us, even if it is brought to us by former generations and foreign peoples." This epistemological pluralism is also echoed in the works of the Iranian modernist intellectual ʿAbd al-Karim Soroush, who states: "I believe that truths everywhere are compatible; no truth clashes with any other truth. . . . Thus, in my search for the truth, I became oblivious to whether an idea originated in the East, or West, or whether it had ancient or modern origins."

The vision of Islam espoused by many modernists is a more liberal, inclusive, humanistic, and even secular interpretation of Islam that is greatly distrustful of Islamist political discourses. By "secular" what is intended is a model of social relations in which the boundaries between religious discourse and political legitimacy are not collapsed, not one in which one would seek an exile of the religious from all of the public domain. The modernists' suspicion of models of government that base themselves on Islamic discourses often provides their critics with ammunition to accuse them of laxness of religious practice. Whether it is warranted or not, modernists have often been perceived as being less observant than their conservative coreligionists.

THE TWENTIETH CENTURY. One of the characteristics of the modernist movement in the twentieth century was its transregional, translinguistic, and transnational character. While figures such as ʿAbduh and Rida worked in Egypt, others such as Sayyīd Aḥmad Khān, Muḥammad Iqbal, and Fazlur Rahman hailed from South Asia. Figures such as Jamāl al-Dīn al-Afghānī moved with seeming ease from Iran and Afghanistan to the Ottoman Empire. One could mention other well-known figures such as the Malaysian Chandra Muzaffar, Indonesians Aḥmad Ḥassan and Nurcholish Madjid, the Algerian/French Mohamed Arkoun, and American Amina Wadud to give a sense of its global reach.

Still, moving toward and into the twentieth century, a few Islamic modernists stood out above the rest. Almost all later modernists engaged the following figures explicitly or implicitly.

Jamāl al-Dīn al-Afghānī (1838–1897). Along with his disciple ʿAbduh, al-Afghānī is seen as the most important of the nineteenth-century Muslim modernists. When in the Sunnī Arab world, he adopted the name Afghānī to distance himself from his Iranian Shīʿī heritage. He was instrumental in arguing for a vision of Islam that adopted modern sciences. He is a good example of the ambiguity many modernists have vis-à-vis realpolitik, now supporting the British imperial forces, now opposing them.

Muhammad ʿAbduh (1849–1905). Along with al-Afghānī, he published the highly influential *al-ʿUrwa al-wuthqa* (*The Firmest Handle*), a title that harkens back to Qurʾān 2:256. Initially exiled from Egypt, ʿAbduh eventually returned to head al-Azhar. Generally considered the most influential of the nineteenth-century Muslim modernists in terms of his impact on later thinkers, ʿAbduh was responsible for many reforms in the educational system.

Rashid Rida (1865–1935). Rida was a link between ʿAbduh and twentieth-century modernists. His *al-Manar* was one of the most important means for disseminating modernist ideas. He too talked explicitly about the need for renewal (*tajdīd*) and renewing (*tajaddud*), connecting it back to the aforementioned *ḥadīth* that God sends a renewer (*mujaddid*) at the beginning of every century.

Muḥammad Iqbāl (1877–1938). Iqbal is widely credited for having been the philosophical inspiration behind the creation of the state of Pakistan. One of the few Islamic modernists with serious interest in poetry and mysticism, he is remembered for having argued for the importance of dynamism in Islamic thought. His widely influential *The Reconstruction of Religious Thought in Islam* simultaneously harkens back to Abū Ḥāmid al-Ghazālī as it pushes the discourse into the twentieth century.

Fazlur Rahman (1919–1988). A British-trained scholar of Islam, he highlighted the importance of educational systems in the reinvigoration of Islam. For the last twenty years of his life he taught at the University of Chicago, beginning a long legacy of exiled Muslim intellectuals who took up teaching posts in Europe and North America. A fierce critic of fundamentalism, Rahman is usually acknowledged as the doyen of Islamic modernism in the latter half of twentieth century. Unlike many modernists, Rahman was profoundly steeped in the tradition of Islamic philosophy, especially that of Mullā Ṣadrā (d. 1632).

PROGRESSIVE ISLAM. The most significant development in modernist Islamic thought in the last generation has been the various understandings of Islam that go under the rubric of "progressive Islam." Fully immersed in postmodern critiques of modernity, progressive Islam both continues and radically departs from the 150-year-old tradition of liberal Islam. Many nineteenth- and early twentieth-century modernists generally displayed an uncritical, almost devotional, identification with modernity and often (though not always) bypassed discussion of colonialism and imperialism. Progressive understandings of Islam, on the other hand, are almost uniformly critical of colonialism, both in its nineteenth-century manifestation and in its current variety. Progressive Muslims develop a critical and nonapologetic "multiple critique" with respect to both Islam and modernity. That double engagement with the varieties of Islam and modernity, plus an emphasis on concrete social action and transformation, is the defining characteristic of progressive Islam today.

Unlike their liberal Muslim forefathers (who usually were fore*fathers*), progressive Muslims represent a broad coalition of female and male Muslim activists and intellectuals. One of the distinguishing features of the progressive Muslim movement as the vanguard of Islamic (post)modernism has been the high level of female participation and leadership. This is particularly the case in Western countries, where a majority of Muslims who self-identify as progressive are female. The majority of progressive Muslims also highlight women's rights as part of a broader engagement with human rights.

Progressives measure their success not in developing new and beatific theologies but rather by the amount of change for good on the ground level that they can produce in Muslim and non-Muslim societies. As Safi and a number of other prominent authors noted in the volume *Progressive Muslims: On Justice, Gender, and Pluralism* (2003), this movement is noted by a number of themes: striving to realize a just and pluralistic society through critically engaging Islam, a relentless pursuit of social justice, an emphasis on gender equality as a foundation of human rights, a vision of religious and ethnic pluralism, and a methodology of nonviolent resistance.

Muslim libera(c)tion. Progressive Muslims perceive of themselves as the advocates of human beings all over this world who through no fault of their own live in situations of perpetual poverty, pollution, oppression, and marginalization. A prominent concern of progressive Muslims is the suffering and poverty, as well as the full humanity, of these marginalized and oppressed human beings of all backgrounds who are called *mustadʿafūn* in the Qurʾanic context. The task of progressives in this context is to give voice to the voiceless, power to the powerless, and confront the "powers that be" who disregard the God-given human dignity of the *mustadʿafūn* all over this earth. Muslim progressives draw on the strong tradition of social justice from within Islam from sources as diverse as Qurʾān and *ḥadīth* (statements of the Prophet Muḥammad) to more recent spokespersons such as ʿAlī Sharīʿatī. The Qurʾān itself specifically links fighting in the cause of God (*Sabīl Allāh*) to the cause of *mustadʿafūn.*

The methodological fluidity of progressive Muslims is apparent in their pluralistic epistemology, which freely and openly draws from sources outside of Islamic tradition, so long as they serve as useful tools in a global pursuit of justice. These external sources include the liberation theology of Leonardo Boff, Gustavo Gutiérrez, and Rebecca Chopp, as well as the secular humanism of Edward Said, Noam Chomsky, and others. Progressive Muslims are likely to combine a Qurʾanic call for serving as "witnesses for God in justice" (Qurʾān 42:15) with the task of a social critic to "speak truth to the powers."

As is the case with many feminists and African-American scholar-activists, progressives do not accept the dichotomy between intellectual pursuit and activism. Whereas many (though not all) of the previous generations of modernist Muslims were at times defined by a purely academic approach that reflected their elite status, progressive Muslims realize that the social injustices around them are reflected in, connected to, and justified in terms of intellectual discourses. They are, in this respect, fully indebted to the majestic criticism of Edward Said. A progressive commitment implies by necessity the willingness to remain engaged with the issues of social justice as they unfold on the ground level, in the lived realities of Muslim and non-Muslim communities.

Progressive Muslims follow squarely in the footsteps of liberation theologians such as Leonardo Boff, who in his *Introducing Liberation Theology* deemed a purely conceptual criticism of theology devoid of real commitment of the oppressed as "radically irrelevant." Boff recognized that *liberação* (liberation) links together the concepts of *liber* ("free") and *ação* ("action"): there is no liberation without action. The aforementioned *Progressive Muslims* (Safi, 2003) volume states: "Vision and activism are both necessary. Activism without vision is doomed from the start. Vision without activism quickly becomes irrelevant" (pp. 6–7).

This informed social activism is visible in the many progressive Muslims organizations and movements, ranging from the work of Chandra Muzaffar with the International Movement for a Just World in Malaysia, the efforts of Farid Esack with HIV-positive Muslims in South Africa, and the work of the 2003 Nobel Peace Prize winner, Shirin Ebadi, with groups such as the Iranian Children's Rights Society. Progressive Muslims are involved in an astonishing array of peace and social justice movements, grassroots organizations, human rights efforts, and the like.

Toward an Islamic humanism. At the heart of a progressive Muslim interpretation is a simple yet radical idea: every human life, female and male, Muslim and non-Muslim, rich or poor, "northern" or "southern," has exactly the same intrinsic worth. The essential value of human life is God given and is in no way connected to culture, geography, or privilege. A progressive Muslim agenda is concerned with the ramifications of the premise that all members of humanity have this same intrinsic worth because each member of humanity has the breath of God breathed into them: "And I breathed into humanity of my own spirit" (*wa nafakhtu fīhi min rūhī*) (Qurʾān 15:29 and 38:72). This identification with the full humanity of all human beings amounts to nothing short of an Islamic humanism. In this global humanistic framework, progressives conceive of a way of being Muslim that engages and affirms the full humanity of all human beings, that actively holds all responsible for a fair and just distribution of God-given natural resources, and that seeks to live in harmony with the natural world.

Engaging tradition. Progressive Muslims insist on a serious engagement with the full spectrum of Islamic thought and practices. There can be no progressive Muslim movement that does not engage the textual and material sources of the Islamic tradition, even if progressives themselves debate what those sources should be and how they ought to be interpreted. Progressives generally hold that it is imperative to work through inherited traditions of thought and practice: Sunnī, Shīʿī, Ṣūfī, juridical, philosophical, theological, mystical, poetical, "folk Islam," oral traditions, and others all must be engaged. In particular cases they might conclude that certain preexisting interpretations fail to offer Muslims sufficient guidance today. However, they can only faithfully claim that position after—and not before—a serious engagement with the tradition.

Social justice, gender equality, and pluralism. Justice lies at the heart of Islamic social ethics. Time and again the Qurʾān talks about providing for the marginalized members of society: the poor, the orphan, the downtrodden, the wayfarer, the hungry, and so forth. Progressive Muslims believe that it is imperative to translate the social ideals in the Qurʾān and Islamic teachings in a way that those committed to social justice today can relate to and understand. For all Muslims there is a vibrant memory of the Prophet repeatedly talking about a real believer as one whose neighbor does not go to bed hungry. Progressives hold that in today's global village, it is time to think of all of humanity as one's neighbor.

Progressive Muslims begin with a simple yet radical stance: the Muslim community as a whole cannot achieve justice unless justice is guaranteed for Muslim women. In short, there can be no progressive interpretation of Islam without gender justice. Gender justice is crucial, indispensable, and essential. In the long run, any progressive Muslim interpretation will be judged by the amount of change in gender equality it is able to produce in small and large communities. Gender equality is a measuring stick of the broader concerns for social justice and pluralism. As Shirin Ebadi, the 2003 Nobel Peace Prize winner, stated, "Women's rights *are* human rights."

Progressive Muslims strive for pluralism both inside and outside of the *ummah.* They seek to open up a wider spectrum of interpretations and practices marked as Muslim and epistemologically follow a pluralistic approach to pursuit of knowledge and truth. In their interactions with other religious and ethnic communities, they seek to transcend the arcane notion of "tolerance" and instead strive for profound engagement through both commonalities and differences.

Progressives and *jihād*. The pervasive discourse of *jihād* has become thoroughly associated with Islam, to the point that one may legitimately ask whether the term can be redeemed. Both Muslim extremist groups such as al-Qāʿidah and Western Islamophobes in fact do use the term to mean a holy war. On the Muslim side, one can point to the public statement of Usāmah bin Lādin: "In compliance with God's order, we issue the following *fatwa* to all Muslims: The ruling to kill the Americans and their allies—civilians and military—is an individual duty for every Muslim who can do it in any country. . . ." Scholars of Islamic law have been quick to point out that the very parameters of this alleged "*fatwa*" violate both the letter and the spirit of Islamic law. At the same time, one has to acknowledge that bin Lādin supports his own recourse to violence through the discourse of *jihād.* This same sentiment is reflected on the Western Islamophobic side, where many Christian evangelicals are recasting centuries old polemic against Islam in a new guise.

Progressive Muslims counter both the Muslim extremists' and the Western Islamophobes' definition of *jihād.* Instead, they hold firmly to the notion that *jihād* is key, not in the sense of holy war and violence but rather in its root meaning of resistance and struggle. In this regard, progressives in the Muslim community emphasize the responsibility to engage the wider social order by confronting injustice and inequality, while always remembering that one must do so in a nonviolent way. In doing so, they are the heirs of both Muslim visionaries such as the mystic Rūmī ("Washing away blood with blood is impossible, even absurd!") as well as exemplars of nonviolence such as Gandhi, Martin Luther King Jr., and the Dalai Lama. This new understanding of *jihād,* which seeks to uphold resistance to well-entrenched systems of inequality and injustice through nonviolent means, is one of the key contributions of progressive Muslims. Building on the comments of religious figures such as the Dalai Lama (in his Nobel acceptance speech), they recognize that even terms like "peace" are insufficient when peace is not connected to justice and the well-being of humanity. The goal is not simply peace in the sense of absence of war but rather a peace that is rooted in justice.

Also revealing their indebtedness to American voices of social justice, many progressive Muslims are also inspired by Martin Luther King Jr. For these Muslims, King embodies speaking out for justice from the depth of a religious commitment, from the very midst of a faith community to that community and beyond. Thus, he is a great source of inspiration for many progressive Muslims to be voices of conscience speaking not in the wilderness but in the very midst of society. Progressives thus seek to be voices for global justice speaking firmly and powerfully to the powers that be while perpetually affirming the dignity of all human beings.

An Islamic Reformation? Modernist Muslims are often asked whether their project constitutes an "Islamic reformation." They answer the question in both the affirmative and the negative. It is undeniably true that there are serious economic, social, and political issues in the Muslim world that need urgent remedying. Much of the Muslim world is bound to a deeply disturbing economic structure in which it provides natural resources such as oil for the global market while at the same time remaining dependent on Western labor, technological know-how, and staple goods. This economic situation is exacerbated in many parts of the modern Muslim world by atrocious human rights situations, crumbling educational systems, and worn-out economies. Most modernist Muslims would readily support the reform of all those institutions.

However, the term *reformation* carries considerably more baggage than that. In speaking of the "Islamic reformation," many people have in mind the Protestant Reformation. It is this understanding that leaves many Muslims uneasy. Theirs is not a project of developing a "Protestant" Islam distinct from a "Catholic" Islam. Most insist that they are not looking to create a further split within the Muslim community so much as to heal it and to urge it along. For this reason, iconic figures such as Shirin Ebadi eschew the language of "reform" and "reformation," instead calling for a return to a real, just Islam.

A global phenomenon or a Western Islam? It would be a clear mistake to somehow reduce the emergence of progressive Islam to a new "American/Western Islam." Progressive Muslims are found everywhere in the global Muslim *ummah.* When it comes to actually implementing a progressive understanding of Islam in Muslim communities, particular communities in Iran, Malaysia, and South Africa *lead,* not follow, the United States. Many American Muslim communities—and much of the leadership represented in groups such as Islamic Circle of North America, the Islamic Society of North America, and the Council on American-Islamic Relations—are far too uncritical of Salafī (if not outright Wahhābī) tendencies that progressives oppose.

Wahhabism is by now a well-known, puritanical reading of Islam that originated in eighteenth-century Saudi Arabia. It was not until the discovery of oil in Saudi Arabia that Wahhabism had the financial resources necessary to import its evangelical mission all over the world, including to the United States. In spite of their exclusivist ideology, Wahhābīs have had a great working relationship first with the British and since the 1930s with the U.S. administration. Lesser known is the Salafī movement, which represents an important school of Islamic revivalism. Salafīs espouse a "return" to the ways of the first few generations of Muslims, the "righteous forefathers." Central to their methodology has been a recentering of Qurʾān and *sunnah* of Prophet Muḥammad. It would be a mistake to view American Muslim organizations such as ISNA and ICNA as Wahhābī. On the other hand, interpretations of Islam such as Shiism and Sufism are largely absent from these organizations, and the representation of important and contested issues such as gender constructions tends to reflect a conservative, Salafī orientation as well. It is in opposition to both Wahhabism and Salafism that many Muslim progressives define themselves.

One also has to acknowledge that the European and more importantly the North American context has provided a fertile ground for the blossoming of progressive Islam. Many participants in this young movement have found a more hospitable and open environment in the North American milieu than in Muslim-majority areas. Even the contested public world of post-9/11 America still offers great possibilities for conducting public conversations about difficult matters of religion and politics. It would be hard to imagine those critical conversations taking place freely and openly in many Muslim countries. Also one has to acknowledge the significance of North American educational establishments, as well as many fruitful cross-pollinations with liberal religious institutions, human rights groups, and the like.

Challenges to Islamic modernism. Muslim modernists face a whole host of challenges. Many modernists have profound internal disagreements about issues ranging from hermeneutical approaches to Qurʾān and *ḥadīth,* women's rights, and others. More problematic is the ongoing question of modernity versus the hegemony of the West. Many modernists have wrestled with the question of how to incorporate political institutions, science, and the like from the same Western civilizations that have continued to colonize and exploit much of the Third World, including many Muslim-majority countries.

Some initial phases of Islamic modernism became entangled in apologetic presentations of Islam in which Islam was idealized and imagined as an initially perfect system that had only been sullied through the misogyny and stagnation of later Muslim generations. That presupposition does not enable one to deal constructively with problematic questions in the Qurʾān or the lifetime of the Prophet and the early companions, even as it dismisses useful resources in later developments.

Other challenges are external. Muslim modernists do not have a natural institutional home other than academia and some media outlets. They have continuously struggled to find a home in the *madrasah* systems, although in some places they have achieved a measure of success because of the efforts of Muḥammad ʿAbduh and others. In other cases, they live in exile (Fazlur Rahman and Naṣr Abū Zayd, for example) for having been persecuted in their homeland. Politically they have often come under attack from a number of directions: state authorities who find the modernists' political critiques disturbing; secularists who are puzzled by the modernists' continued involvement with Islam; traditional religious authorities whose own understanding of Islam is undermined by the modernists. In spite of all the above, some modernists such as Fazlur Rahman and Iqbal have the strange designation of being the target of persecution as well as large-scale admiration.

In conclusion, it is clear that Muslims are entering yet another age of critical self-reflection. Given the level of polemics and apologetics, it is extraordinarily difficult to sustain a critical level of subtle discourse. Yet these Muslims today are not merely initiating social transformation, they are reflecting much wider processes at the same time. They are well situated to provide the most balanced and critical synthesis of Islam and modernity.

SEE ALSO Jamāʿat-i Islāmī; Muslim Brotherhood; Wahhābīyah.

BIBLIOGRAPHY

There are some classical studies for each phase of Islamic modernism, but to get a sense of the flavor and methodology of modernists, there is no substitute for actually reading the primary sources.

The finest place to begin a study of Islam in the contemporary world is Carl Ernst, *Following Muhammad: Rethinking Islam in the Contemporary World* (Chapel Hill, N.C., 2003). For an encyclopedic reference, the four-volume *The Oxford Encyclopedia of the Modern Islamic World* (New York, 1995), edited by John L. Esposito, is a useful resource. The often neglected eighteenth-century context can be studied through N. Levtzion and J. Voll's *Eighteenth Century Renewal and Reform in Islam* (Syracuse, N.Y., 1987). For nineteenth-century and early twentieth-century figures, the classic study remains Albert Hourani's masterpiece, *Arabic Thought in a Liberal Age: 1798–1939* (1962; reprint, Oxford, 1983). It can be supplemented with as Ibrahim M. Abu-Rabi's *Intellectual Origins of Islamic Resurgence in the Modern Arab World* (Albany, N.Y., 1996).

For anthologies of primary sources with useful introductions, there is no better source than the two volumes edited by Charles Kurzman. *Liberal Islam: A Sourcebook.* (New York, 1998) deals more or less with twentieth-century figures, and *Modernist Islam 1840–1940: A Sourcebook* (New York, 2002) with slightly earlier intellectuals. Both are worth going through in detail.

For an overview of Muḥammad ʿAbduh, see his *The Theology of Unity* (London, 1955). A good secondary study is Malcolm H. Kerr's *Islamic Reform: The Political and Legal Theories of Muhammad ʿAbduh and Rashid Rida* (Berkeley, Calif., 1966). Muhammad Iqbal's widely influential *The Reconstruction of Religious Thought in Islam* (Lahore, Pakistan, 1951), reprinted numerous times, is a ubiquitous study of modernist Islam. Another master of Islamic modernism, Fazlur Rahman, can best be approached through two of his works, *Islam and Modernity: Transformation of an Intellectual Tradition* (Chicago, 1984) and *Revival and Reform in Islam: A Study of Islamic Fundamentalism,* edited by Ebrahim Moosa (Oxford, 2000).

Important feminist reevaluations of Islamic history and the rise of the women's movement include Leila Ahmed's *Women and Gender in Islam: Historical Roots of a Modern Debate* (New Haven, Conn., 1992). A more positive reading of the possibility of incorporating feminism into Qurʾanic hermeneutics is Amina Wadud's *Qurʾān and Woman* (Oxford, 1989; reprint 1999). For modernist revaluation of Islamic law, particularly in the area of gender, the classic study is Khaled Abou El Fadl's *Speaking in God's Name: Islamic Law, Authority and Women* (Oxford, 2001).

A critical evaluation of Wahhabism is Hamid Algar's *Wahhabism* (Oneonta, N.Y., 2002). A less polemical study is Ahmad Dallal's "The Origins and Objectives of Islamic Revivalist Thought, 1750–1850," *Journal of the American Oriental Society* 113, no. 3 (1993): 341–359. Also worth consulting is Michael Cook's "On the Origins of Wahhabism," *Journal of the Royal Asiatic Society* 2 (1992): 191–202.

A brilliant anthology of how Neoconservatives, Western Triumphalists, and Christian Evangelicals define Islam as the latest "other" against which the "West" is defined is *The New Crusades: Constructing the Muslim Enemy,* edited by Emran Qureshi and Michael A. Sells, (New York, 2003). The classic study that deconstructs the meta-discourse of "Islam and violence" is Bruce Lawrence, *Shattering the Myth: Islam beyond Violence* (Princeton, N.J., 2000). A prominent intellectual who argues for the necessity of incorporating a Western identity into Islamic consciousness is Tariq Ramadan, author of *Western Muslims and the Future of Islam* (New York, 2003). A useful study of pluralistic readings of the Qur'ān is Abdulaziz Sachedina's *The Islamic Roots of Democratic Pluralism* (New York, 2001) and Suha Taji-Farouki, ed. *Modern Muslim Intellectuals and the Quran* (Oxford, 2004).

Lastly, Omid Safi's edited volume, *Progressive Muslims: On Justice, Gender, and Pluralism* (Oxford, 2003), features the writings of fifteen prominent Muslim intellectuals and activists in areas ranging from social justice to religious pluralism and gender equality. The study marks the full turning point from uncritical engagements with modernity in Islamic liberalism and modernism to a progressive understanding that adopts a critical stance vis-à-vis both Islam and modernity.

OMID SAFI (2005)

MODERNISM: CHRISTIAN MODERNISM

The related terms *liberalism* and *modernism,* when occurring in a religious or theological context, are usually no less imprecise than when used with other references. As T. S. Eliot put it: "Liberalism is something which tends to release energy rather than accumulate it, to relax, rather than to fortify. It is a movement not so much defined by its end, as by its starting point; away from, rather than towards, something definite." Accordingly the content of a set of doctrines or principles described as liberal depends upon that of the "orthodoxy" from which such liberalism diverges, or which it relaxes or qualifies. Much the same applies to *modernism,* which refers not simply to what exists today but to something deemed to be distinctive of today or of the more recent past, and so to be commended as such, in contrast to what represents a settled tradition or a historic inheritance. Defining both terms therefore presents difficulties, and an understanding of what either signifies is best reached by observing how in fact the word has been used, and in particular by recording agreement as to what it at least denotes.

The word *liberalism* was employed early in the nineteenth century to designate "the holding of liberal opinions in politics or theology." Theologically the word did not at first have a favorable connotation. Thus Edward Irving stated in 1826 that whereas "religion is the very name of obligation . . . liberalism is the very name of want of obligation." John Henry Newman went further and spoke in 1841 of "the most serious thinkers among us" as regarding "the spirit of liberalism as characteristic of the destined Antichrist." Liberalism itself he stigmatized in 1864 as "false liberty of thought, or the exercize of thought upon matters in which, from the constitution of the human mind, thought cannot be brought to any successful issue, and therefore is out of place." More succinctly, Newman condemned it as "the antidogmatic principle."

Gradually, however, this view point changed with the broader adoption by theologians of opinions more or less critical of received dogma or traditional interpretations of scripture. Employment of the word *liberalist* came instead to be a mark of approval, in opposition to attitudes referred to pejoratively as traditionalist, dogmatist, or even obscurantist. Moreover, liberalism was taken to signify a readiness not only to modify or actually negate certain doctrines or beliefs usually associated with received religious teaching but also to propagate views of a more positive nature, such as the necessity for freedom of inquiry and research and the conviction that new knowledge, when soundly based, will not prove subversive of fundamental religious truth but rather be a light by which to clarify and enhance such truth. Hence to be identified as "liberal" was regarded as a compliment by an increasing number of Protestant thinkers and scholars in the later nineteenth and early twentieth centuries.

At about the same time the term *modernism* gained currency, especially in Anglican circles, as an alternative, and preferable, designation for such theological liberalism. However, *modernism* has long been accepted in a stricter sense as indicating a type of "progressive" theological opinion to be found in the Roman Catholic Church during the pontificates of Leo XIII and Pius X, and many would now consider usage of the word best limited to this latter sense. "Liberal Catholicism" also designates certain tendencies in nineteenth-century Roman Catholicism, notably in France. Its concern, however, was more political and social than theological.

Attitudes that could in some sense be characterized as liberal or modernist have been recurrent throughout the history of Christian thought, but the movements or tendencies that usually carry one of these epithets are of nineteenth- or twentieth-century occurrence, and in the interest of clarity the present entry will observe this restriction.

The immediate intellectual background of theological liberalism was the Enlightenment of the eighteenth century, with its striving for political, social, and cultural liberty. The criterion of "enlightened" judgment was the use of reason, in which the mysteries of religious faith were prone to seem mere relics of the ignorance and superstition of the past. Deism became the widely prevalent expression of this largely negative standpoint. A new era opened with the later philosophy of the century's greatest thinker, Immanuel Kant, who sought by an analysis of the nature of knowledge itself to offer a rational justification for faith. But the answer he produced in the *Critique of Pure Reason* (1781) was such as to destroy the long-established "natural" theology that most Deist as well as orthodox thinkers regarded as fundamental. In its place he put the witness of the moral consciousness: belief in God was to be seen, philosophically, as a postulate of "practical," or moral, reason. The scientific understanding could not prove the existence of God, but the will, as the faculty of the moral life, required it. Kant's own philosophy of religion—or, more correctly, his philosophy of the Christian religion—was embodied in his suitably entitled *Religion within the Limits of Reason Alone,* one of the main sources from which modern theological liberalism derives. Indeed, Paul Tillich is right in claiming Kant's teaching as "decisive for the theology of the nineteenth century" (*Perspectives on Nineteenth and Twentieth Century Protestant Theology,* London, 1967, p. 64).

The perspective within which Kant views religion appears, on the face of it, narrow. Religion, he maintains, is morality; or at all events morality is of its very substance, albeit construed in terms of divine command. In other words, the religious problem is not a speculative one in which the religious object is validated primarily at the metaphysical level; it is a practical problem, pertaining wholly to man's ethical nature. "The illusion of being able to accomplish anything in the way of justifying ourselves before God through religious acts of worship is *superstition*" (*Religion within the Limits of Reason Alone,* New York, 1960, p. 162). The reductionism that this implies therefore necessitates a critique of traditional beliefs and institutions in anticipation of a more positive statement of what a genuinely rational Christianity must involve. Such insistence on the need for distinguishing between the essential and the nonessential—reason and conscience providing the criteria—was to become the guiding principle of all forms of liberal Christianity, and especially of German nineteenth-century Protestantism.

LIBERAL PROTESTANTISM. Nevertheless, if liberalism is to attain any sort of useful definition, some discrimination has to be made. "Liberal Protestantism," that is to say, is not simply to be equated with "Protestant liberalism." "A moderately orthodox believer," said the French liberal theologian Jean Réville, "may practise liberalism; he will not thereby become a liberal Protestant" (*Liberal Christianity,* London, 1903, p. 17). Protestant liberalism is in fact no more than the conception of Christianity of those who combine a liberal turn of mind with a broadly Protestant type of religious conviction. Such a position is subject, obviously, to many different sources of influence and offers a wide variety of opinion. Liberal Protestantism, on the other hand, is a designation best applied to the kind of theological thinking that, against a generally Lutheran background, developed in Germany during the nineteenth century under the stimulus first of Friedrich Schleiermacher and then of Albrecht Ritschl. Not that it remained confined to Germany: in France, Auguste Sabatier (1839–1901) and Jean Réville (1854–1908) himself, for example, may fairly be classed as liberal Protestants, as are such men as the Presbyterian William Adams Brown in the United States and the Congregationalists T. R. Glover and C. J. Cadoux in Great Britain. Again, Kantian reverberations are as a rule clearly audible in liberal Protestantism, whereas in Protestant liberalism (at all events, in an English and Anglican setting) the prevailing spirit is more that of the seventeenth-century Cambridge Platonists or the latitudinarianism associated with archbishop John Tillotson (1630–1694) than that of Kant or, still less, of Schleiermacher.

Yet to press such distinctions too far would be to obscure the very large amount of common ground that liberals of all shades of opinion occupy in contrast to traditionalist, let alone "fundamentalist," views. Differences are less of kind than of degree, and they are inevitably marked by national and denominational characteristics. Thus all liberals desire, first, a broad interpretation of dogmatic formularies, where these exist and retain some authority. Second, they are cool toward theological speculation that appears to have no particular ethical relevance. And third, they are especially sensitive to the impact on traditional belief of new knowledge in the sciences, both natural and historical. Indeed, in the more recent phases of liberal religious thought, a determining factor has been the historical criticism of the Bible and the effect that this criticism is bound to have upon the understanding and use of scripture—always for Protestants the ultimate source of Christian doctrine. Hence the varieties of liberalism arise in the main from differing responses on the part of individual religious thinkers to each of these leading considerations.

The starting point for a study of liberal Protestantism is the work of Schleiermacher (1768–1834), "the father of modern theology," as he has fitly been called. Kant, for all his anticipation of subsequent trends of thought, was very much an eighteenth-century figure, in whom the individualist note of ethical rationalism was all-pervasive. Schleiermacher, on the other hand, brought to religious reflection a different spirit. For him religion was primarily a condition of the heart; its essence is feeling *(Gefühl).* Without a deep emotional impulse it cannot be sustained in its true character and becomes either dogmatism or moralism. Authentic religion is, rather, a "submission to be moved by the Whole that stands over against man," a "sense and taste for the Infinite." In his great work on systematic theology, *The Christian Faith* (1821–1822; 2d ed., 1830), Schleiermacher called religion a "feeling of absolute dependence" or, for the Christian specifically, a feeling of absolute dependence upon "God in Christ." Thus in Schleiermacher's religious philosophy a fundamental principle of liberalism is already evident, namely, the appeal to inward experience, and therewith an element of subjectivism from which the liberal standpoint can never be dissociated. In this, indeed, Schleiermacher had been anticipated by Kant; but whereas for Kant the subjective determinant was moral, for Schleiermacher it could best be described as aesthetic. In the subsequent development of liberal Protestantism, the moral factor was consistently the more potent.

This is especially so in the teaching of Ritschl (1822–1889), the most influential German theologian of his era, who for the greater part of his career held the chair of theology at the University of Göttingen. His main literary work was *The Christian Doctrine of Justification and Reconciliation* (1870–1874). Ritschl disliked Schleiermacher's emphasis on feeling, and although his own concern was strongly ethical, he believed also that faith must have an objective basis. Such objectivity, however, he found not in metaphysics, Hellenic or Hegelian (for which, as far as theology was concerned,

Ritschl had no use), but in history, or rather in the unique historical events of the New Testament. In his younger days he had come under the influence of the eminent Tübingen historian of early Christianity, Ferdinand Christian Baur (1792–1860), whose skeptical conclusions in this field had to a large extent been dictated by his Hegelian presuppositions. But by 1856 Ritschl had repudiated the Tübingen position, although he welcomed historical criticism as such since he believed that recourse to the original salvific events would bypass the metaphysical Christology of Catholic dogma, which to the genuinely religious mind had become an impediment. In short, he saw Christianity as essentially a life devoted to action, both Godward and manward, in which the ethical imperative is supreme. The corollary of this was that religious doctrines are not assertions of fact, in the ordinary meaning of the word, but "value judgments" *(Werturteile)* expressive of humanity's attitude to the world about it and relating to its moral and spiritual ends. For the human claim to moral freedom and the responsibility that this entails is, in Ritschl's mind, the necessary counterbalance to the determinism of nature as described by modern science, and the primary role of religion is to uphold this claim. To quote Ritschl: "In every religion what is sought, with the help of the supernatural power reverenced by man, is a solution of the contradiction in which humanity finds itself, as both a part of the world of nature and a spiritual personality claiming to dominate nature" (*Justification and Reconciliation,* Edinburgh, 1874–1900, p. 199).

For Ritschl, the distinctiveness of Christianity lay in the unique clue to an understanding of the divine nature and purposes offered by Jesus, who for the Christian is the sole medium of salvation. And Jesus as the Christ is to be known not through any abstruse theology of his person, but by his work—that is, by his own consciousness of God communicated in turn to us, whereby one experiences forgiveness of sin and restoration of the desire and power to do the will of God. The church, to which Ritschl attached high importance, is the only sphere in which justification and reconciliation are experienced. As such, it is the community of the redeemed.

Ritschlianism, however, includes more than the personal teaching of Ritschl himself and comprises the thinking of a number of theologians prominent in German Protestantism down to at least the outbreak of World War I. It also was not without its representatives in the Anglo-Saxon world. Of the German Ritschlians, the most distinguished were Wilhelm Herrmann (1846–1922), Julius Kaftan (1848–1926), and Adolf von Harnack (1851–1930). Indeed, Herrmann's *The Communion of the Christian with God* (1886) is perhaps the most typical as well as the most sympathetic expression of the Ritschlian viewpoint one could cite. Its author, who was professor of theology at the University of Marburg, was if anything even more anxious than Ritschl to sunder Christian doctrine from all traffic with metaphysical philosophy. For him, as for Ritschl, the heart of the gospel is an ethical ideal, and confessions of theological belief are altogether secondary. The object of a Christian's faith is Jesus as he lived. The more radical side of Ritschlianism is represented by Harnack, for many years professor of church history at the University of Berlin. Here again the bedrock of faith is the historical Jesus. In his well-known *What Is Christianity?* (1900), Harnack sets aside the entire Catholic tradition of dogma, hierarchy, and cult; indeed, under the guiding light of modern criticism, he goes far beyond Reformation Protestantism in negating the past. To discover the *Wesen,* the essence, of the Christian religion, the theologian of today must return not merely to the New Testament—theological distortion had already begun with Paul—but to the teaching of Jesus as preserved in the Synoptic Gospels, the heart of which is the principle of the fatherhood of God and the brotherhood of man. The "kingdom" that Jesus preached, shorn of its apocalyptic trappings, must therefore be understood in a purely ethical sense. "The individual is called upon to listen to the glad message of mercy and of God's Fatherhood, and to make up his mind whether he will be on God's side as the Eternal's, or on the side of the world and time."

The final phase of liberal Protestantism is really post-Ritschlian and centers upon the *religionsgeschichtliche Schule* (history of religions school), typified in the work of Ernst Troeltsch (1865–1923) and Wilhelm Bousset (1865–1920). Troeltsch, at first professor of theology at the University of Heidelberg and afterward professor of the history of philosophy at the University of Berlin, was much influenced by the sociologists Wilhelm Dilthey and Max Weber. The fact, as Troeltsch saw it, that Christianity, like any other cultural phenomenon, must be understood primarily in relation to its attendant historical conditions inevitably posed the problem of the absoluteness of its claims in respect not only to the world's other religions but to cultural change generally. The proper approach to Christianity appeared to be by way of the history and philosophy of religion; dogmatic theology acquired relevance only within this broader scholarly framework. Not surprisingly, it was an opinion that to the more traditionally minded placed divine revelation at the disposal of a relativistic historicism. This, along with the persistent anthropocentrism of liberal theology, was to lead, by the end of World War I in 1918, to the antiliberalist reaction of Karl Barth, whose *Epistle to the Romans* appeared in the following year, and to the so-called neoorthodox movement generally.

But despite the powerful Barthian influence that lasted for at least four decades into the twentieth century, the liberal aim of communicating the Christian message to modern humanity in terms of its own modernity was not revoked. This aim is evident enough in the work of two of Barth's most outstanding Protestant contemporaries, Paul Tillich and Rudolf Bultmann, albeit that the associated philosophy here is existentialism rather than post-Hegelian idealism. Moreover, the distinctively humanist tone that since about 1960 has come more or less to pervade virtually all Western theological thinking is clearly continuous with the older liberalizing attitudes.

In the English-speaking world, liberal Protestantism did not form so clearly defined a force as it did in Germany. At any rate it is more difficult to distinguish between liberal Protestants, in Réville's meaning of the term, and theological liberals in a broader sense. But in this broader sense liberalism is multifarious, depending on varying denominational allegiances, although also to a large extent on individual interests and idiosyncrasies. Classification therefore demands much tact.

The antecedents of English liberalism, particularly within the Anglican context, are to be located in eighteenth-century latitudinarianism, in the "noetic" school at Oxford University in the early nineteenth century—whose chief exponents are Richard Whately (1787–1863), Renn Dickson Hampden (1793–1868), and Thomas Arnold (1795–1842)—and in the midcentury "broad church" as represented by H. H. Milman (1791–1868), A. P. Stanley (1815–1881), and Benjamin Jowett (1817–1893), as indeed by all the authors of *Essays and Reviews* (1860), including Jowett. Frederick Denison Maurice (1805–1872), in some ways the most fertile theological mind of his time in England, eschewed the name "broad church," but his teaching, permeated as it was with the influence of Samuel Taylor Coleridge, had a broadening effect within the Church of England and undoubtedly contributed substantially to the shaping of modern Anglicanism. Maurice himself seems scarcely to have appreciated the unsettling effect on orthodox thinking of the historical criticism of the Bible.

A more self-consciously innovative type of liberalism, however, made its appearance toward the end of the century. It was associated with the names of Percy Gardner (1846–1937), professor of classicial archaeology at Oxford University; Hastings Rashdall (1858–1924), dean of Carlisle; W. R. Inge (1860–1954), dean of Saint Paul's, London; H. D. A. Major (1871–1961), principal of Ripon Hall, Oxford; and E. W. Barnes (1874–1953), bishop of Birmingham. All of them were connected with the Modern Churchmen's Union, founded in 1898, and with its organ the *Modern Churchman.* But their "modernism"—to use their own preferred designation—had little theological coherence. Such unity as it possessed stemmed chiefly from a marked opposition to the doctrine and practices of the Anglo-Catholic party within the established church. The Union achieved its highest public notice with its Cambridge conference of 1921 on the general theme of "Christ and the Creeds." Rashdall's paper "Christ as the Logos and Son of God" aroused sharp controversy with such statements as the following: "It is impossible to maintain that God is fully incarnate in Christ, and not incarnate at all in any one else." But by the end of the 1930s Anglican modernism was in decline and is now but the merest wraith of its former self. Indeed, the very name has been virtually abandoned.

A liberalism more akin to continental liberal Protestantism was to be found among the English Nonconformists, or "Free Churchmen," rather than among Anglicans. In the main, however, the Free Church theologians, of whom the most distinguished representatives included P. T. Forsyth and A. E. Garvie (the latter a close student of Ritschlianism), were less inclined to doctrinal novelty than were some of their Anglican contemporaries. The Congregationalist R. J. Campbell (1867–1956), author of *The New Theology* (1907), was an exception. So too was T. R. Glover (1869–1943), a Cambridge classical scholar and author of the popular *Jesus of History* (1917), the thesis of which is much the same as that of Harnack's *What Is Christianity?* Another exception was C. J. Cadoux (1883–1947), whose *Catholicism and Christianity* (1928) propounded a radical critique of Catholic orthodoxy from a liberal angle. The Unitarian tradition, maintained with high repute throughout the nineteenth century by James Martineau (1805–1900)—perhaps the greatest Protestant liberal of his era in England—was also represented, if somewhat journalistically, by L. P. Jacks (1860–1955).

In America the liberal movement in religious thought may be said to have begun with William Ellery Channing (1780–1842). Brought up in the strict ways of New England Calvinism, Channing came to be considered a Unitarian. But critical though he was of traditional doctrines, he believed Christ to have been the perfect revelation of God and the living ideal of humanity. Against Calvinism he set a confident faith in an individual's freedom and inherent capacity for good as a child of God. The leader of the New England Transcendentalist movement, Ralph Waldo Emerson (1803–1882), whom Matthew Arnold, addressing an American audience, described as "your Newman, your man of soul and genius," remains the best-known American religious thinker of the nineteenth century. His religious views are expounded in *Nature* (1836) and the two volumes of *Essays* (1841–1843). The basis of his position was belief in the essential divinity of man; redemption was to be sought in the individual's possession of his or her own soul by original thought and effort. Jesus, he held, was best honored by following his example. A liberal of more orthodox persuasion was Horace Bushnell (1802–1876), who for much of his career was pastor of the North Church at Hartford, Connecticut. His *Discourse on Christian Nurture* (1847) took a mediating line between the old orthodoxy, with its preoccupation with Original Sin and human depravity, and Enlightenment theories of human perfectibility. In *God in Christ* (1849) he applied the moral criterion to dogma, and he insisted that even in scripture the "soul" must be distinguished from the "body."

Nearer the close of the century European influences—and not least Ritschlianism—are discernible in American theology, notably in the writings of H. C. King (1858–1934), president of Oberlin College, Ohio, and William Adams Brown (1865–1943) of Union Theological Seminary, New York, whose work *The Essence of Christianity* appeared in 1902. Among historical scholars of a liberal bent was A. C. McGiffert (1861–1933), also of Union Theological Seminary, who believed religious certitude to be, in the last resort, independent of historical events. Other prominent liberals of the early twentieth century include the well-known New York preacher Harry Emerson Fosdick; Shailer Mathews, whose book *The Faith of Modernism* (1925) is as forthright a statement of liberal ideals as could be wished; and H. N. Wieman, author of *The Wrestle of Religion with Truth* (1927).

Roman Catholic Modernism. The use of the word *Modernism* in restricted reference (hence the capitalization of its initial letter) to a movement of a theologically "modernizing" or liberalizing character in the Roman Catholic Church at the turn of the twentieth century has already been alluded to. But it should at once be said that to describe Roman Catholic Modernism as a movement at all is somewhat misleading, as it had little cohesion, and those to whom the designation "Modernist" has usually been applied do not in any sense constitute a school. As the most famous of them, Alfred Loisy (1857–1940), expressly stated, they were only "a quite limited number of persons" who individually shared "the desire to adapt the Catholic religion to the intellectual, moral and social needs of the present time." But the exact determination of their overall aim differed from one writer to another, according to his particular interest. Thus the only satisfactory way of studying Modernism is not to attempt to impose upon it a schematization like that of Pius X, by whose encyclical *Pascendi dominici gregis* it was condemned in 1907, but to examine and assess each author's contribution to the cause as a whole. The countries where Modernist tendencies were most in evidence were France, Italy, and England. Germany, rather surprisingly, was less affected, and in the United States it had no real following at all.

The task that, in one way or another, the Modernists undertook was that of presenting the world of their day with a defense of Catholicism, in both its doctrinal and institutional aspects, which could be accepted as intellectually plausible. In other words, what Protestant liberals had done for the Reformation tradition they would attempt for the post-Tridentine, and their procedure was often no less radical. Thus Loisy, in *The Gospel and the Church* (1902), approached the whole problem of historical Catholicism—its dogmas, its hierarchy, its cult—along evolutionary lines as a natural growth responsive to spiritual and social needs and determined by the continuously changing cultural environment. A direct reply to Harnack's *What Is Christianity?*, Loisy's book denied that the essence of Christianity could be located at any one stage or identified with any single element within its historical life. The entire historical life of Christianity, he maintained, alone provided the data for a true—because empirically grounded—estimate of what the Christian religion is. In this context, Catholicism will be seen to be justified—so Loisy argued—by the sheer fullness and diversity of its content. Similar arguments were used by the Anglo-Irish Jesuit George Tyrrell (1861–1909), notably in his posthumous work *Christianity at the Cross Roads* (1910).

The peculiar difficulty facing the Modernists lay in seeking to validate a form of Christianity that appeared fatally vulnerable to historical criticism. Indeed, they felt that the main pressure upon faith came from precisely this quarter, and the familiar type of Catholic apologetic, tied as it was to biblical fundamentalism, was incapable of meeting it. Moreover, the question of dogma also raised other issues, of a philosophical order. Catholic philosophy, by official direction, meant Thomism, although more often than not Thomism conceived in a narrow, unhistorical, and scholastic form. A more dynamic religious philosophy was wanted, according to Modernists like the French Oratorian Lucien Laberthonnière (1860–1932), a disciple of Maurice Blondel (1861–1949), as well as to the Bergsonian Édouard Le Roy (1870–1954) and to Ernesto Buonaiuti (1881–1946), protagonist of the Italians and author of *The Program of Modernism* (1907). For a more dynamic philosophy they looked not to Kant, as Pius's *Pascendi* had alleged, but rather to the voluntarist tradition of much nineteenth-century French thought and even to American pragmatism. Tyrrell and Laberthonnière both stressed the role of the will in belief and were disposed to understand doctrine in terms of an ethical symbolism. Le Roy's account of dogma (*Dogme et critique,* 1907), in particular, represented it primarily as *une règle de conduite pratique* ("a rule for practical conduct"), without intrinsic speculative content. Thus the doctrine of the divine personality means in effect "Conduct yourself in your relations with God as you would in your relations with a human person." The vindication of dogma, therefore, will rest on its capacity to induce the experience in which it is itself grounded.

However, the Modernist apologetic, whether historical or philosophical, won no approval at Rome, and the movement was summarily suppressed. In 1910 a specifically anti-Modernist oath was imposed on the clergy, or at least those engaged in teaching. The result of the Vatican's action was to retard Catholic biblical scholarship, as well as practically all non-Thomist theological thinking, for many years to come.

Assessment of Liberalism. The strength of liberalism lay in its conviction that the Christian gospel can be offered to modern individuals without affront to their intelligence. It recognized frankly that Christian belief arose, developed, and was formulated in an era and a culture vastly different from that of nineteenth- and twentieth-century Western society, and that both its intellectual presuppositions and the language in which it came to be articulated are inevitably alien and even in large measure unintelligible to this age. Unless therefore one tries to seal oneself off from all contemporary influences, one is bound to reassess the basics of faith in the light of the radically altered ways of thinking that the post-Reformation era has brought about. Especially must Christianity be seen in the perspective of scientific history, even though this may no longer support forms of belief that have persisted over centuries. Indeed, it is difficult to see how on this score the liberal case can be refuted; the facts speak for themselves, and any modernized version of the Christian religion has to take account of them from the outset.

Nevertheless, liberalism has had its critics from at least the beginning of this century, and not merely among the partisans of a crass traditionalism. To many, its immanentist theology greatly overemphasized the continuity between the world and God and between humanity and God, at the expense of the received belief, on which the whole scheme of redemption turned, that as between finite and infinite, human and divine, there is a qualitative and not merely a quantitative disparity. (The liberal Christology is usually circumscribed by the humanity of Jesus.) In keeping with this, liberalism seemed to its critics if not altogether to minimize sin and evil, yet to interpret these too easily in terms of ignorance, immaturity, and simple maladjustment, while overlooking the sheer heinousness of sin. In fact, liberalism's view of humankind exhibited an optimism stemming from a combination of Enlightenment notions of human perfectibility and the nineteenth-century ideal of progress. Such optimism is encouraged neither by the traditional Christian doctrine of the "natural" human condition as corrupted by the fall nor by the cumulative evidence of sin to that humankind's historical life bears sorry witness. It is also possible to consider as in principle subjective the liberal conception of the church itself: a fellowship of those who share the same or a similar experience, in recognition of which they meet together in worship, hence expressing the social character of religion. Tolerance is applauded because opinions in religious matters inevitably differ. In sum, the values of liberalism, so its critics complain, are essentially those of a bourgeois ethicism having little or nothing of that sense of the eschatological *kairos* ("time") and impending judgment that characterizes the New Testament and persists as a motif in all traditional doctrine.

It was the serious inadequacies of liberalism—as he felt them to be—that led the young Swiss theologian Karl Barth (1886–1968), who had been deeply influenced by Kierkegaard, to protest against the anthropocentrism of liberal theologies in the name of the uncompromising theocentrism of the biblical revelation. The starting point of theology, he urged, must not be subjective "religiousness" but rather God's own self-disclosure through his Word: "God is known by God alone" (*Church Dogmatics* 2.1). Thus neither "religious experience" nor speculative natural theology provides any necessary prolegomena to faith. Instead of the Thomist *analogia entis* ("analogy of being"), Barth offered the *analogia fidei* ("analogy of faith"), that is, the insights of faith based on revelation.

The upshot of the Barthian theological revolution was that all forms of liberalism fell more or less into discredit. This "Barthian captivity," as Reinhold Niebuhr called it, of twentieth-century religious thought persisted for some four decades, and only in the years immediately preceding Barth's death in 1968 did its end become manifest. The neoorthodox reaction, although it has not ceased to exert its pull on some minds—conservative evangelicalism unquestionably gained heart from it—now appears to have been less a recovery of the old certainties than a temporary *arrêt* in a process that is actually part of modernity itself. In other words, the theological difficulties that liberalism had sought to resolve remain, inasmuch as orthodoxy, if it is to uphold its claim to intellectual respectability, cannot avoid the challenge of criticism, whether philosophical or historical. A serious fault in Barth himself was his evasiveness on the historical authenticity of Christianity. These unresolved difficulties have no doubt influenced theologians' disposition to reconsider the achievements of liberalism in a more sympathetic light.

SEE ALSO Evangelical and Fundamental Christianity; Neoorthodoxy; Pentecostal and Charismatic Christianity; Petre, Maude Dominica; Vatican Councils, article on Vatican I.

BIBLIOGRAPHY

For an understanding of liberalism and modernism, Protestant and Catholic, all the primary works cited in the foregoing article should be studied. Of secondary works, Karl Barth's *Protestant Theology in the Nineteenth Century* (1952; translated by Brian Cozens and John Bowden, Valley Forge, Pa., 1973) offers an account of nineteenth-century German theological thinking in general that is of magisterial weight, although its whole approach to liberalism is critical. H. R. Mackintosh's *Types of Modern Theology* (1937; 2d ed., New York, 1958), Barthian also in its viewpoint, is still useful, as is John Macquarrie's *Twentieth Century Religious Thought* (New York, 1963), which covers much ground but makes only summary presentations of individual thinkers.

Claude Welch's *Protestant Thought in the Nineteenth Century* (New Haven, 1972) fills in a good deal of the background of the liberal movement, though as yet only the first volume, covering 1790–1870, has appeared. One of my own books, *Liberal Protestantism* (Stanford, Calif., 1968), provides an extended introduction dealing with most aspects of the movement and a selection of texts. *Ritschl: A Reappraisal* (London, 1978), by James Richmond, offers a fairly full study of a writer whom English-speaking readers have always been apt to find difficult, and *Ernst Troeltsch and the Future of Theology* (Cambridge, 1976), edited by John Powell Clayton, treats at length the last great representative of liberal Protestantism.

Sidney E. Ahlstrom's *Theology in America: The Major Protestant Voices from Puritanism to Neo-Orthodoxy* (Indianapolis, 1967) surveys the American scene. H. D. A. Major's *English Modernism: Its Origin, Methods, Aims* (Cambridge, Mass., 1927), more a manifesto than a history, confines itself principally to Anglicanism. Oliver Chase Quick's *Liberalism, Modernism and Tradition* (London, 1922) discusses the liberal Protestant and Catholic modernist doctrines of Christ in relation to orthodoxy.

The most authoritative of more recent works on Roman Catholic modernism is Émile Poulat's *Histoire, dogme et critique dans la crise moderniste* (Paris, 1962), although Jean Rivière's *Le modernisme dans l'église* (Paris, 1929), the work of a relatively "liberal" Roman Catholic, still provides the most comprehensive survey. In *Roman Catholic Modernism* (London, 1970), I have again supplied a longish introduction and a selection of texts, including excerpts from the Vatican documents condemning modernism. Thomas M. Loome's *Liberal Catholicism, Reform Catholicism, Modernism: A Contribution to a New Orientation in Modernist Research* (Mainz, 1979) is especially valuable for its bibliographical material. Also deserving of mention is Gabriel Daly's *Transcendence and Immanence: A Study of Catholic Modernism and Integralism* (Oxford and New York, 1980).

BERNARD M. G. REARDON (1987 AND 2005)

MODERNITY.

Many factors working together have generated interest in modernity and religion. Among these are an increasing consciousness of the many human societies that now exist, an awareness of previous societies recorded in history, and a recognition of the overwhelming variety of cultures associated with them. The constellation of cultural characteristics associated with the modern period is very different from that normally associated with an isolated tribal culture, a medieval peasant society, or a transitional society of the early modern period. To talk of religion is to identify a particular set of cultural attitudes and activities that point to the deep sources of power in a culture, how humans relate to that power, and the corresponding, codified beliefs and behaviors surrounding it. Each concept is highly complex; to discuss the relationship between them compounds the challenge.

For some time it has been a sophisticated convention to assume that the progressive extension of scientific knowledge sparked the emergence of dynamic Western societies and the extension of their influence. The subsequent triumph of reason and rational behavior over ways of thought and patterns of action associated with traditional cultures was more or less taken for granted. Thus it seemed logical to expect that religious beliefs and behaviors would be forced to the periphery of societies that were becoming modern. By extension it seemed conceivable that religion would disappear altogether. Yet in fact, evidence has suggested that religion, far from disappearing or losing influence, has a prominent place in modern societies. Indeed, religions play many different roles in modern societies, and these societies in turn play back upon religion a wide variety of effects. The term *modernity* refers to the cultural conditions that set the terms for all thought and action in a particular culture. Religious beliefs and behavior cannot be unaffected, even when those who espouse some religion consider themselves untouched by their cultural location. Just as religion remains a cultural reality in modernity, so there can be no escape from modernity, even through a wholehearted appropriation of a comprehensive religious tradition.

DEFINING MODERNITY. *Modern, modernism, modernization, modernity*, and related terms, taken alone, qualified, or compounded, are used every day in the popular media as well as in specialized journals and technical exchanges. The ubiquity of these terms is due in part to the shifting sets of meaning they carry. To clarify the current discussion, I propose certain distinctions between these terms.

First, *modern* is a correlative term; it implies what is new as opposed to what is ancient, what is innovative as opposed to what is traditional or handed down. However, what is judged modern at a particular time and place in a culture will not necessarily be defined as such either in the future or in some other context. Students of religion, especially, who by definition are interested in cultural patterns viewed in a long-term framework, must not fail to put in perspective changing perceptions of what is "new" and what is "old." Since a judgment about what is modern is a matter of the perspective of the observer, phenomena that appear similar may in fact vary considerably depending on their context. Thus, "modern architecture" of the mid-twentieth century now has a distinctly dated look. Similarly, nineteenth-century symphonic music must have seemed "modern" to those brought up on the baroque, but outmoded to those brought up on Stravinsky and Hindemith.

Second, the terms *modernism* and *modernization* represent, respectively, cultural and social attitudes or programs dedicated to supporting what is perceived as modern. Modernism entails a kind of explicit and self-conscious commitment to the modern in intellectual and cultural spheres. It involves a commitment to support the tenets of the "new" in the face of critics, opponents, and detractors. In this it parallels the commitment to modernization, a programmatic remaking of the political and economic aspects of society in support of the "new." This distinction implies that it is more appropriate to speak of modernism in nineteenth-century French Roman Catholicism, or in twentieth-century American Protestantism, or even among those who espouse contemporary versions of ancient Indian traditions, than it is to refer to the "modernization" of a religious tradition. Conversely, it is appropriate to refer to the modernization of a factory plant or its organization of production, or of a tax structure. *Modernism* would normally not be a useful designation with respect to such matters—unless we speak about factory architecture in the one case or art objects as shelters under the tax code in the other.

Thus it is inappropriate to refer to the "modernization" of a religion unless we mean as part of a self-conscious, perhaps largely social and political, program. On the other hand, *modernism* in this context implies a commitment (and usually a cultural program in addition) to render religion compatible with more general commitments in other areas. But is modernism divisible? Attitudes toward art, music, drama, religion, and so forth usually hang together and form a powerful set of interactive commitments. Indeed, such a set of cultural ideals may be related to economic and political change as designated by modernization. The conviction that cultural modernism is often associated with programs for social modernization frequently evolves into a more general belief that secularization is relentlessly supplanting the old with the new. In its extreme form this argument concludes that a process of secularization makes claims upon those involved with it that exhibit a religious character, or that seem like religion in that they are ultimate, unqualified, and beyond review.

Only at this point does the term *modernity* enter our discussion. It explicitly identifies an openness and a commitment to the new as opposed to the old. Our move to the term *modernity* brings us to the consciousness of cultural change. Yet a further move attributes a congruence to the many aspects of a modern culture that makes them appear to be the expression of an entity powerful and coherent in its own right. This third step effectively serves to reify the term *modernity.* To take this step will generally promote confusion in our thinking. It is not helpful to use the term *modernity* as if it referred to a spiritual medium in contemporary life that necessarily rivals religious traditions. It is much more helpful to use it in a prereified or nonreified way as a means of recognizing that cultural change and awareness of that change are pervasive in contemporary societies. What depends upon this distinction between reified and nonreified uses of *modernity*?

One unfortunate consequence of reifying the term *modernity* is that it settles by definition an issue that ought to remain under discussion. To conceive of modernity as a spiritual medium that envelops and interconnects all particular instances of commitment to the modern, whether through modernism or modernization, is to posit an implicitly religious phenomenon, for it assumes that modernity plays the cultural role or roles characteristic of religion. As a consequence, modernity is seen as a rival to traditional or "authentic" religion. An important implication of this view is that religion in a modern society is regarded dichotomously. Either an individual or group is thought to be "for" modernity (and thus against traditional religious commitments) or "for" traditional religion (and thus antipathetic toward modernity in any and all forms). In its most intense version, this dichotomy is characteristic of every period of cultural change known to us and especially of the period we know as the modern one. Under conditions of social and cultural change, and of modernity in particular, one of many responses will be an attempt to reaffirm traditional cultural forms, albeit in highly selective and often strident versions.

CULTURAL CHANGE AND MODERNITY. It is important to explore, at least briefly, the distinction between cultural change and modernism. Stated exactly, the latter is a special case of the former. Cultural change has been a given in human societies throughout every period of which we have knowledge. There have been some periods of more, and others of less, intensive social and cultural change; but certainly no society we know anything about has been altogether free of cultural change. Records of ancient societies and cultures do not permit refined distinctions, but access to more recent historic examples allows some generalizations. Certainly it is possible to identify characteristic religious responses to periods of intensive cultural change. One is the development of the dichotomous view of the world upon which we have already remarked—"civilized" versus "barbarian," "believers" versus "heretics," and so forth. Another response has been the enhancement of orthodoxy, orthopraxy, or tradition in both ancient and recent examples of interaction between cultures as well as within a single culture. A third is the frequently recurring millenarian or apocalyptic response to cultural change. Here change is experienced as so threatening and intense that it is believed a "big change" will necessarily occur.

Cast in this framework, modernity, too, is a special category of social and cultural change. It is, to be precise, social and cultural change embraced self-consciously in the contemporary world. Some characteristic attitudes toward religion mark modernity, but they tend to be special cases of the more general attitudes toward change and not exclusively related to religion. For example, modernity includes a systematic commitment to rationality, that is, a conviction that logically consistent and universalizable principles ought to be the basis for change. Again, modernity tends to undervalue the role of symbols and the subconscious. A third and related attitude is that human life is highly malleable. This set, and the preceding enumeration, is certainly not a full set and is surely a special case of attitudes to social and cultural change. But it is also a special case, because it is self-conscious, of conceivable responses to that larger and more universal phenomenon of social change. Hostility on the part of religious traditions to the modern, especially when cast as a rejection of modernity, is itself as much a characteristic response to social change as its opposite, the enthusiastic acceptance of change by a confirmed modernist. An explicit and positive attitude toward social change is no more directly related to the experience of change than is a negative response. Both are typical attitudes of individuals and groups throughout history who have been religiously sensitive to social and cultural change.

If modernity is not reified as a spiritual entity, and if modernism is recognized as a special and self-conscious case of positive response to social and cultural changes, our proper subject is how religion appears to respond and vary under the conditions of self-conscious social and cultural change in the contemporary world. If we distinguish the fact of cultural change from a postulated, spiritualized, and thus reified modernity as the controlling commitment, we are then in a position to review what seems to happen to religion under the conditions of prolonged change—or at least what has happened in social contexts that have been so characterized. Specifically, in an era that is conscious of the new, are there characteristic changes in religion, especially in relationship to the modern?

THE IMPACT OF MODERNITY ON RELIGION. If we take modernity in this descriptive sense, the decisive commitment to modernization socially and to modernism culturally is first to be observed as a coherent process in the United States. It may be thought that revolutionary France in the last decades of the eighteenth century or Japan in the late twentieth century represent more thoroughgoing examples of commitment to the "modern." Certainly, for brief periods other societies may well have manifested an intense and thoroughgoing commitment to change. But over time, at least to date, American society has set about more thoroughly than other societies to overcome traditional ways and self-consciously to replace them with new ones. It is here that the best exhibits are available, and exhibits over time, of the kinds of cultural changes attendant upon the systematic modernization of society. Further, the actual changes we can observe in religion seem to be remarkably heterogeneous, that is, the changes by no means run in one direction only. How can we best summarize what happens to religion under conditions of modernity?

One useful distinction at this point is between responses to modernity that are explicitly keyed to the whole scope of a religious tradition, and those effects that represent the taking on of a coloration from modern society or that are evidence for generalized, nonspecific influence of modernity. It is preferable to consider the latter kind first, since these effects are ubiquitous; this will enable us in turn to review without confusion explicit religious responses to modern life.

Bureaucratization and rationalization. Some of the changes to be observed in religion relating to the modern world clearly derive from the permeation of religious institutions by techniques and procedures developed in other sectors of the society. For example, European-derived (and certainly American-begun) church traditions have adopted much from the business world. These techniques or procedures are inevitably centralizing. This is apparent, for example, in communications: telephone calls have taken the place of pastoral letters, written reports preempt personal visits, revivals and healing services are often televised rather than held locally. Other consequential changes have to do with the liquidity of wealth; even as successful a promoter as the evangelical John Wesley could not have imagined the means available to the contemporary Methodist (or Roman Catholic) church to generate financial resources and shift their allocations throughout a worldwide, well-organized structure.

Adoption of these kinds of management technique potentially strengthens the hands of central religious leaders. But the same modern society also extends to laity the knowledge and ability to challenge such a transfer of power to central authorities. Countervailing trends, then, are at work, leading both to enhanced localism in the parishes and to the creation of extraecclesial religious organizations. Like centralized religious organizations, the latter make use of techniques widely used in the modern world (media appeals, direct mail campaigns) to raise and dispense funds and to exercise influence. These techniques often are used independently of, if not against, more established ecclesiastical authorities whose power is thus countered.

Other kinds of changes characteristic of the modern world also permeate religious behavior. Many have to do with the high degree of rationality required to function in societies of the scale and complexity characteristic of the contemporary world. One example of this concerns the ordering of time. In the past, traditional religions imposed, or at least sanctioned, a structuring of time to include myriad festivals and feasts. In our society such patterns are in tension with broad social (and especially economic) objectives, so they no longer carry much weight. Thus we can observe certain new constraints or limitations on traditional religion as it impinges on the modern public world. Correspondingly, however, the relevance and influence of religious traditions in the realm of private time and space receive greater emphasis.

These are examples of what we might term the "coloration" through which "new" or modern societies influence all kinds of religious behaviors and beliefs in very basic ways. This "coloration" is thoroughly comparable to the codification of religions in the idioms and through the symbols of particular periods and societies, whether nomadic, pastoral, or urban. The *degree* of penetration by context is different in the contemporary world in some respects, but it is not a different *kind* of penetration. Thus religion is generally affected in the modern era but not solely in terms of conscious response to social and cultural change as represented in modernity.

Religious responses to modernity. There is, however, a contrast between this coloration or permeation of religious traditions and much more explicit religious responses to social change as represented in modern society. Especially as exhibited in American society, these responses may be seen to fall into five categories.

1. One kind of response is the advocacy of new religious ideas or the claim to new insights into ancient religious traditions. This frequently entails embracing the "new" in the name of correctly understanding the old. One dramatic example of this response in North America is the Oneida Community of the nineteenth century. Its founder, John Humphrey Noyes, believed that the spiritual sources for the new modern common life of his community flowed from early Christianity, whose tenets the community claimed to fulfill. Another interesting case is that of Christian Science. Its founder, Mary Baker Eddy, believed that she had correctly interpreted Jesus' teaching, indeed the essential message of early Christianity, which she thought to yield "modern" insights into healing. Many contemporary religiously innovative groups find their sources not so much in Western traditions as in Eastern lore and ritual. (In these cases, too, the connection with healing is often pronounced.)

2. Another response is self-conscious accommodation of religious traditions to modern society, often in very explicit terms. Indeed, here the term *modernist* is frequently used pejoratively with respect to religion. Into this category fall such well-known adaptations as Protestant liberalism (with European as well as New World ver-

sions), the Jewish Reform tradition (which of course had its origins in accommodation to modern European culture at the time of the Emancipation), and Roman Catholic Americanism in the late nineteenth century (a largely indigenous movement).

3. A third pattern of response is the determined attempt to preserve the continuing tradition, albeit self-consciously within limits posed by the new framework. In many respects this strategy undergirds various churchly responses of the nineteenth and twentieth centuries to modern societies, ranging from the proliferation of mainstream Protestant denominations to the careful and restrained Roman Catholic updating of tradition that became highly visible as a result of the Second Vatican Council and to the self-conscious but limited case of the isolated Mercersburg Movement of antebellum nineteenth-century America.
4. A still different pattern, infrequently recognized as equally a response to modernity, is the strident reassertion of a presumed tradition in a condensed, purified, or even reductionist form. The strands of "fundamentalism" in most of the major religious traditions of the globe are to be interpreted in this light. In this perspective, fundamentalisms, as the simultaneous reduction and enhancement of particular traditions, are no less than modernisms determined by the modern culture that they so stridently reject. Here also American society provides the most fully developed instances of fundamentalism, specifically within denominations with a self-consciously British heritage and especially among Presbyterians and Baptists.
5. A final pattern in the religious response to social change in the modern world is the generation of wholly new traditions. This entails celebration of the modern in often bizarre and idiosyncratic ways, although it may also take the form of recovering pagan traditions or exploiting exotic or esoteric beliefs. These new religions are explicit attempts to reject old traditions rather than to accommodate them. But in the larger sense they are also a response to the intense social and cultural changes experienced by people living in the modern era.

This fivefold pattern is, to be sure, an arbitrary division, for the lines between these five types are always shifting. But it serves to point out that the explicit relationships between modern cultures and religions are not single or of one kind only. They vary greatly. Indeed, the relationships are so plural that respective religious movements responding to perceptions of modernity in different ways may in fact be directly opposed to each other. The classical confrontation between liberalism (or modernism) and fundamentalism in American culture is a prime exhibit of this antagonism between essentially related, though very different, responses to a common cultural experience.

CONCLUSIONS. Modernity has proven to affect religion in heterogeneous ways, both explicit and implicit. The various explicit religious responses range from a strong and strident reassertion of traditions, frequently on a reduced basis, to outright and uncritical celebration of cultural change. In this the term *modernity* most usefully refers to the kind of intense social, and hence cultural, change that especially characterizes Europe and America, of the nineteenth and twentieth centuries, but that has extended to other cultural areas a well. This period is not unique, however, for in earlier periods something like the same pattern of a range of religious responses to social change has been evident. Religious life within the Roman Empire may be a useful parallel. With respect to the second kind of response—the implicit level of coloration provided by purely technological aspects of contemporary society—it does seem helpful to identify a peculiar cultural configuration exclusively with "modernity." But this coloration extends as much to the activities of critics of the modern as it does to its partisans. Finally, a significant point is that the modern is not to be seen as itself a spiritual medium, that is to say, a unique religious stance.

When taken together, the concepts of modernity and religion identify the broad range of religious responses to intense and self-conscious social change in the contemporary world. What is uniquely modern is not the particular religious responses to change per se but their variety, intensity, and duration in the contemporary world. Crucial is the insight that religion is not so much threatened by modernity as challenged by it. And the challenge involves an inevitable and implicit coloration of virtually all religious behavior as well as a forcing of responses of many kinds, some direct, some indirect, all to some degree explicit, in the realm of religious belief. In these terms, the concepts of modernity and religion encompass a subject as fascinating as it is complex.

BIBLIOGRAPHY

The subject of modernity has been most fully explored in the social sciences because it has offered a rubric under which scholars can analyze the relentless social change characteristic of the contemporary world. This field looks back to the work of Max Weber, who first gave substantial attention to the relationships between religion and the emergence of modern societies. His *Protestant Ethic and the Spirit of Capitalism*, translated by Talcott Parsons (London, 1930), has continued to provoke strongly positive and negative scholarly responses. The following general discussions of modernity may be particularly useful in the current context: David E. Apter's *The Politics of Modernization* (Chicago, 1965); Cyril E. Black's *The Dynamics of Modernization* (New York, 1966); and Shmuel N. Eisenstadt's *Tradition, Change and Modernity* (New York, 1973). For a different treatment of the question, see *Becoming Modern: Individual Change in Six Developing Countries* (Cambridge, Mass., 1974), by Alex Inkeles and David H. Smith. An interpretation of American history under the same rubric is available as *Modernization: The Transformation of American Life, 1600–1865* (New York, 1976) by Richard D. Brown.

Recent discussions of religion depend heavily on anthropological and sociological perspectives, each of which introduces its own implicitly comparative framework. See the essays (especially that by Clifford Geertz) in *Anthropological Approaches to the Study of Religion*, edited by Michael Banton (London, 1966). Anthony F. C. Wallace's *Religion: An Anthropological View* (New York, 1966) is also useful.

Peter Berger and Thomas Luckmann collaborated on an influential study, *The Social Construction of Reality* (Garden City, N.Y., 1966), but subsequently have explored somewhat different sociological perspectives on religion in the modern world. Berger's *The Sacred Canopy* (Garden City, N.Y., 1967) and Luckmann's *The Invisible Religion* (New York, 1967) give different estimates of the status of religion in contemporary society. Berger also collaborated with Brigitte Berger and Hansfried Kellner in *The Homeless Mind* (New York, 1973), an explicit consideration of how religion is affected by modernization.

Among studies of particular episodes of religious change in modern societies, William R. Hutchison's *The Modernist Impulse in American Protestantism* (Cambridge, Mass., 1976) is a fine study of liberalism in American culture of the nineteenth and twentieth centuries. On this topic also see Kenneth Cauthen's *The Impact of American Religious Liberalism* (New York, 1962). Ernest R. Sandeen's *The Roots of Fundamentalism: British and American Millenarianism, 1800–1930* (Chicago, 1970), sharply focuses on the question of sources. George M. Marsden's *Fundamentalism and American Culture* (New York, 1980) is a superb study that suggests the broader sources of this movement and its implications.

Whitney R. Cross's *The Burned-Over District* (Ithaca, N.Y., 1950), an older case study of religious responses to the extreme social change of upper New York State in the early nineteenth century, suggests how religious movements as diverse as revivalism, Mormonism, and the Oneida Community could originate under the same social conditions. See also Paul E. Johnson's *A Shopkeeper's Millennium* (New York, 1978), a case study of the Rochester Revivals, for one model that explicitly relates religion to rapid social change. *Religious Movements in Contemporary America*, edited by Irving I. Zaretsky and Mark P. Leone (Princeton, 1974), is a compendium of essays on new religious movements.

On the expectation of "big changes" induced in a society whose culture is threatened, see Kenelm Burridge's *New Heaven, New Earth* (New York, 1969). *Millennial Dreams in Action*, edited by Sylvia L. Thrupp (New York, 1970), a broader discussion of millenarianism, suggests additional perspectives on this phenomenon.

New Sources

Ali, Tariq. *The Clash of Fundamentalisms: Crusades, Jihads, and Modernity.* London, 2002.

Ardis, Ann, and Leslie Lewis, eds. *Women's Experience of Modernity, 1875–1945.* Stanford, Calif., 2003.

Asad, Talal. *Formations of the Secular: Christianity, Islam, and Modernity.* Stanford, Calif., 2003.

Fawaz, Leila, and C. A. Bailey, eds. *Modernity and Culture: From the Mediterranean to the Indian Ocean.* New York, 2002.

Hess, Jonathan. *Germans, Jews, and the Claims of Modernity.* New Haven, 2002.

Latour, Bruno. *We Have Never Been Modern.* Translated by Catherine Porter. New York, 1993.

Seligman, Adam. *Modernity's Wager: Authority, the Self, and Transcendence.* Princeton, 2000.

Smith, David. *Hinduism and Modernity.* Oxford, U.K., 2003.

John F. Wilson (1987)
Revised Bibliography

MOGGALIPUTTATISSA, Buddhist elder and *arahant* leader of the monastic order (*saṃgha*) in India during the reign of Aśoka (274–232 BCE). According to the chronicles of the Theravāda tradition (*Mahāvaṃsa* and *Dīpavaṃsa*), he was the chief Buddhist adviser to Aśoka. After Aśoka became a generous supporter of Buddhism, he asked Moggaliputtatissa whether anyone had ever been a greater kinsman of the Buddha's religion. Moggaliputtatissa responded that a true kinsman of the Buddha must let his son or daughter enter the *saṃgha.* As a result, Aśoka encouraged one of his sons, Mahinda, to become a monk and one of his daughters, Saṃghamitta, to become a nun. Moggaliputtatissa subsequently became Mahinda's teacher in the *saṃgha.*

The primary work of Moggaliputtatissa is reported to have been the purification of the *saṃgha* and the organization of the Third Buddhist Council. Because Aśoka supported the *saṃgha* with lavish patronage, the *saṃgha* became corrupt and filled with undisciplined monks. When Aśoka's ministers, sent to ascertain what was wrong within the *saṃgha,* rashly executed some of the monks, Aśoka feared that the blame for the sin would accrue to him. Moggaliputtatissa, however, reassured Aśoka that he was not to blame for the act. Then, seated beside Aśoka, Moggaliputtatissa questioned all the monks and purged the *saṃgha* of those who did not subscribe to the Vibhhajjavāda interpretation of the teachings. The chronicles relate that he then chose a thousand *arahants* and held the Third Council, at which the Tipiṭaka was recited and committed to memory in its complete and final form. Moggaliputtatissa himself recited the *Kathāvatthuppakaraṇa* at this council.

Moggaliputtatissa also arranged for Buddhist monks to be sent as missionaries to other countries. The most notable of these missionaries was Mahinda, who is credited with the introduction of Buddhism to Sri Lanka.

See Also Aśoka.

Bibliography

The primary source for Moggaliputtatissa is *The Mahāvaṃsa, or, The Great Chronicle of Ceylon*, translated and edited by Wilhelm Geiger (1912; reprint, Colombo, 1950). An important secondary source is Walpola Rahula's *History of Buddhism in Ceylon: The Anuradhapura Period* (Colombo, 1956).

New Sources

Bullis, Douglas. *The Mahavamsa: The Great Chronicle of Sri Lanka.* Fremont, Calif., 1999.

George D. Bond (1987)
Revised Bibliography

MOGHILA, PETR See PETR MOGHILA

MOHENJO-DARO See INDUS VALLEY RELIGION

MOHILEVER, SHEMU'EL

MOHILEVER, SHEMU'EL (1824–1898), a leader of the proto-Zionist movement Ḥibbat Tsiyyon. Born in Lithuania, Mohilever served as rabbi in various communities in Lithuania and Poland. In the 1860s and 1870s, he wrote articles in the religious periodical *Ha-Levanon,* in which he advocated cooperation between the Orthodox and the *maskilim,* the followers of the Jewish Enlightenment. Relations between these two groups were extremely bitter, and Mohilever's attempt to create a bridge between them remained ahead of its time.

Like some of the *maskilim,* Mohilever was attracted to the idea of settlement of Jews in the Land of Israel even before the pogroms of 1881. Following the pogroms and the beginnings of mass emigration, he joined with others in creating the Ḥibbat Tsiyyon movement to divert the emigrants to Palestine. Mohilever was the honorary president of the Kattowitz conference of 1884, and his closing speech became a classic Zionist sermon. Ḥibbat Tsiyyon was torn from the outset by tensions between its religious and secular members, and these ultimately led to a withdrawal of support by many Orthodox Jews who had initially favored the movement. True to his belief in working with the *maskilim,* Mohilever remained in Ḥibbat Tsiyyon. However, in order to further religious interests in the movement, Mohilever suggested establishment of a "spiritual center" (*merkaz ruḥani*) which, following his death in 1898, became the foundation for Mizraḥi, the religious Zionist faction within Theodor Herzl's Zionist movement.

Mohilever worked intensively on developing Jewish colonies in Palestine and influenced Baron Edmond de Rothschild to contribute money toward this end. He also headed a tour of agricultural colonies in 1890. These settlement activities, although small and often failures, laid the groundwork for the later Zionist settlement.

Mohilever joined Herzl's World Zionist Organization when it was founded in 1897, but because of his infirm condition, he played no role in its activities. Nonetheless, he made an important contribution to the later Zionist movement with his insistence on an alliance between religious and secular Jewish nationalism.

SEE ALSO Zionism.

BIBLIOGRAPHY

Appraisals of Mohilever's life and work can be found in David Vital's *The Origins of Zionism* (Oxford, 1975), chapter 6. Additional biographical information on Mohilever appears in *The Zionist Idea,* edited by Arthur Hertzberg (Philadelphia, 1959), pp. 398–405.

New Sources

Hovav, Yamimah. *Ha-Rav Shemu'el Mohiliver.* Jerusalem, 1999.

DAVID BIALE (1987)
Revised Bibliography

MÖHLER, JOHANN ADAM

MÖHLER, JOHANN ADAM (1796–1838), German Roman Catholic theologian. Möhler was born on May 6 in Igersheim, Germany, near Mergetheim, about fifty miles from Stuttgart. Having determined to become a priest, he entered the seminary at Ellwangen, which seminary was incorporated by the government of Württemberg into the University of Tübingen in 1817. Möhler was ordained in 1819, and after a year in parish work he returned to Tübingen, to continue his studies in classical philology. Because the seminary authorities experienced continuing difficulty finding a suitable instructor in church history, Möhler found himself appointed privatdocent in church history in 1822 and instructed to prepare himself as best he could. He was given leave in 1822–1823 to travel to various German universities, the high point of his trip being brief contacts with Johann August Wilhelm Neander, Philipp Marheineke, and Friedrich Schleiermacher in Berlin. In the summer of 1823, Möhler began to teach church history, patristics, and canon law at Tübingen. He also contributed articles and reviews to the *Tübinger theologische Quartalschrift,* founded in 1819 by his principal mentor, Johann Sebastian Drey.

Möhler's first major work appeared in 1825: *Einheit in der Kirche, oder Das Prinzip des Katholizismus, dar-gestellt im Geiste der Kirchenväter der drei ersten Jahrhunderte* (Unity in the Church, or the principle of Catholicism, as presented in the spirit of the fathers of the first three centuries). Following the path of Drey's interest in, but by no means full acceptance of, the views of Schleiermacher and Schelling, Möhler in effect locates the Romantic concern for the organic unity of man with man and man with God in the writers of the first Christian centuries. This unity is traceable to the working of the inner spirit of the church, although, like Drey, Möhler retains a clear distinction between the divine and the human. (It should be noted that throughout his theological career Möhler tended to a somewhat Jansenistic view of the anticipatory, or initiating, role of divine grace.) Möhler differed with what later in the century would be standard Roman Catholic teaching in his conception of the church: the outward forms of Christianity are simply produced, as needed, by the spirit, with no assurance that the forms thus produced will always be the same. He wrote, for example, that "the Church is the body belonging to the spirit of the faithful, a spirit that forms itself from inward out." This and similar expressions earned Möhler the mistrust of those German Catholics who lived under Prussian rule, frustrating his attempt to move to one of the Prussian universities. Later some Catholic commentators, such as Edmond Vermeil, saw in Möhler a progenitor of modernism. In 1827 Möhler's *Athanasius der Grosse und die Kirche seiner Zeit* (Athanasius the Great and the church of his time) appeared, in which he criticizes Schleiermacher's Sabellianism and his tendency to blur the God-man distinction. In the following year Möhler was made *professor ordinarius* and doctor of theology.

With Marheineke's *Institutiones symbolicae* as his apparent model, and answering to the renewed German interest in the doctrinal differences arising from the Reformation, Möhler published in 1832 the first of five editions of *Symbolik, oder Darstellung der dogmatischen Gegensätze der Katholiken und Protestanten* (Symbolics, or presentation of the dogmatic differences of Catholics and Protestants). The title refers not to religious symbols but to the Latin *symbolum*, that is, creedal statement. His characterization of Protestant churches drew a number of sharp replies from that quarter, the most significant being the work of his university colleague (on the Protestant theological faculty) Ferdinand Christian Baur, *Der Gegensatz des Katholicismus und Protestantismus . . . mit besonderer Rücksicht auf Herrn Dr. Möhlers Symbolik.* Besides these two works in their various editions, Möhler and Baur each addressed an additional book-length reply to the other, Möhler's *Neue Untersuchungen* and Baur's *Erwiederung auf. . . Möhlers neueste Polemik.* It would appear that the controversy upset both the peace of the university and Möhler's health, with the result that Möhler moved to Munich, where he began teaching in the university in 1835 and where he died on April 12, 1838. His lectures on church history, patristics, and Paul's *Letter to the Romans* were published posthumously.

Möhler's *Symbolik* is divided into two books. After an introduction, book 1 compares Roman Catholic with Lutheran and Reformed teaching in the areas of original sin, justification, the sacraments and the church, and eschatology. Book 2 takes up "the smaller Protestant sects," namely, those of the radical Reformers, Quakers, Pietists, Methodists, Swedenborgians, Socinians, and Arminians. Möhler's conception of comparative dogmatics goes far beyond merely recording divergent views. It is necessary, he writes, "to decompose a dogma into the elements out of which it has been formed and to reduce it to the ultimate principles whereby its author had been determined." On the other hand, it is also necessary that all "parts of the system be viewed in their relation to the whole, . . . to the fundamental and all-pervading idea." Whereas the spirit of the church led Catholicism, as a collectivity, to produce Catholic dogma, the teachings of the reformers were their individual productions. In Luther's mind and teaching, remarks Möhler, there was only "the inordinate pretension of an individuality which wished to constitute itself the arbitrary centre round which all should gather." In this apotheosis of the human, Schleiermacher is "the only genuine disciple of the Reformers." (Interestingly, Baur basically accepted Möhler's assessment of Protestantism. What he objected to was Möhler's denial of Protestantism's right to doctrinal development.) Paradoxically, the germ of Luther's error lay in his theological anthropology, in his understanding of original sin, wherein the total loss of human freedom leads to the affirmation of universal divine necessitation. Viewed systematically, Protestantism displays the fatal flaw of the disappearance of the merely finite human. By 1832 Möhler had sufficiently mastered church history to recognize and accept fundamental theses of the Council of Trent: synergism in justification and good works, and the positive, outward role of Jesus Christ in the institution of the church and the seven sacraments.

In its immediate effect Möhler's work was a noteworthy contribution to increased self-respect and intellectual respectability among mid-nineteenth-century German Catholics. The long-term effect of Möhler's work arose less from his polemical thrusts than from his essentially Romantic vision of the place of Christ in the church. If the whole life of Jesus Christ is "one mighty action," then "the Church is the living figure of Christ manifesting himself and working through all ages. . . . He is eternally living in his Church, and in the sacrament of the altar he has manifested this in a sensible manner to creatures endowed with sense." Möhler's interest in the organic nature of reality and in the dignity of the human as a finite symbol of the divine can be traced, for example, in M. J. Scheeben's *The Mysteries of Christianity* (1865) and Henri de Lubac's ecclesiological studies—and ultimately in papal and conciliar documents, namely, Pius XII's *Mediator Dei* and *Mystici corporis* and the Constitution on the Liturgy of Vatican II.

Bibliography

Works by Möhler

Die Einheit in der Kirche, oder Das Prinzip des Katholizismus. Edited by Josef Rupert Geiselmann. Cologne, 1957. Contains extensive commentary by the editor.

Gesammelte Aktenstücke und Briefe. Edited by Stephan Lösch. Munich, 1928.

Symbolik. 2 vols. Edited by Josef Rupert Geiselmann. Cologne, 1960–1961. Translated by James Burton Robertson as *Symbolism* (London, 1843). Contains Geiselmann's extensive commentary.

Most of Möhler's other writings have been published in photographic reprint (Frankfurt, 1968).

Works about Möhler

Baur, Ferdinand Christian. *Der Gegensatz des Katholicismus und Protestantismus nach den Principien und Hauptdogmen der beiden Lehrbegriffe mit besonderer Rücksicht auf Herrn Dr. Möhlers Symbolik.* 2d ed. Tübingen, 1836.

Chaillet, Pierre, ed. *L'église est une: Hommage à Möhler.* Paris, 1939.

Dupuy, B. D. "Schisme et primauté chez J. A. Möhler." *Revue des sciences philosophiques et théologiques* 34 (1960): 197–231.

Fitzer, Joseph. *Moehler and Baur in Controversy, 1832–38: Romantic-Idealist Assessment of the Reformation and Counter-Reformation.* American Academy of Religion Studies in Religion, no. 7. Tallahassee, 1974.

Geiselmann, Josef Rupert. *Die katholische Tübinger Schule.* Freiburg, 1964.

Goyau, Georges. *L'Allemagne religieuse: Le catholicisme.* 2 vols. Paris, 1910.

Vermeil, Edmond. *Jean-Adam Möhler et l'école catholique de Tubingue, 1815–1840.* Paris, 1913.

JOSEPH FITZER (1987)

MOKOSH is the life-giving goddess in ancient Slavic mythology, inherited from the pre-Indo-European pantheon and debased during the early Christian era. She is the only female deity mentioned in the Kievan pantheon established by Vladimir I in 980 CE. In northern Russia, she has survived as a house spirit, Mokysha or Mokusha; a tall woman with a large head and long arms, she shears sheep at night and spins flax and wool. Her name is connected with spinning and plaiting (Lithuanian *meksti, makstyti,* "to plait," and *mākas,* "shirt"; Russian *meshok,* "sack, bag," *moshna,* "pouch") and with moisture (**mok-* or **mokr-*, "wet, moist"). These associations suggest her ties with the life-giving and life-taking goddess of Old Europe—that is, with Fate, the spinner of the thread of life and the dispenser of the water of life. Menhirs (*kamennye baby*), venerated in some Slavic areas into the twentieth century (and some now called *Maria*), seem to be connected with this ancient goddess, who possessed healing powers. Paralytics, the blind, and the deaf offered flax, wool, and sheep to these stones.

In the Christian era, Mokosh was superseded by Paraskeva-Piatnitsa ("Friday, fifth day") or Lianitsa ("linen washer"). In the Russian Orthodox tradition she is identified as Saint Paraskeviia (from the Greek *paraskevi,* "Friday"). Friday was a day sacred to the goddess and was characterized by taboos on women's work. In Carnival processions, the saint's image was that of a woman adorned with flax, her hair hanging loose and her hands extended. Legends speak of the miraculous powers of healing springs or river sources associated with Paraskeva-Piatnitsa. In the Russian ritual called *mokrida* (from *mokr-*, "wet"), a sacrifice to her consisted of flax, wool, thread, or woven articles such as towels and shirts. Her most important holiday fell on October 28, a day within the annual period of flax preparation. Women may not work on this day. Disregard of this rule may bring on blindness or some other malady, or may even result in death. Piatnitsa may transform intransigent women into frogs. Posts and shrines in her honor were built at crossroads, and wooden images of her were erected as late as the twentieth century.

In northern Russia, old icons testify to the continuing importance of this pre-Indo-European goddess in Christian guise. In them, Saint Paraskeviia, who replaced Mokosh, is shown as one of a saintly triad, along with Saint Elijah (Il'ia), who replaced the Indo-European deity Perun, and Saint Blasius (Vlasii), who replaced the Indo-European deity Veles-Volos.

BIBLIOGRAPHY

Filatov, V. V. "Riazanskaia ikon 'Paraskeva Piatnitsa.'" *Sovetskaia arkheologiia* 1 (1971): 173–190.

Matorin, N. M. *Zhenskoe bozhestvo v pravoslavnom kul'te.* Moscow, 1931.

Tokarev, S. A. *Religioznye verovaniia vostochnoslavianskikh narodov.* Moscow, 1957.

New Sources

Kapica, F. S. *Slavyanskije tradicionnije verovanija, prazdniki i rituali* [Slavic traditional beliefs, festivities and rituals]. Moscow, 2001.

Shaparova, N. S. *Kratkaya enciklopedija slavyanskoj mifologii* [A short dictionary of Slavic mythology]. Moscow, 2001.

Tokarev, S. A. "Moskva Mifi narodov mira (World myths)." *Bolshaya Rossijskaya Enciklopedija,* vols.1–2, 1998.

MARIJA GIMBUTAS (1987)
Revised Bibliography

MOKṢA. The term *mokṣa,* a Sanskrit masculine substantive, and its feminine synonym *mukti,* are derived from the linguistic etymon *muc,* meaning "release." Both terms have always been employed in an exclusively religious sense, denoting release from the tedious and painful cycle of transmigration (*saṃsāra*). Such a notion first appears in Indian thought with the oldest Upaniṣad, as well as in early Buddhism.

The notion of *mokṣa* is found neither in old Vedic literature, nor in the Saṃhitās ("collections"), nor in the Brāhmaṇas, the commentaries referring to sacrificial rites. Indeed, the oldest known Vedic texts are concerned with enjoyment *(bhukti)* of the earthly world, not with release from it. The metaphysical, moral, and soteriological associations of the concept of *mokṣa* are based on a religious sensibility that places absolute priority on the experience of being liberated from those very structures and patterns.

It was not until the sixth century BCE that texts began to give evidence of what would come to be the main concern of Indian religious thought, that is, release from the cycle of rebirth or *saṃsāra,* which is generated by the weight of actions (*karman*) fulfilled during the present life or during previous ones. Such a preoccupation arose at the same time in Brahmanism and Buddhism, and eventually extended throughout the Indian subcontinent. It lies at the very base not only of the Upaniṣads but of the teachings of the Buddha and of his contemporary, the other great religious reformer, Mahāvīra.

The concept of *mokṣa* becomes more elaborately developed in both the *Mahābhārata* and the *Laws of Manu.* The idea also appears in the early Upaniṣads, but is expressed with the synonymous term *mukti.* When *mokṣa* appears, it is under its compound *vimokṣa,* but with the same meaning. Early Buddhism employes the Pali form *mokkha.*

The *Bhagavadgītā,* which very likely constitutes one of the earlier parts of the *Mahābhārata,* does not yet employ the word *mokṣa,* but the etymon *muc* provides substitutes to specify those who have a mind to gain release (4.4); the one who is released is referred to with the adjective form *mukta* (5.28) and, as in the *Chāndogya Upaniṣad,* which predates the *Gītā* by three centuries, the substantive form appears only as *vimokṣa* (16.5) or *nirvimokṣa,* with the same meaning.

Often, where *mokṣa* might be expected, other words are substituted for it. A word derived from Vedism, *amṛta,* is used to introduce the notion of immortality; in that case, however, it takes on a particular significance, putting the stress on the fact that *mokṣa* results in a privileged position, the major effect of which is to avoid rebirth. The essential point is that *mokṣa* is liberation from the ties of action (*karman*) and from *saṃsāra,* the endless chain with no beginning.

By using a different vocabulary, the later systems derived from Brahmanic thought give a different coloration to their conception of release. For instance, the Yoga system proposes *apavarga,* which emphasizes escape from the cycle of rebirths; the Sāṃkhya chooses the word *kaivalya,* that state of being in which one regains primitive unity. However, in spite of a different wording, the aim remains the same, that is, the liberation of the *jīva,* or the individual soul.

In the Vedānta texts of the Middle Ages, composed by the commentators on the *Brahma Sūtra,* it is the substantive term *mokṣa* that is preferred. The most influential of these commentators are Śaṅkara (eighth century CE), Rāmānuja (c. eleventh to twelfth century), Nimbārka (thirteenth century), Madhva (fourteenth century), and Vallabha (fifteenth century). Following them, modern Indian philosophers of the nineteenth century as well as contemporary thinkers adhered to the same term.

Mokṣa is a perennial word in the Indian religious vocabulary; the notion it conveys in every case is the assurance that the practitioner is never to come back to this world again. Various ascetic traditions throughout Indian history have taught that the release from the world can actually take place before one's physical death. Such traditions speak then of the *jīvanmukta,* that person who is "released while still alive."

Writings colored by Tantric influences, particularly those connected to the Vaiṣṇava Pāñcarātra, mention three ways to liberation. The first is based on a full differentiation between the god and his worshiper. The second is based on a theory of union between the two of them: Self and self make one; God and soul are one. The third way to liberation consists of an attempt to reintegrate the Supreme Self through complete identification with it. In Tantric Vaiṣṇavism, that expectation is named inmost union, or *sayujya.*

The *Bhagavadgītā* delineates three paths of self-discipline leading to freedom: through action (*karmayoga*), through knowledge (*jñānayoga*), and through devotion (*bhaktiyoga*). In the first, one is deemed bound by each good or evil deed yet can win appropriate reincarnation through actions or deeds. On the face of it, it seems impossible to place *karman* and *mokṣa* together; good deeds may only be valued as preliminary steps to liberation. But we must consider here the particular context of *karman* in its primitive significance as a ritual act, an act specially consecrated. The word *karman* is, of course, basically related to action. However, one will not be tied up by one's actions if one bears in mind the all-important rule not to expect a reward in this world or later on. Only acts with no self-concern may open the kingdom of the *brahman.*

The main characteristic of *jñānayoga* is the cognition that *ātman* and *brahman* are identical. It is cognition or insight that grants man real freedom, for the individual soul is considered free but fails to recognize it.

The *Bhagavadgītā,* together with all of the theistic systems, also espouses a third way to reach emancipation, that is, through *bhakti,* or devotion. Originating in Vaiṣṇavism, *bhakti* spread forth into other religious traditions of India, and became particularly important in Tantric Śaivism.

With regard to cognition or meditation as a path to *mokṣa,* both the Upaniṣads and Śaṅkara hold that there is a procedure of mind bound to an intuitive recognition between the *ātman* and the *brahman,* that is, the identity of the self within the Self, or the Primary Energy from whom all energies proceed. Through mere concentration of mind one should seize that identification content as the intuitive recognition of the famous *tat tvam asi:* "that thou art."

In the theistic systems, the meditation process, rather than relying upon abstractions, rests on a personification of the Ultimate. Meditation is achieved by concentrating on the god's performances such as they are reported in the sacred texts. The gods are invoked through prayer formulations known as mantras, which are expected to be impregnated by the very energy of the One invoked. The foundations of a relationship with the Lord are built on love and confidence. In return, the Lord, through his benevolence, grants his worshiper the deliverance others achieve only through the course of multiple lifetimes. Sometimes, *mokṣa* appears as a favor granted by the god, owing nothing at all to human effort. The notion of delivery is conceived of quite differently by theistic and nontheistic systems. If such a quest is evident in the Indian current of thought, it is out of a theistic conception that it acquires its full religious significance.

Indian writings with a political tendency often mention the three traditionally recognized objects (*vargas*) of earthly life: *dharma* (moral duty or law), *kāma* (enjoyment), and *artha* (material wealth). In a combined philosophical and religious context, a fourth object, *mokṣa,* is added. Philosophically, it is recognized as the most important, for it expresses the human being's supreme object, his return to the primary cause, the Ultimate.

In the Upaniṣadic context, *mokṣa* is the cause of little mythological elaboration. It is from traditions where *mokṣa* is won by worshiping a personified god that the myth takes strength in literature as well as in iconography. From the epic poems (i.e., the *Mahābhārata* and the *Rāmāyaṇa*) onward, the notion of liberation is given a mythological context. One of the most striking examples is provided by Kṛṣṇaism. In the separate forms of a child, a warrior, and a lover, the hero Kṛṣṇais a permanent actor in the quest for salvation of his worshipers.

The Vedānta circles that issued from Rāmānuja and Nimbārka, and later from Vallabha, emphasized the combined worship of Kṛṣṇa and of his favorite shepherdess, Rādhā, for the predominance of love over any other feeling may in itself lead to emancipation. Because every iconic image keeps a fragment of divinity after ritual ceremonies have been practiced, worshiping images is a definite step in adoration; more potent than the rite itself are the images, charged with a salvific power. The Śaiva tradition also recognizes the efficacy of worshiping the images of the god (Śiva) and the goddess (Devī or Kālī or the Great Goddess).

When people beg for material valuables, the one "who knows," as it is said in the Upaniṣads, is aware that only through the benevolence of God may he reach the Ultimate, which is the way out of the cycle of rebirths.

See Also Bhagavadgītā; Bhakti; Jīvanmukti; Jñāna; Karman, article on Hindu and Jain Concepts; Madhva; Mūrti; Nimbārka; Rāmānuja; Sāṃkhya; Saṃsāra; Śaṅkara; Vallabha.

Bibliography

An excellent introduction to the subject can be found in *Karma and Rebirth in Classical Indian Traditions,* edited by Wendy Doniger O'Flaherty (Berkeley, 1980). See also the "Mokṣadharmaparvan" (Chapter on the Rules of Emancipation) in book 12 of the *Mahābhārata,* translated by Pratap Chandra Roy and K. M. Ganguli (1884–1896; Calcutta, 1963).

New Sources

Fort, Andrew O. *Jivanmukti in Transformation: Embodied Liberation in Advaita and Neo-Vedanta.* Albany, N.Y., 1998.

Living Liberation in Hindu Thought. Edited by Andrew O. Fort and Patricia Y. Mumme. Albany, N.Y., 1996.

Singh, Darham. *Sikh Theology of Liberation.* New Delhi, 1991.

A. M. Esnoul (1987)
Revised Bibliography

MONASTERY.

[*This entry discusses the architecture of Christian monasteries. For discussion of monasteries in Asian religions, see* Temple, *articles on* Buddhist Temple Compounds, Daoist Temple Compounds, *and* Confucian Temple Compounds. *For further discussion of the monastic way of life, see* Religious Communities.]

A monastery is a building or group of buildings arranged for the members of a religious order to live as a community apart from the world in work, study, and prayer dedicated to God. The term *monastery* will be broadly used here to mean not only the houses of monks but also the houses of nuns (convents) and friars (friaries); the term *monk* will be used to mean both male and female residents of monasteries.

The practice of Christian monasticism has its origins in Egypt where, beginning in the late third century, men withdrew to the deserts and mountains to meditate and fast in solitude. Soon these hermits (Lat., *eremites*) formed groups of cells adjacent to a small oratory or church (*laura*). Pachomius (c. 292–346) was the first to organize hermits into a cenobitic community (*coenobium*), where each monk lived alone in a room or a cell but joined with the other monks for prayer and meals. Nothing is known about the physical appearance of these monasteries except that the informally disposed buildings were surrounded by a wall, and the monks grouped according to skills or crafts. In Asia Minor, Basil the Great (c. 329–379) added charitable works such as establishing orphanages, hospitals, and workshops to the monks' activities. Some monastic communities included buildings for travelers and pilgrims.

By the fifth century, the cenobitic system had spread throughout the Mediterranean world and north through Europe. The organization of the buildings varied from monastery to monastery, according to what activities were performed and at what times of the day and night. A coherent and logical architectural scheme was worked out only after the monks' day was strictly regulated.

In 529, Benedict of Nursia (c. 480–547) established a community at Monte Cassino, in Italy, where he composed a rule to govern its life. The rule demanded a blend of liturgy, study, meditation, and manual labor under the close direction of an abbot (*abbas*). While not prescribing the physical features of the monastery, the rule profoundly influenced its design by touching on all aspects of monastic activity, including the monastery's services to society.

The Benedictine Schema. By the late eighth century, Benedict's rule was the accepted code for western European monasteries. The first monastic plan is known as the Plan of Saint Gall—it is extant and now resides in Saint Gall, Switzerland. This plan is a copy from about 820 of a lost scheme for an ideal monastic complex formulated during the reform synods of Aachen in the years 816 and 817. The plan did not designate a specific monastery and was never built as such; rather, it was a statement of policy showing what buildings should make up an ideal monastery and the relationship of these buildings to one another. The Plan of Saint Gall provided a model for later monasteries where the rule of Saint Benedict could be lived in the most rational manner.

Designed to accommodate 110 monks and 150 to 170 serfs and workmen, the Saint Gall plan clearly defines the different activities of the monastic community within separate buildings. Broadly described, these buildings comprise the church; the cloister and its buildings for the monks; the buildings for the sick, the elderly, and the novices; the buildings for the monastery's secular responsibilities; and the domestic buildings serving the community. Each building on the plan is labeled, and these labels are sometimes complemented by a reference to the spiritual significance of the building. The order and logic of the plan both served and reflected the order of the monks' lives as prescribed by Benedict's rule—a perfect life required a perfect monastery.

COMPONENTS. The monastery, a self-contained and self-sustaining community within the larger community of empire, kingdom, or nation, was enclosed by a high wall with only one means of access. Its physical and spiritual heart was the church. Whereas in the eastern Mediterranean, the centralized, or cross, plan was more popular, in the West, as the Saint Gall plan shows, the basilical plan was preferred. East or West, the church was always the most resplendent building in the monastery, invariably constructed of stone or brick and richly ornamented. The church served the local parish, pilgrims, and guests as well as the monastic community. The lay community and visitors were restricted to the western end of the church, located closest to the monastery's entrance.

The monks, housed in their own group of buildings, were isolated from serfs and workmen and from the secular activities of the monastery. Located alongside the eastern half of the church, the monks' quarters consisted of three ranges of large, often double-storied buildings tightly locked around a square or rectangular courtyard that was the cloister. This cloistral complex was usually sited on the south side of the church in cooler northern climates and on the north side in southern climates; site constraints also influenced its location.

A continuous covered arcade surrounded the open court and so gave direct access to all the buildings. The walk closest to the church often was used for reading or study and from the fifteenth century contained recesses or carrels to hold the monks' desks. The origin of the cloister as an architectural unit is still unclear, but the square-shaped cloister surrounded by the monks' quarters was an invention of the Carolingian age; its development was dependent on the adoption of the highly controlled and ordered life prescribed by Benedict.

On the eastern side of the cloister, the dormitory was placed at right angles to the church and, joined to it at the transept, provided direct access for the monks during night services. Monks slept communally in the early Benedictine monasteries, although the dormitory often was divided into separate cubicles by wooden partitions. After Pope Martin V conceded single cells to the Benedictines in 1419, the common dormitory became rare. Taking up a greater area than a dormitory, single cells probably led to the two-story cloister composed of cells on all three sides of the upper floor. On the Saint Gall plan, the dormitory was raised above the monks' warming, or day, room. Located near the dormitory was the reredorter, or latrine, which was linked by a covered passage to protect the monks in inclement weather.

The refectory was placed at right angles to the dormitory, parallel to the church, with the vestiary, or wardrobe, above. While most refectories were at ground level, some were raised on undercrofts, which were used for food storage. Like the dormitory, the refectory had to be large enough to accommodate all the monks at one time. Monks ate at long tables while listening to scriptural readings given from a pulpit. A fountain or basin for the monks to wash in before eating was located near the refectory, often in the south walk of the cloister. From the twelfth century, the fountain was commonly an independent structure projecting into the cloister opposite the refectory. The kitchen was located near the refectory but usually outside the cloister.

On the west side, for easy access to the outer world, was the cellar, located on the ground floor, with a larder above. Between the cellar and the church, the sole formal exit from the cloistral area was through the monks' parlor, where monks, when permitted, met guests. Except for the time they spent working, the monks spent their entire lives in the cloistral complex. This complex, an architecturally conceived whole, provided a self-contained world for the monks within an already separate world.

From the eleventh century, one other building or room not included on the Saint Gall plan became a standard feature of the cloistral area: the chapter house. Used for business matters of the monastery and as a burial place for the abbots, the chapter house was located either next to the church or under the dormitory. In England, it was sometimes a separate circular or polygonal building.

The other buildings that made up a typical medieval monastery, as shown on the Saint Gall plan, were sited and grouped according to their function and their relationship with the secular world. Attached to the north side of the church were rooms for the porter and visiting monks. Flanking the apse was the scriptorium, where selected monks copied and illuminated manuscripts, with the library above it. By the twelfth century, the library frequently was located under the dormitory, alongside the chapter house. Also on the north side of the church, but freestanding, were the buildings that served the monastery's obligations of hospitality and education. These included the house and kitchen for visitors of rank; a school for children of the local nobility; and a house and kitchen for the abbot, whose social responsibilities included such secular activities as entertaining guests. The inscription on the Saint Gall plan notes that the ideal abbot's house is constructed of stone; in many monasteries, except for the church, the abbot's house was the most splendid building.

Isolated to the northeast of the church was the infirmary. This infirmary, also used as a nursing home for aged monks, often was designed as a monastery in miniature, with its own refectory, dormitory, bath house, and chapel arranged around a cloister. Completing this unit was the doctor's house, the house for bloodletting, and a medicinal herb garden. Nearby was the cemetery, which in the Saint Gall plan doubled as an orchard. The novitiate, also planned as a monastery in miniature, was to the south of the infirmary.

The L-shaped tract of land on the south and west was occupied by the service buildings. These included chicken and goose houses, a granary, a mortar and mill, workshops, houses for livestock and their keepers, and facilities for visiting pilgrims, paupers, and servants of distinguished guests.

Careful attention was paid to sanitation. In the Saint Gall plan, most of the latrines were placed on the perimeter. Whenever possible, monasteries were located near flowing water, which was channeled both to provide fresh water and to carry away waste. The importance of the water supply and drainage in medieval monasteries is attested to by a plan, drawn up around 1160, for the installation of a new water system at the Canterbury Cathedral monastery.

There is a coherent and logical organizing principle underlying the plan of Saint Gall. The hierarchical division and separation of buildings by function that is integral to the plan is clearly realized in all later monasteries. The plan provided a highly generalized statement adaptable to highly particularized site conditions, needs, and size. The clarity and unity of the plan served the monastery at a symbolic as well as a practical level, reflecting the order of the Benedictine rule and, by extension, the divine order and rule. For many centuries, the scheme of Saint Gall remained the guiding principle for the layout of a monastery, easily adapted to meet the requirements of orders other than the Benedictine.

Other Developments. The monasteries of the Carthusian order are a variation on the carefully conceived scheme of Saint Gall. In 1084, Bruno of Cologne (c. 1030–1101) fused the eremetic life with the cenobitic in one complex at Chartreuse, France, soon called La Grande Chartreuse. It was designed to house twelve monks and a prior, with each living alone in a cell and working alone in the private garden attached to his cell. The only communal activities in these Carthusian monasteries were mass, matins, vespers, and occasional meals. To ensure the monks' solitude, the cells and gardens were arranged around a large cloister and separated from the ancillary activities of the monastery by the church, refectory, chapter house, library, and prior's cell, all of which were organized around a second and smaller cloister. The quarters for the lay brothers *(conversi)*, who ministered to the needs of the monks, and for the guests were arranged around a separate cloister. Because their tasks required more frequent contact with the outside world, lay brothers inhabited either the western range of the cloister or a duplicate cloistral complex to the west. The Certosa di Pavia, the charter house in Pavia, Italy, founded in 1396, is typical of the layout and, like many Carthusian monasteries, housed twice the ideal number of twelve monks. Despite the adoption of single cells and private gardens, there was no substantive alteration in the ideal monastic scheme since there was no fundamental change in the monk's world of prayer, study, and work.

The Cistercians, founded in 1098 by Stephen Harding, dedicated themselves to restoring the original concept of Benedict's rule—self-sustaining communities based on a life of hard manual labor and prayer. They built their first monastery at Cîteaux, France, but it was later, under the leadership of Bernard of Clairvaux (1090–1153), that the order grew rapidly. Uniformity of activities and liturgy within the order resulted in uniformity in plan and design. For example, all the early churches followed the so-called Bernardine plan of a long nave and a rectangular apse in imitation of the church at Clairvaux. The Abbey of Maulbronn, Germany, founded in 1139, exemplifies Cistercian planning as a whole as well as the early design of the church. Located in secluded valleys, Cistercian monasteries possessed small guest quarters and no outer school. The lay brothers, in the western range of the cloister, were physically separated from the cloister by a walk known as the lane. The monks' refectory was usually at right angles rather than parallel to the church, probably to provide space for the kitchen between the refectory and the quarters of the lay brothers. Extensive and often distant land exploitation required granges consisting of living quarters, a chapel, and barns.

Over the centuries, Benedictine monasteries increasingly were adorned with figural sculpture and painting intended to instruct the faithful in Christian doctrine. For Bernard, this architectural ornament achieved an aesthetic and emotional power inappropriate for monks. Cistercian architecture was without figural sculpture and was minimally embellished, but the unplastered stone buildings achieved an austere monumentality reflective of Cistercian ideals. Cistercian monasteries were structurally innovative and influential in the dissemination of the pointed arch and vault throughout Europe.

The Franciscans (founded by Francis of Assisi, c. 1181–1226), the Dominicans (founded by Dominic of Osma, c. 1170–1221), and the Augustinians (late eleventh century) adapted the Benedictine schema to serve their synthesis of the contemplative life and active ministry. Located in cities and towns, their churches were large and spacious to serve better the new emphasis on preaching. From the 1520s, these three orders played a crucial role in the colonization and conversion of the Americas. In Mexico alone, nearly sixty monasteries were built in the sixteenth century. The early monasteries consisted of a church, often of single nave, and accommodations for the friars grouped around a cloister. For the enormous number of converts, the friars built a large walled courtyard that was attached to a side or corner of the church; this served as a temporary outdoor nave for the huge congregations. A typical courtyard consisted of a vaulted structure with a triple-arched façade to house the Sacrament on the side opposite the entrance and small square structures known as *posas* (Span., *posar*) at the corners. Pauses were made at the *posas* during liturgical processions around the courtyard, and they were used by the friars when teaching separate groups in the corners. The Dominican Monastery of Tepotzlan, Mexico, built in the sixteenth century, shows this ensemble. Both the open court and the *posas* appear to be an original architectural solution, probably invented by the Franciscans, for the particular spatial needs of the early Mexican monasteries. By the mid-sixteenth century, it was normal for these nontraditional open courtyards to be roofed, using traditional European techniques.

As early as the seventh century, and as formalized in the Saint Gall plan, many monasteries served the dual needs of both the monks and the larger community. In England, for example, in ten of the seventeen dioceses, the bishop's residence was in a monastery, and the monastery church also served as the cathedral church. Built within cities, the monks' buildings were set apart by a high wall. The church formed a physical and spiritual link between the conventual buildings and the bishop's palace, court, and administrative buildings outside.

The alliance of secular power with the monastery was demonstrated most influentially in the Escorial palace-monastery in Madrid, built between 1563 and 1584. It was conceived and endowed by Philip II as a retreat for himself and as a mausoleum for his father, Charles V; the monks, in this case of the Hieronymite order, performed daily rituals of commemoration for dead and living royalty. The Escorial was built on a plan of axial symmetry, with the church and crypt at the center and the monastic community housed around five cloisters on the south side of the church and its forecourt. To the north were the palace, a college and seminary, and lodgings for guests. A radical innovation was the king's apartment wrapped around the sanctuary of the church; its location simultaneously stated the power of the monarchy and affirmed monarchal piety. The absolute order of the design of the Escorial, where even the cruciform church echoes the overall grid, reiterates this union of church and monarchy.

The union of religion and state achieved its greatest architectural grandeur in the eighteenth-century Baroque monasteries, especially in central Europe. Adopting a symmetrical and axial plan in emulation of the Escorial, both monastic and secular precincts also were built around their own cloisters. Imperial apartments usually possessed a monumental, ceremonial staircase leading to the imperial hall, a large library to assert the monastery's role as a center of learning, and often a theater. These colossal and ostentatious monastery-palaces had magnificent façades and, sometimes, vast forecourts.

From the beginning, Byzantine and Russian monasteries showed less uniformity of plan than did those in the West. Although the church was normally in the center of the complex, the support buildings were variously arranged. But in the Baroque period, many newly founded monasteries followed the symmetrically planned and sumptuously appointed models of central Europe.

MODERN TIMES. Following the Protestant Reformation of the sixteenth century and the French Revolution of 1789, many monasteries were dissolved or suppressed, and the buildings were destroyed. A monastic revival in mid-nineteenth-century Europe, coupled with colonization and increased missionary activity, saw the establishment of monasteries in Africa, the United States, and, by the end of the century, Japan. In the twentieth century, and especially after World War II, many monastic communities launched extensive building programs, often selecting internationally renowned architects. Emphasis was on mission and on hospital and educational work, including higher education. Some monasteries extended the concept of hospitality to serve as temporary retreats for the laity. As before, the church acted as the spiritual unifier and the physical separator; the cloistral area was located on the side farthest from the visitor's area, and the school and other buildings were on the other.

Even before the Second Vatican Council of 1965, monastic churches were designed to emphasize the unity of monks and laity. The Benedictine Abbey of Saint John in Collegeville, Minnesota, founded in 1856 and redesigned by Marcel Breuer in 1953, preserves traditional plan organization while epitomizing the new trends. The entire complex of conventual buildings, a seminary, a university, and a high school, center on and revolve around the church. Scholastic zones are grouped to the north and west, and the conventional buildings are to the south. But the bell-shaped church has a centrally located altar, which allows the monks' choir to be visible to the laity, and new materials and structural forms directly express contemporary technology and ideas.

The monastery provides a physical environment to serve the contemplative and active dimensions of the monk's life and has, therefore, a continuity in overall planning concepts and building type irrespective of the circumstances of time and place. At the same time, within the type, monastic architecture shows the persistent experimentation and variation necessary for the particular requirements of the different orders.

BIBLIOGRAPHY

Bazin, Germain. *Les palais de la foi.* 2 vols. Fribourg, 1980–1981. A comprehensive and well-illustrated study of Baroque monasteries in Europe, Russia, and Latin America.

Braunfels, Wolfgang. *Monasteries of Western Europe: The Architecture of the Orders.* London, 1972. The basic analysis of Western monastic architecture from its beginnings to the present.

Horn, Walter, and Ernest Born. *The Plan of St. Gall: A Study of the Architecture and Economy of, and Life in a Paradigmatic Carolingian Monastery.* 3 vols. Berkeley and London, 1979. The definitive interpretation of the first monastic plan and a comprehensive study of all aspects of medieval Benedictine monastic architecture and life. Beautifully illustrated, fully documented, and very readable.

Le Bras, Gabriel. *Les ordres religieux: La vie et l'art.* 2 vols. Paris, 1979–1980. A survey of all the monastic orders throughout the world. Particularly useful for its hundreds of illustrations, many in color.

New Sources

Abdel Sayed, Gawdat Gabra, and Tim Vivian. *Coptic Monasteries: Egypt's Monastic Art and Architecture.* Cairo, 2002.

Cassidy-Welch, Megan. *Monastic Spaces and Their Meanings: Thirteenth-Century English Cistercian Monasteries.* Turnhout, Belgium, 2001.

Gerson, Paula Lieber. *Abbot Suger and Saint-Denis: A Symposium.* New York, 1986.

Hanawalt, Barbara, and Michal Kobialka, eds. *Medieval Practices of Space.* Minneapolis, 2000.

Keevill, G., Michael Aston, and Teresa Anne Hall, eds. *Monastic Archaeology: Papers on the Study of Medieval Monasteries.* Oxford, 2001.

Kinder, Terryl Nancy, ed. *Cistercian Europe: Architecture of Contemplation.* Grand Rapids, Mich., 2002.

King, James Cecil, and Werner Vogler, eds. *The Culture of the Abbey of St. Gall: An Overview.* Stuttgart and Zürich, 1991.

Stalley, R. A. *Early Medieval Architecture.* Oxford, 1999.

Verdon, Timothy, and John Dally, eds. *Monasticism and the Arts.* Syracuse, N.Y., 1984.

KAREN KINGSLEY (1987)
Revised Bibliography

MONASTICISM

This entry consists of the following articles:

AN OVERVIEW
BUDDHIST MONASTICISM
CHRISTIAN MONASTICISM

MONASTICISM: AN OVERVIEW

The Greek word *monos,* from which *monasticism* and all its cognates derive, means "one, alone." According to this etymology, therefore, the basic monastic person may be a hermit, a wandering ascetic, or simply someone who is not married or a member of a household. However, the term *monastic* normally refers to people living in community and thus embraces the cenobitic as well as the eremitic and peripatetic lifestyles. In Western societies, the definition of *monasticism* has often been restricted to its classic manifestations, especially the Benedictine tradition. By this definition clergy who adopt some aspects of monastic life and rule (canons regular or regular clerks), mendicant orders (Franciscan, Dominican, and like associations), and other religious orders are not properly called "monastic." Furthermore, within the classic definition one might be able to include some kinds of non-Christian monasticism—that is, those with goals and life patterns fairly similar to the Benedictines—but not others.

Nevertheless, many religious traditions feature (with varying degrees of formal institutionalization) a recognizable type of social structure for which *monasticism* is an appropriate name. The Buddhist *saṃgha,* the Christian religious and monastic orders, Jain monasticism, and Hindu *sādhus* or *saṃnyāsins* provide the most obvious examples. Daoist associations and Muslim Ṣūfī orders share many of the essential features of monasticism, although they also have some atypical aspects. Among primitive peoples something like monasticism exists in the phenomenon of secret societies. Other traditions, for example, Judaism and Protestant Christianity, have little expression of this religious possibility. Even within these religions, however, there have been associations much like monastic communities: among the Essenes, for example, and various sixteenth-century Lutheran groups, through the deaconess movement, to a current interest, most notably in the community at Taize, France.

With all these examples in mind, in the following paragraphs I shall attempt to develop a comprehensive analysis of the monastic phenomenon. In order to avoid the gender specificity of *monk* and *nun,* persons who exhibit and represent the monastic phenomenon will be called "monastics."

DEFINING FEATURES. First and most prominent of the essential features of monasticism is the monastic's distinctive social status and pattern of social relationships. The monastic person is identified as one whose self-perception and public role include membership in a special religious category of persons, a status which is deliberate and extraordinary. In some cases the monastic lives with other monastics, but in other cases participation in a communal life may only be sporadic. Most monastics are at least theoretically members of a group, but they may not live with that group for most of their monastic existence. The monastic status can involve either a new home or homelessness.

The second defining feature of the monastic situation is a specific program or discipline of life. The most obvious examples of formal regulations for the monastic life are the Vinaya of Buddhism and the Benedictine rule, but even less clearly defined categories set up expectations concerning appropriate behavior and activities for monastics. Monastic life, in contrast to the rest of human life, is entirely oriented toward a personal religious goal. Hence, the monastic adopts special patterns of living in order to achieve that goal.

Monastic status is differentiated from other religious roles, offices, and functions in that it is not primarily based on performing some service to others in the religious tradition or to the larger society but on the more private cultivation of a path of transformation. A minister, priest, shaman, or similar expert in sacred procedures exhibits a kind of religious leadership dependent on a community to which sacred values are transmitted. Certainly these roles can be merged: some religious professionals also live like monastics. Likewise the monastic person or community can take on many and varied tasks of service, only some of which may be obviously connected to the pursuit of the personal religious goal. Nevertheless, the essential element in any monastic situation is the longterm focus of the monastic life: separation from normal human existence in the pursuit of individual aspirations.

Third, monastic status is celebrated and publicized in various ways. A process of initiation marked by ceremony is very important to public perception as well as to monastic self-consciousness. Monastic status is also often indicated by distinctive clothing, modifications of the body (such as tonsure), and symbolic accoutrements (for example, the Buddhist staff and begging bowl). In many traditions the monastic leaves the arena of family, clan, or similar "natural" grouping and lives in a deserted place. The difference between monastics and others can be expressed through such factors as a different daily schedule: many monastic rules call for interrupted sleep or early rising. A specific diet may be prescribed. In all cases the monastic status represents a new or added identity expressed by specific behaviors, signs, and patterns of relationship to others.

Finally, it is important to note the presence of a larger religious tradition and set of institutions within which the monastic phenomenon takes place. We do not call those institutions "monastic" when the religious community in question is the whole legitimate religious tradition. The Shakers, for example, had many of the patterns of monastic life but constituted a whole church in and of themselves. This is the phenomenon that is more often termed a "sect" or "cult." Monasticism, by contrast, exists as an option within a wider grouping or identity; it is a special possibility that not everyone in that religious group adopts or is expected to adopt.

The optional monastic identity may be central or peripheral to the larger tradition. Christianity can exist without monasticism because, in the "secular" priesthood and episcopal office, it has a social structure and forms of leadership independent of monastic patterns. Such patterns are even less central in Islam, where much of the tradition disowns monasticism completely. By contrast, monasticism is central to Buddhism and Jainism; indeed, the monastic is sometimes thought to be the only true representative of these traditions and the lay community no more than a subordinate support group. Jainism and Buddhism began with monasticism, whereas Christianity manifested this pattern clearly only after a few centuries of existence.

The basic, common features of monasticism, therefore, can be reduced to these four: special status; dedication of monastics to the practice of personal religious disciplines; ritual entry and ongoing identification marked by special appearance; the role of monasticism as an option for some persons within a larger tradition and community. In addition to these features, however, there are many other frequent characteristics of the monastic situation that are not found in all examples.

FREQUENT CHARACTERISTICS. Even though the most careful definition of *monasticism* could not include communal life as a necessary factor, there can be no doubt that monastic existence is rarely completely solitary. Even wandering or hermit monks assemble periodically. These assemblies and the buildings constructed for longterm residence constitute the most visible aspects of monasticism and therefore might assume a larger place in one's perception of the phenomenon than they should. Much that is important to monastic life is personal, private, mental, or otherwise difficult for outsiders to gain access to. It is often only in public ceremonies or visible features such as the monastery itself that the outsider observes the monastic phenomenon. However, any adequate comprehension of monasticism requires a knowledge of the lives, conversations, and writings of monastics.

Sometimes monastic status is lifelong; this would seem to be the normal implication of the initiation into a higher realm. In some situations, however, temporary affiliation with a permanent community or temporary communities is a possibility. In Thailand many young men enter the preliminary stages of monastic life with no intention of persevering. A few months of monastic existence is better than none from their point of view. The Hindu phenomenon of the ashram is also deliberately temporary yet has many of the characteristics of a monastic community. The ashram may be thought of as the stage of life through which a pious Hindu man proceeds on his way from being a householder with a family to becoming a *saṃnyāsin*, a wandering, homeless, holy man. The ashram may also be thought of purely in terms of a forest dwelling place of such a man and the community that may gather around him.

Christian religious orders often have some arrangement whereby laypeople can become affiliated with the order without becoming full members. The third order of the Franciscan tradition and the Benedictine oblates are two such orders. In some instances a residential oblate may live just like the other members of the community or order. Certain Ṣūfīs live a kind of monastic existence in addition to being married, and several contemporary Christian religious communities are experimenting with such an arrangement.

Another frequent feature of monastic life and a major dynamic in its communal form is the phenomenon of discipleship and obedience. Monastic aspirants gather around a spiritual master, *guru,* or initiator who becomes their model and guide. The starets in the Russian Orthodox Christian tradition, the *shaykh* or *murshid* in Sufism, and the Zen Buddhist master are prominent examples. The relationship of master and disciple also can be found in nonmonastic situations. In all examples this type of association is much more intense and personal than that normally experienced between teacher and pupil. The master embodies the lesson and mediates transcendent power; radical obedience is an important discipline in the attainment of the monastic goal. Monastics sometimes validate their doctrine and practice by reference to their masters and their masters' masters, forming lineages back to the founders of their traditions.

Another important aspect of much monasticism, yet one not essential to it, is poverty or simplicity of lifestyle. The constitutive factors of distinction from normal or prevailing forms of life and the adoption of a specific rule and discipline are often expressed in the rejection of comforts or luxuries enjoyed by the rest of society. It is ironic that, despite the attempt to be ascetic or plain, monasteries often become quite wealthy. In order to participate in the holiness of the monastic community, the surrounding community characteristically bestows its valuables on the monastery, hoping to exchange them for the treasures of merit, wisdom, and piety cultivated by the monastics. Also the industry and discipline of monastic work has occasionally produced significant wealth. Such accumulation of wealth, as well as other factors that may lead to a change in the character of a monastic community's life over a period of time, have produced successive reforms within long monastic traditions. Benedictine history is a story of reforms: the first notable one took efficacious images

EFFICACIOUS IMAGES

As odd or superstitious as it may appear to a scientific, secular view of nature, many religious images and objects are capable of great efficacy and able to protect against evil or misfortune, promote prosperity, heal illness, prompt fecundity, communicate favorably with the dead, or secure divine blessing. In fact, it may even be that such purposes constitute the greatest occasion for images in religious life. The reasons for attributing this kind of power to images or sculptures are as diverse as the psychological and sociological models for explaining their appeal. To those engaged in the visual practices of efficacious images, the reason is probably straightforward: properly crafted and consecrated, images are connected by virtue of tradition, ritual, and likeness to the realities to which they refer. They direct devotion, petition, and desire toward their intended end. And when that end is not achieved, it is not due to the failure of the image as a metaphysical device, but to the inappropriate ritual preparation of the image or the petitioner, or to the intervention of another will, human or divine. Even failure affirms the cultural system of efficacy—in the same way that a failed bridge does not move people in an industrial society to scrap bridge-making, but to reapply the principles of engineering and the methods of construction to create a more reliable bridge.

The horrific appearance of the Hindu goddess Kālī in the sculptural relief shown here **(a)** does not generate fear or revulsion toward the goddess among the faithful who bring their petitions and children before the image. Her fearsome countenance and brutal disemboweling of a figure actually suggest her vicious treatment of the evil afflicting those brought to her for healing, who will

(a) A family views a sculpture of Kālī, a Hindu goddess, Kaalo Bhairab, Kathmandu, Nepal. *[©Macduff Everton/Corbis]*

receive from her the strength she expends against the violated figure of evil upon which she stands. Likewise, the angry intensity of a wooden figure placed on the gable of a home in New Zealand **(b)** was not meant to deter family or friends from entering the home, but malicious spirits. Images charged with such tasks do so by communicating their intention and function to their human users in a routine of efficacy in which intention performs an important role. The medium of their efficacy is thought and feeling. Their very presence affirms the cultural logic of an entire way of life as the objects are viewed daily by their users and their neighbors.

Images are used for a great variety of purposes. Neolithic peoples in northern Europe probably used hand-held fertility figures like the so-called Venus of Willendorf **(c)** to enhance fecundity or secure safe child-

(b) LEFT. Gable figure used to thwart malicious spirits and protect inhabitants of the house, c. eighteenth century, carved wood, shell, human teeth, traces of red pigment, New Zealand. *[Masco Collection; photograph by Dirk Baker]* **(c)** BELOW. Venus of Willendorf, a hand-held female fertility figure, c. 28,000–25,000 BCE, carved limestone. Willendorf, Austria. *[©Archivo Iconografico, S.A./Corbis]*

birth. Ancient Egyptians had themselves buried with small ceramic or wooden figures called *shawabtis* **(d)**, which in the afterlife provided necessary service with food production and preparation. They were incised with magical formulae and hieroglyphics that identified their purpose and ownership. Some Jews and Muslims use the emblematic figure of a hand—called *hamsa* in Hebrew **(e)** and Arabic for "five," often with scriptural texts inscribed on them—to shield them from the pernicious gaze of the evil eye. The origin of the *hamsa* pre-

(d) RIGHT. Ushebti statue of Tshahorpata, chief of the conjurors of the goddess Sekhmet, faience, c. fourth century BCE. *[©Erich Lessing/Art Resource, N.Y.]* **(e)** BELOW. Jewish *hamsa* amulets, used as shields against evil, nineteenth and twentieth centuries, silver, enamel, silver on brass. *[©The Jewish Museum, N.Y./Art Resource, N.Y.]*

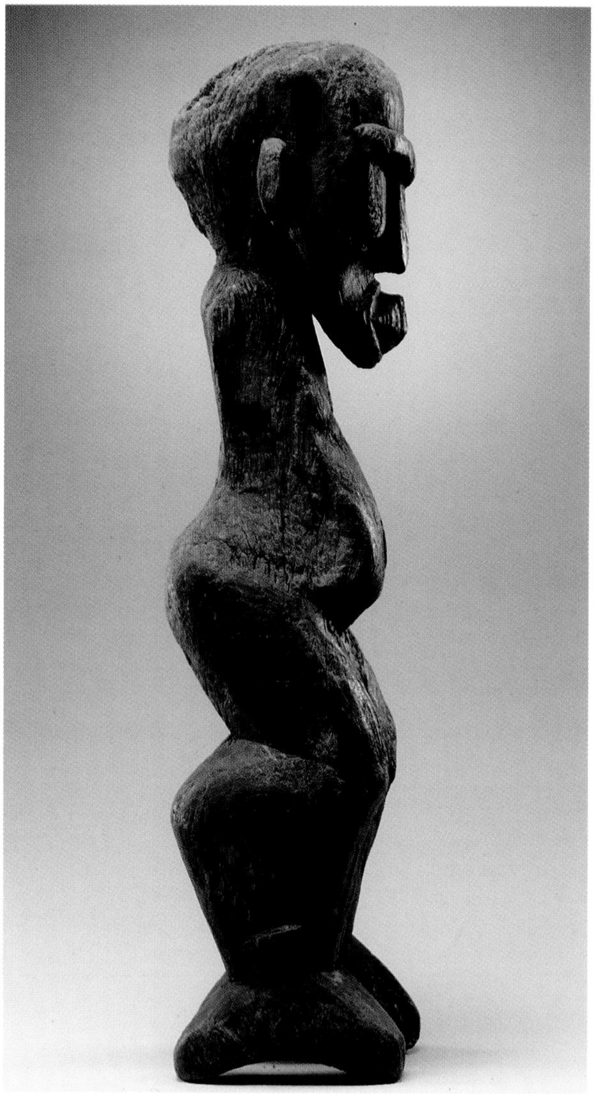

dates both Judaism and Islam. In Hawai'i, figures were erected in male lodges for the purpose of protection **(f)**.

Other images operate primarily as the means of directing petitions to divine forces or ancestors. For example, throughout India and among Hindus around the world, Gaṇeśa **(g)** is a favorite resource for overcoming obstacles associated with any aspect of life. In a like manner, practitioners of Santería create altars to the *orishas*, or deities whom they worship, such as the one shown here **(h)**. Roman Catholics direct their petitions to Saint Jude. Buddhists in Thailand and elsewhere apply gold leaf to sculptures of the Buddha **(i)** as acts of personal devotion and prayer that can solicit a portion of the Buddha's merit. Thai Buddhists hope that such a favorable karmic act will generate a beneficial consequence in this life or higher

(f) LEFT. Carved *aumakua* image, a Hawaiian deity of personal protection, found in 1917, wood, Maui. *[Masco Collection; photograph by Dirk Baker]* **(g)** BELOW. Dancing Gaṇeśa, Hindu remover of obstacles, tenth century, carved stone. *[©Philadelphia Museum of Art/Corbis]*

(h) **ABOVE.** Santería altar in Havana, Cuba. *[©Robert van der Hilst/Corbis]* **(i)** **LEFT.** Buddhists apply gold leaf to statues of the Buddha, Bangkok, Thailand. *[©Nik Wheeler/Corbis]*

rebirth in the next. Tibetan Buddhists make use of prayer wheels **(j)**, which generate prayers at a multiplied rate as they are spun by the faithful. In addition to these uses, images serve as devices for directing influence (malicious or benevolent) toward another. A Congolese charm or spirit container **(k)**, for example, is a receptacle invested with items belonging to a petitioner or those of a targeted party and charged with the task of exerting influence.

Images are often made and used to assist with burial, memorial, and grief. Nineteenth-century American parents often had postmortem photographs made of their children. One of these is paired here with a photograph

(j) ABOVE. Buddhist pilgrims in Lhasa, Tibet, spin prayer wheels, which generate prayers at a multiplied rate. *[©Galen Rowell/Corbis]* **(k) LEFT.** A nineteenth-century African Bakongo sculpture of a male figure, made from wood, glass, fiber, nails, and bone. The figure includes a spirit container (*nkisi*) used to instruct or admonish spirits. *[©Burstein Collection/Corbis]*

of the child taken during life **(l)**. The image on the left is the deceased, whose horizontal position in death has been changed to appear vertical, as if the child has not died, but poses peacefully asleep. Such imagery may have denied the death for grieving parents, or may have mitigated it to a peaceful slumber. If such images bring to mind the carefully prepared image of the corpse and in some vitally therapeutic manner replace the dead body and lost person with a memory image, traditional inhabitants of the Melanesian island of New Ireland used elaborate mortuary masks **(m)** to remove the spiritual traces of the deceased from his or her household. Dancers wearing such masks

(l) ABOVE. Paired photographs of a young girl who lived in the United States during the nineteenth century. The photograph on the left was taken shortly after her death. *[Courtesy of Jay Ruby, Center for Visual Communication]* **(m) RIGHT.** A Murua mask from New Ireland in Papua New Guinea, made from carved wood, sea sponge, and snail opercula. Such mortuary masks were used to remove traces of deceased relatives from the home. *[Masco Collection; photograph by Dirk Baker]*

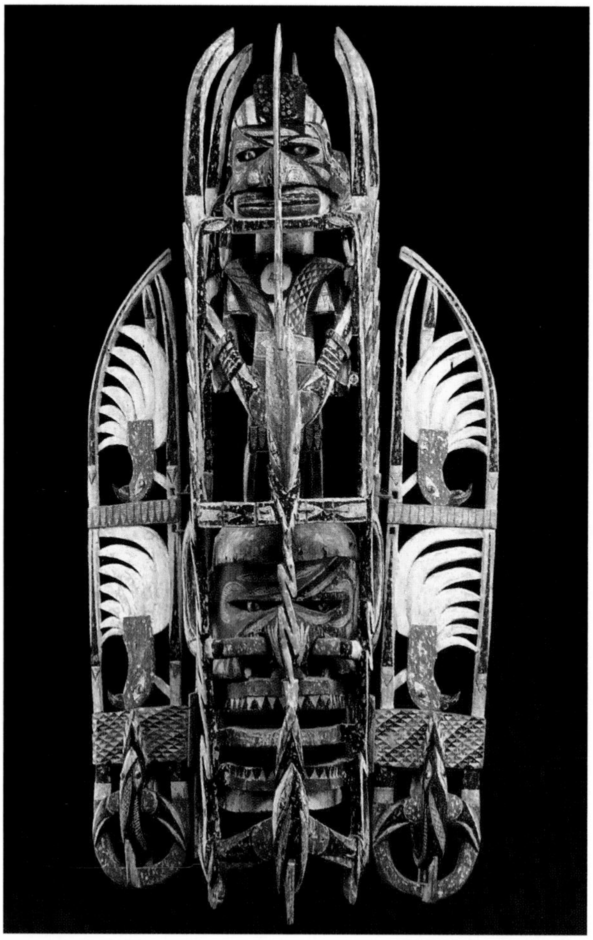

(**n**) A carved wood figurehead, used in initiation ceremonies by the Avelam people from East Sepik province in Papua New Guinea. *[Masco Collection; photograph by Dirk Baker]*

appeared at the home of the deceased in order to cleanse it of taboos by attracting any aspect of the dead away from the home to the site where the body had been cremated.

Perhaps the most common use of imagery is among rites of passage, when members of a society undergo crucial transpositions from one status or age to another. Images often serve to commemorate the event or to assist in the metaphysics of change. In the case of Papuan peoples, ancestors must be engaged to bless and guide the passage, to confer the new status, and to legitimate the change by bringing the initiate into the presence of the extended clan, represented by the totemic figures often included with such figures as the one reproduced here (**n**).

Bibliography

Cox, J. Halley, with William H. Davenport. *Hawaiian Sculpture.* Rev. ed. Honolulu, 1988.

Fazzini, Richard A., James F. Romano, and Madeleine E. Cody. *Art For Eternity: Masterworks from Ancient Egypt.* Brooklyn, N.Y., 1999.

Huyler, Stephen P. *Meeting God: Elements of Hindu Devotion.* New Haven, 1999.

Pal, Pratapaditya. *Desire and Devotion: Art from India, Nepal, and Tibet in the John and Berthe Ford Collection.* Baltimore, Md., 2001.

Wardwell, Allen. *Island Ancestors: Oceanic Art from the Masco Collection.* Seattle and Detroit, 1994.

David Morgan (2005)

place under the aegis of Benedict of Aniane about three hundred years after Benedict of Nursia founded the order. This was followed by the reform programs of Cluny, the Cistercians, the Trappists, and so on.

Monastic clothing has had great significance in some traditions. In many cases the origin of such clothing was merely an extension of the emphasis on simplicity—the garments of the poor were adopted. Ṣūfīs are so called because of their affirmation of simple wool *(ṣūf)* in contrast to the silks of the rich. The ocher robe in India and the various colors of the Christian communities have been important means of identification. There has also been a "romance of the cowl." The monastic garment itself has had a fascination and religious significance, for example in the desire to be buried in a cowl through deathbed profession. In Jain monastic practice we find the unusual phenomenon of nakedness as monastic "clothing." The Digamambara Jain monks are thus "sky-clad" as a precaution against harming even a body louse and as an ascetic discipline, and at the same time to signify their monastic status by departing from the normal way of dressing.

According to one interpretation, monasticism can be understood basically in terms of asceticism; self-denial and the acceptance of pain are the basic reasons for the existence of the institution, from this point of view. Insofar as "asceticism" can refer to any kind of discipline, one cannot argue with this approach. "Asceticism," however, is usually associated with painful and rigorous disciplines, and not all monastic systems prescribe difficult or unusually painful practices. The range is very broad between mild ascetic disciplines and self-denial on a heroic scale, although it is rare that a monastic is not self-conscious about avoiding and rejecting many human potentials and comforts. At the least sleep and eating are usually regulated and reduced. Silence is kept for extended periods. However, ascetic practice is also always a matter of perspective and degree: what seems like suffering to one person might not disturb the comfort of another. If a monastic thinks that suffering must be cultivated in order to achieve a religious goal, many and various techniques may be used. In other situations what might seem like asceticism to the outsider may be understood and experienced more as simplicity and the reorganization of life.

Most monastics in the history of world monasticism have been men; indeed, the founders of monastic orders, including the Buddha, have allowed women to be monastics only reluctantly. This probably has been due more to surrounding cultural factors than to anything intrinsic to monasticism. The avoidance of sexual activity and arousal, however, has been an important aspect of much monastic asceticism. Some monks apparently have thought of women primarily as temptresses, and their literature sounds misogynist. The Orthodox Christian monastic center on Mount Athos, in Greece, forbids entrance to women. By contrast, there is greater interest today in mixed communities and in lessening the isolation of monastics from the rest of society.

MONASTIC ACTIVITY. The program, rule, or discipline that is so important in monastic life varies widely between traditions and monasteries. Some monastics spend their time in liturgical activities, others in devotional or yogic exercises, and many in work that does not seem to be religious at all. The monastic performs any task with its religious effects in mind no matter what its other benefits. The basic monastic purpose is to achieve a religious goal, even if the activities performed by monastics may seem somewhat incidental to such a goal. Apparently irrelevant activity often looms large in specific situations and may provide much motivation for the monastic and support from the larger community. The list of monastic disciplines and activities contains none that are absolutely unique to monasticism but many that have been especially prominent and perhaps easier to pursue within a monastic context.

Meditation and prayer, in their various forms, have been the most important activities in most monasteries: meditation may be discursive, ecstatic, yogic; prayer can be spontaneous, formal, communal, solitary. However, all kinds of religious practice are cultivated in monastic situations. Formal liturgical ceremonies (monastic profession or initiation, sacrifices, and sacred dramas) are frequent and conspicuous aspects of monastic life. Monasteries are known for their communal chanting of sacred texts, as certain Ṣūfī orders are known for their dancing rites; other arts are also developed by monastics in the interests of their religious application. Some monastic traditions have been suspicious of particular art forms, associating them with the luxuries of the world or seeing them as distractions; but even simplicity has artistic intention and power. The stark beauty of a Zen garden or a Cistercian church exemplifies a use of the arts in the service of monasticism as much as more ornate and elaborate artistic expressions.

A special kind of meditation or reflection is important to the monastic endeavor in many places and ways. This is the attention given to every detail of life, both physical and mental. Not only are monastics intent on orienting everything in their lives toward the achievement of religious transformation; their heightened consciousness about the motions and thoughts of everyday life becomes itself a transforming mental discipline. They argue that too much human life is lived unconsciously and thus without purpose or organization. By consciously acknowledging and reflecting on such commonplace activities as breathing, walking, or thinking, the monastic gains a new perspective on the human phenomenon. The smallest building blocks of life may be used to evoke ever-deeper awareness and ultimately enlightenment.

The whole of cenobitic monastic life is choreographed by the rules of the order. Times of sleeping, eating, praying, meditating, and working are all prescribed, and these actions are performed by the monastics in unison. The sounds of bells and other signals punctuate the day and coordinate the many lives of the monastics into a single harmonious program. This attempt to blend individual lives into a larger social unity has been influential as a model for utopian theorists and represents to many lay people an attractive aspect of monastic existence. Religious symbols of unity, harmony, and peace are reinforced by the living of the monastic pattern.

It is not difficult to recognize prayer, meditation, and rituals, which are important in any religious situation, as being important as well in the monastic pursuit of religious transformation. However, monastics also do other works that are not so obviously religious. Many monastic rules demand that the monastic perform menial, common chores, not only because work of that sort must be done by someone in any community of human beings but also because of the meaning that is attached to it within the monastic framework: menial labor may give a form to humility, its rhythms may be seen as an aid in meditation, its performance may be an act of service and obedience to the master, and so on. An emphasis on self-sufficiency and isolation has led monastics and monasteries to be pioneers in foreign and remote areas, performing a service in civilizing or proselytizing. Monasteries have also functioned as hotels and hospitals in remote places.

Some monastic work involves intellectual activity. Benedict's rule emphasizes reading *(lectio divina)* as a major component of the monastic life along with prayer and work. The path to perfection or religious transformation is often an intellectual path that requires a new understanding of the self and the world. Reading and study in the monastic context is a means of salvation, a technique for the reconstruction of one's worldview. Also, because the rule, religious texts, and other written guides to meditation, prayer, and discipline must be available to monastics, much of their effort has been put to copying, studying, and teaching these materials. Their educational task starts with that monastic necessity, easily comes to include other religious scholarship, and may extend to more "secular" knowledge as well. Wisdom and religious insight may be cultivated for their role in religious transformation, but here, as elsewhere, there is the potential for great benefit to the rest of society incidental to the main goal. The role of Christian monasteries in preserving classical Greek and Latin writings is a famous example of the intellectual by-products of monasticism. Buddhist *vihāras* in India and elsewhere have been important centers of learning.

In some situations charitable acts are held to be more important for the monastic than more individual disciplines. A distinction is made within Christian communities between contemplative orders, where activities like those mentioned above predominate, and active orders, where emphasis is placed on work with beneficial effects for others. In the active monastic styles the way to attain deeper or higher religious status is associated with the merit and value of meeting people's needs, in addition to or instead of the cultivation of private pieties. Thus a monastic belonging to an active order may be a teacher, nurse, priest, or support person in some beneficial institution, but with an interest or investment in the work that is beyond that of nonmonastic colleagues. For the monastic such work is part of a discipline or rule, a means toward a religious goal.

The services of monasteries to society as schools, hospitals, and places of hospitality to travelers have been mentioned. Monastics have often provided priestly or pastoral services for their larger communities. Monasteries have also served as orphanages, places of burial, research institutes, and pilgrimage centers. They have provided places of reflection and restoration for individual and communal visits and retreats. It may also be important to people preoccupied with daily, practical concerns that monasteries simply exist; the knowledge that somewhere people are praying and meditating can in itself be beneficial.

A number of answers can be given to the question "Why do people become monastics?" Some of these answers might be given by the monastics themselves; others could be provided by students of human behavior attempting to see beneath and beyond the self-consciousness of participants in a social phenomenon. Some of these responses might seem pejorative or critical of the monastic endeavor, while others would be admiring and adulatory. Some answers are psychological and personal, others more social or historical in focus, and most are complex and ambiguous.

Many people have associated the monastic with words like *escape* and *retreat.* This manner of speaking reflects a perception of the monastic world as a realm dominated by an inability or unwillingness to cope with normal life or "the world." This view might lead one to a conception of monastic life as a refuge for the weak or the scrupulous. Insofar as one understands the world and "normal life" to be diabolical or illusory, however, the monastic retreat is the more courageous and realistic option, calling for extraordinary strength and dedication. Monasticism has also been significant as a preserver of culture and civilization in eras when the political structures of the world were weak. Certainly during the disintegration of the Roman Empire monasteries provided islands of tranquillity and an opportunity for the pursuit of intellectual activity that was unavailable in the surrounding society.

The adoption of a markedly different way of living cannot but imply some criticism of the alternatives. Thus some observers have emphasized the role of monastic life as a protest against the prevailing patterns of the world or of the religious tradition. Even without a specific aim of reforming or transforming their traditions, monastics have offered an alternative set of ideals to their coreligionists and in so doing have often, perhaps unwittingly, inspired change.

The meaning of monastic life in specifically religious or theological terms goes beyond the analysis presented above. By means of symbols and doctrines the visible rites and practices of monastic life are understood to be much more significant than is apparent to the outside observer. The theme of death, for example, is prominent in various ways. Through profession or initiation the monastic technically attains a status comparable to that of the dead. Indeed, the death and rebirth symbolism in these rites is often quite clear. Through the transformation of joining the monastic community or adopting monastic status, one enters the realm of being of the angels, the ancestors, or those who have achieved enlightenment. Furthermore, it has been noted that Christian monasticism began when martyrdom ceased, indicating that it took over as the arena of ultimate commitment, the new form in which one could die to the world for one's faith. Buddhist monasticism is also a way of death in that the *dharma* provides a program for eliminating all attachment to the world as well as any desire to be reborn.

When ascetic activities are stressed in a monastic life they may be understood as penance and sacrifice to atone for sinfulness. Suffering can be thought beneficial to oneself or to others, the latter leading to the possibility of merit and its transfer in the thought of the monastics or their surrounding community. Ascetic practice may be seen as a means of gaining power, not only over oneself but also over others, even the gods, for example in the ideas associated with *tapas* in Hinduism.

Monastics as well as scholars have understood monastic life primarily as a pursuit of mystical experience. The *ṭarīqah* in Ṣūfī monasteries can be seen both as a rule and as a method for attaining advanced spiritual life. Many monastics praise and cultivate special states of mind and body, states in which enlightenment, ecstasy, or union with the divine is said to be reached. No matter how advanced the person or the community, however, such states are bound to be rare. Thus, much that is monastic is at best only oriented toward those rare moments, and perhaps quite irrelevant to them. Furthermore, the broad definition and description of monasticism developed in this article includes possibilities for the orientation of monastic existence in other directions. In other words, many monastics may have a conception of the ideal spiritual state that does not center on mystical experiences or realizations, but could instead be focused on charitable, liturgical, or scholarly work to the neglect or exclusion of private mysticism.

One of the criticisms of monasticism has been that it is selfish, that it is in essence a private, individualistic religiosity. That assertion may be true in some instances, but there is much to counter it. Monastic works of charity offer one kind of counterevidence. The social environment of the monastery represents another. Few, if any, monastics have ever been unknown to at least some other people in their environment, and the very fact of their existence has been influential on others. Even if monasticism is centered on the self and its transformation, there has rarely been a monastic for whom the Dominican motto has not been true: "Contemplata aliis tradere" ("To give to others the fruits of contemplation").

CONTEMPORARY MONASTICISM. In recent decades monastics from various religious traditions have become more aware of each other. Toward the end of his life the famous Trappist monk Thomas Merton wrote and spoke of the many similarities among the world's monastic systems. Roman Catholic monasteries in traditionally non-Christian areas have been interested in this consanguinity and have produced some writing on monasticism as an interreligious phenomenon. Since 1960 an organization known as Aide Inter-Monastères has encouraged dialogue between monastics of various religions. Some Christian monastics and monasteries now practice techniques borrowed from Hinduism and Buddhism.

In the United States many experimental as well as traditional new religious communities have been established. A monastic impulse seems to have been a part of the "counterculture" revolution of the sixties and seventies. Monasticism apparently continues to be a persistent and beneficial social and religious structure. In the seriousness with which the monastic reexamines life and its goals, in the rigor with which a discipline of life is pursued, the monastic phenomenon offers an alternative way of life and view of the world to the rest of society.

SEE ALSO Asceticism; Eremitism; Merit; Secret Societies; Spiritual Discipline.

BIBLIOGRAPHY

Studies of monasticism that take into consideration more than one religious tradition are a fairly recent phenomenon. The best book of this kind is *Blessed Simplicity: The Monk as Universal Archetype* by Raimundo Panikkar and others (New York, 1982). For an informal comparative survey of religious communities, see Charles A. Fracchia's *Living Together Alone: The New American Monasticism* (San Francisco, 1979).

A careful analysis of the theology and practice of Christian monasticism is provided by Louis Bouyer in *The Meaning of the Monastic Life* (London, 1955). The standard teaching and reflection of Christian monks is presented by Claude J. Peifer in *Monastic Spirituality* (New York, 1966). Good books on Christian monasticism and religious orders abound; see especially David Knowles's *The Monastic Order in England*, 2d ed. (Cambridge, 1963), and *The Religious Orders in England*, 3 vols. (Cambridge, 1948–1959). A critical view of medieval monasticism is presented in George G. Coulton's *Five Centuries of Religion*, 4 vols. (Cambridge, 1923–1950). The Benedictine rule, along with indexes and informative articles, is available in *RB 1980: The Rule of St. Benedict in Latin and English, with Notes*, edited by Timothy Fry and others (Collegeville, Minn., 1981).

Hindu monasticism is covered by G. S. Ghurye in *Indian Sadhus*, 2d ed. (Bombay, 1964). Sukumar Dutt's *Buddhist Monks and Monasteries of India* (London, 1962) is the best source on Buddhist monasticism in India. For Chinese Buddhism, see Holmes Welch's *The Practice of Chinese Buddhism, 1900–1950* (Cambridge, Mass., 1967). The Buddhist monastic rule is treated in Charles S. Prebish's *Buddhist Monastic Discipline: The Sanskrit Prātimokṣa Sūtras of the Mahāsāṃghikas and Mūlasarvāstivādins* (University Park, Pa., 1975).

On monasticism in Islam, see J. Spencer Trimingham's *The Sufi Orders in Islam* (New York, 1971). An older standard reference is John K. Birge's study of a Ṣūfī order in Turkey, *The Bektashi Order of Dervishes* (1937; New York, 1982). An abridged translation of a Ṣūfī rule is found in Menahem Milson's *A Sufi Rule for Novices* (Cambridge, Mass., 1975).

On Protestant monasticism, see François Biot's *The Rise of Protestant Monasticism* (Baltimore, 1963). Peter F. Anson surveys Anglican communities in his *The Call of the Cloister*, 4th ed., rev. (London, 1964).

New Sources

Dreyfus, Georges B. J. *The Sound of Two Hands Clapping: The Education of a Tibetan Buddhist Monk.* Berkeley, 2003.

Kieschnick, John. *The Eminent Monk: Buddhist Ideals in Medieval Chinese Hagiography.* Honolulu, 1997.

King, Peter. *Western Monasticism: A History of the Monastic Movement in the Latin Church.* Kalamazoo, 1999.

Lawrence, Clifford H. *Medieval Monasticism: Forms of Religious Life in Western Europe in the Middle Ages.* London, 2001.

McGregor, Richard. *Sanctity and Mysticism in Medieval Egypt: The Wafa' Sufi Order and the Legacy of Ibn 'Arabi.* Albany, 2004.

Olivelle, Patrick. *Rules and Regulations of Brahmanical Asceticism: Yatidharmasamuccaya of Yādava Prakāśa.* Albany, 1995.

Schopen, Gregory. *Bones, Stones, and Buddhist Monks: Collected Papers on the Archaeology, Epigraphy, and Texts of Monastic Buddhism in India.* Honolulu, 1997.

Sterk, Andrea. *Renouncing the World Yet Leading the Church: The Monk-Bishop in Late Antiquity.* Cambridge, 2004.

GEORGE WECKMAN (1987)
Revised Bibliography

MONASTICISM: BUDDHIST MONASTICISM

The myth of the historical Buddha's life provides the basic model for Buddhist monasticism. Prince Siddhārtha Gautama went, in Buddhist language, on the "Middle Way," a life of moderate asceticism, between lay life and extreme asceticism. His practices were based on the belief in the existence and attainability of a transcendent reality, enlightenment more profoundly real, powerful, and blissful than the world as experienced in a nonenlightened state. The exercise of meditation, learning, ethical conduct, and progress on the path to liberation were thought to be best managed in solitude, or at least in single-gender communities that did not engage society in traditionally accepted, lay-oriented ways.

Buddhists believe that the best way to follow the path to enlightenment is to live a disciplined lifestyle, one conducive to generating awareness of one's mental states and the causally produced nature of all elements of existence. Sexual relations, marriage, procreation, family life, career, and personal concerns are distractions from religious concerns and thus rejected as preconditions for admission to the Buddhist monastic communities. Buddhists monks and nuns who take vows are, in canonical terms, "pleased" (*prasādita*) by their vows. Joining the monastic order has a tempering or "cooling" (*śītala*) effect on the passions, anger, and delusions of monks and nuns. According to Buddhist doctrine, to be rid of the bonds of habitual thought and behavior is a happy and pleasing thing; monastic life is not supposed to be oppressive or restrictive.

In the monastic literature, whenever the Buddha prohibited an action and instituted a rule, he did so to please his disciples. Buddhist monastic life is considered a liberation from mental and physical bondage and conducive to religious development. In the monastic literary corpus there are many examples of the advantages of monastic life. In one episode from the Pali Vinaya, translated by Isaline B. Horner in *The Book of the Discipline*, the parents of a young man named Upāli were confused about how to educate, care for, and provide for the best interests of their beloved son:

> "By what means could Upāli, after our demise, live at ease and not be in want?" Then it occurred to Upāli's parents: "If Upāli should learn writing . . . his fingers will become painful. If Upāli should learn calculation . . . his breast will become painful. If Upāli should learn money-changing . . . his eyes will become painful. . . . Now if Upāli should go forth among the recluses, the sons of the Śākyans, so would Upāli, after our demise, live at ease and not be in want." (Horner, 1938–1966, vol. 3, pp. 10–11)

When Upāli heard of his parents' plan, he was delighted and encouraged his friends to join him in the Buddhist order. Entry into the monastic order was socially acceptable and advantageous, not a punishment or life-denying exile. Commitment to, or at least proximity to, religious mysteries brought social and political status, and for this reason monks and nuns gained prestige and power in their support communities.

Fully developed Buddhist monasticism likely did not originate during the historical Buddha's lifetime. Still, Buddhist monks and nuns use the example of the Buddha's life story as a behavioral model. Through Buddhist history, in communities of celibate Buddhist men and women there were two ideal modes of behavior, reflecting the origins and historical developments preserved in the Buddha's story. The two are eremitic asceticism, likely taken from the earliest years of the order, and cenobitic community life, in which monks and nuns are engaged with monastic brethren and lay society. Some monks continued the practice of strictly renunciative solitary retreats in sometimes remote areas, affirming the ancient eremitic roots of Buddhism, while others, often from the same monastery, were concerned with active monastery affairs, community academic studies, and ritual practices—a cenobitic lifestyle. Similarly, solitary or group pilgrimage to sacred sites, for example, was an accepted practice for Buddhist monks, as long as the monks stayed within the ethical and behavioral parameters. Both modes of behavior were validated by the life story of the Buddha: the renunciative mode by Siddhārtha leaving his home, family, and birthright; and the active mode of behavior by his activities after his enlightenment, when he returned to public life as a teacher and monastic community developer. This apparent duality of active behavior and renunciative behavior, even in the context of settled monastic life, is one of the characteristics of Buddhist monastic behavior that continues throughout the history of the institution in many if not all its manifestations.

The Spread of Buddhist Monasticism. One of the important factors in the spread and growth of Buddhist monasticism was its adaptability. As long as monks and nuns preserved the basic teachings and social behavior patterns, Buddhism could be translated into any language or culture. That is, as long as monks obeyed the monastic laws and engaged in the ritual and meditative practices, Buddhism could and did appear in manifold forms through history. This flexibility served the Buddhist "conquest" of Asia well and stimulated the growth of a massive religious institution with broad sociological diversity, extensive literature, philosophy, ritual, and considerable political power. Indeed, in addition to places for meditation and worship, monasteries were centers for the study and practice of medicine, for writing and building library collections, for Buddhist arts, for adjudicating community disputes, and in general for serving the needs of host communities. Buddhism was and remains an international religion and was intended for transmission into different languages and cultures.

The first example of Buddhism's adaptability to its cultural environment is in India itself. Buddhism was a new innovation that adapted as India grew and developed. The early Buddhist Vinaya collections record the growth and evolution in an Indian cultural context. In the first years of Buddhism, like their Upaniṣad-motivated brethren, Buddha's followers were strictly eremitic, following an extreme ascetic lifestyle. The Vinaya monastic literature records that early monks and nuns wandered from place to place, even through the rainy season. These Buddhist wandering mendicants practiced firm renunciation of worldly concerns. With the success of Buddha's system, however, problems developed because of the sheer numbers of converts. Farmers began to complain about crops destroyed by Buddhists wandering in the monsoon, poorly nourished and weak monks and nuns began to develop illnesses, and the large numbers were difficult to manage. Buddha therefore instructed his communities to set up shelters and temporary residences (*ārāma*) for the duration of the monsoon season. Two sections of the Vinaya deal with the realities of feeding, housing, and occupying itinerant Buddhist monks and nuns during the four-month Indian monsoon season.

The new residences soon increased in size, quantity, and quality, thanks in part to continuing donations of buildings and land by the lay populations and political authorities. Buddhist authorities were soon faced with the problems of retreat conduct, and they needed an effective method to propagate the teachings during the retreat time, when monks and nuns did not wander. The earliest solutions for the communities were the *Poṣadha* (the twice-monthly rules *[prātimokṣa]* recitation ceremony) and, eventually, regular collective meetings for group rituals, practice, and instruction. The recitation meetings were not a Buddhist innovation; other Indian religious groups kept the ancient Vedic tradition of meeting on the days of the full and new moon, a practice common to religions of that era, Buddhist and non-Buddhist. It was nonetheless one of the significant steps in the development of collective Buddhist monastic practice and a demonstration of the order's adaptability to local conditions.

The corpus of Indian Buddhist ritual practices and philosophies grew as the order spread and encountered different environments, languages, and social structures. Buddhist monasteries maintained the fundamental teachings and moderate ascetic lifestyle, but Buddhists soon elaborated on the basic doctrines and accommodated new ritual practices current in its own and in new host cultures. Buddhist monasteries became centers for the production of an extensive literary corpus that was often translated into new host languages and subsequently expanded. Though restricted at various times by adverse sociological, economic, and political conditions, Buddhist monasteries were centers for teaching and learning, for medical study and practice, and for elaboration of Buddhist doctrines and associated rituals.

With regional developments in India and gradually elsewhere, first in tropical Śrī Laṅkā and Southeast Asia and later in high-altitude Northwest India, disputes over points of doctrine and monastic discipline arose. These controversies and resolutions were sometimes recorded in detail and sometimes not, with the result that there is a huge body of often fragmented information about early Buddhist monasticism recorded and transmitted out of its original contexts. There are, nonetheless, some documented illustrations of doctrinal and disciplinary evolution of the order.

The process of institutional development can be seen in recorded events. After Buddha's death in the fourth century BCE, his disciples held a meeting at Rājagṛha, which is historically regarded as the First Council. It is plausible that the faithful would hold a meeting after the death of Buddha to formalize the doctrines and the ethical rules and to eulogize the late Buddha. According to the tradition, after the death of the great teacher the disciples gathered to collect and preserve his teachings. Other meetings followed the First Council. The number of these councils is, however, uncertain, and it is probable that there were many more such meetings than are recorded in the standard histories. The point is that there were general meetings at which the doctrinal and disciplinary teachings were reviewed, codified, and sometimes modified to meet the exigencies of changing conditions. While there were obviously developments of major significance resulting in schisms in the community and the development of historical sects, little of the data in the accounts of the early Buddhist conventions and institutions can be confirmed. All of the specifics of the First, Second, and later Councils—the dates, the places, the topics, the resolutions, the participants—are subject to questions. The interest in the councils lie in what philosophical, ethical, and social questions they raised and how those were resolved to support the evolution of the doctrine and spread of the community.

After the first meeting on the occasion of Buddha's death, there were councils at Vaiśālī and later at Pāṭaliputra (Patna). There was eventually a division in the Buddhist monastic order (between Mahāsāṃghika and Sthavira), but the divisive issues are not well understood. These meetings were either concerned with ten points of monastic discipline or with five points of doctrine attributed to one Mahādeva. The list of ten points includes rather trivial matters, and it is probable that these were in themselves indicators of larger issues.

Indeed, a probable cause of the early schism in Buddhism was a controversy between the majority Mahāsāṃghikas and the Sthaviras over expansion of the Vinaya. The Sthaviras evidently saw a need to expand the Vinaya to meet changing conditions. The Mahāsāṃghikas disagreed and were accused of laxity in discipline, which led to the sectarian dispute.

The early schism in Buddhist monasticism is alternatively attributed to five issues of doctrine called the "heresies of Mahādeva." The five points, which may have been issues of the Third Council, clearly involve points of doctrine, including the status of an enlightened being (*arhat*), but their importance and any significant outcomes are unclear. The sequence, chronology, specific philosophical positions, and importance of the specific points are uncertain, but nonetheless the matters involved monastic life. Later sectarian disputes and divisions likewise were over matters of the inviolability of received scriptures, doctrine, and discipline. The main point is that, as Buddhist monasticism developed, there were disruptive forces in the community. These, however, did not impede the growth of Buddhism; they instead signal how Buddhism adapted to different conditions and ideologies and grew larger as a result.

The early councils and schisms were followed by modifications in later times and other places. Mahāyāna Buddhism developed soon after the early schisms, and new theories, rituals, literature, and engagement with lay society were accommodated by and institutionalized in Buddhist monasteries. Monasticism flourished in Northwest India under the Kūṣāṇa kings, and as time went on Buddhist monasticism spread along the central Asian trade routes into China, Korea, Japan, Southeast Asia, and Tibet. Through all of its manifestations it adapted to local cultures and environments and at the same time preserved its basic doctrinal message and its moderate ascetic lifestyle.

BUDDHIST MONASTICISM AND POLITICS. A key factor in the historical success of the Buddhist monastic institution was its ability to function together with political authorities. Even though monks and monasteries were outside of temporal society and did not recognize conventional social and political authority structures, relationships between monasteries and governments were often symbiotic. Buddhist monasteries enjoyed the extensive support and protection of political authorities, and in turn monasteries offered religious services, education, and public legitimization. Monasteries were often civic institutions and served the needs of local communities, generating considerable political influence. It was in a government's best interest to support and be validated by these institutions, and many of the most famous monasteries were built during the major dynastic periods throughout Asia.

The monastic literature includes accounts of imperial support for Indian Buddhist monasteries even during the Buddha's lifetime. The story of Anāthapiṇḍika tells of support by wealthy merchants and kings, King Bimbisāra in particular, who donated the Jeta Grove near Rājagṛha in Māgadha to the Buddha and his community of followers. In her translation of the Vinaya, Horner reports that "[t]he householder Anāthapiṇḍika had dwelling places made, he had cells made, porches, attendance halls, fire halls, huts for what is allowable, privies, places for pacing, wells, halls at the wells, bathing halls, lotus ponds, etc. . . . [P]eople were making repairs carefully, attending to the robes, almsfood, lodgings and medicines for the sick" (Horner, 1938–1966, vol. 5, pp. 222–223). Such lavish support brought merit to the wealthy and royal classes. Royal support also brought the kings legitimacy and provided lay and monastic communities education, medical and hospice care, and religious services.

Royal and wealthy lay political support is evident throughout Buddhist history. Monasteries spread with official support in Māgadha, Bihar, Śrī Laṅkā, and Southeast Asia in the early years after Buddha's death. India was experiencing new growth and had close contacts with Persia and Bactria, Central Asia, and locales even further. In India monasticism survived and grew with local political support, especially under the Mauryan king Aśoka (c. 269–236 BCE). According to the legend, this king was particularly aggressive in his conquest of the Indian subcontinent and subsequently converted to Buddhism. After his conversion he was an avid supporter of religion, especially Buddhist monastic institutions. Buddhism, and specifically the interests of Buddhist monasteries, became factors in national policymaking. As a result, monasteries grew in number and in strength in India, in the far northwest as far as the Greek colonies, to the north in the Himalayas, and in Southeast Asia.

After the fall of the Mauryas, Buddhism continued to develop with government support from central Asian kingdoms. There was a succession of kings, including the Buddhist supporter King Milinda (r. 160–140 BCE). The short-lived Śuṅga (187–151 BCE) and Kāṇva (151–106 BCE) dynasties sponsored a great deal of construction of stupas, temples, and Buddhist institutions. The Kūṣāṇa dynasty was the next major dynasty to officially endorse and sponsor Buddhist institutions. The first of the major transmissions of Buddhist monasticism to China began during the Kūṣāṇa dynasty. Their kings sponsored Buddhist monasteries that stretched from Afghanistan into Samarkand and through modern Pakistan. The kingdom included all of northern India and was influential in Khotan, Yarkand, Kashgar, and further east. Kaṇiska, the best known of the Kūṣāṇa kings, supported Buddhist monasticism. In these times there was extensive growth of Buddhist ritual, Mahāyāna philosophy, sūtra literature, and institutional expansion.

During the Gupta dynasty (320–580 CE), Buddhist monasticism was supported by the royal courts and by craft guilds. Monasteries were well endowed and became centers of learning and religious practice, and often of community life. Some of the most famous monastic scholars lived in the Gupta period, and monasteries were built throughout India on a grand scale with much political and social support. Religion and politics became so closely related in this period that kings who sponsored building projects often took on nearly divine status. Monasteries also increased their wealth and political power. Some of the most renowned Buddhist monasteries in history were built in the Gupta period. Nālandā Monastery in Bihar, for example, was known throughout classical Asia and was a source of doctrine and monasticism for important Southeast Asian communities.

During the division of India into small kingdoms in the Pāla era (650–1250), Buddhist monasteries consolidated into larger monastic institutions because of a lack of pan-Indian institutionalized support structures and because of the destruction of major Gupta monastic centers by invading armies. Nonetheless, monasticism became the vehicle for the transmission of Buddhism to Tibet, China, and Japan, and to new monastic sites in Cambodia, Pagan, Burma, Java, and elsewhere. Pāla era kings especially established and legitimized their imperial rule by resorting to Buddhist religious models and extensive support of Buddhist monasteries. The practice of religiously legitimizing kingship continued in Tibet and Southeast Asia, notably in the Qing dynasty (1644–1911) during the reign of the Qianlong emperor in the late eighteenth century. As a result, monastic institutions increased, for example, in Tibet and Mongolia, where thousands of new Buddhist monasteries were built in the seventeenth to nineteenth centuries.

Because Buddhist monasteries enjoyed popular support and often wielded political power, Buddhism was sometimes criticized and even persecuted or regulated by lay authorities. In Tang China (618–907); Buddhism was persecuted, powerful Buddhist monasteries were secularized in Meiji Japan (1868–1912); and monasteries were targeted in Tibet in the modern period under Chinese rule. Monasteries often accumulated so much influence that they threatened the integrity and credibility of lay governments and were thus a threat to established lay political authority.

Monasticism, and its special relationship with political authority, was present in all of its support cultures. The Buddhist community's moderate asceticism and Middle Way doctrines were transmitted intact into an enormous variety of cultures, preserving monasticism as the constant, the vehicle and foundation necessary to reestablish itself in a foreign environment. Its survival and prosperity often depended on local political authorities, and it did indeed survive and prosper.

BUDDHIST MONASTICISM AND ECONOMICS. The Buddhist order was founded and based on metaphysical principles, but its functions were based on the truth of conventional operations in the world. Accordingly, Buddhist monks and monasteries accepted donations of cash, land, and material of all kinds, and they sometimes became rich and powerful. In spite of the injunctions against individual monks owning money, the monastic literature allows the collective ownership of donated and community wealth. Some monks managed their own finances, and in some places a special lay office was established at monasteries to handle donations and finances for monks. Permanent endowments of land and tax rights; endowments of properties with guaranteed long-term agricultural, pastoral, or other income; rights to impose corvée; and constant donations from the lay communities made some monks and monasteries extremely wealthy.

Monasteries were given land, buildings, novice sponsorship, and donations by political authorities and wealthy businesspersons as a matter of routine. Wealthy persons often willed their properties to monasteries or individual monks further increasing monastic holdings. Local laypeople offered food and materials appropriate to their means. Monasteries and monks had other sources of income, depending on the wealth and circumstances of their support communities. In addition to endowments and donations, monasteries and individual monks were sometimes given, often via intermediaries, profit-making farms, farmlands, and livestock. In Tibet and elsewhere, for example, monasteries received regular payments from profits and percentages of commodities produced or sold. Some monasteries lent money and land rights, receiving interest income and payment in kind. The understanding or basic principal at work here was that monastic income, donated and entrepreneurial, was to be used for religious purposes, even if personal and institutional interests coincided. Scholarship has shown that the monastery and individual monks were involved in a broad range of economic activities and that some monasteries and monks became wealthy.

MONASTICISM AND LAW. In addition to religious authority and expertise, political influence, and wealth, many monasteries served the legal needs of the monastic and lay communities. The Buddhist order had a fully developed internal legal system. The monastic law codes divide offenses according to severity and include detailed definitions and case examples for what constitutes each kind of transgression. In addition to internal monastic law codes, Buddhist canonical law was often a validating instrument for lay law. For example, Burmese monastic leaders produced, implemented, and preserved a fully developed lay legal system based on Buddhist law. Monastic law codes were a source of law and legal authority in Southeast Asian cultures and elsewhere, affirming the Buddhist monastic commitment to engagement in worldly matters. Direct involvement in lay legal matters on all social levels shows further that monasteries and lay political, social, economic, and legal institutions interacted closely in symbiotic relationships.

As time went on, Buddhist monasticism was fully integrated into societies in Southeast Asia and in Tang and, especially, Song China. Chinese monasteries interacted closely with government and influenced legal guidelines in politics, business, and lay life. In Tibet, monasteries were often seats of religious and lay power. The Tibetan practice of combining religious and lay authority put political and legal power in the hands of monastic leaders. There are many examples of religious authorities adjudicating lay disputes over civil and criminal law in addition to laws for monastic behavior.

WOMEN IN BUDDHIST MONASTICISM. The history of women in Buddhist monasticism is varied. Patriarchal societies and gender values took their toll on women's institutions. Though according to mainstream doctrine women can be enlightened, in the canonical versions of Buddhist monastic literature women are often cast in unflattering roles. The number of vows nuns must keep is larger than that for men, and there are specific rules that establish the subordinate status of nuns. There are some early literary collections, the *Therīgātha* hymns, and later writings, but there were few women writers. Women most often did not have access to monastic education. In many countries, moreover, women's ordination lineages did not survive. In modern Tibet and in parts of Southeast Asia, for example, there are no unbroken lineages of full ordination from nun to nun, and nuns are able to take only a brief list of vows.

However, it is also true that women in Asian Buddhist cultures had extensive and important roles in local communities in addition to positive, historical human and divine role models. The status of women varied, depending on specific cultural contexts, economies, and historical periods. There were successes for Buddhist women, including women's ordination lineages. For example, modern scholarship gives evidence of well-established and well-endowed nunneries in India in the Gupta dynasty, though these went into decline in the following centuries. In China, women's ordination lineages were preserved intact.

When women's monasteries were in decline, women reestablished monastic life as they were able. In Tibet, for example, where there was no lineage for full ordination, there were nonetheless many nunneries. Women did not have the educational opportunities that were available for men, but they were able to engage in Buddhist meditations and rituals in celibate monastic institutions. In Tibet there were traditions of women pilgrims, ascetics, and even community leaders and teachers who were recognized by the community at large. Thus, whereas women's monasticism was not preserved in Tibet according to ancient Indian models, there were still vibrant women's communities throughout Tibetan history. Educational standards and facilities were not as developed as in men's monasteries, but women built and maintained strong traditions of meditation, ritual, and community solidarity. Indeed, in twentieth-century Amdo, Northeast Tibet (modern Gansu province), the greater Labrang Monastery community supported women's monasteries even without full ordination.

SEE ALSO Priesthood, article on Buddhist Priesthood; Saṃgha, overview article.

BIBLIOGRAPHY

Davidson, Ronald M. *Indian Esoteric Buddhism: A Social History of the Tantric Movement.* New York, 2002. This work includes much data on the context of monasticism in Pāla India.

French, Rebecca Redwood. *The Golden Yoke: The Legal Cosmology of Buddhist Tibet.* Ithaca, N.Y., 1995. A description of lay and monastic law in Tibet.

Heirman, Ann. "Some Remarks for the Rise of the Bhikṣuṇīsaṅgha and on the Ordination Ceremony for Bhikṣuṇīs according to the Dharmaguptaka Vinaya." *Journal of the International Association of Buddhist Studies* 20, no. 2 (1997): 33–86.

Henry, Patrick G., and Donald K. Swearer. *For the Sake of the World: The Spirit of Buddhist and Christian Monasticism.* Minneapolis, 1989. A study of the functions of monastic life in society.

Holt, John Clifford. *Discipline: The Canonical Buddhism of the Vinayapitaka.* Delhi, 1981. A study of Buddhist doctrines and monastic codes.

Horner, Isaline B., trans. *The Book of the Discipline (Vinayapitaka).* 6 vols. London, 1938–1966. A translation of the Pali Vinaya.

Huxley, Andrew. "How Buddhist Is Theravāda Buddhist Law? A Survey of Legal Literature in Pāli-land." *Buddhist Forum* 1 (1990): 41–85.

Huxley, Andrew. "Buddhist Case Law on Theft: The *Vinītavatthu* on the Second *Pārājika.*" *Journal of Buddhist Ethics* 6 (1999) 313–330.

Huxley, Andrew. "Buddhist Law as Religious System?" In *Religion, Law, and Tradition: Comparative Studies in Religious Law,* edited by Andrew Huxley, pp. 127–148. London, 2002.

Lamotte, Étienne. *History of Indian Buddhism: From the Origins to the Śaka Era.* Translated from the French by Sara Webb-Boin. Louvain, 1988. A dated but useful reference for the history of the Buddhist order.

Schopen, Gregory. *Bones, Stones, and Buddhist Monks: Collected Papers on the Archeology, Epigraphy, and Texts of Monastic Buddhism in India.* Honolulu, 1997. This and other writings by Schopen are authoritative studies on social, economic, and doctrinal issues in Indian Buddhist monasticism.

Von Hinuber, Oskar. "Buddhist Law according to the Theravāda-Vinaya: A Survey of Theory and Practice." *Journal of the International Association of Buddhist Studies* 18, no. 1 (1995): 7–45.

Wijayaratna, Mohan. *Buddhist Monastic Life.* Cambridge, U.K., 1990. A canonical account of early monastic life.

Yifa. *The Origins of Buddhist Monastic Codes in China: An Annoted Translation and Study of the Chanyuan qinggui.* Honolulu, 2002.

Zysk, Kenneth. *Asceticism and Healing in Ancient India: Medicine in the Buddhist Monastery.* Oxford, 1991.

PAUL K. NIETUPSKI (2005)

MONASTICISM: CHRISTIAN MONASTICISM

Christian monasticism does not differ from monasticism in other world religions in its most basic motivation: to allow those who consider themselves capable of practicing a form of religious life that is beyond the means of ordinary believers to do so. The goal and purpose of such extraordinary achievements in Christianity derive from the evangelical counsels of fasting, chastity, and the renunciation of property. With the renunciation of secular attachments, the nun or monk begins a journey of continuous self-mortification with the goal of contemplative unity with God through prayer. Such renunciation has to be practiced and trained for, which requires both abstention and continuous exercise. Abstention is core to the term *monachos,* which means a single, independent, or solitary person. Continuous refinement of practice is core to the term *askesis,* which means training or exercise. Yet whereas singularity through ascetic abstention can highlight the status of religious virtuosi, it may also marginalize them and signify a precarious, even heretical, existence. As such, the salience and permanency of ascetic religious-virtuoso status depends on the reactions of the community and ecclesiastical and political authorities.

BEGINNINGS OF MONASTICISM AND THE "AGE OF THE DESERT" (C. 200–C. 500 CE). Recent research has shown that at the beginning of monasticism, Christian monastic ascetics were only a part of a larger ascetic landscape that was populated by a variety of holy men from different religious traditions in the Roman Empire. It also has become increasingly clear that Christian monasticism does not a have a single beginning, but originated in a variety of communities in different areas. Structural heterogeneity spans the familiar forms of anchorites, who live alone, and cenobites, who live in a stable community, but also the Syrian wandering beggar-ascetics and small communal groups within existing inhabited zones in Egypt; moreover, domestic forms of early monasticism existed that were particularly common among women, which shall be addressed further below. It appears, in fact, that the long-held model of the emergence of Christian monasticism out of the prototypical Egyptian recluse must be abandoned. Egyptian Christian monasticism, in its earliest ascetic forms, was located in urban spaces, and it did not inspire, or was not an apparent model for, monastic developments in the Christian world. Monasticism in Palestine, too, was not about eremitical withdrawal into remote desert regions but rather an integral part of Christian life there from early on. One of the main sources of the traditional view of the eremitical/desert beginnings of monasticism, Athanasius's *Life of Antony,* which portrayed Anthony of Egypt (c. 251–356) as an exemplary Christian person who perfected his sanctity through solitary life in the desert, is now understood as a discursive strategy with the purpose (and result) of homogenizing different forms of monasticism and consolidating them into a type that could be more easily demarcated from other forms that were, in the eyes of ecclesiastical authorities, less desirable. The common characterization of this monastic era as the "Age of the Desert" is therefore questionable at best.

The cenobitic form of monasticism can be traced back to Pachomius of Egypt (c. 290–346). It was based on the consideration that the ascetics' heroic virtue could be bolstered and more easily sustained if they lived in a communal setting, allowing them to create a Christian community of love (*koinōnia,* hence "cenobitic"). This community required both stability in a fixed abode (claustration) and governing principles and guidelines, or a *rule,* which became the hallmarks of monasticism. Neither as removed from society nor as regimented and strictly disciplined as it was once believed they were, Pachomian communities spread in the fourth century and were the precursors to later cenobitic forms of monasticism in the monastic age.

THE WESTERN MONASTIC ERA (C. 500–C. 1200). After the turbulences of the fifth century associated with the onslaught of the barbarian tribes, which ended the Age of the Desert, monastic establishments in Western Christianity were given a normative foundation by the sixth-century Rule of St. Benedict. Named after Benedict of Nursia (c. 480–c. 547) and likely based in part on the earlier *Rule of the Master,* the Rule of St. Benedict emphasized stability, peacefulness, order, and collective self-sufficiency. Confronted with often unstable political conditions and a yet largely untamed natural environment, monks and nuns achieved stability by living in a permanent setting that offered shelter from these conditions. Removed from an outside world of violence and warfare, these "athletes of God" fought a more peaceful, spiritual battle instead. This task necessitated order and a structured, methodical way of life.

The prologue to the Rule calls on monks and nuns to "establish a school for the Lord's service" (Fry, 1981, p. 165), which offered training in the virtues of obedience and discipline. Obedience meant subservience to the abbess or abbot, who had authority over monastic communities' secular and spiritual matters yet was an elected leader and governed by precise mandates of conduct. Discipline both reflected and facilitated commitment to a principled, methodical way of life, which was, because "idleness is the enemy of the soul" (Fry, 1981, p. 249), precisely structured with daily routines. For the most part, these routines focused on collective prayer, *lectio* (the study of texts and private meditation), and work. Collective prayer was organized around a daily round of divine service, the *Opus Dei.* It was complemented by *lectio,* which led to the emergence of Benedictine monasteries as perhaps the foremost centers of learning, scholarship, and literary production from about the eighth century until at least the eleventh century.

Work was also considered one of the constitutive elements of the monastic profession: "When they live by the labor of their hands, as our fathers and the apostles did, then they are really monks" (Fry, 1981, pp. 249, 251). The valorization of work came out of a tradition that viewed labor both as a means of subsistence and charity and as a way to combat the temptation of *acedia,* or sloth and lethargy brought on by idleness. It enabled the members of a monastic community to aid the poor and sick, prevented them from falling into idleness, and contributed to their material self-sufficiency.

The Rule stated that because for members of monastic communities it was "not all good for their souls" to leave the stable and disciplined environment of the monastery, "the monastery should, if possible, be so constructed that within it all necessities, such as water, mill and garden are contained, and the various crafts are practiced" (Fry, 1981, p. 289). The combination of advancing education and craft skills with improving technologies for cultivating land enabled the monastic communities to achieve a high degree of self-sufficiency.

Monastic houses commonly followed a mixed rule, or a combination of observations taken from different rules, until the Rule of St. Benedict ascended to dominance in the early eighth century. Local customs and conventions continued to be accommodated through so-called customaries.

Cluniac and Cistercian monasticism. The term *Cluniac monasticism* denotes a movement to revive and restore Benedictine monastic life after the decline of the Carolingians and the plundering and pillaging of monasteries by the Vikings and Saracens. The tenth-century reforms that emanated from Cluny and a large number of affiliated or similar reform-minded monastic houses such as Gorze, Hirsau, and Bec led to a ceremonialization of the monastic life and much closer affiliation with nobility. Whereas the Rule of St. Benedict prescribed about three and a half hours a day of prayer and recitation of psalms, Cluniac monastic communities engaged in such activities to a much greater extent. As the number of recited psalms increased from 15 to 170, most of the day was spent in the choir, and the celebration of private and commemorative masses further added to the liturgical demands on the monks.

At the same time, Cluniac monasticism represented a closer affinity with the upper, noble strata of society, in that monks performed religious services for nobles in return for material endowments and protection. The Cluniacs' link to the nobility was further strengthened by the fact that many nuns and monks came from noble families and that the higher ranks of the Cluniac organization were populated by men of aristocratic origins. For members of the nobility, the endowment of a monastery in land was thought to secure the donor's temporal and eternal welfare, and noble patronage of monasteries continued to provide privileges and means of influence on the administration of monastic life even after the Gregorian reform movement and canon law curtailed lay proprietorship of cloisters. In part, this was a utilitarian *do ut des* transaction within an economy dominated by gift and barter, a transaction by which secular wealth and status were traded for spiritual assistance in this life and what was to follow thereafter; in part, however, gift transactions and transfers, as newer historical studies have shown, also served to establish, affirm, and deepen lasting social commitments and moral bonds between donors, donees, mediating agents, and their surrounding communities, thereby integrating these parties into a network of relations and encompassing the realms of both the sacred and the profane.

A different, less feudalized and ceremonialized type of spirituality was embraced by the Cistercians. In reaction to changes within the larger society, such as political consolidation and the expansion of commercial markets, they developed a spiritual program that strongly stressed simplicity, poverty, manual labor, and charity. These goals were to be achieved by rejecting worldly entanglements and restoring a strict, literal adherence of the Rule of St. Benedict. Within 150 years the Cistercians expanded from the "new monastery" formed by two dozen monks around Robert of Molesme (c. 1027–1110) and guided by the charismatic Bernard of Clairvaux (d. 1153) to an organization with perhaps over twenty thousand members by the mid-thirteenth century.

The Cistercians' economic achievements are well known. They include opening up uncultivated frontiers, converting rural hinterlands into flourishing farmlands, and enhancing the agricultural productivity of already developed estates. Frugality and a distinct economic organization were at the root of their success in transforming the rural economy. The Cistercians emphasized simplicity and austerity, reflected in a comparatively brief and modest liturgy, plain architecture, and the absence of ornaments in their churches. Intrinsic to Cistercian austerity was an emphasis on manual work, to be performed with vehemence and regularity and viewed as the principal means for supporting a monastic community—an approach in stark contrast to the dominant practices in Benedictine monasticism at the time. This religious attitude was complemented by the rationalized economic organization of Cistercian *granges*—or estates composed of contiguous fields and farms obtained through a combination of gifts, leases, pawns, and purchases. Organized into a single unit for agricultural production, a grange allowed a much more methodical estate management than did the previously fragmented patches of land. Granges were exempt from ecclesiastical tithes and other agricultural taxes, and local markets in the countryside and urban settings (if available) provided a ready outlet for their agricultural and pastoral products.

Having few outlets for expenditure beyond charity and subsistence, the Cistercians could re-invest their wealth in the acquisition of monastic estates, and thus further the basis of their economic success. But in the second part of the thirteenth century, Cistercian land acquisition came to a halt. The peasantry had fewer material incentives to join the order, with serfdom disappearing, markets for agricultural products expanding, and cultivation methods improving by the late twelfth century. Burghers and knights, too, found other spiritual avenues, and the burghers of the cities were differently served by the urban mendicant orders. By the thirteenth century the "new monastery, " a highly aristocratic order, in some ways looked like the monastery of old.

The Mendicant Era (c. 1200–c. 1500). During the twelfth century, monasticism was both revived and altered, developments which occurred in the context of rapid social change. An expanding commercial economy, the revival of the cities, a newly found individualism, and increasing levels of lay literacy altered established social traditions—and with them religious life.

In Italy and France an early response to this change came in the form of religious hermits. Drawing on traditions of eremitical poverty in early Christian monasticism, charismatic hermits such as Romuald of Ravenna (950–1027) or Norbert of Xanten (1080–1134) rejected the stability of the monastery and lived their lives as wandering ascetics. Committed to austerity and noninvolvement with a commercializing, more individualist society, the hermits ushered in a new type of religious eremiticism by not seeking a life of solitude but rather associating with loose groups of followers and supporters. Many of these groups disbanded after the death of their leader, while others assimilated into monastic groups where they continued their serene eremitical life.

A different response came in the form of lay religious movements, which also embraced apostolic poverty but lived in small communities seeking to emulate the life of early Christian communities. Groups such as the Italian Humiliati and the early French and Italian Waldensians rejected the monastic traditions of concentrating on spiritual labor and withdrawing from the world. Combining preaching with itinerancy and austerity, they formed the model for a revival of Christian monasticism in the form of the mendicant orders.

The mendicants. The Franciscans and Dominicans responded to changing socioeconomic conditions by radically breaking with received monastic traditions. They did not question the contemplative life as the ultimate form of Christian perfection, or prayer as the pivotal means to achieve it. They dispensed, however, with the life in a stable, enclosed residence that had been the hallmark of traditional monasticism, and they were governed by ecclesiastical rules whose explicit raison d'être was preaching to the populace. As popular preachers admonishing the laity to repent and to seek inner conversion, they left the seclusion of the cloister for the busy streets of the city, voluntarily renouncing all forms of property, be it personal, as their monastic predecessors had done, or corporate. Instead of collective stability and withdrawal from society, they chose individual mobility and participation in secular affairs.

With this turn, monastic spirituality opened itself to the world. The mendicants rejected the legacy of world flight in monasticism and recentered the meaning of asceticism on notions of strict poverty and active ministry. The attraction of the mendicants was extraordinary: in the first one hundred years they grew from a few men around Francis of Assisi (1181/82–1226) and Domingo de Guzmán (c. 1170–1221), the two founders of the major mendicant orders, to a total of about twenty-eight thousand Franciscans and about twelve thousand Dominicans.

Rapid organizational growth, however, brought about significant changes in mendicant spirituality within the first fifty years, during which some of their early ideals were significantly changed or even abandoned. In the case of the Franciscans, the first friars who joined Francis of Assisi shared his ideal of imitating the simple, austere life of the apostles. Much like other religious charismatics at the time, Francis renounced the vanities of the world, which in his case meant the comfortable lifestyle of a wealthy merchant's son, for the transient existence of an itinerant preacher. Money was not even to be touched, and academic studies were not encouraged. Yet whereas the early Franciscans were expected to support themselves by working and begging, within a span of less than forty years the Franciscans' commitment to manual labor changed, together with their views on the futility of learnedness and absolute avoidance of money. Manual labor was abandoned, as growth in numbers and the inevitable routinization of Franciscan charisma necessitated changes in the order's structure and some of its defining spiritual characteristics. The precarious existence of itinerant beggars and laborers was difficult to reconcile with the need for some institutional and economic stability. It became necessary to impose organizational structures onto the order and to regulate the avenues of admission and advancement, as well as to adopt a less unworldly stance toward money. Furthermore, a great number of priests joined the order, and heresy continued to be viewed as a primary threat. The rustic views of Francis on learning and the unresolved relation of the friars-priests to the secular clergy were at odds with the view shared by many clerics and more-learned members of the order that active ministry required a trained, professional apostolate and the definition of rights and duties vis-à-vis the parish priests. By about the mid-thirteenth century, the Friars Minor were a highly clericalized and learned order, steeped in university life. Earlier notions of absolute poverty gave way to the permission for corporate use, if not ownership, of property, and full control over it.

The other major mendicant order, the Dominicans, did not experience the same organizational dilemmas and shifts in spiritual orientation or emphasis. From the beginning it was conceived to be a priestly order devoted to preaching. The meaning and extent of poverty, while important, was not as contested as among the Franciscans, and intellectual training was considered paramount for an active apostolate. For the professional pastors and preachers who stood at the forefront of the defense of the church as inquisitors and who attended to the spiritual needs of the laity, a solid foundation in theology and the art of preaching was essential. Because the nature of the order was clerical and its orientation priestly, there was no place for work. In the daily routine, manual toil and meditative reading—two of the pillars of the Rule of St. Benedict—gave way to a brief liturgy and the occupations of preaching, studying, and teaching. In both orders, therefore, asceticism was channeled toward the methodical training of the intellect and endured in corporeal and social renunciations such as chastity and penury.

In the later Middle Ages the monasticization of the mendicants and persistent debates over the role of wealth were indicative of significant challenges to religious life. Such challenges were also obvious in traditional religious orders, where abuses and discipline problems as well as declining numbers reflected a crisis in monastic life.

The Reformation, Protestantism, and the Enlightenment. Laxity in spiritual discipline in religious life was one of the issues that prompted the Augustinian friar Martin Luther (1483–1546) to question the foundations of monastic life. Luther, as well as other reformers, ushered in a period in which Protestant authorities disbanded existing houses and disallowed the establishment of new ones. Monastic property was seized and distributed into secular channels.

Ever since the Reformation, the notion of the priesthood of the believer, which exalts each believer to the status of religious virtuoso, has remained one of the pillars of Protestantism. This notion mitigates against the establishment of religious orders whose members enjoy a fundamentally different religious status from that of other members of the church.

A second challenge to monastic life after the Reformation came in the form of the Enlightenment. Enlightenment thinkers tended to equate monastic rituals and traditions with unenlightened superstition and tied them to the society of old. In the wake of the French Revolution and Napoleon Bonaparte's rule, most monastic communities were disbanded or destroyed.

The Apostolic Orders and Teaching Congregations. Reform in the Catholic Church took its own shape in its reformations of religious life in the sixteenth century. One of more than a dozen new apostolic orders that emerged and prospered in that period, the Jesuits represented a new form of order that replaced the emphases in traditional monasticism on contemplation and in the mendicant orders on poverty with a stress on ministry, discipline, and commitment to furthering the church's causes. Founded by Ignatius Loyola (1491–1556), the order grew rapidly. Within a hundred years of their papal approval in 1540, they represented an organization of over 15,000 members. A precipitous decline occurred in the late eighteenth century, however. This decline affected them as well as the traditional monastic groups and the friars. Within a period of fifty years after Pope Clement XIV disbanded the order in 1773, the number of male monks, friars, and members of apostolic orders has been estimated to have dropped to only 70,000, and only about forty of more than one thousand monasteries of the traditional monastic communities survived.

A reversal of such decline was made possible through the revival of traditional monasticism's appeal in the nineteenth century, which led to a revival of Benedictine and Cistercian communities. Numerically more significant, however, was the emergence of hundreds of new religious communities, particularly religious congregations that substituted an active charitable agenda for the traditional contemplative orientation. In practice, this often involved teaching, nursing, and social services. These brothers and sisters in congregations contributed tremendously to the renewal of Catholic religious orders up to the second part of the twentieth century.

The Challenges of Secularization. In an attempt to bring about the *aggiornamento* modernization of Catholic faith, the Second Vatican Council (1962–1965) initiated various changes in the Catholic Church. This occurred at a time when theologians presumed that modern societies underwent a process of secularization that required religious communities to evolve in order to better meet the demands of modern life. Distinctions between laity and priesthood were reduced, and the leveling of status also affected the religious vocation of a member of a monastic community. A steep decline in the number of Catholics entering religious communities ensued. In the United States, by 1990 the annual number of women who entered a religious order was about one-seventh of what it had been three decades earlier, and the number of men in a religious order had been reduced to less than half. Whereas Canada and western European countries experienced a similar decline (with concomitant financial exigencies and geriatrification of membership), the opposite is true for sub-Saharan Africa and South Asia. Catholic religious communities in those areas have grown significantly, to the extent that for some orders these countries produce a very significant portion of novices. So far, no reversal of these trends is in sight for the twenty-first century.

Monasticism and Gender. The role of women in Christian monasticism has undergone many changes. The predominance of teaching congregations over contemplative communities since the second part of the nineteenth century is a reflection of one of the most fundamental changes in monasticism, the increasing involvement of women, as women have joined active congregations in much greater numbers than their male counterparts. When Catholic religious communities reached their numerical peak in the United States in 1965, sisters outnumbered brothers by a ratio of about five to one. Worldwide, the vast majority of Catholic religious today are women.

Women, however, have not always been so strongly represented in Christian monasticism, nor has the cloistered life always been encouraged for female religious. In early monasticism, female religious virtuosity was related to the celibacy of virgins and widows. For women, separation from the world often did not mean withdrawal from the community and living a life of self-mortification in the desert or wilderness (although for some women, it did), but rather a selective abstention from worldly life (sex, marriage, and food) within a family, house, and community. The structure of early female Christian asceticism was heterogeneous: some women lived in informal ascetic groups, others lived an anchorite life, while most remained in their families and communities or joined a household with a clergyman. By the fifth century the claustration of women in cenobitic communities was under way and set the stage for the institutionalization of women under the Rule of St. Benedict.

Following a period of expansion and the flowering of new monastic foundations for women in the seventh century, especially in the form of double monasteries, the proportion of houses dedicated to women declined steadily until the end of the eleventh century. The first Cluniac cloister for women was not founded until about a century and a half after the foundation of Cluny itself. Similarly, while recent scholarship no longer contends that there were no Cistercian establishments for women, the early Cistercians did anything but welcome women with open arms. Further, when women joined they had to maintain strict lifelong enclosure. Nevertheless, half of the about 850 nunneries that were founded for women in France and England between 410 and 1350 appear to have been founded in the period between the late eleventh century and the late twelfth century, including women-centered monastic communities such as Fontevraud and the Gilbertines.

The tradition of claustration continued among the Franciscans and the Dominicans in the later Middle Ages. In 1206, some nine years before the first male Dominican community was founded, Dominic established a cloister for women at Prouille—as an imitation of Cathar houses for women—with the purpose of winning over converts from the Cathars. Unlike Francis, who remained reserved toward the idea of women affiliating with his order, Dominic appears to have been open to women's wishes to join the religious life. The establishment of other monasteries for Dominican nuns followed, and their numbers increased significantly, even though a quota system was put in place to regulate demand. Franciscan convents, inspired by the saintly example of Clare of Assisi (1194–1253), proliferated as well. Yet the nuns lived a religious life quite different from that of the friars. Most importantly, they continued the monastic tradition of strict enclosure for women. Their claustration prevented them from preaching and begging, and no provisions were made for organized study. It required considerable pressure from the papacy to ensure that communities of women were properly integrated into the mendicant orders, if only in thoroughly regulated and well-defined terms. The restrictions on women's access to the apostolic life and on the ways in which they were allowed to live it led them to focus on contemplation. Medieval nuns contributed greatly to the mystical and devotional literature of the later Middle Ages.

In the apostolic era, apostolic orders for women flourished. This was the case for both cloistered and uncloistered communities, even though the latter often had difficulty with ecclesiastical authorities when insisting on performing charitable work for the poor. It was not until the decline of apostolic orders in the late eighteenth century and the revival of monastic communities in the teaching and nursing congregations that active worldly services would become a predominant focus of women religious.

Christian Monasticism in Comparative Perspective. With the exception of Max Weber, few scholars have attempted a comparative study of monasticism in different religious traditions. Weber's writings in the sociology of religion, which focused on the economic ethics of the world religions, revealed that monastic groups generally attracted followers of religious traditions who were best suited for, and most committed to, stringent ascetic practices. The stringency and direction of such ascetic practices varies, however. Compared to its counterparts in Confucianism, Daoism, Hinduism, and Buddhism, Weber argued, Christian monasticism is comparatively unique in two aspects: (1) its relatively modest ascetic requirements, and (2) its stronger inner-worldly focus. Even though Christian monasticism knew of extremely demanding ascetic practices, such as those displayed by the stylites (fifth- and sixth-century Syrian ascetics who solitarily dwelled on a pillar for up to several decades, themselves influenced by Eastern precedents), its practices never quite equaled those required of Hindu ascetics, who may have produced some of the most extraordinary religious forms of world renunciation and bodily abnegation known to humankind. In contrast, Western Christian monasticism, especially as it became guided by the Benedictine rule, aimed for consistency, not supererogatory achievements possible only for a very select few. The emphasis on consistency contributed to Western monasticism's methodical character, and its less stringent ascetic demands coincided with a stronger inner-worldly focus. In other words, Christian monastics were not expected to leave the world behind in contemplation nearly as much as Hindu or Buddhist monks were, but rather embraced manual labor as an ascetic practice.

In practice, the tension between contemplative and ascetic practices proved difficult to resolve. On the one hand, tedious practices of manual labor tended to be given over to monastic affiliates of lesser status to free the monks and nuns proper to engage in contemplative practices, which lessened monasticism's inner-worldly focus. For example, in Cluniac and Cistercian monasticism, most of the manual chores fell on the *conversi,* or lay brothers. On the other hand, reformations of monastic life periodically restored manual labor's status and contributed to important technological advances, such as the use of the watermill and the rationalization of agriculture (particularly on Cistercian estates), or moved it close to the center of monastic spirituality, as happened in the early Franciscan groups. While all forms of monasticism in the world's major religions were much more concerned with transcending the secular spheres than with mastering or rationalizing them, the tension between the two directions appears to have been more pronounced in Christian monasticism; attempts to resolve it brought about a variegated monastic landscape over time.

More recent scholarship has broadened this perspective and led to significant revisions. For example, Mayeul de Dreuille's overview of the monastic traditions in Hinduism, Buddhism, Judaism, and Egyptian religions provides a much-needed newer comparative perspective and reminds the reader of the possible influences of these traditions on Western monasticism. Ilana Friedrich Silber's comparative study of Theravāda Buddhism and medieval Catholicism points to patterns of lay support and interaction with laity as well as to political patronage as factors shaping monasticism's societal impact and the direction of its spirituality—thus indicating a more dynamic relationship between monasticism and society than is suggested by Weber. In spite of these newer studies, research on comparative monasticism and asceticism remains in its infancy.

SEE ALSO Monastery; Nuns, article on Christian Nuns; Religious Communities, article on Christian Religious Orders.

BIBLIOGRAPHY

For a general overview of Western Christian monasticism, the best studies are Peter King's *Western Monasticism: A History of the Monastic Movement in the Latin Church* (Kalamazoo, Mich., 1999) and, with a focus on the Middle Ages, C. H. Lawrence's *Medieval Monasticism: Forms of Religious Life in Western Europe in the Middle Ages* (3d ed., New York, 2001).

Important new studies on early monasticism include James E. Goehring's *Ascetics, Society, and the Desert: Studies in Early Egyptian Monasticism* (Harrisburg, Pa., 1999) and Daniel Caner's *Wandering, Begging Monks: Spiritual Authority and the Promotion of Monasticism in Late Antiquity* (Berkeley, Calif., 2002). The varieties of monasticism in Palestine are addressed in John Binns's *Ascetics and Ambassadors of Christ: The Monasteries of Palestine, 314–631* (Oxford, 1995). On Athanasius and Pachomius and their ecclesiastical position and interpretation, see David Brakke's *Athanasius and the Politics of Asceticism* (Oxford, 1996) and Philip Rousseau's *Pachomius: The Making of a Community in Fourth-Century Egypt* (Berkeley, Calif., 1985).

The Rule of St. Benedict is contained in *R[egula] B[enedicti] 1980: The Rule of St. Benedict,* edited by Timothy Fry, OSB (Collegeville, Minn., 1981). For monastic customaries, see Kassius Hallinger's "Consuetudo: Begriff, Formen, Forschungsgeschichte, Inhalt," in *Untersuchungen zu Kloster und Stift,* edited by the Max-Planck-Institut für Geschichte (Göttingen, Germany, 1980), pp. 140–166. For Cluniac monasticism, see Barbara H. Rosenwein's *Rhinoceros Bound: Cluny in the Tenth Century* (Philadelphia, 1982); for the Cistercians, Louis J. Lekai's *The Cistercians: Ideals and Reality* (Kent, Ohio, 1977). For the moral character of and extensive social relationships entailed by noble donations in the case of Cluny, see Barbara H. Rosenwein's *To Be the Neighbor of Saint Peter: The Social Meaning of Cluny's Property, 909–1049* (Ithaca, N.Y., 1989).

The new eremitical groups in the twelfth centuries are discussed in Henrietta Leyser's *Hermits and the New Monasticism: A Study of Religious Communities in Western Europe, 1000–1150* (New York, 1984). Lester K. Little discusses changes in social conditions and their effects on religious life in *Religious Poverty and the Profit Economy in Medieval Europe* (Ithaca, N.Y., 1978).

For a history of the Franciscans and Dominicans, see John Moorman's *The History of the Franciscan Order* (Oxford, 1968) and William A. Hinnebusch's *The History of the Dominican Order* (Staten Island, N.Y., 1966–1973).

A very readable, up-to-date account of changes and directions in Catholic religious orders since the Reformation is provided by Patricia Wittberg's *The Rise and Fall of Catholic Religious Orders: A Social Movement Perspective* (Albany, N.Y., 1994). Steve Bruce's *God Is Dead: Secularization in the West* (Oxford, 2002) addresses causes and consequences of secularization from a comparative perspective.

The best study of women in monasticism is Jo Ann McNamara's *Sisters in Arms: Catholic Nuns through Two Millennia* (Cambridge, Mass., 1996). Susanna Elms's *Virgins of God: The Making of Asceticism in Late Antiquity* (Oxford, 1993) addresses early monasticism and women. Helen Rose Ebaugh's *Women in the Vanishing Cloister: Organizational Decline in Catholic Religious Orders in the United States* (New Brunswick, N.J., 1993) focuses on current transformations among American female religious.

Max Weber's thoughts on monasticism in the world religions are scattered throughout his *Gesammelte Aufsätze zur Religionssoziologie,* vols. 1–3 (Tübingen, Germany, 1920–1921). Newer scholarship on this topic includes Mayeul de Dreuille, OSB, *From East to West: A History of Monasticism* (New York, 1999), and Ilana F. Silber, *Virtuosity, Charisma, and Social Order: A Comparative Sociological Study of Monasticism in Theravada Buddhism and Medieval Catholicism* (Cambridge, UK, 1995). The role of asceticism in different religious traditions is discussed in *Asceticism,* edited by Vincent L. Wimbush and Richard Valantasis (Oxford, 1995).

Differing strains of asceticism in medieval monasticism are addressed in Lutz Kaelber's *Schools of Asceticism: Ideology and Organization in Medieval Religious Communities* (University Park, Pa., 1998), chapter 2, which contains an earlier version of sections of this article, as well as a more extensive discussion of some issues raised here.

LUTZ KAELBER (2005)

MONEY.

In examining the significance of money in the history of religions, one must begin by making a distinction between the commercial use of money in societies that have developed a market economy and the uses of money in societies with nonmarket economies. In the former, money is used primarily as a medium of exchange and standard of value in the marketplace, and its value lies in its abstractness, in its ability to mediate the exchange of goods between all persons who desire to engage in exchange, regardless of their social status and regardless of the nature of the goods involved. In this context money plays a major role in the economy, and the economic sphere is relatively independent of the social and religious spheres. When money is used in the context of a nonmarket economy, on the other hand, its use is more intimately connected with social and religious institutions. Whereas in a market economy money is used primarily for the commercial exchange of essential goods, in nonmarket economies such exchanges are often accomplished through nonmonetary means (such as barter or redistribution by a political authority), and money is reserved for a more exclusive set of exchanges that are at once social and religious in significance. This article will accordingly focus on the social and religious significance of money in communities with nonmarket economies.

Marcel Mauss (1914) was one of the first scholars to call attention to the religious significance of money in so-called primitive and archaic societies. In 1914 Mauss noted the use of objects like shells and precious metals as means of exchange and payment by peoples who were without a system of coinage. Drawing on evidence from Africa, Oceania, and North America, he insisted, against the anthropologist Bronislaw Malinowski, that such objects are rightly described as money, but he added that they are to be distinguished from modern money in being used only in specific social contexts and in being endowed with numinous or sacred value over and above their economic worth.

One of the most famous examples of such money is provided by the *kula* ring of the Trobriand Islanders, studied by Malinowski and discussed as well by Mauss. The *kula* ring is a complex system of exchange by which armbands and necklaces made of shells, collectively called *vaygu'a,* are traded around a large ring of islands just east of New Guinea. The armbands and necklaces, items of high value but of little practical use (they are seldom used even as ornaments), are traded in opposite directions around the circle by various sets of trading partners who make periodic voyages between their respective islands. The complex system of gifts and countergifts that develops is closely connected with the social order. The higher a person's social status, the more trading partners that person is liable to have, and the more generous he or she may be expected to be in gift giving. Not only is status an important factor in the giver, but the *vaygu'a* themselves develop a kind of status. The more a particular necklace or armband is traded, the more valuable it becomes, receiving a name and personal history and taking on a certain numinous quality. This trade in *vaygu'a* forms the heart of a more extensive trade between the islands that includes trade in ordinary commodities as well as in the valuable shell ornaments. Furthermore, the *vaygu'a* themselves can be given a definite price, in terms of baskets of yams, and in some specific circumstances can serve as a means of payment for services. Mauss argued that they could therefore be considered as a form of money, although clearly not the impersonal medium of exchange normally intended by that word. The *kula* ring thus provides a good example of money in a nonmarket economy, where it is an integral part of the economic system and yet still has a definite social and magico-religious value.

The use of shells as money goes far beyond the Trobriand Islands. The commonest form of shell money is the cowrie shell, which is found in China, India, the Near East, Africa, Europe, and the Americas. This small, attractive shell is well suited to serve as money because of its portability, countability, and immunity to counterfeiting. However, the use of the cowrie as money was originally motivated by more than its practicality. Mircea Eliade (1969) has pointed out the rich symbolism of shells in general, and the cowrie is no exception. It has been used widely as a talisman and is commonly viewed as a symbol of fertility, while among certain Indian tribes of North America it was treated as a sacred object. Like gold and jade, both rich in symbolism, cowries were also quite commonly buried with the dead. In China, cowries were placed in the mouth of the dead person, perhaps as a kind of passage money, similar to the obol for Charon in ancient Greece. The association of cowries with gold is evidenced by the fact that cowries actually made of gold have been found in Egypt and Cyprus. The popularity of the cowrie as a form of money is thus also due to its intrinsic symbolic properties.

Another widespread form of money is the glass bead. These seem to have been particularly common in Africa, where they were believed to grow naturally in the ground and thus to partake of the sacrality of the earth. Like the cowrie, they provided a convenient form of currency that was also endowed with numinous and magical properties. They were used not only as money but also in various rituals. Among some African peoples they were ground up, mixed with water, and rubbed on children to aid their growth. Again like the cowrie, they are often found in graves.

Not only were many types of primitive or archaic money endowed with an intrinsic numinous quality; some were also used as the specified means of payment for various religious services. This is seen clearly in ancient India, where the *Śatapatha Brāhmaṇa* enjoins that the payment (*daksina*) of the priests officiating at a sacrifice be made in gold, cattle, clothing, or horses. With the possible exception of clothing, all these objects are laden with religious symbolic significance. Their value was at least partly intrinsic, and it was this intrinsic worth and not their raw economic value that made them fit for the remuneration of priests. Their economic value was located within a broader context of social and religious value.

A particularly interesting case of an exclusively religious use of money is the Chinese custom of making offerings of paper money to gods, ghosts, and ancestors. Four centuries before paper money began to be used for commercial exchange in China, it was already being used as a sacrificial offering. The money itself consisted of pieces of paper in varying sizes and colors, decorated with designs, depictions of gods, or Chinese characters. A small piece of tin foil was sometimes attached to the center of the paper in order to represent silver or, when dabbed with yellow tint, gold. Obviously this paper money had little real economic value, but this was in fact intentional, because it was believed that what was a mere imitation in this world would become, when transformed by the sacrificial fire, a genuine treasure in heaven. There it would be added to the Celestial Treasury for the benefit of the person making the offering. This paper money is still in use in Taiwan, where four principal types are found: "gold" paper money, offered to the gods; "silver" money, offered to ghosts and ancestors; "treasure money" for repaying the "debt of life"; and "money for the resolving of crisis," used primarily in rites of exorcism.

It goes without saying that gold and silver have been favorite forms of money from earliest times. Long before they came to be used for commercial exchange, however, they were used for gift exchange and as a standard of value among various political, social, and religious elites. Exchanges of articles made of these precious metals were a primary means of asserting and maintaining one's status. The cups, tripods, bowls, and arms exchanged among the ruling elite of Homeric society, for instance, were often made of precious metals and were endowed with the numinous quality that is associated with these metals more generally. A king's treasury could express not only his political sovereignty and personal wealth but also an intrinsic sacred power that could come to the aid of his kingdom in times of crisis.

The close association of gold and silver with royalty, on the one hand, and with religious values, on the other, did not cease when these metals eventually began to be used in the manufacture of coins. Although it has been customary in textbooks on economics to attribute the introduction of coinage or "real" money to a merchant class seeking to overcome an awkward system of barter, this hypothetical reconstruction contains little historical truth. In fact, as illustrated above, the use of money cannot be equated with the use of currency in a market. Furthermore, the transition from a nonmarket to a market economy is a gradual one that is not identical with the introduction of coinage. According to Édouard Will (1954), who builds upon the earlier work of Bernhard Laum (1924), the introduction of coinage in ancient Greece must be understood in the context of the social and legal reforms of the time of Solon (c. 630–560 BCE). Far from being intended to facilitate trade (which was in fact not a Greek but a Phoenician concern), coinage was introduced by the state in order to provide a new standard for an older system of exchange that had become decadent and unjust, and to provide a standard means for payments made to the state such as taxes, fines, port fees, and the like. The introduction of coinage was thus the initiative of the same group with which gold and silver were already associated, namely, the royalty.

The religious significance of the earliest coins must be seen in this larger political context. Although it was argued in the nineteenth century, in particular by Thomas Burgon and Ernst Curtius, that early Greek coinage had a direct religious origin, it seems more likely today that the numerous religious symbols found on these coins are to be understood both as symbols of the issuing city-state and as symbols of the divine sanction behind a specific issuing body and hence behind the value of its coinage as well. This is not to deny that religious representations have been favorite themes on coins throughout history; but these representations are to be understood as expressing the religious values of the issuing body and not necessarily as implying an intrinsic value in the material coin itself.

With the introduction of coinage, therefore, a gradual movement began away from the more archaic pattern of attributing sacral value directly to the material objects used as money and toward the highly abstract forms of money used today, which are valued purely on the basis of their usefulness as indirect media of exchange in commercial markets.

With the introduction of fully monetized market economies, one begins to encounter a reversal in religious attitudes toward money. Whereas the earliest forms of money had a positive numinous quality for many archaic peoples, the disruptive effects that moneys and markets can have on the social structure of previously nonmarket societies can lead to negative evaluations of money as an evil. This can be seen clearly in the medieval West, where the introduction of markets and the increased use of money from the eleventh century onward led to a variety of religious protests. Money was increasingly represented as demonic. Feelings of awe before the numinous qualities of gold and silver were transformed into feelings of disgust for gold and silver coins, which were increasingly compared to excrement. By the end of the thirteenth century, depictions of apes defecating coins begin to appear in the margins of manuscripts. One also finds a picture of the head of a monster vomiting gold coins into a golden bowl. In less extreme forms this religious suspicion of the role of money in a market economy has persisted into the modern era.

See Also Economics and Religion; Gold and Silver; Wealth.

Bibliography

A good introduction to money considered in its social contexts is provided in Walter C. Neale's *Monies in Societies* (San Francisco, 1976). Numerous studies of money in nonmarket economies, including two of Malinowski's essays on the Trobriand Islanders, have been collected by George Dalton in *Tribal and Peasant Economies: Readings in Economic Anthropology* (Garden City, N.Y., 1967). Both Neale and Dalton are students of Karl Polanyi, some of whose more important essays have been edited by Dalton in *Primitive, Archaic, and Modern Economics: Essays of Karl Polanyi* (Garden City, N.Y., 1968). The two standard studies of "primitive money" are Paul Einzig's *Primitive Money,* 2d rev. ed. (Oxford, 1966), and A. Hingston Quiggin's *A Survey of Primitive Money* (London, 1949). These two books are mines of information but need to be supplemented by the more theoretical works listed above.

The symbolism of shells has been studied in Mircea Eliade's "Observations on the Symbolism of Shells," chapter 4 of his *Im-*

ages and Symbols: Studies in Religious Symbolism (New York, 1969), pp. 125–150. Chinese paper money has been studied recently in Hou Jinglang's *Monnaies d'offrande et la notion de trésorerie dans la religion chinoise* (Paris, 1975). On the origins of Greek coinage, see both Ernst Curtius's "On the Religious Character of Greek Coins," *Numismatic Chronicle* 10 (1870): 91–111, and Édouard Will's "De l'aspect éthique des origines grecques de la monnaie," *Revue historique* 212 (July–September 1954): 209–231. The classic work on the origins of Greek money remains Bernhard Laum's *Heiliges Geld: Eine historische Untersuchung über den sakralen Ursprung des Geldes* (Tübingen, 1924). Marcel Mauss's groundbreaking article, "Les origines de la notion de monnaie," first published in 1914, has been reprinted in his *Œuvres,* vol. 2, edited by Victor Karady (Paris, 1969), pp. 106–112. Also to be consulted is his classic study *The Gift: Forms and Functions of Exchange in Archaic Societies* (1954; New York, 1967).

DAVID CARPENTER (1987)

MONGKUT (1804–1868), Thai Buddhist reformer and later king of Thailand. A son of the second king of the Cakkrī dynasty (1782–), Mongkut was heir apparent to the throne. However, when his father (later known as Rama II) died before Mongkut had reached his twentieth birthday, his claims were passed over in favor of those of his uncle (Rama III). Having entered the Buddhist monastic order for a temporary stay only two weeks prior to his father's death, he decided to remain a monk. Mongkut's monastic career did not end until more than a quarter of a century later when, following his uncle's death in 1851, he was chosen to succeed to the throne. At that point he left the order, became king (Rama IV), and began a reign that continued until his death.

Mongkut began his monastic career at Wat Samorai, a forest monastery near Bangkok that was renowned for its emphasis on ascetic practice and meditation. After a year of apprenticeship there he became increasingly dissatisfied because no adequate intellectual grounding or justification was being provided for the practices in which he was engaged. For this reason he left to become associated with a monastery in Bangkok, Wat Mahāthāt, which emphasized the study of the sacred texts written in the Pali language. There he quickly demonstrated his intellectual ability, becoming a leading expert in Pali studies.

Despite his increasing erudition, however, Mongkut remained skeptical about the authenticity of the tradition in which he was participating. At a certain moment during his stay at Wat Mahāthāt he reached a point of spiritual crisis (so the story goes) and vowed that if his doubts were not resolved within the week he would give up the struggle and leave the order. Before Mongkut's self-imposed time limit had expired, the answer that he was seeking came to him during an encounter with a Mon monk. (The Mon were an ethnic group with a long and venerable history in both Thailand and Burma.) This teacher was able to convince Mongkut that the Theravāda tradition as preserved and practiced by the Mons was the authentic tradition, the one remaining truly faithful to the teachings of the Buddha and to the testimony of the Pali scriptures (the Tipiṭaka). The obvious correlary was that the Thai version of the Theravāda tradition was inauthentic, misguided, and in need of reform.

Soon after his encounter with the Mon monk, Mongkut returned to Wat Samorai, where he launched his reform movement. Having initiated his own program of Pali studies at this forest monastery, he soon "discovered" that the boundary stones that established and set off the sacred precincts (*sīmā*) were not in accord with the requirements set forth in the Vinaya (the portion of the Pali Tipiṭaka that deals with the behavior of monks and the proper ordering of monastic life). Thus, he concluded, the ordinations that had taken place at this monastery, which for many years had been an ordination center for the Thai *sangha* as a whole, were invalid. In order to rectify the situation Mongkut arranged for the proper consecration of the sacred precincts at the Wat, and for his own reordination by monks who had been ordained in the Mon tradition. Through these formal ecclesiastical acts Mongkut made an irrevocable break with the traditionally oriented community of Thai monks (the Mahanikai; Pali, Mahānikāya) and established a new, reformist Thai lineage that later came to be known as the Thammayut (Dhammayuttika) Nikāya.

During Mongkut's remaining years in the order, he gradually built the new lineage into a small but distinctive and distinguished community. This community came to include within its ranks a number of serious and intellectually creative young monks, most of them from high-ranking families in the kingdom. It gained the support of many laymen and laywomen, including prestigious and influential members of the nobility. It also gained widespread popular recognition through an active program of teaching, not only in the capital city but also in the countryside.

Like many reformers who have emerged in traditions that have preserved sacred scriptures from the distant past, Mongkut appealed to the authority of those scriptures in order to purge supposed accretions that had, from his perspective, come to compromise the purity of the original tradition. He also combined his emphasis on scripturalist reform with an openness to the new modes of scientific rationality (and the accompanying rejection of inherited "superstitions") that were then being introduced from the West. The effect of these reforms on religious practice was the adherence, by the monks, to more canonical forms of monastic discipline and ritual. Doctrinally, the reforms resulted in a new modernist form of Buddhist teaching that emphasized the humanity of the Buddha and highlighted the ethical and humanitarian aspects of his message.

When, at the age of forty-seven, Mongkut left the order and became king, he assumed the traditional royal responsibility for the support of the *sangha* as a whole. In this new role he provided patronage and protection for the older and much larger Mahanikai lineage, but he clearly favored the reform-minded Thammayut lineage that he himself had founded.

By the time of Mongkut's death in 1868 the reform movement that he had originated was well established. During his long career as a monk he had provided the intellectual and organizational leadership that had enabled the new Thammayut lineage to become a coherent community with its own distinctive emphases and goals. Subsequently, during his seventeen years as king, he fostered both the religious and intellectual atmosphere and the institutional ecclesiastical adjustments that enabled the new movement to consolidate its position and extend its influence. In so doing, Mongkut has contributed, more than any other individual of his era, to the establishment of the gradual but pervasive process of modernist reform that characterized the development of Thai Buddhism during the late nineteenth and early twentieth centuries.

See Also Buddhism, article on Buddhism in Southeast Asia; Buddhism, Schools of, article on Theravāda Buddhism.

Bibliography

The most accessible biographies of Mongkut are A. L. Moffat's *Mongkut, the King of Siam* (Ithaca, N.Y., 1961) and A. B. Griswold's *King Mongkut of Siam* (New York, 1961). These treatments may be supplemented by an indigenous perspective that can be found in the relevant sections of Chula Chakrabongse's *Lords of Life: The Paternal Monarchy of Bangkok, 1782–1932* (New York, 1960). Those who seek a more critical approach with greater historical detail should consult Craig J. Reynolds's "The Buddhist Monkhood in Nineteenth Century Thailand" (Ph.D. diss., Cornell University, 1973).

New Sources

Finestone, J. *Somdet phrarup phraratcha orot phraratchathida læ phraratchanatta nai phrabat somdet phra chomklao chaoyuhua, ratchakan thi si (A Royal Album: The Children and Grandchildren of King Mongkut, Rama IV, of Siam).* Bangkok, 2000.

Narathipphongpraphan, I. Vijavat. *A Diplomatic History of Thailand.* Bangkok, 1991.

Pallegoix, J. B., and W. E. J. Tips. *Description of the Thai Kingdom or Siam: Thailand under King Mongkut.* Bangkok, 2000.

Phiphat, P., et al. *Phapmumkwang khong Krung Thep Phra Maha Nakhon nai samai Ratchakan thi 4: kankhonphop mai (Panorama of Bangkok in the Reign of King Rama IV: A New Discovery).* Krung Thep, 2001.

Thipakonwongmahakosathibodi, et al. *The Dynastic Chronicles. Bangkok Era, the Fourth Reign, B.E. 2394–2411 (A.D. 1851–1868).* Tokyo, 1965.

Frank E. Reynolds (1987)
Revised Bibliography

MONGOL RELIGIONS.

If stereotypical reports from early times are taken into account, the religious forms of the Mongols have been influenced by the religions professed by all ethnic groups who have lived in what later was to become Mongolian territory prior to the emergence of the Mongols. The oldest of these religious forms was shamanism, which was the religion of the Liao empire of the Kitan (907–1125) and their usurping successors, the Jurchen (1115–1234). There have been accounts of Buddhist influences in the steppes since the Chinese Han period (206 BCE–220 CE), while Iranian influences are attested among the Turkic peoples of the region. Nestorian Christianity is reported as early as the twelfth century among the Turkic neighbors and later compatriots of the Mongols, the Kereit, Naiman, and Önggüt. This nourished contemporary Western beliefs that located the realm of the fabulous Prester John in their territory. Later conversions of Mongols by Catholics even led to the foundation of a bishopric in Khanbaliq (Beijing), but this development was short-lived. Renewed Christian missionary attempts in the nineteenth and twentieth centuries have again failed to leave recognizable traces in Mongol popular religions.

In addition to the influences of Nestorianism, Manichaeism, with its dualistic ideas of light and darkness and good and evil, also played a role in the religious history of the region. It had strong footholds in the oasis towns of the Uighurs, which were incorporated into the Mongol Empire under Chinggis Khan (1162–1227). The Zoroastrian deity Ahura Mazdā was an Iranian import who in Mongol popular religion became Khormusta Tengri, with a retinue of thirty-three heavenly beings (*tengri*). All these professions have been of temporary influence, however, while shamanism has remained the perennial dominant religious practice of the Mongols.

In contrast to the abundance of studies on the shamanism of the Siberian ethnic groups and of the Buriats, shamanism in Mongolia has not yet received the scientific treatment needed to form a well-founded opinion of this religious manifestation. Following the trends of research on Siberian shamanism, the emphasis of investigation has been placed on such external paraphernalia as drums, ceremonial dresses, and idols. But unlike the Yakut and Buriat shaman songs, both of which show important Mongolian components, only a very small number of invocations from Mongolia proper have been published; an even smaller number of these incantations have been translated. Recently published materials, however, show shamanism still in existence in the northwestern parts of the Mongolian People's Republic and in eastern Mongolia. A number of invocations gathered in 1982 in the eastern part of Inner Mongolia and among the Daghurs of northwestern Manchuria also testify to the continued existence of shamanism. Some studies on these forms of shamanism have been published.

Mongol shamanism developed into its current state in various phases. In the original phase, fear of natural powers that were thought to be caused by evil forces led to the worship of the spirits of ancestors. One of the few remaining chronicles about the origin of shamanism, a text from the Chahar region, states that the living "made offerings of one wooden bowl of tea, one wooden bowl of water, and one bowl of milk brandy on the first, seventh, and ninth days of each new moon; saluted; and worshiped," attempting thereby to obtain the protection of the ancestral spirits. Through these actions one would combine forces with the masters of places and the waters, thus becoming powerful enough to fight the detrimental forces. The shamans (male, *böge;* female, *idughan/udaghan*), however, by their worship and incantations became the mediators and the means of communication with the forces to which all life was exposed. In addition to the spirits of ancestors, the spirits of unfortunate people who had not found a natural end, having been killed by accident, murder, or suicide, were thought of as possessing particular powers. They were added to the group of helpful powers that were manifest in the venerated idols called *ongons*. Because personal *ongons* were transferred into a greater unit through the merger of smaller ethnic groups or through marriage, the number of *ongons* of the individual shaman increased. (A shaman who marries obtains the *ongons* of his wife's clan.) The more *ongons* a shaman possesses, the greater is his power. This explains the diversity of incantations and the varying names of the invoked spirits and *ongons*. The functions of shamanism, as explained by the shamans themselves, are to invoke the *ongons*, to shamanize with their help, to intercede on behalf of ill persons, to exorcise evil and the powers creating calamities and illness, to expel these into effigies that are then destroyed, and to pronounce charms and prognostications by scapulimancy and other divinatory methods.

Shamanism thus appears to have developed out of the needs of a primitive economic society for the preservation and protection of the means of subsistence (health, fire, food, game, and livestock, as well as human labor, i.e., children), all of which were obtained through the help of the ancestors. People seek shamanic assistance for immediate concerns; there is no belief in its efficacy for retaliation or reward in another world or in a future life. Shamanism, lacking any moral incentive, is a matter of this world, using combinations of natural means to achieve supernatural results. The culmination of all shamanic practice is the ecstasy the shaman experiences when the protective spirit enters his body. The shaman then acts in the spirit's power and speaks in its voice. The ecstatic state is achieved in part by self-hypnosis, and in part by constant turning around in circles, inhaling burning juniper, and gulping large doses of alcohol; no other use of drugs and stimulants is traceable among Mongol shamans. In this state the shaman travels into another world, searching for the soul of the ill person, fighting with evil powers for it, and trying to win back the victim's health. The fate of the person in whose behalf the shaman acts is uttered by the protective genius through the mouth of the shaman.

The shaman's drum serves as the vehicle of this spiritual journey, having the function of a horse or a boat. Some Mongol shamans explain the streamers on their vestments as feathers enabling them to fly on the spiritual journey. Others call these streamers snakes. To transport themselves to the spirit world, certain shamans from Inner Mongolian tribes use wooden or iron staffs, each crowned with a horsehead and terminated with a carved hoof, and adorned with rattling iron rings and little stirrups. Beating the drum and shouting and singing loudly with the assistance of helpers is part of the shaman's ritual; these actions are intended to frighten and scare away the evil spirits and demons. Such an aim is already attested for the Kitan shamans of the tenth and eleventh centuries. Once exorcised, the evil originators of the illness are banished into effigies that are burned or buried.

To become a shaman a person must have the calling. The mental instability, resulting in a long period of initiatory illness, that is often reported for the Siberian and northern Eurasian shamans is rarely mentioned in Mongolia. Such a nervous and feeble condition would not accord with the historical fact that until the time of Chinggis Khan, the shaman (*böge/bägi*) often was the head of the clan and therefore was not only its spiritual leader but also its political and military leader. Mongol shamans seem to be perfectly healthy individuals. The prospective shaman is singled out by an old shaman who becomes his teacher (*bagši*). From the *bagši* the student learns the names of all the ancestral spirits, which eventually are all bequeathed to him. The young shaman thus becomes a link in an age-old chain of religious and ethnic tradition. The continued existence and activity of the *bagši* is still being reported. One famous *bagši* died as recently as 1970 in the Bulghan district of northern Mongolia; in 1983 the incantations of a sixty-one-year-old *bagši* and his pupil (*šabi böge*) were recorded in eastern Mongolia. The costumes of Mongol shamans furthermore lack any of the female symbols and emblems reportedly common among Siberian and Central Asian shamans.

In the thirteenth century Mongol shamanism was influenced by administrative measures when the first Mongol emperor in China, Khubilai Khan (r. 1260–1294), established by imperial decree the office of the state shamans. These shamans were responsible for offerings in memory of Chinggis Khan and his house as well as for the worship of fire. According to the *Yuanshi*, the official Chinese history of the Yüan dynasty, these shamans pronounced their prayers and invocations in the Mongolian language. Judged by the evident longevity of the Mongolian oral tradition and its extraordinary reliability, it seems certain that some of the prayers still used today at the so-called Eight White Yurts, the center of worship of the deified Chinggis Khan in the Ordos territory, contain remnants of these early shamanic prayers and supplications. Tradition has outlived the destructive influences of the fratricidal warfare of the Mongols in the fifteenth and sixteenth centuries as well as more recent attempts at annihilation. The faithful handing down of the clan-bound names of the ancestral spirits from one generation of shamans to the next is proof of the age of the many different extant samples of shaman invocations and poetry. The Yuan government's early administrative measures regulating religious affairs may also account for a certain conformity of expression in the shamanic supplications. The mention in invocations of Chinggis Khan's son, Čagadai, and Čangqulang, one of Čagadai's spouses, testifies to the continued inclusion of historical personages of the Mongol imperial line in the realm of the powerful ancestral spirits and *ongons*. The same holds true for the mention of members of the Mongol imperial family among the persons lauded in the fire prayers for having brought the flame to life by striking sparks from flint and steel.

The ephemeral contacts of Buddhism with the ruling strata of the Mongol nobility during the twelfth and thirteenth centuries and later did not lead to any decisive intrusion of Buddhist notions into the religious conceptions of the bulk of the Mongol populations. Shamanism remained dominant. Only when Buddhist missionary work began among the Mongols in the sixteenth century did shamanism come under heavy attacks. Biographies of Buddhist missionaries such as Neyiči Toyin (1557–1653), who converted the eastern Mongol tribes; the lamas who were active in the southern part of Mongolia ruled by Altan Khan of the Tümet (1507–1583); and the western Mongol Zaya Paṇḍita (1599–1622), who spread Lamaism among the northwestern Mongol groups, show clearly the methods of conversion. All of these missionaries had recourse to the persecution of shamanism and the shamans and to the sequestration and destruction of their idols, vestments, and paraphernalia, using ruthless force, persuasion, and bribes. The conversion aimed particularly at prohibiting bloody offerings of animals and the worship of the *ongot*, the collective term for *ongon* figurines. Princes and overlords sustained the missionaries by donating horses and cows to converts while burning the confiscated shamanic idols in iconoclastic purges. Thousands of the idols were destroyed in this period, and the shamans had to renounce their profession and faith. Many fled during the sixteenth century into more remote regions, even as far as the territory inhabited by the Buriats.

Considered by both the Lamaist clergy and most princes to be a meritorious deed that would further the spread of Buddhism, such persecution has been repeated again and again up to the beginning of the twentieth century. Cases of rounding up, mistreating, and burning shamans were reported among the eastern Khalkha Mongols in the nineteenth century and in the remote northwest of Mongolia in 1904. Yet shamanism and related forms of popular religious worship have not been totally subdued. Forced during the periods of worst suppression into some camouflaged forms, it found a new, more syncretic expression by adding and adapting objects and forms of Buddhist veneration. The old, true forms of "black" and "white" shamanism were supplemented by a third, "yellow" shamanism or semi-shamanism that included praying to Buddhist and shamanic numinous representations. In addition to the traditional objects of veneration (the *ongons*; the sun and moon; Köke Möngke Tengri, the "eternal blue sky"; Khormusta and his thirty-three *tengri;* and the lords of the places, mountains, and waters), a new pantheon was worshiped.

While shamanism calls itself a "faith without scriptures," there exist a great number of written prayers and invocations for this other group of venerated numinous images. Most of these are directed toward obtaining help, blessings, and consecration through the instrument of incense offerings (*sang*). The structure of the *sang* follows the pattern of Buddhist incense offerings, but, shrouded in some Buddhist phrases and verses, contains ancient pre-Buddhist conceptions. This development was due to the necessity of creating a prayer that would appear to be a genuine work of Buddhist liturgy, a practice engaged in by both famous Buddhist ritualists and stout shamanic believers. The former intended to use these new scriptures to expel shamanic ideas completely, while the latter hoped to preserve essential parts of the old belief under the veneer of the new Buddhist religion. The Buriat scholar Dorzi Banzarov, the first to study the popular religion of the Mongols, described this practice: "The Lamas collected prayers which survived on the lips of the people, added to them new ones more in conformity with the new religion, and again distributed them among the people" (Banzarov, 1891, p. 2). In the sixteenth century a process thus began that resulted in the creation of numerous prayers and hymns of semi-Buddhist character, which became an inexhaustible mine of information concerning the conceptions of old Mongol religion. The Hungarian scholar Alice Sárközi has aptly stated the importance of these texts for the history of religions: "Every new text, or even new variants of already known texts can enlarge our knowledge of popular native beliefs and can shed a light on details which up to now have not been quite intelligible" (Sárközi, 1984). Analysis of such materials has yielded insights into the rather complex figure of a fire goddess who developed out of one of the oldest rituals into the worship of mountains and heights (*obogha*) and into the existence of a triad or pentad of gods of fate, headed by Möngke Tengri and Atagha Tengri, all considered to be "a late hypostasis of Eternal Heaven," as Sergei Iu. Nekliudov phrased it (Nekliudov, 1982, p. 500).

These divine representations, as well as those of Chinggis Khan and Geser Khan, the hero of a widely known epic, present an iconography related to the Tibetan "enemy gods" (*gra lha*), wearing the armor of Central Asian warriors of the first millennium CE and mounted on horses of varying color. All of these equestrian deities have protective functions. In addition to Köke Möngke Tengri, Čaghan Ebügen ("white old man") is venerated as the personified creative power, the lord of all earth and water, protector of animals and guarantor of longevity. He is certainly one of the oldest deities of the Mongol pantheon. Prayers to him refer to a legendary meeting between the White Old Man and the Buddha in which the Buddha confirmed him in his functions, testifying to this deity's pre-Buddhist origins. All requests addressed to these numinous representations of the popular religion are requisite to the nomadic/seminomadic pastoral way of life and its additional economics. The prayers ask for the same things as the shamanic invocations do: health; fertility and children; multiplication of livestock; protection against evil, dangers, war, and robbers; prevention of droughts, inundations, and blizzards; and safe roads, journeys, and caravan travel. In regions of additional or expanding agriculture, requests for augmentation and protection of crops are added, but the formulas of the prayer remain the same.

In more recent times the healing activities of the shamans have been more and more predominant, the shaman personnel being divided into real shamans (*böge/udaghan*) and non-shamanic healers and singers. The method of healing employed tends toward a kind of group therapeutic treatment of psychic illness (*andai*), which consists of shamans, helpers, and a crowd of laymen singing and arguing with the patient as a means of restoring him to his normal psychic state. In eastern Mongolia this singing therapy has been practiced since at least the mid-nineteenth century.

SEE ALSO Buddhism, article on Buddhism in Mongolia; Chinggis Khan; Erlik; Gesar; Ongon; Shamanism; Tengri; Ülgen.

BIBLIOGRAPHY

Banzarov, Dorzi. "*Chernaia vera, ili Shamanstvo u Mongolov*" *i drugie stat'i.* Edited by G. N. Potanin. Saint Petersburg, 1891. Translated by Jan Nattier and J. R. Krueger as "The Black Faith, or Shamanism among the Mongols," *Mongolian Studies* 7 (1981–1982): 51–91.

Buyanbatu, G. *Mongghol-un böge-yin šasin-u učir.* Kökekhota, 1985.

Dalai, C. "Mongolyn böögijn mörgölijn tovč tüüh." *Studia Ethnographica* (Ulan Bator) 1 (1959).

Heissig, Walther. "Schamanen und Geisterbeschwörer im Küriye-Banner." *Folklore Studies* (Beijing) 3 (1944): 39–72.

Heissig, Walther. "A Mongolian Source to the Lamaist Suppression of Shamanism in the Seventeenth Century." *Anthropos* 48 (1953): 1–29, 493–536.

Heissig, Walther. *The Religions of Mongolia.* Translated by Geoffrey Samuel. Berkeley, 1980.

Hoppál, Mihály. "Shamanism: An Archaic and/or Recent System of Beliefs." *Ural-Altaische Jahrbücher* 57 (1985): 121–140.

Nekliudov, Sergei Iu. "Tengri." In *Mify narodov mira,* edited by S. A. Tokarev, vol. 2. Moscow, 1982.

Poppe, Nicholas N. "Zum Feuerkultus bei den Mongolen." *Asia Major* 2 (1925): 130–145.

Sárközi, Alice. "Symbolism in Exorcising the Evil Spirits." Paper delivered at the meeting of the Permanent International Altaistic Conference, 1984.

Sodnam, B. "Mongolyn kharyn böögijn duudlagyn tukhaj." *Studia Mongolica* (Ulan Bator) 4 (1962): 59–112.

Tatár, Magdalena. "Tragic and Stranger Ongons among the Altaic Peoples." In *Altaistic Studies,* edited by Gunnar Jarring and Staffan Rosén, pp. 165–171. Stockholm, 1985.

Zhukovskaia, Nataliia L. *Lamaizm i rannie formy religii.* Moscow, 1977.

New Sources

Bold, Bat-Ochir. *Mongolian Nomadic Society: A Reconstruction of the "Medieval" History of Mongolia.* Richmond, U.K., 2001.

Nassen-Bayer, and K. Stuart. "Mongol Creation Stories." *Asian Fold Studies* 51 (1992): 523–534.

Young, R. F. "Deus unus or dei plures sunt? The Function of Inclusivism in the Buddhist Defense of Mongol Folk Religion against William of Rubruck." *Journal of Ecumenical Studies* 26 (1989): 100–137.

WALTHER HEISSIG (1987)
Revised Bibliography

MONISM is a term applied to a group of thinkers or to philosophical systems that emphasize the oneness or unity of reality. Thinkers ordinarily regarded as monists do not themselves use this label, and do not refer to an agreed-upon monistic model. Unlike philosophical systems such as Platonism or Daoism, however, examples of monism cannot be identified by means of an accepted source or criterion. Moreover, in contrast to philosophical schools of thought such as pragmatism or existentialism, monism lacks an identifiable point of origin and a historical framework. In this respect, monism is a conceptual label, like idealism, realism, or determinism. It might be more appropriate to use only the adjectival form: thus, rather than regard a philosophical system as an example of monism, we should understand that, in a variety of ways, philosophical and religious systems are more or less monistic. In view of the arguable character of monism, perhaps the most useful task of the present essay would be to establish one or more definite examples of a monistic system and to abstract from such examples the specific features that render them monistic.

Philosophies frequently regarded as monistic are found in both Asian and Western traditions and are rather evenly distributed among ancient, modern, and contemporary sustems. Many philosophical systems ordinarily regarded as monistic are influenced by mystical experience. Even though there are monistic systems that are not mystical, as well as mystical systems that are nonmonistic, there is a close affinity between monistic and mystical systems of thought. Most of the systems referred to in this article exhibit a mystical as much as a monistic emphasis. The decided influence of mysticism on monistic systems, as well as the considerable frequency with which mystical experience is expressed in a monistic system, would seem to be due to the unitive quality of the mystical experience itself. The great mystics, especially those of the Indian and Christian traditions, emphasize that their blissful experience of oneness with or in the divine renders all particulars insignificant, and in some cases, relatively unreal and illusory. This tendency of monistic thinking to favor unity and oneness at the expense of the particular has confined monism per se to a minority position in philosophy and religion, both Asian and Western. Even in India, ordinarily regarded as uniformly monistic in philosophic and religious outlook, the monistic system of Śaṅkara (traditional dates 788–820) is but one of several competing interpretations of the Hindu scriptures. Similarly, in the Western tradition, philosophical thinkers such as Plotinus (204–270) and Spinoza (1632–1677), and others who espouse an unabashed monism, have proven unable to gain a dominant position in the tradition. Despite significant differences, Śaṅkara, Plotinus, and Spinoza individually and collectively show the essential strength as well as the typical weaknesses of monism as a philosophical position.

ASIAN TRADITIONS. Perhaps of all claimants to the label "monist," the paradigmatic system is that of the ninth-century mystic philosopher Śaṅkara, who stands in the Indian tradition as the foremost interpreter of the ancient scriptures and the creator of an original philosophy of *brahman*, the Absolute, "one without a second." Śaṅkara's *advaita* (nondual) system is one of several alternatives within Vendānta, the religious-philosophical tradition consisting in systematic exposition and speculation based on the Vedas (c. 800–400 BCE) and the Upaniṣads (c. 800–400 BCE), mystical and quasi-philosophical texts in the Sanskrit of the *ṛṣis* (seers) of ancient India.

The dialectic between Śaṅkara and his competitors, both Vedāntins and proponents of other Indian philosophical schools, has helped to establish Śaṅkara's system as a model of monistic thinking. Because his sources are evident, because his arguments on behalf of an absolute oneness of reality are systematic, ingenious, and influential, and because his interpreters and opponents have shown his position to be committed to an unambiguous epistemological and metaphysical monism, Śaṅkara serves, in Wittgenstein's terminology, as a "home base" for the "family resemblances" that monistic systems would seem to share. Whatever else monistic systems have in common, they all seem committed to a conception of reality that resembles Śaṅkara's idea of *brahman* in its oneness and in its contrast to the unreal or less real particulars of the spatial and temporal world, all of which are, according to Śaṅkara, ordinarily and erroneously experienced as separate from *brahman*.

Of the thirteen Upaniṣads that have survived and have been commented upon by sages such as Śaṅkara, Rāmānuja, and Madhva, some tend toward theism, but most contain passages that have placed a definite monistic stamp on the Indian philosophical tradition. The *Bṛhadāraṇyaka* and *Chāndogya* Upaniṣads offer some of the strongest texts for the monistic position:

> Brahman indeed was this in the beginning. It knew itself only as "I am Brahman." Therefore it became all. Whoever among the gods became awakened to this, he, indeed, became that. . . . Whoever knows thus, "I am Brahman," becomes this all. (*Bṛhadāraṇyaka Upaniṣad* 1.4.10)

> Verily, this whole world is Brahman, from which he comes forth, without which he will be dissolved and in which he breathes. (*Chāndogya Upaniṣad* 14.1.1)

According to Śaṅkara, the concept of *brahman* in the Upaniṣads teaches that all particulars of the spatial or temporal world—all objects, thoughts, spirits, and gods (since gods are temporal, they are less than *brahman*)—are real only with respect to, only by virtue of being one with, *brahman*. Particulars that appear real to the observer independent of *brahman* do so because of an all-pervasive ignorance (*avidyā*). Although the universal self and God (in whatever form, by whatever name) is *brahman*, the ignorant perceiver, or believer, habitually regards these and lesser entities, or appearances, as independent realities.

Śaṅkara follows the Upaniṣads in distinguishing two aspects of *brahman*, namely, *nirguṇa* (indeterminate) and *saguṇa* (determinate), and identifies Īśvara (God) as the personification of *saguṇa brahman*. In itself, (*nirguṇa*) *brahman* is beyond qualities—not only beyond description, but beyond any specificity, including the temporal nature of God. *Saguṇa brahman*, which includes everything that is not *brahman* per se—from the most ephemeral entity or musing to the most perfect concept of God—issues from *brahman*, has its reality by virtue of *brahman*, and in the end is gathered into *brahman*. Or rather, *saguṇa brahman* in all of its multiplicity is finally—or once again—realized as the one indivisible (*nirguṇa*) *brahman*, which it never ceased to be even though it most assuredly appeared to be separate from (*nirguṇa*) *brahman*. That is, *saguṇa brahman* appeared real as *saguṇa* (having qualities, particularized, pluralized) even while its true identity as *nirguṇa brahman* ("one without a second") was hidden not only from human consciousness but, presumably, even from higher beings and perhaps from God as well. Obviously, the terrible burden (or flaw) of a system that is so strongly on the side of oneness is to establish a degree of reality for particulars, which range from fleeting moments to God the creator of the universe.

The most effective alternative interpretation to Śaṅkara was provided by the South Indian philosopher-saint Rāmānuja (c. 1017–1137), who argued that the level below *brahman* must also be counted as real. Rāmānuja's position is within Vedānta, but it is closer to traditional theism as developed in the Jewish, Christian, and Muslim traditions. Rāmānuja's criticism of Śaṅkara's advaitist (nondual) conception of *brahman*, however, does not lead him to deny either the *nirguṇa brahman* or Śaṅkara's contention that the reality of *saguṇa brahman* is entirely dependent on *nirguṇa brahman*. In this respect, Rāmānuja's position is closer to that of a theist who affirms, in addition to a God involved in the world, a conception of God or godhead that is beyond and ultimately unaffected by the temporal experiences of God and humanity.

The twentieth-century philosopher-statesman Sarvepalli Radhakrishnan (1888–1975) tried to combine the merits of Śaṅkara's absolute nondualism and Rāmānuja's qualified nondualism by attempting to reconcile, in a polar relationship, the two natures of *brahman*—absolutely one and beyond, on the one side, and pluralistic and particular on the other. It must be admitted that Radhakrishnan's view is very close to that of Śaṅkara except that he forcefully affirms the reality of the world. As he notes in his semiautiobiographical essay *The Religion of the Spirit and the World's Need: Fragments of a Confession* (1952), his intent is to "save the world and give it a real meaning"; it is *brahman* that gives the world its true meaning, but only if *brahman* is understood in a positive relation to the world.

Radhakrishnan's metaphysics shows the influence of both Plotinus's description of the One/Intellect (*nous*)/Soul/World and Whitehead's conception of the divine in process:

> [The *Taittirīya Upaniṣad*] affirms that Brahman on which all else depends, to which all existences aspire, Brahman which is sufficient to itself, aspiring to no other, without any need, is the source of all other beings, the intellectual principle, the perceiving mind, life and body. It is the principle which unifies the world of the physicist, the biologist, the psychologist, the logician, the moralist and the artist. (Radharkrishnan, 1953, p. 59)

> We have (1) the Absolute, (2) God as a Creative power, (3) God immanent in this world. These are not to be regarded as separate entities. They are arranged in this order because there is a logical priority. The Absolute must be there with all its possibilities before the Divine Creativity can choose one. The divine choice must be there before there can be the Divine immanent in this world. This is a logical succession and not a temporal one. The world-spirit must be there before there can be the world. We thus get the four poises or statuses of reality, (1) the Absolute, Brahman, (2) the Creative Spirit, Īśvara, (3) the World-Spirit, Hiranyagarbha, and (4) the World. This is the way in which the Hindu thinkers interpret the integral nature of the Supreme Reality. (ibid., p. 65)

In his attempt to articulate the integral nature of the Supreme Reality, Radhakrishnan argues that *brahman* includes Īśvara, and Īśvara is the concrete manifestation of *brahman:* "There is nothing else than the Absolute which is the presupposition of all else. The central mystery is that of Being itself. We should not think that emphasis on Being overlooks the fact of Becoming" (intro. *The Brahma Sutra*, New York, 1960, p. 119). This fact of becoming is none other than *saguṇa brahman* or Isvra: "The Absolute is a living reality with a creative urge. When this aspect is stressed, the Absolute becomes a Personal God, Īśvara" (ibid., p. 126). Īśvara is not something other than or in addition to *brahman;* Īśvara is *brahman* itself: "The creative thought 'let me be many' belongs to Brahman. It is not simply imagined in him. The energy that manifests itself in Brahman is one with and different from Brahman" (ibid., p. 142).

Despite Radhakrishnan's determination to reconcile Śaṅkara's conception of the *brahman* with the reality and value of the world, he nevertheless admits, with the Upaniṣads and Śaṅkara, that the absolute oneness of (*nirguṇa*) *brahman* is unaffected by God and creation:

> So far as the Absolute is concerned, the creation of the world makes no difference to it. It cannot add anything to or take anything from the Absolute. All the sources of its being are found within itself. The world of change does not disturb the perfection of the Absolute. (Radhakrishnan, in Muirhead, 1958, p. 502)

It is possible to find in some of the Buddhist schools metaphysical and epistemological teachings that seem to be examples of monism, though if one keeps in mind the aim of all Buddhist teaching—to attain enlightenment, *nirvāṇa* (eternal peace), or Buddhahood—such teachings will be seen to be only incidentally and superficially monistic. The concept of *śūnya* or *śūnyatā* as developed by Nāgārjuna (second or third century BCE) offers a vivid example of the way in which Buddhist teaching can be, though perhaps should not be, interpreted monistically. Zen Buddhism (or, in Chinese, Chan Buddhism) offers a second, equally ambiguous example of apparent monism. In both cases, as in the Buddhist tradition generally—to the extent that any generalization can be made accurately for the full variety of Buddhist teachings—the monism affirmed is intended primarily as a mere philosophical or conceptual stage on the way to an enlightenment experience concerning which no statements can be stable or adequate. According to Nāgārjuna, absolute reality can be positively experienced but only negatively expressed: "There is no death, no birth, no destruction, no persistence, no oneness, no manyness, no coming, no departing" (*Madhyamakakārikā* 1).

D. T. Suzuki (1870–1966), the prolific interpreter of Mahāyāna Buddhism and exponent of Zen Buddhism in the West, offers a more explicit account of the paradoxical character of the extent to which Zen may—and may not—be regarded as monistic:

> We may say that Christianity is monotheistic, and the Vedānta [the dominant school of Indian philosophy, based on the Upaniṣads] pantheistic; but we cannot make a similar assertion about Zen. Zen is neither monotheistic nor pantheistic; Zen defies all such designations. Hence there is no object upon which to fix the thought. Zen is a wafting cloud in the sky. No screw fastens it, no string holds it; it moves as it lists. *No amount of meditation will help Zen in one place.* Meditation is not Zen. Neither pantheism nor monotheism provides Zen with its subjects of concentration. . . . Zen wants to have one's mind free and unobstructed; even the idea of oneness or allness is a stumbling block and a strangling snare which threatens the original freedom of the spirit. (Suzuki, 1974, p. 40)

The Mādhyamika (Middle Way) of Nāgārjuna and Zen Buddhism share with monistic philosophies a systematic and highly effective assault on the apparent self-sufficiency and presumed reality of all particulars, but as expressions of Buddhist spiritual wisdom, they move beyond the monistic consequence of this assault to the silence of enlightenment.

In the Chinese tradition, particularly in the writings of Laozi (traditionally, sixth century BCE?) and Zhuangzi (latter fourth to early third century BCE), the illusive but uniquely formative concept of the Dao performs a function similar to the concept of *śūnyatā* in Mādhyamika Buddhism. According to the *Dao de jing* (*The Way and Its Power*), the poetic-philosophical text attributed to Laozi but in actuality compiled by his followers in approximately the early fourth century BCE, the Dao is the unity and the creative principle underlying all particulars. In contrast to an absolute monism such as defended by Śaṅkara, the Daoism of Laozi and Zhuangzi does not threaten, and in fact celebrates, the reality and value of particulars. Space and time, persons and nature, life and death, and all shades of being and becoming arise in and return to the Dao. But the Dao is not a principle or concept to be thought; it is a mysterious, ineffable reality to be experienced—and to the extent experienced, expressed only indirectly and inadequately. The Dao cannot be grasped or defined, but it can be received and hinted at by artful, seemingly effortless, action. The Dao is above concepts, above either being or nonbeing, and yet it runs through all realities named by concepts. It is the One behind the many—but not the One that can be named, thought, or delineated. Like the butterfly, which ceases to be itself when caught and mounted, human attempts to catch the Dao can catch expressions of the Dao, but not the Dao itself.

WESTERN TRADITION. There are perhaps a dozen thinkers spread throughout the history of Western thought who would likely be included in any survey of monistic systems. Among the ancient Greeks, probable candidates include Parmenides for his enigmatic but highly influential definition of reality as One. If monism were to be regarded as a theory of one kind of reality (as distinct from the more usual conception of monism as defining reality as singular), Democritus would be included for his definition of reality as consisting in atoms. Plotinus, the Neoplatonic mystic of the third century, articulated a philosophy of the One that stands as an obvious model of monistic thinking in the history of Western philosophy. The Christian period is steadfastly theistic—that is, maintaining a real separation between creator and creation—with the notable exceptions of the ninth-century Irish theologian John Scottus Eriugena and the fourteenth-century Rhineland mystic Meister Eckhart.

In Judaic and Muslim thought, orthodox theism and its attendant resistance to monism proved effective except for Ibn ʿArabī, the thirteenth-century Spanish Ṣūfī Muslim, who taught that God, or reality, is absolutely singular, and that the human soul is indistinguishable from God. It is important for anyone unfamiliar with Islamic thought to understand that the Muslim thinkers of the Middle Ages were using the same philosophical sources—primarily Plato and the Neoplatonists—as were medieval Jewish and Christian thinkers. Obviously, thinkers in each of these three religious and cultural traditions also drew from—and in turn influenced—their respective religious traditions. In the case of Ibn ʿArabī, his Muslim experience took the form of mysticism known as Ṣūfism. As R. C. Zaehner notes: "The introduction of Neoplatonic ideas into Ṣūfism from philosophy was, of course, made much of by Ibn al ʿArabī who systematized them into something very like Śaṅkara's version of the Vedānta" (*Hindu and Muslim Mysticism*, New York, 1969, p. 174). Although Ibn ʿArabī's system is generally regarded as heretical by orthodox Muslims, his writings—perhaps because of his vast erudition and manifest saintliness—were influential on subsequent Muslim and Christian thinkers.

In the modern period the two most important monistic philosophers have been the seventeenth-century Sefardic Jew Barukh Spinoza, who defines reality as one substance, calling it either God or Nature, and the nineteenth-century German idealist G. W. F. Hegel, whose concept of the Absolute continues to hold its place in the modern West as the dominant monistic philosophical system. Within the present century there are at least four philosophers, all American or British, who have extended the Hegelian, or absolute idealist, variety of monistic philosophy: Josiah Royce and F. H. Bradley, who wrote at the turn of the century, and W. T. Stace and J. N. Findlay, both Hegel scholars and metaphysicians who wrote at midcentury.

Virtually all of these philosophers, religious thinkers, and mystics, as well as others who could be added to the list, can be understood as a variation or subset of one of the following five influential figures: Plotinus, Eriugena, Eckhart, Spinoza, and Hegel.

Plotinus (c. 205–270), the last great thinker of antiquity, combined a profound knowledge of Plato, Aristotle, and the Stoics with an equally profound mystical experience of absolute oneness. Although Plotinus thought that he was faithfully interpreting the philosophy of Plato, he is rightly credited with founding a new school of philosophy, that is, Neoplatonism. Moreover, although Plotinus's writings, and therefore the tenets of Neoplatonism of which he was the first and greatest exponent, were neither influenced by Christian teachings nor read by medieval Christian theologians, nevertheless they exercised a significant influence on Christian thinking indirectly through Augustine (354–430) and Dionysius the Areopagite (fl. c. 500). By the time Plotinus's *Enneads* were rediscovered by Marsilio Ficino, the fifteenth-century head of the Platonic Academy of Florence, Meister Eckhart (1260–1327?) had articulated a novel monistic system, fashioned equally by Neoplatonism and by his spiritual life and thought as a German Dominican monk. The Neoplatonic—or Plotinian—cast of Eckhart's mystical monism accounts for its distinctiveness and for his difficulties with defenders of orthodox Christian theism. A close look at Plotinus's idea of the One will show both its affinities and its ultimate incompatibility with Christian doctrine; not surprisingly, Eckhart's use of Neoplatonic monism led his writings to be censored as heretical.

Plotinus's concept of the One is comparable to, and in part derived from, the absolute One of Parmenides, the Good of Plato's *Republic*, Aristotle's First Cause, and the immanent God of the Stoics. In affirming the absoluteness and transcendence of the One, however, Plotinus is speaking from a compelling mystical experience of Unity. Throughout the *Enneads*, which Plotinus's student Porphyry arranged in six sets of nine treatises each (Gr., *ennea*, "nine"), all of his references to the One, particularly those in the final tractate (6.9), "On the Good, or the One," emphasize that the One cannot be described or characterized, but can only be pointed to as the ineffable source and goal of mystical experience. In terms comparable to the Upaniṣadic concept of *brahman*—though with a greater affirmation of the value and beauty of the individual soul and the physical world—Plotinus conceives of the One as the absolute unity and harmony underlying all particularity and all polarities. The One is the source of the other two principles, or levels, of reality, both of which exist within the One and share completely in its divinity. But the One is not less absolute for their existence. Since the second and third principles, Mind or Intellect (*nous*) and Soul, are also real (though not absolute in their own right), it is not easy, as Plotinus admits, to state in what the One, or the Unity, consists. Unity can be experienced, but not described. Plotinus tells us:

> We are in search of unity; we are to come to know the principle of all, the Good and First; therefore we may not stand away from the realm of Firsts and lie prostrate among the lasts: we must strike for those Firsts, rising form things of sense which are the lasts. Cleared of all evil in our intention towards The Good, we must ascend to the Principle within ourselves; from many, we must become one; only so do we attain to knowledge of that which is Principle and Unity. . . . The Unity, then, is not Intellectual-Principle but something higher still: Intellectual-Principle is still a being but that First is no being but precedent to all Being: it cannot be a being, for a being has what we may call the shape of its reality but The Unity is without shape, even shape Intellectual. (*Enneads* 6.9.3)

In this tractate, Plotinus continues with a series of negative definitions: the One is not merely the Good, nor merely Mind, nor Soul, but is the indivisible source and perfect goal of all of these limited realities. While all characterizations of the One must be negative, experience of the One cannot but be overwhelmingly positive. This experience is more than an intuition or a vision; it is "a unity apprehended":

> The man formed by this mingling with the Supreme must—if he only remember—carry its image impressed upon him: he is become the Unity, nothing within him or without inducing any diversity; no movement now, no passion, no outlooking desire, once this ascent is achieved; reasoning is in abeyance and all Intellection and even, to dare the word, the very self: caught away, filled with God, he has in perfect stillness attained isolation; all the being calmed, he turns neither to this side nor to that, not even inwards to himself; utterly resting he has become very rest. (ibid., 6.9.11)

As this passage shows, it is difficult to separate the mystical from the philosophical assertions in Plotinus's philosophy, and in this respect, although he was not a Christian, Plotinus stands at the head of a line of Christian mystical philosopher-theologians for whom the concept of God, or the Absolute, is equally the object of mystical experience and philosophical reflection.

In his work *On the Division of Nature*, for example, the Irish theologian John Scottus Eriugena (810–877) affirmed and extended several Plotinian tenets: the absolute ineffability of God—a concept expressed in Christian theological language almost identical to descriptions of the One of Plotinus; a dual process of emanation from, and return to, the One of lower stages of reality—stages that also resemble those articulated in the *Enneads*. At the same time, Eriugena also used Christian ideas as developed by Dionysius the Areopagite and Gregory of Nyssa, both of whose works he translated from Greek to Latin. For Eriugena as for Plotinus, God or the One is not only beyond human thought, but equally beyond his own thought: God is incomprehensible even to himself because in his oneness he does not think at all. In fact, the reason for creation, which is accomplished through his ideas (*nous* in Plotinus's system, the divine attributes in Eriugena's), is to manifest the otherwise absolute and eternally hidden nature of God. Thus, the God of Eriugena is virtually identical to the One of Plotinus in that he (or it, in view of its absolute and transpersonal nature) is the source of being and knowledge but absolutely transcends both.

Meister Eckhart (1260–1327?) drew from Eriugena, and through him from Plotinus and early Neoplatonic Christian thinkers. He developed a concept of the Absolute, or God, that he called godhead, from the two points of view developed by Plotinus and Eriugena and comparable to the unqualified (*nirguṇa*) and qualified (*saguṇa*) dual conception of *brahman* in Advaita Vedānta. According to Eckhart, God is Being per se, or all that is, but is also inexplicably above and beyond Being, totally other and absolutely one. Existence or Being can be seen from two points of view, as the mysterious source of being and as being (or creation) itself, but ultimately there is only one existence. This affirmation of absolute unity of being, on the one hand, and on the other, the idea that all beings, including the human soul, are none other than God or Being from the perspective of creation, shows why Eckhart's teaching was regarded as too monist not to be at odds with orthodox Christianity. Eckhart's conception of the unity of God follows Eriugena's negative characterization of God and resembles Nāgārjuna's conception of the ultimate as *śūnyatā*, emptiness or nonbeing. Clearly, there is a point in the monist position at which the absolute fullness and the absolute emptiness of being appear to be indistinguishable—they are equally true and equally inadequate ways of expressing the absolute otherness of the One, the ultimate ineffable source of all particularity.

The same need to see the Absolute from two perspectives—as it is in itself and as it is from the perspective of creation—recurs in the metaphysical system of Barukh Spinoza (1632–1677), according to which the Absolute is referred to as Substance, God, or Nature. These three terms are declared to be perfectly synonymous, infinite, and absolutely necessary: "God, or substance, consisting of infinite attributes, of which each expresses eternal and infinite essentiality, necessarily exists" (Proposition 11). God (or Substance or Nature) manifests itself through an infinity of attributes, two of which, thought and extension (or ideas and bodies), are intelligible to man and constitutive of his experience. These two attributes, which are capable of infinite combinations, are related to each other (in contradistinction to Descartes's dualism of mind and body) through their common source in one divine Substance. Spinoza's solution to the Cartesian dualism, however, generates the same problem that attends all monistic systems—the difficulty in establishing the reality of particulars, which Spinoza refers to as modes, within the one indivisible Substance. Although Spinoza may be thought to have generated his metaphysics from a religious or mystical impulse, his conception of the divine as impersonal and absolutely necessary was clearly not influenced (except perhaps negatively) by either Jewish or Christian theological orthodoxy.

In conceiving of the world as God's manifestation of himself within his inviolable unity, Spinoza is in general agreement with other absolute monists like Advaita Vedānta (of the Upaniṣads and Śaṅkara), Plotinus, Eriugena, and Eckhart, but he is unique in attributing absolute determinism to the divine substance. On this point Spinoza is rigorously consistent even if his terminology gives the impression of inconsistency or paradox: he refers to the necessity of the divine Substance as both freedom and determinism because God is free to do what is required by his nature. God is free because of what he is—or because of the necessity which is the essential character of his existence. Since only God must be, and must be what He is, only God is free. Further, all of God's attributes and modes are what they are necessarily as part of God's essence. Without violating its unity and necessity, one can conceive of God, or Nature in polar terms, as the creator, or *natura naturans* ("Nature naturing"), and as creation, *natura naturata* ("Nature natured"), which consists in the infinite combinations of attributes and modes of the one divine Substance, God, or Nature. Within this Substance, all things that exist do so, and do so in the way that they do, because they are not other than God, and God's nature is absolutely necessary.

In the conclusion of *Ethics* Spinoza asserts that this Substance—which, it must be remembered, is the one and only reality regardless of how plural and diverse it appears to a human perspective—can be known by the third or highest form of knowledge, the intellectual love of God. This love, which is knowledge of a particular in relation to its divine cause (or divine nature), is in effect a direct knowledge of God, or Nature, in its infinity, eternality, and necessity. In this discussion of the intellectual love of God, which occurs in part 5 of *Ethics*, "Of Human Freedom," Spinoza's monistic conception of Substance (God or Nature) reveals a reverence and a personal experiential depth that would appear to be mystical even if not religious in the usual sense. While the overall force of *Ethics* would seem to represent an atheistic monism that allows no room for the God of Western religion, the profoundly mystical love of divine necessity, which is the goal and perhaps the source of Spinoza's entire system, would seem to justify Novalis's often-quoted reference to him as "a God-intoxicated man." W. T. Stace holds to both of these interpretations and suggests that Spinoza "exhibited in himself the living paradox of being a God-intoxicated atheist" (*Mysticism and Philosophy*, p. 217).

In that his philosophy of the absolute Spirit is the result of philosophical reflection rather than the product of his own mystical experience, G. W. F. Hegel is closer to Spinoza than to Plotinus or Eckhart. Hegel would also seem to resemble Spinoza in that his philosophy of the Absolute is an expression, however partial and indirect, of the experience and understanding of absolute Unity for which the great mystics, of both Asia and the West, are the primary source. In explaining the relation between mysticism and philosophy in Hegel, Frederick Copleston wisely remarks that Hegel was not a mystic and did not look to mysticism to solve the problems of philosophy, but rather "he saw in mysticism the intuitive grasp of a truth which it was the business of philosophy to understand and exhibit in a systematic manner" (*Religion and the One*, p. 135).

While Hegel's conception of the Absolute combines elements of many predecessors, including Plotinus, Eriugena, Eckhart, and Spinoza, in his original synthesis he introduces novel conceptions so as to create a uniquely profound and modern monistic philosophy. In terms similar to the conception of God in Eriugena or Eckhart, Hegel conceives of the absolute Spirit as revealing itself through spatial and temporal creation. For Hegel, however, the Absolute is neither empty nor so totally transcendent as to be characterized as nonbeing. Rather, the absolute Spirit of Hegel more closely resembles Spinoza's conception of Substance in that it is intelligible to human consciousness. In fact, it is through human rationality that the Absolute has its being: the Absolute exists through its self-knowing, which is none other than its being known through speculative philosophy. In this respect, Hegel's conception of absolute Spirit may be said to exhibit a radical temporality characteristic of process philosophy and other modern philosophical systems influenced by the theory of evolution. Spirit itself evolves through human consciousness, without which it cannot be said to be intelligible—or real, which comes to the same, according to Hegel's identification of the rational and the real.

Is Hegel's system, then, monistic? In what does his principle of unity, or oneness, consist? Since Hegel's system precludes univocal summations, two responses may fittingly be offered: in that the absolute Idea is single, rational, and the sole reality, Hegel's system clearly resembles monistic systems such as those of Plotinus, Eriugena, Eckhart, and Spinoza; since, however, the absolute Idea cannot be thought to exist in its own right as a full or finished reality separable from the process of human consciousness by which it knows itself, there is a sense in which the One in question, the absolute Idea, is equally plural and temporal. Absolute Spirit is there in the beginning, and without it, there would be no beginning—but it is equally the case that it comes to be, or comes into being, by being thought—as all human reflection is advancing, or making real, the actual content of the divine Idea. In Hegel's view, his *Phenomenology of Spirit* was itself a significant contribution toward the self-realization of absolute Spirit.

Delineating the relationship between these two perspectives—absolute Spirit as the one source of all and as the temporal-spatial process—required thousands of torturous pages by Hegel and continues to produce countless volumes of interpretation by his followers and critics. While it might be possible to solve the problem of the one and the many in contemporary terms without recourse to Hegel, most of the important work on this problem in the present century is demonstrably traceable to one or another interpretation of the Hegelian system. The most promising effort would seem to be that of J. N. Findlay, whose Gifford Lectures, *The Discipline of the Cave* and *The Transcendence of the Cave*, given from 1964 to 1966, represent a reformulation, by phenomenological and dialectical methods, of problems first set forth by Plotinus and Hegel.

CONCLUSION. A survey of monistic systems ranges from the uncompromising Advaita ("nondual") Vedānta of Śaṅkara to those thinkers, such as Radhakrishnan and Hegel, who have attempted to affirm the unity or oneness of reality without jeopardizing the reality or value of the many. In this regard, Radhakrishnan's response to, and restatement of, Śaṅkara's conception of *brahman* "so as to save the world and give it a real meaning" would seem to be a telling critique of the absolute monist position: the stronger the affirmation of oneness, the more difficult it is to affirm particulars in their own right. Within the context of absolute unity, all particulars are relegated to a quasi reality. If all is *brahman*—or Being, or the Absolute, or the One by any other name—then sticks and stones, civilizations and planets, ideas and gods must all share, and perhaps lose, their distinctive reality within the all-inclusive (or all-consuming) reality of the One.

Given the extent to which a monistic system jeopardizes the reality of the ordinary world, it is perhaps not surprising that it typically has drawn its inspiration from, and in turn lends its formulations to, mystical experience. The three most formidable monistic systems—those of Śaṅkara, Plotinus, and Spinoza—are all dependent on mystical awareness, however rational may be their respective processes of articulation. In view of the monistic tendency to devalue the full range of particulars, it is understandable that throughout the history of Western thought, monism has been countered not only by orthodox theologies (of Judaism, Christianity, and Islam) but equally by dominant philosophies. In Asia, and particularly in India, monism may appear to have enjoyed greater success historically, but most Asian thought systems—for example, Confucianism in China, theism and Yoga in India, and various forms of Buddhism throughout Asia—have not been monistic. Further, the remarkable influence of Advaita Vedānta in India may be due as much to its apparent mystical source and hermeneutical power as to its philosophical argumentation. The monist affirmation of the One (in whatever terminology) may well be truer than the myriad religious and philosophical positions that hold to the reality of the many, but while the vast majority of religious thinkers and philosophers fall short of mystical insight, it seems probable that in the future of philosophy and religion monism will continue to be a strongly opposed minority position.

SEE ALSO Dualism; Images; Neoplatonism; Pantheism and Panentheism; Transcendence and Immanence.

BIBLIOGRAPHY

The most useful survey of monistic philosophies is Frederick Copleston's Gifford Lectures, 1980, published as *Religion and the One: Philosophies East and West* (New York, 1982). Although it is less focused on monism, Karl Jaspers's brilliant interpretive study, *The Great Philosophers*, 2 vols. (New York, 1962–1966), treats virtually all of the philosophical contributors to the monist position. Volume 2 is especially recommended for its chapters on Laozi and Nāgārjuna, Heraclitus and Parmenides, Plotinus, Nicholas of Cusa and Spinoza. W. T. Stace's *Mysticism and Philosophy* (Philadelphia, 1960) is a study of the implications of mysticism for philosophy, particularly monistic philosophies. Nine articles on the philosophy of mysticism are collected in *The Monist* 59 (October 1976). Surveys on monism and pantheism are to be found in *The Encyclopedia of Philosophy* (New York, 1967) and *Encyclopaedia Britannica* (Chicago, 1968).

There are several virtually indistinguishable editions of the Upaniṣads, one of which is *The Principal Upaniṣads*, edited and translated by Sarvepalli Radhakrishnan (New York, 1953). Radhakrishnan's metaphysics is most fully articulated in *An Idealist View of Life*, 2d ed. (London, 1957); see also his "Spirit in Man," in *Contemporary Indian Philosophy*, edited by J. J. Muirhead (London, 1958). For a contemporary exposition and defense of Śaṅkara's nondualist system, see Eliot Deutsch's *Advaita Vedānta: A Philosophical Reconstruction* (Honolulu, 1969). For Nāgārjuna and early (or Indian) Mahāyāna Buddhism, see especially *Emptiness: A Study in Religious Meaning* (New York, 1967), by Frederick J. Streng, and *Nagarjuna: A Translation of His Mūlamadhhyamakakārikā with an Introductory Essay*, translated and edited by Kenneth K. Inada (Tokyo, 1970). D. T. Suzuki's *Introduction to Zen Buddhism* (New York, 1974) is one of the many introductions and surveys he has written that are relevant for the paradoxically monistic character of Zen Buddhism; *Zen Buddhism: Selected Writings of D. T. Suzuki*, edited by William Barrett (Garden City, N.Y., 1956), is particularly useful. There are numerous translations of *Laozi's Dao de jing* and of the writings of Zhuangzi, including Wing-tsit Chan's *The Way of Lao Tzu* (Indianapolis, 1963), Burton Watson's *Chuang-tzu: Basic Writings* (New York, 1964), and Raymond M. Smullyan's *The Dao Is Silent* (New York, 1977).

The best translation of Plotinus's *Enneads* remains Stephan MacKenna's *The Enneads*, 3d ed. (New York, 1957). Selections from John Scottus Eriugena's *De divisione naturae* are reprinted in *Selections from Medieval Philosophers*, edited by Richard McKeon, vol. 1 (New York, 1930); in *Medieval Philosophy*, edited by Herman Shapiro (New York, 1964); and in *Medieval Philosophy*, edited by John F. Wippel and Allan B. Wolter (New York, 1969). There are several English-language translations of Meister Eckhart: James M. Clark and John V. Skinner's *Meister Eckhart: Selected Treatises and Sermons* (London, 1958); Raymond B. Blakney's *Meister Eckhart: A Modern Translation* (New York, 1941); Matthew Fox's *Breakthrough: Meister Eckhart's Creation Spirituality* (New York, 1980), with introduction and commentary; and a brilliant philosophical interpretation, Reiner Schürmann's *Meister Eckhart, Mystic and Philosopher* (Bloomington, Ind., 1978). The most scholarly and substantial interpretation of Ibn ʿArabī is Henry Corbin's *Creative Imagination in the Ṣūfism of Ibn ʿArabī* (Princeton, 1969).

Spinoza's metaphysics is fully articulated in one volume, *Ethics*, volume 2 of *The Chief Works of Benedict de Spinoza*, translated by R. H. M. Elwes (New York, 1951). For Hegel, the indispensable—and famously difficult—volume is *The Phenomenology of Mind*. The translation by J. B. Baillie (1910; rev. ed., New York, 1949) has been superseded by a far more readable edition: *Phenomenology of Spirit*, translated by A. V. Miller, with foreword and textual analysis by J. N. Findlay (Oxford, 1977). There are three important restatements of the Hegelian Absolute: Josiah Royce's *The World and the Individual*, 2 vols. (New York, 1901–1902), the Gifford Lectures, 1900–1901; Francis H. Bradley's *Appearance and Reality: A Metaphysical Essay* (1893; 2d rev. ed., Oxford, 1930); and J. N. Findlay's Gifford Lectures, 1964–1966, published in two volumes: *The Discipline of the Cave* (London, 1966) and *The Transcendence of the Cave* (London, 1967). Findlay's neo-Hegelianism, or (in his term) Neo-neo-Platonism, is further developed in his *Ascent to the Absolute: Metaphysical Papers and Lectures* (London, 1970) and is given a precise summation in Douglas P. Lackey's "An Examination of Findlay's Neoplatonism," *The Monist* 59 (October 1976): 563–573.

New Sources

Cooper, John W. *Body, Soul and Life Everlasting*. 1989; rpt. Grand Rapids, Mich., 2000.

Curd, Patricia. *The Legacy of Parmenides: Eleatic Monism and Later Presocratic Thought*. Princeton, 1997.

Gasman, Daniel. "Haeckel's Monism and the Birth of Fascist Ideology." *Studies in Modern European History*, vol. 33. New York, 1998.

Kirby, David K. *Sun Rises in the Evening: Monism and Quietism in Western Culture*. Metuchen, N.J., 1982.

Loy, David. *Nonduality: A Study in Comparative Philosophy*. 1988; rpt. Amherst, N.Y., 1999.

Satlow, Michael. "Jewish Knowing: Monism and Its Ramifications." *Judaism* 45 (Fall 1996): 483–490.

van Gelder, T. J. "Monism, Dualism, Pluralism." *Mind and Language* 13 (1988): 76–97.

Zoetmulder, P. J., and M. C. Ricklefs, eds. *Pantheism and Monism in Javanese Suluk Literature: Islamic and Indian Mysticism in an Indonesian Setting*. Franklin, Mich., 1995.

ROBERT A. MCDERMOTT (1987)
Revised Bibliography

MONKEYS. Monkeys have played a complex and ambiguous role in the religion and folklore of diverse cultures. Although deities in monkey form have occasionally been venerated as psychopomps, tricksters, or intercessors, simians have more commonly been viewed as comical or degenerate simulacra of human beings. Both responses suggest a perception of these animals as challenging boundaries and categories, a theme that in the modern world remains implicit in much visual representation and fictional and scientific narrative. Despite a tendency among premodern authors and artists to be vague and generic about nonhuman primates (a confusion that persists in nontechnical discourse conflating, for example, tailed "monkeys" and tailless "apes"), human responses to simians, especially in regions in which the latter abound, have often been species-specific, reflecting characteristic features or behaviors of particular primate groups.

Perhaps the most widely attested response to anthropoid primates has been the notion that they are degraded or fallen humans, whose bestial status reflects punishment for a transgression. Thus a Jewish legend holds that the men who contrived to place idols atop the tower of Babel were turned by God into apes, and in a Greco-Roman tale a diminutive race of humans who attempted to deceive Hercules were punished by the gods by becoming "tailed ones" *(cercopes)*. A Muslim story holds that apes originated when a group of Jews were cursed for violating the Sabbath, and an Algerian tradition traces them to a human group deprived of speech by divine wrath. According to a medieval European legend, when God visited Adam and Eve after the fall, Eve concealed some of her numerous progeny out of shame over her sexual activity, and, as punishment, God transformed the hidden children into monkeys. Although such tales reflect the anthropocentric prejudices of monotheist religions, they are not confined to Europe and the Middle East. The motif of transgression and metamorphosis into a simian is preserved in the Mayan *Popol Vuh,* and it also occurs in Southeast Asia, in the tale of a wicked couple who are tricked by a god into squatting on red-hot bricks; when their backsides are burned red, they flee in shame into the forest. Similar stories, often involving punishment for sexual license, are the commonest explanations of simian origins among tribal groups in India, and cast doubt on the frequent assertion that Hinduism's now-robust cult of Hanumān derives from a hoary and indigenous tradition of "monkey worship." Comparable tales have been reported concerning the orangutans of Indonesia and the chimpanzees of the Ivory Coast. Japanese folktales involve many instances of cross-species transformation, yet those involving monkeys nearly always feature the one-way metamorphosis of a human who has incurred divine punishment. Even in the case of Hanumān, a sense of transgression of divine powers and of being "marked" as simian in punishment is found in the tale of his jaw (Sanskrit, *hanu*) being disfigured by Indra's thunderbolt. The abundance of such stories confirms Horst Janson's assertion that, when faced with the discomfort aroused by the similitude of simians, humans in general have tended to become "Darwinists in reverse" (Janson, 1952, p. 13).

Veneration of monkeys has been more sporadic. The earliest attested instance, in ancient Egypt, was directed toward a single species of baboon known to Greco-Roman authors as *cynocephalus* or "dog-head" because of its canine facial appearance. In contrast to other monkeys who appear in Egyptian art as leashed pets or performing grotesques, this animal was considered sacred and associated with both sun and moon. Images of seated male baboons, hands raised in adoration of the rising sun, adorn the columns of several temples, and mummified animals were commonly interred in a seated posture. Sculpted baboon images often display erect penises—a mark of lasciviousness in the view of later observers—that probably indicated the connection of both the sun and the animal with fertility. Yet the baboon was also associated with the moon and sacred to the moon god Thoth, a healer and magician, scribe of the gods, and guide of deceased souls. In some myths, the baboon taught hieroglyphics to Thoth and wore his lunar orb on its head. Its image regularly appeared atop scales, signifying postmortem judgment, over which Thoth presided. The god himself was sometimes depicted in the form, or with the head, of a baboon. The humanlike menstrual cycle of the female cynocephalus, which further linked the animal to cosmic rhythms, was noted by some ancient writers, as were temples where troops of semidomesticated baboons were fed by priests.

Elements of Thoth worship were transposed onto the Greco-Roman mystery cult of Hermes Trismegistos—who was likewise a magician, healer, and psychopomp—and gemstone rings carved with images of ithyphallic baboons enjoyed a vogue in the late Roman Empire, possibly as aphrodisiac charms. But the more common response to the Egyptian baboon-deity in classical Mediterranean cultures was scorn and ridicule. A minor decorative motif in Greek art, monkeys appear to have had no sacral significance; rather, they commonly represented ugliness, sycophancy, and immorality. Aristotle's brief observation that anthropoid primates constitute a morphological category situated between humans and quadruped animals would later definitively establish the "link" occupied by these animals in the medieval "great chain of being." The Romans sometimes kept monkeys as pets, but held the sight of one in a dream to be an evil omen. Roman writings, including Galen's accounts of his dissections of Barbary apes (a nearly tailless macaque native to North Africa and Gibraltar, and the best-known monkey in the ancient West), reveal discomfort with their likeness to men, exemplified in the punning aphorism of the second century BCE poet Ennius: "The ape, that vile beast, so similar to us" *(Simia quam similis turpissuma bestia nobis).*

Simian semblance took on ominous implications for religions whose scriptures declared the human form to be the "image of God." The stump-tailed posterior of the Barbary macaque was especially problematic, for God had declared in *Leviticus* 22:23 that all animals were to have tails. A Jewish legend declared that Adam himself was created with a tail, which God later removed as a sign of exaltation over bestial creation. The macaque was hence viewed as a duplicitous beast trying to "ape" human rank. A variant on the story claimed that God himself had cut off the ape's tail as punishment for its presumption, leaving "scars" on its backside—the ischial callosities, or "sitting pads," common to Old World monkeys. The Patristic writings of early Christianity are strident in their denunciation of "idolatrous" Egyptian religion and often focus on "ape worship" as its most loathsome practice. In medieval sources, the devil was called "God's ape" *(simia Dei)* because he tried unsuccessfully to imitate God's creative acts, and the monkey in turn was labeled "likeness of the devil" *(figura diaboli).* Renaissance paintings of the "fall of man" sometimes feature an ape slyly munching one of the forbidden apples; the gullible Eve points to the beast in order to sway her consort's resolve to uphold God's commandment—one instance of a common patriarchal tendency to associate women (as less-than-men) with monkeys.

In time, the Christian morphological preoccupation with monstrous *similitudines* and "hybrid races" that threatened to erase the boundary between the human self and the feral "other" would influence the response of Europeans to newly discovered primates and people in other parts of the world, contributing both to the racism of the colonial era and to the pseudoscience of eugenics that arose in the wake of Darwin's *On the Origin of Species* (1859). The association of simians with the "primitive" and "savage" as well as with the infantile and feminine, and the caricaturing of subject peoples and human enemies as "monkeys," has long persisted in Western discourse, as has the whimsical portrayal of simians as human surrogates in visual art. A recurrent theme in popular culture (reflected in such works as the Danish Baron Hollberg's eighteenth-century novel *Nicolai Climii iter subterraneum,* and the twentieth-century American *Planet of the Apes* films) has been the discovery of a realm in which simians and humans trade places and confront the contingency of species roles. Late-twentieth-century scholarship has also critiqued the burgeoning scientific literature of primatology as (in feminist Donna Haraway's phrase) "simian orientalism," and asserted that its ostensibly "objective" discourse contains numerous elements of disguised mythos (Haraway, 1989, p. 10).

The rich traditions of monkey gods and heroes found in South, Southeast, and East Asia all appear indebted, to varying degrees, to the ancient Indian epic *Rāmāyaṇa* (c. fourth century BCE), in which a race of magical, talking monkeys befriend the human hero Rāma and assist him in recovering his kidnapped wife, Sītā. This tale probably penetrated much of Asia in the early centuries of the common era and may have become interwoven with local monkey lore. In many Southeast Asian Buddhist versions of the story, Rāma's principal helper, Hanumān, here identified as a magical White Monkey, is portrayed as a resourceful but lascivious trickster whose amorous and martial adventures sometimes eclipse those of his human master. The tale of his liaison with the Fish Queen, resulting in a marvelous hybrid son, remains a favorite in the dance theater traditions of Thailand and Cambodia and in the visual art of Malaysia.

In Japan's indigenous Shintō tradition, a "monkey deity" *(saru gami)* named Saruta Biko is attested in texts dating to the eighth century. He belongs to the category of gods associated with liminal spaces such as village boundaries, functions as a messenger between the heavenly and earthly worlds, and serves as mediator between humans and the *kami,* or spirits, particularly the powerful Mountain Deity. He has a special connection with horses and is used in rites intended to protect them from disease. In later Japanese lore, the monkey is primarily portrayed as a trickster and clown, and is associated with human "outcastes" who, like him, mediate between people and gods, yet serve as bearers of pollution. Today, a highly adaptive local species of macaque is considered the "national monkey" of Japan and is said to be the only animal referred to with the honorific *san,* otherwise reserved for humans. The work of twentieth-century Japanese primatologists has been cited for its more emotional and sympathetic response to these animals, exemplified by the monkey funerals sometimes held at research labs.

In China, the popular "monkey king" Sun Wukong of Daoist and Buddhist legend, Ming-period fiction, and modern Beijing opera, probably combines elements of the *Rāmāyaṇa* and of Southeast Asian White Monkey tales with indigenous lore concerning gibbons and macaques. As the most endearing character in the hundred-chapter novel *Xiyou Ji* (Record of the westward journey, 1592), Monkey aids a Buddhist monk in a perilous pilgrimage to India in quest of scriptures, displaying the supernatural powers he acquired by stealing peaches and pills of immortality from the Jade Emperor of the Daoist heaven. Plucky and exuberant, he represents both the Buddhist concept of the restive "monkey mind" that must be tamed to achieve enlightenment and the pragmatism and resourcefulness of a homegrown Chinese culture hero. Despite the centuries-long effort of the literati to suppress non-elite lore and the postrevolutionary crackdown on religious expression, a folk Daoist cult of Monkey survives on Taiwan and in Singapore, where he is revered as a trickster, esoteric preceptor, and healer (especially of children and horses), and as an exorcist sometimes invoked through rites of possession.

The origins of the immensely popular Hindu monkey-god Hanumān, also known as Māruti and Āñjaneya, are obscure. Ceramic monkey figurines from Indus Valley sites and a single Vedic hymn featuring a "virile monkey" have led to speculation that an earthy folk deity *(yakṣa)* in simian form may have preceded Hanumān's literary debut in Vālmīki's *Rāmāyaṇa.* Born of the union of the wind god Vāyu with a celestial nymph who was cursed to assume monkey form, the epic's Hanumān has a rambunctious childhood in which he nearly devours the sun and is wounded and then blessed by the gods. He matures into a sagacious and powerful ally of Rāma who leaps across the ocean carrying his master's ring and message to the captive Sītā, burns the demon city of Lanka with his flaming tail, fetches a Himalayan summit covered with healing herbs to save Rāma's wounded brother during the climactic battle, and ultimately receives the boon of physical immortality as well as Rāma's boundless gratitude. His role expanded in later vernacular retellings of the story, and his independent worship, well attested from roughly the tenth century CE, has undergone dramatic growth in modern times.

Though understood as a devotee of Viṣṇu in the Rāma-incarnation, Hanumān is also regarded as an avatar of Śiva, especially in the latter's awesome and destructive persona as Rudra, and is sometimes paired with local mother goddesses as a guardian or familiar. His propitiation by villagers as a boundary protector, by Śaiva ascetics as an immortal yogi, by the mentally afflicted as a shamanlike exorcist, and by wrestlers as the patron of martial arts may reflect ancient practices only marginally associated with the Rāma narrative. His shrines are ubiquitous in many regions of India and draw huge crowds, especially on Tuesday and Saturday, when worshipers seek his protection from malefic planetary influences. Although Hanumān's visual representation spans the gamut from fully simian to humanlike (though invariably tailed) icons, the deity's celibacy and sagacity pointedly contradict the normal Indian perception of simians, and earthly monkeys, especially the black-faced "hanuman langur" and (less commonly) the reddish rhesus macaque, receive only wary respect and occasional protection as his somewhat debased relatives. A god who is said to combine self-assertive *śakti* (power) and self-effacing *bhakti* (devotion), Hanumān may be read, especially in the discourse of Hindu nationalism, as a subaltern enforcer of traditional high-caste authority, yet he has more typically expressed the upwardly mobile aspirations of lower- and middle-status groups. At once comic and cosmic, subhuman and supernatural, aggressive and contemplative, earthy and divine, Hanumān exemplifies and theologically transfigures the boundary-challenging role that simians have so often played for human cultures.

BIBLIOGRAPHY

Aryan, K. C., and Subhashini Aryan. *Hanumān in Art and Mythology.* Delhi, 1975. A valuable reference for Hanumān iconography.

Corbey, Raymond, and Bert Theunissen, eds. *Ape, Man, Apeman: Changing Views since 1600.* Leiden, 1995. A wide-ranging anthology that critically examines the discourse of the emerging sciences of primatology and paleoanthropology in modern Europe and Japan.

Haraway, Donna. *Primate Visions: Gender, Race, and Nature in the World of Modern Science.* New York, 1989. A feminist historian of science provocatively detects hidden agendas and submerged mythologies in twentieth-century American primate research.

Janson, Horst W. *Apes and Ape Lore in the Middle Ages and the Renaissance.* London, 1952. A signal study of premodern European responses to anthropoid primates.

Lutgendorf, Philip. "My Hanumān Is Bigger Than Yours." *History of Religions* 33, no. 3 (1994): 211–245.

Lutgendorf, Philip. "Monkey in the Middle: The Status of Hanumān in Popular Hinduism." *Religion* 27, no. 4 (1997): 311–332.

Lutgendorf, Philip. "Five Heads and No Tale: Hanumān and the Popularization of Tantra." *International Journal of Hindu Studies* 5, no. 3 (2001): 269–296.

Mair, Victor H. "Suen wu-kung = Hanumat? The Progress of a Scholarly Debate." In *Proceedings of the Second International Conference on Sinology,* pp. 659–752. Taipei, 1989. A magisterial review of the controversy over the origins of the Chinese Monkey King, this article reveals what is at stake in the claims of indigenous origin and revealingly documents the historical spread of the Rāma tale through Southeast and East Asia.

McDermott, William Coffman. *The Ape in Antiquity.* Baltimore, 1938. An unsurpassed study of Egyptian, Greek, and Roman materials.

Narula, Joginder. *Hanumān, God, and Epic Hero.* New Delhi, 1991. The best short work on the subject in English by an Indian scholar.

Ohnuki-Tierney, Emiko. *The Monkey as Mirror.* Princeton, N.J., 1987. A study by a noted anthropologist of human responses to monkeys in Japan.

Yu, Anthony C., ed. and trans. *The Journey to the West.* 4 vols. Chicago, 1977–1983. A complete translation of *Xiyou Ji,* the Ming-period novel concerning the adventures of Monkey and his companions.

PHILIP LUTGENDORF (2005)

MONKS SEE MONASTICISM; RELIGIOUS COMMUNITIES

MONOLATRY SEE HENOTHEISM; MONOTHEISM

MONOPHYSITISM, meaning "one nature" and referring to the person of Jesus Christ, is the name given to the rift that gradually developed in Eastern Christendom after the Council of Chalcedon in 451. While the definition agreed upon at the council laid down that Christ should be acknowledged "in two natures," human and divine, the properties of each nature retaining their identity, the Monophysites held that after the incarnation the two natures became one, so that all the thoughts and acts of the Savior were those of a single unitary being, God in Christ.

The germ of Monophysitism may be found in the *logos-sarx* (Word-flesh) theology of the Alexandrian church. The question of how Christ's personality should be acknowledged could not be avoided, however, once the Creed of Nicaea (325) confessed that he was "of one substance with the Father." If this was so, how was Christ to be considered of one substance with man? Fifty years later, the answer was given uncompromisingly by Apollinaris, bishop of Laodicea in Syria, a friend of Athanasius and an Alexandrian-trained theologian. Scripture, he maintained, emphasized that Christ was "one." In *De fide et incarnatione* he wrote, "There is no distinction in Holy Scripture between the Word and His flesh; He is one energy, one person, one *hypostasis* [individuality], at once wholly God and wholly man." This exactly summed up what was to become the Monophysite position: Christ was "out of two natures," one.

Apollinaris's opinions aroused the opposition of the Cappadocian fathers and were condemned at the Council of Constantinople in 381, but his works circulated widely under the names of orthodox personalities, and as such they influenced profoundly the theology of Cyril of Alexandria (412–444). Cyril, however, was willing to admit at least the mystical reality of the two natures after the incarnation. His successor as patriarch of Alexandria, Dioscorus (444–451), less subtle and more impetuously ambitious for his see, made an uncompromising one-nature Christology the basis of his theology, and enunciated it in his vindication of the archimandrite Eutyches at the Second Council of Ephesus in August 449 (the "Robber Council"). The Council of Chalcedon reversed this situation, and Dioscorus himself was condemned (though for indiscipline rather than for heresy) and exiled. However, a large proportion of Eastern Christians, especially in Egypt, showed that they supported the one-nature Christology and rejected Chalcedon.

Dioscorus died in exile at Gangra in Paphlagonia in 454. Three years later his supplanter, the former archpriest Proterius, who had been consecrated by Egyptian bishops at Chalcedon, was lynched. Another former presbyter of Cyril, Timothy Ailuros (d. 477), was consecrated bishop by the anti-Chalcedonians. Although Timothy was also exiled, until 482 the Church of Alexandria was divided between an anti-Chalcedon majority and a Chalcedonian minority.

Schism, in the sense of establishing a rival church with its own hierarchy, was far from the minds of Timothy and his supporters. They were entirely loyal to the empire politically, but they aimed at persuading the emperor and his advisers to abandon the *Tome* of Leo and the Council of Chalcedon in favor of their one-nature interpretation of the theology of Cyril. Timothy opposed Eutyches' belief that Christ's human nature was not the same as that of ordinary man. In 475 the anti-Chalcedonians came near to success when the usurper Basiliscus, who had forced the legitimate emperor Zeno (474–491) into exile, issued an edict declaring his adherence to the councils of Nicaea and Constantinople and *both* councils of Ephesus, and declaring as anathema the

Tome of Leo and "all that was said and done at Chalcedon in innovation of the holy symbol of Nicaea."

In 476 Basiliscus fell, largely because of the support given to Zeno by the patriarch of Constantinople, Acacius, who was determined to protect the prerogatives of his see against possible renewal of threats from Alexandria. On July 28, 482, in an attempt to reunite the church in Egypt and reconcile it to communion with Constantinople, Zeno issued a circular letter, known as the *Henotikon*, to the "bishops, monks, and laity of Alexandria, Egypt, and Cyrenaica." This letter, drafted on Acacius's advice, reaffirmed the creedal statements of Nicaea, Constantinople, and the first council at Ephesus (431), condemned Nestorius and Eutyches, accepted the Twelve Anathemas of Cyril (which tended toward one-nature Christology), and proclaimed that Jesus Christ, consubstantial with both God and man, and "incarnate from the Holy Spirit and the Virgin Mary and *Theotokos* is one and not two." Anyone who thought differently was anathema. The *Henotikon* avoided denouncing Chalcedon as such, which would have removed from Constantinople its legal superiority, grounded in Canon 28 of that council, over the other sees in the East; but the letter went just far enough to secure the uneasy agreement of Alexandria, Antioch, and Jerusalem. The popes, however, refused to accept the *Henotikon* and denounced the restoration of communion between Acacius and Peter Mongus, patriarch of Alexandria (482–490), as "double-dealing."

The Acacian Schism lasted from 484 to 519. During this time Monophysite opinions hardened in Egypt and Syria, while the emperor Anastasius (491–518) personally favored them. The Monophysites found a spokesman in Severus, a monk from a noble ecclesiastical family in Pisidia who in November 512 was promoted to be patriarch of Antioch. During his six years of rule he evolved a theology based almost entirely on Cyril's teachings. Severus's Christological beliefs, expressed repeatedly in tracts and a massive correspondence (of which four thousand letters and fragments have survived), might be summed up as follows: "The Fathers have taught us that God, the Word, the Unique One begotten by his Father without beginning, eternally, impassably, and incorporeally, did in the last times for our salvation take flesh of the Holy Spirit and of the holy *Theotokos* and ever-virgin Mary, flesh consubstantial with us, animated by an intelligent and reasoning soul." Christ was both God and man, of one single nature; the ideas of Eutyches and Dioscorus, and the *Tome* of Leo and the definition of Chalcedon, were alike repudiated. In the last years of Anastasius's reign, the empire was moving rapidly toward Monophysitism. Communion between the four Eastern patriarchates was maintained, at the expense of communion with Rome.

The death of Anastasius in July and the succession of the Latin-speaking and pro-Chalcedonian Justin I (518–527) brought about an immediate change. Communion between Rome and Constantinople was restored in 519. Severus was exiled, along with his chief supporter, Philoxenus, bishop of Hierapolis (Mabbug) in Mesopotamia, and some fifty-five other bishops. Gradually it became clear that if the Monophysite congregations were to survive, a hierarchy would have to be created to administer sacraments to them. Severus, in exile in Alexandria, reluctantly assented to the ordination of presbyters and deacons in 529/30. Great numbers of volunteers came forward. The schism between the Monophysites and Byzantine orthodoxy may be said to date from that moment.

During the reign of Justinian (527–565), the Monophysite movement assumed the form it was to retain through the centuries. In 532 the emperor tried to settle the controversy through a conference aimed at agreeing upon a statement of doctrine based on the Theopaschite interpretation of Christology, that is, that "one of the Trinity suffered in the flesh and was God." Although this came near to the Monophysite position, the emperor's insistence on the canonical status of Chalcedon wrecked the possibility of agreement. Between that time and the death of Theodora in 548, however, the Monophysites had a firm ally in the empress. At the end of 534, Severus was invited to the capital by the emperor, and the following year Theodora secured the election of a new Monophysite patriarch of Alexandria, Theodosius (535–566), and a pro-Monophysite patriarch of Constantinople, Anthimus, bishop of Trebizend (535–536). This was too much for the emperor, the pope, and the Chalcedonians. Anthimus was replaced, and Severus was condemned by a powerful synod held at Constantinople on June 10, 536; the condemnation was confirmed by edict on August 6.

Severus died at Alexandria in February 538. By that time, Justinian, urged on by the papacy, had restored the Chalcedonian line of patriarchs in Alexandria, a factor that more than any other associated the Monophysite patriarch with the Coptic Christians as a national representative of the Egyptians. Though their patriarch, Theodosius, was ordered to Constantinople at the end of 537, the Monophysites, thanks to Theodora, were not without means of reply. A mission under the presbyter Julian was fitted out by the empress and arrived in the kingdom of Nobatia (Nubia) to convert the royal court to Monophysite Christianity. Even more effective was the series of missions carried out by Jacob Baradai (Burd'ana), who had been consecrated bishop of Edessa by Patriarch Theodosius. Between 542 and his death in 578 he crossed and recrossed the whole area between the Bosporus and the Persian frontier, establishing congregations and a Monophysite hierarchy to govern them. The eventual tally of twenty-seven metropolitans and 100,000 clergy all over the eastern part of the Roman Empire given by Baradai's contemporary John of Ephesus (d. 585) may be exaggerated, but clearly Baradai's missions established the Monophysite church on a permanent footing. Not for nothing did the Syrian Monophysites take the name Jacobites, which they have retained to this day.

On the emperor's side, the Fifth General Council held at Constantinople during 553 may be reckoned as another effort to placate the Monophysites, through its condemnation of the Three Chapters (treatises criticizing Cyril's theology by the Antiochene theologians Theodore of Mopsuestia and Ibas of Edessa). In 573 Justin II (565–578) issued a second *Henotikon,* which again stressed the oneness of Christ, without, however, repudiating Chalcedon. Under Heraclius (610–641), what proved to be the final, though at first the most promising, effort to find a settlement failed. Intrinsically the Monophysites could accept the formula proposed to them by the emperor: that there was one will and one energizing activity in Christ, even if two natures were confessed. For three years following the restoration of the True Cross in Jerusalem in 630, it looked as though this compromise doctrine, known as monoenergism, was providing common ground between Monophysites and Chalcedonians. But once more, suspicion of any formulas that left a shred of authority to Chalcedon, Egyptian distrust of Cyrus "the Caucasian," the emperor's nominee as patriarch of Alexandria, and cleverly orchestrated opposition to monoenergism by Sophronius, patriarch of Jerusalem (634–638), brought the plan to nought. When, within a few years, Egypt, Palestine, and Syria were lost to the Arabs, the Monophysites saw the hand of God in their success against the Byzantines.

By this time, Monophysitism was a missionary faith that had assumed many forms. On the one hand, it rejected outright any idea that the flesh of Christ was liable to suffering—preached by the followers of Julian of Halicarnassus (fl. 520–530)—that is, acceptance of the views of Eutyches; on the other, it accepted the theology of Cyril of Alexandria combined with rejection of the Council of Chalcedon as incompatible with it—represented by the Armenian and Ethiopian churches. The Coptic church and what is known of the Nubian church followed Severus of Antioch more closely and seemed to have been more hostile to Chalcedon and the two-nature Christology enunciated in the *Tome* of Leo. The Syrian church looked back to its great protagonist, Jacob Baradai. Rejection of Chalcedon, on the one hand, and of the two-nature Christology held in the West and by the Nestorians, on the other, has formed the common ground between various national and regional churches known to other traditions as the Monophysite churches. Reluctantly, these have remained separate from the Eastern Orthodox churches and from the West to form one of the four main divisions of Christianity that have survived to our day.

SEE ALSO Councils, article on Christian Councils; Eastern Christianity.

BIBLIOGRAPHY

Atiya, A. S. *A History of Eastern Christianity (1969).* Reprint, Millwood, N. Y., 1980.

Charanis, Peter. *Church and State in the Later Roman Empire: The Religious Policy of Anastasius I, 491–518.* Madison, Wis., 1939.

Devreesse, Robert. *Le patriarchat d'Antioche depuis la Paix de l'Église jusqu'à la conquête arabe.* Paris, 1945.

Dinkler, Erich, ed. *Kunst und Geschichte Nubiens in christlicher Zeit.* Recklinghausen, 1970.

Draguet, René. *Julien d'Halicarnasse et sa controverse avec Sévère d'Antioche sur l'incorruptibilité du corps de Christ.* Louvain, 1924.

Duchesne, Louis. *L'église au sixième siècle.* Paris, 1925.

Frend, W. H. C. *The Rise of the Monophysite Movement.* Cambridge, 1979. Includes sources and bibliography.

Grillmeier, Aloys, and Heinrich Bacht. *Das Konzil von Chalkedon: Geschichte und Gegenwart.* 3 vols. Würzburg, 1951–1962. Contains essays indispensable for studying Monophysitism and its controversies with Chalcedonian orthodoxy.

Halleaux, André de. *Philoxène de Mabbog: Sa vie, ses écrits, sa théologie.* Louvain, 1963.

Honigmann, Ernest. "La hiérarchie monophysite au temps de Jacques Baradée, 542–578." In *Évêques et Évêchés monophysites d'Asie Antérieure au sixième siècle.* Corpus Scriptorum Christianorum Orientalium, no. 127. Louvain, 1951.

Jugie, Martin. "Monophysisme." In *Dictionnaire de théologie catholique,* vol. 10. Paris, 1929.

Lebon, Joseph. *Le monophysisme sévérien.* Louvain, 1909.

Meyendorff, John. *Christ in Eastern Christian Thought.* Crestwood, N. Y., 1975.

Sarkissian, Karekin. *The Council of Chalcedon and the Armenian Church.* London, 1965.

Schwartz, Eduard. "Codex Vaticanus gr. 1431, eine antichalkedonische Sammlung aus der Zeit Kaiser Zenos." *Abhandlungen der bayerisch Akademie der Wissenschaften: Philosophisch-philologische und historische Klasse* 32 (1927): 1–152.

Sellers, R. V. *The Council of Chalcedon: A Historical and Doctrinal Survey.* London, 1953.

Woodward, E. L. *Christianity and Nationalism in the Later Roman Empire.* London, 1916.

New Sources

Harries, Jill. *Sidonius Apollnaris and the Fall of Rome, A.D. 407–485.* Oxford, 1994.

Harvey, Susan Ashbrook. *Asceticism and Society in Crisis: John of Ephesus and the Lives of the Eastern Saints.* Berkeley, 1990.

Kaplan, Steven. *The Monastic Holy Man and the Christianization of Early Solomonic Ethiopia.* Wiesbaden, 1984.

Torrance, Iain R. *Christology after Chalcedon: Severus of Antioch and Sergious the Monophysite.* Norwich, U.K., 1988.

W. H. C. FREND (1987)
Revised Bibliography

MONOTHEISM. Derived from the Greek *mono* ("single") and *theos* ("God"), the term *monotheism* refers to the religious experience and the philosophical perception that emphasize God as one, perfect, immutable, creator of the world from nothing, distinct from the world, all-powerfully involved in the world, personal, and worthy of being worshiped by all creatures. Some forms of monotheism, however, differ about the notions of God as distinct from the world and as personal.

The term *monotheism* has generally been used theologically rather than for philosophical or cross-cultural descriptions of religion. Philosophers have used the term *theism* with the same meaning as *monotheism*, and cross-cultural descriptions find categories like *monotheism* and *polytheism* to be inappropriate in describing some religious traditions. The term *monotheism* presupposes the idea of *theos*—a divine being with mind and will, fully personal, conceivable in images drawn from human life, and approachable through prayer. In this respect monotheism differs from deism and from the various forms of monism. It also presupposes the unity of the divine and raises one *theos* exclusively to absolute supremacy and power, producing and governing everything according to the divine will. In this respect monotheism differs from those views that accept a plurality of divine beings. In the strict sense, *monotheism* best describes the idea of God in Judaism, Christianity, and Islam, and in the philosophical systems based on these traditions. But one may extend the term to include conceptions of deity in certain other traditions such as Zoroastrianism, Sikhism, and some forms of Hinduism and Buddhism, even though these traditions include somewhat different conceptions, such as the existence of evil forces alongside God, the nonpersonal nature of God, God's complete immanence in the world, or the fundamental unreality of the world. In this article, the basic requirement for a religious tradition to be considered monotheistic is that it emphasize both *theos* and *monos*.

MONOTHEISM IN RELIGIOUS HISTORY. Whereas monotheism is most often associated with the Jewish, Christian, and Islamic religions and philosophies, tendencies contributing toward a monotheistic outlook have long been present in human religious history. Monotheism is like a river with many springs and many tributaries. The course of the river is difficult to map, for monotheistic beliefs are often put forward in protest against other beliefs and practices.

Obscure as they are, springs of monotheism can be discerned at the very earliest levels of known human cultural life, in the primordial high god of the archaic hunters. The theory of *Urmonotheismus* ("original monotheism") as put forth by Wilhelm Schmidt and others held that a primordial monotheism was the earliest form of human perception of deity, and that the plurality of gods and spirits found in most primal religions was a degeneration from this original perception. While that theory cannot be substantiated in the history of religions, research in recent years has made it clear that a great many primal or archaic peoples have conceptions of a high god who is creator of the world, has supreme authority over other gods and spirits, and presides over human morality. Some of the most archaic peoples, such as certain groups in Africa, Australian Aborigines, and the nomadic hunters of Tierra del Fuego, have definite conceptions of a supreme god associated with the sky who is changeless, invisible, and all-powerful and who gives morality. The supreme high god characteristically is a remote god (*deus otiosus*), too distant, all-powerful, good, and just to need worship or to be intimately involved in ordinary existence; there are lesser gods and spirits who play a much more active role in the lives of the people.

The streams of the monotheistic vision run dimly through the fertile valleys of archaic agricultural religions with their pluralistic experience of the forces of nature centered on Mother Earth. Here the high god tends to become head of the divine pantheon; pushed into the background by earth gods of fecundity, the high god could hardly be the focus of a unifying perception of deity. But a few high gods developed with supreme sovereignty and autonomy, as sources of fecundating power and guarantors of the order and norms of the world and of human society. For example, Zeus and Jupiter were ruling high gods fashioned in accord with the Greek and Roman notions of norm and law. In India, Varuṇa was sovereign guardian of *ṛta*, cosmic order, a role taken over later by the great gods Viṣṇu and Śiva. Yahveh, the high god of the ancient Hebrews, was known as all-powerful creator, absolute sovereign, and author of all norms and laws by which the earth functions. Belief in these high gods did not necessarily exclude lesser divine forces, but it did provide the opportunity for reflections on the unity of divine reality, as will be seen in the following examples from ancient Greece, Hinduism, and Buddhism.

Greek religion. Among Greek thinkers, ideas of a unitary divine reality were expressed as a means of showing the order and reasonableness of the world. Already in pre-Socratic times, it seems, philosophers like Xenophanes depicted the spiritual unity of the whole world in the notion of the All-One, uncreated, unchangeable, and immanent in all things. Plato stressed the unity of the Good and identified God with that: God must be perfectly good, changeless, and the maker of the best possible world. Aristotle also made the idea of goodness central to his concept of God, the causal principle of all. The unicity of the supreme First Mover follows from the unity of the physical world: God is one, eternal, and immutable. God is defined as pure mind (*nous*), who always thinks one and the same subject, namely himself—and thus this view is not really theism. Later in the Hellenistic religions, the sense of God's unicity was expressed by raising one god or goddess to supremacy, encompassing all others. For example, Apuleius described Isis as the one Great Mother of all, by whatever name she may be called in different areas (*Metamorphoses* 11).

Hinduism. Hinduism is characterized by monistic (*advaita*, or nondualistic) thought, which merges the divine reality with the world in a unity called *brahman*. Here the unifying principle is strong, but the theistic quality of the unified divine reality is of lesser importance. There have always been theistic tendencies in Hinduism, but these have been associated with a variety of divine beings. Yet intense concerns of *bhakti* (devotion to a god) have sometimes led Hindus to raise up one god as supreme ruler, or to see the various gods as manifestations of one God. "They call it Indra, Mitra, Varuṇa, and Agni . . .; but the real is one, although the sages give different names" (*Ṛgveda* 1.169).

Among Vaiṣṇavas, Viṣṇu tends to become all, and the same is true of Śiva among Śaivas. Kṛṣṇa, *avatāra* of Viṣṇu, can be put forth as the supreme God behind all names: "Many are the paths people follow, but they all in the end come to me" (*Bhagavadgītā* 4.11). One theistic strand in Hinduism identifies ultimate reality with Devī, the Great Goddess, in one of her many forms. Thus Hinduism does recognize the oneness of the divine, and it includes theistic forms of worship, even worship of one God exclusively, without denying the reality of other gods.

Buddhism. Buddhism, like Hinduism, is based on monistic or nondualistic thought and posits only an inferior role for those born at the level of gods, trapped as they are like all living beings in the cycles of rebirth. But in Mahāyāna Buddhism, the idea has arisen that beings who have realized their Buddhahood (that is, Buddhas and *bodhisattvas*) can function similarly to gods in theistic religions. Generally Mahāyāna Buddhism holds to the multiplicity of these powerful beings, but in certain schools one such Buddha becomes supreme and is worshiped exclusively. Such is the case with Amitābha (Jpn., Amida) Buddha in Pure Land Buddhism, a soteriological monolatry offering the one hope of salvation for this degenerate age. Esoteric (Vajrayāna) Buddhism has developed a unified cosmotheism, according to which the whole universe is the body of Mahāvairocana, the Great Sun Buddha, with all Buddhas and *bodhisattvas*—and thus all reality—united in this supreme Buddha-reality.

Egyptian religion. One of the earliest forms of exclusive monotheism apparently developed in ancient Egypt. Within the elaborate and complicated polytheism of Egyptian religion there had long been rationalistic tendencies toward seeing various gods as different forms of one particular God, with an emphasis on the supremacy of the Sun God, who tended to absorb other gods. Around 1375 BCE Pharoah Amunhotep IV repudiated the authority of the old gods and their priests and devoted himself exclusively to Aton, the god appearing as the sun disk. He proclaimed himself the son of Aton, taking the name *Akhenaton* ("devoted to Aton"), and he imposed this worship on others. By royal decree Aton became the only God who exists, king not only of Egypt but of the whole world, embodying in his character and essence all the attributes of the other gods. Akhenaton even had the names of the other gods effaced from inscriptions and replaced with the name of Aton. Akhenaton's monotheism was related to protest against abuses in the cults of the gods, but it does not appear to have led to new ethical standards. Within twenty-five years Akhenaton was gone, and his successors restored the old cults.

Zoroastrianism. Growing from the ancient Indo-Iranian polytheistic religion, Zoroastrianism unified all divine reality in the high god Ahura Mazdā. Zarathushtra (Zoroaster), who probably lived sometime between 1700 and 1000 BCE, was a priest who turned against some of the traditional cultic rituals and proclaimed the overthrow of polytheism. In his teaching, Ahura Mazdā (Pahl., Ōhrmazd) is the one God who, to implement the divine will in the world, associates with the six Amesha Spentas ("holy immortals"), spirits or angels that represent moral attitudes and principles. Ahura Mazdā, the Wise Lord, is good, just, and moral, one who creates only good things and gives only blessings to worshipers. The one God is sovereign over history, working out the divine plan for the world. Humans are to assist God through upright deeds, and there will be a final judgment in which every soul will be judged to see if it is worthy of entering Paradise. Conflict is accounted for as the hostility of two primordial spirits: Spenta Mainyu, the good spirit, and Angra Mainyu (Pahl., Ahriman), the evil spirit. Ahura Mazdā apparently fathered these two spirits; the struggle between them has been going on since the beginning of time, when they chose between good and evil. It appears, then, that Ahura Mazdā cannot be called omnipotent, for the realm of evil is beyond his control; in that sense it may be said that this is not a complete monotheism. Yet there is no doubt that Zoroastrianism considers the realm of Ahura Mazdā to be ultimately victorious. Further, in this eschatological religion the conflict between good and evil is understood not so much metaphysically as ethically, involving the free choice of humans either for the rule of the Wise Lord or for that of Angra Mainyu. It is true that later Zoroastrianism brought some of the other gods back into the picture again. But in the teaching of Zarathushtra in the *Gāthās* is found a unique type of monotheism with an ethico-dualistic accent and an eschatological monotheistic fulfillment.

Judaism, Christianity, and Islam. The three religions that generally are held to be the full expressions of monotheism, Judaism, Christianity, and Islam, also arose against the background of the polytheism of the ancient Near East. These three religions are closely related in that they grew from the Semitic cultural background and the foundations of the religion of ancient Israel.

Although it was the fountainhead of this type of monotheism, the religion of ancient Israel was not actually monotheistic in early times. Stories of the patriarch Abraham show that he worshiped the Canaanite high god ʾEl in a variety of forms in addition to the god of the clan, and when the people of Israel entered into a covenant with the high god Yahveh they did not exclude the existence of other gods. One might call early Israelite religion henotheistic or monolatrous in the sense that exclusive loyalty was to be given to Yahveh, but Yahveh's power was limited because other nations had their own gods. Some Israelites lived with a polytheistic vision, giving loyalty to Yahveh as the god of the covenant but also worshiping Baʿal and the other gods of fecundity as they settled in Canaan and became agriculturalists. But the covenant relationship with Yahveh contained the seeds of monotheism; the Israelites experienced Yahveh as personal, being revealed in historical events and demanding exclusive loyalty and ethical behavior according to the covenant law. Prophets arose who challenged the polytheistic notion that various gods controlled the functions of nature. Elijah and Hosea, for example, held that it is only Yahveh who has power in all areas of existence, as the creator of all and the one God who sends corn at the harvest and wine at the vintage. Just as polytheistic ideas were overcome, the prophets also struggled to overcome the limitations of a henotheistic view of God. At one time it was accepted that one could not worship Yahveh outside the land of Israel. But Amos insisted that the one God, Yahveh, had not only brought Israel out of Egypt, but had also brought the Philistines from Caphtor and the Arameans from Kir (*Amos* 9:7). And Second Isaiah, the prophet of the Babylonian exile, went so far as to describe Cyrus II, the mighty king of the Medes and Persians, as "the anointed one of Yahveh" whom Yahveh had taken by the hand (*Is.* 45:1). In the vision of these prophets, Yahveh is no tribal god sharing power with other nations' gods but is in fact the universal creator of all and the director of the history of all peoples, according to Yahveh's own design.

Jews, Christians, and Muslims drew on the fundamental monotheistic vision of ancient Israel, each group filling out the picture of God with colorings and shapes drawn from its own particular culture. The dimensions of the Jewish, Christian, and Muslim type of monotheism will be discussed at more length below.

Sikhism. One more expression of monotheism should be mentioned in this religio-historical survey: Sikhism. Starting with Gurū Nānak (1469–1539 CE), an Indian type of monotheism developed that synthesizes the mystical monotheistic tendency found in Hinduism and the ethical, personal monotheism brought into India by Islam. In Gurū Nānak's teaching, there is only one God, who is immortal, unborn, self-existent, creator of all the universe, omniscient, formless, just, and loving. God is both transcendent as pure potentiality and immanent as world-embodiment. Thus God is contained in everything. God is personal but is beyond complete knowledge, to be worshiped mainly in rituals of repeating his name. Revelation comes through *gurūs* who speak the divine word. Humans attain heaven or hell at the end of a lifetime, although they are involved in many rounds of births and deaths. Final salvation for humans is *nirvāṇa*, absorption into God's being like water blending with water.

Summing up this cross-cultural religio-historical survey, it is clear that monotheism has arisen in a number of ways. In some areas it came through rationalization, seeing the logic of unified divine power. In other traditions, mystical experience of everything as one and unified with the divine gave rise to monotheistic expressions. In still other traditions, historical experiences of one powerful, personal God led toward formulations of monotheistic belief.

MONOTHEISM IN CONTRAST TO NONMONOTHEISTIC VIEWS. Monotheism often arises in opposition to other views of divine reality. One of the most obvious contexts against which monotheism defines itself is a plurality of divine beings or forces, which is commonly called polytheism. Central to polytheism is the notion of *theoi*, personal divine beings within nature and society. These gods have personal wills, control specific spheres, and interact with one another to make up a functioning organism. The functioning of nature is seen as the operation of a plurality of divine wills, and this plurality and conflict are extended to human life and society. Typically there is a head of the pantheon, but this high god is limited in power and authority and often is thought of as old or impotent.

Monotheism distinguishes itself from the various forms of polytheism in that the whole realm of divine power is unified, with no conflicting wills or limitations. God has unlimited authority and power but still is *theos*, possessing personal will and relationship to the world. The plural forces are seen as qualities and attributes of God or as subservient beings of the created world. In the monotheistic view, God transcends the world of nature and human society; the world is not the locus of divine power, for God is the universal creator of everything out of nothing (*ex nihilo*). Humans find value and integration of meaning by realizing their common creaturehood and serving this one universal God. Revelation from God is the source of unified, universal meaning.

Related to polytheism is what F. Max Müller called henotheism and what others have called monolatry: worshiping one god at a time or raising up one most powerful God as the only one to be worshiped. The other gods, while real, are downgraded before this supreme God. Monolatry means one God is worshiped as supreme, though the lesser gods of other peoples are recognized. Henotheism (kathenotheism) would be the view that different gods can be worshiped as the supreme God one at a time without implying that the other gods do not exist.

In contrast to monolatry and henotheism, monotheism universalizes the power and authority of the one God exclusively, for even sharing power with lesser gods would be a limitation that cannot apply. Monotheism is intrinsically universal, transcending tribal or nationalistic limitations; the one God has authority and power over all peoples, friends and enemies alike. And monotheism refuses the henotheistic idea that one god can be worshiped as supreme at one time and another at another time, although it does allow for the experience of various aspects of the one God at different times.

A form of thought close to monotheism but still related to polytheism and henotheism is theistic dualism. Typically, this experience of the divine reality separates out the hurtful or evil elements and associates these with another divine power, thus setting up a divine struggle with echoes in human life. One unified supreme God is posited as the good divine force, and the source of evil can be thought of as many beings or as one evil being.

Strictly speaking, monotheism does not allow the one God to be limited even by the causes of destruction and evil; these causes cannot be divine forces outside the will of the one God. Ultimately the one God must be the source of all reality and all events, including those that humans experience as evil and destructive. Some forms of monotheistic thought do allow for evil beings as creatures of God, permitted to cause destruction and evil for various purposes within the overall authority of the one God. But these demons, devils, and satans are only part of the panorama of human existence, and they cannot limit or act against God's power, authority, and will.

Monism in the history of religions refers to a broad category of thought and experience that emphasizes the oneness or unity of all reality, so that no ontological separation exists between the divine and the world itself. All reality, including humans, share in the divine nature. Hindus and Buddhists have preferred the term nondualism, emphasizing that multiplicity arises from a single basis, and that there is no ultimate duality between self and other. Monism and nondualism tend to be nontheistic, for qualities of personal will and otherness from the world do not fit this perception of the divine. The world is not what it appears to be in the multiplicity of one's perceptions. Rather, either the world is in essence one divine reality, or it is fundamentally an illusion, or it consists of forms and expressions that emanate from the one divine source. Further, monism and nondualism tend to be nonhistorical, in the sense that a cyclical rhythm of time expresses the experience of the one divine reality. The religious path is one of mystical discipline and meditation, bringing progressively higher stages of knowledge and ultimate liberation in union with the one divine reality. Of course, provision is made for theistic practices at the lower levels of spiritual perfection.

Monotheism distinguishes itself from the various forms of monism and nondualism by positing a definite separation between the one divine reality and the world that God brought into existence. In this sense there is a dualistic emphasis in monotheism, for there are two distinct realms of reality, the divine and the created world. Only God is eternal and transcendent, having created the world out of nothing (*ex nihilo*). At the same time, most forms of monotheism hold God not only as transcendent but also as immanent in the world: God's presence, power, and operation are immediately present in human experience. The world is a creature, real and good as part of God's design. Revelation from God is important as guidance; prophetic and devotional emphases predominate over the mystical and meditative ones. God is a personal *theos* who confronts one in historical existence as an Other, to whom one relates through obedience and service. And God works in the history of the world, directing events toward an eschaton in which there will be evaluation and judgment. History has a beginning and an end, and God transcends it all.

DIMENSIONS OF MONOTHEISTIC BELIEF AND PRACTICE. In setting up a typology of monotheism to show the ideal types toward which the various monotheistic religious traditions seem to point, it is important to realize that even within one tradition there will be different experiences and philosophies of monotheism. Thus, while a tradition may be dominated by a certain type, its particular coloration may be affected by hues drawn from other types. Further, monotheistic thought focuses especially on the theoretical or verbal dimension of religious experience. In moving to the practical and the social spheres one encounters a variety of phenomena that at times may not be distinctively monotheistic. Worship, law, customs, and social forms may show striking parallels in different religions without regard to the theoretical stance on monotheism, polytheism, or monism. For example, visual images of the divine reality are used in Christianity as well as in Hinduism, but not in Islam or Judaism—and also not in polytheistic Shintō. Some Muslim mosques are as bare and simple as Buddhist meditation centers, while some Christian churches gleam with golden brocade, candles, images, and saints that rival Hindu or Daoist temples. Orders of priests, monks, and nuns bring some Christian groups close to Buddhism, while the rabbi and imam of Jews and Muslims resemble more the learned teacher of a Hindu ashram. The veneration of saints in some sectors of Islam and Christianity appears similar to the veneration of spiritual beings in traditional African religions, but other sectors of Islam and Christianity strongly reject these practices. Thus care needs to be taken in setting up a monotheistic typology, so that religious traditions are not fitted in too tightly, doing damage to the integrity and richness of the particular religion.

The following typology of dominant emphases in the monotheistic religions includes elements from some religious traditions that may not be fully monotheistic, yet they all put forth the two essential ingredients of monotheism: *monos* and *theos*.

Monarchic monotheism. Monarchic monotheism, the belief in one God who rules over many gods, is close to polytheism and grows out of a cosmic religious context. One high God rises to supreme authority and unlimited power, forcing the other powers to total submission. Akhenaton's monotheistic movement in ancient Egypt was of this type; and Yahvism in early Israel displays this form, with Yahveh pictured as "a great king above all the gods" (*Ps.* 95:3). The attitude that subjugates other religions and imposes a monolithic system on all may be a result of this type of monotheism.

A subtype of monarchic monotheism would be dualistic monotheism: one God opposed against evil forces. In this view there is one ruler God, all-good and all-just, who tends to become distant, watching over the struggle within existence in which evil divine forces play a part. The distinctive quality of this type of monotheism is that it takes evil away from the being of the one God, accounting for it through demons or devils. Zoroastrianism is a classic example of dualistic monotheism: although the one God, Ahura Mazdā, is supreme, the evil spirit Angra Mainyu struggles throughout the history of the world, to be overcome only at the end. Popular forms of Judaism, Christianity, and Islam have sometimes approached this type of dualistic monotheism with ideas of Satan or the devil defying God's will, although generally these religions see the evil one as a creature permitted by the one God to perform evil within creation. The struggle between God and evil forces can be seen as a cosmic struggle, as in the Hindu Purāṇas, in which demonic powers arise anew in each new age and Viṣṇu is incarnated anew in an *avatāra* to do battle and realign the cosmic order. Some traditions in Judaism and Christianity describe God's struggle with Satan or the Antichrist as taking place on a transhistorical, cosmic plane. More commonly, however, dualistic monotheism has strong ties to the historical plane of human existence and provides an ethical dimension for human involvement in God's struggle against evil.

Emanational mystical monotheism. Emanational mystical monotheism may be divided into two subtypes: the worship of one God through many gods, or the worship of one God as the world soul. The first subtype, congenial especially to a monistic context, recognizes many gods but sees them as emanations of the one divine source, which is conceived of in theistic terms. Some ancient Greeks rationalized the plurality of the gods in relation to a particular supreme high god in this way. Hindu theistic cults sometimes offer this explanation of the relation of the many gods to the one great god worshiped in that cult. Viṣṇu, for example, can also be worshiped in many *avatāras* and with many different names. Another example would be Esoteric (Vajrayāna) Buddhism, in which all Buddhas and *bodhisattvas* can be seen as emanations of the Great Sun Buddha, Mahāvairocana.

Another type of monotheism related to the monistic worldview is the mystical view of the one God as the world soul. This type of monotheism holds that there is one personal *theos* who is not sharply separate from the world but rather is the creative divine force in everything. Again, the great theistic cults of Hinduism and Buddhism often show this type. For example, Rāmānuja's "Qualified Nondualism" holds Viṣṇu to be the absolute, supreme God to whom the worshiper relates in *bhakti* as qualitatively different from the worshiper himself; yet Viṣṇu and the worshiper are united as soul and body are united. In the theistic Kṛṣṇa cults, Kṛṣṇa as the supreme personality of God can be experienced as different from the world, yet in the highest mystical experiences these differences fade away and Kṛṣṇa becomes all, as expressed in Arjuna's vision (*Bhagavadgītā*, chap. 11). Sikhism is a monotheism that emphasizes God as absolute creator, self-sufficient and unchanging; yet God is embodied in the world, and the believer who finally reaches *nirvāṇa* becomes absorbed in God. Sikh monotheism, like Hindu monotheistic forms, tends to be nonhistorical, looking on existence as a countless series of cycles until finally the separation is overcome and the worshiper achieves complete union with the one God. Certain mystical movements within Judaism, Christianity, and Islam have also approached this type of monotheism without displaying the ahistorical feature. For example, the "panentheism" ("everything is in God") of Ṣūfī mystics like Ibn al-ʿArabī (1165–1240 CE) or of medieval Jewish mystics tended to see the whole universe as an emanation of God's own being, a reflection of the divine, while maintaining a view of God as distinct from the world.

Historical ethical monotheism. Historical ethical monotheism, the belief in one God guiding the historical design, characteristically describes God as personal, having a will for the historical design of the world, guiding all events as the creator, separate from the world yet immanently involved in human history as the God whose law governs all, who gives value to all and holds all accountable at the end of history, and who is revealed through pivotal prophets, events, and scriptures. Humans are expected to follow God's design by establishing goodness and justice in human society. God makes total demands, controls political history, is intolerant of other gods or other ultimate commitments, and is to be worshiped by all exclusively.

Zoroastrianism contains most of these monotheistic features, although it makes the dualism of good and evil central to the conception of the divine and thereby assigns some limits to the power of God. Sikhism also contains many of the features of ethical monotheism, but it gives central place to a cyclical view of existence and the goal of mystical absorption into God.

The family of religions made up of Judaism, Christianity, and Islam most fully expresses this type of monotheism and places it at the center of religious thought and practice. Each of these three traditions also adds its particular hue to the universal monotheistic vision. Judaism places a strong emphasis on the personal character of God, encountered in an "I-Thou" relationship and providing an ethical design for life as spelled out in the Torah and Talmud. The universal character of the one God is seen as turned toward humankind, especially in the very specific form of the covenant relationship with the Jews as "chosen people." The particular nature of this covenant and its demands does not negate God's universality, in the Jewish view. God's design for the world is to be fulfilled especially through the covenant with the Jews and thus a great responsibility is placed on them. Further, all non-Jews who fulfill in their lives the basic human principles known as the "seven commandments of the children of Noah" will have a share in the life of the world to come. Thus the religion of Judaism expresses a universal monotheism that focuses on God's particular relationship to humans through the covenant with the Jews.

Christians have modulated historical ethical monotheism into concrete, existential terms by emphasizing the personal character of the one God revealed in human history. Resisting tendencies of *tritheism*, Christian tradition has worked out a *triunity* that makes God concretely immanent in this world as Father, Son, and Holy Spirit. Central to this vision is the incarnation of God in the person of Jesus Christ, a historical particularization of the universal God that provides a pivot for all of human history and points to the fulfillment of God's whole design in the eschaton. Christians insist that their Christology is monotheistic; Christ is one substance (*homoousios*) with God the Father. Jews and Muslims, of course, find this doctrine of the incarnation of God in Christ to be out of line with their understanding of monotheism.

Muslims have made the unity *(tawḥīd)* of God the central statement of their confession of faith: "There is no god but God." Islam puts forth a very radical monotheism in insisting on the utter transcendence and sovereignty of God, all-powerful in every aspect of the universe, to be likened to nothing. The greatest sin is *shirk*, associating anything else with God. The universal God is particularized in Islam by making the Qur'ān the concrete revelation by which God relates to all humans and gives them guidance. While the final revelation came through the prophet Muḥammad, it is intended for all humans in all ages as their guide to the ethical life and to the blessings that God intends for faithful creatures.

CURRENT REFLECTIONS ON MONOTHEISM. Monotheism is the long-established religious tradition in the cultures informed by Judaism, Christianity, and Islam, but still a considerable amount of searching and rethinking goes on. Philosophers and theologians continue to draw out the implications of the monotheistic vision for thought and society. For example, an influential work by H. Richard Niebuhr, *Radical Monotheism and Western Culture* (New York, 1960), argues that modern society tends toward henotheism, making one particular society into the center of value and the object of loyalty; in contrast, radical monotheism has as its reference the One, beyond all the many, from whom all reality receives its value. Contemporary Jewish and Muslim writers have also stressed radical monotheism as a critique of the polytheistic or henotheistic tendencies of modern society.

Modern thinkers have also been wrestling with some of the central characteristics of traditional monotheism that seem to be problematic. Difficulties revolve around issues such as God's personality, God's immutability, God's strict separation from the world, the theocratic overtones of monotheism, its patriarchal associations, its seeming suppression of human freedom, and its supposed tendency toward exclusion and violence toward others. Recent critiques of traditional monotheism have come particularly from analyses of the type of ideology and society associated with monotheism. In 1935 Erik Peterson, in an treatise called *Der Monotheismus als politisches Problem* (Leipzig, 1935), described monotheism as a political ideology linked with the notion of divine kingship and leading to totalitarianism, and this line of criticism has recently been renewed. For example, Regina M. Schwartz in *The Curse of Cain: The Violent Legacy of Monotheism* provides a strong indictment of traditional monotheism for the way it has supported various forms of oppression and violence. Feminist thinkers, especially in the Christian and Jewish traditions, have criticized monotheism as a model of the highest form of patriarchal power and authority; in monotheism, God is imaged as male, omnipotent with unilateral power and authority over the world, separate and autonomous, exclusive, and opposed to everything related to change, sensuality, nature, feeling, and femininity. Disillusioned by the effects of secularism, thinkers such as Alain de Benoist and Manuel de Diéguez blame monotheistic ideology for suppressing human freedom and forcing people to adopt atheism as the only alternative. They seek a neopagan resurgence as a new location of the sacred in the plurality and freedom of human life rather than in the monolithic totalitarian rule of monotheism. David Miller likewise has suggested that monotheism can no longer sustain and provide creativity for modern culture, calling for a return to the creative sources of polytheism.

Without surveying all the recent reinterpretations of the idea of monotheism among philosophers and theologians, several lines of thought may be mentioned here. In general, theologians and other thinkers have attempted to be more careful in the use of conventional dualisms like monotheism-polytheism, personal-impersonal, and transcendent-immanent, recognizing that religious traditions, including those labeled monotheistic, are complex and embody elements from both sides of these conceptual dualities. For example, feeling that the traditional view of God as personal tends to make God another being in additional to those known in the world, John Macquarrie and Paul Tillich speak of the divine reality as "Being" or the "Ground of Being," avoiding pantheism but holding God to be not one being but the *source* of all being.

The movement known as process philosophy or theology has attempted to move to a *via media* between an untenable unipolar theism in which God is immutable and completely separate from the world, and an equally untenable pantheism. Alfred North Whitehead and Charles Hartshorne maintain that God includes and penetrates the world, while still being distinct from the being of the world. This bipolar view sees God as infinite personal existence and thus independent of the actual world in abstract identity but including the actual world in concrete existence. God is the source of love and the cause of nature's order and has an overall design for the world. Since God is personal, change and growth take place in God as well as in the world.

Many Christian theologians, like Jürgen Moltmann and Colin Gunton, recognizing the problems with a monarchical, patriarchal monotheism, stress God's liberating relation to humans by reemphasizing the trinitarian conception—though such emphasis widens the gulf between Christian thought and that of Judaism and Islam. Feminist thinkers have produced far-reaching reinterpretations of monotheism, making extensive use of feminine experiences and symbols. For example, Elizabeth Johnson re-envisions the patriarchal God and the attendant hierarchical world order by a theology "from below," drawing on women's life experiences and focusing on the biblical Sophia (Wisdom) tradition as a way of bringing out feminine aspects and qualities of God.

Some scholars continue to defend the value of the traditional monotheistic perspective. For example, Bernard-Henri Lévy turns to the Jewish tradition to show that the monotheistic ideal of eternal, universal law actually has a liberating function, safeguarding against totalitarianism and all the idols of nature, ideology, and the state. In contrast to the criticism that monotheism represses human freedom and creativity, Lenn Goodman draws on Jewish and Islamic philosophy to bring out the interplay of human values and the idea of monotheism, arguing that the monotheistic idea of God illuminates one's social, moral, cultural, and aesthetic life and guides one toward a genuinely humanistic philosophy.

This ongoing discussion makes it clear that monotheistic thought, while often challenged by and in tension with alternate and modified religious understandings, is still central to most of the Western world and will continue to be a dominant mode of experiencing and expressing the divine reality.

SEE ALSO Deism; Dualism; Henotheism; Monism; Theism; Transcendence and Immanence.

BIBLIOGRAPHY

The classic study that marshaled much evidence for an *Urmonotheismus* among archaic peoples is Wilhelm Schmidt's *Der Ursprung der Gottesidee: Eine historisch-kritische und positive Studie*, 12 vols. (Münster, 1912–1955); although Schmidt's theory is no longer accepted, much of the material is still useful. John S. Mbiti gathers and synthesizes concepts about the unity of the high god from all over Africa in *Concepts of God in Africa* (New York, 1970). Arvind Sharma, *Classical Hindu Thought: An Introduction* (New Delhi, 2000), discusses the tendencies toward monotheism alongside monism in Hindu thought and practice; and Tracy Pintchman, *The Rise of the Goddess in the Hindu Tradition* (Albany, N. Y., 1994), shows that various forms of the great Goddess often become a unifying focus in the theistic traditions. Paul Williams, *Mahāyāna Buddhism: The Doctrinal Foundations* (London, 1989), describes tendencies in Mahāyāna Buddhism to raise one or another form of the Buddha to supreme status. Rajinder Kaur Rohi, *Semitic and Sikh Monotheism: A Comparative Study* (Patiala, 1999), explores monotheism in the Sikh tradition.

Erik Hornung, *Akhenaten and the Religion of Light* (translated by David Lorton; Ithaca, N. Y., 1999), examines Akhenaten's brief monotheistic era in ancient Egypt. Tendencies toward a monotheistic view in Greece, Rome, and the Near East are described in *Pagan Monotheism in Late Antiquity*, edited by Polymnia Athanassiadi and Maichael Frede (Oxford, 1999); and John Peter Kenney, *Mystical Monotheism: A Study in Ancient Platonic Theology* (Hanover, N. H. 1991). Peter Clark, *Zoroastrianism: An Introduction to an Ancient Faith* (Brighton, U. K., 1998), discusses the unique interplay of dualistic and monotheistic ideas within Zoroastrianism.

William F. Albright's *From the Stone Age to Christianity: Monotheism and the Historical Process*, 2d ed. (Garden City, N. Y., 1957), is a well-known study of the development of monotheism in ancient Israel viewed against the background of ancient Near Eastern cultures. Two studies emphasizing that the development of monotheism in Israel was a long and complex process are Stanley Rosenbaum, *Understanding Biblical Israel: A Reexamination of the Origins of Monotheism* (Atlanta, 2002); and Robert Karl Gnuse, *No Other Gods: Emergent Monotheism in Israel* (Sheffield, 1997). The Jewish rabbinic conception of the oneness of God is presented by Louis Jacobs in *A Jewish Theology* (New York, 1973). A forceful exposition of monotheism in the Jewish view is found in Abraham Heschel's *Man Is Not Alone: A Philosophy of Religion* (New York, 1951). Paul Tillich presents a monotheistic theology related to his view of God as the "Ground of Being" in his *Systematic Theology*, vol. 1 (Chicago, 1951). *Radical Monotheism and Western Civilization* (New York, 1960) by H. Richard Niebuhr has been very influential in discussing the relevance of monotheism for Christian societal ideals. The central importance of the unity of God in Islam is presented by Muḥammad ʿAbduh in *The Theology of Unity* (London, 1966). The articles in *Islamic Spirituality: Foundations*, edited by Seyyed Hossein Nasr (New York, 1987), look at the oneness of God in relation to many other aspects of Muslim spiritual experience. A rich sampling of philosophical ideas about God, with a typology of theistic views, is found in Charles Hartshorne and William L. Reese's *Philosophers Speak of God* (Chicago, 1953). H. P. Owen surveys the various philosophical approaches to God as he defends traditional theism in *Concepts of Deity* (New York, 1971).

Among many critical views of traditional monotheism, Regina M. Schwartz, *The Curse of Cain: The Violent Legacy of Monotheism* (Chicago, 1997), presents a strong discussion of the relationship of monotheism to various forms of violence and oppression. Material on feminist critiques of traditional theistic concepts can be found in Rosemary R. Ruether's *Sexism and God Talk: Toward a Feminist Theology* (Boston, 1983), and in Judith Plaskow, *Standing Again at Sinai: Judaism from a Feminist Perspective* (New York, 1990). Thinkers as different as Alain de Benoist, *Comment peut-on être païen?* (Paris, 1981), and David L. Miller, *The New Polytheism: Rebirth of the Gods and Goddesses* (New York, 1974, revised ed. 1981), suggest that monotheism fails to provide freedom and religious creativity for the modern age and a return to polytheism is needed. Jan Assmann, in *Moses the Egyptian: The Memory of Egypt in Western Monotheism* (Cambridge, 1997), shows how the idea of monotheism fostered the dichotomy of true religion and false religion in Western intellectual history, while alternate forms of cultural memory more favorable to ancient Egypt continued to persist. And Rodney Stark, in his *One True God: Historical Consequences of Monotheism* (Princeton, N. J., 2001), presents a far-ranging discussion of the historical and sociological repercussions, both negative and positive, that monotheism has had in Western culture.

Presenting monotheism in a positive view, Bernard-Henri Lévy in *Le testament de Dieu* (Paris, 1979) attempts to show that the monotheistic ideal of a universal moral law can be a liberating safeguard against all forms of totalitarianism. *Monotheism*, edited by Claude Geffré and Jean-Pierre Jossua (Edinburgh, 1985), is devoted to the theological discussion of the criticisms of monotheism and the need to rethink and renew this theological concept. Jürgen Moltmann counters oppressive monarchical monotheism with a liberating trinitarian model of God in *The Trinity and the Kingdom: The Doctrine of God* (London, 1981); and Colin E. Gunton, *The One, the Three and the Many: God, Creation and the Culture of Moder-*

nity (Cambridge, 1993), argues that both trinitarian and monotheistic perspectives are necessary for upholding human freedom. Elizabeth A. Johnson, in *She Who Is: The Mystery of God in Feminist Theological Discourse* (New York, 1992), is representative of many feminist scholars as she reinterprets the "one living God" with metaphors and images suggesting relationship and communion. Drawing on extensive studies in Jewish and Islamic philosophy, Lenn E. Goodman presents philosophical investigations of monotheism with respect to ethics and human values, notably in *Monotheism: A Philosophical Inquiry into the Foundations of Theology and Ethics* (Totowa, N. J., 1981); and also in *God of Abraham* (Oxford, 1996).

THEODORE M. LUDWIG (1987 AND 2005)

MONSTERS. Strictly speaking, a monster is a mythical being and may be human or animal or a combination of both; it may be huge, misshapen, or grotesque, malevolent, savage, or terrifying. Such creatures have been a feature of popular lore and religious cult in all parts of the world from earliest times. The term is applied also to human "freaks," or "monstrous births," that is, persons with more or less than the normal number of limbs or organs, Siamese twins, hermaphrodites, and even albinos.

In popular legend, monsters are commonly portrayed as both stupid and gluttonous. What they have in brawn, they lack in brain, and when they devour their victims, it is not because they are innately hostile to the human race but because they possess insatiable appetites. It is often their obtuseness and greed that prove their undoing.

One kind of mythical monster is the dragon, the embodiment of primordial chaos, who is believed to have been subdued in battle by a leading god before the world order could be established. The Sumerians of Mesopotamia spoke of such a combat between the monster Azag ("demon") and the god Ninurta; the Babylonians, of the defeat of the rebellious Tiamat by their supreme god Marduk; the Hittites, of the defeat of a sea serpent named Illuyankas by the combined efforts of the goddess Inaras and a mortal hero; the Hebrews, of Yahveh's rout of Leviathan; the Hindus, of Indra's subjugation of Vṛtra; the Iranians, of the dispatch of the serpentine Azhi Dahaka; and the Greeks, of the triumph of Zeus over the contumacious Typhon.

The primordial monster appears not only in myth but also in ritual. It is a widespread custom to inaugurate a new year or season by staging a mimetic combat between two antagonists who represent respectively the old year and the new, winter and summer, drought and rainfall, and the like—a combat that survives, albeit in distorted form, in the English Mummers' Play and similar seasonal performances elsewhere. What thus inaugurates each separate year or season is thought to have inaugurated the entire procession of years and seasons in any given era and to be destined to happen again before a further era can begin. The defeat of the monster is therefore retrojected into cosmogony and projected into eschatology: Leviathan, Vṛtra, Azhi Dahaka, and Fenrisúlfr of Norse mythology, for instance, are said to be imprisoned but not slain and will eventually burst their bonds and have to be subdued again.

In several myths, the monster personifies the swollen rivers or winter squalls that threaten to inundate the earth unless properly channeled. In Chinese folklore, the subjugation of raging streams is called "caging the dragon." Conversely, however, the monster sometimes personifies a malevolent power who impounds the subterranean waters that have to be released in order to prevent drought.

Adverse natural phenomena are also personified as monsters, though it is sometimes difficult to determine whether these represent the phenomena themselves or the demonic powers that are believed to cause them. One such monster is the gigantic North American deity called the Thunderbird, the flapping of whose wings is believed to cause storms. The ancient Sumerians spoke likewise of a gigantic bird named Heavy Wind (Im Dugud) who caused storms; the Teutons spoke of Hraesvelgr. Analogous figures appear in the folklore of such diverse peoples as the Chinese, the Burmese, and several American Indian tribes.

Hurricanes are often attributed to the rampages of monsters. In the Mesopotamian creation epic *Enuma elish*, the rebellious Tiamat is accompanied into battle by a cohort of gruesome monsters that includes Stormwind, Cyclone, and the like. The Seneca Indians saw in hurricanes the activity of a monstrous bear named Ya-o-gah. According to some scholars, the English word for this phenomenon derives ultimately from *Hurucán*, the name of a monstrous wind god of the Quiché Indians of Central America.

Equally widespread is the belief that eclipses are caused by a monster's swallowing and then disgorging the sun or moon. The Hindus spoke of a dragon called Svarbhanu; analogous figures appear almost universally. In the language of the Turkic-speaking Chuvash and of Estonian folklore, a verbal form translated into English as "eaten" is used to describe an eclipse. Drums and gongs are beaten, bells rung, and trumpets blown in many parts of the world to scare away the dire adversary. A variant of this notion asserts that the sun is pursued nightly by a voracious monster—in ancient Egypt by the serpent Apopis and in Norse mythology by the wolf Skoll.

Another natural phenomenon personified as a monster is the whirlpool, which is said by some scholars to be the original referent of the word *gargoyle* (from the Latin *gurges*). In Arabic a waterspout is popularly termed *tinnīn* ("dragon"); in the Old Testament the sea monster Leviathan is sometimes referred to by the term *tannin.* So, too, Edmund Spenser describes a whirlpool as a whale.

Not only natural phenomena but also human situations and infirmities are personified as monsters or are attributed to their activities. In Babylonian magical incantations, epilepsy and palsy are represented as a demonic monster with a bird's head and human hands and feet, and impotence as one with a lion's mouth, a dragon's teeth, and an eagle's talons. In Jewish folklore, noontime sunstroke and dizziness are attributed to an ogre who has the head of a calf with a revolving horn in the center, one eye in its breast, and a body covered with scales, hair, and eyes.

Sexual dreams are commonly represented in popular lore as due to the assaults of monsters who consort with sleeping men and women. Those that assail men are known as succubi; however monstrous their activities, they are usually portrayed not as grotesque harridans but as voluptuous sylphs or *femmes fatales.* Those that assail women are known as incubi. Belief in such creatures was widespread especially in the Middle Ages and was held even by such noted churchmen as Augustine. They were thought to be the demon lovers of witches, and intercourse with them was said to produce "monstrous births," deformed persons, hermaphrodites, and sometimes albinos. Indeed, according to many medieval commentators the "sons of God," who are said in the *Book of Genesis* (6:1–4) to have consorted with mortal women and thus engendered a race of giants, were in fact incubi.

Fairly universal is the belief in a monstrous beldam who seizes and strangles newborn babes and kills their mothers or drains the mothers' milk. In ancient Mesopotamia, she was known as Lamashtu and was portrayed with a lion's head, a woman's body, and bird's feet. She held serpents in both hands and suckled a black hound and a pig at her breasts. The Hittites knew her as Wesurya ("strangler"); known among the Greeks as Gello, Lamia, or Strix, she could take the form of a screech owl or bat. The Arabs saw her as a goggle-eyed hag whose one foot was that of an ass and the other that of an ostrich. In German folklore, she is a sharp-nosed, scrawny harridan. Superstitious Jews identify her with Lilith, the legendary first wife of Adam, who was expelled childless from Eden for her rebellious behavior and who is therefore envious of all new mothers. In many parts of the world plaques and amulets are hung up to ward her off.

Not only diseases and human infirmities but also death and the netherworld are portrayed as monsters. In several passages of the Old Testament (*Is.* 5:14, *Hb.* 2:5, *Prv.* 1:12) hell is depicted as a being with jaws agape, a portrayal frequent in medieval art, for example, in the east window of York Minster. Supay, the Peruvian deity of the nether regions, is similarly characterized.

There are also animal monsters, creatures that combine the parts of several different beasts or of beasts and human beings. Not all of them are regarded as harmful; some, despite their grotesque forms, represent beneficent spirits or deities. Many of these monsters acquired acceptance through descriptions of them in medieval and later bestiaries, which in turn derive largely from a book about animals known as the *Physiologus,* compiled (probably in Greek) between the third and fifth centuries CE by an unidentified writer and subsequently translated into many European and Oriental languages. Under the hands of Christian redactors, symbolic and allegorical meanings were given to the fabulous beasts, and they were thus incorporated into heraldry (e.g., the lion and the unicorn of British heraldry). Prominent among such creatures are the unicorn, the phoenix, the griffin, and the manticore.

The unicorn is first mentioned by the Greek writer Ctesias (third century BCE) as native to India and akin to the rhinoceros. It was later portrayed in art and literature as a white horse with a single horn protruding from the middle of its forehead. It is identified by some early translators of the Old Testament with the *re'em,* a beast mentioned in several passages, and on the basis of this identification it became prominent in Christian symbolism. The *re'em,* however, is said explicitly to have more than one horn (*Dt.* 33:17, *Ps.* 22:21) probably it is the now extinct aurochs. Legend asserted that the unicorn could be caught only if it leapt into the lap of a virgin sent into the woods to entice it.

The phoenix, a red bird variously identified as an egret or flamingo, is said to be native to Arabia. It was believed to live for five hundred years and then to burn itself in its nest. Out of the ashes arose a new phoenix. Modern scholars believe that this is simply a Greek transmogrification of the Egyptian mythical *bennu* bird, who represented the resurgent sun and rose daily from a flaming tree at Heliopolis.

The griffin is a creature with a lion's head and the wings of an eagle who, in Greek mythology, guarded the gold in the north. It is probably to be identified (even in name) with the biblical *cherub* (Babylonian *karūbu*), who was not an angel, as is commonly supposed, but a monster who guarded the entrance of ancient Mesopotamian palaces and who is also related to the legendary dragon who guards the pot of gold.

The manticore is a hybrid monster described in the bestiaries as possessing a lion's face, a man's body, and a tail with a serpent's head and a scorpion's sting. It has gleaming eyes and can leap prodigious lengths. It is said to be native to the Far East but may in fact derive from the fabulous Indian monster *makara.*

In general, harmful demons are often portrayed as monstrous beasts. A representative example is the Russian Zmei Gorynych, a snake that typifies all evil and is prone to run off with mortal girls.

One example of a beneficent animal monster is the Iranian Senmurv, part dog, part bird, and sometimes part reptile, who gave mankind seeds scattered from a tree in which it lived. Another is the Chinese Qilin, a spirit of good luck who has a deer's body, a bushy tail, cloven hoofs, and horns.

Besides these individual theriomorphic monsters there are also classes of such beings, for example, centaurs, Gorgons, and harpies. Centaurs are most commonly described in Greek literature and portrayed in Greek art as half human and half horse. It should be observed, however, that this is but one variety of them, for their human parts are said to be combined alternatively with those of asses and other beasts. It has therefore been suggested by some modern scholars that centaurs are really the mythical counterpart of the bands of wild men who are said to rampage in animal pelts and perform ritual dances at certain seasons in Balkan countries and who find their congeners in the hobbyhorse performers of English folk custom. The Gorgons are, in Greek mythology, three horrendous sisters whose glance petrifies the beholder. Their hair consists of serpents, and they possess golden wings, brazen claws, and huge teeth. One of them, Medusa, is mortal. Harpies ("snatchers") are filthy winged monsters, part woman and part bird, who defile whatever they encounter and who, according to Hesiod, also carry off newborn babies. In the latter capacity, they have their counterpart in Canaanite lore. Hesiod calls two of them by the names *Aello* ("stormwind") and *Ocypete* ("swift flier"). These names are included to this day in the Jewish amuletic plaques mentioned above as a device for averting the child-stealing beldam.

Human "monsters" or freaks are popularly attributed to the union of mortal women (especially witches) with incubi, or demons. Included among them are misshapen children and adults, androgynes, and persons with extra limbs and organs. An outstanding example is the Pig-faced Lady, Tanakin Skinner, who appeared in London in the early seventeenth century. An otherwise gracious person, she was said to have the head of a sow and to eat from a trough. Her grotesque form was attributed to divine vengeance on her mother, who had refused alms to a poor woman begging for the sustenance of her child. Another example is the Elephant Man, the subject of a well-known play by Bernard Pomerance. Albinos too fall into this class, although the popular attitude toward them is ambivalent. In Senegal, for instance, they are regarded as ominous; in Gabon they are killed at birth, whereas in New Guinea they are deemed holy.

Remote, "outlandish" peoples are often depicted as monsters in traveler's yarns, medieval romances, and the writings of various ancient authors. Herodotus (485?–425 BCE) and Pliny the Elder (23–79 BCE), for example, mention a legendary people of the far North named the Arimaspeans, who have no heads but have eyes in their stomachs. Japanese legend tells of Jon-li, a remote island inhabited by people whose bodies are half human and half dog. Marco Polo says that the inhabitants of the Andaman Islands are dog-headed, and other writers similarly describe the Karen of Burma. The Jewish traveler Binyamin of Tudela (twelfth century) reports that men who live in the Turkish steppes have no noses, although this may refer to flat-nosed Mongolians. In the same vein, Jean Struys (1650) asserts that tailed men are to be found on the southern side of Formosa, and a similar statement is made by later writers about an allegedly cannibal race called the Nuam-ni'aros who lived between the Gulf of Benin and Ethiopia. Jews during the Middle Ages were also commonly accused of cannibalism.

Some monsters are not objects of actual belief but are deliberately invented to scare unruly children. The outstanding monster of this type is the Greek figure Mormo ("bogey"), also called Mormolukeion ("bogeywolf"), who survived in British nurseries as late as the nineteenth century. Similar creatures are the beldam Bebau in central France and the *windigo* of the Ojibwa Indians of North America.

The conquest of a draconic monster who ravages a country or holds a princess or other fair maiden captive is a standard motif in heroic legend. One is the Chimera, a fire-breathing monster, part lion, part dragon, and part goat, who ravaged Lycia and the neighboring lands but was slain by the hero Bellerophon mounted on the winged horse Pegasus. Typhon, a hundred-headed, fiery being, challenged the sovereignty of Zeus but was destroyed by a thunderbolt and buried under Mount Etna. The Minotaur, half bull and half man, was kept in a labyrinth by King Minos of Crete to devour the youths and maidens demanded of Athens as periodic tribute. He was eventually defeated by the hero Theseus with the aid of the princess Ariadne. (The exaction of periodic tribute by water spirits as the price of averting inundation is a not uncommon theme in world folklore.) The Hydra was a hundred-headed monster of the Peloponnese who was slain by Herakles as one of his twelve labors. Whenever one head was severed two grew in its place, but the hero eventually scorched the growth with a firebrand. Geryon was a monster with three heads or three bodies whose herds near Gades (Cadiz) Herakles carried off as his tenth labor, slaying their guardians, the giant Eurytion and the two-headed hound Orthros, as well as the Geryon itself. Fenrisúlfr (Fenriswolf) was the monstrous offspring of Loki in Norse mythology. The gods eventually bound him with a fetter made by dwarfs from the sound of a cat's footfall, the breath of a fish, and the spittle of a bird, and then imprisoned him in the depths of the earth. He will break forth, however, at the final twilight of the gods (Ragnarǫk) and slay Óðinn (Odin), only to be himself slain by Óðinn's son Víðarr. Battles against monstrous dragons are familiar also from the legends of Perseus, Beowulf, Saint George, and many other heroes.

From time to time—especially in the present century—reports have circulated of gigantic prehistoric monsters sighted in various parts of the world. These are commonly termed "monsters," but that designation is misleading, for a monster is essentially abnormal, whereas these creatures are supposedly surviving specimens of mammoths, mastodons, and the like. To this class belongs especially the celebrated Loch Ness monster of Scotland, said to have been seen sporadically throughout the ages, but a subject of public interest only since 1933. It is reputed to have been seen since then by no fewer than four thousand witnesses, and several scientific expeditions have attempted to photograph and identify it. A group of sonar and photographic images obtained in 1973 by the Academy of Applied Science has, for some, lent credence to its existence. It is usually described as being dark gray or brownish black in color, about fifteen to twenty feet long, with a thin neck, small head, long tail, four paddles or fins, and several humps. Another such alleged prehistoric monster is the Yeti, or Abominable Snowman, said to have been sighted or to have left gigantic footprints in remote areas of the Himalayas. He is described as resembling an ape, standing nearly six feet tall, shaggy in appearance, with huge teeth in a large mouth, and a head tapering to a point. However, native Sherpas declare that he is far smaller and has red or black tufts of hair and the face of a monkey. He has no tail and apparently walks on two legs.

Cousin to the Yeti is Sasquatch, or Bigfoot, a hypothetical species of primates said, since 1840, to have been sighted in the mountains of the Pacific Northwest. This creature is reported to be between seven and nine feet in height and to weigh from six hundred to nine hundred pounds. He is not ferocious. He looks like a furry ape, walks upright, and leaves footprints sixteen inches long and six inches wide. Sasquatch plays a role in the folklore of the Northwest Coast Indians and in turn has a cousin in the Mono Grande of the Andes. It has been suggested that the Abominable Snowman, Sasquatch, and Mono Grande may be surviving specimens of a prehistoric ape-man known as *Gigantopithecus,* fossils of which have been discovered in China and other parts of Asia.

Monsters and ogres survive also in popular lore in such figures as Frankenstein's monster, King Kong, and the like—staples of horror movies, television, and comic strips. An interesting development in this respect is the circulation of stories about visitors from outer space allegedly seen emerging from flying saucers. Significantly, many of these stories come from rapporteurs of Irish descent, and the creatures are described as having a form closely resembling that of the leprechauns of Irish folklore.

Finally, it may be observed that monsters also appear as figures of political propaganda. An outstanding instance is the protrayal of the Japanese in World War II as "monkeys"—a tendentious revival of the old practice (mentioned above) of so characterizing remote, unfamiliar peoples. Similarly, barbaric historical personages are commonly designated "monsters," for example, Attila and, in our own day, Adolf Hitler and Joseph Mengele. In such characterizations, the essential nature of a monster is effectively expressed; huge, savage, and hostile, he is the direct opposite of the diminutive dwarf, elf, or gremlin, who, albeit mischievous, is essentially benevolent.

SEE ALSO Dragons; Therianthropism.

BIBLIOGRAPHY

For general works on the theme of monsters, see Charles Gould's *Mythical Monsters* (London, 1886) and C. J. S. Thompson's *The Mystery and Lore of Monsters* (London, 1930). On the cosmogonic dragon, see my *Thespis: Ritual, Myth, and Drama in the Ancient Near East,* 2d ed. (1961; New York, 1977), pp. 137–153. Animal monsters are the subject of Peter Lum's *Fabulous Beasts* (London, 1952) and T. H. White's *The Book of Beasts* (London, 1956); more particularly, see, on the unicorn, Odell Shepard's *The Lore of the Unicorn* (New York, 1930) and, on centaurs, John Cuthbert Lawson's *Modern Greek Folklore and Ancient Greek Religion* (1910; New York, 1964), pp. 190–225. On the child-stealing beldam, see my *The Holy and the Profane* (New York, 1980); on bogeys, see Elizabeth M. Wright's *Rustic Speech and Folklore* (Oxford, 1913). Sabine Baring-Gould discusses tailed men in *Curious Myths of the Middle Ages* (1866; New York, 1884), pp. 86–89, and Richard Andree treats albinos in *Ethnographische Parallelen und Vergleiche* (Leipzig, 1881), pp. 278–280. John Napier discusses Sasquatch in *Bigfoot* (London, 1972) and the Yeti in *The Abominable Snowman* (New York, 1973).

New Sources

Daston, Lorraine, and Katharine Park. *Wonders and the Order of Nature, 1150–1750.* New York, 1998.

Davidson, Hilda Ellis, and Anna Chaudhri, eds. *Supernatural Enemies.* Durham, N.C., 2001.

Friedman, John Block. *The Monstrous Races in Medieval Art and Thought. Medieval Studies.* Syracuse, N.Y., 2000.

Gilmore, David D. *Monsters: Evil Beings, Mythical Beasts, and All Manner of Imaginary Terrors.* Philadelphia, 2003.

Jones, Timothy S., and David A. Sprunger, eds. *Marvels, Monsters, and Miracles: Studies in the Medieval and Early Modern Imaginations.* Kalamazoo, Mich, 2002.

Platt, Peter G., ed. *Wonders, Marvels, and Monsters in Early Modern Culture.* Newark and London, 1999.

THEODOR H. GASTER (1987)
Revised Bibliography

MONTAGU, LILY (1873–1963), founder of the Liberal Jewish movement in England. Born in London on December 22, 1873, Lily H. Montagu was the sixth child of Ellen Cohen Montagu and Samuel Montagu. Her father was a wealthy banker and leading member of the Orthodox Anglo-Jewish community. Convinced that Orthodoxy offered her, and other women, little room for religious self-expression, she found in the works of Claude Montefiore a vision of Judaism that mirrored her own understanding of true religion as personal in nature, universal in outlook, and best revealed through daily conduct.

In the January 1899 issue of the *Jewish Quarterly Review,* Montagu published "The Spiritual Possibilities of Judaism Today," an essay in which she asked all religiously committed Jews to help her form an association aimed at strengthening the religious life of the Anglo-Jewish community through the propagation of Liberal Jewish teachings. Membership would not necessarily demonstrate allegiance to what Montefiore identified as Liberal Judaism but simply would demonstrate the recognition of its ability to awaken within many Jews a sense of spirituality and personal responsibility to God. The Jewish Religious Union (JRU), established by Lily Montagu in February 1902, instituted Sabbath afternoon worship services conducted along Liberal Jewish lines and propaganda meetings, led by Montagu, to clarify and spread its teachings. Though Montefiore agreed to serve as the group's official leader, Montagu assumed responsibility for its major activities and daily affairs.

By 1909, acknowledging the failure of its initial, all-inclusive vision, the union declared itself to be a movement specifically committed to the advancement of Liberal Judaism. During the next few decades, Lily Montagu helped form Liberal Jewish synagogues throughout Great Britain, frequently serving as their chairman or president, and became lay minister of the West Central Liberal Jewish Congregation in 1928, a position to which she was formally inducted in November, 1944. Following Montefiore's death, in 1938, she assumed the presidency of the JRU, later renamed the Union of Liberal and Progressive Synagogues. Having conceived of the idea for an international JRU as early as 1925, Montagu also helped found and eventually became president of the World Union for Progressive Judaism.

Montagu was the author of eleven books, including *Thoughts on Judaism*, a theological treatise published in 1902, and her autobiography, *The Faith of a Jewish Woman*, published in 1943.

BIBLIOGRAPHY

Little has been written either on the history of the Liberal Jewish movement in England or on Lily Montagu herself. The only critical study of Montagu's life and thought published to date is my book *Lily Montagu and the Advancement of Liberal Judaism: From Vision to Vocation* (Lewiston, N.Y., 1983). A second volume, *Lily Montagu: Sermons, Addresses, Letters and Prayers*, edited and with introductions by me (Lewiston, N.Y., 1985), includes a fully annotated selection of her unpublished writings. Finally, for a more detailed account of Montagu's contribution to the development of Liberal Judaism, see my essay "The Origins of Liberal Judaism in England: The Contribution of Lily H. Montagu," *Hebrew Union College Annual* 55 (1984): 309–322.

New Sources

Jacobi, Margaret. "Lily Montagu—A Pioneer in Religious Leadership." In *Hear Our Voice: Women in the British Rabbinate*, edited by Sybil Sheridan, pp. 9–15. Columbia, S.C., 1998.

ELLEN M. UMANSKY (1987)
Revised Bibliography

MONTANISM. Although there are various reports (e.g., Hippolytus, *Refutatio* 8.19.1; Eusebius, *Church History* 6.20.3) that the leaders of Montanism composed many writings, none of these has come down to us. As a result, special importance attaches to the approximately twenty-five surviving fragments of their prophecies and oracles (see new edition in *Kirchengeschichtliche Entwürfe*, 1960) and a few inscriptions, as well as to the writings from Tertullian's Montanist period, although the latter reflect essentially the later development of Montanism. Even the writings of the adversaries of Montanism have disappeared and are known to us only from citations by the fathers of the church. Especially important are Eusebius's account in his *Church History* and the *Panarion* of Epiphanius of Salamis, both of which are based on numerous sources. By contrast, what we know of Montanism from Jerome and Augustine has significantly less value as a source.

According to the sources, Montanism arose in Asia Minor in 156/7 CE and was centered there, at least in its first period. Its founder was Montanus, but he was evidently accompanied from an early date by prophetesses, among whom Priscilla (or Prisca) and especially Maximilla were particularly important. After they had first attracted attention by speaking in tongues, Montanus and his associates made use of intelligible oracles and prophecies to proclaim the final revelation and the will of the Holy Spirit. The Spirit was calling for an intensified expectation of the end, since the Parousia (the second coming of Christ) was imminent. The thousand-year reign would descend to earth at Pepuza (and Tymion?) in Phrygia, and the faithful were to travel there in order to share in it as soon as it appeared. They were to prepare themselves by intensified asceticism.

Glossolalia and the claim of a communication of the Spirit were at this time just as suspect to the official church in Asia Minor as was the expectation of an imminent end. The bishops endeavored in vain through exorcisms to resist the "new prophecy," as the apparently tightly organized movement was called, and they tried to coordinate their activity against the "Cataphrygians" (so called after their place of origin) at the first provincial synods. Despite these efforts, Montanism spread far beyond Asia Minor. Only with great difficulty was its recognition by the bishop of Rome prevented, and approximately in the year 207 in North Africa it made a convert of Tertullian, who became a passionate proselytizer for Montanism.

The fight against the movement was difficult because early Montanism was orthodox in its doctrine and exemplary in its ethics. Its characteristic traits—a heightened expectation of an imminent Parousia and a resultant intense asceticism (to the point of seeking martyrdom)—were basic elements of early Christianity, as were speaking in tongues and the claim to immediate revelation from the Holy Spirit. Montanus claimed that in him the Paraclete had made his appearance. After all, the coming of the Spirit was expressly announced in the *Gospel of John*. In addition, millenarianism found justification in the *Revelation to John* and was especially widespread in Asia Minor, and this even in the subsequent period. The *Revelation to John* and the *Gospel of John* were evidently among the spiritual sources from which Montanism was derived.

By the second half of the second century the official church and its theology had moved beyond the expectation of an imminent Parousia and had made room for the idea of postponement of the end. The *Second Letter of Peter* and the *Shepherd of Hermas* are clear proof of this. In the community at large, however, the expectation of an imminent end was still alive, at least in a latent form, and was given new life by Montanism. It was this expectation that made it possible for the movement to spread so quickly and so widely. The church's opposition to Montanism began to be effective only when the predicted return of the Lord did not occur and the prophetic energies of the movement fell off. Maximilla's oracle, "After me there will be no further prophet but only the end" (Epiphanius, *Panarion* 48.12.4), gave the church a weapon that became all the more effective as time passed after the death of Maximilla and neither the predicted end nor even the disturbances and wars preceding the end came to pass. During the second half of the second century, Montanism underwent the same kind of development that official Christianity had experienced: there was a withering of the prophetic element, cessation of glossolalia, and a decline in ethical standards.

It was the ethical rigorism of Montanism that converted Tertullian. When he became a Montanist in about 207, he evidently had been in conflict with the official church, which in his opinion was too lax, for some time. The gift of prophecy was still alive in Montanism at that time, as was eschatological expectation, though this was no longer as intense as in the beginning. The gift of tongues had disappeared, and the Lord's thousand-year reign was expected to come no longer in Asia Minor but in Jerusalem.

It is not possible to say for certain to what extent Montanism had spread in the West and how long it persisted there. Modern writers often rely too much on the lists of heresies, in which Montanism soon acquired its fixed place, as proof that the movement actually existed in a given area. Although Augustine wrote of "Tertullianists" in Africa, it is uncertain to what extent they are to be identified with Montanism. On the other hand, in the East the laws against heretics give the impression down to the beginning of the fifth century that Montanism was still a living reality there.

The attempt (by Wilhelm E. Schepelern and, later, B. W. Goree Jr., for example) to explain Montanism in terms of the paganism of Asia Minor and especially the cult of Cybele is not a promising one in view of the state of the sources. What these writers view as a tradition peculiar to Asia Minor (e.g., emphasis on ecstasy, the special place of women, intense asceticism) was in fact the common possession of early Christianity.

Bibliography

My contributions to *Kirchengeschichtliche Entwürfe* (Gütersloh, 1960) expand on themes treated above: "Bemerkungen zum Montanismus und zur frühchristlichen Eschatologie" (pp. 105–148) and "Augustin und der Montanismus" (pp. 149–164). See also Heinrich Kraft's "Die altkirchliche Prophetie und die Entstehung des Montanismus," *Theologische Zeitschrift* 11 (1955): 249–271; Douglas Powell's "Tertullianists and Cataphrygians," *Vigiliae Christianae* 29 (1975): 33–54; W. E. Schepelern's *Der Montanismus und die phrygischen Kulte: Eine religionsgeschichtliche Untersuchung* (Tübingen, 1929); and B. W. Goree Jr.'s "The Cultural Bases of Montanism" (Ph. D. diss., Baylor University, 1980). Pierre de Labriolle's *Les sources de l'histoire du montanisme* (Paris, 1913) is still fundamental, even though the editions used are largely outdated.

KURT ALAND (1987)
Translated from German by Matthew J. O'Connell

MONTANUS, second-century Christian schismatic. For information on the life of Montanus we are dependent on statements made by the Christian controversialists of the time, as transmitted by the fathers of the church. Only a few utterances of Montanus himself have come down to us: "I am the Father and I am the Son and I am the Paraclete," as in the *Dialogue between a Montanist and an Orthodox Christian* (J. Ficker, 1905, pp. 447ff.) and according to Didymus of Alexandria (*De Trinitate* 3.41) and Epiphanius (*Panarion* 48.11.1). "The Paraclete" is sometimes replaced by "the Spirit" or "the Holy Spirit" or some expanded form of this. Man is like a lyre, and Montanus is described as the plectrum that sweeps across the strings. Extraordinary promises are made to the faithful, but no concrete indications are given of Montanus's teaching or ethical demands in any of the extant sources concerning him.

Montanus reportedly first attracted notice in the time of the proconsulate of Gratus (Quadratus?), in Ardabau (on the Phrygian border of Mysia), as promulgator of the "new prophecy." When combined with data provided by Eusebius and Epiphanius of Salamis, this information suggests the date 156/157 as the approximate beginning of this movement. Montanus is also reported to have been a recent convert to Christianity (in Eusebius's *Church History* 5.16.17) and to have previously been a priest of Apollo (this designation appears in the *Dialogue*) or, more generally, a priest of idols (in the *Dialogue* and in Didymus's *De Trinitate* 3.41). Jerome speaks of him (*Letters* 41, to Marcella) as *abscisum et semivirum* (castrated and half a man), that is, a priest of Cybele. Montanus is reported to have hanged himself (*Church History* 5.16.13). Since the same story is told of Maximilla, the prophetess and close associate of Montanus, the report is evidently a piece of antiheretical polemic, passed on by an anonymous writer simply as a rumor (cited in *Church History* 5.16.15). We cannot say for certain whether the report is true that Montanus was originally a pagan priest, but the contradictory claims suggest that early Christian polemics played a role in the report, especially since there is no reference to this pagan background of Montanus among the writings of the anti-Montanists of the second century.

Augustine (*De haeresibus liber* 26) reports that Montanus celebrated the Lord's Supper with bread that had been prepared using the blood of a one-year-old infant. The blood had been extracted by means of countless tiny punctures. The same story is told by numerous church fathers (Epiphanius, Filastrius, Cyril of Jerusalem, Jerome), but it represents nothing more than the acceptance into antiheretical Christian polemics of the pagan legend of the orthodox Christian Lord's Supper as involving the ritualistic sacrifice of an infant. This story was told at the end of the second century (cf. Minucius Felix, *Octavius* 9.5). Because they did not recognize this, some scholars saw the story as reflecting the influence of an orgiastic culture in Asia Minor and considered it as justification for looking into the matter further. Montanus's contemporary adversaries knew nothing about the story, or they gladly would have used it in arguments against him. Also, Eusebius, who summarizes virtually everything of the anti-Montanist writings, would undoubtedly have passed the story on.

There was nothing about Montanism that could not have been found, at least in the form of tendencies, in the early Christian church. Montanism was a movement of renewal that sought to revive, in the second half of the second century, certain elements of worship, doctrine, and ethics that had gradually died out in the church at large during the first half of the century. Montanism itself eventually underwent the same kind of development that official Christianity had experienced (cessation of glossolalia, withering of the prophetic element, nonfulfillment of the expectation of the second coming of Christ, decline in ethical standards), so that in the third century Montanism's internal energies were gradually exhausted and nothing was left but a sect that, from the fourth century on, was exposed to ecclesiastical and civil persecution and was doomed to extinction.

BIBLIOGRAPHY

Barnes, Timothy D. "The Chronology of Montanism." *Journal of Theological Studies,* n.s. 20 (1970): 403–408.

Ford, J. Massingberd. "Was Montanism a Jewish-Christian Heresy?" *Journal of Ecclesiastical History* 17 (1966): 145–158.

Gero, Stephen. "Montanus and Montanism according to a Medieval Syriac Source." *Journal of Theological Studies,* n.s. 28 (1977): 520–524.

KURT ALAND (1987)
Translated from German by Matthew J. O'Connell

MOODY, DWIGHT L.

MOODY, DWIGHT L. (1837–1899), American revivalist preacher. Dwight Lyman Moody was born in Northfield, Massachusetts. Like many Americans of his era, he left home as a teenager for the city—first Boston, then Chicago. In each city he quickly established a reputation as an aggressive boot and shoe salesman, but in Chicago he soon turned his organizational talents to religious endeavors, especially those of the local YMCA. During the nearly two decades he lived in Chicago, Moody moved from volunteer to full-time religious work, developed his techniques as an urban evangelist, and began to establish a national reputation as a leader in church circles. After several tentative, exploratory trips overseas, Moody in 1873 launched a career in England as a full-time revivalist. Within two years he had established himself as a highly effective revivalist, able to stir religious feelings in large numbers of people during lengthy revival "campaigns" conducted in the principal cities of England and Scotland.

Moody parlayed his fame overseas into even greater public acclaim in the United States. Beginning in 1875 he conducted a series of lengthy revivals, carefully planned and orchestrated, in most major American cities. True religious sentiment and feeling were to be found in these revivals, even though Moody's activism, efficient organization, and rough-hewn appearance seemed also to exemplify the emerging materialism of industrial America.

By 1880 Moody had established a permanent residence at his birthplace, Northfield, Massachusetts. This act, combined with the evangelist's continuing round of annual urban revivals, exemplified the tension many late nineteenth-century Americans felt in living between the two worlds of small-town origins and big city realities. Moody broadened his concerns beyond mass revivalism in the 1880s. Shifting part of his energy and interest into education, he founded Mount Hermon and Northfield academies in his hometown, and the Moody Bible Institute, for training urban evangelists, in Chicago.

In the last years of Moody's life, growing divisions between liberals and conservatives in American Protestantism somewhat undermined his leadership. His personal integrity and his irenic temperament, however, made it possible for him to bridge the gap between these divergent groups, and only after his death in 1899 did tensions grow so great that open conflict erupted.

In numerous ways Moody epitomized popular American Protestantism in the second half of the nineteenth century. His family life and personal values reflected evangelical Protestant ideals of personal piety and morality. In the public realm, also, Moody embodied key characteristics of the evangelical world. He had transformed that world by adapting the revival tradition to the new urban, industrial context of late nineteenth-century America. His public activities in his later years also offer fascinating glimpses of the breakup of the cultural synthesis evangelism had provided in the nineteenth century. To the end of his life, Moody remained one of the best representatives and reflectors of popular Protestant culture and practice in the United States.

BIBLIOGRAPHY

Findlay, James F. *Dwight L. Moody, American Evangelist, 1837–1899.* Chicago, 1969.

Marsden, George M. *Fundamentalism in American Culture: The Shaping of Twentieth-Century Evangelicalism, 1870–1925.* New York, 1980.

McLoughlin, William G. *Modern Revivalism: Charles Grandison Finney to Billy Graham.* New York, 1959.

Sizer, Sandra S. *Gospel Hymns and Social Religion: The Rhetoric of Nineteenth-Century Revivalism.* Philadelphia, 1978.

Weisberger, Bernard A. *They Gathered at the River: The Story of the Great Revivalists and Their Impact upon Religion in America.* Boston, 1958.

JAMES F. FINDLAY (1987)

MOON. To observers on earth, the moon appears to be the most changeable of celestial phenomena. In earlier times the appearance of the new crescent was often greeted with joy as a return of the moon from the dead; the full moon was considered an occasion for celebration, the waning a time of anxiety, and the eclipse a cause for dread. In religion and mythology the moon plays a variety of roles. It is personified as a male or female divinity, or, like the sun, thought to be an object thrown up into the sky by some supernatural being. It may be thought of as kindly or malicious, male or female, pursued or pursuer, a god of destruction or of birth and growth.

An early recognition of a connection with menstruation gave rise to the conception of the moon as the guardian of the female cycle and of birth or, alternatively, as a male god who monthly defiles women. In connection with dew, rain, or tides, the moon may promote the growth of vegetation or bring disastrous floods.

The moon has been a measure of time from early times, especially for hunting societies. In tropical climates, where the sun is cruel, the moon is considered beneficent, especially by nomads and caravan drivers. As a male god the moon appears as the Strong Bull of Heaven who cares for his cows, the stars; or as the sacrificed god, the son or lover of the mother goddess.

As a goddess, the moon brings cures and eases childbirth or, on the other hand, helps to rot corpses and receives the dead. The waxing and waning of the moon led to the idea that it dies and is reborn, and thus the moon became a part of funeral ceremonies and rites of resurrection. The discovery that the moon is the closest celestial body to the earth led to the idea that the moon was the "abode of souls," a way station to immortality.

The phases of the moon seem to echo the life cycles of women and therefore connect the moon with the Triple Goddess who presided over birth, initiation, and death. The Moon became part of a triad with Hekate, goddess of the underworld, and with Artemis, the divine huntress, whose hounds were the stars. Sometimes even the Egyptian goddess Isis joined the grouping. In this connection the qualities of the moon are fertility, moisture, change, darkness, and magic. In the ancient Chinese division of the universe into *yang* (hot, dry, strong, male) and *yin* (cool, moist, weak, female) the moon is considered *yin.*

Usually the waxing moon is a fortunate omen and waning moon a dangerous one. In the Andaman Islands the waxing moon is male and the waning moon female. The dark of the moon is the time for gathering herbs to be used in spells and curses. The new or full moon is the time for white magic. In some systems, however, the moon rushes to conjunction with the sun to be refreshed by his light.

In poetry, the dying god, who is related to the divine powers of the plant world, is often compared to the moon. Intoxicating liquors used in many religious ceremonies are said to drip forth from the moon. As spider, spinner, and weaver, the moon is likened to the three Fates, who spin and weave man's destiny.

The moon is often paired with the sun, as either father, son, wife, sister, or daughter. Sometimes the moon and sun are twins, and the weaker one, usually the moon, is doomed to live in the underworld, while the other rides on high. Frequently both are thought of as boats riding through the ether as on the ocean. Often, the sun rides in a chariot pulled by four white horses. The moon is pulled by two white horses, or by a bull, a stag, or a cock.

The moon's animal is often the bull, because of the crescent shape formed by its horns, or the hare, because of its fertility or because the "man in the moon" is thought to resemble a hare. The bear is also associated with the moon, because its hibernation and waking are like death and resurrection; the snail, because it retreats and reappears; or the frog, because it is an aquatic creature.

The Moon as a Measure of Time. Aside from night and day, the moon is the most obvious natural measure of time. The Indo-European root is the same for the *moon, month,* and *measure.* There exist what may be notations of the moon's phases in Paleolithic caves in Spain from 7000 BCE. Stonehenge in Great Britain (c. 3000 BCE) may have been used to measure the movements of the moon as well as those of the sun. There are still primitive peoples who use only the moon to measure time. Before the arrival of Europeans, American Indians counted the lunations as "war month," "month of flowers," and so forth. The dark of the moon was the "naked time"; its first appearance, the "coming to life."

Agricultural people, however, needed to have their times of planting and reaping coincide with the seasons—that is, with the sun. Thus began the long effort to correlate twelve lunations (too few) or thirteen lunations (too many) with the solar year. Accounts from republican Rome show the problems associated with this effort. We are told that from earliest times a *pontifex minor* would watch for the new moon from the Capitoline Hill, and when it was sighted, call out to Juno, the queen of the gods. The first of the month was called the calends from the verb "to call out." Juno is in this way identified with the new moon, as her husband, Jupiter, is with the ides, or full moon. The priest then announced the series of festivals for the coming month and whether the nones (the half-moon) would fall on the fifth or the seventh. The festivals, sponsored by the state, were instituted as a means of keeping the agricultural, military, and civil activities in order. It was necessary for all farmers to come into the city to learn on what days they could not work but must keep festival. On calendars that have come down to us, festival days are marked *nefas,* meaning that no work could be done; 109 out of the 355 days of the year were designated *nefas.*

The priesthoods, like the early magistracies, were in the hands of the patricians. The inconvenience of not knowing the feast days was one of the problems that led to the "struggle of the orders." Eventually the *fasti* (calendars) were published, in 304 BCE. The year began in March, and any time that had to be intercalated to bring the months into line with the seasons was added in February, after the Terminalia (a festival of boundaries and the year's end, celebrated on February 23).

Until the end of the republic the work of intercalation was the duty of the pontifices, who were often inefficient or corrupt. For instance, the date of court cases could be shifted by altering the intercalations. By the end of the republic, the whole calendar was out of harmony with both the sun and the moon. Cicero, writing to his friend Atticus, says he is not sure whether or not there will be an intercalation. There was a clause in contracts that read "si intercalat" ("in case of an intercalation").

Julius Caesar, aided by his Egyptian astronomer, made a clean sweep of the quasi-lunar calendar, extended the year 45 BCE from 355 to 445 days, and started anew on January 1, 45 BCE, with a cycle of 365 days, adding another day on the fourth year, after the Terminalia. This, with a few adjustments, is the solar calendar under which we live.

The ancient Greeks sent out criers to announce the sighting of the new moon. At some unknown point in history, the Greeks had limited the length of the year to twelve lunations of "full" or "hollow" months (comprised of thirty and twenty-nine days respectively), with an intercalary month every two years. We learn from Geminus that "they sought for a period which should, as to years agree with the Sun, as to months, with the Moon." The first period they constructed was an eight-year cycle called the *octaeteris.*

A nineteen-year cycle was suggested by the astronomer Meton in 432 BCE but was apparently not accepted by the cities, which went their own way, creating their own calendars and even inventing their own names for the months. In *The Clouds* of Aristophanes, the Moon complains, "You subvert the calendar and fail to observe her days. When the sacred days are unobserved, the gods go hungry, and it is the Moon they threaten." In this confusion, many citizens returned to direct personal observation of the rising moon. Beginning in the second century BCE, two sets of dates were recorded, "according to the state and according to the deity [Selene]."

In Mesopotamia the month began with the sighting of the new moon. A letter to the Assyrian king Esarhaddon (r. 680–669 BCE) states, "On the thirtieth I saw the moon. It was in a high position. The king should wait for the report from the city of Assur and then may determine the first day of the month." There are indications that in some cities months alternated between thirty and twenty-nine days in a nineteen-year cycle with regular intercalations. By the time of the Seleucids (third century BCE), it was possible to calculate the appearance of the new moon and to predict eclipses.

In India, religious festivals are still regulated by the lunar calendar, as are such domestic events as marriages. The moon festivals—two days for the new moon, one for the full moon—are considered important, even by Buddhists. The present names of the months are derived from the *nakshatras* ("lunar mansions"), twenty-seven or twenty-eight conspicuous stars along the ecliptic through which the moon passes.

The early Hebrews celebrated the new moon with a feast, which was a family gathering at which animals were sacrificed. The months were identified by the agricultural activity taking place at the time. The beginning of the month, after being attested to by observers, was announced to various communities by fire signals at first, and later by messengers. Since messengers could not always reach the outlying groups in a day, festivals often went on for two days. Since Passover, celebrated at the full moon, was originally a feast of the first fruits, it had to occur after the reaping of the grain. Thus it became necessary to add another month after Adar (approximately March). After the exile the calendar followed the Babylonian system, using Babylonian names for the months, counting the days from the evening, and intercalating an extra month on a regular basis. After the third century there was increasing dependence on calculation of the beginning of the month, though some sects from time to time insisted on reverting to direct observation.

The lunar year to which Muslims adhere was not established until 631 CE, when Muhammad made his last pilgrimage to Mecca. There he proclaimed that the year should consist of twelve lunar months and that intercalation should be forbidden. As Arabs before that time had probably had a combination lunar and solar calendar, it is likely that Muhammad intended to discourage old pagan festivals. His system won acceptance by the Arabs, who since ancient times held the moon in special reverence. The festivals now run through the whole year and come back to the same solar season in about thirty-three years. The new month begins when two trustworthy Muslims notify the authorities that they have observed the new moon from a mountaintop or from an open field. The crescent motif (the *hilal)* has been much used throughout the centuries in Islamic art and in the last two hundred years has appeared on the standard of Islam.

Early Christians attached importance to celebrating Easter at the time of the Jewish Passover but agreed that Easter should fall on a Sunday. In the third century Christians began to frame lunar calculations for themselves. The Easter controversy raged in the early church and still exists between the Western and Eastern churches. The final conditions arrived at in the West are that Easter must be kept on the Sunday after the paschal moon (the calendar moon whose fourteenth day falls on or after the vernal equinox), reckoned from the day of the new moon inclusive.

THE MOON AS DEITY. Only once, so far as is known, did the moon as divinity command political power and an influential priesthood, but it did so for about three thousand years, through changes of race, language, and regime. The place was the area between the Tigris and Euphrates rivers, known as Mesopotamia ("between the rivers"), and the cult spread or grew independently in Syria, Palestine, Arabia, and Anatolia.

In the southern part of the Land between the Rivers there appeared around 5000 BCE the first urban civilization—a group of cities in which trade, division of labor, metalworking, organized religion, and writing were developed by a people whom history knows as Sumerians. Each of the cities was under the protection of a high god and in the beginning was probably ruled by the priesthood of the god. By the time the first records appear, these gods are all related. An is the creator-sky god. His son, Enlil, the Air, carries on most of the business of controlling the other gods and resides in the holy city of Nippur. The first son of Enlil is Nanna, the Moon, patron of the important city of Ur. His wife is Ningal, daughter of the Lady of the Reeds, a moisture goddess from the marshes. The children of Enlil and Ningal are Utu, the Sun, and Inanna, warrior goddess of love and the Evening Star. The trio of Moon, Sun, and Evening Star are often found together on royal stelae down through Babylonian times.

The Semitic-speaking peoples who succeeded the Sumerians—Akkadians, Assyrians, and Babylonians—took over most of their inventions and adopted the Sumerian pantheon, giving the gods Semitic names. Nanna became Sin; Utu, Shamash; and Inanna, Ishtar.

C. Leonard Woolley, excavating at Ur in 1922–1934, found the famous royal tombs, containing the bodies of mass suicides, royal ladies (who Woolley surmised might have been priestesses of the Moon), and a harp with a bull's head and a lapis lazuli beard, the Strong Bull of Nanna. He also describes the ziggurat of Ur, dedicated to the Moon, the best preserved of its kind in the Near East. At the top of the ziggurat, a high staged tower terraced with trees, was a shrine where the god rested, gave dream oracles, or took part in a sacred marriage. This last is suggested by a hymn in which Ningal addresses Nanna, "In your house on high I will come to you, Nanna. In your perfumed cedar mountain, in your mansion of Ur, I will come to live."

At the base of the ziggurat was a large temple, the real home of the god, where he was fed and clothed daily. Probably the people saw the god only when he was paraded at each phase of the moon—on the first, seventh, and fifteenth days of the month. The temple was a huge complex of storehouses, kitchens, and rooms for priests and slaves. It was a landowner and received rent in kind, which was used for sacrifices and for feeding the enormous staff. Slaves were employed in smelting, weaving, and preparing goods for sale. The high priestess of Nanna was traditionally a king's daughter.

A text describes how Nanna made a pilgrimage to visit his father Enlil at the holy city of Nippur, taking agricultural products and receiving in return Enlil's blessing. Enlil confirmed his son in power as Nanna, the king of Ur. It is likely that the king acted out the life of the god. During the dark days of the moon, called the "days of lying down," the queen conducted the rituals.

The temple complex at Ur was destroyed and reconstructed many times over the centuries, by Assyrians, Babylonians, even by alien Kassites, and finally by Cyrus, the Persian invader. The complex was rebuilt not to conciliate the people but to preserve good relations with the god.

The Assyrians, who took over from the Sumerians the worship of the moon under the name of Sin, built another moon city, Haran, on the Euphrates. The Assyrian kings came to Haran to "take the hand" of Sin after they had been confirmed by their own god, Ashur. In the sanctuary at Haran was a dream oracle, where Esarhaddon (r. 680–669 BCE) was told to proceed to the conquest of Egypt, which he did. Moon worship continued at Haran well into Islamic times when it was the center for a planet-worshiping people called the Sabaeans. The emperor Julian worshiped the moon at the temple in Haran in 365 CE.

In the early sixth century BCE, Babylon was the area's greatest city. Its founder, Nebuchadrezzar, set about rebuilding Ur. His successor, Nabonidus, was an antiquarian and a devoted worshiper of the moon. His mother (or grandmother) had been governor of Haran, and he was perhaps partly of West Semitic origin. In records of Ur, Nabonidus found the inscription of Ur-Namma, founder of the third dynasty of Ur (2100 BCE), whom he called "a king before me." Upon the ancient foundation he rebuilt the ziggurat "as in old times." He also rebuilt the temple at Haran and one in the Arabian city of Tema, where he remained for eleven years. Many critics in Babylon claimed he was putting his god Sin above Marduk.

The name of the moon in Canaan was Yarih. A Canaanite text tells of his wedding to Nikkal (related to Ningal, wife of the Sumerian moon god): "I shall make her field into vineyards, the field of their love an orchard" (Samuel Noah Kramer, *Ugaritic Manual*, 1955, no. 77). There is no doubt that the golden calf worshiped in *Genesis* was a figure of the moon and that Mount Sinai was his home.

Throughout Anatolia there are depictions of and inscriptions to the Anatolian moon god, called Men, from the Indo-European root for *moon* and *measure*. He was known as Menotyrannus ("lord of the moon"), Men Ouranios ("lord of the sky"), or Katachonios ("lord of the underworld"), suggesting that he was a god of death and rebirth. We cannot be sure whether he arrived along the trade routes from the Near East or was an indigenous deity. Later Men became confused with the "dying and rising god" Attis, the castrated follower, son, or lover of the Great Mother of Phrygia, Cybele, as well as with Dionysos and Sabazios of Thrace, two other dying and rising gods.

THE MOON IN MYTHOLOGY. In ancient India, Soma was the deification of a sacred plant that, when pressed, strained, and mixed with milk and barley, became an intoxicating drink for men and gods. The whole ninth book of the *Ṛgveda* is devoted to the praise of the yellow drink, which it identifies with the yellow moon. There is a marriage hymn in which the god Soma is married to the Sun, Sūrya, and has his head in the laps of the Nakṣatras ("lunar mansions"). Soma is celestial and bright, dispelling darkness and dwelling in the waters. In a later hymn, Soma is said to have married all twenty-seven Nakṣatras, daughters of the creator god, but he prefers one, Rohiṇī (possibly identified with the evening star). The other wives complain to their father, who afflicts the moon with a wasting sickness, causing his waning and disappearance. The Moon promises to reform and then grows back again, but always he relapses. In this problem the Moon is aided by Śiva, like Soma an ancient god of change, fertility, and destruction. Śiva wears the Moon's crest on his head; Soma is known as the "crest of Śiva." In a wheeled chariot drawn by a horse or an antelope, Soma leaves the sky to visit the earth at the new moon to revitalize plants and animals. *Soma* as an intoxicating drink has been compared to the wine of the Greek Dionysos, which the playwright Euripides described as "a drink that is poured out, a god for a god."

In Iran there is also a ritual of the sacred drink, there called *haoma*, which is not identified with the moon. In one hymn, the Moon is one of a triad of divinities, the lowest one being the sacred ox, who is sacrificed. The seed of the ox enters the Moon, where it is purified and divides into all the species of plants and animals. Iranians dedicated the right eye of every sacrificed animal to the Moon. They believed that when all things were put in motion by Angra Mainyu, or Evil, the Moon created time, which will run until Angra Mainyu is overthrown.

The ancient Greeks had only one myth concerning the moon, there called Selene, "the bright one." It is the story of how she fell in love with Endymion, a prince of Elis, while he was sleeping on Mount Latmos in Asia Minor. She begged Zeus to give Endymion eternal sleep so that she could visit him every night. In this way she managed to have fifty children by him, the number of the lunations between Olympic games, or equal to one-half of the eight-year cycle. Though there are almost no rituals associated with the moon in Greece, there are traces of moon worship from earlier times and in outlying regions. The Endymion myth connects Asia Minor with western Greece. According to Plato, mothers and nurses in ancient times taught children to bow down to the new moon. Torchlight parades for Selene are mentioned. A dream oracle in the Peloponnese, frequented by ephors from Sparta, was dedicated to Helios (the Sun) and to Pasiphae (the name, meaning "shining on all," is an epithet of the Moon). There was a queen named Pasiphae in Crete, where there are many traces of bull worship. In the myth, this Pasiphae fell in love with a white bull and from their union produced the Minotaur, who was half man and half bull. Another bull brought Europa (whose name, meaning "broad-faced," is another epithet for the Moon) from Phoenicia to Crete.

In Baltic mythology the sun is feminine and the moon masculine. The Balts say that the Sun was once married to the Moon, but he left her for the Morning Star. This so enraged the storm god, the most important Baltic god, that he beat the Moon with his sword, thus reducing the latter's size. The Sun and Moon have many children, the stars, but the Morning Star is a product of a union of the Sun with the storm god himself. The Moon, in shame and anger, avoids his wife, and they never appear together.

In Japan, the Sun, the most important divinity, is feminine; the Moon, her brother, plays only a minor role. Once the Sun ordered the Moon to go down to earth to find out what the goddess of food was doing. When the Moon arrived on earth, the goddess of food, meaning to please him, turned her face toward the land and from her mouth poured out boiled rice; toward the sea, all kinds of fish; and toward the mountains, all kinds of game. The Moon, instead of being pleased, was so enraged that she had offered him things from her mouth that he killed her. Out of her corpse were born the horse, the cow, and the silkworm. Back in Heaven the Sun, angry with her brother for what he had done, said, "I'll see you no more," and so they never meet.

Another myth of plant discovery is told by the Machiganga of Peru. It relates that the Moon gave mortals cultivated plants, giving instructions about them to a mortal girl whom he eventually married. He caused his wife to be fertilized by a fish, and she produced four sons: the daytime Sun, the planet Venus, the Sun Under the Earth (i.e., the sun at night), and the nocturnal Sun, invisible to all but shedding its light on the stars. This fourth child was so hot that he scorched his mother's womb, and she died. The Moon's mother-in-law reproached him, saying that there was nothing left for him to do but to eat the corpse. His wife, disgusted with life on earth, had left her body there and taken her soul to the underworld. The Moon was distressed but obeyed his mother-in-law. Thus the Moon became an eater of corpses and decided to move far away from the earth.

All types of creation myths explain the origin of the moon, usually together with the sun. The cosmic egg motif occurs in the Finnish epic *Kalevala:* the egg falls from heaven onto the knee of the creator goddess as she floats in the cosmic waters, and from it emerge all the aspects of the universe. The sun was made out of the yellow of the egg and the moon out of the white. In Greenland, the Sun and Moon are a mortal pair, sister and brother. In a house with no light they lay together. When the sister discovered that she had committed incest, she tore off her breasts and threw them at her brother; the holes they left became sunspots. Then she flew away and he after her, both carrying torches. The sister's torch burned brighter so she became the sun, and her brother, the moon.

To the type of myth in which the world is created out of the body of a primal being belongs the Huron story of Ataentsic. She was a creation mother goddess who was thrown down from heaven through the hole in the sky she had made by tearing up the world tree. Landing on earth, she gave birth to twins, one good and one evil. The evil son killed her, but the good one made the sun from her face and the moon from her breasts.

In the Aztec pantheon, Huitzilopochtli is a warrior god, culture hero, and the sun. When Mother Earth became pregnant with him (her last child), her other children, the stars, were angry and pursued her to kill her. But one, called Golden Bells, ran ahead to warn her mother. The sun god sprang fully armed from the womb and beheaded Golden Bells. Learning that she had meant well, in compensation he put her head in the sky as the moon, but he chased the other stars away, as the sun does at rising.

The Greek Hesiod (seventh century BCE) describes all creation as the result of sexual union. From the original parents, Earth and Sky, were born twelve Titans, who paired off and produced most of the natural objects as well as the gods. One pair, Theia and Hyperion, become the parents of the Sun (Helios), the Moon (Selene), and the Dawn (Eos). Another pair of Titans became the grandparents of Hekate, goddess of the underworld, and of Artemis, the huntress. Hekate and Artemis later became identified with the moon. In the Homeric *Hymn to the Moon* (sixth century BCE), the Moon has a daughter, Pandia, by Zeus. There was a festival at Athens called the Pandia where round moon cakes were sold and eaten.

In one of the emergence myths characteristic of the southwestern United States, the Pueblo tell how mortals came up in several stages to the surface of the earth. Finding it in darkness, they tossed into the sky the moon and sun, which they had brought with them. A variant of the emergence myth is found in Oceania, in which mankind or the gods are originally enclosed in a shell that they have to pry open. In a Micronesian story, the creator god, Ancient Spider, encased in such a shell, found two snails; after he opened the shell he used the smaller for the moon and the larger for the sun.

In Queensland, the Sun is a woman made by the Moon; although she has two legs, she has a number of arms, which can be seen as the sun's rays. Among the Aranda (Arunta) of Australia, a man of the Opossum totem carried the Moon around with him in a shield, keeping it hidden in a cleft of the rocks all day. One day a man of another totem saw the Moon shining and ran away with it. The Opossum man, unable to catch the thief, called out to the Moon to rise into the sky and shed light on everyone. This it did, and it has remained in the sky ever since.

According to the Pima Indians of North America, the Sun and Moon are parents of Coyote, the famous trickster figure in mythology. In another story, it is Coyote who invents the Sun and Moon. Some Altaic-speaking peoples of Siberia believe that in the beginning there was no sun or moon, but people themselves flew around in the air and gave out light. A high god sent a spirit to help them. Stirring the primeval waters, he found two mirrors, which he set up in the sky as the sun and the moon. Mirrors are often used in rituals by Siberian shamans, and in their out-of-body travels they frequently reach the moon.

The Moon and Death. Because of its monthly disappearance and return, the moon is often connected with the idea of mortal death and rebirth. In the Caroline Islands it is believed that in the beginning men rose from the dead, as did the moon. Every month they fell into a deep sleep when the moon became dark and awoke when the moon returned. An evil spirit disapproved of this and arranged for men to stay dead. In New Zealand, in a similar story, it is the culture hero Maui who wished men to live forever, but the moon said, "No, let them die and become like the soil."

In western Ceram, an island westward of New Guinea, a divine maiden was desired in marriage by the sun god. When her parents, disapproving, put a dead pig in her marriage bed as a substitute for her (perhaps a vestige of a changeover from human to animal sacrifice), the Sun caused her to sink into the ground. The girl called out to her parents, "Slaughter a pig and make a feast. In three days, look into the sky where I will be shining like a light." Thus the feast of the dead was instituted, and mortals for the first time saw the moon rising.

To the Siberian Inuit (Eskimo), death is conceived as loss of one's soul, which travels up to the moon and finally to the sun. This upward flight of the soul through the planets and stars is a widespread motif, found earliest among the Sumerians. It turns up again in Plato's *Republic* and in Cicero's *Somnium scipionis*, where the younger Scipio Africanus dreams he visits his grandfather in the heavens and looks down on all the celestial spheres. Below the moon, his grandfather tells him, all is chaos, but up here all is pure and serene.

The fullest account of the moon as the "abode of souls" is found in the essay *De facie lunae* by Plutarch (second century CE). Pythagorean philosophers had already taught that the Elysian Fields, the Greek isles of the dead, were situated on the sun and moon. In his essay Plutarch describes mortals as consisting of three parts: body, soul, and reason. In death the body is dissolved by Demeter, who stands for Mother Earth. The soul, together with reason, floats upward and, if pure, reaches the moon. If corrupt, it must wander between the earth and the moon until it is purified. The moon is ruled by Persephone, the Greek queen of the underworld, now transferred to the upper spheres. The souls who remain on the moon become beneficent spirits who return to earth to give oracles and help mortals in other ways. Gradually they are dissolved into pure reason and reach the sun.

In one of the earliest Indian Upanisads we are told that there are two roads open to souls after death: the road of flame and the road of smoke. The road of flame leads to the sun and the gods; the road of smoke to the moon, the ancestors, and reincarnation.

In the teaching of Mani, founder of the Manichaeans, the souls of those who have learned the truth during their lives are taken up to the wheel of the sun, where they are purified and passed on to the moon, here described as the superior station. Both of the luminaries are pictured as boats sailing to and fro in the upper atmosphere. When the moon becomes full of souls, it ferries them toward the East to the "aeons of light," who place them in the "pillar of glory," their final resting place. Then the moon, greatly reduced in size, returns for another load of souls.

THE MOON AND THE OCCULT. Witches' meetings are held at the full moon, but the dark of the moon is the time for black sorcery. A practice known as "drawing down the moon" is pictured on Greek vases. In the *Voyage of the Argo* (Apollonius Rhodius, third century BCE), Medea, the priestess of Hekate, is gathering herbs when the Moon addresses her, saying "How often have you disorbed me, making the nights moonless so you might practice your incantations." In this case the Moon would seem to be guiltless in the magic rites.

The lucky rabbit's foot must be taken in the dark of the moon, perhaps because the hare is one of the Moon's animals and she might protect it. According to Aelianos, a Greek writer of the third century CE, the moon causes epilepsy, which may be cured by a special kind of peony that, like the mandrake root, cannot be seen by day but must be gathered at night by tying to it a dog who pulls up the root and then dies (*On Animals* 24). This plant also cures afflictions of the eyes "in which moisture congeals and robs the eyes of their sight." Spells to reunite lovers are especially effective when cast by moonlight. In Theocritus (third century BCE) a lovesick girl calls on the moon for help in her enchantment. The Roman poet Catullus (first century BCE), in his hymn to Diana, calls her Trivia, Lady of the Crossroads (i.e., Hekate), and the "moon with counterfeit light." In the Middle Ages Diana was considered the ruler of witches, together with the "horned god." Pope John XII (tenth century) accused witches of "riding with Diana."

In dream divination, according to Artemidorus (*Interpretation of Dreams*, second century CE), "Intercourse with the Moon is entirely auspicious for shipmasters, pilots, merchants, astronomers, vagabonds and people fond of travelling. But for others it means dropsy. . . . Selene the Moon represents both the wife and mother of the dreamer. She also represents prosperity, business ventures and navigation."

Thoth, the Egyptian god of measure and writing, was appointed by the sun god Re to take his place in the underworld as the moon. Thoth is also the god of magic and spells, like the Greek Hermes. In the Hellenistic period, the two were combined as authors of a series of magico-mystical writings under the name of Hermes Trismegistos.

In the astrology that took form in Alexandria around the second century BCEas a combination of Near Eastern star lore and Greek mathematics, the moon, "when at its northern or southern limits helps in the direction of greater versatility, resourcefulness and capacity for change; in its rising, toward greater natural endowments, firmness and frankness; in its waning, towards dullness, less fixity of purpose and less renown" (Ptolemy, *Tetrabiblos*, second century CE).

In modern astrology, the moon "stands for the feminine, indrawn, receptive, and imaginative side. It tends toward carefulness, prudence, timidity, shyness, and the secluded life, though the lunar person is shrewd and practical in business" (Charles E. Carter, *Principles of Astrology*, London, 1969, p. 50).

THE MOON IN FOLKLORE. Almost universal are cautions and devices to take advantage of the beneficent (and to avoid the unlucky) aspects of the moon, as well as theories to explain the moon spots. It has seemed an obvious ritual to farmers all over the world to plant during the waxing moon and reap during the waning moon, and this is still done in many parts of the United States. In pre-revolutionary France the law required trees to be felled during the waxing moon so that their wood would be drier. Hair, on the other hand, should be cut at the waning moon to make it thick. In England, shingles laid during the waning moon tend to swell. All over Europe, money, especially silver, the moon's metal, is exposed to the waxing moon or turned over in the pocket to make it grow. In Uganda, potters wait for the waxing moon before firing their pots. Warts are everywhere believed to grow as the moon waxes and to decrease at the wane.

Some Muslims in India practice a ritual called "drinking the moon." They fill a silver basin with water, let it reflect the light of the full moon, and drink it at a gulp as a remedy for palpitations and nervous disorders. Mothers in many places present their babies to the full moon so they will grow. In New Guinea, men on a hunting expedition leave their women at home to sing to the new moon for the success of the hunt. Natives of Greenland believe that women can become pregnant from sleeping in the light of the full moon. To prevent this, women wipe their abdomens with spittle. Weddings are variously believed to be lucky if held at the full moon or at the dark of the moon. The latter is explained by Plutarch (*De facie lunae*), who claimed that the moon rushed to conjunction with the sun so that she might be refreshed by his light.

There are innumerable explanations for the spots that the West calls the "Man in the Moon." Some South American Indians believe they are ashes or menstrual blood smeared on the (male) Moon when he raped his sister the Sun. The Selk'nam of South America say they are the results of a beating the (female) Moon received when the Sun discovered that she had disclosed her initiation rites. The same spots are often described as a hare, a frog, a snail, or some other animal or as some mortal lured up to the moon. In Scandinavian mythology they are a boy and girl carrying water, supposed to be the prototypes of Jack and Jill. The Shawnee Indians see in the spots their creator goddess bending over a cooking pot. Among the Malay, they are an old man making a fishing line under a banyan tree. At the other end of the line is a rat, who is eating the line as fast as the man can make it. When the old man is finished, he will use the line to catch everything on the earth and reel it up to the moon.

There is widespread belief that the light of the full moon turns humans who are so disposed into werewolves and causes lunacy if one sleeps in its beams. Very common in Europe and America is the idea that, during the night of the full moon, more crimes are committed, more children are born, and more patients committed to mental hospitals than at other times.

SEE ALSO Feminine Sacrality.

BIBLIOGRAPHY

Since there are few books devoted to the religious and mythological aspects of the moon, most information on the subject must be extracted from religious writings and from histories of the religions of different areas. The most important source for ancient Mesopotamia and Egypt is volume 1 of *The Ancient Near East,* edited by James B. Pritchard (Princeton, 1973). For the origin of the calendar, an excellent account is Elias J. Bickerman's *Chronology in the Ancient World* (Ithaca, N.Y., 1968). By far the most complete book on the development of astrology is still Auguste Bouché-Leclerq's *L'astrologie grecque* (Paris, 1899). Franz Cumont's *Recherche sur le symbolisme funeraire des Romains* contains an unusual amount of data on alien sects of the Hellenistic and Roman periods. An essay by Mircea Eliade entitled "The Moon and Its Mystique," in *Patterns in Comparative Religion* (New York, 1958), provides many insights into the symbolism and iconography of the moon. The same author's *Shamanism: Archaic Techniques of Ecstasy,* rev. & enl. ed. (New York, 1964), gives a background for the religions of Siberia and the American Indians. For folklore on the moon a good source is the Funk and Wagnall's *Dictionary of Folklore, Mythology and Legend* (New York, 1950). Åke Hultkrantz, in *Religions of the American Indians* (Los Angeles, 1979), gives a concise but thorough summary of the beliefs of the Indians of North and South America. The most recent and fullest account of the religions of the Near East is found in Thorkild Jacobsen's *The Treasures of Darkness: A History of Mesopotamian Religion* (New Haven, 1976). The best, most complete book on the subject of the moon is *La lune: Mythes et rites,* edited by Denise Berndt (Paris, 1962), with essays by separate authors on various areas of the world. Some new insights and original research appear in Julius Lewy's "The Late Assyro-Babylonian Cult of the Moon and Its Culmination at the Time of Nabonidus," *Hebrew Union College Annual* (1945–1946): 405–489. An extremely useful collection of material from all over the world is *The Mythology of All Races,* 13 vols., edited by Louis Herbert Gray and George Foot Moore (Boston, 1916–1932), under the auspices of the Archaeological Institute of America. Martin P. Nilsson brings to his *Geschichte der griechischen Religion* (Munich, 1955) a wealth of information on archaeology and comparative religion. Still the most complete collection of mythological material is *Ausführliches Lexikon der griechischen und römischen Mythologie,* 7 vols. in 10, edited by W. H. Roscher (1866–1893; Hildesheim, 1965). The series "Sacred Books of the East" (1879–1910), containing the sacred writings of India and Persia collected by F. Max Müller, was reissued at Delhi in 1965.

New Sources

Beaulieu, Paul-Alain. "The Babylonian Man in the Moon." *Journal of Cuneiform Studies* 51 (1999): 91–99.

Keel, Othmar. *Goddesses and Trees, New Moon and Yahweh: Ancient Near Eastern Art and the Hebrew Bible.* Sheffield, U.K., 1998.

Komaroff, Katherine. *Sky Gods: The Sun and Moon in Art and Myth.* New York, 1974.

López Austin, Alfredo. *Rabbit on the Face of the Moon: Mythology in the Mesoamerican Tradition.* Salt Lake City, 1996.

Neyrolles, Olivier. *Lune (Moon).* Paris, 1999.

Ornan, Tallay. "The Bull and Its Two Masters: Moon and Storm Dieties in Relation to the Bull in Ancient Near Eastern Art." *Israel Exploration Journal* 51/1 (2001): 1–26.

Sermonetti, Giuseppe. *Fiabe di luna: simboli lunari nella favola, nel mito, nella scienza (Moon stories: moon symbols in fable, myth and science).* Milan, 1986.

Theuer, Gabriele. *Der Mondgott in den Religionen Syrien-Palästinas.* Freiburg, Switzerland, 2000.

JEAN RHYS BRAM (1987)
Revised Bibliography

MOORE, GEORGE FOOT.

MOORE, GEORGE FOOT. George Foot Moore (1851–1931) was an American scholar of Hebrew scriptures, Judaism, and the history of religions. Born of Scottish-Irish ancestry in West Chester, Pennsylvania, Moore received his B.A. degree from Yale University (1872) and his B.D. degree from Union Theological Seminary, New York (1877). Following ordination as a Presbyterian clergyman (1878), he served a five-year pastorate in Zanesville, Ohio. Moore's academic career began with his appointment as professor of Hebrew language and literature at Andover Theological Seminary (1883). Moore became professor of theology at Harvard University (1902) and later professor of the history of religions there (1904), a position in which he remained until his retirement in 1928.

Moore's reputation in biblical studies was established with the publication of *A Critical and Exegetical Commentary on Judges* (1895) and *The Literature of the Old Testament* (1913). His *Judaism in the First Centuries of the Christian Era, the Age of Tannaim* (1927–1930) is still the finest description of the religion of the rabbis of the Mishnah in existence. Moore's work is in line with the then regnant paradigm among Jewish scholars (e.g., Solomon Schechter, Louis Ginzberg) for study of the Pharisees/rabbis. This approach focused primarily upon the religion and literature of the Rabbinic elite and its construction of Judaism. *Judaism in the First Centuries of the Christian Era* has been criticized by more recent scholars, principally Morton Smith and his school, for treating the rabbis as representative of what Morton Smith called "Normative Judaism," without focusing on the mystical, magical, or apocalyptic in Judaism beyond the rabbis. Morton Smith's approach is well in line with Moore's general interest in religious elites.

Moore's two-volume *History of Religions* (1913–1919) filled the need for a new handbook on the history of religions with the unity and continuity that single authorship could provide. In this work, Moore limits his treatment to the religions of the "civilized" peoples, omitting any discussion of "primitive" (i.e., tribal) religions. Moore's treatment of the various religions manifests an impressive capacity to master the best current scholarship. Two uncritical assumptions underlie his work, neither of which was uncommon in his day: an evolutionary theory concerning the development of religion and a basic methodological distinction between the religions of "civilized peoples" and "other" (i.e., "primitive" or tribal) religions.

His contributions as a historian of religions were marked by two notable qualities. First, he demonstrated the possibility of pursuing work in the history of religions in a manner that was characterized by openness to the richness of diverse religious traditions (among the "civilized" peoples) on the one hand and by disciplined scholarship on the other. Second, it was singularly important to the study of religion in North America that, even though most work in comparative religion and the history of religions had tended to focus attention on religious traditions other than Judaism and Christianity, his *History of Religions* extended equivalence of treatment and analytical criticism to these "higher" religions. This approach was significant for the development of the study of religion in America and in the communal realm for the ecumenical movement between Christians and Jews.

Moore made frequent contributions to scholarly journals, writing almost forty articles for the *Encyclopedia Biblica* (1899–1903) alone. He was instrumental in the establishment of the *Harvard Theological Review,* contributed to it often, and twice was its editor (1908–1914 and 1921–1931). Moore held presidencies in such notable professional societies as the American Academy of Arts and Sciences (of which he was a fellow), the American Oriental Society, the Society of Biblical Literature and Exegesis, and the Massachusetts Historical Society.

BIBLIOGRAPHY

Bibliographical information concerning Moore can be found in W. W. Fenn's "George Foot Moore: A Memoir," *Proceedings of the Massachusetts Historical Society* 64 (February 1932). The most profound reader and interpreter of Moore was Morton Smith. See Smith's discussion of this scholar in *Harvard Library Bulletin,* 15 (1967), 169–179.

Major Works by Moore

A Critical and Exegetical Commentary on Judges. New York, 1895. This important volume of the International Critical Commentary is still useful and demonstrates Moore's reputation as a careful and diligent scholar of the Hebrew Bible.

The Literature of the Old Testament. New York, 1913. This modest volume in the Home University Library series presents in lucid and concise form both a discourse on the sources, formation, and structure of the Pentateuch and a discussion of every book of the Hebrew Bible, informed by the most careful scholarship of the period and intended for the general reader.

History of Religions. 2 vols. New York, 1913–1919. Volume one discusses the religions of China, Japan, Egypt, Babylonia, Assyria, India, ancient Greece, ancient Rome, and Persia, while volume two discusses Judaism, Christianity, and Islam. Moore's succinct survey of major religious traditions is informed by his mastery of the most competent scholarship in each field and by his special competence in Christianity and Judaism. The approach is characterized more by an interest in the history and thought of each tradition than by a consideration of their sociological and anthropological aspects. A remarkable accomplishment in its time, the work has enduring value.

The Birth and Growth of Religion. New York, 1923. This publication of the Morse Lectures of 1922 presents Moore's theory that religion is grounded in the universal impulse for self-preservation and is developed in an evolutionary fashion, ultimately manifesting an aspiration for self-realization.

"The Rise of Normative Judaism: To the Reorganization of Jamnia." *Harvard Theological Review* 17 (October 1924): 307–373.

"The Rise of Normative Judaism: To the Close of the Mishnah." *Harvard Theological Review* 18 (January 1925): 1–38.

Judaism in the First Centuries of the Christian Era, the Age of Tannaim. 3 vols. Cambridge, Mass., 1927–1930. This introduction to the religion of the early rabbis has not been surpassed.

F. Stanley Lusby (1987)
Steven Fine (2005)

MORALITY AND RELIGION. In the minds of many people, the terms *morality* and *religion* signal two related but distinct ideas. Morality is thought to pertain to the conduct of human affairs and relations between persons, while religion primarily involves the relationship between human beings and a transcendent reality. In fact, this distinction between religion and morality is a relatively modern one. Although tension between religion and morality is already evident in the writings of Plato and other Greek philosophers, the popular modern conception that religion and morality are separate phenomena is probably traceable to the Enlightenment. At that time, a number of thinkers, reflecting Europe's weariness with centuries of religious strife, sought to elaborate ethical theories based on reason or on widely shared human sentiments. In so doing they established the assumption that the norms governing conduct, morality, and ethics (that is, the effort to reason about or justify these norms) were separable from matters of religious belief.

This same cultural context also gave rise to a number of efforts to explain the relationship between morality and religion. Since it was now possible to conceive ways of thinking and acting morally that were not dependent upon religious revelation, it became natural to ask why these two phenomena have usually been so closely linked in human history. Answers to this question were diverse, but they might be broadly divided between those that were friendly to religion and those that were hostile. Kant's thinking epitomized the views of those who believed that religion and morality are mutually necessary: although he was willing to criticize religious excesses and fanaticism, he was convinced that belief in a God who rewards the righteous and punishes the wicked was necessary to ensure full moral commitment.

In the hands of thinkers less friendly to religion, this claim—that religion involves the assumption of a morally governed world—became the simpler assertion that religion represents the effort to buttress morality by adding to its ordinary social sanctions a concocted series of supernaturally mediated rewards and punishments. This was not a new idea. It had already been stated in antiquity by some Greek, Roman, and Chinese philosophers. Although compatible with a respect for religious belief, it generally laid the foundation for a series of stinging critiques of traditional religion. Since morality could be understood in human or rational terms, it seemed to follow that the use of religious sanctions to support moral conduct was appropriate only where primitive, gullible, or morally weak persons were involved. By this reasoning, religion was at best useful during an early stage of human cultural evolution where it provided the "matrix" for moral concepts; in time, it was bound to be replaced by more rational modes of thought.

Some thinkers doubted the usefulness of religion in any context. A social critic like Marx, for example, viewed religion as the effort to support the moral norms and codes of privileged strata and ruling groups, while also masking worldly wrongs with the false allure of otherworldly rewards. Marx did not usually justify this view and his opposition to religion in moral terms. Indeed, he was equally critical of the moral systems and moral philosophies of his day, believing that they, too, were deeply involved with and compromised by the social and material conditions of the era. Yet, in many ways his attitude toward religion is similar to that of the critical Enlightenment philosophers: religion is to be rejected because it is ultimately opposed to the development of full human freedom and moral responsibility.

Decades later, Freud makes this point even more explicitly in *The Future of an Illusion* (1927), arguing that religion must be put aside because it undermines moral responsibility and encourages fanaticism. Individuals or groups whose only reason for being moral is fear of supernatural punishments cannot be counted upon to respect other persons once these fears lose their hold, as they inevitably must before the advance of reason. Furthermore, religious promises of forgiveness of sin and absolution are an encouragement to morally irresponsible behavior. For a mature and morally healthy world to emerge, Freud concluded, men and women of good will must meet together on the common ground of reason and atheism.

Not surprisingly, criticisms of this sort engendered a reaction. Often accepting the claim that religion and morality were only problematically linked, thinkers more sympathetic to religion like Friedrich Schleiermacher or Rudolf Otto sought to develop an abiding place for religion independent of its moral significance. Schleiermacher found this in the emotional state of "God-consciousness," while Otto found it in an essentially nonmoral sense of awe before the mysterious and transcendent. This reaction probably reached its zenith in the writings of Søren Kierkegaard, particularly in *Fear and Trembling* (1843). Although Kierkegaard was fully appreciative of the value of morality, he believed that religious faith ultimately transcended ordinary human moral considerations. In the story of God's command to Abraham to sacrifice Isaac, Kierkegaard discerned a "teleological suspension of the ethical," according to which morality was essentially subordinated to religious concerns. "Duty," he concluded, "is precisely the will of God."

Theoretical Assumptions of Western Ethical Theory To an outside observer, these debates among Western philosophers and theologians concerning the relationship between religion and morality may seem culture-bound. The emergence of ethics as a separate field of inquiry, the effort to distinguish morality from religion, and the countervailing effort to reassert a place for religion in human life all arise from a very particular cultural and social context. Nevertheless, the fact that systematic thinking about ethics emerged in the West, and that it generated a series of divergent explorations of the relationship between religion and morality, does not mean that this thinking or aspects of these views have no validity across cultural lines. The physical sciences, too, have been most fully developed in the Western context, but the value of their findings, and even of their different hypotheses, is not limited to this setting. In trying to understand the relationship between religion and morality, therefore, it may be useful to employ concepts and approaches developed over the past centuries by Western philosophers, theologians, and social scientists. If one keeps in mind that concepts or ideas developed in a Western context are at best tentative efforts to penetrate complex realities and that they may not be wholly applicable to moral and religious traditions elsewhere, this approach can provide an interpretive guide through diverse religious and moral traditions.

Definitions of Religion and Morality. Surveying the modern body of thinking about religion and morality, one can identify a number of distinctive ideas. Foremost among these is an idea already mentioned: that morality and religion, however intertwined, are at least conceptually distinct phenomena. Religion involves beliefs, attitudes, and practices that relate human beings to supernatural agencies or sacred realities. It addresses what has been called the problem of interpretability, which includes such persistent questions as the ultimate nature and purpose of the natural world and the meaning of death and suffering. In contrast, morality has usually been thought of as a way of regulating the conduct of individuals in communities. It represents a response to the problem of cooperation among competing persons or groups and aims at settling disputes that may arise in social contexts.

Force also represents a method of adjudicating conflict, but morality differs from force by appealing to principles or rules of conduct that are regarded as legitimate, that is, as having a justification potentially acceptable to each member of the community. The complex interrelationship between religion and morality is illustrated by the fact that moral legitimation may sometimes involve appeal to shared beliefs involving the supernatural or the sacred. But this is not a necessary aspect of moral justification, which can appeal to reason or to considerations of human welfare.

The Superiority and Logical Independence of Moral Norms. Philosophical analysis has also led to a series of more specific ideas about morality and ethics. For example, moral norms are regarded as among the most authoritative guides to conduct. This means that the dictates of morality are superior to and take precedence over self-oriented, or "prudential," considerations. The fact that something is morally wrong is thus held to be a sufficient grounds for refraining from doing it. Moral philosophers have disagreed over the questions of whether self-interest may play any role in moral decision and whether moral rules may ever be qualified or suspended to protect oneself or those one personally cares for. They have also disagreed over the larger question of whether these rules are absolute or permit exceptions. But that the dictates of morality have considerable authoritativeness and superiority is widely acknowledged.

A tradition of philosophical analysis, beginning with Plato's dialogue *Euthyphro* and culminating in the writings of Kant, has also insisted on the logical independence of moral norms and their conceptual priority over religious and other requirements. According to this line of thinking, human reason and conscience must be the final arbiter of right and wrong. Even religious norms and divine commands must be tested by the "autonomous" individual conscience. Recent discussions by philosophers and theologians have softened the contours of this view. Early rationalist claims that, to be acceptable, every religious command or requirement must conform to existing moral beliefs have been replaced by a recognition that religious teachings, in a dialogue with reasoned morality, can instruct and inform conscience. But the point made by Plato centuries ago, that human reason is the final forum of judgment, is still widely accepted, since to subordinate reason to other considerations is to renounce the very possibility of rational discourse and justification.

The Universality of Moral Norms. The writings of Western moral philosophers also reveal broad lines of agreement about the nature and content of morality. By and large, for example, these thinkers have not been impressed by the position known as "ethical relativism," which holds that basic moral principles or modes of reasoning differ substantially from culture to culture. While ethicists do acknowledge the truth of "cultural relativism," the view that accepted or prohibited modes of conduct vary among cultures, they have pointed out that this does not necessarily mean that fundamental principles are dissimilar. Different technical and social situations can cause common basic principles to yield different results in specific circumstances. For example, a general principle of respect for parents may produce a stringent ban on parricide in a technically advanced civilization but may lead to a custom of abandoning infirm or very elderly parents in hunter-gatherer cultures where there is no provision for sustaining the disabled and where dependency is regarded by all as shameful.

In contrast to the position of ethical relativism, most Western philosophers have subscribed to the essential universality of moral principles. This understanding, in fact, has several important meanings. First, it implies the descriptive point just made: at their most basic level, very similar basic moral rules and principles are understood and respected by human beings everywhere. Second, it implies the normative claim that not only is this so but that it ought to be so. There is a universal standard of morality to which all persons are accountable. This standard is sensitive enough to the reality of specific circumstances to justify broad tolerance of differing social practices, but even so there are limits. Thus, where a strict ethical relativist might conclude that "right" and "wrong" are definable only by the norms of a particular culture, nonrelativists have pointed out that certain cultural practices are so heinous that they cannot be judged morally acceptable without violating human beings' deepest moral self-understanding. For example, the fact that some societies have practiced genocide against minorities in their midst cannot be thought of as making this conduct right. Some things are wrong no matter how widely they are accepted in particular societies. Finally, morality has been regarded as universal in the sense that its rules and protection extend to all who are human. Precisely because it is a reasoned method of settling social disputes and, hence, superior to force or coercion, moral discourse remains the preferred method of relating to all who are capable of this method of social adjudication. G. J. Warnock has expressed the logic behind this view:

> If conduct is to be seen as regulated only *within* groups, we have still the possibility of unrestricted hostility and conflict *between* groups—which is liable, indeed, to be effectively ferocious and damaging in proportion as relations between individuals within each group are effectively ordered toward harmonious co-operative action. Thus, just as one may think that a Hobbesian recipe for 'peace' could securely achieve its end only if all Hobbesian individuals were engrossed within a single irresistible Leviathan, there is reason to think that the principles of morality must, if the object of morality is not to be frustrated, give consideration to *any* human, of whatever special group or none he may in fact be a member. (Warnock, 1971, p. 150)

Warnock and other philosophers who share this view would of course concede that it has more often been honored in the breach than in practice, but we shall soon see that the theoretical assumption that morality embraces the entire human community has special importance for the understanding of religious ethics.

The Moral Rules. Moral philosophers also display wide agreement on the most fundamental rules of morality. These include rules prohibiting persons from killing other persons, from inflicting injury on them, or from depriving them of freedom and opportunity. Other rules prohibit deception or the breaking of promises. All these rules presume that the recipient of the action in question has not voluntarily consented to it. Thus, a surgeon is not regarded as wronging a patient by cutting into his flesh, nor is a stage actor regarded as practicing immoral deception. In addition, these rules are clearly held to apply only where the persons affected by one's choice have not acted immorally in a way that necessitates breaking a rule with respect to them. While killing others or depriving them of their freedom is ordinarily viewed as wrong, for example, it may be justified when individuals threaten harm to others, as in criminal conduct or aggressive war.

These rules for personal conduct constitute only the minimum requirement for moral conduct. They are largely negative in character, prohibiting certain forms of behavior but not requiring positive efforts on others' behalf. In addition to this, however, ethicists recognize supererogatory actions, performance of which is an occasion for moral praise but omission of which does not ordinarily merit condemnation or blame. These actions include forms of mutual aid, generosity, and self-sacrifice. Along with respect for the basic rules, attention to these supererogatory requirements is ordinarily held to enter into the character ideals or standards of virtue that form part of a full system of ethics. Such ideals are separate from, but conceptually dependent upon, the understanding of right acts, since virtuous individuals are those who can be counted upon habitually to do what is right. Kant's famous statement that the only thing that can be called "good without qualification" is the morally good will is not meant to identify the norm of right or wrong conduct (for that, Kant believed, the test of the categorical imperative is required); rather, it is directed to the assessment of individual moral worth. In this connection, it is important to note that the intention of the agent plays a major role in evaluating conduct in terms of such character ideals. Since it is pointless to hold individuals morally responsible for the unforeseeable or uncontrollable consequences of their actions, the moral worth of persons is usually assessed in terms of what they intended to do, although morally acceptable intentions are ordinarily held to encompass reasonable prevision for consequences.

While moral theorists are widely agreed on at least the basic principles governing individual conduct and defining individual virtue, there is far less agreement on the norms or principles that ought to guide the conduct of social and economic institutions. At least for the context of industrialized societies, various competing theories have been advanced to justify everything from laissez-faire through welfare state societies to fully socialist and egalitarian systems. This is no place to settle a debate that continues to be one of the most heated in contemporary moral literature. It is important to note, however, that the very basic condition that moral principles be potentially acceptable to all persons tends to support views acknowledging a significant degree of social responsibility toward those who, through no fault of their own, are seriously disadvantaged. Thus, even thinkers who minimize society's responsibility for social justice tend to endorse efforts to ensure equal opportunity and hardship relief.

The "Moral Point of View." Behind these specific rules, many philosophers have also discerned a way of reasoning that is basic to moral judgment. This involves, first of all, an element of imaginative empathy for the other persons affected by one's choices and a willingness to consider the impact of one's conduct on their welfare. In addition, it calls for a willingness to reason about moral choices in an impartial way, as though the agent were only one interest among all of those affected by a choice. This perspective of impartiality is sometimes called "the moral point of view." Various moral theories have tried to integrate this way of thinking into decision procedures for moral choice. Views that derive moral decisions from the presumed judgments of an ideal sympathetic spectator and those that see such choices as arising from the decisions of self-interested but impartial contractors are examples.

Why Should One Be Moral? Delineation and justification of the moral rules have been the principal focuses of most moral theory. Yet, beyond specific normative issues, a series of persisting questions has stood at the far side of ethical discussion and has been dealt with increasingly by ethicists, as the nature and content of the moral reasoning process have become better understood. One of the most important of these questions is why one should be moral. Because this question can easily be misunderstood, its full significance and the difficulty of answering it may not be appreciated. If it is asked in the sense of why people in general should think and act morally, why morality itself should exist, then, to answer the question, it is necessary only to point to the general usefulness of morality as a method of settling social disputes. In this sense morality is in everyone's interests. Again, if one who has adopted the moral viewpoint of impartiality and empathy for others asks why he or she should obey the moral rules, then it is necessary only to point out that impartial persons would certainly advocate obeying the rules they would choose. But if this question is asked in its sharpest sense of why one should adopt the moral point of view in the first place, it becomes exceedingly difficult to answer. This is especially true whenever acting morally occasions serious loss for the individual agent.

Some philosophers have tried to answer this question in terms of the demonstrable longterm interest and welfare of the moral agent: they have argued that it is, by and large, advantageous to be a morally upright person and disadvantageous to be an immoral one. They point to the social and psychic costs that openly immoral conduct or covert and hypocritical behavior can entail. But others have rejected this approach either on the grounds that it is often not correct (immoral people sometimes do very well) or because it introduces essentially nonmoral motives into one's reasons for being moral. Some who argue this way have contended that no self-interested reasons should be given for being moral: that one's decisions to be moral must rest on a respect for moral reasoning requiring no further justification. For these thinkers the voice of duty, in the words of George Eliot, is "peremptory and absolute." Still others, rejecting both the appeal to personal advantage and the claim that no further justification need be given, have stressed the importance of various metaphysical or religious views in grounding, explaining, and justifying commitment to the moral life. These thinkers have argued that without at least some metaphysical or religious basis moral striving makes no sense. This basis may range from the minimal belief that morality is not pointless or futile, that one's efforts do make a difference, to the stronger belief that, however much it may appear true that good people suffer for their commitments, moral acts and dispositions are, in the ultimate scheme of things, acknowledged and rewarded.

It is noteworthy that discussion of the question "Why should one be moral?" returns ethics to basic matters of religious belief. Hence, the separation of ethical theory from theology and philosophy of religion, which ethical theorists effected during the modern period, has to some extent been reconsidered. It is interesting that this development was anticipated strongly in the work of Kant. To be sure, Kant is well known for his emphasis on the rational accessibility of moral norms and for his insistence that moral commitment must be autonomous, in the sense that it must be based on respect for the dictates of reason and conscience rather than on norms imposed from without and enforced by external rewards or punishments. Nevertheless, Kant's later writings, especially the *Critique of Practical Reason* (1788) and *Religion within the Limits of Reason Alone* (1793), were focused largely on questions concerning the philosophy of religion. In these writings, Kant developed the position that, to make sense, moral striving requires belief in a morally intentioned governor of the universe (this was Kant's "moral proof" of the existence of God), and he began to explore the relationship between ethics and themes in biblical theology. Foremost among these were the issues of sin, repentance, and the possibility of moral righteousness. Kant's discussions here are dense, but it can be said that, in perceiving the need to ground moral commitment in voluntarily assumed religious beliefs, Kant also recognized the difficulty of providing any clear and incontestable rational justification for being moral. Thus his work highlighted the difficulty of sustaining moral commitment and opened up, as never before, the prospect of rational persons' defecting from morality. Discussing this problem under the rubric of the "radical evil" of the human heart, Kant introduced themes that were later developed by Christian theologians like Kierkegaard, Barth, and Niebuhr.

MORAL THEORY AND RELIGIOUS TRADITIONS This body of reasoned reflection on basic issues in morality and ethics provides a useful background for exploring the variety of concrete traditions of religious ethics. Regarded superficially, these traditions display a bewildering variety of teachings and beliefs, making difficult any general conclusions about the relationship between religion and the moral life. But when they are assessed against the framework of concepts just presented, religious traditions display some common patterns. Moreover, identifying these common patterns also helps highlight some of the important differences between traditions. In approaching these concrete traditions with the framework of ethical assumptions as a guide, one should keep in mind one other important consideration: religious traditions are not static entities that display finished form at any moment in time; rather, like most human creations, they develop in the course of history. In his book *Beyond Belief* (1970), the sociologist Robert Bellah has suggested that religious evolution, like the evolution of other complex systems, often involves movement from simplicity to greater differentiation of structure (pp. 20–50). In terms of moral ideas, this suggests a development of greater sensitivity to the full gamut of specific issues and questions identified by systematic ethical theory. We shall see that questions or distinctions barely occurring to thinkers or writers within a tradition during its earliest phases emerge as important issues later in the tradition's life. In addition to looking at traditions synchronically in terms of their structure at any given moment, therefore, we must also look at them diachronically over the course of their development.

The Superiority of Moral Norms and Independence of Moral Reasoning. As we look at the variety of religio-ethical traditions, it is striking that a sense of the distinction between religious, ethical, and even legal norms is often not present, and that when it is, it is often a late development. Furthermore, because the very distinctions are lacking, traditions do not always assert the superiority of moral norms over specifically ritual or religious requirements. This does not mean that these ideas are not present; often they are implicit and can be discerned only by a careful examination of how conflicts between norms are handled.

As I have already observed, most historical traditions tend to see the normative structures bearing on human life as an integrated whole, wherein moral requirements are fused with religious, ritual, and legal norms. In this respect it is often strained to speak of Jewish, Hindu, or Islamic "ethics." In Judaism, for example, the sacred norms for human life constitute *halakhah.* Incompletely understood as "law," *halakhah* is more properly thought of as sacred teaching or guidance, although it is also "law" in the sense that many of its specific requirements were upheld by public sanctions and punishments, when Jews were politically able to govern themselves. In all, *halakhah* discusses 613 specific commandments or normative prescriptions identified by commentators in scripture, including the Ten Commandments. While this body of norms does contain many requirements that are recognizably "moral," these are not clearly distinguished from what we would identify as ritual or religious norms. At a fairly late date in the development of the tradition, commentators would puzzle over why specific ritual commandments (for example, the requirement that only the ashes of a red heifer be used in a specific ritual of expiation) had been placed on a par with obviously important moral norms. But the early tradition tends not to make distinctions of this sort, and even later commentators who were rooted in this tradition agreed that all the norms of *halakhah* were equally sacred and equally incumbent upon the pious Jew. What is true for Judaism in this case, however, may also be said for *sharīʿah* in the Muslim tradition or *dharma* in the Hindu and Buddhist traditions. In each case we have a legal-moral-religious teaching containing the totality of enjoined actions in an undifferentiated unity.

Neither can it be said that many traditions display ethical theorizing in the contemporary sense of an effort to work out and to justify moral norms in rational terms. Commentators on early Christian ethics have noted the striking difference between the tone of early Christian ethical writing and that of the surrounding Greco-Roman world. Whereas Greek and Roman thinkers were concerned with such questions as what constitutes "the good" for man and what patterns of conduct are most conducive to individual and communal well-being, Christian writers commonly established rules for conduct by citing biblical commandments, or by holding up as models for behavior exemplary persons in scripture. Throughout, it is the hope for God's approval (or the avoidance of his wrath) that is pointed to as the principal reason for living a Christian life. As is also true for Judaism and Islam, not human reason but God's will remains the source and sanction for moral conduct.

It is true that in our era each of the biblically based traditions has developed bodies of systematic ethical reflection, and it is also possible today to find treatises on Buddhist, Hindu, or Jain ethics. Yet the separation of moral reasoning from other dimensions of the religious life is largely alien to all these traditions. In Judaism, Christianity, and Islam, the appearance of ethical theorizing initially represents a response to the authority of Greek and Roman philosophy. Thus, some of the earliest thinking about the relationship between religious and rational norms in these traditions—as for instance Sa'adyah Gaon's *Book of Beliefs and Opinions* (933 CE) and Thomas Aquinas's discussion of the forms of the law in his *Summa theologiae* (2.1.90–97)—emerges during the medieval period, when classical philosophy was rediscovered. Similarly, modern efforts to develop statements of Jewish, Christian, or Islamic ethics are very much a response to initiatives in philosophical ethical theory. The authority of Western thought has had a corresponding effect in stimulating thinkers in African and Asian religious traditions to develop systematic approaches to ethics. But in all these cases, writers are usually compelled to begin their discussions with the observation that the moral teachings of their tradition are inseparable from its theological, metaphysical, or ritual dimensions.

Are we to conclude, then, that the separation of ethics from these other aspects of religion is only a Western phenomenon, and one largely traceable to the classical philosophers of Greece and Rome? It is true that systematic, rational thinking about morality—ethics in the modern sense—does emerge primarily in the Greco-Roman world, although one might also speak of ancient Chinese ethics in this sense. Interestingly, in both these cases it was partly the breakdown of an older religious ideal that prompted rational reflection on the human good (a theme we shall return to later). But while ethical theorizing per se may be culturally localized, a sense of the independence, special significance, and even superiority of moral norms with respect to other normative requirements is present throughout many of these diverse traditions.

Criticism of purely ritual efforts to please God, for example, is one of the hallmarks of the Hebrew prophetic tradition. *Amos* 5:21ff. gives classic expression to the theme: "I hate, I despise your feasts, and take no delight in your solemn assemblies. . . . But let justice roll down like waters, and righteousness like an ever-flowing stream." In less impassioned but equally serious tones, Confucius would criticize members of the Chinese elite who believed that Heaven was satisfied with outward displays of piety and ritual in lieu of sincere efforts at righteousness and benevolence: "A man who is not good, what can he have to do with ritual? A man who is not good, what can he have to do with music?" (*Analects* 3.3). Neither the prophets nor Confucius, of course, would eliminate ritual from the life they believed human beings were called to live. For both traditions of thought, a fulfilled human existence was a moral and religious whole. But their opposition to efforts to reduce morality to one lesser aspect of the religious life evidences their sensitivity to the importance and relative priority of the moral norms.

This point could be further illustrated within a number of diverse traditions, but it becomes even clearer when we survey the historical development of religious thought. Not only do traditions tend to highlight moral requirements as they develop over time, but major religious controversies and schisms giving rise to new religious traditions usually effect dramatic ethicization of aspects of the older traditions, thus indicating how important the issue is for diverse religious communities. Many examples from the history of religions could be given: early Christianity's prophetic denunciation of Jewish religious observance and its replacement of the many ritual requirements of Jewish law with a simplified set of primarily moral norms; Protestantism's revolt against Catholic sacramentalism and against the idea that God's favor could be won by religious observance devoid of moral or religious sincerity; Buddhism's deliberate rejection of the heavily ritualized Indian caste order, and its replacement of that order with an ethicized hierarchy based on moral and spiritual attainment; and Daoism's repudiation of alleged Confucian formalism in the name of a simplified religious and moral ideal of spontaneous selflessness.

To be sure, each of these important moments of religious change involves more than moral reform (nor are the allegations of the "reformist" tradition always correct). But it is noteworthy that in each of these cultural contexts the effort to highlight and assert the priority of the moral norms is of such urgency that it could well be an important contributing factor to major religious change. It is also noteworthy that in these quite different contexts change is always unidirectional; religions do not efface the distinction between religious and moral norms as they develop, nor do they subordinate moral requirements over time. On the contrary, just as a theoretical appreciation of the importance of moral norms would suggest, traditions move toward greater clarity about the distinctiveness and relative superiority of moral requirements.

One final matter deserves attention: the claim that the basic derivation of norms in some traditions is religious, not moral. The supreme guide to conduct in these traditions, it is said, is God's command, and because this command is not always moral, these traditions are fundamentally opposed to any idea of the distinctiveness or superiority of moral norms. This viewpoint is associated with forms of divine command ethics in Judaism, Christianity, and Islam. Many believe it finds its strongest biblical support in God's command to Abraham to sacrifice his son Isaac (*Gn.* 22:1–19).

In fact, the issue of divine command ethics is a complicated one. Theoretical defenses of this position (as voiced by al-Ghazali in Islam and by William of Ockham, Duns Scotus, and Kierkegaard in Christianity) usually arise in contexts where the very authority of the tradition is under attack by rationalist critics. These defenses may seek less to represent the tradition in its integrity, therefore, than to place it beyond assault. Examined with less apologetic interests in mind, the traditions themselves do not necessarily support the religiously authoritarian reading they are given. While biblically based traditions trace their norms to God's will, this will is usually viewed in such ethicized terms as to render it unthinkable that God could ever require anything fundamentally wicked or immoral.

The Abraham-Isaac story in *Genesis* 22 is no exception to this rule. Readings based on this passage alone (such as Kierkegaard's) tend to omit the fact that, several chapters earlier, in *Genesis* 18:23–33, Abraham has questioned God concerning the possible destruction of innocent persons along with the wicked in Sodom and Gomorrah, asking boldly, "Shall not the judge of all the earth do right?" Abraham's willingness to question God in moral terms and God's willingness to enter into dialogue with Abraham do not support an understanding of the divine character as arbitrary or nonmoral. In many ways, the episode in *Genesis* 22 reinforces this impression: though a supreme demand is made, the sacrifice itself is not required. The God of the Hebrew scriptures, unlike deities worshiped by idolators, does not demand the slaughter of children. Indeed, this was precisely the lesson drawn by most later Jewish, Christian, and Muslim commentators. In this single text, therefore, we see both sides of the biblical tradition: its emphasis on obedience to God's will and its essential faith that this will is trustworthy and righteous. Taken together, these ideas do not suggest a religious attitude that would subordinate morality, but one that discovers moral intentionality at the tradition's highest level of authority.

Universality and the Moral Rules. We have seen that the term *universality* has several distinct meanings when used in reference to moral rules. It signifies the fact that at least the basic rules of morality are the same across cultures. It also signifies that these rules are to be regarded as applying across cultural lines presumably to every human being. All who are human are members of the moral community and bear the rights and responsibilities of this status. A survey of different historical traditions bears out the presence of these ideas, although historical development and other considerations sometimes render matters complex.

Common moral principles. One of the most striking impressions produced by comparative study of religious ethics is the similarity in basic moral codes and teachings. The Ten Commandments of Hebrew faith, the teachings of Jesus in the Sermon on the Mount and of Paul in his epistles, the requirements of *sādhāraṇa,* or universal *dharma,* in Hinduism (*Laws of Manu,* 10.63), Buddhism's Five Precepts, and Islam's decalogue in the Qurʾān (17:22–39) constitute a very common set of normative requirements. These prohibit killing, injury, deception, or the violation of solemn oaths. C. S. Lewis has called basic moral rules like these "the ultimate platitudes of practical reason," and their presence and givenness in such diverse traditions supports his characterization. Also remarkably similar are norms bearing on social and institutional life, especially economic relations. While none of these traditions condemns private property (though common possession is sometimes viewed as appropriate for the religious elite, or is thought to have prevailed during a utopian era at the beginning of time), all are solicitous of the needs of the disadvantaged or powerless and, in different ways, all encourage active assistance to the poor. Judaism and Islam institutionalize this ethic through rules requiring tithing and charitable donation (indeed, *zakāt,* almsgiving, is one of Islam's Five Pillars of Faith). Christianity accomplishes the same end by encouraging extreme sensitivity to the plight of the weak or needy. Despite their other differences, Confucianism and Daoism share the Chinese conviction that the mark of just rule is a prosperous and happy peasantry. Both laud generosity by the rich and powerful, and both vigorously condemn economic oppression and rapaciousness. The caste system of Hinduism, though opposed to any notions of social equality, aims at ensuring a livelihood and a share in the social product for all members of the community. This was accomplished by means of the *jajmani* patronage system, involving the exchange among castes of services and goods at socially established and protected rates. Finally, while charitable giving in Buddhism goes largely to the monastic community and is directed toward spiritual attainment and not toward economic need, this community itself often has been a refuge for the poor and for orphans and widows. Furthermore, Buddhism espouses a vigorous ideal of shared prosperity in its conception of the duties of the righteous monarch *(cakravartin)*.

Similar assessments of individual moral worth. Beyond these common moral principles, interesting normative similarities may also be identified with respect to the role played by individual decision and intention in the evaluation of moral worth. We have seen that while intention does not figure into the rightness or wrongness of a particular act, it is a crucial consideration in estimating the merit or blame of the moral agent. This aspect of moral reasoning, as well as the centrality of the individual agent as moral subject, is apparently well appreciated by the major traditions under discussion, although again some historical perspective is needed. Very often during their earliest periods, traditions evidence an objective assessment of moral culpability: individuals may suffer social or religious penalties for wrongs accidentally committed. Similarly, the earliest strata of some traditions at times display notions of collective guilt whereby all members of a community are regarded as meriting punishment for the wrongdoing of a few.

Characteristically, however, these less differentiated ideas give way over time to greater precision in the assessment or apportionment of blame. In the Hebrew faith, Ezekiel's rejection of collective punishment (*Ez.* 18:1ff.) represents a watershed in the development of biblical ethics (similar changes in attitude can be discerned in *Deuteronomy* 24:16 and *2 Kings* 14:6). This process of differentiation becomes particularly apparent during moments of radical religious change. None of the "daughter traditions"—neither Buddhism, Christianity, nor Islam—defends the idea of corporate punishment, whereas all put much stress on intention in assessing individuals' deeds. Jesus' criticism of religious and moral hypocrisy may not be fair to the Jewish tradition from which he sprang, but it is fully consistent with the spirit of greater interiority in the assessment of worth that marks the development of biblical faith. Much the same might be said of the Buddhist remolding of the doctrine of *karman* to the effect that karmic consequences are seen to derive from the willing of the agent rather than from the outward deed. The importance of intention *(niyah)* in validating religious and moral observance in Islam and of the kindred concept of *kavvanah* in rabbinic Judaism exemplifies this same process of increasing precision in the assessment of individual worth.

Differences between traditions. Despite all these remarkable similarities, there are also important differences among the codes and teachings of these traditions. Thus, the permitted range of sexual conduct differs from tradition to tradition, with the concept of sexual chastity apparently not ruling out polygamy in some cases (ancient Israelite religion, Islam, Confucianism) but requiring monogamy and even recommending celibacy in others (monastic Christianity and Buddhism). Wrongful killing, too, is variously defined. For Jews and Muslims, killing is permissible if done in self-defense or to punish wrongdoers whose conduct is believed to threaten the community. The New Testament, however, suggests a stance in which even self-defensive killing of other human beings is prohibited. Buddhism and Jainism take this position one step further by discouraging the killing not only of human beings but of all sentient creatures.

Differences of this sort represent an important object of study. Why is it that traditions whose moral attitudes and teachings are in some ways similar tend to differ in other respects? But the significance of these differences for our basic understanding of the relationship between religion and morality should not be exaggerated. For one thing, these differences are manifested against a background of basic similarities in moral teaching. It is sometimes assumed, because religious traditions hold widely different religious beliefs, that their ethics must correspondingly differ; what is remarkable, however, is that these great differences in beliefs apparently do not affect adherence to at least the fundamental moral rules. Furthermore, where moral differences do occur, they do so within the permitted range of moral disagreement. For example, even though Western religious moralists have vested sexual conduct with great importance (often intolerantly imposing their norms on other cultures), there are many different ways in which societies can organize sexual conduct so as to fulfill the more basic moral objective of protecting human beings from injury. In some circumstances the welfare of women and children might seem best accomplished by polygamous relations; in others, monogamy might be desirable. Changing circumstances within a single tradition can even recommend a movement from one pattern to the next, as has been the case for Judaism and, to a lesser extent, Islam. That traditions would differ over a difficult moral issue like this is almost predictable. What would be surprising, and what would throw open to question any claim that religions are basically respectful of the moral rules, would be teachings that permit rape or other violently abusive sexual acts. But no major historical tradition tolerates anything of the kind.

Some differences in these teachings are also traceable to differing moral ideals or standards of supererogation. We have seen that, above and beyond the basic moral rules (which are largely negative and prohibitory), there are a variety of positive encouragements to generosity, sharing, and self-sacrifice. Since views of what is "above and beyond the call of duty" normally differ even within cultures and between individuals, it is not surprising that differences among religious traditions should be marked. Indeed, some of the disagreements with respect to sexual conduct and killing just mentioned are also differences of this sort. New Testament

Christianity, for example, would interpret self-sacrifice to imply celibacy, disregard for material wealth, and abstention from physical self-defense. Buddhists and Jains adopt very similar norms (possibly less for reasons of self-sacrifice or altruism than as part of a vision of spiritual self-cultivation), whereas Judaism and Islam tend to associate self-sacrifice with unstinting obedience to every provision of their respective religious laws. This may require extreme efforts at charity and the willingness to accept martyrdom in the name of the faith, though neither tradition advocates poverty, celibacy, or the renunciation of self-defense. As important as they may be for the study of comparative religious ethics, however, these differences with respect to supererogatory ideals are matters about which reasonable and morally well-intentioned persons can disagree, and they do not affect the traditions' agreement about the basic moral rules.

"Omnipartiality." Probably nothing makes this agreement clearer than the ways in which diverse religious traditions communicate to their adherents the perspective I have called "the moral point of view." We have seen that this requires imaginative empathy for others, an ability to put oneself in their shoes, and the willingness to make moral decisions from a standpoint of objectivity and impartiality. The element of reciprocity here is aptly expressed by the Golden Rule of Christianity (*Mt.* 7:12). While Christians are justly proud of the moral wisdom represented by this simple decision procedure, the Golden Rule is by no means limited to Christianity. Jesus' teaching is initially drawn from Hebrew scriptures (*Lv.* 19:18). Within rabbinic Judaism a negative form of the Golden Rule ("Do not do unto others. . . .") is presented by the sage Hillel as a virtual synopsis of the law. In the *Analects* (12.2), Confucius utters this same negative form of the Golden Rule, and variants of both the negative and positive forms are to be found in Buddhism's *Dhammapada* (10.129–130). Parallels like these led early missionaries and scholars to speculate on the possibility of historical borrowing or even parallel divine revelation in the East and the West. But this similarity of moral perspective does not have to be attributed to anything more than the essential and universal logic of the moral reasoning process.

While the Golden Rule is an impressive intuitive guide to responsible moral decision, its focus is too narrow. In making moral choices, we must consider not only the immediate neighbor but all other persons affected by our conduct or choice. Hence the requirements of universality, objectivity, and impartiality in moral reasoning. In fact, the term *impartiality,* though widely used in moral theory today, is inappropriate, because it suggests detachment and distance in reasoning when what is really required is genuine empathetic concern for all those affected by our decisions. In this respect either *omnipartiality* or *omnicompassion* would be a better term.

When we examine the very highest reaches of religious thought, we are struck by the ways in which adoption of this perspective is encouraged. In the Western traditions believers are called upon to imitate God while trying to develop their own moral and religious lives. The various metaphors for God that express the traits to which believers should aspire convey this moral point of view: God is the creator and king of all the world, the righteous ruler in whom there is neither partiality nor injustice. He is also a parent who loves his creatures with tender mercy and concern. Modeling their behavior on God's, Jews, Christians, and Muslims are thus called to distance themselves from selfish interests and to adopt an omnipartial point of view. Some Asian religions share this teaching. Adherents of the *bhakti* (devotional) tradition of Hinduism find a model in the god (often embodied in the figure of Kṛṣṇa) whose love transcends social distinctions of caste, wealth, or gender. In the ancient Chinese and Confucian traditions, Shangdi ("lord on high") and Tian ("heaven") represent the standard of impartial justice. Knowing no favorites, Heaven judges by merit alone and casts out the unworthy.

Mystical traditions, which often place less emphasis on obedience to God and more on the adherent's experience of a transcendent reality, arrive at this standpoint in a different way. Characteristically, once a person has joined with or is in contact with transcendent reality (whether as *brahman, nirvāṇa,* or the Dao), the ego assumes reduced importance. No longer clinging to the self, one participates sympathetically in all of reality. In Mahāyāna Buddhism this experience eventuates in compassion *(karuṇā)* for all sentient beings and the desire to help extricate them from suffering. The Daoist adept, in achieving mystical insight into the Way, participates in its spontaneity, generosity, and support of all living creatures.

It may be objected that the picture of universal compassion presented here is one-sided: that while the historical religions sometimes counsel universality of perspective, they have also been seedbeds of intolerance, persecution, and cruelty, and that under the guise of religious devotion, all sorts of nationalisms and even tribalisms have flourished. Certainly these things are true. But once again, historical perspective is in order. One of the salient features of all traditional cultures is their tendency to view themselves as human, while outsiders, often all those beyond the narrowest boundaries of a local community, are looked upon as enemies, barbarians, or less than fully human. Frequently this assessment has a real basis in self-perpetuating conditions of conflict and vendetta that render every outsider untrustworthy and dangerous. To some extent, we see this mentality in the early strata of many of the literate traditions, although even there universalist elements are discernible. For example, *Genesis* contains many passages in which Yahveh is depicted as little more than a tribal deity who fights without quarter on behalf of his people, whereas other passages display remarkable universality of perspective. Sometimes the two impulses are joined. A poignant example occurs in *Genesis* 21 when the working of the divine plan on behalf of Isaac's lineage leads Abraham to expel Hagar and her son Ishmael into the desert.

In a moving passage, Yahveh personally intervenes to save the lives of the abandoned pair. Though his first loyalties may be to Israel, the chosen instrument of his purpose in history, Yahveh reveals himself as a God whose compassion and concern transcend national lines.

As traditions develop, one finds an almost invariant movement from relative particularity to greater universalism. Examples include the lofty visions of prophetic faith, where Israel's chosenness comes to be viewed in terms of a mission of universal instruction and redemption; the emergence of *bhakti,* the devotional strain, in later Hinduism, with its perception of the sanctity of all human beings; and the development of various forms of messianism in Mahāyāna Buddhism, placing salvation within the reach of all and rendering every person potentially an enlightened being, or *bodhisattva.* If such development can be found within the traditions, it once again shows itself most dramatically at moments of decisive religious change. Christianity's abandonment of Jewish religious law, for example, opened its community, "the new Israel," to a membership drawn from the entire ancient world. Paul's statement in *Galatians* 3:28 that in Christ "there is neither Jew nor Greek . . . slave nor free . . . male nor female" fully expresses Christianity's universalizing impulse. Similarly, Buddhism, by rejecting Hindu notions of caste, severed the geographical ties to India that had characterized Hinduism and, as a result, Buddhism became a world religion. By expanding the possibility of salvation beyond the narrow community of mendicants, religious developments in later Mahāyāna Buddhism merely accentuated a tendency implicit in Buddhism from the outset.

But probably no tradition better illustrates this tendency to universalism coupled with the possibility of intolerance than Islam. Over the centuries, Muslims' willingness to use the sword in defense of their faith has earned Islam a reputation, especially among Christians, as a paradigm of religious intolerance and persecution. In fact, Islam's record in this regard is much more complex than its foes admit. Not only is the idea of holy struggle *(jihād)* a less bellicose and more defensive concept in the classic Muslim sources than it is often thought to be, but in many ways Islam's record of religious toleration is enviable. And even if some Muslims have promoted their faith through violence, it must be remembered that, in its essence, this faith has the most universalistic aspirations. The object of Islam is precisely to bring all human beings, whatever their race or nationality, into submission to God's will. Islam would create one human community in which all share obedience to a high moral and religious standard and in which all merit the protection embodied by that standard. The fact that some Muslims have at times been prone to excess in promoting this objective may be thought of as an unfortunate consequence of the breadth of their moral and religious vision. This vision is representative of the tendency of other major world religions to fulfill the promise of universality implicit in the moral point of view.

Why Should One Be Moral? Religions are not just bodies of teaching about right and wrong; they are total ways of life. As a result, it is not surprising that they provide answers, whether explicit or implicit, to some of the more urgent "transnormative" questions of morality, among them the questions of why one should be a moral person and how one can attain a morally estimable character. In many ways, these questions are central in religious teaching. While standards of right or wrong conduct are readily elaborated by traditions, efforts to secure full adherence to these standards are a major preoccupation.

Retribution. Religious traditions commonly provide answers to the question "Why should I be moral?" by affirming the existence of an order in which moral retribution (reward and punishment) is assured. Those raised in the West are familiar with some of the standard forms of this belief: God is consummately righteous; he is the omniscient judge of human acts and intentions; he upholds the moral law by punishing the wicked and rewarding the righteous; and, in some cases, he metes out reward and punishment directly in the course of a person's life. But since there is an apparent discrepancy between moral conduct and one's worldly fate—too often the good suffer and the wicked prosper—divine retribution is usually consigned to an eschatological realm, whether a personal afterlife, a period of judgment at the end of history (the kingdom of God), or some combination of these two.

Although this retributive scheme prevails in Judaism, Christianity, and Islam, it is not the only one that religions (including these same Western traditions) have elaborated. The idea of eschatological retribution is absent from many nonliterate traditions, and even in biblical faith it is a relatively late development. More common is a perception of death as departure to a state where the discarnate soul suffers neither punishment nor reward. The principal expectation for virtuous conduct, therefore, lies in the hope of worldly prosperity, numerous progeny, good health, and long life, so as to "come in sturdy old age to the grave," as the *Book of Job* (5:26) says. It may be that more explicitly eschatological thinking arises, as it did in Hebrew faith, only after massive and repeated frustration of these expectations and, even then, only within a context of historical expectation and sustained reflection and writing about this experience.

Neither is the apportionment of reward and punishment always accomplished by a supreme, morally intentioned deity. In some traditions the sincerity of oath takers is tested by requiring them to undergo a quasi-magical ordeal such as ingesting a poison that is expected to prove fatal only if they are guilty of deception. (An instance of such an ordeal is found in *Numbers* 5:11ff., where an accused adulteress is required to vindicate herself by consuming a draft of "bitter waters.")

In many of the nonliterate traditions of Africa and in some Native American religions, lesser supernatural agents such as witches and sorcerers also play a role—indeed, a complex one—in upholding the moral order. These agents are often "negative exemplars," embodying attitudes of selfishness and resentment that are the opposite of the open and generous attitudes expected of a good member of the community. Since witches and sorcerers can themselves expect to be punished for their behavior, the lesson to all is clear: avoid becoming persons of this sort. But the presence of these malign agents also reinforces the moral conduct of others. Anyone who neglects hospitality obligations and treats a stranger unkindly, or who deals unfairly with one of his several wives, or who fails to be generous to others while himself experiencing prosperity may easily fall prey to the destructive powers of a witch. Indeed, since witches and sorcerers are masters of deception, combining outward benevolence with inward wrath (and so, once again, are consummate examples of how *not* to be), it is possible that, if mistreated, one's nearest kin or neighbors may become a threat.

Among the traditions of India, moral reward and punishment are also the province of religious thought, but (at least in the post-Vedic period) they are accomplished by means very different from those in the West. In Indian thought the operative mode is the impersonal, natural-moral law of *karman:* the certainty of moral punishment or reward in combination with a belief in metempsychosis or the transmigration of the individual soul. In the world of *karman,* each act and each volition entails consequences for the welfare of the agent. In a sense, it is misleading to label these consequences rewards or punishments, since they do not result from the action of any judge but are part of the natural law of occurrences in the world. As such, these consequences may be experienced within the lifetime of an individual. More commonly they take many successive lifetimes to work their effect as one's *karman* "ripens." When morally caused suffering does occur, it is often suited to the crime. One who habitually lies, for example, may become the victim of slander in some future life; one who drinks to excess may be reborn insane. Just because it is an impersonal, natural law, *karman* is inescapable. As the *Dhammapada* (9.127) says, "Not in the sky, not in the midst of the sea, not if one enters into the clefts of the mountains" can one be freed from the consequences of evil deeds.

Belief in *karman* is so widely shared among the Indian traditions—Jainism, Hinduism, and Buddhism—that it may be called the principal dogma of Indian religious belief. For these traditions, to reject *karman* is to put oneself outside the religious pale. Indeed, the one intellectual tradition of ancient India that did just this, the Carvaka or materialist school, lives on, like the Sophists of ancient Greece, only as an object of ridicule by the other traditions. It is further testimony to the centrality of this belief in Indian religion that Buddhism, whose doctrine of *anattā* ("nonself") opens to question who or what agent could be the inheritor of continuing karmic forces, nevertheless continues strongly to affirm the reality and significance of this natural-moral law.

One of the future tasks of comparative religious ethics is to better understand why retributive doctrines evolve and take the different forms that they do. It is also important to understand why, in some cases, religious doctrines of retribution lose their power or vanish altogether. To a large extent, but probably for different reasons, this occurred in ancient Greece and China.

In the case of Greek religion, confidence in a reliable religious-moral order may have been eroded, in an increasingly complex society, by repeated frustration of moral expectations. Furthermore, the traditional religion was based on a panoply of deities whose moral integrity and power had been open to question from an early date. The result was a withering of religious confidence and its replacement with an effort to ground moral obedience in an understanding of the relationship between virtue and personal welfare *(eudaimonia).* Thus the rational discipline of ethics, as found in the writings of the great classical philosophers, arose amid the crisis of a religious-moral culture.

In China an opposite series of events seems to have led to the same result. From an early date, Chinese religious thinkers correctly linked human well-being, in the form of a stable, secure, and prosperous society, to moral conduct on the part of rulers. Misrule, it was believed, would manifest itself in popular unrest, rebellion, and susceptibility to invasion. "Heaven sees and hears as our people see and hear" (*Book of Documents* 3.74) was the teaching of the various Chinese traditions. It may be that, in time, this direct, demonstrable, innerworldly link between virtue and welfare largely obviated the need for an impassioned affirmation of religious retribution (at least among the intellectuals who were shaping the tradition). In the Chinese experience, in a very direct and material way, virtue may have reasonably been thought to bring its reward. This was not always to remain true, of course, and at a later date Buddhist eschatology filled a void left by the earlier tradition.

In these respects, the course of Greek and Chinese religious thought contrasts markedly with that of ancient Israel, where an emphasis on religious retribution was magnified by successive and intense experiences of both failure and vindication of moral expectations. This leads one to conjecture that strong schemes of religious retribution are most likely to flourish where confidence in moral retribution is neither too secure nor too imperiled.

The uncertain link between moral conduct and moral reward has a further very important consequence for religious thought: it contributes to the development of sustained reflection on the problem of human sin and wrongdoing. Earlier, I noted how difficult it is to provide answers to the question "Why should one be moral?" If moral or immoral conduct were always followed by its appropriate reward or punishment, not only would this question be easy to answer but individuals would have little temptation to pursue selfish goals. The fact, however, that this is not the case, and that moral commitment may have to rest on uncertain religious beliefs or on metaphysical beliefs, leads to the recurrent possibility of moral weakness and moral failure.

Redemption. It is important to note that strong affirmation by religious traditions of the existence of a morally retributive order, while it relieves this problem in some ways (by reinforcing confidence in retribution), accentuates it in others. It does so first of all because, in a world assumed to be governed by moral considerations, ordinary forms of suffering (sickness, famine, or premature death) are naturally attributed to moral and religious failures on the part of the individual or community. Not surprisingly, therefore, we find a concern with the expiation of sin present in many nonliterate traditions, and even the earliest documents of the literate traditions (such as the cultic ordinances in *Leviticus,* the *Ṛgveda,* or the Chinese *Book of Rites*) emphasize these matters. But as traditions develop, a further problem emerges that often leads into the most subtle and paradoxical reaches of religious thought. Earlier I noted that moral reasoning, though it may lead to a recognition of the need for some confidence in moral retribution, is nevertheless opposed to basing moral commitment on crass considerations of personal benefit or gain. Indeed, not only are individuals who calculate their commitments in this way morally unreliable (since expediential considerations can easily lead them to be immoral), but they do not attain to the highest standard of moral virtue, in which a spontaneous and pure love of righteousness is the principal motivating ground of conduct.

But since religions inevitably hold out the promise of reward, how are they, at the same time, to lead their adherents into such an elevated level of moral attainment? Or, as the outward behavior of adherents becomes more refined, how are religions to prevent egoism from corrupting the inner core of intention? To answer these questions fully would require an extensive exploration of various traditions' conceptions of sin and redemption. We can, however, identify a very common direction taken by religious thought at this point. Simply stated, in coming to terms with this problem, traditions tend to qualify and soften their own insistence on moral retribution. The world may be a moral order, but ultimate redemption does not necessarily rest on the moral performance or accomplishments of the individual agent. The effect of this teaching is twofold: it relieves the inevitable self-condemnation of the morally conscientious yet knowingly frail person, but at the same time it eliminates any vestiges of cloying self-regard that might corrupt the moral life and make it an instrument of pride and self-assertion.

Traditions affect this qualification of the retributive scheme differently. Judaism, Christianity, and Islam emphasize God's grace and the recurrent possibility of repentance. Pauline Christianity takes this teaching to the extreme conclusion that salvation comes not by works of the moral and religious law, but through God's free, unnecessitated love. Similar conceptions are found in the devotional *(bhakti)* tradition of Hindu thought, but in the Indian-derived traditions the retributive order is more commonly qualified differently: ultimate redemption requires one to attain the consciousness that full liberation *(mokṣa, nirvāṇa)* is open only to those who transcend attachment to *saṃsāra,* the karmic realm of merit and demerit.

On the surface, all these teachings appear to undermine the significance of morality and moral striving—indeed, of the very retributive order these faiths have affirmed—and it is true that, at one time or another, teachings such as these have been taken to antinomian conclusions. But religious thinkers or traditions advancing such "transmoral" ideas often seem to have the opposite intent: namely, to free conscientious and morally committed individuals from the last vestiges of self-regard in order to make possible a spontaneous, joyful, and sincere moral life. Thus Paul, after stating his doctrine of justification through grace in *Romans* 5 and posing the rhetorical question "Shall we continue in sin that grace may abound?" (6:1), replies "By no means!" To draw an antinomian or immoralist lesson from this teaching, in Paul's view, would miss the point that it both presupposes and aims at devoted moral commitment.

Hindus and Buddhists are equally vehement in rejecting the idea that, according to their teachings, the religiously liberated person acts immorally. Liberation may take one beyond the moral order of *dharma,* but it is by no means the same thing as *adharma,* or lawlessness. On the contrary, attaining liberation requires a disciplined, righteous life as preparation; for most Hindu and Buddhist thinkers, furthermore, it issues in the most consummately moral existence. Precisely because the liberated person has put all vestiges of egoism behind, he has attained a state of mind where, without regard for personal benefit, he acts out of a free compassion for other beings. This is exactly the state achieved by Arjuna in the *Bhagavadgītā.* Perplexed over the terrible implications for himself and his kinsman if he performs his warrior's duty, Arjuna is unable to act until, in a series of religious encounters, he learns from Kṛṣṇa-Visnu that one's true self is not stained by moral good or evil. This instruction frees him to do his duty and thereby help sustain the cosmic-moral order. Far from being antinomian or immoral, therefore, this teaching of "detached action" *(niskama karman),* as Max Weber observed, is one of the loftiest achievements of Indian moral and religious thought.

CONCLUSION As far back as the historical record allows us to see, religion and morality have been intertwined. This collaboration has not always been fruitful. Such Western critics as Marx and Freud regarded the link between religion and morality as unfortunate. Among other things, they criticized it for producing immoral teachings (whether in the economic or sexual realms) and dubious or morally questionable eschatological schemes, for basing morality on fear of punishment, and for using doctrines of forgiveness for manipulative or immoral purposes. All these criticisms were valid, not just for Western religion in this late period but for all traditions at one moment or another in their history. Religions engage some of the most fundamental and most difficult questions of the moral life, and it is no wonder that their failure to deal adequately with these questions can have the most serious consequences. In the effort to transcend narrow tribalism, for example, a religion can contribute to the reinsertion of tribal attitudes at an ever higher and more dangerous level.

Nevertheless, this critical word is not all that can be said. Religions, whether nonliterate or literate, characteristically emerge and develop in a process of intense dialogue with the requirements of the moral life. They elaborate codes of conduct, procedures for reasoning morally, and standards of virtue. To support commitment to the moral life, they help configure the world as a moral order. Finally, they are prepared to qualify or refine this order so as to permit anyone to attain the highest level of moral excellence. In all these ways, religious traditions have contributed to human moral development and self-understanding. Religion is not reducible to morality, as some nineteenth-century thinkers argued, because religions address a variety of human interests and concerns. Aesthetic propensities, historical or scientific curiosity, speculative and ritual tendencies—all find expression in religious faith. But no one can deny that moral concerns in their fullest sense have been a central aspect of religious life.

SEE ALSO Buddhist Ethics; Chinese Philosophy; Christian Ethics; Confucianism; Dharma; Enlightenment, The; Evil; Freud, Sigmund; Good, The; Halakhah; Islamic Law; Israelite Law; Karman; Kierkegaard, Søren; Law and Religion; Marx, Karl; Neoorthodoxy; Nonviolence; Otto, Rudolf; Relativism; Schleiermacher, Friedrich; Suffering.

BIBLIOGRAPHY

Among the more important classical discussions of the relationship between religion and morality are Plato's *Euthyphro*, Thomas Aquinas's "Treatise on the Law" (*Summa theologiae*, 2.7.90–97), Immanuel Kant's *Critique of Practical Reason* and *Religion within the Limits of Reason Alone*, Søren Kierkegaard's *Fear and Trembling*, and John Stuart Mill's *Three Essays on Religion*. More recent discussions of the relationship between religion and morality include *Religion and Morality: A Collection of Essays*, edited by John P. Reeder, Jr., and Gene H. Outka (New York, 1973), W. G. Maclagen's *The Theological Frontier of Ethics* (New York, 1961), and W. W. Bartley II's *Morality and Religion* (New York, 1971).

Contemporary ethical theory comprises a large domain of views. Good, brief treatments of a number of basic issues can be found in G. J. Warnock's *The Object of Morality* (London, 1971), in William K. Frankena's *Ethics*, 2d ed. (Englewood Cliffs, N.J., 1973), and in Paul W. Taylor's *Principles of Ethics: An Introduction* (Encino, Calif., 1975). Among widely regarded contemporary rationalist approaches to normative ethical theory are Kurt Baier's *The Moral Point of View* (Ithaca, N.Y., 1958), John Rawls's *A Theory of Justice* (Cambridge, Mass., 1971), Bernard Gert's *The Moral Rules* (New York, 1970), and Alan Gewirth's *Reason and Morality* (Chicago, 1978). For treatments of some key moral issues related to religious ethics, see the collections *Ethical Relativism*, edited by John Ladd (Belmont, Calif., 1973), and *Supererogation: Its Status in Ethical Theory*, by David Heyd (New York, 1982).

Much Western thinking about the relationship between religion and morality has focused on the question of whether morality may be based on a divine command. Two recent collections gather together many of the classical and contemporary discussions of this issue: *Divine Command Morality*, edited by Janine Marie Idziak (Lewiston, N.Y., 1980), and *Divine Commands and Morality*, edited by Paul Helms (Oxford, 1981).

Unfortunately, while there are a number of good specific discussions of Christian, Jewish, Hindu, or Buddhist ethics, relatively little work has been done on the comparative analysis of religious traditions in a way comprising not just their specific normative teachings but also their doctrines of retribution and their fundamental ways of relating ethics to other features of the religious life. Two classic discussions in this area are Edward A. Westermarck's *The Origin and Development of the Moral Ideas*, 2 vols., 2d ed. (London, 1924), and his *Christianity and Morals* (1939; reprint, Freeport, N.Y., 1969). These works provide a wealth of information about the moral and religious beliefs of preliterate and literate cultures, though the moral perspective is colored by Westermarck's moral relativism. Even more systematic comparative discussion of specific traditions can be found in Max Weber's pioneering studies of 1915–1919: *Ancient Judaism* (Glencoe, Ill., 1952), *The Religion of India: The Sociology of Hinduism and Buddhism* (Glencoe, Ill., 1958), and *The Religion of China: Confucianism and Daoism* (Glencoe, Ill., 1951), all translated and edited by Hans H. Gerth and Don Martindale. More recent treatments of comparative ethics include my own study *Religious Reason* (Oxford, 1978) and David Little and Sumner B. Twiss Jr.'s *Comparative Religious Ethics: A New Method* (San Francisco, 1978).

New Sources

Brown, Donald. *The Evolution of Morality and Religion.* New York, 2003.

McDonald, James. *The Crucible of Christian Morality.* New York, 1998.

Moody-Adams, Michele. *Fieldwork in Familiar Places; Morality, Culture, and Philosophy.* Cambridge, Mass., 2002.

Oakeshott, Michael Joseph. *Religion, Politics, and the Moral Life.* New Haven, 1993.

Phillips, D. Z. *Religion, and Morality.* London, 1996.

Polkinghorne, John. *Belief in God in an Age of Science.* New Haven, 1998.

Richardson, W. M., and W. J. Wildman, eds. *Religion and Science.* New York, 1996.

Rudd Anthony. *Kierkegaard and the Limits of the Ethical.* New York, 1993.

Schweiker, William. *Mimetic Reflections: A Study in Hermeneutics, Theology, and Ethics.* New York, 1990.

Warner, Martin, ed. *Religion and Philosophy.* Philosophy and Religion series. New York, 1992.

RONALD M. GREEN (1987)
Revised Bibliography

MORAL THEOLOGY

SEE CHRISTIAN ETHICS

MORAVIANS. The Moravian church, as the Unitas Fratrum (Unity of Brethren) is popularly known, is a Protestant denomination with roots in the fifteenth-century Hussite reformation and the eighteenth-century German Pietist movement. By the late nineteenth century, these influences had coalesced to give the denomination its contemporary form and character.

The Unity of Brethren was founded in March 1457 in Kunwald, Bohemia, as the Jednota Bratrská (Society of Brethren), but the issues behind this event stretch back more than a century. From the mid-fourteenth century there had been growing demands for reform within the Roman Catholic Church of Bohemia and neighboring Moravia. The reform movement was centered in the capital city of Prague and the newly established Charles University (1348). Persistent Waldensian influences as well as newer Wyclifite influences from England were evident in this movement.

The calls for reform finally found their most eloquent voice in Jan Hus, priest, university professor, and popular preacher. Although attracted to the doctrines of Wyclif, Hus claimed to advocate independently a return to apostolic simplicity in the church, and he vigorously attacked the lax morality of the clergy. As Hus's popularity increased, so did controversy about his ideas and his difficulties with the hierarchy. He was excommunicated by Pope John XXIII in 1411 but eventually appealed his case to the Council of Constance then in session. After his trial, deemed irregular by later historians, he was burned at the stake as a heretic on July 6, 1415.

Hus's death served to arouse his followers in Bohemia. His ideas soon became entwined with a developing Bohemian nationalism, and Hus himself became something of a folk hero. When civil war erupted, a series of unsuccessful crusades were launched, with the blessings of the papacy, in an attempt to subdue the heretics. Among the most ardent Bohemians, highly respected for their military zeal, were a group of radical religious and political reformers headquartered in the town of Tabor. Although they were destroyed as a separate party by the late 1430s, many of their religious ideas lingered on in the population. Bohemia's political situation would remain unstable for a century after Hus's death until 1526, when the crown was acquired by the Habsburg Ferdinand I.

Upheavals occurred also in the religious life of the Bohemians and Moravians as several groups claiming the heritage of Hus emerged alongside the Roman Catholic Church. One such group, the Utraquists, represented a conservative attempt at reformation, finally insisting only on the right of all believers to receive the bread and wine at Communion and continuing to hope for a reunion with a purified Roman Catholic Church. It was the Utraquist archbishop-elect Jan z Rokycan (c. 1390–1471) whose preaching inspired one of the founders of the Brethren, his nephew Gregory (d. 1474), to pursue more vigorously the goal of reformation. Jan z Rokycan also introduced Gregory to the writings of the radical reformer Petr Chelčický (c. 1380–c. 1460).

Within ten years of the founding of their society, the Brethren felt the need to establish their own clerical orders to insure the efficaciousness of their ministry. They chose deacons, presbyters, and bishops from among their membership. One of the candidates was a former Roman Catholic priest, and some Waldensians may have participated in the establishment of the new orders. Modern historians see in these events an attempt by the Brethren to reconstitute the style of ministry of the New Testament church. Any attempt by the Brethren to claim apostolic succession as traditionally understood must be laid to a faulty reading of Waldensian history on their part. The orders established in 1467 have been carried on into the contemporary Moravian church.

The first decades of the Brethren organization were marked by sectarian characteristics including pacifism, rejection of oaths, communal organization, use of the titles brother and sister for all members, suspicion of advanced education, reluctance to admit members of the nobility to membership, and a preference for rural living. This trend was reversed under the leadership of Bishop Luke of Prague (c. 1460–1528), who succeeded in 1494 in having the works of Chelčický and Gregory reduced to nondogmatic status. The group gave up much of their exclusiveness and moved into the mainstream of society, though not without the defection of a conservative minority. The majority, although retaining a strict church discipline, grew rapidly. It has been estimated that by the 1520s there were from 150,000 to 200,000 members located in 400 congregations in Bohemia and Moravia.

Under the leadership of such bishops as Jan Augusta (1500–1572) and Jan Blahoslav (1523–1571), the Brethren maintained generally friendly contacts with Luther (who wrote favorably about them) and later with leaders of the Reformed churches. Although ecumenical in spirit and experiencing strong influences from first Lutheran and later Reformed theology, the Brethren maintained their own course. They structured their church with dioceses headed by bishops, abandoned clerical celibacy, and eventually accepted a general Reformed understanding of the sacraments of baptism and the Eucharist.

In worship, while ritual was simplified, the church year was retained and lay involvement encouraged through the publication of hymnals and the Czech-language Kralitz Bible (1579–1593) in six volumes with commentary. The church sponsored schools and encouraged the training of clergy in foreign universities.

Since their legal status was often in doubt, the Brethren endured periodic persecutions by the Utraquists and the Roman Catholics. But they continued to maintain their vitality and established congregations in Poland, which later merged with the Reformed church.

The involvement in political affairs of members who were of the nobility helped to bring about disastrous consequences for the Brethren in the opening phase of the Thirty Years' War (1618–1648). With the defeat of the Protestant forces at the Battle of the White Mountain (1620), suppression of Protestantism in Bohemia and Moravia began. The events of this era are highlighted in the career of Bishop Johannes Amos Comenius (1592–1670), the renowned educational theorist. He spent much of his life in exile developing his reforms of education and despite several personal tragedies never lost his belief in the power of the educated mind to serve God's purposes for humanity.

The traditions of the Brethren survived in Bohemia and Moravia through secret meetings and the laxity of government officials in enforcing conformity. Sporadic contacts with Lutherans in border areas also helped to sustain morale.

A group of these secret Brethren were led in 1722 to the German estate of Count Nikolaus Zinzendorf (1700–1760) by the lay evangelist Christian David (1690–1751). There they established the village of Herrnhut. A creative theologian and gifted leader, Zinzendorf became the driving force behind the merger of the Brethren's traditions with the emphases of the Pietist movement.

After initial difficulties, the growing community experienced a series of unifying experiences in the summer of 1727, culminating in a service of Holy Communion on August 13. The fellowship now developed the unique characteristics that would mark its second phase. The residents were organized into residential groups based on age, sex, and marital status ("the choirs"). The intent was to foster spiritual experience appropriate to one's stage in life and to utilize the resources of a concentrated labor force. From Zinzendorf's Christocentric emphasis flowed a rich liturgical life with stress upon the Advent–Christmas and Holy Week–Easter cycles. The Moravian understanding of the joyous nature of the relationship between the believer and the Savior enabled them to develop education and the arts in his praise, sponsoring schools and producing musicians and artists of note. The Brethren's clerical orders were continued through new ordinations by the two remaining bishops in exile. Since the church developed a conferential form of government, however, the bishops became primarily spiritual leaders.

Worship was characterized by a simplified liturgical ritual that observed the festivals of the Christian calendar with particular attention to the Advent–Christmas and Holy Week–Easter cycles. Unique features included the singing of many hymns, with the minister clad in a surplice for the celebration of the sacraments of baptism and Holy Communion. The Lovefeast, patterned after the *agapē* meals of the early Christians, developed as a significant service. In it participants were served a simple meal as an expression of their fellowship with one another.

Under the leadership of Zinzendorf and his de facto successor Bishop Augustus Gottlieb Spangenberg (1703–1792), Herrnhut became the model for some twenty similar communities established in Europe, England, and the eastern United States. These self-sufficient "settlement congregations" were to serve as the home base for two types of outreach developed by the Brethren.

Beginning in 1727 the Moravians sent forth members to serve in their "diaspora" through establishing Pietist renewal societies within existing state churches. This practice is supported by European Moravians today. In 1732, after Zinzendorf's presentation of the plight of the West Indian slaves to the community, the Brethren Leonard Dober (1706–1766) and David Nitschmann (1696–1772) went to Saint Thomas. By 1760 the Moravians had sent out 226 missionaries to the non-European world. This effort introduced into Protestantism the idea that missionary outreach is the responsibility of the whole church, brought the Moravians into significant ecumenical contacts, such as that with John Wesley (1703–1791) in Georgia and England, and helped shape the contemporary Moravian church.

By the mid-nineteenth century, the settlement congregations were given up as no longer viable and the towns opened to all who wished to settle in them. German and Scandinavian immigration to North America in the last century brought new Moravian congregations into being in the eastern and midwestern United States and western Canada. The end of World War II found Herrnhut and the older settlements in East Germany and, through the movement of refugees, a stronger Moravian presence in western Europe. Immigration continues to affect the Moravian church through the recent movements of Surinamese members to the Netherlands and Caribbean-area members to cities in England and North America.

The Moravians have also experienced constitutional changes as they have moved beyond their European origins. The British and American areas of the church gained independence from the German in the mid-nineteenth century, but the foreign missions continued under control of an international board that met in Germany until the end of World War I. Responsibility for the work was then divided among the European, British, and American areas of the church. A major constitutional change in 1957 resulted in the creation of the present seventeen autonomous provinces located in Europe, England, North America, Central America, and Africa, and the undertaking of educational work in India and Israel. The provinces constitute the Moravian Unity and send delegates to periodic meetings of the Unity Synod. The late twentieth century witnessed the rapid growth of the church in Africa and Central America. In America, the Moravian church did not experience significant growth until after the mid-nineteenth century. Earlier attempts at "diaspora"-style outreach had proved unsuited to America, since there was no religious establishment within which to work. Groups gathered by diaspora workers simply became congregations of other denominations. The retention of the exclusive settlement congregations until the 1840s also retarded outreach.

The church has continued to honor many of its traditions of worship and practice. While eschewing a formal dogmatic theological tradition of its own, it affirms the historic creeds of the Christian faith, continues to emphasize the believer's relationship with Christ, and to encourage fellowship among its members. Both men and women are ordained as pastors. The church's historical ecumenical stance is reflected in its participation as a founding member of the World Council of Churches and in the activities of the various provinces in regional councils of churches. Total worldwide membership in the late 1990s was around 720,000.

See Also Comenius, Johannes Amos; Hus, Jan; Pietism; Zinzendorf, Nikolaus.

Bibliography

The most comprehensive bibliography for the early history of the Moravians is Jarold K. Zeman's *The Hussite Movement and the Reformation in Bohemia, Moravia and Slovakia, 1350–1650: A Bibliographical Study Guide* (Ann Arbor, Mich., 1977). Peter Brock discusses *The Political and Social Doctrines of the Unity of Czech Brethren in the Fifteenth and Early Sixteenth Centuries* (The Hague, Netherlands, 1957), while the whole history of the early Moravians is dealt with in Edmund A. De Schweinitz's old but comprehensive *History of the Church Known as the Unitas Fratrum or the Unity of the Brethren*, 2d ed. (Bethlehem, Pa., 1901). The later history of the church is found in J. Taylor Hamilton and Kenneth G. Hamilton's *History of the Moravian Church: The Renewed Unitas Fratrum, 1722–1957* (Bethlehem, Pa., 1967). The best recent biographies of central figures in Moravian church history include two works by Matthew Spinka: *John Hus: A Biography* (Princeton, N.J., 1968) and *John Amos Comenius: That Incomparable Moravian* (Chicago, 1943). Zinzendorf is the subject of John R. Weinlick's *Count Zinzendorf* (Nashville, 1956) and Arthur J. Lewis's *Zinzendorf: The Ecumenical Pioneer* (Philadelphia, 1962).

New Sources

Mason, J. C. S. *The Moravian Church and the Missionary Awakening in England, 1760–1800.* Woodbridge, U.K., 2001.

Sommer, Elisabeth W. *Serving Two Masters: Moravian Brethren in Germany and North Carolina, 1727–1801.* Lexington, Ky., 2000.

Vogt, P. A. "A Voice for Themselves: Women as Participants in Congregational Discourse in the Eighteenth-Century Moravian Movement." In *Women Preachers and Prophets through Two Millennia of Christianity*, edited by Beverly Mayne Kienzle and Pamela J. Walker, pp. 227–247. Berkeley, Calif., 1998.

David A. Schattschneider (1987)
Revised Bibliography

MORDVIN RELIGIONS See MARI AND MORDVIN RELIGION

MORMONISM.

The religious movement popularly known as Mormonism encompasses several denominations and sects, the largest of which is the Church of Jesus Christ of Latter-day Saints, which is headquartered in Salt Lake City, Utah, and had a worldwide membership of about twelve million in 2003. The second largest organization is the Community of Christ (formerly known as the Reorganized Church of Jesus Christ of Latter Day Saints) with headquarters in Independence, Missouri, and a membership of about 250,000. Perhaps the smallest of numerous Mormon splinter groups is the Church of Jesus Christ of Latter Day Saints (Strangite) in Burlington, Wisconsin—composed of followers of James T. Strang (1813–1856)—with about two hundred members. All of these churches trace their origins to founder Joseph Smith Jr. (1805–1844).

Origins of Mormonism. Mormonism began in western New York in the 1820s, a time when the fires of the Second Great Awakening were sweeping across the "burned-over district," and America's most important nineteenth-century waterway, the Erie Canal, was being completed there. Such a mingling of spiritual and physical developments was a perfect expression of the symbiosis between evangelical religion and an emerging industrial order that radically transformed American society, leaving many Americans bewildered and confused. Among those passed by in the rush for progress was the family of Joseph and Lucy Mack Smith, who had left New England with their children in 1816 in search of better economic opportunities in western New York. They settled in the village of Palmyra, directly on the canal route. Though skeptical of the religious enthusiasms of the revivalists, the Smiths were persuaded of the need for religious affiliation. However, they found it difficult to make a choice among competing denominations. Their third eldest son, Joseph Smith Jr., was particularly confused in his search for the one true church. According to a later official church account, in the spring of 1820 the boy, aged fourteen, retired to a grove on his father's farm, where he prayed for divine guidance. In a vision he beheld two personages. One of these spoke to him, pointing to the other, saying "This is my beloved son, hear him!" He was told to join none of the existing denominations, for they were "all wrong."

As young Joseph matured, he had a number of subsequent visions and revelations that convinced him that God had chosen him as his instrument to restore the true church of Christ, which through the course of history had been corrupted by fallible and evil people. In preparation for this restoration, Smith was directed by an angel to unearth a set of golden records from a hill near his parents' farm. He then translated these records with divine aid and published them in 1830 as the *Book of Mormon,* a sacred history of three groups of pre-Columbian migrants to America, including the ancestors of some American Indian tribes. According to the *Book of Mormon,* Christ had visited the inhabitants of the Western Hemisphere after his crucifixion, taught the gospel, and instituted a church "to the convincing of the Jew and Gentile that Jesus is the Christ, the Eternal God, manifesting himself to all nations" (*Book of Mormon,* title page). Although accepted as scripture by believing Mormons, and popularly called the Mormon Bible by nonbelievers, Smith regarded the *Book of Mormon* as a supplement rather than a substitute for the Bible.

Smith also believed that no scripture, ancient or modern, was sufficient for the restoration of the gospel. More than anything else, mankind needed divine authority to act in the name of God, an authority that had vanished after a great falling away in the early days of Christianity. This authority was restored in the spring and summer of 1829, when the powers of the priesthood of the early church—which included the authority to baptize and the gift of the Holy Ghost—were conferred upon Smith and his associate Oliver Cowdery by John the Baptist and the apostles Peter, James, and John. Smith now felt authorized to restore the church of Christ, which he officially organized under the laws of the state of New York on April 6, 1830, shortly after publication of the *Book of Mormon.* In 1838 the name was changed from Church of Jesus Christ to Church of Jesus Christ of Latter-day Saints.

Although the new religion initially met with skepticism and persecution, it succeeded in attracting a substantial following among restorationists, who saw in Mormonism the fulfillment of the awaited return of the true church of Christ led by a divinely ordained priesthood. Perhaps the most prominent and influential of these early converts was Sidney Rigdon (1793–1876), erstwhile associate of Alexander Campbell (1788–1866). Rigdon brought virtually his entire Ohio congregation over to the new religion, thus inducing Smith and most of his New York followers to establish a Mormon settlement in 1831 in Kirtland, Ohio. There Smith greatly amplified and broadened his theological and organizational principles in a series of revelations first published in 1833 as *A Book of Commandments* and later enlarged into the canonical *Doctrine and Covenants.* The Saints were enjoined to gather in communities as God's chosen people under an egalitarian economic order called the Law of Consecration and Stewardship and to build a temple that was, literally and symbolically, the sacred center of the community. Jesus, Moses, Elias, and Elijah then appeared to Smith and Cowdery in the temple in 1836. These revelations initiated a patriarchal order that harkened back to Old Testament traditions and established the nucleus of a kingdom of God in which the temporal and the sacred became indistinguishable.

These innovations—radical departures from traditional Protestantism—while attracting many new converts, strained the loyalty of some early Saints and also began to arouse the hostility of non-Mormons. When the Saints were forced to leave Kirtland in 1838, it was largely the result of internal conflict; however, as early as 1833 a Mormon settlement in Jackson County, Missouri, had to be abandoned because of persecution. When the Mormons were completely driven out of Missouri in 1839, it was primarily because of opposition to their kingdom. Internal conflict also intensified as Smith continued to move beyond his early restorationist impulse in favor of a kingdom of God that achieved its fullest expression in Nauvoo. Founded in 1839 for refugees from Missouri, Nauvoo became Illinois's largest city in its day, with a population of about eleven thousand by 1844. It was a city under the full religious, social, economic, and political control of the Mormon kingdom. Much of this development was the result of the spectacular success of missionaries in Great Britain who, beginning in 1837, sent a steady stream of converts to the American settlements.

The success of Nauvoo may well have led Smith to overreach himself. He assumed the leadership of the Mormon militia and announced his candidacy for the presidency of the United States. Smith ostensibly made this gesture to avoid having to make an inexpedient choice between the Whigs and the Democrats, who attracted the majority of voters, but he was also imbued with the millennial belief that, if God wished him to become president and establish Mormon dominion over the United States, who would hinder him? The temple in the center of Nauvoo was much more Hebraic in design and ritual (with Masonic borrowings) than the one in Kirtland, which resembled a New England meetinghouse. Innovative doctrines and ordinances, such as baptism for the dead and especially plural marriage for time and eternity, with Smith and his closest associates secretly taking numerous wives, offended the religious sensibilities of many Saints, who believed they had joined a more traditional, more Protestant kind of Mormonism. Similarly controversial doctrines, such as belief in the preexistence of humans, metaphysical materialism with its attendant denial of the belief in creation *ex nihilo,* eternal progression, a plurality of gods, and the capacity for humans to achieve divinity through obedience to the principles of Mormonism, outraged not only nonbelievers but tested the faith of some of the more traditionally oriented Latter-day Saints. A group of alarmed anti-Mormons effectively capitalized on internal dissent and formed a mob that killed Smith and his brother Hyrum on June 27, 1844.

History has shown that the killers of the Mormon prophet were wrong in thinking that they had delivered a mortal blow to Mormonism. Although Smith's energy and genius started the new religion and kept it going in the face of nearly insurmountable external and internal opposition, a number of able leaders had been attracted to the young religion. They helped ensure its survival after Smith's death. As early as 1834, Smith had organized some of his most loyal lieutenants into a council of twelve apostles in restorationist emulation of the primitive church. In 1840, Brigham Young (1801–1877) became president of this powerful and prestigious group. In this capacity Young was sustained as leader by those Mormons who had unquestioningly accepted Smith's Nauvoo innovations. Most of those devotees followed Young to the Rocky Mountains, while most of the more traditional Saints, who rejected plural marriage and kingdom building, remained in the Midwest. In 1860, Smith's son Joseph Smith (1832–1914) became president of the Reorganized Church of Jesus Christ of Latter Day Saints, which established its headquarters in Independence, Missouri.

Settlement in Utah. Young's advance pioneering party arrived in the valley of the Great Salt Lake in July 1847 and immediately began to survey a site for a city with a temple at the center. Aided by a steady stream of immigrants, Young built an inland empire, including Utah and parts of present-day Idaho, Wyoming, Arizona, Nevada, and California, which boasted a population of over 100,000 by the time of his death in 1877. A practical leader not given to visions and revelations, he insisted throughout his life that he was implementing the plans that Smith had been unable to realize fully in Nauvoo. Plural marriage, practiced secretly in Nauvoo, was publicly announced to the world from Salt Lake City in 1852. Most of the church leaders took numerous wives to set an example for their somewhat reluctant followers, and by the 1860s more than 30 percent of the Mormon population lived in polygamous households. Temporal government was placed in the hands of ecclesiastical leaders under the auspices of a political kingdom of God whose theocratic model was ancient Israel. An ambitious attempt to establish a Mormon State of Deseret failed, but home rule for the Mormons was only partly thwarted, as the federal government, under the Compromise of 1850, created the Utah Territory with Young as governor.

In 1857, however, President James Buchanan (1791–1868) felt compelled to act on reports by territorial officials, who had accused Young and his followers of disloyalty to the United States and of immoral polygamous liaisons. The president sent an expeditionary force of the U.S. Army to Utah to prove to a reform-minded North that the Democrats were at least against one of the "twin relics of barbarism" (meaning slavery and polygamy), whose elimination had been the rallying cry of the Republican Party platform in 1856. "Buchanan's blunder," however, did not gain him any political advantage and ended in a negotiated settlement. Although Alfred Cumming, a non-Mormon, was officially installed as the new governor, the Mormons regarded Young as *de facto* governor of Utah. Nevertheless, the handwriting was on the wall for Young's Mormon kingdom; further government attacks on polygamy and the political kingdom were delayed only by the Civil War. Beginning in the 1870s, the U.S. Congress exerted increasing pressure on the Mormons, who in 1890 were forced to relinquish polygamy and the political kingdom as the price of their religion's survival. Mormon president Wilford Woodruff (1807–1898) issued a manifesto disavowing any further sanctioning of plural marriages by the church, symbolizing the passing of an era and the beginning of the reconciliation of Mormonism with the world—a transformation reinforced by a "second manifesto" issued by church president Joseph F. Smith (1838–1918), a grand-nephew of the founding prophet, in 1904.

Modern Mormonism. Throughout most of the nineteenth century, Mormonism had been an antimodern, antipluralist religious movement in a modernizing, pluralistic world. The latter was represented perhaps most significantly by the symbiosis between evangelical religion, entrepreneurial capitalism, and political pluralism. Religion, like politics, had become a commodity in the free marketplace of ideas and beliefs. Democrats and Whigs might disagree about means but not about ends. The same was true of Protestant religious denominations, who agreed that ultimately they would all arrive at the same truth, if by different routes. This was a world alien to Smith and most of those who became Mormons. Smith's original quest, which had sent him to pray in his father's grove, was for the one true church. Because truth ultimately could not be divided, "correct principles" also applied to economics, society, and government—principles that were incompatible with an emerging, competitive, capitalist American society. Here then was a fundamental source of conflict between the Saints and their adversaries, in which the former were sustained by their millennial expectations of the near advent of their Savior and the eventual triumph of the kingdom of God over its enemies.

When the Saints voted on October 6, 1890, to accept Woodruff's manifesto, they may not have perceived the full significance of their decision. Yet this event was a watershed in Mormon history, as the Saints then had to jettison some of their most distinctive institutions and beliefs: economic communitarianism, plural marriage, and the political kingdom. Mormons now followed their erstwhile evangelical adversaries into the pluralistic American cultural mainstream, joining what the historian Martin Marty has called "a nation of behavers." In search of new boundaries and symbols of identification, the Mormons, much like the evangelicals, placed greater emphasis on strict codes of behavior: abstinence from alcohol, tobacco, tea, and coffee; acceptance of regulated dress norms; and more intensive monitoring of sexual morality. These codes reflect the very values that had aided nineteenth-century evangelicals in their adaptation to an emerging capitalist industrial order requiring work discipline that was effectively sustained by internalized behavioral norms. Nevertheless, the question of how close modern Mormonism has moved to the Protestant mainstream remains controversial. In spite of Mormon protestations to the contrary, major conservative evangelical groups continue to reject the Mormon claim to be Christian.

In any case, Mormons found modern values congenial in their own adaptation to a competitive, individualistic social and economic order. They prepared the rising generation to meet this change not only through the family but also through a growing number of church auxiliaries: primary associations for the very young, young men's and women's organizations, Sunday schools, priesthood quorums, and women's auxiliaries. Such institutions were all designed to keep Mormons active in their church from the cradle to the grave, while at the same time allowing them to become productive members of the larger American society. Religion thus became a springboard for social and economic success in the world (though not intentionally so), which was further facilitated by the Mormons' increasing commitment to education. In the early years of the third millennium CE some fifty thousand Latter-day Saints (LDS) attended church-sponsored institutions of higher learning, such as the flagship Brigham Young University as well as church colleges in Idaho and Hawai'i. Many thousands more studied at secular universities throughout the United States and the Western world, receiving religious instruction at LDS institutes adjacent to such campuses. Mormons serve in prominent positions in the federal government, in the military, in major business corporations, and in major universities.

Many of these Mormons are third- to fifth-generation Latter-day Saints who have a strong cultural identification with their religion that is enhanced by closely-knit family ties. The strong Mormon emphasis on family solidarity finds theological and institutional expression in the belief in the eternal nature of the family when family ties have been solemnized within the sacred precincts of the temple. Temple ordinances, conducted not only for the living but also vicariously for the dead, are intended to bind families and ultimately the entire human race through sacred covenants. Only those Mormons who observe their religion's strict rules of conduct are allowed to enter the temple and participate in these ordinances and rituals. Temples, then, are not ordinary church buildings but are regarded as special edifices and are found only in major population centers. There are more than a hundred of these in various parts of the world. Meetinghouses, on the other hand, are functional buildings where congregations of several hundred members hold simple worship as well as social and athletic events—all open to non-Mormon visitors. Often two congregations share one building.

Modern Mormonism has succeeded in extending its appeal to members of diverse racial, social, and cultural backgrounds around the world. Missionaries who serve the church at their own expense for two years (mostly young men and women of college age) are increasingly successful in attracting converts in Asia, Latin America, and Africa. Many of these converts are attracted by a lay church that offers active participation to all of its members and provides an instant, socially cohesive group whose authoritarian male leaders set boundaries while providing recognition for behavior that conforms to group standards. Many converts are especially drawn to the Mormon family ideal.

This rapid expansion of Mormonism beyond its traditional culture region as it becomes a world religion brings with it some potential for conflict. Some multigenerational Mormons are apprehensive about the erosion of traditional symbols, such as architecture, in favor of a generic utilitarian building style. Others see this as a necessary accommodation of their religion to the cultural needs of new converts. Prophet President Spencer W. Kimball's 1978 revelation extending the lay priesthood to all Mormon males, irrespective of race or color (blacks had been denied the priesthood prior to that date), can be seen as a clear message indicating recognition of the need for major change. This is not to say, however, that tradition had suddenly lost its hold on a conservative hierarchy. Rather, it could be said Mormonism is cautiously backing into the future. A telling example of continuing conservatism is the persistent opposition to changes in the role of women, who are admonished to remain at home to raise children while partaking of the priesthood only through the male heads of families. (By contrast, the Community of Christ, which had never withheld the priesthood from blacks, announced that women were eligible for ordination to the priesthood.) This emphasis on "family values" is also reflected in continuing resistance to tolerance of homosexuality. At the same time, while not condoning abortion, Mormon leaders are less visible in their opposition than the Catholic hierarchy. They have also refrained from getting involved in the public controversy over stem-cell research, having adopted a wait-and-see attitude. Thus, if their history is a reliable guide to the future, the Mormon hierarchy in Utah will not allow its conservatism to hinder the progress of the Church of Jesus Christ of Latter-day Saints in the twenty-first century.

SEE ALSO Smith, Joseph; Young, Brigham.

BIBLIOGRAPHY

For more than a century, studies of Mormonism were highly polemical, divided by a simple dichotomy between believers and nonbelievers. The first sophisticated modern study of Mormonism was by the Catholic sociologist Thomas F. O'Dea, *The Mormons* (Chicago, 1957). For factual detail, a comprehensive and reliable scholarly account is James B. Allen and Glen M. Leonard, *The Story of the Latter-day Saints* (Salt Lake City, Utah, 1976). An interpretive synthesis from a scholarly Mormon perspective is Leonard J. Arrington and Davis Bitton, *The Mormon Experience: A History of the Latter-day Saints* (New York, 1979). An informative and evenhanded interpretation from a non-Mormon perspective is Richard N. Ostling and Joan K. Ostling, *Mormon America: The Power and the Promise* (San Francisco, 1999). A scholarly history of the Reorganized Church and the Community of Christ is Richard P. Howard, *The Church through the Years;* vol. 1: *RLDS Beginnings, to 1860;* vol. 2: *The Reorganization Comes of Age, 1860–1992* (Independence, Mo., 1992–1993). This should be supplemented by Alma R. Blair's "Reorganized Church of Jesus Christ of Latter Day Saints: Moderate Mormonism," in *The Restoration Movement: Essays in Mormon History,* edited by F. Mark McKiernan, Alma R. Blair, and Paul M. Edwards (Lawrence, Kans., 1973), pp. 207–230. For a perceptive discussion of the problems associated with modernization, see Armand L. Mauss, *The Angel and the Beehive: The Mormon Struggle with Assimilation* (Urbana, Ill., and Chicago, 1994). Klaus J. Hansen, *Mormonism and the American Experience* (Chicago, 1981), attempts to place Mormonism in the broader context of American culture. Jan Shipps's *Mormonism: The Story of a New Religious Tradition* (Urbana, Ill., 1985) is written from the perspective of a sympathetic non-Mormon scholar; hers is a successful attempt to transcend the polemical dichotomy.

KLAUS J. HANSEN (1987 AND 2005)

MORRISON, ROBERT

MORRISON, ROBERT (1782–1834), first Protestant missionary to China. Morrison was born in Morpeth, Northumberland, England, on January 15, 1782, of humble Scottish parentage. At an early age he became an apprentice to his father in making wooden boot trees. During these years he joined the Church of Scotland (1798) and soon began studying Latin, Hebrew, and theology. In 1802 he entered the Congregational Theological College at Hoxton (now Highbury College). His Christian upbringing and studies inclined him toward missionary service and in 1804 he offered himself to the London Missionary Society, which, though not yet ten years old, was beginning to prepare workers for China. Morrison spent the next two years at the Missionary College at Gosport. While there he began an intensive study of the Chinese language using a Chinese tutor and a Catholic translation of part of the New Testament into Chinese kept in the British Museum.

Shortly after his ordination on January 8, 1807, Morrison began making final arrangements for his departure for China on January 31. Because the British East India Company (BEIC) was hesitant to promote Protestant missions to China at that time, Morrison could only gain passage to New York. After receiving a personal written recommendation from James Madison, the American secretary of state, to the American consul in China, he set sail from New York and arrived in Canton on September 7, 1807.

Upon arrival, Morrison found the English-Chinese political situation tenuous. The propagation of Christianity was prohibited by the reigning Ch'ing dynasty. The Missionary Society knew this and had instructed Morrison not to preach openly but rather to concentrate on learning Chinese and to make the necessary preparations for publishing religious literature that would be used for long-range evangelism. Morrison stayed in various Western trade houses in Canton, where he assumed Chinese dress and dietary customs while studying the language with two Roman Catholic Chinese. Pressure from the government, however, eventually forced him to seek refuge in Portuguese Macao, where he stayed for one year with an English family, marrying their oldest daughter in 1809. During that same year he became employed by the BEIC as an interpreter. Having thus been able to acquire permanent residency, Morrison began to turn his efforts to ways in which to propagate the gospel. Realizing that under the current circumstances literature was virtually the only open avenue, he focused his attention on the printed word. The BEIC provided invaluable assistance at this point by allowing Morrison to use their press. His works were prolific and diverse: in 1810, his translation of *Acts* became the first portion of scripture translated into Chinese by a Protestant missionary; *Luke* (1812); the New Testament (1814); a Chinese grammar (1815); *A View of China for Philological Purposes* (1817); the entire Bible (written in 1818, published by 1823, 21 vols.); his magnum opus, a Chinese-English dictionary (3 vols., 1815, 1822, 1823); and catechisms (1812) as well as portions of *The Book of Common Prayer* (1833).

Morrison's wife died in China in 1822. He returned to England in 1824 and became a well-received lecturer able to generate interest for Chinese missions. Shortly before returning to China in 1826, Morrison married Eliza Armstrong.

Morrison witnessed his first Chinese baptism on July 16, 1814. After twenty-five years, his Society co-workers and he had baptized only ten individuals. Yet, in spite of difficulties that he encountered in his work, Morrison succeeded in laying down a foundation for others who were to follow. William Milne (1774–1822) came with his wife to assist Morrison in 1813 and was instrumental in helping translate and publish the Chinese Bible. Later, building upon Milne's school for Chinese established in Malacca (1816), Morrison founded the Anglo-Chinese College (1818). The purpose of this institution, besides providing a context for evangelism, was to establish reciprocal cultivation and respect of Chinese and European culture, language, and literature.

For his efforts, Robert Morrison was awarded an honorary degree from the University of Glasgow (1817); he became a Fellow of the Royal Society in 1824. After his death in Canton on August 1, 1834, his eldest son, John Robert Morrison (1814–1843), succeeded his father as Chinese secretary and interpreter for the British authorities in Canton.

BIBLIOGRAPHY

The principal archival sources are those of the London Missionary Society and the Morrison Library (and related collections) at the University of Hong Kong.

A primary source for any study of Robert Morrison is the two-volume *Memoirs of the Life and Labours of Robert Morrison* (London, 1839), compiled by his widow, Eliza, and published five years after his death. It is the main published authority for Morrison's life and contains much firsthand material. Also included are critical notices of his Chinese works as well as an appendix of original documents. Before the turn of the century William Townsend published a biography, *Robert Morrison, the Pioneer of Chinese Missions* (London, 1888). Later, more comprehensive works appeared such as Marshall Broomhall's *Robert Morrison: A Master-Builder* (New York, 1924), which has a list of his publications, and more recently a study with a more limited focus, Lindsay Ride's *Robert Morrison: The Scholar and the Man* (Hong Kong, 1957).

K. S. Latourette, in *A History of Christian Missions in China* (New York, 1929), reviews Morrison's work in the context of overall Protestant missions, as does Suzanne W. Barnett's article "Silent Evangelism: Presbyterians and the Mission Press in China, 1807–1860," *Journal of Presbyterian History* 49 (Winter 1971): 287–302.

PAUL V. MARTINSON (1987)

MORTIFICATION

MORTIFICATION. The term *mortification* derives from the church Latin *mortificare* ("to put to death"), a term that appears several times in the Latin New Testament. In the *Letter to the Romans*, Paul counseled the early Christians, "if you live according to the flesh you will die, but if by the Spirit you put to death [*mortificetis*] the deeds of the body you will live" (8:13). In the *Letter to the Colossians* the Christian is exhorted: "Put to death [*mortificate*] what is earthly in you: fornication, impurity, passion, evil desire, and covetousness, which is idolatry" (3:5). This "mortification of the flesh" was intimately connected with the "mortification" of Jesus Christ, that is to say, with his crucifixion. According to Paul, Christians carry this death (*mortificatio*) of Jesus in their bodies so that the life of Jesus might also be manifest in them (2 *Cor.* 4:10). All who belong to Christ have "crucified" the flesh with its passions (*Gal.* 5:24). The Christian notion of mortification thus derives from this originally Pauline ideal of participation in the passion of Christ through the putting to death of the inordinate desires of the flesh. This ideal was exemplified by the early martyrs, and when the persecutions eventually came to an end mortification began to function as a sort of self-imposed martyrdom. Thus the adoption of practices of mortification made it possible for future generations of Christians, living in more or less settled times, to recapture some of the self-sacrificing intensity of the early church.

In the general history of religions the term *mortification*, despite its specifically Christian origins, may be extended by way of analogy to refer to a wide variety of practices that aim at the religious transformation of the individual through specific forms of bodily discipline, often entailing a degree of actual physical pain or suffering. Mortification is to be distinct from asceticism in that it is one of the latter's possible components. The term *asceticism* usually refers to a general regimen or way of life that may or may not include specific forms of mortification. Indeed, if mortification is understood as involving the deliberate infliction of actual physical suffering, then it may be altogether absent from some forms of ascetic life, such as that practiced in Buddhism.

For the sake of the following exposition I will distinguish two general types of mortification: the ascetic type, which is more or less integrated into a general form of religious life (and may include, for example, the wearing of rough or inadequate clothing), and the initiatory type, which is occasioned by specific ritual initiations and is more likely to involve the temporary infliction of pain.

ASCETIC MORTIFICATION. In Christianity, mortification usually has been an element in a more general practice of the ascetic life. Among its most extreme forms are self-flagellation and the wearing of a hair shirt. Flagellation is intended to reproduce the scourging of Christ, while the hair shirt, an ancient penitential symbol, can function as a kind of continuous flagellation. The semantic history of the hair shirt is informative. Originally it was simply a garment made of very rough cloth. In the *Book of Daniel* (9:3) the wearing of rough cloth garments is associated with fasting and with strewing ashes on one's head in order to entreat God. In the *Gospel of Matthew* (11:23), such garments are associated with strewing ashes on the head as a sign of conversion. In primitive Christianity they were the dress required of catechumens; from the fourth century on they were adopted by monks as a means of mortification. In the sixteenth century the name *hair shirt* was given to what was really a scourge worn as a belt against the naked flesh, the rope made more painful by being knotted or by the addition of metal nails. This type of hair shirt was first used by certain mendicant orders and became a form of private mortification.

These and other less extreme forms of mortification, such as fasting, could be used as means of individual penance for particular sins or as a more general form of asceticism associated in particular with the monastic orders. In both cases mortification was ideally intended to have a transformative effect, aiding in the transition from a life devoted to the gratification of the desires of the body to a higher, sanctified life in the spirit.

The forms of mortification that one finds in various Hindu religious traditions also aim at a radical transformation of the practitioner, but there is a marked difference in the attitude taken to the suffering that this entails. Whereas in the Christian tradition, the suffering is connected with the sufferings of Christ as an *imitatio Christi*, in Hinduism the suffering lacks this positive aspect and is used negatively as an inducement to rise above the human condition. The practices of Yoga, for instance, aim primarily at the suppression of suffering or at the cultivation of an attitude of complete indifference to it. In itself the suffering involved in mortification has no positive religious significance. The ideal is to reach a state of detachment that is in many respects similar to the Stoic ideal of *apatheia* and is thus quite different from the intense involvement implied in the notion of the *imitatio Christi.*

Buddhism is quite similar in this regard, although the Buddhist ideal of the Middle Way served to moderate some of the more extreme forms of mortification found among the ascetics of the Buddha's day. The Buddha's own engagement in mortification led him to death's door before he renounced such extreme practices. To the extent that the idea of mortification implies immoderation it cannot be accepted as a Buddhist ideal. Nevertheless, Buddhist ascetic practices may still be regarded as forms of mortification to the extent that they aim at the cessation of *saṃsāra*, the cycle of life.

INITIATORY MORTIFICATION. In a wide variety of archaic religious traditions mortification occurs in the context of initiation rituals. In some of these cases, practices of mortification seem intended symbolically to assimilate the initiate into a deathlike condition that is to precede an initiatory rebirth. Such practices thus place the initiate temporarily outside of the normal human order. The practices include a number of temporary dietary restrictions, ranging from fasting to complete abstinence, and various forms of imposed deprivations, such as deprivation of water and of sleep. This may also be the motivation behind several practices designed to test the initiate's endurance of extremes of heat and cold.

The keeping of watches and vigils is widespread. Such practices have been attested to among the Andaman Islanders and peoples of New Guinea (the Siana), Africa (the Venda), and South America (the Ocaina). Deprivation of sleep, food, and drink seem to be ways of symbolizing death: the dead do not eat, drink, or sleep.

Other forms of mortification associated with initiation rituals are more difficult to interpret. A number of practices of a punitive character, such as flogging, for one reason or another form an integral part of the initiation process. Some involve torture, such as the practice of biting the initiate's head through to the bone (Australia) or that of hanging the initiate from a rope that passes through a hole made between the muscle and the shoulder bone (as among some Plains and Northwest Coast tribal groups of North America).

Ritual forms of abuse are usually interpreted as endurance tests, an interpretation at times suggested by the requirement that the painful ordeal be undergone without complaint lest the rite be invalidated. But there are also cases in which the initiate is not forbidden to cry out, and even cases in which a cry of pain must be heard by those who are present. If, when faced with such cases, we refuse to characterize such ritual abuses as purposeful (for example, as tests of endurance), all that remains is to characterize them as expressions of violence. Violence may serve to separate the initiate from his earlier natural state (the infantile) and to introduce him to the social status of an adult. It is violence of this sort that the smith, a common initiator among many African peoples, exerts upon the natural elements in order to transform them into the tools of culture, through a kind of symbolic mortification. Violence may have a similar purpose in rituals of initiation. In the ritual hanging mentioned above, for instance, the initiate is made to spin around as he hangs until he faints. This loss of consciousness, which is precisely the attainment of a state similar to death, may well be the final goal of this rather grim form of mortification.

In general, however, violence is of secondary importance; it is not strictly required in order to act out an initiatory death. In some cases symbolic death may be achieved merely by conducting funeral rites over the initiate or over something that represents him. The initiate may be mourned, spoken of as deceased, subjected to a fake interment, or in other ways treated like a corpse.

Initiatory forms of mortification that involve the creation of a symbolic state of death may also be detected in baptismal rites that call for the complete immersion of the initiate. The passage from impurity to purity implies not only a rebirth but also a death of the old condition. Immersion in water may signify a mortification through a reimmersion in the primordial waters of chaos prior to rebirth. From this perspective, one can say with Mircea Eliade (1958) that the same logic has produced both baptismal rites and myths of inundation, both involving initiatory forms of mortification endowed with cosmic significance.

Mortification of the King. There is a cosmic dimension as well in the "mortification of the king," a rite of periodic cosmic renewal. In Babylonia, this annual ritual consisted merely of stripping the king of his regal insignia, slapping his face, and pulling his ears. However, as James G. Frazer argued in *The Golden Bough*, this seemingly harmless "mortification" may be merely a survival of an earlier practice in which the king was actually put to death.

The practice of the mortification of the king recalls the passion of Christ, who was crucified with the title *Rex Judeorum:* Christ "mortified" as a worldly king so that he could rise again as the heavenly king. The death of Christ also marks the end of a cycle and the initiation of a new order. It is in this death that the Christian participates, both through the initiation of baptism and through the practice of mortification. The initiatory type of mortification, though not prominent, is nevertheless discernible in Christianity in a somewhat attenuated form. This is but one indication that the types of ascetic and initiatory mortification that I have presented here need not be viewed as mutually exclusive.

As a final note, it is interesting that the expression "mortification of the king" (*mortificatio regis*) appears in the literature of alchemy as one of the most frequent symbols of the disintegration of matter. Interpreted spiritually, this *mortification regis* is a part of what Renaissance alchemists called the "saving Christian mystery." Meditation on the *mortificatio regis*, therefore, was comparable to meditation on the *mistero doloroso* of the passion of Christ in the Catholic practice of the recitation of the rosary.

Bibliography

No specific bibliography exists. The reader is referred to the bibliography of *Asceticism* for sources of more information about mortification of the ascetic type and to the bibliographies of the articles on *Initiation* for sources of more information about the initiatory type. Also, for the latter category, see especially Mircea Eliade's *Birth and Rebirth: The Religious Meaning of Initiation in Human Culture* (London, 1958), which places initiatory mortification in the general dialectic between the precosmic and the cosmic. Following this same exegetical line, Eliade's *The Forge and the Crucible: The Origins and Structures of Alchemy*, 2d ed. (Chicago, 1978) discusses the smith as "maître d'initiation" and offers an introduction to the alchemist's mystical theology of *mortificatio.* For a historical overview of the "mortification of the king," see my *Il mito, il rito e la storia* (Rome, 1978), pp. 329–477.

New Sources

Camporesi, Piero. *The Incorruptible Flesh: Bodily Mutation and Mortification in Religion and Folklore.* New York, 1988.

Diamond, Eliezer. *Holy Men and Hunger Artists: Fasting and Asceticism in Rabbinic Culture.* New York, 2004.

Gleason, Randall C. *John Calvin and John Owen on Mortification: A Comparative Study in Reformed Spirituality.* Studies in Church History 3. New York, 1995.

Oddie, Geoffrey A. *Popular Religion, Elites, and Reforms: Hook-Swinging and Its Prohibition in Colonial India, 1800–1894.* New Delhi, 1995.

Schlabach, Gerald. *For the Joy Set before Us: Augustine and Self-Defying Love.* Notre Dame, Ind., 2001.

DARIO SABBATUCCI (1987)
Translated from Italian by J. C. Binzen
Revised Bibliography

MOSES (c. thirteenth century BCE, but date uncertain), or, in Hebrew, Mosheh, was the leader of the Hebrews in the Exodus from Egypt and giver of the Law at Sinai. Tradition regards Moses as the founder of Israel's religion—the mediator of its covenant with God (Yahveh) and its cultic institutions.

HISTORICITY OF MOSES. Any discussion about the historicity of Moses is entirely dependent upon an evaluation of the biblical account of his life and activity. There are no extant records from Egypt that make any reference to him or to the Exodus. Yet most scholars believe that a person named Moses existed and had a connection with the events of the Exodus and the wilderness journey as described in the four biblical books from *Exodus* to *Deuteronomy.* But there is little agreement about how much can be known about Moses or what role he played in the events, because the biblical accounts have been modified and embellished, and Moses' place in some of the traditions may be secondary.

The one point that seems to argue for regarding Moses as historical is his Egyptian name. An explanation of the name *Moses* that few would dispute is that it derives from the Egyptian verb *msy* ("to give birth"), a very common element in Egyptian names. This verb is usually combined with the name of a god (e.g., *Re,* as in *Remesses,* i.e., *Ramses*), and the shortened form, *Moses,* is in the nature of a nickname. But whether in the long or short form, the name is common in Egypt from the mid-second millennium onward. None of the persons in Egyptian historical records bearing the name Moses can justifiably be identified with the biblical Moses, and to do so is quite arbitrary. The only argument for historicity to be derived from Moses' Egyptian name is its appropriateness to the background of Israel's sojourn in Egypt. Other examples of Egyptian names occur among the Israelites, particularly within the ranks of the priests and Levites. Such names may have survived in Canaan at sanctuaries and urban centers from the time of Egyptian control of the region in the Late Bronze Age.

A name by itself, however appropriate to the time and events described, does not make a historical personality. The various elements of the Exodus story do not correspond with known Egyptian history, and historians have usually set about reconstructing the events to make a better fit between the Bible and contemporary records. For instance, the presence of numerous Asiatic slaves in Egypt during the eighteenth and nineteenth dynasties (1550–1200 BCE) was not the result of an enslavement, out of fear and hatred, of a specific people already resident in Egypt, as pictured in *Exodus.* Slaves were brought into Egypt in large numbers as prisoners of war from many different peoples and social classes and were dispersed throughout Egypt to serve in many different capacities. Many Asiatics became free persons within Egyptian society and were found at various levels of rank and status. The nineteenth dynasty in particular was one of great assimilation of Asiatic religion and culture in Egypt. Furthermore, while bedouin were allowed certain grazing rights in the eastern Delta, there is no suggestion that they were enslaved or made to do menial labor. Nothing in the Egyptian records suggests any acts of genocide or any distinct group of state slaves resident in the eastern Delta.

None of the pharaohs in *Exodus* is named, but the reference in *Exodus* 1:11 to the Israelites' building the store cities of Pithom and Ramses is enough evidence for many to date the events to the nineteenth dynasty. Yet Pithom (Tell el-Maskhuta), in the Wadi Tumilat, was not built until the end of the seventh century BCE, and the reference to Ramses and the "land of Ramses" hardly suggests the royal residence. The name *Goshen,* as the region where the Israelites were said to reside, is known only from the latest geographic texts. The few specific names and details, therefore, do not point to a particular period of Egyptian history, and scholars differ on the dating and background of the Exodus precisely because so many details must be radically redrawn to make any connection possible. The quest for the historical Moses is a futile exercise. He now belongs only to legend.

LITERARY TRADITION. The traditions about Moses are contained in the Pentateuch from *Exodus* to *Deuteronomy,* and all other biblical references to Moses are probably dependent upon these. The view of most critical scholars for the past century has been that the Pentateuch's presentation of Moses is not the result of a single author but the combination of at least four sources, known as the Yahvist (J), the Elohist (E), Deuteronomy (D), and the Priestly writer (P), and composed in that order. The existence of E as a separate work from J has long been disputed; at best it is very fragmentary. It is best to treat J and E as a single corpus, JE, as will be done below. The usual dating for these sources places them in a range from the tenth to the fifth century BCE, although there is a strong tendency, which the author of this article supports, to view D (from the seventh century) as the earliest work, JE (from the sixth century) as exilic, and P (from the fifth century) as postexilic. This would account for the fact that so little is made of the Moses tradition outside of the Pentateuch.

Whether one adopts the older scheme or the later date for the Pentateuchal sources, a long period of time separates any historical figure from the written presentation of Moses in the Bible. To bridge this gap one is faced with evaluating the diversity of traditions within the Moses legend and with tracing their history of transmission prior to their use by the later authors, as well as with considering the shape and color the authors themselves gave to the Moses tradition as a reflection of their own times and concerns. The history of the preliterary tradition has occupied a lot of attention but with few convincing results because it is so difficult to control any reconstruction of the various stages of oral tradition. One is therefore left with an examination of the traditions about Moses in their present literary forms within the larger context of the Hebrew scriptures.

Moses as deliverer from Egypt. The general background for the deliverance of the people through Moses is the theme of the oppression and enslavement in Egypt. This theme of Israel's oppression is often mentioned elsewhere in the Hebrew scriptures as the condition of the people from which God "redeemed" them, often without any reference to Moses (note, e.g., *Ez.* 20). The Pentateuch continues to stress God as deliverer but now makes Moses the human agent.

Within the tradition of enslavement the JE writer introduces a special theme of attempted genocide (*Ex.* 1:8–22), which provides the context for the story of Moses' birth and his rescue from the Nile by the Egyptian princess (*Ex.* 2:1–10). But once this story is told, the theme of genocide disappears, and the issue becomes again that of enslavement and hard labor. The story of Moses as a threatened child rescued from the basket of reeds and reared under the very nose of Pharaoh to become the deliverer of his people corresponds to a very common folkloric motif of antiquity. Similar stories were told about Sargon of Akkad and Cyrus the Persian. However, Moses' initial attempt at deliverance (*Ex.* 2:11–15), whereby he kills an Egyptian for beating a Hebrew, is antiheroic because it ends in failure and leads only to his flight to the land of Midian, where he becomes a shepherd (*Ex.* 2:16–22, 3:1). This prepares the way for the author (JE) to present Moses as a most unheroic leader, totally dependent on the divine word from Yahveh for each action he takes.

The story of Moses' experience of the burning bush theophany at Sinai/Horeb, in the land of Midian (*Ex.* 3–4), has all the marks of a new beginning. It resembles that of the prophetic-call narratives in which the prophet experiences a theophany and then is given his commission (*Is.* 6, *Ez.* 1–3). Moses' protest is similar to that of Jeremiah in his call (*Jer.* 1:6–10), but the author in *Exodus* develops it into an elaborate motif. At the same time Moses' call bears some resemblance to the commissioning of a military leader whose task it is to deliver his people from oppression (*Jgs.* 6, *1 Sm.* 9). But Moses is not given the task of being a military leader, nor are the signs he receives meant to give him confidence of victory. The primary concern in the dialogue between Moses and Yahveh is in Moses' role as a spokesman whom the people will believe and who can speak on behalf of the people to the foreign ruler. The author (JE) has drawn upon both the tradition of classical prophecy and the literary history of Gideon and Saul to fashion his rather composite presentation of Moses' call and commission as Israel's deliverer.

The plague stories (*Ex.* 7:14–11:10) carry out the image of Moses as deliverer through the prophetic word of judgment and salvation. But they also add the element of the prophet as a wonder-worker similar to Elijah and Elisha. Yet in the plagues tradition the wonders are all carefully circumscribed by divine commands so that Moses and Aaron—aside from a slight gesture—are almost completely passive and unconnected to them (see also *Ps.* 78:43–51, 105:26–36). The notion of the man of God as miracle worker has been largely absorbed by the view of the prophet as messenger and spokesman. The P writer, however, introduces the notion of a contest between Aaron and the magicians of Egypt (7:8–12). The plague stories as a whole are intended to emphasize the greatness and power of Yahveh and add very little to the Moses tradition.

The climax of Israel's deliverance is at the Red Sea (*Ex.* 13:17–14:31), and here again Moses' role is to announce judgment on the Egyptians and salvation for Israel. In the JE account Moses and Israel do nothing but witness the divine rescue, while in the P version Moses, at God's command, splits the sea with his rod to create a path for the Israelites and, again at divine command, makes the sea come back upon their pursuers. The effect is that the people fear Yahveh and believe in him and in his servant Moses. It is remarkable that except for one late addition to *Deuteronomy* (11:4) there are no references to the Red Sea event in this source even though the Exodus is mentioned many times. This suggests that the Red Sea episode is really secondary to the Exodus tradition. In its present form it constitutes a transition to the wilderness themes and to Moses' direct leadership of his people.

Moses as leader. Apart from an initial contact with Israel's elders in Egypt, which did not turn out very well (*Ex.* 5), Moses' direct leadership of the people begins only when they depart from Egypt. As their leader he is the one to whom the people complain about their hardships in the wilderness. But it is always God who meets their needs, with manna from heaven, or quails, or water from a rock. In the case of the people's complaints or rebellions, sometimes directed at Moses (and Aaron), God answers with judgment, and Moses must act as intercessor to mitigate the severity of the punishment. In all of this Moses is primarily a spiritual leader, a kind of prophetic mediator between the people and God with no other form of authority or legitimation.

Moses is also the supreme judge and head of the administrative functions of the wilderness community. In these capacities the tradition tells of two occasions in which Moses sets up civil institutions, one a system of courts for the purpose of sharing the judicial responsibility of the people (*Ex.* 18, *Dt.* 1:9–18) and the other a council of seventy elders for a sharing of the governance (*Nm.* 11:16–30). But these stories merely represent etiologies of later Israelite institutions. Moses' authority is his endowment of the prophetic spirit and the means by which God speaks and directs the people in every decision.

On a few occasions the Israelites are involved in military encounters, but Moses' role in these is very limited. In their fight against the Amalekites (*Ex.* 17:8–16) Joshua is the military captain, while Moses raises his hands as if to receive divine aid. When Moses sends spies to survey the land of Canaan, it is Joshua and Caleb who play the major role in support of a military campaign and against the negative report of the other spies. When the people finally attempt a southern assault, Moses does not go with them, and they are defeated. In the campaign against the Midianites (*Nm.* 31 [P]) it is Phinehas the priest who takes charge of the army while Moses remains in the camp. In the campaign against Sihon and Og (*Nm.* 21:21–35, *Dt.* 2:24–3:11) Moses appears to lead the forces in the D account, but in JE he recedes into the background. Moses is not a military hero in these traditions.

Moses as lawgiver. The theme of Moses as lawgiver is more closely associated with the theophany at Sinai/Horeb (*Ex.* 19–20, *Dt.* 4–5), and with the prolonged stay at the mountain of God, during which the Law was given to Israel through Moses. Many scholars have argued that the giving of the Law at Sinai originated as a separate tradition. In many respects it represents a detour on the way from Egypt to Canaan and is parallel to another law-giving tradition, which is reflected in *Exodus* 15:25–26. But the matter is hotly debated and still unresolved.

Within the corpus of laws in the Pentateuch there is great variation of type and function reflecting different social settings and historical perspectives. Some of these laws represent the casuistic style of civil law used in the settled life of Israelite society in the land of Canaan. Others are apodictic commands that express universal principles of ethics and religion. There are also laws regarding cultic observances and regulations. Each category of law contains examples of parallel versions among the various Pentateuchal sources, and the law codes of the various sources can be correlated with certain periods of Israelite history. Thus the comparative study of the laws of the Pentateuch has become an important aspect of the study of Israel's social and religious history far removed from the wilderness period, which is their present narrative setting.

Nevertheless Moses has often been viewed as the author of the Ten Commandments. But the two forms, in *Deuteronomy* 5 and *Exodus* 20, are in the sources D and P respectively, and their language is so characteristic of D that there seems little reason to believe that they are any older than the seventh century BCE. Even in these two sources the "ten words" are said to have been given to the people directly without the mediation of Moses and only later written by the finger of God upon the two tables of stone. Furthermore, the JE corpus does not regard the Ten Commandments as a distinct series and has quite a different set of laws and instructions written on the two tables of stone (*Ex.* 34).

The JE corpus of laws in *Exodus* 20:22–23:33, usually designated as the Book of the Covenant (24:7), is a mixture of all types of law, religious and civil regulations, absolute principles of religion and ethics, and paraenesis. These are all given through Moses at one time on Sinai and constitute the basis of the covenant between the people and their God (*Ex.* 24:3–8). Portions of the civil laws are generally regarded as quite old in origin and perhaps taken over from the earlier Canaanite society, but this corpus of laws in its present form derives from the exilic period. The Deuteronomic code (*Dt.* 12–26) is the body of instructions given to Moses *after* the Ten Commandments were proclaimed. The D code was delivered to the people in written form in the land of Moab as preparation for their entry into the promised land. In actual fact the code represents a cultic reform movement of purification and centralization of worship in the time of Josiah (c. 625 BCE). The Priestly code is primarily concerned with setting out an elaborate program of cultic regulations to form the basis for the cult of the Second Temple during the restoration. Its view of Judean society is strongly theocratic, with the high priest as the real head of state—hence the elevation of Aaron alongside of Moses. The P writer has much of this code revealed to Moses at Sinai (*Ex.* 25–31, 35–40; *Lv.; Nm.* 1–10), but some instructions are given during the remaining part of the wilderness journey. In P, Moses' role as the revealer and instructor in divine law is the most dominant.

For all the biblical writers the wilderness period was the constitutional age, the time of Israel's beginning. Whatever was most fundamental to Israelite society was deemed to have arisen in this period. And Moses as the leader, the prophet, the founder, was regarded as the one through whom all this came about. Modern historical criticism, however, has made the Moses tradition problematic by identifying its anachronisms and by dating its materials to later ages. While some scholars have tried to find some elements of the tradition, particularly within the Decalogue, that may go back to Moses, there are others who dispute that any of the laws and customs of the Pentateuch derive from Moses or the wilderness period.

MOSES AS THE FOUNDER OF ISRAELITE RELIGION. Many scholars believe that Moses is the founder of Israel's religion, at least in the form of a worship of Yahveh alone and, ultimately, in the form of monotheism. This position is based upon a number of arguments. First, the P source explicitly states (*Ex.* 6:2–3) that the name of Yahveh was not known before the time of Moses and that the forefathers worshiped God as El Shaddai. In *Genesis* there are also frequent references to forms of El worship among the patriarchs. Yet the JE corpus clearly regards the patriarchs as worshipers of Yahveh and the El epithets as merely titles for Yahveh. It is the P writer who has created a periodization of revelation out of the El references. The use of *El* as a designation for Yahveh becomes particularly frequent in the exilic period (see *Is.* 40–55) and says nothing about early Israelite forms of worship.

Second, in the call narrative of *Exodus* 3:13 Moses inquires about God's name and is given an answer that seeks to explain the name *Yahveh* (actually YHVH in the unvocalized Hebrew text) in terms of its supposed etymology from the verb *hyh* ("to be"). This could be interpreted as signifying that Moses introduced a new understanding of the name and character of Yahveh and Yahveh's relations with his people. Yet this piece of dialogue is unrelated to anything else that follows in the tradition and has the character of theological speculation and interests in the author's own time. It tells nothing about Moses.

Third, the first and second commandments of the Decalogue emphasize the exclusive worship of Yahveh and an imageless cult. Those who attribute the Decalogue to Moses also use it as a basis for their view that Moses was the founder of monotheism. But it is unlikely that these laws predate the seventh century BCE. Archaeological evidence confirms the fact that as late as the eighth century BCE Yahveh was regarded by some Israelites as having a divine consort. At Kuntillat ʿAjrud, a Judean sanctuary in eastern Sinai, two inscriptions were found containing blessings "by Yahveh and his Asherah" (a female deity). One of these inscriptions was accompanied by a drawing of a seated female deity alongside two male divinities(?). At Khirbet el Qôm in western Judah a similar inscription referring to Yahveh and his consort Asherah was also found. The first commandment of the Decalogue may be understood as a direct protest against such a consort being placed or named "beside" Yahveh.

Fourth, there are those who would see in the Sinai covenant Moses' achievement in creating a unique politico-religious union centered upon commitment to Yahveh and a new social order among his fellow Israelites. These scholars point to the Hittite suzerainty treaty model of the Late Bronze Age, which emphasizes absolute loyalty to the great king based upon past favors and complete obedience to a series of stipulations regulating relations between king and vassal as well as between vassal states. The force of the argument lies in the attempt to establish parallels between this model and the giving of the law and covenant ratification at Sinai in *Exodus* 19–24, as well as in the fact that the time of Moses and the time of the Hittite empire are relatively close. The theory, however, has come under criticism because the parallels are too forced to be convincing, the treaty form is not so restricted in time, and the greatest correspondences to such a treaty-covenant form is to be found in *Deuteronomy*—very likely written shortly after Judah had experienced such vassalage to Assyria. In fact, it has been strongly argued that the notion of such a Sinai/Horeb covenant between Yahveh and his people is no older than D and cannot be traced back to Moses.

While the critical scholar may doubt that a historical figure, Moses, living in the thirteenth century BCE was the founder of Israelite religion in anything like the form reflected in the Pentateuch, the tradition itself has clearly regarded him as such, and thus he remained in all the subsequent developments of that tradition in later times.

MOSES IN POSTBIBLICAL JUDAISM. The great diversity within Jewish piety and religion in the centuries that followed the Hebrew scriptures does not allow for a simple statement about the development of the Moses tradition in this period. Nor is it possible to do justice to all the sources or varying viewpoints. Yet a few common features are shared by most of them and may be listed as follows. (1) The Law of Moses, the Torah, becomes understood as the whole of the Pentateuch and not just the laws within it. This means that God revealed to Moses past history as well as future events, in addition to law. (2) The legend of Moses, especially details about his birth and youth, was greatly expanded. (3) Moses is consistently viewed as the greatest prophet of Israel, although the understanding of this "office" and the nature of the revelation he received were not always the same. (4) Moses is the great intercessor and defender on Israel's behalf and the one responsible for mitigating God's punishment for the people's sins. This article now considers some of the special developments of the Moses tradition.

Moses in Hellenistic Judaism. One of the characteristics of Hellenistic Judaism in the period from 200 BCE to 100 CE was its strong apologetic character. A number of pagan writings represented Judaism and its history in a bad light and included Moses in this vilification. In order to counteract this, Jewish writers presented their history in a way that would have special appeal for Gentile audiences and win support for their religion and way of life. Thus Moses was portrayed as a great culture hero and inventor of the arts of civilization, including writing, philosophy, statesmanship, and religion. Moses' early life was modeled after the Hellenistic biography of the divine man, with prophecies about his birth and greatness, accounts of his beauty and royal upbringing, and his great military exploits on behalf of the pharoah. In all these embellishments of the tradition the authors were responding to criticisms of Moses.

Josephus Flavius, the Jewish historian writing at the end of the first century CE, stands in this stream of Hellenistic historiography. Moses is both the Hellenistic "divine man" and the Hebrew "man of God." As lawgiver he is presented in Greek terms as legislator and founder of the ideal constitution—a theocracy (*Jewish Antiquities* 2.6–24, 3.180, 4.13, 150, 156; *Against Apion* 2.75, 145, 154ff.). At the same time Moses is the greatest of the prophets as the "apostle" of God and interpreter of the words of God (*Antiquities* 4.165, 329; 3.85–87).

Philo Judaeus of Alexandria, who also lived in the first century CE, stands in the tradition of Judeo-Greek philosophy and mystical religion. He identifies Moses as the ideal king of Hellenistic ideology and combines in this role most of Moses' task (*Life of Moses* 1). Moses, with his special qualities as divine man, his royal upbringing, and his life as a shepherd, is prepared to become the king of Israel in the wilderness period. To his role as king is related his function as legislator, because the king is the embodiment of law (2.8ff.). The priesthood is also part of the royal office, and Moses is priest, according to Philo, in his establishment of the cult and in his role as intercessor (2.66ff.). Moses is also *the* prophet for Philo but in the special sense of the ecstatic who gains direct intuition of the truth through the mystical experience (2.187ff.). The theophany of Sinai was such an experience for Moses whereby he ascended to heaven itself and became a divine king through divinization. In some of Philo's writings he describes Moses as a hierophant, and the Torah is interpreted as a guide into the mysteries of God (*On the Decalogue* 18; *Allegorical Interpretation* 3.173).

The apocalyptic tradition. In two apocalyptic works, the *Assumption of Moses* and *Jubilees,* Moses receives special and secret knowledge about both past and future as well as the unseen worlds of heaven and hell (*Jub.* 1.26; *Asm. Mos.* 1.16–18). The apocalyptic literature reveals this information with special emphasis on the events of the end of time. Great emphasis is also placed upon Moses as intercessor, but this is not restricted to the wilderness period. Because Moses' death is understood as an assumption into heaven, his role as defender of Israel continues throughout Israel's history up to the Last Judgment (*Jub.* 1.18–21; *Asm. Mos.* 11.17).

The Essenes living at Qumran on the shores of the Dead Sea in the first centuries BCE and CE were a community dedicated to living by the Torah. They regarded themselves as the true Israel, who withdrew to the desert "to prepare the way of the Lord" for the last days (*1 Qumran Scrolls* 8.14f.). The biblical wilderness period was a model for their own experience, and a study of the Law was intended to yield an eschatological revelation for their own times. Moses was the great prophet whose words were the primary revelation for this apocalyptic community (*1 QS* 1.3, 8.15; *Code of Damascus* 5.21).

Rabbinic view of Moses. The rabbinic tradition represents a vast array of sources from the second century to the Middle Ages, containing a wide spectrum of belief and opinion. At the same time it fell heir to many of those traditions and impulses in the Moses tradition that has already been noted above.

In the legal tradition (*halakhah*) Moses represents the great "teacher" by which Israel was instructed in the Torah. This includes not only the laws of the Pentateuch but all the subsequent oral Torah, which was handed down from Moses to Joshua and in succession to the rabbis. All students of the law were really disciples of Moses.

The homiletic tradition (*aggadah*) brought to the fore those other aspects of the Moses tradition that were a part of Jewish piety. It continued to embellish the biography of Moses as the "man of God," but more central is his role as the servant of God. As such he was God's agent for bringing about the rescue from Egypt, for mediating the covenant and the laws to Israel at Sinai, and for leading the Israelites to the Promised Land. The role of servant emphasized Moses' function as intercessor for his people and as one who suffered and died on their behalf. Through his death in the wilderness instead of in Canaan Moses was identified with the sinful generation of the wilderness and thus ensured its salvation in the resurrection.

Moses was the supreme prophet as revealer of the words of God and the one to inaugurate the succession of prophets. The traditions about Moses as king and priest were viewed in a more limited fashion, for while he may have been king during the wilderness period and priest in the dedication of the Tabernacle rites, he was not able to pass on this succession to his heirs, and it remained for David as king and Aaron as high priest to found these lines of succession.

There is also a tradition within the *aggadah* about Moses' heavenly ascent at Sinai that elaborates on his vision of God and his struggles with the angels to acquire the Torah for Israel. These stories have much in common with the ascension materials called *heikhalot,* which Gershom Scholem has seen as reflecting ecstatic mystical experiences. There was a certain reticence expressed by some rabbis toward this form of piety and the rather speculative character of its traditions.

MOSES IN THE NEW TESTAMENT. The New Testament accepts Moses as the author of the Pentateuch (*Mt.* 8:4, *Mk.* 7:10, *Jn.* 1:17), but the real significance of the Pentateuch is as a prophecy that discloses the origins of Christianity (*Lk.* 24:25–27). Yet the whole of the institutional and ritual forms of Judaism as well as the Pharisaic-rabbinic tradition is associated with Moses, so that Moses reflects the ambivalent feelings of Christianity's continuity and discontinuity with Judaism.

In the Gospels, elements in the life of Jesus are parallel to those in the expanded legend of Moses. The infancy narrative in *Matthew* (chap. 2), with its predictions and warnings to king and father, its slaughter of the innocents, its recognition of Jesus' royalty, and the flight into exile until the king's death, is modeled on the Moses biographies. The scene on the mount of transfiguration where Jesus appears with Moses and Elijah has many allusions to the Sinai theophany (*Mt.* 17:1–8, *Mk.* 9:2–8, *Lk.* 9:28–36); Jesus' feeding of the five thousand (*Mt.* 14:13–21, *Mk.* 6:32–44, *Lk.* 9:10–17, *Jn.* 6:1–14) is directly associated in John's gospel with Moses giving the manna in the wilderness (6:25–34); and his forty days of fasting in the wilderness parallel Moses' fast at Sinai (*Mt.* 4:1–2, *Lk.* 4:1–3; cf. *Dt.* 9:9). The story of Jesus' ascension in *Luke* and *Acts* has similarities to the traditions of Moses' assumption (*Lk.* 24:51, *Acts* 1:9–11).

The ministry of Jesus is also compared with that of Moses. In Matthew's gospel, Jesus' teachings are given a setting—that of the Sermon on the Mount—that is parallel to the receiving of the law at Sinai. In *Luke,* Jesus as prophet is a second Moses who has come to redeem his people. In *John,* the comparison with Moses is especially pronounced: "The law came through Moses but grace and truth came through Jesus Christ" (1:17). John's message to Jewish believers is that Jesus is superior to Moses and supplants him so that one must make a choice between Moses and Jesus.

The apostle Paul, using the methods of Hellenistic Jewish exegesis, interprets the time of Moses typologically as a reference to Christianity (*1 Cor.* 10:1–11). But for Paul generally Moses represents a religion of the law, to which he compares his religion of grace.

The *Letter to the Hebrews* draws parallels between Jesus and Moses in order to demonstrate that Jesus is superior. Moses as the servant of God is inferior to Jesus, who is the son of God. Moses instituted the earthly sanctuary, which is only a copy and a shadow of the heavenly, and in this earthly sanctuary the Levitical priesthood ministers according to the law. But Jesus is the eternal high priest who ministers in the heavenly sanctuary by interceding for the faithful (*Heb.* 8:1–6). In the same way Moses is the author of the old covenant, but this was only a preparation for and a foreshadowing of the new covenant through Jesus (*Heb.* 8:7–10:18).

MOSES IN ISLAM. Moses is highly regarded in Islam as the great prophet who foretold the coming of Muḥammad, his successor. Details about Moses' life from the *aggadah* are to be found in the Qurʾān, but there are additional details with parallels from folklore as well as borrowed from other biblical stories and applied to Moses (see especially *sūrah* 28:4–43; also 7:104–158, 20:10–98, 26:11–69). Apart from explicit references there is much in the life of Muḥammad that is implicitly reminiscent of the Moses tradition. This is particularly true of the notions about a dictated revelation received through angels and the experience of an ascent to heaven, in Muḥammad's case, from Jerusalem.

SEE ALSO Israelite Law.

BIBLIOGRAPHY

The vast literature on the figure of Moses makes any selection difficult. The following list is an attempt to provide a fairly broad range of scholarly opinion on this subject. Some general treatments of the life and work of Moses, based upon a critical appraisal of the biblical traditions, are Elias Auerbach's *Moses* (Amsterdam, 1953), translated from the German and edited by Robert A. Barclay and Israel O. Lehman as *Moses* (Detroit, 1975); Fred V. Winnett's *The Mosaic Tradition* (Toronto, 1949); Martin Buber's *Moses: The Revelation and the Covenant* (Oxford, 1946); and a more technical monograph by Herbert Schmid, *Mose: Überlieferung und Geschichte,* "Beihefte zur Zeitschrift für die alttestamentliche Wissenschaft," no. 110 (Berlin, 1968). A classical and still very influential study of the biblical traditions is the one by Hugo Gressmann, *Mose und seine Zeit: Ein Kommentar zu den Mose-sagen* (Göttingen, 1913).

The history of modern research on Moses is treated in Eva Osswald's *Das Bild des Moses in der kritischen alttestamentlichen Wissenschaft seit Julius Wellhausen,* "Theologische Arbeiten," vol. 18 (Berlin, 1962); and R. J. Thompson's *Moses and the Law in a Century of Criticism since Graf,* "Supplements to Vetus Testamentum," vol. 19 (Leiden, 1970).

On the question of Moses' place in history see Roland de Vaux's *Historie ancienne d'Israël* (Paris, 1971), which has been translated by David Smith as *The Early History of Israel* (Philadelphia, 1978); John Bright's *A History of Israel,* 3d ed. (Philadelphia, 1981); and Siegfried Herrmann's *Israels Aufenhalt in Ägypten* (Stuttgart, 1970), translated by Margaret Kohl as *Israel in Egypt* (London, 1973).

Two works that deal with the way in which Moses is used as a paradigm for certain religious and political roles are Gerhard von Rad's *Moses* (New York, 1960) and J. R. Porter's *Moses and Monarchy: A Study in the Biblical Tradition of Moses* (Oxford, 1963). A book that is especially helpful for the treatment of Moses in Judaism, Christianity, and Islam is a collection of essays published under the title *Moïse, l'homme de l'alliance* (Paris, 1955). On the *aggadah,* see especially Louis Ginzberg's *The Legends of the Bible* (New York, 1956), pp. 277–506. This book is an abridgment of the earlier work *The Legends of the Jews,* 7 vols., translated by Henrietta Szold et al. (1909–1938). On Moses in the New Testament and early Judaism, see also Wayne A. Meeks's *The Prophet-King: Moses Traditions and the Johannine Christology* (Leiden, 1967).

JOHN VAN SETERS (1987)

MOSES BEN MAIMON SEE MAIMONIDES, MOSES

MOSES BEN NAHMAN SEE MAIMONIDES, MOSES

MOSQUE

This entry consists of the following articles:

MOSQUE: HISTORY AND TRADITION

The mosque is a built facility with certain unique characteristics for Muslim prayer, as well as an institution dedicated to maintaining community life. As a building its primary and minimal role is to accommodate a congregation that performs its ritual prayers in formation while oriented toward Kaʿbah in Mecca. As an institution it marks the sociocultural existence of a Muslim community, acting both as its center and its emblem.

ETYMOLOGY. The original Arabic word for mosque is *masjid* (plural, *masājid*), meaning a place of *sujūd,* the highly symbolic act of prostration (before God) during *ṣalāt* (ritual prayer), when the whole body reaches its lowest position and the forehead is placed on the earth in a prescribed manner. Since *ṣalāt* is universally performed in Arabic, its constituent stages, including *sujūd,* and its place, *masjid,* have maintained their Arabic form in Persian, Urdu, Turkish and other dialects of the Muslim world. The anglicized word *mosque* is widely used, and its transformation from *masjid* can be traced through the Egyptian *masqid,* Italian *moscheta* or *moschea,* Spanish *mezquita,* and French *mousquaie* or *mosquee.* The etymological source for *masjid* can be traced back to the Aramaic verbal root *s-g-d* and the word *msgd* used for Nabatean and Abyssinian sacred places.

THE TWO SANCTUARIES OF SACRED HISTORY. The Qurʾān presented itself as a continuation and completion of earlier monotheistic revelations through Abrahamic messengers, including Moses and Jesus. The people holding on to those revelations were called *ahl al-kitāb* (People of the Book), and they asserted that they were in posession of revealed books that preceded the Qur᾽ān. These messengers were introduced as followers of the path of submission (*s-l-m,* the root word for Islam) to the same One God to whom Muḥammad was inviting everyone (Qur᾽ān 3:66). It is little wonder then that Kaʿbah in Mecca, whose construction is directly associated with Abraham and his son Ishmael, is identified in verses in the Qur᾽ān, as *bayt* (house), and the precinct around it as *al-Masjid al-ḥaram* (the sanctified mosque). Beyond the historical existence of the word *masjid* before Islam, these verses suggest Muḥammad's mission to restore the sanctity of *Masjid al-ḥaram* and reestablish the centrality of Abrahamic Kaʿbah as *bayt Allāh* (the house of God) for all the People of the Book, including Muslims (Qur᾽ān 2:125–128, 3:96–97, 5:97).

Masjid al-aksa (the remotest mosque) is mentioned in the Qur᾽ān (7:1): " Praise be to Him who made His servant (Muḥammad) journey in the night from *al-Masjid al-ḥaram* to *al-Masjid al-aqsa* which We have surrounded with blessings to show him of our signs." This verse was revealed during the last year in Mecca before *hijrah* (migration) to Medina. There have been disagreements among historians and Qur᾽anic scholars as to the exact identity and location of this "remotest mosque." It is possible to conclude, however, that the term *masjid* here has been used for a place that existed at the time of this revelation but was not built by Muḥammad or his followers, as they were still in Mecca. If it refers to the destination of *Miʿrāj* (ascension) as a heavenly precinct of the throne of God, then it can only be imagined in a metaphoric sense and not as an earthly mosque. If it refers to the Temple Mount in Jerusalem, then it could only be referring to the memory and continued sanctity of the site associated with the devotions of the prophets Elijah, Abraham, David, and Solomon and not the actual physical presence of the Temple of the Lord (*2 Chr.* 3:1), which had been detroyed in 586 BCE and then again in 70 CE. The *Masjid al-aqsa* verse revealed around 621 CE, and Muḥammad's elaborations of his miraculous journey to the Temple Mount and then ascension to heaven *(Miʿrāj),* brought Jerusalem and its sanctuary (Hebrew, *Har Hebayit*; Arabic, *Haram esh-Sharif*) into Muslim consciousness as a remote though unseen place of prostrations (*masjid*) of earlier prophets. Jerusalem, the city of David and Solomon, thus became analogous to Mecca, the city honored as the "first house" of God built by Abraham and Ismael (Qur᾽ān 3:96–97). The two *ḥarams* (sanctuaries) of Mecca and Jerusalem had thus defined for Muḥammad and his followers the goal of an Abrahamic axis and a shared religious geography of the monotheism. In this context the sequential adoption of Jerusalem and then Mecca for the *qiblah* (prayer orientations) from Medina makes more sense than the oft-implied political strategy in Muḥammad's choice and then rejection of Jerusalem in favor of "his" ancestral Mecca. In fact, early Islam's ecumenical attitude toward *ahl al-kitāb* of Syria is demonstrated through the rebuilding of the Temple Mount and accommodating policies of Jewish and Christian prayer during the first century after the conquest in 638 CE, especially when compared with the pre-Islamic treatment by their Byzantine and Roman predecessors.

The Prophet's Mosque in Medina. In Mecca, Muḥammad and his followers became progressively disenfranchised by the ones whose pagan and tribal traditions were challenged by Islam. Muslims who called for return to the One God of Abraham could not pray without harassment in the *Masjid al-ḥaram* around the sanctuary of Kaʿbah, whose very existence was credited to monotheism (Qur᾽ān 2:214, 5:3, 8:34, 22:25). They prayed alone or in small numbers in residences. The Prophet sometimes led a group prayer at the houses of Muḥammad's wife Khadījah and his friend Abū Bakr, but they never had what could justifiably be called a mosque.

Having failed to dissuade Muḥammad from his mission for over a decade, the Meccans planned his assassination. He decided to migrate to a welcoming settlement called Yathrib (later Medina), some three hundred miles north. The year was 620 CE, and the event is called *hijrah* (migration), which marks the beginning of the new Muslim lunar calendar. There are different traditions about what has come to be known as the first mosque in Medina, *masjid al-Kuba.* One tradition suggests that it was used as a place of prayer by those who anticipated Muḥammad's arrival and that he stayed there for some days. Another tradition suggests that the Prophet founded this mosque himself, and even after he established the main mosque in Medina, he made a practice of praying there every Saturday. The Qur᾽anic reference to this mosque as the one "whose foundation was laid from the first day on piety (*taqwa*)," especially when it is presented in contrast with *masjid al-dhirar* (mischief), later constructed to create infidelity and division in the community, makes it a reference point in ethical intentions rather than the physical fact of a mosque (Qur᾽ān 9:107–110). Having arrived in Medina, Muḥammad purchased, rather than accepted as a gift, a piece of land for the mosque from the two orphans who owned it. With the help of his companions he built a modest four-sided enclosure of stone foundations and sun-dried mud bricks. On the outside of the eastern boundary he placed his private chambers (*hujurāt,* Qur᾽ān 49:4), whose curtained doors opened into the mosque courtyard. On the north toward Jerusalem, and later on the south side as the *qiblah* shifted to Mecca, he built shaded porticos (*riwāq*) of palm tree trunks and dried palm leaves and clay. There was no *miḥrāb* (niche) in the north or the south wall yet. Muḥammad's presence as leader of the community—and his staff, which he leaned on while delivering sermons—established the *qiblah* orientation. There was no minaret, as the call to prayer was either from the courtyard or from a nearby roof. There was no formal *mimbar* (stepped pulpit), though he did use makeshift platforms to raise himself to be seen while speaking to large gatherings. In spite of an apparent lack of formality in religious practices, political protocol, communal gatherings, and architectural furnishings in this austere compound, the *ḥadīth* literature and the corresponding verses of the Qurʾān suggest much intensity in this mosque as the formative principles of *sharīʿah,* the structure of Islamic life, were being formed. There Muḥammad taught the Qurʾān as revealed to him, elaborated upon the commandments, led the ritual prayers, received delegations, settled disputes, planned campaigns, assigned tasks, and socialized with his family and community. This place became the crucible for genetic codes that are at the core of continuity in basic religious practices and institutions, especially the mosque, all across the Muslim world.

Beyond the Prophet's Mosque. The historical distance between Muḥammad's death (632 CE) and the formalization of both his *ḥadīth* (sayings) and *sīra* (life) literature, especially considering the internal strifes and partisanships during that period, can justifiably stir some doubts about the accuracy of some narrations about the happenings in the *Masjid al-Nabi.* It is noteworthy, however, that the patterns, if not the exact details, associated with that mosque have become widely accepted as the reference for the purest forms of Islam as intended by God and lived out by his messenger. It is this memory of Muḥammad, constructed with direct reference to his mosque and his city, that is fundamental to the codification of Islamic practices. And if the leader, the state, and the city as Islamic polity is absent, the mosque becomes its primary home and essential ecology. It is little wonder then that any Muslim community idealizes its mosque as a place where there is an *imām* (leader) worthy of the Qurʾanic knowledge, where *ḥadīth* is rehearsed, where *jamaʿat* (congregation) is established, and where a communal life is modeled on Muḥammad's example and the legacy of his companions. The development of mosque in history can thus be presented briefly as a mostly positive but sometimes negative interpretation of one or more of the traditions of the Prophet's mosque.

***Dār al-Imāra* and *Masjid al-Jamī*ʿ.** During Muḥammad's time the intimacy between the leader and his community was maintained by his unique status and was facilitated by the physical adjacency of his residence and the mosque. When the new settlements of al-Basra and al-Kufa in Iraq and al-Fustat in Egypt were established, the Muslim governors, who represented the *Khalīfa* in Medina, maintained the pattern of the Prophet's mosque as both the religious and administrative center. However, factors like local histories of conquered lands, sheer increase of numbers, tribal tensions within the army, ethnic diversity among new converts, and increasing fear of assasinations led to the development of the more secure *dār al-Imāra* (residence of the commander) with a prison and *dīwān* (treasury) that formed one complex in the heart of the new city. In Syria, where the existing structures of Damascus were adapted as the capital of the dynastic caliphate of Umayyads, the existing Roman and Byzantine church was transformed into the Umayyad Mosque and the adjacent palace converted to the *dār al-Imāra* with a secure connection for the ruler-commander-caliph to enter the mosque from his *qiblah* wall side, avoiding having to walk through the congregation and risking assassination attempts. *Maqsūra,* the secure enclosure, was introduced for the ruler to speak from. While the symbolic unity of the place of communal prayer and the place of governance was maintained through sermons and edicts in the name of the ruler, the two started to develop clearer and harder boundaries and ultimately started to become different buildings.

Impractical distances between the original center of the city with its great mosque and the ruler's palace (as in the newly founded Abbasid city of Baghdad) and the expanded periphery of Muslim settlements, as well as a dramatic increase in population, led to the evolution of a religious geography of primary and secondary centers. Primary were the mosques in which the community formed the obligatory Friday congregation (Qurʾān 62: 9–11) and took the name *masjid al-jamaʿah* (also *masjid al-jumʿah* or *masjid al-jamiʿ*, "place of assembly"). Later they were called *al-jamīʿ* or simply *jamīʿ*, meaning the place where the Friday *khuṭbah* (sermon) is delivered. Secondary centers were small mosques (*masājid*) where the immediate neighborhood could conveniently offer the daily prayers.

Seats of Learning and Academies for Training. Because it was in the capital city, the central *masjid* often had the patronage of the ruler or that of a high-ranking minister of the court, and it usually expanded into a complex with colleges, libraries, hostels, kitchens, and infirmaries. Among many similiar cases, the example of *Jamia al-Azhar,* founded in Cairo by the Fāṭimids (970 CE), illustrates such an interpretation of the legacy of the Prophet's mosque as a seat of learning. It is instructive to note that *Jamia* in this sense implies a gathering of faculties (*kulliye*), much like a modern university. However, as various sects and schools of law hardened in their respective interpretations of Islam, the mosques started to get identified as such. The character of their associated institution transformed from a university-like environment to that of *madrasah,* where the aim was less to nurture an inquiring and critical scholar and more to train an evangelical protagonist of a particular *madhab* (sect) and *fiqh* (jurisprudence). Many governments in Muslim history supported such mosque-*madrasah* institutions to prepare individuals trained in particular Muslim schools of thought.

For Remembrance of God. Perhaps the most enduring legacy of the Prophet and his mosque is rooted in the Verses of Light (Qurʾān 24:36–37). The first verse, through a rich yet imaginable parable, introduces the likeness of God's light as an unearthly, dreamlike "lamp in a niche." The second verse states that this light resides in the "houses which God has permitted to be elevated to honored status; for the celebration in them of His name and His glorification in the mornings and the evenings, again and again." In the verses that follow one can see the distinctions created between those who remember in these mosques and those who are distracted or even deny the necessity of this rememberance. Beyond having provided sustained inspiration for the ambience of interior mosque space from the *qiblah* wall to the *miḥrāb*, the light in the *miḥrāb*, the lights in the prayer hall, the niches for keeping the Qurʾān, and the designs of the prayer rugs (*sijjādah*), the Verse of Light is one of the most frequently calligraphed in the mosques. This attitude toward the mosque as a place where a totally noncorporeal omnipresent God could "reside" through individual and collective rememberance of believing humans is corroborated by many other verses (Qurʾān 2:114, 9:17–18, 72:18), which has led to the pervasive belief among Muslims that every mosque is the "house of God." The understandable desire to build a "house" for God, especially with the *ḥadīth* promise that for anyone who builds a mosque on this earth God will build an equivalent house in paradise, led to many mosques commemorating his blessings. Kings, conquerors, princes, and successful businesspeople commissioned such projects with revenue-generating endowments *(awqāf)* to maintain the building and charitable services like kitchens and the staff who kept such a complex alive. Often such projects encompassed a mausoleum-graveyard of the patron's family, with the idea that the grace of the mosque and charity will help deliverance of their souls on the Day of Judgment. It is important to note that whereas the state mosque continued the Prophet's legacy as the governing leader of the community, the devotional mosque preserved those aspects of Islam's spiritual legacy that had started to become victims of political contingencies. Thus the Prophet's mosque, while maintaining some fundamental ritual and formal structure, had to metamorphose into specialized categories.

MOSQUES, PROPHETS, AND SAINTS. There is a fine line between a location—especially the burial place of a prophet, an *imām*, a saint, or a martyr—remaining a place of commemoration or becoming a focus for worship parallel with the worship of God. Muslim history has walked a fine and careful line between the veneration of sites that preserve the sacred memories of a great religious personality or even a *qiblah*-oriented congregation in a mosque with an unshared intention to pray to no one except God. With reference to the Qurʾanic story of the *ashāb al-kahf* (companions of the cave) (Qurʾān 18:2–22), it is important to note that the prevailing party of believers erected a *masjid* over the place to memorialize them while making sure that it was the mosque that was used for prayers to God, rather than the "cave," which could have become the object of idolatory. Likewise, while the Prophet's mausoleum continues to assert his historical presence in his own mosque, the activities of the mosque are totally aimed at the continuation of his mission to establish and maintain a God-conscious, God-directed community based on the Abrahamic monotheistic axis. It is also in this sense that all mosques of the world, whatever particular national, cultural, or historical motivations they have been built upon, maintain the continuity of Muḥammad's Abrahamic mission.

SEE ALSO Ḥaram and Hawtah; Madrasah; Ṣalāt; Worship and Devotional Life, article on Muslim Worship.

BIBLIOGRAPHY

The classic study is Johannes Pedersen's article "Masdjid," in *The Encyclopaedia of Islam* (Leiden, 1913–1936). A basic study of the monument is Jean Sauvaget's *La mosquée omeyyade de Médine* (Paris, 1947); and a brief survey is Lucien Golvin's *La mosquée* (Algiers, 1960). See also K. A. C. Creswell's *Early Muslim Architecture*, 2d ed., vol. 1 (Oxford, 1969); Oleg Grabar's "Islamic Religious Art: The Mosque," in *The Formation of Islamic Art* (New Haven, Conn., 1973), and "The Architecture of the Middle Eastern City from Past to Present: The Case of the Mosque," in *Middle Eastern Cities*, edited by Ira M. Lapidus (Berkeley, Calif., 1979); Doğan Kuban's *Muslim Religious Architecture*, pts. 1–2 (Leiden, 1974–1985); J. S. Thomine's "La mosquée et la madrasa," *Cahiers de civilisation médiévale* 13 (1970): 97–115; James Dickie's "Allah and Eternity: Mosques, Madrasahs, and Tombs," in *Architecture of the Islamic World*, edited by George Michell (London, 1978); Rashid Ahmad's *Mosque: Its Importance in the Life of a Muslim* (London, 1982); Robert Hillenbrand's *Islamic Architecture* (New York, 1994); Martin Frishman and Hasan-Uddin Khan, eds., *The Mosque* (London, 1994); and Renata Holod and Hasan-Uddin Khan, *The Mosque and the Modern World* (London, 1997).

SYED GULZAR HAIDER (2005)

MOSQUE: ARCHITECTURAL ASPECTS

The mosque (from the Arabic *masjid*, meaning "place of prostrations") has been the place of congregational prayer for Muslims since the formation of Islam in 622 CE. It takes on numerous regional styles and varies greatly in size from that of the congregational Friday mosque, called in Arabic *masjid al-jamiʿ*, in Persian and Urdu (*masjid al-jumʿah*), or in Turkish (*ulu çami*), to a simple oratory (*masjid*), to an outdoor space for large assemblies (*musalla*) for special times such as Eid festivals.

Formal ritual prayer (*ṣalāt*)—a sequence of standing, kneeling, and prostration—is one of the "pillars" of Islam. Muslims often pray alone, but the *ummah*, the community of believers, is basic to the mosque. Since Islam does not distinguish between the spiritual and the secular, the mosque is a center for both. It is the emblematic building of Islam.

For a Muslim the building of a mosque is a pious act. The prophet Muḥammad said, "whoever builds for Allāh a mosque, seeking by it Allāh's grace, Allāh will build for him a house in paradise" (related by al-Bukhārī and Muslim). Most mosques are endowed through the creation of a pious trust or *waqf* established by the mosque's builder. In most Muslim countries the state has by now taken over many of the trusts, usually with a ministry of *awqāf* to manage the properties.

All mosques are places of worship, but they are not sacred or consecrated spaces. In the Qurʾān the word *masjid*, although used many times, is applied only to three specific buildings (usually considered sacred), the most holy place being the Kaʿbah in Mecca and its surrounding mosque, al-

Masjid al-ḥaram. It is, according to the Qurʾān, "the very first house of prayer established for humanity. . . . The place where Abraham stood. . . ." (Qurʾān III: 95–97). The other places are the Dome of the Rock in Jerusalem with the Al-Aqsa Mosque (built originally in 715, in its present form around 1350) and the Mosque of Quba in Medina built by the Prophet himself.

The mosque also often incorporates a variety of other functions. Most common is a *madrasah,* or religious school, and small library, a soup kitchen to feed the poor, and a medical facility. Often there may be a public drinking fountain or well. Sometimes there is a shrine to a saint or ruler, but the dead are usually buried elsewhere. Graveyards adjacent to mosques do occur, notably in Eastern Europe. In urban areas shops often form the periphery of the mosque and subsidize the expenses of the facility.

Architectural and Liturgical Elements. Architectural elements of the mosque are not prescribed except for the requirement that worshipers pray facing Mecca, the spiritual center of the Islamic world, and that the surface they pray on be clean. Worshipers pray in straight rows, generally making the prayer space wide and shallow. Islam has two main sects, the Sunnī (around 90 percent of Muslims worldwide) and the Shīʿah, but their mosques are generally architecturally indistinguishable. The most apparent differences lie in the choice of Qurʾanic verses that are displayed in the building.

The direction of Mecca in the prayer hall or space itself is denoted by a *qiblah* wall and niche (*miḥrāb*). The *qiblah* may be simply marked by a line on the sand or can be part of a building. The *miḥrāb* is usually outlined and embellished with calligraphy from Qurʾanic passages. The *imām,* who leads the prayers, stands by the *miḥrāb* in front of the congregation.

A pool, fountain, or simply running water for ritual cleansing (ablutions) before praying is usually provided, as are prayer mats to maintain the cleanliness of the floor surface and define individual areas. Worshipers often bring their own rugs to the mosque. Indeed, the prayer hall of the mosque can be regarded as a modular space based on the dimensions of a prayer mat.

The minaret or *minar* (from *minara,* or lighthouse) is usually a tower from which the *muezzin* (*muʾadhdhān*), a specially delegated person, gives the call to prayer (*adhān*). Traditionally the human voice has carried the *adhān,* but in contemporary times the voice is amplified by loudspeakers to rise above the general cacophony of the city. The minaret also acts as a visual marker for the mosque.

Other physical elements commonly used are the entrance portal marking the transition into the mosque from the outside world, the circular dome, an abstraction of the heavens, and the courtyard (*sahn*), also used as an overflow prayer space. In a large mosque, there is often a *dikka,* or raised platform, on which one person or a small group of worshipers transmit the *imām*'s postures to those unable to see or hear the *imām* himself.

Inside the mosque adjacent to the *miḥrāb* is the *mimbar,* or pulpit, from which the sermon is delivered after the Friday prayers. It consists of a movable platform with steps, usually made of elaborately carved wood.

Islamic civilization has made significant contributions to architecture. One is the use of two- and three-dimensional geometry at all scales, which not only organizes space but also imparts symbolic meanings. The three-dimensional *muqarnas,* the so-called stalactite form, is unique to Islam. This device is usually used as a transitional element between two surfaces (for example, at a corner) and acts to "dematerialize" space. Calligraphy, the word of God expressed in written form, is another important contribution. Such texts on buildings—epigraphy—signal the presence of Islam and add beauty and complexity to surfaces. Gardens have always been important reminders to Muslims to be stewards of the earth. They follow geometric principles of design and scientific and engineering principles dealing with sustainability and nature, for example, in the recycling of water. Water features are present in almost all gardens, seen as places of pleasure and individual contemplation, but gardens do not occur frequently in mosques.

Typology of the Mosque. Each region of the Islamic world combines these elements to express a local architecture in which vernacular and historic traditions are distinguished. Architecturally, the mosque may be divided into five main types corresponding to historical and regional manifestations.

The first type, the *hypostyle* mosque, originated in the Arabian Peninsula. It also occurs elsewhere, with varied form and construction materials. The mosque consists of a rectangular hypostyle, or many-columned covered hall, usually in wood and earth block or brick, with a flat roof. It is perhaps the most ancient construction method. One enters first into an enclosed courtyard with its ablutions facility, then into the hall from the side opposite the *qiblah* wall. A single square minaret with an internal staircase rises above the building. The hypostyle mosque was the most dominant form from the seventh to the thirteenth centuries and has not significantly altered over the ages. Its model was the Mosque of the Prophet—the Masjid an-Nabi—which as far as we can tell started off as the Prophet's house in Medina, a simple courtyard with rooms on two sides. In 707 CE the caliph al-Walid replaced it with a new building with minarets added as visual markers or to carry the *adhān.* Because of its symbolic importance, it has expanded over the centuries to accommodate the multitudes that pray in it, until today the early mosque is unrecognizable.

The Umayyad Great Mosque (715) in Damascus encompasses the former Church of St. John, itself built on the site of a Roman temple. The Great Mosque of Córdoba, Spain (786–990), has elegant double-horseshoe arches, into which a cathedral was inserted in the sixteenth century. Other prominent examples of hypostyle mosques include the

Mosque of Ibn Tulun (879) in Cairo, and the Kutubiyya (twelfth century) in Marrakech, Morocco.

A different hypostyle earth building tradition is found in Northern Africa, especially in Sudan, and was transmitted by Muslim Arab traders across the African continent to the western sub-Saharan region. Commonly referred to as the Hausa-Fulani tradition, it combines the use of the hypostyle hall with buttressed walls and towers to produce a vernacular common to both monumental and rural buildings. Mosques incorporate older African symbols, such as ancestor pillar fertility symbols and tops covered in ostrich eggs for strength. Construction methods use reinforcing stick scaffolding that remains embedded in the structure. It is a living tradition, which makes these mosques difficult to date. The present building of the Great Mosque of Djenne in Mali was built in 1909, although the mosque is much older. A recent earth mosque in Yaama (1962–1982), Niger, uses the same architectural language and appears to be timeless.

There are two interesting exceptions in Africa. In East Africa, where Islam was brought from India and Oman and rooted itself in the coastal area, there is Indian-inspired mosque architecture. The second is the Afro-Brazilian mosque, so named for West African slaves in Brazil who worked as church builders. In the late nineteenth century they returned to Niger and surrounding countries, where they produced mosques that are clearly Portuguese Catholic baroque. Local people regard them as traditionally Islamic.

The next type is the mosque with four *iwans,* which occurs mainly in Iran, Central Asia, and Afghanistan, developed from the indigenous Iranian building used for houses, *madrasahs,* and caravansaries. In Iran the traditional vault-and-dome building was used to develop *iwans,* or vaulted open porches, encompassed by a giant portal (*pishtaq*) arranged around a central courtyard. Off one *iwan* is the prayer hall. The local tile-making techniques transferred from China produced blue-and-white ceramics to cover the important entrance portals and the *miḥrāb.* Epigraphy attained artistic heights.

The *iwan* mosque coalesced during the Seljuk dynasty (1038–1194) and penetrated Egypt under the rule of Salah ad-Din (Saladin) and his Ayyūbid dynasty (1171–1250). Under the patronage of Mamlūk sultans (1250–1517) elaborate mosque complexes marked the power and wealth of the rulers. The Tilakari Mosque-Madrasah (1660) in Samarkand, Uzbekistan, is a fine example of this style, but the pinnacle of perfection is the Masjid-i Shah (1637) in Isfahan, Iran. This type remained in the architecture of the region and was also transmitted to Central Asia and India, where it was transformed.

The third type is the *Indian mosque,* fully developed by the Imperial Moguls (1526–1828). It is characterized by a wide rectangular prayer hall covered with triple domes, a courtyard with a pool of water surrounded by colonnades, and a monumental entrance. Building material in the Indo-Pakistani subcontinent was mainly brick, and construction techniques and decorative schemes combined the Persian and Hindu traditions. Mosques varied in scale from the small Moti (Pearl) Masjid of 1662 in the Delhi Red Fort to the magnificent large Badshahi Mosque (1674) in Lahore.

The Ottomans (1281–1922) in Anatolia developed in the sixteenth century the fourth type, the *central domed mosque,* that has become the dominant model for contemporary architecture. It is characterized by a large central domed space without columns. It places pencil-thin minarets at the building's corners. The origins of this form lie in the Byzantine centralized basilica plan of the Hagia Sophia in Istanbul (then Constantinople). It was taken to unprecedented heights by the great architect Sinan in the Sulemaniye Complex (1557) in Edirne, and in the picturesque Sultan Ahmet or Blue Mosque (early seventeenth century) of Istanbul, designed by his disciple Mehemet Agha. Both the courtyard and prayer hall are square in plan, with the courtyard open to the sky and surrounded by domed porches.

The same typology occurs again in Indonesia and Malaysia, where there is essentially a unified central space but in a very different style and in wood construction. Islam spread via the sea routes to Southeast Asia in the eighteenth century. The buildings in this region retained their own traditional forms based on the Javanese pavilion with its central two- to five-tiered pyramidal roof. The structure of the main hall is supported by four columns (*saka-guru*), with the roof covered with either wood shingles or clay tiles. The ablutions space is usually housed in a separate pavilion. The minaret, when present, is a freestanding structure, made usually of brick. The complex is often surrounded by a compound wall. Mosques throughout the archipelago adhere to this model, with variations such as elevation onto stilts. A good example is the Masjid Agung (1474) in Demak, Central Java, the oldest extant mosque in the region. Until the nineteenth century Javanese mosques were often not oriented toward Mecca but retained the culturally auspicious east-west axis: this, however, has changed. Minarets too, perhaps to be more normative, are now commonplace. (However, some of the coastal towns reveal clearly their Indian antecedents.)

The last type is the Chinese *pavilion* mosque, developed using architecture associated with Chinese culture. (The exception is the western Xinjiang region, where wood and brick building traditions of Central Asia prevail.) The first Muslims appeared in China during the Tang dynasty (618–907) and soon began building with indigenous Chinese architecture. The Chinese mosque employs the traditional pitched roof form with upturned ends, a timber structure, and a rectangular columnar prayer hall. As in Southeast Asia, the complex consists of independent structures, each housing a different function. Even the gateway and the minaret are separate structures. The minaret is a square to octagonal several-tiered pagoda. The mosque form is essentially indistinguishable from other public buildings. The surrounding high wall encloses Chinese gardens, where the transition between one area and another is marked by traditional Chinese moon gates. The most famous example of this type is the Great Mosque of Xian (eighth century, in present form from 1392). It has a minaret-pagoda, a series of pavilions and gardens, and a *qiblah* wall with a very ornate *miḥrāb* made of wood. Another example is the Niu Jie (Ox Street) Mosque (1362) in Beijing. Islam adapted the techniques and meaning of local architecture while bringing in new elements.

Some Contemporary Issues. The contemporary mosque often expresses the identity of its users—especially true where Muslims are in the minority. There are three streams of design—the vernacular, historic, and modern.

A fine mud-brick mosque was designed in the vernacular mode by Hassan Fathy at New Gourna (1948) near Luxor in Egypt as an alternative to the pan-Islamic modern architecture.

Perhaps the greatest recent historicist mosque is the Hassan II Mosque (1993) in Casablanca, Morocco. It is the largest contemporary mosque in the world, built on the edge of the city on reclaimed land. The location was inspired by the verse from the Qurʾān that states: "the throne of God lies on the water" (Qurʾān XI: 7). It uses forms of twelfth-century Moroccan architecture, scaled up several times, in a very ornate structure. Its 650-foot-tall minaret has a laser beam projecting twenty miles in the direction of Mecca. The prayer hall can accommodate 25,000 worshipers. The structure's center acts as a courtyard when the roof slides open. There are some rather fantastic features, such as a swimming pool and the most elaborate ablutions facility anywhere. The craftsmanship of the whole complex reflects some extraordinary features. It is a modern building in the guise of tradition.

Contemporary mosques that proclaim modernity together with Islam can be found worldwide. The Shah Faisal Mosque (1970–1986) in Islamabad, Pakistan, was conceived as a national mosque to reflect the then progressive modern state. The Sherefuddin Mosque (1980) in Visoko, Bosnia, is uncompromisingly modern, and the Manhattan Islamic Center Mosque (1991) in New York skillfully abstracts the Ottoman mosque.

The way in which architecture reflects society is observed in the spaces designated for women's prayer. Usually 10 to 15 percent of the prayer area is demarcated for women, in a balcony or to the sides, separated from the men. One mosque that places women in a central location is in Kingston, Ontario, Canada. Perhaps this was due to the fact that women were on the mosque building committee—itself a rare occurrence—and that the community is formed of a liberal university population. In their debate over the physical position for women, some one hundred letters were written to *imāms* all over the world to get their opinions. There was no consensus and the community had to make its own decision.

Women in many countries attend mosque for prayer but also for educational and social functions. In Europe and the United States, women and children are increasingly frequenting mosques, where the use of the complex is changing. This may affect the design of mosques, which have usually been centers for men.

Mosque design is undergoing a "globalizing" influence in terms of using elements thought to be normative. Indeed, a dome on a mosque built in 2000 in Shanghai, China, is used only as a sign. It has no relationship whatsoever to the building's structure or interior spaces—it merely sits atop the flat roof. In Indonesia, ready-made tin domes sold along the sides of roads are replacing the indigenous pyramidal roof. It is the dome and the minaret that have become the desirable symbols for the mosque, leading to the neglect of regional architectural traditions. Largely because of the current influence of the Arab Middle East, especially Saudi Arabia, such elements become the expression of an Islam that tries to be universal.

The architecture of the mosque is not just about design and place making. Its importance lies also in the collective meanings it transmits over time. To understand mosques is to understand the architecture of the region and place, and even more significantly, the culture to which it belongs. The mosque reflects the pluralism of Islam while remaining unchanged in its ritualistic aspects. Modernity and internationalism with their own tenets have created new mosque styles, but in the main mosques today continue to emulate either vernacular or historicist models in order to give them legitimacy and instant recognition in the eyes of a global *ummah*-community.

See Also Calligraphy, article on Islamic Calligraphy; Iconography, article on Islamic Iconography; Ṣalāt; Worship and Devotional Life, article on Muslim Worship.

Bibliography

Brend, Barbara. *Islamic Art.* Cambridge, Mass., 1991. A good overall introduction to the field.

Davidson, Cynthia, ed. *Architecture beyond Architecture.* London, 1995.

Frishman, Martin, and Hasan-Uddin Khan, eds. *The Mosque: History, Architectural Development and Regional Diversity.* London and New York, 1994. An important collection of essays by prominent scholars arranged in part thematically and in part by coverage of mosques by region.

Grabar, Oleg. *The Formation of Islamic Art.* New Haven, Conn., 1973. An analytical study by a prominent scholar and historian of art, with an essay on the mosque.

Holod, Renata, and Hasan-Uddin Khan. *The Contemporary Mosque: Architects, Clients, and Designs Since the 1950s.* New York, 1997. Coverage of new mosques worldwide divided by who commissioned the project.

Michell, George, ed. *Architecture of the Islamic World: Its History and Social Meaning.* London and New York, 1978. A collection of essays on various building types, with a useful appendix cataloging key monuments.

Hasan-Uddin Khan (2005)

MOTHER GODDESS SEE GODDESS WORSHIP

MOTOORI NORINAGA

MOTOORI NORINAGA (1730–1801), regarded as the preeminent scholar of the Kokugaku ("national learning") school of premodern Japan. Born Ozu Yoshisada to a merchant-class family in Matsuzaka, Norinaga became interested in literature as a young man. Following the death of his brother-in-law in 1751, Norinaga's mother skillfully juggled the family finances in order to send her son to the capital, Kyoto, to continue his education. In 1752 he became the student of Hori Keizan, a Confucian scholar, with whom he studied Chinese literature. That same year he also discovered a book on Japanese poetry written by the Shingon monk Keichu, the first Kokugaku scholar (*kokugakusha*). This experience moved Norinaga to undertake the study of the earliest Japanese documents, an occupation that he complemented with the study of practical medicine. As a result of his reading, which inculcated in him a growing awareness of, and sensitivity to, Japan's long cultural and religious history, he abandoned the name Ozu in favor of his family's ancestral name, Motoori. Later, he took Norinaga as his personal name.

Norinaga returned to Matsuzaka in 1757 and began to practice internal medicine, but his main interest continued to center on "ancient learning" (*kogaku*), the literary and historical heritage of the early Japanese state. His early works include *Ashiwake obune* (A small boat on a reedy river), which discusses the nature of *waka* poetry; *Shibun yōryō* (The essence of *Genji*), an analysis of the *Genji monogatari* (Tale of Genji); and *Isonokami sasamegoto* (Whisperings of Isonokami), in which he developed the celebrated concept of *mono no aware*. This term, which literally means the sentiments or affections felt immediately after experiencing something, Norinaga considered to be the integrating concept of the *Genji monogatari*. Using this notion, he attempted to free the analysis of literature from the moralism of contemporary criticism. His emphasis on human experience for its own sake was fundamental to his existential outlook on life; it was from this standpoint that he would later explore his own cultural identity within the Shintō tradition.

Norinaga's major work, the *Kojikiden* (Commentary on the *Kojiki*), was begun in 1763, soon after Norinaga's first and only meeting with Kamo no Mabuchi (1697–1769), a disciple of Kada Azumamaro (1668–1736) and a major figure in the Kokugaku movement. Their meeting took place as Mabuchi was passing through Matsuzaka on a pilgrimage to the Grand Shrine at Ise. Prior to this, Norinaga had already begun to read the works of Mabuchi, intending to study the *Kojiki* with him sometime in the future. After their fortuitous meeting, Mabuchi accepted Norinaga as his student; through a lively correspondence that continued until Mabuchi's death, Norinaga gradually laid claim to the intellectual successorship of the Kokugaku movement. Some thirty-five years elapsed between the time Norinaga began work on the *Kojikiden* and its completion in 1798. During that time he produced a number of other important works. These include the most representative of his treatises on Shintō, *Naobi no mitama* (The Spirit of Naobi; 1771); *Hihon tamakushige* (Special Edition of *The Spirit Box;* 1787), a discussion of Japanese politics presented to the Kii (one of three collateral Tokugawa families); and *Uiyamabumi* (Introductory Remarks for Scholastic Beginners; 1798), which marked the end of his scholarly career. In that year he began to draw a pension from the daimyo of Kii in response to an earlier request.

In the year preceding his death Norinaga wrote *Shokki rekichō Shōshikai* (Commentaries on Imperial Edicts in the *Shoku Nihongi*) and his will, which described in detail the procedures to be followed at his funeral. He also purchased land at the top of Mount Yamamuro to be used for his burial plot. Many have interpreted these actions as a rejection of Buddhism and an affirmation of his conviction that his spirit would remain on this earth forever.

In his many works Norinaga combined philological acumen with a keen sense of the primacy of the ancient texts of Japan, providing a basis on which scholars of his generation could forge a new appreciation of Shintō myth. He regarded Shintō as the way of the *kami* (which he defined as anything possessing awe-inspiring or superior power) and thus essentially the way of the emperor, the direct descendant of the deity Amaterasu. According to Norinaga, it is not our fate after death that should be our concern but rather a spontaneous and natural appreciation of life itself. In this life-affirming ethic he advocated a joyous reliance on the will of the *kami*, and maintained that each person was possessed of an innate sense of moral rectitude that renders manmade ethical systems unnecessary. For Norinaga, these attitudes were the very essence of the received traditions of antiquity. He himself eschewed the word *kokugaku*, holding that "learning" could not but refer to the study of the ancient texts and traditions of Japan.

SEE ALSO Kokugaku.

BIBLIOGRAPHY

Motoori Norinaga's complete works are contained in the twenty-two-volume *Motoori Norinaga zenshū* (Tokyo, 1977). Studies of his life and thought include Kobayashi Hideo's *Motoori Norinaga* (Tokyo, 1977) and Muraoka Tsunetsugu's work by the same name (Tokyo, 1928). See also Maruyama Masao's *Studies in the Intellectual History of Tokugawa Japan*, translated by Mikiso Hane (Princeton, 1975).

New Sources

Nosco, Peter. *Remembering Paradise: Nativism and Nostalgia in Eighteenth-Century Japan*. Cambridge, Mass, 1990.

UEDA KENJI (1987)
Revised Bibliography

MO-TZU SEE MOZI

MOUNTAINS have an important place in the symbolic geography of religious traditions the world over, although the ways in which mountains are significant have differed. Some have been seen as cosmic mountains, central to an entire worldview; others have been distinguished as places of revelation and vision, as divine dwelling places, or even as geographical manifestations of the divine.

Attitudes toward mountains in general have varied widely. Chinese poets such as Xie Lingyun (fourth to fifth century CE) and Hanshan (eighth to ninth century CE) were attracted by mountains through a sense that these peaks piled one upon the other led not only to the clouds, but to heaven. And yet in the West, the image of jutting mountain peaks touching the clouds has not always had a positive symbolic valence. In the sixteenth and seventeenth centuries, for example, Luther and others held the view that mountains appeared in an otherwise pleasingly symmetrical world only after the flood, which scarred the surface of the earth with "warts and pockmarks" and signaled the fall and decay of nature. Mountains were, in the view of the sixteenth-century English writer Edward Burnet, the ruins of the postdiluvial world, a sign of chaos and fractured creation. However, in the late seventeenth century with the "aesthetics of the infinite" came a new appreciation of the splendor and height of mountains as stretching the imagination toward God. One writer of the time described his response to the Alps as "a delightful Horrour, a terrible Joy, and at the same time, that I was infinitely pleas'd, I trembled" (quoted in Nicolson, 1959, p. 277).

THE COSMIC MOUNTAIN AS SACRED CENTER. As the center of the world, linking heaven and earth and anchoring the cardinal directions, the mountain often functions as an *axis mundi*—the centerpost of the world; it is a cosmic mountain, central to the order and stability of the cosmos. One of the most important such mountains is Mount Meru, or Sumeru, the mythical mountain that has "centered" the world of the majority of Asians—Hindu, Buddhist, and Jain. According to Hindu cosmology, four lotus-petal continents spread out from Mount Meru at the center and beyond them the seven ring-shaped seas and ring-shaped continents of the wider universe. Mount Meru rises heavenward as the seed cup of the world lotus. As an *axis mundi,* this mountain, rooted deep in the netherworld, rises high through the realms of heaven, where it spreads out to accommodate the cities of all the gods. Interestingly, Meru does not form a peak, for the geographical texts of the Purāṇas agree that Meru is wider at top than at bottom, true to both its seed-cup prototype and the polytheistic consciousness that accommodates many gods at the top. Meru has four sides of different colors (*varṇas*) and is flanked by four directional mountains. Above Meru stands the polestar, and daily the sun drives his chariot around the mountain. The heavenly Ganges in its descent to earth first touches the top of Meru and then divides into four rivers that run in the four cardinal directions to water the earth.

As the center of the world-circle, or *maṇḍala,* Mount Meru is symbolically repeated in many Hindu temples that take the mountain as an architectural prototype. The *śikhara* (spire or peak) of the temple rises high above the cavelike womb-chamber of the sanctum and is capped with the cogged, ring-shaped *āmalaka,* the sun itself, a symbol of the heavens. The mountain is also repeated in the architecture of the Buddhist stupa, the reliquary dome with gateways in the four directions and a multileveled mast at the top marking the *bhūmi*s ("worlds") that lead to heaven. The mountain symbolism is most elaborately seen in the stupa of Borobudur in Java, which is actually built over a small hill. There one sequentially circumambulates the nine *bhūmi*s of the cosmos to reach the top. In China and Japan, the vertical dimension of the stupa became attenuated in the structure of the pagoda and came to predominate over the dome-shaped tumulus of the reliquary. Even so, the pagodas of the Far East preserve the basic mountain symbolism of the stupa. In Southeast Asia, one of the many duplicates of Meru is Mount Gunung Agung, the great volcanic mountain that is at the center of the island of Bali. Throughout Bali, individual temples repeat the mountain symbolism and are called *meru*s. Their nine roof-layers again signify the vertical dimensions of the cosmic mountain linking heaven and earth.

Like Meru, other mountains have been seen as cosmic centers. Mount Hara has a central place in the ancient cosmology of the Zoroastrian tradition. According to the *Zamyad Yasht,* it was the earth's first mountain, and its roots the source of the other mountains of Iran. Like other cosmic centers, it is the pivot around which the sun and the stars revolve, and like many other sacred mountains, it is also considered to be the source of heavenly waters. In Japan, the great volcanic peaks, among which Fuji is the most famous, have been thought to link earth and heaven. In Morocco, the great Atlas range in the territory of the Berbers is sometimes called the "pillar of heaven." Mountains that center and stand at the quarters of a fourfold cosmos are numerous, as can be seen in the quadrant mountains of China and in the "Encircled Mountain" of the Navajo, around which stand four peaks, each identified with a direction and a color.

Mountains not considered "centers" in any cosmology still share this image of stability and permanence, of both height and unshakable depth. The *Book of Psalms* speaks of the "foundations" of the mountains and hills. Among the Yoruba, myths stress the durability of the hills and, therefore, their ability to protect. The Yoruba say "Ota oki iku," meaning "The rock never dies." In East Africa, one might receive the blessing "Endure, like Kibo." Kibo is the peak of Mount Kilimanjaro and marks, for the Chagga people, the direction of all that is powerful and honorable.

In a similar vein, there are many traditions of the mountain that stood firm during a great flood. Mount Ararat in Turkey is known as the mountain where Noah found land and the ark came to rest. Among the Native American peoples of the Pacific Northwest, Mount Rainier was a pillar of stability during the flood. Peruvian myths from the Sierran highlands claim the same for several of the high peaks of the Andes.

The mountain as nature's great link between heaven and earth has also been widely symbolized architecturally, as in the case of Meru. In ancient Mesopotamia, the seven-storied ziggurat, with its high temple at the top and its low temple at the bottom, allows for the descent of the divine. The pyramids of Mesoamerican civilization, such as the ruins at Teotihuacán, are clearly aligned to stand at the center of ceremonial avenues. The Pyramid of the Moon at Teotihuacán is further aligned with Mount Cerro Gordo, which it duplicates.

MOUNTAINS OF REVELATION AND VISION. There are many mountains that may not have a central role in cosmology but that are, nonetheless, places of powerful contact between the divine and the human. For example, on top of Adam's Peak, or Śrī Pada ("auspicious foot"), in Sri Lanka is a large indentation said to be a footprint. According to Buddhists, it is the footprint of the Buddha himself, matched by a similar imprint at Phra Sat in Thailand. For Hindus, it is the imprint of Śiva; for Muslims, that of Adam; for Christians, that of the apostle Thomas. In any case, the belief that the peak was once trod by one larger than life is held by the people of all four traditions who climb to the top on pilgrimage.

In the Islamic tradition, it was on Mount Hira on the outskirts of Mecca that Muḥammad heard the revealed word of the Qur'ān. At nearby Mount Arafat, the entire assembly of pilgrims stands from noon to sunset on the ninth day of the *ḥājj* pilgrimage. This collective act of standing, before God and around Arafat, is considered by many to be the most powerful moment of the *ḥājj.*

Mount Sinai, where Moses encountered Yahveh face to face, is one of the most striking examples of the mountain of revelation. There Yahveh appeared to the Hebrews as a storm, with fire and lightning, or as a cloud that covered the peak. And there Yahveh also appeared directly, when Moses and the elders ascended the mountain and "saw the God of Israel" (*Ex.* 24:10). In the Elohist and Deuteronomic traditions, Yahveh appeared on Mount Horeb. There Moses enountered Yahveh in the burning bush. And there Elijah stood before the Lord, who, after the rock-breaking wind, the fire, and the earthquake, spoke to him as "a still small voice" (*1 Kgs.* 19:11–12). And Jesus was transfigured upon a high mountain, sometimes said to be Mount Hermon, and appeared to Peter, John, and James with a glowing countenance, in dazzling raiment, and flanked by Moses and Elijah (*Mt.* 17:1–8; *Mk.* 9:2–8; *Lk.* 9:28–36).

The mountain top is a revelatory landscape, its height offering both the vision of heaven and a broad perspective on earth. Mountain ascent is associated with vision and the acquisition of power, as is clear in the vision quest of many of the Native American traditions and in the ascents of the *yamabushi,* the mountain ascetics of Japan. In both cases, transformation, including spiritual insight, is part of the mountain experience. For the pilgrim who is not an adept, a shaman, or an initiate, the mountaintop still affords ecstatic vision. In the words of the great Chinese mountain poet Hanshan, "High, high from the summit of the peak, / Whatever way I look, no limit in sight" (*Cold Mountain,* trans. Burton Watson, New York, 1970, p. 46).

THE DWELLING PLACE OF THE DIVINE. For the Hebrews, God's "dwelling place" was surely not Sinai, the place of revelation, but Mount Zion, the sturdy, rocky mount of Jerusalem. Zion, neither lofty nor dramatic, was the firm foundation of Jerusalem, the "City on a hill." Here God was said to dwell in the midst of the people. The awesome mountaintop, where God appears in fire and lightning, is replaced with the security and protection of a fortress mountain.

The hills of Canaan were the high places of powerful local *baalim,* and Mount Zaphon was the abode of the great Baal Hadad. In the *Ras Shamra* Ugaritic texts, Baal describes his dwelling place "in the midst of my mountain, the godly Zaphon, in the holy place, the mountain of my heritage, in the chosen spot, the hill of victory" (Clifford, 1972, p. 138). Many of Zaphon's traditions have likely become attached to Zion.

Perhaps the earliest evidence for mountaintop sanctuaries is in the Middle Minoan period (2100–1900 BCE) on Crete, where peak and cave sanctuaries such as those at Mount Juktas, Mount Dikte, and Mount Ida have been found, along with evidence of votive offerings to the goddess. In the Greek mythological tradition, Olympus is the dwelling place of the gods, especially of Zeus, whose cult was widely associated with mountaintops. Hermes, Apollo, Artemis, and Pan had mountain sanctuaries as well.

The hilltop and mountain shrines of both local and widely known gods are also important in the sacred geography of India. Śiva is called Giriśa, the "lord of the mountains." He dwells upon Mount Kailash in the Himalayas and has mountain shrines all over India, such as Śrī Śaila in Andhra Pradesh and Kedara in the Himalayas. Śiva's consort, Pārvatī, is the daughter of the mountain (*parvat*), and she too dwells on mountaintops in countless local forms—as Vindhyavāsinī in central North India or as Ambikā at Girnār in Gujarat. Similarly, in South India, Skanda has hilltop shrines at Palṇi and Tirutaṇi, Ayyappan dwells on Mount Śabari in Kerala, and Śri Veṅkateśvara dwells on the Seven Hills of Tirupati.

In China, there are four mountains that came to be associated with the four directions and four prominent *bodhisattvas.* Most famous among them is the northern peak, Wutai Shan, associated with Mañjusri, the *bodhisattva* of wisdom. When the Japanese monk Ennin visited Mount Wutai in the ninth century CE, it was a bustling center of monastic learning and of lay pilgrimage. The others are Mount Jiuhua in the south, Mount Emei in the west, and the hilly island of Putuo Shan off the Zhejiang coast in the east. According to popular tradition, the *bodhisattvas* associated with these mountains were to be seen not merely in the temples but would take human form and appear as a beggar or an elderly monk to pilgrims along the way.

In addition to this group of four Buddhist mountains there are the five mountains of the Daoist tradition, again situated at the four compass points, with a center mountain shrine at Song Shan in Henan Province. Tai Shan in Shandong Province is perhaps the most famous of the five, with seven thousand stone stairs leading to the top where, next to the Daoist temple, a stone monument stands uninscribed but for the word *di* ("god"). The poet who was supposed to honor the mountain on this tablet was silenced by its splendor.

Mountains Charged with Divine Power. Japanese traditions recognize many mountain divinities—the *yama no kami.* In a sense, they dwell upon the mountain, but it might be more correct to say that the *yama no kami* are not really distinct from the mountain itself. In the Shintō traditions of Japan the separation of nature from spirit would be artificial. In the spring, the *yama no kami* descend from the mountains and become *ta no kami, kami* of the paddy fields, where they remain for the seasons of planting, growth, and harvest, returning to the mountain in the autumn. Even as the *kami* change locus, they remain part of the nature they inhabit.

In the Heian period, with increasing Shintō-Buddhist syncretism, the mountain *kami* came to be seen as forms of Amida Buddha and the various *bodhisattvas*, and the Shugendō tradition of mountain ascetism began. Among Japan's important mountain sanctuaries are Mount Haguro, Mount Gassan, Mount Yoshino, Mount Omine, and the Kumano mountains, identified with the Pure Land of Amida Buddha. Religious associations called *ko* organize locally or regionally for the ascent of particular mountains, taking the name of the mountain itself (Fujikō, Kumanokō, etc.).

Many Native American traditions share this sense of the inseparability of mountain and spirit power. The peoples of the Pacific Northwest, for instance, often begin their tales with "Long ago, when the mountains were people. . . ." The mountains, such as Tacoma, now known as Rainier, are the mighty ancestors of the past. Farther south, the divine personification of mountains can be seen in Popocatépetl and his spouse Iztaccíhuatl in Mexico or in Chimborazo and his spouse Tungurahua in Ecuador. The Zinacantecos of Chiapas still honor the tutelary ancestors, the Fathers and the Mothers, in shrines at both the foot and summit of their sacred hills. Among the Inca, the localization of power is called *huaca,* and is often manifest in stones or on mountains, such as the great Mount Huanacauri above Cuzco.

The mountain *is* the temple. Mount Cuchama in southern California, known as the Place of Creation, was one of the four exalted high places of the native peoples. For worship and initiation, it had no temple, for it was itself nature's own temple. India has many such striking examples of divine mountains, among which is Aruṇācala (Dawn Mountain) in the Tamil lands of South India. This holy hill is said to be the incandescent hierophany of Śiva and is reverently circumambulated as a temple would be.

Life and Death. As givers of life, mountains are the source of rivers and, thus, the source of fertility. This is made explicit in the relation of the mountain and rice-field *kami* in Japan. On the south side of Mount Atlas in Morocco, fruits are said to grow spontaneously. And on the mythical Mount Meru the divine trees are said to yield fruits as big as elephants, which burst into streams of nectar when they fall and water the earth with divine waters. As the prophet Amos said of the Land of Israel, "The mountains shall drip sweet wine, and all the hills will flow with it" (*Am.* 9:13).

Mountains are the source not only of nourishing waters but also of rains and lightning. Storm gods are often associated with mountains: Zeus, Rudra/Śiva, Baal Hadad of Ugarit, Catiquilla of the Inca, and many more.

Mountains, the source of the waters of life, are also seen as the abode of the dead or the path to heaven for the dead. Among the Shoshoni of the Wyoming, for instance, the Teton Mountains were seen primarily as the dangerous place of the dead. The Comanche and Arapaho, who practiced hill burial, held similar beliefs. The Japanese elegy literature makes many references to the mountain resting place of the souls of the dead. A coffin is called a "mountain box," choosing a burial site is called "choosing the mountain," and the funeral procession chants "We go to the mountain!" Throughout the Buddhist world, the stupa, which originally is said to have housed the relics of the Buddha, has become on a miniature scale the symbolic form in which the ashes of the dead are housed.

The Persistence of the Mountain. Through the ages many sacred mountains have accumulated many-layered traditions of myth and pilgrimage. Moriah, the mount of the Temple in Jerusalem, is a good example. First, it was an early Canaanite high place, a threshing floor and sanctuary for harvest offerings. According to tradition, it was there that Abraham came to sacrifice Isaac. And it was there that Solomon built the great Temple, and Nehemiah rebuilt it after the Babylonian exile. And much later, according to Islamic tradition, it was there that Muḥammad began his ascent from earth to heaven on his mystical "night journey" to the throne of God.

In Mexico, Tepeyac, the hill of the Aztec goddess Tonantzin, became the very place of the apparition of Our Lady of Guadalupe when the Catholic tradition was layered upon indigenous traditions. Similarly, the great mountain-shaped pyramid of Quetzalcoatl at Cholula became, in the age following the conquest, the site of Our Lady of Remedios. In Japan, Mount Koua and Mount Hiei, both charged with the power of their particular *kami,* became in Buddhist times the respective centers of the Shingon and the Tendai traditions. In countless such cases, the mountain persists as a sacred center, while myths and traditions change.

See Also Architecture; Center of the World; Cosmology, articles on Buddhist, Hindu, and Jain Cosmologies; Geography; Iconography, article on Buddhist Iconography; Pyramids; Stupa Worship; Temple, articles on Buddhist Temple Compounds, Mesoamerican Temples.

Bibliography

Benson, Elizabeth P., ed. *Mesoamerican Sites and World-Views.* Washington, D.C., 1981. A collection of essays on the worldview of the ancient Aztec and Maya civilizations by Doris Heyden, Horst Hartung, Linda Schele, and others, along with an essay on the sacred geography of highland Chiapas by Evon Vogt.

Clifford, Richard J. *The Cosmic Mountain in Canaan and the Old Testament.* Cambridge, Mass., 1972. A study of cosmic mountain traditions of El and Baal in Canaan; the *Genesis,* Sinai, and Zion traditions of the Old Testament; and the cosmic center in intertestamental literature. Background also provided on the cosmic center and mountain in the ancient Near Eastern traditions of Egypt and Mesopotamia.

Cohn, Robert L. *The Shape of Sacred Space: Four Biblical Studies.* Chico, Calif., 1981. Four essays on sacred space in the Hebrew Bible: "Liminality in the Wilderness"; "Mountains in the Biblical Cosmos"; "The Sinai Symbol"; and "The Senses of a Center."

Eliade, Mircea. "The Symbolism of the Centre." In *Images and Symbols: Studies in Religious Symbolism* (1952), translated from the French by Philip Mairet, New York, 1969. One of the several places where Eliade discusses the cosmic mountain and its homologies in the symbolization of the world center.

Evans-Wentz, W. Y. *Cuchama and Sacred Mountains.* Edited by Frank Waters and Charles L. Adams. Chicago, 1981. An exploration of the significance of Mount Cuchuma in southern California, sacred to the Cochimi, Yuma, and other Native American peoples. Included also is a long chapter titled "Other Sacred Mountains throughout the World" that focuses primarily on the mountains of Japan, India, Central Asia, and North America.

Hori, Ichiro. "Mountains and Their Importance for the Idea of the Other World." In *Folk Religion in Japan: Continuity and Change,* edited by Joseph M. Kitagawa and Allan L. Miller. Chicago, 1968. A general essay on the significance of mountains in Japan, including their role in cosmology, their rites and pilgrimages, and their sacred waters.

Mullikin, Mary Augusta, and Anna M. Hotchkis. *The Nine Sacred Mountains of China.* Hong Kong, 1973. An illustrated record of the pilgrimages made by these two women in 1935 and 1936 to the five sacred mountains of the Daoists and the four sacred mountains of the Buddhists in China.

Nicholson, Marjorie Hope. *Mountain Gloom and Mountain Glory: The Development of the Aesthetics of the Infinite.* Ithaca, N.Y., 1959. The classic Western study of attitudes toward mountains, including theological, philosophical, and emerging scientific dimensions. The focus of the study is the change in the view of mountains in the literature of seventeenth- and eighteenth-century England, from the view that mountains are the "Warts, Wens, Blisters, Imposthumes" on the face of Nature to the view that mountains are the grand natural cathedrals of the divine.

Diana L. Eck (1987)

MOVEMENT FOR THE RESTORATION OF THE TEN COMMANDMENTS OF GOD.

On March 17, 2000, several hundred followers (estimates vary, but there may well have been more than three hundred, including seventy-eight children) of the Ugandan Movement for the Restoration of the Ten Commandments of God (MRTCG) died in Kanungu, Uganda, when their church was burned, in what was alternately called a mass suicide or a homicide perpetrated by the movement's leaders. The subsequent discovery, in various locations, of mass graves containing the remains of people believed to be murdered (most of them stabbed) raised the death toll to 780 and possibly more, the largest such incident in recent history at that time.

The MRTCG, a fringe Catholic group, had been established among an epidemic of apparitions of the Virgin Mary and Jesus in Catholic circles in Africa, most of them not recognized by the Roman Catholic Church. These apparitions occurred during and after a series of famous apparitions in Kibeho, Rwanda, from 1981 to 1989. There, seven "seers" were encouraged and approved by the Catholic hierarchy. The apparitions that led to the formation of the MRTCG started in 1987, when a number of Catholics claimed to have had visions of Jesus and the Virgin Mary in southwestern Uganda after Specioza Mukantabana, a Rwandan girl who claimed a connection with Kibeho (although she was not one of the seven "approved" seers) moved in 1986 to the Ugandan diocese of Mbarara and later to the diocese of Masaka, starting a movement in Mbuye. Among the new Ugandan seers were Paul Kashaku (1890–1991) and his daughter Credonia Mwerinde (1952–2000), a barmaid with a reputation for sexual promiscuity. Mwerinde later claimed to be a former prostitute—probably a false claim and a conscious attempt to replicate the role of Mary Magdalene. Kashaku had a past as a visionary and claimed to have seen, as early as 1960, an apparition of his deceased daughter Evangelista.

Kashaku claimed to have had a particularly important vision in 1988, and he impressed, among others, Joseph Kibwetere (1931–2000), who claimed to have himself received visions since 1984. Kibwetere was a solid member of the Catholic community in Uganda. He had been a politician and a locally prominent member of the Catholic-based Democratic Party in the 1970s. Eventually, a community was established in Kibwetere's home in 1989. The newly formed group attempted to merge the movement with other "apparitionist" groups, including the one established in Mbuye by Mukantabana (a group that had been condemned by the local Catholic bishop). These attempts failed however. A group of twelve apostles (six of them women) was appointed, and Kibwetere became their leader after Kashaku's death in 1991.

The seers claimed to have seen Jesus, Mary, and Joseph in several different visions, which were heavily influenced by recognized Catholic apparitions, such as those at La Salette and Fatima. The visions were also influenced by unofficial Catholic sources, including the messages of the Italian visionary priest Father Stefano Gobbi, several visionaries based in the United States, and William Kamm ("Little Pebble"), a marginal Catholic prophet who claimed that he would eventually become pope. The messages of the seer's visions addressed typical Ugandan themes, such as the AIDS epidemic and government corruption.

Eventually, the village of Kanungu was designated *ishayuriro rya Maria* (rescue place for the Virgin Mary), and the seers moved there in 1994. The group converted to their prophetic visions a handful of Catholic priests and nuns, including Father Dominic Kataribaabo (1967–2000), a Ugandan Dominican priest who was educated in the United States. The MRTCG developed an archconservative brand of Catholicism, and some of its leaders and members were eventually excommunicated by the Roman Catholic Church, although the priests were only suspended from their priestly functions rather than excommunicated. The MRTCG broke with the Ugandan Catholic Bishops on questions of reliability of apparitions (including their own), clerical garb, and the proper ways of taking communion. They regarded as licit only communion taken kneeling, and rejected the practice of the communicant taking the host in his or her hands. Unlike other Catholic traditionalist movements, however, the MRTCG did accept ecumenism and the new ritual of the Mass introduced after Vatican II. The MRTCG's Masses were celebrated in vernacular rather than Latin. The movement's publications strongly denied that the MRTCG was a new religious movement, and claimed that it was simply a conservative Catholic group. The Ugandan Catholic Bishops, however, concluded otherwise.

The Movement for the Restoration of the Ten Commandments of God was legally incorporated with this name in 1994, and a boarding school was licensed until 1998, when the license was revoked by the government on the grounds that its teachings that were contrary to the Ugandan constitution. The government also expressed concern over breaches of public health regulations and possible mistreatment of children. In fact, the main message of the MRTCG was that the Ten Commandments had been distorted and needed to be restored in their full value. The third edition of the handbook *A Timely Message from Heaven: The End of the Present Times* (1996), mainly written by Kataribaabo, proclaimed: "Ours is not a religion but a movement that endeavors to make the people aware of the fact that the Commandments of God have been abandoned, and it gives what should be done for their observance." Additional comments in the book about morality refer to themes common in traditionalist and other Catholic archconservative circles. For example, inappropriate dress is seen as a sign of immorality in the statement: "girls prefer wearing men's trousers to wearing their own dresses." The message was also apocalyptic:

> All of you living on the Planet, listen to what I'm going to say: When the year 2000 is completed, the year that will follow will not be year 2001. The year that will follow shall be called Year One in a generation that will follow the present generation; the generation that will follow will have few or many people depending on who will repent. . . .The Lord told me that hurricanes of fire would rain forth from heaven and spread over all those who would not have repented.

It is worth noting that these MRTCG visions are very similar to those of the church-approved Kibeho visionaries, who saw rivers of blood, great fires, and decapitated corpses. The Kibeho seers warned, on the basis of what the Virgin Mary had told them, that "there isn't much time left in preparing for the Last Judgment. We must change our lives, renounce sin. Pray and prepare for our own deaths and for the end of the world" (Maindron, 1985, p. 107). Of course in Kibeho, church approval also meant church control, and the apocalyptic elements were given approved and centuries-old metaphorical interpretations. But once the MRTCG left the Catholic fold, the group acted out some of the Kibeho images literally.

The approximately five thousand members of the MRTCG (the movement had branches in several small Ugandan towns) were said to avoid sex and to rarely talk for fear of breaking the commandment about not bearing false witness, and they were reported to have developed a sign language (reports of their unusual behavior may have been exaggerated after the tragedy). Although most members were former Catholics, the group also included some from the African Initiated Churches (AIC, formerly called African Independent Churches) and from local spiritualist groups.

The MRTCG was considered to be among the less violent local apocalyptic movements in Uganda. However, the group did predict the end of the world for December 31, 1999, later revising the date and claiming that on March 17, 2000, the Virgin Mary would appear and take members to heaven. The prophetic failure may have induced a number of members to doubt the leaders and ask for the return of money they had contributed. This development (similar to what occurred in the Order of the Solar Temple prior to the homicides and suicides of 1994) may have created a category of "traitors" who were killed in various waves prior to March 17 and whose bodies have been found in several mass graves. On the other hand, the mass graves remain in many respects a mystery, and it is also possible that some "weak" members, regarded as not fully prepared to commit suicide, were killed without being regarded as "traitors."

Shortly before March 17, Kibwetere wrote to his wife Theresa (not a member of the MRTCG), urging her to carry on the movement after his departure. A nun visited nearby villages announcing the coming of the Virgin Mary for March 17. Apparently, while some members did know about the suicide plan, others were simply told about an imminent supernatural event and did not expect to die. As in the case of the Solar Temple (and notwithstanding the obvious differences) there were three categories of victims: those who knew about the suicide and regarded it as a "rational" way to escape a doomed world (a minority); those who expected to go to heaven but did not know how; and the "traitors" who doubted Kibwetere after the prophetic failure. The latter may have been assassinated before the church fire. The presence of three, rather than two, categories of victims creates a continuum between homicide and suicide.

Among the leaders, Kataribaabo was originally identified among the dead, but later the Ugandan government issued a warrant for his arrest, along with warrants for Kibwetere and Mwerinde. Dental records for the three are unavailable, and it has been impossible to determine whether they died in the fire (as their families believe) or escaped with the movement's money (as some witnesses suggest and the Ugandan government apparently believes). The idea that the leaders were con artists who escaped with the money was also the explanation preferred by the media and some members of the law enforcement community in the Solar Temple case, before dental records proved this theory wrong. Most scholars believe that the leadership of the MRTCG died in the 2000 fire, and the leaders' behavior prior to these events supports this conclusion.

Uganda is home to hundreds of religious movements, many of them apocalyptic and millenarian. This is not surprising since Uganda experienced a virtual apocalypse during the bloody regime of Idi Amin Dada (1925–2003) and given the atrocities of the civil war. Followers of apocalyptic movements in Uganda expect justice to come with the end of the world, not through politics. Scholarship about Uganda's apocalyptic movements warns against applying Western models to situations peculiar to that country. In fact, conflict between "cults" and the national army, as well as protest and violence (even suicide), are often manifestations of preexisting ethnic, tribal, and political conflicts.

In general, tragedies in Uganda also confirm that violence connected to new religious movements erupts because of a combination of factors internal and external to the groups. In the MRTCG case, internal factors included the personalities of the leaders, their literal interpretations of prophecies about the end of the world (as exemplified by Kibeho and Gobbi), and the crises within society and the Roman Catholic Church. Once dissociated from the church's time-tested metaphorical interpretations, apocalyptic revelations may be taken literally and acted upon. External factors include the difficult situation prevailing in Uganda, particularly in areas ravaged by disaster, famine, and civil war.

After the tragedy of Kanungu, some African governments reacted strongly against "cults." The risk is that they will engage in witch-hunts, failing to acknowledge that most apocalyptic movements throughout the world are law-abiding and nonviolent. In Africa, as elsewhere, claims that all millenarian and apocalyptic movements are heading for mass suicide are grossly inaccurate. These assumptions may in fact amplify tension and deviance, thus operating as self-fulfilling prophecies, helping to cause the very evils people claim they want to prevent.

SEE ALSO Cults and Sects; New Religious Movements, overview article, article on New Religious Movements and Millennialism, article on New Religious Movements and Violence; Temple Solaire.

BIBLIOGRAPHY

Kabazzi-Kisirinya, S., R. K. Nkurunziza, and Banura Gerard Deusdedit, eds. *The Kanungu Cult-Saga: Suicide, Murder, or Salvation?* Kisubi, Uganda, 2000. An interpretation by local scholars.

Maindron, Gabriel. *Apparizioni a Kibeho: Annuncio di Maria nel cuore dell'Africa.* Brescia, Italy, 1985. A primary source for the apparitions in Kibeho.

Mayer, Jean François. "Field Notes: The Movement for the Restoration of the Ten Commandments of God." *Nova Religio* 5 (2001): 203–210. A scholarly account and interpretation.

Movement for the Restoration of the Ten Commandments of God. *A Timely Message from Heaven: The End of the Present Times.* 3d ed. Karuhinda, Rukungiri; Rubiziri, Bushenyi, Uganda, 1996. The only book published by the movement.

MASSIMO INTROVIGNE (2005)

MOZI. Very little is known about the life of the fifth-century BCE Chinese thinker Mozi (Master Mo), although a number of clues suggest that he may have been trained as an artisan. He was the first major thinker to challenge the heritage of Confucius (551–479 BCE) and is best known as the founder of the Mohist school or lineage of thinkers that flourished in the fourth and third centuries BCE, but he fell into obscurity soon after. Although the teachings attributed to Mozi, under the eponymous title Mozi (the core of which is held to represent Mozi's own writings rather than elaborations and accretions by later Mohists), were transmitted to posterity, they exercised little influence after the third century BCE and were largely ignored until the nineteenth century.

Whereas in early Confucian writings it is the figures of the ruler and the father that served as authority models, Mozi appealed to a higher authority: *tian* (heaven). For him, it was the ideal model of what is constant, reliable, objective, measurable, and equally accessible to all (Hansen, 1992, p. 100). Many of Mozi's arguments are backed by an appeal to *tian* or *(shang) (supreme ancestor).* This is one of the reasons that Mohism has often been described as a religion. Mozi's concept of *tian* is conventionally understood as a morally normative force with authority above the ruler, which expressed its wishes through a variety of mechanisms, including portents and the appearance of spirits.

There is, however, a real question as to whether Mozi did, in fact, believe in a normative *tian.* A more pragmatic interpretation would be that he actually believed that if people act as if *tian* is a normative force, then they will be more inclined to act in ways that conform with Mozi's own philosophical principles. It is important to note that Mozi does not talk of tian's decrees *(ming),* but only of its intentions or goals *(zhi).* From a moral point of view this affords people the responsibility to make their own moral choices. Further supporting the pragmatic interpretation is the fact that order in the world is only achievable through strenuous effort on the part of both humans and *tian.* For Mozi there is no preexistent order of things: an ordered human society is produced and maintained by the purposeful cooperation of *tian,* spirits, and humans, who work together in the face of the constant propensity of things to revert to a state of chaos (Schwartz, 1985, p. 141). The social upheavals of the times would certainly have reinforced this view.

The message is clear: if humans want order, they, like *tian,* must work at it, and the model they should follow is the one that *tian* itself has shown them: favoring utility and benefit over harm. Moral conduct was defined as acting so as to benefit others, which ultimately will benefit oneself. For Mozi's utilitarianism to work, it is crucial that people believe that their efforts can make it work. Utility/benefit provides a measurable standard that anyone can use with accuracy. For Mozi, utility included such things as food and shelter, peace, and the material conditions of life. The benefit-harm distinction also appeals as being a standard that is natural or pre-social rather than conventional. As such, it seems to offer a neutral basis for ranking alternative proposals about what is the best course of action. Confucian moral standards, by contrast, are derived from the teachings of so-called sages, or culled from tradition. Another weakness with Confucian ethics is that moral concern is graded according to one's relationship with someone, and family members always come first. Mozi argues that morality must involve equal concern for all people. Indeed, Mozi's most celebrated doctrine is the doctrine of ungraded concern for others *(jian ai).* He maintained that the world's disorders are the product of human selfishness and a lack of mutual concern. Mozi's panacea for these ills requires people to be as concerned about others as they are for themselves.

Mozi had four main criticisms of early Confucians: (1) they did not believe in the existence of *shangdi* (supreme ancestor) or spirits, thus incurring the displeasure of these anthropomorphic powers; (2) they insisted on elaborate funerals and practiced three years of mourning when a parent died, resulting in a waste of resources and energy; (3) they attached great importance to music, another extravagant waste of resources; and (4) they believed in predetermined fate, which leads to laziness and resignation.

Mozi applied three standards to gauge the value of any doctrine: its basis, its verifiability, and its applicability. Take the example of fatalism, which Mozi criticizes on the following grounds: (1) Fatalism is not in accord with the intentions of *tian* or the teachings of the ancient sage kings. This is proved by quoting ancient writings that record the teachings of the ancient sage kings. (2) The real existence of fate cannot be proven by any means. It cannot be proven empirically by the senses of hearing and sight, for no one from the beginning of time to the present could testify that they had ever seen or heard directly from such a thing as fate. Moreover it cannot be proven using moral arguments because moral arguments require the nonexistence of fate. (3) Fatalism is the creation of tyrants, used by bandits and other wrongdoers, and welcomed by lazy people. Although it has been claimed that these three standards are the earliest known example of an attempt to formulate principles of reasoned argument in early China, it should be noted that the appeal to ancient authorities still occupies first place (Graham, 1978, p. 11).

Although Mozi's writings have often been criticized for being dull and repetitive, he did use consistent and rigorous arguments. Positive assessments of his legacy note his attempts to justify his philosophical ideas; his efforts to submit traditional morality to the test of social utility; his defense of innovation; his support for the new kind of centralized state, with merit rather than birth as the grounds for preferment; and for introducing reasoned argument into classical Chinese thought (Graham, 1978, p. 4).

BIBLIOGRAPHY

Fraser, Chris. "Mohism." In *The Stanford Encyclopedia of Philosophy,* edited by Edward N. Zalta. Stanford, Calif., 2002. Available at: plato.stanford.edu/archives/win2002/entries/mohism. Authoritative and informative overall of the Mohist school and its doctrines.

Graham, A. C. "Introduction." In *Later Mohist Logic, Ethic and Science,* pp. 3–72. Hong Kong, 1978. Succinct and authoritative introduction to the historical background of the Mohist school and its canon.

Hansen, Chad. *A Daoist Theory of Chinese Thought: A Philosophical Interpretation.* New York, 1992. See chapter 4 for an impassioned analysis that provides Mozi with his strongest philosophical voice in English.

Mei, Y. P., trans. *Ethical and Political Works of Motse.* London, 1929; reprint, Westport, Conn., 1973. Translation of chapters that are held to represent the thought of Mozi.

Schwartz, Benjamin. *The World of Thought in Early China.* Cambridge, Mass., 1985. Comprehensive introductory overview of Mozi's thought.

Watson, Burton, trans. *Mo Tzu: Basic Writings.* New York, 1963. Partial translation of chapters that are held to represent the thought of Mozi.

Wong, David B. "Universalism versus Love with Distinctions: An Ancient Debate Revived." *Journal of Chinese Philosophy* 16 (1989): 251–272. A philosophically insightful partial defense of Mozi's ungraded concern *(jian ai)* thesis.

Wong, David B. "Mohism: The Founder, Mozi (Mo Tzu)." In *Encyclopedia of Chinese Philosophy,* edited by Antonio S. Cua, pp. 453–460. New York, 2003. A balanced and succinct overview of Mozi's thought.

JOHN MAKEHAM (2005)

MUDRĀ. *Mudrā* in Sanskrit means seal or stamp of authority. In ordinary Sanskrit this meaning has always been in use. For instance, a political play written by Viśākhadatta (c. 7 CE) is called *Mudrā-rākṣasa* (The signet [ring] of Rākṣasa). Rākṣasa was the chief minister of the Imperial Nandas, the enemies of Candragupta Maurya, king of Magadha, and this ring was his seal of office.

However, in the medieval Brahmanic tradition, especially in religious practice, another meaning of the term *mudrā* became prevalent. In this context *mudrā* is a symbolic representation of a concrete form, or an idea, presented through gestures *(hastas)* and, sometimes, facial expression. It thus becomes closely associated with hand gestures used in dance and acting. *Mudrā* can also refer to hand gesture in an iconographical context, though this is a late innovation (see Colas). For example, in the Buddhist Tantra the term *mudrā* is sometimes used to describe hand postures found in images of the Buddha and Bodhisattva. Some esoteric Buddhist Tantras, such as the *Guhyasiddhi* written by Padmavajra during the seventh century, call the adept's female partner mudrå. According to the *Siddha Tantras,* supreme Sakti who is nameless (*anakhya*) is designated as mudrå. As the term means divine authority and as Sakti is indeed the manifest divine authority, it is correct to call her *mudrå.* Tantric's partner is taken in rituals as a representative of the supreme Sakti and thus the divine authority incarnate (White, 2003).

In early Indian religious understanding, the term *mudrā* refers exclusively to ritual hand gestures symbolizing a variety of meanings and conferring legitimacy on a ritual act. The *Viṣṇudharmottara Purāṇa,* a famous early work on iconography, interestingly associates *mudrā* with esoteric rituals *(rahasya-mudrā).* In book III (the book on dance), it describes techniques of dance, including hand gestures *(nṛtta-hasta).* Not until the middle of the book does it turn to a discussion of the *mudrā* hand gestures *(mudrā-hastān vyākhyāsyāma),* which are presented as being in a separate category from the other hand gestures. Although the whole section on the performing arts in this Purāṇa concerns ritual worship, the mention of "esoteric" *(rahasya)* in relation to the *mudrā-hastas* clearly indicates that such *mudrās* were reserved for esoteric worship and not intended for use in the forms of public worship that incorporated dance along with gestures and mimesis. This esoteric quality becomes obvious when one takes into account the sorts of things that are represented by *mudrā-hastas*. Often these are abstract ideas like the mystic syllable *"Oṃ"* or the esoteric use of the vowels (Beyer, 1973, pp. 101–102). The same Purāṇa introduces a type of *mudrā* known as *śāstra-mudrā* (3.33.15–16). These gestures depict deities in the special characteristic postures described in the *mantras* associated with them. *Śāstra-mudrās* also include a not particularly esoteric group of gestures used to represent the vehicles of these deities.

It is clear that a gesture is called *mudrā* when it accompanies a *mantra* and has an explanatory mimetic connection with what the *mantra* expresses. It may mime some salient features of the deity of the *mantra,* or it may mime the abstract idea expressed in the *mantra;* for example, the *mantra "aḥ,"* which depicts the deity of the primal point of creation, must be uttered along with prescribed hand gestures. *Mudrā* also is seen as an agent that invests the *mantra* with the energy of its associated deity, and thus invests the worshipper with that deity's power. During the ritual investment of divine power, a process known as *nyāsa,* the ritual hand gestures indicate the divesting of power from each part of the deity's body to the corresponding part of the worshipper's body. Finally, one may deduce from the *Viṣṇudharmottara Purāṇa* that *mudrā* not only refers to a type of hand gesture but also symbolizes the seal of approval of the deity whose *mantra* the *mudrā* accompanies. It seals the *mantra's* efficacy with divine authority.

The formulation of *mudrās* in a ritual context has been elaborately systematized. Indeed, all the major religious systems of classical India record the correct formulation of these hand gestures in their canonical texts and exegetical works. *Mudrās* are divided into three categories, each associated with different stages of a ritual. The first consists of *mudrās* associated with ritual purification of the worshipper's person, of the place of worship, and of the ingredients of offerings. These are called purificatory gestures, and are used at the beginning and end of a ritual. The second category is made up of those hand gestures known as *saṃskāra mudrā.* These are associated with the part of a ritual in which the worshipper envisages a cosmogonic sequence through which the deity gradually assumes a personal form and takes up residence in the worshipper's innermost core. This is the adept's heart conceived as a lotus, the seat of the deity, and is known as the lotus-heart. The worshipper invites the deity to emerge from his lotus-heart to sit upon the divine pedestal set up in front of the worshipper, so that offerings may be made. The third category of *mudrās, pūjā-mudrā,* comes into play when the worshipper makes offerings and imagines them being received by the deity. The final offering is of the worshipper's own self. A ritual ends with the worshipper envisaging the deity taking leave and being reabsorbed into the worshipper's heart.

The *Mudrās* form a secret system of sign or symbolic language known only to sectarian participants in various rituals. Buddhist, Śaiva, Śākta, and Vaiṣṇava tantric sects each have some sets of *mudrās* that are different from those used by other sects. In fact, members of one tantric sect can communicate with each other secretly by using *mudrās* unknown to an enemy sect.

In general, though, when the same type of object is being referred to, sectarian variation in *mudrā* use is not extreme. Furthermore, some *mudrās* do not vary, at least significantly, from sect to sect. For example, the *mudrā* used to welcome a deity (extrapolated from the everyday gesture used to welcome a revered guest) is almost the same in the Śaiva, Śākta, and Vaiṣṇava sects. Likewise, all sects use an identical *mudrā* called *surabhī* when a jug of water or other drink that is being offered to the deity is mentally identified with divine nectar. (The name of this *mudrā* is derived from the celestial cow Surabhī, whose milk is nectar.)

Ritual hand gestures are acts of elaborate mimesis. An act of warning toward any malevolent agent is played out either by imitating a weapon, for instance an arrow, or by making an explosive sound by snapping fingers or clapping hands. The ritual worshipper is an actor creating a totally supernatural world of religious reality through focused meditation, vivid imagination, and total understanding of his religious ideology and aims. That is why his gestures carry an authority invested by long religious tradition.

See Also Buddhism, Schools of; Hands; Mantra.

Bibliography

Beyer, Stephen. *The Cult of Tārā: Magic and Ritual in Tibet.* London, 1973.

Colas, Gérard. "Variation sur la pâmoison dévote: A propos d'un poème de Vedânta Deshika et du théâtre des araiyar." In *Images du corps dans le monde hindou,* edited by Véronique Bouillier and Gilles Tarabout, pp. 275-314. Paris, 2002.

Ghosh, Manomohan, ed. and trans. *Bharata's Nāṭya-śāstra.* Calcutta, 1967. See chapter 9.

Gupta, Sanjukta, Dirk Jan Hoens, and Teun Goudriaan. *Hindu Tantrism.* Leiden, Netherlands, 1979.

Janaki, S. S., ed. and trans. *Mudrālakṣṇam, Cited in Nirmalamaṇi's Commentary on Aghora śivācārya-paddhati.* Madras, India, 1986.

White, David Gordon. *Kiss of the Yogini: "Tantric Sex" in Its South Asian Contexts.* Chicago, 2003.

Sanjukta Gupta (2005)

MUḤAMMAD ibn ʿAbdullāh (c. 570–632 CE) is revered by Muslims as the prophet to whom the Qurʾān, the sacred scripture of Islam, was revealed. Apart from the Qurʾān and the *ḥadīth,* the main sources for his life history are the biographies written by four early Muslim historians: Muḥammad ibn Isḥāq (d. c. 767), Muḥammad ibn Ṣaʿd (d. c. 845), Abū Jaʿfar al-Ṭabarī (d. c. 923), and Muḥammad ibn ʿUmar al-Waqīdī (d. c. 820).

Early Life (c. 570–610). Born in Mecca, in the Arabian Ḥijāz, in about 570, Muḥammad was a member of the Quraysh, the ruling tribe of Mecca, but of the clan of Hāshim, one of its less influential family groups. Orphaned early in life, he was brought up by his uncle Abū Ṭālib, and although he was treated kindly, the experience of deprivation made an indelible impression on Muḥammad, who remained poor throughout his youth and a marginal figure in the thriving city of Mecca. Mecca had long been the holiest city in Arabia. The Kaʿbah, the cube-shaped shrine in the heart of the town, was of great antiquity. It was a place of pilgrimage. Each year, Arabs came from all over the peninsula to perform the arcane rites of the *ḥājj* pilgrimage, whose original significance had been forgotten but which still yielded a powerful religious experience. Because of the great sanctity of the Kaʿbah, all violence was forbidden in Mecca and its environs, and this made it possible for the Arabs to trade peacefully there, away from the endemic tribal warfare that engulfed the Arabian steppes. During the sixth century, the Quraysh had made Mecca a vital station in the spice trade, and they had become rich by trading in the surrounding countries.

Little is known about Muḥammad's early years. After his death, legends developed that indicated that he had been marked out from birth for future greatness, but until he was about twenty-five there was little sign of this glorious future. He grew up to be a very able young man and was known in Mecca as al-Amīn, the reliable one. He was handsome, with a compact, solid body of average height. His hair and beard were thick and curly, and he had a strikingly luminous expression. Yet his orphaned status held him back. He could get no position commensurate with his talents, but became a merchant, whose job it was to lead the trading caravans to Syria and Mesopotamia. But in about 595, his luck changed. Khadījah bint Khuwaylid, a wealthy businesswoman, hired Muḥammad to take some merchandise into Syria, and she was so impressed that she proposed marriage. Even though she was considerably older than he, this was no mere marriage of convenience. Muḥammad sincerely loved Khadījah and together the couple bore a son, who died in infancy, and four daughters who survived: Fāṭimah, Zaynab, Ruqayyah, and Umm Kulthūm.

But by the time he was forty years old, Muḥammad had become deeply concerned about the malaise that was apparent in Mecca. The Quraysh had become rich beyond their wildest dreams and had left the desperate nomadic life of the steppes behind. But in the new stampede for wealth some of the old tribal values had been lost. In the desert, most Arabs lived on the brink of malnutrition, taking their herds from one watering hole to another and competing desperately with the other tribes for food and sustenance. Throughout Arabia, one tribe fought another in a murderous cycle of vendetta and counter-vendetta. In this brutal existence, the unity of the tribe was essential for its very survival, and a strict nomadic code insisted upon the importance of protecting its weaker and more vulnerable members. But the aggressive capitalism of Mecca had resulted in some of the Quraysh making money at the expense of some of the tribe's poorer clans, including Muḥammad's own clan of Hāshim. The old values were disappearing, nothing new had yet appeared to take its place, and while the more successful members of the Quraysh were naturally happy with these developments, the weaker clans felt endangered and lost.

There was also spiritual restlessness in Mecca and throughout the peninsula. Arabs knew that Judaism and Christianity, which were practiced in the neighboring Byzantine and Persian empires, were more sophisticated than their own pagan traditions. Some had come to believe that the high God of their pantheon, *al-Lāh* (whose name simply meant "the God"), was the deity worshiped by Jews and Christians, but he had sent the Arabs no prophet and no scripture in their own language. Indeed, the Jews and Christians often taunted the Arabs for being left out of the divine plan. Intent on finding a solution, Muḥammad used to retire to a cave on the summit of Mount Ḥirāʾ, just outside Mecca, during the month of Ramaḍān, where he prayed, fasted, and gave alms to the poor. It was in this cave that on 17 Ramaḍān 610 Muḥammad woke to find himself overwhelmed by a devastating presence, and heard the first words of a new Arabic scripture pouring from his lips.

THE MESSAGE OF MUḤAMMAD. For the first two years, Muḥammad kept quiet about this revelation, confiding only in his wife Khadījah and her cousin, Waraqa ibn Nawfal, who had converted to Christianity. Both encouraged him to believe that this was a genuine revelation from God, who had chosen him to bring the old religion of the Jews and the Christians to the Arabs. In 612, after another powerfully endorsing revelation, Muḥammad began to preach in Mecca, and he gradually gained converts, including his young cousin ʿAlī ibn Abī Ṭālib, his friend Abū Bakr, and the young merchant ʿUthmān ibn ʿAffān from the powerful Umayyad family. Many of the converts, including a significant number of women, were members of the poorer clans; others were unhappy about the new inequality in Mecca, which was alien to the Arab spirit.

Muḥammad's message was simple. He taught the Arabs no new doctrines about God: like the Jews and Christians, most of the Quraysh already believed that Allāh had created the world and would judge humanity in the Last Days. Muḥammad had no intention of founding a new religion, but saw himself as the latest in a long line of prophets that included Adam, Noah, Abraham, Moses, and Jesus (Qurʾān 2:129–132). Muḥammad was not attempting to contradict or supersede these prophets, and he never required Jews or Christians to convert to his new Arab faith, because they had received authentic revelations of their own. Constantly, the revelations that he received from God insist that Muḥammad's followers must respect the *ahl al-kitāb* (People of the Book). God commands them to speak to the Jews and Christians with courtesy: "Say to them: We believe what you believe; your God and our God is one" (Qurʾān 29:46). God had sent one prophet after another to every people on the face of the earth, each of which had expressed the divine message in its own language and cultural idiom (Qurʾān 35:22). In principle, one cult, one tradition, one scripture was as good as another (Qurʾān 6:160). What mattered was the quality of one's surrender (*islām*) to God, not to any mere human expression of his will.

The essence of Muḥammad's message was, therefore, not doctrinal but social and ethical. It was wrong to build up a private fortune, but good to share wealth and create a society where the weak and vulnerable were treated with respect. If the Quraysh did not mend their ways, their society would collapse (like other unjust societies in the past) because they were violating the fundamental laws of existence.

MUḤAMMAD AND THE QURʾĀN. This was the core teaching of the new scripture, which became known as the *qurʾān* (recitation) because it was an aural revelation, designed to be listened to for the music of its language, rather than perused page by page. Most of the believers, including Muḥammad himself, were not learned, and they absorbed its teachings by listening to public recitation of its chapters (*sūrahs*). The Qurʾān was revealed to Muḥammad piecemeal, verse by verse, *sūrah* by *sūrah*, during the next twenty-one years, often in response to a crisis or a problem that had arisen in the little community of the faithful. These revelations were very painful to Muḥammad, who used to say: "Never once did I receive a revelation without thinking that my soul had been torn away from my body." In the early days, the impact was so frightening that his whole body was convulsed; he would sweat profusely, experience a peculiar heaviness, or hear strange sounds, such as the tolling of a bell. The great prophets of Israel also felt the divine impact as a near lethal blow and found it almost impossibly painful and difficult to utter the word of God.

Muḥammad had perceived the great problems of his people at a deeper level than most of his contemporaries, and when he "listened" to events as they unfolded, he had to delve deeply into his inner self to find a solution that was not only politically viable but also spiritually sound. He was also communicating a new literary form and a masterpiece of Arab poetry and prose. The extraordinary beauty of the Qurʾān was in fact responsible for the conversion of many of Muḥammad's first disciples. One of the most dramatic of these conversions was that of ʿUmar ibn al-Khaṭṭāb, who was passionately devoted to the old paganism and initially opposed to Muḥammad's message. But he was also deeply versed in Arabic poetry, and the first time he heard the language of the Qurʾān, it broke down all his reservations. "When I heard the Qurʾān, my heart was softened and I wept, and Islam entered into me."

THE MISSION IN MECCA (612–622). The new teaching would eventually be called *islām* (surrender), and a *muslim* was a man or a woman who had made this existential submission of their entire selves to Allāh and his demand that human beings behave towards one another with justice and compassion. It was an attitude expressed in the prostrations of the ritual prayer (*ṣalāt*), which Muslims were required to make three times a day, facing Jerusalem, the city of the Jews and Christians. Thus at first Muslims were turning their backs on the pagan religion, symbolized by the Kaʿbah, and reaching out towards the monotheistic tradition that they were now determined to follow. The posture of their prayer was thus designed to change their fundamental attitude and orientation. The old tribal ethic had been egalitarian. Arabs did not approve of kingship, and it was abhorrent to them to grovel on the ground like a slave. But the prostrations were designed to teach their bodies, at a level deeper than the rational, to counter the hard arrogance and self-sufficiency that was rife in mercantile Mecca, to lay aside their selfishness, and to accept that before God they were as nothing. Muslims were also required to give a regular proportion of their income to the poor in alms (*zakāt*) and to fast during the month of Ramaḍān, reminding themselves of the privations of those who were too impoverished to eat and drink when they wished.

Social justice was, therefore, the cardinal virtue of Islam. Muslims were commanded, as their first duty, to build a community (*ummah*) in which wealth was fairly distributed. This was far more crucial than any doctrinal teaching about God. The political and social welfare of the *ummah* would have sacred value for Muslims, and would become the chief sign that Muslims were living according to God's will. This habit of mind has persisted to the present day. Muslims would be profoundly affected by any misfortune or humiliation suffered by the *ummah*. Its spiritual and political health is as crucial to Muslims' religious lives as theological doctrines have been to Christians.

Muḥammad found the Christian preoccupation with doctrine difficult to understand. The Qurʾān tends to regard such speculation as self-indulgent guesswork (*ẓannah*). It seemed pointless to argue about abstruse dogmas that nobody could prove one way or the other. He did have to take up certain theological positions, of course. By the sixth century, most of the Arabs were tending towards monotheism, and even though the Kaʿbah was officially dedicated to Hubal, a Nabatean deity, and was surrounded by effigies of some 360 gods, many Arabs believed that it had originally been dedicated to Allāh. Indeed, those Arabs who had converted to Christianity felt comfortable making the *ḥājj* pilgrimage because they saw the Kaʿbah as the shrine of their own God, and Muḥammad and the Muslims continued to perform the old rites there. Some of the Quraysh, however, were still happy with the old paganism, and they were especially devoted to three Arabian goddesses: Manāt, Allāt, and al-ʿUzzah. Muḥammad forbade his followers to take part in their cults, comparing the pagan deities to weak tribal chiefs who were a liability for their people because they could no longer give them adequate protection. The Qurʾān put forward no philosophical arguments in favor of monotheism. Its approach was strictly practical, and appealed to the pragmatic Arabs. The old religion was simply not working (Qurʾān 25:3; 29:17; 44:47). This was evident in the spiritual malaise, the chronic tribal warfare that was tearing the peninsula apart, and an injustice that violated the highest Arab traditions. The way forward was to be found in the worship of a single God, the creation of a united *ummah*, and the pursuit of justice and equity that alone would bring peace to Arabia. But the Qurʾān insisted that it was teaching nothing new. Its message was simply a "reminder" of truths that everybody knew already (Qurʾān 80:11). This was the primordial faith that had been preached to the whole of humanity by all the prophets of the past.

Muḥammad gradually acquired a small following, and eventually about seventy families converted to Islam. At first the most powerful and successful men in Mecca ignored the Muslims, but by 616 they had become extremely angry with Muḥammad, who, they claimed, reviled the faith of their fathers and was obviously a charlatan who only pretended to be a prophet. They were especially irritated by the Qurʾān's description of the Last Judgment, which they dismissed as primitive fairy stories. But their greatest fear was its condemnation of their ruthless capitalism. On the Last Day, Arabs were warned that their wealth would not help them, nor would the power and influence of their family connections. Everybody would be tried on his or her own merits. Had they looked after the poor? Why had they built up private fortunes instead of sharing their money? The Quraysh, who had become rich and prosperous as a result of the new economy, did not appreciate this kind of talk, and an opposition party developed, led by Abū al-Ḥakam, who is called Abū Jahl (Father of Lies) in the Qurʾān. Muḥammad's old friend, Abū Sufyān, an extremely able and intelligent man, and the devout pagan Suhayl ibn ʿAmr also joined the opposition. All had relatives who had converted to Islam, and all feared that Muḥammad was plotting to take over the leadership of Mecca. At this stage, the Qurʾān insisted that Muḥammad should have no political function in the city; he was simply a *nādhir* (a warner). But how long would it be before a man who claimed to receive instructions directly from Allāh would feel inspired to seize supreme power for himself?

PERSECUTION IN MECCA. By 617 the Muslims' relationship with some of the Meccan establishment had deteriorated beyond repair. Abū Jahl imposed a boycott on Muḥammad's clan of Hāshim, forbidding the people of Mecca to marry or trade with the Muslims. This meant that nobody could sell them food. This ban lasted for two years, and the food shortages may have caused the death of Muḥammad's beloved wife Khadījah. The ban certainly ruined some of the Muslims, such as Abū Bakr, financially. Slaves who had converted to Islam were particularly badly treated, tied up, and left to burn in the blazing sun. Most seriously, in 619, after the ban had been lifted, Abū Ṭālib, Muḥammad's uncle and protector (*wālī*) died. This made Muḥammad's position untenable. As an orphan, he was now entirely without powerful family backing. According to the tribal laws of vendetta that still prevailed in Mecca, without a patron who could avenge his death, a man could be killed with impunity. It took Muḥammad a long time to find a chieftain in the city who would become his *wālī*. Clearly he had to find a new solution for himself and the community of Muslims.

Tradition has it that it was during this dark period that Muḥammad experienced his mystical flight (*isrāʾ*) to the Temple mount in Jerusalem. There he was welcomed by all the great prophets of the past, who invited him to preach to them. This vision represents Muḥammad's longing to bring the Arabs, who had apparently been left off the map of salvation, from far-off Arabia into the heart of the monotheistic family. After his sermon, Muḥammad made the *miʿrāj*, ascending through the seven heavens to the throne of God.

In Mecca, however, the Muslims' position had become so untenable that Muḥammad was ready to listen to a delegation of chiefs from Yathrib, an agricultural settlement some 240 miles north of Mecca, who approached him in 620 with a novel proposal. A number of different tribes had settled in Yathrib, abandoning the nomadic lifestyle, but the habits of tribal warfare were so engrained that they found it impossible to live peacefully together. As a result, Yathrib was caught up in one deadly feud after another. Some of these tribes had either converted to Judaism or were of Jewish descent, and so the people of Yathrib were used to monotheistic ideas, were not so wedded to the old paganism as some of the Meccan families, and were desperate to find a means of living together in a single community. They had heard of the prophet in Mecca who claimed to be the messenger of the one God, and thought that he might be what they were looking for. During the *ḥājj* of 620, delegates from Yathrib approached Muḥammad, converted to Islam, and made a pledge with the Muslims. Each side vowed that it would not fight the other, and they would defend each other from common enemies. There were further negotiations and discussions. Finally Muḥammad reached a momentous decision. In 622, the Muslim families slipped quietly out of Mecca, one by one, and made the migration (*hijrah*) to Yathrib. Muḥammad, whose new protector had recently died, narrowly escaped assassination, and he and Abū Bakr were the last of the Muslims to escape.

THE *HIJRAH* (622). The *hijrah* marks the start of the Muslim era, because it was at this point that Muḥammad was able to implement the Qurʾanic ideal fully in a social setting. It was a revolutionary step. The *hijrah* was no mere change of address. In Arabia, the tribe was the most sacred value of all. To abandon your own kin to join forces with another group, with whom you had no blood relationship, was not only absolutely unheard of, it violated a strong taboo and was essentially treasonable. The Quraysh, shocked to the core by this extraordinary defection, were outraged, and they had no means of accommodating a development that had no precedent in their world. They vowed to exterminate the *ummah* in Yathrib, which had flouted the deepest and strongest sanctities of Arabia.

The Muslims themselves found the migration a wrenching, painful experience. They were not going forward eagerly into a new life, like other emigrants, but were primarily aware only of the trauma of severance. This is clear in the word they used to describe their radical departure from their tribe. The first stem of the Arabic root word *HJR, hajarahhu,* can be translated: "he cut himself off from friendly or loving communion or intercourse. He ceased to associate with them." The people of Yathrib were also aware that they were engaged in a highly controversial and precarious experiment in promising to give protection (*awliyah*) and help (*naṣr*) on a permanent basis to people who were not kin. Henceforth, they would be known as the Anṣār, the "helpers" of the Prophet, but the English translation gives rather a feeble impression of what was involved. *Naṣr* meant that one had to be ready to back up one's "help" with force, if necessary. The pledge that the Anṣār had made with the Muslims was therefore called the "Pledge of War."

Muḥammad had not expected to hold political office, and initially had no intention of founding a new polity. But the force of circumstances that he could not have foreseen meant that overnight he had become the head of a collection of tribal groups that had no blood ties but were bound together by a shared ideology—an astonishing innovation in Arabia. Nobody in Yathrib was forced to convert to the religion of the Qurʾān, which forbids any coercion in religious matters in the strongest terms (2:256). But on his arrival, Muḥammad drew the people of Yathrib together in a covenant. The Muslims, Jewish tribes, and those who preferred to stay with the old paganism all belonged to a single *ummah,* could not attack one another, and vowed to give one another protection. They were all to be "helpers" to each other. News of this extraordinary new "supertribe" spread, and though at the outset nobody in Arabia believed that it would survive, it proved to be the inspiration that would bring peace to Arabia, just ten years after the *hijrah.*

Yathrib would become known as al-Madīnah (*the* City) because it became the archetype of the perfect Muslim society in Islamic thought. Throughout history, many Muslims have looked back on the Prophet's sojourn in Medina as a golden age, when the ideals of Islam were fully incarnated in society. They have idealized this period, much as Christians have idealized the primitive church. In fact, however, these were hard and difficult years, full of darkness and danger for Muḥammad. When he arrived in Medina, one of his first actions was to build a simple mosque (*masjid;* literally, a place of prostration). It was a rough building, which expressed the austerity of the early Islamic ideal. The roof was supported by tree trunks, a stone marked the *qiblah* (the direction of prayer), and the Prophet stood on a tree trunk to preach. Future mosques would be inspired by this model. There was also a courtyard where Muslims met to discuss all the concerns of the *ummah*—social, political, and military, as well as religious. Muḥammad and his wives lived in small huts around the edge of the courtyard. Unlike holy places in other traditions, the mosque was not separated from secular activities and devoted only to worship. In the Qurʾanic vision, there is no dichotomy between the sacred and the profane, the religious and the political, sexuality and ritual. The whole of life is potentially holy and must be brought into the ambit of the divine. From the start, the aim was *tawḥīd* (making one), a holistic vision that would give Muslims intimations of the unity that is God.

MUḤAMMAD'S WIVES. In Mecca, Muḥammad had remained monogamous, married only to Khadījah, even though polygamy was common in Arabia. In Medina, however, Muḥammad became a great *sayyid* (chief) and was expected to have multiple wives, but most of the marriages he contracted were politically motivated. The tie of blood was still important, and as he formed his supertribe, Muḥammad bound some of his closest companions to him by marriage. His favorite new wife was ʿĀʾishah, the daughter of Abū Bakr. He also married Ḥafṣah, the daughter of ʿUmar ibn al-Khaṭṭāb, and arranged the marriages of two of his own daughters to ʿUthmān ibn ʿAffān and ʿAlī ibn Abī Ṭālib, his cousins. Many of his other wives were older women who were without protectors or were related to the chiefs of tribes that became the allies of the *ummah.* None of these wives bore the Prophet any children.

In the West, Muḥammad's wives have occasioned a good deal of prurient interest, but they were sometimes more of a worry than a pleasure. On one occasion, when he found them quarrelling about the division of booty after a raid, he threatened to divorce them all unless they lived more strictly in accordance with Islamic values (Qurʾān 33:28–29). Muḥammad was no chauvinist, but he genuinely enjoyed women's company. ʿUmar and some of his other companions were shocked by the way he allowed his wives to stand up to him and answer him back. Muḥammad regularly helped with household chores, mended his own clothes, and took his wives' advice very seriously. On one occasion Umm Salāmah, the most intelligent of his wives, helped him to prevent a mutiny.

The Qurʾān gave women rights of inheritance and divorce centuries before women in other cultures, including the West, were accorded such legal status. The emancipation of women was one of Muḥammad's objectives. In pre-Islamic Arabia, elite women, like Khadījah, enjoyed a degree of power and independence, but the vast majority of women had virtually no human rights and were treated little better than slaves or animals. The Qurʾān prescribes some degree of segregation for the Prophet's wives, as a matter of protocol, but there is nothing in the Qurʾān that commands the veiling and segregation of all women in a separate part of the house. These customs were adopted some three or four generations after Muḥammad's death, when Muslims imitated the customs of the Greek Orthodox Christians of Byzantium (also Iran), who had long veiled and segregated their women in this way. The Qurʾān is an egalitarian faith, and sees men and women as partners before God, with identical duties and responsibilities (Qurʾān 33:35). The women of Medina played an active role in public life, and some even fought alongside the men in battle. It was only later that Muslim men dragged the faith back to the old patriarchy (the same process happened in Christianity).

THE CHANGE OF THE *QIBLAH* FROM JERUSALEM TO MECCA. When he arrived in Medina, Muḥammad eagerly anticipated the prospect of working alongside the Jewish tribes, believing that they would welcome him as a prophet in their own tradition. Shortly before the *hijrah,* he had introduced some practices that would make the connection with Judaism more explicit, such as communal prayer on Friday afternoon, while Jews would be preparing for the Sabbath, and a fast on Yom Kippur. He was therefore greatly disappointed when the Jews of Medina refused to accept him as an authentic prophet. Some of the Qurʾanic accounts of such figures as Noah or Moses were different from the biblical stories, and many of the Jews scoffed when these were recited in the mosque. Like many of the pagan Arabs of Medina, the three main Jewish tribes also resented Muḥammad's political ascendancy. They had formed a powerful bloc before his arrival, and now felt their position threatened.

But some Jews in the smaller clans were friendly and increased Muḥammad's knowledge of their scriptures. He was especially excited to hear that in the book of *Genesis,* Abraham had two sons, and that Ishmael, the child of his concubine Hagar, was said to be the father of the Arab nation (*Gn.* 16; 18:18–20). Abraham had cast Ishmael and Hagar out into the wilderness at God's command, and the Jews and Christians of Arabia believed that they had settled in Mecca, that Abraham had visited them there, and that together Abraham and Ismāʿīl had built the Kaʿbah. Muḥammad was delighted to hear this, since it showed that Arabs had not been left out of the divine plan after all, and that the Kaʿbah was not really a pagan shrine, but had been the first temple of the true God in Arabia.

By 624 it was clear that most of Medina's Jews would never accept Muḥammad, who was also shocked to learn that Jews and Christians, whom he had assumed to belong to a single faith, actually had serious theological disagreements. It seemed disgraceful to split the unity of God's religion into warring sects because of abstruse speculations that nobody could prove definitively. Such sectarianism was idolatrous in erecting a human theological system to the unity that was essential to the faith of Allāh. It made people quarrelsome and unkind, and Muḥammad wanted no part of this sectarianism. So, in January 624, he made one of his most creative innovations. During prayers, he told the congregation to turn around so that they faced Mecca rather than Jerusalem. This change of *qiblah* was a declaration of independence. By turning towards the Kaʿbah, which had been built by Abraham, who had lived before the revelation of the Torah and the Gospels, Muslims were tacitly reverting to the original pure monotheism that had pertained before the divisions in God's religion. Muslims were turning to God alone, not to one of the established faiths; they were abjuring divisive sectarianism and would take their own direct route to God (Qurʾān 6:159, 161–162).

JIHĀD. A few weeks after the change of the *qiblah,* Muḥammad took yet another decisive step. The Emigrants who had made the *hijrah* had no means of earning a living in Medina. There was no land left for them to farm, and most of them were merchants and businessmen, with no experience of date cultivation. The Anṣār, as the helpers in Medina were called, could not be expected to feed and support this large community, because their own resources were stretched to the limit, so Muḥammad resorted to the tradition of the *ghazw* (colloquial, *ghazū*; "raid"). The *ghazū* was rather like a national sport and a crude means of redistributing resources in a region where there were simply not enough of the necessities of life to go round. Raiding parties would attack the herds or trading caravans of a rival tribe and carry off booty and livestock. The trick was to avoid taking human life, because this would automatically trigger a vendetta, and nobody wanted that. It was forbidden to conduct a *ghazū* against a tribe that had become an ally or "client" (a weaker tribal group that had sought protection from one of the stronger tribes).

In order to earn their keep in Medina, some of the Emigrants began to conduct raids, attacking the rich caravans from Mecca. But this was a shocking departure from tradition, because it was unheard of to initiate a *ghazū* against your own tribe. But the Emigrants saw themselves as the victims of the Quraysh, who had persecuted them and forced them to leave their homes. The traumatic breach of the *hijrah* meant that they had been cast out of their tribe. The Anṣār, who had no quarrel with the Quraysh, took no part in these first raids. At first the raiding parties enjoyed some success, but in March 624 Muḥammad led a large band of Emigrants to the coast in order to intercept the largest Meccan caravan of the year. When the Quraysh heard of this shocking project they dispatched an army to defend the caravan, but even though they were heavily outnumbered, the Muslims were able to inflict a defeat on the Meccans at the well of Badr. The Quraysh fought in the old Arab style, with careless bravado, and had no overall strategy, but the Muslims fought under Muḥammad's unified command with greater discipline. The victory made a great impression on the nomadic tribes, who were not displeased to see the haughty Quraysh humiliated in this way. They began to look with interest at the prophet who seemed to be the coming man in Arabia.

But the Quraysh were certain to retaliate, and Muḥammad now found himself engaged in a full-scale war with Mecca. During the five years of hostilities, the Qurʾān gives instructions about proper conduct on the battlefield, and develops a theory of warfare that is similar to the Christian ideal of the just war. The Qurʾān permits only a war of self-defense; Muslims must never initiate hostilities (2:191). Warfare is always abhorrent (2:217), but sometimes it is necessary to fight in order to bring the kind of persecution the Muslims had endured in Mecca to an end or to preserve decent values (2:217:22:40). As long as the fighting continues, Muslims must dedicate themselves to the war wholeheartedly in order to bring hostilities to a speedy conclusion, but the second the enemy makes a peaceful overture, all hostilities must cease (2:192). But it is always better to avoid warfare, to forgive injuries, to talk rather than to fight, and to forgive (5:45).

The word *jihād* does not mean "holy war," as Western people often imagine. It means "struggle" or "effort." It is difficult to put God's will into practice in a flawed and violent world, and Islam demands that Muslims make an effort on all fronts: physical, moral, political, social, spiritual, and intellectual. Sometimes it may be necessary to fight, but far more important is the interior *jihād*, the personal struggle to eradicate greed, hatred, and egotism from one's own heart. Thus, after the Battle of Badr, Muḥammad is said to have told his companions: "We are returning from the lesser *jihād* (the battle) to the greater *jihād*," the more crucial and demanding effort to reform one's own society and one's own self.

But for five years after the Battle of Badr, the Muslims had to fight in order to survive. Abu Sufyān launched two major offensives against the Muslims in Medina, vowing not merely to defeat the Muslims but also to exterminate the entire community, as Arab tradition demanded. Muḥammad also had to contend with hostility within Medina, since some of the pagans in Medina resented the power of the Emigrants and were determined to expel them. In 625, Mecca inflicted a severe defeat on the *ummah* at the Battle of ʿUhud, but two years later the Muslims overcame the numerically superior Meccan army at the Battle of the Trench, so called because Muḥammad had protected the settlement by digging a ditch around it. This victory was a turning point because it convinced most of the nomadic tribes that the supremacy of the Quraysh was over. The old religion seemed discredited because the gods were clearly unable or unwilling to come to the aid of Mecca. Many of the tribes allied themselves to Muḥammad, who began to build a powerful confederacy whose members swore not to attack one another and to avenge attacks on one another. Some of the Meccans also began to defect and made the *hijrah* to Medina. After five years of deadly danger, it seemed that the *ummah* would survive.

THE MASSACRE OF THE JEWISH TRIBE OF QURAYẒAH. Three of the most powerful Jewish tribes of Medina—Qaynuqāʿ, Naḍīr, and Qurayẓah—had joined the disaffected pagans of the settlement and plotted the overthrow of Muḥammad. To this end, the Jewish tribes had formed alliances with Mecca. They were a security threat, since the location of their territory meant that they could easily join a besieging Meccan army and attack the *ummah* from within. When the Qaynuqāʿ staged an unsuccessful coup against Muḥammad in 625, they were expelled from Medina. Muḥammad tried to reassure the Naḍīr and made a special alliance with them, but when they attempted to assassinate him, he sent them into exile too. The exiles joined the nearby Jewish settlement of Khaybar, and helped to build support for Abū Sufyān from the northern Arab tribes. When the remaining tribe of Qurayẓah sided with Mecca during the Battle of the Trench, Muḥammad showed no mercy. The seven hundred men of Qurayẓah were killed and their women and children sold as slaves.

This was an appalling incident, and Muḥammad was acting exactly like a traditional Arab chieftain, retaliating mercilessly to ensure the survival of his own people. An Arab *sayyid* was not expected to spare surviving enemies. Had Muḥammad simply exiled the Qurayẓah, they would have swelled the Jewish opposition in Khaybar and brought another war upon the *ummah.* The executions sent a grim message to Khaybar and helped to quell pagan opposition in Medina. Muḥammad acted according to the old tribal ethic in an attempt to bring hostilities to an end as soon as possible. This had been a fight to the death, and both sides had understood that the stakes were high.

The struggle did not indicate any hostility towards Jews in general, however, and showed no antipathy to Jewish religion. The Jews of Medina who had not sided with Mecca continued to be a part of the *ummah* and to enjoy Muslim protection. The Qurʾān continued to command Muslims to respect the People of the Book and to revere the Jewish prophets. Later, Jews, like Christians, enjoyed full religious liberty in the Islamic empires. Hatred of Jews became marked in the Muslim world only after the creation of the State of Israel in 1948 and the subsequent loss of Arab Palestine. As a result of this originally secular conflict, some Muslims now quote the passages in the Qurʾān that refer to Muḥammad's struggle with the three rebellious Jewish tribes, thus distorting both the message of the Qurʾān and the attitude of the Prophet himself, who felt no antagonism toward the Jewish people.

A Peace Offensive (628–630). The massacre of the Qurayẓah may have been a personal watershed for Muḥammad himself. His struggle with Mecca had followed the old patterns of violence in Arabia. The persecution of Muslims in Mecca had led to the *hijrah* and subsequent Muslim raids on the Meccan caravans. *Ghazū* had led to full-scale warfare. Attack had led to counterattack, injury to reprisal and retaliation. There had been atrocities on both sides. This had long been the chronic problem of Arabia. As long as Muḥammad continued to behave like a traditional Arab chieftain, he and his Muslims would be caught in an escalating spiral of violence, vendetta, and counter-vendetta. After his victory at the Battle of the Trench in 627, therefore, Muḥammad felt that it was time to break this vicious cycle.

In March 628, Muḥammad initiated an audacious campaign of nonviolence that eventually brought the conflict to an end. He announced that he was going to make the *ḥājj* pilgrimage to Mecca and asked for volunteers to accompany him. Since pilgrims were forbidden to bear arms during the *ḥājj,* the Muslims would be walking directly into the lions' den and putting themselves at the mercy of the Quraysh. Nevertheless about a thousand Muslims set out for Mecca with the Prophet, attired in the traditional white pilgrim robes and performing the rites of the *ḥājj* meticulously. Muḥammad was well aware that he was putting the Quraysh in a difficult position. If they attacked unarmed Arab pilgrims, they would violate the most sacred principles of Arabia and would be reviled as unworthy guardians of the Kaʿbah. The Quraysh did dispatch their cavalry to attack the pilgrims, but with the help of friendly local tribes the Prophet evaded them and managed to reach the well of Ḥudaybiyah, at the edge of the Meccan sanctuary, where all violence was forbidden. The Muslims then dismounted from their camels and sat down peacefully to await developments. Eventually the Quraysh were pressured to send a delegation and to sign a treaty with Muḥammad.

The treaty was extremely unpopular with the Muslims because Muḥammad appeared to throw away all the advantages that he had gained in the course of the long conflict. Even though Muḥammad could easily have forced the issue, he agreed to waive his right to complete the *ḥājj,* on the condition that the Muslims could make the pilgrimage the following year. There would be a truce between Mecca and Medina. This meant that Muḥammad had to abandon the economic blockade that was beginning to strangle the Meccan economy and that the Muslims could no longer engage in lucrative raids on the Meccan caravans. Muḥammad also promised to return any Meccan who converted to Islam and made the *hijrah* to Medina. The treaty so enraged the Muslims that there was danger of mutiny. But the Qurʾān insists that as soon as the enemy sues for peace, Muslims must bring hostilities to an end and sign a treaty, no matter how disadvantageous the terms. The Qurʾān refers to the treaty of Ḥudaybiyah as a "manifest victory": it was the spirit of peace that distinguished the true believer from the violence of paganism (48:1, 26–27)

Ḥudaybiyah was another turning point. More tribes came over to Muḥammad's confederacy, and conversion to Islam became an irreversible trend. Arabs were pragmatic people: once the old religion had shown itself to be inadequate, they would not remain committed to it. Many of the new members of the confederacy, however, joined for political reasons and did not alter their religious conviction. Muḥammad was well aware of this and did not press for conversion in these cases.

Eventually, in 630, the Quraysh violated the treaty of Ḥudaybiyah by attacking one of Muḥammad's tribal allies. The Prophet was then free to march on Mecca with an army of ten thousand men. Faced with this overwhelming evidence of the change in their fortunes, the Quraysh conceded defeat, opened the city gates, and Muḥammad took Mecca without bloodshed. He destroyed the idols around the Kaʿbah, but nobody was forced to enter Islam against their will, according to Qurʾanic principles. Muḥammad's victory, however, convinced some of his most dedicated opponents, such as Abū Sufyān, that the old faith had failed, and they became Muslims.

Last Days (630–632). After his victory, Muḥammad returned to Medina. He had promised the Anṣār that he would never abandon them in order to return to his native city, and Medina remained the administrative capital of the Islamic polity for another thirty years. His most significant act during these final years was the farewell pilgrimage to Mecca in 632, during which he reinterpreted the old pagan rituals of the *ḥājj* and gave them a Muslim significance by linking them to episodes in the story of Abraham, Hagar, and Ishmael. Therefore, when Muslims make the *ḥājj*, which is the peak experience of their religious lives, they are not reminded of Muḥammad but symbolically rehearse their relationship with the whole monotheistic family, returning to the roots of this faith. Shortly after this last pilgrimage, Muḥammad died in ʿĀʾishah's arms on June 8, 632. He was buried in her little hut in the courtyard of the mosque of Medina by members of his immediate family.

MUḤAMMAD IN MUSLIM PIETY. The Qurʾān warns Muslims against the dangers of idolatry (*shirk*); they must not give to any mere creature the honor due to God alone. Constantly Muḥammad had warned the *ummah* against deifying him, as the Christians had deified Jesus. Muḥammad was a mere mortal, like themselves. Nevertheless, devotion to the Prophet is crucial to Muslim spirituality. Muslims call him the "perfect man" because his life represents the ideal of *islām*, a wholehearted surrender to God. Just as Christians attempt to imitate Christ, Muslims imitate Muḥammad in their lives in order to approximate as far as possible this perfection, and to come as close as they can to God himself. The *sharīʿah*, the corpus of Islamic law, was developed on the basis of the Qurʾān and the daily practice of the Prophet. During the ninth century, scholars began a process of research and compiled the great collections of Muḥammad's maxims (*ḥadīth*) and accounts of his customary behavior, traveling throughout the Islamic empire to discover as much evidence as they could.

The *sunnah* (i.e., the model conduct of the Prophet) and *sharīʿah* taught Muslims to imitate the way Muḥammad spoke, ate, loved, washed, and worshiped, so that in the smallest details of their external lives they reproduce his actions in the hope of attaining his interior submission to God. This means that throughout the Islamic world, Muslims have acquired a clear identity, which draws them together. The way they pray or wash, as well as their table manners and personal hygiene, follow a common distinctive pattern. Muslims from China, Indonesia, and the Middle East, for example, all perform the prostrations of *ṣalāt* in the same way. This devotion also means that Muslims internalize the Prophet at a profound level and identify with him deeply. As a result, if Muḥammad is attacked or denigrated in any way, Muslims may feel personally violated.

The imitation of Muḥammad has also influenced many of the various political movements in Islam. Muḥammad did not retire to a cave or mountaintop, but was a man of the world, who worked incessantly to change his society. The society of Medina in Muḥammad's time has become the blueprint of the ideal Muslim society and has always been the starting point of political science in Islam. Because of the Qurʾān's emphasis on the paramount importance of social justice, politics has an inescapably religious dimension in Islam, and from a very early date Muslims have followed the example of Muḥammad's own life when they have sought to reform the *ummah*. From the early seventh century to the present day, Muslim reformers have first withdrawn from mainstream society in imitation of the Prophet's *hijrah*, and then engaged in a *jihād*, a struggle that may or may not include military action, to bring their fellow Muslims back to the Islamic ideal. The pattern of migration and struggle has become an archetypal form of engaging in political action. Most recently, the Egyptian activist Sayyid Quṭb (1906–1966) developed a fundamentalist ideology based entirely on Muḥammad's life, and he followed this archetypal pattern closely in his seminal book *Milestones* (1964). Quṭb's vision has inspired almost every single fundamentalist movement in the Sunnī world. Usāmah bin Lādin, the founder of the terrorist organization al-Qāʿidah, whose members attacked the Pentagon and the World Trade Center in New York on September 11, 2001, is a disciple of Quṭb. Unfortunately, Quṭb's ideology has distorted the Prophet's life by reducing the meaning of *jihād* to "holy war" and making this the climax of Muḥammad's career, forgetting that the Prophet finally abjured armed struggle and won victory by an ingenious policy of nonviolence.

The example of Muḥammad also informs Sufism, the mystical dimension of Islam. From the eighth century, Muslims who were disturbed by the growing wealth and luxury of the Islamic empire withdrew from the mainstream and imitated the simple lifestyle of the Prophet. The Ṣūfīs may even derive their name from their practice of wearing the kind of coarse woolen cloth *(taṣawwuf)* preferred by Muḥammad. In their spiritual exercises, Ṣūfīs hope to put themselves into the same receptive state of mind as the Prophet when he received the revelations of the Qurʾān, and they see the story of the *miʿrāj* as the archetype of the return that everybody must make to God, the source of their being. The *miʿrāj* is regarded as the supreme example of Muḥammad's surrender to the divine. But Ṣūfīs do not withdraw from the world in the same way as Christian or Buddhist monks. Their mystic call is often experienced as an inner rebellion against social or political injustices, and like Muḥammad they engage in a campaign of spiritual effort, which they call the "greater *jihād*." To this day, an intense spirituality modulates easily into political activism in the Muslim world. Ṣūfīs have often been at the forefront of many reform movements or in the vanguard of opposition to anything that threatens the *ummah*, externally or internally.

The prophet Muḥammad is equally venerated in the Shīʿah. Indeed, because of their devotion to the Prophet they also venerate his descendants, whom they believe should be the political leaders of the Muslim community. According to the traditional ethos of Arabia, the special gifts of a chieftain was handed down to his sons and descendants, and after the Prophet's death many of the Muslims believed that Muḥammad's prophetic quality would have been inherited by his male descendants. Because he had no surviving sons, these Muslims believed that some of his prophetic charisma had passed to ʿAlī, Muḥammad's cousin and son-in-law, to his sons—Ḥasan and Ḥusayn—and, following Ḥusayn's tragic murder by the Umayyad caliph, to the descendants of Ḥusayn, until the line finally died out in the ninth century. Each of these inspired *imāms* were the spiritual "leaders" of their people; each had inherited a secret knowledge (*ilm*) of divine truth. Each, as it were, kept some of Muḥammad's unique prophetic qualities alive, and in some mysterious way, kept the Prophet alive in each generation.

See Also Ḥadīth; Islam, overview article; Islamic Law, article on Sharīʿah; Miʿrāj; Qurʾān, overview article; Shiism, overview article; Sunnah.

Bibliography

Ahmed, Leila. *Women and Gender in Islam: Historical Roots of a Modern Debate.* New Haven and London, 1992.

Armstrong, Karen. *Muhammad: A Biography of the Prophet.* New York and London, 1991.

Armstrong, Karen. *Islam: A Short History.* London and New York, 2000.

Crone, Patricia. *Meccan Trade and the Rise of Islam.* Princeton, 1987.

Esposito, John L. *Islam: The Straight Path.* 3d ed. Oxford and New York, 1998.

Gabrieli, Francesco. *Muhammad and the Conquests of Islam.* Translated by Virginia Luling and Rosamund Linell. London, 1968.

Haykal, Muḥammad Ḥusayn. *The Life of Muhammad.* Translated from the 8th ed. by Ismāʿīl Rāgī A. al Fārūqī. 1976.

Hodgson, Marshall G. S. "Muḥammad's Challenge." In *The Venture of Islam: Conscience and History in a World Civilization,* 3 vols. Chicago and London. 1974. See vol. 1, pages 146–187.

Ibn Isḥāq, Muḥammad. *The Life of Muḥammad: A Translation of Isḥāq's Sīrat Rasūl Allāh.* Edited and translated by Alfred Guillaume. London, 1955.

Lewis, Bernard. *The Arabs in History.* London, 1950; 6th ed., 1993.

Lings, Martin. *Muhammad: His Life Based on the Earliest Sources.* London, 1983; rev. ed., 1991.

Mernissi, Fatima. *Women and Islam: An Historical and Theological Enquiry.* Translated by Mary Jo Lakeland. Oxford, 1991.

Nasr, Sayyid Hossein. *Muḥammad: Man of Allāh.* London, 1982.

Rodinson, Maxime. *Mohammed.* Translated by Anne Carter. London, 1971.

Schimmel, Annemarie. *And Muhammad Is His Messenger: The Veneration of the Prophet in Islamic Piety.* Chapel Hill, N.C., 1995.

Ṭabarī, al-. *Taʾrīkh al-rusul wa-al-mulūk* (The history of al-Ṭabarī), vol. 7, *The Foundation of the Community.* Translated and edited by W. Montgomery Watt and M. V. McDonald. Albany, N.Y., 1987.

Watt, W. Montgomery. *Muhammad at Mecca.* Oxford, 1953.

Watt, W. Montgomery. *Muhammad at Medina.* Oxford, 1956.

Watt, W. Montgomery. *Muhammad's Mecca: History in the Quran.* London, 1988.

Karen Armstrong (2005)

MUḤAMMAD AḤMAD

MUḤAMMAD AḤMAD (AH 1260–1302/1844–1885 CE), Sudanese preacher and mystic who claimed to be the Mahdi of Islam. Muḥammad Aḥmad ibn ʿAbd Allāh was born at Labab Island on the Nile in Dongola province of a Nubian family claiming descent from the Prophet and was brought up at Karari, just north of Omdurman. He received a traditional Islamic education and at age seventeen became apprenticed to Muḥammad Sharīf Nūr al-Dāʾim, a shaykh of the Sammānīyah Ṣūfī order. He spent seven years serving and imbibing mystical wisdom from his master who then authorized him to teach the doctrines of the order and to initiate others.

In 1870 he took up residence on Aba Island on the White Nile just north of Kosti, along with his three brothers, who were engaged in the family trade of boat building. Once settled there his growing reputation as a Ṣūfī teacher and ascetic began to gain him a considerable following among the local peoples. His teacher, Muḥammad Sharīf, also established himself nearby in 1288/1872, but before long the two men fell out, perhaps because of the elder man's jealousy at this pupil's acclaim. Muḥammad Sharīf announced Muḥammad Aḥmad's expulsion from the Sammānīyah order, whereupon the latter declared his allegiance to a rival shaykh of the order and denounced his former shaykh as a man who flouted the *sharīʿah.*

In 1878 his new shaykh, al-Qurashī wad al-Zayn, died, and Muḥammad Aḥmad was immediately recognized as his successor. Shortly afterward he received a visit from the man who was to be his political successor, the *khalīfah* ʿAbd Allāh (ʿAbdullāhi) ibn Muḥammad Ādam. ʿAbd Allāh's attachment to Muḥammad Aḥmad, however, was more than that of a Ṣūfī disciple to his master. He recognized him as the expected Mahdi, the final regenerator of Islam who, it was believed, would appear shortly before the end time to usher in a period of justice and Sammānīyah equity and unite the whole world under the banner of Islam.

Up to this point there is no indication that Muḥammad Aḥmad had considered the possibility that he might be the Mahdi, though he must have been aware of the widespread belief in the Sudan and West Africa that the Mahdi would appear in the thirteenth century of the Hijrah (1785–1882 CE). Even now he hesitated, but following a series of visions he became convinced in 1881 that God had designated him as the Mahdi. For three months his Mahdihood was a secret, revealed at first only to trusted disciples and then, on a visit to al-Ubayyiḍ (El Obeid) in Kordofan, to religious scholars and finally, to the common people. Finally, on June 29, 1881, his public manifestation (*ẓuhūr*) as the expected Mahdi took place on Aba Island, and he called upon his adherents to rally to him.

Events now moved rapidly. In keeping with the Prophet's practice to muster his followers and distinguish the true believers, he undertook an "emigration" (*hijrah*) from Aba Island to Jabal Qadīr in the Nuba Mountains of southern Kordofan, naming those who rallied to him the "helpers" (*al-anṣār*) after the Prophet's allies in Medina. While encamped at Jabal Qadīr, his supporters won two resounding victories against forces sent by the Turco-Egyptian government of the Sudan, gaining for the Mahdi enormous prestige and a considerable quantity of arms and other booty. The Mahdi now turned his attention to central Kordofan, where he had been warmly received before his manifestation and where there was already a body of believers in his mission. An initial attack by Mahdist forces on al-Ubayyiḍ in September 1882 was repulsed by government troops with heavy losses, but a siege resulted in the town's fall to the Mahdi early in 1883.

The universal implications of the Mahdi's mission were now made plain. A vision assured him that he would eventually offer prayer in Cairo, Mecca, Jerusalem, and Kufa. The first step was to strike at the heart of the Turco-Egyptian administration, Khartoum, and this city was duly occupied after considerable bloodshed in January 1885.

Following this triumph the Mahdi established his headquarters in nearby Omdurman, but he was destined to survive for only six months, dying, it is generally believed, from typhus. The Islamic state he was in the process of establishing, however, lasted for a further fourteen years until the forces of the Anglo-Egyptian "reconquest" mowed down the *khalīfah* ʿAbd Allāh in 1899.

The mission of the Mahdi, however, had not been to establish a lasting political structure. His claim to Mahdihood implied that the apocalypse was at hand, and he constantly exhorted his followers to reject the world and its deceits and to prepare for the life to come. As a divinely appointed leader he claimed a status only a little short of that of a prophet. While preaching strict adherence to the Qurʾān and the prophetic *sunnah*, he placed himself above the interpretations of the *madhhab*s, the Islamic law schools, and issued authoritative pronouncements on ritual, social, and economic matters through a series of written proclamations (*manshūrāt*) and oral rulings issued in public gatherings (*majālis;* sg., *majlis*). Though a Ṣūfī and shaykh of a suborder, he ordained that belief in his mission overrode all other loyalties and that his prayer manual, the *Rā-tib*, superseded the litanies of the orders. Mystical ideas, however, pervaded all his thinking. His mission was announced in visions in which the Prophet invested him as Mahdi in the presence of Khiḍr, the legendary immortal "man of God," and other "saints" (*awliyāʾ*). He was told by the Prophet that he had been created from the light of the core of his heart, an allusion to the preexistent light before creation that God made incarnate in Adam and other prophets and, finally, in Muḥammad and his descendants.

Although his claims to be the Mahdi must be judged to have been unsubstantiated, many Sudanese remained loyal to Muḥammad Aḥmad's memory. His posthumous son, Sayyid ʿAbd al-Raḥmān, was won over by the British administration and was able to benefit from popular pro-Mahdist sentiment (especially among the Baqqārah) to establish grassroots support for a national political party. The Ummah party, which he founded in 1945, played the dominant role in Sudanese politics in both the first republic (1956–1958) and the second (1964–1969). The Mahdi's great-grandson, Sayyid al-Ṣādiq, a Western-educated Islamic modernist, remains an influential thinker and a key political personality.

SEE ALSO Messianism, article on Messianism in the Muslim Tradition.

BIBLIOGRAPHY

No full-length critical biography of the Mahdi has yet been published in any European language. Ismāʿīl ʿAbd al-Qādir's hagiographical life, *Kitāb saʿādat al-mustahdī bi-sīrat al-Imām al-Mahdī*, has now been partially translated in Haim Shaked's *The Life of the Sudanese Mahdi* (New Brunswick, N. J., 1978). The best account of the period as a whole is P. M. Holt's *The Mahdist State in the Sudan, 1881–1898,* 2d ed. (Oxford, 1970). The autobiography of a Sudanese participant in the Mahdīyah (and later a pioneer of modern education in the Sudan) has been translated in Jousef Bedri and George Scott's *The Memoirs of Babikr Bedri* (Oxford, 1969), as have the memoirs of a European administrator in the Turco-Egyptian government, *The Sudanese Memoirs of Carl Christian Giegler Pasha, 1873–1883,* edited by Richard Hill (Oxford, 1984). No study has yet been made of the Mahdi's religious thought, but ample material exists in the four volumes of his proclamations, rulings, and letters in M. I. Abu Salīm's *Manshūrāt al-Imām al-Mahdī* (Khartoum, 1963–1964).

JOHN O. HUNWICK (1987)

MUḤAMMAD ʿALĪ LĀHORĪ SEE LĀHORĪ, MUḤAMMAD ʿALĪ

MUISCA RELIGION.

Located high on the Colombian plateau, the territory of the Muisca people extended a scarce 300 kilometers long by 125 kilometers wide. To history, the Muisca have become known as the Chibcha, a name derived from Chibchacum, one of their major deities (Von Hagen, 1974, p. 78). Their state comprised two principal kingdoms that, for four generations of rulers preceding the Spanish conquest of this area in 1537, were ruled by two hereditary monarchs, the Zipa from Bacata in the south and the Zaque from Hunsa in the north. Independent allied territories bordered the northern region. The city of Sugamuxi, which was governed by an elected *cacique* ("leader") was an important religious center (Falchetti and Plazas de Nieto, 1973, pp. 39–45).

Unlike the theocratic empires of Mexico and Peru, the fledgling Muisca state had no stone pyramids, temples, or sculpture. In common with the religions of other American theocracies, however, that of the Muisca placed special emphasis on the adoration of the sun. In Muisca cosmology, the supreme deity, Chiminigagua, was equated with light. Myth recounts how, in the beginning, darkness and silence reigned over a sterile world. Light existed only as the omniscient Chiminigagua within an impenetrable shell of clay. On the occasion of the first dawn, the god broke the shell and illuminated with beauty all that had previously been chaos. He then dispatched two ravens to the ends of the earth. As the birds flew, bright light emanated from their beaks, revealing all the creations of the omnipotent god: the sun, the moon, the vivid birds that animate the sky, and the animals and plants of the earth (Pérez de Barradas, 1950–1951, vol. 2, p. 372; Samper, in Camargo Pérez, 1937, p. 186).

Complementing this dawn-creation myth is the legend of Bachue, fecund mother and matrilineal deity. One spring morning, the sun's rays, like a luminescent emerald, projected sparkling colors over the bleak moor. Warm breezes cleared the early mists as brightly hued birds skimmed over Lake Iguaque. With the gentle murmur of waves, Bachue and her three-year-old son appeared from the waters. Bachue raised her son to maturity, at which point they married. With each pregnancy the prolific Bachue gave birth to five or six children and peopled the entire Muisca realm. With her consort, Bachue instructed the Muisca in the moral precepts of society. Finally, after many years, the couple returned to Iguaque, where they changed into snakes and disappeared into the depths of the lake. Thus Chiminigagua is the energizing power of the universe and Bachue is the progenetor of the Muisca people (Arango Cano, 1970, pp. 29–40).

Bochica, the envoy of Chiminigagua, was a protective deity who saved the Muisca from a disastrous flood inflicted by the irate god Chibchacum (Triana, 1970, p. 82). From a rainbow Bochica hurled a golden staff that dispersed the menacing storm clouds and shattered the mountain below, allowing the flood waters to escape into the Tequendama Falls. For the cruelty he inflicted on the Muisca, Chibchacum was condemned for eternity to carry the earth on his shoulders; as he shifts the weight from one shoulder to another, earth tremors are felt (Arango Cano, 1970, pp. 65–72). The conflict between the two deities is thought to symbolize the rivalry between the chiefs, whose patron was Bochica, and the merchant class, which was protected by Chibchacum (Pérez de Barradas, 1950–1951, vol. 2, p. 401).

Muisca gods were worshiped at the streams, lakes, waterfalls, and mountains of the territory. Rocks bearing the footprints of Bochica were venerated, and many cliff and rock surfaces were carved or painted with sacred designs (Pérez de Barradas, 1950–1951, vol. 2, pp. 340–354). The holiest shrine was the Temple of the Sun, a circular building with cane walls that were whitened with mud daub and floors covered with fine esparto mats. On platforms against the walls lay the mummies of illustrious ancestors. In tribute to their forefathers, the faithful brought to the temple offerings of emeralds and gold that were placed in hollow wood or ceramic sculptures. The gold or *tumbaga* (an alloy of gold and copper) objects, known as *tunjas*, were anthropomorphic or zoomorphic, in the form of snakes, lizards, birds, monkeys, or felines. Kneeling reverently in the temple with arms held high, the supplicant chanted hymns to the omnipotent spirit of the Sun (Camargo Pérez, 1937, pp. 53–59; Samper, in Camargo Pérez, 1937, p. 190).

Birds were sacrificed in the temple in great numbers. Especially valued were macaws and parrots that were taught to speak; after the sacrifice their heads were preserved. Human sacrifice took place prior to departure for war, and head trophies were taken from the enemy to adorn the temples. During the construction of a temple, posts were driven into the ground through the bodies of living slaves. In honor of the Sun, young boys known as *moxas* were procured from alien territories and reared in the temples as priests. Believed capable of conversing with the Sun in song, these youths were considered sacred, and their movements were circumscribed by strict taboo. Sexually innocent, they were sacrificed in early puberty. To the chanting of hymns, the heart and viscera of a *moxa* were removed, his head severed, and his blood sprinkled on the temple posts. To placate the Sun in times of drought, a youth would be sacrificed before sunrise on a mountain peak, the east-facing rocks anointed with blood, and the body exposed on the mountain to be devoured by the Sun (Kroeber, 1946, p. 907).

Another important ceremonial offering took place at the Lake of Guatavita in commemoration of a legendary princess. Long ago, a ruler, upon discovering his wife's adulterous liaison with a young warrior, tortured and impaled the man and forced his wife to eat the heart and genitals of her lover. Grief stricken, the princess fled, seeking refuge with the guardian spirits of the sacred lake. Full of remorse, the ruler sent priests to reclaim his wife, but they found her in an enchanted palace protected by a great snake. In memory of his abused wife, the ruler promised to give bountiful gifts; thus, on nights of full moon, the princess appears above the waters of the lake to remind people of their obligation and to bring prosperity to the Muisca.

At the investiture of a ruler, offerings were made to obtain the benevolence of the lake's tutelary spirits. Before sunrise, to the sound of flutes and drums, the ruler, carried on the shoulders of painted warriors, approached the Lake of Guatavita. Boarding a raft, he shed his cloak and stood naked, his body anointed with fragrant resin and coated with gold dust. Accompanied by nobles and priests, the raft proceeded to the center of the lake, as worshipers along the banks intoned sacred hymns. When the first rays broke across the horizon, the gilded monarch, resplendent in the Sun's divine light, emitted a joyful cry that was echoed by his reverent subjects. Placing in the waters offerings of gold and emeralds, the ruler finally immersed himself in the lake to wash away the precious gold particles. And on his triumphant return to shore he was received with acclaim and celebration (Arango Cano, 1970, pp. 101–119).

BIBLIOGRAPHY

Arango Cano, Jesús. *Mitos, leyendas y dioses Chibchas.* Manizales, Colombia, 1970.

Camargo Pérez, Gabriel. *La roma de los Chibchas.* Boyacá, Colombia, 1937. This book also contains the article "El culto del sol," by G. Samper, pp. 184–192.

Falchetti, Ana María, and Clemencia Plazas de Nieto. *El territorio de los Muiscas a la llegada de los Españoles.* Bogotá, 1973.

Kroeber, A. L. "The Chibcha." In *Handbook of South American Indians,* edited by Julian H. Steward, vol. 2, pp. 887–909. Washington, D.C., 1946.

Pérez de Barradas, José. *Los Muiscas antes de la Conquista.* 2 vols. Madrid, 1950–1951.

Triana, Miguel. *La civilización Chibcha* (1922). Bogotá, 1970.

Von Hagen, Victor W. *The Golden Man: A Quest for El Dorado.* London, 1974.

New Sources

Llano Restrepo, María Clara. *La Chicha, una Bebida Fermentata a Través de la Historia.* Bogotá, 1994.

Rozo Gautá, José. *Espacio y Tiempo entre los Muiscas.* Bogotá, 1997.

Rozo Gautá, José. *Mito y Rito entre los Muiscas.* Santafé de Bogotá, 1997.

Rueda, Carl Henrik Langebaek. *Regional Archaeology in the Muisca Territory: A Study of the Fúquene and Susa Valleys.* Pittsburgh, Pa., 1995.

Urbina Rangel, Fernando, and Púa M. Giovanni. *Vita Cotidiana de Las Culturas Amerindias. Aztecas, Muiscas, Uitatos, Araucanos.* Bogotá, 2001.

PITA KELEKNA (1987)
Revised Bibliography

MULLĀ ṢADRĀ (AH 979/80–1050, 1571/2–1641 CE),

popular name of Muḥammad ibn Ibrāhīm al-Shīrāzī; Persian philosopher, theologian, and mystic. As his name indicates, Muḥammad, titled Ṣadr al-Dīn ("breast-plate [defender] of the faith") was born in Shiraz; his father, Ibrāhīm ibn Yaḥyā, is said to have been a governor of the province of Fārs.

LIFE. Little is known of the details of Mullā Ṣadrā's life. He came at a young age to Isfahan, which was the Safavid capital and the center of a flourishing school of philosophy established by Muḥammad Bāqir Mīr Dāmād (d. 1631), Mullā Ṣadrā's mentor and a philosophic thinker of fairly high caliber. Ṣadrā also studied theology with Bahā᾽ al-Dīn al-ʿĀmilī (d. 1621), a theologian, mathematician, and architect whose treatises on mathematics and science were taught at al-Azhar University in Cairo. His third teacher, Mīr Findiriskī (who died the same year as Mullā Ṣadrā), is believed to have taught Ṣadrā the Peripatetic philosophy of Ibn Sīnā (Avicenna).

Sometime in his youth, most likely during his middle twenties, Mullā Ṣadrā left Isfahan under persecution from certain traditionalist circles who, probably among other things, accused him of pantheism; he was also impelled by a strong inner need to base his thought on a more solid footing than the superficial method of debates and "verbal quibbles," as he calls them. He settled in the village of Kahak in the mountains near Qom (an important center of religious learning in Iran), where he led a solitary life, devoting himself to deep contemplation of the basic problems of truth and life, particularly of human destiny. This was accompanied by strenuous religious exercises as a means of spiritual catharsis, as he avers, and as preparation for the reception of truth. It is not certain how long he stayed in Kahak: reports vary from seven to fifteen years, but the latter figure appears to be more accurate within the periodization of his life suggested below. In any event, Ṣadrā informs us that during this stay, as he resigned himself to God and passively submitted to truth, his mind was "flooded with invasions of intuitive truth." This infused new life into him; he had gone into seclusion troubled and brokenhearted, but he came out of it with a new philosophical discovery, a discovery that was to serve him as the master principle for the solution of all philosophical problems, from the theory of movement, through epistemology, to the nature of the self and God. This was the principle of the reality of existence and the fictitiousness of essences. To expound this principle he wrote various works, including his *magnum opus, Al-asfār al-arbaʿah* (The four journeys).

After his stay in Kahak, Ṣadrā returned to his native town, Shiraz, where it is said a mosque school was built for him by Allāhwirdī Khan under orders from Shah ʿAbbās II. This was the "Khan School" mentioned by the seventeenth-century traveler Thomas Herbert as the most prominent school in Iran; it offered courses in philosophy, astrology (that is, astronomy: astrology is prohibited in orthodox Islam), physics, chemistry, and mathematics. The building, though badly in need of restoration, still stands today. Here Ṣadrā wrote practically all of his works and trained scholars, the most famous of whom were Mullā Fayḍ Kāshānī and ʿAbd al-Razzāq Lāhījī. He is said to have died in Basra on a return from his seventh pilgrimage to Mecca; he was buried there. If reports are to be believed, he made several pilgrimages to Mecca on foot. Such a journey is not uncommon among Muslims, but in the case of a busy intellectual leader it would have been an almost incredible feat.

The life of Ṣadrā thus falls into three broad periods. The first covers his childhood and his period of study in Shiraz and Isfahan—up to his early or middle twenties; the second is the period of his self-imposed exile in the village of Kahak, which, if it spanned fifteen years, would bring him to the age of almost forty, and the last period covers the last thirty lunar years of his life, which would give him a total of seventy lunar or sixty-eight solar years.

THOUGHT. Mullā Ṣadrā tells us that in his early youth he held to the primary reality of essences and considered existence to be a "secondary attribute" contributed by the mind to external reality. This doctrine of "essentialism" arose with Suhrawardī al-Maqtūl, "the Martyr" (d. 1191), who criticized the view of Ibn Sīnā that existence is a "real" attribute of existents. Suhrawardī held that in reality there are only essences, and that existence is a most general attribute contributed only by the mind and with no counterpart in the external world. This doctrine became very popular after Suhrawardī and gave rise to the doctrine of the "unity of being" *(waḥdat al-wujūd),* according to which all beings share existence equally but differ in their essences, a doctrine often linked with pantheism since it asserts the unity of the existence of God with all beings. At some point during his period of seclusion, however, Ṣadrā abandoned this view in favor of the idea of the primary or sole reality of existence, which he then used as his master principle in all fields of philosophic inquiry.

The doctrine of the sole reality of existence implies (1) that essences are not real but are produced only in the mind by the impact of outside reality upon it and (2) that existence is in eternal progressive motion, which at each point assumes all previous grades of movement and transcends them. Let us now consider the fuller impact of each of these propositions. First, existence is "something whose nature it is to be in the external world," while mind is the natural home of essences. The moment we conceptualize existence, therefore, it becomes an essence and falsifies real existence; thus, existence cannot be known through conceptual reason but only through direct intuition, just as we know ourselves. As Ṣadrā puts it, "That which is directly experienced is existence, but that which is understood by the mind are essences." Even so, however, the concept of existence differs from all other concepts or essences, in that it alone presupposes real existence. Essences are dysfunctional to existence: the more something has of existence, the less it has of essence. God, the most perfect being, is therefore pure and absolute existence without any essence, although this fact does not, in Ṣadrā's view, negate God's attributes, because each of them, as an infinite and concrete entity, is identical with God's existence and is only conceptually distinguishable from the others, while essences are closed and mutually exclusive. Existence alone is all-inclusive; from it, the mind somehow partitions and carves essences for certain practical purposes, but the continuum of reality is falsified in the process.

Second, this continuum of reality is the continuum of eternal progressive motion, which is unidirectional and irreversible. This movement, which Ṣadrā calls "substantive movement," occurs in the very substance of everything and not just in its accidents or extrinsic attributes, such as color, shape, locus, and so on. This latter kind of movement is reversible in quality and quantity—hot can become cold or vice versa—but such extrinsic motion is dependent upon an inner, intrinsic one that is irreversible. This intrinsic or substantive motion is so imperceptible that we become aware of it only after a great deal of cumulative change has occurred and a critical point is reached. In view of his doctrine of "substantive motion," Ṣadrā, of course, denies that real motion has any enduring substratum. But contrary to the theologians (*mutakallimūn*), who believe in atomism, he spends a good deal of effort to prove continuity, without which the whole idea of process would become impossible, and he would end up denying the very motion that he wants to establish. He therefore concludes by asserting that while the idea of a fixed and enduring substratum is real with regard to accidental movements, it is fictional with regard to substantive movement, which is itself a veritable unity wherein the potential and the actual or the "active" and the "passive" principles are one and the same. In a self-actualizing process, any dualism between that which produces change and that which is receptive of change vanishes.

In the entire field of reality, it is only existence that is characterized by substantive change. Existence alone is therefore "systematically ambiguous" (*mutashakkik*) because it is "that which, by virtue of sameness, creates difference"; other phenomena, like extrinsic motion and time, are so only because they are contingent upon this substantive change. This substantive movement of the world process always proceeds from the general to the specific, from the genus to the differentia, from the abstract to the concrete, and every subsequent development contains the prior developments and transcends them. Ṣadrā also describes the process as movement from mutually exclusive to mutually inclusive parts of being, or from the "composite" to the "simple" being. He thus enunciates the principle: "The truly simple is all reality." A consequence of this principle is that what appears contradictory at a lower level of being appears as a synthetic unity at a higher level, since mutually exclusive factors progressively become mutually inclusive.

Whereas God is absolute existence, the perpetually and progressively moving grades of existence are the "modes" of existence; these modes, in proportion to the measure of existence they realize, are organized according to the principle of "more or less," or *ad priorem et posteriorem*, a principle that Ṣadrā borrowed from Suhrawardī. But while for Suhrawardī the principle of "more or less" applies to essences, according to Ṣadrā it applies to existence alone, and that is, as we have seen, the "systematic ambiguity" (*tashkīk*) of existence. On the basis of this *tashkīk* of existence, moreover, Ṣadrā asserts that although in this life all humans partake of one species, thanks to the progressive motion from abstract to concrete in the evolutionary process, in future life every human will become a species unto himself. Strictly speaking, on this principle, every form or mode of being has an irreducible reality of its own, which cannot be dissolved without residue: each being, Ṣadrā tirelessly repeats, exists in its own right as a unique and unanalyzable particular (*fard*). Yet so strong is the pull of the pantheistic-monistic worldview of his earlier days that Ṣadrā emphatically tells us that only God is real and truly existent; every other being is only a chimera, a pseudo-being beside God. Here lies the most basic tension in Ṣadrā's thought, one which he never seems able to overcome; it is the tension between his philosophical and his religious motivations. Thus, while he tells us that the question "why does the world move?" is a meaningless one, like the question, "why does fire burn?"—for the only answer is "because this is its very nature"—in the same breath, he insists that it is God who creates change at every moment in the world process, that nothing other than him has any reality whatever, and that all contingent beings are not just things related to him, but mere relations, a hardly intelligible proposition.

Nonetheless, Ṣadrā applies his fundamental theory of existence and its evolution to various traditional problems of philosophy with an amazing degree of consistency and success. Thus, in his theory of knowledge he argues strongly against the Peripatetic view that knowledge comes about by way of gradual abstraction of the object of knowledge from matter and its relationships until pure intellective knowlege is attained. If this is the case, then our intellective knowledge of an animal, for example, since it is abstracted from the matter of the animal, must falsify the object of knowledge, because the real animal has matter, and "concepts in the mind would become like engravings on the wall." Knowledge, in fact, since it is at a higher plane of being than material things, is more concrete, simple, and inclusive, until, at the highest level, the full knowledge-being equation is reached as in God.

In his eschatology, Ṣadrā rejects the doctrine of the transmigration of souls, giving as one reason, among others, that when a soul has developed in a body it cannot regress and start from scratch, which it would have to do if it joined a newborn body. Applying his doctrine of the systematic ambiguity of existence to the problem of will, Ṣadrā asserts that will (like knowledge and other intrinsic attributes) is commensurate with a particular form of existence. Fire, for example, has a certain tendency (like other natural objects) but no will; humans have a will with choice between alternatives. They have to choose because they are a mixture of power and powerlessness, knowledge and ignorance; their "free will" means that they have choice, but also that this choice has determinants. Philosophers who hanker after an "absolutely free will" for humans are running after a mirage. God has a free will without choice since, in his case, there is no question of alternatives to choose from; nevertheless, he does not work under constraint. Thus, an individual can say, "If I will, I will write; otherwise not," and God can say, "If I will, I will create; otherwise not," even if God must always create, given his nature; but fire cannot say, "If I will, I will burn; otherwise not." These differences are due to the nature of existence in each case.

WORKS. The editor of *Al-asfār al-arbaʿah* (Tehran, 1958) puts the number of Ṣadrā's works at thirty-two or thirty-three; S. H. Nasr, in his study *Mullā Ṣadrā and His Transcendent Philosophy,* mentions forty-six, although he includes a number of items entitled "Answers to Questions." Although Ṣadrā wrote works of religion as well as philosophy, the latter are by far the more important, since the former are products of the application of his philosophical hermeneutics to religious tenets. His writings can also be divided into original works and commentaries; the commentaries on Ibn Sīnā's *Metaphysics* and Suhrawardī's *Ḥikmat al-Ishrāq* are very important and certainly more influential even than most of Ṣadrā's smaller original pieces. His most important and comprehensive work is undoubtedly *Al-asfār al-arbaʿah.* The first part deals with ontology, discussing questions of existence, essence, and movement. The second, apparently addressing the categories of substance and accidents, deals with his natural philosophy. The third "journey" is devoted to a discussion of God's being and attributes, while the last deals with humanity and its destiny, which is the final purpose of the entire work. Two other important late works are *Al-mabdaʾ wa-al-maʿād* (The Origin and the Return, that is, of all being from and to God) and *Al-shawāhid al-rubūbīyah* (Divine Witnesses), held to be his last work; these are both in the nature of summaries of the *Asfār.*

Despite his fame, Ṣadrā had little influence in his own lifetime. As mentioned earlier, two of his pupils gained prominence. It appears that since he had synthesized several schools of Islamic thought and also wrote commentaries on some of their prominent texts, his works gradually became a focal point of philosophic studies in Iran and subsequently in the Indian subcontinent, where Ṣadrā's commentary on Ibn Sīnā's *Metaphysics* was taught and where numerous manuscripts of his works still exist uncataloged.

BIBLIOGRAPHY

The latest edition of the *Asfār* (Tehran, 1960–) so far includes three "journeys" in nine volumes; the publication of the second "journey," which exists only in the 1865 Tehran lithograph edition, is still awaited. The first great commentator on the *Asfār* was ʿAlī Nūrī (d. 1831), followed by a series of other commentators, the most able and prominent of whom was Hādī Sabzawārī (d. 1871). A list of important commentaries (which have never been published independently of the text) is given in the publisher's introduction to the recent edition of the *Asfār* mentioned above. Ṣadrā has had many "debunkers" as well, particularly Abū al-Ḥasan Jalwah (d. 1894), who claimed that Ṣadrā "stole" practically all of his characteristic ideas without naming his sources, a claim that of course cannot be taken seriously. For the past few decades, Iran has witnessed reinvigorated interest in Ṣadrā. The celebration of his four hundredth anniversary in 1961 occasioned the publication of some valuable information about him and his writings, along with editions of some of his previously unpublished works.

In the West, the first book on Ṣadrā's thought, *Das philosophische System von Schirāzi* (Strassburg, 1913), was published by Max Horten. This was followed by Henry Corbin's translation of *Al-mashāʿir* as *Le livre des pénétrations métaphysique* (Tehran, 1964). I have published a detailed critical analysis of Ṣadrā's philosophy based primarily on the *Asfār* entitled *The Philosophy of Mullā Ṣadrā* (Albany, N. Y., 1975). Seyyed Hossein Nasr's *Mullā Ṣadrā and His Transcendent Philosophy* (Tehran, 1978) contains useful information on the life and works of Ṣadrā. James Winston Morris has published an annotated English translation of Ṣadrā's treatise *Al-ḥikmah al-ʿarshīyah* entitled *The Wisdom of the Throne* (Princeton, 1981), with a lengthy introduction from an esoteric angle.

For general bibliography, see Seyyed Hossein Nasr's work cited above.

New Sources

Dakake, Maria Massi. "The Soul as Barzakh: Substantial Motion and Mulla Sadra's Theory of Becoming." *Muslim World* 94 (January 2004): 107–131.

Nasr, Seyyed Hossein, "Mulla Sadra: His Teachings." In Seyyed Hossein Nasr and Oliver Leaman, eds. *History of Islamic Philosophy.* New York, 1996, pp. 643–652.

Kalin, Ibrahim. "Mulla Sadra's Religious Ontology of the Intelligibles and Theory of Knowledges." *Muslim World* 94 (January 2004): 81–107.

Ziai, Hossein. "Mulla Sadra: His Life and Works." In Seyyed Hossein Nasr and Oliver Leaman, eds. *History of Islamic Philosophy.* New York, 1996, pp. 635–642.

FAZLUR RAHMAN (1987)
Revised Bibliography

MÜLLER, F. MAX (1823–1900), German-born philologist and Vedic scholar, professor at Oxford University and celebrated public lecturer in the comparative study of language, mythology, and religion, editor of the *Rig-Veda Samhitâ* (6 vols.), and editor of *The Sacred Books of the East* (50 vols.).

Friedrich Max Müller was born December 6, 1823, in Dessau, in the small German Duchy of Anhalt-Dessau. His father, Wilhelm Müller (1794–1827), had been a distinguished young Romantic poet known to many as the "Byron of Germany" for his *Griechen Lieder,* written in support of Greek nationalism. Before Wilhelm's untimely death, Franz Schubert had composed a pair of song cycles—*Winterreise* and *Die Schöne Müllerin*—that immortalized two of Wilhelm's best sets of poems. Max Müller's mother, Adelheide Müller (c.1799–1883), had been the eldest daughter of Ludwig von Basedow, a chief minister of Anhalt-Dessau. Max Müller was educated in nearby Leipzig, at the Nicolai-Schule where Leibniz also had been a student, and then at the University of Leipzig, where his father's memory opened doors for Müller into the city's artistic circles. Müller at first considered a career as a poet and musician before settling upon the life of a scholar. Although he studied philosophy with Christian Weisse and M. W. Drobisch, Müller proved to be an especially gifted student of languages, mastering Greek and Latin as well as Arabic, Persian, and Sanskrit, the latter of which he had taken under Hermann Brockhaus.

After completing a Ph.D. in philosophy in 1843, Müller continued his studies in Sanskrit and comparative philology at Berlin under Franz Bopp, who had been famous for examining the linguistic links among the so-called Aryan family of languages, and Friedrich Schelling, under whose influence Müller himself began to see striking parallels between the history of language and the history of religion. In early 1845, Müller traveled to Paris to study Sanskrit under Eugène Burnouf. Although Müller's brief stay in Berlin saw the publication of his first book, a German translation of ancient Indian fables known as the *Hitopadesa* (1844; Eng. trans., 1866), it was in Paris where Müller received the research direction he needed. At Burnouf's urging, and with the diplomatic support of Baron Christian von Bunsen, Müller was commissioned by the East India Company and Oxford University Press to edit a critical edition of the *Rg Veda,* a project that would take him twenty-four years to complete and would culminate in the six-volume *Rig-Veda Samhitâ,* with Sānaya's commentary (1849–1873). In 1846, Müller traveled to London, where a complete set of the Vedas was archived. Bunsen also helped Müller secure his first teaching and research positions at Oxford. Except for brief excursions to the Continent, Müller worked and resided at Oxford for the remainder of his life.

In 1856, Müller achieved broad public recognition when he published his book-length essay "Comparative Mythology." In this essay, Müller applied current linguistic analysis to the study of mythology in order "to account in a more intelligible manner for the creation of myths" (1909, p. 17). According to Müller, the sun in its various phenomenal modes was the chief source of ancient mythology. In myths Müller saw not simply the personification of the sun, the dawn, the twilight, and so on, but a metaphysical correspondence that human thought and human language drew between the perception of nature and the analogies that the ancient Indo-Europeans had used when communicating what they perceived. The names that people gave to these phenomena, the *nomina* (sing. *nomen*), were later mistaken for divine beings, or *numina* (sing. *numen*), and myths began to develop around these names to account for their existence. Thus, for Müller, mythology represented an earlier "mythopoeic" period or strata in the evolution of human thought and, as such, was viewed by him as a vestige of the past that still impressed itself on the thought and language of the present. Though Müller appears to have borrowed this and other ideas from Burnouf, including his assertion that mythology is a "disease" or weakness of language, the solar thesis that Müller had advanced as a young scholar came in time to overshadow much of his later, more original, thought. Beginning in the 1870s, critics, such as Andrew Lang, savagely attacked Müller's views on mythology. Indeed, it was Lang's relentless barrage against Müller that seemed to have had the most deleterious effect on the respect and influence that Müller's views on mythology had earlier enjoyed.

In 1858 Müller was elected fellow of All Souls College, which, along with his stipend as deputy Taylorian professor of modern European languages, provided a sufficient income for him to marry and raise a family. In 1859, he published his most scholarly work to that point, *A History of Ancient Sanskrit Literature.* Although in 1860 Müller had lost a bitter election bid to fill Oxford's Boden Chair in Sanskrit, in 1861 and again in 1863 he presented a series of celebrated lectures on the study of language that were published in two volumes as *Lectures on the Science of Language.* By now Müller had become a leading voice in his field and, in recognition of his achievements, Oxford University created for him a chair in comparative philology, which he occupied from 1868 until his retirement in 1875.

In his lifetime Max Müller achieved renown not only for his work in comparative philology and mythology, but also as a champion for the comparative study of religion as a "science" apart from theology. But, despite his best efforts, Müller's work would never gain the lasting success for which he had hoped. After his death in 1900, a *Times* of London obituary mourned his loss, acclaiming him "one of the most brilliant and prolific writers of our time; one whose voice has charmed several generations of Englishmen; who was a great scholar . . . possessing . . . a power of breathing human interest into dry bones, a curiously sympathetic intelligence and a rare mixture of the talents of the poet and the savant" (quoted in Voigt, p. 81). But others were much less effusive, such as Louis Henry Jordan, who called Müller's work in comparative religion "incomplete and strangely defective." Jordan believed that Müller had "attempted to be an investigator in far too many departments" and thus "was able to devote only such fragmentary leisure as he could manage to command. It was for this reason that he never really found time to apply himself, with resolute and persistent purpose, to the promotion of Comparative Religion" (pp. 153–154).

Although Müller could not resist the temptation to open every door that invited his curiosity, he had in fact outlined for himself a specific research program that focused on questions concerning the origins and development of religion, mythology, and philosophy (or rather, cognitive thought) through a "scientific," that is, comparative and historical, examination of language. It was near the end of his life, in his *Contributions to the Science of Mythology* (1897), that Müller laid out for his readers the logic behind the four sciences to which he had devoted much of his fifty-year career at Oxford. Following the method of analyzing and clarifying concepts that he adopted from the German philosophers Johann Herbart and Friedrich Schelling, Müller's aim was to trace the Indo-European (or Aryan) languages back to their common word roots, layer by layer, in order to uncover and comprehend "the whole sphere of activity of the human mind from the earliest period within the reach of our knowledge to the present day" (p. v). As he explained further:

> There is nothing more ancient in the world than language. The history of man begins, not with rude flints, rock temples or pyramids, but with language. The second stage is represented by myths as the first attempts at translating the phenomena of nature into thought. The third stage is that of religion or the recognition of moral powers, and in the end of One Moral Power behind and above all nature. The fourth and last is philosophy, or a critique of the powers of reason in their legitimate working on the data of experience. (p. v)

Müller believed that in the ancient Vedic scriptures, especially in its mythology, he had found the roots of human thought and the earliest form of religion. As he had proclaimed in his *Autobiography* (1901):

> All knowledge, whether individual or possessed by mankind at large, must have begun with what the senses can perceive, before it could rise to signify something unperceived by the senses. Only after the blue aether had been perceived and named, was it possible to conceive and speak of the sky as active, as an agent, as a god. The step from the visible to the invisible, from the perceived to the conceived, from nature to nature's gods, and from nature's god to a more sublime unseen and spiritual power. All this seemed to pass before our very eyes in the Veda, and then to be reflected in Homer and Pindar (pp. 149, 150).

Over three decades earlier, in the preface to his multi-volume collection of essays, *Chips from a German Workshop* (1867), Müller had already arrived at the interconnection among language, mythology, religion, and thought and the need for scholars to examine these connections historically and comparatively. As he wrote: "There is to my mind no subject more absorbing than tracing the origin and first growth of human thought—not theoretically, but historically" (p. ix). At times he likened his linguistic work to that of an archaeologist and at other times to a geologist, digging down through the rock and shale to find the bottom layer of human conscious perception upon which the whole history of the evolution of human thought, mythology, and religion had been founded. "Language," he continued, "still bears the impress of the earliest thoughts of man . . . buried under new thoughts, yet here and there still recoverable in their sharp original outline. . . . [B]y continuing our researches backward from the most modern to the most ancient strata, the very elements and roots of human speech have been reached, and with them the elements and roots of human thought" (p. ix). As with the roots of language, so with the roots of religion: "The elements and roots of religion were there as far back as we can trace the history of man; and the history of religion, like the history of language, shows us throughout a succession of new combinations of the same radical [or root] elements" (p. x). For Müller, that foundation was the first conscious perception of the Infinite, this "One Moral Power behind and above all nature" mentioned earlier. Müller was convinced that it was from this perception of the Infinite that the root elements of all religions emerged, which included "a sense of human weakness and dependence, a belief in a Divine government of the world, a distinction between good and evil, and a hope of a better life" (p. x).

During his long career, Müller was engaged in nearly every intellectual debate that stirred up controversy, the most important of which was the debate over Darwin's *On the Origin of Species* (1859). In his *Lectures on the Science of Language,* Müller argued forcefully that the distinction between human- and animal-kind was the possession of language by the former. So strong was Müller's position that when his younger Oxonian colleague Edward Tylor defended Darwin's position, Müller took it as a breach of their otherwise friendly rivalry. Then, when Darwin's book *The Descent of Man* appeared in 1871, Müller responded in 1873 with his *Lectures on Mr. Darwin's Philosophy of Language,* aimed largely to counter Darwin's supporters. Müller reiterated his views more systematically in *The Science of Thought* (1887), and once more in his *Three Lectures on the Science of Language* (1889). It should be noted that in all these works, Müller's main concern had been over the threat that Darwin's ideas posed, not to religion, but to natural science. Müller, for his part, had already accepted the idea of an evolutionary development of religion, rejecting special revelation or any religious faculty or instinct in humankind as the source of religion or religious ideas. As Müller saw it, unless apes could speak and hence reason, Darwin was flatly wrong. For, as Müller declared, "language forms an impassable barrier between man and beast" (1899, p. 5; see 1887, pp. 152–178).

Finally, in addition to his public stand against Darwinism, Müller also began to present to the English public his ideas on the comparative study of religion. Although Müller had been recognized chiefly for his work in comparative philology and mythology, it was his lectures in the "science" of religion that would prove to be his most provocative, earning him praise in some circles, but denunciation in others as being little more than an atheist in academic disguise. For instance, one clergyman condemned Müller's 1888 Gifford Lectures as "nothing less than a crusade against Divine revelation, against Jesus Christ, and against Christianity."

Müller's first lecture series on religion, which he titled "Lectures on the Science of Religion," were given in 1870 and published in 1872 with a later dedication to Ralph Waldo Emerson. His second series of lectures, published in 1878 as *Lectures on the Origin and Growth of Religion, as Illustrated by the Religions of India,* was presented at Westminster Abbey as the inaugural Hibbert Lectures. During this same period, Müller began work as editor of the monumental series *The Sacred Books of the East,* the highly acclaimed fifty-volume collection of sacred scriptures. For this collection, Müller offered several of his own translations, notably of the *Upanisads* (2 vols., 1879–1884) and of the *Dhammapada* (1881), both of which remain in print.

During the last decade of his life, Müller returned once more to his views on the natural, or evolutionary, development of religion in four sets of Gifford Lectures, presented in Glasgow between 1888 and 1892. He published these lectures under the titles *Natural Religion* (1889), *Physical Religion* (1891), *Anthropological Religion* (1892), and *Theosophy or Psychological Religion* (1893). As Müller explained anew, religion began with humanity's first perception of the Infinite in and beyond nature and natural phenomena. The Infinite has always existed but remained unnoticed until human consciousness rose above that of a brute animal. This awareness came, not by a divine revelation, but through human reflection upon the Infinite in nature, in humanity, and in the self. In essence, this is what Müller meant by natural, not nature, religion.

Though almost wholly ignored by most modern critics of Müller's work, these four series of lectures encapsulate Müller's most complete and developed views, which had originated a half-century earlier. And though Müller believed that in his Science of Religion he was moving beyond theology to history, in the end his views were perhaps too heavily imbued with the language of theology—European as well as non-European—to enable him to work out a truly comparative science of religion.

SEE ALSO Indo-European Religions, article on History of Study; Lang, Andrew.

BIBLIOGRAPHY

Byrne, Peter. *Natural Religion and the Nature of Religion: The Legacy of Deism.* London and New York, 1989. A very helpful secondary source that, among other things, examines the philosophical and anthropological context of the academic study of religion in Europe; it features a splendid chapter on Müller and Tylor.

Chaudhuri, Nirad C. *Scholar Extraordinary: The Life of Professor the Rt Hon. Friedrich Max Müller.* New York, 1974. A sympathetic biography of Max Müller that quotes liberally from relevant primary sources, but without citations.

Jordan, Louis Henry. *Comparative Religion: Its Genesis and Growth.* Edinburgh, 1905; reprint, Atlanta, 1986. A contemporary overview and assessment of the main thinkers and schools of thought in the nascent field of comparative religion.

Kitagawa, Joseph M., and John S. Strong. "Friedrich Max Müller and the Comparative Study of Religion." In *Nineteenth Century Religious Thought in the West,* vol. 3, edited by Ninian Smart, John Clayton, Stephen Katz, and Patrick Sherry, pp. 179–213. Cambridge, 1985. A detailed intellectual biography of Max Müller that outlines Müller's ideas and assesses his contribution to the academic study of religion.

Müller, F. Max. *Chips from a German Workshop,* vol. 1. London, 1867. A collection of Müller's essays on mythology and religion published during his early period.

Müller, F. Max. *The Science of Thought.* London, 1887. A useful summary of Müller's thought on the philosophy of language, with a critique of Darwin's theory of human descent.

Müller, F. Max. *Contributions to the Science of Mythology.* 2 vols. London, 1897. A massive two-volume reprise of Müller's linguistic theory on the origin of myth; lengthy and technical, but clearly written.

Müller, F. Max. *Three Lectures on the Science of Language, etc., with a Supplement, My Predecessors.* 3rd ed. Chicago, 1899. A series of public lectures attacking Darwin and his disciples from the perspective of Müller's philosophy of language.

Müller, F. Max. *My Autobiography: A Fragment.* New York, 1901. A personal reflection by Müller on the cultural and intellectual climate of the Victorian era and his own place within that period.

Müller, F. Max. *The Life and Letters of the Right Honorable Friedrich Max Müller, edited by his wife.* 2 vols. London: Longmans, Green, 1902. A valuable two-volume primary-source collection of Müller's personal and professional correspondence, as edited by his wife, Georgina.

Müller, F. Max. *Comparative Mythology: An Essay.* New York, 1909. Müller's most celebrated essay.

Neufeldt, Ronald W. *F. Max Müller and the Rg-Veda.* Columbia, Mo., 1980. A critical reassessment of the life and work of Max Müller from the perspective of the role and influence of the *Rg Veda* in Müller's thought.

Noiré, Ludwig. *Max Müller and the Philosophy of Language.* London, 1879. A contemporary and sympathetic assessment of Müller's philosophy of language that includes a chapter on the debate between Darwin and Müller as well as the author's own views on the origin of language.

Stone, Jon R., ed. *The Essential Max Müller: On Language, Mythology, and Religion.* New York, 2002. A collection of nineteen essays, articles, and addresses that span nearly forty years of Müller's scholarly career.

Trompf, G. W. *Friedrich Max Müller: As a Theorist of Comparative Religion.* Bombay, 1978. A sympathetic overview and assessment of Müller's life and works that lays stress on the Kantian influences in Müller's thought.

Voigt, Johannes H. *Max Mueller: The Man and His Ideas.* Calcutta, 1967. A sympathetic but balanced overview of Müller's life and works.

JON R. STONE (2005)

MÜLLER, KARL O. (1797–1840), German classical historian and mythologist. Karl Otfried Müller was educated at Breslau and at Berlin under the classical philologist August Böckh. In 1819 he was appointed adjunct professor of ancient art and literature at Göttingen and taught there until 1839, when he left Germany to study and travel. He died of fever in Athens the next year.

Müller may be claimed as the most balanced and versatile classical historian of his time, especially in the area of Greek religion and myth. None before him had portrayed this ancient religion and mythology within such a broad and unfolding historical context. Müller's innovation, as Henri Pinard de la Boullaye said, was "not a thesis but a method." Müller related cult and myth, for example, to such complex matters as the shift from agriculture to war and hunting, the founding of cities and colonization, the movement of tribes, and the way differences in locale and climate affect ritual and belief. His many-sided approach gave scholarly rigor to Johann von Herder's emphasis, a generation earlier, on seeing national culture as an organic whole, developing from its own historical roots, language, customs, and geography. Müller thus opposed the Romantic view, common in his time, of Greek religion as patently derived from India and the East, usually by way of migrating priests. He treated Greek civilization in its own terms and applied any useful method: philology, the history of religions, aesthetics, cartography, archaeology. By this variety of means, he clarified what might be called the historical topography of Greek cults and myths as they arose, flourished, and spread. He traced the way this changed over time, and he tried to assign causes, explaining, for example, how a single deity (such as Demeter) was replaced by the Homeric pantheon, how earlier cults remained visible in later and different forms, why the role of local sanctuaries changed, and why mystery religions emerged.

Müller postulated that cult originates in symbol, which is both a transcending and a material representation; myth comes afterward, as an explanation of the cult. He treated myth mainly as a historical document, a clue that the Greeks themselves gave to the meaning of existing customs, beliefs, and important events. He took myth to be a most reliable guide, however, and he was convinced that the folk mind speaking in myth does not falsify or even invent. (Here he reflected the influence of his friends the famous German folklorists Jakob and Wilhelm Grimm.) The most exalted role Müller allowed myth was that of giving an ideal representation to otherwise realistic matters.

BIBLIOGRAPHY

Müller's major works are *Prolegomena zu einer wissenschaftlichen Mythologie* (1825), translated as *Introduction to a Scientific System of Mythology* (London, 1844); *Geschichten hellenischer Stämme und Städte*, 3 vols. (Breslau, 1820–1824), translated as *The History and Antiquities of the Doric Race*, 2 vols. (Oxford, 1830); and *A History of the Literature of Ancient Greece*, 2 vols. (London, 1840). First published in English, this last work is a translation of Müller's *Geschichte der griechischen Literatur bis auf das Zeitalter Alexanders*, 2 vols. (Breslau, 1841).

For a general discussion of Müller and other classical historians of his time, see G. P. Gooch's *History and Historians in the Nineteenth Century* (London, 1952), chap. 3. A sympathetic view of Müller in the context of history of religions is given by Henri Pinard de la Boullaye in his *L'étude comparée des religions*, vol. 1 (Paris, 1922), pp. 268–276 and 389. A condensed and learned account of Müller and his disciples and opponents is Otto Gruppe's *Geschichte der klassischen Mythologie und Religionsgeschichte* (Leipzig, 1921), pp. 157–165. Müller as a mythologist is discussed, with translated selections, in *The Rise of Modern Mythology, 1680–1860*, compiled by me and Robert Richardson (Bloomington, Ind., 1972), pp. 416–425.

New Sources

Calder, William M., and Renate Schlesier. *Zwischen Rationalismus und Romantik. K. O. Müller und die antike.* (Hildesheim, 1998).

Calder, William M., R. Scott Smith, and John Vaio. *Teaching the English Wissenschaft: The Letters of Sir George Cornewall to Karl Otfried Müller (1828–1839).* New York, 2002.

Fittschen, Klaus. "Karl Otfried Müller zum 150. Todestag: Ansprache anlässlich der Gedenkfeier am 25. Oktober 1990." *Mitteilungen des Deutschen Archäologischen Instituts. Athenische Abteilung* 106 (1991): 1–7.

Gercke, Hans-Joachim. "Karl Otfried Müller und das Land der Griechen." *Mitteilungen des Deutschen Archäologischen Instituts. Athenische Abteilung* 106 (1991): 9–35.

Momigliano, Arnald. "K. O. Müller's Prolegomena zu einer wissenschaftlichen Mythologie and the meaning of Myth."

Annali della Scuoloa Normale Superiore di Pisa 13 (1983): 673–689. Momigliano was also the editor of a monographic issue of the same journal entirely devoted to this German scholar (*Annali della Scuola Normale Superiore di Pisa* 14, 1984).

Nickau, Klaus. "Karl Otfried Müller, Professor der Klassischen Philologie 1819–1840." In *Die klassischen Altertumswissenschaften an der Georg-August-Universität Göttingen. Eine Ringvorlesung zu ihrer Geschichte,* edited by Carl Joachim Classen, pp. 27–50. Göttingen, 1989.

Unte, Wolfhart, and Helmut Rohlfing. *Quellën fur eine Biographie Karl Otfried Müller (1797–1840): Bibliographie und Nachlass.* New York, 1997.

BURTON FELDMAN (1987)
Revised Bibliography

MÜNTZER, THOMAS (1488?–1525), also known as Münzer; radical Protestant reformer involved in the German Peasants' War of 1524–1525. Little is known about Müntzer's early life. His name first appears in the 1506 matriculation records of the University of Leipzig, which required entering students to be at least seventeen years old. Attempts to demonstrate that Müntzer was born earlier than 1488—perhaps as early as 1468—on the basis of records reporting his membership in a religious order have been successfully refuted by Walter Elliger in his detailed biography, *Thomas Müntzer* (Göttingen, 1975, pp. 10–11). Born of a well-to-do family in the Saxon town of Stolberg, Müntzer attended the universities of Leipzig (1506–1512) and Frankfurt an der Oder (1512–1516), where he received the master of arts degree. He was ordained, perhaps in 1513.

Increasingly curious about the relationship of faith to history, Müntzer learned Hebrew and Greek. He studied Eusebius's *Church History,* Augustine, Jerome, the apocalyptic speculations of the Italian Cistercian abbot Joachim of Fiore, the German mystics (especially Johannes Tauler), the records of the reform councils of Constance (1414–1418) and Basel (1431–1449), and canon law. Between 1516 and 1520, Müntzer was an itinerant priest and scholar, for a brief period taking the positions of provost and father confessor in the convents of Frose and Beuditz. In 1518, he traveled to Wittenberg, where he may have met Luther, then north to Jüterbog, where he became known as "emulator of Martin." In 1520, on Luther's recommendation, he became pastor of Zwickau, the "pearl of Saxony."

Zwickau had become the center of the silver trade, with a large influx of tradesmen hoping to make a fortune. There Müntzer began a reform program to eliminate socioeconomic differences between the rich and the poor. He organized meetings of small groups of common people, mostly weavers who had lost their jobs in the wake of the silver boom. Nicholas Storch, the leader of the unemployed weavers and a member of a radical Christian group known as the Zwickau Prophets, persuaded Müntzer that there was sufficient evidence to suggest that the end of the world was near. The city council soon accused the Zwickau Prophets and their pastor, Müntzer, of fomenting rebellion. Müntzer tried to enlist the support of Luther who, however, did not respond.

In 1521, the Zwickau council dismissed Müntzer from the pastorate of Saint Catharine's Church. Müntzer went to Prague, hoping for the support of the Hussites, who were well-known enemies of the Roman papacy. There he posted a handwritten declaration (later known as the Prague Manifesto) on the doors of various churches. Written in German, Latin, and Czech, this manifesto attacked the status quo and announced the beginning of a final reformation leading to a "renewed apostolic church" in which only the Holy Spirit would reign. Müntzer called on the people of Prague to support him in communicating the new "living word" and to oppose anyone defending the status quo. The Prague authorities first placed Müntzer under house arrest and then banned him from Prague.

Once again Müntzer took to the road, traveling through Saxony with brief stops in Erfurt, Halle, and Nordhausen; by 1523 he was penniless and nearly starved. However, he was convinced that his personal suffering was but a prelude to the final tribulations of the world. He met and married the apostate nun Ottilie of Gersen in 1523, the same year he received a call to the pastorate in Allstedt, a small town in electoral Saxony. In 1524, the Müntzers became parents of a son.

In Allstedt, Müntzer implemented his new vision of church and world. First, he reformed congregational life by creating a German church order, a German Evangelical mass, and the German Order of Allstedt, this last to help "poor and collapsing Christendom." He wrote Luther, his Stolberg friends, and Karlstadt that he had become the advocate of the Holy Spirit, who would radically change Germany and the world. In addition, Müntzer wrote several revolutionary tracts. Published in 1524, the tracts *Concerning the Invented Faith, Protestation, A Clear Disclosure of the False Faith of an Unfaithful World,* and *A Highly Necessary Defense and Answer against the Soft-Living Flesh of Wittenberg* (all written in German) declared that the "elect of God" must experience the "bitter Christ" in the "depth of the soul" in order to be purified for the final battle between good and evil, the final struggle between the status quo and new life in the Holy Spirit. Müntzer now called himself the "new Daniel," the leader of a "league of the elect" who would smash the opponents of the Holy Spirit. Those who refused to accept the Holy Spirit in their souls, Müntzer proclaimed repeatedly, would have to be forced to do so, if necessary by the sword. No "ungodly" could be tolerated among the "elect."

When Müntzer led a small band of "elect" in destroying a small Catholic chapel outside Allstedt, Saxon authorities became alarmed. Having been warned by Luther against the "restless spirit of Allstedt," representatives of the Saxon court met with Müntzer in Allstedt, where he preached a radical sermon to them. They then summoned him to Weimar and ordered him to stop his agitations. When the authorities confiscated copies of his treatises, Müntzer was convinced that the time had come to oppose the status quo with force. But, in a letter of September 5, 1524, the Anabaptist reformer Conrad Grebel warned Müntzer against the use of violence.

Müntzer never received the letter because he had left Allstedt vainly seeking support in Switzerland, especially in Basel. He then joined bands of rebellious peasants in Mühlhausen. He and the radical priest Henry Pfaiffer tried once again to create a model of reform, but the Mühlhausen authorities banned both of them. By the spring of 1525, Müntzer had joined the rebelling peasants in Thuringia and had become their chaplain. In May of 1525, the peasants were cruelly defeated at Frankenhausen, and Müntzer, who had fled before the massacre, was captured, tortured, and beheaded. Luther approved of Müntzer's execution, calling it a "just and terrible judgment of God."

Müntzer was the first Protestant theocrat who advocated a Christian crusade to liberate the world from sin, death, and evil. He was a spiritualist who could no longer endure the compromise between internal spiritual experience and living in an imperfect external world; a truly apocalyptic thinker, he tried to transform theological ideas into revolutionary action. Reformers like Luther and Calvin made him the symbol of villainy, and Anabaptists and other radical reformers refused to support him. Ironically, he would become a hero in the nineteenth and twentieth centuries to Marxists and other communist groups who advocated revolution, although of course without Müntzer's theological foundation.

BIBLIOGRAPHY

A treatment of Müntzer's life and thought and a translation of some of his writings are offered in my book *Reformer without a Church* (Philadelphia, 1967). The most detailed analysis of Müntzer's life and work is available only in German: Walter Elliger's *Thomas Müntzer* (Göttingen, 1975). Müntzer's entire literary production, including letters and notes, has been collected and critically edited by Günther Franz with the collaboration of Paul Kirn in *Thomas Müntzer: Kritische Gesamtausgabe* (Gütersloh, 1968).

Müntzer's language is difficult, since he wrote in medieval Latin and in sixteenth-century German, often using a particular dialect. Two of his works are available in English: "Sermon before the Princes" (1524), in *Spiritual and Anabaptist Writers,* edited by George H. Williams, "Library of Christian Classics," vol. 25 (Philadelphia, 1957); and "Highly Necessary Defense and Answer against the Soft-Living Flesh of Wittenberg" (1524), in Hans J. Hillerbrand's "Thomas Müntzer's Last Tract against Luther," *Mennonite Quarterly Review* 38 (1964): 20–36. Some excerpts from these two works and a portion of his "Confession and Recantation" (1525) have been translated by Lowell H. Zuck in a collection he has edited, *Christianity and Revolution: Radical Christian Testimonies, 1520–1650* (Philadelphia, 1975), pp. 36–44, 46–47. The British Reformation historian E. Gordon Rupp has written a comprehensive essay on Müntzer, "Thomas Müntzer: The Reformer as Rebel," in *Patterns of Reformation* (Philadelphia, 1969), pp. 157–353. There are also two American historical sketches depicting Müntzer as dissenter and revolutionary: "Thomas Müntzer," in Steven E. Ozment's *Mysticism and Dissent* (New Haven, 1973), pp. 61–97; and "Thomas Müntzer," in Hans J. Hillerbrand's *A Fellowship of Discontent* (Philadelphia, 1967), pp. 1–30.

ERIC W. GRITSCH (1987)

MŪRTI. According to many Hindu religious traditions, *mūrti* is a god's form, its infinite metaphysical reality manifested visibly. Aside from a limited class of objects called *svayambhū* (self-created or natural), *mūrtis* are mainly anthropomorphic figures or symbols. They are the ritually consecrated cult images at the center of *pūjā* (worship), which is the dominant form of Hindu religious practice.

In Vedic sacrifice the deity is unseen, being represented only by the chanted *mantras* of the priests as they move among the abstract geometric forms of the altars that represent the cosmos. The deity's form first emerges in the practice of the orthodox tradition with the later, theistic Upaniṣads, where a vision of the *mūrti* of the personalized deity is summoned through meditation. In the epics, image worship is mentioned and accepted, but it is given only marginal and fleeting notice, while major interest is centered upon the fire sacrifice. Only with the emergence of sectarian Agamic and Puranic literature, from the fourth century CE on, did the notion of *mūrti* and its use in *pūjā* become systematically formulated. There, for the first time, the claim is made that worship of *mūrti* succeeds or even supplants the sacrifice.

Paralleling this textual record are inscriptions and fragmentary temple and image remains from as early as the second century BCE. Very few images of orthodox Puranic deities have survived from before the third century CE, however, and not until the fifth and sixth centuries were *mūrtis* and the temples that house them committed to the permanence of stone throughout the subcontinent. Nearly all earlier images, and most later ones, were made of perishable materials, and so lost.

An image is a *mūrti,* not by virtue of looking like the deity it represents, but because it conforms to prescribed measurements and symbolic conventions and is accorded orthodox consecration (*pratiṣṭhā*) and authentic devotion by those whose activities create it, the initiated artist (*sthapati*), priest (*ācārya*), and devotee (*bhakta*). This process is expounded in two sets of authoritative texts. Requirements as to materials, measurements, proportion, decoration, and symbolism according to which the *mūrti* is shaped are provided in technical manuals known as the Śilpaśāstras. Explanation of the metaphysical significance of each stage of manufacture and the prescription of specific *mantras* to sanctify the process and lodge the power of the deity in the image are found in the Agamas and Tantras, liturgical handbooks. The process is modeled on the instructions found in the Brāhmaṇas for building fire altars.

Mūrti worship also, partially patterned after the fire sacrifice, takes place in the complementary contexts of household and public altars. Images of *iṣṭadevatā* and *kuladevatā,* family deities who are treated as honored guests, are found in a discrete location in every household. The *mūrtis* of public cults are established in palatial temples, where they are served by an attached priesthood and may be visited by their devotees. As material extensions of the *mūrti* and descendants of the sacrificial altar, such temples are created in accordance with the same technical and liturgical prescriptions as the *mūrtis* themselves.

See Also Iconography, article on Hindu Iconography; Temple, article on Hindu Temples.

Bibliography

Along with a consideration of the full range of Hindu deities, going back as far as the Vedas, Alain Daniélou's *Hindu Polytheism* (New York, 1964) contains a section on the representation and worship of deities, in which the discussion of *mūrti* is set in its broader context. T. A. Gopinatha Rao's venerable *Elements of Hindu Iconography,* 2 vols. (1914; reprint, New York, 1968), offers a compendium of Agamic and Puranic lore about deities compared with examples of *mūrtis* and illustrative images. Its general introduction offers a wealth of information, including a discussion of various systems of classifying *mūrtis*. Jitendra Nath Banerjea's *Development of Hindu Iconography,* 2d ed. (Calcutta, 1956), provides a detailed explanation of the origin of *mūrti* worship in both the texts and in the material record. It also presents the historical development of *mūrti* largely based on material findings. To approach an authentic understanding of the richness of textual thought on *mūrti* more closely, one may read a translation of one of the liturgical handbooks: *Kāśyapa's Book of Wisdom (Kāśyapa-Jñānakāṇḍaḥ: A Ritual Handbook of the Vaikhānasas),* translated and annotated by Teun Goudriaan (The Hague, 1965).

Gary Michael Tartakov (1987)

MURUKAN̲, the Tamil name for the Hindu deity also known by such names as Skanda, Kumāra, Subrahmaṇyam, or Kārttikeya. The name is sometimes transcribed as Murugan. While Murukan̲ is the most popular god in present-day Tamil India, he has been worshiped in a variety of forms from at least the third or second century BCE. In his earliest South Indian form, Murukan̲ was described in classical (or Caṅkam) literature as a god of hill and hunt, who was worshiped by hill people, the *kuriñcis*, as a possessor of young damsels and avenger of *anaṅku* and *cūr,* malevolent spirits of the hills.

In North India, Skanda was depicted in epic mythology as the son of Rudra-Śiva or Agni, and as a warrior deity patronized by such dynasties as the Śakas, Ikśvaku, and Guptas. By the eighth century CE, and throughout the medieval period, these earlier attributes of the god seem to have merged, as subsequent literature, iconography, and temple architecture attest to Murukan̲'s worship in South India as a high god and the son of Śiva.

Murukan̲ was especially extolled by such medieval Tamil *bhakti* (devotional) poets as Aruṇakirinatha of the fifteenth century and Kacciyapaciva of the seventeenth. Late in the nineteenth century, worship of Murukan̲ was given new impetus by a Tamil renaissance, during and after which temples to Murukan̲ were renovated, pilgrimages to these centers increased, and the god came to be viewed as the quintessential Tamil deity.

The basic myth of Skanda-Murukan̲'s life and exploits is found in the *Mahābhārata* (3.223–232; 9.46–47; 13.130–133). It is repeated in the *Ramāyāṇa* (1.36–37), and further embellished in a wide range of Sanskrit and Tamil literature, especially in Kālidāsa's (fourth century CE?) *Kumārasambhava* and the *Skanda Purāṇa.*

According to Kālidāsa's version of the myth of Skanda's birth, the deity is born of Śiva's semen when the latter marries Pārvatī following an extensive period of meditation and austerities (*tapas*) on Mount Himavat. Later accounts, as in the *Skanda Purāṇa,* say Skanda is born of sparks emanating from Śiva's brow. According to the *Mahābhārata,* Skanda is born of Agni's love-play with Svāhā while she is impersonating the wives of six *ṛṣis*. Once born, Skanda is suckled by the six Kṛttikā (Pleiades) maidens and engages in a variety of childhood exploits, including the defeat of Indra, the humiliation of Brahmā, and the instruction of Śiva as to the meaning of the sacred syllable *oṃ*. On the sixth day of his life, he is made general of the divine army and conquers the *asuras* headed by Tāraka (or, in South Indian accounts, Surapadma). After the battle, according to the epic myths, he is given in marriage to Devasenā (literally, "army of the gods"); in southern versions, Murukan̲ woos Vaḷḷi, a hunter damsel who becomes the god's second consort.

Murukan̲ is the most widely worshiped god among Tamil Hindus in the early twenty-first century, and three of the six most popular pilgrimage centers in Tamil Nadu are temples consecrated to him. One of these, Palani, is the second largest pilgrimage complex in South India. Six major festivals celebrating events in the god's life attract millions of worshipers, from the festivals of Skanda-Ṣaṣṭi in October-November to Vaikāci Vicākam in May-June. The cultus incorporates a whole spectrum of rituals, from classical fire sacrifices and Tantric invocations as prescribed in the Śaivagāmas to folk forms of possession and dancing with the *kāvaṭi,* or peacock arch. In addition, the god is popularly perceived to be the inspirational source of Tamil literature, vanquisher of cosmic and personal malaise, and the embodiment of Śaiva thought and religion.

See Also Tamil Religions.

Bibliography

Clothey, Fred W. *The Many Faces of Murukan̲: The History and Meaning of a South Indian God.* The Hague, 1978.

Clothey, Fred W. *Rhythm and Intent: Ritual Studies from South India.* Madras, 1983.

First International Conference on Skanda-Murukan. "Research Papers on the Cult of Skandra-Murukan." Available from http://murugan.org/research/98papers.htm.

Zvelebil, Kamil. *Tiru Murugan.* Madras, 1982.

FRED W. CLOTHEY (1987 AND 2005)

MUSAR MOVEMENT. The Musar movement for individual self-examination and ethical renewal spread among mid-nineteenth-century Lithuanian Jewry after its founding by Yisraʾel Salanter (1810–1883). So called from the Hebrew term *musar* ("ethics, instruction"), the Musar movement can be viewed as one of the first attempts in eastern Europe to organize traditionalist circles within Jewish society in modern forms, although its long-term legacy and influence remained limited to the Lithuanian *yeshivot.*

The Musar ideology was formed during the young Yisraʾel Salanter's fifteen-year sojourn in Salant during the 1820s and 1830s. There, in addition to achieving mastery of Talmud in the standard manner, Salanter came under the influence of the saintly reclusive figure Yosef Zundel of Salant. Zundel devoted his attention to the ethical aspects of Jewish law, which in his view had been neglected. He believed that in order to overcome the temptations of evil, special actions were necessary beyond a theoretical knowledge of one's legal obligations. To this end Zundel developed a system of regular self-analysis and study of ethical texts, and he introduced such innovations as the repetition of Talmudic statements on ethical issues as a way to induce the proper mood for soul-searching. Yisraʾel Salanter built upon the system of his master, but unlike Zundel he attempted to present the Musar doctrine to the community at large within an organizational framework.

In Vilna in the mid-1840s, Salanter made his first efforts to establish a mass Musar movement. Departing from the standard practice for heads of *yeshivot,* he presented a series of public talks addressed not only to scholars but also to artisans and most particularly to affluent educated businessmen. Salanter called for the inclusion of ethical works in the curriculum of Torah study that is incumbent upon every Jew. Such study, besides making the individual aware of the ethical responsibilities stipulated by Jewish law, would also help him recognize and struggle with his unconscious impulses and bring them under control. For this purpose, Salanter set up a *musar-shṭibl* (Yi., "house of moral instruction") where, through the combined practice of meditation and the somber repetition of moral texts, an appropriately ecstatic-fearful mood could be created for the encounter with elemental passions and drives. During this Vilna period, Salanter arranged for the reprinting of classic ethical texts and attracted the first of his key disciples.

By all indications, Salanter intended the Musar movement to answer the threat to traditional Jewry posed by the Haskalah, the movement for Jewish Enlightenment, one of whose major centers was in Vilna. Believing that existing institutions could not meet this danger, Salanter instead tried to bolster the religious loyalties of the individual Jew. His emphasis on ethical behavior indicates that Salanter shared many of the Haskalah's criticisms of the social and economic ills of Jewish society, but unlike proponents of Haskalah he did not prescribe a thorough educational and economic reform of Jewry as the proper solution for these problems. In Salanter's view, a revival of the standards for social and economic relations demanded by Jewish law would redress the imbalances in Jewish society.

In 1849, rather than accept a teaching position offered him in a government-sponsored rabbinical seminary in Vilna, Yisraʾel Salanter transferred his base of operations to Kovno (modern-day Kaunas). He succeeded in establishing *musar-shṭiblekh* there and in several other towns. Yet the immense personal prestige that Salanter enjoyed in his lifetime was not reflected in a corresponding success for his planned mass movement. By the 1850s *musar-shṭiblekh* existed in only five communities, with an estimated following in the hundreds. More lasting achievements of the Kovno period include the model of a Musar *yeshivah,* where self-examination and the study of ethical tracts formed regular parts of the curriculum, and where responsibility for the students' spiritual development was assigned to a *mashgiaḥ* ("supervisor"), who functioned alongside the normal teaching staff. Salanter's disciples from this period spread this model to most of the major Lithuanian *yeshivot,* among whose students the movement found its greatest success. Salanter's letters to his disciples, later collected and published, laid down the basic ideological direction of the Musar phenomenon.

Despite Salanter's unassailable personal moral and scholarly credentials, his innovations aroused no little criticism in rabbinical circles. Some claimed that the stress on ethics undermined the centrality of Torah study, while others worried that the elitist spirit of the Musar groups carried a potential for sectarianism. This polemic over the Musar movement continued into the twentieth century.

After 1857, when Yisraʾel Salanter moved to Germany, although he maintained his personal influence over his students, the practical work of spreading the movement's teachings was carried on by the disciples. Through their efforts Musar became the dominant mode in the Lithuanian *yeshivot,* despite occasional strong resistance on the part of more traditional *yeshivah* leaders. Among the major successors of Yisraʾel Salanter were Simḥa Zisl Broyda of Kelem (1824–1898), who in the schools under his supervision tried to develop a systematic educational method based on Musar principles; Yitsḥaq Blazer (1837–1907), former rabbi of Saint Petersburg and interpreter and publisher of Salanter's teachings, who served as head of the Kovno *kollel* (an advanced *yeshivah* providing stipends for married students); Eliʿezer Gordon (1840–1910), rabbi of Telz and head of its noted *yeshivah;* Note Hirsh (Natan Tsevi) Finkel (1849–1927), known as the Old Man of Slobodka, spiritual director of the central Musar *yeshivah* in Slobodka. Each of these figures put his personal stamp on the basic Musar doctrine and thus helped to evolve variations of its teachings on the nature of man, the nature of evil, and the ways to struggle with evil. All of the Musar *yeshivot,* however, featured daily Musar studies (often at twilight) and the role of the *mashgiaḥ,* whose responsibilities included regular talks to the student body as well as individual guidance. Most extreme among the Musar schools was that directed by Yosef Yosl Hurwitz, the Novaradok (Nowogródek) school, where students were required to pursue intense Musar study and to perform unusual (i. e., socially unacceptable) actions in public as a way of subduing the lower instincts.

The expansion of the Musar *yeshivot* continued in the period following World War I, but was cut off by the Nazi Holocaust. The Slobodka and Novaradok Musar approaches live on, however, in *yeshivot* set up in Israel and the United States.

SEE ALSO Jewish Thought and Philosophy, article on Jewish Ethical Literature; Salanter, Yisra'el; Yeshivah.

BIBLIOGRAPHY

The best historical study of the early stages of the development of the Musar movement is in Hebrew, Immanuel Etkes's *R. Yisra'el Salanter ve-re'shitah shel tenu'at ha-Musar* (Jerusalem, 1982). The only full-length study of the movement is the hagiographic and apologetic *Tenu'at ha-Musar,* 5th ed., 5 vols. (Jerusalem, 1974) by Dov Katz. Volume 1 of Katz's work has been translated by Leonard Oschry as *The Musar Movement: Its History, Leading Personalities and Doctrines* (Tel Aviv, 1977). An interesting supplementary volume by Katz entitled *Pulmus ha-Musar* (Jerusalem, 1972) reviews the long-running public controversy over the Musar doctrine. For a short but somewhat superficial survey of the movement, see Abraham Menes's "Patterns of Jewish Scholarship in Eastern Europe," in volume 2 of *The Jews,* 4th ed., edited by Louis Finkelstein (New York, 1973), pp. 177–227. On the inner life of the Lithuanian *yeshivot,* see Gedalyahu Alon's "The Lithuanian Yeshivah," in *The Jewish Expression,* edited by Judah Goldin (New Haven, 1976), pp. 452–468, and Shaul Stampfer's *The Lithuanian Yeshiva* (Hebrew; Jerusalem, 1995). On the Novaredok school, see David Fishman's "Musar and Modernity: The Case of Novaredok," *Modern Judaism* 8: 1 (1988), pp. 41–64. For a vivid but jaundiced portrayal of the director of a Musar *yeshivah,* see Chaim Grade's novel, *The Yeshiva,* 2 vols. (New York, 1977). For personal portraits of some of the figures associated with the movement, see the idiosyncratic and controversial *Making of a Godol: A Study of Episodes in the Lives of Great Torah Personalities* (Jerusalem, 2002), by Noson Kamenetsky.

GERSHON C. BACON (1987 AND 2005)

MUSES. Near the highest peak of snowy Olympus, the nine Muses—Clio, Euterpe, Thalia, Melpomene, Terpsichore, Erato, Polyhymnia, Ourania, and Calliope, daughters of Zeus and Mnemosyne (Memory)—were born to be, in Hesiod's words, "the forgetting of misfortunes and respite from sorrow" (*Theogony* 55). Like-minded virgins, free from grief, their only concern is song. Always accompanied by the Graces and Desire, they dance in chorus on delicate feet on the mountaintops, bathe in springs with violet glints, and make their way to the radiant abodes of Zeus, which laugh under the spell of their sweet voices (*Theogony* 1ff.).

What the Muses sing is *mnēmosunē*—memory of what is, what was, and what will be. And for the Greeks, memory is truth. The subject of their song is the kingdom of Zeus the father, he who subdued the Titans, who restored his brothers' power and imposed a harsh fate on their father Kronos, and who bestowed honors on all the gods. The Muses sing the victory of the cosmos, of harmony over chaos, and their sweet accents make Zeus's enemies tremble in the depths of the earth (*Theogony* 68ff.; Pindar, *Pythia* 1.13). They also sing the miserable fate of mortals, who live in bewilderment, unable to find a cure for death or a remedy for old age (Homeric *Hymn to Apollo* 190ff.).

With Apollo, the Muses select and inspire the men they cherish. These are the lyre players and singers, and they, too, are able to make sorrow and grief disappear from mortal hearts with the sweet strains that flow from their lips. Thus when poets sing to Apollo and the Muses at the beginning of their songs, they put themselves under divine protection and make an offering at the same time. Invoking the Muses is the price the poet pays in order for his song to be called veracious and in order that he may breathe the imperishable memory and knowledge that the Muses alone bestow. Those who disdain this inspiration and pride themselves on being capable of creating and fashioning their songs without the Muses are punished; they are made to sing untruths and soon become mute, like the poet Thamyris (*Iliad* 2.594ff.).

Each of the nine Muses presides over one of the arts. According to one scheme, Clio is linked with history, Euterpe with music, Thalia with comedy, Melpomene with tragedy, Terpsichore with dance, Erato with elegy, Polyhymnia with lyric poetry, Ourania with astronomy, and Calliope with eloquence. Only Calliope, first among the Muses, has a role in the courts of kings (*Theogony* 80ff.); it is she who gives them wisdom and mellow voices. If the political initiation resembles poetic initiation, the music that Calliope teaches kings can in no case be confused with that of the poet. The Muse inspires kings with the knowledge of the kingdom of Zeus, so that the divine cosmos may be recreated among men.

The spirit that emanates from the Muses is the springlike freshness that allows mortals to derive some fortune from divine nature and to forget death. That may be why the Muses warn poets that they know how to sing untruth just as well as truth.

BIBLIOGRAPHY

Boyancé, Pierre. *Le culte des Muses chez les philosophes grecs.* Paris, 1937.

Pearson, A. C. "Muses." In *Encyclopaedia of Religion and Ethics*, edited by James Hastings, vol. 9. Edinburgh, 1917.

Svenbro, Jesper. *La parole et le marbre: Aux origines de la poétique grecque.* Lund, 1976.

New Sources

Bing, Peter. *The Well-Read Muse: Present and Past in Callimachus and the Hellenistic Poets.* Göttingen, 1988.

Camilloni, Maria Teresa. *Le Muse.* Rome, 1998.

JEANNIE CARLIER (1987)
SILVIA MILANEZI (1987)
Translated from French by Alice Otis
Revised Bibliography

MUSEUMS AND RELIGION. The last generations of the twentieth century saw a huge increase in the number of museums worldwide; one estimate suggests ten thousand in 1950 and ten times that number fifty years later. In the more developed countries of the world they took on a dramatic new importance and public recognition. In many of the new museums the emphasis has been on attracting new visitors and offering them both entertainment and education rather than on scholarship and on their collections. So far, though, most have shown little interest in religion.

The first two great modern museums were perhaps the British Museum in London and the Museé du Louvre in Paris. The first was formed in 1759 from the collection of Sir Hans Sloane, who described it as "tending many ways to the manifestation of the glory of God [and] the confutation of atheism and its consequences" (quoted in Altick, 1978, p. 229). The second was formed in 1793 by France's atheist revolutionary government from artworks seized from the church, the king, and the aristocracy. These two traditions—respect for, and hostility to, religion—continue in the modern museum, but even stronger is the Enlightenment heritage of indifference to "traditional" faith. One observer commented that "the message of galleries and museums is that religion is a thing of the past, but that if there is anything sacred in society, it is art" (O'Neill, 1996, p. 191).

THE VICTORIAN MUSEUM: SCIENTIFIC COLLECTING AND PUBLIC IMPROVEMENT. As both urbanization and democracy rapidly grew in Europe and North America in the nineteenth century, the museum became an important expression of emerging national and civic identities, aimed at assertion to the world outside and production of loyal and educated citizens within. The later nineteenth-century museum was not only part of what Habermas (1989) called the "bourgeois public sphere," but a "new apparatus for the production of knowledge" (Hooper-Greenhill, 1992); it took on the job of informal public education, aimed sometimes at the proletariat but more often at the middle and upper working classes. In this new seriousness of purpose, museums were frequently in alliance with the churches and often used the language of faith, even of mission, to describe their efforts not only to improve the lot of the poor but to improve society itself. Visitors were encouraged to consider the wonderful works of the Creator, as well as offered opportunities for self-improvement. The most radical efforts were an attempt to help the poor to "see," in John Ruskin's sense that "To see clearly is poetry, prophecy and religion" (Koven, 1994, p. 25). We should note too the plethora of commercial attractions with a biblical theme (such as panoramas of the Holy Land) Victorian London offered, whose "sacred interest . . . attracted thousands of visitors who were not profane enough to enjoy ordinary sights" (quoted in Altick, 1978, p. 182).

RELIGION AND SCIENCE. The British Association for the Advancement of Science met in 1860 in the newly completed University Museum at Oxford. At this meeting took place the famous exchange between Bishop Samuel Wilberforce and scientist T. H. Huxley, which ever since has been taken (however unjustly) as a symbol of the clash between religion and the theory of evolution. The issue had been caricatured as a question of whether human beings were descended from apes, and the popular version has it that Wilberforce asked Huxley if he was descended from apes on his grandfather's or grandmother's side. Huxley is supposed to have replied that he would sooner be descended from an ape than from a "divine who employed authority to stifle the truth."

It was appropriate that this famous exchange took place in a museum, for museums in the urbanized West were in the later nineteenth century the forums for public debate on fundamental questions in a way in which, perhaps, they have never been since. While for some Victorian curators "the study of natural science was a kind of religious contemplation, and the scope of the museum's displays was thus enormously important in communicating that religious purpose" (Yanni, 1999, p. 65), a sizable proportion of visitors now probably saw specimens as emblems of evolution rather than as evidence of God's handiwork. This tension remains today; in the late twentieth century one half of all U.S. college students were alleged to believe in creationism, that is, that God created the earth and all that is in it pretty much as it is today, so the caution displayed by the Field Museum in Chicago when they wanted to set up a new gallery devoted to evolution is understandable (Asma, 2001).

AMBIGUITY AND RESOLUTION? In 1941 the *New Yorker* published a cartoon by the famous comic artist Charles Addams (Paine, 2000, frontispiece). It depicted a dark-skinned man wearing a suit and tie but also a headband, standing quietly in front of a huge and mysterious statue, holding a goat. One museum guard says to another: "He wants to know if he may make a small sacrifice in front of it." The joke is threefold: firstly, the very idea that a "native person," however respectable, could still have any rights over an object in a museum; secondly, the idea that a once-holy object could continue any longer to retain any of its holiness once it had been transferred to a museum; thirdly, the notion of a goat being sacrificed in a neat and tidy museum. It demonstrates starkly the ambiguity of the sacred object in the profane museum.

Half a century later, in 1990, the Dalai Lama personally consecrated a Tibetan altar, designed and built by a Tibetan trained at a monastery in Sikkim, in the Newark Museum in New Jersey (Gaskell, 2003, p. 149). Those fifty years had seen a radical change in the approach of museums to objects in their care regarded as "sacred" by some. The key to this turnaround of consciousness was the political—and thence cultural—demands being made by the indigenous peoples of "settler" countries, particularly in North America and Australia. In the United States these demands climaxed in the 1990 Native American Graves Protection and Repatriation Act, which required museums to list, and to return when asked, a wide range of significant cultural objects, as well as human remains. Australia had in part led the way with the Aboriginal and Torres Strait Islander Heritage Protection Act, 1984.

At both a legal and ethical level, debate about the care of sacred objects has been closely bound up with debate about the care of human remains, about the restitution of looted property, and—in some countries—about the treatment of sacred sites. The International Council of Museums' Code of Ethics, adopted in 1986, demanded that material of sacred significance be looked after "in a manner consistent with professional standards and the interests and beliefs of members of the community, ethnic or religious groups from which the objects originated."

Museums have responded in four ways to the realization that a museum object may also be a sacred object. Many museums have decided that secular values must prevail; that the museum must continue to treat it as a specimen, historical document, material evidence in a framework of scientific inquiry that discounts nonscientific or nonaesthetic explanations.

The second way is to return the object to those who would treat it as sacred. Glasgow Museum in Scotland returned a Ghost Dance Shirt to the Lakota Sioux, with much support from local opinion in the city. In both North America and Australia objects of religious and other cultural significance have been returned to local museums and "keeping places" run by indigenous communities (Simpson, 1996).

The third way is to retain the object in the museum but to house and treat it in ways that those who see it as sacred would approve. Rotorua Museum in New Zealand offers a bowl of water for purification to visitors to their display of Te Arawa treasures. The National Museum of the American Indian in Washington State provides in its Cultural Resources Center a ceremonial room with a fire pit where objects can be "smudged" with burning sweetgrass.

The fourth way of responding is to allow the object to move regularly between the sacred and the secular. In Moscow the Tretyakov Gallery displays the supremely important and powerful Virgin of Vladimir icon in a church attached to the museum, but on three great feast days a year it is removed from its showcase and displayed for veneration; moreover, the patriarch of Moscow has been accorded curatorial status within the museum (Gaskell, 2003, p. 154).

Art Museums. Art museums worldwide are full of religious images, very many of them produced for formal liturgical use, as altarpieces or cult statues, or as the decoration of places of worship or the paraphernalia of a cult; the museums of such countries as Italy and India, with a rich heritage of religious art, are famous for their extensive collections. Yet seldom is the original religious purpose of these objects given much prominence in the museum's presentation: labels will give date, artist, and a brief summary of the iconography but little if any explanation of a work's liturgical function or religious significance.

The same approach is found even where the title of a gallery, "Islamic Art," for example, might lead the visitor to expect some explanation of what it is about Islam that informs the works of art displayed and the role they played in Muslim praxis. In reality, religion here is being used simply as a label for a culture, and it is very seldom that an "Islamic Art" gallery gives much attention even to any liturgical use its exhibits may once have had.

Though many modern artists tackle religious themes or more or less consciously incorporate and express spiritual values in their work, it is seldom that these influence either the design of the overall building in which they are displayed or the museums' public programming. Two exceptional art museums are the Museum of Contemporary Religious Art in St. Louis and the Museum of Biblical Art in New York. Very special is the Rothko Chapel in Houston, Texas, which was opened in 1971 to house a series of fourteen great contemplative abstract paintings by the American artist Mark Rothko, which were designed as a group to create a numinous space. The chapel was intended from the start to be a multifaith center and focus of religious debate.

Human History Museums. There is a constant debate among curators of human history museums: should the exhibits concentrate on presenting the objects the museum holds, or should the objects be used to help tell a story? In other words, which comes first, object or story? The majority of museums worldwide probably say "the object," which is one reason religion too seldom features largely in museums of local history. Even in museums that say "the story," religion appears as a very minor aspect of local history. With some commendable exceptions (Paine, 2000, p. 157), museums seldom try to analyze the role of religion in local society and in popular culture, in the way that the best of them examine the local economy or try to analyze the role of class and gender.

It is particularly disappointing that social history museums, which aim to present the life of their communities, so seldom include the popular religion that always accompanies and underlies official religion. Museums dedicated to the ethnography of non-European societies are in a different situation, not least because their curators are firmly grounded in the academic study of anthropology and because religious paraphernalia have attracted the attention of collectors. As a result, ethnography museums have generally treated indigenous religions with great seriousness, though Museon in The Hague is one of very few that address religion as a worldwide phenomenon.

When a human history museum has collected prominent examples of the material culture of religion for other reasons, it may find itself having to tackle the issue. Skansen, the hugely influential open-air museum established near Stockholm, Sweden, in 1891, received its first church in 1916. Today many open-air museums include places of worship reconstructed or moved from elsewhere, and these are very commonly actually used for worship; one African example is the Ghana National Cultural Centre in Kumasi, Ghana, which includes both a chapel and a traditional Ashante shrine (Duah, 1995, p. 110). By contrast with open-air museums where buildings from elsewhere are reconstructed, "ecomuseums" comprise an alliance of buildings, sites, and object collections still in their original places, and very often these include places of worship. The ecomuseum of Hiranocho in Japan, founded by the Ryonin Kawaguchi, priest of the Senkouji Buddhist Temple, comprises fifteen different attractions, including a number of active temples and shrines (Davis, 2004, p. 98).

THE TEMPLE AS MUSEUM. There is no hard-and-fast distinction between museums and historic monuments. Many of these monuments, in countries around the world, are religious, and increasingly they are being subject to the same type of visitor-oriented—sometimes even commercial—management as conventional museums. Inevitably this gives rise to special problems, especially where the site is still regarded as "sacred" by a local population. Indeed, one can see an increasing convergence between museums and sacred spaces—from York Minster charging entrance fees to Druids wanting to perform ceremonies at Stonehenge. These issues are interestingly discussed by Shackley (2001).

Larger places of worship tend to amass treasures, sometimes very rich treasures indeed. The huge Venkateswara temple at Tirupati in eastern India, which sees over ten million pilgrims a year, for example, houses a massive number of valuable items. Many traditional treasuries have evolved into modern museums. Thus, the sacristy of the Cathedral of the Assumption of the Virgin at Dubrovnik, Croatia, was designed in 1712 to display the relics of Saint Blaise and 138 other reliquaries; the intention was both to display relics for veneration and also to display precious gold and silverwork in honor of the saint. The display is very like an early museum.

Throughout Catholic Europe there are diocesan museums; in England many cathedrals have "treasuries" to display gold and silver plate from churches in the diocese. In most of these museums, though, the emphasis has now come to be on the "decorative arts" aspects of the objects; statues of saints are arranged by period and artistic school, silverware by makers. Seldom is there much attempt to explain to visitors the religious significance and function of the object. Even at the Antivouniotissa Museum in Corfu the labels tend to explain the icons in this wonderful collection in terms of Byzantine art history rather than as spiritually powerful tools. A notable exception to this pattern is St. Catharine's Convent Museum at Utrecht in the Netherlands. Here the story of religion in the Netherlands is told through its artifacts, from an early ninth-century chalice to late nineteenth-century Catholic and Protestant labor union banners.

THE MUSEUM AS TEMPLE. The rhetoric that later nineteenth-century museums shared with churches has continued to be used ever since. Throughout the later nineteenth century and much of the twentieth, art museums in particular were called "temples of art," "cathedrals," in which works of art were "enshrined" and some of which became "sacred places of pilgrimage for museum-goers." For some observers museums do not merely share a rhetoric with religious shrines but actually share many of their functions. Art museums, in particular, share with shrines a separateness from the mundane world, an expectation that visitors will adopt a particular receptive frame of mind and a particular pattern of reverent behavior, that they will follow a ceremonial path. Museums are the forums for a ritual associated with rational, scientific thought. (Duncan, 1990, p. 92; 1995, p. 12). The visitor comes away—or is expected to come away—transformed by communion with immortal spirits of the past, with a sense of being enlightened, spiritually uplifted.

Sometimes museums and shrines converge more literally. Commemorative museums often take on the character of shrines; examples include many Holocaust museums; the Nikko Toshogu Shrine, burial place of Tokugawa Iegasu, the first modern shogun of Japan; and the Tuol Sleng Museum (museum of genocide) in Phnom Penh, Cambodia.

FAITH COMMUNITY MUSEUMS. Faith communities, especially minority communities, often create museums to explain their faith and its history to their own community and to others. Many Jain temples, in India and now also elsewhere, have attached "museums" that—through a series of dioramas—show historical incidents in, and aspects of, their faith. Jewish museums fall into two distinct categories: those that exhibit the paraphernalia of synagogue or domestic worship and balance art history and religious practice and belief, and those that tell the story of the local Jewish communities. The Jewish Museum in London has two sites: one for the former, one for the latter.

Some faith communities maintain museums dedicated to their founder or leaders; an example is John Knox's House in Edinburgh, dedicated to the sixteenth-century Scottish Protestant leader. In the Buddhist tradition visitors to such museums can gain merit. Wat Tham Khlong Paen, a sacred site near Nong Bua Lamphu in Thailand, was the meditation ground of the late Luang Phu Khao, a highly revered monk. A small museum there exhibits his few personal possessions and a life-size wax figure, and "opens daily to public for merit-making and homage-paying."

World Religion Museums. The German philosopher of religion Rudolf Otto, professor of theology at Philipps-Universität in Marburg, Germany, set up the Religionskundliche Sammlung in 1927, devoted to the academic study of religion as a worldwide phenomenon. Sadly, Otto "felt obliged, like most curators, to present the objects in a 'rational' and 'scientific' manner, with no attempt to evoke the 'feeling for the numinous' which was at the heart of his own great contribution to the study of religion" (O'Neill, 1996, p. 195). In the 1990s the Musée des Religions was opened in Nicolet, Quebec, and the St. Mungo Museum of Religious Art and Life, in Glasgow, Scotland; the motive for both was the encouragement of mutual respect and understanding among mixed populations.

Other museums that seek to address religion on a worldwide basis stem from faith backgrounds but ones that accept that there are many paths to the truth and that an understanding of their different routes will help everyone on the journey. The earliest of these was surely Glencairn Museum at Bryn Athyn, Pennsylvania, established by the Swedenborgian bishop William Henry Benade in 1879. The Eternal Heritage Museum is part of the Sai Baba Ashram at Puttaparthy, Andhra Pradesh, India, while the Museum of World Religions in Taipei, Taiwan, was founded in 2001 by Buddhist Master Shih Hsin-tao. The Museum of the History of Religion in St. Petersburg, Russia, is a museum whose declared purpose has changed dramatically. In 1932 the Kazan Cathedral was turned by the Soviet state into a Museum of Atheism; after the fall of the Soviet Union the cathedral was returned to the Russian Orthodox Church, and the museum has become the Museum of the History of Religion, housed in a new building.

Museums and Their Publics. Museums today are making a bigger effort than at any time since the mid-nineteenth century to engage with their communities and to attract wider audiences. The fashionable terms are access, social inclusion, and outreach, and if museums seem reluctant to tackle religion in their permanent displays, the situation is improving in their public programming. In Europe and North America, at least, there is a growing number of temporary exhibitions that treat aspects of religion. Some—notably the 2000 Seeing Salvation exhibition at London's National Gallery—take their theme to a new level of serious debate and public response. Education programs, too, regularly tackle religious subjects, sometimes deliberately underpinning the school curriculum but often seeking to address cultural diversity issues.

Museums have adopted a variety of methods of consulting with their publics and encouraging their participation. St. Mungo's Museum in Glasgow uses a "feed-back board" on which visitors are encouraged to pin their comments and remarks; these have been the subject of a fascinating analysis by the French sociologist of religion Patrick Michel (Michel, 1999).

The impact of mass population movement from the later twentieth century has led many Western museums to celebrate diversity of local cultures, including religions, with the aim of promoting a more tolerant society. The museums of cities like Bradford, Leicester, and Liverpool in the United Kingdom have included Islam, Sikhism, and—to a lesser extent—Chinese religions in their local history exhibits and have promoted educational programs and temporary exhibitions to celebrate and interpret immigrant faiths. This approach has its dangers, not least that the "host" majority community will feel alienated, and this may particularly be true where "their" museums pay little attention to what many may still see as "their" faith (Hooper-Greenhill, 1997; Paine, 2000).

Museums and Religious Change. Museums have long had a role in religious change. Nineteenth-century European missionaries frequently sent home items relating to the former religions of their converts; in their new homes these objects took on a new life, often symbolizing the dark Other and feeding racism as much as commitment to mission. Today many of these objects survive in European and North American ethnography museums, like the Royal Museum for Central Africa at Tervuren in Belgium (Wastiau, 2000), or, less often, in museums set up by missionary societies themselves, like the Norwegian Missionary Society's Museum of Mission in Stavanger, Norway. Much more research is needed into the role these religious objects took on in their new homes: to what extent was their "religious" function remembered, or were they regarded simply as "works of art"?

What kind of new material culture was adopted by converts has been even less explored by museums until recently. Fieldwork carried out by the British Museum in the New Guinea Highlands in 1990, presented in a book and an exhibition, contrasted the incorporation of much traditional culture by Wahgi converts to Roman Catholicism, while evangelical converts were urged to make a radical break (O'Hanlon, 1990, p. 35). Nor has much attention—at least in English-language literature—been given to change in the perspective of those studying religion. So far there has been little attention given to changes brought to the way religion is interpreted in museums by the collapse of Marxism in the countries of the former Soviet Union.

During the Civil War in Bosnia many museums and many mosques and churches were damaged and destroyed. Often the heritage of the enemy becomes a target for hatred and destruction, and where intercommunal struggle is also religious conflict, museums can seldom escape becoming involved, even if they try hard to remain even-handed and above the fray—although too often they enthusiastically take sides. Museums, too, are often deeply involved in struggles between religious and secular interests and can be created to assert secular values over religious. The great Byzantine church of Hagia Sophia in Istanbul was turned into a mosque in 1453, but in 1932 it was turned into a museum as part of Atatürk's secularization campaign (Tunbridge and

Ashworth, 1996). The nearby sultan's palace was also turned into a museum, so that the relics of the Prophet, brought from Cairo in 1517, are now cared for by a secular museum.

FURTHER PERSPECTIVES ON MUSEUMS AND RELIGION. Museums aspire to tell the story—stories—of humankind, to celebrate human creativity, to inspire, to be a forum for public debate, to research every aspect of material culture, and to raise people's awareness of their environment and history. There is scarcely an aspect of human life and endeavor, or of the natural world in which we live, that museums have not at some time or other claimed to explore and reflect upon. Traditionally, museums have been about acquisitions, preservation, and presentation of both the works in their permanent collections and special exhibitions. They have been the centers for explanations and explorations of the ways in which art, in its many forms and varieties, has influenced, shaped, or reflected human history and achievements. The stories of diverse communities—social, ethnic, and religious—have been told in museums; individual artists and curators have presented traditional and controversial opinions about religion, politics, and gender through special exhibitions or permanent displays. Globally, museums have become the storage sites for objects once created for religious purposes but now rendered mundane.

As the idea of taste has been transformed from the concept of selection and decision with moral valuing to that of connoisseurship reflective of class and, thereby, economic and social distinctions, there has been a parallel evolution in the idea of the museum from its beginnings in the Enlightenment into the twenty-first century. However, in recent years, the irony has become that as ethically charged issues confront museums each successive day—from the question of the repatriation of sacred objects to that of the censorship of displays or exhibitions in response to religiously motivated critiques, as, for example, in the outcries surrounding the exhibitions of Edwina Sandys's sculptures to Andres Serrano's photography to Chris Offili's paintings—museums face challenges related to or inspired by religion. As the twenty-first century unfolds, museums will continue to play significant roles in the lives of individuals, communities, and nations; thereby cultural and religious values will continue to impinge upon, to illuminate, and to question each other.

As the role and purpose of the arts, including performance and display, garners more attention from scholars of religion, the museum both as an individual entity and as an institutional repository of religious and sacred art will become a focus for research and a conversation partner. Critical to both museum studies and religious studies, if not to the day-to-day practicality of museums, is the relationship between publicly or privately funded institutions in their displays, presentations, research, and programs for religious and sacred art. The curatorial responsibility in recognizing and privileging the religious history and values of works of art presents a profound responsibility. The questions of distinguishing between religious art and sacred art and the modes of display and preservation accorded to each further requires sensitivity and knowledge of religion not simply as a historical entity but as a living reality. A working partnership between museum professionals and religion scholars will be necessary to face the challenge of maintaining within the museum environment the individual integrity of the two working principles of museums as caretakers of cultural and religious patrimony and of religion as a communicator of social, cultural, or moral values.

SEE ALSO Art and Religion; Iconoclasm; Iconography; Icons; Idolatry; Images; Popular Culture; Visual Culture and Religion.

BIBLIOGRAPHY

The growth in their numbers and repute has been reflected in a significant growth in academic interest in museums: their collections, what prompts people to collect and what is going on when they do, their political context, their social function, their history, their educational role and how people learn in museums. As Pearce (1999, p. 1) puts it, "It is . . . incumbent upon the investigator to try to find ways in which, first, the social meanings of individual objects can be unraveled; second, the significance of the museum as a cultural institution can be understood; and third the process through which objects become component parts of collections, and collections themselves acquire collective significance, can be appreciated." A variety of approaches, derived from other disciplines and philosophies, have informed the growth of the modern discipline of museology, and recent scholarship has been increasingly concerned with ways in which museums display culture, construct difference, and produce relations of power. But there has been disappointingly little crossover between such scholarship and the equally lively field of religious studies. O'Neill (1996), Paine (2000), Clavir (2002), and Gaskell (2003) comprise most of the literature in English on museums and religion, while the wider topic of the material culture of religion is admirably introduced by Plate (2002).

Material Religion: The Journal of Objects, Art and Belief is the only journal devoted to the material culture of religion. Published three times a year, it gives close attention to museum issues. Three leading museum journals, which occasionally cover religious matters, are UNESCO's quarterly *Museum International*, the American Association of Museums' bimonthly *Museum News*, and the (U.K.) Museums Association's monthly *Museums Journal*.

Valuable websites on museums in general include the Canadian Heritage Information Network website at http://www.chin.gc.ca, the J. Paul Getty Trust website at http://www.getty.edu, and the International Council of Museums website at http://www.icom.org. At http://www.icom.org/vlmp is ICOM's invaluable gateway to museum sites throughout the world; a new museum site is added every day.

Altick, Richard D. *The Shows of London*. Cambridge, Mass, 1978.

Arnold, Ken. "Birth and Breeding: Politics on Display at the Wellcome Institute for the History of Medicine." In *The Politics of Display: Museums, Science, Culture*, edited by Sharon MacDonald. London, 1998.

Asma, Stephen T. *Stuffed Animals and Pickled Heads: The Culture and Evolution of Natural History Museums.* New York, 2001.

Clavir, Miriam. *Preserving What Is Valued: Museums, Conservation and First Nations.* Vancouver, 2002.

Davis, Peter. "Ecomuseums and the Democratisation of Japanese Museology." *International Journal of Heritage Studies* 10, no. 1 (March 2004): 93–110.

Duah, Francis Boakye. "Community Initiative and National Support at the Ahante Cultural Centre." In *Museums and the Community in West Africa,* edited by Claude Daniel Ardouin and Emmanuel Arinze. Washington, D.C., 1995.

Duncan, Carol. "Art Museums and the Ritual of Citizenship." In *The Poetics and Politics of Museum Display,* edited by Ivan Karp and Steven D. Lavine, pp. 88–103. Washington, D.C., 1990.

Duncan, Carol. *Civilizing Rituals: Inside Public Art Museums.* London, 1995.

Gaskell, Ivan. "Sacred to Profane and Back Again." In *Art and Its Publics: Museum Studies at the Millennium,* edited by Andrew McClellan. Malden, Mass., 2003.

Habermas, Jurgen. *The Structural Transformation of the Public Sphere: An Inquiry into a Category of Bourgeois Society.* Cambridge, U.K., 1989.

Hooper-Greenhill, Eilean. *Museums and the Shaping of Knowledge.* London, 1992.

Hooper-Greenhill, Eilean, ed. *Cultural Diversity: Developing Museum Audiences in Britain.* London, 1997.

Koven, Seth. "The Whitechapel Picture Exhibitions and the Politics of Seeing." In *Museum Culture: Histories, Discourses, Spectacles,* edited by Daniel J. Sherman and Irit Rogoff, pp. 22–48. Minneapolis, Minn., 1994.

Lorente, J. Pedro. *Cathedrals of Urban Modernity: The First Museums of Contemporary Art, 1830–1930.* Aldershot, U.K., 1998.

Michel, Patrick. *La Religion au Musée: Croire dans l'Europe Contemporaine.* Paris, 1999.

O'Hanlon, Michael. *Paradise: Portraying the New Guinea Highlands.* London, 1990.

O'Neill, Mark. "Making Histories of Religion." In *Making Histories in Museums,* edited by Gaynor Kavanagh. London, 1996.

Paine, Crispin. "Religion in London's Museums." In *Godly Things: Museums, Objects and Religion,* edited by Crispin Paine. London, 2000.

Pearce, Susan M. *Museums, Objects and Collections: A Cultural Study.* Leicester, U.K., 1992.

Pearce, Susan M., ed. *Interpreting Objects and Collections.* London, 1994.

Plate, S. Brent, ed. *Religion, Art and Visual Culture: A Cross-Cultural Reader.* New York, 2002.

Shackley, Myra. *Managing Sacred Sites: Service Provision and Visitor Experience.* London, 2001.

Simpson, Moira G. *Making Representations: Museums in the Post-Colonial Era.* London, 1996.

Study, David, and Martin Henig. *The Gentle Traveller: John Bargrave, Canon of Canterbury, and His Collection.* Abingdon, U.K., n.d.

Tunbridge, J. E., and G. J. Ashworth. *Dissonant Heritage: The Management of the Past as a Resource in Conflict.* Chichester, U.K., 1996.

Wastiau, Boris. *ExitCongoMuseum.* Tervuren, Belgium, 2000.

Williams, Jonathan. "Sacred History? The Difficult Subject of Religion." In *Enlightenment: Discovering the World in the Eighteenth Century,* edited by Kim Sloan with Andrew Burnett. London, 2003.

Wittlin, Alma S. *Museums: In Search of a Useable Future.* Cambridge, U.K., 1970.

Yanni, Carla. *Nature's Museums: Victorian Science and the Architecture of Display.* Baltimore, 1999.

CRISPIN PAINE (2005)

MUSIC

This entry consists of the following articles:

MUSIC: MUSIC AND RELIGION

Music and religion are closely linked in relationships as complex, diverse, and difficult to define as either term in itself. Religious believers have heard music as the voices of gods and the cacophony of devils, praised it as the purest form of spirituality, and condemned it as the ultimate in sensual depravity; with equal enthusiasm they have promoted its use in worship and sought to eradicate it from both religious and secular life. Seldom a neutral phenomenon, music has a high positive or negative value that reflects its near-universal importance in the religious sphere. This importance—perhaps difficult to appreciate for post-industrial-revolution Westerners accustomed to reducing music to the secondary realms of "art," "entertainment," and occasional "religious" music isolated behind sanctuary walls—has nonetheless been pervasive.

Religious "texts" have been sung, not written, throughout most of human history; and religious behavior has found musical articulation in almost every religious tradition. Navajo priests are "singers"; the primary carriers of Sinhala traditional religion are drummers and dancers; and the shamans of northern Eurasia and Inner Asia use music as their principal medium of contact with the spirit world. Through the centuries, priests, monks, and other specialists have sung the Christian masses, Buddhist *pūjās,* Islamic calls to prayer,

Hindu sacrifices, and other ceremonies that form the basis of organized religious observances in the world's major religions.

The values, uses, and forms of religious music are as diverse and culture-specific as the religious traditions in which they are found. Christian liturgical music is generally as characteristically "European" as Hindu devotional music is "Indian"; both use sounds, forms, and instruments from their respective cultures and have contributed greatly to the overall musical life of their own regions. Yet music, like religion, can transcend cultural limits; the religious musical systems of Ethiopia and Tibet, for example, differ almost as greatly from the secular musics of their own respective cultures as the musics of foreign countries.

Religious musical systems may also extend across cultural boundaries. Islam, for example, has forged musical links across vast regions of Asia and Africa; and North American traditions such as the Ghost Dance and the peyote cult have created musical bridges between very diverse ethnic groups. Other well-known intercultural religious musical traditions include Jewish, Christian, Hindu, Buddhist, and West African/Latin American possession music. Additional cases may include (1) the drumming and singing of Asian shamans, perhaps constituting a related tradition stretching from Scandinavia to the Himalayas, and possibly even extending into the Americas; (2) the epic songs, based on improvisatory recombinations of traditional song segments, of Central Asia and eastern Europe; (3) the bronze gong ensembles, associated with cosmological and calendrical symbolism and functions, of Southeast Asia; (4) perhaps the ancient sacrificial chants, linked to modal systems built on tetrachords, of Indo-European peoples extending from India to Greece; and (5) conceivably an even wider connection between Chinese, Indian, and Greek conceptions of music as an embodiment of universal cosmological and mathematical laws.

Yet, second only to its universal occurrence, diversity is the most characteristic feature of religious music, even in the great intercultural religious traditions. Christian music, for example, includes not only Gregorian plainsong, Palestrina masses, Protestant hymns, and Bach oratorios but also the resonant basses of the Russian Orthodox choir, the ornate melodies of Greek Orthodox chant, and the percussion-accompanied dances of Ethiopian Coptic worship; in the postcolonial era, it encompasses West African rhythms, and metallic sonorities of the Javanese *gamelan* orchestra, and the driving beat and electronic tones of the rock band as well. Hindu music aimed at helping to achieve the meditative state of *samādhi* can employ the very non-Indian sounds of Indonesian bronze instruments. Musical diversity in its religious and cultural contexts will be treated in other articles; here, I shall discuss some panreligious and pancultural issues.

Definitions and Concepts. Given the close links between musical and religious concepts, a nonsectarian definition of music may be impossible. For example, one common definition of music as "humanly patterned sound" conflicts with widely held religious beliefs that music is not humanly, but rather, divinely patterned. To members of traditions holding that music or, at least, religious music originates with the gods or with devils, the assertion of the human origin of music must seem the ultimate in Western materialistic dogmatism, however scientifically neutral it may seem to the outsider.

Even definitions as simple as the dictionary staple "art of sounds" carry ethnocentric and sectarian implications. In many religious contexts, music is less an expressive "art" than a technology applied to produce practical results, from the storage and retrieval of information contained in religious narratives and teachings memorized in song to the attraction of animals in hunting, increase of harvests, curing of diseases, communication with the divine, supplication, and control of the various levels of psychocosmic experience. While aesthetic beauty may or may not be integral to such technologies, individual self-expression plays little part in them and may be detrimental to their intended results.

The concept of music as an "art" carries overtones of a late European ideology based on the sanctity of self-expression and individualism, ultimately rooted in Greek and Judeo-Christian notions of ego, self, and soul. For some traditions, music is antithetical to the very notion of an individual self or soul. One group of Buddhist texts takes music as the archetypal embodiment of impermanence and conditioned causality, dependent on external sources and conditions, in order to show that there can be no such thing as an individual self. By contrast, modern Western scholars tend to view music, at least in its ideally purest forms, as fundamentally independent of external causes and conditions; they draw a sharp line between "extramusical" elements such as symbolism, function, purpose, and so forth, and "the music itself," which is supposed to consist of pure arrangements of tones. This concept of music seems to reflect European post-Renaissance religious concepts of an autonomous and inviolable soul wholly contained in the body of the individual. Perhaps it also reflects postfeudal economic concepts of individual entrepreneurial freedom, just as the Buddhist concept of an impermanent music resulting from temporary combinations of causes and conditions reflects basic Buddhist religious beliefs.

Even sound may not play a decisive role in religious concepts of music, at least not in any technical sense. When fundamentalist Muslims ban recordings of Western popular music and fundamentalist Christians burn them, they are not necessarily reacting to the melodic or chordal structures that constitute the essence of music for the technically oriented outsider. The "music of the spheres" extolled by early Christian writers was not sound in the sense of physical waves propagated in a gaseous medium; and, in Tibetan Buddhist thought, music consists of both the "actually present music" produced by sound-making voices and instruments and the "mentally produced music" perceived and imagined by each listener, with different results according to individual differences in experience, skill, and imagination. Religious traditions have by and large no more conceived music to consist of sounds and the "extramusical" than they have considered persons to be made up of the physical body and the "extrapersonal." Hence, even the most basic technical definition of music will ignore or deny essential aspects of music as conceived by many religions, while labels such as "symbolism" applied to nonacoustic aspects may appear misguided or even hostile from a believer's perspective.

The very attempt to define music neutrally and openmindedly might be objectionable from some religious viewpoints. For certain Christians, some kinds of secular music and the musics of other religions are the works of the devil and should not be mentioned without condemnation; on the other hand, for the Mahāyāna Buddhist author Sa Skya Paṇḍita, all music deserves praise because it relieves human suffering. Some Muslims would object to a discussion of Qurʾanic vocalizations and other songs under the same heading and would assign negative connotations to music in general; but some Ṣūfī writers discuss music only in terms of highest praise for its capacity to lead to spiritual fulfillment, and they would consider a neutral approach as evidence of a lack of real understanding or appreciation of music's most important meanings and values.

Many religions and cultures do not have a concept corresponding to "music" or "religious music." For Islam, *al-mūsīqī* ("music") is, in principle, what the West might consider secular music, controversial for its potential to mislead believers into sensual distractions; melodic vocalizations of the Qurʾān and certain religious poetry are not "music," however musical they may seem on technical and aesthetic grounds. To avoid violating the integrity of a tradition by imposing a dissonant external viewpoint, it might help to consider all such cases of performances that sound musical to the outsider, but are not music to the insider, as "paramusical."

Cultures as diverse as those of Ethiopia (Shelemay, 1982) and modern Tibet have distinct terms and concepts for religious and secular music, with no common category of "music" to unite them. The music of the Chinese *chin* (a type of zither), on the other hand, is clearly conceived as music and has strong roots in Confucian and Daoist concepts and practices; but it certainly is not "religious" in the same sense as the singing of monks in Buddhist or Daoist temples. And, although the point lends itself all too easily to distortion and romanticism, it is a well-known fact that in many small-scale kinship-based societies of hunters, nomads, and subsistence farmers, where formal role distinctions are much less prominent than in bureaucratized state civilizations, it is often as difficult to draw a clear line between "sacred" and "secular" musics as it is between religion and everyday life. Are Pygmy honey-gathering songs part of a traditional ritual, a comic entertainment, a social regulatory system designed to ensure and enhance egalitarian universal participation in community life, or an aesthetically exquisite polyphonic art? The question, if not meaningless, is at least inelegant.

Musics, like religions, are most meaningfully defined in their own terms. Along with aspects of musical sounds and their structural relationships, religious definitions frequently take into consideration such factors as cosmological and mathematical laws, divine origin or inspiration, psychological and emotional effects, social and ethical implications, relations or contrasts between religious and secular musics, and a wide range of other elements.

Since the selection of factors varies widely from one religious tradition to another, as does the relative importance assigned to any particular element, an approach that attempted to define all religious musics "in their own terms" would result in a collection of mutually unintelligible approaches to what must on some level be a cosmically, divinely, or humanly universal topic. For want of a better solution, we must discuss music and religion in the terms most widely shared by the full range of musical and religious traditions; and these, in the first place, require attention to the technical elements of music and of the paramusical phenomena found in religious contexts.

TECHNICAL FEATURES. Music has its technical basis in human voices and/or musical instruments that produce sounds with patterned acoustical characteristics. Religious traditions often stress a distinction between vocal and instrumental music and frequently assign higher value to vocal music. This is usually because of its capacity to communicate meanings through the words of song texts, because the human body seems more a part of divine creation than instruments created by human artifice, or because of negative associations of instruments and their music. In some traditions, such as the Mennonite churches and Theravāda Buddhist monasteries, vocal music is performed *a cappella*, without instrumental accompaniment. No cases are known in which vocal music is rejected entirely in favor of instrumental music; but there are significant examples (such as the Siberian shaman's drum) where instruments and their music equal or overshadow vocal music in religious importance.

Patterned human vocalizations take two forms: speech, emphasizing contrastive distinctions between units (phonemes, syllables, words) with distinct meanings, and singing, emphasizing prolonged continuity of sounds with controlled pitch (frequency of vibration). Singing without words produces a melody, a patterned sequence of tones; with words sung to the melody, one has a song. A song may be sung on a single, steady pitch level (monotone); or its melody may rise and fall to any number of higher and lower pitches, the total of which, arranged in ascending or descending order, are its scale; or it may consist of continuous, gradually shifting tone contours without distinctly separate high or low levels. Sets of musical scales may be conceived as modes that incorporate standard melodic patterns, ethical and cosmological implications, and other non-acoustic features.

Religious traditions may place greater value and emphasis on either words or melody; and vocal styles may range from formally simple, with few up-and-down melodic movements to avoid distortion of the words of the texts, to more elaborate, with complex melismatic movements to enhance musical beauty. It was once widely believed that such differences represented an evolutionary sequence from "primitive" chant to musical art; but, as Edith Gerson-Kiwi (1961) has convincingly argued, melodic simplicity may be a deliberately developed stylistic alternative to elaborate secular styles in complex cultures. Varying textual/musical emphasis may reflect varying mythic/ritual applications, stressing either the informational content of religious narratives or the aesthetic beauty or power of a religious offering. Contrasting textual/musical emphases may also reflect differences in communicating with human believers in an intelligible language, or with spirits or gods, who may prefer the special mode of musical communication.

Melodies may be performed as a solo by a single singer or instrument player, in unison by a chorus of singers, or accompanied by other singers or instruments playing independent, distinct musical parts. They may be arranged so as to occur simultaneously with other melodies (polyphony), with a steady-pitch monotone (drone), or with conventionally arranged sequences (harmony) of other pitches or simultaneous-pitch clusters (chords). The most musically complex of these features may occur in the smallest local religions of the sociopolitically and technologically simplest cultures. Generally, such traditions tend toward maximum religious and musical participation by the whole group, while the "great" religions of urban civilizations tend toward complex patterns of religious and musical specialization. However, the existence of religious and musical specialists such as the shaman in small cultures, of complex divisions of musical function in the group performances of hunter-gatherers such as the Pygmies and San, and of movements toward community religious and musical participation such as the growth of the Lutheran chorale and Buddhist monastic chant in urban civilizations in Europe and India, show that even the most general rules may find exceptions in religious and musical traditions.

Rhythms are the product of patterned accents and "long" and "short" durations of sounds. Their patterns may be varying groups of irregular or equal-length beats (abstract or actually played accent/time units) and pulses (shortest units actually played); or patterns may recur in cycles of the same number of beats played again and again. Rhythms and cycles may be classified as appropriate to specific gods and ritual activities, and some traditions (such as Tantric Buddhism) use mathematical beat groups extending into the hundreds to musically embody cosmological and other religious concepts. Rhythms often form a link between music, words, and dance. In songs with prose texts, musical rhythms are often free, varying along with long-short syllable and sentence patterns; while songs with poetic texts often reflect the meter of poetic stanzas, with the same number of syllables and beats recurring in successive lines. However, musical settings may also utilize different rhythmic patterns from the texts set to them. Dance rhythms provide cues of accent and patterning to coincide with movements of the body; they range in style from syncopated (favoring sounds that fall between and overlap beats) and very fast styles associated with some African American possession religions to the asymmetrical, extremely slow rhythms used in Tibetan Buddhist dances.

Musical instruments are scientifically classed into four groups according to the means used to produce sound: idiophones (bells, gongs, etc.), which produce sound by means of a solid vibrating body; membranophones (drums, etc.), which utilize a stretched membrane; chordophones (lutes, harps, etc.), which use strings; and aerophones (flutes, trumpets, etc.), in which vibrating air produces the sound. Instruments of all these classes are widely used in religious music, although one class or another is looked on with special favor or disfavor by various religious traditions. Instruments are often played in groups or ensembles. These are sometimes called "bands" or "orchestras," with the latter term technically implying greater size and more variety of instrument types; but the terms are often used simply to connote a lesser or greater degree of respect on the writer's part.

Some Western writings on religion and music, particularly works by early scholars and missionaries, contain misnomers that convey false technical implications. Most common is the term *primitive*, which implies both "early" and "simple"; in fact, historical evolutionary chronologies of musical types are speculative and controversial, and the term has been indiscriminately applied solely on racial grounds to musics comparable in complexity and sophistication to the music of any known civilization. Words such as *noise*, *din*, and *cacophony* often simply indicate lack of understanding or sympathy.

Instruments are frequently misnamed; for example, *flageolet*, the name of a flute, is widely applied to oboes and trumpets; *tambourine*, a frame drum with jingles, is used for every kind of drum; and *guitar* and *harp*, applied to almost any chordophone. A more ambiguous usage is *chant*, a term that should carry technical implications of free rhythm, limited pitch range, and a relatively simple melodic style. In fact, the term is widely used as a simple synonym for "religious vocalization" or "religious song," even in cases of melodically and rhythmically very complex music; hence, it may impart the misleading impression that a music is of inferior aesthetic quality simply by virtue of its being religious.

ORIGINS, MYTHS, AND SYMBOLISM. The close relationship of music and religion may imply, as some myths and legends claim, a common or related origin. From the eighteenth to the early twentieth century, evolution-oriented scholars debated theories of musical origins in the sounds of birds and animals, emotional cries of grief at funerals, language intonations, stylized recitations of religious texts, and animistic awe of "voices" heard in natural objects such as shells and bamboo tubes, and so forth. All such theories proving no less speculative and resistant to objective investigation than the traditional myths they were meant to replace, the issue gradually lost scientific interest, and it is now all but ignored in musical research. But, as if in discouragement at having failed to construct their own myth of musical origins, scholars also made little effort to explore the origin question in its traditional context of religious mythology; and today we still find ourselves in the "surprising" position of finding, as did Alan P. Merriam (1964, p. 74), "that there seem to be almost no available accounts of beliefs concerning the ultimate origin of music."

Accessible information, while insufficient to allow for generalization or systematic analysis, is abundant enough to show that music is as diverse in myths of origin as in any other of its aspects. Music may be thought to originate in a primordial divine power, as in the *nāda-brahman* "God-as-sound" of Hinduism, or in the efforts and discoveries of such human originators as Jubal and his father Lamech, briefly mentioned in Jewish and Islamic traditions (see *Gn.* 4:21), or Fuxi and Huangdi, in Chinese legend the discoverers of music and its mathematical-cosmological basis. Music may also play a cosmogonic role in the origin or maintenance of the world, as in the drum-playing and cosmic dance of the Hindu god Śiva Nataraja or in widespread stories of gods who "sing" their creations and creatures into existence.

The creation of individual pieces of music and musical instruments may involve contact with the divine. In the vision quest of the Plains Indians, individuals would go out alone into the wilderness to fast and seek divine messages revealed in songs, which they would then bring back to enhance the religious and musical life of the community. The Asian shaman's quest for a drum may take him to the center of the world and the beginning of time, just as the Australian Aborigine's dreaming of songs may provide a link to the primordial Dreaming. Musical creation may even move in the opposite direction, from the human world to the divine, as in the case of the Tibetan composer Milaraspa (1040–1123), whose songs are said to have been "imported" to heaven by the mkha' 'gro ma goddesses who, like their counterparts in many other religions, fill the Tibetan Buddhist heavens with their music.

The idea that music originally belonged to "other" places, times, persons, or beings is found in many myths, sometimes with connotations of conflict and conquest, as in the South American and Melanesian legends of male theft of sacred flutes from the women who originally possessed them. However, the discovery or creation of music is more often a joyful or ecstatic experience, as in the many vocal and instrumental pieces and religious dances of Tantric Buddhism experienced in dreams and meditations as celestial performances and then recomposed by the meditator for performance in the human world. Handel's often-quoted account of seeing God and the angels while composing the "Hallelujah" chorus—to say nothing of the religious experiences the chorus continues to evoke for many of its performers—may indicate the viability of such concepts even in cultures that favor ideas of human composition of music over divine creation and that tend to conceptualize musical "inspiration" in more secular terms.

Specific beliefs in music coming to us from other realms and beings may be a special case of a more general belief in the otherness, the special or extraordinary nature, of music in human experience. Such beliefs are seldom rooted in simple perceptions of music as strange and alien but rather seem based on recognition of the beauty and power of music. Thus, even when some traditions condemn music, they are condemning aspects of it that other traditions find worthy of praise: music exerts a strong appeal on humans, spirits, or gods; it stimulates sensual, bodily, and mental involvement, and so on. Does the power of music come from physical sensations of breath, motion, and vibration, from cognitions of proportion and symmetry as unexpected and serendipitous in the auditory realm as geometric arrays in nature, from socially and culturally conditioned associations? Is there one explanation, or are there separate causes for different kinds of musics and experiences? Whatever the answer, music enhances, intensifies, and—in ways that may elude precise analysis and control but which are nevertheless apparent both to participants and observers—transforms almost any experience into something felt not only as different but also as somehow better. In this transformative power, music resembles religion itself; and when the energies of music and religion are focused on the same object in an isofunctional adaptation of both toward a common meaning and goal, intensification reaches a peak greater perhaps than either might achieve by itself. Thus, the "otherness" of music and the "other" levels of reality and beings encountered in religion merge into a heightened synthesis of religious-musical experience. The possibility of such a synthesis may help to explain the aspect of music in religion that we usually call symbolism.

Symbolism is a problematic concept for both religion and music. Like the gods and spirits who remain invisible to an outside observer or to a camera, music's religious meanings and functional effects that elude capture by microphones and tape recorders may strike the uninitiated outsider as pure symbolism and yet be at least as real as its physical sounds to the aware and sensitive insider. For the Aztec, songs were flowers, birds, pictures, and the spirits of dead warriors called back to earth (Bierhorst, 1985); we ourselves would probably find it easier to agree that a song "is" a picture than that a song *is*, rather than *symbolizes*, a spirit. And if we adopt the kind of viewpoint that reduces the symbolic relationship between symbol and meaning to questions of physical-intangible and real-unreal, thus disposing of the spirits, we still have not decided whether songs are the symbols of flowers or vice versa. One senses that either choice is equally arbitrary; but if both are admissible as the real basis of the symbol, then why not the spirits as well?

Even if we take musical symbolism as a comparative and technical question of meanings attributed to sounds and forms, there are further questions of how so abstract and nondiscursive a medium can symbolize effectively, other than by purely arbitrary association, in the absence of explicit content that would lend itself to unambiguous communication. Some hear the diabolical in sounds that others find sacred; cross-cultural searches for even the most general agreement on music's cognitive or emotional significance have been unrewarding. There even seems to be a contradiction in the attempt to encode or decipher symbolic meanings in music: its aesthetic power seems to rely on the manipulation of abstract forms, however defined by a given culture and style, to the extent that subjecting form to an externally imposed system of meanings and functions might imply conflicts of purpose and musically inferior results.

Yet, if a symbol is that which stands for and reveals something other than itself, then music throughout the world has been accepted as successfully symbolizing the "other" of religion. Part of its success must derive from its generally perceived qualities of otherness and extraordinariness, and perhaps even from the very abstractness that frees it from associations too narrow to be associated with religious goals and meanings. But symbolic effectiveness must also rely on more specific associations than arbitrary applications to meanings or goals, which, even though they may be isofunctionally linked to the goals of religious practice, may still appear extrinsic to the music. If such associations do not arise from explicit musical content, then they must result from specific forms that accord with other meaningful forms in the religious sphere. Isoformalism of shared musical and religious forms, then, may combine with isofunctional applications to produce music that effectively symbolizes a religious object, and moreover without compromising the aesthetic integrity or viability of music as a medium of structured forms. Taking religious inspiration as the primary element in the process, this synthesis would occur when the form of a religious experience, action, image, or statement stimulated the creation of a corresponding musical form appropriate to and effective in the context of the musical system of its particular culture or religious tradition.

When religious and musical forms and purposes thus coincide, we have the kind of congruence that allows religious meaning to pervade every aspect of music from its assumed origin to the forms of individual instruments, songs, and pieces, and at every level of meaning from the most central to the most peripheral, from the most general to the most specific. The synthesis may be so complete as to leave no certainty whether either component, religion or music, takes precedence over the other; and it certainly allows for influence in both directions. There are, for example, not only myths of music, but also musics of myths; and the influence of music on mythology is almost certainly more pervasive and more important than the influence of mythology on music.

Contrary to a famous assertion by Lévi-Strauss, Wagner was far from the first, even in the Judeo-Christian tradition, to structurally "analyze" myths through music, for there are European precedents for the musical structuring of mythic narratives and themes going back to the Middle Ages, and far older examples from other parts of the world. These range in complexity from dramatizations as musically elaborate as Bach's or Wagner's (for example, the many performance genres of the Hindu epics *Rāmāyaṇa* and *Mahābhārata* in South and Southeast Asia), to the almost universal forms of mythic vocalization that utilize a simple binary contrast of sung myth/unsung ordinary discourse, or melodic and rhythmic highlighting of important words and passages to create a musically enhanced structure for a mythic narrative. For most religions throughout history, myths have been embodied not in written literature but in musical performance; and such performances provide one of the most characteristic bridges between religious belief and action, between myth and ritual.

TIME, SPACE, AND RITUAL. Music is widely used as a demarcator of ritual time and space. In traditional settings all over the world, one may enter a community just before or during a ritual performance and be drawn toward the center of religious activity by musical sounds that grow progressively stronger as one moves toward the center. At the ceremonial site, music may emanate from the exact center of action; or musicians may be placed at the borders of the ritual site, creating a boundary zone of maximum sensual stimulation through which one passes to enter the ritual area itself. In either case, the ceremonial space is pervaded by musical sounds that, more than any other element, fill the entire sacred area with a tangible energy and evidence that a special situation has been created.

Sometimes architectural or geographic isolation is used to confine the sound to the ritual space, and the music becomes an intimate or secret experience restricted to ritual participants and unheard by the general public. In other contexts, musical contrasts may mark the boundaries of sacred spaces by reserving different styles or sounds for sacred centers and profane peripheries: for example, Christian churches with bells that ring on the outside and organ music on the inside, or Theravāda Buddhist monastic ordinations with royal processional instruments outside the temple and choral chanting inside.

Unlike works of visual art, which exist in their entirety and all their details at any given moment, music unfolds through time. Thus, it creates a temporal framework that may be synchronized with ritual time in various ways. At the simplest level, the beginning and ending of a musical performance may coincide with the beginning and end of a ritual performance. Music may begin before a ritual and end after it, enclosing the performance in a temporal bracket or frame; or music may be performed selectively at temporal high points in ritual activity, highlighting significant periods of religious action.

But music also structures the experience of time in more complex ways. The tempo of the sounds that constitute the "events" of a musical performance may be considerably faster or slower than the pace of everyday experience, and they may combine in unusual temporal patterns. Music uses formal devices such as cyclicity, repetition, contrast, variation, and development of one pattern of organization into another. Any or all of these devices may be used to create perceptual impressions of the extension or compression of a moment of experience to a longer or shorter time than normal, the return of a previous moment, or the building of intensity toward a climax and emergence of a new structural and experiential framework.

For both time and space, the structuring effect of music and other performance media may thus function in quite distinct ways. The most obvious way is by contrastive marking of boundaries between music-filled sacred space/time and profane space/time without music. The musical preludes and postludes performed before and after Christian services, or the conch-shell trumpet notes sounded before and after many South Asian rituals, often from a temple door or gateway, exemplify the boundary-marking aspect of music used to highlight ritual activity by creating a sonic frame around it in time and space.

A different mode of organization is used when the spatial and temporal centers, rather than the boundaries, of ritual activity are brought into concentrated focus by music. This phenomenon occurs at a conceptual or "symbolic" level when music is perceived as a spatio-temporal *axis mundi*, a channel of communication with spiritual realms and primordial eras. For example, singing the "drum lineage" songs of the Tibetan Bon religion evokes a link with the beginning of time and the center of the world.

More concretely, the central spatiotemporal foci of ritual actions in the physical world may be highlighted by musical intensification, while movement toward or away from the center is marked by gradually changing intensity rather than a sharp boundary. For example, the religious and musical focus of a Sinhala Kohombā Kankāriya ritual is in the drumming, singing, and dancing of the priests themselves; their sound is heard with decreasing intensity as one moves outward through the concentric rows of the audience in the open-walled ritual enclosure, through the streets of the village, and on out through the fields of the surrounding district, which may be the ultimate space consecrated by their performance.

In such cases, the consecrated space is defined by its relation to the ritual action at its center, rather than by a boundary at its edge; and the gradually diminishing intensities of musical sounds emanating from the center serve well to embody this central-focal mode of spatial demarcation. A similar mode of temporal demarcation seems to occur in, for example, the Shona Bira ritual described by Berliner (1978, chap. 8), in which the *mbira* musicians begin their performance with unobtrusive, unelaborate playing and gradually build to a peak of musical and religious interaction with the audience. Both musical intensity of creative improvisation and religious experiences of spirit possession occur within this focal period, and both gradually fade away to more ordinary levels as the ritual draws to an end. In such modes of application, music ceases to be a simple boundary marker, enhancer, or accompaniment to ritual action and religious experience: musical and ritual structure and content begin to take on more vital and significant relationships.

The most basic and widespread musical and ritual time-structuring device is repetition, often carried to such lengths as to perplex or bore the outside observer. It may be that repetition and redundancy serve to impart sensations of continuity, stability, and security, that they aid concentration and provide safeguards against distraction, or that they simply allow continuation of a "state of music" to enhance a ritual performance. Whatever the cause, the use of repetition is surely wide enough to show the importance of this little-understood formal device. However, except in unusual cases such as South Asian *mantra*, Japanese Nembutsu chanting, and some kinds of instrumental accompaniments to rituals, which may involve very prolonged repetitions, musical repetition is almost always found in conjunction with variation, and each depends on the other.

For example, we might consider three possible musical settings for the beginning of the Christian Mass, "Kyrie eleison / Christe eleison / Kyrie eleison." (1) The same melody, musical form, and so forth, is repeated in all three phrases. This would appear to minimize the effect of the textual variation "Kyrie . . . / Christe . . . / Kyrie" and create a musical analogue of the textual continuity provided by the triple repetition of "eleison," reinforcing the conceptual unity of the plea for mercy expressed in all three phrases. (2) Each phrase is set to a different melody or form. Here, the formal analogue is with the variation of initial words, rather than continuity and repetition, and the cognitive effect might be a heightened awareness that each phrase represents a new act of asking mercy, even though there is textual repetition in the first and third phrases. (3) The beginning and ending "Kyrie . . ." phrases are set to the same or a similar melody or form, with the intervening "Christe . . ." set to a different one.

Here, the use of musical variation and repetition corresponds exactly with the variation and repetition of "Kyrie . . . / Christe . . . / Kyrie"; continuity and conceptual unity are given cyclic expression in the identity of the beginning and ending phrases, while the middle phrase receives the special treatment of being given its own individual musical setting. Both repetition and variation in this context acquire a different significance than in (1), with its triple repetition, or (2), with its ongoing changes. The individualized setting in the second phrase is likely to be experienced by performers and observers alike as a special or climactic moment between the pattern established in the first phrase and repeated at the end; and a participant might experience it as a special enhancement of asking mercy in the name of Christ, without special attention to the role played by musical forms. But the formal differences remain: (1) with its repetition and sense of continuity and prolongation of a moment and action already begun, (2) with its emphasis on change and newness, and (3) with its variation-repetition structure and sense of return to a previous moment when the text and music of the first phrase are repeated at the end.

Similar cases can be found in many religious traditions; for example, in the various settings of the Buddhist Triple Refuge, with its three-phrase invocation of Buddha, Dharma (teaching), and Saṃgha (religious community). The actual use of musical structuring through repetition and variation is frequently much more complex, and each tradition tends to develop its own characteristic styles. For example, many Christian Mass settings use extensive repetitions of text phrases such as "Kyrie eleison" with increasingly different variations of the melody, developing it into new forms, and building to climaxes of musical intensity. Buddhist settings of the Triple Refuge, on the other hand, tend to use melodic variation in more restrained ways, and concentrate instead on text/music repetitions that build to mathematical or exponential permutations such as triple repetitions of a three-phrase structure, resulting in a 32 formal structure, and perhaps a sense of transcending cyclic repetition to reach a more abstractly perfect state. However such structures may be felt or interpreted in their own traditions, it is clear that they make equally sophisticated but formally quite different use of such features as continuity, change, and development of basic elements into more complex forms. And since each in its own context is only a small part of a much longer ritual performance, opportunities for complex structuring of musical time are obviously great.

Yet, however natural the concept "musical time" may appear to us, we must treat the issue with caution. Westerners may not be the only ones to conceive of music and its structures in temporal terms. For example, the Javanese prince Mangkunegara VII (1957) and others see the *wayang kulit* (shadow play) in such terms. For them, this all-night performance, with its chronological ordering of musical modes and its complex alterations of repeating sections and new developments, encapsulates the experience of progress through a prolonged state of *samādhi* meditation and through life from birth to spiritual fulfillment. And Judith Becker (1979, 1981), in a series of provocative articles, suggests that Javanese music embodies local and Hindu-Buddhist time concepts from cyclicity to the coincidence of differently ordered calendars.

Alan P. Merriam (1981) has warned that we may be imposing our own prejudices on African music by discussing it in terms of a "musical time" for which African languages have no corresponding terms. Nevertheless, we find areas in Africa with both musical coincidence of different-length beat cycles and calendrical coincidence of different-length week cycles, and the parallel seems too exact and complex to be unrelated. Perhaps one solution would be, in studying a culture, to adopt a comparative perspective that takes musical time as one of the fundamental modes of human time perception and organization, whether or not the culture calls it by a term that also applies to calendrical or experiential time, just as we continue to identify and study "music" and "religion" in cultures that have no equivalent terms. Since each culture and religion has its own concept of time, some such artificially neutral viewpoint may be necessary to think clearly about questions of musical and ritual durations and structures, questions that transcend both cultural and religious boundaries.

See Also Chanting; Drums; Percussion and Noise.

Bibliography

There is no integrated study of this subject on a worldwide scale. Older studies tended either toward ethnographic-scrapbook approaches, indiscriminately assembling all kinds of traveler's remarks on music hastily encountered and little understood, or to evolutionist approaches meant to "explain" the superiority of European religion and music. The articles on music in the *Encyclopaedia of Religion and Ethics*, edited by James Hastings, vol. 9 (Edinburgh, 1917), exemplify both approaches. More recent research has favored field studies of single communities or ethnic groups. Although such studies have resulted in intensive exposure and considerably more extensive and accurate firsthand information, they have also produced works that frequently tend to one-sided emphasis of either religious or musical factors with inadequate attention to their mutual relationships. Readers who want to learn more about the religious music of a given tradition should consult not only the bibliographies of the articles on music that follow but also the general articles on the same religious traditions elsewhere in the encyclopedia.

The most extensive collection of studies of religious music by individual authors writing on different areas and religions is the *Encyclopédie des musiques sacrées*, edited by Jacques Porte (Paris, 1968), and, in English, articles listed under the names of individual religions and countries in the *New Grove Dictionary of Music and Musicians*, 20 vols., edited by Stanley Sadie (London, 1980). Other collections of recent studies are found in two special "Sacred Music" issues of the journal *World of Music* (Berlin; vol. 24, no. 3, 1982, and vol. 26, no. 3, 1984), and in *Sacred Sound: Music in Religious Thought and Practice*, edited by Joyce Irwin (Decatur, Ga., 1984). Standard works on the theory and method of research on world musics, including religious music, include Bruno Nettl's *The Study of Ethnomusicology* (Urbana, 1983), in which see especially chapters 11, 12, and 15, and Alan P. Merriam's *The Anthropology of Music* (Evanston, Ill., 1964), in which see chapters 4, 11, and 12. The most comprehensive cross-cultural theoretical approach to a single aspect of religious music is Gilbert Rouget's *Music and Trance: A Theory of the Relations between Music and Possession* (Chicago, 1985). Less helpful applications of cross-cultural theory are found in works such as *Man, Magic and Musical Occasions* by Charles L. Boilès (Columbus, Ohio, 1978), which subsumes all kinds of religious practices under "magic," or Arnold Perris's *Music as Propaganda* (Westport, Conn., 1985), which evaluates the musics of other religions by European Christian standards.

A number of studies of religious music in specific traditions make effective use of anthropological approaches to religion, particularly those approaches that focus on language and symbolism. Classic anthropological studies include works by David P. McAllester on the Navajo, *Enemy Way Music* (Cambridge, Mass., 1954), and on the peyote cult, *Peyote Music* (New York, 1949). A broadbased anthropological approach is used in *Horses, Musicians, and Gods: The Hausa Cult of Spirit Possession* by Fremont E. Besmer (South Hadley, Mass., 1983), while a focus on symbolism marks Steven Feld's work on the Kaluli of Papua New Guinea, *Sound and Sentiment* (Philadelphia, 1982). Works in the emerging category of "performance studies" place less emphasis on technical description and analysis of music but give it an important place in a multidimensional exploration of the multimedia world of cultural and religious performances; examples include Bruce Kapferer's study of Sinhala lowland possession cults, *A Celebration of Demons* (Bloomington, Ind., 1983), and Ellen B. Basso's study on the Kalapalo Indians of Brazil, *A Musical View of the Universe* (Philadelphia, 1985). These newer studies often show a sophisticated approach to the sung and narrated "texts" of oral traditions that may eventually enable more meaningful comparisons with traditionally text-oriented studies of the literate religions of Asia and the Mediterranean.

Studies of musical and ritual time include Judith Becker's "Time and Tune in Java," in *The Imagination of Reality*, edited by Aram A. Yengoyan and A. L. Becker (Norwood, N.J., 1979), pp. 197–210, and "Hindu-Buddhist Time in Javanese Gamelan Music," in *The Study of Time*, edited by J. T. Fraser et al., vol. 4 (New York, 1981); Alan P. Merriam's "African Musical Rhythm and Concepts of Time-Reckoning," in *Music East and West*, edited by Thomas Noblitt (New York, 1981), pp. 123–141; and Lawrence E. Sullivan's "Sacred Music and Sacred Time," *World of Music* 26, no. 3 (1984): 33–52. Other works cited in this article include Paul Berliner's *The Soul of Mbira* (Berkeley, 1978); John Bierhorst's *Cantares Mexicanos: Songs of the Aztecs* (Stanford, Calif., 1985); Edith Gerson-Kiwi's "Religious Chant: A Pan-Asiatic Conception of Music," *Journal of the International Folk Music Council* 13 (1961): 64–67, which has an overstated but important thesis; Prince Mangkunegara VII's *On the Wayang Kulit (Purwa) and Its Symbolic and Mystic Elements* (Ithaca, N.Y., 1957); and Kay Kaufman Shelemay's "Zēmā: A Concept of Sacred Music in Ethiopia," *World of Music* 24, no. 3 (1982): 52–67.

New Sources

Brulé, Pierre, and Christophe Vendries. *Chanter les dieux: musique et religion dans l'antiquité grecque et romaine: actes du colloque des 16, 17 et 18 décembre 1999, Rennes et Lorient.* Rennes, 2001.

Collins, Mary, David Noel Power, and Mellonee V. Burnim. *Music and the Experience of God.* Edinburgh, 1989.

Danielson, Virginia, Scott Lloyd Marcus, and Dwight Fletcher Reynolds. "The Middle East." In *Garland Encyclopedia of World Music*, vol. 6. New York, 2002.

Leonard, Neil. *Jazz: Myth and Religion.* New York, 1987.

Marini, Stephen A. *Sacred Song in America: Religion, Music, and Public Culture.* Urbana, 2003.

Moody, Ivan. *Contemporary Music and Religion.* Reading, U.K., 1995.

Reed, Teresa L. *The Holy Profane: Religion in Black Popular Music.* Lexington, Ky., 2003.

Shelemy, Kay Kaufman. *Music as Culture.* New York, 1990.

Sylvan, Robin. *Traces of the Spirit: The Religious Dimensions of Popular Music.* New York, 2002.

Wuthnow, Robert. *All in Sync: How Music and Art Are Revitalizing American Religion.* Berkeley, 2003.

TER ELLINGSON (1987)
Revised Bibliography

MUSIC: MUSIC AND RELIGION IN SUB-SAHARAN AFRICA

The most compelling reason for music making in Africa derives from religious experience, for it is generally believed that the spiritual world is responsive to music and deeply affected by it. Acting through human mediums, the gods are known to object to the singing of particular songs and to express dissatisfaction when performances are slipshod or lacking in animation. Now and then they also bring new songs or themes of songs to their worshipers. Hence worship always finds its most intense expression in music making, which can go on for hours or days during major religious festivals, for performing sacred music in this manner gives not only aesthetic satisfaction but also the assurance of continuous contact with the spiritual world. Accordingly, those who worship particular gods often describe themselves in songs as the children of those gods and may distinguish themselves from other members of the community, among other ways, by their repertoire of songs, instruments, and dances.

Ancestral spirits, as well as gods, generate repertoires of songs and instrumental forms. The scale and intensity of expressions related to ancestral spirits, however, varies considerably in relation to the perspective from which they are viewed. While some societies emphasize the spiritual and behavioral aspects of ancestors in the performance of rain rites, curative rites, initiation and other rites of passage and special rites for the dead, others focus on the philosophical aspects of the concept of the ancestor. Celebrations of life or the triumph of life over death indicated by the continuing presence of the dead is given scope in special festivals involving displays of ancestral masks and dramatic enactments accompanied by music and dance. Some centralized traditional states employ music and ritual for political ends.

ORGANIZATION OF SACRED MUSIC. Because the spiritual world is believed to be sensitive to music, performances of sacred music are usually controlled. Accordingly there are occasions during which (1) little or no music is performed (such as personal ritual and worship); (2) music other than the sacred music of the gods is performed (such as events during which social rather than religious values are emphasized); (3) both sacred and nonsacred music may be performed (for example, the funeral of a priest or priest-medium or religious festivals that incorporate the singing of songs of insult sanctioned by the gods for the release of tension in society); and (4) sacred music is performed (such as fixed days of worship, festivals, and other special occasions on which dramatic enactments, including trance and spirit possession, take place). The repertoire of sacred music used on ritual occasions usually includes either songs and instrumental pieces or sound events that function as codes or signals for indicating divine presence or for inviting undivided attention.

As in many cultures of the world, African songs provide avenues for making references to the sources of religious experience and to the values that hold a community of worshipers together. Marion Kilson shows in her study of Ga songs and symbols that a homogeneous body of sacred songs may include references to the supreme being, individual lesser gods and their interrelations, creatures and objects of nature connected with the religious experience, the seasons, ritual symbols, interpersonal relations, and events in the life of the community of worshipers. Africans sing about their gods and their own social history in their sacred songs because their gods accompany them during their migrations as well as in their encounters with other societies.

Sacred song repertoires usually include items that fulfill special functions related to the details of worship or a ritual occasion. Some songs are sung for the opening and closing of worship while others accompany, precede, or follow particular rites or provide the link between different phases of a ritual occasion. Getting in and out of trance or remaining in a state of trance can be aided by particular songs, while changes in the mood of worship can be effected not only through the content of songs but also through variations in form and singing style, including the occasional use of spoken verse; changes from speechlike chants in free rhythm or recitative style to songs in strict rhythm; and differentiations between simple litany types of songs and songs that utilize more complex forms or occasionally songs in strophic form.

Group singing is invariably led by cantors, who may not necessarily be priests or priest-mediums. Special chants performed as solos that require mastery of particular vocal techniques and repertoire may be performed by specialists in the religious community. In some societies the songs of public worship are performed by a select group of singers well versed in the tradition and not by the entire congregation.

Sacred songs may be sung unaccompanied (especially when they are in free rhythm) or they may be accompanied by handclapping, bells, rattles, friction sticks, or by more complex percussion on drums or tuned idiophones (*mbira* and xylophones). Chordophones such as lutes, harp-lutes, and arched harps are also used in religious contexts in some societies.

In general, instruments that can play complex melodic and rhythmic patterns are treated not only as accompanying instruments but also as instruments that can stand on their own in ensembles. They may be assigned their own limited repertoire of pieces that are specific not only in their basic materials but also in style and tempo, so that they can be correlated with various songs, movement, and dance. During performances it is the instrumental ensemble that provides the required energy levels for movement expression and more especially for trance and spirit possession.

Because of the different roles performed by vocal and instrumental pieces and the dance, it is customary to combine all three in a full performance. Where this is done, all that a priest-medium who wants to perform a particular dance while in trance needs to do is start a song in the set for the particular dance. The instrumentalists will switch automatically to the rhythms he needs. The singers will similarly take up the song he started and continue with others in the same set.

A number of conventions are used to distinguish the sacred from the secular. For example, a simple ritual act of dedication or the use of external symbols of sacralization, such as marks of white clay, special drapes, pendants, or symbolic carvings, might distinguish sacred instruments from their secular counterparts. There are a few instances where the distinction is made in the form, structure, and tuning of instruments. For example, among the Lobrifor of Ghana, there is a xylophone used in sacred rituals that has fourteen bars, like other xylophones; however, only twelve bars are played, and a tetratonic tuning is used instead of the usual pentatonic. Similarly the *mbira dzavadzimu*, a tuned idiophone (*sansa*, or hand piano) of the Shona of Zimbabwe, used for playing music connected with ancestral rituals, is distinguished from those tuned idiophones played for entertainment, such as the *mbira dzavandau* and the *karimba*. It has twenty-two keys that are generally wider and thicker than those of other instruments and a keyboard with three manuals.

The organization of sound events that function as signals or codes follows similar conventions. Instead of the clapperless bells used in musical ensembles, clapper bells may be used in ritual contexts. Instead of a regular flute made of bamboo, a flute made out of the tip of an animal horn may be used. Instead of an instrument, voice masks and whistling may be used to indicate the presence of particular gods or spirits. Ankle buzzers and similar devices normally used in the context of the dance may be worn by a novice, a ritual expert, or a medium when he is in ritual contact with his god so that anyone approaching him might take a different route.

Similar functions may be performed by instruments set aside for this purpose. Thus the bull-roarer (or thunder stick) is used in some societies to represent the voice of the ancestor (for example, among the Dogon of Mali) or the voice of a god (such as Oro of the Yoruba of Nigeria). The major god of the Poro initiation society of the Senufo is represented not only by the sound of an eland's horn incorporated into an aerophone ensemble but also by the bull-roarer. Here and there one finds sacred drums that function in the same manner, drums such as the *digoma* of the Lovedu of the Transvaal, beaten twice a year in a ritual addressed to the ancestors; the drums of the Lozi of Zambia associated with chiefship; and the *bagyendanwa* drum in the Ankole region of Uganda.

Coded sounds are not always played as independent sound events. They can also be incorporated into regular pieces. For example, where the gods are worshiped collectively, the entrance and exit of each god can be indicated aurally through changes in rhythm or instrumentation or by a song functioning as a code.

Impact of Religion on Musical Life. Because music makers, artists, and crafters are also carriers of the religious beliefs of their societies, religious concepts and practices extend to artistic behavior in the public domain. A music club or association that performs recreational music may begin with libation, a song of invocation, or an instrumental prelude from the sacred repertoire in order to ensure that nothing goes wrong in the course of the performance. Some societies ban all musical performances for a few days after rites performed at the beginning of the planting season or before the annual harvest festival, while others prohibit the performance of certain musical types outside prescribed contexts. The making of instruments such as xylophones and drums begins and ends with rituals irrespective of the contexts in which they will be used. In some societies the rituals continue at various stages in the process of manufacture and on each occasion on which the finished product is used. There are also instances where musicians seek ritual protection not only for their instruments but also for themselves and their art. Belief in ancestors also sometimes plays a role in the recruitment and training of musical specialists, such as the royal musicians (*ingombe*) of the Bemba of Zambia and the royal drummers and fiddlers of the Dagomba of Ghana.

Because sacred music is held in high esteem, the borrowing and adaptation of instruments or musical items of particular aesthetic or verbal interest occurs now and then in the music performed in the public domain. While in the past this was done with discretion, social change now seems to have opened the door to conscious exploitation of the aesthetic potential of sacred music, both in traditional music practice and in the new forms of African popular and art music. The reverse process, whereby traditional sacred music is influenced by secular music, does not seem to be common, although a few notable examples can be cited. The emergence of centralized states in Ghana in the pre-European period, which developed royal court music of a complex order, seems to have encouraged the incorporation of the talking drum (*atumpan*), an instrument of kingly command, and the royal heavy drum (*bommaa*) into the ensemble of gods regarded as state gods.

Similarly, the advent of new cults that worship in the traditional manner has led to the development of new repertoires of traditional sacred music that utilize the recitative song style of traditional hunters' associations. These songs are used partly because of their affective character and partly because the gods of the new associations are regarded as hunter gods who specialize in the neutralization of evil forces such as witchcraft and sorcery.

Introduced Religions. Although indigenous religions have continued to maintain the vigor and vitality of their beliefs and expressive forms, both Islam and Christianity are also well established in many parts of Africa in spite of the alien modes of worship they brought with them.

Islam. Because Islamic religion does not view the sensuous qualities of music with favor and therefore tends to discriminate between what is admissible in religious life and what is not, the connection between music and Islamic religious observances in Africa has been marginal, in contrast to traditional African religions in which music is integral to worship and ritual observance. Apart from the call to prayer and the Qurʾanic recitations that are at the core of Islamic worship and that have been maintained in sub-Saharan Africa, it is religious events in the life of Islamic communities that provide outlets for music. The type of music used in these contexts depends on the community, in particular whether it is an Arab or Afro-Arab community, an African community ruled by an Islamic aristocracy, or an African community with Islamic leaders and a traditional aristocracy.

In all three types of communities the Qurʾān is chanted in the original Arabic during worship and on other occasions, while nonliturgical music may be in the local language and idiom. Friday services are observed, while the Prophet's birthday and his ascent to heaven or particular episodes in his life are commemorated in the form of festivals at which music in the local idiom may be performed. The end of Ramaḍān, the period of daytime fasting, is marked by feasts and music, while the routine pilgrimage to Mecca also provides a pretext for music making for the pilgrims, both on the occasion of their departure and on their return.

There is a general tendency in Islamic communities for a simple musical event that satisfies the Islamic ideal to grow into a more elaborate and sometimes inadmissible form, a process that leads to its secularization as entertainment music. The Yoruba Islamic musical types *apala*, *waka*, *fuji*, and *sakara*, for example, which started as modest forms of pilgrimage music, have become part of the general entertainment repertoire. Similarly among the Dagomba of Ghana *damba* music and dance performed at the *damba* festival, which celebrates the birth of the Prophet, is now performed in other contexts by *lunsi* drummers. Sectarianism and syncretic tendencies have similarly encouraged the use of African musical resources at *dhikr* gatherings as well as modifications in liturgical practice that allow for the development of a corpus of songs based on local models.

Christianity. A different picture presents itself when one turns to Christianity in Africa, for it has been less compromising than Islam as far as the use of local musical resources is concerned. Like traditional African religion, Christianity regards music as an integral rather than a marginal aspect of worship. Accordingly they share a similar approach to the organization of the content of sacred songs.

However, the values that guide the selection and use of music and musical instruments in Christian worship as well as performance organization and musical behavior are very different from those of traditional African worship. Until recently, African modes of expression and behavior seemed to the leaders of the Christian church not only unsuitable for Christian worship, but also not conducive to the restrained Christian life expected of converts. African drumming and dancing and the exuberance of African celebrations such as festivals and rituals of the life cycle were not tolerated. The problem that Christianity in Africa has had to face, therefore, is how to integrate Christian worship with indigenous cultures and preserve at the same time the basic Christian beliefs, values, and norms of behavior that characterize the religion. Although the Ethiopian church could have been used as a model of integration, it was ignored for quite a long time because it did not conform to the norms and values of the Western church.

The most obvious practical step toward indigenization of music widely adopted in the nineteenth century was the translation of hymns in European languages into African languages. It was not generally realized, however, that indigenization, in a fuller sense, would have also meant setting the translated texts of hymns to tunes that reflect African rhythmic and melodic characteristics or that follow the intonational contour and rhythm of texts, since many African languages are tone languages (that is, languages in which tones or pitches distinguish meaning or tend to be fixed for particular words, phrases, and sentences). The retention of the Western tunes invariably led to the distortion of the words, a situation that has not been fully remedied in many parts of Africa.

A few missionaries and African church leaders who became aware of this problem tried to provide other solutions. The Livingstonia Mission in Malawi, for example, encouraged local Ngoni people to adapt their traditional songs for church use, and also arranged for traditional instruments such as bells, drums, and horns to be used for calling worshipers to church. Elsewhere songs in the traditional style emerged (such as the Fanti lyrics of the Methodist Church of Ghana) that could be sung as spirituals or anthems.

The search for solutions to this problem, and to the whole question of Christianity in relation to African cultures, continued in the early decades of the twentieth century with the formation of the International Missionary Council. A more liberal attitude toward African cultures as well as to the indigenization of Christian liturgies and music emerged. This has encouraged not only African contributions to Western hymnody in African languages but also the development of new forms of syncretic church music that combine African and Western resources. Songs and anthems as well as a number of new settings of the Mass that use drums and other traditional African instruments as accompaniment have become fashionable in Roman Catholic churches. The All African Conference of Churches and local church music associations are also giving encouragement to the creation and dissemination of new African hymns.

African Independent Churches have also grappled with the problem. Beginning with hymns in translation and original compositions in the same style, leaders of these churches give scope to songs in the style of traditional African music as well as songs based on the style of marching songs and African popular music. Both African drums and Western band instruments not generally used in ecumenical churches are utilized by independent churches, since physical movement and expressions of ecstasy are encouraged.

As might be expected, there is a close relationship between trends in African church music and trends in contemporary African secular music, for many contemporary composers of art music are also composers of church music and of music for educational institutions formerly run largely by churches. Church choirs and singing bands as well as school choral groups are the main performers of African choral music in the art music tradition, while the repertoires of the few independent choral societies often include new African church music. Because of the large number of independent churches that have sprung up, composers of African popular music now include religious themes and tunes sung by such churches in their repertoire of dance music, a practice that enables their songs to be performed not only in independent churches but also in ballrooms, cafes, night clubs, and on social occasions.

SEE ALSO African Religions, article on New Religious Movements; Bull-Roarers; Drama, article on African Religious Drama; Drums; Percussion and Noise.

BIBLIOGRAPHY

Ekwueme, Lazarus Nnanyelu. "African Music in Christian Liturgy: The Igbo Experiment." *African Music* 5 (1973–1974): 12–33.

Euba, Akin. "Islamic Musical Culture among the Yoruba: A Preliminary Survey." In *Essays on Music and History in Africa*, edited by Klaus P. Wachsmann, p. 171. Evanston, Ill., 1971.

Jones, A. M. *African Hymnody in Christian Worship.* Gwelo, Rhodesia, 1976.

Kilson, Marion. *Kpele Lala: Ga Religious Songs and Symbols.* Cambridge, Mass., 1971.

Mapoma, Isaiah Mwesa. "The Use of Folk Music among Some Bemba Church Congregations in Zambia." *Yearbook of the International Folk Music Council* 1 (1969): 72–88.

Nketia, J. H. Kwabena. "Possession Dances in African Societies." *Journal of the International Folk Music Council* 9 (1957): 4–8.

Oosthuizen, G. C. *The Theology of a South African Messiah: An Analysis of the Hymnal of "The Church of the Nazarenes."* Leiden, Netherlands, 1967.

Turnbull, Colin M. *The Forest People: A Study of the Pygmies of the Congo.* New York, 1961.

Weman, Henry. *African Music and the Church in Africa.* Translated by Eric J. Sharpe. Uppsala, Sweden, 1960.

New Sources

Akpabot, Samuel Ekpe. *Form, Function and Style in African Music.* Ibadan, Nigeria, 1998.

Charry, Eric S. *Mande Music: Traditional and Modern Music of the Maninka and Mandinka of Western Africa.* Chicago, 2000.

Dagan, Esther A., ed. *Drums, the Heartbeat of Africa.* Montreal, 1993.

Erlmann,Veit. *Nightsong: Performance, Power and Practice in South Africa.* Chicago, 1996.

Euba, Akin. *Essays on Music in Africa.* Bayreuth, Germany, 1988.

Ewens, Graeme. *Africa O-Ye!: A Celebration of African Music.* New York, 1992.

Kivnick, Helen Q. *Where Is the Way: Song and Struggle in South Africa.* New York, 1990.

Kofie, Nicholas N. *Contemporary African Music in World Perspectives: Some Thoughts on Systematic Musicology and Acculturation.* Accra, Ghana, 1994.

Locke, David. *Kpegisu: A War Drum of the Ewe.* Tempe, Ariz., 1992.

J. H. KWABENA NKETIA (1987)
Revised Bibliography

MUSIC: MUSIC AND RELIGION IN INDIGENOUS AUSTRALIA

In indigenous Australia music and religion are discussed with reference to the concept of the dreaming. The term *dreaming* is an English way of describing the era of creation in indigenous Australian belief when great ancestral beings walked the earth, experiencing, interacting and creating landscape and life. A senior Yanyuwa man from the Aboriginal community at Borroloola in the southwest Gulf of Carpentaria of the Northern Territory explains the dreaming in the following way:

> In our language, in Yanyuwa, we call the Dreaming Yijan. The Dreamings made our Law or narnu-Yuwa. This Law is the way we live, our rules. This Law is our ceremonies, our songs, our stories; all of these things come from the Dreaming. . . . The Law was made by the Dreamings many, many years ago and given to our ancestors and they gave it to us. . . . The Dreamings were the first to dance our ceremonies and sing our songs. Some of these songs are dangerous, they are secret and sacred, women and children are not allowed to see them. Others are not secret, everyone can look at them, but they are still sacred. . . . The Dreamings named all of the country and the sea as they travelled, they named everything that they saw. The Dreamings gave us our songs. These songs are sacred and we call them kujika. These songs tell the story of the Dreaming as they travelled over the country, everything the Dreaming did is in the songs. . . . These songs are like maps, they tell us about the country, they are maps which we carry in our heads. (Mussolini Harvey, in Bradley, 1988, p. xi)

His words clearly illustrate the integral relationship of song to *Yijan,* or the dreaming, of song to country and place, of music to religion and to an Aboriginal sense of spirit or spirituality in Yanyuwa culture. Indigenous Australian language and cultural groups show basic similarities in their understandings of the relationship between music and the dreaming, although each has its own unique and specific stories, language, and discourses of creation and ceremony linked to country and geographical region. For example, Pitjtantjatjara-speaking peoples of the Western Desert region in Australia refer to the dreaming as *Tjukurrpa.* The diversity of indigenous understandings and performance of music and religion is enormous. For the purposes of this article, examples will be drawn from Yanyuwa culture to illustrate broader concepts of performance practice and religious belief.

Indigenous Australia has no equivalent term for "spirituality" or "religion" as it is used in English. There are, for example, a number of generic and specific terms that translate as "spirit being," there are terms for the creative ancestral beings, and there are also terms that speak of one's spirit having a source; but none of these terms is used to create a term that speaks of the spirit as it is used in spirituality and as such must be used with trepidation (Rose, 1992, p. 59). The words *spiritual* and *spirit* are open to many interpretations. From a Western perspective such terms have their roots in Greek and Christian thought and imply a split between the secular material world and the realm of the spirit. This binary view subtly suggests that enactment of spirituality means leaving the everyday world of the body behind to enter into a separate and disembodied sacred or holy domain. For example, as we have discussed elsewhere (Bradley and Mackinlay, 2000, 2003), in the Yanyuwa context the boundaries between the sacred and the secular are necessarily blurred. For Yanyuwa there is only one world, one environment, one country that is simultaneously material and spiritual. The spiritual is tied to everyday lived reality and immersed in seemingly mundane pragmatic activities. Practices such as singing clearly establish an immutable relationship of what could be called the spirit of place to the spirit of people. Yanyuwa cosmology therefore allows the Western terms *spirit* and *spirituality* to be used in many circumstances but always tightly bound to the expression and performativity of people's relationship to kin and country.

In many indigenous Australian cultures, a distinction is made between those phenomena, experiences, and knowledges that are considered restricted and unrestricted. These terms delineate who can access the knowledge and information contained within performance through participation. The term "restricted" refers to performance that limits the participants on the basis of gender, age, and/or kinship affiliation. In contrast, the term "unrestricted" denotes performance that does not have any conditions attached on who may participate. The Yanyuwa have two terms, *kurdukurdu* and *lhamarnda,* that could be seen as synonymous with the above terms and by extension with the Western terms "sacred" and "secular." Yanyuwa people often explain *kurdukurdu* as a correlate to the terms "secret" and "sacred" and therefore restricted, while *lhamarnda* is described as "free," or not secret and sacred.

In many ways the Yanyuwa terms *kurdukurdu* and *lhamarnda* resonate with discussions of "inside" and "outside" knowledge in Yolngu culture by both Keen (1994) and Morphy (1991). While we do not want to suggest that Yanyuwa and Yolngu systems of knowledge are the same, it is useful to consider briefly the overlap between them and therefore contextualize Yanyuwa knowledge in relation to other indigenous Australian cultures. Morphy (1991, p. 78) asserts that the concepts of inside and outside in Yolngu culture operate as a continuum and are central to understanding the structure, rationale, and existence of levels of knowledge in Yolngu culture. He also describes "inside" sacred knowledge as "restricted" and "outside" mundane knowledge as "unrestricted" (1991, p. 79) and emphasizes that there is great fluidity between them insofar as "the ancestral world extends into the everyday world, the inside flows into the outside" (1991, p. 80).

Importantly, Morphy acknowledges that there is much interaction and interconnection between inside and outside realms and suggests that "outside forms are in a sense generated by inside forms and not separate from them." This can generate, as Keen (1994, p. 226) contends, the performance and realization of inside concepts in outside spaces or "secrecy in public." In such performances, the restricted esoteric "inside" knowledge has clear referents, but the subjects or their significance is not inferred discursively (1994, p. 227).

In most indigenous Australian cultures there is not one singular translatable word for music, and categorization of performance into styles and genres by people is determined according to a complex set of interrelationships between the origins of songs, the purposes they serve, and the people who may participate in performance (Bradley and Mackinlay, 2000, p. 2). Conversations about categories of music often begin with a distinction being made on the basis of whether the creative source of the music resides in ancestral or human beings. For example, in Yanyuwa culture songs from ancestral beings are described as *kujika*, belong to *kurdukurdu* (restricted) forms of performance, and have their basis in the actions of the Spirit ancestors who lived their lives by traveling, marking, and singing the landscape into being during the creative period, which the Yanyuwa call *Yijan* (generally translated into English as "dreaming"). Songs made by human beings (when composed by men, these songs are called *walaba;* by women, *a-kurija*) are *lhamarnda* (unrestricted) and contrast directly with the big history of the ancestral beings in that they document little history or individual and community memory of events within living recollection.

Knowledge of song, both restricted and unrestricted, is but one way people give order to their country and to their history of human and nonhuman kin. Such songs are ultimately concerned with attachment to place and contain many emotional dimensions. It is these emotional dimensions that become the means by which groups of people and individuals are in constant negotiation with each other, for songs are not just free to anyone. All song and music in indigenous Australian performance traditions are bound by negotiations. These negotiations include the legitimacy of claims to knowledge and connections to place and people, to the past, to the present, and also to the future. Thus, even in relation to songs life becomes much more than the pragmatics of singing and performing, or even the often alluded to mystical/religious and historical conceptions; rather, it is about the union of all these things.

The songs of the dreaming ancestors are said by indigenous people to hold and carry the knowledge of the ancestral beings as they walked across the country, and each song verse becomes one footprint in the songline of that Spirit ancestor. In Aboriginal ceremony and ritual, performers aim to recreate the actions of the ancestors by tapping into the power of the dreaming through correct presentation of all the elements of the song cycle, including song text, melodic line, rhythmic pattern, and other ritual behavior such as the painting of body designs, the use of ceremonial objects, the preparation of and performance on ceremony ground, and the actions of performers. In Yanyuwa, song cycles are called by the generic term *kujika,* a word that has widespread use throughout the Gulf region and even into northeast Arnhem Land (Avery, 1985; Merlan, 1987; Trigger, 1992; Keen, 1994), and by its cognate form in the Victoria River region of the Northern Territory (Wild, 1987, Rose, 1992). When people sing a song cycle, they are described as *wandayarra* (following) or *yinbarraya* (singing) the road.

There is no one term for *kujika* verse in Yanyuwa; people use the Kriol term "leg," a term also recorded by Merlan (1987). Singers or knowledgeable people reference the song verses by what the actual song verse is about; in many instances each song verse has a key word by which that verse is known. In addition, song verses are also tied to the landscape via named places. In Yanyuwa, *kujika* song texts are always described using the present participle form of the verb; thus, they are described as *jiwini ki-awarala* (constantly being in country), *wulumantharra* (running), *wingkayarra* (moving, going), or even in some instances as *wujbantharra* (flowing); when the singers near a place name or a particular species, it is described as *rdumatharra* (getting). The songs are also *windirrinjarra* (ascending) and *lhankanbayarra* (descending) and are always accompanied by a cardinal direction marker. When the song is nearing completion, it is then described as *yibarrantharra* (placing). There is a sense that these songlines are ever present on the country like flowing conduits of meaning. If the code is known, they can be tapped into and followed, and then voice is given to that which is always on or in the country and the sea.

Of importance to any understanding of music and religion in indigenous Australian cultures is the concept of "taste," "skin," or "essence." In Yanyuwa the term for essence is *ngalki* (Kirton and Timothy, 1977). *Ngalki* is best described as that thing which marks the individual identity or essence of something. It can refer to the taste or smell of food, one's own particular body smell, or the positioning of people, flora, fauna, and natural phenomena into the four semi-moieties that exist in Yanyuwa society. Broadly speaking, *ngalki* as a concept presents the Yanyuwa way of making sense of the complex relationship between the people who make music, the process of music making, and the sound that is music. In terms of musical structure, the *ngalki* of a particular song is often described by Yanyuwa people as the melody or voice. It also includes the type of beating accompaniment used, the particular types of rhythmic patterns attached to song text, the way these are fitted onto a specific melodic shape, and the way all three components are combined during the act of musical performance. Thus, the correct interlocking of all performance elements gives each Yanyuwa song style its unique identity, and it is through the act of performance that the embedded power within genres is given meaning, accessed, and utilized by performers.

When used in relation to song, the term *ngalki* is often prefixed by a descriptive marker that marks the perceived quality of the performance or a person's opinion of the tune that is associated with a song. Thus *yabi ngalki* (literally, "good essence") can refer to both a good performance or a song that is seen to have an enjoyable tune; *wardi ngalki* (literally, "bad essence"), to a song that is quite plainly not being well performed; *jirda ngalki* (literally, "bitter/bad-tasting essence"), to a song that is not being performed properly because the tune is incorrect or the singers are discordant; *daburrdaburr ngalki* (literally, "rough/troubled essence"), to the tune of a song that is considered hard to learn and requires a long time spent with older accomplished singers. This is a term often used by men to describe a number of songs associated with various ceremonies and ritual actions. The term has a special relevance to songs that are considered powerful enough to affect other human beings or impact upon the order of the natural world and where the correct tune is considered to be the conveyer of the song's inherent power or *wirrimalaru.*

Within a Yanyuwa understanding of good performance, especially of *kujika,* a person who is seen to be performing song cycles at a high level of emotional engagement and technical skill is often described as *jarrilu-ngalkiwunjayarra,* "he is drinking the essence of the road." It is felt that he has embodied the song to such an extent that it is if the country that is being sung is through him and sustaining him. It is interesting that song knowledge is described in terms of "food," where the ability to learn and acquire song knowledge, especially that relating to the sacred knowledge of the land, is something that ones needs, like food, in order to survive. This survival can be seen at both the level of the singer and the country itself; perhaps the inverse of this is that if one does not sing and refuses to "drink the essence," then both the individual and country will not be truly seen to live.

To know and to sing in Aboriginal culture is to also know and acknowledge kin and country, to be aware where one fits in the family, the history of the family, and the country and sea that one's family has moved across and also calls home. While *kujika* may speak of how one belongs to land in terms of a cosmological understanding, there are the other more intimate, humanly composed songs that speak of the totally human dimension to experience. These songs are an excellent example of what Fox (1997, pp. 6–7) terms "social knowledge," a kind of knowledge that allows people constantly to comprehend, interact, and interpret their place-world. These songs are an important part of connectivity between people and place, and in many respects these songs are the containers that hold memories that connect people and places. This genre of new or unrestricted songs in Yanyuwa culture, and more generally across indigenous Australia, includes the diversity of contemporary rock and popular musics—these forms of performance too hold important individual, social, historical, emotional, and spiritual relationships, memories, and meanings. For example, the appearance of specific and nonspecific places, notions of place, and attachment to place (Dunbar-Hall, 1997, p. 62) within the song texts of these new songs plays an important role in naming, knowing, and remembering country in this unrestricted performance genre. This naming of places in unrestricted forms of Aboriginal performance resonates with the texts of restricted songs "[w]here singing about sites and events of the past associated with them are a means of affirming group and individual identity and of stating relationships to places. In this way, Aboriginal sites become songs" (Dunbar-Hall, 1997, p. 62). By specifically naming place in unrestricted singing, the composer reveals the personal, emotional, and spiritual significance implied in a particular locality.

Today, many indigenous Australian peoples and communities fight daily to survive against the contemporary realities of colonial and historical legacy, social upheaval, and cultural dispossession. Many indigenous communities suffer from high rates of family violence and alarmingly high alcohol and substance abuse statistics. Age expectancy is low for both men and women, and suicide among young people is increasing. Combined with increasingly poor health (for example, diabetes, renal failure, heart conditions, disease related to poor nutrition) and inadequate housing conditions, indigenous peoples are struggling to exist under the impact of dramatic social upheaval and change and Western systems of domination and oppression. Beneath these daily experiences of trauma, however, performance remains a powerful way to sustain a strong cultural and spiritual identity for Aboriginal people. Music is a religion in indigenous Australia in the sense that it is the central way to sing, know, and embody relationships to family, place, and spirituality. In the worldview of many indigenous Australian peoples, landscape and song are integrally related whereby knowledge and memories of landscape are named, encoded, and embodied in music performance. Through performance of place and country in restricted and unrestricted contexts, singers negotiate and evoke memory and emotion to continually create and re-create the knowledge associated with landscape and what it means to be an Aboriginal person in body, mind, and spirit—a unified, complete, and whole person. Understandings of sacred and secular, inside and outside knowledge, and restricted and unrestricted performance are integrally connected and the lines of distinction between them blurred. Lived experience of song, kin, and country enacts a performative memory and knowledge of time, space, and location that connect spirit of place to the spirit of indigenous Australian peoples.

SEE ALSO Australian Indigenous Religions, overview article.

BIBLIOGRAPHY

Avery, J. "The Law People: History, Society and Initiation in the Borroloola Area of the Northern Territory. " Ph.D. diss., University of Sydney, 1985.

Bradley, J. *Yanyuwa Country: The Yanyuwa People of Borroloola Tell the History of Their Land.* Richmond, Va., 1988.

Bradley, J., and E. Mackinlay. *Songs from a Plastic Water Rat: An Introduction to the Musical Traditions of the Yanyuwa Community of the Southwest Gulf of Carpentaria. Ngulaig 17.* St. Lucia, 2000.

Bradley, J., and E. Mackinlay. "Many Songs, Many Voices, and Many Dialogues: A Conversation about Yanyuwa Performance Practice in a Remote Aboriginal Community." *Rural Society.* 2003.

Dunbar-Hall, P. "Site as Song—Song as Site: Constructions of Meaning in an Aboriginal Rock Song." *Perfect Beat* 3, no. 3 (1997): 58–76.

Fox, J. "Place and Landscape in Comparative Austronesian Perspective." In *The Poetic Power of Place: Comparative Perspectives on Austronesian Ideas of Locality,* edited by J. Fox. Canberra, 1997.

Keen, I. *Knowledge and Secrecy in an Aboriginal Religion.* Oxford, 1994.

Kirton, J., and N. Timothy. "Yanyuwa Concepts Relating to 'Skin.'" *Oceania* 47, no. 2 (1977): 320–322.

Merlan, F. "Catfish and Alligator: Totemic Songs of the Western Roper River, Northern Territory." In *Songs of Aboriginal Australia,* edited by M. Clunies-Ross, T. Donaldson, and S. Wild, pp. 143–167. Oceania Monograph 32. Sydney, 1987.

Morphy, H. *Ancestral Connections: Art and an Aboriginal System of Knowledge.* Chicago, 1991.

Rose, D. B. *Dingo Makes Us Human: Life and Land in an Aboriginal Australian Culture.* Cambridge, 1992.

Trigger, D. *Whitefella Comin': Aboriginal Responses to Colonialism in Northern Australia.* Cambridge, 1992.

Wild, S. A. "Recreating the Jukurrpa: Adaptation and Innovation of Songs and Ceremonies in Warlpiri Society." In *Songs of Aboriginal Australia,* edited by M. Clunies-Ross, T. Donaldson, and S. Wild, pp. 97–120. Oceania Monograph 32. Sydney, 1987

ELIZABETH MACKINLAY (2005)
JOHN BRADLEY (2005)

MUSIC: MUSIC AND RELIGION IN OCEANIA

The uttering of formulaic texts, the sounding of musical instruments, and the enactment of physical movements are all integral to the expression of religious beliefs throughout Oceania. The supernatural beings that were contacted varied widely in the extent of their powers and the nature of their physical embodiments, but much human activity was intended to open lines of contact with that other world. Music was not and is not a self-contained art, nor merely the vehicle for communication with the other world, but in many instances it is the means of opening such lines of communication, and it is intended both to express and to reveal. Singing at a predetermined location and appropriate time enables contact with beings somehow residing outside space and time. For participants, religious rituals exist primarily to be perpetuated. A personal understanding of the theological or mystical bases for rituals, or the meanings of song poetry, or the symbolism of their myriad of sacra, is secondary. Essentially, process takes precedence over product.

POLYNESIA. Accounts of the origins of the universe established the first associations between humans and gods. Rituals maintained such links through a body of sacred lore administered through both individual and group expressions of worship, supplication, instruction, and appeasement. Polynesian pantheons consist of named categories of supernatural beings and named individuals within those categories. Major deities—Tāne, Tū, Rongo, and Tangaroa in East Polynesia; Tangaloa and Maui in West Polynesia —were associated with land creation and elements of nature. References in oral tradition to such beings tended to be confined to spoken accounts or recited poetry. East Polynesia, particularly Tahiti and Hawai'i, saw the development of religious specialists in the form of an established priesthood, and religious buildings in the form of temples. The carvings on pre-European East Polynesian drums, particularly those beaten during temple-based rituals, often included representations of major deities. The priesthood also held responsibility for the many years of teaching chants and dances to neophytes. In the many and varied contexts of performance, the agent activating the human-superhuman link was the uttered word.

Mythology credits the importation of the first *pahu* temple drums and their associated sacred dances from Tahiti to Kauai Island, whence its use in *heiau* temples spread to Hawai'i's other islands. The primary use of this sharkskin-covered wooden drum was to signal major events within the temple, summoning gods to enter the precincts and to speak through its sound. It also accompanied sacred dances. On Tahiti itself, such a drum was used both for signaling and for accompanying religious rituals. In both areas, the drums were given personal names.

The areas of association and influence of minor deities included natural events, local topography, and specific domestic activities. Such beings were considered contactable during periods of heightened emotion, particularly at moments of danger, such as illness and warfare. In Samoa, people of two villages used a song to summon the deadly Nifoloa to avenge any major insult to local residents. In another village the locally based god Te'e was appeased through a song in its honor. To cure certain ailments, Samoan traditional healers may still resort to exorcism, singing their command to the malign spirit believed responsible to leave the patient's body.

Throughout East Polynesia, minor gods were routinely contacted to ensure ongoing maintenance of the normally benign social relationship with local communities. In this context, the gods were held to share human pleasure in the performing arts, most notably singing and dancing, together with the sight and fragrance of costumed and perfumed bodies in action. The practice of performance as god appeasement was most developed in Hawai'i, where Pele and Laka were considered divine patrons of dancing. Much song poetry was dedicated to these beings—and still is, as part of the ongoing renaissance of Hawaiian culture. Whether invisible or existing in emblematic form, the gods were believed to be present during performances. The religious goal of hula performances was additionally based on a belief in sympathetic magic. By presenting an act in the context of dance, one gains power over it. One can thus govern the outcome of a future act or cause a past act to happen again.

The elevated nature of such expressive arts was emphasized by a corresponding expectation of performance perfection. If such perfection was not achieved due to accidental error, the result was held to be personal disaster. The accidental omission of a word in an incantation performed at the birth of the Maori mythological character Maui resulted ultimately in his death and failure to win immortality for humanity. Avoidance of breath breaks in the melodic flow was a feature of traditional Maori incantations and group chant on the grounds that the consequences were death or disaster. A system in which the group leader, having snatched an early breath, continued singing wordlessly at the ends of poetic lines while the group took breath overcame such concern.

In some regions ancient song poetry addressing gods survived Christian missionizing through prompt transcription, but it exists now more as an artifact of culture than an instrument of religion. In Tokelau, a handful of songs referring to the supreme god Tui Tokelau are now sung at festivals as affirmations of corporate ethnicity, and on Niue a song addressing the god of the ocean, Tagaroa, is routinely featured in cultural displays and competitions. The revival in the 1970s of oceangoing voyaging in reconstructions of traditional East Polynesian canoes stimulated a return of interest in associated rituals and performance styles. A convergence of such canoes at the sacred Tahitian site of Taputapuatea in 1995 signaled the formal reconnection of ancestral relationships among several Polynesian island groups. The renewed interest in cultural activities, also began in the 1970s in Hawai'i, French Polynesia, and New Zealand—possibly influenced by the newly established South Pacific Arts Festival—has seen the incorporation into public performances of various reconstructions of practices associated with indigenous religion. In Hawai'i, the construction and use of *pahu* drums, revived performances of chants and dances honoring named gods, and the performance of chants at the opening of the state legislature and other major public events all testify to the renaissance. Recitation of *karakia* incantations to national gods is a routine feature of major Maori activities, such as the openings of new public buildings and museum exhibitions.

In several parts of urban Polynesia, an ironic shift in attitudes has recently occurred. In the nineteenth and twentieth centuries, Christian missionaries strove hard and successfully to ban many performances of dancing on the grounds that the activity was heathen. Now, however, among both island homeland and expatriate communities of Polynesians, Christian churches may include dance tuition among their cultural programs and even numerically dominate competitions of traditional dance at local and national levels.

Although details of most Polynesian religions are now recounted in the past tense following almost two hundred years of intensive and successful Christian missionizing, a few Polynesian-populated outlier islands in Melanesia have attempted to maintain their indigenous practices in a reaction against what they consider the culturally damaging activities of missionaries and Christian churches. Communities on the islands of Takū (Mortlock Islands), Nukumanu (Tasman Islands), and Mungiki (Bellona Island) have participated in such a movement. Although some activities are now restricted to some extent by national legislation, others flourish. On these small, fragile, and remote islands, ongoing supernatural assistance is considered a survival necessity for which the formal performance of a variety of songs and dances is offered as a gesture of gratitude. Men may call on their dead ancestors while fishing, and, in the poetry of songs composed to mark their subsequent success, duly name their ancestors and acknowledge their supernatural assistance. In preparation for formal dances on the ritual arena, both men and women may wear emblems of their clan's founding ancestor as protection against the malevolent spirits believed to be in attendance during the performance. Also on the ritual arena in front of the assembled community, senior men take turns to intone long invocations to clan spirits and ancestors in order both to ensure continuation of clement weather and bountiful fish stocks, and also to avert crop diseases. The poetry of such invocations tends to be fixed by tradition and contains semantically dense language.

MICRONESIA. Preliminary findings from the few published studies of Micronesian religion indicate that religious activities incorporating singing (with or without dancing) tend to focus on village or matriclan efforts to ensure the maintenance of personal health, food production, and travelers' safety. The Micronesian pantheon contains no recognized paramount individual. Typical group religious activities have a patron god possessing limited geographical authority. Shamans sing to establish contact with such beings and to obtain advice and admonition, using incantations to lay a mantle of divine protection over hazardous occupations. At shrines, priests lead performances of humanly or divinely composed songs and dances to entertain a village or district god whose reaction in turn is conveyed by the priests.

ISLAND MELANESIA. Diversity features strongly among the many religious practices of Island Melanesia, where speech rather than song tends to be the chief medium of communication with the supernatural realm. Both here and in Papua New Guinea there is no sharp distinction between religion and magic. Human ancestors function not only as genealogical markers of the historical past but also as points of supportive contact for living descendants. Musical performances are featured in ancestor worship rituals in the Solomon Islands, New Caledonia, and Vanuatu. Dances and songs assist families of the recent dead to ensure that the physical severance occurring at death is accompanied by the spirit's enduring departure from the region, since a lingering presence can be mischievous. By contrast, in other regions the ability of the recent dead to maintain useful and essentially benign contact with the world of the living is ritually emphasized as elderly relatives sing in imitation of spirit voices while living descendants dance.

In contrast to Polynesia, specific sound quality itself may assume religious significance in both Island Melanesia and Papua New Guinea. Blasts from conch trumpets may be believed to expel unwanted spirits at a funeral or to represent actual spirit voices. It is a widespread belief that the ghost of a local person influences local affairs, causing or curing sickness, prophesying, and controlling the weather and crops. In regions where male initiation still assumes cultural significance, the real origin of the sounds of conches and flutes is initially kept secret from initiates (who are told that they are hearing spirit voices) and only later revealed as sound-producing devices. Until the mid-twentieth century, secret societies flourished in Vanuatu, where men (and sometimes women) achieved social elevation through competitive grade-taking that culminated in large-scale performances of song and dance.

Until it was sanitized by missionaries to become primarily a social activity in New Caledonia, the round dance was the means of contacting ancestors at the culmination of the large-scale *pilou-pilou* ritual. Processing around a central pole that symbolized the material connection between the living and the dead, Kanak men and women believed themselves to be the very bodies of their own ancestors as they danced. Other Kanak men's dances are totemic, giving visual expression to an association with either a maternal or paternal clan. The totemic ancestors' world, characterized by black land, a rancid smell, and ashes, can be entered only by persons possessing those same features. Dancers therefore plaster themselves with layers of earth and ashes as part of an effort to acquire the ancestors' restorative powers. The totemic bonds between paternal and maternal clans may similarly be given visual expression through dancing.

PAPUA NEW GUINEA. Papua New Guinea represents a maze of sociocultural groups and extreme linguistic complexity. Published information on cultural practices is marginal for many regions and may be nonexistent for others. The following generalized comments are therefore necessarily tentative.

Much New Guinea music is associated with various types of revelation in the context of religious ritual. Religious experience and understanding are the intended results of enhanced sensation and heightened emotion, states that are frequently instigated and sustained by periods of singing and dancing. The sense of mystery may be additionally intensified by the use of lyrics that are ungrammatical, archaic, foreign, or even secret. Men's formal activities tend to be held inside communal longhouses over a period of several days and nights. In contrast with other regions of Oceania, one goal of religious activity here may be the invocation of benign spirits, who are invited to meet with the living and so strengthen them.

Sacred instrumental music tends to be valued more for its sonic qualities than its aesthetic content as such. Flutes and bull roarers are widely used to produce sounds understood by the uninitiated to be spirit voices. Only after their physical ordeal are the real sources revealed to male novices, but even then under pain of secrecy. Slit drums and bull roarers are prominent in this respect in New Britain and New Ireland. Slit drums and paired flutes predominate in the central Highlands, Papua Gulf, and Huon Gulf areas. The absence of finger holes on these end-blown or side-blown flutes from the Sepik and Highlands, whose unequal size represents male and female identities, allows only the fundamentals and selected harmonic pitches to be sounded. The so-called fanfare melodies produced result from a sharing between the two instruments of individual notes in the melodic line. Acoustic continuity is one goal of both the paired flutes and other sound-producing devices, fostering the illusion of a nonhuman source of the sounds. For a similar purpose of subterfuge, men may modify their voices by singing into empty containers such as gourds, bamboo, or conches. In some regions the handles of the hourglass-shaped drums that men carry to accompany their own dancing may be carved with ancestral figures or combine human and avian forms to emphasize mythological connections. Bird symbolism is also common for paired flutes and their repertoires, and is visually represented through men's knee-bending dance movements. Much ritual dancing is more participatory than presentational, constituting statements of entitlement intended for fellow participants rather than acts of entertainment intended for an audience.

Among the Kaluli of the Southern Highlands province, bird calls are simultaneously avian identifiers and talk from the dead, since birds are a frequent visible form of a spirit reflection. In particular, *gisalo* dance songs, whose tonal organization is identical to that of musical representations of the call of a fruit dove, are composed with the intention of moving a male audience to tears. Women's response to the men's weeping is to break into song, thus creating a culturally activated cycle based on the belief that the *gisalo* performer is transformed into a bird during song and dance performance.

Ancestor appeasement through singing is widely practiced, using a limited repertoire of music that those ancestors themselves either composed or transmitted. Easing the passage of the human spirit from the human world is also a part of religious ritual life in the Trobriand Islands. Songs sung in what is believed to be the language of the dead describe in glowing and erotic terms the quality of life in the afterworld, thus facilitating the departure. These (and other related) activities confirm the spirit's retention after death of aesthetic preferences and values espoused during life.

Mythology frequently attributes the invention or discovery of specific musical instruments to women, who later yielded them to men. Men subsequently appropriated the instruments for themselves and continue to monopolize their use through stealth and deception in an apparent gesture of male self-enhancement. A prime focus of religious music in New Guinea and islands to the immediate east is the widespread practice of puberty rites, in which singing and dancing are integral to each stage of the rituals. In some regions the structure of male initiation rituals suggests the processes of menstruation, impregnation, gestation, and parturition, as men further attempt to obtain for themselves through ritual the female life-imparting capabilities denied to them in reality. In other areas the initiation ritual, together with its complex of songs and dances, may reflect and validate sex-role social structures.

SUMMARY. It is not possible to generalize in a temporal sense for all of Oceania, since continuation of religious beliefs and practices is no longer universal, largely as a result of Christian missionizing. Whereas Polynesia and Micronesia have favored the undisguised human voice in vocal contributions to religious ritual, Island Melanesia and Papua New Guinea seek to disguise it as being of nonhuman origin, furthering the notion of deception by restricting knowledge of the real source of instrumental sounds. In the one region, musical sound is an elevated and consciously refined form of the uttered word, and in the other it was and is a vocal means to an essentially nonmusical end. In much of Oceania, careful contact with the spirit realm was considered expedient, if not essential, for the achievement of essentially positive social outcomes.

Whether through family heads or specialists within the society, contact with a variety of supernatural beings was couched in terms of individuals whose personal identity was known and acknowledged in song poetry. Some activities were preemptive from a position of social balance and were intended to achieve ongoing physical and mental health, continued sexual attractiveness, and the availability of adequate food resources. By contrast, remedial activities such as healing and forceful victory over adversaries arose as a result of perceived social imbalance. In all such spheres of activity, whether by invocation or entertainment or supplication, the gods' potentially benevolent powers were exploited and their potentially malevolent attributes avoided. And one major means by which peaceful and productive coexistence with the gods was managed was—and in some regions still is—through the performance of song and dance.

BIBLIOGRAPHY

Ammann, Raymond. *Kanak Dance and Music.* Nouméa, New Caledonia, 1997. A survey of the music and dance output of the culturally diverse nation of New Caledonia.

Feld, Steven. *Sound and Sentiment: Birds, Weeping, Poetics, and Song in Kaluli Expression.* 2d ed. Philadelphia, 1990.

Handy, E. S. Craighill. *Polynesian Religion.* Honolulu, Hawaii, 1927; reprint, New York, 1971. Includes a section on music and dancing and a comprehensive regional bibliography.

Kaeppler, Adrienne L., and J. W. Love, eds. *The Garland Encyclopedia of World Music,* vol. 9, *Australia and the Pacific Islands.* New York, 1998. Contains several articles on the links between religious belief and musical performance.

McLean, Mervyn. *Maori Music.* Auckland, New Zealand, 1996. The most comprehensive publication on Maori music, including references to religious beliefs.

Rossen, Jane Mink. *Songs of Bellona Island.* 2 vols. Copenhagen, 1987.

Tatar, Elizabeth. *Hula Pahu: Hawaiian Drum Dances,* vol. 2, *The Pahu: Sounds of Power.* Honolulu, Hawaii, 1993.

RICHARD M. MOYLE (2005)

MUSIC: MUSIC AND RELIGION IN MESOAMERICA

In Mesoamerica, multifaceted music cultures were characterized by an ancient substratum of shared function and meaning. Common to all cultures is the ritualization of both vocal and instrumental music, as well as dance practices. Many studies have dealt with pre-Hispanic musical traditions, starting with "Aztec Music" (1883) by Hilborne T. Cresson and "Altmexikanische Knochenrasseln" ("Bone-rattles of ancient Mexico," 1898), by Eduard Seler. However, only a few explicitly discuss the autochthonal understanding and underlying religious aspects of these traditions (Stanford, 1984; Stevenson, 1996).

METHODS. A rich volume of source material is available for research in the ancient music cultures of Mesoamerica. There are not only numerous preserved musical instruments, but also a large quantity of depictions in art showing ritual functions of music. Written documents from the early colonial period (sixteenth century and early seventeenth century) also provide enlightening information. Moreover, it is possible to make ethnomusicological comparisons on the basis of cultural continuities.

Archaeology. Archaeological information, such as the context of unearthed sound artifacts, is of great importance, since it provides insight into invaluable information on the function and meaning of music in pre-Hispanic cultures in precise chronological order. Depositing musical instruments into burials indicates a use in death cults, whereas using them as offerings in the fills of superimposed temple structures indicates a use by the cults practiced at these locations. Both cases reflect the concept of music in the spiritual realm. In this way the instruments, which possibly represented the personal property of the deceased, were taken with him or her into the world of the dead. Offerings such as those at the Aztec Templo Mayor in the Valley of Mexico (1325–1521 CE) represent cosmograms that reflect the notion of numinous spheres filled with specific sounds.

Music iconography. From an iconographic point of view, of interest are both the preserved musical instruments and other archaeological findings, such as figurines of musicians and figurative votive representations of musical instruments, particularly the representation of musicians and dancers in stone relief, mural and vase painting, and picture manuscripts. On the basis of these sources, specific functions of the instrumentary and the context of musical practices can be meticulously reconstructed. Sound scrolls or volutes provide a pictographic clue about instrumental music and recitative song, which attained the level of a complex, incompletely decrypted symbolism in Teotihuacán in the Mexican Highlands (c. 150 BCE–750 CE) (LaGamma, 1991). In Mesoamerica, volutes also symbolized scents, smoke, and precious liquids, such as water or blood, and in the depiction of offerings and sacrificial acts they stood for the connection with the spiritual world (Heyden, 1979; Houston and Taube, 2000).

Ethnohistory. The written sources from the early colonial period provide extensive insight into the musical traditions of Mesoamerica. Because Spanish missionaries mainly composed these sources, a critical interpretation is essential to avoid misinterpretations or disinformation. Valuable information is contained within the descriptions of indigenous musical practices with regard to ceremonial dances, processions, and temple rituals but also comes from traditional myths, in which musical instruments play an integral role (see section on Music in Aztec Myth, below). Dictionaries and bilingual chronicles also provide an important contribution to the understanding of autochthonous musical traditions. In addition to Aztec terminology, Mixtec and other terminologies point to a uniform concept of music in Mesoamerica (Stanford, 1966).

Ethnomusicology. Despite multilayered syncretism, certain musical practices of contemporary ethnic groups in Mexico and Guatemala contain pre-Hispanic elements. Thus, ethnomusicological studies can be highly informative. On the other hand, it should be pointed out that the process is increasingly more difficult the more distant the temporal, spatial, and cultural reference points are from one another. The problem becomes clear when looking at the function of wooden rasps among Mexican ethnic groups, such as the Tarahumara (Sierra Madre Occidental, Chihuahua), in comparison to the function of similar instruments made from human thighbones by the Aztecs. While the wooden rasps are played on a wooden resonator and on the head of the sick person in a Tarahumara peyote ceremony (Deimel, 2000), bone rasps were played on a skull resonator in the Aztec death cult to help the deceased on his or her difficult journey into the underworld (Seler, 1898). The rasp, called *omichicahuaztli* (instrument for strengthening the bones) by the Aztecs, has maintained a magical function until the twenty-first century, though its culture-specific meanings must be clearly differentiated.

THE HISTORY OF MUSIC IN MESOAMERICA. Some percussion instruments (idiophones and membranophones) and wind instruments (aerophones) used in Mesoamerica are unique in the world with regard to their shape and technical functions. A historical survey shows that the music cultures of Mesoamerica reflected a more than three-thousand-year-old history prior to the Spanish conquest (Castellanos, 1970; Dultzin Dubín and Nava Gómez Tagle, 1984).

Archaic period (prior to 2500 BCE). It can be assumed that the knowledge of bone flutes was brought into the New World when America was first populated, as these instruments were already produced in the Old World during the Upper Palaeolithic Era (c. 40,000–10,000 BCE). Among the prehistoric musical instruments of Mesoamerica that were made by hunters and gatherers around 10,000 BCE are whistles from the toe bones of ungulates as well as ribs with simple perforations that were possibly used to produce calls (Schöndube, 1986, p. 91, photos 1–2). The ability to imitate specific sounds from the natural environment using the human breath with the aide of acoustical tools represented an effective medium of communication with the outside world with which the environment could be commanded and controlled—as with the imitation of animal calls for the hunt. Sound association must have played an increasingly larger role when making instruments that could produce sounds not present in nature. Among the first instruments in Mesoamerica that required sound association were percussion instruments, such as conch tinkles, bone rasps made from the shoulder blades of deer, and turtle shells that were struck with deer antlers, with which complex rhythms could be created.

Preclassic period (c. 2500 BCE–150 CE). Archaeological finds confirm that pre-Hispanic instrumentary was extensively expanded in the Preclassic period, during which the first large ceremonial centers were erected. Simultaneous with the first use of ceramics, sophisticated whistles and flutes were produced, which can hardly be differentiated from subsequent instruments (Martí, 1968). This suggests similar instruments made out of perishable materials, such as cane flutes, were already in existence centuries earlier. Shell trumpets are among the earliest burial findings of musical instruments in Tlatilco, Valley of Mexico, dated to around 1400–1200 BCE, revealing the existence of complex trade relations (García Moll et al., 1991, p. 220). They possibly assumed an important role as ceremonial signaling instruments whose potent, vibrating sounds could be heard over long distances. In Tlatilco, spherical rattles made from ceramics that could have served as simple hand rattles were also unearthed (García Moll et al., 1991). As suggested by ceramic figurines, they were perhaps attached to the dancers' ritual clothing as row rattles (Feuchtwanger, 1980, p. 140, Figures 28–29). Other figurines show gourd rattles, tripod drums, and flute players (Feuchtwanger, 1980, p. 141, Fig. 32–36). These finds attest to the complexity that musical and dance practices had already attained in the Middle Preclassic period (c. 1200–300 BCE). Among the remarkable instruments that were produced in Tlatilco are whistling bottles, which function on the principle of air pressure against a whistle that is initiated by the movement of water within the axially shaken vase (Martí, 1968, pp. 110–119). Because the instruments seem to sound of their own accord, they must have been related to a particular ritual function with unknown implications. The production of flutes and whistles in the shape of birds and other animals, such as snakes, also suggests a specific cult use, as animals were seen as manifestations of supernatural beings and the instruments cannot always imitate the animal represented.

Mass findings of elaborately decorated shell trumpets in West Mexican shaft tombs, dated to the Late Preclassic period (300 BCE–150 CE), suggest that certain musical instruments became status symbols for high-ranked individuals (Furst, 1966; López Mestas Camberos and Ramos de la Vega, 1998). On the basis of West Mexican figurines that show musicians riding on drums, Peter T. Furst made the interpretation that drums served as vehicles with which the path into the spiritual world was taken (Furst, 1998, pp. 183–185). The high importance of rattles and wooden drums in shamanic practices, which continue in the twenty-first century in the ceremonies of various Mexican ethnic groups, can possibly be attributed to the creation of repetitive rhythmic structures to put the musicians, dancers, and singers into a trance. The high tone frequency of many ceramic wind instruments that lies in a sensitive hearing range and leads to interference effects when played simultaneously can also produce strong psychological effects (Both, 2002b). Among other techniques for selectively evoking altered states of consciousness are hyperventilation and ritual intoxication with highly psychoactive substances obtained from various plants associated with the deities of music (Wasson, 1980, pp. 56–78; Heyden, 1985, pp. 21–39).

Classic period (c. 150–750/900 CE). In the Classic period, in which many important cultures developed in Mesoamerica, the existing instrumentary was further expanded. The large quantity of musical instruments found in ceremonial centers and preserved depictions in mural and relief art show the important position attributed to ritual musical and dance practices. On the basis of the widely distributed production of various ceramic flutes and whistles, it can be seen that even smaller regional centers were characterized by their own unmistakable music. Several findings, including a large find of ceramic flutes in a burial in Tres Zapotes, Veracruz, suggest the use of panpipes in the Early Classic period (Martí, 1968, pp. 95–106). The production of multi-tubular duct flutes, which reached a climax in Teotihuacán, suggests the development of complex scale systems (Martí, 1968, pp. 191–213). The use of slit-drums in the Early Classic period is suggested by findings of figurative votive representations in West Mexico and at Monte Albán, Oaxaca (Furst, 1998, p. 184, Fig. 23; Martí, 1970, p. 104, Fig. 88). The instruments initially exhibit a box shape with four feet, as indicated also by stone sculptures from the Mayan region (Castellanos, 1970, pp. 47–48, Figs. 7.B–8.A).

Also proven to have been used in the Classic period are ceramic trumpets and long tubular trumpets made out of vegetative material that were used for various occasions, such as battles, processions, and autosacrificial rites, according to the preserved depictions. In the mural paintings of Structure 1 in Bonampak, Chiapas (790 CE), there is a preserved mural of a Mayan court ceremony, in which musicians are depicted with tubular trumpets, turtle shells, a tripod drum, and gourd rattles. Shell trumpets were especially important, so much so that sanctuaries were erected for them. An example of this is the Temple of the Plumed Conches in Teotihuacán, dated to 200 CE (Bernal, 1963, photos 15–16, Lám 7). In the Jaguar Compound in Teotihuacán (c. 450–700 CE), mural paintings of forward-walking cats of prey playing shell trumpets were uncovered, which suggests a procession of jaguar impersonators (Fuente, 1996, vol. 1, pp. 115–119). Other murals in Teotihuacán show shell trumpets playing of their own accord and calling certain divine beings associated with the fertility cult (Séjourné, 1966, Fig. 142; Kubler, 1967, Fig. 5). In Teotihuacán the ceremonial instrument was decorated with the iridescent tail plumes of the quetzal bird, and mouthpieces were attached that possibly consisted of circular ear spools. Also in the Mayan region, organological modifications were made to shell trumpets, with the perforation of up to two finger holes. The instruments were possibly deified both in Teotihuacán and in the Maya culture and were closely related to the fertility cult, sacrificial practices, and the underworld. Unusual instruments that were perhaps also associated with the underworld are huge bone rasps made from whale ribs, which were discovered in an offering at Monte Albán (Caso et al., 1967, p. 103, Figs. 70–71). Even if the conceptual implications of the instruments cannot be determined with absolute certainty, it can be assumed that whale bones were considered to be the remains of gigantic beings from bygone eras, such as the bones of mammoths and other prehistoric animals.

Postclassic period (900–1521 CE). In Postclassic Mesoamerica the ancient concepts were further developed. The instrumentary was expanded with bells and metal discs that could have served as gongs (Flores Dorantes, 1979). Bells made out of copper alloys and gold were found in the Sacred Cenote at Chichén Itzá, Yucatán (750/900–1200 CE) and in the tombs reused by Zapotecs and Mixtecs at Monte Albán

(900–1400 CE). Fine metallic sounds became an expression of stately power (Hosler, 1994).

Aztec music culture finally developed in the Late Postclassic period (1325–1521 CE). Rattle sticks became important instruments and were attributed with a magical function in cults dedicated to rain, water, and mountain gods (Neumann, 1976, pp. 247–248). The preserved slit-drums, which either exhibited an elaborately decorated box shape or zoomorphic and anthropomorphic shapes, suggest high craftsmanship in the production of wooden drums (Castañeda and Mendoza, 1933). On the famous tripod drum from Malinalco, the "four-movement" (*nahui ollin*) sign for the fifth world era and a representation of the deity of music Xochipilli (Flower Prince) in a bird costume are depicted. The drum is additionally ornamented with Aztec war imagery, such as dancing jaguars and eagles as well as volutes in the form of the *atl-tlachinolli* sign, the metaphor for war (Seler, 1904). A stone representation of a slit-drum to scale, on the other hand, shows Macuilxochitl (Five Flower), a deity of music closely related to Xochipilli. The imagery of his eyes is noteworthy, into which the palms of two hands are incorporated, as are the flowers surrounding the mouth, a metaphor for music and sacrifice. In addition, jaguar pelts are represented on the sides of the drum, thus indicating the existence of a hybrid instrument consisting of a slit-drum and a double-sided cylindrical drum, which could have been played by two priests simultaneously.

In the excavations of the previous Aztec temple precinct of Tenochtitlán in the center of Mexico City, many musical instruments were unearthed, such as metal bells, conch tinkles, ceramic flutes, shell trumpets, fragments of shell trumpets, and incense ladles with rattles built into the handles (López Luján, 1993). The context of the findings provides highly informative data about ritual music practiced in the temple cult of the Aztecs and reflects the association of specific sounds with the aquatic underworld or the paradisiacal spheres of the rain god Tlaloc.

In several shrines called the Red Temples, the Aztec deities of music and musical instruments were honored in the form of figurative votive representations (Olmedo Vera, 2002). In a court east of the Templo Mayor, the monumental representation of a shell trumpet was found next to an altar, from which it possibly was knocked down (Luna Erreguerena, 1982). The sculpture underscores the high position of the trumpet, because no other instrument was sculpted in a comparable size.

Written sources from the early colonial period suggest that in Late Postclassic Mesoamerica a differentiation was made between temple music practiced by specialized priests and court and palace music practiced by professional musicians (Both, 2001). It can be assumed that similar differentiations were made in earlier cultures. The priests responsible for the temple music of Tenochtitlán introduced the nightly sacrificial practices with shell trumpets in the *tlatlapitzaliztli* ritual, the "frequent sounding of wind instruments" (Sahagún, 1997, p. 80). At midnight began the *tozohualiztli* ritual, the night watch of the drummers, which was connected with songs and astronomical observations from atop the temples (Sahagún, 1997, p. 80). The ritual human sacrifice was accompanied by shell trumpets and tripod drums (Sahagún, 1950–1982, vol. 3, bk. 2, p. 28). In a temple designated as "house of mist" (*ayauhcalli*), priests sounded shell trumpets and gongs during ritual cleansing (Sahagún, 1950–1982, vol. 3, bk. 2, p. 77). Ritual music was also practiced by women, who played slit-drums or rattle sticks as representatives of female deities and appeared as temple singers and dancers in various ceremonies.

While the priest-musicians lived in the temple precinct of Tenochtitlán, the professional musicians formed a group that resided at the court. They were responsible for providing music in the ruler's palace and for large ceremonial dances in the temple precinct, in which cult activities such as ritual human sacrifices were interwoven (Both, 2001). From the depiction of circle dances in picture manuscripts, it can be seen that dancers often carried gourd rattles decorated with feathers, whereas the drummers were positioned in the center of the dancers (Martí and Prokosch Kurath, 1964). In addition, there are reports of music by trumpets, pipes, and portable drums during battles, which served as distraction noise for surprise attacks and for giving signals (Moreno, 1961). It is unclear whether priests or court musicians were responsible for the noise, or whether there was a third group of specialized musicians among the eagle and jaguar warriors.

MUSIC IN AZTEC MYTH. In the Aztec cosmogony some key information shines light on the ritual function and meaning of musical instruments in Mesoamerica. The Legend of the Suns tells of the origin of the shell trumpet while discussing the creation of humankind (Johansson, 1997). At the beginning of the fifth world era the divine creator Quetzalcoatl (Feathered Snake) travels down into the underworld into the kingdom of the ruler of the dead, Mictlantecuhtli. Quetzalcoatl is supposed to procure the bones of the beings of foregone eras, which is to be ground up and mingled with the sacrificed blood of deities to create humankind. In order to be allowed to take the bones, Quetzalcoatl is to blow on the shell of the ruler of the underworld four times and turn to the four corners of the world when doing so. However, Quetzalcoatl must first create the shell trumpet by removing the tip of the spire of the shell thus producing the embouchure. Quetzalcoatl accomplishes what seems impossible through his magical powers with the aide of caterpillars and black bees, which bore a channel into the shell. After Quetzalcoatl performs the shell trumpet ritual, Mictlantecuhtli must let his opponent leave with the bones.

Noteworthy about this myth is that the creation of humankind was announced in the underworld with the shell trumpet, and thus tremendous creative potential is attributed to its sound. As a wind instrument with a spiral-shaped channel, the trumpet was closely related to the magical powers of Quetzalcoatl (Corona Núñez, 1966). The myth additionally provides an explanation for why musical instruments had to be played four times facing the four corners of the world to guarantee the effectiveness of a ritual. This musical practice was paraphrased with a metaphor that can be translated as "carry something [i.e., the musical instrument or the sound] four times in all directions around the precious circular greenstone [i.e., the center of the world]" (*nauhpa xictlayahualochti in chalchiuhteyahualco*). It is important to ascertain that numerical symbolism and musical directionalism, even in conjunction with other instruments, such as in the flute ritual of the deity Tezcatlipoca (Smoking Mirror), played an important role (Both, 2002a).

Another myth that has been handed down in two versions explains the history of the origins of the tripod drum (*huehuetl*) and the slit-drum (*teponaztli*) (Ceballos Novelo, 1956). At a time when music still did not exist on the earth, the instruments lived as singers at the court of the sun; one had three feet and the other had large ears. To give humans the ability to conduct ceremonies and thus connect with the deities, a representative of Tezcatlipoca in one version and the wind god Ehecatl in the other takes up the journey to the sun with ritual songs to induce the singers to manifest themselves as drums on earth. For this purpose they call up whales and turtles that form a bridge over the ocean to the sun. The sun forbids the singers to hear the song, but it is so powerful that they are enticed to come to earth.

In this myth the drums are described as divine creatures that originate from the sun. Based on the imagery on preserved instruments, these beings could have been Xochipilli and Macuilxochitl. It is therefore assumed that drums represented sounding idols—"vessels" in which the respective deities resided during the ritual. In this regard, music was possibly seen as the ritual voices of divine beings. This principle is still present in the twenty-first century in ethnic groups in Mexico. Thus, the deified ceramic drums of the Maya-Lacandón (Selva Lacandona, Chiapas) exhibit sounding holes that are so situated that the sound emanates from behind the effigy of the deity K'ayom (Ochoa Cabrera et al., 1998, p. 70), and the holes situated in the body of the tripod drum of the Huichol (Sierra Madre Occidental, Nayarit und Jalisco) are considered to be the mouth of the deity T'epu (Berrin, 1978, pp. 180–181). In Mesoamerica this concept was also extended to other instruments, in particular ceramic flutes (Both, 2002a). According to ethnohistorical sources, Tezcatlipoca spoke through the flute to announce his will (Sahagún, 1950–1982, vol. 7, bk. 6, p. 50).

In Mesoamerica, musicians assumed the position of expert mediators. They established a form of communication with the spiritual world that helped the voices of the gods to be heard, and they were therefore attributed high reverence. The autochthonal understanding also explains the high degree of formalization of musical practices, which looked back upon a three-thousand-year varied history at the time of the Spanish Conquest. Even shortly after the Conquest, Spanish missionaries prohibited their practice because it represented an integral component of religious activities.

SEE ALSO Afterlife, article on Mesoamerican Concepts; Aztec Religion; Deification; Drama, article on Mesoamerican Dance and Drama; Funeral Rites, article on Mesoamerican Funeral Rites; Human Sacrifice, article on Aztec Rites; Iconography, article on Mesoamerican Iconography; Maya Religion; Mesoamerican Religions, article on Classic Cultures; Shamanism, overview articles; Tezcatlipoca; Tlaloc; Underworld.

BIBLIOGRAPHY

Bernal, Ignacio. *Teotihuacan.* Mexico City, 1963.

Berrin, Kathleen, ed. *Art of the Huichol Indians.* New York, 1978.

Both, Arnd Adje. "Die Musikkultur der Azteken." *Mitteilungen der Berliner Gesellschaft für Anthropologie, Ethnologie und Urgeschichte* 22 (2001): 43–48.

Both, Arnd Adje. "Aztec Flower-Flutes: The Symbolic Organization of Sound in Late Postclassic Mesoamerica." In *Studien zur Musikarchäologie,* vol. 3, edited by Ellen Hickmann, Anne D. Kilmer, and Ricardo Eichmann, pp. 279–289. Rahden, Germany, 2002a.

Both, Arnd Adje. "The Songs of Tlaloc: Interference of Ten Ceramic Duct Flutes, Offering 89 of the Aztec Templo Mayor." *Journal of the Acoustical Society of America* 112, no. 5 (2002b): 2367.

Caso, Alfonso, Ignacio Bernal, and Jorge R. Acosta. *La cerámica de Monte Alban.* Mexico City, 1967.

Castañeda, Daniel, and Vincente T. Mendoza. *Instrumental precortesiano: Instrumentos de percusión.* Vol. 1. Mexico City, 1933.

Castellanos, Pablo. *Horizontes de la música precortesiana.* Mexico City, 1970.

Ceballos Novelo, Roque C. "Los instrumentos musicales: Su origen legendario." In *Estudios Antropológicos publicados en homenaje al doctor Manuel Gamio,* pp. 317–320. Mexico City, 1956.

Corona Núñez, José. "La palabra creadora representada por el joyel del viento" In *Summa Antropológica en homenaje a Roberto J. Weitlaner,* pp. 187–192. Mexico City, 1966.

Cresson, Hilborne T. "Aztec Music." *Proceedings of the Academy of Natural Sciences of Philadelphia* (1883): 86–94.

Deimel, Claus. "Der Peyote-Schraper der Rarámuri (Tarahumara)." In *Jaguar und Schlange: Der Kosmos der Indianer in Mittel- und Südamerika,* edited by Niedersächsisches Landesmuseum Hannover and Ethnologisches Museum, SMB PK, pp. 169–180. Berlin, 2000.

Dultzin Dubín, Susana, and José Antonio Nava Gómez Tagle. "La música en el panorama histórico de Mesoamérica." In *La música de México,* vol. 1, *Historia,* pt. 1, *Periodo prehispánico (ca. 1500 A.C. a 1521 D.C.),* edited by Julio Estrada, pp. 16–34. Mexico City, 1984.

Feuchtwanger, Franz. "Tlatilco-Terrakotten von Akrobaten, Ballspielern, Musikanten, und Tanzenden." *Baessler-Archiv,* n.s., 28 (1980): 131–153.

Flores Dorantes, Felipe de Jesús. "Los instrumentos musicales de metal en Mesoamérica." In *Los procesos de cambio: XV Mesa Redonda,* vol. 2. Mexico City, 1979.

Fuente, Beatriz de la, ed. *La pintura mural prehispánica en México.* Vol. 1, *Teotihuacán.* Mexico City, 1996.

Furst, Peter T. "Shaft Tombs, Shell Trumpets, and Shamanism: A Culture-Historical Approach to West Mexican Archaeology." Ph.D. diss., University of California, Los Angeles, 1966.

Furst, Peter T. "Shamanistic Symbolism, Transformation, and Deities in West Mexican Funerary Art." In *Ancient West Mexico: Art and Archaeology of the Unknown Past*, edited by Richard F. Townsend, pp. 168–203. Chicago, 1998.

García Moll, Roberto, Daniel Juárez Cossio, Carmen Pijoan Aguade, M. Elena Salas Cuesta, and Marcela Salas Cuesta. *Catálogo de entierros de San Luis Tlatilco, México: Temporada IV.* Mexico City, 1991.

Heyden, Doris. *La comunicación no verbal en el ritual prehispánico.* Cuadernos de Trabajo 25. Mexico City, 1979.

Heyden, Doris. *Mitología y simbolismo de la flora en el México prehipánico.* Mexico City, 1985.

Hosler, Dorothy. *The Sounds and Colors of Power: The Sacred Metallurgical Technology of Ancient West Mexico.* Cambridge, Mass., 1994.

Houston, Stephen, and Karl Taube. "An Archaeology of the Senses: Perception and Cultural Expression in Ancient Mesoamerica." *Cambridge Archaeological Journal* 10, no. 2 (2000): 261–294.

Johansson, Patrick K. "La fecundación del hombre en el mictlan y el origen de la vida breve." *Estudios de Cultura Náhuatl* 27 (1997): 69–88.

Kubler, George. *The Iconography of the Art of Teotihuacán.* Studies in Pre-Columbian Art and Archaeology no. 4. Washington, D.C., 1967.

LaGamma, Alisa. "A Visual Sonata at Teotihuacan." *Ancient Mesoamerica* 2, no. 2 (1991): 275–284.

López Luján, Leonardo. *Las ofrendas del Templo Mayor de Tenochtitlán.* Mexico City, 1993.

López Mestas Camberos, Lorenza, and Jorge Ramos de la Vega. "Excavating the Tomb at Huitzilapa." In *Ancient West Mexico: Art and Archaeology of the Unknown Past*, edited by Richard F. Townsend, pp. 52–70. Chicago, 1998.

Luna Erreguerena, Pilar. "El caracol marino de piedra rosa." In *El Templo Mayor: Excavaciones y estudios*, edited by Eduardo Matos Moctezuma, pp. 241–244. Mexico City, 1982.

Martí, Samuel. *Instrumentos musicales precortesianos.* Mexico City, 1968.

Martí, Samuel. *Alt-Amerika: Musik der Indianer in präkolumbischer Zeit.* Musik des Altertums, vol. 2, Musikgeschichte in Bildern: Altamerika. Leipzig, 1970.

Martí, Samuel, and Gertrude Prokosch Kurath. *Dances of Anáhuac: The Choreography and Music of Precortesian Dances.* Viking Fund Publications in Anthropology no. 38. Chicago, 1964.

Moreno, Salvador. "La música en la Historia Verdadera de la Conquista de la Nueva España." *Cuadernos Hispanoamericanos* 134 (1961): 201–215.

Neumann, Frank J. "The Rattle-Stick of Xipe Totec: A Shamanic Element in Pre-Hispanic Mesoamerican Religion." In *Actas del XII Congreso International de Americanistas* 2 (1976): 243–251.

Ochoa Cabrera, José Antonio, Claudia Linda Cortés Hernández, and Nancy Cortés Hernández. *Los oficios de k'ayom: Música Hach Winik (Lacandona).* Mexico City, 1998.

Olmedo Vera, Bertina. *Los Templos Rojos del Recinto Sagrado de Tenochtitlan.* Colección Científica 439. Mexico City, 2002.

Sahagún, Fray Bernardino de. *The Florentine Codex.* Translated from the Aztec into English by Arthur J. O. Anderson and Charles E. Dibble. Santa Fe, N. Mex., 1950–1982. Sixteenth-century manuscript.

Sahagún, Fray Bernardino de. *Primeros Memoriales.* Paleography of Nahuatl text and English translation by Thelma D. Sullivan; completed and revised, with additions, by H. B. Nicholson, Arthur J. O. Anderson, Charles E. Dibble, Eloise Quiñones Keber, and Wayne Ruwet. Norman, Okla., 1997. Sixteenth-century manuscript.

Schöndube Baumbach, Otto. "Instrumentos musicales del occidente de México: Las Tumbas de Tiro y otras evidencias." *Relaciones: Estudios de Historia y Sociedad* 7, no. 28 (1986): 85–110.

Séjourné, Laurette. *Arquitéctura y pintura en Teotihuacán.* Mexico City, 1966.

Seler, Eduard. "Altmexikanische Knochenrasseln." *Globus* 74, no. 6 (1898): 85–93.

Seler, Eduard. "Die holzgeschnitzte Pauke von Malinalco und das Zeichen atl-tlachinolli." *Mitteilungen der Anthropologischen Gesellschaft in Wien* 34 (1904): 222–274.

Stanford, Thomas. "A Linguistic Analysis of Music and Dance Terms from Three Sixteenth-Century Dictionaries of Mexican Indian Languages." *Inter-American Institute for Musical Research Yearbook* 2 (1966): 101–159.

Stanford, Thomas. "El concepto indígena de la música, el canto y la danza." In *La música de México,* vol. 1 *Historia,* pt. 1, *Periodo prehispánico (ca. 1500 A.C. a 1521 D.C.),* edited by Julio Estrada, pp. 63–76. Mexico City, 1984.

Stevenson, Robert M. "Reflexiones sobre el concepto de música precortesiana en México." *Heterofonía* 114–115 (1996): 25–37.

Wasson, R. Gordon. *The Wondrous Mushroom: Mycolatry in Mesoamerica.* New York, 1980.

ARND ADJE BOTH (2005)

MUSIC: MUSIC AND RELIGION IN SOUTH AMERICA

South America is a remarkably musical and religious continent. All of its countries show vigorous popular and indigenous traditions, which have music and dance as its core. Catholicism is the predominant official religion in all of South America, but the continental religious scenarios are diverse and constantly changing, especially with the recent growth of evangelic churches and with the development of many alternative religions, most of them derived from local and syncretic practices. One common trait in the majority of these South American religious practices is the role of music in religiosity in communicating with spiritual beings.

The centrality of music in South American sacred rituals has been indicated not only by ethnological and ethnohistorical research, but also by archeological evidences of pre-

Columbian musical instruments. During the last decades, the knowledge about South American pre-Columbian societies has changed the vision of these groups as simple survivals of Andean complex societies. According to recent archeological research, the settlements around the Amazon River were densely inhabited complex societies, organized in agricultural chieftains with intense ritual life. These findings will change the perceptions of Amazonian societies of the past and also of their music. In Brazil, due to climatic conditions and to the fact that most of the musical instruments were made of perishable materials, few archeological evidences have been found until now. One exception is the deer bone flute found at the Northeastern Zona da Mata's Madre do Brejo site, estimated to be two thousand years old. On the other hand, from the Andes and the Pacific coast there are several archeological records of musical instruments such as pottery rattles, metal cymbals, stone and pottery horns and flutes, and leather and wood membranophones.

Rich ethnographical material comes from the writings of the first voyagers who visited South America during the sixteenth and seventeenth centuries. One example is Jean de Léry's description of the religious musical rituals of the Tupi Indians of the Brazilian coast, considered to be the first ethnomusicological account. Voyagers who crossed the continent from the Brazilian coast to Peru through a pre-colonial path named Peabiru provided descriptions of the Guarani Indians' large religious festivals. There are accounts of such musical rituals in various South American lowlands societies, and archeological research reinforces these descriptions with the discovery of enormous pottery vessels used in drinking rituals.

Since the beginning of the invasion of South America by European peoples, missionaries made a systematic and strategic effort to convert indigenous societies to Christianity, trying to make them abandon their beliefs and native cults. The procedures of the missionaries were sometimes violent, involving even the destruction of musical instruments and the demonization of certain music repertoires. European Church music was largely used for this goal, including translation of Christian texts into native languages. Music was largely used to attract indigenous peoples to the missions. A remarkable example of the dimension of these missions is the so-called Sete Povos das Missões (Missions' seven peoples), a conglomerate of Jesuit missions founded in the region of southern Brazil and northern Argentina in the seventeenth century. In these *reduções* (reductions, as those missions are called), hundreds of Indians were taught to construct and play European early Baroque music. At the end of the seventeenth century, Sepp, a Jesuit missionary especially dedicated to musical activities, wrote a letter in which he reported that music was played daily by the Indian musicians at mass and that if all those musicians were assembled, they would amount to 3,000 people. This strategy was largely employed in South America in general.

During the Brazilian colonial period (1500–1822), large populations of people were brought from western Africa to work as slaves. The religious practices of these people and their Afro-American descendents are very musical, and this religious musicality influenced much of Brazilian contemporary music and culture. Much historical data about the Afro-Brazilian religious and musical practices was preserved. In contrast, in Peru, the music of African descendents was ignored and emphasis was placed upon the Indigenous musical heritage. However, both cases show that the Colonial period was crucial in the construction of South American popular religiosity. The colonial heritage is usually analysed through the idea of syncretism in all South American popular celebrations, many of them part of the Catholic calendar, though there are notable regional differences.

Many popular contemporary Brazilian festivals have dance and music as their central axis. For example, there is the Festa do Divino Espírito Santo (Holy Spirit's Feast), which occurs seven weeks after Easter, in which several musical genres are represented, such as *congadas* and *catiras.* During this ritual, a group of singers visits a villager's house asking for donations. Between Christmas and January 6, hundreds of cities in Brazil celebrate the Folia de Reis (Companies of Kings), their songs recalling the Three Kings' journey to welcome the baby Jesus. Musicians playing *viola* (five-stringed guitar), *pandeiro* (tambourine) and *cavaquinho* (four-stringed mandolin-like guitar) accompany the singers. During the Festas Juninas (June Festivals), which celebrate Saint Peter, Saint Anthony and Saint John, the musical genre played the most is *forró,* which originated in northeastern Brazil and is usually played by a trio of accordionist-singers, a triangle player, and a *zabumba* player (the *zabumba* is a sort of bass drum).

If Brazilian popular religiosity expresses itself through musical practices, one may say the same happens in all of South America, considering its common cultural heritage from the indigenous peoples and the colonizers and immigrants from Europe. Other examples are the Señor de los temblores (Cuzco, Peru), the Señor de los Milagros (Lima, Peru) and the *Cuasimodo* (Chile), this last example a religious procession that takes place on the Sunday after Easter. There is great variability concerning the musical instruments employed and their repertoires.

In Peru, Catholic and agricultural popular festivals are the center of community life in Andean villages like Conima, where they occur at least once a month. In the rituals of *t'inka* and *ch'alla,* Aymara Peruvians worship local deities and also sacred places, such as certain rivers that are conceived as animate and powerful. The maker of the musical instruments is a community member who is considered to be the owner of esoteric knowledge. Recent investigations of similar rites have identified symbols of Indian identity and subversion codified in music, choreography and mask styles.

Since the second half of the twentieth century, ethnological research has shown that shamanism constitutes not only a curing system but a fundamentally religious practice, facilitating the interaction between humans and supernatural beings. South American lowlands indigenous societies' worldviews reveal simultaneously a deep religious sense and a musical hearing of the world. In all these peoples, there is a central role of the shaman both as curer and mediator between human and spiritual beings. The connection between mythic beliefs and everyday life makes it possible to think of these cosmologies as native systems of thought about the universe, or, in other words, as religions.

The indigenous peoples who live in central Brazil's Upper Xingu Park believe their cosmos is populated by spiritual beings that severely interfere in human lives. They are monstrous invisible spirits, related to certain animals,, plants, and other natural beings, and can only be seen by the shaman through his tobacco-induced trance. For the Xinguanos, all human sicknesses originate from these spirits' actions on the body, into which they throw an invisible object in order to provoke sickness and death and steal the precious human souls. The cure of a sick person is highly related to the aesthetic dimension in such a way that the restoration of health may be equated with the restoration of the original condition of beauty. A ritual must be performed in which the music of the specific spirit causing the sickness is played. All native music belongs to these spirits, and it is played in curing rituals in order to please the spirits and to transform them from the sick person's enemy to his life-enduring ally.

The Guarani compose one of the largest indigenous societies of South America, the total population amounting to about 150,000 people living in Paraguay, Bolivia, Brazil, Argentina and Uruguay. After more than five hundred years of contact with European colonizers, of submission to forced labor by Portuguese and Spanish invaders and of threats to eradicate their religious beliefs by Jesuit missionaries, the Guarani continue to speak their language and perform their music in daily rituals. In daily shamanistic rituals, as the Sun, the creator hero, sets in the horizon, the Guarani sing, play and dance, for music is the path to reach the divinities. The communication with the spiritual beings is a means for the Guarani to express their orphaned state, for their ancestors were abandoned by the Gods as they left this earth. Guarani rituals serve to ward off sadness and exercise the body,, and at the same time serve to care for the health of the entire earth. The Kaiowa Guarani use maraca rattles and rhythmic sticks, and the Mbyá Guarani use also guitar, fiddle and drum. The Chiriguano Guarani from Bolivia, adorned with leather or wooden masks, play the *quena* flute during the extended festival calendar. The Mbyá use of guitar and violin is an example of how musical instruments introduced by the European colonizers in the early years of contact were appropriated by the Indians into their native mythology. As early as the seventeenth century, a dictionary of Guarani language, elaborated by the Jesuits, presents a definition of *mbaraka* that includes, beside the rattle, string instruments such as the guitar and fiddle. Currently the Guarani in southeastern Brazil and Argentina use in their rituals a five-stringed guitar that is tuned in a special way.

All indigenous rituals show a central role of music, and in fact they may be considered music rituals. At the same time, these ritual activities concern spiritual or supernatural beings, myths and mythic beliefs, or in other words, their cosmology. Ethnologists have been studying Amerindian cosmologies as essentially shamanic, arguing that the figure of the shaman centers all ritual and mythic thought, for he is the subject who can perceive different perspectives to the universe. Several ethnographies emphasize the shamanic practice as both healing and musical, such as the Shipibo-Conibo of the Peruvian Amazon, whose shamanic songs are transformed into invisible drawings that are printed on the patient's skin.

In the last few decades, South American indigenous societies have experienced the reinforcement of native identities and, at the same time, faced the increasing presence of various protestant churches in their villages. In this scenario, in which native cosmologies reveal both adaptation and appropriation of elements of these churches, the role of music remains strategic, as has been shown for the Wichi of Argentina.

In fact, since the 1990s there has been a noticeable growth of evangelic churches—especially the Pentacostal movement—throughout all South America. This growth parallels the retraction of Catholicism, even in Brazil, which is considered the largest Catholic country in the world. A reaction of the Catholic Church has been its so-called Movimento Carismático (Charismatic Movement), which largely employs typically evangelic strategies directly related to music. In this sense, there is a stimulation of musical practices and an opening to a variety of musical genres, particularly those appreciated by the younger generations, such as rock and rap music. This is a model imported from North American protestant churches, widely adopted in Brazil and all South American countries. American black music, like gospel, has been a fundamental influence on this popularization of the evangelic music movement. The Catholic charismatic movement has been trying to adopt the use of popular music genres, but the church's conservative leadership does not approve of this modification. For example, the Vatican released a document ordering the return to the earlier mass ceremony, condemning the use of popular music.

In Brazilian culture, the official and the popular, as much as the religious and the superstitious, intermingle in such a way that there is a generative process that is constantly re-elaborated. Brazilian religiosity is a composite of distinct approaches to the sacred that is simultaneously inclusive and exclusive, moving towards syncretism. New religious centers develop alongside the official religions, creating an ever changing and growing religious field, especially among the poorest classes. A similar movement happens in Brazilian music in general, constantly and creatively transforming itself and generating new musical genres, as if religion and music constitute a means of expressing both the protest for the social condition and the meaning of existence. Recent studies show that, instead of over-emphasizing the African components in South American black musical traditions, one should envision all the rich dialectics of these practices.

A famous example of Brazilian syncretism is Candomblé, an African American religion organized around the cult of African mythic ancestors called *orixás,* but also with reference to indigenous figures (the so-called *caboclas*) and to Catholic saints. The music of its cults, understood as a fundamental element of Candomblé, is the only means of getting in touch with these ancestor spirits through trance and possession. Candomblé cults have been growing in Argentina and Uruguay. In Uruguay, African descendent populations take to the streets of the capital, Montevideo, many times per year with their drum orchestras. These are rituals of renewing the cultural identity that are marked by a warrior ethos, all these meanings being generated through music.

In South American cities, young generations following the New Age movement of the eighties are still searching for new ways of developing their religiosity. Due to this, there has been an important growth of practitioners of oriental religions, like Buddhism. However, there is also a vigorous valorization of local and regional identities which points to more authentic local practices, for example, those that mix spirituality and the indigenous world. One example in this direction is the recent psychotropic plants-based religions, like União do Vegetal (Union of the Vegetal) and Santo Daime (Saint Daime), which largely use *ayahuasca* (*Banisteriopsis caapi*).The former religion has in its musical repertoire the master's *hinos* (hymns), which are sung for the purpose of teaching and leading the collective hallucinogenic experience. Santo Daime and União do Vegetal churches, as well as the practice of *mestizo* shamans and *vegetalistas* (vegetalists), have been spreading in many locations all over Brazil and neighboring countries, not only around the Amazonian villages from where they originated, but also in large cities. According to Peruvian Amazon *vegetalistas,* the power of curing and traveling through time and space is acquired through the memorization of magical melodies and songs called *icaros.* These songs are learned from plant, animal and stone spirits during dreams or visions.

In northeastern Brazil, the *toadas* and *cantigas* lead the religious rituals in which the participants drink a psychotropic plant called *Jurema.* Amongst indigenous peoples of this region, similar rituals are called *toré.* The *toré* rituals exhibit different configurations according to the group. During the drinking of *jurema,* the Xukurú Indians sing the *toré* songs accompanied by rattle and flutes made of plastic. In the African-indigenous ritual called *catimbó-jurema,* the singers are accompanied by drums. Both of these *jurema* drinking rituals reveal striking Catholic elements.

All the musical performances mentioned here, and others like Carnaval, are expanding the connotations of the religious field to other social and political domains. Though they may not be seen by its agents as instruments to make politics, these rituals reinforce the bonds of social identity by joining religious and ethnic symbols. Thus, many groups that have suffered social prejudice throughout their history recognize that their culture was preserved through the performance of their religious rituals, as the case of Brazilian northeastern Indians, for whom these practices function today as an affirmation of their emerging ethnicity. This particular mixture of the ethnic and the religious is certainly a characteristic of the relationship between music and religion in South America.

BIBLIOGRAPHY

Arinze, Francis Card. *Redemptionis Sacramentum: On Certain Matters to Be Observed or to Be Avoided Regarding the Most Holy Eucharistic.* Rome, 2004.

Basso, Ellen. *Musical View of the Universe: Kalapalo Myth and Ritual Performances.* Philadelphia, 1985.

Bastide, Roger. *As Religiões Africanas no Brasil* (The African religions in Brazil). São Paulo, 1985.

Béhague, Gerard H. "Introduction." In *Music and Black Ethnicity: The Caribbean and South America.* Miami, 1992.

Bigenho, Michelle. *Sounding Indigenous: Authenticity in Bolivian Music Performance.* New York, 2002.

Birman, Patrícia, ed. *Religião e Espaço Público* (Religion and public space). São Paulo, 2003.

Carvalho, J. J. *Ritual and Music of the Sango Cults of Recife, Brazil.* Ph.D. dissertation. Belfast, 1984.

Cooley, Timothy. "Casting shadows in the field: an introduction." In *Shadows in the Field: New Perspectives for Fieldwork in Ethnomusicology,* edited by Gregory Barz and Timothy Cooley. New York, 1997.

DaMatta, Roberto. *Carnivals, Rogues, and Heroes: An Anthropological Interpretation of the Brazilian Dilemma.* Notre Dame, Ind., 1992.

D'Harcourt, R. and D'Harcourt, M. *La música de los incas y sus supervivencias.* Lima, 1990 [1925].

Ferreira, Luis. *Los Tambores del Candombe.* Montevideo, 1997.

Ferretti, Sérgio. *Repensando o sincretismo* (Rethinking syncretism). São Paulo, 1995.

Garcia, Miguel. "Conversión religiosa y cambio cultural." *Latin American Music Review,* 19 (1998): 2.

Gebhart-Sayer, Angelika. "Una terapia estética de los diseños visionarios del ayahuasca entre los Shipibo-Conibo." *América Indígena* 46, no. 1 (1986).

Geertz, Clifford. "Religion as a Cultural System." In *The Interpretation of Cultures. Selected Essays.* New York, 2000.

Grünewald, Rodrigo (Org.). *Toré: Regime encantado dos índios do Nordeste* (Toré: the enchanted regime of the Northeastern Indians). Recife, Brazil, 2004.

Guss, David M. "'Indianness' and the Construction of Ethnicity in the Day of the Monkey." *Latin American Studies Series.* No. 9 (1995).

Langdon, E. J. and Baer, G., eds. *Portals of Power: Shamanism in South America.* Albuquerque, 1992.

Lucas, Glaura. *Os Sons do Rosário: O Congado Mineiro dos Arturos e Jatobá* (The sounds of Rosário: the Congado Mineiro of Arturos and Jatobá). Belo Horizonte, Brazil, 2002.

Luna, Luis E. "Icaros: Magic Melodies." In: *Portals of Power: Shamanism in South America,* edited by Jean Langdon and Gerhard Baer. Albuquerque, 1992.

Menezes Bastos, Rafael José. "Apùap World Hearing: On the Kamayurá Phono-Auditory System and the Anthropological Concept of Culture." *The World of Music* 41, no.1 (1999): 85–96.

Montardo, Deise Lucy. *Através do "Mbaraka": Música e Xamanismo Guarani* (Through the *Mbaraka:* Guarani music and shamanism). Doctoral dissertation in anthropology. São Paulo, Brazil, 2002.

Novaes, Regina. "Errantes do Novo Milênio: salmos e versículos bíblicos noespaço público." In: *Religião e Espaço Público,* edited by Patrícia Birman. São Paulo, Brazil, 2003.

Piedade, Acácio. *O Canto do Kaw̲oká: Música, Cosmologia e Filosofia entre os Wauja do Alto X̲ingu* (The chant of Kawoká: Music, cosmology and philosophy among the Wauja from the Upper Xingu). Doctoral dissertation in anthropology. Florianópolis, Brazil, 2004.

Reily, Suzel Ana. *Voices of the Magi: Enchanted Journeys in Southeast Brazil.* Chicago, 2002.

Romero, Raúl R., ed. *Musica, danzas y mascaras en los Andes.* Lima, 1993.

Rondon, Víctor. "Música y ritualidad misional en el Chile colonial: raíces de la religiosidad popular actual." *Série estudos 4.* Porto Alegre, Brazil, 2000.

Roosevelt, Anna. C., ed. *Amazonian Indians from Prehistory to the Present: Anthropological Perspectives.* Tucson, Ariz., 1994.

Sánchez, Wálter. "La Plaza Tomada: Proceso histórico y etnogénesis musical entre los Chiriguano de Bolivia." *Latin American Music Review* 19 (1998): 2.

Sepp, Antônio. *Viagem às Missões jesuíticas e trabalhos apostólicos* (Journey to Jesuit missions and apostolic work; 1698). São Paulo, 1980.

Turino, Thomas. *Moving Away from Silence: Music of the Peruvian Altiplano and the Experience of Urban Migration.* Chicago, 1993.

Vianna, Hermano. *The Mystery of Samba: Popular Music and National Identity in Brazil.* Durham, N.C., 1999.

Viveiros de Castro, Eduardo. "Cosmological Deixis and Amerindian Perspectivism." *Journal of the Royal Anthropological Institute* (September 1998).

Wright, Robin M., ed. *Transformando os Deuses: os múltiplos sentidos da conversão* (Transforming the Gods: multiple senses of conversion). Campinas, Brazil, 1999.

Acácio Tadeu de Camargo Piedade (2005)
Deise Lucy Oliveira Montardo (2005)

MUSIC: MUSIC AND RELIGION IN THE MIDDLE EAST

Highly developed musical cultures entirely devoted to religious worship flourished in ancient Mesopotamia and Egypt. Each was distinguished by a well-organized ritual, a rich hymnody, numerous musical instruments, and an established musical theory. In Mesopotamia cuneiform texts, artworks, reliefs, plaques, and seals provide a wealth of information concerning the musical culture. In Egypt musical scenes frequently appear on the walls of tombs because the Egyptians believed that pictorial reproductions of domestic life secured a pleasurable existence in the other life. Few musical instruments have been excavated in Mesopotamia, but a great many have been found in Egypt, where the aridity of the desert has preserved them from decomposition.

Despite the great variety of cultures in the region, the general approach to sacred music, its nature, function, and meaning, was imbued with a spirit of unity. The music has been characterized as normative and refined, and as giving primacy to such diverse performing styles as singing to a solo instrumental accompaniment, performing with an instrumental group, dancing, and other ritual gestures. Performances were confined to a distinct class of well-trained male and female musicians and dancers.

It is tempting to conclude that this music lacked the freshness, spontaneity, and devotional expression characteristic of folk worship, yet despite its refinement and professionalism it remained linked in many ways to its magical antecedents and the divine origins from which it drew its vitality. Being essentially associated with worship, sacred music served to honor the gods in the performance of the daily liturgy in temples and to accompany the traditional funeral rites and the annual festivals. The link between past and present and between humanity and the cosmos is evident in this music in many respects. Thus the Babylonian New Year festival symbolized the reduction of the primordial epoch to a scale of annual duration. This annual celebration of plant life and fertility has been associated with a wedding of the gods and with the epic of the creation of the world, recited on the fourth day of the festival.

Both in Mesopotamia and Egypt, sacred music has been associated with divinities and celestial protectors. The head of Hathor, the Egyptian goddess of heaven, love, and sacred music, was usually surmounted by the sistrum. This shaken musical instrument, consisting of a handle and a frame with jingling crossbars, was used to accompany ritual ceremonies associated particularly with the goddess. The bull, a symbol of fertility and divine power, shown frequently in the gigantic Assyrian reliefs surmounted by a human head as a guardian against misfortune, was associated in the Ur period (2600–2350 BCE) with the lyre, whose sound box was modeled after the body of a bull. The lyre had a yoke-shaped frame consisting of two arms and a variable number of strings stretched over the frontal soundboard. In a later stylized form, only the bull's head remained as an embellishment. Three precious specimens of the instrument have been excavated at the royal cemetery in Ur.

Any attempt to figure out how this music sounded would be fruitless. It is true that the earliest form of musical writing was the cuneiform system used from the middle of the fourth millennium BCE by the Sumerians, Babylonians, and Assyrians. However, the few written examples that have been deciphered in recent years do not alter the basic fact that sacred music of the ancient civilizations was oral by nature and conception and regarded as a priestly secret not to be divulged. Hence, like other musical traditions transmitted orally, it did not lend itself to a fixed definite version. However, regarding performance practices and particularly the numerous instruments and their functions researchers are on firmer ground.

Vocal music, which predominated, emphasized the religious texts through varying modes of expression, from a solemn recitation performed in a tense voice to a well-constructed song with instrumental accompaniment. Hymns were sung either by a solo performer or by a chorus in responsorial and alternating rendition. As with the superscriptions of the biblical psalms, Mesopotamian and Egyptian texts frequently included musical instructions whose meanings are still largely unknown. The most significant information concerns musical instruments and their ample usage in worship. They range from the rudimentary to the highly sophisticated. Among the simpler instruments, used mainly for ritual or apotropaic purposes in both Mesopotamia and Egypt, are various small clay or metal bells embellished with symbols of gods; clay rattles in the form of animals; clappers with animal heads or in the form of a human hand, found in Egypt; bronze cymbals of various sizes that can be struck in a vertical or horizontal movement and were used at sacrifices and funerals; and the sistrum.

Drums in various shapes and sizes were also used in worship, particularly in Babylonia where they attained great importance. A table of sacerdotal instructions from Erech, dating from the Seleucid period, gives precise details for making the sizable goblet-shaped drum *lilissu,* as well as a description of its ritual. Made of metal in the shape of a perfectly formed bull, this drum was prepared by means of a long ceremonial process accompanied by sacrifices, libations, and prayers. The instrument was used to raise lamentations of grief for the darkened moon and served as an object of worship in itself. The bronze trumpet made its first appearance in association with cult during the reign of Ramses II (1304–1237 BCE). Two trumpets, richly decorated with bells, were found in the tomb of Tutankhamen. Pipes were rather common in Egypt but rare in Mesopotamia where strings were preferred. The same is true of side-blown flutes, which appeared in the Old Kingdom (c. 3000–2200 BCE).

The richest and most highly developed category of instruments was that of the various harps and lyres. Harps appeared in two main types, one in which the body of the instrument forms an arch and the other in which the neck and body forms an angle. In both types the strings were either vertical or horizontal to the soundboard and were plucked either with or without a plectrum. The arched harp, the earlier type, first appeared in the Sumerian period. The vertical arched harp was most common in Egypt, where it is found in tombs of the Old Kingdom together with flutes and pipes. The lyre arrived relatively late in Egypt, not earlier than the New Kingdom (c. 1569–1085 BCE).

MUSIC IN THE BIBLE. The Bible is the chief and richest source of information about music and musical activity in ancient Israel. It seems that in the earliest nomadic period and during desert travel music did not play a significant role in worship. However, the biblical texts provide many references to certain types of folk music used for various popular occasions of rejoicing, such as the celebration of the arrival of the sacred ark in Jerusalem (*2 Sm.* 6:5), the singing of the canticle of the sea, which marked the victory over the Egyptians (*Ex.* 15:20, 15:21), and the welcoming of a hero on his return from the battlefield by dancing and drum-playing women (*Jgs.* 11:34, *1 Sm.* 18:6–7). A magical character is associated with the various uses of the ram's horn, or *shofar,* the effects of which are depicted in relation to the theophany (*Ex.* 19:13–19, 20:18) and to the fall of Jericho (*Jos.* 6:6–20). Two references reveal the important role music played in ecstatic prophecies (*1 Sm.* 10:5, *2 Kgs.* 3:15). From the reproachful sayings of the prophets Isaiah and Amos concerning banquets and music, the existence may be inferred of a secular art music (*Is.* 5:12, *Am.* 6:5).

The bulk of biblical references concern sacred music associated with temple worship. This music was similar in many ways to the traditions mentioned above in its ceremonial aspect, organization, and performance practices. It also was confined to a distinct class of highly trained professional musicians, the Levites. The *Book of Psalms* contains many instructions regarding musical performance, as well as the names of the leaders who conducted the ensembles of singers and instrumentalists playing lyres, cymbals, rattles, clappers, and other instruments. However, this music excluded dance from worship and was exempted form all associations with deities or celestial protectors. As to the ultimate origin of music, the Bible ascribes its invention, in antediluvian times, to a human hero, Jubal "the father of them that play upon the harp and the organ" (*Gn.* 4:21). This statement occurs in a passage also naming other inventions including the products of bronze and iron.

MUSIC UNDER JEWISH AND MUSLIM RELIGIOUS AUTHORITIES. After the destruction of the Second Temple by the Romans (70 CE) and the dispersion of the Jewish people, the attitude toward music in worship underwent a significant change. Individual and communal intimate prayer replaced the Temple's ceremonial worship, and theologians became more and more involved in the revision of norms regarding the place and nature of music in the synagogue service. The first consequence of this new attitude was the total banishment of musical instruments except for the *shofar.*

The exclusion of instruments usually has been justified as being an aspect of ongoing mourning over the Temple's destruction. The reasoning involved in the long-lasting debate over the use of sophisticated musical forms in synagogal singing was of a rather ideological nature. It is interesting to note in this regard that the basic views expressed in the rabbinical arguments, with reference to the scriptures, have much in common with those expounded by Muslim theologians very soon after the emergence of Islam (622 CE). In relation to *samāʿ* (Arabic for "hearing"; often also meaning the thing heard, for example, music) there developed a large polemical literature dealing with the question of the lawfulness of music from a theological point of view. The term *samāʿ* has been contrasted with *ghināʾ*, which means "singing," and, by extension, secular art music. This identification led the authorities of both religions to assign the concept of music to secular entertainment music. The resulting frictions and conflicts with that flourishing urban music, echoed in the literature, have determined to a large extent the intransigence of those who oppose music.

Another argument found in this polemical literature concerns the respect for the holy texts and for their adequate rendition. Beautifully composed melodies with instrumental accompaniment and dancing were considered distractions that prevented the faithful from concentrating on the message in the text. Those having the most extreme form of this attitude considered music harmful, capable of affecting adversely the behavior and judgment of the hearer. Some authorities went so far as to attribute the origin of music to satanic forces and held that its direct influence on the listener's soul was basically a temptation of the devil or a delusion.

A Jewish Midrashic exegesis of the biblical verse concerning the invention of musical instruments singled out the fact that the inventor, Jubal, belonged to the posterity of Cain. Cain's descendants were plunged into amusements that combined music, adultery, and drinking of intoxicating liquors. This combination of music making and depravity was said to have incurred God's wrath and thereby contributed to bringing about the flood. (See Louis Ginzberg, *The Legends of the Jews,* vol. 1, Philadelphia, 1956, pp. 116–118.) Some Muslim theologians, referring to this exegesis, actually included Satan among the inventors or promoters of music.

An interesting Arabic version of the origin of music, cited by several writers, attributes the invention of music to Jubal's father, Lamech. It relates that Lamech, at an advanced age, lost his only son. In his grief he refused to be separated from the boy and hung his corpse in a tree so that he could be near him and see him. He later made a *ʿūd* (lute) from a leg of the corpse and sang laments to its accompaniment. Lamech's invention and the lament corresponding to the first biblical song (*Gn.* 4:19) may refer to ideas concerning the making of a musical instrument out of human bones, thus suggesting the incorruptibility of the corpse, the rebirth of the defunct spirit, and the identification of that spirit with the sound of the instrument within which it continues to vibrate.

MUSIC AND THE MYSTICAL EXPERIENCE. The Jewish and Muslim mystical movements concerned themselves with various complex views regarding music, its role, effects, and origin. In qabbalistic literature all musical topics are interwoven with a multitude of qabbalistic symbols that are correlated with the whole of creation. Islamic mysticism, or Sufism, which can be traced back to the eighth century, developed complex congregational ritual and spiritual exercises in which music and dance play a determinant role. A related system of symbolism has been elaborated in the appropriate literature.

As to the question of music's origin, both Jewish and Muslim mystics advanced in different formulations the idea that music is neither monogenetic nor monovalent, that is, it oscillates between the divine and the satanic, the celestial and the terrestrial. The impact of music on the listener depends on the individual's virtue as well as the degree of mystical cognition of God and his revelation. In its highest form the listening experience becomes entirely spiritual, according to the Spanish Muslim mystic Ibn al-ʿArabī (1165–1240). He claimed that this form of the listening experience consists of hearing with a spiritual ear the singing of all things in creation praising the glory of God, and in seizing and enjoying the significance of this. The role assigned to music as leading to knowledge and the constant repetition of music's revelation through mystical intention indicates, according to the qabbalists, that music was God's creation. He created it on the third day, making angels out of his own breath to sing his glory day and night. This highly spiritual function of music led the founder of the Mawlawīyah order, the poet Jalāl al-Dīn Rūmī (1207–1273), to declare: "There are many ways leading to God; I have chosen that of music and dance."

The analogy between humankind and the universe and the sought-after resonance and harmony between them are frequent themes in mystical speculation. The music created by human beings is considered a pale reflection of the most exalted and perfect harmony embodied in the heavenly spheres. Therefore whoever sets out to learn to enjoy the pleasures of the celestial music will find that in order to do so he must first shake himself free of the defilement of matter and release himself from the shackles of this world. On the level of individual experience, music helps the devotee untie the knots that bind the soul to matter, allowing it to go beyond the barriers of its own personal existence. Indeed, human spirits, whose origin is the superior world, recall their homeland when hearing music. The ascent of the soul from its earthly existence to its divine home, which signifies redemption, has been symbolized in the mystical imagery of certain Ṣūfī orders by dance and movement. It is said that dance uproots the foot of the worshiper, transporting him to the summit of the world.

Qabbalah went further by introducing the idea that the power of human sacred music exerts an influence in the celestial realm. Thus humankind is a protagonist in the cosmic drama. It is said in this regard that everything done by the individual or the community in the mundane sphere is magically reflected in the upper region, that the impulse from below calls forth one from above. Hence the singing of hymns on earth causes an immediate resonance in the upper spheres; by means of his mystical intention the devotee contributes to the establishment of perfect tuning and harmony between himself and the macrocosm. However, the ideal perfection, the harmony that signifies salvation, is hard to obtain. This is because the way leading to it is constantly obstructed by evil forces. Adam's fall and the interference of Satan have been the causes of the contamination of divine music and the disturbance of the original harmony. To overcome these obstacles and restore the original harmony, the realm of darkness must first be defeated. Sacred music and prayer directed by mystical intention are the most formidable weapons in the combat for salvation.

See Also Chanting; Samāʿ.

Bibliography

Curt Sach's *The History of Musical Instruments* (New York, 1940) is an authoritative work on the history and morphology of instruments; it includes chapters on Mesopotamia, Egypt, and ancient Israel. Different forms of instruments are discussed in the following museum catalogs: R. D. Anderson's *Catalogue of Egyptian Antiquities in the British Museum,* vol. 3, *Musical Instruments* (London, 1976); Joan Rimmer's *Ancient Musical Instruments of Western Asia in the British Museum* (London, 1969); and Christiane Ziegler's *Catalogue des instruments de musique égyptiens du Musée du Louvre* (Paris, 1979).

Important contributions to the study of different aspects of Mesopotamian music include Wilhelm Stauder's "Die Musik der Sumerer, Babylonier und Assyrer," in *Orientalische Musik,* in the series "Handbuch der Orientalistik," edited by Hans Hickman (Leiden, 1970), and the same author's article "Mesopotamia" in the *New Grove Dictionary of Music and Musicians,* edited by Stanley Sadie (London, 1980). Among the various studies dealing with music theory and notation, I recommend Anne Draffkorn Kilmer's "The Discovery of an Ancient Mesopotamian Theory of Music," *Proceedings of the American Philosophical Society* 115 (1971): 131–149, and Marcelle Duchesne-Guillemin's "Sur la restitution de la musique hourrite," *Revue de musicologie* 66 (1980): 5–26.

For discussion of Egyptian music, see Hans Hickmann's *Quarante-cinq siècles de musique dans l'Égypte ancienne* (Paris, 1956). A good general survey on biblical music is Esther Gerson-Kiwi's "Musique," in *Dictionnaire de la Bible,* supp. vol. 5 (Paris, 1957), cols. 1411–1468. Recent specific studies are Bathja Bayer's "The Biblical 'Nebel,'" *Yuval* (Jerusalem) 1 (1968): 89–131, and "The Titles of the Psalms," *Yuval* 4 (1982): 29–123. The institution of synagogal music and its development are studied in depth in Eric Werner's *The Sacred Bridge,* 2 vols. (New York, 1959–1984). On the rabbinical attitude toward music, see Israel Adler's *La pratique musicale savante dans quelques communautés juives,* 2 vols. (Paris, 1966), and the same author's "Histoire de la musique religieuse juive," in *Encylopédie des musiques sacrées,* edited by Jaques Porte, vol. 1 (Paris, 1968). The question concerning the ideological attitude of the Jewish religious authorities has been treated in my "Der Judaismus" in *Religiöse Autoritäten und Musik,* edited by Dorothea Baumann and Kurt Fischer (Kassel, 1984), pp. 67–83. For discussion of the story of Lamech and Jubal, see my "The *ʿūd* and the Origin of Music," in *Studia Orientalia Memoriae D. H. Baneth Dedicata* (Jerusalem, 1979). The most important sources dealing with the lawfulness of *samāʿ* are analyzed in my *The Theory of Music in Arabic Writings (c. 900–1900)* (Munich, 1979).

Amnon Shiloah (1987)

MUSIC: MUSIC AND RELIGION IN INDIA

Music has historically given unity to Indian society and civilization, often doing so in contrast to the discord among the dominant religions and multiple sects of South Asia. The symbolic meanings of music provide common musical substance and practice, and they are shared across sacred boundaries of many kinds. The religious and philosophical unity embodied through musical practice, therefore, has deep historical roots, which has meant that music and religion share many aspects of a common ontology. South Asian musical practices, moreover, have often mediated the conflicts between religions, responding to new possibilities for shared dialogue and intensifying worship. It is, therefore, virtually impossible to separate music from religion in India, for religious meaning, concrete and abstract, is present in South Asian music at every level.

Sound in its infinite varieties is of crucial importance to Indian religious thought. The universe itself is constituted of and by sound, and the omnipresence of sound envelops daily life. Hearing and listening to sound, therefore, are required of the individual to negotiate a path through life. Accordingly, the ontology of music depends on the physical perception of sound as a means of contemplation and worship. In Hinduism the primacy of hearing and listening for devotion is clearly evident in the term given to the foundational sacred scriptures, *śruti* (literally, "something that is heard"), which also refers to the fine divisions of pitch in Indian melodic modes, or *rāgas.* The aural perception of music also serves as the central ontology of music in Islam, in which the term *samaʿ* (both "hearing" and "listening") refers to music making and establishes the importance of aural perceptions, rather than sound production.

Just as the universe of sound is omnipresent, it is also dense, often even loud and cacophonous. The music of the Hindu temple, for example, is not limited to the sounds of instruments performing discrete pieces in a ritual performance. The general commotion of worshipers usually joins an instrumentarium consisting of percussion instruments of all kinds, as well as horns and woodwind instruments, fashioned to produce the loudest possible volume. The amplification of this sound universe is extreme throughout India, with loudspeakers broadcasting Hindu temple music into the streets or the Muslim *adhān,* or call-to-prayer, across the urban landscape. The density of sound is central to an epistemology of sacred experience through music. Sustaining the universe of sound is possible because of the multitude of musical experiences that channel devotion and join human beings together in communal worship. That epistemology of sacred experience through music crosses religious, linguistic, and socioeconomic boundaries, providing some measure of unity, both real and idealized, to the subcontinent of India.

Core Concepts about the Relation of Music to Religion. Organized and articulated as music, sacred sound has the power to represent the order of the universe and by extension symbolically to sustain human existence. The metaphorical unity of music lies in the capacity to sustain a central pitch, the *ōm* of Hindu metaphysics, the drone of the Indian music. Like the *ōm,* a drone displays characteristics of centrality and unbrokenness. Both characteristics are evident in the most ancient musical practice of Brahmanic Hinduism, the performance of passages from the *Ṛgveda,* in which chanters sing melodies that surround and return to the symbolically central pitch, which itself is intoned to the syllable, *ōm.* Virtually every Indian musical practice has adapted the symbolic use of sound to articulate the order of the universe, concentrating it in the drone pitch, which is not only played without break by a drone-producing instrument (e.g., the *ṭambūra* in the classical traditions), but provides the pitch to which the percussion instruments are tuned. Around the drone pitch there is a constellation of pitches in the melodic modes, or *rāgas,* which focus on the drone through their melodic motion. Accordingly, the organization of the universe is symbolically present in virtually every manifestation of sound in Indian music, linking music and religion through shared traits of a common metaphysics.

The temporal organization of Indian music also expresses many fundamental aspects of South Asian religious and philosophical thought. Meter in Indian music relies extensively on cyclical patterns, and rhythm results from additive principles, rather than the division into smaller and smaller units found in Western musical theory. Meter, or *tāla,* unfolds as a hierarchy of patterns, smaller ones embedded in larger ones, which return again and again to the same point of beginning. Musical structure, therefore, does not result from a unidirectional teleology leading toward conclusion—that is, there is no forward movement, no development in the Western classical sense. The cyclical character of musical time reflects the aspects of life and history that are fundamental to Indian religions. The absence of a strict impulse toward a telos of ending reflects many aspects of soteriology in religious thought; that is, it mirrors beliefs in the continuation of both human and musical life in an afterlife. Many musical forms, as well as individual pieces and performances, can be extended through improvisation that reiterates and embellishes the basic cyclical units. In a more practical sense, the epistemological extension of the life of a musical piece can enhance devotion and contemplation; for example, the standard South Indian compositional form, *kriti,* revolves around texts which repeatedly enjoin the musician to reflect on the name of a god (and at times on the life-giving acts of the *kriti's* composer).

Cyclical concepts of sacred time and the soteriological relation between birth and rebirth also influence the broader patterns of music history in South Asia. Music does not change through radical innovation and growing complexity, but rather retains connections to musical principles that have constituted musical theory and thought since at least the eighth century CE. New traditions and new pieces enter Indian music history, but they do so not by displacing the old, but rather by expanding repertoires and musical ideas that already have a long historical presence. This is particularly evident in the retention of many aspects of Hinduism in the musical styles and practices of Muslim North India and Pakistan. The Hindu narratives that provide a representational template for *rāga,* for example, remain no less important in Hindustani music in the Muslim North, even when used for devotional purposes in Islam. Similarly, musical influences from the Middle East, especially from Persia, came to serve Indian musical ends in Mughal India, for example, in the shaping of the Hindustani instrumentarium (e.g., with the integration of the plucked-lute *[sitār]* and pair of drums *[tablā]* associated by some with the fourteenth-century Ṣūfī, Amīr Khusraw). The epistemological relatedness of musical and religious thought in India historically underlies many of the transformations described by the term *Indianization.*

Just as music is inseparable from most rituals in Indian religions, so too is ritual meaning densely present in much musical activity. Music has the potential to recalibrate the temporal and social components of ritual, transposing them from the everyday to the sacred world. In tribal societies, music making is highly ritualistic, accompanying virtually all seasonal and life-cycle events. Generally speaking, music is most efficacious during ritual when it enhances participation. Ritual music making, therefore, encourages congregational devotion and often accompanies processions and dance. Because certain types of music making are suspect in Muslim rituals, and because Brahmanic tradition suggests a preference for silence in certain Hindu rituals, such as funerals, the use of music in specific rituals can also dispel polemics against music itself. Musical performance, even in the classical tradition, would be unthinkable without the expressive presence of ritual. The choice of *rāga,* the order of genres, and the interaction of musicians from different castes and religions influence the performance itself and account for the ways in which musical and religious connections remain intact.

Religious difference in South Asia is represented by music and mediated, even ameliorated, through musical practice. Musical historiographies, both Indian and Western, divide Indian musical practices, including devotional music, between North and South. That division has both musical and religious distinctions. In the South, Hinduism plays the overwhelming role in determining sacred meaning and musical structure. In the North, Islam is critical for the shaping of music. Despite the musical divisions between North and South, the distinction between Muslim and Hindu ontologies can only be partial, for the musical borders between North and South, as well as between the religions and sectarian groups in all parts of India, have been very fluid.

A more accurate distinction, particularly from a musical perspective, might instead be based on the contrast between change that accommodates religious and social difference and that which more conservatively retains the hierarchical structure of older religious traditions, Hindu and non-Hindu. The tension between these two patterns of religio-social difference does not obey a strict division between North and South, Muslim and Hindu. Religious accommodation in northern India—for example, Vaiṣṇava movements in the Bengali-speaking regions—has led to sweeping changes in music, from the emergence of a new music culture among the mendicant Bauls in Bengal to the crucial presence of musical "houses," or *gharānās*, with origins in Bengal, such as the Benares *gharānā* in which Ravi Shankar and Ali Akbar Khan are principal members.

Indian music and religion share a common distribution of specialist roles across a hierarchy. This hierarchy is most apparent in Hinduism, in which the most respected musical specialists—those who chant the Vedic hymns or play the *vīṇā,* the classical instrument with the highest status in Karṇāṭak (South Indian) art music—have traditionally been restricted to the Brāhmaṇ castes. In contrast, musicians with the lowest status in Karṇāṭak music, drummers who touch the skins of animals, or *paṟaiyar*s (Tamil for "drum maker"), are literally low caste and figuratively outcasts. The sacred priesthood is in many ways interchangeable with the musical specialists of the classical instrumental tradition. In contrast, the nonspecialist sacred repertoires, such as *bhajan*s, have the potential to level hierarchical differences, and thus create a common repertoire.

The distinction between musical specialization and everyday music making extends to the nature of the musical repertoires themselves and to their transmission. The religious priesthood and musical specialists perform from written traditions, most often in a "high" sacred language, such as Sanskrit. Nonspecialized traditions, however, are entirely oral, and the texts of songs or hymns constituting ritual and everyday repertoires are regional and vernacular. Though this tension between the classical and the quotidian subsided to some degree in the twentieth century, it remains one of the distinguishing characteristics of the ways in which music reflects the structure of South Asian religions.

Religious narrative inscribes meaning directly and indirectly on the structures of Indian music and musical instruments. Gods and goddesses, real and apocryphal saints, assume many and varied forms throughout the great epic cycles of Hinduism and the genealogies of Muslim shrines. The most frequently appearing musician-god in the Hindu epic *Mahābhārata* is Kṛṣṇa. Kṛṣṇa represents a constellation of divine attributes, among them divine love and beauty *(prema* and *rupa),* but even more important for his symbolic role in musical narrative are the many episodes in his life during which he is associated with *gopīs,* female cowherds, in a grouping that allegorically symbolizes the relation of the soul to god. That relation appears in countless images of Kṛṣṇa playing the flute to the *gopīs,* in the myths that associate narratives with specific *rāgas,* and in iconography used to depict divine love.

The musical representation of Sarasvatī specifies the different mythological and narrative roles she plays as a Hindu goddess. In Hindu writings Sarasvatī represents an ontology of human understanding, *vidyā,* that allows the human to transcend the cycle of death and rebirth, and it is this ontology that she brings to the most fundamental of all Indian musical instruments, the *vīṇā.* So basic is the meaning of the *vīṇā* to Hinduism that its very physical shape, with a head and vocal cords that sing and a gourd body that resonates as the human body, is regarded as metaphysically human. To enhance Sarasvatī's ability to effect *vidyā,* she appears frequently in the iconography appearing on *vīṇās* themselves. The *vīṇā* of Karṇāṭak classical music is, in fact, often referred to as the *sarasvatī vīṇā.*

The sacred music of South Asia maps place and identity in complex sacred geographies. Fundamental to the sacred geographies of all South Asian religions is the relation between centers and peripheries. Sacred musical centers coalesce around Hindu temples, Muslim shrines, and Buddhist monasteries. Musical activity at these centers is intensive and usually highly ritualized. Though the musical activity at a temple or shrine may be in the hands of a religious priesthood or musical specialists, it nonetheless depends on the participation of the devout who travel from elsewhere to worship at the center. Musical activity at the centers of the sacred geography is also the densest, and music itself concentrates sensory experiences to heighten the awareness of god and the efficacy of devotion.

The sacred journey from the periphery to the center usually involves pilgrimage, a form of ritual journey and community-formation common to all South Asian religions. The music of pilgrims is communal and congregational, practiced not by specialists but by the devout, who learn and adapt new songs, usually from oral tradition, to their sacred journeys. Folk and regional musical practices characterize peripheries, serving local functions and producing local liturgies and repertoires. Music in particular connects the sacred journey to the shrine at which worship is concentrated, multiplying the ways in which diverse genres of music collectively underlie religious experience. The sacred geographies of India, therefore, create possibilities for unity through the musical practices that reflect their dynamic quality and coalesce through ritual and performance at temples and shrines.

HINDUISM. Historically, Hinduism has provided the body of religious thought that has most fundamentally shaped Indian musical practices. Music, either possessing a discrete ontology or embedded in other sacred and performative practices (e.g., devotion and dance), appears in the earliest sacred texts, such as in the Upaniṣads and the Vedas. The evidence of Hindu influence on musical thought has remained clear, even profound, until the present day, even in those repertoires and styles that now characterize other religions, including Islam. The historiography of Indian musical thought, in certain fundamental ways, runs parallel to the history of Hinduism, with its dynamic relation between central principles and texts, and variant denominations and interpretations. Just as Hinduism itself has not always prescribed a single religious orthodoxy, musical practices that arise from Indian religious thought do not always prescribe canonic classical traditions of music.

Surveying the diverse musics that embody and articulate Hinduism requires an understanding of the ways in which hierarchy and egalitarianism yield two contrasting domains of musical practice. Within the hierarchy there are those, notably Brāhmaṇs, endowed with particular power to practice religious and musical specialties. The resilience of a religious hierarchy is evident in the long history of classical music in India, a tradition based on complex texts and highly developed performance skills. It is not by chance that the classical tradition is full of religious overtones. Until the modern era, for example, some practices of classical music, such as playing the *vīṇā* in the South and singing *dhrupad* in the North, were the restricted domains of high-caste Hindus or high-status Muslims. If the influence of Hinduism on Indian music seems to display a top-down trajectory, it also produces the tension that generates the need for musical egalitarianism. It is for this reason that the most widespread practice of Hindu devotional music, the singing of *bhajans*, attracts the broadest participation from Indian society and spreads across religious and sectarian boundaries. Any discussion of music and Hinduism must therefore account for both highly specialized and broadly egalitarian musical practices.

The mythological concepts concerning the creation of the world and the human position in it that are recounted in the foundational texts of Hindu thought and Brahmanic tradition, the Vedas, are profoundly musical. The Vedas are recognized as a body of revealed texts, compiled during the millennium or so of Aryan invasion and ascendancy in South Asia, from around 1500 BCE to 500 BCE. Although the four basic texts of the Veda—*Ṛgveda, Yajurveda, Sāmaveda, Atharvaveda*—differ in function and historical appearance, all Hindus recognize that they embody fundamental aspects of Hindu thought. The formal aspects of the Vedas are musical, and the texts are often referred to as "hymns," compiled into hymnals. *Rc* glosses most often as "hymn," that is, as a body of songs, employing repetitive patterns, that to some degree rely on collective, even congregational, performance. Other English terms used to describe the Vedas range from "incantation" to "chant," all of them recognizing the performative foundation in song.

Unlike many religions, Hinduism employs musical concepts in the discourse about and practice of its foundational sacred texts. Performance of the Vedic hymns relies on specific pitch structures, with specific pitch patterns and tonal hierarchies, usually a group of two or three pitches surrounding a central pitch, the sustaining of which symbolizes the unbroken order of the universe. Similarly, the metrical performance of Vedic hymns generates a temporal framework that is rendered musical through the repetition of stress patterns. As foundational sacred texts, therefore, the Vedas generate identifiable musical parameters, and many of these remain central to the structure of music in South Asia until the present, especially: (1) The sustained presence and focus provided by a fundamental tone or drone; (2) a hierarchy of pitches, in which some pitches have greater tonal significance than others; and (3) the logogenic, or word-generated, nature of musical rhythm and meter.

The Vedic hymns are inseparable from Brahmanic ritual, which they transformed into the enactment of everyday Hindu practice. Ideally, the performance of the Vedas is ceaseless and seamless, the ultimate realization of everyday devotion through music. The ritual of performing the Vedic hymns, moreover, gave rise to other texts, specifically the Brāhmaṇas and the Upaniṣads. Of the two bodies of text, the Upaniṣads are more speculative and philosophical, whereas the Brāhmaṇas are more expository, developing principles set forth in the four Vedic canons. The Brāhmaṇas, thus, have performative functions, realized through the articulation of ritual through prayer and song. A Brāhmaṇ literally is "one who prays."

Already in the second millennium BCE, the Vedas and Brahmanic tradition succeeded in establishing and maintaining fundamental musical concepts, and they historically represent a first instance of the ontological unity afforded to Indian religion through music. Performance of the Vedas established a direct relation between the religious text and the manner of its performance. By extension, a logogenic relation between text and performance emerges. Music becomes a medium or vehicle for the more complete expression of words. The music that serves as such a medium, furthermore, is immanent in the words of a sacred text. The music embodies some aspect of meaning contained in the words, and therefore music is never separable from words, even when words are absent—such as in South Indian instrumental music, in which the composed melody, the *kriti,* is always based on a song with a specific text. The logogenic meaning of music may be direct (e.g., when enforced by specific metrical rules) or indirect (e.g., when reflecting the same sense of cosmological order with which the texts of the Vedic hymns concern themselves). Together, musical performance and religious ritual are wedded as music and text become inseparable.

Early Hindu and Brahmanic tradition generated fundamental ideas about music, such as concepts concerning composition and improvisation, and the identity of discrete forms, genres, and pieces of music. Music in the Brahmanic tradition conveys stories, indeed fundamental narratives from Hindu mythology and cosmology. Though a piece of music, such as one of the *kritis* of South Indian classical music, may not be literally "about" a particular story, knowing the story in question is critical to understanding the music. The Vedic hymns are the source of music's formal structures, which are developed in performance through improvisation within a system of pitches and patterns functioning in predetermined ways. As with the sacred texts, music contains the *ōm,* the fundamental pitch that focuses the Vedic text and sustains the order of the universe. The fundamental structure and symbolic meaning of music in sacred practice was present from the beginnings of Hindu practice.

Devotion in Hinduism intensifies unity and is itself intensified through congregational prayer and song. The unity of devotion resides in the possibility of evoking *rasa,* a constellation of emotional moods, among them yearning and compassion, but also wonder and fear, through performance. The primary genres of Hindu vocal music enhance *rasa* through their power to facilitate emotional unity and congregational participation. Hindu devotional music is both specific to South Indian regions because of its frequent use of vernacular languages and malleable enough in some genres, notably *kīrtana* and *bhajans*, to extend its egalitarian notion of devotion, or *bhakti,* to other religions and to regional practices in North India and Pakistan.

Beginning roughly in the fourteenth century CE, poet-saints created repertoires of Hindu devotional songs that combined both musical and poetic properties of *rasa.* The emergence of the devotional repertoires was significant for the spread of vernacular musical practice across regional, linguistic, and sectarian borders. The great devotional singer-composers of the early era of *kīrtana* singing came from Kannada (e.g., Narahari Tīrtha, fourteenth century), Bengal (e.g., Caitanya, 1486–1533), and Telugu-speaking regions (e.g., Tallapakku Annamāchārya, b. 1424). Devotional repertoires spread across India, moreover, because of the activities of *haridāsa* singers, devotees of Vaiṣṇava Hinduism, who visited shrines and festivals, and integrated *kīrtana*-singing with pilgrimages. *Kīrtana* were quickly accessible to the diverse communal and linguistic groups who sang them because of their reliance on composed refrains, or *pallavi,* often with repeated meditations on the names of god, and then the unfolding of a series of strophes, or *caraṇam,* that worshipers without previous knowledge could quickly learn.

The most widespread form of Hindu devotional music is *bhajan*-singing. The concept of *bhajan* relates both to a specific vocal genre and to the performance practices necessary for communal singing. As genre and repertoire, the *bhajan* is remarkably accessible, consisting often of a very brief text, in which textual formulae, particularly forms of the names of Hindu deities (e.g., Rāma or Śiva), and even non-Hindu deities (e.g., Allah), will serve as the basis of repeated reflection. The relatively simple texts also ensure mobility, making it possible to move *bhajan* repertoires across linguistic borders and to gather them in such ways that they could become the primary song form accompanying Hindu pilgrims. Musically, too, formulae, such as antiphonal patterns in which a leader is followed by a chorus singing the same text and melody, invite rather than encumber participation.

The social context of *bhajan*-singing is communal, both when performed privately and when performed publicly. Homes, temples, and community centers (sometimes called *bhajan* halls) serve as the gathering place for the intensive performances. Modern technologies, particularly the widespread and inexpensive dissemination of *bhajans* on audio cassette, continue to make devotional song one of the most widely practiced of all musical genres in South Asia at the beginning of the twenty-first century.

BUDDHISM. Buddhist music is important in modern South Asia not so much because of extensive presence, but rather because of the ways it contains fundamental historical-aesthetic concepts about the ontology of music and because its practices provide bridges to the music of East and Southeast Asia. Buddhism survives into the twenty-first century primarily in the north and the northeast, especially Tibet, and in the south, almost entirely in Sri Lanka. The musical practices of the two areas of South Asian Buddhism differ considerably. Monasticism dominates Tibet, and musical practices there represent the ritual practices of monastic life, itself an epistemological realization of the cycles of birth and rebirth. Theravāda Buddhism provides the framework for ritual and musical practice in Sri Lanka, where the interaction of monks and lay practitioners is much more extensive.

Historically, Buddhism has provided a theological impetus for unity and egalitarianism in Indian religion. The rise of Buddhist thought in the centuries following the Buddha's life (c. 485–405 BCE) provided a theological and philosophical counterpoint to the domination of the Brahmanic tradition and the Upaniṣads. From the earliest centuries, Buddhism opened up new possibilities for the contemplation of the external world primarily through mental and spiritual processes. Contemplation, moreover, achieved its highest form through various practices that required discipline, in particular that which takes place in monastic settings. Ritualized and inscribed in treatises, such as the *Śvaraśāstra* (Treatise on melody) and the *Vādyaśāstra* (Treatise on instrumental music), Buddhist concepts of music rely on the intensity and the unity achieved through contemplation that can be both individual and communal. For Indian musical practices, the fundamental principles of Buddhism have been significant for several reasons. Aesthetically, Buddhist thought opened epistemological possibilities for resolving the tensions between elite and vernacular musical practices.

In Buddhist devotion, contemplating sound itself is the most efficacious form of meditation. The sound universe of Buddhist devotion is encountered through various forms of ritual and worship. Early Buddhist texts, for example, stress that the contemplation of sound allows the individual to transcend the limitations of individual being through *srotra vijñāna,* or "aural knowledge." The bells and other percussion instruments that accompany monastic ritual, moreover, have direct religious significance, as they recall the ways in which the Buddha entered the world into which he was reborn as Siddhārtha. The contemplation of sound requires both the listening to and the production of music. Chanting is particularly important as a communal experience, in which vocal performance requires an intense awareness of the relation between individual melody lines and the overall texture of the group's chants; in other words, Buddhist chanting entails heterophonic singing, in which individuality and communality are at once distinct and merged.

Theravāda Buddhists in Sri Lanka base their chanting on oral interpretation of the Pali canon of sacred texts. Melodic ideas remain anchored in an understanding of the Buddha's teachings, that is, in a practice known as *sarabhanna,* in which a sustained choral sound elongates text across slowly moving pitches virtually devoid of ornaments. At the same time, Buddhist musical practice contains many of the structural features of Indian music. Critically important, for example, is that sound be unbroken, which in turn means that chanters employ overlapping phrases. Weighted tones, moreover, anchor chanting, and because of the seeming absence of phrases, the sound of chanting produces a sense of deployment around a drone pitch.

Sustained choral chanting and the maintenance of an unbroken flow of sound characterize Tibetan Buddhist worship. In Tibet, however, percussion instruments—bells, cymbals, and drums—produce a much more articulated feeling of pulse and rhythm, in which the temporal qualities of music are not entirely anchored to sacred texts. Tibetan instrumental ensembles may become quite large, and monastic repertoires may become highly stylized and distinct from chanting. Though Buddhist religious and musical thinking so emphatically provides a framework for music in South Asia, musical practice is by no means unchanging. Buddhist repertoires are diverse, as are the ways Buddhists achieve unity and devotion through the contemplation of sound and music.

ISLAM. From the first settlements of Muslim peoples in South Asia in the eighth century CE until the sixteenth century, when the Persian-speaking Mughal Empire established a firm foothold in North India, Islam became an increasing presence in South Asian culture and music. Despite its proscriptions against music in some contexts, Islam offered South Asians an alternative approach to the cultivation and performance of music. As a whole, Muslim music making was more egalitarian than that of Hinduism, and just as Islam attracted converts because of the openness of its religious doctrines, so too did it multiply the possibilities of music making, in both sacred and secular domains of society. In many areas of cultural and musical life, Islam proved to be flexible, encouraging regional diversity in the music of Afghanistan, Pakistan, Kashmir, and Bengal, all of which can claim classical music systems of their own in the twenty-first century. The Muslim regions also fostered extensive musical exchange with the Middle East and Central Asia, which enriched the diversity of musical genres and introducing new instruments and instrumental ensembles.

The Indianization of music that has led to unity throughout India has an historical counterpoint in the Muslim areas of the North, namely Islamicization. Roughly speaking, Islamicization results when a musical concept, form, theoretical system, or ensemble structure undergoes a transformation allowing it to express the cultural distinctiveness of North India or Pakistan. One of the earliest forms of Islamicization is evident in the cultivation of Mughal miniature paintings from the sixteenth century onward. Imported with the Mughal settlement from Persia, miniature-painting frequently included musical subject matter revealing the many ways in which music and musicians were crossing religion-based musical boundaries. Miniature-painting even influenced the visual representation of Hindu myth in *rāgmālā*-painting, which also depicted the *rāga* classification of North Indian classical music. Islamicization is particularly prominent in the modern era—for example, in the modes of popular music that make room for devotional practice (e.g., *qawwālī*) and in pan-Islamic musico-poetic genres (e.g., *ghazal*). In this sense, Islamicization is far less a process of restricting musical activity than a means of expanding the religious significance that South Asian musics have worldwide.

The musical genres of Muslim South Asia fall into two general categories: (1) genres common to devotional practices throughout the Islamic world; and (2) genres with musical, linguistic, and historical roots in South Asia itself. In the case of both categories it is critical to understand just how music finds its place in Islam. Scriptural pronouncements about musical practice in Islam are very much open to interpretation, both because of their ambivalence and because of their paucity. Orthodox interpretations found in the commentaries on the Qurʾān, the *aḥādīth,* are conclusive only insofar as they show the Prophet to have found some musical practices acceptable and others suspect. South Asian practice, especially in Pakistan, where Islam is also the state religion, suggests a fairly orthodox and literal interpretation of the position of music in Islamic society. On one hand, music in the strictest sense, especially music including instruments, does not have an official place in the institutions of public worship. Though the Qurʾān employs melody and modes, reciting is considered "reading" *(qirāʾah)* and never "singing." On the other hand, the aural experience of music, *samaʿ,* or "listening," is fully sanctioned, especially when the music in question is used to accompany recitation of the Qurʾān or takes the form of devotional song. Sacred musics in Muslim South Asia respond to these positions in various ways, and their reception throughout the world thus varies as well.

Devotional music in Muslim South India is very widespread, and it provides aesthetic and cultural continuity across the borders of the three largest nations with Muslim populations, namely India, Pakistan, and Bangladesh. Many sacred musical genres are common to the three countries, such as *qawwālī.* The shrines and saintly lineages around which certain repertoires coalesce have local and international aspects, which reveals the extent to which the borders of the northern parts of South Asia have remained contested through history. Whereas repertoires may be similar, individual practices may differ extensively. Differences are particularly evident in the use of various languages in performances of devotional song, not only due to the prevalence of regional languages and folk melodies in *kāfī,* or "devotional song," but also on account of the mix and hybrid use of languages and musical styles in *qawwālī.* Instrumental ensembles may also be at once local and global, as seen, for example, in *qawwālī* with its use of the hand-pumped organ, or harmonium, and in the use of variants of the bowed spiked fiddle, or *sāraṅgī,* in Rajasthani and Pakistani devotional musics. Muslim devotional musics, therefore, are never static, bounded repertoires, but rather are fluid musical practices that constantly respond to change and the shifting attitudes toward music within Islam.

Local practices of Muslim devotional music are largely encompassed by the term *kāfī. Kāfī* is not one style or genre of devotional music, but many, whose common characteristics reflect musical influences and change from below. The texts of *kāfī* appear to come from regional narratives, often featuring heroes and heroines associated with historical events. In the songs themselves, however, the regional stories and characters take on a larger, symbolic meaning, especially with regard to the ways in which the devout achieve spiritual union. Though the roots of *kāfī* are to be found in the use of folk instruments and strophic structures, they have moved stylistically toward the classical traditions. The string instrument commonly employed with *kāfī,* the *sāraṅgī,* has become a classical instrument only in the past century, but has definitively won its position in the classical instrumentarium of North Indian, or Hindustani, classical music. Even the term *kāfī* has found its way into Hindustani classical music, where it has become the name of a *rāga.*

The most global Muslim devotional music of South Asia is *qawwālī,* which since its introduction to the West by the Sabri Brothers in the mid-1970s and its popularization on an international scale in the 1980s and 1990s, principally by Nusrat Fateh Ali Khan, has become the world music of South Asian Sufism. Like other devotional genres in South Asia, *qawwālī* is not a single style, but rather embodies a constellation of sacred practices and musical sounds that together give it identity. *Qawwālī* is, first of all, a poetic genre, lending itself to an expansive musical repertoire. It is played by specialists, who are also often professionals, namely *qawwāls* ("fluent" or "eloquent" ones), a term that refers to the primacy of the text and is derived from the Arabic word *qaul,* "to speak or to say."

Qawwālī also has a specific function and venue. Its performances constitute the musical and spiritual life of a shrine dedicated to a specific Ṣūfī saint. Through performance, therefore, *qawwālī* expresses a specific history and tradition. For Chishtī Ṣūfīs, the spiritual lineage extends back to Amīr Khusraw (1244–1325), a *qawwāl* and poet himself, who was a disciple of the Ṣūfī saint and great spiritual founder of Chishtī Ṣūfīs, Nizāmuddīn Auliyā. The tradition of devotional song thus follows a specific path, made possible by the succession of sheikhs who supported shrines in Pakistan and North India.

The compositional nature and musical structure of *qawwālī* is no less specific, for it is possible to talk about individual pieces transmitted with discrete identities through oral tradition. For example, one of the best-known *qawwālī* songs, "Man kunto Maulā" (see the recorded examples on tracks 1 and 2 of the CD accompanying Qureshi, 1995), contains the following constellation of musical and symbolic meanings and references:

1. "Man kunto Maulā" refers to the Chishtī Ṣūfī lineage, and is performed at shrines dedicated to both Amīr Khusraw and Nizāmuddīn Auliyā.
2. The text is in Persian, which connects the song to Islam in the Middle East.
3. It contains an example of a subgenre known as *basant,* which here serves to signify a specific aspect of a saint's life, Amīr Khusraw's reflections on Nizāmuddīn Auliyā's love for his deceased nephew.
4. The melody consists of two segments, one ascending *(asthāyī)* and the other descending *(antharā),* which together provide the structural framework for almost all melodies in Hindustani music.
5. The *rāga* is a hybrid form, *megh-ushshaq,* which has both North Indian *(megh)* and Middle Eastern *(ushshaq)* connotations.
6. The structure of the *rāga,* which features mixed tetrachords, reflects techniques associated with Amīr Khusraw.

Though technical, this brief analysis of a single *qawwālī* song reveals the ways in which musical ends can provide a direct link to Ṣūfī religious thought and comment on the genealogy of Muslim South Asia and its historical roots in the Middle East. Symbolic power also moves from religious signification to music in "Man kunto Maula." Amīr Khusraw, for example, in addition to being a spiritual leader in Chishtī Sufism is recognized as the legendary inventor of the *sitār* and the *tablā,* canonic melodic and percussion instruments in Hindustani classical music. Such associations further suggest an interchange between music and religion, leading some to claim that Hindustani music itself formed from Ṣūfī practices. If such a claim is in large part untenable, it nonetheless deserves attention for pointing out the religious dimension of musical thought in North India and Pakistan, and for illustrating the ways in which Sufism and its most widely recognized tradition of devotional music, *qawwālī,* has historically established an appropriate place for music in Islam.

OTHER SOUTH ASIAN RELIGIONS AND RELIGIOUS PRACTICES. The religious diversity of South Asia is far greater than the usual concentration of musicological and theological surveys on Hinduism, Buddhism, and Islam suggests. An understanding of religion in South Asia requires the survey of tribal and regional religious practices, some of them religions in their own right, others local variants of the larger religions. The musical practices of such religions and sects also fall generally into two categories. In the first of these, music takes place primarily as the expression of ritual, and its structure and style are linked to function and the efficacy of ritual-musical activity. Regarded in this way, the music of ritual is secondary to the ritual itself, thus limiting the extent to which a musical system with its own structures and independent form can evolve.

In the second category, the music of tribal and regional religions possesses the dominant systemic qualities of a larger Indian music cultures, for example *rāga* and *tāla,* but the variants of these are simpler than in the classical systems, and local inflection often determines the ways in which the music itself functions. Neither of these categories has historically explained the diversity of tribal music with sufficient thoroughness. The study of tribal, regional, and sectarian music, nonetheless, began attracting considerable ethnographic and ethnomusicological attention in the 1980s and 1990s, so much so that scholarship in the first decade of the twenty-first century holds the promise of reformulating the basic study and understanding of Indian music.

The potentially unifying influence of music on Indian religious thought remains present even across the sacred landscapes of smaller religions. Religions that distinguish themselves primarily from Hinduism frequently have embraced hymns, even *bhajans* from the Hindu tradition, as a repertoire for congregational performance. The primary body of songs in Jainism, for example, consists of hymns whose texts and functions owe an historical debt to Hindu devotional music. The Ṣūfī musical tradition of Kashmir *(ṣūfyānā mūsīqī)* embodies both Middle Eastern and Indian classical traditions, producing a classical tradition of its own, which is suited to performance in mosques and temples alike, as well as in the special shrines of Kashmiri Ṣūfīs, the *tekke.* Sikhism and Zoroastrianism, too, make extensive use of styles and repertoires borrowed from Hindustani classical music, adapting them to their own ritual practices rather than radically breaking from them. These specific cases of sectarian religious tradition in South Asia make it clear that Indianization of religious musics requires the transformation of similarities no less then differences.

Historically, musical influences have been introduced into South Asia by smaller religions and religious sectors that have arrived from elsewhere. Jewish communities established themselves in India as early as the first millennium CE, making communities such as the Cochin Jews some of the oldest in the Jewish Diaspora. Jewish musical traditions remained both relatively isolated and intact, but also sometimes integrated with Indian music—for example, in the theater ensembles in urban centers such as Mumbai.

Christian communities can also claim long and complex histories in South India. Among the oldest Christian sects are those that descend from the Christian Orthodox traditions of the Middle East, especially the Syrian Orthodox church. In some parts of India, especially in Kerala, the Christian population is comparable in size to other religious groups, making it no longer possible to consider them as simply a minority religious community. Christian musical traditions have distinctive qualities, but they also reflect the unifying sound aesthetic of Indian music as a whole. Christian worship is extensively liturgical, lending itself to the congregational performance of hymns. As a result, Indian Christian churches are capable of adapting Christian hymn repertoires from Europe and North America, but are no less disposed to draw upon *bhajan* repertoires.

South Asia has long attracted intensive missionary activity, some of it at the behest of colonial forces, and some under the auspices of Christian denominations in the West. Anglican and evangelical Protestant traditions are therefore present in the cities and regions of English domination, whereas Catholicism is more common in areas of Portuguese colonialism, particularly in Goa and some parts of Sri Lanka. Evangelical Protestantism also has an especially strong presence in Sri Lanka.

The musical traces and transformations produced by the presence of Christianity in South Asia are considerable. During the twentieth century, the publication of hymnals with regional Indian languages supplanting European texts became so extensive that it is possible to speak of an Indianization of Christian hymnody. The instrumentarium of South Asian music, moreover, also reflects missionary and colonial influences, as can be seen in the widespread use of brass bands, including for rituals of various kinds. Another example of this influence is the Indianization of the harmonium, a portable organ of European origin with hand-pumped bellows that has encroached into South Asian music—for example, into *qawwālī,* which would be unthinkable without the harmonium.

Whatever the influences from Christianity and Western religious incursions into India, it is still necessary to recognize the resilience of Indian music itself. Rather than rejecting hymn traditions and Western instruments as foreign, Indian musical traditions have transformed them and integrated them so that they play unifying roles in the interaction between music and religion in India.

POSTCOLONIAL AND GLOBAL SITES FOR MUSIC AND RELIGION. Religious musical practices in South Asia have embraced rather than rejected modernization, with its changing technologies and diverse media. Even the most basic ontologies of sound and its density in the universe have benefited from technologies, not least among them electronic amplification and recording. In the sound universe of the Indian city, the broadcasting of music from loudspeakers, radios, and cassette recorders produces a texture comprised of competing voices and traditions. Extreme volume itself has become a medium for enhancing the contemplation of devotional music in the public sphere.

Modern technology and mediation have also proved particularly useful for the popularization of South Asian religious music. In the vast industry of Indian film-making, for example, the reconciliation of religious difference has long provided one of the most fundamental themes. Whether focusing on the virtually irreconcilable relationships between the families of Hindu-Muslim lovers or on past and present moments of sectarian violence (e.g., Mani Ratnam's *Bombay,* which won international acclaim in 1995), Indian filmmakers and composers draw upon music to signify religious unity, even to effect it symbolically on the screen. In the twenty-first century film is perhaps the preeminent site in which religious themes are expressed through the unifying power of Indian music.

The religious musics of South Asia have also achieved global distribution as world music. The globalization of religious music began during the British colonial era, not least because of the successful establishment of a colonial recording industry by British firms. Recordings broadened the audience base both in South Asia and abroad, creating processes of exchange and hybridity. The first vocalists to achieve global status were the *dhrupad* singers, Faiyazuddin Dagar (1934–1989) and Zahiruddin Dagar (1932–1994) Few musicians anywhere have achieved the global stardom of Nusrat Fateh Ali Khan (1948–1997), whose performances of *qawwālī* wove traditional motifs of devotion into a world-music mix.

The globalization of religious music has further benefited from the South Asian Diaspora, with its extensive patterns of settlement and exchange with India itself. The musical styles of the Diaspora integrate religious musics in complex ways, from the merging of folk and ritual musics in *bhangra,* to the *bhajans* and other devotional practices that provide the template for the styles known as *chutney* in Indo-Caribbean popular music. Throughout the history of India, sacred musics have accommodated religious influences from outside the subcontinent, and they have themselves extended across Asia with the spread of Hinduism and Buddhism, and with the colonial dispersion of Indians to South Africa, the Pacific, Europe, and the Americas. At the beginning of the twenty-first century, the religious musics of India thrive in the Diaspora. Even as they respond to the pressures of globalization, they retain their vigor and their significance in South Asian society, providing unity to the Diaspora no less than during the millennia of religious diversity in India itself.

Bibliography

Theological and Philosophical Issues

Blackburn, Stuart. *Singing of Birth and Death: Texts in Performance.* Philadelphia, 1988.

Hamilton, Sue. *Indian Philosophy: A Very Short Introduction.* Oxford, 2001.

Roche, David. "Music and Trance." In *The Garland Encyclopedia of World Music,* vol. 5, *South Asia: The Indian Subcontinent,* edited by Alison Arnold. New York, 2000.

Rowell, Lewis. *Music and Musical Thought in Early India.* Chicago, 1992.

Ritual and Tribal Practices

Babiracki, Carol. "Music and the History of Tribe-Caste Interaction in Chotanagpur." In *Ethnomusicology and Modern Music History,* edited by Stephen Blum, Philip V. Bohlman, and Daniel Neuman, pp. 207–228. Urbana, Ill., 1991.

Gaston, Anne-Marie. *Krishna's Musicians: Musicians and Music Making in the Temples of Nathdvara Rajasthan.* New Delhi, 1997.

Gold, Ann Grodzins. *Fruitful Journeys: The Ways of Rajasthani Pilgrims.* Berkeley, Calif., 1988.

Gurung, Kishor. *Ghamtu: A Narrative Ritual Music Tradition as Observed by the Gurungs of Nepal.* Kathmandu, Nepal, 1996.

Roche, David. "Devi Amba's Drum: Mina Miracle Chant and the Ritual Ostinato of Spirit-Possession Performance in Southern Rajasthan." Ph.D. diss., University of California, Berkeley, 1996.

Wolf, Richard K. "Of God and Death—Music in Ritual and Everyday Life: A Musical Ethnography of the Kotas of South India." Ph.D. diss., University of Illinois at Urbana-Champaign, 1997.

Wolf, Richard K. "Music in Seasonal and Life-Cycle Rituals." In *The Garland Encyclopedia of World Music.* Vol. 5: *South Asia: The Indian Subcontinent,* edited by Alison Arnold. New York, 2000.

Hinduism

Hopkins, Steven Paul. *Singing the Body of God: The Hymns of Vedantādeśika in Their South Indian Tradition.* New York and Oxford, 2002.

Howard, Wayne. *Sāmavedic Chant.* New Haven, Conn., 1977.

Jackson, William. "Religious and Devotional Music: Southern Area." In *The Garland Encyclopedia of World Music.* Vol. 5: *South Asia: The Indian Subcontinent,* edited by Alison Arnold. New York, 2000.

Morinis, E. Alan. *Pilgrimage in the Hindu Tradition: A Case Study of West Bengal.* Delhi, 1984.

Staal, J. Frits. *Nambudiri Veda Recitation.* The Hague, 1961.

Buddhism

Ellingson, Ter. "The Mandala of Sound: Concepts and Sound Structures in Tibetan Ritual Music." Ph.D. diss., University of Wisconsin, Madison, 1979.

Trewin, Mark. "Rhythms of the Gods: The Musical Symbolics of Power and Authority in the Buddhist Kingdom of Ladakh." Ph.D. diss., City University of London, 1996.

Greene, Paul D. "Sounding the Body in Buddhist Nepal: *Neku* Horns, Himalayan Shamanism, and the Transmigration of the Disembodied Spirit." *World of Music* 4, no. 2 (2002): 93–114.

Islam

Beck, Guy. "Religious and Devotional Music: Northern Area." In *The Garland Encyclopedia of World Music,* vol. 5, *South Asia: The Indian Subcontinent,* edited by Alison Arnold. New York, 2000.

Qureshi, Regula Burckhardt. *Sufi Music of India and Pakistan: Sound, Context, and Meaning in Qawwali.* Chicago, 1995.

Sakata, Hiromi Lorraine. "Devotional Music." In *The Garland Encyclopedia of World Music,* vol. 5, *South Asia: The Indian Subcontinent,* edited by Alison Arnold. New York 2000.

Further Religious Traditions

Dimock, Edward D., Jr., and Denise Levertov, eds. and trans. *In Praise of Krishna: Songs from the Bengali.* Garden City, N.Y., 1967.

Henry, Edward O. *Chant the Names of God: Musical Culture in Bhojpuri-Speaking India.* San Diego, Calif., 1988.

Kelting, M. Whitney. *Singing to the Jinas: Jain Laywomen, Maṇḍaḷ Singing, and the Negotiations of Jain Devotion.* New York and Oxford, 2001.

Maskarinec, Gregory G. *The Rulings of the Night: An Ethnography of Nepalese Shaman Oral Texts.* Madison, Wis., 1995.

Myers, Helen. *Music of Hindu Trinidad: Songs from the India Diaspora.* Chicago, 1997.

Tingey, Carol. *Auspicious Music in a Changing Society: The Damāi Musicians of Nepal.* London, 1994.

Weisethaunet, Hans. *The Performance of Everyday Life: The Gaine of Nepal.* Oslo, 1998.

PHILIP V. BOHLMAN (2005)

MUSIC: MUSIC AND RELIGION IN SOUTHEAST ASIA

The ten nation-states of Southeast Asia, namely Brunei, Burma, Cambodia, Indonesia, Laos, Malaysia, the Philippines, Singapore, Thailand, and Vietnam, contain many hundreds of ethnic groups. These regional groups speak thousands of different languages practice various religions, and perform thousands of styles of music. Although many of the Southeast Asian countries are trying to build national cultures, regionalism is usually accepted, sometimes celebrated, and occasionally suppressed. Major faiths practiced in Southeast Asia include Islam, Buddhism, Christianity, and Hinduism.

Vocal and instrumental music has been central to the religious life of the region from antiquity to the present. Most of this music shares some common characteristics that distinguishes it from compositions found in other areas of the world. Separating music strictly by country can be misleading. The mainland countries of Thailand, Laos, and Cambodia, for example, all celebrate certain ceremonial traditions (such as the *wai kruu* ritual) that honor teachers, ancestral spirits, and the Buddha, whereas Malaysia and Indonesia, most of whose residents are Muslim, share several contemporary Islamic musical styles. Vietnam's religious music shares more similarities with the Chinese music of East Asia than with ritual songs in other neighboring countries.

Southeast Asians belong to all of the major world religions. In the past, the religious rituals practiced within any particular faith differed markedly by country. Mass communications and education throughout the region, however, have reduced or eliminated local adaptations. Reform movements and urbanization also have helped to standardize religious and musical practices. For example, Muslims in southern Thailand or Vietnam now worship in much the same way as do their counterparts in the southern Philippines and the Lesser Sunda Islands of Indonesia.

Despite the modernization that threatens the unique regional traditions, most Southeast Asian countries maintain distinctive strata that represent various periods of cultural developments and belief systems. In central Java, for example, in the courtyards of the royal mosques during the week-long Muslim celebration called Mawlid that commemorates the birth of the prophet Muḥammad, musicians still play the *gamelan* called *sekaten,* a musical ensemble that was first developed in the 1600s to help spread Islam. Oddly enough, these performances occur near the headquarters of a Muslim reformist organization Laskar Jihad, which pointedly rejects such music, as it seeks to transform most of Southeast Asia into an Islamic super state. Such unique regional traditions seemingly in contrast to modernist movements are often contested and may disappear or secularize to survive.

Indigenous faiths—once widely practiced—are gradually decreasing as evangelism, modernization, and deforestation encroach on the rural environment. Most premodern ethnic groups are converting, adapting, or moving to urban centers and giving up their rich ritual and musical traditions. Several groups in remote areas of each country, however, have maintained their ancestral beliefs. The Temiar people of Malaysia, for instance, continue to practice their traditional songs of healing, gender relationships, and trance mediums.

Musical activity in Southeast Asia ranges from frequent to rare. In Bali, Indonesia, creating art—dance, sculpture, and painting in addition to music—is a fundamental part of the Hindu religion. In some parts of Malaysia, by contrast, Islamic leaders may prohibit music.

NOTIONS OF POWER. Transformational ideas of spiritual and political power have had a long history in numerous religious traditions. These notions are usually centered on a person, place, or object. Great leaders and artists, for example, are often perceived to have become more spiritually powerful after a religious experience; in Muslim regions, for example, a musician may become purer after having visited the holy city of Mecca. Moreover, many famous composers and compositions often are considered to have been divinely inspired; in Bali, this concept is described by a standard term: *taksu.* Ancient places thought to be invested with spiritual force, such as Cambodia's Angkor Wat and Java's Borobudur, also can be viewed as centers of power. Similarly, certain objects, such as heirlooms and musical instruments, may be believed to contain or emanate divine power.

Gong-chime musical ensembles have often been viewed as vessels of power and as vehicles for ennobling rulers or framing ceremonial events. These ensembles usually feature hanging or horizontally-mounted knobbed gongs (as distinguished from vertical East Asian flat gongs), sometimes accompanied by wind or stringed instruments or drums. The craft of metallurgy, which has been practiced for thousands of years, was initially developed in Vietnam. Bronze musical instruments gradually assumed ritual prominence throughout the region; religious ceremonies incorporated bronze drums, for instance, as early as 100 BCE. Later artisans constructed foundries in order to manufacture instruments; by the second millennium CE, the smiths who crafted these instruments were being hailed as artists that could harness the power of the earth.

Examples of these ensembles include the various gamelans of Java, Bali, and Lombok, in Indonesia; the *kulintang* of the southern Philippines; the Thai *piphat*; the Burmese *hsaìñwaìñ*; the Cambodian *pinn peat*; and various others found in Malaysia, Laos, and elsewhere. According to their believers, these ensembles frequently mediate power. For example, in some ensembles musical instruments or elements that unite male and female (in counterpart pairs) or other cosmological symbolism may be thought to invoke the divine or balance the world through performance. Similarly, in Thailand, worshipers believe that elder *piphat* musicians can access power through a sacred repertoire and then manifest the divine while they play.

Many Southeast Asians also believe that these gong-chime ensembles possess a residing spirit; faithful listeners will provide offerings on a regular basis. In Indonesia, older ensembles are generally thought to be more sacred; the greater the age of the instruments, the greater their interaction with the ancestors, and therefore the greater reverence and power the ensemble commands. In these gamelans, the gong is the spiritual center; it may receive a title or name during a consecration ceremony on behalf of the ensemble. Some scholars have asserted that gamelans are symbolic depictions of macrocosm and microcosm, and that they represent a tripartite universe or anthropomorphism of head, body, and foot; others note that some of the ensembles are considered to be living organisms. Reports in Java, of particularly "alive" gamelans playing on their own without human musicians, add to the ensembles' identity and mystique.

Gong-chime compositions also are believed to be powerful, able to influence nature, time, places, people and objects. For example, some Javanese believe that a composition called *Anglir Mendung* (Like storm clouds) can cause rainfall if it is performed at the proper time. Many scholars have also suggested that the cyclic nature of the gong-punctuated music produced by gamelans in Java and Bali echoes the passage of time; they compare it to the region's complex calendar systems and interpret the music as a powerful metaphor of the structure of life and the cosmos.

Most of the ancient concepts of power and music were originally based on Hindu-Buddhist ideas; they were widely adopted in the region partially because early monarchs found these notions appealing. Later, Muslim evangelists who traveled to the region appropriated these ideas as they sought to gain converts in areas like the southern Philippines and Java. They also developed new instrumental, vocal, and dramatic musical forms in order to spread Islam; similarly, Christian missionaries adapted Western hymns to the regional musical genres to draw converts to their faith.

Poetry in song form—intended to communicate new teachings, sacred stories, and prayers—has been central to Southeast Asian religious life for generations. Sacred texts sung in many different sacred languages—Hinduism in Sanskrit, Buddhism in Pali, Islam in Arabic, and Catholicism in Latin—accompanied these new religions into Southeast Asia. At first, these languages were used solely in the courts, in order to legitimize authority through sung poetry and chant. Stories from religious texts—such as the *Rāmāyaṇa*, the *Mahābhārata*, the Qurʾ ān, or the Bible—often became songs that were sung in either the local or the imported language; these songs, in turn, popularized the new beliefs. Some songs that blended the old and the new had particular powers; in Java, for example, certain songs could be sung to stop heavy rains, tame crocodiles, or to exorcise malevolent spirits. In Sumatra, a shaman trained in black-and-white magic could use eleven different grades of song to entice and capture renegade tigers that had trespassed onto human lands.

One powerful musical ritual celebrated in several countries is the shadow puppet theater. In many cultures, it carries cosmological significance, particularly in the Indonesian areas of Java, Bali, and Lombok. There, puppeteers (*dalang*) are greatly respected for their power to re-create the universe, restore spiritual balance, achieve healing, and perform other transformations. The accompanying music is also powerful; in Java, the gamelan compositions played during the overture symbolize the span of a human life, while in Lombok, the opening gamelan pieces invoke the elements of life (fire, air, water) to help re-create the world. A *dalang* transmits the morals of a story and imparts spiritual and ethical values while entertaining and educating the audience. Moreover, a puppet theater performance might affect the environment. In Cambodia, the Reamker shadow theater, a local appropriation of the *Rāmāyaṇa*, is believed to attract rain.

AUTHENTICITY AND ACCULTURATION. Musical ideas frequently accompanied new religions into the region; these either were retained fairly intact, such as the Buddhist chants that were adopted in mainland Southeast Asia, or absorbed into local forms. Religious influences from India came to Southeast Asia unevenly and over many centuries; most of the regions modified a particular faith's notions of hierarchy, city-state, ruler, and texts to suit the local environment. Musical incorporations are much less obvious, though some scholars have suggested that the cyclic metric cycles used in the gong-chime ensembles may have originated with Indian *tala* systems, and some Sanskrit terms have become part of the musical vocabulary.

The texts of Hinduism and Buddhism have been inspiring and powerful influences, and the scriptures have stimulated dance dramas based on epics such as the *Rāmāyaṇa* and the *Mahābhārata*, as well as poetry and song. The forms that developed were generally indigenous and based on preexisting frameworks. For example, artists in some mainland Southeast Asian areas, such as Laos, constructed unique courtship songs to transmit Buddhist *Jātaka* tales and Hindu-Buddhist cosmological stories. In the lowland Philippines, the passion of the Christ (*Pasyon*) was recited or sung following performances of older, pre-Christian epics, and the all-night singing that recounts the birth of Muḥammad in the southern Philippines adopted the same framework.

Influences from China, too, have been widespread and particularly prominent in Vietnam, where many Buddhist texts have been translated and maintained in classical Chinese. Chinese instruments have found favor in several areas, and some Chinese narratives have spread as far away as Bali. Chinese immigrants throughout Southeast Asia (the fewest of whom live in Laos, with the majority in Singapore) have maintained or adapted their religious and musical traditions to their particular context. Though India and China have been religious "donor" countries to some extent, it is unwise to suggest that Southeast Asia merely adopted their influences. Each ethnic group and country has changed over time; in addition to exporting socioreligious ideology, India and China also have actively borrowed beliefs from Southeast Asia.

Southeast Asian countries have exploited each other for millennia. Victors in early Siam often carried off Cambodian music organizations following a conquest, and then institutionalized Cambodian music in Thai courts; Thai musicians, in turn, were often kidnapped and taken to Burma; Laotian court music is thought to have originated in Cambodia; and monks from these countries frequently visited Buddhist centers in other nations, thus spreading and sharing liturgical and musical ideas. Javanese religio-cultural influence was imposed upon much of the archipelago during the reign of dynasties such as the Hindu-Buddhist Majapahit and the early Islamic Mataram. Religious and cultural concepts and musical instruments thus moved frequently throughout the region, inspiring local artistic responses to Hinduism, Buddhism, Christianity, and Islam. Reform movements, found primarily within Islamic societies, have fought against such heterogeneity and striven for purity in religious and musical practices.

Islam in Southeast Asia is often termed moderate by scholars. In rural areas, Islamic events may still be celebrated with local music, though in coastal and urban areas, orthodox or standardized forms of worship are the norm. The Islamic Minangkabau people in west Sumatra, who live in coastal and inland areas, are a case in point. While the coastal Minangkabau have discontinued most of their indigenous poetic forms, gong-chime ensembles, and matrilineal family patterns to follow Islam, most of those that live inland have retained them.

The Christian Batak in north Sumatra faced a similar dilemma. Barred from using indigenous music in church, many of them switched to German-style brass bands in conforming to so-called Christian notions of proper music. These ensembles, however, soon lost favor; coupled with a change to local control and a revival movement, the "traditional" drum-gong ensemble, *gondang sembilan*, was then brought into the church for services. Much earlier, in fact, Catholics in Central Java had featured masses that were accompanied by gamelans. Such blending of the local music with the adopted religion is often contested, however, particularly within the Islamic communities.

Though the relationship between music and Islam has been complicated, many Southeast Asian Muslims regularly enjoy music. Several instruments have become associated with pan-Islam in the region, including barrel drums, frame drums, plucked lutes, and oboes. The two musical-like behaviors directly associated with Islam—Qurʾanic recitation and call to prayer—are fairly uniform throughout the region. Earlier distinctions in practice seem to have largely disappeared, with the development of telecommunications, Islamic schools, recordings, and the visits of specialists from countries such as Egypt. Many Southeast Asian Muslims also travel to the Middle East to study these prayer forms, and participate in frequent national and international contests designed to standardize these activities. In some areas, such as Indonesia, chant is accepted as a form of "music"; a separate genre (*seni musik Islam*, or Islamic musical art) can promote music as an agent of *dakwah* (bringing people to Islam); while in other areas (similar to Arabic countries), chant is not considered to be music because it is based on the divine word of the Qurʾ ān, and music in Islam is rarely approved. One intriguing development in Malaysia and Indonesia is participation of women and girls in Qurʾanic recitation. They perform in public and on television, and, in modern Indonesia, even in the company of men. In these respects—allowing women to publicly perform recitation and generally accepting music—Islam in Southeast Asia appears to be more moderate than in most of the Middle East and South Asia.

The spread of Islam to many areas has led to a marked decrease or a secularization of non-Islamic musical forms. For example, the shadow puppet theater has disappeared in several parts of Malaysia (where it conveyed Hindu epics), while that on the Indonesian island of Lombok has further secularized and is frequently aimed at tourists. Other forms have had to become more Islamic to survive; for example, many poetic forms in Sumatra are now prefaced by Arabic prayers. Modernization and globalization have also affected these and hundreds of other genres. Forms that used to be "functional" (ritually transformative or educational) are now "aesthetic" (placed on a formal stage for appreciation) and compete with television for an audience, or are repackaged for tourism. The Cambodian Reamker shadow theater, for example, once performed as a part of various complex rituals over several nights, now is staged only as a one-hour presentation at universities. Younger generations of Southeast Asians have not generally been interested in retaining ritual music traditions different from orthodox or modernized forms.

Orthodoxy, Traditionalism, and Popular Movements. Some tension exists between orthodox and local practices in most of Southeast Asia, not only in the Muslim regions but also among Christians, Buddhists, and Hindus. For centuries, people throughout much of Southeast Asia believed that the landscape was populated by ancestral or natural spirits, who were the original owners of the land, water, and trees; these notions have been fundamental in creating and systematizing rice culture and associated ritual practices featuring music. External religions have acculturated to the context and contributed new inspiration and meaning to the arts. In some areas, indigenous and external beliefs were constructed into a complementary duality of female and male; local faiths (female) functioned in fertility and healing and often involved female officials, while imported ones operated in royal houses and formal places of worship and were dominated by men.

Even today, many mainland Southeast Asians perceive no contradiction in honoring Buddha [Siddhārtha Gautama (c. 563–c. 483 BCE)] in addition to a supreme being and a pantheon of deities; similarly, some Catholics in Vietnam, Muslims in Java, and Hindus in Bali include altars for spirits or deities. In this model of acculturation, earlier music practices are often incorporated into syncretic rites. For example, traditional gong ensembles have become part of animistic funeral practices in upland Christianized Vietnam; the sacred gamelan *Mawlid* is performed during the ceremony of the same name to honor Muḥammad in north Lombok in Indonesia, while a different sacred gamelan, *jerujeng,* is used for Buddhist festivals in the western part of the island. A free-reed mouth organ accompanies female spirit mediums who intervene in the curing rituals performed in the Buddhist areas of northeast Thailand and Laos; the *hsaìñwaìñ* ensemble accompanies possession trances held at Burmese temples; the *kulintang* ensemble accompanies Islamic rites in parts of Mindanau and the Sulu Archipelago in the Philippines, while a gong marks the hours during Ramaḍān in Datu Piang. In Indonesia, gamelans direct Muslim performers of hobbyhorse trance dancing in East Java, and Roman Catholic Torajans in Sulawesi dance in large circles as part of elaborate funerals to send the spirit of the deceased to the next world. Among those who practice the pure forms of world religions, indigenous music and ritual may be invited as a last resort. Orthodox Muslims in Sumbawa, Indonesia, have incorporated female performers, gong ensembles, and pre-Islamic ritual forms when Western medicines and Islamic prayers are not enough for their congregations. Similarly, Indonesians say that, although most of them are practicing Muslims, they all worship the volcano deities whenever a nearby volcano threatens to erupt.

Colonization by European powers profoundly affected every Southeast Asian country except Thailand, which has never been subject to Western rule. Europeans introduced Christianity, established missions, and imported and modified hymns; the new religion found favor in the Philippines and in parts of mainland Southeast Asia and Indonesia. Movements since the late twentieth century have aimed at developing "indigenous hymnody" (hymns based on scripture in local languages with local music elements) to maintain and multiply the faithful. Warfare and communism have exerted equal forces on the music of the region, despite the fact that many countries were not directly involved in either disruption. Buddhist and Christian music and services in the affected mainland countries (namely, Laos, Cambodia, and Vietnam) were largely restricted, and sometimes allowed to be performed only in service to the state. In Cambodia, court music quickly disappeared in the 1970s; after the disastrous Khmer Rouge leadership, many other musical forms also vanished, along with thousands of musicians. Due to poverty, isolation, and political conservatism, sponsored music activities in Laos are similarly lacking.

Beginning in the late nineteenth century, Islam in Southeast Asia, once tremendously varied, began to assume a recognizable shape. In Indonesia, Malaysia, and Brunei, a reformist movement took hold and began to enforce the pillars of Islam, establishing schools taught by Arab specialists or returning Ḥājji (pilgrims who had traveled to Mecca). A number of pan-Islamic musical forms soon developed, including *hadrah* (Ṣūfī-related music/ritual events), *burdah* (hymn singing), and *zikir, dabus,* or *dhikr* (Ṣūfī ritual music involving repetitive phrases), generally accompanied by frame drums and often stimulating trance. Many of the early Muslim evangelists were Ṣūfī and their legacies remain; perhaps this fact has contributed to a more permissive attitude toward music in the region. As the language of the Qurʾān, Arabic has a special status in all Muslim areas of Southeast Asia. Songs in Arabic, regardless their source or meaning, are generally considered proper and spiritually meritorious.

What Arabic has been for Islam, the language of Pali has been for Buddhism. Chant assemblies, convoked by signals played on bells, gongs, drums, and other percussion instruments, perform the Pali canon of liturgy. Music during services, however, varies by country. In Vietnam, monks often perform on a lute, and lay musicians may be asked to accompany funeral ceremonies; in Burma, tempo is marked by a bell and clappers, in Laos by bells and a drum; the Chinese diaspora communities use a diversity of ritual instruments in numerous Buddhist, neo-Confucian, or other ceremonies. Buddhist reform movements are not known, though some Thai communities are concerned about a Hindu layer (found throughout much of mainland Buddhism) underlying many rites and music. Furthermore, isolated Buddhist groups today often wish to be part of a larger community, and they may ultimately sacrifice local traditions for their identity and survival. The Boda of Lombok, for example, frequently invite Javanese and occasionally Japanese Buddhist monks to update their training, chants, and services as they coexist with a strong society of Muslims.

Popular religious music is widespread in Malaysia and island Southeast Asia. In Indonesia, *pop rohani* is Christian pop; *qasidah moderen* and some styles of *dangdut* (combining national, Western, Arabic, and Hindi film music elements) are Islamic. The performer Rhoma Irama pioneered *dangdut* in the 1970s. Commentators have credited or accused Irama of proselytizing for Islam; most artists, however, do not promote Islam. Singer and dancer Inul Daratista rose from poverty to become one of the most popular and controversial *dangdut* artists in twenty-first-century Indonesia. She became a superstar through music videos that showcased her erotic dance movements. She was soon censured by a conservative Muslim organization, the Indonesian Ulemas Council. The public rose to her defense, however, and created a backlash against the council, demonstrating the limited popularity of reformist Islam. In other areas, Balinese popular music frequently discusses issues of Hindu experience, and in Singapore and Malaysia, videos and video CDs of Buddhist songs in a karaoke format are produced for national and international markets.

BIBLIOGRAPHY

For detailed surveys of music and related issues in Southeast Asia, see *Southeast Asia–Garland Encyclopedia of World Music*, vol. 4, edited by Sean Williams and Terry Miller, New York and London, 1998. For shorter surveys, see the *New Grove Dictionary of Music and Musicians*, edited by Stanley Sadie, London, 2001. A useful annotated bibliography on performing arts and religion is *The Music and Dance of the World's Religions* by E. Gardner Rust, Westport, Conn., 1996. Books that feature chapters on musical culture in Southeast Asia include *Essays on Southeast Asian Performing Arts: Local Manifestations and Cross-Cultural Implications*, edited by Kathy Foley, Berkeley, Calif., 1992; *Balinese Music in Context: a Sixty-Fifth Birthday Tribute to Hans Oesch*, edited by Danker Schaareman, Winterthur, Switzerland, 1992; and *Performance in Java and Bali: Studies of Narrative, Theatre, Music, and Dance*, edited by Bernard Arps, London, 1993. A periodical focusing on music in Vietnam, Cambodia, and Laos is *Selected Reports in Ethnomusicology*, Vol. IX, edited by Amy Catlin, Los Angeles, 1992.

Anderson, Benedict. "The Idea of Power in Javanese Culture." In *Culture and Politics in Indonesia*, edited by Clare Holt et al., pp. 1–69. Ithaca, N.Y., 1972. A look at Javanese sultans and the ways they construct and manipulate spiritual and political power through symbolic and ritual action.

Bakan, Michael B. *Music of Death and New Creation: Experiences in the World of Balinese Gamelan Beleganjur*. Chicago, 1999. A reflexive ethnography describing political uses, contests, and rituals of processional *beleganjur* ensembles.

Becker, Judith. "Hindu-Buddhist Time in Javanese Gamelan Music." In *The Study of Time, Papers from the Fourth Conference of the International Society for the Study of Time, Alpbach-Austria*, edited by J. T. Fraser, N. Lawrence, and D. Park, pp. 162–172. New York, 1981. An article that explores numerology and cyclic time in gamelan music, calendar systems, and Hindu-Buddhist Javanese cosmology.

Becker, Judith. *Gamelan Stories: Tantrism, Islam, and Aesthetics in Central Java*. Tempe, Ariz., 1993. A work that explores the diverse religious background and spiritual significance of Javanese gamelan and dance dramas.

Becker, J. and A. L. Becker. "A Musical Icon: Power and Meaning in Javanese Gamelan Music." In *The Sign in Music and Literature*, edited by Wendy Steiner, pp. 203–215. Austin, Tex., 1981. A theoretical study combining linguistics and meaning in the articulation of power in Javanese gamelan performance, in which gamelan music is iconic of time and cosmology.

Brinner, Benjamin. *Knowing Music, Making Music: Javanese Gamelan and the Theory of Musical Competence and Interaction*. Chicago, 1995. An ethnography of Javanese music competence and its location in self-perceptions, mutual assessments, ritual and context, and cognition.

DeVale, Sue Carole, and I Wayan Dibia. "*Sekar Anjar*: An Exploration of Meaning in Balinese Gamelan." *The World of Music* 33 (1) (1991): 5–51. A thorough and structural investigation into the cosmological design motives, symbolism, and architecture of Balinese instruments and gamelan music.

Geertz, Clifford. *The Religion of Java*. New York, 1960. A classic study that categorizes differing practices and views of Islam in Java; Indonesian scholars often refer to this book in their own studies.

Geertz, Clifford. *The Interpretation of Cultures*. New York, 1973. A collection of essays featuring penetrating analyses on person and time in Bali, the Balinese cockfight, Balinese social inversion, and Javanese ritual and social change, among other topics.

Geertz, Clifford. *Negara: The Balinese Theater State in the Nineteenth Century*. Princeton, N.J., 1980. An interpretive analysis of theatric Hindu political imagery, symbolism, and the state.

Gold, Lisa Rachel. "The Gender Wayang Repertoire in Theater and Ritual: A Study of Balinese Musical Meaning." Ph.D. diss., University of California, Berkeley, 1998. A detailed look at the ritual significance of the Balinese shadow puppet theater and its music in the construction of spiritual meaning and narrative.

Harnish, David. "Religion and Music: Syncretism, Orthodox Islam, and Musical Change in Lombok." *Selected Reports in Ethnomusicology* 7 (1988): 123–138. An overview of music changes among Muslims in Lombok, Indonesia as a result of increasing Islamification.

Harnish, David. "The Future Meets the Past in the Present: Music and Buddhism in Lombok." *Asian Music* 25, nos. 1–2 (1994): 29–50. An analysis of a particular Buddhist festival in Lombok, its negotiations with indigenous beliefs and music, and the Indonesian national drive for monotheism.

Harnish, David. "Music, Myth, and Liturgy at the Lingsar Temple Festival in Lombok, Indonesia." *Yearbook for Traditional Music* 29 (1997): 80–106. A detailed structural and interpretive overview of an annual religious festival in Lombok combining migrant Hindu Balinese and local Sasak Muslims, their debates on myth, and their music.

Harnish, David. "Worlds of Wayang Sasak: Music, Performance, and Negotiations of Religion and Modernity." *Asian Music*

34, no. 2 (2003): 91–120. A discussion on the history of the shadow puppet theater in Lombok, its relationship to changing Islamic orientations, and adjustments made by puppeteers to religious and commercial forces.

Hatch, Martin. "Music and Religion in Southeast Asia." In *The Encyclopedia of Religion*, edited by Mircea Eliade, vol. 10. New York, 1987. This article emphasizes Javanese traditions.

Heimarck, Brita Renée. *Balinese Discourses on Music and Modernization: Village Voices and Urban Views.* New York and London, 2003. An ethnography that traces the tensions between village and urban views on music and ritual significance, including an analysis of the transformation of music in conservatories.

Herbst, Edward. *Voices in Bali: Energies and Perceptions in Vocal Music and Dance Theater.* London, 1997. An ethnography of performance, highlighting the spiritual preparedness of performers and their interactions with ritual context.

Ramseyer, Urs. *The Art and Culture of Bali.* Singapore, 1986. A comprehensive look at the role of religion in Balinese artistic culture.

Rasmussen, Anne K. "The Qur' ān in Indonesian Daily Life: The Public Project of Musical Oratory." *Ethnomusicology* 45 (1) (2001): 30–57. A descriptive ethnography of the position of Qur'anic recitation in contemporary Indonesia; the author offers many insightful reflections on her studies on recitation with other women and her interaction with performers, as well as her own performances.

Roseman, Marina. *Healing Sounds from the Malaysia Rainforest: Temiar Music and Medicine.* Berkeley, Calif., 1991. A deeply contextualized study on the religious culture and music of Temiar, with emphases on trance, healing and gender.

Sarkissian, Margaret. *D'Albuquerque's Children: Performing Tradition in Malaysia's Portuguese Settlements.* Chicago, 2000. A comprehensive music ethnography of the minority Portuguese descendents in Malaysia, their negotiations with history and the contemporary state, and cultural/spiritual elements of performance.

Sumarsam. *Gamelan: Cultural Interaction and Musical Development in Central Java.* Chicago, 1995. An analysis of Hindu, Islamic, European, Chinese, and Malay forces and their influence on the development of Javanese gamelan over the centuries.

Sutton, R. Anderson. *Calling Back the Spirit: Music, Dance, and Cultural Politics in Lowland South Sulawesi.* New York, 2002. An exploration of the way Makassarese performers seek to empower local music and dance by reinvesting spiritual significance in response to broader Indonesian and international cultural influences.

Tenzer, Michael. *Balinese Music.* Berkeley, Calif. and Singapore, 1998. An overview of Balinese music styles and their roles in Balinese culture and religion.

Walton, Susan. "Heavenly Nymphs and Earthly Delights: Javanese Female Singers, Their Music and Their Lives." Ph.D. diss., University of Michigan, Ann Arbor, 1996. An exploration of the spiritual and sometimes erotic imagery of Javanese female gamelan singers and their negotiations and manipulations of that position; the author, a fine gamelan singer herself, also illuminates the decisions that singers make during performances.

Wong, Deborah. *Sounding the Center: History and Aesthetics in Thai Buddhist Performance.* Chicago, 2001. A sometimes reflexive ethnography on the Thai *piphat* ensemble, ritual authority and the *wai kruu* ceremony from a performance studies' perspective.

Wong, Deborah, and René T. A. Lysloff. "Threshold to the Sacred: The Overture in Thai and Javanese Ritual Performance." *Ethnomusicology* 35 (3) (1991): 315–348. An article that examines overtures in Javanese shadow puppet theater and Thai Hindu-Buddhist ritual; both establish ritual time and space for the audience and invoke divine presence.

DAVID HARNISH (2005)

MUSIC: MUSIC AND RELIGION IN CHINA, KOREA, AND TIBET

The three main streams of religion in East Asia—Confucianism, Buddhism, and Daoism—all employ music to express beliefs and ideas. Ancient shamanic practices as well as Christianity and Islam also play a part in the musical histories of China, Korea, and Tibet.

CHINA. Popular religion in China has for centuries drawn from Confucianist, Daoist, Buddhist, and animist elements. Extremely diverse in their local practices, the various forms of popular religion serve as vehicles for intense spiritual expression. Music is an integral part of this local structure. Festivals of popular religion almost always include processions accompanied by outdoor bands, and lion or dragon dances. Performances of music drama dedicated to the gods also form a key part of these festivals.

Aside from the three major groups, numerous minor religious communities also exist in China, Taiwan, and Hong Kong. Islam, for example, is practiced by about 3 percent of the population in China. No systematic report on Chinese Islamic practice is available to this author, but while conducting research on Chinese theater in China during the early 1980s, this author observed an evening service in a local mosque in Hangzhou celebrated by a small group of Chinese Sunnī Muslims. The service lasted about an hour and consisted of a cappella chanting of Qur'anic texts in Arabic by the congregation, lead by a mullah with appropriate obeisances.

Christianity also has a small following in China. Chinese Christian liturgies, whether of the Catholic or the Protestant church, follow their Western models closely. Hymnals used in the Chinese Protestant churches contain primarily hymn tunes from the West with Chinese texts, but "acculturated" hymns by Chinese composers based on Western models are occasionally included in Chinese Protestant hymnals. Protestant hymn tunes became one of the important predecessors of the modern Chinese song genre known as *geming geju* ("revolutionary song").

Imperial ancestral cult rites. *Yayue* ("elegant music") was the music used in solemn state rites. The term may be used broadly to denote music used in court rituals and entertainments, as well as that performed in secular government ceremonies. Since the Han dynasty (206 BCE–220 CE), however, the term has come to be used more narrowly to denote music used in solemn sacrificial rites with religious overtones, such as the imperial ancestral cult rites, Confucian rites, and rites dedicated to Heaven and Earth. It is in the latter, more restrictive, sense that the term *yayue* is used here.

Even though the repertory and musical styles of *yayue* changed from one dynasty to the next, it has always been performed by chorus and instrumental ensemble. The *yayue* chorus, called *dengge,* varied in size from one dynasty to the next. The *yayue* instrumental ensemble is sometimes called *bayin* ("eight sounds") because its instruments represent eight essential kinds of timbres: metal (bell), stone (chime), clay (ocarina), wood (pounded wooden box and wooden scraper), gourd (mouth organ whose base was made of gourd), silk (zither), bamboo (flute), and leather (drum). A partial list of *yayue* instruments, according to modern classification, includes, among the idiophones: the *zhong,* suspended clapperless bronze bells of varying sizes struck with a mallet; the *xing,* suspended stone chimes of varying sizes struck with a mallet; the *zhu,* a pounded wooden box; and the *yu,* a tiger-shaped wooden scraper scraped with a bamboo whisk; among the membranophones: the *gu,* suspended drums of varying sizes and shapes; the *bofu,* a two-headed barrel drum placed on a wooden stand, played with bare hands; among the aerophones: the *xun,* an ocarina; the *zhi* and the *di,* transverse bamboo flutes; the *dongxiao,* an end-blown notched bamboo flute; the *paixiao,* a panpipe; and the *sheng,* a mouth organ whose sound box was first made of gourd, now of wood; and among the chordophones: the *qin,* a bridgeless zither with seven strings; and the *se,* a twenty-five string zither with bridges. The number of individual instruments included in the yayue orchestra varied from period to period. Qin with one, two, three, five, and nine strings at various times have been included.

Dance was also an integral part of solemn state sacrificial rites. Two kinds of dances were performed: the *wenwu* (civil dance), and the *wuwu* (military dance). The number of dancers prescribed was thirty-six in six lines of six persons (*liuyi,* "six rows of six dancers") or in eight lines of eight persons (*bayi,* "eight rows of eight dancers"). *Liuyi* was prescribed for rites for emperors, and *bayi* for rites for lesser personages. Occasionally more than sixty-four dancers were used, but such an occurrence was rare and was usually viewed as an aberration. All dancers were male. The *wenwu* dancers, dressed in civilian clothes, held long pheasant feathers in their right hands and flutes in their left hands; the *wuwu* dancers, dressed in military clothes, bore swords in their right hands and shields in their left hands.

In addition to the use of music and dance in solemn state rites, other important ceremonial features included animal sacrifice and the offering of vegetarian food and wine to the personage being honored. Two kinds of animal sacrifice were defined: the *tailao,* or "great sacrifice," involving the sacrificial killing and offering of oxens, sheep, and pigs; and the *xiaolao,* or "lesser sacrifice," involving the sacrificial killing and offering of oxen and sheep only. *Tailao* represented the highest honor to be bestowed and was prescribed only for the rites for emperors and Confucius.

Confucian rites. Shidian, a state sacrificial ritual held in spring and autumn in honor of Confucius, was established by the first emperor of the Han dynasty, Gaozu (r. 206–193 BCE), who made Confucianism the state ideology. Ceremonial features of Shidian rites conducted by the emperor were similar to those of the imperial ancestral cult rites, and like them they underwent many changes over the centuries. Four components remained basic: *tailao,* the Great Sacrifice; three rounds of offering of food and wine to Confucius, known as *sanxian* ("three offerings"); *yayue* performance; and *wenwu.*

Prior to the middle of the Qing dynasty, two ensembles made up the *yayue* orchestra. One, called *tangshangyue* ("ensemble on the terrace"), sat on the terrace adjacent to the main shrine hall where the rite took place; the other, called *tangxiayue* ("ensemble on the ground"), was performed in the courtyard below. After the mid-Qing period (around 1766), however, only the *tangshangyue* was used.

In Shidian rites conducted by the emperor, the *wenwu* was always performed by thirty-six dancers (i.e., *liuyi*), except during the mid-Ming period, from about 1477 to 1531 CE, when the prescribed number of dancers increased first to sixty-four (i.e., *bayi*), then to seventy-two. After 1531 the number of prescribed dancers of Shidian was reduced once again to thirty-six.

Yayue compositions played at Shidian rites are referred to collectively as *dachengyue* ("music of completeness"), a term derived from the name customarily given to Confucian temples, *dachengmiao* ("temple of completeness"). The musical styles and repertoire of *dachengyue,* as well as its tunings and modes, changed frequently over the centuries. The most recent *dachengyue* was commissioned in 1742 by the emperor Qian Long of the Qing dynasty (r. 1736–1796). The Qing repertory consisted of six compositions and their transpositions. The original and the transposed versions were played in the spring and autumn rites respectively. All six compositions are for chorus with accompaniment by *yayue* orchestra. The chorus was made up of twelve male voices.

The texts of the six compositions are hymns of praise to Confucius uniformly composed in eight lines of four words each. Individual words are set syllabically to pitches of equal duration. Melodically, all the compositions are pentatonic with disjunct melodic movement; they were sung in unison in a slow, stately manner.

The vocal melodies were accompanied in unison by bell and stone chime sets and by the entire body of chordophones and aerophones. All the drums and single bells and stone chimes, as well as the *zhu* and the *yu,* perform colotomic, that is, structure-marking, functions. Three strokes on the *zhu* signaled the beginning of a piece; three strokes on the *yu* signaled the end. The melodic phrase setting of each four-word line was initiated by one stroke on the *bozhong* ("big bell"), and concluded with three strokes on the *jiangu* ("big drum") and three more on the *bofu;* these three-stroke *bofu* patterns consisted of a light first beat played by the left hand, an accented second beat played by the right hand, and a concluding beat by both hands. Preceding the singing of each word, the pitch was sounded on one bell of the bell set; afterward the same pitch was struck on a stone chime of the chime set. The dances were accompanied by chorus and orchestra.

Buddhist liturgical music. Traditional Buddhist services comprise four major categories: regular services; rites for the dead; rites for special services; and services commemorating birthdays of Buddhist deities. Regular services are conducted in two types of Buddhist institutions: monasteries and lay Buddhist organizations. In the monasteries, morning and evening services are held daily; in the lay institutions, regular services (modeled after those of the monasteries) are held once or twice weekly.

In all categories of Buddhist services, music, both vocal and instrumental, plays an integral part. Vocal and instrumental items follow one another without break in any given service. In general, Buddhist liturgical music can be characterized as simple, serene, and solemn. Liturgical texts used in Buddhist services are always chanted or sung, either solo or in chorus. *Fanbei* is the generic term for all vocal liturgical music. *Fanbei* is a distinctively Chinese style of liturgical song, though it may have been inspired by the Indian principle of syllabic, monotonic recitation.

Eight types of liturgical texts, some in verse format and some in prose, are used in Buddhist services:

(1) Sūtra (*jing*)—Buddhist scripture in Chinese verse translation with ten syllables to the line. This type contains discourses of the Buddha and the *bodhisattvas*.

(2) *Mantra* (*zhou*)—Central Asian, Pali, or Sanskrit devotional incantations in Chinese syllabic transliteration; *mantra* texts are meaningless to Chinese, though their general import may be known.

(3) Hymn (*zan*)—eulogy in verse having irregular meter.

(4) *Gātha* (*ji*)—verse exposition organized in eight-stanza structure, each stanza having four lines of equal length and each line containing either five or four syllables.

(5) *Nianfo*—chanting the names of the Buddha or *bodhisattvas*. The length of a line is determined by the number of syllables that make up a name.

(6) Prayer (*xuanshu* or *wen*)—prayers in verse to Buddhist deities.

(7) Invocation (*shangyin* or *zuofan*)—verse text calling the congregation to worship.

(8) Instruction (*shisong*)—priest's address to a deity; in verse.

Fanbei music is pentatonic. Some items, such as hymn and *gātha,* feature a wide melodic range and varying melodic contour; others, such as sūtra, *nianfo,* and prayer, have a narrower range and a somewhat static melodic contour. The *mantra* tends to be monotonal. A dominant feature of *fanbei* music is the consistent use of repetitive motifs or pairs of motifs. Variation of motifs is also frequent.

In regular services, each *fanbei* item is begun by the precentor (*weina*), who sings the first phrase and is then joined by the congregation of monks or laypeople. A vocal piece always begins slowly and gradually gets faster. Heterophony frequently results as some members of the congregation sing variants of the melody according to their different abilities. Instruments are always used to accompany singing in regular services. *Fanbei* are frequently chanted or sung by a solo voice in special services, but responsorial and antiphonal singing may also be used. Instrumental accompaniment may be absent in solo chanting in special services.

Three melodic styles of *fanbei* are distinguished by modern writers: syllabic, neumatic, and melismatic. *Fanbei* in syllabic style have one or two notes to each syllable of the text. To this type belong sūtra, *mantra,* prayer, and some *nianfo* chants. *Fanbei* in neumatic style feature three, four, or more notes to each syllable. *Gātha* and some *nianfo* used specifically to accompany the obligatory circumambulation in regular services belong to this type. *Fanbei* in melismatic style have ten or more notes set to one syllable. To this type belongs the hymn.

In traditional Buddhist services, nonpitched idiophones and membranophones are used to accompany *fanbei* singing. Instruments are also used to play the preludes, interludes, and postludes of services. In contemporary practice seven types of instruments are used: the *dagu,* a suspended two-headed barrel drum played with a mallet; the *dazhong,* a suspended bell played with a stick; the *daqing,* a large inverted metal bowl-shaped bell resting on a cushion and struck with a mallet; the *yinqing,* a small inverted bell fastened to a wooden handle and struck with a stick; the *muyu,* a wooden slit drum in the shape of a stylized fish head, struck with a wooden stick; the *danzi,* a small framed gong fastened to a handle and struck with a stick; and the *hazi,* a pair of cymbals. These instruments are made in various sizes to suit the demands of different ritual contexts. Those used in monasteries, for example, are usually larger than those used in lay institutions.

Buddhist worship manuals provide instrumental notation indicating the usage of musical instruments. Duration of notes and dynamics are not indicated in such manuals but are transmitted orally. Vocal melodies are transmitted entirely by oral means.

The arrangement of percussion patterns in a given vocal piece can be divided into three kinds: regular meter, in 4/4 or 3/4; composite meters, alternating between 4/4, 3/4, or 1/4; and unmeasured pieces, having no fixed temporal units. Some instruments use specific rhythmic patterns known by particular names. For example, the *muyu* (slit drum) pattern, known as "Eighty-eight Buddhas," is characterized by a series of accelerated strokes in diminishing volume. Another pattern, "Nine Bells and Fifteen Drums" (referring to the number of strokes on each), is used for the *bozhong* and *jiangu.* This pattern is made up of an initial slow section consisting of alternating drum and bell strokes, a fast central section consisting of simultaneous strokes on both instruments (with the drum being played twice as fast as the bell), and an accented drum stroke to conclude the pattern. During a regular service this pattern is played several times as an interlude and thereby performs a structural function for the entire service similar to that of the ritornello in Western compositions.

Music in Daoist rituals. The role of music in Daoist ritual practices has not been studied systematically by musicologists. Hence any discussion of music in Daoist rituals will necessarily be highly tentative. The following remarks are based primarily on the examination of a limited number of samples recorded in Taiwan, where monastic Daoism (such as it existed in China prior to the 1950s) does not exist. These examples are from rituals performed by different groups of ordained or lay priests belonging to a variety of orders. In addition, some of the description provided here is based on my observations in Hong Kong.

In contemporary Taiwan and Hong Kong, the most frequently performed Daoist rituals are funeral rites, exorcist rites, and the community rite of purification (Jiao). These rites are normally performed by a chief Daoist priest, the *daoshi,* with a small group of assistant priests and a few lay instrumentalists. Performances of rituals usually take place in the local Daoist temple or in the local temple of a popular religion, such as the Temple of Mazu (a goddess protector of seafarers) in Taiwan or the Temple of Tianhou ("heavenly mother") in Hong Kong. Funeral rites may be performed at the home of the bereaved family. Some rites are performed in full view of the public, while others (e.g., certain purification rites) are performed behind closed doors to shut out the profane in order that the ritual purpose of purification may be fulfilled.

Music and dance play a central role in Daoist rituals. Both vocal and instrumental music are used. Vocal music, with or without instrumental accompaniment, includes passages in heightened speech, monotonal incantation, chants, and hymn tunes. Texts, in Chinese or Sino-Sanskrit prose or verse, are set syllabically or melismatically to pentatonic or heptatonic melodies; both measured and unmeasured melodies are found. Structurally, most compositions are in strophic form, but some are through-composed. In chants and hymn tunes, repetition of a motif or a phrase appears to be a prominent feature.

Vocal pieces are recited or sung mainly by a solo voice; occasionally responsorial singing and ensemble singing in unison are also employed. Singing is commonly done in a relaxed manner; use of special vocal techniques such as shouts, groans, microtonal vocal inflection or glides, and falsetto are not uncommon. A characteristic opening glissando often precedes a vocal piece, and the insertion of vocable passages are by no means rare.

Instruments are used either singularly or in a group. These include, among the nonpitched idiophones: the *daqing,* an inverted bowl-shaped bell struck with a mallet; the *muyu,* a wooden slit drum struck by a stick; the hand bell; cymbals; and the gong; among the membranophones: the *fagu,* the ritual drum, which is a barrel drum played with two sticks; among the chordophones: the *sanxian,* a three-stringed, unfretted, plucked lute; and the *erhu,* a two-stringed, bowed fiddle; and among the aerophones: the *suona,* a shawm, and the buffalo horn.

Symbolically, the *daqing* represents heaven and the male principle, *yang,* while the *muyu* represents earth and the female principle, *yin.* When the ritual drum plays a certain pattern, it signals the beginning of a significant phase of a given ritual. Musically, all the idiophones beat time as well as mark off sections of music. Beats of the ritual drum also serve to regulate the tempo in passages where varying tempi occur. In addition to serving a colotomic (structure-marking) function, the cymbals are also used as a solo instrument playing various rhythmic patterns in a virtuosic manner as overtures, interludes, or postludes. One of the special cymbal playing techniques involves the manipulation of the dynamics of the sound after a clash by varying the degree of proximity between the two cymbal plates, resulting in a voicelike quality that can be quite eerie. This technique is used in funeral rites.

Instrumental melodies are played by the *suona*(s) and *erhu;* when serving as accompaniment to the vocal melodies, these instruments play a heterophonic version of the vocal melodies. The *sanxian* is used mainly as a colotomic instrument; it plays tremolo or chords to mark off vocal sections.

In ritual performances Daoist priests not only sing but also dance either alone or in groups. All dance gestures, as well as choreographic formations, have symbolic meanings.

To a believer, a Daoist priest is an indispensable intermediary between the human world and the spirit world. His presence is therefore necessary at a funeral in order to perform rites that ensure repose for the deceased. His presence is also required at exorcism or purification rites in order to perform rituals that will render evil ghosts harmless or to restore health, tranquillity, and purity to a community.

One of the most important community purification rites is the Jiao. Dividing into several phases, Jiao rituals may last three to five days or more, depending on the requests of the sponsors. The introductory part of Jiao is known as *qingsheng* ("inviting the spirits"). It is initiated with a liturgical item called *buxu* ("dancing in the void"), a generic term for an opening ceremony in which dance and hymn singing serve as preparation for ritual meditation. Both dance and hymns are accompanied by an instrumental ensemble of shawms, gong, drum, and *muyu.* The introductory part of Jiao also includes a liturgical item called "Flower Offering," accompanied by voices alone. In the middle part of Jiao the key ritual feature is a liturgy for the souls in purgatory, known as Pudu ("salvation"); it is a sung liturgy accompanied by an instrumental ensemble. The most colorful part of Jiao is an exorcist rite for the community called Dawanghang. To the accompaniment of shawms, gongs, and cymbals, the *daoshi* makes preparations to launch a paper boat, the vehicle that is to transport demons of infectious diseases away from the human world. When preparations are complete, the sounding of a series of water buffalo horn calls, accompanied by the ritual drum and gong strokes in accelerated speed, signals the actual launching of the paper boat. When the music stops, the *daoshi* calls upon the demons by name to board the boat and is answered by his assistant. Once this roll call is completed the *daoshi* plays the water buffalo horn, a signal to launch the boat by burning it.

The final phase of Jiao is a celebration of the restoration of health and purity to the community through the marriage of yin and yang. In heightened speech the *daoshi* offers incense to heavenly spirits. He then states the purpose of the Jiao and names the sponsors; both statements are chanted. A prayer whose text is written on a piece of paper is chanted next; it is a petition to the heavenly spirits on behalf of the community. When the prayer is finished, the written text is burned. Thereupon the sounding of drum rolls indicates that the climax of the ritual is to be unfolded. The *daoshi* calls out the name of Laozi three times, inviting him to visit the site of the altar; each call ends with an abrupt vocal leap encompassing the interval of an eleventh, followed by a long drum roll. Then eight drum beats are sounded three times. The number three symbolizes heaven, earth, and water, the three elements of the cosmos, and also the head, chest, and abdomen, the three essential parts of a person. These drum beats summon the spirit of the *daoshi* to offer tea and incense to Laozi. He first chants and then dances, using stylized and symbolic gestures simulating the acts of offering tea and incense to Laozi.

KOREA. Shamanism, the oldest of Korean religions, consists of a group of unorganized beliefs about the supernatural world. It still has some following today, particularly among the rural population. In modern times, the two major social and religious forces existing in the Republic of Korea (South Korea) are Confucianism and Christianity. Christianity was introduced into Korea as early as the late sixteenth century, but it was not until the late nineteenth century that missionaries from the West—both Protestant (mostly Methodist and Presbyterian) and Roman Catholic—began full-fledged missionary work. Korean Christian liturgies follow their Western models closely. Western hymn tunes with Korean texts are used in services. Occasionally, hymns composed by modern Korean composers are also included in the Korean hymnals. Some of these hymns are set in triple meter, a characteristic feature of indigenous Korean music.

Mahāyāna Buddhism was introduced to Korea from China during the late fourth century CE. Today Buddhist rituals, if performed at all, usually take place in a few temples staffed by a handful of married priests. Some of these priests conduct classes for the laity in Buddhist chanting and in so doing have become the sole perpetuators of the now fragile Buddhist ritual tradition in Korea. The survey given below of Buddhist ritual music is based on field reports conducted by Korean musicologists among married Buddhist priests.

Sacrifice to Confucius. Music used in the rite of sacrifice to Confucius is called *a-ak.* This term is the Korean pronunciation of the Chinese term *yayue* ("elegant music"). In contemporary usage the term *a-ak* denotes the whole repertory of court music, but in the Yi dynasty (during which *a-ak* was first codified) the term denoted music performed in a number of sacrificial rites observed by the royal court and in government ceremonies. It is in this latter, more restricted sense that the term *a-ak* is used here.

The Korean *a-ak* tradition began in 1116, when the Chinese emperor Huizong (r. 1101–1125) of the Song dynasty sent a large number of *yayue* instruments to the Korean emperor Yejong (r. 1105–1125) of the Koryo dynasty, as a political gesture. Subsequently, during the Yi dynasty, and particularly during the reign of Emperor Sejong (1455–1468), *a-ak* was codified and expanded. Its codification was directed by the music theorist Pak Yon (1378–1458), who undertook not only the theoretical clarification of *a-ak* based on Chinese sources but proceeded also to construct a large number of musical instruments based on Chinese models. In addition, Pak Yon reconstructed music for the *a-ak* ensemble based on a limited number of notated Chinese ritual melodies, adding to these melodies his own interpretation of Chinese musical concepts and tunings. The result was a body of music with a mixture of Chinese and Korean elements but essentially Confucian in spirit. *A-ak* has been performed continuously from the fifteenth century till the present, with no evidence of decline.

Reflecting the Confucian doctrine of universal harmony, the *a-ak* orchestra employs eight kinds of instruments representing the eight essential kinds of instrumental timbres: metal (bells), stone (chimes), silk (zithers), wood (pounded wooden box and wooden scraper), bamboo (flutes), clay (ocarina), leather (drum), and gourd (mouth organ). In the modern *a-ak* orchestra the gourd category is missing, and wooden clappers (*pak*) have been added; this latter instrument performs a very limited function.

According to present-day performance practices, *a-ak* played in the rite of sacrifice to Confucius is performed antiphonally by two orchestras, one placed on the terrace of the main shrine building and the other placed in the courtyard below the terrace. The terrace orchestra, called *tŭngga,* consists of seventeen players; the courtyard orchestra, called *hōn'ga,* consists of fifteen players. During Emperor Sejong's reign the number of players in both orchestras was much larger, and vocal items were included. But today *a-ak* is purely instrumental. Two ritual dances are performed in the sacrifice to Confucius, the *munmu* (civil dance) and the *mumu* (military dance). Sixty-four dancers are prescribed for this ritual.

The overall musical characteristics of *a-ak* are refinement, serenity, and simplicity. The repertory consists of two basic heptatonic compositions and their transpositions. Structurally, each composition has eight phrases of equal length, each phrase consisting of four notes of equal duration. The tempo is exceedingly slow. Melody instruments including flutes, panpipes, ocarinas, and stone chimes play in unison; the flute, however, ends each note with an upward slide of about a semitone from each pitch. The drums and bells perform purely a colotomic function by marking off sections of each composition.

Royal ancestral shrine music. The music repertory for this ritual contains a limited number of compositions said to be chosen by Emperor Sejong. In terms of musical style they reflect an acculturated mixture of Chinese and Korean music; native Korean music (*hyangak*) current in the fifteenth century is also represented. These compositions are vocal pieces in Chinese with orchestral accompaniment arranged in suite form. Two orchestras are used to perform this ritual. These orchestras are also called *tŭngga* and *hŏn'ga,* as in the *a-ak* orchestra, but their instrumentation is different.

Buddhist rituals. Traditional Korean Buddhist rites consist of three components or performing genres: ritual chant with or without instrumental accompaniment, outdoor band music and ritual dance with vocal and instrumental accompaniment. Of the three, ritual chant is by far the most important.

Five categories of special Buddhist rites in which music plays a prominent role are distinguished: Kakpae-je, a rite in praise of ten Buddhist deities whose rituals call for the largest repertory of chants and dances; Saengjŏn yesu-je, a purification rite; Sangju kwŏn'gong-je, a rite dedicated solely to Buddha; Surguk-che, a rite for the spirits of water and earth; and Yŏngsan-je, a tribute rite. In addition a number of small-scale rituals associated with rites for the dead also employ music and dance. Today large-scale special rites are held only at the demand of sponsors. A rite may last from one to several days depending upon the request of the sponsors.

Three categories of ritual chants are differentiated: sūtra (Buddhist invocation), *hwach'ŏng* (chant based on folk style), and *pŏmp'ae* (a long solemn chant). Sūtra chants, also called *yŏmbul* ("invocation"), are of two kinds, each having different texts and employing different instrumental accompaniment. Texts of the first type are Chinese transliterations of Sanskrit and hence are unintelligible to laypeople. Texts of the second type are Chinese translations from Sanskrit whose general import may be understood by the laity. In the following discussion the first type of chant will be called "Sanskrit sūtra" and the second type "Chinese sūtra."

The repertory of Sanskrit sūtra is small. The music is for unison chorus with instrumental accompaniment. The vocal part consists of the repetition of a few sets of syllabic phrases. The instrumental part, played by an ensemble of reeds, drums, large gong, and a wooden slit drum called *mok'tak*, consists of the repetition of a melody independent of the vocal one and played by the reeds, with isorhythmic patterns played by drum and gong and the constant beats of the *mok'tak*. There is a subtle relationship between the accentuation of the vocal melody and the instrumental rhythm. Chinese sūtra chants are also performed by unison chorus, which sings repeated sets of texts having a limited compass. The constant beats of the *mok'tak* accompany the voices, each beat coinciding with the utterance of a textual syllable. The repertoire of Chinese sūtra is relatively large. While Sanskrit sūtra chants are employed mostly in special rites, Chinese sūtra chants are employed in both regular and special rites.

Hwach'ŏng (lit., "humble request") are chants for solo voice with texts in vernacular Korean. The singer traditionally accompanies himself with strokes played on a small gong; another accompanying instrument used is a suspended barrel drum (*puk*) played by someone other than the singer. The drum player strikes the bottom of the drum with one bare hand while at the same time striking the wooden frame of the right side of the drum with two sticks. Triple meter, a common feature of Korean indigenous music, is usually found in *hwach'ŏng*. *Hwach'ŏng* texts, expounding the benefits of Buddhist enlightenment, are set in verse form.

The third category of Buddhist chants, the *pŏmp'ae*, is said to derive from the Chinese *fanbei*. *Pŏmp'ae* texts are in Chinese verse, but Chinese rhyming schemes and tonal patterns are not observed in these texts. *Pŏmp'ae* music is made up of repetition, variation, and structural rearrangement of a basic set of stereotyped motifs or phrases. As performed today, *pŏmp'ae* is always sung in free rhythm and in a low register. The meaning of the texts is frequently difficult to grasp because each syllable is set melismatically to notes of long duration. In addition, the practice of liberal insertion of passages of vocables further obscures the meaning of the texts.

Two types of compositions are found in the *pŏmp'ae* repertory: the *hossori* (short chant) and the *chissori* (long chant). Each type is characterized by a distinct melodic and textual organization, as well as by the employment of different styles of performance. *Hossori* consists of solo, choral, and responsorial chants, all of which are sung in a relaxed, open-throated manner to the accompaniment of a small hand bell. Structurally, *hossori* texts are organized in quatrain form with lines of equal length. These four lines are set to a pair of melodic phrases in repetition; thus musically the structure of *hossori* is in binary form: *a b a b*. *Hossori* are always sung slowly at first, then faster, and then slowly again to conclude. In the fast sections the motifs within each phrase undergo a process of rhythmic reduction.

For special rites *hossori* may be performed in conjunction with a ritual dance, accompanied by an outdoor band made up of one or two conical double-reed instruments (*t'aep'yongson*) and a large gong (*ching*). A barrel drum (*puk*), a pair of cymbals (*chegum*), a long trumpet (*nepal*), and a conch shell (*nagak*) may also be added to the band. The band plays repetitions of a long melodic cycle that has only a tenuous correlation with the vocal melody.

The other type of *pŏmp'ae*, the *chissori*, is regarded as the most important and sophisticated of all Korean Buddhist chants. It is seldom performed today; when performed, *chissori* is always used in conjunction with large-scale special rites. Music for the *chissori* is drawn from a pool of stereotyped melodic phrases, each in turn built on a series of motifs. The way in which these motifs are organized into a piece defines the individuality of a *chissori* composition. The entire repertory of *chissori* contains seventy-two compositions.

Like that of *hossori*, the performance of *chissori* begins slowly and then speeds up; in the fast section the motifs undergo a process of rhythmic reduction; it then concludes slowly. Most *chissori* are performed primarily by an ensemble of voices in unison. But a few compositions may have one or two solo sections inserted either at the beginning, in the middle, or at the end. These solo interpolations (*hŏdŏlp'um*) are optional groups of fixed melodies independent of those of the ensemble and made up of stereotyped motifs. Depending on the time available, *chissori* may be sung either with measured rhythm, or with unmeasured rhythm in which the duration of each note is greatly prolonged. Consistent use of microtonal glides characterizes *chissori* performance. A special feature is the application of a microtonal upward glide prefixed to a given note; this note is then followed suddenly by a falling glide encompassing the interval of an octave. *Chissori* is sung in a tense-throated manner. For notes in the high register, falsetto technique is used.

TIBET. The indigenous religion of Tibet is Bon, which evolved from northern and Inner Asian shamanism. During the periods of the first kings (seventh–tenth century CE), North Indian Mahāyāna Tantric Buddhism was introduced to Tibet. Subsequently Bon and Tantric Buddhism merged and resulted in a highly syncretic form of Tibetan Buddhism.

Music in Bon ritual. Monastic forms of Bon have been largely assimilated by Tantric Buddhism. Many ritual practices of Bon have also been influenced by Buddhism. Bon ritual music employs chanting and instrumental music; the chief instruments are the indigenous *phyedrṅa* (single-headed drum) and the *gshaṅ* ("flute bell"). Flutes and trumpets made of animal bones are also used. In the instrumental part of the ritual the drum occupies a central place. According to legend, when a Bon priest plays a drum he is thought of as mounting a flying steed to heaven to communicate with the gods. Bon chants are organized in strophic form, and in performance a large variety of vocal techniques are used, such as gliding before and after a given note, whistling, shouting, or masking the voice. Some of these sounds are said to represent the voices of spirits heard through the singer as medium. As the ritual progresses, the tempo of chanting and instrumental music accelerate, and the volume also increases; great intensity is generated as a result.

Buddhist liturgy. Tibetan Buddhists hold that music prepares the mind for spiritual enlightenment. Accordingly, music (vocal as well as instrumental) is employed in the monastic routines that focus on five daily assemblies held in the monastery shrine hall between sunrise and sunset. The daily services consist predominantly of choral chants, with or without instrumental accompaniment, and antiphony between choral chant and instrumental interludes. All music is notated. Important liturgical items include the monks' "invitation" to the deities to visit the place of worship, the ritual of offering, thanksgiving hymns, and hymns of praise to the Buddha and the *bodhisattvas.*

Monks participating in the daily services sit cross-legged in paired rows facing one another. The music of the service proceeds under the direction of the *dbumdza* (chant leader). The choral chant is normally sung in unison in a quiet and restrained manner; heterophony occasionally occurs. Texts for choral chants are drawn mostly from the sacred scripture known as the Bka' 'gyur (Kanjur, doctrine attributed to Buddha) and from Bstan 'gyur (Tanjur, commentaries). Three main chant styles are distinguished: solo parlando recitation, *gdaṅ* (hymn), and *abyaṅs* (sustained chant).

Solo parlando recitation, in measured or unmeasured rhythm, is usually employed in short introductory passages. The *gdaṅ* is chanted in a series of meters (duple, triple, or asymmetrical meter such as 11/8), depending on the textual structure. Melodically, sections of *gdaṅ* are made up of repetitions of one or two pairs of phrases having a limited range in predominantly conjunct motion. The chant may also be monotonal. Words in *gdaṅ* are set either syllabically or melismatically. In performance a variety of ornaments, such as glissando and glides before and after a note, are used. *Gdaṅ* is accompanied by a cymbal and drum whose function is simply to beat time.

The *abyaṅs* is chanted in an extremely low register and essentially in a monotone. Words are set syllabically to notes of long duration prefixed or affixed by a variety of microtonal inflections or vocal glides. A special vocal technique has been cultivated by two monasteries of the Dge-lugs-pa order in which each chanter simultaneously sings two pitches, a deep fundamental and a clear harmonic (either the fifth or the sixth harmonic), resulting in a choral effect. The *abyaṅs* is chanted in a quiet manner.

In contrast to the quiet vocal chanting of *abyaṅs*, instrumental interludes of *abyaṅs* are played loudly. The aerophones are always played in pairs. One of the two *rgya gliṅs*, which are shawms, plays the main melody in an unadorned manner while the other plays the main melody with ornamentation. The other aerophones, the *duṅ*—a trumpet of varying sizes with a low tone quality, the *rkaṅ glin*—a trumpet made of animal femur or of metal, and the *duṅ dkar*—a conch, play long, sustained notes and repeat chords of two pitches, a two-note ostinato figure. The *domaru,* a rattle drum, and the *dril bu,* a handbell, are played by one person whose strokes serve mainly as signals marking sections of the chants. The cymbals (*gsil snyan* and *rol mo*) and the two *ruga* drums, untuned double-headed drums each struck with a crooked stick, play a variety of rhythmic figures as well as beating time. The resultant instrumental texture is complex and its timbre full of subtle nuances. In contrast to the rhythmic complexity and subtlety of the percussion part, the music for the shawms—the only melody instruments in the ensemble—is rather simple and straightforward; it is played in a rhythmically fixed manner with penetrating volume. Circular breathing is employed in shawm playing so that a continuous line is achieved.

Liturgical drama. The *'cham* is a quasi-liturgical ritual drama performed to exorcise evil spirits. The ritual is performed outdoors and involves the use of music (both vocal and instrumental), mime, and dance, as well as elaborate costumes and masks. The music ensemble consists of groups of chanters and an instrumental ensemble similar to that used in monastic liturgical services, with the addition of special sound effects not found in those services.

SEE ALSO Chanting; Drama, article on East Asian Dance and Theater; Mantra; Nianfo; Sūtra Literature.

BIBLIOGRAPHY

China

Bian, Rulan Zhao. *Song Dynasty Musical Sources and Their Interpretation.* Cambridge, Mass., 1967.

Bian, Rulan Zhao, et al. "China." In *New Grove Dictionary of Music and Musicians,* edited by Stanley Sadie, vol. 4, pp. 245–283. London, 1980.

Granet, Marcel. *Festivals and Songs of Ancient China* (1919). New York, 1932.

Kishibe Shigeo. "La danse du Confucianisme," "Rites du Taô," "Musique religieuse en Chine." In *Encyclopédie des musiques sacrées,* vol. 1, pp. 265–267, 268–271, 272–274. Paris, 1968.

Kuttner, Fritz A. "Musique des sacrifices confucéens." In *Encyclopédie des musiques sacrées,* vol. 1, pp. 250–264. Paris, 1968.

Li, Chunren. "An Outline of the History of Chinese Buddhist Music." *Journal of Buddhist Culture* 1 (1972): 123–130.

Liu, Zhunruo. "Five Major Chant Types of the Buddhist Service, Gongdian." In *Chinoperl Papers,* no. 8, pp. 130–160. Ithaca, N. Y., 1978.

Prip-Møller, Johannes. *Chinese Buddhist Monasteries: Their Plan and Function as a Setting for Buddhist Monastic Life* (1937). Hong Kong, 1982.

Van Aalst, J. A. *Chinese Music* (1884). Reprint, New York, 1964.

Wong, Isabel. "Geming Gequ: Songs for the Education of the Masses." In *Popular Chinese Literature and Performing Arts in the People's Republic of China 1949–1979,* edited by Bonnie S. McDougall, pp. 114–143. Berkeley, Calif., 1984.

Yank Yinliu. *Zhongguo gudai yinyue shigao,* vol. 1. Beijing, 1980.

Korea

Byong Won Lee. "Korea." In *New Grove Dictionary of Music and Musicians,* vol. 10, pp. 192–208. London, 1980.

Byong Won Lee. "Korean Court Music and Dance." *World of Music* 23 (1981): 35–51.

Hahn, Man-young. "The Four Musical Types of Buddhist Chant in Korea." *Yearbook for Traditional Music* 15 (1983): 45–58.

Provine, Robert C., Jr. "The Treatise on Ceremonial Music (1430) in the Annals of the Korean King Sejong." *Ethnomusicology* 18 (January 1974): 1–30.

Provine, Robert C., Jr. "'Chinese' Ritual Music in Korea: The Origins, Codification, and Cultural Role of Aak." *Korean Journal* 20 (February 1980): 16–25.

Provine, Robert C., Jr. "'Chinese' Ritual Music in Korea." In *Traditional Korean Music,* edited by the Korean National Commission of UNESCO. Arch Cape, Oreg., 1983.

Survey of Korean Arts: Traditional Music. 2 vols. Edited by The Korean National Academy of Arts. Seoul, 1971–1974.

Tibet

Crossley-Holland, Peter. "rGy-gling Hymns of the Kamu-Kagyu: The Rhythmitonal Architecture of Some Tibetan Instrumental Airs." *Selected Reports in Ethnomusicology* 1 (1970): 79–114.

Crossley-Holland, Peter. "Tibet." In *New Grove Dictionary of Music and Musicians,* vol. 18, pp. 799–811. London, 1980.

Ellingson, Ter. "'*Don rta dbyangs gsum:* Tibetan Chant and Melodic Categories." Asian Music 10 (1979): 112–156.

Kaufmann, Walter. "The Notation of the Buddhist Chant (Tibet)." In his *Musical Notations of the Orient,* pp. 355–417. Bloomington, Ind., 1967.

Lerner, Lin. "Two Tibetan Ritual Dances: A Comparative Study." *Tibetan Journal* 8 (Winter 1983): 50–57.

DISCOGRAPHY

China

Levy, John. *Chinese Buddhist Music.* Introduction by Laurence Picken; notes by Laurence Picken and John Levy. Lyrichord LLST 7222.

Levy, John. *Chinese Daoist Music.* Introduction and notes by Laurence Picken. Lyrichord LLST 7723.

Migot, A. *Musique religieuse chinoise et tibétaine.* La boïte à musique BAM LD 383.

Korea

Levy, John. *Korean Court Music.* Lyrichord LL 7206.

Levy, John. *Musique bouddhique de Corée.* Vogue LVLX 253.

Tibet

Crosseley-Holland, Peter. *The Music of Tibetan Buddhism.* Bärenreiter Musicaphon BM 2008-11

Crossley-Holland, Peter. *Tibetan Ritual Music.* Lyrichord LL 181 and LLST 7181.

Musique de l'Asie traditionelle, vol. 4, *Tibet: Rituel du soir.* Playa Sound PS 33504.

ISABEL WONG (1987)

MUSIC: MUSIC AND RELIGION IN JAPAN

Traditionally, religious music in Japan consisted of songs and dances that were performed as offerings to various gods.

Songs and dances also served to work performers into trances in *kamiasobi* (singing songs and dancing for gods) in order to call a god or gods into attendance. During the Tumulus period (third to seventh century CE), songs and dances were performed by virgins consecrated to deities, continuing a tradition of shamanistic music from the Yayoi period (fourth century BCE to third century CE). Such performances were accompanied by koto (a long four- or eight-stringed zither) and *tsuzumi* (a hand-beaten drum). These instruments appear in clay figures of consecrated virgins and the songs and dances are described in several ancient texts, including *Kojiki* (712 CE), *Nihonshoki* (720 CE), and *Fudoki* (first half of the eighth century). The songs incorporated into these works were probably sung for feasts, funerals, and similar occasions.

Kagura (music of the gods) refers to the music and dance used in Shintō ceremonies. *Kagura,* called *kamiasobi* in old times, originated in the song and dance of ancient religious services. *Kagura* can be divided into the two forms: *mikagura* and *okagura* (*satokagura*). *Mikagura* is performed at the imperial palace, whereas *okagura* is performed at local shrines. *Mikagura* originated in *kinkashinen* (religious feasts), which were held in Seishodo Palace during the reign of Emperor Seiwa (r. 858–876) of the Heian era. Singers were accompanied by a type of koto (probably a *wagon,* a long six-stringed zither). In the reign of the Emperor Ichijyo (r. 986–1011), *mikagura* was performed in the Naishidokoro (Kashikodokoro) Palace to the accompaniment of *kagurabue* (a bamboo transverse flute), *hichiriki* (a double-reed pipe), and *wagon.*

Mikagura performers sang several types of songs, including: (1) *niwabiuta* (songs of the garden bonfire), consisting of chants of *niwabi* and *ajimesahō;* (2) *torimonouta* (songs of holding hands for dance), consisting of *sakaki, mitegura, tsue, sasa, yumi, tachi, hoko, hisago, kazura,* and *karakami;* (3) *saibaraburi* (songs of *saibara*), which are folk songs collected from various regions and which includes forms known as *ajime, oosaibari, kosaibari, senzai,* and *hayauta;* (4) *hoshiuta* (songs of stars); and (5) *zōka* (songs of various kinds), including *akaboshi, tokuzeniko, yuuzukuru, hirume, yutate, kamiage* and *asakura, sonokoma, hetsuiasobi,* and *sakadono.* The chant, sung in slow tempo, is rich in melismatic style. Singers were divided into two groups called *motokata,* which faced the shrine from the left, and *suekata,* which faced the shrine from the right. Each one of the principal singers, called *ondō,* beat a *shakubyōshi* (a wooden clapper). The *ninjyō* (a male dancer) performed in the evening at the small shrine in Kashikodokoro Palace with the emperor in attendance.

Okagura has been performed at shrines during folk ceremonies since the modern period. There are several forms of *okagura: mikokagura* (dance of a maiden in the service of a shrine); *izumokagura* (dances using mats, bells, sacred trees, swords, and other objects with mythical significance); *isekagura,* which consists of *yudateshinji* (sprinkling hot water of an iron pot) and dances illustrating various stories; and *shishikagura* (dances with lion's mask). In *ōmotokagura* (worship of ancestors called *Ōmoto*), which is performed in Shimane prefecture, a spiritualistic male medium works himself into a trance and reports the oracle of the god concerning that year's harvest.

Some shamanistic practices persist among shamans called *itako* (Aomori prefecture) and *yuta* (Amami Island and Okinawa). Here the spirit of the dead possesses a *miko* (female shaman) and speaks through her in simple chanting.

The authentic music of Chinese Confucian ceremonies was never performed in Japan, but the spirit of Confucianism can be found in the music of the *ch'in* (a long seven-stringed zither), an instrument favored by the intelligentsia interested in Chinese philosophy and literature during the Edo period (1603–1867).

When Buddhism was introduced from Kudara on the Korean peninsula by King Kinmē in the early sixth century, dances called *gigaku,* which originated in China, were performed in order to dedicate temples to the Buddha. The masked characters of *gigaku* performed to the accompaniment of a *yokobue* (a bamboo transverse flute), a *shōban* (a gong), and ten *yōko* (hand drums hung at waists).

Kenzuishi and Kentoshi, Japanese envoys to Sui and Tang dynasty China, introduced Buddhist chanting (*shōmyō*) and *gagaku* (court music and dance) to Japan. In 752, to celebrate the completion of a colossal bronze statue of Vairocana Buddha at Tōdaiji, the principal national temple in Nara, a magnificent Buddhist service was held. A thousand or more monks sang *shikahōyō,* composed of four Buddhist chants (*bonnon, shakujyō, bai,* and *sange*), and performances of *gagaku, gigaku,* and other types of music and dance were presented. Eighteen types of instruments, *gigaku* masks, and a number of the costumes that were used in this service have been preserved in the Shōsōin (the treasure house of Tōdaiji) in Nara. In 861, *mushataie* (another type of Buddhist service) was held in Tōdaiji to celebrate the completion of repair work on the head of the Vairocana Buddha, which had been damaged during an earthquake. On a stage in front of the Daibutsuden (the large building housing the statue of Vairocana Buddha) *gagaku* and *bonnbai* (a form of *shōmyō*) were performed, and Buddhist chanting called *narashōmyō* or *nantoshōmyō* was conducted in several Nara temples.

When in the early years of the ninth century the Tendai and Shingon sects were introduced by the monks Saichō, Ennin, and Kūkai from Tang dynasty China, *shōmyō* was newly reformulated as the *tendaishōmyō* and *shingonshōmyō.* The *goenembutsu*—repeating the *nembutsu* (chanting of the name of Amida/Amitabha Buddha) in five kinds of voice—that Ennin brought to Japan from China was performed as *inzēnembutsu* (drawing voice *nembutsu*) on Mount Hie, the headquarters of the Tendai sect. The *fudannembutsu* (*nembutsu* ceremony) was developed by the monk Sōō in the Mudōji temple and handed down by the monks Sengan and Genshin, who also developed a form of chant praising the Buddha called *wasan.* In addition, Shōrinin, which the monk Jakugen set up in Ōhara (Kyoto), and Raigoin, founded by the monk Ryōnin in Ōhara, served as *shōmyō* fundamental schools. Ryōnin contributed to the reunification of *tendaishōmyō*, which had split into branches after Ennin. *Gyozan shōmyō rokkanjyō*, a book expounding the theoretical and practical principles of the music, was edited by the monk Kekan, a pupil of Ryōnin. *Shōmyōfyojinshū*, a work edited by the monk Tanchi, established the basis of modern *shōmyō* by applying the musical theory of *gagaku*. The monk Kanchō established the basis for *shingonshōmyō*, although this style later developed into several schools, including *ninnajisōōinryū*, *nakanokawadaijyōshōninryū*, and *daigoryū*.

Various Buddhist sects that were opened to membership from the wider public were formed during the Kamakura period (1185–1333). Hōnen, the founder of the Jōdo sect, emphasized the importance of the *nembutsu*: "Namu Amida Butsu." Ippen, founder of the Ji sect (a branch of Jōdo), propagated *nembutsu* through the *odori-nembutsu* (dancing *nembutsu*). The forms of chanting practiced by the Jōdo, Jyōdo-shin (founded by Shinran, a pupil of Hōnen), and the Ji sects were influenced by Tendai Buddhism. On the other hand, the chants of the Rinzai and Sōtō Zen sects, newly transmitted from China by Ēsai and Dōgen respectively, were influenced by Chinese practices.

The general term for Buddhist chanting is *shōmyō*, or *bonbai*. *Shōmyō* texts can be classified into three types based on the language used: Sanskrit, Chinese, or Japanese. *Bongosan* are Sanskrit chants. Several types of chants are performed using classical Chinese (*kangosan*). Chinese-language chants include *bai* and *kada* (verse chants praising a blessing of Buddha); *nyoraibai* (a *tathagata* chant); *gobai* (a later chant); *sōrēkada* (all-praising chant); *ekōkada* (chant to hold a memorial service); *sange* (verse chant performed while scattering flowers); *bonnon* (verse chant for a memorial service before the principal image of Buddha); *shakujyō* (verse chant involving a priest's staff); and *sange* (chant to repent sins). Japanese-language chants include *wasan* (verse chant praising a blessing of Buddha); *saimon* (prose chant repaying Buddha or the founder of a sect); *hyōbyaku* (prose chant explaining the purpose of a Buddhist service); *kyōshaku* (prose chant explaining the content of a sūtra); *kōshiki* (prose chant praising the Buddha), and *rongi* (prose chant summarizing content of a sūtra).

Bongosan texts are written in Chinese characters that yield phonetic approximations of the Sanskrit. *Kangosan* is a system of chanting Chinese texts according to their *kan* reading (i.e., according to the Japanese equivalents of the sounds of the Chinese graphs). *Wasan* consists of Chinese texts translated into Japanese.

Shōmyō influenced various forms of chanting directly or indirectly. *Kōshiki* and *Rongi*, forms of narrative *shōmyō*, musically influenced *Heikyoku* (the recitation of the *Tale of the Heike*). Musical terms associated with *shōmyō* include *shojyū* (the lower set of notes), *sanjyū* (the upper set of notes), *chūon* (the middle set of notes), *sashigoe* (the chanting of syllables smoothly), *shiragoe* (chanting in conversational style), and *yōkyoku* (the chanting of Nō dramas). *Shōmyō* also includes *sashi* (chanting in rhythm as speech), *sanjyū* (the opening style), *yōkyoku* (the chanting of Nō dramas), and *jyōruri* (a dramatic narrative chant). *Jyōruri* was originally the recitation of the romance of Minamoto Yoshitsune (a military commander) and the princess Jyōrurihime, chanted to time kept by tapping a fan or by *biwa* (a four-stringed lute) accompaniment. *Jyōruri* was accompanied by the *shamisen* (a three-stringed plucked lute) after that instrument was introduced to Japan from the Ryukyu Islands in the sixteenth century. This style was later adapted to the puppet theater.

Another chant form called *fushidansekkyō* was developed from *sekkyō* (sermons or discourses). Such sermons were chanted in singsong tones in order to more easily educate the people. Iterant chanters and performers also recited *sekkyōbushi* (a parable or story of karmic destiny). These popular performers used *sasara* (a scraper), *kane* (a small gong), and *kakko* (a small horizontally-held drum). During the Edo period, itinerant troupes performed *sekkyōbushi* with puppets.

During the Heian period (794–1185), *gagaku* and *shōmyō* were adapted to Japanese styles. In the court, *saibara* (folk songs collected from various regions) were performed to the accompaniment of the instruments used in *gagaku*, including *ryūteki* (a bamboo transverse flute), *hichiriki* (a double-reed pipe), *shō* (an wind instrument with seventeen bamboo pipes), *sō* (a long thirteen-stringed zither), *biwa*, and *shakubyōshi* (wooden clappers). The court chant known as *rōei* (chanting a Chinese and Japanese poem) was accompanied by *ryūteki*, *hichiriki*, and *shō* in a free rhythm.

During the Heian period, *imayō* (modern chanting or songs of the present age) were performed by *asobime*. *Asobime* or *asobi* were itinerant female singers and dancers, sometimes associated with prostitution. *Kugutsume* were similar performers who used puppets beginning in the middle of the Heian era. The retired emperor Go Shirakawa (1127–1192) and his vassals were taught *imayō* by *asobime*. This is remarkable in that members of the highest elite apprenticed themselves to gypsy-like women. The *asobime* practice of singing *imayō* was held to be an efficacious means of achieving enlightenment. Go Shirakawa compiled *Ryōjinhishō*, an anthology of *zōgē* (various chants) and oral instructions on *imayō*. There were broadly several kinds of songs: *imayō* in the narrow sense; *hōmonka* (songs influenced by Buddhist chanting); *kamiuta* (songs of the *kami*), *chōka* (long chants), and *koyanagi* (free-form chants). These were sometimes performed to the accompaniment of a fan beat or a hand drum. According to the *Ryōjinhishō*, Go Shirakawa received twelve years of training in *imayō* from Otomae, an *asobime* from Aohaka in Mino province. *Imayō* chanted by monks to the accompaniment of *sō* (the zither used in *gagaku*) in temples were called *etenrakuimayō* or *etenrakuutaimono*.

In the late Muromachi era (mid-sixteenth century), the monk Kenjyun of Zendō temple in northern Kyushu developed *tsukushisō*, a solo chant performed while accompanying oneself on the *sō*. Yatsuhashi Kengyo (a high-ranking blind performer) reformed *tsukushisō* into *sōkyoku* (koto music). In the Edo period, *sōkyoku* consisted of *kumiuta* sung to the accompaniment of *sō*.

During the Kamakura period, the *fukeshakuhachi* (a vertical bamboo flute) was played as part of the training of monks called *komusō* of Fukeshū, one of the Chinese Zen sects. In the Edo period the Tokugawa shogunate authorized Fukeshū and made use of *komusō* as secret agents, who toured the country during their training.

Heikyoku was a narrative form of vocal music performed by *biwahōshi*, blind monks who performed with the *biwa*. They chanted the military epic *Heike monogatari*, describing the famous history of the Heike (one of two great political families of twelfth-century Japan). Another group of blind biwa-playing monks were *jijinmōsō* in Kyushu. *Jijinmōsō* performed *mōsōbiwa* (a genre of *biwa* music) as they visited individual houses to calm the violent *dokōjin* (gods of the earth) and pray for bountiful harvests.

Most songs were sung in unison, with occasional use of the intervals of the fourth or fifth separating two voice parts moving in parallel. The scale, consisting of twelve tones, varied according to the period and the genre. Generally, intervallic skips of the fourth and fifth characterize the melodic pattern. The singing could be either melismatic in free rhythm, or it could consist of one tone sung in metric rhythm. Noteworthy is the fact that the melodic structure of *shōmyō* influenced other forms of Japanese music. For example, both *Heikyoku* and the singing in Nō drama were influenced by chant forms.

The notation of Buddhist chants falls into three categories. The oldest is called *ko hakase* (old *hakase;* musical notation), which indicates the melody with marks representing the four Chinese tonal accents. The second system, called *go-on hakase* (five-tone *hakase*), is represented by short vertical and horizontal bars, one for each letter of the text, showing five tones. The newest category of chant notation, *meyasu hakase* (literally, "*hakase* for easy understanding"), presents the melodic line in more detail by drawing curved lines in addition to the marks for tone pitches. This system resembles the neumic system of medieval Europe. *Meyasu hakase* is preserved in a manuscript dated 1311 written by Ryōnin, the founder of this chant notation.

A comparison between Buddhist music in Japan and other Asian countries reveals both similarities and differences. A chanting style based on one tone and the use of percussion instruments is common to all, but the use of the double-reed pipe and trumpet is not found in Japan. Vocalization in deep voice is also common to many Asian Buddhist societies. The biggest difference is in regard to melody. Chinese chants, more popular in character than Japanese chants, tended to adapt the melodies of folk and popular music. By contrast, Japanese chant has preserved the older style of Buddhist music.

See Also Chanting.

Bibliography

Giesen, Walter. *Zur Geschichte des Buddhistisches Ritualgesangs in Japan*. Kassel, Germany, 1977.

Harich-schneider, Eta. *A History of Japanese Music*. Oxford, 1973.

Hirano Kenji, Kamisango Sukeyasu, and Gamo Satoaki, eds. *Nihon Ongaku Daijiten* (Encyclopedia of Japanese Music). Tokyo, 1989.

Kikkawa Eishi. *Kamigami no ongaku* (Music of Shintō). Toshiba TW–8004–7. Tokyo, 1976. Sound recording in Japanese, with English summary.

Kikkawa Eishi, Kindaichi Haruhiko, Koizumi Fumio, and Yokomichi Mario, eds. *Nihon Koten Ongaku Taikei* (An Outline of Japanese Classical Music), vols. 1–8. Tokyo, 1982.

Malm, William P. *Traditional Japanese Music and Musical Instruments*. New ed. Tokyo, 2000. Originally published in 1959.

Kishibe Shigeo (1987)
Ogi Mitsuo (2005)

MUSIC: MUSIC AND RELIGION IN GREECE, ROME, AND BYZANTIUM

This survey of the interrelation of religion and music in Western antiquity from the Homeric age to the age of Justinian (c. 1000 BCE–500 CE) will examine the religious dimensions of the music of Greece and Rome, the music of the early church, and the liturgical music of Byzantium.

Greek Music. The word *music* (*mousikē*) originated in the Greek language. However, to the Greeks it meant more than the art of tones sung or played on instruments. It encompassed education, science, and proper behavior, as well as singing and the playing of instruments. To modern man this ancient music—the very little that has come down to us—sounds simple, unmelodious, and occasionally even dull, but in the broader conception of *mousikē* we may recognize the basis for the magical, ritual, and ethical dimensions that characterize Greek music and relate it to Greek religion. This discussion of Greek music during the period from the Homeric epics (eighth century BCE) to the age of the Roman emperor Augustus (first century BCE) will treat, together with religious function, its theory, and main styles and forms.

Pre-Christian Greek religions. Greek religions were polytheistic and based upon popular mythologies. Followers of Homeric religion adored and feared the Olympian gods, who frequently behaved like humans, possessed of very human virtues and vices. Their cult was sacrificial, and its liturgy proceeded by sacrificial action. Sacrifice served in rituals of atonement, imprecation, and thanksgiving, in ceremonies for the dead, and in the fearful adoration of the chthonic divinities of the netherworld. Its aims were gratification of the gods and apotropaic protection from adversary gods or demonic forces. In the seventh and sixth centuries BCE Orphism arose, a mystic movement taking as founder the fabled musician Orpheus. Closely related to Orphism, and also originating in Thrace, was the cult of Dionysos, which worshiped with wine and song in wild bacchanalia its god Dionysos-Bacchus. Beginning with the fifth century BCE and thereafter, a more philosophical, less ecstatic type of religion emerged under the impact of Pythagorean, Platonic, Aristotelian, and Stoic philosophies. Connection with ethical principles characterized this conception of religion. We may see it in the still polytheistic context of Sophocles' Oedipus trilogy in Antigone's defense of "the infallible, unwritten eternal laws of heaven, which no mortal can overrule." Socrates, who lived by this doctrine, like Sophocles' heroine, paid with his life. Yet Socrates' teachings were carried on by Plato, whose systematization of Socratic thought wholly reshaped Greek religion.

Musical principles. From earliest times the Greeks took interest in the theory of music, and subsequent to Pythagorean concern with the mathematico-philosophical aspects of music they occupied themselves with it continuously. Their most important achievements were their acoustic discoveries, which were basic to the development of Western music.

From the infinity of tones, sounds, and rhythms with which nature surrounds man, the Greeks selected a limited number of tones, which they ordered, identified, and categorized according to *harmoniai*, or species of scales. In Greek music theory the term *harmony* refers to the various divisions of the octave into scales. The Greeks knew Dorian, Phrygian, Lydian, Mixolydian, and other scales, each of which consisted of two conjunct or disjunct tetrachords. Tetrachords composing the scales were divided into three distinct genera: the harmonic, the chromatic, and the enharmonic. (Greek tetrachords and scales progressed downward from a higher tonic rather than upward as in medieval and modern music.) Scales were precise, mathematically constructed systems. The scope of these *harmoniai*, however, was much greater than that of simple scales. The Doric "harmony" was the yardstick by which all melodies were judged. Its strict simplicity was understood as the ideal of moral straightforwardness, indeed, of Spartan fortitude and austerity. Within their various scales, the Greeks also knew certain tropes (*tropoi*), which characterized the mode of any given melody. The meaning of "mode" in Greek musical theory has been a matter of considerable scholarly debate; I take it to refer to complex melodic types or structures of melodic motives on the order of the Indian *rāgas* or Arabian *maqamat*.

The theory of tone-word relationship is basic to an understanding of Greek music. Poetry and music were closely bound, with the words of the text defining rhythmic structure through the quantities of metrical pattern. The role of stress or accent in relation to meter and music, controversial in late antiquity, remains problematic.

Magic power of music. The Greeks ascribed to music magic and therapeutic powers. It could heal wounds (Homer, *Odyssey* 19.437ff.), and it could move blocks of stone; the singing of Amphion, son of Zeus, was said to have enchanted stones to build of their own accord the walls of Thebes. The historical figure Thaletas of Gortyn (seventh century BCE) tried to drive the plague from Sparta by singing.

Ritual use of music. I have referred to the rituals of sacrifice in Homeric religion. The first canto of the *Iliad* gives a good description of priestly *thusia*, or sacrifice, made by the priest Chryses to his god Apollo (1.447–473). After Chryses has burned pieces of meat and fat and tasted them, a libation is spent accompanied by song. Only the chthonic deities were adored in strict silence. Several ancient inscriptions, as that from Dodona, speak of the ritual of praying, or more properly "vowing," and sacrificing; on such occasions music, at least a kind of hymnic chant, was obligatory. The dedication of a new temple was always a festivity during which vows and sacrifices were offered and hymns or other music heard. At marriages *thusia*, prayers, and hymns inaugurated a happy espousal, at least in the circles of the nobility, as we read in Apollonis of Rhodes (fl. 222–181 BCE).

The aforementioned tone-word relationship has special significance for the ritual use of music. Lamentations for the dead Hector show clearly certain ritualistic traits (*Iliad* 24.720ff.). The choric odes of Pindar (518–438 BCE) served in official worship. Special reverence was paid the Delphic hymns; according to Plutarch (c. 46–after 120 CE), several were so celebrated that they were repeated every year.

The musical *ēthos*. To the Greeks, *mousikē* meant more than mere music. Hence it was judged not only by its audible beauty but also by its moral effect upon the listener. This principle, which the Greeks shared with many great ancient civilizations, constituted the doctrine of *ēthos*; in Greek music theory this doctrine reached its highest expression.

There was extensive philosophical reflection upon musical *ēthos*, that is, the character, nature, or moral effect of a musical work. Every melody, in each of its aspects, was subject to the postulates of its *ēthos*; the *ēthos* was determined by all components of its respective melody. Each scale, rhythm, and trope, when performed at the "right" spot and at the "just" time, has a concrete, predictable influence on the listener's emotions, behavior, and character.

Plato gave the doctrine of *ēthos* its most radical formulation in his *Republic*. According to his thesis, certain scales turn men into cowards and make women unable to bear healthy children; other scales inspire courage, fear, piety, nobility, and so forth (376d, 398b ff.). In the *Laws*, it is really in terms of the doctrine of *ēthos* that he criticizes the professional music of his day (700a ff.). The *nomos*, literally the "law" or "set," had become the main form used by professional singer-composers in musical contests. Consisting of several movements without strophic repetition, and characterized by its *harmonia* and its specific rhythm as musical representation of meter, it might depict the exploits of some god, such as the famous Pythian *nomos*, which glorified Apollo's battle with the Pythian dragon. Plato decried the musical license that violated the laws (*nomoi*) dividing music into several distinct kinds. The hymn, the lament, the paean, the dithyramb, and the lyric song, each ought be true to its form. Their admixture could only bring disorder to the society in which such confused and irregular music was heard.

The philosophy of musical *ēthos* did not remain undisputed. Its sharpest opponents were Philodemus of Gadara (first century BCE) and an anonymous rhetorician, a sophist whose arguments have come down to us in the *Papyrus Hibbeh.* Even Plutarch, the historian of Greek music, and Aristoxenus (fourth century BCE), its main theorist, speak in rather cautious terms about the doctrine of *ēthos.* Despite these controversies, the *ēthos* doctrine was cultivated by the Neoplatonists and by the church fathers and was championed by as influential a philosopher as Boethius.

Tragedy as musical drama. Attic tragedy originated in ritual, especially in that of Dionysos. The term *tragedy* derives from *tragōidia,* or "song of the goat," in celebration of a totemistic element in the Dionysian cult. The link between tragedy and ritual is clearly discernible in the tragedies of Aeschylus and Sophocles; it is less intimate in those of Euripides, the poet of the Greek enlightenment.

The ritual origin of tragedy is well known. Less known are the philosophical treatises devoted to its meaning, parts, and effects, and to the music that best represented the *ēthos* of the drama and its protagonists. According to Aristotle's celebrated *Poetics,* an effective drama has six parts, among which the *melopoia,* or musical composition, was not the least important. In its heyday, the tragedy contained a number of musical forms: the entrance of the choir (*parodos*), the standing song (*stasimon*), the song of the choir's exit (*exodos*), a song with pantomime (*huporchēma*), a lament (*kommos*), and the chanted recitatives of the main actors. Certain *harmoniai* were preferred for the drama, for example, the Mixolydian, because of its sorrowful *ēthos,* and the Doric, because of its solemn character.

Musical instruments. The musical instruments most significant for Greek religious practice may be named briefly. The main instruments were the lyre and its variants, such as the *kithara, barbitos, phorminx, trigōnon,* and *psaltērion.* They were all stringed instruments, to be plucked with or without a plectrum. The harp was probably imported from Egypt. They served chiefly the highly regulated Apollonian rite or style, which eschewed all ecstatic or orgiastic expression. Their music was strict, even severe; they were used by priests and the nobility. The hymns of Pindar, composed for accompaniment by lyre, were sacred to Apollo.

More appropriate to the unrestrained Dionysian style were such wind instruments as the *aulos,* a shrill-sounding primitive clarinet that was usually played as a double instrument with two mouthpieces. Sacred to Dionysos, it engendered violent merriment, wild breast-beating, or hopeless mourning. The distinction between Apollonian and Dionysian thus marks contrasting currents both musical and religious.

Relics of Greek music. Fifteen pieces of Greek music are known, of which three were carved in stone (two of these were found in Delphi and one in Tralles, in Asia Minor). Most of these pieces are only fragments. Their transcription into modern notation is, in certain details, controversial. An example of one of those carved in stone is the *skolion,* or libation song, of Seikilos, originating in the first century BCE.

ROMAN MUSIC. No written musical document of the early days of Roman history has come down to us; we must depend upon archaeological evidence. Ancient Rome was built upon three civilizations: Etruscan, Greek, and, finally, Near Eastern. In general Greek music came to Rome as a study to be learned and exercised. Eventually the powerful influence of Hellenistic music began to recede as the influence of Egyptian, Syrian, and Hebrew music increased.

Pre-Christian Roman religions. Roman cultic and popular customs were invariably accompanied by chanted and played music. Thus, according to the first-century historian Livy, the sodalities of the Salian priesthood regularly used chants at their rites. Numa, the legendary second king of Rome, provided the Salii, or "leapers," with arms and decreed that they chant hymns and dance at the appointed festivals of the martial god Mars. Their heavy-footed dance of arms in triple time was sacred to the god of war. Vergil (70–19 BCE) indicates that the songs of the Salii were executed responsorially (Vergil, *Aeneid* 8.285). The precentor of the priests, the *vates* ("poet" or "seer"), was considered divinely inspired.

Under the leadership of Livius Andronicus, Roman poet of the third century BCE, rites of atonement and consecration sacred to the goddess Juno were celebrated by choirs of virgins. Many of their hymns appear to have had apotropaic functions: to banish death, illness, and danger, and to establish peace between gods and mortals. The poet Horace (first century BCE) refers to the function of the *vates* in such rites, asking, "Where would innocent boys and girls learn their prayers, had not the Muse granted them a poet?" The customarily noisy *nenies,* or lamentations, functioned according to the principle "The greater the noise, the greater the loss"; they were disliked by Horace and later Roman poets, who were inclined to prefer the refinement of Greek poetry.

Music and poetry. Statius, a poet of the first century CE, no less than the poet Catullus a generation before him, took for granted the chanted performance of his poems. The poet Horace was probably the best-trained musician of his day, for he was commissioned by the emperor Augustus to create the words and music of the *Carmen saeculare.* It appears that Horace also taught its melody to the choir. In the first century BCE Greek dominance was as yet unchallenged, as evidenced by the existence of a Roman association, the Societas Cantorum Graecorum, yet Horace took pride in "having introduced Aeolian verses" to the culture of Rome.

Musical instruments. Because it had an expansive and militaristic culture, Rome used musical instruments more for its army than for its sanctuaries, although the ancient festivals, the Parilia and the Saturnalia, were certainly not celebrated without chants and popular music. The *tibia*, a primitive oboe comparable to the *aulos*; the *tuba*, a kind of trumpet; the Greek *kithara* and lyre; and, later, Asiatic instruments such as the Phrygian *curva tibia*, were heard on many cultic occasions. Wind instrument players were organized into the union of *tibicines*, stringed instrument players into that of the *fidicines*. Noise-making rattles, cymbals, and so forth were played by corybants and priests at Bacchanalian revels and were also heard at funerals.

Musical importations. Mystery cults imported from Asia featured bloody rites of initiation accompanied by the wild sound of noisemaking instruments and the Phrygian *tibia*. From Persia, borne by the legionnaires, came the cult of Mithra, with its ceremony of blood-baptism. The rattling of sistrums and the tinkling of harps accompanied the more peaceful cult of Isis, imported from Egypt. This multitude of foreign sounds was, like the *nenies*, condemned by Horace and later writers.

EARLY CHRISTIAN MUSIC. Foreign musics and mythologies were a horror and an abomination to the early Christians, or, rather, Judeo-Christians of the first two centuries, as were any pagan practices. The question of influence by Roman popular songs upon the chants of the early church has been raised, but all too few facts in favor of such a hypothesis can be adduced. The first Latin Church Fathers were so strongly biased against anything that smacked of paganism that they may well have suppressed any real evidence. Further, the Romans did not invent a musical notation of their own, nor were they interested in musical theory, so that any question of influence is difficult to judge.

The last part of Augustine's philosophical work *De musica* is now lost; it may have contained important views about the music of his contemporaries. Nonetheless, we are in possession of many, often contradictory testimonies of Christian chant in the Roman Empire, as it originated in Greece, Palestine, Italy, and other parts of the empire. Among them is just one piece of notated music, the *Oxyrhynchus hymnus*, and a veritable host of descriptions, speculations, and comparisons, ancient and medieval. Possibly some oral traditions were preserved until the ninth century, during which time a musical notation was developed in Europe. Some insights have resulted from this—rarely authentic—material, mainly in modern studies. A few examples will illustrate the state of this research:

1. *Hosanna filio David.* This antiphon for Palm Sunday is of ancient origin. Amédée Gastoué ascribes its intonation to the resemblance of the word *hosanna* with *hoson zēs*, the beginning words of a libation song.
2. Tropos Spondeiakos. Clement of Alexandria, second-century Church Father, recommended in his work on Christian education, the *Pedagogue*, that Christians should sing psalms before retiring, as the Jews of Alexandria did, and mentioned the Tropos Spondeiakos, or mode of libation, as the most suitable one. Pseudo-Plutarch, a contemporary of Clement, described this Doric-spondaic mode in his book on music and thus made possible its reconstruction. Years ago, I demonstrated that this mode occurs in some of the oldest Christian chants (in Latin, Greek, and Syriac) and in ancient prayers of the Yemeni Jews (*The Sacred Bridge*, vol. 1, 1959).
3. The tune of the *Te Deum*. This tune belongs to the very same family of melodies as the Tropos Spondeiakos and is equally old.
4. *Oxyrhynchus hymnus*. Written in the third century, this work is a praise of Christ that paraphrases a passage from Psalm 93. It represents a perfect mixture of Greek syllabic chant and Hebrew melismatic elements. This interpenetration of Greek and Hebrew elements was characteristic of most chants before the fourth century, when the Council of Laodicea set certain theological standards, which determined the split between Eastern and Roman Catholic liturgies.

Early Christian music thus preserved Greek and Hebrew sources of influence. Emphasis on the Greek elements in this music was made mainly by Boethius in his *De institutione musica*. Peter Wagner, the great expert on Gregorian chant, submitted a number of explanations for the role of Judeo-Christians as transmitters of Hebrew musical tradition to early Christian chants. The epitaphs of Deusdedit (Jonathan) and Redemptus (Yigael), singers whom Pope Damasus brought to Rome from Jerusalem, contain such remarks as "he sounded his ancient prophet [David] in sweet songs."

BYZANTINE MUSIC. While the Byzantine Empire was a well-defined entity both historically and geographically, its music belongs to its specific liturgy and so must be more closely circumscribed. The music of Byzantium will be sketched here as it developed in its first stage, from its origin in the fourth century during the reign of Constantine the Great until 565, the year of the death of Justinian I, who disbanded the Academy of Athens. The date is significant, for it marks the gradual separation of Byzantine culture from its Greek patrimony.

Music and Byzantine Christianity. We have no traces of early Byzantine secular music aside from reports of the great festivities held in honor of the emperor and his court, and about these noisy occasions we know most details from the tenth-century book of ceremonies by Constantine VII. No Byzantine music antedating the ninth century has come down to us. The term *Byzantine music* is, moreover, limited to liturgical chants. Although Syriac and Hebrew elements were probably integrated, definite evidence of these influences is not available, as the scholarship in this field is barely a hundred years old.

Musical notation. The Byzantine liturgy used two kinds of rhetorical notation. The first, the ancient ekphonetic notation, served the priests in reciting the sacred scriptures in a prescribed system of cantillation. Its connection with Syriac and Hebrew accents is quite obvious, as Egon Wellesz and I have shown. This kind of symbolism did not represent real musical pitches or intervals; instead, it punctuated the sentences and indicated pauses and the rise and fall of the voice. The second kind of notation was not established before the ninth century and so stands outside the scope of this description. This musical notation grew out of ekphonetic and rhetoric beginnings, and came to be applied to the chanted parts of the liturgy, especially to the *troparia*, centos of psalm verses and new poetry; the *heirmologia*, containing the models of traditional melodies; and the *kanones*, poetic paraphrases of nine biblical canticles: two songs of Moses, the prayer of Hannah, the prayer of Habakkuk, the hymn of Isaiah, the hymn of Jonah, the prayer of the three youths in the furnace, the apocryphal continuation of this prayer, and the Magnificat. The second ode was usually omitted in order to make a number equal to the eight modes, or *ēchoi* (Octoechos). From each of the original biblical texts, only a number of verses were chanted, and these were interwoven with poems by Byzantine authors.

The Octoechos. The Octoechos is a system of eight modes (originally not scales), whose names were erroneously borrowed from the classic Greek *harmoniai.* The concept of the Octoechos is very ancient; its origin has been linked to the Babylonian-Akkadian calendar. As a musical term, *ʿal-ha-sheminit* occurs in the superscriptions to two Hebrew psalms (sixth and twelfth) and, in the Greek literature, in Yohanan Rufos's sixth-century *Plerophoriai.* Under the name "Octoechos" many hymns of the Byzantine and Syrian churches were collected and ordered according to the eight modes and the seven-plus-one Sundays between Easter and Pentecost. Their texts were first published in about 540 by Severus, patriarch of Antioch. This work became the exemplar for many ritual books of the Byzantine Church. These books became repositories of an enormous number of liturgical melodies, whose influence enriched many of the chants of the Near East, even after the collapse of the empire in 1453.

SEE ALSO Aristotle; Chanting; Dionysos; Orpheus; Plato; Pythagoras; Socrates.

BIBLIOGRAPHY

For a full, mostly reliable study of Greek music, see "Greece, Ancient" by R. P. Winningham-Ingram and others in the *New Grove Dictionary of Music and Musicians*, edited by Stanley Sadie (London, 1980). For the advanced reader, Isobel Henderson's "Ancient Greek Music" in the *New Oxford History of Music* (Oxford, 1957) is recommended, although it neglects the Asiatic elements. Curt Sach's writings, especially his *Rise of Music in the Ancient World, East and West* (New York, 1943), contain the best available scholarship on ancient music, easily readable by the layman. See also Edward A. Lippman's *Musical Thought in Ancient Greece* (New York, 1964). Hermann J. Abert's study of *ēthos* in Greek music, *Die Lehre vom Ethos in der Musik des griechischen Altertums*, 2d ed. (Tutzing, 1968) is still the best presentation of this difficult subject, but it requires some philosophical background. *Antiquity and the Middle Ages* (New York, 1950), volume 1 of *Source Readings in Music History*, edited by Oliver Strunk, gives several Greek sources in good translation but is somewhat opinionated in its selection. My "The Origin of the Eight Modes in Music (Octoechos)," *Hebrew Union College Annual* 21 (1948): 211–255, presents most of the ancient sources of the system of musical modes.

For data on music in Rome, see "Rome, Ancient" by Günter Heischhauer in the *New Grove Dictionary of Music and Musicians.* J. E. Scott's "Roman Music" in the *New Oxford History of Music* presents a solid and scholarly evaluation.

The first chapter in volume 1 of Karl Gustav Fellerer's *The History of Catholic Music* (Baltimore, 1961) offers discussion of early Christian music. See also my *The Sacred Bridge*, 2 vols. (New York, 1959–1984), which examines the interdependence of liturgy and music in the Jewish and Christian traditions during the first millennium.

For a complete survey of Byzantine music in all its aspects, see "Byzantine Rite, Music of the," by Kenneth Levy in the *New Grove Dictionary of Music and Musicians.* Egon Wellesz's *A History of Byzantine Music and Hymnography*, 2d ed. (Oxford, 1961) is the standard work on the subject. For the more advanced reader, Wellesz's study "Word and Music in Byzantine Liturgy," *Musical Quarterly* 23 (July 1937): 297–310, gives a fine presentation of the most problematic aspects. For the reader familiar with classical literature, Carsten Høeg's profound study "Les rapport de la musique chrétienne et de la musique de l'antiquité classique," *Byzantion* 25–27 (1955–1957): 383–412, is highly recommended. For discussion of ancient musical instruments, Curt Sachs's *The History of Musical Instruments* (New York, 1940) is still the standard reference work.

New Sources

Anderson, Warren. *Music and Musicians in Ancient Greece.* Ithaca, N.Y., 1994.

Belis, Annie. *Les Musiciens dans l'Antiquité.* Paris, 1999.

Brulé, Pierre, and Christophe Vendriès, eds. *Chanter les dieux: musique et religion dans l'antiquité grecque et romaine.* Rennes, Zool.

Comotti, Giovanni. *Music in Greek and Roman Culture.* Baltimore, Md., 1989.

Landels, John G. *Music in Ancient Greece and Rome.* New York, 1999.

McKinnon, James, ed. *Antiquity and the Middle Ages: From Ancient Greece to the 15th Century.* Music and Society Series, vol. 1. Englewood Cliffs, N.J., 1991.

Mathiesen, Thomas J. *Apollo's Lyre: Greek Music and Music Theory in Antiquity and the Middle Ages.* Lincoln, 1999.

Scott, William C. *Musical Design in Sophoclean Theater.* Hanover, N.H., 1996.

West, M. L. *Ancient Greek Music.* New York, 2001.

ERIC WERNER (1987)
Revised Bibliography

MUSIC: RELIGIOUS MUSIC IN THE WEST

The religious music that is commonly considered Western had its beginnings in the Middle East and the Mediterranean, as did Western religions themselves. As that music developed over the centuries, it shaped and was shaped by a variety of musical cultures, most notably those of Europe and North America. Primarily Jewish or Christian in character, Western religious music has also been influenced at times by Islamic practices.

Different groups of Jews and Christians have been identified in the West partly by the kinds of music they have cultivated or prohibited. Much music, however, has crossed denominational and religious lines. Furthermore secular and sacred styles have been mutually influential, even if sometimes controversially so. Since the late eighteenth century Western music of a religious or spiritual nature has often appeared in a relatively secular guise.

From Temple to Synagogue and Church. Given the importance of the *Book of Psalms* to both Jewish and Christian worship and in view of references in *Psalms* to a variety of musical instruments, laments, and songs of praise, one might suppose that in later times Jews and Christians alike would have felt free to make music with virtually every means imaginable. But in the first few centuries of the common era dramatic changes in the context of worship for both groups made that kind of musical license virtually unthinkable.

In 70 CE the Roman army under Titus destroyed the Second Temple in Jerusalem; shortly thereafter Jews were deprived of their homeland. Accordingly the center of Jewish worship shifted from the Temple (originally the primary locus of *Psalms*) to the synagogue and the home.

Having started out as a Jewish sect, Christians likewise experienced in their first few centuries major, if less traumatic, shifts in the context and content of worship. With the missionary efforts of Paul and others, an ever-increasing percentage of the followers of Jesus were Gentiles. In addition Christians were often, albeit intermittently, targets of Roman persecution and were consequently constrained in their worship. Then in 313 CE the social situation of Christianity changed dramatically with the conversion of Constantine. Christianity became a legal and then privileged religion of the Roman Empire itself.

For both Jews and Christians there was considerable contrast between temple psalmody and their own liturgical practices. It is uncertain when synagogues originated; they may have begun in some form as far back as the exilic period or earlier. In any case, when worship took place in the synagogue, it never entailed sacrifice, as temple worship did. Nor did it make use of priests or a choir or any musical instruments except (later) the shofar, which had always had a limited ritual role—mainly on Ro'sh ha-Shanah. Some scholars believe that, until 70 CE, psalmody itself had no part at all in the synagogue and that psalm singing may not, in fact, have reappeared until around the fourth century CE In any case, the synagogue service was essentially a service of the word, with prayers and readings from Scripture.

Consistent with the principles of rabbinic Judaism, which were to remain normative until the eighteenth century, the musical simplicity of the synagogue apparently derived from three sources: rules (*halakhah*) for observing the Sabbath, which would be violated by the tuning and carrying of instruments; mourning over the Temple's destruction, which meant a ban on instrumental music until the coming of the messiah; and concern over the ostensibly sensual qualities of women's voices, with the result that only men were permitted to sing.

None of this is to imply that synagogue worship in its formative stages was unmusical. By the latter part of the first millennium if not before, the synagogue service employed three genres of chant: psalmody (responsorial or antiphonal), cantillation of Scripture, and liturgical chant for prayers. The liturgy in that way was musical through and through.

For their part, Christians during the apostolic age (first century CE) sang "psalms, hymns, and spiritual songs," as stated in *Ephesians* 5:19 and *Colossians* 3:16. While those terms are vague, many scholars believe that the sung texts included the biblical psalms (though that has been disputed), canticles such as those in *Exodus* 15 and *Habakkuk* 3, and hymns written by poets and composers who have not been identified. That the terms for the genres are left imprecise is not surprising; the New Testament spells out few details regarding either music or worship. One is told that Jesus and his disciples sang a hymn at the conclusion of the last supper, but scholars are left to speculate that the supper may have been a Passover seder and that the hymn may have been the Hallel.

It seems to have been a foregone conclusion among early Christians that instruments had no place in public worship. For their service of the word, Christians were still accustomed to the pattern of the synagogue, the music of which was strictly vocal. Whereas it is no longer assumed that there was an extended period of continuity with synagogue practice, Christians must have continued intoning prayers and chanting Scriptures. How and what Christians sang during the Eucharist (Communion) or at common meals is uncertain. The service of the Eucharist was probably indebted to Jewish and pagan traditions surrounding domestic meals and ritual banquets. None of the music survives, however—nor any other music from late antiquity.

Scholars formerly thought that Christians initially approached matters of music in a puritanical spirit that only gradually relaxed over the next several centuries as Christians became more sophisticated. Closer inspection of texts and dates has shown, however, that, whereas concerns over musical propriety and practice were a minor matter at first, they actually increased in the patristic period (roughly the second through the fifth centuries).

It was in response to pagan ritual and entertainment practices, which often combined song, drama, and dance, that church fathers raised objections to licentious singing and the use of instruments—the "senseless sounds" of drums and cymbals and the "clamor" of the trumpets. Clement of Alexandria summoned Christians to struggle against the "music of idols," especially instrumental music. He admitted that God permitted the Jews to use instruments in former times but insisted that this indulgence was a temporary concession to their weakness. John Chrysostom and others interpreted the instruments of the psalms allegorically, as symbolic of how harmony is produced in the soul. Tertullian, Augustine, and Chrysostom all said that Christian psalmody should serve as an antidote to sensuous excitement and a positive cure. When done moderately and with understanding, singing was said to lay the passions to rest, to still the body, and to calm and order the soul.

In making those claims about music, Christian pastoral theologians during the patristic era set the tone for the church for centuries to come. Yet doubtless aware of similar criticisms within the educated pagan world itself, they were not only recalling the ancient example of the harpist David playing for the fitful Saul. They were also mirroring and aligning themselves with the views of music held by esteemed pagan philosophers from Plato to Plotinus. According to such philosophy, whereas some instruments and modes of music making feed the passions, earthly music of the right kind reflects a divinely beautiful order. The highest music is intellectual and spiritual: inaudible. Hence the ambivalence of Augustine in a famous passage in Book 10 of the *Confessions.* There he admits having been moved to tears by psalms sung in church, and he acknowledges the "ardent piety" to which the singing can give rise. But he repents having in former years been moved more by the singing, the "delights of the ear," than by the truth of what was sung. And he wavers even as he consents to psalm singing in church.

When the church sang, the congregation as a whole participated, often responsively, guided by some sort of leader or "cantor." Clement of Alexandria emphasized the unity of many voices, all singing in unison. Women participated—and not in separate choirs, as in pagan rituals. But following a phase in which Christian women were indeed formed into choirs, a reaction set in. In the third and fourth centuries women's voices began to be silenced altogether in church—a practice that, despite the objections of Ambrose in particular, became prevalent.

MEDIEVAL DEVELOPMENTS. Already by the time of the destruction of the Second Temple, more Jews were living in the Diaspora than in Palestine, with especially large communities to be found in Babylonia and in Alexandria, Egypt. Subsequently the rapid conquests in the Middle East, North Africa, and the Iberian Peninsula by the armies of Islam (seventh to eighth centuries CE) created the framework for the basically uniform character of medieval Judaism. Regarded by Muslims as a "people of the Book" (as were the Christians), Jews in Muslim lands were permitted to have relative autonomy.

Singing, in the form of chant and cantillation, was vital to synagogue worship as it developed. Scripture, prayer, and words of praise were not merely read but variously intoned or chanted. In synagogues between approximately the seventh and ninth centuries CE, a system of signs (*te'amim*) was created to aid proper accentuation, verse division, and appropriate melodic patterns in chanting the text of Scripture. This process culminated in the Tiberias Massoretic system, the interpretation of which eventually resulted in the eight regional traditions of cantillation that now exist.

As time passed the need for a more or less professional singer, or cantor (*hazzan*), became evident. Traveling from one community to another, cantors shaped melodic patterns of prayer that later were regarded as sacred. Those chants came to be known as *nusach.* Although a lay precentor, then as now, would have presented the chant strictly as preserved and transmitted, the professional cantor rendered the melodic prayer with a greater measure of improvisatory freedom. Thenceforth the singing of the cantor was one of the glories of worship, although also periodically subject to criticisms of excessive virtuosity.

As synagogue services became more standardized from the fifth through the ninth centuries CE, complex poetic additions to, and substitutes for, fixed prayers became popular. Known as *piyyutim,* these liturgical poems included short refrains for congregational singing as well as more intricate refrains that could be given to a choir. The best known *piyyut* of all comes from the sixteenth century: *Lecha Dodi,* "Come, my Beloved, to meet the Bride; let us welcome the Sabbath," by Solomon Alkabetz (1505–c. 1572).

Two major branches of Judaism developed in Europe: Ashkenazi and Sefardi. Ashkenazic Jews moved outward from Italy to German-speaking lands, Russia, France, and England. They made use of special tunes, thought to be ancient, which were sung on solemn occasions. Those tunes were called *misinai,* which means "from Sinai," the most famous being the *Alenu* and the *Kol Nidre.*

Sefardic communities thrived in medieval Spain, where, after a golden age under Muslim rulers, they were forced by Muslims and then Christians to retreat to parts of northern Europe or back to North Africa and Palestine. In the Sefardic tradition, cantors paid greater attention to diction than to embellishment. In Spain, Arabic poetry, which was lyrical and characteristically even in meter, influenced both the secular and sacred Hebrew poetry of Yehudah ha-Levi, among others. Sefardic song borrowed Arabic modes and musical phrases, encouraging congregational singing. One form of Andalusian suite called *nuba* became popular, typically employing instruments except on the Sabbath. During the gradual reconquest of Spain by Christians, leading up to the expulsion of the Jews in 1492, Christian and Jewish styles blended, using Ladino dialect. Popular, rhythmic songs were enjoyed at such informal Jewish functions as Sabbath meals. A number of *cantica* melodies were adapted to hymns such as *Adon Olam* and *Yigdal* and even to the Qaddish doxology.

Christian chants may have developed relatively independently from Jewish practices, after a period of contact. Chant was particularly important to daily prayer in monastic communities. Even before the fall of Rome in 476 CE, which by convention marks the beginning of the early medieval period, the Christian monastic movement provided an alternative to the more worldly forms of Christianity newly ascendant in the Roman world of the fourth century. The Divine Office made extensive use of chant for reciting psalms and other sacred texts, in accordance with the rule established by Benedict of Nursia (c. 480–c. 547). Musically the most important of the eight canonical hours were matins, lauds, and vespers, the last incorporating the *Magnificat* canticle from *Luke* 1:46–55.

Sunday Eucharist in churches everywhere gave rise to a variety of regional "rites," all of which involved plainchant settings both of the pertinent variable texts (the Proper) for the Mass and invariable, fixed texts (the Ordinary): the Kyrie, Gloria, Credo, Sanctus, Benedictus, Agnus Dei, and Ite, missa est (often omitted from musical settings). The responsive psalmody and liturgy from Milan, which took the name Ambrosian, persisted after other local variations such as Gallican and Mozarabic had given way to Rome. By the eighth century CE Rome had a *Schola cantorum* for training church musicians. Tradition has it that Pope Gregory I (c. 540–604 CE) regulated and standardized the various liturgical chants, but that was more likely carried out over the next two centuries. The form of chant that eventually prevailed, which came to be called Gregorian, was imported and codified by Charlemagne (742–814 CE) in Frankish lands, superceding a form of Roman chant known as Old Roman.

Because plainchant evolved orally, it made considerable use of melodic formulas and simple structures. With quiet beauty, it formed a kind of stream on which to float prayer and praise. It served the word but without dramatic gestures or conspicuous attempts to illustrate the meaning of the texts. Chants employed melodic formulas called psalm tones, one for each of eight church scales, called modes, plus a *tonus peregrinus*, or "wandering tone." The singing was often antiphonal. Long melodies that were given hymn texts in couplets were known as sequences, two of the most famous being the *Dies irae* (heard in the Requiem Mass), and *Veni Sancte Spiritus.* Hildegard of Bingen (1098–1179) composed notable sequences in addition to antiphons and a musical morality play in plainchant, *Ordo virtutum* (The virtues).

Chant notation appeared for the first time in the ninth century CE, at which point it indicated only the rise and fall of pitches; in the eleventh century the use of staff lines finally specified pitch exactly. Probably the invention of notation contributed to the rise of multilinear singing, or polyphony, the earliest form of which was organum—initially a simple parallel motion between two or more vocal parts. In the twelfth century at Notre Dame Cathedral of Paris, Lenonin and Perotin composed rhythmically complex, multilayered forms of organum, which led shortly to motets that employed different sets of words simultaneously. In the fourteenth century there appears the first polyphonic setting of the entire Ordinary of the Mass by a single composer: the *Messe de Notre Dame* by the leading composer of the *Ars nova* in France, Guillaume de Machaut (c. 1300–1377).

If Gregorian chant by the High Middle Ages comprised the most extensive body of religious music in the West (and possibly anywhere on earth), polyphony was to become, over the next few centuries, one of the most intricately artistic achievements in all of sacred art. In the hands of such composers as John Dunstable (c.1390–1453), Guillaume Dufay (c. 1400–1474), Johannes Ockeghem (c. 1420–1497), and Josquin des Prez (c. 1450–1521), polyphonic music provided a vertically and horizontally ordered, well proportioned, and harmonious world of sound. Polyphony thus fulfilled venerable ideas of how human music could mirror or imitate the divine order of the cosmos—ideas that were adumbrated long before by Boethius (c. 480–524 CE) and still earlier by Augustine in his incomplete treatise *De musica* (c. 409 CE). Although music as studied in the medieval universities was essentially a theoretical branch of mathematics linked to astronomy, the making of polyphonic music itself could be regarded as both rational and theological.

In the meantime in Byzantium—the eastern part of the former Roman Empire that flourished long after the western part of the Empire fell—the plainchant of the liturgy had continued for centuries relatively unchanged. In Constantinople this music was characterized by ancient antiphonal psalmody and by a strophic form of hymnody known as the *kontakion*, a poetic elaboration on a biblical text. Yet in the last phase of the Byzantine Empire a new style of music emerged, the *kalophonic*, or "beautiful sounding." Whereas monophonic in the manner of plainchant, it was unusually florid. With the fall of Constantinople to the Turks in 1453, the Middle Ages came to a spectacular close.

RENAISSANCE AND BAROQUE. By the dawn of the European Renaissance (1453–1600), which was roughly concurrent in time with the Protestant Reformation, Jews had suffered massively from a wave of expulsions, forced conversions, and persecutions, climaxing in their fateful expulsion from Spain in 1492. Although the primary features of rabbinic Judaism remained relatively unchanged until the middle of the eighteenth century, messianic hopes intensified, along with mystical impulses and practices.

Qabbalistic mysticism, which had its roots in the Middle Ages, entered a new phase under the inspiration of Isaac Luria (1534–1572). He taught that the sparks of the godhead had fallen into captivity. Music was one of the spiritual means by which to liberate imprisoned elements of divinity and to contribute to the anticipated reparation, or *tikkun*, whereby creation could be restored to its intended harmony. An important aspect of *tikkun* was the practice of taking non-Jewish and secular tunes and transforming them into sacred songs.

In a related development over a century and a half later, eastern European Hasidism, under the leadership of Baʿal Shem Tov (c.1700–1760), emphasized the importance of joyful worship. Drawing on qabbalistic ideas, Hasidic music theory promoted the concept that even a melody without words, called a *niggun,* can contain divine sparks. The highest melodies, created by Hasidic saints, or *tsaddiqim,* were said to be like pure souls, their forms conveying mystical meaning and constituting an elevated form of prayer. The influence of Hasidic music was felt, eventually, in virtually all forms of Judaism. Hasidic-style music, mostly nonliturgical, remains popular in the twenty-first century, as in the central European style known as klezmer (from klezmorim, or "music makers").

Polyphonic art music did not find a home in the synagogue before around 1600. The polyphony introduced by Salomone Rossi (c. 1570–c. 1628) and published as *The Songs of Solomon* in Mantua, Italy, was remarkable but atypical. In Italian synagogues of the seventeenth century one could sometimes hear baroque cantatas on special occasions. In Amsterdam and Prague certain synagogues likewise introduced instrumental music, including the organ.

No such use of instruments was allowed to invade the more traditional synagogues—nor the churches of Eastern Orthodox Christianity. With the fall of Constantinople, Russian Orthodoxy became the main inheritor of the Byzantine tradition. The sung liturgy, while translated into Russian, continued to be exclusively vocal and remains so. While a wide-ranging, melismatic way of chanting arose in the sixteenth century, along with polyphony in two or three voices, the more decisive change came in the mid-1650s, when the patriarchy and the official Russian Church adopted polyphony on a broad scale. Although schismatic groups led by the Old Believers resisted that development as smacking of Roman Catholicism, the exclusive use of monophonic chant faded into a small minority tradition by the eighteenth century. At that time Dimitry Bortnyansky (1751–1825) set the dominant tone by composing elegant sacred choral concertos.

Within western Europe the Protestant Reformers of the sixteenth century differed considerably among themselves when it came to music. But for virtually all of them, music was a matter of consequence. It was part of what they thought they needed to reform. By their era the Ordinary of the Catholic Mass had been left to the choir and clergy, congregational response had been sharply curtailed, and morning and evening prayer had become choral as well. Because the choir itself was made up of clergy (often minor orders) and was exclusively male, there was little sense of the whole people's involvement in the liturgy and its music.

Martin Luther (1483–1546) emphasized vernacular, congregational hymnody not only as a way of retrieving the practice of the early church but also as a corollary to the doctrine of the priesthood of all believers. Luther himself wrote numerous metrical psalms and such hymns as the famous "Ein feste Burg" ("A Mighty Fortress"), for which he may also have composed the melody. Luther and his colleagues translated traditional Latin hymns, supplied sacred words for popular songs (as long as they had not been too intimately connected with brothels and inebriation), and took over popular vernacular hymns. Wanting to employ good and memorable tunes, Luther also took art songs of the day as a model. One of the main achievements of Lutheran music was the strophic, congregational hymn, or chorale, which in subsequent centuries became popular in four-part harmonizations. At the same time Luther had a great fondness for polyphony—especially that of Josquin—and envisioned a place for choral polyphony in the Mass, the liturgy of which he retained in modified form, both in Latin and in German. Convinced that, next to theology, music deserves the "highest honor," Luther considered music a great gift of God to be used as a vehicle of worship, as an aid to piety, and as a means of education.

In contrast to Luther, the Swiss reformer Huldrych Zwingli (1484–1531), although an accomplished musician, banished even congregational singing from the church, arguing that the biblical principle of "making music in your hearts" excluded using the voice itself. In Geneva, John Calvin (1509–1564) oversaw the production of a complete metrical psalter, edited in large part by Louis Bourgeois. Highly influential, the *Genevan Psalter* set the pattern for unaccompanied unison singing of metrical psalms in many different lands and was soon arranged in instrumental and polyphonic versions for domestic use.

In sixteenth-century England the book of metrical psalms compiled by Thomas Sternhold, and subsequently edited and supplemented by John Hopkins, provided the official basis for Anglican hymnody until the early nineteenth century. In the seventeenth century it was supplemented by Anglican chant, which called for singing psalm tones in harmony. In America the New England Puritans used the Scottish *Psalms of David in Meter* (1650) and, to a lesser extent, the *Bay Psalm Book* (1640).

In the eighteenth century Dissenters in England established an alternative hymnody that, besides making use of paraphrases of Scripture, incorporated songs of "human composure." Isaac Watts (1674–1748) showed the way with hymns such as "When I Survey the Wondrous Cross," followed by the Charles Wesley (1707–1788), whose five thousand hymns, including "Love Divine, All Loves Excelling," not only were intended to be a musical practical theology but also an emotional inspiration. Soon those hymns were a beloved feature not only of Methodist hymnody but of Protestant and evangelical hymnody in general.

Whereas hymn singing could claim roots in New Testament practice (without anyone knowing exactly what that had sounded like), other forms of church music during the

Renaissance and baroque eras were far removed from anything early Christians would have recognized. In England choral music within a Catholic orbit often employed a rich texture of five or six voices. Thomas Tallis (c. 1505–1585) went so far as to compose an elaborate motet with forty independent parts, *Spem in alium.* Various European Catholic composers of polyphony, such as Tomas Luis de Victoria (c. 1548–1611) and Orlando di Lasso (1532–1594), treated texts in a highly expressive, even passionate, manner.

Whether polyphonic textures could render sacred texts in a sufficiently intelligible fashion had long been an issue, however, and became so again. Many centuries earlier church leaders such as Pope John XXII (1316–1334) and John of Salisbury (1120–1180) had already complained not only about ostentatious singing but also about the incomprehensibility of texts when sung in multiple, overlapping lines of music, "some taking high and others low parts, some singing in advance, some following in the rear, others with pauses and interludes," all sounding like a "concert of sirens." The Protestants of the Reformation era definitely gave priority to the word, both spoken and sung. Thus King Edward VI of England in 1548 prescribed music that, in setting a text, would provide a "playn and distincte note, for every sillable one." Partly in response to such Protestant attempts at directness and simplicity, the Catholic Counter-Reformation, promoted by the Council of Trent, likewise criticized complicated polyphony for obscuring sacred texts, although the main concern was to discourage everything "impure or lascivious." Legend has it that the Italian Giovanni Pierluigi da Palestrina (c. 1525–1594) saved the future of polyphonic church music by composing his *Missa Papae Marcelli* in such a way as to demonstrate that restrained polyphony could indeed support the sacred word.

Nevertheless during the following era—commonly known as the baroque (roughly 1600–1750)—church music could be quite theatrical and exuberant. That is immediately apparent from the splendid variety of the *Vespers of the Blessed Virgin* (1610), composed by Claudio Monteverdi (1567–1643), which opens with instrumental fanfares drawn from his opera *L'Orfeo.* Yet the baroque, which saw the beginnings of opera, had its own ways of honoring the text. According to Monteverdi, music in the predominant modern style was meant, in fact, to serve the text. That modern style employed expressive dissonances, angular melodic lines, and rhythmic drive and freedom to dramatize the meaning of the words. It thus appealed directly to the "affections." Indeed the baroque anticipated the emphasis on the expressive function of music that later pervaded romanticism in a more personal way. Music of the baroque also included new forms of counterpoint, anchored in dramatic and often fast-moving chord progressions.

Church music of the baroque era made much use of newly evolved instruments: strings, woodwinds, trumpets, timpani, and certainly the organ. The organ up until then had mostly been employed modestly. Between the ninth and the twelfth centuries small organs (portative and positive) had migrated into the church from secular settings, along with a few large and unwieldy ones. Organs during the Reformation period were used extensively to introduce hymns and to alternate with—and eventually to accompany—congregational song as well as to provide preludes and postludes or Communion music. In the baroque era organs became much more complex mechanically and far grander and more versatile, especially in German-speaking lands. By the time of J. S. Bach (1685–1750) organ music included toccatas and fantasies, lengthy preludes and fugues, and numerous other forms that appear to have been designed primarily for concerts or instruction, although influencing sacred style as well.

Musical settings of the Mass grew increasingly varied. In France especially the organ sometimes took for itself parts of the Mass that might otherwise have been sung, elaborating on the pertinent chant tunes. In the Venetian-Viennese tradition of the Mass, instrumental figurations and sectional contrasts became a prominent feature, along with passages for solo voice. Late in this same period the concerted Mass in the so-called Neapolitan style unfolded on a larger scale than ever before, each of the parts of the Ordinary being subdivided into separate movements. Such Masses reflected a strong influence from opera, both in their emotional character and in their musical forms, such as duets and arias. At the same time Palestrina's works were preserved and imitated as classic models.

New forms of sacred music were born during the baroque: the sacred concerto, which Heinrich Schütz (1585–1672) raised to a high level, and more importantly the oratorio, the cantata, and the passion. Oratorio began in a Catholic place of prayer—the Oratory of Philip Neri in late-sixteenth-century Rome. Soon it became a religious counterpart to opera, adopted widely by Catholics in Italy and by Protestants in Germany, allowing them to present biblical stories in concert form, rather than being staged. Oratorio was particularly popular during Lent, when opera houses were closed. George Frideric Handel (1685–1759) brought oratorio to England, where its combination of narratives (recitatives), solos, and choruses became immensely popular. In England, however, oratorio was usually kept out of church, due to puritanical opposition to anything smacking of the theater. Thus Handel's many oratorios, including *Samson*, *Jephtha*, and the atypical but extraordinarily popular *Messiah*, were presented mainly in theaters and concert halls.

Although many Protestant composers tried their hands at cantatas or passions, the spiritual depth, intellectual craft, and sheer artistry of the many settings by J. S. Bach were beyond compare. Such cantatas, which were sometimes criticized for sounding too secular, borrowed stylistic features from Italian opera as they offered a musical commentary on the Gospel lesson for a given Sunday. The passion music that Bach composed for Good Friday services was far more extended in scale, lasting between two and three hours compared with the typical twenty minutes of a cantata. The *Saint Matthew Passion* together with Bach's lengthy *Mass in B Minor*—a kind of summa of the genre—can be counted among the greatest classics of Western religious music.

Enlightenment Era to the Twenty-First Century. For Jewish composers since the European Enlightenment period of the late seventeenth century and eighteenth century (overlapping the artistic baroque), the most salient feature of modernity was the struggle for emancipation and the concomitant question of assimilation—first in German-speaking countries of central Europe and then, a century later, in eastern Europe. In Westphalia, Berlin, and Hamburg in the early nineteenth century the aesthetic norms that guided Reform synagogue worship as it attempted to conform to a predominantly Christian culture were derived from Protestant Christianity: the reading of the Bible, rather than chanting, and the use of organs and Gentile-style hymns. In Vienna the cantor Salomon Sulzer (1804–1890) took a less-extreme approach. He purified the chant of the excess operatic embellishments that had accrued, and he made use of a choir of a dozen voices of men and boys, to the acclaim of visitors such as Franz Liszt and the critic Eduard Hanslick. Sulzer's contemporary Louis Lewandowski (1823–1894) composed and arranged simpler music for congregational singing in smaller synagogues. Choirs were also introduced in eastern Europe but only rarely included mixed voices at a time when men and women in the synagogue were still almost always seated separately. Organs remained controversial, yet many were installed in synagogues by midcentury, sometimes with the stipulation that they could be played only by Gentiles.

In the United States, Reform synagogues made decisive changes in liturgy and music, minimizing the role of the cantor and of chant. The music of the *Union Hymnal* of 1897 was more Protestant in style than identifiably Jewish—albeit intended for use by a professional choir and rabbi rather than the congregation. The 1932 edition, by contrast, reflected a desire to recover a distinctly Jewish sound, as Reform Jews had become more comfortable with their Jewish identity in the American context. By 1950s the Reform, Conservative, and Orthodox movements had all established schools of sacred music to train cantors. Yet the following decades, in which Sefardic Hebrew replaced Ashkenazic as the dominant dialect in liturgy, also saw a more populist and eclectic approach to liturgical music, tapping into the idioms of folk music and dance. Subsequently, within Reform Judaism itself, there has been a call for greater attention to traditional forms as well.

During the modern era numerous "classical" composers produced works of distinctly Jewish provenance whose primary context was intended to be the concert hall. These include such figures as Arnold Schoenberg (1874–1951), Ernest Bloch (1880–1959), Samuel Adler (b. 1928), Alexander Goehr (b. 1932), Leonard Bernstein (1918–1990), and Aaron Jay Kernis (b. 1960).

Russian Orthodox composers in the previous century were similarly active in the secular music world. Some of them, such as Mikhail Glinka (1804–1857), also wrote liturgical music, but there they faced the added challenge that the Russian Church repertoire remained exclusively vocal. Glinka himself, for instance, turned to modal harmonies and simple chordal structures when writing for the liturgy. Pieter Ilyich Tchaikovsky (1840–1893) and Sergei Rachmaninov (1873–1943) made more distinctive contributions, the latter with his choral *Vespers* (properly an "All Night Vigil"), which disturbed traditional church leaders at the time but is often regarded as the apogee of modern Russian liturgical music.

The center of musical life in the modern era clearly moved from liturgical settings (of whatever sort) to secular venues. Accordingly much of the development in Roman Catholic and Protestant music also became a story of interaction with, or reaction to, secular styles. The operatic influence that had been audible even in the case of Bach's cantatas became unmistakable, for example, in the Masses of Franz Joseph Haydn (1732–1809) and of Wolfgang Amadeus Mozart (1756–1791). Haydn's oratorios *The Creation* and *The Seasons,* while incorporating scriptural and religious themes, had a largely genial and buoyant manner, wearing their religious garb lightly. The high seriousness of Ludwig van Beethoven (1770–1827) in his *Missa Solemnis* could not be doubted. But that long and involving work was liturgically impractical, and the music became a virtual Mass in itself.

The trend continued with the gigantic Requiem Masses of Hector Berlioz (1803–1869) and Giuseppe Verdi (1813–1901), two composers who were by no means known as devout Catholics. The works themselves used theatrical means to convey powerful visions of eschatological hopes and fears. Richard Wagner (1813–1883) mined Christian myth in his opera *Parsifal* but without embracing Christian doctrine. Similarly Gustav Mahler (1860–1911) in his *Resurrection Symphony* (Second Symphony) and *Symphony of a Thousand* (Eighth Symphony) evidently found it spiritually empowering not to be restricted, textually, to any one specific religion. The same could be said earlier of the more conservative Johannes Brahms (1833–1897), whose *German Requiem* was essentially a concert work that avoided specifically Christian language while using biblical texts compiled by Brahms himself.

Certain classical composers nonetheless worked for the renewal of church music as such and of music related directly to the church. These included Franz Liszt (1811–1886), whose poetic oratorio *Christus* remains an unduly neglected masterpiece, and Felix Mendelssohn (1809–1847), who revived Bach's music and gathered a popular following with his own oratorios *Saint Paul* and *Elijah.* Anton Bruckner (1824–1896) wrote Masses and motets in addition to his monumental symphonies.

It was also in the nineteenth century, in a movement centered in Germany, that Catholic clergy and musicians promoted a new Cecilian Society, which was dedicated to reviving Gregorian chant and polyphony in the style of Palestrina. Other Catholics, led by the Benedictines at Solesmes, France, made efforts to restore the truer and more ancient forms of Gregorian chant. In England the Oxford Movement (1833–1845), emphasizing the broadly Catholic origins of the Church of England, recovered patristic hymnody and revived the medium of chant, usually in the English language.

Such endeavors anticipated the wider liturgical movement of the next century, in which various Roman Catholics and Protestants alike sought to renew worship by attending to its early paradigms as well as by emphasizing greater lay participation. The Second Vatican Council (1962–1965) ratified many of those themes, with the result that much of the music for the Ordinary of the Mass was returned to the congregation, Catholic hymnody came to life, and soon virtually everything was sung in the vernacular. The ensuing outburst of liturgical music in a wide array of popular guises brought both excitement and dismay. The music of the church became diverse and inclusive, yet the quality was uneven. Meanwhile much of the vast treasury of historical sacred music was orphaned, at least for the time being.

Congregational song had already expanded considerably in the nineteenth century and early twentieth century, even as mixed choirs and paid quartets became popular. The Church of England was enriched by two hymnals in particular, *Hymns Ancient and Modern* (1861) and *The English Hymnal* (1906), both of which have contemporary successors. Protestants in nineteenth-century America not only produced indigenous hymnbooks, such as the *Sacred Harp* and *Southern Harmony,* they later thrived on popular urban gospel songs, such as the hymns of Fanny Crosby (1820–1915), and on revival music that entered the evangelical mainstream.

African Americans at first adopted the hymns of the European-American churches. But by the middle of the nineteenth century, after emancipation, they produced their own hymnals. Long before then they had created their own tradition of shouts, spirituals, and "sorrow songs," often employing call-and-response patterns hearkening back to African idioms. Blending those traditions with many others, black gospel songs later in the century could be either jubilant or prayerfully protracted—as in "Precious Lord, Take My Hand" by Thomas A. Dorsey (1899–1993). The music of African American worshippers has since exhibited, by and large, great improvisatory freedom and rhythmic vitality. Inspired in part by Pentecostal movements, many African American churches have welcomed a variety of instruments, including percussion, and have made special use of the expressive possibilities of the Hammond organ. Whereas African American church music has often existed in tension with the more "worldly" styles of jazz and blues, the interaction between church and secular styles has been conspicuous. Duke Ellington (1899–1974) and John Coltrane (1926–1967) were able to infuse jazz with religious meaning. And contemporary gospel styles have absorbed elements of rock and rap.

In the last decades of the twentieth century Christian denominations produced an unprecedented number of new hymnals, drawing on music in a wide array of styles and from the worldwide Christian community. Some committees were guided specifically by concerns for social justice and inclusive language. Other groups, exploring alternative worship patterns, abandoned hymnals altogether in favor of projecting onto a screen the words of praise and worship choruses and contemporary Christian music. In the Catholic tradition the Saint Louis Jesuits led the way in the 1970s by providing scripturally based and accessible worship music. Ecumenically the music of the Taizé community in France, composed by Jacques Berthier (1923–1994), spread abroad a more meditative spirituality.

In relation specifically to modern classical music, churches utilized the works of a small number of recognized composers such as Ralph Vaughan Williams (1872–1958), Randall Thompson (1899–1984), and John Rutter (b. 1945). Unbeknownst to most churchgoers, many other modern composers—including Igor Stravinsky (1882–1971), Francis Poulenc (1899–1963), Frank Martin (1890–1974), Benjamin Britten (1913–1976), and Olivier Messiaen (1908–1992)—continued to produce major religious works. Such music typically made exceptional demands on both listener and performer, however. A large gap widened between modernist works, which often bristled with difficulties, and the sensibilities of most churchgoers. That gap only increased as churches turned more and more to the idioms of popular culture and began mixing styles in "blended worship." With spiritually attuned listeners also being drawn to New Age and world music, the classical establishment often seemed remote.

It is thus noteworthy from a religious perspective that, in the present era, or postmodernity, the differences between Eastern and Western music and between "elite" and "popular" have begun to erode, even in the concert hall. Some of the finest recordings of Bach cantatas have been originating in Japan. And among the latest classical styles are a spiritually centered minimalism and a tonally based (and often multicultural) eclecticism that have both shown considerable "crossover" potential. Works by composers such as Arvo Pärt (b. 1935), John Tavener (b. 1944), James MacMillan (b. 1959), John Adams (b. 1947), Tan Dun (b. 1957), and Osvoldo Golijov (b. 1960) appear to hold out promise for new kinds of artfully wrought religious music that might grow alongside, and interact with, the burgeoning indigenous and popular traditions.

SEE ALSO Chanting; Christianity, overview article; Islam, overview article; Judaism, overview article.

BIBLIOGRAPHY

There is as of 2004 no truly encompassing survey of Western religious music. A comprehensive and virtually indispensable resource is Stanley Sadie and John Tyrell, eds., *New Grove Dictionary of Music and Musicians*, 2d ed., 29 vols. (New York, 2001), also available online. More succinct articles representing the new socially and culturally informed musicology are in Alison Latham, ed., *Oxford Companion to Music* (Oxford, U.K., 2002). Useful at a general level are Paul Henry Lang, *Music in Western Civilization* (New York, 1941); and the more up-to-date Donald Jay Grout and Claude V. Palisca, *A History of Western Music*, 6th ed. (New York, 2000). The eight volumes of the series *Music and Society* (Englewood Cliffs, N.J., 1986–1999), Stanley Sadie, general ed., are exceptionally good resources. Two anthologies of readings are pertinent: W. Oliver Strunk's *Source Readings in Music History*, rev. ed., edited by Leo Treitler (New York, 1998); and Piero Weiss and Richard Taruskin, eds., *Music in the Western World: A History in Documents* (New York, 1984).

A volume that represents both Jewish and Christian perspectives is Lawrence A. Hoffman and Janet R. Walton, eds., *Sacred Sound and Social Change: Liturgical Music in Jewish and Christian Experience* (Notre Dame, Ind., 1992), which has been an important resource for this entry. Eric Werner's *The Sacred Bridge: The Interdependence of Liturgy and Music in Synagogue and Church during the First Millennium*, 2 vols. (New York, 1959), is a classic discussion of the liturgical and musical relations between synagogue and church, though often debatable in its conclusions. Uniquely valuable but also dated is Abraham Zvi Idelsohn, *Jewish Music in Its Historical Development* (New York, 1929). On the cantorial tradition, two works stand out: Eric Werner, *A Voice Still Heard: The Sacred Songs of the Ashkenazic Jews* (University Park, Pa., 1976); and Mark Slobin, *Chosen Voices: The Story of the American Cantorate* (Urbana, Ill., 1989). Jeffrey A. Summit provides a rich ethnographic study in *The Lord's Song in a Strange Land: Music and Identity in Contemporary Jewish Worship* (New York, 2000).

For early Christian ideas and uses of music, see Johannes Quasten, *Music and Worship in Pagan and Christian Antiquity*, translated by Boniface Ramsey (Washington, D.C., 1983); and James McKinnon, ed., *Music in Early Christian Literature* (Cambridge, U.K., 1987). A valuable resource for later viewpoints on Catholic Christian music is Robert F. Hayburn, ed., *Papal Legislation on Sacred Music, 95 A.D. to 1977 A.D.* (Collegeville, Minn., 1979). Christian theologies of music are well presented in Quentin Faulkner, *Wiser than Despair: The Evolution of Ideas in the Relationship of Music and the Christian Church* (Westport, Conn., 1996); Joyce L. Irwin, *Neither Voice nor Heart Alone: German Lutheran Theology of Music in the Age of the Baroque* (New York, 1993); Albert L. Blackwell, *The Sacred in Music* (Louisville, Ky., 1999); and Jeremy Begbie, *Theology, Music, and Time* (Cambridge, U.K., 2000).

Karl Gustav Fellerer gives a good account of Catholic music in *The History of Catholic Church Music*, translated by Francis A. Brunner (Baltimore, Md., 1961). A detailed survey of Protestant music is Friedrich Blume, *Protestant Church Music: A History* (New York, 1974). Paul Westermeyer's *Te Deum: The Church and Music* (Minneapolis, Minn., 1998) emphasizes vocal and specifically congregational music. On hymnody, a useful resource is David W. Music, ed., *Hymnology: A Collection of Source Readings* (Lanham, Md., 1996). Richard Arnold's *The English Hymn: Studies in a Genre* (New York, 1995) is unsurpassed. African American hymnody and religious music is treated in Eileen Southern, *The Music of Black Americans: A History*, 3d ed. (New York, 1997); Jon Michael Spencer, *Protest and Praise: Sacred Music of Black Religion* (Minneapolis, Minn., 1990); and Jon Michael Spencer, *Black Hymnody: A Hymnological History of the African American Church* (Knoxville, Tenn., 1992). For religious music in the United States generally, see Stephen A. Marini, *Sacred Song in America: Religion, Music, and Public Culture* (Urbana, Ill., 2003). The articles in Edward Foley, ed., *Worship Music: A Concise Dictionary* (Collegeville, Minn., 2000), are brief but wide-ranging and reliable. Edward Foley's *Ritual Music: Studies in Liturgical Musicology* (Beltsville, Md., 1995) contains a detailed bibliographical essay on music and liturgy.

FRANK BURCH BROWN (2005)

MUSLIM BROTHERHOOD. Founded in 1928 by Ḥasan al-Bannāʾ (1906–1949), the Society of Muslim Brothers (al-Ikhwān al-Muslimūn) was created to bring Egyptian Muslims back to an awareness of the objectives of religion within a society that had, in the view of al-Bannāʾ, been corrupted by alien ideologies and a materialist philosophy imported from the West.

HISTORICAL BACKGROUND. The British occupation of Egypt in 1882 had fueled a nationalist movement seeking independence from British rule; these aspirations culminated in the revolt of 1919 under the leadership of the aging politician Saʿd Zaghlūl and the newly formed Wafd ("delegation") party. The decade of the 1920s offered the Egyptians constitutional government and hopes of an impending settlement between Britain and Egypt through a negotiated treaty. When Zaghlūl died in 1927, these hopes were eroded, and a number of movements appeared as alternatives to the liberal notions of government that had not been successful, partly through interference on the part of the king and the British authorities in Egypt and partly through ineptness on the part of the parliamentarians. In addition to the fascists and the communists, these movements included the Society of Muslim Brothers, who believed that the path of reforming the country's social and political problems lay in the islamization of institutions.

Ḥasan al-Bannāʾ, a primary school teacher who was the son of a small-town religious teacher, was early attracted to Sufism, which, along with classical Islamic studies, formed his major intellectual foundations and became the linchpins of his group. He described the Muslim Brotherhood as a "Salafīyah movement [espousing return to the early principles of Islam], a Sunnī [orthodox] way, a Ṣūfī [mystical] truth, a political organization, an athletic group, a cultural and educational union, an economic company, and a social idea." The movement spread rapidly, representing every segment of society from newly urbanized rural immigrants to high government officials. In its heyday in the 1940s, the Muslim Brotherhood claimed to represent one million members; later estimates are difficult to establish.

The structure of the organization was spelled out in the Fundamental Law of the Organization of the Muslim Brothers, promulgated in 1945 and later amended. Leading the organization was the general guide, who chaired the General Guidance Council (the policy-making body) and the Consultative or General Assembly, both of which were elective bodies. A secretary general was in charge of a secretariat linking the council and the rest of the organization. Two further subdivisions dealt with various committees (press, peasants, students, etc.) and with an administrative body supervising branches outside the capital. A chain of command was thus established over the entire membership.

SPREAD OF THE MOVEMENT. Weekly lectures, preaching in mosques, and periodic conferences allowed for popular participation, and the establishment of a press soon spread the message of the Society of Muslim Brothers further. Unconcerned with doctrinal differences, the participants concentrated on growth, action, and organization, and by 1939 they were ready for political activity. The war years were to provide them with a forum.

Nationalist agitation against the British continued with labor strikes and student demonstrations until, in 1942, the British threatened King Fārūq (Farouk) with deposition and forced him to appoint a Wafd government under Muṣṭafā al-Naḥḥās. This incident generated further support for the Muslim Brotherhood, by then the only other grouping with a mass base to rival the Wafd. Even among the Wafd leadership there were many who approved of the society as a bulwark against the spread of communism among the working class. For the next few years the society established links with disaffected officers within the army (who were later to carry out the revolution of 1952), and, unknown to even his closest colleagues, al-Bannāʾ stockpiled weapons and created a secret apparatus trained in the use of armed violence for tactical operations.

With the end of the war, agitation for the evacuation of British forces from Egypt started once again, with frequent student demonstrations and acts of violence until the British garrison was finally withdrawn to the Canal Zone. The situation in Palestine and the war against Israel in 1948 provided the Muslim Brotherhood with an opportunity to collect more arms as members volunteered during the war and remained in the forefront of the fighting until their organization was dissolved in December 1948. The immediate cause for the government's action against the society was the death of the Egyptian chief of police, Salīm Zakī, who was killed by a bomb thrown at him during student demonstrations protesting the armistice with Israel. Mass arrests followed as the government, fearing the society's growing influence, sought to proscribe it. Three weeks later, the prime minister, Maḥūmud Fahmī al-Nuqrāshī, was assassinated by a Muslim Brother. In February 1949 Ḥasan al-Bannā' was himself assassinated, probably with the complicity, if not the actual participation, of the government of the day.

After the Muslim Brotherhood was proscribed, its property confiscated, and its members put on trial, many of its remaining members fled to other Arab countries, where they founded autonomous branches of the society. In 1951 a Wafd government, seeking a buffer against rising leftist movements, allowed the society to reconvene. A judge with palace connections, Ḥasan Ismāʿil al-Huḍaybī, was chosen as new leader. That same year the Wafd government unilaterally abrogated the treaty of 1936 with England, and Egyptian youth, including the Muslim Brothers, were encouraged to harass British camps in the Canal Zone. In January 1952 British forces attacked the Ismailia police station, and forty Egyptian policemen were killed. On the following day Cairo was set on fire in a monstrous riot that gutted the heart of the city. The Muslim Brothers were suspected of planning the riot, which they had not, although some of them were among the many participants. From then on the country was virtually without effective government until July 23, 1952, when the Free Officers movement, which included future Egyptian presidents Jamāl ʿAbd al-Nāṣir (Gamal Abdel Nasser) and Anwar al-Sādāt, seized power and three days later sent the king into exile.

There had been strong links between the Muslim Brotherhood and the Free Officers—Nasser and Sadat had both been members of the society. Once all political parties had been disbanded, the only focus for mass support lay with the society. Nasser knew that it represented the lone challenge to his authority and that its leaders expected to share power with the officers; a power struggle was inevitable. In 1954 a member of the Muslim Brotherhood allegedly attempted to shoot Nasser during a public rally, and once again the society was proscribed and its members arrested.

The society remained underground throughout the Nasser era. When Sadat came to power in 1970 all prisoners were released, including the Muslim Brothers, and, to combat the Nasserite current, Sadat allowed the society to reestablish itself under the leadership of an *ʿālim* (religious scholar), Shaykh al-Tilimsānī, and to publish its own newspapers. Meanwhile newer associations patterned after the society, the Islamic *jamāʿāt* ("groups"), had appeared. Some of these were extensions of the Muslim Brotherhood; others regarded the society as retrograde and beholden to the government. It was a member of one of the latter, more extremist groups who assassinated Sadat in 1981.

DOCTRINES AND IMPACT. According to the program of al-Bannā', the Society of Muslim Brothers was given a mission to restore the rule of the *sharīʿah* (Islamic law) to Egypt, and to all other Muslim countries where their missionary activities had set up affiliates. Rule of the *sharīʿah* rendered inadmissible the separation of church and state, for the state, they believed, existed in order to serve religion and to facilitate the fulfillment of Islamic religious duties. The Islamic state had the Qur'ān as its constitution; its government operated through *shūrā*, or consultation, and the executive branch, guided by the will of the people, ruled through Islamic principles. The ruler, chosen by the people, was responsible to them and not above the law, with no special privileges. Should he fail in his duties he was to be ousted. Freedom of thought, of worship, and of expression were vital, as was freedom of education. Finally, freedom of possessions was to be maintained within the limits set by Islamic law, which frowns upon the excessive accumulation of wealth and enjoins *zākāt* ("alms") as a basic religious duty. Social justice was to be the guiding principle of government.

The significance of the Society of Muslim Brothers and of its modern offshoots, the *jamāʿāt*, is that they represent a protest movement couched in a traditional Islamic idiom that expresses the ethos of a people. The society arose in protest against a foreign occupation that threatened the identity of a people and the dissolution of its culture and religion. It spoke to people in the language they understood and appreciated, that of Islam and its historical past, and it did not posit newfangled notions derived from a Western idiom, although the society did use Western techniques of mass communications and of assembly, even ideas of government, which were garbed in Muslim idiom. As such it was comprehensible to the masses who suffered political discrimination and economic exploitation by a government that was largely indifferent to their welfare, especially during periods of economic recession. Those who were disillusioned with Western ideologies and their ability to solve Egypt's problems, or indeed the problems of any Muslim country, turned to the precepts of the society, or to similar movements that they identified with their roots and cultural authenticity (*aṣā-lah*), for guidance and spiritual consolation. The same phenomenon was reproduced during the Sadat regime (1970–1981) when the "Open Door" (*infitāḥ*) policy disrupted society and led to rampant consumerism, which, exacerbated by the influx of oil money, raised fears of becoming engulfed by westernization.

Organizations such as the Muslim Brotherhood or the *jamāʿāt* are regarded by some Muslim regimes as dangerous foci of opposition and have thus met with violent repression. In 1982, under the regime of president Ḥāfiẓ al-Asad, the Syrian army shelled the city of Hama, a Muslim Brotherhood stronghold; portions of the city were leveled and casualties were variously estimated at ten thousand to twenty thousand. Similar attacks were repeated in Aleppo, Homs, and Latakia. In Iraq the regime of Ṣadām Ḥusayn waged a relentless campaign against the Shīʿī group al-Daʿwah al-Islāmīyah. In Saudi Arabia Muslim militants seized the Grand Mosque in Mecca for several days in 1979. In Sudan the Muslim Brotherhood forced the regime of Muḥammad Jaʿfar al-Numayrī (Numeiri) to adopt Islamic policies in 1977. Comparable militant groups have spread to most Muslim countries irrespective of their forms of government.

BIBLIOGRAPHY

Enayat, Hamid. *Modern Islamic Political Thought.* Austin, 1982. A thoughtful interpretation of political ideas from major Muslim countries.

Harris, Christina Phelps. *Nationalism and Revolution in Egypt.* The Hague, 1964. An early study of the Muslim Brotherhood, written before much interesting material had been uncovered but useful nonetheless.

Husaini, Ishak Musa. *The Moslem Brethren: The Greatest of Modern Islamic Movements.* Translated by John F. Brown and John Racy. Beirut, 1956. The first account of the society, written by an uncritical admirer but containing many quotes from al-Bannāʾ.

Ibrahim, Saad Eddin. *The New Arab Social Order.* Boulder, 1982. A study of the effect of oil riches on Middle East society, with an excellent discussion of militant movements.

Kotb, Sayed (Quṭb, Sayyid). *Social Justice in Islam.* Translated by John B. Hardie. Washington, D. C., 1953. A major work written by a leading Muslim intellectual.

Mitchell, Richard P. *The Society of the Muslim Brothers.* Oxford, 1969. The definitive work on the society. The author died before he could bring his work up to date, but it remains the only critical account of the movement.

Wendell, Charles, trans. and ed. *Five Tracts of Hasan al-Banna (1906–1949).* Berkeley, 1978. Basic source documents with annotations.

AFAF LUTFI AL-SAYYUD MARSOT (1987)

MUSŌ SŌSEKI (1275–1351), a monk of the Rinzai school of Zen Buddhism in medieval Japan. Born into an aristocratic family, he entered the religious life at an early age, rose to become head of some of Japan's most influential Zen monasteries, and left his stamp on Rinzai Zen and medieval culture.

Musō's earliest Buddhist training was not in Zen, but in esoteric Tendai and Shingon Buddhism. He was drawn to Zen at about the age of twenty and went to study under the Chinese Zen master Yishan Yining at the monastery of Engakuji in Kamakura. Although an able pupil, Musō was unable to convince Yishan that he had attained a valid enlightenment experience. Finally, he left Engakuji to seek his understanding of the buddha-nature in a life of solitary wandering and meditation, and to test his Zen with other masters. He attained his enlightenment one night, deep in a forest, watching the embers of his campfire. This enlightenment experience was formally recognized *(inka)* by the Japanese Zen master Kōhō Kennichi, with whom Musō studied for several years.

After Kōhō's death in 1314, Musō returned to his solitary wanderings, deepening his insight through meditation in mountain hermitages. His spiritual reputation eventually reached Kyoto and Kamakura. In 1325, at the age of fifty-one, he was invited by the emperor Go-Daigo to head the important Kyoto monastery of Nanzenji. Musō also came to the attention of the Hōjō regents in Kamakura and the early Ashikaga shoguns, all of whom were eager to patronize the monk and study Zen under his guidance. After Nanzenji, Musō went on to head several other important Rinzai *gozan* monasteries. By the close of his life, he was regarded as the most eminent monk in Japan, had become the leader of a rapidly growing band of disciples, and had seven times been the recipient of the prestigious title of *kokushi,* or National Master.

Musō's considerable contributions to medieval Zen and Japanese culture were made in several areas. As a Zen master, with a large following of monks and laymen, Musō advocated a kind of Zen practice that was readily accessible to the Japanese of his day. Although he studied under Chinese Zen masters, Musō himself never visited China. His Zen incorporated the traditional Rinzai practices of seated meditation and *kōan* study, but its Chinese character was tempered by his own early religious training, his continued devotion to Japanese Esoteric Buddhism, and his strong interest in Japanese poetry and culture. In his book *Muchu mondo* (Dialogues in a dream), Musō tried to explain Zen in straightforward, everyday language as he responded to the questions raised by the warrior Ashikaga Tadayoshi.

Musō also played an important role as a monastic leader and regulator who shaped the character of Rinzai Zen monastic life in medieval Japan. Although his Zen was easily accessible to monks and laymen, he set high standards for his monks. He divided them into three categories: those few who singlemindedly pursued enlightenment, those whose Zen practice was diluted by a taste for scholarship, and those who merely read about Zen and never threw themselves into a search for self-understanding. To help and discipline the practice of all his followers, Musō laid down strict rules for his communities in codes such as the *Rinsen kakun,* a set of regulations for Rinsenji. In this, Musō was setting himself in the tradition of such famous Chinese and Japanese monastic leaders as Baizhang and Dōgen Kigen, both of whom had devoted considerable attention to the proper practice of Zen community life.

Musō was also an intellectual and a man of culture. Schooled in Chinese, he wrote poetry in both Chinese and Japanese. He is also renowned as a garden designer. In addition, Musō was a major political figure in his day. He served as confidant and go-between for the emperor Go-Daigo, the Hōjō, and the Ashikaga, encouraged the sending of trading missions to China and the building of new Zen monasteries, and raised Rinzai Zen to a position of political prominence in medieval Japanese society.

SEE ALSO Gozan Zen.

BIBLIOGRAPHY

Collcutt, Martin. *Five Mountains: The Rinzai Zen Monastic Institution in Medieval Japan.* Cambridge, Mass., 1981.

Fontein, Jan, and Money L. Hickman, eds. *Zen Painting and Calligraphy.* Boston, 1970.

Kraft, Kenneth L., trans. "Musō Kokushi's Dialogues in a Dream." *The Eastern Buddhist,* n.s. 14 (Spring 1981): 75–93.

MARTIN COLLCUTT (1987)

MUʿTAZILAH.

A religious movement in early Islam, the Muʿtazilah turned into a theological school that become dominant in the third and fourth centuries AH (ninth to tenth century CE) and persisted in certain areas until the Mongol invasion at the beginning of the thirteenth century CE. The history of the movement is comprised of three different phases: (1) an incubation period that lasted roughly through the eighth century; (2) a short period of less than half a century (c. 815–850) when the Muʿtazilī school, after having defined its identity, developed an astonishing variety of individual, sometimes contradictory ideas and permeated the intellectual life at the Abbasid court; and finally (3) several centuries of scholastic systematization channeled into two branches or schools that were named after the towns of Basra and Baghdad respectively.

Each of these phases presents its own problems for the researcher: the first is badly documented and can only be reconstructed on the basis of later reports, which are frequently distorted and tendentious; the second is better attested but needs detailed monographical treatment; and the third has only recently begun to attract scholarly attention. On the whole, knowledge of this movement is still rudimentary. Detailed research is hampered by the lack of original texts. This is due to the fact that, after the middle of the ninth century, the Muʿtazilī movement was gradually driven into the position of a heresy; in the areas where it was considered "unorthodox" its books were no longer copied. Therefore we have to rely, at least up to the third phase, mainly on heresiographical reports. For the later centuries we possess a few texts, some of which reach the size of a *summa theologica,* but they belong to a rather restricted period; outside of this limit, many of the thinkers still remain mere names to us.

HISTORY.

The Muʿtazilī movement is usually traced back to the end of the Umayyad period, the years between 740 and 750. But during the first century of its existence the movement was far from the most important factor in the development of Islamic theology.

Origins. The Muʿtazilah began in Iraq, but there the Shīʿah (in Kufa) and the Ibāḍīyah (in Basra and Kufa) initially had the better thinkers, while the school of Abū Hanīfah, which combined juridical competence with an "ecumenical" outlook in theology, enjoyed greater missionary success. We are not even sure whether we can assume—as all of our sources do—that a real continuity existed between the first and second phases: there seems to be almost no doubt that the great thinkers of the second phase did not have any precise knowledge about their spiritual ancestors. When they moved from the old intellectual centers, Basra and Kufa, to the Abbasid court in Baghdad they felt the urge to preserve the memory of their past, but they evidently could not rely on any established historical tradition of the "school." The gap was widened by the fact that they disagreed with certain opinions held in the preceding generation and therefore tried to keep their immediate predecessors out of the picture. Under these circumstances we must reckon with the possibility that they constructed a past which never belonged to them or was only partially true. We should also not forget that the historical reports that were transmitted at that time were not collected and written down until some time later, from the middle of the second half of the ninth century onward.

The lack of historical recollection is amply demonstrated by the discovery that no Muʿtazilī author had any precise information about the original meaning of the name *Muʿtazilah*. Our sources offer a number of explanations, but all of them are secondary guesses and beside the point; some are blatantly tendentious. Modern scholarship has contributed a few more suggestions, but the question still remains open. All that we can prove is that the movement bore this name when it became involved in an insurrection against the caliph al-Manṣūr in 762. But the name does not seem to have been invented at that time, for it does not fit the situation. It means "those who dissociate themselves" or "those who keep themselves apart" and thus calls for political neutrality rather than revolutionary activism. The name already existed in the first century AH (seventh century CE), with this connotation, as a term designating some renowned companions of the Prophet who abstained from any participation in the first civil war (the Battle of the Camel in 656 and the Battle of Ṣiffīn in 657). It was then probably applied to the first Muʿtazilī thinkers since they, too, did not side with any political party of their time.

This attitude was distinctive insofar as it was adopted in a period when almost everybody had to make personal alignments clear, namely during the last years of the Umayyad caliphate, which saw the breakdown of the political order in Iraq and elsewhere. The founder of the movement, a cloth merchant from Basra by the name of Wāṣil ibn ʿAṭāʾ, intended to create a missionary organization working inside Islam; he sent his disciples, as "propagandists," to the most remote regions of the Islamic empire—the Arabian Peninsula, Armenia, Iran, India (the Punjab), and the Maghreb—so that they could interpret the Muslim creed and win people over to his own cause. Unfortunately, we do not know what this "cause" really implied. We cannot exclude the possibility that it was originally political, for Wāṣil copied a model that clearly had a political character, that is, the network of agents built up by the Ibāḍīyah, with whom he lived closely in Basra. Most of our information, however, contradicts this hypothesis: Wāṣil wanted reform, not revolution. Islam, was, after all, still the religion of a minority; outside the great centers, the knowledge of what Islam really meant was rather limited, and its definition differed from area to area. It any case, Wāṣil did not live to see the fruit of his efforts; he died in 749, one year before the triumph of the Abbasids.

Wāṣil's "propagandists" were mostly merchants like himself, and when they traveled, they combined business with missionary zeal. This pattern explains how the movement financed itself but does not say much about its spiritual impetus. The inner motivation of Wāṣil's circle seems to have derived from a certain feeling of inferiority: all of the participants were non-Arabs, that is, they did not enjoy the natural prestige of the aristocracy but came, as "clients," from Iranian or Aramaean families who had been converted to Islam one or two generations before. They possessed considerable wealth and were, as a matter of fact, recognized in their society, but they had to rely on Islam as the basis of their identity. They knew something about Islamic law, for Wāṣil advised them to win the favor of their audience by delivering *fatwās* ("legal opinions") to demonstrate their juridical expertise. But they also deliberately distinguished themselves from normal, "worldly" people: they clipped their mustaches and wore turbans (which, at that time, were characteristic of certain nomadic tribes but not of the urban population); they also wore special sandals and wide sleeves. This was the attire of ascetics; it gave them a certain "alternative" touch.

The organization was taken over by Wāṣil's colleague ʿAmr ibn ʿUbayd (d. 761), a prominent disciple of Ḥasan al-Baṣrī, the great figure of religious life in Basra during the preceding generation. ʿAmr had to cope with the new situation created by the Abbasid seizure of power. He seems to have given up all relations with the cells outside Iraq and in Basra, where he controlled a considerable number of adherents (who possibly formed youth groups), he kept quiet. This position became increasingly precarious at the end of his life as discontent with the Abbasid government mounted in Iraq. After his death the activists among the Muʿtazilah followed the call of the Shīʿī pretender Muḥammad ibn ʿAbd Allāh al-Nafs al-Zakīyah (or rather, that of his brother Ibrāhīm) and took part in the revolt of 762. When the attempt failed, the Muʿtazilah were persecuted and went into hiding; those who had compromised themselves mostly fled to Morocco.

This event seems to be a decisive turning point. We hear that afterward the Muʿtazilah still possessed a mosque of their own in Basra, but we do not know of any leading personality for at least thirty years. Above all, there is no hint of any specific theological activity. Then, toward the end of the eighth century, two figures emerged: al-Aṣamm in Basra and Ḍirār ibn ʿAmr in Kufa. But neither of them was a typical Muʿtazilī; as a matter of fact, the later school kept a certain distance from them. Al-Aṣamm was obviously an Ibāḍī, whereas Ḍirār, a judge by profession and one of the most original thinkers of this period, differed from the *communis opinio* of the following generation in his ideas concerning free will and therefore fell victim to a *damnatio memoriae.* The original concept of the Muʿtazilah as a popular missionary movement seems to have survived best in Baghdad where, during the same period, Bishr ibn al-Muʿtamir, a slave merchant by profession, exhorted the masses by expressing his theological ideas in simple poetry. That was appropriate for the social climate in the newly founded capital; the town had attracted many people who came to make their fortune and ended up by being uprooted.

The period of success. The Muʿtazilah were propelled from provinciality to prime importance by the theological interest which emerged at the Abbasid court. The change came in two shifts, first through the influence of the Barmakids, the viziers of Hārūn al-Rashīd (r. 786–802), and then, after a short setback caused by their downfall, thanks to the initiative of the caliph al-Maʾmūn (813–833). Both the Barmakids and al-Maʾmūn were not so much interested in theology itself as in listening to disputations: they liked to have representatives of different religions and confessions argue against each other. This predilection may have been stimulated by a non-Iraqi environment: the Barmakids originally came from Balkh, and al-Maʾmūn first resided in Merv; in Transoxiana, where both towns were situated, Islam coexisted with Zoroastrianism, Buddhism, Christianity, and Judaism.

However, the main stimulus came from the intellectual atmosphere of the capital itself. Islam was no longer the religion of a minority, as in the time of Wāṣil, but a creed which had rapidly expanded at the expense of other religions. The conversions to Islam had been prompted mostly by social considerations, but theology had to furnish an *a posteriori* justification: thus the outlook of the new theology was strongly apologetic and its style predominantly dialectical. The Muslims were not entirely unprepared; they had experienced enough internal strife between different "sects" in order to know what methods to use in disputes. Therefore, the Muʿtazilah were not the only ones to sharpen these weapons for the fight with their pagan adversaries. But besides being skillful dialecticians (*mutakallimūn*) they offered a concept of Islam which, by its rationality, transcended the divisions among the old theologico-political factions (Shīʿah, Murjiʿah, and others) and therefore had broad appeal, at least among the intellectuals. The Muʿtazilah thus became the first overall, "orthodox" school of theology.

Their path to success can still be traced. Ḍirār ibn ʿAmr took part in the sessions arranged by the Barmakids, but there he was only one among many. In Merv, one generation later, the situation was different; the Muʿtazilī Thumāmah ibn Ashras acted as a kind of counselor to al-Maʾmūn, and Bishr ibn al-Muʿtamir was among those who put their signature as witnesses to the document in which the caliph nominated the Shīʿī imam ʿAlī al-Riḍā as his successor. The real breakthrough came when, in 820, al-Maʾmūn moved the court back to Baghdad. Two figures dominated the scene there: the Basran theologian Abū al-Hudhayl al-ʿAllāf, who was already about seventy (he died a centenarian in about 840), and his nephew al-Naẓẓām. The latter showed all the features of a courtier: he mocked at asceticism and excelled in light and imaginative poems which celebrated wine and the beauty of youths. He therefore acquired the reputation of being a drunkard and a homosexual. He was not necessarily either, since poetry is not reality, but these characterizations demonstrate that, with their success, the Muʿtazilah also came under scrutiny. Al-Naẓẓām's open identification with the ideals of high society did not tally with Bishr ibn al-Muʿtamir's earlier attempt to convert the masses. The split deepened when those who still understood the Muʿtazilah as a popular movement and kept to the old ascetic tradition started adopting Ṣūfī tendencies: they dressed in wool and asserted that the Muslim community should abstain from electing a caliph (a merely symbolic viewpoint, for the community did not have any influence in this respect anyway). In their view, however, court life was a scandal and the entire Muslim world corrupt, full of injustice and violence.

For the moment, the court party had the upper hand. But enjoying the favor of the caliph also meant supporting his policies. When al-Maʾmūn, in a decree sent throughout the empire in 833, asked his governors to enforce the doctrine of the createdness of the Qurʾān as a kind of state dogma, the Muʿtazilah were immediately identified with this measure. This evaluation was only partly justified. The caliph had certainly made the decision by himself, as a demonstration of his spiritual leadership of the community, and his main adviser had been a theologian by the name of Bishr al-Marīsī, who, through his belief in determinism, stood apart from the Muʿtazilah. But the Muʿtazilah subsequently had to lend their intellectual support to the measure. When the policy of the caliphs led to a persecution (the so-called *miḥnah*, or "inquisition") the chief judge was a Muʿtazilī: Ibn Abī Duwād. The *miḥnah* lasted for fifteen years, and the government succeeded in purging the ranks of the state officials of any opposition. Resistance remained strong, however, among the population of Baghdad who, with a clear anti-intellectual bias, rejected rational theology in favor of the prophetic tradition (*ḥadīth*). Therefore the caliph al-Mutawakkil, the third successor of al-Maʾmūn, decided to steer another course. In 848 he ordered some traditionists to preach about (spurious) sayings in which the Prophet allegedly condemned the Muʿtazilah and similar groupings; a few years later, any occupation with dialectical theology was prohibited. The Muʿtazilah were removed from the court.

But the movement was still very strong. Measures taken in Baghdad did not always have consequences outside the capital, and the Muʿtazilah had established themselves in almost all parts of the Islamic world: in Upper Mesopotamia and in the Syrian Desert (among the Kalb); in several suburbs of Damascus and in Lebanon (for instance in Baalbek); in Bahrein and even in the Maghreb (again among certain tribes in what is today Morocco and Algeria); in Armenia; above all in western Iran, in the provinces of Kerman, Fārs (for instance in Arradjān and in Sirāf), and Khuzistan (for instance in Shūshtar, Susa, ʿAskar Mukram, and Gundē-shāpūr, at that time the seat of a famous medical academy directed by the Nestorians); and finally in India, in the area along the shore of the Indian Ocean to the west of the Indus Delta. In these centers the trend toward individualistic thinking and dialectical pyrotechnics had certainly not been as predominant as in Baghdad. Many of the Iranian towns mentioned are situated on the main trade routes: it seems that the common theological outlook created an atmosphere of confidence essential for better business.

This extended geographical base helped the Muʿtazilah to survive. However, it also fostered misunderstandings and tensions which came about through separate regional developments. In Baghdad, the caliph al-Mutawakkil had not only acted against the Muʿtazilah but also—and even more violently—against the Shīʿah. Consequently al-Jāḥiẓ (d. 869), a prominent Muʿtazilī author who had maintained close relations with Ibn Abī Duwād and other high state officials, wrote a book in which he praised the Muʿtazilah and at the same time attacked the Shīʿah. This opportunistic turn irritated a colleague of his by the name of Ibn al-Rāwandī (d. about 910), who had just come from the East, where he had acquired a sound reputation within and outside of his school. Iran was governed by the dynasty of the Tahirids, who did not follow al-Mutawakkil's anti-Shiʿah policy. Ibn al-Rāwandī therefore joined the Shīʿah in Baghdad and refuted al-Jāḥiẓ's book. But he did more than that: in a series of treatises he showed that some of the axioms accepted by the Muʿtazilah, such as the createdness of the world or the justice of God, that is, theodicy, were not based on solid premises and that the Qurʾān was full of contradictions. His enemies within the school called him a freethinker for those views, but he apparently wanted only to point out that, with respect to certain positions, the dialectical method allowed for arguments pro and con which simply neutralized each other. Thus the Muʿtazilah, shortly after being deprived of political power, were also faced with the inadequacy of their intellectual instruments.

The scholastic phase. Ibn al-Rāwandī's pinpricks produced a shock. His books were refuted by several authors, in Baghdad as well as in Basra. Although these two towns were far from the only strongholds of Muʿtazilī theology, their names served as labels for the two different schools that took up Ibn al-Rāwandī's challenge and, going beyond mere refutation, began systematizing the material accumulated in the past. At the beginning of the tenth century their main representatives were Abū al-Qāsim al-Kaʿbī (d. 931), who was identified with Baghdad although he only studied there and then taught in his hometown of Balkh in eastern Iran, and for Basra, al-Jubbāʾī (d. 915) with his son Abū Hāshim (d. 933). In their efforts to build up a coherent theological framework they had to care more than their predecessors about epistemological and terminological problems; this accounts for their growing interest in precise definitions and questions of logic.

The range of the Basran school, which, like the school of Baghdad, gradually shifted to Iran, is well attested by the work of the *qāḍī* ʿAbd al-Jabbār (d. 1024/5), chief judge at Rayy (near modern Tehran). His *Mughnī ([The Book] That Makes [Other Books] Superfluous)*, a twenty-volume *summa theologiae*, has recently been edited as far as it is preserved and also subjected to some research. Besides this valuable source, further texts written by his pupils and other theologians who followed his views are also available. For Muʿtazilī hermeneutics our best source is Abū al-Ḥusayn al-Baṣrī (d. 1044), with his *Kitāb al-muʿtamad* (The Reliable Book), although this book is concerned with the criteria of jurisprudence, not those of theology.

For the school of Baghdad, on the contrary, we lack extensive original documentation. But its ideas are relatively clear to us thanks to a development that deeply influenced the later history of the Muʿtazilah: the winning over of the Shīʿah. This process took place within two of the three main branches of Shīʿī theology; the Zaydīyah and the Twelver Shīʿah. Only the Ismāʿīlīyah preferred to seek support in Neoplatonic philosophy instead. Among the Zaydīyah the door had already been opened to Muʿtazilī thought by the imam al-Qāsim ibn Ibrāhīm (d. 860), though he did not intend to be a Muʿtazilī himself. The final decision was taken somewhat later and in two different regions: first by his grandson al-Hādī ilā al-Ḥaqq (d. 911), who founded a Zaydī principality, an imamate, in Yemen; second, though with certain setbacks, by the Zaydī pretenders in northern Iran, in the area near the Caspian Sea. Among the Twelvers, Muʿtazilī theology was introduced by two members of the Banū Nawbakht, a famous family of state officials and scholars: Abū Sahl Ismāʿīl al-Nawbakhtī (d. 924) and his nephew Ḥasan ibn Mūsā (d. between 912 and 922). The trend originally met strong resistance there, especially from the traditionist theologian Ibn Bābawayhī (d. 991), but then it prevailed because of the influence of Shaykh al-Mufīd (d. 1022).

The motives for these dogmatic shifts are not altogether clear. The Muʿtazilah still retained, among their theological principles, the obligation to spread the right belief; this may explain their usefulness for the Zaydī pretenders. The Twelvers had lost their spiritual leader through the disappearance (*ghaybah*) of the twelfth imam in 874 and may have clung to rational theology for new reliable guidance. In Baghdad, Muʿtazilī theologians had always had moderate Shīʿī leanings, although they did not normally side with the Rawāfiḍ (i.e., the Twelvers). At the end of the ninth century, even a Basran like al-Jubbāʾī recognized ʿAlī's son Ḥusayn as a righteous ruler. Abū al-Qāsim al-Kaʿbī was the secretary of an early Zaydī pretender in Iran. Later on, the crisis of the caliphate revived the hopes for political support. The Muʿtazilah in Baghdad entertained relations with Sayf al-Dawlah (r. 944–967), the Hamdanid ruler of Aleppo, and then with the Buyids; both dynasties had Shīʿī leanings. A Buyid vizier, al-Ṣāḥib ibn ʿAbbaād (d. 995), promoted the *qāḍī* ʿAbd al-Jabbār in Rayy.

The Baghdad school exerted its strongest influence among the Zaydīyah, though only in its Yemeni wing. The Caspian imams were under Basran influence, but their principality did not survive. However, theological works of the Iranian wing were taken over into the Yemen, for instance the great Qurʾān commentary written by al-Ḥākim al-Jushamī (d. 1101). Among the Twelvers, al-Mufīd followed the Baghdad school, but in the generation after him a pupil of the *qāḍī* ʿAbd al-Jabbār, Sharīf al-Murtaḍā

(d. 1044), turned to Basran ideas and determined the Twelver outlook for the centuries to come. On the whole, the Zaydīyah adopted Muʿtazilī doctrine more fully than the Twelvers.

Outside of the Shīʿī areas, the Muʿtazilah were in retreat. But their impact persisted in at least two places. I have mentioned the Berber tribes in the Maghreb; some of them remained Muʿtazilī even after the Fatimid invasion, at least up to the second half of the eleventh century. They called themselves Wāṣilīyah, with reference to Wāṣil ibn ʿAṭāʾ. In fact, they seem to have lost contact with the Iraqi Muʿtazilah very early and did not participate in the move toward intellectualism instigated by the Abbasid court. We find scarcely any traces of theological activity; the claim to be Wasiliyah merely constituted a symbol of identity, the implications of which we do not know. In addition, Muʿtazilī theology continued to exert a certain attraction in Baghdad and in Iran, among jurists belonging to the school of Abū Hanīfah. In Baghdad, this combination became precarious after the weakening of Buyid power. In 1017, the caliph al-Qadīr forced the Ḥanafī judges and witnesses to make a public disavowal; pressure from traditionist, especially Hanbali, circles increased steadily. Eastern Iran, with its fragmented political landscape, offered better conditions. Muʿtazilī thought flourished under the Khwārizm-shāhs up to the beginning of the thirteenth century. We even know about a Muʿtazilī in the environment of Timur Lenk (Tamerlane, d. 1405). He, however, seems to have been an exception; generally speaking, the end of Muʿtazilī influence on Sunnī circles in Iran came earlier, with the Mongol invasion in the first half of the thirteenth century.

In the contemporary Muslim world, Muʿtazilī ideas are evaluated in different ways. In Iran, they still permeate theological thinking, especially after the revival of Shiism. In Yemen, they belong to the Zaydī heritage, but have lost all reproductive vigor. In certain Sunnī countries undergoing the impact of modernist movements, they have been thought of as giving witness to the essentially rational character of Islam; this has led, especially in Egypt during the last two generations, to a certain scholarly interest which was sometimes hailed as a "renaissance." Modern fundamentalism, however, has proved that view premature. Muʿtazilī ideas are again pushed back into the corner of heresy.

DOCTRINE. That Muʿtazilī doctrine changed over the centuries should go without saying. What is perhaps more important is the fact that its function also changed. During the incubation phase doctrine was less important than group solidarity; at the Abbasid court, Muʿtazilī theology represented the first attempt at a rational and universal description of Sunnī Islam; and in the later centuries certain basic positions, especially the doctrine of free will, served as a label which indicated that a person belonged to the Muʿtazilī "school."

The "five principles." The decisive step toward creating a reliable "dogmatic" framework was apparently taken rather late, by Abū al-Hudhayl, who defined five principles that he considered indispensable to Muʿtazilī identity. These have determined the structure of Muʿtazilī theological works for centuries, in spite of the fact that two or even three of these principles did not retain much importance in later discussion. One of them was already dated when Abū al-Hudhayl took it up: the princple of "enjoining what is good and forbidding what is evil" (*al-amr bi-al-maʿrūf wa-al-nahy ʿan al-munkar*), that is, active admonition to follow the right path and resist impiety. This had been the device of the revolution against al-Manṣūr in 762 and was probably the justification for Wāṣil's missionary projects, but it was rather out of place at the Abassid court.

The second principle, concerned with the intermediate state of the Muslim sinner, was still valid at that time, but derived its importance from an earlier debate that had its roots in the period before Wāṣil. It was a compromise between two attitudes that had arisen in the seventh century, on the one hand the rigorist belief that every Muslim who commits a grave sin excludes himself or herself from the community, and on the other, an "ecumenical," communitarian position which understood the revelation of the *kerygma* as the decisive event by which every Muslim, whether sinner or not, was ultimately saved. Wāṣil was rigorist enough to abhor any laxity or minimalism, but he lived late enough to realize that the exclusiveness practiced by the rigorists could not serve as the basis of the world religion that Islam had meanwhile become. He wanted the grave sinner to remain a member of the Muslim community, with all the rights that involved (safety of life and property, inheritance from other Muslims, etc.), but he insisted that the sinner would be condemned to eternal punishment in Hell like the pagans if that person did not repent. Thus, the grave sinner is to be treated neither as an unbeliever nor as a true believer. This doctrinal position was apparently not far from that taken by Wāṣil's teacher, Ḥasan al-Baṣrī, but it was Wāṣil who brought it into focus and sharpened it by changing the terminology. Ḥasan had called the Muslim sinner a *munāfiq* ("hypocrite"), using a word taken from the Qurʾān, where it referred to enemies of Muḥammad who had not openly sided with the unbelievers. This led to exegetical problems; the Qurʾanic context was not always appropriate for the theological definition wanted. Therefore Wāṣil used the term *fāsiq* ("transgressor") instead. This term was equally Qurʾanic but had merely moral and no historical connotations.

The eternal punishment of the "transgressor" was Abū al-Hudhayl's third principle. It turned out to be somewhat flexible. The school sometimes tolerated members who only believed in a kind of prolonged purgatory; the dogma was also mitigated among the Twelvers. This tolerance derived from the fact that the discussion shifted to a related issue that had been Abū al-Hudhayl's fourth (or, according to his own counting, second) principle: God's justice. God does not do wrong: he punishes the sinner and rewards the good. He has the right to do so because he has put human beings under an obligation; he has revealed the law, and men and women have the choice to obey or to disobey. This choice presupposes two things: freedom of decision and an instrument to grasp this possibility of decision, that is, reason. However, the fact that man is an intelligent being then implies that the obligation already existed before revelation; the prophets are sent to confirm what reason knows, or should have known, beforehand. To a certain extent, revelation is merely a sign of God's mercy or favoring help which makes insight easier for man. It may, however, add new commandments; there are rational laws (e.g., the interdiction of lying) and revealed laws (e.g., the prohibition of the eating of pork).

Abū al-Hudhayl's last principle was the unity of God. This had always been an indispensable postulate for Islam, as opposed to the Christian trinitarian beliefs and the dualism of Iranian religions such as Zoroastrianism or Manichaeism. But this unity had been understood in different ways. Early anthropomorphists such as the Qurʾān commentator Muqātil ibn Sulaymān (d. 767 or later) had found it sufficient to assert that God is one and not two or three, which did not exclude his having human shape. They merely held that God's body is compact, not hollow, for he neither eats nor drinks. He is thus one in number and consistence but he is not one in form, for he has limbs like man. The Muʿtazilah, on the contrary, understood unity as incorporeity, unity in essence: God is beyond time and place, he is unchangeable. They did not even agree when some Shīʿī anthropomorphists in Kufa, Hishām ibn al-Ḥakam among others, refined their position so far as to conceive of God as a body of light that radiates like an ingot of silver. For the Muʿtazilah, God is not a body at all but only "something," a being that cannot be perceived by the senses but is exclusively known to us through revelation or through reason, by the effect of his creative will in nature. God will therefore not even be seen in Paradise: he is unlike all other beings.

Divine attributes. Unity then also means that the attributes ascribed to God in the Qurʾān are identical with him and not different entities or hypostases. This is true at least for "essential attributes" such as knowledge, power, or life; they are eternal and unchangeable like God himself and merely tell us something about certain aspects of his nature. "When one states that the Creator is knowing," said Abū al-Hudhayl, "he has asserted the reality of an act of knowing that is God and has denied ignorance in God and has indicated [that there is] some object known [to God] that has been or will be." However, in addition to "essential attributes" there are also "attributes of action" such as willing, hearing, seeing, or speaking, which describe God's temporal relationship with his creation; they are other than God and subject to change, for they come into being when God acts and cease when his action ceases. They do not subsist in him. This is why the caliph al-Maʾmūn declared the Qurʾān to be created: the Qurʾān is God's "speech" or "discourse" and came into being at a certain historical moment.

This theory presented certain problems. The attributes were inferred from Qurʾanic statements, where they normally took the form of predicates or "names," in sentences like "God is knowing," "God is (all) mighty," and so on. These sentences then had to be reformulated as, for example, "God has knowledge" and "God has power." How could this be done without reifying the attributes and transforming them into independent entities? And if knowledge really was God, as Abū al-Hudhayl seemed to say, how could it be differentiated from his power and other attributes? Finally, the question of whether there are attributes beyond revelation that have to be deduced rationally must be asked; predicates like "eternal" or "existent" were absent from the Qurʾān.

Since these questions referred to statements contained in the holy text, they were answered by linguistic analysis. The doctrine of attributes is based not on metaphysics but on grammar. Our understanding must therefore proceed from the Arabic language and medieval grammatical theory. The first differentiation can already be found in the translation of Abū al-Hudhayl's statement mentioned above: instead of "God has knowledge" we have to say "There is an act of knowing belonging to God"; Arabic linguistic feeling and Muʿtazilī theology insisted that "knowledge" is "knowing," that is, an infinitive rather than a noun, and as such not necessarily permanent or independent. This was not, however, a definitive solution. One could still, as did certain opponents of the Muʿtazilah such as Ibn Kullāb (d. 855?), conclude that this formulation referred to a separate entity that subsists in God. Al-Jubbāʾī therefore rephrased Abū al-Hudhayl's doctrine in the following way: "The meaning of one's describing God as knowing is (1) the assertion of [God's] reality, (2) that [God] is contrary to whatever cannot know, (3) that he who says that [God] is ignorant states a false proposition, and (4) an indication that there are things that [God] knows." Here, the act of knowing is completely excluded: what is asserted is only God's reality. This was enough to protect God against any plurality, but there was some reason for doubting whether it was enough to affirm his knowledge.

Al-Jubbāʾī's son Abū Hāshim then established a compromise by going back to the original Qurʾanic statements and inserting a copula into them (which is normally absent from nontemporal statements in Arabic): *Allahu ʿālimun* thus became *kāna Allāhu ʿāliman,* "God is knowing." The copula was then understood as a "complete verb," that is, it gained existential meaning: "God is"; the assertion of God's reality had been made explicit. The participle for "knowing," however, now put into the accusative instead of the nominative, was no longer interpreted as a predicate but as a *ḥāl,* a "state" of the subject instead of an attribute. In the words of Abū Hāshim himself: "Since it is true that [God] has a state in his being knowing, the knowledge that he is knowing is a knowledge of the thing itself [that is, the subject as] in this state rather than a knowledge of the act of knowing or of the thing itself." This theory allowed the above statements to be understood univocally of all knowers; a theological problem had been put into the general frame of grammatical analysis.

However, since the purpose of this description was ontological we find the later authors unfolding a whole range of different ways of predication and attribution. There are, for example, besides the "essential attributes" also "attributes of the essence," that is, attributes which not only make some statement about the essence but denote the essence itself and thus are not shared by anything else (in the case of God, a word like *eternal).* Then there are attributes grounded in the presence of an accident. They were subdivided by the *qāḍī* ʿAbd al-Jabbār into several categories: for example, those that specifically qualify the substrate (or object) and necessitate a state in it as a whole, like motion or rest; and those which specifically qualify the substrate but do not necessitate a state of it as a whole, as, for example, colors (which may inhere in a few single atoms of the substrate, but not the whole of it). From them we may distinguish attributes determined by the agent who causes the existence of the thing, like "well ordered" or "skillfully wrought" (with respect to the creation, for instance); attributes directly derived from his action, like "speaking," "commanding," and so on; and finally attributes that are grounded neither in the essence nor in an accident, like "self-sufficient" said with respect to God (since this word which, in Arabic, originally means "rich" is positive only in its form of expression whereas "its strict sense is the denial of need on the part of one who is specifically characterized by a state having which need and self-sufficiency are actually possible").

The Muʿtazilī worldview. The way in which the theory of the divine attributes developed shows that the achievement of Muʿtazilī theology consisted not only in defining basic tenets by which it distinguished itself from other schools but also in the conceptual and systematic framework through which these tenets were expressed. Another case in point is the atomistic model by which the relationship between God and his creation was explained. This model had been conceived as early as the eighth century by Ḍirār ibn ʿAmr, but the theologian who gave it its final form was again apparently Abū al-Hudhayl. He thought of atoms as mathematical points that do not have any spatial extension until they touch each other. Atoms therefore are not three-dimensional; only bodies are. Normally it is only in spatial existence, that is, in combination with each other, that atoms take on accidents: color, for instance, and consequently visibility. Only a few accidents are connected with atoms when they are still isolated, namely those that, in the form of an alternative, make combination possible: composition versus separation and, as the medium through which composition and separation take place, motion versus rest. Motion then means that the atoms join each other and receive extension, or that they part and thus lose their corporeity again; rest means that they retain their status of being isolated and therefore cannot be perceived, or of being composite and therefore remain spatial.

What is decisive, however, is that the atoms do not join by themselves, for their composition is an "accident," and accidents, by definition, are created by God. A body exists therefore only as long as God allows this accident of composition to endure. This is Greek atomism turned upside down. Democritus and Epicurus intended to explain nature by the principle of chance (therefore the church fathers abhorred their philosophy). For the Muʿtazilah, on the contrary, atomism served as an accomplice of divine omnipotence. As mere conglomerates, things do not possess any essence of their own; this demonstrates their dependence on God. However, although objects are reduced to purely material composites, this was not a materialistic theory. The Greek atomists were searching for the monad: they wanted to explain nature. The Muʿtazilī atomists were searching for the pivot of God's will and power: they wanted to explain creation.

That is why, in contrast to the Greeks, the Muʿtazilah extended atomism to the realm of human action. The freedom of choice that is necessary for human responsibility is based upon a capacity which the individual receives from God. This capacity is not a permanent quality, an inborn power of acting, but a momentary capability to do one specific act. The Muʿtazilah shared this basic assumption with their determinist or predestinarian opponents. What made the difference was merely the fact that they did not think that this capacity was given simultaneously with the act, as the determinists did, but one moment before, leaving an interval of one time atom so that people have the chance to make their decisions, to choose whether to perform the action, to leave it, or to do something else. There were Muʿtazilah, especially in the Baghdad school, who believed that the capacity for action was not merely momentary since it was identical with health and the intact functioning of the body, but even they understood this continuum as a mere accumulation of single isolated moments.

Continuity was a factor that never came first in this model. With respect to the physical world, consequences had to be taken into account especially regarding the explanation of movement, for in the context of atomism movement meant only that the atoms of a moving body were, at different moments, opposite to the subsequent atoms of the surface on which this body was moving. Consequently, one had to discuss the problem of when movement takes place at all, whether during the first moment, when it begins, or during the second, when it has already ceased to exist. Movement, it could be said, is only a convention of language; in reality, bodies are always at rest, though at subsequently different places. Continuity is then only an illusion of our senses, as in a film.

With respect to human existence, this lack of continuity comes to the fore in the Muʿtazilī concept of person. For Abū al-Hudhayl the human being was first a mere complex of atoms and "accidents." It is true that he or she is alive whereas other bodies are not, but life is again only an "accident," a quality added to the conglomerate of atoms which form the body. There is something like a soul, but it is conceived of merely as a kind of breath that permeates the body as long as that body is alive. The soul may leave the body during sleep; this explains the phenomenon of dreaming. But the soul is not immortal: it guarantees life and it disappears together with it. What Abū al-Hudhayl and his colleagues wanted to explain was not the continuity or uniqueness of the human person, but God's power to create human beings anew in the hereafter. God adds the "accident" of life to the atoms that form them when God creates them; God withdraws this accident when he makes them die; and adds it again when he resurrects them.

This concept of a fundamentally disjointed world seems to exclude causality. But the Muʿtazilah usually did not go so far as to deny causality completely. To begin with, they gave it a different name: "production," which they defined as the dependence of one act on another. The examples they adduced show, however, that they thought in terms of human actions alone. They did not want to formulate a law of nature but to bind the human being to the consequences of his or her own behavior. They were mainly interested in man and his responsibility; their approach was juridical rather than metaphysical, for they started from man's obligation toward God. Later on, they recognized that they could not neglect the universe completely and would have to give an explanation for the phenomenon of a world that functions in an orderly and foreseeable way in spite of its being dependent on God's will at each moment. Abū al-Qāsim al-Kaʿbī spoke of God's "habit" in this respect, the *coutume de Dieu* that changes only in the case of a miracle.

Abū al-Hudhayl's worldview that I have described so far mainly influenced the Basran school, through al-Jubbāʾī. But during his lifetime he was already contradicted by his nephew al-Naẓẓām, who did not believe in atomism but proceeded from the infinite divisibility of bodies. Al-Naẓẓām also reduced God's immediate omnipotence. According to him, inanimate things now have a nature of their own that is independent in its activity, although ultimately created by God. They are still composites of different elements; however, these elements do not simply agglomerate like atoms but mix and grow into organic units. Nor do they depend on God's will at each moment of their existence; they are rather created all at once and then behave according to their own character. The human being, too, is no longer merely unique because of outward form but possesses a soul which, though still material, persists beyond death; al-Naẓẓām was the first Islamic theologian to take over the Platonic proofs for the immortality of the soul. This soul, a "subtle body," permeates all the limbs and keeps them alive. It can mix with other "bodies" that come to it from outside, such as sounds; this explains sense perception.

For some time, al-Naẓẓām's alternative approach had enormous success. But there were certain excesses that discredited it. Ultimately it did not supplant atomism. Nevertheless, it was not without influence on the Baghdad school. The Baghdadis continued to believe in atomism, but they held that the atoms have extension and endure by themselves, as do their basic accidents. Characteristically enough, it was a Baghdadi like Kaʿbī who relied on the concept of the *coutume de Dieu;* like al-Naẓẓām, he believed in the existence of natural qualities that determine the functioning of bodies and guarantee the preservation of the species. However, his natural philosophy was closer to Greek concepts than was al-Naẓẓām's; he followed the classical doctrine of the elements. In most of these points he was attacked by the followers of al-Jubbāʾī, who stuck to the Basran system.

Epistemology. Arguments for the existence of God were used within the circle of the Muʿtazilah at least from the time of Abū al-Hudhayl. The cosmological proof was known from Christian sources. But the Muʿtazilah preferred by far the argument *e novitate mundi;* deriving the existence of God from the "accidental" character of creation corresponded to their atomistic worldview. Originally, the notion of God had been considered as *a priori,* "necessary," as one said. Abū al-Hudhayl even believed that the "proof" for God's existence, namely the createdness of the world, was also immediately evident. This insight then implied, as he thought, the obligation to speculate further about God's nature and to look out for his commandments; it had juridical consequences. When later theologians, in an attempt to create an overall rational system, gave up the *a priori* character of the notion of God, they were confronted, just because of the juridical aspect mentioned, with a very typical problem: how can man be obliged to know God if he does not already know him, that is, is it not that the obligation to recognize God's existence presupposes that man already possesses a notion of God? Al-Jubbāʾī then answered this question by assuming that man necessarily feel the obligation to know God because when he reaches intellectual maturity he becomes aware of being constantly exposed to the merciful assistance of an unknown reality and then realizes that in order to be grateful for this anonymous help he should know where it comes from; otherwise his benefactor might become angry at being unduly ignored. Man, as it were, awakens with an existential feeling of fear that only ceases when he has recognized that there is a God who will be just and merciful if his commandments are fulfilled. This cognition then grants that "tranquillity of the soul" that always results from knowing the truth.

Influence and originality. Muʿtazilī theology certainly participated in the process of the hellenization of Arabo-Islamic thought that started in the eighth century. But we should not forget that Abū al-Hudhayl and even al-Naẓẓām developed their ideas when most Greek texts were not yet available in Arabic or were just being translated. Obviously neither Aristotle nor the Neoplatonists exerted any impact on their thought. Al-Naz-zam's system reminds us in some places of the Stoics (especially their theory of *krāsis di holōn,* "total mixture"), but that influence was filtered through Iranian intermediaries and reached him not in the form of a written translation but through his contacts with followers of Bardesanes or Manichaeans who lived in Iraq.

It will not be possible to judge the overall situation adequately until we have further studies of individual Muʿtazilī thinkers and the "dark period" between the great Hellenistic philosophers, up to the time of Proclus (410?–485 CE) and Iamblichus, and the arrival of Islam. What cannot be doubted, however, is the originality of the Muʿtazilī approach: Ḍirār's and Abū al-Hudhayl's atomistic theory is a case in point. They took Greek *spolia* but used them for an edifice that was entirely theirs, a theological system that was juridical in its outlook rather than metaphysical. They rarely quoted the Qurʾān because they wanted to rely on reason, but nevertheless they always took the Qurʾān as their guide. They offered a coherent worldview that was different from that of the later Muslim philosophers. These therefore reacted with reticence and, finally, contempt. Al-Kindī still tried to adjust his thinking to Muʿtazilī axioms in certain points, but al-Fārābi treated the Muʿtazilī theologians as "dialecticians" who used the wrong method. The Muʿtazilah, on the other hand, never changed their approach. A few of them, like Abū al-Ḥusayn al-Baṣrī, became interested in Aristotelian philosophy, but ultimately they did not adopt Aristotle's basic categories in either logic or metaphysics.

SEE ALSO Attributes of God, article on Islamic Concepts; Free Will and Predestination, article on Islamic Concept; God, article on God in Islam; Kalām; Occasionalism.

BIBLIOGRAPHY

There is no satisfactory work on the Muʿtazilah as a whole. Albert Nasri Nader's *Le système philosophique des Muʿtazila* (Beirut, 1956) treats the development up to the beginning of the scholastic (third) phase, but this work is marred by philological misunderstandings and gives almost no biographical information. W. Montgomery Watt's *The Formative Period of Islamic Thought* (Edinburgh, 1973) is an introduction to early Muslim theology where the Muʿtazilah appear in the context of the other theological movements existing during the first three centuries of Islam (until al-Ashʿarī). Harry A. Wolfson's *The Philosophy of the Kalam* (Cambridge, Mass., 1976) follows the author's earlier works on Philo and the church fathers: it presents stimulating ideas but ignores some recent editions and secondary literature. My article "Une lecture à rebours de l'histoire du muʿtazilisme," in *Revue des études islamiques* 46 (1978): 163–240 and 47 (1979): 19–69, gives a biographical and systematic account of the period between Wāṣil and Ibn al-Rāwandī.

For the rest, one has to resort to monographs, of which there are not many. Abū al-Hudhayl's system has been analyzed in a perceptive way by R. M. Frank in his study *The Metaphysics of Created Being according to abû l-Hudhayl al-ʿAllâf* (Istanbul, 1966) and in an article in *Le Muséon* 82 (1969): 451–506, "The Divine Attributes according to the Teaching of Abû l-Hudhayl al-ʿAllâf." Hans Daiber's *Das theologisch-philosophische System des Muʿammar ibn ʿAbbād as-Sulamī* (Beirut, 1975) treats another early thinker but also presents much material about his contemporaries. The *qāḍī* ʿAbd al-Jabbār has been dealt with most extensively in J. R. T. M. Peters's *God's Created Speech* (Leiden, 1976). For the Muʿtazilī influence on the Zaydīyah, see Wilferd Madelung's *Der Imām al-Qāsim ibn Ibrāhīm und die Glaubenslehre der Zaiditen* (Berlin, 1965). The relationship with the Twelvers is analyzed in detail, at least as far as the beginnings are concerned, by Martin J. McDermott in *The Theology of al-Shaikh al-Mufīd* (Beirut, 1978). Much information on individual thinkers is hidden in the relevant articles in *The Encyclopaedia of Islam*, new ed. (Leiden, 1960–), and in the *Encyclopaedia Iranica* (Leiden, 1982–), but it is not easy for the nonspecialist to find this.

Studies of specific problems of Muʿtazilī theology tend to compare the Muʿtazilah with other "schools," especially the Ashʿarīyah. On the doctrine of attributes we have Michel Allard's *Le problème des attributs divins* (Beirut, 1965), which contains a chapter on al-Jubbāʾī, and especially R. M. Frank's *Beings and Their Attributes* (Albany, N. Y., 1978), which gives a subtle analysis of the teaching of the Basran school. The arguments for and against the doctrine of free will are listed and treated in detail by Daniel Gimaret in *Théories de l'acte humain en théologie musulmane* (Paris, 1980). Gimaret's interpretation of the Muʿtazilī model is modified by R. M. Frank in his article "The Autonomy of the Human Agent in the Teaching of Abd-al-Djabbar," *Le Muséon* 95 (1982): 323–355. The consequences for Muʿtazilī ethics are described in George F. Hourani's *Islamic Rationalism* (Oxford, 1971). The corresponding physical ideas become clear in Judith Katz Hecker's "Reason and Responsibility: An Explanatory Translation of Kitab al-Tawlid from al-Mughni fi Abwab al-Tawhid wa-l-Adl by Qadi Abd-al-Jabbār al-Hamadhani" (Ph. D. diss., University of California, Berkeley, 1975). For atomism, Salomon Pines's *Beiträge zur islamischen Atomenlehre* (Berlin, 1936) still retains its value; it has now to be compared with Frank's book on Abū al-Hudhayl. Carmela Baffioni's *Atomismo e antiatomismo nel pensiero islamico* (Naples, 1982) attempts a new comparison with Greek atomism, but unfortunately ignores Frank's study. On epistemology, see Marie Bernand's *Le problème de la connaissance d'après le Mugni du cadi ʿAbd al-Ǧabbār* (Algiers, 1982). Muʿtazilī polemics against dualism have been treated by Guy Monnot in *Penseurs musulmans et religions iraniennes* (Paris, 1974).

JOSEF VAN ESS (1987)

MUTILATION SEE BODILY MARKS

MYCENAEAN RELIGION SEE AEGEAN RELIGIONS

MYERHOFF, BARBARA G.

MYERHOFF, BARBARA G. (1935–1985), American anthropologist and scholar of religion, myth, ritual, and symbolism. Born in Cleveland, Ohio, and raised there and in Los Angeles, Myerhoff received her bachelor's degree in sociology and her doctorate in anthropology from the University of California at Los Angeles; her master's degree in human development was awarded by the University of Chicago. Her entire professional career was spent as a member of the University of Southern California's department of anthropology. Writing and conducting research since the sixties, Myerhoff studied a variety of types of social groups. She distinguished herself through her contributions to the development and application of symbolic anthropology.

Myerhoff's scholarly writings analyze those morphological features of ritual that allow it to be effective in secular as well as sacred settings and in pre- and post-colonial societies, as well as modern and post modern ones. She understood ritual and its constituent symbols to be capable of formulating experience for its participants and of allowing them to transform their daily roles and statuses by encountering alternate social relations and versions of reality. She eventually ascribed the efficacy of ritual to its feature of repetitive action and to its sensory components, which create certainty through performance. Rituals are the medium for enacting the system of meanings—primarily ideological—that constitutes a religion. These ideas found their earliest expression in her doctoral research on the shamanic religion of the Huichol Indians of Mexico's Sierra Madre Occidental, whose results were published as *The Peyote Hunt of the Huichol Indians* (1975).

Following this work, Myerhoff turned to the study of ritual in modern society. She explored the commonalities and differences between rituals in complex and primitive societies, indicating that ritual continues even in modern societies to provide messages of order and predictability as well as to set the stage on which cultures and individuals can create and present themselves to themselves. These themes are explored in *Secular Ritual: Forms and Meanings* (1977), which Myerhoff coedited with Sally Falk Moore (see especially their introduction, "Ritual Work and the Problem of Meaning," pp. 3–24).

Her subsequent ethnographic research on the place of religion in complex society led her to claim that, although most men and women continue to require what religion had traditionally provided them, this cultural system is now lacking and hence they are on their own to seek out such experiences where they may. Thus, she analyzed ritual-like expressive and reflexive genres in contemporary society: journal keeping, storytelling, and autobiography. All are areas in which the religious function of self-presentation and the creation of meaning occur.

Myerhoff's study of elderly California Jews, *Number Our Days* (1979), focused on improvised or "nonce" (i. e., nonrecurring) rituals that wed traditional and secular, and open and closed, features (see also her paper "We Don't Wrap Herring in a Printed Page: Fusions, Fictions and Continuity," in *Secular Ritual,* pp. 199–226). She demonstrated that such rituals provide meaning for people by their evocation of childhood and domesticity, creating an orderly sense of personal as well as cultural continuity in their lives. Myerhoff's work on elderly Jews was the subject of an Academy Award-winning film by Lynn Littman (with whom Myerhoff collaborated), also called *Number Our Days* (1977). Their second collaboration, *In Her Own Time* (1985), concerned her final fieldwork with Orthodox Jews in the Fairfax community of Los Angeles and focused on her relationship with the community during the last months of her life.

Myerhoff's symbolic anthropology, while always culturally specific, paid an unusual amount of attention to universal problems of meaning in human life. She saw these problems—including the need for self-reflection and the urge to create an orderly world—as the substance of religion across cultures, and along with anthropologist Victor Turner and others, she formulated a dynamic view of religion as a symbolic process in society.

Bibliography

Other publications by Myerhoff concerning her work among the Huichol Indians are "Return to Wirikuta: Ritual Reversal and Symbolic Continuity in the Peyote Hunt of the Huichol Indians," in *The Reversible World: Symbolic Inversion in Art and Society,* edited by Barbara A. Babcock (Ithaca, N. Y., 1978), pp. 225–239, and "The Huichol and the Quest for Paradise," *Parabola* 1 (Winter 1976): 22–29. Myerhoff's work on autobiography and related genres is represented by an essay she wrote with Deena Metzger, "The Journal as Activity and Genre, or Listening to the Silent Laughter of Mozart," *Semiotica* 30 (1980): 97–114, and by her introduction to *A Crack in the Mirror: Reflexive Studies,* edited by Jay Ruby (Philadelphia, 1982), in which her essay "Life History among the Elderly: Performance, Visibility, and Re-Membering" also appears (pp. 99–117). A number of Myerhoff's essays were collected posthumously in a volume edited and with an introduction by Marc Kaminsky, *Remembered Lives: The Work of Ritual, Storytelling and Growing Older* (Ann Arbor, Mich., 1992). In 2000 Myerhoff was named a Woman of Valor by the Jewish Women's Archive. The Woman of Valor website about her and her work can be found at www.jwa.org by following the link to exhibits.

RIV-ELLEN PRELL (1987 AND 2005)

MYSTERY PLAYS SEE DRAMA, *ARTICLE ON* EUROPEAN RELIGIOUS DRAMA

MYSTERY RELIGIONS.

Like many other terms that represent concepts in the history of religions, *mysteries,* or *mystery religions,* serves as an umbrella term covering a wide variety of referents. Since the word had its own origin and history, its use needs to be analyzed carefully, especially in the context of comparative studies.

DEFINITION OF TERMS. The Greek word *mustēria* refers initially only to the "mysteries" of Eleusis and signifies a secret celebration or secret worship that is accessible only to initiates (*mustai*), who have had themselves initiated (*muein* or *telein*) into it. Other terms used for the celebration are *teletē* and *orgia;* Latin writers either use the Greek word or translate it as *initia.* Originally, then, *mysteries* denotes a specific religious manifestation that is essentially different in character from other, official cultic functions; the mysteries are not open to everyone but require a special initiation. But in Greek, *mustēria* is already applied to comparable rituals of initiation (see below) and thus acquires a general meaning. When taken over by philosophy (especially Neoplatonism and Neo-Pythagoreanism) and Christianity, the term increasingly loses its original concrete religious referent and acquires instead the sense of a revealed or mysterious divine wisdom ("mysteriosophy") that is only available to or attainable by adepts.

The term *mysteries* was familiar, of course, to classical philologists, who knew it from the ancient tradition, but it was not until the nineteenth century that it again became a technical term in the history of religions for secret cults or ceremonies of initiation (owing especially to James G. Frazer). In particular it was much used by the history of religions school, most often by Richard Reitzenstein and Wilhelm Bousset, in their attempt to render comprehensible the multiplicity that marked the history of religions in the Hellenistic period and late antiquity, as well as to demonstrate the connections between that world and early Christianity. In the view of the history of religions school, the mysteries were an expression of popular piety that drew sustenance especially from the so-called Oriental mystery religions of the Roman imperial age; in the long run, it was claimed, even the early church could not escape the influence of those religions. Discussion of the beginnings of Christianity was carried on for a long time under the sign of the mysteries, which were regarded as one of Christianity's roots; this approach can still be found today.

There can be no objection to a general use of the term *mysteries* provided that its original meaning continues to resonate even as its application is extended. The problem here is the same as with *gnosis* or *gnosticism.* These technical terms have been given a broader meaning, but scholars have not on that account ceased to use them in a restricted regional sense: *gnōsis* as a Greek word meaning "esoteric knowledge" and referring to religious groups of late antiquity. My own inclination is not to detach these terms from the historical context in which they exercised historical influence but to continue to use them primarily in their restricted sense, without, however, forgetting that the history of religions needs such umbrella terms—especially in comparative studies. The danger otherwise is that the terminology will become blurred and cease to be of help in describing original religious phenomena and will serve only for a religious typology that lacks historical depth.

Thus, for example, Buddhism has been explained by Paul Lévy (1957) as a "mystery religion," simply because of certain ritual factors that play a part in the consecration of Buddhist monks and resemble to some extent ritual elements in the Greek and Oriental mysteries. This demonstration I regard as an unsuccessful venture into dangerous territory. Certainly, Buddhism (especially Tibetan Mahāyāna or Vajrayāna Buddhism) has its "mysteries" in the sense of esoteric rituals, just as do most of the other great religions (especially Hinduism). But such instances occur during later historical stages that presuppose a developed hierarchy and represent a kind of ritualization of esoteric teachings that can in turn be traced back in part to older foundations. It is possible in the same way to give the name *mysteries* to various disputed early Mesopotamian and early Egyptian rituals.

We really have no choice but to understand the term *mysteries* as a historical category that registers a specific historico-religious content and that relates in particular to the Greco-Roman age. The general, typological use of the word must be measured against that standard. Mysteries, then, are special initiation ceremonies that are esoteric in character and often connected with the yearly agricultural cycle. Usually they involve the destiny of the divine powers being venerated and the communication of religious wisdom that enables the initiates to conquer death. The mysteries are part of the general religious life, but they are to a special degree separated from the public cult that is accessible to all, and on this account they are also called "secret cults."

THE "PHENOMENOLOGY" OF THE MYSTERIES. *Mysteries,* then, refers primarily to the content as found in the history of Greco-Roman and Near Eastern religions. At the cultic-ritual level, which is the dominant level, the discipline of the *arcanum* (the obligation of strict secrecy) means that we know very little more about the mysteries than the ancient sources—including ancient Roman literature—occasionally pass on as supposedly reliable information. Our historical knowledge is limited because Christian writers (such as Clement of Alexandria and Firmicus Maternus) who reported on the mysteries allowed their own polemical or apologetic interpretations to color their accounts.

We are relatively well informed about the general structure of the ceremonies (Eleusis, Samothrace, Isis, Mithras). Processions and public functions (sacrifices, dances, music) framed the actual celebration, which was held in closed rooms (*telestērion, spelunca,* temple) and usually comprised two or three acts: the dramatic action (*drōmenon*) with the "producing and showing" of certain symbols (*deiknumena*) and the interpretation (exegesis), through a communication of the myth (*legomena*) and its attendant formulas, of what had been experienced. The sacred action (*drōmenon*) and the sacred narrative (*legomenon, muthos, logos*) were closely connected. We are still rather ignorant regarding the central ceremony, that is, the initiation proper. Any interpretation of it can be hypothetical only, never certain. In my opinion, the heart of the celebration was the linking of the initiate with the destiny of the divinity or divinities, as expressed in performance and word, and the resultant bestowal of hope for some kind of survival after death. This interpretation is also suggested by burial gifts for the deceased (e.g., the "Orphic" gold plate from southern Italy). The ancient human problems of suffering, death, and guilt undoubtedly played an important part in the efficacy of the mysteries. The idea of rebirth can be documented only in later Hellenism. In any case, there is no evidence of a unitary theology of the mysteries that was common to all the mysteries; the origins and historical course of the several mysteries were too discrepant for that. Even the later philosophical explanation of the *logos* of the mysteries was not everywhere the same.

A word must be said here about the connection often made between the mysteries and the idea of "dying and rising divinities," who are linked to the vegetation cycle. James G. Frazer, who accepted the ideas of Wilhelm Mannhardt on nature myths and folk myths, was the leader and main influence in this area. In addition to an uninhibited use of terminology (e.g., *resurrection* is usually understood in the biblical and Christian sense), the chief defect of this theory is its utter neglect of source criticism. Strictly speaking, the "vegetation theory" is a theory at two removes that, as Carsten Colpe has shown, simply takes a theory at one remove, namely, the ancient *interpretatio Graeca,* and prolongs it in the spirit of nineteenth-century Romanticism. The nineteenth-century scholars did not further analyze the ancient use of symbols and metaphors in which the vegetative processes of withering and blooming (in the myth of Adonis) were already described (especially from the second century on) by such terms as *dying, declining, disappearing,* and *being renewed, reappearing, rising.* I say nothing of the fact that these same scholars made no distinction between primary, cult-related myth and secondary, literary mythology. A whole series of so-called vegetation divinities, such as Adonis, Attis, and Osiris, or Tammuz, were interpreted according to the same pattern, namely, as dying and rising gods; their cults, with their "mystery" character, supposedly served to communicate to the "initiates" the powers associated with the "fruitfulness" of nature.

As we know today, there is no evidence at all that any of these gods was thought of as "rising" in any proper sense of the term. In actual fact, there were great differences in mythology and ritual; only secondarily (often as early as late antiquity) were the divinities assimilated to one another (e.g., Osiris to Adonis and Attis). The often only fragmentary mythology centering on these divinities told of the disappearance or stay of the god in the lower world, where he lived on (as lord of the lower world or, in the case of Osiris, as judge of the dead) or from which in one or another manner he returned to the light of day (on earth, in the air, or in heaven) and resumed his role as a god (which he had never abandoned). The connection with rituals was also quite diverse; there was by no means always a question of mysteries in the sense of secret cults (see below). We must also allow for the possibility that some of the so-called Oriental mysteries acquired their mystery character only secondarily, under the influence of Greek and especially the Eleusinian mysteries (this was certainly the case with Osiris in relation to Adonis). The interpretation of the mysteries as being, without distinction, ancient vegetation cults should therefore no longer be used as a magic hermeneutical key.

In view of this critique, the historical and phenomenological problem of the origin of the mysteries remains unresolved. Repeated attempts have been made to move beyond the now-outdated nature-myth theory. Ethnologists in particular have repeatedly focused on the mysteries and interpreted them as survivals of ancient "rites of passage" (Arnold van Gennep); in our day this theory has been maintained especially by Mircea Eliade. There is much that is correct in it. The ethnological contributions that play a role in it come in part from the morphology of culture school (Frobenius), in part from the history of culture school of Vienna. The latter, represented by Wilhelm Schmidt and Wilhelm Koppers, sees the initiation of young men or boys and the whole organization of adult male society as one of the important roots of the mysteries. In cultural and historical terminology the mysteries reflect the agrarian, matriarchal stage, in which for the first time the male sector of society, as distinct from the female sector, developed secret societies and initiation ceremonies (as a protest against matriarchal tyranny, according to Koppers). That stage would be located chronologically in the Mesolithic period. The Greek mysteries are not directly linked to that stage and its events, but they are pre-Indo-Germanic and ultimately have their roots in it.

The history of culture theory as developed by Wilhelm Schmidt has been largely abandoned today. It has left behind only the idea—itself not new—that the origin of the mysteries is to be sought in some stage of primitive agricultural development. Even this, however, does not apply to Osiris, who from the beginning was associated with pastoral symbols, thus reflecting a nomadic culture, and had close ties with the Egyptian ideology of kingship; the later Corn Osiris has been assimilated to Adonis, and the Hellenistic mysteries of Osiris, which focus primarily on Isis, have in turn been influenced by the Eleusinian mysteries of Demeter and Persephone (Kore). The role played by female divinities need not be linked to a hypothetical matriarchy; these goddesses are phenomena belonging to an agrarian culture (Mother Earth). Among modern philologists Walter Burkert is the chief proponent of the view that the root of the mysteries is to be looked for in agrarian culture and specifically in secret society ceremonies (with their tests of courage and their sexual, orgiastic traits) and that they originated in the Neolithic age; the dawning Greek individualism of the seventh and sixth centuries BCE took over these ancient cults and turned them into a deliberately adopted religion centered on the conquest of death.

Adolf E. Jensen has suggested a different ethnological approach. He sees behind the Greek mysteries (especially those of Eleusis) a conception of the world proper to the culture of early food growers; this conception centered on the death or possibly the sacrifice of a female prototypical being (or divinity) who was the source of the life-sustaining cultivated vegetation, and thus it thematized for the first time the mystery of death and life ("the slain god"). There has since been occasional criticism of the interpretation of the Melanesian starting point (the myth of Hainuwele; see Jonathan Z. Smith's "A Pearl of Great Price and a Cargo of Yams: A Study in Situational Incongruity" in *History of Religions* 16, 1976, pp. 1–19, and his *Imagining Religion*, Chicago, 1982, pp. 90–101); nonetheless it is a legitimate question whether earlier food-cultivation stages are to be glimpsed behind the mysteries. The answer can be found only through cooperative study by ethnologists, prehistorians, philologists, and historians of religion. In any case an answer is not directly required for understanding our historical and philological material, which comes to us primarily from Greek sources. All our ancient informants confirm the view that the mysteries in general took their character primarily from the Greek mysteries and became widespread only as a result of hellenization.

THE HISTORICAL MULTIPLICITY OF MYSTERIES. Within the confines of this article it is necessary to start with the ancient Greek mysteries and move on to related Oriental mysteries.

The Greek mysteries. The Greek mysteries were from the outset cults of clan or tribe. They can in many cases be traced back to the pre-Greek Mycenaean period and were probably ancient rituals of initiation into a clan or an "association." The most important were the mysteries of Eleusis, which in fact provided the pattern for the idea of mysteries. The independent town of Eleusis (there is evidence of a prehistoric settlement there in the third millennium BCE) became an Athenian dependency in the seventh century BCE and thereby acquired, especially from the sixth century on, a pan-Hellenic role that in the Roman imperial age attracted the attention of Rome. Augustus, Hadrian, Marcus Aurelius, Commodus, and Gallienus had themselves initiated into the Eleusinian mysteries. An attempt under Claudius (r. 41–54) to move the celebration to Rome failed. The destruction of the sanctuary came under Alaric's Christian Goths in 395 CE. The mythological background for the Eleusinian mysteries was provided by the story of the goddesses Demeter and Kore, preserved in the Homeric *Hymn to Demeter*. The pair were presented as mother and daughter. Their relationship developed in a gripping manner the theme of loss (death), grief, search, and (re)discovery (life). The interpretation of the story as purely a nature myth and specifically a vegetation myth is actually an old one and can appeal to ancient witnesses for support; nonetheless it is oversimplified precisely because it loses sight of the human and social content of the myth.

The public ceremonies of the annual Eleusinian ritual are well known to us and confirmed from archaeological findings. The director was the hierophant, who from time immemorial had been a member of the Eumolpides, a noble family that had held the kingship of old. The Kerukes family filled the other offices. All classes, including slaves, were admitted to the cult. According to degree of participation, a distinction was made between the *mustēs* ("initiate") and the *epoptēs* ("viewer"); only the latter was regarded as fully initiated. But this distinction was not original and came in when the Eleusinian mysteries were combined with the mysteries of Agrai on the Ilissos (near Athens) in the seventh century BCE. The Lesser Mysteries at Agrai took place annually in February (the month Anthesterion) and were regarded as a preliminary stage leading to the Greater Mysteries held at Eleusis in September (16–20 Boe-dromion). Sacrifices, libations, baths, ablutions, fasts, processions (especially bringing the "holy things," the cult symbols, to Eleusis), and torches all played an important role in both feasts. The center of all activity was the ceremony that was not open to the public. It was held in the "place of consecration" known as the *telestērion*, which is not to be confused with the temple of Demeter at the same location.

We know that at the ceremonies at Agrai the initiate knelt down with a ram's skin draped around him and held an unlit torch in his hand. The priestess shook a winnowing fan (*liknon*) over him, and he handled a serpent (sacred to Demeter and Kore). Finally water was poured over him. In the Eleusinian ceremony, of which we know less, the initiation took place at night. It included the handling of an object, not identified with certainty, which was taken from a "coffer" (perhaps the instrument—mortar and pestle—used in preparing the sacred potion; other interpretations see the coffer as an image of the womb). In addition, there was a "viewing" (*epopteia*) of the (rescued?) Kore, probably in dramatic form (*drōmenon*). The cry that the hierophant uttered at this point suggests as much: "The Lady bore a holy boy-child: Brimo bore Brimos" (Hippolytus, *Refutations* 5.8.40). The reference is probably to the birth of Ploutos, the personification of wealth, from Demeter; yet it is questionable whether this was intended as a symbol of the new birth of the initiate and not as a symbol of the limited power of the lower world or death. The latter meaning seems to be suggested by the concluding rite: the showing of an ear of grain by the priest (Hippolytus, ibid.). This must have signified that life is "Mother" Demeter's gift to human beings. A fragment of Pindar (Bowra 121) says of the initiates: "Happy they who see it and then descend beneath the earth. They know life's end but also a new beginning from the gods." To them alone is life given in the underworld; all others encounter evil (see Sophocles, frag. 837, Pearson).

In addition to the mysteries of Eleusis, there was a series of others about which there is unsatisfactory information. Almost all of them were very ancient. They include the mysteries at Phenas in Arcadia (also mysteries of Demeter); those at Andania in Messenia, in which Demeter and Hermes were venerated as great gods; those at Phyle, dedicated to "Earth, the great mother"; and those on Paros and Thasos, which were again mysteries of Demeter. More important were the mysteries of the great gods, or Kabeiroi, on the island of Samo-thrace, where there was an ancient place of worship until the fourth century CEthat attracted many, especially in the second century BCE. The gods in question were probably a pair of Phrygian divinities, father and son (*kabeiros* is a Semitic word). The ceremonies had a pronounced orgiastic and burlesque character and were probably connected with what had originally been associations of smiths (iron rings played a role). Later, however, the Kabeiroi were regarded as helpers in distress at sea. Practically nothing is known of these mysteries; there are hints of links with Demeter and Orpheus.

More important were the Dionysian mysteries, information on which has come down to us from as early as the fifth century BCE (see Euripides, *The Bacchae*). As is well known, Dionysos was an unusual god who represented a side of Greek life long regarded as un-Greek—a view that has caused interpreters many difficulties. His *thiasos* ("company") was probably originally an association of women that spread throughout Greece, especially the islands, and carried on a real proselytizing activity by means of itinerant priestesses. There was no one central sanctuary, but there were centers in southern Italy (Cumae), Asia Minor, and Egypt. Ecstatic and orgiastic activity remained characteristic of this cult as late as the second century BCE and only then assumed more strictly regulated, esoteric forms, as can be seen from the laws of the Iobacchant community at Athens, where the cult of Dionysos (Bacchus) had become a kind of club. The myth of Dionysos had for its focus the divine forces hidden in nature and human beings; these forces were thematized and applied chiefly by women. The ecstatic nocturnal celebrations showed traits of promiscuity (Maenads and satyrs) and took place in the open air. It is uncertain to what extent the paintings in the Villa Item at Pompeii and in the Casa Omerica reproduce the later ritual of the Dionysian mysteries. These paintings are more likely a mysteriosophic interpretation within the framework of a bridal mysticism in which the soul (the immortal element as part of the god Dionysos) presents the pattern of a cycle of purifications. The myth of Dionysos was at an early stage combined with the Orphic mysteries. The hope of another world that was promised and confirmed in the rites is well attested by burial gifts (gold plates) from Greece and southern Italy. Even after death, the initiate remained under the protection of the god.

The Orphic mysteries are a difficult phenomenon to deal with. Often they are not easily distinguished from the Dionysian mysteries. Also, it is not certain whether they were actually mysteries and, if they were, where we should look for their origin. Testimonies do not go back beyond the sixth century BCE and vary widely. It is certain that at an early date Orpheus was turned into the founder of the Eleusinian, Dionysian, and Samo-thracian mysteries. Orphism therefore had no central sanctuary. It seems to have been more of a missionary religion that, unlike the official cults, devoted itself to the theme of the immortal soul *(psuchē)* and its deliverance from the present world. It had an ethical view of the relation between initiation and behavior. A way of life that was shaped by certain rules served to liberate the soul or the divine in human beings. The anthropogonic and cosmogonic myth that provided an explanation of the hybrid human condition also showed the way to redemption; cosmology and soteriology were thus already closely connected. As a result, Orphism broke away from the religion of the *polis*, not only because it possessed holy books that contained its teachings, but also because the idea of the immortality of the soul made the official cult superfluous. Greek philosophy, beginning with Socrates and Plato, gave a theoretical justification for all this.

The Oriental mysteries. Narrowly understood, the Oriental mysteries comprised only the mysteries of Isis and of Mithras. But since the ancient Alexandrian reporters applied the technical terms *mustēria* and *teletai* in their proper sense to any orgiastic cult or ritual, and especially to the numerous and often quite exotic Oriental cults of the imperial period, a whole series of these religions came to be classified as mysteries; this usage has prevailed down to our own time.

Mysteries of Cybele are attested on the Greek mainland and islands from the third century BCE. Oddly, no mention is made of Attis. Pausanias, in the second century CE, is the first witness to the connection; the mythological relation is attested by Catullus in his "Poem 63" (first century BCE). We know nothing about the structure and content of these mysteries; perhaps they were an imitation of the Eleusinian mysteries. In any case, the Roman cult of Cybele, who was worshiped on the Palatine from 204 BCE on, was not a mystery religion. Beginning in the second century CE and down to the fifth century, the literature speaks of the mysteries of Mater Magna (Mētēr Megalē) but tells us no more about them. On the supposition that we are not dealing simply with a misleading terminology, these mysteries may have focused on the ritual castration of novices (Galli) and its deeper meaning. With regard to Attis, inscriptions in Asia Minor dating from the first century CEspeak of the "initiates of Attis" (Attabokaoi). Some formulas, preserved by Clement of Alexandria and Firmicus Maternus, show that the reference is to a participation in the destiny of the divinity whereby the faithful are promised deliverance: "Be consoled, O initiates, for the god is delivered; therefore we too shall have deliverance from our troubles" (Firmicus Maternus, *De erroribus profanarum religionum* 22.1–3).

The initiation involved an anointing; there is also reference to a kind of sacred meal (eating from a tambourine, drinking from a cymbal). The meaning of an accompanying formula is uncertain in the version given by Clement of Alexandria (*Protrepticus* 15): "I have entered the *aduton* [bridal chamber?]." Firmicus Maternus has a simpler version: "I have become an initiate of Attis." At the end of the fourth century CE, the cult of Cybele and Attis also included baptism in bull's blood (*taurobolium*). This ceremony had developed out of an older sacrifice of a bull, attested from the middle of the second century on. It was supposed to bring renewal to the initiates; only a single inscription interprets the renewal as a "new birth." The baptism was a onetime rite and perhaps was intended to compete with Christian baptism.

The Hellenistic cult of Isis in late antiquity undoubtedly involved secret initiatory celebrations. We learn something about them from Apuleius's famous novel, *Metamorphoses*, or *The Golden Ass* (second century CE). Greek influence is especially clear here: it was only through the identification of Isis with Demeter (attested in Herodotus, 2.59) and the hellenization of the cult of Isis that the latter came to include mysteries (first attested c. 220 BCE on Delos). In this form it spread, despite occasional opposition, throughout the whole civilized world of the time, reaching Rome in the first century BCE. It became one of the most widely disseminated Oriental religions of late antiquity, especially from the second century BCE on. Isis became the great thousand-named, universal goddess (*panthea*) who had conquered destiny and was invoked in numerous hymns and aretalogies that display a remarkable Greco-Egyptian atmosphere and tone.

This successful hellenization was probably due to the introduction of the cult of Sarapis under Ptolemy I, son of Lagus (305–283 BCE), when this novel Greco-Egyptian cult (*Sarapis* combines *Osiris* and *Apis*) was celebrated with both an Eleusinian priest (Timothy, a Eumolpid) and an Egyptian priest (Manetho) participating. Isis, Thoth, and Anubis were naturally linked with Sarapis (Osiris). The well-known story of Isis, Osiris, and Horus (Harpocrates) acquired its complete form only in Greek and in this version was probably a product of Hellenism (Osiris being assimilated to Adonis). The ancient Egyptian cult of Osiris was originally connected with the monarchy and displayed the character of a mystery religion only to the extent that the dead pharaoh was looked upon as Osiris and brought to Abydos not simply to be buried but also to be greeted by the people as one restored to life in the form of a new statue in the temple. The hope of survival *as* or *with* or *like* Osiris was the predominant form that the hope of another world took in ancient Egypt, and it continued uninterrupted in the Greco-Roman period; it provided a point of attachment for the mysteries of Isis.

The cult of Isis had its official place in the Roman festal calendar (beginning in the second century CE) and comprised two principal feasts: the Iseia, which was celebrated from October 26 to November 3 and included the *dromenon* of the myth, with the "finding" (*heuresis, inventio*) of Osiris as its climax; and the sea-journey feast (Navigium Isidis, Ploiaphesia) on March 5, the beginning of the season for seafaring, of which Isis had become the patron deity. According to Apuleius (*Metamorphoses* 11) the actual mysteries began with preliminary rites such as baptism (sprinkling), a ten-day fast, and being clothed in a linen robe. At sunset the initiates entered the *aduton* for further ceremonies to which only allusions are made: a journey through the lower world and the upper world (the twelve houses of the zodiac, which represented the power of destiny) and a vesting of the initiate as the sun god (*instar solis*); the initiate was *renatus* ("reborn") and became *sol* ("the sun"), or in other words experienced a deification (*theomorphōsis*). He thereby became a "servant" of Isis and "triumphed over his destiny [*fortuna*]." In addition to a consecration to Isis, there was evidently also a consecration to Osiris, but we know even less about this ceremony.

The cult of Mithras (Mithra) in the Roman imperial age, like that of Isis, was not originally Oriental but was a creation of Hellenistic syncretism. It is true that the name of the god Mithras is Indo-Iranian in origin and originally meant "contract" (*mithra, mitra*) and that some Iranian-Zoroastrian elements are recognizable in the iconographic and epigraphic sources; these facts, however, do not point to a Persian origin of the cult. No testimonies to the existence of Mithraea in Iran have as yet been discovered. On the other hand, the vast majority of these sanctuaries have been found in the Roman military provinces of central and eastern Europe, especially in Dalmatia and the Danube Valley. The Mithraeum at Dura-Europos on the Euphrates is the most eastern. It was built by Roman soldiers from Syria in 168 CE, rebuilt in 209 CE, and expanded in 240 CE. It was thus not the creation of a native community. The "Parthian" style is simply a matter of adaptation to local tradition and no proof of an Iranian origin of the mysteries. There is as yet no evidence of Mithraea in Babylonia (Mesopotamia); three Mithraea have been found in Asia Minor, one in Syria. The oldest Mithraea are from the middle of the second century CE; most are from the third and fourth centuries. Thus an Eastern origin for the Mithraic mysteries is most uncertain.

According to Plutarch (*Life of Pompey* 24) they were introduced into the West by Syrian pirates in the first century BCE. This report may have a historical basis because the veneration of Mithras in Syria, Pontus, and Commagene is well attested, though no reference is made to any mysteries of Mithras. It is likely that soldiers from this area, where Greeks and Orientals came in contact, brought the cult of Mithras to the West in the first century CE. In the second century CE, however, the cult was transformed into mysteries in the proper sense and widely disseminated as a soldiers' religion, until finally Mithras was elevated to the position of Sol Invictus, the god of the empire, under Diocletian (r. 284–305). As in the case of the cult of Isis, the Hellenistic worshipers of Mithras transformed the foreign god and his cult along lines inspired by the awakening individualism of the time with its rejection of the traditional official cult and its longing for liberation from death and fate—a longing especially understandable in soldiers. In addition, the exotic elements (Egyptian, Persian) are to be attributed to the contemporary tendency to emphasize and cultivate such traits as being especially efficacious.

We are, once again, poorly informed about the myth and rites of the Mithraic mysteries. We have no account by an Apuleius as we do for the mysteries of Isis. Instead we have a large mass of archaeological documents that are not always easy to interpret. The so-called *Mithraic Liturgy* is a magical text concerned only marginally with the mysteries of Mithras. What Porphyry has to say about these mysteries in his *Cave of the Nymph* is philosophical exegesis in the Neoplatonic vein.

The Mithraic mysteries took place in small cavelike rooms that were usually decorated with the characteristic relief or cult statue of Mithras Tauroctonus ("bull-slayer" or "bull-sacrificer"). In form, this representation and its accompanying astrological symbols is Greco-Roman; its content has some relation to cosmology and soteriology, that is, the sacrifice of a bull is thought of as life-giving. Other iconographic evidence indicates that the god was a model for the faithful and wanted them to share his destiny: birth from a rock, combats like those of Herakles, ascent to the sun, dominion over time and the cosmos. Acceptance into the community of initiates (*consecranei*) or brothers (*fratres*) was achieved through consecratory rites in which baptisms or ablutions, purifications (with honey), meals (bread, water, wine, meat), crownings with garlands, costumes, tests of valor, and blessings played a part. There were seven degrees of initiation (Corax, Nymphus, Miles, Leo, Perses, Heliodromus, Pater), which were connected with the planetary deities and certain symbols or insignia. Surviving inscriptions attest the profound seriousness of the mysteries. Mithras is addressed: "You have rescued us, too, by shedding the blood that makes us immortal." Since these groups accepted only men (mostly soldiers), they can be considered true religious associations of males. Also worth noting is the close link between Mithras and Saturn (Kronos) as god of the universe and of time (Aion, Saeculum, Aevum); Saturn is the father of Mithras and the one who commissions him, while Mithras is in turn connected with the sun god (Sol, Apollo). (There is still a good deal of obscurity in this area.) Christian apologists (Justin, Tertullian, Jerome, Firmicus Maternus) regarded the mysteries of Mithras as a serious rival of early Christianity; several Christian churches were built over Mithraea.

IMPACT OF THE MYSTERIES. Because the Greek mysteries, especially the Eleusinian and the Dionysian, exerted a growing attraction and influence, Hellenistic literature accepted and developed in varying ways the ideas and representations proper to the mysteries. An effort has been made (Kerényi, 1927; Merkelbach, 1984) to extend our knowledge of the mysteries, and especially of the ritual concealed from us by the discipline of the secret (*arcanum*), by examining the novels of late antiquity. Such fictional themes as loss, search, and recovery, (apparent) death and return to life, the passing of tests, transformations (metamorphoses), hints of "mysteries," and so on may very well have been reflections of the mysteries. Ambiguity, allegory, and symbolism served as codes that could be broken only by initiates (and in our day by scholars). Reinhold Merkelbach speaks in this context of an "Isis novel" (in Apuleius, Xenophon of Ephesus, Achilles Tatius, the *Historia Apollonii Regis Tyri*, and parts of the pseudo-Clementine literature as reworked by Christian gnostics); a "Mithras novel" (Syrian Iamblichus, *Babylonica*); a Dionysos novel (Longus, *Daphne and Chloe*); and, in the *Aethiopiaca* of Heliodorus, a "syncretistic Helios novel" that combines the mysteries of Isis, Mithras, and Dionysos.

The philosophical and religious literature of the Hellenistic age was also affected by the mysteries. The *Corpus Hermeticum*, for example, is filled with reminiscences of the terminology of the mysteries, and we are quite justified in assuming that the circles responsible for the corpus had "mysteries" that were given ritual expression. The same holds for some of the gnostic writings, which not only frequently discuss the concept of *musterion*/*mysterium* but also adopt in their rituals various aspects of the mysteries and especially the notion of a *disciplina arcani* (see below). Even Hellenistic Judaism, especially in the person of Philo Judaeus (first century CE), underwent the same influence. A work like *Joseph and Aseneth* is unintelligible without a knowledge of the mysteries. Even the Greek translation (the Septuagint) of the Hebrew Bible does not escape their influence, any more than the subsequent writings of the Christian community. The language of Christ's apostle Paul (especially in *1 Corinthians* and *2 Corinthians*) and of his disciples (in *Ephesians* and *Colossians*) betrays this environment, as does, no doubt, the *First Letter of Peter.*

The impact of the mysteries became more concrete beginning in the second century CE, as the Christian church found itself increasingly in competition with these forms of worship. The cultic area of the church's life, especially baptism and eucharist, underwent a profound transformation as the sacraments became "mysteries" to which not everyone had immediate access. Preparation (initiation) was now required in the form of fasts, instructions, purifications. The unbaptized and those on the way to baptism (catechumens) were not admitted to the sacred Christian cultic meal, which was regarded as the "remedy bringing immortality" and acquired its efficacy through the epiclesis (invocation) of the priest; in other words, the cultic meal was placed under a kind of discipline of secrecy. As the church became hierarchically organized (especially from the third century on) and as it became an established church under Constantine in the fourth century, it not only won greater publicity to the detriment of the old established religion but at the same time acquired an aspect of mystery whereby it sought to give a Christian direction to a new phenomenon, the religiosity of the masses. *Mystery* now became not only a cultic term but also, following a path blazed by ancient philosophy, made its way into Christian theology, where *mysticism* came to mean a kind of knowledge of God that is not available to everyone.

"MYSTERIOSOPHY." A typically Hellenic spiritualization of the language of the mysteries had been going on in Greek philosophy since Plato; in the ensuing period, as the mysteries spread, *mysterium* and *sophia* became more and more closely associated, and in late antiquity the distinction between religion and philosophy became ever more tenuous. The parallelism of the two was due to the fact that, according to Greek philosophy, knowledge of God was attainable only by a path resembling the one followed in the mysteries at the ritual and religious level: that is, there was need of preparations, instructions, and even a kind of authorization (*katharsis*). For Plato, knowledge of God is identical with the vision of supreme and utterly pure being; the vision brings a participation in that being and even bestows immortality. For this reason, terms taken from the mysteries were often used in philosophy: *epopteia, teletē, mustēria.* Platonic and Stoic philosophers began to impose their own meaning on the available myths connected with the mysteries; they began to "mythologize" them, that is, to link *muthos* and *logos.* Preliminary steps in this direction, or at least parallel manifestations, were already to be found in Orphism, which posited a "hidden" (mystic) link between the cosmos and human beings and made use in addition of the doctrine of the soul (a divine element located in the body). This paraphilosophical explanation has been called "mysteriosophy" (Bianchi, 1979); we met it earlier in the traditions concerned with Eleusis, where it already bore a strong Orphic impress.

Insofar as the philosophy of the Hellenistic age and late antiquity was interested in the mysteries, it took the often bizarre mythical traditions associated with them and sought to extract their rational (logical) nucleus by interpreting them as pieces of natural philosophy or as nature myths (this was especially the case with the Stoics). Unfortunately, we possess only fragmentary examples of such interpretations of the mysteries. Thus Cybele (Magna Mater) was interpreted as Mother Earth (Lucretius, Varro) and as the origin of being, and Attis as the instrument of creation (i.e., of becoming) or as Logos and Savior (Emperor Julian). Isis, understood as mother of the gods and universal goddess (*panthea*), was identified with Demeter (Plutarch). Mithras (the Sun) became principle ("Creator and Father") of the universe (Porphyry); his identification with Aion ("eternal time") probably also goes back to a philosophical interpretation.

The influence of this kind of philosophical interpretation on the later theology of the mysteries cannot simply be rejected out of hand. Traditions such as Hermetism, a Greco-Egyptian revelatory religion, show the path followed in this alignment of philosophy and religion, which the Neo-Phythagoreanism and late Platonism (Plotinus) led to philosophy being turned into religion, philosophical knowledge into the vision of God, and the life of the philosopher into a religious *bios* ("life"). At work in this process was the conviction that behind both religion (the mysteries) and philosophy was the "ineffable," the "mystery," or "being," as opposed to everything transient or to "becoming," and that this ultimate reality was to be approached not simply through thought (*theōria*) but also through one's way of life (*praxis*); only the two together could lead one to vision, enlightenment, and immortality (see especially Iamblichus, *De mysteriis*).

This current of thought provided the matrix for gnosticism, a movement that not only continued to some extent the ritual practices of the mysteries, such as cultic meals, baptisms, purifications, anointings, and *drōmena* and was organized as a mystery-association (*thiasos*) but also borrowed from the mysteries at the level of ideology (mythology). The so-called Naassene sermon "On Man" (Hippolytus, *Refutatious* 5.6, 4–10, 2) is an instructive example of this borrowing and, at the same time, one of the few sources that preserve authentic citations from the Eleusinian mysteries. Among other things, Attis is here interpreted as the gnostic Primal Man (Anthropos); his castration by Cybele becomes a deliverance from what is earthly. Osiris, Adonis, and Adam are likewise variants of the perfect human being or of the immortal soul. According to this gnostic sermon, the mysteries of Isis are the root of all nongnostic cults, and Persephone-Kore, in the form of Aphrodite, represents transient becoming. For this reason, all these mysteries are looked upon as the "lesser mysteries," while the mysteries of gnosticism become the "greater mysteries" or the "heavenly mysteries." This synoptic view of all mysteries in the service of a mysteriosophic and gnostic interpretation was a path by which the traditions embodied in the ancient mysteries made their way into late antiquity. Thus transformed and preserved, they became part of the heritage left by heathen and Christian antiquity and, to that extent, remained alive even after the cessation of the cultic practices that had once been their true reality.

SEE ALSO Dionysos; Dying and Rising Gods; Eleusinian Mysteries; Isis; Mithra; Mithraism; Orpheus.

BIBLIOGRAPHY

General Works

Bornkamm, Günther. "Mustērion." In *Theological Dictionary of the New Testament,* edited by Gerhard Kittel, vol. 4. Grand Rapids, Mich., 1967.

Campbell, Joseph, ed. *Papers from the Eranos Yearbooks,* vol. 2, *The Mysteries.* Princeton, 1955.

Lévy, Paul. *Buddhism: A "Mystery Religion"?* London, 1957.

Metzger, Bruce. "Bibliography of Mystery Religions." In *Aufstieg und Niedergang der römischen Welt,* vol. 2.17.3, pp. 1259–1423. Berlin and New York, 1984.

Greek Mysteries

Bianchi, Ugo. *The Greek Mysteries.* Leiden, 1976.

Burkert, Walter. *Griechische Religion der archaischen und klassischen Epoche.* Stuttgart, 1977. Translated as *Greek Religion* (Cambridge, Mass., 1985).

Casadio, G. "Per un'indagine storico-religioso sui culti di Dioniso in relazione alla fenomenologia dei misteri, I." *Studi storico-religiosi* 6 (1982): 210–234 and 7 (1983): 123–149.

Foucart, Paul-François. *Les mystères d'Eleusis* (1914). New York, 1975.

Guthrie, W. K. C. *Orpheus and Greek Religion: A Study of the Orphic Movement.* 2d ed., rev. London, 1952.

Hemberg, Bengt. *Die Kabiren.* Uppsala, 1950.

Kern, Otto. *Die griechischen Mysterien der klassischen Zeit.* Berlin, 1927. Amended in *Die Antike* 6 (1930): 302–323.

Nilsson, Martin P. *The Dionysiac Mysteries of the Hellenistic and Roman Age* (1957). New York, 1975.

Nilsson, Martin P. *Geschichte der griechischen Religion* (1941–1957). 2 vols. 3d rev. ed. Munich, 1967–1974.

Otto, Walter F. *Dionysos: Myth and Cult.* Bloomington, Ind., 1965.

Turchi, Nicola. *Fontes historiae mysteriorum aevi hellenistici.* Rome, 1923.

Oriental Mysteries

Bianchi, Ugo, ed. *Mysteria Mithrae.* Leiden, 1979.

Bianchi, Ugo, and Maarten J. Vermaseren, eds. *La soteriologia dei culti orientali nell'Impero Romano.* Leiden, 1982.

Colpe, Carsten. "Zur mythologischen Struktur der Adonis-, Attis- und Osiris-Überlieferungen." In *Lisan mithurti: Festschrift Wolfram Freiherr von Soden,* edited by Wolfgang Röllig, pp. 23–44. Neukirchen-Vluyn, 1969.

Cumont, Franz. *The Mysteries of Mithra* (1903). New York, 1956.

Cumont, Franz. *The Oriental Religions in Roman Paganism* (1911). New York, 1956.

Hepding, Hugo. *Attis: Seine Mythen und sein Kult* (1903). Berlin, 1967.

Hinnel, John R., ed. *Mithraic Studies.* 2 vols. Totowa, N. J., 1975.

Kerényi, Károly. *Die griechisch-orientalische Romanliteratur in religionsgeschichtlicher Beleuchtung.* Tübingen, 1927.

Merkelbach, Reinhold. *Mithras.* Konigstein, 1984.

Reitzenstein, Richard. *Die hellenistischen Mysterienreligionen nach ihren Grundgedanken und Wirkungen.* Berlin, 1927. Translated as *The Hellenistic Mystery Religions* (Pittsburgh, 1978).

Vermaseren, Maarten J. *Die orientalischen Religionen im Römerreich.* Leiden, 1981.

Christianity and Gnosticism

Angus, S. *The Mystery-Religions and Christianity.* 2d ed. London, 1928. Reprinted as *The Mystery-Religions: A Study in the Religious Background of Early Christianity* (New York, 1975).

Frickel, J. *Hellenistische Erlösung in christlicher Deutung.* Leiden, 1984.

Loisy, Alfred. *Les mystères païens et le mystère chrètiens.* 2d ed. Paris, 1930.

Wagner, Günter. *Das religionsgeschichtliche Problem von Römer 6,1–11.* Zurich, 1962.

New Sources

General Works

Burkert, Walter. *Ancient Mystery Cults.* Cambridge, Mass., and London, 1987.

Gordon, Richard. "Mysteries." In *The Oxford Classical Dictionary,* pp. 1017–1018. Oxford, 1996.

Pettazzoni, Raffaele. *I misteri. Saggio di una teoria storico-religiosa* (1924). 2d edition with a foreword by Dario Sabbatucci and bibliographical updates by Giovanni Casadio. Cosenza, Italy, 1997.

Sfameni Gasparro, Giulia. *Misteri e teologie. Per la storia dei culti mistici e misterici nel mondo antico.* Cosenza, Italy, 2003.

Turcan, Robert. "Initiation." In *Reallexikon für Antike und Christentum,* vol. 18, pp. 87–159. Stuttgart, 1996.

Zeller, Dieter. "Mysterien/Mysterienreligionen." In *Theologische Realenzyklopädie,* vol. 23. Berlin and New York, 1994.

Greek Mysteries

Cosmopoulos, Michael B., ed. *Greek Mysteries. The Archaeology and Ritual of Ancient Greek Secret Cults.* London and New York, 2003.

Oriental Mysteries

Turcan, Robert. *Les cultes orientaux dans le monde romain.* Paris, 1989. English translation *The Cults of the Roman Empire.* Cambridge, Mass., 1996.

Christianity and Gnosticism

Burkert, Walter. *Antichità classica e cristianesimo antico. Problemi di una scienza comprensiva delle religioni.* Cosenza, Italy, 1996.

Smith, Jonathan Z. *Drudgery Divine. On the Comparison of Early Christianity and the Religions of Late Antiquity.* Chicago, 1990.

KURT RUDOLPH (1987)
Translated from German by Matthew J. O'Connell
Revised Bibliography

MYSTICAL UNION IN JUDAISM, CHRISTIANITY, AND ISLAM.

MYSTICAL UNION IN JUDAISM, CHRISTIANITY, AND ISLAM. To describe the nature of mystical union in the three monotheistic faiths is a task fraught with difficulties and ambiguities both conceptual and real. First, the term *unio mystica* is primarily a modern expression; though the phrase does occur in Christian mysticism, its appearance is relatively rare. Various words for and descriptions of union or uniting with God, however, are important in the history of Christian mysticism, and accounts of union with God are also prominent in Judaism and Islam. Second, even the term *mysticism* itself, another modern creation, has come under attack. To what extent, for example, does the use of a term created in the modern Christian West distort the meaning of key figures, movements, and texts from the traditions of Judaism and Islam? The question is a real one, but the position adopted here is that, if mysticism is understood broadly as the preparation for, the consciousness of, and the effect engendered by what mystics describe as a direct and immediate transformative contact with the divine presence, then it is useful to speak of a strong mystical element in each of the three faiths. Third, if one allows that mysticism is a helpful term in the study of religion, is mystical union to be conceived of as its essence? Though some investigators have so claimed, the study of mystical traditions indicates that the language of union is only one of the linguistic strategies used by mystics to try to describe, or at least to point to, what they contend is the ultimately ineffable nature of their contact with God. Unitive mysticism is one of a group of interactive and nonexclusive semantic fields found in the traditions of Judaism, Christianity, and Islam. There are mystics in each tradition who either explicitly avoid union language (e.g., Augustine of Hippo) or else who tend to relegate such language to the margin in favor of other modes of mystical expression, such as those related to the vision of God or to theurgical action in the divine realm.

CHARACTERISTICS OF UNITIVE MYSTICISM. Treatments of mystical union have often employed the terms *pantheism* and *monism* to characterize unitive expressions, but pantheism and monism are not adequate categories for discerning the import of unitive language. God is certainly all things in the monotheistic faiths, in the sense that the world is a manifestation of God; but God is also transcendentally more than the world, so the simple identification between God and world implied in pantheism is not an accurate term. Monism, understood as the belief that there is one basic principle underlying all reality, is true of most forms of mysticism of the monotheistic religions (though not of Qabbalah). But monism tells little more than this and hence is an empty category for serious investigation of mysticism.

Previous scholarship on mysticism often employed oppositional terminology, such as impersonal versus personal union, absorptive versus nonabsorptive union, habitual versus ecstatic union, essential union versus intentional union, and the like. Such typologizing, however, should not be applied in any crude way, as if mystics could easily be pigeonholed into one or the other category. The comparative dimensions of mystical union emerge from attention to some of the profound issues at work in unitive texts. The persistence across traditions of particular doctrinal and ethical issues concerning union and the employment of certain distinctive forms of language to describe unitive states points to a fruitful realm of comparative dynamics.

Among these issues is the question of what kinds of language are used to present union. Rather than being easily classifiable by opposed types, most mystical texts feature an oscillation and interaction between two poles that need not be seen as expressing opposition. On the one hand, there is what can be called *mystical uniting*, that is, an intentional union of God and human that emphasizes the ongoing distinction of the two; on the other hand, there is a deeper union understood as *mystical identity*, expressing indistinction between God and human, at least at some level of reality. The pole of mystical uniting is more common and doctrinally more acceptable; the pole of mystical identity is daring and debatable, yet many noted mystics in all three faiths have insisted that indistinction is the ultimate goal of the journey to God. Whereas some mystics tend to use only one of these forms of language, many use formulations that reflect subtle variations in the range of expressions between both ways of presenting the divine-human conjunction.

Mystics make use of a variety of images and symbols, as well as distinctive expressions and forms of technical discourse, in their attempts to suggest through language what lies beyond language. Images of erotic love—the kiss, the embrace, the memory of encounter, even sexual intercourse—are favored ways of expressing mystical union. Three images for mixing substances that originated in ancient philosophical writings are also popular among the mystics: the drop of water in a vat of wine, the bar of iron in fire, and air illuminated by the sun. Some images lend themselves more aptly to symbolizing the absorption that leads to mystical identity, such as the ocean, the desert, the mirror, the abyss, cloud and darkness, and the identical eye (Meister Eckhart: "The eye with which I see God is the same eye with which God sees me"). Another powerful image for absorption is eating and being eaten. There are also distinctive linguistic expressions and strategies found across the three traditions: ecstatic identity pronouncements (especially in Islam); forms of dialectical language expressing fusion and indistinction; the language of the return to the pre-creational state; and reduplication discourses, often involving referential ambiguity, especially in dealing with pronouns signifying God and the human.

Intimately allied with the difference between mystical uniting and mystical identity is the issue of annihilation. Many mystics have insisted that union-identity can only be found through annihilation of the self, but the meaning of annihilation is complex and open to a host of questions. What self is being annihilated: the created self or also a deeper, pre-creational self found in God? Is the ego annihilation total and final or only in certain respects and for particular times and circumstances? Finally, is the annihilation in some way a mutual one in which both God and human lose themselves in some deeper reality? Annihilation is not a simple or univocal category but is, rather, analogical, dialogical, and paradoxical. Furthermore when annihilation language is used in texts that stress mystical identity, it is often accompanied by strategies of qualification that must be taken into account to get the full measure of the meaning of annihilation. Some of these strategies are dialectical in the sense that they insist on the coexistence of indistinction and distinction in the relation between God and human—from one perspective union is total identity; from another, it coexists with an ongoing real difference between the two. Other qualifications are more perspectival, claiming that annihilation is essentially a matter of the consciousness of the mystic and not the structures of reality themselves.

In the monotheistic faiths the God of creation, revelation, and redemption is not a static and indifferent First Principle but a loving and all-knowing God, who creates humans whose likeness to him consists precisely in their ability to know and to love. The various ways of expressing mystical union are intimately connected with the relation between knowing and loving, both in the path to union and in its realization. Here too important comparative issues arise. Most mystics claim that both knowing and loving are necessary in the way to God, but many mystics stress the superiority of love, often expressed in highly erotic ways, whereas others conceive of union as attaining mental identity with the Divine Intellect. In unitive states some mystics contend that one reaches a higher divine way of knowing (*gnōsis*); other mystics see all loving and knowing, at least as most people conceive them, as abrogated when union or identity is attained. The variations found in Judaism, Christianity, and Islam on this essential problematic are too multiple to be easily characterized, but it is difficult to appreciate the dynamics of union unless one addresses the relation between unitive expressions and the roles of love and knowledge.

Among the other persistent issues concerning the comparative dimensions of mystical union is that of the ethical implications of claims of having attained union-identity with God. If mystics think they have become in some sense one with God, what does this mean for their behavior and their relation to the wider community of faith? Does this indicate, for instance, that the ordinary religious practices, and perhaps even the moral code, no longer are binding on mystics? In both Christianity and Islam mystics, especially those who claimed identity with God, have been suspected of holding such views. These mystics were at times subject to persecution, imprisonment, and even death, as shown by the examples of al-Ḥallāj and ʿAyn al-Quḍāt al-Hamadhānī in Islam and Marguerite Porete, Meister Eckhart, and Miguel de Molinos in Christianity. Do these incidents prove that there is always an inherent challenge to institutional and dogmatic religion in the mystical impetus to become one with God? Some have argued this case, but a careful study of even the strongest claims for mystical identity with God across the three traditions demonstrates that few mystics have consciously adopted an antinomian stance or broken with the common religious practices and institutional claims of their tradition, however much they may have come to see these as secondary. There seems to be no inherent conflict between unitive claims and common religious and ethical practice as long as the mystic sees both faith and union as coming from the same divine source.

In a brief essay it is not possible to pursue these issues across the three monotheistic faiths. What follows is a sketch of some of the major unitive mystics in Christianity, Islam, and Judaism, designed to provide a road map for those who wish to investigate unitive mysticism further. Because the language of mysticism and mystical union arose in Christianity, this article looks at Christian expressions first. Strong forms of unitive mysticism appeared as early as the second century of Islam (eighth century CE). Although Judaism was deeply influential on the origins of both Christianity and Islam, because unitive language emerged in Jewish mysticism relatively late, it will be treated last.

UNION IN CHRISTIAN MYSTICISM. The Greek qualifier *mustikos* is derived from the verb *muein*, meaning "to close the mouth or eyes." Ancient writers used the term in the sense of something hidden, as in the case of the mystery cults, but from the second century CE Christians adopted *mustikos* to signify the inner realities of their beliefs and practices. The word was most often used to describe the hidden spiritual meaning of the Bible, but it was also employed in speaking of the Sacraments and of the vision of God (*thēoria mustikē*). Around the year 500 CE Pseudo-Dionysius coined the term *theologia mustikē* to indicate the knowledge (or better, superknowledge) by which mystics attain God. The earliest uses of the term *mystical union* (*sunousia mustikē, koinōnia mustikē*) are found in the *Spiritual Homilies* ascribed to the Egyptian monk Macarius but actually written in Messalian circles in Syria in the late fourth century CE (see *Hom.* 10.2, 15.2, and 47.17). Pseudo-Dionysius was the first to use the term *henōsis mustikē* (*Divine Names* 2.9). The Latin translators of the Dionysian corpus employed various terms for Dionysius's *henōsis*, but use of *unio mystica* was rare, despite the many discussions of union found in the medieval and early modern periods. The term did emerge in some of the textbooks on mysticism of the sixteenth and seventeenth centuries (e.g., L. Blosius and M. Sandaeus).

Mystical union in Christianity to 1200. If the term mystical union is rare, the reality of union with God is old in Christianity. The earliest Christian mystical system, that found in the Alexandrian exegete Origen (d. 254 CE), already displays a rich teaching on the union between the loving soul and the Incarnate Logos, especially as found in the spiritual reading of the *Song of Songs*. Commenting on *Song of Songs* 2:10–13, Origen says, "For the Word of God would not otherwise say that the soul was his neighbor, did he not join himself to her and become one spirit with her." Here Origen is referencing a text from Paul (*1 Cor.* 6:17: "Whoever is joined to the Lord becomes one spirit with him"), a passage that became the leitmotif for those forms of Christian mysticism that emphasize mystical uniting. For Origen and others, the soul burning with love for Christ is divinized by grace to enjoy a union of loving conformity with the Logos that introduces it to the delights of "mystical and ineffable contemplation."

Origen's younger contemporary, the pagan philosopher and creator of Neoplatonism Plotinus (d. 270 CE), had a powerful effect on later mysticism in all three traditions. Many of the characteristic ways in which mystics sought to present identity with God are already found in the passages where Plotinus talks about the soul attaining *henōsis*, first with the Supreme Intellect (nous), where some duality still remains, and finally with the ultimate and unknowable One (*to hen*). Throughout his *Enneads*, but especially in *Ennead* 6.9, Plotinus explores with unrivaled subtlety and deep personal concern how the soul must lose or annihilate its present identity to find a transcendent self in the One. "When it [the soul] is not anything else, it is nothing but itself. Yet, when it is itself alone and not in a being, it is in That [the One]" (*Ennead* 6.9.11). Plotinus's view of mystical union is fundamentally dialectical. The One always is the soul in a transcendental sense, but because the One is also always more than the soul, the two can never be totally identified in an absolute way. Plotinus's apophatic treatment of the First Principle and his dialectical notion of union were developed by later Neoplatonists, such as Proclus (d. 485 CE), whose philosophy also had an impact on Christian and Islamic mysticism.

Forms of language that explore the possibility of attaining identity with God, especially God conceived of as one and three in the dynamic relationship of Father, Son, and Holy Spirit, begin to appear in Christianity in the late fourth century CE in the writings of Evagrius (d. 399 CE), a learned Origenist who became a desert monk. With Evagrius one finds a variety of forms of language, images, and metaphors, both for loving union with God and for merging into identity with the Trinity. Evagrius appears to be the first Christian to use one of the favored metaphors for mystical identity, that of rivers returning to the sea. In speaking of how created minds return to the Trinity to attain their pre-creational state, he says: "When minds flow back to him like torrents into the sea, he changes them all completely into his own nature, color, and taste. They will no longer be many but one in his unending and inseparable unity, because they are united and joined with him" (*Letter to Melania* 6). About a century later the anagogic mysticism of Pseudo-Dionysius also uses diverse images and linguistic strategies to present a mysticism of identity that lies beyond all knowing and loving. Describing the ascent of Moses, an archetypal mystic for Jews, Christians, and Muslims, Dionysius says: "Renouncing all that the mind may conceive, wrapped entirely in the intangible and invisible, he belongs completely to Him who is beyond everything. Here, being neither oneself nor someone else, one is united to the wholly Unknown by an inactivity of all knowledge, for the best, knowing beyond the mind in knowing nothing" (*Mystical Theology* 1.3).

The twelfth century was the golden age of speculation on oneness of spirit (*unitas spiritus*), following the Pauline-Origenist tradition. Intense discussion of the modalities of union and the role of love and knowledge in unitive states was carried on by Cistercian authors, such as William of Saint Thierry (d. 1148) and Bernard of Clairvaux (d. 1153), as well as the early scholastic systematizers of mysticism of the school of Saint Victor, such as Hugh (d. 1141) and Richard (d. 1173). Bernard is unrivaled in his subtle expositions of how the love between the soul and the Incarnate Word leads to a complete conformity of wills imaged in spousal union. Nevertheless Bernard insisted that oneness in loving (*unus*) is different from the oneness of essence (*unum*) enjoyed by the three persons of the Trinity (*Sermons on the Song of Songs* 71.6–9). Bernard's friend William of Saint Thierry did not abandon the Pauline language of union of spirit, but his profound treatment of how the Holy Spirit, transcendent Love itself, becomes the love by which one loves God moves in the direction of mystical identity. William was also significant for the ways in which he explored the transformation of the love-knowledge relation in the path to union. Love is more powerful than knowing on the way to God, but the height of love found in mystical union includes a transformed knowledge, what William called the *intelligentia amoris.*

Mystical union in Christianity, 1200–1700. In the thirteenth century new forms of mysticism burst upon the scene in Western Christendom. Attaining God in mystical uniting continued to be widely discussed (e.g., Bonaventure), but what is striking about the new mysticism of the later Middle Ages is the way in which many of its practitioners turned to the language of mystical identity to express their oneness with God. The move is first evident in some of the women mystics of the thirteenth century, especially the beguines Hadewijch, Mechthild of Magdeburg, and Marguerite Porete. Porete's *Mirror of Simple Annihilated Souls,* one of the most striking presentations of mystical identity in the history of Christianity, employs an impressive range of forms of discourse to suggest how God, the "Farnear," takes the place of the soul that has perfectly annihilated itself: "Now he possesses the will without a why in the same way that he possessed it before she [the soul] was made a lady by it. There is nothing except him. No one loves except him, for nothing is except him, and thus he alone completely loves, and sees himself alone completely, and praises alone completely by his being itself" (*Mirror,* chap. 91).

Whereas the women mystics continued to employ both the language of mystical uniting and that of mystical identity, Meister Eckhart (d. 1327/8) was the foremost spokesperson for a pure mysticism of indistinct, or identical, union in the history of Christianity. Eckhart used the dialectical language of Neoplatonic philosophy to explore the distinct-indistinction of the ground of identity where "God's ground is the soul's ground and the soul's ground is God's ground" (*German Sermon* 6). Some passages even suggest attaining indistinction with the God-beyond-God, as in *German Sermon* 48, which says that the soul is not content with the Trinity of persons or the divine essence, "but it wants to know the source of this essence, it wants to go into the simple ground, into the quiet desert where distinction never gazed, not the Father, nor the Son, nor the Holy Spirit." The teachings of Porete and Eckhart were too daring for the institutional church of the time. Porete was executed for heresy in 1310, and Eckhart was posthumously condemned in 1329.

Eckhart's language of indistinction was always qualified by his dialectical insistence on the continued distinction between God and creature. His followers Henry Suso and John Tauler continued to use the dialectic of distinction-indistinction, but they also introduced qualifications not found in Eckhart. Suso, for example, echoing what can be found in many Ṣūfī mystics, carefully distinguished between the ongoing ontological difference between God and human and the perception of this difference. One can lose the latter in moments of mystical rapture but never the former, according to Suso. A particularly intricate solution to the problem of mystical union is found in the Dutch mystic Jan van Ruusbroec (d. 1381). According to his *Little Book of Enlightenment,* union with God exists on three interpenetrating levels: union with an intermediary achieved through grace and the ordinary means of salvation; union without an intermediary achieved through the excess of love, the level of *unitas spiritus;* and finally, union without difference or distinction, "where the three Persons [of the Trinity] give way to the essential unity . . . . There all the elevated spirits in their superessence are one enjoyment and one beatitude with God without difference." These levels always coexist, here and hereafter.

The debate over mystical union continued. In the fifteenth century Jean Gerson attacked false views of mystical union, not only of the Eckhartian variety but also those found in the writings of Ruusbroec and even some of the formulations of Bernard of Clairvaux. In the sixteenth century some of the radical reformers employed the language of mystical identity taken over from late medieval figures. The great

Spanish mystics Teresa of Avila (d. 1582) and John of the Cross (d. 1591) display a rich teaching on mystical union that cannot be explored here. Though each makes use of expressions that taken out of context might suggest some form of mystical identity, viewed synoptically they insist that the loving union that can be found in this life involves only conformity of the transformed self with God, not indistinction or identity. As John put it in his *Spiritual Canticle* 31.1: "This thread of love binds the two . . . with such firmness and so unites and transforms them and makes them one in love, that, although they differ in substance, yet in glory and appearance the soul seems to be God and God the soul." In the mysticism of the seventeenth century that led to the condemnations of quietism (1687 and 1699), it was not so much the doctrine of union itself, as the teaching on annihilation and the supposed indifference to sin that resulted from this that was the focus of objections to mystical teaching.

MYSTICAL UNION IN ISLAM. What is striking about Islam is the way in which strong forms of mystical identity emerged quite early in the development of the Ṣūfī tradition. In part this reflects the impact of the noted union ḥadīth (an extra-Qurʾanic divine statement): "I became the hearing with which he hears, the seeing with which he sees, the hand with which he grasps, and the foot with which he walks." The emphasis on identity coexists along with highly developed forms of erotic union language. Through the absorption and transposition of themes from pre-Qurʾanic Arabian love poetry, the Ṣūfī mystics, in both prose and verse, stand out among the most fervent proponents of the role of absolute, single-minded love in the pursuit of God, as such figures as Rābiʿah al-ʿAdawīyah (d. 810 CE), Jalāl al-Dīn Rūmī (d. 1273), and Fakhr al-Dīn ʿIrāqī (d. 1289) demonstrate. The Ṣūfīs also explored the special characteristics of mystical knowing (*maʿrifa*) with subtlety equal to that found in any tradition.

Tawḥīd, "to declare that God is one," is the central duty of all Muslims. The recognition that God alone is, that he is the sole agent, and that he alone can truly say "I" emphasizes that the absolute unity and simplicity of the transcendent creator also constitutes the immanent reality of all things, as the union ḥadīth indicates. The eleventh-century Iranian mystic Ibn Hawāzin al-Qushayrī, whose *Treatise on Sufism* is among the most popular explanations of Ṣūfī terms, put it thus: "For the appearance of the real, Most Praised, is the disappearance of the creature" (Sells, 1996, p. 132). Annihilation and identity are central to Islamic belief and the mysticism based upon it.

A variety of special terms with subtle connotations express various aspects of this identity mysticism. Among the most important are the twin terms *fanāʾ* and *baqāʾ*, conceived of as two crucial stages (*maqāmat*) in the Ṣūfī path. *Fanāʾ*, or passing away, is the annihilation of the ego consciousness, absolute nullification in the presence of the divine. (It has been compared to the Middle High German verb *entwerden*, "unbecoming," used by Eckhart [Schimmel, 1975, p. 142].) But *fanāʾ* is inseparable from *baqāʾ*, or subsisting, because when the human ceases to be, what remains is only the divine reality in which all things subsist. It is in this state that some Ṣūfī mystics made ecstatic statements that belong properly to God, such as al-Ḥallāj's "I am the Truth" and al-Bisṭāmī's "Glory be to Me."

Closely related to *fanāʾ* and *baqāʾ* are two other sets of terms. The Arabic root *w-j-d* gives rise to a series of words expressing various forms of ecstasy in the sense of being found, or drawn out, by God (*tawājud, wajd, wujūd*; Sells, 1996, pp. 110–116). These can be described as states of intensification of existence achieved through passing away into pure divine existence. Another set of terms denotes different ways of speaking of union, or oneness (*jamʿ*). According to Qushayrī's *Treatise*, both union in the sense of God's action in humans and separation, what the human does through acts of worship, are necessary. Beyond this duality lies what he and other Ṣūfīs call the "union of union" (*jamʿ al-jamʿ*), which Qushayrī says is "the utter perishing and passing away of all perception of any other-than-God, Most Glorious and Sublime, through the onslaughts of reality" (Sells, 1996, p. 118). The Ṣūfīs denied that such expressions of mystical identity were to be thought of as forms of unification (*ittiḥād*), as if God and human were two things mixed together. They also abjured *ḥulūl*, that is, indwelling or incarnationalism, by which God is conceived of as inside the human spirit, coexisting with it. However, in Islam, as in Christianity, some community leaders, and even some moderate Ṣūfīs, accused other Ṣūfīs of incarnationalism and improper expressions of union as well as of the antinomianism (*ibahah*) some Christian mystics were said to have propounded. Such Ṣūfīs as al-Sarrāj (d. 933 CE) and Rūzbihān Baqlī (d. 1209) worked out detailed defenses of the ecstatic statements of identity with God (*shathiyat*) made by mystics like al-Ḥallāj and al-Bisṭāmī (see Ernst, 1985). Significant to this defense was the distinction between pronouncements made in the state of mystical intoxication (*sukr*) and what could be legitimately said in ordinary consciousness, or the state of sobriety (*ṣaḥw*).

Important Ṣūfī mystics. Of the host of names of Ṣūfī mystics it is possible only to mention a few here. Jaʿfar as-Ṣādiq (d. 765 CE), the sixth imam of the Shiite tradition, is among the earliest commentators on the Qurʾān. His treatment of the story of Moses (Mūsā) as told in *Surā* 7 treats the patriarch's experience of God on Sinai as an intimate conversation (*munājāt*) that led to annihilation of the ego and divine self-proclamation: "Mūsā heard words coming forth from his humanity and attributed the words to him [the deity] and he spoke to him from the selfhood of Mūsā and his servanthood. Mūsā was hidden from himself and passed away from his attributes" (Sells, 1996, p. 80). Another early figure is the greatest female mystic of the Islamic tradition, Rābiʿah. The stories and sayings attributed to her in Farīd al-Dīn ʿAṭṭār's *Memorial of the Friends of God* testify not only to the power of her longing for God but also to her desire to worship God without intermediary.

The third and fourth centuries of Islam (ninth and tenth centuries CE) witnessed some of the strongest proponents of mystical identity in the history of monotheistic religion. The most famous figure is doubtless Ibn Manṣūr al-Ḥallāj, whose martyrdom in 922 CE made him a paradigmatic figure in Islam for debates over mysticism. But from the point of view of the comparative study of mystical union, no less important are two somewhat older contemporaries of Ḥallāj. Abū Yazīd al-Bisṭāmī (Bāyazīd in the Persian tradition) expressed identity with God in ways that were no less challenging than those of Ḥallāj. His writings contain remarkable forms of reduplicated expressions of total annihilation, the "passing away of passing away" (*fanāʾ al-fanāʾ*). Like Muḥammad, who was credited with a celestial journey (*Miʿrāj;* see *Surā* 17), al-Bisṭāmī dreamed he underwent an ascent through all the heavenly spheres to attain a vision of God in which he "melted away like lead" into indescribable union. Many of al-Bisṭāmī's sayings express the broken forms of discourse that often characterize mystical identity: "My I am is not I am. Because I am he, and I am he is he" (Ernst, 1985, p. 26).

No less daring, and perhaps more theoretically rich in his discussions of union, is the Baghdad Ṣūfī, Abū al-Qāsim al-Junayd (d. 910 CE). In his writings one finds not only a mind of great originality but also a moving personal witness. In discussing *tawḥīd,* for example, he says: "Fear grips me. Hope unfolds me. Reality draws me together. The real sets me apart. When he seizes me with fear, he annihilates me from myself through my existence, then preserves me from myself. . . . From the reality of my annihilation, he annihilated me from both my abiding and my annihilation" (Sells, 1996, p. 254).

In the twelfth century the most famous of Muslim teachers, Abū Ḥāmid al-Ghazālī, a convert to the Ṣūfī path, helped integrate the mystical impetus into the broad stream of tradition through such works as his treatise *The Niche of Lights,* which emphasized the distinction between mystical speech and ordinary discourse. The limits were tested again in the thirteenth century with the writings of three classic mystics, Ibn al-Fāriḍ (d. 1235), Ibn al-ʿArabī (d. 1240), and Rūmī (d. 1273). Al-Fāriḍ and Rūmī, supreme mystical poets, were more easily incorporated into the tradition than Ibn al-ʿArabī. This Spanish Ṣūfī was a philosopher, mystic, and poet who not only synthesized earlier mystical traditions but also raised them to a new level of profundity through his mystical philosophy of the unity of existence (*wahdat al-wujūd*) in such works as his *Bezels of Wisdom* and the vast *Meccan Revelations.* Although Ibn al-ʿArabī was suspicious of divine identity statements made in ecstasy, his use of dialectical language in which references to God and human are inextricably fused was attacked both in his time and in later Islamic history. Each of these three figures, as well as a number of their successors in the later history of Sufism, would deserve extended treatment in a more ample account of the story of mystical union in Islam.

JEWISH CONCEPTIONS OF MYSTICAL UNION. The significance of unitive language in Jewish mystical traditions has been the subject of contention. Scholarly study of Judaism, born in the Enlightenment, relegated mysticism to the margins, seeking to demonstrate that Judaism was a rational form of moral monotheism. Even Gershom Scholem (1941 and 1971), who resurrected mysticism as central to Jewish history, sought to distinguish Jewish mysticism from Christian and Islamic forms, because its strict sense of the gulf between God and human made claims for mystical union, and especially mystical identity, suspect and secondary. Since the 1980s, however, new research by Moshe Idel (1988a, 1988b), Idel and Bernard McGinn (1996), and Rachel Elior (1993) has shown that unitive language, even expressions of mystical identity, is not at all foreign to Jewish mysticism, though it is late.

The earliest stages of Jewish mysticism represented by the Merkavah literature (c. second to tenth centuries CE) do not feature the language of union but concentrate on heavenly ascensions to a vision of the throne of God. Unitive language first appears in the mid-twelfth century in the early stages of Qabbalah. Though Jewish forms of unitive mysticism show important analogies to Christian and Muslim forms, the distinctive practices and linguistic character of Jewish mysticism, both in the various types of Qabbalah and in the later Hasidic mysticism, have their own hermeneutics.

Deuteronomy 4:4 states, "You who cleave to the Lord God are all alive this day" (cf. *Dt.* 10:20 and 13:5). The notion of "cleaving" (*devekut*) provided a biblical warrant for later unitive forms of Jewish mysticism, not only those of mystical uniting but also stronger connotations of mystical identity. Moshe Idel (Idel and McGinn, 1996) has suggested that unitive understandings of *devekut* and related terms, such as *hitahed* (uniting) and *yiḥud* (union), express two models of mystical union: a universalizing type in which the soul of the mystic becomes all-embracing by cleaving to the Universal Object; and an annihilative-integrative model in which the mystic's ego is annihilated (as in Ṣūfī *fanāʾ*) in order to be perfectly integrated into the divine realm. The qabbalistic and Hasidic mystics who used strong forms of mystical identity, like their Christian and Muslim counterparts, usually qualified their statements by insisting that identity with God was not total; the ego remains or returns, at least in some way. Similarly even the most powerful proponents of identity language never broke with Jewish *halakhic* practice or lapsed into an antinomian posture. The only real heresy in the past eight centuries of Jewish history, that of Shabbetai Tsevi, was messianic in origin, not mystical.

Jewish unitive mystics. Among the earliest Jewish thinkers who spoke of mystical union was the mid-twelfth-century philosopher Abraham ibn Ezra, who saw Moses' cleaving to God as a model for the soul's return to its primordial state of universality. This theme continued on in Qabbalah, for example in ʾEzra of Gerona (c. 1250), who held that the soul of a prophet ascends until it is united to the "supernal soul in a complete union" (Idel, 1988a, p. 42), a formulation that seems to be influenced by Neoplatonic views. The most impressive work of Spanish Qabbalah, the *Zohar,* produced by mystical groups centered around Mosheh de Léon in the late thirteenth century, did not use extensive language of union, though the appearance of some unitive expressions (e.g., *Zohar* III.288a) became a proof text for later mystics. Other theosophical qabbalists, however, did employ considerable unitive language. For example, Isaac of Acre (active c. 1300) understood cleaving as the means for attaining the gift of prophecy in the soul's ascent to union with the hidden godhead of Qabbalah, the Ein Sof. Commenting on *Leviticus* 19:24, he says that the years of the maturation of fruit trees mentioned in the text are to be understood as the advance of the soul through mystical stages until, "'And in the fifth year,' which refers to the *'Eiyn Sof* which surrounds everything, this soul will cleave to the *'Eiyn Sof* and will become total and universal, after she had been individual, due to her palace, while she was yet imprisoned in it, and she will become universal, because of her source" (Idel, 1988a, p. 48). This reference to attaining a pre-creational state echoes a theme found in contemporary Christianity and Islam.

The most extreme formulations of identity mysticism in Qabbalah occur in the writing of Abraham Abulafia in the late thirteenth century. Abulafia's ecstatic form of Qabbalah, based upon practices of meditation and number manipulations, was fundamentally intellectualist. Like Plotinus, he envisaged an ascent to union with the Agent Intellect and finally to the Hidden God. Abulafia expresses this last stage in reduplicating language of fused pronouns comparable to some of the most extreme Muslim mystics: "For now he is no longer separated from his Master, and behold he is his Master and his Master is he; for he is so intimately united with him, that he cannot by any means be separated from him, for he is he" (Idel, 1988b, p. 10).

The Safedian qabbalism of the sixteenth and seventeenth centuries also employed unitive language, as the examples of Mosheh Cordovero and Eliyyahu de Vidas indicate. Nevertheless it is fair to say that unitive mysticism was at its strongest in some of the forms of Hasidic mysticism that began in eastern Europe in the eighteenth century and that continue to flourish in the twenty-first century. The Hasidic mystics were deeply influenced by Qabbalah, but the qabbalists were generally more concerned with repairing the structures of the divine world, whereas the Hasidic masters stressed personal experiences of union.

Amid a wealth of unitive statements found in Hasidic mysticism, the materials from the Habad movement, founded by Dov Ber, the maggid of Mezhirich (d. 1772), stand out. In a disciple of the maggid, Shne'ur Zalman of Liadi (d. 1813), one finds extreme statements of annihilation and identity with the divine. In explaining the meaning of mystical interpenetration (*hitkalelut*), Shne'ur says: "When man cleaves to God, it is very delightful for Him, and savorous for Him, so much so that He will swallow it into his heart, . . . as the corporeal throat swallows. And this is the true cleaving, as he becomes one substance with God in whom he was swallowed, without being separate [from God] to be considered as a distinct entity at all" (Idel and McGinn, 1996, p. 43). Dov Ber of Lubavitch, Shne'ur's son, wrote *Tract on Ecstasy,* which carefully discriminated five levels of ecstatic progression in which the fourth level, one of annihilation, leads to the fifth form of ecstasy, "actual essential *yeḥidah,*" which is "called 'ecstasy of the whole essence,' that is to say his whole being is so absorbed that nothing remains and he has no self-consciousness whatsoever" (Jacobs, 1963, pp. 136–139). Other Habad mystics, such as Aharon Halevi Horowitz of Staroselye (d. 1828), were even more daring in their claims for attaining mystical identity, but this is not the place to pursue mystical union in Habad, or among other Hasidic leaders, such as the famous Naḥman of Bratslav (d. 1810).

CONCLUSION. Union, whether conceived of as the uniting of God and human or in a deeper way as some form of identity with God, has been a key feature of the mystical traditions of Judaism, Christianity, and Islam. Although direct links between the mysticisms of the three faiths have been relatively rare, the common dynamics of monotheistic attempts to express their consciousness of becoming one with God display analogies that invite further investigation and promise important contributions to ecumenical understanding.

BIBLIOGRAPHY

Beierwaltes, Werner. *Denken des Einen: Studien zur neuplatonischen Philosophie und ihrer Wirkungsgeschichte.* Frankfurt, Germany, 1985. A major study of Neoplatonic mysticism with a fine chapter on *henōsis* in Plotinus.

Dupuy, Michel. "L'union à Dieu." In *Dictionnaire de spiritualité: Ascétique et mystique, doctrine et histoire,* edited by Marcel Viller et al., vol. 16, cols. 40–61. Paris, 1992. A survey of Christian materials.

Elior, Rachel. *The Paradoxical Ascent to God: The Kabbalistic Theosophy of Habad Hasidism.* Albany, N.Y., 1993. An introduction to Habad Hasidism and its language of union.

Ernst, Carl W. *Words of Ecstasy in Sufism.* Albany, N.Y., 1985. Important study of the role of ecstatic utterances in Sufism.

Gardet, Louis. "Theólogie de la mystique." *Revue Thomiste* 71 (1971): 571–588.

Haas, Alois M. "Unio mystica." In *Historisches Wörterbuch der Philosophie,* edited by Joachim Ritter, Karlfried Gründer, and Gottfried Gabriel, vol. 11, cols. 176–179. Basel, Switzerland, 2001. A detailed study of the term.

Idel, Moshe. *Kabbalah: New Perspectives.* New Haven, Conn., 1988a. Fundamental to recent work on Qabbalah, with two chapters on mystical union.

Idel, Moshe. *Studies in Ecstatic Kabbalah.* Albany, N.Y., 1988b. See the first essay, "Abraham Abulafia and *Unio Mystica.*"

Idel, Moshe, and Bernard McGinn, eds. *Mystical Union in Judaism, Christianity, and Islam: An Ecumenical Dialogue.* 2d ed.

New York, 1996. See especially the essays by Idel, McGinn, and Michael A. Sells on unitive language in Judaism, Christianity, and Islam.

Jacobs, Louis, trans. and ed. *Dobh Baer of Lubavitch: "Tract on Ecstasy."* London, 1963.

Jantzen, Grace. "Chang'anWhere Two Are to Become One': Mysticism and Monism." In *The Philosophy in Christianity*, edited by Godfrey Vesey, pp. 147–166. Cambridge, U.K., 1989.

McGinn, Bernard. *The Presence of God: A History of Western Christian Mysticism.* New York, 1991–. Three volumes have appeared as of 2004. Unitive language is studied in all of them.

McGinn, Bernard. "Ocean and Desert as Symbols of Mystical Absorption in the Christian Tradition." *Journal of Religion* 74 (1994): 155–181.

Merkur, Dan. *Mystical Moments and Unitive Thinking.* Albany, N.Y., 1999. Argues for a new psychological approach to unitive thinking and contains a useful survey of modern theories of *unio mystica.*

Pépin, Jean. "'Stilla aquae modica multo infusa vino, ferrum ignitum, luce perfusus aere': L'origine de trois comparisons familières à la théologie mystique médiévale." *Divinitas* 11 (1967): 331–375. Classic article on history of three images for mystical union.

Schimmel, Annemarie. *Mystical Dimensions of Islam.* Chapel Hill, N.C., 1975. A classic work on Sufism with consideration of unitive language.

Scholem, Gershom. *Major Trends in Jewish Mysticism.* New York, 1941. Classic work, though Scholem's view of the role of union in Judaism is contested.

Scholem, Gershom. *The Messianic Idea in Judaism and Other Essays on Jewish Spirituality.* New York, 1971. See the essay "*Devekut,* or Communion with God."

Sells, Michael A. *Mystical Languages of Unsaying.* Chicago, 1994. A challenging analysis of strong identity statements in Neoplatonism, Christianity, and Islam.

Sells, Michael A., trans. and ed. *Early Islamic Mysticism: Sufi, Qur'an, Miraj, Poetic and Theological Writings.* New York, 1996. A fine anthology of early Islamic mystical texts with insightful discussions of the role of mystical union.

BERNARD MCGINN (2005)

MYSTICISM [FIRST EDITION].

No definition could be both meaningful and sufficiently comprehensive to include all experiences that, at some point or other, have been described as "mystical." In 1899 Dean W. R. Inge listed twenty-five definitions. Since then the study of world religions has considerably expanded, and new, allegedly mystical cults have sprung up everywhere. The etymological lineage of the term provides little assistance in formulating an unambiguous definition. In the Greek mystery cults, *muein* ("to remain silent") probably referred to the secrecy of the initiation rites. But later, especially in Neoplatonic theory, the "mystical" silence came to mean wordless contemplation. Even this "contemplation" does not coincide with our own usage of that term, since *theōria* denotes speculative knowledge as well as what we call contemplation.

Nor does the early Christian term *mustikos* correspond to our present understanding, since it referred to the spiritual meaning that Christians, in the light of revelation, detected under the original, literal meaning of the scriptures. Eventually the idea of a meaning hidden underneath surface appearances was extended to all spiritual reality (the sacraments, especially the Eucharist, even nature itself as expressive of God's majesty). Yet the strictly private character that we so readily associate with the term *mystical* was never part of it.

Sometime between the fourth and the fifth centuries, the Christian meaning began to absorb the Greek connotations of silence and secrecy. For Dionysius the Areopagite, the influential Syrian (?) theologian, mystical theory consisted of the spiritual awareness of the ineffable Absolute beyond the theology of divine names. Still, even for him, mystical insight belonged essentially to the Christian community, not to private speculation or subjective experience. Contrary to this objective, communal meaning, Western Christianity, mostly under Augustine's impact, eventually came to understand the mystical as related to a subjective state of mind. Thus Jean de Gerson, the fifteenth-century chancellor of the Sorbonne, described mystical theology as "experimental knowledge of God through the embrace of unitive love." Here we witness the formulation of the modern usage of a state of consciousness that surpasses ordinary experience through the union with a transcendent reality.

CHARACTERISTICS. With such a wide range of meanings, it is not surprising that commentators disagree about the characteristics of the mystical experience. Those mentioned in William James's *The Varieties of Religious Experience* rank among the most commonly accepted. *Ineffability* emphasizes the private, or at least incommunicable, quality of the experience. Mystics have, of course, written quite openly and often abundantly about their experience. But, by their own testimony, words can never capture their full meaning. This raises a delicate problem of interpretation to which we shall return. Secondly, James mentions the *noetic* quality of the experience. To be sure, mystical insight hardly ever augments theoretical knowledge. Nevertheless its insight suffuses a person's knowledge with a unique, all-encompassing sense of integration that definitely belongs to the noetic order. This point deserves emphasis against those who assert that mysticism is the same everywhere and that only the postmystical interpretation accounts for the difference. Distinctions begin with the noetic qualities of the experiences themselves. The *pasivity* of the mystical experience may well be its most distinctive characteristic. Its gratuitous, undeserved nature stands out, however much the privileged subject may have applied himself to ascetic exercises or meditative techniques. Once the higher power takes possession, all voluntary preparation appears to lose its efficacy. *Transiency*, a more controversial characteristic, has, I think justifiably, been challenged, for great mystics have remained for prolonged periods in enhanced states of consciousness. Intermittent intensive experiences figured therein as moments of a more comprehensive surpassing awareness. Perhaps we should speak of the *rhythmic*, rather than the transient, quality of mystical life.

To James's four characteristics we may add a fifth: *integration.* Expanded beyond its ordinary limits, the mystical consciousness somehow succeeds in overcoming previously existing opposition in its integration with a higher reality. This, however, should not be interpreted to mean that all restrictions cease to exist. Some of them clearly maintain a sense of transcendence within the union. This is precisely what gives them their distinctly religious character.

IDENTITY AND DIFFERENCE. That a "common factor" underlies the most diverse spiritual theologies has been asserted with great emphasis by such writers as René Guénon, Aldous Huxley, Frithjof Schuon, and Alan Watts. Some assumption of identity also seems to direct the thought of several Indian philosophers. In the West at least, the theory rests on the general principle that only subsequent interpretations distinguish one mysticism from another. Each mystic unquestionably tends to interpret his experience in the light of the theological or philosophical universe to which be belongs. Moreover, the nature of his spiritual quest usually shapes the experience. But to conclude therefrom that the interpretation remains extrinsic is to deny the experience a specific, ideal content of its own and to reduce it to mere sensation. Experience itself is distinctly cognitive and intentionally unique. As Gershom Scholem once pointed out, there is no mysticism-in-general; there are only particular mystical systems and individuals, Hindu, Buddhist, Muslim, Jewish, Christian, and so forth.

The specific quality of the experience in mystical individuals or schools does not, of course, exclude a kind of family resemblance in this variety. A denial of similarity has induced traditional interpretations to study mystical schools exclusively from the perspective of their own theological principles. Thus, for example, R. C. Zaehner's controversial *Mysticism* (1957) ranks mystical schools according to their proximity to orthodox Christian love mysticism. Alternatively, the assumption of a genuine similarity of experiences enables us to consider a variety of phenomena under some general categories without reducing them to simple identity. Such a general discussion would include nonreligious as well as religious mysticism, even though basic differences separate them. The present essay focuses only on religious mysticism. But a few words must be said about so-called nature mysticism, a term unrelated to the distinction, current in Roman Catholic theology, between "natural" (or acquired) and "supernatural" (or infused) mysticism. Nature mysticism refers to the kind of intense experience whereby the subject feels himself merging with the cosmic totality. Now, a mystical experience of the cosmos may also be religious. But in the religious experience a sense of transcendence persists throughout the experience of cosmic union either with regard to nature as a whole or to its underlying principle. Some descriptions of romantic writers (John F. Cooper, William Wordsworth, Jean Paul) seem to express such a mystical awareness of nature. We also find traces of it in Turner and in the nineteenth-century painters of the Hudson River school. The artist most remembered for his mystical descriptions of nature may well be Richard Jeffries. In his case the distinction between the religious and the nonreligious is particularly hard to maintain. In other cases any religious equation of cosmic-mystical experiences with what John of the Cross or the *Bhagavadgītā* expressed would be clearly inappropriate. Nevertheless, to deny any resemblance between the intense, unifying experience of nature and that of a transcendent presence would be absurd.

At this point the problem of narcotically induced states presents itself. Must we dismiss them as not mystical or at least as not religiously mystical because of their chemical origin? Such a simplistic categorization would be a blatant instance of the "genetic" fallacy. Instead of describing the phenomenon itself, we would then be satisfied to evaluate it according to its presumed origin. Of course, any mental state introduced without spiritual preparation is unlikely to foster spiritual development, and, if habitual, the reliance on chemical means may permanently obstruct growth. But however beneficial or detrimental this eventual impact upon personality may be, there can be no doubt that in a religious context chemicals may induce states of undeniably religious-mystical character. Thus the ritual consumption of peyote cactus buttons, dating back to pre-Columbian times, has undoubtedly played a significant role in the religious awareness of native Americans and has since the end of the nineteenth century been instrumental in remythologizing the cult.

Similarly, experiences resulting from pathological psychic conditions (e.g., manic depression, hysteria) should not per se be excluded from the mystical. Nor should these or drug-induced states be considered separately from "nature" or religious mysticism. On the latter alone we shall concentrate. The typology here presented considers only the mystical aspect of various religions: it claims neither adequacy in the general area of religion nor completeness in the classification of mystical religion.

MYSTICISM OF THE SELF. Mysticism belongs to the core of all religion. Those religions that had a historical founder all started with a powerful personal experience of immediate contact. But all religions, regardless of their origin, retain their vitality only as long as their members continue to believe in a transcendent reality with which they can in some way communicate by direct experience. The significance of such an experience, though present in all religion, varies in importance. Christianity, especially in its reformed churches, attaches less significance to the element of experience than other faiths do. In Vedantic and Sāṃkhya Hinduism, on the contrary, religion itself coincides with the kind of insight that can come only from mystical experience. Their particular concept of redemption consists in a liberation from change and from the vicissitudes of birth and death. Their craving for a state of changeless permanence aims not at some sort of unending protraction of the present life but rather at the extinction of all desire in this life. Hindu spirituality in all its forms displays an uncommonly strong awareness of the sorrowful quality of the human condition. Apart from this common temper and an acceptance of the authority of the Vedas, Hinduism presents such a variety of religious doctrines and practices that a single name hardly applies. Still, a similar, inward-directed mystical tendency warrants discussion under a single title.

The original Vedic religion with its emphasis on sacrifice and rite appears rather remote from what we usually associate with the term *mysticism*. Yet two elements in its development strongly influenced the later, more obviously mystical direction. First, forms of meditation became at some point acceptable substitutes for the performance of the actual sacrifice and were held to yield equally desirable benefits. Though such forms of concentration had little in common with what we understand today by contemplation, they nevertheless initiated an interiorization that Hinduism would pursue further than any other religion (Dasgupta, 1972, p. 19). Second, the term *brahman*, which originally referred to the sacred power present in ritual and sacrifice, gradually came to mean a single, abstractly conceived Absolute. The search for a primal unity is already obvious in some Vedic texts (e.g., the Creation Song, which speaks of "that one thing, breathless, breathed by its own nature"). The subordinate status of the gods ("The gods are later than this world's production," *Ṛgveda* 10.129) may have favored the drive toward unity. Polytheism, though abundantly present, had remained spiritually so undeveloped that it did not obstruct the road toward spiritual unity.

In the Upaniṣads (eighth to fifth century BCE) the unifying and the spiritualizing tendencies eventually merged in the idea of an inner soul (*ātman*), the Absolute at the heart of all reality to which only the mind has access.

> The inner Soul of all things, the One Controller, Who makes his one form manifold— The wise who perceive Him as standing in oneself, They, and no others, have eternal happiness! (*Kaṭha Upaniṣad* 5.12)

This is not a metaphysical theory, but a mystical path to liberation. It requires ascetical training and mental discipline to overcome the desires, oppositions, and limitations of individual selfhood. "As a man, when in the embrace of a beloved wife, knows nothing within or without, so this person, when in the embrace of the intelligent Soul, knows nothing within or without" (*Bṛhadāraṇyaka* 4,3.22). Here lies the origin of the *advaita* (nondualist monism that would become dominant in classical Hinduism). The *Māṇḍukya Upaniṣad* anticipates the later, radical expressions in its description of the highest state of consciousness as one beyond dreamless sleep. Above all, it equated the deeper self (*ātman*) thus discovered with *brahman* itself. This deeper self tolerates no subject-object opposition. If taken literally, this state would eliminate consciousness itself and with it the very possibility of a "mystical" state. Yet such a total elimination of personal consciousness remains an asymptotic ideal never to be reached but to be approached ever more closely. The three aspects of *brahman* (*sat-cit-ānanda*) that even extreme monists distinguish include two that are clearly conscious. Even if any distinction beyond the One were to be a mere illusion, as in the extreme interpretation of *māyā* (originally, the created world itself) given by Śaṅkara (eighth century CE), it still remains an opposition to indiscriminate Unity. Metaphysical speculation in classical Hinduism may occasionally have surpassed its mystical tendency. But that there *was* a religious experience at the basis of this extreme monism cannot be doubted.

> The starting-point of Śaṅkara and the Sāṃkhya-Yoga is the *experience* of the immortality of the soul; and immortality in this case does not mean the infinite prolongation of human life in time: that is *Samsāra* which the Hindus regard rather as a living death; it is death-in-life, not life-in-death. It means rather an unconditioned and absolutely static condition which knows nothing of time and space and upon which death has no hold; and because it is not only pure Being, but also pure consciousness and pure bliss, it must be analogous to life. (Zaehner, 1962, p. 74)

Of course, not all the Upaniṣads were radically monist in their expression (*Śvetāśvatara* is clearly not), nor was the Vedantic theology the only mysticism of the self in India. The Sāṃkhya-Yoga mentioned in the above passage advocates a radical dualism. It recognizes two irreducible principles of reality: *prakṛti*, the material principle and source of energy, cause of both the material world and psychic experience, and *puruṣa*, discrete units of pure consciousness similar to the *ātman* of the Upaniṣads. In contrast to cosmic intellect (*mahat*), ego-consciousness (*ahaṁkāra*), and mind (*manas*) as the source of perception and action, the multiplicity of individual *puruṣa*s exists independently of the cosmic forces altogether. Yet *puruṣa* must be liberated from a confusion with *prakrti* by means of concentrated effort. Sāṃkhya thought, although it has no place for deity and is specifically atheistic, was assimilated into the age-old tradition of yoga, providing the practice with a soteriological and cosmological framework. This mystical self-isolation recognizes no absolute One (*brahman*/*ātman*) beyond the individual spirit. Liberation here means the opposite of merging with a transcendent Self. In its pure form, Sāṃkhya-Yoga, far from leaning toward pantheist monism (as Vedantic spirituality does), results in the most extreme individualism. If the idea of God appears at all, it is as that of one *puruṣa* next to all others, their model insofar as God is entirely free of cosmic contamination. But we must avoid tying the Yoga techniques to the later Sāṃkhya theology: they were practiced also in non-dualist or in the so-called qualified-dualistic (Viśistādvaita) systems.

What are these qualified-dualistic systems that make up the third school of Hindu mysticism? It seems hazardous to ground them in theological theories. To be sure, each mystical system contains an interpretation as an essential part of the experience, but these interpretations cannot be simply transferred into the kind of logically coherent systems for which we usually reserve the name *theology*. A mystical theology is less concerned about logical consistency and sharply defined concepts than about adequate translations of the actual experience. This is particularly the case in a tradition wherein the mystical element constitutes most of the core of the religion itself. Hence in describing such later writers as Rāmānuja (eleventh century CE) as "qualified dualists," we should be aware that we are referring more to a practical-devotional than a speculative-metaphysical attitude. Rāmānuja may never have abandoned the metaphysical assumptions of the monist tradition in which he grew up. But finding absolute monism inadequate for the practice of spiritual life, he reaffirmed the traditional concept of a God endowed with personal attributes (*saguṇa brahman*), instead of the attributeless absolute substance (*nirguṇa brahman*). God thereby is not merely a model but also a redeemer who assists the soul on its path to liberation.

In thus qualifying the monist doctrine, Rāmānuja was inspired by what the *Bhagavadgītā* (c. second century BCE) had assumed throughout. This mystical poem, perhaps the finest spiritual work to come from the East, is hard to classify by Western canons. The narrative assumes a clearly theistic position: the god Viṣṇu incarnated in Kṛṣṇa exhorts the hero Arjuna on the eve of battle with his stepbrother to take heart and fight. But the message he delivers ranges from traditional piety and observance of the ancient rites to the monism of the Vedānta, combined with the dualistic cosmology of Sāṃkhya-Yoga. The work is a synthesis in all respects. Not only does it unite the monist and theistic strands, but it also presents a method of combining the active with the contemplative life. It advises a mental discipline that enables a person to act with total detachment from the fruits of his deed. By itself, the active life (*karman*) weaves its own web of causes and effects, entailing an endless cycle of birth and death—the very essence of what a person seeks to be liberated from. Yet various kinds of yoga detach the mind from this natural determination, while still allowing a person to fulfill the obligations of his station in life. Through equanimity of emotions, holy indifference, and purity of heart, even the active person will come to detect the one presence of *brahman* in all things. The *Gītā* is not a manual of yogic practice. It is a mystical work that culminates in a vision of God. A most powerful theophany completes Kṛṣṇa's description of God's presence in the world (chap. 11). Still the poem concludes with the sobering advice to seek God in the ordinary way of piety rather than through self-concentration. The advice was taken up by the *bhakti* movement, which produced some of the finest flowers of Hindu spirituality and which continues to nourish much of Indian piety today.

The Mysticism of Emptiness: Buddhism. It seems difficult to conceive of two religious doctrines more different from one another than Hinduism, especially Sāṃkhya, and Buddhism. In one, we find a quest for an absolute self (*ātman, puruṣa*); in the other, the obliteration of the self (anatman/anatta—no soul). Yet upon closer inspection the two appear to have a great deal in common. Both are systems of salvation, rooted in a profoundly pessimistic attitude about the changing world of everyday existence, and they aim at a condition of changelessness that surpasses that existence. Moreover, their adherents mostly hope to attain this salvation through enlightenment prepared by moral discipline and mental concentration. In the more radical schools the quest for a unified state of mind leads to some form of practical monism and, in Indian Mahayana Buddhism no less than in "classical" Hinduism, a theoretical monism. Any kind of "grace"—which would introduce a new dualism—is thereby excluded. Even those parts of the tradition that deviate from these rigorous principles appear to have some common features. Amida Buddhism advocates a faith in the "saving Buddha" that strongly resembles *bhakti* Hinduism.

Meanwhile, the goal of enlightenment is conceived in very different ways. The Buddhist description both of the experience and of the path that leads to it is characterized by a spare simplicity as well as by a persistent reluctance to use any but negative predicates. For our purposes it is not necessary to enter into the basic tenets of the theory. Their development varies from the Hīnayāna to the Mahāyāna doctrines. But even in the Theravada tradition, the Eightfold Path of virtue concludes with "right concentration," which, in turn, must be obtained in eight successive forms of mental discipline (the *dhyānas*). Once again we are confronted with a faith that from its origins is headed in a mystical direction. The three negative terms—nonattainment, nonassertion, nonreliance—define a state of utmost emptiness by which Nāgārjuna's Mādhyamika school (150 CE) described enlightenment. Emptiness appears, of course, also in Hīnayāna schools, as the principal quality of *nirvāṇa*, the supreme enlightenment. But with the Mahāyāna schools the emphasis on emptiness, even in the preparatory stages, becomes particularly strong. *Nirvāṇa* itself thereby ceases to be an independent realm of being: it becomes a particular vision of the phenomenal world. Nonattainment consists in emptying the self of all personal qualities, desires, and thoughts, indeed of all that might be considered to comprise a "self." For ultimate reality is unconditioned and void of all defining distinctions. If this concept is understood ontologically, there is no substantial soul; if understood epistemologically, there is no way of knowing reality as long as the notion of subject remains; if understood ethically, there is no expression of ultimate reality as long as one's desires condition one's existence. As the late Mahāyāna poet Śāntideva wrote:

> The Stillness (*Nirvāṇa*) lies in surrender of all things, and my spirit longs for the Stillness; if I must surrender all, it is best to give it for fellow-creatures. I yield myself to all living creatures to deal with me as they choose; they may smite or revile me for ever, cover me with dust, play with my body, laugh and wanton; I have given them my body, why shall I care. Let them make me do whatever works bring them pleasure; but may mishap never befall any of them by reason of me. (quoted in Ananda Coomaraswamy's *Buddha and the Gospel of Buddhism*, New York, 1964, p. 321)

Beyond wisdom, then, the Buddhist ideal requires compassion, an attitude rooted in the deep awareness that all beings are interconnected. It is this compassion that inspired the *bodhisattva* vocation in Mahāyāna Buddhism.

As Nāgārjuna defined it, nonassertion became the logical counterpart of the emptiness doctrine. The Madhya-mika paradoxes reveal an intense awareness of the ineffable quality of ultimate truth. No expression is definitive, not even the Four Noble Truths on which Buddhism is founded. The entire Dharma itself, the doctrine, is no more than a dream, a vague echo. To be sure, the conception of an ineffable absolute is also present in Hīnayāna Buddhism, as the following *Udāna* statement clearly asserts: "There is, monks, an unborn, not become, not made, uncompounded; and were it not, monks, for this unborn, not become, not made, uncompounded, no escape could be shown here for what is born, has become, is made, is compounded" (*Buddhist Texts through the Ages*, ed. Edward Conze, Oxford, 1954, p. 95).

Yet the Mahāyāna schools drew more radical conclusions. For the Mādhyamika *nirvāṇa* consists mostly of sets of contradictories, both of which are negated. To Nāgārjuna, *nirvāṇa* is logical "nonsense" to which the principle of contradiction does not apply. One may read this as a program of extreme skeptical philosophy. It is, in fact, a powerful assertion of transcendence in which all distinctions vanish. For the Mādhyamika masters, *nirvāṇa* lies beyond the total peace experience: it has become the Absolute *in itself*, the undivided Oneness of the ultimate reality. No longer separated from conditioned existence, the Mahāyāna *nirvāṇa* becomes indistinguishable from the samsaric realm of phenomenal (and therefore illusory) reality. The Buddhist negation, far more radical than a mere declaration of absence, leaves no common space wherein the Absolute could be compared with any positive qualities. It attempts the logically impossible, namely, to overcome the very interconnectedness of all dependent being and, since all that exists is dependent, of existence itself. Nothing remains here but the road to total silence. Salvation comes through wisdom, but clearly the wisdom here is the opposite of cognitive—it consists in mystical silence.

The ways to emptiness vary. Mental training by the confrontation of paradoxes has been mentioned. Other ways, especially Yogācāra Buddhism, emphasize the attainment of "pure thought." This consists not in thinking *about* something but rather in the insight that thought is not in any object but in a subject free of all objects. Yogācāra pursues the basic truth of emptiness in a practical rather than a logico-metaphysical way.

Of particular importance here is Chan (Jpn., Zen) Buddhism, a doctrine imported into China by the Indian Bodhidharma that later spread to Japan. Most consistent of all in its pursuit of emptiness, it rejected all dependence (nonreliance), including the one based on the Buddha's own words. Indeed, the very desire for enlightenment must be abandoned, according to the famous Zen master Dōgen. The name Chan, or Zen, derived from dhyāna (Pali *jhāna*), indicates the importance of mental concentration. But Zen also requires a systematic surpassing of reason. At an early stage in his training the disciple is given a *kōan*, a paradoxical statement that baffles reason and for which he must find a "higher" sense. Once the mind has become cleared of the ordinary apparatus of conscious thought, unconscious elements emerge from its subliminal depths. Zen masters refer to this stage of hallucinations as makyō—the demonic universe—and advise the student not to dwell on any extraordinary experiences. Their advice agrees with the attitude recommended by Christian spiritual directors to mystics passing through the so-called "illumination" stage with regard to visions and voices. All this prepares a state of unification in which the mind gradually sheds the patterns of oppositional consciousness present in desire, fear, prejudice, or even objective conceptualization. C. G. Jung once suggestively described it as "a breakthrough by a consciousness limited to the ego-form, into the non-ego-like self." In the experience of total unity the self becomes reduced to a state of pure perceptiveness. This occurs in the final stage, *satori*, enlightenment itself, often referred to as *kenshō*, the ability to see the essence of things. We might perhaps translate it as "suchness" or "ultimate reality" (the Sanskrit term *tathatā*, used for the one reality that constitutes the entire universe, coincides in Mahāyāna Buddhism with *nirvāṇa* itself).

Most typical of that final state of emptiness as Zen Buddhists conceive of it is that it results not in a withdrawal from the real but in an enhanced ability to see the real as it is and to act in it unhampered by passion and attachment. Thus emptiness creates a new worldliness. Can such a state be called mystical? Not if one reserves the term for a direct contact with an Absolute that can be described by positive attributes. But such a restriction is not warranted. Any form of religious mysticism claims a direct contact with the Absolute. How it defines this Absolute depends on its particular outlook. Judaism and Christianity are religions of the word; Buddhism is a religion of silence that renounces all ways of naming the Absolute. Even to demand the presence of grace as a specific expression of a divine benevolence is to deny Buddhism the right to conceive of the Absolute as lying beyond any form of expression. Meanwhile, the function of what Christians call "grace" does not remain unfulfilled, as appears in the attitude of thanksgiving that shapes the Buddhist monk's life as much as that of his Western counterpart. In thanking the nameless source of all goodness, the Buddhist professes the presence of a benevolent Absolute.

Of course, here as in other cases the outsider is unable to decide to what extent religion blossoms into actual mystical experience. What counts is the possibility it presents of an intense, direct contact with the Absolute, and the methodic way that a particular religion offers for realizing this encounter. Not every form of Zen may be called mystical or even religious, any more than the practice of yoga in Hindu culture or, for that matter, the study of Neoplatonic theory.

Mysticism of the Image: Eastern and Early Western Christianity. Unlike some other religions, Christianity has never equated its ideal of holiness with the attainment of mystical states. Nor did it encourage seeking such states for their own sake. Nevertheless, a mystical impulse undeniably propelled it in its origin and determined much of its later development. The synoptic Gospels present Jesus as dwelling in the continuous, intimate presence of God. His public life begins with a prayer and a vision: "While Jesus after his baptism was at prayer, heaven opened and the Holy Spirit descended on him in bodily shape like a dove" (*Lk.* 3:21–22). It ends with a prayer of total abandonment: "Father, into your hands I commend my spirit" (*Lk.* 23:46). Jesus initiates all important public acts with a prayer. He often withdraws from the crowd for long periods of solitary prayer. He interprets his entire existence through its reference to God, whom he calls Father. To himself he applies Isaiah's messianic words: "The Spirit of the Lord is upon me." The same Spirit he promises to those who pray in his name.

The mystical quality of Jesus' life is most clearly stated in the Fourth Gospel. Some of the words attributed to him may have originated in theological reflection rather than in his own expression. But they thereby witness all the more powerfully to the mystical impulse he was able to transmit to his followers. Biblical speculations on the Word of God are reinterpreted as expressions of God's personal revelation in an incarnated divine Logos. The intimate union between the Father and the Word is, through the Holy Spirit, granted to all true believers. Indeed, the presence of the Spirit entitles them to the same love with which God loves his Son. In John's gospel the two principal currents of Christian mysticism have their source: the theology of the divine image that calls the Christian to conformity, and the theology that presents the intimacy with God as a relation of universal love.

The letters of Paul develop the idea of life in the Spirit. "We all reflect as in a mirror the splendor of the Lord; thus we are transfigured into his likeness, from splendor to splendor: such is the influence of the Lord who is Spirit" (*2 Cor.* 3:18). The Spirit's principal gift, in the understanding of Paul, consists in *gnōsis*, that insight into the "mystery of Christ" that enables the believer to understand the scriptures in a deeper, "revealed" sense. This insight into the hidden meaning of the scriptures led to the Alexandrian interpretation of the term *mystical* discussed earlier. Yet the practice long preceded the term. The entire *Letter to the Hebrews* consists of an allegorical reading of the Yom Kippur sacrifice as foreshadowing Christ's definitive sacrifice on the cross.

The tenor of early Christian mysticism was determined by the New Testament and by trends in Hellenistic Judaism (especially Philo Judaeus's scriptural theology and the late Judaic meaning of *gnōsis*). A third factor, usually referred to as Neoplatonism, must be added. Yet that movement, though influential in the development of Christian spirituality, may be too restricted an account of its beginnings; Origen (and, to some extent, even Clement) had already developed a mystical theology of the image before Plotinus. It might be more accurate, then, to look to the entire philosophically Platonic, religiously syncretic, and generally Gnostic culture of Alexandria at the end of the second century. In that climate Ammonius Saccas himself, Origen's and Plotinus's common master, grew up and taught. But soon Plotinus's philosophy was to provide much of the ideological apparatus for a Christian theology of the image. Though Plotinus's thought leaves no doubts about its Platonic origins, it was profoundly affected by such religious influences as the mystery religions, Gnosticism, Philo's Judaism, and that syncretism of Hellenistic currents and older Egyptian traditions that is usually referred to as Hermetism. Plotinus's philosophy as exposed in his nine treatises (the *Enneads*) is often presented as an emanational process that originates in an undetermined Absolute (the One), becomes intelligible in a realm of mind (the *nous*), and arrives at its final hypostasis in a world soul (the *psuchē*) shared by all individual souls. Such a presentation misses Plotinus's central insight and the source of its mystical fertility, namely, the immanence of the One in all the lower hypostases. The mystical-intellectual process for him consists in a return to that ever-present One, beyond the vision of the intelligible forms. A crucial role in this process is played by the notion of image, so important in early Christian mysticism. For Plotinus each emanation reflects the previous one as an image. Even the world, though steeped in opaque matter that allows no further emanations, reflects the soul and the mind. Clearly, in this context being an image is more than being an external copy. It implies that each sphere of reality refers in its very essence to a higher one. As such, the image presents, rather than represents. Man alone is able to read his world and his own soul as an appeal to turn inward to mind and, beyond mind, to the One. By a process of asceticism and contemplation, he may overcome the dispersion of time and of all that separates him from the total simplicity (the One) of his inner core. The Plotinian union with the One has been called *ecstatic*, but the term *instatic* might be more appropriate for describing a movement of inwardization and simplification. Plotinus's spiritual theology strikes us as decidedly cool: no sensuous feeling, no "visions," and no emotion. Yet more than any other master (outside the scriptures) did this last of the great pagan philosophers influence subsequent Christian mysticism.

The first attempt at a systematic theology of the mystical life in Christ was written by Plotinus's fellow Alexandrian and codisciple, Origen. In his *Twenty-seventh Homily on Numbers* Origen compares spiritual life to the Jews' exodus through the desert of Egypt. Having withdrawn from the pagan idols of vice, the soul crosses the Red Sea in a new baptism of conversion. She passes next through the bitter waters of temptation and the distorted visions of utopia until, fully purged and illuminated, she reaches Terah, the place of union with God. In his commentary on the *Song of Songs*, Origen initiated a long tradition of mystical interpretations that see in the erotic biblical poem just such a divine union. His commentary also presents the first developed theology of the image: the soul is an image of God because she houses the primal image of God that is the divine Word. Even as that word is an image of the Father through its presence to him, the soul is an image through the word's presence in her, that is, through her (at least partial) identity with it. The entire mystical process thus comes to consist in a conversion to the image, that is, to ever greater identity with the indwelling Word. The emphasis on the ontological character of the image of God in man (as opposed to the external copy) persists throughout the entire Christian tradition and holds the secret of its amazing mystical power.

The privileged place of love distinguishes Origen's theology from Neoplatonic philosophy. This emphasis on love becomes even more pronounced in the writings of Gregory of Nyssa, the fourth-century Cappadocian bishop. Under Neoplatonic influence Gregory describes the mystical life as a process of *gnōsis* initiated by a divine eros, which results in the fulfillment of the soul's natural desire for union with the God of whom she bears the image. Though akin to God from the beginning, the soul's mystical ascent is a slow and painful process that ends in a dark unknowing—the mystical night of love.

This theology of darkness, or "negative theology," would be developed to its extreme limits by a mysterious, Greek-writing Syrian of the sixth century who presented himself as the Dionysius whom Paul converted on the Areopagus. His enormous (though in the West not immediate) impact steered the theology of the image in a wholly new direction. Neoplatonic as no Christian theologian had ever dared to be, he identified God with the nameless One. Even the divine relations of the Trinity were ultimate only in the order of manifestation. Beyond all names and even beyond being itself lies the dark reality of a divine superessence. The mystical ascent moves toward that nameless unity. Throughout this thoroughgoing negation, Dionysius preserves the core of the image theology, for precisely the primordial union of the soul with God serves as the moving principle of the mystical ascent. Through constant negation the soul overcomes the created world, which prevents the mind from reaching its ultimate destiny. Yet Dionysius's *Mystical Theology* is ecstatic rather than introspective in its concept: the soul can achieve her vocation of union with God only by losing herself in the recesses of the divine superessence. In this respect it differs from the Western mysticism that it so deeply influenced.

Augustine (354–430), the towering figure who stands at the beginning of all Western theology (also, and especially, spiritual theology), described the divine image rather in psychological terms. God remains present to the soul as both origin and supreme goal. She is attracted by him and bears his image. But, unlike its definition by the Greek Fathers, that image remains for Augustine mostly the external effect of a divine cause. Augustine's treatise *On the Trinity* abounds with speculations on the soul's similarity to the Trinity, such as her constituting one mind out of the three faculties of intellect, will, and memory. They would amount to no more than superficial analogies were it not that God's presence in that same inner realm invites the soul to turn inward and convert the static resemblance into an ecstatic union. "Now this Trinity of the mind is God's image, not because the mind resembles, understands and loves itself [the superficial analogy], but because it has the power also to remember, understand and love its Maker" (*On the Trinity* 14.12.15). In actualizing the divine potential of its external resemblance, in allowing it to be directed to its archetype, the soul is gradually united with God. While the Greeks assert the initial identity, Augustine starts from a creator-creature analogy, which the divine attraction and man's following of it transform into an identity.

Unfortunately, this rich theology of identity remained largely unexplored by Augustine's spiritual followers until, in the twelfth century, the Cistercians and the Benedictines of Saint Victor Abbey combined it with the mystical theology of the Greeks. This fertile synthesis of Augustinian psychology with Greek spiritual ontology culminated in the two movements of Rhineland mysticism and Flemish spirituality. We shall here consider only their chief representatives: Eckhart and Ruusbroec.

Johannes Eckhart, possibly the most powerful mystical theologian of the Christian Middle Ages, synthesized the Greek and Augustinian theories of the image with a daring negative theology in one grandiose system. His mystical vision became the basis of an entire theology and, indeed, of a metaphysics of being. He was a subtle dialectician in his systematic Latin works and a paradoxical preacher in his vernacular sermons, so that his spiritual identity remains even today a subject of controversy. Few have succeeded in harmonizing the two parts of his prodigious output. Yet they do belong together. For Eckhart's endeavor was precisely to present the mystical union not as a privilege of the few but as the very vocation and ultimate realization of humanity. The mystical theory of the divine image holds the key to his theological ontology.

God is Being, and being in the strict sense is only God. With this bold principle, Eckhart reinterprets a Thomist tradition that "analogously" attributed being to God and finite existence. For Eckhart, the creature *qua* creature does not exist. Whatever being it possesses is not its own, but remains God's property. Both its limited essence (what determines it as this being rather than that) and its contingent existence (that it happens to be) are no more than the negative limits of its capacity to receive God's own being. "Every creature," Eckhart wrote, "radically and positively possesses Being, life and wisdom from and in God, and not in itself." Hence, God is totally immanent in the creature as its very being, while totally transcending it as the *only* being. By this presence God is totally like the creature; yet, lacking any of its determinations, he is totally unlike it. On these productive antinomies Eckhart builds his densely rich concept of image. The entire content of the creaturely image of God consists in the divine presence, while the fact that the creature's limitation reduces this identity to a likeness (hence including difference) accounts for the image's total directedness toward the divine exemplar: "Every image has two properties. One is that it takes its Being immediately from that of which it is the image. . . . The second property of the image is to be observed in the image's likeness. And here especially note two things; an image is, firstly, not *of* itself and (secondly) not *for* itself" (*Meister Eckhart*, trans. Maurice O. Walshe, London, 1979, vol. 1, pp. 124–125).

Since the finite subject conveys nothing positive to the image but rather obscures it by its limitations, only God's unlimited self-expression in his eternal Word (the Son) is his perfect image. The quality of the creature's image depends on the presence of that divine image in it, or, more correctly, on the degree of its own immanence in that archetype. The mind—specifically the spiritual mind—fully actualizes that immanence. Eckhart appears to join earlier (Greek) theologians who had defined the image through the presence of God's Word in the soul. But he gives it a more radical turn by declaring that divine Word the soul's very being. Rather than presence, Eckhart speaks of identity. Of course, as a creature the soul totally differs from the divine image. But its created nature contains God's own, uncreated being. In that being the soul coincides with God. "There is something in the soul that is so near akin to God that it is one and not united [to him]. . . . If man were wholly thus, he would be wholly uncreated and uncreatable" (ibid., vol. 2, p. 85).

The soul's being is generated in an eternal now with (indeed, within) the divine Word: "The Father bears his Son in eternity like himself. 'The Word was with God, and God was the Word' (*Jn* 1:1): the same in the same nature. I say more: He has borne him in my soul. Not only is she with him and he equally with her, but he is in her: the Father in eternity, and no differently" (ibid., p. 135). The mystical process then consists in a person's becoming conscious of his divine being. But this is far more than a cognitive process. It demands that utmost poverty and total detachment whereby he gives up his entire created existence "as he was when he was not [that is, before his birth]" (ibid., p. 271). Indeed, the spiritual soul no longer prepares a "place" for God, for "God is himself the place where He works." Only through that ultimate detachment, that waylessness in which there are neither names nor methods, does the soul come to resemble the image that she was in God "and between which and God there was no distinction before God created."

Farther than Eckhart the mysticism of the image could not go. Yet the identity that he so powerfully affirmed excluded any positive consideration of difference. Must the creature's difference remain without any spiritual significance? Was this no more than the circle of nothingness drawn around God's own being? Were even the trinitarian distinctions in God destined to be surpassed in a permanent rest in nameless unity? These were the questions that confronted later mystics of the Rhineland and the Low Countries. No one answered them with more balance and deeper insight than Jan van Ruusbroec (1293–1381), a Brussels parish priest and later a hermit in the wooded solitude of Groenendaal. Unlike Eckhart's theology, Ruusbroec's majestic summa of Christian life in the spirit did not conclude in a darkness beyond distinction. For Ruusbroec also the soul must move into God's nameless unity. But this divine desert is not a terminal resting ground. God's own being, as the mystery of the Trinity discloses, is dynamic, never at rest nor permanently withdrawn into its own darkness. Its silence is pregnant with God's revelatory Word. And so the contemplative, after having reached the divine silence, moves into God's self-revelation in the image of the Son and, with the Son, out into the otherness of creation. For Ruusbroec also, God dwells in darkness. But "in this darkness there shines and is born an incomprehensible light, which is the Son of God, in whom we behold eternal life; and in this light one becomes seeing" (*Spiritual Espousals* 3.1). Ruusbroec postulated no unity beyond the Trinity. The One is the Father—that is, a fertile unity, a silence that must speak, a darkness that yields light. Through its union with God the soul partakes in the movements within God. Once arrived in the empty desert of the Godhead, she is carried by the divine dynamism and moves with the Father into his divine image and into the multiplicity of creation. At that point the creatures appear both in their divine foundation within the image and also in their divinely constituted otherness. Not only their divine core but also their limited creaturehood are to be respected and cherished. Unlike Eckhart, Ruusbroec included in his mysticism of the image a mysticism of creation. Finitude itself, however different, is never separate from the divine image. Thus his theory of contemplation culminates in the ideal of the "common life," a rhythmic balance between withdrawing into interior life and flowing out into charitable practice.

Toward the end of the Middle Ages the mysticism of the image receded in favor of the more personal but also more private mysticism of love. Yet the theology of the image never died. It survived in the theological theories of uncreated grace (e.g., Lessius, De la Taille, Rahner), in patristic studies (Petavius, de Regnon), and in Cistercian spirituality. Today it enjoys a genuine revival, as the success of Thomas Merton's work witnesses.

MYSTICISM OF LOVE: MODERN CHRISTIAN MYSTICISM AND SUFISM. All Western religions have produced mystics of love. Judaism, Christianity, and Islam have known each its own kind of spiritual eros. In singling out love as characteristic of some movements in particular, I restrict the term to those in which personal love of God dominated—namely, Sufism and the spiritual movements that gradually came to prevail in Western Christendom since the late Middle Ages. Chronologically, Sufism precedes Christian love mysticism. Yet I shall discuss the latter first in order to maintain the continuity with the earlier type of Christian spirituality.

Christianity. Some time during the twelfth century, Christian piety underwent a basic change: its approach to

God became more human and affective. Love had, of course, always been an essential ingredient. But now it became the whole thing. At first it appeared in conjunction with the newly recovered trinitarian mysticism. The same Cistercians who reintroduced the Greek theology of the image to the West also initiated love mysticism. Thus in William of Saint-Thierry's influential works, the two currents of contemplation and affection, of image-identity and love-likeness appear simultaneously, occasionally in the same sentence. "When the object of thought is God and the will reaches the stage at which it becomes love, the Holy Spirit at once infuses Himself by way of love. . . . The understanding of the one thinking becomes the contemplation of one loving" (*Golden Epistle* 249–250). The duality persisted for centuries. Ruusbroec brought both trends to a powerful synthesis in his *Spiritual Marriage,* a work that incorporates Greek trinitarian mysticism in the scheme of a treatise on spiritual love by subordinating the more extrinsic assimilation through love to the more intrinsic inhabitation of God in the soul.

The emphasis on love is part of a more general tendency to involve the entire personality in the religious act. The new spiritual humanism (partly influenced by the Spanish Islamic culture) would revive interest in the psychological theory of Augustine and pay an unprecedented spiritual attention to the created world. The first great name to emerge was Bernard of Clairvaux. No Christian mystic has ever surpassed "the mellifluous doctor," as he is called, in the eloquent praise of spiritual love. Still, in many ways he remained a transitional figure: his Christocentric love is directed at the divine person of the Word, rather than at the human nature of the Christ, focus of later medieval spirituality. But the tradition he established clearly differs from that of image mysticism. In a famous sermon on the *Song of Songs,* he defines the unity of the spirit with God as resulting rather "from a concurrence of wills than from a union of essences." Here likeness firmly replaces image-identity. Does it mean that Bernard accepts only an external union with God? Not really, for in his treatise *On Loving God* he describes the highest degree of love as the condition of a drop of water disappearing in a quantity of wine. Experience itself becomes transformed. "To love yourself as if you no longer existed, to cease completely to experience yourself, to reduce yourself to nothing, is not a human sentiment but a divine experience" (10.27). Nevertheless, the transient quality of ecstatic love, its submission to the psychic rhythm of the soul, its affinity with human eros, all herald the advent of a different type of spirituality.

The humanization of man's relation to God transforms man's attitude toward a creation in which God now comes to be more intimately present. An interpersonal, and hence more creaturely, relation to God is ready to accept each creature on its own terms and for its own sake. In this respect its attitude differs essentially from the image mysticism that holds the creature worthy of spiritual love only in its divine core, where it remains rooted in God. The love mystic also cherishes its finite, imperfect being, which, resulting from a divine act of creation, is endowed with a sacred quality of its own. The mystery of the divine incarnation here attains a more universal level of meaning, as if Christians suddenly understood how much the creation must matter to a God who himself has become flesh. The new awareness gave rise to the powerful humanism that since the thirteenth century has characterized Western Christendom. Francis of Assisi taught his contemporaries to regard nature with a different eye and to love the deformed and the sick as much as the hale and the sound. His attitude found a uniquely poetic expression in the *Canticle of Brother Sun* and in Jacopone da Todi's lyricism. But the discovery of God's presence in creation was capable of systematic treatment, as one of Francis's followers, Bonaventure, demonstrated in *The Journey of the Mind to God.* By now the Christocentric orientation of the new spirituality had moved to Christ's humanity—the perfect creature so intimately united to God that loving could never detract the soul from loving God himself. Soon that humanity came to fulfill an essential mediating function in spiritual life. Teresa of Ávila would accuse herself of having neglected this link with the divine in her early years.

As the incarnational consciousness spread to all creation, divine transcendence ceased to imply a negation of the created world. Thenceforth God's presence has been found *within* rather than *beyond* creation. Precisely this immanentization of the divine accounts for the earthly quality of Christian love mysticism and for its followers' deep involvement with human cares and worldly concerns. Catherine of Siena, Ignatius of Loyola, and Teresa of Ávila, among many others, led extremely active lives and deeply influenced the culture of their age. This orientation toward the creature created new spiritual problems. For it requires uncommon virtue not to become attached to a creature one loves for its own sake. By no coincidence did most love mystics become "saints," that is, persons who, by heroic virtue, learned to love without possessiveness. All mysticism demands mental purity. But for those whose love of God passes through creation, the purifying process proves especially exacting. Besides renouncing the superfluous, an essential condition of spiritual growth, mystics so deeply involved with creation have to move against the grain of their natural inclination in order to establish the precarious balance of love and detachment. What al-Ghazālī writes about Ṣūfī mortification is a task for all love mystics: "The uprooting from the soul of all violent passions, the extirpation from it of vicious desires and evil qualities so that the heart may become detached from all that is not God." But when the mystical state proper begins, spiritual men and women tend to stop or reduce this active mortification.

Significantly, John of the Cross, one of the most articulate mystics of love, describes the entire spiritual process as an increasing purification, a "night" that starts with the senses, spreads to the understanding, and concludes in the total darkness of union with God. Most mystics would, perhaps more appropriately, refer to the second and third stages as illumination and union. But they equally emphasize the increased need for detachment. Followers of this tradition tend to equate the beginning of the mystical life with a state of passive prayer that excludes the ability to meditate. John of the Cross distinguishes the night of the senses, common to all who enter the mystical life, from the "horrible and awful" passive purgation of the spirit in the advanced. Not all agree with this description, but all stress the need for total passivity with respect to the divine operation. An entire school has taken what Teresa of Ávila calls the prayer of "quiet" to be the goal of spiritual life itself. As practiced by Miguel de Molinos (1628–1696) and Jeanne Guyon (1648–1717), this controversial concept drew upon itself a number of official condemnations. The debate began with the question whether the spiritual person should remain passive with regard to temptations, especially carnal temptations. The quietist attitude, the adversaries claimed, led to gross immorality—as in the case of Molinos. But the discussion then moved toward the more central issue of whether quiet is acquired or infused. The quietists failed to make adequate distinctions and thereby appeared to present mystical graces available to all, while allowing the pious to neglect the pursuit of common virtue and the practice of good works. Finally, with the French bishop Fénelon, both pupil and director of Jeanne Guyon, the dispute turned to the problem of "pure love": only the love that loves God exclusively because of himself is worthy of a spiritual person. Once the mystic has attained this state of pure love, he or she abandons the methodic pursuit of virtue and, eventually, all control over the spiritual process. None of the charges against the quietists was ever fully substantiated. Yet the entire controversy reveals how sensitive the issue of active or passive quiet had become. The question whether the "higher states of prayer" are available to all could hardly have been raised in an earlier, less psychological age.

The "illumination" that normally follows the period of purgation should not be thought of as a succession of new insights. John of the Cross refers to it as a darkness of the understanding caused by the excessive light of faith (*Ascent of Mount Carmel* 3.3.1). Still, the light is often reflected in unusual cognitive states—hallucinatory perceptions, intensively imagined visions or voices, nonrepresentational intuitions—which in unpredictable ways testify to the profound transformation the mind undergoes in the higher stages of mysticism. They are often hard to interpret, and spiritual masters have traditionally adopted a cautious attitude toward them. Yet we should not place them all on an equal footing. John of the Cross distinguishes concrete visions (either sensational or imaginary) from so-called spiritual apprehensions. While he dismisses the former as a breeding ground of moral illusions, among the latter he finds the most direct expressions of God's experienced presence. John equates such "intellectual" (nonrepresentational) visions (ibid., 2.24) with revelations of God's being "in the naked understanding" of the soul that has attained the state of union—"for they are themselves that union" (ibid., 2.26)—and with the spiritual "feelings" that emerge "in the substance of the soul" (ibid., 2.32). In such states illumination has in fact turned into union.

It is in terms of union that Teresa of Ávila discusses the matter in her *Interior Mansions* (Fifth and Sixth Mansions). What characterizes this final stage of love mysticism—whether defined in cognitive or in affective terms—is its permanence. Hence Teresa refers to it as a "marriage." Here the distinction between the "likeness" of love mysticism and the "identity" of image mysticism ceases to exist—even in the terminology. In the highest love union, intentional intermediacy yields to substantial presence. The trend from likeness to unity appears even more clearly in Ṣūfī mysticism.

Sufism. With its stern emphasis on law and orthodoxy, Islam hardly seems to present a fertile soil for intensive personal experience of the love of God. Yet Islam assumes the entire social system, *sharīʿah* (the way), into a privileged communal relation with God. Moreover, the Qurʾān states that, next to the ordinary believers who serve their creator according to the precepts of the law, there are some to whom God communicates his essential mystery inwardly in peace of the soul and friendship with God (Qurʾān 17:27). Here the Prophet allows for the possibility of a realm of personal religion. The possibility was soon actualized and eventually flowered into unparalleled mystical beauty. Even the unique authority of the Qurʾān has in an indirect way contributed to Islam's mystical wealth, for precisely because it remains the supreme norm of its interpretation, pious readers may find in it whatever meaning divinely inspired insight (*istinbāṭ*) privately reveals to them. Only when personal interpretation openly clashes with established doctrine (especially its rigorous monotheism) could religious authorities interfere. Thus, paradoxically, Islam, the "religion of the book," allows greater freedom of interpretation than religions that place less emphasis on the written word. Though early Muslim mysticism stayed in close connection with the Islamic community, conflicts arose. Already at the time of Ḥasan al-Baṣrī (d. 728), the patriarch of Islamic mysticism, Sunnī traditionalists objected to his attempt to go beyond the letter of law and doctrine. Thus began the opposition between "internal" and "external" religion that, from the tenth century on, led to increasingly severe confrontations. Nevertheless, a deep personal piety remained an essential element of the Islam that substantially contributed to rendering it a world religion.

Most Islamic mysticism could be characterized as love mysticism. Many texts show an amazing similarity in spirit and even expression with later Christian mysticism. Certain passages in the poetry of Rābiʿah al-ʿAdawīyah (d. 801) appear to throw a bridge across the centuries to Teresa of Ávila, while John of the Cross's *Dark Night* echoes some of Shaykh al-Junayd's poems. The similarity becomes somewhat intelligible through the established influence of Syrian monasticism (especially the hesychastic movement) upon the early

Ṣūfīs, and the strong Muslim impact upon Spanish culture as a whole and upon its mystics in particular. The resemblance has often tempted Western scholars to interpret Ṣūfī writings by means of Christian concepts. Yet the difference is substantial and appears with increasing clarity in some later Ṣūfī developments toward monism. Here love no longer represents the highest union with God but is merely a way station on the road to a more total identity. Still, early Ṣūfīs adopted models of asceticism that had closer ties with the spirituality of the Desert Fathers than with the worldly luxury of the expanding Muslim empire. Even the wool dress (*ṣūf*) from which they probably derived their name may well have had a Christian symbolic meaning. At any rate, the passive asceticism of the early Ṣūfīs stood in sharp contrast with the outgoing, active attitude of the Prophet's early followers. Not until the eighth century, however, did the emphasis shift from an asceticism inspired by a fear of judgment to a mysticism of love for which fasting and poverty served as means to a higher end.

The most attractive figure in this early love mysticism is certainly the former slave Rābiʿah. To her we owe some of the purest mystical love poetry of all time, such as her famous prayer at night: "Oh, my Lord, the stars are shining and the eyes of men are closed, and kings have shut their doors, and every lover is alone with his beloved, and here am I alone with Thee" (Margaret Smith, *Rābiʿa the Mystic*, Cambridge, 1928, p. 22). Her "pure" love, even as the love of later mystics possessing that quality, refuses to act or pray out of self-interest, "If I worship Thee from fear of hell, burn me in hell; and if I worship Thee in hope of paradise, exclude me from paradise; but if I worship Thee for Thine own sake, then do not withhold from me Thine eternal loveliness." Only repentance inspired by sorrow for having offended the Beloved is worthy of the spiritual person. For all its erotic exuberance, this and similar love mysticism remained doctrinally "sober." It developed elaborate schemes of the stages (*maqāmāt*) of the love of God. Eventually it used Neoplatonic categories, which strengthened it theoretically but may have favored its later development toward monism.

In Shaykh al-Junayd (d. 910), Ṣūfī mystical theology reached full maturity as well as a systematic unity. Though this religious leader went far in adopting Plotinus's theory, his orthodoxy was never questioned. Louis Massignon, the famous student of Islamic mysticism, describes al-Junayd as "clever, prudent and timid, conscious of the danger of heterodoxy which is peculiar to mysticism," and as a wise spiritual director "who suspends his judgment and defers the question so long as experience does not seem to him decisive and crucial" (Massignon, 1954, p. 275). Still, his theory of emanation from a preexistence in God to a separate existence in time daringly reinterpreted the creation doctrine. In *Kitāb al-Fanāʾ* he writes, "He annihilated me [in my divine preexistence] in creating me even as, in the beginning, He created me [in my separate existence in time] when I was not," and "He was the source of their existence, encompassing them, calling them to witness when still their eternal life was utterly negated, a state in which they were from all pre-eternity" (Zaehner, 1957, pp. 165–166).

By following this principle of emanation to its ultimate consequences al-Junayd's disciple, al-Ḥallāj, ended up with the allegedly monist theory for which he was executed in the year 922. With al-Ḥallāj begins a wholly new phase in Ṣūfī mysticism that continued to use the language of love, but frequently in a more symbolic sense than had the earlier Ṣūfīs. Meanwhile it remains very doubtful whether al-Ḥallāj, despite his strong expressions, ever considered himself fully identical with God. His claim of divinization refers to a passive, transient state—not to a permanent self-deification. Such ecstatic exclamations as "I am the Truth," by no means unique to him, express a temporary, divinely granted awareness of identity with God. He probably remained a love mystic always longing for a union that was only occasionally attained, as in the following oft-quoted verses: "Between me and Thee lingers an 'it is I' that torments me. Ah, of Thy grace, take this 'I' from between us." Even the supreme expression of union still indicates a remnant of duality. "I am He whom I love, and He whom I love is I. We are two Spirits dwelling in one body" (Nicholson, 1939, p. 218). Elsewhere al-Ḥallāj firmly upholds God's transcendence with respect to his creation, as in the words quoted by al-Qushayrī: "He has bound the whole to contingency, for transcendence is His own. . . . He remains far from the states of his creation, in Him there is no mingling with His creation, His act permits of no amendment, He is withdrawn from them by His transcendence as they are withdrawn from Him in their contingency" (Louis Massignon, *La passion d'al Hossayn-ibn-Mansoûr al Hallaj*, Paris, 1922, p. 638).

After al-Ḥallāj, Ṣūfī piety reached a temporary truce with orthodox learning in al-Ghazālī (d. 1111), the greatest of the theologians. A learned teacher of law and doctrine, he abandoned his chair to spend eleven years as a wandering Ṣūfī, and at the end of his life retired to a Ṣūfī monastery. Bypassing the antinomian trends that emerged after al-Ḥallāj, he returned to a more traditional attempt to emphasize experience over the letter of the law. With Ibn al-ʿArabī (d. 1240) the dependence on Neoplatonism (especially the so-called *Theology of Aristotle*) and, with it, the movement toward monism became more pronounced than ever. He provided the link between Western classical culture and Eastern Islamic mysticism that culminated in Jalāl al-Dīn Rūmī. Ṣūfī mysticism, however much inclined toward monism, never abandoned the language and imagery of love. Ibn al-ʿArabī, with al-Ghazālī the most philosophical of all Muslim mystics, never ceases to integrate his Neoplatonic vision with the Qurʾān's dualistic doctrine of man's relation to God. Still one may doubt whether he did more than adapt the terminology of traditional Ṣūfī love mysticism to his own kind of monism. The Absolute for him is an indistinct One that, overcome by the desire to be known, projects itself through creative imagination into apparent otherness. In this projection the relation of the One to the created world, specifically to man, determines that of the Absolute to the differentiated idea of God, the intellectual pole as opposed to the cosmic pole of finite being. All that the creature is, is divine, yet God always exceeds creation. Through man's mediation the dependent, created world returns to its primordial unity. As the image of God, man imposes that image upon the cosmos and reflects it back to its original. In fulfilling this mediating task he approaches the (Gnostic?) archetype of the Perfect Man, the ideal link that restores the broken oneness. Only the Muslim saint realizes the model in its fullness.

All of this appears far removed from Islamic love mysticism and even from monotheism. But the same Ibn al-ʿArabī also wrote a collection of sensual love poetry to which he later added a mystical interpretation. Even his "monist" *Bezels of Wisdom* concludes with a dithyramb on spiritualized sexual love as providing access to the perfect love of God. It states that in woman, man most perfectly contemplates God. "The greatest union is that between man and woman, corresponding as it does to the turning of God toward the one He has created in His own image, to make him His vice regent, so that He might behold Himself in him. . . . If he [man] knew the truth, he would know Whom it is he is enjoying and Who it is Who is the enjoyer; then he would be perfected" (*The Bezels of Wisdom*, in *The Classics of Western Spirituality*, ed. John Farina, New York, 1980, pp. 275–276). However thorough Ibn al-ʿArabī doctrinal monism may have been, it never prevented him from attributing to love a primary role in the practical process of reunification with God. His readers, both inside and outside Islam, have always emphasized this dualism of mystical praxis. This explains his impact both on Spanish Catholic (Ramon Lull, John of the Cross) and on Persian Ṣūfī mystics.

In the refined mystical poetry that constitutes the glory of Persian Sufism, the same drift toward monism is frequently expressed in erotic language. Here the undisputed master is Jalāl al-Dīn Rūmī (d. 1273). He himself was influenced by others (such as ʿAṭṭār, and Ibn al-ʿArabī's disciple in Konya, al-Qunawī, and especially his strange mentor, al-Tabrīzī), yet sang, with a voice uniquely his own, of the longing for the Beloved.

> I am not the kingdom of ʿIraquain, nor of the country of Khorasan, I am not of this world, nor of the next, nor of Paradise, nor of hell. My place is the Placeless, my trace is the Traceless; 'Tis neither body nor soul, for I belong to the soul of the Beloved. I have put duality away, I have seen that the two worlds are one: One I seek, One I know, One I see, One I call. He is the first, He is the last, He is the outward, He is the inward. (*Dīvānī Shamsi Tabrīz*,trans. R. A. Nicholson, Cambridge, 1898, p. 125)

Persian poets after Rūmī expressed a similar synthesis of monist reality and erotic longing, none with more force and evocative power than ʿAbd al-Raḥmān Jāmī (d. 1492):

> Beware! Say not, "He is All Beautiful, And we His lovers? Thou art but the glass, And He the face confronting it, which casts Its image on the mirror. He alone Is manifest, and thou in truth art hid, Pure Love, like Beauty, coming but from Him, Reveals itself in thee." (E. G. Brown, *A Year amongst the Persians*, Cambridge, 1926, p. 138)

Yet most important for the later mystical life of Islam in Iran were the flourishing Ṣūfī orders of dervishes (one of them founded by Rūmī himself). As they spread, mystical life reached all layers of the population, and the search for mystical trance reached unprecedented proportions. After the fifteenth century, Persian mysticism produced no more great writers. Generally speaking, the trend of the past three centuries in Islam has been more toward communal piety and law than toward personal devotion. Yet in our own day we witness a revival of Ṣūfī movements.

ESCHATOLOGICAL MYSTICISM: JEWISH MYSTICS. The section headings in this article do not capture the full meaning of the content. At best they approximate a definition of a dominant trend in a particular, more or less unified mystical school. In the case of Jewish mysticism the description may not even serve this minimal purpose: Judaism has produced forms of mysticism so unlike any other and so variant among themselves that no common characteristic marks them all. At most we can say that they "commune" with one another, not that they share an identical spirit. Gershom Scholem wisely embedded this irreducible diversity, reflective of a spiritual Diaspora, in the very title of his authoritative work *Major Trends in Jewish Mysticism* (1941). The closest he comes to a general characteristic is the point at which he draws attention to the persistent presence of eschatological traits in Jewish mysticism: "This eschatological nature of mystical knowledge becomes of paramount importance in the writings of many Jewish mystics, from the anonymous authors of the early He-khaloth tracts to Rabbi Naham of Brazlav" (p. 20). The eschatological element most clearly appears in the earliest trend: the often Gnostically influenced mythical speculation on Ezekiel's vision of the throne-chariot, the *merkavah*. Mysticism around this theme began in the first centuries of the common era. It consisted of an attempt to ascend to the divine throne beyond the various intermediate spheres (the *heikhalot*). Except for its biblical starting point (first developed in the Ethiopic *Apocalypse of Enoch*), the impact of Gnostic *plērōma* mythology dominates this spiritual "throne world." But also the typically Hellenistic connection of mysticism and magic appears to have been strong. *Merkavah* mysticism declined after the seventh century, but enjoyed a steady revival in Italy in the ninth and tenth centuries, which, in turn, may have influenced medieval German Hasidism.

Whereas *merkavah* mysticism had been esoteric, Hasidism (from *ḥasid*, "pious one") began in the twelfth century as a popular movement closely connected with the *halakhah* (law). The early development has been fixed in the *Sefer Ḥasidim* (Book of the Pious), which contains the spiritual testaments of the prolific Yehudah the Pious and of two other early writers. The eschatological element, present from the beginning, gradually became more pronounced. Yet various other elements appear as well, among them an almost monastic emphasis on the religious virtues of simplicity, humility, and indifference. While *merkavah* mysticism attained its goal by contemplation, Hasidism did so primarily by prayer and spiritual practice. To pure transcendence it opposes the intensive awareness of an omnipresent creator accessible to the *Ḥasid* even in his daily activities. Finally, while *merkavah* mysticism displays Gnostic traits, Hasidic "theology" shows a resemblance to Neoplatonism even in its Greek Christian development. God's glory *(kavod)* is distinct from God's being as a first manifestation of his presence (*shekhinah*), which mediates between this hidden essence and the fully manifest creation. The Hasidim indulged in elaborate speculation about the inner and outer glory of God, and about the kingdom of his created yet hidden presence.

These daring speculations seldom developed into a coherent theology. In that respect they differed from the spiritual movement that, from the fourteenth century on, would largely replace it—Qabbalah. It originated in thirteenth-century Spain as a highly esoteric doctrine, one that its followers were reluctant to divulge. After the expulsion of the Jews from Spain (1492), however, it developed into a theology of exile that spread to large segments of the Jewish world. More speculative than ecstatic (though methods for ecstasy were not absent), it was deeply influenced by Gnostic theologies. Its masterwork, the *Zohar*, by its daring adoption of Gnostic cosmogonies surpassed in this respect even *merkavah* mysticism. In addition, it absorbed the Neoplatonic currents that had swept through the Arabic and Jewish culture of twelfth- and thirteenth-century Spain. Considering the hazardous nature of its thought, its relation to normative tradition and official authority remained, on the whole, remarkably peaceful, if not always amiable. Indeed, the branch that produced the most daring speculation found its expression mostly in traditional rabbinical commentaries on the sacred text. Another trend of Qabbalah, culminating in Avraham ben Shemu'el Abulafia (1240–after 1291), is more prophetic. It combines in a highly original way philosophical theory—much of it derived from Maimonides (Mosheh ben Maimon, 1135/8–1204)—with mystical speculations on the divine names. Abulafia left his native Saragossa early in life to travel all over the Near East and to settle down in Sicily, where he wrote most of his many works. They all aim at assisting the soul to untie the "knots" that bind it to this world of multiplicity and to allow it to return to its original unity (surprisingly named after Aristotle's Agent Intellect). This union may be attained through contemplation of a sufficiently abstract object, such as the letters of the Hebrew alphabet. Any combination of letters results in word figures that in some way refer to the sacred tetragrammaton of the divine name, *YHVH*. In meditating upon them—somewhat as the yogin uses a *mantra*—consciousness moves to a higher state of unity that releases man's prophetic faculty.

Wholly different is the theophysical mysticism that resulted in that unsurpassed masterpiece of mystical speculation, the *Zohar* (Book of Splendor). Its origin remains mysterious, because the anonymous author has carefully covered his tracks (even to the point of writing in Aramaic rather than Hebrew) and attributed his work to earlier authorities. Yet internal criticism suggests that it was written in Spain in the last third of the thirteenth century, probably by one author. The writer, familiar with the philosophies of Maimonides and of Neoplatonism, has, above all, undergone the influence of unknown Gnostic sources. Synthesizing all qabbalistic writings of the century, he attempts to stem the rationalist trend by giving traditional Judaism a hidden mystical interpretation. Thus this highly esoteric work was, in fact, written for the enlightened Jewish intelligentsia of late-fourteenth-century Spain. Central in the *Zohar* doctrine is the theology of the *sefirot*, the ten "regions" into which the divine emanation extends itself. Importantly, the divine *plērōma* of these *sefirot* does not emanate *from* God: it remains *within* God as his manifest being, in contrast to the "hidden God." Gershom Scholem writes: "The point to keep in mind is that the *sefirot* are not secondary or intermediary spheres which interpose between God and the universe . . . not steps of a ladder between God and the world, but various planes in the manifestation of the Divinity which proceed from and succeed each other" (Scholem, 1961, pp. 208–209). Here also language fulfills a crucial function: the *sefirot*, the creative names God gives himself, anticipate the faculty of speech in man. The ultimate manifestation consists of God's simple, immanent presence in the entire creation, the *shekhinah*. In becoming aware of this divine presence, man comes to understand his own deeper self.

Creation takes place *within* God as a transition from the divine *Nothing*, the mathematical point frequently identified with God's Wisdom (the *ḥokhmah* of *Proverbs*). Even evil proceeds from a negative principle in God himself that has become isolated from the rest of the divine organism. Man's reaction consists in restoring creation to its original union within God.

The idea of an immanent creation was taken one step further by some sixteenth-century mystics of Safad in Palestine, exiled from Spain after the expulsion decree. The new Diaspora gave Qabbalah a distinctly messianic, eschatological aspect that had been less prominent in the *Zohar*. Thus the mystical return to the aboriginal creation now came to be seen as anticipating the messianic era. According to Isaac Luria (1534–1572), the most important mystic of the school, creation originates through a process of self-emptying whereby God withdraws from a mystical space within himself in order to establish the possibility for a reality other than his own omnipresent being. The concept of *tsimtsum* (withdrawal) allows Luria to distinguish the world of creation from the emanations that occur *within* God's own being and to prevent creation from collapsing into a pantheistic oneness.

The Gnostic idea of the primordial man, *adam qadmon,* which models God's manifest being on the human organism, provides a transition between the sphere of the *sefirot* and the created world, while, at the same time, explaining the origin of evil. The light of the divine being is refracted through this supreme emanation. The first six *sefirot* receive and reflect the divine light radiated by *adam qadmon.* But the lower six are not powerful enough to retain the light, and it "shatters the vessels" (*shevirat ha-kalim*). Here evil begins to exist as a separate entity. Through the breaking of the vessels, the forces of evil that were mixed with the divine light become segregated from the good. This purgative event, good in itself, would have allowed the total elimination of evil in the final reintegration of the last sefirah. But Adam's fall, once again, reintroduced chaos into the cosmos. The Diaspora symbolizes this general disarray in which the *shekhinah* itself is sent into exile.

Luria's mystical theory culminates in his idea of redemption, a redemption, mystically conceived, that coincides with the messianic era. Through prayer, spiritual man plays an active role in restoring the original order of the universe. Mystical piety will recall the *shekhinah* back to the spiritual *plērōma* and prepare the world for the messianic coming. The powerful concept of *tikkun* (reintegration) conveyed meaning to the bitter experience of the exile. Yet, combined with messianic expectations, it also created a tense and potentially explosive sense of anticipation. Luria's mystical theology therefore prepared the terrain for the pseudomessiahs and the antinomian movements of the seventeenth and eighteenth centuries. Thus the unstable Shabbetai Tsevi (1625–1676) was able (largely through the efforts of his "prophet," Natan of Gaza) to render himself accepted as the Messiah and even to retain many of his followers when he himself apostasized to Islam. Was this not part of the Messiah's vocation in a world that had exiled him to the realm of darkness? Large groups of Shabbateans apostasized publicly while secretly preserving their messianic faith—thus repeating voluntarily what Marrano Jews had been compelled to do involuntarily. The exile among the infidels initiated the condition for the final separation of good and evil of the messianic era. At the same time, antinomian behavior inaugurated a reign in which the restrictions of the Law would be abolished and the primordial state of freedom restored.

Qabbalah was not to end in this state of general disintegration. A new Hasidism on the rise in eighteenth-century Poland incorporated much of its mystical piety while rejecting its messianic excesses. It was neither esoteric nor elitist. More emotional than intellectual, it appears more as a revivalist movement than as a theological school. Yet its nonsystematic character has not prevented it from occasionally attaining speculative peaks. It honored the charismatic leader more than the learned rabbi, even though most of its leaders were rabbis and all endeavored to remain within rabbinical orthodoxy. The new Hasidism began with two inspired men: the Besht (Yisra'el ben Eli'ezer, 1700–1760) and his disciple, Dov Baer, the Maggid of Mezhirich. They, like all their major followers, distinguished themselves more by the striking gesture, the memorable story, than by interpretation of the Torah. It is hard to evaluate the precise "mystical" significance of so popular a movement. Yet the intensive religious experience of its greatest writers leaves no doubt. Here particularly we should restrain ourselves from imposing too narrow limits on the term *mystical.* Hasidism may be more practical and certainly more social than earlier spiritual movements, but its emphasis upon a joyful spirit and moral living derives from a mystical source.

Jewish mysticism shows an unparalleled variety of forms ranging from deep speculation to purely emotional experience. It consistently appeals to scriptural authority, yet no mystical movement ever strayed further from theological orthodoxy than late messianic Qabbalah. And still for all the variety of its forms and of the external influences to which it was exposed, Jewish mysticism unquestionably possesses a powerful unity of its own. In it the word dominates, and the often tragic experience of the present lives in constant expectation of the future.

See Also Aesthetics, article on Philosophical Aesthetics; Attention; Consciousness, States of; Esotericism; Psychedelic Drugs; Religious Experience.

Bibliography

A popular edition of many Christian, Muslim, and Jewish mystics with generally good introductions is the series "Classics of Western Spirituality" under the editorship of Richard J. Payne (New York, 1978–).

The best works on mysticism in general remain William James's *The Varieties of Religious Experience* (New York, 1902) and Evelyn Underhill's *Mysticism* (New York, 1911).

Mysticism: Sacred and Profane (Oxford, 1957) by R. C. Zaehner is a biased work, but the author knows the subject well, especially Hindu mysticism. A collection of essays on the mystical experience is *Studies in the Psychology of the Mystics,* edited by Joseph Maréchal (Albany, N. Y., 1964). A sampling of essays on various aspects and schools of mysticism is found in *Understanding Mysticism,* edited by Richard Woods (Garden City, N.Y., 1980).

Two important books on Hindu mysticism are R. C. Zaehner's *Hinduism* (London, 1962) and, older but still valuable, Surendranath Dasgupta's *Hindu Mysticism* (New York, 1927).

A number of good studies on mysticism in Buddhism are available: Edward Conze's *Buddhism: Its Essence and Development* (Oxford, 1951) and D. T. Suzuki's *On Indian Mahāyāna Buddhism,* translated and edited by Edward Conze (New York, 1968), are two. Frederick J. Streng has published a valuable study of Nāgārjuna in his book *Emptiness: A Study in Religious Meaning* (New York, 1967).

For discussions of Christian mysticism, the reader may consult the introductions to many volumes of the "Classics of Western Spirituality" and the three-volume *A History of Christian Spirituality* (New York, 1963–1969) by Louis Bouyer, Jean Leclercq, François Vandenbroucke, and Louis Cognet. An older history is Pierre Pourrat's *Christian Spirituality* (Westminster, Md., 1953–1955), a four-volume work. On French spirituality of the modern age, Henri Brémond's twelve-volume *Histoire litté-raire du sentiment religieux en France*, 2d ed., edited by René Taveneaux (Paris, 1967–1968), remains unsurpassed. On Protestant spirituality, see *The Protestant Mystics*, edited by Anne Fremantle (London, 1964); in addition, volume 3 of the *History of Christian Spirituality* deals with Protestant, Orthodox, and Anglican forms of mysticism. A further discussion of Orthodox mysticism is George P. Fedotov's *A Treasury of Russian Spirituality* (1950; Belmont, Mass., 1975).

For a study of Islamic mysticism, see Annemarie Schimmel's *Mystical Dimensions of Islam* (Chapel Hill, N.C., 1975); Louis Massignon's *Essai sur les origines du lexique technique de la mystique musulmane*, 3d ed. (Paris, 1968); Reynold A. Nicholson's *Legacy of Islam* (London, 1939); and Margaret Smith's *Way of the Mystics: The Early Christian Mystics and the Rise of the Sufis* (London, 1976).

The choice of general works on Jewish mysticism is limited, but the best is a classic by Gershom Scholem, *Major Trends in Jewish Mysticism* (1941; reprint, New York, 1961).

LOUIS DUPRÉ (1987)

MYSTICISM [FURTHER CONSIDERATIONS].

The term *mysticism,* like the term *religion* itself, is a problematic but indispensable one. Identifying a broad spectrum of ideas, experiences, and practices across a diversity of cultures and traditions, it is a generic term rather than the name for any particular doctrine or mode of life. The application of appropriate epithets yields terminology for specific categories of mysticism (theistic mysticism, nature mysticism, and eschatological mysticism) and for distinct cultural or doctrinal traditions (e.g., Hindu mysticism, bhakti mysticism, Jewish mysticism, merkavah mysticism). The term mysticism is also a modern one, serving the purpose of comparative study and theoretical analysis, drawing into a single arena ideas and practices otherwise isolated within their own local names and histories.

Inevitably, however, the term remains colored if not hampered by the complexity of its own history: by its original Greek etymology (meaning "silence, secrecy, initiation, ineffability"), by the early Christian use of the word *mystical* to describe the deeper significance of Scripture and liturgy, by the later Christian definition of *mystical theology* as loving union with God by grace, and by popular uses of mysticism as a label for anything nebulous, esoteric, occult, or supernatural. Although mysticism is now firmly entrenched within the vocabulary of the modern study of religions, its usage overlaps and to some extent competes with its employment in specifically theological contexts. Christian or at least theistic mysticism continues to be given prominence even in studies treating the subject at a more generic or theoretical level (e.g., in much philosophy of religion). Given its persistently Christian associations and the fact that the term has no real counterpart in other traditions, it is not surprising that the suitability of mysticism as a neutral, global term has been questioned by some scholars. Others, more radically, have challenged the authenticity of the concept itself, viewing it as a product of post-Enlightenment universalism.

SCOPE AND DEFINITION OF THE TERM MYSTICISM. Louis Dupré, in his survey of mysticism in world religions in this encyclopedia, acknowledges the difficulty of any overall definition of mysticism, but some sort of definition must be possible if one is to accept the category of the mystical as coherent and illuminating. By way of a broad definition, one can say that the term mysticism relates to traditions affirming direct knowledge of or communion with the source or ground of ultimate reality, as variously experienced in visionary, ecstatic, contemplative, or unitive states of consciousness and as diversely embodied in doctrines and practices expressing a unitary and compassionate view of the cosmos and human existence. The profound transcendental experiences that empower mystics and inform their ideas and actions are typically characterized by paradox: they are personal yet self-transcending, noetic while in some sense ineffable, striven after but also recognized as independent of human effort.

To move from a general to a more specific definition is either to defer to this or that doctrinal interpretation or historical tradition or to engage creatively in some religiously or metaphysically inspired synthesis or syncretism. The former move tends to obscure cross-cultural insights in the interests of protecting the coherence of a particular cultural or theological tradition; the latter tends to overlook the concrete embodiment within a given culture characteristic of even the most universalistic mysticism. Both moves, though legitimate, lie beyond the agenda of a strictly scientific study of religion. Alternatively, one might allow a definition to become so qualified or all-embracing that mysticism becomes virtually synonymous with *spirituality* (a much vaguer term than mysticism) or even with a selective history of religion in general.

There is no advantage in conflating mysticism, even in its broadest definition, with other types of or currents within religion, such as prophecy, theurgy, divination, mediumship, shamanism, spirit possession, occultism, spiritualism, or charismatic enthusiasm. It is possible to affirm mysticism as a distinctive strand within religion while not denying its multiple connections with other forms of practice and experience. Nor does the distinctive nature of mystical states mean that their investigation should be segregated from that of other traditions of extraordinary experience. In this connection the category of "altered states of consciousness" is a useful one within which to locate mystical states, whether for the sake of making connections or for drawing contrasts. The continuities of the mystical with such varied categories as the aesthetic, the psychic, or the pathological are certainly closer than has been acknowledged in the past. Two areas where mysticism has both illuminated and been illuminated by juxtaposition with other phenomena are shamanism and the near-death experience.

Any modern treatment of mysticism must satisfy two negative and two positive criteria. First, it must avoid reifying mysticism into some kind of uniform system or tradition standing outside the historical traditions of religion. Second, it must avoid making the forms or truths of the mysticism of any one tradition a touchstone for the evaluation of mysticism more generally. Third, it must take into account the global diversity of mysticism; it must embrace Nagarjuna as well as Teresa of Ávila, Isaac Luria as well as Shankara, Mirabai as well as Plotinus. Finally, it must take into account what may be called the four "dimensions" of mysticism: the experiential, the theoretical, the practical, and the social. That is, the varieties of mystical experience are intimately linked with a body of disciplines and techniques, which in turn are informed by a body of ideas expressed in doctrine and philosophy, symbolism and speculation, all of which have social embodiment within particular historical communities and traditions. To these a fifth dimension could be added—even where "bracketed out"—the ontological dimension, covering the transcendental causes or realities implicit in mystical experience. To acknowledge these dimensions and the multiple connections between them enriches but also complicates the study of mysticism, particularly in the case of comparative studies. How can one consider Buddhist enlightenment without reference to Buddhist meditation, the language of Christian mysticism without knowledge of the Bible or liturgy, or Hindu yoga without adverting to Vedic sacrifice and cosmology? Again, how is one to structure a comparison between the stages of contemplative prayer in Spanish Carmelite mysticism and the stages of transic concentration in Theravāda Buddhism or between the language of negation in Meister Eckhart and the language of emptiness in Nagarjuna?

Mystical Experience. It is generally accepted that "mystical experience" is a subcategory of the broader category of "religious experience." But whereas all mystical experience may be "religious," it is not necessarily religious in the explicit sense of being closely associated with some established doctrine, practice, or tradition. Since Dupré's survey limits itself to mysticism in religious traditions, it is important to acknowledge the prevalence of what might be termed "natural" mysticism: the fact that mystical experience is often reported as supervening quite suddenly and unexpectedly in the lives of secular individuals not committed to any doctrine or discipline. These "unattached" mystics do not necessarily interpret their experiences in conventional religious terms or indeed possess the language for any systematic interpretation. But the imperative to interpretation is strong, and some individuals make their own experiences (or the experiences of others) the starting point for some new system of belief or practice.

Although it is generally agreed that central to mysticism is some sort of profound religious experience, there are striking differences in how scholars characterize and evaluate such experience. There are broadly three positions here. To begin with there is the view that mysticism involves states of consciousness that while extraordinary are different only in degree from other states of consciousness. Then there is the view that mystical states are not only extraordinary but also completely different from any other kind of human experience. In both views mystical experience lends itself to appropriate scrutiny from the various scholarly disciplines, allowing theologians and metaphysicians to focus on its doctrinal implications, phenomenologists and philosophers on its structure and cognitive significance, psychologists and sociologists on its emotional and behavioral features, scientists on its physiological conditions and correlates, and so on.

A third and more radical view to have emerged in recent years is that it is fundamentally misconceived to think of the mystical life as based upon the cultivation and interpretation of special episodes or states of consciousness, whether or not different in kind from other types of experience. In this view mysticism is not about having extraordinary kinds of experience that, having been reported by mystics, can be studied at one remove by theologians and other scholars in order for their real meaning to be understood. Rather, mysticism is about a transformed and transforming way of experiencing the world as a whole through a life shaped by the intellectual, liturgical, and communal structures of a particular tradition. Mystical states of consciousness do not offer the mystic, let alone the observer, privileged shortcuts to ultimate truth independently of these structures.

The view that one can learn something important about mysticism through a detailed scrutiny of mystical states on the basis of their literary expression goes back to the persistently influential work *The Varieties of Religious Experience* by William James (1902). This view led directly to the work of R. C. Zaehner (*Mysticism Sacred and Profane,* 1957) and W. T. Stace (*Mysticism and Philosophy,* 1960), which fueled debates about the variety or uniformity of mystical experience throughout the 1960s and 1970s. Where Zaehner insisted on a hierarchy of substantially distinct types of mystical experience, Stace emphasized a phenomenological and indeed ontological common core of experience underlying what for him was a relatively superficial doctrinal and literary diversity. With far more mystical texts now available and a wealth of contributions from a wide range of scholarly disciplines, the weaknesses both of the empirical basis and of the methodology of this earlier debate are all too apparent. The complexity of the distinction between the content of an experience and the forms of its interpretation is now approached in a much more sophisticated way, and the diversity of mystical experience is no longer ignored even by those who argue for an underlying unity.

Through the 1980s and 1990s, however, a new debate emerged. In one camp are those who argue that the distinctions between different types of mysticism and mystical experience are largely if not wholly constructed through the ideas, symbols, and practices defining the traditions mystics inhabit. This "constructivist" analysis of mysticism is associated above all with a series of highly influential collections of essays edited by Steven Katz. Milder versions of constructivism allow for an unconstructed core of experience (not necessarily Stace's "universal core") as a necessary basis around which the cultural construction of those more accessible features of mystical experience takes place; stronger versions hold, reductionistically, that mystical experience is a construction per se. In the other camp are those who insist that mysticism, beneath its cultural forms, is based on an unmediated experience, a "pure consciousness event" or "zero experience" immune to cultural determination and representing an "innate capacity." This view, to some extent a development of Stace's position, could be called the "purist" view. Leading the way here are the writings of Robert Forman. Where the constructivist emphasis tends to see mystical experience as just another form of human experience, albeit an intense and influential one, the purist view stretches the ordinary notion of human experience to the breaking point, raising the question whether an experience of transcendence is not in effect a transcendence of experience.

Constructivism as a theory of mysticism should not be confused with "contextualism," which usefully names an approach to mysticism (common to most contemporary scholars) that takes full account of the intellectual, practical, and institutional contexts within which mystical experience arises. As a general approach, contextualism is compatible with either a constructivist or a purist reading of mystical traditions. But it is also made the basis for a critique of the emphasis on "mystical experience" that characterizes so much writing on mysticism—an emphasis commonly denigrated as "experientialism." The idea of a "private" or "inner" experience that can somehow become the "object" of scholarly study is, according to antiexperientialist scholars, both conceptually confused and untrue to the mystical traditions themselves—though it is also conceded that some mystical traditions have themselves become "experientialist." The antiexperientialist critique (especially prominent among Christian theologians) has been a useful corrective to an approach to the study of mysticism long dominated by psychological and phenomenological analysis—an approach that frequently relies upon trawling through world religions for insights and experiences thought to be too good to be left imprisoned within alien rituals, doctrines, and institutions. Thus harvested, these insights and experiences are then served up as the "essence" of mysticism.

Antiexperientialism also harmonizes with the warnings given in most mystical traditions that mystics should not crave or become attached to experiences qua psychological states and feelings. Even so, it is impossible to deny that great importance has been attached to the cultivation and interpretation of mystical states of consciousness in the world's religious traditions, albeit within the protective and hermeneutic framework of the beliefs and disciplines of these traditions. One only has to think of the Buddhist techniques of mindfulness, transic concentration, intuitive insight, and visualization, all of which can be traced back to the practices and enlightenment experience of the Buddha himself. Or again, one might think of the ecstatic and visionary experiences that play a key role within the mysticism of the Qabbalah.

Mystical Doctrine and Practice. The contextualist emphasis of modern scholarship focuses attention on the subtle relationships between experience, doctrine, and text in the life of mystical traditions and above all on language as the key to these relationships. Mystical texts are no longer seen merely as vehicles for the expression of ideas but as integral parts of the experiential process—of its initiation, assimilation, and exegesis. An important element in this renewed understanding of the instrumental and performative as distinct from purely descriptive function of mystical texts is a new appreciation of the apophatic, or "unsaying," function of mystical language. Apophatic language is a cross-cultural feature of mysticism. Similarities in the nature and use of mystical language may well turn out to be at least as significant for the comparative study of mysticism as similarities in the phenomenology of mystical states of consciousness.

Mystics, contrary to what is often assumed, have been nourished rather than restricted by the doctrines and disciplines of their traditions. This is not to say that some mystics have not aroused suspicion or hostility as a result of their sayings, speculations, or activities. But many of the world's greatest religious leaders, thinkers, and defenders of tradition have also been mystics. Mysticism has the potential to manifest either a conservative or a revolutionary character.

The varieties of mystical practice tend to receive less scholarly attention than the varieties of experience or doctrine, partly through persistent stereotypes of mysticism as "otherworldly" and indifferent to the body and to the "externals" of religion. Mystical practices cover anything pertaining to the training of body and mind, whether as elements of a mystic's general way of life or as part of the more immediate conditions of the mystical experience; they include prayer and worship, solitude and wandering, chanting and reading, bodily postures and breathing techniques, diet and fasting, ritual dance or disciplined movement, and the use of intoxicants. But of particular interest because of their intimate connection with the cultivation (or at least supervention) of mystical states are the specialized techniques often lumped together as meditation but better differentiated as meditation and contemplation. These terms, notwithstanding their Greek and Christian associations, correspond to a distinction found within many mystical traditions. Meditative techniques are those that engage intellect, emotion, and imagination in the systematic exploration of a doctrinal theme or devotional focus. Contemplative techniques, though often arising out of meditation, involve suspending or transcending all normal mental operations in the development of one-pointed consciousness or intuitive absorption. The term *contemplation* is appropriate even in its ambiguity, connoting as it does both an activity and an experience. Arguably, the varieties of mystical technique offer a better point of entry to the comparative study of mysticism than abstract ontologies or phenomenologies (monistic, dualistic).

The Social Dimension of Mysticism. The social dimension of mysticism covers both the institutional embodiment of mysticism in groups and movements and the influence of mysticism upon the wider society and vice versa. Moreover, there are not just social but also political aspects to mysticism. Mystics have played prominent roles in the doctrinal development of their traditions, in reform, in renewal and protest, and sometimes in sectarian, messianic, and millenarian movements.

Issues of gender have become prominent in the study of mysticism since the 1980s. This is only partly a reflection of the attention to such issues within the study of religion as a whole. More significantly it is because, within many mystical traditions, women are better represented and have made more distinctive contributions than in other religious contexts. Leaving aside the unbidden nature of mystical experience, environments and ways of life associated with mysticism (such as asceticism, monasticism, and writing) have also favored women, even in patriarchal societies, because these contexts have been less subject to the restrictive customs of ordinary society. Acknowledging the presence and contributions of women mystics is only part of the story, however. There are also specifically feminist critiques of how the lives, writings, and influence of women mystics continue to be evaluated in ways that fail to do justice to their distinctive contributions. A number of French women thinkers have taken particular interest in how some women mystics have been able to work beyond the restricting oppositions dogging so much of Western culture (male-female, body-soul, reason-emotion).

Mysticism in the Study of Religion. The study of mysticism both benefits and suffers from the specialist nature of modern scholarship. The subject is well represented across the whole range of the humanities and social sciences and also in much scientific and medical literature. But academic specialism, and the theoretical agenda inhabiting it, have encouraged scholars to focus on one dimension of mysticism to the neglect of other dimensions. Thus sociologists not only emphasize the social aspects of mysticism but are also liable to produce sociological explanations of mysticism, and likewise in the case of other disciplines, including those of theology or metaphysics, where theories of mysticism may underestimate social, psychological, and cultural aspects.

Yet because mysticism by its very nature looks toward what is universal or transcendental, it tends to elicit these elements in those who engage with it. Scholars as well as practitioners have recognized mysticism not just as a constant motif within religions but as a key to what is most important in religion. It is at least as common for mysticism to be identified as the heart of religion as for ethics or worship or ritual to be so regarded. As such, mysticism tends to figure prominently in revisionist global theologies, metaphysical system building, New Age thought, debates about the relationship between world religions, and interdisciplinary approaches to art, language, and human consciousness.

See Also Breath and Breathing; Consciousness, States of; Feminism, article on French Feminists on Religion; Meditation; Monasticism, overview article; Religious Experience; Shamanism, overview article.

Bibliography

The literature on mysticism is voluminous. The development of the subject through the years is best tracked through periodical literature. This bibliography restricts itself to a selection of general and comparative studies in book form published since 1978. It excludes studies of individual mystics and editions or anthologies of mystical texts.

Austin, James H. *Zen and the Brain: Toward an Understanding of Meditation and Consciousness.* Cambridge, Mass., 1998.

Barnard, G. William. *Exploring Unseen Worlds: Williams James and the Philosophy of Mysticism.* Albany, N.Y., 1997.

Barnard, G. William, and Jeffrey John Kripal, eds. *Crossing Boundaries: Essays on the Ethical Status of Mysticism.* New York, 2002.

Bishop, Donald H., ed. *Mysticism and the Mystical Experience: East and West.* London and Toronto, 1995. A useful collection of essays surveying mysticism in various traditions.

Brainard, F. Samuel. *Reality and Mystical Experience.* University Park, Pa., 2000.

D'Aquili, Eugene, and Andrew B. Newberg. *The Mystical Mind: Probing the Biology of Religious Experience.* Minneapolis, Minn., 1999.

Ellwood, Robert S. *Mysticism and Religion.* 2d ed. New York and Oxford, U.K., 1999. One of the few introductory surveys of major issues and positions in the study of mysticism, stressing the inseparability of mysticism from the rest of religion.

Forman, Robert K. C., ed. *The Problem of Pure Consciousness: Mysticism and Philosophy.* New York and Oxford, U.K., 1990. The first of three volumes by the leading proponent of the nonconstructivist analysis of mysticism.

Forman, Robert K. C., ed. *The Innate Capacity: Mysticism, Psychology, Philosophy.* New York, 1998.

Forman, Robert K. C. *Mysticism, Mind, Consciousness.* Albany, N.Y., 1999.

Franks Davis, Caroline. *The Evidential Force of Religious Experience.* Oxford, 1989.

Gellman, Jerome. *Mystical Experience of God: A Philosophical Enquiry.* Aldershot, U.K., 2001. A critical survey of objections to the argument that mystical experience provides evidence for theism.

Hollenback, Jess Byron. *Mysticism: Experience, Response, and Empowerment.* University Park, Pa., 1996.

Hollywood, Amy. *The Soul as Virgin Wife: Mechthild of Magdeburg, Marguerite Porete, and Meister Eckhart.* Notre Dame, Ind., 1995.

Hollywood, Amy. *Sensible Ecstasy: Mysticism, Sexual Difference, and the Demands of History.* Chicago, 2001.

Hunt, Harry T. *Lives in Spirit: Precursors and Dilemmas of a Secular Western Mysticism.* Albany, N.Y., 2003.

Idel, Moshe. *Kabbalah: New Perspectives.* New Haven, Conn., 1988.

Idel, Moshe, and Bernard McGinn, eds. *Mystical Union in Judaism, Christianity, and Islam: An Ecumenical Dialogue.* New York, 1996.

James, William. *The Varieties of Religious Experience* (1902). New York, 1929.

Jantzen, Grace. *Power, Gender, and Christian Mysticism.* Cambridge, U.K., 1995.

Jones, Richard H., ed. *Mysticism Examined: Philosophical Enquiries into Mysticism.* Albany, N.Y., 1993.

Katz, Steven T., ed. *Mysticism and Philosophical Analysis.* New York, 1978. The first of four volumes by the leading proponent of constructivism.

Katz, Steven T., ed. *Mysticism and Religious Traditions.* New York, 1983.

Katz, Steven T., ed. *Mysticism and Language.* New York, 1992.

Katz, Steven T., ed. *Mysticism and Sacred Scripture.* New York, 2000.

McGinn, Bernard. *The Presence of God: A History of Western Christian Mysticism.* New York, 1994–. An ongoing project in several volumes, already established as the standard history of Christian mysticism.

McIntosh, Mark A. *Mystical Theology: The Integrity of Spirituality and Theology.* Cambridge, U.K., 1998.

Merkur, Dan. *Mystical Moments and Unitive Thinking.* Albany, N.Y., 1999.

Mommaers, Paul, and Jan van Bragt. *Mysticism Buddhist and Christian: Encounters with Jan van Ruusbroec.* New York, 1995.

Newell, William Lloyd. *Struggle and Submission: R. C. Zaehner on Mysticism.* Washington, D.C., 1981.

Nieto, José C. *Religious Experience and Mysticism: Otherness as Experience of Transcendence.* Lanham, Md., and New York, 1997.

Petroff, Elizabeth Avilda. *Body and Soul: Essays on Medieval Women and Mysticism.* New York, 1994.

Pike, Nelson. *Mystic Union: An Essay in the Phenomenology of Mysticism.* Ithaca, N.Y., 1992.

Roy, Louis. *Transcendent Experiences: Phenomenology and Critique.* Toronto, 2001.

Roy, Louis. *Mystical Consciousness: Western Perspectives and Dialogue with Japanese Thinkers.* New York, 2002.

Ruffing, Janet K., ed. *Mysticism and Social Transformation.* Syracuse, N.Y., 2001.

Sells, Michael A. *Mystical Languages of Unsaying.* Chicago and London, 1994. A study of the apophatic approach in four different mystical traditions.

Stace, W. T. *Mysticism and Philosophy.* Philadelphia, 1960.

Stoeber, Michael. *Theo-Monistic Mysticism: A Hindu-Christian Comparison.* New York, 1994.

Turner, Denys. *The Darkness of God: Negativity in Christian Mysticism.* Cambridge, U.K., 1995.

Wainwright, William J. *Mysticism: A Study of Its Nature, Cognitive Value, and Moral Implications.* Madison, Wis., 1981.

Wiethaus, U., ed. *Maps of Flesh and Light: The Religious Experience of Medieval Women Mystics.* Syracuse, N.Y., 1993.

Zaehner, R. C. *Mysticism Sacred and Profane: An Inquiry into Some Varieties of Praeternatural Experience.* London, 1957.

PETER MOORE (2005)

MYTH

This entry consists of the following articles:

MYTH: AN OVERVIEW

The English word *myth* comes from the Greek *muthos,* meaning "word" or "speech." It owes its significance to its contrast with *logos,* which can also be translated as "word," but is used especially in the sense of a word that elicits discussion or an argument. The reference to Jesus Christ as the Logos (Word) of God is well known from the Gospel of John; this is a necessary reminder that the lines separating *logos* and *muthos* are not rigid. *Muthos* in its meaning of "myth" describes a story about gods and superhuman beings. A myth is an expression of the sacred in words: it reports realities and events from the origin of the world that remain valid as the basis and purpose of all there is. Consequently, a myth functions as a model for human activity, society, wisdom, and knowledge. The word *mythology* is used for the entire body of myths found in a given tradition. It is also used as a term for the study of myths.

The definition given here contains elements on which not all specialists would agree or place the same emphasis. The use of the word *sacred* might impress some as defining the subject of myth with a word that lacks more clarity than the term being defined. For the historian of religions, however, no confusion occurs. The distinction between the sacred and the profane emphasized by the philosophically inclined French sociologist Émile Durkheim (1858–1917) is based on a sober observation: all human traditions and societies heed the sacred and mark it in one way or another. Its ultimate or metaphysical reality is not the issue.

The most general characteristic of the sacred is not that it is exalted, although in many instances that may be the case, but that it is distinct from ordinary, profane, everyday worldly things. In communicating the sacred, a myth makes available in words what is available by no other means, and its words are different from other words: the words of myth have an extraordinary authority and are in that perceivable manner distinct from common speech. The language of myth does not induce discussion; it does not argue, but presents. The most familiar example in the West, the opening words of Genesis, "In the beginning God created the heavens and the earth," is very different from the words in any theological chapter on the doctrine of creation, precisely because the latter are meant to analyze, to systematize, or to discuss God's creative acts, not to present them. The words have to make a case for their validity, while the myth is its validity. A myth, whether its subject is the acts of deities or other extraordinary events, always takes us back to the beginnings of all things; hence cosmogony, the birth of the world, is a principal theme. In each case, the age to which the myth transports us is very different from our own; it is in fact a time beyond any human being's ken, and hence the events and realities dealt with are literally altogether different from the facts people are concerned with in their everyday human lives. The authority of myth is more than an analogy to authorities on earth.

Myth relies on one of the three forms of religious expression: sacred speech, sacred acts, and sacred places. As such, it occurs side by side in most traditions with sacred places or objects (symbols) and sacred acts (that is, cult, rituals, sacrifices, and ceremonial acts and performances). The chief reason myths attract scholarly attention is their medium: words. They can be expected to elucidate the entire religious life of a community, shedding light especially on the ritual acts and sacred objects that by themselves do not speak at all, or certainly not often, and not as clearly. For instance, a central temple or a sacred pole may be of paramount significance in the religious life of a community, yet it is the recorded myth that is most likely to explain its pivotal role in the community's religious life.

MYTH, SYMBOL, AND RITUAL. The fact that the mode of a mythical expression is words may account, to quite an extent, for the problems the subject has caused for intellectuals from antiquity to the present age. Myths have been looked upon as conscious efforts to veil rational propositions, as allegories for historical events, as poetic imageries, as unconscious verbalizations of inner desires, as mental classificatory schemes, and as social structures. Many scholarly attempts have been helpful in highlighting such relationships, yet each of these attempts has failed to arrive at an overall explanation. Admittedly, none may be possible.

To understand myth, we must do more than accumulate the results of specialized approaches and fragmentary methodological views. Rather, a determined inquiry, and any true science of mythology, should take into serious consideration also the whole of religious expressiveness within which myths function. Of course, myths are language and speech and literature. Of course, myths may reveal something of the society in which they were formulated. Of course, myths may manifest deeper human drives than those displayed in civilized life. Nevertheless, human religious expressiveness in its threefold form of sacred speech, sacred acts, and sacred places remains essentially one, and the three forms we distinguish had best be considered as merely the aspects visible to us; our differentiation of the three forms is external, conceptual, formal. The three always occur together, in any culture. We can only observe that, as a rule, one of the three has a dominant role; some civilizations have a wealth of myths, some of rituals, and some of sacred places.

A sociological, psychological, or other special scholarly view may provide illumination, yet the coherency of a religious tradition should not be allowed to fall between the cracks. As in the case of the computer, where output depends structurally upon the questions asked, each of our sciences and scholarly disciplines can only provide answers in accordance with its own definition of problems. For instance, the semantic problem facing historians of religions is not a mere extension of linguistics. Whatever the definition of religion may be, it must have something to do with the totality of human orientation, hence with the underlying certainties or assumptions concerning each particular activity or creation. The history of religions deals with such totality not in the manner of philosophy, by reflecting on premises for coherent and defensible thought and action, but by studying the evidence of religious documents in human tradition. The principal question is not "What is true?" but "What have societies, civilizations, and communities found necessary to point to and preserve as true?" Here the study of myths becomes the obvious source out of the entire store of religious documentation.

THE UNITY OF MYTH AND THE VARIABILITY OF CULTURE. The variety of cultures, of their languages, means of production, and evaluation of what is essential, is overwhelming. This variety invites us to look for an explanation of myths in the specificity of each society, and certainly many an answer to many a question can be obtained in this manner. Ignoring the specificity of a tradition would be the worst methodological error. Given this, however, it is essential to remember that by our definition myth emphasizes realities and events from the origin and foundation of the world. This presents a certain difficulty that lies hidden just below the surface. "The world" suggests a oneness, but the myths from the world's myriad cultures and ages are manifold. It would be easy to conclude that the oneness of the world depicted by myths is in each case at most a collective fiction peculiar to an isolated tribe, and yet such a conclusion would be questionable. For one thing, there is too much contact, exchange, and mutual understanding between different tribes and nations to permit such a conclusion.

Resolving the issue of the origin of the world, and what it is that remains fundamental to the world, does not call for one immutable formula. The question does not demand an answer that prohibits variety but rather one that includes it. Not only do myths vary from culture to culture; each one is itself open to transformation. Staple foods, basic provisions, and tools are among the topics that occur in cosmogonic myths, but these fundamental elements in human existence vary from the hunting and gathering communities and the early peasant and pastoral societies to the most complex urban centers. How essential are these elements to the cosmogonic myth? The answer is that they are at the same time essential and completely insufficient, because the issue goes far beyond nutrition and tool-making and all the other culturally specific human concerns. Just the same, myths take account of these absolute necessities and can even assign them a direct role in the origin of the world. The multiplicity of mythologies has immediate and important methodological consequences from the outset of any inquiry: the multiplicity is observed from the beginning and is not merely a methodologically inconsequential by-product of our final conclusions. It concerns the very nature of the primary documents of the object of our discipline. Hence, for instance, the history of religions must take the variety in the very first items of nutrition in origin myths seriously; we cannot disregard the choices made by the narrator.

A most important consequence of the multiplicity of mythologies is that by necessity, the investigator has a particular position vis-à-vis a given mythological tradition; and indeed this orientation is necessary in order to gain any perspective on any myth. There is no such thing as objectivity that amounts to neutrality; there is no understanding where the subject has eliminated herself or himself. This absolutely necessary subjectivity is not a whimsical individual stance or solipsism but the recognition of the only ground from which a religious phenomenon can be traced.

One may also state that the world of religions, spawning its myths, is not as remote from the natural sciences as has been supposed in the humanities and the social studies that developed in the wake of the German philosopher Wilhelm Dilthey's work; furthermore, the world of science may be affected by mythology in spite of the intentions of scientists.

It is noteworthy for the historian of religions that the ancient problem of the unity of nature is eliciting new interest among scientists. There is no reason to jump to conclusions and equate that interest with the expression of age-old myths, yet the revival by itself is fascinating and promises to overcome unnecessary barriers between the humanities and the sciences. Students of subatomic particles theorize on a possible "supersymmetry" in nature. These theoretical considerations are hard to separate altogether from the ancient and universal mythological interest in the mystery of oneness (whether of the world or God or the Ultimate). Still a reservation is in order here. What distinguishes modern scientists is that they search for mathematical formulation, a direction that cannot be applied to the mythical narration and poetry available to us. To scientists, a serious object of study is principally an invitation to a precise, calculable demonstration of relationships.

The topic of symmetry has received much attention in aesthetics, and has deeper roots there than in physics. Here also ties to mythology are visible, even if difficult to define. For the church father Augustine, symmetry was a rational entity, because it does not occur in nature but does occurs in human creations. It exists in human reason itself; through it God created humans in his own image. Whether one speaks about Augustine's reasoning as philosophy, science, or mythology will depend on one's intellectual frame of reference.

Myth and politics. In the study of politics, power is a necessary concept. It is, of course, an abstraction. Wielders of power are not sterile laboratory tubes filled with that element. Religion and hence mythological elements play a great part in the exertion of political control over others; and since the nineteenth century there has been a steady growth of ideological theories affiliated with as well as opposed to religious factors. Religion and myth, like power, never occur in pristine purity, but always in admixtures. The fact that people are religious (as well as political, philosophizing, and knowledge-gathering) beings is not necessarily a pleasant or attractive fact. To say that humans are *Homo religiosus* is not a compliment. The unity of myth in various cultures and human inquiries is accordingly the statement of a problem, rather than of a supposed mysterious, pure, dialogic core of all human existence.

In recent times, serious scholars have turned to political power as to some extent explanatory of myth (as well as sacrifice). Even if some of their reasoning may be open to criticism, it certainly cannot be denied that notions of justice—as well as revenge—not infrequently are rooted in myth. Until this very day, Justice is depicted as a blindfolded goddess, wielding scales. In texts, as in speech, justice and myth are frequently inseparable. The expulsion of the first humans from paradise and Cain's punishment for the first murder as depicted in the book of Genesis are well-known models. True justice seems everywhere most concisely embedded in myth. In Hinduism, Dharma ("justice," and in this context in particular, "the right tradition"), is also a god, and Pāṇḍavas Yudhiṣṭira, who is entitled to the throne in the epic *Mahābhārata,* is said to be Dharma's son. When Buddhism spread through Asia from India to Korea, it was accepted and propagated by the elite, who reformed the juridical system in accordance with the new Buddhist teachings. In ancient Greece, Themis, a consort of Zeus, is called on as the goddess of Justice.

Cosmogonic imagery. Another point should be noted: each society, culture, or historical epoch has nothing but its own vocabulary to tell even its most basic myths. This point is so obvious as to run the risk of being overlooked. A comparison with modern science is illuminating. Twentieth- and twenty-first-century astronomers and physicists have discussed a theory of the origin of the universe they have labeled the big bang, as distinct from the steady state theory. Irrespective of mathematical calculations, the discussion could not very well be carried on without labels taken from the common speech of our age: in the final analysis, these are poetic similes that have taken on a life of their own; they have a pregnant metaphorical significance like the imageries in traditional cosmogonic myths.

One of the many accomplishments of Raffaele Pettazzoni, the great Italian historian of religions, is his huge collection of myths and legends from all continents. Included are many cosmogonic myths. Mircea Eliade occupied himself with the supreme significance of cosmogonic myths. That significance is evident in most traditions. Whatever other myths are told—about the origin of animals, plants, institutions, or anything else—they take for granted the basis provided in some myth of the creation of the universe. Even eschatological myths, seemingly positing the end of the world as if in contrast to the beginnings of the world, do not abandon their relationship to the cosmogony. This abiding relation is not paradoxical. All thoroughgoing eschatologies express themselves as renewals of the real, truly intended origin. The reference to Jesus Christ as the new Adam is a well-known example. In the history of Christianity, the Protestant movement saw itself as engaged in reestablishing the pure, original form of the religion. In Marxism (and in the ideas of the young Marx himself) even the most typical eschatological myth of the classless society is expressly concerned with the restoration of the human race as it was originally—without private property.

Character and Content of Myth. At first sight, myths may seem to have much in common with other forms of folk literature. They deal with supernatural events, as fairy tales do; they deal with extraordinary figures comparable to those in legends and sagas. The authority of myths, however, distinguishes them clearly from other sorts of narratives. Typically, the myth tells of a time altogether different from the time of our experience ("in the beginning . . ." or "before heaven and earth were created . . ."), whereas the typical fairy tale, no matter how wonderful its events, begins "Once upon a time . . . ," which is to say, a time like ours. The saga's hero and the legend's sacred protagonist are no doubt superior to all normal human beings, yet their time resembles the historical time of our experience.

Epics present a special case, for they are often a prime source for our knowledge of myths: the *Iliad* and *Odyssey* of Homer are celebrated instances in the Western tradition. Nevertheless, epics as such do not have the authority of myths, no matter how they function as educational tools held in the highest esteem by a society. The myths they narrate in the body of their texts and the mythological references they make can be seen as part of an educational pattern: this is how people should understand the basic, authoritative models in the religious tradition. Moreover, in addition to instruction, epics provide entertainment for their audience. One cannot say this of myths, even though there are good reasons to speak of the narrative style of myths, which can be truly arresting and spellbinding. Raffaele Pettazzoni went so far as to see in epics the first clear signs of a process of secularization.

The themes of myths are innumerable. Often the characters are gods and goddesses, sometimes animals, plants, mountains, rivers. . . . In each case, the myth directly or by implication links its striking presentation of events to an altogether different time and thereby posits its authority. Nevertheless, the astounding variety of myths can best be discussed not in terms of their protagonists or the events they describe, but rather in terms of their various structures and their cultures of origin.

The Function of Myth in the Tradition of Cities and Civilizations. Many a modern city-dwellers makes the mistake of thinking that myths belong only to a dim, unsophisticated past. Yet not only is there no religious tradition on earth today without its identifiable myths, but the history of cities and urban life itself, which began thousands of years ago, is steeped in myths and rituals. Ancient temples everywhere are spoken of in terms of the mythical traditions with which they are imbued. To understand this properly we have to divest ourselves of the modern habit of viewing religion as something distinct, separate from the "ordinary" things of life. The duties of elected officials in ancient Athens always involved functions they were expected to perform in rituals. Even earlier, in Mesopotamian civilization, temples served purposes we would immediately identify as religious, such as sacrifice, and for administrative matters we would look upon as by nature secular or bureaucratic.

Additional and abundant evidence comes from civilizations in the New World: the Aztecs in Central America and the Incas in South America. The mythologies at the heart of these civilizations generally support a pronounced class structure and a powerful central ruling elite. Adding to the complexity and fascination of mythological development in Central America and South America is the socio-mythological complexity of the Spanish invaders, who themselves emerged from turbulent centuries of Christian, Muslim, and various ancient local traditions. An example of the new, fascinating mythological interweaving appears in the cult of Our Lady of Guadalupe. The emphasis on the religious roots of authority is most striking in the intertwined myths of the New World, with their roots on both sides of the Atlantic. We should add that in spite of great religious upheavals and reforms, remnants of the ancient traditions still remain.

The function of myth is particularly striking in periods when large-scale religious change occurred. One such case has been studied in an exemplary manner. It occurred with the new retelling of local tribal myths in Central Asia and was instrumental in the area's conversion to Islam. The retelling by Muslim missionaries was so effective that Islam became fully accepted, indeed rooted in a large part of Central Asia. History makes it clear that myths, whether or not they are clearly cosmogonic, do not merely relate to explanations of the world's beginnings. They reveal their force and function when history shows their role in renewing life, in a city, a society, a civilization. In each religious tradition such a force of renewal is the most striking manifestation of a myth's function.

Structure and Style. What characterizes mythical recitations, and what is their purpose? Contrary to the assumption of much traditional scholarship, myths are not essentially etiological (from Greek *aitia,* "cause") in the sense of explaining origins or causes. It is true that the word *etiology* could be used, with some caution, but only if one adheres to the sense the Greeks themselves sometimes gave to the term *aitia:* a primeval condition. Hence the term could also refer to primary states or first principles. This meaning of the term, however, was not usually in the minds of the scholars who thought of myth in terms of etiology. Until recently many students saw in myths a prescientific endeavor to establish causes for the universe, natural phenomena, and everything else that preoccupies modern science, thereby overlooking the fact that this scientific preoccupation with causality is a very precisely determined feature of modern history, as much as the attendant confidence in technological progress. For instance, it is certainly no coincidence that the very influential folklorist and classicist James G. Frazer launched his idea of fertility as the principal explanation for most of the world's myths and rituals shortly after artificial fertilizer was marketed for the first time in the nineteenth century.

The supposed prescientific nature of myths was incongruous with another view sometimes held at the same time by the same theorists, namely that myths contained the texts necessary to accompany rituals, after the manner of a libretto to an opera. Since the latter theory generally entailed the idea that rituals were only magical acts, all these theories, incongruous or not, were really variations on the theoretical theme of a prelogical mentality, one of the most enduring products of cultural evolutionism and best known through its articulation by the French philosopher Lucien Lévy-Bruhl (1857–1939).

Yet myths are not attempts at causality foreshadowing nineteenth-century scientific discussion. Their notion of an origin and basis of all things should be taken quite seriously. If indeed the isolated and desiccated notion of first causes was the central issue in myths—if the myth's only concern was epistemology—one could not very well imagine any need for ritual related to myth. Instead, an academic-style presentation would suffice. Obviously, no myths in that style exist. And that is precisely the issue. A myth does something else, and something more encompassing than presenting a reasonable (or even pre-reasonable) explanation of things. This is the reason Eliade has rightly emphasized cosmogony as the fundamental myth. In whatever cultural or religious tradition a creation myth is recited, it is paradigmatic in a special, one might even say pregnant manner, because of the many things to which its sheer force as a model is able to give birth.

In many instances, creation myths are recited in a special, archaic language, different from the vernacular. One such case is a creation myth in the Ngaju-Dayak tradition (South Kalimantan, Borneo). Its unusual language is not meant to keep it secret but rather serves to underline its significance, preserved by experts in the community. The narrative itself establishes the land, orienting the villages and their mirror-image counterparts in the heavenly realms; it creates the social divisions and their functions, as well as the principles of the legal system. The myth is couched in lyrical poetry, as are many myths in Southeast Asia, including those expressed in the vernacular. Sometimes, a cosmogonic myth is recited on special occasions, as in the ancient Near East on the enthronement of a king or for the renewal of life and kingship together in the New Year festival. Elsewhere instances occur where the cosmogony functions to cure the sick or renew a poet's inspiration. In all these examples the creation of the world is invoked for its fundamental and founding power.

In simple terms, how does human speech succeed in expressing the underlying reality of existence; how can something so ungraspable be expressed at all? All myths can be seen as coming to terms in their own way, within their culture, within their necessities of life, with this question. The special features of myth, in spite of great cultural diversity, result from the unusual task it sets for speech itself to go beyond the ordinary limits of knowledge and perception.

An archaic language for myth is a feature found throughout the world. The phenomenon occurs in very different civilizations and circumstances: the use of Latin in the liturgy of the Roman Catholic church; the importance of the Church Slavonic liturgical language in the history of the Orthodox church, the use and cultivation of Sanskrit in Hinduism, and the attention given to the study and use of Sumerian in ancient Babylon many centuries after that language had ceased to be spoken. Although far from universal, such eccentricities of language are a feature of myth that indicate an awareness of a tradition deserving special protection.

Another feature in many traditions is the special care taken that myths shall be recited only at specific times and places. This points out clearly that myths are not like other stories. This awareness of the special nature of myths is illustrated in a folk tale of the North American Wichita Indians concerning a contest between Coyote and an opponent. The two contestants tell stories, and the winner will be the one who knows the most stories. Coyote wins because his store of stories is inexhaustible: he can make them up at will. His opponent restricts himself to stories that have not been made up. He tells only true stories, and those are limited in number. True stories, are, of course, what in our study are called myths.

Humor in myth. One feature of myths that is indeed universal can best be indicated by the word *humor.* This does not refer to jokes or quick-wittedness, and least of all is it a spur to uproarious laughter. It is closer perhaps to what the German Romantics, who were intrigued by the experience of humor, seemed to think of as a smile that liberates us from anxieties, and especially from the doldrums, of our existence. If successful, myths, setting out to do what ordinary speech cannot reach, have to break through a barrier that is set for our normal understanding, and hence *liberation* is an apt word for what is envisaged.

An alternative to seeing the humor of myths is to view myth as a primitive form of doctrinal system in the general evolution of the world of thought, as evidence that the primitive ancients could not think like modern people do, or in some other way to force myth into some scheme of logic that satisfies our contemporary sense of what reason and empirical reality are really all about. In all cases, these distortions neglect the actuality and the immediate presentation of the myths themselves.

A myth of the Brazilian Ge begins by stating that in former times the Indians had neither corn nor fire. It describes how one member of the tribe takes his wife to a distant place in the forest, where they set up a plantation and plant corn and other staple foods. The wife's lover visits her secretly, and later returns with another man from the village. The husband turns into a man-eating snake, and devours the visitor. Thereupon the villagers kill the snake and bring to their village corn and the other cultivated plants, as well as fire. In the course of the story, the wife gives birth twice to a number of snakes, first in the forest, later in the village, and finally goes back into the forest, where she orders her offspring to bite people forevermore.

Whatever one may want to say about the origins of the enmity between humans and snakes, or about hidden logical systems, or about the frequently attested relation between the acquiring of a civilized life and violence, the myth conforms to other myths in that it contains events that strike the listener as strange or contradictory, beginning with the juxtaposition of the people without corn or fire and the departure of one couple to a forest where they run a plantation and suddenly master fire. Not all etiology is discarded, not all logic made superfluous; no less attention should be paid to cultural patterns and conditioning. Nevertheless, something that liberates, something that shakes listeners loose from their customary habits of mind, is given form in myth.

One need not look far to find other examples. In the familiar story in *Genesis,* God creates light on the first day of creation, yet the sun, the moon, and the other heavenly bodies do not come into being until the fourth day. By the end of the chapter, on the sixth day, God gives to the wild animals, to the birds of heaven, the reptiles, to every living creature, all of the green plants for food. Obviously, this is at odds with the knowledge possessed by every listener who is familiar with the eating habits of such animals as lions. One may argue that the narrative is not really a creation story but rather a paradise story. Whether we are convinced by this argument or by the realization that, according to the story, the creator god is something other than a prime mover, we are more shocked than persuaded into that novel idea. The accepted lines of thought are ruptured and replaced by new ones.

Of course, adherents of a tradition develop their own explanations, and it is characteristic that for instance the rabbinical commentaries embroider on puzzling texts not merely by analyzing them logically, but by participating in the same mythical vein in which the texts tell their stories. Thus the ancient rabbis tell us that the light created on the first day was not the ordinary light of the sun that we see. Instead, it was light by which one would have been able to see the entire world in a glance from one end to the other. God, in his wisdom, foreseeing human wickedness, hid that extraordinary light—and will not reveal it until the new world to come.

The German writer Jean Paul (pseudonym of Johann Paul Friedrich Richter, 1763–1825), known for his literary essays, was thoroughly aware that humor does not deal with trifling matters but, on the contrary, with matters of ultimate importance. The four forms of humor he defined do not need much modification to be applied to mythical literature. All of them are characterized by their defiance of the wooden habits of human minds.

The first, the Dimming of Opposites, is probably present in most myths. Imageries abound such as that of a time before creation when heaven and earth were not yet separated, or of a beginning in which the two were so close that people could not stand up straight, or as in *Genesis,* when it was necessary to separate the waters below from the waters above.

The second variety of humor depicts an Inverse Effect. Somehow, a disastrous event leads to infinite bliss that could not have been anticipated by the listener. Consider the Hindu cosmogonic story of the churning of the ocean. Before all ordinary time, in fact before the creation of the world, the gods and the demons exist in some apparent harmony. Then the gods raise the question of how they may attain immortality. Together with the demons they begin their quest for it by churning the ocean. Completely unexpectedly, instead of immortality a most deadly poison turns up. All variants of the myth state that the great god Śiva rescues the world (which, curiously, has not been born yet) from the poison by swallowing it. The *Rāmāyaṇa* version has the interesting detail that it is the god Viṣṇu who suggests that Śiva drink the poison on the grounds that the first offering is duly his. The accounts and their interpretations vary, but Śiva does drink the poison, and the world is established. The seriousness of the humor involved is evident, as is also the case with the crucifixion of Jesus Christ at the origin of Christianity, followed—without anyone among the human actors and witnesses involved anticipating it—by the resurrection.

A third category of humor, Subjective Reservedness, may be the best formula to denote the awareness in mythic narration of the curious union of the human voice that narrates and the sacred, more-than-human reality narrated. This awareness is expressed in many ways, sometimes elaborately, sometimes matter-of-factly. The standard beginning of a Buddhist sutra, which tells of the wonderful teachings and miracles of the Buddha that make freedom, or *nirvāṇa,* accessible, is the following: "Thus have I heard. . . ." Many myths are interspersed with phrases such as "it is said that," or "they say." Part of the tradition of many a Hindu is that he reveres his spiritual teacher, who in turn has his teacher, and so on, until the line finally reaches God. Tradition requires that the entire list of names be recited regularly. Thus, the mere individual quite consciously elaborates on his relationship to the absolute divine ruler.

A fourth category of humor is Grotesque, a term not generally associated with sacred tradition. Yet it describes the most striking form of humor—in any tradition other than one's own. Some myths speak of worlds that were created before the present one, and that were failures. For instance, in the tradition of the Hill Saora in India, the first world was a world made of a resinous substance; in that world some brothers set up a still and made liquor. The liquor was not merely excellent, it was too excellent; when it flowed it burst into flames, and as a result the entire world burned up and sank back into the primordial ocean. We may also recall the snakes of the Ge in Brazil and the Hindu story of the churning of the ocean. Often, the grotesque is a matter of exaggerated attention to detail or measurement. Grotesqueness helps to emphasize the complete otherness of that time at the beginning of the world or that time on which all liberation, salvation, or bliss hinges.

Change and disappearance of mythical traditions? There is no doubt that myths change in the course of time. In addition, the spread of the great missionary religions, mainly Islam and Christianity, has no doubt contributed to the neglect and disappearance of many a mythological heritage. We are however far from a dependable assessment of the entire globe's mythological state at the present moment. We do know that the role of myths has been important in many periods in which large-scale religious change occurred, as it was in the conversion of Central Asia to Islam. The revision of the old myths by Muslim missionaries was not destructive but fruitful, and led to full acceptance of Islam.

HISTORY OF STUDY. Questions about religion, including the subject of myth, are undoubtedly older than recorded history, and hence a full history of the study of myths would have to begin a very long time ago, in that undatable period hidden from us in which religion originated. Explicit intellectual discussions on the subject are closer to us and have an important beginning with the ancient Greeks. Some of the standard methods of explaining myths owe their first formulation to the Greeks, so a rapid survey of mythology, in the sense of the study of myths, ought to commence with them. The concentrated intellectual discipline of a religio-historical study is, however, much more recent, not coming into its own until the early nineteenth century.

The classical world. Greek thinkers developed three modes of accounting for myth, each of which can be distinguished clearly. Each continued in the scholarship of later centuries. Hence, in Western civilization the Greek ideas on the subject of myth do not merely represent a start but form the roots that nourished systems devised by later scholars.

In the first place, allegorical explanations served to extract the meaning of myths for many thinkers in classical civilization. The text of myths was explained not by what it said literally but as depicting or concealing in poetic images a reality behind the text, if the text could only be properly understood. A good example may be found in the widely accepted interpretation in classical Greece of Homer's *Iliad* as intending not the physical involvement of the gods in the war that the epic describes but instead the inner human struggle between good and evil.

The allegorizing of myth has occurred all over the world and in many periods, often when texts or customs that could not be summarily dismissed are no longer understood or perhaps have taken on an offensive quality in a new age. Many of the well-known classical thinkers, beginning with Theagenes (seventh century BCE), Heracleitus (c. 540–480 BCE), Parmenides (born c. 515 BCE), Empedocles (c. 490–430 BCE), and including Plato (c. 429–347 BCE), employed allegorical explanations of myths. An interesting feature, not only surviving since the classical period but expanded into an elaborate system in nineteenth-century nature mythology, was the assumption that many myths could be read as allegorical accounts for natural phenomena.

Rational explanations of various sorts also occur throughout the classical texts. One of these which often strikes the modern reader as far ahead of its time is found in a famous fragment from Xenophanes (c. 560–478 BCE):

> Mortals suppose that the gods are born, and that they wear men's clothing and have human voice and body, . . . but if cattle or lions had hands, so as to paint with their hands and produce works of art as men do, they would paint their gods and give them bodies in form like their own, horses like horses, cattle like cattle.

We should see this passage in a proper perspective. Xenophanes, though we know him only from some fragments, must have had in common with the majority of classical thinkers the desire not merely to destroy prevalent assumptions by means of some rational analysis but to make room for a philosophy worthy of the name; in the case of Xenophanes this philosophical concern was to create a proper understanding of the idea of transcendence. There were some classical thinkers, nevertheless, who spent great effort to demonstrate the worthlessness of traditional myths. The eclectic Latin writer Cicero (106–43 BCE) is quite critical in this regard; and the Latin didactic poet Lucretius (c. 99–55 BCE) is very sharp in his rational criticism.

A manner of explaining myths called euhemerism is named for the Greek writer Euhemerus (c. 340–260 BCE). Euhemerus was not a philosopher or a scholar, but the author of an imaginative story in which the narrator tells of a voyage to an island in the east whose kings bestowed gifts of lasting cultural value (such as the calendar, granted by Ouranos in the tale) and were elevated to the status of gods by their grateful subjects. Hence *euhemerism* depicts divinities as mortals who came to be venerated because of their contributions to the human race. This interpretation was to have a life which no one could have foreseen, in the classical world and long thereafter.

The Christian world. With regard to mythology, the intellectual world of Christianity was in most respects an immediate continuation of the Greek. Allegorical and rational explanations as well as euhemeristic reasoning abounded for centuries. Nevertheless, especially in euhemerism, the apologists and church fathers introduced a change. Where the classical world told admiringly of men whose great exploits caused them to be worshipped as deities, the Christian world speaks of the gods of classical myth as mere men remembered because of their excessively evil deeds and vices. This change came about as result of a larger shift in orientation—one that Plato, Aristotle, or any of the ancient thinkers could never have foreseen. The new Christian world makes much of the distinction between true and false religion. For Christian thinkers, true and false religion was not simply a topic for discussion, as it had been for the ancients. The Christians believed that theirs was the true knowledge of God, and other traditions were seen as false and pagan. Thus pagan gods were not gods at all, but demonic beings.

This twist in euhemerism filled an intellectual need and was generally accepted. Nevertheless, during the Middle Ages a narrative tradition of many streams, akin to the euhemerism of the classics, also continued. Thus the Norse gods could be categorized by tracing them through stories of kinship from the heroes in the *Iliad* and ultimately linking them by the same procedure to the creation story in the book of Genesis.

The eighteenth century. The eighteenth century is the prelude to the modern study of myth. For the first time serious efforts were made to assess the discoveries by voyagers of the Renaissance. One very important assemblage of myth was collected by Jesuit missionaries in North America. Questions of revelation and of falsehood and truth raised in the Christian tradition were revived and given new, complex forms. In the work of Bernard Le Bovier de Fontenelle (1657–1757), old and new ideas intermingle. Like other authors of the period, he begins by assuming the factual reality of God's revelation in the Old Testament and speculating on the intellectual inability of other nations to accept that original knowledge. The new age is visible in his effort to show the similarity between myths found among American Indians and those of the ancient Greeks and in his view that the inability of those peoples to accept true religion reflected an intellectual childishness. The childishness of the ancient and so-called savage races becomes a standard image in many of the explanations that follow in the eighteenth and nineteenth centuries.

Fontenelle's most original idea, next to his insistence on comparing different pagans, is his inference that all peoples have the same mental disposition and that, as a result, comparable developments occur in different parts of the world. More clearly than Fontenelle, Charles de Brosses (1709–1777) makes a case for comparative studies and shows an interest in questions of origins that would characterize much of the scholarship of the next century. His studies led him to the conclusion that elements of West African religion in his time could explain Greek mythological conceptions. Hence, in his view, the study of later "savages" can reveal much about earlier traditions.

Besides an expanding knowledge of the world, an even more significant factor marked the eighteenth century and made it a watershed: the rationalism of the Enlightenment. This change within the history of philosophy made it possible to narrow down the narrative euhemeristic expositions into a principle of explanation. For the study of myths this new intellectual direction was of course a mixed blessing. The new mood demanded laws of causation rather than seeking the coherencies present in myths. Although the greatest legacy of the philosopher David Hume (1711–1776) is his critique of overconfidence in reason, his *Dialogues Concerning Natural Religion* (1779) contains many passages that typify the eighteenth-century obsession with definitions. De Brosses, who was certainly a man of the Enlightenment, made extensive use of Hume's ideas in his own work.

The Romantics. The Romantic movement that swept Europe and America had its strongest exponents in Germany, and the movement's influence on the study of myths, historical linguistics, and other related comparative studies such as art, law, and culture, was profound. Indeed, many of these disciplines were initiated under the Romantic influence. While the Enlightenment had sharpened the tools of the intellect in its resistance to the ancien régime politically and to the church religiously, the Romantic movement, without rejecting the Enlightenment's accomplishments, created a very different center of attention that can be captured by such words as *emotion, vision,* and *genius.* Emotion came to be seen as at least of equal importance to the rationalism of the previous age.

The theologian Friedrich Schleiermacher (1768–1834), who left his mark on all areas in the study of religion in the nineteenth century and beyond, was of the opinion that the divine, in itself ungraspable, was represented mythically; the mythical he explained as "a historical representation of the supra-historical." As was typical in the Romantic outlook, the emphasis fell on a vision of something eternal, not subject to the vicissitudes of history, yet expressed in history. The age that saw the Faustian creativity of Beethoven, the fully Romantic works of Mendelssohn, Chopin, Schubert, and Schumann, the writings of the young Goethe, Blake, and the German poets Friedrich Hölderlin and Novalis, as well as the paintings of Delacroix, Turner, and Théodore Géricault, saw also the philosophical creations of Georg Wilhelm Friedrich Hegel (1770–1831).

Hegel's thought was the first since late antiquity (most especially, that of the non-Christian Roman thinker Plotinus, 205–270 CE) to develop a system free from the Christian philosophical opposition between true and false religion. Another idealistic, Romantic philosopher, Friedrich Wilhelm Joseph von Schelling (1775–1854), wrote a philosophy of mythology centered on a totality of human vision. Johann Gottfried von Herder (1744–1803) was an important early Romantic, especially for his essays on poetry and mythology. During the Romantic period, many works of scholarly intent were written on symbolism and mythology. A few of these made a lasting mark, among them the writings of Karl Otfried Müller (1797–1840) and the brothers Jacob (1785–1863) and Wilhelm (1786–1859) Grimm.

Nineteenth-century evolutionism. Without the Romantic impulse, the astounding nineteenth-century scholarly achievements in mythology and religion would be inconceivable. In the nineteenth century much new data became available, through ethnology, archaeology, and the study of ancient and distant civilizations and their languages. Compiling dictionaries, constructing grammars, and investigating Indo-European linguistics all demanded an extraordinary effort, and this effort, whether among government administrators in the colonies acquired by Western powers, in the expansion of newly established missionary societies, in the laboratories of science, or in historians' scrutiny and classification of documents, owed its principal inspiration to the Romantic thinkers. The idea of evolution—of development from low to high, simple to complex—that became so enormously influential in nineteenth-century thought is inseparable from the Romantic movement, predating the influence of Charles Darwin's *On the Origin of Species by Means of Natural Selection* (1859) in the work of Hegel, and also the much more positivistic works of the English social theorist Herbert Spencer (1820–1903) and the French philosopher Auguste Comte (1798–1857).

The cumbersome examination of facts and their compilation united with a Romantic attitude is perhaps nowhere as clearly to be seen as in the person of the Vedic scholar F. Max Müller (1823–1900). In his theories on the origin and development of language and myth, Müller posits as a beginning a pure awe in human experience before nature—especially in viewing the dawn—which he thought he had documented in the Vedic hymns. He marshaled all his knowledge of ancient Indo-European languages and literatures as a basis for a theory that a "disease of language" accounts for the formation of misunderstandings, which are deposited in myths such as those of the Hindu Purāṇas. The finishing touch is provided by the general idea of evolution, according to which religions evolve to ever higher and purer forms.

Modern studies. The nineteenth century saw greater and greater complexity in materials available for study and the methods that could be employed. The achievements in the area of mythology by anthropologists, folklorists, psychologists, philologists, sociologists, and historians of religions were innumerable. Nevertheless, for a general intellectual orientation, it is possible and helpful to speak of variations on the theme which was set with the opposition and complementarity of rationalism and romanticism. And certainly in the study of myths the rationalists and the Romantics gave such a wide view of things that all later labors can sometimes seem like mere embellishments to their discussions. We can definitely speak about a constitutional or structural contrast between scholarly concerns for the problems and scholarly concerns for unity in the study of myths.

The earliest Romantics, in the 1770s, known in German literary history by their association with Sturm und Drang (storm and stress), can be understood in their opposition to the rationalism ushered in by the French philosophers. Even the influential ideas of Johann Gottfried von Herder concerning the origin of language and myths, composed in his ecstatic writings about nature, can be read for their reaction against an intellectualist attitude which prevailed in Herder's day. The growing Romantic movement, however, was not engaged in combating the progress the Enlightenment had brought about and so frequently invoked. The new expressions we find among such Romantics as Schleiermacher point more to a transformation than an opposition, allowing subjects such as myth and history to be approached in fruitful ways.

More extreme Romantic scholarly work, such as that by Georg Friedrich Creuzer (1771–1858), elicited stern criticism from Christian A. Lobeck (1781–1860) because of its speculative features, its lack of evidence. In F. Max Müller's work and, as we must infer, in his personal make-up, the rational and the Romantic existed harmoniously.

Since the late nineteenth century the non-Romantic side has predominated. Scholars such as the classicist Theodor Mommsen (1817–1903), Franz Cumont (1886–1949), and Martin P. Nilsson (1874–1967), who have contributed greatly to our knowledge of mythology, are splendid examples of this type. Fewer in number, scholars with an avowed Romantic outlook have included the German classicist Walter F. Otto (1874–1958) and the Dutch historian and phenomenologist of religion Gerardus van der Leeuw (1890–1950).

Sometimes the two attitudes are openly discussed, yet more often they are not. Whatever names are given to the two sides may not be accepted by one or the other party involved. Mircea Eliade preferred the term *morphology of religion* to *phenomenology,* which was employed by Van der Leeuw. Whichever term one likes, it is easy to see that in Eliade as well as Van der Leeuw the emphasis is on the sacred, and the study of its manifestations. This interest goes back to Rudolf Otto (1869–1937) and to Friedrich Schleiermacher. The reaction to this keen interest in the sacred itself is not difficult to detect, though it is multifarious. Many historians (such as Raffaele Pettazzoni) have been more concerned with a proper understanding of the variety of myths than with what seemed speculation on a unity behind the variety; such scholars have been suspicious of theologically inspired apologetic tendencies as well. Many an anthropologist, especially in the school of Franz Boas (1858–1942), has been too preoccupied with the puzzling coherencies of specific cultures in all their creations to pay much attention to an underlying ultimate significance of myths.

A generalization that can be made, with caution, is that the beginning of the third millennium seems characterized by a longing for unspeculative, concrete results.

An increasing number of studies have come to focus on the social and political aspects of religion and storytelling rather than on ultimate meanings of myths. Together with this focus goes a decreased interest in philosophical aspects of religion. This tendency might make the study of myth in days to come different from what characterized previous eras in mythology and the history of religions.

The occurrence of problems and disagreements in the study of myth and religion is of course nothing to be unduly worried about. What we have referred to as an opposition/complementarity is a natural feature in any discipline concerned with people and their cultures and societies. Next to structural anthropology, historical anthropology makes its voice heard. Whereas the former, if not concerned with an ultimate unity, is at the very least concerned with coherencies in myths and other human creations, the latter spends more time on the specificities and changes in any culture. An issue that has received no profound discussion is the difference, or rather, lack of contact, between the search for unity pursued by phenomenologists (or morphologists) and by structuralist anthropologists. That both are searching for coherencies in myths is clear, yet the nature of a unifying goal is assumed in two very different manners. The choice of rationalism and romanticism as labels may be helpful in this case, yet they are not telling us the whole story.

It is striking, however, that Eliade's conception of the sacred is missing in the work of the field's foremost anthropological structuralist, Claude Lévi-Strauss (born 1908); instead, Lévi-Strauss shows an obvious interest in the very visible yet long overlooked, typically human, ceaseless drive to reconcile empirical knowledge with the equally human drive for control over the world. Translators like to leave the term *bricolage* untranslated; it is the term Lévi-Strauss uses to describe the widespread process at work all over the world in tribal traditions to build up knowledge; the closest equivalent in English is *tinkering*. Lévi-Strauss is a gifted author and wrote several books that present not only his theories, but the living context in which his theories developed. No doubt his early philosophical interest accounts for the fact that his theories on structuralism are so well thought-out. A voracious reader, he was also well aware of the use of the term *structuralism* in other fields of study before he himself adopted it. Its use was common in anthropology, and Lévi-Strauss repeatedly makes reference to the work of the Dutch structuralist anthropologist J. P. B. Josselin de Jong, and contributed to a book in his honor. In his perhaps most autobiographical and certainly most eminently readable book, *Tristes Tropiques: An Anthropological Study of Primitive Societies in Brazil,* he writes most directly about his impatience with the disorder in the still rather recent study of anthropology. In *The Savage Mind* he writes with fervor and with obvious delight about the knowledge fostered in "primitive" societies.

The knowledge that the then-traditional practice in anthropology, with its emphasis on the supposedly primitive or even savage elements it perceived among the natives was in fact the science of the concrete. It seems likely that Lévi-Strauss sees in the science of the concrete, built up through a tinkering process, something that is not all that far away from the good French scientific, sober, rationalist tradition, not only of Descartes, but also with a taste of Auguste Comte.

The absence of any notion of the sacred in Claude Lévi-Strauss's work cannot be ignored. In *Tristes Tropiques* Lévi-Strauss writes about his youthful experiences during World War I in the house of his grandfather, who was the rabbi in Versailles. The corridor leading from the house to the synagogue had to be negotiated in absolute silence. It seems obvious that for him "the sacred" retained a tone he had difficulty with. At the time, he says, "I was already an unbeliever." An unbeliever at the age of nine or ten? He relates this to the experience of amazement he would have later in Buddhist temples where monks slept in the same room where services were held and did not mind caressing their pupils between lessons in the alphabet. In the same work he refers disdainfully to the philosophy as taught in France in his student years as "mental gymnastics."

Dutch anthropologist J. van Baal, who served as the last governor of Dutch New Guinea, learned much from J. P. B. Josselin de Jong, who was one of his teachers, and was himself a splendid observer of various societies in Southeast Asia and their ceremonial interactions. As an administrator, he was less given to theoretical expositions than Claude Lévi-Strauss. At the same time, like other structuralists, he was hesitant to attribute "reality" to religion, yet was not averse to dealing with great problems in society. In 1972 he published a small, very interesting book, *De boodschap der drie illusies* (The message of the three illusions). The illusions are respectively religion, art, and the element of play in all human culture. No human society exists without these three, van Baal suggests, yet they do not have the reality of a concept like physics.

MYTHS AND THE MODERN WORLD. Myths and mythmaking have certainly not disappeared from the modern world. That notion, still rather popular, was fostered by nineteenth-century evolutionists who posited a decline of religion as part of some general world-wide progression. The process of history does not give up its most basic constituents, including its mythological creativity, because prevailing ideas change. The fact that in common parlance the word *myth* has a derogatory meaning has no bearing on the issue. Antiquity was already familiar with that same use of the term. The apostle Paul is among those on record as despisers of mere myths. Two religions of India, Buddhism and Jainism, have expressed strong misgivings about prevailing religious ideas, and these misgivings are another kind of depreciation of myths. Myths have continued to flourish, however, and the misgivings of any given religion, religious grouping, or age do not change that fact today any more than in the past.

In entering upon the study of myths, we should quickly reject the illusion that we are entitled to speak of the mythology, in the sense of the entire body of myths, of any group, whether they be ancient Mesopotamians or an African people or the citizens of the United States of America. In none of these cases are we ever looking objectively at a total belief system. We are never in a position to do so. All we have before us are at best good selections by a scholar or a good sampling by a field worker. The availability of a collection in print between two covers does not make our position that of an objective observer readying himself for complete understanding. We look only at a fragment in time and place. The nature, structure, and style of myths points not merely to the existence of bodies of material, but to living traditions. The humor in myths changes in time, together with everything else in history, but it also indicates a universal human propensity. The erroneous idea that our own world is largely devoid of myths or is rapidly purified of such things rests largely on the assumption that our world, in whatever way that term is defined, is real and does not depend on fiction. Every age, however, and every civilization, rests on a foundation of mythic fictions. The philosopher Alphonse de Waelhens, in Castelli, *Mythe et Foi,* has rightly pointed out that we are able to see quite clearly the outline of a myth only after that myth has ceased to function unassailed and unquestioned, that is to say, as an expression of supposed reality.

In our own world, we lack the distance necessary for clear views of our own myths, and the question of which ones will stand out as central can be discussed seriously only by later generations. These future scholars also will have to make up their minds on the basis of fragmentary information, just as our scholarship must always remain conscious of the inadequacy of our information about mythology in ancient Mesopotamia or present-day Iran, or the nineteenth-century myths of evolutionism, materialism, missionary optimism, colonialism, or Marxism. Our own world with respect to its mythology is completed by the manner in which we orient ourselves not only within our transcendencies, but also vis-à-vis other people in our endeavors to define and interpret their myths. This, one might say, concludes our circle of interpretation.

The Danish thinker Søren Kierkegaard (1813–1855) once conjured up the image of a man with his mouth so full of food that he could not swallow. Kierkegaard raised the question of whether one might better help that man by stuffing more food into his mouth or by taking some out. Obviously, only the latter could be a solution. In the same way, Kierkegaard argued, a man can be so filled with information, which he mistakes for useful knowledge, that even in the face of his own protests and his insistence on adding even more to his store of learning, the only cure is to take some of that knowledge away. This is the task Kierkegaard assigned himself in using the comical to make the overburdened man see the uselessness of what he knew. Kierkegaard's parable is a perfect illustration of the unceasing propensity toward myth-making in modern times and, at the same time, of the need for the mature intellect to occupy itself with the issue of mythology.

Endeavors to explain religion (or explain it away) have been a by-product of culture since antiquity, if not earlier. In the nineteenth century such endeavors were part of Marxism, and they became part of the educational curriculum in the twentieth-century Soviet Union and People's Republic of China. The trend in this direction is actually part of life in all industrial nations. Claude Lévi-Strauss dismisses religion, and yet he also makes efforts to understand myths scientifically, that is to say, in a way that as objectively as possible makes sense out of them. Several scholars have objected to the dismissal of religion, among them anthropologists such as Adam Kuper and Clifford Geertz. Nevertheless, the modern aversion to scholars like Rudolf Otto, who emphasized the religious experience as the key element in religion, is much more general, and certainly affects notable historians of religions as well.

An adequate assessment of the present-day situation in the study of myths would require extraordinary talent. It is, however, not easy to avoid one impression: the study of religion and religions has not been flourishing in recent times, and—with notable exceptions—no longer has a strong basis in linguistics and philology, the traditional basis of the history of religions.

See Also African Religions, article on Mythic Themes; Australian Indigenous Religions, article on Mythic Themes; Cargo Cults; Chinese Religion: Mythic Themes; Cosmogony; Euhemerus and Euhemerism; Humor and Religion; Indian Religions, article on Mythic Themes; Intuition; Japanese Religions, article on The Study of Myths; Logos; Mesoamerican Religions, article on Mythic Themes; Millenarianism, overview article; Myth and Ritual School; North American Indian Religions, article on Mythic Themes; South American Indian Religions, article on Mythic Themes; Structuralism.

Bibliography

Andrews, James T. *Science for the Masses: The Bolshevik State, Public Science, and the Popular Imagination in Soviet Russia, 1917–1934.* College Station, Tex., 2003.

Asimov, Isaac, George Zebrowski, and Martin H. Greenberg, eds. *Creations: The Quest for Origins in Story and Science.* New York, 1983. Useful reading for students of myth, reminding us at the very least of the complexities in the exact sciences in telling us of the origins of the universe.

Baal, J. van. *Dema: Description and Analysis of Marind-anim Culture.* The Hague, 1966.

Baumann, Hermann. "Mythos in ethnologischer Sicht." *Studium Generale* (1959): 1–17, 583–597.

Beemer, Margaret Anne. *Godly Interchange: The Appropriation of Non-Christian Symbols in the Development of Christianity in Spain and the Valley of Mexico.* Ann Arbor, Mich., 1988.

Bell, Catherine. *Ritual Theory, Ritual Practice.* New York, 1992.

Bianchi, Ugo. *The History of Religions.* Leiden, 1975.

Blair, Sheila S., and Jonathan M. Bloom. *The Art and Architecture of Islam 1250–1800.* New Haven, Conn., 1994.

Bolle, Kees W. "The Myth of Our Materialism." In *Religion and Politics in the Modern World,* edited by Peter H. Merkl and Ninian Smart. New York, 1983. "Few things are as exclusively 'material' as they seem" might sum up the essay.

Bolle, Kees W. "Myths and Other Religious Texts." In *Contemporary Approaches to the Study of Religion,* vol. 1, edited by Frank Whaling. Berlin, 1984. Surveys the study of myths since World War II and includes an extensive bibliography.

Bolle, Kees W. *The Freedom of Man in Myth.* Nashville, 1993. Deals with myth and mysticism and tries to show the presence and importance of humor in religion.

Bolle, Kees W. *The Enticement of Religion.* Notre Dame, Ind., 2002. Concentrates on the basics of religion, and evidence found in places or things, in acts (rituals, things done), and in words (myths). The author feels justified in extending this view to society and politics as well as poetry. In fact, he leaves little space for wholly non-religious things.

Bottéro, Jean. *Mesopotamia: Writing, Reasoning, and the Gods.* Chicago, 1992. Of special importance for its treatment of the mythology of death.

Bottéro, Jean. *The Birth of God: The Bible and the Historian.* University Park, Pa., 2000.

Bottéro, Jean, and Samuel Noah Kramer. *Lorsque les dieux faisaient l'homme: Mythologie mésopotamienne.* Paris, 1989.

Broda, Johanna, Davíd Carrasco, and Eduardo Matos Moctezuma. *The Great Temple of Tenochtitlan: Center and Periphery in the Aztec World.* Berkeley, Calif., 1987.

Castelli, Enrico, ed. *Mythe et Foi.* Paris, 1966. See especially "Le mythe de la démythification" by Alphonse de Waelhens.

DeWeese, Devin. *Islamization and Native Religion in the Golden Horde: Baba Tükles and Conversion to Islam in Historical and Epic Tradition.* University Park, Pa., 1994.

Dundes, Alan, ed. *Sacred Narrative.* Berkeley, Calif., 1984. An illuminating collection of studies on mythology.

Eliade, Mircea. Most of Mircea Eliade's books are relevant to the study of myth: *Birth and Rebirth* (Chicago, 1958) deals with initiation ceremonies and their myths; *From Primitives to Zen* (New York, 1967) presents a wide selection of mythological materials; *Myths, Dreams, and Mysteries* (New York, 1961) discusses myth, psychoanalysis, and relations between myths and modern society; *Myth and Reality* (New York, 1963) sums up the author's main ideas on myths, their structure, and their continuation in modern times; *The Myth of the Eternal Return* (rev. ed., New York, 1965), also published under the title *Cosmos and History* (New York, 1959), deals with the problem of mythical time and history.

Feldman, Burton, and Robert D. Richardson, eds., *The Rise of Modern Mythology, 1680–1860.* Bloomington, Ind., 1972. Excellent summaries of scholarly interpretations of myths together with representative excerpts.

Geertz, Clifford. *The Interpretation of Cultures: Selected Essays.* New York, 1973. Geertz is a master of common sense. *The Interpretation of Cultures* reflects on the sense of various interpretive systems dealing with cultures, including the ideas of Claude Lévi-Strauss, as well as on his own findings in Indonesia.

Ginzberg, Louis. *Legends of the Bible.* Philadelphia, 1956.

Gray, Louis H., and George Foot Moore, eds. *Mythology of All Races.* 13 vols. Boston, 1916–1932. Though dated in some of its discussions, still one of the best collections of myths available in English.

Griaule, Marcel. *Dieu d'eau. Entretiens avec Ogotemmêli.* Paris, 1948. The religious world of the Dogon takes on clear, often unexpectedly philosophical form. Ralph Butler, Audrey I. Richards, and Beatrice Hooke created a very good translation entitled *Conversations with Ogotemmêli: An Introduction to Dogon Religious Ideas.* London, 1965.

Gusdorf, Georges. *Mythe et Métaphysique.* Paris, 1953. This French philosopher deals explicitly with the relationship between philosophy and myth.

Haber, Howard E., and Gordon L. Kane. "Is Nature Supersymmetric?" *Scientific American 254* (June 1986). A lucid description of a problem of physics, this essay is also illuminating in its implications for the use of ordinary words, suggesting comparisons with mythological language. For an equally suggestive example from developments in biochemistry, see Marc Lappe's *Broken Code.*

Jaspers, Karl. *Truth and Symbol.* New York, 1959. Still one of the most concise philosophical discussions of the symbolic nature of language and inquiry.

Jensen, Adolf E., ed. *Mythe, Mensch, und Umwelt.* New York, 1978. A reprint of a special volume of the journal *Paideuma* (vol. 4, 1950). Contains an important collection of essays by various specialists about myths and their environment in nonliterate and classical traditions. Among the important contributions are essays by the Africanist Hermann Baumann, the ethnologist Martin Gusinde, the classicists Walter F. Otto and Franz Altheim, and, among other students of classical civilizations, the Indologist Hermann Lommel and the Americanists Walter Krickeberg and Hermann Trimborn.

Jung, Carl G., and Karl Kerenyi. *Essays on a Science of Mythology.* Princeton, N.J., 1969. This work is important because of Kerenyi's interpretations of classical mythical themes; it presents at the same time an introduction to Jung's psychological approach.

Kuhn, Thomas S. *The Structure of Scientific Revolutions.* 2d ed. Chicago, 1970. Both this book and his *The Essential Tension* (Chicago, 1979), although without explicit reference to myths, provide insights into the change of science within its historical and social environs.

Kuper, Adam. *Anthropology and Anthropologists.* London, 1993. A critical assessment of anthropological achievement in England and elsewhere. Critical of Claude Lévi-Strauss.

Langer, Suzanne K. *Philosophy in a New Key: A Study in the Symbolism of Reason, Rite, and Art.* 3rd ed. Cambridge, Mass., 1957. One of the superb classics in the study of symbolism.

Lappe, Marc. *Broken Code: The Exploitation of DNA.* San Francisco, 1984.

Leeuw, Gerardus van der. *Religion in Essence and Manifestation: A Study in Phenomenology.* New York, 1963. This is the best known work by the principal founder of the phenomenology of religion. See also his "Primordial Time and Final Time," in *Man and Time,* edited by Joseph Campbell. New York, 1959.

Lévi-Strauss, Claude. *Structural Anthropology,* translated by Claire Jacobson and Brooke Grundfest Schoepf. New York, 1963; *Introduction to a Science of Mythology,* translated by John and Doreen Weightman. New York, 1969: vol. 1, *The Raw and the Cooked;* vol. 2, *From Honey to Ashes;* vol. 3, *The Origin of Table Manners;* vol. 4, *The Naked Man;* Claude Lévi-Strauss. *Tristes Tropiques: An Anthropological Study of Primitive Societies in Brazil,* translated by John Russell. New York, 1964.

Lévi-Strauss, Claude, and Didier Eribon. *Conversations with Claude Lévi-Strauss,* translated by Paula Wissing. Chicago, 1991.

Lincoln, Bruce. *Priests, Warriors, and Cattle: A Study in the Ecology of Religions.* Berkeley, Calif., 1981; *Emerging from the Chrysalis: Rituals of Women's Initiation.* New York, 1991; *Death, War, and Sacrifice.* Chicago, 1991; *Theorizing Myth: Narrative, Ideology, and Scholarship.* Chicago, 1999; *Holy Terrors: Thinking About Religion After September 11.* Chicago, 2003. Without any harmful intention in mind, I believe one could sum up the strength of Lincoln's work not merely by the solidity of his dealings with sources, the evidence on which all worthwhile study should rest, but also with a term such as *fiery justice.* Hence he does not deal only with matters of the past, but is attracted to great issues of the present. Even if one is not always certain whether he takes religious data wholly seriously, the sense of justice he brings to bear on all issues, especially political ones, is unmistakable.

Long, Charles H. *Alpha: The Myths of Creation.* New York, 1963. Long was one of the first doctoral students of Eliade. In this work, more than elsewhere, he is also closest to his master. In *Significations: Signs, Symbols, and Images in the Interpretation of Religion* (Philadelphia, 1986), one sees a greater interest in the role of myth and other forms of religious symbolism in their relation to historical and social problems than Eliade ever displayed.

Maquet, Jacques. *The Aesthetic Experience: An Anthropologist Looks at the Visual Arts.* New Haven, Conn., 1986. Illuminates the evidence of beauty as a universal feature in human existence.

Maranda, Pierre, ed. *Mythology.* Baltimore, 1972. An anthology of various schools in the study of myths, with special attention to structuralism.

Merleau-Ponty, Jacques, and Bruno Morando. *The Rebirth of Cosmology.* New York, 1976. A discussion between a philosopher and a scientist; of interest for a modern understanding of the *raison d'être* of mythology.

Nilsson, Martin P. *Geschichte der griechischen Religion,* 2 vols. 2d ed.; Munich, 1955. Splendid, indeed classical work on ancient Greek religion.

Orzech, Charles D. *Politics and Transcendent Wisdom: The Scripture for Humane Kings in the Creation of Chinese Buddhism.* University Park, Pa., 1998. Of great significance in understanding the rarely discussed relationship between Buddhism and politics.

Pettazoni, Raffaele. *Essays on the History of Religions.* Leiden, the Netherlands, 1954. Of special significance for its essays "The Truth of Myth," and "Myths of Beginnings and Creation Myths." See also his four-volume *Miti e Leggende* (Turin, 1948–1959). Geographically organized, it is the most representative collection of myths in nonliterate traditions from the entire world.

Plessner, Hellmuth. "Elemente menschlichen Verhaltens." *Merkur* 15 (1961): 603–614.

Schneider, Laurence. *Biology and Revolution in Twentieth Century China.* Lanham, Md., 2003. This work seems almost a companion volume to the work by James T. Andrews mentioned above. Both in Soviet Russia and Communist China religion was imagined to disappear under the evidence and weight of modern science, but it did not happen. It is useful to point out that neither work, in spite of its historical accuracy, tells us very much about the strength of specific religious traditions in Russia or China.

Sebeok, Thomas A., ed. *Myth: A Symposium.* Bloomington, Ind., 1955. Presents nine scholars' divergent views on myths.

Smith, Jonathan Z. *Map Is Not Territory: Studies in the History of Religions.* Chicago, 1978; *Imagining Religion: From Babylon to Jonestown.* Chicago, 1982; *Drudgery Divine: On the Comparison of Early Christianities and the Religions of Late Antiquity.* Chicago, 1990. Most of Smith's books are collections of essays, but each has a special theme, and each one is a challenge to the reader, and as a rule sheds a new light on the interpretation of a myth or a specific religious problem. And at the very least, each essay shows a new difficulty to the reader.

Thompson, Stith. *Motif-Index of Folk-Literature.* 6 vols. Rev. ed.; Helsinki, 1955–1958. In the tradition of folklore studies; it does not make a sharp distinction between myths and other forms of folk literature. For the complexity of differences between genres, see also his *The Folktale* (Berkeley, 1977) and his essay "Myth and Folktales" in *The History of a Myth: Pacariqtambo and the Origin of the Inkas,* edited by Gary Urton (Austin, Tex., 1990).

Vries, Jan de. *Perspectives in the History of Religions.* Berkeley, 1977. Concentrates on the study of myths in the history of Western thought since classical antiquity.

Wach, Joachim. *Religionswissenschaft.* Leipzig, 1924. Of no direct interest to the study of myths, but of lasting importance for its discussion of the problem of false objectivity in the study of religious phenomena.

KEES W. BOLLE (1987 AND 2005)

MYTH: MYTH AND HISTORY

At first glance, myth and history appear to be complete opposites. To be sure, they are both narratives, that is to say, arrangements of events into unified stories, which can then be recounted. But myth is a narrative of origins, taking place in a primordial time, a time other than that of everyday reality; history is a narrative of recent events, extending progressively to include events that are further in the past but that are, nonetheless, situated in human time.

This initial definition, however, calls for a series of qualifying remarks that reveal a network of more complex relations in the place of this stark opposition. Let us first consider the fact that our very model of myth has come down to us from the stories of the gods in ancient Greece. Furthermore, a transition from myth to history can be seen in the

Greek myths themselves, as they extend to include the history of heroes and the histories of ancestors. These are more properly termed legendary narratives, unfolding in a time lying between the time of origins and that of recent events. History will encroach on this legendary time, extending its grasp to include an ever more distant past.

An even more significant intersection between myth and history has been brought to light through the extension, familiar from contemporary anthropology, of the notion of myth to types of narrative that are extremely widespread in contemporary archaic societies. These narratives are characterized by being anonymous, and so without any determinant origin. They are received through tradition and accepted as credible by all the members of the group, with no guarantee of authenticity other than the belief of those who transmit them. History will mark an "epistemological break" with this mode of transmission and reception, but only after an evolution involving many intermediate stages, as we shall see later.

A source of even more serious conflict between myth and history, and therefore also an occasion for more complex forms of transition or compromise, has to do with the object of myth itself, which we temporarily designated as a narrative of origins. The concern with origins extends far beyond the history of gods, heroes, and ancestors. The questions pertaining to the origins of things extend to all the entities of individual and social life. Thus myths can reply to any of the following types of question. How did a particular society come to exist? What is the sense of this institution? Why does this event or that rite exist? Why are certain things forbidden? What legitimizes a particular authority? Why is the human condition so miserable; why do we suffer and die? Myth replies to these questions by recounting how these things began. It recounts the creation of the world and the appearance of humans in their present physical, moral, and social condition. With myth therefore we are dealing with a very particular type of explanation, which will maintain a complex relation to history. This type of explanation essentially consists in myth's foundational function: the myth recounts founding events. Its tie and subsequent conflict with history result from this function. On the one hand, myth exists only when the founding event has no place in history but is situated in a time before all history: *in illo tempore,* to borrow Mircea Eliade's now classic expression. On the other hand, what is at stake in any such foundation is to relate our own time to this other time, whether this be in the form of participation, imitation, decadence, or abandonment. It is precisely this relation between our time and the time of the myth that is the essential factor constituting the myth, rather than the types of things founded by it, whether the latter include the whole of reality—the world—or a fragment of reality—an ethical rule, a political institution, or even the existence of man in a particular condition, fallen or innocent.

In the light of this brief phenomenology of myth, it appears that the relation of myth to history can be situated on three different levels. In a limited, narrow sense, myth and history are two different kinds of narrative. Myth is a narrative concerning the origin of everything that can worry, frighten, or surprise us. History, on the other hand, is a precise literary genre, namely the writing of history or historiography. Taken in this strict sense, history can enter into a variety of relations with myth; history's own origin from myth is not the only such relation. The genetic point of view must not blind us to other possible viewpoints. If, as we shall see, history does not necessarily take the place of myth but may exist alongside it within the same culture, together with other types of narrative, then the question of the relation between myth and historiography must be approached from the perspective of a classification of the various kinds of narratives that are produced by a particular society at a particular moment. The genetic and taxonomical perspectives must each be allowed both to complement and to limit the exclusive claims of the other.

As a backdrop to this well-defined problem a vaster one arises, related to a second meaning of the term *history.* History is not only a literary product; it is also what men do or suffer. Many languages preserve these two meanings of their word for "history": history (or story) as the narrative of the events of the past, and history as the whole of these events themselves, as human beings make them or are affected by them. Beyond the question of the writing of history is the question of how a given culture interprets its historical mode of existence. A number of problems arise in this connection. How, for instance, is the stability or change affecting a culture's mores or institutions perceived? What value is attributed to it? Does change itself have meaning? That is to say, is change at once meaningful and directed toward an end, or is it incoherent, given to disorder, chance, and meaninglessness? And, if there is a sense to it, is it an improvement, a form of progress, or a degeneration, a decadence?

To move from the first sense of *history* to the second is not difficult. The writing of history as an essentially literary activity is after all one of the ways a society accounts for its own past. It inevitably leads to the more general question of the sense that that society ascribes to its own historical development. This interrelationship between history as literary activity and history as lived experience gives a new meaning to the question of the relation between history and myth. Myth, to the extent that it is defined by its foundational role, can function to ascribe a positive or negative value to history in general, to the extent that the latter is understood as a mode of human existence.

When dealing with myth and history at this level, we must avoid the temptation to engage in simplistic oppositions between types of civilizations or to employ genetic interpretations that are overly linear. A single society may in fact have both myths of decadence and myths of progress, whether in different epochs or in the same period. This competition of myths may express the uncertainty that a society experiences concerning the meaning of the changes that it undergoes. Furthermore, in a given culture, historiography may be intended to provide only partial explanations that make no claim to be comprehensive, while the broader question of the meaning of history is left to legends and myths. As a result, two cultures may differ as to their most fundamental myths and yet present striking similarities in both the techniques and goals of their historiography. This was true of the Greeks and Hebrews, as will be shown below.

Finally, in the background of the question of the meaning of history, we find the question of a society's interpretation of the time in which its history—and all history—unfolds. This third question is implicit in the two preceding ones. In the first place, historiography can be defined as the narrative of human actions in the past. Since this interest in the past is inseparable from an interest in the present and from expectations about the future, historiography necessarily includes in its definition a reference to time. It is knowledge of societies and people in time.

This reference to time cannot help but affect the first and second senses of *history:* both the meaning that a class of literati gives to the act of writing history and the meaning that a particular society gives to its history through narrative activity imply a specific perception of time. The evaluation of time may even become the object of reflection, or it may remain implicit, in much the same way that change may be evaluated positively or negatively. It is at this level that the so-called cyclical and linear conceptions of time oppose one another.

The question of the supposed opposition between cyclical and linear conceptions of time is a thorny one. To begin with, it is not certain that the notion of cyclical time has but one meaning. In addition to the paradigmatic case of the periodical regeneration of time by specific rites, there are many other ways of conceiving the periodical return of the same situations and the same events; a number of periodicities are to be distinguished here. Nor is it certain that the notion of linear time was clearly perceived as a global alternative to that of cyclical time before modern astronomy and cosmology or the even more recent ideologies of progress. Last but not least, a single culture can give rise to contrary myths concerning the cyclical or linear character of time. This is part of the uncertainty that a particular society may foster concerning its own historical condition and that of the human race as a whole. Then too, the culture that produces myths of cyclical time or of linear time may also produce a historiography that is deliberately developed outside of this framework, limiting its scope to restricted temporal segments that can be inserted in either of those versions of time. For these reasons, the problem of the apparent split between cyclical and linear time should not be tackled head-on. Instead, this debate should be carried on within the horizon of the two preceding investigations.

Ancient Greece. To guide us in this problem, it will be helpful to take as our reference the relations between myth and history in ancient Greece. In the cultural sphere of the ancient Near East and the Mediterranean, they alone—along with ancient Israel—produced a historiography worthy of the name. In addition, the variety of the relations that this production maintained with myth (a Greek term if ever there was one!) permits us to verify the extreme complexity of the problem and the validity of the three-stage model that we have just suggested.

If we adhere to the definition of history as historiography, then history's relation to myth is determined in its essential features by the birth of a type of knowledge and a type of discourse (prose narrative) that make a series of decisive breaks with the mythical mode of thought and with its privileged mode of literary expression, versified poetry. The earliest witness that we have to history's break with myth was provided by Herodotos in the middle of the fifth century BCE, whose work stands as a literary landmark. Its title—*Historiē* in the Ionian dialect—has ever since determined not only the name of the discipline that he inaugurated but also the principal meaning of this term, namely investigation. These "histories" are in fact investigations into the causes of the wars fought between the Greeks and the Persians. Unlike myths of origin and heroic tales situated in distant times, the histories of Herodotos are concerned with recent events. Herodotos was interested in the causal role of antecedent events and in the role of responsible agents in the events that he investigated. His writings are thus far more than mere descriptions. They are expressions of a mode of thinking that characterizes what has been called the Ionic Enlightenment and so take their place within a vaster ensemble of investigations into cosmology, geography, and ethnography. They find their speculative equivalent in philosophy as such, where *phusis*, a term we translate as "nature," constitutes at once the field of exploration and the key word. In Ionian philosophy the notion of *archē* in the sense of "principle" decisively splits off from *arche* in the sense of "beginning." This bifurcation of the notion of origin is of great importance for the understanding of the separation of history from myth.

The epistemological break with myth that marks the emergence of history, geography, ethnology, cosmology, and the philosophy of nature does not entitle us to represent the process as simply genetic and linear, however. This would be to overlook the intermediate stages that exist in the transition from myth to history, as well as the continued dependence of the new mode of thought on the earlier mythical mode. In addition, we would thereby overlook the simultaneous existence of several different types of narrative within the same culture.

In contrast to a simplistic representation of the "Greek miracle," we should be attentive instead to this phenomenon of transition, which preserves a sense of the different elements that went to make up the "event" of the Ionic Enlightenment. Herodotos was in fact preceded by an entire series of prose writers who paved the way for him. The most important of these was certainly Hecataeus of Miletus, whom we know only through a few surviving quotations. Already in the second half of the sixth century, this prose writer was the author of a *periēgēsis,* a realistic account of a voyage around the world that relates history to geography, cartography, and ethnology, and of the *Genealogies,* which constructed the great family tree of the heroic age. The break between myth and history did not, therefore, take place all at once, but only gradually. Herodotos's *Histories* themselves did not cut every tie with the stories of the heroic age, as can be seen from his attempts at a general chronology dating back to the Trojan War. And if Herodotos was concerned so specifically with the Persian Wars, this was because, in his opinion, they deserved to be reported as much as had the Trojan War. Finally, the epic dimension of Herodotos's work, which allows him to preserve the chronological and analogical ties between heroic and historical times, must be attributed to the influence of the versified epic of Homer.

The twofold relation of break and filiation between myth and history on the level of narrative form becomes clearer when we consider the end or goal assigned to this new kind of literature. Here we move from the first to the second senses of *history.* The end that Herodotos assigned to his investigations can be found in the prologue of the *Histories:* "Here are set forth the researches (*historiē*) of Herodotos of Halicarnassus, that men's actions may not be forgotten, nor things great and wonderful, whether accomplished by Greeks or barbarians, go without report, nor especially the causes (*aītiē*) of the wars between one and another."

Three features of this prefatory remark deserve emphasis. The struggle against forgetfulness is cited first; later we shall discuss the conception of time that is implied here. It is then to the great deeds of the Greeks and the barbarians that this exercise of memory is applied. The very notion of great deeds marks a tie with the epic of the age of heroes, even though it is being applied here to recent times. But, in particular, this cult of memory binds history to the self-understanding that a people acquires by giving an account of its past. The memory that history cultivates is therefore that of a people taken as a single body. In this way, history takes its place within the body of traditions that together constitute what could be called the narrative identity of a culture. To be sure, it does this within a critical mode that is entirely different from mythical traditions, since the latter draw their authority from the very act of transmitting the immemorial. But the opposition between the critical mode of historiography introduced here by Herodotos and the authoritative mode of the reception of myth in Homer occurs within the larger phenomenon of tradition: the poet and the man of letters are united within the single great melting pot of culture.

The third feature of Herodotos's project points in the same direction: the object of his research is to discover the cause of an essentially conflictual event, namely the Persian Wars. These wars not only served to oppose Greek and barbarian but fundamentally threatened a whole configuration of peoples, just as the Trojan War had done in heroic times. This is the major crisis for which history now seeks a cause. By attributing this cause to a responsible agent, the *Histories* give an ethical coloration to the entire course of events, which at the same time attests to a striking kinship between history and tragedy. It was the *hubris* of Cresus that endangered the harmony of a people, and even the victory of the Greeks appears as a retribution (*tisis*) that reestablishes this lost harmony. In this way, a certain divine justice is effected by the course of events. One cannot help thinking here of a fragment from Anaximander: "for (existing things) pay penalty and retribution to each other for their injustice according to the assessment of Time." This fragment displays a manner of thinking halfway between myth and what, with the Sophists, Socrates, and Plato, will be termed *sophia* ("wisdom").

From this threefold analysis we can see that the passage from myth to history cannot be reduced to the mere substitution of the latter for the former. In competition with this linear evolution, we must make room for an accumulation of literary genres and the modes of thinking related to them: theogonic myths written in the style of scholarly and literary mythology, myths of the heroic age cast in the literary mode of the epic and of tragedy, and, finally, history. So little did history replace myth that Plato still wages war against myths in his dialogues, though not without including here and there some *palaios logos* received from the Orphic tradition or from alleged Egyptian wisdom. What is more, he invents certain myths himself, in the form of philosophical tales.

A third problem now remains. This is the problem of the representation of time that underlies history, a problem that forms the backdrop to the debate between history and myth. If Greek historiography holds some importance in this area, it is less in relation to the so-called opposition between cyclical time and linear time than to the dividing line between the time of the gods and the time of men.

With respect to the debate concerning the Greeks' supposed opposition of cyclical and linear conceptions of time, opened by Thorleif Boman in *Hebrew Thought Compared with Greek* (1960), it is clear that historiography not only does not provide any confirmation of the thesis that holds Hellenism to be massively in favor of a cyclical conception of time but in fact refuses to take either side. As Arnaldo Momigliano stresses, to the extent that Herodotos concentrates his attention on a limited segment of history, he is entirely unaware of an historical cycle, much less an eternal return. Of course, he believes that there are forces operating in history, forces that are ordinarily tied to the intervention of the gods in human life, which become visible only at the end of a long chain of events. Such was the *hubris* against which Solon warned. Nothing, however, indicates that these interventions attest to a cyclical time. Herodotos "attributed to the Persian War a unique, non-cyclical significance, chiefly as a conflict between free men and slaves" (Momigliano, 1977, p. 187).

It is instead to the second problem, that of the split between the time of the gods and the time of men, that the earliest Greek historiography makes the most decisive contribution. The comparison with Homer, Hesiod, and the tragedians is instructive here. In Homer, the little substance that human time takes on is due still to the family tie that unites most of the heroes to the gods. In order to evoke these heroic times ordinary memory is not enough: it is not a mere literary convention when in book 2 of the *Iliad* (lines 484–487), the poet asks the Muses, the daughters of Memory (Mnemosyne), to guide him through the confusion of human time and space. "And now, tell me, Muses, dwelling on Olympus, for you are indeed goddesses: present everywhere, you know all things; we hear only noises, we ourselves know nothing. Tell me who were the guides, the leaders of the Danaans?" It is because time is utter confusion for the human observer that the poet calls upon a Muse to unite him with the higher vision of the gods. In Hesiodic myth, the ages and the races that live in them are inserted between the time of the gods and human time, serving as much to separate them as to connect them. This is a history of decadence, interrupted only by the fourth race, that of heroes. The fate of the race of the last age, the iron age, is to suffer fatigue and hardships and hence to live painfully in time. The only remedy for this is the monotonous repetition of work in the fields. Nevertheless, the cycle of time is already that of a human time.

In the works of the tragedians, man is defined as "ephemeral." This is not because man's life is short but because his condition is tied to the accidents of time. The "sovereign time" sung by the chorus can at the same time be the "avenging time" that will reestablish justice. Historiography, on the other hand, by virtue of the task that it sets for itself, introduces a certain consistency into the time of men, relating it to the human time of the "first inventor" (*protos euretēs*). On the one hand, Herodotos recognizes these first inventors in those who first gave offense to the Greeks and thereby brought on the Persian Wars. On the other hand, the historian himself, by naming himself, by giving the reasons he has for recalling the past, and by seeking the sense of past events, establishes himself as a first inventor. It is in this double manner that he gives human time its consistency. Despite its linear framework, however, this human time still leaves room for analogies and correspondences that elevate the characters above and beyond time.

It is only with Thucydides that a logical time will govern the disorder of historical time that stems from the repetition of the same dissensions between cities, which make innumerable and terrible evils "occur and recur unendingly." The second great Greek historian is then able to define his work as a means of "seeing clearly into events of the past and those yet to come by reason of the human character they possess, offering similarities or analogies" (*History of the Peloponnesian War* 1.22). This is the sense of the famous expression *ktēma eis aei* ("acquisition for all times"): human time will take on consistency in the face of the time of the gods only when the narrative is anchored to a sort of logic of action.

ANCIENT ISRAEL. Following the majority of exegetes and cultural historians, we have adopted the working hypothesis that only the Greeks and the Hebrews developed a historiography comparable to that of the moderns. It is therefore in reference to the birth of history in Greece that we shall discuss the similar phenomenon in ancient Israel. Obstacles to this sort of comparative undertaking are by no means lacking, however.

The first source of difficulty lies in a difference of literary genre. Literary genres such as epic, tragedy, lyric poetry, and history, which are represented in Greece by distinct works and authors, are found grouped together and often interwoven in the Hebrew Bible, a book that is itself actually a collection of books. Therefore, if we are to find in the Hebrew scriptures a collection of texts comparable to Herodotos's *Histories*, we will have to ignore the important question of context at the risk of serious distortions. This is the case, for instance, with the story of David's rise (*1 Sm.* 16:14–*2 Sm.* 5:25) and the succession story (*2 Sm.* 7, 9–20; *1 Kgs.* 1–2).

A second difficulty lies in the complexity of narrative as a genre. The narrative genre is represented by such a wide variety of forms that we cannot restrict our classification merely to an opposition between history and myth. It is necessary to work out a typology of narrative forms, however rudimentary and merely provisional, before we can inquire into the possible filiations between one form and another.

There is still another difficulty. In addition to the variety of literary genres surrounding the narrative core and the diversity of narrative forms themselves, the Hebrew scriptures present a hierarchy of different texts. First-order units that represent the entire range of narrative forms are incorporated into larger ensembles such as the compositions of the Yahvist, which present narrative features that differ from those of the first-order units. In order to account for the difference of level and structure between these larger narratives and their smaller, properly historiographic segments, it is advisable to refer to the former as "history-like *narratives.*"

Finally, concerning the specific problem of myth and history, we must be prepared to confront the paradoxical situation that, in contrast to the evolution that led from myth to history in Greece, in Israel the quasi myths or myth fragments borrowed from neighboring cultures were incorporated into the great narrative ensembles mentioned above in the form of historicized myths, as is the case in *Genesis* 1–11. This reinterpretation of myth on the basis of history appears quite specific to the literary sphere of ancient Israel.

We can navigate our investigation through the reefs of these difficulties by proceeding along the lines of the three levels of inquiry outlined in the first paragraph: namely, a typology of narrative forms, an analysis of the historical mode of understanding of the community that produces these narratives, and, finally, a brief look at the conception of time that may be implicit either in the literary forms or in the self-understanding revealed in ancient Israel.

With respect to the typology of narrative forms, in which history and myth take their place at the two opposite poles of the spectrum, it is important to note that genetic investigations, stemming principally from the work of Hermann Gunkel and Hugo Gressmann, have employed structural analysis to establish criteria for the identification of narrative forms and then gone on to work out their filiation. Gunkel (1928) himself argued that the historiography illustrated by the two narratives concerning David mentioned above stemmed from legends (*Sagen*), rather than from the myths of the ancient Middle East or from the lists, annals, and chronicles that were widespread among Israel's neighbors. In order to establish this thesis, Gunkel had to work out a brief typology that allowed him to distinguish legends from other types of stories. He first distinguished legends (*Sagen*), which refer to characters in the real world but living in times gone by, both from myths, which are origin narratives, taking place in a time different from that of ordinary experience, and tales (*Märchen*), which are pure fictions intended for amusement. Then, within the *Sagen* themselves, he distinguished between father legends (*Vatersagen*) and hero legends (*Heldensagen*). Father legends are tied to family leaders who are representative of their social group. They are sometimes related in a series, like the stories of Joseph; Gunkel calls these "novellas" (*Novellen*). Hero legends (*Heldensagen*), to the extent that they concern public figures like Moses, Joshua, Saul, and David, can contain a genuinely historical element. According to Gunkel, it is within this subgroup that we can follow the evolution from the pure heroic legend, illustrated by the story of Gideon, to history in a sense similar to that of Herodotus, as in the two narratives of David referred to above. Gressmann (1910) then carried this approach further by calling attention to the prophetic legends, whose purpose is devotional and edifying.

Gressmann's major contribution, however, was his tripartite division of history. First there is the history that concerns recent events (it is assumed that the narratives relating to David were written shortly after the events recounted). Then come legends, concerning distant events, and, finally, myths, relating to primordial times. The advantage of this threefold division is that it brackets the question of the presumed degree of veracity, as measured by our modern notion of documentary proof. Nevertheless, in Gunkel and Gressmann the concern for typology is immediately swallowed up by the interest in genesis: their major interest is in determining how historiography as a scholarly genre arose out of legend.

The same question is considered by Gerhard von Rad (1962), but on the basis of different preoccupations. He too asks about the preconditions for the emergence of historiography, but whereas Gunkel stresses the decisive role of the emergence of a monarchic state, von Rad focuses on the demand for explanation present in the etiological function of legends, on the formation of a prose literature, and especially on the organizing role played by a theological vision of history. It is under the influence of this third and decisive factor that the narrative organization prevails over the parataxic presentation of the heroic legends. By the same token, the relation of filiation between the legend and the myth appears even weaker. And it is an enlightenment similar to that in Ionia that permits the passage from the novella, which itself is already relatively complex, to even larger ensembles, such as the stories of David and the Yahvist document, which are thus placed on the same level as the historiographical core, at least as far as their organization is concerned.

Armed with these sketchy typological criteria for distinguishing between genres, Hebrew exegesis set out to examine the question of their filiation, a question held to be fundamental. It is within this framework that Gunkel's continuist hypothesis has been tested by his successors (Gerhard von Rad, Martin Noth, William F. Albright, Umberto Cassuto, Claus Westermann, and John van Seters). This hypothesis can include a number of different emphases. Emphasis can be placed on the political factor, on the enlightened spirit of the age assumed to be close to the reported events, or on the degree of organization in the legends themselves prior to their literary phase. One can emphasize the possible existence of early Israelite epics influenced by Mesopotamian and Canaanite epics, the constitution of court archives, lists, annals, and other documents similar to those found among Israel's neighbors, and finally and most especially the organizing power exerted by the theological motif. In fact, however, these rival genetic hypotheses have shown themselves to be practically unverifiable in the absence of Israelite sources distinct from the canonical texts of the Hebrew scriptures. It is not even certain that the texts that appear closest to Greek historiography were actually written at a period close to that of the events reported, or even that there was an Israelite literature prior to the writing of *Deuteronomy.*

The responses of scholars to these doubts have taken three forms. Some have sought a renewal of genetic investigations on the basis of new hypotheses. Others have accorded a privilege to a more detailed structural analysis of narrative forms, and still others have undertaken a properly literary study of the narrative art, which is found in all narrative forms.

The first orientation is illustrated in particular by the works of John Van Seters and Hans H. Schmid, who date the first Israelite writings five or six centuries later than previous scholarship did and thereby overthrow all the earlier hypotheses concerning filiation.

The second orientation is illustrated by the taxonomical concern that presides over the works of George W. Coats on *Genesis.* Coats divides the main narrative genres into the saga, the tale, the novella, legends, histories, reports, fables, etiological narratives, and, finally, myths. The term *saga* (not to be confused with the German *Sage,* "legend") here refers to the Icelandic and Nordic sagas of the Middle Ages, which are long, traditional narratives in prose, subdivided into family sagas and heroic sagas. The tale is characterized by the fact that it has few characters, a single setting, and a simple plot. The novella, in turn, is a complex tale with a plot involving tension and its resolution. Legends are static narratives with no plot in praise of the virtues of a hero. A history is intended to report events that actually took place; a report describes an isolated event. Fables depict a fictional world, while etiological narratives purport to explain a situation, to name a place or a character. Finally, myths are reduced to the sphere that remains, namely the imaginative domain relating to the activity of the gods in the divine world (hence *Genesis* 6:1–4).

A noteworthy example of the third orientation is given by Robert Alter and Adele Berlin. These authors, unhampered by typological concerns, have studied the art of narrative composition, basing their studies on the poetic model applied to the modern novel. So-called primitive and naive narratives suddenly appear to be works of consummate refinement in the use of dialogue and in the handling of events with reticence and understatement. At the same time, the literary analysis enhances the theological import of these texts and suggests that the conflict between the inevitability of the divine plan and human recalcitrance is in itself the source of narrative developments.

The development of structural analysis has tended to obscure the problem of the relations between myth and history behind its more detailed typologies. Nevertheless, the problem reemerges at another level as the problem of the self-understanding of a culture as this is expressed through its traditions. This new line of questioning is called for by the typology itself, to the extent that the aim of any narrative form is to contribute to self-understanding. Here, then, in the context of the Hebrew scriptures, we confront the second sense of *history:* history as it refers to the historical mind of ancient Israel, its manner of conducting itself historically. In this regard, most exegetes agree in characterizing the self-understanding of ancient Israel as globally historical, something that cannot be said of the Greeks. If the latter did indeed produce a historiography that is more clearly set out on the level of its works and more deliberately critical with respect to received traditions, they nevertheless sought their identity—without perhaps ever actually finding it—more in the political sphere of their existence. At the same time, their philosophers developed a cosmological and nonhistorical philosophy of reality as a whole. Israel alone understood itself principally through the traditions of which it was at once the author and recipient. This is essentially what von Rad wanted to stress in his *The Theology of Israel's Historical Traditions* (1962), the first volume of his *Old Testament Theology.* With Israel, the act of narrating had from the outset a theological value, and the theological intention was instilled in the collection of traditions, which the theologian could not help but retell.

This second level of investigation must not be confused with the first; the "historical" understanding of a people through its literature is not exclusively, nor even principally, expressed in historiographic writings. It may instead be expressed through an entire range of narrative forms and even, little by little, by all the other literary genres inasmuch as they are historicized or, better, "narrativized." This expansion of the historical mind beyond the narrative form characteristic of historiography finds its expression in the internal hierarchy characteristic of the narrative literature of the Hebrew scriptures, through which the narrative units distinguished by the typology are subordinated to larger ensembles, of which the Yahvist document is a good model. Not only does this vast composition reach back before the monarchy, before the settlement, before the patriarchs, to the very creation of the world; it also encompasses units that represent the entire range of narrative forms distinguished above, as well as vast nonnarrative texts, such as laws, sapiential segments, praises, curses, and blessings—in short, a wide variety of literary forms and "language games." As noted above, in order to preserve this internal variety and difference of level, it is advisable to reserve the term *history* for those units that display a structural and thematic kinship with early Greek historiography and to refer to other narratives as "history-like," following Hans W. Frei in his *The Eclipse of Biblical Narrative* (1974).

It is on the level of this vast history-like narrative, and on that of the different narratives superimposed on the great Yahvist narrative, that the theological design of narrative literature itself is revealed. In this regard, there has been noticeable evolution in interpretation since Gunkel sought to save the ancient historiography that he considered to be contemporary with the epoch of Solomon from the regretted influence of the prophets. Von Rad considerably reworked the problem by seeing in the great Yahvist construction the expansion of the confessional recital that can be read in *Deuteronomy* 24:5–9 and *Joshua* 24:2–13. According to von Rad, this "historical credo," with its own distinctive liturgical roots, governed the history of the settlement, leading the people from Egypt to the Promised Land. It then incorporated into itself the Sinai tradition, which, as a distinct cult-legend with its revealed commandments and its theology of the covenant, had heretofore had a separate existence. Around this core was clustered the history of the patriarchs, prefaced by the majestic history of the creation of the world and the origin of humanity. The Yahvist would then be the writer of genius who, due to the shifting of the myths from their original matrix, used the theological motif inherent in the tradition of the settlement to give coherence to this collection of heterogeneous narratives. With the Yahvist, we are no longer dealing with a storyteller but with a theologian-narrator who expresses his vision of the relations between God and his people by means of a continuous history, in which the history of the chosen people is bound up with the universal history of humankind and with the history of the world itself.

Starting from the historiographic pole, von Rad's successors have asked how the historical recital of the settlement relates to the narratives of the succession and to those of David's rise to power. What exchanges took place between the sacred and political vision of God's sovereignty over history and the idea of a divine guidance operating throughout the migration and the settlement? Did the former serve as a structural model for the latter, and the latter as a theological model for the former? It is in this connection that Robert Alter's suggestion takes on its full importance: he asks whether the paradox of the inevitability of the divine plan and human recalcitrance is not revealed in even the smallest narrative units when these are examined in the light of the art of biblical narrative. The most significant narratives turn out to be those in which the divine intention is realized, not through divine intervention, but through the very play of human passions, after the fashion of a *nemesis* inherent in human conduct.

We move from the historiographic pole back to the mythical by inquiring into the theology of history that is evinced in the large narrative units, or even in the smaller ones. Actually, we should speak of theologies of history, for it is not certain that what has been called salvation history (*Heilsgeschichte*) covers all the intentions of the biblical writers. We must be careful not to project the biblical theology of today onto the Hebrew scriptures. The interweaving of a number of different theological themes must be respected: the covenant, the promise and its fulfillment, ethical instruction through the narrative, and so forth. Aside from this plurality of the theologies of history, there is the question of the function of the theological plan as a whole. As a kind of counterpart to the historicizing of the origin myths, could it not itself function as a myth, in the sense of the transcendent founding of present history on the basis of a more fundamental history? More precisely, it seems that the theology of traditions has been assimilated into an etiological myth of the settlement in a foreign land, hence of the gift of the soil. After the catastrophe of the exile, this myth was itself capable of being transformed into an etiological myth of the loss of the land. This second etiological use of the myth results in a new theology of history, centered around the theme of retribution—in short, a theodicy. In the Deuteronomic narrative, this new theodicy finds an expression that may be weak historiographically but is strong in its moral resources. Nevertheless, we must admit that by calling salvation history itself a myth, we are stretching the notion of myth beyond its strict sense of a history of origins *in illo tempore.* Salvation history unfolds in the time of men rather than in the time of the gods. This fundamental difference must make us more careful in using the term *myth* to characterize theological interpretations like those of salvation history.

We must reserve for a third level of analysis the controversial question of whether the conception of time in ancient Israel was explicit or merely implicit. James Barr, in *Biblical Words for Time* (2d rev. ed., 1969), warns us of the temptation to seek information on the Hebrew conception of time at the level of the language itself, in its vocabulary and semantics, or in the etymology of individual words. The meaning of words, Barr observes, results from their use in determined contexts. Thus in our attempt to discover a Hebraic conception of time we are led back to the contexts provided by the narrative forms considered above and to the historical mentality discussed earlier.

An initial question arises: is a specific conception of time implicit in the narrative forms used in the Hebrew Bible? The reply would seem to be negative. The various types of narrative taken separately include very different temporal implications. No general view of time can be extracted from the historiography of *Samuel* and *Kings;* it concerns a given segment of time that permits no extrapolation. To be sure, we can admit that the historiography of the Hebrew Bible, like that of the Greeks, assumes a certain familiarity with temporal succession and chronology. But this relation to time is purely pragmatic. In addition, and this is the most important point, other narrative forms, such as the saga and the legend, on the one hand, and the origin myth, on the other, take place in qualitatively different times, which can be usefully described as "recent," "distant," or "primordial." Thus the "days" of creation are incommensurable with the years in which the monarchs reign; the same is true concerning the patriarchs, who are situated, so to speak, "between" primordial times and historical time. It is therefore advisable to respect the specific temporal qualities belonging to the various classes of narrative.

If we now consider the great narrative compositions, like that of the Yahvist, in which the historical mind of ancient Israel is expressed, it cannot be denied that the various traditions with their heterogeneous durations are submitted to a single temporal order that we should probably represent as a rectilinear and irreversible time underlying a universal history that stretches from creation to the end of the monarchy and to the period of the return from the Babylonian exile. However, besides the fact that this representation is never made explicit by the brilliant composer of the Yahvist document, it would be sorely inadequate for the narrative style of this quasi-historical narrative even if it had been made explicit. This is so for several reasons.

First of all, the time unfolded by the great narrative remains a creation of the narrative art itself. The time immanent in the great narrative configuration by no means abolishes the differences between the heterogeneous time-spans that it encompasses. Thus we cannot say that the election of Abraham occurs after the seven days of creation. The mere succession of narratives does not allow us to project along a single time scale the time of origins, that of the patriarchs, that of the settlement in Canaan, and that of the monarchical period. The idea of a single narrative scale common to all the time-spans is a modern idea foreign to the thinking of ancient Israel and even to that of ancient Greece.

In addition, a series of correspondences and analogies are added to the temporal succession in which one event follows another, as for instance between the various covenants and the various laws, and even the various theophanies. In this regard one could speak of a cumulative aspect of time in the Hebrew Bible rather than of a purely successive one.

Finally, and what is most important, the relation between God's faithfulness and man's recalcitrance, which is illustrated in so many different ways by the special narrative art of the Hebrew storytellers, narrators, and historians, does not lend itself to interpretation in terms of the categories inherited from Platonism and Neoplatonism, where divine immutability is diametrically opposed to the mutability of all things human. God's faithfulness, which marks the history of men, suggests the idea of an omnitemporality rather than that of a supratemporality. This omnitemporality, moreover, is in perfect agreement with the sort of cumulative history we have just mentioned. In order to be able to speak of a biblical time, we would have to take all of the literary genres into account and not only the genre of narrative. There is an immemorial time of the laws, a proleptic time of prophecy, an everyday time of wisdom, a "nowness" of hymnic complaint and praise. Biblical time—if this expression has any meaning—is made up of the interweaving of all the temporal values that are added onto the numerous temporal qualities preserved by the variety of narrative forms. The representation of a linear and irreversible time is wholly inadequate for this chorus of voices.

Would we then be justified in speaking of a return to mythical time by way of a history-like narrative, on the basis of the theologies presiding over the narrative composition itself, as, for example, in the conception of history as salvation history? This could be done only by ascribing to the term *myth* the extremely broad sense of a founding narrative that is related to everyday existence. In fact, it is just as important to stress the historicization of myth as it is to emphasize the mythologization of history. The position of the origin myth in *Genesis* 1–11 attests to this decisive subordination of myth to history. It is only as a broken myth that the archaic myth is reasserted within the gravitational space displayed by the historiography of the monarchic period and by the narrative of the conquest and settlement.

Perhaps it is in this that the hidden kinship between Greek thought and Hebrew thought resides. Each of them in its own way breaks with myth. Each, too, reinvents myth, one as a philosophical tale, as we saw in Plato, and the other as a broken and historicized myth, as in the Yahvist account of creation.

SEE ALSO Cosmogony; Historiography; Sacred Time.

BIBLIOGRAPHY

Albright, William F. *Yahweh and the Gods of Canaan: A Historical Analysis of Two Contrasting Faiths.* Jordan Lectures in Comparative Religion, no. 7. London, 1968.

Boman, Thorleif. *Hebrew Thought Compared with Greek.* Philadelphia, 1960.

Cassuto, Umberto. "The Beginning of Historiography among the Israelites." In his *Biblical and Oriental Studies,* vol. 1, pp. 7–16. Jerusalem, 1973.

Frei, Hans W. *The Eclipse of Biblical Narrative: A Study in Eighteenth and Nineteenth Century Hermeneutics.* New Haven, 1974.

Fritz, Kurt von. "Herodotus and the Growth of Greek Historiography." *Transactions of the American Philological Association* 67 (1936): 315–340.

Gressmann, Hugo, ed. *Die älteste Geschichtsschreibung und Prophetie Israels.* Göttingen, 1910.

Gunkel, Hermann. "Geschichtsschreibung im Alt Testament." In *Die Religion in Geschichte und Gegenwart,* vol. 2. Tübingen, 1928.

Huizinga, Johan. "A Definition of the Concept of History." In *Philosophy and History: Essays Presented to E. Cassirer,* edited by Raymond Klibansky and Herbert J. Paton, pp. 1–10. Oxford, 1936.

Lévi-Strauss, Claude. *Mythologiques.* 4 vols. Paris, 1964–1971.

Malinowski, Bronislaw. *Myth in Primitive Psychology.* New York, 1926.

Momigliano, Arnaldo. "Time in Ancient Historiography." In his *Essays in Ancient and Modern Historiography,* pp. 179–204. Oxford, 1977.

Noth, Martin. "Geschichtsschreibung im Alt Testament." In *Die Religion in Geschichte und Gegenwart,* 3d ed., vol. 2. Tübingen, 1958.

Pearson, Lionel. *Early Ionian Historians.* Oxford, 1939.

Rad, Gerhard von. *Old Testament Theology,* vol. 1, *The Theology of Israel's Historical Traditions.* New York, 1962.

Rad, Gerhard von. "The Beginnings of Historical Writing in Ancient Israel." In his *The Problem of the Hexateuch and Other Essays,* pp. 166–204. London, 1966.

Romilly, Jacqueline de. *Histoire et raison chez Thucydide.* Paris, 1956.

Schmid, Hans H. "Das alttestamentliche Verständnis von Geschichte in seinem Verhältnis zum gemeinorientalischen Denken." *Wort und Dienst: Jahrbuch der Theologischen Schule Bethel* 13 (1975): 9–21.

Van Seters, John. *In Search of History: Historiography in the Ancient World and the Origins of Biblical History.* New Haven, 1983.

Vernant, Jean-Pierre. "Mythical Aspects of Memory and Time." In his *Myth and Thought among the Greeks.* London, 1983.

Vidal-Naquet, Pierre. "Temps des dieux et temps des hommes." *Revue de l'histoire des religions* 157 (January–March 1960): 55–80.

Westermann, Claus. "Zum Geschichtsverständnis des Alten Testaments." In *Probleme Biblischer Theologie,* edited by Hans Walter Wolff, pp. 611–619. Munich, 1971.

New Sources

Binder, Gerhard, and Bernd Effe. *Mythos: erzählende Weltdeutung im Spannungsfeld von Ritual, Geschichte und Rationalität.* Trier, 1990.

Campbell, Joseph, and Bill Moyers. *Power of Myth.* New York, 1988.

Chandler, Tertius. "Can Greek Myths Be History?" *Patristic and Byzantine Review* 18–19 (2000–2001): 271–272.

Israeli, Raphael. "Myth as Memory: Muslims in China between Myth and History." *Muslim World* 91, nos. 1–2 (2001): 185–208.

McKenzie, Steven L., and Thomas Römer, eds. *Rethinking the Foundations: Historiography in the Ancient World and in the Bible.* Berlin, 2000.

Noegel, Scott B. "Adam in Myth and History: Ancient Israelite Perspectives on the Primal Human." *Biblica* 83/4 (2002): 583–586.

Ruedas, Javier. "Social Context and Creation of Meaning in Indigenous Amazonian Performances of Myth and Oral History." *Journal of Ritual Studies* 17, no. 2 (2003): 35–71.

Van Seters, John. *Prologue to History: The Yahwist as Historian in Genesis.* Louisville, 1992.

Von Hendy, Andrew. *Modern Construction of Myth.* Bloomington, Ind., 2002.

PAUL RICOEUR (1987)
Revised Bibliography

MYTH AND RITUAL SCHOOL. The term *Myth and Ritual school* refers to two movements, one in Great Britain in the second quarter of the twentieth century, connected with the name of S. H. Hooke of the University of London, and the other, less clearly identifiable, appearing at about the same time in Scandinavia. The "school" or movement arose in reaction against an evolutionary approach to the study of ancient religions, although it depended upon data collected by scholars holding to the evolutionary outlook. It arose also as a result of a growing recognition in many circles of the central importance of ritual acts for ancient peoples and of the accompanying texts—the myths. The movement thus was rightly designated the "Myth and Ritual school," for it sought to show how pervasive were the central ritual acts of ancient societies and how inseparable from these acts were the accompanying words. The school gave great prominence to the religions of the ancient Near East; the most weighty applications of the school's findings were made to the study of the Hebrew scriptures and the New Testament.

The pattern of religious activity identified by the school was focused upon the celebration of New Year's Day and upon the place of the king in that celebration. The community was enabled to participate in the actual renewal of the cosmos as the various elements of the ritual were observed. The Myth and Ritual school thus stressed the enormous cultural significance of right observance of the ritual; ritual and its accompanying words were, according to the Myth and Ritual theorists, at the heart of an ancient society's self-understanding.

BACKGROUND. Many elements contributed to the appearance of the Myth and Ritual school. The gathering of data on religious practices by ethnologists and anthropologists such as was carried out, for example, by James G. Frazer and reported in his multivolume work, *The Golden Bough,* 12 vols. (1911–1915), provided vast comparative materials for the school's use. Specialized studies of the social and psychological aspects of the life of ancient Israel, in particular the work of the Danish scholar Johannes Pedersen (*Israel, Its Life and Culture,* 2 vols., 1926–1940), proved influential in Great Britain and in Scandinavia. And the studies of the great Danish historian of religion and specialist in Germanic religion Vilhelm Grönbech were a highly influential factor in shaping the school's appreciation of the dynamism and power of cultic life, with its many-faceted ritual acts. Also influential were the studies of the German scholar Wilhelm Mannhardt on cultic practices related to agriculture and the agricultural year (see especially his *Wald- und Feldkulte,* 2 vols., 1874–1876, 2d ed., 1904–1905).

BEGINNINGS. Both branches of the school originate in association with the work of the great Hermann Gunkel, founder of the method of form criticism. An Old Testament specialist whose work firmly rooted the study of the Old Testament in the cultic practices of the ancient Near East, Gunkel also saw the connection between ritual and myth, especially in his studies of the myths and legends of *Genesis* (*Genesis,* 1901; 2d ed., 1922). But it was the Norwegian scholar Sigmund Mowinckel who first applied the insights and approach of Gunkel to the cultic materials of the Hebrew Psalter in a series of studies (*Psalmen-Studien,* 4 vols., 1921–1925).

For Mowinckel the early Israelite cult was a living reality, marked by the existence of wonder-workers and mischief makers who had to be dealt with by means of ritual acts and formulas. The New Year's Day celebrations saw the Israelite God Yahveh enthroned afresh as lord of the universe, with whom the earthly king was cultically associated. Details of this celebration would later be worked out by the Myth and Ritual school, but Mowinckel gave the basic structure of the celebration in this early study of the Israelite cult. Mowinckel gave examples from the surrounding religious practices to show that this cult of Yahveh in Israel had very close similarities with those of its neighbors. Many other scholars would join in the search for parallels and for further evidence of the influence of ancient Near Eastern myth and ritual upon the religion and cult of early Israel.

THE BRITISH SCHOOL. The Myth and Ritual school in Great Britain was a remarkable instance of scholarly collaboration in an age in which individual scholars tended to work in relative independence of one another. The moving force within the school was S. H. Hooke, longtime professor of Old Testament studies in the University of London. He edited a series of studies during a twenty-five-year period in which he and his colleagues sought to identify the connection between ritual acts and the words that accompanied them—that is, the myths, the "libretto" of the ritual score. The first study appeared in 1933 under the title *Myth and Ritual.* The second, *The Labyrinth,* was published two years later. These two works covered the rites of the peoples of ancient Mesopotamia, Egypt, Anatolia, and Canaan, and dealt at length with the myth and ritual of ancient Israel and of early Christianity. The third of the volumes came out in 1958: *Myth, Ritual, and Kingship.* It included an essay by H. H. Rowley, "Ritual and the Hebrew Prophets," in which

Rowley indicated reservations about aspects of the school. It also included an important critical assessment of the school by S. G. F. Brandon, which called attention to certain critics of the school and included several points of sharp disagreement by Brandon himself. This chapter in the book is addressed by Hooke in his introductory essay. It was a salutary thing that this open debate on the school's view was furthered by publications in which the school's central positions were espoused.

For the British school, the central undertaking seemed to be to show how many of the cultic practices and the motifs of ancient Near Eastern myths and sagas had their counterpart in texts of the Hebrew scriptures. The reconstruction of the annual festival in ancient Israel produced an amazing richness: recitation of the story of creation; humiliation and ritual murder of the king; descent of the king into the underworld; resurrection from death and restoration to the throne; the sacred marriage of the king and his consort, representing the divine pair; the reestablishment of the cosmos and the historical order; and the recitation of the divine law. The pattern was derived from the New Year ritual text preserved in the Akkadian language and dating to Seleucid times, augmented by many texts from other times and societies.

Critics pointed out that these elements were actually drawn from many places in the Hebrew scriptures, never appearing together, if indeed some of the elements actually appeared at all. Critics also made the point that Israel's earthly king is a latecomer in Israel to the historical scene and is often under the most severe challenge and indictment by the prophets. But for about three decades the British Myth and Ritual school pressed its viewpoint, enlisted scholars of great learning and influence into its ranks, and sought to refine its position.

THE SCANDINAVIAN SCHOOL. Less formally associated with one another than were those of the British group, the Scandinavian specialists dealing with myth and ritual also gained much of their initial perspective from the work of Hermann Gunkel and from the early writings of Sigmund Mowinckel. Other works of special importance for the Scandinavian school included a study of *Exodus* 1–15 by Johannes Pedersen in which the author saw these chapters to be a text that accompanied the celebration of the Passover festival in early Israel. The whole drama of the call of Moses, the move to Egypt to effect deliverance, the plagues, the last dreadful night as the Passover was observed, closing with the legend of the crossing at the Red Sea, the defeat of Egypt's forces, and the triumph song of the Israelites, would have been recited as the libretto of the Exodus celebration. Early stages of the text that accompanied the ritual could to some degree be distinguished from the later stages of the tradition; but the character of *Exodus* 1–15, said Pedersen, was better explained as the Passover ritual text than on the basis of separate literary sources or traditions. Pedersen recognized Passover to be a nature festival of pastoralists that, by means of the annual celebration with its accompanying legend, rooted the natural festivity in Israel's historical consciousness.

The work of the Swedish scholar H. S. Nyberg on the *Book of Hosea* also greatly influenced the Scandinavian school. In *Studien zum Hoseabuche* (1935) Nyberg argued that the text of *Hosea* was probably preserved orally until the time of the Babylonian exile, but he also argued, on the basis of analogies from the ancient Near East, that oral tradition is very reliable indeed. Thus Nyberg spoke for the value of the cultic community of ancient Israel in the preservation of the words of its leaders and for their reuse in the cult, thereby (like Pedersen) expressing mistrust of the "bookish" approach of western European and North American scholars. In addition, the comparisons drawn by Nyberg to early Arabic practices would prove useful in the later work of the Scandinavian Myth and Ritual school.

Other studies followed. Alfred Haldar examined the relations of ancient prophets to the cult and came to the conclusion that although prophets were often critical of the cult, they were themselves usually the product of the cult as well, functionaries who had their regular place in the ceremonies and rituals by means of which the society's life was renewed. Aage Bentzen of Denmark, in one of his very influential writings (*King and Messiah,* 1955), dealt with later eschatological writings, showing that the kingship ritual of early times continued to exercise influence in postexilic times, as Israelite messianism developed. Richard Reitzenstein (1978) did the same for Hellenistic religious rites and practices, bringing to the study and evaluation of the New Testament a wealth of history-of-religions materials reflecting cultic practices believed to illuminate the world of the New Testament. A lengthy commentary on the *First Letter of Peter* by Frank Leslie Cross (1954) presented this New Testament book as the text to accompany the celebration of the Christian "Passover," Easter.

Ivan Engnell and Sigmund Mowinckel, in quite different ways, brought the work of the Myth and Ritual school in Scandinavia to a new level. Engnell was a vigorous exponent of the king's central position in the cult. He probably overstated the case for the accuracy of oral tradition and related too many biblical texts to the royal cult, thus producing a reaction against the entire position of the school. An essay by Martin Noth was considered by many scholars to have offered the definitive refutation of the Scandinavian approach to the place of the king in the Israelite cult ("God, King, and Nation," in *The Laws in the Pentateuch and Other Essays,* 1966). Noth pointed out how late kingship appears on the scene. Israel's very identity as a people is formed in the Israelite traditions long before there is a king. The kings are held under constant surveillance by the ancient prophets, according to the biblical record. And the eschatological pictures of the king of the time of consummation offer such a picture of this "last" king that further judgment is expressed against all incumbents. Mowinckel, in his major work on Israelite messianism and eschatology, *He That Cometh* (1955), provided a seasoned and thoughtful critical assessment of the work of the Myth and Ritual school in both its British and its Scandinavian forms. At the same time, Geo Widengren continued his specialized studies dealing with the relation of myth and ritual, refining the outlook of the Myth and Ritual school and making it evident that in most particulars the school's outlook had stood the test of time.

CONTINUING INFLUENCE. Despite the weaknesses of the school, as pointed out by Henri Frankfort (*Kingship and the Gods,* 1948), Martin Noth, and many others, the result of the work of these scholars has been on the whole very positive. The Myth and Ritual school presented a forceful critique of evolutionistic schemes employed in the study of religion. It kept critical scholarship continuingly alerted to the need to take the actual practices of a religion at least as seriously as it took that religion's ideas and its literary heritage. It underscored the significance of the king for the entire life of ancient societies. Moreover, the comparative approach of the school has endured and become characteristic of the study of religion. Historical, comparative, structural, and systematic studies of religion all have their place in the study of religion, and the Myth and Ritual school contributed much to the enlargement of the vision of scholars engaged in the study of religion.

The school was able to bring together specialists from many backgrounds, linguistic interests, skills, and schools of interpretation, forging a working team (as in Great Britain) or furthering collaboration on several interlocking problems (as in Scandinavia), offering creative and comprehensive interpretations of central features of religion, especially the religions of the eastern Mediterranean area and Mesopotamia.

The school claimed too much for the pervasiveness of the pattern of ritual observance in the societies studied. It did not sufficiently allow for the differences in the understanding of kingship in the different lands. It seems also to have reconstructed patterns that turned out to be not nearly so widespread as its members thought, such as ritual marriage and the death and resurrection motif. But the school also brought to prominence several features of religious understanding and cultic practice that are unmistakable as the study of religion and religions continues.

Some of the critics of the Myth and Ritual school also went too far in their contentions. The differences between the historical consciousness of ancient Israel and that of Israel's neighbors were exaggerated by Martin Noth and others. And if the chief festival in the life of ancient Israel was centered upon the covenant rite or upon Jerusalem, rather than upon the king as representative of the deity, even so the role of the king in the cult of ancient Israel was very prominent indeed.

Two aspects of scholarship characterize the study of myth and ritual in the early twenty-first century. The first is the extent of collaborative work on myth and ritual by scholars in many fields: philologists, historians, anthropologists, ethnologists, sociologists, philosophers, archaeologists, along with specialists in religion. Indeed, the study of religion today is unthinkable without such collaborative work. It is important to remember, however, that the Myth and Ritual school did much to further this collaboration and to display its fruitfulness.

The second aspect is the comparison of texts in religious studies. Not only does the comparison of texts help to clarify the varied meanings of ritual acts; it also helps scholars to see the strength and meaning of the texts as literature. Here the interest of the Myth and Ritual school was too narrow. The story of creation does belong in association with ritual acts, but it also has a life outside its ritual use. The great prayers and hymns of the ancient world and of Israel are cultic texts to be used as the community participates in the recreation and reestablishment of its world and of the cosmos, but they too have a life of their own. These cultic texts offer perspectives, a worldview, an understanding of certain fundamental realities upon which the social existence of the peoples depended. Nevertheless, the school's insistence that these cultic texts were to be seen as actual parts of the ritual life of the people was an invaluable recognition.

BIBLIOGRAPHY

Cross, Frank Leslie. *I Peter: A Paschal Liturgy.* London, 1954.

Doty, William G. *Mythography: The Study of Myths and Rituals.* Tuscaloosa, Ala., 1986, 2000.

Fontenrose, Joseph. *The Ritual Theory of Myth.* Berkeley, Calif., and Los Angeles, 1966.

Gaster, T. H. "Myth, Mythology." In *Interpreter's Dictionary of the Bible,* vol. III., ed. George W. Buttrick, pp. 481–487. New York and Nashville, 1962.

Grönbech, Vilhelm. *The Culture of the Teutons (1909–1912).* 3 vols. Translated by William Worster. London, 1931.

Hooke, S. H., ed. *Myth and Ritual.* Oxford, 1933.

Hooke, S. H., ed. *The Labyrinth.* New York, 1935.

Hooke, S. H., ed. *Myth, Ritual and Kingship.* Oxford, 1958.

James, E. O. *Christian Myth and Ritual.* London, 1933.

Müller, Gerhard, ed. *Theologische Realencyclopädie,* vol. 23. Berlin & New York, 1994, pp. 597–665.

Oden, Jr., Robert A. "Myth and Mythology." In *The Anchor Bible Dictionary,* vol. IV, ed. David Noel Freedman, pp. 946–960. New York and London, 1992.

Patton, Laurie L., and Wendy Doniger, eds. *Myth and Method.* Charlottesville, N. C., and London, 1996.

Porter, J. R. "Myth and Ritual School." In *Dictionary of Biblical Interpretation,* ed. John H. Hayes. Nashville, 1999.

Reisenfeld, Harald. "Kultgeshichtliche Methode." In *Die Religion in Geschichte und Gegenwart,* 3d ed., vol. 4. Tübingen, 1960.

Reitzenstein, Richard. *The Hellenistic Mystery Religions* (1910). Translated by John E. Steely. Pittsburgh, 1978.

Segal, Robert A., ed. *The Myth ane Ritual Theory: An Anthology.* Malden, Mass., and Oxford, 1998.

Sienkewicz, Thomas J. *Theories of Myth: An Annotated Bibliography.* Magill Bibliographies. Lanham, Md. & London. Also Pasadena, Calif., and Englewood Cliffs, N. J., 1997.

Westermann, Claus. "Kultgeschichtliche Schule." In *Die Religion in Geschichte und Gegenwart,* 3d ed., vol. 4. Tübingen, 1960.

Widengren, Geo. "Die religionswissenschaftliche Forschung in Skandinavien in den letzten zwanzig Jahre." *Zeitschrift für Religions- und Geistesgeschichte* 5 (1953): 193–222, 320–334.

Widengren, Geo, et al., eds. *La Regalita Sacra/The Sacred Kingship.* Leiden, 1959. See the historical chapter by Carl-Martin Edsman, "Zum sakralen Königtum in der Forschung der letzten hundert Jahre," pp. 3-17.

WALTER HARRELSON (1987 AND 2005)

MYTHIC ANCESTORS SEE ANCESTORS, *ARTICLE ON* MYTHIC ANCESTORS

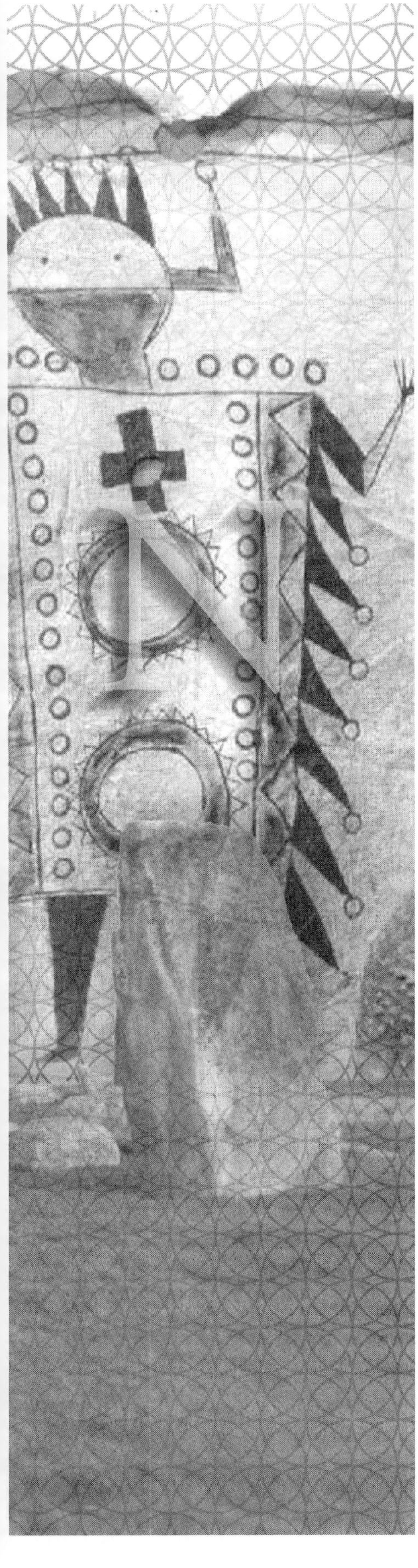

N

NABATEAN RELIGION. The scholarly consensus is that the Nabateans, whose kingdom flourished from about 400 BCE to 106 CE and whose capital was Petra in Jordan, were in part the descendants of the earlier inhabitants of southern Jordan, though apparently ruled by a dynasty of north Arabian background. At its most extensive, the Nabatean kingdom also incorporated other populations, including many of Aramean descent in southern Syria. In discussing Nabatean religion, therefore, one needs to take account of the fact that some peoples under Nabatean rule may only have adopted the traditions of Petra superficially, while basically retaining their own traditional cults. A "new" deity could be assimilated into or merged with a well-established local deity. Also, distinct Nabatean regions can be detected in which the deities worshiped vary along with other cultural markers (such as language and personal names).

NABATEAN HISTORY. The history of the Nabatean kingdom can only be traced in part, the sources being principally epigraphic, literary, and numismatic. Archaeology and iconography provide some evidence in relation to religion but add little to Nabatean history.

The epigraphic corpus consists of thousands of inscriptions and a few papyri written in the Nabatean version of the Aramaic language (widely used from the Achaemenid era) and in a distinctive local variety of the Achaemenid Aramaic script. Although the number of Nabatean inscriptions is large (over five thousand), many come from regions well outside the Nabatean heartland and were probably written by people who had only a tenuous connection with the Nabatean state (and its religion). Also, many were written after the fall of the Nabatean kingdom in 106 CE and thus provide only secondary evidence for the period of the kingdom itself.

Although the prestigious literary language, Aramaic, was used for inscriptions, it is generally agreed that the Petran élite, and probably large swathes of the populations of the southern and eastern parts of the kingdom, used some early form of Arabic as a vernacular. The evidence for this is provided by Arabic loanwords in Nabatean Aramaic and by the fact that many of the peoples in eastern Jordan used a form of early Arabic (Safaitic).

CLOCKWISE FROM TOP LEFT CORNER. Thai bronze Buddha in meditation under a *nāga. [©Michael Freeman/Corbis]*; A lion-headed Imdugud bird above two stags in a twenty-fifth-century BCE Mesopotamian relief from the temple of Ninhursaga. British Museum, London. *[©Erich Lessing/Art Resource, N.Y.]*; Detail of an Apache "Kan" god painted on a warrior's cloak. Smithsonian Institution, Washington, D.C. *[©Werner Forman/Art Resource, N.Y.]*; Stonehenge. Wiltshire County, England. *[©Roger Ressmeyer/Corbis]*; Double-headed Neolithic idol, 5000–2000 BCE. Historical Museum, Targoviste, Romania. *[©Erich Lessing/Art Resource, N.Y.]* .

Literary evidence for Nabatean history is entirely nonnative and mostly in Greek. Still, little historical detail is recorded, though Diodorus Siculus includes important anecdotes on the Nabatean contact with the Seleucids, and Josephus makes passing comment on Judaean dealings with the Nabateans. Other authors, writing in Greek (Strabo) and Latin (Pliny), confine themselves largely to describing aspects of Nabatean society (including religious aspects). These various sources make it clear that the basis of Nabatean prosperity was control of the overland routes of the Arabian incense trade: the trade was heavily taxed.

The Nabateans first appear in a historical context in 312 BCE in conflict with the Seleucids (Diodorus). Thereafter their independent kingdom is mentioned in the books of Maccabees, mostly in conflict with, though sometimes in alliance with, the Judaeans. From c. 100 BCE we have a tolerably clear king list, reconstructed in part on the basis of Nabatean inscriptions and coins and in part on the basis of authors like Josephus, who detailed ongoing relations with the Judaeans. On the wider stage, the involvement of the Nabatean Syllaeus (later pretender to the Nabatean throne) in Aelius Gallus's largely abortive campaign in 24 BCE against southern Arabia is recorded by Strabo (blaming Syllaeus). After a dispute over the throne, Aretas IV ruled from 9 BCE to 40 CE, and it was under this king that Petra and Nabataea enjoyed a period of evident success, with most of the great buildings of Petra being built at this time. Aretas appears to have had a nationalistic policy, and he took the title "lover of his own people." Rabel II (from 70 CE) is the last of the kings. Nabatean control over the trade routes was in decline and there was a (peaceful?) Roman takeover in 106 CE, at which point Nabataea was incorportated into the Province of Arabia with its center at Boṣrā.

NABATEAN SITES. The main Nabatean sites have yielded evidence of religious architecture that throws some light on practice. Petra and Madā'in Ṣāliḥ in Saudi Arabia (ancient Ḥegra) are also notable for their visible monuments that did not require excavation, being carved into rock faces. For reasons of space, the concentration here is on the main sites: there is a full gazetteer in Wenning (1987) and a survey in Healey (2001).

At Petra, even the rock defile, the so-called Sīq, which is the most usual access point to the city, was at least in part religious, as is suggested by religious carvings in it, some with inscriptions, and it may have been used for processions connecting Petra itself with Gaya (later named al-Jī, Wādī Mūsā), which is known to have had at least one important temple.

At the other end of the Sīq, the narrow defile opens out in front of the Khazneh, a monumental façade carved out of the rock. There has long been ambiguity about the original purpose of the Khazneh, but it is most likely a tomb of a king, though no inscription exists to confirm its function. The Khazneh's baroque decoration is the result of Alexandrian influence.

After the Khazneh, the space in which Petra itself is located opens out and the city is dominated by two principal features: monumental tombs (some probably royal) carved out of the steep rock faces, and a main street that terminates at the gateway of a major temple, passing other religious and nonreligious monuments on its way. The only inscribed tomb in the central area, Qabr al-Turkmān, does not name the person for whom it was carved. Some have seen the absence of inscribed tombs at Petra (by contrast with Ḥegra) as arising from a taboo against names on tombs at Petra. A more likely explanation is that some impermanent material like wood was used for the inscriptions on Petran tombs (and a tomb outside the Sīq does have a name).

The temple at the end of the main street is surrounded by a *temenos*. The sanctuary itself, to the left of the axis of the main street, is square and has an inner sanctum in which the object of worship was placed on a podium against the rear wall. The front was open, and directly opposite the entrance stood an altar surrounded by a large enclosure suitable for the gathering of crowds.

Only fragmentary inscriptions from the immediate area give any clue to the deity to whom the temple was dedicated. There are two hypotheses. As the probable main temple of the city, it is often assumed to be dedicated to the main god, Dushara (below), and in support of this we may note a fragmentary post-Nabatean inscription with a dedication to Zeus: Dushara came to be identified with Zeus. The other hypothesis notes that the traditional Arabic name of the temple, Qaṣr al-Bint, "castle of the girl," might be an echo of the temple of Aphrodite, which existed later at Petra (as we know from one of the documents in the "Babatha" archive found to the west of the Dead Sea [papyrus Yadin 12]) and suggests the temple was dedicated to a Nabatean goddess (on Allāt/al-ʿUzzā, see below).

Just outside the *temenos* gate, to the north, lies the Temple of the Winged Lions (so named because of decorative features discovered there). This is a complex structure at the center of which is a *cella* of a very different type than that of the Qaṣr al-Bint, one that allowed movement *around* the podium on which the cult object stood. Hammond suggested that this central podium was surrounded by curtains and elaborated this suggestion in terms of a "mystery" cult similar to that of Isis (as described in Apuleius's *Golden Ass*). In support of the Isis link is a beautiful votive figure with Isiac iconography. The inscription on the figure does not, however, name the goddess, only the dedicator of the offering involved, and while we know that Isis *was* worshiped at Petra, this cult seems to have been practiced in remote rock sanctuaries around the city. In any case, all the goddesses of the Roman world and adjacent areas were susceptible to Isis influences because of her extreme popularity. It seems most likely, therefore, that the Temple of the Winged Lions was dedicated to Allāt/al-ʿUzzā in Isis mode. Unfortunately, the one extensive inscription from the temple deals with tithes for priests but throws no light on the identity of the goddess.

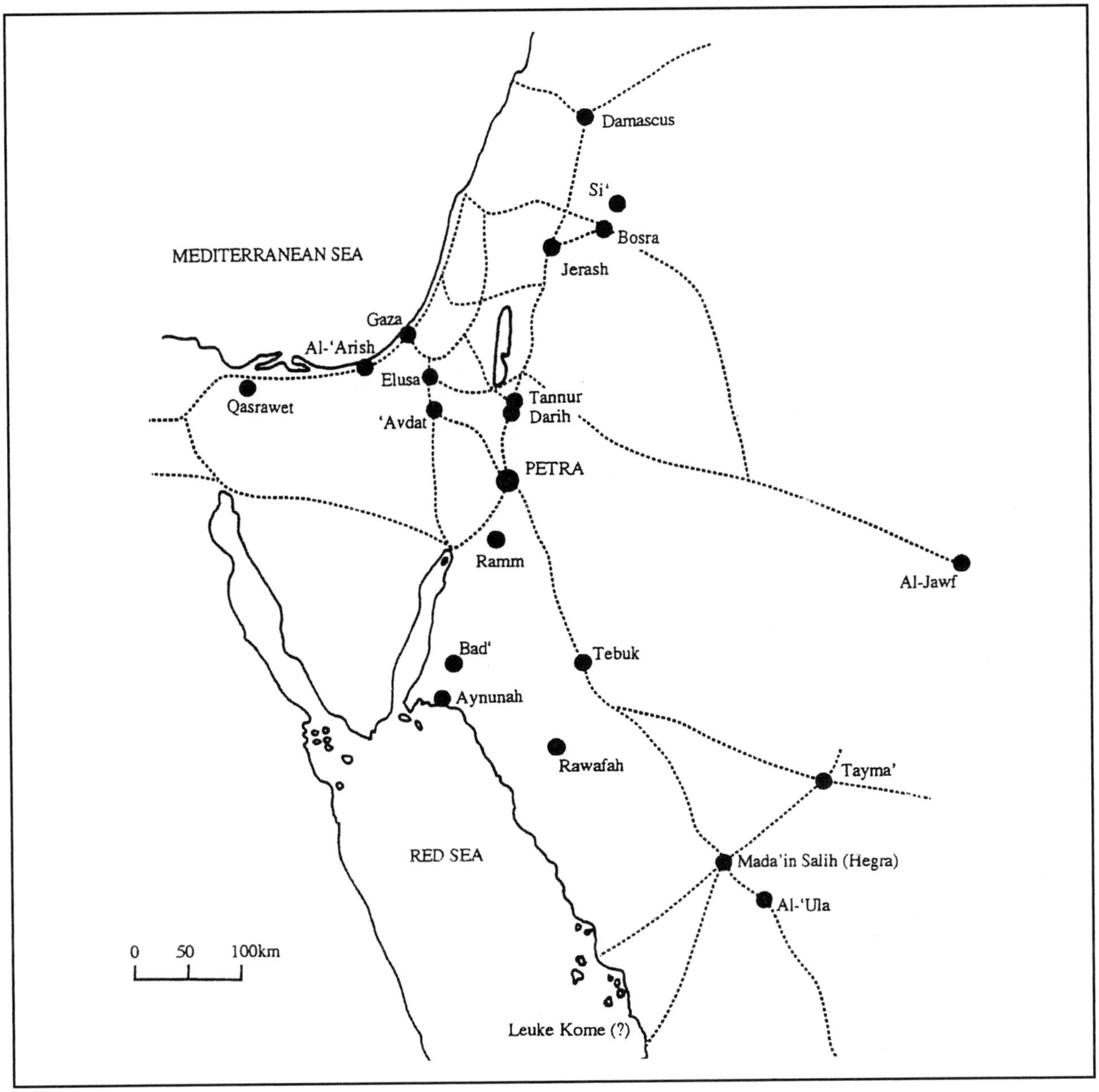

FIGURE 1. Nabatean Sites. *Illustration courtesy of the author.*

The third building to note here is the so-called "Great Temple" or "Large Temple" to the south. Again we have an elaborate building that *may* have been a temple, but the presence in its midst of a theater suggests it was used for some other purpose.

RELIGIOUS INSTALLATIONS. Temples ascribed to the Nabateans are found at a number of neighboring sites, the most important of which are Dhariḥ and Tannūr to the north and in Wādī Ramm to the south. It is not easy to be sure that others, for example, in southern Syria, are Nabatean in design: the Nabatean colonization of southern Syria was culturally superficial. Of the Nabatean temples proper there are two types. One (Qaṣr al-Bint) has a podium against the rear wall. The other type has a pillared gallery around the podium (Winged Lions, Dhariḥ, Ramm). The suggestion has been made that this latter arrangement would have allowed circumambulation, but there is no direct evidence of such a ritual, and the space available would not allow for more that a few cult officials.

Apart from built temples, the Nabateans were also fond of open-air sanctuaries on the tops of mountains. The most striking of these is the so-called High Place on the Madbaḥ outcrop at Petra. Here we find an elaborate installation involving podia, steps, reservoirs, and drainage channels. Arabic *madbaḥ* means "altar" or "place of sacrifice," and the installation, which overlooks the center of the city, is usually

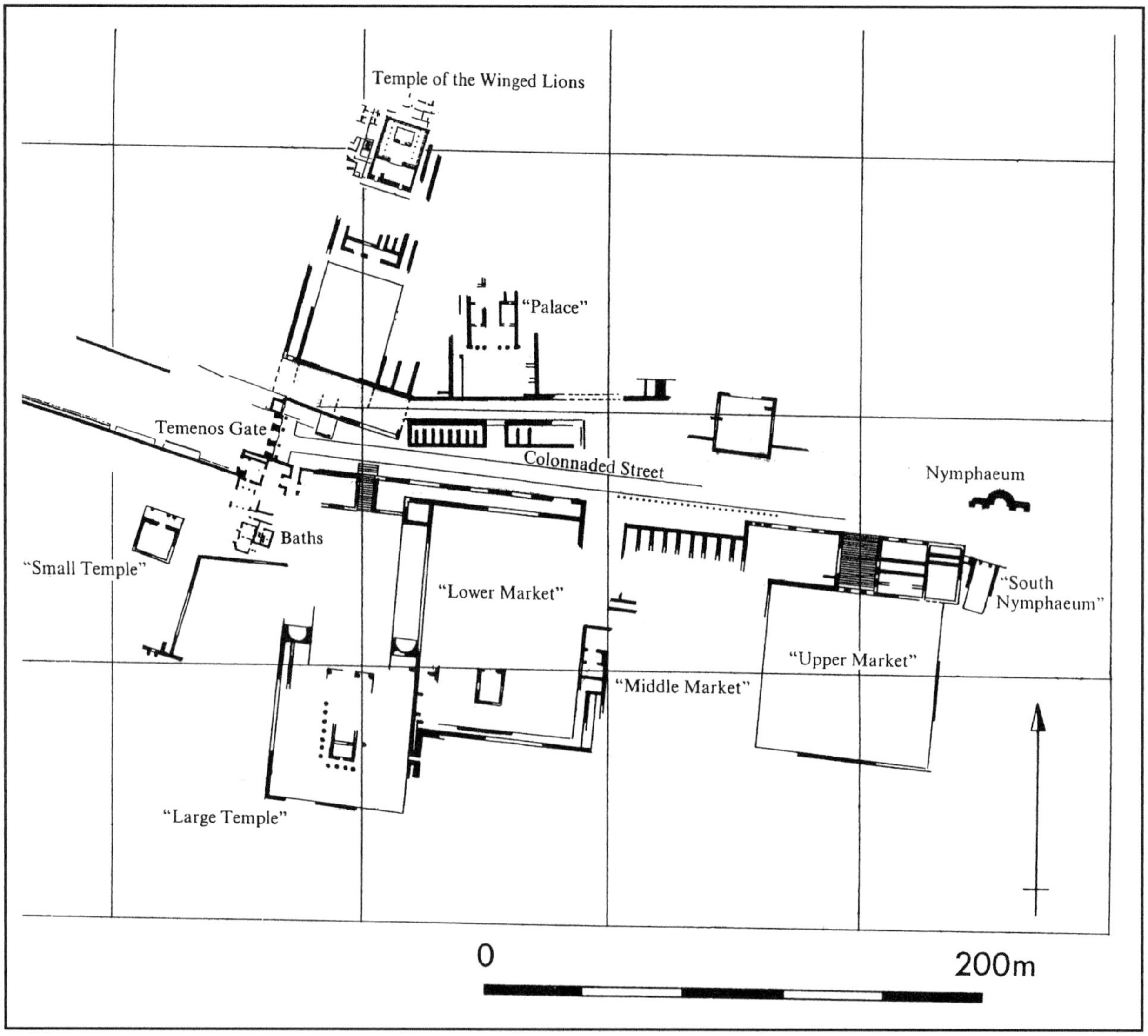

FIGURE 2. Plan of Petra. *(from J. McKenzie, The Architecture of Petra).*

interpreted in this light. Its religious significance is confirmed by the monumental stairway that leads to it and by the religious niches, some with inscriptions and distinctive religious iconography, that surround it. One niche carved nearby has crescent moons and was probably dedicated to a moon deity, while another, farther away, has a remarkable dual representation (probably) of Dushara both as a bearded "classical" god and as a plain *betyl* or stone pillar.

Cult niches are a common religious artifact of the Nabatean tradition. They were often podia for *betyls* (cult-stones). The latter are usually plain and unmarked, but some have minimalist representations of a face. Some were movable, while others were carved *in situ* out of the rock face, with up to three *betyls* of different sizes, apparently representing a "divine family."

That the Nabateans believed in an afterlife is suggested by hundreds of monumental tombs. In some cases these are provided with *triclinia,* ritual banqueting rooms, suggestive of a commemorative ceremony. Some *triclinia* are not related to the dead but were the locus of special cults *(mrzḥy')* adhered to by guilds or sodalities.

THE DEITIES. Dushara appears to be the main Nabatean god, his primacy being evident in the phrase "Dushara and all the gods" in several inscriptions and in the fact that wherever gods are listed he appears first. His name *(dwšr')* is in origin an epithet meaning "the One of (Mount) Shara" (located in southern Jordan). The same analysis of the name appears in Islamic sources, which call him *D̲ū al-Šarā(t).* The name's structure is paralleled in northern and southern Arabia. Dushara's close link with the Petra area is clear from his epithet "god of Gaya," this being an old name of the village at the entrance to Petra.

Of the few indications of specific characteristics of Dushara, we may note the title "the one who separates night from day" in an inscription, which suggests an astral character. Scholars have favored the planet Venus (male in southern Arabia), Mercury (the Arabian god Ruḍā) or the sun (Strabo hints at such a cult in Nabataea, and a solstice aspect of Dushara is suggested later by Epiphanius). Roman identifications of Dushara, for example, with Zeus and Dionysos, are secondary.

Names of other male deities occur, such as Baalshamin (an import from Nabatean Syria), Qōs (Edomite and worshiped at Tannūr) and Hubal (only in northern Arabia), but there is such a concentration on Dushara that it can be argued that he was, in practice, the supreme Nabatean deity. Certainly he was the dynastic deity of the royal house, "the god of our lord (the king)," and because of this his cult spread wherever Nabatean rule extended. In the different localities he was connected with established local gods, such as Baalshamin in Syria.

On the female side, there is evidence of worship of a number of goddesses: Allāt, al-ʿUzzā, and Isis and Atargatis (these last two being foreign). There are also some goddesses who appear only in particular localities within the Nabatean realm (for example, Manōtu only in Ḥegra; specific manifestations of Allāt localized in Boṣrā, the Ḥawrān and Ramm).

The two principal female divine names that occur (though never together) are Allāt and al-ʿUzzā. The distribution of these in the inscriptions suggests that they were never worshiped side by side. There is no explicit evidence of Allāt at Petra and little of al-ʿUzzā at Ramm and in southern Syria. When account is taken, therefore, of the fact that al-ʿUzzā is in fact an epithet, not a personal name, meaning in Arabic "the Mighty One," it is possible to conclude tentatively that al-ʿUzzā was for the Nabateans an epithet of Allāt. The latter enjoyed much wider popularity in Syria and Jordan, while the title al-ʿUzzā is more restricted in use and of Arabian background. The two were, however, distinguished in later tradition in northern Arabia. A final resolution of this may be provided in the future by further epigraphic evidence identifying or distinguishing the two.

Little can be said of characteristics of Allāt and al-ʿUzzā. The former is described in inscriptions as "mother of the gods" (reading uncertain) and "the great goddess." Herodotos identified her with Aphrodite, though in the Ḥawrān she was identified with Athena. al-ʿUzzā is the northern Arabian goddess of the planet Venus and is identified with Aphrodite in a Nabatean inscription from the island of Cos.

Of the various other deities who have some degree of prominence, note may be made of: (1) al-Kutbā, a deity in the Thoth/Nabu tradition, but apparently worshiped in both male and female forms; (2) other deities with north Arabian affiliations such as Shayʿal-Qawm and Hubal; and (3) the god ʿObodat, apparently the divinization of one of the kings of Petra, whose tomb was reportedly located at ʿAvdat in the Negev (Uranius).

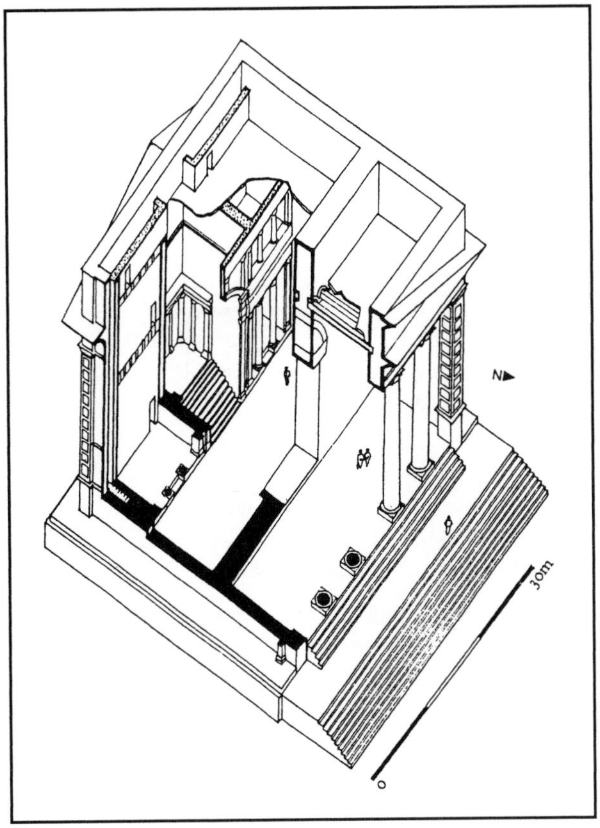

FIGURE 3. The Qasr al-Bint Temple, Petra. *(from J. McKenzie, The Architecture of Petra [after Gibson]).*

ANICONISM AND ARABIA. Reference has already been made to a Nabatean (and wider northern Arabian) tradition of representing deities not as human beings but as *betyls*. This is part of the Nabateans' northern Arabian heritage, but it was not in itself a matter of rigid religious principle, as can be see from the fact that under Greek and Roman influence the Nabateans soon got used to making statues. Reference has been made earlier to the combined representation of Dushara both as a plain *betyl* and as a bearded male figure.

Aniconism (reluctance about or rejection of images) constitutes one of the cultural links between the Nabateans and their contemporary Judaean neighbors on the one hand and the later Muslims on the other, though in the case of Judaism and Islam, aniconism became a central part of religious ideology. There are other points of contact with Jewish practice (such as the probable use of secondary burial), but the northern Arabian coloring of Nabatean religion is much stronger. Apart from the use of *betyls*, major deities such as Dushara and al-ʿUzzā /Allāt, as well as the minor deities such as Hubal and Manōtu (= Manāt), have a clear north Arabian background and they re-emerge later as the pre-Islamic idols destroyed by order of Muḥammad. The most likely explanation of this phenomenon of Arabianism is that at least the higher strata of Nabatean society were of northern Arabian origin: this would also explain the probable use of a form of Arabic as a vernacular and the predominance of Arabian-type personal names.

Because of the sparsity of the evidence, there are few aspects of Nabatean religiosity on a personal level that can be teased out in any detail. A certain fondness among a minority for devotional cults associated with particular gods (Isis and others) may reflect personal religion. The repeated use in graffiti of the religious formula "Remembered be . . ." envisages a pious passer-by bringing blessing on himself by mentioning the name of the inscriber "before the god."

Nabatean religious tradition was heavily influenced by northern Arabian religion, both in the particular gods venerated and in some of the forms that veneration took: the reluctance to depict deities in human form is a good example.

Historically more important, perhaps, is the distinct tendency to restrict attention and worship to the main deities, Dushara and Allāt/al-ʿUzzā (if the latter is a single deity, as argued above). Other gods were worshiped by specialist groups (special ethnically, geographically, socially), but Dushara and Allāt formed a divine pair par excellence, and the cult of these two appears to be the official cult of the state. This is a modified form of monotheism, though involving a pair of deities rather than just one. This type of "dyotheism" was not new—even the Old Testament Yahweh was regarded by many Israelites as having a spouse.

Bibliography

Hackl, Ursula, Hanna Jenni, and Christoph Schneider. *Quellen zur Geschichte der Nabatäer: Textsammlung mit Übersetzung und Kommentar* (*Novum Testamentum et Orbis Antiquus* 51). Freiburg and Göttingen, 2003.

Healey, John. *The Nabatean Tomb Inscriptions of Mada'in Salih* (*Journal of Semitic Studies* Supplement 1). Oxford, 1993.

Healey, John. *The Religion of the Nabateans: A Conspectus* (*Religions in the Graeco-Roman World*, 136). Leiden, 2001.

Starcky, Jean. "Pétra et la Nabatène." In *Dictionnaire de la Bible: Supplément*, edited by Henri Cazelles et al., vol. 7, cols. 886-1017. Paris, 1966.

Tholbecq, Laurent. "Les Sanctuaires des Nabatéens: état de la question à la lumière de recherches archéologiques récentes." *Topoi* 7, no. 2 (1997): 1069–1095.

Wenning, Robert. *Die Nabatäer—Denkmäler und Geschichte* (*Novum Testamentum et Orbis Antiquus* 3). Freiburg/Göttingen, 1987.

Wenning, Robert. "Bemerkungen zur Gesellschaft und Religion der Nabatäer." In *Religion und Gesellschaft: Studien zu ihrer Wechselbeziehung in den Kulturen des Antiken Vorderen Orients* I (*Alter Orient und Altes Testament* 248), edited by Rainer Albertz, pp. 177–201. Münster, 1997.

JOHN F. HEALEY (2005)

NABU was a god, possibly of West Semitic origin, who became a major divine figure in Babylonia and Assyria of the first millennium BCE. He is first mentioned in official Babylonian documents of the time of Hammurabi (c. 1760 BCE) and may have been brought to Babylonia by the West Semites, who migrated there in large numbers in 2000–1800 BCE. Nabu was closely aligned with Marduk, whose minister, scribe, and ultimately son he was considered to be. The cult of Nabu began to spread in the Old Babylonian period. He grew in importance, becoming the god of the Ezida temple and the city of Borsippa by the beginning of the first millennium BCE. Nabu and Marduk are frequently mentioned together as the major pair of gods in Babylonia. *Nabu* appears in many personal names, including *Nabu-Kudurri-usur* (the biblical Nebuchadrezzar), which means "Nabu protect our boundaries." In Assyria, Nabu was revered as one of the most important gods, and his popularity was still increasing at the end of the Assyrian empire.

Nabu appeared in several important cultic festivals of the first millennium BCE. The most important was the Akitu, the spring New Year festival, which began when Nabu came in solemn procession from Borsippa to Babylon. The festival celebrated the reign of Marduk, but Nabu's participation was important enough that the absence of the festival during a period of political disturbance was referred to as "when Nabu did not come from Borsippa." He also appeared in the Babylonian celebration of his marriage to Nana and the Assyrian celebration of his marriage to Tashmetum.

Nabu is best known as the god of writing. He was the patron of scribes, displacing Nisaba, who played this role until the Old Babylonian period (1800–1590 BCE). As Marduk's scribe, Nabu was the writer of the tablets of destiny. He was associated with Marduk and Ea and consequently was considered a god of wisdom. By the end of Assyrian history Nabu was also assuming some of the characteristics of the hero figure Ninurta.

SEE ALSO Akitu; Marduk; Ninurta.

Bibliography

For further information on Nabu, see Francesco Pomponio's *Nabû: Il culto e la figura di un dio del pantheon babilonese ed assiro* (Rome, 1978).

New Sources

Wiseman, D. J., and J. A. Black. *Literary Texts from the Temple of Nabû.* London, 1996.

TIKVA FRYMER-KENSKY (1987)
Revised Bibliography

NĀGĀRJUNA, best known as the first Mahāyāna philosopher in India, is a highly complex figure whose philosophical works, iconic image, and esoteric meditations are studied, honored, and practiced in many Mahāyāna traditions to this day. He developed his systematic philosophy of "emptiness" *(śūnyatā)* some time during the second century CE. According to most hagiographic traditions, however, he attained the alchemical ability to extend his life, and the esoteric texts that some traditions attribute to him were apparently composed several generations after his philosophical works. In Tibet, where his philosophical texts were widely studied, these esoteric writings also became revered and widespread. Whatever the historical reality of Nāgārjuna's life and authorship may be, the great span of his life and the great breadth of his alleged corpus stand as metaphors for his prominence within Mahāyāna Buddhism.

Many of Nāgārjuna's hagiographies, all of which come from China and Tibet, recount an episode that illustrates Nāgārjuna's importance for the Mahāyāna. Probably the earliest texts of the Mahāyāna were in a style that came to be known as Perfection of Wisdom *(prajñāpāramitā)*. These texts teach a challenging theory: addressing much of what early Buddhists held to be ultimately true and real, Perfection of Wisdom claims that such things actually are not ultimately true or real at all. According to Mahāyāna accounts, these texts were taught by the Buddha himself, but they were so challenging that they were kept secret for several centuries after the Buddha's passing; otherwise, their radical doctrines might have led some disciples astray. For their safekeeping, the Perfection of Wisdom texts were conveyed to the land of the *nāgas*, usually depicted as serpent-spirits, who secretly guarded the texts until the world was ready to receive the Perfection of Wisdom. Eventually, Nāgārjuna's fame became known to the *nāga* king, and he invited Nāgārjuna to come teach his philosophy to his subjects. Having traveled magically to the *nāga* kingdom, Nāgārjuna taught the king and his subjects the philosophy of emptiness, and his hosts were so delighted that they conferred on him the long hidden texts. With Nāgārjuna on hand to explain the text's meaning, it was clear that the world was ready to receive these difficult teachings.

While Nāgārjuna's journey to the *nāga* world may be difficult to confirm, there is no doubt that he did indeed champion the Perfection of Wisdom by explaining and defending the notion of emptiness *(śūnyatā)*, the central theme of those texts. His philosophy of emptiness is one of Nāgārjuna's main contributions to the Mahāyāna, and to understand that philosophy, one must see how it is rooted in the previous Buddhist theories that emptiness challenges.

PHILOSOPHY OF EMPTINESS (*ŚŪNYATĀ*). From its earliest period, Buddhist thought rested on the notion that humans seek above all to eliminate suffering, and that the only way to eliminate suffering is to eliminate its causes. According to the strand of Buddhist thought that most concerns Nāgārjuna, suffering is caused by "ignorance" *(avidyā)*, a way of seeing the world that distorts all of one's cognitions. Centered on an erroneous view of one's personal identity as fixed and absolute, ignorance is said to afflict all of the mental states of all ordinary persons. And since one's actions are therefore guided by erroneous and distorted mental states, they cannot fully succeed; hence, all attempts to eliminate suffering end in frustration.

To resolve this problem, one must eliminate ignorance, that is, the pervasive error about one's personal identity that distorts one's experiences. In conceptual terms, this error is the belief that, in some fashion or another, one has an essentially real and immutable identity, a personal "self" or *ātman*. One way to eliminate that belief is to demonstrate convincingly that its object, the alleged self, does not truly exist. And to negate the self, early Buddhist thinkers used a type of reductive analysis: one exhaustively categorizes all of the constituents of mind and body so as to leave no item unexamined, and one then carefully examines those constituents or "elements" (*dharmas*) in order to determine whether any—singly or in combination—could be the self. Using various contemplative techniques, one's thorough search demonstrates that no such self is to be found anywhere in body and mind, and knowing that nothing other than the constituents of mind and body could be a self, one is convinced that no such self exists. One proceeds to deepen this realization of "no-self" (*anātman*) in meditation, and eventually, ignorance is completely overcome. One thus attains *nirvāṇa*, utter freedom from suffering.

Nāgārjuna accepts this model, and he is also familiar with the early Buddhist style of reductive analysis. To put it simply, one analyzes an entity by attempting to break it into its component parts, and if it cannot be broken down further, the entity is ultimately real. The traditional example, a water-jug, is not ultimately real because it can be broken down into more fundamental parts existing at discrete moments of time. Eventually, the analytical process reaches its conclusion: one discovers the irreducible elements that are the stuff of the mental and physical universe. Only these elements are ultimately or truly real.

It is important to note that, while a reductive analysis of this kind leads to the conclusion that entities such as water-jugs are not ultimately real, it does not totally deny the reality of such entities. That is, in ultimate terms a water-jug is actually just irreducible bits of matter; only those irreducible elements are *ultimately* real (*paramārthasat*); the water-jug is not. Nevertheless, in practical and linguistic terms, one can still use the term *water-jug* successfully. Hence, a water-jug is *conventionally* real (*saṃvṛtisat*).

This notion of the two realities—the ultimate and the conventional—is crucial for Nāgārjuna's thought, and he readily accepts it as well. He is not satisfied, however, with simple reduction as a way to discover what is ultimately real. His main critique focuses on the notion of "essence" (*svabhāva*) that the aforementioned reductive analysis assumes. Essence is implicated in the reductive analysis because, in order to truly know that there is no self in mind and body, one must be able to say what mind and body truly are. Since mind and body are just a bundle of elements, this comes down to knowing what the elements truly are. And in order to know what each element truly is, one must know what kind of thing it is—that is, one must recognize its true nature or essence (*svabhāva*).

Nāgārjuna responds to this emphasis on essence by redefining the notion of ultimate reality. He appears to draw on an intuition about parts and wholes in the reductive approach. In order for that analysis to succeed, one must call into question the relation between, for example, the water-jug as a whole and the irreducible particles of matter that are its parts. The analysis concludes that such a whole-part relation cannot be rationally defended; hence, since wholes clearly cannot exist without parts, they must be unreal. The intuition here is that, rather than directly critiquing the notion of a whole such as a water-jug, the analysis attacks the reality of the relation that allegedly ties the whole to its parts. Whether or not this intuition directly inspires Nāgārjuna, it is clear that he supplants the reductive approach with a relational analysis that, moving beyond just the whole-part relation, critiques all forms of relationality and ends in the denial of all essences.

Nāgārjuna's relational analysis begins by admitting that, if an entity were ultimately real, it would indeed need to have an essence or *svabhāva*, but he argues that for an entity to have an essence, it is not sufficient that it be irreducible. Instead, when one says that an entity has an essence, one actually means that the entity's identity is utterly devoid of any dependence on other entities. Thus, to have an essence, the entity must have an utterly independent or nonrelational identity. Since only an entity with such an essence can be ultimately real, to know whether an entity ultimately exists, one need only determine whether its identity is in any way dependent; in other words, can one know what this thing truly is without referring to something other than that thing? If one can know that entity's identity without referring to other entities, then that entity is indeed utterly independent and, hence, ultimately real. But if the entity's identity is inextricably linked to other entities, then that entity is dependent, and as such, the entity has no essence. Hence, that entity is not ultimately real; it can only be conventionally real, at best.

Nāgārjuna applies this relational analysis especially to all those allegedly elemental things that are the mental and physical stuff of the universe according to most early Buddhist thinkers. And he finds that all those things, even the most cherished elements of the Buddhist path, are utterly lacking in essence because none exist independently. Even *nirvāṇa* itself lacks any essential, nonrelational identity, for it depends upon its opposition to *saṃsāra*, the world of suffering. And since *nirvāṇa*, as with all things, lacks essence, it is not ultimately true or real.

For Nāgārjuna, the realization that all things lack essence is the cure for ignorance, which he construes as any "grasping" (*grāha*) to essential, fixed identities, whether of persons or things. The realization that counteracts ignorance comes in the meditation on "emptiness," the metaphor that he uses to evoke this utter lack of essence. His detailed arguments for emptiness examine many forms of relationality. His best known text, for example, begins with an analysis of causality which demonstrates that any entity produced by causes cannot be ultimately real because its existence depends on its causes. These arguments, however, are not themselves sufficient to eliminate ignorance because, as a deeply ingrained cognitive state, ignorance requires more than just argumentation for its elimination. Instead, the conclusion of the arguments—namely, that all entities are utterly empty of any essence—must be cultivated in a contemplative experience through which one becomes fully absorbed in that emptiness.

Nāgārjuna never clearly specifies the way in which one must meditate on emptiness; this and other thorny details are left to later Mahāyāna thinkers. One issue, however, is clear: whether in meditation or in argument, emptiness itself must not be essentialized, for in that case, one would fall into an incurable nihilism. In other words, emptiness is the conclusion to the question, "What is this entity really or truly?" It is the discovery that there is no ultimately real or true identity to be discovered. But if that discovery (i.e., the emptiness of essence) is itself thought to be ultimately or essentially real, then one will have interpreted it as a kind of absolute nothingness at the core of all things. To do so would be to contradict Nāgārjuna; he specifies that no entity has any essence, but if emptiness is interpreted as an absolute nothingness, then one has made emptiness into every entity's essence, albeit in an utterly nihilistic way. Nāgārjuna sees the danger of such an interpretation, and he therefore speaks of emptiness itself as not really being emptiness. In other words, just as a person, being empty of any essence, is not really or ultimately a person, so too emptiness, lacking any essence, is not truly or ultimately emptiness. In this way, Nāgārjuna avoids the nihilism that would ensue from construing emptiness as an absolute nothingness that is the essence of all things.

Using his relational analysis, Nāgārjuna argues that all entities are empty of essence and, thus, that no entity (not even emptiness) is ultimately real. Following, however, the paradigm of the two realities mentioned above, Nāgārjuna does accept that we can speak intelligibly of many things as *conventionally* real. Thus, even though the stuff of the universe does not ultimately exist, it most certainly does exist conventionally in terms of our practical actions and our use of language. A key issue for Nāgārjuna is seeing that the *way* in which entities exist conventionally is deeply linked to his notion of emptiness. In short, emptiness describes things' ultimate mode of existence: they are not ultimately real because they are empty of any fixed, nonrelational identity. Things' conventional mode of existence must be the inverse: they *are* conventionally real because they are filled with fluid, relational identities. Speaking of this fluid relationality that characterizes conventional reality, Nāgārjuna calls it "interdependence" or *pratītya-samutpāda.*

The relationship between emptiness and interdependence is central to Nāgārjuna's thought, as is exemplified by an exchange in Nāgārjuna's best known text, the *Mūlamadhyamaka-kārikā* (Fundamental wisdom of the Middle Way). Raising an objection to the philosophy of emptiness, an opponent asks, if everything is empty of essence, then how is reality possible? That is, if no entity is ultimately real because every entity is empty of essence, then how can a seed produce a sprout? Or, more significantly, how can the practice of the Buddhist path lead to *nirvāṇa*? According to Nāgārjuna, seeds are not truly real, but how then could they produce anything? And if the Buddhist path is also not truly real, how could it lead one to spiritual freedom?

Nāgārjuna's response is to turn the question on its head: if everything were *not* empty of essence, then how could reality be possible? If a cause had an essence, then being ultimately real, it would have an utterly nonrelational identity: what it is in and of itself could in no way be dependent on anything else. But an entity is a cause only in relation to an effect; if the effect were irrelevant to the cause's identity, then clearly anything would be a cause for anything. In short, identities such as "seed" or "path" are clearly relational, and as such, they cannot be ultimate. If they were ultimate, then they would be nonrelational, and a nonrelational world is an utterly inert, unchanging world. Seeds would never produce sprouts, and the path would never lead to *nirvāṇa.*

***Nirvāṇa* and Compassion.** Nāgārjuna's philosophy of emptiness correlates with a significant change in the conception of *nirvāṇa* as it becomes articulated in Mahāyāna Buddhism. In early Buddhism, *nirvāṇa* stands in strict opposition to *saṃsāra,* the world of suffering. As Mahāyāna develops, however, this duality is called into question, such that Perfection of Wisdom texts include episodes in which *saṃsāra* itself is transformed into *nirvāṇa.* Thus, as Nāgārjuna puts it, in ultimate terms there is no distinction between *saṃsāra* and *nirvāṇa.*

Two prerequisites for this shift in the alterity of *nirvāṇa* are found in Nāgārjuna's work. The first is the combination of emptiness and interdependence discussed above. If *saṃsāra* itself is to be the locus of *nirvāṇa,* then *saṃsāra* cannot be composed of irreducible elements that are immutable in their fixed and ultimate essences. They must instead be capable of radical transformation, and this possibility is expressed in philosophical terms through Nāgārjuna's notions of emptiness and interdependence: being empty, things are not fixed in any particular essence, and being interdependent, they can assume new identities in accord with the new, interdependent context in which they are located. The second prerequisite is that there must be some means to achieve that transformation, or to put it more accurately, there must be some principle that guides the transformative process such that it ends in *nirvāṇa.* For Nāgārjuna, that principle is great compassion (*mahākaruṇā*).

Nāgārjuna does not treat compassion as a philosophical concept for which one must argue; instead, it is an indispensable ethical principle that, on his view, distinguishes Mahāyāna Buddhism. Although he never provides a precise definition, later commentators specify that great compassion is an overwhelming need to eliminate the suffering of all beings. Nāgārjuna maintains that, for the Mahāyāna path to be effective, it must combine the philosophy of emptiness with that type of powerful motivation, in part because without such an intense driving force, one could not attain the final goal of the Mahāyāna, namely, the state of buddhahood itself.

In stressing the cultivation of compassion, Nāgārjuna carefully links it with early Buddhist ethical practices, such as adherence to monastic discipline. In this way, Nāgārjuna's radical denial of the ultimate reality of Buddhist notions is accompanied by a consistent, even vigorous defense of Buddhist ethical norms. If one were to examine only Nāgārjuna's best known philosophical texts, one might not get this impression, and it is therefore important to recall that, even if one examines only the works of Nāgārjuna the philosopher (and not the esoteric adept), one still encounters a wide range of writings.

Literary Contributions and Esoteric Writings. Putting aside the question of Nāgārjuna's Tantric esoterica, the philosopher Nāgārjuna, who was active during the second century CE, wrote a large number of texts, some philosophical, some ethical and prescriptive, and others poetic. These texts are all composed in Sanskrit, and this itself is unusual. Prior to Nāgārjuna, Buddhist thinkers wrote in languages such as Pāli that were most likely rooted in earlier, regional dialects. Nāgārjuna may have been the first Buddhist thinker to compose a philosophical text in Sanskrit, and all Mahāyāna thinkers follow his example.

Stylistically, Nāgārjuna's works were also original, in that he composed nearly all of his works in verse and chapter. Buddhists prior to Nāgārjuna certainly employed verse to compose philosophical texts, but Nāgārjuna generally divided his texts into chapters, each of which generally contains a sustained argument in verse. This style, which Nāgārjuna may have borrowed from non-Buddhist authors, also becomes the norm for later Mahāyāna philosophers.

Although neither ornate nor metrically sophisticated, Nāgārjuna's poems are also influential for later thinkers. Cast as "praises" (*stotra*) to the Buddha, his poetical works convey his philosophy in a manner that is not possible through systematic argument. Using various tropes, such as antithesis and paradox, Nāgārjuna's praises become a model for Mahāyāna philosophers, many of whom follow his lead in writing both systematic philosophy and poetical praises.

In later Indian Buddhism and especially in Tibet, the image of Nāgārjuna as poet-philosopher expands to include Nāgārjuna the Tantric adept. From an historical standpoint, it is difficult to accept that the author of Nāgārjuna's philosophical texts is also the author of the much later Tantric texts. Nevertheless, the Tibetan Buddhist traditions do see the authors as identical, and as a result, Nāgārjuna becomes an awesome figure whose philosophical prowess is easily matched by his magical powers. The esoteric texts in question are especially important for the forms of Tibetan Tantra that developed after the eleventh century CE. In detailed but highly abstruse language, Nāgārjuna the adept recounts the means to reproduce the death process so as to enter into the subtlest state of mind, namely, the form of mind that transfers from one life to the next. While in that subtle state, one is to realize the emptiness of even this most basic form of consciousness, thus greatly accelerating the process of eliminating ignorance. In this way, the image of Nāgārjuna combines for Tibetans the most advanced meditative practices with the most sublime form of Buddhist thought.

SEE ALSO Mādhyamika; Nirvāṇa; Pratītya-samutpāda; Śūnyam and Śūnyata.

BIBLIOGRAPHY

Burton, David F. *Emptiness Appraised: A Critical Study of Nāgārjuna's Philosophy.* Richmond, U.K., 1999. A useful critique of Nāgārjuna.

Dreyfus, Georges, and Sara L. McClintock, eds. *The Svātantrika-Prāsaṅgika Distinction: What Difference Does a Difference Make?* Boston, 2002. Focuses on later interpretations of Nāgārjuna's thought.

Galloway, Brian. "Some Logical Issues in Madhyamaka Thought." *Journal of Indian Philosophy* 17 (1989): 1–35. A difficult but very useful analysis of Nāgārjuna's style of reasoning.

Garfield, Jay L., trans. and commentator. *The Fundamental Wisdom of the Middle Way: Nāgārjuna's Mūlamadhyamakakārikā.* Oxford, 1995. A complete translation of Nāgārjuna's main text, along with a philosophical commentary.

Hayes, Richard P. "Nāgārjuna's Appeal." *Journal of Indian Philosophy* 22 (1994): 299–378. A somewhat hyperbolic but insightful critique of modern scholarship on Nāgārjuna.

Siderits, Mark. "Nāgārjuna as Anti-realist." *Journal of Indian Philosophy* 16 (1988): 311–325. Interprets Nāgārjuna's thought in relation to contemporary philosophy.

Williams, Paul, and Anthony Tribe. *Buddhist Thought: A Complete Introduction to the Indian Tradition.* London, 2000. An accessible presentation of Mahāyāna thought that helps to locate Nāgārjuna within a wider context.

JOHN D. DUNNE (2005)

NĀGAS AND YAKṢAS and their female counterparts, *nāgīs* and *yakṣīs*, are pre-Aryan fertility deities of the Indian subcontinent whose fundamental relationship with agricultural pursuits has led to their incorporation into the Hindu and Buddhist pantheons as low-level *devas* (gods), or as a separate category of deities between *devas* and demons and ghosts. In addition, *nāgas* and *yakṣas*, often likened to the guardian *nats* of Thailand and *phi* of Burma, are intimately related with kingship symbolism and play a significant role in the myths and rituals of the Buddhists of South and Southeast Asia.

Early Hindu and Buddhist texts state that *nāgas* and *yakṣas* reside in *caityas*, ancient places of worship marked by a tree, stone altar, pool, or stream, and a railing to designate sacred territory. From these sacred sites, *nāgas* and *yakṣas* are believed to determine the fertility and wealth of a bounded territory as small as a paddy field or as large as a state. If properly worshiped, these deities can guarantee abundance and health to a region through their control over water and its essences, such as semen and sap. They can also bestow gems and the wealth of the underworld, which they are believed to protect. If, however, these territorial fertility deities are slighted, they can withdraw their gifts, bringing famine and spreading disease. This ambivalent power over life and death is revealed in many sculptures in which a *nāga* or *yakṣa* in human form wields in the right hand a sword to protect or chastise and in the left a jar of fertilizing liquids.

In myths and art, *nāgas* are represented as living among the roots of trees or on anthills—entrances to the underworld. They appear as cobras with one or many hoods or can metamorphose into humanlike creatures with dilated cobra hoods springing from the neck and spreading over the head. *Yakṣas,* who are said to live in tree trunks, can also take human forms that may disguise a demonic side. The female *yaksis* are often portrayed as voluptuous maidens, with large breasts and hips, clinging to trees in full bloom—an important fertility motif in India.

As guardians of a region's abundance, *nāgas* and *yakṣas* have come to be intimately associated with kingship in South Asia. In ancient India the *caitya* altar was used as a place of coronation, a practice suggesting that the king's authority was guaranteed or enhanced by deities such as *nāgas* and *yakṣas.* This thesis is supported by *Jātaka* tales and many dynastic myths in which kings are granted rule over a region by forming an agreement with a *nāgarāja* (*nāga* king) or a liaison with a *nāgī* or *yakṣī.* If the king fails in his duties, these deities withdraw their fertilizing powers and bring an end to the king's reign.

The portrayal of *nāgas* and *yakṣas* in the Theravada canon and in the Buddhist myths and rituals of Southeast Asia suggests the incorporation of the symbolism of kingship into the figure of the Buddha and the taming of the powers of nature through the Buddha's *dharma.* These themes reveal an interesting relationship between the otherworldly thrust of Buddhism and the importance of Buddhism for this-worldly existence. In widespread myths the Buddha confronts evil *nāgas* and *yakṣas* who are ravishing a region, reveals his greater command of the forces of nature in combat with these deities, converts the deities with the force of his virtues, and leaves behind a relic as a symbol of the contract that guarantees the good behavior of the deities. These myths, which parallel the Buddha's confrontation with the *yaksa*-like Māra, seem to emphasize the chaotic powers of *nāgas* and *yakṣas* in order to reveal the Buddha's virtues and assert his continuing rule over a region. It appears that very early in Buddhism worshipers honored the Buddha's relics placed in stupas and then went to nearby shrines of *nāgas* and *yakṣas,* to remind these deities of their obligations. Such contracts are recalled in Sri Lankan exorcism rituals in the early twenty-first century, to assure that *yakṣas* leave the person they are possessing. In this manner the Buddha, while withdrawn, remains a lord or ruler of this existence through the power of his *dharma.*

The incorporation of kingship symbolism by the figure of the Buddha can also be seen in his association with the *nāgarāja* Mucilinda. In myth and art, after the Buddha attains *nirvāṇa* he is protected from the weather by the coils and hoods of Mucilinda. Such protection designates kingship in South Asia. These myths help to explain why *nāgas* and *yakṣas* become guardians of the Buddha's relics. They are offering not only their protection but their powers over nature to the Buddha and his followers.

The relationship of the this-worldly powers of the *nāga* and the world-denying view of Buddhism is also revealed in the fascinating figure of Upagupta and in the ordination ceremony. In Burma and Thailand, the monk Upagupta is said to have been born of a *nāgī* maiden. This association allows the fertility powers of the *nāga* to be controlled by the rigorous meditative discipline of the monk, and Upagupta is called upon in rituals to tame the forces of nature. It also can be speculated that the reason a candidate for ordination into the monkhood is called a *nāg* is that he is about to tame his physical desires for the good of society and for the higher goal of Buddhism.

See Also Nats.

Bibliography

The best single work on *yakṣas* is Ananda K. Coomaraswamy's *Yakṣas,* 2 pts. (Washington, D.C., 1928–1931). Jean P. Vogel's *Indian Serpent-Lore, or the Nāgas in Hindu Legend and Art* (London, 1926) gives a wealth of information on the *nāga.* My article "The Buddha and the Nāga: A Study in Buddhist Folk Religiosity," *History of Religion* 13 (August 1973): 36–53, surveys the symbolism of the *naga* and *yakṣa* in Buddhist literature. My article, "The Taming of Māra: Witnessing to the Buddha's Virtues," *History of Religion* 15 (November 1978), speaks of the monk Upagupta and his relationship with a *nāgī,* Māra, and the Buddha.

Lowell W. Bloss (1987 and 2005)

NAG HAMMADI.

Unearthed in 1945 by a group of Egyptians digging for fertilizer, the so-called Nag Hammadi codices were one of the most important manuscript discoveries of the twentieth century for the study of religion in the late ancient Mediterranean world, particularly formative Christianity and Judaism. The forty-six different tractates that the codices contain have provided scholars with a wealth of new data for understanding the development of early Christian traditions about Jesus; Gnostic, Valentinian, and other streams of Christian thought later considered to be heretical; and Coptic grammar, orthography, and codicology. For the most part, however, these sources have not resulted in settled opinions or certain knowledge, but in sharpened debate and new avenues of investigation. Many questions about the codices and their contents remain unanswered.

The Discovery and Publication of the Codices. A group of Egyptian peasants discovered a jar containing the codices in December 1945 at the base of the Jabal al-Tarīf on the east bank of the Nile, across the river from the town of Nag Hammadi. One of the group, Muhammad ʿAlī, broke the jar and found within it thirteen leather-bound codices, which he brought home. There his mother used some of the leaves as fuel for an oven. The codices then passed into the hands of different antiquities dealers. Most famously, Codex I ended up at the Jung Institute in Zurich; also known as the Jung Codex, it was one of the first codices whose tractates were published. Eventually all the codices (except for a fragment) were deposited in the Coptic Museum in Old Cairo, where they are now preserved. Although ʿAlī reports that he found thirteen codices in the jar, the present "Codex XIII" consists actually of leaves that had been removed from a codex in antiquity and placed into the cover of Codex VI. The fate of the thirteenth codex seen by ʿAlī remains unknown.

Especially in comparison to the fate of the Dead Sea Scrolls, the publication of the Nag Hammadi codices was efficient and a model of international cooperation. The political circumstances of Egypt in the 1950s delayed some early publication efforts, but during the 1950s and 1960s some of the texts, especially from Codex I, were published, among which was the *Gospel of Thomas* from Codex II. With the support of UNESCO, a complete facsimile edition was published over the course of the 1970s and completed with an introduction in 1984. James M. Robinson, the American New Testament scholar, organized an international team of scholars to produce an English-language edition and translation. The first English translation appeared in 1977, and volumes of editions of the Coptic texts, with extensive introductions and notes appeared gradually, until the so-called Coptic Gnostic Library was complete; the entire set was reissued in five large paperback volumes in 2000.

As they did their work, most of the editors generously circulated photocopied transcriptions of the texts, so that interested scholars could read them even before the official edition appeared. Meanwhile, two other publishing projects have contributed significantly to the study of the codices. The Berliner Arbeitskreis für koptische-gnostische Schriften, founded and directed by the late Hans-Martin Schenke, has produced a series of important translations, monographs, and commentaries in German. The Bibliothèque copte de Nag Hammadi, based at the University of Laval in Québec and directed by Louis Painchaud, continues to issue high-quality editions of the Coptic texts with translations and commentary in French. Other scholars have published editions and translations independently. Today many of the

Nag Hammadi works can be studied in multiple critical editions and modern translations. In 1971 David Scholer published a comprehensive bibliography of scholarship on Nag Hammadi and Gnosticism, which he updates annually in the journal *Novum Testamentum.*

The Codices and their Origins. Although the hoard of manuscripts is often referred to as a "library," scholars have no definitive evidence for the context of the manuscripts' creation and collection. The scripts, writing materials, and dialects of the manuscripts are diverse. It has been estimated that the handwriting of as many as fourteen different scribes can be detected in the codices. Although all the texts are in Coptic, some are in the Sahidic dialect and others in Subakhmimic, with great variation even within these two broad categories. It seems likely, therefore, that the manuscripts were copied at different locations and subsequently collected by a person or group. In addition to their importance for the history of religions, the codices have contributed to a revival in the study of Coptic philology and codicology. Several of the leather covers contain *cartonnage,* scraps of discarded papyrus glued together to make the cover firm: the latest of the scraps can be dated to 348 CE, and thus it is believed that the codices were constructed around 350 CE and buried sometime in the following decades.

Scholars continue to debate who might have ordered the copying of the manuscripts, collected them, and buried them. Most have suggested Christian monks. The discovery was made near the site of ancient Pbou, the location of a major Pachomian monastery during the fourth century; the cartonnage of Codex VII contains scraps of letters written by solitary (not Pachomian) monks; some of the manuscripts contain scribal notes with Christian prayers or blessings; and at least some of the tractates can be understood to support an ascetic lifestyle. Some scholars have suggested that the order of the tractates in individual codices reflects interests in liturgy, eschatology, and contemplative ascent that are characteristic of Egyptian monks. On the other hand, monks were not the only religiously interested persons in fourth-century Egypt with the wherewithal to finance the production and collection of such books: literate and well-off persons, Christians and not, clerical and lay, could be found in many of the cities and towns along the Nile. Since cartonnage could have been simply gathered from a local trash heap by the makers of the covers, it provides no evidence for the identity of the person or persons who paid for their creation. It is not clear that the original owner(s), the collector(s), and the burier(s) of the codices were identical. Some scholars have speculated that the codices were buried in the wake of Bishop Athanasius of Alexandria's declaration of an official canon of the Bible for the Egyptian church in a letter of 367 CE. Despite these theories, the social context of the codices and the circumstances of their burial remain unknown.

The Contents of the Codices. The forty-six different tractates contained in the Nag Hammadi codices vary widely in their genres and theologies. Although most can be considered Jewish or Christian in the sense that they draw on the Hebrew Bible, the New Testament, and other Jewish and Christian literature, others, such as a fragment of Plato's *Republic,* certainly did not derive from a Jewish or Christian milieu. All of the texts were originally composed in Greek and subsequently translated into Coptic; thus, they could have originated in locations throughout the eastern Mediterranean or among Greek-speaking communities in the West. Many of the tractates are apocalypses or revelations, in which a divine figure (e.g., Jesus) or authoritative human being (e.g., Adam) reveals future events, cosmological secrets, or theological doctrines to an elect person or group. In the *Apocryphon of James,* for example, Jesus appears after his resurrection and teaches a small group of disciples, and in the *Apocalypse of Adam,* Adam reveals to his son Seth the true story of his origin and predicts future events. Other works are or include theological treatises (e.g., *Tripartite Tractate*), sermons (e.g., *Gospel of Truth*), prayers *(Prayer of the Apostle Paul),* hymns (e.g., *The Three Tablets of Seth*), wisdom books (e.g., *Teachings of Silvanus*), a philosophical epistle (*Treatise on Resurrection*), and an anthology of excerpts from theological works (*Gospel of Philip*). Several tractates call themselves "gospels," but none resemble the Gospels of the New Testament, which present a narrative of Jesus' ministry emphasizing his passion and death. The *Gospel of Thomas,* for example, presents a collection of Jesus' sayings, in the manner of the biblical book of *Proverbs,* without any narrative.

Like other manuscripts from antiquity, the codices contain works that appealed to the collector(s), but that also represent diverse theologies and original social and religious contexts. Scholars have only begun the task of categorizing the tractates and attempting to reconstruct their original milieus, and certainty in these areas is probably impossible. Nonetheless, a scholarly consensus appears to have emerged that at least four corpora of literature can be identified. First, scholars call a set of approximately twelve Nag Hammadi tractates "Sethian Gnostic." Although the precise contents of this grouping is debated, it usually includes *The Apocryphon of John, The Hypostasis of the Archons, The Egyptian Gospel, The Apocalypse of Adam, The Three Steles of Seth, Zostrianos, Allogenes, Melchizedek, The Thought of Norea, Marsanes, Trimorphic Protennoia,* and sometimes *Thunder—Perfect Intellect.* Although these treatises differ from one another in genre and some mythic and theological details, they share an underlying myth of origins, in which Adam's son Seth, four divine caregivers called luminaries, and the (according to the myth) ignorant and foolish God of *Genesis* (sometimes called Ialdabaoth) play prominent roles. In his anti-heretical work *Detection and Overthrow of Gnosis, Falsely So-Called* (*Haer.,* c. 180 CE), Bishop Irenaeus of Lyons attributes this same myth to "the gnostic school of thought" and to "the gnostics" (*Haer.* 1.11, 29). For this reason, some scholars believe that these works originated in the only ancient religious group that should be called "Gnostic."

Related to the (Sethian) Gnostic text group is another set of treatises that scholars assign to the Valentinian school of thought, an important Christian theological tradition of the second through fourth centuries. According to Irenaeus, the Christian teacher Valentinus, who died around 175, adapted the Gnostic myth in creating his own system of thought. In the decades following Valentinus's death, Christian theologians teaching in his tradition formed study circles of interested Christians alongside and sometimes in competition with Christian churches. Like its (Sethian) Gnostic counterpart, the Valentinian myth was open to creative revision and elaboration, but it generally took a less negative attitude toward the God of *Genesis* and emphasized themes of integration and recovery of original cosmic and psychic unity; Valentinian theologians devoted considerable attention to such traditional Christian topics as sin and salvation, the resurrection of the dead, and the sacraments. Valentinian works found at Nag Hammadi include *Prayer of the Apostle Paul, The Gospel of Truth, Treatise on Resurrection, Tripartite Tractate,* and *The Gospel of Philip,* among others. Some argue that Valentinus himself is the author of *The Gospel of Truth.*

Two tractates, *The Gospel of Thomas* and *The Book of Thomas the Contender,* grant special authority to the apostle Didymus Judas Thomas, whom Christian tradition credits with bringing Christianity to Mesopotamia and India and sometimes identifies as Jesus' twin brother. Since these works share literary connections and theological affinities with each other and with *The Acts of Thomas,* a text that survives in Greek and Syriac and was not found in the Nag Hammadi cache, some scholars consider them evidence for a "Thomas Christianity," similar to the Pauline Christianity and Johannine Christianity associated with other sets of early Christian literature. Thomas Christianity is believed to have been centered in Edessa, a city in northern Mesopotamia, and to have run from the first century down to the third and perhaps fourth. Thomas theology was highly ascetic, emphasizing the divine origin of the soul, its fall into matter and the body, and its return to its origin and reunion with its true self. Other scholars, however, doubt this reconstruction of an organized Thomas branch of Christianity. Although it is often referred to as the most prominent of the "Gnostic gospels," *The Gospel of Thomas* lacks evidence of the kind of elaborate myth found in the (Sethian) Gnostic works, and thus scholars are increasingly reluctant to refer to it as "Gnostic."

In three tractates from Codex VI—*The Discourse on the Eighth and Ninth, The Prayer of Thanksgiving,* and *Asclepius*—the divine revealer is "thrice great Hermes" or Hermes Trismegistus, a composite of the native Egyptian god Thoth and the Greek god Hermes. These tractates belong, therefore, to a body of pseudepigraphic literature composed in Greek centered around Hermes, now called the Corpus Hermeticum, which may have originated in religious and philosophical circles active in Greco-Roman and late ancient Egypt. Both *The Prayer of Thanksgiving* and *Asclepius* were known before the Nag Hammadi discovery, while *The Discourse on the Eighth and Ninth* is a new addition to the corpus.

Most of the remaining Nag Hammadi tractates are simply miscellaneous Christian literature, the precise doctrinal, sectarian, or theological affiliations of which are unclear or debated. To be sure, some are not Christian in their origin at all (e.g., the fragment of Plato's *Republic* in Codex VI), and some scholars question the "Christian" character of others (e.g., *Authoritative Teaching*). But most are Christian works of an astonishing variety, underlining the impressive diversity of early Christianity in the centuries before Constantine.

THE SIGNIFICANCE OF THE DISCOVERY. The Nag Hammadi discovery has made an enormous impact on several areas of the religious history of the ancient Mediterranean world, even if the results of the impact are not entirely clear. After decades of editing and translating the tractates, scholars are still engaged in sorting out the implications of the new data for such fields as Gnosticism, Jesus traditions and the New Testament, early church history, and late ancient Platonism.

Certainly the codices have contributed the most to the study of Gnosticism. Before the discovery, except for a handful of other recently published texts in Coptic, scholars' knowledge of "Gnosticism" was limited to the statements made by Christian heresiologists, such as Irenaeus. The parallel between *The Apocryphon of John* and Irenaeus's description of the myth of "the gnostics" (*Haer.* 1.29) showed that this work (which is found also in a previously known Coptic manuscript) and the texts closely related to it came from a circle that was known as Gnostic. At last scholars could read (in Coptic translation) works composed by the presumed Gnostics themselves, rather than depend solely on the reports of their "orthodox" opponents, and thus several clichéd charges against the Gnostics (e.g., their lack of interest in ethics) could be evaluated more fully. On the other hand, scholars have found few other correspondences between the Nag Hammadi tractates and the myths and sects described by such anti-Gnostic authors as Irenaeus, Hippolytus of Rome, and Epiphanius of Salamis, and so they have increasingly questioned the value of the heresiological reports, which still provide the only evidence for the social history of such groups.

The tractates have not resolved the protracted debate over the definition of *Gnostic* and *Gnosticism.* Impressed by the variety of the texts and their mismatch with the heresiologists, some scholars argue that these terms should be abandoned altogether and the surviving texts analyzed individually and on their own terms, apart from these categories. Others point to the correspondence between the myth found in *The Apocryphon of John* and that in Irenaeus's account of "the gnostics" (*Haer.* 1.29) and suggest that the term *Gnostic* be applied only to the group responsible for the texts belonging to the "Sethian Gnostic" group; perhaps the Valentinians can be called "Gnostic," but only in a derivative sense, because they adapted the myth of the Gnostics. Still other scholars believe that, despite their variety on several points, many (if not most) of the Nag Hammadi tractates exhibit a set of characteristics that are usefully gathered under the category "Gnosticism." In this case, the Nag Hammadi tractates have not led to a scholarly consensus, but the terms of the debate are perhaps clearer than they were before.

Debate also surrounds the significance of Nag Hammadi works that include sayings attributed to Jesus or that parallel writings of the New Testament. One question is whether such works as *The Gospel of Thomas, The Dialogue of the Savior,* and *The Apocryphon of James* preserve oral or written traditions of Jesus' sayings that are independent of the New Testament Gospels, and thus provide additional information about the historical Jesus and the development of early Christian gospels. Of the relevant tractates, *The Gospel of Thomas* has received the most attention and seems most likely to contain traditions independent of the canonical Gospels, and perhaps even sayings that can be attributed to the historical Jesus. Passages in *Trimorphic Protennoia* and *The Apocryphon of John* parallel sections of the *Gospel of John,* especially the prologue, and some scholars have suggested that they can be used to reconstruct earlier written sources that were available to the author of the Fourth Gospel. The Nag Hammadi texts also have provided new material for the discussion of whether Gnosticism, however it is defined, existed during the first century CE and thus may stand behind the opponents criticized by New Testament authors like Paul. Most scholars now reject the identification of Paul's opponents as Gnostics.

The codices have raised or affected numerous other issues in the study of early church history. These include the development of a Christian canon of scripture. What status did these writings have for the Christians who produced and read them? Were they considered scriptural, equivalent in authority to the texts that were emerging in some churches as "the New Testament"? The tractates' extensive use and revision of the Hebrew Bible (in the form of its Greek translation, the Septuagint) have provided new insights into conflicts among early Christians over the interpretation of the Bible and have suggested links between early Christian and Jewish exegeses of the same biblical texts. Scholars have discovered connections also between certain Nag Hammadi works—especially some Valentinian writings and "wisdom texts" like *The Teachings of Silvanus*—and the literature of early Egyptian monasticism, particularly those letters attributed to Antony the Great and Paul of Tamma.

It appears that Plotinus, the great Neoplatonist philosopher (d. 269/270), knew *Zostrianos* and *Allogenes* or at least persons in the circles in which these works circulated. These two tractates, along with *Marsanes* and others, show contact with the issues and terminology that characterized Platonist philosophical discussions in the second and third centuries. Scholars have now been able to construct a fuller and more detailed narrative of the development of Platonism in this period, one that more extensively documents the interchanges between "Christian" and "pagan" circles and the centrality of "mystical" or "esoteric" themes that scholars once saw as marginal.

The study of the Nag Hammadi codices is still an emerging and relatively new field in comparison to the study of most other sources for ancient Mediterranean religions. In the sixty years since their discovery, scholars have edited and translated the texts, making them available to a wide range of interested readers. Although many questions remain open, especially about the authors of the tractates and the collector(s) of the codices, the thirteen books found by Muhammad ʿAlī and his friends have already creatively unsettled traditional ways of understanding the religious history of the first four centuries after Jesus Christ.

SEE ALSO Gnosticism.

BIBLIOGRAPHY

Hedrick, Charles W., and Robert Hodgson Jr., eds. *Nag Hammadi, Gnosticism, and Early Christianity.* Peabody, Mass., 1986.

King, Karen L. *What Is Gnosticism?* Cambridge, Mass., 2003.

Koester, Helmut. *Ancient Christian Gospels: Their History and Development.* Philadelphia, 1990.

Layton, Bentley, ed. *The Rediscovery of Gnosticism: Proceedings of the International Conference on Gnosticism at Yale, New Haven, Connecticut, March 28–31, 1978.* 2 vols. Leiden, 1980–1981.

Layton, Bentley. *The Gnostic Scriptures.* Garden City, N.Y., 1987.

Layton, Bentley. "Prolegomena to the Study of Ancient Gnosticism." In *The Social World of the First Christians: Essays in Honor of Wayne A. Meeks,* edited by L. Michael White and O. Larry Yarbrough, pp. 334–50. Minneapolis, 1995.

Lease, Gary. "Nag Hammadi: Archaeology." In *Anchor Bible Dictionary,* edited by David Noel Freedman, vol. 4. New York, 1992.

Painchaud, Louis, and Anne Pasquier, eds. *Les textes de Nag Hammadi et le problème de leur classification: Actes du colloque tenu à Québec du 15 au 19 septembre 1993.* Québec, 1995.

Pearson, Birger. "Nag Hammadi Codices." In *Anchor Bible Dictionary,* edited by David Noel Freedman, Vol. 4. New York, 1992.

Pearson, Birger, and James E. Goehring, eds. *The Roots of Egyptian Christianity.* Philadelphia, 1986.

Perkins, Pheme. *Gnosticism and the New Testament.* Minneapolis, 1993.

Robinson, James M. "From Cliff to Cairo: The Story of the Discoverers and Middlemen of the Nag Hammadi Codices." In *Colloque international sur les textes de Nag Hammadi (Québec, 22–25 août 1978),* edited by Dernard Barc, pp. 21–58. Québec, 1981.

Robinson, James M., ed. *The Facsimile Edition of the Nag Hammadi Codices.* 15 vols. in 11. Leiden, 1972–1984.

Robinson, James M., ed. *The Hag Hammadi Library in English.* 3d rev. ed. San Francisco, 1988.

Robinson, James M., ed. *The Coptic Gnostic Library: A Complete Edition of the Nag Hammadi Codices.* 5 vols. Leiden, 2000.

Scholer, David M. *Nag Hammadi Bibliography 1948–69.* Leiden, 1971.

Scholer, David M. "Bibliographica Gnostica: Supplementum I." *Novum Testamentum* 13 (1971): 322–336. Updated annually thereafter, except for 1976.

Turner, John D., and Anne McGuire, eds. *The Nag Hammadi Library after Fifty Years: Proceedings of the 1995 Society of Biblical Literature Commemoration.* Leiden, 1997.

Turner, John D., and Ruth Majercik, eds. *Gnosticism and Later Platonism: Themes, Figures, and Texts.* Atlanta, 2000.

Williams, Michael A. *Rethinking "Gnosticism": An Argument for Dismantling a Dubious Category.* Princeton, 1996.

Wisse, Frederik. "The Nag Hammadi Library and the Heresiologists." *Vigiliae Christianae* 25 (1971): 205–223.

DAVID BRAKKE (2005)

NAHMANIDES, MOSES (c. 1194–c. 1270), also known by the acronym RaMBaN (Rabbi Mosheh ben Naḥman); Spanish name, Bonastrug da Porta; Talmudist, biblical exegete, mystic, and polemicist. Born in Gerona, Catalonia, in a period of cultural transition and controversy, Nahmanides confronted the traditions and attitudes of Spanish, Provençal, and northern Ashkenazic Jewry in a wide range of intellectual pursuits.

His Talmudic education with Yehudah ben Yaqar in Barcelona and with Me'ir ben Yitsḥaq of Trinquetaille exposed him to the dialectical methodology of the Tosafists of northern France, which had penetrated into Languedoc and was revolutionizing the study of the Babylonian Talmud, the central text in the Jewish curriculum. Nahmanides adopted this methodology, which he enriched with the Talmudic studies of Provençal scholars and the textual traditions of Spanish Jewry, to produce *novellae* and legal monographs that would establish the dominant school of rabbinics in Spain until the expulsion of 1492. Aside from his *novellae,* Talmudic commentaries that served as standard texts in medieval Spain, Nahmanides' works in this field include *Milḥamot ha-Shem,* a defense of Yitsḥaq Alfasi's code against the strictures of Zeraḥiah ha-Levi, in which Nahmanides presented what is essentially a complex commentary on selected portions of the Talmud; a critique of Maimonides' *Book of the Commandments* which was also a defense of the Geonic *Halakhot gedolot; Torat ha-adam,* a lengthy monograph on the laws of mourning; a series of studies on other aspects of Talmudic law such as vows, menstrual impurity, and indirect causation of damages, some of which were modeled after Alfasi's code; and, of course, *responsa.*

Although Nahmanides is a towering figure in the history of Talmudic study, his greatest direct impact on the masses of Jews probably came through his wide-ranging and enormously influential commentary on the Pentateuch, which was to become one of the first printed Hebrew books. Nahmanides was persuaded that all knowledge could be found in the Torah, and his efforts to explicate the text touched upon all the areas of his intellectual interest. He was, first of all, deeply concerned with the plain meaning of the text. This concern went beyond questions of philology and syntax; Nahmanides was extraordinarily interested in the structure and order of biblical narrative, which he perceived, despite an apparent rabbinic statement to the contrary, as carefully chronological. The commentary contains nuanced and richly textured observations about the morality, motivations, and personalities of biblical characters; Nahmanides did not hesitate, for example, to question the moral legitimacy of Abraham's apologia to Abimelech that Sarah was indeed his half sister (*Gn.* 20:12). Though he provided an ongoing critique of the commentary of Avraham ibn ʿEzra,ʾ often accusing him of insufficient respect for rabbinic exegesis, Nahmanides allowed himself considerable independence in areas that do not touch upon legal norms, and his frequent deviations from Rashi's interpretations can involve a rejection of their rabbinic sources as well.

Nevertheless, for Nahmanides, the straightforward meaning of the Bible, however complex, does not begin to plumb its depths. He stressed the typological understanding of scripture, which, despite Midrashic precedent, was rather unusual among medieval Jews. Thus, the patriarchal settlement of the Land of Israel is taken to foreshadow the later conquest and remains a source of assurance that Jewish rule will be restored at the end of days.

The profoundest level of meaning in scripture, however, is not typological but mystical. This layer of meaning is the one that Nahmanides discusses at the very beginning of his commentary, where he asserts that the Torah consists entirely of esoteric names of God. Nevertheless, neither this extreme esotericism nor his conviction that mystical doctrines could be known only through tradition prevented him from finding these doctrines in the "plain" meaning of scripture as well, so that straightforward exegesis and what Nahmanides called "hidden wisdom" intersected in a fashion that legitimated the teachings of the Gerona qabbalists by an appeal to the biblical text itself. Although Nahmanides' allusions to esoteric lore remained brief, elusive, and inaccessible to the uninitiated, these doctrines move toward center stage in his commentary to *Job,* where belief in transmigration of souls emerges as the only satisfactory resolution of the problem of evil. This problem and its qabbalistic solution are also at the heart of the theological monograph *Shaʿar ha-gemul,* which Nahmanides appended to *Torat ha-adam* and which treats theodicy both exoterically and esoterically.

In the final analysis, Nahmanides' crucial role in the history of Qabbalah does not lie primarily in the content of these passages and similar, sometimes more elaborate discussions in his sermons (*The Law of the Lord Is Perfect, Sermon for a Wedding, Sermon on Ecclesiastes, Sermon for Roʾsh ha-Shanah*), nor is it to be sought in his partially preserved commentary on *Sefer yetsirah* (Book of creation). His key contribution was the legitimation of Qabbalah by the very fact that he advocated it; the problems raised by this system for Jewish theology could not readily be pressed if the critic would thereby be raising questions about the orthodoxy of so unimpeachable a figure as Nahmanides. Consequently, the mere fact that Nahmanides was a mystic was a significant factor in the triumphant progress of Qabbalah in late medieval and Renaissance Jewish history.

Aside from his mystical, exegetical, and homiletical writings, Nahmanides produced two other influential works on non-halakhic topics. *Sefer ha-ge'ullah* (Book of the redemption) was prompted by some signs of messianic skepticism among Spanish Jews. Although Nahmanides did not consider the redemption to be in the first rank of Jewish dogmas—one could, after all, expect greater heavenly rewards for observing the Torah under James I of Aragon than under the much more benevolent messianic king—defense of the belief in redemption was important theologically and crucial for the collective psyche of medieval Jewry. Nahmanides insisted on the continuing relevance of eschatological passages in the Bible, which, he said, are both unfulfilled and unconditional. Finally, he joined the ranks of messianic calculators, arguing eloquently that a straightforward reading of the end of *Daniel* points to the arrival of the ultimate redeemer in 1403, a date sufficiently close to buttress Jewish morale yet sufficiently removed to discourage messianic hysteria.

Any discussion of exile and redemption inevitably had polemical implications for Jews in Christian Europe, but Nahmanides' major polemical work was thrust upon him late in life under extraordinary circumstances. A Jewish convert to Christianity began to engage in vigorous missionary activity utilizing the relatively new argument that Talmudic passages demonstrate the truth of Christianity. In 1263 in Barcelona, Nahmanides was forced to defend the Jewish position in a disputation witnessed by James I. Despite the reservations of some scholars, there is every reason to believe that Nahmanides, who received an award from the king after the debate, acquitted himself with distinction; he later recorded his version of the proceedings in a work that lifted Jewish spirits and influenced subsequent polemicists through the medieval period and beyond.

His boldest and most controversial argument, which was probably sincere, maintained that rabbinic *midrash* was not dogmatically binding; hence, the Jewish polemicist was free to reject some uncongenial statements of the rabbis. The reaction of later Jews to this approach was profoundly ambivalent, and they wondered both about Nahmanides' sincerity and about the ultimate utility of an approach that undercut Christian arguments and respect for the rabbis at the same time. Nahmanides' own reverence for the rabbis even while differing from them is illustrated in his one other foray into Jewish-Christian polemic—a brief commentary on *Isaiah* 53 in which he asserted his conviction that the suffering servant is the Jewish people, but devoted the work to explaining how the Talmud could have understood the figure messianically without drawing Christian conclusions.

The disputation at Barcelona was not Nahmanides' first encounter with controversy of significant historical dimensions. In 1232, he had played a major role in the dispute over the writings of Maimonides and the legitimacy of philosophical inquiry. Some rabbis in northern France, responding to complaints by Provençal antirationalists, had proclaimed a ban against the study of Maimonides' *Guide of the Perplexed* and the first section of his code, while Maimonists had reacted by placing the Provençal anti-Maimonists under the ban. Nahmanides, who admired Maimonides but had deep reservations about the standard form of philosophical study, proposed a compromise to the rabbis of northern France that may well have persuaded them to withdraw from further involvement in this dispute. The code, including its first section, should be studied with enthusiasm; public study of the *Guide* should be banned; private study of both the *Guide* and philosophy in general should gently be discouraged.

Modern scholarly views of Nahmanides' position in this controversy as well as of his overall philosophical posture reflect considerable disagreement. Many scholars perceive him as a thoroughgoing antirationalist who despised philosophy and saw a world of omnipresent miracles in which no natural order existed; others, with greater justice, see a far more complex figure who absorbed much of the medieval philosophical legacy, made his living as a physician, saw a naturalistic world punctuated by miracles, and espoused disciplined theological inquiry within carefully delineated limits.

The Land of Israel had always played a particularly significant role in Nahmanides' thought, and when he found himself under pressure in the wake of the Barcelona disputation, he went there to spend his remaining years. This was no placid retirement. Nahmanides revived the Jewish community of Jerusalem, which had been decimated by the invasion of the Khwarazan Turks in 1244. He became the head of the Jewish community in Acre, and it was in Israel that he put the finishing touches on his *magnum opus* on the Pentateuch.

SEE ALSO Tosafot.

BIBLIOGRAPHY

Works by Nahmanides

The standard edition of Nahmanides' novellae is *Ḥiddushei ha-Ramban,* 2 vols. (Jerusalem, 1928). Charles B. Chavel has edited *Perushei ha-Torah le-Rabbenu Mosheh ben Naḥman (Ramban),* 2 vols. (Jerusalem, 1962), and *Kitvei Rabbenu Mosheh ben Nahman,* 2 vols. (Jerusalem, 1963), and is the editor and translator of *Ramban (Nachmanides): Commentary on the Torah,* 5 vols. (New York, 1971–1976), and *Writings and Discourses,* 2 vols. (New York, 1978). Despite drawbacks, Chavel's are the standard editions of these novellae and also contain commentary by the editor.

Works about Nahmanides

The best of several short books on Nahmanides that contain both biographical information and analysis of his thought is Heymann Chone's German work, *Nachmanides* (Nuremberg, 1930), while Chavel's *Ramban: His Life and Teachings* (New York, 1960) is the only such work in English. The characterization in Solomon Schechter's *Studies in Judaism,* vol. 1

(1896; reprint, Cleveland, 1958), remains useful. The most elaborate volume on aspects of Nahmanides' thought is Chayim Henoch's *Ha-Ramban ke-ḥoqer ve-khi-mequbbal* (Jerusalem, 1978). For an important collection of new studies, see *Rabbi Moses Naḥmanides*, edited by Isadore Twersky (Cambridge, Mass., 1983).

New Sources

Chazan, Robert. *Barcelona and Beyond: The Disputation of 1263 and Its Aftermath.* Berkeley, 1992.

Henoch, Chayim. *Ramban: Philosopher and Kabbalist on the Basis of His Exegesis to the Mitzvoth.* Northvale, N.J., 1998.

Novak, David. *The Theology of Nahmanides Systematically Presented.* Atlanta, 1992.

Pedaya, Haviva. *Ha-Ramban: hit'alut zeman mahzori vetekst kadosh.* Tel Aviv, Israel, 2003.

Stern, Josef. *Problems and Parables of Law: Maimonides and Nahmanides on Reasons for the Commandments (ta'amei ha-mitzvot).* Albany, N.Y., 1998.

DAVID BERGER (1987)
Revised Bibliography

NAḤMAN OF BRATSLAV (1772–1810), Hasidic master and founder of the Bratslav sect, born in Medzhibozh, Ukraine. A great-grandson of Yisra'el ben Eli'ezer (1700–1760), the BeSHT, the first central figure of Hasidism, Naḥman proclaimed a path that stood in direct opposition to that of his esteemed forebear. Naḥman's complex and tortuous struggle for faith stood in sharp contrast to the BeSHT's ideal of simplicity and wholeness: theologically, Hasidism's earlier enthusiastic proclamation of the all-pervasive presence of God is replaced in Bratslav Hasidism by a painful awareness of his absence. The relative "neutralization" of messianic energies, characteristic especially of the Mezhirich school, is also reversed in Bratslav, where Naḥman, whom Bratslavers consider the only true *tsaddiq* ("righteous man"), is clearly depicted at least as a proto-messianic figure.

Given the family into which he was born, it was probably expected of Naḥman that he lead a Hasidic following in a movement that was becoming firmly entrenched in a pattern of dynastic succession. In his early years he refused this role, feeling himself inadequate to it and perhaps disdaining Hasidism as it was popularly practiced in his surroundings.

In 1798 Naḥman undertook a pilgrimage from the Ukraine to the Holy Land. Arriving in the Galilee right in the midst of Napoleon's battle with the Turks, he suffered numerous hardships and was at times close to death. He saw this journey as a private rite of passage, and later in life often looked back on it as a source of inspiration. Only on his return from the Land of Israel was he ready to assume the mantle of leadership, and this he did in a highly selective manner. Gathering around himself an elite cadre of disciples dedicated to a revitalization of the Hasidic movement, Naḥman issued an open challenge to such popular figures as Aryeh Leib of Shpola and his own uncle, Baruch of Medzhibozh. He saw Hasidism as having grown self-satisfied, compromised by the shallow assurances of blessing such self-proclaimed *tsaddiqim* would offer in exchange for the rather considerable gifts they were receiving. In Naḥman's community poverty was the ideal, miracles were disdained, and the master was not to be bothered with such small matters as material blessings. The disciples were to devote themselves to an intense regimen of private devotion and penitence. In the early years of his leadership, Naḥman insisted that each new disciple confess all of his sins to him. Sin was taken quite seriously in Bratslav, where earlier Hasidic warnings against excessive guilt were set aside.

The essential practice that Naḥman demanded of his disciples was *hitbodedut,* which in Bratslav meant a daily "conversation" that each Hasid was to have with God. *Hitbodedut* had to be practiced for an hour each day, spoken aloud in one's native tongue, and performed by each Ḥasid in private, preferably outdoors. During this hour the disciple was instructed to "break his heart" and confess before God his most secret thoughts. While the Bratslav sect remained fully within Jewish orthodoxy, including full observance of the law and recital of daily liturgy, it was this new practice of *hitbodedut* that was the true focus of its spiritual attention.

Naḥman was filled with ambivalence about his role as leader. Some of his statements exude an exaggerated sense of self-importance, a claim that he is the only true *tsaddiq* of his generation, and an air of megalomania. Others reflect just the opposite: an acute sense of unworthiness, a feeling of personal emptiness, and a regret at having allowed himself to accept a mantle of which he was unworthy. These alternating attitudes fit in with Naḥman's well-documented alternating states of elation and melancholy, a pattern that would today probably be diagnosed as manic-depression. It was in the course of his recurrent bouts with depression and guilt that Naḥman came to articulate his distinctive theological position.

The absence of God from human life is a reality that must be treated seriously. The religious person must come to terms with the fact that he lives in a world from which God has absented himself. Moments of doubt, inevitable in such a situation, must be treated as recording a valid aspect of human experience, and the notion of faith must be so expanded as to dialectically encompass doubt and denial within it. The seeker must struggle constantly with the eternal questions; one who does so will ascend through a constant spiral of doubt, denial, longing, faith, renewed challenge, doubt and denial, a higher rung of faith, and so forth. The great danger to such a quest is complacency; its highest ideal, that of constant growth. The nature of faith becomes ever more complex as it seeks to contain within itself ever more serious questions and conflicts.

Faith, a term more prevalent in Bratslav than in any other premodern Jewish ideology, is defined as a constant longing for God, an outcry of the broken heart aware of his distance. Such faith can only be cultivated, Naḥman taught, in a world where God's absence is real and where no easy answers are available to fill the painful void. Thus the absence of God is paradoxically God's greatest gift, allowing people the psychological room in which to build up the reservoir of faith that is the most important human asset. The awareness that this self-absenting (*tsimtsum,* as the older qabbalistic term is read in Bratslav) is itself a divine gift allows one to suffer life in the void, but does not alter its reality.

The sharp inner tensions that drove Naḥman to seek a path of redemption for himself, his disciples, and the Hasidic movement as a whole culminated in a brief messianic attempt in the year 1806. Once that attempt had failed (Naḥman saw the death of his infant son as a sure sign from heaven), a new and more subtle way to deliver the message of redemption was sought. This led Naḥman to the telling of his tales, now collected, symbolic fantasies that give fresh and vital expression to the mythic themes of qabbalistic thought. Redemption is the central underlying motif in most of these tales, the purpose of which seems to have been the preparing of his hearers' minds for the great events to come. Published in 1815, the tales take their place alongside Naḥman's collected teachings, *Liqquṭei Moharan* (1809, 1811), as unique classics in the Hasidic corpus.

Naḥman died tragically of tuberculosis at the age of thirty-eight, leaving no male heir. His faithful disciple, Natan of Nemirov, led the community after him but always acted as the master's surrogate rather than his successor. Bratslav is unique in surviving as a Hasidic community that has no living master; in later times, when they were much persecuted within the Hasidic world, they were referred to by others as the "dead Ḥasidim." The small but hardy band of Bratslavers treated this as a badge of honor, however, as they remained true to the memory of the one master who had been theirs and who, according to some Bratslav sources, was yet to come again.

BIBLIOGRAPHY

Naḥman's *Tales* exist in several English translations, the most useful that by Arnold J. Band (New York, 1978), which also contains introductions and notes to each tale. Arthur Green's *Tormented Master: A Life of Rabbi Nahman of Bratslav* (University, Ala., 1979) is the first full-length critical biography. Hebrew readers will also want to consult Joseph G. Weiss's *Meḥqarim ba-Ḥasidut Bratslav* (Jerusalem, 1974) and Mendel Piekarz's *Ḥasidut Bratslav* (Jerusalem, 1972).

New Sources

Cohen, Laurent. *Le maître des frontières incertaines: Rabbi Nahman de Bratslav.* Paris, 1994.

Danieli, Natascia. "La 'restaurazione universale' ('tiqqun ha-kelali') nell'insegnamento de Nahman di Bratslav." *Henoch* 23 (2001): 97–112.

Magid, Shaul, ed. *God's Voice from the Void: Old and New Studies in Bratslav Hasidism.* Albany, N.Y., 2002.

Niborski, Itzhok (Isidoro). "Mysticisme et modernité dans la littérature Yiddish: Rabbi Nahman de Braslev et Aaron Zeitlin." *Yod* 31–32 (1992): 159–170.

Verman, Mark. "Aliyah and Yeridah: The Journeys of the Besht and R. Nachman to Israel." *AJMT* 3 (1988): 159–171.

ARTHUR GREEN (1987)
Revised Bibliography

NAHUATL RELIGION.

The speakers of Nahuatl dialects compose the largest group of indigenous people in Mexico. Numbering about 800,000, they live primarily in the Federal District and the states of México, Morelos, Puebla, Tlaxcala, Guerrero, Veracruz, and San Luis Potosí. Smaller populations can be found in Jalisco, Nayarit, Oaxaca, and Tabasco. The proportion of Nahuatl speakers in central Mexico is declining, but their absolute number is fairly stable and is augmented by millions of Spanish-speaking villagers who preserve elements of Nahuatl heritage. Among both these groups, remnants of pre-Hispanic Nahuatl religion persist in combination with a Catholicism that retains much of the character of its sixteenth-century Hispanic origins.

Folk Catholicism in most Nahuatl villages is more than a superficial veneer on a pre-Hispanic substratum; it constitutes the very meaning of village life. Social solidarity is expressed in terms of spiritual kinship, that is, as godparenthood and ritual commensality. Godparenthood is associated not only with the sacraments of baptism, first communion, confirmation, and marriage but also with many nonsacramental events ranging from the blessing of dwellings, stores, tractors, and trucks to curing ceremonies and graduation from sixth grade. Baptism, the other sacraments, and blessings sanctify persons and objects and so recruit them into the spiritual family (i.e., the village or neighborhood conceptualized as a sacred community).

Life within the spiritual family is symbolized by the fiesta, which bears an obvious similarity to the Eucharist and the agape (love feast) of early Christians. The fiesta, or ritual meal, consists of three courses—rice, turkey in mole sauce, and beans—accompanied by alcoholic beverages. Fiestas honor the patron saints of neighborhoods and villages and mark the sacramental rites of passage. The festivities occasion momentary conviviality, and their preparation promotes enduring amity by requiring villagers to give generously of their time and resources for the benefit of others. The familial symbolism and sentiments associated with the fiesta system come into sharp focus during the Christmas-Candlemas season, at which time festivities center on the Holy Family—the Christ Child, Mary, and Joseph.

On or about the third of May, fiestas are held to honor mountainside crosses that protect communities and neighborhoods during the rainy season. In a weather-working cult in northern Morelos, crosses are associated with San Miguel Arcángel, four lightning-hurling saints, and groups of "rain dwarfs" (*awaque*). The weather-working shamans hold their own ceremonies at mountainside shrines at the beginning of May and again in early November, or roughly at the start and the end of the rainy season.

In contrast to the saints and members of the Holy Family are many evil and Adamic beings who threaten the villagers. Some of these beings are satirized by dancers at carnivals and fairs, where the Devil may be represented by a figure in a red suit with horns. In apparitions, the Devil may appear as a Spanish gentleman, or *hacendado*, mounted on horseback. Other sinister beings include Death; goblins (the spirits of unbaptized children) who offer women bribes for sexual favors; were-animals called *naguales*, who molest drunkards and women on unlit paths after nightfall; La Llorona, also known as La Malinche, a sirenlike apparition who aborted or murdered her children after being abandoned by a lover who is sometimes identified as the Spanish conqueror Cortés; witches who cause illness and poverty, and who suck blood from children's necks; Water Snake and Little Bull, two supernatural animals that bring forth crop-damaging winds and rain; and harmful spirits called *ehecame* ("winds") or *los aires*. *Ehecame* cause paralysis, tics and twitches, neuralgia, loss of sensation, skin disorders, and other afflictions. Witches use a technique called *aire echado* ("thrown air") in which dirt from a grave containing a *tonalli*, or shadow-soul, is mixed with other ingredients and hurled against the victim's house.

Ehecame can also cause *susto* ("fright"), an emotional reaction that affects the shadow-soul of a living person and results in depression, insomnia, and loss of appetite. The parts of the shadow-soul are dispersed throughout the bloodstream, but in response to fright they retreat toward the heart or leave the body. In some communities the shadow-soul fragments are likened to animals or are said to take animal form when outside the body. Persons with weak natures are more vulnerable than others to fright-illness.

Fright-illness and various other beliefs indicate that persons having strong—even tainted—natures enjoy more protection against evil than do persons with weak or sensitive natures. Indeed, nature as well as spirit is seen as a necessary and inevitable part of a person's total makeup. Thus Nahuatl rituals repeatedly express the place of evil and nature in the overall scheme of things. Ritual impersonations of La Malinche, Cortés, Huehuenches ("old ones"), Tenanchis (the grandmothers of the Christ Child), and the figures of the bull and the deer testify to the importance of the Adamic. In mock bull slayings and deer hunts, the killer/hunter assumes a role analogous to that of the serpent who tempts Adam and Eve. The Tenanchis appear during the Christmas-Candlemas season as enticing, tempting figures suggestive of Eve. Huehuenches dance during Carnival, also evoking the Adamic, but in more sinister fashion: as Herod's agents they are enemies of the Christ Child. In some communities the struggle between the forces of good and evil is dramatized during local fairs by mock battles between "Christians" and "Moors."

The Nahuatl ritual complex thus includes various vestiges of the pre-Hispanic pantheon, but its basic armature is nonetheless recognizably Catholic: Eve and, through her, Adam are deceived by the serpent and so denied immortality, but they generate natural life; by contrast, Christ is killed by the agents of the devil, yet his death offers spiritual immortality. The appeal of these conceptual polarities for Nahuatl villagers may be grounded in the realities and contradictions of peasant existence. The villagers subscribe to spiritual values, but the exigencies of daily life continually remind them of the importance of nature and the ever-present problem of evil.

Bibliography

For a classic ethnographic monograph on a Nahuatl community with information on religion, see William Madsen's *The Virgin's Children* (Austin, 1960). Hugo G. Nutini and Betty Bell provide a comprehensive description of godparenthood in *Ritual Kinship: The Structure and Historical Development of the Compadrazgo System in Rural Tlaxcala* (Princeton, 1980). An authoritative treatment of ancient and contemporary Nahuatl conceptions of the soul and related issues can be found in Alfredo López Austin's *Cuerpo humano e ideología: Las concepciones de los antiguos nahuas* (Mexico City, 1980). Donald Cordry's *Mexican Masks* (Austin, 1980) illustrates and interprets ritual masks and costumes from various areas, including the Nahuatl region.

New Sources

Alcina Frank, José. *Mitos y literatura azteca (Aztec myths and literature)*. Madrid, 1989.

Burkhart, Louise M. "A Nahuatl Religious Drama of c. 1590." In *Latin American Indian Literatures Journal* 7 (1991): 153–171.

Burkhart, Louise M. "The Aesthetic of Paradise in Nahuatl Devotional Literature." *Res: Anthropology and Aesthetics* (1992): 89–109.

History and Mythology of the Aztecs: The Codex Chimalpopoca. Translated by John Bierhorst. Tucson, 1992.

Neumann, Franke J. "Experience of Time in Nahuatl Religion," *Journal of the American Academy of Religion* 44 (1976): 255–263.

JOHN M. INGHAM (1987)
Revised Bibliography

NAKAE TŌJU

NAKAE TŌJU (1608–1648), Japanese Neo-Confucian thinker. Tōju, often called the Sage of Ōmi, was born in Ogawa in Ōmi Province on Lake Biwa in central Japan. With the exception of sixteen years spent in Ōzu on the island of Shikoku, he passed his life in Omi engaged in studying, teaching, and writing. His grandfather, who had adopted him at the age of nine, took him to Shikoku and encouraged his early education. After his grandfather's death, when Tōju was fifteen, he attended lectures on the *Analects* by a visiting Zen priest. After this he began serious study of the Four Books (*Analects, Great Learning, Doctrine of the Mean, Mencius*) and of Zhu Xi's commentaries on them. In 1634, citing as motives his own ill health and his desire to be with his widowed mother, he returned to Ōmi. Although some sources indicate that another motive may have been the desire to escape political entanglements, most accounts mark this as the beginning of his focus on the virtue of filial piety.

In 1636 he set up a school called the Tōju Shoin and accepted pupils of all classes and backgrounds. The Four Books and Zhu Xi's commentaries were the core of the curriculum, but Tōju wished to avoid the behavioral formalism sometimes associated with the transmission of Zhu Xi's thought. Instead, he stressed the need to adapt Neo-Confucianism to time, place, and rank. It was during this period that he studied the Five Classics (*History, Odes, Rites, Changes, Spring and Autumn Annals*). Inspired by them, he wrote two works on moral cultivation, both in 1638: *Jikei zusetsu* (The diagram of holding fast to reverence, explained) and *Genjin* (Inquiry into man). In the following year he wrote *Rongo kyotō keimō iden* (Resolving obscurities concerning the Hsiang-tang chapter of the *Analects*), in which he discussed the reverential attitude displayed by Confucius in daily activities and in religious rituals.

Tōju had been moved by this aspect of Confucius's character and wished to return to the religious spirit he saw in Confucius and in the Five Classics. He began to recite each morning the *Hsiao ching* (Classic of filial piety), and he subsequently became increasingly convinced of its profound implications. In 1641 he wrote *Kōkyō keimō* (The true meaning of the classic of filial piety). His other major work, written a year earlier and continually revised until his death, was *Okina mondō* (Dialogues with an old man). Here, in addition to discussing filiality, Tōju noted how Confucian morality was essential for the samurai class.

Tōju has been considered the founder of the Wang Yang-ming school in Japan, but it was not until three years before his death that he acquired Wang's complete works. Although deeply affected by them, he had already been exposed to the writings of late Ming thinkers such as Wangji, who some scholars feel may have had an even stronger influence on him. It is clear that his doubts about Zhu Xi's thought arose from his aversion to its formalistic interpreters. The appeal of the Ming Confucians was their emphasis on interiority, innate knowledge, universal sagehood, and a religious sense of reverence.

Tōju's principal religious ideas can be summarized as a profound reverence for the Supreme Being (*jōten*), manifested in an optimistic doctrine of moral self-cultivation based on the innate knowledge of the good. Tōju taught that the heart of self-cultivation was filiality, for it was the "root of the human" and an intricate part of the transformative processes of nature itself. As the dynamic reciprocity between all created things, he saw filiality as the basis of social relations and as a nurturing principle in the natural order. Thus Tōju's distinctive religiosity drew on various strains of Confucian and Neo-Confucian thought, and combined a reverent theism, interior cultivation, and filial devotion.

SEE ALSO Confucianism in Japan.

BIBLIOGRAPHY

Works by Nakae Tōju are collected in three sources: *Tōju sensei zenshū*, 5 vols. (Shiga-ken, 1928–1929), edited by the Tōju Jinga Sōritsu Kyōsankai; *Nakae Tōju bunshū* (Tokyo, 1926), edited by Mukasa San and others; and *Nakae Tōju* (Tokyo, 1974), edited by Yamanoi Yū as volume 29 of "Nihon shisō taikei." Tōju thought is the subject of a recent study by Yamamoto Makoto, *Nakae Tōju no jugaku* (Tokyo, 1977).

New Sources

Soum, Jean-François. *Nakae Tôju (1608–1648) et Kumazawa Banzan (1619–1691): Deux Penseurs de l'Epoque d'Edo.* Paris, 2002.

MARY EVELYN TUCKER (1987)
Revised Bibliography

NAKAYAMA MIKI (1798–1887) was the founder of Tenrikyō ("The Teaching of Divine Wisdom"), which is one of Japan's best known "new religions" (*shin shūkyō*), with over two million members at the beginning of the twenty-first century. Miki's story is important not only for understanding Tenrikyō, but also for understanding what is novel about the many new religious movements that arose and flourished in Japan since the end of the nineteenth century.

The church's sacred biographies present a sanctified image of Miki as a shrine of God who was also a divine model for all who sought salvation. She was born into a wealthy farming family in the small village of Sanmaiden in what is now Nara prefecture on April 18, 1798. As a child she showed a remarkable generosity of spirit as well as unusual devotion to the *nembutsu* faith of Pure Land (Jôdo) Buddhism. Miki was a spiritual seeker whose quest for the truth almost led her to become a Buddhist nun.

In 1810, however, her family forced her to marry Zenbei Nakayama (1788–1853), the eldest son of the prosperous village chief of Shoyashiki village, now known as Tenri City near Nara, Tenrikyō's headquarters. According to Miki's revelations, Shoyashiki was also the sacred center where humanity was first created (*jiba*) by God. She was put in charge of Nakayama family affairs at the age of sixteen. She became a paragon of virtue through obedience and hard work—the "good wife and wise mother" according to the contemporary Confucian feminine ideal.

Nevertheless, Miki endured intense personal suffering. Her mother-in-law constantly bullied her, while her husband Zenbei led a dissolute life that almost led to her death when his lover Okano, the family maid, tried to poison her. In 1828 yet another tragedy occurred when a neighbor's child she was caring for became ill with smallpox. Miki vowed to the gods that she would sacrifice her own life as well as her children's to save him. Indeed, two of her own children died after the neighbor's child miraculously recovered.

Miki's turning point occurred on October 23, 1838, when she was forty years old. Life was uncertain after one of the worst famines to affect Japan in the nineteenth century, followed by an unsuccessful political revolt by the samurai Ōshio Heihachirō. Miki, who was physically and emotionally drained after the birth of her last child, Kokan, faced further misery when her eldest son Shūji (1821–1881) was afflicted with unbearable pain in his left leg. His condition gradually worsened in spite of consultations with physicians. As a last resort, a mountain ascetic *(yamabushi)* was called to perform an exorcism *(yosekaji)* on Shūji. The normal procedure for an exorcism required the ascetic to recite incantations that forced the evil spirit to enter a female medium. There it would announce its identity and its reasons for afflicting the child. In Shūji's case, however, something extraordinary happened. Because the ascetic's normal medium was not available, he asked Miki to serve in her stead. When Miki went into a trance, however, instead of an evil spirit, an august voice spoke through her, saying, "I am the general of heaven. I am the true and original God. . . . I have descended from heaven to save all human beings, and I want Miki to be the shrine of God." Despite initial opposition, Miki's family acceded to the god's demand, and Miki embarked on her career as a living *kami (ikigami)*, or deity. In 1841 her god, whom she addressed as Tenri-Ō-no-Mikoto, commanded her to live a life of poverty as the first stage of her mission to relieve human suffering. She gave the family treasures to those in need, even going so far as to tear down the Nakayama mansion. After Zenbei died in 1853, she began to proclaim her new faith by reciting the simple prayer *Namu Tenri-Ō-no-Mikoto* ("Honor to the Lord of Divine Wisdom") on the street corners of Osaka. She also began to attract many converts because of her miraculous healing powers, especially her ability to grant a painless passage through childbirth *(obiya yurushi)*. In 1863 she met Izō Iburi, a master carpenter who became her most devoted disciple and built the first worship hall on the Nakayama estate. Following the roof raising, however, an incident at a local shrine led to Miki's disciples being arrested for disturbing the peace. This episode began a long period of persecution by the Shintō priests, Buddhist authorities, and local police who feared the new religion.

From 1866 to 1882, Miki wrote down the two major scriptures of Tenrikyō containing the revelations of God, the *Ofudesaki* (The tip of the divine writing brush), and the *Mikagura Uta* (The songs of the *Tsutome* service), followed by a third scripture known as *Osashizu* (Divine instructions). *Osashizu* was written down by Izō as Miki's spiritual intermediary after her death. Miki also taught a ritual dance called *Teodori,* which is still performed as a regular part of Tenrikyō services.

Miki's revelations and her sacred dance were intended to convey the central doctrines of Tenrikyō. Miki believed that voluntary poverty is necessary to achieve salvation, and that true happiness is found only through consecrated labor when a devotee acts with no thought of reward. Unhappiness is caused by dust settling on the heart from past evil *karma.* A joyful life *(yōki gurashi)* can be attained by having true faith in God the parent *(oyagami)*, who has the power to sweep away the evil dust. The laughter, songs, and *Teodori* dance are concrete realizations of this joy in ritual form. Miki ardently believed that the entire world could be renewed *(yo naoshi)* by following her method of salvation. Although her son Shūji won official recognition from the Shintō authorities in 1867, government persecution of Tenrikyō continued throughout the Meiji period (1868–1912). The Meiji authorities tried to stamp out "evil religions" in order to promote "enlightenment and progress" (*bunmei kaika*) through modern rational principles. They also saw Tenrikyō, which was popular among the peasantry, as a direct threat to Shintō and its nationalistic faith in the emperor. Miki was arrested over eighteen times for her heretical beliefs until her death in 1887 at the age of eighty-nine.

Miki's biography is significant to contemporary students of religion for three reasons. First, it shows the typical features associated with the rise of Japanese new religions. Tenrikyō arose outside the priestly establishment in a time of social unrest. It is also a syncretic mix of Shintō, Buddhist and folk religious elements that reflects the religious dynamism of Japanese religions. Moreover, Miki's belief system is typical in its claim to reveal a previously hidden truth from a hitherto unknown god for the spiritual benefit of humankind and the renewal of the world *(yo naoshi).*

Second, Tenrikyō, like many other new religions, was founded by a charismatic woman who fit the ancient Japanese pattern of the female shamanic medium (*miko*). Shimazono Susumu has noted, however, that Nakayama Miki and other charismatic founders like her displayed a new trait. Rather than simply filling the traditional role of a spirit medium as an assistant to a Buddhist ascetic, Miki acted on her own behalf throughout her life. After her death, she still continued to serve as a mouthpiece for God through her male assistant Izō. Moreover, the *kami* who possessed Miki was not an ordinary malevolent fox or snake spirit but an all-powerful and benevolent parent god. Tenri-Ō-no-Mikoto not only created the world and humanity but was also a caring deity promising universal salvation. Miki also differed from the traditional spirit medium in another respect, according to Shimazono. As a "shrine of God," Miki was a vehicle for the divine in every aspect of her life, not only when she was in a trance state. She thus became a model of human fellowship with the divine for the faithful to emulate. Founders who were living *kami* like Miki played an important role in emerging nineteenth-century Japanese religious movements.

Third, several scholars have called attention to Miki's special role as a savior of poor and oppressed women. Traditional Buddhist teachings denigrated women as polluted and spiritually inferior beings. Tenri-Ō-no-Mikoto, however, taught that men and women are spiritual equals. Indeed, the god's other names, "parent god" *(oyagami)* and Sun-Moon *(tsuki-hi)*, convey Miki's revelation that the sacred is both male and female. Miki also taught women that childbirth is not polluting, but rather a joyful experience protected by God's power—a controversial teaching given the old restrictive Japanese customs surrounding childbirth.

SEE ALSO Japanese Religions, article on Popular Religion; New Religious Movements, article on New Religious Movements and Women; Tenrikyō.

BIBLIOGRAPHY

Ellwood, Robert S. *Tenrikyo: A Pilgrimage Faith: The Structure and Meanings of a Modern Japanese Religion.* Nara, Japan, 1982.

Gössmann, Elizabeth. *Frauen und Neue Religionen: Die Religionsgründerinnen Nakayama Miki und Deguchi Nao.* Vienna, 1989.

Kasahara Kazuo, ed. *A History of Japanese Religion.* Tokyo, 2001.

Morishita, Saburo Shawn. *Teodori: Cosmological Building and Social Consolidation in a Ritual Dance.* Rome, 2001.

Nakayama Miki. *Ofudesaki: The Tip of the Writing Brush.* 6th ed. Tenri, Japan, 1993.

Nakayama Yoshikazu. *My Oyasama.* 2 vols. Nara, Japan, 1984–1986.

Reader, Ian. *Religion in Contemporary Japan.* Honolulu, 1991.

Shimazono Susumu. "The Living Kami Idea in the New Religions of Japan." *Japanese Journal of Religious Studies* 6 (1979): 389–409.

Shimazono Susumu. "Charisma and the Evolution of Religious Consciousness: The Rise of the Early New Religions of Japan." *Annual Review of the Social Sciences of Religions* 6 (1982): 153–176.

Van Straelen, Henry. *The Religion of Divine Wisdom: Japan's Most Powerful Religious Movement.* Tokyo, 1954.

Yamashita Akiko. "Tenrin-Ō and Henjō-nansi: Two Women Founders of New Religions." *Japanese Religions* 16 (1990): 1–23.

MARK W. MACWILLIAMS (2005)

NAMĀZ SEE ṢALĀT

NAMES AND NAMING

NAMES AND NAMING activities are central to human symbolic and communicative processes. To be human is to name, and be named, and thereby to possess full being and the ability to relate to the world in meaningful ways. In the Bible, God is said to have brought all the newly created animals to the first human, "to see what he would call them" (*Gn.* 2:19). In all human communities there is thought to be a close relationship between the name of a person or other phenomenon and its character, status, and very being.

Names often have a mysterious quality, whether they refer to sacred beings of a transcendent nature or to humans and other concrete entities. There is power in names, because they both participate in the reality named and give definition and identity to that reality. That is, name and named exist in a mutual relationship in which the power of the former is shared with the being of the latter. Being without name has a very marginal status in the world of phenomena. For example, traditional Christian teaching holds that unbaptized children who die go to limbo. They have no clearly defined status because they have been given no name by the proper ceremonial means. The act of christening during baptism renders a new life human in the religio-cultural sense, which is more significant than mere biological humanness. Similarly, among the Netsilik, in a traditional Inuit (Eskimo) context, once a female infant had received a name it was absolutely forbidden to kill her, though female children were often considered superfluous.

Persons have often been thought to persist after death through the remembrance of their names. In ancient Egypt, children had the solemn duty to preserve the names of their parents through ritual means. The Old Kingdom Pyramid Text of Pharaoh Pepi I refers to his continued existence by means of the repetition of his name: "Thy name which is on earth lives; thy name which is on earth lasts; thou wilt not disappear; thou wilt not be destroyed in all eternity" (cited by Henri Frankfort, *Kingship and the Gods*, Chicago, 1948, p. 113).

Not only humans, whether of high or low degree, but also gods exist and express their power, presence, and will by means of their names. In ancient Israel, God was believed to dwell in his Temple through his name (*shem*), while he himself dwelt in heaven. That is, by his name, *YHVH* (probably then pronounced as *Yahveh*), God resided in revealed form among his creatures. In this case, Yahveh's inner being was not coterminous with his name; but his power, will, and presence were made manifest in his sanctuary through it. Islamic belief holds that Allāh likes to be called upon by his names, which provide vehicles for communication and even union between Allāh and his human servants. In Hinduism, the mention of a god's name has soteriological value. One view even holds that the name of God is greater than its referent, because sound (*sphoṭa*) is absolute. But not all traditions have a name for God, nor is it always considered proper, because of their holiness, to utter those names that are associated with divinity.

NAMES OF GODS AND OTHER SACRED ENTITIES. It is common to nearly all religious practices that in order to communicate with a deity one must know its name. Knowledge of a divine name gives the knower both power and an avenue of communication with its source. This intimate relationship between knowing a name and participating in its power has both religious and magical aspects.

Ancient Israel and Judaism. Moses asked the voice from the burning bush, identified as "the god of your fathers," what his name was, and was answered "I am" (*ehyeh*), which, in a different Hebrew grammatical form, is rendered *Yahveh* (approximately, "He causes to be"; *Ex.* 3:13–14). In keeping with this most mysterious and potent of God's names in the Hebrew tradition is the conviction that God's names are, generally speaking, according to his acts. Causing to be is the greatest of acts and thus the name *Yahveh* is the most sublime name. Yahveh, as name and as theological concept, affirms both God's eternal reality and his reliable presence with his covenant people, Israel.

There are many names for God in the Hebrew scriptures; some of them appear to be very archaic, and some were shared by other Semitic peoples in antiquity. Other names came into being during the long covenant history of Israel, both through contact with neighboring peoples and through the deepening insights of Hebrew prophets and poets. *Baal* ("lord"), a term common to Canaanite religion and Hebrew faith, came to be associated with Yahveh for a time, only to be repudiated later. *Adon*, which also means "lord," did not earn the opprobrium of *Baal* and continues to the present to be an honorific substitution for *Yahveh*, the name that postexilic Jews considered too holy to utter. *Adonai* ("my lord") came to be a potent religious term because of its referent, whose real name was different. Here sacred names can be seen operating on different levels, with one gracious name serving as a protective shield for another, more sacred name. Certain other divine titles and names emerged from Israel's cumulative experiences and convictions: political ones meaning "king," "judge," "shepherd"; kinship terms meaning "father," "brother," "kinsman"; and metaphors from nature with such meanings as "rock."

Christianity. The New Testament community inherited most of the Israelite names and convictions associated with God but never developed the strong sense of taboo connected with the holiest name, *Yahveh*. Jesus took the Hebrew name of God as "father" but rendered it in the familiar form *Abba* ("daddy"), which astonished people because it is ordinarily used only between an actual begotten child and its father. *Father* has remained the most characteristic Christian appellation for God, used especially when the speaker draws near to him in prayer, worship, and praise. All other names for God, whether inherited from the biblical tradition of the Jews or generated within the Christian movement, have been tempered by the intimate personal dimension that Jesus emphasized.

The Christians accepted the older Hebraic custom of speaking or acting "in the name of" someone, whether God or a human, as a representative or witness. The New Testament sometimes uses the names of God and Jesus almost interchangeably as the ultimate divine authority, while never suggesting directly that Jesus is other than the mediator between God and humankind, and not to be worshiped himself. The identification between Father and Son, however, becomes almost total in later christological developments, when Christians came increasingly to conceive of God in terms of Jesus' incarnation. "At the name of Jesus, every knee should bow" (*Phil.* 2:10) is one way in which the New Testament expresses the exalted nature of Christ, whose name is holy.

Islam. In characteristic Abrahamic fashion, the religion of Muḥammad and the Qurʾān places heavy emphasis on the name of God. All utterances, written or spoken, should be prefaced by the phrase "In the name of Allāh, the merciful, the compassionate" (Arab., "Bismillāh al-raḥmān al-raḥīm"). The word *Allāh* is probably an archaic contraction of the Arabic definite article *al-* and *ʿilāh*, "deity" (cf. Heb. *el*, *eloh*, "god"). Allāh, "the god," or God, was central in the pre-Islamic pantheon but as the highest and not the sole divinity. The ancient Arabs believed that Allāh had three daughters, but this as well as other views of Allāh's relatedness and contingency were swept away by the prophetic activity of Muḥammad and the message of the Qurʾān. The Islamic scripture emphasizes Allāh's incomparable uniqueness. It also provides many names and titles of Allāh, sometimes outright but often in the sense of derivations of divine attributes and activities (e.g., *Knower*, *Provider*, *Relenting*). Later Islam developed out of the Qurʾān a list of the "most beautiful names of Allāh " (*al-asmaʾ, al-ḥusnā*), which are traditionally believed to number ninety-nine. The names are recited by Muslims, often with the aid of a string of beads called a *subḥa*. Each name has a particular power and should be recited according to the spiritual station of the seeker.

In addition to *Allāh*, two other names figure prominently in the Qurʾān. The first is *Rabb* ("lord"), a term that occurs most frequently in passages containing material about Jews and Christians. The message of Allāh's uniqueness and sovereignty is often declared with the use of *Rabb*, beginning with what is commonly considered to be the first passage to have been revealed: "Recite: In the name of thy Lord *[rabbika]*, who created man of a blood clot" (surah 96:1–2). The second frequent Qurʾanic name besides *Allāh* is *al-Raḥmān* ("the merciful"), which is the same as the old South Arabian Jewish name for God. The Qurʾān commands the believers to "call upon Allāh, or call upon al-Raḥmān; whichsoever you call upon, to him belong the names most beautiful" (17:110).

Muslims have never observed a taboo respecting the name of God. Instead, they have preferred to utter their praises with as many divine names and attributes as possible, following the Qurʾanic command: "O believers, remember God oft [by means of *dhikr*, "mentioning" his names], and give him glory at the dawn and in the evening" (33:41).

Sikhism. The Indian combination of devotional Hindu and Ṣūfī Islamic doctrines founded by Gurū Nānak (d. 1539) emphasizes the magnification of God by his name in a special form of devotion known as *nām mārga* ("the path of the name"). A variety of names for God are recognized and uttered by Sikhs, including both Muslim and Hindu ones, but the most common is *Sat Nām* ("the true name"). Although Sikhs believe that it is beyond humankind's capacity to describe and define God, people can become purified and free of their egos by means of the veneration of his names, with intelligent awareness and detachment from the world.

Hinduism. There is a persistent conviction within the rich and complex Hindu worldview that the mysterious, unknowable ultimate reality, *brahman* (which literally means "expansion, swelling, growth"), transcends and undergirds all. *Brahman* is the holiest of beings, the most real being, and the source and goal of all being. Hindus have developed highly abstract pantheistic and theistic philosophical doctrines of *brahman.* At bottom, the name *brahman* means "prayer," in the sense of sacred utterance, so that by speaking the word one participates in its reality as power and speech. The believer is able to meditate on divine themes by means of *mantras*, special patterns and techniques of oral utterance that center on the name of a deity, or on a sacred syllable or sound. A *mantra* is not limited to divine names as words only but may be rooted in the whole realm of sound and breath. *Mantras* are recited under the guidance of a guru, or preceptor, who knows the correct pronunciation of the formulas and other aspects of ritual performance, such as posture and breath control.

It is of the utmost importance in Hinduism that the correct name for a deity be used, depending on the purpose and status of the worshiper. The many named divinities of Hinduism, although never universally regarded as belonging to a single system, nevertheless can be identified as components of a comprehensive and balanced worldview, with prominent social and cultural dimensions.

The invocation of names of gods is especially prominent in devotional (*bhakti*) Hinduism. Singing and recitation of the divine names, especially that of Kṛṣṇa, is believed to bring release (*mokṣa*) from the round of rebirth (*saṃsāra*). Some Hindus meet regularly to perform *nāma vali*, a "necklace of names" in which an emotionally charged congregation and its leader sing the name of a deity, beginning slowly, and building up to a spirited climax. The Purāṇas contain much on name praise, such as the following passage: "Hari's Name, Hari's Name, and Hari's Name alone is my vocation. In the Kali age there is no other, no other, indeed no other course [for *mokṣa*]" (cited in Singer, 1966, pp. 143–144).

Mahāyāna Buddhism. Mahāyāna Buddhism places considerable emphasis upon the soteriological efficacy of invoking the Buddha's name. The Pure Land schools of East Asia stress faith in Amitābha (called Amida in Japan), focusing on the simple ritual of reciting the name of the Buddha in order to be saved and enter paradise.

Nembutsu. The devout repetition of the phrase "Namu Amida Butsu" ("Homage to Amida Buddha") is believed to deliver one from sins and, if uttered on the threshold of death, will effect one's rebirth in the Pure Land of Amida. There are different schools of the ritual remembrance of the Buddha's name, called *nembutsu* in Japanese and *nien-fo* in Chinese. The Japanese monk Hōnen (1133–1212) taught that one should repeat the name of Amida with faith, a practice open to practically anyone, not requiring long apprenticeship in meditation. Hōnen and some of his disciples insisted that the *nembutsu* formula should be repeated continuously, as many as seventy thousand times in one day. Shinran (1173–1262), who followed his master Hōnen in *nembutsu*, considered a single recitation of the ritual invocation, "with faith," as sufficient for salvation. In Japan, the name is a key dimension, whereas in China and India, invoking the name of Amitābha Buddha has been associated with the less central contemplation of the gigantic features of the Buddha's cosmic body.

The Lotus Sūtra. Another ritual naming practice in Mahāyāna Buddhism is the invocation of the *Lotus Sūtra*, a major book in the Buddhist canon that became a central scripture of Tendai Buddhism in China and Japan. Nichiren (1232–1282), a Japanese seeker who studied Tendai, Zen, and Pure Land Buddhism, concluded his spiritual training with the discovery that enlightenment could be achieved by anyone who has sincere faith in the teaching of the *Lotus Sūtra.* This faith was then to be expressed in the formula "Namu Myōhōrengekyō" ("Homage to the *Sūtra of the Lotus of the Wonderful Law*"). Implicit in this Japanese statement of affirmation is the sense of humble submission to the power of what is named, which is also somehow the name itself. Nichiren chanted the name of the *Lotus Sūtra* to the accompaniment of a drum.

China. The Chinese have traditionally stressed the importance of names, whether in the Confucian doctrine of the "rectification of names," a philosophy of balance, propriety, and equity in the universe, or at the practical level of naming gods, humans, and other beings. Confucianism has always emphasized the veneration of ancestors, but the Way of Heaven (*tʿien-dao*) has traditionally been ultimate. *Tʿien* ("heaven") is sometimes a name for the impersonal sky that overarches all things; at other times *tʿien* has taken on a somewhat more personal meaning, as the divine ruler of events on earth. A variant is *shang-ti* ("supreme ruler," or God). But *tʿien*, even when it means "deity," is subordinate to *dao*, the universally acknowledged ultimate reality in Chinese religious thought. *Dao* cannot be named, nor can it be translated. To characterize the term as the impersonal, creative, and regulating power of the universe is to approach its essence, which in any case is mysterious and transcendent. But, paradoxically, *dao* is also immanent and natural. Laotzu's classic treatise, *Dao-te ching*, opens: "The way *[dao]* that can be spoken of is not the constant way; the name that can be named is not the constant name. The nameless was the beginning of heaven and earth; the named was the mother of the myriad creatures" (trans. D. C. Lau, Baltimore, 1963).

Nonliterate and archaic traditions. The appellations for divinity and humankind alike among nonliterate peoples are often extremely varied and complex. Names and naming are frequently surrounded by taboos and employed only with specified ritual procedures, including considerations of status, relationship, season, age, place, and power.

Australia. Among the Aborigines of southeastern Australia, before Europeans arrived, there was a fully developed belief in a "high god," as scholars have named the category of supreme being in archaic religion. In Australia, the high god's names, myths, activities, and associated rituals were closely guarded secrets, known only to the initiated males of high status. *Baiame* is one of the names for the Australian high god, who is believed to have created the world, given moral laws, and established the initiation rites by means of which humans attain their full being and come into contact with ultimate reality. The Australian high god is a sky divinity who performed his greatest labors at the beginning of things, but who nevertheless continues to live and have influence. *Baiame, Daramulun, Nurunderi, Bunjil,* and *Biral* are some of the names for the "sky-hero," as A. P. Elkin (1954) calls the Australian high god. The secret name of this deity was divulged during initiation rites, when his voice was heard in the sound of the bull-roarer.

Africa. Celestial supreme beings are also known in traditional African religions. Some are distant and uninvolved in human affairs, as in Australia. But others are active and engaged in the world, especially on the moral plane. The Yoruba believe in a high god called Ọlọrun ("lord of the sky"). Ọlọrun is not directly involved in historical existence, but rules through intermediaries. Among the Dinka, on the other hand, Nhialac, whose name means "above," is honored as both creator and sustainer of the world. The Dinka tend to identify all other gods and sacred forces with Nhialac, who thus becomes a sort of only god, in the monotheistic sense, as well as supreme being. The Nuer have no special name for God, but simply use the term *kwoth* ("spirit"), together with appropriate qualifying words or clauses.

Ancient Egypt. The celestial type of deity is clearly discernible in ancient Egyptian religion, where the pharaoh was believed to be the divine embodiment of Horus, the falcon god, and Re, the sun god. Celestial names and attributes are always reserved for royalty in such traditions as that of Egypt, in which the close relationship, even identification, of the divine and human realms is bound up with rule and cosmic order. Ancient Egyptian sources indicate a great concern for names and their power. The most powerful name for a god was his or her unknown name, as is evident in the famous story of how Isis tricked the supreme god Re into revealing his secret name, which resulted in the goddess's appropriation of his power. Name magic became highly developed in ancient Egypt, especially with respect to deities, who exercised direct power over humans for good or ill.

Ancient Rome. The naming of deities in Roman times was a highly complex and carefully regulated affair. The Romans kept long lists of divinities, both known and unknown; and they also preserved secret lists of divine names. Hermann Usener wrote a celebrated book called *Götternamen* (Names of Gods; 1896) in which he argued that the Romans distinguished both "momentary" and "functional" deities, who received names according to their times and kinds of activities. Every time, place, thing, and event had its own deity, according to this theory, and the myriad deities that inevitably resulted from such a view were arranged hierarchically. Usener's thesis that momentary and functional gods gave rise to more pervasive, overarching gods, and finally to God, has not fared well in recent times, although his researches still provide a detailed review of the naming systems employed by the ancient Romans.

HUMAN NAMES AND NAMING PROCESSES. Human names and naming practices are often as important ritually and symbolically as those connected with deities. For example, in ancient Egypt, the name of a god, person, or object was equivalent to its inner being; without *ren,* "name," there was no existence. In the case of humans, *ren* came to be equal in importance to the *ka,* the individual's "spirit" or "vital force." Likewise, in traditional China the name and its owner were identical. In Confucian ancestral rites, the deceased had a "spirit tablet" or a gravestone engraved with his or her name. If the name were omitted or effaced, then there was thought to be no spirit in the grave, and the person utterly ceased to exist. Similar ideas, with different specific rites and behavior patterns, can be found in other traditions (e.g., in Africa, Oceania, and the Americas).

Judaism. Jews have traditionally employed biblical names, which in turn were derived from many sources: kinship (e.g., *Yehoshuʿa ben Nun,* "Joshua the son of Nun"), animals (e.g., *Raḥel* or *Rachel,* "ewe"), plants (e.g., *Tamar,* "palm"), personal characteristics (e.g., *Esav* or *Esau,* "hairy"), circumstances of birth (e.g., *Yaʿaqov* or *Jacob,* "he who takes by the heel"), and relationship to God (e.g., *ʿOvadyah* or *Obadiah,* "servant of Yahveh"). In biblical times, the Hebrews practiced name changing because of status changes or special circumstances and experiences. Yaʿaqov's (Jacob's) name was changed to *Yisraʿel* (*Israel,* "let God contend" or "he who strives with God") after his struggle with the angel (*Gn.* 32:29). Avram's (Abram's) name was changed to *Avraham* (*Abraham*) and Sarai's to *Sarah* when they were commissioned with their auspicious roles as parents of multitudes (*Gn.* 17:5, 17:15). Jews have also adopted foreign names in certain periods. In medieval Europe, they adopted both sacred and secular names, a practice that endures.

Christianity. Christians have sometimes insisted on specifically Christian names for their children, but they have often also adopted names current in the countries where they have lived. Where Christians have constituted a minority, for example in Islamic regions, "Christian" names (like *Peter, George, Paul, Mark,* and *Thomas*) have been important factors in preserving religious and social identity. Although it has rarely been required that children take biblical names, it has often been done. More common has been the practice of giving a child the name of a saint. Persons entering holy orders or elevated to high ecclesiastical office have also taken saints' names. During the Reformation, Protestants began using Old Testament names for their children, to distinguish themselves from Roman Catholics. The Council of Trent decreed that all baptized infants must be given a saint's name.

Islam. The conversion to Islam is accompanied by a change of name. Muslim names are partly based on ancient

Arabic or other (Persian, Turkish, or Indian) usages, partly upon the sayings of Muḥammad reported in the body of traditions known as *ḥadīth.* Muḥammad taught that the best names are *ʿAbd Allāh* ("God's servant") and *ʿAbd ar-Raḥmān* ("servant of the merciful"). From this basis, the use of *ʿabd* with any of the ninety-nine "most beautiful names" of God became very common. The name *Muḥammad* and its parallels are widely used for males, for according to tradition every man with the name of Muḥammad will go to paradise. The Muslims developed a list of ninety-nine names of the Prophet *(asmāʾ sharīfah)* to parallel the ninety-nine names of God. Among them are *Aḥmad* ("most praised"), *Tāhā* (the first word of surah 20), *Mudaththir* ("wrapped," the opening word of surah 74), *Munīr* ("radiant," surah 33:45), and so forth. Also popular are the names of the Prophet's family and his companions, although in Shīʿī circles one will never find the names of the first three caliphs or of ʿĀʾishah but will very frequently find those of Fāṭimah and the imams, from ʿAlī to Taqī or Riḍā. Names of the Qurʾanic prophets are widely used, including those of Mūsā (Moses) and ʿĪsā (Jesus).

Traditionally, a Muslim name has several different parts, among them the *ism,* the *nisbah,* and the *kun-yah.* The *ism* is the religious name, like those mentioned above. The *nisbah* shows the relation to one's birthplace, tribe, or line of thought; in Arabic, it ends in *ī,* as in *Makkī* ("from Mecca"), *Thaqafī* ("from the Thaqīf tribe"), and *Ḥanafī* ("belonging to the Ḥanafī school of law"). The *kunyah* indicates the relation of a parent to a child; either *Abū* ("father of") or *Umm* ("mother of") is given to a firstborn child, as in *Abū ʿAlī,* or is used in a more general sense, as in *Abū al-Fawāris* ("father of the riders"). The *kunyah* is the name of honor by which one ought to be addressed.

A Muslim name is often complemented by a *laqab,* a nickname pointing to some special quality, as in *al-Aʿraj* ("the lame one"). Often, composites with *al-dīn* ("of the religion") are added to the *ism,* as in *Jalal al-Dīn* ("majesty of religion"). To people in political positions compounds with *al-dawlah* ("of the state") may be given as honorific titles, as in *Sayf al-Dawlah* ("sword of the state"). Rulers surrounded themselves with long chains of honorific names, the central one pointing to their relation with God, as in *al-Mutawakkil ʿalā Allāh* ("who trusts in God"). Male children were sometimes given repellent names to avert the evil eye, but slaves were often given such delightful names as *Marjān* ("coral") and *Kāfūr* ("camphor").

Non-Arab Muslims traditionally continued using their inherited names, complemented by Muslim names; in countries under Persian cultural influence, such as Turkey and India, Persian names were often used among the upper classes. Indo-Pakistan has produced unusually colorful names, which are often incompatible with Arabic grammar.

Names are often given by an elder member of the family or a venerated master. If a child is born on an auspicious day or in a sacred month, he or she may be named accordingly: by *Ramaḍān,* for instance, or *Mawlidīyah* (for a girl born on the birthday, *mawlid,* of the Prophet). If the child is the result of a special prayer he may be given the name *Nabi-Bakhsh* ("gift of the Prophet"), *Dād-ʿAlī* ("Ali's gift"), or *Ghauth-Bakhsh* ("given by Ghauth," i.e., *ʿAbd al-Qādir Jīlānā*). Often, especially in India, the Qurʾān is opened and the first meaningful word found is taken for a name. Family names were long unknown in some parts of the Muslim world, or have only recently been introduced, as in Turkey; in such cases the *nisbah* or the *laqab* may develop into a family name.

Hinduism. Hindu names are extremely varied and numerous. They often include the names of deities, as in *Devadatta* ("given by God"). A Hindu name should reflect the bearer's place within the caste hierarchy. Sometimes a secret name is given to a boy and will remain as part of what survives of him after his death. A close relationship exists between name and personality, and so one's name must be guarded and respected. A traditional Hindu wife never calls out the name of her husband or utters it to others, nor will her husband use her name aloud. The more names a person has, the more secure he or she is from evil and harm. A change of name occurs when status is altered, as when a person becomes a ruler or is recognized as a great spiritual leader.

The ritual of name giving is an important family event, requiring new clothes, an auspicious spatial orientation for the ceremony, the bestowing of a consecrated gold object on the child, and anointing. The name is selected by a family priest or astrologer. Careful attention is given to the number of syllables in the selected name (an even number for boys, odd for girls), its source, and other similar matters.

China. There is an intimate relationship in Chinese tradition between a person's name and his essential being. After a person's death, if no spirit tablet is attached to the grave, there is no continuing inhabitant of the grave in the sense of a distinct personality. The spirit tablet, or "soul silk," is inscribed with the taboo name of the deceased and receives the prayers and veneration of his family. Although names are maintained for generations, the real name of the deceased is never uttered aloud; rather, another name or title is used. This applies also to living persons, who are commonly referred to by inferior names, which are often apotropaic, considered capable of warding off evil because of their unattractive associations. A demon is unlikely to take an interest in a child with a name meaning "stupid dog" or "sweet potato." Inferior names are known in other cultures, too, such as those of Africa and of ancient Greece. Paired with the inferior name is a "fate name" *(ta ming),* which bears an auspicious meaning (prosperity, happiness, success). The fate name is also never uttered. In traditional China, each name was thought to require an adequate portion of each of the five elements of the universe, which were symbolized by certain Chinese characters. The precise determination of a new name was made by consulting the horoscope.

The naming of persons, especially males, has been a complex matter in China. The "milk name," given a month after birth, remains with the person for life. It is used by relatives and others close to the person. Additional names include a "book name," bestowed upon starting school; a "great name," received at marriage; a name to be used by friends outside the family circle; a "studio name," for scholars; and a posthumous, or taboo, name, inscribed on the spirit tablet. Females receive fewer names than males, but they, too, have a milk name, a surname, a marriage name, and nicknames.

Chinese emperors had many names, some connected with their years of rule and any favorable factors connected with them. A ruler's personal name was taboo during his lifetime. At the domestic level, a child was forbidden to utter the name of his father, and wives avoided using their husbands' names, as in India.

Nonliterate traditions. The use of secret names has been widespread among otherwise very distinct and dispersed cultures. In Aboriginal Australia, name taboos were associated with secret rituals featuring the names of sacred and totemic beings. A person's secret name was never uttered beyond the ritual setting, when the *tjurunga* was being examined, and it was not known beyond the circle of initiated males of his local totem group. Even when the secret name was spoken, it was whispered, lest an enemy learn it and work evil magic by it. The secret name among Aboriginals represented the real self, linked with the past, present, and future in the timeless Dreaming.

Among the Inuit (Eskimo) of North America, the Netsilik distinguished between a personal soul and a name soul. The former was the source of health and energy but was vulnerable to attacks by evil spirits and wicked shamans. A name soul was an actual name, with life and power of its own, and it could protect the person who bore it. Therefore, people acquired as many names as possible, because they served as guardians. Males and females bore names without regard to sex, and the names often came from nonhuman categories such as animals, natural objects, and activities. Hunters liked to have additional names for greater strength, and women obtained them in order to have healthier children. When giving birth, a mother would often call out various names; if the birth was made easier after the mention of a particular name, then it was believed that a name soul had already entered the baby's body, and that would be its name.

In Native American cultures, names were thought to shape and influence the personalities and characters of individuals. Names might serve as an ideal or goal if they were auspicious or represented some virtue. Or names were given that reflected failings and character flaws. It was common for a person to earn a series of names during his lifetime. Among the Blackfeet, a man normally had at least three names: he received the first at birth and used it until he went to war for the first time. The second was a nickname given to him in boyhood by his playmates. It was often unflattering and would sometimes remain attached to its bearer for life. The third was the tribal name, bestowed after the young man had fought his first enemy. The tribal name was based on the outcome of that fateful experience and he bore it for life, whether it reflected honor or dishonor. If a person earned an unflattering name because of his first battle, he could possibly redeem himself through later exploits and then be awarded a meritorious name by the tribe. An individual might earn as many as a dozen names during his lifetime, all of which were his exclusive possessions, forbidden to others. It has also been traditional among Native Americans not to divulge their own names when asked. Someone else must utter the name, because it would be boastful as well as inauspicious to speak one's own name aloud. In many Native American cultures, names were drawn from the totemic and animal worlds, as well as from incidents in life. Names of deities were rarely used in connection with human names.

SEE ALSO Attributes of God; Dhikr; God; Nianfo; Supreme Beings.

BIBLIOGRAPHY

The articles collected under the general title "Names" in the *Encyclopaedia of Religion and Ethics*, edited by James Hastings, vol. 9 (Edinburgh, 1917), continue to be useful, although not all of them provide much information on the religious and magical significance of names. A balanced and informative collection of interpretive articles on several traditions is *Der Name Gottes*, edited by Heinrich von Stietencron (Düsseldorf, 1975). There are a number of penetrating observations on the religious dimensions of names in volume 1 of Gerardus van der Leeuw's *Religion in Essence and Manifestation* (1938; Gloucester, Mass., 1967), pp. 148–149, 152, 155–170, 184, 198–199, 287, 422.

Names from Hebrew scriptures have received much attention in modern scholarship. A suggestive historical and cultural survey is contained in Johannes Pedersen's *Israel: Its Life and Culture* (1926–1947; Oxford, 1959), pp. 245–259. Philological and theological analyses are considered in Edmund Jacob's *Theology of the Old Testament* (New York, 1958), in which see especially pages 43–63 and 82–85. The articles "God, Names of," by Bernhard W. Anderson, and "Name," by Raymond Abba, in the *Interpreter's Dictionary of the Bible*, 4 vols. (Nashville, 1962), are thorough, technical summaries with good bibliographies. They treat both Old and New Testaments. A more specialized study is Vincent Taylor's *The Names of Jesus* (New York, 1953).

Arabic and Islamic names and titles are defined and explained in the erudite but accessible article "Names (Arabic)," by David S. Margoliouth, in the *Encyclopaedia of Religion and Ethics*, vol. 9. The "most beautiful names" of Allāh are listed and discussed under their Qur'anic Arabic title, "Al-asmā' al-ḥusnā," by Louis Gardet, in *The Encyclopaedia of Islam*, new ed. (Leiden, 1960–). Other relevant articles in the new edition include "Ism," "Kunya," and "Laḳab," which contain valuable material for further study of Islamic nomenclature and titulature, especially the comprehensive entry "Lakab." August Fischer's "Vergöttlichung und Tabuisierung der Namen Muḥammads," in *Studien zur Arabistik, Semitistik und Islam-kunde*, edited by Richard Hartmann and Helmuth Scheel (Leipzig, 1943), provides a good survey of the use of the name *Muḥammad* and the changes introduced in its pronunciation so that its purity would not be compromised by too frequent use. See also Annemarie Schimmel's *And Muhammad Is His Messenger* (Chapel Hill, N.C., 1985), chapter 5, for the names of the Prophet and their application.

The vast field of Hindu names has not been studied as much as it deserves. A good brief survey is found under the entry "Names" in Benjamin Walker's *The Hindu World: An Encyclopedic Survey of Hinduism,* vol. 2 (New York, 1968), pp. 116–121. See also the article "Nāman," in Margaret Stutley and James Stutley's *A Dictionary of Hinduism* (London, 1977), pp. 201–203. There are highly significant data and discussions pertaining to name veneration in *bhakti* Hinduism in the articles by Milton Singer and T. K. Venkateswaran in *Krishna: Myths, Rites, and Attitudes,* edited by Milton Singer (Chicago, 1966), pp. 91, 143–144, 166, 169, 170. Most of the article "Names (Indo-European)," by Louis H. Gray, in the *Encyclopaedia of Religion and Ethics,* vol. 9, deals with Hindu sources and examples.

For the significance of the Buddha's name in Mahāyāna Buddhism, see Hajime Nakamura's *Ways of Thinking of Eastern Peoples* (Honolulu, 1964), pp. 444, 461, 558–559, 566–567. Original texts in translation can be found in *The Buddhist Tradition in India, China and Japan,* edited by William Theodore de Bary, Yoshito S. Hakeda, and Philip B. Yampolski (New York, 1969), pp. 345–348, and in *The Buddhist Experience: Sources and Interpretations,* translated and edited by Stephan Beyer (Encino, Calif., 1974), p. 124.

Chinese traditional naming is surveyed in the absorbing entry "Names," in J. Dyer Ball's *Things Chinese, or Notes Connected with China,* 5th ed., revised by E. Chalmers Werner (1926; Detroit, 1971), pp. 413–418. See also Ball's article "Names (Chinese)," in the *Encyclopaedia of Religion and Ethics,* vol. 9. The religious and magical aspects of names are surveyed, with generous quotation from original sources, in the classic of J. J. M. de Groot, *The Religious System of China,* 6 vols. (1892–1910; Taipei, 1974), especially the chapters in volume 6, book 2, part 4, "The War against Spectres" and "Use and Disuse of Names," pp. 1109–1142. The role of the name in the veneration of ancestors is described in Laurence G. Thompson's *Chinese Religion: An Introduction,* 3d ed. (Belmont, Calif., 1979), pp. 48, 52.

A classification of types and uses of names was attempted by George B. Foucart in his article "Names (Primitive)," in the *Encyclopaedia of Religion and Ethics,* vol. 9. Much research on names has appeared since in the anthropological literature. See, for example, Claude Lévi-Strauss's stimulating analysis of primitive naming in his *The Savage Mind* (London, 1966), pp. 172–216. See also the collection of papers titled *Naming Systems,* 1980 Proceedings of the American Ethnological Society, edited by Elisabeth Tooker (Washington, D.C., 1984).

Australian name taboos are described in A. P. Elkin's book *The Australian Aborigines,* 3d ed. (Sydney, 1954), pp. 129–130, and in Baldwin Spencer and F. J. Gillen's classic, *The Native Tribes of Central Australia* (1899; London, 1938), p. 139. Names and naming in selected African contexts are treated in Benjamin C. Ray's *African Religions: Symbol, Ritual, and Community* (Englewood Cliffs, N.J., 1976). Ancient Egyptian texts in which names are featured have been translated by E. A. Wallis Budge in *The Book of the Dead,* 2d ed. (London, 1960), in which see especially chapter 28. Inuit naming is described in Asen Balikci's *The Netsilik Eskimo* (New York, 1970), pp. 199–200. American Indian naming practices are discussed in original sources collected by Sam D. Gill in his *Native American Traditions: Sources and Interpretations* (Belmont, Calif., 1983), pp. 82–90.

FREDERICK MATHEWSON DENNY (1987)

NĀNAK,

NĀNAK, Gurū (1469–1539), was the founder of the Sikh religion and the first of a succession of ten gurūs or spiritual prophets.

LIFE. Born in 1469, in Talwandi, a small village in northern India (now in Pakistan), Nānak grew up in a religiously diverse atmosphere. A plurality of Hindu, Muslim, Buddhist, and Jain philosophies and practices circulated in the Punjab of his time. During Nānak's lifetime Babur defeated the Lodi dynasty in the Battle of Panipat (1526) and established the Mughal Empire. Nānak was born into a Bedi family of *kṣatriya* Hindus. His father, Kalyan Chand, worked as an accountant for the local Muslim landlord. His mother, Tripta, was a pious woman. The parents named him after their older daughter Nānaki. The love and understanding Nānak received from his sister during his formative years were vital to his consciousness. Later he went to live with Nānaki and her husband Jairam in Sultanpur and worked at the local grocery shop. He married Sulakhni, and they had two sons, Sri Chand (b. 1494) and Lakhmi Das (b. 1497).

In Sultanpur, Nānak had a revelation of the oneness of reality. With his proclamation, "There is no Hindu; there is no Musalman," Nānak began his religious mission. Thereafter for twenty-four years he traveled throughout India and beyond spreading his message of divine unity. During most of his travels, his Muslim companion Mardana played on the rebec, while Gurū Nānak sang songs of intense love addressing the ultimate One in everyday Punjabi. The direct and simple style of Gurū Nānak's teaching drew people from different religious and social backgrounds. Those who accepted him as their "gurū" and followed his teachings came to be known as Sikhs, a Punjabi word that means "disciple" or "seeker" (Sanskrit, *śiṣya;* Pali, *sikha*).

At the end of his travels, Gurū Nānak settled in Kartarpur, a village he founded by the river Ravi. A community of disciples grew around him here. Engaged in ordinary occupations of life, they denied monastic practices and affirmed a new sense of family. Their pattern of *sevā* (voluntary service), *langar* (cooking and eating irrespective of caste, religion, or sex), and *sangat* (congregation) created the blueprint for Sikh doctrine and practice. In his own lifetime Nānak appointed his disciple Lahina as his successor, renaming him Angad (my limb). Gurū Nānak died in Kartarpur in 1539.

Though there is little historical documentation dating from Nānak's lifetime, his own hymns in the *Gurū Granth* have survived. He is vividly remembered in the *janamsākhīs* and the ballads of Bhai Gurdas.

JANAMSĀKHĪS. These "birth stories" are short narratives depicting the birth and life of Gurū Nānak. Combining myth, legend, and history, they portray the divine dispensation of Nānak, his concern for kindness and social cohesiveness, and his stress on divine unity and the consequent unity of humanity. The *janamsākhīs* disclose the illustrious advent of Nānak's birth. In their central concern and luminous descriptions, the accounts of Nānak's birth have a great deal in common with those of Christ, Buddha, and Kṛṣṇa. Just as baby Jesus' stable was lit up by the bright Star of Bethlehem, the humble mud hut in which Nānak was born was flooded with light at the moment of his birth. But Mata Tripta goes through a normal pregnancy, and her Muslim midwife, Daultan, is struck by the extraordinary qualities of the child she delivers.

The *janamsākhīs* continue to provide fabulous details of Gurū Nānak's entire life. They depict scenes in which dreadful and dangerous elements of nature either protect him (like the cobra offering his shade to a sleeping Nānak) or are controlled by him (with his outstretched palm Nānak stops a huge rock hurled at him). They depict Nānak's divine configuration. At his death, the shroud is left without the body and flowers are found in its place; both Hindus and Muslims carry away the fragrant flowers to cremate or bury according to their respective customs. The quick and vigorous style of the *janamsākhīs* lent itself easily to oral circulation, and they became popular. The *janamsākhīs* have also been painted and brightly illustrated. The *janamsākhīs* provide Sikhs with their first literary and visual introduction to their heritage, and the stories continue to nurture them for the rest of their lives.

BHAI GURDAS. The ballads of Bhai Gurdas celebrate Gurū Nānak as the axial point between the human and the divine and as the founder of a unique ethical and spiritual legacy. Bhai Gurdas (1551–1636), born twelve years after the death of Nānak, is the first theologian of the Sikh religion. His depiction of Nānak's advent holds special significance in the communal memory of the Sikhs. As Gurū Nānak made his appearance, mist lifted, "light filling the world / Like the stars vanish and darkness recedes as the sun rises." Bhai Gurdas powerfully portrays Nānak as the medium of divine revelation whose inspired utterances *(bani)* radically changed the world. He focuses on the transcendent aspect of Nānak's personality and his liberating message for his stratified society. Nānak's critique of asceticism, macho behavior, and superstitious observances comes out effectively through Bhai Gurdas's wit and lively meters.

THE *GURŪ GRANTH.* The Sikh scripture compiled in 1604 contains 974 hymns by Nānak on a wide range of themes. The opening hymn is Nānak's *Japu,* which is the quintessence of Sikh philosophy. Nānak's metaphysical vision of the divine, his ethical stress on social equality, and his aesthetic approach form the basis for the entire Sikh scripture.

Metaphysics. The *Gurū Granth* begins with Nānak's formulation, *"Ik Oaṅkār"* (literally, "1 Being Is"). Without using any terms, Nānak designates the divine as the numeral 1. *Oan* is the primal syllable of Indian thought. Nānak's character for the word *oan* has an arc flying off, as though it were a geometric symbol for the infinity of the numeral 1. In a milieu seething with Hindu-Muslim conflict, the realization of the divine One was critical for Nānak. But his view differed from Hinduism in which the singular reality can be incarnated in myriad ways. Nānak explicitly qualifies that the One cannot be installed (*thapia na jae*), cannot be made (*kita na hoe*). Nānak's "Oneness" did not correspond with the Islamic notion of one God either, because his vision of the One includes a plurality of approaches to the divine. In his Baburvani hymns, Nānak specifically criticizes the narrow religious worldview that was imposed by Babur's Mughal regime on the people of India.

Ethics. More than a theological belief, "Oneness" is an active and dynamic awareness of the infinite within the human self. Such a consciousness gets rid of dualities (*dubida*) and petty selfishness *(huamai).* The One pervades each being, says Nānak: "there is a light in all and that Light is That One." How then could there be hegemonies of caste, race, religion, or gender? Nānak's metaphysical insight aimed to reproduce an egalitarian ethical system. He rejected the fourfold caste system in which a *śūdra* was below the *brahman.* He rejected notions and practices that relegated women below men. He spoke against beliefs concerning the pollution associated with menstruation and childbirth and against the sexist practices of sati and purdah. Nānak's fivefold spiritual journey (in the finale of his *Japu*) urges men and women to:

1. live morally in this diverse and variegated planet earth—*dharam*;
2. expand their knowledge—*gian*;
3. refine psychological and intellectual faculties—*saram*;
4. work vigorously—*karam*;
5. bring into their daily activities the truth (*sach*) that is present in all the continents and constellations alike.

Nānak boldly affirms life on earth and makes personal, economic, social, and political concerns a part of his religious worldview.

Aesthetics. Nānak provides no proofs, arguments, rules, theories, or prescriptions. In order to bring about a real change in his divisive society, he wanted to reach into the very consciousness of his people. Inspired poetry *(bani* or *shabad)* was his means. Aesthetics was his approach. "Only the relisher of fragrance can recognize the flower," he claimed (*Gurū Granth* 725). His passionate utterances celebrate the singular creator and exult in wonder at the beauty and vastness of the cosmos. Through his aesthetic discourse, Nānak tried to awaken his followers and revitalize their senses, psyche, imagination, and spirit.

LEGACY. For the twenty million Sikhs living around the globe, Nānak is a continuing reality. Their day begins by reciting his sublime poetry. Sikh homes, places of business, and sacred spots display his images. Wearing an outfit combining Hindu and Muslim styles, his eyes rapt in divine contemplation, and his right palm imprinted with the symbol of the singular reality, Gurū Nānak inspires his viewers to discover "That One" for themselves.

SEE ALSO Ādi Granth; Sikhism.

BIBLIOGRAPHY

For Gurū Nānak's biography, see Hew McLeod, *Gurū Nānak and the Sikh Religion* (Oxford, 1968; reprint, 1996); and Harbans Singh, *Guru Nanak and Origins of the Sikh Faith* (Bombay, India, 1969). Mcleod analyzes *janamsākhī* literature in *The B40 Janamsakhi* (Amritsar, India, 1981). Translations of Nānak's poetry include Gopal Singh, *Sri Guru Granth Sahib: English Version* (Chandigarh, India, 1978); G. S. Talib, *Sri Guru Granth Sahib: In English Translation* (Patiala, India, 1987); and Nikky-Guninder Kaur Singh, *Name of My Beloved: Verses of the Sikh Gurus* (Delhi, 2001). C. Shackle analyzes Nānak's language in *A Gurū Nānak Glossary* (London, 1981). Nikky-Guninder Kaur Singh, *Feminine Principle in the Sikh Vision of the Transcendent* (Cambridge, U.K., 1993), is a feminist interpretation of Nānak's work.

NIKKY-GUNINDER KAUR SINGH (2005)

NANJŌ BUNYŪ

NANJŌ BUNYŪ (1849–1927), also transliterated Nanjio Bunyiu; Japanese Buddhist scholar who first introduced Sanskrit into Japan from Europe and laid the foundation for Western-style Sanskrit and Buddhist studies in Japan. Nanjō was born in Gifu prefecture on May 12, 1849, and was educated in a school run by the Higashi-Honganji. In 1876 he was selected by the abbot Gennyo to study Sanskrit and Sanskrit Buddhist texts in England. F. Max Müller, whom he visited at Oxford in 1879, advised him to study Sanskrit there under A. A. Macdonell, one of Müller's students. Nanjō returned to Japan with an M.A. degree in 1884, and the following year he began to teach Sanskrit at the University of Tokyo.

During his stay in England Nanjō helped Müller to publish Buddhist Sanskrit manuscripts that had been preserved in such Japanese temples as the Hōryūji and the Kōkiji. Their collaboration resulted in the publication of *Buddhist Texts from Japan* (Oxford, 1881), published under Müller's name, and the two other volumes published jointly by Müller and Nanjō: *Sukhâvatī-vyûha, Description of Sukhâvatī, the Land of Bliss* (Oxford, 1883) and *The Ancient Palm-Leaves Containing the Pragñāpâramitâ-hridaya-sûtra and the Ushnīsha-vigaya-dhâranī* (Oxford, 1884). These were the first contributions Japanese scholars had made to the international field of Sanskrit studies.

Nanjō's most significant contribution to Sanskrit and Buddhist studies was *A Catalogue of the Chinese Translation of the Buddhist Tripitaka, the Sacred Canon of the Buddhists in China and Japan* (Oxford, 1883), which has long served as the only guide to the Chinese version of the Buddhist Tripiṭaka for European and American scholars who do not read Asian languages. Nanjō also rendered valuable service to the study of Buddhist Hybrid Sanskrit. His work here includes publication, with H. Kern, of the text of the *Saddharmapuṇḍarīka Sūtra* (Saint Petersburg, 1908–1912), the *Laṅkāvatāra Sūtra* (Kyoto, 1923), and the *Suvarṇaprabhāsa Sūtra* (Kyoto, 1931), with Izumi Hokei.

In 1888 Nanjō received the D.Litt. degree from the University of Tokyo; he was appointed a member of the Imperial Academy of Japan in 1906. In 1914 he became president of Ōtani University and in 1923 professor emeritus at the same university. He devoted himself to research, education, and administrative duties and the propagation of Jōdo Shinshū until he passed away at the age of seventy-eight on November 9, 1927.

SEE ALSO Müller, F. Max.

BIBLIOGRAPHY

Miyamoto Shōson's *Meihi Bukkyōno schichō—Inoue Enryōno jiseki* (Tokyo, 1975), an interesting essay on the leading Buddhist thinkers of the Meiji era, contains a discussion of Nanjō and his work on pages 100–123. Nanjō's autobiography, written at the age of seventy-five, has been published as *Nanjō Bunyū jijoden* (Kyoto, 1924).

MAYEDA SENGAKU (1987)

NANNA

NANNA is the Sumerian name of the Mesopotamian moon god; his Akkadian name is Sin. Depending on different theologies, he was considered either the son of An (Anu), the nominal head of the pantheon, or of Enlil, the pantheon's real head. In cuneiform, Nanna's name was commonly represented by his sacred number, thirty, corresponding to the number of days in the lunar month. The Sumerian myth *Enlil and Ninlil* explains how the moon god came to have his dwelling in the sky. Originally he was to be born in the netherworld, but Enlil worked out an ingenious scheme whereby three other gods would be substituted in Nanna's place. Hence he was free to inhabit the sky.

Nanna's consort was Ningal ("great queen"), called Nikkal in Aramaic and Phoenician. Their children were the two other great astral deities, Inanna (Ishtar) and the sun god, Utu (Shamash). In southern Babylonia Nanna's principal cultic place of worship was Ur, while in northwestern Mesopotamia his center was Haran. It is curious that both these cities are associated with traditions about the patriarch Abraham before he entered Canaan (*Gn.* 11:27–32).

Although the moon cult rose with the political fortunes of Ur, particularly during its third dynasty, founded by Naram Sin ("beloved of Sin") circa 2000 BCE, Nanna maintained his popularity throughout the entire history of Mesopotamian civilization. The great diffusion of the moon religion in Mesopotamia is attested by the frequent occurrence of Nanna's name in theophoric personal names in all periods and by the numerous hymns and prayers praising him as a friendly and beloved god. Notwithstanding Nanna's popularity, the attempt of the last Neo-Babylonian king, Nabonidus, to place Nanna at the head of the pantheon in place of Marduk did not gain acceptance and indeed met with strong opposition.

Nanna's cosmic function intimately concerned mankind. The moon god lit up the night and measured time. Hence he was viewed as the controller of the night, the month, and the entire lunar calendar. Similarly, observations of the moon and, in particular, reports of the moon's appearances and disappearances constituted the basis for many omens that directly affected the land, the king, and the people. The enigmatic phenomenon of the constant rising and setting of the moon found its echo in the Akkadian epithet of the moon god as "a fruit that arises from itself and produces itself."

A cause for considerable anxiety was the occasional occurrence of an eclipse, which was considered a bad prognosis and spelled nothing but trouble. In the so-called eclipse myth, the phenomenon is explained as resulting from an attack on the moon by seven evil demons. The moon's capture by these demons causes its light to become cloudy. Prayers and sacrifices are therefore necessary to strengthen the moon and keep it free from future attack (i.e., from another eclipse).

In the hymns and prayers there is a tendency to ascribe to Nanna nearly all the qualities attributed to the other celestial deities. He is unfathomably wise, the organizer of life, guardian and leader of mankind, judge of heaven and earth, master of destinies, helper of the destitute and the lonely, and so forth. He is also associated with royalty. Nanna has the ability to confer royalty on kings by means of a divine halo, the same luminous halo that was observed to surround the moon. Furthermore, kings often expressed the wish that the great gods would confer on them a life renewable every month like the moon.

In the moon god's honor a special month of the year, Siwan (the summer solstice month), was dedicated to him. During the third dynasty of Ur, festivals called *eshesh* ("all-temple" or "general" festivals) were celebrated on the first, seventh, and fifteenth days of the month, corresponding to the phases of the moon.

The symbol of Nanna on cylinder seals and boundary stones was the crescent moon. Because the crescent moon appeared in Mesopotamia with its convexity at the bottom, the idea arose that the crescent was a boat carrying the moon god across the skies. This idea was furthered by the fact that the crescent shape was similar to the shape of the long, graceful boats which were—and are today—the chief means of transportation in the Mesopotamian (modern-day Iraqi) marshes (Jacobsen, 1976). Not surprisingly, then, another of Nanna's common epithets was "the shining boat of heaven."

BIBLIOGRAPHY

There is to date no full-length treatment of Nanna. Åke Sjöberg's *Der Mondgott Nanna-Suen in der sumerischen Überliefe-rung* (Stockholm, 1960) deals primarily with texts of Sumerian prayers to the moon god up till the end of the Old Babylonian period. The best surveys are still those by Édouard Dhorme, *Les religions de Babylonie et d'Assyrie* (Paris, 1945), pp. 54–60, 83–86; by D. O. Edzard, "Mondgott," in *Wörterbuch der Mythologie*, edited by Hans Wilhelm Haussig, vol. 1, *Götter und Mythen im Vorderen Orient* (Stuttgart, 1965), pp. 101–103; and by Thorkild Jacobsen, *The Treasures of Darkness: A History of Mesopotamian Religion* (New Haven, 1976), pp. 121–127.

New Sources

Black, Jeremy, and Anthony Green. *Gods, Demons and Symbols of Ancient Mesopotamia: An Illustrated Dictionary.* Austin, Tex., 1992.

Bottéro, Jean. *Religion in Ancient Mesopotamia.* Chicago, Ill., 2001.

Dalley, Stephanie, trans. and ed. *Myths from Mesopotamia: Creation, The Flood, Gilgamesh and Others.* New York, 1989.

DAVID MARCUS (1987)
Revised Bibliography

NAOMI SEE RUTH AND NAOMI

NARCOTICS SEE PSYCHEDELIC DRUGS

NĀ RO PA (1016–1100), also known as Nāḍapāda and Nāroṭapa; one of the eighty-four Indian Vajrayāna *mahāsiddhas* ("completely perfected ones"). Nā ro pa was the chief disciple of the *siddha* Ti lo pa (988–1069) and the second human member of the Vajrayāna lineage. This lineage runs from the celestial Buddha Vajradhāra to Ti lo pa, thence to Nā ro pa and his Tibetan disciple Mar pa (1012–1096), and then to the Tibetan Mi la ras pa (1040–1123), with whom the Bka' brgyud pa, one of the four major schools of Tibetan Buddhism, properly begins. Although the Bka' brgyud pa lays special claim to Nā ro pa, he is highly regarded throughout Tibet; in fact, most of the major Tibetan schools have over the course of time integrated his major transmissions and teachings into their own doctrinal formulations.

The earliest and one of the most important biographies of Nā ro pa (approximately twelfth century) outlines the major movements of his life. This biography is a typical example of Vajrayāna hagiography in its intermingling of the ordinary and tangible with the cosmic, magical, and supernatural. Within the genre, however, this biography of Nā ro pa emphasizes the spiritual development of its subject, concentrating on the earlier phases of his career where he is presented as an ordinary, struggling human being seeking spiritual awakening. Only toward the end of his biography do we find Nā ro pa emerging as a fully enlightened *siddha*, majestic in demeanor and surrounded by miracles.

According to his biography Nā ro pa was born in Bengal of the *kṣatriya*, or royal caste. At the age of eleven he went to Kashmir for three years of formal study of Buddhism, a study that continued with tutors upon his return to Bengal. His Buddhist education was cut short when, at the age of sixteen, he was forced by his father to marry a brahman girl named Ni gu ma. The marriage lasted eight years, and was then dissolved by mutual agreement so that Nā ro pa could further his religious training. Ni gu ma was also spiritually inclined, took up Buddhist training herself, and in due course became the founder of an important Vajrayāna and Tibetan lineage.

After the divorce, Nā ro pa returned to his Buddhist training, taking ordination and continuing his study for nine more years, becoming accomplished in the various major areas of Buddhist learning. In 1049 Nā ro pa went to the famous Buddhist monastic university of Nālandā in northeast India and successfully participated in a religio-philosophical debate. As a result, he was elected to the powerful and prestigious position of abbot or gate-keeper, thus fulfilling the ideals of conventional monastic Buddhism and receiving his recognition within that world.

Eight years later a shift occurred in Nā ro pa's spiritual development, from satisfaction with a predominantly intellectual understanding of Buddhism to the search for greater depth of comprehension, and from the monastic life of conventional Buddhism to the nonmonastic form of the Tantric yogin. Such a shift is described in the lives of several other of the eighty-four *siddhas* and we may suppose that it was not entirely uncommon in those days. Nā ro pa's biography tells us that one day while studying a Buddhist philosophical text he suddenly had a vision of an ugly old hag. She made it clear to him that while he understood the text he was reading on a conceptual level, he had no inner understanding of it at all. She further revealed that if he wanted to attain genuine understanding, Nā ro pa should seek one Ti lo pa, who alone could help him.

Nā ro pa was devastated by the vision, and was unable to discount the truth it revealed. His response to the hag's revelation was to give up his position at Nālandā and to abandon the monastic life, wandering forth in search of the *siddha* Ti lo pa. He experienced eleven further visions, which he dismissed as worthless because they contradicted his preconceptions about spirituality, but which in retrospect were revealed to him to have been manifestations of Ti lo pa himself. In despair over his failure to find his teacher, Nā ro pa came to the brink of suicide; at just this moment, he met Ti lo pa.

As depicted in Nā ro pa's biography, Ti lo pa is a strange, enigmatic figure, anonymous in his context and unnoticed by others, but recognized by Nā ro pa as a powerful and uncompromising teacher and, most important, as his authentic *guru.* However, as Guenther rightly comments, Ti lo pa "is more than the individual who happened to become Nā ro pa's Guru. In a certain sense, Tilopa is Nā ro pa's total self which summons him to find himself" (Guenther, 1963, p. iv). Nā ro pa committed himself unreservedly to serve Ti lo pa, and attended him for twelve years, until the latter's death in 1069. During this time Nā ro pa underwent a rigorous training marked by much hardship and ordeal, and was put through twelve major trials by his teacher. These trials, depicted as external, literal events, no doubt epitomize moments in Nā ro pa's inner spiritual journey: at Ti lo pa's behest, he hurls himself from the top of a three-story temple roof; he leaps into a blazing fire; he is beaten senseless on several occasions by people he deliberately provokes at his master's command; he offers his body to leeches; and so on. Finally, he cuts off his own head and limbs and offers them as a fit offering to his master. At each offering Ti lo pa restores his disciple and instructs him in the next stage of his Tantric training.

By the time of Ti lo pa's death, Nā ro pa had purified his being and achieved realization, possessing a rich array of Tantric teachings to pass to his disciples. These teachings included the "six *yogas* of Nā ro pa" (*Nā ro chos drug*), practices particularly associated with the Bka' brgyud pa lineage but which subsequently became known and practiced among the other Tibetan schools. Nā ro pa had seven chief disciples among the many he trained, including Maitri pa, Ḍombhi pa, and Mar pa. His chief legacy is his consolidation of the teachings received from Ti lo pa, which he then passed on to his chief disciple, the Tibetan Mar pa, thus enabling their flowering within Tibet in the Bka' brgyud lineage and other Tibetan traditions. Nineteen works in the Tibetan Bstan 'gyur (Tanjur) are attributed to Nā ro pa, including several Tantric *sādhanas* (liturgical meditations) on the Vajrayāna deities Vajrayoginī, Hevajra, and others particularly important to the Bka' brgyud tradition, two collections of Tantric realization songs (*vajragīti*), and a number of commentaries on Vajrayāna topics.

SEE ALSO Buddhism, article on Buddhism in Tibet; Buddhism, Schools of, article on Tibetan and Mongolian Buddhism; Mahāsiddhas; Mar-pa.

BIBLIOGRAPHY

The Life and Teachings of Nāropa, translated by Herbert V. Guenther (Oxford, 1963), provides a translation of an important Tibetan biography of Nā ro pa written by Lha'i btsun pa Rin chen rnam rgyal of Brag dkar (twelfth century). Included is Guenther's difficult but sometimes very helpful commentary. Nā ro pa's historical and religious context is discussed in David Snellgrove and Hugh Richardson's *Cultural History of Tibet* (1968; reprint, Boulder, 1980), pp. 313ff., and his well-known yogic legacy of the "six yogas" is discussed in Giuseppe Tucci's *The Religions of Tibet*, translated by Geoffrey Samuel (Berkeley, 1980), pp. 98–101.

New Sources

Trungpa, Chogyam. *Illusion's Game: The Life and Teaching of Naropa.* Edited by Sherab Chödzin. Boston, 1994.

REGINALD RAY (1987)
Revised Bibliography

NASIʾ SEE PATRIARCHATE

NĀṢIR-I KHUSRAW is best known as a Persian poet, philosopher, and traveler, as well as for his efforts in spreading the Ismāʿīlī form of Islam in Central Asia. Born in 1004 in Qubadiyan in present-day Tajikistan, he is buried in the Yumgan Valley of Afghan Badakhshan, where he spent the most creative period of his life in exile.

Educated in the major sciences of the day, Khusraw served as an official in the Ghaznawid Court. In his autobiography he describes a life of indulgence and social rounds. In 1045 he dramatically resigned from his post and set out on a pilgrimage to Mecca. He describes his travels along the Silk Road, the performance of his pilgrimage, and his journey to Cairo, the capital of the Fāṭimid Ismāʿīlī empire, after leaving Mecca. He writes admiringly of the civic, administrative, and cultural achievements of Egypt, and during his stay he became immersed in the study of Ismāʿīlī philosophy.

Khusraw benefited from the presence of many of the scholars who studied and taught at the institutions of learning, such as Al-Azhar and *Dār* al Hikmah, and joined the da'wa, the organization responsible for the spread and preaching of Islam among the Fāṭimids. After more travels, including two pilgrimages, he was appointed to be in charge of the da'wa in Khurāsān. Successful in his mission, Khusraw nonetheless became the target of intense hostility and was forced to find refuge in the Pamir mountains, where he spent the rest of his life.

Khusraw's writings reflect the broad range of his intellectual interests and abilities. His *Dīwān* contains his best poems, which draw on the imagery of the place and the encompassing themes of quest, ethics, the foibles of daily life, and even the anguish of exile. The poems are coloured by a strong sense of devotion to the cause of the Prophet and his heirs, the Imams. There are other, more philosophical, writings that reflect Khusraw's primary interests: intellectual exposition of Islamic thought, esoteric hermeneutic of the Qurʾān, and the inner quest for spirituality and personal enlightenment. His *Safer nama*, an account of his travels, is a classic of detailed and trenchant observations of places, persons, and society.

Perhaps Khusraw's most important contribution was the commitment to developing and sustaining the use of the Persian language. He ranks among the foremost writers of his generation in preserving writing in Persian prose and poetry, and his writings have had a significant impact on Persian-speaking peoples across the region.

Khusraw's teaching and works have been preserved by the Ismāʿīlīs of the region who remember and commemorate him in their literature, music, and practices as the founder of their community. More recently his works have become widely available through new editions and translations.

BIBLIOGRAPHY

The most recent general study is Alice Hunsberger's *Nasir Khusraw: Ruby of Badakhshan* (London, 2000). Portions of his *Dīwān* have been translated in A. Schimmel's *Make a Shield from Wisdom* (London, 1993). The *Safar nama* has been translated as *Naser-e-Khosraw's Book of Travels*, by W. M. Thackston, (Albany, N.Y., 1986). See also H. Corbin, "Nasir-i-Khusran and Iranian Ismailism," in the *Cambridge History of Iran*, Vol. 4, (Cambridge, U.K., 1975), pp. 520–542. An increasing number of studies have been undertaken recently in Iran and Tajikistan, including newer editions of many of his works.

NOZIR ARABZODA (2005)

NĀTARĀJI SEE ICONOGRAPHY, *ARTICLE ON* HINDU ICONOGRAPHY; ŚIVA

NATHAN (tenth century BCE), or, in Hebrew, Natan; a prophet in the court of King David. Nathan is presented in the Hebrew scriptures as a prophet and intimate of David's court, appearing in three different scenes. In the first scene (*2 Sm.* 7:1–17), Nathan is consulted by David about the king's plans to build a temple for Yahveh. Nathan approves of the plan, which will be carried out by David's son, and also promises David by divine oracle the establishment of a perpetual dynasty. This scene constitutes the climax of the Deuteronomist's account of David's reign, in which Nathan acts as the spokesman for the historian's royal ideology.

In the second scene (*2 Sm.* 12:1–15), Nathan presents to David the divine reprimand for his adultery with Bathsheba and his murder of Uriah. By means of a parable about an unjust rich man who robbed a poor man of his only lamb he is able to get David to condemn himself. He also predicts future troubles for David's household.

In the third story (*1 Kgs.* 1), Nathan is part of a court conspiracy in which he advises Bathsheba of a plan to persuade the senile David to make Solomon king instead of his older brother Adonijah. The plan is successful, and Nathan and Zadok anoint Solomon even before David's death. Here divine guidance plays no part in the events, only human ambition.

These last two scenes are part of a literary work known to modern scholars as the succession story, which some would date to the time of Solomon and thus have it reflect a historical memory of these events. But there are reasons to believe that the succession story is a late fiction and tells nothing about the nature of prophecy in the time of David. Also suspect is the Chronicler's attribution to Nathan of historical chronicles that he suggests are his sources for the reigns of David and Solomon (*1 Chr.* 29:29, *2 Chr.* 9:29).

SEE ALSO David.

BIBLIOGRAPHY

Treatments of the prophet Nathan are invariably included in the broader studies of King David. A more detailed review of the scholarly discussion on these texts may be found in my book *In Search of History: Historiography in the Ancient World and the Origins of Biblical History* (New Haven, 1983), chap. 8.

New Sources

Bodner, Keith. "Nathan: Prophet, Politician and Novelist?" *Journal for the Study of the Old Testament* 95 (2001): 43–54.

JOHN VAN SETERS (1987)
Revised Bibliography

NATIONALISM SEE CIVIL RELIGION

NATION OF ISLAM.

The first several decades of the twentieth century marked a continuing challenge for African Americans. Attempting to carve out a viable socioeconomic, political, and cultural space was difficult in light of disenfranchisement, mob violence, and the scarcity of good jobs. Hearing rumors of increased opportunities, many African Americans participated in the "Great Migration" that marked the movement of African Americans into northern and southern cities in search of better life options. However, in places like Chicago and Detroit, African Americans quickly came to realize that racial discrimination could not be escaped through migration.

MASTER FARD AND THE BEGINNING OF A MOVEMENT. W. D. Fard (Master Fard Muhammad; 1891?–1934?) appeared in Detroit in 1930, selling scarves and other goods, and engaging eager listeners in conversations that involved a history lesson concerning their true status as Asiatics, originally from Mecca. His teachings perplexed and intrigued listeners and, while his theories seemed fantastic, his audience grew as blacks in Detroit gained from his teachings a new sense of self-worth and a way to critique oppression encountered during the course of daily existence.

To secure the greatness blacks were meant to exhibit, it was necessary to reject the teachings, or "tricknology," of whites, and embrace Islam—the black community's true religion. Black Americans were lost within the wilderness of the United States, but Master Fard had been sent to restore them to their former glory through his teachings and written materials—the Supreme Lessons—a blending of basic educational skills and metaphysics.

This, of course, was not the first time an articulation of Islamic teachings was expressed within the context of African American communities. Scholars have recently recognized an early Muslim presence in North America that might represent roughly 10 percent of the African population in North America during slavery. Diary accounts, autobiographies, and Works Progress Administration (WPA) documents all attest to such Islamic practices as prayer while facing east, dietary restrictions, and Islamic names given to children in early African American communities. This early Islamic presence serves as a cultural memory upon which more recent practices developed. For example, the Moorish Science Temple, developed roughly a decade before the Nation of Islam, espoused doctrines that combined Islamic teachings with other theological orientations. Members of the Moorish Science Temple believe Noble Drew Ali (1886–1929), the organization's founder, is reincarnated in subsequent leaders. Some suggest that Master Fard was Noble Drew Ali reincarnated, an argument rejected by the Nation of Islam. Master Fard maintained a degree of mystery by suggesting that he was from the East, sent on a special mission, with more information to be revealed in time.

Some estimates suggest that Master Fard's temple grew to roughly eight thousand members, one of the most important being Elijah Muhammad (born Elijah Poole; 1897–1975). As part of the Great Migration, Poole came to Detroit from the South. But with a limited education, Poole found it difficult to secure employment that met the needs of his growing family. This economic situation, combined with his unfulfilled interest in church ministry, left him frustrated but open to the inspiring teachings of Master Fard. Upon first hearing Master Fard, there was a quick connection between the two that culminated in Poole's name change to Elijah Muhammad and his being called to minister in Fard's movement. With the mysterious disappearance of Master Fard in 1934, a power struggle emerged, centered on Elijah Muhammad. Forced to leave Detroit for a period, he traveled to cities such as Chicago, presenting the teachings of Master Fard.

ELIJAH MUHAMMAD'S TEACHINGS. The conversion of new members did not involve an emotional response as happened in so many black churches. It entailed an intellectual and psychologically deliberate acceptance of the teachings of the Honorable Elijah Muhammad. The completion of this transformation, this acceptance of the black person's true nature and destiny, was presented by the convert in a letter to Elijah Muhammad's headquarters in Chicago. In this letter, the person seeking membership indicated participation in several meetings and a firm belief in the doctrines. The letter included a request for full participation in the life of the Nation and asked the Honorable Elijah Muhammad to provide the writer with the person's original name. Until a new name was given, members made use of *X,* which represented the unknown. The old name represented the white race and the damaging effects of slavery (and a slave mentality) on the identity of black Americans. The *X* involved a rejection of the former self and the embrace of a new identity associated with a new relationship with Allah and his messenger, Elijah Muhammad.

Self-sufficiency was one of the Nation of Islam's mantras, and it was expressed practically through the organization's various business ventures, which included restaurants, bakeries, and a farm. This attention to economic self-determination as a step toward complete knowledge of self is in keeping with the organization's push for separation from whites through the development of an independent black nation comprised of several states with rich farming land. In order to finance this new nation, the Honorable Elijah Muhammad called for the U. S. government to provide enough funds to sustain the black nation for twenty to twenty-five years. From the Nation's perspective this was neither a loan nor a handout. It was overdue wages for centuries of uncompensated slave labor. According to the Nation of Islam, it was a small price to pay when one considered the institutions and accumulated wealth that resulted from centuries of chattel slavery.

In lectures Elijah Muhammad proclaimed that Fard was God (Allah) incarnate and that he, Elijah Muhammad, was the messenger of God commissioned to teach black Americans about their true nature as the original people of the earth, godlike and destined to rule the universe. The most troubling dimension of this teaching was the reference to white people as devils who were made by a wise, yet mad, scientist named Mr. Yakub as a predestined part of the 25,000-year cycle of history in which we currently live. This actual and historical devil race, the story goes, will rule blacks for a set number of years. Such a period of domination and destruction, the Nation taught, serves as a pedagogical tool by which blacks, who strayed from their original religion of Islam, are corrected and prepared for their future glory. The Nation of Islam would ultimately soften the more harsh dimensions of its theology, arguing that the devil doctrine entailed a metaphorical attack on white supremacy and discrimination as opposed to an attack on white Americans. While remaining controversial, this rethinking of the Nation of Islam's more charged view is most notable as of the 1990s.

The Nation of Islam's task entailed enlightenment, the presentation of the true nature of blacks and whites, and the tools necessary for blacks to transform themselves. Once blacks in America—the Lost/Found Nation—gained knowledge of self and accepted the teachings of the Honorable Elijah Muhammad as the "Spiritual Head of the Muslims in the West," judgment would occur through which whites would be punished and the earth purged by fire, and blacks would then regain control over the universe. The faithful of God (i.e., the Nation's members) would construct a new civilization guided by principles of truth, freedom, justice, and equality.

Nation of Islam doctrine fluctuates between the complete destruction of whites and a measure of hope for the redemption of whites. The Nation's concern with issues of justice begs the question concerning an inherent contradiction: Should a community be punished for fulfilling its destiny, even when this involves the oppression of other groups? Is it proper, as a matter of justice, to condemn a community for its actions when it has no choice but to behave in a certain way because it has no free will?

Inconsistencies in the Nation's theology and rhetoric did not prevent growth and the alteration of the organizational framework to accommodate new members of various economic classes. For example, each local temple contained a minister who spread the Honorable Elijah Muhammad's teachings. To facilitate increased work and opportunities, the local minister was assisted by the captains of the Fruit of Islam (the collective of men who handed down discipline and provided security) and the Muslim Girl's Training and General Civilization Class, and so on. In addition, Elijah Muhammad expanded his network of ministers to maximize national exposure made available through television, including documentaries such as *The Hate That Hate Produced* (broadcast in 1959), and also the Nation's radio broadcasts and newspaper.

Aggressively seeking out members of the black community and the prison system, a process called "fishing," provided the Nation with its greatest source of growth and visibility. Through personal contact with black prisoners, the Nation gained one of its best-known leaders—Malcolm X (1925–1965)—whose charisma and media appeal benefited the Nation of Islam as both its national and international profile increased in importance and prominence within popular imagination. The Honorable Elijah Muhammad's personal moral failures, combined with the Nation of Islam's lack of participation in the civil rights movement, resulted in Malcolm's break with the Nation and his conversion to Sunnī Islam in 1964. Malcolm X embraced racial equality as a basic element of Islam in light of his encounter with Muslims from various ethnic and racial groups during his pilgrimage to Mecca. This perspective would result in new strategies for the obtainment of social justice as a dimension of human rights discourse. He established the Organization of Afro-American Unity and Muslim Mosque Incorporated shortly before his death in 1965.

The Nation of Islam Transformed. After the Honorable Elijah Muhammad's death in 1975, his son, Wallace Deen Muhammad (Imam Warith Deen Muhammad, b. 1933), was named head of the Nation of Islam. Attempting to bring the Nation into line with the larger, worldwide Islamic community, he rethought the aesthetics of the temples. He removed the Christian church trappings, such as pews (or chairs), and he replaced framed sayings by Elijah Muhammad with more Islamic ornamentation. Of more significance, the organization's practices were altered radically through a quick effort to enforce the five pillars of Islamic faith, the practices and attitudes embraced by all orthodox Muslims. In keeping with this shift, the presentation of Master Fard as Allah and Elijah Muhammad as the final Messenger was removed because of conflict with the orthodox understanding of Allah and the role of the prophet Muḥammad as the final prophet. In place of his more exalted role, Elijah Muhammad was presented as someone who, although misguided at points, sought to help black Americans achieve better life options. As a symbol of theological and aesthetic change, the name of the organization was changed to the World Community of Islam in the West, and changed again in 1982 to the American Muslim Mission. Imam Warith Deen Muhammad ultimately established a council of religious leaders, known as imams, to assist with religious and organizational questions, and members were told to consider themselves as simply members of the world community of Islam.

The Nation of Islam had been prone to schism. Notable among these various organizations is the Five Percent Nation (also known as the Nation of Gods and Earths), founded by Clarence 13X (1928–1969) in 1964 among young New Yorkers and based on a radical interpretation of the Nation's theology that presented blacks as gods with special knowledge based upon divine wisdom, often revealed through mathematics. However, the most visible and perhaps important of these splinter groups developed in 1978, when Minister Louis Farrakhan (b. 1933) formed a new organization named the Nation of Islam. Farrakhan affirmed the doctrines presented by Elijah Muhammad, including the teaching that Fard was Allah, and that the Honorable Elijah Muhammad was the messiah, with one significant addition. Farrakhan argued, based on a vision, that he himself was the prophet carrying on the work until the return of the messiah and judgment.

With time, the theology of the Nation of Islam under Minister Farrakhan would again change to include the institution of fasting during the month of Ramaḍān, as opposed to the more limited restriction instituted by the Honorable Elijah Muhammad. Furthermore, members of the Nation are currently encouraged to play a role in politics. Farrakhan modeled this through his participation in the Reverend Jesse Jackson's first run for the U.S. presidency in 1988, as well as his encouragement of Nation of Islam members to run for political office. This is clearly a break with the Honorable Elijah Muhammad's rejections of political involvement in a society that is marked for destruction.

While relations with the Jewish community remain tense at best, Farrakhan has worked to improve connections to the larger Islamic world. For example, his participation in the *ḥājj* (the pilgrimage to Mecca made by all financial and able-bodied Muslims) in 1985, as well as the availability of membership in the Nation without regard to race and ethnicity, speak to important shifts that make possible a repositioning of the Nation of Islam within the religious and political landscape of the United States and the world. However, this repositioning is not without significant tensions, as expressed, for example, through the Nation of Islam's sympathetic relationship with Libya's Muammar Qadhafi and the Libyan leader's efforts to provide the Nation with financial assistance.

Periods of tension and questionable allegiances have been mixed with more productive moments. Minister Farrakhan and the Nation of Islam, for instance, have sought to maintain a high level of viability through efforts such as the Million Man March in 1995. This was a gathering in Washington, D.C., of black men from various religious, social, and economic backgrounds. The purpose behind the gathering was repentance for misdeeds that have damaged the unity and vitality of black America, and a commitment to restoring themselves to their proper role as black men within the black community. While this event was successful, with participation estimated by some to have reached well over one million, the Nation of Islam has not been able to sustain positive attention. To some extent it remains a marginal religious tradition with a membership that is difficult to state with accuracy. Membership estimates typically range between thirty thousand and seventy thousand. By contrast, there are roughly four million African American Sunnī Muslims in the United States.

SEE ALSO Elijah Muhammad; Islam, article on Islam in the Americas; Malcolm X.

BIBLIOGRAPHY

Ansari, Zafar Ishaq. "Aspects of Black Muslim Theology." *Studia Islamica* 53 (1981): 137–176. Ansari provides a brief discussion of major theological themes within the teachings of the Nation of Islam, based on a concern with understanding its development within the context of the larger Islamic community.

Austin, Allan D. *African Muslims in Antebellum America: Transatlantic Stories and Spiritual Struggles.* New York, 1997. Austin presents the early Islamic presence in North America through biographical portraits of African Muslims enslaved between 1730 and 1860.

Clegg, Claude Andrew. *An Original Man: The Life and Times of Elijah Muhammad.* Boston, 1996. This book provides an analysis of the Nation of Islam's development through a biographical discussion of Elijah Muhammad, highlighting the manner in which Nation of Islam doctrine grew out of his personal convictions and struggles.

Essien-Udom, E. U. *Black Nationalism: A Search for an Identity in America.* Chicago, 1962. This is one of the early studies of the Nation of Islam. It provides analysis of nationalism within black communities through attention to the Nation of Islam's method of conversion, doctrine, and social location.

Gardell, Mattias. *In the Name of Elijah Muhammad: Louis Farrakhan and the Nation of Islam.* Durham, N.C., 1996. Using social history as a framework, this text explores the Nation of Islam. It moves from Elijah Muhammad through the alterations to the Nation's doctrine and platform initiated by Louis Farrakhan.

Gomez, Michael A. "Muslims in Early America." *Journal of Southern History* 60, no. 4 (1994): 670–710. This article is a history of Muslim practices in the United States, beginning with the presence of African Muslims early in the slave trade. The author discusses this history within the larger context of African American religious and cultural life.

Lee, Martha F. *The Nation of Islam: An American Millenarian Movement.* Lewiston, Maine, 1988; reprint, Syracuse, N.Y., 1996. This book explores the Nation of Islam's development in light of its rhetoric regarding the eventual destruction of whites and the coming greatness of blacks.

Lincoln, C. Eric. *Black Muslims in America.* 3d ed. Grand Rapids, Mich., 1994. Using a sociological lens, Lincoln provides the first detailed treatment of the Nation of Islam from its initial presence through the beginning of Farrakhan's leadership.

Mamiya, Lawrence H. "From Black Muslim to Bilalian: The Evolution of a Movement." *Journal for the Scientific Study of Religion* 4 (1982): 138–152. Mamiya outlines and discusses shifts in African American Islamic identity from the Nation of Islam to the presence of African American Sunnī Muslims seeking connection to Muslims across the globe.

McCloud, Aminah Beverly. *African American Islam.* New York, 1995. This book is a survey of various African American Islamic communities. It also addresses such key issues as the role of women within the Islamic community.

Nuruddin, Yusuf. "The Five Percenters: A Teenage Nation of Gods and Earths." In *Muslim Communities in North America,* edited by Yvonne Yazbeck Haddad and Jane Idleman Smith, pp. 109–132. Albany, N.Y., 1994. This article provides a concise history of the Five Percent Nation, highlighting its connections to and impact on popular culture.

Pinn, Anthony B. "The Great Mahdi Has Come!" In *Varieties of African American Religious Experience,* pp. 104–153. Minneapolis, 1998. Pinn provides a theological history of the Nation of Islam, giving primary attention to its development in light of its depiction of and response to moral evil.

Tate, Sonsyrea. *Little X: Growing Up in the Nation of Islam.* San Francisco, 1997. Tate's book is a personal reflection on the Nation of Islam's doctrinal shifts as Warith Deen Muhammad took over. Using the story of her family, Tate explores the impact of the Nation's changing teachings.

Turner, Richard Brent. *Islam in the African American Experience.* Bloomington, Ind., 1997. Turner provides a history of the Islamic presence in North America, beginning with West Africa and moving through the Nation of Islam and African American involvement in Sunnī Islam.

White, Vibert L., Jr. *Inside the Nation of Islam: A Historical and Personal Testimony by a Black Muslim.* Gainesville, Fla., 2001. White uses his personal history with the Nation of Islam as a means of critique, pointing out the Nation's flaws and inconsistencies.

Wormer, Richard. *American Islam: Growing Up Muslim in America.* New York, 1994. Wormer discusses Islam from the perspective of young Muslims and the challenges they face growing up in the United States.

ANTHONY B. PINN (2005)

NATIVE AMERICAN CHRISTIANITIES.

Heretofore scholars have not fully appreciated the rich variety and complex textures of Christian beliefs and practices among Native Americans. Specialists of indigenous religions largely have left the study of Native Christianity to missions historians. Historians of missions, in turn, lacking the linguistic and ethnographic training to otherwise interpret the subtleties, have understood Native Christianity largely as the straightforward outcome of missionary intentions and efforts. But a broader examination of the range of ways that different Native communities have variously engaged the missionaries' message and a more focused examination of how Native people have improvised locally on the missionary tradition suggest that the Christian tradition thus engaged bears consideration not simply as a subset of missiology or church history but as a Native American religious tradition among other Native American religions. The attempt here will be to briefly remark on the circumstances of the missions if only to underscore the ironic nature of the outcome: the transformations and improvisations through which various Native peoples have made the beliefs and practices of the tradition their own. A range of contemporary concerns facing Native Christians will also be surveyed.

The variousness of Native Christianities is due, in part, to the great diversity of aboriginal Native religions. The United States has recognized within its borders more than five hundred distinct Native tribes, speaking more than two hundred different first languages. Generalizations across the diversity of these traditions are often more facile than they are helpful, for each tribal religion has been tied to a variety of traditional lifeways on a variety of landscapes and invokes a variety of symbols of the sacred, each with a complexity and sophistication of its own.

That said, one can be sure of one commonality: along with the shared experience of colonization and Christian missionization, each Native community has shared the consequent burden of balancing continuity of tradition with the cultural and religious changes necessary to adapt to those colonizing realities. Whether such religious changes are best encapsulated as conversion, consolidated resistance, revitalization, or hybridity, they were all shaped by social, political, economic, and environmental realities even as they were formed by internal factors, such as visions, beliefs, and a need for meaning making.

Even these colonial realities, however, are diverse in themselves. Native communities in what became the United States have operated under nearly three hundred different treaties and have been missionized by nearly every institutional branch of Roman Catholic, Protestant, and Orthodox Christianity. The meeting of a diverse group of aboriginal religions with a diverse group of Christian missionaries produced a bewildering range of idiosyncratic Native Christianities, but as Bonnie Sue Lewis has observed, this is not simply due to the diverse missionary encounters that missions historians have long noted; it also results from what indigenous Americans variously did with the Christian beliefs and practices exchanged in missionary encounters. And here one finds the key pattern that gives shape to the range of idiosyncratic Native Christianities. To varying degrees, depending on relative levels of autonomy, all Native Christians have been active agents in their religious histories. In paying attention to how they made the Christian tradition their own, one finds that these communities often have drawn resourcefully on their indigenous traditions and idioms not so much to translate Christianity but to transpose the narratives and practices of the Christian tradition into distinctive idioms and structures of Native religions, oftentimes in ironic relation to the intentions of European American missionaries. For this reason, consideration of the fuller diversity and texture of Native Christianities cannot content itself with the history of missions proper, though of course it must begin there.

ROOTS IN MISSIONARY CONTACT. From the sixteenth century on, European economic, geopolitical, and colonial designs on North America were often conjoined with missionary designs. Missionaries were often in full complicity with other colonizing interests; sometimes they were in considerable tension. Similarly some missionaries were more invested than others in yoking cultural revolution to adherence to Christian practices, beliefs, and communities. Still, as George Tinker has importantly observed, whatever their intentions, missionaries of all denominations were "partners" in cultural "genocide," complicit in, if not directly responsible for, "the effective destruction of a people by systematically or systemically (intentionally or unintentionally in order to achieve other goals) destroying, eroding, or undermining the integrity of the culture and system of values that defines a people and gives them life" (Tinker, 1993, pp. 4, 6). Several examples, though by no means exhaustive, will perhaps be suggestive of the range of possibilities.

In the high Valley of Mexico claimed as New Spain in the 1520s, while some Spaniards questioned to what degree Indians were human, Dominican friars with millennial expectations imagined the promise of ideal Christian communities among peoples they took to be innocent noble savages as yet untainted by Europe's vices. By the early seventeenth century, Franciscan friars associated with explorers in what would become the American Southwest had established a network of mission stations in and around Santa Fe on the upper Rio Grande and later along the California coast, baptizing many and making often-divisive inroads in Native communities, even as European disease and compulsory labor were fragmenting them. In 1680 a movement known as the Pueblo Revolt gathered people of various eastern Pueblos under the direction of Popé, a visionary prophet, killed many of the missionaries and drove the Spaniards from the region for a time. Diminishing attention to the North by Spanish authorities and later those of Mexico, from the mid–eighteenth century to its absorption into the United States in 1848, meant that Christians in the various Pueblos were left relatively free of clerical control and thus could articulate Christian practices and beliefs in their own idiom.

In the fur-trading region claimed as New France, Catholic missionaries worked among communities speaking Algonkian and Iroquoian languages from the 1630s on. Jesuits certainly carried European assumptions about savagery and civilization, but they also studied Native languages and ceremonial customs assiduously and accommodated many Native practices in their effort to extend the Sacraments. In important respects, celibate priests identified themselves, and were so identified, with the healers and shamanic ritual specialists in Native communities with whom they consciously competed in ceremonial displays. With time, Jesuits came to view such aboriginal traditions more as obstacles than as conduits to the Christian faith. After the expulsion of Jesuits from North America in 1763, however, these Native communities, like the Native peoples of New Spain, were largely free of clerical control and enjoyed considerable autonomy in the shaping of their faith (Vecsey, 1997, pp. 23–26).

In the Pacific fur-trading region claimed as New Russia, from the late eighteenth century on, Orthodox priests with even more pronounced liturgical proclivities promoted the faith among Tlingit and other coastal peoples, less concerned with fomenting a complete cultural revolution than with incorporating Native peoples into the sacramental community.

In New England missionaries took a more Protestant view—and one more consistent with settler colonies—that the process of becoming Christian necessitated a demonstrable inner conversion that would be manifested not only in professed Christian belief but also in demonstrable radical cultural conversion. To be sure, even Protestant missionaries took a variety of positions on the precise relationship between Christianity and culture and did not uniformly preach the "gospel of soap." Moravians, Mennonites, and Quakers could point to considerable continuities between Native communal commitments and the Christian life. Still, with the Protestant insistence on a rigorous inner religious life, becoming Christian for some bespoke radical change away from aboriginal custom.

NATIVE TRANSFORMATIONS OF BELIEF AND PRACTICE. If the degree to which Native Christians could shape missionary Christianity varied, depending on missionaries' commitments to other colonizing interests, to wedding the faith with cultural change, and to developing a Native clergy, amid varying circumstances of dispossession and disease, Native Christianities as a whole developed at a considerable, often ironic, distance from the missionaries' intentions. Catholic, Protestant, and Orthodox missionaries alike were left to scrutinize the sincerity of professed conversions; although prone to welcome any signs that their efforts were bearing fruit, they remained conspicuously uneasy with hybrid practices, which they often considered to be evidence of backsliding.

In any case, one ought to question, following Kenneth Morrison, the worth of "conversion" as an analytical term in any discussion of Native Christianities. In the seventeenth century, for example, Montagnais/Naskapi, Micmac, and Huron/Wendat peoples were surely changed by their encounters with Jesuits in New France, and Native Americans affiliated with the missions stood in no small tension with fellow tribes people. But the Sacraments, especially baptism and extreme unction, that Jesuits proffered and the notion of God that Jesuits preached were transformed in Native religious idioms that focused on the cosmological centrality of sacred power, where the workings of power mattered more than the orthodoxies of abstract theology. Here "religious change" rather than conversion better describes the way the power accessed through Christianity was embraced by those left with "religious uncertainty" in light of disease and concomitant social chaos (Morrison, 2002, pp. 131, 145).

Having developed largely outside the discipline of Euro-American clergy, Catholicism in the upper Rio Grande Pueblos has brought traditional seasonal corn dances and ceremonials into hybrid forms intermingled with devotion to Christian saints. In Cochiti Pueblo, for example, on the feast day of its patron saint, deer heads and conifer boughs adorn an arbor at one end of the Pueblo's plaza housing an image of the saint along with the Franciscan brother and village elders, as the brother and the elders preside over drummers, dancers, Kiva society members, and "sacred clowns" performing ancient indigenous dances of thanksgiving for corn.

Among Native people missionized by Protestants, such transformations are typically subtler, sprouting between the cracks of missionary discipline concerning the congruence of the Christian gospel and Euro-American culture. Still, they are significant for their indication that even here Native Christians could assert some degree of agency in the creation of their own traditions. Given the intentions of Baptist and Methodist missionaries among the Mississippi Choctaw, the historian Clara Sue Kidwell finds it ironic that mission churches and schools became havens for the sustained public practice of distinctive Choctaw traditions and core values. "Choctaws took advantage of mission churches," she writes, "as places where they could congregate and be themselves, where they could speak their own language and visit and play stickball, with its attendant gambling and drinking" (Kidwell, 2001, p. 183).

Among the Ojibwas (known to some scholars as Ojibwe), missionaries of various Protestant persuasions in the western Great Lakes began in the 1830s to vigorously promote the singing of hymns translated into the Native tongue. The Ojibwas, they learned, were more interested in the singing of songs than in the reading of translated Scripture or listening to unwieldy sermons through a translator. But pedagogical theory of the era understood hymnody to be a particularly useful tool in the moral education of children, and missionaries, having construed their Ojibwa charges to be like children, promoted and disciplined Native hymnody as a tool for eradicating Ojibwa culture and planting the seeds of Christian civilization. For their part, Ojibwas who affiliated with the Episcopalian mission—or more precisely with the Native clergy and lay sodalities (religious associations) nurtured in part by the mission itself—sang hymns in ways that betokened an indigenized Christianity shaped but not determined by the mission.

While there are occasional references in the missionary record to hymnody in worship, the ritualized singing of which missionaries frequently wrote belonged far from the mission church in the semiautonomous spaces of Ojibwa homes, in all-night prayer meetings and funeral wakes. Missionaries hastened to applaud this development, but they also noted that the ritualized nature of this singing placed it, along with other funerary practices, quite outside their discipline. Hymn singing was ritualized, the province of sodalities of men and women respectively, led by elders, in deathbed scenes or in all-night funeral wakes. By the late twentieth century, on certain Minnesota reservations, such ritualized hymn singing by groups of elders was considered by many—even many non-Christian Ojibwas—as a "traditional" rite of mourning, fully Christian but also fully Ojibwa (McNally).

The Tlingit communities of Southeast Alaska also sing Native-language hymns associated with Presbyterian missionaries of the late nineteenth century and early twentieth century. But before the Presbyterians came, most Tlingits had become incorporated into the Christian faith by Russian Orthodox priests whose liturgical tradition, especially after the U.S. purchase of Alaska from Russia, paid far less attention to repressing any continuities of Tlingit culture within Tlingit Christian practice, particularly elements of the elaborate funerary ritual complex known commonly as the potlatch. Indeed as Sergei Kan finds in *Memory Eternal,* the Orthodox emphasis on the ongoing relations between the living and the dead and the elaborate ritualizing around death and mourning allowed Tlingits to assign "their own meanings to Orthodox symbols" and to make Orthodoxy "meaningful to them without deviating in any major way . . . [from] Orthodox ritual practice" (Kan, 1999, p. 419). By the late twentieth century, even non-Orthodox Tlingits would categorize the elaborate Orthodox ceremonies of the forty-day funerary feast as "traditional" Tlingit activities.

One should also note a wide range of important religious transformations that drew on and improvised on Christian practices and beliefs (especially those concerning heaven and hell) in light of indigenous traditions but distinctively through the authority of visionary prophets—such as Handsome Lake (1735–1815) among the Seneca or Smohalla (c. 1815–1895) among the peoples of the Plateau in Washington Territory, whose Indian Shaker religion continues to the early twenty-first century—and the peyotist traditions of the Native American Church. These movements ought to be classified as new religious movements rather than as Native Christianity, given that their center of gravity lay not in Christian narratives and institutions but in the charismatic authority of prophets or in the transformative power of ritual as in the Native American Church.

Surely one can find many examples of more straightforward conversions among Native people that represent an utter discontinuity between traditional and Christian beliefs and practices, but the previous examples suggest that a consideration of Native Christianity cannot content itself with the history of missionaries and their intentions.

ISSUES OF INTERPRETATION. Scholarly reappraisals of Native Christianity in the late twentieth century and early twenty-first century have focused on what Native peoples did with the beliefs and practices that missionaries introduced. But they interpret the nature of those transformations in a variety of ways. Perhaps the idiosyncrasies of various Native Christianities themselves account for the range of interpretive frameworks. But by 2004 older models based on the concept of acculturation, through which Native culture systems, static and unified prior to contact, were seen to collide with Euro-American Christian ones and gradually to erode and acculturate, had yielded to more fluid models based on processual notions of culture. Interpretations based on the notion of acculturation could effectively account for the frequent violence and dispossession associated with culture change generally and Christianization in particular. But they could not account for the puzzling ways traditional practices and beliefs became woven tightly into the fabric of Native Christianity. At best these were seen as evidence of "syncretism," cultural aggregates pressed together by external circumstances but lacking stability or a logic of their own. Or alternatively they were seen as only nominally Christian, evidence really of disingenuous Native uses of Christian forms to promote an indigenous agenda.

By 2000 the literature had come to appreciate cultural change as something other than an oxymoron and had begun to attend seriously to the hybridity of Native Christianities. More importantly, this literature also may have begun to appreciate how at least some Native Christians remarkably have made their own a tradition whose missionary legacy had meant "continued bondage to a culture that is both alien and alienating, and even genocidal" (Tinker, 1993, p. 5). Building on Victor Turner's notion of the multivocality of religious symbols (see Kan) or Pierre Bourdieu's concept of the logic of practice as distinct from the logic of discursive thought (see McNally), some observers have noted that the indigenization of Christianity happens less through the more conventional discursive media of theology and creed and more in and through ritual practices that can more deftly address the potential contradictions of embracing a tradition associated with a colonizing history. For affirming an identity at once "Native" and "Christian" has posed considerable problems, social and existential, to Native Christians (see Treat).

CONTEMPORARY NATIVE CHRISTIANITIES. Even if, as the Cherokee theologian William Baldridge has put it, "doing theology, thinking theologically, is a decidedly non-Indian thing to do," Native thinkers have begun in earnest to develop a Christian theology that incorporates distinctively Native religious idioms, just as indigenized Christian liturgical practices have incorporated traditional Native religious elements (Treat, 1996, p. 12). But these efforts often did not resemble formal theology; they were often local, collaborative endeavors, found in dialogues between Christian and "traditional" spiritual leaders or rooted in indigenous theological institutions (Vecsey, 1999). In 2001, however, Clara Sue Kidwell, Homer Noley, and George Tinker published *A Native American Theology,* revisiting the themes of systematic theology, such as creation, Christology, sin, and eschatology, and proposing new ones, like "land" and "trickster," in order to "create a dialogue in which Indian people can speak as equals to Christians," encouraging them to "recognize the uniqueness of their practices with regard to Christianity" and to challenge "Indian people to examine their beliefs" whereby "some may reaffirm their faith" and "others may decide to abandon churches in order to maintain their national ceremonial traditions in lieu of participation even in Indian Christianity" (Kidwell, Noley, and Tinker, 2001, pp. 3–4).

Implicit here is an observation that many Native Christians have not squared their Christianity with their traditional "Native" identities. To be sure, some Christian denominations, perhaps especially Evangelical and Pentecostal traditions growing quickly among Natives as among Americans as a whole, do not emphasize continuity between indigenous traditions and the Christian faith. Other denominations with missionary legacies, and notably the Roman Catholic Church since the theological and liturgical sea changes of the Second Vatican Council in the 1960s, have emphasized the "inculturation" of the gospel into the theological and ceremonial vernaculars of various Native traditions, have staged interreligious dialogues with non-Christian spiritual leaders, and have promoted indigenous leadership (see Vecsey; Peelman; Treat). Still, since the broad rekindling of traditional Native American religions from the 1970s on, many Native people, even the baptized, have imagined the terms *Native* and *Christian* to be mutually exclusive and have decidedly chosen not to affiliate with the beliefs, practices, and institutions of Native Christianity. Thus just as it was in the missionary heyday of the nineteenth century but even more fully as a result of Native peoples' improvisation on and transformation of the missionary tradition, a wide range of Native Christianities obtains in the early twenty-first century.

SEE ALSO Black Elk; Wovoka.

BIBLIOGRAPHY

Axtell, James. *The Invasion Within: The Contest of Cultures in Colonial North America.* New York, 1985.

Bowden, Henry Warner. *American Indians and Christian Missions: Studies in Cultural Conflict.* Chicago, 1981.

Fienup-Riordan, Ann. *The Real People and the Children of Thunder: The Yup'ik Eskimo Encounter with Moravian Missionaries.* Norman, Okla., 1991.

Kan, Sergei. *Memory Eternal: Tlingit Culture and Russian Orthodox Christianity through Two Centuries.* Seattle, Wash., 1999.

Kidwell, Clara Sue. *Choctaws and Missionaries in Mississippi, 1818–1918.* Norman, Okla., 1995.

Kidwell, Clara Sue, Homer Noley, and George Tinker. *A Native American Theology.* Maryknoll, N.Y., 2001.

Lewis, Bonnie Sue. *Creating Christian Indians: Native Clergy in the Presbyterian Church.* Norman, Okla., 2003.

McLoughlin, William G. *The Cherokees and Christianity, 1794–1870: Essays on Acculturation and Cultural Persistence.* Athens, Ga., 1994.

McNally, Michael D. *Ojibwa Singers: Hymns, Grief, and a Native Culture in Motion.* New York, 2000.

McNally, Michael D. "The Practice of Native American Christianity." *Church History* 69 (December 2000): 834–859.

Morrison, Kenneth. *The Solidarity of Kin: Ethnohistory, Religious Studies, and the Algonkian-French Religious Encounter.* Albany, N.Y., 2002.

Peelman, Achiel. *Christ Is a Native American.* Ottawa, Ontario, Canada, 1995.

Tinker, George. *Missionary Conquest: The Gospel and Native American Cultural Genocide.* Minneapolis, Minn., 1993.

Treat, James, ed. *Native and Christian: Indigenous Voices on Religious Identity in the United States and Canada.* New York, 1996.

Vecsey, Christopher. *On the Padres' Trail.* Notre Dame, Ind., 1996.

Vecsey, Christopher. *The Paths of Kateri's Kin.* Notre Dame, Ind., 1997.

Vecsey, Christopher. *Where the Two Roads Meet.* Notre Dame, Ind., 1999.

MICHAEL D. MCNALLY (2005)

NATIVE AMERICAN SCIENCE.

NATIVE AMERICAN SCIENCE. A comprehensive understanding of Native American science presents a challenge because it is difficult to draw meaningful conclusions from the ideas, practices, and observations of hundreds of separate societies. Adding to the challenge is that Native American traditions were oral.

THE VALIDITY OF ORAL TRADITIONS. The oral histories of American Indians are knowledge systems about the natural environment and how they sustain a social structure of mutual dependence that ensures the survival of future generations. These oral narratives lay out a background on which further descriptions weave a picture that originated in the minds of the ancients. The ability to visualize the narrative provides a sturdy framework on which to build an age-old lesson of ideologies and conceptual understanding. In this way Native Americans passed on a culture that sustained life for thousands of years. These narratives were not passed on by rote. Rather, they provided knowledge that was experienced and became embedded in the conscience. Often, skillfully articulated Native American knowledge was associated in complex ways with ritual or ceremony. The inhabitants of the Americas before European contact, in hundreds of distinct societies, maintained knowledge banks of such sophistication that modern scholars who study human antiquity are mystified as to the origin of such a keen understanding of nature.

Confidence in the historical authenticity of ancient narratives is seen to be weak because of a lack of written evidence, sanctioned genocide, and removal of children to missionary and government boarding schools thereby distorting American Indian cultural traditions. Yet faulting oral traditions because they are not set in stone is applying too high a standard. Even in contemporary interpretations of translated ancient texts there are frequent conceptual misunderstandings. Misconceptions arise from struggles with foreign vernaculars expressing foreign worldviews and are compounded by provincial colloquialisms lacking modern equivalents.

TWO WAYS OF UNDERSTANDING THE NATURAL WORLD. The scientific method provides its practitioners with the authority to validate knowledge as objective truth. Objectivity, based on the absence of personal bias, is the foundation for the integrity of Western science. Some would argue, however, that objectivity is not a strength of the scientific enterprise; rather, it is its greatest weakness because it allows the experimenter to do "science for the sake of science," unencumbered by a subjective personal bias consisting of ethical and moral considerations. Advocates of science use the preemptive disclaimer that benefits outweigh risks to justify profit-driven research even where there are negative outcomes. As long as "objectivity" is equated with integrity, one can justify anything with equal impartiality, even making a nuclear bomb to destroy evil. The western scientific mind, in just a few hundred years, leaves behind the most imposing legacy of all time, a world full of side effects that generations to come will be forced to cope with, not the least of which is environmental degradation on a global scale.

Native Americans for thousands of years maintained a completely different worldview of ancient systems of subjective knowledge, orally transmitted. In these traditions, respect for life and caring for the land was and is a cultural imperative to insure the survival of future generations. Despite bloody conflicts and the loss of land, integral to the survival of a society and its customs, many groups maintained some semblance of their ancient knowledge systems by means of their traditions of oral history. Skilled orators have preserved ancient knowledge to the present. Now Native American scholars convey knowledge in images using the written word, despite the difficulty of precisely illustrating a concept. The orator, who has many visual props at hand, can be sure of precisely illustrating a concept for an audience, whereas the writer most likely will never know this about the reader.

In the spirit of the scientific method, the following hypothesis offers a tangible approach to begin piecing together an understanding of how oral history might work at the physiological level. Modern cognitive neuroscientists, using functional magnetic resonance imaging (fMRI), map brain activities associated with the movement of limbs, the five major senses, thought, perception, and memory. Ancient wisdom endures as thoughts and perceptions of the mind, not as squiggles of a pen. The physical manifestations of thought and even perception remain elusive (we cannot put either in a petri dish), but fMRI at least reveals the location in the brain of the activity of mental imagery or visualization. One might intuitively associate such activity with the visual cortex, but this is not the case. The fMRI data indicate that mental imagery and visualization are more closely associated with the seat of memory in the brain.

It is tempting to conclude that using imagery and visualization enhances the memory of details. The evidence seems to confirm that the mental image relays specific knowledge in the telling of a story. By letting an image do the talking rather than a narrative memorized by rote, orators, when called upon to relay the knowledge, are free to pass on the tradition in their own words. The Western scientific mind is uncomfortable with this practice because the orator has freedom of expression to embellish or omit key features of the knowledge. However, the trained orator knows that if the person on the receiving end has not grasped the idea to the fullest, if an exact copy of the image has not transferred from one mind to the next, it could compromise the very survival of the tribe. Even if the information that the orator learned in one day took several days to paint for the mind's eye of the receiver, the transfer was precise.

Humans within a community are drawn down different life paths. As an example, one person might be an excellent astronomer and will hone that skill, while another might have a talent to heal and will pursue that career path. Celebration of each milestone in life, from the time of birth, through childhood, adolescence, adulthood, and old age, is ceremonially guided, thus maintaining the continuity of knowledge and a sense of community. Ultimately, community members serve the needs of the community not solely for purposes of that day or season but rather because they operate within a framework designed to insure the survival of generations into the future.

ANCIENT WISDOM AND THE SCIENTIFIC REVOLUTION. Education in the Western tradition convinces its audience that it is risky to commit a story to memory, say nothing of the workings of a whole society, because it will inevitably suffer corruption. So memory cannot be trusted to represent the truth, whole and entire. Yet Native Americans have devised and orally transmitted superior innovations and inventions that persist to the present day.

Emory Keoke and Kay Porterfield (2002) document hundreds of Native American innovations and inventions demonstrating the superiority of the American Indian intellect at the time of European contact. Old World explorers reaped many inventions and innovations from the highly intelligent inhabitants of the New World. The gifts fostered a greed that, within twenty years, set the stage of a betrayal that spanned five centuries, remnants of which persist today. The dehumanizing stereotype of "savage wild heathens" rationalized European expropriation from the New World of intellectual property in the form of inventions, processes, philosophies, and political or religious social systems. Europeans returned to the Old World and often claimed that innovations were accidental discoveries, thus relieving themselves of the burden of crediting ancient intellectual property as a source. There is evidence of appropriated knowledge in the areas of agriculture, medicine, transportation, architecture, psychology, military strategy, government, and language.

Keoke and Poterfield claim, "A case can be made that contact with American Indians actually served as one of the catalysts for the Scientific Revolution in Europe [during the sixteenth century]" (2002, p. xi). In view of this historical relationship between the Scientific Revolution and ancient Native American knowledge, the modern Western mind is naturally tempted to locate ancient knowledge of natural phenomena squarely in the domain of modern science. Were it otherwise, our tradition would have to teach that the Scientific Revolution is an outgrowth of ancient knowledge—a concept that the contemporary scientific community is not likely to embrace. Regardless, at the point of European contact, American Natives had in place meaningful understandings of the function and utility of the natural environment.

TRANSFERRING BETWEEN THE SYSTEMS. It is intriguing how ancient minds conceived of the innovations. People everywhere, throughout time, have desired to understand the complexities, beauty, and utility of the natural world within a spiritual domain. Intellectual maneuvers within a spiritual domain limit knowledge acquisition to a realm bound by subjectivity. It is in this realm that the ancients as well as moderns operated in the quest for the knowledge of how to sustain both the people and the life-giving environment. However, the objective mind finds it impossible to rationalize the mechanism that reveals knowledge.

Modern anthropologists and archaeologists have put forth several hypotheses of how the ancients acquired knowledge. The two most popular ideas reflect easy-to-recognize attitudes: Perhaps Native Americans stumbled upon their knowledge by accident, since there is no record of their using the European scientific method. Or perhaps Native Americans used a variation of the scientific method over a long period, since it provides a logical way to gain knowledge. Both ideas impose preconceived ideas on American Indians that presume methods foreign to the ancient cultural experience. Neither is adequate to define an entire continent of people. The first idea is a stereotypical assumption that American Indians are intellectually inferior. The second educated guess assumes that ancient ancestors were no more intelligent than the Ken Keyes's hundredth monkey, who learned simply by observing.

But consider this: Einstein himself said that one of the keys to his intelligence lay in his ability to visualize the problems he was working on and then to translate those visual images into the abstract language of mathematics. One of the most famous examples of this is the story that he developed his special theory of relativity out of daydreams visualizing what it would be like to ride through the universe on a beam of light (Cardoso).

With this in mind, an important question arises. Why does the human brain occupy more space than it needs, since by some estimates, the average person uses only ten percent of its potential? If the theory of evolution is true, why has natural selection not phased out the excess folds of our gray matter? Contrary to expectations, the excess gray matter is used for visualization, and visualization, as described by many Native American elders, is a vehicle that reveals knowledge of the natural world, as illustrated by Einstein's daydreams. If the concept of Einstein's daydreams brings forth in the mind of the reader a mental image of a gaze beyond the windowpane, then the reader has acquired knowledge based on mental imagery. This is the whole point of oral history, a tradition rooted in mental imagery and visualization.

Sons and daughters of Manifest Destiny whittle away at a terrible legacy left by their ancestors, as strength returns slowly to the sons and daughters whose ancestors survived. Together, a vision of the future that reveals to the world the inalienable right of full recognition is possible. The right of self-determination and the implicit right to self-govern and unite as a sovereign nation is on the horizon. Native Americans all over the continent are embracing sovereignty on a path leading to the unity of their nations, with the ultimate goal of picking up the chards of a broken vessel and replenishing a parched dream.

See Also Aesthetics, article on Visual Aesthetics; North American Indian Religions, overview article; Oral Tradition; Poetry, article on Native American Poetry and Religion; Politics and Religion, article on Politics and Native American Religious Traditions; Rites of Passage, article on North American Indian Rites; Shamanism, article on North American Shamanism; Study of Religion, article on The Academic Study of Religion in North America; Visual Culture and Religion, overview article.

Bibliography

Abram, David. *The Spell of the Sensuous: Perception and Language in a More-Than-Human World.* New York, 1996.

Basso, Kieth H. *Wisdom Sits in Places: Landscape and Language among the Western Apache.* Albuquerque, 1996.

Cajete, Gregory. *Look to the Mountain: An Ecology of Indigenous Education.* Skyland, N.C., 1994.

Cajete, Gregory, ed. *A People's Ecology: Explorations in Sustainable Living.* Santa Fe, 1999.

Cajete, Gregory. *Native Science: Natural Laws of Interdependence.* Santa Fe, 2000.

Deloria, Barbara, Kristen Foehner, and Sam Scinta, eds. *Spirit and Reason: The Vine Deloria, Jr., Reader.* Golden, Colo., 1999.

Gornick, Vivian. *Women in Science: 100 Journeys into the Territory.* New York, 1990.

Jaimes, M. Annette, ed. *The State of Native America: Genocide, Colonization, and Resistance.* Boston, 1992.

James, Keith. *Science and Native American Communities: Legacies of Pain, Visions of Promise.* Lincoln, Neb., 2001.

Keoke, Emory D., and Kay M. Porterfield. *Encyclopedia of American Indian Contributions to the World: 15,000 Years of Inventions and Innovations.* New York, 2002.

Keyes, Ken, Jr. "The Hundredth Monkey." Available from http://www.spiritual-endeavors.org/free/.

Nelson, Richard K. *Make Prayers to the Raven: A Koyukon View of the Northern Forest.* Chicago, 1983.

Peat, F. David. *Blackfoot Physics: A Journey into the Native American Worldview.* Grand Rapids, Mich., 2002.

Roberts, Royston M. *Serendipity: Accidental Discoveries in Science.* New York, 1989.

Suzuki, David, and Peter Knudtson. *Wisdom of the Elders: Honoring Sacred Native Visions of Nature.* New York, 1992.

Williamson, Ray A. *Living the Sky: The Cosmos of the American Indian.* Norman, Okla., 1984.

MARIA CATALINA (2005)

NATS. The *nats* of Burma make up a structured system of animistic spirits, predating the advent of Theravāda Buddhism but coexisting with it and with other systems of divination and prediction such as astronomy and alchemy. The *nat* cult is oriented to handling immediate and personal crises and avoiding evil, whereas Buddhism, the dominant higher religious ideology in Burma, is concerned chiefly with rebirth and eventually with salvation. Most students of Burmese religion agree that the term *nat* refers to any one of a host of animistic spirits, including human beings who have died violent deaths; former royal figures; spirits in fields, trees, and rivers; and regional, territorial overlords. The *nats* that are propitiated in Burma are the *auk nats,* the lower active spirits. The *devas* of Hinduism are also called *nats,* but they are not a ritual entity in Burma. In the time of King Anawratha (c. 1044 CE), an official list of *nats* was compiled. Since then, the members of the list have changed, but the number, thirty-seven, remains constant. The thirty-seven official *nats* share with the remaining *nats* the capacity to cause harm and, sometimes, to offer protection. They need to be respected and propitiated if evil is to be warded off.

Anthropological studies of Burmese religion have discovered the surprising fact that the *nats* of Burma form a structured system. This is in contrast to similar systems of animistic spirits in other Theravāda Buddhist countries, Thailand, Sri Lanka, Laos, and Cambodia. The Thai *phī* and the Sinhala *yakā* spirits, which play the same role as the *nats,* do not form a structure as they do in the Burmese system. Here, the *nats* are differentiated on four levels: the territorial *nats* reign over a region; the village *nats* guard a human settlement; the *mizaing* and *hpazaing* are *nats* at the family level inherited from the mother and father, respectively; and finally there are *nats* connected with special activities such as travel, domestic protection, and other frequent and mundane activities.

Nats are often represented in carved figures or other symbolic modes such as the coconut and red cloth of the house-protecting nat, Min Maha Giri, found on a house pole in every Burmese home. There are also festivals held to honor certain *nats.* The most important *nat* festival, of national prominence, is the celebration consecrated to the Taungbyon brothers, a pair of *nats.* At some *nat* festivals, and at other occasions where many people are gathered, there is often dancing by *natgadaws.* These *nat* wives are said to be possessed by their *nat* spouses, and in the trance of possession they offer prognostications for onlookers who feed them strong drink and tobacco. The *natgadaws* do not take actual husbands, since the *nats* are said to fill that particular role.

SEE ALSO Burmese Religion.

BIBLIOGRAPHY

Brown, R. Grant. "The Taungbyon Festival." *Journal of the Royal Anthropological Institute* 45 (1915): 355–363.

Htin Aung. "The Thirty-seven Lords." *Journal of the Burma Research Society* 39 (1956): 81–100.

Nash, June C. "Living with Nats: An Analysis of Animism in Burman Village Social Relations." In *Anthropological Studies in Theravada Buddhism,* edited by Manning Nash. See pages 117–136. New Haven, 1966.

Nash, Manning. *The Golden Road to Modernity: Village Life in Contemporary Burma.* New York, 1965.

Spiro, Melford E. *Burmese Supernaturalism.* Exp. ed. Philadelphia, 1978.

Temple, R. C. *The Thirty-seven Nats: A Phase of Spirit-Worship Prevailing in Burma.* London, 1906.

New Sources

Brac del Perrière, Bénedicte. *Les Rituels de Possession en Bermanie: du Culte d'Etat aux Cérémonies Privées.* Paris, 1989.

Rodrigue, Yves. *Nat-pwe: Burma's Supernatural Subculture.* Translated by Roser Flotats. Gartmore, U.K., 1992.

MANNING NASH (1987)
Revised Bibliography

NATURALISM. In the broadest sense, *naturalism* can denote any philosophy in which "nature" or "the natural" functions as the most general explanatory or normative concept. What counts as naturalism in a particular context depends upon how the term *nature* and its cognates are used. Given the long and varied history of such terms in Western thought, it should not be surprising that any two doctrines named "naturalism" may have little more than etymological connections in common.

HISTORY AND DEFINITIONS. Even in ancient Greece, "naturalism" designated several distinct positions. For the Cynics, naturalism consisted in severe condemnation of conventional values and artificial virtues. The virtuous man is one who lives naturally, but living naturally requires a rigorously ascetic practice in which all conventional and artificial goods are shunned. Stoic naturalism also sought detachment from the conventional and the artificial, and agreed that the virtuous man is one who lives naturally, but its conception of nature was articulated in an elaborate cosmology. Human nature, for the Stoics, is part of cosmic nature, and virtue is identified with conformity to natural law. Both Cynicism and Stoicism take us a great distance from Aristotle (384–322 BCE), who resisted any attempt to abstract the virtuous life from the *polis* but who nonetheless looked with favor upon something called "naturalism." Man, according to Aristotle, is by nature political, and this conviction leaves no room for the contrasts Cynics and Stoics need to define their positions. His naturalism, unlike theirs, was directed mainly against Eleatic skepticism about change and against the denial of "nature" and "natural motion" by Democritus (460–363? BCE) and others. Aristotle aimed to develop and defend natural science as knowledge of what exists "by nature." The nature of a thing, for him, is its power of acting in a particular determinate way, as defined by its end. The study of man is thus continuous with physics, for to study man is to study a specific kind of natural body by seeking out its nature. Man stands within nature, which is an intelligible, teleological order of motions. If Aristotle's philosophy is definitive of classical naturalism, then Democritus would surely qualify as an antinaturalist, despite his materialism, though both are routinely referred to as naturalists by modern writers. "Naturalism" later acquires specifically pejorative connotations in some Platonic, gnostic, and Christian writings, where the natural is contrasted with the spiritual in a way foreign to Aristotle and Democritus alike.

These ancient usages have had some impact on recent discussions of naturalism, mainly via Christianity, which transmitted an unstable amalgam of Hebraic, Stoic, Platonic, and Aristotelian conceptions of nature to the modern world. Nor can the rediscovery and dissemination of ancient writings since the late medieval period be entirely discounted as an influence. Still, modern debates over naturalism are best viewed as responses to the rise of modern science. The central point at issue is the scope of scientific inquiry as it is now practiced, and the basic terms of debate are set by the development of the sciences since 1600, not by conceptions of nature inherited from antiquity.

"Naturalism," when used as the name of a general philosophical outlook in contemporary discussion, usually signifies the view that all objects, truths, and facts fall within the scope of scientific inquiry, that nothing is in principle insusceptible to scientific explanation. This view may usefully be termed unrestricted naturalism. It differs from restricted forms of naturalism in that its thesis is not confined to a specific domain of inquiry, such as ethics. An ethical naturalist holds that ethical truths, facts, or values fall within the scope of scientific inquiry. As a form of restricted naturalism, ethical naturalism can be defended without committing oneself to the unrestricted position. Furthermore, one can accept a form of unrestricted naturalism without committing oneself to, say, ethical naturalism, provided one is prepared to deny that there are ethical truths, facts, or values in the relevant sense. To adopt a naturalistic attitude toward something is to maintain that it falls within the scope of scientific inquiry. Unrestricted naturalists sometimes argue, however, that failure to bring a domain of putative truths or facts within the scope of scientific inquiry shows only that there are no truths or facts to be found there, thus calling that domain, rather than the scope of science, into question. Such arguments can bring unrestricted naturalists into conflict with those defending naturalistic approaches in a specific area, a fact responsible for much terminological confusion, not least of all in debates over religion.

Many different conceptions of scientific inquiry and its findings have flourished in the modern period, and the content of both restricted and unrestricted forms of naturalism has varied accordingly. Where materialism has reigned as a philosophy of science, "naturalism" and "materialism" have tended to be used interchangeably, and Democritus has made his way onto lists of early naturalists. Materialist versions of naturalism define themselves polemically over against supernaturalism and idealism, neither of which is compatible with an ontology designed to reduce everything that exists and happens to matter in motion. That is, both supernaturalism and idealism postulate entities and occurrences that fall outside the scope of scientific inquiry as materialists conceive it. But it is important to see that scientific inquiry can be conceived in other ways and associated with other sorts of ontological assumptions.

A group of twentieth-century American philosophers known as critical naturalists has consistently gone out of its way to deny materialist methodological and ontological principles. Critical naturalists often cite Aristotle and Barukh Spinoza (1632–1677) as the great representatives of the naturalistic tradition. Some, like Frederick Woodbridge (1867–1940), have made extensive use of ideas from such figures in their own constructive projects. Many have tried to make room, within a naturalistic outlook, for the human phenomena—such as mind, intention, and culture—formerly claimed as the special province of the idealists. Some have argued that, because naturalistic methods place no *a priori* constraints on the types of hypotheses one may consider in science, acceptance of naturalism involves no bias against supernaturalist ontologies as such. Hence, in recent philosophy, as in the remainder of this article, "naturalism" is not tied to a particular ontology, though a naturalist in this sense remains bound to embrace whatever ontological scruples and commitments the course of scientific inquiry, rightly understood, entails.

Debates over Naturalism. The most common general charge leveled in the literature of the middle and late twentieth century against versions of unrestricted naturalism is that they cannot successfully account for themselves. Can naturalism account for itself without either falling into contradiction or arguing in a circle? Does naturalism in fact presuppose something that cannot be brought within the scope of scientific inquiry as naturalists construe it?

Taking these questions as their point of departure, some antinaturalists argue as follows. Naturalism is, in its unrestricted forms, a philosophical thesis about the validity and scope of scientific inquiry. How, then, is naturalism to be justified as a philosophical thesis? By appealing to scientific inquiry? That would be consistent with the naturalistic thesis, but it also seems circular. How can the validity and limitless scope of scientific inquiry be established by appealing to scientific inquiry itself without begging the question? It seems that it cannot, and what this shows is that any attempt to vindicate the naturalist's thesis without arguing in a circle necessarily makes an appeal to standards of judgment that do not belong to scientific inquiry per se. Hence, naturalism cannot be justified; the only noncircular means one could use in trying to justify it obviously contradicts it.

This line of argument may seem compelling, but it hardly forces naturalists to abandon their position. Does not the same problem arise for any standards or principles anyone might propose as valid and ultimate? If so, then naturalists are at least no worse off than their critics. The real question, naturalists will argue, is how critics intend to stop the regress of standards short of infinity without themselves arguing in a circle.

The antinaturalist can stop the regress, it would seem, only by invoking a set of standards that are self-justified, intuitively known, or demonstrably indispensable to rational thought as such. What, then, prevents naturalists from claiming similar status for the principles implicit in scientific practice? Once this question has been raised, naturalist and critic seem on equal footing: each seems to require arguments capable of certifying some set of principles as fundamental in the relevant sense. Furthermore, the debate can easily degenerate into a merely verbal dispute at this point, for it is not necessarily clear why the antinaturalist's principles cannot be said to be part of scientific method—namely, the foundational part.

Increasingly, however, naturalists have expressed skepticism about such notions as self-justification and intuitive knowledge, whether defended by other naturalists or by their critics. So they have sought a more radical response to the problem, arguing that scientific inquiry is just the honorific title given to the continuing process of rational criticism and revision of inherited theory and practice. This process, while perhaps best exemplified in the natural sciences, is not confined to them and is essentially continuous from field to field. It derives its justification not from foundational principles on which it rests but rather from the way it helps adaption to the environment through progressive self-correction. Justification is a dialectical affair directed toward the pragmatic resolution of problems. In this view, humankind is saved from infinite regress in justificatory arguments not by foundational principles but by the settling of real doubts, and if the process as a whole is circular, it is not viciously so. Naturalistic philosophy is simply scientific inquiry gone self-conscious, reflecting on itself. The great pragmatist, John Dewey (1859–1952), offered something like this defense and reformulation of naturalism, restated eloquently by W. V. O. Quine (1908–2000).

When some critics have charged naturalism with an inability to account for itself, they have argued somewhat differently from the way considered thus far. Their point is that defending naturalism and practicing science are human activities involving thought and purposeful behavior in the pursuit of values, and that naturalism is unequipped to account for any such activity. This argument challenges naturalists to show that they can explain thought, intention, and value without violating naturalistic scruples. But then unrestricted naturalism, to be vindicated, must ultimately be prepared to either explain or explain away every domain of putative objects, truths, or facts in naturalistic terms. So the appraisal of unrestricted naturalism must sooner or later take up each member in a long series of analyses of restricted topics, one of which is religion.

NATURALISM AND RELIGION. What can naturalists make of traditional religious utterances, such as the theist's discourse about God? Assume for the moment that some of what the theist says is to be interpreted as asserting the existence of a supernatural being who created the universe. If the theist is right in making this assertion, presumably, the naturalist will be obliged to show that God can be brought within the scope of scientific inquiry. The naturalist will, in other words, have to construct a "natural theology." Some naturalists, such as the eighteenth-century Deists, have adopted this strategy, but most have deemed it unsuccessful, concluding instead that no supernatural being exists. If no such being exists, naturalists need not be held responsible to account for its existence scientifically. The task, in that event, would be to explain God's existence away while still making sense of religious behavior, including the theist's utterances about God, reports of religious experience, and so on.

If, however, the theist's utterances about God are not to be taken as true assertions about a supernatural being, how shall they be taken? One alternative is to say that they are true but elliptical assertions about something else, something that does fall within the scope of science. Some followers of the French sociologist Émile Durkheim (1859–1917) argue, along these lines, that religious utterances are best interpreted as symbolic assertions about society, that the actual object of religious worship is the social group, and that religious behavior can be fully explained in a systematic science of society. Similar proposals have been developed by other theorists who take economics or psychology, not sociology, as the appropriate idiom of reduction.

A second alternative is to claim that the problematic religious utterances are not properly viewed as assertions in the strict sense at all. Instead, they are to be assimilated to some other class of speech-acts, such as expressions of emotions, wishes, or moral prescriptions. An example of this approach would be the emotivist theory of religious language popular among logical positivists.

Third, a naturalist may take the apparent assertions in religious discourse at face value while ascribing false beliefs to those who utter them, a strategy much simpler than the others but also one that raises the additional question of how these allegedly false beliefs came to be accepted. Here again at least two options suggest themselves. It may be argued, on the one hand, that religious assertions—while not to be construed as nonpropositional expressions of emotions or desires—are nonetheless determined by essentially nonrational forces in the human personality, society, or history. On the other hand, one could argue that religious beliefs, though now known to be false, arose under circumstances that tended to make them seem reasonable to reasonable people.

Those committed to defending traditional religious claims as true are not the only people interested in opposing the naturalist's attempts to explain religion. The other major source of antinaturalism in the study of religion is the claim, often made by thinkers in the hermeneutical tradition of Wilhelm Dilthey (1833–1911), that the objective procedures of scientific inquiry are insufficient for use in the study of human beings, least of all their religious and artistic self-expression. Human beings are, of course, objects within nature, and the naturalist's methods can teach a great deal about humankind as a natural species. But human beings are also spiritual, self-creating subjects. Understanding them involves determining the meaning that their behavior, verbal and nonverbal, has for them, and therefore calls for an interpretive approach distinct from the naturalist's explanatory methods.

Naturalists have responded to the hermeneutical tradition's antinaturalism in several ways. The most common sort of response can be seen in various attempts to reduce much of what hermeneutical theorists want to say about meaning and understanding to the languages of natural science. Critical and pragmatic naturalists move in another direction, accusing Dilthey and his followers of uncritically taking over unduly narrow conceptions of scientific inquiry from the materialists and positivists they otherwise oppose. Broaden the conception of scientific inquiry enough, and the line hermeneutical theorists have drawn between the natural sciences and humanistic studies (*Naturwissenschaften* and *Geisteswissenschaften*) will disappear—as will the rationale for viewing hermeneutical philosophy and naturalism as exclusive alternatives.

Finally, it should be noted that some naturalists have been as interested in reconstructing religion as they have been in criticizing or explaining it. Dissatisfied with traditional religion on naturalistic grounds, they have attempted to devise religious systems capable of fulfilling the essential personal or social functions they assign to religion without departing from naturalism as a creed. The most ambitious such attempt was that of Auguste Comte (1798–1857), the French positivist, who took the rituals of Roman Catholicism as models for his own conception of the sacraments and identified humanity as the proper object of religious devotion and service. Dewey's proposals, in contrast, were much less ambitious and involved no attempt to found an organized religion. According to Dewey, any ultimate end that serves to unify one's life and actions takes on a religious quality. Dewey's aim was to portray this-worldly concern with "the problems of men" as the optimal religious ideal. There have been other recent attempts to reconstruct religion in naturalistic terms, but none has won much of a following.

SEE ALSO Analytic Philosophy; Deism; Hermeneutics; Logical Positivism; Materialism; Nature, article on Religious and Philosophical Speculations; Positivism; Science and Religion; Sociology; Supernatural, The.

BIBLIOGRAPHY

The best place to begin a study of naturalism is with *Naturalism and the Human Spirit*, edited by Yervant H. Krikorian (New York, 1944), which includes characteristic essays by John Dewey, Sidney Hook, and John Herman Randall Jr., as well as an essay titled "Naturalism and Religion" by Sterling P. Lamprecht. No study of naturalism should end before taking up O. K. Bouwsma's essay "Naturalism," in his *Philosophical Essays* (Lincoln, Neb., 1965), pp. 71–83. George Santayana's five-volume work *The Life of Reason, or the Phases of Human Progress* (New York, 1905–1906) exerted considerable influence on American naturalism in the early twentieth century and includes a notable treatment of religion. John Dewey's account of naturalized religion appears in his book *A Common Faith* (New Haven, 1934). The most comprehensive recent naturalistic reconstruction of religion is probably Julian Huxley's *Religion without Revelation* (1927; reprint, New York, 1958). The most influential twentieth-century attack on naturalism may well be Edmund Husserl's "Philosophie als strenge Wissenschaft," *Logos* 1 (1910): 289–314. For classic statements of the hermeneutical tradition's antinaturalism, see Wilhelm Dilthey's *Gesammelte Schriften*, 2d ed. (Stuttgart, 1957–1960). W. V. O. Quine's pragmatic naturalism can be sampled in his *Ontological Relativity and Other Essays* (New York, 1969). The concerns of the hermeneutical tradition from Dilthey to Hans-Georg Gadamer and of pragmatic naturalism from Dewey to Quine come together most clearly in Richard Rorty's *Philosophy and the Mirror of Nature* (Princeton, 1979).

New Sources

Griffin, David Ray. *Religion and Scientific Naturalism: Overcoming the Conflicts.* Albany, N.Y., 2000.

Hardwick, Charley. *Events of Grace: Naturalism, Existentialism, and Theology.* New York, 1996.

Lawlor, Mary. *Recalling the Wild: Naturalism and the Closing of the American West.* New Brunswick, N.J., 2000.

Mitchell, Lee Clark. *Determined Fictions: American Literary Naturalism.* New York, 1989.

Nielsen, Kai. *Naturalism and Religion.* Amherst, N.Y., 2001.

Pizer, Donald. *The Theory and Practice of American Naturalism: Selected Essays and Reviews.* Carbondale, Ill., 1993.

Reich, Lou. *Hume's Religious Naturalism.* Lanham, Md., 1998.

JEFFREY STOUT (1987)
Revised Bibliography

NATURE

This entry consists of the following articles:

NATURE: RELIGIOUS AND PHILOSOPHICAL SPECULATIONS

In the West, "natural philosophy" and "philosophy of nature" have developed side-by-side and at times have been confused. The first has been defined by Galileo, Auguste Comte, and Charles Darwin as the pursuit of a total but essentially objective knowledge of phenomena, whereas the second has oriented such thinkers as Gottfried W. Leibniz, Georg W. F. Hegel, and Henri Bergson toward an intuitive approach that nevertheless strives to be rigorous regarding the reality that underlies data derived from observation. Among the thinkers of this second category, those who have come more and more to be labeled *Naturphilosophen*, or "philosophers of nature," since the time of German Romanticism occupy a special place.

Since antiquity, the representatives of that tendency are generally committed to grasping the concrete character of nonmechanical, nonphysical reality or, as F. J. W. Schelling put it, the "productivity" concealed behind sensible appearances, without, as a rule, neglecting the study of appearances themselves. They are not satisfied with a natural philosophy based on empiricism alone. Their ideas indisputably bear the mark of the religious, indeed of Gnosticism—not in the dualistic sense this word evokes when it is applied to the Gnostics of the beginning of our own era, but in the sense of a frame of mind fixed on defining the nature of the relationships linking God, human beings, and the universe by means not relevant solely to the experimental method.

PRE-SOCRATICS, STOICISM, HERMETISM, AND THE EARLY MIDDLE AGES. The pre-Socratics hardly opposed matter to mind, soul to body, or subject to object, but they had a tendency to approach nature with a nondualistic, noncategorical attitude. In such a view, all being is concrete. Yet their thinking contained dynamic and creative contradictions. Cosmologies and anthropologies rested on pairs of opposites. The pre-Socratics had a sense of analogy and homology insofar as they did not think in purely Aristotelian categories. Their imaginary world was grounded in concrete nature, interpreting and molding it into living structures. Hence the importance of the elements (whose rich symbolism would later be taken up again by the alchemists): water for Thales, air for Anaximenes, fire for Heraclitus. For these physicist-metaphysicians, especially Heraclitus, the logic of antagonism was primordial. "Night and day," he said, "they are one." Hence the pre-Socratics' labyrinthine style, which seems obscure because it is made of paradoxes. Parmenides was already moving away from such categories of nature with his linear thought, his *doxa*, which tended to annul these contradictions. Thus, too, Anaxagoras, who saw in nature a thinking principle that is copresent in the ordering of the world, but that also separates the human being from the rest of the cosmos. But later, Empedocles affirmed six principles—reassemblage and dispersion, plus the four elements—and presented the history of the world as the reconstitution of a dislocated unity.

Stoicism, over almost six centuries, paved the way for Neoplatonism and certain Gnostic and Hermetic currents. Indeed, it placed emphasis on the need to know the concrete universe, harmoniously blending wisdom and technique, and taught the necessity of a savoir-faire that rejects pure speculation and must lead to the knowledge of an organic whole, thus assuring the accord between things heavenly and terrestrial. That trait appeared again and again in a more systematic manner as one of the important aspects of Alexandrine Hermetism, whose teachings often affirm that God is known through the contemplation of the world. Hence the preference of the *Hermetica* texts for the particular, the *mirabilia,* over the abstract and the general; science is not "disinterested" but aims to rediscover the general by means of an enriching detour through the concrete and through individual objects

This focus on the concrete hardly occurs in Neoplatonism, where the intelligible reality, the realm of the mind to which one strives to gain access, has no purpose in explaining the world of the senses. Instead, it aids us in quitting this world in order to help us to enter the pure region where knowledge and happiness are possible. The essential thing is to go beyond the sensual, up to the world of ideas. Within diverse branches of early Gnosticism, the belief prevailed that the world is the work of an evil entity.

The ninth-century theologian John Scotus Eriugena, who was born in Ireland and lived at the court of Charles the Bald, authored *De divisione naturae* (or *Periphyseon*), which was to nourish much of subsequent Theosophical speculation up to the age of German idealism in the nineteenth century. The two kinds of nature he distinguished, namely *natura naturans* and *natura naturata* (i.e., creative nature and created nature), were later to inspire Jewish qaballistic literature.

In the same century, the Arabs translated many ancient texts and, inspired by Aristotle, wrote commentaries on them. But together with the rationalistic empiricism of Aristotle, and in the margins of a form of positivism, we see Arab thought also expressing a highly mythicized vision of a world ruled by spiritual forces that only intuition can aspire to grasp. The medieval West received this teaching by way of the Latin translations of Arabic texts that were often concerned with the theory and practice of medicine and magic.

The twelfth century saw a return to the cosmological themes of Greco-Roman antiquity, in other words, to a universe conceived and represented as an organic whole, subject to laws that must be sought in the light of analogy. But the "discovery" of laws would entail twofold consequences: on the one hand, a powerful process of secularization was set in motion, at the expense of a sense of the sacred. On the other hand, and conversely, a lasting renewal of what might be called the feeling of cosmic participation took place. This latter corresponded to the systematic and poetic elaboration of a network of relations between the visible and invisible realms of creation. The universe was approached by form of philosophical speculation that was committed to deciphering living, concrete meanings. According to Jean de Meung, nature became the "chamberlain," or vicar, of God—a God who, as it turned out, incarnated in stone in this age that saw the emergence of a great sacred art of the West.

Nature, its unity and its laws, is what interested the Platonism of the school of Chartres as it appeared in the works of William of Conches, who was much concerned with physics, propagated the teachings of Eriugena on the world soul, and undertook, like Bernard Silvester of Tours (*De Mundi universitate,* 1147), to integrate a Platonic philosophy of nature within Christianity. The Platonic doctrine of ideas, and the reflection on numbers, were of a nature to incite the intellect to remove from the sensible world any form of reality judged to be absolute, and to place it in the realm of the archetypes or *exempla.* But the school of Chartres did not succumb to this temptation inherent in classical Platonism. It rather tended to integrate the intellect with the material world and the natural sciences. Its debt to Arabic science in this respect is quite evident—especially in medical science, which had only recently been made accessible to the West.

In the thirteenth century two opposing tendencies divided philosophical and religious reflection. The Franciscan orientation, represented mainly by Bonaventure, showed renewed interest in all things in nature. This was followed by the Dominican orientation, derived from Aristotle and represented by Albertus Magnus and Thomas Aquinas, who elaborated a philosophy based mainly on concepts rather than on living, inter-related symbolic images. From another source came a third tendency, that of the school of Oxford, which shared with the spirit of Chartres a desire for universal intuition. Nature holds the largest place in the thought of Bonaventure, along with his mystical leanings. The "Seraphic Doctor" considered nature equal to the Bible and as a book to be deciphered. The spirit of Oxford blossomed further in the work of the early thirteenth-century bishop Robert Grosseteste. Neoplatonism and an interest in the sciences, two traits characteristic of both these English masters, appeared clearly in Grosseteste. His preferred subject, speculations on the nature of light, was to enjoy a long posterity. The nature of light as the "first corporeal form" *(lux)* accounts for the presence of all of the bodies of the universe and the constitution of the world by its expansion, its condensation, or its rarefaction. Grosseteste imagined that a point of light created by God was diffused in such a manner that a sphere of a finite radius was formed, which was to become the universe (a hypothesis that has been, duly or not, paralleled to the Big Bang theory). The limit of its power of diffusion determined the firmament, which in turn sent back a light *(lumen),* which in turn engendered the celestial spheres and the spheres of the elements. Adam Pulchrae Mulieris, another theologian of the light, prefigured several of Grosseteste's intuitions with his *Liber de intelligentiis.*

Roger Bacon, a thirteenth-century Franciscan of Paris and Oxford, has been often presented as a rationalist precursor of the experimental method of modern science. Nevertheless, what Bacon called "experience" *(experimentum)* should be taken not in its current, modern sense, but in the sense of "the work of an expert." In this understanding, the practices of the alchemist and the astrologer as well fall under the heading of *experimentumi.* Paracelsus would later go along similar paths when dealing with "experience" in medicine, by which he understood the study and knowledge of concealed natural forces. For Bacon, experimental science meant secret and traditional science, with the condition that concrete science not be separated from the Holy Scriptures but that the two be complementarily linked together.

To these works must be added what became a well-known genre in the thirteenth century, that of the *summae* ("sums") and *specula* ("mirrors"), of which Alexander Neckam's *De naturis rerum* is the first example. To this genre belong such works as the *Speculum majus* of Vincent of Beauvais, an exposé of natural history in the form of a commentary on the first chapters of *Genesis.* Aside from this, other works of the same sort worthy of note include *De natura rerum* by Thomas of Cantimpré, and Bartholomew the Englishman's *De proprietatibus rerum.* Only occasionally do these works offer a philosophy of nature in the full sense of the term, but since they are replete with lots of histories and observations on the powers of plants, animals, and minerals, as well as on the heavenly signs, they prepared the way for the occult philosophy of the Renaissance.

From the Late Middle Ages to the Renaissance. The problem of nominalism versus realism, which was posed sharply in the fourteenth century, entailed a debate with high stakes for the construction of a philosophy of nature. Nominalism (contrary to realism) is loath to see in the laws and the realities of the sensible world a collection of analogous/homologous replicas of realities on high, or *exempla.* Nominalism emerged victorious from the debate, clearing the field for the development of modern science, beginning with physics. Thus the continuity between a spiritually structured universe and self-sufficient, purely physical laws, which had been sustained by "traditional" philosophies, was broken. At the same time, the influence of nominalism joined with that of Averroism and, in bringing about the downfall of the Avicennian concept of the universe, paved the way for an ongoing secularization of the cosmos.

The *Ars magna* of Ramón Lull, written in 1308 and inspired by Qabbalah, was an instrument of knowledge that claimed to be applicable at all possible and imaginable levels, from God himself down to the lowest orders of nature, by way of the angels, the stars, and the four elements. Lull's *Ars* played the role of a channel through which a part of the medieval Neoplatonism revived by Eriugena passed, in other words, a dynamic Platonism close to the Jewish mysticism that was to flourish in Florence and Spain. It was interpreted, along with other writings falsely attributed to him, as a form of Qabbalah, although it was hardly so. A grandiose conception of nature is also found in the contemporary writings of Peter of Abano. Astrological Hermetism makes up half of his encyclopedic work, of which the *Conciliator* is the most important volume. Here, nature is seen as controlled by the stars, and objects are filled with spirits.

In addition, alchemy played a big role. It had begun to regain currency in the West in the twelfth century. It assumed three forms, which may have been complementary in the minds of many alchemists, but which it is convenient to distinguish. These were, first, research into procedures of metallic transmutation (for example, the production of gold); second, a "spiritual" alchemy, in which the chemical metaphors served as an aid to meditation, with a conscious or unconscious transformation of the experimenter himself as the goal; and third, an alchemy presented as a philosophy of nature, as in Petrus Bonus's *Pretiosa margarita novella.* In the middle of the fourteenth century, the Franciscan Jean De Rupescissa (or Jean de Roquetaillade) developed at length the idea that a "quintessence" is at work in each object, and he proposed theories on the four elements and the "three principles." All such speculations herald Paracelsus's work, but before him another great name emerged in the thought of the fifteenth-century: Nicholas of Cusa, the apostle of a total science in which the *ars coincidentiarum* is clearly distinguished from the *ars conjecturarum* of common science. The first corresponds to the principle of the intellectual knowledge of objects, the second to the principle of a purely rational knowledge. What he called the *docta ignorantia* is a form of superior knowledge, a gnosis of the coincidence of opposites, or state of the unity of all things.

The Renaissance promoted the revival of a philosophy of nature, primarily in Germanic countries, which were thenceforth the preserver of holistic worldviews; that is, embracing the fullness of the world. In the seventeenth century, the term *pansophy* was often bestowed on them, in order to emphasize their universalizing character. As early as the sixteenth century, Paracelsus, the famous physician of Einsiedeln, Basel, and Salzburg, played a decisive role, with his immense oeuvre and his abundant posterity. While preserving the Neoplatonic idea of intermediaries between humankind and the divine, he did so less as a spiritualist meditating on the nature of intermediary intellects than as a practitioner seeking to discover the analogical relationships between a concrete, living, dynamic heaven and the human being studied in all his constituent parts.

In opposition to Neoplatonism, nature for Paracelsus emerged directly from divine power. He distinguished two orders of suprasensible realities, or "lights." There is the "light of grace," of a uniquely spiritual order, a divine world to which human beings are related through their immortal spirit. This is the domain of mysticism proper; he hardly ventured to occupy himself with it, except in order to stress its ontological preeminence and existence. His domain of research was the other "light," that of nature, or *philosophia sagax,* which he described as an autonomous power of revelation. Between these two lights he placed astronomy or astrology as a third area or term. Everything that concerns these three realms, as well as biology, human psychology, and even the arts, emerges from nature's light and obeys the laws of analogy. Hence the focus on deciphering correspondences among metals, planets, parts of the human body, and so forth, with a view to improving, through observation and experimentation, our understanding of the complexity of nature's divinely created unity. Chemistry and medicine are emphasized in the search for such a comprehension. One must, as Paracelsus himself said, "acquire the wonders of God through the mediation of Nature."

Paracelsism spread through Germany and the rest of Europe at the end of the sixteenth century and the beginning of the seventeenth, at least two generations after the death of its initiator, whose work was not well known nor widely published until then. Among his successors and disciples, Gerhard Dorn, Alexander von Suchten, and Oswald Croll occupy an important place. Their philosophy, like their master's, is not autonomous but is set within a theology; it has a dynamic character bearing on all levels, up to the level of God himself, by no means a *deus otiosus.* The manner in which they conceive the organic unity of the world with its multiple hypostases always results in a kind of "sacred physics" far from the dryness that characterizes many cosmologies of the Middle Ages. Paracelsism corresponds to a new and influential irruption of a "physiological" cosmology—or cosmosophy, rather—in the West, and in the seventeenth century was to lead to developments operating in several directions: notably, a "chemical philosophy," more or less influenced by alchemy, and which the new scientific paradigms struggled to get rid of throughout the seventeenth and eighteenth centuries.

These pansophic outlooks fueled the inspiration of the Rosicrucian movement, whose first manifestations were the *Fama Fraternitatis* (1614) and the *Confessio Fraternitatis* (1615)—which were almost simultaneous with those of thinkers like Robert Fludd and Jakob Boehme. With Boehme, a new esoteric current appeared, namely the so-called Theosophical one (see below).

THE ROOTS OF ROMANTIC *NATURPHILOSOPHIE.* Among the precursors of Romantic *Naturphilosophie* are, in particular, Christian Theosophy, "mosaic physics," "physico-theology," the so-called "theology of electricity," the first experiments in animal magnetism, and also three new orientations that appeared toward the end of the eighteenth century on the stage of philosophy in general, and will be further explained below.

To begin with Christian Theosophy, an esoteric current that flourished from the beginning of the seventeenth century onward (notably with Boehme), one of its prevailing aspects is the search for dynamic correspondences between nature, human beings, and God (or divine entities) through an ongoing "illuminative" speculation bearing on the complex and dramatic relationships between these three, envisaged as *dramatis personae.* In the eighteenth century, Theosophical discourses dealt more and more with the notion of "higher physics," or "sacred physics," as opposed to a merely rational variety. Such sacred physics set itself up against the desacralization of the universe. It was a matter of resacralizing both science and the world. Theosophy *stricto sensu* starts from a speculation that bears on the divine, whereas *Naturphilosophie* proper begins with an observation of natural phenomena, which it then tries to integrate into a holistic and spiritual worldview. But since Theosophers often transferred to the spirit or the divine itself the proprieties of physics, it is scarcely surprising that in some authors the distinction between *Naturphilosophie* and Theosophy tends to get blurred.

Mosaic physics also flourished in the seventeenth century. The term *physica sacra,* often linked to it, served to designate a reading of the Bible considered as the key to understanding another book, that of nature. The contents of both books were supposed to coincide. Jan Amos Comenius, for instance, represents this tendency. In the pre-Enlightenment era, at the end of the seventeenth century, first in England, then in other European countries, there arose a so-called physico-theology, which endeavored to reconcile scientific discoveries with faith (not necessarily with the Bible) as a reaction to mechanistic worldviews and Cartesian rationalism. Physico-theologians (for example, Friedrich Christian Lesser, *Lithotheologie,* 1735) were lavish in descriptions of animals (bees, mollusks, spiders, birds, etc.), plants, and natural phenomena (lightning, storms), to which they attributed symbolic and spiritual, albeit generally static, meanings.

In the context of the later widespread craze for experimentation with electricity and galvanism (1789, experiments of Galvani; 1800, Voltaic pile), the pre-Romantic period witnessed the success of Franz Anton Mesmer's theories, and the development of animal magnetism by Armand Marie de Puységur and his followers. Another result of the belief in a magnetic fluid pervading human beings and the whole universe was the so-called "theology of electricity." The latter was marked by a kind of spiritual realism represented by the Theosopher Friedrich Christoph Oetinger and other figures like Prokop Divisch, Johann Ludwig Fricker, Gottlieb Friedrich Rösler (e.g., their book *Theorie der meteorologischen Elektrizität,* 1765). This "theology" may be considered, at least with regard to Oetinger, as a kind of proto-*Naturphilosophie.*

Besides these three precursors, three further factors pertaining to the history of philosophy proper, are also relevant to the appearance of *Naturphilosophie.*

The influence of French naturalism. With Georges-Louis de Buffon's theoretical works and Denis Diderot's *Le rêve de d'Alembert* (1769), a new way of considering physics had begun to emerge. It began as a kind of literary exercise rather than a strictly scientific discourse, but as it became more popular it pervaded the culture of the time. Buffon, in particular, fostered a taste for synthesis (a typical trait of Romantic thought, along with the painful experience of human limits) and promoted the theme of the soul of the world *(anima mundi)*.

The philosophies of Immanuel Kant and Johann Gottlieb Fichte. In *Metaphysische Anfangsgründe der Naturwissenschaft* (Metaphysical foundations of natural science, 1786), which discussed the necessity of discovering the a priori principles at work behind empirical data, Kant presented as a constitutive characteristic of nature the two forces of Newtonian physics, attraction and repulsion, at a time when the notion of polarity was already spreading outside esoteric circles and flowing into various domains, including medicine. Leaning on some of Kant's ideas, which he extended to the utmost, Fichte proceeded to spread the idea that the world is a product of imagination (notably in *Grundlage der gesamten Wissenschaftslehre* [Foundations of the entire doctrine of science, 1794–1795]). Imagination was understood as resulting from a synthetic and spontaneous activity of the spirit (i.e., the thing in itself and our representation of it are identical).

Spinozan philosophy. Having been considered an atheist during most of the eighteenth century, Spinoza's religious ideas returned to center stage at the turn of the century, but were now interpreted as those of a man intoxicated with God. His "*Deus sive natura*" was no longer read as a disguised profession of materialistic faith, but as the affirmation that nature is something divine. At this time, there was a prevailing tendency to conceive of God as not identical with things but as the primordial center of energy from which the development of organic forms and the entire finite world proceeded. Indeed, *Naturphilosophie* generally avoids pantheism in favor of this panentheism (i.e., God is everywhere in nature, but outside also).

THE ESSENTIALS OF ROMANTIC *NATURPHILOSOPHIE*. *Naturphilosophie* proper appeared during the last years of the eighteenth century, heralded by two groundbreaking works, published almost simultaneously in 1798: F. J. W. Schelling's *Von der Weltseele* (On the soul of the world) and Franz von Baader's *Über das pythagoräische Quadrat in der Natur* (About the Pythagorean square in nature). Besides these two, mention must be made of the first writings of the theoretician in animal magnetism, Carl August von Eschenmayer (e.g., *Sätze aus der Naturmetaphysik auf chemiche und medicinische Gegenstände angewandt* [Elements of the metaphysics of nature, applied to chemical and medical objects], 1797). Along with Baader, and even more than Schelling, Eschenmayer combined the data of the pansophic-esoteric legacy with the new spirit of Kantian philosophy. Among the further representatives of *Naturphilosophie*, the following authors and their representative works stand out: Karl Friedrich Burdach (*Blicke ins Leben* [Glimpses into life], 1842–1848); Wilhelm Butte (*Arithmetik des menschlichen Lebens* [Arithmetic of human life], 1811); Carl Gustav Carus (*Natur und Idee*, 1862); Joseph Ennemoser (*Der Magnetismus im Verhältnis zur Natur und Religion* [Magnetism as related to nature and religion], 1842); Gustav Theodor Fechner (*Zend-Avesta*, 1851), Joseph Görres (*Aphorismen über Kunst, als Einleitung zu künftigen Aphorismen über Organonomie, Physik, Psychologie und Anthropologie* [Aphorisms on art, as an introduction to future aphorisms on organonomy, physics, psychology, and anthropology], 1802); Justinus Kerner (*Eine Erscheinung aus dem Nachtgebiete der Natur* [A manifestation from the night-side of nature], 1836); Dietrich Georg Kieser (in particular his contributions in the 1820s to the journal *Archiv für den Thierischen Magnetismus*); Giovanni Malfatti (*Studien über Anarchie und Hierarchie des Wissens* [Studies about anarchy and hierarchy of knowledge], 1843); Johann Friedrich von Meyer (in particular his contributions in the 1820s and 1830s to *Blätter für höhere Wahrheit* [Journal for higher truth]); Adam Müller (*Lehre vom Gegensatz* [The contradiction theory], 1804); Novalis (pseudonym of Friedrich von Hardenberg, *Das allgemeine Brouillon: Materialien zur Enzyklopädistik* [The general draft: Materials for my encyclopedic project], 1798–1799); Hans Christian Oersted (*Der Geist der Natur* [The spirit of nature], 1850–1851); Lorenz Oken (*Lehrbuch der Naturphilosophie* [Coursebook on *Naturphilosophie*], 1809); Johann Wilhelm Ritter (*Fragmente aus der Nachlasse eines jungen Physikers* [Fragments from the legacy of a young physicist], 1810); the painter Philipp Otto Runge (*Farbenkugel* [Ball of colors], 1810); Gotthilf Heinrich von Schubert (*Ansichten über die Nachtseite der Naturwissenschaft* [Views on the night sides of the science of nature], 1808); Henrik Steffens (*Grundzüge der philosophischen Naturwissenschaften* [The main traits of the philosophical science of nature], 1806); Gottfried Reinhold Trevisarus (*Die Erscheinungen und Gesetze des organischenn Lebens* [The manifestations and laws of organic life], 1831–1833); Ignaz Troxler (*Über das Leben und sein Problem* [On life and its problem], 1806); Johann Jakob Wagner (*Organon der menschlichen Erkenntniss* [Organon of human knowledge], 1830). One should also mention, with respect to other cultural fields, such names as Louis-Claude de Saint-Martin (*L'Esprit des choses* [The spirit of things], 1802), William Paley (*Natural Theology*, 1802), and Sir Humphrey Davy (*Consolations in Travel*, 1830).

The Theosophical orientation proper is far from being the rule amongst these figures. It is conspicuous in Baader, Meyer, and Schubert, for example, but almost absent from the works of such authors as Burdach, Oken, and Wagner. However, most *Naturphilosophen* share three common tenets, which are explicitly or implicitly present in their discourse, and account for their proximity to esotericism in general, and to Theosophy in particular:

First, nature has a history of a mythical order. This ontological postulate functions as a poetic mainspring for research and speculation. The world is not made of eternal, immutable things but is, like the spirit, engaged in a process of a highly dramatic character. A quadruple polar structure underlies most of these speculations. The first pole is the undifferentiated chaos, or primordial light. From that, two opposite poles emerge, which are both opposed and complementary to one another and assume various forms, like fire and water, fire and light, masculine and feminine, attraction and repulsion. A fourth term then manifests, which reflects the first one and is the common product within which the two opposing terms combine. Such a quaternary is the basic structure, in fact a mythical narrative, identified by Schelling as "the repressed mystery of Christianity." It is the story of the "Redeemed Redeemer," that is, the metahistory of a captive light awakened by another light that had remained free. Hence the frequent use of the two notions of light and gravity (rather than darkness), the latter being understood as something by which the primitive energies have been engulfed, but from which they are still likely to reemerge. In a similar vein, Jakob Boehme had described nature as a fire whose embers human beings should rekindle and which in turn would redeem them.

The second tenet concerns the identity of spirit and nature, first expressed by Schelling. "Spirit" is understood as the universal, even divine one, in its relation to nature and to the human beings. Ontologically, this identity rests on a mythical conception of the history of nature, based on an epistemological plane where the negative or destructive opposition of the two is surmounted: Spirit becomes nature, nature becomes spiritualized. Oersted wrote: "The more you advance toward [the] agreement between Nature and Spirit. . .the more perfect you will find it and [the more you will see that] these two Natures are the seeds of one common root" (*Betrachtungen über die Geschichte der Chemie* [Considerations on the history of chemistry], 1807). This "philosophy of identity" (viz., Schelling) has remained the most suggestive idea of *Naturphilosophie,* because it bears on the perennial metaphysical question of the relationship between nature and spirit. By the same token, self-knowledge and knowledge of the world go hand in hand. Both are an initiatory journey and immersion into "the becoming" *(das Werden).* But this *Werden* is dramatic because it implies both order and disorder. The world that surrounds us, and we ourselves, bear witness to an ancient order that has been disrupted. The idea is conspicuous also in Romantic art and literature, which lavishly depict natural landscapes resulting from cataclysmic events, thus reflecting one of the essential themes developed by Theosophy, namely the belief in an original fall of human beings and nature. The interdependence of human being and nature, including the entire cosmos and the soul of the world, is the central idea underlying the research of such *Naturphilosophen* as Baader, Schubert, and Kerner in mesmerism, animal magnetism, and dreams.

Third, nature as a whole is a living net of correspondences to be deciphered and integrated into a holistic worldview. Nature is to be read as a text replete with symbolic implications, whose meaning lies beyond itself. A spirit speaks through it. As a consequence, rigorous experimental science is never more than an obligatory first step toward a comprehensive, holistic knowledge encompassing both *natura naturans* and *natura naturata* (i.e., the invisible as well as the visible processes at work within nature and the whole cosmos). Things always present themselves as symbols, which bring back to both the warp and woof of a universal web. Living structures are detected in crystals, celestial constellations, and electric phenomena. Mechanistic imaginary and the compartmentalization of science into sectors cut off from one another are replaced by an organic merging of all disciplines. Thus concrete science and metaphysics, or experimentation and meditation, are two sides of the same coin. Almost all representatives of this current were scholars with at least one scientific specialty, like chemistry, physics, geology, mine engineering, or medicine. The fragments of empirical reality require a "second reading." Once reality has been subjected to scientific analysis, it needs to be deciphered symbolically in order to yield clusters of meaning. Consequently, a scientific fact is perceived as a sign, and signs respond to each other. Concepts borrowed from chemistry are transferred to astronomy or human psychology; notions pertaining to botany are used to describe inorganic processes or vice versa. It is not surprising that the Romantic image of the wise physician, characteristic of period literature, enjoyed a great success, based as it was on the analogy between medicine and poetry. In literature, such transfers from one domain to another often took the form of aphorisms (e.g., Novalis), a genre generally praised by German Romanticism. The Romantic writer Friedrich Schlegel claimed that "the combinatorial mind is truly prophetic," and Schelling advocated a form of nondogmatic polytheism: "Monotheism of the mind and of the heart, and polytheism of the imagination and of art, this is what we need" (1962, vol. 1, p. 70).

Goethe's philosophy of nature is somewhat distinct from the current of *Naturphilosophie.* Admittedly, throughout his life he certainly maintained the notion of a vital universe, and his scientific works, especially those on the metamorphosis of plants and on colors, place him close to some leanings of the *Naturphilosophen.* But he was more interested in trying to grasp eternity in an instant, or infinity in an object (William Blake), than in discovering commonalities or correspondences between things, or in what the latter symbolize of the invisible. More generally, he remained aloof from Romanticism. Apart from brilliant exceptions like Ritter and Oersted, the *Naturphilosophen* did not make significant discoveries themselves, but they were keen to find and express truths of a different order, that of the absolute.

In the wake of Romantic *Naturphilosophie.* After about sixty years, the current of *Naturphilosophie* faded away in the 1850s. It was probably the last period in which people—or, at least, the savants—had felt at home on earth. Gradually, an estrangement from nature had made headway: the view had begun to prevail that nature is hostile, and not a place where they could feel at home. Nature came to represent either "the other," linked to a feeling of no longer being "at home in the world," or conversely to a reflexive response against the increasing disenchantment of the world (a kind of last-ditch attempt at exorcizing the specter of disenchantment). This process had already been smoldering for quite a few decades, as exemplified by Arthur Schopenhauer's *Die Welt als Wille und Vorstellung* (The world as will and representation, 1819), in which nature is considered as being outside the categories of understanding. In the second half of the nineteenth century, *Naturphilosophie* was definitely superseded by the advent of scientistic, materialistic worldviews. However, it left numerous legacies. A number of celebrated philosophers in the twentieth century, like Ludwig Klages, Hermann Keyerling, and Max Scheler, have reclaimed some of its heritage, but in an essentially speculative manner, since very few of them were chemists, astrophysicists, or physicians.

Originally inspired by Goethe, Rudolf Steiner followed an orientation more akin to *Naturphilosophie* proper, which has consequently left its imprint upon the teachings and literature of the Anthroposophical Society until the present. Less directly but more importantly, the most obvious survival of *Naturphilosophie* is to be found in the theories of the unconscious. In this respect, works like Schubert's *Die Symbolik des Traums* (Symbolism of dreams, 1814), and perhaps even more Carus's *Psyche: Entwicklungsgeschichte der Seele* (Psyche: The historical development of the soul, 1846), certainly influenced the ideas of late nineteenth-century thinkers like Eduard von Hartmann (*Philosophie des Unbewussten* [Philosophy of the unconscious], 1869). Even more importantly, these theorists of the unconscious represent the historical roots of psychoanalysis, leading to the theories of Sigmund Freud (for whom the unconscious is rather monolithic, as it had been for Arthur Schopenhauer) and those of Carl Gustav Jung, who described the unconscious as a dynamically functioning quaternary. Jung may be considered the latest major representative of *Naturphilosophie*, given his views of alchemy (namely, that what alchemists saw in their crucible was a constellation of their own unconscious), and his theories on synchronicity as well.

Over the last decades, members of several scientific communities have adopted some conceptions pertaining to *Naturphilosophie*, whether they were aware of this tradition or not. For example, the idea of intelligent matter has been addressed by scientists like Valdemar Axel Firsoff (*Life, Mind, and Galaxies*, 1967) and Jean Charon (*L'Homme et l'Univers* [Man and the universe], 1974). The hypothesis that matter is modeled on the spirit has been developed in Arthur Koestler's *The Roots of Coincidence* (1972). Authors like David Bohm (*Wholeness and the Implicate Order*, 1980) and Fritjof Capra (*The Tao of Physics*, 1975) have developed "holistic" interpretations of modern physics, thus fostering a sort of visionary physics that has gained entrance into the literature of the New Age (see Hanegraaff) in the form of various speculations on the relationship between "science" and "conscience," "science" and "tradition," and so on.

BIBLIOGRAPHY

Ayrault, Roger. *La genèse du romantisme allemand: Situation spirituelle de l'Allemagne dans la deuxième moitié du XVIIIe siècle.* Paris, 1964. See vol. 4, pages 13–167.

Benz, Ernst. *Theologie der Elektrizität: Zur Begegnung und Auseinandersetzung von Theologie und Naturwissenschaft im 17ten und 18ten Jahrhundert.* Mainz, Germany, 1970.

Bernoulli, Christoph, and Hans Kern, ed. *Romantische Naturphilosophie.* Jena, Germany, 1926.

Brinkmann, Richard, ed. *Romantik in Deutschland: Ein interdisziplinäres Symposium.* Stuttgart, Germany, 1978. See the section entitled "Romantik im Spanungsfeld von Naturgefühl, Naturwissenschaft und Philosophie, " pp. 167–330.

Cazenave, Michel, ed. *Science et conscience: Les deux lectures de l'universe.* Paris, 1980.

Engelhardt, Dietrich von. "Bibliographie der Sekundärliteratur zur romantischen Naturforschung und Medizin, 1950–1975." In *Romantik in Deutschland: Ein interdisziplinäres Symposium*, edited by Richard Brinkmann, pp. 307–330. Stuttgart, Germany, 1978.

Debus, Allen G. *The Chemical Philosophy: Paracelsian Science and Medicine in the Sixteenth and Seventeenth Centuries.* 2 vols. New York, 1977.

Engelhardt, Dietrich von. "Romantische Naturforschung." In *Historisches Bewusstsein in der Naturwissenschaft von der Aufklärung bis zum Positivismus*, edited by Dietrich von Engelhardt, pp. 103–157. Freiburg, Germany, 1979.

Faivre, Antoine. *Philosophie de la nature: Physique sacrée et théosophie, XVIIIème-XIXème siècles.* Paris, 1998.

Faivre, Antoine, and Rolf Christian Zimmerman, eds. *Epochen der Naturmystik: Hermetische Tradition im wissenschaftlichen Fortschritt.* Berlin, 1979.

Gilson, Étienne. *La philosophie au moyen âge: Des origines patristiques à la fin du XVe siècle.* 2d ed. Paris, 1944.

Gode von Aesch, Alexander. *Natural Science in German Romanticism.* New York, 1941; reprint, 1966.

Gusdorf, Georges. *Le savoir romantique de la nature.* Paris, 1985.

Hanegraaff, Wouter. *New Age Religion and Western Culture: Esotericism in the Mirror of Secular Thought.* Albany, N.Y., 1996. See pages 64–76.

Joël, Karl. *Der Ursprung der Naturphilosophie aus dem Geiste der Mystik.* Jena, Germany, 1906.

Leibbrand, Werner. *Die spekulative Medizin der Romantk.* Hamburg, Germany, 1956.

Lenoble, Robert. *Histoire de l'idée de nature.* Paris, 1969.

Pagel, Walter. *Paracelsus: An Introduction to Philosophical Medicine in the Era of the Renaissance.* Basel, Switzerland, 1958; 2d ed., 1982.

Schelling, F. W. J. *Briefe und Dokumente.* Edited by Horst Fuhrmans. 2 vols. Bonn, Germany, 1962.

Sladek, Mirko. *Fragmente der hermetischen Philosophie in der Naturphilosophie der Neuzeit.* Frankfurt, Germany, 1984.

Stebbins, Sara. *Maxima in Minimis: Zum Empirie- und Autoritätsverständnis in der physico-theologschen Literatur der Frühaufklärung.* Frankfurt, Germany, 1980.

ANTOINE FAIVRE (1987 AND 2005)

NATURE: WORSHIP OF NATURE

What is ordinarily spoken of as "nature"—the physical world, including all living beings beyond the control of human culture—often appears to the religious consciousness as a manifestation of the sacred. Through nature, modes of being quite different from the specifically human reveal themselves to the religious imagination. The sun, the moon, and the earth, for example, can symbolize realities that transcend human experience. Throughout the history of religions, "nature" frequently is perceived as initiating a relationship with humankind, a relationship that is the foundation of human existence and well-being. In large part, this relationship is expressed in forms of adoration, a response of the total personality, or of an entire religious community, to the phenomena of nature.

The worship of nature underscores the fact that the sacred can appear in any guise. The religious person is confronted by the paradox that the sacred can manifest itself in material form without losing its essential character. In the worship of nature, radically different levels of existence are felt to interpenetrate and coexist. The possibilities of the human spirit become coextensive with the sacred capacities of the rest of the physical universe. The worship of nature thus highlights both the freedom of the sacred to appear in any form, and the capacity of the human being to recognize it for what it is in any expression. It also underlines the capacity of profane reality itself to become a transparent symbol of something other than itself, even while remaining what it is. In such a religious perception of the universe, nature transcends its brute physicality. It becomes a cipher, a symbol of something beyond itself. From this point of view, nature's existence is like the human situation in the world. Its modes of being as a manifestation of the sacred become resources for understanding the human religious condition. In many traditions, in fact, the belief in the shared destiny of nature and humanity is highly elaborated, so that the objects of nature are held to possess the same essential qualities as human beings: emotions, life cycles, personalities, volition, and so on.

The value and function of nature thus goes beyond the concrete sphere to the mystery of the sacred as it appears in the fuller reaches of religious experience. Only by keeping this in mind will people understand the forms in which communities respond to powers revealed in the physical universe. The following provide a series of suggestive illustrations of worship of nature.

The sky is often revered as a manifestation of divinity or venerated as the locus of the gods. The Konde of east-central Africa adored Mbamba (also named Kiara or Kyala), a divinity who dwelt with his family in the heights above the sky. The Konde offer prayer and sacrifice to the god who dwells in the sky, especially at times when rain is called for. Many divinities of the sky originally lived on earth or with the first human beings. Eventually, they withdrew on high. Not much is recounted about them in myth. The Samoyed peoples adored Num, a god who lived in the seventh heaven and whose name means "sky." Num overspreads the entire universe and is identified not only with the sky but with the sea and the earth. Tengri (Sky) is the supreme being among Mongols (Tengeri among the Buriats).

Baiame is the supreme god among tribes of southeastern Australia (Kamilaroi, Euahlayi, and Wiradjuri). He welcomes the souls of the dead into his dwelling place beside the flowing waters of the Milky Way. His voice is thunder; he is omniscient. Although supreme beings of the sky like Baiame reveal important mysteries to the first ancestors before they withdraw on high, and although they play a major part in initiation ceremonies, they do not usually dominate liturgical life.

Objects fallen from the sky come from the sacred locus of the heavens and often become the objects of religious cults. For example, the Numana of the Niger River valley in West Africa, who accord an important place to the divinity of the sky, vernerate small pebbles, which they believe have fallen from the sky. They install these sacred pebbles on top of cones of beaten earth some three feet high and offer sacrifices to them. Since the pebbles have fallen from the sky, they are believed to be fragments of the sky god. Actual meteorites are frequently the center of a cult associated with sky gods. In the same way, flints and other species of "thunder stones" or "rain stones" fallen from the sky are treated as sacred, for they are believed to be the arrowpoints shot by the god of lightning or by other celestial divinities.

Worship of the sun is widespread, especially at the times of the solstices. The Chukchi of northern Asia, for example, offer sacrifices to the light of the sun. Among the Chagga of Mount Kilimanjaro in Tanzania, Ruwa (Sun) is the supreme being, who receives sacrificial offerings in times of crisis. In societies engaged in intensive agriculture, the sun is worshiped in connection with the fertility of the crops and regenerative life of the cosmos. Such is the case with Inti in the Inca pantheon. The sun's power in such cases is not limited to the fertility of foodstuffs but extends also to human progeny. Privileged groups of human beings reckon their descent from the sun as did the Inca nobles, the Egyptian pharaoh, and important chiefly families on the island of Timor that reckon they are the "children of the sun." In many cultures the sun is believed to traverse the underworld at night. Therefore the sun becomes a sacred guide for the soul's journey through the land of the dead. In the Harvey Islands, the dead cluster in groups to await the biannual postmortem trek. During the solstices the sun leads these groups through the netherworld. Veneration of the sun takes the form of following his tracks when he sets. The sun carries into heaven the warriors who have fallen in battle.

Frequently the sun is worshiped because of its heroic achievements, including the creation of human beings. The sun and the moon created human beings from gourds, according to the tradition of the Apinagé people of South America. In the tradition of the Desána, a Tucano-speaking group of southern Colombia, the sun inseminated his daughter with light (through her eye) and caused the creation of the universe.

The moon is one of the most fascinating and rich religious characters. It has long been an object of worship in many cultures. The moon's shifting shape and changing disposition in the sky at various times of the night, day, and month makes it the focus of a wide range of associations that have led to its veneration. Sin, the Babylonian god of the moon, had important connections with the waters of the earth. Their ebb and flow were connected with the rhythmic capacities and periodic nature of Sin. Sin also created the grasses of the world.

The moon is frequently a lascivious being associated with the wanton powers of fertility. Often the moon is venerated as the source of sexual life and originator of reproductive processes such as menstruation and intercourse. The Canelos Quichua of eastern Ecuador, for example, treat Quilla, the moon, as a central supernatural being. When the new moon is immature, it is called *llullu Quilla,* the "green" or "unripe" moon. During these phases it is a prepubescent girl unable to conceive offspring or fashion pottery or prepare beer. The adult moon, *pucushca Quilla,* however, is a lascivious male whose incestuous exploits are recounted in myth. The moon's illicit exploits with his sister, the bird Jilucu, engendered the stars. When they discovered their origins, the stars wept and flooded the earth (Norman Whitten, *Sacha Runa: Ethnicity and Adaptation of Ecuadorian Jungle Quichua,* Urbana, Ill., 1976, p. 45).

Among the Siriono of eastern Bolivia, Yasi (Moon) is the most important supernatural being. He once lived on earth as a chief, but after creating the first human beings and teaching them the fundamentals of culture, he ascended into heaven. The waxing of the moon occurs as Yasi washes his face clean by degrees after returning from the hunt. The Siriono build lean-tos made of leaves in order to protect sleepers from exposure to the dangerous rays of the moon. These would cause blindness. Yasi provokes thunder and lightning by throwing jaguars and peccaries down to earth (Holmberg, 1960).

Mountains are a ubiquitous object of cult. In the Kunisaki Peninsula of Japan, for example, a tradition that dates back to the Heian period establishes a systematic, metaphorical relationship between the image of the mountain and the salvific power of the *Lotus Sūtra* (Grapard, 1986, pp. 21–50). The sacred mountain of this peninsula represents the nine regions of the Pure Land and is an important pilgrimage center. Its eight valleys are the eight petals of the lotus blossom that represents the Diamond Mandala and the Womb Mandala. These structures become the basis for the architecture of temples, the divisions of the text of the *Lotus Sūtra of the Wondrous Law,* and the program for the spiritual lives and geographic travels of pilgrims. All of these isomorphic structures represent the Pure Land of the Dainichi Nyorai. "This mountain is the permanent residence of the heart-mind of the Marvelous Law. It is the Lotus Pedestal on which the Buddha rests" (verses attributed to Enchin and quoted in Grapard, 1986, p. 50). The sacred mountain embodies the six realms *(rokudō)* of existence: that of the gods, human beings, titans, animals, hungry ghosts, and hells. Within these realms, arranged in a vertical hierarchy, all beings and all forms of rebirth have their place. Mount Haguro, another sacred mountain on the northern part of the Japanese island of Honshu, serves as the center of worship during four seasonal feasts. The New Year celebration is one of the most important and dramatic of these, for at that time the sacred combat between the old and the new year determines the outcome of the future year (Earhart, 1970; Blacker, 1975, chap. 2).

In South America, offerings are made to the mountains of the Andes throughout the year to sustain and stimulate the life of the community. The mountain is a divine body in whose life all beings participate and from whose abundance and well-being all benefit. The community cultivates food from the body of the mountain. It gives forth fluids (water, semen, milk, and blood) that sustain life. Sacrifices and offerings placed in specific holy sites on the mountain replenish the fat, the power source, of the mountain body (Bastien, 1985, pp. 595–611).

Waters are frequently presented as supernatural beings worthy of worship. Water, according to mythic accounts, is often the source of primal life. Such is the case in the Babylonian creation story recorded in the *Enuma elish,* wherein Apsu and Tiamat (fresh water and sea water, aspects of the primordial ocean) mingle chaotically to give rise to all subsequent forms of life. Springs, rivers, and irrigation waters are the centers of religious attention throughout the world. They are celebrated not only during the episodes of the agricultural cycle but also at moments of rebirth into initiatory societies and at moments of initiation into culture itself. Immersion water, standing in a stream or under a waterfall, or other forms of extended exposure to water serve as ordeals commonly associated with initiation. For the Akwẽ and Chavante peoples of Brazil, for example, the lengthy exposure of initiands to water recalls the time when mythical heroes created the world's contents at the time of the flood.

In Scandinavian mythology Ægir (the Sea) is the boundless ocean. His wife, Ran, casts her net through the ocean and drags human beings into its depths as sacrificial offerings. The nine daughters of Ægir and Ran represent the various modes and moments of the sea. All of these divine beings dwell in the magnificent castle at the bottom of the ocean where the gods occasionally gather around a miraculous caldron. Apparently the cult of disposing of caldrons at the bottom of seas or lakes is associated with this mythology.

Water monsters are also the object of cultic action. They are placated or combated to stave off a repetition of the cosmic deluge. Aquatic dragons embody the fertile principles manifest in moisture. They must be slain or tamed to release their fecund powers and to prevent drought. Thus the Chinese dragon Yin gathers together all the waters of the world and controls the rain. Images of Yin were fashioned at times of drought and at the onset of the rains (Granet, 1926, vol. 1, pp. 353–356).

The earth is sacred in many traditions and is the object of devotion and affection. As the source of life, Pachamama (Mother Earth) of the Andes is worshiped on various occasions throughout the year. The agricultural cycle is coordinated with her menstrual periods, the times when she is open for conception. The earth is frequently a partner of the sky or of some other celestial fertilizing divinity. Among the Kumana of southern Africa, for example, the marriage of the sky and the earth makes the cosmos fertile. Liturgical life is directed toward the fruitful accomplishment of this union. Among North American Indian peoples such as the Pawnee, the Lakota, the Huron, the Zuni, and the Hopi, the earth is the fertile partner of the sky and the source of abundant life. The care extended to the earth takes involved forms of worship. The earth is also frequently the locus of burial. As such the earth becomes an ambivalent source of regenerative life, for it is a regeneration accomplished through devouring. All that is buried in the earth and rises to new life must undergo the decomposition of the seed. Rituals associated with the earth, such as agricultural orgies, frequently reenact this furious and destructive episode of degeneration in imitation of the experience of the seed in the earth.

Plants, trees, and vegetation also have their place in worship. The tree of life or the cosmic tree expresses the sacredness of the entire world. Scandinavian myth offers the example of Yggdrasill, the cosmic tree. Yggdrasill sinks its roots into the earth and into the netherworld where giants dwell. Divinities meet daily near the tree to pass judgment on the world's affairs. The Fountain of Wisdom flows from a spot near the tree as does the Fountain of Memory. Yggdrasill miraculously renews itself in spite of the fact that an enormous serpent named Níðhoggr (Nidhogg) gnaws at its roots. The universe will continue to exist because Yggdrasill perdures. An enormous eagle defends it from its enemies and the god Óðinn (Odin) tethers his horse to its branches.

Other kinds of vegetation also manifest sacred powers and divinities. Thus the Vedic and Puranic creation accounts identify the lotus floating upon the water as a manifestation of the divinity and of the universe. Miraculous trees, flowers, and fruits reveal the presence of divine powers. Rites of spring frequently center on plants, boughs, or trees that are treated as sacred. The fertility of the cosmos is symbolized by the union of male and female plants or by the blossoming of a bough from a specific species of plants. Around the world, the agricultural cycle is hedged around with religious acts directed toward the furthering of the powers of fertility manifest in various crops. In particular, the moments of sowing and reaping are marked by sacrifices. The seeds themselves undergo a form of sacrificial death as do the harvested stalks at the end of the growing season. The picking of first fruits and the gathering of the last sheaf of the fields is frequently the occasion for religious festival and ceremony.

Animals have also stimulated the religious imagination in such a way as to warrant devotion. Animals, birds, fish, snakes, and even insects have all become the focus of adoration in one culture or another. Often their bodies represent the transformed expression of supernatural beings that underwent metamorphosis at the beginning of time (Goldman, 1979).

Examples of the worship of nature could be multiplied endlessly. There is hardly any object in the natural cosmos that has not become the center of cult somewhere at one time or in one place or another. How this should be interpreted is a matter of extreme delicacy. In general modern interpreters have failed to settle on a satisfactory explanation. Even the term *nature* carries a range of connotations that obscure the meaning of sacred objects of cult in many cultures. Each generation of scholars in the last century spawned a number of interpretive theories in which the worship of nature figured as a large element in the assessment of religion in general. In fact, the effort to desacralize nature in the Western perception and to identify the perception of nature as sacred with "primitive" peoples played a large role in the foundation of the social sciences and in the self-understanding of the modern West (Cocchiara, 1948). Offering a nuanced interpretation of the worship of nature would require a detailed deconstruction of the cultural sciences as well as a subtle appreciation of the religious terminology of each culture in question. James G. Frazer contended that the worship of nature and the worship of the dead were the two most fundamental forms of natural religion (1926, pp. 16–17). F. Max Müller founded his school of comparative religious studies on the principle that myths spoke about nature. E. B. Tylor also established his influential theory of animism, a still-lingering interpretation of religion on the notion that human beings projected onto nature certain animate qualities of their own character, visible especially in dream and in the rational explanations of death. Claude Lévi-Strauss pushes this intellectualized perception of nature in the formation of religion even further, contending that religion involved the humanization of the laws of nature (Lévi-Strauss, 1966, p. 221). A politico-economic interpretation of religion points to the intricate unity between nature and human beings, bound together by common origins and by reciprocities visible in ritual. According to Michael Taussig (1980), it is ritual action that aligns human beings with the helping spirits of nature. These rituals are extended in the modern rites of labor, such as those associated with miners and farmhands. The rituals dedicated to nature are aimed at enlisting nature's power in the cause of liberation of human being in the cosmos. The worship of nature, in this view, is an example of cosmological principles and the rituals dedicated to nature are also the arenas where these principles are created, renewed, and reformed (Taussig, 1980). The worship of nature has also become an important object of scholarly study in order to study nature as a category in the conceptual schemes of different cultures (Ortner, 1974; MacCormack and Strathern, 1980).

See Also Animals; Center of the World; Deus Otiosus; Earth; Ecology and Religion; Hierophany; Moon; Sky; Sun; Supreme Beings; Vegetation; Water.

BIBLIOGRAPHY

General Works

The classic study of the sacral experience that underlies the worship of nature remains Mircea Eliade's *Patterns in Comparative Religion* (New York, 1958), which contains extensive discussions and bibliographies on many of the themes treated briefly above (sun, moon, water, earth, vegetation, et al.). For earlier discussions, see F. Max Müller's *Natural Religion* (London, 1888), E. B. Tylor's *Primitive Culture,* 2 vols. (1871; reprint, New York, 1970), and James G. Frazer's *The Worship of Nature* (London, 1926). Other helpful studies include *The Savage Mind* by Claude Lévi-Strauss (London, 1966) and *Menschenbilder früher Gesellschaften: Ethnologische Studien zum Verhältnis von Mensch und Natur,* edited by Klaus E. Müller (Frankfurt, 1983), which gathers together a number of essays on various aspects of nature (forests, stones, cultivated plants, and pastoral animals) and includes a bibliography.

Specialized Studies

Bastien, Joseph W. "Qollahuaya-Andean Body Concepts: A Topographical-Hydraulic Model of Physiology." *American Anthropologist* 87 (September 1985): 595–711.

Blacker, Carmen. *The Catalpa Bow: A Study of Shamanistic Practices in Japan.* London, 1975.

Cocchiara, Giuseppe. *Il mito del buon selvaggio: Introduzione alla storia delle teorie etnologiche.* Messina, 1948.

Earhart, H. Byron. *A Religious Study of the Mount Haguro Sect of Shugendo.* Tokyo, 1970.

Goldman, Irving. *The Cubeo: Indians of the Northwest Amazon* (1963). Urbana, Ill., 1979.

Granet, Marcel. *Danses et légendes de la Chine ancienne.* 2 vols. Paris, 1926.

Grapard, Allan G. "Lotus in the Mountain, Mountain in the Lotus: *Rokugō kaizan nimmon daibosatsu hongi.*" *Monumenta Nipponica* 41 (Spring 1986): 21–50.

Holmberg, Allan R. *Nomads of the Long Bow: The Siriono of Eastern Bolivia.* Washington, D.C., 1960.

MacCormack, Carol P., and Marilyn Strathern, eds. *Nature, Culture, and Gender.* Cambridge, 1980.

Ortner, Sherry. "Is Female to Male as Nature Is to Culture?" In *Women, Culture, and Society,* edited by Michelle Zimbalist Rosaldo and Louise Lamphere. Stanford, Calif., 1974.

Tambiah, Stanley J. "Animals Are Good to Think and Good to Prohibit." *Ethnology* 8 (October 1969): 423–459.

Taussig, Michael T. *The Devil and Commodity Fetishism in South America.* Chapel Hill, N.C., 1980.

Zolla, Elemire. "Korean Shamanism." *Res* 9 (Spring 1985): 101–113.

New Sources

Albanese, Catherine L. *Nature Religion in America: From the Algonkian Indians to the New Age.* Chicago, 1990.

Burton, Lloyd. *Worship and Wilderness: Culture, Religion, and Law in the Management of Public Lands and Resources.* Madison, Wis., 2002.

Suzuki, David T., and Peter Knudtson. *Wisdom of the Elders: Honoring Sacred Native Visions of Nature.* New York, 1992.

Lawrence E. Sullivan (1987)
Revised Bibliography

NAVĀ'Ī, 'ALĪ SHĪR See 'ALĪ SHĪR NAVĀ'Ī

NAVAJO RELIGIOUS TRADITIONS.

Because of it colonial origin, the designation *Navajo* is in the process of being replaced by the term *Diné,* a word derived from the phrase *Diyin Dine'é* (people with supernatural powers). For this reason, *Diné* will be used throughout this article. The Diné, whose population in the 2000s has been estimated at 180,462, now live primarily on the Diné Nation (a land reserve approximately 270,000 square miles in size) located within the four corners of northeastern Arizona, northwestern New Mexico, southeastern Utah, and southwestern Colorado. Archaeological and linguistic evidence suggests that the Diné were latecomers to the American Southwest, arriving between 1000 and 1525 CE. Through contact with the Spanish and Pueblo peoples they acquired horses, sheep, goats, and agriculture. Anthropologists generally attribute similarities between Diné and Pueblo cosmologies and practices to the fact that many Pueblo refugees began to live among the Diné following the Pueblo Revolt of 1680. Many Diné elders describe this period as one of mutual exchange, rather than of unilateral influence.

Cosmology and Worldview. The path of walking in beauty and harmony, known as *Hózhóójí,* is the basic philosophy of the Diné Nation and is the foundation for their culture, beliefs, and traditions. The path of *K'e* is based on a reciprocal relationship of kinship with the surrounding environment and the universe. The Diné *bá'ólta'í* (teacher, messenger) Wilson Aronilth Jr. explains: "According to our great forefathers' teaching, our clan system is the foundation of how we learn about our self image and self identity. . . . A wise Diné can look back into the values of his clan and see his true self" (Aronilth, 1991, p. 76). The Diné were instructed by the Diyin Dine'é to live within the boundaries of the four mountains located in New Mexico, Arizona, and Colorado. Instruction were given by the Diyin Dine'é to build a *hooghan* (round house). The primary function of the *hooghan* was as a place for ceremonies and prayers.

The Diné origin myth recounts the Diné *hajíínáí* (emergence) from a series of underworlds onto *Nahasdzáán* (the Earth's surface). Using a medicine bundle brought from the underworlds, in an all-night ceremony at the place of emergence, First Man, First Woman, and other Diyin Dine'é set in place the "inner forms" of natural phenomena (earth, sky, the sacred mountains, plants, and animals), creating the present world (the fourth world). The Diné creation story recounts that it is in the fourth world that 'Asdzáá Nádleehé (Changing Woman) was born; she was impregnated by

Jónaa'éí (Sun) and gave birth to twin sons, who killed various monsters that had been endangering the Diyin Dine'é. Using the medicine bundle First Man had given her, 'Asdzáá Náleehé created maize. She also created the Diné (Earth-Surface People), from epidermal waste rubbed from her skin.

The Diné creation myth indicates that there is no dichotomy between the natural and supernatural in Diné religion. Furthermore, humans (the Earth-Surface People) and the Diyin Dine'é are conceived of in terms of the same set of motivating forces: the notion of *nílch'i* (wind), the concept of *bii'gistiin* (inner form) or *bii'siziinii* (in-lying one), and the opposing notions of *hózhó* (harmony, balance) and *hóchó* (disharmony, disorder).

Wind is a unitary phenomenon that is the source of all life, movement, and behavior. However, wind has various aspects that have different functions and, hence, different names. Before the Emergence, winds are said to have given the means of life (i.e., breath) to the inhabitants of the underworlds. After the Emergence, mists of lights were placed along each of the cardinal directions and four sacred mountains were created in each direction. Each direction is said to have an "inner form" *(bii'gistiin)* as well as a closely associated wind. From the four directions these winds give the means of life, movement, thought, and communication to the natural phenomena, the Diyin Dine'é, and the Diné. Wind's Child is sent to guide and advise the Earth-Surface People. Finally, each Diné also has a "wind within one" *(nílch'i biisíinii)* that enters at birth and guides the individual.

Thus both natural phenomena and humans have inner forms or "in-lying ones" animated by wind. As Gary Witherspoon has written, "In most cases the Holy People of the fifth world are those who are the inner forms of various natural phenomena and forces, including animals. These in-lying ones are the controlling and animating powers of nature. Diné ritual is designed to control the Holy People who are the inner forms and controlling agents of natural phenomena" (Witherspoon, 1983, p. 575).

The Diyin Dine'é are immune to danger, destruction, and death. They are not holy in the sense that they are virtuous, but rather in the sense that they are powerful. It is the responsibility of each Diné to maintain harmonious relations with the Diyin Dine'é, though the Diyin Dine'é may be persuaded to aid in the restoration of a person who has become ill through improper contact with them.

In Diné belief the term *hózhó* refers to a positive or ideal environment. As Witherspoon puts it, "The goal of Diné life in this world is to live to maturity in the condition described as *hózhó,* and to die of old age, the end result of which incorporates one into the universal beauty, harmony, and happiness described as *'Sa'áh naagháí, Bik'eh hózhó'* " (Witherspoon, 1983, p. 573). The phrase *"Sa'áh naagháí, bik'eh hózhó"* (long life, filled with happiness and harmony) occurs in most ritual songs and prayers and clearly exemplifies the Diné ideal. The foundation of the philosophy is the reciprocal relationship between the Diné and all of the entities in the universe, including animals, plants, the cosmos, and the earth that sustains all living things.

Illness is thought to be a state of *hóchó* that has resulted from the patient's contact with something "dangerous." Leland C. Wyman and Clyde Kluckhohn (1938, pp. 13–14) list four groups of "etiological factors" that can produce sickness:

1. Natural phenomena such as lightning, wind, and thunder.
2. Some kinds of animals, including bears, deer, coyotes, porcupines, snakes, eagles, and fish.
3. Coming into contact with ceremonial paraphernalia at inappropriate times.
4. Diné ghosts, aliens, witches, or werewolves.

Following such an encounter, a ceremony is required to restore the individual to the state of *hózhóójí.*

CHANTS AND CEREMONIES. Anthropologists have identified twenty-four chant complexes; only about eight were well known and frequently performed in the 1970s, while six were extinct and four were obsolete. There has been little agreement among either Diné consultants or anthropologists as to how these chants might be ordered into a system. (See Wyman and Kluckhohn, 1938; Haile, 1938; Reichard, 1950; Wyman, 1983; Witherspoon, 1983; and Werner et al., 1983, for various possibilities.)

Chants are associated with a number of rituals, the most important of which are the Hózhóójí and Enemyway ceremonies. The Hózhóójí (Blessingway) ceremony is of central importance for the Diné, and is intended to preserve a beautiful, peaceful, harmonious state of balance *(hózhó).* It is the foundation of the Kinaaldá ceremony, a puberty ritual for young girls. The Enemyway ceremony *('anna'jí),* in contrast, is designed to counteract the evil effects of contact with non-Diné people killed in battle and is used to exorcise their spirits (ghosts). According to Wyman (1983, p. 541), it is one of a mostly obsolete group of ancient war ceremonials and is now classed together with other ceremonies collectively labeled Evilway *(hóchó'ojí).*

The Diné model of the cosmos is expressed in the setting of the ceremony itself. The chant takes place in the *hooghan,* which is circular like the horizon. Movement during a ritual is always clockwise or "in the direction of the sun." Men sit on the south side of the *hooghan;* women on the north side. The singer sits on the southwest side and the patient, when resting, sits on the northwest side. The east (where the door is located) is associated with the Hayoołkááł Hastiin Diyin (Dawn Spirit Talking).

COMPARISONS. Although Diné elders do not make cross-cultural comparisons between Diné traditions and the traditions of other Native American Indians, some scholars, such as Louise Lamphere, note striking similarities between Diné ceremonialism and that of both the Apache and the Pueblo. Both the Diné and the Apache place great emphasis on the goal of achieving long life, and both center their ceremonies on the individual—that is, on changing his or her state through prestation, the removal of evil objects, and identification with supernatural power. Like Pueblo religion, Diné religion entails a view of a cosmos that is structured as a bounded universe in which the present world is at the top of several layered worlds through which the ancestors emerged. While Diné ritual replicates the cosmos differently than Apache ritual, its use of color, sex, and directional symbolism find many parallels in Pueblo ritual and in the Pueblo worldview (see Heib, 1979; Tedlock, 1979; and Ortiz, 1969).

The similarities between the ceremonies of the Diné, the Apache, and the Pueblo suggest that there are unifying features to ceremonialism in native Southwest cultures. Southwest religion, like that of other Native American cultures; is closely tied to the natural environment. Native cosmologies are rooted in conceptions of time and space that imbue the local terrain with supernatural meaning. Natural objects are made into ritual objects and are used to attract positive supernatural power, to remove dangerous power, and to represent sacred presence. A ceremonial specialist using these objects and ritual actions communicates with the supernatural in order to ensure that natural and cultivated plant and animal life will continue to be abundant and that individual and communal health and prosperity are maintained.

Although many books are available with specific descriptions of ceremonies, rituals, chants, and prayers, the Diné emphasis on orality and holistic understanding suggests that long-term fieldwork and language acquisition are the most reliable and responsible methods of research.

See Also Athapaskan Religious Traditions.

BIBLIOGRAPHY

Aberle, David F. "'The Navajo Singer's Fee': Payment of Prestation?" In *Studies in Southwestern Ethnolinguistics: Meaning and History in the Languages of the American Southwest,* edited by Dell H. Hymes with William E. Bittle, pp. 15–32. The Hague, 1967.

Aronilth, Wilson, Jr. *Foundation of Navajo Culture.* Navajoland, U.S.A., 1991.

Haile, Berard. "Navaho Chantways and Ceremonials." *American Anthropologist* 40, no. 4 (January–March 1938): 639–652.

Heib, Louis. "Hopi World View." In *Handbook of North American Indians,* vol. 9: *Southwest,* edited by Alfonso Ortiz. Washington, D.C., 1979.

Kaplan, Bert, and Dale Johnson. "The Social Meaning of Navajo Psychopathology and Psychotherapy." In *Magic, Faith, and Healing,* edited by Ari Kieve, pp. 203–229. New York, 1964.

Lamphere, Louise. "Symbolic Elements in Navajo Ritual." *Southwestern Journal of Anthropology* 25, no. 3 (1969): 279–305.

Lamphere, Louise. "Southwestern Ceremonialism." In *Handbook of North American Indians,* vol. 10, *Southwest,* edited by Alfonso Ortiz. Washington, D.C., 1983.

McNeley, James K. *Holy Wind in Navajo Philosophy.* Tucson, Ariz., 1981.

Ortiz, Alfonso. *The Tewa World: Space, Time, Being, and Becoming in a Pueblo Society.* Chicago, 1969.

Reichard, Gladys A. *Navaho Religion: A Study of Symbolism.* 2 vols. New York, 1950.

Tedlock, Dennis. "Zuni Religion and World View." In *Handbook of North American Indians,* vol. 10, *Southwest,* edited by Alfonso Ortiz. Washington, D.C., 1979.

Werner, Oswald, Allen Manning, and Kenneth Y. Begishe. "A Taxonomic View of the Traditional Navajo Universe." In *Handbook of North American Indians,* vol. 10, *Southwest,* edited by Alfonso Ortiz. Washington, D.C., 1983.

Witherspoon, Gary. *Navajo Kinship and Marriage.* Chicago, 1975.

Witherspoon, Gary. "Language and Reality in Navajo World View." In *Handbook of North American Indians,* vol. 10, *Southwest,* edited by Alfonso Ortiz. Washington, D.C., 1983.

Wyman, Leland C. *Blessingway: With Three Versions of the Myth Recorded and Translated from the Navajo by Father Berard Haile.* Tucson, Ariz., 1970.

Wyman, Leland C. "Navajo Ceremonial System." In *Handbook of North American Indians,* vol. 10, *Southwest,* edited by Alfonso Ortiz. Washington, D.C., 1983.

Wyman, Leland C., and Flora L. Bailey. "Idea and Action Patterns in Navaho Flintway." *Southwestern Journal of Anthropology* 1 (1945): 356–377.

Wyman, Leland C., and Clyde Kluckhohn. *Navajo Classification of Their Song Ceremonials. Memoirs of the American Anthropological Association* 50. Menasha, Wis., 1938.

Louise Lamphere (1987)
Marilyn Notah Verney (2005)

NAVARĀTRI ("nine nights"), also known as Durgotsava ("festival of the goddess Durgā"), is a festival celebrated in India and Nepal at the time of the vernal and autumnal equinoxes. The nine nights are followed by a festival known both as Daśarā (or Daśaharā, "destroying the ten [sins]") and as Vijayādaśamī ("victory on the tenth [day]"). Although the festival of the vernal equinox is not celebrated in all regions of India, it appears in modified form in local festivals dedicated to the Goddess. The great autumnal Navarātri, which takes place during the nine nights following the new moon in the lunar month of October-November, is pan-Indian and is regarded as an important rite performed to benefit a variety of aspects of Hindu life (see Kane, 1958, vol. 5, pt. 5, pp. 156–157).

The theology and function of the Goddess, particularly of Durgā and of all popular female deities, find expression in the Navarātri (Biardeau, 1981, pp. 142–156). Its main textual source is the *Devīmāhātmya* (Glorification of the Goddess), which is a section of the *Mar-kaṇḍeya Purāṇa* often extracted and regarded as a text in its own right. According to that text, the demons (*asuras*) at one time overcame the gods, and Mahiṣāsura, the Buffalo Demon, took the place of the king of the gods. From the palpable anger of the gods was formed the body of the Goddess, known variously as Mahāmāyā ("great illusion"), Caṇḍī ("the cruel"), Durgā ("unattainable"), and by other names. The Goddess, incarnate at the energy (*śakti*) of the gods, obtained weapons from the gods and in her various forms fought against the multifarious *asuras*, whose archetype is Mahiṣa.

When she is regarded as a virgin, as distinct from any male consorts, or as the supreme deity, the Goddess in India is depicted as a fearsome and terrible deity who demands blood sacrifices. From the defeated Buffalo Demon springs a *puruṣa*, a "man" who when sacrificed becomes a devotee of the Goddess. Navarātri is thus closely associated with sacrificial themes, although in most regions vegetable substitutes now take the place of sacrificial animals in the ritual. The many forms and aspects of the Goddess and of the *asuras* correspond with the various interests and evils of this earth, for the continuation of which she manifests herself. What is more precisely at stake in the story of the *Devīmāhātmya*, however, is Mahiṣāsura's usurpation of the gods' power over the world. Hence it follows that the Goddess's close relationship with the king is a crucial element for the preservation of the Hindu cosmo-social order and for the prosperity of the kingdom as well.

The Navarātri is more complex in some regions of India than in others. In some areas it is primarily a festival marking the growing season. In others, it centers mostly around the worship of a local goddess, who may be thought of as the spouse of an untouchable. It may also be a highly ceremonialized and intricate festival, as in the former princely states, where the king was required to perform the Buffalo Sacrifice.

The main Navarātri ritual consists of installing the Goddess in the home and in the temple throughout the nine nights of the ceremony. In Tamil Nadu the Goddess is seated among many other images in a royal audience and is visited daily by women singing devotional songs; there, the ninth night is consecrated to the worship of Sarasvatī, the goddess of learning, and to *āyudhapūjā*, the worship of weapons and tools. In other regions young girls are worshiped as embodiments of the virgin Goddess. In Mysore (modern-day Karnataka) and Bastar the nine nights were a time of ascetic practices for the king.

In Bengal, the installation of the Goddess in a royal temple is an elaborate life-giving rite (see Östör, 1980, pp. 71ff.). The night between the eighth and ninth days serves as the climax to the ceremony as a whole. Nava-ratri is also an important popular festival in which the Bengalis build huge, richly decorated images of the Goddess. These icons of Devī are destroyed during the Vijayādaśamī rites. Large and excited crowds of people (who at times transgress the norms of conduct) parade the many images of the Goddess to bodies of water, where they are immersed.

Vijayādaśamī concerns primarily the *kṣatriya* caste. In royal states and in Nepal the king performs *āyudhapūjā*, officiates at parades of soldiers astride horses and elephants, and symbolically conquers the world by throwing arrows to the four directions. Ritually crossing the boundaries, the king goes toward the northeast to perform *śamīpūjā*, the worship of the *śamī* tree, traditionally associated with the sacred fire. This appears to be a ritual restatement of an event recounted in the *Mahābhārata* in which the heroes of the epic retrieve the weapons they had hidden in that tree. Seated in a royal audience, the king receives the renewed allegiance of his subjects. In some regions there are dramatic enactments of the victory of Viṣṇu's incarnation as Rāma over Rāvaṇa, the demon-king of Sri Lanka. In former times, the end of Navarātri, which coincides with the end of the monsoon, marked the time for kings to return to their wars. Moreover, the close association between the *asura*-slayer, Devī, and the kingdom, which is under her protection, symbolically restores prosperity to everyone in the domain.

See Also Durgā Hinduism; Hindu Religious Year.

Bibliography

Madeleine Biardeau's *L'hindouisme: Anthropologie d'une civilisation* (Paris, 1981) gives an accurate idea of the Goddess in the Hindu conceptions. P. V. Kane's *History of Dharmaśāstra (Ancient and Medieval Religious and Civil Law)*, vol. 5, pt. 1 (Poona, 1958), pp. 154–194, remains useful for its textual references. For *Navarātri* celebrations in Bengal, Ákos Östör's *The Play of the Gods: Locality, Ideology, Structure, and Time in the Festivals of a Bengali Town* (Chicago, 1980) is the most detailed and interesting study. See also Oscar Lewis's *Village Life in Northern India* (Urbana, Ill., 1958) and Lawrence A. Babb's *The Divine Hierarchy: Popular Hinduism in Central India* (New York, 1975).

Marie-Louise Reiniche (1987)

NAẒẒĀM, AL-. Abū Isḥāq Ibrāhīm ibn Sayyār al-Naẓẓām (c. AH 165–221/c. 782–836 CE) was an early Muslim theologian of the rationalist Muʿtazilī school.

Born in poverty in the city of Basra, al-Naẓẓām rose to literary prominence through his keen wit and rhetorical skills, and eventually moved to Baghdad where he was granted a large salary by the state. His most notable poetry employed abstract theological terms and metaphors in praise of wine and the beauties of youths, but he was remembered (and criticized) especially for his theological views. He studied theology under his uncle, Abū al-Hudhayl al-ʿAllāf (d. c. 841 CE), the founder of the Basra school of speculative Muʿtazilī theology. He is also said to have applied his prodigious memory to the study of traditions (*ḥadīth*), Jewish and Christian scriptures and commentaries, Greek philosophy, and Iranian dualistic traditions. In Baghdad he caused a stir with his "new philosophy," a non-atomistic system in which infinitely divisible bodies move by discrete instantaneous leaps. He attracted a proverbially large number of disciples, who perpetuated aspects of his teaching for a century or so; but although the Baghdad school of the Muʿtazilah drew on some of his ideas, his physical theory soon lost out to Abū al-Hudhayl's atomism, and his thought was largely rejected by the Basra school. His own books are lost, but Josef van Ess has pieced together a broad, if still partly tentative, sketch of his thought from citations by later writers, including most notably his famous pupil, the celebrated litterateur and theologian, al-Jāḥiẓ (d. 869 CE).

Seeking common ground from which to debate dualists such as the Manichaeans, al-Naẓẓām adopted an ontology akin to their view of the world as a mixture of opposites. He rejected Abū al-Hudhayl's view that the world consists of indivisible atoms in which qualities inhere as accidents, proposing instead that objects are combinations of perceptible, corporeal qualities that pervade one another and become hidden or manifest as things change. For example, coldness is among the normally manifest qualities of wood, but when it is set ablaze the previously latent quality of fire, itself composed of warmth and brightness, becomes manifest. Human beings cannot create or destroy such qualities, but the human spirit is capable of initiating changes in their arrangements (i.e., movements or actions, which are the only accidents recognized by al-Naẓẓām). The spirit, a subtle body, by nature wills only what is good, but because it is trapped in a perceptible body permeated by conflicting motivations, it can choose evil. The body implements the actions willed by the spirit, and God creates the effects of those actions in their objects, in accordance with the qualities he gave each object at creation.

Although al-Naẓẓām's ontology had many points in common with Stoic philosophy and Iranian dualistic traditions, he employed it in the defense of Islamic doctrines, citing the intermingling of opposite qualities, for example, as proof of a creator who brings them together. He proposed radical formulations of several cardinal Muʿtazilī principles: God's justice, God's oneness, and the createdness of the Qurʾān. Prompted by debates with dualists over the problem of evil, al-Naẓẓām went beyond the disputed Muʿtazilī thesis that God always does what is best (*aṣlaḥ*), to claim that God is not even capable of injustice, or indeed of anything less than what is most salutary for his creatures (including animals). God does not will or create either good or bad human actions, except in the sense that he commands certain acts, and creates their effects in their objects. Against Christians, dualists, and even some Muslims who seemed to vitiate God's oneness by ascribing to him eternal partners, al-Naẓẓām adopted an extreme form of the Muʿtazilī teaching that God does not have real attributes coeternal with himself. He argued that to affirm one of God's attributes is not to ascribe a positive quality to God's essence, but merely to affirm that essence and to deny that it has the opposite quality. Only God's actions upon the created world can be described positively. One such action is his speech, the Qurʾān, which the Muʿtazilah claimed is created rather than eternal. Al-Naẓẓām agreed, but whereas he considered human speech an attribute of the speaker (an accident and a movement by which the speaker breaks up and articulates a previously existent but formless sound), he claimed that God's speech is itself sound created in articulated form. Thus he could not describe God as speaking, or say that human recitation of the Qurʾān is itself the Qurʾān. Although he formalized the doctrine that the Qurʾān is a miraculous proof of Muḥammad's prophethood, he did not claim, as would later theologians, that its rhetorical style is intrinsically inimitable; instead he argued that Muḥammad's opponents had failed to match the Qurʾān's eloquence only because God had temporarily rendered them unable to do so. What he considered probative was the Qurʾān's content—its revelation of things that a human being could not otherwise know.

In theology al-Naẓẓām insisted that knowledge of God be arrived at through doubt and reason, but on rationally inscrutable points of law he insisted on following the letter of the Qurʾān. He blamed the prevailing chaos of conflicting legal opinions on those prominent companions of the prophet Muḥammad who had followed their own opinions in their rulings. His older contemporary, the famous jurist al-Shāfiʿī (d. 820 CE), had sought to bring Islamic law into full harmony with the Qurʾān by interpreting the Qurʾān almost exclusively in light of reports from the Prophet himself, by extending the reach of its provisions through reasoning by analogy, and by exploiting its linguistic ambiguities to resolve contradictions. Al-Naẓẓām took a diametrically opposite approach. He rejected the independent legal authority of reports (*ḥadīth*)—even those that the Muslim community accepted by consensus (*ijmāʿ*)—arguing that reports give certainty only when corroborated by rational or perceptual evidence, regardless of how many people transmit them. He also rejected most, if not all, analogical reasoning (*qiyās*), and insisted that the language of the Qurʾān be applied absolutely literally in the absence of specific qualifying evidence (which may, however, include reports or consensus). Some aspects of this approach were soon taken up by the Ẓāhirī school of law (now institutionally defunct), and he was much quoted by Shīʿī legal theorists, who shared his rejection of analogy and consensus and his antipathy for certain companions of the Prophet. Mainstream Sunnī legal theory, however, followed al-Shāfiʿī's lead.

BIBLIOGRAPHY

The only comprehensive European-language study of al-Naẓẓām is in Josef van Ess, *Theologie und Gesellschaft im 2. und 3. Jahrhundert Hidschra: Eine Geschichte des religiösen Denkens im frühen Islam* (Berlin, 1991–1997), vol. 3, pp. 296–418. Vol. 6, pp. 1–204, provides an annotated German translation of the citations on which van Ess based his study. The most detailed English overview is van Ess's article "Abū Esḥāq. . .Naẓẓām" in *Encyclopaedia Iranica,* edited by Ehsan Yarshater (New York and London, 1982). Helpful works on specific aspects of al-Naẓẓām's thought include:

Bernand, Marie. "Le savoir entre la volonté et la spontanéité selon an-Naẓẓām et al-Ǧāḥiẓ." *Studia Islamica* 39 (1974): 25–57.

Ess, Josef van. "Ein unbekanntes Fragment des Naẓẓām." In *Der Orient in der Forschung: Festschrift für Otto Spies zum 5.* April 1966, edited by Wilhelm Hoenerbach, pp. 170–201. Wiesbaden, Germany, 1967. On al-Naẓẓām's legal theory, principally reports and consensus.

Ess, Josef van. *Das Kitāb al-Nakt des Naẓẓām und seine Rezeption im Kitāb al-Futyā des Ǧāḥiẓ: Eine Sammlung der Fragmente mit Übersetzung und Kommentar.* Göttingen, Germany, 1972. On al-Naẓẓām's legal theory, principally his criticisms of companions of the Prophet.

Ess, Josef van. *Theology and Science: The Case of Abū Isḥāq an-Naẓẓām.* Ann Arbor, Mich., 1978. On al-Naẓẓām's theories of bodies and movement.

Ess, Josef van. "Wrongdoing and Divine Omnipotence in the Theology of Abū Isḥāq an-Naẓẓām." In *Divine Omniscience and Omnipotence in Medieval Philosophy: Islamic, Jewish, and Christian Perspectives,* edited by Tamar Rudavsky, pp. 53–67. Dordrecht, Netherlands, 1985. This is followed by a response by Richard Frank entitled "Can God Do What Is Wrong?" (pp. 69–79).

Wolfson, Harry Austryn. "The *Ḫāṭirāni* in the Kalam and Ghazālī as Inner Motive Powers of Human Actions." In *Studies in Mysticism and Religion, Presented to Gershom G. Scholem,* edited by Efraim E. Urbach, R. J. Zwi Werblowsky, and Chaim Wirszubski, pp. 363–379. Jerusalem, 1967.

DAVID R. VISHANOFF (2005)

NDEMBU RELIGION. The Ndembu, also called the Lunda, number about sixty thousand and inhabit small villages in the district of Mwinilunga in the northwestern province of Zambia. Although their descent system is matrilineal, women leave home to marry into their husbands' villages, a system that sets up social tensions and, before the advent of Christianity, used to result in a high divorce rate. In this conflict-torn society, cult associations formerly had a great unifying power, calling together members from many different kinship groups to cooperate in rituals that gave moments of spiritual revelation, which in turn resolved conflicts and healed illness.

CULTS OF AFFLICTION. Among the Ndembu, affliction was seen as having a spiritual cause: the spirit of a dead matrilineal relative *(mukishi)* afflicted a living descendant, "coming out" in a range of different modes of spirit visitation. Thus the spirit might "come out in Nkula," the mode of menstrual troubles; Wubwang'u, the mode of twins; Isoma, the miscarriage mode; Ihamba, a spirit tooth wandering in the patient's body, needing ritual extraction; Wuyang'a, the mode for hunters; Tukuka, the mode of Western diseases; or Chihamba, the mode of the demigod of thunder. Wu-bwang'u and Ihamba afflictions still exist today.

The spirit "caught" a living relative in the first place because he or she had not honored the spirit's memory. When afflicted, an individual required a complex ritual, the mode of which was determined by the consideration of symptoms and by divination. The ritual (*n'goma,* "drum") was performed by a cult association consisting of those who had already been afflicted in that mode. The aim was to bring the spirit up out of the ground (the place where the spirits dwell) so that by recognizing its existence and giving it a concrete form—as a figure, effigy, tooth, or voice—it could be revealed. *Ku-solola,* "to reveal," was a basic element of Ndembu religion and curative ritual. The religion taught: "what hurts you, when discovered and propitiated, helps you." Through the use of medicines, drumming and singing, and distinctive rites appropriate to each mode, the spirit was brought once more into the social milieu and would, at a switch point in the ritual, begin to do good instead of harm to the patient. Often what triggered the change was a sacrifice, which might be the beheading of a fowl or a blow on an effigy, signifying killing; while the victim embodied the spirit, the act gave a sense of innocence and *communitas.* Ndembu sacrifice was the point where the visible and invisible components of the cosmic order interpenetrated and exchanged qualities. When the spirit world and the world of the living were at one, the patient was healed.

LIFE-CRISIS RITUALS. A young girl or boy could not become a full member of the Ndembu people without an initiation ritual. The matrilineal character of the descent system emphasized the bond of breast feeding; thus, a forest shrub called *mudyi,* which has milky sap, was a dominant symbol for both girls' and boys' initiations. *Mudyi* represented the matrilineage itself and the virtues of good family living; its "milk" was the sensory pole of the symbol's meaning, hinting at the satisfactions associated with mother's milk—a pole that gave power to the ideological pole of goodness.

Both girls' and boys' initiations were rites of passage, and they are still performed in a truncated form. The novice passes ritually from childhood into a liminal time of seclusion when she or he is neither child nor adult. Finally the initiate is reincorporated into society as a full member.

Girls are initiated singly, at puberty; the initiate used to be laid down under a blanket at the foot of a milk tree for an entire day, while the women danced around her. At evening she was carried into a seclusion hut, where she received training for three months. At the end she performed a public dance and might then be married.

Boys from five to fifteen years of age are still circumcised in groups in a sacred enclosure away from the village. They are secluded there during healing, and in former times used to be visited by an *ikishi* dancer, a spirit from ancient times (not an ancestor spirit). Finally the boys would rejoin society in a public celebration that used to include a triumphal dance before the chief. In both rituals the place of ordeal and humiliation used to be called "the place of death"; symbolic death and rebirth were basic features of these and many of the curative rites.

Death itself was celebrated by a masked dancer (*kadang'u*) who was both mourner and clown. Among the funerary symbols were three trenches filled with white-, red-, and black-colored water, representing goodness, blood and ambivalence, and death; these trenches were known as "rivers" proceeding from Nzambi, the creator god. Formerly, a stilt walker, the head of the funerary society, would come to beat and initiate the small boys of the mourning camp. Medicines and rituals are still used to keep the ghost of the dead person quiet.

Thus Ndembu religion was directly concerned with human events, whether sickness, bad luck in hunting, conflict in the village, or phases in the maturation of an individual. It was mainly through sickness that an individual began to sense the presence of an ancestor spirit; thus it was the very irregularities of life, its negative events, that created the positive sense of the supernatural, especially when the spirit possessed a patient and she swayed, her body physically released by its presence. The palpable existence of spirits developed in the course of the experience of misfortune. This is not to be explained as a compensation mechanism; misfortune did more than arouse fantasies, for it triggered well-recognized faculties (*wanga*) that needed the stimulus of trouble, and then of social cooperation, in order to flower. Senior doctors still train their apprentices in those faculties and teach the appropriate material accompaniments of medicine, drumming, confession, and trance in order to exorcise evil spirits. In spite of the growth of Christianity, traditional healers are increasing in numbers. Owing to the suppression of ancestor cults, they do not appeal to the ancestor spirits of the patients, but instead are helped by tutelary spirits from among their own ancestors or from some strong departed personality. Formerly a doctor entered his vocation after being sick himself. In the case of an incipient diviner he might be troubled in his breathing until he gave in to the demands of his spirit and underwent the Kayong'u initiation.

SPIRITS. In the past, Ndembu religion centered upon ancestor spirits who communicated with humans frequently but unpredictably. Like the people's own lives, their domain was process, not the absolute. Continually involved in human life, they could heal their descendants and make them sexually potent. Such spirits could also be reborn in their patrilateral descendants. They were often whimsical, difficult, and easily offended when forgotten, but beneficent when treated with respect. Thus all of humanity, past, present, and future, was strongly knit together. *Mukishi* ancestor spirits and the ancient *ikishi* spirits, however, are no longer recognized as necessary agents of healing or change in rites of passage.

The Ndembu also believed in the *mwevulu,* the spirit shadow that was thought to leave a person and wander about when he or she was asleep and dreaming. It was this "shadow" that left a person when he or she died. Certain evil spirits are still feared, principally the *mufu,* the dangerous ghost that arises when funerary rites have not been properly fulfilled, and the harmful *andumba* (sg., *ndumba*), familiars sent by witches in the shape of little men with their feet reversed, or in the form of hyenas, jackals, owls, or small rodents. Two other types of beings are also feared: the leader of the *andumba,* the *kahwehu,* often the ghost of the witch's murdered husband, who is said to have continued intercourse with her, and the *musalu,* or zombie, which can be raised from a corpse by a witch and sent out to kill.

GOD. The pre-Christian Ndembu recognized a creator god who was known as Nzambi. Having once created the world Nzambi never intervened in the lives of humans, and his role in religion was exiguous except in a negative sense. The Ndembu girl during her sacralization and seclusion was carefully shielded from his sight—as represented by the sun. This male god, the sun, and men and boys, must be absent from her scenes of rebirth. Nzambi's place was far away above the world. He was thought to be connected with rain, animals, and fertility, and also with the moral order, which decreed piety to the dead and compassion to the living. Christians have appropriated the name *Nzambi* to translate the term *God;* and now even traditional healers pray to Nzambi, just as Ndembu Christians have been doing for decades.

BIBLIOGRAPHY

The works of Victor Turner are central to understanding Ndembu religion. His early study "Lunda Rites and Ceremonies" (1953), reprinted in *The Occasional Papers of the Rhodes-Livingstone Museum* (Manchester, 1974), provides a factual account of each Ndembu ritual. Four subsequent books provide analysis. *The Forest of Symbols: Aspects of Ndembu Ritual* (Ithaca, N. Y., 1967) is a collection of essays including discussions of the rite of circumcision, the funerary cult, initiation of a doctor, and hunters' rites. *The Drums of Affliction: A Study of Religious Processes among the Ndembu of Zambia* (London, 1968) analyzes rites associated with menstruation, teeth, and girl's initiation. *The Ritual Process: Structure and Anti-Structure* (Chicago, 1969) studies curative rites and the twin ritual. *Revelation and Divination in Ndembu Ritual* (Ithaca, N. Y., 1975) analyzes the ritual drama Chihamba and compares its symbolism with that of Western religion. I have recently analyzed the work of a modern Ndembu doctor-priest in "Philip Kabwita, Ghost Doctor: The Ndembu in 1985," *Drama Review* 10, no. 4 (1986).

New Sources

Jordan, Manuel. "Art and Divination among Chokwe, Lunda, Luvale and other Related Peoples of Northwestern Zambia." In *Insight and Artistry in African Divination,* edited by John Pemberton. Washington, D.C., 2000.

Pritchett, James Anthony. *Continuity and Change in an African Society: The Kanongesha Lunda of Mwinilunga, Zambia.* Ph.D. thesis, Harvard University, 1990.

Pritchett, James Anthony. *The Lunda-Ndembu: Style, Change and Social Transformation in South Central Africa.* Madison, Wis., 2001.

Turner, Edith L. B. *Experiencing Ritual: A New Interpretation of African Healing,* Philadelphia, 1992.

Turner, Victor Witter. *The Ritual Process: Structure and Anti-Structure.* New York: Aldine de Gruyter, 1995.

Turner, Victor Witter. *Schism and Continuity in an African Society: A Study of Ndembu Village Life.* Oxford and Washington, D.C., 1996.

EDITH TURNER (1987)
Revised Bibliography